Baseball Prospectus 2009

WILLIAM BURKE • CLIFFORD J. CORCORAN • CLAY DAVENPORT

NEIL DEMAUSE • STEVEN GOLDMAN • KEVIN GOLDSTEIN

GARY HUCKABAY • DEREK JACQUES • JAY JAFFE

CHRISTINA KAHRL • DAVID LAURILA • BEN LINDBERGH

MARC NORMANDIN • CALEB PEIFFER

JOHN PERROTTO • NATE SILVER

A PLUME BOOK

PLUME
Published by Penguin Group
Penguin Group (USA) Inc., 375 Hudson Street, New York, New York 10014, U.S.A.
Penguin Group (Canada), 90 Eglinton Avenue East, Suite 700, Toronto, Ontario, Canada M4P 2Y3
(a division of Pearson Penguin Canada Inc.)
Penguin Books Ltd., 80 Strand, London WC2R 0RL, England
Penguin Ireland, 25 St. Stephen's Green, Dublin 2, Ireland (a division of Penguin Books Ltd.)
Penguin Group (Australia), 250 Camberwell Road, Camberwell, Victoria 3124, Australia
(a division of Pearson Australia Group Pty. Ltd.)
Penguin Books India Pvt. Ltd., 11 Community Centre, Panchsheel Park, New Delhi – 110 017, India
Penguin Group (NZ), 67 Apollo Drive, Mairangi Bay, Auckland 1311, New Zealand
(a division of Pearson New Zealand Ltd.)
Penguin Books (South Africa) (Pty.) Ltd., 24 Sturdee Avenue, Rosebank, Johannesburg 2196, South Africa

Penguin Books Ltd., Registered Offices:
80 Strand, London WC2R 0RL, England

First published by Plume, a member of Penguin Group (USA) Inc.

First Printing (2009 edition), February 2009
1 3 5 7 9 10 8 6 4 2

ISBN 978-0-452-29011-2

Printed in the United States of America
Set in Utopia
Design by Jane Raese

Contents

Fungoes

Foreword

You know what just hit me? What would be *so* great? If you could, like, know in advance what was going to *happen!* How cool would *that* be?

All snark aside, there is no claim or warranty made, either by *Baseball Prospectus* or by this foreword, that this is actually Biff Tannen's copy of *Grey's Sports Almanac*. But it'll do.

There are probably better matches produced by the rules of statistical probability, mathematical reduction, and the hard work of the denizens of the *BP* sweatshop, but if you are now what I was a year ago—a first-time practitioner in these dark arts—let me pull a sufficiently chilling set of numbers from page 490 of last year's edition. There, it is foretold that in 2008, Evan Longoria would most likely bat .266, on-base .339, slug .459, rap out 31 doubles, a pair of triples, and 25 homers. Probability suggested he would also drive in 87 runs, strike out 130 times, and steal six bases.

As you can see, the numbers were wildly off. Longoria actually batted .272, on-based .343, slugged .531, rapped out 31 doubles, *three* triples, and 27 homers. Reality proved he would also drive in 85 runs, strike out 122 times, and steal seven bases.

If you throw out the significant overspill in slugging (as if Longoria or the Rays are going to send it back) and pretend the percentage points are whole numbers, then the variation between *BP*'s Evan Longoria and the real-life version is 24 points. *Baseball Prospectus* was off by *24 points*, spread over seven statistics. It basically got everything right except whether Longoria, while wearing one of those goofy flap-caps in the Series last October, would look more like Johnny Carson's Floyd R. Turbo or Elmer J. Fudd.

How does *BP* do it? I don't know, and moreover, I don't want to know. Believe it or not, I used to be a math prodigy. I mean a serious, take-this-kid-to-the-experts, math prodigy. Then they started mixing in algebra and trigonometry and then something called Math 5. If the teacher hadn't let me take that course pass/fail, I'd still be a senior at Hackley School in Tarrytown, New York. Apparently, I was just an addition-and-subtraction prodigy.

I bore you with this, because the *real* joy within these pages is not just predictions unmatched in baseball history; it's that these bona fide prodigies have done all the heavy lifting. You, the Braves fan, should not have had to wonder about what was going to happen next after Tim Hudson opened up 11-7 last year, but the *Baseball Prospectus* forecast had him finishing around 12-10. The book just *told* you what was going to happen; it became your responsibility only to assume the crash position and await (a) Hud's sudden retirement, (b) Hud's unexpected trade to the Inchon Sammi Superstars, or (c) a ligament in Hud's elbow to blow like an overtuned guitar string.

Shout out almost anything that would have surprised you about last season (or if this is the first time you've read this book, *did* surprise you): The Mariners melting before your eyes and J. J. Putz being too good and too healthy to be true? Pages 465-478 (the book left out the stuff about how Putz would wind up going to the Mets as setup man; I suppose you have to leave the reader something to guess at). Josh Hamilton's 130 RBI season? Page 118, wherein a tidy 17-73-.283 campaign is forecast, but the text notes, "if he can learn to hit left-handers, he'll go from very good to outright dangerous" (and then Hamilton hit .288 off lefties last season). K-Rod's record 62 saves? Page 250: "given the Angels' run context most years, he may get a shot at Bobby Thigpen's single-season mark of 57."

I've been trying to find good, credible baseball forecasting, especially to extrapolate major league performance from minor league numbers—not perfect, and this *isn't* perfect, as it didn't see Cliff Lee's resurgence, for instance—since 1968. That was when Tony Solaita hit 51 home runs at High Point–Thomasville of the Carolina League. Watching him in a home run contest at Yankee Stadium that September, I dreamed of him leading my boyhood team out of the wilderness, and it dawned on me that whatever 51 home runs in the Carolina League meant, they probably didn't mean 51 home runs in Yankee Stadium.

And here, I dare say, *is* that credible forecasting. It is useful in more ways than you can imagine, from simply giving you insight about what has come before, to enabling you to delight as reality catches up with the forecasts in these pages, to allowing you to destroy the other owners in your fantasy league. I used to be a full-timer. By 1994, we were so deeply in the woods that we used to hold an amateur draft the week before the ac-

tual amateur draft. I mean, this was the tertiary syphilis version of what we then still called Rotisserie. And then came the strike and the threat of having to draft Pedro Borbon the Elder and I got out, until two years ago. I left, enlarging the newspaper's weekly stats on a photocopier and hand-entering them into my Mac. I returned to a world of Internet-driven, instantaneous decision-making. And I couldn't shake off the rust fast enough.

And then I met *BP*. Mine is a 10-team, clean-start, National League–only operation. I'll spare you the details, but despite having the last pick, I won the league going away. Then more or less the same group of guys drafted a 10-team NFL league and I got *that* last pick, too, and I won *that* as well, running the table from Week 7 on. Every time I needed to make either team better, the information was there for me, whether in black-and-white predictions or the more nuanced thought-provoking clues spread like fortune cookie fortunes all through this book and its football counterpart. If you try this, you will notice things like the top 50 guys on your "list" bearing only passing resemblance to those on everybody else's. You will shudder and say "this can't be right." Trust me: it probably is.

You may have noticed that one of the *BP* boys, Mr. Silver, has now spread out into picking elections and getting them righter than they got Evan Longoria. So now we have to worry about this crowd somehow gaining control of the weather or, in my case, of being able to predict television news ratings.

But for now, the rest of world is still safe and, quaintly, relatively unpredictable. So you can enjoy what you read here in *Baseball Prospectus*. Or you can ignore it. At your everlasting peril.

Keith Olbermann
New York, New York
December 2008

Statistical Introduction

In our 2005 book, *Mind Game*, we began with a page titled "A Comforting Note About Statistics." The comforting message was, "You can enjoy this book without an advanced degree in mathematics." We've subsequently repeated that message in every book we've done except previous editions of the one that you're holding your hands, the Baseball Prospectus annual. That's because the ratio of numbers to letters is higher in this series than it is in our one-off projects such as *Baseball Between the Numbers* or *It Ain't Over 'Til It's Over*. Open to almost any page and you'll see it: big chunks of text alternating with big chunks of numbers. Despite this, the comforting note still applies: if you're not familiar with any statistics that aren't on the back of a baseball card, and even if you're not even familiar with *those*, you can find just as much information about the state of baseball today between these covers as if you had just walked out of the astrophysics lab at NASA.

For those readers who do want to know more about the statistics we utilize within these pages, this section of the book is designed to introduce you to the tools we use for player analysis and to explain how they fit together. We'll start by introducing a few key concepts, including our PECOTA projection system, then we'll go over the statistics used in the thirty team chapters that follow, including a few new features we're unveiling this year.

Types of Statistics

In this book we refer to two distinct types of baseball metrics: cumulative statistics and rate statistics. **Cumulative statistics** tally individual events such as hits, walks, strikeouts, home runs, errors, or wins over the course of the season. Cumulative statistics are the backbone of all the other baseball metrics because they represent a record of the events that happened on the field. Knowing that a player hit 12 home runs, however, does us little good on its own. We need to place our cumulative statistics in context. If he hit those 12 dingers over the course of a single month—as four major leaguers did in 2008—he might look over that span like the second coming of Hank Aaron. If the player in question hit his 12 home runs over the course of a season, he

might also resemble Hank Aaron...as he was in 1975, playing out the twilight of his career with the Brewers. On the other hand, if he hit 12 homers over the course of a 13-year career, that total would indicate he's likely the type that needs a strong tailwind just to get the ball to the warning track, not much of a slugger at all.

That brings us to **rate statistics**, which measure the frequency of events and are thus often expressed as percentages, averages, or ratios. Slugging percentage, for example, is a measure of a hitter's power determined by total bases divided by at-bats. Returning to our example of 12 home runs. In his next-to-last season in the majors, Aaron had a .355 slugging percentage to go with his dozen dingers, below the National League average and well below his career mark of .555. On the other hand, the four major leaguers who hit a dozen homers in a month last season—Dan Uggla, J.D. Drew, Adam Dunn, and Ty Wigginton—posted slugging percentages in those months that ranged from .762 to .848. While the cumulative statistic needs context to show us the difference between these performances, the rate statistic does it all by itself.

Of course, rate statistics sometimes need a context of their own. Each of the dozen-homer months mentioned above featured a slugging percentage that if, carried out over the course of a full season, would place in the top 10 seasons of all time, a rarified country occupied only by Barry Bonds and Babe Ruth. However, the four players who had those outstanding months didn't wind up posting historic slugging percentages—indeed, none of them even finished in the top 10 in slugging percentage for their respective leagues! The point is that performance is extremely variable, which makes the concept of **sample size** important. Wigginton followed up his .806 slugging percentage in August by posting an anemic .305 slugging percentage in September. Similarly, sometimes you'll flip a coin and the result will be heads four times in a row. This is not a reason to think you have a magical coin that only comes up heads. As you gather a larger sample—400, 500 coin flips—you should see results that more closely resemble the actual probabilities of the coin flip, 50 percent per side. With ballplayers, that means sometimes we'll discount the rate statistic performance of a player who was extremely hot or extremely cold for 100 plate appearances or 50 innings as a "small-sample fluke," electing instead to rely on larger samples of a whole season or more worth of data to make our analyses.

Translating Baseball Performance

While statistics become increasingly more informative when placed in the context of frequency and sample size, there is yet another context to be considered, and that is the environment in which they were achieved. As a player rises through the minor leagues, plays in foreign leagues, or even simply moves around the majors, the quality of his competition changes, as do the physical environments in which he performs, whether it be a small ball park at a high elevation in a dry climate in which batted balls seem to rocket over the fence, or a cavernous park on the water in which potential home runs get hung up by the thick sea air or lake-effect winds. What's more, the effects of a ballpark's environment or the competition level of a given league can fluctuate from year to year, and can vary quite significantly over a period of several years. As a result, players' statistical records are awash with distortions and statistical noise. The need to correct these distortions has given rise to an entire family of advanced statistics that attempts to translate performance compiled in different contexts to a common standard. Our translated statistics (sometimes called "normalized" or "adjusted" statistics) were devised by Clay Davenport and are typically signified by the prefix "Equivalent," such as Equivalent Slugging Percentage (EqSLG). These statistics adjust every player's performance—whether it took place in the major leagues, minor leagues, Japanese or Mexican leagues—to show us what it would have looked like had it happened in a neutral ballpark (one that doesn't favor either pitchers or hitters) in the major leagues, in a season in which the average hitter hit for a .260 batting average, .330 on-base percentage, and .420 slugging percentage. Translated statistics are found in the gray shaded areas on the right side of the statistical tables in the player comments in the team chapters.

Predicting Future Performance with PECOTA

Having translated all player performances to a neutral context we have a uniform body of data that allows us to see trends and to forecast performance. Our main tool for this purpose is **PECOTA** (which stands for **P**layer **E**mpirical **C**omparison and **O**ptimization **T**est **A**lgorithm), a system created by Nate Silver that proj-

ects future player performance based on existing trends in the historical record. PECOTA works by analyzing a number of quantifiable factors, including production metrics (batting average, isolated power), usage metrics (plate appearances, major league career length, minor league level), phenotypic attributes (handedness, height, and weight), and a player's defensive position. For minor leaguers, the player's amateur signing bonus—adjusted for inflation—is added to the mix for comparison with other prospects. With this data, PECOTA identifies as many as a hundred of the hitters or pitchers who are most comparable to the player being projected. The career trends of those players are then used in producing that player's forecast.

The PECOTA projections also incorporate an adjustment for the discrepancy of difficulty between the National and American Leagues, as the American League is currently quite a bit tougher than the National League (roughly 10 points worth of EqA, or 25 points of EqERA above and beyond the adjustment required by the inclusion of the designated hitter in place of the pitcher in opposing lineups). A player migrating from the AL to the NL can expect a boost in his projection, while a player moving from the senior to the junior circuit can expect a corresponding drop in production; in both cases, that change will be reflected in his PECOTA projection. Similarly, the system adjusts for platoon splits (a player moving from a platoon role to a full-time role can be expected to experience a decline), ballpark component factors (for example, a left-handed batter Miller Park can expect an increase in the number of triples they hit) and for first/second half splits (a player who performed better in the second half than in the first can expected to perform better the following season). These adjustments help to place the player's performance in a context-neutral environment for the most accurate comparison to other ballplayers and career paths, and the adjustments are then made to the player's projection to reflect the effects of changes of league, home ballpark, or role.

The Team Prospectus

The bulk of this book is composed of thirty team chapters, one for each major league franchise. On the first page of each chapter, you'll find the Team Prospectus box which looks like our sample.

2008 Record is quite simply the team's win-loss record for last season, their final place in their division, and postseason results, if any. **Pythagenport record** is an adjusted win-loss record based on the team's runs

ORIOLES PROSPECTUS

2008 record: 68-93; Fifth place, AL East

Pythagenpot record: 72-89

Runs scored per game: 4.86 (8th in AL)

Runs allowed per game: 5.40 (13th in AL)

Team EqA: .259 (Tied for 8th in AL)

2008 Batters Age: 30.6 (5th-oldest in AL)

2008 Pitchers Age: 27.9 (4th-youngest in AL)

Ballpark: Oriole Park at Camden Yards; Slight hitter's park; Park Factor of 1.023

2008: To paraphrase Thomas Jefferson, every rotation degenerates when entrusted to Jeremy Guthrie alone.

2009: The arrival of Matt Wieters eases another lost year, but the team's young positional talent can't take the next step sans pitching help.

Example of a Team Prospectus box

scored and allowed that better represents the actual performance of the team in question by correcting for some of the luck involved in its actual record. The relationship between run differential and winning percentage was first demonstrated by Bill James in his 1980 *Baseball Abstract*. James dubbed his translation of runs scored and allowed into wins and losses "Pythagorean record" because of the resemblance of the use of squares in his equation to the Pythagorean theorem ($a^2 + c^2 = b^2$); subsequent research refined the coefficients in the equation even further. Our version, created by Clay Davenport (thus "Pythag*enport*"), uses the context-neutral Equivalent Runs in place of actual runs scored and allowed, for an even more accurate measure of a team's expected wins and losses. Indeed, Pythagenport record correlates better to a team's performance in the coming season than its actual record.

Runs scored/allowed per game are the team's actual runs scored/allowed divided by total games played, followed by their league ranking in parentheses (with the top figure in the league being the highest runs-scored total, but the lowest runs-allowed total). While runs scored per game gives us a basic sense of the team's offensive prowess, the next line, **Team EqA**, gives us a more advanced measure. Equivalent Average (EqA) is a rate statistic that combines all of the components of offense, including baserunning, into a number on the same scale as batting average. For teams, a .260 EqA is

league average, a .280 EqA is very good, and a .240 EqA is very poor. Like other Equivalent statistics, EqA is normalized for ballpark and league offensive levels.

2008 Pitchers/Batters Age give the weighted average ages for each team, using the players' "baseball ages"—that is, the age each player was as of July 1 of the given season—weighted by playing time (plate appearances for batters, batters faced for pitchers) so that outliers don't skew the average disproportionately to the role they played on the team. In other words, weighted averaging ensures that if a team were to sign baseball's Methuselah, Julio Franco, for a couple of dozen plate appearances, it wouldn't necessarily make them the oldest team in the league.

The **Ballpark** line in the team box tells us the name of the team's home park for the previous season as well as both a description and a **Park Factor** indicating that park's effect on run scoring. Park Factor is calculated by comparing the differences in run scoring by the park's team and their opponents both at and away from the ballpark in question. A neutral ballpark that doesn't favor hitters or pitchers gets a rating of 1.000, while a park that favors hitters has a higher rating, and a park that favors pitchers has a lower rating. It is important to note that a ballpark can sometimes boost home run output without increasing run scoring overall. Accordingly, while the World Champs' Citizens Bank Park is considered somewhat of a bandbox, only three ballparks got closer to being purely neutral than Philadelphia's in 2008, all in the National League: Miller Park, AT&T Park and Minute Maid Park. The two most extreme parks in the majors were Petco Park (an extreme pitcher's park, 0.902 park factor) and Colorado's Coors Field (an extreme hitter's park, 1.067 factor).

The Hitters' Statistics

After an opening essay, each chapter moves on to the player comments. Position players are listed first, in alphabetical order, and each player is listed with the major league team with which he finished the 2008 season. So, for example Emilio Bonifacio, who started the 2008 season with Arizona, was traded to Washington at midseason, and was then dealt to the Marlins in November, is listed as an National. If you can't quite remember where a player ended up last September, there's an index in the back. Each player is represented by his statistics from every significant stint in the majors, minors, or prominent international leagues (Japanese and Mexican) between 2006 and 2008. Let's use the 2008 AL Rookie of the Year as an example.

Evan Longoria			3B								Bats: R		Throws: R		Height: 6' 2"		Weight: 180		Born: October 7, 1985			Age: 23
YEAR	TEAM	LVL	AGE	PA	R	2B	3B	HR	RBI	BB	SO	SB	CS	EqBRR	AVG	OBP	SLG	EqAVG	EqOBP	EqSLG	EqA	VORP	WARP	DEFENSE
2006	VIS	A+	20	128	22	8	0	8	28	13	19	1	1	-0.5	.327	.402	.618	.252	.312	.487	.267	4.1	0.5	22-3B	0
2006	HUD	A-	20	39	5	1	1	4	11	5	5	1	0	-0.1	.424	.487	.879	.353	.410	.735	.360	15.8	0.7	6-3B	-1
2006	MNT	AA	20	109	14	5	0	6	19	1	20	2	1	0.1	.267	.266	.486	.248	.248	.457	.236	-1.1	0.5	25-3B	4
2007	MNT	AA	21	447	78	21	0	21	76	51	81	4	0	0.0	.307	.403	.528	.269	.350	.472	.282	22.3	2.7	96-3B	1
2007	DUR	AAA	21	128	19	8	0	5	19	22	29	0	0	0.0	.269	.398	.490	.236	.364	.443	.280	5.1	0.5	27-3B	-1
2008	TBA	MLB	22	508	67	31	2	27	85	46	122	7	0	0.4	.272	.343	.531	.274	.347	.553	.300	35.7	4.3	116-3B	3
2009	TBA	MLB	23	604	80	31	2	27	88	58	133	7	2	0.5	.266	.342	.482	.270	.346	.507	.289	28.4	4.2	141-3B	4

Breakout: 20%   Improve: 59%   Collapse: 14%   Attrition: 8%   Comparables: Ron Hansen, Eric Chavez, Jeff Burroughs, Ryan Zimmerman

Hitter Statistics Example

The first line of the entry contains the player's name and some basic biographical information. The next line shows the headers for the columns of data that follow, with each horizontal line representing one season or fraction of a season with a given team. If a player had significant playing time both statistical lines will be listed. Note that extremely short stints, such as rehab assignments or year-end cups of coffee in a higher league—such as Longoria's April stint in the International League—have been trimmed out in the interest of space and because of the lack of meaningful data provided by those small samples.

The first few columns of data show time and assignment data—the year (**YEAR**), team (**TM**), and level (**LVL**) at which the hitter played. Levels are designated as the major leagues (MLB), the Japanese Leagues (JPL, JCL), Mexican League (MEX), Triple-A (AAA), Double-A (AA), High A-ball (A+), A-ball (A), Short-Season A-ball (A-), and Rookie ball (Rk). For each season, we also show how old the player was at the time using his baseball **Age** that season as per the team age information in the Team Prospectus boxes.

The next few columns—**PA** (Plate Appearances), **R** (Runs), **2B** (doubles), **3B** (triples), **HR** (home runs), **RBI** (runs batted in), **BB** (walks), **SO** (strikeouts), **SB** (stolen bases), and **CS** (caught stealing)—show the actual and familiar statistical totals the player compiled in those cumulative categories during the given playing stint. Like the other items in the "unshaded" side of the statistical table, these are raw, untranslated statistics.

Next is Equivalent Baserunning Runs (**EqBRR**), which measures how often a player takes an extra base relative to the average player—be it on a hit, a groundball, a fly ball, a passed ball or wild pitch, a stolen base, or even a balk—as well as how often a player is thrown out attempting to take that extra base and translates those extra bases gained and lost into Equivalent Runs (thus Equivalent Baserunning Runs).

The next three columns show the three most commonly used rate statistics in their raw, unadjusted form: batting average (**BA**), on base percentage (**OBP**), and slugging percentage (**SLG**). Throughout the book you may see these three statistics presented as what we call the "slash stats." For example, "Last year, Longoria hit .272/.343/.531," by which we mean he had a .272 batting average, a .343 on-base percentage, and a .531 slugging percentage. These three statistics are the best short-hand summary of a hitter's season as they tell us how often he got a hit, how often he reached base (or, inversely, avoided making an out), and how successful he was at hitting for extra bases by measuring the total bases he gained on a per-at-bat basis.

The remaining columns contain Baseball Prospectus's most useful original statistics. The next three columns are **EqBA**, **EqOBP**, **EqSLG**. These are our "translated" versions of the three slash stats discussed before. **EqA** is the same stat that appears in the Team Prospectus boxes, but whereas team totals generally fall between .280 and .240, individual hitters' EqAs show a much wider spread, again reflecting typical batting averages. Something in the area of .350 is a typical league-leading total—last year the NL leader was a little higher (Albert Pujols, .371) and the AL leader was a little bit lower (Milton Bradley, .337). A .400 EqA is exceptionally rare, but the greatest hitters in history—Babe Ruth, Mickey Mantle, Ted Williams, Bonds—have pulled it off in their best seasons. On the other hand, if your EqA is .220, you'd better be a great defensive player, or you'll be heading back to the minors.

The next column in the statistical record is **VORP**, which stands for Value Over Replacement Level. VORP is an estimate of total player value, which builds on a MLVr, a rate-based version of Marginal Lineup Value (MLV), a measure of offensive production created by David Tate and further developed by Keith Woolner. MLV is an estimate of the additional number of runs a given player will contribute to a lineup that otherwise consists of average offensive performers. MLVr is approximately equal to MLV per game; the league average MLVr is zero (0.000). MLVr and incorporates the position the player plays, how many games he played, and what "replacement level" is for his position. Replacement level is a concept discussed in great detail in the article "Understanding and Measuring Replacement Level" by Keith Woolner, which was published in *Baseball Prospectus 2002*, so we'll only summarize the main points here. We define replacement level as "the expected level of performance a major league team can receive from one or more of the best available players who substitute for a suddenly unavailable starting player at the same position and who can be (or were) obtained with minimal expenditure of team resources." Metrics such as MLVr, which compare a player to league-average offense, are incomplete because they do not account for the value of having a player healthy and in the lineup. Losing a starting player typically results in more starts being given to a bench player who is significantly below average (like Nick Punto). By comparing a player's production to the level of a typical bench player or "Quadruple-A" journeyman (which we dub replacement level), we recognize the value of a player's durability. The concept of VORP is equally applicable to position players and pitchers.

VORP is available on BaseballProspectus.com for all players and seasons going back over 50 years, and is updated daily during the season. A couple of additional details about how VORP is presented for *minor* league players:

- VORP for minor leaguers is computed using their translated rates of production, and so should be considered to be their major-league equivalent VORP, not their VORP relative to the minor league they actually played in.
- Minor league players are rated at their most frequently played position, rather than a weighted average across all positions they appeared at (as is done with major league players). That is, if a minor league player plays 100 games at second base, and 20 at shortstop, he would be considered to be purely a second baseman in calculating his VORP. (This is *not* true for major league players: If a major league player played 100 games at second, and 20 at shortstop, we would his compute his VORP on a weighted average basis, with second base having five times the weight of shortstop).
- Minor leagues have shorter seasons than the majors do, and as a result, even excellent translated

rates of production may not produce as high a VORP as for a player with the benefit of a 162-game schedule.

Although VORP looks at what position a player plays, it does not directly consider how well he fields that position. Thus we turn to the next column in hitter table, WARP, which stands for Wins Above Replacement Player. WARP is explained in much greater detail in Clay Davenport's essay in the back of this book, along with his explanations of a few other tweaks and adaptations to his system. In brief, it is a different take on the replacement level, which differs from VORP in two significant ways. First, as its name implies, WARP is measured in wins rather than runs. Longoria's 4.3 WARP means that if all of Longoria's playing time last year had been replaced from the world of freely available talent, we'd expect the Rays to have won 93 games last season, rather than 97. Second, WARP aggregates a player's performance as a hitter, fielder, and even pitcher into a single number. So unlike VORP, which applies a uniform positional adjustment that says that a shortstop is more valuable than a first baseman, WARP looks at the quality of each player's performance, so that a good-fielding first baseman is more valuable than a bad-fielding shortstop, all other things being equal. We'll go over how the players' defense is measured below, but first, a note of warning to our readers who may be familiar with WARP coming in: the WARP values you see in this book are slightly different from what you've seen over the past several years on the Baseball Prospectus web site. Due to changes in methodology explained in Clay's essay, the WARP replacement level has risen by about two wins, across the board. In other words, 2008 WARP leader Albert Pujols has a WARP of 11.3; using the previous methodology, that would have been 13.5. The changes are across the board, so the relative values between players remain the same—Pujols is seven wins better than Longoria, and 15 wins better than the Royals' Tony Peña, Jr.—but the scale is different. Longoria's 4.3 WARP would be unimpressive under the old methodology, so you might have to keep in mind that it's equivalent to an old WARP in the sixes.

The final column, Defense, shows the position, number of games, and fielding rating for the player at his primary position(s). Although we've featured fielding ratings in the past several editions of this book, there have been significant improvements in the methodology used to calculate these ratings this year. Once again, the details are in Clay Davenport's essay later in this book, but in a nutshell, the previous iterations of our defensive metric used mathematical assumptions to estimate how many plays each fielder potentially could have made, then compared that to the plays the fielder actually made to establish the fielder's performance. Although these estimates were pretty good, modern play-by-play data, available for both the major and minor leagues, gives us a much more accurate tally of where each ball was hit, and what type of batted ball it was (groundball, line drive, fly ball, etc.), making our new ratings much more accurate. As in previous seasons, the fielding rating is denominated in runs, so Longoria's 2008 line which reads "116-3B 3" means he played the equivalent of 116 full games at the hot corner, with a defensive performance that was three runs above average for third basemen.

The 2009 line is the PECOTA projection for the player in the upcoming season. Note that the player is projected into the league and park context as indicated by his team abbreviation; for example, Nick Swisher is projected as a Yankee, even though he appears in the White Sox chapter. All PECOTAs represent a player's projected major league performance.

The numbers beneath the 2009 forecast line—Breakout, Improve, Collapse, and Attrition—are also a part of PECOTA, and estimate the likelihood of changes in performance relative to a player's previously established level of production. PECOTA differs from other projection systems in that it uses historical comparables data to generate a probability distribution, rather than just a single forecast line. History might tell us, for example, that an old, slow hitter will manage just fine eighty percent of the time, but will have a disastrous, career-ending season (a "collapse") twenty percent of the time. Conversely, a young pitcher with a high walk rate might show a sudden and marked improvement (a "breakout") fifteen percent of the time, while failing to improve much at all in his other seasons. The Breakout, Collapse, Improve, and Attrition numbers are an attempt to quantify these sorts of performance changes. To be more precise about it:

- **Breakout Rate** is the percent chance that a hitter's equivalent runs produced per PA, or a pitcher's EqERA (see more on our pitcher stats below), will improve by at least 20 percent relative to the weighted average of his performance over his most recent seasons of 2006-2008 (with 2008 performance weighted more heavily). High breakout rates are indicative of upside potential.
- **Improve Rate** is the percent chance that a hitter's equivalent runs produced per PA, or a pitcher's EqERA, will improve *at all* relative to his baseline performance. A player who is expected to perform just the same as he has in the recent past will have an Improve Rate of 50 percent. Note that Breakout Rate is a subset of Improve Rate; Improve Rate is the chance that a player improves *at all*; Breakout Rate is the chance that he improves *a lot*.
- **Collapse Rate** is the percent chance that a position player's equivalent runs produced per PA, or a pitcher's EqERA, will decline by at least 25 percent relative to his baseline performance over his past three seasons. High collapse rates are indicative of downside risk.
- **Attrition Rate** operates on playing time rather than performance. Specifically, it measures the likelihood that a hitter's plate appearances, or a pitcher's innings pitched, will decrease by at least 50 percent relative to his established level. Attrition Rate captures any reason for substantial playing time decline, including catastrophic injuries, but also a player being benched, retiring in mid-season, or anything similar.

Breakout Rate and Collapse Rate can sometimes be counterintuitive for players who have already experienced a radical change in their performance levels. It's also worth noting that the projected decline in his rate performances is not indicative of an expected decline in underlying ability or skill, but rather something of an anticipated correction following his spectacular rookie season. PECOTAs projections will almost always correct for such extreme performances, much like Pythagenport record does at the team level.

The final piece of information, listed just to the right of the hitter's Attrition Rate, are his four highest scoring comparable players, as determined by PECOTA. Note that these are simply the four most similar comparables, and not the entire sample from which PECOTA generates its projection. Occasionally, a player's top comparables will not be representative of the larger sample that PECOTA uses. It's also important to note that established major leaguers are compared to other major leaguers only, while minor league players may be compared to major league or minor league players, with PECOTA strongly preferring the latter (in fact, PECOTA prefers to compare a player at the same level of competition: a Double-A player to other Double-A players, for example). All comparables represent a snapshot of how the listed player was performing at the same age as the current player, so if a 23-year-old hitter is compared to Sammy Sosa, he's actually being compared to a 23-year-old Sammy Sosa, which is much different than being compared to Sosa at the age of 31, when he was one of the best hitters on the planet, or 38, when he was an adequate DH who could stand to be platooned, though one could infer from the comparison that the current player has at least some chance of following Sosa's career path.

The Pitchers' Statistics

Now let's take a look at a sample pitcher's entry, this time from last season's NL Cy Young winner.

The first line and the **YEAR**, **TM**, **LVL**, and **AGE** columns are the same as in the hitter's example above, and should be self-explanatory. The next set of columns—**W** (Wins), **L** (Losses), **SV** (Saves), **G** (Games pitched), **GS** (Games Started), **IP** (Innings Pitched), **H** (Hits), **BB**, **SO**, **HR**—are the actual, unadjusted cumulative stats compiled by the pitcher during his stint.

Next is **GB%**, which is the percentage of all batted balls that were hit on the ground, including both outs and base hits. Because ground balls are more likely to be turned into outs than fly balls, the average GB% measured only from outs will be higher than for all batted balls. Furthermore, measuring GB% using just outs can be skewed by having an unusually good (or bad) infield or outfield defense. Therefore, we prefer to measure GB% using all batted balls, including both outs and hits. The average GB% for a major league pitcher in 2007 was about 45%; a pitcher with a GB% anywhere north of 50% can be considered a good groundball pitcher.

BABIP is batting average on balls in play, a statistic recently popularized by research indicating that pitchers exert a relatively small influence over the outcomes of balls in play (everything except home runs, strikeouts, walks, and times hit by pitch). A high BABIP is most likely due to a poor defense, or bad luck, rather than a pitcher's own abilities, and may be a good indicator of a potential rebound. A typical league-average BABIP is about .290, although in 2008, that number was .303. BABIP is not necessarily a strong indicator of a pitcher's overall performance—Mike Mussina, with a .327 BABIP, did a better job of preventing runs than the holder of the lowest BABIP in the majors, Detroit's Armando Galarraga (.239)—but it can help explain performances that exceed or fall short of expectations.

The next column is **STUFF**. Our definition of STUFF is a mathematical formula and not quite the same as the scouting term "stuff"; we aren't using radar guns or trying to evaluate the break on a curveball. STUFF is a shorthand rating of a pitcher's demonstrated skills, relative to his age and level; its primary use is to evaluate prospects, not established major league pitchers. An average major league starter, or a minor league pitcher who has shown the talent to develop into an average major league starter, will score a 10. Pitchers who score above 20 are excellent prospects; those above 30 belong the ranks of the truly elite. Lincecum's **STUFF** ratings in his short time in the minors justified the anticipation that he could succeed despite his slight stature and unorthodox mechanics. The largest single component of STUFF is strikeout rate, but walk rate, home run rate, hit rate, ERA, innings pitched per game, age, and age relative to league all figure into the final STUFF rating.

The **WHIP** and **ERA** columns are familiar to most fans, particularly those who play fantasy baseball. WHIP is the number of baserunners allowed per inning ([Walks + Hits] / IP), which makes it analogous to OBP. ERA is the pitcher's earned run average. Both of these statistics are unadjusted and untranslated.

The next column is Defense-Adjusted ERA, abbreviated as DERA. DERA is a version of Equivalent ERA that adjusts for the quality of the defense playing behind the pitcher when he's on the mound. This neutralizes the advantage enjoyed by a pitcher who plays in front of an exceptional group of glovemen, and the disadvantage suffered by a pitcher whose defense is less than competent. It is important not to confuse DERA with a different concept, DIPS ERA, which was created by Voros McCracken. DIPS ERA focuses on those elements of pitching performance that do not involve the defense,

Tim Lincecum — Bats: L   Throws: R   Height: 5' 11"   Weight: 170   Born: June 15, 1984   Age: 25

YEAR	TEAM	LVL	AGE	W	L	SV	G	GS	IP	H	BB	SO	HR	GB%	BABIP	STUFF	WHIP	ERA	DERA	EqH9	EqBB9	EqSO9	EqHR9	DEF	VORP	SN/WX
2006	SJO	A+	22	2	0	0	6	6	27	13	12	48	3	50.0%	.246	25	0.93	2.00	3.24	6.8	5.0	9.4	2.2	-2	6.6	—
2007	FRE	AAA	23	4	0	0	5	5	31	12	11	46	0	53.6%	.218	29	0.74	0.29	2.15	4.3	3.4	9.5	0.3	4	11.2	—
2007	SFN	MLB	23	7	5	0	24	24	146¹	122	65	150	12	48.1%	.292	36	1.28	4.00	3.86	7.3	3.5	8.5	0.7	0	26.0	3.87
2008	SFN	MLB	24	18	5	0	34	33	227	182	84	265	11	44.7%	.312	49	1.17	2.62	2.70	7.2	2.9	9.3	0.4	-3	72.3	8.70
2009	SFN	MLB	25	13	9	0	30	30	206	169	77	220	16	45.0%	.290	37	1.19	3.25	3.47	7.3	3.0	8.4	0.7	-0	48.4	6.83

Breakout: 7%   Improve: 21%   Collapse: 42%   Attrition: 9%   Comparables: Johnny Antonelli, Jim Maloney, Andy Messersmith, Cliff Fannin

Pitcher Statistics Example

taking the quality of defense out of the equation. DERA also takes the quality of defense out of the equation, but by measuring it and adjusting for it. The key to this adjustment is found in the next column, labeled **DEF**. DEF is a personal measure of the quality of the defense that played behind the pitcher, and its impact on run scoring. This metric uses the individual defensive ratings of each defender who played behind the pitcher when he was on the mound, adjusted for the pitcher's ground ball/fly ball tendencies (for example, a ground ball pitcher would be more affected by the quality of his infielders than his outfielders) to asses the total impact of defense on his performance.

The next four columns, all starting with "Eq," are the pitcher's rates of production (hits allowed per nine innings, strikeouts per nine innings, etc.) based on his "translated" statistics. As with the hitter example above, a pitcher's raw statistics are adjusted and converted to a neutral-park major league equivalent performance. We present the translated (or equivalent) per 9 inning rates of hits allowed (**EqH9**), walks issued (**EqBB9**), strikeouts recorded (**EqSO9**), and home runs surrendered (**EqHR9**).

VORP, again, is Value Over Replacement Player. A pitcher's VORP is the number of extra runs that a replacement level pitcher would have allowed to score if he pitched the same number of innings as this pitcher, based on his translated statistics. Slightly different standards are applied for starting and relief pitchers because of the different replacement levels for the two roles.

The final column, **SN/WX**, actually represents two statistics, each of which tell us how many wins the pitcher contributed to his team by applying a concept called "Win Expectation," which was discussed in the 2005 and 2006 editions of this book. The **WX** is short for **WXRL**, which refers to "**W**ins e**X**pected above **R**eplacement and adjusted for **L**ineup faced" for relief pitchers. For each bullpen appearance, Win Expectation looks at the situation the reliever faced when he entered the game—the score; the number and placement of men on base, if any; the inning and number of outs—and compares that to the situation when the reliever leaves the game, whether because he was replaced by another pitcher or because the game ended. By measuring the chances of his team winning at the beginning and the end of the appearance and taking the difference, Win Expectation determines the percentage of a win that the reliever contributed during his appearance. Since a 100 percent chance equals a win and a zero percent chance equals a loss, all chances in between follow suit. Thus if a reliever enters a game when his team has an 85 percent chance of winning and leaves with them

holding a 95 percent chance, as determined by Win Expectation, he contributed 0.1 wins. If he left with his team holding a 75 percent chance he would have contributed -0.1 wins. All of these fractional wins are then adjusted for the strength of the actual hitters faced, compared to replacement level, then added up to produce the pitcher's cumulative season total of expected wins above replacement adjusted for lineup, or WXRL.

WXRL has benefits over other statistics used to evaluate bullpen performance. Because it relies on the Win Expectation framework, it is sensitive to leverage, and will assign more value to a reliever who pitches well in a close game than to a reliever who is just as effective in a blowout. Unlike ERA, WXRL rewards a reliever for keeping any runners he inherits from scoring—it also punishes a reliever for leaving runners on base for the next pitcher to take care of, regardless of whether or not those runners come around to score. In this way, the reliever's contribution is isolated from that of both the pitcher that preceded him and the one that that followed him.

The **SN** in this final column is short for **SNLVAR**, which stands for "Support Neutral Lineup-adjusted Value Added above Replacement" and measures the performance of starting pitchers. Like WXRL, SNLVAR is based on Win Expectation is adjusted according to the actual hitters faced, and is compared to replacement level. For example, facing the slugging lineups of the AL East in the majority of his starts, Roy Halladay pitched against batters who averaged a .266/.342/.425 line last year; Brandon Webb, pitching in the weaker National League and the particularly weak NL West, faced opposing hitters who batted .254/.325/.393. Both SNLVAR and WXRL adjust for such differences, and both statistics are only listed for a player's major league appearances.

As with hitters, the pitcher's 2008 line and the one below it represent his PECOTA projection for the upcoming season and list his four most comparable pitchers.

The Managers' Statistics

Each team chapter ends with a manager's comment. Fact-based analysis of managers has been a sketchy proposition throughout baseball history. There are many aspects of a manager's job that defy enumeration, and as a result, few bother to try. For the most part, only two statistics are ever brought to bear in evaluating managers' performances: wins and losses.

However, we're a stubborn lot, so we've devised a series of statistics to look at various aspects of managerial performance. Most of these statistics fall into two broad categories: managerial decisions—that is, how long did the manager stick with his starters, how often did he use pinch-hitters and relievers, how frequently did his teams sacrifice and steal—and some of the results of those decisions. While the manager is not directly in control of the results—a good manager can be done in by poor execution on his team's part—those statistics can provide insight as to the manager's ability to identify and adapt to his team's strengths and weaknesses. Let's take a look at the reigning AL Manager of the Year, Joe Maddon.

Taking the columns from left to right, we start off with the **YEAR**, **TEAM**, and the team's actual record (**W-L**). **Pythag +/-** tells us by how many games the team under or over performed its Pythagenport record. As you can see above, Maddon's Rays were the rare team that actually hit their Pythagenport record on the head. That shouldn't be held against him—keep in mind that Pythag +/- is a mathematical expression of team performance, not an interpretation of the manager's work. That being said, it can be interesting to try to figure out how or why a team greatly under or over performed its Pythagenport record.

Next comes a group of statistics that measure a manager's use of and success with his pitching staff. **Avg PC** is the average pitch count of his starting pitchers in that particular year, and **100+P** and **120+P** are the numbers of games in which a manager had his starter exceed 100 or 120 pitches. **QS** is the total number of quality starts a manager received from his starting pitchers. We define a quality start as any game in which the starter lasted a minimum of six innings pitched and allowed no more than three runs. We prefer to use runs instead of the more commonly accepted unearned runs because the former are irrefutable fact—the runs scored—as opposed to a statistic dependent on judgment calls made by individual official scorers. **BQS** is Blown Quality Starts, a Baseball Prospectus invention that measures games in which the starter delivered a quality start through six innings, then lost it in the seventh inning or

later by allowing a fourth run. The fault for a Blown Quality Start lies primarily at the feet of the manager who left his starter in the game after the minimum requirements of the Quality Start had met. That said, a Blown Quality Start is not necessarily an indictment of the manager's abilities or tactics—a number of factors ranging from excellent offensive support to extremely poor bullpen support, can lead a manager to leave his starter in a game after they've thrown six quality innings. Conversely, the decision by a manager to "bank" quality starts by restricting his starters to only six innings can have downsides as well as it increases his bullpen's workload and increases the opportunity for the pen to blow a game in which a starter was cruising. Jim Leyland's Tigers had the most BQS in the majors last year, with 13, while Kansas City's Trey Hillman was the full-time manager who was most protective of his starters' quality starts, allowing only 3.8% of them to be blown.

Speaking of bullpen support, the next stats in the manager table tally how many pitching changes a manager made over the course of the season (**REL**) and how many times the reliever called upon didn't allow any runners, be they his own or inherited, to score (**REL w Zero R**). Bequeathed runners also count against REL w Zero R, which means even if a reliever did not allow a run to score on his watch, but left the game with a man on base, and the pitcher who replaced him allowed that runner to score, he does not earn his manager a tick in this column. Concluding the pitching section **IBB** is quite simply the number of intentional walks the manager ordered during the given season. Like some other strategic elements, you'll see large differences between leagues and between specific managers: Hillman called for four wide only 15 times in 2008, while Bobby Cox's Braves gave out free passes more than five times as often (80 intentional walks, the second straight year that the Braves led the league).

The next group of statistics deals with the manager's use of his bench. The first stat is **Subs**, which is the number of defensive substitutes the manager employed dur-

MANAGER: JOE MADDON

YEAR	TEAM	W-L	Pythag +/-	Avg PC	100+ P	120+ P	QS	BQS	REL	REL w Zero R	IBB	Subs	PH	PH Avg	PH HR	SB2	CS2	SB3	CS3	SAC Att	SAC %	POS SAC	Squeeze	Swing	In Play
2006	TBA	61-101	-3	93.0	49	1	62	5	444	228	39	68	80	.225	1	109	45	24	7	64	54.7%	32	4	153	112
2007	TBA	66-96	0	97.1	80	0	69	12	483	258	31	16	80	.159	1	114	43	16	4	48	70.8%	33	4	129	92
2008	TBA	97-65	5	96.0	71	0	77	4	448	289	29	50	131	.186	3	113	38	28	10	41	56.1%	20	1	135	94

Manager Statistics Example

ing the season. The next three stats tell us how often the manager used pinch-hitters (**PH**), the combined batting average of those pinch-hitters (**PH Avg**), and how many home runs they hit (**PH HR**). Again, these aren't reflective of any particular genius or lack of it; some managers simply like to pinch hit more than others. It's also important to keep in mind the differences between leagues; on average, NL managers pinch hit almost three times as often as their AL counterparts.

We then turn to the so-called "small ball" tactics, starting with the running game. The manager's aggressiveness on the bases is broken down by successful steals of second base (**SB2**) and times caught (**CS2**) and the times hit team was successful and not successful stealing third (**SB3** and **CS3**). Bunts, perhaps the most controversial tactic in the book, come next. We provide the number of sacrifices a team attempted (**SAC Att**) and their success rate (**SAC %**). Again, be sure to keep in mind the differences between leagues, as National League sacrifice attempts are greatly inflated by the fact that the pitchers hit in the senior circuit. To correct for this, we list the number of times a manager got a successful sacrifice from a position player (**POS SAC**), which allows for comparisons between the two leagues. For example, the Minnesota Twins finished behind 12 National League teams in sacrifice hits last year, but when we look at only sacrifices by position players, Ron Gardenhire's team led the majors by a wide margin with 47. We finish up with **Squeeze**, which counts the number of successful squeeze plays the team executed over the season. Joe Torre succeeded 2007 squeeze play leader Grady Little as manager of the Dodgers, and there must be something in the water at Chavez Ravine, because Torre blew away the field with 10 squeeze plays in 2008. Finally, we have a couple of statistics that attempt to measure the manager's investment in hit-and-run tactics and how well his team executed them. **Swing** is the number of times a hitter swung at a pitch while the runners were in motion, while **In Play** reflects how many times his hitters swung and made contact while those runners were off to the races.

The better you understand the statistical tools detailed above, the more you'll get out of this book. If you want more details about the statistics we use, you can consult the glossary at BaseballProspectus.com (www.baseballprospectus.com/glossary), or read our book *Baseball Between the Numbers*. BaseballProspectus.com also features daily articles and statistics updated throughout the regular season.

Derek Jacques with
Nate Silver, Clay Davenport, and Christina Kahrl

Arizona Diamondbacks

After the 2007 season, much was made of the observation that the Diamondbacks had finished significantly better than expected. If you drill all the way down to what Clay Davenport refers to as third-order wins, or what a team's record should have been after you adjust for its expected runs scored and allowed, league, and schedule, the Diamondbacks were an impressive 12 games better than you would have predicted. Sabermetric orthodoxy posits the old Bill James "Plexiglas Principle," suggesting that the D'backs would have returned whence they came in 2008, sliding back down toward the 78 wins we would have expected them to have won in 2007 instead of hanging around the 90 they did win.

In this instance as in so many others, however, orthodoxy is perhaps better seen as a suggestion; the Snakes did very nearly mount a successful defense of their division title, although they won just 82 games instead of the 84 they were expected to by third-order adjustments. They certainly hadn't sat still and accepted their inexorable sabermetrically ordained fate to slide backward: the December deal to land A's ace Danny Haren was indicative of an intent to contend. Haren, added to Brandon Webb and an interesting collection of young hitters, seemed to promise good things, and to some degree, this was correct: the lineup improved marginally in terms of team Equivalent Average (EqA), performing slightly better than expected in both years (five runs above in 2007, seven in 2008). A Haren-enhanced rotation saw its Support-Neutral Lineup-adjusted Value Added Rate (SNLVAR) move up from .528 and sixth best in the league to .541 (and fifth). A better lineup and a better rotation would leave you wondering: How did they come up short?

Perhaps predictably, a lot of attention went to the bullpen, in no small part because bullpen performance is unpredictable and because Arizona enjoyed the benefit of an especially effective pen in 2007, with a staff WXRL (reliever expected wins added) of 14.5 that rated second in the major leagues. Between seasons, general manager Josh Byrnes traded away fragile closer Jose Valverde to acquire the less-famous Chad Qualls from the Astros. This seemed to herald a potential unit-wide problem if you were inclined to get worked up over roles and "established closers"; Qualls certainly wasn't one, nor was first choice Brandon Lyon, and Tony Pena's breakthrough in 2007 was widely suspected of being a one-shot deal. All of these concerns proved to be reasonable, and management was inspired to deal for Nationals reliever Jon Rauch to shore up a pen that seemed to be delivering less than it had.

Nevertheless, as is too often the case with teams that didn't have enough famous people to engender a conceit that they were covered in the pen, the relief problems were overstated. The Snakes didn't slump in their relief pitching in 2008 relative to 2007: their Fair Runs Allowed (FRA) dropped from 4.39 and 15th in the majors to 4.65 and 19th. Their Adjusted Runs Prevented (ARP) went from 17th in the majors to 20th. The bullpen was no more a great strength in 2007 than it was a problem in 2008.

The real problem was that this wasn't a very good offensive ballclub, and the rotation, while improved, wasn't good enough to make up the difference. Getting hung up on the vagaries of relief pitching can help you lose the forest for the trees: by team EqA, the 2007 division-winning D'backs were 15th in the National

League; last year's second-place team was 13th. If quantitative analysis has proven one thing accepted inside the industry and out, it's that relief pitching performance is going to bounce around, and the absence or presence of an "established closer," however easy to get worked up over, can't make up for a critical component that is fundamentally bad. That was the lineup, not the bullpen.

In a competitive ecology that features unbalanced schedules, it's worth reevaluating the entire concept of the Plexiglas Principle. The D'backs were entirely in control of their own destiny, 4½ games up with little more than a month to go, after taking the first game of three from the Dodgers on August 29. If fielding a bad lineup is what provided the Windex, what made Arizona an easily observed fly on history's windscreen was losing the next two games and then a subsequent three-game set against the eventual division winners a week later.

An evaluation based upon general tendencies toward slip-sliding away cannot depend on such granularity. The pen was a mediocre unit in 2007, and a mediocre unit in 2008. The lineup was lousy, and that's even after making allowances for Josh Byrnes and company's active attempts to fix it after both Eric Byrnes and later Orlando Hudson were lost to injury for the balance of the season. Having already swung their preseason deal to land a starter of Haren's caliber and seen their club get off to a terrific start (21-9 through 30 games), the brass wasn't about to let this opportunity slip by if they could avoid it. After wasting a month on trying to play Alexis Romero in Justin Upton's place while the latter was on the disabled list, they traded for slugger Adam Dunn with three weeks left in August; after nearly two weeks of winging it at second after losing Hudson, they added David Eckstein with a month to go. So slender were the margins by which the Diamondbacks were beaten by the Dodgers that the timeliness of these moves is of more significance than any other factor. Romero, Chris Burke, and Augie Ojeda are not good options with which to shore up a weak lineup, and they never were.

Note that once they lost Eric Byrnes, the Snakes were largely a station-to-station team; only the Padres and Pirates attempted fewer steals. This might seem odd, given that this is a young team, but despite the presence of so many high-profile youngsters, Arizona is not really your classic collection of blue-chip prospects doing the fleet and agile sorts of things classically associated with young players. The D'backs posted the third-best unintentional walk rate in the NL, drawing a free pass in 8.7 percent of all plate appearances, while post-

ing the second-worst mark in the majors for their strikeout rate (behind only the free-swinging Fish). Those are what you might normally consider the hallmarks of an old team, with a heavy tilt toward a certain Ben Grieve-ness that might frighten Arizona fans for good reason.

While there are chicken/egg issues with causation—do the Rays not run much because they don't have speed, or because they're the sort of smart outfit that understands the limits of the virtues of running when you play in a bandbox?—a number of the Snakes' young hitters possess what are usually considered "old player" skills. Mark Reynolds and Justin Upton ranked among the top 10 players in the majors in their Three True Outcomes (TTO) percentages of all plate appearances (homers, walks, and strikeouts), and Chris Snyder ranked 17th. Chris B. Young generated a lot of the three outcomes, but because he also had 699 plate appearances (PA), his overall TTO percentage ranked a relatively modest 67th among all hitters with 200 or more PA.

Table 1. Everything Happens at Home Plate: Baseball's Three True Outcomes Leaders

Rk	Player	PA	BB%	K%	HR%	TTO%
1.	Jack Cust, OAK	598	18.6	32.9	5.5	57.0
2.	Adam Dunn, CIN-ARI	651	18.7	25.2	6.1	50.1
3.	Mark Reynolds, ARI	613	10.4	33.3	4.6	48.3
4.	Carlos Pena, TBA	607	15.8	27.4	5.1	48.3
5.	Kelly Shoppach, CLE	403	8.9	33.0	5.2	47.1
6.	Jarrod Saltalamacchia, TEX	230	13.5	32.2	1.3	46.9
7.	Ryan Howard, PHI	700	11.6	28.4	6.9	46.9
8.	Mike Napoli, LAA	274	12.8	25.6	7.3	45.6d
9.	Justin Upton, ARI	417	12.9	29.0	3.6	45.6
10.	Dan Uggla, FLO	619	12.4	27.6	5.2	45.2

Few deals seemed better suited for keeping with a team's established skills than the decision to trade for Dunn, one of only two men in the game who finished ahead of Reynolds in his ability to do something decisive without putting a ball in play. But acquiring Dunn while helping make up for the absences of both Byrnes and Justin Upton also helped Arizona secure a place in history. We were treated to two of the 10 most TTO-oriented teams in the 40-year era of divisional play just this past season. While the Marlins finished with the second-best mark by delivering a walk, strikeout, or homer in 34.2 percent of all of their PA, coming up just short of the 34.5 percent achieved by the '94 Tigers, the 2008 Diamondbacks finished 10th overall with 33.0 percent. To round out the rest of the top 10, you find the

2001 Brewers (who set the team record for strikeouts, with 1,399), the McGwire-aided 2000 Cardinals, the Dunn-led 2004 and 2005 Reds, the 2001 Padres, and the 1999 and 2000 Oakland A's, busily a-birthing Moneyball powered by Jason Giambi, Matt Stairs, and Ben Grieve. (For the curious, the high-water marks in the 1980s were the '86 editions of the Phillies and Mariners at 30.5 and 30.4 percent, respectively; in the 1970s, no team had a TTO higher than 30 percent, although the 1970 Padres and Mets came closest.)

To no small extent, the home runs are a product of the team's environment, as the Snakes play in one of the latter-day bandboxes that populate the NL. The walk rates of hitters like Reynolds (10.4 percent), Upton (12.9), and Snyder (13.9) are what we generally consider positives, and Young (8.9 percent) and Conor Jackson (9.6) were certainly both chipping in goodly numbers of base-running opportunities when they weren't putting the ball in play.

The club's offensive problems are most visibly reflected in the teamwide strikeout rate. The park doesn't have a bad rap for visibility issues; indeed, like Coors Field, not only does Chase Field suppress strikeouts, but given the number of good things that happen on balls in play, including the greater likelihood of extra bases, the free-swinging Snakes aren't doing nearly enough to exploit their environment. Away from home, their inability to make contact became crippling. The D'backs were absolutely awful on the road, hitting a paltry .234/.309/.385 away from Chase, against .268/.345/.446 at home. Obviously, there was a significant drop-off in terms of the outcomes on balls in play, and that, combined with their jump in strikeouts from 19.6 percent of all PA at home to 22.2 percent of all PA on the road, meant fewer balls in play to help drive their averages in the right direction.

Add in that the D'backs are among the more popup-happy lineups in baseball, ranking third in the NL in 2008 and 2006, and tops in the majors in 2007, and you start to get a sense of the scope of the problem: Arizona's offense falls victim to an especially large number of bad at-bats, and that's not a park problem, but something much more fundamentally creditable to who's playing and what they're capable of. Given the scope of the problem, you can have a lot of sympathy for the hitting coach Rick Schu.

Can the Diamondbacks fix it, given that we shouldn't anticipate a lot of turnover within their collection of youngsters in the immediate future? While Stephen Drew has blossomed into the sort of stardom that was expected of him, and Upton's ascendance to superstardom seems assured, it remains to be seen if experience is going to help fix players as gifted yet flawed as Reynolds and Young. Reynolds' combination of skills might conjure up comparisons to Matt Williams or Dean Palmer in the earlier stages of their careers, but both of those hitters established themselves as future stars in their age-24 seasons, whereas Reynolds took a step backward in his. Nor did Chris Young improve on his mildly disappointing rookie season. Both have the kind of talent that might see them step forward as firmly as Drew did in his age-25 season last year; that would be normal, but the problem with Young and Reynolds is that they're anything but normal as young players go. In addition, if Chad Tracy is healthy in 2009, he doesn't really fix the problem as much as exacerbate it, both in terms of his strengths (power against right-handed pitching) and in terms of his problems (a modest OBP, lots of strikeouts).

If the Diamondbacks do fix the lineup, it won't be a moment too soon. They have the rotation to win now, even after dealing Micah Owings in the Dunn deal and watching Randy Johnson depart as a free agent. Brandon Webb and Danny Haren match up with any team's top starting duo, Doug Davis makes a solid midrotation starter, and while an additional veteran might be reassuring, Max Scherzer and Yusmeiro Petit have the potential to round things out.

In the absence of cold, hard cash, however, it appears that the D'backs are going to invest in a new crop of second-rate second-base patches to replace departing free agent Hudson, and barring their finding a taker for the debilitated Byrnes or Tracy, they're pretty well stuck with the same deficient lineup. As a result, the outcome of the 2009 season depends on how well and how quickly several young players mature: Scherzer and perhaps also Petit in the rotation; Young and Reynolds in the lineup; and, perhaps most importantly, Upton representing a true wild card, a player who might explode on the league and give Arizona a real prime-time player in the everyday lineup. In 2008, he showed signs of the player he could become both before and after an epic slump and a quad injury. Just 21 this year, his time could now be upon us.

Failing that, the Diamondbacks will struggle to win 90 games, and while that doesn't necessarily keep them out of contention in the NL West, without a big offensive improvement, their chances of adding to 2007's brief bit of glory are rather remote.

HITTERS

Chris Burke | 2B/OF | Bats: R | Throws: R | Height: 5' 11" | Weight: 180 | Born: March 11, 1980 | Age: 29

YEAR	TEAM	LVL	AGE	PA	R	2B	3B	HR	RBI	BB	SO	SB	CS	EqBRR	AVG	OBP	SLG	EqAVG	EqOBP	EqSLG	EqA	VORP	WARP	DEFENSE				
2006	HOU	MLB	26	413	58	23	1	9	40	27	77	11	1	1.6	.276	.347	.418	.276	.345	.416	.270	14.6	0.8	38-2B	4	32-CF	-6	
2007	HOU	MLB	27	363	39	19	2	6	28	27	52	9	3	-1.0	.229	.304	.357	.233	.309	.370	.240	-4.6	0.1	34-2B	2	22-CF	0	
2008	ARI	MLB	28	199	20	5	1	2	12	27	33	5	0	0.1	.194	.310	.273	.182	.302	.255	.217	-7.9	0.3	13-LF	8	10-2B	1	
2009	ARI	MLB	29	142	16	6	1	3	13	13	22	3	1	0.2	.245	.323	.369	.239	.316	.360	.238	0.2	0.3	37-2B	-1			

Breakout: 28% Improve: 43% Collapse: 39% Attrition: 47%   Comparables: Carl Warwick, Reid Nichols, Steve Lombardozzi, James Mouton

It seems clear that Burke will never be the player we once thought he was. The question is, what happened? He put up some nice numbers in the minors, and as the 10th overall pick in the 2001 draft, he had the scouting reports to match. Perhaps Burke is just a Quad-A guy, and maybe he was damaged by Houston when Craig Biggio's quest for 3,000 hits stopped the team from giving him a fair shake when his time came. We'll never know, and at this point, it's probably too late for him to turn it around. Nontendered in December, his second act, if he has one, will come elsewhere.

Eric Byrnes | OF | Bats: R | Throws: R | Height: 6' 2" | Weight: 210 | Born: February 16, 1976 | Age: 33

YEAR	TEAM	LVL	AGE	PA	R	2B	3B	HR	RBI	BB	SO	SB	CS	EqBRR	AVG	OBP	SLG	EqAVG	EqOBP	EqSLG	EqA	VORP	WARP	DEFENSE			
2006	ARI	MLB	30	606	82	37	3	26	79	34	88	25	3	3.1	.267	.313	.482	.258	.306	.463	.265	24.3	2.5	116-CF	1	10-RF	-1
2007	ARI	MLB	31	698	103	30	8	21	83	57	98	50	7	6.7	.286	.353	.460	.276	.347	.452	.282	35.7	6.6	109-LF	21	28-RF	1
2008	ARI	MLB	32	224	28	13	1	6	23	16	36	4	4	-1.4	.209	.272	.369	.209	.272	.379	.219	-9.5	-0.6	47-LF	1		
2009	ARI	MLB	33	389	51	21	2	12	48	29	59	12	4	0.8	.266	.327	.442	.259	.319	.431	.260	5.4	1.4	93-LF	4		

Breakout: 19% Improve: 53% Collapse: 20% Attrition: 27%   Comparables: Emil Brown, Jeffrey Leonard, Glenallen Hill, Al Cowens

Arizona's biggest mistake heading into 2008 was the compound boner of trading Carlos Quentin to ensure playing time for Byrnes while making things even worse by committing $30 million to Byrnes through 2010. The veteran responded by having a horrible year, mostly because of hamstring injuries. Actually, "hamstring injury" is putting it lightly, as one of Byrne's was nearly torn off the bone. Arizona fans have a minimum of two more years to let this particular decision bother them, but as a speed player with busted wheels, you can anticipate how well this turns out.

Tony Clark | 1B | Bats: S | Throws: R | Height: 6' 7" | Weight: 245 | Born: June 15, 1972 | Age: 37

YEAR	TEAM	LVL	AGE	PA	R	2B	3B	HR	RBI	BB	SO	SB	CS	EqBRR	AVG	OBP	SLG	EqAVG	EqOBP	EqSLG	EqA	VORP	WARP	DEFENSE	
2006	ARI	MLB	34	147	13	4	0	6	16	13	40	0	0	-0.7	.197	.279	.364	.189	.277	.348	.217	-6.7	-0.9	29-1B	-3
2007	ARI	MLB	35	245	31	5	1	17	51	21	59	0	0	-0.6	.249	.310	.511	.237	.303	.502	.269	7.5	0.8	51-1B	2
2008	SDN	MLB	36	107	5	3	0	1	11	19	32	0	0	-0.5	.239	.374	.307	.250	.383	.318	.261	1.2	0.1		
2008	ARI	MLB	36	77	7	2	0	2	13	12	23	0	0	0.2	.206	.338	.333	.190	.325	.317	.236	-1.5	-0.1	15-1B	0
2009	ARI	MLB	37	120	13	5	0	4	14	16	30	0	0	-1.0	.250	.353	.406	.243	.345	.396	.260	2.1	0.1	33-1B	-1

Breakout: 32% Improve: 53% Collapse: 34% Attrition: 44%   Comparables: Dick Stuart, Bobby Bonilla, Jim Hickman, Greg Myers

Last year was one of those seasons where Clark's performance couldn't overcome his reputation as a clubhouse leader and role model to young players. As easy as it would be to write him off, Clark has become something like the Bret Saberhagen of bench bats, seemingly only producing in every other year. It's not like it's going to cost a lot to see if you can find that odd-year magic again, which is why the Snakes re-upped him for a year and $800,000.

Stephen Drew — SS

Bats: L   Throws: R   Height: 6' 1"   Weight: 185   Born: March 16, 1983   Age: 26

YEAR	TEAM	LVL	AGE	PA	R	2B	3B	HR	RBI	BB	SO	SB	CS	EqBRR	AVG	OBP	SLG	EqAVG	EqOBP	EqSLG	EqA	VORP	WARP	DEFENSE
2006	TUC	AAA	23	383	55	16	3	13	51	33	50	3	3	1.5	.284	.340	.462	.239	.295	.395	.239	-4.4	0.6	80-SS -2
2006	ARI	MLB	23	226	27	13	7	5	23	14	50	2	0	1.5	.316	.357	.517	.301	.347	.488	.284	17.7	1.4	54-SS -2
2007	ARI	MLB	24	619	60	28	4	12	60	60	100	9	0	2.5	.238	.313	.370	.227	.308	.360	.241	3.3	-0.5	144-SS -17
2008	ARI	MLB	25	663	91	44	11	21	67	41	109	3	3	-4.8	.291	.333	.502	.284	.327	.502	.277	42.8	2.3	146-SS -19
2009	ARI	MLB	26	608	80	34	5	20	77	52	98	6	2	0.7	.278	.342	.470	.271	.334	.458	.270	29.6	2.6	142-SS -6

Breakout: 39% Improve: 58% Collapse: 14% Attrition: 10%   Comparables: Kurt Stillwell, Jay Bell, Todd Walker, Russ Adams

This really is just the beginning for Drew, because his raw talent is unquestionable, he's just turning 26, and he hit .326/.372/.556 after the 2008 All-Star break. If you can think of any reason to be pessimistic about Drew's future, we'd love to hear it. Until then, we'll keep projecting stardom, and that's on the modest side. If he's a legitimate MVP candidate at some point over the next three years, you shouldn't be shocked in the least.

Adam Dunn — OF/1B

Bats: L   Throws: R   Height: 6' 6"   Weight: 275   Born: November 9, 1979   Age: 29

YEAR	TEAM	LVL	AGE	PA	R	2B	3B	HR	RBI	BB	SO	SB	CS	EqBRR	AVG	OBP	SLG	EqAVG	EqOBP	EqSLG	EqA	VORP	WARP	DEFENSE		
2006	CIN	MLB	26	683	99	24	0	40	92	112	194	7	0	-0.7	.234	.365	.490	.220	.358	.466	.285	21.9	3.1	148-LF -3		
2007	CIN	MLB	27	632	101	27	2	40	106	101	165	9	2	1.5	.264	.386	.554	.254	.384	.545	.310	45.9	4.3	133-LF -8		
2008	CIN	MLB	28	464	58	14	0	32	74	80	120	1	1	-2.0	.233	.373	.528	.229	.371	.534	.303	27.2	2.3	103-LF -10		
2008	ARI	MLB	28	187	21	9	0	8	26	42	44	1	0	-0.6	.243	.417	.472	.231	.412	.441	.303	10.2	1.4	21-RF -1	15-1B -4
2009	ARI	MLB	29	601	97	25	1	36	98	105	141	4	1	-2.8	.262	.396	.541	.255	.387	.528	.308	34.6	3.8	141-LF -10		

Breakout: 28% Improve: 62% Collapse: 9% Attrition: 14%   Comparables: Troy Glaus, Jim Thome, Mike Epstein, Pat Burrell

You certainly can't call Dunn unreliable, because in the last four years he's walked over 100 times while hitting 40 home runs on the nose. The trade to Arizona gave him the opportunity to make a ton of money in his free-agency walk year, but he was still the same player, striking out a ton, not hitting for average, showing limited mobility in the field, and, oh yeah, those walks and homers. While the low batting averages tend to obscure Dunn's value among the traditionally minded, back-of-the-bubblegum-card crowd, he does play back some of the runs on defense. Somewhere and someday, there's an American League team's DH spot with Dunn's name on it.

David Eckstein — MI

Bats: R   Throws: R   Height: 5' 7"   Weight: 175   Born: January 20, 1975   Age: 34

YEAR	TEAM	LVL	AGE	PA	R	2B	3B	HR	RBI	BB	SO	SB	CS	EqBRR	AVG	OBP	SLG	EqAVG	EqOBP	EqSLG	EqA	VORP	WARP	DEFENSE		
2006	SLN	MLB	31	552	68	18	1	2	23	31	41	7	6	-1.9	.292	.350	.344	.296	.352	.346	.248	8.3	2.2	117-SS 5		
2007	SLN	MLB	32	484	58	23	0	3	31	24	22	10	1	-1.7	.309	.356	.382	.317	.363	.401	.274	22.3	1.7	107-SS -10		
2008	TOR	MLB	33	303	27	18	0	1	23	24	27	2	1	-2.5	.277	.354	.358	.278	.357	.375	.262	8.2	1.4	54-SS 1	5-2B 1
2008	ARI	MLB	33	73	5	3	0	1	4	7	5	0	0	1.0	.219	.301	.313	.219	.301	.312	.221	-2.2	0.4	17-2B 4		
2009	ARI	MLB	34	285	31	14	1	2	24	20	22	3	1	-0.6	.279	.341	.361	.272	.334	.352	.243	7.2	0.9	70-SS -1		

Breakout: 12% Improve: 33% Collapse: 43% Attrition: 40%   Comparables: Cookie Rojas, Jeff Frye, Roberto Peña, Rey Sanchez

As Eckstein reaches his middle 30s and his skills degrade, the best he can hope for is sticking around a few more years as the mini-me middle-infield version of Tony Clark, where people decide that he's such a great guy to have around that they'll put up with the soft production. It's rarely a good idea, but it works here and there. Eckstein is enthusiastic about continuing his career as a second baseman (his position in college and the minors), but the fact that he's not a shortstop anymore might hurt his value too much for his effort and attitude to matter.

Orlando Hudson — 2B

Bats: S   Throws: R   Height: 6' 0"   Weight: 185   Born: December 12, 1977   Age: 31

YEAR	TEAM	LVL	AGE	PA	R	2B	3B	HR	RBI	BB	SO	SB	CS	EqBRR	AVG	OBP	SLG	EqAVG	EqOBP	EqSLG	EqA	VORP	WARP	DEFENSE
2006	ARI	MLB	28	650	87	34	9	15	67	61	78	9	6	3.8	.287	.354	.454	.275	.347	.436	.270	29.9	4.6	150-2B 15
2007	ARI	MLB	29	601	69	28	9	10	63	70	87	10	2	2.7	.294	.376	.441	.282	.371	.428	.282	33.4	5.0	133-2B 13
2008	ARI	MLB	30	455	54	29	3	8	41	40	62	4	1	0.2	.305	.367	.450	.297	.361	.445	.281	25.6	2.7	102-2B 1
2009	ARI	MLB	31	524	69	28	3	9	54	50	68	7	2	0.3	.291	.360	.420	.283	.352	.410	.267	20.4	2.6	123-2B 2

Breakout: 6% Improve: 31% Collapse: 28% Attrition: 12%   Comparables: Tom Herr, Jose Vidro, Bill Mueller, Johnny Ray

For the second straight year, the O-Dog was playing Gold Glove–level defense at second while having a very nice year offensively (that despite being miscast as a three-hole hitter), and then was unavailable during the stretch run, due to injury. (In 2008, it was a thumb; the year before, it was a wrist.) Hudson is a free agent at press time and healthy; interested teams should note that though he seemed to become a two-way player during his time in Arizona, hitting .294/.365/.448 overall, there was a good deal of park-generated production at work, with Hudson batting .315/.393/.509 in 832 PA in the cozy confines at Chase Field and .274/.339/.392 in 874 PA in the cold, uncaring outside world.

Conor Jackson — 1B/LF — Bats: R Throws: R Height: 6' 2" Weight: 225 Born: May 7, 1982 Age: 27

YEAR	TEAM	LVL	AGE	PA	R	2B	3B	HR	RBI	BB	SO	SB	CS	EqBRR	AVG	OBP	SLG	EqAVG	EqOBP	EqSLG	EqA	VORP	WARP	DEFENSE			
2006	ARI	MLB	24	556	75	26	1	15	79	54	73	1	0	-1.4	.291	.368	.441	.279	.357	.426	.275	13.3	0.4	120-1B	-11		
2007	ARI	MLB	25	477	56	29	1	15	60	53	50	2	2	-0.4	.284	.368	.467	.274	.362	.458	.281	21.0	1.3	98-1B	-4		
2008	ARI	MLB	26	612	87	31	6	12	75	59	61	10	2	2.0	.300	.376	.446	.293	.370	.447	.285	28.9	3.7	74-LF	9	65-1B	-1
2009	ARI	MLB	27	602	85	34	3	16	76	63	66	8	3	-0.9	.295	.373	.461	.287	.365	.450	.283	21.7	2.9	141-1B	4		

Breakout: 19% Improve: 44% Collapse: 20% Attrition: 4%   Comparables: Carlos Lee, Garrett Atkins, John Ellis, Gabe Kapler

Finally given a platoon-free job at first base, Jackson had a year that was solid but unspectacular. His ability to hit for average has never been in question, and he draws a decent number of walks, but doubts about his power potential have persisted throughout his career. He didn't do much to help refute those concerns with just 12 bombs, including none in the last 51 games of the season (hitting just .260/.323/.335 over that span). Basically, Jackson is a right-handed Mark Grace without the glove work in a league that has evolved to a point where that ain't worth terribly much. The Snakes attempted to rectify this situation by moving Jackson to left so that Chad Tracy could play first base—not that Tracy profiles any better at the position.

Miguel Montero — C — Bats: L Throws: R Height: 5' 11" Weight: 195 Born: July 9, 1983 Age: 25

YEAR	TEAM	LVL	AGE	PA	R	2B	3B	HR	RBI	BB	SO	SB	CS	EqBRR	AVG	OBP	SLG	EqAVG	EqOBP	EqSLG	EqA	VORP	WARP	DEFENSE	
2006	TEN	AA	22	337	24	18	0	10	46	39	44	0	3	0.0	.270	.362	.436	.244	.326	.410	.255	3.6	1.3	73-C	-1
2006	TUC	AAA	22	154	21	5	0	7	29	14	21	1	1	-3.2	.321	.396	.515	.277	.348	.460	.277	6.7	0.7	28-C	-3
2006	ARI	MLB	22	17	0	1	0	0	3	1	3	0	0	-0.1	.250	.294	.313	.250	.294	.312	.211	-0.6	0.0	5-C	0
2007	ARI	MLB	23	244	30	7	0	10	37	20	35	0	0	-1.1	.224	.292	.397	.216	.288	.380	.236	0.7	-0.3	57-C	-5
2008	ARI	MLB	24	207	24	16	1	5	18	19	49	0	0	0.8	.255	.330	.435	.245	.320	.435	.260	6.5	0.6	46-C	-1
2009	ARI	MLB	25	281	34	15	1	11	40	28	45	0	0	-0.9	.269	.351	.468	.262	.343	.456	.273	14.5	2.0	69-C	-3

Breakout: 48% Improve: 70% Collapse: 13% Attrition: 25%   Comparables: Joe Garagiola, Ed Herrmann, Ron Hodges, Eddie Taubensee

With Chris Snyder's emergence, Montero became a backup who got some extra at-bats because he was also Randy Johnson's personal catcher. In truth, there's not a huge difference between these two backstops; Snyder has the defensive edge and a bit more power, but Montero is the better all-around hitter. Other teams recognize this, which is why Montero was high on this winter's wish list for teams looking for catching help. Pending a trade, Montero has been taking some ground balls at third base in hopes of becoming the next Todd Zeile or something more lucrative than being the exclusive caddy for a pitcher who is no longer with the team.

Augie Ojeda — INF — Bats: S Throws: R Height: 5' 8" Weight: 170 Born: December 20, 1974 Age: 34

YEAR	TEAM	LVL	AGE	PA	R	2B	3B	HR	RBI	BB	SO	SB	CS	EqBRR	AVG	OBP	SLG	EqAVG	EqOBP	EqSLG	EqA	VORP	WARP	DEFENSE			
2006	IOW	AAA	31	378	40	11	1	3	25	46	38	4	1	1.0	.248	.356	.320	.196	.289	.264	.202	-25.2	-2.0	90-SS	-9		
2007	TUC	AAA	32	118	20	8	0	0	17	10	11	1	0	0.6	.323	.395	.404	.243	.310	.301	.225	-4.2	0.7	28-SS	6		
2007	ARI	MLB	32	132	16	2	2	1	12	15	13	1	0	0.7	.274	.354	.354	.257	.344	.336	.250	2.1	-0.1	19-2B	1	9-SS	-3
2008	ARI	MLB	33	272	27	9	2	0	17	26	24	0	0	1.4	.242	.343	.299	.236	.337	.288	.230	-3.2	0.2	32-2B	0	14-SS	2
2009	ARI	MLB	34	172	17	6	1	0	12	16	19	1	0	0.1	.249	.332	.310	.242	.324	.302	.224	-0.2	0.2	44-2B	1		

Breakout: 27% Improve: 53% Collapse: 35% Attrition: 48%   Comparables: Ted Kubiak, Dennis Hocking, Jamey Carroll, Jeff Reboulet

Ojeda was so valuable in filling in for Hudson at the end of 2007 that the D'backs brought him back as a utility player. He quickly showed why he'd bounced from Triple-A team to Triple-A team when he was in his late 20s—

though Ojeda is willing to take a walk, slugging percentages of under .300 just don't make you a keeper. Re-signed in September before arbitration, if he's kept to a reserve role behind even Felipe Lopez at the keystone, he's an adequate acquired taste.

Gerardo Parra   OF

Bats: L   Throws: L   Height: 6' 1"   Weight: 186   Born: May 6, 1987   Age: 22

YEAR	TEAM	LVL	AGE	PA	R	2B	3B	HR	RBI	BB	SO	SB	CS	EqBRR	AVG	OBP	SLG	EqAVG	EqOBP	EqSLG	EqA	VORP	WARP	DEFENSE		
2006	MSO	Rk	19	303	46	18	4	4	43	25	30	23	7	2.7	.328	.386	.469	.232	.271	.338	.213	-26.9	-2.2	65-RF	-4	
2007	SBN	A	20	488	64	25	4	6	57	30	51	24	8	0.0	.320	.370	.435	.252	.292	.351	.226	-14.1	-2.0	91-RF	-7	15-CF -1
2007	VIS	A+	20	109	11	2	1	2	14	4	17	2	3	-1.4	.284	.303	.382	.221	.239	.317	.187	-8.1	-0.7	20-CF	0	
2008	VIS	A+	21	224	26	8	4	2	19	23	31	12	4	-1.7	.301	.381	.413	.234	.308	.328	.229	-7.1	-0.8	41-CF	-5	8-RF 0
2008	MOB	AA	21	302	35	14	6	4	33	24	34	16	9	-1.3	.275	.341	.419	.234	.286	.358	.227	-10.0	-1.2	59-CF	-7	12-RF 0
2009	ARI	MLB	22	572	69	31	6	7	50	39	84	20	8	1.2	.266	.320	.386	.259	.313	.377	.241	-0.1	0.7	134-CF	-7	

Breakout: 57% Improve: 78% Collapse: 12% Attrition: 14%   Comparables: Rafael Alvarez, Melky Cabrera, Alejandro De Aza, Alex Romero

Parra won the Midwest League batting title in 2007 and entered the year as a top 100 prospect. He followed that up by hitting pretty well in the Cal League, and he held his own at Double-A. Unfortunately, Parra's power didn't develop, and scouts now see him as more of a guy who can only play center field in a pinch, instead of being a legitimate defender at the position. That kind of profile has a lot of people wondering if he's just a classic tweener, which equals fourth outfielder, which equals an uncertain future.

Tim Raines Jr.   OF

Bats: S   Throws: R   Height: 5' 10"   Weight: 195   Born: August 31, 1979   Age: 29

YEAR	TEAM	LVL	AGE	PA	R	2B	3B	HR	RBI	BB	SO	SB	CS	EqBRR	AVG	OBP	SLG	EqAVG	EqOBP	EqSLG	EqA	VORP	WARP	DEFENSE		
2006	HAR	AA	26	269	40	11	0	6	23	23	54	25	5	1.8	.292	.352	.413	.211	.263	.312	.207	-18.2	-1.7	27-CF	2	15-RF 0
2006	NWO	AAA	26	70	8	4	0	1	5	3	13	5	0	1.8	.227	.261	.333	.194	.229	.284	.185	-6.8	-0.4	12-2B	1	
2007	CCH	AA	27	92	15	2	1	1	7	7	18	4	2	0.0	.244	.319	.329	.163	.217	.244	.155	-11.5	-1.0	20-CF	-2	
2007	ROU	AAA	27	309	43	14	3	11	49	15	47	21	2	0.0	.333	.368	.519	.272	.306	.431	.259	4.4	0.9	46-LF	4	
2008	TUC	AAA	28	540	96	30	13	18	78	26	96	28	8	1.6	.311	.346	.530	.227	.259	.384	.224	-19.4	-2.3	83-CF	-10	22-RF -2
2009	ARI	MLB	29	438	49	22	5	10	43	23	103	15	5	1.6	.244	.288	.393	.237	.281	.383	.230	-5.5	0.6	104-CF	0	

Breakout: 39% Improve: 63% Collapse: 24% Attrition: 22%   Comparables: Tito Landrum, Butch Davis, Alex Diaz, Chris Jones

Raines had his peak, age-28 year in 2008; too bad it was in Triple-A. He established career highs in nearly every offensive category except for stolen bases (he ripped off 81 in the Carolina League way, *way* back in the day), but never got the call. If he had picked up a thing or two about plate discipline from his dad, Raines might have had some semblance of a major league career. Instead, all his big year probably bought him is another year of making a decent living at Triple-A.

Mark Reynolds   3B

Bats: R   Throws: R   Height: 6' 1"   Weight: 200   Born: August 3, 1983   Age: 25

YEAR	TEAM	LVL	AGE	PA	R	2B	3B	HR	RBI	BB	SO	SB	CS	EqBRR	AVG	OBP	SLG	EqAVG	EqOBP	EqSLG	EqA	VORP	WARP	DEFENSE		
2006	LNC	A+	22	322	64	18	2	23	77	41	72	1	1	-1.0	.337	.422	.670	.239	.314	.484	.269	9.7	0.6	29-SS	-5	15-3B -2
2006	TEN	AA	22	127	23	7	0	8	21	11	37	0	1	1.0	.272	.346	.544	.259	.323	.509	.274	6.6	0.4	12-LF	0	9-3B 0
2007	MOB	AA	23	155	28	9	2	6	22	20	32	2	1	0.3	.306	.394	.537	.268	.346	.471	.278	7.9	-0.1	31-3B	-7	6-2B -1
2007	ARI	MLB	23	414	62	20	4	17	62	37	129	0	1	-0.9	.279	.349	.495	.266	.340	.478	.278	19.3	2.5	95-3B	5	
2008	ARI	MLB	24	613	87	28	3	28	97	64	204	11	2	2.7	.239	.320	.458	.233	.315	.458	.266	14.9	2.0	146-3B	-1	
2009	ARI	MLB	25	567	79	30	3	29	84	60	153	9	3	0.4	.260	.344	.506	.253	.336	.494	.280	23.5	2.9	133-3B	0	

Breakout: 32% Improve: 58% Collapse: 11% Attrition: 21%   Comparables: Dean Palmer, Jay Buhner, Mike Pagliarulo, Nick Esasky

Let's not get too caught up on that one number. Yes, 204 strikeouts is ridiculous. Sure, it's like eight percent of all-time strikeout leader Reggie Jackson's career total, and Reynolds got there in just one season. Nevertheless, it's only five more than Ryan Howard's total in 2008, and just 10 more than Adam Dunn's career high. The thing is, when you can hit 40-plus home runs and draw 100 walks, as those gentlemen do, you can make up for 204 strikeouts. Unfortunately, Reynolds has about two-thirds that much power and half the plate discipline, and that just isn't going to cut it. Have we mentioned that he stinks defensively at third, too, and that's really his only position?

Alex Romero   OF   Bats: L   Throws: R   Height: 6′ 1″   Weight: 185   Born: September 9, 1983   Age: 25

YEAR	TEAM	LVL	AGE	PA	R	2B	3B	HR	RBI	BB	SO	SB	CS	EqBRR	AVG	OBP	SLG	EqAVG	EqOBP	EqSLG	EqA	VORP	WARP	DEFENSE
2006	NBR	AA	22	200	29	11	2	5	16	26	19	15	7	1.7	.281	.384	.461	.250	.342	.430	.267	5.6	0.4	44-LF -2
2006	ROC	AAA	22	262	20	8	2	0	26	15	22	6	2	-0.4	.250	.300	.301	.222	.270	.268	.192	-19.7	-1.7	43-LF 2 22-RF -3
2007	TUC	AAA	23	584	82	32	6	5	66	37	53	12	10	-4.3	.310	.354	.421	.257	.302	.357	.228	-11.2	-0.4	97-RF 1 16-LF 3
2008	TUC	AAA	24	186	28	9	2	3	19	11	19	4	3	0.4	.324	.368	.451	.269	.312	.389	.240	0.1	-0.1	25-CF -5 10-RF 2
2008	ARI	MLB	24	142	13	8	2	1	12	3	20	4	0	-0.9	.230	.250	.341	.228	.248	.338	.207	-6.0	-1.1	25-RF -1 5-LF -3
2009	ARI	MLB	25	386	43	20	3	5	34	26	47	7	3	0.6	.258	.312	.375	.251	.305	.366	.233	-5.4	-0.2	92-RF -2

Breakout: 36% Improve: 53% Collapse: 21% Attrition: 19%   Comparables: Trent Oeltjen, Tim Leiper, Matty Alou, Endy Chavez

Once upon a time, a "Free Alex Romero" campaign briefly flowered, as he consistently put up solid numbers in the minors, yet rarely showed up on any prospect lists. There was a reason for that absence, as he lacked tools and secondary skills. While he's a better hitter than he showed in his big-league debut, he's really no more than your classic Triple-A insurance type. Fortunately, fans don't take to "Recapture Alex Romero"-type campaigns with the same enthusiasm.

Jeff Salazar   OF   Bats: L   Throws: L   Height: 6′ 0″   Weight: 190   Born: November 24, 1980   Age: 28

YEAR	TEAM	LVL	AGE	PA	R	2B	3B	HR	RBI	BB	SO	SB	CS	EqBRR	AVG	OBP	SLG	EqAVG	EqOBP	EqSLG	EqA	VORP	WARP	DEFENSE
2006	CSP	AAA	25	381	62	14	7	9	39	46	64	12	5	0.0	.265	.357	.433	.212	.298	.361	.233	-10.6	-2.1	82-CF -18
2006	COL	MLB	25	67	13	4	0	1	8	11	16	2	0	1.8	.283	.409	.415	.264	.403	.377	.292	3.9	-0.1	12-CF -5
2007	TUC	AAA	26	472	76	31	9	10	68	56	56	18	5	1.4	.299	.385	.495	.237	.323	.395	.255	0.8	3.4	91-CF 14 12-LF 4
2007	ARI	MLB	26	103	13	6	1	1	10	9	19	2	0	1.0	.277	.340	.394	.269	.340	.387	.259	1.3	0.5	20-RF 3
2008	TUC	AAA	27	115	29	6	3	4	18	14	14	3	0	0.6	.364	.439	.606	.275	.348	.451	.279	4.8	0.4	8-CF 0 5-RF -1
2008	ARI	MLB	27	152	17	5	3	2	12	21	41	0	2	0.0	.211	.331	.344	.203	.329	.336	.235	-3.7	-0.7	15-LF -4 10-RF 0
2009	PIT	MLB	28	174	24	9	2	5	19	21	33	3	1	0.8	.252	.347	.436	.251	.347	.451	.275	7.9	1.0	45-CF -3

Breakout: 48% Improve: 64% Collapse: 22% Attrition: 31%   Comparables: Brady Anderson, Jim Dwyer, John Vander Wal, Bob Speake

Salazar has gotten much further than was expected when he was an eighth-round pick out of college in 2002. He nearly went 30-30 in his full-season debut in the minors, but he's nowhere near that good. The Diamondbacks went back and forth between him and Romero as the primary extra outfielder (an oxymoronic term, we know), but Salazar offers more value as he runs better, works the count better, and has a little more pop. Still, he's not starting material. The D'backs nontendered him in December, making him a free agent at press time.

Chris Snyder   C   Bats: R   Throws: R   Height: 6′ 3″   Weight: 230   Born: February 12, 1981   Age: 28

YEAR	TEAM	LVL	AGE	PA	R	2B	3B	HR	RBI	BB	SO	SB	CS	EqBRR	AVG	OBP	SLG	EqAVG	EqOBP	EqSLG	EqA	VORP	WARP	DEFENSE
2006	ARI	MLB	25	213	19	9	0	6	32	22	39	0	0	-0.4	.277	.349	.424	.262	.338	.410	.265	5.8	1.7	54-C 6
2007	ARI	MLB	26	380	37	20	0	13	47	40	67	0	1	-3.5	.252	.342	.433	.240	.336	.422	.264	14.4	2.9	100-C 9
2008	ARI	MLB	27	404	47	22	1	16	64	56	101	0	0	-0.5	.237	.348	.452	.228	.342	.440	.272	16.6	3.2	104-C 7
2009	ARI	MLB	28	372	44	19	1	13	48	46	78	0	0	-1.6	.254	.355	.451	.248	.347	.440	.271	15.7	2.8	89-C 3

Breakout: 21% Improve: 45% Collapse: 27% Attrition: 28%   Comparables: Gene Oliver, Todd Pratt, Charles Johnson, Chris Hoiles

Snyder is the best .237-hitting catcher around, as he walks, nearly half of his hits go for extra bases, and he's a good defender who played error-free ball last year while being the fifth-best catcher in the National League in throwing out runners (31 percent). He's the kind of player who will get more attention once he stays healthy and goes deep 20 times, as he missed about a month last year recovering from a "testicular fracture." Quick word of advice: don't ask Will Carroll to give you an in-depth explanation of that injury—you'll lose sleep for weeks. Giving him a three-year, $14.25 million extension with a club option for 2012 locks him up through his best years.

Chad Tracy — 1B

Bats: L Throws: R Height: 6' 2" Weight: 200 Born: May 22, 1980 Age: 29

YEAR	TEAM	LVL	AGE	PA	R	2B	3B	HR	RBI	BB	SO	SB	CS	EqBRR	AVG	OBP	SLG	EqAVG	EqOBP	EqSLG	EqA	VORP	WARP	DEFENSE			
2006	ARI	MLB	26	662	91	41	0	20	80	54	129	5	1	-0.2	.281	.343	.451	.270	.334	.435	.267	15.4	2.4	142-3B	1		
2007	ARI	MLB	27	260	30	18	2	7	35	29	43	0	0	-1.4	.264	.346	.454	.249	.338	.444	.271	7.9	1.3	42-3B	2	13-1B	2
2008	ARI	MLB	28	292	25	16	0	8	39	16	49	0	0	0.5	.267	.308	.414	.261	.302	.412	.245	0.4	-0.3	59-1B	-1		
2009	ARI	MLB	29	328	39	19	1	12	47	29	56	1	0	-0.8	.274	.341	.467	.267	.333	.456	.269	9.5	1.1	79-1B	3		

Breakout: 35% Improve: 66% Collapse: 15% Attrition: 23%   Comparables: Jim Spencer, Henry Rodriguez, Dick Nen, Gail Harris

Since showing so much promise in his second full season—which is now four years ago—Tracy's skills have been eroded by injuries, specifically a microfractured knee that required extensive surgery. He's now immobile and without much leverage in his swing, leaving him a powerless first baseman when Arizona was hoping he could come back to play third base to spot for the struggling Reynolds. It's hard to discern how much value is left here, but Arizona still is committed to $4.75 million to him for 2009 and will almost assuredly not pick up his option the following year.

Justin Upton — RF

Bats: R Throws: R Height: 6' 3" Weight: 205 Born: August 25, 1987 Age: 21

YEAR	TEAM	LVL	AGE	PA	R	2B	3B	HR	RBI	BB	SO	SB	CS	EqBRR	AVG	OBP	SLG	EqAVG	EqOBP	EqSLG	EqA	VORP	WARP	DEFENSE			
2006	SBN	A	18	501	71	28	1	12	66	52	96	15	7	-5.0	.263	.343	.413	.205	.269	.328	.210	-29.6	-3.4	103-CF	-16		
2007	VIS	A+	19	150	27	6	2	5	17	19	28	9	4	-1.1	.341	.433	.540	.258	.336	.402	.258	2.3	0.4	28-CF	0		
2007	MOB	AA	19	306	48	17	4	13	53	37	51	10	7	1.3	.309	.399	.556	.269	.346	.496	.282	18.2	1.5	58-CF	-3	8-RF	0
2007	ARI	MLB	19	152	17	8	3	2	11	11	37	2	0	-0.4	.221	.283	.364	.209	.276	.353	.221	-5.3	-0.8	35-RF	-3		
2008	TUC	AAA	20	68	13	3	1	3	10	7	26	2	0	1.3	.279	.353	.508	.242	.309	.484	.267	1.9	0.1	12-RF	-1		
2008	ARI	MLB	20	417	52	19	6	15	42	54	121	1	4	-0.8	.250	.353	.463	.242	.347	.454	.272	8.7	1.0	97-RF	-4		
2009	ARI	MLB	21	504	76	28	4	21	73	56	112	11	4	0.8	.278	.361	.506	.270	.353	.494	.286	21.3	2.5	119-RF	-1		

Breakout: 59% Improve: 82% Collapse: 12% Attrition: 21%   Comparables: Bob Horner, B.J. Upton, Darryl Strawberry, Jeff Burroughs

In the first 11 games of the season, Upton hit .415 with five home runs and pretty much looked like the greatest thing since sliced bread. His final numbers turned out to be simply decent, but sliced bread still just might need to give up the crown before all's said and done. Upton's 2008 was basically the equivalent of Ken Griffey Jr.'s first season—a year filled with greatness and rawness in equal doses. Griffey improved the next year, and two years later, he was a top 10 MVP finisher. Don't be surprised if Upton follows the same route.

Josh Whitesell — 1B

Bats: L Throws: L Height: 6' 3" Weight: 220 Born: April 14, 1982 Age: 27

YEAR	TEAM	LVL	AGE	PA	R	2B	3B	HR	RBI	BB	SO	SB	CS	EqBRR	AVG	OBP	SLG	EqAVG	EqOBP	EqSLG	EqA	VORP	WARP	DEFENSE	
2006	HAR	AA	24	467	47	11	0	19	56	53	125	2	6	-6.8	.264	.354	.433	.225	.304	.370	.233	-9.4	-1.1	84-1B	0
2007	HAR	AA	25	487	70	23	1	21	74	87	107	6	2	1.4	.284	.425	.512	.215	.337	.394	.258	2.3	0.4	87-1B	0
2008	TUC	AAA	26	560	86	36	0	26	110	74	136	1	2	-0.1	.328	.425	.568	.262	.350	.448	.275	21.7	-0.1	115-1B	-16
2009	ARI	MLB	27	477	51	22	1	17	59	51	138	1	1	-1.5	.238	.327	.418	.232	.319	.408	.250	0.1	-0.1	113-1B	-4

Breakout: 14% Improve: 32% Collapse: 38% Attrition: 23%   Comparables: Pat Dodson, Larry Broadway, Troy Neel, Eric Crozier

Whitesell was previously an organizational solider in the Nationals' system; he was always a little old for his level, but also drew a ton of walks and hit for solid power. The D'backs picked him up to fill out their Triple-A roster, and he ended up finishing among the Pacific Coast League's leaders in several categories and finally getting to the big leagues. Arizona thinks he's for real, and they'll give him a legitimate shot at a bench job this spring.

Chris Young   CF

Bats: R   Throws: R   Height: 6' 2"   Weight: 180   Born: September 5, 1983   Age: 25

YEAR	TEAM	LVL	AGE	PA	R	2B	3B	HR	RBI	BB	SO	SB	CS	EqBRR	AVG	OBP	SLG	EqAVG	EqOBP	EqSLG	EqA	VORP	WARP	DEFENSE	
2006	TUC	AAA	22	466	78	32	4	21	77	52	71	17	5	0.9	.276	.363	.532	.237	.318	.466	.268	11.2	2.7	100-CF	5
2006	ARI	MLB	22	78	10	4	0	2	10	6	12	2	1	0.4	.243	.308	.386	.229	.295	.357	.232	-0.1	0.1	17-CF	2
2007	ARI	MLB	23	624	85	29	3	32	68	43	141	27	6	0.8	.237	.295	.467	.229	.291	.464	.258	16.0	0.8	142-CF	-9
2008	ARI	MLB	24	699	85	42	7	22	85	62	165	14	5	0.8	.248	.315	.443	.241	.309	.442	.258	15.9	2.0	157-CF	0
2009	ARI	MLB	25	601	85	36	4	24	82	56	114	19	5	1.9	.268	.341	.487	.261	.334	.475	.276	24.5	3.8	141-CF	3

Breakout: 43%   Improve: 67%   Collapse: 10%   Attrition: 16%   Comparables: Mike Cameron, Reggie Sanders, Woodie Held, Ron Gant

Sophomore slump, or cause for concern? There are still more questions than answers here. The power drop can be attributed to a nagging wrist injury, and the decline in steals might be explained by his losing the leadoff job, but to fully write off the season requires those excuses and more. Young still strikes out a ton. So, to become the star people thought he would be, he needs to keep improving his plate discipline and turn more of 2008's doubles back into balls that go over the fence. A very good second half last year (.278/.343/.508) gives cause for optimism.

PITCHERS

Tony Barnette

Bats: R   Throws: R   Height: 6' 2"   Weight: 190   Born: November 9, 1983   Age: 25

YEAR	TEAM	LVL	AGE	W	L	SV	G	GS	IP	H	BB	SO	HR	GB%	BABIP	STUFF	WHIP	ERA	DERA	EqH9	EqBB9	EqSO9	EqHR9	DEF	VORP	SN/WX
2006	MSO	Rk	22	6	4	0	15	15	76[1]	81	20	74	9	41.5%	.307	-52	1.33	3.90	8.21	15.2	4.2	3.5	3.5	-4	-18.8	—
2007	SBN	A	23	8	8	1	26	25	160	160	28	108	11	44.8%	.301	-42	1.18	3.60	7.40	12.3	3.0	2.3	1.9	-6	-27.7	—
2008	MOB	AA	24	11	7	0	27	27	153[2]	143	42	133	17	43.1%	.292	-20	1.20	3.86	6.05	9.8	2.7	4.8	1.7	11	-7.3	—
2009	ARI	MLB	25	5	10	0	32	21	123	163	48	76	27	43.0%	.330	-3	1.71	7.01	6.83	11.5	3.0	4.9	1.9	1	-13.3	-0.62

Breakout: 6%   Improve: 42%   Collapse: 22%   Attrition: 16%   Comparables: Dan Rambo, Mark DiFelice, Allen Morlock, Ryan Franklin

In 2007, Barnette was "just" one of those polished college guys who pitched well in the Midwest League, so nobody took notice. Arizona jumped him up two levels in '08, and after a slow start, he was Double-A Mobile's best pitcher during the second half of the season, making himself a prospect in the process. This is a something-for-nothing deal, where a low draft pick is better than you thought, because his average stuff plays up due to command and a fearless approach. His ceiling is as a fifth starter or middle reliever, but hey, you can't argue with something for nothing.

Billy Buckner

Bats: R   Throws: R   Height: 6' 2"   Weight: 215   Born: August 27, 1983   Age: 25

YEAR	TEAM	LVL	AGE	W	L	SV	G	GS	IP	H	BB	SO	HR	GB%	BABIP	STUFF	WHIP	ERA	DERA	EqH9	EqBB9	EqSO9	EqHR9	DEF	VORP	SN/WX
2006	HDS	A+	22	7	1	0	16	16	90[1]	92	47	85	6	56.6%	.328	-8	1.54	3.90	6.27	11.3	5.9	4.5	1.3	5	-6.0	—
2006	WIC	AA	22	5	3	0	13	13	75[2]	78	39	63	7	57.1%	.308	-8	1.56	4.67	7.07	10.9	5.0	4.5	1.4	6	-11.6	—
2007	WIC	AA	23	1	3	0	4	3	19[1]	20	6	13	4	53.0%	.258	-24	1.35	4.66	7.58	9.9	3.3	3.3	2.8	3	-4.2	—
2007	OMA	AAA	23	9	7	0	27	15	104[2]	108	26	83	11	48.9%	.319	-5	1.28	3.78	4.55	10.8	2.5	5.3	1.2	-1	11.3	—
2007	KCA	MLB	23	1	2	0	7	5	34	37	16	17	5	41.8%	.308	-15	1.56	5.29	5.52	10.2	4.4	4.1	1.5	2	3.1	0.23
2008	TUC	AAA	24	5	10	0	21	20	116[1]	136	43	69	9	46.9%	.332	-11	1.54	4.95	5.80	10.4	3.4	3.3	0.9	-4	-2.5	—
2008	ARI	MLB	24	1	0	0	10	0	14	16	4	11	3	39.5%	.325	-2	1.43	3.21	3.46	11.1	2.1	6.9	2.1	1	3.9	0.10
2009	ARI	MLB	25	4	6	0	32	12	83[1]	107	39	51	14	47.0%	.330	-5	1.75	6.24	6.14	11.2	3.7	4.9	1.5	1	-3.4	0.12

Breakout: 5%   Improve: 23%   Collapse: 45%   Attrition: 28%   Comparables: John Habyan, Ryan Hancock, Bruce Tanner, Steve Cummings

Acquired from the Royals prior to the season for Alberto Callaspo, Buckner is the type of pitcher who throws strikes and succeeds by mixing his pitches effectively. Pitchers of this make and model have little margin for error, as Buckner demonstrated last year, when his control took a step backward. He pitched well at the end of the year in a relief role; the dimensions of the bullpen probably define the boundaries of his future.

Juan Cruz

Bats: R Throws: R Height: 6' 2" Weight: 155 Born: October 15, 1978 Age: 30

YEAR	TEAM	LVL	AGE	W	L	SV	G	GS	IP	H	BB	SO	HR	GB%	BABIP	STUFF	WHIP	ERA	DERA	EqH9	EqBB9	EqSO9	EqHR9	DEF	VORP	SN/WX
2006	ARI	MLB	27	5	6	0	31	15	94²	80	47	88	7	43.1%	.289	20	1.34	4.18	3.86	7.2	3.9	7.5	0.6	1	19.7	2.94
2007	ARI	MLB	28	6	1	0	53	0	61	45	32	87	7	35.0%	.302	25	1.26	3.10	3.25	6.9	4.1	10.8	0.9	-2	12.2	0.79
2008	ARI	MLB	29	4	0	0	57	0	51²	34	31	71	5	30.0%	.287	26	1.26	2.61	2.70	6.5	4.7	10.4	0.9	0	15.9	1.17
2009	ARI	MLB	30	3	3	3	45	1	57	50	32	67	7	37.0%	.300	19	1.44	4.33	4.27	7.5	4.5	9.4	1.1	0	9.3	0.87

Breakout: 5% Improve: 20% Collapse: 52% Attrition: 8% Comparables: Scott Williamson, Armando Benitez, Matt Mantei, Octavio Dotel

For the past seven years, Cruz has been one of those guys who, if you saw him on the right day, you'd be convinced was one of the premier relievers in the game, because when he's on, his overpowering fastball/slider combination is truly closer-worthy. Occasional control issues remain his bugaboo, but he saved his best year for the right time, and as a free agent with a reputation that is less than his talent and production, the team that signs him is going to get a steal.

Doug Davis

Bats: R Throws: L Height: 6' 4" Weight: 210 Born: September 21, 1975 Age: 33

YEAR	TEAM	LVL	AGE	W	L	SV	G	GS	IP	H	BB	SO	HR	GB%	BABIP	STUFF	WHIP	ERA	DERA	EqH9	EqBB9	EqSO9	EqHR9	DEF	VORP	SN/WX
2006	MIL	MLB	30	11	11	0	34	34	203¹	206	102	159	19	46.7%	.314	14	1.51	4.91	4.58	8.8	3.9	6.4	0.7	-2	18.2	2.85
2007	ARI	MLB	31	13	12	0	33	33	192²	211	95	144	21	48.7%	.325	11	1.59	4.25	3.97	9.6	3.9	6.4	0.9	1	28.7	3.99
2008	ARI	MLB	32	6	8	0	26	26	146	160	64	112	13	48.9%	.332	14	1.53	4.32	3.72	9.7	3.3	6.1	0.7	-7	19.4	2.97
2009	ARI	MLB	33	7	8	0	22	22	124	133	54	92	15	48.0%	.310	12	1.50	4.82	4.84	9.3	3.4	5.9	1.0	1	12.0	2.29

Breakout: 5% Improve: 22% Collapse: 41% Attrition: 31% Comparables: Rudy May, Gary Peters, Pat Rapp, Kenny Rogers

We all know what Doug Davis is—he's the same thing he's been for years, a guy who depends on a curve, and when it's on, he can give you six or seven solid innings and keep you in the ballgame but never dominate. None of that matters a bit. What matters is that the dude did it having come back from cancer, and that's way cool. Rock on, Doug Davis. Rock on.

Juan Gutierrez

Bats: R Throws: R Height: 6' 3" Weight: 200 Born: July 14, 1983 Age: 25

YEAR	TEAM	LVL	AGE	W	L	SV	G	GS	IP	H	BB	SO	HR	GB%	BABIP	STUFF	WHIP	ERA	DERA	EqH9	EqBB9	EqSO9	EqHR9	DEF	VORP	SN/WX
2006	CCH	AA	22	8	4	0	20	20	103	94	34	106	10	41.5%	.288	6	1.24	3.06	4.82	10.0	3.3	5.9	1.4	2	8.4	—
2007	ROU	AAA	23	5	10	0	26	25	156	154	63	108	17	48.6%	.295	-12	1.39	4.15	6.26	9.4	3.9	4.4	1.3	11	-10.9	—
2007	HOU	MLB	23	1	1	0	7	3	21¹	25	6	16	3	32.4%	.338	4	1.45	5.92	5.48	10.1	2.1	6.3	1.3	0	-0.0	-0.08
2008	TUC	AAA	24	5	11	0	25	22	116²	152	44	87	11	47.9%	.371	-15	1.68	6.09	6.79	12.0	3.5	4.3	1.0	-13	-14.9	—
2009	ARI	MLB	25	4	8	0	25	16	95²	118	40	62	15	46.0%	.320	2	1.65	6.09	6.04	10.7	3.3	5.1	1.4	1	-2.8	0.35

Breakout: 17% Improve: 47% Collapse: 20% Attrition: 25% Comparables: Beltran Perez, Esteban Loaiza, Jose Mesa, Rodrigo Lopez

Gutierrez was one of the key elements in the deal that sent Jose Valverde to Houston. The big-bodied power righty with a good sinker was seen as nearly big-league ready when Arizona added him. Instead, he was arguably the most frustrating prospect in the Snakes' system. He was maddeningly inconsistent, often sandwiching one good start between two in which he'd fail to get out of the fourth inning. He has those occasional successes to cling to, but his spot on the totem pole is nonetheless much lower.

Dan Haren

Bats: R Throws: R Height: 6' 5" Weight: 220 Born: September 17, 1980 Age: 28

YEAR	TEAM	LVL	AGE	W	L	SV	G	GS	IP	H	BB	SO	HR	GB%	BABIP	STUFF	WHIP	ERA	DERA	EqH9	EqBB9	EqSO9	EqHR9	DEF	VORP	SN/WX
2006	OAK	MLB	25	14	13	0	34	34	223	224	45	176	31	45.4%	.292	11	1.21	4.12	4.76	8.7	1.8	6.3	1.2	9	40.8	5.39
2007	OAK	MLB	26	15	9	0	34	34	222²	214	55	192	24	45.4%	.292	18	1.21	3.07	3.95	8.5	2.1	6.7	1.0	5	55.6	6.23
2008	ARI	MLB	27	16	8	0	33	33	216	204	40	206	19	44.7%	.308	33	1.13	3.33	3.65	8.3	1.4	7.5	0.7	9	53.7	6.35
2009	ARI	MLB	28	14	9	0	31	31	210¹	200	45	189	24	46.0%	.290	29	1.16	3.53	3.56	8.3	1.7	7.1	1.0	2	49.4	6.96

Breakout: 14% Improve: 51% Collapse: 11% Attrition: 5% Comparables: Gaylord Perry, Shane Reynolds, Frank Sullivan, Aaron Harang

Once you adjust for park and the lack of a designated hitter, Dan Haren was almost the same pitcher he was in 2007—merely one of the better pitchers in baseball. Whether or not the deal that brought him to Arizona was a good deal for the Diamondbacks is still an open issue. A critic might note that nearly every prospect they sent to Oakland looked mighty good in the minors, while Haren didn't pitch his team into the postseason and looked downright tired by the time August rolled around. One has to wonder if staying healthy has almost worked against him, as he hasn't missed a turn for four years while tossing almost 900 innings in the process. Color us a bit concerned.

Randy Johnson

Bats: R   Throws: L   Height: 6' 10"   Weight: 231   Born: September 10, 1963   Age: 45

YEAR	TEAM	LVL	AGE	W	L	SV	G	GS	IP	H	BB	SO	HR	GB%	BABIP	STUFF	WHIP	ERA	DERA	EqH9	EqBB9	EqSO9	EqHR9	DEF	VORP	SN/WX
2006	NYA	MLB	42	17	11	0	33	33	205	194	60	172	28	42.7%	.288	11	1.24	5.00	5.17	8.7	2.6	6.8	1.2	-4	13.8	2.48
2007	ARI	MLB	43	4	3	0	10	10	56²	52	13	72	7	43.1%	.338	39	1.15	3.81	3.58	8.6	1.8	10.1	1.0	1	12.3	1.46
2008	ARI	MLB	44	11	10	0	30	30	184	184	44	173	24	42.7%	.313	22	1.24	3.91	3.68	8.7	1.8	7.3	1.1	-7	27.2	3.46
2009	*SFN*	*MLB*	*45*	*8*	*7*	*0*	*21*	*21*	*127¹*	*126*	*37*	*111*	*14*	*43.0%*	*.300*	*22*	*1.28*	*3.82*	*4.01*	*8.8*	*2.4*	*6.9*	*1.0*	*-0*	*25.6*	*3.44*

Breakout: 34% Improve: 70% Collapse: 30% Attrition: 32%   *Comparables: Phil Niekro, Jamie Moyer, Tommy John, Hoyt Wilhelm*

Sure, Johnson is well into his 40s and has a bad back and a bad haircut and needs some extra rest here and there, but every once in a while, especially toward the end of the year, when the back bothered him less, he still kind of looked like the Big Unit of old. He's clearly a fraction of his former self, but he wants to get to 300 wins (he's just five away), and he still puts people away. The Giants certainly didn't sign him for one year and $8 million for charity's sake; they signed someone who can help them win ballgames.

Wil Ledezma

Bats: L   Throws: L   Height: 6' 4"   Weight: 210   Born: January 21, 1981   Age: 28

YEAR	TEAM	LVL	AGE	W	L	SV	G	GS	IP	H	BB	SO	HR	GB%	BABIP	STUFF	WHIP	ERA	DERA	EqH9	EqBB9	EqSO9	EqHR9	DEF	VORP	SN/WX
2006	TOL	AAA	25	4	3	0	12	12	71²	60	23	66	6	39.4%	.295	-1	1.17	2.53	4.22	9.8	3.7	5.9	1.4	-1	9.8	—
2006	DET	MLB	25	3	3	0	24	7	60¹	60	23	39	5	36.5%	.286	-2	1.38	3.58	3.75	9.0	3.3	5.1	0.8	-2	13.0	1.04
2007	DET	MLB	26	3	1	0	23	0	35²	38	26	24	4	42.2%	.312	-11	1.79	4.79	5.19	9.9	6.2	5.5	1.0	0	3.0	-0.03
2007	ATL	MLB	26	0	2	0	12	0	9¹	12	4	7	1	58.8%	.344	-13	1.71	7.74	6.30	10.8	2.7	6.3	0.9	-3	-4.1	-0.24
2007	SDN	MLB	26	0	0	0	9	1	14¹	20	8	16	2	33.3%	.429	6	1.95	6.29	5.14	12.9	4.5	9.6	1.3	-2	-2.1	0.12
2008	SDN	MLB	27	0	2	0	25	6	54¹	49	38	49	4	39.6%	.306	8	1.60	4.48	5.07	8.0	5.2	7.0	0.7	1	3.5	0.49
2008	ARI	MLB	27	0	0	0	3	0	4	2	3	4	0	27.3%	.200	4	1.25	0.00	0.00	4.5	6.8	6.8	0.0	0	2.5	0.01
2009	*WAS*	*MLB*	*28*	*2*	*3*	*1*	*32*	*2*	*44¹*	*44*	*24*	*38*	*5*	*41.0%*	*.297*	*4*	*1.51*	*4.71*	*5.10*	*8.9*	*4.2*	*6.6*	*1.0*	*0*	*3.3*	*0.30*

Breakout: 16% Improve: 35% Collapse: 33% Attrition: 42%   *Comparables: Dean Stone, Mike Kilkenny, Brad Havens, Mike Stanton*

The Padres got Ledezma through waivers at the middle of the season in order to send him to Triple-A, but when they tried it again in September, the bullpen-desperate D'backs couldn't resist grabbing him. He's long been frustrating to scouts, as left-handers who can get it up into the mid-90s don't exactly grow on trees, but his lack of control and a reliable secondary offering make job security unlikely. As if to demonstrate this point, Arizona nontendered him, but somebody will bite on the hard-throwing lefty, because some team always does.

Brandon Lyon

Bats: R   Throws: R   Height: 6' 1"   Weight: 195   Born: August 10, 1979   Age: 29

YEAR	TEAM	LVL	AGE	W	L	SV	G	GS	IP	H	BB	SO	HR	GB%	BABIP	STUFF	WHIP	ERA	DERA	EqH9	EqBB9	EqSO9	EqHR9	DEF	VORP	SN/WX
2006	ARI	MLB	26	2	4	0	68	0	69¹	68	22	46	7	44.0%	.289	-2	1.30	3.90	4.11	8.2	2.4	5.4	0.8	4	15.3	1.74
2007	ARI	MLB	27	6	4	2	73	0	74	70	22	40	2	43.4%	.287	6	1.24	2.68	2.81	8.1	2.3	4.6	0.2	2	24.0	4.32
2008	ARI	MLB	28	3	5	26	61	0	59¹	75	13	44	7	40.9%	.343	-2	1.48	4.70	3.41	10.7	1.6	5.8	0.9	-7	4.3	1.31
2009	*ARI*	*MLB*	*29*	*3*	*4*	*12*	*47*	*0*	*54¹*	*59*	*16*	*37*	*7*	*44.0%*	*.300*	*1*	*1.38*	*4.33*	*4.33*	*9.5*	*2.3*	*5.4*	*1.2*	*1*	*9.0*	*0.98*

Breakout: 8% Improve: 22% Collapse: 49% Attrition: 24%   *Comparables: Dave Heaverlo, Matt Whiteside, Chuck Crim, Carlos Reyes*

Somebody somewhere is going to do something very stupid this winter and give Brandon Lyon a big chunk of change because of those 26 saves. They're going to ignore the 4.78 ERA and the .301 opponent's batting average for the double-digit number in the saves column while saying to themselves, "Now, there's a proven guy who can help us." And they're going to get what they deserve.

Reid Mahon

Bats: R **Throws: R** **Height: 6' 3"** **Weight: 215** **Born: June 1, 1983** **Age: 26**

YEAR	TEAM	LVL	AGE	W	L	SV	G	GS	IP	H	BB	SO	HR	GB%	BABIP	STUFF	WHIP	ERA	DERA	EqH9	EqBB9	EqSO9	EqHR9	DEF	VORP	SN/WX
2006	YAK	A-	23	2	3	4	22	0	36²	32	14	25	4	61.2%	.252	-56	1.27	4.23	10.02	11.4	5.3	1.9	3.3	2	-15.9	—
2007	SBN	A	24	4	4	11	32	0	45²	34	8	28	1	65.5%	.239	-30	0.92	1.77	5.86	8.0	2.7	1.9	0.8	0	-1.2	—
2007	VIS	A+	24	1	1	8	11	0	14	10	2	9	1	52.4%	.220	-21	0.86	1.29	4.15	7.6	2.1	2.8	1.4	2	2.1	—
2008	MOB	AA	25	0	0	18	33	0	41	45	10	33	5	55.6%	.317	-28	1.34	3.07	5.82	11.6	2.6	4.4	1.9	1	-0.9	—
2008	TUC	AAA	25	0	2	6	19	0	24	22	14	18	3	45.9%	.271	-20	1.50	5.25	6.85	8.0	5.3	4.2	1.1	2	-3.3	—
2009	ARI	MLB	26	2	4	0	24	6	53²	67	25	27	9	51.0%	.310	-11	1.71	6.38	6.36	10.9	3.6	4.0	1.5	1	-3.5	-0.13

Breakout: 14% Improve: 45% Collapse: 29% Attrition: 9%   **Comparables: Mike DeJean, Dave Paveloff, Ryan Smith, Jason Martines**

Mahon is a great story: he went undrafted as a position player, but an area scout remembered seeing him throw a mop-up game and signed him for $500, good money for a kid who was working at a golf course at the time. It was a good call, too, as the big-bodied Mahon has become a sleeper prospect, thanks to an outstanding sinker that reaches the mid-90s at times. His inability yet to find a dependable second pitch has hampered him in the upper levels, but team officials are convinced that he'll eventually be a big-league bullpen fixture.

Jarrod Parker

Bats: R **Throws: R** **Height: 6' 1"** **Weight: 180** **Born: November 24, 1988** **Age: 20**

YEAR	TEAM	LVL	AGE	W	L	SV	G	GS	IP	H	BB	SO	HR	GB%	BABIP	STUFF	WHIP	ERA	DERA	EqH9	EqBB9	EqSO9	EqHR9	DEF	VORP	SN/WX
2008	SBN	A	19	12	5	0	24	24	117²	113	33	117	8	46.0%	.315	-7	1.24	3.44	6.88	13.0	4.0	4.5	1.8	-3	-14.5	—
2009	ARI	MLB	20	3	8	0	19	19	94	128	46	60	18	45.0%	.340	3	1.85	7.24	7.09	11.8	3.9	5.1	1.7	1	-12.8	-0.66

Breakout: 19% Improve: 56% Collapse: 15% Attrition: 12%   **Comparables: Oscar Dechavez, Steve Maye, Luis Cota, Chris George**

Expectations are a funny thing. Parker was Arizona's first-round pick in 2007 and was generally considered the best high-school arm in the draft, after Rick Porcello. Then everyone finally got to see him pitch, and he was really good, but he wasn't great, or just not as great as was promised. Legends had been spun of the 97 mph fastball and the devastating slider; instead, we got 92-95 mph and a *good* slider. The thing is, those qualities mean Parker is still a great prospect, easily the best in the Arizona system, and projects as a star-level starter. Yet, because he wasn't quite what was advertised, he still bears the stigma of being a disappointment.

Jailen Peguero

Bats: R **Throws: R** **Height: 6' 0"** **Weight: 195** **Born: January 4, 1981** **Age: 28**

YEAR	TEAM	LVL	AGE	W	L	SV	G	GS	IP	H	BB	SO	HR	GB%	BABIP	STUFF	WHIP	ERA	DERA	EqH9	EqBB9	EqSO9	EqHR9	DEF	VORP	SN/WX
2006	CCH	AA	25	2	0	14	27	0	38²	18	16	48	0	39.2%	.234	14	0.89	0.71	2.55	5.6	4.3	7.6	0.3	3	12.0	—
2006	ROU	AAA	25	1	2	1	21	0	36	34	18	30	3	48.0%	.299	-14	1.44	3.50	4.11	9.8	4.6	4.9	1.0	-6	5.8	—
2007	TUC	AAA	26	6	2	4	53	0	66²	47	26	68	5	50.0%	.261	2	1.09	1.89	4.43	6.1	3.6	6.6	0.8	11	8.5	—
2007	ARI	MLB	26	1	0	0	18	0	14²	17	13	9	2	29.2%	.341	-11	2.05	9.18	7.71	10.9	7.1	5.1	1.3	0	-4.9	0.13
2008	TUC	AAA	27	6	4	5	51	0	70¹	71	40	68	5	45.0%	.332	-5	1.58	4.22	4.83	9.3	5.1	5.7	0.8	-6	5.9	—
2008	ARI	MLB	27	0	0	0	7	0	9¹	9	4	5	0	46.4%	.333	-9	1.39	4.84	3.24	9.7	3.2	4.3	0.0	-2	0.0	-0.01
2009	ARI	MLB	28	3	4	1	45	4	54²	56	32	43	7	43.0%	.300	-1	1.60	5.27	5.27	9.0	4.5	6.2	1.1	0	3.2	0.43

Breakout: 12% Improve: 29% Collapse: 38% Attrition: 12%   **Comparables: Jose Paniagua, Geremi Gonzalez, Brandon Medders, Jesus Colome**

Signed off the scrapheap after the 2006 season, Peguero put together a couple of nice years at Triple-A and got a handful of fill-in innings in the big leagues each time. He's an undersized righty with a sinker/slider combination and occasional control problems, and at 28, it's not like he's suddenly going to get better. Expect a handful of major league innings scattered over the next few years, but not much more.

Tony Pena

Bats: R   Throws: R   Height: 6' 1"   Weight: 220   Born: January 9, 1982   Age: 27

YEAR	TEAM	LVL	AGE	W	L	SV	G	GS	IP	H	BB	SO	HR	GB%	BABIP	STUFF	WHIP	ERA	DERA	EqH9	EqBB9	EqSO9	EqHR9	DEF	VORP	SN/WX
2006	TEN	AA	24	2	0	0	6	17	20²	18	5	17	0	60.3%	.295	-5	1.14	0.89	2.21	8.4	2.2	4.4	0.4	1	7.6	—
2006	TUC	AAA	24	3	1	7	24	0	26²	17	2	21	1	45.9%	.222	2	0.73	1.72	4.56	6.0	0.7	4.9	0.7	5	3.0	—
2006	ARI	MLB	24	3	4	1	25	0	30²	36	8	21	6	41.5%	.309	-10	1.43	5.57	4.88	9.8	2.0	5.5	1.4	-2	0.2	0.94
2007	ARI	MLB	25	5	4	2	75	0	85¹	63	31	63	8	48.6%	.236	6	1.10	3.27	3.74	6.4	2.9	6.3	0.7	5	20.7	4.14
2008	ARI	MLB	26	3	2	3	72	0	72²	80	17	52	5	49.8%	.329	5	1.33	4.33	3.82	9.5	1.7	5.7	0.6	-3	8.7	1.61
2009	ARI	MLB	27	3	3	3	54	0	60²	61	18	43	7	47.0%	.290	4	1.30	3.91	3.97	8.8	2.3	5.7	1.0	1	12.9	1.05

Breakout: 8%   Improve: 25%   Collapse: 44%   Attrition: 19%   Comparables: Dave Heaverlo, Jesse Crain, Chuck Crim, Randy St. Claire

Pena became a different pitcher in 2008, reducing his walk rate dramatically while also giving up many more hits. The problem? His once-excellent fastball dropped to the 90-93 mph range. He tinkered with his mechanics throughout the season, delivering occasional spurts of dominance, but overall his season left most scratching their heads about a guy who once looked like he might be the answer at closer, but clearly wasn't, last year.

Yusmeiro Petit

Bats: R   Throws: R   Height: 6' 0"   Weight: 230   Born: November 22, 1984   Age: 24

YEAR	TEAM	LVL	AGE	W	L	SV	G	GS	IP	H	BB	SO	HR	GB%	BABIP	STUFF	WHIP	ERA	DERA	EqH9	EqBB9	EqSO9	EqHR9	DEF	VORP	SN/WX
2006	ABQ	AAA	21	4	6	0	17	17	96²	101	20	68	14	42.5%	.295	2	1.26	4.30	5.55	9.6	2.0	4.1	1.7	4	0.5	—
2006	FLO	MLB	21	1	1	0	15	1	26¹	46	9	20	7	32.0%	.429	-3	2.09	9.58	6.31	15.4	2.8	6.3	2.1	-8	-11.0	-0.38
2007	TUC	AAA	22	8	4	0	17	17	93²	83	38	60	11	27.4%	.258	-5	1.29	4.03	5.74	7.3	3.6	3.8	1.2	9	-1.5	—
2007	ARI	MLB	22	3	4	0	14	10	57	58	18	40	12	34.1%	.269	7	1.33	4.58	3.92	8.6	2.5	5.8	1.7	0	7.8	1.09
2008	TUC	AAA	23	3	3	0	11	11	60	64	8	67	7	36.8%	.350	17	1.20	4.80	4.94	10.0	1.4	6.9	1.2	-4	4.3	—
2008	ARI	MLB	23	3	5	0	19	8	56¹	45	14	42	12	34.9%	.214	-3	1.05	4.32	5.43	6.5	1.9	5.7	1.7	8	7.4	1.24
2009	ARI	MLB	24	6	8	1	35	17	113	119	32	87	20	38.0%	.290	11	1.33	4.76	4.69	9.1	2.2	6.1	1.5	1	14.3	2.02

Breakout: 15%   Improve: 37%   Collapse: 30%   Attrition: 27%   Comparables: Edgar Gonzalez, Fernando Nieve, Leo Nuñez, Carlos Villanueva

Petit has been a huge star in the minors, putting up some silly numbers, but it just hasn't translated well in the big leagues. Petit succeeds on a highly deceptive delivery and pinpoint control. The problem is, he only throws in the upper 80s, so his strikes are quite hittable. He pitched with equal inconsistency and mediocrity in both starting and relief roles, and while he has value in the big leagues, it's nothing more than as an extra arm at the back end of the pen or a rotation.

Chad Qualls

Bats: R   Throws: R   Height: 6' 5"   Weight: 225   Born: August 17, 1978   Age: 30

YEAR	TEAM	LVL	AGE	W	L	SV	G	GS	IP	H	BB	SO	HR	GB%	BABIP	STUFF	WHIP	ERA	DERA	EqH9	EqBB9	EqSO9	EqHR9	DEF	VORP	SN/WX
2006	HOU	MLB	27	7	3	0	81	0	88²	76	28	56	10	60.5%	.266	-5	1.17	3.75	4.39	8.0	2.6	5.5	1.0	8	21.5	2.84
2007	HOU	MLB	28	6	5	5	79	0	82²	84	25	78	10	57.7%	.335	13	1.32	3.05	2.58	9.0	2.5	8.2	1.0	-3	25.0	3.56
2008	ARI	MLB	29	4	8	9	77	0	73²	61	18	71	4	58.7%	.289	21	1.07	2.81	3.51	7.1	1.8	7.5	0.5	2	18.1	1.95
2009	ARI	MLB	30	4	3	6	58	0	64¹	63	21	53	6	55.0%	.300	9	1.31	3.54	3.62	8.5	2.6	6.5	0.8	1	16.0	1.44

Breakout: 13%   Improve: 36%   Collapse: 30%   Attrition: 11%   Comparables: Mike Timlin, Greg McMichael, Braden Looper, Bob Locker

Another transfer from Houston in the Valverde deal, Qualls is an underrated commodity at this point, as he's one of the hardest things to find: a consistent reliever. Qualls has had four straight years of fine performances while pitching in 77 or more games and had his best year in 2008 with a career-high strikeout rate and career-low walk rate. He has two plus pitches, beginning with a monster sinker that also has 92-95 mph velocity and causes as many swings and misses as it does ground balls, as well as a solid slider. There's no reason he can't be good for years to come.

Jon Rauch

Bats: R   Throws: R   Height: 6' 11"   Weight: 250   Born: September 27, 1978   Age: 30

YEAR	TEAM	LVL	AGE	W	L	SV	G	GS	IP	H	BB	SO	HR	GB%	BABIP	STUFF	WHIP	ERA	DERA	EqH9	EqBB9	EqSO9	EqHR9	DEF	VORP	SN/WX
2006	WAS	MLB	27	4	5	2	85	0	91¹	78	36	86	13	31.3%	.272	3	1.25	3.35	4.14	7.5	3.1	7.7	1.2	6	23.3	1.68
2007	WAS	MLB	28	8	4	4	88	0	87¹	75	21	71	7	35.9%	.274	14	1.10	3.61	2.99	7.5	1.9	6.8	0.7	-6	19.0	2.90
2008	WAS	MLB	29	4	2	17	48	0	48¹	42	7	44	5	34.0%	.280	13	1.01	2.98	3.70	7.6	1.1	7.2	0.9	4	12.5	2.20
2008	ARI	MLB	29	0	6	1	26	0	23¹	27	9	22	6	34.7%	.344	-8	1.54	6.57	5.48	10.2	3.1	7.4	2.3	-1	-3.0	-0.62
2009	ARI	MLB	30	3	4	8	52	0	59	58	19	50	9	37.0%	.280	7	1.29	4.24	4.20	8.5	2.5	6.7	1.3	1	10.3	1.03

Breakout: 14%   Improve: 31%   Collapse: 42%   Attrition: 22%   Comparables: Jerry Spradlin, Justin Speier, Scott Sanders, Bill Dawley

The Diamondbacks needed some bullpen help down the stretch, so they sent minor league speedster Emilio Bonafacio to the Nats for Rauch, who had assumed the closing duties in Washington and was doing pretty well there. Once he got to Arizona, things didn't go so well, as he tried to pitch through some forearm stiffness. He was only closing in our nation's capital because there were no other options; in reality, he's just another decent fastball/slider guy worthy of a middle relief role who also gets to be a trivia footnote as the tallest player ever.

Connor Robertson

Bats: R   Throws: R   Height: 6' 2"   Weight: 215   Born: September 10, 1981   Age: 27

YEAR	TEAM	LVL	AGE	W	L	SV	G	GS	IP	H	BB	SO	HR	GB%	BABIP	STUFF	WHIP	ERA	DERA	EqH9	EqBB9	EqSO9	EqHR9	DEF	VORP	SN/WX
2006	MID	AA	24	7	2	6	55	0	83	73	22	97	1	48.8%	.362	16	1.14	2.82	3.75	10.4	3.0	7.6	0.4	-3	14.8	—
2007	SAC	AAA	25	4	1	2	31	0	39¹	43	21	40	3	39.5%	.367	-4	1.63	4.35	5.80	11.9	5.3	7.1	1.0	-4	-0.8	—
2008	TUC	AAA	26	7	4	1	47	0	71²	69	30	72	7	44.3%	.332	-10	1.38	5.02	5.82	9.3	4.0	6.2	1.1	-2	-1.7	—
2008	ARI	MLB	26	0	1	0	6	0	7	8	2	2	1	37.0%	.280	-27	1.43	5.14	6.14	9.8	2.5	2.5	1.2	1	0.5	-0.29
2009	NYN	MLB	27	3	3	1	45	3	51	55	25	42	6	44.0%	.320	2	1.55	5.04	5.51	9.7	3.8	6.4	1.1	0	1.4	0.23

Breakout: 17%   Improve: 53%   Collapse: 20%   Attrition: 16%   Comparables: Dan Hubbs, Dana Ridenour, Jim Lewis, Darryl Scott

Robertson came to Arizona with Haren to even up the number of bodies in the deal a bit and pitched much better than his Triple-A ERA, with solid ratios across the board. He's very similar to Petit, only with less control and maybe even more deception—his natural motion is a twisting delivery that hides the ball behind his body and head until just moments before its release. It should work enough to get him a few more shots, but his ceiling ends there. Dealt to the Mets in December for Scott Schoeneweis, Robertson will be in the mix for the trash-time brigade in Flushing.

Wes Roemer

Bats: R   Throws: R   Height: 6' 0"   Weight: 190   Born: October 7, 1986   Age: 22

YEAR	TEAM	LVL	AGE	W	L	SV	G	GS	IP	H	BB	SO	HR	GB%	BABIP	STUFF	WHIP	ERA	DERA	EqH9	EqBB9	EqSO9	EqHR9	DEF	VORP	SN/WX
2007	YAK	A-	20	1	0	0	8	0	12	11	2	18	1	36.7%	.357	10	1.08	4.50	7.59	12.7	2.5	5.9	2.5	-1	-2.4	—
2008	VIS	A+	21	7	12	0	28	28	162²	199	33	122	25	46.4%	.349	-35	1.43	4.59	5.80	13.9	2.8	3.5	2.8	-19	-3.2	—
2009	ARI	MLB	22	4	8	0	25	17	95¹	138	35	52	25	43.0%	.340	-6	1.82	7.37	7.08	12.6	2.9	4.3	2.2	1	-12.6	-0.74

Breakout: 15%   Improve: 49%   Collapse: 17%   Attrition: 10%   Comparables: Brian Cooper, Charles McHugh, Ricky Rojas, Rick Balabon

Roemer was one of the best control specialists in the history of college baseball—in 2006, he struck out 145 in 155 innings while walking just seven. That was enough to make him a supplemental first-round pick, but his full-season debut was a bit of a mess. The Cal League hit .308 against him as his precision wasn't enough to make up for pedestrian velocity and a slider that is merely average. Still, every once in a while, he'd be perfectly dominant, and if he can change "every once in a while" to "often," he'll have some kind of career.

Leo Rosales

Bats: R   Throws: R   Height: 6' 1"   Weight: 185   Born: May 28, 1981   Age: 28

YEAR	TEAM	LVL	AGE	W	L	SV	G	GS	IP	H	BB	SO	HR	GB%	BABIP	STUFF	WHIP	ERA	DERA	EqH9	EqBB9	EqSO9	EqHR9	DEF	VORP	SN/WX
2006	MOB	AA	25	5	6	0	53	0	61	53	18	54	6	44.7%	.264	-29	1.16	3.25	6.97	9.0	2.8	4.6	1.6	-1	-9.2	—
2007	POR	AAA	26	1	1	14	24	0	24²	23	10	27	3	43.3%	.313	-2	1.34	3.28	3.80	8.7	3.8	7.2	1.5	-1	4.7	—
2008	TUC	AAA	27	2	2	9	29	0	36¹	39	14	28	5	36.8%	.312	-24	1.46	4.46	5.80	9.6	3.5	4.5	1.5	0	-0.8	—
2008	ARI	MLB	27	1	1	0	27	0	30	32	15	18	2	46.1%	.306	-10	1.57	4.20	3.23	9.1	3.8	4.7	0.6	-3	4.1	0.44
2009	ARI	MLB	28	1	2	1	30	0	30¹	32	13	20	4	43.0%	.290	-4	1.47	4.81	4.82	9.3	3.3	5.1	1.2	0	3.7	0.26

Breakout: 17%   Improve: 34%   Collapse: 42%   Attrition: 47%   Comparables: Jack Cressend, Max Surkont, Juan Acevedo, Rob Stanifer

When Rosales was in the Padres' system, he closed at every level and did it well. This inspired dreams of his becoming the next Trevor Hoffman, a ninth-inning guy with a ridiculously good changeup. While Rosales's change is that good a pitch, he doesn't really have anything to set it up with—all he can do is try to keep hitters' timing off-kilter. That works if you're Doug Jones and can throw about 12 different changeups, but Rosales has just one and less command.

Max Scherzer

										Bats: R		Throws: R		Height: 6' 3"		Weight: 190		Born: July 27, 1984			Age: 24	
YEAR	TEAM	LVL	AGE	W	L	SV	G	GS	IP	H	BB	SO	HR	GB%	BABIP	STUFF	WHIP	ERA	DERA	EqH9	EqBB9	EqSO9	EqHR9	DEF	VORP	SN/WX
2007	VIS	A+	22	2	0	0	3	3	17	5	2	30	0	53.8%	.192	16	0.41	0.53	2.25	4.5	1.7	9.0	0.6	2	6.0	—
2007	MOB	AA	22	4	4	0	14	14	73²	64	40	76	3	50.7%	.316	12	1.41	3.91	6.06	9.6	5.3	5.7	0.8	-1	-3.5	—
2008	TUC	AAA	23	1	1	0	13	10	53	35	22	79	2	53.4%	.297	34	1.08	2.72	3.76	6.3	3.8	9.2	0.5	0	10.8	—
2008	ARI	MLB	23	0	4	0	16	7	56	48	21	66	5	42.8%	.321	31	1.23	3.05	3.56	7.8	2.9	9.4	0.8	0	12.1	1.06
2009	ARI	MLB	24	10	9	1	37	26	158	138	65	168	14	46.0%	.300	29	1.28	3.77	3.81	7.6	3.2	8.4	0.8	1	33.9	4.56

Breakout: 16%   Improve: 35%   Collapse: 21%   Attrition: 10%   Comparables: Josh Beckett, Mike Moore, Mark Prior, Ralph Branca

Scherzer failed to make the big-league club out of camp, but forced his way back up by not allowing an earned run in his first 17 innings while striking out 29. In his first appearance in the majors, he retired all 13 batters he faced while striking out seven of them, but from there, he was more inconsistent. Being merely mortal, Scherzer would almost have to be more inconsistent than that, but he was either dominant or mediocre, depending on his command and the quality of his slider. He also missed some time with a sore shoulder. His fastball is a monster, at 93-97 mph, and if the slider goes from one that flashes as plus to a consistent plus, he's an All-Star.

Daniel Schlereth

										Bats: L		Throws: L		Height: 6' 0"		Weight: 210		Born: May 9, 1986			Age: 23	
YEAR	TEAM	LVL	AGE	W	L	SV	G	GS	IP	H	BB	SO	HR	GB%	BABIP	STUFF	WHIP	ERA	DERA	EqH9	EqBB9	EqSO9	EqHR9	DEF	VORP	SN/WX
2008	SBN	A	22	1	0	0	7	0	9	3	4	14	0	59.1%	.136	8	0.78	2.00	5.87	5.9	5.9	8.2	0.0	1	-0.2	—
2009	ARI	MLB	23	3	5	1	34	7	68¹	71	45	56	8	47.0%	.310	3	1.68	5.57	5.60	9.0	5.1	6.5	1.0	1	1.5	0.35

Breakout: 0%   Improve: 0%   Collapse: 0%   Attrition: 0%   Comparables: Ritchie Moody, Royce Ring, Steve Howe, Jesse Crain

Schlereth became Arizona's closer of the future the moment it used its first-round pick on him last June. He's a left-hander who can touch 97 mph, and he backs it up with a hard curve; he had no problems carving up minor league hitters. The son of a former NFL player, he brings a football mentality to the mound and is as aggressive as it gets. The only knock against him is that he's a health risk, as his is a violent delivery and he's already had a Tommy John surgery.

Doug Slaten

										Bats: L		Throws: L		Height: 6' 5"		Weight: 200		Born: February 4, 1980			Age: 29	
YEAR	TEAM	LVL	AGE	W	L	SV	G	GS	IP	H	BB	SO	HR	GB%	BABIP	STUFF	WHIP	ERA	DERA	EqH9	EqBB9	EqSO9	EqHR9	DEF	VORP	SN/WX
2006	TEN	AA	26	2	3	8	40	0	43	31	15	59	1	46.2%	.341	13	1.07	1.88	3.55	9.0	3.6	8.5	0.5	-1	8.7	—
2006	TUC	AAA	26	2	1	2	18	0	20²	10	7	21	0	51.0%	.213	9	0.84	0.45	2.25	4.5	3.2	6.3	0.0	2	7.4	—
2006	ARI	MLB	26	0	0	0	9	0	5²	3	2	3	0	43.8%	.200	-6	0.88	0.00	3.18	4.8	3.2	4.8	0.0	2	3.8	0.38
2007	ARI	MLB	27	3	2	0	61	0	36¹	41	14	28	4	43.8%	.316	-1	1.51	2.73	2.68	9.5	2.9	6.3	1.0	-2	9.1	0.05
2008	ARI	MLB	28	0	3	0	45	0	32¹	33	14	20	4	39.4%	.282	-14	1.45	4.74	4.86	8.6	3.2	4.9	1.1	0	0.7	0.15
2009	ARI	MLB	29	2	2	2	48	0	42¹	42	18	32	5	43.0%	.290	2	1.42	4.32	4.32	8.6	3.4	6.1	1.0	0	7.2	0.58

Breakout: 8%   Improve: 23%   Collapse: 53%   Attrition: 28%   Comparables: Gary Wayne, Scott Ruskin, Jeremy Hernandez, Andrew Lorraine

Slaten has got an "L" next to his throw column and has pitched in 115 big league games, yet has just 74⅓ innings. That's the template for a situational reliever, and that's exactly what Slaten is. Still, he's probably not going to be around forever, Fossas-style. He's good against lefties, but that's about it; he's not a total shutdown type as much as he was often the only option Bob Melvin had, and even then, the Snakes got by without him at times. The Snakes' trading for Schoeneweis puts Slaten in a fight for any kind of job.

Daniel Stange

												Bats: R		Throws: R		Height: 6' 3"		Weight: 185		Born: December 22, 1985		Age: 23	

YEAR	TEAM	LVL	AGE	W	L	SV	G	GS	IP	H	BB	SO	HR	GB%	BABIP	STUFF	WHIP	ERA	DERA	EqH9	EqBB9	EqSO9	EqHR9	DEF	VORP	SN/WX
2006	MSO	Rk	20	5	2	13	27	0	36²	39	17	48	2	52.8%	.370	-7	1.55	4.23	6.23	16.0	6.5	5.6	2.1	-7	-2.1	—
2007	VIS	A+	21	4	5	16	38	0	42¹	37	18	53	3	63.2%	.324	-1	1.30	3.19	5.95	10.5	4.8	6.2	1.1	-5	-1.5	—
2007	MOB	AA	21	1	0	1	5	0	6²	9	2	5	1	52.2%	.364	-13	1.64	5.37	7.50	15.0	3.0	4.5	3.0	0	-1.3	—
2008	SBN	A	22	1	0	1	11	0	17	11	1	17	0	34.1%	.256	4	0.71	1.59	4.11	8.8	1.2	4.7	0.6	1	2.5	—
2008	VIS	A+	22	1	2	0	11	0	13²	10	6	14	2	41.7%	.242	-16	1.17	3.94	7.82	8.5	5.0	5.0	2.1	3	-3.1	—
2009	ARI	MLB	23	2	4	0	27	5	55	69	28	38	10	44.0%	.330	-4	1.76	6.83	6.73	10.9	3.9	5.4	1.6	1	-6.4	-0.37

Breakout: 11% Improve: 39% Collapse: 26% Attrition: 9%   Comparables: John Trautwein, Neil Jamison, Ricky Steik, Jim Austin

One of the better relief prospects in the system before his elbow popped and required Tommy John surgery, Stange looked sharp on his return, and he should start the year at Double-A with the chance to move up quickly. His velocity is already back in the mid-90s, and he'd gotten up to 98 mph presurgery, a level that some think he can return to. His slider is another wipeout offering, and many in the Arizona organization think he's the best sleeper in the system.

Matt Torra

												Bats: R		Throws: R		Height: 6' 3"		Weight: 225		Born: June 29, 1984		Age: 25	

YEAR	TEAM	LVL	AGE	W	L	SV	G	GS	IP	H	BB	SO	HR	GB%	BABIP	STUFF	WHIP	ERA	DERA	EqH9	EqBB9	EqSO9	EqHR9	DEF	VORP	SN/WX
2006	SBN	A	22	0	1	0	7	7	25²	24	5	20	0	46.9%	.313	-11	1.15	1.79	4.79	12.6	3.5	3.5	0.4	-1	1.9	—
2007	VIS	A+	23	12	10	0	28	28	158²	186	43	137	15	46.7%	.351	-27	1.44	6.01	7.13	13.9	3.4	4.0	1.6	-22	-24.0	—
2008	MOB	AA	24	5	5	0	13	13	79	91	12	50	5	47.8%	.326	-5	1.30	2.85	3.58	11.6	1.7	3.2	1.1	-11	16.9	—
2008	TUC	AAA	24	5	5	0	14	13	78¹	97	19	46	13	43.0%	.319	-23	1.48	4.71	5.95	10.6	2.3	3.1	1.6	-1	-3.1	—
2009	ARI	MLB	25	5	10	0	31	20	122	163	39	66	24	44.0%	.330	-3	1.66	6.50	6.38	11.6	2.5	4.3	1.7	1	-7.7	0.00

Breakout: 17% Improve: 52% Collapse: 19% Attrition: 15%   Comparables: Tim Stauffer, Mark Knudson, Joe Kucharski, Josh Pearce

You have to give it to a guy like Torra: a first-round pick in 2005 as a big-bodied power pitcher with rough mechanics, he lasted a grand total of 10 pro innings before he completely destroyed his shoulder. That would be the end for most guys, but Torra re-invented himself as a finesse guy. He rarely gets out of the 80s anymore, but he fills the strike zone with three pitches and depends on his defense. It hasn't been an especially successful approach for Torra, and he'll never be more than a fifth starter, but you can't help rooting for him.

Cesar Valdez

												Bats: R		Throws: R		Height: 6' 1"		Weight: 175		Born: March 17, 1985		Age: 24	

YEAR	TEAM	LVL	AGE	W	L	SV	G	GS	IP	H	BB	SO	HR	GB%	BABIP	STUFF	WHIP	ERA	DERA	EqH9	EqBB9	EqSO9	EqHR9	DEF	VORP	SN/WX
2006	YAK	A-	21	7	5	0	16	16	97¹	97	20	81	5	57.3%	.316	-17	1.20	3.15	6.83	12.8	3.4	3.1	1.8	-9	-11.5	—
2007	SBN	A	22	7	10	0	25	25	148	130	32	106	11	58.8%	.273	-38	1.09	3.41	7.65	10.9	3.4	2.5	2.1	6	-29.5	—
2008	VIS	A+	23	10	3	0	15	15	96	88	16	80	5	54.6%	.292	1	1.08	2.53	4.18	9.5	2.2	3.9	1.0	-5	14.2	—
2008	MOB	AA	23	3	5	0	12	12	64¹	63	23	60	2	55.7%	.341	6	1.34	4.06	5.37	10.7	3.5	5.5	0.6	0	1.5	—
2009	ARI	MLB	24	6	11	0	25	25	135	167	51	78	21	51.0%	.320	5	1.62	5.99	5.98	10.7	3.0	4.6	1.3	1	-2.6	0.76

Breakout: 14% Improve: 49% Collapse: 15% Attrition: 16%   Comparables: Rodrigo Lopez, Enrique Gonzalez, Ramiro Mendoza, Chris Mason

Valdez was never an especially bright blip on anyone's prospect radar, but Arizona keeps moving him up, and he keeps getting batters out, so the ranks of his naysayers are dwindling. He has a pretty good sinker, a decent curve, and two plus changeups—one a classic change, and one that's more of a harder pitch that acts as a splitter. That combination is brought up by his excellent control, and if everything works out, he could be in the back end of the rotation by 2010.

Brandon Webb

| | | | | Bats: R | | | Throws: R | | Height: 6' 2" | | Weight: 230 | | Born: May 9, 1979 | | | Age: 30 |

YEAR	TEAM	LVL	AGE	W	L	SV	G	GS	IP	H	BB	SO	HR	GB%	BABIP	STUFF	WHIP	ERA	DERA	EqH9	EqBB9	EqSO9	EqHR9	DEF	VORP	SN/WX
2006	ARI	MLB	27	16	8	0	33	33	235	216	50	178	15	67.3%	.293	31	1.13	3.10	3.44	7.9	1.7	6.3	0.5	10	68.7	7.12
2007	ARI	MLB	28	18	10	0	34	34	236¹	209	72	194	12	63.6%	.291	34	1.19	3.01	3.43	7.7	2.4	6.9	0.4	11	66.0	7.12
2008	ARI	MLB	29	22	7	0	34	34	226²	206	65	183	13	65.9%	.295	31	1.20	3.30	3.22	7.9	2.2	6.4	0.5	-4	51.0	6.50
2009	*ARI*	*MLB*	*30*	*14*	*9*	*0*	*31*	*31*	*212*	*202*	*61*	*168*	*14*	*60.0%*	*.300*	*23*	*1.24*	*3.29*	*3.40*	*8.3*	*2.3*	*6.3*	*0.6*	*2*	*56.0*	*7.39*

Breakout: 7%   Improve: 27%   Collapse: 16%   Attrition: 4%   *Comparables: Rick Reuschel, Orel Hershiser, Roy Halladay, Charles Nagy*

The NL Cy Young Award winner of 2006 has finished as the runner-up in each of the last two years, and he serves as a bit of a lesson for those who get obsessed with radar gun readings—Webb is one of the best pitchers in the game while sitting at 88-91 mph. He also serves as a cause for frustration among prospect people—now, whenever some big sinkerballer comes up but doesn't throw very hard, people think they have the next Brandon Webb on their hands. They don't; Webb is an exception, not a precedent. His sinker is excellent, featuring more vertical movement than do either of his secondary pitches, both of which are quality offerings. Webb's sinker is up there with Nolan Ryan's fastball and Mariano Rivera's cutter when it comes to iconic pitches of their type.

LINEOUTS

Hitters

PLAYER	TEAM	LVL	AGE	PA	R	2B	3B	HR	RBI	BB	SO	SB-CS	EqBRR	AVG/OBP/SLG	EqAVG/EqOBP/EqSLG	EqA	VORP	WARP
OF C. Cowgill	YAK	A-	22	95	21	3	1	11	28	12	17	5-0	2.0	.304/.415/.785	.195/.263/.460	.243	-2.3	0.1
	SBN	A	22	231	31	13	3	1	17	25	61	1-0	-0.0	.249/.346/.358	.197/.277/.293	.199	-15.7	-0.9
4C J. D'Antona	TUC	AAA	26	454	69	35	1	21	79	30	64	1-0	-1.8	.365/.405/.604	.287/.325/.471	.271	19.0	-1.9
	ARI	MLB	26	19	2	0	0	0	1	2	4	0-0	0.0	.176/.263/.176	.176/.263/.176	.143	-1.7	-0.2
C R. Hammock	TUC	AAA	31	242	29	6	2	5	27	18	47	1-0	1.3	.240/.297/.355	.176/.225/.261	.165	-25.5	-2.1
	ARI	MLB	31	48	4	1	0	0	2	5	9	0-0	0.3	.190/.292/.214	.190/.292/.214	.181	-2.9	-0.4
SS J. Merchan	TUC	AAA	27	477	50	23	5	4	72	18	44	2-2	-3.7	.339/.373/.443	.259/.291/.338	.220	-14.5	-1.9
SS R. Navarro#	MSO	Rk	18	323	42	17	7	2	31	25	77	17-9	-3.0	.258/.323/.385	.169/.214/.245	.149	-73.2	-5.2
OF T. Oeltjen*	TUC	AAA	25	491	75	28	10	6	60	24	68	15-7	-0.5	.317/.357/.466	.256/.293/.376	.236	-7.9	-0.2
2/3 R. Ryal	MOB	AA	25	509	65	22	4	16	66	35	96	4-4	-0.8	.274/.334/.443	.200/.246/.328	.196	-37.7	-2.4
MI Y. Sanchez#	MOB	AA	24	523	61	20	3	0	22	23	41	8-13	-2.4	.296/.333/.348	.235/.264/.284	.182	-40.4	-2.9

Collin Cowgill is a fifth-round pick who hit 11 home runs in his first 16 pro games and then hit one in 50 Midwest League games. The truth of what he'll be is, as always, somewhere in between. ⊘ Once part of the minor league Three Amigos with Connor Jackson and Carlos Quentin, **Jamie D'Antona** had problems finding a defensive home and took too long to hit at the upper levels; Arizona didn't have much use for him, and now he's off to hit for the Yakult Swallows. ⊘ With a good pair of catchers on hand, there just wasn't much room left at the inn for **Robby Hammock**, a career up-and-down guy who deserves the key to the city of Tucson after spending parts of the last six years there. He was nontendered in December, so he may have to become mayor of another town. ⊘ **Jesus Merchan** is a minor league journeyman who suddenly put up monster numbers in Tucson—and that's a total mirage. ⊘ Shortstop **Reynaldo Navarro** has yet to do much, production-wise, but scouts love his tools. ⊘ **Trent Oeltjen** hit .238 in Rochester two years ago, but raised that average 79 points last year in Tucson, so we're guessing he likes the weather. ⊘ **Rusty Ryal** can play second or third and has a bit of power; he might get to "The Show" as a bench player. ⊘ It seems as if light-hitting, slick-fielding shortstops from Cuba grow on trees, and **Yunesky Sanchez** is part of the latest crop to wash up on our shores.

Pitchers

PLAYER	TEAM	LVL	AGE	W	L	SV	IP	H	BB	SO	HR	GB%	BABIP	STUFF	WHIP	ERA	DERA	EqH9	EqBB9	EqSO9	EqHR9	DEF	VORP
B. Augenstein	SBN	A	21	5	1	0	87¹	73	9	69	2	59.1%	.278	14	0.94	2.16	5.03	10.6	1.8	3.4	0.8	8	4.9
	VIS	A+	21	2	4	0	44	57	5	30	5	61.8%	.361	-12	1.41	3.89	6.64	14.2	1.8	3.0	2.1	-2	-4.5
B. Brown	MOB	AA	23	6	15	0	144¹	152	67	112	8	52.1%	.338	-7	1.52	4.18	5.12	11.6	4.6	4.4	1.0	-7	6.9
B. Enright	VIS	A+	22	12	8	0	164¹	185	35	143	17	43.2%	.337	-18	1.34	4.44	4.98	12.3	2.8	4.1	1.9	-24	10.3
E. Gonzalez	ARI	MLB	25	1	3	0	48	58	21	32	8	42.4%	.329	-12	1.65	6.00	4.50	10.5	3.4	5.2	1.3	-6	-2.5
A. Shappi	MOB	AA	25	0	1	1	29¹	25	4	27	1	53.5%	.286	-1	0.99	1.54	4.13	8.6	1.6	5.1	0.6	3	4.6
	TUC	AAA	25	2	5	0	55¹	81	15	39	11	45.5%	.374	-33	1.74	6.02	6.20	13.4	2.5	4.0	2.0	-9	-3.6
E. Vasquez	TUC	AAA	24	3	6	0	83	79	73	57	11	37.1%	.292	-19	1.83	6.72	8.29	8.6	7.7	3.9	1.3	4	-24.0
C. Zavada*	SBN	A	24	3	1	8	35¹	6	5	54	1	52.5%	.119	18	0.31	0.51	3.34	2.8	1.9	7.5	0.8	6	8.1

Bryan Augenstein is a strike thrower who dominated the Midwest League and then got hit hard after a move up. He doesn't have much in the way of stuff, so this might be a trend. ⊘ **Brooks Brown** entered the year as one of the better pitching prospects in the system, but he hit a wall at Double-A, and many scouts now see him as a reliever. ⊘ Lefty **Jon Coutlangus** has set-up-man potential, but missed most of the year with an injury. Announcers are hoping he doesn't make it back, for fear of what happens when you only slightly mispronounce his name. ⊘ Arizona's third-round pick last June, righty **Kevin Eichhorn** is Mark's son, but he's not a sidearmer or a reliever; instead, Kevin has midrotation potential. ⊘ **Barry Enright** is a finesse pitcher who got hit hard in the California League by trying to overpower people; let that be a warning to you. ⊘ Between Doug Davis's thyroid and Randy Johnson's back, **Edgar Gonzalez** had a golden opportunity to establish himself as part of Arizona's future, but ineffectiveness and elbow problems destroyed his season. He'll get chances as a guy with good stuff and command, but his outlook is limited. ⊘ **A. J. Shappi** has one of the better sliders in the system, but that's really his only pitch, and it didn't stop Triple-A hitters from crushing him. ⊘ **Esmerling Vasquez** has a lot of arm strength and can touch 95 mph, but he completely stopped throwing strikes last year; his career is at a crossroads. ⊘ Signed out of the indy leagues, **Clay Zavada** put up some PlayStation numbers in Low-A, but he's a trick pitcher with a Bugs Bunny changeup and little else.

MANAGER: BOB MELVIN

YEAR	TEAM	W-L	Pythag +/−	Avg PC	100+ P	120+ P	QS	BQS	REL	REL w Zero R	IBB	Subs	PH	PH Avg	PH HR	SB2	CS2	SB3	CS3	SAC Att	SAC %	POS SAC	Squeeze	Swing	In Play
2006	ARI	76-86	-3	95.2	70	3	76	13	461	299	44	56	275	.193	7	64	26	11	4	84	72.6%	21	1	105	80
2007	ARI	90-72	11	94.9	68	4	80	9	469	314	38	77	240	.243	12	90	16	18	8	79	69.6%	26	0	118	89
2008	ARI	82-80	-1	95.8	56	3	94	6	443	292	41	52	257	.226	3	46	16	12	5	97	70.1%	29	1	121	89

Melvin is an interesting manager in that he's an inveterate tinkerer *before* the game, treating his lineup card with an elaborate care that might have left set-lineup doyen Ralph Houk wondering how the young man ever gets out of the office. *During* the game, however, Melvin is not an especially aggressive tactician, although he got more involved with one-out strategies on the road last season. This is one of those tendencies that can help make a bad situation just that wee bit worse, and Melvin is just one of many managers who has tried to "help" in the face of mounting frustration. It would be easy to bash the man for the way Lyon-as-closer flopped, but the pen was going to come down a peg regardless, and he didn't freak out once it became obvious he didn't have a reliable lefty reliever.

Atlanta Braves

Generally speaking, there are two types of playoff teams. There are the one-year wonders, the teams for whom everything fleetingly comes together. Such teams include the 2007 Rockies, the 2006 Tigers, the 2003 and 1997 Marlins, the 1998 Padres, the 1993 Phillies, and the wire-to-wire world champion 1990 Reds. Then there are the perennial contenders, teams such as the current Red Sox and Angels, the A's and Cardinals from earlier this decade, and the Yankees prior to last year.

Of course, the greatest perennial contenders in baseball history were the Atlanta Braves of 1991 to 2005. Their streak of 14 playoff appearances in 15 years—interrupted by the strike of 1994—came to an end in 2006, but the Braves appeared poised to make that look like a fluke at the 2007 trading deadline. Trailing by just 3½ games in the NL East and a mere 1½ in the wild-card race, they acquired first baseman Mark Teixeira and reliever Ron Mahay from the Rangers for a quintet of prospects. Both players excelled in Atlanta—the Braves' offense scored 5.7 runs per game during Teixeira's first month with the team—but poor starting pitching and an overcrowded field of contenders conspired to leave the Braves on the outside looking in yet again. Nonetheless, with Teixeira (albeit in his walk year) in place, the Braves had high hopes for 2008. Those hopes and Teixeira would both be gone before the trading deadline came around again.

It is tempting to write off the Braves' 2008 season as a perfect storm in which everything that could have gone wrong did. The top three men in Atlanta's Opening Day rotation had their seasons ended early by surgery, as did one of their replacements. Another member of that Opening Day staff injured himself before his first start

and didn't reappear until late July. Their right fielder followed a pair of 100 RBI seasons by posting the third-worst VORP (value over replacement player) in baseball, costing the team nearly two wins against what a replacement-level player would have contributed. One-half of the Braves' intended left-field platoon suffered a season-ending injury in late May, while the other half struggled to hit in Triple-A. Their closer saved just three games before having season-ending elbow surgery. Their primary set-up man from 2007 had Tommy John surgery in May, and his replacement was so overworked that he posted a 9.55 ERA over the season's final three months. Adding insult to those many injuries, the Double-A debut of the organization's top center-field prospect was delayed by 50 games by a human-growth-hormone-related drug suspension.

It would seem unfair to hold a team that had all of that happen to it fully accountable for its failures, but if you look at the names associated with those assorted maladies, the fate of the 2008 Braves can be said to have been as much the result of flaws with the design itself as from any misfortune. The sub-replacement right fielder was Jeff Francoeur, whose hack-tastic approach at the plate in previous seasons made such a collapse a distinct possibility. The intended left-field platoon of Matt Diaz and rookie Brandon Jones was a compromise to begin with, unexceptional offensively or defensively. The injured closer was Rafael Soriano, who has been plagued by elbow problems throughout his career. The beleaguered set-up men were Peter Moylan, who had been out of the game for nine years prior to the last World Baseball Classic, and Blaine Boyer, who missed all of 2006 due to a shoulder injury.

BRAVES PROSPECTUS

2008 record: 72-90; Fourth place, NL East

Pythagenport record: 78-84

Runs scored per game: 4.66 (6th in NL)

Runs allowed per game: 4.86 (12th in NL)

Team EqA: .266 (5th in NL)

2008 Batters Age: 27.3 (3rd-youngest in NL)

2008 Pitchers Age: 25.8 (youngest in NL)

Ballpark: Turner Field; Slight pitcher's park; Park Factor of .982

2008: The middle infielders outhit the corner outfielders, the rotation ain't what it used to be, and one-run games prove a bridge too far.

2009: Young pitching will define the Braves' new world, but the arms aren't ready for prime time.

The top four men in the 2008 Braves' Opening Day rotation were Tim Hudson, John Smoltz, Tom Glavine, and Mike Hampton. Some might look at those names and see a quartet of past-20 game winners, but the quartet was perhaps best described, as they were in the previous edition of this book, as "Tim Hudson, two old guys, and 'staff.'" Smoltz was 41, Glavine was 42, and Mike Hampton hadn't thrown a regular-season pitch since 2005. There was no guarantee that any of those three would make it through the season, and none of them did. Losing Hudson to Tommy John surgery was legitimately a bad break, but that was balanced by the surprisingly strong showings of 22-year-old rookie Jair Jurrjens, who was acquired during the offseason for veteran shortstop Edgar Renteria, and Mexican League veteran/Mariners castoff Jorge Campillo, an astute minor league signing.

Jurrjens and Campillo were just two things that went *right* for the Braves last year. There were others. Chipper Jones continued to abuse National League pitching, setting career highs in batting average and on-base percentage, despite his annual trip to the DL. Brian McCann rebounded from a sophomore slump to lead NL catchers in VORP at the still-tender age of 24. Yunel Escobar had filled in ably for an injured Renteria in August 2007 and proved to be a valuable major league shortstop in his first full season. Kelly Johnson remained solid at second base, and Mike Gonzalez made a successful late-season return from Tommy John surgery to reclaim the closer's job that his 2007 elbow injury had briefly yielded to Soriano.

Indeed, the 2008 Braves weren't quite as bad as they seemed. Using our third-order wins (which are based on run differential and adjusted for the strength of competition), the Braves' performance was that of a 79-win team instead of their actual 72. The difference was largely attributable to the Braves' abysmal 11-30 (.268) record in one-run games. Had they simply managed a .500 record in those games, they would have gone 81-81 on the season.

Still, once again the Braves were not without blame for their failings. The reason the Braves were so bad in one-run games, and thus fell so far short of their Pythagorean promise, was that their bullpen was flat awful, ranking 22nd in WXRL. The 2008 Braves converted just 59 percent of their save opportunities; only six teams were less effective in preserving slim leads. As a unit, the Braves' bullpen saw its ERA increase by 0.7 from 2007, despite the fact that the league as a whole scored nearly 0.2 of a run less per game overall in 2008.

Soriano's elbow was a big reason for this decline, but so was Bobby Cox's abuse of his few effective relievers. The Braves' best reliever in 2007 was Australian recla-mation project Moylan, who had just returned to the States the year before on the heels of his eye-catching performance in the first World Baseball Classic. Cox had Moylan throw 90 innings of relief in 2007. After just 5⅔ more in 2008, Moylan's elbow gave out and he underwent Tommy John surgery. The man who assumed Moylan's place as the primary set-up man last year was Boyer, who had missed all of 2006 with a shoulder injury and had thrown just 53⅔ innings in 2007. As Cox's new go-to man, Boyer threw 44⅔ innings over just the first three months of the 2008 season before collapsing thereafter. Without Soriano, Moylan, or Boyer, and with Mike Gonzalez still rehabbing in the minors, Cox leaned heavily on LOOGY Will Ohman (83 games) and minor league veteran Jeff Bennett (80⅔ relief innings in addition to four starts). Both weathered the strain admirably, but Bennett now bears a red flag to match those of Boyer and Soriano. The prospects of a full season of Gonzalez and a surgically repaired Soriano pitching in his walk year suggest that the Braves can expect significant improvement from their bullpen this year, but the track records of those pitchers and their manager's heavy hand should mute that optimism considerably.

The Braves hopes for improvement elsewhere are similarly muted. To begin with, the infield and catching positions, as a group, are more likely to regress than improve. Chipper Jones and McCann had huge years last year that will be hard to top, Escobar and Johnson are unlikely to show much significant improvement, and new first baseman Casey Kotchman will be charged with replacing the production of Teixeira, the man for whom he was acquired. Teixeira contributed 30.3 runs above replacement to the Braves in 2008 before being traded; in his best full major league season, Kotchman was 26.2 runs above replacement. Even in the best-case scenario, the Braves will lose ground in the infield, and that will undermine whatever production they recover in the outfield corners (thanks in part to the impossibly low baseline that was set last year).

The only significant change in personnel they stand to make on offense this year is in center field, where Jordan Schafer will get a chance to win the job out of spring training and is likely to assume the job later in the year, even if he isn't the team's Opening Day center fielder. Schafer is a legitimate blue-chip prospect, an all-around talent who is a terrific fielder and combines 20/20 potential with solid on-base skills at the plate. Still, he's a 22-year-old kid who will enter the 2009 season having had just 297 at-bats above A-ball. He'll star for the Braves in the future, but as their biggest hope for an improved offense entering this season, he's too little, and he could arrive too late.

The Braves have a similar situation in the starting rotation with Tommy Hanson, the team's top pitching prospect. Hanson dominated the Arizona Fall League last November, but has made just 18 starts above A-ball. Even more than Schafer, Hanson will need an adjustment period upon reaching the majors, and is projected as more of a solid second starter than a shutdown ace.

The one meaningful improvement to the rotation that the Braves had made as of press time was the acquisition of veteran Javier Vazquez from the White Sox. Vazquez is likely to benefit from the move to the weaker league and the opportunity to face opposing pitchers rather than designated hitters once every nine batters, but the greatest benefit he offers the team will be his durability: Vazquez has averaged 216 innings a year over the last nine seasons. That alone could help ease the strain on the Braves' bullpen, which was third in baseball in total innings pitched last year. Beyond Vazquez and Hanson, however, the Braves face likely regression from 2008 rookie revelations Jurrjens and Campillo and have left themselves to fill in any remaining gaps in the rotation with the usual gaggle of unestablished, low-ceiling prospects or the surgically repaired arms of their past greats, who are now yet another year older.

None of this adds up to a team that is significantly better than the .500 record a simple recovery in their one-run fortunes would yield. Though National League teams certainly need not be much better than .500 to consider themselves contenders these days, any further patching of the team as currently constructed in pursuit of a quick return to the playoffs would be misguided and would probably result in little more than one-year wonder contention, accompanied by an early playoff exit.

Rather than focus on the near miss of 2007, the team should look toward the long-term promise of players such as Schafer, Hanson, Jurrjens, McCann, and Escobar, of whom the last is the oldest at 26, to which you could add Johnson (27) and perhaps still Francoeur (25). Beyond that good group, the Braves have another wave of prospects on the way, led by outfielder Jason Heyward, who could prove to be the best hitter on the team soon after his arrival. They also have first baseman Freddie Freeman, who's due to arrive just in time to replace Kotchman after the latter departs for free agency, and lefty starters Cole Rohrbough and Jeff Locke. With a little patience, the Braves could have all these players in place and established by 2012. Complemented by a free-agent ace and perhaps one more big bat in left or in place of a by-then-retired Chipper Jones at third, the Braves would have a team that could emerge as a perennial contender in the next decade. That sounds a lot better than grasping after a chance to lose another NL Division Series, but the Braves need to ask themselves what kind of playoff team they want to be.

HITTERS

Josh Anderson   CF   Bats: L   Throws: R   Height: 6' 2"   Weight: 195   Born: August 10, 1982   Age: 26

YEAR	TEAM	LVL	AGE	PA	R	2B	3B	HR	RBI	BB	SO	SB	CS	EqBRR	AVG	OBP	SLG	EqAVG	EqOBP	EqSLG	EqA	VORP	WARP	DEFENSE			
2006	CCH	AA	23	610	83	26	4	3	50	27	73	43	13	-0.3	.308	.349	.385	.265	.296	.333	.227	-18.8	0.2	117-CF	4	8-LF	3
2007	ROU	AAA	24	564	64	17	6	2	43	32	75	40	8	0.0	.273	.325	.341	.242	.290	.307	.219	-26.6	-1.5	55-RF	-1	38-CF	2
2007	HOU	MLB	24	75	10	3	0	0	11	5	6	1	1	-0.0	.358	.413	.403	.358	.413	.403	.286	5.3	-0.2	15-CF	-6		
2008	RIC	AAA	25	541	77	25	4	4	40	30	57	42	7	4.2	.314	.358	.405	.270	.313	.360	.244	-5.6	-2.2	111-CF	-24	5-LF	0
2008	ATL	MLB	25	146	21	7	1	3	12	8	33	10	1	3.0	.294	.338	.426	.301	.345	.456	.284	7.5	0.7	27-CF	-1		
2009	ATL	MLB	26	541	68	23	4	3	41	30	72	33	9	2.3	.273	.318	.352	.273	.316	.363	.243	2.7	0.7	127-CF	-8		

Breakout: 32%   Improve: 52%   Collapse: 18%   Attrition: 14%   Comparables: Tike Redman, Tyrell Godwin, Kerry Robinson, Trench Davis

Acquired from the Astros for reliever Oscar Villarreal following the 2007 season, Anderson showed some batting-average-driven improvement at Triple-A and finished the year as the Braves' center fielder after Mark Kotsay was traded to Boston. A year older than Gregor Blanco, Anderson is a much better basestealer and has more power than his Venezuelan counterpart, but lacks Blanco's plate discipline. Of course, having more power than Blanco is a rather meaningless achievement, and Anderson's lack of patience more than undermines that advantage. Now 26, he's still nothing more than a fifth outfielder.

Gregor Blanco   CF

Bats: L   Throws: L   Height: 5' 11"   Weight: 170   Born: December 24, 1983   Age: 25

YEAR	TEAM	LVL	AGE	PA	R	2B	3B	HR	RBI	BB	SO	SB	CS	EqBRR	AVG	OBP	SLG	EqAVG	EqOBP	EqSLG	EqA	VORP	WARP	DEFENSE			
2006	MIS	AA	22	302	45	16	3	0	9	43	57	17	6	1.7	.287	.397	.375	.269	.367	.369	.266	6.6	1.2	66-CF	0		
2006	RIC	AAA	22	327	43	12	1	0	19	52	53	14	9	-1.4	.294	.408	.346	.264	.378	.315	.255	2.1	-0.5	64-CF	-10	5-LF	-1
2007	RIC	AAA	23	545	81	18	5	3	35	63	85	23	18	-3.2	.282	.369	.362	.253	.335	.335	.239	-6.2	-0.3	118-CF	-5		
2008	ATL	MLB	24	519	52	14	4	1	38	74	99	13	5	0.8	.251	.366	.309	.260	.375	.320	.259	0.7	-0.1	58-LF	-8	56-CF	-2
2009	ATL	MLB	25	373	51	13	2	3	28	47	64	11	5	1.9	.263	.360	.344	.263	.358	.355	.258	4.8	1.2	89-CF	-3		

Breakout: 22%   Improve: 43%   Collapse: 22%   Attrition: 28%   Comparables: Brett Butler, Elliott Maddox, Shin-Soo Choo, Darren Lewis

Blanco's speed and patience make him a useful fourth outfielder. He'll get on base, he covers huge swaths of whichever part of the pasture he's asked to roam, and he can be a weapon on the bases. However, his utter lack of power makes him problematic as a starter, particularly in a corner. That he returned to a part-time role over the final two months of last season suggests that the Braves have learned that lesson. He and Anderson are likely to share time in center field until Jordan Schafer's arrival.

Matt Diaz   LF

Bats: R   Throws: R   Height: 6' 1"   Weight: 205   Born: March 3, 1978   Age: 31

YEAR	TEAM	LVL	AGE	PA	R	2B	3B	HR	RBI	BB	SO	SB	CS	EqBRR	AVG	OBP	SLG	EqAVG	EqOBP	EqSLG	EqA	VORP	WARP	DEFENSE
2006	ATL	MLB	28	322	37	15	4	7	32	11	49	5	5	-1.5	.327	.364	.475	.331	.366	.482	.286	16.9	3.6	66-LF 18
2007	ATL	MLB	29	384	44	21	0	12	45	16	63	4	0	-1.5	.338	.368	.497	.341	.371	.511	.301	28.9	3.0	76-LF 3
2008	ATL	MLB	30	140	9	2	0	2	14	3	32	4	2	0.8	.244	.264	.304	.252	.271	.311	.202	-7.1	-1.0	33-LF -3
2009	ATL	MLB	31	225	25	10	1	5	28	11	41	4	2	-0.5	.282	.324	.414	.282	.322	.427	.257	3.7	0.8	56-LF 2

Breakout: 12%   Improve: 32%   Collapse: 32%   Attrition: 28%   Comparables: Jose Morales, Art Schult, Greg Colbrunn, Carmen Castillo

Diaz's 2008 season was a complete loss after he tore the posterior cruciate ligament in his left knee in a collision with the wall in Milwaukee on May 27, effectively finishing his season. He didn't hit in 11 rehab games in July and August, appeared in just one more game for the Braves, and would have been a nontendered candidate if the Braves had even one reliable outfielder coming out of the 2008 season. Although a platoon asset (.328/.361/.508 career vs. left-handed pitchers), Diaz's days in the majors could be numbered.

Yunel Escobar   SS

Bats: R   Throws: R   Height: 6' 2"   Weight: 200   Born: November 2, 1982   Age: 26

YEAR	TEAM	LVL	AGE	PA	R	2B	3B	HR	RBI	BB	SO	SB	CS	EqBRR	AVG	OBP	SLG	EqAVG	EqOBP	EqSLG	EqA	VORP	WARP	DEFENSE			
2006	MIS	AA	23	501	55	21	4	2	45	59	77	7	9	-0.5	.264	.361	.346	.246	.331	.339	.239	-6.8	0.2	60-SS	-4	33-3B	1
2007	RIC	AAA	24	195	20	10	3	2	29	14	27	7	3	0.8	.333	.379	.456	.298	.344	.425	.268	7.5	1.2	45-SS	1		
2007	ATL	MLB	24	355	54	25	0	5	28	27	44	5	3	0.6	.326	.385	.451	.332	.393	.473	.296	25.5	2.8	40-SS	1	18-3B	-1
2008	ATL	MLB	25	587	71	24	2	10	60	59	62	2	5	1.0	.288	.366	.401	.297	.374	.419	.275	24.9	3.5	124-SS	1		
2009	ATL	MLB	26	548	66	27	2	6	53	50	68	5	3	0.2	.287	.357	.387	.287	.356	.399	.264	23.5	2.4	129-SS	-1		

Breakout: 10%   Improve: 31%   Collapse: 28%   Attrition: 15%   Comparables: Mike Lansing, Al Gallagher, Danny Thompson, Johnny Lipon

Escobar wasn't expected to repeat the power he showed down the stretch in 2007, and he didn't, but he did show an unexpected improvement in his plate discipline, improving his K/BB ratio from 1.6 to 1.1. A strong defensive shortstop who hits for solid averages, who can pop double digits in homers, and who will draw an unintentional walk once every 10 plate appearances or so (as he did last year) is a very handy thing to have. Escobar joins keystone partner Kelly Johnson, McCann behind the plate, and eventually Schafer in center to give the Braves a strong, young core up the middle to build around.

Tyler Flowers   C

Bats: R   Throws: R   Height: 6' 4"   Weight: 220   Born: January 24, 1986   Age: 23

YEAR	TEAM	LVL	AGE	PA	R	2B	3B	HR	RBI	BB	SO	SB	CS	EqBRR	AVG	OBP	SLG	EqAVG	EqOBP	EqSLG	EqA	VORP	WARP	DEFENSE			
2006	DNV	Rk	20	150	24	9	0	5	16	16	30	0	0	-2.5	.279	.373	.465	.203	.260	.312	.197	-21.5	-1.8	22-1B	-3	7-C	0
2007	ROM	A	21	445	65	34	2	12	70	49	74	3	4	-6.1	.298	.378	.488	.236	.301	.385	.237	-6.1	-1.7	64-1B	-5	14-C	-5
2008	MYR	A+	22	520	72	32	1	17	88	98	102	8	7	-5.6	.288	.427	.494	.262	.388	.454	.292	32.2	4.0	85-C	-1		
2009	CHA	MLB	23	574	68	28	1	17	66	68	138	4	2	-2.0	.247	.340	.410	.247	.341	.419	.266	11.2	2.5	135-C	-15		

Breakout: 26%   Improve: 56%   Collapse: 16%   Attrition: 6%   Comparables: Chris Ashby, Mike Sweeney, Eddy Martinez-Esteve, Val Pascucci

The key player acquired by the White Sox in the Javier Vazquez trade, Flowers is a masher who should arrive in the majors just in time to replace A. J. Pierzynski when the latter's contract expires after the 2010 season. The problem is that Flowers' ability to remain a catcher is in doubt. He has a strong arm but is tall and heavy, and doesn't move well behind the plate. Flowers spent most of his first two professional seasons at first base (in part due to a 2007 knee surgery) and could return there. Fortunately, Paul Konerko's contract expires at the same time as Pierzynski's, and Flowers has the bat to carry the position. Playing his home games at pitching-friendly Myrtle Beach last year, Flowers drew 98 walks and slugged .494, then followed up with 12 homers in 20 games in the hitting-friendly Arizona Fall League, slugging .973 (yes, really). He'll love the Cell.

Jeff Francoeur　　RF　　Bats: R　Throws: R　Height: 6' 4"　Weight: 220　Born: January 8, 1984　Age: 25

YEAR	TEAM	LVL	AGE	PA	R	2B	3B	HR	RBI	BB	SO	SB	CS	EqBRR	AVG	OBP	SLG	EqAVG	EqOBP	EqSLG	EqA	VORP	WARP	DEFENSE	
2006	ATL	MLB	22	686	83	24	6	29	103	23	132	1	6	-0.5	.260	.293	.449	.261	.293	.452	.248	0.4	0.3	160-RF	-1
2007	ATL	MLB	23	696	84	40	0	19	105	42	129	5	2	-0.0	.293	.338	.444	.294	.341	.452	.273	20.0	2.5	160-RF	0
2008	ATL	MLB	24	652	70	33	3	11	71	39	111	0	1	0.7	.239	.294	.359	.241	.296	.370	.231	-17.8	-0.9	149-RF	0
2009	ATL	MLB	25	596	68	31	2	19	81	39	100	3	2	-0.6	.275	.328	.444	.275	.326	.458	.265	11.9	1.9	140-RF	0

Breakout: 35%　Improve: 71%　Collapse: 11%　Attrition: 13%　　　Comparables: Charlie Spikes, Glenn Braggs, Joe Adcock, Ollie Brown

Francoeur's poor plate discipline has long been a concern of ours, but after he showed improvement in that department in his age-23 season in 2007, we were ready to jump on the Frenchy bandwagon. Oops. Francoeur got off to a solid start last year, hitting .294/.321/.500 through April 27, but over the next four months, he hit just .213/.279/.308, earning a brief demotion to Double-A in early July to clear his mind and fix his swing. (It didn't work.) Francoeur didn't swing a bat for most of the winter leading up to 2008 and came to camp having added 20 pounds of bulk, which slowed his swing. Because he lacks the ability to work counts and get on base through other means, when the bottom fell out, he just kept on falling. Francoeur showed signs of recovery in September (.286/.333/.418), but the lack of power in those rates remains troubling. He hit just three homers over his final 70 games, and his isolated power has declined in each of the last three seasons. After last year, he has nowhere to go but up, but a full recovery in 2009 seems unlikely.

Freddie Freeman　　1B　　Bats: L　Throws: R　Height: 6' 5"　Weight: 220　Born: September 12, 1989　Age: 19

YEAR	TEAM	LVL	AGE	PA	R	2B	3B	HR	RBI	BB	SO	SB	CS	EqBRR	AVG	OBP	SLG	EqAVG	EqOBP	EqSLG	EqA	VORP	WARP	DEFENSE			
2007	BRA	Rk	17	234	24	7	0	6	30	7	33	1	2	-2.2	.268	.295	.379	.202	.221	.289	.163	-59.2	-4.4	49-1B	-2	6-3B	-2
2008	ROM	A	18	540	70	33	7	18	95	46	84	5	5	-4.8	.316	.378	.521	.265	.322	.447	.261	15.5	0.6	120-1B	-1		
2009	ATL	MLB	19	617	63	33	3	15	68	47	116	2	3	-0.8	.252	.312	.399	.252	.311	.411	.245	-1.4	0.4	144-1B	2		

Breakout: 50%　Improve: 72%　Collapse: 10%　Attrition: 6%　　　Comparables: Ryan Klesko, Dernell Stenson, James Loney, Scott Rolen

The Braves' second-round pick in 2007, Freeman established himself as their first baseman of the future, with a monster full-season debut last year. A good defender with a strong arm, he has the potential to be a middle-of-the-order hitter for the next contending Braves team, as his swing is built for both average and increasing power. He also shares a secret identity with Captain Marvel Jr., which probably didn't get much play in his high school but would have been a big thing had he been born about 1930.

Gorkys Hernandez　　CF　　Bats: R　Throws: R　Height: 6' 0"　Weight: 175　Born: September 7, 1987　Age: 21

YEAR	TEAM	LVL	AGE	PA	R	2B	3B	HR	RBI	BB	SO	SB	CS	EqBRR	AVG	OBP	SLG	EqAVG	EqOBP	EqSLG	EqA	VORP	WARP	DEFENSE	
2006	TGR	Rk	18	217	41	9	2	5	23	10	27	20	4	1.0	.327	.356	.463	.254	.276	.383	.228	-15.1	-1.1	49-CF	-4
2007	WMI	A	19	533	84	25	5	4	50	36	69	54	11	10.2	.293	.344	.391	.233	.274	.312	.212	-30.1	0.1	119-CF	13
2008	MYR	A+	20	467	75	23	6	5	42	48	79	20	4	5.9	.264	.348	.387	.236	.308	.356	.237	-9.7	2.0	94-CF	15
2009	ATL	MLB	21	582	70	28	5	6	45	46	101	20	7	4.0	.261	.323	.363	.261	.321	.375	.245	4.4	3.1	136-CF	12

Breakout: 57%　Improve: 78%　Collapse: 8%　Attrition: 8%　　　Comparables: Carlos Gomez, Willie Cañate, Desmond Jennings, Gregor Blanco

A speed-and-defense center fielder, Hernandez is stuck behind Jordan Schafer on the Braves' depth chart and thus is as likely to be used as a trade chip as to continue his climb through the Braves' system. He got off to a great start in the offense-stifling environment of Myrtle Beach last year before hamstring trouble brought down his numbers. He nevertheless managed to repeat his production from 2007 by compensating for the resulting loss in average with improved plate discipline, which could be the key to his eventual big-league success.

Jason Heyward — RF

Bats: L   Throws: L   Height: 6' 4"   Weight: 220   Born: August 9, 1989   Age: 19

YEAR	TEAM	LVL	AGE	PA	R	2B	3B	HR	RBI	BB	SO	SB	CS	EqBRR	AVG	OBP	SLG	EqAVG	EqOBP	EqSLG	EqA	VORP	WARP	DEFENSE		
2007	BRA	Rk	17	31	1	4	0	1	5	2	4	1	1	-0.7	.296	.355	.556	.241	.258	.414	.231	-1.8	-0.1	6-RF	0	
2007	DNV	Rk	17	17	3	1	0	0	1	1	5	0	0	-0.2	.313	.353	.375	.188	.235	.188	.121	-4.7	-0.3	4-RF	0	
2008	ROM	A	18	508	88	27	6	11	52	49	74	15	3	4.0	.323	.388	.483	.271	.332	.417	.262	11.6	1.0	99-RF	-2	4-CF 0
2008	MYR	A+	18	25	3	2	0	0	4	2	4	0	0	0.4	.182	.240	.273	.182	.240	.273	.183	-2.4	-0.2			
2009	*ATL*	*MLB*	*19*	*617*	*77*	*37*	*4*	*12*	*61*	*53*	*102*	*9*	*5*	*2.1*	*.270*	*.334*	*.416*	*.270*	*.333*	*.429*	*.261*	*9.4*	*1.9*	*144-RF*	*-1*	

Breakout: 58%   Improve: 77%   Collapse: 3%   Attrition: 7%   *Comparables: Al Chambers, Chipper Jones, James Loney, Casey Kotchman*

The Braves' top pick in 2007, Heyward excelled in the full-season Sally League at the age of 18 last year, and he's expected to develop more power as his big frame fills out. A solid right fielder with a strong arm, Heyward's the team's top hitting prospect, and he should be a top run producer on the Braves' next contending team.

Omar Infante — UT

Bats: R   Throws: R   Height: 6' 0"   Weight: 180   Born: December 26, 1981   Age: 27

YEAR	TEAM	LVL	AGE	PA	R	2B	3B	HR	RBI	BB	SO	SB	CS	EqBRR	AVG	OBP	SLG	EqAVG	EqOBP	EqSLG	EqA	VORP	WARP	DEFENSE		
2006	DET	MLB	24	245	35	11	4	4	25	14	45	3	2	0.4	.277	.325	.415	.265	.317	.399	.248	5.2	0.8	34-2B	2	6-3B 0
2007	DET	MLB	25	178	24	6	1	2	17	9	29	4	1	1.0	.271	.307	.355	.267	.307	.370	.239	-0.9	-0.1	14-2B	0	9-SS -1
2008	ATL	MLB	26	348	45	24	3	3	40	22	44	0	1	-3.4	.293	.338	.416	.300	.345	.435	.270	9.5	0.9	26-3B	-1	25-LF -6
2009	*ATL*	*MLB*	*27*	*382*	*45*	*21*	*2*	*7*	*40*	*28*	*52*	*3*	*2*	*0.5*	*.275*	*.332*	*.408*	*.275*	*.330*	*.421*	*.259*	*10.4*	*1.3*	*92-3B*	*1*	

Breakout: 18%   Improve: 47%   Collapse: 26%   Attrition: 16%   *Comparables: Pat Kelly, Jim Davenport, Rich Aurilia, Aaron Boone*

A handy utilityman who can play the three infield skill positions and spot in the outfield, Infante saw too much action in left last year due to the Braves' dearth of viable alternatives. Still, he had one of his better years at the plate, showing increased contact and some doubles power. He's still young enough for those improvements to be real, and he previously showed some pop in his lone season as the Tigers' starting second baseman back in 2004. Spotted in the infield against lefty pitching, he's an asset.

Cody Johnson — LF

Bats: L   Throws: R   Height: 6' 4"   Weight: 195   Born: August 18, 1988   Age: 20

YEAR	TEAM	LVL	AGE	PA	R	2B	3B	HR	RBI	BB	SO	SB	CS	EqBRR	AVG	OBP	SLG	EqAVG	EqOBP	EqSLG	EqA	VORP	WARP	DEFENSE	
2006	BRA	Rk	17	127	13	6	1	1	16	12	49	2	0	0.7	.184	.260	.281	.136	.189	.229	.124	-53.3	-3.5	23-LF	-4
2007	DNV	Rk	18	270	51	18	5	17	57	26	72	7	0	-1.0	.305	.374	.630	.209	.259	.399	.223	-19.8	-1.6	50-LF	-3
2008	ROM	A	19	514	62	26	1	26	89	40	177	8	3	-2.1	.252	.307	.479	.215	.267	.405	.230	-15.0	-4.0	105-LF	-25
2009	*ATL*	*MLB*	*20*	*603*	*61*	*32*	*2*	*22*	*74*	*50*	*190*	*6*	*3*	*-0.0*	*.227*	*.292*	*.415*	*.227*	*.291*	*.428*	*.244*	*-4.1*	*-1.0*	*141-LF*	*-17*

Breakout: 60%   Improve: 84%   Collapse: 4%   Attrition: 4%   *Comparables: Rob Nelson, Eric Duncan, Matt Winters, Ian Stewart*

The Braves' top pick in 2006, Johnson has tremendous power, but that was all he had going for him in his full-season debut last year. Superficially, he's an Adam Dunn type, except that he doesn't draw nearly as many walks as Dunn did, and Johnson strikes out far more often than Dunn ever did in the minor leagues. Unless Johnson can close the huge holes in his swing, he's unlikely to have much of a major league career.

Kelly Johnson — 2B

Bats: L   Throws: R   Height: 6' 1"   Weight: 205   Born: February 22, 1982   Age: 27

YEAR	TEAM	LVL	AGE	PA	R	2B	3B	HR	RBI	BB	SO	SB	CS	EqBRR	AVG	OBP	SLG	EqAVG	EqOBP	EqSLG	EqA	VORP	WARP	DEFENSE	
2007	ATL	MLB	25	608	91	26	10	16	68	79	117	9	5	0.4	.276	.375	.457	.279	.381	.472	.292	35.3	5.0	128-2B	7
2008	ATL	MLB	26	614	86	39	6	12	69	52	113	11	6	-0.8	.287	.349	.446	.295	.356	.470	.281	27.1	5.2	135-2B	14
2009	*ATL*	*MLB*	*27*	*625*	*92*	*36*	*5*	*17*	*75*	*70*	*108*	*12*	*6*	*2.4*	*.287*	*.370*	*.467*	*.287*	*.369*	*.481*	*.290*	*41.2*	*5.0*	*146-2B*	*5*

Breakout: 18%   Improve: 55%   Collapse: 10%   Attrition: 8%   *Comparables: Eric Hinske, Chase Utley, Pete Ward, Dan Uggla*

After a strong debut as the Braves' second baseman in 2007, Johnson regressed last year, losing power and walks. He showed some improvement against his fellow lefties, but that was largely based on a jump in batting average. It seems that Johnson just is what he is. A .281/.364/.464 hitter in the minors who was thrown out on 34 percent of his steal attempts, he has hit .282/.362/.451 in his two seasons as the Braves' second baseman while being thrown out on 36 percent of his steal attempts. If the Braves give him a red light on the bases, he'll continue to make a solid contribution to the lineup, though his limited defense at the keystone drags down his overall value.

Brandon Jones   **LF**   Bats: L   Throws: R   Height: 6' 2"   Weight: 195   Born: December 10, 1983   Age: 25

YEAR	TEAM	LVL	AGE	PA	R	2B	3B	HR	RBI	BB	SO	SB	CS	EqBRR	AVG	OBP	SLG	EqAVG	EqOBP	EqSLG	EqA	VORP	WARP	DEFENSE			
2006	MYR	A+	22	255	27	10	3	7	35	25	49	11	6	-1.2	.257	.329	.420	.214	.271	.342	.213	-13.1	-1.4	49-LF	-3		
2006	MIS	AA	22	194	18	9	3	7	25	15	38	4	2	-2.1	.273	.326	.477	.257	.304	.475	.263	5.5	1.2	30-RF	2	17-LF	4
2007	MIS	AA	23	418	58	21	6	15	74	44	84	12	7	0.0	.293	.368	.507	.265	.329	.465	.270	15.7	2.1	89-LF	5		
2007	RIC	AAA	23	191	26	12	1	4	26	17	36	5	0	2.0	.300	.363	.453	.273	.335	.442	.271	6.5	0.8	43-LF	1		
2007	ATL	MLB	23	21	0	1	0	0	4	0	8	0	0	-0.1	.158	.190	.211	.158	.190	.211	.127	-2.6	-0.3	5-LF	-1		
2008	RIC	AAA	24	396	44	24	1	8	52	46	76	9	6	0.3	.260	.343	.405	.233	.318	.378	.244	-3.2	-0.2	55-LF	-4	30-RF	2
2008	ATL	MLB	24	128	16	10	1	1	17	7	28	1	0	0.5	.267	.312	.397	.274	.317	.402	.252	0.4	-0.1	25-LF	-2		
2009	ATL	MLB	25	486	56	25	3	11	56	44	106	9	4	0.6	.253	.323	.396	.253	.321	.409	.252	1.3	1.1	115-LF	2		

Breakout: 29% Improve: 52% Collapse: 22% Attrition: 12%   Comparables: Jeff Wetherby, Tommy Dunbar, Keith Hughes, Shawn Hare

The Braves hoped that Jones would crack their starting outfield last year, but outside of five games in June in which he went 10-for-19 as their left fielder, his season was almost as lost as Diaz's. Starting the year at Triple-A for the first time, Jones struggled through his worst season, one marked by a near-complete loss of power. Jones claims he was putting too much pressure on himself, but now that he's entering his age-25 season, the pressure will only increase as the Braves are again hoping he can serve as Diaz's platoon partner.

Chipper Jones   **3B**   Bats: S   Throws: R   Height: 6' 4"   Weight: 210   Born: April 24, 1972   Age: 37

YEAR	TEAM	LVL	AGE	PA	R	2B	3B	HR	RBI	BB	SO	SB	CS	EqBRR	AVG	OBP	SLG	EqAVG	EqOBP	EqSLG	EqA	VORP	WARP	DEFENSE	
2006	ATL	MLB	34	477	87	28	3	26	86	61	73	6	1	-1.8	.324	.409	.596	.324	.412	.596	.334	54.9	4.2	100-3B	-12
2007	ATL	MLB	35	600	108	42	4	29	102	82	75	5	1	1.3	.337	.425	.604	.337	.430	.616	.344	78.3	8.5	120-3B	7
2008	ATL	MLB	36	534	82	24	1	22	75	90	61	4	0	-0.0	.364	.470	.574	.371	.476	.593	.363	74.7	8.2	111-3B	5
2009	ATL	MLB	37	567	104	33	2	23	90	88	67	5	1	-1.9	.341	.443	.564	.341	.441	.582	.342	65.1	6.3	133-3B	-2

Breakout: 7% Improve: 38% Collapse: 30% Attrition: 16%   Comparables: Frank Robinson, Ellis Burks, Stan Musial, Edgar Martinez

Jones has hit an astounding .332/.430/.585 over the last four seasons, but entering the last year of his contract at the age of 37, he's no sure bet to be on the next contending Braves team. Jones has never been a good defensive third baseman, and the injuries that have prevented him from playing more than 137 games in a single season since 2003 are sure to catch up to him as he approaches his 40th birthday. With Kotchman occupying first base, the only place for Jones to go might be to another team. If the Braves aren't contending by the trading deadline, they'd be better off selling high on the future Hall of Famer than holding on to him for a run at 500 homers, a mark he'll reach more easily as a first baseman or DH. Of course, they won't deal him, but they should.

Kala Ka'aihue   **1B**   Bats: R   Throws: R   Height: 6' 2"   Weight: 230   Born: March 29, 1985   Age: 24

YEAR	TEAM	LVL	AGE	PA	R	2B	3B	HR	RBI	BB	SO	SB	CS	EqBRR	AVG	OBP	SLG	EqAVG	EqOBP	EqSLG	EqA	VORP	WARP	DEFENSE	
2006	ROM	A	21	284	44	16	2	15	49	52	66	3	0	-1.0	.329	.458	.614	.247	.352	.457	.279	12.3	0.1	64-1B	-8
2006	MYR	A+	21	222	37	8	0	13	31	30	49	0	1	-2.8	.223	.342	.473	.187	.278	.379	.225	-8.4	-1.1	49-1B	-3
2007	MYR	A+	22	376	57	20	1	22	61	53	92	2	0	-3.2	.298	.410	.583	.242	.330	.465	.272	12.4	0.1	81-1B	-8
2007	MIS	AA	22	133	14	5	1	0	8	11	51	0	0	0.0	.127	.211	.186	.124	.188	.182	.088	-22.1	-2.5	32-1B	-4
2008	MIS	AA	23	475	63	23	2	14	61	88	119	0	4	-3.5	.274	.417	.457	.237	.354	.398	.265	9.3	1.1	94-1B	2
2009	ATL	MLB	24	523	56	24	1	19	66	67	155	1	1	-2.2	.232	.336	.418	.232	.334	.431	.263	5.5	1.0	123-1B	-1

Breakout: 40% Improve: 72% Collapse: 13% Attrition: 8%   Comparables: Vito Chiaravalloti, Brandon Sing, John Jaha, Mike Napoli

Ka'aihue refined his approach entering his first full season at Double-A, trading off some power for increased plate discipline. As a result, the big man got his K/BB ratio back to its A-ball level, but he nearly halved his home-run rate in the process. Playing winter ball in his native Hawaii, Ka'aihue's plate judgment regressed without a concurrent resurgence of power. He'll have to find a happy medium to become a viable major leaguer.

Casey Kotchman 1B

Bats: L   Throws: L   Height: 6' 3"   Weight: 215   Born: February 22, 1983   Age: 26

YEAR	TEAM	LVL	AGE	PA	R	2B	3B	HR	RBI	BB	SO	SB	CS	EqBRR	AVG	OBP	SLG	EqAVG	EqOBP	EqSLG	EqA	VORP	WARP	DEFENSE	
2006	ANA	MLB	23	88	6	2	0	1	6	7	13	0	1	-0.7	.152	.221	.215	.141	.221	.205	.132	-11.6	-0.8	22-1B	2
2007	ANA	MLB	24	508	64	37	3	11	68	53	43	2	4	-6.2	.296	.372	.467	.289	.369	.470	.286	22.6	3.1	117-1B	8
2008	ANA	MLB	25	398	47	24	0	12	54	18	23	2	1	-4.6	.287	.327	.448	.282	.322	.460	.266	10.0	2.5	96-1B	16
2008	ATL	MLB	25	175	18	4	1	2	20	18	16	0	0	-1.2	.237	.331	.316	.237	.331	.316	.235	-3.9	-0.7	40-1B	-3
2009	ATL	MLB	26	538	64	30	2	11	66	45	48	1	3	-2.0	.288	.353	.423	.288	.351	.437	.269	13.9	2.0	127-1B	6

Breakout: 25% Improve: 59% Collapse: 16% Attrition: 17%   Comparables: Derrick May, Frank Torre, Tino Martinez, Bruce Bochte

August was a tough month for Casey Kotchman. An Angels brat since his father became one of the club's minor league managers when Casey was just a year old, Kotchman was traded to the Braves at the trading deadline and immediately sunk into an awful slump, hitting .157/.259/.214 in his first 20 games with Atlanta. Then, his mother suffered a nonfatal brain aneurysm. After a two-week absence from the team, Kotchman returned having put things in perspective and hit .305/.394/.402. Prior to the trade, Kotchman's unintentional walk rate was way down (26.5 PA/UIBB), the result of a misguided attempt to hit for more power, but with the Braves, it returned to normal (10.9 PA/UIBB vs. 11.1 career entering the year). Having regained the plate approach that is the key to his offensive game, and with that emotional summer behind him, Kotchman should return to his 2007 form this year, solidly occupying first base until Freeman's arrival, which should sync up with Kotchman's free agency.

Brent Lillibridge SS

Bats: R   Throws: R   Height: 5' 11"   Weight: 190   Born: September 18, 1983   Age: 25

YEAR	TEAM	LVL	AGE	PA	R	2B	3B	HR	RBI	BB	SO	SB	CS	EqBRR	AVG	OBP	SLG	EqAVG	EqOBP	EqSLG	EqA	VORP	WARP	DEFENSE	
2006	HIC	A	22	333	59	18	5	11	43	51	61	29	8	4.1	.299	.414	.522	.216	.304	.370	.240	-7.3	1.8	72-SS	8
2006	LYN	A+	22	252	47	10	3	2	28	36	43	24	5	7.2	.313	.426	.423	.255	.343	.343	.252	-0.9	1.3	54-SS	3
2007	MIS	AA	23	237	31	8	3	3	17	20	60	14	7	0.0	.275	.355	.387	.244	.311	.362	.236	-3.6	0.7	52-SS	2
2007	RIC	AAA	23	355	47	14	2	10	41	20	59	28	5	7.4	.287	.331	.436	.260	.302	.416	.254	1.4	0.8	84-SS	-6
2008	RIC	AAA	24	403	46	18	7	4	39	33	90	23	7	0.1	.220	.294	.344	.201	.273	.329	.218	-22.3	-0.6	91-SS	-4
2008	ATL	MLB	24	85	9	6	1	1	8	3	23	2	0	1.4	.200	.238	.338	.198	.235	.333	.199	-2.3	-0.3	21-SS	0
2009	CHA	MLB	25	456	53	21	3	8	36	38	106	22	7	3.2	.231	.303	.359	.231	.304	.366	.242	1.0	1.5	108-SS	3

Breakout: 34% Improve: 58% Collapse: 17% Attrition: 14%   Comparables: Eric Owens, Antonio Perez, Brian Bixler, Greg Gagne

Lillibridge's strong age-22 season in A-ball is starting to look like an outlier rather than the measure of his true potential. Expected to pressure Escobar for the shortstop job last year, Lillibridge instead suffered an all-out collapse in his first full season at Triple-A, which in turn drew attention to how much of his 2007 production was dependent on his batting average. His defense and foot speed held, but if he can't pull his bat out of its current nosedive, he'll have to lean on his athleticism to eke out a major league career as a utilityman. The good news is that having been included in the Javier Vazquez trade, his options are more plentiful with the White Sox, who could use him in center field and will allow him to compete for the jobs at second and third base in spring training. Still, he's blocked at shortstop by Alexei Ramirez and is unlikely to beat out Chris Getz or Josh Fields at the other two infield spots.

Brian McCann C

Bats: L   Throws: R   Height: 6' 3"   Weight: 210   Born: February 20, 1984   Age: 25

YEAR	TEAM	LVL	AGE	PA	R	2B	3B	HR	RBI	BB	SO	SB	CS	EqBRR	AVG	OBP	SLG	EqAVG	EqOBP	EqSLG	EqA	VORP	WARP	DEFENSE	
2006	ATL	MLB	22	492	61	34	0	24	93	41	54	2	0	-4.4	.333	.388	.572	.332	.388	.568	.319	56.2	5.6	114-C	-1
2007	ATL	MLB	23	552	51	38	0	18	92	35	74	0	1	-4.1	.270	.320	.452	.268	.320	.463	.266	24.4	2.9	127-C	-1
2008	ATL	MLB	24	573	68	42	1	23	87	57	64	5	0	-2.3	.301	.373	.523	.307	.380	.543	.311	51.0	5.5	129-C	-5
2009	ATL	MLB	25	564	77	34	1	23	94	55	64	4	1	-2.7	.299	.371	.511	.299	.369	.527	.299	48.8	5.9	132-C	0

Breakout: 15% Improve: 50% Collapse: 23% Attrition: 7%   Comparables: Matt Nokes, Joe Torre, Gary Carter, Ted Simmons

After a sophomore slump in 2007, McCann rebounded with a strong third season as the Braves' principal catcher, emerging as the team's second-best hitter after Mark Teixeira was traded to Anaheim. Only two catchers allowed more stolen bases than McCann did last year, but that had as much do to with his constant presence behind the plate and Jair Jurrjens's total inability to hold runners as it did with McCann's admittedly subpar arm.

Greg Norton   UT

Bats: S   Throws: R   Height: 6' 1"   Weight: 205   Born: July 6, 1972   Age: 36

YEAR	TEAM	LVL	AGE	PA	R	2B	3B	HR	RBI	BB	SO	SB	CS	EqBRR	AVG	OBP	SLG	EqAVG	EqOBP	EqSLG	EqA	VORP	WARP	DEFENSE
2006	TBA	MLB	33	335	47	15	0	17	45	35	69	1	5	-2.3	.296	.374	.520	.289	.374	.519	.293	20.5	1.4	24-RF -1 20-1B -3
2007	TBA	MLB	34	240	25	9	0	4	23	37	55	1	1	-1.4	.243	.358	.347	.240	.363	.345	.257	-0.8	0.2	
2008	SEA	MLB	35	18	2	2	0	0	4	2	4	0	0	-0.2	.438	.500	.563	.438	.500	.562	.369	3.3	0.2	
2008	ATL	MLB	35	202	27	10	0	7	31	31	40	0	0	-0.5	.246	.361	.427	.246	.365	.427	.277	6.0	0.2	16-LF -2 7-1B -2
2009	ATL	MLB	36	144	17	7	0	4	18	20	29	1	1	-0.6	.254	.359	.403	.254	.357	.415	.269	4.2	0.2	38-DH

Breakout: 17%   Improve: 41%   Collapse: 34%   Attrition: 44%   Comparables: Champ Summers, David Segui, John Vander Wal, Mike Jorgensen

A switch-hitter who can't hit right-handed and a four-corner utility man who can no longer play third base, Norton continues to hang on to his major league career, thanks to out-of-character surges in production in the last two even-numbered years. Purchased from the Mariners at the beginning of May to help round out the Atlanta bench, Norton hit .316/.473/.526 as a pinch-hitter last year (74 plate appearances), a fluke of fortune that will probably find him another bench job in which he's sure to disappoint.

Martin Prado   INF

Bats: R   Throws: R   Height: 6' 1"   Weight: 190   Born: October 27, 1983   Age: 25

YEAR	TEAM	LVL	AGE	PA	R	2B	3B	HR	RBI	BB	SO	SB	CS	EqBRR	AVG	OBP	SLG	EqAVG	EqOBP	EqSLG	EqA	VORP	WARP	DEFENSE
2006	MIS	AA	22	191	17	6	2	1	15	14	35	2	2	-1.3	.278	.330	.352	.258	.304	.331	.223	-5.8	-1.1	27-2B -6 16-3B -1
2006	RIC	AAA	22	257	30	12	1	2	23	12	28	2	2	1.0	.282	.314	.365	.252	.282	.331	.211	-10.7	-1.3	45-2B -8 13-3B 2
2006	ATL	MLB	22	49	3	1	1	1	9	5	7	0	0	-1.7	.262	.340	.405	.256	.333	.395	.255	1.2	-0.5	7-2B -2 4-3B -3
2007	RIC	AAA	23	443	61	23	3	4	41	34	41	5	4	5.2	.316	.374	.420	.284	.339	.388	.255	7.6	0.2	85-2B -4 8-3B -1
2007	ATL	MLB	23	62	5	3	0	0	2	3	6	0	0	0.4	.288	.323	.339	.288	.323	.339	.232	-0.0	0.4	7-2B 3 5-3B 1
2008	ATL	MLB	24	254	36	18	4	2	33	21	29	3	1	-1.1	.320	.377	.461	.329	.385	.487	.300	16.1	1.9	18-3B 1 16-2B 3
2009	ATL	MLB	25	380	44	19	2	4	36	29	46	4	2	0.6	.281	.339	.386	.281	.337	.398	.256	9.3	1.2	91-2B -1

Breakout: 13%   Improve: 45%   Collapse: 30%   Attrition: 26%   Comparables: Gil Flores, Julio Gotay, Jose Castillo, Al Gallagher

Prado looks like a younger, better version of Infante, but while he is a solid second baseman and finished the year in Chipper's stead at third base, he isn't really viable at shortstop, and most of his production at the plate is average-driven. Still, that production was steady on either side of the sprained thumb he suffered in May, and given that he's just 25, the Braves would be wise to find out if the extra doubles power he showed in the majors last year was real.

Clint Sammons   C

Bats: R   Throws: R   Height: 6' 0"   Weight: 200   Born: May 15, 1983   Age: 26

YEAR	TEAM	LVL	AGE	PA	R	2B	3B	HR	RBI	BB	SO	SB	CS	EqBRR	AVG	OBP	SLG	EqAVG	EqOBP	EqSLG	EqA	VORP	WARP	DEFENSE
2006	MYR	A+	23	407	36	21	0	8	56	32	65	4	4	0.0	.258	.323	.383	.205	.252	.301	.191	-31.7	-1.7	94-C -4
2007	MYR	A+	24	91	13	6	0	4	13	10	14	1	1	-0.5	.269	.363	.500	.195	.264	.341	.211	-5.3	0.3	18-C 4
2007	MIS	AA	24	328	27	10	0	5	36	26	72	1	1	0.0	.243	.304	.328	.201	.253	.267	.179	-29.7	-0.9	80-C 3
2008	RIC	AAA	25	305	23	18	0	1	22	21	60	7	2	0.3	.237	.295	.313	.206	.261	.274	.188	-25.4	-1.5	77-C -5
2008	ATL	MLB	25	59	2	0	0	1	4	5	12	0	0	-0.1	.148	.220	.204	.148	.220	.204	.125	-5.5	-0.8	15-C -3
2009	ATL	MLB	26	298	20	12	0	4	26	20	70	3	1	-0.5	.196	.254	.289	.196	.253	.298	.186	-13.2	-0.2	73-C 0

Breakout: 36%   Improve: 50%   Collapse: 32%   Attrition: 27%   Comparables: Steven Liddle, Ronn Reynolds, Brian Loyd, Rick Guarno

A catch-and-throw guy, Sammons jumped from High-A to the majors over the last two seasons, finishing 2008 as McCann's backup. That's about all he'll ever be, despite a strong throwing arm (32 percent caught stealing in 2008). He'll probably be squeezed out by the two-year deal handed to Dave Ross.

Jordan Schafer   CF

Bats: L   Throws: L   Height: 6' 1"   Weight: 190   Born: September 4, 1986   Age: 22

YEAR	TEAM	LVL	AGE	PA	R	2B	3B	HR	RBI	BB	SO	SB	CS	EqBRR	AVG	OBP	SLG	EqAVG	EqOBP	EqSLG	EqA	VORP	WARP	DEFENSE
2006	ROM	A	19	422	49	15	7	8	60	28	95	15	9	-2.7	.240	.293	.376	.191	.230	.291	.173	-41.7	-5.9	106-CF -25
2007	ROM	A	20	145	16	15	2	5	20	16	31	4	4	-3.0	.372	.441	.636	.278	.338	.474	.273	7.2	-0.2	32-CF -7
2007	MYR	A+	20	481	70	34	8	10	43	40	95	19	11	0.7	.294	.354	.477	.232	.280	.382	.226	-13.2	-1.9	101-CF -12
2008	MIS	AA	21	349	46	18	6	10	51	49	88	12	5	-2.2	.269	.378	.471	.233	.321	.408	.254	1.8	-0.2	78-CF -9
2009	ATL	MLB	22	513	57	27	4	12	55	45	136	13	6	1.1	.238	.308	.391	.238	.307	.404	.245	3.6	0.6	121-CF -7

Breakout: 44%   Improve: 63%   Collapse: 13%   Attrition: 7%   Comparables: Jimmy White, Louie Meadows, John Vander Wal, Richard Brown

A drug suspension (for human growth hormone) cut into Schafer's Double-A debut last year, but it was still a successful campaign for the 21-year-old, who survived the jump with his speed, power, and patience intact. After shaking off the rust from his suspension, Schafer hit .303/.387/.526 in the second half. A stellar defensive center fielder with a strong arm, he could get a shot at the major league job this spring, or he could hit his way into the job with a strong early showing at Triple-A. The only lingering concern is his inability to hit lefties.

PITCHERS

Manny Acosta

Bats: R   Throws: R   Height: 6' 4"   Weight: 170   Born: May 1, 1981   Age: 28

YEAR	TEAM	LVL	AGE	W	L	SV	G	GS	IP	H	BB	SO	HR	GB%	BABIP	STUFF	WHIP	ERA	DERA	EqH9	EqBB9	EqSO9	EqHR9	DEF	VORP	SN/WX
2006	MIS	AA	25	0	0	4	13	0	15¹	7	15	13	1	63.2%	.162	-7	1.46	2.38	5.02	5.0	9.4	4.4	1.3	1	0.9	—
2006	RIC	AAA	25	1	6	17	38	0	44¹	38	32	44	4	59.7%	.304	-8	1.59	3.67	5.40	9.1	7.3	6.0	1.5	0	0.9	—
2007	RIC	AAA	26	9	3	12	40	0	59²	46	35	56	0	56.7%	.297	7	1.36	2.26	4.02	8.4	5.9	6.0	0.3	1	9.4	—
2007	ATL	MLB	26	1	1	0	21	0	23²	13	14	22	2	59.6%	.200	12	1.14	2.28	3.57	5.2	4.8	7.9	0.8	3	9.4	0.61
2008	ATL	MLB	27	3	5	3	46	0	53	48	26	31	7	54.2%	.263	-17	1.40	3.57	4.33	8.1	3.8	4.7	1.2	1	8.1	0.09
2009	ATL	MLB	28	2	2	2	32	0	37²	37	21	27	3	49.0%	.290	-2	1.53	4.33	4.62	8.7	4.4	5.6	0.7	0	5.0	0.37

Breakout: 10% Improve: 29% Collapse: 50% Attrition: 38%   Comparables: Franklyn German, Jim Todd, Gary Wagner, Rodney Myers

A skinny Panamanian out of the Yankees system, Acosta got a shot at closing during Rafael Soriano's early-season stints on the disabled list. Acosta had a 1.61 ERA and allowed just one inherited runner to score in April and May, but was awful in June and tore his right hamstring in early July, resulting in a seven-week stay on the DL. Acosta made just five appearances for the Braves after his late-August return, but, with his high-90s heat, could emerge as a valuable late-inning reliever for them in 2009.

Jeff Bennett

Bats: R   Throws: R   Height: 6' 3"   Weight: 200   Born: June 10, 1980   Age: 29

YEAR	TEAM	LVL	AGE	W	L	SV	G	GS	IP	H	BB	SO	HR	GB%	BABIP	STUFF	WHIP	ERA	DERA	EqH9	EqBB9	EqSO9	EqHR9	DEF	VORP	SN/WX
2007	RIC	AAA	27	3	5	1	36	6	86	84	34	45	5	56.0%	.281	-27	1.37	3.35	6.46	10.2	4.0	3.0	0.9	17	-7.5	—
2007	ATL	MLB	27	2	1	0	3	2	13	14	3	14	3	57.5%	.314	14	1.31	3.46	3.95	9.2	2.0	8.6	2.0	1	3.5	0.39
2008	ATL	MLB	28	3	7	3	72	4	97¹	86	47	68	5	64.6%	.288	5	1.37	3.70	4.22	8.0	3.8	5.6	0.5	4	17.0	2.03
2009	ATL	MLB	29	3	3	2	45	1	59	62	27	39	4	57.0%	.310	-1	1.51	4.41	4.77	9.4	3.5	5.1	0.7	0	5.9	0.55

Breakout: 11% Improve: 29% Collapse: 48% Attrition: 36%   Comparables: Gary Wagner, Jim Winn, Mike Fetters, Dave Gumpert

Bennett dislocated his pitching shoulder in early July, but missed just three weeks and was better after he returned than before the injury. Despite the time on the shelf, he appeared in 72 games, starting four and adding 80⅔ innings out of the pen, a workload similar to the one he bore for Triple-A Richmond in 2007. That durability and flexibility, combined with a tight slider and a spike in his ground-ball rate (opponents slugged just .333), made him a very valuable pitcher to have on staff. If Bennett can reduce his walks and keep inducing grounders, he could have a breakout season in 2009—if those workloads don't make it a break*down* season.

Blaine Boyer

Bats: R   Throws: R   Height: 6' 3"   Weight: 215   Born: July 11, 1981   Age: 27

YEAR	TEAM	LVL	AGE	W	L	SV	G	GS	IP	H	BB	SO	HR	GB%	BABIP	STUFF	WHIP	ERA	DERA	EqH9	EqBB9	EqSO9	EqHR9	DEF	VORP	SN/WX
2007	RIC	AAA	25	4	3	2	21	12	73¹	76	50	62	1	48.4%	.359	5	1.72	4.30	6.37	11.5	6.9	5.4	0.3	1	-5.6	—
2007	ATL	MLB	25	0	0	0	5	0	5¹	10	1	3	0	59.1%	.476	-5	2.06	3.40	0.00	18.0	1.8	5.4	0.0	-3	0.4	0.07
2008	ATL	MLB	26	2	6	1	76	0	72	73	25	67	10	46.1%	.312	-2	1.36	5.88	5.45	8.9	2.6	7.3	1.2	-5	-6.2	-0.83
2009	ATL	MLB	27	2	2	2	38	1	47²	47	20	41	5	45.0%	.300	8	1.39	4.30	4.58	8.7	3.2	6.6	0.9	0	6.5	0.56

Breakout: 50% Improve: 68% Collapse: 16% Attrition: 36%   Comparables: Todd Ritchie, Thad Tillotson, Mike Fetters, Don Johnson

Speaking of heavy workloads, Boyer lost most of 2006 to shoulder surgery and struggled with his control in 2007. He emerged as the Braves' eighth-inning guy in the first half of 2008, but having thrown 44⅔ innings by the end of June (including appearances in both games of a doubleheader in late May), he fell apart when the calendar flipped to

July. He pitched in just two Braves wins in August (one of which saw him surrender four runs in less than an inning) and gave up eight runs in just 3⅓ innings of work in September. The good news is that his control was never the issue; he simply got smacked around. Given the winter to rest, he could be an asset in a more balanced bullpen this year, as he held opposing batters to a .228/.293/.377 line during those first three months.

Jorge Campillo

Bats: R   Throws: R   Height: 6' 1"   Weight: 190   Born: August 10, 1978   Age: 30

YEAR	TEAM	LVL	AGE	W	L	SV	G	GS	IP	H	BB	SO	HR	GB%	BABIP	STUFF	WHIP	ERA	DERA	EqH9	EqBB9	EqSO9	EqHR9	DEF	VORP	SN/WX
2007	TAC	AAA	28	9	6	0	24	22	149¹	151	39	99	11	40.0%	.302	2	1.27	3.07	4.90	8.9	2.5	4.1	0.9	14	11.3	—
2007	SEA	MLB	28	0	0	0	5	0	13¹	18	6	9	2	34.0%	.372	-15	1.80	6.77	6.08	11.5	4.1	5.4	1.4	-3	-3.3	-0.18
2008	ATL	MLB	29	8	7	0	39	25	158²	158	38	107	18	40.6%	.294	5	1.24	3.91	4.15	8.9	1.8	5.4	1.0	1	25.7	3.56
2009	ATL	MLB	30	5	6	1	32	13	97²	107	29	64	13	42.0%	.300	4	1.40	4.74	4.96	9.8	2.3	5.1	1.2	0	8.1	1.31

Breakout: 3%   Improve: 20%   Collapse: 51%   Attrition: 27%   Comparables: George Zuverink, Armando Reynoso, Mike Oquist, Chris Brock

The primary beneficiary of the plague of season-ending surgeries that afflicted the rotation, Campillo was originally signed by the Braves out of his native Mexico as a 17-year-old back in 1996. He was released just a year later and spent most of his 20s as a star in the Mexican League. The Mariners were enticed by his league-leading ERA in 2004, but his first stateside season ended in Tommy John surgery. Recovered, Campillo turned in a solid season in the hitter-friendly Pacific Coast League in 2007 and signed as nonroster invitee with the Braves last spring. Called up in mid-April, he posted a 1.27 ERA out of the bullpen before getting his shot at the rotation. Before long, Campillo was the Braves' default second starter, though a poor finish (6.75 ERA over his last 10 starts) puts that status in doubt. A wily moundsman whose best weapon is a changeup that acts like a screwball, he's a great find as a back-end starter; as anything more, he's a sign of weakness.

Buddy Carlyle

Bats: L   Throws: R   Height: 6' 3"   Weight: 185   Born: December 21, 1977   Age: 31

YEAR	TEAM	LVL	AGE	W	L	SV	G	GS	IP	H	BB	SO	HR	GB%	BABIP	STUFF	WHIP	ERA	DERA	EqH9	EqBB9	EqSO9	EqHR9	DEF	VORP	SN/WX
2006	ABQ	AAA	28	3	1	0	13	2	28¹	17	7	22	3	34.1%	.171	-4	0.85	1.92	3.62	5.3	2.3	4.6	1.3	4	6.0	—
2007	RIC	AAA	29	5	2	0	9	9	48²	40	9	56	5	46.7%	.299	14	1.01	2.59	4.50	9.2	2.0	7.6	1.6	3	5.4	—
2007	ATL	MLB	29	8	7	0	22	20	107	117	32	74	19	35.0%	.307	-5	1.39	5.21	4.57	9.6	2.4	5.8	1.5	-7	2.0	1.27
2008	ATL	MLB	30	2	0	0	45	0	62²	52	26	59	5	45.1%	.287	11	1.24	3.59	3.82	7.6	3.2	7.6	0.7	1	12.9	1.28
2009	ATL	MLB	31	3	3	1	34	3	56²	57	20	44	8	41.0%	.290	4	1.36	4.34	4.57	9.0	2.8	6.0	1.2	0	7.0	0.74

Breakout: 20%   Improve: 45%   Collapse: 36%   Attrition: 32%   Comparables: Donne Wall, Woody Main, Hal Brown, Ernie Johnson

The injury that cost Carlyle most of May was a sprained neck resulting from a collision with a runner on the first-base line. A starter for most of his 12-year journeyman career (eight organizations in two hemispheres), Carlyle was used exclusively in relief after his mid-April promotion and responded with his best major league season. Still, it's an indication of his value that even in his best year, 37 of his 45 appearances came with the Braves either losing or winning by more than four runs.

Tom Glavine

Bats: L   Throws: L   Height: 6' 0"   Weight: 205   Born: March 25, 1966   Age: 43

YEAR	TEAM	LVL	AGE	W	L	SV	G	GS	IP	H	BB	SO	HR	GB%	BABIP	STUFF	WHIP	ERA	DERA	EqH9	EqBB9	EqSO9	EqHR9	DEF	VORP	SN/WX
2006	NYN	MLB	40	15	7	0	32	32	198	202	62	131	22	46.7%	.299	10	1.33	3.82	4.58	9.3	2.5	5.5	0.9	11	36.9	4.98
2007	NYN	MLB	41	13	8	0	34	34	200¹	219	64	89	23	44.1%	.293	-4	1.41	4.45	5.05	9.9	2.5	3.9	1.0	16	27.7	5.56
2008	ATL	MLB	42	2	4	0	13	13	63¹	67	37	37	11	49.3%	.303	-15	1.64	5.55	5.75	9.7	4.7	4.9	1.6	2	0.4	0.91
2009	ATL	MLB	43	3	4	0	20	8	56¹	67	22	33	8	48.0%	.310	-7	1.58	5.31	5.58	10.6	3.0	4.5	1.2	0	0.8	0.38

Breakout: 13%   Improve: 26%   Collapse: 56%   Attrition: 47%   Comparables: Dennis Martinez, Kenny Rogers, Joe Niekro, Jeff Fassero

Just three starts into his victory lap with the Braves, Glavine pulled up lame with a strained hamstring. Though he only missed the minimum due to that injury, he was inconsistent after his return and landed back on the DL in mid-June with elbow pain. After one more try in mid-August, Glavine went under the knife to have a torn flexor tendon in his pitching elbow repaired and some tissue cleaned up around his labrum. His comfort level during his off-season throwing program will determine if he gives it one more try with the Braves this year or joins Greg Maddux in Cooperstown in 2014.

Mike Gonzalez

Bats: R   Throws: L   Height: 6' 2"   Weight: 215   Born: May 23, 1978   Age: 31

YEAR	TEAM	LVL	AGE	W	L	SV	G	GS	IP	H	BB	SO	HR	GB%	BABIP	STUFF	WHIP	ERA	DERA	EqH9	EqBB9	EqSO9	EqHR9	DEF	VORP	SN/WX
2006	PIT	MLB	28	3	4	24	54	0	54	42	31	64	1	40.1%	.311	30	1.35	2.17	2.44	6.5	4.4	9.4	0.2	2	23.1	3.49
2007	ATL	MLB	29	2	0	2	18	0	17	15	8	13	0	40.8%	.313	6	1.35	1.59	1.69	8.4	3.9	6.8	0.0	0	8.1	1.10
2008	ATL	MLB	30	0	3	14	36	0	33²	26	14	44	6	32.5%	.270	11	1.19	4.27	6.03	7.1	3.1	9.7	1.6	3	-0.3	1.12
2009	ATL	MLB	31	2	2	10	40	0	38	33	18	41	4	40.0%	.300	17	1.34	3.69	3.88	7.9	3.6	8.4	0.9	0	7.9	0.86

Breakout: 8%   Improve: 24%   Collapse: 43%   Attrition: 6%   Comparables: Brian Fuentes, Jason Christiansen, Randy Myers, Arthur Rhodes

The sore elbow that ended Gonzalez's 2006 campaign early led to ligament-replacement surgery in 2007. Back in action last June, he stepped into the vacant closing role and pitched as well as could have been expected. His ERA inflated a bit in September due to a spike in his home-run rate, but having shaken off the rust, he should finally emerge this year as the dominant closer the Braves thought they had acquired from the Pirates two years ago.

Mike Hampton

Bats: R   Throws: L   Height: 5' 10"   Weight: 195   Born: September 9, 1972   Age: 36

YEAR	TEAM	LVL	AGE	W	L	SV	G	GS	IP	H	BB	SO	HR	GB%	BABIP	STUFF	WHIP	ERA	DERA	EqH9	EqBB9	EqSO9	EqHR9	DEF	VORP	SN/WX
2008	ATL	MLB	35	3	4	0	13	13	78	83	28	38	10	53.8%	.296	-7	1.42	4.85	5.14	9.6	2.9	4.1	1.2	2	4.1	1.03
2009	HOU	MLB	36	4	5	0	26	12	79	88	25	42	9	53.0%	.300	-3	1.43	4.57	4.88	10.2	2.5	4.1	1.1	-0	7.0	1.12

Breakout: 23%   Improve: 50%   Collapse: 23%   Attrition: 40%   Comparables: Wilbur Wood, Ed Lopat, Johnny Podres, Andy Ashby

Entering the 2008 season, Mike Hampton hadn't thrown a competitive pitch since having Tommy John surgery in late 2005. A torn flexor tendon required additional surgery in 2007, he tore a hamstring in his first start in the Mexican winter league before last season, and ten minutes before his first start of the 2008 season, Hampton tore his left pectoral muscle while warming up in the bullpen. It took him eight rehab starts across five levels to finally make it back to the majors, and four more with the Braves to get his sea legs back, but once he did he was surprisingly effective and efficient. Seven of his last nine appearances resulted in quality starts, and all nine lasted at least six full innings, in which he posted a respectable 3.72 ERA. Walk years really do work wonders, but dramatically low strikeout rates undo them, as the Astros are about to discover after signing Hampton to a one-year contract.

Tommy Hanson

Bats: R   Throws: R   Height: 6' 6"   Weight: 210   Born: August 28, 1986   Age: 22

YEAR	TEAM	LVL	AGE	W	L	SV	G	GS	IP	H	BB	SO	HR	GB%	BABIP	STUFF	WHIP	ERA	DERA	EqH9	EqBB9	EqSO9	EqHR9	DEF	VORP	SN/WX
2006	DNV	Ind	19	4	1	0	13	8	51¹	42	9	56	2	41.1%	.302	10	1.00	2.11	7.05	11.5	3.2	3.8	1.8	3	-7.2	—
2007	ROM	A	20	2	6	0	15	14	73	51	26	90	6	44.3%	.269	18	1.05	2.59	5.40	9.0	4.6	6.0	1.8	-3	1.4	—
2007	MYR	A+	20	3	3	0	11	11	60	53	32	64	10	39.4%	.299	-10	1.42	4.20	7.99	12.1	6.6	5.9	3.7	0	-13.5	—
2008	MYR	A+	21	3	1	0	7	7	40	15	11	49	0	32.1%	.188	38	0.65	0.90	3.32	4.5	2.8	7.3	0.2	5	9.6	—
2008	MIS	AA	21	8	4	0	18	18	98	70	41	114	9	43.0%	.283	14	1.13	3.03	5.55	7.8	3.9	6.8	1.5	6	0.5	—
2009	ATL	MLB	22	7	8	0	31	20	129	124	63	116	18	40.0%	.290	17	1.45	4.90	5.13	8.6	3.8	7.0	1.2	0	7.9	1.70

Breakout: 8%   Improve: 30%   Collapse: 28%   Attrition: 19%   Comparables: Mike Meyers, John Maine, Jesse Foppert, Sam Militello

Dug out of the late rounds of the 2005 draft as a draft-and-follow, Hanson has emerged as the Braves' top pitching prospect. A big righty with a four-pitch assortment (fastball, curve, slider, change), he excelled in Double-A last year for the Southern League champions and flat-out dominated the Arizona Fall League. Some of his minor league career numbers—10.4 K/9, 1.09 WHIP, 6.5 H/9—are mouthwatering, but he's just shy of ace material, as he lacks one unhittable pitch. The Braves would be wise to give Hanson a few starts at Triple-A to start the year, but he could get big-league hitters out now and should mature into a front-end stalwart for the next contending Braves team's rotation.

Tim Hudson

Bats: R   Throws: R   Height: 6' 1"   Weight: 170   Born: July 14, 1975   Age: 33

YEAR	TEAM	LVL	AGE	W	L	SV	G	GS	IP	H	BB	SO	HR	GB%	BABIP	STUFF	WHIP	ERA	DERA	EqH9	EqBB9	EqSO9	EqHR9	DEF	VORP	SN/WX
2006	ATL	MLB	30	13	12	0	35	35	218¹	235	79	141	25	58.6%	.303	7	1.44	4.86	4.78	9.1	2.8	5.3	0.9	-2	16.3	3.44
2007	ATL	MLB	31	16	10	0	34	34	224¹	221	53	132	10	62.7%	.299	24	1.22	3.33	3.65	8.8	1.9	5.1	0.4	8	59.0	7.94
2008	ATL	MLB	32	11	7	0	23	22	142	125	40	85	11	60.5%	.268	14	1.16	3.17	4.27	7.8	2.2	4.9	0.6	15	36.8	4.55
2009	ATL	MLB	33	9	7	0	23	23	139¹	146	42	88	12	56.0%	.300	14	1.35	4.04	4.35	9.4	2.3	4.9	0.7	0	19.6	3.24

Breakout: 2%   Improve: 29%   Collapse: 34%   Attrition: 23%   Comparables: Bill Swift, John Denny, Larry Jackson, Joe Horlen

Hudson was cruising along having another typically solid season when, six shutout innings and 68 pitches into a late-July start against the Marlins, his elbow unexpectedly went *sproing!* A couple of weeks later, he was having Tommy John surgery. Hudson hopes to return in August and pitch well enough to convince the Braves to pick up his $12 million mutual option for 2010.

Chuck James

Bats: L   Throws: L   Height: 6' 0"   Weight: 170   Born: November 9, 1981   Age: 27

YEAR	TEAM	LVL	AGE	W	L	SV	G	GS	IP	H	BB	SO	HR	GB%	BABIP	STUFF	WHIP	ERA	DERA	EqH9	EqBB9	EqSO9	EqHR9	DEF	VORP	SN/WX
2006	RIC	AAA	24	1	0	0	7	6	33	30	6	25	3	37.5%	.273	-4	1.09	2.73	3.94	9.0	2.0	4.2	1.4	0	5.9	—
2006	ATL	MLB	24	11	4	0	25	18	119	101	47	91	20	29.5%	.250	0	1.24	3.78	5.12	7.0	3.0	6.2	1.3	17	24.9	3.08
2007	ATL	MLB	25	11	10	0	30	30	161¹	164	58	116	32	32.8%	.280	-8	1.38	4.24	4.84	8.9	2.8	6.1	1.7	16	27.9	4.26
2008	RIC	AAA	26	5	5	0	16	15	86¹	76	39	74	5	30.2%	.293	3	1.33	2.92	4.32	7.8	4.2	4.9	0.7	1	12.1	—
2008	ATL	MLB	26	2	5	0	7	7	29²	36	20	22	10	30.7%	.310	-21	1.89	9.09	8.31	10.7	5.0	5.6	3.0	-1	-11.3	-0.58
2009	ATL	MLB	27	4	5	0	26	13	77	80	36	56	13	36.0%	.290	3	1.50	5.15	5.33	9.2	3.6	5.6	1.4	0	3.5	0.77

Breakout: 7%   Improve: 29%   Collapse: 44%   Attrition: 34%   Comparables: Vic Albury, Rich Folkers, Jesus Sanchez, Dennis Cook

Complaining of fatigue in his pitching shoulder, James posted a 6.04 ERA over his final nine starts in 2007, skipping two late-August turns along the way. The shoulder flared up again in spring training last year, and James never made more than two consecutive starts for the Braves all year, instead bouncing between the DL, the majors, and Triple-A. In September, he became the fourth Braves starter to go under Dr. James Andrews' knife, as the good doctor repaired his labrum and torn rotator cuff. The only encouraging thing about James' season was how well he pitched in Richmond amid all his other struggles. A smart, deceptive lefty with a good changeup but a scary fly-ball rate, he should return midyear to restart his career as a swingman. The Braves declined to tender him a 2009 contract, giving the formerly promising lefty a chance to become someone else's rehab project.

Jair Jurrjens

Bats: R   Throws: R   Height: 6' 1"   Weight: 160   Born: January 29, 1986   Age: 23

YEAR	TEAM	LVL	AGE	W	L	SV	G	GS	IP	H	BB	SO	HR	GB%	BABIP	STUFF	WHIP	ERA	DERA	EqH9	EqBB9	EqSO9	EqHR9	DEF	VORP	SN/WX
2006	LAK	A+	20	5	0	0	12	12	73²	53	10	59	4	54.8%	.239	27	0.86	2.09	5.56	9.0	2.0	3.8	1.2	7	0.3	—
2006	ERI	AA	20	4	3	0	12	12	67¹	71	21	53	7	51.7%	.327	2	1.37	3.35	5.80	12.1	3.7	4.1	1.8	0	-1.3	—
2007	ERI	AA	21	7	5	0	19	19	112²	112	31	94	7	49.3%	.314	19	1.27	3.19	4.41	11.3	3.0	4.9	1.1	-1	13.5	—
2007	DET	MLB	21	3	1	0	7	7	30²	24	11	13	4	37.1%	.217	3	1.14	4.69	6.14	7.1	3.1	3.4	1.2	5	4.6	0.67
2008	ATL	MLB	22	13	10	0	31	31	188¹	188	70	139	11	51.7%	.309	32	1.37	3.68	4.01	8.8	2.8	5.8	0.5	0	32.4	4.16
2009	ATL	MLB	23	10	8	0	25	25	156¹	159	53	115	15	50.0%	.300	21	1.35	4.06	4.33	9.1	2.6	5.7	0.8	0	22.6	3.67

Breakout: 11%   Improve: 33%   Collapse: 32%   Attrition: 16%   Comparables: Greg Maddux, Lee Tunnell, Dave Stieb, Dan Larson

A command and control pitcher with a good changeup and a solid ground-ball rate but unexceptional stuff overall, Jurrjens is unlikely to improve on his breakout 2008 season, but with talent like Hanson on the way, he won't have to. Jurrjens is young enough and good enough to be a midrotation rock on the next contending Braves team. He faded a bit down the stretch last year as his workload piled up, but having been stretched out, he shouldn't have that problem again. Still, the Braves should be mindful that he's just 23 years old and not out of the injury nexus just yet.

Jeff Locke

Bats: L   Throws: L   Height: 6' 2"   Weight: 180   Born: November 20, 1987   Age: 21

YEAR	TEAM	LVL	AGE	W	L	SV	G	GS	IP	H	BB	SO	HR	GB%	BABIP	STUFF	WHIP	ERA	DERA	EqH9	EqBB9	EqSO9	EqHR9	DEF	VORP	SN/WX
2006	BRA	Ind	18	4	3	0	10	5	32	38	5	38	4	33.8%	.427	-21	1.34	4.22	9.93	22.6	3.6	6.0	6.4	0	-10.9	—
2007	DNV	Rk	19	7	1	1	13	11	61	48	8	74	2	54.0%	.318	4	0.92	2.66	7.56	12.4	2.9	4.5	1.6	0	-10.9	—
2008	ROM	A	20	5	12	0	25	24	139²	150	38	113	6	56.5%	.328	12	1.35	4.06	7.45	10.9	3.6	3.1	1.0	-3	-27.1	—
2009	ATL	MLB	21	4	7	0	17	17	90	116	41	46	12	52.0%	.330	1	1.74	6.56	6.98	11.5	3.5	4.0	1.2	0	-12.5	-0.60

Breakout: 15%   Improve: 45%   Collapse: 14%   Attrition: 9%   Comparables: Aaron Thompson, Andy Van Hekken, Mike Kusiewicz, Michael Hinckley

The team's second-round pick in 2006, Locke was undermined by some dreadful team defense and poor run support with the Braves' Sally League team in Rome last year. Still, Locke posted strong peripherals and remains one of the team's top pitching prospects. A lefty who throws in the low 90s with a strong curve and a developing changeup, he should impress at pitching-friendly Myrtle Beach this year and follow Cole Rohrbough into the 2012 rotation.

Stephen Marek

Bats: R   **Throws:** R   **Height:** 6′ 2″   **Weight:** 200   **Born:** September 3, 1983   **Age:** 25

YEAR	TEAM	LVL	AGE	W	L	SV	G	GS	IP	H	BB	SO	HR	GB%	BABIP	STUFF	WHIP	ERA	DERA	EqH9	EqBB9	EqSO9	EqHR9	DEF	VORP	SN/WX
2006	CDR	A	22	10	2	0	19	19	119²	95	24	100	8	49.0%	.262	-27	1.00	1.96	5.33	10.6	3.2	3.4	2.1	12	3.1	—
2006	RCU	A+	22	2	3	0	6	6	32	26	13	33	4	45.2%	.289	-7	1.22	3.94	6.43	10.0	4.8	5.1	2.2	2	-2.6	—
2007	RCU	A+	23	8	10	0	25	25	134	133	49	106	17	49.6%	.294	-40	1.36	4.30	6.51	11.4	4.3	3.6	2.1	-9	-12.2	—
2008	ARK	AA	24	2	6	3	34	0	46²	39	21	57	2	53.3%	.319	-1	1.28	3.66	5.28	8.9	4.5	7.1	0.8	0	1.6	—
2009	*ATL*	*MLB*	*25*	*3*	*4*	*1*	*24*	*6*	*56¹*	*60*	*29*	*43*	*7*	*48.0%*	*.310*	*3*	*1.58*	*5.33*	*5.65*	*9.5*	*4.0*	*5.9*	*1.1*	*0*	*0.3*	*0.25*

Breakout: 30%   Improve: 53%   Collapse: 16%   Attrition: 16%   *Comparables: Brian Wood, Jim Jefferson, Matt Kinzer, Ruddy Lugo*

The pitcher obtained from the Angels with Casey Kotchman for Mark Teixeira, Marek was converted from starting to relief last year as he made the leap to Double-A. A thick-bodied, max-effort righty with three solid pitches (a fastball that reaches 95 mph, curve, changeup), he dominated in the Arizona Fall League, was added to the 40-man roster, and could find himself in the major league pen before the year is out.

Kris Medlen

Bats: S   **Throws:** R   **Height:** 5′ 10″   **Weight:** 175   **Born:** October 7, 1985   **Age:** 23

YEAR	TEAM	LVL	AGE	W	L	SV	G	GS	IP	H	BB	SO	HR	GB%	BABIP	STUFF	WHIP	ERA	DERA	EqH9	EqBB9	EqSO9	EqHR9	DEF	VORP	SN/WX
2006	DNV	Ind	20	1	0	10	20	0	22²	14	2	36	0	61.7%	.298	19	0.72	0.41	4.34	10.6	2.4	7.2	1.0	3	2.6	—
2007	ROM	A	21	0	1	8	17	0	20²	13	3	33	1	54.5%	.279	19	0.77	0.87	2.33	7.9	2.3	7.9	0.9	-2	7.0	—
2007	MYR	A+	21	2	0	2	18	0	24	22	7	28	1	53.0%	.333	6	1.21	1.13	3.74	11.2	3.7	6.2	1.2	-3	4.5	—
2008	MIS	AA	22	7	8	1	36	17	120¹	121	27	120	8	45.0%	.340	6	1.23	3.52	5.02	11.3	2.4	6.1	1.2	2	6.9	—
2009	*ATL*	*MLB*	*23*	*4*	*5*	*0*	*22*	*11*	*75*	*86*	*24*	*59*	*9*	*46.0%*	*.320*	*14*	*1.46*	*4.85*	*5.10*	*10.2*	*2.5*	*6.1*	*1.1*	*0*	*4.8*	*0.94*

Breakout: 9%   Improve: 27%   Collapse: 36%   Attrition: 18%   *Comparables: Lloyd Peever, Roy Oswalt, Tommy Shimp, David Nied*

A college shortstop who hit .308/.333/.577 in Double-A last year (26 at-bats), Medlen spent his first two pro seasons pitching exclusively in relief, but was moved into the Double-A rotation last June and rose to the challenge, thanks in large part to his great changeup. His small frame leaves doubts about his ability to hold up over a full season as a starter, but despite pitching in relief in the Arizona Fall League, he will start the 2009 season in the Triple-A rotation.

Charlie Morton

Bats: R   **Throws:** R   **Height:** 6′ 5″   **Weight:** 218   **Born:** November 12, 1983   **Age:** 25

YEAR	TEAM	LVL	AGE	W	L	SV	G	GS	IP	H	BB	SO	HR	GB%	BABIP	STUFF	WHIP	ERA	DERA	EqH9	EqBB9	EqSO9	EqHR9	DEF	VORP	SN/WX
2006	MYR	A+	22	6	7	2	30	14	100¹	116	54	75	14	45.9%	.330	-63	1.70	5.39	9.31	14.3	6.1	3.5	3.1	-5	-36.3	—
2007	MIS	AA	23	4	6	0	41	6	79²	80	37	67	3	48.1%	.331	-15	1.47	4.29	7.24	10.8	4.5	4.5	0.7	8	-13.4	—
2008	RIC	AAA	24	5	2	0	13	12	79	51	27	72	0	58.3%	.244	22	0.99	2.05	4.38	5.7	3.2	5.3	0.2	12	10.6	—
2008	ATL	MLB	24	4	8	0	16	15	74²	80	41	48	9	52.5%	.301	-9	1.62	6.14	6.10	9.3	4.1	4.9	1.1	-3	-9.3	0.53
2009	*ATL*	*MLB*	*25*	*4*	*5*	*0*	*25*	*12*	*77²*	*80*	*35*	*54*	*8*	*49.0%*	*.300*	*6*	*1.48*	*4.83*	*5.16*	*9.2*	*3.5*	*5.4*	*0.9*	*0*	*5.2*	*0.91*

Breakout: 31%   Improve: 60%   Collapse: 16%   Attrition: 35%   *Comparables: Joe Slusarski, Ryan Glynn, Doug Konieczny, Jose Mesa*

After spending most of the 2007 season pitching in relief for Double-A Mississippi, Morton returned to starting in the Arizona Fall League and responded with a breakout performance. He followed that with an equally impressive Triple-A debut, earning a mid-June promotion to the decimated major league rotation. In the majors, he was inconsistent, undermined by a back injury that took the edge off his stuff, pared 25 pounds off his lanky frame, and ultimately cost him most of September. The Braves think very highly of his mid-90s heat and four-pitch arsenal (plus curve and change, average slider), so after putting the weight back on this winter, he'll get another crack at the rotation in spring training.

Will Ohman

Bats: L   **Throws:** L   **Height:** 6′ 2″   **Weight:** 205   **Born:** August 13, 1977   **Age:** 31

YEAR	TEAM	LVL	AGE	W	L	SV	G	GS	IP	H	BB	SO	HR	GB%	BABIP	STUFF	WHIP	ERA	DERA	EqH9	EqBB9	EqSO9	EqHR9	DEF	VORP	SN/WX
2006	CHN	MLB	28	1	1	0	78	0	65¹	51	34	74	6	34.1%	.273	16	1.30	4.13	4.43	7.0	4.0	9.0	0.7	6	14.2	1.66
2007	CHN	MLB	29	2	4	1	56	0	36¹	42	16	33	3	41.5%	.345	6	1.60	4.96	2.68	10.2	3.4	7.5	0.7	-6	4.2	-0.77
2008	ATL	MLB	30	4	1	1	83	0	58²	51	22	53	3	38.4%	.289	10	1.24	3.68	4.55	7.6	2.9	7.0	0.5	4	9.4	1.64
2009	*ATL*	*MLB*	*31*	*2*	*2*	*3*	*51*	*0*	*45²*	*42*	*19*	*41*	*5*	*40.0%*	*.290*	*9*	*1.34*	*3.79*	*4.01*	*8.3*	*3.2*	*7.0*	*0.9*	*0*	*8.4*	*0.76*

Breakout: 20%   Improve: 45%   Collapse: 31%   Attrition: 23%   *Comparables: Alan Embree, Ken Dayley, Jesse Orosco, Bill Kennedy*

Ohman turned in another fine year as a LOOGY in 2008, holding southpaws to a .200/.257/.314 line. He also allowed just 17 percent of his inherited runners to score, which became the best mark in the National League after Damaso Marte was traded to the Yankees. A free agent, Ohman is one of the few matchup relievers who deserves a multiyear contract.

James Parr

Bats: R　Throws: R　Height: 6′ 1″　Weight: 185　Born: February 27, 1986　Age: 23

YEAR	TEAM	LVL	AGE	W	L	SV	G	GS	IP	H	BB	SO	HR	GB%	BABIP	STUFF	WHIP	ERA	DERA	EqH9	EqBB9	EqSO9	EqHR9	DEF	VORP	SN/WX
2006	MYR	A+	20	7	8	1	24	22	134²	138	37	90	14	37.4%	.303	-18	1.30	4.83	7.99	12.2	3.3	3.1	2.3	-2	-31.7	—
2007	MYR	A+	21	3	4	0	8	8	39²	36	6	37	1	36.4%	.333	22	1.06	3.17	4.54	11.5	2.4	5.1	0.8	-3	4.0	—
2007	MIS	AA	21	4	5	0	18	16	98	111	25	75	8	39.7%	.353	0	1.39	4.59	6.47	12.2	2.7	4.1	1.4	1	-8.6	—
2008	MIS	AA	22	8	4	0	18	17	95	87	37	81	9	32.1%	.297	-8	1.31	3.69	5.85	9.9	3.8	4.9	1.6	6	-2.4	—
2008	RIC	AAA	22	5	3	0	10	9	55²	49	14	44	9	38.9%	.278	12	1.13	3.23	4.14	7.8	2.5	4.5	1.0	1	8.8	—
2008	ATL	MLB	22	1	0	0	5	5	22¹	29	9	14	4	27.5%	.338	2	1.70	4.84	4.50	11.5	3.3	4.9	1.6	-1	1.0	0.49
2009	*ATL*	*MLB*	*23*	*6*	*9*	*0*	*36*	*23*	*124¹*	*141*	*50*	*88*	*23*	*37.0%*	*.300*	*5*	*1.54*	*5.51*	*5.66*	*10.2*	*3.1*	*5.5*	*1.6*	*0*	*0.7*	*0.86*

Breakout: 0%　Improve: 11%　Collapse: 56%　Attrition: 11%　　Comparables: Chad Ogea, Jeff Brantley, Tom Kramer, Adam Peterson

Parr kicked off his major league career last September with a pair of six-inning starts in which he didn't allow a run; he then allowed 13 tallies in his last 10⅓ frames on the year. A midsized righty with weak stuff, Parr relies on a deceptive delivery and received his promotion largely due to the Braves' desperation. He's unlikely to mature into much more than a utility pitcher.

Jo-Jo Reyes

Bats: L　Throws: L　Height: 6′ 2″　Weight: 230　Born: November 20, 1984　Age: 24

YEAR	TEAM	LVL	AGE	W	L	SV	G	GS	IP	H	BB	SO	HR	GB%	BABIP	STUFF	WHIP	ERA	DERA	EqH9	EqBB9	EqSO9	EqHR9	DEF	VORP	SN/WX
2006	ROM	A	21	8	1	0	13	13	75²	62	25	84	5	50.8%	.305	2	1.16	2.99	6.02	11.2	4.6	5.0	2.0	-1	-3.0	—
2006	MYR	A+	21	4	4	0	14	14	65²	52	36	58	0	41.3%	.292	10	1.35	4.14	7.43	9.4	5.9	4.4	0.5	-4	-12.1	—
2007	MIS	AA	22	8	1	0	13	13	73¹	63	35	71	5	46.5%	.310	4	1.34	3.56	5.54	9.6	4.7	5.4	1.2	2	0.4	—
2007	RIC	AAA	22	4	0	0	6	6	36	25	12	39	2	53.3%	.258	30	1.03	1.00	3.41	7.3	3.1	6.8	0.8	3	8.3	—
2007	ATL	MLB	22	2	2	0	11	10	50²	55	30	27	9	45.3%	.295	-10	1.68	6.21	6.34	9.8	4.7	4.7	1.4	0	-6.2	0.28
2008	RIC	AAA	23	1	1	0	8	8	39	31	16	38	2	53.7%	.284	9	1.21	2.31	4.03	7.3	4.0	5.7	0.7	4	6.6	—
2008	ATL	MLB	23	3	11	0	23	22	113	134	52	78	18	49.7%	.332	-8	1.65	5.81	5.19	10.7	3.6	5.6	1.4	-8	-6.1	0.81
2009	*ATL*	*MLB*	*24*	*5*	*6*	*1*	*32*	*15*	*98¹*	*102*	*44*	*72*	*11*	*49.0%*	*.300*	*8*	*1.48*	*4.64*	*4.93*	*9.3*	*3.5*	*5.7*	*1.0*	*0*	*8.5*	*1.41*

Breakout: 23%　Improve: 53%　Collapse: 24%　Attrition: 29%　　Comparables: Brian Bohanon, Arthur Rhodes, Allen Watson, Colby Lewis

In 2007, Joseph Albert "Jo-Jo" Reyes was rushed into the big-league rotation at the age of 22 with just six Triple-A starts under his belt. Last May, after just eight more Triple-A starts, he was back again to take the place of an injured John Smoltz. Reyes has excelled in his brief time at Triple-A (1.68 ERA, 9.24 K/9, 2.75 K/BB), but his major league performances tell us that 14 Triple-A starts spread out over two stints hasn't been enough to prepare him for the majors. In "The Show," he appears to be pitching away from contact, due to a lack of confidence, but he's still young and left-handed, with a fastball that can hit 95 and a pair of solid breaking pitches. The Braves need to show some patience with him if they want him to fulfill his potential as a midrotation starter.

Cole Rohrbough

Bats: L　Throws: L　Height: 6′ 3″　Weight: 205　Born: May 23, 1987　Age: 22

YEAR	TEAM	LVL	AGE	W	L	SV	G	GS	IP	H	BB	SO	HR	GB%	BABIP	STUFF	WHIP	ERA	DERA	EqH9	EqBB9	EqSO9	EqHR9	DEF	VORP	SN/WX
2007	ROM	A	20	2	0	0	6	6	28	13	12	38	1	33.9%	.218	25	0.89	1.29	4.68	6.1	5.4	6.8	1.1	1	2.6	—
2007	DNV	Rk	20	3	2	0	8	7	33¹	20	8	58	1	55.6%	.311	28	0.84	1.08	5.20	11.1	4.2	7.2	1.6	0	1.2	—
2008	ROM	A	21	3	4	0	13	12	58¹	55	31	76	3	51.0%	.364	3	1.48	4.94	7.94	11.5	6.9	6.4	1.2	-5	-13.3	—
2008	MYR	A+	21	2	2	0	5	5	31²	27	8	28	0	40.8%	.292	27	1.10	3.41	6.52	9.9	2.8	5.0	0.3	2	-3.0	—
2009	*ATL*	*MLB*	*22*	*4*	*8*	*0*	*25*	*17*	*97¹*	*110*	*61*	*82*	*14*	*44.0%*	*.330*	*8*	*1.76*	*6.40*	*6.73*	*10.1*	*4.9*	*6.6*	*1.3*	*0*	*-11.1*	*-0.45*

Breakout: 25%　Improve: 54%　Collapse: 13%　Attrition: 10%　　Comparables: Colin Charland, Blaise Ilsley, Arthur Rhodes, Jon Lester

A power lefty with a great curve, Rohrbough was hampered by shoulder and ankle injuries in 2008, the latter of which required off-season surgery. He was also undermined by Rome's poor defense, as can be seen by the 1.5 runs he shed from his ERA on his promotion to High-A Myrtle Beach. Rohrbough needs more consistency with his changeup and will repeat at Myrtle Beach to start the season, but could make the leap to Double-A by midyear and could emerge as a strong midrotation starter, provided his body holds up.

John Smoltz

Bats: R   Throws: R   Height: 6' 3"   Weight: 220   Born: May 15, 1967   Age: 42

YEAR	TEAM	LVL	AGE	W	L	SV	G	GS	IP	H	BB	SO	HR	GB%	BABIP	STUFF	WHIP	ERA	DERA	EqH9	EqBB9	EqSO9	EqHR9	DEF	VORP	SN/WX
2006	ATL	MLB	39	16	9	0	35	35	232	221	55	211	23	47.6%	.306	29	1.19	3.49	3.73	8.2	1.9	7.5	0.8	8	61.3	7.43
2007	ATL	MLB	40	14	8	0	32	32	205^2	196	47	197	18	47.0%	.312	36	1.18	3.11	3.11	8.4	1.8	8.0	0.7	-3	56.1	7.03
2008	ATL	MLB	41	3	2	0	6	5	28	25	8	36	2	49.3%	.324	28	1.18	2.57	1.29	8.4	2.2	9.6	0.6	-4	9.7	0.77
2009	BOS	MLB	42	8	5	1	25	17	108	103	29	91	10	45.8%	.291	17	1.21	3.57	3.62	8.1	2.1	7.1	0.8	2	22.8	3.30

Breakout: 0%   Improve: 21%   Collapse: 34%   Attrition: 40%   Comparables: Roger Clemens, Hoyt Wilhelm, Gaylord Perry, Ron Reed

Smoltz was dominant in his first four starts last year, but hit the DL at the end of April after an abbreviated fifth turn with what was described as a "severely inflamed biceps muscle and an inflamed rotator cuff." An attempted comeback as a closer with a new three-quarters delivery produced three dominant rehab outings in late May and one blown save for the major league club in June. A week later, Smoltz had arthroscopic shoulder surgery, which found "significant" damage, particularly to his labrum, though nothing wildly out of sorts for a 41-year-old pitcher with more than 3,000 innings under his belt. Like Glavine, he'll use his off-season throwing program to decide whether he wants to return to the Braves or increase his workload for TBS. If he's done, the Braves' great starting trio of Maddux, Glavine, and Smoltz could reunite in Cooperstown in 2014.

Rafael Soriano

Bats: R   Throws: R   Height: 6' 1"   Weight: 220   Born: December 19, 1979   Age: 29

YEAR	TEAM	LVL	AGE	W	L	SV	G	GS	IP	H	BB	SO	HR	GB%	BABIP	STUFF	WHIP	ERA	DERA	EqH9	EqBB9	EqSO9	EqHR9	DEF	VORP	SN/WX
2006	SEA	MLB	26	1	2	2	53	0	60	44	21	65	6	28.8%	.262	19	1.08	2.25	2.91	6.6	3.1	8.9	0.9	3	25.4	3.17
2007	ATL	MLB	27	3	3	9	71	0	72	47	15	70	12	33.3%	.198	10	0.86	3.00	4.00	5.6	1.6	8.1	1.4	8	20.8	3.60
2008	ATL	MLB	28	0	1	3	14	0	14	7	9	16	1	22.6%	.200	14	1.14	2.57	5.93	4.6	5.3	9.2	0.7	4	3.7	0.39
2009	ATL	MLB	29	3	2	6	37	0	43	35	17	43	6	33.0%	.260	14	1.20	3.46	3.59	7.2	3.0	7.7	1.2	0	9.8	1.02

Breakout: 8%   Improve: 21%   Collapse: 53%   Attrition: 13%   Comparables: Bill Risley, Joe Nathan, Trevor Hoffman, Chris Schroder

Just four appearances into his 2008 season, Soriano hit the disabled list with elbow pain. Twice he returned to pitch in just five games before again complaining of pain in his pitching elbow and landing back on the DL. Finally, in late August, he went under the knife for an ulnar nerve transposition and to have a bone spur removed. The surgery revealed no ligament damage, so Soriano is expected to be all the way back to start the year as Gonzalez's primary setup man. Pitching in his walk year, he'll have the added incentive of setting himself up to land a closer's job as a free agent.

Julian Tavarez

Bats: L   Throws: R   Height: 6' 2"   Weight: 195   Born: May 22, 1973   Age: 36

YEAR	TEAM	LVL	AGE	W	L	SV	G	GS	IP	H	BB	SO	HR	GB%	BABIP	STUFF	WHIP	ERA	DERA	EqH9	EqBB9	EqSO9	EqHR9	DEF	VORP	SN/WX
2006	BOS	MLB	33	5	4	1	58	6	98^2	110	44	56	10	58.5%	.324	-14	1.56	4.56	4.98	9.8	4.0	4.7	0.9	3	12.9	0.38
2007	BOS	MLB	34	7	11	0	34	23	134^2	151	51	77	14	54.8%	.306	-9	1.50	5.14	5.36	10.4	3.2	4.5	0.9	-2	2.8	0.97
2008	BOS	MLB	35	0	1	0	9	0	12^2	18	9	6	0	60.4%	.391	-27	2.13	6.38	7.30	13.1	5.8	3.6	0.0	-1	-3.7	-0.25
2008	MIL	MLB	35	0	1	0	7	0	7^1	13	5	10	0	65.4%	.520	7	2.45	8.63	4.70	16.4	4.7	10.6	0.0	-6	-5.4	-0.40
2008	ATL	MLB	35	1	3	0	36	0	34^2	42	14	35	5	51.8%	.363	3	1.62	3.89	3.57	10.7	3.1	7.9	1.3	-5	1.5	0.55
2009	ATL	MLB	36	3	3	1	36	2	52^2	56	23	38	5	51.0%	.310	-1	1.50	4.57	4.91	9.5	3.4	5.6	0.8	0	4.5	0.45

Breakout: 25%   Improve: 57%   Collapse: 24%   Attrition: 36%   Comparables: Dave Weathers, Todd Jones, Mike DeJean, Clem Labine

After being released by a pair of playoff-bound teams in the Red Sox and Brewers, Tavarez landed in Atlanta and pitched well out of the pen, though not well enough for the team to want to bring back the notoriously temperamental free agent for his age-36 season. The next team Tavarez signs with will be the 12th in his 17-year big-league career.

LINEOUTS

Hitters

PLAYER	TEAM	LVL	AGE	PA	R	2B	3B	HR	RBI	BB	SO	SB-CS	EqBRR	AVG/OBP/SLG	EqAVG/EqOBP/EqSLG	EqA	VORP	WARP
3B E. Campbell	MYR	A+	22	390	56	15	1	19	67	50	58	4-1	-0.6	.255/.362/.479	.230/.323/.440	.262	6.7	0.4
3B J. Gilmore	ROM	A	19	104	6	1	0	0	4	2	20	1-0	0.8	.186/.202/.196	.147/.163/.157	.000	-20.9	-1.9
	DNV	Rk	19	277	27	23	0	4	31	13	41	0-3	-6.1	.337/.365/.473	.251/.274/.350	.215	-22.7	-2.9
INF R. Gotay#	ATL	MLB	25	117	10	5	0	2	8	13	32	1-1	-0.3	.235/.322/.343	.243/.328/.369	.245	-1.0	-0.2
INF D. Hernandez	MIS	AA	24	85	8	3	1	2	8	6	8	1-4	-1.6	.286/.341/.429	.241/.291/.380	.228	-1.7	-0.5
	RIC	AAA	24	490	46	23	3	5	53	20	73	7-5	-2.3	.288/.317/.383	.255/.285/.351	.220	-15.6	-0.4
SS B. Hicks	MYR	A+	22	400	68	23	2	19	56	45	122	14-3	-0.1	.234/.335/.480	.224/.311/.452	.262	5.7	2.4
	MIS	AA	22	64	9	3	1	1	7	7	17	0-0	0.1	.241/.333/.389	.211/.292/.368	.229	-1.9	0.1
1B S. Thorman*	RIC	AAA	26	411	47	22	2	19	56	19	83	7-1	2.0	.251/.283/.465	.213/.246/.406	.223	-16.2	-1.6
OF M. Young*	MIS	AA	25	577	74	16	11	3	50	68	62	30-12	1.7	.289/.384/.385	.222/.296/.301	.215	-29.5	-2.1

Something of a problem child, **Eric Campbell** has moved slowly since being drafted in the second round in 2004, but he finally managed to combine plate discipline and power in 2008. With **Jon Gilmore** (included in the Vazquez trade) out of the way, a successful jump to Double-A this year would make him a reasonable in-house candidate to replace Chipper at the hot corner. ⦸ A 2007 supplemental first-round pick, Gilmore now enters the race to salve the White Sox' festering hot corner vacancy, though he's a long-range solution at best, given that the top line on his résumé is a batting-average-driven half-season at rookie ball. ⦸ Subutility man **Ruben Gotay** isn't viable at shortstop or at the plate, yet he keeps getting major league opportunities. ⦸ A utility prospect if there is such a thing, **Diory Hernandez** provides solid defense at the three infield skill positions, and average-driven production at the plate, but he's a brutal basestealer (55 percent career success rate). ⦸ Given Lillibridge's fall from grace, **Brandon Hicks**, the Braves' 2007 third-round pick out of Texas A&M, becomes the most likely eventual challenger to Escobar at shortstop. He has power, patience, good hands, and a bit of speed, but has to make more contact to survive the jump to Double-A. ⦸ Having hit .235/.271/.452 against righties across parts of two big-league seasons, **Scott Thorman** failed to stick as a platoon player. Having posted similar numbers across the board in Triple-A last year prior to becoming a minor league free agent, he may fail to stick as a baseball player. ⦸ **Matt Young** is a smallish Gregor Blanco type—speed, patience, and no power—who can spot at the keystone, but he is less viable in center and has yet to see Triple-A at age 26.

Pitchers

PLAYER	TEAM	LVL	AGE	W	L	SV	IP	H	BB	SO	HR	GB%	BABIP	STUFF	WHIP	ERA	DERA	EqH9	EqBB9	EqSO9	EqHR9	DEF	VORP
F. Bueno*	RIC	AAA	27	2	6	0	84¹	100	29	59	8	42.6%	.341	-19	1.53	5.23	5.86	10.8	3.3	3.9	1.2	-4	-2.3
R. Delgado	DNV	Rk	18	3	8	0	69	63	30	81	5	52.8%	.347	-18	1.35	3.13	8.15	14.4	7.8	4.4	2.5	0	-15.0
B. DeVall*	BRA	Rk	18	0	0	0	9²	4	2	7	1	56.0%	.125	-4	0.62	0.93	4.50	7.9	3.4	2.2	4.5	0	1.0
S. Evarts*	ROM	A	20	2	0	0	18	15	1	14	0	68.0%	.300	16	0.89	1.50	3.45	9.2	1.1	3.4	0.6	-1	3.8
J. Julio	CLE	MLB	29	0	0	0	17²	18	11	15	3	32.7%	.319	-7	1.64	5.59	5.40	9.7	5.4	7.0	1.6	0	0.4
	ATL	MLB	29	3	0	0	12¹	9	8	19	0	65.4%	.346	12	1.38	0.73	0.00	7.5	5.2	11.2	0.0	-1	6.7
C. Kimbrel	DNV	Rk	20	1	2	6	19	5	10	27	0	73.2%	.128	9	0.79	0.47	4.19	2.8	7.0	4.2	0.5	0	3.0
	ROM	A	20	2	0	4	12²	6	4	26	0	50.0%	.353	11	0.79	0.71	1.64	8.2	4.1	10.6	0.8	0	4.8
A. Lerew	RIC	AAA	25	1	4	0	37	43	20	22	5	53.2%	.319	-28	1.70	4.14	6.88	10.7	5.1	3.3	1.8	1	-5.0
V. Nuñez	RIC	AAA	33	3	1	3	57¹	54	28	61	1	47.8%	.346	5	1.43	3.46	3.90	8.9	4.7	6.3	0.3	-2	10.4
	ATL	MLB	33	1	2	0	32²	32	19	24	0	41.2%	.323	1	1.56	3.85	3.90	8.9	4.5	5.8	0.0	1	6.4
T. Redmond	MIS	AA	23	13	5	0	166¹	164	33	133	17	37.2%	.301	-14	1.18	3.52	5.54	10.3	2.1	4.4	1.7	3	1.0
J. Ridgway*	RIC	AAA	27	4	0	4	52²	67	26	57	3	53.1%	.418	-9	1.76	5.46	5.88	12.9	5.0	6.6	0.7	-8	-1.5
	ATL	MLB	27	1	0	0	9²	7	1	8	3	57.1%	.160	0	0.83	3.71	6.30	6.3	0.9	6.3	2.7	3	2.1
R. Ring*	ATL	MLB	27	2	1	0	22¹	32	10	16	2	57.6%	.385	-16	1.88	8.48	6.08	12.2	3.0	5.3	0.8	-8	-11.2
S. Rodriguez*	BRA	Rk	20	1	2	5	29	16	13	45	0	45.9%	.276	18	1.00	2.79	7.96	8.3	6.6	6.2	0.7	0	-6.8
P. Stockman	RIC	AAA	28	1	1	2	30	15	18	26	3	38.2%	.164	-7	1.10	2.10	4.91	4.3	5.5	4.9	1.2	7	2.2
	ATL	MLB	28	0	0	0	7¹	2	4	9	0	42.9%	.143	7	0.82	0.00	1.23	2.5	3.7	8.6	0.0	1	4.6
J. Teheran	DNV	Rk	17	1	2	0	15	18	4	17	2	53.5%	.400	-26	1.47	6.60	13.50	19.9	5.6	4.0	4.0	0	-9.9
L. Valdez	MIS	AA	24	4	3	28	65¹	48	36	77	3	44.6%	.284	-3	1.29	2.76	6.32	7.9	5.0	6.9	0.9	5	-5.0
C. Vines	MYR	A+	23	4	1	2	86	86	21	77	6	50.4%	.320	-7	1.24	3.98	5.31	11.7	2.7	5.2	1.3	-7	2.5

Soft-tossing lefty starter **Francisley Bueno** defected from Cuba just before Escobar did in the summer of 2004, but Bueno doesn't have the stuff to remain teammates with him stateside. ⊘ A skinny 19-year-old Panamanian, **Randall Delgado** has a low-90s sinker and a plus curve, but lacks an effective third pitch and is a long way from the majors. ⊘ The Braves' top pick in 2008 as a supplemental first-rounder, lefty **Brett DeVall** doesn't have the highest ceiling in the game, but his above-average stuff and command make him highly polished for a teenager. ⊘ The Braves' second pick in the supplemental first round of the 2006 draft, **Steven Evarts** had Tommy John surgery last summer and will spend 2009 rehabilitating his left arm. ⊘ The Braves were **Jorge Julio**'s sixth organization in the last three years, and no matter what uniform he wears, the results are always the same: lots of strikeouts, but too many walks and homers. ⊘ A third-round pick out of an Alabama community college in last year's draft, **Craig Kimbrel** is a stocky power reliever who sprang into action last year by being unhittable across three levels, though his low three-quarters delivery could leave him susceptible to lefties as he continues to rise. ⊘ Righty starter **Anthony Lerew** spent last year rehabbing from his own May 2007 ligament-replacement surgery and was last seen in the Puerto Rican winter league. ⊘ Aussie World Baseball Classic reclamation project **Peter Moylan** had Tommy John surgery last May, but hopes to return before the All-Star break this year. ⊘ **Vladimir Nuñez**'s return to the major leagues last year after a three-year absence was more a symptom of the Braves' myriad pitching injuries than a solution. ⊘ Acquired from the Pirates late in spring training for Tyler Yates, **Todd Redmond** won Southern League Pitcher of the Year honors in his first full season in Double-A, but his extreme fly-ball rate mutes our optimism for his future. ⊘ When the Braves traded Willy Aybar to the Rays prior to the season, they received **Jeff Ridgway**, a hard-throwing lefty who's still hoping to eke out a big-league career as somebody's second lefty in the bullpen. ⊘ Ridgway couldn't be much worse than last year's second lefty, **Royce Ring**, who pitched himself off the team and out of the organization, in part by allowing righties to hit .419/.471/.674. ⊘ The last piece sent to Chicago in the Vazquez deal, **Santos Rodriguez** is a tall, lanky 21-year-old Dominican lefty who can reach 93 mph on the gun and dominated out of the pen in a brief repeat of rookie ball last year. ⊘ Big Aussie **Phil Stockman**'s hip sidelined him last year. He's dominant out of the pen when healthy, but has appeared in 30 games in a season just once since turning pro in 1998. ⊘ Colombian beanpole **Julio Teheran** just turned 18, but he has tremendous potential: he can reach the upper 90s with his fastball, has a good curve, and is already developing a changeup. ⊘ Signed away from the Pirates as a six-year minor league free agent, Dominican righty **Luis Valdez** excelled in relief at Double-A and was added to the roster in October. ⊘ **Chris Vines** pitched well in seven relief appearances but less so in 13 starts as a 23-year-old in High-A at pitching-friendly Myrtle Beach.

MANAGER: BOBBY COX

YEAR	TEAM	W-L	Pythag +/−	Avg PC	100+ P	120+ P	QS	BQS	REL	REL w Zero R	IBB	Subs	PH	PH Avg	PH HR	SB2	CS2	SB3	CS3	SAC Att	SAC %	POS SAC	Squeeze	Swing	In Play
2006	ATL	79-83	-6	92.6	61	8	70	6	522	342	69	51	299	.277	8	49	34	4	1	105	74.3%	25	6	106	78
2007	ATL	84-78	-5	89.2	43	2	78	6	527	346	89	36	288	.213	3	60	25	4	3	77	71.4%	16	2	110	82
2008	ATL	72-90	-6	89.0	41	1	70	10	545	357	80	38	288	.265	8	53	20	5	4	108	63.9%	36	2	130	102

Like Chipper, Bobby Cox is a sure-fire Hall of Famer and an Atlanta institution who may not be in an Atlanta uniform the next time the Braves make the playoffs. Cox, who will be 68 in May, is unlikely to rise above his current fourth place on the all-time managerial wins list without managing deep into his 70s (he's 436 wins behind second-place John McGraw and chasing younger Tony La Russa for third). With the Braves foundering, Cox has shown a tendency to ride his pitchers hard, particularly his relievers, and the overused arms are starting to pile up behind him. One-third of the top dozen single-season games-pitched totals amassed during Cox's Braves tenure have come in the last two seasons. Of those four pitchers, Peter Moylan followed his 80-game season by having Tommy John surgery, Blaine Boyer burned out halfway through his 76 games in 2008 (posting a 9.55 ERA over the season's final three months), and Tyler Yates was dumped after making 75 appearances in 2007. That top dozen doesn't include Rafael Soriano's 71 appearances in 2007 (before a 2008 season scuttled by elbow problems) or the 72 games Jeff Bennett pitched in last year. Cox led NL skippers in pitching changes and relievers used on no rest in 2008 and was among the league leaders in those categories the previous two years (and the Braves' staff was *good* in 2007). The arms Cox is burning through are neither young enough nor good enough to bother saving, but with more promising prospects on the way, the Braves need to make sure Cox doesn't overuse the wrong guys in the pursuit of one last playoff run.

Baltimore Orioles

It happened again. Despite running last in the ultra-competitive American League East, the Orioles were a respectable 61-63 through August 17, outscoring their opponents by seven runs to that point. Then the bottom dropped out, as the team went into a 2-15 nosedive and wound up losing 30 of its final 37 games by a combined margin of 94 runs, as if to prove that the Orioles could finish in last place on merit alone.

The season-ending skid was all too reminiscent of the previous year, in which an infamous 30-3 drubbing by the Rangers on August 21 tossed the Orioles into a season-ending 11-28 freefall; where they had been 58-65 with a +11 run differential, they finished 11-28, outscored by 123 runs in that span. In fact, this is a recurring problem for the Orioles, as five times in the last seven years, they've played respectably for over half a season, with a positive run differential if not quite a winning record, only to tank the rest of the way (see Table 1).

It's true that the 2008 Orioles had the misfortune of playing in a division that featured four teams with at least 86 wins, making for the strongest five-team division of the wild-card era. The Orioles were actually 46-43 with a +32 run differential outside the AL East, but against those East beasts, they went a combined 22-50 with a -119 run differential, both major league worsts, and 25 of those intradivision games came within their final 37-game span. The result of this slide was the Orioles' 11th consecutive losing season, and the fourth straight year they've declined in total victories.

If the question is whether 2008 represented anything beyond more of the same business as usual, the answer is a qualified yes. This past season marked Andy MacPhail's first full year running the team (he was hired

in late June 2007), and he got a solid start on a long-overdue rebuilding effort, trimming the team's Opening Day payroll from $93.6 million (10th in 2007) to $67.2 million (22nd in 2008). Much of that had to do with the two major trades MacPhail made last winter.

In November, MacPhail shipped Miguel Tejada to Houston for pitchers Matt Albers, Troy Patton, and Dennis Sarfate, third baseman Mike Costanzo, and outfielder Luke Scott. The personnel returns weren't overwhelming, but the Orioles did shed the $26 million remaining on Tejada's contract. Scott set career highs in every major category but was overexposed as a full-time player, Costanzo struggled in Triple-A, Sarfate stayed busy in low-leverage relief stints, and Albers and Patton both suffered torn labrums, the former after a solid half-season in the bullpen, the latter in spring training. Still, that's a pretty penny saved by sending out a declining player.

In February, MacPhail netted five more players from the Mariners in exchange for Erik Bedard, receiving center fielder Adam Jones and pitchers George Sherrill, Chris Tillman, Kam Mickolio, and Tony Butler. Sherrill, a situational lefty who had never closed before, moved into the role and earned All-Star honors with 28 saves in a strong first half; his ERA ballooned after the break as he missed a month due to shoulder inflammation and collected just three more saves. Jones hit .270/.311/.400, numbers that don't look like much but still offer optimism for the 23-year-old's future. Tillman emerged as a potential star after escaping from the California League and improving his changeup. Meanwhile, the ever-fragile Bedard was limited to 15 starts for Seattle and needed surgery to remove a shoulder cyst.

ORIOLES PROSPECTUS

2008 record: 68-93; Fifth place, AL East

Pythagenpot record: 72-89

Runs scored per game: 4.86 (8th in AL)

Runs allowed per game: 5.40 (13th in AL)

Team EqA: .259 (Tied for 8th in AL)

2008 Batters Age: 30.6 (5th-oldest in AL)

2008 Pitchers Age: 27.9 (4th-youngest in AL)

Ballpark: Oriole Park at Camden Yards; Slight hitter's park; Park Factor of 1.023

2008: To paraphrase Thomas Jefferson, every rotation degenerates when entrusted to Jeremy Guthrie alone.

2009: The arrival of Matt Wieters eases another lost year, but the team's young positional talent can't take the next step sans pitching help.

Table 1. A Brief History of Amazing Orioles Meltdowns

Year	W-L	RD	Date	W-L	RD*
2008	61-63	+7	8/17	7-30	-94
2007	58-65	+11	8/21	11-28	-123
2005	49-40	+27	7/15	25-48	-98
2003	57-59	+16	8/10	14-32	-93
2002	63-63	+1	8/23	4-32	-107

*RD: Run Differential

Those two moves saved the Orioles millions in past and future contracts (especially had they tried to re-sign Bedard) while restocking the organization with talent. But as well as MacPhail did with those two trades, it's difficult to deny that he could have done even more. He missed the narrow window of opportunity to flip Sherrill before the trade deadline; held on to Aubrey Huff and Melvin Mora amid their first good seasons since 2004 and 2005, respectively; and during the season, he found no takers on Ramon Hernandez, Kevin Millar, Melvin Mora, or Jay Payton, not that all were equally tradable. The good players had more money remaining on their contracts than the Orioles were willing to eat, while the fate of the not-so-good ones is self-explanatory.

The one who got away from getting away was Brian Roberts. Signed through 2009 with a limited no-trade clause, Roberts may have set a major league record for the most rampant speculation ever surrounding a player *not* traded; in spring training, updates on a potential trade to the Cubs appeared hourly, but no deal was ever consummated. The reported package offered by Chicago was admittedly short of top-tier prospects, but that may have had to do with the perception that Roberts wasn't truly available, either via his own wishes or those of owner Peter Angelos, who speaks of Roberts in reverential, Ripkenesque terms.

Go back to that table above. The history of late-season meltdowns makes for an ugly track record, one that speaks ill of a team beyond simple wins and losses. Chronic season-ending slumps like those aren't the result of random chance or a few bad breaks. They're failures of the organizational culture, the result of too many veterans with thousand-yard stares playing out the string on dead-end ballclubs—all the more reason for MacPhail to have moved more aggressively last summer.

As it was, the 2008 Orioles were an old team, with Jones and right fielder Nick Markakis the only regulars under 30; Roberts and Scott were in their age-30 seasons. The offense ranked eighth in the league in raw scoring and eighth in EqA (.259), but it did rank fifth in slugging percentage, in part because Roberts, Huff, and Markakis all cracked at least 48 doubles. The lineup's least-productive slots were at shortstop, where five players made between 26 and 46 starts and hit a combined .218/.259/.276 (a .200 EqA), and first base, where Millar hit just .234/.323/.394.

The O's were seventh in the league in Defensive Efficiency (.688) and ninth in Park-Adjusted Defensive Efficiency (0.72 percent below average). Again, shortstop was a real problem. Among assorted advanced metrics, of the 28 shortstops to play at least 200 innings, Luis Hernandez, Juan Castro, Brandon Fahey, and Alex Cintron all ranked among the bottom six in Revised Zone Rating; Freddie Bynum, surprisingly, was second. All five finished with negatives in John Dewan's Plus/Minus system, with Fahey (-9) and Cintron (-12) leading the way. The team's raw Defensive Efficiency fell by a staggering 35 points in the second half, from .703 to .668, while Castro started 46 of those 67 games after the All-Star break.

Such defensive inefficiency represented a major problem for a pitching staff that was dead worst in the league in both strikeouts and walks. The rotation lacked a single starter with a strikeout rate better than league average, so it was no wonder this unit finished last in the majors, with a 5.51 ERA, and second-to-last in the American League in SNLVAR. "Ace" Jeremy Guthrie was the only member of the unit with at least a dozen starts and an ERA below 5.25. Brian Burres, Garrett Olsen, and Radhames Liz combined for 65 starts and a 6.43 ERA, all finishing above 6.00. In that context, the perpetually maddening Daniel Cabrera starts to look like a staff savior with his 5.25 ERA over 180 innings, but even as he cut his walk rate to 4.5 per nine, his strikeout rate fell from 7.3 to 4.8. The bullpen wasn't much better, finishing 12th in the league in WXRL, just 0.3 wins above replacement level. Rookie Jim Johnson placed 13th in the league at 3.2 WXRL, but he's not got dominant stuff, and nobody thinks he can assume a larger role on the staff. The bottom line is that the Orioles simply lacked enough major league arms to fill out the schedule.

The good news is that their future is brightest in that department. Tillman and 2008 first-round pick Brian Matusz both project as front-end starters in a big-league rotation, and 2007 fifth-rounder Jake Arrieta, who had a strong year at High-A Frederick, should make the majors as a starter as well. Brandon Erbe, the team's third-round pick from 2005, is back on track after repeating at Frederick, though his ceiling doesn't appear as high as that for the aforementioned trio. David Hernandez, a 2005 16th-rounder, took a big step forward at Double-A Bowie. All are at least a couple of years away from "The Show." Immediate help from within being slim pickings, the Orioles threw $1.5 million at Mark Hendrickson and imported 34-year-old right-hander Koji Uehara from the Japanese leagues on a two-year deal to help provide a crust of experience to tide them over in the meantime.

The long-term outlook isn't so rosy when it comes to hitters, at least beyond catcher Matt Wieters. The Orioles' first-round pick in 2007, Wieters ranks as one of the top prospects in the minors. He hit a combined .355/.454/.600, splitting time between High-A and Double-A, and he should be up with the big club in 2009. Beyond him, however, the pickings are slim. Outfielder Nolan Reimold rebounded from injuries to post a strong season at Bowie, but he's now 25 and doesn't rate as an impact bat, and neither does first baseman Brandon Snyder, the O's 2005 first-rounder. Third baseman Billy Rowell, their 2006 first-rounder, has flaws with his swing and concerns about his effort afield.

The Orioles aren't likely to be competitive in 2009, and let's face it, 2010 isn't looking all that realistic, either, particularly in a division where the Rays' youth movement has only begun to flower, the Red Sox have strong prospects as well, and the Yankees will continue to spend their way into contention. The Orioles need to avoid the temptation of going about their winter business as usual, patching various holes with midpriced options who give them an upside of about 75 wins—a level the Orioles have actually reached just once in this millennium. To do so only forestalls the more extensive rebuilding effort MacPhail was brought in to launch; they need to remain disciplined when it comes to doling out contracts to mediocrities who won't be part of the next winning Orioles club.

If they're itching to spend a few dollars on free agents, an investment in their infield defense would make the most prudent course. The Rays set a record with a 54-point year-to-year-improvement in Defensive Efficiency, and it did wonders for the development of their pitching staff. For the Orioles, signing strong defensive shortstop Cesar Izturis is a commonsensical move that will pay disproportionate dividends—after last season's debacle at the position, they have nowhere to go but up, but what's more important, as in the case of the Rays, the added stability will have teamwide effects. Glove men come cheaper than hitters on the open market or in trade, and they're a low-cost means of keeping runs off the board for a team desperately in need of same.

In all, the good news for Orioles fans is that while the 2009 season certainly won't be pretty, the bottom of the trough has been reached. The team has begun taking solid steps in the right direction, and that's more than can be said for them over the better part of the last decade.

HITTERS

| Mike Costanzo | | | | | 3B | | | | | | | | Bats: L | | Throws: R | | Height: 6' 3" | | Weight: 215 | | Born: September 9, 1983 | | Age: 25 |

YEAR	TEAM	LVL	AGE	PA	R	2B	3B	HR	RBI	BB	SO	SB	CS	EqBRR	AVG	OBP	SLG	EqAVG	EqOBP	EqSLG	EqA	VORP	WARP	DEFENSE
2006	CLR	A+	22	593	72	33	1	14	81	74	133	3	2	-2.5	.258	.364	.411	.216	.307	.358	.234	-14.3	-0.8	131-3B -4
2007	REA	AA	23	595	92	29	1	27	86	75	157	2	0	1.0	.270	.368	.490	.238	.323	.433	.261	9.7	0.6	134-3B -10
2008	NOR	AAA	24	538	56	28	2	11	63	52	159	2	2	-1.1	.261	.333	.395	.258	.328	.402	.254	6.1	-0.1	72-3B -6 34-1B 1
2009	BAL	MLB	25	510	51	24	1	15	59	48	150	2	1	-0.7	.230	.306	.384	.228	.307	.390	.243	-4.7	0.3	120-3B -5

Breakout: 11%   Improve: 41%   Collapse: 27%   Attrition: 8%   Comparables: Scott Stahoviak, Jason Grabowski, Brad Nelson, John Vander Wal

Costanzo was a popular guy last offseason; the Astros got him from the Phillies in the Lidge deal, and then the Orioles got him in the Tejada trade. Unfortunately, the 2007 power burst that made him desirable evaporated as quickly as gasoline on a blacktop road in August. We'd normally say something about Norfolk being a tough park to hit in, but the fact is that Costanzo hit pretty much the same at home (.263/.337/.386) as on the road (.259/.328/.405); the strikeouts, not the park, are what's holding him back. He was trying to learn to catch in the spring, an accomplishment that would certainly raise his value, but it never translated into any games played. The Orioles left him unprotected in the Rule 5 draft, but no one bit; what a difference a year makes.

Tyler Henson   3B   Bats: R   Throws: R   Height: 6' 1"   Weight: 190   Born: December 15, 1987   Age: 21

YEAR	TEAM	LVL	AGE	PA	R	2B	3B	HR	RBI	BB	SO	SB	CS	EqBRR	AVG	OBP	SLG	EqAVG	EqOBP	EqSLG	EqA	VORP	WARP	DEFENSE			
2006	BLU	Rk	18	170	21	5	2	0	13	18	49	1	1	1.9	.230	.314	.291	.160	.213	.199	.122	-51.2	-4.0	23-SS	-6	10-3B	-4
2007	ABE	A-	19	289	44	18	4	5	31	22	68	20	2	4.1	.289	.353	.449	.233	.280	.383	.233	-13.9	-2.6	63-SS	-20		
2008	DEL	A	20	541	71	25	3	11	62	25	121	20	3	2.3	.265	.310	.392	.231	.269	.352	.216	-24.2	-1.2	118-3B	2		
2009	BAL	MLB	21	591	56	31	3	11	56	32	151	12	4	1.6	.233	.279	.361	.231	.279	.366	.225	-13.0	-0.2	138-3B	1		

Breakout: 59%   Improve: 77%   Collapse: 10%   Attrition: 5%   Comparables: Josh Barfield, Eddie Lantigua, Frank Valdez, Victor Diaz

As Hensons go, Tyler is better than Drew, but still not as cool as Jim. A terrific all-around athlete, Henson led his high school to state championships in football (quarterback) and baseball (shortstop/pitcher). His limitations are his bat and strike-zone judgment. After seeming to break out in 2007, he gave the progress back at Delmarva—pitchers realized that he'd swing at anything, so why throw a strike? Henson lifted his profile a bit with a strong performance in Hawaiian winter ball, but "small sample" caveats definitely apply.

Luis Hernandez   SS   Bats: S   Throws: R   Height: 5' 10"   Weight: 180   Born: June 26, 1984   Age: 25

YEAR	TEAM	LVL	AGE	PA	R	2B	3B	HR	RBI	BB	SO	SB	CS	EqBRR	AVG	OBP	SLG	EqAVG	EqOBP	EqSLG	EqA	VORP	WARP	DEFENSE			
2006	MIS	AA	22	413	39	12	4	1	29	20	46	4	4	-1.0	.268	.308	.329	.248	.281	.313	.206	-21.3	-1.7	65-SS	-4	33-2B	-3
2006	RIC	AAA	22	74	3	4	0	1	5	0	8	0	1	-0.8	.192	.192	.288	.178	.178	.260	.117	-10.2	-0.3	19-SS	3		
2007	BOW	AA	23	393	42	15	6	0	37	18	50	6	5	0.2	.242	.276	.316	.216	.247	.289	.184	-33.0	-0.1	89-SS	12		
2007	NOR	AAA	23	34	4	0	0	0	3	0	5	0	0	-0.1	.273	.273	.273	.265	.265	.265	.178	-2.5	0.2	9-SS	3		
2007	BAL	MLB	23	71	5	2	0	1	7	1	10	2	2	-0.7	.290	.300	.362	.290	.300	.362	.222	-0.5	0.3	16-SS	4		
2008	NOR	AAA	24	216	18	7	0	0	11	8	27	2	2	-1.0	.185	.216	.220	.175	.206	.204	.108	-31.0	-2.7	54-SS	-5		
2008	BAL	MLB	24	91	9	1	0	0	3	7	11	2	0	-1.1	.241	.295	.253	.244	.299	.256	.213	-2.7	-0.2	25-SS	0		
2009	KCA	MLB	25	349	26	12	2	1	23	15	48	4	3	0.5	.224	.259	.278	.221	.257	.286	.186	-15.7	-0.7	84-SS	1		

Breakout: 54%   Improve: 66%   Collapse: 24%   Attrition: 16%   Comparables: Juan Lorenzo, Thomas Soto, Pat Maxwell, Tomas Perez

Hernandez had the first crack at the shortstop job last year, didn't hit—yeah, like that was a surprise to anyone with firing synapses—and wound up in Norfolk for the rest of the year. That responsible people made decisions about him based on 69 at-bats in 2007 demonstrates that for all the inroads sabermetrics has made into front offices, there is still a great deal of work to do. The inability of the front office to solve its shortstop problem before the season or even create any viable alternative led to a season-long rotation of dreck, dross, flotsam, and frass where Ripken once roamed. Cesar Izturis is an improvement, mostly by virtue of the stability he'll bring.

Ramon Hernandez   C   Bats: R   Throws: R   Height: 6' 0"   Weight: 235   Born: May 20, 1976   Age: 33

YEAR	TEAM	LVL	AGE	PA	R	2B	3B	HR	RBI	BB	SO	SB	CS	EqBRR	AVG	OBP	SLG	EqAVG	EqOBP	EqSLG	EqA	VORP	WARP	DEFENSE	
2006	BAL	MLB	30	560	66	29	2	23	91	43	79	1	0	-0.7	.275	.343	.479	.265	.338	.470	.276	28.9	3.8	125-C	2
2007	BAL	MLB	31	409	40	18	0	9	62	36	59	1	3	-2.6	.258	.333	.382	.253	.330	.386	.249	6.3	0.6	96-C	-6
2008	BAL	MLB	32	507	49	22	1	15	65	32	62	0	0	-3.5	.257	.308	.406	.254	.307	.414	.249	8.3	0.8	118-C	-8
2009	CIN	MLB	33	365	40	17	1	10	44	31	53	0	1	-1.8	.264	.331	.412	.263	.329	.412	.254	11.8	1.8	88-C	-3

Breakout: 18%   Improve: 43%   Collapse: 30%   Attrition: 28%   Comparables: Javy Lopez, Don Leppert, Joe Oliver, Bengie Molina

Neither Hernandez nor the Orioles were happy with each other in 2008, and with Wietersmania building, the Orioles pawned him off on the Reds for Ryan Freel and a couple of minor leaguers. He got off to a bad start in 2008, entering June with a .229 EqA, but rebounded with a .271 mark the rest of the way. He's set a new career low in caught-stealing percentage two years in a row, with a career-worst 99 stolen bases allowed last year. Hernandez clearly isn't what he was in his late 20s, but Camden Yards loves its righty hitters and might have camouflaged a more precipitous decline: in his three seasons at Orioles Park, Hernandez hit .291/.351/.485 with 31 home runs in 660 at-bats, and on the road, he batted .238/.305/.370 with 16 home runs in 668 at-bats. His new home, the Gap, also favors righties, so the illusion might persist for another year or two.

Aubrey Huff   DH

Bats: L   Throws: R   Height: 6' 4"   Weight: 235   Born: December 20, 1976   Age: 32

YEAR	TEAM	LVL	AGE	PA	R	2B	3B	HR	RBI	BB	SO	SB	CS	EqBRR	AVG	OBP	SLG	EqAVG	EqOBP	EqSLG	EqA	VORP	WARP	DEFENSE
2006	TBA	MLB	29	256	26	15	1	8	28	24	25	0	0	1.2	.283	.348	.461	.272	.344	.447	.273	9.1	1.1	55-3B 1
2006	HOU	MLB	29	261	31	10	1	13	38	26	39	0	0	-0.2	.250	.341	.478	.246	.335	.469	.275	7.1	0.3	29-RF -4 24-3B -3
2007	BAL	MLB	30	603	68	34	5	15	72	48	87	1	1	1.8	.280	.337	.442	.272	.333	.448	.268	12.4	0.7	47-1B -4 14-3B -2
2008	BAL	MLB	31	661	96	48	2	32	108	53	89	4	0	-2.3	.304	.360	.552	.297	.358	.556	.304	55.6	4.4	31-3B -4 22-1B 1
2009	BAL	MLB	32	580	73	32	2	20	83	48	85	3	1	-1.5	.275	.338	.457	.273	.339	.464	.276	17.3	1.9	136-DH

Breakout: 4%   Improve: 24%   Collapse: 28%   Attrition: 11%   Comparables: Ted Kluszewski, Chris Chambliss, Tino Martinez, Kent Hrbek

In the last 10 years, there have been 10 players who were over 30 and who had an EqA at least 30 points higher than in any of their previous three seasons. Huff, the only player to do it in 2008, makes 11. Nine of those 10 players saw their EqAs drop in their next season, by an average of 38 points; the 10th was Barry Bonds, 2002. So the odds are pretty high that Huff's power surge will quietly dissipate in 2009, returning him to his 2005-2007 condition as a somewhat inadequate producer who slightly increases his value by possessing the versatility to play three corners badly.

Adam Jones   CF

Bats: R   Throws: R   Height: 6' 2"   Weight: 200   Born: August 1, 1985   Age: 23

YEAR	TEAM	LVL	AGE	PA	R	2B	3B	HR	RBI	BB	SO	SB	CS	EqBRR	AVG	OBP	SLG	EqAVG	EqOBP	EqSLG	EqA	VORP	WARP	DEFENSE
2006	TAC	AAA	20	416	69	19	4	16	62	28	78	13	4	2.9	.287	.345	.484	.265	.316	.455	.263	11.2	1.4	83-CF 0 12-RF -1
2006	SEA	MLB	20	76	6	4	0	1	8	2	22	3	1	-0.3	.216	.237	.311	.216	.237	.297	.185	-4.0	-0.5	22-CF -1
2007	TAC	AAA	21	469	75	27	6	25	84	36	106	8	7	1.5	.314	.382	.586	.285	.349	.536	.291	35.1	3.6	93-CF 2 8-RF -1
2007	SEA	MLB	21	71	16	2	1	2	4	4	21	2	1	2.0	.246	.300	.400	.246	.300	.446	.254	-0.4	0.2	13-LF 1
2008	BAL	MLB	22	514	61	21	7	9	57	23	108	10	3	0.8	.270	.311	.400	.271	.312	.412	.252	7.2	2.2	125-CF 10
2009	BAL	MLB	23	488	66	24	4	18	67	31	105	10	4	1.6	.278	.331	.470	.276	.332	.477	.277	19.3	3.3	115-CF 3

Breakout: 35%   Improve: 61%   Collapse: 18%   Attrition: 17%   Comparables: Andre Dawson, Ellis Burks, Dwight Evans, Garry Maddox

There's a lot of promise here, more than enough to make the Bedard trade worthwhile to the O's without even considering the other players involved. There are also lingering questions that, if they remain unaddressed, could render Jones more into the next Corey Patterson than into a Grady Sizemore. His control of the strike zone is decidedly weak, and he didn't show as much power last year as he had before. These are not unrelated problems. Some of the blame can plausibly be connected to the broken foot Jones suffered in August; he missed a month and wasn't sharp after he returned. His defense continues to improve; remember, this was only his third season in the outfield.

Nick Markakis   RF

Bats: L   Throws: L   Height: 6' 2"   Weight: 215   Born: November 17, 1983   Age: 25

YEAR	TEAM	LVL	AGE	PA	R	2B	3B	HR	RBI	BB	SO	SB	CS	EqBRR	AVG	OBP	SLG	EqAVG	EqOBP	EqSLG	EqA	VORP	WARP	DEFENSE
2006	BAL	MLB	22	542	72	25	2	16	62	43	72	2	0	2.2	.291	.351	.448	.279	.345	.439	.272	19.6	2.2	105-RF 1 23-LF 5
2007	BAL	MLB	23	710	97	43	3	23	112	61	112	18	6	0.3	.300	.362	.485	.292	.358	.491	.289	34.2	4.7	158-RF 6
2008	BAL	MLB	24	697	106	48	1	20	87	99	113	10	7	-2.5	.306	.406	.491	.301	.407	.497	.307	47.0	6.2	155-RF 7
2009	BAL	MLB	25	661	96	36	3	21	89	73	107	10	3	0.1	.286	.368	.466	.284	.369	.473	.292	23.5	4.3	154-RF 5

Breakout: 15%   Improve: 40%   Collapse: 14%   Attrition: 7%   Comparables: Steve Kemp, Ben Grieve, Leon Durham, Keith Hernandez

Markakis continued his streak of raising his EqA and EqR in every season of his pro career to date, starting from his Aberdeen debut in 2003. Extend that into 2009, and you're looking at a serious MVP candidate. There's really nothing about him to dislike—he had too many caught stealings, if you want to get nitpicky—and he's just now entering his prime. Hitting 40 doubles in consecutive years by his age-24 season puts him on a list that's littered with Hall of Famers: Musial, Yastrzemski, Williams, Medwick, Gehrig, Greenberg. On the downside, it also includes Ben Grieve.

Kevin Millar   **1B**   Bats: R   Throws: R   Height: 6' 0"   Weight: 215   Born: September 24, 1971   Age: 37

YEAR	TEAM	LVL	AGE	PA	R	2B	3B	HR	RBI	BB	SO	SB	CS	EqBRR	AVG	OBP	SLG	EqAVG	EqOBP	EqSLG	EqA	VORP	WARP	DEFENSE
2006	BAL	MLB	34	503	64	26	0	15	64	59	74	1	1	-3.1	.272	.374	.437	.261	.370	.427	.279	15.6	0.9	91-1B -7
2007	BAL	MLB	35	562	63	26	1	17	63	76	94	1	1	-2.4	.254	.365	.420	.245	.362	.421	.275	11.3	1.0	98-1B -6
2008	BAL	MLB	36	610	73	25	0	20	72	71	93	0	1	-4.7	.234	.323	.394	.228	.325	.401	.254	-2.4	0.4	128-1B 2
2009	BAL	MLB	37	393	42	17	1	14	51	44	66	1	1	-2.0	.231	.320	.407	.229	.321	.413	.257	-0.3	0.4	94-1B -2

Breakout: 14% Improve: 40% Collapse: 34% Attrition: 41%   Comparables: Andre Thornton, Roy Sievers, Tino Martinez, Tim Wallach

Hmm, how about a checklist? BABIP? Declining. Double-to-homer ratio? Dropping. Batting average? Dropping as the season goes on. If those aren't indicators of a guy who was never fast losing what little foot speed he had left, then nothing is. Millar can still drive a cripple pitch, he can still work a walk, and he's still regarded as a clubhouse inspiration. He's testing the free-agent market, trying to wring another few paychecks out of veteran presence.

Lou Montanez   **LF**   Bats: R   Throws: R   Height: 6' 2"   Weight: 200   Born: December 15, 1981   Age: 27

YEAR	TEAM	LVL	AGE	PA	R	2B	3B	HR	RBI	BB	SO	SB	CS	EqBRR	AVG	OBP	SLG	EqAVG	EqOBP	EqSLG	EqA	VORP	WARP	DEFENSE			
2006	WTN	AA	24	162	24	11	0	2	25	15	26	5	3	-0.7	.369	.438	.489	.310	.373	.428	.279	9.1	1.0	26-RF	1	11-LF	1
2006	IOW	AAA	24	269	23	12	0	8	31	17	44	0	1	-2.1	.224	.281	.371	.201	.250	.329	.197	-17.9	-3.0	56-LF -12			
2007	BOW	AA	25	135	24	2	0	3	11	10	16	3	2	0.2	.339	.398	.430	.272	.321	.352	.237	-1.2	-0.5	31-CF -5			
2007	NOR	AAA	25	241	27	11	0	7	26	22	35	1	3	-0.1	.259	.332	.410	.245	.310	.394	.243	-0.9	-0.7	32-LF	-6	27-RF	0
2008	BOW	AA	26	501	90	32	5	26	97	36	63	4	4	2.1	.335	.385	.601	.266	.309	.489	.268	18.5	1.2	85-LF	-5	13-RF	1
2008	BAL	MLB	26	117	18	6	1	3	14	4	20	0	0	-0.2	.295	.316	.446	.295	.316	.473	.267	2.9	-0.5	20-LF -7			
2009	BAL	MLB	27	503	56	23	2	16	65	31	88	3	2	0.1	.261	.310	.423	.259	.311	.429	.255	0.6	0.5	119-LF -6			

Breakout: 28% Improve: 49% Collapse: 29% Attrition: 10%   Comparables: Barry Bonnell, Larry Littleton, Sean Berry, Glenn Wilson

Montanez has been around the block a few times. He was the third overall pick in the 2000 draft and, as such, can certainly be called a late bloomer. He won the triple crown in the Eastern League despite missing the last month of Bowie's season when he was called up to replace Adam Jones and his broken foot. He homered in his first at-bat in the majors, which is always a nice thing to be able to tell the grandkids. Montanez needs to keep every bit of his newfound hitting going forward; between his position and weak defense, the value bar is set awfully high, and the addition of Ryan Freel might crowd him off of the roster.

Scott Moore   **INF**   Bats: L   Throws: R   Height: 6' 2"   Weight: 195   Born: November 17, 1983   Age: 25

YEAR	TEAM	LVL	AGE	PA	R	2B	3B	HR	RBI	BB	SO	SB	CS	EqBRR	AVG	OBP	SLG	EqAVG	EqOBP	EqSLG	EqA	VORP	WARP	DEFENSE			
2006	WTN	AA	22	532	52	28	0	22	75	55	126	12	7	-0.4	.276	.360	.479	.258	.331	.465	.271	20.0	2.2	121-3B	-1		
2006	CHN	MLB	22	42	6	2	0	2	5	2	10	0	0	-0.1	.263	.317	.474	.256	.310	.462	.260	0.6	0.0	5-1B	0		
2007	IOW	AAA	23	382	61	19	4	19	69	48	100	4	3	3.1	.265	.373	.526	.235	.338	.462	.273	12.2	0.3	73-3B	-13	16-LF	2
2007	BAL	MLB	23	50	2	2	0	1	11	1	15	0	1	-1.1	.255	.260	.362	.255	.260	.362	.212	-2.4	-0.7	9-3B	-5		
2008	NOR	AAA	24	318	41	21	2	7	44	23	67	3	0	-0.5	.247	.321	.408	.238	.307	.407	.246	-0.5	-0.2	36-3B	-3	16-1B	1
2009	BAL	MLB	25	397	46	20	1	14	51	34	98	6	2	0.3	.240	.315	.421	.238	.316	.427	.258	3.8	1.1	95-3B	-3		

Breakout: 16% Improve: 44% Collapse: 26% Attrition: 17%   Comparables: Clint Hurdle, Brad Snyder, Orsino Hill, Tim Thompson

It was a lost season for Moore. Although he initially stuck with the Orioles coming out of spring training, he couldn't fill their desperate need for shortstop help and was sent down-bay to Norfolk. There, he had to fight knee and hand injuries to stay in the lineup. He'll need every scrap of offense he can muster to get past the fringe-player stage, because he's not an asset on defense. Moore and Mora could be a dance team, the waltz being how performances and decisions about each affect the other.

Melvin Mora   3B

Bats: R   Throws: R   Height: 5' 11"   Weight: 200   Born: February 2, 1972   Age: 37

YEAR	TEAM	LVL	AGE	PA	R	2B	3B	HR	RBI	BB	SO	SB	CS	EqBRR	AVG	OBP	SLG	EqAVG	EqOBP	EqSLG	EqA	VORP	WARP	DEFENSE
2006	BAL	MLB	34	705	96	25	0	16	83	54	99	11	1	1.3	.274	.342	.391	.265	.337	.385	.258	9.1	0.2	151-3B -14
2007	BAL	MLB	35	527	67	23	1	14	58	47	83	9	3	-0.9	.274	.341	.418	.267	.339	.422	.266	10.4	2.2	118-3B 4
2008	BAL	MLB	36	570	77	29	2	23	104	37	70	3	7	0.5	.285	.342	.483	.283	.343	.500	.280	24.6	3.0	120-3B 1
2009	BAL	MLB	37	391	47	20	1	12	53	29	57	3	2	-0.6	.271	.331	.437	.269	.332	.443	.268	10.5	1.3	93-3B -2

Breakout: 14% Improve: 37% Collapse: 22% Attrition: 33%   Comparables: Ken Boyer, Phil Garner, Vinny Castilla, Mike Bordick

If the season started at the All-Star break, Mora would have won himself a batting title and just missed on an RBI crown as well. But the first half counts, too, and Mora didn't produce much then. You could it say it was because he was favoring a sore shoulder out of spring; you could also say that he's getting older and that stretches like the first half are going to become more and more common. He's another Oriole for whom 2009 is the last year of his contract, but the problem is, there's no prospect of note ready to take over at third.

Jay Payton   OF

Bats: R   Throws: R   Height: 5' 10"   Weight: 205   Born: November 22, 1972   Age: 36

YEAR	TEAM	LVL	AGE	PA	R	2B	3B	HR	RBI	BB	SO	SB	CS	EqBRR	AVG	OBP	SLG	EqAVG	EqOBP	EqSLG	EqA	VORP	WARP	DEFENSE	
2006	OAK	MLB	33	588	78	32	3	10	59	22	52	8	4	0.8	.296	.325	.418	.290	.321	.416	.255	12.3	0.8	51-LF 2	43-CF -8
2007	BAL	MLB	34	470	48	21	5	7	58	22	42	5	2	-1.2	.256	.292	.376	.252	.292	.383	.235	-10.4	0.7	102-LF 8	12-CF 2
2008	BAL	MLB	35	363	41	10	2	7	41	22	53	8	1	2.2	.243	.291	.346	.240	.293	.350	.229	-7.0	1.3	46-LF 20	34-CF -3
2009	BAL	MLB	36	218	23	9	1	4	22	12	29	4	1	0.0	.256	.301	.362	.254	.301	.367	.236	-3.1	0.5	55-LF 5	

Breakout: 17% Improve: 42% Collapse: 35% Attrition: 47%   Comparables: Andy Pafko, Darrin Jackson, Bill Virdon, Lenny Harris

Yes, Payton does a great job in the outfield; a marginal center fielder will tend to do very well in left, as you can see by looking at Payton, or David DeJesus, or Johnny Damon. Payton has become a strictly leather player, unable to swing with any authority, particularly against right-handed pitchers, against whom he "slugged" .288 last year, extending a four-year downward trend in that stat. He retains some pop against lefties, but with a .287 OBP against them, he's really not helping much against anybody. A free agent at this writing, he shouldn't and won't attract a great deal of interest.

Guillermo Quiroz   C

Bats: R   Throws: R   Height: 6' 1"   Weight: 200   Born: November 29, 1981   Age: 27

YEAR	TEAM	LVL	AGE	PA	R	2B	3B	HR	RBI	BB	SO	SB	CS	EqBRR	AVG	OBP	SLG	EqAVG	EqOBP	EqSLG	EqA	VORP	WARP	DEFENSE
2006	SAN	AA	24	68	5	3	0	3	9	3	15	0	0	-0.4	.188	.235	.375	.154	.191	.277	.142	-8.9	-0.6	15-C -1
2006	TAC	AAA	24	153	15	8	0	3	28	11	29	0	0	-1.4	.304	.359	.428	.286	.333	.407	.259	3.3	0.7	29-C 1
2007	OKL	AAA	25	278	22	16	0	6	33	15	52	0	0	0.0	.266	.307	.398	.230	.270	.345	.212	-12.5	-1.4	70-C -11
2008	BAL	MLB	26	148	12	5	0	2	14	12	34	0	0	-0.6	.187	.259	.269	.188	.265	.286	.191	-8.6	-0.7	40-C -2
2009	BAL	MLB	27	172	13	7	0	4	19	11	38	0	0	-0.9	.223	.275	.346	.221	.276	.351	.217	-3.0	0.2	44-C -2

Breakout: 43% Improve: 55% Collapse: 35% Attrition: 49%   Comparables: Tom Pagnozzi, Luis Pujols, Tom Nieto, Ken Rudolph

You don't expect much offense from a backup catcher; it's in the nature of the beast. Orioles fans have gotten used to an exceptionally uninspiring display, as Quiroz becomes the fourth Orioles backup backstop in five years who failed to deliver even a .200 EqA. It isn't clear whether he'll be an O or an ex-O in 2009, but you can be pretty sure that he'll remain an offensive zero.

Nolan Reimold   RF

Bats: R   Throws: R   Height: 6' 4"   Weight: 207   Born: October 12, 1983   Age: 25

YEAR	TEAM	LVL	AGE	PA	R	2B	3B	HR	RBI	BB	SO	SB	CS	EqBRR	AVG	OBP	SLG	EqAVG	EqOBP	EqSLG	EqA	VORP	WARP	DEFENSE	
2006	FRD	A+	22	504	73	26	0	19	75	76	107	14	8	-0.9	.255	.379	.455	.207	.304	.374	.237	-10.9	-0.9	94-RF -7	19-CF 2
2007	BOW	AA	23	203	30	15	0	11	34	17	47	2	3	-1.8	.306	.365	.565	.265	.315	.497	.267	9.1	0.4	45-RF -2	
2008	BOW	AA	24	586	87	29	3	25	84	63	82	7	3	0.6	.284	.367	.501	.257	.330	.465	.271	20.9	2.9	126-RF 4	5-LF 2
2009	BAL	MLB	25	557	63	26	1	21	73	49	116	5	2	-0.1	.240	.313	.421	.238	.313	.427	.257	-3.1	1.3	131-RF 2	

Breakout: 20% Improve: 50% Collapse: 25% Attrition: 10%   Comparables: Mike Fuentes, Joe Mather, Jeff Baker, Marcus Thames

A slugging outfielder who's fought nagging injuries on his way up, Reimold finished second in the Eastern League in homers (to teammate Lou Montanez), and that earned him a spot on the team's 40-man roster. At the very least, you would expect him to be the first outfielder called up in event of injury in 2009, and don't count out a possible job platooning with Luke Scott in left.

Brian Roberts 2B

Bats: S Throws: R Height: 5' 9" Weight: 180 Born: October 9, 1977 Age: 31

YEAR	TEAM	LVL	AGE	PA	R	2B	3B	HR	RBI	BB	SO	SB	CS	EqBRR	AVG	OBP	SLG	EqAVG	EqOBP	EqSLG	EqA	VORP	WARP	DEFENSE	
2006	BAL	MLB	28	629	85	34	3	10	55	55	66	36	7	3.7	.286	.347	.410	.275	.342	.402	.268	31.4	2.8	133-2B	1
2007	BAL	MLB	29	716	103	42	5	12	57	89	99	50	7	8.9	.290	.377	.432	.281	.374	.435	.290	44.6	5.7	150-2B	6
2008	BAL	MLB	30	704	107	51	8	9	57	82	104	40	10	0.7	.296	.378	.450	.294	.381	.457	.293	47.8	4.0	150-2B	-11
2009	BAL	MLB	31	630	95	35	5	13	64	69	90	31	8	3.1	.274	.355	.428	.272	.356	.434	.282	27.3	3.9	147-2B	-1

Breakout: 13% Improve: 37% Collapse: 23% Attrition: 5%   Comparables: Ray Durham, Don Buford, Jose Offerman, Chuck Knoblauch

Perhaps the biggest surprise of the season was that Roberts stayed with the Orioles all year, despite frequent rumors that had him headed somewhere for something (usually Wrigleyville, for lots, or little, or anything else in between). The talk this winter is about getting him signed to a contract extension. This presents a thorny dilemma. As one of the top leadoff men in baseball right now, Roberts would be very hard to replace, particularly as the Orioles have no one in their system remotely comparable. He's also very popular. On the other hand, his age is such that he may not be a valuable contributor by the time the Orioles are in contention (whenever that will be), and it's unlikely his market value will be any higher than it is now.

Billy Rowell 3B

Bats: L Throws: R Height: 6' 5" Weight: 205 Born: September 10, 1988 Age: 20

YEAR	TEAM	LVL	AGE	PA	R	2B	3B	HR	RBI	BB	SO	SB	CS	EqBRR	AVG	OBP	SLG	EqAVG	EqOBP	EqSLG	EqA	VORP	WARP	DEFENSE	
2006	ABE	A-	17	49	8	4	0	1	6	4	12	0	0	1.2	.326	.388	.488	.244	.286	.356	.225	-2.8	-0.7	11-3B	-4
2006	BLU	Rk	17	180	38	15	3	2	26	25	47	3	0	1.4	.329	.422	.507	.210	.278	.327	.214	-20.0	-2.3	36-3B	-9
2007	DEL	A	18	388	47	21	3	9	57	31	104	3	2	-3.6	.273	.335	.426	.216	.265	.335	.207	-22.1	-3.0	80-3B	-12
2008	FRD	A+	19	414	39	24	0	7	50	36	104	1	4	-5.1	.248	.315	.368	.218	.278	.339	.212	-20.4	-0.7	100-3B	5
2009	BAL	MLB	20	542	50	26	2	12	56	39	144	2	2	-1.2	.236	.294	.371	.234	.295	.376	.232	-8.2	-0.1	127 3B	-2

Breakout: 53% Improve: 72% Collapse: 10% Attrition: 2%   Comparables: Ian Stewart, Greg Blosser, Ben Grieve, Mike Laga

Rowell has been a first-round bust so far, but it really is hard to write off someone who can't legally drink yet. His swing still impresses scouts, but there's been no translation of it into success at the plate; he's piled up a lot of strikeouts, shown precious little power for a 6' 5" hulk, and there have been no signs of improvement to hang your hat on through his third year as a pro.

Oscar Salazar UT

Bats: R Throws: R Height: 6' 1" Weight: 220 Born: June 27, 1978 Age: 31

YEAR	TEAM	LVL	AGE	PA	R	2B	3B	HR	RBI	BB	SO	SB	CS	EqBRR	AVG	OBP	SLG	EqAVG	EqOBP	EqSLG	EqA	VORP	WARP	DEFENSE				
2007	BOW	AA	29	566	73	39	2	22	96	26	77	3	3	-3.0	.289	.324	.494	.176	.202	.294	.158	-64.9	-7.9	74-3B	-12	19-2B	-8	
2008	NOR	AAA	30	491	73	42	3	13	85	42	56	8	2	-2.7	.316	.371	.512	.268	.322	.446	.264	13.5	0.2	82-1B	-7	5-3B	1	
2008	BAL	MLB	30	94	13	3	0	5	15	12	13	0	1	-0.1	.284	.372	.506	.275	.372	.525	.298	5.4	0.6	9-1B	1	6-3B	-1	
2009	BAL	MLB	31	428	41	24	1	10	51	27	79	3	1	-0.7	.237	.286	.381	.235	.286	.387	.233	-8.4	-0.8	102-1B	-2			

Breakout: 32% Improve: 49% Collapse: 30% Attrition: 25%   Comparables: Chris Truby, Russ Morman, Jorge Toca, Brian Lesher

Years back, Salazar was signed by the A's out of Venezuela in 1994 and seemed a promising hitter, but one without a defensive home on the diamond. Then he started bouncing around on waivers, washing up in the Orioles' system in '07. His outstanding work in the Venezuelan winter league suggests that his recent good stickwork is no isolated event, and as one of the very few position players on the 40-man, he might finally get a chance to stick around.

Luke Scott   LF   Bats: L   Throws: R   Height: 6' 0"   Weight: 210   Born: June 25, 1978   Age: 31

YEAR	TEAM	LVL	AGE	PA	R	2B	3B	HR	RBI	BB	SO	SB	CS	EqBRR	AVG	OBP	SLG	EqAVG	EqOBP	EqSLG	EqA	VORP	WARP	DEFENSE			
2006	ROU	AAA	28	381	63	15	1	20	63	52	66	6	1	-1.9	.299	.400	.541	.242	.333	.442	.269	9.4	2.2	82-LF	8		
2006	HOU	MLB	28	249	31	19	6	10	37	30	43	2	1	-1.6	.336	.426	.621	.332	.422	.617	.340	29.4	2.9	45-LF	1	9-RF	-2
2007	HOU	MLB	29	425	49	28	5	18	64	53	95	3	1	-0.1	.255	.351	.504	.254	.355	.508	.290	19.3	3.0	90-RF	6		
2008	BAL	MLB	30	536	67	29	2	23	65	53	102	2	2	0.2	.257	.336	.472	.250	.334	.477	.274	17.2	2.3	95-LF	4		
2009	BAL	MLB	31	429	56	21	2	17	62	46	87	3	1	-0.5	.255	.340	.458	.253	.340	.465	.276	9.7	1.9	102-LF	-1		

Breakout: 16% Improve: 42% Collapse: 31% Attrition: 20%   Comparables: Dan Pasqua, Raul Ibañez, Walt Moryn, Jim King

Scott quickly endeared himself to his new team, going 8-for-16 and keying two wins in the first week of the season. The inevitable return to reality was not quite so kind, but he was still a solid contributor at the plate and in the field. He comes with a pair of drawbacks to him: first, he needs a platoon partner, as left-handed pitchers eat him up, but Ryan Freel is expected to help with that in 2009. Second, still shy of three full years of major league service, he's already 31 years old.

Brandon Snyder   1B   Bats: R   Throws: R   Height: 6' 2"   Weight: 205   Born: November 23, 1986   Age: 22

YEAR	TEAM	LVL	AGE	PA	R	2B	3B	HR	RBI	BB	SO	SB	CS	EqBRR	AVG	OBP	SLG	EqAVG	EqOBP	EqSLG	EqA	VORP	WARP	DEFENSE			
2006	DEL	A	19	159	12	12	0	3	20	9	55	0	0	-1.5	.194	.237	.340	.162	.196	.277	.152	-20.2	-1.6	23-C	-2		
2006	ABE	A-	19	131	14	8	1	1	11	5	43	2	1	0.2	.234	.267	.339	.183	.206	.278	.156	-28.7	-1.9	26-C	-4		
2007	DEL	A	20	501	63	23	3	11	58	44	107	0	2	-3.0	.283	.354	.422	.227	.283	.340	.216	-21.5	-2.2	63-1B	1		
2008	FRD	A+	21	476	70	33	2	13	80	29	83	3	2	-0.8	.315	.358	.490	.272	.310	.438	.256	9.5	0.5	81-1B	2	6-3B	-1
2009	BAL	MLB	22	582	57	30	2	17	71	35	131	3	2	-0.9	.249	.298	.406	.247	.299	.412	.246	-5.4	0.1	136-1B	0		

Breakout: 45% Improve: 72% Collapse: 10% Attrition: 3%   Comparables: Craig Worthington, Bob Zupcic, Javier Ortiz, Jim Maler

The former first-round pick showed signs of life as a prospect last year, turning into one of the Carolina League's top hitters. He's another year removed from the shoulder injury that ended his days as a catcher (and nearly his baseball career). As nice as it was, he's still not showing enough power to cut it as a major league first baseman.

Matt Wieters   C   Bats: S   Throws: R   Height: 6' 5"   Weight: 230   Born: May 21, 1986   Age: 23

YEAR	TEAM	LVL	AGE	PA	R	2B	3B	HR	RBI	BB	SO	SB	CS	EqBRR	AVG	OBP	SLG	EqAVG	EqOBP	EqSLG	EqA	VORP	WARP	DEFENSE	
2008	FRD	A+	22	280	48	8	0	15	40	44	47	1	2	-1.3	.345	.448	.576	.301	.396	.513	.310	28.2	3.7	47-C	7
2008	BOW	AA	22	250	41	14	2	12	51	38	29	1	0	0.5	.365	.460	.625	.349	.436	.627	.351	43.1	4.1	44-C	2
2009	BAL	MLB	23	649	105	33	2	31	102	77	102	4	2	-1.0	.311	.395	.544	.308	.396	.552	.319	59.6	7.9	151-C	-3

Breakout: 15% Improve: 41% Collapse: 23% Attrition: 2%   Comparables: Mark Teixeira, J.D. Drew, Alex Gordon, Ben Grieve

No matter what happens in Wieters' major league career—which should start very soon with Ramon Hernandez traded away—he can bask in the glory of what was arguably the best minor league performance of the last 40 years. If we set a 200 at-bat requirement, Wieters picked up the highest known translated EqA in both the Carolina and the Eastern leagues. His combined EqA, .329, is the third-highest mark in any league, behind Ryan Howard (.338, 2005, Triple-A) and Glenn Braggs (.335, 1986, Triple-A), both of whom had fewer plate appearances. And, oh yeah, he's a catcher. An excellent catcher. Take anything we've said about any player in any year of the Baseball Prospectus, and Wieters had a better year than that guy. So how lucky was Clay Davenport that the two games he went to see him play, Wieters went 0-for-7 with a walk and three popups?

PITCHERS

Matt Albers

| | Bats: L | Throws: R | Height: 6' 0" | Weight: 205 | Born: January 20, 1983 | Age: 26 |

YEAR	TEAM	LVL	AGE	W	L	SV	G	GS	IP	H	BB	SO	HR	GB%	BABIP	STUFF	WHIP	ERA	DERA	EqH9	EqBB9	EqSO9	EqHR9	DEF	VORP	SN/WX
2006	CCH	AA	23	10	2	0	19	19	116¹	96	47	95	4	53.5%	.277	8	1.23	2.17	4.55	8.7	4.0	4.5	0.7	4	12.9	—
2006	ROU	AAA	23	2	1	0	4	4	25²	24	10	26	2	40.2%	.304	10	1.35	3.93	5.16	11.1	4.0	6.8	1.2	1	1.1	—
2006	HOU	MLB	23	0	2	0	4	2	15	17	7	11	1	45.8%	.356	3	1.60	6.00	5.02	10.7	3.8	6.3	0.6	0	-0.3	-0.12
2007	ROU	AAA	24	2	3	0	9	9	53	50	22	43	6	53.8%	.301	-6	1.36	3.74	6.20	9.3	4.0	5.5	1.3	5	-3.3	—
2007	HOU	MLB	24	4	11	0	31	18	110²	127	50	71	18	49.5%	.313	-14	1.60	5.85	5.34	9.6	3.5	5.3	1.4	-3	-5.3	1.85
2008	BAL	MLB	25	3	3	0	28	3	49	43	22	26	4	54.1%	.262	-12	1.33	3.49	4.28	7.6	3.7	4.3	0.7	3	10.6	0.92
2009	BAL	MLB	26	3	3	1	29	4	55	59	24	33	6	49.0%	.300	0	1.50	4.77	4.66	9.4	3.5	5.1	1.0	0	5.4	0.60

Breakout: 19% Improve: 45% Collapse: 33% Attrition: 30%   Comparables: George Susce, Marc Wilkins, Rafael Carmona, Chuck Seelbach

Part of the Tejada trade, Albers did a solid job in long relief before shoulder woes cut his season short in June. Diagnosed with a torn labrum, he is attempting to rehab it without surgery. If it works, he'll be ready for spring; if not, he'll miss all of 2009 in addition to the half of 2008 already gone. Albers is in serious contention for a spot in the projected Orioles rotation, which tells you more about the Orioles' options than about him.

Jake Arrieta

| | Bats: R | Throws: R | Height: 6' 4" | Weight: 225 | Born: March 6, 1986 | Age: 23 |

YEAR	TEAM	LVL	AGE	W	L	SV	G	GS	IP	H	BB	SO	HR	GB%	BABIP	STUFF	WHIP	ERA	DERA	EqH9	EqBB9	EqSO9	EqHR9	DEF	VORP	SN/WX
2008	FRD	A+	22	6	5	0	20	20	113	80	51	120	7	49.7%	.265	14	1.16	2.87	4.63	8.5	4.6	6.4	1.1	3	11.1	—
2009	BAL	MLB	23	5	7	0	19	19	100²	112	59	76	15	44.0%	.310	12	1.69	5.84	5.61	9.7	4.8	6.3	1.3	0	-2.3	0.50

Breakout: 1% Improve: 16% Collapse: 47% Attrition: 16%   Comparables: Ryan Bradley, Rod Henderson, Jay Witasick, Thomas Diamond

Arrieta had flashed dominant stuff in college, but had a poor season going into the 2007 draft. That performance deterred teams, so the Orioles were able to steal him in the fifth round, and he's since recovered the first-round stuff from prior years. He made his debut in High-A and promptly led the league in ERA, mainly by overpowering the circuit with a power fastball that gets into the upper 90s. His season was a little short, though not because of injury—he was part of the US Olympic team and had six shutout innings in Beijing.

Danys Baez

| | Bats: R | Throws: R | Height: 6' 1" | Weight: 235 | Born: September 10, 1977 | Age: 31 |

YEAR	TEAM	LVL	AGE	W	L	SV	G	GS	IP	H	BB	SO	HR	GB%	BABIP	STUFF	WHIP	ERA	DERA	EqH9	EqBB9	EqSO9	EqHR9	DEF	VORP	SN/WX
2006	LAN	MLB	28	5	5	9	46	0	49²	53	11	29	3	40.7%	.323	-2	1.29	4.35	4.71	9.1	1.8	4.7	0.5	-1	4.0	-0.03
2006	ATL	MLB	28	0	1	0	11	0	10	7	6	10	0	37.0%	.259	5	1.30	5.40	5.23	6.1	4.4	7.8	0.0	1	0.6	0.07
2007	BAL	MLB	29	0	6	3	53	0	50¹	50	29	29	8	52.4%	.269	-26	1.57	6.44	6.88	8.5	4.8	4.4	1.4	5	-1.2	0.12
2009	BAL	MLB	31	2	2	1	25	1	34¹	38	13	20	4	45.0%	.290	-4	1.47	4.86	4.73	9.6	3.1	4.9	1.1	0	2.9	0.30

Breakout: 37% Improve: 57% Collapse: 25% Attrition: 36%   Comparables: Rich Monteleone, Galen Cisco, Bruce Dal Canton, Juan Acevedo

After missing all of the second year of his three-year deal recovering from elbow surgery, Baez will be back in time for spring training. The Cuban checked the lay of the land, noted the crowded bullpen, and has gamely announced a desire to return to starting, something he hasn't done in the majors since 2002. But since the Orioles are paying him either way and need the help, it can't hurt to give it a try. Set your expectations on "low," and be stunned if he turns out any better than that.

Brian Bass

Bats: R   Throws: R   Height: 6' 0"   Weight: 215   Born: January 6, 1982   Age: 27

YEAR	TEAM	LVL	AGE	W	L	SV	G	GS	IP	H	BB	SO	HR	GB%	BABIP	STUFF	WHIP	ERA	DERA	EqH9	EqBB9	EqSO9	EqHR9	DEF	VORP	SN/WX
2006	WIC	AA	24	4	1	0	6	5	27	29	6	18	2	60.0%	.307	-15	1.30	4.00	6.31	10.9	2.5	3.5	1.1	0	-2.0	—
2006	OMA	AAA	24	1	5	0	7	7	32²	49	14	11	7	48.9%	.341	-56	1.96	7.55	9.58	14.5	4.1	1.5	2.6	-7	-13.7	—
2006	ROY	Rk	24	1	1	0	3	3	12¹	15	0	9	0	59.5%	.357	-38	1.24	4.46	10.45	15.7	1.7	1.7	0.9	0	-5.6	—
2007	ROC	AAA	25	7	3	1	37	10	103¹	96	24	80	8	57.1%	.290	-13	1.16	3.49	5.34	9.9	2.4	4.7	1.1	3	2.8	—
2008	MIN	MLB	26	3	4	1	44	0	68¹	84	22	32	11	59.8%	.312	-28	1.55	4.88	4.73	10.9	2.7	3.8	1.5	-6	1.1	0.55
2008	BAL	MLB	26	1	0	0	5	4	21	14	9	13	1	52.5%	.220	-2	1.10	4.71	6.97	5.7	3.5	4.8	0.4	4	0.7	0.61
2009	BAL	MLB	27	2	3	1	31	3	53	60	18	30	7	51.0%	.300	-1	1.47	4.75	4.65	9.8	2.8	4.7	1.1	0	5.2	0.50

Breakout: 48%   Improve: 67%   Collapse: 24%   Attrition: 42%   Comparables: Mike Lincoln, Scott Winchester, Jon Adkins, Ricky Trlicek

The Orioles were pretty close to recruiting pitchers from their sales department, the security guards, the crowd … some of those peanut vendors have good arms … as the injuries piled up late last season. They found a warm body with a pedigree in getting Bass from the Twins. It was a classic replacement-level acquisition, and that's pretty much what Bass has been throughout his career.

Brad Bergesen

Bats: L   Throws: R   Height: 6' 2"   Weight: 205   Born: September 25, 1985   Age: 23

YEAR	TEAM	LVL	AGE	W	L	SV	G	GS	IP	H	BB	SO	HR	GB%	BABIP	STUFF	WHIP	ERA	DERA	EqH9	EqBB9	EqSO9	EqHR9	DEF	VORP	SN/WX
2006	DEL	A	20	5	4	0	18	14	86¹	97	10	49	6	46.0%	.313	-27	1.24	4.29	8.69	13.6	2.1	1.6	2.0	1	-26.3	—
2007	DEL	A	21	7	3	0	15	15	94¹	75	17	73	3	58.4%	.262	8	0.98	2.20	6.01	9.7	2.6	3.2	0.9	8	-3.9	—
2007	FRD	A+	21	3	6	0	10	10	56¹	78	9	35	4	55.0%	.364	-18	1.55	5.75	7.74	16.0	2.3	2.5	1.6	-9	-11.9	—
2008	FRD	A+	22	1	1	0	4	3	17¹	15	6	15	2	64.7%	.265	2	1.21	2.08	3.94	10.1	3.4	5.1	1.7	0	3.0	—
2008	BOW	AA	22	15	6	0	24	23	148	143	27	72	11	53.6%	.268	-2	1.15	3.22	5.29	9.6	1.7	2.9	1.0	12	4.9	—
2009	BAL	MLB	23	6	11	0	25	25	139²	189	39	56	23	48.0%	.320	1	1.63	6.22	6.00	11.8	2.3	3.4	1.4	0	-9.0	0.10

Breakout: 4%   Improve: 26%   Collapse: 39%   Attrition: 11%   Comparables: Wally Whitehurst, Brandon Hynick, Hector Trinidad, Tim Dillard

Bergesen was an afterthought going into last season, but he rocketed up the team's prospect charts with a 16-win performance that earned him recognition as the Orioles' minor league Pitcher of the Year. His best pitch is a sinking fastball, and the Orioles can hope that he'll get enough grounders from it for him to develop into a back-end starter in the rotation. A worrisome sign for his prospect status was his getting +12 runs of defensive support, the third-highest total of any pitcher in the Eastern League.

Brian Burres

Bats: L   Throws: L   Height: 6' 1"   Weight: 180   Born: April 8, 1981   Age: 28

YEAR	TEAM	LVL	AGE	W	L	SV	G	GS	IP	H	BB	SO	HR	GB%	BABIP	STUFF	WHIP	ERA	DERA	EqH9	EqBB9	EqSO9	EqHR9	DEF	VORP	SN/WX
2006	OTT	AAA	25	10	6	0	26	26	139²	133	57	110	14	42.9%	.300	-23	1.36	3.75	6.64	10.2	4.4	4.8	1.6	13	-14.7	—
2006	BAL	MLB	25	0	0	0	11	0	8	6	1	6	1	54.2%	.217	3	0.88	2.25	4.32	5.4	1.1	5.4	1.1	2	3.5	0.51
2007	BAL	MLB	26	6	8	0	37	17	121	140	66	96	14	39.0%	.335	-5	1.70	5.95	5.60	10.4	4.6	6.3	1.1	-1	0.4	1.67
2008	BAL	MLB	27	7	10	0	31	22	129²	165	50	63	17	36.9%	.328	-20	1.66	6.04	6.09	11.2	3.1	3.8	1.2	2	-4.9	1.03
2009	BAL	MLB	28	2	4	0	26	6	50²	62	22	30	8	41.0%	.320	-5	1.66	6.02	5.76	10.7	3.6	5.0	1.4	0	-2.6	0.00

Breakout: 22%   Improve: 47%   Collapse: 27%   Attrition: 53%   Comparables: Mike Kekich, Mike Mimbs, Wandy Rodriguez, Lance Painter

Burres had a couple of good stretches in 2008. One of them was in the spring, when he beat Albers and others out to win the fifth starter's slot, and he then proceeded to dance his way out of trouble through April and May. After that, he was just a disaster; the last 12 games he pitched in were all Orioles losses, and by an average of six runs. There just isn't much margin for error when you're a fly-ball pitcher without overpowering stuff.

Daniel Cabrera

Bats: R   Throws: R   Height: 6' 9"   Weight: 270   Born: May 28, 1981   Age: 28

YEAR	TEAM	LVL	AGE	W	L	SV	G	GS	IP	H	BB	SO	HR	GB%	BABIP	STUFF	WHIP	ERA	DERA	EqH9	EqBB9	EqSO9	EqHR9	DEF	VORP	SN/WX
2006	BAL	MLB	25	9	10	0	26	26	148	130	104	157	11	42.4%	.320	34	1.58	4.74	4.99	7.8	6.2	8.7	0.6	3	18.7	3.38
2007	BAL	MLB	26	9	18	0	34	34	204¹	207	108	166	25	50.7%	.308	4	1.54	5.55	5.37	9.0	4.4	6.4	1.1	-3	4.8	2.41
2008	BAL	MLB	27	8	10	0	30	30	180	199	90	95	24	49.4%	.303	-13	1.61	5.25	5.59	9.8	4.1	4.2	1.2	8	8.5	2.06
2009	WAS	MLB	28	8	9	0	23	23	138	133	67	112	12	48.0%	.300	19	1.45	4.31	4.72	8.7	3.8	6.3	0.8	0	13.4	2.70

Breakout: 34% Improve: 63% Collapse: 18% Attrition: 31%   Comparables: Jeff Juden, Stan Williams, Joey Jay, Aaron Sele

What can we add to the story of Daniel Cabrera? He's been the permanent tease, always showing you a little hint of some amazing talent, and we're all suckers who want to believe that this time, it's for real, that he's really figured it out this time, that he's gonna be gooooood … and before you know it, you're walking back to the MARC train with another loss. We thought this at the end of May, when he was 5-1, 3.74 ERA, and walking less than four men per nine. You can see how things had to go after that to arrive at his final record. The Orioles finally had enough of him, nontendering him in December; the Nats apparently had enough self-loathing to take their chances, spending $2.6 million for a year's worth of maddening moundsmanship.

Fernando Cabrera

Bats: R   Throws: R   Height: 6' 4"   Weight: 220   Born: November 16, 1981   Age: 27

YEAR	TEAM	LVL	AGE	W	L	SV	G	GS	IP	H	BB	SO	HR	GB%	BABIP	STUFF	WHIP	ERA	DERA	EqH9	EqBB9	EqSO9	EqHR9	DEF	VORP	SN/WX
2006	CLE	MLB	24	3	3	0	51	0	60²	53	32	71	12	34.9%	.304	6	1.40	5.19	5.12	7.9	4.8	9.8	1.7	-1	5.1	0.02
2007	CLE	MLB	25	1	2	0	24	0	33²	38	22	39	7	35.4%	.356	4	1.78	5.61	5.45	10.4	5.5	9.3	1.9	-1	0.6	0.02
2007	BAL	MLB	25	0	0	1	9	0	10	12	9	9	2	21.9%	.333	-11	2.10	12.60	11.70	10.8	7.2	7.2	1.8	0	-7.2	0.11
2008	NOR	AAA	26	0	0	0	11	0	13	11	7	13	0	34.3%	.314	5	1.38	0.69	0.75	9.0	5.2	6.0	0.0	-1	6.5	—
2008	BAL	MLB	26	2	1	0	22	0	28¹	32	17	31	9	23.8%	.315	-10	1.73	5.41	5.40	10.2	4.8	8.6	2.9	0	0.5	0.02
2009	BAL	MLB	27	1	2	1	27	0	32²	30	19	33	5	35.0%	.290	12	1.49	4.73	4.51	8.0	4.7	8.4	1.3	0	3.7	0.30

Breakout: 44% Improve: 69% Collapse: 18% Attrition: 38%   Comparables: Rocky Coppinger, Kurt Knudsen, Wayne Rosenthal, Wes Gardner

Cabrera brought his brief Orioles career to a screeching halt by flipping the ball to his manager instead of handing it to him as he was being taken out. Showing up your manager is a big no-no, especially when you're recent waiver bait, and he was released a couple of days later. The best split-fingered pitch (and Cabrera's is really good) is useless if you can't get ahead in the count, and he hasn't shown any control in four years.

Lance Cormier

Bats: R   Throws: R   Height: 6' 1"   Weight: 200   Born: August 19, 1980   Age: 28

YEAR	TEAM	LVL	AGE	W	L	SV	G	GS	IP	H	BB	SO	HR	GB%	BABIP	STUFF	WHIP	ERA	DERA	EqH9	EqBB9	EqSO9	EqHR9	DEF	VORP	SN/WX
2006	ATL	MLB	25	4	5	0	29	9	73²	90	39	43	8	50.6%	.347	-12	1.75	4.88	4.73	11.0	4.4	5.0	0.9	-2	4.7	1.33
2007	RIC	AAA	26	4	2	0	10	10	52	56	15	31	4	67.3%	.325	-17	1.37	3.46	5.96	11.7	3.2	3.8	1.2	4	-1.8	—
2007	ATL	MLB	26	2	6	0	10	9	45⁷	56	22	27	16	51.6%	.282	-35	1.71	7.09	7.49	10.6	3.7	4.9	3.0	4	-8.3	-0.02
2008	NOR	AAA	27	1	1	0	9	0	18²	12	5	12	0	72.7%	.222	-8	0.91	0.96	3.93	5.9	2.5	3.4	0.0	3	3.4	—
2008	BAL	MLB	27	3	3	1	45	1	71²	78	34	46	4	58.8%	.322	-5	1.56	4.02	4.08	9.7	3.9	5.1	0.5	-2	10.5	0.55
2009	BAL	MLB	28	2	3	1	33	2	50¹	57	21	31	6	53.0%	.310	0	1.54	4.72	4.62	9.9	3.4	5.2	0.9	0	5.1	0.50

Breakout: 30% Improve: 47% Collapse: 32% Attrition: 39%   Comparables: Kirk Saarloos, George Culver, Clay Carroll, Jack Aker

Cormier more or less took over Albers' long relief role on the latter's injury, and he was just as surprisingly effective at it. It was a little bit of a surprise that he was nontendered, but his age and history combine to make him a long shot for continued success. He's been exactly the type of guy the Orioles have made foolish commitments to in the past, so take his departure as a sign that they're learning.

Brandon Erbe

Bats: R   Throws: R   Height: 6' 4"   Weight: 180   Born: December 25, 1987   Age: 21

YEAR	TEAM	LVL	AGE	W	L	SV	G	GS	IP	H	BB	SO	HR	GB%	BABIP	STUFF	WHIP	ERA	DERA	EqH9	EqBB9	EqSO9	EqHR9	DEF	VORP	SN/WX
2006	DEL	A	18	5	9	0	28	27	114^1	88	47	133	2	36.0%	.319	19	1.18	3.23	6.92	10.9	5.7	5.6	0.9	-1	-13.9	—
2007	FRD	A+	19	6	8	0	25	25	119^1	127	62	111	14	47.8%	.331	-32	1.58	6.26	10.32	13.2	6.2	4.6	2.6	-8	-54.9	—
2008	FRD	A+	20	10	12	0	28	28	150^2	120	50	151	21	40.8%	.258	2	1.13	4.30	6.41	9.5	3.5	5.9	2.3	7	-12.4	—
2009	BAL	MLB	21	5	10	0	31	22	128^2	155	60	96	28	39.0%	.310	8	1.67	6.66	6.30	10.5	3.8	6.2	1.9	0	-12.5	-0.50

Breakout: 26% Improve: 68% Collapse: 12% Attrition: 10%   Comparables: Eric Hurley, Kyle Davies, Will Inman, Tyler Clippard

The optimistic will look at Erbe's repeat of the Carolina League and see improvement across the board, a pitcher who's still pretty young, and one who has a strong fastball and a plus slider. The less charitable will point out that it still doesn't rate as a good performance, the fastball is rated 3-4 mph lower than a couple of years ago, the home runs are way too frequent, and there's no third pitch. That's a description of a guy who should be shifting to the bullpen.

Jeremy Guthrie

Bats: R   Throws: R   Height: 6' 1"   Weight: 195   Born: April 8, 1979   Age: 30

YEAR	TEAM	LVL	AGE	W	L	SV	G	GS	IP	H	BB	SO	HR	GB%	BABIP	STUFF	WHIP	ERA	DERA	EqH9	EqBB9	EqSO9	EqHR9	DEF	VORP	SN/WX
2006	BUF	AAA	27	9	5	0	21	20	123	104	48	88	6	53.0%	.271	-4	1.24	3.15	5.94	9.2	4.2	4.2	0.9	11	-4.3	—
2006	CLE	MLB	27	0	0	0	9	1	19^1	24	15	14	2	48.4%	.367	-4	2.02	6.99	5.50	11.5	7.0	6.0	1.0	-3	-2.0	-0.17
2007	BAL	MLB	28	7	5	0	32	26	175^1	165	47	123	23	43.7%	.275	3	1.21	3.70	4.68	8.2	2.2	5.5	1.2	16	39.4	4.18
2008	BAL	MLB	29	10	12	0	30	30	190^2	176	58	120	24	44.7%	.261	3	1.23	3.63	4.51	8.0	2.5	4.9	1.1	15	41.9	5.13
2009	BAL	MLB	30	9	10	0	26	26	159	171	56	101	23	44.0%	.290	13	1.42	4.77	4.61	9.4	2.8	5.3	1.2	0	14.1	2.80

Breakout: 5% Improve: 32% Collapse: 39% Attrition: 16%   Comparables: Fred Sanford, Max Surkont, Dave Wickersham, Bob Porterfield

"Ace" is stretching it, but as the owner of the only credible performance in the Orioles' big-league rotation, it's tough to escape hanging the handle on him. Guthrie's been a successful convert to the Mazzone-inspired "low and away" school of pitching, generating plenty of weakly hit balls to the opposite field. Even with a plausible explanation in hand, it's worrisome to find him near the top of the charts in defensive support (fifth best in the American League, at +15) and in hit differential (23 less than expected, fourth highest). He also had shoulder trouble at the end of the year, getting pounded in his final three starts.

David Hernandez

Bats: R   Throws: R   Height: 6' 3"   Weight: 214   Born: May 13, 1985   Age: 24

YEAR	TEAM	LVL	AGE	W	L	SV	G	GS	IP	H	BB	SO	HR	GB%	BABIP	STUFF	WHIP	ERA	DERA	EqH9	EqBB9	EqSO9	EqHR9	DEF	VORP	SN/WX
2006	DEL	A	21	7	8	0	28	28	145	134	71	154	13	39.0%	.316	-33	1.41	4.16	9.17	12.9	6.6	4.7	2.5	-4	-48.7	—
2007	FRD	A+	22	7	11	0	28	27	145^1	139	47	168	16	37.7%	.323	-24	1.28	4.96	7.95	12.2	4.1	6.2	2.4	-3	-33.4	—
2008	BOW	AA	23	10	4	0	27	27	141	112	71	166	10	37.4%	.305	20	1.30	2.68	4.13	8.7	4.5	8.0	1.0	-2	21.7	—
2009	BAL	MLB	24	5	9	0	30	19	113	130	66	97	23	37.0%	.320	10	1.73	6.41	6.05	10.0	4.7	7.2	1.7	0	-8.3	-0.10

Breakout: 17% Improve: 48% Collapse: 22% Attrition: 17%   Comparables: Duff Brumley, Eric Gagné, Jose DeJesus, James McDonald

With Hernandez, you have a player who set school records in juco ball for strikeouts, led the Carolina League in strikeouts in 2007, led the Eastern League in strikeouts in 2008, and yet still isn't seen as an especially good prospect. That's because he's got a strange, deceptive delivery that scouts think won't play in the majors. He's also had a bad habit of grooving pitches when he gets behind in the count; he still gets behind, but at least he gave in a lot less often in 2008.

Jim Johnson

Bats: R   Throws: R   Height: 6' 5"   Weight: 245   Born: June 27, 1983   Age: 26

YEAR	TEAM	LVL	AGE	W	L	SV	G	GS	IP	H	BB	SO	HR	GB%	BABIP	STUFF	WHIP	ERA	DERA	EqH9	EqBB9	EqSO9	EqHR9	DEF	VORP	SN/WX
2006	BOW	AA	23	13	6	0	27	26	156^2	165	57	124	13	53.0%	.327	-23	1.42	4.44	6.44	12.3	4.2	4.2	1.6	-8	-12.9	—
2007	NOR	AAA	24	6	12	0	26	25	148	164	48	109	15	47.7%	.320	-23	1.43	4.07	6.96	11.5	3.2	4.3	1.5	5	-21.1	—
2008	BAL	MLB	25	2	4	1	54	0	68^2	54	28	38	0	59.0%	.258	3	1.19	2.23	3.36	7.0	3.4	4.4	0.1	7	26.2	3.20
2009	BAL	MLB	26	2	3	1	38	1	51^2	55	22	33	5	51.0%	.300	2	1.50	4.45	4.38	9.3	3.5	5.4	0.8	0	7.1	0.60

Breakout: 28% Improve: 59% Collapse: 12% Attrition: 24%   Comparables: Barry Jones, Rick Bauer, Jim Hannan, T.J. Tucker

Called up from Norfolk, Johnson established himself by running off 16 scoreless innings over 10 games. His performance earned him a move through the bullpen roles, settling in as the primary set-up man and, briefly, as closer when Sherrill was injured. There were occasional noises about having him start a game, but Trembley preferred to keep him in a role where he was thriving, and intends to keep him there in '09. His season was cut short by a shoulder injury—a distressingly common phrase in this chapter—but he should recover by spring.

Radhames Liz

Bats: R **Throws: R** **Height: 6' 2"** **Weight: 185** **Born: June 10, 1983** **Age: 26**

YEAR	TEAM	LVL	AGE	W	L	SV	G	GS	IP	H	BB	SO	HR	GB%	BABIP	STUFF	WHIP	ERA	DERA	EqH9	EqBB9	EqSO9	EqHR9	DEF	VORP	SN/WX
2006	FRD	A+	23	6	5	0	16	16	83²	57	44	95	8	41.6%	.261	-9	1.21	2.81	6.06	9.6	6.1	6.6	2.1	5	-3.6	—
2006	BOW	AA	23	3	1	0	10	10	50²	55	31	54	9	42.0%	.346	-19	1.71	5.38	6.54	14.1	7.2	6.1	3.2	-8	-4.5	—
2007	BOW	AA	24	11	4	0	25	25	137	101	70	161	13	37.5%	.273	-2	1.25	3.22	5.94	8.5	5.2	7.1	1.6	6	-4.8	—
2007	BAL	MLB	24	0	2	0	9	4	24²	25	23	24	3	23.0%	.319	6	1.95	6.92	7.56	9.0	7.6	7.6	1.1	1	-4.3	-0.53
2008	NOR	AAA	25	3	7	0	15	15	87	77	32	85	6	35.4%	.309	4	1.25	3.62	5.93	8.9	3.6	5.9	1.0	3	-3.0	—
2008	BAL	MLB	25	6	6	0	17	17	84¹	99	51	57	16	35.0%	.317	-19	1.78	6.73	6.56	10.6	5.0	5.5	1.7	-2	-11.2	0.37
2009	BAL	MLB	26	3	4	0	20	10	63	68	33	47	11	37.0%	.300	5	1.61	5.79	5.51	9.5	4.2	6.3	1.5	0	-0.9	0.30

Breakout: 42% Improve: 68% Collapse: 18% Attrition: 47%   Comparables: *Robinson Tejeda, Renie Martin, Dan Pfister, Kevin Correia*

Performance-wise, Liz is reminiscent of Daniel Cabrera, with the dynamic fastball, wildness, and lack of progress all present and accounted for, but physically, the gangly Liz would never be mistaken for the hulking Cabrera. In Liz's case, the problem seems to be his release point; he's inconsistent and usually early, which leads to high pitches, which makes for his almost never getting a ground ball while generating the high home-run totals that have plagued his career.

Brian Matusz

Bats: L **Throws: L** **Height: 6' 5"** **Weight: 200** **Born: February 11, 1987** **Age: 22**

YEAR	TEAM	LVL	AGE	W	L	SV	G	GS	IP	H	BB	SO	HR	GB%	BABIP	STUFF	WHIP	ERA	DERA	EqH9	EqBB9	EqSO9	EqHR9	DEF	VORP	SN/WX
2009	BAL	MLB	22	4	12	0	26	26	129¹	184	82	73	27	43.9%	.346	-4	2.06	8.13	7.72	12.5	5.1	4.7	1.8	0	-32.8	-2.60

Breakout: N/A Improve: N/A Collapse: N/A Attrition: N/A   Comparables: *Drew Hall, Kyle Abbott, Bryan Oelkers, Tony Blasucci*

Matusz spent all spring carrying the title of "top college pitcher in the draft," and he ultimately went fourth overall before signing for a $3.2 million bonus. He's not the overpowering type, but he's greater than the sum of his parts because he has no real weakness. His fastball sits in the low 90s, and his curveball is outstanding, as is his changeup. He even mixes in a pretty good slider, and all the pitches are brought up a grade because of pinpoint control. Although he missed regular-season competition, he debuted in the Arizona Fall League, and after having little trouble getting people out there, he could begin his career as high as Double-A and be part of the Orioles' rotation in 2010.

Kameron Mickolio

Bats: R **Throws: R** **Height: 6' 9"** **Weight: 256** **Born: May 10, 1984** **Age: 25**

YEAR	TEAM	LVL	AGE	W	L	SV	G	GS	IP	H	BB	SO	HR	GB%	BABIP	STUFF	WHIP	ERA	DERA	EqH9	EqBB9	EqSO9	EqHR9	DEF	VORP	SN/WX
2006	EVE	A-	22	1	0	0	4	21	0	32²	34	7	26	1	67.3%	.324	-28	1.27	2.80	5.40	13.3	3.5	2.9	1.3	-6	0.6	—
2007	WTN	AA	23	3	1	2	18	0	29²	24	12	27	0	39.0%	.300	-6	1.21	1.82	4.55	8.5	3.9	4.9	0.3	2	3.2	—
2007	TAC	AAA	23	3	3	1	14	0	24	19	10	28	3	45.2%	.276	3	1.21	3.75	6.46	7.2	3.8	7.6	1.5	3	-2.3	—
2008	BOW	AA	24	2	1	1	28	0	38¹	39	22	40	2	58.4%	.346	-2	1.59	4.70	4.86	10.7	4.9	6.8	0.7	-4	3.0	—
2008	NOR	AAA	24	1	0	2	17	0	20	13	9	23	0	61.1%	.250	2	1.10	1.80	3.92	6.1	3.9	6.5	0.0	-1	3.9	—
2008	BAL	MLB	24	0	1	0	9	0	7²	8	4	8	0	37.5%	.364	3	1.57	5.84	4.50	9.0	4.5	7.9	0.0	-1	-0.0	-0.53
2009	BAL	MLB	25	2	3	1	29	3	52¹	56	27	42	5	48.0%	.320	7	1.59	5.16	5.04	9.4	4.2	6.7	0.9	0	2.4	0.30

Breakout: 84% Improve: 95% Collapse: 1% Attrition: 10%   Comparables: *Toby Borland, Michael Nix, Curt Schmidt, Steve Rain*

A giant of a man, Mickolio goes after hitters with an unorthodox, nearly sidearm, cross-body motion. No pitching coach can see that motion without cringing, but since Mickolio can get the ball up to 98 or so, no one wants to mess with it, either. His control is better than most of the hard throwers in the minors, but it's still something of a liability. In an ideal world, he would be a Bobby Jenks–like closer. In this one, he's fighting for a spot in a bullpen that's crowded with warm bodies and desperate for someone to break out and star.

Jim Miller

| | | | | | | | Bats: R | | Throws: R | | Height: 6' 1" | | Weight: 200 | | Born: April 28, 1982 | | | Age: 27 | |

YEAR	TEAM	LVL	AGE	W	L	SV	G	GS	IP	H	BB	SO	HR	GB%	BABIP	STUFF	WHIP	ERA	DERA	EqH9	EqBB9	EqSO9	EqHR9	DEF	VORP	SN/WX
2006	TUL	AA	24	0	3	12	45	0	44¹	50	14	41	10	28.7%	.316	-39	1.45	3.88	5.48	12.4	3.2	5.1	3.0	-2	0.6	—
2007	BOW	AA	25	2	3	4	30	0	38²	26	25	49	0	34.4%	.292	14	1.32	2.79	4.00	7.8	6.5	7.8	0.2	-1	6.4	—
2007	NOR	AAA	25	1	2	3	22	0	27²	25	16	30	3	39.2%	.297	-11	1.48	4.22	6.00	9.3	5.3	6.3	1.7	1	-1.2	—
2008	BOW	AA	26	0	1	0	7	0	13	11	5	17	1	43.8%	.333	12	1.23	3.46	2.92	9.5	3.6	8.8	0.7	-2	3.7	—
2008	NOR	AAA	26	3	5	10	49	0	67	50	22	79	4	38.2%	.286	3	1.07	3.09	5.29	7.5	3.2	7.1	0.8	5	2.2	—
2008	BAL	MLB	26	0	2	1	8	0	7²	9	5	8	0	52.0%	.391	8	1.83	1.17	0.00	9.7	5.4	7.6	0.0	-3	2.0	-0.28
2009	BAL	MLB	27	3	3	1	30	4	56	59	27	49	9	38.0%	.310	10	1.52	4.86	4.63	9.1	3.9	7.4	1.3	0	5.3	0.60

Breakout: 29% Improve: 52% Collapse: 28% Attrition: 17%   Comparables: Greg Jones, Kurt Knudsen, Chad Orvella, Jim Mann

As part of what the Orioles got back from the Rockies when the O's needed to make Rodrigo Lopez go away, Miller gave them their first return on that investment beyond addition by subtraction when Miller filled in for a depleted September bullpen. If you're a bottom-line guy, you'll look at the 1.17 ERA and say he did great. If you're into process, you'll look at the 1.83 WHIP and steer clear. He's another pitcher whose chief problem has been keeping the ball down in the zone.

Garrett Olson

| | | | | | | | Bats: R | | Throws: L | | Height: 6' 1" | | Weight: 195 | | Born: October 18, 1983 | | | Age: 25 | |

YEAR	TEAM	LVL	AGE	W	L	SV	G	GS	IP	H	BB	SO	HR	GB%	BABIP	STUFF	WHIP	ERA	DERA	EqH9	EqBB9	EqSO9	EqHR9	DEF	VORP	SN/WX
2006	FRD	A+	22	4	4	0	14	14	81	81	19	77	7	46.4%	.336	-8	1.23	2.78	4.99	12.9	3.1	5.1	1.9	-4	4.8	—
2006	BOW	AA	22	6	5	0	14	14	84	78	31	85	5	46.8%	.327	7	1.30	3.43	5.04	11.0	4.2	5.6	1.2	-3	4.7	—
2007	NOR	AAA	23	9	7	0	22	22	128	95	39	120	13	45.1%	.253	-3	1.05	3.16	5.87	8.0	3.1	5.9	1.6	12	-3.6	—
2007	BAL	MLB	23	1	3	0	7	7	32¹	42	28	28	4	34.6%	.392	9	2.16	7.80	6.68	12.2	7.5	7.0	1.2	-3	-5.9	-0.34
2008	NOR	AAA	24	1	2	0	7	7	36¹	35	16	39	1	43.7%	.362	7	1.40	2.98	5.45	9.6	4.4	6.5	0.5	4	0.6	—
2008	BAL	MLB	24	9	10	0	26	26	132²	168	62	83	17	44.0%	.341	-11	1.73	6.65	5.35	11.2	3.8	4.9	1.2	-15	-13.2	0.67
2009	BAL	MLB	25	4	6	0	26	14	87²	99	41	60	13	43.0%	.310	6	1.59	5.51	5.29	9.9	3.7	5.7	1.3	0	1.3	0.70

Breakout: 36% Improve: 53% Collapse: 18% Attrition: 34%   Comparables: Chris Haney, Taylor Phillips, Alex Kellner, Jamie Moyer

The survey says that the defense behind Olson was 15 runs below average last year. Only two major league pitchers, Javier Vazquez and Nate Robertson, fared worse, and both of them had at least 30 innings on Olson. By far the key location was third base, which earned a -9.3 behind Olson—and only Olson—compared with a +7.9 rating on the rest of the Orioles' staff. Part of that would be having Aubrey Huff at third 50 percent more often than O's pitchers had to endure on average; another part is that an above-average number of Olson's "ground" balls are scorched, quasi-line drives. But on a deeper level, it doesn't make that much difference. Assign all possible responsibility to the fielders, and Olson is still a below-average pitcher who doesn't have an out pitch with which to finish off a major league hitter.

Troy Patton

| | | | | | | | Bats: S | | Throws: L | | Height: 6' 1" | | Weight: 185 | | Born: September 3, 1985 | | | Age: 23 | |

YEAR	TEAM	LVL	AGE	W	L	SV	G	GS	IP	H	BB	SO	HR	GB%	BABIP	STUFF	WHIP	ERA	DERA	EqH9	EqBB9	EqSO9	EqHR9	DEF	VORP	SN/WX
2006	SLM	A+	20	7	7	0	19	19	101	92	37	102	4	45.7%	.318	19	1.28	2.94	6.50	11.3	4.2	5.2	1.1	-7	-9.1	—
2006	CCH	AA	20	2	5	0	8	8	45	48	13	37	6	36.1%	.327	9	1.36	4.40	7.07	11.6	3.0	4.5	1.9	2	-6.9	—
2007	CCH	AA	21	6	6	0	16	16	102¹	96	33	69	10	43.7%	.278	-2	1.26	2.99	5.79	9.9	3.5	3.6	1.4	11	-2.0	—
2007	ROU	AAA	21	4	2	0	8	8	49	44	11	25	5	40.0%	.264	6	1.12	4.59	5.85	8.1	2.3	3.0	1.1	2	-1.3	—
2007	HOU	MLB	21	0	2	0	3	2	12²	10	4	8	3	30.0%	.194	13	1.11	3.54	6.08	6.1	2.0	5.4	2.0	3	2.4	0.17
2009	BAL	MLB	23	4	7	0	32	13	87²	114	37	46	20	41.0%	.310	-7	1.73	6.80	6.42	11.4	3.4	4.4	1.9	0	-10.8	-0.60

Breakout: 3% Improve: 26% Collapse: 41% Attrition: 24%   Comparables: Ryan Ketchner, Steve Bast, Troy Brohawn, Horacio Estrada

Like Albers, Patton came from Houston in the Tejada trade. Also like Albers, he has a labrum tear. Unlike Albers, the Orioles knew he had it when they got him; they liked him enough, regardless, and felt they had enough cover in the trade that they were willing to take the chance on him. He did need surgery, missing all of 2008, and that's never good for a pitcher, but since he was a finesse guy in the first place, they're hopeful that it won't be as bad for him as it would be for a pure gas type. The shoulder's been a problem for several years; it's possible that nothing in these stat lines is relevant.

Chris Ray

| | Bats: R | Throws: R | Height: 6' 3" | Weight: 215 | Born: January 12, 1982 | Age: 27 |

YEAR	TEAM	LVL	AGE	W	L	SV	G	GS	IP	H	BB	SO	HR	GB%	BABIP	STUFF	WHIP	ERA	DERA	EqH9	EqBB9	EqSO9	EqHR9	DEF	VORP	SN/WX
2006	BAL	MLB	24	4	4	33	61	0	66	45	27	51	10	37.2%	.203	-8	1.09	2.73	4.73	5.4	3.5	6.1	1.2	13	22.9	4.31
2007	BAL	MLB	25	5	6	16	43	0	42²	35	18	44	5	45.2%	.275	6	1.24	4.43	4.68	7.2	3.6	8.1	1.1	2	6.6	-0.19
2009	BAL	MLB	27	3	3	2	37	2	53¹	53	18	44	7	41.0%	.290	12	1.33	4.16	4.01	8.7	2.7	6.9	1.1	0	9.1	0.90

Breakout: 15% Improve: 30% Collapse: 40% Attrition: 21%   Comparables: Bill Simas, Matt Turner, Scott Sullivan, Jim Coates

Ray went down in mid-2007 with torn ligaments and only came back long enough in 2008 to tour the Orioles minor league system an inning at a time. He is now pain-fee, which is good, and should be close to full strength by spring. Assuming this, how does Trembley handle having two closers? The best guess right now is that Ray will have to prove himself more than George Sherrill might, but there's a very good chance Ray will get into at least a saves-sharing arrangement by August.

Dennis Sarfate

| | Bats: R | Throws: R | Height: 6' 4" | Weight: 225 | Born: April 9, 1981 | Age: 28 |

YEAR	TEAM	LVL	AGE	W	L	SV	G	GS	IP	H	BB	SO	HR	GB%	BABIP	STUFF	WHIP	ERA	DERA	EqH9	EqBB9	EqSO9	EqHR9	DEF	VORP	SN/WX
2006	NAS	AAA	25	10	7	0	34	21	125¹	125	78	117	7	51.6%	.340	3	1.62	3.67	5.61	11.2	6.1	6.1	0.9	1	-0.1	—
2006	MIL	MLB	25	0	0	0	8	0	8¹	9	4	11	0	30.4%	.391	8	1.56	4.34	2.16	9.7	3.2	10.8	0.0	-1	1.6	0.05
2007	NAS	AAA	26	2	7	4	45	1	61²	61	47	68	6	55.4%	.362	2	1.75	4.52	5.34	11.0	7.4	7.8	1.3	-3	1.6	—
2007	HOU	MLB	26	1	0	0	7	0	8¹	5	1	14	0	62.5%	.333	8	0.72	1.08	0.00	6.8	1.1	11.2	0.0	-1	4.4	0.44
2008	BAL	MLB	27	4	3	0	57	4	79²	62	62	86	8	41.7%	.283	14	1.56	4.74	4.94	7.1	6.4	8.6	0.9	-1	5.0	-0.48
2009	BAL	MLB	28	2	3	1	34	3	53¹	52	35	53	6	44.0%	.310	12	1.63	4.89	4.73	8.5	5.4	8.3	0.9	0	5.0	0.50

Breakout: 26% Improve: 45% Collapse: 19% Attrition: 34%   Comparables: John Briscoe, Bill Kelso, Paul Shuey, Earl Wilson

The most impressive thing about Sarfate's season was that he broke his collarbone in April, didn't tell anyone about it, and pitched all year. Here's the not-for-the-squeamish part: it didn't heal properly (uh, maybe because it hadn't been treated properly?), so an edge of it was sticking out and digging into the muscle every time he threw. Just writing about it hurts. Sarfate is another one of the "throw it as hard as you can, maybe it will be a strike" school that helped the O's lead the majors in walks—and hit batsmen, a Sarfate specialty.

George Sherrill

| | Bats: L | Throws: L | Height: 6' 0" | Weight: 225 | Born: April 19, 1977 | Age: 32 |

YEAR	TEAM	LVL	AGE	W	L	SV	G	GS	IP	H	BB	SO	HR	GB%	BABIP	STUFF	WHIP	ERA	DERA	EqH9	EqBB9	EqSO9	EqHR9	DEF	VORP	SN/WX
2006	SEA	MLB	29	2	4	1	72	0	40	30	27	42	0	33.3%	.303	20	1.43	4.28	3.66	6.9	5.9	8.5	0.2	-2	7.8	1.51
2007	SEA	MLB	30	2	0	3	73	0	45²	28	17	56	4	29.6%	.250	20	0.99	2.36	3.30	5.1	3.1	9.1	0.8	4	18.3	1.62
2008	BAL	MLB	31	3	5	31	57	0	53¹	47	33	58	6	34.0%	.299	9	1.50	4.73	4.36	7.9	5.0	8.6	1.0	-1	6.5	1.45
2009	BAL	MLB	32	3	4	21	54	0	51¹	45	25	53	7	34.0%	.280	16	1.36	3.91	3.74	7.7	3.9	8.7	1.1	0	10.0	1.30

Breakout: 26% Improve: 56% Collapse: 20% Attrition: 17%   Comparables: Aurelio Lopez, Juan Berenguer, Ricardo Rincon, Brian Fuentes

Sherrill is a good situational lefty who did an adequate job of getting right-handed people out often enough to make a passable closer, which says a lot about how a reliever who doesn't lose his cool can pretty much rack up saves just by doing his thing. Now that his label has changed from "lefty set-up dude" to "closer," we'll see how much labels matter as the Orioles try to sort through their bullpen roles for 2009. Here's a hint: decide according to proven skills, not labels. Sherrill's best skill remains getting lefties out.

Chris Tillman

| | Bats: R | Throws: R | Height: 6' 5" | Weight: 195 | Born: April 15, 1988 | Age: 21 |

YEAR	TEAM	LVL	AGE	W	L	SV	G	GS	IP	H	BB	SO	HR	GB%	BABIP	STUFF	WHIP	ERA	DERA	EqH9	EqBB9	EqSO9	EqHR9	DEF	VORP	SN/WX
2006	EVE	A-	18	1	3	0	5	5	19¹	25	15	29	4	48.0%	.477	-7	2.09	8.01	11.08	25.6	13.2	8.3	7.6	-4	-7.9	—
2006	MRN	Rk	18	2	0	1	5	0	11	9	5	16	0	50.0%	.346	8	1.27	0.82	6.75	12.5	6.8	5.8	1.0	0	-1.2	—
2007	WIS	A	19	1	4	0	8	8	33	31	13	34	1	43.3%	.316	-4	1.33	3.55	10.55	12.1	5.6	4.0	1.2	1	-16.0	—
2007	HDS	A+	19	6	7	0	20	20	102²	107	48	105	12	40.4%	.332	-5	1.51	5.26	8.16	10.9	5.1	4.7	1.8	-3	-27.6	—
2008	BOW	AA	20	11	4	0	28	28	135²	115	65	154	10	40.0%	.306	44	1.33	3.18	4.41	9.2	4.2	7.6	1.0	0	17.0	—
2009	BAL	MLB	21	6	9	0	34	20	128¹	138	70	115	20	39.0%	.320	17	1.62	5.72	5.47	9.4	4.4	7.5	1.3	0	-0.9	0.70

Breakout: 19% Improve: 45% Collapse: 17% Attrition: 12%   Comparables: Scott Garrelts, Will Inman, Hector Fajardo, Yovani Gallardo

Thank you once again, Mr. Bavasi. Yet another piece of the Bedard trade, the tall, thin Tillman brought his act to Bowie and did not disappoint people expecting a top prospect. The youngest pitcher to start the year in Double-A, Tillman throws in the low 90s, with a very good curve and a … well, OK, he's not perfect, he's still working on the changeup. Tillman has made progress on control, but still has some work to do there as well. Something that sets him apart from other pitching prospects is that nebulous, unquantifiable "presence" that's part attitude, part confidence, and part intelligence. Scouts and opposing hitters say he has it.

Jamie Walker

Bats: L   Throws: L   Height: 6' 2"   Weight: 195   Born: July 1, 1971   Age: 38

YEAR	TEAM	LVL	AGE	W	L	SV	G	GS	IP	H	BB	SO	HR	GB%	BABIP	STUFF	WHIP	ERA	DERA	EqH9	EqBB9	EqSO9	EqHR9	DEF	VORP	SN/WX
2006	DET	MLB	35	0	1	0	56	0	48	47	8	37	8	33.8%	.275	-1	1.15	2.81	2.87	9.0	1.5	6.1	1.3	0	17.6	0.80
2007	BAL	MLB	36	3	2	7	81	0	61¹	57	17	41	6	34.8%	.273	-6	1.21	3.23	4.06	7.8	2.3	5.1	0.9	3	15.1	1.58
2008	BAL	MLB	37	1	3	0	59	0	38	53	11	24	12	36.4%	.323	-35	1.68	6.87	5.82	11.9	2.3	4.9	2.8	-4	-6.3	-2.03
2009	BAL	MLB	37	2	2	2	37	0	35	38	9	22	5	37.0%	.290	-3	1.34	4.34	4.14	9.5	2.1	5.2	1.3	0	5.3	0.40

Breakout: 35% Improve: 57% Collapse: 16% Attrition: 26%   Comparables: Eddie Guardado, Alan Embree, Rich Rodriguez, Grant Jackson

Walker missed a month with elbow inflammation, but should have taken the rest of the year off. He was already off his game before hitting the disabled list, with an ERA of around 5.00, but after coming back, he couldn't throw a ball through a tissue, and hitters, even the lefties he's supposed to get out, teed off. Tests couldn't find anything structurally wrong with the elbow, which leads to the idea that age may be catching up to Walker and that the Orioles might be forced to eat the remaining $4 million or so due him in 2009.

Chris Waters

Bats: L   Throws: L   Height: 6' 0"   Weight: 170   Born: August 17, 1980   Age: 28

YEAR	TEAM	LVL	AGE	W	L	SV	G	GS	IP	H	BB	SO	HR	GB%	BABIP	STUFF	WHIP	ERA	DERA	EqH9	EqBB9	EqSO9	EqHR9	DEF	VORP	SN/WX
2006	MIS	AA	25	8	14	0	27	27	155¹	152	79	117	24	39.6%	.294	-58	1.49	4.82	8.59	11.5	5.2	4.2	2.9	14	-45.9	—
2007	BOW	AA	26	8	9	0	27	27	152¹	144	86	117	17	43.1%	.288	-28	1.51	4.49	6.86	10.5	5.8	4.3	1.8	2	-19.5	—
2008	BOW	AA	27	5	0	0	6	6	32	20	8	22	2	55.6%	.205	6	0.88	1.69	3.56	6.2	2.4	4.5	0.9	3	6.9	—
2008	NOR	AAA	27	3	6	0	18	16	90	97	43	72	10	39.1%	.327	-24	1.56	5.70	8.79	10.7	4.7	4.7	1.5	9	-30.1	—
2008	BAL	MLB	27	3	5	0	11	11	64²	70	29	33	9	48.7%	.285	-11	1.53	5.01	5.12	9.3	3.6	4.0	1.2	0	4.3	0.65
2009	BAL	MLB	28	4	9	0	43	18	110¹	140	63	61	21	43.0%	.320	-11	1.84	6.81	6.48	11.1	4.6	4.6	1.6	0	-14.6	-0.80

Breakout: 12% Improve: 42% Collapse: 25% Attrition: 30%   Comparables: Les Strode, Stan Clarke, Steve Davis, Gino Minutelli

An organizational arm, the kind of guy who's been providing depth to minor league rosters for years, Waters was struggling in Norfolk when he got a most unexpected call to come to Baltimore. Let's be honest: only a team desperate for warm bodies would have called up a player who was pitching the way Waters was. To his credit, he made the most of it (with some luck—note the low BABIP), pitching a little over his head and picking up a few wins. Don't expect a repeat.

LINEOUTS

Hitters

PLAYER	TEAM	LVL	AGE	PA	R	2B	3B	HR	RBI	BB	SO	SB-CS	EqBRR	AVG/OBP/SLG	EqAVG/EqOBP/EqSLG	EqA	VORP	WARP
INF R. Adams	DEL	A	21	497	68	26	5	11	57	36	109	12-5	-0.4	.308/.367/.462	.254/.305/.396	.242	-1.9	0.1
UT F. Bynum*	NOR	AAA	28	155	15	4	3	0	15	20	39	8-1	1.5	.246/.342/.323	.211/.301/.271	.217	-9.1	-0.9
	BAL	MLB	28	121	13	3	1	0	8	5	31	2-3	-1.3	.179/.220/.223	.188/.229/.232	.147	-11.6	-1.2
SS J. Castro	BAL	MLB	36	166	15	6	0	2	16	10	26	0-0	-1.1	.205/.256/.285	.207/.262/.293	.195	-8.0	-0.5
INF A. Cintron#	NOR	AAA	29	71	9	1	0	2	10	2	11	0-0	-0.5	.288/.329/.394	.254/.286/.358	.222	-2.0	0.1
	BAL	MLB	29	144	12	5	1	1	10	7	15	0-2	-2.2	.286/.321/.361	.288/.329/.364	.239	0.7	-0.4
SS B. Davis*	BOW	AA	24	497	57	22	7	4	53	26	80	8-7	-0.7	.284/.324/.389	.252/.287/.358	.223	-13.9	-0.1
UT B. Fahey*	NOR	AAA	27	248	26	7	0	1	23	21	47	1-4	-0.8	.252/.317/.297	.222/.283/.267	.191	-17.3	-2.7
	BAL	MLB	27	113	8	9	2	0	12	3	25	0-0	-1.2	.226/.252/.349	.226/.252/.349	.206	-3.2	-1.0
C O. Santos	NOR	AAA	27	332	31	13	0	1	36	20	57	1-2	-1.3	.269/.328/.323	.235/.290/.281	.202	-19.1	-1.1
INF E. Torres#	NOR	AAA	25	525	69	20	6	1	46	38	60	28-11	-6.6	.307/.357/.381	.280/.331/.353	.244	-0.9	1.2

While **Ryan Adams** hit well enough to capture your attention, his 52 errors—including a five-error game and three separate three-error days at the office—should encourage you to avert your eyes lest he hit you in one. ⊘ **Freddie Bynum** missed the first month of the season with a knee injury and spent the rest of the year missing pitches; he's now a National. ⊘ When your shortstop isn't producing, you can always trade for **Juan Castro** and have him not produce for you, too. ⊘ Among Orioles shortstops last year, **Alex Cintron** was the best hitter. That's kind of like being the best Freddie Prinze movie. ⊘ **Blake Davis** is a younger, shorter copy of Brandon Fahey, but every bit as desirable as the original. ⊘ The organizational veteran among the handful of people who played shortstop for the O's, **Brandon Fahey** is still overmatched at the plate and marginal in the field. ⊘ **Omir Santos** has yet to record a full-season EqA higher than his weight, and he only weighs 200. ⊘ **Eider Torres** kept waiting in vain for Brian Roberts to be traded, but this was one Tide that never turned, and given his limited ability at the plate, it's just as well.

Pitchers

PLAYER	TEAM	LVL	AGE	W	L	SV	IP	H	BB	SO	HR	GB%	BABIP	STUFF	WHIP	ERA	DERA	EqH9	EqBB9	EqSO9	EqHR9	DEF	VORP
G. Aquino	NOR	AAA	30	2	2	9	25²	23	6	29	2	46.5%	.323	0	1.13	2.45	4.74	9.1	2.2	6.9	1.1	0	2.4
	BAL	MLB	30	0	0	0	9¹	17	9	9	1	38.2%	.516	-3	2.79	12.58	7.00	17.0	8.0	8.0	1.0	-4	-6.8
R. Bierd	BAL	MLB	24	0	2	0	36²	48	19	25	3	42.0%	.363	-12	1.83	4.90	3.65	11.4	4.1	5.4	0.7	-5	2.8
A. Castillo*	NOR	AAA	32	3	1	0	26¹	16	6	26	2	41.8%	.215	-1	0.84	2.05	5.26	6.0	2.1	6.0	1.1	6	1.0
	BAL	MLB	32	1	0	0	26	27	10	23	3	45.7%	.308	2	1.42	3.81	2.73	9.2	3.1	6.8	1.0	-3	5.9
R. Cherry	NOR	AAA	28	0	1	0	37¹	35	9	37	3	44.4%	.323	-7	1.18	2.90	5.55	9.3	2.5	6.1	1.0	4	0.2
	BAL	MLB	28	0	3	1	17	15	16	15	3	43.4%	.255	-6	1.82	6.35	6.87	7.4	6.9	6.4	1.5	-1	-3.8
B. McCrory	NOR	AAA	26	2	3	5	45	41	24	35	1	62.3%	.313	-12	1.44	3.80	7.01	8.7	5.2	4.3	0.4	7	-6.8
	BAL	MLB	26	0	0	0	6¹	10	8	5	0	62.5%	.455	-16	2.84	15.71	13.50	13.5	9.4	5.4	0.0	-2	-7.6
H. Penn	NOR	AAA	23	6	7	0	99²	110	35	65	14	49.0%	.307	-35	1.45	4.78	7.65	10.7	3.5	3.7	1.9	9	-21.7
W. Perez*	FRD	A+	23	2	4	2	56¹	44	30	69	5	59.1%	.305	2	1.31	2.88	4.29	9.8	5.5	7.7	1.6	0	7.3
	BOW	AA	23	0	0	1	23¹	16	8	23	1	54.0%	.246	8	1.03	2.32	3.68	7.4	3.3	6.5	0.8	2	4.7
A. Simon	MTR	MEX	27	7	2	0	81	66	20	61	5	47.2%	.281	-3	1.06	2.67	5.75	8.3	2.8	5.4	1.3	9	-1.3
	BAL	MLB	27	0	0	0	13	16	2	8	4	61.7%	.286	-10	1.38	6.23	5.40	10.1	1.4	4.7	2.7	-2	-1.4
C. Spoone	BOW	AA	22	3	3	0	41¹	40	27	32	4	62.5%	.293	-1	1.62	4.58	5.26	10.1	5.7	5.0	1.4	-3	1.5

Talk of **Greg Aquino** becoming the closer evaporated after a quick bit of April nastiness and a bad hamstring; he'll be in the Indians' camp. ⊘ A Rule 5 pick, the Orioles hid **Randor Bierd** away, almost never letting him into any contested games and shelving him with a shoulder injury. ⊘ A Cuban refugee who'd been playing in the Atlantic League prior to last season, **Alberto Castillo** is a good LOOGY candidate. ⊘ **Rocky Cherry**, a generic hard thrower with control issues, was taken away from Baltimore in the Rule 5 draft by the Mets; wherever he's at, he'll fight for the last spot in a bullpen somewhere. ⊘ After missing all of 2008 recovering from shoulder surgery after already losing time to elbow surgery in the past, it's unclear what's left of **Jim Hoey**'s once-promising career and blazing fastball. ⊘ **Bob McCrory** is yet another guy with a good fastball and next to no idea of where it's going, but he's in the bullpen mix all the same. ⊘ While it seems as if he's been on the cusp of sticking forever, **Hayden Penn**'s latest bid for a job was shelved by shoulder soreness that shut him down in the first week of August, but the O's are still desperate for starters, and he's still in the organization. ⊘ **Wilfrido Perez** is an undersized lefty who's thrived since being moved to relief; he held opposing hitters to a .211 average last year and earned a spot on the Orioles' 40-man roster. ⊘ After getting ditched by the Dodgers in April, **Alfredo Simon** spent his summer south of the border, slinging strikes in the Mexican League. Big-bodied or not, the Birds will take what they can get. ⊘ Biceps tendonitis and then shoulder problems that required surgery in the fall will keep former top prospect **Chorye Spoone** out of action until the second half, but if he can still mix low-90s heat and a plus curve, he'll still be a prospect.

MANAGER: DAVE TREMBLEY

YEAR	TEAM	W-L	Pythag +/−	Avg PC	100+ P	120+ P	QS	BQS	REL	REL w Zero R	IBB	Subs	PH	PH Avg	PH HR	SB2	CS2	SB3	CS3	SAC Att	SAC %	POS SAC	Squeeze	Swing	In Play
2007	BAL	40-53	2	94.0	43	1	38	3	279	149	29	24	62	.190	0	76	29	16	3	38	52.6%	19	2	83	63
2008	BAL	68-93	-4	92.6	64	0	56	11	492	265	44	37	117	.218	3	69	32	12	3	42	64.3%	26	2	147	117

Given how much the bullpen in particular and the pitching staff in general kept Trembley busy, it's a wonder he had time for much in-game management. But he was also among the skippers most likely to get cute with the hit-and-run, which might at least have been a way to break up the tedium of managing a weak lineup to a certain doom. It's hard to cite Trembley for much of anything, given how the lurching from one disaster on the mound to the next would keep almost anybody on their heels, but to the positive, Adam Jones did well as a rookie on the skipper's watch. This winter's pause will do more to put Trembley on the spot in terms of picking a pitching staff and really sorting through what he's got. But if 2009 ends up resembling another exercise in cat herding the pitchers and waiting around for the veterans' contracts to run out, all it'll take is a bad patch and he could be as readily scapegoated as Sam Perlozzo and Lee Mazzilli were.

Boston Red Sox

Perhaps Boston's 2008 season seemed on the surface a disappointment, given that it failed to yield a third championship for the Terry Francona/Theo Epstein-led version of the franchise, but let's play one of those "If you had said" games. If, prior to the season, you had said that all of the following would take place:

- Jason Varitek's bat would pancake.
- Manny Ramirez would wear out his welcome and be traded out of town.
- David Ortiz, Mike Lowell, J. D. Drew, Julio Lugo, and Josh Beckett would lose both time and productivity to injuries.
- Jacoby Ellsbury would play every day but would demonstrate that his 2007 hot cup of coffee would have the same transient heat as a cup of joe from Starbucks.
- Curt Schilling would retire, having failed to throw even a single pitch in anger.
- Clay Buchholz would be booted from the rotation with a wholly deserved 2-9 record.
- A total of 16 starts would be made by Paul Byrd, Bartolo Colon, and Charlie Zink.

... and you then concluded with, "but the team will still win 95 games and go to the playoffs," you might have been institutionalized. Though it hadn't been planned in advance, 2008 turned out to be a transition year for the Red Sox, and not only did the club handle it with aplomb, it emerged better prepared to continue its run of contention into the future.

The center of this crucible, as ever, was Manny Ramirez, who demonstrated that "Manny being Manny" could be more than just harmless eccentricity and could take on a more pernicious meaning. While most teams would probably like to have a whole roster of hitters who hit .299/.398/.529, who played in 100 of 109 team games while being accused of "jaking it," and who went on a .347/.473/.587 tear during the same month they were supposedly phoning it in, it is clear that Ramirez's floating knee injuries and dramatically lifeless at-bats were having a detrimental effect in the clubhouse.

To the credit of general manager Theo Epstein and the rest of the organization's leadership, when the Red Sox decided that dealing Ramirez would be more productive than a suspension and protracted appeals process, they did not simply dump him; they recognized that some effort would be needed to replace his extraordinary production. The three-team trade that was made on July 31 with the Dodgers and Pirates not only achieved this goal by bringing in Jason Bay to replace Manny, but also brought in a player who was both offensively accomplished and more than six years younger and already under contract through the 2009 season.

Becoming younger was no small part of the deal's success. As much as poor decision-making, faulty talent evaluation, and burgeoning salaries, age is the great enemy of dynastic teams. While the 2008 Red Sox were not a particularly old team—their hitters averaged 29.8 years of age (sixth oldest) and their pitchers averaged 29.2 (fourth oldest)—age was on the cusp of becoming a problem, as some of the team's lineup mainstays, particularly Ramirez, Mike Lowell, and Jason Varitek, were firmly ensconced in the thirtysomething career danger zone, with 32-year-olds David Ortiz, J. D. Drew, and Julio

---

RED SOX PROSPECTUS

2008 record: 95-67; Second place, AL East

Pythagenport record: 96-66

Runs scored per game: 5.22 (2nd in AL)

Runs allowed per game: 4.32 (3rd in AL)

Team EqA: .270 (2nd in AL)

2008 Batters Age: 30.4 (6th-oldest in AL)

2008 Pitchers Age: 28.5 (7th-youngest in AL)

Ballpark: Fenway Park; Strong hitter's park; Park Factor of 1.049

2008: The best team in baseball settles for the Wild Card and an ALCS exit.

2009: A quality backstop would do wonders, but even a lawn chair with a catcher's mitt would keep the Sox in the thick of another tight AL East race.

Lugo not far behind. Indeed, declining performance or injuries afflicted five of these six players in 2008, and six of six if you accept Ramirez's knee injury as fact.

By the end of the season, most of the answers to where the new generation of Sox run producers would come from had been made known, or at least hinted at. Second baseman Dustin Pedroia blossomed into a top run producer at his position en route to winning the American League's MVP Award. In Lowell's absence, first baseman Kevin Youkilis, who'd worked his way through the minors as a third baseman, showed he could play the hot corner well enough that the Sox had the option (pending takers) of dispensing with Lowell altogether and shopping for an upgrade at first base. Ellsbury initially suffered through what seemed like a potentially career-altering slump, but adjusted in late July and finished the season by hitting .317/.352/.462 over his last 50 games, enough to revise hopes that he might give the team its first all-around center fielder since Johnny Damon defected to the Yankees. At shortstop, rookie Jed Lowrie showed that at the very least, he could play Lugo to a draw.

The pitching staff also received a needed infusion of youth, with 24-year-old Jon Lester emerging as a staff ace and 23-year-old rookie Justin Masterson demonstrating that he might be an asset in the bullpen or the starting rotation. The only disappointment was top right-handed prospect Clay Buchholz, who spent the season in full reverse after a promising debut in late 2007. Still, 2009 will be just his age-24 season, and he seemingly remains a tweak or two away from giving the Red Sox another strikeout pitcher to add to a staff that already led the American League in that category.

What makes this retooling all the more impressive is that the game is supposed to be rigged against dynastic clubs. The draft, of course, rewards those teams with losing records while punishing those that win. The Red Sox have not had a losing record since 1997 and have won over 90 games in eight of the 11 seasons since. As a result, the Sox have not had a pick in the top half of the draft's first round since 1998, when they selected Adam Everett with the 12th overall pick. (The Red Sox have not picked in the first round's top 10 since 1993.) Between high finishes and draft picks forfeited after free-agent signings, the Red Sox have drafted as high as number 17 just twice in that period and have sometimes been shut out of the first round altogether, not picking until the second round in 2001, 2002, and 2004. In 2007, they picked only slightly ahead of the second round, starting the draft with the 15th pick of the supplemental round.

Despite shopping in the player development market with this handicap, the Sox have done almost spectacu-

larly well in the draft. Though they have not hesitated to sign veterans and have made something of a specialty out of forging working truces with such temperamental types as Ramirez and Pedro Martinez, they also know when to move on. This has meant risking heavy criticism in their very angst-y market. They traded the popular but stiffening and fragile Nomar Garciappara when he was a 30-year-old batting .321. They refused to buy one or two more good seasons from a declining Pedro Martinez at the cost of four, a price the Mets ultimately paid. Ramirez, as evidenced by his Ruthian production with the Dodgers, was not moved when he *had* to be, but only when he *should* have been. After the 2004 triumph, Derek Lowe and Orlando Cabrera were also allowed to fly away as free agents. Arguably the only exception made to this cold-eyed policy was the four-year deal Jason Varitek signed in December of that year, one consummated in obeisance to intangibles that one suspects the Red Sox will not soon see again in another player.

This posture on the part of management is unusual, to say the least. Traditionally, a championship has meant a sinecure for almost every player involved, as all the local heroes get jobs for life. Not so with the Red Sox, and this lack of sentimentality has been the key to their continuing excellence. Note how this policy provided the team a bonanza in the 2005 draft. Despite the loss of their first-round pick (28th overall) to the Cardinals as a result of the ill-fated decision to sign free-agent shortstop Edgar Renteria, the Red Sox drafted Ellsbury with a compensation pick from the Angels for the loss of Orlando Cabrera, selected Craig Hansen at 26th overall with a compensation pick from the Dodgers for Derek Lowe, and took Clay Buchholz with a supplemental pick awarded for the loss of Pedro Martinez. Shortstop Jed Lowrie and pitcher Michael Bowden were also taken in the supplemental round (with picks awarded for the loss of Orlando Cabrera and Derek Lowe, respectively). While the futures of Ellsbury, Buchholz, Lowrie, and Bowden are not written in stone, they have all reached the big leagues with the potential of becoming regulars and, in some cases, stars. That's all a team can ask of its player development staff and its farm system.

The 2006 draft class is more impressive still. Though the Sox have apparently missed with first-round pick Jason Place—a power hitter who has struggled to control the strike zone—they scored with Daniel Bard (now that he has found a home in the bullpen), Justin Masterson, and four additional players who now rank among the organization's top prospects: Kris Johnson (first-round supplemental number 10), Ryan Kalish (9th round), Josh Reddick (17th round), and Lars Anderson (18th round). Note the team's success in finding promising talents in the late rounds, a point in the draft at which most of the players selected are ticketed as minor league roster filler, not coming stars. It is not enough to merely put a club in the position to receive draft picks; the Red Sox have drafted wisely as well. The constellation of Pedroia, Lowrie, and Ellsbury could evolve into the up-the-middle spine of the club, one that allows the team to build around them with easier-to-find corner players, as well as the offensive punch at traditionally inoffensive positions sufficient to pursue the same unsentimental policy with David Ortiz and J. D. Drew should that become advantageous.

All in all, the Red Sox have had an extraordinary run of major league success coupled with unusually efficient minor league production. They most closely resemble the dynastic Yankees of the late 1940s and 1950s (more so, ironically, than do the Yankees themselves),

and like that team, they are well situated to overcome, indeed have overcome, the dangers of age. Those old Yankees kept their dynasty fresh by ruthlessly turning over the roster, something they could do, in those pre-draft days, because they used their financial advantages in the areas of scouting and player development. Having thwarted the diminishing returns of low-draft positions, the Red Sox are in a position to do the same thing.

The Yankees were ultimately stopped by the imposition of the draft, coupled with ownership's diminishing interest in reinvesting in scouting and amateur bonuses. In the Red Sox' case, the continuation of their run depends on their ongoing ability to make more of the draft than their position and frequent pursuit of top free agents should allow. They may not be able to do this, and yet, they have done it for so long that there is arguably as much skill on display as luck.

HITTERS

Lars Anderson 1B   Bats: L   Throws: L   Height: 6' 4"   Weight: 215   Born: September 25, 1987   Age: 21

YEAR	TEAM	LVL	AGE	PA	R	2B	3B	HR	RBI	BB	SO	SB	CS	EqBRR	AVG	OBP	SLG	EqAVG	EqOBP	EqSLG	EqA	VORP	WARP	DEFENSE
2007	GRN	A	19	533	69	35	3	10	69	71	112	2	4	0.0	.288	.385	.443	.216	.298	.336	.223	-19.8	-3.9	110-1B -17
2007	LNC	A+	19	47	13	2	0	1	9	11	9	0	0	0.2	.343	.489	.486	.243	.383	.351	773	0.8	0.1	8-1B 0
2008	LNC	A+	20	358	58	19	1	13	50	46	64	0	0	-2.2	.317	.408	.513	.226	.316	.379	.244	-3.4	-0.7	70-1B -3
2008	PME	AA	20	163	27	13	0	5	30	29	43	1	0	-0.3	.316	.436	.526	.301	.411	.529	.319	17.8	1.3	21-1B -1
2009	BOS	MLB	21	597	67	36	2	13	67	66	145	3	2	-0.9	.250	.336	.400	.242	.330	.403	.258	-2.0	0.3	140-1B -5

Breakout: 33% Improve: 63% Collapse: 10% Attrition: 2%   Comparables: Joey Votto, Bo Dodson, Steve Cox, Eric Duncan

Though Anderson was projected as a slugger after being drafted in 2006, his first professional season saw him leave the power in batting practice and take the strikeouts into the games. His second season was almost a reversal, thanks to a significant jump in isolated power and a reduction in punchouts at Lancaster. While Lancaster is a hitter's paradise, Anderson's power came with him to Double-A Portland, but the high strikeout rate returned. To some degree, this is a consequence of his selectivity, for good and bad. Given his youth, there's no reason not to look to the future with anticipation. Anderson has middle-of-the-order potential and should get a look in 2009 with the expectation that he'll be Boston's everyday first baseman the following year.

Jeff Bailey 1B   Bats: R   Throws: R   Height: 6' 2"   Weight: 200   Born: November 19, 1978   Age: 30

YEAR	TEAM	LVL	AGE	PA	R	2B	3B	HR	RBI	BB	SO	SB	CS	EqBRR	AVG	OBP	SLG	EqAVG	EqOBP	EqSLG	EqA	VORP	WARP	DEFENSE			
2006	PAW	AAA	27	548	64	22	5	22	82	74	116	1	2	-4.6	.275	.383	.489	.224	.327	.415	.259	4.7	0.2	75-1B	-6	15-LF	3
2007	PAW	AAA	28	478	64	22	1	15	60	59	99	9	6	1.3	.245	.358	.416	.192	.291	.338	.222	-20.5	-2.3	84-1B	-4	12-LF	-1
2008	PAW	AAA	29	494	88	28	3	25	75	62	90	5	2	-1.2	.301	.405	.562	.241	.338	.458	.273	16.0	0.9	61-1B	-4	23-RF	0
2008	BOS	MLB	29	59	10	1	1	2	6	9	17	0	0	-0.1	.280	.390	.460	.265	.390	.449	.293	2.9	0.3	8-1B	0		
2009	BOS	MLB	30	410	44	21	1	12	50	44	101	3	1	-0.6	.229	.319	.394	.222	.314	.398	.249	-5.0	0.2	98-1B	0		

Breakout: 15% Improve: 41% Collapse: 38% Attrition: 19%   Comparables: Dick Gernert, Bill Moore, Deron Johnson, Jeff Manto

With the ghosts of Sean Casey and Mark Kotsay patrolling roster spots for the Sox, it's a wonder that minor league vet and International League MVP Bailey wasn't called up sooner. Sure, Bailey was 29 years old this season and in his sixth stint at Triple-A, but there's no reason not to take a chance on a guy approaching .300/.400/.600 when your other options are actively killing your offense.

Jason Bay   LF

Bats: R   Throws: R   Height: 6' 2"   Weight: 205   Born: September 20, 1978   Age: 30

YEAR	TEAM	LVL	AGE	PA	R	2B	3B	HR	RBI	BB	SO	SB	CS	EqBRR	AVG	OBP	SLG	EqAVG	EqOBP	EqSLG	EqA	VORP	WARP	DEFENSE
2006	PIT	MLB	27	689	101	29	3	35	109	102	156	11	2	1.4	.286	.396	.532	.282	.395	.526	.314	48.7	5.8	155-LF -1
2007	PIT	MLB	28	614	78	25	2	21	84	59	141	4	1	-2.1	.247	.327	.418	.249	.332	.428	.265	5.6	0.0	138-LF -14
2008	PIT	MLB	29	459	72	23	2	22	64	59	86	7	0	2.7	.282	.375	.519	.294	.386	.552	.316	34.9	2.3	103-LF -17
2008	BOS	MLB	29	211	39	12	2	9	37	22	51	3	0	0.6	.293	.370	.527	.279	.363	.519	.300	14.5	0.2	47-LF -12
2009	BOS	MLB	30	626	90	35	3	26	96	76	137	7	2	-0.0	.271	.364	.493	.264	.358	.498	.293	22.0	2.2	146-LF -15

Breakout: 12%   Improve: 37%   Collapse: 25%   Attrition: 8%   Comparables: Dwight Evans, Jay Buhner, Tim Salmon, Bernard Gilkey

Bay's return to form cleared him of accusations that his slowing bat was an issue of skill rather than the knee injury he battled through in 2007. This was good news for a Bucs team looking to deal him, and better news for a Sox club desperate to move Manny Ramirez. Not only did Bay bump his walk rate back up, but his power returned to his '06 levels. He wasn't as productive at Fenway as elsewhere, as most of the balls he pulled turned into singles or groundouts. Though this is most likely a small-sample issue, if it's provoked by the swing-altering presence of the Green Monster, the loss of pull power would be bad news for his production.

Dusty Brown   C

Bats: R   Throws: R   Height: 6' 0"   Weight: 180   Born: June 19, 1982   Age: 27

YEAR	TEAM	LVL	AGE	PA	R	2B	3B	HR	RBI	BB	SO	SB	CS	EqBRR	AVG	OBP	SLG	EqAVG	EqOBP	EqSLG	EqA	VORP	WARP	DEFENSE
2006	PME	AA	24	331	32	17	0	5	40	24	65	2	1	-1.5	.224	.284	.332	.189	.242	.281	.181	-31.0	-1.0	79-C 3
2007	PME	AA	25	285	43	16	2	9	43	28	64	0	0	0.0	.268	.344	.453	.203	.267	.341	.210	-15.3	-0.1	70-C 1
2008	PAW	AAA	26	350	39	14	2	12	55	40	81	0	0	1.0	.290	.377	.471	.248	.334	.414	.263	5.6	1.6	70-C -1
2009	BOS	MLB	27	334	25	16	1	6	33	27	93	1	0	-0.3	.203	.272	.322	.197	.268	.325	.206	-12.3	0.2	81-C -1

Breakout: 14%   Improve: 27%   Collapse: 56%   Attrition: 29%   Comparables: Kevin Cash, Tom Prince, Terry McGriff, Rey Palacios

If the Red Sox decide to forgo the pleasure of a repeat engagement with Varitek behind the dish, Brown could be part of a decent bit of homegrown getting by. He can hurt lefties (.337/.411/.584) and will take a walk, and his ability to throw out 27 percent of opposing basestealers makes him a better-throwing complement to the lefty-swinging Kottaras (19 percent). Not that the Sox would automatically go the cheap route, having signed Josh Bard, but we're just sayin' ...

Chris Carter   LF

Bats: L   Throws: L   Height: 6' 0"   Weight: 210   Born: September 16, 1982   Age: 26

YEAR	TEAM	LVL	AGE	PA	R	2B	3B	HR	RBI	BB	SO	SB	CS	EqBRR	AVG	OBP	SLG	EqAVG	EqOBP	EqSLG	EqA	VORP	WARP	DEFENSE	
2006	TUC	AAA	23	588	87	30	3	19	97	78	69	10	4	-6.3	.301	.395	.483	.255	.345	.420	.267	14.6	-0.8	118-1B -17	
2007	TUC	AAA	24	561	74	39	3	18	84	50	68	2	0	-7.1	.324	.383	.521	.270	.332	.444	.268	17.4	-1.7	82-1B -20	20-LF -6
2007	PAW	AAA	24	52	6	1	0	1	4	4	7	0	0	-0.2	.234	.308	.319	.208	.283	.292	.201	-3.2	-0.4	12-1B -1	
2008	PAW	AAA	25	522	65	25	2	24	81	41	84	0	0	-2.7	.300	.356	.515	.262	.319	.463	.266	15.8	1.3	73-LF -1	
2008	BOS	MLB	25	20	5	0	0	0	3	2	5	0	0	-0.1	.333	.400	.333	.333	.400	.333	.268	0.5	0.0		
2009	BOS	MLB	26	504	55	29	1	13	65	41	84	2	1	-1.6	.260	.324	.413	.253	.318	.417	.256	0.8	0.2	119-LF -11	

Breakout: 15%   Improve: 36%   Collapse: 35%   Attrition: 17%   Comparables: Benny DiStefano, John Harris, Matt Watson, Shawn Hare

Carter's production in 2007 was partly the product of a high BABIP and the environment he played in, but his 2008 Pawtucket campaign was not too far removed from that level. He hit for more power, and though he saw an increase in his strikeouts, his whiff rate is still well below the danger zone at which batting average threatens to collapse. With the Sox most likely not bringing back Casey or Kotsay, Carter may earn a bench job. There's some urgency to this for Carter because, at age 26, a third stint at Triple-A would stain his future with the dreaded "minor league slugger" label.

Sean Casey 1B

Bats: L Throws: R Height: 6' 4" Weight: 235 Born: July 2, 1974 Age: 34

YEAR	TEAM	LVL	AGE	PA	R	2B	3B	HR	RBI	BB	SO	SB	CS	EqBRR	AVG	OBP	SLG	EqAVG	EqOBP	EqSLG	EqA	VORP	WARP	DEFENSE	
2006	PIT	MLB	31	244	30	15	0	3	29	23	22	0	0	-1.8	.296	.377	.408	.291	.373	.408	.277	5.2	0.9	52-1B	1
2006	DET	MLB	31	196	17	7	0	5	30	10	21	0	1	-1.5	.245	.286	.364	.230	.276	.355	.216	-8.2	-0.4	46-1B	4
2007	DET	MLB	32	496	40	30	1	4	54	39	42	2	2	-2.2	.296	.353	.393	.286	.347	.390	.258	7.5	0.6	111-1B	2
2008	BOS	MLB	33	218	14	14	0	0	17	17	25	1	0	-3.4	.322	.381	.392	.308	.372	.394	.272	7.6	0.5	38-1B	0
2009	BOS	MLB	34	223	22	14	0	2	26	17	26	1	0	-1.8	.280	.341	.389	.272	.335	.392	.255	0.8	0.4	56-1B	1

Breakout: 23% Improve: 44% Collapse: 30% Attrition: 33%   Comparables: Ted Kluszewski, Hal Morris, Larry Biittner, Terry Kennedy

Injuries to Mike Lowell meant Casey saw more playing time than the Red Sox would have preferred, but the Mayor initially held his own, thanks to a rash of singles that propped up the rest of his slash stats. Most of that came prior to the All-Star break, as he hit all of .233/.300/.247 afterward. Given that the Sox have younger, less expensive options wasting away in Pawtucket, while Casey can no longer slug over .400, chances that he has value to anybody as a free agent, let alone Boston, seem slight.

Kevin Cash C

Bats: R Throws: R Height: 6' 0" Weight: 190 Born: December 6, 1977 Age: 31

YEAR	TEAM	LVL	AGE	PA	R	2B	3B	HR	RBI	BB	SO	SB	CS	EqBRR	AVG	OBP	SLG	EqAVG	EqOBP	EqSLG	EqA	VORP	WARP	DEFENSE			
2006	DUR	AAA	28	273	17	10	1	2	21	24	74	1	2	-2.0	.183	.270	.258	.146	.221	.220	.139	-35.8	-2.5	48-C	0	4-3B	-1
2007	PAW	AAA	29	208	22	7	0	7	25	23	56	0	0	-0.1	.176	.276	.335	.143	.229	.269	.173	-22.1	-0.4	52-C	5		
2007	BOS	MLB	29	33	2	1	0	0	4	4	13	0	0	-0.1	.111	.242	.148	.111	.242	.148	.140	-3.5	-0.2	9-C	0		
2008	BOS	MLB	30	162	11	7	0	3	15	18	50	0	0	-0.7	.225	.309	.338	.213	.302	.333	.227	-2.0	0.0	42-C	0		
2009	BOS	MLB	31	119	7	6	0	2	11	10	35	0	0	-0.6	.194	.266	.303	.188	.262	.306	.197	-5.6	-0.1	32-C	-1		

Breakout: 53% Improve: 58% Collapse: 38% Attrition: 64%   Comparables: Joe Lonnett, Bill Plummer, Jimmie Schaffer, Mike Ryan

Tease Cash for playing the sucker's role of Tim Wakefield's caddy (which paid $400,000) all you like, but his batting line was not all that much different from that of starting catcher Jason Varitek—though that says more about Varitek's decline than it does anything positive about Cash. He's now had 557 major league plate appearances, something like a single season's worth, and has batted .184/.248/.285. If the Red Sox need a designated backstop for Wakefield, given the production of Cash, Doug Mirabelli, and others since 2005 (.199/.271/.320 in 607 PA), they've paid a particularly high price for the privilege.

Alex Cora INF

Bats: L Throws: R Height: 6' 0" Weight: 200 Born: October 18, 1975 Age: 33

YEAR	TEAM	LVL	AGE	PA	R	2B	3B	HR	RBI	BB	SO	SB	CS	EqBRR	AVG	OBP	SLG	EqAVG	EqOBP	EqSLG	EqA	VORP	WARP	DEFENSE			
2006	BOS	MLB	30	264	31	7	2	1	18	19	29	6	2	1.0	.238	.312	.298	.226	.304	.286	.215	-5.1	-1.1	49-SS	-1	11-2B	-4
2007	BOS	MLB	31	232	30	10	5	3	18	7	23	1	1	-0.0	.246	.298	.386	.236	.288	.389	.235	-1.4	1.1	34-2B	7	23-SS	3
2008	BOS	MLB	32	179	14	8	2	0	9	16	13	1	1	-1.5	.270	.371	.349	.263	.365	.342	.257	4.6	-0.1	43-SS	-5		
2009	BOS	MLB	33	157	17	7	1	1	14	11	17	2	1	0.0	.254	.320	.340	.247	.315	.344	.235	0.7	0.3	41-SS	0		

Breakout: 32% Improve: 50% Collapse: 31% Attrition: 43%   Comparables: Rob Wilfong, Chuck Hiller, Lenny Harris, Jose Vizcaino

Though he did not log too many plate appearances overall, Cora was useful when he played, putting together his best walk rate since 2004 with the Dodgers while also posting the lowest strikeout rate of his career. As long as he can take a walk, he has his uses as a reserve, but shoppers looking at him as a free agent shouldn't stretch him to everyday play, especially anywhere besides Fenway, where he has hit .271/.333/.354 since 2006 while batting just .229/.313/.330 everywhere else.

Covelli "Coco" Crisp CF

Bats: S Throws: R Height: 6' 0" Weight: 180 Born: November 1, 1979 Age: 29

YEAR	TEAM	LVL	AGE	PA	R	2B	3B	HR	RBI	BB	SO	SB	CS	EqBRR	AVG	OBP	SLG	EqAVG	EqOBP	EqSLG	EqA	VORP	WARP	DEFENSE	
2006	BOS	MLB	26	452	58	22	2	8	36	31	67	22	4	3.3	.264	.317	.385	.249	.308	.366	.243	8.1	0.5	101-CF	0
2007	BOS	MLB	27	591	85	28	7	6	60	50	84	28	6	8.4	.268	.330	.382	.256	.323	.375	.252	9.5	5.2	137-CF	35
2008	BOS	MLB	28	409	55	18	3	7	41	35	59	20	7	1.2	.283	.344	.407	.277	.343	.408	.265	13.1	1.4	99-CF	0
2009	KCA	MLB	29	402	51	18	3	6	36	33	60	16	5	2.5	.264	.328	.381	.261	.326	.393	.257	4.2	1.9	96-CF	3

Breakout: 20% Improve: 54% Collapse: 18% Attrition: 19%   Comparables: Chuck Carr, Stan Javier, Derrel Thomas, Roger Cedeño

Deficient in one aspect of his game or another during his time in Boston, Crisp's value is primarily housed beyond his batsmanship, in his baserunning and his fielding. Even so, last year he was an average center fielder offensively, thanks in part to boosting his liner rates, one that finally put him back around the numbers of his Cleveland days. The Royals will find out if Crisp's return from the offensive abyss is legitimate or if, much like Crisp's attempts to fight the much larger James Shields this year, they are rushing headfirst into something they don't quite understand.

J. D. Drew — RF

Bats: L   Throws: R   Height: 6' 1"   Weight: 200   Born: November 20, 1975   Age: 33

YEAR	TEAM	LVL	AGE	PA	R	2B	3B	HR	RBI	BB	SO	SB	CS	EqBRR	AVG	OBP	SLG	EqAVG	EqOBP	EqSLG	EqA	VORP	WARP	DEFENSE	
2006	LAN	MLB	30	594	84	34	6	20	100	89	106	2	3	1.4	.283	.393	.498	.279	.392	.491	.302	33.4	3.6	125-RF	-5
2007	BOS	MLB	31	552	84	30	4	11	64	79	100	4	2	-0.1	.270	.373	.423	.252	.364	.412	.274	12.7	2.9	120-RF	8
2008	BOS	MLB	32	456	79	23	4	19	64	79	80	4	1	2.1	.280	.408	.519	.264	.401	.511	.312	32.3	3.6	99-RF	-2
2009	BOS	MLB	33	464	67	25	3	13	60	65	85	4	2	0.2	.269	.374	.451	.261	.368	.456	.288	12.7	2.4	110-RF	-2

Breakout: 8%   Improve: 38%   Collapse: 20%   Attrition: 11%   Comparables: Roger Maris, Fred Lynn, Bobby Abreu, Ryan Klesko

Despite accumulating nearly 100 fewer plate appearances than in 2007, Drew hit for more power, doubling of his HR/FB rate. While his fly-ball rate itself only jumped up slightly, the distance he hit them increased dramatically, which allowed him to surpass even his 90th-percentile PECOTA forecast last year. He missed time to various back maladies, a knee and a thigh, but his back injury was the most serious. After the All-Star break, Drew hit all of .211/.395/.356, thanks to the back issues. That still made him more productive than his sometime replacement, Kotsay. Though the back problem is not supposed to be chronic, there always seems to be one injury or another hampering Drew, which could be more of a problem with Manny gone and Papi declining.

Jacoby Ellsbury — CF

Bats: L   Throws: L   Height: 6' 1"   Weight: 185   Born: September 11, 1983   Age: 25

YEAR	TEAM	LVL	AGE	PA	R	2B	3B	HR	RBI	BB	SO	SB	CS	EqBRR	AVG	OBP	SLG	EqAVG	EqOBP	EqSLG	EqA	VORP	WARP	DEFENSE			
2006	WIL	A+	22	281	35	7	5	4	32	25	28	25	9	1.9	.299	.379	.418	.254	.312	.359	.237	-4.0	1.1	58-CF	8		
2006	PME	AA	22	225	29	10	3	3	19	24	25	16	8	-1.7	.308	.387	.434	.272	.342	.386	.256	3.6	1.0	47-CF	3		
2007	PME	AA	23	83	16	10	2	0	13	6	7	8	1	0.0	.452	.518	.644	.387	.439	.560	.342	12.8	1.8	18-CF	6		
2007	PAW	AAA	23	401	66	14	5	2	28	32	47	33	6	4.3	.298	.360	.380	.262	.322	.346	.246	-5.0	-0.6	66-CF	-3	12-LF	-5
2007	BOS	MLB	23	127	20	7	1	3	18	8	15	9	0	1.8	.353	.394	.509	.336	.383	.509	.314	12.8	2.1	16-LF	7	12-CF	1
2008	BOS	MLB	24	609	98	22	7	9	47	41	80	50	11	8.0	.280	.336	.394	.272	.331	.393	.261	16.1	5.1	61-CF	9	39-LF	16
2009	BOS	MLB	25	569	87	30	5	7	53	42	75	42	12	4.0	.291	.348	.409	.283	.343	.413	.272	11.6	4.2	133-CF	13		

Breakout: 30%   Improve: 59%   Collapse: 17%   Attrition: 15%   Comparables: Del Unser, Pat Kelly, Steve Hovley, Johnny Damon

Despite not having a set position in the outfield, Ellsbury accumulated the most playing time of any Boston out-fielder by virtue of staying healthy (and not being traded). This season was a learning experience for the speedy 24-year-old: he started out hot, but pitchers quickly figured out that he lacked the muscle or the swing to be a power threat, and they began to bust him inside. The result was an awful run through June and July, during which he hit .246/.271/.308. He did finally adjust, hitting .314/.352/.463 over the final two months by switching to an all-fields approach. The Red Sox believe he's turned a corner.

Ryan Kalish — OF

Bats: L   Throws: L   Height: 6' 1"   Weight: 205   Born: March 28, 1988   Age: 21

YEAR	TEAM	LVL	AGE	PA	R	2B	3B	HR	RBI	BB	SO	SB	CS	EqBRR	AVG	OBP	SLG	EqAVG	EqOBP	EqSLG	EqA	VORP	WARP	DEFENSE			
2006	LOW	A-	18	40	8	0	1	0	4	2	14	2	0	0.6	.200	.275	.257	.162	.220	.216	.155	-9.5	-1.0	10-RF	-3		
2007	LOW	A-	19	104	27	4	1	3	13	16	12	18	3	2.5	.368	.471	.540	.304	.385	.467	.298	14.6	0.4	22-CF	-5		
2008	GRN	A	20	420	51	16	1	3	32	53	76	18	4	2.9	.281	.376	.356	.222	.310	.290	.221	-19.7	-1.2	51-RF	-1	41-CF	-1
2008	LNC	A+	20	82	6	6	0	2	14	8	23	1	0	0.3	.233	.305	.397	.176	.244	.311	.196	-6.5	-0.8	18-RF	-3		
2009	BOS	MLB	21	580	68	31	3	5	48	55	126	17	6	2.4	.248	.322	.352	.241	.317	.355	.241	-10.7	0.8	136-RF	4		

Breakout: 32%   Improve: 59%   Collapse: 14%   Attrition: 5%   Comparables: Peter Bergeron, Bert Flores, Lars Anderson, Shin-Soo Choo

Though athletic and sporting some tools both offensively and defensively, Kalish is still quite raw, and the after-effects of a 2007 wrist injury seemed to drag down his most recent campaign. He struggled to hit for power at both

Greenville and Lancaster, and whether he ends up in a corner or in center has a lot to do with how much he fills out and if his power potential is ever fulfilled. Kalish gets a free pass for now, due to his youth and the wrist issues, but he will need to show something soon in a full-season league.

Casey Kelly — SS

Bats: R Throws: R Height: 6' 3" Weight: 194 Born: October 4, 1989 Age: 19

YEAR	TEAM	LVL	AGE	PA	R	2B	3B	HR	RBI	BB	SO	SB	CS	EqBRR	AVG	OBP	SLG	EqAVG	EqOBP	EqSLG	EqA	VORP	WARP	DEFENSE	
2008	LOW	A-	18	32	5	5	1	0	4	0	8	0	1	-1.1	.344	.344	.563	.250	.250	.438	.228	-1.0	-0.3	8-SS	-2
2008	RSX	Rk	18	109	10	5	0	1	9	6	34	1	0	0.7	.173	.229	.255	.136	.173	.194	.075	-49.3	-2.7	21-SS	-3
2009	BOS	MLB	19	564	37	32	3	5	44	28	162	6	3	0.8	.203	.246	.302	.197	.242	.305	.185	-27.3	-2.1	132-SS	-7

Breakout: 93% Improve: 93% Collapse: 5% Attrition: 1%   Comparables: Benji Gil, Brandon Wood, Mark Lewis, Eddie Williams

Boston's 2008 first-round pick, Kelly has a lot of potential defensively, although he may need to move to third base because of his large frame. Production at the plate was a problem during his professional debut, as he struggled to make contact in rookie ball, but he did get the bat on the ball once he moved to Lowell. There is still a chance that he will be converted to pitching if he cannot make it as a hitter, and given his numbers on the mound in high school along with the attention paid to him by Tennessee to play quarterback, he has the arm for it.

Mark Kotsay — OF

Bats: L Throws: L Height: 6' 0" Weight: 205 Born: December 2, 1975 Age: 33

YEAR	TEAM	LVL	AGE	PA	R	2B	3B	HR	RBI	BB	SO	SB	CS	EqBRR	AVG	OBP	SLG	EqAVG	EqOBP	EqSLG	EqA	VORP	WARP	DEFENSE			
2006	OAK	MLB	30	558	57	29	3	7	59	44	55	6	3	-4.8	.275	.332	.386	.267	.330	.384	.252	11.2	-1.0	117-CF	-19		
2007	OAK	MLB	31	226	20	14	0	1	20	19	20	1	1	-0.6	.214	.279	.296	.210	.279	.298	.202	-9.2	-1.2	53-CF	-4		
2008	ATL	MLB	32	345	39	17	3	6	37	25	34	2	3	-0.5	.289	.340	.418	.296	.348	.434	.267	10.4	0.6	78-CF	-6		
2008	BOS	MLB	32	91	6	8	1	0	12	7	11	0	1	-0.1	.226	.286	.345	.214	.283	.333	.210	-4.3	-0.4	17-RF	1	4-1B	-1
2009	BOS	MLB	33	341	35	20	2	4	36	24	38	2	2	-0.9	.269	.321	.380	.261	.316	.383	.245	0.3	0.4	82-CF	-5		

Breakout: 32% Improve: 59% Collapse: 21% Attrition: 28%   Comparables: Joe Orsulak, Gus Bell, Bill Virdon, Darin Erstad

After a solid performance for the Braves that was broken up by yet another bout of back soreness, Kotsay hit feebly for the Sox while splitting time between first and right, covering for Lowell and Drew. This underwhelming performance was capped in the playoffs when he showed a national audience that there was no way he could catch up with an elite fastball anymore, as Rays rookie David Price made him look far older than his 32 years. Kotsay's defense is not what it used to be, either, meaning that he has one foot (and a few toes TBNL on the other) out the door marked "Exit Major Leagues."

George Kottaras — C

Bats: L Throws: R Height: 6' 0" Weight: 185 Born: May 16, 1983 Age: 26

YEAR	TEAM	LVL	AGE	PA	R	2B	3B	HR	RBI	BB	SO	SB	CS	EqBRR	AVG	OBP	SLG	EqAVG	EqOBP	EqSLG	EqA	VORP	WARP	DEFENSE	
2006	MOB	AA	23	310	40	19	1	8	33	50	68	0	1	-0.9	.276	.394	.451	.258	.363	.443	.280	14.4	1.1	67-C	-9
2006	POR	AAA	23	133	14	10	1	2	17	12	30	0	0	0.0	.210	.286	.361	.190	.261	.331	.205	-8.0	-0.8	28-C	-5
2007	PAW	AAA	24	334	32	22	0	9	39	32	71	1	1	-1.6	.241	.316	.408	.218	.288	.383	.233	-8.1	-0.8	82-C	-12
2008	PAW	AAA	25	462	63	18	0	22	65	64	110	0	0	1.0	.243	.348	.456	.214	.318	.407	.253	-0.3	0.5	71-C	-7
2009	BOS	MLB	26	406	38	20	1	11	49	44	106	0	0	-0.6	.215	.304	.373	.209	.299	.377	.237	-3.1	0.7	97-C	-10

Breakout: 19% Improve: 39% Collapse: 40% Attrition: 20%   Comparables: Pete Laforest, Sal Rende, Brad Gulden, Mike Hocutt

Two years and one organization later, Kottaras finally found his bat again. His power output revived the potential he flashed at Double-A in 2006, and this time, his line looked solid without the aid of an unrealistic BABIP. Being an offense-first catcher who doesn't hit is like being a sushi restaurant that's run out of fish, so this was a positive development. Patience at the plate has always been a virtue for Kottaras, but he may need to take the bat off his shoulder to stick. Whether or not Varitek leaves, don't expect Kottaras to get the first call to replace him now that Josh Bard's been brought back.

Che-Hsuan Lin   CF   Bats: R   Throws: R   Height: 6' 0"   Weight: 180   Born: September 21, 1988   Age: 20

YEAR	TEAM	LVL	AGE	PA	R	2B	3B	HR	RBI	BB	SO	SB	CS	EqBRR	AVG	OBP	SLG	EqAVG	EqOBP	EqSLG	EqA	VORP	WARP	DEFENSE			
2007	RSX	Rk	18	200	33	10	6	4	22	17	42	14	3	0.6	.263	.330	.457	.190	.235	.321	.195	-41.1	-2.9	28-CF	-5	14-RF	-2
2007	LOW	A-	18	50	7	2	0	0	3	5	10	3	2	-0.9	.163	.265	.209	.133	.204	.178	.113	-14.3	-0.6	11-CF	1		
2008	GRN	A	19	415	60	13	6	5	37	43	62	33	7	2.2	.249	.342	.359	.202	.284	.301	.213	-24.8	-1.4	77-CF	-1	9-RF	-1
2009	BOS	MLB	20	522	54	26	4	5	38	39	106	21	9	2.5	.223	.288	.328	.217	.283	.331	.220	-16.7	0.4	123-CF	4		

Breakout: 54%   Improve: 76%   Collapse: 12%   Attrition: 11%   Comparables: Oscar Jiminez, Rogearvin Bernadina, Jose Leiva, Brian Hunter

A member of the 2008 Taiwanese Olympic team, Lin has not progressed much since his 2007 debut in the Gulf Coast League. He's incredibly athletic, but has trouble making contact, as evidenced by his consistently low batting averages and high strikeout rates. He cut down on the K's in '08 in the Sally League, but he's still a work in progress with more tools than production.

Mike Lowell   3B   Bats: R   Throws: R   Height: 6' 3"   Weight: 210   Born: February 24, 1974   Age: 35

YEAR	TEAM	LVL	AGE	PA	R	2B	3B	HR	RBI	BB	SO	SB	CS	EqBRR	AVG	OBP	SLG	EqAVG	EqOBP	EqSLG	EqA	VORP	WARP	DEFENSE	
2006	BOS	MLB	32	631	79	47	1	20	80	47	61	2	2	-1.4	.284	.339	.475	.267	.328	.455	.267	21.7	5.0	146-3B	24
2007	BOS	MLB	33	653	79	37	2	21	120	53	71	3	2	-6.2	.324	.378	.501	.307	.366	.491	.292	42.9	6.1	149-3B	16
2008	BOS	MLB	34	468	58	27	0	17	73	38	61	2	2	-5.7	.274	.338	.461	.264	.331	.458	.269	15.8	3.6	105-3B	16
2009	BOS	MLB	35	469	51	27	1	14	69	37	62	2	1	-2.7	.272	.332	.442	.264	.327	.446	.267	10.6	2.6	111-3B	7

Breakout: 14%   Improve: 40%   Collapse: 24%   Attrition: 12%   Comparables: Doug DeCinces, Matt Williams, Jeff Conine, Brooks Robinson

Even with the partially torn labrum in his right hip, Lowell was still an asset on defense, at least until it got to the point where just standing around was a painful experience for him. Mixed in with the health problems were a few months when Lowell was one of the better hitters in the game (.324/.381/.581 May-June), along with other times when he could barely keep things above the Mendoza line. Injuries aside, the overall line was a near twin of 2006, something that might have been expected, given that Lowell's 2007 campaign was fueled by BABIP excess. As long as the hip is healthy—and it is expected to be healed up in time for spring training after arthroscopic surgery—you can expect more good work.

Jed Lowrie   SS   Bats: S   Throws: R   Height: 6' 0"   Weight: 180   Born: April 17, 1984   Age: 25

YEAR	TEAM	LVL	AGE	PA	R	2B	3B	HR	RBI	BB	SO	SB	CS	EqBRR	AVG	OBP	SLG	EqAVG	EqOBP	EqSLG	EqA	VORP	WARP	DEFENSE			
2006	WIL	A+	22	438	43	21	6	3	50	54	65	2	2	-1.6	.262	.352	.374	.218	.290	.321	.216	-20.7	-1.4	88-SS	-9		
2007	PME	AA	23	408	61	31	7	8	49	65	58	5	3	0.0	.297	.410	.501	.256	.359	.443	.278	16.9	1.8	84-SS	-8		
2007	PAW	AAA	23	177	21	16	1	5	21	12	33	0	1	-2.1	.300	.356	.506	.272	.322	.481	.270	7.3	2.0	31-SS	7	7-2B	1
2008	PAW	AAA	24	234	35	14	2	5	32	31	43	1	0	-0.8	.268	.359	.434	.241	.333	.407	.263	2.8	1.1	47-SS	0		
2008	BOS	MLB	24	306	34	25	3	2	46	35	68	1	0	-2.5	.258	.339	.400	.248	.336	.403	.263	7.3	2.0	43-SS	6	27-3B	1
2009	BOS	MLB	25	414	50	29	2	9	49	44	77	3	1	0.0	.260	.341	.432	.253	.336	.436	.269	14.8	2.4	99-SS	2		

Breakout: 29%   Improve: 52%   Collapse: 25%   Attrition: 27%   Comparables: Howard Johnson, Jason Bates, Roy Smalley, Darrell Evans

Boston fans wanted to embrace Lowrie as a scrappy Dustin Pedroia Lite, but as of right now, he's a player who hit just .258 despite posting a well-above-average .342 BABIP and an unsustainably high line-drive rate. Couple this with the switch-hitter's just managing a .222/.308/.344 against right handers, and you see why slotting him in as the starting shortstop—especially with his lack of range—is a risky proposition. More time in the majors could patch up his punchout problems, but could just as easily expose him as a future member of the Reserve Players of America.

Julio Lugo — SS

Bats: R Throws: R Height: 6' 1" Weight: 175 Born: November 16, 1975 Age: 33

YEAR	TEAM	LVL	AGE	PA	R	2B	3B	HR	RBI	BB	SO	SB	CS	EqBRR	AVG	OBP	SLG	EqAVG	EqOBP	EqSLG	EqA	VORP	WARP	DEFENSE		
2006	TBA	MLB	30	322	53	17	1	12	27	27	47	18	4	1.8	.308	.373	.498	.300	.372	.495	.297	31.1	2.5	71-SS	-4	
2006	LAN	MLB	30	164	16	5	1	0	10	12	29	6	5	-1.5	.219	.278	.267	.219	.282	.267	.198	-10.6	-1.0	18-2B	1	13-3B -3
2007	BOS	MLB	31	630	71	36	2	8	73	48	82	33	6	1.9	.237	.294	.349	.226	.288	.344	.231	-3.7	-0.1	138-SS	-7	
2008	BOS	MLB	32	307	27	13	0	1	22	34	51	12	4	-1.2	.268	.355	.330	.263	.353	.324	.253	6.0	0.0	75-SS	-9	
2009	BOS	MLB	33	286	35	13	1	3	24	25	44	13	3	0.6	.255	.325	.347	.248	.320	.350	.246	2.9	0.6	70-SS	-2	

Breakout: 19% Improve: 47% Collapse: 28% Attrition: 33% Comparables: Royce Clayton, Bobby Adams, Ivan DeJesus, Tony Taylor

During the 2007 season, Lugo's ability to hit did not just drop off a cliff: it was bound, locked in a safe, and thrown off the cliff into the bottom of a lake filled with flesh-eating piranhas. He improved slightly this year, but most of that work was done at home, where he hit .305/.384/.391, against .233/.327/.271 on the road. His defense cratered, with both the conventional and the advanced metrics marking him as one of the worst shortstops in the game. He ended the year on the 60-day DL, and though he should be healthy come 2009, the main thing binding him to a Red Sox roster spot is the two years left on his contract.

David Ortiz — DH

Bats: L Throws: L Height: 6' 4" Weight: 230 Born: November 18, 1975 Age: 33

YEAR	TEAM	LVL	AGE	PA	R	2B	3B	HR	RBI	BB	SO	SB	CS	EqBRR	AVG	OBP	SLG	EqAVG	EqOBP	EqSLG	EqA	VORP	WARP	DEFENSE	
2006	BOS	MLB	30	686	115	29	2	54	137	119	117	1	0	-2.3	.287	.413	.636	.259	.400	.583	.325	77.8	6.6	8-1B	2
2007	BOS	MLB	31	667	116	52	1	35	117	111	103	3	1	-2.1	.332	.445	.621	.308	.431	.593	.340	82.4	7.4	5-1B	0
2008	BOS	MLB	32	491	74	30	1	23	89	70	74	1	0	-1.8	.264	.369	.507	.248	.361	.488	.290	30.0	2.4		
2009	BOS	MLB	33	569	82	31	1	27	94	81	96	1	0	-2.4	.269	.375	.504	.262	.369	.509	.299	28.7	3.2	134-DH	

Breakout: 3% Improve: 21% Collapse: 31% Attrition: 10% Comparables: Carlos Delgado, Jim Thome, John Mayberry, Jason Giambi

Though Manny Ramirez's messy exit got all the attention, Ortiz's dip in power had at least as significant an impact on Boston's season. Ortiz had just recovered from a painfully slow start (.184/.294/.350 in April) when he tore a tendon sheath in his left wrist and landed on the disabled list. Though he showed few ill effects statistically when he returned after nearly 50 games on the shelf (batting .277/.385/.529 in 55 games), the intimidating stroke of old was absent; he missed on pitches he used to crush and became noticeably more patient, trying to get on base however he could, despite his diminished swing. Ortiz believes the wrist will be healthy for 2009 after a prolonged rest. As Ortiz goes, so go the Red Sox, so they can only hope he's correct.

Dustin Pedroia — 2B

Bats: R Throws: R Height: 5' 9" Weight: 180 Born: August 17, 1983 Age: 25

YEAR	TEAM	LVL	AGE	PA	R	2B	3B	HR	RBI	BB	SO	SB	CS	EqBRR	AVG	OBP	SLG	EqAVG	EqOBP	EqSLG	EqA	VORP	WARP	DEFENSE		
2006	PAW	AAA	22	493	55	30	3	5	50	48	27	1	4	-6.7	.305	.384	.426	.274	.349	.397	.262	11.1	1.5	74-SS	-10	32-2B 4
2006	BOS	MLB	22	98	5	4	0	2	7	7	7	0	1	-2.7	.191	.258	.303	.182	.258	.284	.184	-5.3	-0.2	19-2B	4	5-SS -2
2007	BOS	MLB	23	581	86	39	1	8	50	47	42	7	1	0.0	.317	.380	.442	.303	.370	.434	.282	32.7	4.6	129-2B	11	
2008	BOS	MLB	24	726	118	54	2	17	83	50	52	20	1	3.5	.326	.376	.493	.314	.367	.488	.296	59.8	7.6	154-2B	17	
2009	BOS	MLB	25	649	90	42	3	12	75	51	53	12	4	0.9	.303	.364	.447	.294	.358	.451	.283	31.8	4.7	151-2B	8	

Breakout: 16% Improve: 49% Collapse: 13% Attrition: 7% Comparables: Ron Hunt, Rick Burleson, Davey Johnson, Rich Rollins

Pedroia's nabbing Rookie of the Year and Most Valuable Player awards in consecutive seasons is a nifty trick, one that puts him alongside Cal Ripken Jr. and Ryan Howard as the only players to accomplish the feat. He also had more doubles (54) than punchouts (52); he's the seventh player since 1977 with a minimum of 50 doubles to pull that off. Though Pedroia was far more productive at home—.344/.393/.519 with 35 of those doubles—he was no slouch on the road, with an impressive .309/.359/.468 that many teams would kill to get out of their second baseman. Pedroia's numbers lack any kind of BABIP-related concerns, meaning that as long as he keeps on using Fenway to his advantage, he's going to put up impressive campaigns at the plate.

Josh Reddick — OF

Bats: L   Throws: R   Height: 6' 2"   Weight: 180   Born: February 19, 1987   Age: 22

YEAR	TEAM	LVL	AGE	PA	R	2B	3B	HR	RBI	BB	SO	SB	CS	EqBRR	AVG	OBP	SLG	EqAVG	EqOBP	EqSLG	EqA	VORP	WARP	DEFENSE			
2007	GRN	A	20	403	60	17	6	18	72	26	51	8	5	0.0	.306	.352	.531	.235	.273	.407	.231	-7.9	-1.9	86-RF	-10	6-CF	-1
2008	GRN	A	21	58	7	4	2	0	9	5	8	2	1	-0.3	.340	.397	.491	.278	.328	.426	.256	1.5	0.0	12-RF	-1		
2008	LNC	A+	21	331	60	11	8	17	57	17	49	9	1	3.3	.343	.375	.593	.251	.283	.454	.250	2.3	-0.1	59-RF	-3	8-CF	0
2008	PME	AA	21	132	22	4	2	6	25	12	25	3	1	-0.2	.214	.290	.436	.202	.273	.429	.239	-2.4	-0.5	31-CF	-5		
2009	BOS	MLB	22	556	61	32	6	15	68	35	102	7	4	2.6	.251	.300	.423	.243	.295	.427	.248	-3.9	0.5	130-RF	-1		

Breakout: 40% Improve: 58% Collapse: 19% Attrition: 10%   Comparables: Rob Ducey, Nigel Wilson, Carlos Gonzalez, Daryl Sconiers

Reddick killed at hitter-friendly Lancaster, launching 17 homers in a half-season's work while posting a .250 ISO. More impressive was the low strikeout rate (just under 16 percent) that he brought along with that power; that's a good sign for his future, especially given his tendency to be overly aggressive at the plate. Portland was not as kind to him; his strikeout rate shot up while his batting average did the reverse. Still, he managed to keep most of the power despite his struggles, no small victory for a 21-year-old tossed into Double-A at midseason. Reddick's combination of tools and baseball skills has some in the organization feeling that he's a good comp to Jason Bay, the man he might take over for in a couple of years.

Dave Ross — C

Bats: R   Throws: R   Height: 6' 2"   Weight: 240   Born: March 19, 1977   Age: 32

YEAR	TEAM	LVL	AGE	PA	R	2B	3B	HR	RBI	BB	SO	SB	CS	EqBRR	AVG	OBP	SLG	EqAVG	EqOBP	EqSLG	EqA	VORP	WARP	DEFENSE	
2006	CIN	MLB	29	296	37	15	1	21	52	37	75	0	0	-1.2	.255	.353	.579	.243	.344	.559	.298	21.8	3.0	70-C	3
2007	CIN	MLB	30	348	32	10	0	17	39	30	92	0	0	-1.4	.203	.271	.399	.196	.270	.395	.228	-2.7	1.5	94-C	11
2008	CIN	MLB	31	173	17	9	0	3	13	32	36	0	1	-1.6	.231	.381	.366	.222	.376	.363	.268	4.9	0.8	42-C	0
2009	ATL	MLB	32	168	17	7	0	6	21	21	42	1	0	-1.0	.220	.321	.395	.220	.319	.407	.250	4.1	1.1	43-C	0

Breakout: 29% Improve: 58% Collapse: 28% Attrition: 48%   Comparables: Doug Mirabelli, Ron Karkovice, Steve Bilko, Mark Parent

Released by the Reds in August, Ross was signed by the Red Sox and called up just before rosters expanded, but he was an afterthought, restricted to late-inning mop-up duty. He's a known quantity, a hitter who struggles to maintain his batting average while popping just enough home runs to keep things interesting. He did throw in a new wrinkle in 2008, dramatically upping his walk rate despite seeing the same number of pitches per plate appearance as the year before; this should probably be regarded as a fluke. The Braves signed him to a two-year deal to be Brian McCann's caddy, hoping he can at least outhit Corky Miller and Clint Sammons' combined .114 average in 2008.

Jon Van Every — OF

Bats: L   Throws: L   Height: 6' 1"   Weight: 195   Born: November 27, 1979   Age: 29

YEAR	TEAM	LVL	AGE	PA	R	2B	3B	HR	RBI	BB	SO	SB	CS	EqBRR	AVG	OBP	SLG	EqAVG	EqOBP	EqSLG	EqA	VORP	WARP	DEFENSE			
2006	AKR	AA	26	272	35	16	5	10	40	26	80	5	1	0.0	.258	.338	.496	.196	.264	.363	.219	-13.0	-0.6	50-CF	2	9-LF	-2
2006	BUF	AAA	26	171	23	9	2	5	16	16	51	5	2	-1.2	.258	.339	.444	.229	.304	.405	.245	-1.0	0.1	42-CF	-1		
2007	AKR	AA	27	176	27	14	5	4	34	19	48	4	5	-1.6	.344	.416	.583	.233	.297	.396	.237	-2.1	0.9	27-CF	8		
2007	BUF	AAA	27	186	17	5	1	8	23	23	57	2	3	-2.2	.272	.370	.468	.228	.315	.395	.246	-0.7	1.5	48-CF	10		
2008	PAW	AAA	28	442	84	15	3	26	70	54	157	6	1	3.6	.263	.360	.524	.224	.315	.446	.260	6.1	2.6	116-CF	9		
2008	BOS	MLB	28	18	0	0	1	0	5	1	6	0	0	-0.5	.235	.278	.353	.235	.278	.353	.216	-0.7	-0.1				
2009	BOS	MLB	29	449	46	23	3	13	50	43	158	5	3	0.6	.213	.293	.385	.206	.288	.389	.235	-7.1	1.3	106-CF	5		

Breakout: 20% Improve: 32% Collapse: 36% Attrition: 24%   Comparables: Rob Ducey, Brad Tyler, Jim Eisenreich, Ty Van Burkleo

Van Every's first year with the Sox organization was a good one, as the aspiring fourth outfielder beat up Triple-A pitching and posted some impressive power numbers. The problem that has kept him in the minors since 2001 is that he also struck out over 41 percent of the time. Despite Van Every's power, when a hitter misses that often, he's a stretch to succeed over long periods against major league pitching, even more so in a reserve role.

Jason Varitek — C

Bats: S Throws: R Height: 6' 2" Weight: 230 Born: April 11, 1972 Age: 37

YEAR	TEAM	LVL	AGE	PA	R	2B	3B	HR	RBI	BB	SO	SB	CS	EqBRR	AVG	OBP	SLG	EqAVG	EqOBP	EqSLG	EqA	VORP	WARP	DEFENSE	
2006	BOS	MLB	34	416	46	19	2	12	55	46	87	1	2	-1.9	.238	.325	.400	.222	.318	.380	.244	3.3	1.2	92-C	1
2007	BOS	MLB	35	518	57	15	3	17	68	71	122	1	2	-3.6	.255	.367	.421	.236	.355	.405	.268	21.0	3.5	120-C	7
2008	BOS	MLB	36	483	37	20	0	13	43	52	122	0	1	-3.2	.220	.313	.359	.212	.311	.360	.236	-2.1	1.5	117-C	6
2009	BOS	MLB	37	258	23	12	0	7	32	28	63	0	0	-2.0	.234	.323	.388	.227	.318	.392	.248	3.3	1.4	64-C	0

Breakout: 16% Improve: 45% Collapse: 29% Attrition: 50%   Comparables: Lance Parrish, Terry Steinbach, Damian Miller, Greg Myers

The slow-swinged shadow of his former self hit .201/.293/.323 against right handers, suggesting that he should either stick to batting right-handed or take up the short end of a catching platoon, perhaps the perfect way to move into the role of player/coach or player/manager. Agent Scott Boras has said that neither of those options is in Varitek's plans, though, as Tek intends to catch full-time for somebody. Taken with Boras' initial demand that Varitek reel in a contract like Jorge Posada's current four-year, $52.4 million deal, these considerations have ensured that for Tek, the newswire is filled with the sounds of crickets rather than ongoing negotiations.

Kevin Youkilis — 4C

Bats: R Throws: R Height: 6' 1" Weight: 220 Born: March 15, 1979 Age: 30

YEAR	TEAM	LVL	AGE	PA	R	2B	3B	HR	RBI	BB	SO	SB	CS	EqBRR	AVG	OBP	SLG	EqAVG	EqOBP	EqSLG	EqA	VORP	WARP	DEFENSE			
2006	BOS	MLB	27	680	100	42	2	13	72	91	120	5	2	0.5	.279	.381	.429	.260	.372	.406	.278	20.4	3.1	116-1B	8	15-LF	2
2007	BOS	MLB	28	625	85	35	2	16	83	77	105	4	2	4.8	.288	.390	.453	.272	.381	.446	.289	27.9	3.8	123-1B	8	12-3B	0
2008	BOS	MLB	29	621	91	43	4	29	115	62	108	3	5	-0.3	.312	.390	.569	.299	.381	.563	.310	53.4	6.1	110-1B	4	28-3B	7
2009	BOS	MLB	30	597	81	36	2	21	84	70	109	3	2	-0.6	.275	.366	.475	.267	.360	.480	.290	20.3	3.3	140-1B	6		

Breakout: 6% Improve: 35% Collapse: 22% Attrition: 9%   Comparables: Tim Salmon, Jeff Conine, Eric Karros, Nick Esasky

The fan favorite jumped from an above-average, patient hitter into a legitimate power threat with serious patience—at least at first glance. His walk rate actually dropped for the fourth straight season, but his strikeouts remained around the 20 percent mark, and he not only swung at more pitches but made contact with a higher percentage of them as well, meaning he was waiting on pitches he could not do anything with and swinging at those he could. Normally, we might caution that his .347 BABIP would suggest a lot of luck and a regression in 2009, but his liner rate of 22 percent is both typical for Youkilis and correlative with that kind of success rate. The biggest gain came from his rate of homers on fly balls; with roughly the same percentage of fly balls, Youk hit almost twice as many of them for homers. Whether this will be an enduring change is another question; Youkilis had plenty of long balls that just cleared the wall, tying for fifth in the majors in homers that cleared the fence by less than 10 vertical feet with 11 fence scrapers.

PITCHERS

David Aardsma

Bats: R Throws: R Height: 6' 4" Weight: 205 Born: December 27, 1981 Age: 27

YEAR	TEAM	LVL	AGE	W	L	SV	G	GS	IP	H	BB	SO	HR	GB%	BABIP	STUFF	WHIP	ERA	DERA	EqH9	EqBB9	EqSO9	EqHR9	DEF	VORP	SN/WX
2006	IOW	AAA	24	2	3	8	29	0	36	31	15	36	1	55.6%	.326	-2	1.28	3.25	4.50	8.7	4.0	6.4	0.5	0	4.2	—
2006	CHN	MLB	24	3	0	0	45	0	53	41	28	49	9	38.1%	.239	-3	1.30	4.08	4.92	6.8	4.1	7.6	1.4	7	11.0	1.28
2007	CHR	AAA	25	3	2	15	28	0	35¹	26	11	45	7	32.2%	.241	-12	1.05	4.33	6.68	8.3	3.2	8.0	2.7	4	-4.0	—
2007	CHA	MLB	25	2	1	0	25	0	32¹	39	17	36	4	39.2%	.389	7	1.73	6.41	4.22	11.0	4.5	8.7	1.1	-7	-2.0	-0.05
2008	BOS	MLB	26	4	2	0	47	0	48²	49	35	49	4	45.3%	.346	8	1.73	5.54	4.98	9.8	6.1	8.2	0.8	-3	-0.0	-0.11
2009	BOS	MLB	27	2	2	2	39	0	44¹	41	24	42	5	42.0%	.300	12	1.46	4.32	4.33	7.9	4.4	8.0	0.9	1	7.0	0.56

Breakout: 29% Improve: 51% Collapse: 33% Attrition: 32%   Comparables: Jeff Parrett, Tim Scott, Jesus Colome, Shawn Hillegas

Aardsma will take another shot at consistency this year, which would be a first, but there were plenty of positive signs in 2008. Though never an asset, his control had never before been as bad as it was in 2008, to some extent negating his high strikeout rate and improved ground-ball rate. Despite the wildness, the former first-round pick actually pitched reasonably well through mid-July, posting a 2.75 ERA in 39⅓ innings. It was only after coming back from a groin-inspired stay on the DL that he truly got hammered, giving up 18 runs in his final 9⅓ innings of the season, including three home runs allowed.

Daniel Bard

Bats: R   Throws: R   Height: 6' 4"   Weight: 195   Born: June 25, 1985   Age: 24

YEAR	TEAM	LVL	AGE	W	L	SV	G	GS	IP	H	BB	SO	HR	GB%	BABIP	STUFF	WHIP	ERA	DERA	EqH9	EqBB9	EqSO9	EqHR9	DEF	VORP	SN/WX
2007	GRN	A	22	3	5	0	17	17	61²	55	56	38	3	44.4%	.291	-23	1.80	6.42	10.80	10.0	11.0	2.0	1.4	0	-30.8	—
2007	LNC	A+	22	0	2	0	5	5	13¹	21	22	9	2	51.9%	.388	-29	3.23	10.15	17.31	15.9	15.9	2.1	2.1	-3	-16.9	—
2008	GRN	A	23	1	0	0	15	0	28	12	4	43	1	66.0%	.224	21	0.57	0.64	2.88	6.1	2.2	7.9	1.1	3	7.6	—
2008	PME	AA	23	4	1	7	31	0	49²	30	26	64	3	60.0%	.255	16	1.13	1.99	4.34	6.4	4.5	8.7	0.8	6	6.7	—
2009	BOS	MLB	24	3	3	1	22	5	50¹	48	34	44	4	50.0%	.300	9	1.62	4.75	4.78	8.2	5.4	7.3	0.7	1	5.6	0.65

Breakout: 40%   Improve: 74%   Collapse: 9%   Attrition: 13%   Comparables: Jay Powell, Duane Ward, Wayne Gomes, Charlie Kerfeld

After struggling as a starter, the 2006 first-rounder's move to the pen generated spectacular results: 107 strikeouts in 77⅔ innings of work, though his old struggles with control resumed at Double-A. Short of secondary stuff in the past, his slider finally showed promise as part of his relief arsenal. He could be shoring up the big-league club's shaky pen with his 96-plus fastball by midseason, if not sooner.

Josh Beckett

Bats: R   Throws: R   Height: 6' 5"   Weight: 220   Born: May 15, 1980   Age: 29

YEAR	TEAM	LVL	AGE	W	L	SV	G	GS	IP	H	BB	SO	HR	GB%	BABIP	STUFF	WHIP	ERA	DERA	EqH9	EqBB9	EqSO9	EqHR9	DEF	VORP	SN/WX
2006	BOS	MLB	26	16	11	0	33	33	204²	191	73	158	36	46.4%	.265	-1	1.29	5.01	5.44	7.6	3.1	6.1	1.4	12	20.9	3.91
2007	BOS	MLB	27	20	7	0	30	30	200²	189	40	194	17	47.9%	.307	32	1.14	3.27	3.23	9.0	1.7	7.7	0.8	-1	59.9	6.17
2008	BOS	MLB	28	12	10	0	27	27	174¹	173	34	172	18	42.5%	.320	28	1.19	4.03	4.23	9.2	1.6	7.9	1.0	6	34.6	4.66
2009	BOS	MLB	29	13	8	0	29	29	190²	180	51	167	21	44.0%	.290	25	1.21	3.72	3.73	8.1	2.1	7.4	0.9	4	40.1	5.80

Breakout: 24%   Improve: 70%   Collapse: 7%   Attrition: 9%   Comparables: Turk Farrell, Larry Dierker, Mike Mussina, Len Barker

Both Beckett and the Red Sox denied that he was injured for much of the season, but it was apparent that something was amiss, as his velocity was often well below past averages; this was noticeable during the playoffs, when Beckett was topping out in the low 90s. He spent time on the DL in August with right elbow inflammation, but except for the velocity issue, he was effective upon his return. Despite the health issue, Beckett's season was much like his '07, when he was a legitimate Cy Young candidate, as his peripherals were almost identical; he stranded fewer runners but gave up a few more homers, and saw his ground-ball rate dip, with those balls in play becoming liners. Better luck in 2009 may be all he needs, but that dip in velocity is a bit disconcerting.

Michael Bowden

Bats: R   Throws: R   Height: 6' 3"   Weight: 215   Born: September 9, 1986   Age: 22

YEAR	TEAM	LVL	AGE	W	L	SV	G	GS	IP	H	BB	SO	HR	GB%	BABIP	STUFF	WHIP	ERA	DERA	EqH9	EqBB9	EqSO9	EqHR9	DEF	VORP	SN/WX
2006	GRN	A	19	9	6	0	24	24	107²	91	31	118	9	52.7%	.293	-14	1.14	3.53	7.91	12.6	4.2	5.0	2.3	5	-23.4	—
2007	LNC	A+	20	2	0	0	8	8	46	35	8	46	1	45.9%	.288	35	0.93	1.37	3.86	8.4	2.4	4.9	0.6	5	8.1	—
2007	PME	AA	20	8	6	0	19	19	96²	105	33	82	9	36.5%	.340	8	1.43	4.28	5.03	11.9	3.7	4.9	1.5	-12	5.6	—
2008	PME	AA	21	9	4	0	19	19	104¹	72	24	101	5	42.8%	.249	38	0.92	2.33	3.54	6.6	2.0	6.3	0.7	2	23.3	—
2008	PAW	AAA	21	0	3	0	7	6	40	40	5	29	5	38.3%	.296	13	1.13	3.38	5.35	10.7	1.5	4.4	1.7	4	1.0	—
2008	BOS	MLB	21	1	0	0	1	1	5	7	1	3	0	16.7%	.389	5	1.60	3.60	0.00	13.5	1.9	5.8	0.0	-2	1.3	0.18
2009	BOS	MLB	22	9	8	0	36	22	147¹	157	47	101	20	39.0%	.300	9	1.38	4.75	4.71	9.2	2.6	5.8	1.1	4	15.3	2.57

Breakout: 7%   Improve: 25%   Collapse: 22%   Attrition: 12%   Comparables: Kevin Slowey, Jeff Suppan, Larry Christenson, Don Robinson

The 2005 first-round pick was dominant at Double-A Portland, holding opposing batters to a .191 average and keeping his walk rate down near two per nine innings. He was not quite as impressive after his promotion to Pawtucket, suffering a steep drop in his strikeout rate and a corresponding rise in home runs allowed. On the other hand, his walk rate improved from stingy to downright penurious, and he wasn't embarrassed in his sole major league start. He needs to improve his changeup further to better complement his low-90s heat and sharp curve, but 2008 was a step in the right direction.

Clay Buchholz

Bats: L   Throws: R   Height: 6' 3"   Weight: 190   Born: August 14, 1984   Age: 24

YEAR	TEAM	LVL	AGE	W	L	SV	G	GS	IP	H	BB	SO	HR	GB%	BABIP	STUFF	WHIP	ERA	DERA	EqH9	EqBB9	EqSO9	EqHR9	DEF	VORP	SN/WX
2006	GRN	A	21	9	4	0	21	21	103	78	29	117	10	46.5%	.281	-14	1.04	2.62	5.88	11.8	4.2	5.4	2.6	4	-2.7	—
2006	WIL	A+	21	2	0	0	3	3	16¹	10	4	23	0	53.3%	.302	14	0.87	1.12	3.77	8.2	3.1	8.2	0.6	-1	2.9	—
2007	PME	AA	22	7	2	0	16	15	86²	55	22	116	4	46.9%	.276	37	0.89	1.76	3.25	7.3	2.7	8.3	0.8	3	21.0	—
2007	PAW	AAA	22	1	3	0	8	8	38²	32	13	55	5	47.4%	.318	20	1.16	3.95	7.05	9.2	3.4	9.0	1.7	4	-6.0	—
2007	BOS	MLB	22	3	1	0	4	3	22²	14	10	22	0	40.0%	.259	21	1.06	1.59	3.86	6.4	3.9	8.1	0.0	0	9.3	1.00
2008	PME	AA	23	1	0	0	2	2	15	7	1	18	0	53.1%	.255	15	0.53	1.80	4.20	4.2	0.6	7.8	0.0	2	2.3	—
2008	PAW	AAA	23	4	2	0	9	9	43²	36	17	43	3	41.7%	.303	6	1.21	2.47	4.89	9.8	4.2	6.3	0.9	6	3.1	—
2008	BOS	MLB	23	2	9	0	16	15	76	93	41	72	11	49.2%	.360	6	1.76	6.75	5.81	11.5	4.5	7.6	1.3	-9	-12.9	-0.19
2009	BOS	MLB	24	10	9	0	30	30	164²	163	73	146	17	45.0%	.310	21	1.43	4.56	4.56	8.5	3.5	7.4	0.9	4	19.3	3.38

Breakout: 44% Improve: 76% Collapse: 10% Attrition: 24%   Comparables: Pete Smith, Dennis Leonard, Don Cardwell, Len Barker

Things did not go quite so well this time around for Buchholz in the face of high expectations, though there is hope. His ERA is far off from his adjusted runs allowed numbers, as he stranded far fewer runners than is normal and had a much higher BABIP (.366) than expected, given his league-average liner tendencies. He also looked great in his nine starts at Pawtucket, whiffing just under a batter per inning while keeping his free passes in a tolerable range, and his stint in the Arizona Fall League also went well. As long as he can rein in his walk rate—even keeping it at the league average would be acceptable—he will be an asset to Boston's rotation.

Paul Byrd

Bats: R   Throws: R   Height: 6' 1"   Weight: 190   Born: December 3, 1970   Age: 38

YEAR	TEAM	LVL	AGE	W	L	SV	G	GS	IP	H	BB	SO	HR	GB%	BABIP	STUFF	WHIP	ERA	DERA	EqH9	EqBB9	EqSO9	EqHR9	DEF	VORP	SN/WX
2006	CLE	MLB	35	10	9	0	31	31	179	232	38	88	26	41.3%	.322	-10	1.51	4.88	5.63	10.7	1.8	3.8	1.2	-5	1.1	1.94
2007	CLE	MLB	36	15	8	0	31	31	192¹	239	28	88	27	40.1%	.313	-9	1.39	4.59	4.92	10.6	1.2	3.5	1.3	3	21.9	2.46
2008	CLE	MLB	37	7	10	0	22	22	131	146	24	56	23	38.2%	.281	-18	1.30	4.53	5.62	9.6	1.5	3.3	1.6	13	14.8	2.35
2008	BOS	MLB	37	4	2	0	8	8	49	58	10	26	8	35.3%	.311	-5	1.39	4.78	4.82	11.0	1.7	4.4	1.5	2	6.3	0.58
2009	BOS	MLB	38	7	7	0	28	19	121	147	29	53	17	40.0%	.300	-7	1.45	5.06	5.01	10.4	1.9	3.7	1.2	3	8.8	1.74

Breakout: 13% Improve: 40% Collapse: 28% Attrition: 31%   Comparables: Bob Forsch, Sid Hudson, Doyle Alexander, Murry Dickson

Byrd's ERA in 2008 may be almost identical to that of 2007, but looking a little deeper suggests that the 13-year vet may be on the way out. His home-run rate, already higher than was safe, given his pitch-to-contact style, increased further, and his BABIP was lower than it should have been, a blessing in the present that could haunt Byrd in the future. Lefties tomahawked him at a .317/.361/.529 clip, and he survived by holding right handers to a .283 OBP, but everybody hit him hard: left handers had an isolated power of .212, righties .169, and his overall ISO of .191 ranked ninth in the majors (150-innings-and-up division). As he heads into his age-38 season, the most to be hoped for is that Byrd continues to crank out innings at modest cost and doesn't decline any further from his already precarious position.

Bartolo Colon

Bats: R   Throws: R   Height: 5' 11"   Weight: 245   Born: May 24, 1973   Age: 36

YEAR	TEAM	LVL	AGE	W	L	SV	G	GS	IP	H	BB	SO	HR	GB%	BABIP	STUFF	WHIP	ERA	DERA	EqH9	EqBB9	EqSO9	EqHR9	DEF	VORP	SN/WX
2006	LAA	MLB	33	1	5	0	10	10	56¹	71	11	31	11	42.2%	.316	-12	1.46	5.12	6.11	11.1	1.8	4.3	1.6	1	-1.2	0.22
2007	LAA	MLB	34	6	8	0	19	18	99¹	132	29	76	15	42.3%	.364	-5	1.62	6.34	5.49	11.6	2.5	5.9	1.4	-10	-7.2	0.39
2008	BOS	MLB	35	4	2	0	7	7	39	44	10	27	5	42.5%	.315	4	1.38	3.92	5.03	10.1	2.1	5.3	1.1	0	2.7	0.35
2009	BOS	MLB	36	5	5	0	22	13	77¹	89	22	48	10	44.0%	.310	2	1.43	4.92	4.90	9.9	2.3	5.2	1.1	2	7.4	1.16

Breakout: 25% Improve: 53% Collapse: 23% Attrition: 40%   Comparables: Mike Garcia, Larry Jansen, Tiny Bonham, John Burkett

Colon was not half-bad during his time with the Red Sox, short though it was. His ERA was roughly a half-run better than it should have been, given his peripherals, and his velocity was roughly the same as it has been for the past few seasons with the Angels. The Red Sox took a chance on him in spring training, signing him despite a long history of physical problems and an equator-like waistline. Although they patiently nursed him through various injuries, Colon jumped the Sox in September because he was averse to pitching out of the bullpen. Though it has now been over three years since both Colon's Cy Young and his last healthy season, chances are he'll find another team to pay for another crash diet/rehab combo by March.

Manny Delcarmen

Bats: R   Throws: R   Height: 6' 2"   Weight: 190   Born: February 16, 1982   Age: 27

YEAR	TEAM	LVL	AGE	W	L	SV	G	GS	IP	H	BB	SO	HR	GB%	BABIP	STUFF	WHIP	ERA	DERA	EqH9	EqBB9	EqSO9	EqHR9	DEF	VORP	SN/WX
2006	BOS	MLB	24	2	0	0	50	0	53¹	68	17	45	2	46.9%	.382	6	1.59	5.07	4.39	10.8	2.7	6.8	0.3	-3	4.6	0.63
2007	PAW	AAA	25	3	2	0	20	0	29¹	28	14	37	1	46.8%	.351	6	1.43	3.38	4.55	10.4	4.6	8.1	0.7	-2	3.2	—
2007	BOS	MLB	25	0	0	1	44	0	44	28	17	41	4	47.4%	.222	7	1.02	2.05	4.15	6.0	3.3	7.3	0.8	9	18.6	1.62
2008	BOS	MLB	26	1	2	2	73	0	74¹	55	28	72	5	52.9%	.262	15	1.12	3.27	3.38	6.8	3.0	7.6	0.6	2	20.2	1.29
2009	BOS	MLB	27	3	2	3	53	0	58²	54	24	54	5	47.0%	.300	15	1.33	3.59	3.65	7.9	3.3	7.7	0.7	1	14.3	1.19

Breakout: 25%   Improve: 53%   Collapse: 17%   Attrition: 12%   Comparables: Greg Harris, Bill Campbell, Dave Smith, Jose Paniagua

Though Delcarmen's ERA was not as shiny as it was in 2007, his overall performance improved, with slightly more of the good stuff (strikeouts, grounders) and a little less of the bad (walks, homers). His strand rate returned to the realm of mortals, which was the reason for the large shift in his stats. It's tough to project relievers, but given Delcarmen's solid peripherals and pure stuff, he should be able to deliver another successful campaign in 2009.

Devern Hansack

Bats: R   Throws: R   Height: 6' 2"   Weight: 185   Born: February 5, 1978   Age: 31

YEAR	TEAM	LVL	AGE	W	L	SV	G	GS	IP	H	BB	SO	HR	GB%	BABIP	STUFF	WHIP	ERA	DERA	EqH9	EqBB9	EqSO9	EqHR9	DEF	VORP	SN/WX
2006	PME	AA	28	8	7	1	31	18	132	122	36	124	14	40.4%	.287	-27	1.20	3.27	5.88	11.2	3.2	5.1	1.8	3	-3.7	—
2006	BOS	MLB	28	1	1	0	2	2	10	6	1	8	2	48.1%	.160	10	0.70	2.70	4.50	4.5	0.9	6.3	1.8	2	3.8	0.44
2007	PAW	AAA	29	10	7	0	25	23	139²	126	40	131	16	43.3%	.292	-12	1.19	3.61	6.06	9.7	2.9	5.9	1.7	14	-6.7	—
2007	BOS	MLB	29	0	1	0	3	1	7²	9	5	5	2	46.4%	.269	-10	1.83	4.68	4.50	10.1	5.6	4.5	2.2	-1	0.2	-0.05
2008	PAW	AAA	30	6	10	0	25	25	139	123	41	128	16	39.8%	.276	-9	1.18	4.08	5.41	9.9	3.0	5.7	1.5	2	2.7	—
2008	BOS	MLB	30	1	0	0	4	0	6²	6	1	5	0	45.0%	.316	6	1.05	4.03	4.26	8.5	1.4	5.7	0.0	-2	-0.5	0.13
2009	BOS	MLB	31	4	5	0	28	11	80²	94	31	56	14	40.0%	.310	1	1.54	5.70	5.56	10.0	3.1	5.8	1.4	2	0.8	0.49

Breakout: 12%   Improve: 38%   Collapse: 39%   Attrition: 32%   Comparables: Josias Manzanillo, Ramon Ortiz, Mike Gardiner, Derek Botelho

Given the problems the Sox experienced with their bullpen, it's surprising that Hansack has not been given more of a role. He has thrown 24⅓ innings in the majors, with 18 strikeouts against seven walks; the sample is small, but he has shown promise in the minors, and his fastball/slider combination lends itself well to relief, especially to help out a pen as dilapidated as that of Boston's.

Kris Johnson

Bats: L   Throws: L   Height: 6' 4"   Weight: 170   Born: October 14, 1984   Age: 24

YEAR	TEAM	LVL	AGE	W	L	SV	G	GS	IP	H	BB	SO	HR	GB%	BABIP	STUFF	WHIP	ERA	DERA	EqH9	EqBB9	EqSO9	EqHR9	DEF	VORP	SN/WX
2006	LOW	A-	21	0	2	0	14	13	30²	25	7	27	0	63.4%	.305	-5	1.06	0.89	4.74	11.7	4.0	3.6	0.7	-1	2.4	—
2007	LNC	A+	22	9	7	0	27	27	136	148	57	100	20	46.5%	.305	-46	1.51	5.56	8.43	12.1	4.9	3.2	2.2	13	-38.3	—
2008	PME	AA	23	8	9	0	27	27	136¹	147	56	108	5	51.1%	.333	9	1.49	3.63	4.93	10.7	3.6	5.1	0.6	-7	9.7	—
2009	BOS	MLB	24	6	8	0	29	19	113¹	144	56	67	14	47.0%	.330	-1	1.76	6.22	6.16	10.9	3.9	5.0	1.1	3	-6.7	0.10

Breakout: 11%   Improve: 36%   Collapse: 22%   Attrition: 18%   Comparables: Matt Young, Mike Milchin, Zach Jackson, Danny Borrell

Johnson underwent Tommy John surgery back in 2005, and his curveball has yet to recover, leaving him to use his fastball and changeup as his go-to pitches. His 2008 season provided some progress, as a promotion to Double-A Portland saw him increase his strikeout rate while lopping an entire homer per nine off (though leaving Lancaster behind may have a lot to do with the latter). His future will be in relief unless the curveball reemerges.

Jon Lester

Bats: L   Throws: L   Height: 6' 2"   Weight: 190   Born: January 7, 1984   Age: 25

YEAR	TEAM	LVL	AGE	W	L	SV	G	GS	IP	H	BB	SO	HR	GB%	BABIP	STUFF	WHIP	ERA	DERA	EqH9	EqBB9	EqSO9	EqHR9	DEF	VORP	SN/WX
2006	PAW	AAA	22	3	4	0	11	11	46	43	25	43	5	43.9%	.290	-1	1.48	2.74	5.28	9.7	5.5	5.5	1.6	3	1.6	—
2006	BOS	MLB	22	7	2	0	15	15	81¹	91	43	60	7	40.5%	.347	17	1.65	4.76	4.23	9.7	4.7	5.9	0.7	-2	12.8	1.77
2007	PAW	AAA	23	4	5	0	14	14	71²	67	31	51	4	45.9%	.296	-5	1.37	3.89	5.02	9.8	4.3	4.2	0.9	-1	4.3	—
2007	BOS	MLB	23	4	0	0	12	11	63	61	31	50	10	35.8%	.288	-1	1.46	4.57	5.46	9.3	4.1	6.3	1.5	7	9.5	1.14
2008	BOS	MLB	24	16	6	0	33	33	210¹	202	66	152	14	50.0%	.302	21	1.27	3.21	3.54	9.0	2.7	5.9	0.6	8	59.6	6.32
2009	BOS	MLB	25	10	8	0	27	27	162	171	62	114	18	45.0%	.300	14	1.44	4.45	4.45	9.1	3.1	5.9	0.9	4	22.2	3.57

Breakout: 4%   Improve: 21%   Collapse: 38%   Attrition: 9%   Comparables: Bob Knepper, Noah Lowry, Tom Gorzelanny, Jim O'Toole

Lester *arrived* in 2008, serving notice with his May 19 no-hitter against the Royals that he had become the pitcher many thought he could be back when he was breezing through the minors. His velocity rocketed back to its precancer level, while his command finally blossomed at the major league level (its belated manifestation not being atypical of young southpaws). Lester's brush with mortality and subsequent success is just the latest example of baseball's being a game of redeeming features and makes the 25-year-old one of the easiest players in the game to root for, regardless of team preference. Assuming he maintains his control, Lester should continue to reward his well-wishers in coming seasons.

Javier Lopez — Bats: L — Throws: L — Height: 6' 4" — Weight: 220 — Born: July 11, 1977 — Age: 31

YEAR	TEAM	LVL	AGE	W	L	SV	G	GS	IP	H	BB	SO	HR	GB%	BABIP	STUFF	WHIP	ERA	DERA	EqH9	EqBB9	EqSO9	EqHR9	DEF	VORP	SN/WX
2006	CHR	AAA	28	2	1	12	26	0	33	28	6	26	1	73.1%	.293	-1	1.03	0.55	1.88	10.0	2.2	5.0	0.6	1	11.9	—
2006	PAW	AAA	28	0	0	4	13	0	16	20	8	12	1	61.4%	.352	-25	1.75	5.06	6.32	12.1	5.2	4.0	1.1	-2	-1.3	—
2006	BOS	MLB	28	1	0	1	27	0	16²	13	10	11	1	67.4%	.273	-10	1.38	2.69	5.87	7.0	5.9	5.9	0.6	2	1.5	0.82
2007	PAW	AAA	29	2	1	0	17	0	16²	19	8	15	0	70.6%	.396	-10	1.62	3.77	5.40	12.6	4.8	5.4	0.0	1	0.3	—
2007	BOS	MLB	29	2	1	0	61	0	40²	36	18	26	2	53.2%	.279	-9	1.33	3.10	4.62	8.5	3.9	5.1	0.5	5	11.5	0.44
2008	BOS	MLB	30	2	0	0	70	0	59¹	53	27	38	4	60.6%	.282	-5	1.35	2.43	3.05	8.5	3.9	5.3	0.6	3	20.5	1.60
2009	BOS	MLB	31	2	2	1	51	0	45²	49	21	29	3	55.0%	.310	-3	1.52	4.33	4.45	9.2	3.7	5.3	0.5	1	6.5	0.53

Breakout: 5% — Improve: 22% — Collapse: 53% — Attrition: 23% — Comparables: Ray King, Jay Powell, Buddy Groom, Juan Agosto

Lopez finished second on the Red Sox in WXRL, a surprising development that says far more about the state of Boston's depleted pen than it does about the merits of the lefty spot reliever. Lopez doesn't strike out many hitters, walks more than his fair share, and cannot stop right handers from crushing him. Lefties found him unhittable, failing to a .182/.305/.282 beat and batting just .217 when they put the ball in play. Keeping the ball on the ground helped (his 2.7 G/F was his highest over a full season), as did strong support from the many pitchers who followed him—as a LOOGY who either got his man or was pulled, Lopez bequeathed the ninth-most baserunners in the majors last year. This is an overlooked aspect of bullpen strategy: successful use of a pitcher like Lopez requires quality righties to follow him, because 20 to 30 percent of the time, the southpaw is going to fail and force another pitching change.

Justin Masterson — Bats: R — Throws: R — Height: 6' 6" — Weight: 250 — Born: March 22, 1985 — Age: 24

YEAR	TEAM	LVL	AGE	W	L	SV	G	GS	IP	H	BB	SO	HR	GB%	BABIP	STUFF	WHIP	ERA	DERA	EqH9	EqBB9	EqSO9	EqHR9	DEF	VORP	SN/WX
2006	LOW	A-	21	3	1	0	14	0	31	20	2	33	0	74.4%	.244	13	0.71	0.87	3.45	8.5	1.6	4.1	0.6	1	6.9	—
2007	LNC	A+	22	8	5	0	17	17	95²	103	22	56	4	54.9%	.314	-11	1.31	4.33	6.65	11.1	2.8	2.2	0.8	1	-10.4	—
2007	PME	AA	22	4	3	0	10	10	58	49	18	59	4	68.3%	.297	14	1.16	4.34	5.96	9.1	3.3	6.0	1.2	0	-2.2	—
2008	PME	AA	23	1	3	0	8	8	38¹	37	16	37	0	68.1%	.330	13	1.38	4.23	5.06	9.4	3.6	6.3	0.2	-4	2.2	—
2008	BOS	MLB	23	6	5	0	36	9	88¹	68	40	68	10	55.0%	.245	2	1.22	3.16	4.46	7.2	3.8	6.3	1.1	14	26.7	2.66
2009	BOS	MLB	24	7	6	1	37	16	107¹	109	44	80	9	53.0%	.300	10	1.43	4.20	4.28	8.7	3.3	6.3	0.7	3	17.2	2.30

Breakout: 16% — Improve: 45% — Collapse: 22% — Attrition: 15% — Comparables: Josh Johnson, Mark Gubicza, Jim Gott, Jim Lonborg

Masterson was serviceable as a starter, though 28 walks over 54 innings is a bit much, even for a side-arming ground-ball specialist. Relief was where he shone, with 7.6 whiffs and 3.1 walks per nine over his 27 appearances. Still, perhaps the greatest share of his success was due to delivery that rings up righties, limiting them to just .196/.274/.298. He was also successful against left-handed hitters, but although southpaw swingers hit only .238, too many of their hits went for extra bases. This raises an interesting question for Masterson's future: he was more effective as a reliever, but he has the endurance to start, and as a starter, the impact of the occasional home run allowed to a left hander would be diminished. Masterson's current lack of a reliable third pitch may ultimately resolve this question in favor of the bullpen.

Daisuke Matsuzaka

| | Bats: R | Throws: R | Height: 6' 0" | Weight: 190 | Born: September 13, 1980 | Age: 28 |

YEAR	TEAM	LVL	AGE	W	L	SV	G	GS	IP	H	BB	SO	HR	GB%	BABIP	STUFF	WHIP	ERA	DERA	EqH9	EqBB9	EqSO9	EqHR9	DEF	VORP	SN/WX
2007	BOS	MLB	26	15	12	0	32	32	204²	191	80	201	25	39.3%	.302	17	1.32	4.40	4.29	9.0	3.4	7.9	1.1	4	38.3	5.01
2008	BOS	MLB	27	18	3	0	29	29	167²	128	94	154	12	39.5%	.262	26	1.32	2.90	3.87	7.1	4.6	7.3	0.7	16	51.4	5.83
2009	BOS	MLB	28	10	8	0	26	26	155	145	67	135	18	40.0%	.290	21	1.37	4.32	4.29	8.1	3.5	7.3	1.0	3	22.4	3.67

Breakout: 3%   Improve: 28%   Collapse: 33%   Attrition: 18%   Comparables: Andy Messersmith, Chan Ho Park, Juan Guzman, Bob Gibson

Dice-K was maddening last season, brilliant at times while shutting down the opposition for innings at a time, yet each frame seemed like watching the ninth of an important game with an unreliable closer on the mound, as Matsuzaka would nibble with pitch after pitch rather than putting the hitters away or forcing them into contact. His P/PA increased, as did his walk rate, but fewer home runs and a low BABIP helped him survive that. Dice-K stranded nearly 81 percent of his baserunners, thanks to a .164/.285/.288 line with runners in scoring position. Relying on both that and his BABIP to hold up in '09 is just asking for trouble.

Hideki Okajima

| | Bats: L | Throws: L | Height: 6' 1" | Weight: 194 | Born: December 25, 1975 | Age: 33 |

YEAR	TEAM	LVL	AGE	W	L	SV	G	GS	IP	H	BB	SO	HR	GB%	BABIP	STUFF	WHIP	ERA	DERA	EqH9	EqBB9	EqSO9	EqHR9	DEF	VORP	SN/WX
2007	BOS	MLB	31	3	2	5	66	0	69	50	17	63	6	47.1%	.246	12	0.97	2.22	3.84	6.8	2.1	7.3	0.8	12	29.5	4.47
2008	BOS	MLB	32	3	2	1	64	0	62	49	23	60	6	35.1%	.261	9	1.16	2.61	3.90	7.1	3.0	7.5	0.9	9	22.1	1.31
2009	BOS	MLB	33	3	2	3	56	0	54²	52	20	48	6	41.0%	.290	11	1.31	3.72	3.74	8.1	3.0	7.4	0.9	1	11.9	1.07

Breakout: 11%   Improve: 24%   Collapse: 43%   Attrition: 17%   Comparables: Mike Stanton, Jesse Orosco, Tug McGraw, Ricardo Rincon

Okajima appeared fatigued when the year began, and it did not help things that the opposition was not falling for the deceptive movement on his splitter/changeup hybrid as much as they had when first introduced to it. Okajima adjusted by throwing "the Oki Doke" less often, instead mixing in a few more fastballs and many more curveballs. When all was said and done, Okajima's campaign looked much the same as '07 as far as peripherals, though his G/F ratio dropped; at least his homer rate did not increase much, despite the large bump in fly balls. Were the long ball to become an issue after his nearly two-thirds drop in WXRL from one year to the next, his value would become mostly speculative.

Jonathan Papelbon

| | Bats: R | Throws: R | Height: 6' 4" | Weight: 230 | Born: November 23, 1980 | Age: 28 |

YEAR	TEAM	LVL	AGE	W	L	SV	G	GS	IP	H	BB	SO	HR	GB%	BABIP	STUFF	WHIP	ERA	DERA	EqH9	EqBB9	EqSO9	EqHR9	DEF	VORP	SN/WX
2006	BOS	MLB	25	4	2	35	59	0	68¹	40	13	75	3	38.7%	.228	34	0.78	0.92	1.96	4.7	1.7	8.5	0.4	6	38.6	6.74
2007	BOS	MLB	26	1	3	37	59	0	58¹	30	15	84	5	28.9%	.216	31	0.77	1.85	2.97	5.3	2.2	10.0	0.8	7	27.2	5.10
2008	BOS	MLB	27	5	4	41	67	0	69¹	58	8	77	4	51.1%	.302	30	0.95	2.34	3.13	7.7	0.9	8.7	0.5	1	20.9	3.22
2009	BOS	MLB	28	5	4	33	54	0	61¹	47	15	67	5	43.0%	.270	29	1.01	2.49	2.56	6.6	1.9	9.2	0.7	1	22.9	3.54

Breakout: 16%   Improve: 21%   Collapse: 40%   Attrition: 11%   Comparables: Eric Gagné, Bryan Harvey, Roberto Hernandez, Dick Radatz

At times, Papelbon is a one-pitch closer, since he mostly throws fastballs, with only the occasional splitter to finish off a hitter. That trend was even more pronounced in 2008, as Papelbon threw even more fastballs, partly to combat the lack of swings and misses on splitters in the dirt. His declining strikeout rate reflects the change in hitters' approaches to the pitch, but he compensated by dramatically improving his ground-ball rate. The dip in splitters and wasted pitches dropped his pitches per plate appearance from 4.1 to 3.8, which also helped him lower his walk rate. As long as he displays this level of control, Sox fans will have nothing to worry about.

David Pauley

Bats: R **Throws: R** **Height: 6′ 2″** **Weight: 185** **Born: June 17, 1983** **Age: 26**

YEAR	TEAM	LVL	AGE	W	L	SV	G	GS	IP	H	BB	SO	HR	GB%	BABIP	STUFF	WHIP	ERA	DERA	EqH9	EqBB9	EqSO9	EqHR9	DEF	VORP	SN/WX
2006	PME	AA	23	2	3	0	10	10	60²	54	17	47	6	54.7%	.291	-13	1.18	2.39	4.92	11.0	3.4	4.1	1.7	2	4.0	—
2006	PAW	AAA	23	1	3	0	9	9	50²	60	18	25	10	50.3%	.307	-46	1.55	5.56	9.20	12.7	3.9	2.5	2.9	-1	-18.4	—
2006	BOS	MLB	23	0	2	0	3	3	16	31	6	10	1	46.9%	.476	-3	2.31	7.88	4.20	18.0	3.6	5.4	0.6	-6	-3.0	-0.06
2007	PAW	AAA	24	6	6	0	27	26	153²	164	49	110	18	55.3%	.304	-26	1.39	4.33	6.81	11.1	3.2	4.1	1.7	4	-19.5	—
2008	PAW	AAA	25	14	4	0	25	25	147	147	41	103	10	52.4%	.308	-5	1.28	3.55	5.51	10.9	3.0	4.2	0.9	8	1.3	—
2008	BOS	MLB	25	0	1	0	6	2	12¹	23	5	11	2	44.0%	.447	-13	2.27	11.71	7.11	16.3	3.6	7.1	1.4	-6	-8.5	-0.38
2009	BOS	MLB	26	6	8	0	34	18	115¹	153	48	59	17	48.0%	.330	-8	1.74	6.47	6.39	11.4	3.3	4.3	1.2	3	-9.9	-0.29

Breakout: 10% Improve: 45% Collapse: 18% Attrition: 16% Comparables: *Tim Harikkala, Kevin Jarvis, Ed Wojna, Mike Birkbeck*

Pauley is one of Boston's "Break Glass in Case of Emergency" starters in Pawtucket, and he was called up for the first time since 2006, with predictably disastrous results. He has been average at best in Pawtucket—those 2008 numbers lose a bit of their gloss when you realize this is his third go-round in Rhode Island. Yes, Pauley has barely been given a sniff of the majors during his time in the organization, but between his ho-hum minor league campaigns and his awful stints in Boston, he has not earned much more than that.

Chris Smith

Bats: R **Throws: R** **Height: 6′ 2″** **Weight: 200** **Born: April 9, 1981** **Age: 28**

YEAR	TEAM	LVL	AGE	W	L	SV	G	GS	IP	H	BB	SO	HR	GB%	BABIP	STUFF	WHIP	ERA	DERA	EqH9	EqBB9	EqSO9	EqHR9	DEF	VORP	SN/WX
2006	PME	AA	25	9	6	0	20	20	115	114	29	78	9	47.7%	.295	-23	1.24	4.07	6.73	11.4	3.0	3.2	1.4	2	-13.3	—
2006	PAW	AAA	25	1	1	0	7	6	33	33	9	23	2	36.0%	.290	-12	1.27	3.27	6.61	9.6	2.8	3.9	0.8	3	-3.7	—
2007	PME	AA	26	6	9	1	30	14	104	126	42	80	10	42.3%	.365	-31	1.62	4.41	5.09	13.6	4.4	4.4	1.7	-15	5.2	—
2008	PAW	AAA	27	1	5	15	37	4	59¹	54	11	52	6	44.8%	.291	-10	1.10	3.19	4.45	10.0	2.0	5.4	1.3	2	7.0	—
2008	BOS	MLB	27	1	0	0	12	0	18¹	18	7	13	6	27.6%	.240	-25	1.36	7.87	8.00	9.0	3.0	5.5	3.0	2	-4.0	-0.01
2009	MIL	MLB	28	3	4	1	40	5	55²	68	22	39	10	40.0%	.320	-5	1.60	5.56	5.78	11.0	2.9	5.2	1.6	1	0.1	0.16

Breakout: 20% Improve: 57% Collapse: 16% Attrition: 23% Comparables: *Brian Sanches, Steve Montgomery, Jason Rakers, Jim Austin*

Another victim of the team's decision to almost randomly sort through relievers in the bottom of their bullpen, Smith is a soft-tossing right hander who complements his fastball with a slider and a change. This combination was not enough to keep the Sox' attention, as the team designated him for assignment in October. He elected to become a free agent rather than return to the minors.

Tim Wakefield

Bats: R **Throws: R** **Height: 6′ 2″** **Weight: 210** **Born: August 2, 1966** **Age: 42**

YEAR	TEAM	LVL	AGE	W	L	SV	G	GS	IP	H	BB	SO	HR	GB%	BABIP	STUFF	WHIP	ERA	DERA	EqH9	EqBB9	EqSO9	EqHR9	DEF	VORP	SN/WX
2006	BOS	MLB	39	7	11	0	23	23	140	135	51	90	19	40.1%	.266	0	1.33	4.63	5.65	7.7	3.1	4.9	1.1	13	16.1	2.11
2007	BOS	MLB	40	17	12	0	31	31	189	191	64	110	22	40.8%	.285	-3	1.35	4.76	5.31	9.6	2.9	4.7	1.1	14	24.1	3.86
2008	BOS	MLB	41	10	11	0	30	30	181	154	60	117	25	36.2%	.242	-1	1.18	4.13	5.44	7.7	2.7	5.1	1.3	24	29.8	4.17
2009	BOS	MLB	42	6	6	0	17	17	97²	105	34	61	13	39.0%	.290	5	1.43	4.98	4.93	9.3	2.8	5.2	1.2	2	9.5	1.59

Breakout: 8% Improve: 35% Collapse: 18% Attrition: 42% Comparables: *Phil Niekro, Charlie Hough, Early Wynn, Don Sutton*

In 2008, Wakefield was the same pitcher he has been in recent seasons, with enough butterfly-induced strikeouts to get by and lower walk totals than in his younger days. Though the arm of a knuckleballer may seem as if it should last forever, shoulder tendonitis caused him problems in August. The Sox picked up his perpetual $4 million option for 2009—even with back and shoulder issues, Wake's contract makes him an inexpensive proposition to stock the back end of the rotation with. There have been whispers of a possible retirement this winter, but they have become nothing more than that as of press time.

Charlie Zink

Bats: R   Throws: R   Height: 6' 1"   Weight: 190   Born: August 26, 1979   Age: 29

YEAR	TEAM	LVL	AGE	W	L	SV	G	GS	IP	H	BB	SO	HR	GB%	BABIP	STUFF	WHIP	ERA	DERA	EqH9	EqBB9	EqSO9	EqHR9	DEF	VORP	SN/WX
2006	PAW	AAA	26	9	4	0	23	15	109¹	100	60	58	7	44.2%	.274	-19	1.47	4.04	6.93	9.4	5.8	2.9	1.1	11	-14.8	—
2007	PME	AA	27	9	3	0	16	16	92²	92	44	55	6	53.1%	.293	-19	1.47	3.98	6.67	10.4	4.9	3.1	1.2	2	-10.1	—
2007	PAW	AAA	27	2	3	0	8	8	47¹	51	27	23	8	42.6%	.269	-41	1.65	5.90	10.17	10.8	5.3	2.3	2.3	8	-23.4	—
2008	PAW	AAA	28	14	6	0	28	28	174¹	144	49	106	13	43.1%	.252	-8	1.11	2.84	5.98	8.6	2.8	3.4	1.0	26	-7.0	—
2008	BOS	MLB	28	0	0	0	1	1	4¹	11	1	1	0	39.1%	.478	-39	2.77	16.74	8.31	22.8	2.1	2.1	0.0	-4	-4.8	-0.21
2009	BOS	MLB	29	5	8	0	29	19	112²	141	52	51	16	42.0%	.310	-11	1.72	6.41	6.32	10.8	3.7	3.8	1.2	3	-8.2	-0.12

Breakout: 11%   Improve: 46%   Collapse: 21%   Attrition: 13%   Comparables: Jerry Reed, Henry Bonilla, Dave Johnson, Reid Cornelius

Though blooming a bit late at the age of 29, Zink is a knuckleballer, after all, and the rules that apply to all other pitchers just don't apply to the breed. He had his most successful campaign in what seems like ages, as he more than cut his walk and homer rates in half while tacking on nearly a full strikeout per nine. His sole major league start was less encouraging and, given the skepticism with which knuckleballers must contend, may serve to keep him buried. Still, Zink is back in the picture as a potential major league pitcher; he only awaits a team desperate enough to give him a sustained opportunity.

LINEOUTS

Hitters

PLAYER	TEAM	LVL	AGE	PA	R	2B	3B	HR	RBI	BB	SO	SB-CS	EqBRR	AVG/OBP/SLG	EqAVG/EqOBP/EqSLG	EqA	VORP	WARP
3B M. Almanzar	RSX	Rk	17	99	16	6	1	1	11	8	15	3-3	-1.5	.348/.414/.472	.237/.283/.333	.209	-11.6	-0.3
	GRN	A	17	147	12	5	2	2	11	5	39	0-1	-2.4	.207/.238/.314	.170/.197/.270	.141	-18.4	-1.1
SS A. Diaz	LNC	A+	21	282	31	9	6	0	29	20	60	3-2	-0.4	.281/.330/.363	.192/.241/.258	.169	-27.3	-2.8
	PME	AA	21	153	20	8	2	2	23	10	30	0-1	0.2	.288/.336/.417	.270/.314/.418	.251	1.9	0.5
C L. Exposito	GRN	A	21	204	34	8	1	11	31	12	42	1-1	-1.4	.283/.328/.508	.223/.265/.415	.226	-4.8	-0.5
	LNC	A+	21	239	31	13	2	10	37	9	47	0-1	-1.9	.301/.331/.509	.218/.246/.389	.213	-10.1	0.4
3B W. Middlebrooks	LOW	A-	19	226	21	17	2	1	21	12	73	10-0	0.7	.254/.298/.368	.202/.236/.305	.189	-36.7	-2.7
SS Y. Navarro	GRN	A	20	361	46	14	4	7	54	29	73	3-2	0.2	.280/.341/.412	.224/.279/.347	.218	-15.1	-0.8
	LNC	A+	20	196	33	13	2	4	23	12	30	3-2	-0.5	.348/.393/.508	.250/.291/.386	.233	-2.9	-0.8
SS O. Tejeda	GRN	A	18	396	44	18	1	4	38	20	76	11-5	-1.2	.261/.301/.347	.207/.242/.285	.179	-35.5	-5.4
INF G. Velazquez	PAW	AAA	28	386	54	17	4	10	46	22	73	3-3	-0.9	.260/.310/.417	.205/.251/.340	.203	-23.2	-1.3
C M. Wagner	PME	AA	24	393	44	19	0	10	48	38	78	0-0	0.7	.219/.304/.363	.195/.270/.327	.210	-22.5	0.0

Another in what has turned into a long line of raw, teenage players up the middle in the organization, **Michael Almanzar** is an elite talent signed out of the Dominican Baseball Academy in 2007. He tore up the GCL for the short time he was there, but was humbled by the Sally League. Rushed, he remains a prospect with a very high ceiling. ⊘ Aggressive at the plate and afield, free-swinging **Argenis Diaz** is a bare step ahead of the other shortstop prospects in the organization, and with the Fermin suite of skills, he's not a big-time upside guy. ⊘ **Luis Exposito's** strike zone judgment needs some serious tuning, and curveballs occasionally give him trouble, but his power is promising, and catchers who can hit are always in fashion. ⊘ A sleeper in the Boston system, '07 fifth-rounder **Will Middlebrooks** has the ability to an above-average fielder thanks to a strong arm and solid range, but his bat did not show the same kind of development during his first year as a pro. ⊘ Defensively gifted shortstop **Yamaico Navarro** can be overly aggressive at the plate, but he managed to drop his punchouts a bit at Lancaster in 2008. His walks also fell though, and much of his slugging bump was just batting average. Luckily, he has a swing that generates liners, so expect at least doubles power in his future. ⊘ **Oscar Tejeda** has the tools, but are they ever raw: he has speed, but is not good at swiping bases, and he has potential at the plate, but his unrefined command of the zone is keeping him back. Once Navarro was promoted to Lancaster, Tejeda took on shortstop duties full-time, allowing him to focus on his primary position rather than wherever they had room for him that day. ⊘ **Gil Velazquez** was on the Sox roster twice, once to replace Colon, once when Lowell was taken off of the playoff roster; he's 29 and holds career minor league rates of .230/.290/.308. His 15 minutes have now come and gone. ⊘ Whether the Red Sox sort out their catching situation at the highest level or not, slick-fielding **Mark Wagner** is going to have to bounce back from the second-half slump that nearly killed his prospect status last summer.

Pitchers

PLAYER	TEAM	LVL	AGE	W	L	SV	IP	H	BB	SO	HR	GB%	BABIP	STUFF	WHIP	ERA	DERA	EqH9	EqBB9	EqSO9	EqHR9	DEF	VORP
F. Doubront*	GRN	A	20	12	8	0	115¹	115	24	118	9	45.9%	.337	0	1.21	3.67	5.76	12.4	3.1	4.8	1.8	-8	-1.8
	LNC	A+	20	1	1	0	14	15	4	20	1	40.6%	.373	12	1.36	3.86	0.75	13.5	3.8	8.2	1.5	-6	6.5
N. Hagadone*	GRN	A	22	1	1	0	10	5	6	12	0	68.0%	.200	7	1.10	0.00	4.50	5.4	6.3	5.4	0.0	0	1.2
H. Jones*	PME	AA	24	0	1	4	22²	21	4	26	0	61.9%	.344	21	1.10	1.19	1.61	9.3	1.6	7.3	0.0	-1	9.9
	PAW	AAA	24	7	2	8	50²	55	14	50	3	42.4%	.349	-2	1.36	3.02	2.91	12.2	2.9	6.2	0.8	-7	13.8
K. Snyder	PAW	AAA	30	1	4	1	37²	34	12	30	5	41.3%	.280	-22	1.22	5.25	7.68	9.7	3.2	4.5	1.7	5	-8.4
M. Timlin	BOS	MLB	42	4	4	1	49¹	60	20	32	9	44.8%	.323	-23	1.62	5.66	4.74	10.9	3.3	5.1	1.6	-4	0.3

A stick-thin Venezuelan lefty, **Felix Doubront** was the best performer in Greenville's rotation, changing speeds effectively with an easy delivery and pitching his way onto the 40-man roster. ⊘ A sandwich-round pick in '07, **Nick Hagadone** impressed in early camps and during spring training, but Tommy John surgery in April derailed his season. Prior to the injury, he had solid control and fantastic velocity for a left-hander, hitting the mid-90s. He may be able to return to the mound in High-A by May. ⊘ "LOOGY prospect" sounds more like an oxymoron than a dubious compliment, but **Hunter Jones** is a big-bodied lefty with adequate velocity and pitched his way onto the 40-man after signing as a non-drafted free agent. ⊘ Designated for assignment early on, **Kyle Snyder** never did much of anything at Pawtucket to inspire a recall, a bad sign for a veteran pitcher. Minor league free agency most likely brings his time with the Red Sox to a close. ⊘ Much-touted Japanese amateur **Junichi Tazawa** signed on with Boston in December for a $3 million, three-year big-league deal which translates into an accelerated developmental timetable; hopefully his low-90s heat, splitter, and change are as good as advertised. ⊘ Finally relied on for the low-leverage situations he should have been reserved for the last few years, **Mike Timlin** was nevertheless terrible when he wasn't spending time on the DL for various minor injuries. The sink on his fastball has not been as pronounced since 2006, which in turn has dropped his ground-ball rates; without the grounders, Timlin's utility is nonexistent.

MANAGER: TERRY FRANCONA

YEAR	TEAM	W-L	Pythag +/-	Avg PC	100+ P	120+ P	QS	BQS	REL	REL w Zero R	IBB	Subs	PH	PH Avg	PH HR	SB2	CS2	SB3	CS3	SAC Att	SAC %	POS SAC	Squeeze	Swing	In Play
2006	BOS	86-76	5	95.6	64	2	67	11	453	263	25	71	93	.221	0	46	22	5	1	39	56.4%	22	0	126	106
2007	BOS	96-66	-7	97.9	68	4	81	10	451	323	20	43	83	.203	0	83	20	13	4	54	55.6%	30	3	149	100
2000	BOS	95-67	-2	95.9	69	1	78	10	466	298	17	52	60	.236	2	99	32	21	2	48	58.3%	27	0	114	90

The idea that Tito is the most successful manager in Red Sox history continues to build up a head of steam. He handled the bullpen very well, considering it lacked depth, but the poorer pitchers were used in the lowest of low-leverage situations, while his better relievers were utilized to good effect, and he's not afraid to have former starters like Papelbon or Masterson work longer than most managers lean on their key relievers. As far as offensive tactics, Francona is sabermetrically sensible, not bunting much or getting too cute; the three speedsters (Ellsbury, Crisp, and Lugo) get the green light, along with Pedroia, but everyone else sits still. If there's a cause for complaint, it's that Varitek was not lifted for a pinch-hitter once during the regular season, although he was pulled three times in October. This may not be an issue in 2009 (depending on where Tek winds up), but it points to Francona's over-committed loyalty to certain players. Given the weight of the pros versus that single con, it's difficult to complain about his performance, let alone the results.

Chicago Cubs

It's easy to understate the challenge of winning with a team that's supposed to win. For example, the Braves and Mets haven't won lately, despite considerable financial commitments, and just look at what was expected of the "thousand-runs" Tigers in 2008. Certainly, the disappointment of consecutive quick exits from the Division Series puts a bit of a damper on expectations that the Cubs would bring on the eschaton with their first title in a century. Nevertheless, in terms of execution and results, and in light of the crapshoot that postseason matchups can be, it should be taken at face value that the Cubs aimed to win now, and by a reasonable standard drawn in broad strokes, they have.

In the money the Cubs have committed in recent seasons to a crew of win-now veteran players in their late primes and a win-now skipper also on the downslope of an exceptional career, the old canard that the Cubs might merely play at relevance while really just settling in to reap their Wrigley riches seems as dead as Julius Caesar. As conspiracy theories went, that was always an overdrawn caricature of the days of Ed Lynch or Andy MacPhail, Dallas Green or Don Grenesko, crafted by people investing too much time watching *The X Files*. There was no shakedown conspiracy, just bad plans or poorly executed ones. And where the Cubs used to have to settle for unusual combinations of events to make a run at a pennant, it is to the credit of everyone from Jim Hendry on down that this team is nothing like those fitful forays. Where MacPhail might have hemmed and hawed over grabbing Gary Gaetti in 1998 to fix an obvious lineup problem, Hendry moved on Jim Edmonds in May when the opportunity arose; when the Brewers acquired C. C. Sabathia in July, Hendry promptly dealt a backlog of

---

CUBS PROSPECTUS

2008 record: 97-64; First place, NL Central

Pythagenport record: 99-62

Runs scored per game: 5.32 (1st in NL)

Runs allowed per game: 4.16 (2nd in NL)

Team EqA: .271 (3rd in NL)

2008 Batters Age: 30.4 (3rd-oldest in NL)

2008 Pitchers Age: 29.4 (8th-oldest in NL)

Ballpark: Wrigley Field; Hitter's park; Park Factor of 1.042

2008: Smooth sailing from April through September, but the NL's best offense disappears in October.

2009: Sweet Lou guides the Billy Goat out to pasture despite a bullpen transition.

---

dodgy prospects to roll the dice with Rich Harden. The Cubs don't just want to win a few ballgames; they've gunned for it all.

This deserves mention because not every team has taken its opportunities as seriously as the Cubs presently do their own. The early-aughties Twins, for example, were ever ready to talk about how happy they were just to be there during their brief run of relevance. In contrast, Hendry's Cubs didn't simply settle for the assembly of a team probably good enough to defend their NL Central title. Instead, in adapting that design, Hendry expended no little effort in-season to assemble a squad that was supposed to be strong enough to beat all comers. That it did not, even after these efforts, is nothing short of agony, a stele erected to the age-old proposition that the game is supposed to break your heart, and then staked through the sternums of the most forgiving faithful in the industry. Poor them.

When it comes to that drive to deliver the one thing that hasn't been done since 1908, Hendry has perhaps found his perfect on-field foil in veteran skipper Lou Piniella. As we've noted in the past, Hendry's gifts as an evaluator and player-development guy tend to dovetail neatly with a manager of strong opinions about what to do with the big-league club. Where Dusty Baker's paucity of ideas and inability to adapt left the club a bit directionless once 2003's false spring forward died on a surgeon's table or two, that failure paved the way for Piniella, a skipper who's already suffered his share of near misses in high-profile jobs, and perhaps therefore a man without interest in adding too many more to his record.

Piniella is something of an artifact, a product of the 1980s, a period that our former colleague Keith Woolner might describe as a competitive ecology, where considerable tactical diversity bred a brand of baseball far more differentiated than today's staid skippering and relentless bullpen quadrilles. He was not singled out for any particular brand of genius at a time when his rivals and role models included Earl Weaver and Sparky Anderson and Billy Martin, Whitey Herzog and Davey Johnson, La Russa, Leyland, and Lasorda, lions, tigers, and bears. As it often is with teams, so it goes with managers—you play to the level of the competition. When managers platooned or ran or bunted or gunned for big innings but above all else invested as much care on offensive tactics as today's skippers devote to the tedium of bullpen overmanagement, you had to roll with it, lest you wind up one of the era's idlers, a John McNamara or a Jim Frey.

As a result, Piniella's roots from those more complicated times puts him in pretty stark contrast the younger managers, and it serves him in good stead today. Most managers might have responded to losing Alfonso Soriano early (and then again in June) by throwing up their hands and plugging in some near-adequate Todd Hollandsworth type because he's an outfielder and you've lost an outfielder and you need an outfielder. But Piniella responded as only a product of the problem-solving generation could. He adapted to the talent on hand and to the circumstances, taking a bad situation like losing your presumptive best ballplayer and instead employing his best available players to best effect. Why go looking for a Hollandsworth when you can instead create a more regular role for Mike Fontenot, get Ronny Cedeño some at-bats, and get everything you need in terms of power in a pinch right there?

Mark DeRosa's positional flexibility helped make that possible, of course, not to mention his past utility role with the Braves playing for another of the game's great living fossils, Bobby Cox. Not that anyone's going to start referring to DeRosa as the new Tony Phillips, but beyond getting the lion's share of playing time at second, DeRosa was also the Cubs' second-most-often used player at third and both outfield corners. Usually when a second baseman becomes a "utility" player, it's because he isn't good enough to play regularly, but in DeRosa's case, he's the rare player who is and does. When Soriano went down, the solution was to play DeRosa in the outfield and build a cross-positional lineup platoon of Fontenot and Reed Johnson. What might have been a handicap instead became a differentiated asset that reflected a certain nimbleness with player usage.

This wasn't Piniella's first creative solution, representing as it does an echo of 1992, when he similarly moved Bip Roberts around the diamond, or just eight

or nine years ago, when he did likewise with Mark McLemore. It wasn't necessarily his most inspired bit of mixing and matching—which might have been his desperate lineup-card machinations with the Mariners of 1995, the team that achieved the impossible, forgotten feat of catching the Angels from behind to force a tiebreaker. The year 2008 may not even be Piniella's most disappointing one, not when the single-season record for wins was achieved by his '01 Mariners team, a team that was torched in the AL Championship Series by the Yankees.

On some level, Fontenot might be the signature player by whom to describe Piniella's adaptive player usage patterns with the Cubs last summer, in the same way that Tony La Russa seemed to leach value out of Rick Honeycutt; or Jim Leyland had Lloyd McClendon, Gary Varsho, or John Wehner; or Earl Weaver had John Lowenstein; and Gene Mauch seemed to carry Rob Wilfong around like a piece of lucky luggage. It's fascinating to see how a skipper carves out a role for a player whom other people might not value, and then employs him to good effect.

There's no revelation in suggesting that a manager has his guys—that's human nature, to identify somebody you like to have around, because you know what he can do. But it does say something about the players a manager finds a way to make useful, and the kind of player he does. With his years of working around the cages as a player, coach, and manager, Piniella saw a guy who could hit, and he needed a hitter. Where so few managers these days find ways to wedge in that extra left-handed bat, Piniella did. So many managerial stats fall short as evaluative tools of a skipper's skill, because of their failure to capture elective decision-making on the operational level: how well a manager designs a roster, a lineup card, a bullpen, a bench. Picking who plays and why, and enjoying the benefits of that decision, instead of hiding behind the performances, the successes and the failures. These are things that may never be captured as easily as how many times a man asks his pitchers to bunt, and calling that informative; it's where sabermetrics as a tool leaves off and historical analysis must step in.

Now that DeRosa's been dealt to the Indians, Fontenot will be on the spot as someone the Cubs are depending on, but the trade helped make other things possible, primarily affording Jim Hendry the opportunity to address the team's right-wards lean in the lineup by signing the unpredictable, fragile, and tremendously gifted Milton Bradley to a three-year, $30 million contract. Bradley's ability to stay healthy is always going to be in question, but his ability to hit is not. The GM and skipper also sought out additional help on the left side of the plate for the bench by signing Joey Gathright and Aaron Miles.

In managing his pitching staff, Piniella, we can safely say, has come a long way. The manager who exercised such care in how he handled Carlos Zambrano, Rich Harden, and Ryan Dempster and who kept Jason Marquis on a short leash and used within his limits—this is not the same man who took hold of the fragile veteran staff of the 1988 Yankees and blew it to smithereens, obliterating an equally fragile bid for contention. The capacity to adapt may not be readily identified with Piniella, but the manager of 20 years ago would not have acted with the same prudence that the older Lou delivered. It's also worth crediting him with crafting a bullpen that more properly resembles the better units of his career, whether it's the Nasty Boys of 1990 or the equally murderous Mariners trio of Kaz Sasaki, Jeff Nelson, and Arthur Rhodes. The combination of Kerry Wood and Carlos Marmol, however, lacked that third man those other combos boasted, and replacing Wood with Kevin Gregg in the top tandem unsettles things that much

more, but as Piniella has adapted to other challenges, perhaps he will with this one as well.

The recent curse-breaking triumphs of the Red Sox and White Sox might have engendered a certain millenarian expectation that 2008 was the Cubs' turn, but that's why they play the games, and the task is as yet undone. With a certain grim purpose, you can understand the readiness to cast last year as a failure, but it was not; it was instead a reflection of an organizational commitment to get the thing done, and if they do or don't, it won't be for want of trying. Dispensing with the children's crusades of the past was overdue here as in no other organization. In an industry populated with franchises designed to grind down and crush the opposition and contend again and again, the fact that you can count on the Cubs making their way to join them is progress. While much depends on who buys the ballclub and what the purchasers wish of their new toy, the challenge for the win-now Cubs is to win now. With the means and the ambition, who's to say third time isn't the charm?

HITTERS

Henry Blanco C Bats: R Throws: R Height: 5' 11" Weight: 220 Born: August 29, 1971 Age: 37

YEAR	TEAM	LVL	AGE	PA	R	2B	3B	HR	RBI	BB	SO	SB	CS	EqBRR	AVG	OBP	SLG	EqAVG	EqOBP	EqSLG	EqA	VORP	WARP	DEFENSE			
2006	CHN	MLB	34	261	23	15	2	6	37	14	38	0	0	-1.5	.266	.304	.419	.260	.301	.409	.245	1.4	1.7	59-C	8	5-1B	1
2007	CHN	MLB	35	58	3	3	0	0	4	2	12	0	0	0.0	.167	.193	.222	.167	.193	.222	.123	-6.2	-0.5	12-C	1		
2008	CHN	MLB	36	128	15	3	0	3	12	6	22	0	0	-0.1	.292	.325	.392	.289	.323	.380	.244	3.2	0.6	29-C	4		
2009	CHN	MLB	37	110	9	4	0	2	11	7	20	0	0	-0.4	.242	.289	.344	.239	.287	.344	.216	-1.0	0.4	30-C	1		

Breakout: 29% Improve: 46% Collapse: 31% Attrition: 34%   Comparables: Sandy Alomar, Charlie O'Brien, Clyde McCullough, Pat Borders

Junior Ortiz himself would have to approve of Blanco's sense of timing in delivering a nice, hollow batting average, right in time for free agency, which the Cubs were intent on immanent-izing instead of picking up a 2009 option. Blanco still does the things you expect from him: pound the odd left-handed weakling, and throw so well that he deters the running game from even happening on his watch. When asked to do these things no more than occasionally, he's an asset.

Welington Castillo C Bats: R Throws: R Height: 6' 0" Weight: 200 Born: April 24, 1987 Age: 22

YEAR	TEAM	LVL	AGE	PA	R	2B	3B	HR	RBI	BB	SO	SB	CS	EqBRR	AVG	OBP	SLG	EqAVG	EqOBP	EqSLG	EqA	VORP	WARP	DEFENSE	
2007	PEO	A	20	353	41	11	2	11	44	23	77	1	3	-3.9	.271	.334	.423	.217	.265	.336	.207	-20.0	-0.7	82-C	-1
2008	DAY	A+	21	127	15	8	0	0	12	4	23	1	0	-2.8	.273	.299	.339	.213	.236	.262	.166	-13.7	-1.3	28-C	-5
2008	TEN	AA	21	220	25	11	0	4	24	14	50	0	0	-1.5	.298	.362	.414	.244	.292	.346	.222	-6.9	-0.5	48-C	-4
2009	CHN	MLB	22	384	29	16	1	7	37	21	97	1	1	-1.3	.227	.276	.332	.225	.273	.332	.205	-8.3	0.1	92-C	-3

Breakout: 38% Improve: 59% Collapse: 20% Attrition: 19%   Comparables: Robert Machado, Yorvit Torrealba, Jose Peña, Gilberto Reyes

Notionally a catching prospect, Castillo's prospect status is defined by the tools of ignorance and his ability to wear them well. Unfortunately, he's a haphazard receiver with sloppy footwork. A strong arm and a quick release make him a good deterrent against the running game, but he's not yet a good catcher, and his blend of hack-happiness and merely modest pop doesn't translate into the kind of talent who might play regularly someday.

Ronny Cedeño   SS

Bats: R   Throws: R   Height: 6' 0"   Weight: 180   Born: February 2, 1983   Age: 26

YEAR	TEAM	LVL	AGE	PA	R	2B	3B	HR	RBI	BB	SO	SB	CS	EqBRR	AVG	OBP	SLG	EqAVG	EqOBP	EqSLG	EqA	VORP	WARP	DEFENSE			
2006	CHN	MLB	23	572	51	18	7	6	41	17	109	8	8	-0.9	.245	.271	.339	.244	.270	.338	.207	-18.4	-0.7	127-SS	2	14-2B	0
2007	IOW	AAA	24	327	52	15	3	10	37	30	46	6	4	-0.4	.359	.422	.537	.312	.375	.473	.288	23.1	3.0	72-SS	3		
2007	CHN	MLB	24	80	6	2	0	4	13	3	18	2	1	-0.1	.203	.231	.392	.200	.228	.387	.207	-2.9	-0.1	12-SS	2		
2008	CHN	MLB	25	236	36	12	0	2	28	18	41	4	1	-1.1	.269	.328	.352	.264	.323	.343	.238	2.2	0.2	30-2B	0	20-SS	2
2009	CHN	MLB	26	271	30	12	1	5	27	18	45	5	2	0.4	.262	.316	.385	.259	.313	.385	.242	5.3	0.8	67-SS	0		

Breakout: 26% Improve: 47% Collapse: 27% Attrition: 29%   Comparables: Fred Manrique, Doug Flynn, Julio Gotay, Frank Duffy

Cedeño remains ready to be at least a second-division starter at short for somebody, but has to settle for reserve duties as long as he's in Wrigleyville. Were he given a full-time job, he'd not only provide plus defense, but a decent amount of sock and enough steals to chip in better than the slappy Felix Fermin types. The DeRosa deal might mean more at-bats for him at second, but he'll be contending with Fontenot and free-agent addition Aaron Miles.

Tyler Colvin   CF

Bats: L   Throws: L   Height: 6' 3"   Weight: 190   Born: September 5, 1985   Age: 23

YEAR	TEAM	LVL	AGE	PA	R	2B	3B	HR	RBI	BB	SO	SB	CS	EqBRR	AVG	OBP	SLG	EqAVG	EqOBP	EqSLG	EqA	VORP	WARP	DEFENSE			
2006	BOI	A-	20	288	50	12	6	11	53	17	55	12	5	-1.4	.268	.313	.483	.201	.235	.359	.202	-34.6	-3.7	46-LF	-9	18-CF	-2
2007	DAY	A+	21	262	38	24	3	7	50	10	47	10	4	0.0	.306	.336	.514	.242	.271	.431	.237	-2.8	0.6	61-CF	4		
2007	TEN	AA	21	257	34	11	2	9	31	5	54	7	1	2.6	.291	.313	.462	.244	.261	.400	.226	-7.0	0.6	44-CF	9	12-RF	-1
2008	TEN	AA	22	602	68	27	11	14	80	44	101	7	4	-0.7	.256	.312	.424	.205	.250	.351	.207	-35.2	-3.5	65-LF	-1	54-CF	-7
2009	CHN	MLB	23	586	61	34	3	15	67	34	130	8	4	1.8	.242	.290	.399	.239	.287	.399	.234	-6.1	0.8	137-CF	-1		

Breakout: 64% Improve: 74% Collapse: 13% Attrition: 3%   Comparables: Mitch Maier, Miguel Negron, Terrence Long, Randy Byers

A toolsy maybe, Colvin made big strides in the second half, when he learned to start ripping the pitches he could hit instead of waiting for a walk to just happen. Pitch identification is an issue, but at some point, it's going to boil down to what he can do as opposed to trying to make him do what he can't. Poor instincts might keep him out of center, and while he has the arm for right, he'll need to hit a lot better than his slugging over .500 after the Southern League's all-star break, as promising as that was in his age-23 season. In short, he's still shy of a finished product, and he will need to build on a good second half to deliver as something more than just an extra outfielder.

Mark DeRosa   2B

Bats: R   Throws: R   Height: 6' 1"   Weight: 205   Born: February 26, 1975   Age: 34

YEAR	TEAM	LVL	AGE	PA	R	2B	3B	HR	RBI	BB	SO	SB	CS	EqBRR	AVG	OBP	SLG	EqAVG	EqOBP	EqSLG	EqA	VORP	WARP	DEFENSE			
2006	TEX	MLB	31	572	78	40	2	13	74	44	102	4	4	-2.8	.296	.357	.456	.280	.346	.437	.269	22.5	2.6	58-RF	0	39-3B	0
2007	CHN	MLB	32	574	64	28	3	10	72	58	93	1	2	0.4	.293	.371	.420	.284	.367	.414	.273	20.2	3.9	79-2B	5	32-3B	7
2008	CHN	MLB	33	593	103	30	3	21	87	69	106	6	0	3.8	.285	.376	.481	.280	.371	.482	.295	36.7	5.0	74-2B	6	30-RF	-1
2009	CLE	MLB	34	497	63	24	2	12	58	54	87	5	2	-0.3	.269	.354	.414	.267	.353	.431	.275	14.0	2.4	117-2B	-2		

Breakout: 13% Improve: 32% Collapse: 32% Attrition: 20%   Comparables: Don Hoak, Chuck Hinton, Ken Boyer, Melvin Mora

Although last year's power spike shouldn't be expected every season, DeRosa wasn't especially hit-lucky, is a good power-on-contact type, and doesn't seem to be fazed by any of the innumerable new responsibilities he gets handed. That super-utilityman might have seemed indispensable, but the Cubs decided they'd rather make room on their payroll and take their chances with Fontenot, Aaron Miles, and Cedeño at second, dealing DeRosa in his last contract year to the Tribe. For the Indians, he ought to provide a ready excuse to move Jhonny Peralta to third and Asdrubal Cabrera to short, but it appears they'll put DeRosa at third and simultaneously play three infielders at their second-best positions.

Jim Edmonds — CF

Bats: L　Throws: L　Height: 6' 1"　Weight: 210　Born: June 27, 1970　Age: 39

YEAR	TEAM	LVL	AGE	PA	R	2B	3B	HR	RBI	BB	SO	SB	CS	EqBRR	AVG	OBP	SLG	EqAVG	EqOBP	EqSLG	EqA	VORP	WARP	DEFENSE			
2006	SLN	MLB	36	408	52	18	0	19	70	53	101	4	0	-0.0	.257	.350	.471	.254	.350	.470	.284	19.9	2.1	90-CF	0	5-1B	-2
2007	SLN	MLB	37	411	39	15	2	12	53	41	75	0	2	-1.7	.252	.325	.403	.253	.332	.419	.259	6.3	0.4	94-CF	-6		
2008	SDN	MLB	38	103	6	2	0	1	6	10	24	2	1	-0.5	.178	.265	.233	.178	.265	.233	.182	-6.8	-1.3	24-CF	-7		
2008	CHN	MLB	38	298	47	17	2	19	49	45	58	0	1	-2.8	.256	.369	.568	.249	.366	.566	.306	23.4	2.1	70-CF	-4		
2009	CHN	MLB	39	370	50	19	1	17	56	48	73	2	1	-1.7	.265	.363	.491	.262	.360	.491	.288	20.7	2.0	89-CF	-8		

Breakout: 41%　Improve: 74%　Collapse: 11%　Attrition: 29%　　Comparables: Ken Griffey, Luis Gonzalez, Graig Nettles, Willie McCovey

Released a bare month into his ghastly stint with San Diego, Edmonds landed with the Cubs and slugged at a clip he hasn't matched since 2004—his last serious shot at MVP consideration. He has lost more than a half-dozen steps in center, but if he can slug over .500 against right-handers—and he managed .612 for the Cubs—and man a corner, he could be the short-term free-agent steal of the winter. On the other hand, if he's made an everyday center fielder and paid like one should be, he'll be a serious stumbling block beyond the first year of a deal.

Ryan Flaherty — SS

Bats: L　Throws: R　Height: 6' 3"　Weight: 200　Born: July 27, 1986　Age: 22

YEAR	TEAM	LVL	AGE	PA	R	2B	3B	HR	RBI	BB	SO	SB	CS	EqBRR	AVG	OBP	SLG	EqAVG	EqOBP	EqSLG	EqA	VORP	WARP	DEFENSE	
2008	BOI	A-	21	245	39	19	2	8	26	24	51	4	2	-1.5	.297	.369	.511	.199	.245	.346	.199	-28.3	-1.7	51-SS	-5
2009	CHN	MLB	22	530	47	31	2	12	55	36	155	5	3	0.6	.221	.278	.365	.219	.275	.364	.217	-4.5	-0.1	125-SS	0

Breakout: 61%　Improve: 74%　Collapse: 14%　Attrition: 8%　　Comparables: Mike Costanzo, Jeff Branson, John Toale, Mike Gulan

A big shortstop who shined at Vanderbilt playing alongside Pedro Alvarez, Flaherty was a 2008 first-round pick for a Cubs organization that understands that his future really lies at second—where he'd be a relative hulk—or third, where his offense is going to have to pan out. As a baseball rat with a smooth swing and good instincts, he will at least have a utility player's upside, but could pan out as more if he comes through as a hitter.

Mike Fontenot — 2B

Bats: L　Throws: R　Height: 5' 8"　Weight: 170　Born: June 9, 1980　Age: 29

YEAR	TEAM	LVL	AGE	PA	R	2B	3B	HR	RBI	BB	SO	SB	CS	EqBRR	AVG	OBP	SLG	EqAVG	EqOBP	EqSLG	EqA	VORP	WARP	DEFENSE			
2006	IOW	AAA	26	418	54	28	2	8	36	47	64	5	4	-3.5	.296	.375	.450	.246	.320	.392	.248	0.4	1.7	87-2B	9		
2007	IOW	AAA	27	231	46	17	4	6	34	16	32	3	1	1.9	.336	.384	.540	.266	.313	.430	.256	3.6	1.2	20-SS	2	18-2B	0
2007	CHN	MLB	27	260	32	12	4	3	29	22	43	5	4	0.6	.278	.336	.402	.275	.336	.408	.255	4.0	0.8	52-2B	3		
2008	CHN	MLB	28	284	42	22	1	9	40	34	51	2	0	-0.3	.305	.395	.514	.295	.389	.504	.305	24.4	2.8	55-2B	5		
2009	CHN	MLB	29	259	35	16	1	6	31	26	46	2	1	0.6	.278	.356	.440	.275	.352	.440	.273	14.5	1.7	64-2B	2		

Breakout: 16%　Improve: 49%　Collapse: 30%　Attrition: 33%　　Comparables: Mike Cubbage, Tim Jones, Craig Counsell, Tim Flannery

As wonderful as Fontenot's development as a spare second baseman has been, it's important to keep his success in context—make him an everyday player, and you'll start seeing the things he can't do, like handle the better power right-handers. Spot use against midrotation starters as the oft-used caddy for a rover like DeRosa was probably the perfect role for him, but with DeRosa dealt, he could either be on the spot as a regular or could stay in a keystone rotation with free agents Aaron Miles and Cedeño.

Jake Fox — 1B

Bats: R　Throws: R　Height: 6' 0"　Weight: 210　Born: July 20, 1982　Age: 26

YEAR	TEAM	LVL	AGE	PA	R	2B	3B	HR	RBI	BB	SO	SB	CS	EqBRR	AVG	OBP	SLG	EqAVG	EqOBP	EqSLG	EqA	VORP	WARP	DEFENSE			
2006	DAY	A+	23	291	45	15	1	16	61	27	49	4	1	-2.6	.313	.383	.574	.243	.302	.459	.261	4.9	0.8	48-C	-4		
2006	WTN	AA	23	204	20	17	0	5	25	9	44	0	0	-0.6	.269	.304	.435	.251	.283	.415	.239	-1.7	0.2	41-C	-1		
2007	TEN	AA	24	388	60	23	1	18	60	17	72	6	2	-3.4	.284	.327	.504	.227	.261	.418	.231	-9.1	-0.4	35-1B	3	17-LF	3
2007	IOW	AAA	24	108	18	7	0	6	19	5	23	2	0	0.2	.283	.343	.535	.250	.306	.480	.267	2.9	0.0	13-RF	-1	6-LF	-1
2007	CHN	MLB	24	15	3	2	0	0	1	1	2	0	0	-0.0	.143	.200	.286	.143	.200	.214	.112	-1.6	-0.2				
2008	TEN	AA	25	459	76	29	1	25	79	46	73	4	2	-2.6	.307	.397	.580	.222	.291	.427	.247	-2.5	-1.4	47-1B	-4	35-LF	-7
2008	IOW	AAA	25	120	17	10	1	6	26	2	31	3	0	0.4	.222	.242	.479	.186	.207	.407	.206	-7.7	-0.5	25-1B	2		
2009	CHN	MLB	26	447	45	22	1	17	61	28	111	3	1	-1.0	.233	.288	.412	.230	.285	.412	.237	-4.4	-0.1	106-1B	2		

Breakout: 25%　Improve: 42%　Collapse: 30%　Attrition: 18%　　Comparables: Dave Hengel, Tim McIntosh, Mitch Lyden, Aaron Herr

Not exactly a prospect any more than he was ever really a catcher, Fox has bopped as the old-timer in younger men's leagues and settled into playing first or left while the organization sorts out if he'll pan out into something more than a minor league slugger. The happy news is that he finished strong, slugging .707 in roughly his last 200 personal appearances in Double-A. If the Cubs were in the DH league and this was 20 years ago, he'd make a neat platoon partner with Micah Hoffpauir, but they aren't and it isn't.

Kosuke Fukudome RF · Bats: L · Throws: R · Height: 6' 0" · Weight: 190 · Born: April 26, 1977 · Age: 32

YEAR	TEAM	LVL	AGE	PA	R	2B	3B	HR	RBI	BB	SO	SB	CS	EqBRR	AVG	OBP	SLG	EqAVG	EqOBP	EqSLG	EqA	VORP	WARP	DEFENSE			
2006	CHU	JP	29	578	117	47	5	31	104	76	94	11	2	—	.351	.438	.653	.332	.415	.567	.328	75.9	5.9				
2007	CHU	JP	30	348	64	22	0	13	48	69	66	5	2	—	.294	.443	.520	.279	.408	.425	.296	21.9	2.0				
2008	CHN	MLB	31	590	79	25	3	10	58	81	104	12	4	2.6	.257	.359	.379	.250	.354	.374	.263	6.1	1.1	123-RF	3	7-CF	-5
2009	CHN	MLB	32	465	71	26	2	10	53	64	79	8	3	0.8	.286	.386	.439	.282	.382	.438	.287	18.3	2.7	110-RF	1		

Breakout: 14% Improve: 47% Collapse: 24% Attrition: 19%   Comparables: J.D. Drew, Gene Hermanski, Pat Kelly, Joe Cunningham

In the crosstown battle of much-anticipated imports, the Cubs' adding Fukudome initially seemed the winning choice over the Sox' Cubano, Alexei Ramirez. For three months, Kosuke was the toast of the town, hitting .296/.404/.430, but from July 1 onward, he hit .207/.297/.313, increasingly losing lineup space to Fontenot as Piniella gave up on his famous free agent. Fukudome's contract is effectively unmovable, and barring a major turnaround, he may have trouble fending off Joey Gathright in a bid to share playing time in center with Reed Johnson. Right now, he's as big a mistake of the 2008 shopping season as a Hummer H3, with equally nonexistent trade-in value.

Sam Fuld CF · Bats: L · Throws: L · Height: 5' 10" · Weight: 180 · Born: November 20, 1981 · Age: 27

YEAR	TEAM	LVL	AGE	PA	R	2B	3B	HR	RBI	BB	SO	SB	CS	EqBRR	AVG	OBP	SLG	EqAVG	EqOBP	EqSLG	EqA	VORP	WARP	DEFENSE			
2006	DAY	A+	24	405	63	19	6	4	40	40	54	22	3	7.9	.300	.378	.422	.213	.277	.305	.209	-25.4	-0.9	84-CF	3		
2007	TEN	AA	25	392	56	23	2	2	27	41	38	10	3	0.8	.290	.372	.388	.214	.284	.293	.207	-23.9	-1.5	57-CF	-1	20-RF	1
2007	IOW	AAA	25	63	13	4	1	1	2	9	5	2	0	2.0	.269	.397	.442	.226	.349	.377	.265	0.4	0.0	6-RF	0	5-LF	1
2008	TEN	AA	26	397	48	16	3	5	48	50	40	7	8	-2.6	.271	.366	.381	.182	.253	.263	.178	-37.3	-3.0	81-CF	-4		
2008	IOW	AAA	26	76	11	3	0	1	4	8	12	3	2	-0.7	.222	.310	.317	.182	.260	.258	.186	-6.6	-0.3	13-CF	2		
2009	CHN	MLB	27	428	35	18	2	2	28	35	77	6	3	1.1	.199	.268	.272	.197	.266	.272	.184	-23.5	-0.9	102-CF	2		

Breakout: 25% Improve: 40% Collapse: 37% Attrition: 17%   Comparables: Kevin Long, John Jackson, Bruce Dostal, Vernon Spearman

Fuld had a nice camp, and that's a reminder that lots of people have nice camps, especially in Arizona, where the air is thin and the competition a bit sparse. At the end of the day, we're talking about a guy who just turned 27, isn't a plus center fielder, and doesn't run well enough to fit in as a reserve. You know how this story ends: out in the cornfields of Iowa. Leave the gun, take the cannolis, and move on.

Micah Hoffpauir 1B · Bats: L · Throws: L · Height: 6' 3" · Weight: 195 · Born: March 1, 1980 · Age: 29

YEAR	TEAM	LVL	AGE	PA	R	2B	3B	HR	RBI	BB	SO	SB	CS	EqBRR	AVG	OBP	SLG	EqAVG	EqOBP	EqSLG	EqA	VORP	WARP	DEFENSE			
2006	WTN	AA	26	163	28	11	2	10	31	20	29	0	0	-0.3	.268	.362	.594	.201	.276	.444	.246	-1.9	-0.5	37-1B	-3		
2006	IOW	AAA	26	297	34	9	1	12	49	33	59	1	2	0.3	.267	.345	.451	.222	.296	.391	.240	-4.8	-0.9	59-1B	-4		
2007	IOW	AAA	27	342	56	24	0	16	73	24	34	2	1	0.6	.319	.365	.552	.258	.304	.446	.256	5.3	0.6	65-1B	-2	10-LF	-5
2008	IOW	AAA	28	313	63	34	2	25	100	17	46	2	0	0.2	.362	.393	.752	.278	.309	.563	.286	21.9	1.0	55-1B	-10	8-LF	4
2008	CHN	MLB	28	80	14	8	0	2	8	6	24	1	0	0.0	.342	.400	.534	.329	.387	.534	.312	7.7	0.3	5-1B	-2	4-RF	0
2009	CHN	MLB	29	423	53	26	1	19	65	36	85	2	1	0.0	.261	.327	.489	.258	.323	.489	.273	12.4	1.0	101-1B	-4		

Breakout: 21% Improve: 53% Collapse: 20% Attrition: 14%   Comparables: Gary Rajsich, Brian Daubach, Greg Walker, Dave Revering

Hoffpauir's breakout should be enough to get him Daryle Ward's job as the primary power source off the bench, but he could come in handy as a regularly employed spot starter for Derrek Lee if the big first baseman's slump extends into 2009. Beyond that, he's an outfielder only in the sense that he'll play there if asked, so his opportunities are directly related to Lee's fortunes.

Reed Johnson   **OF**   Bats: R   Throws: R   Height: 5' 10"   Weight: 180   Born: December 8, 1976   Age: 32

YEAR	TEAM	LVL	AGE	PA	R	2B	3B	HR	RBI	BB	SO	SB	CS	EqBRR	AVG	OBP	SLG	EqAVG	EqOBP	EqSLG	EqA	VORP	WARP	DEFENSE		
2006	TOR	MLB	29	517	86	34	2	12	49	33	81	8	2	0.2	.317	.388	.477	.302	.376	.463	.291	32.9	3.4	72-LF	7	28-RF 2
2007	TOR	MLB	30	307	31	13	2	2	14	16	56	4	2	-0.4	.236	.305	.320	.236	.302	.331	.224	-11.4	0.0	56-LF	8	8-RF -1
2008	CHN	MLB	31	374	52	21	0	6	50	19	68	5	6	-1.2	.303	.358	.420	.304	.358	.430	.270	12.8	0.9	63-CF	-8	14-LF 4
2009	CHN	MLB	32	289	35	14	1	6	33	19	49	3	2	0.1	.276	.337	.405	.273	.334	.405	.256	6.0	0.9	71-CF	-3	

Breakout: 12%   Improve: 31%   Collapse: 39%   Attrition: 27%   Comparables: Danny Bautista, Ken Berry, Mike McCormick, Roberto Kelly

It's a reflection of odd local standards that Johnson was seen as a speed player and a center fielder when the Cubs picked him up. It would have been swell if true, but Johnson's not fast (those eight bags swiped in 2006 were a career high), nor can he really play center all that well. Perhaps after the Corey Patterson experience, people were only too quick to play make-believe, but luckily, Edmonds landed in their laps. Like Fontenot, if pressed into full-time play, Johnson becomes a problem, but he's adequate in a role where he sees lefties more often than not.

Derrek Lee   **1B**   Bats: R   Throws: R   Height: 6' 5"   Weight: 245   Born: September 6, 1975   Age: 33

YEAR	TEAM	LVL	AGE	PA	R	2B	3B	HR	RBI	BB	SO	SB	CS	EqBRR	AVG	OBP	SLG	EqAVG	EqOBP	EqSLG	EqA	VORP	WARP	DEFENSE	
2006	CHN	MLB	30	204	30	9	0	8	30	25	41	8	4	-0.1	.286	.368	.474	.276	.363	.448	.281	7.1	1.2	44-1B	4
2007	CHN	MLB	31	650	91	43	1	22	82	71	114	6	5	-5.5	.317	.400	.513	.307	.395	.506	.305	47.4	4.1	143-1B	-2
2008	CHN	MLB	32	698	93	41	3	20	90	71	119	8	2	-2.6	.291	.361	.462	.285	.357	.462	.282	30.4	3.5	149-1B	7
2009	CHN	MLB	33	612	84	35	2	19	85	67	105	8	3	-2.7	.289	.369	.464	.286	.365	.464	.285	24.3	2.8	143-1B	1

Breakout: 10%   Improve: 42%   Collapse: 20%   Attrition: 7%   Comparables: Joe Torre, John Olerud, Eric Karros, Bob Watson

Lee was once an MVP-caliber player, but that was on the other side of a few injuries, and it's important to take a step back and ask where he'll be going forward as he heads into his age-33 season. After a hot April, he hit .275/.344/.415, way below what you want from a first baseman, and while his athleticism might encourage you to expect that he'll age gracefully, graceful and mediocre isn't going to keep the lineup firing on all cylinders.

Felix Pie   **CF**   Bats: L   Throws: L   Height: 6' 2"   Weight: 170   Born: February 8, 1985   Age: 24

YEAR	TEAM	LVL	AGE	PA	R	2B	3B	HR	RBI	BB	SO	SB	CS	EqBRR	AVG	OBP	SLG	EqAVG	EqOBP	EqSLG	EqA	VORP	WARP	DEFENSE		
2006	IOW	AAA	21	623	78	33	8	15	57	46	126	17	11	-1.8	.283	.341	.451	.251	.303	.407	.244	-0.7	-0.5	122-CF	-10	13-RF 0
2007	IOW	AAA	22	250	51	9	5	9	43	19	40	9	6	2.7	.362	.410	.563	.316	.364	.502	.289	19.9	0.7	49-CF	-7	4-RF -2
2007	CHN	MLB	22	194	26	9	3	2	20	14	43	8	1	2.8	.215	.271	.333	.209	.269	.328	.217	-5.7	0.8	48-CF	12	
2008	IOW	AAA	23	368	57	20	5	10	55	23	54	11	7	1.4	.287	.336	.466	.249	.293	.408	.239	-2.3	-0.1	79-CF	-3	
2008	CHN	MLB	23	93	9	2	1	1	10	7	29	3	0	0.3	.241	.312	.325	.241	.312	.325	.236	-0.6	-0.2	22-CF	-1	
2009	CHN	MLB	24	492	65	28	3	13	55	38	97	14	6	2.8	.274	.333	.435	.271	.329	.435	.263	15.8	2.6	116-CF	3	

Breakout: 41%   Improve: 65%   Collapse: 11%   Attrition: 13%   Comparables: Jose Moreno, Mike Davis, Carlos Beltran, Pedro Valdes

Initially given an opportunity to share the job in center, Pie never ended up inspiring confidence in his manager, who instead got carried away with Reed Johnson. The tools that made Pie the favorite flavor of 2006 on prospect lists are all still there, but that's part of the problem—he hasn't really made progress. Dangled in almost every rumored deal this winter, if he's still a Cub in March and can't beat out Fukudome or Gathright, it's an open question if he's going to fulfill the expectations people had for him.

Aramis Ramirez   **3B**   Bats: R   Throws: R   Height: 6' 1"   Weight: 215   Born: June 25, 1978   Age: 31

YEAR	TEAM	LVL	AGE	PA	R	2B	3B	HR	RBI	BB	SO	SB	CS	EqBRR	AVG	OBP	SLG	EqAVG	EqOBP	EqSLG	EqA	VORP	WARP	DEFENSE	
2006	CHN	MLB	28	660	93	38	4	38	119	50	63	2	1	-1.7	.291	.352	.561	.283	.344	.548	.296	43.4	4.3	152-3B	-5
2007	CHN	MLB	29	558	72	35	4	26	101	43	66	0	0	-1.5	.310	.366	.549	.298	.357	.539	.299	42.6	5.9	122-3B	15
2008	CHN	MLB	30	645	97	44	1	27	111	74	94	2	2	-3.1	.289	.380	.518	.283	.374	.516	.300	45.4	4.8	142-3B	-1
2009	CHN	MLB	31	615	85	37	2	26	101	59	79	2	1	-1.9	.288	.363	.509	.285	.359	.509	.292	37.8	4.5	144-3B	3

Breakout: 10%   Improve: 42%   Collapse: 23%   Attrition: 7%   Comparables: Mike Lowell, Don Money, Brooks Robinson, Sal Bando

On a visceral level, A-Ram is seen as *the* bopper in a lineup where so many other players seem to come and go or run hot and cold. Last year's odd random development was his failure to hurt lefties (.239/.333/.388), when he has more often smote them (.287/.352/.534 career, including 2008). Jeff Bagwell had odd interruptions like that as well, but it shouldn't persist, part of the reason why you can anticipate a continued good run, albeit one short of nearing 40 homers again, as Ramirez did during his age 26-28 peak.

Alfonso Soriano — LF

Bats: R Throws: R Height: 6' 1" Weight: 180 Born: January 7, 1976 Age: 33

YEAR	TEAM	LVL	AGE	PA	R	2B	3B	HR	RBI	BB	SO	SB	CS	EqBRR	AVG	OBP	SLG	EqAVG	EqOBP	EqSLG	EqA	VORP	WARP	DEFENSE			
2006	WAS	MLB	30	728	119	41	2	46	95	67	160	41	17	-4.7	.277	.351	.560	.286	.360	.580	.303	47.7	7.5	156-LF	15		
2007	CHN	MLB	31	617	97	42	5	33	70	31	130	19	6	-0.1	.299	.337	.560	.291	.331	.556	.290	40.8	6.6	119-LF	22	11-CF	2
2008	CHN	MLB	32	503	76	27	0	29	75	43	103	19	3	-0.6	.280	.344	.532	.272	.337	.527	.291	33.0	3.2	104-LF	1		
2009	CHN	MLB	33	596	90	34	2	33	103	52	121	21	6	0.6	.281	.348	.538	.278	.345	.537	.294	31.1	4.0	140-LF	1		

Breakout: 23% Improve: 44% Collapse: 19% Attrition: 9%   Comparables: Don Baylor, Roy Sievers, Andre Dawson, Dusty Baker

The race to call Soriano a great defender flies in the face of what's actually involved—he's as aggressive a left fielder as you'll find when it comes to throwing, but his combination of bad routes, poor instincts, and sloppy play adds up to something well short of an obvious asset on defense. Like his defense, his performance on the bases and at the plate is a spectacle, but not exactly spectacular, useful but hard to fit easily into any archetypal role, and his wheels seem to be aging faster than his other working parts. He gets a bad rap for hitting with men on (slugging .503, and .595 with RISP), in part as a reaction formation against his not being anyone's classic idea of a leadoff hitter.

Geovany Soto — C

Bats: R Throws: R Height: 6' 1" Weight: 230 Born: January 20, 1983 Age: 26

YEAR	TEAM	LVL	AGE	PA	R	2B	3B	HR	RBI	BB	SO	SB	CS	EqBRR	AVG	OBP	SLG	EqAVG	EqOBP	EqSLG	EqA	VORP	WARP	DEFENSE			
2006	IOW	AAA	23	391	34	21	0	6	38	41	74	0	1	-0.5	.272	.353	.386	.244	.318	.350	.236	-6.3	0.2	96-C	-4		
2006	CHN	MLB	23	26	1	1	0	0	2	0	5	0	0	-0.1	.200	.231	.240	.200	.231	.240	.145	-2.3	-0.2	6-C	0		
2007	IOW	AAA	24	449	75	31	3	26	109	53	94	0	0	-3.1	.353	.424	.652	.308	.381	.569	.316	48.6	4.4	70-C	-2	20-1B	-3
2007	CHN	MLB	24	60	12	6	0	3	8	5	14	0	0	-0.3	.389	.433	.667	.370	.417	.667	.351	10.6	1.1	14-C	2		
2008	CHN	MLB	25	563	66	35	2	23	86	62	121	0	1	-4.0	.285	.364	.504	.278	.359	.500	.291	39.9	5.1	128-C	4		
2009	CHN	MLB	26	551	76	32	1	25	85	61	116	1	1	-2.5	.288	.370	.519	.284	.367	.518	.297	42.5	5.8	129-C	2		

Breakout: 26% Improve: 63% Collapse: 15% Attrition: 11%   Comparables: John Orsino, Johnny Romano, Earl Battey, Lance Parrish

En route to handily winning the NL Rookie of the Year Award, the beefy backstop fulfilled every Hector Villanueva fan's wildest fantasies, generating the best season by a Cubs catcher (as measured by VORP) in more than half a century, Rick Wilkins' single brush with stardom in 1993 aside. Perhaps predictably, the list of best Cubs catchers since 1954 is a bit of a rogue's gallery: Wilkins in one big year, three Michael Barrett seasons, Randy Hundley in 1967, and Jody Davis in 1983. And Soto, who isn't exactly a Greek golden god in double knits, but we can hope this doesn't catch up with him too quickly.

Ryan Theriot — SS

Bats: R Throws: R Height: 5' 11" Weight: 175 Born: December 7, 1979 Age: 29

YEAR	TEAM	LVL	AGE	PA	R	2B	3B	HR	RBI	BB	SO	SB	CS	EqBRR	AVG	OBP	SLG	EqAVG	EqOBP	EqSLG	EqA	VORP	WARP	DEFENSE			
2006	IOW	AAA	26	312	41	11	5	0	22	27	34	14	3	2.0	.304	.367	.379	.249	.305	.316	.225	-10.9	-0.6	40-SS	-7	19-2B	2
2006	CHN	MLB	26	159	34	11	3	3	16	17	18	13	2	1.5	.328	.412	.522	.314	.401	.504	.314	19.0	1.3	32-2B	-2		
2007	CHN	MLB	27	597	80	30	2	3	45	49	50	28	4	1.3	.266	.326	.346	.261	.324	.345	.246	5.8	2.0	96-SS	1	26-2B	5
2008	CHN	MLB	28	661	85	19	4	1	38	73	58	22	13	-0.2	.307	.387	.359	.307	.388	.359	.267	27.9	2.8	141-SS	-4		
2009	CHN	MLB	29	582	81	23	3	1	40	59	54	21	6	1.9	.283	.359	.350	.280	.356	.350	.256	17.2	2.4	136-SS	1		

Breakout: 20% Improve: 45% Collapse: 25% Attrition: 13%   Comparables: Scott Fletcher, Johnny Temple, Ricky Gutierrez, David Eckstein

It's easy to cherry-pick things to fret about—Theriot doesn't run as well as you might wish, and he presents a bit of a problem hitting second, since he hits so many grounders that twin killings are unavoidable. Theriot rated 20th in the majors in NetDP (essentially, double plays hit into above average). Despite those sorts of nagging concerns, though, it's important to focus on how, Eckstein-like, he made himself into a playable shortstop, and his improved patience makes him an offensive asset at a position where too many teams have punted getting anything. It isn't going to be a long and brilliant career, but for a guy who wasn't necessarily expected to make it as a utility type, you've come a long way, baby.

Tony Thomas   **2B**   Bats: R   Throws: R   Height: 5' 10"   Weight: 180   Born: July 10, 1986   Age: 22

YEAR	TEAM	LVL	AGE	PA	R	2B	3B	HR	RBI	BB	SO	SB	CS	EqBRR	AVG	OBP	SLG	EqAVG	EqOBP	EqSLG	EqA	VORP	WARP	DEFENSE	
2007	BOI	A-	20	214	44	12	8	5	33	25	41	28	2	6.9	.308	.404	.544	.210	.272	.369	.227	-15.3	-0.2	40-2B	0
2008	DAY	A+	21	493	62	30	4	7	43	34	113	22	10	-0.5	.266	.320	.400	.216	.263	.347	.214	-27.0	0.4	103-2B	12
2009	CHN	MLB	22	562	59	33	5	11	55	38	143	19	7	2.4	.232	.288	.377	.229	.285	.377	.231	-2.5	1.2	132-2B	7

Breakout: 47% Improve: 74% Collapse: 11% Attrition: 4%   Comparables: Jay Canizaro, Kevin Flora, Terry Shumpert, Marco Scutaro

Pushed aggressively—and appropriately—to High-A in his first full season after being picked in the third round of 2007, the former Florida State star didn't blossom or blow it, he simply sort of … was. Thomas ran out of steam in the second half, but the Florida State League is a tough assignment for a young hitter, and he did win series MVP when Daytona took the FSL title. Thomas has a weak arm and limited defensive playability anywhere but second, so to escape a future as an organizational type, he's going to have to develop at the plate.

Josh Vitters   **3B**   Bats: R   Throws: R   Height: 6' 3"   Weight: 200   Born: August 27, 1989   Age: 19

YEAR	TEAM	LVL	AGE	PA	R	2B	3B	HR	RBI	BB	SO	SB	CS	EqBRR	AVG	OBP	SLG	EqAVG	EqOBP	EqSLG	EqA	VORP	WARP	DEFENSE	
2007	CUB	Rk	17	32	0	0	0	0	2	1	9	0	0	0.0	.067	.094	.067	.065	.091	.065	.000	-20.9	-1.0		
2007	BOI	A-	17	23	2	0	0	0	1	2	5	1	1	-0.5	.190	.261	.190	.136	.174	.136	.000	-8.2	-0.5	4-3B	0
2008	PEO	A	18	14	1	3	0	0	1	0	5	0	0	-0.1	.214	.214	.429	.214	.214	.357	.186	-1.1	-0.1		
2008	BOI	A-	18	277	38	25	2	5	37	13	45	1	3	-4.9	.328	.365	.498	.228	.249	.352	.202	-27.1	-1.7	57-3B	0
2009	CHN	MLB	19	574	41	36	2	9	54	26	138	2	3	-0.7	.225	.264	.348	.222	.261	.348	.204	-19.2	-1.2	135-3B	2

Breakout: 60% Improve: 79% Collapse: 13% Attrition: 3%   Comparables: Craig Repoz, Eddie Williams, Mark Lewis, Kelly Gruber

The much-loved top pick of the team in 2007 worked his way through an initial hand issue to shine in the Northwest League, showing power and a smooth stroke before his 19th birthday. He still has a lot to learn in terms of hitting for power and his footwork around the bag, but a good work ethic should give the organization and fans alike reason to look forward to his first full season with Low-A Peoria.

Daryle Ward   **1B**   Bats: L   Throws: L   Height: 6' 2"   Weight: 240   Born: June 27, 1975   Age: 34

YEAR	TEAM	LVL	AGE	PA	R	2B	3B	HR	RBI	BB	SO	SB	CS	EqBRR	AVG	OBP	SLG	EqAVG	EqOBP	EqSLG	EqA	VORP	WARP	DEFENSE			
2006	WAS	MLB	31	123	15	9	0	6	19	14	21	0	1	-0.3	.308	.390	.567	.317	.403	.587	.325	11.9	1.0	8-RF	-2		
2006	ATL	MLB	31	27	2	1	0	1	7	1	6	0	0	0.1	.308	.333	.462	.308	.333	.462	.270	1.2	0.1				
2007	CHN	MLB	32	133	16	13	0	3	19	22	23	0	0	-0.1	.327	.436	.527	.303	.421	.495	.318	13.4	1.1	10-1B	-1	8-RF	1
2008	CHN	MLB	33	119	8	7	0	4	17	16	24	0	0	-1.9	.216	.319	.402	.206	.311	.402	.249	0.1	0.2	7-1B	2		
2009	CHN	MLB	34	131	16	8	0	5	20	18	24	0	0	-0.9	.271	.371	.464	.268	.367	.464	.284	5.9	0.6	35-1B	0		

Breakout: 33% Improve: 57% Collapse: 27% Attrition: 39%   Comparables: Sid Bream, Dale Long, Doug Mientkiewicz, Dave Clark

Now years past the dream that he might someday pan out as somebody's DH, Ward has managed to put together a nice little career by adapting to the difficulties of life as a professional pinch-hitter. That doesn't automatically equal reliable results, but it goes with the territory when your playing time is sporadic at best. His bat is slowing down, which will increasingly militate against his remaining a manager's late-innings game-breaker off the bench, but a familiarity with the job will keep him in circulation for a while yet.

PITCHERS

Jose Ascanio

Bats: R   Throws: R   Height: 6′ 0″   Weight: 170   Born: May 2, 1985   Age: 24

YEAR	TEAM	LVL	AGE	W	L	SV	G	GS	IP	H	BB	SO	HR	GB%	BABIP	STUFF	WHIP	ERA	DERA	EqH9	EqBB9	EqSO9	EqHR9	DEF	VORP	SN/WX
2006	MYR	A+	21	1	1	0	8	6	31¹	38	20	23	0	36.6%	.388	-7	1.86	4.92	6.49	15.4	7.5	3.4	0.7	-5	-2.6	—
2006	MIS	AA	21	4	2	0	24	0	38	37	17	37	2	35.1%	.327	5	1.42	4.26	6.88	11.0	4.3	5.3	1.0	0	-5.0	—
2007	MIS	AA	22	2	2	10	44	1	78	66	18	71	1	46.8%	.310	11	1.08	2.54	5.42	8.9	2.3	4.9	0.4	9	1.5	—
2007	ATL	MLB	22	1	1	0	13	0	16	17	6	13	3	30.9%	.275	5	1.44	5.06	5.71	8.8	2.6	6.2	1.6	0	-0.8	0.04
2008	IOW	AAA	23	2	1	11	40	0	54²	54	23	58	10	42.4%	.321	-17	1.41	5.10	6.24	9.8	3.9	6.4	1.9	-2	-3.8	—
2008	CHN	MLB	23	0	0	0	6	0	5²	8	4	3	1	36.4%	.368	-26	2.12	7.89	4.50	12.0	4.5	4.5	1.5	-2	-1.4	0.06
2009	CHN	MLB	24	2	3	1	42	3	49¹	56	23	39	9	42.0%	.310	-1	1.58	5.77	5.95	10.0	3.6	6.0	1.5	1	-0.7	0.03

Breakout: 16%   Improve: 45%   Collapse: 14%   Attrition: 11%   Comparables: Leo Nuñez, Ramon Peña, Jose Arredondo, Johann Lopez

The hard-throwing Ascanio had opportunities to sneak into the back end of the bullpen, but tendencies toward high strikes and too many cookies—especially to left-handed hitters—bode ill. If he can keep pumping gas in the mid-90s, he'll get looked at, but the Venezuelan has to be consistent at the right time during the team's moment of need to pan out.

Mitch Atkins

Bats: R   Throws: R   Height: 6′ 3″   Weight: 230   Born: October 1, 1985   Age: 23

YEAR	TEAM	LVL	AGE	W	L	SV	G	GS	IP	H	BB	SO	HR	GB%	BABIP	STUFF	WHIP	ERA	DERA	EqH9	EqBB9	EqSO9	EqHR9	DEF	VORP	SN/WX
2006	PEO	A	20	13	4	0	25	25	138	110	53	127	10	40.4%	.267	-10	1.18	2.41	6.73	11.4	5.5	3.9	2.3	7	-14.6	—
2007	DAY	A+	21	8	7	0	20	20	115	99	31	88	14	36.8%	.266	-23	1.13	3.13	5.80	10.1	3.4	3.9	2.5	0	-2.3	—
2007	TEN	AA	21	1	1	0	7	4	26	30	11	18	5	40.0%	.333	-17	1.58	5.54	6.85	13.3	4.2	3.4	3.0	-2	-3.3	—
2008	TEN	AA	22	9	6	0	18	18	110	107	27	88	14	40.8%	.285	-16	1.22	3.76	6.25	10.4	2.4	4.4	2.0	4	-7.5	—
2008	IOW	AAA	22	8	1	0	10	10	54¹	48	23	44	11	30.7%	.250	-9	1.31	4.48	7.18	8.5	3.9	4.8	2.1	10	-9.3	—
2009	CHN	MLB	23	6	9	0	24	24	127	151	51	82	29	39.0%	.300	2	1.59	6.25	6.33	10.5	3.1	4.9	2.0	2	-6.6	0.28

Breakout: 8%   Improve: 45%   Collapse: 25%   Attrition: 9%   Comparables: Kent Bottenfield, Todd Burns, Ryan Vogelsong, Matt Wise

Winning 17 games across two levels helped Atkins win the organization's minor league pitcher of the year award, but the more impressive development was a fleshed-out arsenal, as he complemented consistent low-90s velocity with a solid curve and change. In another organization, he'd draw more attention, but he has the talent to wind up at the back end of a big-league rotation.

Jose Ceda

Bats: R   Throws: R   Height: 6′ 4″   Weight: 205   Born: January 28, 1987   Age: 22

YEAR	TEAM	LVL	AGE	W	L	SV	G	GS	IP	H	BB	SO	HR	GB%	BABIP	STUFF	WHIP	ERA	DERA	EqH9	EqBB9	EqSO9	EqHR9	DEF	VORP	SN/WX
2006	PDR	Rk	19	2	0	0	8	4	23¹	20	13	31	1	30.9%	.358	-9	1.43	5.06	10.19	15.3	8.7	5.6	3.1	0	-9.0	—
2006	CUB	Rk	19	0	0	0	5	3	12²	6	7	21	0	36.8%	.333	9	1.07	0.74	3.86	9.6	8.7	8.7	1.0	0	1.8	—
2006	BOI	A-	19	1	0	0	3	3	11²	5	2	11	1	28.6%	.250	9	0.63	3.21	6.75	7.7	2.9	4.8	2.9	1	-1.2	—
2007	PEO	A	20	2	2	0	21	6	46¹	14	31	66	1	49.4%	.155	20	0.97	3.11	8.34	4.8	8.8	6.6	0.9	7	-12.5	—
2008	DAY	A+	21	2	2	0	15	12	54¹	41	28	53	4	37.5%	.272	0	1.27	4.81	7.09	10.3	5.9	5.4	1.7	-8	-7.8	—
2008	TEN	AA	21	2	1	9	22	0	30¹	26	14	42	2	36.1%	.358	25	1.32	2.08	2.30	10.5	4.6	8.9	1.3	-2	10.0	—
2009	FLO	MLB	22	3	5	1	22	9	62¹	64	45	62	9	39.0%	.310	8	1.73	5.91	6.26	9.3	5.6	7.3	1.3	0	-4.0	-0.05

Breakout: 19%   Improve: 41%   Collapse: 23%   Attrition: 18%   Comparables: Fernando Cabrera, Rafael Medina, Cecilio Guante, Ubaldo Jimenez

Genuine closer prospects are rare animals. It's like casting starlets for directors hunting for Marlene Dietrich types who refuse to look at anything else—either you've got it or you don't, and it's really up to the director as to whether you do or you don't. Happily, Ceda has the right things to flash on anybody's casting couch: triple-digit velocity and a slider with the right kind of wiggle to turn heads if the heat didn't get your attention. Flipped to the Fish for Kevin Gregg in an unfortunate rush to turn the page from the days of Kerry Wood's closing, he's an excellent bet to wind up saving games for the Marlins by 2010, perhaps no matter what Matt Lindstrom achieves in the meantime.

Neal Cotts

Bats: L   Throws: L   Height: 6' 1"   Weight: 200   Born: March 25, 1980   Age: 29

YEAR	TEAM	LVL	AGE	W	L	SV	G	GS	IP	H	BB	SO	HR	GB%	BABIP	STUFF	WHIP	ERA	DERA	EqH9	EqBB9	EqSO9	EqHR9	DEF	VORP	SN/WX
2006	CHA	MLB	26	1	2	1	70	0	54	64	24	43	12	43.6%	.315	-20	1.63	5.17	4.47	10.3	3.8	6.3	1.8	-4	4.3	0.14
2007	IOW	AAA	27	2	2	0	24	6	50¹	43	30	48	4	47.8%	.300	-4	1.45	4.83	6.38	7.9	5.6	6.4	0.9	4	-4.2	—
2007	CHN	MLB	27	0	1	0	16	0	16²	15	9	14	1	46.0%	.304	3	1.44	4.85	2.70	8.1	4.3	7.0	0.5	-3	2.1	0.16
2008	IOW	AAA	28	2	0	3	19	0	27	23	10	33	0	53.7%	.348	13	1.22	2.00	3.28	9.5	3.6	8.0	0.4	1	6.4	—
2008	CHN	MLB	28	0	2	0	50	0	35²	38	13	43	7	37.9%	.333	9	1.43	4.29	3.96	9.7	2.7	9.4	1.7	-1	4.6	0.00
2009	CHN	MLB	29	2	2	2	43	0	37	35	16	35	5	43.0%	.290	9	1.37	3.96	4.14	8.4	3.3	7.2	1.1	0	7.3	0.61

Breakout: 34%   Improve: 57%   Collapse: 15%   Attrition: 30%   Comparables: Alan Embree, Frank DiPino, Mike Myers, Aaron Fultz

An arbitration-inflated-illionaire as a result of the Cubs' faith that a lefty with a sharp slider and 90-plus velocity has to turn into something someday, Cotts has yet to really inspire confidence for any length of time. But the talent is there, even if he is pushing 30 and has all the reliability of a blind date.

Ryan Dempster

Bats: R   Throws: R   Height: 6' 2"   Weight: 215   Born: May 3, 1977   Age: 32

YEAR	TEAM	LVL	AGE	W	L	SV	G	GS	IP	H	BB	SO	HR	GB%	BABIP	STUFF	WHIP	ERA	DERA	EqH9	EqBB9	EqSO9	EqHR9	DEF	VORP	SN/WX
2006	CHN	MLB	29	1	9	24	74	0	75	77	36	67	5	55.1%	.324	8	1.51	4.80	4.44	9.0	3.6	7.1	0.5	-3	4.0	-1.32
2007	CHN	MLB	30	2	7	28	66	0	66²	59	30	55	8	49.5%	.279	-2	1.34	4.72	5.37	8.1	3.6	7.0	1.0	9	8.3	2.64
2008	CHN	MLB	31	17	6	0	33	33	206²	174	76	187	14	48.6%	.283	31	1.21	2.96	3.25	8.0	2.9	7.3	0.6	4	58.2	6.85
2009	CHN	MLB	32	11	9	1	39	25	168¹	165	67	143	16	49.0%	.300	13	1.38	4.10	4.32	8.7	3.1	6.5	0.8	2	25.0	3.99

Breakout: 3%   Improve: 21%   Collapse: 33%   Attrition: 14%   Comparables: Mike Moore, Dave Stieb, Bobby Witt, Dave Stewart

Teams get so worked up over exotic items like pitching imports from Japan or Cuba, but if you prefer to shop domestic, is there anything that inspires more jibber-jabbery enthusiasm than Marlins moundsmen? Big-game Fishing has made hurlers like Carl Pavano, Dontrelle Willis, Kevin Brown, and A. J. Burnett rich beyond their wildest dreams of avarice, but not one of them has topped his single best professional seasons, all of which were made in Marlins uniforms. Last year, though, Dempster managed to become just the second high-profile former Fish to exceed his best year in Miami (as per SNLVAR), and where Josh Beckett's 2007 with the Red Sox was a predictable bit of blossoming by the youngster, Dempster's long and winding road back from surgery, failure, relief work, and wildness is a bit more inspiring. The move back into the rotation after years of bullpen work was a risk, but Dempster held up well, and he didn't even lose significant velocity starting. If anything, he simplified his repertoire instead of expanding it, relying on pounding the zone with his fastball and moving it around. Re-signed for four years and $52 million, he might yet be cause for Pavano- or Willis-like heartburn. But in light of the non-Sabathias on the market, the years in the pen may reasonably give Dempster the durability to deliver on that deal. Add in an above-replacement-level Harry Caray impression and the new, distinctive, distracting glove flip in his delivery, and Dempster has made himself a popular player on a sports scene that loves a bit of personality.

Chad Gaudin

Bats: R   Throws: R   Height: 5' 10"   Weight: 180   Born: March 24, 1983   Age: 26

YEAR	TEAM	LVL	AGE	W	L	SV	G	GS	IP	H	BB	SO	HR	GB%	BABIP	STUFF	WHIP	ERA	DERA	EqH9	EqBB9	EqSO9	EqHR9	DEF	VORP	SN/WX
2006	SAC	AAA	23	3	0	0	4	4	24¹	14	8	26	0	52.2%	.246	23	0.91	0.37	2.78	5.6	3.2	7.1	0.4	-1	7.1	—
2006	OAK	MLB	23	4	2	2	55	0	64	51	42	36	3	40.1%	.251	-1	1.45	3.09	4.04	6.9	5.8	4.5	0.4	4	19.2	1.59
2007	OAK	MLB	24	11	13	0	34	34	199¹	205	100	154	21	51.1%	.310	5	1.53	4.43	4.72	9.4	4.3	6.2	1.0	-3	23.3	3.71
2008	OAK	MLB	25	5	3	0	26	6	62²	63	17	44	6	41.7%	.300	0	1.28	3.59	4.30	9.3	2.2	5.6	0.9	0	10.9	1.05
2008	CHN	MLB	25	4	2	0	24	0	27¹	29	10	27	5	33.3%	.320	-2	1.43	6.26	6.33	10.0	2.7	8.0	1.7	1	-3.4	-0.13
2009	CHN	MLB	26	5	4	1	40	6	77²	75	30	65	9	45.0%	.290	8	1.36	4.14	4.35	8.5	3.0	6.4	1.0	1	13.9	1.43

Breakout: 20%   Improve: 48%   Collapse: 22%   Attrition: 21%   Comparables: Dennis Martinez, Cliff Fannin, Gene Nelson, Gary Bell

On the crowded list of potential fifth starters who might replace Jason Marquis, Gaudin rates behind Sean Marshall but ahead of Rich Hill and Charlie Root. That's something of a shame, given his successes as a starter (including four quality starts in six for the A's last year), but he's a bit Marquis-like in his profligate generation of baserunners, and short right-handed starters scare too many people in the industry, even when they throw in the low 90s. At least the Cajun can count on being in demand as a roommate for his cooking skills, but he's wasted as just an extra arm.

Angel Guzman

Bats: R   Throws: R   Height: 6' 3"   Weight: 195   Born: December 14, 1981   Age: 27

YEAR	TEAM	LVL	AGE	W	L	SV	G	GS	IP	H	BB	SO	HR	GB%	BABIP	STUFF	WHIP	ERA	DERA	EqH9	EqBB9	EqSO9	EqHR9	DEF	VORP	SN/WX
2006	IOW	AAA	24	4	4	0	15	15	75²	72	24	77	5	40.6%	.328	8	1.28	4.07	5.57	9.4	3.1	6.4	0.9	2	0.2	—
2006	CHN	MLB	24	0	6	0	15	10	56	68	37	60	9	34.9%	.388	10	1.88	7.39	6.02	11.4	5.2	8.9	1.3	-4	-9.5	0.26
2007	CHN	MLB	25	0	1	0	12	3	30¹	32	9	26	2	47.3%	.345	16	1.35	3.56	2.83	10.0	2.5	7.5	0.6	-1	8.0	0.38
2008	CHN	MLB	26	0	0	0	6	1	9²	10	4	10	1	30.0%	.321	6	1.45	5.57	5.59	9.3	2.8	8.4	0.9	0	0.2	0.18
2009	CHN	MLB	27	3	3	1	27	5	56²	54	24	54	7	43.0%	.300	13	1.36	4.25	4.45	8.4	3.2	7.2	1.0	1	9.7	0.98

Breakout: 29%   Improve: 48%   Collapse: 27%   Attrition: 29%   Comparables: Tim Scott, Mike Adams, Paul Shuey, Jason Isringhausen

Healthy slightly less often than Rich Harden, Guzman's latest comeback—from Tommy John surgery this time—got him all the way back to the majors at season's end, and he yet again flashed plus stuff. Guzman's been flirting with possibilities for about as many years as Niles Crane mooned over Daphne, but after a few too many teases, you can forgive people who'd like to see him finally get around to the bonking already. If healthy in consecutive months, he might yet turn into a quality reliever, but that's a big *if*.

Rich Harden

Bats: L   Throws: R   Height: 6' 1"   Weight: 190   Born: November 30, 1981   Age: 27

YEAR	TEAM	LVL	AGE	W	L	SV	G	GS	IP	H	BB	SO	HR	GB%	BABIP	STUFF	WHIP	ERA	DERA	EqH9	EqBB9	EqSO9	EqHR9	DEF	VORP	SN/WX
2006	OAK	MLB	24	4	0	0	9	9	46²	31	26	49	5	43.5%	.241	21	1.22	4.24	6.00	6.0	5.0	8.6	1.0	9	9.0	1.38
2007	OAK	MLB	25	1	2	0	7	4	25²	18	11	27	3	38.7%	.254	20	1.13	2.45	3.00	6.8	3.8	8.6	1.1	1	9.9	1.04
2008	OAK	MLB	26	5	1	0	13	13	77	57	31	92	5	30.5%	.289	41	1.14	2.34	2.68	7.3	3.4	9.6	0.6	0	28.2	3.63
2008	CHN	MLB	26	5	1	0	12	12	71	39	30	89	6	31.1%	.214	40	0.97	1.77	2.89	5.3	3.3	9.3	0.8	6	28.5	3.27
2009	CHN	MLB	27	13	6	0	28	28	182²	133	71	235	21	37.0%	.270	41	1.12	3.04	3.16	6.4	3.0	9.8	1.0	2	51.0	6.91

Breakout: 10%   Improve: 24%   Collapse: 50%   Attrition: 13%   Comparables: Hideo Nomo, Nolan Ryan, Kevin Appier, Sandy Koufax

While getting Harden from the A's drew less attention than Milwaukee's pickup of C. C. Sabathia, it cost the Cubs less in talent and came with a 2009 option that kept him under control and tilting the division's balance of power Wrigley-ward an additional season. The question of whether he'll be healthy enough long enough is going to be asked—and needs to be—for years to come, but as a power pitcher in the weaker league, he'll thrive if managed carefully. Piniella has experience and success handling the type, having gotten good work out of Jose Rijo with the Reds back in the day.

Kevin Hart

Bats: R   Throws: R   Height: 6' 4"   Weight: 215   Born: November 29, 1982   Age: 26

YEAR	TEAM	LVL	AGE	W	L	SV	G	GS	IP	H	BB	SO	HR	GB%	BABIP	STUFF	WHIP	ERA	DERA	EqH9	EqBB9	EqSO9	EqHR9	DEF	VORP	SN/WX
2006	FRD	A+	23	6	11	0	28	27	148¹	149	65	122	18	50.5%	.297	-52	1.44	4.62	8.77	12.5	5.0	4.0	2.6	-3	-46.6	—
2007	TEN	AA	24	8	5	0	18	17	102	100	27	92	13	52.8%	.303	-27	1.25	4.24	7.21	11.3	2.8	5.0	2.0	7	-16.8	—
2007	IOW	AAA	24	4	1	0	9	8	56	56	23	39	6	50.3%	.309	-8	1.41	3.54	5.00	8.8	3.8	4.3	1.2	5	3.6	—
2007	CHN	MLB	24	0	0	0	8	0	11	7	4	13	0	40.0%	.292	10	1.00	0.82	0.87	6.1	2.6	9.6	0.0	0	6.2	0.37
2008	IOW	AAA	25	4	2	5	26	10	57²	38	20	63	3	44.0%	.255	8	1.01	2.81	5.43	6.8	3.3	6.9	0.7	11	1.0	—
2008	CHN	MLB	25	2	2	0	21	0	27²	39	18	23	2	59.6%	.389	-5	2.06	6.50	4.18	12.9	4.8	6.4	0.6	-9	-6.3	-0.61
2009	CHN	MLB	26	5	6	2	61	7	96	105	43	72	14	48.0%	.310	-2	1.54	5.38	5.62	9.7	3.5	5.7	1.3	1	2.3	0.45

Breakout: 40%   Improve: 68%   Collapse: 7%   Attrition: 22%   Comparables: Steve Watkins, Steve Shields, Charlie Mitchell, Albie Lopez

Already something of a steal—the Cubs got him from the Orioles for Freddie Bynum, for Pete (Gammons') sake—Hart has bounced around a bit in his role, but his mix of low-90s heat and a cutter seems to be pointing him pen-ward. He's not going to break out, but a guy good enough to be an extra arm in the pen is always worth having, and his coming this far is a tribute to the team's scouting effort.

Rich Hill

| | | | Bats: L | | Throws: L | | Height: 6' 5" | | Weight: 205 | | Born: March 11, 1980 | | Age: 29 |

YEAR	TEAM	LVL	AGE	W	L	SV	G	GS	IP	H	BB	SO	HR	GB%	BABIP	STUFF	WHIP	ERA	DERA	EqH9	EqBB9	EqSO9	EqHR9	DEF	VORP	SN/WX
2006	IOW	AAA	26	7	1	0	15	15	100²	62	21	135	3	48.4%	.282	47	0.83	1.80	3.21	6.5	2.1	8.9	0.5	5	25.3	—
2006	CHN	MLB	26	6	7	0	17	16	99¹	83	39	90	16	33.2%	.259	12	1.23	4.17	4.77	7.4	3.1	7.4	1.3	8	17.0	2.45
2007	CHN	MLB	27	11	8	0	32	32	195	170	63	183	27	39.4%	.278	21	1.19	3.92	4.35	8.0	2.6	8.0	1.1	17	40.4	4.83
2008	CHN	MLB	28	1	0	0	5	5	19²	13	18	15	2	36.4%	.216	7	1.58	4.11	5.03	5.9	6.9	5.9	0.9	3	3.8	0.70
2008	IOW	AAA	28	2	4	0	7	7	26	22	28	32	4	41.5%	.310	12	1.92	5.88	7.30	9.1	9.5	7.7	1.8	-1	-4.7	—
2008	DAY	A+	28	1	2	0	3	3	12¹	12	11	14	0	36.4%	.387	2	1.87	8.05	13.06	13.9	10.5	6.1	0.9	0	-8.5	—
2009	CHN	MLB	29	4	5	0	27	11	78	76	42	69	10	41.0%	.290	7	1.50	4.98	5.16	8.5	4.2	6.8	1.1	1	5.5	0.98

Breakout: 4%   Improve: 17%   Collapse: 48%   Attrition: 40%   Comparables: David West, Al Osuna, Mickey Mahler, Don Larsen

Nobody wants to be the pitcher who comes into the game to the strains of "Pop Goes the World" by Men Without Hats, but how else can you capture the mystery of Rich Hill? Can we put all of this on his tendency to lose his always-tenuous grip on the strike zone, or did the Cubs' quick decision to ditch him from the rotation a month into the season and send him down to work on his command make matters worse? He never did get better, not after rest, not at any level, and not in winter ball. Blass-itis is no laughing matter, and it's telling that in all of the Cubs' trade talks, nobody was asking after the guy who did what Hill did in 2007. That's because nobody is sure that guy even exists anymore.

Bob Howry

| | | | Bats: L | | Throws: R | | Height: 6' 5" | | Weight: 220 | | Born: August 4, 1973 | | Age: 35 |

YEAR	TEAM	LVL	AGE	W	L	SV	G	GS	IP	H	BB	SO	HR	GB%	BABIP	STUFF	WHIP	ERA	DERA	EqH9	EqBB9	EqSO9	EqHR9	DEF	VORP	SN/WX
2006	CHN	MLB	32	4	5	5	84	0	76²	70	17	71	8	39.9%	.300	16	1.13	3.17	2.84	8.3	1.8	7.6	0.8	0	23.9	2.11
2007	CHN	MLB	33	6	7	8	78	0	81¹	76	19	72	8	32.9%	.296	14	1.17	3.32	3.24	8.5	1.8	7.5	0.8	3	22.9	3.12
2008	CHN	MLB	34	7	5	1	72	0	70²	90	13	59	13	35.3%	.352	-7	1.46	5.35	3.52	11.9	1.4	6.8	1.6	-11	1.2	-0.09
2009	SFN	MLB	35	3	3	3	49	0	56²	59	14	44	7	38.0%	.300	6	1.29	4.02	4.22	9.3	2.0	6.1	1.1	-0	8.2	0.78

Breakout: 17%   Improve: 33%   Collapse: 40%   Attrition: 24%   Comparables: Rick White, Dick Hall, Jose Mesa, Eddie Fisher

Howry's welcome to Wrigleyville was already well worn out, as he made far too many mistakes in the zone, but a 59/8 ratio of strikeouts to unintentional walks reflects his doing something right. He's signed a one-year deal with his original organization, the Giants, who sent him to the White Sox in the locally infamous "White Flag" trade of 1997, so at least he's got both sides of town gnashing their teeth at the mention of his name.

Jon Lieber

| | | | Bats: L | | Throws: R | | Height: 6' 2" | | Weight: 240 | | Born: April 2, 1970 | | Age: 39 |

YEAR	TEAM	LVL	AGE	W	L	SV	G	GS	IP	H	BB	SO	HR	GB%	BABIP	STUFF	WHIP	ERA	DERA	EqH9	EqBB9	EqSO9	EqHR9	DEF	VORP	SN/WX
2006	PHI	MLB	36	9	11	0	27	27	168	196	24	100	27	44.7%	.309	2	1.31	4.93	4.52	9.6	1.1	4.8	1.2	-4	13.1	2.69
2007	PHI	MLB	37	3	6	0	14	12	78	91	22	54	7	45.2%	.336	15	1.45	4.73	4.14	9.9	2.2	5.9	0.7	-4	7.6	1.04
2008	CHN	MLB	38	2	3	0	26	1	46²	59	6	27	10	41.4%	.314	-14	1.39	4.05	3.33	11.5	1.0	4.7	1.8	-4	5.6	0.32
2009	CHN	MLB	39	3	3	1	30	3	54²	65	11	31	8	44.0%	.310	-5	1.39	4.69	4.90	10.5	1.5	4.4	1.2	1	5.1	0.60

Breakout: 21%   Improve: 36%   Collapse: 33%   Attrition: 32%   Comparables: Mike Jackson, Tim Worrell, Terry Mulholland, Jerry Staley

As fun as it is to remember when Lieber was stolen from the Pirates for Brant Brown—the "outfielder" who gave us Ron Santo's famous shriek of "Oh nooo!"—that was 10 years ago. Lieber no longer has the ability to fool enough people on the right often enough to have a future in talk radio, and he fools those on the left less often than Bill O'Reilly. A free agent, he'll go wherever desperation cries out for succor and give it his best shot.

Ted Lilly

| | | | Bats: L | | Throws: L | | Height: 6' 1" | | Weight: 190 | | Born: January 4, 1976 | | Age: 33 |

YEAR	TEAM	LVL	AGE	W	L	SV	G	GS	IP	H	BB	SO	HR	GB%	BABIP	STUFF	WHIP	ERA	DERA	EqH9	EqBB9	EqSO9	EqHR9	DEF	VORP	SN/WX
2006	TOR	MLB	30	15	13	0	32	32	181²	179	81	160	28	38.9%	.292	4	1.43	4.31	4.81	8.9	3.9	7.1	1.3	4	25.9	3.90
2007	CHN	MLB	31	15	8	0	34	34	207	181	55	174	28	36.2%	.270	18	1.14	3.83	4.38	7.9	2.1	7.1	1.1	21	47.2	5.43
2008	CHN	MLB	32	17	9	0	34	34	204²	187	64	184	32	34.9%	.274	12	1.23	4.09	4.20	8.4	2.4	7.1	1.3	8	35.3	4.80
2009	CHN	MLB	33	10	8	0	26	26	161²	156	53	139	24	39.0%	.280	18	1.29	4.26	4.41	8.5	2.6	6.6	1.3	2	23.4	3.85

Breakout: 11%   Improve: 46%   Collapse: 23%   Attrition: 21%   Comparables: Floyd Bannister, Jerry Koosman, Gary Peters, Chris Short

Theodore Roosevelt Lilly might not charge up the hill like his namesake or even Craig Lefferts, but he's an underrated craftsman in a rotation built around talents more dramatic. His tateriffic tendencies and bass-ackwardness make him someone to handle with care, but halfway through his four-year contract, he's given the Cubs 20 quality starts or more in each season. He's not a star, but he's also a lot better than the fourth horseman he rates here. Add in his ability to cut down the running game and help himself out a bit at the plate, and he's an eminently likable little lefty.

Carlos Marmol

														Bats: R		Throws: R		Height: 6' 2"		Weight: 180		Born: October 14, 1982		Age: 26	

YEAR	TEAM	LVL	AGE	W	L	SV	G	GS	IP	H	BB	SO	HR	GB%	BABIP	STUFF	WHIP	ERA	DERA	EqH9	EqBB9	EqSO9	EqHR9	DEF	VORP	SN/WX
2006	WTN	AA	23	3	2	0	11	11	58	42	25	67	1	46.8%	.304	19	1.16	2.33	4.64	8.6	4.3	6.9	0.5	2	5.6	—
2006	CHN	MLB	23	5	7	0	19	13	77	71	59	59	14	33.0%	.270	-1	1.69	6.08	6.10	8.3	6.1	6.3	1.4	6	-1.3	0.41
2007	IOW	AAA	24	4	1	0	8	7	41	30	12	48	4	30.2%	.274	18	1.02	3.95	5.23	6.5	2.6	7.4	1.1	3	1.7	—
2007	CHN	MLB	24	5	1	1	59	0	69¹	41	35	96	3	32.7%	.264	37	1.10	1.43	1.57	5.9	4.1	10.5	0.4	2	34.6	3.70
2008	CHN	MLB	25	2	4	7	82	0	87¹	40	41	114	10	36.4%	.174	21	0.93	2.68	3.67	4.4	3.6	9.5	0.9	7	25.3	5.12
2009	CHN	MLB	26	4	3	6	56	2	71	52	36	86	8	35.0%	.270	22	1.23	3.42	3.57	6.5	3.9	9.2	0.9	1	17.7	1.74

Breakout: 19% Improve: 37% Collapse: 42% Attrition: 12%   Comparables: Armando Benitez, Steve Bedrosian, Ugueth Urbina, Bryan Harvey

The NL leader in Adjusted Runs Prevented, Marmol has served his apprenticeship and should be ready to step into a power closer's role that extends beyond merely logging ninth-inning saves and collecting high-fives. What that should mean is slightly fewer appearances but no real drop in his innings pitched, as he comes into tight games earlier than someone straightjacketed into the Eck role. He'll have to go through the drill of "winning" the job in competition with journeyman Kevin Gregg, but talent will be less the driving factor than Piniella's adapting to the new order.

Jason Marquis

														Bats: L		Throws: R		Height: 6' 1"		Weight: 210		Born: August 21, 1978		Age: 30	

YEAR	TEAM	LVL	AGE	W	L	SV	G	GS	IP	H	BB	SO	HR	GB%	BABIP	STUFF	WHIP	ERA	DERA	EqH9	EqBB9	EqSO9	EqHR9	DEF	VORP	SN/WX
2006	SLN	MLB	27	14	16	0	33	33	194¹	221	75	96	35	44.5%	.294	-17	1.52	6.02	5.85	10.1	3.0	4.1	1.5	1	-7.0	2.06
2007	CHN	MLB	28	12	9	0	34	33	191²	190	76	109	22	52.5%	.275	2	1.39	4.60	4.74	8.8	3.1	4.8	0.9	6	16.9	3.09
2008	CHN	MLB	29	11	9	0	29	28	167	172	70	91	15	49.0%	.292	3	1.45	4.53	4.66	9.4	3.2	4.3	0.8	7	20.8	2.55
2009	COL	MLB	30	6	10	0	32	21	133¹	160	55	78	19	46.4%	.315	1	1.61	5.57	5.23	10.0	3.2	4.7	1.2	1	7.6	1.70

Breakout: 11% Improve: 37% Collapse: 25% Attrition: 21%   Comparables: Richard Dotson, Walt Terrell, Stan Bahnsen, Omar Olivares

Marquis is always going to be a bit of a punching bag, on and off the field, because there's not a lot of glamour in being an overpaid innings sponge. He was on a Cubs team that got that's what he's for and didn't bang on him for what he isn't. Despite his considerable postseason experience, they sensibly skip him in the playoffs, for instance. Put all that together, and he's a solid bit of regular-season filler, but he'll be sorely tested pitching in Coors Field regularly after getting dealt to the Rockies for Luis Vizcaino. The all-time high for a pitcher who hit and allowed career highs in homers in the same season is 42, set by Don Newcombe in 1955 (7 hit, 35 allowed)—what do you think the odds are Marquis takes his best shot at that tally?

Sean Marshall

														Bats: L		Throws: L		Height: 6' 7"		Weight: 205		Born: August 30, 1982		Age: 26	

YEAR	TEAM	LVL	AGE	W	L	SV	G	GS	IP	H	BB	SO	HR	GB%	BABIP	STUFF	WHIP	ERA	DERA	EqH9	EqBB9	EqSO9	EqHR9	DEF	VORP	SN/WX
2006	IOW	AAA	23	0	2	0	4	4	21²	17	14	21	1	57.9%	.291	10	1.46	3.40	6.30	8.1	6.3	6.3	0.9	2	-1.6	—
2006	CHN	MLB	23	6	9	0	24	24	125²	132	59	77	20	48.6%	.286	-7	1.52	5.58	5.67	9.3	3.7	5.0	1.2	6	0.1	1.50
2007	IOW	AAA	24	2	0	0	4	4	24²	17	8	15	2	47.3%	.208	-2	1.01	1.82	5.11	5.5	2.9	3.6	0.7	6	1.3	—
2007	CHN	MLB	24	7	8	0	21	19	103¹	107	35	67	13	49.9%	.293	3	1.37	3.92	4.72	9.3	2.6	5.5	1.0	9	16.9	2.64
2008	IOW	AAA	25	1	1	0	7	7	31²	26	6	25	2	51.6%	.264	3	1.01	3.41	5.28	7.9	1.8	4.7	0.6	4	1.1	—
2008	CHN	MLB	25	3	5	1	34	7	65¹	60	23	58	9	42.8%	.287	5	1.27	3.86	3.46	8.4	2.8	7.1	1.1	-1	13.8	1.64
2009	CHN	MLB	26	5	4	2	42	9	77²	78	29	59	9	46.0%	.290	4	1.38	4.29	4.51	8.9	2.9	5.8	1.0	1	11.4	1.41

Breakout: 15% Improve: 38% Collapse: 44% Attrition: 29%   Comparables: Hank Aguirre, Steve Cooke, Dennis Bennett, Chuck Finley

Marshall seems to be the one young starter the Cubs won't let get away, but also the one everyone asks after in trade talks. He's not overpowering in any literal sense, but his command of breaking stuff and knowledge of how, when, and where to mix in an entirely average left-hander's fastball seem to do just fine in leaving opponents flailing. His upside is as a solid midrotation starter, but if he settles for being a solid innings-eater in middle relief with occasional use as an emergency starter, that works as well.

Jeff Samardzija

Bats: R   Throws: R   Height: 6' 5"   Weight: 220   Born: January 23, 1985   Age: 24

YEAR	TEAM	LVL	AGE	W	L	SV	G	GS	IP	H	BB	SO	HR	GB%	BABIP	STUFF	WHIP	ERA	DERA	EqH9	EqBB9	EqSO9	EqHR9	DEF	VORP	SN/WX
2006	BOI	A-	21	1	1	0	5	5	19	18	6	13	1	58.3%	.288	-21	1.26	2.37	4.96	13.2	5.0	2.2	1.7	1	1.2	—
2006	PEO	A	21	0	1	0	2	2	11¹	6	6	4	1	54.5%	.161	-28	1.08	3.24	11.00	8.0	8.0	1.0	3.0	3	-5.4	—
2007	DAY	A+	22	3	8	0	24	20	107¹	142	35	45	8	52.8%	.347	-50	1.65	4.95	8.17	14.8	4.1	1.4	1.6	0	-26.8	—
2007	TEN	AA	22	3	3	0	6	6	34¹	33	9	20	8	38.3%	.262	-24	1.22	3.41	5.91	10.7	2.8	2.8	3.4	4	-1.1	—
2008	TEN	AA	23	3	5	0	16	15	76	71	42	44	6	41.0%	.280	-24	1.49	4.86	7.00	9.9	5.2	2.9	1.3	5	-11.0	—
2008	IOW	AAA	23	4	1	0	6	6	37¹	32	16	40	5	47.4%	.307	9	1.29	3.14	5.35	9.4	4.3	7.2	1.6	6	0.9	—
2008	CHN	MLB	23	1	0	1	26	0	27²	24	15	25	0	47.0%	.296	7	1.41	2.27	4.45	7.9	4.1	7.0	0.0	3	5.6	0.39
2009	CHN	MLB	24	6	9	1	55	19	123¹	146	68	80	19	45.0%	.310	-8	1.73	6.29	6.52	10.4	4.3	5.0	1.4	2	-8.6	-0.32

Breakout: 2%   Improve: 23%   Collapse: 49%   Attrition: 21%   Comparables: Ray Ricken, Larry Luebbers, Chris Gissell, Eric Ludwick

Believers are no doubt still worked up over the former Domer wideout making it to "The Show" and shining in August. But as much as his obvious gifts—high-90s heat and a plus slider—were on display, when the calendar flipped to September, Cubs fans got to see the maddening inconsistency and wildness that make him something less than a sure thing. Samardzija is an inconsistent mechanical mess who gets sloppy, turning sizzling stuff into offerings both flat and fat. If he irons that out, he'll give the organization the last laugh on everyone—ourselves among them—who second-guessed his $10 million deal to give up football.

Donald Veal

Bats: L   Throws: L   Height: 6' 4"   Weight: 215   Born: September 18, 1984   Age: 24

YEAR	TEAM	LVL	AGE	W	L	SV	G	GS	IP	H	BB	SO	HR	GB%	BABIP	STUFF	WHIP	ERA	DERA	EqH9	EqBB9	EqSO9	EqHR9	DEF	VORP	SN/WX
2006	PEO	A	21	5	3	0	14	14	73²	45	40	86	4	36.3%	.255	5	1.16	2.70	7.39	9.7	7.7	5.7	2.0	7	-11.9	—
2006	DAY	A+	21	6	2	0	14	14	80²	46	42	88	3	41.1%	.240	24	1.10	1.68	5.27	7.2	6.3	5.8	1.0	14	2.6	—
2007	TEN	AA	22	8	10	0	28	27	130¹	126	73	131	11	43.6%	.331	-7	1.53	4.97	7.34	11.4	5.5	5.6	1.4	6	-23.0	—
2008	TEN	AA	23	5	10	0	29	29	145¹	150	81	123	19	45.7%	.326	-32	1.59	4.52	6.96	12.0	5.5	4.9	2.2	3	-19.5	—
2009	PIT	MLB	24	3	8	0	27	16	92²	117	59	70	14	42.0%	.340	4	1.89	6.70	6.86	11.2	5.0	6.0	1.3	-1	-13.3	-0.75

Breakout: 14%   Improve: 41%   Collapse: 22%   Attrition: 18%   Comparables: Kirt Ojala, Norm Charlton, Steve Engel, Dan Plesac

Once a top prospect in the system, Veal's repeated failure to advance represents a massive disappointment, one surrounded by questions about his effort. Even so, he's gifted with a power arsenal: a reliably low-90s fastball and an overhand curve that flits from dominant offering to "ball!" The Cubs decided not to make room for him on the 40-man, and the Pirates snapped him up via the Rule 5 draft on the off chance that plus stuff and a spot in the pen might be a nice match of player and possibility.

Randy Wells

Bats: R   Throws: R   Height: 6' 5"   Weight: 230   Born: August 28, 1982   Age: 26

YEAR	TEAM	LVL	AGE	W	L	SV	G	GS	IP	H	BB	SO	HR	GB%	BABIP	STUFF	WHIP	ERA	DERA	EqH9	EqBB9	EqSO9	EqHR9	DEF	VORP	SN/WX
2006	WTN	AA	23	4	2	0	12	12	62¹	45	13	54	2	48.6%	.253	10	0.93	1.59	4.68	7.7	2.1	4.7	0.6	10	6.1	—
2006	IOW	AAA	23	5	5	0	13	12	69²	87	23	59	7	46.3%	.370	-6	1.59	4.94	5.43	12.3	3.3	5.2	1.4	-7	1.3	—
2007	IOW	AAA	24	5	6	2	40	9	95²	100	41	101	11	46.8%	.341	-9	1.47	4.51	5.23	9.7	4.0	6.9	1.3	-5	3.8	—
2008	IOW	AAA	25	10	4	0	27	19	118²	127	34	102	15	46.6%	.309	-13	1.36	4.02	5.97	10.4	2.7	5.2	1.3	5	-4.7	—
2008	CHN	MLB	25	0	0	0	3	0	4¹	0	2	1	0	63.6%	.000	-22	0.46	0.00	4.50	0.0	4.5	2.2	0.0	2	2.7	0.11
2009	CHN	MLB	26	5	6	1	31	11	88²	99	32	64	12	46.0%	.310	4	1.48	5.15	5.38	9.8	2.8	5.5	1.2	1	4.3	0.88

Breakout: 13%   Improve: 38%   Collapse: 20%   Attrition: 23%   Comparables: Oscar Munoz, Mauro Gozzo, Dan Wright, Jose Silva

Though a former catcher, Wells shows excellent touch on a decent assortment of sliders, changeups, and low-90s heat. He keeps impressing people with his moxie, but a stress fracture cost him a shot at a postseason roster spot. A pity for the Jays that they didn't keep him as a Rule 5 pick last season; he'll never be more than an extra guy for the Cubs, but he'd be Toronto's third starter the way things are going up there.

Kerry Wood

Bats: R   Throws: R   Height: 6' 5"   Weight: 225   Born: June 16, 1977   Age: 32

YEAR	TEAM	LVL	AGE	W	L	SV	G	GS	IP	H	BB	SO	HR	GB%	BABIP	STUFF	WHIP	ERA	DERA	EqH9	EqBB9	EqSO9	EqHR9	DEF	VORP	SN/WX
2006	CHN	MLB	29	1	2	0	4	4	19²	19	8	13	5	42.2%	.246	-5	1.37	4.11	5.40	8.1	3.2	5.4	1.8	1	0.3	0.16
2007	CHN	MLB	30	1	1	0	22	0	24¹	18	13	24	0	35.9%	.286	15	1.27	3.33	3.42	7.2	4.2	8.4	0.0	1	7.1	0.02
2008	CHN	MLB	31	5	4	34	65	0	66¹	54	18	84	3	43.1%	.319	35	1.09	3.26	2.33	7.9	2.1	9.7	0.4	-5	18.0	2.18
2009	CLE	MLB	32	4	4	19	49	0	56	53	21	55	6	41.0%	.300	17	1.30	3.68	3.62	8.2	2.9	8.1	1.0	0	12.6	1.58

Breakout: 16%   Improve: 42%   Collapse: 31%   Attrition: 8%   Comparables: Eric Plunk, Lee Smith, Eric Gagné, Rick Aguilera

Finally healthy and finally present for a full season for the first time since 2003, Woody rose to the challenge of closing, flashing better velocity than he's had in years, setting up his slider extremely well (or the odd, still-nasty curve now and again), and still pitching with that wee bit of the old mean streak that produces a few more hit batsmen than might seem necessary. There's a genuine bit of heartbreak to see him depart after 14 years in the organization, but Marmol is the better pitcher, and the Indians gave Wood a pretty tasty two-year deal with a vesting option for a third that he'll have a hard time keeping from vesting. If you want to get upset about something, let it be Ceda-for-Gregg, not Wood working his way back diligently enough to land himself a good score.

Michael Wuertz

Bats: R   Throws: R   Height: 6' 3"   Weight: 205   Born: December 15, 1978   Age: 30

YEAR	TEAM	LVL	AGE	W	L	SV	G	GS	IP	H	BB	SO	HR	GB%	BABIP	STUFF	WHIP	ERA	DERA	EqH9	EqBB9	EqSO9	EqHR9	DEF	VORP	SN/WX
2006	IOW	AAA	27	6	0	10	30	0	41	30	9	67	2	44.0%	.318	29	0.95	1.76	2.88	7.7	2.0	9.7	0.7	0	12.3	—
2006	CHN	MLB	27	3	1	0	41	0	40²	35	16	42	5	55.2%	.278	14	1.25	2.65	2.38	7.6	3.0	8.2	0.9	-2	13.5	0.22
2007	CHN	MLB	28	2	3	0	73	0	72¹	64	35	79	8	46.5%	.301	16	1.37	3.49	2.86	8.1	3.9	9.1	0.9	-3	18.0	0.89
2008	IOW	AAA	29	0	1	4	17	0	20	13	14	29	2	55.8%	.282	18	1.35	3.60	5.59	7.0	6.1	9.3	0.9	2	0.0	—
2008	CHN	MLB	29	1	1	0	45	0	44²	44	20	30	4	46.0%	.305	-10	1.43	3.62	4.89	9.6	3.6	5.5	0.9	3	5.4	0.12
2009	CHN	MLB	30	2	2	2	42	0	44²	43	21	41	5	46.0%	.300	7	1.44	4.14	4.35	8.4	3.7	7.1	1.0	1	7.3	0.61

Breakout: 7%   Improve: 30%   Collapse: 40%   Attrition: 19%   Comparables: Tyler Yates, Joe Boever, Jerry Johnson, Vicente Romo

What do you think hurts Wuertz, the fact that he keeps getting opportunities or that the Cubs keep kicking him to Iowa, seemingly no matter how well he pitches? Admittedly, he's something of a one-trick pony, a slider king with bass-ackward virtues best used when and where a simple situational southpaw won't do. Even in today's hyperspecialized relief environment, that's a pretty fidgety bit.

Carlos Zambrano

Bats: S   Throws: R   Height: 6' 5"   Weight: 255   Born: June 1, 1981   Age: 28

YEAR	TEAM	LVL	AGE	W	L	SV	G	GS	IP	H	BB	SO	HR	GB%	BABIP	STUFF	WHIP	ERA	DERA	EqH9	EqBB9	EqSO9	EqHR9	DEF	VORP	SN/WX
2006	CHN	MLB	25	16	7	0	33	33	214	162	115	210	20	49.2%	.259	28	1.29	3.41	3.76	6.8	4.2	8.0	0.7	10	54.3	6.14
2007	CHN	MLB	26	18	13	0	34	34	216¹	187	101	177	23	48.2%	.273	17	1.33	3.95	4.23	8.0	3.7	7.0	0.9	14	43.8	5.61
2008	CHN	MLB	27	14	6	0	30	30	188²	172	72	130	18	48.1%	.273	13	1.29	3.91	3.89	8.5	3.0	5.5	0.8	4	36.1	5.02
2009	CHN	MLB	28	11	8	0	27	27	169²	159	77	141	17	47.0%	.290	17	1.39	4.12	4.34	8.3	3.5	6.3	0.9	2	25.1	4.19

Breakout: 3%   Improve: 20%   Collapse: 45%   Attrition: 19%   Comparables: Joey Jay, Stan Williams, Wilson Alvarez, Jason Jennings

Big Z isn't quite the workhorse he'd been in years past. While some of it was a matter of the club's taking precautions as it eased its way down the stretch, Zambrano started wrestling with shoulder pain in June and was complaining of a dead arm by the end of August. Especially troubling was his stretch-drive kick, which alternated exceptional and execrable outings (and a few too many of the latter) with very little in between. The question is whether there's a ticking time bomb in his right arm, if it's in his elbow or shoulder, and how soon it blows up. On a lighter note, he's had 221 PAs since his last walk as a hitter, but he's hit 11 homers in that span. It's as if Shawon Dunston never left, except now he pitches.

LINEOUTS

Hitters

PLAYER	TEAM	LVL	AGE	PA	R	2B	3B	HR	RBI	BB	SO	SB-CS	EqBRR	AVG/OBP/SLG	EqAVG/EqOBP/EqSLG	EqA	VORP	WARP
RF K. Burke*	PEO	A	20	144	12	5	1	2	8	11	34	3-0	-0.8	.206/.278/.305	.179/.236/.269	.170	-15.3	-1.5
	BOI	A-	20	280	46	18	2	7	41	28	70	6-3	-1.3	.261/.336/.437	.189/.238/.320	.193	-39.3	-3.0
C K. Hill#	IOW	AAA	29	412	56	24	2	17	64	40	77	3-2	-2.4	.275/.350/.492	.206/.271/.361	.218	-18.0	-0.3
	CHN	MLB	29	22	0	1	0	0	1	0	12	0-0	-0.1	.095/.095/.143	.136/.136/.182	.000	-3.7	-0.4
OF D. Johnston*	PEO	A	21	298	39	17	1	15	50	22	87	4-8	-3.7	.288/.349/.524	.245/.298/.451	.250	3.8	-0.1
OF J. Kroeger*	IOW	AAA	25	480	73	38	3	15	69	43	82	12-3	-2.4	.307/.373/.514	.258/.318/.425	.258	7.2	0.4
3B C. McGehee	IOW	AAA	25	550	68	30	0	12	92	40	89	0-3	-4.2	.296/.345/.429	.251/.296/.362	.229	-12.1	-0.2
	CHN	MLB	25	25	1	1	0	0	5	0	8	0-0	0.0	.167/.160/.208	.167/.160/.208	.078	-3.2	-0.1
OF B. Snyder*	BUF	AAA	26	446	52	28	5	12	61	27	123	7-3	1.3	.246/.297/.426	.212/.260/.378	.218	-18.8	-0.6
2B N. Spears*	TEN	AA	23	473	71	22	5	7	51	58	72	6-5	-1.4	.299/.394/.438	.243/.322/.365	.244	-4.0	0.5

Repeating a cycle of flailing in Low-A followed by modest productivity in Boise isn't propelling **Kyler Burke** toward a big-league career, but he is the kind of athletic outfielder the organization loves. Even so, he needs to show something resembling progress. ⦿ With very little fanfare, **Koyie Hill** came back from an off-season accident in which he severed four fingers from his right hand with a table saw. With the fingers reattached, he shook off assertions he'd never again play, hit more than well enough, and now stands a decent chance at backing up Soto behind the plate. ⦿ A former high school shortstop picked in the fourth round of the 2005 draft, **Dylan Johnston** found his promise of power potential hampered by injuries, but he just took a big step forward. ⦿ Already a well-traveled minor league vet going into his age-26 season, **Josh Kroeger** chips in with a bit of pop and an arm strong enough for right, but he'll have to win a popularity contest with a big-league skipper to land a job. ⦿ The Cubs' expanding commitment to scouting the Far East netted another catch in Korean teen **Hak-Ju Lee**, an unpolished, toolsy shortstop years removed from showing up on big-league radars. ⦿ With slick glove work and a contact-oriented stroke, **Casey McGehee** could help out on the right bench as a defensive replacement at third and pinch-hitter; that may be in Milwaukee, where he signed after the season. ⦿ Discarded by an Indians organization desperate for outfield help, former Ball State star **Brad Snyder** was picked up on waivers, the thinking being that his athleticism and power potential might finally develop with a change of scenery. For this to happen, his command of the strike zone has to improve. ⦿ **Nate Spears,** a refugee from the Orioles' organization, has never failed to get on base, but his walks, bunting skills, and poor footspeed make for a blend that's been out of fashion for years.

Pitchers

PLAYER	TEAM	LVL	AGE	W	L	SV	IP	H	BB	SO	HR	GB%	BABIP	STUFF	WHIP	ERA	DERA	EqH9	EqBB9	EqSO9	EqHR9	DEF	VORP
J. Berg	TEN	AA	24	0	3	0	28¹	29	11	10	1	73.8%	.283	-22	1.41	3.50	5.27	10.2	3.6	1.3	0.7	-1	1.0
	IOW	AAA	24	4	6	0	90¹	91	48	49	11	62.2%	.288	-33	1.54	5.68	8.29	9.9	5.0	3.1	1.4	10	-25.3
M. Carrillo	DAY	A+	21	7	6	0	115²	82	33	71	9	40.6%	.221	-15	0.99	2.88	5.05	9.1	3.4	2.9	1.7	0	6.3
	TEN	AA	21	2	2	0	24¹	32	10	22	4	44.6%	.368	-1	1.73	7.04	8.46	14.9	4.0	5.2	2.4	-6	-7.1
A. Cashner	BOI	A-	21	1	1	0	16¹	19	19	16	1	49.0%	.391	-22	2.33	4.97	9.69	17.3	13.8	3.5	2.8	-2	-5.9
J. Jackson	BOI	A-	20	0	0	0	9	7	1	14	1	47.4%	.333	7	0.89	5.00	7.36	13.5	2.5	7.4	3.7	-1	-1.4
	PEO	A	20	2	2	0	24	22	5	37	3	37.7%	.404	19	1.13	3.00	5.79	15.4	3.4	8.7	3.4	0	-0.4
	DAY	A+	20	2	0	0	17	11	7	21	0	32.1%	.268	15	1.06	1.59	3.68	9.2	4.9	7.4	0.6	0	3.1
M. Mateo	PEO	A	24	1	0	1	15	4	7	20	1	44.4%	.115	-3	0.73	1.20	6.08	4.1	6.1	6.8	1.4	3	-0.7
	DAY	A+	24	4	3	0	88¹	87	29	65	6	42.3%	.310	-34	1.31	3.57	6.40	12.6	4.0	3.6	1.5	0	-6.9
D. McDaniel	BOI	A-	20	2	0	7	32¹	14	17	45	1	64.6%	.206	14	0.96	1.67	5.16	6.4	5.8	5.8	1.2	5	1.5
B. Muldowney	PEO	A	23	1	0	0	31	17	10	25	2	50.0%	.176	-21	0.87	2.61	7.50	6.0	3.9	3.0	1.5	7	-6.3
	DAY	A+	23	5	3	0	54¹	47	13	39	7	43.8%	.260	-28	1.10	2.98	4.86	11.7	3.1	3.7	2.7	0	3.8
D. Rhee	PEO	A	19	4	1	0	40	28	16	33	0	61.6%	.252	19	1.10	1.80	6.00	8.0	5.0	3.5	0.5	2	-1.6
B. Schlitter	CLR	A+	22	4	3	6	48²	39	21	58	1	54.0%	.306	7	1.23	2.22	4.20	9.2	4.8	6.4	0.6	0	7.0
	DAY	A+	22	0	1	3	8¹	9	3	9	0	40.0%	.400	-1	1.45	2.17	4.05	14.9	4.1	6.8	0.0	0	1.2

A beefy sinkerballer, **Justin Berg** has been added to the 40-man roster in recognition of his abilities to reduce the game to infield patty-cake, but problems against lefties and struggles in winter ball reflect a far-from-certain future. ⦿ If you're worried about where to get your Big Z fix in the years to come, chunky Mexican import **Marco Carrillo** might just be your man. ⊘ After a breakout season closing for Texas Christian, **Andrew Cashner** was picked 19th overall by the Cubs in last June's draft. They're converting him to starting for the time being; his high-90s velocity and wipeout slider headline a full arsenal that projects well. ⊘ A steal in the ninth round of the 2008 draft, **Jay Jackson** offers mid-90s heat and a plus slider that has the organization drooling in anticipation. ⊘ A live-armed Dominican stringbean, **Marcos Mateo** was added to the 40-man to keep him in-house after a strong second half, but he was old for his level, and he's still a bit raw. ⊘ A juco pitcher most teams shied away from, thinking he was going to Oklahoma State, **Dan McDaniel** had a price after all, and the Cubs paid it after picking him in the 14th round last June. Armed with mid-90s heat, he could move up fast as a reliever. ⊘ A gutty sinker/slider type picked out of Pitt in 2006, **Billy Muldowney** bounced back from an injury-riddled '07 to show some promise. ⊘ Another Korean prospect signed just last year, **Dae-Eun Rhee** is a power lefty with breaking stuff that will need work once he bounces back from Tommy John surgery; watch for his return to a stateside mound in the second half. ⊘ Not to be mistaken for an ill-considered malted laxative concept, **Brian Schlitter** is big, throws hard, and was the door prize from the Phillies for taking Scott Eyre off the Cubs' hands.

MANAGER: LOU PINIELLA

YEAR	TEAM	W-L	Pythag +/-	Avg PC	100+ P	120+ P	QS	BQS	REL	REL w Zero R	IBB	Subs	PH	PH Avg	PH HR	SB2	CS2	SB3	CS3	SAC Att	SAC %	POS SAC	Squeeze	Swing	In Play
2007	CHN	85-77	-3	95.0	69	6	81	4	478	323	46	85	257	.208	6	78	24	8	9	64	75.0%	28	4	126	98
2008	CHN	97-64	-3	96.0	72	3	83	5	478	298	45	48	271	.198	5	66	27	20	7	109	59.6%	21	3	173	142

Since we've talked about Piniella's gifts more than enough in the team essay, there is perhaps no better space to note how lucky the Windy City is. In contrast with a generation of polite gray men in dugouts across the industry, all politely providing the media with antiseptic observations about their responsibilities and aspirations, Piniella and Ozzie Guillen reflect how canny tacticians can also do their jobs screening the media without leaching personality out of the exercise. A certain genuine quality in both men has become a fundamental part of promoting their teams as entertainment. In a city that worships Mike Ditka and Phil Jackson to this day, it's a lovely thing for both ballclubs to have two such skippers, and years from now, when fans on both sides of town are back to being stuck with the facile, polite, and dull, we'll miss these days.

Chicago White Sox

Who doesn't like a nice surprise? After their bull's-eye landing on 72 wins in 2007, the White Sox didn't take that as a hint to tear down and start over. Instead, Kenny Williams elected to make a serious play at giving their core talent another bite of the apple, shoring up the lineup by trading for Nick Swisher and Orlando Cabrera in high-profile deals, while adding Alexei Ramirez and swapping in Carlos Quentin in less splashy moves. Much would depend on how well young starters John Danks and Gavin Floyd panned out, but that bet had already been made.

While this was generally seen as a dubious exercise, the risk was clearly worth the payoff, as the Sox brawled their way to an AL Central title. Snobs might note that a good amount of the drama was self-inflicted (no less than Carlos Quentin's season-ending injury was), as a sweep at the Twins' hands with a week to go made matters unnecessarily exciting. Fair enough, but the double-dare play-ins immediately after the season, without a single day's pause—first a Monday makeup game against the luckless Tigers to try to tie the Twins and then, that done, a Tuesday one-game playoff against Minnesota that clinched the matter—was as unusual a high-wire act as you could imagine. This baseball riff on March Madness–style win-or-die matchups made for attention-grabbing good times in a sport where buzzer-beaters are almost automatically out of the question because of the six-month marathon of the regular season. That the Sox delivered on it made for that much more interesting a contrast with the Cubs' almost actuarial ascendance to October (and subsequent almost-instant elimination by the Dodgers).

After the Sox notched this gratuitous, tasty little division title, the happy upshot of what Williams has been up to since is that he's taken this last hurrah of the 2005 team as historical gravy. A good team built on discrete strengths—a lineup driven by park-aided power, depth, and breadth in the pitching staff, and a quality defense years before the Rays made it fashionable—the Sox gave their fans an entertaining final spasm. Now, with the passage of time, the odds that the Sox might contend again with a lineup keyed on Paul Konerko and Jim Thome and Jermaine Dye, or with a rotation built up around Mark Buehrle, Javier Vazquez, and Jose Contreras, is nearing zero. Williams knows this, which is why, after this team gave the South Side its little division title, he's continued breaking it up, slowly regearing that contender to build up the next one.

As we touched on in last year's edition, Williams has already been busy on this score, acquiring younger players to make over his roster one spot at a time. In his additions of Quentin and Ramirez or Danks and Floyd, it's important to recognize that Williams traded for all of them, and all are twentysomethings with good futures and their peak seasons ahead of them. Dealing away Vazquez to the Braves gave the Sox either their next starting catcher or their next big right-handed slugger at first base, depending on which of the two Tyler Flowers turns into; either way, Flowers is going to be a huge (literally) part of the next really good Sox lineup. Dealing away Nick Swisher is equal parts dispatching a disappointment and adding a third-base bat (Wilson Betemit) to replace Joe Crede, but the acquisition of pitchers Jeff Marquez and Jhonny Nuñez should be evaluated with the understanding that the organization

---

WHITE SOX PROSPECTUS

2008 record: 89-74; First place, AL Central

Pythagenport record: 90-73

Runs scored per game: 4.98 (5th in AL)

Runs allowed per game: 4.50 (6th in AL)

Team EqA: .259 (Tied for 8th in AL)

2008 Batters Age: 31.2 (3rd-oldest in AL)

2008 Pitchers Age: 28.8 (4th-oldest in AL)

Ballpark: U.S. Cellular Field; Hitter's park; Park Factor of 1.039

2008: A durable rotation, an effective bullpen, and a low-OBP, high-HR lineup resemble 2005's title team, without the big trophy.

2009: Recognizing the risk of discovering what happens when players with old-player skills get old, Kenny Williams retools on the fly.

has done a good job of identifying other people's young pitchers who can help them. Williams has been taking offers on Dye as well. If the general manager similarly leverages the right fielder's last year or two under team control into a key piece of the next good Sox squad, he will have achieved exactly what you'd ask of any GM, with or without a *New York Times* best seller as part of his legacy.

At its core, what the Sox have been doing is fundamentally sound big-picture management, using transient success as a stepping-off point to build something with greater staying power. Where most teams might cling to that brief bit of happiness and try to keep the guttering embers of success burning, however dimly, Williams has taken on a much more admirable task: a responsibility to design an uncertain future. His past successes—and Ozzie's—should allow both men time in which to take their next best shot. Although the fruits of Sox player development have been emptied out in recent seasons in service of the team's pursuit of playoff spots, the organization has been open to exploiting outside sources of talent. While you can't exactly hook up a pipeline to Cuba, perhaps one of the additional benefits of employing Jose Contreras is having some brand recognition among the latest émigrés, first Alexei Ramirez and now third-base teen sensation Dayan Viciedo. Nor did Williams just settle for the exotic solutions. His diktat before the 2007 draft, directing the team to shake up its drafting tendencies and start taking some chances instead of collecting low-upside players, seems to have helped as well.

We've already tucked into a bit of Windy City triumphalism in our essay on the Cubs, so let's instead look at one of the more interesting developments of the season in Bridgeport. One operational decision *could* have contributed to the Sox' victory: Ozzie Guillen's flirtations with either a four-man rotation or a five-day rotation down the stretch. Dial back to August 9, 2008, when Jose Contreras came back from the disabled list, started against Boston, shredded his Achilles, and departed for the rest of the season. A game behind the Twins at that point with 36 to play, the Sox did not have an established somebody to step into the fifth slot. From the farm, they had organizational soldier Lance Broadway and Clayton Richard, the guy they'd picked instead of Broadway the first time Contreras got hurt. A power lefty who'd stepped in for Contreras for three starts, Richard failed to get out of the fifth in any of them. From the pen, they might also have turned to D. J. Carrasco; he'd managed nine quality starts in 20 for the Royals in 2005 and had been a starter in Triple-A—albeit a bad one—in 2007. With Scott Linebrink on the

disabled list, however, the bullpen needed Carrasco; robbing Peter to pay Paul carried a potentially heavier cost than one cranky apostle, and Carrasco's spotty track record as a starter made such a move less than a sure proposition.

In this situation, lots of teams might have freaked out and sent out a search party for Jeff Weaver (or worse). The Sox initially responded by floating Broadway and Richard through the slot, winning the first three times the fifth starter's turn came up, against the Royals, Mariners, and Orioles, the league's worst—convenient, that. However, they weren't skipping the slot, and Guillen didn't take advantage of offdays scheduled on three straight Thursdays to keep his front four starting every fourth day, no matter what. The next two times the fifth slot came up, the Sox lost. A trio of rainouts in the second week of September made a hash of things, compressing 15 games into 15 days with one doubleheader and one offday, or 16 games in 16 days if they had to play the rained-out game against the Tigers (as the Sox wound up having to do).

Guillen had already entertained the idea of starting Vazquez on three days' rest in Detroit on the 13th before that game was rained out, so his solution wasn't all that surprising. He had the front three starters (by his lights)—Vazquez, Buehrle, and Floyd—start on three days' rest the next week and pushed Danks back a couple of days so as to line up that trio to face the Twins in their big series on four days' rest. It turned out badly twice over: Vazquez got hammered by the Yankees in his start on short rest, Floyd lost to the Royals on short rest, and both of them got belted around in the Twins' sweep of the series Guillen had so carefully lined them up for. At least Buehrle won his game on short rest and had done well against the Royals. After Danks lost the first game of the final series to the Indians on normal rest, leaving the Sox down a half game, Guillen repeated the short-rest exercise in the final weekend with Vazquez and Buehrle. Vazquez lost yet again, and Buehrle won again, forcing the playoff (which Floyd won on three days' rest) and the playoff (which Danks won on three days' rest). As things turned out, the fifth slot received only one of those 16 assignments (Richard lost a tough game to the Yankees).

Did working guys on short rest help or hurt? Buehrle won his two games on short rest, and he pitched well enough to win in the start against the Twins that was bookended by those games; he also gave the Sox seven good innings in the second game of the Division Series before giving up a pair of hits in the eighth. Floyd put up a quality start through six innings in his first short-rest start against the Royals on the 20th and beat the

Tigers on short rest in the makeup game on the 29th. Danks threw eight shutout innings at the Twins on short rest in the one-game playoff and followed that with a strong game against the Rays in the Sox' only win in the Division Series. On the other hand, in the four games from his first turn on short rest through his Game One assignment against Tampa Bay in the Division Series, Javier Vazquez didn't make it out of the fifth inning.

Is there a moral to this story, besides that starting Javier Vazquez on short rest is a bad idea? We're not dealing with enough data to really draw a substantial conclusion. Using the definition of a quality start as three runs allowed through the first six innings pitched, over the last 20 years, a starter has delivered a quality start 53.9 percent of the time; on less than four days' rest, the number drops to 49.7 percent of the time. In evaluating the difference, keep in mind that it's generally the better starters, those who deliver quality starts more often than 53.9 percent of the time, who make those starts on short rest. In contrast, over the same 20 years, starting on four or five days' rest, pitchers give a quality start—a winnable ballgame—54.8 percent of the time. That's a bit of a difference, and unless you're the White Sox in extremis, this sort of math adds up over 162 games.

Let's go at this from another tack: much of what motivates proposals to go back to the four-man rotation is built on the ready understanding that fifth starters are pitchers you generally want to see a lot less of. You can do that quite a bit without asking your front four to start on short rest, actually. Skipping the fifth starter over the course of six months of regular-season play every time the schedule lets you makes plenty of sense, while keeping the other four starters on their turns every fourth day. If anything, it's relatively historical, because history isn't really replete with four-man rotations where four men got all the starts—it took the 1972 Dodgers to invent not fifth starters per se as much as an established fifth starter, as well as the egalitarianism that the fifth starter was a person who shouldn't be skipped.

Take the 2009 schedule for the White Sox, for instance: begin by trying to start your first starter every fifth day, and you end up with a final spread in which whoever you put in the top slot gets 36 starts, the second and third get 35 apiece, the fourth gets 32, and your fifth gets only 24. That adds up to a lot more quality spread across a much larger chunk of your season, yet you're doing it without asking any of your front four to do anything unusual, just take their turns every fifth day. In contrast, the 2008 Sox had their fifth starters make 32 starts, and that's with some conscious effort to avoid them in the melee of September, with starters having to make starts on short rest. Given that your front three are basically taking on the same workload, what's important is identifying which of the pitchers is the fourth-best starter of the four, since he's the one who will see fewer games than the other three will. Picking your fifth starter can be a Stengel-like exercise of playing matchups, or a space to alternate a few kids, or a bit of both.

Beyond potentially getting a greater number of winnable ballgames from your front four, another virtue of turning the fifth slot into a less stable assignment is what it allows you to do with your roster. Of those 24 starts for the fifth slot, 21 will be before September and roster expansion, and only nine of those 21 would have to be made on four days' rest. This means that many times, you can do as the Sox did with Richard and Broadway tag-teaming in August; you can bounce a guy to the minors when you don't need a fifth starter standing around on his rest days. Whether a manager would rather have an extra bat, a third catcher, a pinch-runner, or a reliever, treating the fifth starter's slot as a floater allows the skipper extra game days to stock the roster with the mix he'd rather have. Teams are already effectively doing this on an ad hoc basis during the regular season, but if they were to plan early for some of the roster churn, they could derive some additional advantages. Take the bullpen: knowing that the fifth starter ships out for a shuttle assignment to Triple-A tomorrow and that you'll have another reliever tomorrow night can influence how you use your relievers in tonight's game.

All of this might seem dryly logistical, but given a game where the wild card has helped narrow the margins between who makes it to October and who doesn't, this kind of broad-stroke proposal for how to maximize value from your rotation doesn't seem especially kooky—if anything, given the stakes, it's almost a necessity. A large segment of the stat-head community is still kidding itself over ever seeing four-man rotations again, but you can treat this as a pragmatic alternative that allows for seeing more of the game's better starters and fewer of the game's worst.

HITTERS

Brandon Allen   1B

Bats: L   Throws: R   Height: 6' 2"   Weight: 235   Born: February 12, 1986   Age: 23

YEAR	TEAM	LVL	AGE	PA	R	2B	3B	HR	RBI	BB	SO	SB	CS	EqBRR	AVG	OBP	SLG	EqAVG	EqOBP	EqSLG	EqA	VORP	WARP	DEFENSE
2006	KAN	A	20	427	36	17	2	15	68	22	126	6	4	-1.2	.213	.257	.380	.170	.202	.291	.159	-51.8	-6.4	96-1B -14
2007	KAN	A	21	561	84	39	5	18	93	39	124	7	4	-2.6	.283	.337	.483	.216	.260	.367	.214	-26.2	-3.1	66-1B -3
2008	WNS	A+	22	366	57	26	4	15	44	41	83	14	3	-0.9	.279	.372	.527	.245	.325	.471	.271	12.8	1.0	83-1B 0
2008	BIR	AA	22	173	30	6	2	14	31	19	41	3	1	0.6	.275	.358	.614	.247	.316	.538	.281	10.0	0.6	39-1B -1
2009	CHA	MLB	23	564	62	27	2	22	73	43	163	9	4	-0.1	.230	.294	.418	.230	.294	.427	.248	-7.2	0.1	132-1B 0

Breakout: 45%   Improve: 65%   Collapse: 19%   Attrition: 7%   Comparables: Eric Hinske, Travis Ishikawa, Luis Gonzalez, Brian Dubose

Allen is the reason that the White Sox hope newly acquired power prospect Tyler Flowers can remain at catcher. A big, left-handed masher drafted out of a Texas high school in the fifth round in 2005, Allen has always had great power, but needed some work on his plate discipline. A repeat of the Sally League in 2007 cut his strikeout-to-unintentional walk rate from 5.7 to 3.4. Last year, he got that ratio down to 2.1, then crushed 14 homers after making the midseason leap to Double-A. The only drag is his poor play in the field, but if the Sox wind up with Flowers at first and Allen at DH in 2011, they'd be unlikely to complain.

Brian Anderson   CF

Bats: R   Throws: R   Height: 6' 2"   Weight: 220   Born: March 11, 1982   Age: 27

YEAR	TEAM	LVL	AGE	PA	R	2B	3B	HR	RBI	BB	SO	SB	CS	EqBRR	AVG	OBP	SLG	EqAVG	EqOBP	EqSLG	EqA	VORP	WARP	DEFENSE
2006	CHA	MLB	24	406	46	23	1	8	33	30	91	4	7	-0.6	.224	.290	.358	.214	.285	.349	.217	-11.4	-0.1	108-CF 7
2007	CHR	AAA	25	223	29	8	2	8	31	19	47	3	2	-1.3	.255	.318	.435	.218	.278	.386	.228	-6.3	0.2	35-CF 5
2007	CHA	MLB	25	19	3	1	0	0	0	2	7	0	0	0.4	.118	.211	.176	.118	.211	.176	.100	-2.5	-0.2	
2008	CHA	MLB	26	193	24	13	0	8	26	10	45	5	1	2.0	.232	.272	.436	.228	.272	.444	.245	0.9	-0.4	50-CF -4
2009	CHA	MLB	27	140	16	7	0	5	17	11	34	2	1	0.1	.239	.302	.420	.240	.303	.429	.252	2.9	0.5	37-CF -1

Breakout: 45%   Improve: 58%   Collapse: 33%   Attrition: 47%   Comparables: Luis Terrero, Brian Lesher, Mark Smith, Jeff Baker

Handed the center field job in 2006, Anderson pancaked. Three years later, he's hit a mere .221/.277/.379 in the majors, and the White Sox still don't have a center fielder. Anderson is still an asset in the field, but it hardly seems worth carrying his bat for his glove. Fortunately, he still has options left. Weird stats fact: Anderson's eight homers last year all came off lefties, but 10 of his 13 doubles came off of righties.

Cole Armstrong   C

Bats: L   Throws: R   Height: 6' 3"   Weight: 210   Born: August 24, 1983   Age: 25

YEAR	TEAM	LVL	AGE	PA	R	2B	3B	HR	RBI	BB	SO	SB	CS	EqBRR	AVG	OBP	SLG	EqAVG	EqOBP	EqSLG	EqA	VORP	WARP	DEFENSE	
2006	WNS	A+	22	149	9	5	0	2	14	17	30	0	0	-2.3	.237	.322	.321	.184	.253	.250	.172	-16.0	-1.2	31-C -3	4-1B 0
2007	WNS	A+	23	316	35	17	0	12	39	23	69	1	1	0.0	.288	.342	.474	.211	.255	.344	.204	-19.2	-1.4	69-C -7	
2007	BIR	AA	23	79	2	6	0	1	12	3	20	0	0	-2.2	.239	.273	.366	.219	.253	.315	.200	-5.3	0.1	20-C 2	
2008	BIR	AA	24	234	27	17	0	6	31	10	31	0	1	-0.5	.252	.293	.413	.215	.245	.341	.198	-15.5	-0.9	53-C -2	
2008	CHR	AAA	24	145	12	12	0	2	17	5	27	0	0	-0.7	.275	.310	.406	.245	.276	.374	.219	-4.3	0.1	36-C 1	
2009	CHA	MLB	25	333	20	13	0	6	33	17	84	0	0	-1.3	.193	.238	.299	.193	.239	.306	.180	-17.8	-0.4	80-C 0	

Breakout: 28%   Improve: 42%   Collapse: 42%   Attrition: 28%   Comparables: Jeff Smith, Matt Merullo, Jeff Banister, Izzy Molina

Coming off a strong showing in the Arizona Fall League, Armstrong could emerge as A. J. Pierzynski's backup this year. He's quite similar to A. J. at the plate (lefty doubles power, no patience), but a superior defender behind it, and he's seven years A. J.'s junior. He's not a future starter, but if Pierzynski's bat goes bad, the Sox could do worse than upgrade to Armstrong's glove in the short term.

Gordon Beckham   SS

Bats: R   Throws: R   Height: 6' 0"   Weight: 185   Born: September 16, 1986   Age: 22

YEAR	TEAM	LVL	AGE	PA	R	2B	3B	HR	RBI	BB	SO	SB	CS	EqBRR	AVG	OBP	SLG	EqAVG	EqOBP	EqSLG	EqA	VORP	WARP	DEFENSE
2008	KAN	A	21	63	11	2	0	3	8	5	7	0	1	-0.4	.310	.365	.500	.254	.302	.424	.242	0.4	0.5	13-SS 3
2009	CHA	MLB	22	581	49	26	2	14	59	41	129	6	4	0.6	.233	.293	.368	.234	.293	.375	.233	-1.6	0.5	136-SS -3

Breakout: 0%   Improve: 0%   Collapse: 0%   Attrition: 0%   Comparables: Ryan Braun, Chris Burke, Gabe Alvarez, Aaron Hill

Beckham emerged as a potential first-round pick when he led the Cape Cod League in home runs during the summer of 2007. He then solidified that status with a .411/.519/.804 University of Georgia campaign that included 28 home runs in 71 games. The White Sox were pleasantly surprised that he was still on the board when their pick, eighth overall, came up last June. Beckham has been even better than expected as a pro, adding a .394/.468/.652 performance in the Arizona Fall League to his Sally League debut. There's no doubt that he'll continue to hit for average and power and draw his share of walks, but some folks question his overall athleticism and thus his ability to remain at shortstop. With Alexei Ramirez shifting to short this spring, some within the organization see Beckham more as the next Chase Utley. He could be Chicago's second baseman as early as 2010.

Orlando Cabrera — SS — Bats: R — Throws: R — Height: 5' 9" — Weight: 185 — Born: November 2, 1974 — Age: 34

YEAR	TEAM	LVL	AGE	PA	R	2B	3B	HR	RBI	BB	SO	SB	CS	EqBRR	AVG	OBP	SLG	EqAVG	EqOBP	EqSLG	EqA	VORP	WARP	DEFENSE	
2006	LAA	MLB	31	675	95	45	1	9	72	51	58	27	3	9.0	.282	.335	.404	.271	.330	.395	.262	30.1	3.1	147-SS	-1
2007	LAA	MLB	32	701	101	35	1	8	86	44	64	20	4	4.7	.301	.345	.397	.296	.342	.401	.265	26.5	3.1	150-SS	-4
2008	CHA	MLB	33	730	93	33	1	8	57	56	71	19	6	2.7	.281	.334	.371	.277	.334	.376	.253	19.0	2.2	155-SS	-4
2009	CHA	MLB	34	555	67	26	2	7	48	41	60	14	4	1.3	.268	.324	.372	.268	.325	.379	.252	10.6	1.7	130-SS	0

Breakout: 12%   Improve: 40%   Collapse: 34%   Attrition: 30%   Comparables: Eric Young, Dick Groat, Johnny Temple, Mike Bordick

Cabrera is admirably consistent. He's a good defensive shortstop who's rarely hurt, and he can steal bases, knock some doubles, and draw enough walks to keep his team in the black at the position. He's a valuable nonstar regular for a playoff-quality team that gets the bulk of its production from other positions, but at age 34, it's not clear how long he'll be able to keep it up. Chances are that the contract Cabrera receives this winter will be a bad one for his new team.

David Cook — OF — Bats: R — Throws: R — Height: 5' 11" — Weight: 195 — Born: July 21, 1981 — Age: 27

YEAR	TEAM	LVL	AGE	PA	R	2B	3B	HR	RBI	BB	SO	SB	CS	EqBRR	AVG	OBP	SLG	EqAVG	EqOBP	EqSLG	EqA	VORP	WARP	DEFENSE			
2006	WNS	A+	24	528	76	24	5	16	58	77	108	17	4	1.1	.233	.352	.421	.163	.252	.292	.193	-48.8	-6.0	128-LF	-24		
2007	WNS	A+	25	400	73	22	3	16	50	51	77	10	8	0.0	.279	.373	.503	.175	.245	.313	.193	-33.9	-3.3	35-LF	3	34-RF	-7
2007	BIR	AA	25	126	19	5	2	8	25	24	22	2	2	0.1	.293	.437	.626	.238	.357	.495	.288	7.1	0.7	27-RF	0		
2008	BIR	AA	26	274	44	15	2	12	30	62	47	8	7	-0.9	.313	.467	.577	.225	.348	.405	.264	4.7	-0.4	36-RF	-7	21-CF	-3
2008	CHR	AAA	26	262	32	11	2	7	26	31	65	6	0	-0.1	.259	.351	.417	.221	.309	.359	.240	-5.8	-0.6	56-RF	-4	8-LF	0
2009	CHA	MLB	27	440	40	18	2	11	41	44	131	6	3	0.1	.195	.279	.331	.195	.279	.338	.218	-21.1	-1.3	104-RF	-4		

Breakout: 11%   Improve: 37%   Collapse: 36%   Attrition: 13%   Comparables: Cliff Brumbaugh, Bo Porter, Pat Casey, Scott Ullger

A Miami of Ohio product who has moved slowly through the system, Cook has passed the expiration date for being an outfield prospect, but he does just keep hitting and could yet emerge as a valuable bench bat, providing power and patience from the right side. He'd be even more valuable if the White Sox stop him from trying to steal bases.

Joe Crede — 3B — Bats: R — Throws: R — Height: 6' 2" — Weight: 230 — Born: April 26, 1978 — Age: 31

YEAR	TEAM	LVL	AGE	PA	R	2B	3B	HR	RBI	BB	SO	SB	CS	EqBRR	AVG	OBP	SLG	EqAVG	EqOBP	EqSLG	EqA	VORP	WARP	DEFENSE	
2006	CHA	MLB	28	586	76	31	0	30	94	28	58	0	2	-3.3	.283	.323	.506	.268	.311	.489	.268	20.0	3.6	141-3B	13
2007	CHA	MLB	29	178	13	5	0	4	22	10	24	0	1	-0.0	.216	.258	.317	.211	.258	.325	.198	-11.0	-0.2	44-3B	5
2008	CHA	MLB	30	373	41	18	1	17	55	30	45	0	3	-1.2	.248	.314	.460	.240	.309	.462	.259	6.2	1.4	93-3B	4
2009	CHA	MLB	31	326	31	15	0	12	44	23	44	0	1	-1.3	.241	.298	.412	.242	.299	.420	.247	0.9	0.8	79-3B	2

Breakout: 27%   Improve: 52%   Collapse: 26%   Attrition: 32%   Comparables: Ed Sprague, Rod Barajas, Dave Roberts, Daryle Ward

Crede announced his return from back surgery with seven home runs in April and proceeded to be very much the same player he was before his herniated disc, albeit one with an expected decline in his defense. There was also a surprising, if subtle, improvement in his plate discipline. Then his back flared up again, forcing him to the DL in late July. He made a week-long attempt to return to the lineup at the end of August, but hit just .174 before yielding to back pain yet again. That's not the best way to enter free agency.

Jermaine Dye   RF

Bats: R   Throws: R   Height: 6' 5"   Weight: 240   Born: January 28, 1974   Age: 35

YEAR	TEAM	LVL	AGE	PA	R	2B	3B	HR	RBI	BB	SO	SB	CS	EqBRR	AVG	OBP	SLG	EqAVG	EqOBP	EqSLG	EqA	VORP	WARP	DEFENSE	
2006	CHA	MLB	32	611	103	27	3	44	120	59	118	7	3	-2.9	.315	.385	.622	.294	.370	.590	.314	64.5	6.3	139-RF	7
2007	CHA	MLB	33	561	68	34	0	28	78	45	107	2	1	-1.6	.254	.317	.486	.243	.310	.484	.267	10.9	2.0	130-RF	3
2008	CHA	MLB	34	645	96	41	2	34	96	44	104	3	2	-1.4	.292	.344	.541	.282	.338	.539	.290	37.7	2.7	147-RF	-10
2009	CHA	MLB	35	500	66	26	1	25	84	40	95	3	1	-2.0	.271	.333	.503	.272	.334	.514	.286	17.1	2.3	118-RF	-3

Breakout: 14%   Improve: 38%   Collapse: 29%   Attrition: 16%   Comparables: Dave Parker, Dave Winfield, Dante Bichette, Bob Allison

Dye's time in Chicago represents a late peak for a player who got off to a slow start on his career and then had his proper peak interrupted by a freak injury. Dye was the World Series MVP in his first season with the Pale Hose and an AL MVP candidate in his second year. And although he slumped badly to start 2007, he hit .298/.368/.579 after that year's All-Star break and nearly equaled that clip over a full season in 2008. Now 35, he's likely to start slowing down soon, but that seems unlikely to happen all at once in this, the last guaranteed year of his contract.

Josh Fields   3B

Bats: R   Throws: R   Height: 6' 1"   Weight: 215   Born: December 14, 1982   Age: 26

YEAR	TEAM	LVL	AGE	PA	R	2B	3B	HR	RBI	BB	SO	SB	CS	EqBRR	AVG	OBP	SLG	EqAVG	EqOBP	EqSLG	EqA	VORP	WARP	DEFENSE			
2006	CHR	AAA	23	526	85	32	4	19	70	54	136	28	5	-0.7	.305	.379	.515	.278	.351	.488	.287	32.0	1.9	113-3B	-13		
2006	CHA	MLB	23	25	4	2	0	1	2	5	8	0	0	-0.0	.150	.320	.400	.150	.320	.400	.253	-0.4	0.5	4-3B	4		
2007	CHR	AAA	24	249	28	14	0	10	37	39	60	8	5	-1.4	.283	.394	.498	.255	.361	.466	.283	12.5	0.4	53-3B	-9		
2007	CHA	MLB	24	418	54	17	1	23	67	35	125	1	1	-2.6	.244	.308	.480	.235	.303	.480	.263	7.3	0.9	78-3B	-4	20-LF	1
2008	CHR	AAA	25	318	41	15	3	10	35	37	98	8	2	-0.1	.246	.341	.431	.226	.318	.394	.250	-1.0	0.3	57-3B	-1		
2008	CHA	MLB	25	35	3	1	0	0	2	3	17	0	0	0.1	.156	.229	.188	.156	.229	.188	.121	-3.8	-0.6	7-3B	-2		
2009	CHA	MLB	26	476	59	21	2	20	61	52	146	9	3	-0.5	.236	.324	.437	.237	.325	.446	.267	8.5	1.5	113-3B	-4		

Breakout: 22%   Improve: 49%   Collapse: 18%   Attrition: 17%   Comparables: Adam Hyzdu, Russ Morman, Steve Hosey, Scott Bryant

The White Sox' top pick in 2004, Fields crushed at Triple-A in 2006 and stepped into the breach left by Crede in 2007, turning in a solid rookie season, particularly in the power department. With Crede back in action last year, Fields got an ego-deflating demotion back to Charlotte, where his struggles were exacerbated by a right knee that required off-season arthroscopic surgery. When Crede's back went out again, it was Juan Uribe who finished the season as the Chicago third baseman, not Fields; he'd underwhelmed Ozzie in a brief six-game tryout prior to Uribe's ascension. This year, with Crede and Uribe both gone and his legs back under him, Fields should pick up where he left off two years ago. Whether that's a good thing depends on one's perception of low OBPs and moderate power production, but in a platoon role with Wilson Betemit—he slugged .698 against big-league lefties in '07—he could shine.

Chris Getz   2B

Bats: L   Throws: R   Height: 6' 0"   Weight: 175   Born: August 30, 1983   Age: 25

YEAR	TEAM	LVL	AGE	PA	R	2B	3B	HR	RBI	BB	SO	SB	CS	EqBRR	AVG	OBP	SLG	EqAVG	EqOBP	EqSLG	EqA	VORP	WARP	DEFENSE			
2006	BIR	AA	22	573	67	15	6	2	36	52	47	19	6	4.4	.256	.326	.321	.240	.301	.313	.221	-23.8	-2.4	127-2B	-15		
2007	BIR	AA	23	319	40	10	2	3	29	36	30	13	7	0.6	.299	.382	.381	.269	.340	.350	.246	-0.1	-0.5	67-2B	-9		
2008	CHR	AAA	24	457	60	24	1	11	52	41	53	11	4	1.5	.302	.366	.448	.268	.333	.415	.261	9.6	1.9	61-2B	6	26-SS	-5
2009	CHA	MLB	25	469	52	19	2	6	37	39	60	8	3	1.8	.251	.316	.344	.251	.317	.351	.238	-1.5	0.4	111-2B	-3		

Breakout: 9%   Improve: 35%   Collapse: 31%   Attrition: 12%   Comparables: Mickey Morandini, Ken Boswell, Ed Giovanola, Jeff Huson

With Alexei Ramirez set to shift over to his natural position of shortstop, Getz gets first dibs on the keystone, threatening Chicago with an onslaught of such puns. Getz's first crack at Triple-A resulted in his best minor league season and his first display of any real power, albeit in a homer-friendly environment. He profiles as an Orlando Cabrera type of hitter, delivering solid averages, enough walks, few strikeouts, and doubles power to the gaps. In the field, he's been prepped as a utility man, but second base is his best position. He's a good fit and shouldn't need a platoon partner.

Ken Griffey Jr.   OF

Bats: L   Throws: L   Height: 6' 3"   Weight: 230   Born: November 21, 1969   Age: 39

YEAR	TEAM	LVL	AGE	PA	R	2B	3B	HR	RBI	BB	SO	SB	CS	EqBRR	AVG	OBP	SLG	EqAVG	EqOBP	EqSLG	EqA	VORP	WARP	DEFENSE
2006	CIN	MLB	36	472	62	19	0	27	72	39	78	0	0	-0.2	.252	.316	.486	.244	.311	.471	.264	14.8	-0.4	98-CF -19
2007	CIN	MLB	37	623	78	24	1	30	93	85	99	6	1	-4.6	.277	.372	.496	.264	.368	.481	.293	31.6	3.1	130-RF -6
2008	CIN	MLB	38	425	51	20	1	15	53	61	64	0	1	-2.5	.245	.355	.432	.237	.350	.425	.271	9.0	1.1	85-RF -2
2008	CHA	MLB	38	150	16	10	0	3	18	17	25	0	0	-2.0	.260	.347	.405	.246	.340	.392	.259	3.5	-0.6	28-CF -9
2009	CHA	MLB	39	442	53	21	1	16	58	53	76	2	1	-2.7	.250	.343	.432	.251	.344	.441	.272	7.2	1.1	105-RF -7

Breakout: 17%   Improve: 45%   Collapse: 22%   Attrition: 21%   Comparables: Fred McGriff, Dwight Evans, Darrell Evans, Dave Winfield

If Kid Griffey hung 'em up now, no one would blame him. After 20 years, 611 homers, and countless leg injuries, he's earned some rest. He finally made it back to the postseason last year, providing a highlight in the Sox' tie-breaking 1-0 win over the Twins by throwing a runner out at home for a season-saving assist, but he hit for less power than in any other season since he was a 19-year-old rookie, and that one moment of clutch defense didn't come near to justifying the uniquely Chicago delusion that he was still a center fielder. Griffey would need three seasons to reach 3,000 hits at his current pace. Unless a playoff team offers him a fourth-outfielder/pinch-hitter spot from which to pursue an elusive championship ring, he'd be better off starting his Cooperstown clock.

Paul Konerko   1B

Bats: R   Throws: R   Height: 6' 2"   Weight: 215   Born: March 5, 1976   Age: 33

YEAR	TEAM	LVL	AGE	PA	R	2B	3B	HR	RBI	BB	SO	SB	CS	EqBRR	AVG	OBP	SLG	EqAVG	EqOBP	EqSLG	EqA	VORP	WARP	DEFENSE
2006	CHA	MLB	30	643	97	30	0	35	113	60	104	1	0	-5.7	.313	.381	.551	.292	.368	.528	.302	47.6	4.0	132-1B -1
2007	CHA	MLB	31	636	71	34	0	31	90	78	102	0	1	-3.2	.259	.351	.490	.244	.344	.479	.280	24.1	2.5	138-1B 2
2008	CHA	MLB	32	514	59	19	1	22	62	65	80	2	0	-2.4	.240	.344	.438	.230	.340	.434	.270	10.5	1.5	111-1B 3
2009	CHA	MLB	33	528	64	23	1	21	76	60	92	1	0	-2.8	.256	.345	.448	.256	.346	.457	.277	9.9	1.7	124-1B 0

Breakout: 9%   Improve: 40%   Collapse: 20%   Attrition: 14%   Comparables: Eric Karros, Gil Hodges, Deron Johnson, Tom Brunansky

Konerko's 2008 looked a lot like Dye's 2007. Hitting just .215/.325/.368 on June 15, Konerko landed on the DL with a strained oblique. After returning on July 8, he hit .267/.366/.514 with 14 homers in 60 games plus two more in the AL Division Series (to give him seven career jacks in 19 post-season games). Like Dye in 2008, Konerko is likely to come close to repeating his second-half numbers this year. That's good news for the Sox, who have Konerko under contract for two more years and can't deal him unless he waives his five-and-ten rights.

Sergio Miranda   SS

Bats: S   Throws: R   Height: 5' 9"   Weight: 169   Born: March 5, 1987   Age: 22

YEAR	TEAM	LVL	AGE	PA	R	2B	3B	HR	RBI	BB	SO	SB	CS	EqBRR	AVG	OBP	SLG	EqAVG	EqOBP	EqSLG	EqA	VORP	WARP	DEFENSE	
2007	KAN	A	20	283	45	9	2	1	30	37	27	5	3	-1.2	.282	.384	.349	.221	.304	.273	.208	-16.0	-0.5	60-SS -1	
2007	GRF	Rk	20	32	2	3	1	0	1	3	4	1	2	-0.9	.464	.516	.643	.310	.355	.448	.265	3.1	-0.1	7-SS -2	
2008	KAN	A	21	250	31	9	0	2	35	23	26	2	7	-2.2	.306	.383	.375	.251	.318	.318	.222	-7.1	-1.5	21-2B -8	21-SS -1
2008	WNS	A+	21	121	11	5	2	0	12	7	15	5	5	-1.0	.209	.250	.291	.179	.215	.259	.162	-14.7	-1.8	27-SS -5	5-2B -3
2009	CHA	MLB	22	498	44	18	2	2	32	37	70	6	6	0.9	.229	.290	.292	.229	.290	.298	.208	-13.9	-1.4	118-SS -12	

Breakout: 41%   Improve: 58%   Collapse: 26%   Attrition: 16%   Comparables: Mark Germann, Timothy Harkrider, Greg Smith, Michael Westbrook

A small, scrappy, switch-hitting shortstop out of Virginia Commonwealth University, Miranda has good plate discipline, but only average speed and no power, the latter of which could reduce the number of pitches out of the zone he sees as he moves up the ladder. In the field, he's sure-handed, but has limited range. He's likely to be a future utility man.

Jerry Owens   CF

Bats: L   Throws: L   Height: 6' 3"   Weight: 190   Born: February 16, 1981   Age: 28

YEAR	TEAM	LVL	AGE	PA	R	2B	3B	HR	RBI	BB	SO	SB	CS	EqBRR	AVG	OBP	SLG	EqAVG	EqOBP	EqSLG	EqA	VORP	WARP	DEFENSE			
2006	CHR	AAA	25	493	75	15	5	4	48	45	61	40	12	6.5	.262	.330	.346	.227	.294	.313	.222	-23.0	0.6	83-CF	5	26-LF	7
2007	CHR	AAA	26	267	39	10	0	3	21	29	37	23	8	2.1	.284	.361	.366	.237	.311	.314	.232	-9.1	0.6	57-LF	8		
2007	CHA	MLB	26	389	44	9	2	1	17	27	63	32	8	3.9	.267	.324	.312	.265	.326	.310	.238	-2.1	0.3	80-CF	3	4-LF	-1
2008	CHR	AAA	27	398	39	11	0	1	21	38	56	30	13	2.7	.276	.346	.316	.222	.290	.256	.202	-28.5	-1.5	87-CF	0		
2008	CHA	MLB	27	17	1	0	0	0	1	0	4	2	1	-0.7	.250	.250	.250	.250	.250	.250	.193	-1.3	-0.1				
2009	CHA	MLB	28	406	39	11	1	1	22	30	73	21	6	2.0	.211	.272	.258	.212	.273	.263	.196	-22.0	-0.6	97-CF	1		

Breakout: 21%   Improve: 30%   Collapse: 47%   Attrition: 20%   Comparables: Jason Tyner, Don Landrum, Tyrell Godwin, Peter Bergeron

Anderson's miserable 2006 made Owens look like a viable center-field option in 2007. Owens' bat shattered that illusion, and he spent most of last year playing an errorless, punchless center field for Triple-A Charlotte. He's fast and thus a useful defensive replacement and pinch-runner, but at his age, he'll never be more than that.

A. J. Pierzynski   C

Bats: L   Throws: R   Height: 6' 3"   Weight: 240   Born: December 30, 1976   Age: 32

YEAR	TEAM	LVL	AGE	PA	R	2B	3B	HR	RBI	BB	SO	SB	CS	EqBRR	AVG	OBP	SLG	EqAVG	EqOBP	EqSLG	EqA	VORP	WARP	DEFENSE	
2006	CHA	MLB	29	543	65	24	0	16	64	22	72	1	0	-2.4	.295	.333	.436	.280	.320	.421	.255	18.2	1.6	126-C	-5
2007	CHA	MLB	30	509	54	24	0	14	50	25	66	1	1	-1.9	.263	.309	.403	.253	.301	.406	.243	8.5	1.6	119-C	3
2008	CHA	MLB	31	570	66	31	1	13	60	19	71	1	0	-1.6	.281	.312	.416	.274	.306	.417	.249	14.5	1.4	127-C	-5
2009	CHA	MLB	32	372	35	17	1	8	44	16	51	1	1	-1.6	.258	.295	.385	.259	.296	.393	.237	2.7	1.3	89-C	-1

Breakout: 14%   Improve: 30%   Collapse: 41%   Attrition: 38%   Comparables: Terry Kennedy, Javy Lopez, Sandy Alomar, Eddie Taubensee

It's curious that a player as disliked as Pierzynski can still manage to be overrated. A heady player, his value is almost completely tied up in his ability to catch 130-plus games and deliver 40-odd extra-base hits annually. Since the Twins traded him, he has hit an extremely consistent .274/.317/.417 while averaging 134 games per year. There's something to be said for reliability, but his middling power is undermined by the fact that he's never drawn more than 20 unintentional walks in a season, and his steady presence behind the plate is diminished by his poor throwing arm (21.6 percent of opposing runners caught stealing over those five seasons, and just 18 percent last year). The result is a 32-year-old catcher with no room for decline. He's signed through 2010; his next team will get burned if it expects him to keep on keeping on.

Carlos Quentin   LF

Bats: R   Throws: R   Height: 6' 2"   Weight: 220   Born: August 28, 1982   Age: 26

YEAR	TEAM	LVL	AGE	PA	R	2B	3B	HR	RBI	BB	SO	SB	CS	EqBRR	AVG	OBP	SLG	EqAVG	EqOBP	EqSLG	EqA	VORP	WARP	DEFENSE			
2006	TUC	AAA	23	396	66	30	3	9	52	45	46	5	0	-1.9	.289	.424	.487	.247	.364	.425	.278	12.4	1.6	73-RF	-2	6-CF	1
2006	ARI	MLB	23	191	23	13	3	9	32	15	34	1	0	0.0	.253	.342	.530	.246	.332	.503	.281	8.1	1.4	42-RF	5		
2007	TUC	AAA	24	135	30	12	1	4	27	9	14	0	1	-0.6	.348	.430	.574	.297	.375	.500	.296	9.9	0.7	26-RF	-2		
2007	ARI	MLB	24	263	29	16	0	5	31	18	54	2	2	-1.4	.214	.298	.349	.210	.294	.349	.226	-10.6	-0.4	65-RF	2		
2008	CHA	MLB	25	569	96	26	1	36	100	66	80	7	3	2.7	.288	.394	.571	.278	.388	.569	.316	51.3	4.5	128-LF	-6		
2009	CHA	MLB	26	539	78	28	1	23	77	53	86	5	2	-0.4	.273	.363	.485	.274	.364	.495	.294	20.9	3.0	127-LF	-2		

Breakout: 21%   Improve: 50%   Collapse: 19%   Attrition: 9%   Comparables: Bob Allison, Gary Roenicke, Frank Thomas, Dwight Evans

A first-round pick out of Stanford in 2003, Quentin made his pro debut at High-A in 2004, was in Triple-A by 2005, and hit .313/.413/.527 over parts of four minor league seasons. Somehow, his poor, injury-laden half-season for the Diamondbacks in 2007 made people forget about all that, so his breakout with the White Sox last year still managed to come as a surprise. The Cell is a great place to be a right-handed power hitter, but Quentin also hit .300/.390/.560 on the road and appeared to be on his way to the league MVP when he suffered a bizarre season-ending injury, breaking his wrist when he hit his bat with his fist in frustration during an at-bat on September 1. Wrist injuries and Quentin's emerging fragility leave lingering concerns, but his production last year was real and will be repeated if he can stay healthy.

Alexei Ramirez　　　　SS　　　　Bats: R　　Throws: R　　Height: 6' 1"　　Weight: 170　　Born: September 22, 1981　　Age: 27

YEAR	TEAM	LVL	AGE	PA	R	2B	3B	HR	RBI	BB	SO	SB	CS	EqBRR	AVG	OBP	SLG	EqAVG	EqOBP	EqSLG	EqA	VORP	WARP	DEFENSE			
2008	CHA	MLB	26	509	65	22	2	21	77	18	61	13	9	0.0	.290	.317	.475	.284	.313	.482	.264	19.9	1.2	114-2B	-5	7-CF	0
2009	CHA	MLB	27	524	66	27	3	16	67	20	67	12	7	1.4	.289	.320	.456	.290	.321	.465	.267	19.9	1.8	123-2B	-6		

Breakout: 24% Improve: 56% Collapse: 19% Attrition: 13%　　　　Comparables: Jerry Adair, Clint Barmes, Dave Stapleton, John Castino

Considering that the Cuban defector was a largely unknown quantity when he signed with the White Sox just before we went to press last year, PECOTA did an awfully good job of predicting Ramirez's debut season. Still, the spindly Ramirez was better than even PECOTA expected. Intended as a center-field safety net and power-hitting utility man, Ramirez settled in at second base following a mid-May injury to Juan Uribe and hit .303/.330/.501 the rest of the way, finishing second in the AL Rookie of the Year voting. An excellent athlete who generates great leverage with his long arms, he needs to be more discerning both at the plate (33.2 PA/UIBB after taking over at the keystone) and on the bases. Otherwise, he should be one of the most valuable shortstops in the American League's weak field after moving back to his natural position this spring.

John Shelby III　　　　OF　　　　Bats: R　　Throws: R　　Height: 5' 10"　　Weight: 185　　Born: August 6, 1985　　Age: 23

YEAR	TEAM	LVL	AGE	PA	R	2B	3B	HR	RBI	BB	SO	SB	CS	EqBRR	AVG	OBP	SLG	EqAVG	EqOBP	EqSLG	EqA	VORP	WARP	DEFENSE			
2006	GRF	Rk	20	279	37	12	3	8	36	18	55	8	4	-2.3	.272	.332	.440	.186	.224	.293	.172	-49.7	-2.9	42-2B	-1	23-SS	-3
2007	KAN	A	21	538	83	35	9	16	79	35	77	19	8	1.0	.301	.352	.508	.234	.274	.393	.229	-13.5	-3.4	61-CF	-10	54-2B	-17
2008	WNS	A+	22	482	81	37	7	15	80	22	98	33	5	4.1	.295	.331	.510	.258	.288	.458	.256	6.5	0.6	67-LF	-2	21-CF	0
2009	CHA	MLB	23	529	54	27	3	14	58	26	127	17	6	1.5	.237	.278	.389	.238	.279	.397	.235	-8.7	-0.4	124-LF	-5		

Breakout: 33% Improve: 55% Collapse: 23% Attrition: 11%　　　　Comparables: Jason Felice, Aaron Rowand, Ray Sadler, Aaron Peel

He's only the second John T. Shelby in major league history, but the third in his family. Son of the 1980s center fielder nicknamed "T-Bone," "Treybone" is a power-and-speed threat, but just like daddy, he could find his lack of plate discipline to be his undoing. Shelby's K/UIBB slipped to 4.7 last year. That's not a good sign for player who finished the year as a 23-year-old in High-A. Also a bad sign: this former second baseman reimagined as the team's future center fielder made most of his starts in the left pasture in 2008. His lack of walks and slow adjustment to the outfield mark him as surprisingly raw for a college product. He'll have to shape up quickly to maintain his prospect status.

Nick Swisher　　　　1B　　　　Bats: S　　Throws: L　　Height: 6' 0"　　Weight: 215　　Born: November 25, 1980　　Age: 28

YEAR	TEAM	LVL	AGE	PA	R	2B	3B	HR	RBI	BB	SO	SB	CS	EqBRR	AVG	OBP	SLG	EqAVG	EqOBP	EqSLG	EqA	VORP	WARP	DEFENSE			
2006	OAK	MLB	25	672	106	24	2	35	95	97	152	1	2	-1.6	.254	.372	.493	.242	.370	.479	.290	30.0	4.8	78-1B	2	73-LF	9
2007	OAK	MLB	26	659	84	36	1	22	78	100	131	3	2	1.3	.262	.381	.455	.260	.386	.468	.296	34.1	4.0	54-CF	-10	46-RF	6
2008	CHA	MLB	27	588	86	21	1	24	69	82	135	3	3	1.1	.219	.332	.410	.209	.329	.404	.256	3.4	-0.8	60-CF	-17	52-1B	0
2009	NYA	MLB	28	524	64	22	1	20	71	70	118	3	1	-0.7	.237	.345	.429	.241	.351	.457	.279	12.3	1.9	123-1B	1		

Breakout: 22% Improve: 45% Collapse: 20% Attrition: 15%　　　　Comparables: Pat Burrell, Chili Davis, Bob Allison, Brad Wilkerson

An investigation into Swisher's lost season suggests that it was the product of little more than bad luck. His walk rate and isolated power were right in line with his career rates, and his line-drive rate was up from his previous two seasons, but his batting average on balls in play fell 52 points from his 2007 mark. That doesn't scan, nor does the fact that he was Nick Swisher at the Cell (.247/.361/.517) and Bob Uecker on the road (.189/.301/.294). Given a fresh start, he should snap back to form with the Yankees, who will do him (and themselves) the additional favor of not asking him to play center field.

Jim Thome — DH

Bats: L Throws: R Height: 6' 3" Weight: 250 Born: August 27, 1970 Age: 38

YEAR	TEAM	LVL	AGE	PA	R	2B	3B	HR	RBI	BB	SO	SB	CS	EqBRR	AVG	OBP	SLG	EqAVG	EqOBP	EqSLG	EqA	VORP	WARP	DEFENSE
2006	CHA	MLB	35	610	108	26	0	42	109	107	147	0	0	-1.6	.288	.416	.598	.259	.403	.552	.321	62.7	5.3	
2007	CHA	MLB	36	536	79	19	0	35	96	95	134	0	1	-2.8	.275	.410	.563	.258	.402	.548	.318	45.9	4.5	
2008	CHA	MLB	37	602	93	28	0	34	90	91	147	1	0	-0.8	.245	.362	.503	.231	.357	.492	.289	33.3	2.9	
2009	CHA	MLB	38	499	67	22	0	24	74	68	126	0	1	-2.7	.249	.357	.477	.249	.358	.487	.288	19.3	1.8	118-DH

Breakout: 6% Improve: 21% Collapse: 28% Attrition: 22%   Comparables: Darrell Evans, Willie McCovey, Frank Thomas, Willie Stargell

Like Dye, Thome has had a good ride on the South Side. He had a monstrous first season in Chicago, picked up his 500th career homer with a game-winning jack at the Cell in late 2007, and hit the solo home run that put the Sox back in the playoffs in 2008's tiebreaker against the Twins. Last year, he played in the most games he's played in since 2003, vesting his 2009 option along the way, and even slugged .521 against lefty pitching. Though he lost a bit of power and a few walks, symptoms of the ice-cold streaks with which he bookended his .288/.399/.604 June-August peak, he was still third in VORP among designated hitters behind the career years of Milton Bradley and Aubrey Huff. Now at 541, he'll pass 600 homers on his way to Cooperstown.

Juan Uribe — INF

Bats: R Throws: R Height: 6' 0" Weight: 220 Born: March 22, 1979 Age: 30

YEAR	TEAM	LVL	AGE	PA	R	2B	3B	HR	RBI	BB	SO	SB	CS	EqBRR	AVG	OBP	SLG	EqAVG	EqOBP	EqSLG	EqA	VORP	WARP	DEFENSE			
2006	CHA	MLB	27	495	53	28	2	21	71	13	82	1	1	-0.1	.235	.257	.441	.223	.247	.430	.229	-0.7	0.8	126-SS	3		
2007	CHA	MLB	28	563	55	18	2	20	68	34	112	1	9	-2.1	.234	.284	.394	.227	.279	.395	.226	-8.0	1.1	147-SS	6		
2008	CHA	MLB	29	353	38	22	1	7	40	22	64	1	3	-0.7	.247	.296	.386	.242	.296	.394	.235	-3.9	0.6	52-3B	6	41-2B	0
2009	CHA	MLB	30	348	33	17	1	10	42	21	69	1	2	-0.6	.239	.290	.401	.240	.291	.409	.240	1.3	0.7	84-SS	-1		

Breakout: 47% Improve: 67% Collapse: 17% Attrition: 32%   Comparables: Ed Sprague, Joe Crede, Dale Berra, Dave Roberts

We still don't understand the quick $4.5 million the Sox gave Uribe within weeks of the 2007 World Series. Yes, he finished 2008 as the third baseman of a playoff team, but that was by default after Crede's back ended his season, Fields' knee sapped his, and Uribe lost his second-base job to a mid-May hamstring tear and Alexei Ramirez. Uribe is a miserable hitter (.241/.284/.409 over the last four seasons) and an overrated fielder, gives away extra outs on the bases (16 steals and 30 times caught stealing with Chicago), and has received poor marks for his conditioning and commitment. He's not yet 30, but he's lucky to have lasted this long.

DeWayne Wise — OF

Bats: L Throws: L Height: 6' 1" Weight: 195 Born: February 24, 1978 Age: 31

YEAR	TEAM	LVL	AGE	PA	R	2B	3B	HR	RBI	BB	SO	SB	CS	EqBRR	AVG	OBP	SLG	EqAVG	EqOBP	EqSLG	EqA	VORP	WARP	DEFENSE			
2006	LOU	AAA	28	180	27	10	4	4	21	13	29	6	2	0.4	.266	.335	.461	.219	.282	.387	.233	-4.5	-0.7	29-CF	-3	11-RF	-2
2006	CIN	MLB	28	40	3	2	0	0	1	0	6	0	0	-0.1	.184	.184	.237	.179	.179	.231	.103	-4.6	-1.0	4-CF	-4		
2007	LOU	AAA	29	222	34	11	7	7	20	8	56	8	2	1.2	.251	.284	.473	.204	.232	.403	.214	-10.4	-0.9	29-CF	1	15-RF	-2
2008	CHR	AAA	30	222	39	14	3	9	23	22	32	15	7	-0.7	.319	.402	.565	.255	.332	.454	.267	7.1	0.9	34-RF	0	11-CF	1
2008	CHA	MLB	30	143	20	4	2	6	18	8	32	9	0	3.1	.248	.293	.450	.242	.293	.461	.268	4.2	0.3	16-CF	3	15-LF	-4
2009	CHA	MLB	31	311	36	15	3	10	36	21	72	10	4	1.2	.240	.297	.416	.240	.297	.425	.251	-0.3	0.7	75-CF	-4		

Breakout: 35% Improve: 55% Collapse: 21% Attrition: 34%   Comparables: Tommy McCraw, Gary Varsho, Larry Stahl, Gil Coan

A now-thirtysomething journeyman, Wise saw his performance for the White Sox last year almost exactly repeat his 175 PA stint for the Braves in 2004, which also ended in a Division Series loss and his last appearance in an edition of *BP*. In between, he made just 46 major league plate appearances. Wise can hit for some power against righties, steal some bases, and sub at all three outfield positions, but he doesn't do any of those things well enough to keep a major league job, and he doesn't do anything else well at all. Nick Swisher had to know the writing was on the wall in Chicago when he was benched in favor of Wise in the ALDS.

PITCHERS

Lance Broadway

| | | | | | | | | | | | | | Bats: R | | Throws: R | | Height: 6' 2" | | Weight: 210 | | Born: August 20, 1983 | | Age: 25 |

YEAR	TEAM	LVL	AGE	W	L	SV	G	GS	IP	H	BB	SO	HR	GB%	BABIP	STUFF	WHIP	ERA	DERA	EqH9	EqBB9	EqSO9	EqHR9	DEF	VORP	SN/WX
2006	BIR	AA	22	8	8	0	25	25	154²	160	40	111	10	48.6%	.316	-5	1.30	2.74	5.97	10.8	2.7	3.8	1.2	11	-5.9	—
2007	CHR	AAA	23	8	9	0	26	26	155	155	78	108	17	49.4%	.299	-22	1.50	4.65	6.69	10.7	5.0	4.2	1.6	6	-17.3	—
2007	CHA	MLB	23	1	1	0	4	1	10¹	5	5	14	0	36.4%	.238	10	0.97	0.87	2.61	4.4	4.4	9.6	0.0	1	5.0	0.55
2008	CHR	AAA	24	11	7	0	24	23	145	166	44	101	24	53.2%	.320	-37	1.45	4.66	6.13	12.1	3.2	4.1	2.2	-2	-7.9	—
2008	CHA	MLB	24	1	0	0	7	1	14	20	5	7	4	53.7%	.320	-29	1.79	7.07	5.79	12.2	3.2	3.9	2.6	-1	-1.7	0.00
2009	CHA	MLB	25	5	8	0	36	16	110	141	48	62	20	48.0%	.320	-2	1.71	6.22	5.86	11.4	3.4	4.6	1.6	-1	-7.3	-0.09

Breakout: 22%　Improve: 54%　Collapse: 19%　Attrition: 16%　　　　Comparables: Dustin Moseley, Joe Kucharski, Tony McKnight, Paul McClellan

Expected to compete for the fifth spot in the rotation, Broadway was torched in spring training last year. With Javier Vazquez in Atlanta, he'll be back in the mix this spring. Broadway's repeat of Triple-A saw him improve his ground-ball and walk rates, but at the expense of becoming more hittable (due to increases in his hit and homer rates), with lefties doing the bulk of the damage. The result was a near repeat of his 2007 WHIP and ERA, which is far from encouraging. He has won both of his major league starts, but both came against the Royals. He's a back-end starter at best and just the first of a string of similar low-ceiling college starters in the White Sox system.

Mark Buehrle

| | | | | | | | | | | | | | Bats: L | | Throws: L | | Height: 6' 2" | | Weight: 220 | | Born: March 23, 1979 | | Age: 30 |

YEAR	TEAM	LVL	AGE	W	L	SV	G	GS	IP	H	BB	SO	HR	GB%	BABIP	STUFF	WHIP	ERA	DERA	EqH9	EqBB9	EqSO9	EqHR9	DEF	VORP	SN/WX
2006	CHA	MLB	27	12	13	0	32	32	204	247	48	98	36	46.0%	.313	-15	1.45	4.99	4.88	11.0	2.2	3.9	1.5	-5	16.7	2.44
2007	CHA	MLB	28	10	9	0	30	30	201	208	45	115	22	45.2%	.292	4	1.26	3.63	4.46	8.9	1.9	4.5	1.0	19	49.8	5.65
2008	CHA	MLB	29	15	12	0	34	34	218²	240	52	140	22	50.7%	.315	10	1.34	3.79	3.70	9.9	2.0	5.2	0.9	-10	37.2	4.85
2009	CHA	MLB	30	11	10	0	29	29	181²	207	49	112	24	48.0%	.310	16	1.40	4.58	4.35	10.1	2.1	4.9	1.2	-2	19.4	3.54

Breakout: 13%　Improve: 46%　Collapse: 24%　Attrition: 13%　　　　Comparables: Jim Kaat, Livan Hernandez, Frank Tanana, Jaime Navarro

One of the most reliable pitchers in baseball, Buehrle enjoys an active streak of eight straight 200-inning seasons—the longest in the game entering 2009. In 2008, the first season of a four-year extension, he posted a career-high ground-ball rate and his highest strikeout rate since 2004, went 4-1 with a 2.29 ERA over his last six starts as the Sox surged into the playoffs, and pitched seven strong frames in his lone ALDS start, only to have the game and his bullpen unravel in the eighth. Buehrle works quickly, neutralizes the running game (only 12 men attempted to steal against him last year, seven were caught, and he picked off two others), and fields his position well. Having him under contract for $14 million per year through the age of 32 looks like a bargain.

D. J. Carrasco

| | | | | | | | | | | | | | Bats: R | | Throws: R | | Height: 6' 1" | | Weight: 215 | | Born: April 12, 1977 | | Age: 32 |

YEAR	TEAM	LVL	AGE	W	L	SV	G	GS	IP	H	BB	SO	HR	GB%	BABIP	STUFF	WHIP	ERA	DERA	EqH9	EqBB9	EqSO9	EqHR9	DEF	VORP	SN/WX
2006	FKU	JP	29	0	3	0	3	3	10¹	22	10	9	3	0.0%	.475	-40	3.11	14.85	22.00	24.0	12.0	6.0	4.0	0	-16.4	—
2007	TUC	AAA	30	5	14	0	34	22	137¹	185	60	103	16	49.8%	.370	-26	1.78	6.69	8.25	11.8	4.0	4.6	1.3	-2	-40.1	—
2008	CHR	AAA	31	2	1	1	8	1	25	24	7	24	0	56.9%	.348	5	1.24	2.88	3.91	10.6	2.7	5.9	0.4	0	4.3	—
2008	CHA	MLB	31	1	0	0	31	0	38²	30	14	30	2	55.5%	.267	5	1.14	3.95	4.10	7.0	3.1	6.3	0.5	1	8.2	1.00
2009	CHA	MLB	32	2	2	1	39	0	44¹	50	20	33	6	49.0%	.320	0	1.59	5.17	4.93	10.0	3.7	6.0	1.1	-0	2.0	0.14

Breakout: 54%　Improve: 70%　Collapse: 14%　Attrition: 34%　　　　Comparables: Masao Kida, Bucky Brandon, Rodney Myers, Matt Whiteside

Prior to last year, Carrasco hadn't pitched in the majors since 2005 and was lit up as a starter in the Pacific Coast League in 2007. Signed to a minor league deal last January, he pitched well in relief for Triple-A Charlotte to start the year, earned a July promotion, and posted a 2.45 ERA in his first 21 appearances before turning back into a pumpkin in September. Carrasco's ground-ball tendencies would seem to make him a solid middle-relief option, but his career path suggests the White Sox would be foolish to expect much out of him in 2009, and plenty of young ground-balling starters in their system could be converted for the same purpose.

Justin Cassel

Bats: R **Throws: R** **Height: 6' 1"** **Weight: 190** **Born: September 25, 1984** **Age: 24**

YEAR	TEAM	LVL	AGE	W	L	SV	G	GS	IP	H	BB	SO	HR	GB%	BABIP	STUFF	WHIP	ERA	DERA	EqH9	EqBB9	EqSO9	EqHR9	DEF	VORP	SN/WX
2006	GRF	Rk	21	3	2	0	13	4	39²	38	10	37	1	60.5%	.327	-13	1.22	2.98	8.02	12.0	4.0	3.5	1.1	3	-9.1	—
2006	WNS	A+	21	1	1	0	4	4	19	28	4	8	2	59.0%	.351	-34	1.68	5.21	8.31	16.6	2.6	1.0	2.1	-4	-5.2	—
2007	WNS	A+	22	4	2	0	10	6	39²	31	17	31	1	65.2%	.268	-8	1.21	2.27	6.00	9.0	5.0	3.8	0.8	5	-1.6	—
2008	BIR	AA	23	10	4	0	28	28	165	171	57	104	7	54.7%	.307	-8	1.38	3.11	5.91	10.9	3.4	3.3	0.8	1	-5.2	—
2009	CHA	MLB	24	4	8	0	27	17	100²	134	47	46	16	51.0%	.330	-5	1.80	6.81	6.52	11.7	3.7	3.7	1.4	-1	-14.2	-0.79

Breakout: 6%   Improve: 37%   Collapse: 32%   Attrition: 8%   Comparables: Steve Falteisek, Frank Seminara, Robert Averette, Alan Johnson

A seventh-round pick out of University of California–Irvine in 2006, Cassel established himself nicely at Double-A last year. He's a fairly pedestrian ground-baller. While he doesn't do anything showy, he's reliably effective across the board and keeps the ball in the park, which makes him projectable as a future innings eater. The problem is that the White Sox are up to their ears in pitchers who fit that description, and Cassel is far from the best of that underwhelming bunch.

Jose Contreras

Bats: R **Throws: R** **Height: 6' 4"** **Weight: 245** **Born: December 6, 1971** **Age: 37**

YEAR	TEAM	LVL	AGE	W	L	SV	G	GS	IP	H	BB	SO	HR	GB%	BABIP	STUFF	WHIP	ERA	DERA	EqH9	EqBB9	EqSO9	EqHR9	DEF	VORP	SN/WX
2006	CHA	MLB	34	13	9	0	30	30	196	194	55	134	20	45.7%	.288	12	1.27	4.27	4.40	8.7	2.5	5.4	0.8	1	33.6	4.22
2007	CHA	MLB	35	10	17	0	32	30	189	232	62	113	21	47.0%	.335	0	1.56	5.57	4.67	10.6	2.7	4.6	1.0	-24	-5.3	0.94
2008	CHA	MLB	36	7	6	0	20	20	121	130	35	70	12	52.7%	.298	5	1.36	4.54	4.31	9.3	2.4	4.5	0.9	-3	15.5	2.48
2009	CHA	MLB	37	4	6	0	24	12	81²	99	26	47	11	47.0%	.320	1	1.53	5.37	5.13	10.7	2.6	4.6	1.2	-1	1.8	0.66

Breakout: 12%   Improve: 33%   Collapse: 41%   Attrition: 48%   Comparables: Don Larsen, Jack Billingham, Sonny Siebert, Ken Forsch

Contreras was 6-3 with a 2.76 ERA after beating the Royals on June 5 of last year, but from there, his season jumped the tracks. After going 1-3 with an 8.60 ERA over his next seven starts, he hit the DL with tendonitis in his pitching elbow. In the second inning of his first start after nearly a month on the shelf, he ruptured his Achilles tendon trying to beat Jacoby Ellsbury to first base. The injury occurred on August 9 and typically takes nine to 12 months to heal, so expect to see Contreras on the comeback trail around midseason. Perhaps the time off will allow his elbow to recover as well. *Something* needs to change, as Contreras's strikeout rate has declined every season of his career since his 2003 stateside debut and is now well below average.

John Danks

Bats: L **Throws: L** **Height: 6' 1"** **Weight: 200** **Born: April 15, 1985** **Age: 24**

YEAR	TEAM	LVL	AGE	W	L	SV	G	GS	IP	H	BB	SO	HR	GB%	BABIP	STUFF	WHIP	ERA	DERA	EqH9	EqBB9	EqSO9	EqHR9	DEF	VORP	SN/WX
2006	FRI	AA	21	5	4	0	13	13	69	74	22	82	11	39.2%	.354	6	1.39	4.17	6.36	11.9	3.4	7.2	2.3	0	-5.4	—
2006	OKL	AAA	21	4	5	0	14	13	70²	67	34	72	11	39.3%	.296	0	1.44	4.36	6.78	9.7	4.5	6.4	2.0	1	-8.9	—
2007	CHA	MLB	22	6	13	0	26	26	139	160	54	109	28	37.6%	.317	-2	1.54	5.50	5.09	10.1	3.3	6.1	1.8	-6	2.3	0.68
2008	CHA	MLB	23	12	9	0	33	33	195	182	57	159	15	43.8%	.296	26	1.23	3.32	3.78	8.4	2.5	6.6	0.7	10	53.3	6.11
2009	CHA	MLB	24	10	9	0	28	28	169	171	57	137	24	43.0%	.290	26	1.34	4.27	4.03	9.0	2.7	6.5	1.2	-2	24.7	3.97

Breakout: 20%   Improve: 40%   Collapse: 29%   Attrition: 15%   Comparables: Adam Eaton, Bob Shirley, Kevin Appier, Ken Holtzman

Kenny Williams said he wouldn't trade Brandon McCarthy unless he was blown away by an offer, but when the Rangers offered Danks, a former first-round pick, Williams jumped. McCarthy has since struggled in Texas, while Danks has emerged as one of the game's better young pitchers. Going 7-4 with a 2.67 in the first half last year, Danks then struggled a bit after the break, but with the Sox chasing the division title in 2008, he held the opposition scoreless in three of his last four starts, including eight innings of two-hit ball in Chicago's 1-0 victory over the Twins in the tiebreaker. In his next turn, he pitched the Sox to their only ALDS victory against the Rays. Danks's improvement from his rookie season was striking: he cut his walk rate by nearly one free pass per nine innings, upped his strikeout rate slightly, got his ground balls to outnumber his fly balls, and reduced his home-run rate by nearly two-thirds. Danks simply became a better pitcher, and given his good velocity, great curve, and mentors such as pitching coach Don Cooper and fellow southpaw Buehrle, he should continue to mature as he enters his mid-20s.

Octavio Dotel

Bats: R   **Throws:** R   **Height:** 6' 0"   **Weight:** 210   **Born:** November 25, 1973   **Age:** 35

YEAR	TEAM	LVL	AGE	W	L	SV	G	GS	IP	H	BB	SO	HR	GB%	BABIP	STUFF	WHIP	ERA	DERA	EqH9	EqBB9	EqSO9	EqHR9	DEF	VORP	SN/WX
2006	NYA	MLB	32	0	0	0	14	0	10	18	11	7	2	36.6%	.421	-20	2.90	10.80	8.10	16.2	9.9	5.4	1.8	-3	-6.3	-0.43
2007	KCA	MLB	33	2	1	11	24	0	23	24	11	29	3	46.0%	.356	14	1.52	3.91	3.09	9.3	3.9	9.6	1.2	-3	4.5	0.51
2007	ATL	MLB	33	0	0	0	9	0	7²	5	1	12	1	17.6%	.250	8	0.78	4.68	4.50	5.6	1.1	10.1	1.1	-1	-0.1	0.18
2008	CHA	MLB	34	4	4	1	72	0	67	52	29	92	12	39.5%	.274	11	1.21	3.76	3.97	7.0	3.4	10.1	1.6	-2	9.7	1.12
2009	CHA	MLB	35	3	2	3	43	0	48	43	20	54	7	39.0%	.290	20	1.31	4.04	3.81	8.0	3.3	9.1	1.2	-0	9.1	0.76

Breakout: 47%   **Improve:** 75%   **Collapse:** 10%   **Attrition:** 25%   **Comparables:** Jeff Brantley, Dan Miceli, Mike Trombley, Juan Berenguer

Finally healthy for a full season and back in his preferred setup role, Dotel largely matched his career rates across the board, an interesting result, given that those rates combine three seasons of total dominance with the Astros, three seasons spent struggling to break through as a late-blooming starter or rehabbing Tommy John patient, and three seasons somewhere in the middle. Where he went off the charts was in allowing 16 of 17 attempted base thieves to advance safely, the result of weak-armed catchers and Dotel's not-unfounded belief that he could strike out the man at the plate before the runner could come all the way around.

Jack Egbert

Bats: L   **Throws:** R   **Height:** 6' 3"   **Weight:** 205   **Born:** May 12, 1983   **Age:** 26

YEAR	TEAM	LVL	AGE	W	L	SV	G	GS	IP	H	BB	SO	HR	GB%	BABIP	STUFF	WHIP	ERA	DERA	EqH9	EqBB9	EqSO9	EqHR9	DEF	VORP	SN/WX
2006	WNS	A+	23	9	8	0	25	25	140	131	46	120	2	58.3%	.315	2	1.26	2.96	5.63	11.4	3.9	4.3	0.6	-1	-0.4	—
2006	BIR	AA	23	0	2	0	4	4	21¹	17	8	24	0	50.0%	.309	16	1.18	0.85	3.15	8.6	3.6	6.3	0.4	0	5.4	—
2007	BIR	AA	24	12	8	0	28	28	161²	138	44	165	3	54.7%	.315	20	1.13	3.06	4.97	9.0	2.8	5.7	0.4	0	10.5	—
2008	CHR	AAA	25	4	12	0	24	22	129²	133	41	117	15	52.6%	.316	-16	1.34	4.65	7.32	10.7	3.1	5.3	1.5	11	-23.5	—
2009	CHA	MLB	26	6	9	0	34	18	122²	144	48	80	16	51.0%	.320	8	1.57	5.42	5.20	10.4	3.1	5.3	1.2	-1	1.6	0.91

Breakout: 26%   **Improve:** 56%   **Collapse:** 11%   **Attrition:** 20%   **Comparables:** Ben Hendrickson, Jason Grimsley, Jason Davis, Sean Bergman

Like Broadway, Egbert is a low-ceiling college arm who is starting to bump his head at Triple-A. A former Rutgers Scarlet Knight who possesses a worm-killing, high-80s fastball, Egbert was underwhelming in his Triple-A debut with the Charlotte Knights last year, turning in his worst minor league season as his walk, hit, and home-run rates swelled, calling into question his viability as a fifth-starter candidate this spring.

John Ely

Bats: R   **Throws:** R   **Height:** 6' 1"   **Weight:** 190   **Born:** May 17, 1986   **Age:** 23

YEAR	TEAM	LVL	AGE	W	L	SV	G	GS	IP	H	BB	SO	HR	GB%	BABIP	STUFF	WHIP	ERA	DERA	EqH9	EqBB9	EqSO9	EqHR9	DEF	VORP	SN/WX
2007	GRF	Rk	21	6	1	0	13	12	56	55	14	56	6	50.0%	.333	-20	1.23	3.86	7.43	13.3	4.3	3.9	2.7	0	-9.4	—
2008	WNS	A+	22	10	12	0	27	27	145¹	142	46	134	18	52.3%	.310	-16	1.29	4.71	6.14	11.0	3.3	5.4	2.0	-1	-7.9	—
2009	CHA	MLB	23	4	8	0	19	19	95²	125	44	61	20	47.0%	.330	5	1.76	6.86	6.44	11.5	3.6	5.1	1.9	-1	-11.9	-0.57

Breakout: 16%   **Improve:** 51%   **Collapse:** 17%   **Attrition:** 14%   **Comparables:** Edinson Volquez, Jeff Hartsock, Mike Hostetler, Paul Menhart

A 2007 third-round pick out of Miami of Ohio, Ely is a tick better than Egbert, Broadway, and Cassell. He throws a bit harder and has a nice curveball, but he's ultimately cut from the same cloth and projects as a fourth starter at best. He'll start the year in Double-A, but probably won't be in the big-league picture until late 2010 at the earliest.

Gavin Floyd

Bats: R   **Throws:** R   **Height:** 6' 4"   **Weight:** 225   **Born:** January 27, 1983   **Age:** 26

YEAR	TEAM	LVL	AGE	W	L	SV	G	GS	IP	H	BB	SO	HR	GB%	BABIP	STUFF	WHIP	ERA	DERA	EqH9	EqBB9	EqSO9	EqHR9	DEF	VORP	SN/WX
2006	SWB	AAA	23	7	4	0	17	17	115	117	38	85	9	42.1%	.320	-15	1.35	4.23	6.95	12.1	3.7	4.6	1.3	8	-15.3	—
2006	PHI	MLB	23	4	3	0	11	11	54¹	70	32	34	14	36.4%	.322	-20	1.88	7.29	7.07	10.6	4.5	5.0	1.9	0	-11.3	-0.22
2007	CHR	AAA	24	7	3	0	17	17	106²	93	35	96	9	43.3%	.288	-3	1.20	3.12	5.45	9.5	3.4	5.6	1.3	12	1.7	—
2007	CHA	MLB	24	1	5	0	16	10	70	85	19	49	17	43.3%	.312	-19	1.49	5.27	4.89	10.5	2.3	5.4	2.2	-3	2.7	0.79
2008	CHA	MLB	25	17	8	0	33	33	206¹	190	70	145	30	42.2%	.261	1	1.26	3.84	4.67	7.9	2.7	5.5	1.3	7	28.3	3.35
2009	CHA	MLB	26	9	10	0	27	27	164¹	177	59	111	25	43.0%	.290	17	1.44	4.90	4.63	9.5	2.8	5.5	1.3	-2	12.7	2.64

Breakout: 16%   **Improve:** 56%   **Collapse:** 20%   **Attrition:** 13%   **Comparables:** Kevin Gross, Todd Stottlemyre, Adam Eaton, Gil Meche

The former Phillies first-round pick finally appeared to deliver on some of his promise last year after winning the fifth-starter's job out of spring training. Unfortunately, Floyd's season was largely an illusion, one the Sox shouldn't plan on seeing again. Begin with Floyd's lucky .259 opponents' average on balls in play, which suppressed his hits allowed; mix in league-average strikeout and walk rates, fly-ball tendencies and a correspondingly high homer rate, a complete inability to hold runners (a major league–high 37 steals allowed against just five men caught stealing), and a ton of run support (5.9 R/G), and you've got a 17-game winner headed for a rude awakening in 2009.

Lucas Harrell

Bats: S   Throws: R   Height: 6' 2"   Weight: 200   Born: June 3, 1985   Age: 24

YEAR	TEAM	LVL	AGE	W	L	SV	G	GS	IP	H	BB	SO	HR	GB%	BABIP	STUFF	WHIP	ERA	DERA	EqH9	EqBB9	EqSO9	EqHR9	DEF	VORP	SN/WX
2006	WNS	A+	21	7	2	0	17	17	91²	58	44	70	3	62.8%	.224	7	1.12	2.47	5.81	7.5	5.3	3.7	0.9	11	-2.0	—
2006	BIR	AA	21	0	2	0	3	3	9²	12	14	4	1	51.4%	.333	-33	2.83	10.76	16.62	13.5	14.5	2.1	2.1	0	-10.7	—
2008	KAN	A	23	1	1	0	3	3	10²	13	4	7	0	70.3%	.361	-35	1.59	5.89	7.45	14.0	4.7	1.9	0.9	-2	-2.0	—
2008	BIR	AA	23	3	3	0	11	10	54²	56	19	34	3	55.9%	.317	-17	1.37	3.46	6.84	11.0	3.4	3.2	1.1	0	-6.9	—
2009	CHA	MLB	24	3	6	0	22	13	77	99	41	36	10	53.0%	.330	-6	1.82	6.67	6.44	11.4	4.2	3.8	1.2	-1	-10.6	-0.55

Breakout: 12%   Improve: 54%   Collapse: 20%   Attrition: 22%   Comparables: Justin Cassel, Jesus Delgado, Dave Graybill, Zachary Ward

After losing 2007 to elbow surgery, Harrell made a strong return last year, finishing the year with a solid run in Double-A before getting in some extra work in the Arizona Fall League. Ironically, the lost time makes Harrell, the rare high school arm drafted by the White Sox in recent years, look a lot like Broadway, Egbert, et al., as he'll turn 24 in June and is still chasing a strong High-A performance from three years ago.

Bobby Jenks

Bats: R   Throws: R   Height: 6' 3"   Weight: 275   Born: March 14, 1981   Age: 28

YEAR	TEAM	LVL	AGE	W	L	SV	G	GS	IP	H	BB	SO	HR	GB%	BABIP	STUFF	WHIP	ERA	DERA	EqH9	EqBB9	EqSO9	EqHR9	DEF	VORP	SN/WX
2006	CHA	MLB	25	3	4	41	67	0	69²	66	31	80	5	60.4%	.347	20	1.39	4.00	3.48	8.8	4.0	9.5	0.7	-3	16.0	3.94
2007	CHA	MLB	26	3	5	40	66	0	65	45	13	56	2	56.4%	.254	19	0.89	2.77	3.62	5.8	1.7	6.7	0.3	7	23.9	2.51
2008	CHA	MLB	27	3	1	30	57	0	61²	51	17	38	3	59.4%	.265	4	1.10	2.63	2.73	7.4	2.3	5.0	0.5	1	21.9	4.50
2009	CHA	MLB	28	3	4	18	48	0	54²	53	18	41	5	54.0%	.290	9	1.30	3.61	3.50	8.6	2.6	6.1	0.8	-1	12.2	1.52

Breakout: 4%   Improve: 12%   Collapse: 60%   Attrition: 9%   Comparables: Jose Jimenez, Greg McMichael, Mark Eichhorn, Aaron Heilman

Jenks's maturation has been fascinating to watch, as he's followed an unusual path. Once a wild, fire-balling starter, he's turned into a contact-pitching closer who doesn't hurt himself with walks and gets his opponents to pound his heater into the ground. Over the past two seasons, Jenks has allowed just five homers and walked just 30 men in 126⅔ innings, while striking out just 6.7 men per nine frames, despite his high-90s heat. Jenks missed three weeks in July with scapula bursitis and had a rough September, but still finished eighth in the majors in WXRL.

Scott Linebrink

Bats: R   Throws: R   Height: 6' 2"   Weight: 200   Born: August 4, 1976   Age: 32

YEAR	TEAM	LVL	AGE	W	L	SV	G	GS	IP	H	BB	SO	HR	GB%	BABIP	STUFF	WHIP	ERA	DERA	EqH9	EqBB9	EqSO9	EqHR9	DEF	VORP	SN/WX
2006	SDN	MLB	29	7	4	2	73	0	75²	70	22	68	9	40.4%	.289	7	1.22	3.57	3.77	8.8	2.3	7.5	1.0	1	18.6	3.92
2007	SDN	MLB	30	3	3	1	44	0	45	41	14	25	9	39.7%	.234	-20	1.22	3.80	5.28	8.1	2.4	4.9	1.8	7	9.5	2.07
2007	MIL	MLB	30	2	3	0	27	0	25¹	27	11	25	3	50.7%	.343	10	1.50	3.56	2.92	9.1	3.6	8.4	1.1	-4	2.7	-0.32
2008	CHA	MLB	31	2	2	1	50	0	46¹	41	9	40	8	40.1%	.260	0	1.08	3.69	4.11	7.8	1.6	6.8	1.6	2	10.1	1.91
2009	CHA	MLB	32	3	2	2	45	0	51	53	17	40	8	41.0%	.290	6	1.36	4.41	4.15	9.1	2.7	6.4	1.3	-1	6.9	0.58

Breakout: 8%   Improve: 24%   Collapse: 49%   Attrition: 20%   Comparables: T.J. Mathews, Mike Trombley, Xavier Hernandez, Tom Buskey

Painting in shades of his Padres peak, Linebrink posted a 1.36 ERA and a 0.82 WHIP as the White Sox' primary eighth-inning setup man during the first three months of the 2008 season, stranding 80 percent of his inherited runners. Then, having averaged 79 innings of relief a year over the previous five seasons and on pace for a similar total again, his shoulder finally gave out. Linebrink hit the DL in mid-July with a sub-scapular strain and was hit hard on his return in September. The four-year deal the Sox gave him after the 2007 season looked foolish at the time; it looks worse now.

Jon Link

| | | | | | | | Bats: R | | Throws: R | | Height: 6' 2" | | Weight: 205 | | Born: March 23, 1984 | | | Age: 25 | |

YEAR	TEAM	LVL	AGE	W	L	SV	G	GS	IP	H	BB	SO	HR	GB%	BABIP	STUFF	WHIP	ERA	DERA	EqH9	EqBB9	EqSO9	EqHR9	DEF	VORP	SN/WX
2006	FTW	A	22	5	5	3	53	0	62	72	24	57	3	48.8%	.356	-42	1.55	4.94	10.27	14.6	5.5	3.6	1.7	-9	-28.2	—
2007	LEL	A+	23	2	1	13	41	0	41	32	11	45	5	61.1%	.262	-19	1.05	3.07	6.39	8.5	3.1	5.4	1.9	6	-3.3	—
2007	WNS	A+	23	1	0	3	14	0	17²	16	4	19	1	65.2%	.333	-7	1.13	2.54	3.68	12.3	3.1	6.1	1.2	-1	3.1	—
2008	BIR	AA	24	5	4	35	56	0	56²	48	27	66	3	56.9%	.311	-5	1.32	3.02	4.58	9.2	4.4	6.7	1.0	-1	6.2	—
2009	CHA	MLB	25	2	4	1	24	5	52¹	61	29	42	7	51.0%	.330	6	1.70	5.69	5.44	10.3	4.3	6.4	1.1	-1	-0.9	0.10

Breakout: 40%　Improve: 71%　Collapse: 8%　Attrition: 9%　　　Comparables: Rocky Roquet, Gary Mielke, Mark Huismann, Heath Bell

Acquired from the Padres for utility man Rob Mackowiak at the 2007 trading deadline, Link had a strong Double-A debut as Birmingham's closer last year, boasting a 2.01 ERA prior to a poor final week of the season. His mid-90s heat and correspondingly impressive strikeout rates could thrust him into the major league pen at some point this season. He's more likely to settle in as a setup man than a closer in the major leagues, which as just as well, given Jenks's dominance.

Boone Logan

| | | | | | | | Bats: R | | Throws: L | | Height: 6' 5" | | Weight: 200 | | Born: August 13, 1984 | | | Age: 24 | |

YEAR	TEAM	LVL	AGE	W	L	SV	G	GS	IP	H	BB	SO	HR	GB%	BABIP	STUFF	WHIP	ERA	DERA	EqH9	EqBB9	EqSO9	EqHR9	DEF	VORP	SN/WX
2006	CHR	AAA	21	3	1	11	38	0	42¹	35	12	57	1	44.7%	.340	30	1.12	3.42	5.08	10.2	3.2	8.8	0.5	-2	2.3	—
2006	CHA	MLB	21	0	0	1	21	0	17¹	21	15	15	2	46.7%	.339	1	2.08	8.32	6.38	10.3	6.9	6.4	1.0	-4	-6.2	-0.55
2007	CHA	MLB	22	2	1	0	68	0	50²	59	20	35	7	52.0%	.333	-5	1.56	4.97	4.11	10.2	3.2	5.4	1.3	-5	4.4	0.25
2008	CHA	MLB	23	2	3	0	55	0	42¹	57	14	42	7	46.5%	.382	2	1.68	5.96	3.83	12.1	2.8	7.9	1.5	-10	-3.4	-0.37
2009	ATL	MLB	24	2	2	3	48	0	43²	43	16	40	5	46.0%	.300	13	1.34	3.95	4.18	8.7	2.8	7.1	0.9	0	8.4	0.64

Breakout: 46%　Improve: 68%　Collapse: 21%　Attrition: 34%　　　Comparables: Jim Crawford, Bob Allen, Ed Farmer, Jim Brewer

Logan had a great first half last year, boasting a 1.95 ERA, a 4.4 K/BB, and 20 of 24 inherited baserunners stranded and holding lefties to a .197/.209/.273 line through July 9. Then it all came crashing down—he pitched only three scoreless outings out of 12 over the next month as opposing batters hit an even .500 against him (lefties hit .459), producing 24 hits in eight innings. After a brief demotion, his return engagement as a September call-up was no better. In reality, the early-season success was as much of a fluke as the late-season collapse. Logan throws a fastball in the mid-90s, a rare thing coming from a lefty, but that's all he offers, so hitters can sit on the heater. Flipped to Atlanta in the Javier Vazquez deal, it's now up to Roger McDowell and the Braves to teach him a second pitch.

Mike MacDougal

| | | | | | | | Bats: S | | Throws: R | | Height: 6' 3" | | Weight: 180 | | Born: March 5, 1977 | | | Age: 32 | |

YEAR	TEAM	LVL	AGE	W	L	SV	G	GS	IP	H	BB	SO	HR	GB%	BABIP	STUFF	WHIP	ERA	DERA	EqH9	EqBB9	EqSO9	EqHR9	DEF	VORP	SN/WX
2006	KCA	MLB	29	0	0	1	4	0	4	2	0	2	0	72.7%	.182	-3	0.50	0.00	4.91	4.9	0.0	4.9	0.0	2	2.7	0.24
2006	CHA	MLB	29	1	1	0	25	0	25	19	6	19	1	63.4%	.261	7	1.00	1.80	3.75	6.8	2.2	6.4	0.4	5	12.1	0.86
2007	CHA	MLB	30	2	5	0	54	0	42¹	50	33	39	3	58.2%	.362	3	1.96	6.81	5.53	10.4	6.4	7.2	0.6	-8	-8.2	-0.14
2008	CHR	AAA	31	0	4	4	38	2	49¹	48	30	65	2	56.9%	.368	11	1.58	3.83	4.27	10.9	6.0	8.2	0.6	-3	6.8	—
2008	CHA	MLB	31	0	0	0	16	0	17	16	12	12	0	48.1%	.308	4	1.65	2.12	1.62	8.6	5.9	5.4	0.0	-1	7.0	-0.02
2009	CHA	MLB	32	2	2	2	45	0	43²	43	26	40	3	53.0%	.310	8	1.57	4.40	4.27	8.7	4.7	7.4	0.7	-0	5.5	0.45

Breakout: 20%　Improve: 46%　Collapse: 29%　Attrition: 23%　　　Comparables: Ted Abernathy, Ed Farmer, Mike Fetters, Todd Jones

MacDougal is a classic hard-throwing reliever with similarly inflated strikeout and walk rates, the kind of pitcher who drives managers crazy. Demoted in late April for walking seven men in eight innings, Ozzie didn't bring him back to the majors until rosters expanded in September. Mac walked five men in his 8⅓ innings that month and was dropped from the 40-man roster after the season. At this point, MacDougal is probably wishing he had been sent to Atlanta in place of Logan, but he'll earn $2.65 million to sit in Guillen's doghouse for another season.

Aaron Poreda

Bats: L   Throws: L   Height: 6' 6"   Weight: 240   Born: October 1, 1986   Age: 22

YEAR	TEAM	LVL	AGE	W	L	SV	G	GS	IP	H	BB	SO	HR	GB%	BABIP	STUFF	WHIP	ERA	DERA	EqH9	EqBB9	EqSO9	EqHR9	DEF	VORP	SN/WX
2007	GRF	Rk	20	4	0	0	12	8	46^1	29	10	48	1	65.1%	.245	30	0.84	1.17	3.10	7.5	3.5	4.0	0.9	0	11.3	—
2008	WNS	A+	21	5	5	0	12	12	73^1	67	18	46	1	55.0%	.281	17	1.16	3.32	5.58	8.9	2.5	3.2	0.4	7	0.2	—
2008	BIR	AA	21	3	4	0	15	15	87^2	81	22	72	5	50.4%	.310	18	1.17	2.98	5.85	10.1	2.6	4.7	1.0	7	-2.2	—
2009	CHA	MLB	22	5	8	0	19	19	105	126	40	58	14	51.0%	.310	9	1.57	5.74	5.53	10.6	3.0	4.5	1.2	-1	-2.6	0.54

Breakout: 5%   Improve: 20%   Collapse: 42%   Attrition: 9%   Comparables: Joe Magrane, Billy Traber, Zach Jackson, Brad Arnsberg

The White Sox' top pick in the 2007 draft, Poreda is another college arm, but he breaks the cycle of mediocrity by being a big, powerful lefty in a system overrun by ordinary right-handers. Not unsurprisingly, he's the organization's top pitching prospect, a status he confirmed last year by excelling at Double-A in the second half of his first full year in the pros. Poreda will get a chance to make the White Sox rotation out of camp, but even if he starts the year in Triple-A, he could find himself in the big-league rotation before long. Given that he threw 170 innings last year (including 9⅓ in relief in the Arizona Fall League), the only thing holding him and his upper-90s heater back is the slow development of his secondary pitches.

Clayton Richard

Bats: L   Throws: L   Height: 6' 5"   Weight: 225   Born: September 12, 1983   Age: 25

YEAR	TEAM	LVL	AGE	W	L	SV	G	GS	IP	H	BB	SO	HR	GB%	BABIP	STUFF	WHIP	ERA	DERA	EqH9	EqBB9	EqSO9	EqHR9	DEF	VORP	SN/WX
2006	KAN	A	22	6	6	0	18	17	95	117	28	54	0	57.2%	.361	-24	1.53	3.69	7.62	14.4	4.2	1.5	0.7	-2	-18.6	—
2006	WNS	A+	22	1	3	0	4	4	23^2	29	6	12	2	67.1%	.346	-30	1.51	4.66	9.15	14.8	3.0	2.2	1.7	-3	-8.2	—
2007	WNS	A+	23	8	12	0	28	27	161^1	159	59	99	11	59.2%	.298	-36	1.35	3.63	7.73	11.7	4.5	2.6	1.6	6	-33.6	—
2008	BIR	AA	24	6	6	0	13	13	83^2	66	16	53	2	52.0%	.257	5	0.98	2.47	5.47	8.0	1.9	3.3	0.6	8	1.1	—
2008	CHR	AAA	24	6	0	0	7	7	44	33	4	33	3	56.6%	.238	10	0.84	2.45	4.07	7.5	1.1	4.3	0.9	4	7.1	—
2008	CHA	MLB	24	2	5	0	13	8	47^2	61	13	29	5	50.6%	.335	-6	1.55	6.04	5.06	11.1	2.2	4.7	0.9	-8	-5.7	0.04
2009	CHA	MLB	25	6	10	0	49	22	137^2	177	50	67	21	50.0%	.320	-4	1.64	6.13	5.86	11.4	2.9	3.9	1.3	-2	-8.7	-0.14

Breakout: 25%   Improve: 56%   Collapse: 11%   Attrition: 28%   Comparables: Bobby Livingston, Bill Latham, Alex Graman, Heath Phillips

An eighth-round pick out of the University of Michigan in 2005, Richard spent his first three pro seasons in A-ball and then shot from Double-A to the majors last year, making quick work of Triple-A in between. A tall lefty sinkerballer with a decent changeup and curve, he was abused by major league right-handers (.320/.365/.523), which suggests his ultimate destination could be the bullpen. For now he's the fourth starter; his current role is also his ceiling.

Derek Rodriguez

Bats: R   Throws: R   Height: 6' 1"   Weight: 190   Born: May 17, 1983   Age: 26

YEAR	TEAM	LVL	AGE	W	L	SV	G	GS	IP	H	BB	SO	HR	GB%	BABIP	STUFF	WHIP	ERA	DERA	EqH9	EqBB9	EqSO9	EqHR9	DEF	VORP	SN/WX
2006	KAN	A	23	6	11	0	25	25	147^2	149	45	109	10	50.2%	.303	-46	1.32	4.65	9.72	11.9	4.1	2.5	1.8	-1	-61.0	—
2006	WNS	A+	23	1	1	0	2	2	11^1	15	3	13	1	54.5%	.438	3	1.62	4.86	3.12	19.7	4.2	7.3	2.1	-4	2.4	—
2007	WNS	A+	24	14	5	0	28	28	161	164	55	124	10	56.3%	.324	-28	1.36	3.69	6.51	12.5	4.3	3.7	1.5	-6	-14.1	—
2008	BIR	AA	25	5	1	1	29	0	42^2	30	18	44	2	43.6%	.275	-8	1.12	3.37	5.98	7.7	4.0	6.0	0.9	4	-1.7	—
2008	CHR	AAA	25	0	1	1	20	1	36^2	24	15	44	5	44.6%	.224	-6	1.06	3.19	5.94	6.7	4.0	6.9	1.7	5	-1.4	—
2009	TBA	MLB	26	3	4	0	24	7	58^2	70	31	39	9	47.0%	.320	-1	1.71	5.86	5.81	10.6	4.1	5.5	1.3	-0	-3.2	-0.05

Breakout: 31%   Improve: 67%   Collapse: 10%   Attrition: 10%   Comparables: Brian Meyer, Scott Medvin, Ed Myers, Kurt Mattson

Yet another midsized college righty, Rodriguez was taken out of the University of Nevada–Las Vegas in the middle rounds of the 2005 draft. The Sox converted him to relief last year with great success; between Double-A, Triple-A, and the Arizona Fall League, Rodriguez struck out 102 men in 92 innings against just 39 walks and seven homers. The conversion worked so well that the Rays grabbed Rodriguez in the Rule 5 draft. Competing for a spot against the weak underbelly of Tampa Bay's bullpen, he is likely to stick.

Adam Russell

Bats: R   Throws: R   Height: 6' 8"   Weight: 250   Born: April 14, 1983   Age: 26

YEAR	TEAM	LVL	AGE	W	L	SV	G	GS	IP	H	BB	SO	HR	GB%	BABIP	STUFF	WHIP	ERA	DERA	EqH9	EqBB9	EqSO9	EqHR9	DEF	VORP	SN/WX
2006	WNS	A+	23	7	3	0	17	17	94	80	39	61	5	60.8%	.273	-21	1.27	2.68	5.86	10.4	4.8	2.9	1.3	6	-2.4	—
2006	BIR	AA	23	3	3	0	10	10	55²	59	19	47	5	49.7%	.323	-17	1.41	4.73	8.06	11.6	3.5	4.6	1.8	1	-14.0	—
2007	BIR	AA	24	9	11	1	38	20	138²	159	58	95	8	53.3%	.339	-26	1.56	4.80	7.16	11.4	4.1	3.4	1.0	0	-22.7	—
2008	CHR	AAA	25	3	2	0	25	0	37¹	28	19	28	3	46.4%	.234	-16	1.26	2.90	5.15	7.4	4.7	4.2	1.0	6	1.8	—
2008	CHA	MLB	25	4	0	0	22	0	26	30	10	22	1	45.2%	.363	4	1.54	5.19	3.12	10.4	3.1	6.6	0.3	-5	2.1	0.07
2009	CHA	MLB	26	2	2	1	33	1	36²	41	18	25	4	47.0%	.310	-0	1.60	5.12	4.90	10.0	3.8	5.6	1.0	-0	2.0	0.17

Breakout: 26%   Improve: 56%   Collapse: 21%   Attrition: 36%   Comparables: Rick Bauer, Jeff Nelson, Barry Jones, Jeremy Griffiths

Like Rodriguez, Russell was a conversion success story in 2008. A massive righty lacking secondary offerings, he was moved to the pen on arrival in Triple-A and posted a 1.74 ERA in his first 21 games, earning a mid-June call-up. A pair of ugly outings around the All-Star break got him returned to Charlotte, and he struggled again on his return to the bigs in early August, but his last nine appearances went well enough to keep him in the mix for this year's pen. Still, his stuff doesn't match his size, and his low three-quarter delivery leaves him susceptible to lefty hitters.

Matt Thornton

Bats: L   Throws: L   Height: 6' 6"   Weight: 230   Born: September 15, 1976   Age: 32

YEAR	TEAM	LVL	AGE	W	L	SV	G	GS	IP	H	BB	SO	HR	GB%	BABIP	STUFF	WHIP	ERA	DERA	EqH9	EqBB9	EqSO9	EqHR9	DEF	VORP	SN/WX
2006	CHA	MLB	29	5	3	2	63	0	54	46	21	49	5	50.0%	.279	6	1.24	3.33	3.69	7.5	3.4	7.2	0.8	3	17.1	1.73
2007	CHA	MLB	30	4	4	2	68	0	56¹	59	26	55	4	45.8%	.344	6	1.51	4.80	3.93	9.5	3.9	7.9	0.7	-4	7.2	0.01
2008	CHA	MLB	31	5	3	1	74	0	67¹	48	19	77	5	53.5%	.264	25	1.00	2.67	3.07	6.3	2.3	9.0	0.7	4	23.4	1.32
2009	CHA	MLB	32	3	3	5	68	0	63	59	23	62	6	49.0%	.300	17	1.30	3.47	3.31	8.2	2.9	8.0	0.9	-1	14.3	1.35

Breakout: 25%   Improve: 51%   Collapse: 32%   Attrition: 14%   Comparables: Doug Brocail, Brian Fuentes, Roberto Hernandez, Jason Christiansen

As expected, Thornton rebounded nicely from his disappointing 2007 campaign. The numbers were pretty across the board. Lefties hit just .170/.256/.223 against him, while righties failed to tally a 600 OPS. Just five of his pitches left the park. The catch is that a lot of that was powered by an abnormally low BABIP, just as his poor 2007 was dragged down by a .344 BABIP. He should settle in the middle in 2009, which should be enough for him to remain valuable.

Javier Vazquez

Bats: R   Throws: R   Height: 6' 1"   Weight: 210   Born: July 25, 1976   Age: 32

YEAR	TEAM	LVL	AGE	W	L	SV	G	GS	IP	H	BB	SO	HR	GB%	BABIP	STUFF	WHIP	ERA	DERA	EqH9	EqBB9	EqSO9	EqHR9	DEF	VORP	SN/WX
2006	CHA	MLB	29	11	12	0	33	32	202²	206	56	184	23	41.7%	.311	21	1.29	4.84	3.99	9.1	2.4	7.3	0.9	-18	23.2	3.22
2007	CHA	MLB	30	15	8	0	32	32	216²	197	50	213	29	41.2%	.294	21	1.14	3.74	3.72	8.1	1.9	7.8	1.2	0	51.5	5.17
2008	CHA	MLB	31	12	16	0	33	33	208¹	214	61	200	25	39.7%	.320	20	1.32	4.67	3.75	9.2	2.4	7.6	1.1	-19	23.8	3.28
2009	ATL	MLB	32	13	9	0	30	30	198	183	57	188	22	41.0%	.290	29	1.21	3.58	3.75	8.2	2.2	7.4	1.0	0	40.9	5.96

Breakout: 26%   Improve: 66%   Collapse: 6%   Attrition: 11%   Comparables: Jack Morris, Bob Feller, Pedro Astacio, Mickey Lolich

Buehrle may hold the longest active 200-inning streak in the majors, but Vazquez is the only man to enter the 2009 season with nine straight seasons of 32 or more starts, and if not for two missing frames in 2004, he would have Buehrle's innings streak beat as well. That kind of consistency has tremendous value, even if Vazquez has settled in as a league-average run-preventer. His stellar peripherals are undermined by his fly-ball/home-run tendencies and his trouble getting through the sixth inning—opposing batters hit .360/.380/.570 against Javy in the sixth inning last year. The Braves hope that being spared from the DH will allow Vazquez to save his bullets and pitch deeper into games. Even if he doesn't (or can't), he'll benefit from Bobby Cox's quicker hook, though not necessarily from leaving the Cell, where he has a career mark of 24-16 with a 4.07 ERA.

Ehren Wasserman

Bats: S   Throws: R   Height: 6' 0"   Weight: 185   Born: December 6, 1980   Age: 28

YEAR	TEAM	LVL	AGE	W	L	SV	G	GS	IP	H	BB	SO	HR	GB%	BABIP	STUFF	WHIP	ERA	DERA	EqH9	EqBB9	EqSO9	EqHR9	DEF	VORP	SN/WX
2006	BIR	AA	25	4	8	22	61	0	63¹	60	25	47	3	55.1%	.305	-24	1.35	2.57	5.61	9.9	3.9	3.9	0.9	0	-0.1	—
2007	CHR	AAA	26	2	4	5	38	0	42²	34	18	33	0	62.6%	.296	-9	1.22	2.11	4.12	8.5	4.1	4.8	0.2	2	6.5	—
2007	CHA	MLB	26	1	1	0	33	0	23	20	7	14	0	70.4%	.286	-3	1.17	2.74	3.63	7.7	2.4	4.8	0.0	1	6.5	1.10
2008	CHR	AAA	27	3	0	7	32	0	39	29	13	42	1	52.0%	.298	7	1.08	1.15	2.72	7.9	3.5	6.7	0.5	1	11.6	—
2008	CHA	MLB	27	1	2	0	24	0	19²	27	14	9	0	44.2%	.375	-22	2.08	7.77	6.20	11.5	5.8	3.5	0.0	-4	-6.2	0.00
2009	CHA	MLB	28	2	2	1	38	0	35	39	16	23	4	50.0%	.310	-2	1.55	4.99	4.81	9.8	3.6	5.3	0.9	0	2.3	0.16

Breakout: 21%   Improve: 41%   Collapse: 42%   Attrition: 39%   Comparables: Marc Valdes, Phil Niekro, Kip Gross, D.J. Carrasco

Side-arming Ehren Wasserman dominated at Triple-A last year, faring even better against lefties than righties, but was beat about the face and neck in the first two of his three stints in the majors. He fared better as a September call-up, but still walked more than he struck out and didn't show any discernable split on the season as a whole. The trouble is that Wasserman's out pitch is a slurve that breaks out of the strike zone. Major league hitters simply stopped swinging at it and had no trouble when he came back with his high-80s fastball. Now 28, he seems unlikely to solve that particular puzzle.

LINEOUTS

Hitters

PLAYER	TEAM	LVL	AGE	PA	R	2B	3B	HR	RBI	BB	SO	SB-CS	EqBRR	AVG/OBP/SLG	EqAVG/EqOBP/EqSLG	EqA	VORP	WARP
3B J. Castillo	BIR	AA	24	435	60	20	9	8	58	42	85	3-0	0.7	.289/.354/.448	.238/.290/.376	.232	-10.3	0.0
	CHR	AAA	24	113	12	7	1	0	18	8	23	1-2	0.7	.287/.327/.376	.255/.298/.343	.227	-3.1	0.1
1B B. Eldred	CHR	AAA	27	469	62	22	1	35	100	28	144	3-3	-3.4	.244/.305/.546	.212/.268/.478	.247	-0.0	-1.0
OF M. Gartrell	BIR	AA	24	466	54	22	2	14	52	45	106	7-1	2.2	.254/.334/.421	.214/.275/.355	.220	-20.7	-1.6
C T. Hall	CHA	MLB	32	136	7	3	0	2	7	6	19	0-0	-1.6	.260/.304/.331	.252/.296/.315	.214	-1.4	-0.7
C F. Hernandez#	WNS	A+	22	288	28	15	0	6	31	32	33	2-2	-2.5	.245/.338/.382	.217/.299/.353	.230	-8.8	1.1
1B C. Marrero*	KAN	A	21	505	53	29	5	10	61	54	89	11-5	-2.7	.273/.355/.431	.219/.294/.351	.229	-17.7	-1.9
OF J. Martinez	KAN	A	19	156	19	5	0	2	18	12	26	7-5	-1.5	.306/.359/.382	.247/.295/.308	.210	-7.5	-1.0
3B C. Retherford	WNS	A+	22	519	66	28	1	16	71	37	78	11-6	-1.1	.295/.350/.464	.259/.306/.418	.250	3.4	1.1

A Panamanian who brings doubles power and who has improved his on-base skills as he has advanced, 25-year-old third baseman **Javier Castillo** will serve as part of Josh Fields' safety net this year. ⊘ At age 27, minor league masher **Brad Eldred** finally produced over a full Triple-A season, but struck out 6.3 times for every unintentional walk. Having signed with the Nats, he might get another chance to take his all-or-nothing swing to "The Show." ⊘ On reaching Double-A, **Maurice Gartrell** lost 45 points off his average with corresponding dips in his OBP and slugging, and he didn't fare much better in the Arizona Fall League before a separated shoulder ended his participation. He has a broad range of skills, but doesn't excel in any one area and can't play center, which lowers his ceiling considerably. ⊘ **Toby Hall** was a solid backup catching option against lefty pitching until he tore the labrum in his throwing shoulder prior to the 2007 season; he's caught just 15 percent of opposing basestealers since. ⊘ Once a precocious prospect, small, switch-hitting catcher **Francisco Hernandez**'s slow progress has seen his age finally catch up to his levels. A contact hitter with a strong arm, he projects as a future backup. ⊘ **Christian Marrero**'s full-season debut exposed his impressive 2007 showing as little more than a 20-year-old repeating rookie ball. ⊘ The tall, toolsy teen son of late ChiSox corner infielder Carlos Martinez, **Jose Martinez** was just catching fire in his full-season debut when a knee injury ended his season in mid-May. He'll be back at full strength this year and remains one of the organization's top prospects. ⊘ A nondrafted free agent out of Arizona State University, the undersized **C. J. Retherford** was a collegiate bully in the prep-dominated Pioneer League in his pro debut in 2007, but was exposed last year in High-A, where the only damage he did came against lefty pitching. ⊘ A teen sensation in Cuba, 20-year-old defector **Dayan Viciedo** signed a major league contract with the White Sox in November. In contrast to the lanky, versatile, and older Alexei Ramirez (with whom he and fellow countryman Jose Contreras share an agent), Viciedo is maturing into a big-bodied slugger with monstrous power but questionable commitment. The

Sox want him to challenge Josh Fields for the third-base job in spring training, but he's more likely to start out in the minors and reemerge as a first baseman.

Pitchers

PLAYER	TEAM	LVL	AGE	W	L	SV	IP	H	BB	SO	HR	GB%	BABIP	STUFF	WHIP	ERA	DERA	EqH9	EqBB9	EqSO9	EqHR9	DEF	VORP
D. Day	BIR	AA	27	1	6	0	47²	51	28	35	3	60.3%	.329	-25	1.66	6.60	9.48	11.5	5.6	3.9	1.2	0	-18.8
	CHR	AAA	27	0	3	0	23²	29	6	25	3	51.3%	.361	-13	1.48	4.56	5.56	12.7	2.4	6.4	1.6	-1	0.1
M. Dubee	WNS	A+	22	5	7	1	103	103	37	90	12	52.5%	.320	-21	1.36	4.37	5.38	11.1	3.7	5.0	1.9	-7	2.3
E. Loaiza	LAN	MLB	36	1	2	0	24	24	5	9	3	37.5%	.256	-13	1.21	5.63	5.40	8.3	1.4	2.9	1.1	0	0.3
	CHA	MLB	36	0	0	0	3	3	0	1	1	41.7%	.182	-28	1.00	3.00	8.10	8.1	0.0	2.7	2.7	1	-0.0
K. McCulloch	BIR	AA	23	8	11	0	156²	188	60	85	9	56.4%	.344	-23	1.58	4.65	6.53	12.7	3.8	2.7	1.1	-11	-14.8
H. Ramirez*	KCA	MLB	28	1	1	0	24¹	21	1	11	1	59.8%	.250	-1	0.90	2.59	3.65	7.3	0.4	3.6	0.4	1	6.7
	CHA	MLB	28	0	3	0	13	24	8	2	0	46.8%	.407	-40	2.46	7.62	5.14	14.8	4.5	1.3	0.0	-3	-2.4
C. Santeliz	WNS	A+	21	3	6	0	68	55	48	60	8	48.0%	.267	-3	1.51	4.90	7.30	9.2	7.2	5.1	2.0	-1	-11.7
	BIR	AA	21	0	1	0	16¹	14	8	6	2	38.5%	.245	-30	1.35	4.42	6.14	9.2	4.9	1.8	1.8	0	-0.9
K. Texeira	WNS	A+	22	3	1	20	38²	28	14	36	0	62.7%	.259	6	1.09	0.93	3.29	7.0	3.5	4.9	0.2	1	9.8
	BIR	AA	22	3	2	1	22¹	18	7	24	2	61.7%	.321	6	1.12	2.02	4.50	9.4	3.2	6.8	1.8	3	2.4
C. Torres	BIR	AA	25	9	5	0	101¹	86	29	93	4	47.1%	.303	4	1.14	3.20	5.73	9.3	2.9	5.4	0.8	7	-1.3
	CHR	AAA	25	0	0	0	19²	23	11	19	2	50.8%	.368	-8	1.73	4.57	5.50	12.5	5.5	6.0	1.5	0	0.2

Career reliever **Dewon Day** appeared to have solved his wildness in Triple-A last spring, only to be demoted to Double-A and moved into the rotation for the first time in his career. Despite disastrous results, he was claimed off waivers by the Red Sox after the season. ⊘ When the White Sox got **Michael Dubee** from the Phillies for Tad Iguchi at the 2007 deadline, Dubee had just been converted to the bullpen. The Sox undid that, but seemed to rethink things after getting a better look at his underwhelming stuff. ⊘ **Esteban Loaiza** didn't have a healthy season among the four covered by the contract he signed with the A's after the 2005 season, and managed just 64⅓ innings with a 5.60 ERA over the last two. Released twice last year and ultimately done in by shoulder inflammation, he's probably finished. ⊘ **Kyle McCulloch** is another of those low-ceiling, right-handed college pitchers with weak peripherals and ground-ball tendencies who will be fortunate to find himself at the back of a rotation someday. He was also the Sox' top draft pick in 2005. Oof. ⊘ Released by the Mariners during spring training, converted to relief by the Royals, and traded to the White Sox for scraps, **Horacio Ramirez** survives due to the arm he throws with and despite his inability to retire lefties or strike anyone out (4.1 K/9 career). The Royals took him back as a free agent in December, signing him to a one-year contract. ⊘ The Sox' decision to add hard-throwing Venezuelan **Clevelan Santeliz**—of whom scouts have observed a disturbing cockiness-to-talent ratio—to the 40-man roster in November cost them Derek Rodriguez, a more advanced pitcher, when the latter was spirited away in the Rule 5 draft. ⊘ Big, fireballing lefty reliever **Andy Sisco** had Tommy John surgery last April and hopes to work his way back to the majors this year. ⊘ Sent to the Yankees in the Nick Swisher deal, side-arming Hawaiian reliever **Kanekoa Texeira** could emerge as another moving part in the Yankees' fungible bullpen of quality team-controlled arms. ⊘ Yet another mediocre college right-hander, Kansas State product **Carlos Torres** would make a good utility pitcher, given his durability and clean mechanics.

MANAGER: OZZIE GUILLEN

YEAR	TEAM	W-L	Pythag +/−	Avg PC	100+ P	120+ P	QS	BQS	REL	REL w Zero R	IBB	Subs	PH	PH Avg	PH HR	SB2	CS2	SB3	CS3	SAC Att	SAC %	POS SAC	Squeeze	Swing	In Play
2006	CHA	90-72	2	100.9	93	4	76	12	398	222	59	51	135	.225	6	83	43	10	4	72	61.1%	39	2	127	100
2007	CHA	72-90	6	100.7	98	2	82	15	463	258	50	31	100	.227	3	75	38	3	6	61	67.2%	36	0	128	108
2008	CHA	89-74	-1	97.3	72	4	86	9	463	286	42	49	75	.281	2	54	29	13	4	47	59.6%	25	1	128	98

Because Guillen was a scrappy, small-ball-style player, he was labeled as a kind of throwback Deadball Era (or at least the 1960s) manager on his arrival as White Sox skipper in 2004. Though the White Sox won the World Series in Ozzie's sophomore season with pitching and power rather than speed and sac bunts, there was still some truth to the Ozzieball epithet. Throwback Guillen pushed his starters deep into games, used his relievers interchangeably, and did bunt and steal more than the average bear. Yet, the style of any manager worth his job is dictated by his players, and as the horses in his rotation have found other pastures and the Scott Podsedniks in his lineup have yielded to still more thumpers, Guillen's style has become more conventional. Consider the trends above: shorter outings for the rotation now staffed by younger arms; fewer blown quality starts, thanks to those quicker hooks; more relievers used on no rest, as favorites have emerged in specific roles; fewer steals, as he had no viable thieves other than Orlando Cabrera; fewer bunts from a lineup with eight men in double digits in homers; and even a decrease in intentional walks, a category in which Guillen led the league in 2005 and 2006. Ozzie's behavior may not have changed, but his managing has.

Cincinnati Reds

In mid-August, Cincinnati's Barcalounger era officially came to a close, as Adam Dunn was dealt to the Arizona Diamondbacks for an underwhelming package of a midrotation pitcher and two marginal prospects. Weeks earlier, at the July trade deadline, Ken Griffey Jr. had been handed off to a contender for a youngish middle reliever and a second-tier infield prospect. Neither package was the king's ransom imagined during the years that the two outfielders were featured in just about every trade rumor out of the Queen City, but then again, both men were just weeks away from free agency and neither was likely to return. Griffey, in particular, seemed to be with the Reds only so that the franchise could "own" his landmark 600th home run, which happened in mid-June. By the time Junior hit the big dinger, he was already mired in a season that was a substantial step back from his resurgent 2007, and between that and his no-trade rights, the market for his services was substantially depressed.

The expectations were different eight years earlier, when Griffey was a superstar added to catapult a 96-win team to the next level of contention. Griffey was acquired in exchange for a package of young players in what was thought to be a steal for the Reds, and the club immediately signed him to a then-mammoth nine-year, $116 million contract. The contract wasn't intended to take Griffey merely through his 600th homer, but also well into his pursuit of Hank Aaron's career home run record. With perennial All-Star Barry Larkin batting in front of Griffey, and a crew of prospects (including Dunn) following close after, the Reds would be a perennial contender when they opened their new ballpark in 2003.

> ## REDS PROSPECTUS
>
> **2008 record:** 74-88; Fifth place in NL Central
>
> **Pythagenport record:** 71-91
>
> **Runs scored per game:** 4.35 (12th in NL)
>
> **Runs allowed per game:** 4.99 (13th in NL)
>
> **Team EqA:** .251 (14th in NL)
>
> **2008 Batters Age:** 28.8 (8th-youngest in NL)
>
> **2008 Pitchers Age:** 28.6 (6th-youngest in NL)
>
> **Ballpark:** Great American Ballpark; Hitter's park; Park Factor of 1.031
>
> **2008:** It was a rare, youth-oriented year for the team's veteran skipper, but Corey Patterson was more indicative of the Dusty road.
>
> **2009:** Walt Jocketty looks to put his stamp on a team that's always at least half a rotation away.

Obviously, some things happened on the way to Big Red Machine 2.0. Larkin, 36 in Griffey's first year with the club, was headed into a steep decline; he would never be simultaneously healthy and good again. Most of the prospects, with the notable exception of Dunn, proved to be great disappointments. Griffey's mighty body broke down, and he wound up missing almost three years' worth of his team's games during the term of his contract. And the losses piled up: an 85-win season in 2000 was as good as the Griffey era got, and since then, the franchise has endured eight consecutive losing seasons. Dunn, the other player most identified with the 21st-century Reds, was blamed more for his faults than he was celebrated for his virtues—though he was a perennial leader in the "Three True Outcomes" (home runs, walks, and strikeouts), his many detractors focused on his high strikeout totals and poor defense, ignoring the things he did to put runs on the board.

Despite the duo's association with the failure and futility of the last nine years, there was something odd but understandable about jettisoning these veterans now. This wasn't a team dismantling to rebuild—the Cincinnati Reds are actually just about to get exciting and may be closer to contending now than they have been at any other time in the new millennium.

The problem with believing Junior Griffey was the last, expensive piece in the championship puzzle was that it ignored so many other problems. During the Griffey years, the team's one constant was its failure to prevent runs from scoring. Beginning with the reign of Jim Bowden, who took over as general manager in October 1992 and remained until October 2003, Reds pitching staffs have been shallow and undertalented. From 2001 on, the team never finished higher than 10th in the National League in runs allowed. Part of that, at least since 2003, was the team's home park: Great American Ballpark has consistently boosted home runs and usually boosted offense during its lifetime. But more importantly, the poor showing was a matter of weak personnel. It was not merely a matter of bad luck with health that the Reds' franchise was the poster child for instability in the starting rotation; fixing this was just not a priority during the Bowden years. Bowden was general manager of the Reds for 11 seasons. In six of nine Bowden seasons not affected by the 1994-1995 labor dispute, just one starter or no starters made 30 or more starts for the club, a problem that hung over into the first year of the Dan O'Brien regime in 2004 (Table 1).

Table 1. Pitchers Making 30 or More Starts for the Reds

Year	Pitcher (Starts)
1993	Jose Rijo (33)
1996	John Smiley (34), Dave Burba (34)
1997	Mike Morgan (30)
1998	Brett Tomko (34), Pete Harnisch (32)
1999	Pete Harnisch (33)
2000	Steve Parris (33)
2001	Elmer Dessens (34)
2002	Jimmy Haynes (34), Elmer Dessens (30)
2003	None
2004	None

At no time during these years did the team have a third pitcher reach 30 starts. That would finally happen in 2005, when Eric Milton, Aaron Harang, and Ramon Ortiz turned the trick. They weren't all good, but the last

time Cincinnati had known such regularity was in 1992, and Tim Belcher, Jose Rijo, and Greg Swindell were still young. Another way of looking at the problem of rotation stability in Cincinnati is continuity. During the period in question, every team except Tampa Bay (which only came into existence in 1998) found at least two starting pitchers whom the club could count on for years at a time (Table 2).

Unsurprisingly, the instability and generally weak personnel produced poor results. By several measures, including strikeout rate and lineup-adjusted support-neutral value over replacement (SNLVAR), a measure of starting pitching quality, Reds staffs have consistently been among the worst (Tables 3-4).

Table 3. Pitching in the Bowden/Griffey Era

Year	K Rate	MLB Rank	NL Rank	PADE	MLB Rank	NL Rank	RA	MLB Rank	NL Rank
1993	16.0	10	6	-2.53	28	14	4.93	22	12
1994	18.1	5	4	-1.13	18	9	4.25	3	3
1995	16.6	11	8	0.20	12	6	4.35	5	4
1996	17.4	8	6	-0.73	14	9	4.82	9	8
1997	18.5	8	5	0.45	8	6	4.75	12	8
1998	17.7	12	9	-0.14	12	7	4.75	12	8
1999	17.4	9	6	4.28	1	1	4.38	4	4
2000	16.0	18	13	1.76	3	2	4.73	7	6
2001	14.9	25	15	-1.09	18	9	5.30	24	14
2002	15.6	23	14	-0.22	15	8	4.79	19	13
2003	14.5	26	15	-1.09	20	11	5.51	27	15
2004	15.4	26	15	-1.42	24	14	5.65	28	15
2005	14.9	25	16	-3.45	29	16	5.58	28	16
2006	16.7	16	11	-2.02	27	16	4.99	19	9
2007	16.8	17	10	-2.12	25	13	5.30	26	15
2008	19.3	6	5	-3.83	30	16	4.99	23	13
Average	16.6	15.3	9.9	-0.82	17.8	9.8	4.94	16.8	10.2

Table 2. Leading Starting Pitchers by Team, 1993–2004

Rank	Team	Pitcher	GS	# Pitchers starting >100 Games	Rank	Team	Pitcher	GS	# Pitchers starting >100 Games
1	Braves	Greg Maddux	333	5	16	Dodgers	Hideo Nomo	191	8
2	Twins	Brad Radke	318	4	17	Expos/Nats	Javier Vazquez	191	5
3	Yankees	Andy Pettitte	276	6	18	Cubs	Steve Trachsel	186	5
4	Mariners	Jamie Moyer	266	3	19	Royals	Kevin Appier	185	4
5	Giants	Kirk Reuter	259	6	20	Padres	Andy Ashby	185	5
6	Orioles	Mike Mussina	244	4	21	A's	Tim Hudson	183	3
7	Astros	Shane Reynolds	243	7	22	Cardinals	Matt Morris	175	3
8	Blue Jays	Pat Hentgen	235	5	23	White Sox	James Baldwin	165	7
9	Indians	Charles Nagy	223	4	24	Brewers	Cal Eldred	152	4
10	Angels	Chuck Finley	219	4	25	Tigers	Brian Moehler	131	3
11	Mets	Al Leiter	213	4	26	Marlins	Brad Penny	130	3
12	Rangers	Kenny Rogers	210	4	27	Rockies	Pedro Astacio	129	4
13	Red Sox	Tim Wakefield	201	5	28	Pirates	Jason Schmidt	129	4
14	Phillies	Curt Schilling	200	2	29	Reds	John Smiley	123	1
15	D'backs	Randy Johnson	192	3	30	Devil Rays	None	-	0

Table 4. Reds SNLVAR, 1993–2008

Year	SNLVAR	MLB Rank	NL Rank
1993	16.9	19	10
1994	15.0	13	6
1995	19.2	9	5
1996	16.5	19	10
1997	16.0	19	11
1998	16.7	17	9
1999	22.6	9	6
2000	22.5	11	8
2001	9.9	28	15
2002	11.6	27	14
2003	7.3	27	14
2004	12.6	26	13
2005	8.1	27	15
2006	18.8	14	9
2007	15.4	23	12
2008	14.0	23	13
Average	15.2	19.4	10.6

Table 5. Top Teams by Defense-Adjusted ERA (DERA), 2008

Team	DERA	ERA	MLB Rank
Cubs	3.86	3.87	5
D'backs	3.87	3.98	7
Blue Jays	3.93	3.49	1
Dodgers	3.94	3.68	2
White Sox	3.95	4.06	11
Reds	4.11	4.55	23
Phillies	4.17	3.88	6
Brewers	4.21	3.85	4
Giants	4.31	4.38	17
Angels	4.32	3.99	8

Even when the Reds have received good individual pitching performances—as with Aaron Harang's emergence and Bronson Arroyo's career year in 2006—those gains have been given back by the staff's supporting members and by the team's defense. The Reds' defense, measured by Park-Adjusted Defensive Efficiency (PADE), was consistently below average since 2001. In recent years, the defense has been abysmal; last year, it was the worst in the game.

At last, the team may have crossed the long pitching desert. Given this cavalcade of negatives, it might be surprising that the most exciting feature of the team's 2008 season was the promise of a new, vastly improved pitching staff. While the results in terms of runs allowed weren't that far outside the 21st-century trend, the strikeout rate leaped into the game's top third. Leading the trend were Edinson Volquez, acquired before the season for Rule 5 pick/reclamation case Josh Hamilton, and rookie Johnny Cueto, but there were also strong contributions by Harang, Arroyo, and even bullpen hands like closer Francisco Cordero and setup men Bill Bray, Jared Burton, and Jeremy Affeldt. Except for Affeldt, all these pitchers will return in 2009, and Harang, Burton, and Bray may see greater playing time as the result of changing roles or recovery from injury. Unlike some other elements of a pitcher's performance, strikeout rate tends to be consistent from one season to the next, and every out secured by strikeout is one less for the defense to register.

Speaking of the defense, this, too, is in line to improve. The departed Dunn and Griffey were both poor defenders; younger replacements should lead to some improvement, although paying Willy Taveras $6.25 million over the next two years is a heavy price to pay in money and in the lineup to get good glove work. Whoever's playing it, the shortstop position should rebound with the return of Alex Gonzalez, or through the efforts of a healthy Jeff Keppinger, or through the work of youngster Paul Janish. A smart acquisition—say, picking up a good defensive third baseman and moving the defensively execrable Edwin Encarnacion to left field—could pay dividends at multiple positions. As the AL champion Tampa Bay Rays have shown, defensive upgrades can quickly pay immense dividends—DERA, a statistic that measures what a team's normalized ERA would have been if the pitchers had a league-average defense behind them, considered the Reds' pitching staff the sixth-*best* in baseball in 2008 (Table 5). The Reds don't have to transform themselves into one of the best defensive ballclubs in baseball, as the Rays did: just providing the pitching staff some mediocre defensive support would make this a completely different ballclub.

The team's offense was also subpar. The Reds finished 23rd in the majors in runs scored, and 25th in team EqA, so whether you adjust for the park (as with EqA) or not, they were pretty bad. Hope for improvement is an uneven proposition; while you might think it unlikely, for example, that the team would again allow an outfielder to have the season with the bat that Corey Patterson did in 2008, the signing of punchless, low-OBP speedster Willy Taveras to take his place is hardly cause for optimism. More happily, it's likely that trade acquisition Ramon Hernandez will outperform the team's 2008 catchers, who collectively performed at the replacement level. Jay Bruce lived down to the very lowest projections of his performance—he should perform better in 2009.

The man charged with capitalizing on all this optimism is general manager Walt Jocketty. He took the organization's reins in April, after already coming aboard as a "special advisor" (or, some might say, official in-house stalking horse) in January. Changing a member of the management crew in April is a phenomenally shoddy move, the type of thing that reflects as poorly on the person doing the firing as it does on the one being fired. After all, in the first 21 games of the season, the team learned nothing about outgoing GM Wayne Krivsky that it didn't already know going into spring training. Regardless of whether Krivsky's dismissal was justified, if the goal is to try to win now, you'0ts6d be admittedly hard-pressed to find a better executive than Jocketty to put in charge of your team. History will probably be kind to Krivsky, who is likely to be remembered more for swiping Hamilton in the Rule 5 draft and acquiring Volquez and Brandon Phillips than for the Austin Kearns trade with the Nationals—a trade that ended in headaches and grievances. With the Cardinals, Jocketty presided over one of the great win-now organizations in sports, seldom writing off a season over a dozen-year span that culminated in six division titles and an 83-win team nonetheless good enough to capture the 2006 World Series title. Although he was criticized for his spending and for the state of the Cardinals' farm system, no one ever accused Jocketty of defeatism on the major league level.

In many ways, Jocketty is the anti-Krivsky. While Krivsky's signature moves involved acquiring unproven talents with high upside, the Cardinals' Jocketty most often targeted players with long track records of steady, if sometimes unexciting, performance. Jocketty has a famous knack for acquiring proven performers in return for large packages of minor leaguers who, all told, usually accomplished little at the major league level. If Jocketty can tap into these skills at least one more time, especially now that the Reds have something of a starting rotation they can count on going forward, the Reds may finally close the book on this long, misguided era.

HITTERS

Yonder Alonso — 1B

Bats: L   Throws: R   Height: 6' 2"   Weight: 215   Born: April 8, 1987   Age: 22

YEAR	TEAM	LVL	AGE	PA	R	2B	3B	HR	RBI	BB	SO	SB	CS	EqBRR	AVG	OBP	SLG	EqAVG	EqOBP	EqSLG	EqA	VORP	WARP	DEFENSE	
2008	SAR	A+	21	25	1	1	0	0	2	5	5	0	0	0.1	.316	.440	.368	.250	.360	.300	.253	-0.3	0.3	4-1B	2
2009	CIN	MLB	22	564	57	28	2	14	62	52	137	9	3	0.3	.239	.312	.389	.238	.310	.389	.243	-3.9	0.4	132-1B	1

Breakout: 0%   Improve: 0%   Collapse: 0%   Attrition: 0%   Comparables: Will Clark, Michael Aubrey, Carlos Peña, Pat Burrell

A 1311 OPS during his junior year at Miami convinced the Reds to take Alonso with the seventh overall pick in the 2008 draft. He has the two skills you look for in a slugging first baseman—tons of power and excellent plate discipline. His position and advanced skills put him on a collision course with current Reds first baseman Joey Votto; the fact that he's already on the 40-man roster (a result of the four-year, $4.5 million big-league contract it took to sign him) means that the reckoning between them will probably come soon. The Reds drew some criticism for taking Alonso because of this, but when you have a pick that high, you really should take the best player and let the rest sort itself out.

Paul Bako — C

Bats: L   Throws: R   Height: 6' 2"   Weight: 205   Born: June 20, 1972   Age: 37

YEAR	TEAM	LVL	AGE	PA	R	2B	3B	HR	RBI	BB	SO	SB	CS	EqBRR	AVG	OBP	SLG	EqAVG	EqOBP	EqSLG	EqA	VORP	WARP	DEFENSE	
2006	KCA	MLB	34	167	7	3	0	0	10	11	46	0	0	-1.5	.209	.261	.229	.204	.261	.224	.166	-13.7	-0.8	45-C	0
2007	BAL	MLB	35	174	13	3	1	1	8	15	50	0	1	-0.8	.205	.277	.256	.206	.283	.258	.191	-9.4	-0.8	47-C	-2
2008	CIN	MLB	36	338	30	11	2	6	35	34	90	0	2	-1.0	.217	.299	.328	.213	.297	.330	.220	-6.9	-0.5	87-C	-4
2009	CIN	MLB	37	153	13	5	1	2	13	15	36	0	1	-0.8	.234	.310	.332	.233	.308	.332	.221	0.1	0.3	40-C	-2

Breakout: 46%   Improve: 62%   Collapse: 29%   Attrition: 56%   Comparables: Jim Sundberg, Ron Hassey, Tom Prince, Del Rice

With his 10th organization in an 11-year career, itinerant catcher Bako was his team's primary backstop for the first time since his rookie year. His season was ugly, even when graded on a generous "for a catcher" curve; tenure and the fact that he makes his outs from the left side of the plate give him a better-than-merited chance of catching on somewhere this season.

Jay Bruce — RF

Bats: L   Throws: L   Height: 6' 2"   Weight: 218   Born: April 3, 1987   Age: 22

YEAR	TEAM	LVL	AGE	PA	R	2B	3B	HR	RBI	BB	SO	SB	CS	EqBRR	AVG	OBP	SLG	EqAVG	EqOBP	EqSLG	EqA	VORP	WARP	DEFENSE			
2006	DYT	A	19	498	69	42	5	16	81	44	106	19	9	-0.9	.291	.355	.516	.225	.279	.406	.235	-9.7	-1.2	52-RF	-3	41-CF	-4
2007	SAR	A+	20	298	49	27	5	11	49	24	67	4	4	0.0	.325	.379	.586	.260	.312	.491	.267	11.5	0.9	49-CF	-3	18-RF	0
2007	CHT	AA	20	74	10	7	1	4	15	8	20	2	1	0.0	.333	.405	.652	.284	.351	.597	.301	7.7	0.4	11-CF	-2		
2007	LOU	AAA	20	204	28	12	2	11	25	15	48	2	2	-1.5	.305	.358	.567	.280	.332	.550	.288	15.2	1.8	40-CF	1	9-RF	2
2008	LOU	AAA	21	201	34	9	5	10	37	12	45	8	1	-0.7	.364	.393	.630	.335	.366	.600	.319	25.0	2.7	26-CF	1	10-RF	0
2008	CIN	MLB	21	452	63	17	1	21	52	33	110	4	6	-0.1	.254	.314	.453	.255	.316	.464	.260	5.4	0.2	66-RF	-3	32-CF	-3
2009	CIN	MLB	22	609	86	34	4	28	90	47	136	12	5	0.8	.283	.342	.509	.282	.339	.510	.284	29.4	3.7	142-RF	2		

Breakout: 35%   Improve: 76%   Collapse: 9%   Attrition: 6%   Comparables: Rick Monday, Tony Conigliaro, Manny Ramirez, Kal Daniels

The big Jay Bruce rollout didn't go exactly as planned. He was like one of those Nick Cage vehicles that opens at the top of the box-office charts but winds up banished from theaters two weeks later—after a torrid first dozen games in the majors, Bruce had a .280 on-base percentage the rest of the way. Lefties didn't seem to bother the phenom much in the minors, but they ate his lunch in "The Show" (.190/.263/.299). Bruce's track record is strong enough that you have to write this off as an adjustment period; still, Dusty Baker isn't known for his patience, and no one's interested in seeing *Bangkok Dangerous 2*.

Wilkin Castillo — C/UT

Bats: S   Throws: R   Height: 6' 0"   Weight: 170   Born: June 1, 1984   Age: 25

YEAR	TEAM	LVL	AGE	PA	R	2B	3B	HR	RBI	BB	SO	SB	CS	EqBRR	AVG	OBP	SLG	EqAVG	EqOBP	EqSLG	EqA	VORP	WARP	DEFENSE			
2006	LNC	A+	22	218	25	10	1	3	19	13	24	9	2	-1.5	.285	.329	.390	.200	.235	.298	.185	-18.6	-1.2	33-C	0		
2006	TEN	AA	22	88	7	3	0	0	5	6	10	1	0	-1.2	.250	.314	.289	.218	.267	.256	.191	-7.3	-0.2	21-C	1		
2007	MOB	AA	23	449	50	31	3	6	46	17	62	18	14	-4.4	.302	.333	.437	.262	.287	.392	.233	-5.8	0.9	68-C	4	19-2B	-2
2008	TUC	AAA	24	425	40	18	2	6	47	24	54	4	1	3.5	.254	.305	.358	.211	.258	.295	.193	-30.0	-2.6	47-C	2	37-3B	-5
2008	LOU	AAA	24	43	2	0	0	0	0	1	5	1	2	-0.3	.190	.209	.190	.167	.186	.167	.000	-7.3	-0.9	6-3B	-2		
2008	CIN	MLB	24	34	6	1	0	0	1	1	5	0	0	0.5	.281	.303	.313	.281	.303	.312	.216	-0.8	-0.1	4-LF	0		
2009	CIN	MLB	25	474	40	22	2	5	40	22	72	8	4	0.8	.234	.273	.328	.233	.271	.329	.205	-12.5	-0.4	112-C	-5		

Breakout: 42%   Improve: 55%   Collapse: 26%   Attrition: 13%   Comparables: Javier Guzman, Cris Colon, Jose Uribe, Felix Molina

Few are born with the mark of the third catcher: the skill to don the tools of ignorance and use them well, combined with the flexibility to play around the infield, the sagacity to stand in the outfield without looking lost, and even a half-teaspoonful of speed thrown in for good measure. Sadly for *Bonileño* Wilkin Castillo, the mark carries with it an awful curse—a lack of pop or patience, which condemns the bearer to watch the starters at all the positions he can play from the bench, but to never join them.

Chris Dickerson — OF

Bats: L   Throws: L   Height: 6' 4"   Weight: 212   Born: April 10, 1982   Age: 27

YEAR	TEAM	LVL	AGE	PA	R	2B	3B	HR	RBI	BB	SO	SB	CS	EqBRR	AVG	OBP	SLG	EqAVG	EqOBP	EqSLG	EqA	VORP	WARP	DEFENSE			
2006	CHT	AA	24	465	65	21	7	12	48	65	129	21	6	1.2	.242	.355	.424	.214	.311	.393	.249	-4.5	0.5	107-CF	-3		
2007	CHT	AA	25	123	11	4	1	1	11	7	31	7	2	0.0	.272	.325	.351	.205	.244	.282	.184	-10.8	-1.1	29-CF	-3		
2007	LOU	AAA	25	416	58	11	6	13	44	52	131	23	5	2.2	.260	.361	.435	.240	.331	.409	.261	4.7	1.6	57-CF	2	27-LF	2
2008	LOU	AAA	26	414	65	16	9	11	53	54	102	26	7	3.6	.287	.384	.479	.248	.343	.431	.271	11.1	3.7	66-CF	12	18-RF	2
2008	CIN	MLB	26	122	20	9	2	6	15	17	35	5	3	-0.4	.304	.413	.608	.304	.413	.627	.328	13.3	0.9	21-LF	-4	5-CF	0
2009	CIN	MLB	27	470	63	21	4	15	50	51	130	17	6	2.1	.247	.333	.427	.246	.331	.428	.263	9.5	2.2	111-CF	-1		

Breakout: 20%   Improve: 48%   Collapse: 22%   Attrition: 17%   Comparables: Al Martin, John Rodriguez, Mike Cameron, Bob Brower

Dickerson had the hottest streak of his entire career take place in the majors. That .300 batting average is likely to be a pure fluke—a .364 BABIP doesn't scream "sustainable." He does, however, have real power, real speed, and—rare for a player who's often described as toolsy—a decent batting eye. Nonetheless, he can't really afford to let off-season ankle surgery slow his momentum. Unfortunately, the Reds' decision to sign Willy Taveras would seem to limit him to a bench role or more time in the sticks. He turns 27 shortly after the season begins, and has already spent enough time in Louisville that he has started to take on side projects there, like getting everyone to recycle.

Edwin Encarnacion — 3B

Bats: R Throws: R Height: 6' 1" Weight: 215 Born: January 7, 1983 Age: 26

YEAR	TEAM	LVL	AGE	PA	R	2B	3B	HR	RBI	BB	SO	SB	CS	EqBRR	AVG	OBP	SLG	EqAVG	EqOBP	EqSLG	EqA	VORP	WARP	DEFENSE	
2006	CIN	MLB	23	463	60	33	1	15	72	41	78	6	3	-0.3	.276	.359	.473	.268	.350	.462	.278	15.7	1.5	104-3B	-6
2007	CIN	MLB	24	556	66	25	1	16	76	39	86	8	1	0.8	.289	.356	.438	.283	.353	.435	.275	20.9	0.9	131-3B	-14
2008	CIN	MLB	25	582	75	29	1	26	68	61	102	1	0	1.2	.251	.340	.466	.250	.338	.471	.277	21.3	0.9	139-3B	-17
2009	CIN	MLB	26	577	82	31	2	24	80	59	92	5	2	-0.4	.283	.365	.493	.282	.363	.493	.290	34.4	3.3	135-3B	-6

Breakout: 37% Improve: 65% Collapse: 7% Attrition: 7% Comparables: Doug Rader, Aramis Ramirez, Tony Perez, Kevin Mitchell

Encarnacion has settled into an uncomfortable groove—his offensive performance is consistent, as are the defensive lapses at the hot corner. He's still young enough and talented enough to break out, but at this point, it seems unlikely that he's ever going to be Graig Nettles. It's time to stop getting frustrated about the things Encarnacion does poorly and focus on what he does well: bring some power to the lineup. Given his iceberg-like nature, bringing his team two wins above replacement with his bat but giving away one with the glove, he might be better utilized in a platoon or other part-time arrangement, depending on the ground-ball/fly-ball mix of the day's pitcher.

Juan Francisco — 3B

Bats: S Throws: R Height: 6' 2" Weight: 180 Born: June 24, 1987 Age: 22

YEAR	TEAM	LVL	AGE	PA	R	2B	3B	HR	RBI	BB	SO	SB	CS	EqBRR	AVG	OBP	SLG	EqAVG	EqOBP	EqSLG	EqA	VORP	WARP	DEFENSE	
2006	RDS	Rk	19	190	24	14	0	3	30	6	35	2	0	1.8	.280	.305	.407	.216	.232	.330	.188	-39.7	-2.5	37-3B	-3
2006	BIL	Rk	19	36	6	3	0	0	2	0	8	2	1	-0.3	.333	.333	.417	.222	.222	.278	.160	-6.6	-0.6	5-3B	-1
2007	DYT	A	20	562	69	21	4	25	90	23	161	12	6	0.0	.268	.301	.463	.211	.237	.357	.200	-36.1	-3.7	116-3B	-8
2008	SAR	A+	21	541	71	34	5	23	92	19	123	1	2	-0.9	.277	.303	.496	.236	.259	.438	.233	-8.3	-1.3	105-3B	-7
2009	CIN	MLB	22	586	58	31	2	21	74	26	159	3	2	0.2	.245	.281	.425	.244	.279	.425	.235	0.6	0.1	137-3B	-6

Breakout: 55% Improve: 76% Collapse: 11% Attrition: 8% Comparables: Andujar Cedeño, Geronimo Berroa, Frank Valdez, Victor Diaz

Talk about a mixed bag. Francisco showed more power and a reduced, if still very high, strikeout rate at Sarasota. At the same time, his defense at the hot corner didn't improve, and fewer strikeouts didn't herald better plate selectivity—he walked less than four percent of the time, a step back from his 2007 level. He put a beating on the Dominican winter league, but if he doesn't learn to take a pitch now and then, this might prove to be his ceiling.

Todd Frazier — INF

Bats: R Throws: R Height: 6' 3" Weight: 215 Born: February 12, 1986 Age: 23

YEAR	TEAM	LVL	AGE	PA	R	2B	3B	HR	RBI	BB	SO	SB	CS	EqBRR	AVG	OBP	SLG	EqAVG	EqOBP	EqSLG	EqA	VORP	WARP	DEFENSE			
2007	BIL	Rk	21	186	29	6	5	5	25	18	22	3	3	0.2	.319	.409	.513	.212	.274	.324	.206	-18.2	-1.8	34-SS	-8		
2007	DYT	A	21	24	4	3	0	2	5	2	4	0	0	0.0	.318	.375	.727	.261	.320	.652	.298	2.6	0.4	6-SS	1		
2008	DYT	A	22	127	25	10	0	7	20	15	28	4	2	-0.4	.321	.402	.598	.243	.315	.461	.261	3.2	0.8	16-SS	1	4-1B	2
2008	SAR	A+	22	414	62	20	3	12	54	41	84	8	4	0.2	.281	.357	.451	.237	.302	.403	.243	-2.6	1.2	55-SS	6	15-1B	-1
2009	CIN	MLB	23	608	73	33	3	21	75	56	144	8	5	0.8	.248	.322	.437	.248	.320	.437	.258	15.4	2.6	142-SS	-3		

Breakout: 54% Improve: 83% Collapse: 2% Attrition: 5% Comparables: Sean Rodriguez, Scott Hairston, Xavier Nady, Chad Huffman

A former Little League world champion, Todd Frazier has been regarded as something of a tweener as a professional: not quick enough afield to stay at shortstop, but not strong enough at the plate to carry his bat at the other end of the defensive spectrum. Third base, the eternal refuge of the tweener, is a stacked position in the Reds' system; he'll have to keep pounding the ball to be considered at the outfield corners.

Ryan Freel — UT

Bats: R Throws: R Height: 5' 10" Weight: 185 Born: March 8, 1976 Age: 33

YEAR	TEAM	LVL	AGE	PA	R	2B	3B	HR	RBI	BB	SO	SB	CS	EqBRR	AVG	OBP	SLG	EqAVG	EqOBP	EqSLG	EqA	VORP	WARP	DEFENSE			
2006	CIN	MLB	30	523	67	30	2	8	27	57	98	37	11	-1.6	.271	.363	.399	.266	.360	.396	.271	15.2	2.2	45-CF	-2	40-RF	5
2007	CIN	MLB	31	304	44	13	3	3	16	18	47	15	8	-0.1	.245	.308	.347	.248	.310	.360	.231	-4.7	-1.6	50-CF	-11	14-3B	-2
2008	CIN	MLB	32	143	17	8	0	0	10	8	18	6	4	-0.9	.298	.340	.359	.303	.345	.356	.246	1.7	-0.7	17-CF	-4	5-LF	-3
2009	BAL	MLB	33	162	20	7	1	2	14	12	23	6	2	0.5	.266	.328	.360	.264	.329	.365	.250	1.3	0.1	42-CF	-4		

Breakout: 22% Improve: 42% Collapse: 38% Attrition: 40% Comparables: Wayne Kirby, John Moses, Mike McCormick, Lonnie Smith

Trading Freel to the Orioles for Ramon Hernandez, the Reds might have sold him at the right time. The utilityman's vaunted flexibility doesn't count for much if he's always on the disabled list, and repeated leg injuries, such as the hamstring tendon tear that ended his season, have decimated his speed. He'll bring the Orioles his one remaining tool, the ability to get on base at a decent clip, albeit in a punchless sort of way.

Alex Gonzalez   SS

Bats: R   Throws: R   Height: 6' 0"   Weight: 200   Born: February 15, 1977   Age: 32

YEAR	TEAM	LVL	AGE	PA	R	2B	3B	HR	RBI	BB	SO	SB	CS	EqBRR	AVG	OBP	SLG	EqAVG	EqOBP	EqSLG	EqA	VORP	WARP	DEFENSE	
2006	BOS	MLB	29	429	48	24	2	9	50	22	67	1	0	0.4	.255	.299	.397	.241	.287	.378	.234	3.7	0.6	109-SS	-1
2007	CIN	MLB	30	430	55	27	1	16	55	24	75	0	1	1.0	.272	.325	.468	.267	.322	.466	.267	18.1	2.2	98-SS	0
2009	CIN	MLB	32	246	25	11	1	7	30	17	43	0	1	-0.2	.250	.309	.406	.249	.307	.407	.244	6.3	0.8	61-SS	1

Breakout: 21%   Improve: 35%   Collapse: 37%   Attrition: 29%   Comparables: Max Alvis, Rich Rollins, Jim Davenport, Randy Jackson

Knee surgery scuttled Alex Gonzalez's season before it could begin. The Reds' league-worst defense felt his absence acutely, or at least, they missed the glove Gonzalez had when he was acquired, before the 2007 season. With the uncertainties of microfracture surgery added to his advancing age, there's no telling which, if any, of Gonzalez's skills will survive a 17-month layoff.

Jerry Hairston Jr.   UT

Bats: R   Throws: R   Height: 5' 10"   Weight: 185   Born: May 29, 1976   Age: 33

YEAR	TEAM	LVL	AGE	PA	R	2B	3B	HR	RBI	BB	SO	SB	CS	EqBRR	AVG	OBP	SLG	EqAVG	EqOBP	EqSLG	EqA	VORP	WARP	DEFENSE				
2006	CHN	MLB	30	92	8	3	0	0	4	4	14	3	0	0.4	.207	.253	.244	.200	.244	.235	.174	-6.1	-0.3	17-2B	3			
2006	TEX	MLB	30	100	17	3	1	0	6	9	20	2	2	-0.2	.205	.286	.261	.195	.286	.253	.191	-7.3	-0.4	16-LF	2	6-CF	0
2007	TEX	MLB	31	184	22	7	0	3	16	11	24	5	1	1.6	.189	.249	.289	.182	.247	.289	.200	-11.5	-0.2	15-CF	2	12-2B	1
2008	LOU	AAA	32	85	11	8	2	4	19	3	9	1	1	-0.0	.380	.405	.684	.312	.341	.562	.297	7.7	0.7	6-SS	0	6-RF	0
2008	CIN	MLB	32	297	47	20	2	6	36	23	36	15	3	0.1	.326	.384	.487	.326	.386	.496	.303	27.7	1.9	30-SS	-7	13-CF	1
2009	CIN	MLB	33	309	42	18	2	8	36	23	41	10	4	1.0	.284	.343	.450	.283	.341	.451	.272	14.6	1.7	75-SS	-4			

Breakout: 30%   Improve: 59%   Collapse: 11%   Attrition: 27%   Comparables: Alan Bannister, Dan Gladden, Tom Brookens, Gerald Williams

This is why it pays to persevere. Between the 2005 All-Star break and the end of the 2007 season, Hairston's major league performance pretty much stated "I don't belong"—more than 500 plate appearances' worth of .212/.274/.291 performance. But just when you thought not only was there a fork in him, but it was also starting to rust, Hairston made his way to the Great American Ballpark and started one of the all-time romances between man and stadium. Bolstered by an amazing offensive assault at home (.410/.471/.590) and the "versatility" to play the outfield and stand at various infield positions during an emergency, Hairston is again in demand.

Ryan Hanigan   C

Bats: R   Throws: R   Height: 6' 0"   Weight: 195   Born: August 16, 1980   Age: 28

YEAR	TEAM	LVL	AGE	PA	R	2B	3B	HR	RBI	BB	SO	SB	CS	EqBRR	AVG	OBP	SLG	EqAVG	EqOBP	EqSLG	EqA	VORP	WARP	DEFENSE	
2006	CHT	AA	25	150	17	2	0	0	14	19	23	0	0	0.6	.246	.347	.262	.191	.273	.214	.172	-15.0	-0.9	23-C	1
2007	CHT	AA	26	247	30	14	1	3	27	41	30	0	2	0.0	.299	.420	.426	.209	.312	.299	.222	-10.5	-0.2	55-C	-2
2007	LOU	AAA	26	150	16	5	0	1	9	14	15	0	0	-0.5	.252	.333	.315	.212	.286	.265	.199	-9.9	0.5	31-C	8
2008	LOU	AAA	27	311	37	14	0	4	35	25	39	1	0	-2.7	.324	.392	.419	.271	.335	.365	.250	1.0	1.7	71-C	5
2008	CIN	MLB	27	98	9	2	0	2	9	10	9	0	0	0.3	.271	.367	.365	.271	.367	.365	.263	2.8	0.7	26-C	2
2009	CIN	MLB	28	310	28	12	1	4	26	30	50	1	1	-0.7	.232	.315	.325	.231	.313	.325	.225	-1.9	1.2	75-C	3

Breakout: 22%   Improve: 39%   Collapse: 37%   Attrition: 31%   Comparables: Greg Olson, Bud Bulling, Dutch Dotterer, Rick Sweet

Hanigan bravely fought his way through the Reds' horde of backstops to become the team's primary catcher at the end of the season, only to see his shot at a starting job fade with the trade that brought Ramon Hernandez over from the Orioles. While the idea of Hanigan as a starter might always have been a stretch—it's tough for an old rookie catcher with his skill set to get much of a shake, let alone a fair one—he did acquit himself well when given the opportunity, showing some good defense and a league-average bat.

Scott Hatteberg   **1B**   Bats: L   Throws: R   Height: 6' 1"   Weight: 210   Born: December 14, 1969   Age: 39

YEAR	TEAM	LVL	AGE	PA	R	2B	3B	HR	RBI	BB	SO	SB	CS	EqBRR	AVG	OBP	SLG	EqAVG	EqOBP	EqSLG	EqA	VORP	WARP	DEFENSE	
2006	CIN	MLB	36	539	62	28	0	13	51	74	41	2	2	-2.5	.289	.389	.436	.280	.384	.423	.284	15.5	2.7	122-1B	5
2007	CIN	MLB	37	417	50	27	1	10	47	49	35	0	0	0.6	.310	.394	.474	.298	.388	.468	.297	25.7	2.3	86-1B	0
2008	CIN	MLB	38	61	3	3	0	0	7	7	7	0	1	-0.9	.173	.262	.231	.173	.262	.231	.176	-5.6	-0.5	10-1B	0
2009	CIN	MLB	39	153	17	7	0	3	16	17	16	0	0	-0.7	.262	.349	.380	.261	.346	.380	.255	1.2	0.2	40-1B	0

Breakout: 12% Improve: 24% Collapse: 47% Attrition: 40% Comparables: Dave Bergman, Chris Chambliss, Ken Griffey, Rusty Staub

The Reds' interest in pickin' machine Scott Hatteberg ended when Joey Votto rightfully won the first-base job. Hatteberg didn't take well to life on the bench: he batted a Hattebergian .308/.355/.423 when he got to start, but getting isolated plate appearances every couple of days didn't agree with him. Released on June 4, he failed to catch on with another club, not surprising, given that the majors aren't generally friendly to starting first basemen who've only cracked a .450 slugging percentage once in their careers. As of this winter, he's still looking for a contract, a nonroster invite, anything, so this could be the end.

Norris Hopper   **OF**   Bats: R   Throws: R   Height: 5' 10"   Weight: 210   Born: March 24, 1979   Age: 30

YEAR	TEAM	LVL	AGE	PA	R	2B	3B	HR	RBI	BB	SO	SB	CS	EqBRR	AVG	OBP	SLG	EqAVG	EqOBP	EqSLG	EqA	VORP	WARP	DEFENSE			
2006	CHT	AA	27	52	7	2	1	0	10	6	3	3	0	1.3	.283	.365	.370	.208	.269	.292	.200	-3.8	-0.3	6-CF	-1	4-RF	1
2006	LOU	AAA	27	410	47	11	3	0	26	20	25	25	7	1.6	.347	.378	.392	.289	.319	.331	.234	-6.3	0.1	56-LF	3	15-CF	0
2006	CIN	MLB	27	47	6	1	0	1	5	6	4	2	2	-0.6	.359	.435	.462	.359	.435	.462	.306	3.2	0.7	8-RF	3		
2007	CIN	MLB	28	335	51	14	2	0	14	20	33	14	6	1.9	.329	.371	.388	.328	.373	.396	.269	12.8	2.2	46-CF	4	13-LF	6
2008	CIN	MLB	29	58	3	0	0	0	1	5	6	1	0	0.3	.200	.286	.200	.196	.281	.196	.176	-4.0	-0.4	5-CF	0		
2009	CIN	MLB	30	114	13	4	1	0	8	8	11	3	1	0.3	.274	.330	.324	.273	.327	.325	.234	-0.4	0.3	31-CF	0		

Breakout: 27% Improve: 43% Collapse: 36% Attrition: 51% Comparables: John Wehner, Hank Allen, Tommie Reynolds, Wallace Johnson

Hopper is the kind of speedy, aggressive player who might have become the apple of Dusty Baker's eye had his ulnar collateral ligament not failed him, requiring surgery. Position players come back pretty well from Tommy John surgery, so his forecast—such as it is—shouldn't change much.

Paul Janish   **SS**   Bats: R   Throws: R   Height: 6' 2"   Weight: 190   Born: October 12, 1982   Age: 26

YEAR	TEAM	LVL	AGE	PA	R	2B	3B	HR	RBI	BB	SO	SB	CS	EqBRR	AVG	OBP	SLG	EqAVG	EqOBP	EqSLG	EqA	VORP	WARP	DEFENSE			
2006	DYT	A	23	108	19	6	0	5	18	7	10	0	0	1.0	.398	.435	.612	.287	.318	.446	.261	3.3	0.3	24-SS	-2		
2006	SAR	A+	23	393	53	17	2	9	55	38	39	8	2	0.6	.278	.355	.421	.221	.285	.341	.224	-16.5	-1.2	83-SS	-11		
2007	CHT	AA	24	391	46	21	2	1	20	50	54	10	3	0.0	.244	.358	.330	.194	.290	.268	.205	-26.1	-0.7	67-SS	1	13-2B	-2
2007	LOU	AAA	24	227	20	8	1	3	19	14	31	2	0	-0.3	.221	.278	.317	.205	.255	.312	.199	-15.0	-1.4	55-SS	-8		
2008	LOU	AAA	25	365	45	20	1	7	42	26	71	2	0	1.2	.252	.324	.387	.225	.291	.357	.228	-10.7	1.2	88-SS	8		
2008	CIN	MLB	25	89	5	2	0	1	6	7	18	0	0	0.1	.188	.270	.250	.188	.270	.250	.180	-4.5	-0.2	23-SS	2		
2009	CIN	MLB	26	448	42	22	1	7	40	37	86	3	1	0.1	.224	.297	.342	.223	.295	.343	.222	-2.7	0.3	106-SS	0		

Breakout: 33% Improve: 61% Collapse: 24% Attrition: 13% Comparables: Chris Martin, Gookie Dawkins, Tim Dulin, Mark DeRosa

Janish doesn't have any wood to go with his cowhide, but given the uncertainty for the Reds over who's available to play short, they may have to bite the bullet and hope that the youngster makes up in the field what he gives away at the plate. While that's not a ringing endorsement, is that plan any worse than giving Juan Castro yet another lease on life? Knowing Dusty Baker, we guess that somewhere, Neifi Perez's pager is beeping.

Jeff Keppinger

INF Bats: R   Throws: R   Height: 6' 0"   Weight: 180   Born: April 21, 1980   Age: 29

YEAR	TEAM	LVL	AGE	PA	R	2B	3B	HR	RBI	BB	SO	SB	CS	EqBRR	AVG	OBP	SLG	EqAVG	EqOBP	EqSLG	EqA	VORP	WARP	DEFENSE		
2006	NOR	AAA	26	366	36	13	0	2	26	28	21	0	4	-0.3	.300	.353	.359	.279	.329	.336	.235	-3.6	0.9	54-2B	7	12-LF -1
2006	OMA	AAA	26	142	21	6	1	2	17	12	9	0	0	-1.2	.354	.407	.465	.300	.348	.408	.264	4.7	0.2	16-2B	-4	9-3B 2
2006	KCA	MLB	26	67	11	2	0	2	8	5	6	0	0	-0.0	.267	.323	.400	.254	.323	.390	.249	-0.2	0.0	12-3B	0	
2007	LOU	AAA	27	261	31	15	1	2	18	23	14	1	1	-1.1	.368	.424	.469	.303	.357	.397	.266	8.4	1.0	19-3B	1	19-2B 4
2007	CIN	MLB	27	276	39	16	2	5	32	24	12	2	1	1.6	.332	.400	.477	.326	.397	.479	.300	22.8	2.1	44-SS	-4	9-3B 2
2008	CIN	MLB	28	502	45	24	2	3	43	30	24	3	1	0.6	.266	.310	.346	.265	.311	.352	.235	1.5	-1.3	99-SS	-17	8-3B 0
2009	CIN	MLB	29	499	54	24	1	4	42	39	31	2	1	-0.2	.286	.343	.372	.285	.341	.373	.250	13.1	0.9	118-SS	-8	

Breakout: 15%   Improve: 40%   Collapse: 30%   Attrition: 17%   Comparables: Scott Fletcher, Bob Randall, Julio Franco, Mike Bordick

For the first six weeks of the season, the "Jeff Keppinger, offensive shortstop" plan seemed to be working, on the strength of a .326 batting average on balls in play (BABIP). Then he fouled a ball off his left kneecap, suffering a fracture in that knee for the second time in his career and becoming the second Reds shortstop to be sidelined by a knee fracture in 2008. Unlike Alex Gonzalez, Keppinger was back on the field in a month, but was a shell of his former self, posting a .236 BABIP the rest of the way. Research by Clay Davenport indicates that at the time of the injury, Keppinger rated as an above-average defender, but afterward, he was one of the worst in the majors. Regardless of the reasons for his failure, it's unlikely that Keppinger will get another opportunity to play short every day.

Devin Mesoraco

C Bats: R   Throws: R   Height: 6' 1"   Weight: 200   Born: June 19, 1988   Age: 21

YEAR	TEAM	LVL	AGE	PA	R	2B	3B	HR	RBI	BB	SO	SB	CS	EqBRR	AVG	OBP	SLG	EqAVG	EqOBP	EqSLG	EqA	VORP	WARP	DEFENSE	
2007	RDS	Rk	19	155	16	4	0	1	8	15	26	2	0	-2.1	.219	.310	.270	.160	.219	.201	.121	-56.3	-3.0	27-C	-3
2008	DYT	A	20	334	29	13	1	9	42	20	64	2	3	-5.2	.261	.311	.399	.215	.257	.346	.206	-19.3	-2.0	71-C	-12
2009	CIN	MLB	21	444	31	20	1	8	42	28	104	1	1	-2.0	.213	.268	.328	.213	.266	.328	.201	-13.5	-0.5	105-C	-8

Breakout: 56%   Improve: 71%   Collapse: 13%   Attrition: 7%   Comparables: Rene Rivera, John Gibbons, Wynn Beck, Lance Jennings

There was improvement for Mesoraco last year, even if it was from abysmal to just plain bad. The scouting classes still see all the tools that made him the 15th pick overall two years ago, just in a somewhat thicker body. High school catchers drafted in the first round get a bum rap—everyone remembers the busts, forgetting the Paul Konerkos and Justin Morneaus who make it to the majors at other positions—but unless Mesoraco's bat comes around, he might get lumped in there with the cautionary tales like Ben Davis and Kurt Brown.

Corey Patterson

CF Bats: L   Throws: R   Height: 5' 9"   Weight: 175   Born: August 13, 1979   Age: 29

YEAR	TEAM	LVL	AGE	PA	R	2B	3B	HR	RBI	BB	SO	SB	CS	EqBRR	AVG	OBP	SLG	EqAVG	EqOBP	EqSLG	EqA	VORP	WARP	DEFENSE	
2006	BAL	MLB	26	498	75	19	5	16	53	21	94	45	9	6.0	.276	.314	.443	.267	.307	.436	.263	23.4	3.9	123-CF	19
2007	BAL	MLB	27	503	65	26	2	8	45	21	65	37	9	2.0	.269	.304	.386	.267	.303	.396	.249	5.7	0.9	119-CF	0
2008	CIN	MLB	28	392	46	17	2	10	34	16	57	14	9	0.5	.205	.238	.344	.207	.239	.360	.204	-18.9	-1.1	90-CF	5
2009	WAS	MLB	29	365	44	18	3	7	36	20	54	23	7	2.2	.261	.306	.391	.264	.309	.408	.252	6.0	1.6	88-CF	2

Breakout: 46%   Improve: 69%   Collapse: 17%   Attrition: 25%   Comparables: Bobby Tolan, Rudy Law, Ty Cline, Willie Smith

The situation looked perfect for Patterson: a veteran-lovin' manager he's worked with before, a good ballpark, and only an unproven phenom and an injury-prone veteran standing between him and the starting job. Piece of cake. However, given full chance to flower in Cincy, Patterson imploded, posting numbers eerily similar to the 2005 performance that got him drummed out of Chicago. Even with his bat threatening to single-handedly derail the offense—in 155 plate appearances as the leadoff hitter, he batted .182/.217/.322—Patterson's legs and glove retained some value; those are the tools that got him his next gig with the Nats, on a minor league deal.

Brandon Phillips 2B Bats: R Throws: R Height: 6' 0" Weight: 195 Born: June 28, 1981 Age: 28

YEAR	TEAM	LVL	AGE	PA	R	2B	3B	HR	RBI	BB	SO	SB	CS	EqBRR	AVG	OBP	SLG	EqAVG	EqOBP	EqSLG	EqA	VORP	WARP	DEFENSE		
2006	CIN	MLB	25	587	65	28	1	17	75	35	88	25	2	3.1	.276	.324	.427	.268	.317	.413	.261	21.2	0.3	136-2B	-16	
2007	CIN	MLB	26	702	107	26	6	30	94	33	109	32	8	1.9	.288	.331	.485	.283	.327	.486	.276	37.7	3.5	153-2B	-4	
2008	CIN	MLB	27	609	80	24	7	21	78	39	93	23	10	0.9	.261	.312	.442	.262	.313	.452	.260	16.4	2.8	139-2B	5	
2009	CIN	MLB	28	605	85	29	4	20	72	42	88	21	7	1.8	.282	.337	.458	.281	.335	.458	.271	29.0	3.0	141-2B	-2	

Breakout: 22% Improve: 59% Collapse: 12% Attrition: 8% Comparables: Mariano Duncan, Dave Concepcion, Michael Young, Phil Garner

Only Dusty Baker could look at a guy who walked in fewer than five percent of his 2007 PAs and say that the problem was that Phillips needed to be *more* aggressive. Phillips's bat never came back from the All-Star break: he was hitting .225/.291/.374 for the second half when a broken finger ended his season in early September. Still, the four-year contract the Reds gave him prior to the season was a good idea—Phillips was one of the team's few defensive stand-outs, and $27 million to cover his remaining prime years was a fine investment.

Danny Richar 2B Bats: L Throws: R Height: 6' 0" Weight: 170 Born: June 9, 1983 Age: 26

YEAR	TEAM	LVL	AGE	PA	R	2B	3B	HR	RBI	BB	SO	SB	CS	EqBRR	AVG	OBP	SLG	EqAVG	EqOBP	EqSLG	EqA	VORP	WARP	DEFENSE				
2006	TEN	AA	23	548	79	25	5	8	42	52	77	15	5	0.9	.292	.360	.415	.261	.321	.389	.251	1.9	0.1	120-2B	-10			
2007	TUC	AAA	24	299	40	20	4	8	46	27	47	4	5	-4.9	.285	.348	.479	.237	.300	.415	.243	-0.7	0.2	50-2B	-2	13-SS	-1
2007	CHR	AAA	24	145	21	5	4	5	15	10	24	4	0	1.0	.346	.400	.556	.313	.361	.530	.301	13.0	0.9	26-2B	-4	6-SS	0
2007	CHA	MLB	24	206	30	9	3	6	15	16	33	1	3	0.9	.230	.289	.406	.226	.289	.414	.235	-2.8	-1.3	55-2B	-13		
2008	CHR	AAA	25	271	35	12	1	9	39	20	45	11	2	-0.1	.262	.321	.427	.228	.284	.388	.235	-6.3	-1.0	47-2B	-7	8-SS	-3
2008	LOU	AAA	25	129	16	9	2	2	16	11	26	3	3	-2.0	.254	.320	.421	.217	.287	.383	.230	-3.1	-0.1	21-2B	-1	5-SS	0
2008	CIN	MLB	25	37	4	2	0	0	3	0	9	1	0	0.3	.222	.222	.278	.216	.216	.270	.166	-2.4	-0.4	6-2B	-1		
2009	CIN	MLB	26	470	56	24	3	11	48	39	87	11	5	1.6	.253	.318	.401	.252	.315	.402	.248	9.2	0.7	111-2B	-6		

Breakout: 28% Improve: 54% Collapse: 16% Attrition: 17% Comparables: German Barranca, Juan Uribe, Carlos Garcia, Antonio Perez

It's a hard life for second-base prospects, particularly on a team that has Brandon Phillips on the roster. Still, Richar, obtained from the White Sox with Nick Masset in the Junior Griffey trade, has pretty good power for a middle in-fielder and bats from the left side, but on-base issues are going to be his bugaboo. If playing shortstop were in his bag of tricks, his future with this club would be more assured. Then again, the Reds were forced to discard the "ability to play shortstop" prerequisite from their "infield help wanted" ads last year and may be forced to do so again.

Adam Rosales INF Bats: R Throws: R Height: 6' 1" Weight: 193 Born: May 20, 1983 Age: 26

YEAR	TEAM	LVL	AGE	PA	R	2B	3B	HR	RBI	BB	SO	SB	CS	EqBRR	AVG	OBP	SLG	EqAVG	EqOBP	EqSLG	EqA	VORP	WARP	DEFENSE				
2006	DYT	A	23	244	36	9	3	6	29	15	40	5	1	2.4	.270	.328	.419	.183	.225	.287	.1/1	-24.8	-2.1	44-SS	-5			
2006	SAR	A+	23	147	15	8	2	2	14	20	27	3	3	-0.5	.213	.329	.361	.165	.260	.291	.192	-12.4	-1.2	21-SS	-4		
2007	SAR	A+	24	300	47	23	5	5	48	31	46	9	2	3.4	.294	.393	.488	.214	.294	.359	.234	-9.0	-0.3	49-1B	3		
2007	CHT	AA	24	302	51	18	6	13	31	37	66	4	4	0.0	.278	.377	.549	.226	.308	.447	.257	3.3	0.0	57-1B	-2		
2008	LOU	AAA	25	473	70	29	7	11	58	22	82	7	1	1.7	.287	.339	.463	.252	.299	.421	.248	1.1	0.9	60-3B	-5	21-SS	3
2008	CIN	MLB	25	30	0	1	0	0	2	1	4	1	0	-0.0	.207	.233	.241	.207	.233	.241	.163	-2.2	-0.3				
2009	CIN	MLB	26	477	51	27	3	12	53	35	107	6	3	1.6	.237	.301	.399	.236	.298	.400	.240	-0.2	0.5	113-3B	-2		

Breakout: 35% Improve: 56% Collapse: 16% Attrition: 13% Comparables: Brian Barden, Marshall McDougall, J.J. Furmaniak, Chris Nyman

Rosales is a victim of the rare and awkward minor league short-to-first position shift, or the Mike Morse Shuffle, as we sometimes call it. Players who go from short to first are usually tall shortstops who are decent with the bat but deemed not to have enough arm for the hot corner or the agility to play second. The problem is that if the guy's bat doesn't have quite enough juice to make the trip all the way across the defensive spectrum intact, he's pigeonholed, a utility guy nobody trusts to play defense anywhere but first base. What Rosales has going for him is a team that was desperate for anyone to play short in 2008 and that may be similarly disposed in 2009.

Neftali Soto　3B

Bats: R　Throws: R　Height: 6' 2"　Weight: 180　Born: February 28, 1989　Age: 20

YEAR	TEAM	LVL	AGE	PA	R	2B	3B	HR	RBI	BB	SO	SB	CS	EqBRR	AVG	OBP	SLG	EqAVG	EqOBP	EqSLG	EqA	VORP	WARP	DEFENSE	
2007	RDS	Rk	18	167	18	7	5	2	28	11	31	2	0	-0.6	.303	.355	.454	.228	.263	.354	.214	-20.5	-1.1	32-SS	-4
2008	BIL	Rk	19	71	12	10	1	4	11	4	10	1	0	0.2	.388	.423	.746	.250	.282	.456	.243	1.0	-0.1	11-3B	-1
2008	DYT	A	19	233	26	15	1	7	36	7	36	1	1	-0.7	.326	.343	.500	.271	.288	.430	.244	1.2	-0.1	29-3B	-1
2009	CIN	MLB	20	554	49	34	2	13	58	29	115	1	2	-0.8	.246	.288	.395	.245	.286	.395	.231	-2.0	-0.1	130-3B	-5

Breakout: 25%　Improve: 54%　Collapse: 19%　Attrition: 10%　　Comparables: Jose Viera, Chris Cassels, Darren Reed, Roberto Zambrano

A third-round pick in 2007 out of Puerto Rico, Soto mashed four home runs in his first six Pioneer League games and was quickly moved to a full-season affiliate at Low-A Dayton, where he continued to impress with his bat. Soto has two tools, a power bat and a cannon for an arm. He's also a big-bodied kid who is already a well-below-average runner. Most think that he's bound for first base or a corner outfield slot at best, with the hope that his bat will be sufficiently juicy that he can meet the higher offensive demands of those positions.

Drew Stubbs　CF

Bats: R　Throws: R　Height: 6' 4"　Weight: 200　Born: October 4, 1984　Age: 24

YEAR	TEAM	LVL	AGE	PA	R	2B	3B	HR	RBI	BB	SO	SB	CS	EqBRR	AVG	OBP	SLG	EqAVG	EqOBP	EqSLG	EqA	VORP	WARP	DEFENSE	
2006	BIL	Rk	21	252	39	7	3	6	24	32	64	19	4	0.9	.252	.368	.400	.175	.243	.266	.179	-43.9	-1.9	52-CF	2
2007	DYT	A	22	575	93	29	5	12	43	69	142	23	15	0.0	.270	.364	.421	.199	.275	.311	.205	-36.0	-2.1	125-CF	-1
2008	SAR	A+	23	358	49	21	4	5	38	50	82	27	8	3.2	.261	.366	.406	.207	.296	.341	.231	-14.1	-0.3	84-CF	-1
2008	CHT	AA	23	106	12	8	0	0	9	11	21	3	1	0.3	.315	.400	.402	.260	.330	.333	.238	-1.5	0.7	24-CF	5
2008	LOU	AAA	23	84	14	4	2	2	10	6	20	3	0	-0.7	.293	.354	.480	.263	.325	.447	.268	2.3	0.5	18-CF	1
2009	CIN	MLB	24	534	60	29	3	11	48	53	160	14	6	1.0	.224	.307	.370	.224	.305	.370	.237	-2.8	1.2	126-CF	0

Breakout: 53%　Improve: 77%　Collapse: 9%　Attrition: 7%　　Comparables: Chad McConnell, Jeff Pyburn, Dante Powell, Mark Bradley

A propensity for strikeouts has been Stubbs' main issue since the Reds selected him with their first pick in the 2006 draft, and while he's made significant progress in that area, it has cost him his plus power. Even if it never returns, he still has enough skill left over to fill the organization's gaping hole in center field. He draws walks and runs extremely well, and some feel he's the best defensive outfielder in the minor leagues. If the power comes back, he's Mike Cameron. If not, his overall value is still above average, given his on-base skills and glove.

Chris Valaika　SS

Bats: R　Throws: R　Height: 6' 1"　Weight: 200　Born: August 14, 1985　Age: 23

YEAR	TEAM	LVL	AGE	PA	R	2B	3B	HR	RBI	BB	SO	SB	CS	EqBRR	AVG	OBP	SLG	EqAVG	EqOBP	EqSLG	EqA	VORP	WARP	DEFENSE	
2006	BIL	Rk	20	315	58	22	4	8	60	24	61	2	2	1.3	.324	.387	.520	.223	.263	.353	.213	-26.4	-0.6	65-SS	-1
2007	DYT	A	21	331	38	20	3	10	56	17	72	1	4	0.0	.307	.353	.493	.233	.269	.382	.222	-10.5	-1.4	71-SS	-12
2007	SAR	A+	21	241	26	9	1	2	23	13	42	0	3	-1.6	.253	.310	.332	.207	.252	.284	.181	-19.9	-1.6	50-SS	-4
2008	SAR	A+	22	145	20	9	0	7	31	7	28	2	0	0.5	.363	.393	.585	.307	.336	.526	.289	11.5	1.7	29-SS	4
2008	CHT	AA	22	417	58	19	1	11	50	28	74	7	4	-0.3	.301	.352	.443	.252	.294	.380	.233	-6.7	0.1	95-SS	-5
2009	CIN	MLB	23	582	60	32	2	18	70	37	138	5	3	-0.3	.252	.303	.418	.251	.301	.419	.246	12.9	1.8	136-SS	0

Breakout: 53%　Improve: 71%　Collapse: 11%　Attrition: 4%　　Comparables: Josh Barfield, Ryan Gripp, Jim Opie, Fran Mullins

Valaika, the Reds' minor leaguer of the year, is the prospect closest to being able to help with the club's shortstop mess. He's not considered a premium defender, and most think that if he makes it to the majors, he'll spend his time on the other side of the keystone. Valaika's offense is dependent on his batting average and his ability to rifle the ball to all fields, although there is a growing sense that the bit of power he's shown in the minors might be for real.

Javier Valentin　C/UT

Bats: S　Throws: R　Height: 5' 10"　Weight: 215　Born: September 19, 1975　Age: 33

YEAR	TEAM	LVL	AGE	PA	R	2B	3B	HR	RBI	BB	SO	SB	CS	EqBRR	AVG	OBP	SLG	EqAVG	EqOBP	EqSLG	EqA	VORP	WARP	DEFENSE			
2006	CIN	MLB	30	201	24	6	1	8	27	13	29	0	0	0.2	.269	.313	.441	.259	.308	.427	.253	4.0	0.6	35-C	2		
2007	CIN	MLB	31	265	19	21	0	2	34	19	25	0	0	-2.9	.276	.328	.387	.269	.325	.380	.247	5.9	-0.4	53-C	-8		
2008	CIN	MLB	32	144	10	8	0	4	18	14	27	0	0	0.1	.256	.326	.411	.256	.326	.419	.258	2.6	0.2	9-1B	0	8-C	0
2009	CIN	MLB	33	114	12	6	0	3	13	11	17	0	0	-0.6	.258	.330	.403	.257	.327	.404	.253	3.3	0.4	31-C	-3		

Breakout: 24%　Improve: 47%　Collapse: 38%　Attrition: 37%　　Comparables: Matt Batts, Carl Sawatski, Ed Fitz Gerald, Sean Berry

It was a hard year to be a Reds catcher—the fight for playing time had a mosh-pit quality. Valentin wound up playing some first base and even standing at third for a few innings to keep occupied, but he didn't get a start behind the plate after July 23, and he barely saw the tools of ignorance thereafter. His bat still plays against right-handers (.271/.342/.430), so there should still be a role for him somewhere.

Joey Votto — 1B

Bats: L Throws: R Height: 6′ 3″ Weight: 220 Born: September 10, 1983 Age: 25

YEAR	TEAM	LVL	AGE	PA	R	2B	3B	HR	RBI	BB	SO	SB	CS	EqBRR	AVG	OBP	SLG	EqAVG	EqOBP	EqSLG	EqA	VORP	WARP	DEFENSE	
2006	CHT	AA	22	590	85	46	2	22	77	78	109	24	7	-6.9	.319	.408	.547	.293	.375	.533	.304	56.4	3.7	134-1B	-5
2007	LOU	AAA	23	580	74	21	2	22	92	70	110	17	10	-5.3	.294	.381	.478	.270	.352	.455	.277	25.9	1.7	90-1B	1 34-LF -5
2007	CIN	MLB	23	89	11	7	0	4	17	5	15	1	0	-2.7	.321	.360	.548	.310	.348	.548	.298	6.7	0.3	15-1B	0 6-LF -2
2008	CIN	MLB	24	589	69	32	3	24	84	59	102	7	5	-6.6	.297	.368	.506	.293	.367	.514	.294	35.3	3.7	137-1B	4
2009	CIN	MLB	25	574	88	31	2	26	86	63	108	11	3	-1.5	.289	.370	.514	.288	.368	.515	.297	32.4	3.9	135-1B	4

Breakout: 28% Improve: 51% Collapse: 19% Attrition: 10%   Comparables: Mel Hall, Wally Joyner, Mike Epstein, Greg Walker

A strong kick down the finish line—he batted .343/.429/.664 from August 16 through the end of the year, with 10 homers—wasn't quite enough for Votto to overtake the Cubs' Geovany Soto in the NL Rookie of the Year race. Votto has had a long development path—he was drafted in 2002—but the result of all that time in the forge is a player who's ridiculously solid, a good defender, a lefty who isn't run out of the lineup by lefties, and a player just coming into his prime. The only downside is his baserunning: Votto wound up in the bottom five in the majors in EqBRR (equivalent base-running runs), roughly on a par with Bengie Molina and the bad-hipped version of Mike Lowell, and you know how Dusty hates those base-cloggers.

PITCHERS

Jeremy Affeldt

Bats: L Throws: L Height: 6′ 4″ Weight: 225 Born: June 6, 1979 Age: 30

YEAR	TEAM	LVL	AGE	W	L	SV	G	GS	IP	H	BB	SO	HR	GB%	BABIP	STUFF	WHIP	ERA	DERA	EqH9	EqBB9	EqSO9	EqHR9	DEF	VORP	SN/WX
2006	KCA	MLB	27	4	6	0	27	9	70	71	42	28	9	49.8%	.265	-26	1.61	5.91	7.16	8.0	5.0	3.0	1.0	8	-3.1	0.15
2006	COL	MLB	27	4	2	1	27	0	27¹	31	13	20	4	54.3%	.307	-11	1.61	6.92	4.97	9.0	3.4	5.6	0.9	-4	-3.7	0.23
2007	COL	MLB	28	4	3	0	75	0	59	47	33	46	3	53.2%	.277	6	1.36	3.51	3.68	7.1	4.4	6.6	0.5	2	13.4	-0.73
2008	CIN	MLB	29	1	1	0	74	0	78¹	78	25	80	9	57.3%	.327	12	1.31	3.33	3.29	8.3	2.4	7.9	0.9	-4	13.8	0.19
2009	SFN	MLB	30	3	3	3	62	0	62¹	61	27	54	5	51.1%	.306	8	1.41	4.03	4.32	8.8	3.5	6.8	0.8	0	9.8	0.80

Breakout: 28% Improve: 59% Collapse: 18% Attrition: 18%   Comparables: Greg Cadaret, Gary Lucas, Andy Hassler, Steve Kline

Hard-throwing Jeremy Affeldt was the most distrusted reliever in the National League last year, given the lowest-leverage opportunities of anyone who'd thrown 50 innings or more out of the pen. Despite overall decent results and peripheral statistics, in more than half of Affeldt's appearances, he entered the game with the Reds leading or trailing by four or more runs. Despite Dusty Baker's year-long no-confidence vote—considering the parties involved, perhaps *because* of it—the Giants gave Affeldt a two-year contract.

Bronson Arroyo

Bats: R Throws: R Height: 6′ 5″ Weight: 195 Born: February 24, 1977 Age: 32

YEAR	TEAM	LVL	AGE	W	L	SV	G	GS	IP	H	BB	SO	HR	GB%	BABIP	STUFF	WHIP	ERA	DERA	EqH9	EqBB9	EqSO9	EqHR9	DEF	VORP	SN/WX
2006	CIN	MLB	29	14	11	0	35	35	240²	222	64	184	31	39.9%	.274	16	1.19	3.29	4.02	7.7	2.1	6.2	1.0	20	64.6	7.27
2007	CIN	MLB	30	9	15	0	34	34	210²	232	63	156	28	37.6%	.317	13	1.40	4.23	3.64	8.8	2.3	6.1	1.0	-8	30.5	4.32
2008	CIN	MLB	31	15	11	0	34	34	200	219	68	163	29	44.4%	.324	8	1.44	4.77	4.38	9.1	2.6	6.4	1.2	-7	12.4	3.51
2009	CIN	MLB	32	10	11	0	29	29	177	193	55	133	25	43.0%	.310	20	1.40	4.65	4.57	9.7	2.5	5.8	1.2	-3	17.6	3.40

Breakout: 6% Improve: 18% Collapse: 37% Attrition: 13%   Comparables: Danny Darwin, Darryl Kile, Bob Rush, Dave Mlicki

For a while last season, it looked as though Arroyo had lost it completely. The lanky junkballer hit rock bottom on June 24, when he had the worst start of his career in Toronto: 10 runs and three homers allowed, all without registering an out in the second inning. After that low point, Arroyo went 11-4 with a 3.42 ERA, finishing with overall peripheral numbers close to what he's had the last four or five seasons. The Reds hope for more league-average innings-eating in 2009.

Homer Bailey

Bats: R Throws: R Height: 6' 4" Weight: 205 Born: May 3, 1986 Age: 23

YEAR	TEAM	LVL	AGE	W	L	SV	G	GS	IP	H	BB	SO	HR	GB%	BABIP	STUFF	WHIP	ERA	DERA	EqH9	EqBB9	EqSO9	EqHR9	DEF	VORP	SN/WX
2006	SAR	A+	20	3	5	0	13	13	70²	49	22	79	6	44.8%	.247	14	1.01	3.33	7.44	8.8	3.9	5.5	1.8	3	-13.4	—
2006	CHT	AA	20	7	1	0	13	13	68¹	50	28	77	1	52.4%	.298	49	1.15	1.59	3.02	8.5	4.2	6.6	0.4	1	18.0	—
2007	LOU	AAA	21	6	3	0	12	12	67¹	49	32	59	4	46.5%	.254	21	1.20	3.08	6.75	7.5	4.6	5.3	0.8	11	-8.2	—
2007	CIN	MLB	21	4	2	0	9	9	45¹	43	28	28	3	47.3%	.294	23	1.57	5.76	5.44	7.6	4.7	5.1	0.6	0	-1.5	0.65
2008	LOU	AAA	22	4	7	0	19	19	111¹	118	46	96	10	46.6%	.337	0	1.47	4.77	5.72	11.4	4.3	5.4	1.3	-2	-1.3	—
2008	CIN	MLB	22	0	6	0	8	8	36¹	59	17	18	8	46.2%	.392	-18	2.09	7.93	7.05	13.4	3.4	3.9	1.7	-5	-12.1	-0.61
2009	CIN	MLB	23	6	9	0	35	22	121²	139	59	92	17	45.0%	.320	10	1.62	5.73	5.69	10.2	3.8	5.8	1.2	-2	-2.1	0.60

Breakout: 30% Improve: 68% Collapse: 16% Attrition: 11%   Comparables: Mark Grant, Andy Hawkins, Mike Harkey, Mike Moore

Some hurlers pitch to the batter, others pitch to the score, and then there are those, like Homer Bailey, who pitch to the radar gun. His constant attempts to make each pitch harder than the last have eroded his stamina and made coaching the young phenom an exercise in frustration. It's indicative of Bailey's approach that when he had two strikes on a batter—a situation in which National Leaguers as a group batted .185/.256/.284—batters were teeing off to the tune of .391/.421/.638. Still, if the Reds grow tired of Bailey's act, there seem to be plenty of teams willing to see if they can do a better job with the youngster.

Bill Bray

Bats: L Throws: L Height: 6' 3" Weight: 220 Born: June 5, 1983 Age: 26

YEAR	TEAM	LVL	AGE	W	L	SV	G	GS	IP	H	BB	SO	HR	GB%	BABIP	STUFF	WHIP	ERA	DERA	EqH9	EqBB9	EqSO9	EqHR9	DEF	VORP	SN/WX
2006	NWO	AAA	23	4	1	5	21	0	31²	26	9	45	5	41.3%	.300	12	1.12	4.04	4.20	9.3	2.7	9.3	2.1	-3	4.7	—
2006	WAS	MLB	23	1	1	0	19	0	23	24	9	16	2	50.0%	.314	-1	1.43	3.91	3.57	9.1	3.2	6.0	0.8	-2	4.1	0.42
2006	CIN	MLB	23	2	1	2	29	0	27²	33	9	23	3	40.7%	.345	4	1.52	4.22	3.86	10.0	2.6	6.8	1.0	-2	2.9	0.76
2007	LOU	AAA	24	1	2	0	18	0	19	19	6	29	1	49.0%	.383	13	1.32	4.26	4.91	10.8	2.9	9.8	1.0	-2	1.4	—
2007	CIN	MLB	24	3	3	1	19	0	14¹	16	5	14	1	43.2%	.357	9	1.47	6.29	4.30	9.2	2.5	8.0	0.6	-2	-0.4	0.01
2008	CIN	MLB	25	2	2	0	63	0	47	50	24	54	4	39.0%	.359	16	1.57	2.87	1.85	8.9	3.7	8.7	0.7	-8	10.6	0.36
2009	CIN	MLB	26	2	2	3	49	0	43²	39	19	46	4	42.0%	.300	18	1.33	3.64	3.60	8.0	3.5	8.1	0.9	-1	11.0	0.80

Breakout: 27% Improve: 50% Collapse: 24% Attrition: 19%   Comparables: Jerry Garvin, Willie Hernandez, Jim York, Bill Simas

Finally experiencing a somewhat injury-free season, Bray proved ill suited for the lefty specialist role in the Reds' bullpen. Despite dominating portsiders in the minors, control issues make him a less-than-ideal LOOGY in "The Show"—in that role, a .360 OBP against fellow lefties is unacceptable. Arthur Rhodes' acquisition should free Baker to use Bray in a less matchup-oriented role, where he can cut loose and use his high-velocity mix to good effect.

Jared Burton

Bats: R Throws: R Height: 6' 5" Weight: 230 Born: June 2, 1981 Age: 28

YEAR	TEAM	LVL	AGE	W	L	SV	G	GS	IP	H	BB	SO	HR	GB%	BABIP	STUFF	WHIP	ERA	DERA	EqH9	EqBB9	EqSO9	EqHR9	DEF	VORP	SN/WX
2006	MID	AA	25	6	5	1	53	0	74²	71	27	66	7	45.5%	.306	-24	1.32	4.12	6.16	10.1	3.8	5.1	1.3	4	-4.3	—
2007	LOU	AAA	26	1	0	1	10	0	14	11	4	13	0	61.1%	.306	2	1.07	0.64	2.92	8.8	2.9	5.8	0.0	2	3.7	—
2007	CIN	MLB	26	4	2	0	47	0	43	28	22	36	2	45.7%	.232	9	1.16	2.51	3.74	5.2	3.9	7.1	0.4	5	13.3	1.27
2008	CIN	MLB	27	5	1	0	54	0	58²	56	25	58	6	50.6%	.311	10	1.38	3.22	2.97	7.7	3.1	7.6	0.9	-3	13.2	0.59
2009	CIN	MLB	28	2	2	2	44	0	50¹	52	22	41	5	46.0%	.310	6	1.46	4.34	4.32	9.1	3.5	6.3	0.9	-1	7.1	0.60

Breakout: 4% Improve: 19% Collapse: 60% Attrition: 22%   Comparables: Tom Davey, Barry Jones, Kevin Gregg, Paul Shuey

A Mariano Rivera pitch-alike, Burton encountered adversity this season in the form of a strained lat muscle—described by some in the media as an injury to his side, but more accurately referred to as his shoulder. The injury cost him nearly two months on the DL, and when he came back in September, he was ineffective (2.23 ERA prior to the injury, 7.84 after). There isn't much data on latissimus injuries for pitchers, but given an off-season's rest, the muscle should be completely healed for this season.

Francisco Cordero

Bats: R | Throws: R | Height: 6' 2" | Weight: 235 | Born: May 11, 1975 | Age: 34

YEAR	TEAM	LVL	AGE	W	L	SV	G	GS	IP	H	BB	SO	HR	GB%	BABIP	STUFF	WHIP	ERA	DERA	EqH9	EqBB9	EqSO9	EqHR9	DEF	VORP	SN/WX
2006	TEX	MLB	31	7	4	6	49	0	48²	48	16	54	5	43.8%	.341	15	1.32	4.80	4.25	8.5	2.8	8.9	0.9	-2	6.5	-0.94
2006	MIL	MLB	31	3	1	16	28	0	26²	20	16	30	2	36.4%	.290	22	1.35	1.69	1.73	6.9	4.8	9.3	0.7	0	12.9	1.69
2007	MIL	MLB	32	0	4	44	66	0	63¹	52	18	86	4	42.3%	.322	36	1.11	2.99	2.24	7.1	2.2	10.1	0.6	-5	18.5	3.22
2008	CIN	MLB	33	5	4	34	72	0	70¹	61	38	78	6	42.6%	.313	15	1.41	3.33	3.41	7.3	4.0	8.6	0.8	1	16.6	3.18
2009	CIN	MLB	34	3	4	17	49	0	55²	52	25	58	6	42.0%	.300	14	1.38	4.03	3.98	8.3	3.6	8.0	1.0	-1	9.9	1.20

Breakout: 4% Improve: 28% Collapse: 45% Attrition: 10%   Comparables: Jim Gott, Jay Howell, Jeff Russell, Hoyt Wilhelm

While most of Cordero's peripherals have been pretty steady over the years, his walk rate has fluctuated, sometimes violently. The surprising thing is that these fluctuations have seldom signaled a substantial change in his performance level—few players have picked up more than two walks per nine innings from one season to the next with less tangible effect. Cordero is a functional closer, whose save conversion rate tends to be on the low side of acceptable. Over the full course of his four-year contract (plus a 2012 club option), he may not fully reward Wayne Krivsky's decision to outbid the Brewers for his services prior to last season, but Walt Jocketty can shrug it off as something that wasn't his call.

Johnny Cueto

Bats: R | Throws: R | Height: 5' 10" | Weight: 198 | Born: February 15, 1986 | Age: 23

YEAR	TEAM	LVL	AGE	W	L	SV	G	GS	IP	H	BB	SO	HR	GB%	BABIP	STUFF	WHIP	ERA	DERA	EqH9	EqBB9	EqSO9	EqHR9	DEF	VORP	SN/WX
2006	DYT	A	20	8	1	0	14	14	76¹	52	15	82	5	53.4%	.254	8	0.88	2.60	5.68	10.0	3.2	5.0	2.1	4	-0.6	—
2006	SAR	A+	20	7	2	0	12	12	61	48	23	61	6	37.0%	.268	4	1.16	3.54	7.00	10.2	4.7	5.0	2.2	7	-8.4	—
2007	SAR	A+	21	4	5	0	14	14	78¹	72	21	72	3	47.4%	.304	17	1.19	3.33	5.77	10.1	3.3	4.7	1.0	-1	-1.4	—
2007	CHT	AA	21	6	3	0	10	10	61	52	11	77	6	37.2%	.324	26	1.03	3.10	5.31	9.5	1.9	7.2	1.6	4	1.9	—
2007	LOU	AAA	21	2	1	0	4	4	22	22	2	21	2	34.4%	.323	20	1.09	2.05	2.66	10.6	1.3	6.2	1.3	-1	6.6	—
2008	CIN	MLB	22	9	14	0	31	31	174	178	68	158	29	40.4%	.307	19	1.41	4.81	4.46	8.4	2.9	7.0	1.4	-6	11.4	2.62
2009	CIN	MLB	23	8	8	0	23	23	136	140	50	122	19	41.0%	.310	27	1.40	4.64	4.54	9.1	2.9	6.9	1.2	-2	14.8	2.60

Breakout: 17% Improve: 44% Collapse: 22% Attrition: 18%   Comparables: Rich Dotson, Jake Peavy, Dan Spillner, Ervin Santana

The physical comparison that Cueto draws is to a young Tom Gordon—Cueto is an undersized guy with longish arms and a big fastball and sharp breaking ball. He's more aggressive about pitching inside than Flash ever was: with Edinson Volquez and Kyle Kendrick, Cueto shared the NL lead in hit batsmen (14). He also hopes to diverge from young Flash's injury history—the end of Cueto's season was marred by elbow soreness, which bears watching going forward. But if he is healthy, he and Volquez could be the best Dominican one-two punch since Pedro Martinez and Carlos Perez teamed up with the Expos. To get there, he'll have to overcome the disadvantage of being a fly-ball pitcher at the Gap—a goodly number of flies allowed by Cueto went over the fences, and he tied with teammate Aaron Harang for the last top 10 spot in the National League in home runs allowed per fly ball.

Aaron Harang

Bats: R | Throws: R | Height: 6' 7" | Weight: 275 | Born: May 9, 1978 | Age: 31

YEAR	TEAM	LVL	AGE	W	L	SV	G	GS	IP	H	BB	SO	HR	GB%	BABIP	STUFF	WHIP	ERA	DERA	EqH9	EqBB9	EqSO9	EqHR9	DEF	VORP	SN/WX
2006	CIN	MLB	28	16	11	0	36	35	234¹	242	56	216	28	42.8%	.326	27	1.27	3.76	3.16	8.8	1.9	7.5	0.9	-13	49.8	5.98
2007	CIN	MLB	29	16	6	0	34	34	231²	213	52	218	28	43.0%	.292	29	1.14	3.73	3.30	7.5	1.7	7.8	1.0	-3	53.6	6.11
2008	CIN	MLB	30	6	17	0	30	29	184¹	205	50	153	35	36.2%	.318	1	1.38	4.79	4.49	9.2	2.0	6.5	1.6	-2	14.8	3.42
2009	CIN	MLB	31	11	10	0	29	29	183	188	44	152	25	41.0%	.300	26	1.27	4.22	4.15	9.1	1.9	6.4	1.2	-3	27.2	4.40

Breakout: 3% Improve: 33% Collapse: 26% Attrition: 13%   Comparables: Don Newcombe, Andy Benes, Freddy Garcia, Mark Clark

Whenever a guy gets labeled as having a rubber arm, the designation is temporary—eventually, even rubber dries up and snaps. In the case of the Reds' workhorse, some regard the four-inning relief appearance Harang made on May 25—working on two days' rest—as the breaking point. Before the relief appearance, Harang was having a fairly normal year, with a 3.50 ERA. In the eight starts that followed, his ERA was more than double that; afterward, the big righty spent a month on the disabled list with "forearm stiffness." Although Harang was effective in September and seemed to be pitching at full velocity in his last two starts, forearm stiffness often graduates to elbow pain. Buyer beware.

Daniel Ray Herrera

Bats: L   Throws: L   Height: 5' 8"   Weight: 145   Born: October 21, 1984   Age: 24

YEAR	TEAM	LVL	AGE	W	L	SV	G	GS	IP	H	BB	SO	HR	GB%	BABIP	STUFF	WHIP	ERA	DERA	EqH9	EqBB9	EqSO9	EqHR9	DEF	VORP	SN/WX
2006	BAK	A+	21	4	2	1	14	5	53¹	39	12	61	0	70.7%	.293	33	0.96	1.36	3.81	8.0	2.7	5.6	0.4	-3	9.9	—
2007	BAK	A+	22	2	0	1	7	1	11	14	5	11	1	58.3%	.371	-15	1.73	3.27	2.70	14.4	5.4	4.5	1.8	-3	3.2	—
2007	FRI	AA	22	5	2	0	34	0	52¹	43	20	64	3	49.6%	.342	7	1.20	3.79	5.76	10.5	4.4	7.9	1.0	0	-0.8	—
2008	CHT	AA	23	3	0	0	10	0	17²	12	7	10	0	58.8%	.255	-18	1.07	2.54	4.41	6.6	3.9	2.8	0.6	1	2.2	—
2008	LOU	AAA	23	4	4	6	47	0	55	47	10	50	4	53.4%	.279	-3	1.04	2.78	5.09	8.7	1.9	5.4	1.0	7	3.0	—
2008	CIN	MLB	23	0	0	0	7	0	7¹	10	3	8	1	66.7%	.429	6	1.77	7.40	5.87	11.7	3.5	8.2	1.2	-2	-2.3	0.06
2009	CIN	MLB	24	3	3	1	30	3	52²	55	20	40	5	51.0%	.310	8	1.43	4.42	4.43	9.4	3.0	5.8	0.9	-1	6.7	0.70

Breakout: 46%   Improve: 76%   Collapse: 6%   Attrition: 18%   Comparables: Steve Frey, Tim Davis, Jeff Innis, Carmen Pignatiello

A mighty mite with a mid-80s fastball, Daniel Herrera was part of the booty brought in by the Josh Hamilton trade with the Rangers. Despite being the sort of fellow who makes AL MVP Dustin Pedroia look big, Herrera cut a swath through the minors with that two-seam fastball, a screwball that comes at the batter in the 60 mph range, and a whole lotta moxie. Since the bullpen's primary lefties are both injury prone, Herrera stands a good chance at some time in "The Show."

Sam LeCure

Bats: R   Throws: R   Height: 6' 1"   Weight: 190   Born: May 4, 1984   Age: 25

YEAR	TEAM	LVL	AGE	W	L	SV	G	GS	IP	H	BB	SO	HR	GB%	BABIP	STUFF	WHIP	ERA	DERA	EqH9	EqBB9	EqSO9	EqHR9	DEF	VORP	SN/WX
2006	SAR	A+	22	7	12	0	27	27	141¹	130	46	115	12	40.9%	.290	-28	1.25	3.44	6.39	11.5	4.1	3.8	1.9	0	-10.9	—
2007	CHT	AA	23	7	5	0	21	21	110	119	46	104	12	45.4%	.347	-22	1.50	4.17	5.22	12.0	4.2	5.2	1.8	-7	4.2	—
2008	CHT	AA	24	9	7	0	27	27	155¹	147	58	128	12	41.0%	.303	-11	1.32	3.42	5.05	9.7	3.6	4.6	1.3	4	8.9	—
2009	CIN	MLB	25	4	8	0	24	17	99¹	116	45	70	18	41.0%	.310	7	1.62	5.99	5.87	10.4	3.6	5.4	1.6	-2	-3.6	0.30

Breakout: 6%   Improve: 21%   Collapse: 27%   Attrition: 12%   Comparables: Brian Boehringer, Turk Wendell, Brian Sikorski, Jeff Brantley

LeCure repeated at Chattanooga, with results not much different from the first time around, and his peripherals were right around his minor league career rates. Nevertheless, he was added to the 40-man roster in November and remains a pitchability prospect, with average stuff across the board but a good sense of how to approach the batter. Like Matt Maloney, he's also an extreme fly-ball pitcher in an organization whose end stop is a bandbox, and that just doesn't bode well.

Mike Lincoln

Bats: R   Throws: R   Height: 6' 2"   Weight: 215   Born: April 10, 1975   Age: 34

YEAR	TEAM	LVL	AGE	W	L	SV	G	GS	IP	H	BB	SO	HR	GB%	BABIP	STUFF	WHIP	ERA	DERA	EqH9	EqBB9	EqSO9	EqHR9	DEF	VORP	SN/WX
2008	CIN	MLB	33	2	5	0	64	0	70¹	66	24	57	10	51.9%	.284	-4	1.28	4.48	4.82	7.7	2.5	6.3	1.1	4	7.6	1.94
2009	CIN	MLB	34	2	2	2	42	0	49¹	53	18	38	6	48.0%	.310	2	1.44	4.73	4.72	9.5	3.0	5.9	1.1	-1	4.3	0.30

Breakout: 13%   Improve: 40%   Collapse: 35%   Attrition: 29%   Comparables: Tom Ferrick, Rick White, Giovanni Carrara, Mike DeJean

It pays to persevere, part two. We had previously described Lincoln as filler, and this was before the injury woes that drove him out of the game four years ago. Already 29 when the injury bug hit and pretty much a fungible middle reliever with a decent curveball at that time, he's not the guy we would have picked to gut his way through two Tommy John surgeries and years of rehab to make it back to the majors. The Reds' reward for giving Lincoln a chance was that he became arguably the best pitcher in their bullpen; Lincoln's reward was a two-year, $4 million contract with the Reds. Good work for a player most had written off.

Kyle Lotzkar

Bats: L   Throws: R   Height: 6' 4"   Weight: 200   Born: October 24, 1989   Age: 19

YEAR	TEAM	LVL	AGE	W	L	SV	G	GS	IP	H	BB	SO	HR	GB%	BABIP	STUFF	WHIP	ERA	DERA	EqH9	EqBB9	EqSO9	EqHR9	DEF	VORP	SN/WX
2007	RDS	Rk	17	0	2	0	7	7	21	21	7	24	2	41.4%	.352	-12	1.33	3.86	8.47	15.4	5.3	4.8	3.7	0	-5.4	—
2007	BIL	Rk	17	0	0	0	2	2	8	1	3	12	1	42.9%	.000	8	0.50	1.13	2.25	1.1	4.5	5.6	2.2	0	3.0	—
2008	DYT	A	18	2	3	0	10	10	37²	29	24	50	2	33.7%	.325	14	1.41	3.58	7.79	10.9	8.1	6.4	1.4	1	-7.9	—
2009	CIN	MLB	19	3	9	0	21	21	95¹	118	85	80	21	40.0%	.340	2	2.13	8.36	8.21	11.0	7.1	6.5	1.9	-2	-26.2	-2.20

Breakout: 4%   Improve: 32%   Collapse: 34%   Attrition: 10%   Comparables: Brandon Erbe, Luis Rivera, Clint Zavaras, Pat Mahomes

A big, raw Canadian, Lotzkar has the best arm in the Reds' system, with a fastball that sits in the low 90s and touches 94 mph consistently and that projects to get even better. His delivery is violent and probably played a part in the elbow fracture that shortened his season in 2008, but the Reds have worked hard on smoothing him out without costing his power arsenal. He's a project, to be sure, but no pitcher in the system matches his ceiling.

Gary Majewski

Bats: R　Throws: R　Height: 6' 1"　Weight: 220　Born: February 26, 1980　Age: 29

YEAR	TEAM	LVL	AGE	W	L	SV	G	GS	IP	H	BB	SO	HR	GB%	BABIP	STUFF	WHIP	ERA	DERA	EqH9	EqBB9	EqSO9	EqHR9	DEF	VORP	SN/WX
2006	WAS	MLB	26	3	2	0	46	0	55¹	49	25	34	4	55.9%	.262	-5	1.34	3.58	4.04	7.6	3.6	5.0	0.6	2	12.6	0.06
2006	CIN	MLB	26	1	2	0	19	0	15	30	4	9	1	55.6%	.492	-10	2.27	8.40	1.23	17.8	1.8	4.9	0.6	-9	-3.7	-1.69
2007	LOU	AAA	27	1	1	4	38	0	38²	33	15	30	2	55.5%	.292	-19	1.24	3.95	5.97	9.3	3.9	4.9	0.8	3	-1.4	—
2007	CIN	MLB	27	0	4	0	32	0	23	43	3	10	3	54.1%	.421	-21	2.00	8.22	5.09	15.7	1.2	3.9	1.2	-5	-6.4	-1.40
2008	LOU	AAA	28	2	1	3	22	0	26¹	27	7	22	2	55.1%	.329	-13	1.29	3.76	4.63	11.2	2.7	5.4	1.2	0	2.5	—
2008	CIN	MLB	28	1	0	0	37	0	40	61	15	27	6	51.0%	.407	-15	1.90	6.53	4.08	12.9	2.9	5.4	1.4	-10	-5.3	-0.04
2009	CIN	MLB	29	2	2	2	38	0	40²	45	15	28	4	50.0%	.310	2	1.48	4.41	4.38	9.9	3.0	5.4	0.9	-1	5.4	0.40

Breakout: 28%　Improve: 56%　Collapse: 25%　Attrition: 39%　Comparables: Jon Adkins, Joe Niekro, Steve Comer, Tom Morgan

Majewski hit arbitration eligibility after the season, and the Reds wisely said "no thanks." Even after shoulder problems, Majewski could still throw pretty hard, but his offerings had no life to them and he was pretty badly mauled by major league hitters. Undeterred by Maj's 7.38 ERA and 134 hits in 78 innings spread over parts of three seasons with the Reds, the Phillies signed him to a minor league deal with a spring training invite. He was a serviceable pitch-to-contact reliever with a 3.27 ERA in 162⅓ innings prior to 2006 shoulder problems; here's hoping this is the year he gets it back. Given that pitchers of his type are not usually long-lived, the odds are against it.

Matt Maloney

Bats: L　Throws: L　Height: 6' 4"　Weight: 220　Born: January 16, 1984　Age: 25

YEAR	TEAM	LVL	AGE	W	L	SV	G	GS	IP	H	BB	SO	HR	GB%	BABIP	STUFF	WHIP	ERA	DERA	EqH9	EqBB9	EqSO9	EqHR9	DEF	VORP	SN/WX
2006	LWD	A	22	16	9	0	27	27	168¹	120	73	180	5	46.2%	.267	1	1.15	2.03	6.24	10.0	5.6	4.6	1.1	6	-10.6	—
2007	REA	AA	23	9	7	0	21	21	125²	117	45	115	13	43.5%	.300	-15	1.29	3.94	6.56	10.4	3.7	5.2	1.6	0	-12.6	—
2007	CHT	AA	23	2	2	0	4	4	28	17	3	39	4	39.3%	.241	25	0.71	2.57	5.47	6.8	1.4	8.2	2.1	5	0.4	—
2007	LOU	AAA	23	2	1	0	3	3	17	10	6	23	2	45.9%	.235	16	0.94	3.18	5.62	6.8	3.4	9.0	1.7	2	-0.0	—
2008	LOU	AAA	24	11	5	0	25	25	140¹	143	39	132	18	40.8%	.310	-15	1.30	4.68	6.66	10.7	2.8	5.6	1.6	13	-15.6	—
2009	CIN	MLB	25	6	9	0	33	19	122²	136	51	96	20	41.0%	.310	12	1.52	5.52	5.44	9.8	3.3	6.1	1.4	-2	1.4	0.90

Breakout: 23%　Improve: 57%　Collapse: 14%　Attrition: 21%　Comparables: Matt Beech, Chris Haney, Chris Capuano, Micah Bowie

Maloney's peripheral numbers continue to impress, even if his stuff doesn't. When people think about finesse pitchers, it's typically ground-ball guys who come to mind—think Tommy John. But Maloney isn't that kind of pitcher; he throws strikes, but primarily in the upper half of the zone, so batters hit balls off him into the air. That gives rise to worries about what will happen when it's major leaguers popping flies off him and Great American Ballpark trying to hold those flies in.

Nick Masset

Bats: R　Throws: R　Height: 6' 4"　Weight: 235　Born: May 17, 1982　Age: 27

YEAR	TEAM	LVL	AGE	W	L	SV	G	GS	IP	H	BB	SO	HR	GB%	BABIP	STUFF	WHIP	ERA	DERA	EqH9	EqBB9	EqSO9	EqHR9	DEF	VORP	SN/WX
2006	FRI	AA	24	2	2	0	8	8	48²	38	20	40	0	64.5%	.275	4	1.20	2.05	5.17	7.7	4.0	4.4	0.4	6	2.2	—
2006	OKL	AAA	24	4	5	3	24	7	67	79	28	65	4	53.9%	.377	-10	1.60	4.84	7.25	12.1	4.0	6.1	0.9	-4	-11.6	—
2006	TEX	MLB	24	0	0	0	8	0	8²	9	2	4	0	53.6%	.346	-8	1.27	4.14	2.25	10.1	2.2	3.4	0.0	-2	1.9	0.06
2007	CHR	AAA	25	0	4	0	11	9	45¹	51	9	33	6	48.0%	.321	-21	1.32	4.57	6.75	12.2	2.2	4.4	2.0	1	-5.3	—
2007	CHA	MLB	25	2	3	0	27	1	39¹	52	26	21	2	43.1%	.362	-15	1.98	7.10	4.85	11.5	5.5	4.2	0.5	-9	-5.0	0.11
2008	CHA	MLB	26	1	0	1	32	1	44²	55	21	32	4	58.1%	.364	-7	1.70	4.63	3.16	11.4	4.0	5.9	0.8	-8	3.0	0.97
2008	CIN	MLB	26	1	0	0	10	0	17¹	16	5	11	3	49.1%	.265	-5	1.21	2.08	3.31	8.3	2.2	5.5	1.7	1	5.1	-0.42
2009	CIN	MLB	27	2	3	1	33	2	51¹	56	21	37	6	50.0%	.310	4	1.50	4.53	4.51	9.7	3.2	5.6	1.0	-1	6.2	0.60

Breakout: 36%　Improve: 57%　Collapse: 23%　Attrition: 34%　Comparables: Mike Fetters, Peter Munro, Todd Coffey, Matt Belisle

Part of the package the Reds received for Griffey, Masset is a reminder that a strong fastball doesn't always lead to big strikeout numbers or a power pitcher's profile. But thanks to wildly varying defensive play behind him, he neither pitched as badly as he appeared to with the White Sox nor as well as he seemed to with the Reds. As with so many things, the truth lies somewhere in the middle. Now that Matt Belisle has been nontendered, Masset could fit into the swingman/emergency starter role.

Micah Owings

Bats: R Throws: R Height: 6' 5" Weight: 220 Born: September 28, 1982 Age: 26

YEAR	TEAM	LVL	AGE	W	L	SV	G	GS	IP	H	BB	SO	HR	GB%	BABIP	STUFF	WHIP	ERA	DERA	EqH9	EqBB9	EqSO9	EqHR9	DEF	VORP	SN/WX
2006	TEN	AA	23	6	2	0	12	12	74	66	17	69	4	46.8%	.318	10	1.12	2.92	4.05	10.0	2.4	5.4	1.1	-1	11.5	—
2006	TUC	AAA	23	10	0	0	15	15	87²	96	34	61	4	39.1%	.332	1	1.49	3.72	4.89	11.0	3.8	4.2	0.7	2	6.4	—
2007	ARI	MLB	24	8	8	0	29	27	152²	146	50	106	20	38.7%	.279	7	1.28	4.30	4.61	8.2	2.5	5.8	1.1	10	21.1	2.94
2008	ARI	MLB	25	6	9	0	22	18	104²	104	41	87	14	35.0%	.294	5	1.39	5.93	5.74	8.5	3.0	6.4	1.1	3	-5.3	0.76
2009	CIN	MLB	26	5	7	1	30	15	103²	109	41	82	15	39.0%	.300	12	1.45	5.07	4.98	9.4	3.1	6.1	1.3	-2	6.2	1.30

Breakout: 13% Improve: 39% Collapse: 35% Attrition: 28% Comparables: Don Larsen, Dick Hall, James Baldwin, Ron Schueler

Owings sometimes gets frustrated that when his name comes up, his hitting is often the first item of discussion. Sadly, his mound exploits last season supplied few other positive things to discuss: at the end of May, he lost his effectiveness, which led to a demotion and a diagnosis of shoulder soreness. After he was dealt to the Reds in the Dunn trade, he couldn't pitch, but the team kept him on the roster … to pinch-hit. If he's healthy in spring training, Owings will have the inside track on the fifth starter's job. If he's not healthy, he might miss the days when what people talked about was his hitting.

Ramon Ramirez

Bats: R Throws: R Height: 5' 10" Weight: 172 Born: September 16, 1982 Age: 26

YEAR	TEAM	LVL	AGE	W	L	SV	G	GS	IP	H	BB	SO	HR	GB%	BABIP	STUFF	WHIP	ERA	DERA	EqH9	EqBB9	EqSO9	EqHR9	DEF	VORP	SN/WX
2006	SAR	A+	23	4	5	0	15	11	65	66	21	53	11	41.6%	.291	-54	1.34	4.29	7.71	13.3	4.2	3.9	3.5	3	-13.1	—
2007	SAR	A+	24	5	2	1	15	12	73¹	64	25	86	5	47.1%	.319	-6	1.21	4.05	5.95	10.7	4.3	6.6	1.5	-5	-2.5	—
2007	CHT	AA	24	5	1	1	16	0	31¹	30	12	35	3	38.8%	.338	-14	1.34	4.60	6.28	10.7	3.8	6.3	1.6	2	-2.2	—
2007	LOU	AAA	24	1	0	0	5	2	14²	7	6	16	0	53.1%	.226	13	0.88	0.00	2.70	5.4	4.1	7.4	0.0	3	4.3	—
2008	CHT	AA	25	2	3	0	11	9	46	41	15	52	6	37.9%	.304	-9	1.22	4.70	6.23	9.8	3.1	6.6	2.1	-5	-3.0	—
2008	LOU	AAA	25	4	5	1	19	15	99¹	76	42	93	8	48.5%	.269	0	1.19	3.08	4.95	8.2	4.3	5.8	1.1	8	6.6	—
2008	CIN	MLB	25	1	1	0	5	4	27	17	11	21	3	44.4%	.203	14	1.04	2.67	3.71	5.1	3.0	6.1	1.0	3	9.3	0.93
2009	CIN	MLB	26	5	7	1	35	16	99	108	48	82	16	43.0%	.310	9	1.58	5.54	5.45	9.7	3.8	6.4	1.4	-2	1.1	0.60

Breakout: 12% Improve: 33% Collapse: 31% Attrition: 23% Comparables: John DeSilva, Jeff Montgomery, Josias Manzanillo, Robinson Checo

Yet another of the Reds' undersized pitchers, Ramirez has gotten good strikeout numbers from an assortment that includes a low-90s fastball and a decent change. He experiences bouts of control problems, especially when facing lefty batters. He will challenge for a rotation spot this spring and is versatile enough to land in the bullpen if he doesn't make it.

Josh Roenicke

Bats: R Throws: R Height: 6' 3" Weight: 195 Born: August 4, 1982 Age: 26

YEAR	TEAM	LVL	AGE	W	L	SV	G	GS	IP	H	BB	SO	HR	GB%	BABIP	STUFF	WHIP	ERA	DERA	EqH9	EqBB9	EqSO9	EqHR9	DEF	VORP	SN/WX
2006	BIL	Rk	23	1	0	6	14	0	15²	10	12	24	1	58.8%	.273	-10	1.45	6.51	12.41	11.7	10.2	7.3	2.2	1	-9.3	—
2007	SAR	A+	24	2	1	16	27	0	27²	23	15	41	1	61.9%	.367	13	1.37	3.25	4.50	10.9	6.8	9.0	1.1	-1	2.9	—
2007	CHT	AA	24	1	1	8	19	0	19	12	6	15	0	49.0%	.240	-10	0.95	0.95	4.08	6.1	3.1	4.1	0.0	3	3.0	—
2008	CHT	AA	25	4	2	10	22	0	22	21	12	28	2	48.3%	.358	-6	1.50	3.27	4.64	10.1	5.1	7.2	1.3	-2	2.3	—
2008	LOU	AAA	25	2	0	3	35	0	39	34	14	43	2	42.6%	.324	1	1.23	2.54	3.72	9.4	3.7	6.9	0.7	1	7.6	—
2008	CIN	MLB	25	0	0	0	5	0	3	6	2	6	0	22.2%	.667	3	2.67	9.00	0.00	21.0	6.0	15.0	0.0	-3	-1.1	-0.21
2009	CIN	MLB	26	2	3	1	28	4	53	60	31	46	7	46.0%	.330	6	1.70	5.34	5.26	10.0	4.6	6.8	1.2	-1	1.7	0.30

Breakout: 5% Improve: 21% Collapse: 37% Attrition: 12% Comparables: Dana Ridenour, Ryan Braun, Bert Roberge, Derrick Turnbow

Roenicke was primarily an outfielder in college—like his father and uncle, former major leaguers Ron and Gary—and was drafted by the Reds in 2006 as a reliever. With a fastball that hits 98 mph, Roenicke is one of the hardest throwers in the organization, and he complements his heat with a power slider. He should get a shot at the bullpen this season and could eventually succeed Cordero as closer.

Daryl Thompson

Bats: R		Throws: R		Height: 6' 1"		Weight: 183		Born: November 2, 1985		Age: 23													

YEAR	TEAM	LVL	AGE	W	L	SV	G	GS	IP	H	BB	SO	HR	GB%	BABIP	STUFF	WHIP	ERA	DERA	EqH9	EqBB9	EqSO9	EqHR9	DEF	VORP	SN/WX
2007	DYT	A	21	5	0	0	5	5	28	16	2	24	1	34.2%	.208	14	0.64	0.96	4.74	7.3	1.5	3.6	1.1	6	2.4	—
2007	SAR	A+	21	9	5	0	22	22	105	106	31	97	19	34.9%	.300	-42	1.30	3.77	6.85	12.5	3.8	5.0	3.7	3	-12.8	—
2008	SAR	A+	22	0	2	0	3	3	15²	20	7	7	2	53.6%	.360	-37	1.72	6.88	10.80	14.9	5.4	1.4	2.7	0	-7.7	—
2008	CHT	AA	22	3	2	0	10	10	61¹	44	14	56	2	37.6%	.273	23	0.95	1.76	4.87	7.2	2.4	5.3	0.6	6	4.6	—
2008	LOU	AAA	22	5	0	0	7	7	45²	39	9	33	4	43.5%	.267	8	1.05	2.76	5.27	8.6	2.1	4.2	1.3	7	1.6	—
2008	CIN	MLB	22	0	2	0	3	3	14¹	20	7	6	3	40.0%	.327	-13	1.88	6.92	6.14	11.0	3.7	3.1	1.8	0	-1.7	0.20
2009	CIN	MLB	23	6	11	0	38	22	139²	170	56	90	29	41.0%	.310	4	1.61	6.11	5.93	10.8	3.2	5.0	1.8	-3	-5.9	0.30

Breakout: 4%   Improve: 21%   Collapse: 34%   Attrition: 15%   Comparables: Todd Burns, Mike Saipe, Mark Brownson, Justin Miller

Thompson made stops at five levels last season, traveling all the way from the Gulf Coast League to Yankee Stadium. He made his way through the minors by pounding the strike zone with mid-90s heat, but this proved more elusive during his brief stint in the majors. Still, the true down note to Thompson's season was shoulder soreness that resulted in a minor league DL stay—not a promising sign for a player who already has an extensive injury history.

Edinson Volquez

Bats: R		Throws: R		Height: 6' 0"		Weight: 200		Born: July 3, 1983		Age: 25													

YEAR	TEAM	LVL	AGE	W	L	SV	G	GS	IP	H	BB	SO	HR	GB%	BABIP	STUFF	WHIP	ERA	DERA	EqH9	EqBB9	EqSO9	EqHR9	DEF	VORP	SN/WX
2006	OKL	AAA	22	6	6	0	21	21	120²	86	72	130	9	45.7%	.273	22	1.31	3.22	5.23	7.4	5.6	7.0	1.0	6	4.7	—
2006	TEX	MLB	22	1	6	0	8	8	33¹	52	17	15	7	43.5%	.366	-21	2.07	7.30	5.79	13.5	4.4	3.6	1.7	-5	-5.1	-0.07
2007	BAK	A+	23	0	4	0	7	7	35¹	27	20	38	4	40.9%	.267	-10	1.33	7.14	10.47	8.5	6.1	5.2	1.9	3	-17.7	—
2007	FRI	AA	23	8	1	0	11	11	58¹	46	19	62	9	45.8%	.253	-6	1.11	3.55	5.37	9.2	3.5	6.4	2.2	1	1.4	—
2007	OKL	AAA	23	6	1	0	8	8	51	25	21	66	0	45.9%	.238	41	0.90	1.41	2.94	5.1	3.9	8.8	0.2	6	14.5	—
2007	TEX	MLB	23	2	1	0	6	6	34	34	15	29	4	37.9%	.309	11	1.44	4.50	5.13	8.9	3.8	6.8	1.1	2	4.7	0.54
2008	CIN	MLB	24	17	6	0	33	32	196	167	93	206	14	47.5%	.306	35	1.33	3.21	3.03	7.2	3.6	8.3	0.6	-9	43.8	5.43
2009	CIN	MLB	25	9	8	0	25	25	151¹	141	68	151	17	44.0%	.300	31	1.38	4.21	4.18	8.3	3.6	7.7	1.0	-2	22.6	3.60

Breakout: 13%   Improve: 36%   Collapse: 30%   Attrition: 17%   Comparablos: Chan Ho Park, Russ Meyer, Pete Harnisch, David Cone

Volquez went from our pick to be the next Dennis Tankersley to earning the nickname "Little Pedro"—as in Martinez, a comparison justified by Volquez's build and power changeup—in a single season. The league caught up with him a bit in the second half (4.60 ERA, after a 2.29 ERA in the first), as he was marked by a resurgence of the gopherball problems that had plagued him in the past. Other than his home run rate, Volquez's other peripherals remained pretty steady, so even if the second half were more representative of the "real" Edinson Volquez, we'd still be looking at a good pitcher. If he could shave one walk per nine off his 2008 performance, we'd be looking at someone special.

Dave Weathers

Bats: R		Throws: R		Height: 6' 3"		Weight: 235		Born: September 25, 1969		Age: 39													

YEAR	TEAM	LVL	AGE	W	L	SV	G	GS	IP	H	BB	SO	HR	GB%	BABIP	STUFF	WHIP	ERA	DERA	EqH9	EqBB9	EqSO9	EqHR9	DEF	VORP	SN/WX
2006	CIN	MLB	36	4	4	12	67	0	73²	61	34	50	12	46.5%	.236	-12	1.29	3.54	4.04	6.7	3.6	5.5	1.2	6	18.9	2.53
2007	CIN	MLB	37	2	6	33	70	0	77²	67	27	48	4	38.3%	.268	6	1.21	3.59	3.81	6.6	2.6	5.0	0.4	4	18.5	3.30
2008	CIN	MLB	38	4	6	0	72	0	69¹	76	30	46	6	44.4%	.314	-3	1.53	3.25	2.54	8.9	3.2	5.2	0.8	-5	17.0	0.69
2009	CIN	MLB	39	2	2	1	41	0	47	52	18	28	7	43.0%	.300	8	1.49	4.90	4.84	9.9	3.1	4.7	1.2	-1	3.6	0.30

Breakout: 1%   Improve: 11%   Collapse: 79%   Attrition: 33%   Comparables: Dennis Lamp, Jose Mesa, Lee Smith, Steve Reed

Weathers made the rare choice by a free agent to accept arbitration from his former club. Even at age 39, "Stormy" could almost certainly have picked up a multiyear deal on the free market. His decision was based in large part on comfort in and with Cincinnati and the Reds' organization—although not necessarily with the Great American Ballpark. Over his four-year tenure with the Reds, Weathers has functioned at a significant disadvantage at home (4.71 runs allowed there as opposed to 2.93 on the road).

LINEOUTS

Hitters

PLAYER	TEAM	LVL	AGE	PA	R	2B	3B	HR	RBI	BB	SO	SB-CS	EqBRR	AVG/OBP/SLG	EqAVG/EqOBP/EqSLG	EqA	VORP	WARP
UT J. Cabrera	LOU	AAA	35	239	26	16	5	4	30	13	39	5-3	-3.0	.288/.340/.465	.228/.277/.388	.230	-6.0	-0.5
	CIN	MLB	35	126	17	6	1	3	12	8	29	2-0	0.1	.252/.310/.400	.252/.310/.400	.250	1.1	-0.5
SS Z. Cozart	DYT	A	22	464	57	20	6	14	49	24	77	3-3	1.0	.280/.330/.457	.218/.257/.364	.213	-22.6	0.4
LF D. Dorn*	CHT	AA	23	388	64	21	2	21	60	42	84	1-0	0.7	.277/.367/.539	.232/.304/.450	.257	4.6	-0.6
OF S. Henry	CHT	AA	22	454	66	22	6	11	62	42	75	16-7	-2.2	.285/.361/.455	.241/.300/.392	.241	-4.7	-1.4
INF A. Phillips	LOU	AAA	31	170	27	9	1	5	22	20	19	2-0	-2.0	.315/.394/.493	.255/.333/.423	.266	3.5	0.3
	CIN	MLB	31	80	11	3	0	3	10	6	14	0-0	-0.7	.233/.300/.397	.233/.300/.397	.240	-0.2	-0.5
C C. Tatum	CHT	AA	25	328	31	18	1	8	57	26	59	1-1	-2.5	.253/.312/.403	.185/.232/.307	.183	-29.3	-1.3
	LOU	AAA	25	40	1	0	0	0	4	0	16	0-0	-0.0	.179/.175/.179	.179/.175/.179	.021	-6.6	-0.4
3B B. Waring	DYT	A	22	503	63	23	2	20	71	43	156	1-0	-2.4	.270/.346/.467	.217/.277/.374	.225	-17.4	-1.4

Jolbert Cabrera may be this year's personification of the replacement level: a guy who's been knocking around the Far East and the minors the past four years and can give you just less-than-adequate production at five positions. ⊘ Shortstop **Zach Cozart** is the best defensive infielder in the system, and while he has questionable hitting skills, he did show surprising power last year. ⊘ **Daniel Dorn** isn't one of the more heralded names in the Reds' system, but he projects as a platoon left fielder after tagging northpaws at a .290/.379/.592 clip in Double-A. ⊘ Signed for $2 million out of the Dominican Republic, outfielder **Juan Duran** has incredible tools that suggested a right-handed Daryl Strawberry to some, although Duran is rawer than the carpaccio at that nice Italian place down the street. ⊘ An athletic former infielder, **Sean Henry** has been remarkably consistent at the plate, and mere survival in this system might breed opportunity. ⊘ As a corner guy who can also play second in a pinch, **Andy Phillips** has some value as a reserve, but unfortunately, he's still a career .297/.363/.512 minor league hitter who has batted .250/.294/.384 in "The Show"; the Pirates will see if he can fit into the Doug Mientkiewicz role from last year. ⊘ As a decent receiver behind the plate with a spray hitter's virtues at it, **Craig Tatum** has some value as a potential backup backstop. ⊘ Traded to the Orioles in the Ramon Hernandez trade, **Brandon Waring** is a potential power bat for the hot corner, but is still a bit raw; he was old for the Midwest League.

Pitchers

PLAYER	TEAM	LVL	AGE	W	L	SV	IP	H	BB	SO	HR	GB%	BABIP	STUFF	WHIP	ERA	DERA	EqH9	EqBB9	EqSO9	EqHR9	DEF	VORP
M. Belisle	CIN	MLB	28	1	4	0	29²	47	6	14	4	51.6%	.374	-11	1.79	7.27	6.03	12.4	1.4	3.4	1.1	-4	-8.8
	LOU	AAA	28	5	1	4	38	43	11	27	1	61.7%	.336	-16	1.42	4.26	6.38	11.0	2.9	3.9	0.5	1	-3.2
D. Buck	SBN	A	23	1	4	0	45²	44	10	24	5	58.4%	.265	-43	1.18	3.94	8.26	12.3	3.1	1.6	2.5	7	-11.9
	SAR	A+	23	0	1	0	13	9	4	9	0	65.8%	.237	-17	1.00	4.15	9.49	7.3	3.6	2.9	0.0	4	-5.3
C. Fisher	CHT	AA	25	1	5	8	50²	52	20	46	3	59.7%	.322	-19	1.42	3.73	6.16	10.1	3.6	4.9	1.1	-2	-3.1
	LOU	AAA	25	5	0	0	17¹	14	9	21	0	59.6%	.320	9	1.33	1.04	2.12	8.5	4.8	7.4	0.0	1	6.6
J. Fogg	SAR	A+	31	1	0	0	19	24	3	14	1	41.3%	.371	-14	1.42	3.32	6.61	14.9	2.2	3.9	1.1	2	-1.8
	LOU	AAA	31	1	1	0	17	14	3	12	0	50.0%	.292	10	1.00	1.59	2.87	8.6	1.7	4.0	0.0	0	4.8
	CIN	MLB	31	2	7	0	78¹	97	27	45	17	39.2%	.309	-25	1.58	7.59	6.28	9.8	2.5	4.4	1.8	-8	-18.4
B. Jukich*	CHT	AA	25	10	4	0	139	147	54	111	6	56.5%	.346	-3	1.45	3.82	5.54	11.2	3.8	4.5	0.9	-4	0.8
	LOU	AAA	25	1	1	0	22²	30	4	15	2	55.3%	.350	-10	1.50	4.36	5.64	12.5	1.6	3.6	1.2	-3	-0.1
R. Manuel	SAR	A+	24	1	0	0	7²	5	3	11	0	27.8%	.278	7	1.04	0.00	2.45	7.4	3.7	7.4	0.0	0	2.6
	CHT	AA	24	5	3	3	77	47	15	92	2	39.5%	.250	19	0.81	1.40	3.04	6.0	1.9	6.8	0.5	2	21.9
Z. Stewart	DYT	A	21	1	2	3	16¹	10	3	13	0	61.4%	.227	0	0.80	0.55	4.30	7.4	2.5	3.1	0.6	3	2.1
	SAR	A+	21	0	2	2	16²	16	11	23	0	37.5%	.421	14	1.62	1.62	4.50	12.9	7.7	8.4	0.6	0	1.7
P. Viola*	CHT	AA	25	4	7	2	82¹	88	36	84	6	48.8%	.361	-21	1.51	4.48	6.61	11.4	4.2	5.8	1.3	-4	-8.7
T. Wood*	SAR	A+	21	3	4	0	46²	39	21	41	2	48.1%	.278	8	1.28	2.70	6.02	9.1	5.0	4.4	1.0	3	-2.0
	CHT	AA	21	4	9	0	80	91	48	58	9	37.5%	.331	-22	1.74	7.09	9.99	11.8	5.6	3.8	1.8	2	-36.9
T. Young	DYT	A	22	1	3	1	25²	25	15	21	1	48.7%	.333	-21	1.56	3.50	5.32	12.3	7.8	3.3	1.2	-3	0.7
	SAR	A+	22	1	2	2	33²	31	13	26	0	47.2%	.295	-18	1.31	2.40	7.03	9.6	4.2	3.7	0.3	5	-5.1

The Reds nontendered the always-fringy **Matt Belisle** after a brutal campaign during which he was demoted in May; he then required knee surgery in August to repair a torn ligament. ⊘ **Dallas Buck**'s value lies in the hopes that he gets his fastball back as he recovers from Tommy John surgery. Before the 2006 draftee got hurt, he was considered one of the best college pitching prospects in the nation. ⊘ Moved to a bullpen role last season, **Carlos Fisher** pounds the bottom half of the zone with a blend of cutters and sinkers and might enter into the big-league picture this year. ⊘ Aside from a September call-up with the White Sox in 2001, **Josh Fogg** has never posted a league-average ERA. Ever. ⊘ A soft-tossing southpaw, **Ben Jukich** succeeds as best he can by keeping the ball down and avoiding cookies. ⊘ A stringy Texan control pitcher with mediocre stuff, **Robert Manuel** pitched his way onto the 40-man with an insanely good 103/12 K/UBB ratio last year; win that many battles at home plate, and your fly-ball tendencies might be survivable in the Gap. ⊘ A third-round pick last June, **Zach Stewart** is one of those college closers who could move quickly through the system, but his big-league ceiling is probably no higher than setup man. ⊘ **Pedro Viola** took a step backward in his mad dash up the minor league ladder, regressing a bit in his second shot at Double-A. ⊘ **Travis Wood**'s sinking fastball and change get raves, but the 2005 second-round pick completely stalled out in Double-A. ⊘ The Nationals looked past makeup issues and the lack of a solid secondary pitch in selecting hard thrower **Terrell Young** with the first pick in the Rule 5 draft; he'll try to stick as a reliever.

MANAGER: DUSTY BAKER

YEAR	TEAM	W-L	Pythag +/−	Avg PC	100+ P	120+ P	QS	BQS	REL	REL w Zero R	IBB	Subs	PH	PH Avg	PH HR	SB2	CS2	SB3	CS3	SAC Att	SAC %	POS SAC	Squeeze	Swing	In Play
2006	CHN	66-96	-3	91.9	57	7	55	5	542	357	44	40	270	.216	5	107	41	13	5	117	71.8%	56	7	145	117
2008	CIN	74-88	3	97.9	80	3	75	5	507	321	40	48	282	.231	5	68	39	17	6	118	61.0%	34	6	136	104

In contrast to earlier managerial stints, Dusty Baker largely let his young charges play—and in the case of Jay Bruce, struggle—without his resorting to veteran substitutes last season. The main exception was outfielder Corey Patterson, who was rumored to be dating Baker's daughter at the same time the skipper was regularly writing the fellow former Cub's nonhitting name into the lineup. Baker was incensed over the Patterson rumor, but the idea of a manager not only *choosing* to rely on an out machine like Patterson, but also batting him *leadoff* impugned Baker's judgment to such an extreme degree that a more nefarious explanation seemed to be required. "Why not Joey Votto? Why not Jay Bruce or Edwin Encarnacion? They're single," Baker asked in September, suggesting that he could not distinguish between productive players, those with the potential to be productive, and Corey Patterson. At least nepotism would have been a face-saving answer. Baker's management of a young pitching staff was somewhat restrained compared with his infamous work with the Cubs. His judgment was called into question when he used his top two starters in an extra-inning game in May, after which Aaron Harang was ineffective, and later injured; while the Reds did finish with the fourth-highest age-adjusted pitcher workload (per the Pitcher Abuse Points system), the workload was a mere fraction of what he put on the ill-fated Cubs rotation in 2003. Whether this suggests a lesson learned or just the manager's not going to the crop once he saw the race was lost is open to interpretation.

Cleveland Indians

The Indians have gone longer without a World Series title than has any other American League team, with the championship flag hoisted by Lou Boudreau's 1948 club their last. While it is therefore understandable if the natives are growing restless, especially in the wake of another season that promised much more than was delivered, such frustration should be tempered with the knowledge that the team's recent failures have been born primarily of misfortune, not bad design. From losing seven of the last eight games in 2005 to miss out on a playoff berth, to finishing 11 wins below Pythagorean expectation in 2006, to squandering a 3-1 lead over the Red Sox in the 2007 AL Championship Series, bad luck has tinged the club's 21st-century disappointments. Last year, misfortune sought out the Tribe right from the beginning, ruining the aspirations of a championship-caliber club before the All-Star break.

It began on Opening Day. Although the Indians won, C. C. Sabathia was touched for five runs by the White Sox. That was the beginning of a horrific four-start stretch in which the defending AL Cy Young winner gave up 27 runs in 18 innings to open his walk year, prompting all manner of diagnoses for what was amiss. The null hypothesis turned out to be the correct one, for Sabathia began shaving runs off his ERA in short order. His surprising slump was nothing but a high-profile fluke and, in that respect, served as a small-scale model for what was to come in Cleveland's season as a whole.

The Indians scuffled through the first month and a half, but things really turned ugly in late May, when a seven-game losing streak dropped them below .500. The squad would not resurface until the second-to-last

day of the season, and it would get a whole lot worse before it began getting better. A 10-game slide starting in late June forced Cleveland to endure the ignominy of viewing the Royals' backside from last place, which the Tribe had not occupied so late in a season at any point during the wild-card era.

On July 6, eight losses into that swoon, the club officially gave up on its October aspirations, dealing Sabathia to the Brewers for prospects. At the time of the trade, Cleveland was 37-51 and 13½ games behind Chicago in the American League Central. The Indians were underachieving, but that record did not reflect how they had actually played, for their run ledger showed 387 scored and 393 allowed. If that -6 differential was properly made manifest in Cleveland's record, the club would have been 43-45 and within reasonable striking distance of first place, which might well have prevented the front office from cashing in its big meal ticket so hastily.

Revisionist history is a futile exercise, but it's hard not to wonder where a more fortunate distribution of first-half runs might have led, given just how well the Tribe played down the stretch. Even without Sabathia and third baseman Casey Blake, Cleveland posted a 40-28 record after the break, five games better than any other AL Central squad, and was the best team in the American League from August 7 onward (32-17). This, surely, was the real version of the Indians, the squad that had been projected to easily win 90-plus games and grapple with the Tigers (an even more ill-fated club, as it turned out) for another AL Central crown.

While there were major problems with the offense (chiefly the injuries to Travis Hafner and Victor Martinez), any postmortem of the team's bitter first half

---

INDIANS PROSPECTUS

2008 record: 81-81; Third place in AL Central

Pythagenport record: 85-77

Runs scored per game: 4.98 (6th in AL)

Runs allowed per game: 4.77 (9th in AL)

Team EqA: .261 (7th in AL)

2008 Batters Age: 28.1 (4th-youngest in AL)

2008 Pitchers Age: 28.6 (7th-oldest in AL)

Ballpark: Jacobs Field; Slight hitter's park; Park Factor of 1.010

2008: If only Cliff Lee could pitch every day, maybe the bullpen wouldn't be quite so vexing.

2009: The team's recent pattern of winning every other year offers hope, but the offense is underpowered and Kerry Wood doesn't solve all their pen problems.

---

must focus on the bullpen. In 2007, the Indians had one of the best pens in the league, a unit that ranked second in the junior circuit with 13.5 wins added above replacement level (WXRL). Manager Eric Wedge had hit upon a working formula: the high-leverage setup innings went to the devastating righty-lefty combo of Rafaels Betancourt and Perez, while veteran closer Joe Borowski came on with the bags clean for the ninth, which led to 45 out of 50 save chances converted despite an ERA north of 5.00. All three of those arms were still in Cleveland in 2008, as were Jensen Lewis and Tom Mastny, who rounded out Cleveland's top five in WXRL.

That group, however, was simply horrific through the first four and a half months last year. Borowski forgot his ABC's (Always Be Closing) and hit the disabled list, but the more surprising collapse belonged to Betancourt, who went from the league's best setup man to a Gasoline Squad All-Star. The waters kept rising throughout the summer, finally reaching their peak on August 14, when Perez and Edward Mujica combined to give up eight runs in the eighth inning to Baltimore. That dropped Cleveland's aggregate WXRL to -3.9, a figure that would have been the second-worst American League mark in history.

Cleveland's pen performance perked up considerably down the stretch, thanks largely to the installation of Lewis to clean up the toxic spillage in the closer role, but the Indians still finished as the only major league bullpen to clock in below replacement level (-0.4). For the suffering Tribe fans, this offered a horrible sense of déjà vu. Just two seasons before, the franchise had been racked by a nearly identical implosion, going from 12.5 WXRL in 2005 to -1.5 in 2006. In fact, the sickening late-innings roller coaster that the squad has ridden during the past four seasons is without precedent in baseball history.

Table 1. The Unbearable Lightness of Bullpens: Top Declines in WXRL, 1954–2008

Team	Year 1	Year 2	Drop
Yankees	1970	1971	-16.8
Royals	1998	1999	-15.2
Indians	2005	2006	-14.2
Indians	2007	2008	-13.9
Astros	1999	2000	-13.6

Cleveland's 2006 and 2008 teams have something else in common, as well, in that both finished well below expectations. This is not a coincidence. The smoking ruins of an underachieving team are usually preceded by blazes originating in the bullpen—as another example, take the 1999 Royals team, which ended 11 wins below its Pythagorean record, with the worst WXRL ever (-7.7). Given the high leverage of the situations in which late relievers are called upon, a few bad outings in a few key spots can have a disproportionately large effect on a team's bottom line. Such destruction is generally evidenced through that team's record in close games, and indeed, the Indians were a combined 14-24 in one- and two-run games during the 2008 first half.

In the past four years, Cleveland has demonstrated the fundamental nature of relief work in a grossly exaggerated fashion. Small sample sizes, which is to say, luck, are inherent in the seasonal performance of relievers. This scarcity of data leads to a greater amount of year-to-year variance than is exhibited in the statistics of starting pitchers or position players. Enough of this negative variation coming together leads to disastrous dives like those that befell the Indians in 2006 and 2008.

The paroxysms that Cleveland has suffered since 2005 raise an important philosophical question: How can one minimize that risk in building a bullpen? From one perspective, it makes sense to pay a premium for the best relievers, as once the effects of leverage are properly accounted for, a great closer can carry the same impact as a top starter can (Brad Lidge, with 7.6 WXRL last year, was about as valuable as Cliff Lee, with 7.7 SNLVAR). But such production from a closer depends so much on in-game usage and the context of appearances, and so few relievers can overcome the volatile nature of their profession to consistently pitch at a high level (there's only one Mariano Rivera). Furthermore, since it is significantly easier to pitch well in short bursts than as a starter, there is a wide spectrum of pitchers capable of serving as decent relievers, many of whom cost little. The prudent approach is therefore to avoid ever handing relievers long-term, big-money deals.

Especially given his squad's recent experience, general manager Mark Shapiro understands the unpredictability of relief work and the sound economics of using playing time and fungibility to inform the assignment of resources. Since taking over before the 2002 season, he has not given any reliever a contract longer than two years, preferring to fill in around farm-bred talent by going season-to-season with lower-cost veterans. After 2006, he made no huge signings to fix the failed pen, instead bringing in Borowski, a second-tier 36-year-old closer; Aaron Fultz, a 33-year-old lefty coming off a 4.54 ERA season; and 42-year-old journeyman Roberto Hernandez—all on one-year deals with club options. Such deals provide a built-in risk-control mechanism that the Indians have used extensively in assembling their relief corps over the past several years. The pen's marked improvement in 2007 was primarily due not to anything this trio did, but to the emergence of Perez and the rebound of Betancourt. If anything, the 2008 conflagration might have only strengthened Shapiro's resolve against offering multiyear contracts, because of the poor showing of Betancourt and Masahide Kobayashi, who before the season were bestowed with the first two-year deals given to Indians' relievers since Mark Wohlers signed one in 2002.

That is not to say that Shapiro and Co. should receive no blame for last year's blowup—the decision to exercise Borowski's $5 million option was arguable, and the club ended up paying dearly for that gamble—but this overall approach to the pen's construction is sound. The Indians can be optimistic about the coming season, as they already had the core of a potentially solid unit on hand: behind Perez, Betancourt, Kobayashi, and Lewis, young arms like Adam Miller, Tony Sipp, and Jeff Stevens are primed to step in from the minors to contribute, and the bevy of lefty starters who do not win a rotation job can be filtered through the late innings as well. Beyond that depth, the decision to give former Cubs closer Kerry Wood a two-year deal (plus a likely vesting option for 2011) is the first and only bet that runs against the organization's understandable caution with relief help, but that's because Wood can be the high-leverage asset that Borowski really couldn't be.

If Cleveland managers deserve some absolution for the bullpen combustion, given management's general adherence to sensible core principles, however, it is only fair to dole out blame for its failure to fulfill another commandment of sabermetrics: thou shalt receive thunder from the corners. Since Shapiro assumed control, the Indians have been unable to scare up reliable production from either left or right field, two positions that generally need to make hay for an offense to function properly.

Table 2. No Average Joes: Indians Outfield Corner Production, 2002–2008

Left Field EqA

Year	MLB Avg	Tribe	Diff
2008	.276	.271	-.005
2007	.269	.254	-.015
2006	.272	.256	-.016
2005	.271	.290	+.019
2004	.277	.282	+.005
2003	.279	.269	-.010
2002	.277	.233	-.044

Right Field EqA

Year	MLB Avg	Tribe	Diff
2008	.276	.276	.000
2007	.272	.262	-.010
2006	.270	.280	+.010
2005	.272	.267	-.005
2004	.272	.262	-.010
2003	.275	.274	-.001
2002	.277	.265	-.012

The Indians have plenty of strength up the middle, but their inability to fill in the corners with reliable bats instead of occasionally adequate ones has held back Cleveland's attack, and last year, when the problems extended to first and third base, as well as DH, there was no extra bopping from the outfield corners to help minimize the damage. This shortcoming speaks to several causes: first, that the club's farm system, while pumping out a number of excellent players, has been unable to produce outfielders (Grady Sizemore was drafted by the Expos), and second, that the Indians have refused to spend their limited cash on overpaying for big-name corners, while doing a poor job targeting cheaper fill-ins (David Dellucci, Jason Michaels, Trot Nixon).

Ironically, the team's bullpen struggles in 2006 and '08 might end up leading indirectly to the procurement of solutions for this corner issue, as well as raw material for a renewed run in the coming decade, through having given the front office an opportunity to implement its shrewd bartering skill. In 2006, Cleveland's fall led to the separate trades of Eduardo Perez and Ben Broussard to the Mariners for second baseman Asdrubal Cabrera and outfielder Shin-Soo Choo, respectively. (Rival GMs will miss having Bill Bavasi in Seattle.) Last year, the haul was even heftier: Sabathia fetched slugging left fielder Matt LaPorta as well as more underrated outfield prospect Michael Brantley; Casey Blake was turned into one of the most exciting young catchers in the game, Carlos Santana; and starter Anthony Reyes was freed from St. Louis after falling out of favor there.

An important backdrop that should not be overlooked in last year's transactions is the stability within the Cleveland front office and its importance in the franchise's long-term health. Shapiro and his top assistants know that they have the full support of the ownership group, which is headed by Lawrence Dolan, and can thus implement a rebuilding plan without any reservations or uncertainty. Management was able to begin taking steps for 2009 and beyond as soon as it estimated that a 2008 playoff berth was out of reach, not even waiting until the All-Star break to unload

Sabathia. In organizations with not as complete a level of trust and security as in Cleveland, it becomes harder for top executives to properly weigh present exigencies against future demands.

For Cleveland, the future arrives this season, as last year's swoon, like that of 2006, promises to be short-lived. The Indians are looking through a new window of opportunity. The division is weaker, and Shapiro's making a play for 2009 beyond just fixing the pen by adding short-term rentals. Trading a trio of extra arms to get Mark DeRosa from the Cubs gives the infield three solid regulars at second, short, and third, if no clear suggestion as to who starts at which spot. Inking Carl Pavano to a one-year, $1.5 million deal is more risk than possi-

ble reward, but it pushes the crowd of non-dominant lefties into a winner-take-all fight for the fifth slot behind Lee, Carmona, Pavano, and Reyes.

That leaves the Twins as the Tribe's chief nemesis, and a healthy battle for the AL Central crown should ensue. It is a battle that Cleveland is well prepared for, both this year and going forward, for last July's stockpiling coupled with the progress made by several of the team's neophytes has given Cleveland the division's best farm system. Once that talent fully blooms, all it will take is—should we dare tempt fate?—a little change in luck, and the persistent drumbeat at Progressive Field could be serving as the pulse of a victory march through Cleveland, the first in over 60 years.

HITTERS

Michael Aubrey — 1B

Bats: L   Throws: L   Height: 6' 0"   Weight: 195   Born: April 15, 1982   Age: 27

YEAR	TEAM	LVL	AGE	PA	R	2B	3B	HR	RBI	BB	SO	SB	CS	EqBRR	AVG	OBP	SLG	EqAVG	EqOBP	EqSLG	EqA	VORP	WARP	DEFENSE	
2006	KIN	A+	24	36	8	3	0	2	10	5	5	0	0	-0.3	.286	.417	.607	.226	.324	.484	.276	1.1	0.0	6-1B	-1
2006	AKR	AA	24	29	3	2	0	1	2	2	4	0	0	0.4	.269	.345	.462	.222	.300	.407	.243	-0.2	0.0	5-1B	0
2007	AKR	AA	25	221	22	11	0	7	34	10	35	0	0	0.6	.248	.290	.403	.190	.225	.310	.178	-20.1	-2.6	31-1B	-5
2008	AKR	AA	26	112	14	10	1	2	16	8	12	0	0	0.9	.282	.330	.456	.210	.250	.371	.212	-5.7	-0.3	16 1B	2
2008	BUF	AAA	26	309	29	18	0	7	37	16	40	0	0	-1.7	.281	.328	.418	.240	.285	.361	.224	-9.3	-1.6	33-1B	-4
2008	CLE	MLB	26	50	2	0	0	2	3	5	5	0	0	-1.3	.200	.280	.333	.200	.280	.333	.214	-2.1	-0.3	11-1B	-1
2009	CLE	MLB	27	360	27	16	1	8	41	19	65	0	0	-1.0	.215	.263	.339	.214	.262	.354	.209	-16.2	-1.7	87-1B	-6

Breakout: 34% Improve: 46% Collapse: 36% Attrition: 23%   Comparables: Bruce Robinson, Greg Smith, Dee Brown, Steve Stanicek

The multitude of past injuries—back, hamstring, oblique—and the accompanying missed developmental time have leached most of the promise from Aubrey's bat. The former first-rounder stayed healthy enough to play in more games than he did the previous three seasons combined and made up for his first major league demitasse, but reversing the trajectory of his stagnant prospect status was too difficult a task. Aubrey's defense is still strong despite a restriction of range from all the ailments, and he could hit his way into a small platoon share of first base at some point this season, but he'll eventually be passed over by the younger first-base options ascending from the sticks.

Michael Brantley — OF

Bats: L   Throws: L   Height: 6' 2"   Weight: 180   Born: May 15, 1987   Age: 22

YEAR	TEAM	LVL	AGE	PA	R	2B	3B	HR	RBI	BB	SO	SB	CS	EqBRR	AVG	OBP	SLG	EqAVG	EqOBP	EqSLG	EqA	VORP	WARP	DEFENSE			
2006	WVA	A	19	435	47	10	2	0	42	61	51	24	7	0.9	.300	.402	.339	.231	.312	.262	.213	-24.2	-2.2	101-LF	-4	6-CF	-1
2007	WVA	A	20	255	41	15	1	2	32	31	22	18	6	-0.3	.335	.413	.440	.260	.327	.352	.243	-2.0	-0.2	30-1B	1	19-LF	-1
2007	HUN	AA	20	223	28	6	1	0	21	29	25	17	3	3.1	.251	.353	.294	.215	.303	.256	.215	-14.7	-0.3	48-LF	4		
2008	HUN	AA	21	479	80	17	2	4	40	50	27	28	8	4.8	.319	.395	.398	.274	.335	.345	.245	-1.8	1.5	60-CF	7	21-1B	1
2009	CLE	MLB	22	553	65	23	2	3	39	47	58	18	7	2.1	.261	.327	.332	.260	.326	.346	.243	-7.3	1.3	130-CF	-3		

Breakout: 40% Improve: 65% Collapse: 17% Attrition: 7%   Comparables: Lee Graham, Rafael Delima, Mark Carreon, Trey Beamon

Because the Brewers made the playoffs, Cleveland got to pick one of two players to be named later in the C. C. Sabathia deal, rather than have Milwaukee choose for the team. The Tribe went with the speedy outfielder Brantley over power-hitting infielder Taylor Green. Brantley already has a remarkably professional approach for a hitter so young: his career OBP in over 1,600 minor league plate appearances is .399, he has walked over 50 more times than he's fanned, and he has stolen at a 78 percent clip. His defense is not of a starting caliber in center field, but with

Sizemore in center and LaPorta eventually in left, Brantley's path to the majors may be fourth outfielder. His lack of power might an issue, but the Indians believe that he can add a decent dose of pop as he ages.

Asdrubal Cabrera   MI

Bats: S   Throws: R   Height: 6' 0"   Weight: 170   Born: November 13, 1985   Age: 23

YEAR	TEAM	LVL	AGE	PA	R	2B	3B	HR	RBI	BB	SO	SB	CS	EqBRR	AVG	OBP	SLG	EqAVG	EqOBP	EqSLG	EqA	VORP	WARP	DEFENSE			
2006	TAC	AAA	20	233	27	12	2	3	22	24	51	7	5	-2.3	.236	.323	.360	.217	.296	.343	.225	-8.1	-0.4	60-SS	-5		
2006	BUF	AAA	20	211	26	11	0	1	14	8	39	5	4	1.0	.263	.295	.337	.238	.268	.311	.205	-12.1	-1.5	52-SS	-10		
2007	AKR	AA	21	425	78	23	3	8	54	45	42	23	7	2.4	.310	.383	.454	.268	.335	.401	.260	7.0	1.5	90-SS	-4		
2007	CLE	MLB	21	186	30	9	2	3	22	17	29	0	0	2.5	.283	.354	.421	.272	.348	.430	.272	6.1	1.5	36-2B	3	5-SS	2
2008	BUF	AAA	22	152	25	7	1	4	13	7	25	2	2	-3.8	.326	.375	.475	.296	.342	.458	.270	7.4	0.4	29-SS	-4	5-2B	0
2008	CLE	MLB	22	418	48	20	0	6	47	46	77	4	4	-1.9	.259	.346	.366	.258	.350	.372	.256	6.2	1.8	88-2B	4	17-SS	1
2009	CLE	MLB	23	519	59	25	2	9	50	43	92	9	4	1.4	.258	.326	.380	.257	.325	.395	.254	9.3	1.9	122-2B	3		

Breakout: 23% Improve: 52% Collapse: 25% Attrition: 7%   Comparables: Luis Alicea, Ruben Gotay, Angel Gonzalez, Kurt Stillwell

Whatever parasitic alien felled Josh Barfield in 2007 found a new host last spring in Cleveland's other young second baseman. After having won the keystone job, thanks to a fantastic second half as a rookie, Cabrera hit an appalling .184/.282/.247 in 185 plate appearances through June 8. An accelerated reeducation in Buffalo had Cabrera back in Cleveland to open the second half, and he was arguably the Indians' best player the rest of the way, hitting .320/.398/.464 in 233 PAs to reestablish himself. Especially after the DeRosa deal, Cabrera's future may still be at shortstop—he's Cleveland's strongest defender at both middle infield spots, and for years the team has talked about moving Jhonny Peralta to third base. If Cabrera does cross over the bag, he could be the best all-purpose shortstop in the American League as early as this season.

Jamey Carroll   INF

Bats: R   Throws: R   Height: 5' 9"   Weight: 170   Born: February 18, 1974   Age: 35

YEAR	TEAM	LVL	AGE	PA	R	2B	3B	HR	RBI	BB	SO	SB	CS	EqBRR	AVG	OBP	SLG	EqAVG	EqOBP	EqSLG	EqA	VORP	WARP	DEFENSE			
2006	COL	MLB	32	534	84	23	5	5	36	56	66	10	12	-3.3	.300	.377	.404	.288	.369	.385	.262	18.9	4.4	101-2B	27	7-SS	-3
2007	COL	MLB	33	268	45	9	1	2	22	28	34	6	2	2.6	.225	.317	.300	.219	.314	.294	.225	-7.1	0.2	48-2B	5	7-3B	-1
2008	CLE	MLB	34	402	60	13	4	1	36	34	65	7	3	1.5	.277	.355	.346	.278	.358	.348	.255	5.9	1.1	65-2B	5	23-3B	-3
2009	CLE	MLB	35	255	30	8	2	2	20	22	41	5	2	1.0	.260	.334	.336	.259	.333	.351	.246	1.5	0.8	63-2B	2		

Breakout: 18% Improve: 37% Collapse: 32% Attrition: 31%   Comparables: Wayne Terwilliger, Scott Fletcher, Rich Amaral, Ed Charles

Signed for infield insurance, Carroll ended up getting 66 starts at second base as a result of Cabrera's first-half flop, and 18 more at third to spell an overwhelmed Andy Marte. He proved that his horrendous 2007 season was not a harbinger of career doom, getting on base at a little better than his career rate. The Indians expressed their gratitude for the patchwork performance by exercising Carroll's $2.5 million option. If he picks up another 400 plate appearances, it will mean something has again gone very wrong.

Lonnie Chisenhall   SS

Bats: L   Throws: R   Height: 6' 1"   Weight: 200   Born: October 4, 1988   Age: 20

YEAR	TEAM	LVL	AGE	PA	R	2B	3B	HR	RBI	BB	SO	SB	CS	EqBRR	AVG	OBP	SLG	EqAVG	EqOBP	EqSLG	EqA	VORP	WARP	DEFENSE	
2008	MHV	A-	19	305	38	20	3	5	45	24	32	7	2	-0.5	.290	.355	.438	.229	.282	.370	.226	-17.2	-0.2	55-SS	-1
2009	CLE	MLB	20	596	59	34	3	9	58	37	95	7	4	0.9	.247	.297	.368	.246	.296	.383	.236	0.7	0.6	140-SS	-5

Breakout: 51% Improve: 68% Collapse: 16% Attrition: 6%   Comparables: Adrian Cardenas, Hank Blalock, Dave Hansen, Brent Butler

The possessor of the best old-school baseball name in the 2008 draft, Chisenhall was also the best juco player in the country. He was expected to go a bit later than 29th in the first round, partly due to a makeup issue—a charge of grand larceny during his freshman year at South Carolina led to dismissal from the team and a transfer to Pitt Junior College (N.C.), where he hit .410 and struck out only eight times all season. Chisenhall had a solid debut, but he'll need to keep smoking the ball as he moves up, for his glove (16 errors) has already put in for a transfer to second or third.

Shin-Soo Choo — RF

Bats: L Throws: L Height: 5' 11" Weight: 205 Born: July 13, 1982 Age: 26

YEAR	TEAM	LVL	AGE	PA	R	2B	3B	HR	RBI	BB	SO	SB	CS	EqBRR	AVG	OBP	SLG	EqAVG	EqOBP	EqSLG	EqA	VORP	WARP	DEFENSE			
2006	TAC	AAA	23	427	71	21	3	13	48	45	73	26	4	3.3	.323	.394	.499	.299	.364	.478	.291	28.8	1.8	50-LF	-4	30-RF	-2
2006	CLE	MLB	23	167	23	11	3	3	22	18	46	5	3	0.1	.295	.373	.473	.285	.373	.458	.284	8.2	1.0	29-RF	3	9-LF	-1
2007	BUF	AAA	24	238	34	11	2	3	26	21	40	10	3	1.6	.260	.328	.375	.232	.294	.360	.237	-6.5	-0.3	31-LF	-2	9-RF	2
2007	CLE	MLB	24	20	5	0	0	0	5	2	5	0	1	-0.1	.294	.350	.294	.235	.300	.235	.189	-1.0	-0.1				
2008	CLE	MLB	25	370	68	28	3	14	66	44	78	4	3	3.4	.309	.397	.549	.305	.397	.556	.316	32.9	2.4	45-RF	-2	25-LF	-6
2009	CLE	MLB	26	471	66	26	2	13	58	47	100	10	4	1.9	.276	.353	.444	.275	.352	.463	.282	13.3	1.8	111-RF	-5		

Breakout: 18% Improve: 48% Collapse: 25% Attrition: 16% Comparables: Willie Crawford, Norm Siebern, Bob Skinner, Ricky Ledee

Hee-Seop Choi, the first South Korean position player to make it to the majors, wasn't given a fair shot to play, and his talents were squandered. Choo is the second of his countrymen to make it, and it appears he's found the right organization. After Franklin Gutierrez failed to hold on to the job in right, Choo was brought back from Tommy John surgery to smash righties, and he obliged with a 992 OPS. He also held his own against lefties (800 OPS in 84 PAs), which was unexpected, considering past returns. The Indians are set to give Choo the majority of playing time in right, and he should help end Cleveland's seven-year run of below-average production from that corner.

Trevor Crowe — OF

Bats: S Throws: R Height: 6' 0" Weight: 190 Born: November 17, 1983 Age: 25

YEAR	TEAM	LVL	AGE	PA	R	2B	3B	HR	RBI	BB	SO	SB	CS	EqBRR	AVG	OBP	SLG	EqAVG	EqOBP	EqSLG	EqA	VORP	WARP	DEFENSE			
2006	KIN	A+	22	273	51	15	2	4	31	48	46	29	6	3.2	.329	.449	.470	.262	.363	.391	.271	7.0	0.7	59-CF	-5		
2006	AKR	AA	22	176	20	7	2	1	13	20	24	16	6	-1.4	.234	.318	.325	.205	.284	.295	.216	-10.9	-1.8	22-CF	-3	6-2B	-8
2007	AKR	AA	23	589	87	26	4	5	50	62	71	28	9	0.1	.259	.341	.353	.223	.294	.308	.218	-28.9	-2.5	99-CF	-9	26-RF	-1
2008	AKR	AA	24	229	45	16	2	4	28	27	29	13	5	3.3	.323	.404	.485	.277	.351	.446	.277	9.9	2.3	22-LF	7	15-CF	3
2008	BUF	AAA	24	164	25	12	2	5	13	15	43	5	2	-0.8	.274	.350	.486	.245	.319	.449	.261	3.6	0.1	21-LF	-5	9-CF	2
2009	CLE	MLB	25	430	51	21	3	6	37	38	85	14	5	1.6	.246	.317	.362	.244	.315	.377	.247	-2.7	0.9	102-CF	-2		

Breakout: 20% Improve: 40% Collapse: 27% Attrition: 20% Comparables: Everett Graham, Thomas Howard, McKay Christensen, Jerome Nelson

Crowe missed more than a month from early April to mid-May with lower back tightness, and started off terribly, hitting .155 in his first 58 at-bats. From then on, he lit the afterburners to thaw his frozen prospect star. A 27-for-49 stretch in late June was followed shortly thereafter by his first trip to Buffalo, where he kept on hitting. Like Brantley, Crowe has the speed but not the natural instinct to man center, and despite last season's outburst, his power potential is still questionable in the corners. As the Crowe flies, however, it shouldn't be a long trip at all from the team's new affiliate in Columbus to Cleveland.

David Dellucci — LF

Bats: L Throws: L Height: 5' 11" Weight: 195 Born: October 31, 1973 Age: 35

YEAR	TEAM	LVL	AGE	PA	R	2B	3B	HR	RBI	BB	SO	SB	CS	EqBRR	AVG	OBP	SLG	EqAVG	EqOBP	EqSLG	EqA	VORP	WARP	DEFENSE			
2006	PHI	MLB	32	301	41	14	5	13	39	28	62	1	3	-1.5	.292	.369	.530	.288	.365	.527	.295	18.0	1.7	31-LF	1	21-RF	-2
2007	CLE	MLB	33	199	25	11	2	4	20	17	40	2	1	0.0	.230	.296	.382	.220	.291	.384	.237	-5.2	-0.5	42-LF	-3		
2008	CLE	MLB	34	375	41	19	2	11	47	24	76	3	2	-0.3	.238	.307	.405	.238	.309	.417	.250	0.3	0.0	43-LF	-1		
2009	CLE	MLB	35	214	24	10	1	7	29	16	45	2	1	-0.3	.254	.316	.425	.252	.315	.442	.260	2.8	0.2	54-LF	-5		

Breakout: 21% Improve: 49% Collapse: 29% Attrition: 47% Comparables: Walt Moryn, Charlie Maxwell, Pat Mullin, Bob Jones

From 2005 to '06, Dellucci posted an OPS near 900 in over 800 PAs for the Rangers and Phillies. Since signing a three-year $11.5 million deal with the Indians, he has seen those numbers shrink to a 700 OPS in 575 PAs. Dellucci no longer hits right handers well enough to be the long side of a corner platoon, making him another fourth outfielder in an organization awash with them. Unlike his competitors, though, Dellucci is close to the end and carries a poor glove and is therefore a serious roster drag. His contract concludes at the end of the season, so there is little reason for Cleveland not to sink this already sunk cost if it needs to free up some space.

Tim Fedroff   CF   Bats: L   Throws: R   Height: 5' 11"   Weight: 220   Born: February 4, 1987   Age: 22

YEAR	TEAM	LVL	AGE	PA	R	2B	3B	HR	RBI	BB	SO	SB	CS	EqBRR	AVG	OBP	SLG	EqAVG	EqOBP	EqSLG	EqA	VORP	WARP	DEFENSE
2008	MHV	A-	21	102	12	6	1	0	12	10	20	1	1	0.8	.319	.382	.407	.223	.282	.298	.201	-11.2	-0.4	23-CF 1
2009	CLE	MLB	22	570	48	28	3	8	52	42	151	6	4	0.4	.223	.284	.334	.222	.282	.348	.220	-15.3	-0.1	134-CF -1

Breakout: 56%   Improve: 77%   Collapse: 16%   Attrition: 2%   Comparables: Andre Ethier, Clint King, Dan Peltier, Marvin Lowrance

A seventh-round pick last year out of University of North Carolina–Chapel Hill, Fedroff batted .404/.468/.642 with 12 homers for the Tar Heels, who advanced to the semifinals of the College World Series before losing to eventual champion Fresno State. He should have gone higher, considering talent and performance, but concerns about his slight build dropped him to the Indians, who went above the recommended slot bonus to ensure signing him. Fedroff's addition was emblematic of a larger trend, as Cleveland spent healthily in the draft to snap up quality college talent that fell lower than expected.

Ben Francisco   OF   Bats: R   Throws: R   Height: 6' 1"   Weight: 190   Born: October 23, 1981   Age: 27

YEAR	TEAM	LVL	AGE	PA	R	2B	3B	HR	RBI	BB	SO	SB	CS	EqBRR	AVG	OBP	SLG	EqAVG	EqOBP	EqSLG	EqA	VORP	WARP	DEFENSE			
2006	BUF	AAA	24	579	80	32	4	17	59	45	72	25	5	3.0	.278	.345	.454	.249	.312	.425	.257	5.7	1.3	38-CF	7	34-RF -1	
2007	BUF	AAA	25	425	60	27	2	12	51	36	66	22	8	-2.5	.318	.382	.496	.273	.334	.451	.270	15.4	1.7	45-CF	-2	29-LF 3	
2007	CLE	MLB	25	66	10	5	0	3	12	3	19	0	2	-2.5	.274	.303	.500	.258	.288	.516	.256	0.5	0.6	11-LF	5		
2008	BUF	AAA	26	104	9	3	1	1	6	11	25	3	0	-0.5	.228	.308	.315	.194	.269	.280	.200	-8.1	-0.2	17-LF	1	6-RF 2	
2008	CLE	MLB	26	499	65	32	0	15	54	40	86	4	3	2.4	.266	.332	.438	.265	.334	.454	.269	10.7	1.8	73-LF	1	26-RF 2	
2009	CLE	MLB	27	491	60	26	2	14	61	41	88	8	3	0.5	.260	.328	.424	.259	.327	.442	.266	6.0	1.7	116-LF	2		

Breakout: 30%   Improve: 48%   Collapse: 22%   Attrition: 22%   Comparables: Lou Clinton, Mike Shannon, Chris James, Scott Hairston

Francisco's solid performance in his first full big-league campaign was a pleasant development, but while the numbers he put up looked brilliant in the light of Jason Michaels' replacement-level stylings, the harsher sun of the American League revealed his bat to be just about average for the position. He's the initial default starter in left, with the Tribe hoping that a little age-27 lightning will strike.

Ryan Garko   1B   Bats: R   Throws: R   Height: 6' 2"   Weight: 225   Born: January 2, 1981   Age: 28

YEAR	TEAM	LVL	AGE	PA	R	2B	3B	HR	RBI	BB	SO	SB	CS	EqBRR	AVG	OBP	SLG	EqAVG	EqOBP	EqSLG	EqA	VORP	WARP	DEFENSE
2006	BUF	AAA	25	437	43	18	0	15	59	45	67	4	5	-4.0	.247	.352	.420	.218	.314	.382	.244	-4.7	-0.6	85-1B -2
2006	CLE	MLB	25	209	28	12	0	7	45	14	37	0	0	-1.3	.292	.359	.470	.283	.351	.457	.279	7.7	0.4	45-1B -3
2007	CLE	MLB	26	541	62	29	1	21	61	34	94	0	1	-9.0	.289	.359	.483	.283	.352	.490	.285	22.6	2.1	118-1B -2
2008	CLE	MLB	27	563	61	21	1	14	90	45	86	0	0	-3.8	.273	.346	.404	.271	.346	.415	.268	10.3	0.1	119-1B -9
2009	CLE	MLB	28	445	47	21	1	13	57	36	78	1	1	-2.6	.261	.333	.420	.260	.331	.437	.266	5.4	0.6	106-1B -3

Breakout: 15%   Improve: 41%   Collapse: 31%   Attrition: 24%   Comparables: Doug Ault, Paul Konerko, Lance Niekro, Dick Sisler

Garko tied for the team lead in RBI, but was a considerably below-average starter at first. He also has to deal with Jason Giambi comparisons of his glovework. Next season will see him begin to lose a sizable chunk of playing time to Victor Martinez at first base whenever Kelly Shoppach catches. This erosion of his playing time will eventually be finished by the tidal power of Beau Mills, Matt LaPorta, Wes Hodges, or Nick Weglarz.

Franklin Gutierrez   OF   Bats: R   Throws: R   Height: 6' 2"   Weight: 180   Born: February 21, 1983   Age: 26

YEAR	TEAM	LVL	AGE	PA	R	2B	3B	HR	RBI	BB	SO	SB	CS	EqBRR	AVG	OBP	SLG	EqAVG	EqOBP	EqSLG	EqA	VORP	WARP	DEFENSE			
2006	BUF	AAA	23	413	63	27	0	9	38	49	84	13	8	-2.0	.278	.373	.433	.254	.344	.408	.263	8.5	2.4	56-CF	8	18-LF 0	
2006	CLE	MLB	23	141	21	9	0	1	8	3	28	0	0	1.5	.272	.288	.360	.265	.281	.360	.219	-3.8	-0.3	24-RF	-2	9-LF 3	
2007	BUF	AAA	24	138	29	7	0	4	16	8	20	7	3	-1.3	.341	.384	.488	.308	.348	.462	.277	7.9	0.8	15-RF	0	13-CF 1	
2007	CLE	MLB	24	301	41	13	2	13	36	21	77	8	3	0.4	.266	.318	.472	.259	.314	.481	.268	5.8	0.7	64-RF	-1	7-LF -1	
2008	CLE	MLB	25	440	54	26	2	8	41	27	87	9	3	1.4	.248	.307	.383	.249	.310	.397	.247	-3.2	0.9	86-RF	7	11-CF 1	
2009	SEA	MLB	26	358	42	18	2	10	42	27	79	8	2	1.0	.256	.318	.412	.259	.321	.436	.263	3.9	1.4	86-RF	3		

Breakout: 33%   Improve: 57%   Collapse: 27%   Attrition: 23%   Comparables: Ron Davis, Mike Shannon, George Thomas, Sam Mele

Gutierrez entered the season as the Indians' starting right fielder on the strength of his slugging in limited 2007 action and his excellent glove, but he hit just .216/.264/.315 in the first half, and that was pretty much the end of that. He's flummoxed by righties (.246/.298/.378 against them in 591 lifetime PAs), and he didn't hit lefties last year, either. Dealt to the Mariners as part of the three-way deal centering on the Mets' acquisition of J. J. Putz, Gutierrez is slated to start for Seattle in center field, where he'll continue to impress as a ball-hawk and disappoint offensively. Note that his career rates away from Cleveland (.248/.294/.357) are nearly identical to his rates against right handers.

Travis Hafner   **DH**   Bats: L   Throws: R   Height: 6' 3"   Weight: 240   Born: June 3, 1977   Age: 32

YEAR	TEAM	LVL	AGE	PA	R	2B	3B	HR	RBI	BB	SO	SB	CS	EqBRR	AVG	OBP	SLG	EqAVG	EqOBP	EqSLG	EqA	VORP	WARP	DEFENSE
2006	CLE	MLB	29	563	100	31	1	42	117	100	111	0	0	-1.8	.308	.439	.659	.291	.434	.632	.348	78.5	6.8	
2007	CLE	MLB	30	659	80	25	2	24	100	102	115	1	1	-1.2	.266	.385	.451	.252	.379	.443	.288	24.6	3.3	10-1B 3
2008	CLE	MLB	31	233	21	10	0	5	24	27	55	1	1	-2.6	.197	.305	.323	.188	.300	.315	.223	-6.6	-0.8	
2009	CLE	MLB	32	394	48	18	1	13	52	50	85	1	1	-1.9	.248	.352	.422	.247	.350	.439	.274	10.1	1.2	94-DH

Breakout: 3%   Improve: 27%   Collapse: 33%   Attrition: 25%   Comparables: Jim Gentile, Sid Bream, Tony Solaita, Don Mincher

Forget 2006—that may as well be ancient history—but can Hafner even repeat his 2007 production? The Indians still have to pay him nearly $52 million through 2012, and the weakened state of his right shoulder inspires little hope for an adequate return on that investment. At the end of May, when Hafner finally gave up fighting against the soreness that had been present since spring training, rest and rehab were thought to be all that was needed for recovery. He went over three months between major league games, trying to build up strength, and then collected five hits in 41 at-bats during his September return. Dr. James Andrews performed surgery on the shoulder in October; oddly, he found no structural damage. Given Hafner's age and skill set—and knowing that players who emerge later tend to burn out quicker—Cleveland fans might soon need to shift the "Mistake by the Lake" label from the old Memorial Stadium to the Pronk-sized albatross now firmly tethered to Chief Wahoo's neck.

Wes Hodges   **3B**   Bats: R   Throws: R   Height: 6' 2"   Weight: 180   Born: September 14, 1984   Age: 24

YEAR	TEAM	LVL	AGE	PA	R	2B	3B	HR	RBI	BB	SO	SB	CS	EqBRR	AVG	OBP	SLG	EqAVG	EqOBP	EqSLG	EqA	VORP	WARP	DEFENSE
2007	KIN	A+	22	450	60	22	3	15	71	44	90	0	0	-0.3	.288	.367	.473	.230	.291	.381	.233	-9.5	-3.0	98-3B -23
2008	AKR	AA	23	573	70	29	3	18	97	52	105	3	1	-0.6	.290	.354	.466	.266	.325	.444	.265	15.5	0.0	125-3B -17
2009	CLE	MLB	24	592	60	31	2	15	73	47	133	2	1	-0.6	.249	.312	.402	.248	.310	.419	.252	3.4	0.2	139-3B -10

Breakout: 24%   Improve: 46%   Collapse: 27%   Attrition: 10%   Comparables: Philip Klimas, Stan Royer, Jim Opie, Tim Teufel

The Indians need a third baseman, and Hodges is chugging his way up through the system. There are few questions about his bat—Hodges legendarily hit .430 as a high school senior after a broken bone forced him to swing left-handed—but as with several of the team's other top offensive assets in the minors (Mills, Weglarz, LaPorta), his defense is rough. Hodges led Eastern League third basemen with 28 errors, and his .899 fielding percentage was the lowest of all regular position players. Most of those miscues were on throws, often the result of poor footwork on relatively routine plays. The Indians believe he can become a serviceable defender and are committed to sticking with him at the hot corner.

Matt LaPorta   **LF**   Bats: R   Throws: R   Height: 6' 2"   Weight: 212   Born: January 8, 1985   Age: 24

YEAR	TEAM	LVL	AGE	PA	R	2B	3B	HR	RBI	BB	SO	SB	CS	EqBRR	AVG	OBP	SLG	EqAVG	EqOBP	EqSLG	EqA	VORP	WARP	DEFENSE	
2007	HEL	Rk	22	28	4	1	0	2	4	1	8	0	0	0.0	.259	.286	.519	.148	.179	.296	.144	-6.7	-0.5		
2007	WVA	A	22	102	18	8	0	10	27	7	22	0	1	-0.4	.318	.392	.750	.226	.275	.516	.259	2.1	0.3	17-LF 1	
2008	HUN	AA	23	366	56	23	2	20	66	45	63	2	1	-0.0	.288	.402	.576	.248	.336	.497	.281	17.3	1.5	70-RF -4	7-LF 1
2008	AKR	AA	23	67	6	1	0	2	8	4	12	0	0	1.0	.233	.299	.350	.213	.279	.328	.214	-3.3	0.9	15-LF 9	
2009	CLE	MLB	24	503	54	26	1	20	72	42	116	1	1	-1.1	.243	.317	.443	.242	.316	.462	.265	3.6	1.7	119-RF 1	

Breakout: 27%   Improve: 54%   Collapse: 18%   Attrition: 12%   Comparables: John Russell, Scott Bryant, Greg Blosser, Mike Laga

The pièce de résistance in the bounty Cleveland received from Milwaukee for Sabathia, LaPorta is the solution to Cleveland's long-standing problem in left field … or maybe its developing problem at DH, for LaPorta's range afield leaves a lot to be desired. People pay to watch LaPorta swing for the fences, however, and he brings a full toolbox to the plate; he was leading the Southern League in homers when the trade occurred. Things didn't go so well afterward, not that a mild concussion after getting nailed in the helmet by a Chinese heater in Beijing helped. (Seriously, are the Olympics good for anything?) Cleveland will start LaPorta off at its new Triple-A affiliate in Columbus, and a return to his first-half form could have him up to "The Show" by midsummer. Though unlikely, a Ryan Braun–level impact isn't completely out of the question.

Andy Marte **3B** Bats: R Throws: R Height: 6' 1" Weight: 190 Born: October 21, 1983 Age: 25

YEAR	TEAM	LVL	AGE	PA	R	2B	3B	HR	RBI	BB	SO	SB	CS	EqBRR	AVG	OBP	SLG	EqAVG	EqOBP	EqSLG	EqA	VORP	WARP	DEFENSE	
2006	BUF	AAA	22	394	49	23	0	15	46	34	81	1	0	-1.6	.261	.322	.451	.234	.294	.415	.244	-2.5	1.4	91-3B	9
2006	CLE	MLB	22	178	20	15	1	5	23	13	38	0	0	-0.2	.226	.287	.421	.215	.281	.405	.234	-2.7	0.5	49-3B	5
2007	BUF	AAA	23	379	47	17	1	16	60	21	64	0	0	0.3	.267	.309	.457	.239	.277	.428	.240	-3.3	-0.3	84-3B	-3
2007	CLE	MLB	23	60	3	4	0	1	8	2	9	0	0	0.1	.193	.233	.316	.193	.233	.298	.175	-4.3	-0.6	15-3B	-2
2008	CLE	MLB	24	257	21	11	1	3	17	14	52	1	2	-1.4	.221	.268	.315	.222	.272	.329	.207	-12.2	-0.3	66-3B	6
2009	CLE	MLB	25	232	23	12	1	8	31	15	46	1	0	-0.4	.243	.297	.414	.242	.295	.431	.249	2.5	0.8	58-3B	2

Breakout: 47% Improve: 64% Collapse: 23% Attrition: 36%   Comparables: Dale Berra, Tucker Ashford, Tony Batista, Kevin Young

Marte got the chance to play every day at third after Casey Blake was dealt, but by year's end, the majority of starts were going to Carroll. It's hard to criticize that decision: among American Leaguers with at least 250 plate appearances, only Yankees catcher Jose Molina had a worse OPS. Marte's fall from grace is one of the more inexplicable developments for a top prospect in recent years, but now that Marte's faults are explicit and indisputable, the Indians will finally have to move on at the hot corner. Out of options, Marte's relative youth and strong glove will allow him additional chances.

Victor Martinez **C** Bats: S Throws: R Height: 6' 2" Weight: 195 Born: December 23, 1978 Age: 30

YEAR	TEAM	LVL	AGE	PA	R	2B	3B	HR	RBI	BB	SO	SB	CS	EqBRR	AVG	OBP	SLG	EqAVG	EqOBP	EqSLG	EqA	VORP	WARP	DEFENSE			
2006	CLE	MLB	27	652	82	37	0	16	93	71	78	0	0	-5.5	.316	.391	.465	.302	.385	.454	.293	46.7	3.7	126-C	-12	19-1B	-1
2007	CLE	MLB	28	645	78	40	0	25	114	62	76	0	0	-1.7	.301	.374	.505	.288	.366	.503	.296	49.0	5.5	116-C	3	25-1B	-2
2008	CLE	MLB	29	294	30	17	0	2	35	24	32	0	0	-0.8	.278	.337	.365	.277	.340	.367	.252	4.9	1.2	50-C	4	9-1B	0
2009	CLE	MLB	30	433	45	22	0	10	52	39	55	0	0	-1.8	.272	.342	.408	.271	.340	.425	.266	12.3	2.3	103-C	-5		

Breakout: 4% Improve: 31% Collapse: 33% Attrition: 14%   Comparables: Earl Battey, Michael Barrett, Alan Ashby, David Segui

Last year was a comedy of injuries for Martinez: he strained his hamstring on Opening Day, missed time in May because of a stiff neck and a cut on his finger, and aggravated his sore right elbow with an awkward swing in early June. The last in that series resulted in surgery to remove bone chips, knocking Martinez out for two and a half months. Martinez's first homer of the year didn't come until September 2, although his line after the operation (.279/.351/.456 in 77 PAs) raises hope for a full recovery. Upon his return, Martinez played a number of games at first base, which provided a glimpse of Cleveland's future plans, given Shoppach's emergence and the devolution of Garko's bat. Martinez should see between 40 and 60 starts at first in 2009 to capitalize on the club's possession of two catchers better than the starter on most clubs.

Beau Mills **1B** Bats: L Throws: R Height: 6' 3" Weight: 220 Born: August 15, 1986 Age: 22

YEAR	TEAM	LVL	AGE	PA	R	2B	3B	HR	RBI	BB	SO	SB	CS	EqBRR	AVG	OBP	SLG	EqAVG	EqOBP	EqSLG	EqA	VORP	WARP	DEFENSE			
2007	MHV	A-	20	33	5	2	0	0	1	3	7	0	0	0.0	.179	.303	.250	.133	.212	.200	.119	-8.8	-0.6				
2007	LKC	A	20	198	32	12	1	5	36	14	38	0	0	0.0	.271	.333	.435	.208	.258	.339	.206	-11.2	-1.1	22-3B	-3	16-1B	2
2007	KIN	A+	20	48	7	6	0	1	5	4	8	0	0	0.2	.275	.375	.500	.233	.292	.395	.240	-0.7	-0.1				
2008	KIN	A+	21	549	78	34	3	21	90	54	105	2	3	0.3	.293	.373	.506	.268	.337	.471	.274	24.6	1.1	98-1B	-6	8-3B	0
2009	CLE	MLB	22	613	66	32	2	19	78	52	138	2	2	-0.4	.248	.317	.417	.247	.316	.435	.258	1.2	0.9	143-1B	0		

Breakout: 31% Improve: 59% Collapse: 16% Attrition: 5%   Comparables: Sam Horn, Carlos Peña, Sid Bream, Andy LaRoche

Former first-round pick "General" Mills showed why he's the best offensive prospect in the system. He scoffed at the pitching-heavy reputation of the Carolina League in his first full pro season, tying for the circuit lead in homers while finishing second in RBI and third in slugging. He's not a great athlete and is rough around the bag at first base—rough enough that he might not wear a glove in the majors—but that won't matter much when he's knocking 30-plus homers out of "the Prog" in a few years' time.

Jhonny Peralta — SS

Bats: R   Throws: R   Height: 6' 1"   Weight: 195   Born: May 28, 1982   Age: 27

YEAR	TEAM	LVL	AGE	PA	R	2B	3B	HR	RBI	BB	SO	SB	CS	EqBRR	AVG	OBP	SLG	EqAVG	EqOBP	EqSLG	EqA	VORP	WARP	DEFENSE	
2006	CLE	MLB	24	632	84	28	3	13	68	56	152	0	1	-2.7	.257	.323	.385	.246	.320	.378	.244	9.5	3.3	145-SS	15
2007	CLE	MLB	25	647	87	27	1	21	72	61	146	4	4	-3.0	.270	.341	.430	.261	.336	.434	.265	20.4	3.4	149-SS	1
2008	CLE	MLB	26	664	104	42	4	23	89	48	126	3	1	0.3	.276	.331	.473	.272	.330	.483	.275	37.5	4.3	143-SS	1
2009	CLE	MLB	27	629	72	31	3	19	78	53	134	4	2	-0.6	.261	.327	.425	.260	.326	.443	.265	20.7	3.3	147-SS	4

Breakout: 20%   Improve: 44%   Collapse: 23%   Attrition: 6%   Comparables: Jay Bell, Gary Gaetti, Clete Boyer, Travis Fryman

After two seasons of frustration, the power that Peralta displayed in 2006 returned as he set a franchise record for extra-base hits by a shortstop (surpassing Hall of Famer Lou Boudreau's 65 from 1940). Peralta was the best offensive shortstop in the weak post-"trinity" American League field and is signed for the next three seasons at just $15 million total. The bad news is that he's growing increasingly immobile at the position. He'll need a move to third at some point, and it's possible that the acquisition of Mark DeRosa from the Cubs might create the impetus to do so, although over the winter the Tribe said it would be DeRosa who would head to the hot corner.

Carlos Rivero — SS

Bats: R   Throws: R   Height: 6' 3"   Weight: 198   Born: May 20, 1988   Age: 21

YEAR	TEAM	LVL	AGE	PA	R	2B	3B	HR	RBI	BB	SO	SB	CS	EqBRR	AVG	OBP	SLG	EqAVG	EqOBP	EqSLG	EqA	VORP	WARP	DEFENSE			
2006	IDN	Rk	18	148	17	6	0	2	22	10	20	0	0	0.0	.284	.338	.373	.223	.262	.317	.198	-26.6	-0.3	34-SS	2		
2006	BNC	Rk	18	73	3	3	0	1	7	5	11	0	1	-1.5	.212	.264	.303	.159	.192	.232	.127	-21.1	-1.7	9-3B	-1	7-SS	-3
2007	LKC	A	19	490	59	26	0	7	62	47	84	1	2	0.0	.261	.332	.369	.203	.260	.287	.189	-37.8	-2.7	111-SS	-9		
2008	KIN	A+	20	455	46	27	1	8	64	36	84	1	2	-2.3	.282	.342	.411	.256	.308	.380	.240	-3.7	-0.4	104-SS	-12		
2009	CLE	MLB	21	534	43	25	1	10	53	37	113	1	1	-1.4	.239	.293	.354	.237	.292	.369	.230	-1.9	0.1	125-SS	-4		

Breakout: 53%   Improve: 70%   Collapse: 9%   Attrition: 9%   Comparables: Jhonny Peralta, Jose Viera, Luis Iglesias, Aarom Baldiris

On the surface, Rivero's numbers don't look that spiffy. But consider that he was a 20-year-old shortstop evolving in probably the toughest offensive environment in the minors and that Kinston's home park is an above-average pitcher's haven, even compared with that standard. In a system that lacks depth in the middle infield, Rivero is the crown jewel. Defensively, he has good hands and a cannon arm, but lacks that strong first step afield. He's also enormous, so like Peralta, he'll probably move to third base eventually—not since A-Rod has a player so large held down short at the major league level. Rivero's bat looks as if it could be an asset even after that shift.

Carlos Santana — C

Bats: S   Throws: R   Height: 5' 11"   Weight: 170   Born: April 8, 1986   Age: 23

YEAR	TEAM	LVL	AGE	PA	R	2B	3B	HR	RBI	BB	SO	SB	CS	EqBRR	AVG	OBP	SLG	EqAVG	EqOBP	EqSLG	EqA	VORP	WARP	DEFENSE			
2006	VRO	A+	20	223	16	10	2	3	18	23	43	0	3	-1.9	.268	.345	.384	.218	.287	.327	.212	-11.2	-2.8	30-3B	-10	21-LF	-7
2006	OGD	Rk	20	168	31	5	1	7	27	30	19	4	0	-0.5	.303	.423	.515	.207	.292	.352	.231	-10.7	-1.3	31-RF	-5	6-3B	-1
2007	GRL	A	21	334	32	20	1	7	36	40	45	5	3	0.0	.223	.318	.370	.179	.256	.299	.191	-27.8	-2.4	64-C	-7	5-3B	-2
2008	SBR	A+	22	434	88	34	4	14	96	69	59	7	4	0.5	.323	.431	.563	.273	.375	.475	.292	27.0	2.6	75-C	-9		
2008	KIN	A+	22	126	34	5	1	6	19	20	24	3	0	1.5	.352	.452	.590	.324	.417	.574	.333	17.5	2.1	24-C	3		
2009	CLE	MLB	23	553	64	29	2	14	62	62	110	5	2	0.9	.246	.333	.403	.245	.332	.420	.263	10.9	2.4	130-C	-13		

Breakout: 19%   Improve: 50%   Collapse: 23%   Attrition: 6%   Comparables: Roberto Petagine, Scotti Madison, Max Ramirez, Jorge Posada

The Sabathia deal got the attention, but Shapiro's ability to leverage Ned Colletti's mistrust of Andy LaRoche could end up ranking among the best trades in team history. By flipping impending free agent Casey Blake, Shapiro brought back a switch-hitting backstop who killed the ball from both sides of the plate last year (919 OPS against left-handed pitchers, 1026 against righties). Santana laid waste to the California League, earning MVP honors while leading the circuit in OBP and finishing second in batting average and slugging. While the Cal League is a hitter's paradise, any doubts about Santana's breakout were erased when he hit even better for Kinston. He ended the season second in all of the minors with 117 RBI and scored more runs (125) than any other bush leaguer in three years. A converted third baseman/outfielder who only started catching in 2007, Santana is still learning the position, but scouts believe he possesses the raw tools to stay behind the plate.

Kelly Shoppach   C

| | | | | | | | | | | | | | | | Bats: R | Throws: R | | Height: 6' 0" | | Weight: 220 | | Born: April 29, 1980 | | Age: 29 |

YEAR	TEAM	LVL	AGE	PA	R	2B	3B	HR	RBI	BB	SO	SB	CS	EqBRR	AVG	OBP	SLG	EqAVG	EqOBP	EqSLG	EqA	VORP	WARP	DEFENSE
2006	BUF	AAA	26	87	11	8	0	4	9	6	25	0	1	-1.4	.282	.356	.538	.253	.322	.468	.263	2.8	0.6	21-C 1
2006	CLE	MLB	26	120	7	6	0	3	16	8	45	0	0	-1.6	.245	.297	.382	.239	.297	.385	.236	-0.7	0.8	32-C 5
2007	CLE	MLB	27	177	26	13	0	7	30	11	56	0	0	0.0	.261	.310	.472	.256	.310	.481	.266	6.6	1.2	47-C 3
2008	CLE	MLB	28	403	67	27	0	21	55	36	133	0	0	0.5	.261	.348	.517	.256	.347	.533	.292	28.3	3.2	98-C -2
2009	CLE	MLB	29	420	48	22	1	20	65	37	135	0	1	-1.2	.248	.324	.468	.246	.322	.488	.273	16.6	3.0	100-C 0

Breakout: 17%   Improve: 36%   Collapse: 35%   Attrition: 16%   Comparables: Dave Duncan, George Mitterwald, Ozzie Virgil, Mike Macfarlane

Victor Martinez's many ailments allowed Shoppach, one of the game's most overqualified reserve catchers, to show that he is among the best catchers in the majors, period. From when Martinez went down on June 11 onward, Shoppach hit .273/.366/.564 in 319 PAs and even tied the single-game record for extra-base hits with a two-homer, three-double night on July 30 (joining Lou Boudreau as the only other AL player to accomplish that feat). It would be difficult for the Tribe to holster its secret weapon, so he should get another 400+ PAs through a creative C/1B/DH rotation. There is some risk that Shoppach will be exposed by a dramatic increase in playing time. He was a prodigious strikeout artist last year, K-ing in 37.8 percent of his at-bats, the same rate as Mr. 204, Mark Reynolds. The reason Shoppach was able to sustain his batting average despite such a low contact rate is that he hit .357 on balls in play, a success rate that is likely to drop. Given this and the team's depth behind the plate, Cleveland might be wise to try to capitalize on Shoppach's emergence by flipping him to one of the many teams in need of a starting catcher.

Grady Sizemore   CF

| | | | | | | | | | | | | | | | Bats: L | Throws: L | | Height: 6' 2" | | Weight: 200 | | Born: August 2, 1982 | | Age: 26 |

YEAR	TEAM	LVL	AGE	PA	R	2B	3B	HR	RBI	BB	SO	SB	CS	EqBRR	AVG	OBP	SLG	EqAVG	EqOBP	EqSLG	EqA	VORP	WARP	DEFENSE
2006	CLE	MLB	23	751	134	53	11	28	76	78	153	22	6	6.8	.290	.375	.533	.279	.371	.521	.300	67.9	7.9	157-CF 16
2007	CLE	MLB	24	748	118	34	5	24	78	101	155	33	10	7.7	.277	.390	.462	.268	.386	.458	.294	46.9	6.6	156-CF 12
2008	CLE	MLB	25	745	101	39	5	33	90	98	130	38	5	5.1	.268	.374	.502	.262	.374	.509	.304	60.7	7.4	151-CF 10
2009	CLE	MLB	26	704	110	36	5	30	98	85	134	27	7	3.9	.269	.368	.494	.268	.366	.515	.301	42.5	7.0	162-CF 8

Breakout: 20%   Improve: 53%   Collapse: 12%   Attrition: 8%   Comparables: Roger Maris, Lloyd Moseby, Bobby Bonds, Barry Bonds

Sizemore carried the stiff carcass of Cleveland's offense through the spring doldrums and midsummer wasteland, serving as the sole Tribesman who spent the entire season on the warpath. If his teammates had played up to expectations, he might have become the first Indian since Al Rosen in 1953 to win the MVP, for he finished second in league VORP, behind Alex Rodriguez. Sizemore doesn't deserve the Gold Gloves that have begun to accumulate, but that's of secondary importance for a player with so unique an offensive skill set—after becoming the second Indian to post a 30-30 season (Joe Carter is the other), Sizemore joined Rodriguez and Bobby Abreu as the only players in major league history to have accomplished all four of the following single-season milestones: 100 walks, 50 doubles, 30 homers, and 30 steals.

Nick Weglarz   LF

| | | | | | | | | | | | | | | | Bats: L | Throws: L | | Height: 6' 3" | | Weight: 215 | | Born: December 16, 1987 | | Age: 21 |

YEAR	TEAM	LVL	AGE	PA	R	2B	3B	HR	RBI	BB	SO	SB	CS	EqBRR	AVG	OBP	SLG	EqAVG	EqOBP	EqSLG	EqA	VORP	WARP	DEFENSE
2007	LKC	A	19	532	75	28	0	23	82	82	129	1	1	0.0	.276	.395	.497	.216	.315	.377	.242	-6.7	-2.0	103-LF -16
2008	KIN	A+	20	454	68	20	5	10	41	71	78	9	5	1.3	.272	.396	.432	.248	.358	.408	.269	12.4	1.6	74-LF 2
2009	CLE	MLB	21	566	67	26	3	14	58	69	129	6	3	1.2	.237	.336	.387	.236	.334	.403	.259	-0.5	0.6	133-LF -11

Breakout: 28%   Improve: 52%   Collapse: 18%   Attrition: 2%   Comparables: Bo Dodson, Dernell Stenson, Joey Votto, Steve Cox

Weglarz led his native Canada in hitting at the summer games, and he possesses the patience and power potential of another Canadian outfielder—Jason Bay. While Weglarz's raw power did not manifest itself in High-A, his walk rate increased slightly and his strikeouts dropped appreciably; such advanced plate discipline from a player so young is rare. The concern is that Weglarz possesses the dreaded "old player skills," as he's big and slow with a clunky glove that might eventually demand a move to first. The bat is shaping up to make an impact at any position, though, and he'll begin next season as one-fourth of a Double-A murderer's row with Mills, Santana, and Rivero.

PITCHERS

Rafael Betancourt

Bats: R   Throws: R   Height: 6' 2"   Weight: 200   Born: April 29, 1975   Age: 34

YEAR	TEAM	LVL	AGE	W	L	SV	G	GS	IP	H	BB	SO	HR	GB%	BABIP	STUFF	WHIP	ERA	DERA	EqH9	EqBB9	EqSO9	EqHR9	DEF	VORP	SN/WX
2006	CLE	MLB	31	3	4	3	50	0	56²	52	11	48	7	25.6%	.280	3	1.11	3.81	4.87	7.5	1.7	6.6	0.9	6	13.5	1.63
2007	CLE	MLB	32	5	1	3	68	0	79¹	51	9	80	4	29.0%	.242	31	0.76	1.48	2.56	5.7	0.9	8.0	0.5	8	40.1	6.85
2008	CLE	MLB	33	3	4	4	69	0	71	76	25	64	11	31.4%	.325	-7	1.42	5.07	4.97	9.4	2.9	7.1	1.4	0	4.9	0.58
2009	CLE	MLB	34	3	3	4	47	0	56	55	14	47	8	33.0%	.290	10	1.23	3.94	3.83	8.6	2.0	6.9	1.3	0	10.6	0.93

Breakout: 19%   Improve: 45%   Collapse: 32%   Attrition: 15%   Comparables: Keith Foulke, Enrique Romo, Justin Speier, Jeff Reardon

After the club bought out his last two arbitration-eligible seasons, Betancourt made the transformation from best firefighter in baseball to purveyor of top-grade lighter fluid. By mid-May, he had already allowed as many runs and homers in 16 innings as he did all of last season. Betancourt started mixing in more sliders and changeups, but nothing much helped. Random variation is the likely culprit, as his velocity was strong, although middle relievers in their 30s are prone to just losing it (see Guillermo Mota, a former Indian who, like Betancourt, was also suspended for steroid use). With a $5.4 million club option on the line, Betancourt has extra incentive to get his mojo back.

Joe Borowski

Bats: R   Throws: R   Height: 6' 2"   Weight: 225   Born: May 4, 1971   Age: 38

YEAR	TEAM	LVL	AGE	W	L	SV	G	GS	IP	H	BB	SO	HR	GB%	BABIP	STUFF	WHIP	ERA	DERA	EqH9	EqBB9	EqSO9	EqHR9	DEF	VORP	SN/WX
2006	FLO	MLB	35	3	3	36	72	0	69²	63	33	64	7	34.6%	.284	6	1.38	3.74	3.93	7.6	3.7	7.4	0.8	1	14.9	2.76
2007	CLE	MLB	36	4	5	45	69	0	65²	77	17	58	9	35.8%	.342	-3	1.43	5.07	4.21	10.2	2.2	6.8	1.2	-7	5.0	2.70
2008	CLE	MLB	37	1	3	6	18	0	16²	24	8	9	4	24.6%	.339	-34	1.92	7.54	6.75	11.9	3.6	4.2	2.1	-1	-3.2	-1.67
2009	CLE	MLB	38	2	2	5	28	0	33²	36	12	24	4	35.0%	.300	-0	1.41	4.42	4.30	9.3	2.8	5.8	1.1	0	4.5	0.45

Breakout: 40%   Improve: 60%   Collapse: 15%   Attrition: 29%   Comparables: Rich Gossage, Aurelio Lopez, Giovanni Carrara, Ted Power

American League hitters were itching for another crack at Borowski following his *Matrix*-esque performance in 2007, and they soon found that his ability to duck bullets had evaporated. In his first four innings, Borowski gave up eight runs and three homers, twice turning Cleveland ninth-inning leads into losses. After the second of those debacles, Borowski shuffled to the DL with a triceps strain. He threw a little harder upon returning, but the Indians finally told him to hit the bricks after he blew another game on July 1. The realization that lightning traveling as slow as Borowksi's heater never strikes twice would have saved the Tribe two wins, by conservative estimation, and perhaps altered the season's trajectory. Borowski finished his Cleveland career with 51 saves in 63 chances, despite a 5.79 RA, which says everything about how overrated the ability to get the game's last three outs is.

Bryan Bullington

Bats: R   Throws: R   Height: 6' 4"   Weight: 220   Born: September 30, 1980   Age: 28

YEAR	TEAM	LVL	AGE	W	L	SV	G	GS	IP	H	BB	SO	HR	GB%	BABIP	STUFF	WHIP	ERA	DERA	EqH9	EqBB9	EqSO9	EqHR9	DEF	VORP	SN/WX
2007	IND	AAA	26	11	9	0	26	26	150²	146	59	89	10	46.3%	.297	-17	1.36	4.00	6.85	9.8	3.9	3.4	1.0	18	-19.3	—
2007	PIT	MLB	26	0	3	0	5	3	17	24	5	7	3	51.6%	.350	-21	1.71	5.29	6.48	11.9	2.2	3.8	1.6	2	-0.0	0.04
2008	IND	AAA	27	4	6	0	15	15	75	90	25	60	8	50.6%	.350	-21	1.53	5.52	7.62	12.7	3.4	4.8	1.4	-3	-15.6	—
2008	BUF	AAA	27	1	3	1	10	8	53	65	13	47	7	59.1%	.360	-10	1.47	4.75	5.11	12.8	2.6	5.3	1.6	-8	2.7	—
2008	CLE	MLB	27	0	2	0	3	2	14²	15	2	12	4	53.3%	.275	7	1.16	4.90	5.65	8.8	1.3	6.3	2.5	0	0.7	0.01
2009	TOR	MLB	28	4	7	0	28	13	91²	110	36	56	14	48.0%	.310	-4	1.59	5.76	5.84	10.6	3.2	4.9	1.4	2	-2.4	0.30

Breakout: 14%   Improve: 46%   Collapse: 22%   Attrition: 21%   Comparables: Seth Greisinger, Jeff Heathcock, Craig McMurtry, Kris Benson

Bearing the stigma of being the first overall pick in the 2002 draft and the scars of 2006 Tommy John surgery, Bullington started what could be a long period of wandering when he moved from the Pirates to the Indians, and then to Toronto on an October waiver claim. He's still searching for his first major league victory, as well as a performance that will prevent his career from serving as a memento of the previous Pittsburgh regime's failures.

Fausto Carmona

Bats: R   Throws: R   Height: 6' 4"   Weight: 220   Born: December 7, 1983   Age: 25

YEAR	TEAM	LVL	AGE	W	L	SV	G	GS	IP	H	BB	SO	HR	GB%	BABIP	STUFF	WHIP	ERA	DERA	EqH9	EqBB9	EqSO9	EqHR9	DEF	VORP	SN/WX
2006	BUF	AAA	22	1	3	0	6	5	27^1	28	8	28	2	49.4%	.342	4	1.33	5.65	9.95	11.4	3.2	6.4	1.1	2	-12.2	—
2006	CLE	MLB	22	1	10	0	38	7	74^2	88	31	58	9	60.1%	.346	6	1.59	5.42	4.52	10.3	3.7	6.2	1.0	-7	4.5	-0.88
2007	CLE	MLB	23	19	8	0	32	32	215	199	61	137	16	64.8%	.282	17	1.21	3.06	3.90	8.2	2.4	5.1	0.7	15	65.9	6.80
2008	CLE	MLB	24	8	7	0	22	22	120^2	126	70	58	7	64.6%	.298	2	1.62	5.44	5.05	9.1	4.8	3.8	0.5	-9	-1.1	1.35
2009	CLE	MLB	25	7	8	0	33	20	128	139	59	77	10	56.0%	.310	6	1.54	4.68	4.73	9.6	3.6	4.9	0.7	0	10.4	1.93

Breakout: 11%   Improve: 37%   Collapse: 25%   Attrition: 18%   Comparables: Scott Erickson, Zach Day, Kevin Brown, Andy Hassler

Carmona was in the midst of a bizarre season when he went on the DL with a hip problem in late May. He had a 3.67 RA with just one homer allowed in 58 innings, but his K/BB ratio was a contorted 23/38. It figured that his command was being thrown off by the injury, but he was even worse after returning. Carmona relies on his ability to discover the right rhythm for his symphony of pounding sinker after sinker into the zone's lower depths, and he never found that repeatable groove. His heavy, bat-biting heater remains deadly, as he led all AL starters with a 2.96 G/F ratio while lowering his home-run rate, and the Indians are confident that with good health and more off-season work (he pitched in his native Dominican Republic's winter league), he will return to form.

Kelvin De La Cruz

Bats: L   Throws: L   Height: 6' 5"   Weight: 187   Born: January 8, 1988   Age: 21

YEAR	TEAM	LVL	AGE	W	L	SV	G	GS	IP	H	BB	SO	HR	GB%	BABIP	STUFF	WHIP	ERA	DERA	EqH9	EqBB9	EqSO9	EqHR9	DEF	VORP	SN/WX
2007	MHV	A-	19	2	4	0	12	12	54^1	41	34	53	5	46.8%	.273	-17	1.38	3.98	8.10	11.8	8.1	4.6	3.1	4	-12.0	—
2007	IDN	Rk	19	3	0	0	3	3	18	7	2	20	1	58.5%	.154	16	0.50	0.50	2.20	6.1	2.2	4.4	2.2	0	6.2	—
2008	LKC	A	20	8	4	0	18	18	95^2	71	34	96	2	56.1%	.282	26	1.10	1.69	3.47	9.8	4.8	4.8	0.7	-3	19.6	—
2008	KIN	A+	20	3	2	0	8	8	29^1	35	25	36	1	47.1%	.410	22	2.05	6.45	6.91	13.5	8.2	7.2	0.7	-5	-4.0	—
2009	CLE	MLB	21	4	9	0	27	19	100^2	127	76	68	15	47.0%	.340	-2	2.01	7.10	6.97	11.1	6.0	5.6	1.3	0	-17.2	-1.15

Breakout: 3%   Improve: 27%   Collapse: 34%   Attrition: 12%   Comparables: Chi-Hung Cheng, Wilfredo Rodriguez, Brian Givens, Franklin Morales

De La Cruz stands out among the many young southpaw starters in the Cleveland system because of his velocity: the lanky lefty throws a low-90s fastball and has surprisingly polished secondary stuff for his age (solid curveball and plus change), giving him more upside than any other pitcher in the organization. The main task for De La Cruz is learning how to repeat his delivery to consistently fire strikes. He'll begin the year at High-A Kinston.

John Gaub

Bats: R   Throws: L   Height: 6' 2"   Weight: 200   Born: April 28, 1985   Age: 24

YEAR	TEAM	LVL	AGE	W	L	SV	G	GS	IP	H	BB	SO	HR	GB%	BABIP	STUFF	WHIP	ERA	DERA	EqH9	EqBB9	EqSO9	EqHR9	DEF	VORP	SN/WX
2007	IDN	Rk	22	0	0	0	4	0	4	4	4	4	0	44.4%	.444	2	2.00	2.25	3.86	19.3	19.3	3.9	0.0	0	0.4	—
2008	LKC	A	23	1	1	2	34	0	64	44	32	100	3	37.9%	.323	8	1.19	3.38	5.83	10.7	6.7	8.3	1.2	-5	-1.4	—
2009	CHN	MLB	24	3	4	0	32	4	56^1	61	43	55	9	40.8%	.329	2	1.85	6.18	6.33	9.6	6.0	7.5	1.3	1	-3.5	-0.20

Breakout: 27%   Improve: 62%   Collapse: 14%   Attrition: 7%   Comparables: Josh Newman, Bill Mendek, Dave Richards, Tyler Johnson

There aren't many 23-year-old prospects in Low-A, but former University of Minnesota closer Gaub makes the cut: you can't ignore 14 strikeouts and six hits per nine in Wiffle ball, let alone the minors, especially from a southpaw. Shoulder surgery in college knocked him down to the 21st round of the 2006 draft, but his low-90s moving fastball and plus slider could lead to a major league career in the pen. Dealt to the Cubs in the DeRosa deal, his opportunities have improved by joining a team without a well-established lefty reliever.

David Huff

Bats: L   Throws: L   Height: 6' 2"   Weight: 190   Born: August 22, 1984   Age: 24

YEAR	TEAM	LVL	AGE	W	L	SV	G	GS	IP	H	BB	SO	HR	GB%	BABIP	STUFF	WHIP	ERA	DERA	EqH9	EqBB9	EqSO9	EqHR9	DEF	VORP	SN/WX
2007	KIN	A+	22	4	2	0	11	11	59^2	57	15	46	4	43.3%	.299	-12	1.21	2.71	5.40	11.6	3.2	3.5	1.5	-3	1.2	—
2008	AKR	AA	23	5	1	0	11	10	65^2	44	14	62	5	51.1%	.235	19	0.88	1.92	4.24	6.6	2.0	6.1	1.0	10	9.6	—
2008	BUF	AAA	23	6	4	0	16	16	80^2	68	15	81	8	53.1%	.280	10	1.03	3.01	3.86	8.5	1.9	6.1	1.3	-3	14.9	—
2009	CLE	MLB	24	5	6	0	25	15	96	103	30	69	11	45.0%	.300	15	1.38	4.46	4.42	9.4	2.5	5.9	1.0	0	11.1	1.79

Breakout: 13%   Improve: 32%   Collapse: 29%   Attrition: 17%   Comparables: Chuck Stobbs, George Stone, Ken Holtzman, Jim O'Toole

After seeing limited action in 2007 due to a sore elbow, Huff blew away hitters in his first crack at the high minors. He led all of Cleveland's qualifying bush leaguers with a 2.52 ERA and finished with more strikeouts than walks plus hits allowed on the season, one of only 11 qualifying minor league starters to do so. Huff throws a high-80s sinking fastball that he controls extremely well, a nasty changeup that serves as his strikeout pitch, and both a curve and a slider. Viewed as polished when selected with the 39th overall pick in 2006 out of UCLA, Huff is ready for the majors, so don't be surprised if he wins the fifth starter's job this spring.

Zach Jackson

Bats: L   Throws: L   Height: 6' 5"   Weight: 220   Born: May 13, 1983   Age: 26

YEAR	TEAM	LVL	AGE	W	L	SV	G	GS	IP	H	BB	SO	HR	GB%	BABIP	STUFF	WHIP	ERA	DERA	EqH9	EqBB9	EqSO9	EqHR9	DEF	VORP	SN/WX
2006	NAS	AAA	23	4	6	0	18	18	107²	106	44	58	11	51.4%	.276	-25	1.40	4.11	7.19	10.7	4.1	3.2	1.4	16	-17.3	—
2006	MIL	MLB	23	2	2	0	8	7	38¹	48	14	22	6	47.1%	.323	-3	1.62	5.40	4.62	10.6	2.8	4.6	1.2	-4	-0.1	-0.07
2007	NAS	AAA	24	11	10	0	29	28	169²	184	64	123	13	49.7%	.337	-5	1.46	4.45	5.92	11.3	3.7	4.8	1.0	2	-5.6	—
2008	NAS	AAA	25	1	5	0	22	6	57¹	81	18	34	10	55.2%	.351	-43	1.73	7.85	8.89	13.3	2.9	3.2	1.7	-5	-20.7	—
2008	BUF	AAA	25	3	1	0	8	4	26²	25	5	20	3	51.8%	.275	-11	1.12	4.04	5.81	8.9	2.1	4.1	1.4	2	-0.6	—
2008	CLE	MLB	25	2	3	0	9	9	54²	64	14	30	7	52.9%	.313	-1	1.43	5.59	4.67	10.2	2.2	4.3	1.2	-6	0.0	0.28
2009	CLE	MLB	26	6	9	0	43	19	122¹	154	50	67	17	47.0%	.320	-3	1.67	5.86	5.77	11.1	3.3	4.5	1.2	0	-4.6	0.21

Breakout: 27%   Improve: 65%   Collapse: 12%   Attrition: 20%   Comparables: Terry Mulholland, Heath Murray, Jeff Mutis, John Rheinecker

A throw-in to the Sabathia haul, Jackson is another lefty who works in the high 80s. His poor performances at Triple-A the last several years peg him as strictly back-end rotation filler. Jackson held his own, however, after joining Cleveland's rotation late in the season and could thus be peddling his five-pitch mix as the long man out of the Indians' pen rather than in the Columbus rotation.

Masahide Kobayashi

Bats: R   Throws: R   Height: 6' 0"   Weight: 195   Born: May 24, 1974   Age: 35

YEAR	TEAM	LVL	AGE	W	L	SV	G	GS	IP	H	BB	SO	HR	GB%	BABIP	STUFF	WHIP	ERA	DERA	EqH9	EqBB9	EqSO9	EqHR9	DEF	VORP	SN/WX
2006	CHB	JP	32	6	2	34	53	0	53²	49	8	48	4	—	.296	-4	1.06	2.68	4.35	9.4	1.8	6.0	1.1	0	6.9	—
2007	CHB	JP	33	2	7	27	49	0	47¹	53	12	35	4	—	.318	-22	1.37	3.62	6.50	10.4	3.0	4.7	1.2	0	-4.6	—
2008	CLE	MLB	34	4	5	6	57	0	55²	65	14	35	8	50.5%	.310	-15	1.42	4.52	4.98	10.0	2.1	4.8	1.3	1	5.9	-1.25
2009	CLE	MLB	35	2	2	2	38	0	43²	51	13	26	5	46.0%	.310	-5	1.47	4.95	4.91	10.3	2.4	4.8	1.1	0	2.5	0.21

Breakout: 21%   Improve: 44%   Collapse: 33%   Attrition: 35%   Comparables: Kirk McCaskill, Eddie Fisher, Matt Herges, Mark Williamson

A dominant closer for Bobby Valentine's Chiba Lotte Marines, Kobayashi was one of three pitchers (along with Kazuhiro Sasaki and Shingo Takatsu) to record 200 saves in the history of Japanese baseball. He once threw in the high-90s, but didn't pack that brand of heat on his trip across the Pacific. Although he was brought in to provide insurance for the probable scenario in which Borowski exploded, the Indians discovered that their pricey policy was unable to pay out when disaster hit. Kobayashi never pitched well enough to take over as stopper, faded badly down the stretch, and threw only three innings in September to stay fresh for 2009. Cleveland owes him $3 million, so he's being counted on to perform better.

Aaron Laffey

Bats: L   Throws: L   Height: 6' 0"   Weight: 170   Born: April 15, 1985   Age: 24

YEAR	TEAM	LVL	AGE	W	L	SV	G	GS	IP	H	BB	SO	HR	GB%	BABIP	STUFF	WHIP	ERA	DERA	EqH9	EqBB9	EqSO9	EqHR9	DEF	VORP	SN/WX
2006	KIN	A+	21	4	1	1	10	4	41²	38	6	24	0	70.8%	.284	-2	1.07	2.18	6.05	10.2	1.9	2.3	0.5	0	-1.9	—
2006	AKR	AA	21	8	3	0	19	19	112²	121	33	61	9	61.6%	.320	-17	1.37	3.53	6.04	12.5	3.6	2.6	1.5	1	-4.8	—
2007	AKR	AA	22	4	1	0	6	6	35	29	7	24	2	61.7%	.262	5	1.03	2.31	5.18	8.7	2.2	3.8	1.1	2	1.5	—
2007	BUF	AAA	22	9	3	0	16	15	96¹	89	23	75	5	63.6%	.293	14	1.16	3.08	5.14	9.4	2.5	4.6	0.8	8	4.7	—
2007	CLE	MLB	22	4	2	0	9	9	49¹	54	12	25	2	64.5%	.323	13	1.34	4.56	4.60	10.0	2.1	4.0	0.4	0	7.0	0.81
2008	BUF	AAA	23	6	2	0	11	11	61²	72	18	47	2	54.7%	.354	2	1.46	4.38	5.71	11.6	2.9	4.5	0.5	1	-0.7	—
2008	CLE	MLB	23	5	7	0	16	16	93²	103	31	43	10	52.5%	.296	-3	1.43	4.23	4.81	9.6	2.7	3.6	1.0	0	9.0	1.86
2009	CLE	MLB	24	8	11	0	30	30	160¹	199	59	85	18	52.0%	.330	7	1.60	5.33	5.30	10.9	2.9	4.4	1.0	1	2.4	1.50

Breakout: 11%   Improve: 41%   Collapse: 28%   Attrition: 20%   Comparables: Claude Osteen, Horacio Ramirez, Jimmy Anderson, Tom Glavine

A soft-tossing sinkerballer, Laffey stepped into the rotation in late April to replace the injured Jake Westbrook and was highly effective for two months, firing nine quality starts in his first 11 tries. He sputtered after that and, on giving up eight runs in back-to-back late-July outings, was shipped to the east side of the lake for some adjustments. Laffey was slated to come back up in September, but instead got shut down with an inflamed left elbow. There was no lasting damage, so he'll be ready to compete for a starting job this spring.

Cliff Lee

Bats: L		Throws: L		Height: 6' 3"		Weight: 190		Born: August 30, 1978		Age: 30														

YEAR	TEAM	LVL	AGE	W	L	SV	G	GS	IP	H	BB	SO	HR	GB%	BABIP	STUFF	WHIP	ERA	DERA	EqH9	EqBB9	EqSO9	EqHR9	DEF	VORP	SN/WX
2006	CLE	MLB	27	14	11	0	33	33	200²	224	58	129	29	33.9%	.300	0	1.41	4.39	4.60	9.2	2.5	4.9	1.2	-9	21.5	2.97
2007	CLE	MLB	28	5	8	0	20	16	97¹	112	36	66	17	37.4%	.304	-16	1.52	6.29	5.84	9.9	3.0	5.2	1.6	-7	-7.5	0.18
2008	CLE	MLB	29	22	3	0	31	31	223¹	214	34	170	12	46.4%	.304	32	1.11	2.54	2.74	8.5	1.3	6.1	0.5	-2	76.5	7.72
2009	CLE	MLB	30	12	10	0	30	30	192	201	52	135	24	42.0%	.300	18	1.32	4.21	4.14	9.2	2.2	5.8	1.1	1	28.0	4.50

Breakout: 10%   Improve: 46%   Collapse: 21%   Attrition: 10%   Comparables: Gary Peters, Terry Mulholland, Denny Neagle, John Smiley

With regard to pure shock value of a performance, Lee's season ranks in the top percentile all-time, as he became the first pitcher in baseball history to post a sub-3.00 ERA in 200 innings a year after having a 6.00-plus mark in over 50. He allowed a total of five runs and four walks in his first seven starts of the year, in the process becoming the only pitcher since the dawn of game-log data in 1956 to throw three straight games with at least eight innings, three or fewer hits, no more than one walk, and at least eight strikeouts. The dream was expected to end at any moment, but it never did: Lee maintained his superb control and kept hitters in the ballpark, while the Indians kept scoring runs to support their unlikely ace, so that by year's end, he had posted the fifth-best winning percentage in American League history. Lee's tremendous season can't be deemed a BABIP-fueled fluke, as his .302 mark was almost exactly league average. The veteran's success stemmed from a league-low walk rate as well as a rise in groundball tendency. Always a fastball pitcher who put his outfielders to work, Lee's G/F ratio rose from 0.76 entering 2008 to 1.38, his homer rate fell from 1.3 to a league-leading 0.5, and he induced 27 double-play grounders. The Cy Young was well deserved, and while it will most likely end up being the only one on his career mantle, Lee should settle down as one of the better AL starters.

Jensen Lewis

Bats: R		Throws: R		Height: 6' 3"		Weight: 195		Born: May 16, 1984		Age: 25														

YEAR	TEAM	LVL	AGE	W	L	SV	G	GS	IP	H	BB	SO	HR	GB%	BABIP	STUFF	WHIP	ERA	DERA	EqH9	EqBB9	EqSO9	EqHR9	DEF	VORP	SN/WX
2006	KIN	A+	22	7	6	0	21	20	108¹	110	29	94	11	40.5%	.313	-31	1.29	4.00	7.37	13.1	3.4	4.5	2.3	-7	-18.5	—
2006	AKR	AA	22	1	2	0	7	7	39²	41	12	44	4	41.4%	.356	8	1.35	3.90	4.98	13.1	3.7	6.3	1.8	-8	2.4	—
2007	AKR	AA	23	2	0	1	24	0	39	27	13	49	2	39.6%	.287	11	1.03	1.85	3.79	8.1	3.5	7.8	1.0	0	7.2	—
2007	BUF	AAA	23	1	0	1	10	0	13	5	4	12	1	31.3%	.133	-2	0.69	1.38	5.54	3.5	2.8	5.5	1.4	5	0.1	—
2007	CLE	MLB	23	1	1	0	26	0	29¹	26	10	34	1	36.3%	.329	27	1.23	2.15	1.52	7.9	2.7	8.8	0.3	-3	11.6	0.62
2008	BUF	AAA	24	1	2	1	11	0	20	16	8	18	2	41.7%	.264	-15	1.20	3.60	6.20	7.5	3.5	4.9	1.3	1	-1.4	—
2008	CLE	MLB	24	0	4	13	51	0	66	68	27	52	8	37.0%	.306	-4	1.44	3.82	3.43	9.0	3.3	6.2	1.1	-4	13.5	1.59
2009	CLE	MLB	25	3	3	6	44	0	52	51	20	44	7	38.0%	.290	10	1.37	4.25	4.16	8.6	3.1	6.9	1.1	0	9.0	0.75

Breakout: 32%   Improve: 57%   Collapse: 26%   Attrition: 32%   Comparables: Steve Kealey, Ray Burris, Rich Yett, Brian Fisher

Fed up with the repeated failures of his other options—first Borowski, then Betancourt, then Kobayashi—Eric Wedge turned to Lewis in early August. Lewis responded by reeling off 13 saves in 13 opportunities to close the season. With a fastball in the high 80s and a strong changeup as his out pitch, Lewis lacks classic closer stuff, but he could be an effective setup option for new closer Kerry Wood.

Scott Lewis

Bats: S		Throws: L		Height: 6' 0"		Weight: 185		Born: September 26, 1983		Age: 25														

YEAR	TEAM	LVL	AGE	W	L	SV	G	GS	IP	H	BB	SO	HR	GB%	BABIP	STUFF	WHIP	ERA	DERA	EqH9	EqBB9	EqSO9	EqHR9	DEF	VORP	SN/WX
2006	KIN	A+	22	3	3	0	27	26	115¹	84	28	123	3	43.4%	.277	19	0.97	1.49	4.06	9.3	3.0	5.9	0.8	5	17.5	—
2007	AKR	AA	23	7	9	0	27	25	134²	135	34	121	13	37.2%	.320	-12	1.25	3.67	5.13	11.4	2.8	5.4	1.6	-1	6.3	—
2008	AKR	AA	24	6	2	0	13	13	73¹	62	9	61	2	39.5%	.279	24	0.97	2.33	3.04	8.2	1.1	5.3	0.4	-2	20.2	—
2008	BUF	AAA	24	2	2	0	4	4	24	19	4	21	2	31.9%	.270	8	0.96	2.63	5.09	7.8	1.6	5.1	1.2	3	1.3	—
2008	CLE	MLB	24	4	0	0	4	4	24	20	6	15	4	38.2%	.225	5	1.08	2.63	4.07	7.0	1.8	4.8	1.5	2	6.7	0.82
2009	CLE	MLB	25	8	9	1	40	24	139²	152	38	95	20	38.0%	.300	10	1.36	4.64	4.53	9.6	2.2	5.6	1.3	0	14.5	2.38

Breakout: 3%   Improve: 11%   Collapse: 65%   Attrition: 19%   Comparables: Ron Bryant, Jarrod Washburn, Scott McGregor, Dave McNally

Tommy John surgery followed by tendonitis caused Lewis to throw just 18⅔ innings combined in 2004-05, his first two minor league seasons, but he has been outstanding at every level since then. A preternatural ability to command his secondary offerings, primarily an excellent Uncle Charlie and plus changeup, trumps Lewis's mediocre velocity. Last year, he walked just 1.4 per nine across three levels and opened his major league career with 15 consecutive scoreless innings. He'll be in the mix for a starting job in camp.

Jonathan Meloan

Bats: R   Throws: R   Height: 6' 3"   Weight: 230   Born: July 11, 1984   Age: 24

YEAR	TEAM	LVL	AGE	W	L	SV	G	GS	IP	H	BB	SO	HR	GB%	BABIP	STUFF	WHIP	ERA	DERA	EqH9	EqBB9	EqSO9	EqHR9	DEF	VORP	SN/WX
2006	CGA	A	21	1	1	1	12	0	23	9	7	41	2	61.1%	.212	20	0.70	1.57	5.31	6.2	4.0	8.9	2.2	3	0.7	—
2006	VRO	A+	21	1	0	0	4	3	18¹	15	4	27	2	67.9%	.346	16	1.05	2.49	3.94	10.7	2.8	7.9	2.2	-2	3.0	—
2006	JAX	AA	21	1	0	0	5	0	10¹	3	5	23	1	43.8%	.214	10	0.79	1.78	3.72	5.6	4.7	11.2	1.9	1	2.0	—
2007	JAX	AA	22	5	2	19	35	0	45¹	24	18	70	3	47.1%	.256	21	0.93	2.19	4.29	6.6	3.9	9.2	1.1	1	6.1	—
2007	LVG	AAA	22	2	0	1	14	0	21¹	12	9	21	2	46.4%	.189	10	0.99	1.69	4.43	4.0	3.6	6.0	0.8	5	2.9	—
2008	LVG	AAA	23	5	10	0	21	20	105	119	60	99	7	43.1%	.366	8	1.70	4.97	5.19	10.7	5.2	5.7	0.7	-12	4.6	—
2008	BUF	AAA	23	0	1	0	12	0	14²	12	9	12	1	50.0%	.289	-18	1.43	4.29	7.24	8.6	5.9	4.6	0.7	2	-2.5	—
2009	CLE	MLB	24	3	5	0	33	11	72²	80	46	53	9	43.0%	.310	0	1.74	5.91	5.82	9.7	5.0	6.0	1.1	0	-3.4	0.07

Breakout: 15%   Improve: 38%   Collapse: 23%   Attrition: 22%   Comparables: Ryan Vogelsong, Dennis Tankersley, Mike Loynd, Albie Lopez

The lesser part of the spoils from mugging Colletti in the Blake deal, Meloan is a live arm with big-time control problems. The Dodgers tried to make him a starter last year, which didn't go well at all, but Cleveland returned him to the relief role that better suits his stuff and approach. If a re-acclimation to the bullpen leads to the calming of his excitable command, Meloan and his big-league heat could prove to be an asset for the Indians later on this season.

Adam Miller

Bats: R   Throws: R   Height: 6' 4"   Weight: 200   Born: November 26, 1984   Age: 24

YEAR	TEAM	LVL	AGE	W	L	SV	G	GS	IP	H	BB	SO	HR	GB%	BABIP	STUFF	WHIP	ERA	DERA	EqH9	EqBB9	EqSO9	EqHR9	DEF	VORP	SN/WX
2006	AKR	AA	21	15	6	0	26	24	153²	129	43	157	9	55.6%	.301	25	1.12	2.76	4.82	10.0	3.3	5.6	1.1	-3	12.1	—
2007	BUF	AAA	22	5	4	0	19	11	65¹	68	21	68	4	53.6%	.346	10	1.36	4.82	6.42	10.9	3.2	6.4	0.9	-1	-5.6	—
2008	BUF	AAA	23	0	1	0	6	6	28²	26	12	20	0	54.4%	.292	-4	1.32	1.88	4.55	8.8	3.9	3.9	0.3	4	3.2	—
2009	CLE	MLB	24	4	6	0	21	13	81	91	36	54	9	51.0%	.320	8	1.57	5.22	5.21	9.9	3.6	5.5	0.9	0	2.3	0.74

Breakout: 25%   Improve: 48%   Collapse: 34%   Attrition: 29%   Comparables: Gary Parmenter, Tom Poholsky, Tommie Sisk, Kyle Money

Miller is the Tribe's answer to Rich Harden, possessing both the sublime stuff and the draining inability to showcase it. He was shut down in late May with what turned out to be a tear in the flexor tendon of his right middle finger. Surgery to reattach the tissue kept him out of game action for the rest of the year, marking a low point in the top prospect's injury-riddled career. Miller began throwing again in August and was sound enough to pitch in the Dominican winter league. Cleveland plans to use him as a reliever in 2009, both to keep him off the shelf and to prevent too large a jump in workload. A healthy Miller could crack the big-league bullpen.

Edward Mujica

Bats: R   Throws: R   Height: 6' 2"   Weight: 220   Born: May 10, 1984   Age: 25

YEAR	TEAM	LVL	AGE	W	L	SV	G	GS	IP	H	BB	SO	HR	GB%	BABIP	STUFF	WHIP	ERA	DERA	EqH9	EqBB9	EqSO9	EqHR9	DEF	VORP	SN/WX
2006	AKR	AA	22	1	0	8	12	0	19²	11	9	17	0	54.0%	.229	0	1.04	0.00	1.53	6.6	5.1	4.6	0.5	0	8.0	—
2006	BUF	AAA	22	3	1	5	22	0	32¹	31	5	29	1	37.9%	.333	8	1.12	2.52	4.60	10.7	1.8	5.5	0.6	2	3.3	—
2006	CLE	MLB	22	0	1	0	10	0	18¹	25	0	12	1	24.6%	.387	17	1.36	2.95	0.51	11.7	0.5	5.1	0.5	-5	6.4	-0.24
2007	BUF	AAA	23	2	1	14	34	0	37²	35	9	44	4	35.0%	.333	-1	1.17	5.01	6.49	10.4	2.6	7.5	1.6	0	-3.4	—
2007	CLE	MLB	23	0	0	0	10	0	13	19	2	7	3	29.4%	.340	-18	1.62	8.31	5.40	12.2	1.4	4.1	2.0	-4	-3.2	-0.01
2008	BUF	AAA	24	0	2	4	18	0	26	29	10	27	2	38.8%	.370	-11	1.50	4.15	5.40	11.2	3.6	6.1	1.1	0	0.6	—
2008	CLE	MLB	24	3	2	0	33	0	38²	46	10	27	5	30.8%	.339	-11	1.45	6.74	5.92	10.4	2.1	5.4	1.2	-2	-4.0	-1.36
2009	CLE	MLB	25	2	2	2	39	0	41	42	12	32	6	37.0%	.290	8	1.31	4.32	4.24	8.9	2.4	6.4	1.2	0	7.3	0.48

Breakout: 46%   Improve: 67%   Collapse: 21%   Attrition: 39%   Comparables: Matt Ginter, Steve Kealey, Ray Burris, Bubba Harris

Mujica contributed more to the Tribe's bullpen flame-out than did all others except Borowski, giving up four or more runs in an inning or less on four occasions. Wedge actually got desperate enough to try him in the closer role in early August—Mujica was handed a 7-4 lead against the Rays and promptly allowed the first three batters he faced to score. Although he was always vulnerable against lefties, last year his power fastball/splitter combo was thumped by righties as well, and he kept getting hammered in his native Venezuela after the season.

Rafael Perez

Bats: L   Throws: L   Height: 6' 3"   Weight: 185   Born: May 15, 1982   Age: 27

YEAR	TEAM	LVL	AGE	W	L	SV	G	GS	IP	H	BB	SO	HR	GB%	BABIP	STUFF	WHIP	ERA	DERA	EqH9	EqBB9	EqSO9	EqHR9	DEF	VORP	SN/WX
2006	AKR	AA	24	4	5	0	12	12	67¹	53	22	53	3	61.2%	.267	-8	1.12	2.82	6.42	8.9	3.6	4.1	0.9	9	-5.6	—
2006	BUF	AAA	24	0	3	0	13	0	27¹	20	8	33	0	71.0%	.303	11	1.03	2.66	5.19	8.3	3.1	7.6	0.3	1	1.2	—
2006	CLE	MLB	24	0	0	0	18	0	12¹	10	6	15	2	60.0%	.250	10	1.30	4.39	3.95	5.9	4.0	8.6	1.3	0	2.4	0.00
2007	BUF	AAA	25	3	3	0	8	7	46²	53	11	31	3	52.6%	.347	-10	1.37	3.66	6.59	11.9	2.6	4.0	1.1	1	-4.7	—
2007	CLE	MLB	25	1	2	1	44	0	60²	41	15	62	5	54.7%	.237	20	0.92	1.78	2.95	5.8	2.1	8.0	0.7	4	25.7	3.25
2008	CLE	MLB	26	4	4	2	73	0	76¹	67	23	86	8	58.4%	.307	18	1.18	3.54	3.50	8.0	2.5	9.0	1.0	-1	17.0	2.35
2009	CLE	MLB	27	4	3	5	65	0	64²	60	23	59	5	51.0%	.300	16	1.28	3.37	3.38	8.1	2.8	7.5	0.7	0	16.2	1.40

Breakout: 29%   Improve: 54%   Collapse: 20%   Attrition: 16%   Comparables: Sparky Lyle, Dave Smith, Bobby Ayala, Fred Scherman

Perez is perhaps the prototypical sinker/slider reliever, mixing equal doses of heaters and hard breakers. He pitched nearly as well as in his rookie campaign, but a return to league average in BABIP hurt his overall numbers. As a left hander who can get out batters on both sides of the plate and fire for multiple frames at a time, he's an extremely valuable commodity and the best bet for the Indians' top setup man in 2009.

Anthony Reyes

Bats: R   Throws: R   Height: 6' 2"   Weight: 230   Born: October 16, 1981   Age: 27

YEAR	TEAM	LVL	AGE	W	L	SV	G	GS	IP	H	BB	SO	HR	GB%	BABIP	STUFF	WHIP	ERA	DERA	EqH9	EqBB9	EqSO9	EqHR9	DEF	VORP	SN/WX
2006	MEM	AAA	24	6	1	0	13	13	84	70	11	82	9	42.0%	.270	9	0.96	2.57	4.32	8.3	1.3	6.1	1.3	5	11.6	—
2006	SLN	MLB	24	5	8	0	17	17	85¹	84	34	72	17	37.0%	.289	0	1.38	5.06	4.29	8.9	3.2	7.0	1.6	-4	9.4	1.87
2007	MEM	AAA	25	1	1	0	6	6	38²	27	11	33	4	46.1%	.245	9	0.98	2.79	4.25	6.8	2.8	5.8	1.2	3	5.4	—
2007	SLN	MLB	25	2	14	0	22	20	107¹	108	43	74	16	36.2%	.284	-4	1.41	6.04	6.21	8.6	3.1	5.7	1.2	4	-7.8	0.43
2008	MEM	AAA	26	2	3	0	11	11	52²	51	21	47	4	49.0%	.324	1	1.37	3.24	4.62	10.0	3.9	5.7	0.9	2	5.3	—
2008	SLN	MLB	26	2	1	1	10	0	14²	16	3	10	2	37.5%	.304	-2	1.30	4.90	3.77	9.4	1.9	5.7	1.3	-1	1.0	0.41
2008	CLE	MLB	26	2	1	0	6	6	34¹	31	12	15	2	46.5%	.261	1	1.25	1.84	3.21	7.8	2.9	3.5	0.5	5	15.2	1.71
2009	CLE	MLB	27	4	5	1	32	10	78	86	30	49	12	42.0%	.300	0	1.49	5.19	5.09	9.7	3.1	5.1	1.3	0	3.4	0.64

Breakout: 5%   Improve: 28%   Collapse: 42%   Attrition: 39%   Comparables: Bob Stoddard, Adam Bernero, Jason Middlebrook, Mike Williams

Reyes simply did not get along with Dave Duncan and Tony La Russa. The USC-educated righty views himself as a high-fastball power pitcher, while Duncan insisted he work down in the zone with two-seamers. The philosophical divide led the Cards to jerk him up and down from Triple-A and back and forth between the rotation and bullpen before they finally shipped him to Cleveland for two tickets to the Rock and Roll Hall of Fame (and minor league reliever Luis Perdomo). Reyes came to the Indians with a bounce in his step and a twinkle in his eye—or at least pitched like he did, allowing no more than two runs in any of his six starts before a sore elbow shut him down in September. The MRI scan was clean, and Reyes is set to begin a successful run as the Tribe's third or fourth starter.

Hector Rondon

Bats: R   Throws: R   Height: 6' 3"   Weight: 165   Born: February 26, 1988   Age: 21

YEAR	TEAM	LVL	AGE	W	L	SV	G	GS	IP	H	BB	SO	HR	GB%	BABIP	STUFF	WHIP	ERA	DERA	EqH9	EqBB9	EqSO9	EqHR9	DEF	VORP	SN/WX
2007	LKC	A	19	7	10	0	27	27	136	143	27	113	13	43.4%	.320	-8	1.25	4.37	8.02	13.2	2.9	3.6	2.0	-1	-32.0	—
2008	KIN	A+	20	11	6	0	27	27	145	130	42	145	12	41.7%	.304	22	1.19	3.60	5.17	9.9	3.0	5.8	1.5	0	6.4	—
2009	CLE	MLB	21	6	10	0	24	24	132²	162	52	95	23	40.0%	.320	14	1.61	6.08	5.90	10.7	3.1	5.9	1.5	0	-7.1	0.29

Breakout: 9%   Improve: 51%   Collapse: 18%   Attrition: 10%   Comparables: Hector Fajardo, Tyler Clippard, Julio Valera, Jose Lima

One of the nice things about signing teenagers is that they're usually still physically developing, and sometimes that leads to a jump in velocity. Rondon pumped his fastball into the mid-90s, which helped result in a highly impressive season and a midsummer showcase in the Futures Game at Yankee Stadium, where he threw a clean inning for the victorious World team. Besides Miller, Rondon is the team's best right-handed pitching prospect, but he needs to work on improving his slider at a season-opening assignment to Double-A.

Rich Rundles

Bats: L   Throws: L   Height: 6' 5"   Weight: 180   Born: June 3, 1981   Age: 28

YEAR	TEAM	LVL	AGE	W	L	SV	G	GS	IP	H	BB	SO	HR	GB%	BABIP	STUFF	WHIP	ERA	DERA	EqH9	EqBB9	EqSO9	EqHR9	DEF	VORP	SN/WX
2006	SLU	A+	25	1	2	0	3	3	19²	27	6	9	2	61.6%	.352	-40	1.72	1.88	4.96	17.6	4.4	1.7	2.2	-2	1.2	—
2006	BIN	AA	25	1	3	0	12	7	43²	53	23	23	4	48.1%	.333	-40	1.76	4.58	8.77	13.8	6.0	2.3	1.6	-3	-13.7	—
2006	SFD	AA	25	5	6	0	15	14	86¹	100	28	47	9	55.3%	.318	-31	1.49	4.60	6.69	12.3	3.4	2.7	1.5	-3	-9.6	—
2007	AKR	AA	26	3	0	2	23	2	34¹	27	10	29	0	54.5%	.299	-5	1.08	1.84	4.50	8.4	3.1	4.8	0.3	2	3.9	—
2007	BUF	AAA	26	2	4	0	17	0	26²	28	16	19	1	63.7%	.307	-19	1.65	2.70	6.33	10.0	5.3	3.7	0.7	0	-2.2	—
2008	BUF	AAA	27	5	4	4	55	0	52²	40	24	60	3	50.0%	.280	-1	1.21	2.90	4.80	7.8	4.4	6.9	0.7	6	4.5	—
2008	CLE	MLB	27	0	0	0	8	0	5	5	3	6	0	53.8%	.385	5	1.60	1.80	0.00	9.6	5.8	9.6	0.0	-1	2.2	0.13
2009	CLE	MLB	28	2	3	0	24	4	44	51	25	33	5	49.0%	.330	1	1.73	5.44	5.37	10.3	4.5	6.1	0.9	0	0.3	0.15

Breakout: 22%   Improve: 53%   Collapse: 18%   Attrition: 20%   Comparables: Ben Van Ryn, Matt Miller, Matt Smith, Mike Muñoz

Drafted by the Red Sox in 1999, Rundles bounced to the Expos, Mets, and Cardinals before making it up with Cleveland in his 10th season. Surprisingly, none of his other clubs did more than dabble with Rundles as a reliever; the Indians decided to move him to the bullpen full-time, which will ensure his long-term financial security. Rundles only rolls his heater up there in the mid-80s, but fends hitters off with a strong slider and curve. His three-quarters delivery has helped him hold lefties to a 526 OPS since joining the Tribe, and he could serve as the LOOGY that Cleveland lacked last year.

Tony Sipp

Bats: L   Throws: L   Height: 6' 0"   Weight: 190   Born: July 12, 1983   Age: 25

YEAR	TEAM	LVL	AGE	W	L	SV	G	GS	IP	H	BB	SO	HR	GB%	BABIP	STUFF	WHIP	ERA	DERA	EqH9	EqBB9	EqSO9	EqHR9	DEF	VORP	SN/WX
2006	AKR	AA	22	4	2	3	29	4	60²	44	21	80	2	38.2%	.309	13	1.08	3.14	5.04	8.9	3.9	7.5	0.7	-1	3.4	—
2008	KIN	A+	24	0	0	0	5	0	8	4	3	10	0	44.4%	.235	8	0.88	1.13	3.52	5.9	3.5	7.0	0.0	1	1.8	—
2008	AKR	AA	24	0	3	1	16	0	21²	19	7	32	4	42.9%	.351	10	1.20	3.73	4.43	9.7	3.1	10.2	2.2	-2	2.6	—
2009	CLE	MLB	25	3	3	1	27	5	57¹	56	24	56	7	41.0%	.300	18	1.39	4.53	4.45	8.6	3.3	8.0	1.1	0	7.9	0.83

Breakout: 31%   Improve: 58%   Collapse: 19%   Attrition: 13%   Comparables: Dick Stigman, Mike Paul, Rod Scurry, Doug Bochtler

Sipp has not yet pitched above Double-A, but already has a fascinating profile. Despite big talent, he was not selected until the 45th round of the 2004 draft after his first season at Clemson, for he put up uneven numbers and most teams believed he wouldn't sign. The Indians gambled, and after a dominant showing in the Cape Cod League threw $130,000 his way—the equivalent of sixth-rounder money—to coax him from college. Sipp posted startling K totals in his first three pro seasons, thanks to a low-90s heater and devastating slider, but then was sidelined by elbow trouble and Tommy John surgery. He was throwing 94 upon returning last June and could reach the majors this year to form a nasty left-handed tag team with Perez.

Jeremy Sowers

Bats: L   Throws: L   Height: 6' 1"   Weight: 180   Born: May 17, 1983   Age: 26

YEAR	TEAM	LVL	AGE	W	L	SV	G	GS	IP	H	BB	SO	HR	GB%	BABIP	STUFF	WHIP	ERA	DERA	EqH9	EqBB9	EqSO9	EqHR9	DEF	VORP	SN/WX
2006	BUF	AAA	23	9	1	0	15	15	97²	78	29	54	1	53.5%	.263	7	1.10	1.39	4.69	8.6	3.3	3.2	0.3	17	8.9	—
2006	CLE	MLB	23	7	4	0	14	14	88¹	85	20	35	10	49.2%	.257	-2	1.19	3.57	4.84	7.9	2.0	3.1	0.9	11	23.6	2.79
2007	BUF	AAA	24	4	5	0	15	15	96²	112	24	61	6	49.0%	.329	-9	1.41	4.10	6.49	11.3	2.5	3.4	1.0	-1	-9.3	—
2007	CLE	MLB	24	1	6	0	13	13	67¹	84	21	24	10	40.9%	.310	-23	1.56	6.42	6.08	10.8	2.6	2.7	1.4	-1	-3.6	0.37
2008	BUF	AAA	25	4	3	0	10	10	60²	56	17	43	4	46.8%	.295	0	1.20	2.08	4.15	9.3	2.9	4.2	1.0	7	9.1	—
2008	CLE	MLB	25	4	9	0	22	22	121	141	39	64	18	44.0%	.306	-16	1.49	5.58	6.58	10.1	2.6	4.1	1.3	8	-4.9	0.56
2009	CLE	MLB	26	6	7	0	29	18	109¹	127	37	56	16	45.0%	.300	1	1.50	5.16	5.08	10.3	2.7	4.2	1.2	0	4.3	1.19

Breakout: 30%   Improve: 55%   Collapse: 24%   Attrition: 24%   Comparables: Brian Anderson, Jerry Augustine, Allan Anderson, Neal Heaton

The Indians were unhappy with the arm strength that Sowers displayed during the 2007 season, as his fastball dropped below 86 mph on average after sitting in the 88-89 range as a rookie. With the help of a preseason throwing program, he turned the heat up to an average of 90, but Sowers' fastball proved to be unsafe at any speed, as it was again hit hard and long. While his velocity returned, Sowers' command of the heater, once a strong point for the former Vanderbilt star, did not follow suit. Without overpowering ability, he badly needs precise location and a better approach to changing speeds to survive. With the luster of his status as the sixth overall selection in 2004 now dulled considerably, Sowers will have to fight with the rest of the club's young southpaws for the fifth rotation spot.

Jeff Stevens

Bats: R   Throws: R   Height: 6' 1"   Weight: 220   Born: September 5, 1983   Age: 25

YEAR	TEAM	LVL	AGE	W	L	SV	G	GS	IP	H	BB	SO	HR	GB%	BABIP	STUFF	WHIP	ERA	DERA	EqH9	EqBB9	EqSO9	EqHR9	DEF	VORP	SN/WX
2006	DYT	A	22	2	4	0	14	6	42²	42	16	43	6	46.2%	.321	-38	1.37	4.48	7.64	15.8	6.0	4.9	4.4	-3	-7.5	—
2006	LKC	A	22	7	3	0	16	15	73¹	65	23	60	4	46.9%	.282	-30	1.20	4.43	9.51	11.7	4.3	3.0	1.7	6	-28.4	—
2007	KIN	A+	23	3	2	0	15	0	35	18	9	37	2	51.2%	.198	-7	0.77	2.31	6.40	6.4	3.1	5.6	1.4	2	-2.9	—
2007	AKR	AA	23	3	1	2	34	0	48¹	40	16	65	4	41.2%	.320	6	1.16	3.17	4.40	9.6	3.4	8.2	1.4	0	6.0	—
2008	AKR	AA	24	5	1	1	17	0	28²	19	11	37	2	47.7%	.274	15	1.05	2.51	4.00	7.3	3.3	9.0	1.0	2	4.8	—
2008	BUF	AAA	24	0	3	5	19	0	29²	19	16	44	3	32.3%	.276	13	1.18	3.94	5.20	7.2	5.2	9.4	1.3	1	1.2	—
2009	CHN	MLB	25	3	3	1	24	5	54	52	28	54	8	41.0%	.299	12	1.48	4.90	5.08	8.5	4.1	7.6	1.3	1	4.7	0.60

Breakout: 32%   Improve: 59%   Collapse: 12%   Attrition: 14%   Comparables: Bo Donaldson, Carlos Guevara, Craig Dingman, Joe Boever

As the player Cleveland got from Cincinnati for Brandon Phillips, Stevens relies on an excellent fastball that sits in the 92-93 range, though it can get up to 95. He's ready for a big-league trial despite getting tagged with two of the three losses in the Olympics, but it will be with the Cubs after he was packaged to Wrigleyville in the DeRosa deal.

Josh Tomlin

Bats: R   Throws: R   Height: 6' 1"   Weight: 175   Born: October 19, 1984   Age: 24

YEAR	TEAM	LVL	AGE	W	L	SV	G	GS	IP	H	BB	SO	HR	GB%	BABIP	STUFF	WHIP	ERA	DERA	EqH9	EqBB9	EqSO9	EqHR9	DEF	VORP	SN/WX
2006	MHV	A-	21	8	2	0	15	15	77¹	56	15	69	5	33.8%	.242	-30	0.92	2.10	7.95	11.2	3.6	3.4	3.0	13	-17.2	—
2007	LKC	A	22	10	3	0	26	15	103²	103	19	89	10	44.2%	.305	-29	1.18	3.30	5.67	12.3	2.7	3.7	2.1	-4	-0.7	—
2007	KIN	A+	22	1	1	0	6	5	27²	24	12	20	0	49.4%	.286	-10	1.30	3.57	6.39	9.9	5.0	3.2	0.4	-2	-2.2	—
2008	KIN	A+	23	9	5	3	40	9	102²	82	16	109	10	43.3%	.287	-8	0.95	2.98	5.69	9.2	1.8	6.5	1.7	10	-0.9	—
2009	CLE	MLB	24	4	6	0	27	11	79	96	27	52	15	41.0%	.320	3	1.56	5.83	5.63	10.7	2.7	5.4	1.6	0	-1.9	0.22

Breakout: 10%   Improve: 34%   Collapse: 26%   Attrition: 14%   Comparables: Tim Reynolds, Keith Troutman, Dan Rambo, Julian Heredia

Tomlin had an impressive season, but he was old for High-A, and without overwhelming stuff (he possesses a high-80s sinking fastball, slider, and change), he still has much to prove in the system's upper rungs. After he pitched mostly from the bullpen, the Tribe sent him to the Arizona Fall League as a starter, where he posted an excellent 28-3 strikeout-to-walk ratio while otherwise taking the obligatory thin-air Arizona pounding. Cleveland will keep him in that role when he opens 2009 at Double-A.

Jake Westbrook

Bats: R   Throws: R   Height: 6' 3"   Weight: 200   Born: September 29, 1977   Age: 31

YEAR	TEAM	LVL	AGE	W	L	SV	G	GS	IP	H	BB	SO	HR	GB%	BABIP	STUFF	WHIP	ERA	DERA	EqH9	EqBB9	EqSO9	EqHR9	DEF	VORP	SN/WX
2006	CLE	MLB	28	15	10	0	32	32	211¹	247	55	109	15	62.4%	.326	8	1.43	4.17	4.16	10.1	2.3	4.1	0.6	-6	36.9	5.04
2007	CLE	MLB	29	6	9	0	25	25	152	159	55	93	13	55.7%	.310	5	1.41	4.32	4.98	9.4	3.1	4.9	0.8	9	24.2	3.23
2008	CLE	MLB	30	1	2	0	5	5	34²	33	7	19	5	58.0%	.267	2	1.15	3.11	4.28	8.3	1.6	4.3	1.3	3	9.4	0.92
2009	CLE	MLB	31	5	5	0	21	14	85	99	30	48	8	54.0%	.310	4	1.51	4.84	4.86	10.2	2.8	4.6	0.9	0	6.4	1.14

Breakout: 9%   Improve: 34%   Collapse: 38%   Attrition: 29%   Comparables: Dennis Lamp, Albie Lopez, Bill Bonham, Bennie Daniels

Westbrook and Victor Martinez formed a snake-bit battery in 2008. After a strong beginning, the sinkerballer went down for a month with a strained ribcage muscle, then lasted just one start in his return before experiencing elbow soreness. That classic kiss of death precipitated the need for a Tommy John reconstruction in June; recovery will knock him out until at least midseason in 2009. Even then, Westbrook didn't get quite enough face time in the operating room. He topped off his lost campaign with arthroscopic hip surgery in early September, but that shouldn't affect his rehab timetable.

LINEOUTS

Hitters

PLAYER	TEAM	LVL	AGE	PA	R	2B	3B	HR	RBI	BB	SO	SB-CS	EqBRR	AVG/OBP/SLG	EqAVG/EqOBP/EqSLG	EqA	VORP	WARP
2B J. Barfield	BUF	AAA	25	320	30	18	1	5	23	15	58	9-5	-2.4	.251/.292/.368	.219/.257/.339	.206	-18.4	-0.9
1B J. Brown*	BUF	AAA	24	460	52	30	3	7	51	35	67	3-3	-3.7	.281/.337/.417	.249/.304/.382	.237	-4.9	-1.5
C S. Fasano	CLE	MLB	36	54	5	4	0	0	6	3	17	0-0	0.0	.261/.340/.348	.261/.340/.348	.250	0.8	0.4
C C. Gimenez	AKR	AA	25	233	46	15	1	6	26	52	33	0-1	0.9	.339/.487/.537	.274/.412/.452	.303	17.4	1.9
	BUF	AAA	25	229	23	9	1	3	19	23	60	2-1	0.4	.272/.354/.374	.237/.317/.333	.235	-5.4	0.6
1B S. Head*	AKR	AA	24	434	50	24	2	13	49	24	75	1-1	-2.4	.290/.325/.455	.250/.281/.409	.236	-5.1	-0.4
OF T. Linden#	SAC	AAA	28	94	13	7	0	3	12	14	22	1-0	0.4	.333/.447/.538	.272/.366/.444	.283	4.4	0.3
	BUF	AAA	28	383	51	20	1	14	50	52	101	3-2	-1.7	.278/.386/.475	.227/.328/.396	.253	1.1	0.1
2B C. Phelps#	MHV	A-	21	157	24	10	2	2	21	15	22	4-3	-2.2	.312/.376/.454	.228/.280/.345	.216	-12.1	-1.5
INF J. Rodriguez	AKR	AA	23	621	75	22	10	7	49	77	122	12-6	-0.7	.241/.335/.359	.221/.307/.343	.232	-17.7	1.8
C W. Toregas	AKR	AA	25	186	22	9	0	12	35	17	20	0-1	-1.2	.296/.371/.574	.247/.312/.488	.268	6.1	1.7
	BUF	AAA	25	178	15	8	0	2	25	15	32	2-0	0.7	.219/.301/.310	.196/.274/.285	.199	-12.5	-0.2
1B M. Whitney	AKR	AA	24	531	57	29	2	10	58	59	93	0-0	-1.4	.268/.356/.404	.230/.310/.364	.237	-9.4	-1.0

Josh Barfield continued to follow the Andy Marte developmental plan, joining his teammate at former-prospect support-group meetings while struggling through a second straight lost season. ⊘ Once seen as a top prospect, **Jordan Brown** can't make any excuses for his 2008 numbers. He doesn't have Aubrey's defensive acumen at first, and a birthday in the first Reagan administration doesn't help. ⊘ **Sal Fasano**, current owner of the best mutton-chops in the game, is in the wrong organization to get full union benefits from his International Brotherhood of Backup Catchers card. ⊘ Fasano's redundancy is partly due to the presence of **Chris Gimenez**, an Astros castoff who might make a useful bench bat. ⊘ Since hitting six homers in the first 10 games of his pro career in 2005, **Stephen Head** has been completely underwhelming. ⊘ Formerly of the Giants and Marlins, **Todd Linden** passed from Oakland to Cleveland last year, spending time at Triple-A for the seventh straight season. That is probably just the beginning of a Captain Cook–like minor league tour. ⊘ A second baseman drafted in the third round out of Stanford, **Cord Phelps** led the Cardinals in OBP and walks last season, an approach he brought with him to the pros. He could move up quickly. ⊘ **Josh Rodriguez** flopped in his first introduction to Double-A after going 20-20 on the Carolina League in 2007, dampening enthusiasm about his potential to be a starting second baseman. ⊘ **Wyatt Toregas** is a defensively promising catcher (he threw out 41 percent of would-be thieves last season) who could make it to "The Show" as a backup. ⊘ **Matt Whitney** was snatched up by the Nationals in the 2007 Rule 5 draft, only to be returned when Jim Bowden realized that he wasn't a toolsy, athletic outfielder. Whitney's power fizzled after leading A-ball with 32 homers in '07, but the Nats followed up by signing him as a minor league free agent this winter.

Pitchers

PLAYER	TEAM	LVL	AGE	W	L	SV	IP	H	BB	SO	HR	GB%	BABIP	STUFF	WHIP	ERA	DERA	EqH9	EqBB9	EqSO9	EqHR9	DEF	VORP
R. Bryson	WVA	A	20	3	2	5	55	43	20	73	3	43.7%	.308	18	1.15	4.25	7.03	10.5	4.8	6.5	1.3	-3	-7.7
	LKC	A	20	0	1	0	12¹	6	6	11	1	45.5%	.161	8	0.98	2.20	7.71	6.2	6.2	3.9	1.5	1	-2.7
B. Donnelly	CLE	MLB	36	1	0	0	13²	20	10	8	2	36.0%	.391	-20	2.20	8.54	6.75	13.5	6.1	4.7	1.4	-2	-4.0
S. Elarton	BUF	AAA	32	1	2	0	25²	21	7	18	2	42.3%	.257	-11	1.09	2.45	2.96	8.1	2.6	4.1	1.1	-2	7.1
	CLE	MLB	32	0	1	0	15¹	16	9	15	0	45.7%	.348	13	1.63	3.53	3.52	9.4	4.7	7.6	0.0	-1	2.9
M. Ginter	BUF	AAA	30	6	6	0	100	109	32	65	10	45.4%	.308	-19	1.41	4.14	6.28	10.6	3.2	3.7	1.3	4	-7.3
	CLE	MLB	30	1	3	0	21	25	3	12	3	43.1%	.324	1	1.33	5.14	4.50	10.8	1.4	4.5	1.4	-1	1.5
C. Lofgren*	AKR	AA	22	2	6	0	85²	93	52	72	9	40.4%	.332	-12	1.69	5.99	6.78	11.0	5.2	5.4	1.4	-2	-10.8
J.D. Martin	AKR	AA	25	11	3	0	79²	73	19	71	5	44.9%	.321	6	1.15	2.48	2.66	9.4	2.2	5.9	0.8	-6	24.3
	BUF	AAA	25	1	0	0	10	6	2	8	2	40.7%	.160	-8	0.80	1.80	4.66	5.6	1.9	4.7	2.8	2	-1.0
T. Mastny	BUF	AAA	27	2	2	0	35¹	26	12	43	1	48.2%	.305	12	1.08	1.78	3.06	8.1	3.6	7.8	0.6	0	9.1
	CLE	MLB	27	2	2	0	20	28	11	19	6	32.9%	.349	-25	1.95	10.80	9.58	12.2	4.4	7.4	2.6	-2	-10.9
J. Rincon	MIN	MLB	29	2	2	0	28	33	16	20	5	41.1%	.318	-19	1.75	6.11	6.04	10.2	4.4	5.4	1.6	-2	-3.2
	CLE	MLB	29	1	1	0	27¹	34	8	19	3	44.1%	.344	-11	1.54	5.60	5.74	11.1	2.4	5.7	1.0	0	-0.4
J. Weaver	NAS	AAA	31	2	4	0	55	64	20	37	9	44.4%	.327	-25	1.53	6.22	7.74	12.1	3.6	4.1	1.8	-2	-11.9
	BUF	AAA	31	2	2	0	29²	38	10	22	7	44.6%	.333	-37	1.62	6.06	5.93	13.2	3.6	4.3	3.0	-4	-1.0

The most obscure member of the four-player Sabathia package, **Rob Bryson** boasts an 11.4 K/9 mark in his two pro seasons. The Tribe will groom him as a potential closer. ⊘ Perhaps the Indians imported **Brendan Donnelly** just to see what would happen when he pitched in the same division as Jose Guillen; Donnelly faced the Royals three times, but did not get to square off against his nemesis. ⊘ **Scott Elarton** was placed on the restricted list in late June for an undisclosed personal reason. It is unclear whether he will return to professional ball, but his ERA this millennium is 5.67; only the immortal Jose Lima (6.00) exceeded him in a comparable number of innings. ⊘ You may know **Matt Ginter** as the journeyman who briefly filled in the gaping rotation hole immediately after Sabathia's departure. ⊘ **Chuck Lofgren** was a big-time prospect after an excellent season for Kinston at age 20, but his stuff has gone south, and the homers and walks north, over the last two years, prompting a demotion to the bullpen. ⊘ A Tommy John surgery survivor who is already an eight-year minor league vet, **J. D. Martin** should eventually make it up to the majors as a reliever. ⊘ The 6'6" **Tom** "Nasty" **Mastny** is the only big-leaguer to be born in Indonesia (where his parents were vacationing). He was sold to Japan's Yokohama BayStars in December, so a return visit to his birthplace just became that much easier. ⊘ For the fourth straight season, **Juan Rincon's** run average and WHIP rose; the Twins cast him off midyear, and Cleveland desperately snapped him up. He didn't pitch appreciably better for the Tribe, and it looks as though he might be finished. ⊘ Speaking of guys who are finished, **Jeff Weaver** hasn't put up an ERA below 5.70 or WHIP below 1.50 since 2005.

MANAGER: ERIC WEDGE

YEAR	TEAM	W-L	Pythag +/−	Avg PC	100+ P	120+ P	QS	BQS	REL	REL w Zero R	IBB	Subs	PH	PH Avg	PH HR	SB2	CS2	SB3	CS3	SAC Att	SAC %	POS SAC	Squeeze	Swing	In Play
2006	CLE	78-84	-12	97.4	81	2	77	14	379	221	35	26	97	.232	2	50	19	5	4	44	68.2%	27	0	121	87
2007	CLE	96-66	4	95.9	69	1	89	10	395	248	42	58	116	.272	4	66	40	6	1	43	74.4%	30	0	136	98
2008	CLE	81-81	-5	94.8	60	1	79	12	397	231	28	31	111	.237	2	73	26	3	3	58	74.1%	42	0	133	90

Among AL managers, only Mike Scioscia and Ron Gardenhire have been with their respective teams longer than has Wedge, who is now entering his seventh season helming the Tribe. Yet at only 41, he remains the youngest skipper in the junior circuit. Wedge has generally displayed a slow hook: he made fewer pitching changes than any other skipper did in both 2006 and 2007, and last year, he finished ahead of only Scioscia. The Indians again got a great deal of length from their starters, who ranked fourth in innings, and the dearth of switches is also a function of having no situational lefty (Rafael Perez being a bit more valuable than that). For an AL manager, Wedge sacrificed frequently last season, with 21 of the 43 successes coming from his second basemen. Beyond that, there's not much smallball being played by the lake, and since Wedge took over in 2003, Cleveland has not cracked the top half of the majors in stolen base percentage (it was 16th overall last year, after finishing 28th in 2007). That's mostly a reflection of the personnel on hand. He's cobbled together platoons, having been forced to mix and match in the outfield corners for the majority of his tenure, especially last season. One other thing that stands out about the Wedge-run Indians is underperformance of Pythagorean expectancy. Since 2003, Cleveland has finished a combined 19 wins below its predicted first-order records. This is probably due to the chronic hemorrhaging in the bullpen and the general lack of a shutdown closer to prevent one-run leads from turning into one-run losses.

Colorado Rockies

As the snows of late December piled high around the ears of baseball's off-season planning division, there were scant signs of activity in Denver. Aside from the November 12 deaccessioning of Matt Holliday, the nontendering of Willy Tavaras a month later, and the almost sotto voce posteructation "excuse me" signing of journeyman southpaw reliever Alan Embree, there has been little movement from the Rockies and almost no sign that they possessed any overarching vision for a return to the World Series.

This hesitancy to make a bold stroke would seem inexcusable in a division as soft and runny as the National League West, one in which the Dodgers coughed and sputtered their way to the postseason with a mere 84-78 record in 2008 and whose division champion hasn't needed to produce more than 90 wins since 2004. Almost any small action has the potential to change the balance of power in the division. And yet, the Rockies' tentative, temporizing winter was understandable as an expression of the common psychological affliction known as "What the Hell Do We Do Now?" Syndrome.

In 2007, Dan O'Dowd and company had seemed finally to have hit on the elusive formula for winning Rockies baseball, one that would allow them to "win at altitude" and to win *everywhere*. (Winning at altitude has always been a bit of a chimerical pursuit—the Rockies have always been winning at home, as their average Coors Field record of 44-37 over the last ten years is identical to the average major league home record.) It involved the commonsense decision to pursue the control of things that could be controlled. Humidors or not, in a high-altitude environment, home runs are going to be hit, whether one employs sinkerballers or changeup

---

> ## ROCKIES PROSPECTUS
>
> **2008 record:** 74-88; Third place in NL West
>
> **Pythagenport record:** 74-88
>
> **Runs scored per game:** 4.61 (8th in NL)
>
> **Runs allowed per game:** 5.12 (14th in NL)
>
> **Team EqA:** .258 (9th in NL)
>
> **2008 Batters Age:** 27.9 (5th-youngest in NL)
>
> **2008 Pitchers Age:** 28.8 (7th-youngest in NL)
>
> **Ballpark:** Coors Field; Strong hitter's park; Park Factor of 1.063
>
> **2008:** Regression, thy name is Rockies.
>
> **2009:** Falling from the peak of a pennant can be painful, but with a pitching rebound the Rockies might not hit bottom.

---

artists or, Heaven forfend, an entire staff of Dave LaRochian La Lobbers. What can be controlled is the number of baserunners a team puts on base, both on offense and on defense, by employing patient hitters, a control-oriented pitching staff, and ball-hawks at as many positions as possible. In this way, when the home runs are inevitably hit by both sides, the home team's round-tripper tallies three runs and the visitors tally two, and so on with all the lesser hits. This the Rockies did very well in 2007. The reason that 2008 was such a disappointment compared with 2007 was that the Rockies, due to injuries and some regression on the part of their players, stopped doing these things.

No recourse to statistically sophisticated sermonizing is necessary to see this; a simple examination of the changes a year had wrought on the Rockies is sufficient to make the case. In 2007, the Rockies led the National League in on-base percentage and unintentional walks received (getting more runners on than the other guy), allowed the third-fewest walks in the league, and ranked fourth in the league and sixth in the majors in defensive efficiency (keeping the other guy off base). The Rockies lost large swaths of ground in each of these categories in 2008. They dropped to fifth in the league on OBP, and 10th in unintentional walks. The pitching staff's control faded, sinking the team to 10th-fewest walks allowed (or seventh-most), and the rate of walks allowed per nine increased from 3.1 to 3.5. Finally, the Rockies sank like a stone in the all-important Defensive Efficiency rankings, the measure of the percentage of balls in play that were turned into outs by the team's gloves. The final rankings saw the Rockies decline to 14th in the league and 27th in the majors.

It took nearly a rosterwide failure to achieve these results. After 2007, it was muttered that Todd Helton's bad back had put him on the downside of his career, and yet he had posted a .434 OBP and a .494 slugging percentage. He saved the real downside for 2008, when all his power and batting average vanished, presaging Helton's own disappearance to the disabled list as of Independence Day. Garrett Atkins batted a wholly inadequate .258/.316/.407 as his substitute.

Second base, abandoned after Kaz Matsui cashed in on his career-reviving run with the Rockies by accepting a gratuitous three-year contract offered by the Astros, was the subject of a long spring training battle that seemed to have resolved itself in favor of Jayson Nix. In fact, to borrow from noted Rockies fan Sir Winston Churchill, when it came to second base, the only thing the Rockies were resolved to be was irresolute. Nix didn't hit, lasting not quite two weeks in the starting role before the Rockies sent him to the bench. (After batting .111 in 45 April at-bats, he was more or less forgotten about and later released.) He was followed by a revolving door of six starters, none of whom played particularly well at the position: Jeff Baker hit well but was a subpar fielder; Omar Quintanilla did a better job with the glove but didn't hit. The result was that Rockies keystoners batted .252/.305/.404 for the season, versus the major league averages of .276/.338/.409 at the position.

Second base might have settled into the lap of Clint Barmes, who spent the season rediscovering his bat after a disastrous 2006 and a 2007 spent mostly in the minors. Unfortunately, he would soon be needed to cover for Troy Tulowitzki at shortstop. Having followed in Barmes' footsteps into the Rockies infield, Tulowitzki seemed determined to reenact the more ignominious segments of Barmes' career. Even before taking time off for a lengthy disabled stay caused by a torn quadriceps, Tulo hadn't hit. Nor did he hit when he briefly returned before—shades of Barmes' 2005 losing bout with a package of venison—he smashed his bat on the ground in frustration, creating shards that lacerated his palm. Barmes saved his best hitting for when he was subbing for Tulowitzki, batting .319/.352/.541 in 144 plate appearances as a shortstop. Still, he could not make up for the defense's loss of Tulowitzki's great range from 2007, when Tulo recorded 561 assists, the highest total in the majors since 1988 and one that would not look out of place in a catalog of Ozzie Smith's fielding achievements.

Third base was doubly compromised, not only because Garrett Atkins saw his EqA dip for the second straight season, but because Helton's absence required Atkins to move across the diamond, finally opening a spot for disappointing 2003 first-round pick Ian Stewart. Oddly enough, Stewart was disappointing, a superficial bit of slugging barely disguising that he failed to hit right-handers (.231/.328/.392 in 244 PAs) or away from Coors (.234/.348/.431).

Worse horrors were yet to come in center field. In 2007, banjo hitter Willy Taveras had shown that under select circumstances, he could actually help a major league team as something more than a pinch-runner and defensive substitute. Unfortunately, those circumstances included slapping .320 in singles, something he had never done before and is unlikely to do ever again. Sadly, the worst season of Taveras's major league career featured far more durability than he had shown the previous season. Taveras was not the worst center fielder in the National League, not when Michael Bourn, Andruw Jones, and Corey Patterson were toiling on the circuit, but this had to be faint comfort, given an outfielder slugging .296 at Coors Field.

These disasters on offense were leavened only by another strong season from Matt Holliday, consistency from Brad Hawpe, and the tardy but satisfying blossoming of catcher Chris Iannetta. These small mercies did not nearly make up for the aforementioned failures on offense, nor could they paper over the even more disappointing pitching staff.

The 2007 starting rotation had not exactly been stable, with only lefty Jeff Francis making more than 30 starts and with the entire pennant-winning effort eventually depending on the last-minute arrival of rookie southpaw Franklin Morales to give it that extra push. Both of these pitchers lost ground in 2008. Francis had given the Rockies over 400 innings from 2006 to 2007, but shoulder problems derailed his season. These things happen, but Morales's vanishing act was not so easily dismissed—he simply went wild, his walks racing upward even as his strikeouts hit the basement floor and kept on going. Though he forged a winning record at Triple-A, his minor league work was of insufficient quality to inspire his recall, the key number being an unsustainable walk rate of 6.7 per nine innings.

The news wasn't all in the pitching department. Aaron Cook showed consistency with his third straight season with a park- and league-adjusted ERA of 116. Ubaldo Jimenez showed ace potential and Jorge de la Rosa, the mystifying power lefty who had failed to establish himself with the Brewers and Royals, finally seemed to overcome his wildness, with a 3.08 ERA in 73 second-half innings. There are too many ifs involved for comfort, but the Rockies' rotation could return to strength this year if several things happen: *if* Jimenez continues to progress; *if* Cook can hold his ground for another year; *if* Jason Marquis eats ... outings; *if* Morales can recover his stuff and his poise; *if* Francis or Jason Hirsh can recover from their injuries in good form; *if* de la Rosa can hold on to his progress; if Greg Smith, acquired in the Holliday deal, can pitch as he did for Oakland; *if* prospect Jhoulys Chacin can make a headlong dash to the majors. If some but not necessarily all of these things happen, the Rockies will have less need to tinker with the dead-end types like Livan Hernandez or Mark Redman.

The bullpen will also probably have to be rebuilt with the free agency of closer Brian Fuentes. Early talk foresees a spring training battle between Manny Corpas and the newly acquired Huston Street, but neither is an ideal candidate, the former having been smoked to the tune of 10.5 hits per nine innings in 2008 and the latter having had health problems as well as demonstrating undue deference to left-handed hitters in the past. The Rockies retain a solid relief piece in Taylor Buchholz, a pitcher whom they had the perspicacity to reenvision as a reliever after years of failed starting assignments. The Buchholz now stops here, with a career ERA of 2.42 in 122⅔ relief innings, compared with a 6.05 ERA in 27 career starts. The signing of Embree seems little more than a desultory gesture toward having a lefty, any lefty, in the pen after the defection of Fuentes.

The Holliday trade itself seems a clear sign that the methods that worked so well for the Rockies in 2007, that of maximizing their own on-base percentage and minimizing that of the opposition, are not something they are able to sustain, and they are inexorably moving, or being moved, away from that model. The trade itself is not the problem, but the return. In addition to Street, who is a good but inessential reliever, the Rockies acquired left-handed starter Greg Smith, whose low strikeout rate and high walk rate make him exactly the kind of pitcher likely to put the home team on the wrong end of some big innings. As for outfielder Carlos Gonzalez, the .273 OBP he recorded with the A's last year was not unrepresentative. For the Rockies' sake, it can only be hoped that Seth Smith and a precocious prospect like Dexter Fowler can combine to keep Gonzalez on the bench or at Colorado Springs.

Even with Holliday in the fold, the Rockies ranked only ninth in the National League in home runs in 2008. With Holliday gone but unreplaced, the Rockies are likely to be overpowered both in their own ballpark and on the road. They badly needed to be in on one of the major power-hitting free agents available on the winter market, but as long as Helton and his balky back consume roughly a quarter of the payroll (as he will continue to do through 2011), their hands are apparently tied. Still, with some mild good luck in the pitching line and a return to form by Tulowitzki, the Rockies could enjoy a rebound season, one sufficient to keep them in the running in the weak NL West.

HITTERS

Garrett Atkins — 3B

Bats: R   Throws: R   Height: 6' 3"   Weight: 215   Born: December 12, 1979   Age: 29

YEAR	TEAM	LVL	AGE	PA	R	2B	3B	HR	RBI	BB	SO	SB	CS	EqBRR	AVG	OBP	SLG	EqAVG	EqOBP	EqSLG	EqA	VORP	WARP	DEFENSE			
2006	COL	MLB	26	695	117	48	1	29	120	79	76	4	0	0.6	.329	.409	.556	.308	.391	.523	.311	63.6	6.2	155-3B	0		
2007	COL	MLB	27	684	83	35	1	25	111	67	96	3	1	-1.6	.301	.367	.486	.287	.358	.473	.286	36.3	2.3	146-3B	-15		
2008	COL	MLB	28	664	86	32	3	21	99	40	100	1	1	-0.3	.286	.328	.452	.281	.323	.452	.266	18.0	1.3	89-3B	1	59-1B	-6
2009	COL	MLB	29	644	90	36	2	26	97	62	89	3	1	-1.7	.302	.371	.510	.283	.353	.483	.285	30.3	3.0	150-3B	-9		

Breakout: 21%   Improve: 51%   Collapse: 18%   Attrition: 8%   Comparables: Mike Lowell, Ken McMullen, Morgan Ensberg, Ray Knight

Few players have taken advantage of Coors Field better than Atkins. In his career, he's hit .337/.394/.527 at home, and a pedestrian (or worse) .260/.328/.424 away from Denver's pinball machine. He's also a maladroit fielder. It's not that he's necessarily a bad player. He's more one who fills a gap and doesn't cause any headaches, but you are always looking for something better—kind of like that girlfriend you had a few years ago. Now traveling through his arbitration-eligible seasons, Atkins is about to reach the point where he can command dollars wholly out of line with his actual abilities. This perhaps explains why the Rockies were rumored to have spent a good deal of the winter Hamlet-ing on about whether to deal or not to deal him.

Jeff Baker   UT

Bats: R   Throws: R   Height: 6' 2"   Weight: 210   Born: June 21, 1981   Age: 28

YEAR	TEAM	LVL	AGE	PA	R	2B	3B	HR	RBI	BB	SO	SB	CS	EqBRR	AVG	OBP	SLG	EqAVG	EqOBP	EqSLG	EqA	VORP	WARP	DEFENSE		
2006	CSP	AAA	25	538	71	30	4	20	108	46	110	7	1	-0.4	.305	.369	.508	.241	.300	.416	.248	-0.7	-0.1	119-RF	-3	
2006	COL	MLB	25	58	13	7	2	5	21	1	14	2	0	0.1	.368	.379	.825	.351	.362	.789	.354	10.9	0.9	9-RF	0	
2007	COL	MLB	26	159	17	2	2	4	12	13	40	0	0	-1.0	.222	.296	.347	.217	.296	.343	.223	-4.8	-0.7	11-1B	-1	10-RF -1
2008	COL	MLB	27	333	55	22	1	12	48	26	85	4	0	-1.3	.268	.322	.468	.262	.318	.463	.270	11.2	1.0	41-2B	0	14-1B -1
2009	COL	MLB	28	290	38	16	2	11	41	23	66	4	1	-0.4	.275	.336	.482	.258	.320	.456	.265	10.1	1.0	71-2B	-6	

Breakout: 30%   Improve: 52%   Collapse: 25%   Attrition: 32%   Comparables: Archi Cianfrocco, Sam Bowens, Dustan Mohr, Ike Brown

When Baker got a monstrous bonus out of college, he was supposed to be much more than a utility player, but he's ended up being both valuable and unique as a multiposition reserve whose calling card is power. Four things hold him back from being an everyday player: trouble with righties (.248/.299/.411 career), trouble on the road (.216/.278/.356 career), defense, and Clint Barmes, who has that gritty/gutsy thing going for him that Clint Hurdle loves.

Clint Barmes   INF

Bats: R   Throws: R   Height: 6' 0"   Weight: 210   Born: March 6, 1979   Age: 30

YEAR	TEAM	LVL	AGE	PA	R	2B	3B	HR	RBI	BB	SO	SB	CS	EqBRR	AVG	OBP	SLG	EqAVG	EqOBP	EqSLG	EqA	VORP	WARP	DEFENSE		
2006	COL	MLB	27	535	57	26	4	7	56	22	72	5	4	2.6	.220	.264	.335	.215	.258	.328	.205	-20.1	0.2	120-SS	11	
2007	CSP	AAA	28	477	68	20	6	11	44	22	52	8	6	-0.4	.299	.364	.451	.210	.268	.326	.206	-25.9	0.9	87-SS	19	5-CF -3
2007	COL	MLB	28	39	5	3	0	0	1	1	13	0	0	1.3	.216	.237	.297	.216	.237	.297	.179	-2.3	-0.3			
2008	COL	MLB	29	417	47	25	6	11	44	17	69	13	4	2.4	.290	.322	.468	.287	.319	.477	.269	19.1	3.0	54-2B	8	32-SS 2
2009	COL	MLB	30	234	26	13	2	5	26	12	35	5	2	0.4	.260	.309	.412	.244	.294	.390	.237	3.3	0.9	58-SS	2	

Breakout: 38%   Improve: 52%   Collapse: 27%   Attrition: 48%   Comparables: Tim Cullen, Billy Hunter, Billy Gardner, Pete Mackanin

Barmes has been given plenty of opportunities to put a choke hold on Colorado's second-base job, and he did so in 2008, despite missing a good chunk of the first half with a knee injury. With this kind of player, you have to live with the good (he makes contact, has gap power, and runs well) and the bad (he's much more dangerous against left-handers, and he's a big-time hacker who rarely walks). When you add it all up, he's only arguably the best option the Rockies have at second, but he's also nothing to hang your hat on.

Dexter Fowler   CF

Bats: S   Throws: R   Height: 6' 4"   Weight: 173   Born: March 22, 1986   Age: 23

YEAR	TEAM	LVL	AGE	PA	R	2B	3B	HR	RBI	BB	SO	SB	CS	EqBRR	AVG	OBP	SLG	EqAVG	EqOBP	EqSLG	EqA	VORP	WARP	DEFENSE	
2006	ASH	A	20	458	92	31	6	8	46	43	79	43	23	0.6	.296	.373	.462	.209	.267	.332	.209	-26.8	-2.5	97-CF	-9
2007	MOD	A+	21	299	43	7	5	2	23	44	64	20	11	-0.6	.273	.397	.367	.221	.320	.298	.225	-11.2	0.4	61-CF	6
2008	TUL	AA	22	505	92	31	9	9	64	65	89	20	8	4.7	.335	.431	.515	.275	.360	.439	.277	21.5	2.5	105-CF	-2
2008	COL	MLB	22	27	3	0	0	0	0	0	5	0	1	-0.0	.154	.185	.154	.154	.185	.154	.000	-4.2	-0.5	6-CF	-1
2009	COL	MLB	23	590	84	35	6	10	54	58	126	21	9	4.2	.277	.353	.426	.259	.336	.403	.258	12.3	2.4	138-CF	-5

Breakout: 49%   Improve: 76%   Collapse: 5%   Attrition: 4%   Comparables: Stan Jefferson, Mike Brumley, Paul Householder, Jerome Nelson

Fowler has always been one of those players about whom, the second he takes the field, the first thing you say to yourself is, "I want me one of those." He's tall, long, athletic, and loaded with tools, and those tools took a dramatic step toward turning into baseball skills with a breakout performance at Double-A before he left to join the Olympic squad. Rockies officials insist that they want Fowler to get some time in Triple-A to begin the year, but his talent is far too great to keep on the farm for too long. As is, he's the reason Willy Taveras was nontendered in December ... well, that and the fact that Taveras stinks.

Brad Hawpe   RF

Bats: L   Throws: L   Height: 6' 3"   Weight: 205   Born: June 22, 1979   Age: 30

YEAR	TEAM	LVL	AGE	PA	R	2B	3B	HR	RBI	BB	SO	SB	CS	EqBRR	AVG	OBP	SLG	EqAVG	EqOBP	EqSLG	EqA	VORP	WARP	DEFENSE	
2006	COL	MLB	27	575	67	33	6	22	84	74	123	5	5	-3.6	.293	.383	.515	.272	.369	.484	.288	32.6	2.5	134-RF	-6
2007	COL	MLB	28	606	80	33	4	29	116	81	137	0	2	-4.3	.291	.387	.539	.271	.376	.514	.300	38.8	3.5	137-RF	-6
2008	COL	MLB	29	569	69	24	3	25	85	76	134	2	2	-1.8	.283	.381	.498	.273	.374	.495	.295	29.7	1.6	131-RF	-18
2009	COL	MLB	30	502	74	26	2	23	76	68	112	2	2	-1.5	.285	.384	.514	.267	.365	.487	.290	21.0	2.2	118-RF	-8

Breakout: 14%   Improve: 42%   Collapse: 18%   Attrition: 13%   Comparables: Paul O'Neill, Pete Ward, Geoff Jenkins, Jay Buhner

If anything, at least Hawpe is dependable, having reeled off three straight seasons of nearly identical performance. This is clearly what he is, a .290 hitter with 25 to 30 home runs annually and 80 walks, and that's largely without having to account for a Coors Field discount, as Hawpe holds a good deal of his value on the road, batting .282/.376/.482 away from home, versus .283/.374/.504 in low-gravity environments. His skill set shouldn't deteriorate over the next two years, over which he is owed a reasonable $13 million. The only caveat is Hawpe's range in the field, which visibly plunged last year (and registered dramatically in all the major fielding metrics, including ours), though this may have been a symptom of the hamstring problems that put him on the disabled list in May.

Todd Helton — 1B

Bats: L   Throws: L   Height: 6' 2"   Weight: 210   Born: August 20, 1973   Age: 35

YEAR	TEAM	LVL	AGE	PA	R	2B	3B	HR	RBI	BB	SO	SB	CS	EqBRR	AVG	OBP	SLG	EqAVG	EqOBP	EqSLG	EqA	VORP	WARP	DEFENSE
2006	COL	MLB	32	649	94	40	5	15	81	91	64	3	2	-2.2	.302	.404	.476	.280	.388	.442	.292	31.8	2.0	142-1B -11
2007	COL	MLB	33	682	86	42	2	17	91	116	74	0	1	-5.4	.320	.434	.494	.298	.423	.471	.314	53.5	6.1	148-1B 9
2008	COL	MLB	34	361	39	16	0	7	29	61	50	0	0	-3.5	.264	.391	.388	.252	.382	.376	.274	8.6	0.8	80-1B -1
2009	COL	MLB	35	444	62	24	1	11	55	71	55	1	1	-2.4	.291	.405	.449	.273	.386	.425	.285	14.4	1.7	105-1B -2

Breakout: 16%   Improve: 30%   Collapse: 36%   Attrition: 31%   Comparables: J.T. Snow, John Olerud, Mike Hargrove, Ryan Klesko

Helton's chronic back troubles finally caught up with him in 2008, as he had his worst season as a pro while missing nearly half the season. He had arthroscopic surgery at the end of September, and all that the Rockies can do right now is hope, because healthy or not, he's owed well over $50 million over the next three years. Hurdle has already promised more time off for Helton to try to ensure that he's available when needed. With a bench full of guys who can play the position, it shouldn't be a big problem. But the Rockies will miss having even the diminished 2006-2007 version of Helton in the lineup if he can't snap back.

Jonathan Herrera — MI

Bats: S   Throws: R   Height: 5' 9"   Weight: 150   Born: November 3, 1984   Age: 24

YEAR	TEAM	LVL	AGE	PA	R	2B	3B	HR	RBI	BB	SO	SB	CS	EqBRR	AVG	OBP	SLG	EqAVG	EqOBP	EqSLG	EqA	VORP	WARP	DEFENSE	
2006	MOD	A+	21	568	87	20	8	7	77	58	67	34	15	-1.3	.310	.382	.427	.245	.306	.342	.232	-14.3	2.0	121-SS 10	
2007	TUL	AA	22	573	65	24	4	3	40	36	68	18	12	-1.9	.257	.315	.338	.219	.266	.295	.197	-40.0	-1.1	124-SS 4	
2008	CSP	AAA	23	250	40	7	0	3	31	19	30	15	2	2.0	.310	.367	.381	.239	.296	.296	.219	-11.8	-0.2	27-SS -1	25-2B 2
2008	COL	MLB	23	66	5	1	1	0	3	4	10	1	1	-0.4	.230	.277	.279	.230	.277	.279	.193	-3.5	0.1	14-2B 4	
2009	COL	MLB	24	408	46	16	3	3	30	29	56	13	5	2.1	.255	.311	.341	.239	.296	.323	.219	-3.8	1.1	97-SS 9	

Breakout: 37%   Improve: 49%   Collapse: 29%   Attrition: 18%   Comparables: Ramon Santiago, Carlos Leon, Bernie Castro, Domingo Ramos

Herrera spent a little more than a month in the big leagues early in the season, when the injury bug hit the infield, and he hit just enough to not get the call again when rosters expanded in September. He's an outstanding defensive player who can play both middle infield positions, but offensively, he's simply a guy who slaps the ball around and runs well. He doesn't work the count well, he possesses a little more power than Jason Tyner has, and his ceiling ends at utility player.

Matt Holliday — LF

Bats: R   Throws: R   Height: 6' 4"   Weight: 235   Born: January 15, 1980   Age: 29

YEAR	TEAM	LVL	AGE	PA	R	2B	3B	HR	RBI	BB	SO	SB	CS	EqBRR	AVG	OBP	SLG	EqAVG	EqOBP	EqSLG	EqA	VORP	WARP	DEFENSE
2006	COL	MLB	26	667	119	45	5	34	114	47	110	10	5	-2.1	.326	.387	.586	.308	.370	.557	.306	57.7	3.4	149-LF -17
2007	COL	MLB	27	713	120	50	6	36	137	63	126	11	4	3.4	.340	.405	.607	.324	.394	.588	.322	76.1	9.4	153-LF 21
2008	COL	MLB	28	623	107	38	2	25	88	74	104	28	2	8.2	.321	.409	.538	.310	.400	.535	.320	61.9	5.6	138-LF -3
2009	OAK	MLB	29	608	89	34	2	23	89	59	105	14	4	0.1	.291	.366	.492	.298	.373	.524	.305	34.6	4.3	142-LF -2

Breakout: 6%   Improve: 25%   Collapse: 25%   Attrition: 7%   Comparables: Dave Winfield, Dave Parker, Bob Watson, Cliff Floyd

If anyone thinks Holliday is going to be able to repeat this kind of production while moving from Colorado to Oakland, that person has another thing coming. In his career, Holliday hit .357/.423/.645 at Coors (roughly Albert Pujols) and .280/.348/.455 on the road (roughly Shane Victorino). Now, he's better than Shane Victorino, but do you really think he's going to hit .320, and in the stronger league? Do you really think he's going to hit 30 bombs? Are you sure about that?

Chris Iannetta   C

Bats: R   **Throws:** R   **Height:** 6' 0"   **Weight:** 225   **Born:** April 8, 1983   **Age:** 26

YEAR	TEAM	LVL	AGE	PA	R	2B	3B	HR	RBI	BB	SO	SB	CS	EqBRR	AVG	OBP	SLG	EqAVG	EqOBP	EqSLG	EqA	VORP	WARP	DEFENSE	
2006	TUL	AA	23	185	38	10	2	11	26	24	26	1	0	-0.5	.321	.418	.622	.272	.357	.537	.298	14.7	1.3	37-C	-4
2006	CSP	AAA	23	180	23	12	1	3	22	24	29	0	0	-3.3	.351	.447	.503	.284	.378	.426	.283	8.9	1.5	36-C	2
2006	COL	MLB	23	93	12	4	0	2	10	13	17	0	1	0.3	.260	.370	.390	.247	.366	.364	.261	1.4	0.2	22-C	-2
2007	COL	MLB	24	234	22	8	3	4	27	29	58	0	0	-1.4	.218	.330	.350	.204	.322	.332	.237	0.7	0.4	55-C	0
2008	COL	MLB	25	407	50	22	2	18	65	56	92	0	0	-0.6	.264	.390	.505	.258	.385	.502	.302	30.4	3.8	94-C	0
2009	COL	MLB	26	421	62	23	2	16	59	55	80	1	1	-1.4	.285	.392	.499	.267	.373	.473	.291	26.8	3.7	100-C	0

Breakout: 24%   **Improve:** 61%   **Collapse:** 21%   **Attrition:** 25%   **Comparables:** Brian Downing, Todd Zeile, Earl Battey, Ed Bailey

We told you he'd be good; it just took an extra year. This happens quite often. Not only is the jump to big-league baseball remarkably difficult on a pure talent level, but there is also so much else to cope with, from the crowds to the media to the travel. It's hard to say exactly why it took Iannetta so long, but that's water under the bridge. This is the real Chris Iannetta, and he'll be one of the National League's better catchers for years to come.

Joe Koshansky   1B

Bats: L   **Throws:** L   **Height:** 6' 4"   **Weight:** 225   **Born:** May 26, 1982   **Age:** 27

YEAR	TEAM	LVL	AGE	PA	R	2B	3B	HR	RBI	BB	SO	SB	CS	EqBRR	AVG	OBP	SLG	EqAVG	EqOBP	EqSLG	EqA	VORP	WARP	DEFENSE	
2006	TUL	AA	24	573	84	28	0	31	109	64	134	3	2	-1.9	.284	.371	.526	.227	.299	.419	.246	-2.0	-0.7	125-1B	-3
2007	CSP	AAA	25	569	79	30	2	21	99	67	128	4	3	-2.1	.295	.380	.490	.224	.309	.381	.240	-7.4	-1.4	130-1B	-5
2008	CSP	AAA	26	526	90	36	4	31	121	60	158	1	0	-2.2	.300	.380	.600	.229	.303	.451	.257	5.5	0.8	117-1B	3
2008	COL	MLB	26	40	5	3	0	3	8	1	17	0	0	-0.2	.211	.250	.526	.211	.250	.526	.252	0.2	0.0	8-1B	0
2009	COL	MLB	27	502	54	28	2	20	68	47	150	2	1	-1.2	.234	.310	.437	.220	.295	.414	.241	-5.5	0.2	118-1B	4

Breakout: 16%   **Improve:** 38%   **Collapse:** 31%   **Attrition:** 17%   **Comparables:** Brian Daubach, Eric Crozier, Troy Neel, Kevin Burns

We don't have the official word from our Warsaw office yet, but we're fairly sure that *Koshansky* translates as "Four-A hitter." He's averaged 37 home runs per 162 games in his minor league career, yet with all of Todd Helton's health issues last year, Koshansky started a grand total of just eight games in his place. That's not exactly a scenario that inspires much confidence in his future.

Michael McKenry   C

Bats: R   **Throws:** R   **Height:** 5' 10"   **Weight:** 200   **Born:** March 4, 1985   **Age:** 24

YEAR	TEAM	LVL	AGE	PA	R	2B	3B	HR	RBI	BB	SO	SB	CS	EqBRR	AVG	OBP	SLG	EqAVG	EqOBP	EqSLG	EqA	VORP	WARP	DEFENSE	
2006	TRI	A-	21	290	28	16	1	4	23	22	49	3	3	-1.0	.216	.303	.339	.164	.220	.256	.160	-59.7	-3.2	46-C	-2
2007	ASH	A	22	485	79	35	1	22	90	66	84	8	9	0.3	.287	.392	.539	.193	.280	.361	.222	-20.1	0.1	84-C	3
2008	MOD	A+	23	472	59	28	1	18	75	55	101	2	4	-2.8	.258	.360	.468	.198	.286	.357	.224	-18.0	0.9	95-C	6
2009	COL	MLB	24	509	50	25	2	15	58	46	128	2	2	-0.0	.222	.299	.387	.208	.284	.366	.224	-5.7	1.5	120-C	1

Breakout: 39%   **Improve:** 67%   **Collapse:** 15%   **Attrition:** 11%   **Comparables:** Lloyd McClendon, Nick Hundley, Giuseppe Chiaramonte, Mike Daniel

The Rockies already have a good young catcher at the big-league level, but they may have found a relatively decent one in McKenry. He has a hitch in his swing and will probably always hit for a lowish average with plenty of strikeouts, but he makes up for that with walks, power, and one of the best defensive packages in the minors, including an outstanding arm. Double-A will be a big test for his bat, and we'll learn just how real this all is.

Matt Miller   OF

Bats: R   **Throws:** R   **Height:** 6' 2"   **Weight:** 210   **Born:** December 26, 1982   **Age:** 26

YEAR	TEAM	LVL	AGE	PA	R	2B	3B	HR	RBI	BB	SO	SB	CS	EqBRR	AVG	OBP	SLG	EqAVG	EqOBP	EqSLG	EqA	VORP	WARP	DEFENSE			
2006	MOD	A+	23	415	52	20	2	12	77	31	37	4	9	-6.2	.323	.381	.486	.246	.290	.377	.230	-8.3	-2.5	41-RF	-3	38-CF	-13
2006	TUL	AA	23	97	14	1	1	1	7	11	13	1	1	0.0	.229	.330	.301	.186	.268	.267	.186	-8.0	-0.3	15-LF	3		
2007	TUL	AA	24	502	59	22	2	11	61	42	69	1	4	-2.4	.262	.337	.395	.209	.269	.320	.203	-30.9	-4.0	111-LF	-12		
2008	TUL	AA	25	461	72	21	0	10	87	44	45	4	2	1.5	.344	.408	.469	.257	.312	.357	.237	-6.4	-1.7	68-LF	-10	13-RF	-1
2008	CSP	AAA	25	144	26	14	0	0	20	15	16	2	0	0.6	.331	.410	.444	.244	.319	.315	.233	-3.9	-1.2	16-LF	-8	14-RF	-1
2009	COL	MLB	26	538	49	23	1	7	51	40	80	3	2	-0.8	.245	.305	.343	.230	.290	.325	.212	-17.8	-1.9	126-LF	-9		

Breakout: 22%   **Improve:** 38%   **Collapse:** 40%   **Attrition:** 14%   **Comparables:** Luis Lopez, Noochie Varner, Bill Ortega, Royce Huffman

Miller seemed like a guy to keep an eye on when he hit 30 home runs in 2005, but that happened at Low-A Asheville, where balls just fly out of the park, and he's yet to top more than 13 home runs in a season since. The good news is that he finished second in the Texas League batting race last year; the bad news is that he's already 26. His most optimistic projection is that he winds up as a big-league bench bat.

Jayson Nix **2B** Bats: R Throws: R Height: 5' 11" Weight: 185 Born: August 26, 1982 Age: 26

YEAR	TEAM	LVL	AGE	PA	R	2B	3B	HR	RBI	BB	SO	SB	CS	EqBRR	AVG	OBP	SLG	EqAVG	EqOBP	EqSLG	EqA	VORP	WARP	DEFENSE			
2006	CSP	AAA	23	397	39	14	1	2	26	32	61	15	3	3.5	.251	.317	.313	.203	.265	.258	.189	-33.6	-1.0	100-2B	7		
2007	CSP	AAA	24	483	80	33	2	11	58	31	79	24	8	4.0	.292	.342	.451	.229	.280	.362	.226	-16.2	1.7	103-2B	20	5-3B	-2
2008	CSP	AAA	25	303	63	21	2	17	51	27	64	11	5	-1.0	.303	.373	.591	.230	.296	.441	.253	1.1	0.6	62-2B	-2		
2008	COL	MLB	25	65	2	2	0	0	2	7	17	1	0	0.4	.125	.234	.161	.125	.234	.161	.135	-6.7	0.0	16-2B	5		
2009	CHA	MLB	26	409	40	19	1	9	39	29	95	10	4	1.2	.215	.276	.346	.215	.277	.354	.222	-8.3	0.7	97-2B	6		

Breakout: 30% Improve: 51% Collapse: 29% Attrition: 23% Comparables: Josh Wilson, Terry Shumpert, Gookie Dawkins, Jed Hansen

Nix won the job at second base in spring training, but it was all downhill from there, as he went just 5-for-45 in April, and that was that. He did put up big numbers in Triple-A while showcasing his always-outstanding defensive skills. The Rockies released him in late October, but he quickly signed a big-league deal with the White Sox, who will pit him in a spring training battle with prospect Chris Getz for their second-base job.

Scott Podsednik **OF** Bats: L Throws: L Height: 6' 1" Weight: 190 Born: March 18, 1976 Age: 33

YEAR	TEAM	LVL	AGE	PA	R	2B	3B	HR	RBI	BB	SO	SB	CS	EqBRR	AVG	OBP	SLG	EqAVG	EqOBP	EqSLG	EqA	VORP	WARP	DEFENSE	
2006	CHA	MLB	30	591	86	27	6	3	45	54	95	40	19	-0.1	.262	.331	.354	.249	.326	.338	.240	-10.0	-0.2	122-LF	1
2007	CHA	MLB	31	235	30	13	4	2	11	13	36	12	5	0.4	.243	.299	.369	.238	.294	.379	.235	-5.3	0.4	52-LF	6
2008	COL	MLB	32	181	22	8	1	1	15	16	28	12	4	1.2	.253	.322	.333	.253	.322	.333	.240	-0.7	-0.3	23-CF	-1
2009	COL	MLB	33	126	17	6	1	1	11	11	19	7	3	0.5	.272	.339	.372	.255	.322	.352	.243	0.2	0.1	34-LF	0

Breakout: 30% Improve: 41% Collapse: 36% Attrition: 40% Comparables: Wayne Kirby, Chris Singleton, Marvin Benard, George Altman

Podsednik won the extra outfield job in Colorado in spring training, but he didn't do much with it. He's the kind of player who needs to hit at least .280 to be valuable, as he has only an average walk rate and zero power; when he hits .250, he's an offensive black hole. Nonetheless, he still runs well and can play all three outfield positions, so the Rockies are thinking of giving him a return invitation. If they don't, somebody else surely will.

Omar Quintanilla **MI** Bats: L Throws: R Height: 5' 9" Weight: 190 Born: October 24, 1981 Age: 27

YEAR	TEAM	LVL	AGE	PA	R	2B	3B	HR	RBI	BB	SO	SB	CS	EqBRR	AVG	OBP	SLG	EqAVG	EqOBP	EqSLG	EqA	VORP	WARP	DEFENSE			
2006	CSP	AAA	24	349	48	23	2	4	29	20	55	4	1	1.1	.276	.342	.403	.225	.287	.343	.223	-13.0	0.2	47-SS	-3	30-2B	5
2006	COL	MLB	24	38	3	1	1	0	3	3	9	1	1	-0.6	.176	.243	.265	.176	.243	.265	.173	-3.0	0.0	7-SS	2		
2007	CSP	AAA	25	393	54	30	4	3	43	31	65	3	1	2.6	.319	.380	.454	.240	.303	.353	.232	-9.0	0.4	46-SS	2	26-2B	1
2007	COL	MLB	25	75	6	4	0	0	5	5	15	0	0	0.7	.229	.280	.286	.214	.267	.271	.183	-3.6	-0.3	18-2B	1		
2008	CSP	AAA	26	91	18	4	0	1	8	16	11	3	0	-0.0	.329	.451	.425	.237	.359	.316	.255	-0.7	0.3	14-SS	1	5-2B	-1
2008	COL	MLB	26	234	28	17	0	2	15	15	46	0	0	4.2	.238	.288	.348	.235	.287	.352	.223	-3.6	-0.6	32-SS	-2	24-2B	-1
2009	COL	MLB	27	245	29	15	1	4	25	20	41	2	1	0.8	.275	.340	.404	.257	.323	.382	.246	6.9	0.8	61-SS	-1		

Breakout: 49% Improve: 67% Collapse: 22% Attrition: 47% Comparables: Marlon Anderson, Jeff Branson, Kiko Garcia, Alex Cora

After waiting patiently for his opportunity, Quintanilla finally got his shot at becoming the team's primary utility infielder in 2008, and he flopped. Playing second when Barmes slid over to short for an injured Tulo, Omar had 10 hits in his first 25 at-bats, but hit just .216 thereafter. He doesn't bring enough other skills—including his glove work—to make up for any bat dysfunction. He's a career .313 hitter in the minors, but not even an iota of that has shown up in the majors. For now, the Quintanilla Shake is still the backup at two positions where, for health or performance issues, there is some instability, but he has zero chance of graduating to a larger role.

Seth Smith — OF

Bats: L Throws: L Height: 6' 3" Weight: 215 Born: September 30, 1982 Age: 26

YEAR	TEAM	LVL	AGE	PA	R	2B	3B	HR	RBI	BB	SO	SB	CS	EqBRR	AVG	OBP	SLG	EqAVG	EqOBP	EqSLG	EqA	VORP	WARP	DEFENSE			
2006	TUL	AA	23	582	79	46	4	15	71	51	74	4	4	0.8	.294	.361	.483	.246	.303	.405	.243	-1.7	0.2	107-RF	2	5-LF	0
2007	CSP	AAA	24	505	68	32	6	17	82	39	73	7	3	-1.1	.317	.381	.528	.252	.315	.430	.257	6.9	1.2	96-RF	3	21-CF	-1
2008	CSP	AAA	25	303	55	16	2	10	53	46	46	11	0	4.1	.323	.426	.524	.242	.343	.395	.268	3.8	1.9	37-LF	9	26-RF	-1
2008	COL	MLB	25	123	13	7	0	4	15	15	23	1	0	-1.3	.259	.350	.435	.250	.341	.435	.270	3.7	0.4	10-RF	0	5-CF	1
2009	COL	MLB	26	405	54	23	2	12	52	39	68	6	2	0.1	.275	.348	.453	.257	.331	.429	.264	6.7	1.9	97-RF	6		

Breakout: 31% Improve: 52% Collapse: 19% Attrition: 21% Comparables: John Vander Wal, Paul O'Neill, Jacob Cruz, Ryan Langerhans

Smith is a high draft pick who was slow to develop, but in his defense, he's hit everywhere, carrying a career minor league line of .313/.379/.524. Even bigger numbers last year at Triple-A finally forced the Rockies' hand, and they installed him as a bench outfielder, where he performed admirably while substituting in at all three outfield positions. Even with more exciting young players like Fowler and the recently acquired Carlos Gonzalez in the mix, there is some thought within Colorado at giving Smith a shot at an everyday job, or at least a semi-everyday job, as he just can't hit left-handers.

Ryan Spilborghs — OF

Bats: R Throws: R Height: 6' 1" Weight: 190 Born: September 5, 1979 Age: 29

YEAR	TEAM	LVL	AGE	PA	R	2B	3B	HR	RBI	BB	SO	SB	CS	EqBRR	AVG	OBP	SLG	EqAVG	EqOBP	EqSLG	EqA	VORP	WARP	DEFENSE			
2006	CSP	AAA	26	306	50	20	1	5	34	30	49	8	2	1.1	.338	.400	.476	.258	.320	.382	.249	-0.2	0.4	40-LF	2	27-CF	-2
2006	COL	MLB	26	186	26	6	3	4	21	14	30	5	2	0.1	.287	.337	.431	.275	.330	.413	.261	4.9	-0.2	19-CF	-8	11-RF	2
2007	CSP	AAA	27	145	25	7	1	5	17	18	19	4	3	-0.1	.323	.410	.516	.228	.317	.386	.247	-0.9	-0.3	19-LF	-2	9-CF	-1
2007	COL	MLB	27	300	40	14	1	11	51	28	45	4	1	-0.3	.299	.363	.485	.286	.357	.477	.288	17.0	2.4	36-CF	5	14-RF	0
2008	COL	MLB	28	275	38	14	2	6	36	38	41	7	4	-2.3	.313	.407	.468	.310	.406	.474	.303	17.7	0.2	19-LF	-4	16-RF	-4
2009	COL	MLB	29	202	29	10	1	5	23	21	32	5	2	0.1	.289	.364	.437	.271	.346	.414	.267	6.0	0.4	51-CF	-7		

Breakout: 13% Improve: 36% Collapse: 39% Attrition: 44% Comparables: Bob Brower, Kevin Sefcik, George Thomas, Larry Harlow

Spilborghs was slowly but surely taking away center-field at-bats from Willy Taveras early in the season, but a strained oblique cost him a huge chunk of time. As a fourth outfielder over the last three years, he's consistently outperformed the starter (his major league career rates stand at .302/.374/.466), and that production is finally going to be rewarded as he enters this spring with the center-field job his to lose. He's solid and not a star, and is likely to be just a placeholder until Fowler is ready, but any upgrade on Taveras is to be celebrated, even if that amounts to no more than workmanlike production.

Ian Stewart — 3B

Bats: L Throws: R Height: 6' 3" Weight: 205 Born: April 5, 1985 Age: 24

YEAR	TEAM	LVL	AGE	PA	R	2B	3B	HR	RBI	BB	SO	SB	CS	EqBRR	AVG	OBP	SLG	EqAVG	EqOBP	EqSLG	EqA	VORP	WARP	DEFENSE			
2006	TUL	AA	21	528	75	41	7	10	71	50	103	3	8	-2.9	.268	.351	.452	.225	.294	.378	.232	-11.5	0.4	113-3B	7		
2007	CSP	AAA	22	474	72	23	2	15	65	49	92	11	2	3.4	.304	.379	.478	.240	.316	.381	.248	-3.0	-0.6	105-3B	-10		
2007	COL	MLB	22	46	3	4	0	1	9	1	17	0	0	-0.0	.209	.261	.372	.209	.261	.349	.208	-1.4	0.1	5-3B	3		
2008	CSP	AAA	23	298	65	15	6	19	57	34	66	7	2	0.2	.280	.372	.607	.217	.304	.464	.261	3.9	-0.2	62-3B	-9		
2008	COL	MLB	23	304	33	18	2	10	41	30	94	1	1	-0.9	.259	.349	.455	.252	.344	.451	.273	10.3	2.3	60-3B	6	10-2B	3
2009	COL	MLB	24	529	70	31	3	19	70	53	127	7	3	0.4	.263	.344	.468	.247	.327	.443	.263	13.9	2.3	125-3B	2		

Breakout: 37% Improve: 64% Collapse: 12% Attrition: 12% Comparables: Scott Moore, Brian Rosinski, Josh Fields, Michael Tucker

The organization's first-round pick in 2003, Stewart was the MVP of the Sally League in his full-season debut and looked like one of the best prospects in the game. For some reason, that reputation stuck, despite his coming nowhere close to replicating those numbers at the upper levels. Triple-A Colorado Springs helped him put up big numbers again, and with 10 home runs in a half-season for Colorado, many folks are acting like the next future star of the Rockies has arrived. Don't buy into it: Stewart's BABIP is completely unsustainable, he didn't really hit right-handed pitching (.231/.328/.392 while striking out 33 percent of the time), and he doesn't do enough otherwise to make up for it. He might play some at third and he might play some in the outfield, but he's not some huge upgrade at either position, and he's not a future star.

Willy Taveras — CF

Bats: R Throws: R Height: 6' 0" Weight: 160 Born: December 25, 1981 Age: 27

YEAR	TEAM	LVL	AGE	PA	R	2B	3B	HR	RBI	BB	SO	SB	CS	EqBRR	AVG	OBP	SLG	EqAVG	EqOBP	EqSLG	EqA	VORP	WARP	DEFENSE	
2006	HOU	MLB	24	587	83	19	5	1	30	34	88	33	9	6.6	.278	.333	.338	.279	.333	.340	.246	4.2	2.7	123-CF	18
2007	COL	MLB	25	408	64	13	2	2	24	21	55	33	9	1.4	.320	.367	.382	.316	.364	.377	.266	17.0	1.3	79-CF	-1
2008	COL	MLB	26	538	64	15	2	1	26	36	79	68	7	11.9	.251	.308	.296	.247	.305	.293	.241	2.0	0.4	111-CF	1
2009	CIN	MLB	27	384	53	12	3	1	24	26	55	39	10	3.2	.264	.320	.325	.263	.318	.325	.241	-0.2	1.3	92-CF	2

Breakout: 15% Improve: 32% Collapse: 39% Attrition: 28%   Comparables: David Hulse, Lance Johnson, Alex Sanchez, Tom Goodwin

After four years as a starting center fielder, two with Houston and two with Colorado, Taveras has few surprises left, yet the Rockies only just figured out that the only thing he can do is run. That skill allows him to cover plenty of ground in center and steal bases, but that's really it—he has little in the way of on-base skills and even less power. The Rockies tried to trade him, but when they realized that nobody was interested, they just let him go, nontendering him. In one of the winter's biggest surprises, he got a two-year, $6.25 million deal with the Reds; apparently their taste for quality in center was ruined by Corey Patterson.

Yorvit Torrealba — C

Bats: R Throws: R Height: 5' 11" Weight: 200 Born: July 19, 1978 Age: 30

YEAR	TEAM	LVL	AGE	PA	R	2B	3B	HR	RBI	BB	SO	SB	CS	EqBRR	AVG	OBP	SLG	EqAVG	EqOBP	EqSLG	EqA	VORP	WARP	DEFENSE	
2006	COL	MLB	27	241	23	16	3	7	43	11	49	4	3	-0.6	.247	.293	.439	.237	.283	.415	.236	0.6	1.2	60-C	6
2007	COL	MLB	28	443	47	22	1	8	47	34	73	2	1	0.3	.255	.323	.376	.247	.318	.368	.241	5.3	1.7	104-C	6
2008	COL	MLB	29	261	19	17	0	6	31	12	44	0	4	-4.1	.246	.293	.394	.244	.290	.395	.231	-1.4	0.2	65-C	-2
2009	COL	MLB	30	220	20	11	1	4	23	14	37	0	1	-0.9	.253	.309	.374	.237	.294	.354	.223	-1.1	0.7	55-C	0

Breakout: 21% Improve: 37% Collapse: 34% Attrition: 41%   Comparables: Gary Bennett, Joe Girardi, Pete Daley, Russ Gibson

Chris Iannetta's first-year struggles cost the Rockies in a few ways. Torrealba stepped up in 2007 as the starter, and while he wasn't even league average, he was all the Rockies had, so they committed a couple of years and $7.25 million dollars to him. While the club is obviously thrilled that Iannetta figured things out, they now have an overpriced backup, and that money could be used for some help in the bullpen or elsewhere. You can't blame the Rockies for doing what they did—at the time, Torrealba was the only catcher they could depend on—but now they're kind of stuck with him, and it hurts the team on more of an economic than a talent level.

Troy Tulowitzki — SS

Bats: R Throws: R Height: 6' 3" Weight: 205 Born: October 10, 1984 Age: 24

YEAR	TEAM	LVL	AGE	PA	R	2B	3B	HR	RBI	BB	SO	SB	CS	EqBRR	AVG	OBP	SLG	EqAVG	EqOBP	EqSLG	EqA	VORP	WARP	DEFENSE	
2006	TUL	AA	21	485	75	34	2	13	61	46	71	6	5	-4.1	.291	.370	.473	.245	.312	.404	.248	0.6	1.4	102-SS	-2
2006	COL	MLB	21	108	15	2	0	1	6	10	25	3	0	1.6	.240	.318	.292	.229	.308	.281	.219	-1.7	-0.4	25-SS	-4
2007	COL	MLB	22	682	104	33	5	24	99	57	130	7	6	0.2	.291	.359	.479	.280	.352	.469	.277	39.2	7.3	152-SS	25
2008	COL	MLB	23	421	48	24	2	8	46	38	56	1	6	-1.1	.263	.332	.401	.257	.329	.401	.249	8.1	1.6	97-SS	3
2009	COL	MLB	24	521	68	29	2	15	66	50	79	4	3	0.1	.283	.356	.452	.265	.339	.428	.264	21.2	2.8	123-SS	3

Breakout: 26% Improve: 49% Collapse: 20% Attrition: 16%   Comparables: Ron Hansen, Ken McMullen, Bob Aspromonte, Larry Parrish

As good a year as Tulo had in 2007—when he finished one vote shy of Rookie of the Year honors and was a top 20 MVP candidate—that's how bad 2008 was. He was hitting as low as .163 in late April, didn't hit a home run until the third week of the season, and then landed on the disabled list a week later with a torn quadriceps. That kept him out until late June, but he lasted a total of about 10 days before a splintered bat tore apart his hand. The good news is that once he was healthy, he was really good again, saving his season averages with a .330/.392/.534 mark in the season's final month. Give him a mulligan—he's still a star.

Eric Young, Jr. — 2B/CF

Bats: S Throws: R Height: 5' 10" Weight: 180 Born: May 25, 1985 Age: 24

YEAR	TEAM	LVL	AGE	PA	R	2B	3B	HR	RBI	BB	SO	SB	CS	EqBRR	AVG	OBP	SLG	EqAVG	EqOBP	EqSLG	EqA	VORP	WARP	DEFENSE		
2006	ASH	A	21	569	92	28	6	5	49	67	75	87	31	2.6	.295	.391	.409	.212	.286	.301	.214	-33.3	-1.3	117-2B	0	
2007	MOD	A+	22	613	113	29	11	8	63	46	105	73	18	0.2	.291	.359	.430	.235	.288	.341	.228	-22.2	1.3	126-2B	13	
2008	TUL	AA	23	476	74	24	4	3	33	61	77	46	16	4.0	.290	.391	.392	.237	.326	.329	.239	-9.6	1.9	92-2B	11	4-CF 1
2009	COL	MLB	24	542	77	27	5	4	38	50	102	42	13	3.8	.263	.337	.370	.247	.321	.350	.245	4.1	2.1	127-2B	7	

Breakout: 38% Improve: 67% Collapse: 15% Attrition: 12%   Comparables: Denny Hocking, Tom Lawless, Quentin Harley, Greg Smith

The Rockies keep moving Young up the ladder, he keeps producing, and the number of doubters in the scouting community keeps decreasing. It's almost impossible to *not* compare him to his father at this point: he's a little guy who slaps the ball around the field enough to hit in the upper .290s, draws his fair share of walks, and steals a bunch of bases. Young is not a great second baseman, but he's acceptable there, and the Rockies have also had him learning to play the outfield to give themselves a few more options with him. He was a 30th-round pick, and he's going to have a career. You don't get to say that a lot.

PITCHERS

Ced Bowers

Bats: R   Throws: L   Height: 6' 2"   Weight: 220   Born: February 10, 1978   Age: 31

YEAR	TEAM	LVL	AGE	W	L	SV	G	GS	IP	H	BB	SO	HR	GB%	BABIP	STUFF	WHIP	ERA	DERA	EqH9	EqBB9	EqSO9	EqHR9	DEF	VORP	SN/WX
2008	CSP	AAA	30	6	1	1	35	2	65	50	43	74	5	50.0%	.288	7	1.43	3.74	4.91	7.5	5.9	7.1	0.9	6	4.8	—
2008	COL	MLB	30	0	0	0	5	0	6²	11	5	5	2	31.8%	.474	-14	2.40	13.43	7.94	17.5	6.4	6.4	3.2	-3	-5.5	-0.07
2009	COL	MLB	31	2	3	1	30	3	49	52	33	43	6	45.0%	.320	4	1.72	5.44	5.10	8.8	5.2	7.2	1.0	0	3.4	0.42

Breakout: 29%   Improve: 54%   Collapse: 24%   Attrition: 25%   Comparables: Mike Muñoz, Kevin Tolar, Greg McCarthy, Jeff Tabaka

Cedrick Bowers is *cool*. A fourth-round pick by the Devil Rays twelve years ago, Bowers spent eight years in the Tampa system, topping out with multiple years at Triple-A with command issues and an overly emotional mound demeanor keeping him from reaching the big leagues. Released, he persevered in Korea and Japan and had an epiphany in the latter place, dedicating himself to keeping his emotions in check in the manner of the usually stoic Japanese players. When Bill Geivett, formerly of the Rays, gave him a shot, Bowers pitched well enough at Triple-A to get the call to "The Show." Even if Bowers never makes it back to the big leagues, he has a book's worth of stories from the Pacific Rim, and he can always say he struck out Rickie Weeks every time he faced him (twice).

Taylor Buchholz

Bats: R   Throws: R   Height: 6' 4"   Weight: 220   Born: October 13, 1981   Age: 27

YEAR	TEAM	LVL	AGE	W	L	SV	G	GS	IP	H	BB	SO	HR	GB%	BABIP	STUFF	WHIP	ERA	DERA	EqH9	EqBB9	EqSO9	EqHR9	DEF	VORP	SN/WX
2006	ROU	AAA	24	1	3	0	7	7	44	47	17	37	2	42.6%	.345	-2	1.45	4.91	6.47	11.8	3.8	5.4	0.7	-2	-3.9	—
2006	HOU	MLB	24	6	10	0	22	19	113	107	34	77	21	45.5%	.258	-8	1.25	5.89	6.61	8.2	2.4	5.5	1.5	11	-4.2	1.31
2007	COL	MLB	25	6	5	0	41	8	93²	105	20	61	8	46.3%	.329	8	1.33	4.23	3.52	9.9	1.7	5.6	0.7	-3	15.5	0.95
2008	COL	MLB	26	6	6	1	63	0	66¹	45	18	56	5	39.6%	.225	12	0.95	2.17	3.80	5.2	2.0	6.4	0.7	7	19.3	2.55
2009	COL	MLB	27	3	3	2	47	2	64²	67	21	50	8	43.0%	.300	8	1.36	4.44	4.20	8.7	2.5	6.3	1.1	1	11.4	1.08

Breakout: 21%   Improve: 51%   Collapse: 23%   Attrition: 20%   Comparables: Turk Farrell, Rich Bordi, Les Lancaster, Scott Sullivan

When Buchholz was used as a trade chip by the Phillies and Astros earlier in the decade, he looked like a solid rotation piece. That hasn't worked out, but the Rockies did turn him into one heck of a reliever. He's effective against both sides, thanks to a 91-94 mph pitch with cutting action that has gone from a trick pitch to his primary offering. He's not quite closer-worthy, but there is no reason he can't be a successful late-innings type for years to come.

Jhoulys Chacin

Bats: R   Throws: R   Height: 6' 1"   Weight: 168   Born: January 7, 1988   Age: 21

YEAR	TEAM	LVL	AGE	W	L	SV	G	GS	IP	H	BB	SO	HR	GB%	BABIP	STUFF	WHIP	ERA	DERA	EqH9	EqBB9	EqSO9	EqHR9	DEF	VORP	SN/WX
2007	CAS	Rk	19	6	5	0	16	16	92	85	26	77	5	62.7%	.307	-1	1.21	3.13	7.22	10.7	4.4	2.8	1.6	0	-14.6	—
2008	ASH	A	20	10	1	0	16	16	111¹	82	30	98	3	66.1%	.264	35	1.01	1.86	4.92	8.7	3.6	3.8	0.8	11	7.6	—
2008	MOD	A+	20	8	2	0	12	12	66¹	61	12	62	3	57.5%	.323	23	1.10	2.31	4.97	11.0	2.5	4.8	1.1	5	4.1	—
2009	COL	MLB	21	5	9	0	21	21	113²	140	50	67	14	55.0%	.330	8	1.67	6.04	5.76	10.3	3.4	4.8	1.0	1	0.3	0.92

Breakout: 0%   Improve: 15%   Collapse: 41%   Attrition: 6%   Comparables: Julian Tavarez, Jair Jurrjens, Oswaldo Sosa, Jose Martinez

Chacin has had the biggest breakout of any Colorado farmhand, leading all the minor leagues with 18 wins while finishing sixth in strikeouts. He's a remarkably mature product for someone who just turned 21, as he pounds the strike zone with as many as five pitches: a sinker, a cutter, two breaking balls, and an outstanding changeup. The only knock against him is that he lacks true ace-level stuff, but there's no reason he couldn't be a second or third starter in the majors in short order, especially if he can repeat last year's success when he moves up to Double-A this season.

Aaron Cook

Bats: R Throws: R Height: 6' 3" Weight: 215 Born: February 8, 1979 Age: 30

YEAR	TEAM	LVL	AGE	W	L	SV	G	GS	IP	H	BB	SO	HR	GB%	BABIP	STUFF	WHIP	ERA	DERA	EqH9	EqBB9	EqSO9	EqHR9	DEF	VORP	SN/WX
2006	COL	MLB	27	9	15	0	32	32	212²	242	55	92	17	58.6%	.308	8	1.40	4.23	4.01	9.4	2.0	3.5	0.6	5	40.1	4.49
2007	COL	MLB	28	8	7	0	25	25	166	178	44	61	15	59.5%	.290	0	1.34	4.12	5.01	9.5	2.1	3.2	0.7	18	24.5	2.85
2008	COL	MLB	29	16	9	0	32	32	211¹	236	48	96	13	57.0%	.313	12	1.34	3.96	3.88	9.3	1.8	3.7	0.5	1	35.4	4.03
2009	COL	MLB	30	9	10	0	26	26	161¹	195	43	81	16	55.0%	.320	8	1.47	4.81	4.61	10.1	2.1	4.1	0.8	1	19.4	3.41

Breakout: 3% Improve: 20% Collapse: 36% Attrition: 19% Comparables: Al Fitzmorris, Jim Barr, Jake Westbrook, Scott Erickson

The All-Star Game demonstrated what Aaron Cook is in a nutshell. He allowed seven base runners over three innings, but didn't allow a single run, because of his knack for inducing grounders. Cook will mix in about 10 to 15 sliders a game, but otherwise, he's all about the sinker, a pitch that he adds and subtracts from to assist in its deception, throwing it anywhere from 87 to 93 mph. He gives up a lot of hits, but he doesn't walk anyone, and again, there are always those ground balls, which truly are a pitcher's best friend. It's a bit of a high-wire act, but Cook is so good at it as to be an honorary Flying Wallenda.

Manuel Corpas

Bats: R Throws: R Height: 6' 3" Weight: 170 Born: December 3, 1982 Age: 26

YEAR	TEAM	LVL	AGE	W	L	SV	G	GS	IP	H	BB	SO	HR	GB%	BABIP	STUFF	WHIP	ERA	DERA	EqH9	EqBB9	EqSO9	EqHR9	DEF	VORP	SN/WX
2006	TUL	AA	23	2	1	19	34	0	36²	22	4	35	0	63.0%	.247	9	0.72	0.99	4.54	7.0	1.3	5.9	0.3	7	4.0	—
2006	COL	MLB	23	1	2	0	35	0	32¹	36	8	27	3	45.5%	.344	12	1.36	3.62	2.61	9.9	2.0	7.3	0.9	-2	9.2	0.21
2007	COL	MLB	24	4	2	19	78	0	78	63	20	58	6	58.4%	.263	12	1.06	2.08	2.99	7.3	2.0	6.5	0.6	8	31.6	4.04
2008	COL	MLB	25	3	4	4	76	0	79²	93	23	50	7	50.6%	.335	-4	1.46	4.52	4.08	9.8	2.2	5.0	0.7	0	10.2	-0.22
2009	COL	MLB	26	3	3	4	57	0	64¹	69	19	44	6	51.0%	.310	5	1.37	3.97	3.80	9.0	2.3	5.5	0.8	1	15.9	1.22

Breakout: 4% Improve: 18% Collapse: 64% Attrition: 14% Comparables: Jose Santiago, Hipolito Pichardo, Luis Ayala, Clay Carroll

Corpas had quite the Jekyll-and-Hyde season in 2008. From June through August, he had a 2.48 ERA in 36 appearances. Unfortunately, that came sandwiched between a first two months and a September that saw him at a 6.58 mark in 40 games. Note that these swings are themselves a reduced version of Corpas's 2007-2008; in the former he was hit-lucky, with a low BABIP, while in the latter he was hit-unlucky. However, mere luck and inadequacy on the part of the fielders doesn't completely explain away 2008, as Corpas apparently earned some of his poundings with a below-average line-drive rate; he was allowing the batters to get their swings in. Despite the acquisition of Huston Street, the Rockies are still talking about Corpas as their closer in 2009, which makes no sense. He's not some raw guy with closer stuff—his fastball sits at around 92-93 mph and his slider is merely solid. The message that he is a closer is either specifically designed to increase his trade value or pure delusion.

Jorge de la Rosa

Bats: L Throws: L Height: 6' 1" Weight: 210 Born: April 5, 1981 Age: 28

YEAR	TEAM	LVL	AGE	W	L	SV	G	GS	IP	H	BB	SO	HR	GB%	BABIP	STUFF	WHIP	ERA	DERA	EqH9	EqBB9	EqSO9	EqHR9	DEF	VORP	SN/WX
2006	MIL	MLB	25	2	2	0	18	3	30¹	32	22	31	4	43.5%	.333	5	1.78	8.32	6.82	8.8	5.4	8.0	1.1	-3	-8.8	0.27
2006	KCA	MLB	25	3	4	0	10	10	48²	49	32	36	10	41.4%	.279	-4	1.66	5.17	5.81	8.4	5.8	5.8	1.7	4	4.1	1.00
2007	KCA	MLB	26	8	12	0	26	23	130	160	53	82	20	41.2%	.329	-15	1.64	5.82	5.06	10.8	3.4	4.9	1.4	-9	0.0	1.23
2008	COL	MLB	27	10	8	0	28	23	130	128	62	128	13	47.3%	.330	18	1.46	4.92	4.36	8.4	3.7	7.8	0.8	-5	8.6	2.19
2009	COL	MLB	28	6	7	1	33	17	108²	116	48	93	15	44.0%	.310	13	1.51	5.04	4.72	8.9	3.4	6.9	1.1	1	12.9	1.93

Breakout: 33% Improve: 60% Collapse: 18% Attrition: 25% Comparables: Gerry Arrigo, Chris Capuano, Kent Mercker, Bo Belinsky

When he was acquired from the Royals at the end of April, it was hoped de la Rosa would shore up the back of the rotation. He did, but it took a while; he was downright awful initially, allowing 25 runs over 23 innings in his first five starts. From there he moved back and forth from the bullpen to the rotation and slowly came around, finishing the year back in a starting role and going 5-2 with a 2.61 ERA in his last eight outings. It's not like the guy is without stuff—he can get his fastball up to 96 mph at times—but he's found more success using a low-90s cutter to complement his slider in his quiver of off-speed offerings. The Rockies are optimistic that they might be on to something here, and de la Rosa will compete for the fifth starter's job this spring.

Jeff Francis

Bats: L   **Throws: L**   **Height: 6' 5"**   **Weight: 205**   **Born: January 8, 1981**   **Age: 28**

YEAR	TEAM	LVL	AGE	W	L	SV	G	GS	IP	H	BB	SO	HR	GB%	BABIP	STUFF	WHIP	ERA	DERA	EqH9	EqBB9	EqSO9	EqHR9	DEF	VORP	SN/WX
2006	COL	MLB	25	13	11	0	32	32	199	187	69	117	18	46.1%	.276	13	1.29	4.16	4.22	7.7	2.7	4.8	0.7	8	35.1	4.06
2007	COL	MLB	26	17	9	0	34	34	215¹	234	63	165	25	46.3%	.321	17	1.38	4.22	3.71	9.7	2.3	6.6	0.9	1	41.6	5.38
2008	COL	MLB	27	4	10	0	24	24	143²	164	49	94	21	45.7%	.312	0	1.48	5.01	4.48	9.3	2.6	5.1	1.2	-2	9.8	1.91
2009	COL	MLB	28	9	9	0	26	26	152²	172	47	116	19	44.0%	.320	19	1.43	4.79	4.50	9.4	2.4	6.2	1.0	1	19.9	3.42

Breakout: 6%   **Improve: 33%**   **Collapse: 28%**   **Attrition: 20%**   Comparables: *Jerry Reuss, Pete Schourek, Denny Neagle, Bob Knepper*

Francis was yet another bottle of milk that spoiled in 2008. While he's hardly an ace, Francis had delivered two years as an above-average innings-eater. He couldn't even perform that role last season, though, as constant shoulder inflammation plagued him throughout the year and his once-average fastball dipped into the 85-87 mph range. The Rockies finally shut him down with a couple of weeks to go in the season, but shoulder issues are the biggest of big red flags, and it's hard to be especially optimistic here.

Christian Friedrich

Bats: R   **Throws: L**   **Height: 6' 3"**   **Weight: 210**   **Born: July 8, 1987**   **Age: 21**

YEAR	TEAM	LVL	AGE	W	L	SV	G	GS	IP	H	BB	SO	HR	GB%	BABIP	STUFF	WHIP	ERA	DERA	EqH9	EqBB9	EqSO9	EqHR9	DEF	VORP	SN/WX
2008	ASH	A	20	0	1	0	3	3	12	14	7	15	2	45.9%	.343	2	1.75	7.50	9.82	14.7	7.4	5.7	3.3	-1	-5.2	—
2008	TRI	A-	20	2	1	0	8	8	36	31	8	50	2	51.1%	.345	18	1.08	3.25	5.93	13.4	3.3	6.2	2.1	-5	-1.1	—
2009	COL	MLB	21	5	12	0	26	26	133	182	73	94	28	44.0%	.350	5	1.92	7.86	7.25	11.5	4.3	5.7	1.7	1	-21.4	-1.19

Breakout: 34%   **Improve: 82%**   **Collapse: 6%**   **Attrition: 2%**   Comparables: *Mike Milchin, Adam Pettyjohn, Kyle Abbott, Mark Langston*

Generally seen as one of the better college arms in the draft, Colorado was pleasantly surprised to see Friedrich on the board with the 25th overall pick and quickly signed him to a $1.35 million bonus. Friedrich's fastball is average to slightly above, but his curveball was the best in the draft and helped him strike out 65 over 48 innings in his pro debut. He's the best starting prospect in the system after Chacin, but at least two or three years away.

Brian Fuentes

Bats: L   **Throws: L**   **Height: 6' 4"**   **Weight: 230**   **Born: August 9, 1975**   **Age: 33**

YEAR	TEAM	LVL	AGE	W	L	SV	G	GS	IP	H	BB	SO	HR	GB%	BABIP	STUFF	WHIP	ERA	DERA	EqH9	EqBB9	EqSO9	EqHR9	DEF	VORP	SN/WX
2006	COL	MLB	30	3	4	30	66	0	65¹	50	26	73	8	35.5%	.266	19	1.16	3.45	2.97	6.3	3.1	8.9	0.9	1	19.7	2.14
2007	COL	MLB	31	3	5	20	64	0	61¹	46	23	56	6	36.7%	.248	10	1.13	3.08	4.67	6.6	2.9	7.6	0.7	10	14.8	0.37
2008	COL	MLB	32	1	5	30	67	0	62²	47	22	82	3	35.8%	.306	32	1.10	2.73	2.70	6.5	2.7	9.7	0.4	-1	18.0	3.62
2009	LAA	MLB	33	4	4	23	64	0	61²	55	22	61	7	37.0%	.290	17	1.24	3.53	3.52	7.8	3.0	8.3	1.0	0	13.7	1.75

Breakout: 10%   **Improve: 36%**   **Collapse: 38%**   **Attrition: 7%**   Comparables: *Todd Worrell, Norm Charlton, Eric Plunk, Roberto Hernandez*

Fuentes saved his best for last, saving 30 of Colorado's 74 wins and putting up career highs in several categories just in time for free agency. He doesn't have classic closer stuff, but his 91-94 mph fastball features both deception and a lot of movement, while his slider is outstanding at times. He was absolutely dominant away from Coors last year, allowing just 14 hits in 29⅓ innings with a 1.84 ERA. The third-best free-agent reliever on the market, he got the third-best deal behind K-Rod's and Kerry Wood's, signing with the Angels for two years (plus a 2011 club option) and $17.5 million.

Jason Grilli

Bats: R   **Throws: R**   **Height: 6' 5"**   **Weight: 225**   **Born: November 11, 1976**   **Age: 32**

YEAR	TEAM	LVL	AGE	W	L	SV	G	GS	IP	H	BB	SO	HR	GB%	BABIP	STUFF	WHIP	ERA	DERA	EqH9	EqBB9	EqSO9	EqHR9	DEF	VORP	SN/WX
2006	DET	MLB	29	2	3	0	51	0	62	61	25	31	6	48.8%	.279	-18	1.39	4.21	4.95	9.1	3.6	4.1	0.9	4	11.1	0.08
2007	DET	MLB	30	5	3	0	57	0	79²	81	32	62	5	45.6%	.315	2	1.42	4.74	4.54	9.1	3.3	6.0	0.6	-4	7.6	0.29
2008	DET	MLB	31	0	1	0	9	0	13²	12	7	10	1	39.0%	.275	-3	1.39	3.28	2.70	8.1	4.1	6.1	0.7	-1	3.9	-0.06
2008	COL	MLB	31	3	2	1	51	0	61¹	55	31	59	1	44.5%	.321	19	1.40	2.94	2.79	7.6	3.8	7.6	0.1	-1	17.3	0.59
2009	COL	MLB	32	3	3	2	47	0	58¹	62	26	48	7	45.0%	.310	6	1.50	4.68	4.42	8.9	3.4	6.7	1.0	0	9.2	0.71

Breakout: 8%   **Improve: 36%**   **Collapse: 40%**   **Attrition: 23%**   Comparables: *Gregg Olson, Mark Wohlers, Ted Power, Jerry Spradlin*

Now more than a decade removed from being the fourth overall pick in the 1997 draft, Grilli never turned into the stud people expected out of college, but slowly, very slowly, he's developed into a pretty nice reliever. Every year, he gets a little bit better, and he enjoyed a career best campaign in 2008, despite the transition to Coors after being traded by the Tigers for pitcher Zach Simons (and despite his former manager slagging him posttrade). He's slowly transformed into a pure power pitcher, sitting at 93-96 mph with his fastball and complementing it with a sharp slider. He's finally arbitration-eligible and in line for his first decent payday, and he's well worth it.

Matt Herges

Bats: L   Throws: R   Height: 6' 0"   Weight: 210   Born: April 1, 1970   Age: 39

YEAR	TEAM	LVL	AGE	W	L	SV	G	GS	IP	H	BB	SO	HR	GB%	BABIP	STUFF	WHIP	ERA	DERA	EqH9	EqBB9	EqSO9	EqHR9	DEF	VORP	SN/WX
2006	FLO	MLB	36	2	3	0	66	0	71	94	28	36	5	47.9%	.353	-10	1.72	4.31	3.69	11.5	3.1	4.2	0.5	-10	3.7	-0.99
2007	CSP	AAA	37	2	1	1	32	0	35¹	24	10	33	2	52.7%	.247	4	0.96	1.27	3.48	6.1	2.7	6.1	0.5	7	7.9	—
2007	COL	MLB	37	5	1	0	35	0	48²	34	15	30	4	48.6%	.217	0	1.01	2.96	4.25	5.9	2.4	5.2	0.7	8	15.4	2.01
2008	COL	MLB	38	3	4	0	58	0	64¹	79	24	46	5	41.6%	.354	-3	1.60	5.04	4.57	10.2	2.8	5.5	0.7	-3	1.7	-0.75
2009	COL	MLB	39	2	2	1	37	0	43²	54	16	27	6	44.0%	.330	-6	1.61	5.48	5.16	10.4	2.9	5.0	1.1	0	3.0	0.22

Breakout: 10%   Improve: 20%   Collapse: 45%   Attrition: 35%   Comparables: Mike Maddux, Jose Mesa, Harry Gumbert, Steve Sparks

Prior to the season, Herges' name showed up in the Mitchell report, and he admitted to performance-enhancing substance use, albeit well in his past. He probably could have better used the boost in 2008, as his stuff took a big dip; back problems didn't help. The Rockies declined his option, making him a free agent. Herges is a fastball/changeup righty without much of a fastball anymore, so there's not much left here.

Livan Hernandez

Bats: R   Throws: R   Height: 6' 2"   Weight: 245   Born: February 20, 1975   Age: 34

YEAR	TEAM	LVL	AGE	W	L	SV	G	GS	IP	H	BB	SO	HR	GB%	BABIP	STUFF	WHIP	ERA	DERA	EqH9	EqBB9	EqSO9	EqHR9	DEF	VORP	SN/WX
2006	WAS	MLB	31	9	8	0	24	24	146²	176	52	89	22	40.0%	.322	-3	1.55	5.34	4.62	10.3	2.7	4.9	1.2	-13	2.0	1.48
2006	ARI	MLB	31	4	5	0	10	10	69¹	70	26	39	7	36.8%	.290	6	1.38	3.77	4.15	8.6	3.0	4.7	0.8	5	16.0	1.64
2007	ARI	MLB	32	11	11	0	33	33	204¹	247	79	90	34	41.5%	.314	-15	1.60	4.93	4.74	10.5	3.1	3.8	1.4	9	20.4	3.09
2008	MIN	MLB	33	10	8	0	23	23	139²	199	29	54	18	45.7%	.354	-15	1.63	5.48	5.28	12.5	1.7	3.0	1.3	-12	-4.1	0.95
2008	COL	MLB	33	3	3	0	8	8	40¹	58	14	13	7	47.8%	.345	24	1.79	8.04	5.95	12.4	2.7	2.7	1.4	-5	-9.3	-0.29
2009	COL	MLB	34	5	8	0	26	18	108¹	142	36	54	18	43.0%	.320	-4	1.64	6.10	5.68	10.9	2.6	4.1	1.4	1	1.4	0.87

Breakout: 8%   Improve: 36%   Collapse: 33%   Attrition: 25%   Comparables: Bill Gullickson, Walt Terrell, Aaron Sele, Matt Morris

Have arm, will travel. The only thing valuable about Hernandez at this point is that you know he's going to take the mound every fifth day. He's made 30-plus starts for 11 straight years now, but he's got nothing left in the tank, with a fastball that sat at 83-87 mph and led to the National League hitting .345 against him with a .571 slugging percentage. His overall rate of hits allowed, 12.9 per nine innings, was something special, representing a level of hittability not exceeded in the major leagues since Jim Walkup of the Browns (whose name should have perhaps been Jim *Hitup*) was pounded for 13.1 hits per nine back in 1937 (150 innings and up division). At this writing, Hernandez is on the hunt for a job, and somebody will probably give him at least a spring invite, as the devil you know …

Jason Hirsh

Bats: R   Throws: R   Height: 6' 8"   Weight: 250   Born: February 20, 1982   Age: 27

YEAR	TEAM	LVL	AGE	W	L	SV	G	GS	IP	H	BB	SO	HR	GB%	BABIP	STUFF	WHIP	ERA	DERA	EqH9	EqBB9	EqSO9	EqHR9	DEF	VORP	SN/WX
2006	ROU	AAA	24	13	2	0	23	23	137¹	94	51	118	5	40.2%	.246	16	1.06	2.10	4.20	7.5	3.6	5.5	0.6	13	20.0	—
2006	HOU	MLB	24	3	4	0	9	9	44²	48	22	29	11	32.2%	.264	-15	1.57	6.04	6.26	9.2	3.7	5.1	2.0	2	-2.0	0.65
2007	COL	MLB	25	5	7	0	19	19	112¹	103	48	75	18	32.7%	.258	-2	1.34	4.81	5.30	7.8	3.3	5.5	1.3	14	12.7	1.41
2008	CSP	AAA	26	4	4	0	18	17	99¹	115	52	51	16	38.4%	.304	-33	1.68	5.80	6.70	10.4	4.7	2.7	1.6	7	-11.8	—
2008	COL	MLB	26	0	0	0	4	1	8²	15	4	6	3	19.4%	.364	-25	2.19	8.28	6.75	13.5	2.9	4.8	2.9	-3	-3.9	0.04
2009	COL	MLB	27	4	7	0	26	14	86	106	41	53	18	38.0%	.310	-3	1.70	6.55	6.02	10.3	3.7	5.0	1.7	1	-2.3	0.29

Breakout: 3%   Improve: 11%   Collapse: 60%   Attrition: 30%   Comparables: Jeremy Griffiths, Gene Conley, Brian Fisher, Pete Broberg

Hirsh seemed to be hitting his stride in 2007 before breaking his leg, but 2008 proved to be a major step backward, as a strained shoulder in spring training turned into an endless bout of soreness that kept him on the shelf almost until June and in Colorado Springs until rosters expanded. Despite early problems with his command, his velocity was nearly all the way back, so at least there's that bit of good news. The rotation is a bit of a blur, but he's in the edges of the picture.

Ubaldo Jimenez

Bats: R   Throws: R   Height: 6' 4"   Weight: 200   Born: January 22, 1984   Age: 25

YEAR	TEAM	LVL	AGE	W	L	SV	G	GS	IP	H	BB	SO	HR	GB%	BABIP	STUFF	WHIP	ERA	DERA	EqH9	EqBB9	EqSO9	EqHR9	DEF	VORP	SN/WX
2006	TUL	AA	22	9	2	0	13	13	73²	49	40	86	2	43.2%	.287	28	1.22	2.46	4.29	8.4	5.7	7.5	0.6	5	9.5	—
2006	CSP	AAA	22	5	2	0	13	13	78¹	74	43	64	7	43.9%	.311	1	1.50	5.07	7.14	8.8	5.0	4.9	1.1	9	-13.0	—
2006	COL	MLB	22	0	0	0	2	1	7²	5	3	3	1	45.8%	.174	-7	1.04	3.51	7.04	4.7	3.5	3.5	1.2	3	1.3	0.25
2007	CSP	AAA	23	8	5	0	19	19	103	110	62	89	9	47.8%	.341	3	1.67	5.85	6.70	10.0	5.7	5.6	1.0	3	-12.0	—
2007	COL	MLB	23	4	4	0	15	15	82	70	37	68	10	47.7%	.262	16	1.30	4.28	4.88	7.4	3.5	6.8	1.0	6	9.3	1.79
2008	COL	MLB	24	12	12	0	34	34	198²	182	103	172	11	56.1%	.305	25	1.43	3.99	4.01	7.7	4.0	6.8	0.4	2	31.6	4.48
2009	COL	MLB	25	9	10	0	28	28	165²	166	80	143	16	50.0%	.310	23	1.48	4.66	4.44	8.4	3.7	7.0	0.8	1	23.1	3.80

Breakout: 13%   Improve: 41%   Collapse: 25%   Attrition: 17%   Comparables: Jim Hughes, Jim Clancy, Tony Armas, Daniel Cabrera

Jimenez's inconsistency drives both Rockies fans and management a little nuts, but he's only 24, and he had more than enough outings to convince that his is a special arm. His violent delivery causes extreme control issues, but his fastball sits at 94-97 mph and touches triple digits once in a while, and when his ability to throw strikes is merely average, he's unstoppable. He's nowhere close to his prime, but made strides during the second half. Jimenez could be poised for a breakout season and a fine career as long as his arm holds up—that last is what keeps our prediction from becoming a lock.

Franklin Morales

Bats: L   Throws: L   Height: 6' 0"   Weight: 170   Born: January 24, 1986   Age: 23

YEAR	TEAM	LVL	AGE	W	L	SV	G	GS	IP	H	BB	SO	HR	GB%	BABIP	STUFF	WHIP	ERA	DERA	EqH9	EqBB9	EqSO9	EqHR9	DEF	VORP	SN/WX
2006	MOD	A+	20	10	9	0	27	26	154²	126	89	179	9	54.5%	.310	19	1.39	3.68	5.98	9.3	6.4	5.7	1.3	-8	-5.9	—
2007	TUL	AA	21	3	4	0	17	17	95²	77	45	77	8	47.6%	.270	6	1.27	3.48	6.65	9.1	5.0	4.7	1.2	13	-10.1	—
2007	CSP	AAA	21	2	0	0	3	3	17	20	13	16	1	41.3%	.422	14	1.94	3.71	3.29	13.8	8.6	7.2	0.7	-2	3.5	—
2007	COL	MLB	21	3	2	0	8	8	39¹	34	14	26	2	57.0%	.283	36	1.22	3.44	3.49	7.7	2.8	5.6	0.5	3	10.9	1.32
2008	COL	MLB	22	1	2	0	5	5	25¹	28	17	9	2	40.9%	.299	-14	1.78	6.40	6.49	8.9	4.8	2.7	0.7	3	-1.2	0.23
2008	CSP	AAA	22	10	5	0	21	21	110¹	108	82	83	14	45.3%	.307	-7	1.72	5.47	7.19	9.5	6.8	4.6	1.3	14	-18.1	—
2009	COL	MLB	23	5	10	0	37	24	117	141	89	83	19	45.0%	.330-4		1.96	6.80	6.31	10.1	5.9	5.8	1.3		1 -6.3	0.06

Breakout: 4%   Improve: 19%   Collapse: 38%   Attrition: 16%   Comparables: Jesus Martinez, Josias Manzanillo, Mike Chris, Mike Potts

On the long list of Colorado's 2008 disappointments, Morales might rank first. The best prospect in the system coming off a season in which he helped pitch his team into the playoffs, Morales tried to work through a variety of injuries with the result that his stuff and control both took big steps backward. After pitching six shutout innings in his initial start, Morales was tagged for 18 runs in his next 19⅓ innings and was sent down. Once sitting in the mid-90s with his fastball, he only occasionally touched that in 2008, and he just didn't throw enough strikes. Colorado Springs continued to be a mixed bag, but reports out of Venezuela this winter were extremely positive, and this is way too good of an arm to give up on.

Juan Morillo

Bats: R   Throws: R   Height: 6' 3"   Weight: 190   Born: November 5, 1983   Age: 25

YEAR	TEAM	LVL	AGE	W	L	SV	G	GS	IP	H	BB	SO	HR	GB%	BABIP	STUFF	WHIP	ERA	DERA	EqH9	EqBB9	EqSO9	EqHR9	DEF	VORP	SN/WX
2006	TUL	AA	22	12	8	0	27	27	140	128	80	132	13	47.9%	.307	-4	1.49	4.63	6.98	10.8	5.8	5.6	1.4	3	-19.4	—
2007	TUL	AA	23	6	4	0	46	0	57¹	44	27	59	2	46.4%	.282	-1	1.24	2.36	4.89	8.8	4.9	6.1	0.7	4	4.2	—
2007	CSP	AAA	23	0	1	0	7	0	9²	7	4	12	0	39.1%	.304	9	1.13	3.71	4.82	6.8	3.9	8.7	0.0	1	0.8	—
2008	CSP	AAA	24	1	0	0	52	0	59²	53	56	55	3	47.6%	.314	0	1.83	5.28	6.21	8.4	8.2	5.4	0.6	3	-3.9	—
2009	COL	MLB	25	2	3	0	24	5	49¹	53	42	41	6	45.0%	.320	-1	1.92	6.38	6.00	9.1	6.6	6.7	1.0	0	-1.2	0.04

Breakout: 15%   Improve: 45%   Collapse: 22%   Attrition: 18%   Comparables: Craig House, Rafael Medina, Jesus Colome, Brian Bowles

In principle, Morillo could be a big-league closer. Not only does he have the best pure arm in the organization, but it's also one of the best in all of baseball. He routinely hits 100 mph, sits at 97-99, and has been clocked by one scout as high as 103 in the past. Nevertheless, this is baseball, not speed trials or the Olympics. The fastball is as straight as an arrow, he has no idea where it's going when it comes out of his hand, and he's yet to find anything close to a reliable secondary offering, as his upper-80s slider is a flat, sweepy pitch. Morillo is a cautionary tale on wasted talent and the futility of trying to live on velocity alone.

Steven Register

						Bats: R		Throws: R		Height: 6' 1"		Weight: 170		Born: May 16, 1983			Age: 26	

YEAR	TEAM	LVL	AGE	W	L	SV	G	GS	IP	H	BB	SO	HR	GB%	BABIP	STUFF	WHIP	ERA	DERA	EqH9	EqBB9	EqSO9	EqHR9	DEF	VORP	SN/WX
2006	TUL	AA	23	4	10	0	27	27	155¹	189	53	77	25	46.8%	.319	-56	1.56	5.57	8.66	13.7	3.7	2.4	2.3	2	-47.4	—
2007	TUL	AA	24	1	3	37	60	0	58	63	16	48	3	50.8%	.341	-19	1.36	4.03	5.74	12.0	3.0	4.7	0.8	0	-0.8	—
2008	CSP	AAA	25	5	3	16	56	0	59	57	19	52	4	47.5%	.314	-8	1.29	3.36	5.34	8.9	3.0	5.3	0.8	8	1.7	—
2008	COL	MLB	25	0	0	0	10	0	10	13	6	8	4	37.1%	.300	-28	1.90	9.00	8.44	10.1	4.2	5.9	3.4	0	-3.3	-0.08
2009	COL	MLB	26	2	3	1	44	3	49¹	63	22	34	9	45.0%	.330	-4	1.72	6.38	5.92	10.7	3.4	5.6	1.5	0	-0.8	0.02

Breakout: 60% Improve: 88% Collapse: 4% Attrition: 20% Comparables: Jon Huber, John Pawlowski, Dario Veras, Matt Kinzer

The Mets plucked Register from the Rockies in the Rule 5 draft in December 2007. When he didn't make the team, they tried to work out a deal with Colorado to keep him, but were ultimately forced to send him back. He's a classic sinker/slider type who grades up a bit due to excellent command and control. That control didn't show up in his brief major league debut, but he should have a solid big-league career without ever approaching stardom.

Greg Reynolds

						Bats: R		Throws: R		Height: 6' 7"		Weight: 225		Born: July 3, 1985			Age: 23	

YEAR	TEAM	LVL	AGE	W	L	SV	G	GS	IP	H	BB	SO	HR	GB%	BABIP	STUFF	WHIP	ERA	DERA	EqH9	EqBB9	EqSO9	EqHR9	DEF	VORP	SN/WX
2006	MOD	A+	20	2	1	0	11	11	48¹	51	14	29	1	57.2%	.316	6	1.35	3.37	5.24	10.5	3.4	2.2	0.6	-4	1.8	—
2007	TUL	AA	21	4	1	0	8	8	50²	32	9	35	2	53.5%	.213	21	0.81	1.42	5.48	6.6	2.1	3.8	0.8	14	0.6	—
2008	CSP	AAA	22	1	3	0	13	13	63¹	84	22	37	4	52.7%	.372	-6	1.67	4.27	5.31	12.6	3.3	3.3	0.8	-1	1.9	—
2008	COL	MLB	22	2	8	0	14	13	62	83	26	22	14	46.3%	.311	-27	1.76	8.13	7.45	10.7	3.1	2.8	1.8	0	-16.8	-0.41
2009	COL	MLB	23	7	11	0	40	25	148¹	185	55	72	21	48.0%	.320	-3	1.62	5.98	5.65	10.4	2.9	4.0	1.2	1	2.1	1.19

Breakout: 18% Improve: 38% Collapse: 22% Attrition: 14% Comparables: Jason Grilli, Justin Wayne, Seth Greisinger, Matt Belisle

You know, 26 walks in 62 innings for a rookie isn't the worst thing in the world, but it looks pathetic when you realize that Reynolds struck out even fewer batters. His minor league strikeout rates are just as troubling. Reynolds has suffered through constant shoulder problems since being drafted. At this point, reminding Colorado fans that this was the guy the Rockies selected with the second overall pick in the 2006 draft instead of Evan Longoria amounts to nothing more than a cruel joke. Even if you had, say, a power sinker that's a combination of Brandon Webb's and Superman's, it is still nearly impossible to get by in the majors while striking out so few batters—and Reynolds doesn't even throw that sinker.

Esmil Rogers

						Bats: R		Throws: R		Height: 6' 1"		Weight: 146		Born: August 14, 1985			Age: 23	

YEAR	TEAM	LVL	AGE	W	L	SV	G	GS	IP	H	BB	SO	HR	GB%	BABIP	STUFF	WHIP	ERA	DERA	EqH9	EqBB9	EqSO9	EqHR9	DEF	VORP	SN/WX
2006	CAS	Rk	20	3	6	0	15	15	63	78	24	40	8	46.8%	.338	-59	1.62	7.00	13.42	16.1	5.5	1.3	3.7	2	-46.7	—
2007	ASH	A	21	7	4	0	19	18	117²	125	42	90	6	49.3%	.327	-9	1.42	3.75	6.31	11.5	4.5	2.9	1.2	-6	-8.4	—
2008	MOD	A+	22	9	7	0	25	25	143²	146	45	116	9	42.8%	.324	-13	1.33	3.95	6.45	11.6	4.0	3.9	1.3	-1	-12.1	—
2009	COL	MLB	23	4	9	0	27	19	103¹	146	53	60	21	44.0%	.340	-5	1.92	7.81	7.21	11.8	4.0	4.7	1.7	1	-15.9	-0.93

Breakout: 21% Improve: 53% Collapse: 19% Attrition: 16% Comparables: Jose Vargas, Geraldo Padua, Les Straker, Wilton Chavez

Rogers' numbers as a 22-year-old in the California League are good, but hardly eye-popping. There are extenuating circumstances, as the guy is just learning how to pitch. A converted shortstop, Rogers entered the year with just 34 games of professional mound experience, but more than held his own, thanks to a low-90s fastball and surprisingly advanced curve. The Rockies think he's one of the best sleepers in the system.

Glendon Rusch

						Bats: L		Throws: L		Height: 6' 1"		Weight: 225		Born: November 7, 1974			Age: 34	

YEAR	TEAM	LVL	AGE	W	L	SV	G	GS	IP	H	BB	SO	HR	GB%	BABIP	STUFF	WHIP	ERA	DERA	EqH9	EqBB9	EqSO9	EqHR9	DEF	VORP	SN/WX
2006	CHN	MLB	31	3	8	0	25	9	66¹	86	33	59	21	38.5%	.344	-27	1.79	7.47	6.34	11.7	4.0	7.4	2.5	-2	-12.0	-0.58
2008	SDN	MLB	33	1	2	0	12	0	19²	22	11	12	2	46.4%	.308	-21	1.68	6.40	6.64	9.7	4.0	4.9	0.9	-1	-3.8	0.16
2008	CSP	AAA	33	1	2	0	7	7	41	48	13	24	4	54.3%	.338	-11	1.49	4.61	4.93	11.0	3.1	3.3	0.9	1	2.9	—
2008	COL	MLB	33	4	3	0	23	9	64	72	14	43	8	42.0%	.317	0	1.34	4.78	4.25	9.0	1.6	5.2	1.0	-1	6.7	0.51
2009	COL	MLB	34	3	4	1	30	7	61²	75	22	41	10	43.0%	.320	-2	1.56	5.71	5.33	10.2	2.7	5.3	1.4	1	3.3	0.51

Breakout: 12% Improve: 44% Collapse: 27% Attrition: 39% Comparables: Johnny Podres, Kent Mercker, Jim Deshaies, Fritz Peterson

Signed to a minor league deal after the Padres sent him down in May, the Rockies initially used him to help out in the rotation before bumping him back to the pen, but whatever the role, he pretty much stunk. Rusch's upside is limited, but even acknowledging this, the Rockies aren't using him correctly. He can't get righties out anymore (they hit .296/.359/.493), but lefties still really struggle against him, managing just a paltry .261 on-base percentage in 2008. The Rockies re-signed him to another minor league contract, and if they can just forgo starting him, he could be a solid LOOGY for the next five years. More power to him; this is a guy who was on the verge of retirement, both from the game and of a more existential kind, after missing all of 2007 while fighting a potentially fatal blood clot in his lung.

Ryan Speier

Bats: R   Throws: R   Height: 6' 7"   Weight: 210   Born: July 24, 1979   Age: 29

YEAR	TEAM	LVL	AGE	W	L	SV	G	GS	IP	H	BB	SO	HR	GB%	BABIP	STUFF	WHIP	ERA	DERA	EqH9	EqBB9	EqSO9	EqHR9	DEF	VORP	SN/WX
2007	CSP	AAA	27	1	4	33	50	0	49¹	47	23	40	3	47.3%	.308	-11	1.42	4.38	5.40	8.6	4.3	5.0	0.7	4	1.1	—
2007	COL	MLB	27	3	1	0	20	0	18	20	8	13	1	43.6%	.358	-1	1.56	4.00	2.70	10.8	3.8	6.5	0.5	-1	4.1	0.25
2008	CSP	AAA	28	1	0	5	11	0	13¹	10	4	9	1	55.0%	.237	-15	1.05	2.03	4.72	6.1	2.7	4.1	0.7	3	1.3	—
2008	COL	MLB	28	2	1	0	43	0	51	52	18	33	3	52.5%	.316	-1	1.37	4.06	3.96	8.6	2.7	5.2	0.5	2	9.5	0.73
2009	COL	MLB	29	2	2	1	36	0	39¹	44	17	27	4	49.0%	.310	0	1.55	4.78	4.53	9.4	3.4	5.6	0.9	0	5.3	0.44

Breakout: 19%   Improve: 44%   Collapse: 37%   Attrition: 33%   Comparables: Mike Fetters, Rick Bauer, Tom Tellmann, Greg Booker

Once one of the top relief prospects in the system, Speier missed all of 2006 with major shoulder surgery. Since then, he's fashioned himself into a big-league-worthy extra arm as a ground-ball pitcher who's stingy with the home run. That's the sum of his skills, and he'll never be up to late-innings work, but there are worse guys to have on your roster.

Luis Vizcaino

Bats: R   Throws: R   Height: 5' 11"   Weight: 210   Born: August 6, 1974   Age: 34

YEAR	TEAM	LVL	AGE	W	L	SV	G	GS	IP	H	BB	SO	HR	GB%	BABIP	STUFF	WHIP	ERA	DERA	EqH9	EqBB9	EqSO9	EqHR9	DEF	VORP	SN/WX
2006	ARI	MLB	31	4	6	0	70	0	65¹	51	29	72	8	46.7%	.274	17	1.22	3.58	3.05	6.8	3.5	9.0	1.0	0	18.5	2.14
2007	NYA	MLB	32	8	2	0	77	0	75¹	66	43	62	6	37.0%	.282	1	1.46	4.30	4.38	7.7	4.6	6.3	0.7	1	12.7	2.08
2008	COL	MLB	33	1	2	0	43	0	46	48	19	49	10	35.1%	.314	0	1.46	5.28	4.05	8.9	3.1	8.3	1.7	-4	1.8	-0.50
2009	CHN	MLB	34	3	2	2	46	0	52¹	47	23	51	7	39.1%	.282	8	1.34	4.06	4.22	8.0	3.4	7.5	1.2	1	9.1	0.80

Breakout: 15%   Improve: 35%   Collapse: 40%   Attrition: 21%   Comparables: Mike Trombley, Doug Bair, Dan Miceli, Curt Leskanic

Vizcaino's basic peripherals are better than his ERA, and he has a slightly above-average fastball and nice changeup, but as a fly-ball pitcher, he's in the worst place for him, pitching in Colorado. Vizcaino's giving up 10 home runs in 203 PAs tested Clint Hurdle's patience—he's supposed to be a key setup reliever, after all. The Rockies were on the hook for another year at $3.5 million, but exchanged one bad contract for another with the Cubs, getting Jason Marquis for Vizcaino, with $875,000 coming to Denver to boot.

Casey Weathers

Bats: R   Throws: R   Height: 6' 1"   Weight: 205   Born: June 10, 1985   Age: 24

YEAR	TEAM	LVL	AGE	W	L	SV	G	GS	IP	H	BB	SO	HR	GB%	BABIP	STUFF	WHIP	ERA	DERA	EqH9	EqBB9	EqSO9	EqHR9	DEF	VORP	SN/WX
2007	ASH	A	22	0	1	2	13	0	13²	6	7	19	2	53.6%	.160	2	0.95	4.60	7.82	5.7	5.7	6.4	2.8	1	-3.1	—
2008	TUL	AA	23	2	1	2	44	0	44¹	34	28	54	1	51.9%	.308	8	1.40	3.05	5.80	9.1	6.5	7.4	0.4	4	-0.9	—
2009	COL	MLB	24	3	4	1	29	6	62¹	67	43	55	8	47.0%	.320	6	1.77	5.94	5.62	9.0	5.4	7.1	1.0	1	1.2	0.31

Breakout: 13%   Improve: 28%   Collapse: 30%   Attrition: 6%   Comparables: Brandon Morrow, Craig Hansen, Robbie Morrison, Jeff Keener

The team's top pick in 2007, Weathers was blowing away Double-A hitters in his full-season debut, thanks to an upper-90s fastball and plus-plus slider, but after playing for Team USA and pitching in the Arizona Fall League, his elbow went pop—he'll miss all of 2009 after Tommy John surgery. The good news is that with today's medical advancements, that's now just a bump in the road.

LINEOUTS

Hitters

PLAYER	TEAM	LVL	AGE	PA	R	2B	3B	HR	RBI	BB	SO	SB-CS	EqBRR	AVG/OBP/SLG	EqAVG/EqOBP/EqSLG	EqA	VORP	WARP
C E. Bellorin	CSP	AAA	26	356	28	27	3	5	65	15	43	1-1	-0.5	.293/.328/.436	.212/.243/.322	.190	-24.7	-0.7
OF C. Blackmon*	TRI	A-	22	321	42	21	5	2	33	16	37	13-7	-1.8	.338/.390/.466	.242/.269/.343	.211	-25.7	-3.4
4C T. Blanco MOD	TUL	AA	26	441	59	34	0	23	88	31	74	6-2	-2.1	.323/.385/.587	.222/.270/.414	.234	-8.8	-3.2
3B D. Holcomb	ASH	A	22	588	89	46	0	14	102	65	60	6-5	1.3	.318/.400/.491	.239/.313/.380	.242	-5.1	0.6
C A. Melhuse#	CSP	AAA	36	107	14	7	0	3	16	15	22	0-0	-1.8	.311/.411/.489	.204/.299/.312	.219	-4.8	-0.3
SS C. Nelson	TUL	AA	22	329	38	18	2	3	42	35	69	6-1	2.1	.237/.324/.346	.192/.269/.296	.202	-22.3	-3.6
C W. Rosario	CAS	Rk	19	291	48	15	3	12	49	24	57	4-3	-0.5	.316/.371/.532	.195/.237/.320	.188	-44.5	-1.7
OF C. Sullivan*	CSP	AAA	28	419	70	32	3	7	47	31	63	13-7	-0.3	.320/.373/.475	.216/.265/.326	.206	-23.4	-2.9
UT C. Wimberly#	TUL	AA	24	449	65	17	2	0	26	41	45	59-16	9.3	.291/.370/.345	.226/.293/.268	.213	-26.9	-1.8

Edwin Bellorin has been the Rockies' insurance catcher for the last two years, and at least he's a plus defender who throws well, finishing third in the PCL in throwing out runners. ⊘ A second-round pick last June, outfielder **Charles Blackmon** is loaded with tools and torched the Northwest League in his pro debut. ⊘ Once a hot prospect in the Boston system, **Tony Blanco** has become a journeyman, but he did open some eyes by finishing second in the Texas League in slugging, and just like you can't teach height in basketball, you can't teach this kind of power either. ⊘ One of the toolsiest players in the system, shortstop **Hector Gomez** played just one game in 2008 due to a variety of injuries, and won't return until May this year as he recovers from Tommy John surgery. ⊘ Third baseman **Darin Holcomb** won Sally League MVP honors in 2008, but he was also old for the league and his power potential is questionable. ⊘ **Adam Melhuse** may be a guy who'll turn 37 before the season starts, but he's also a catcher, so if he wants to keep on going, somebody will give him another Triple-A deal. ⊘ Former top pick **Chris Nelson** hit a wall at Double-A, but the Rockies still have faith in his athleticism, a belief reinforced by signs of life in the Arizona Fall League. ⊘ Teenage catcher **Wilin Rosario** had a monster year in the Pioneer League, and the Rockies think he has superstar potential. ⊘ After spending two years as an occasional big-leaguer, **Cory Sullivan** has spent more time at Colorado Springs over the last two seasons, which doesn't bode well—if you can't out-hit Willy Taveras ... ⊘ **Corey Wimberly** is a minuscule speed demon who can play six positions. You can dream of him becoming the next Chone Figgins, but that's a reach—and a disappointingly limited use of valuable REM sleep.

Pitchers

PLAYER	TEAM	LVL	AGE	W	L	SV	IP	H	BB	SO	HR	GB%	BABIP	STUFF	WHIP	ERA	DERA	EqH9	EqBB9	EqSO9	EqHR9	DEF	VORP
C. Graham	ASH	A	22	12	6	0	147^{1}	99	83	138	3	54.3%	.245	11	1.24	2.26	5.83	7.8	7.0	4.1	0.7	15	-3.4
S. Lindsay	ASH	A	23	1	2	0	24^{1}	30	12	26	1	40.0%	.398	-13	1.73	5.56	8.10	16.2	6.8	5.4	1.4	-1	-5.6
	MOD	A+	23	2	3	0	47^{1}	33	34	56	1	42.2%	.283	12	1.42	4.00	8.65	8.2	8.4	6.1	0.6	4	-14.5
R. Mattheus	TUL	AA	24	2	5	17	57^{2}	50	27	56	5	65.6%	.315	-16	1.33	3.28	4.99	9.8	5.0	5.7	1.4	-3	3.5
M. Redman*	COL	MLB	34	2	5	0	45^{1}	61	16	20	7	49.4%	.335	-18	1.70	7.55	6.17	10.8	2.7	3.5	1.2	-4	-10.5
	CSP	AAA	34	8	4	0	85	96	22	51	5	56.3%	.331	-7	1.39	5.29	6.17	10.4	2.5	3.4	0.7	5	-5.2
C. Roe	MOD	A+	21	2	1	0	19^{2}	24	3	16	1	32.9%	.333	-1	1.37	5.48	10.24	12.6	1.9	3.3	0.9	-2	-10.0
	TUL	AA	21	5	4	0	105^{1}	98	34	70	15	49.6%	.268	-19	1.25	4.27	7.78	10.0	3.5	3.5	2.0	15	-23.8

Sam Deduno is a promising righty with an outstanding curveball, but he missed all of 2008 after an April Tommy John surgery; we'll see how quickly he's spinning yakkers with his old aplomb. ⊘ Right-hander **Connor Graham** is a mountain of a man who can touch 97 mph and who limited Sally League hitters to a .189 batting average, but he also hands out walks like a politician making promises. ⊘ An Australian righty with a golden arm, **Shane Lindsay** has had a career's worth of injuries at 23, but when he's healthy he dominates, so he'll keep getting chances. ⊘ Seen as more of an organizational arm entering the year, **Ryan Mattheus** saw his stuff take a big step forward with his conversion to relief; his heat's now sitting in the mid-90s, and he's generating plenty of grounders, making him a legit relief prospect. ⊘ You know that sentences involving **Mark Redman** and "millions" could mean you're talking either paydays or baserunners, but that didn't stop the Rockies from using him as an initial rotation patch. ⊘ A supplemental first-round pick in 2005, **Chaz Roe** has been slow to develop, but he made some minor strides at Double-A and the Rockies still believe in him.

MANAGER: CLINT HURDLE

YEAR	TEAM	W-L	Pythag +/−	Avg PC	100+ P	120+ P	QS	BQS	REL	REL w Zero R	IBB	Subs	PH	PH Avg	PH HR	SB2	CS2	SB3	CS3	SAC Att	SAC %	POS SAC	Squeeze	Swing	In Play
2006	COL	76-86	-5	95.9	56	2	74	11	498	310	81	34	259	.214	6	80	44	4	3	162	73.5%	64	0	145	111
2007	COL	90-73	-2	90.5	51	0	74	5	529	348	61	52	283	.216	4	98	31	2	0	124	66.9%	37	2	142	104
2008	COL	74-88	1	92.3	53	0	67	4	484	310	49	43	250	.239	4	116	34	25	3	130	69.2%	41	0	108	82

Say this for Hurdle: in his seven seasons as Rockies manager, he's evolved. After years of relentless self-victimization by the profligate issuance of intentional walks, he's cut back dramatically, as if he finally noticed not only the poor results he was getting from the practice, but also the very notion that putting extra runners on base in a hitter's park might be a bad idea. Unfortunately, he's still one of the buntiest skippers in the biz. He's led the majors in sac attempts in four of the last five seasons and three years running. And it's not just the pitchers whom he's asking to drop one down. From 2005 through 2008, no team has bunted its position players as often as Hurdle's Rockies have, though in fairness to the manager, it must be said that if you have Willy Taveras, Cory Sullivan, or Clint Barmes in the lineup, you don't have too many other cards to play. Oddly enough, despite his interest in the bunt, Hurdle almost never pushes the squeeze button. He's all about moving the runner over to create an opportunity for a better bat, not getting a run home. That seems like an insignificant fact, but it hides a choice bit of conflicted thinking: the hitters with which Hurdle was most likely to bunt were also those he was most likely to bat first or second in the lineup. If he had so little confidence in these players as hitters, why the heck did he assign them such prominent roles in the offense?

Detroit Tigers

Almost a quarter of a century ago, Bill James wrote that much of what we perceive to be pitching is actually defense. This statement was lost among the plethora of ideas that James was coming out with in that period, and its true implications were not grasped for years. It was not until Voros McCracken began to explore the idea of defense-independent pitching (now popularly known as DIPs) in 1999 that the interaction between pitching and defense began to be documented.

In retrospect, James' initial observation was simultaneously revolutionary and obvious to the point of being tautological, and yet somehow, no one had ever made that connection before. Put aside the controversy over the nuances of DIPs, which center on the degree to which individual pitchers can control the direction of balls in play, and just approach the issue in a commonsense manner: a ball hit within reach of a fielder is almost always an out, while a ball hit where no fielder happens to be standing generally falls safely. Both areas, the place where no fielder is standing and the places where they are standing, are malleable, varying according to each fielder's range and his original positioning. It is easy, but inaccurate, to concoct generalizations about the fate of batted balls, such as, "A line drive hit directly at the shortstop is always an out," or "A soft grounder to third nearly always results in a 5-3 putout," because in baseball, the fielders are not fixed. There is no such thing as "directly at the shortstop," because the shortstop's positioning varies at the outset of each play. What happens after the ball is struck is also highly dependent on the fielder. If a ball is hit 10 feet to the left of where the shortstop began the play, and the shortstop

in question is Jimmy Rollins, the defense might record an out. If the shortstop is Derek Jeter, the first defender to touch the ball is going to be the center fielder.

Those who believe that pitchers have such determinative power over the direction of batted balls that the best pitchers can steer the ball away from Derek Jeter or Delmon Young and toward the Gold Glovers on the field are exercising a form of faith greater than that demanded by most major religions. Thus, when it comes to run prevention, defense isn't just important; it's almost everything, and it increases in value the fewer strikeout pitchers a staff has, for the simple reason that more balls in play means more chances for a ball to find or evade a fielder. The Tigers' climb up the hill from historic losers in 2003 to 2006 pennant winners and possibly back down the other side of the hill in 2007 and 2008 is a story of improving and declining defense.

A team's ability to convert balls in play into outs is typically rendered as a simple percentage, but several years ago, BP's James Click introduced park adjustments to create a more accurate picture. He aptly named this measure Park-Adjusted Defensive Efficiency, or PADE. As with old-fashioned Defensive Efficiency, PADE is expressed as a percentage, so a PADE of 1.00 means that a team turned one percent more balls in play into outs than the league-average defense, with allowances made for the effects of their park. Note how the Tigers' pitching results and their ability to field balls in play went hand in hand during the years of their rise and fall (Table 1).

General manager Dave Dombrowski noticed the elephant in the room, and the 2008-2009 winter's activities

---

TIGERS PROSPECTUS

2008 record: 74-88; Fifth place in AL Central

Pythagenport record: 78-84

Runs scored per game: 5.07 (4th in AL)

Runs allowed per game: 5.33 (12th in AL)

Team EqA: .264 (Tied for 4th in AL)

2008 Batters Age: 31.0 (4th-oldest in AL)

2008 Pitchers Age: 29.9 (2nd-oldest in AL)

Ballpark: Comerica Park; Slight hitter's park; Park Factor of 1.029

2008: Total systems failure transforms pre-season favorites into cellar-dwellers.

2009: The game of infield musical chairs continues, but this year's contestants remember their gloves and forget their bats.

Table 1. Tigers Burning Bright, Then Out: Defensive Performance, 2003–2008

Year	PADE Rank (AL/MLB)
2003	12/27
2004	12/28
2005	8/15
2006	1/4
2007	3/9
2008	8/18

were devoted to shoring up the defense. Strong defensive catcher Gerald Laird was acquired from Texas, shortstop Adam Everett was signed as a free agent, and Brandon Inge was shifted back to third base. This series of transactions will almost certainly strengthen the defense, at least to a limited extent—with Miguel Cabrera at first base, an orphaned Carlos Guillen in left field, and Magglio Ordoñez in right field, there are going to be some bad days and some missed plays, but assuming Everett can stay healthy, the defense will almost certainly be improved. The offense will suffer proportionately. In 2008, Detroit ranked fourth in the league in runs per game, averaging 5.1 runs per contest. Consider the effect on the four positions that have been changed:

- In 2008, Tigers third basemen hit .259/.344/.430, equivalent to a .285 EqA; this was with Guillen making 87 starts and Inge 33. New/old cornerman Inge is a career .237/.304/.392 hitter who has batted .223/.309/.373 over the last two seasons.
- Tigers shortstops, principally Edgar Renteria, batted .269/.324/.396, equivalent to a .261 EqA. This was considered a terribly disappointing season for Renteria, but the Tigers have replaced him with Everett, a .246/.298/.355 hitter.
- The Tigers employed a congeries of left fielders in 2008, recovering from the ill-fated Jacque Jones acquisition with a rotation that included Marcus Thames, intriguing rookie Matt Joyce, and even a bit of Gary Sheffield. This group combined to hit .238/.316/.450 with 31 home runs and a .261 EqA. If Carlos Guillen maintains his production of the last two seasons, which average out to .292/.365/.474, or a .289 EqA, the Tigers will have improved at the position, but Guillen's general trend is downward, his health is questionable, and his defense at the position impossible to forecast.
- Catcher could conceivably have received a slight offensive upgrade. This is not because Laird is a great hitter, but rather because Inge is such a bad one and Pudge Rodriguez's bat was failing. The Tigers received only .253/.314/.387 rates from

their backstops. Laird batted .276/.329/.398 (.257 EqA) in 2008, though his career rates are only .255/.306/.383.

This is a big downgrade from the 1,000 runs that were predicted for the Tigers beginning on December 5, 2007, when the blockbuster trade brought in Cabrera and Dontrelle Willis from the Marlins. The 1,000-run description of a good offense is used far too glibly, and the case of the Tigers was no exception. It takes not only a collection of great hitters playing in a conducive offensive environment to score 1,000 runs, but also a collection of great, *patient* hitters. Just seven teams have crossed the 1,000-run barrier, five of them during the offensively explosive 1930s, with the two exceptions being the 1950 Red Sox and the 1999 Indians. Six of the seven teams led their league in on-base percentage (the 1930 Cardinals finished second). Four of the seven led their league in walks, and two others finished second—the outlier being the aforementioned Cardinals.

In scoring 887 runs in 2007, the Tigers had drawn 474 walks, "good" for 12th in the league. Expanding the sample still further, of the 27 modern teams to score 950 or more runs in a season, 21 of the clubs drew 600 or more walks. Even with their new additions, the Tigers were unlikely to add the kind of patience to plate 113 additional runs. In the event, amid the majors' offensive downturn and several disappointing offensive seasons—including several that were predictable (notably those of Ordoñez, Polanco, Sheffield, and Renteria)—the Tigers actually slipped to 821 runs.

Thus, the 1,000 runs were chimerical, and more's the pity, because the pitching staff was so disappointing that the Tigers would have needed close to that number (about 960 runs) to overcome the handicap imposed by the mound corps and reach the 90 wins necessary to surpass the division-winning White Sox. In retrospect, the Tigers failed to heed warning signs from 2007, when the staff slipped from 2006's league-leading 4.2 runs allowed per game to a ninth-best (or sixth-worst) 4.9 runs allowed per game. While Justin Verlander had seemed to take a step toward ace-dom in his second full season, the rest of the staff was unraveling around him:

- Kenny Rogers missed most of the season with a blood clot in his shoulder and elbow soreness. Given his age and the decline in his strikeout rate to wing/prayer territory recently, there was good reason to doubt that he had a 20th major league season of any quality left in his arm.
- Nate Robertson, a Kenny Rogers pitch-alike of the let 'em hit it variety, had started out the season

with a dominant April, only to be tagged so badly in a series of May-June starts that he had been disabled with a "tired arm." Results upon his return were equivocal, though he seemed to be improving toward the end of the season. Still, the overall picture was of a pitcher whose strikeout and walk rates were drifting in unwanted directions.

- Jeremy Bonderman posted a 3.34 ERA (with shining peripherals) in nine starts from the start of the season until the end of May, but a sore elbow began eating away at his results thereafter, and he went 1-8 with an 8.23 ERA in his last 10 starts.

- The little matter of a fifth starter: there was none. Both in the success of 2006 and in the less-so of 2007, manager Jim Leyland failed to find a number five. In 2006, the fifth starters (that is, any starter not Verlander, Rogers, Robertson, or Bonderman) posted a run average of 5.05. This was not much of a problem, because the front four were healthy. In 2007, with Rogers hurt and Bonderman and Robertson missing time, starters beyond the quartet pitched 315⅓ innings, with an RA of 5.48. The Tigers actually got lucky in these games, going 21-18.

Even Verlander had occasional problems with wildness, as suggested by his 19 hit batsmen and 17 wild pitches. Dombrowski was not ignorant of the team's problematic starters and lack of second-line pitching, but two of the club's most likely rotation candidates to break through were dealt in off-season deals, as Jair Jurrjens was packaged to the Braves to get Edgar Renteria, while former first-round pick Andrew Miller and nearly ready pitchers Eulogio De La Cruz, Burke Badenhop, and Dallas Trahern were included in the deal to get Willis and Cabrera. Possible staff-filler types like Roman Colon and Jose Capellan were dealt off for little return, and Chad Durbin was nontendered, ultimately signing with the Phillies, for whom he did excellent relief work.

Willis should have rounded out the rotation, but he suffered an epic, perhaps tragic collapse of health and pitching psyche, a big setback for a staff for which everything went bad at once. Rogers stayed old and ineffective, Robertson went to pieces, and Verlander's control took a powder. Bonderman was diagnosed with a career-threatening (and perhaps life-threatening) case of thoracic outlet syndrome, in which a rib must be removed to stop it from impinging blood vessels and causing the formation of blood clots. The rotation's sole saving grace turned out to be what seemed at the time to be a throwaway deal that had brought them Armando Galarraga from the Rangers. Galarraga's minor

league record was hardly inspiring; even we dismissed him in last year's book, noting that while he "flashes a couple of plus pitches at times with his fastball/slider combination," his upside was probably "a decent bullpen career."

In truth, the Tigers initially did not think much of Galaragga, either, ticketing him to Toledo midway through spring training, which is ironic, given the parallel collapse of the bullpen that Galarraga might have helped prevent had he not ultimately been recalled to replace Willis in the rotation. The Tigers' bullpen has been on the same what-goes-up-must-plummet-violently ride that the defense has been on (Table 2).

Table 2. Up in Smoke: Tiger Pen Performance

Year	WXRL
2003	1.01
2004	2.75
2005	7.58
2006	10.39
2007	7.54
2008	0.02

The 2007 pen had gotten its best work from closer Todd Jones and spot lefty Bobby Seay; in 2008, Seay regressed while Jones was soon tearfully declaring for retirement. Joel Zumaya worked his way back from shoulder surgery by June, only to show very little control before being shut down again with a stress fracture in the same shoulder. Off-season efforts to strengthen the unit had included the trading for Denny Bautista and signing Aquilino Lopez, Francisco Cruceta, Casey Fossum, and the forever-hopeful Matt Mantei, who hadn't pitched since 2005 and hadn't been healthy since ever. Lopez was the only one who paid off. There were subsequent regrettable decisions: LOOGY Tim Byrdak, released in spring training, latched on with the Astros and continued to be an effective weapon against left-handers. Jason Grilli fell out of favor by the end of April and was dealt to the Rockies for minor league reliever Zach Simons, and while Simons may prove to have greater long-term value than Grilli, the latter did pitch quite well for Colorado. Later, Pudge was dealt to the Yankees in return for Kyle Farnsworth, a pitcher so nakedly vulnerable to getting bombed that had Edward Teller only lived to see him pitch, his most fervid H-bomb fantasies might finally have been satisfied.

Unlike the assertive efforts made to rebuild the defense this winter, Detroit's efforts to patch up its equally disappointing pitching staff have been on the desultory side. At this writing, Fernando Rodney is expected to open the season as the club's closer, not because he has demonstrated any particular aptitude for the job, but because he's the last man standing, although there is the hope that Zumaya may one day pitch again with his old dominance. The bullpen is again likely to be a nightmare. Similarly, the fate of the rotation has been pinned on hopes of having hope. Verlander must find his way out of his second-half morass. Willis must find himself, period. Bonderman must regain health. There was also the decision to deal Joyce for Rays right-hander Edwin Jackson, a talented 25-year-old pitcher who is forever becoming without ever arriving.

In total, much about the Tigers' 2009 effort, from the decision to trade offense for pure glove work to the embrace of Jackson as staff savior and Rodney as closer, is so nebulously wishful. It wouldn't be surprising if before Opening Day, they brought in Herbert Hoover as a consultant and declared the team slogan to be "Prosperity is just around the corner." Defense is important and likely to take some pressure off the pitching staff, but the Tigers still require three-dimensional players if the team is to compete, and the current plan, which seems aimed at preventing 1,000 runs instead of scoring them, has little chance of working as long as the pitching depth remains thin and the offense compromised by the plan itself.

Recent observations point out that with population loss, many formerly bustling Detroit neighborhoods are rapidly returning to nature, as vacant lots revert to grassland. Grass has grown on the 2006 pennant-winning Tigers, too, to the point that the window has closed on this iteration of the ballclub.

HITTERS

Miguel Cabrera — 1B

Bats: R   Throws: R   Height: 6' 4"   Weight: 240   Born: April 18, 1983   Age: 26

YEAR	TEAM	LVL	AGE	PA	R	2B	3B	HR	RBI	BB	SO	SB	CS	EqBRR	AVG	OBP	SLG	EqAVG	EqOBP	EqSLG	EqA	VORP	WARP	DEFENSE		
2006	FLO	MLB	23	676	112	50	2	26	114	86	108	9	6	-3.2	.339	.430	.568	.340	.433	.571	.334	78.8	7.4	151-3B	-4	
2007	FLO	MLB	24	680	91	38	2	34	119	79	127	2	1	-4.3	.320	.401	.565	.320	.404	.577	.326	67.5	5.8	147-3B	-14	
2008	DET	MLB	25	684	85	36	2	37	127	56	126	1	0	-2.5	.292	.349	.537	.284	.346	.541	.296	42.7	3.0	135-1B -7	13-3B	-2
2009	DET	MLB	26	651	94	33	2	32	111	66	114	3	1	-3.0	.294	.369	.527	.294	.372	.544	.307	43.0	4.6	152-1B	1	

Breakout: 5%   Improve: 43%   Collapse: 20%   Attrition: 0%   Comparables: Cal Ripken, Greg Luzinski, Orlando Cepeda, Kent Hrbek

There was a hint of panic when Cabrera got off to a slow start, batting .284/.349/.489 in the first half, and proved unable to play third base. His work at the hot corner had never been good, but it seemed to go off the cliff early on. Moved to first, he quickly adjusted to his new environment and returned to being one of the best hitters in the game, mashing 26 home runs in the last three months to lead the league with 37 and tying for the circuit lead with 331 total bases (he hit .302/.350/.601 in the second half). You can't talk about how good Cabrera is without also talking about how young he is—the top first-base prospect in the system, Jeff Larish, is six months *older* than Cabrera. If Cabrera stays healthy, there's the potential for some monster counting numbers in his career.

Brent Clevlen — OF

Bats: R   Throws: R   Height: 6' 2"   Weight: 190   Born: October 27, 1983   Age: 25

YEAR	TEAM	LVL	AGE	PA	R	2B	3B	HR	RBI	BB	SO	SB	CS	EqBRR	AVG	OBP	SLG	EqAVG	EqOBP	EqSLG	EqA	VORP	WARP	DEFENSE			
2006	ERI	AA	22	451	47	17	0	11	45	47	138	6	2	0.9	.230	.313	.357	.214	.288	.333	.221	-20.5	-1.6	100-RF -5	8-CF	2	
2006	DET	MLB	22	42	9	1	2	3	6	2	15	0	0	-0.9	.282	.317	.641	.256	.293	.615	.288	4.0	0.1	8-CF	-1		
2007	TOL	AAA	23	366	33	14	5	7	36	39	113	4	4	-1.7	.220	.304	.360	.215	.292	.359	.228	-11.5	-1.5	57-CF -9	31-RF	0	
2008	TOL	AAA	24	540	75	23	7	22	82	54	166	7	2	2.4	.279	.358	.496	.282	.356	.507	.291	37.4	2.5	62-RF -1	39-CF	-9	
2008	DET	MLB	24	28	4	0	0	0	1	3	8	0	0	-0.1	.208	.296	.208	.208	.296	.208	.185	-2.0	0.2	4-LF	3		
2009	DET	MLB	25	494	53	21	3	14	56	42	149	5	2	0.3	.235	.304	.394	.235	.306	.406	.248	-4.6	0.6	116-RF	0		

Breakout: 14%   Improve: 42%   Collapse: 28%   Attrition: 12%   Comparables: Scott Lydy, John Vander Wal, Jeff Baker, Pat Bryant

Clevlen has gotten cups of coffee in the majors in each of the last three years, and he's not in line for a whole pot, even with Joyce dealt away. The former second-round pick was once seen as one of the top prospects in the system after earning Florida State League MVP honors in 2005, but although he put up good numbers last year at Toledo, he is seen as a player with some power and a good arm, but too many strikeouts for it to make enough of a difference.

Curtis Granderson — CF

Bats: L Throws: R Height: 6' 1" Weight: 185 Born: March 16, 1981 Age: 28

YEAR	TEAM	LVL	AGE	PA	R	2B	3B	HR	RBI	BB	SO	SB	CS	EqBRR	AVG	OBP	SLG	EqAVG	EqOBP	EqSLG	EqA	VORP	WARP	DEFENSE	
2006	DET	MLB	25	679	90	31	9	19	68	66	174	8	5	2.0	.260	.335	.438	.247	.330	.427	.262	22.0	2.8	147-CF	5
2007	DET	MLB	26	676	122	38	23	23	74	52	141	26	1	6.4	.302	.361	.552	.291	.352	.550	.303	63.8	5.3	144-CF	-4
2008	DET	MLB	27	629	112	26	13	22	66	71	111	12	4	6.0	.280	.365	.494	.275	.366	.497	.293	40.6	5.1	133-CF	6
2009	DET	MLB	28	613	86	30	8	22	77	61	126	11	4	3.5	.267	.344	.470	.267	.346	.486	.285	26.8	4.3	143-CF	0

Breakout: 14% Improve: 39% Collapse: 15% Attrition: 7%   Comparables: Andy Van Slyke, Ray Lankford, Mike Davis, Kirk Gibson

A broken bone in his hand to shelve him at the start of the year and a miserable September to provide an equally disappointing bookend prevented Granderson from matching his 2007 numbers, but he's still an excellent player whose outstanding work habits contribute to the suspicion that he still hasn't peaked. He's the quintessential center fielder with a broad set of skills, a player who doesn't stand out in any one offensive category so much as he does everything well. Moreover, there is room for optimism as he increased his walk rate in 2008 while slashing his number of strikeouts. There are significant breakout possibilities here.

Carlos Guillen — UT

Bats: S Throws: R Height: 6' 1" Weight: 215 Born: September 30, 1975 Age: 33

YEAR	TEAM	LVL	AGE	PA	R	2B	3B	HR	RBI	BB	SO	SB	CS	EqBRR	AVG	OBP	SLG	EqAVG	EqOBP	EqSLG	EqA	VORP	WARP	DEFENSE				
2006	DET	MLB	30	622	100	41	5	19	85	71	87	20	9	2.1	.320	.400	.519	.304	.392	.503	.303	65.6	6.3	138-SS	5	4-1B	-1	
2007	DET	MLB	31	630	86	35	9	21	102	55	93	13	8	-0.2	.296	.357	.502	.285	.351	.504	.286	42.3	4.2	120-SS	-6	20-1B	3	
2008	DET	MLB	32	489	68	29	2	10	54	60	67	9	3	0.9	.286	.376	.436	.279	.376	.440	.286	22.4	3.2	84-3B	6	18-1B	-1	
2009	DET	MLB	33	535	72	27	3	14	64	56	82	9	3	0.4	.271	.349	.426	.271	.351	.440	.276	18.4	2.7	126-3B	2			

Breakout: 5% Improve: 26% Collapse: 35% Attrition: 10%   Comparables: Bill Mueller, David Segui, Ken Boyer, Joe Torre

Guillen's numbers were great as a shortstop, but now that he's a third baseman turned first baseman turned left fielder (the last being where the Tigers intend to play him in their latest master plan) rapidly approaching his mid-30s and coming off knee and back problems, he's that much less productive as a player. The Tigers owe him $36 million for the next three years on the contract they signed in December 2007, and there's a very good chance that they're not going to get the kind of hitting they expected for the money.

Mike Hessman — 3B

Bats: R Throws: R Height: 6' 5" Weight: 215 Born: March 5, 1978 Age: 31

YEAR	TEAM	LVL	AGE	PA	R	2B	3B	HR	RBI	BB	SO	SB	CS	EqBRR	AVG	OBP	SLG	EqAVG	EqOBP	EqSLG	EqA	VORP	WARP	DEFENSE				
2006	TOL	AAA	28	394	45	11	0	24	49	45	129	3	1	-3.3	.165	.269	.406	.139	.233	.324	.191	-34.7	-2.2	94-3B	0			
2007	TOL	AAA	29	498	71	24	2	31	101	64	153	6	11	-3.1	.254	.356	.540	.224	.314	.470	.261	10.9	1.9	116-3B	3			
2007	DET	MLB	29	57	7	0	0	4	12	5	17	0	0	-0.3	.235	.298	.471	.216	.281	.471	.253	0.5	-0.1	9-1B	-1			
2008	TOL	AAA	30	473	83	20	5	34	72	59	140	3	3	-0.6	.271	.374	.602	.245	.340	.542	.291	30.4	3.1	100-3B	-1	4-SS	-1	
2008	DET	MLB	30	31	6	1	0	5	7	2	9	0	0	-0.0	.296	.387	.889	.296	.387	.926	.378	5.9	0.5	8-3B	-1			
2009	DET	MLB	31	403	48	16	1	23	61	41	130	2	2	-0.7	.217	.303	.464	.217	.305	.479	.265	6.4	1.4	96-3B	-1			

Breakout: 20% Improve: 41% Collapse: 25% Attrition: 27%   Comparables: Rob Deer, Izzy Alcantara, Marcus Thames, Russell Branyan

With 117 home runs over the last four years, Hessman is now one of the all-time greats—in Mud Hens history. Though not a prospect, given his age, Hessman has value. He has very real power and provides solid glove work at the hot corner. In another world, with another organization, he'd be an established below-average starter at the position. The Tigers are going to give him a shot this spring as a corner reserve.

Michael Hollimon — MI

Bats: S Throws: R Height: 6' 1" Weight: 185 Born: June 14, 1982 Age: 27

YEAR	TEAM	LVL	AGE	PA	R	2B	3B	HR	RBI	BB	SO	SB	CS	EqBRR	AVG	OBP	SLG	EqAVG	EqOBP	EqSLG	EqA	VORP	WARP	DEFENSE				
2006	WMI	A	24	537	69	29	13	15	54	77	124	19	5	-0.9	.278	.386	.501	.182	.265	.314	.205	-37.0	-0.9	123-SS	0			
2007	ERI	AA	25	552	91	34	8	14	76	64	121	17	6	0.0	.282	.371	.478	.204	.281	.353	.224	-23.7	-0.2	93-2B	-1	30-SS	2	
2008	TOL	AAA	26	385	56	16	4	15	33	45	109	7	3	0.3	.211	.306	.420	.199	.289	.396	.238	-8.5	-1.4	73-2B	-13	13-SS	-3	
2008	DET	MLB	26	25	4	2	1	1	2	1	6	0	0	0.2	.261	.280	.565	.261	.280	.565	.277	1.5	0.1	5-SS	0			
2009	DET	MLB	27	445	39	19	3	10	40	39	138	6	2	0.9	.186	.262	.326	.186	.263	.337	.210	-14.3	-0.6	106-2B	-1			

Breakout: 13% Improve: 34% Collapse: 41% Attrition: 16%   Comparables: Craig Kuzmic, Chase Lambin, Darrel Deak, Chris Clapinski

With a full four years of college play and a transfer thrown in for good measure, Hollimon was already just days short of 23 when the Tigers drafted him, so his career couldn't really afford any bumps in the road. Everything started off extremely well, with Hollimon proving himself offensively up through Double-A, but 2008 was much more than a bump, it was almost a cul-de-sac. While he got to play in the big leagues briefly, it was more out of necessity than performance as he stopped hitting at Triple-A before succumbing to labrum surgery. He'll be 27 by the time he returns at midseason, and his best hope is to end up as some kind of bench player.

Brandon Inge — 3B/C

Bats: R   Throws: R   Height: 5' 11"   Weight: 190   Born: May 19, 1977   Age: 32

YEAR	TEAM	LVL	AGE	PA	R	2B	3B	HR	RBI	BB	SO	SB	CS	EqBRR	AVG	OBP	SLG	EqAVG	EqOBP	EqSLG	EqA	VORP	WARP	DEFENSE			
2006	DET	MLB	29	601	83	29	2	27	83	43	128	7	4	-1.6	.253	.313	.463	.242	.307	.454	.258	8.9	5.2	156-3B	32		
2007	DET	MLB	30	577	64	25	2	14	71	47	150	9	2	0.3	.236	.312	.376	.229	.308	.377	.242	-5.1	1.8	147-3B	13		
2008	DET	MLB	31	407	41	16	4	11	51	43	94	4	3	-2.3	.205	.303	.369	.203	.306	.380	.241	-5.3	1.3	55-C	2	36-3B	5
2009	DET	MLB	32	378	44	17	2	12	46	34	90	4	2	-0.2	.243	.319	.412	.243	.321	.425	.260	6.7	2.0	90-3B	7		

Breakout: 35%   Improve: 58%   Collapse: 22%   Attrition: 36%   Comparables: Scott Brosius, Tim Hulett, Connie Ryan, Jim Hegan

We've yet to deduce exactly what hypnotic effect Inge exerts on the Tigers, but they're going into the season thinking he's their starting third baseman, even though he hits more like a backup catcher—a position he used to start at, even though again, he hits like a backup. Confounding things even more is the way that Detroit badly overreacted to his fluky 27-homer 2006 season by giving him a four-year extension. As a result, Inge will receive almost $13 million over the next two years. That's $13 million for a guy with a career OPS under 700. Reading the previous sentence again may force you to jab something sharp into your eye—you've been warned.

Cale Iorg — SS

Bats: R   Throws: R   Height: 6' 2"   Weight: 182   Born: September 6, 1985   Age: 23

YEAR	TEAM	LVL	AGE	PA	R	2B	3B	HR	RBI	BB	SO	SB	CS	EqBRR	AVG	OBP	SLG	EqAVG	EqOBP	EqSLG	EqA	VORP	WARP	DEFENSE
2007	TGR	Rk	21	13	1	0	0	0	0	1	6	0	0	0.0	.182	.308	.182	.083	.154	.083	.000	-6.8	-0.3	
2007	LAK	A+	21	19	0	2	0	0	5	1	5	0	0	-0.1	.278	.316	.389	.222	.263	.333	.203	-1.1	-0.1	
2008	LAK	A+	22	431	61	15	7	10	47	35	111	22	11	-2.8	.251	.329	.405	.216	.278	.363	.224	-16.6	-1.4	93-SS -13
2009	DET	MLB	23	541	57	26	6	10	50	33	153	17	9	1.8	.230	.285	.367	.230	.286	.379	.231	-2.3	0.4	127-SS -3

Breakout: 49%   Improve: 71%   Collapse: 11%   Attrition: 11%   Comparables: Tyler Greene, Steve Kiefer, Jim Opie, Austin Manahan

The Tigers took a shot in the 2007 draft by nabbing Iorg when others assumed he'd go back to school after a two-year Mormon mission; it cost nearly $1.5 million to lure him to the pros. He was impressive in his first full season, showing outstanding defensive skills and above-average power potential for his position. At the same time, he's already 23 with less than 100 games of pro experience, and his hitting approach needs work. He's too unusual for PECOTA to understand what to do with him, and some scouts feel the same way.

Matt Joyce — OF

Bats: L   Throws: R   Height: 6' 2"   Weight: 185   Born: August 3, 1984   Age: 24

YEAR	TEAM	LVL	AGE	PA	R	2B	3B	HR	RBI	BB	SO	SB	CS	EqBRR	AVG	OBP	SLG	EqAVG	EqOBP	EqSLG	EqA	VORP	WARP	DEFENSE			
2006	WMI	A	21	530	75	30	5	11	86	56	70	5	4	3.1	.258	.338	.415	.208	.272	.339	.213	-27.5	-2.2	105-RF	-1		
2007	ERI	AA	22	514	61	33	3	17	70	51	127	4	6	0.0	.257	.333	.454	.215	.282	.388	.230	-14.1	-1.8	112-RF	-5	4-CF	-2
2008	TOL	AAA	23	227	36	13	2	13	41	24	62	2	3	-0.2	.270	.352	.550	.269	.345	.547	.291	17.3	1.2	41-RF	-3	14-CF	0
2008	DET	MLB	23	277	40	16	3	12	33	31	65	0	2	-0.7	.252	.339	.492	.246	.339	.504	.281	8.6	1.8	46-LF	5	18-RF	0
2009	TBA	MLB	24	480	51	24	3	15	58	47	120	2	2	0.7	.227	.307	.405	.230	.311	.426	.254	-3.6	0.9	114-RF	1		

Breakout: 23%   Improve: 52%   Collapse: 23%   Attrition: 8%   Comparables: Jim Adduci, Steve Deangelis, Tracy Sanders, Bobby Higginson

Joyce got off to a huge start at Triple-A and an equally huge introduction to the majors, earning a player of the week award in July and slugging nine home runs in his first 94 at-bats. It was a bit downhill from there, as pitchers found ways to exploit the numerous holes in his swing and he hit just .243/.351/.392 in the second half. He still showed enough to be worth Edwin Jackson in a postseason trade, as he moves to the hometown team he rooted for as a kid. He's not without skills, as the power is real, he has a good approach, and he's a very good outfielder with a cannon for an arm, but the strikeouts are likely to be an issue throughout his career, and he needs a platoon partner against lefties.

Jeff Larish — 1B/3B

Bats: L Throws: R Height: 6' 2" Weight: 200 Born: October 11, 1982 Age: 26

YEAR	TEAM	LVL	AGE	PA	R	2B	3B	HR	RBI	BB	SO	SB	CS	EqBRR	AVG	OBP	SLG	EqAVG	EqOBP	EqSLG	EqA	VORP	WARP	DEFENSE			
2006	LAK	A+	23	552	76	34	2	18	65	81	101	9	7	-5.1	.258	.379	.460	.197	.299	.351	.229	-19.6	-1.3	131-1B	2		
2007	ERI	AA	24	556	71	25	2	28	101	87	108	6	2	0.0	.267	.390	.515	.207	.317	.408	.253	-1.2	0.2	120-1B	1		
2008	TOL	AAA	25	440	49	20	2	21	64	50	109	0	1	1.5	.250	.341	.477	.238	.325	.460	.267	11.8	2.4	92-1B	14	8-3B	-2
2008	DET	MLB	25	111	12	6	0	2	16	7	34	2	2	-0.5	.260	.306	.375	.260	.312	.385	.237	-1.3	-0.4	9-3B	-2	4-1B	0
2009	DET	MLB	26	470	45	19	1	14	55	45	127	2	1	-0.7	.212	.292	.362	.212	.294	.373	.232	-12.8	-0.4	111-1B	4		

Breakout: 10% Improve: 31% Collapse: 47% Attrition: 14% Comparables: Pat Dodson, Paul Sorrento, Eric Crozier, Ben Broussard

Larish put up some massive numbers at Arizona State by hitting for average, tons of power, and truckloads of walks. The power and walks have stuck with him as a pro, but the average? Not so much. Despite the kind of numbers that suggest a one-dimensional, plodding slugger, Larish is actual a pretty good athlete, and the Tigers gave him some work at third base in the Arizona Fall League to see if some positional flexibility could give him a bench role. Already 26, he's not going to get any better offensively, and another year at Triple-A would just be a waste of everyone's time.

Magglio Ordoñez — RF

Bats: R Throws: R Height: 6' 0" Weight: 215 Born: January 28, 1974 Age: 35

YEAR	TEAM	LVL	AGE	PA	R	2B	3B	HR	RBI	BB	SO	SB	CS	EqBRR	AVG	OBP	SLG	EqAVG	EqOBP	EqSLG	EqA	VORP	WARP	DEFENSE	
2006	DET	MLB	32	646	82	32	1	24	104	45	87	1	4	-4.6	.298	.350	.477	.285	.342	.463	.273	27.0	1.5	142-RF	-7
2007	DET	MLB	33	678	117	54	0	28	139	76	79	4	1	-1.9	.363	.434	.595	.349	.426	.592	.339	84.0	7.7	137-RF	-2
2008	DET	MLB	34	623	72	32	2	21	103	53	76	1	5	-8.0	.317	.376	.494	.312	.375	.504	.295	34.5	3.0	128-RF	-8
2009	DET	MLB	35	552	70	30	1	17	81	49	74	2	2	-3.0	.296	.360	.468	.295	.362	.483	.290	21.2	2.5	130-RF	-6

Breakout: 4% Improve: 19% Collapse: 30% Attrition: 8% Comparables: Bob Watson, Jim Rice, Carl Furillo, George Hendrick

C'mon, you really didn't think he'd hit .363 again, did you? His 2008 season was labeled by some as a disappointment, but it was a good match for his 2007 numbers and well in line with his career averages. This is what he is—a good player, but not a great one. He's entering what will probably be a walk year, if he's merely good again; his 2010 option costs $18 million with a $3 million buyout. In a city that in many ways is the official mascot of our failing economy, that should be an easy decision.

Placido Polanco — 2B

Bats: R Throws: R Height: 5' 10" Weight: 195 Born: October 10, 1975 Age: 33

YEAR	TEAM	LVL	AGE	PA	R	2B	3B	HR	RBI	BB	SO	SB	CS	EqBRR	AVG	OBP	SLG	EqAVG	EqOBP	EqSLG	EqA	VORP	WARP	DEFENSE	
2006	DET	MLB	30	495	58	18	1	4	52	17	27	1	2	-1.8	.295	.329	.364	.287	.322	.361	.239	7.4	2.1	106-2B	15
2007	DET	MLB	31	641	105	36	3	9	67	37	30	7	3	0.9	.341	.388	.458	.334	.383	.461	.292	46.2	3.4	135-2B	-10
2008	DET	MLB	32	629	90	34	3	8	58	35	43	7	1	2.9	.307	.350	.417	.304	.350	.424	.271	25.5	3.6	135-2B	6
2009	DET	MLB	33	501	59	24	2	5	46	26	35	5	2	0.1	.291	.333	.382	.291	.335	.395	.257	11.9	1.6	118-2B	0

Breakout: 5% Improve: 24% Collapse: 38% Attrition: 20% Comparables: Mark Grudzielanek, Felix Millan, Johnny Ray, Dick Groat

C'mon, you really didn't think he'd hit .341 again, did you? Like Ordoñez, Polanco went back to producing at his normal career rates, and because so much of the rest of the team didn't live up to expectations, Polanco was seen as one of the bad guys, even though he was still an above-average second baseman who played good defense and smacked line drives all over the field. At $4.6 million in the final season of a four-year deal, he's a relative bargain.

Ryan Raburn — UT

Bats: R Throws: R Height: 6' 0" Weight: 185 Born: April 17, 1981 Age: 28

YEAR	TEAM	LVL	AGE	PA	R	2B	3B	HR	RBI	BB	SO	SB	CS	EqBRR	AVG	OBP	SLG	EqAVG	EqOBP	EqSLG	EqA	VORP	WARP	DEFENSE			
2006	TOL	AAA	25	512	68	29	4	20	79	51	120	16	4	1.9	.275	.352	.490	.254	.327	.471	.272	18.3	1.8	73-LF	0	32-2B	-3
2007	TOL	AAA	26	373	60	21	3	17	64	51	73	12	4	2.6	.292	.394	.540	.264	.358	.503	.292	23.9	1.3	45-CF	-4	39-LF	-7
2007	DET	MLB	26	148	28	12	2	4	27	8	33	3	0	2.2	.304	.340	.507	.290	.331	.507	.284	9.0	-0.2	10-RF	1	8-2B	-4
2008	DET	MLB	27	199	26	10	1	4	20	16	49	3	1	2.3	.236	.298	.368	.232	.298	.376	.236	-3.1	-0.8	14-LF	-2	13-2B	-2
2009	DET	MLB	28	243	32	12	1	10	33	22	60	5	1	0.8	.255	.328	.457	.255	.330	.471	.276	8.4	1.0	60-LF	-1		

Breakout: 26% Improve: 48% Collapse: 23% Attrition: 24% Comparables: Scott Hairston, Carmen Castillo, Jeffrey Leonard, Brian Jordan

In what's become his particular career path, Raburn was a jack-of-all-trades in 2008, playing all three outfield postings as well as second and third base, and though he never played there, he was also the club's emergency catcher.

The problem was that he stopped hitting, especially after showing so much promise the previous year. He's not this bad, but he's not as good as his 2007 numbers, either; at least his ability to play anywhere will keep him around for a while.

Wilkin Ramirez

Wilkin Ramirez — OF — Bats: R — Throws: R — Height: 6' 2" — Weight: 190 — Born: October 25, 1985 — Age: 23

YEAR	TEAM	LVL	AGE	PA	R	2B	3B	HR	RBI	BB	SO	SB	CS	EqBRR	AVG	OBP	SLG	EqAVG	EqOBP	EqSLG	EqA	VORP	WARP	DEFENSE
2006	LAK	A+	20	263	31	10	4	8	33	10	69	8	2	-1.0	.225	.259	.394	.190	.217	.349	.192	-22.2	-2.1	65-3B -5
2007	LAK	A+	21	343	48	7	4	10	41	20	86	28	6	5.7	.273	.315	.414	.229	.268	.372	.225	-13.5	-0.4	77-LF 4
2007	ERI	AA	21	133	15	3	1	2	14	8	38	6	2	0.0	.215	.273	.306	.185	.233	.274	.178	-13.7	-1.1	17-LF 0
2008	ERI	AA	22	482	74	24	7	19	73	43	138	26	12	1.1	.303	.371	.522	.273	.336	.490	.277	25.1	2.3	100-LF 1
2008	TOL	AAA	22	38	2	1	0	0	0	1	11	1	0	0.3	.083	.132	.111	.083	.132	.139	.000	-8.0	-0.8	9-LF -2
2009	DET	MLB	23	556	66	26	5	16	60	35	153	21	8	2.8	.246	.299	.410	.246	.301	.424	.252	-3.6	0.9	130-LF -2

Breakout: 54%   Improve: 76%   Collapse: 5%   Attrition: 8%   Comparables: Jose Gonzalez, Yamil Benitez, Ruben Rivera, Braulio Castillo

The Tigers have been extremely patient with Ramirez, who has had one of the best tool packages in the system for years, but he didn't really perform up to expectations until last year. He has above-average power and speed, but his plate discipline has always been a problem and probably always will be. If he somehow figures things out at the plate, he could be pretty good; if he doesn't, he's probably the next Juan Encarnacion—at best.

Edgar Renteria

Edgar Renteria — SS — Bats: R — Throws: R — Height: 6' 1" — Weight: 200 — Born: August 7, 1975 — Age: 33

YEAR	TEAM	LVL	AGE	PA	R	2B	3B	HR	RBI	BB	SO	SB	CS	EqBRR	AVG	OBP	SLG	EqAVG	EqOBP	EqSLG	EqA	VORP	WARP	DEFENSE
2006	ATL	MLB	30	673	100	40	2	14	70	62	89	17	6	-0.2	.293	.361	.436	.293	.363	.440	.279	39.2	3.5	142-SS -9
2007	ATL	MLB	31	543	87	30	1	12	57	46	77	11	2	4.9	.332	.390	.470	.335	.397	.482	.304	49.2	5.0	113-SS 0
2008	DET	MLB	32	547	69	22	2	10	55	37	64	6	3	-0.8	.270	.317	.382	.268	.319	.388	.247	9.6	1.6	132-SS 0
2009	SFN	MLB	33	497	60	24	2	8	51	41	61	8	2	-0.1	.280	.341	.398	.280	.341	.410	.262	19.6	1.9	117-SS -2

Breakout: 8%   Improve: 28%   Collapse: 35%   Attrition: 19%   Comparables: Dick Groat, Carney Lansford, Dave Concepcion, Lou Boudreau

C'mon, you really didn't think he'd hit .332 again, did you? (Yes, we'll keep going to the well on that line, because let's face it, the 1,000-run plan was based on so many batting average-driven fancies.) Unlike Ordoñez and Polanco, Renteria did not simply return to his normal production; he took an actual total nosedive, having what was the worst season of his career once you factor in his rapidly declining defense. The Giants surprised a lot of people by giving him $18.5 million for the next two years, but we've all but given up on trying to figure out what the Giants are doing of late.

Ryan Roberson

Ryan Roberson — 1B — Bats: R — Throws: R — Height: 6' 5" — Weight: 240 — Born: August 1, 1983 — Age: 25

YEAR	TEAM	LVL	AGE	PA	R	2B	3B	HR	RBI	BB	SO	SB	CS	EqBRR	AVG	OBP	SLG	EqAVG	EqOBP	EqSLG	EqA	VORP	WARP	DEFENSE
2006	WMI	A	22	142	11	5	1	0	13	8	42	3	1	-0.5	.233	.282	.286	.176	.211	.221	.127	-19.5	-2.1	26-1B -2
2007	LAK	A+	23	402	47	28	1	15	51	28	107	3	0	1.1	.268	.326	.473	.214	.264	.385	.223	-15.7	-2.3	99-1B -7
2008	ERI	AA	24	485	75	19	1	25	86	34	120	7	4	-1.2	.289	.346	.507	.242	.293	.447	.251	3.5	-1.2	111-1B -10
2008	TOL	AAA	24	25	2	2	0	0	1	0	7	0	0	0.0	.240	.240	.320	.240	.240	.320	.183	-1.8	-0.3	6-1B -1
2009	DET	MLB	25	512	46	22	2	16	62	31	154	5	2	-0.8	.215	.268	.372	.214	.269	.384	.225	-18.2	-1.5	121-1B -3

Breakout: 25%   Improve: 49%   Collapse: 30%   Attrition: 9%   Comparables: Steve Smitherman, Ryan Shealy, Andy Bevins, Rick Lundblade

A 30th-round pick who put up some big numbers at a small school (George Washington), Roberson has turned himself into something of a prospect after finishing among the Double-A Eastern League leaders in home runs and slugging percentage. He's a massive guy with a huge swing, but bad plate discipline and Miguel Cabrera in front of him mean his future is likely to be found in another organization.

Dusty Ryan — C

Bats: R   Throws: R   Height: 6' 4"   Weight: 220   Born: September 2, 1984   Age: 24

YEAR	TEAM	LVL	AGE	PA	R	2B	3B	HR	RBI	BB	SO	SB	CS	EqBRR	AVG	OBP	SLG	EqAVG	EqOBP	EqSLG	EqA	VORP	WARP	DEFENSE			
2006	WMI	A	21	375	49	13	2	6	35	44	102	3	4	-2.9	.245	.344	.354	.196	.273	.283	.193	-27.6	-1.6	85-C	-4		
2007	LAK	A+	22	168	17	0	0	7	22	18	52	0	1	-2.5	.214	.310	.359	.181	.266	.309	.201	-12.2	-0.7	32-C	-2		
2008	ERI	AA	23	338	46	17	2	15	50	38	95	2	1	-0.0	.253	.340	.476	.229	.310	.445	.257	4.1	1.3	65-C	-2	7-1B	1
2008	TOL	AAA	23	81	12	7	2	2	13	6	27	0	0	-0.5	.315	.370	.548	.324	.378	.608	.320	10.5	1.0	17-C	0		
2008	DET	MLB	23	50	6	2	0	2	7	5	13	0	0	0.1	.318	.380	.500	.318	.380	.500	.302	4.2	0.7	14-C	2		
2009	DET	MLB	24	490	49	21	2	14	55	45	147	3	2	-1.0	.223	.299	.378	.222	.301	.391	.241	-0.8	1.8	116-C	-1		

Breakout: 30%   Improve: 46%   Collapse: 28%   Attrition: 9%   Comparables: Justin Towle, Creighton Gubanich, Ozzie Virgil, B.J. Waszgis

A low-profile draft-and-follow who nearly fell off the radar after an injury-plagued 2007 season, Ryan had a breakout campaign at Double-A and finished the season with an impressive big-league debut. He's not an especially adept hitter, but he does have power and an outstanding arm. The Tigers acquired Gerald Laird and Matt Treanor to handle this year's catching responsibilities, but Ryan still could be the backstop of the future in Detroit, or at least a valuable backup.

Ramon Santiago — MI

Bats: S   Throws: R   Height: 5' 11"   Weight: 175   Born: August 31, 1979   Age: 29

YEAR	TEAM	LVL	AGE	PA	R	2B	3B	HR	RBI	BB	SO	SB	CS	EqBRR	AVG	OBP	SLG	EqAVG	EqOBP	EqSLG	EqA	VORP	WARP	DEFENSE			
2006	TOL	AAA	26	100	13	6	0	2	12	9	18	2	1	-0.3	.253	.333	.398	.230	.309	.356	.235	-2.0	-0.1	14-2B	1	12-SS	-2
2006	DET	MLB	26	86	9	1	1	0	3	1	14	2	0	0.4	.225	.244	.263	.213	.232	.250	.171	-5.2	-0.1	15-SS	4	8-2B	0
2007	TOL	AAA	27	402	40	19	4	3	30	16	61	8	9	-4.6	.263	.309	.362	.227	.265	.320	.199	-22.5	1.0	89-SS	16		
2007	DET	MLB	27	74	10	5	1	0	7	1	10	3	0	0.0	.284	.324	.388	.284	.324	.388	.257	2.3	0.8	21-SS	5		
2008	DET	MLB	28	156	30	6	2	4	18	22	17	1	0	1.1	.282	.411	.460	.276	.411	.480	.308	11.9	0.6	26-SS	-5	13-2B	-2
2009	DET	MLB	29	232	24	9	2	3	19	17	39	3	1	0.6	.242	.307	.343	.242	.309	.354	.236	0.4	0.4	58-SS	-1		

Breakout: 33%   Improve: 51%   Collapse: 35%   Attrition: 39%   Comparables: Dennis Hocking, Jose Macias, Mike Ramsey, Walt Weiss

When a guy with a career OPS of barely 600 puts up these kinds of numbers in limited playing time, it's not a breakout; it's a stone fluke. The Tigers know this, which is why they brought in Adam Everett to take the—wait, what? Santiago is a very good defender without much offensive ability (despite that 2008 line), but isn't that exactly what Everett is, too? Color us confused.

Dane Sardinha — C

Bats: R   Throws: R   Height: 6' 0"   Weight: 215   Born: April 8, 1979   Age: 30

YEAR	TEAM	LVL	AGE	PA	R	2B	3B	HR	RBI	BB	SO	SB	CS	EqBRR	AVG	OBP	SLG	EqAVG	EqOBP	EqSLG	EqA	VORP	WARP	DEFENSE	
2006	LOU	AAA	27	249	19	7	0	2	10	15	64	0	0	0.5	.175	.231	.231	.147	.198	.190	.094	-39.4	-2.1	66-C	3
2007	TOL	AAA	28	421	38	15	1	10	47	25	98	2	0	2.0	.202	.255	.325	.170	.215	.278	.164	-44.9	-2.1	112-C	1
2008	TOL	AAA	29	197	19	9	0	6	18	8	59	1	0	-1.1	.202	.238	.350	.183	.215	.312	.177	-18.3	-1.5	52-C	-6
2008	DET	MLB	29	49	2	0	1	0	3	4	11	0	0	-1.3	.159	.229	.205	.159	.229	.205	.139	-4.6	-0.2	14-C	1
2009	DET	MLB	30	235	14	9	0	4	20	13	67	1	0	-0.7	.178	.227	.281	.178	.228	.290	.171	-15.0	-0.4	58-C	1

Breakout: 58%   Improve: 58%   Collapse: 32%   Attrition: 40%   Comparables: Dann Bilardello, John Orton, Ben Davis, Marc Sullivan

One of the best college catchers in recent memory, Sardinha received a guaranteed big-league contract in lieu of a bonus from the budget-minded Reds at the beginning of the decade. But he quickly proved to be a good-glove/no-hit catcher who has spent the last five seasons at Triple-A, giving teams little reason to believe he'll ever be anything more than an emergency catcher. The good news is that Sardinha knows it sure beats working at Sears, so he's set for a return engagement at Toledo next year.

Gary Sheffield   DH   Bats: R   Throws: R   Height: 6' 0"   Weight: 215   Born: November 18, 1968   Age: 40

YEAR	TEAM	LVL	AGE	PA	R	2B	3B	HR	RBI	BB	SO	SB	CS	EqBRR	AVG	OBP	SLG	EqAVG	EqOBP	EqSLG	EqA	VORP	WARP	DEFENSE				
2006	NYA	MLB	37	166	22	5	0	6	25	13	16	5	1	-0.3	.298	.355	.450	.287	.349	.427	.273	7.5	0.9	19-RF	2	6-1B	1	
2007	DET	MLB	38	593	107	20	1	25	75	84	71	22	5	5.0	.265	.378	.462	.255	.374	.463	.292	27.7	3.3	6-RF	1	6-LF	1	
2008	DET	MLB	39	482	52	16	0	19	57	58	83	9	2	-0.1	.225	.326	.400	.219	.326	.400	.256	3.7	0.5	5-LF	2			
2009	DET	MLB	40	411	54	16	1	14	52	50	70	11	4	-0.7	.244	.339	.412	.243	.341	.426	.270	7.4	0.9	98-DH				

Breakout: 13%   Improve: 53%   Collapse: 33%   Attrition: 20%   Comparables: Brian Downing, Darrell Evans, Tony Perez, Rafael Palmeiro

It's easy to put up with Sheffield's antics when he's hitting like an All-Star, but when he hits as he did in 2008, it's far easier to remember that he's a misanthropic jerk. The Tigers tried to trade him during the offseason, but teams wanted Detroit to pick up a big chunk of his $14 million contract, which was kind of the point of wanting to trade him in the first place. If there's anything to be optimistic about, Sheffield has a long track record of producing in final contract years, and now he's playing not just for a deal, but to extend his career.

Jamie Skelton   C   Bats: L   Throws: R   Height: 5' 11"   Weight: 165   Born: October 28, 1985   Age: 23

YEAR	TEAM	LVL	AGE	PA	R	2B	3B	HR	RBI	BB	SO	SB	CS	EqBRR	AVG	OBP	SLG	EqAVG	EqOBP	EqSLG	EqA	VORP	WARP	DEFENSE	
2006	ONE	A-	20	154	20	8	1	1	22	21	29	1	1	-0.3	.300	.403	.400	.221	.310	.309	.224	-11.1	-0.1	21-C	1
2007	WMI	A	21	417	60	24	2	7	52	55	53	18	5	4.6	.309	.402	.448	.248	.326	.362	.246	-2.9	0.6	79-C	-4
2008	LAK	A+	22	282	43	8	2	3	23	64	50	14	5	1.4	.307	.468	.406	.256	.404	.354	.281	9.6	1.6	54-C	-3
2008	ERI	AA	22	106	22	2	0	2	11	19	23	1	1	-0.4	.294	.425	.388	.253	.377	.345	.264	1.6	0.8	23-C	2
2009	ARI	MLB	23	511	66	26	2	9	44	67	111	10	4	1.8	.251	.354	.383	.245	.346	.374	.256	10.9	2.9	120-C	1

Breakout: 19%   Improve: 42%   Collapse: 26%   Attrition: 9%   Comparables: Mike Twardoski, Darren Bragg, Ronald King, Todd Betts

As a catcher with a .416 career on-base percentage and a plus arm, one would think that "Helter" Skelton would be a highly prized prospect. The problem is, he's just too unusual to be taken seriously. At 5-foot-11 and 165 pounds (and that might be generous), he just doesn't *look* like a catcher, certainly not one who could handle a full-season workload. The Tigers tried him out at second base this winter, and the Diamondbacks took him in the Rule 5 draft to kick the tires and see what there is here. There is something here, but nobody is quite sure what it is.

Ryan Strieby   1B   Bats: R   Throws: R   Height: 6' 6"   Weight: 220   Born: August 9, 1985   Age: 23

YEAR	TEAM	LVL	AGE	PA	R	2B	3B	HR	RBI	BB	SO	SB	CS	EqBRR	AVG	OBP	SLG	EqAVG	EqOBP	EqSLG	EqA	VORP	WARP	DEFENSE	
2006	ONE	A-	20	254	26	9	0	4	25	25	58	1	1	-0.4	.241	.319	.335	.185	.251	.276	.181	-41.5	-3.1	49-1B	-1
2007	WMI	A	21	519	65	23	2	16	76	63	78	6	5	-3.4	.253	.347	.422	.198	.276	.322	.211	-29.7	-3.9	112-1B	-11
2008	LAK	A+	22	478	65	19	7	29	94	46	101	0	1	0.2	.278	.352	.563	.236	.300	.486	.263	11.9	-0.5	92-1B	-11
2009	DET	MLB	23	549	52	23	2	18	67	45	142	1	1	-1.2	.224	.292	.388	.223	.294	.401	.240	-11.2	-0.8	129-1B	-4

Breakout: 34%   Improve: 65%   Collapse: 12%   Attrition: 9%   Comparables: Brad Pounders, Cesar Nicolas, Brandon Sing, Kevin Eberwein

Strieby is lost in the shuffle, yet another first-base prospect in a system that doesn't need one, but remember the name. Twenty-nine home runs in just 112 Florida State League games is a phenomenal achievement, even if he was a bit old for the league. Strieby has every bit as much power as you'd expect from a player of his size. Even more intriguing, the power comes with a manageable strikeout rate. The bat is Strieby's ticket to the big leagues, as he's your classic gigantic, plodding first base/DH type, but many scouts think the bat will be enough.

Marcus Thames   OF   Bats: R   Throws: R   Height: 6' 2"   Weight: 220   Born: March 6, 1977   Age: 32

YEAR	TEAM	LVL	AGE	PA	R	2B	3B	HR	RBI	BB	SO	SB	CS	EqBRR	AVG	OBP	SLG	EqAVG	EqOBP	EqSLG	EqA	VORP	WARP	DEFENSE				
2006	DET	MLB	29	390	61	20	2	26	60	37	92	1	1	-2.9	.256	.333	.549	.243	.328	.533	.284	19.3	0.9	45-LF	-9	5-RF	0	
2007	DET	MLB	30	284	37	15	0	18	54	13	72	2	1	-0.1	.242	.278	.498	.235	.275	.500	.256	2.7	1.0	31-LF	5	22-1B	1	
2008	DET	MLB	31	342	50	12	0	25	56	24	95	0	3	-1.5	.241	.292	.516	.236	.292	.522	.266	7.0	0.8	55-LF	1	5-1B	-1	
2009	DET	MLB	32	297	36	12	1	18	50	25	83	0	1	-0.8	.233	.303	.483	.233	.305	.499	.269	5.8	0.8	72-LF	-4			

Breakout: 30%   Improve: 51%   Collapse: 27%   Attrition: 29%   Comparables: Dave Kingman, Andy Kosco, Pete Incaviglia, Steve Balboni

Once seen as merely a Quadruple-A player in the Yankees and Rangers systems, Thames has fashioned a career as a fourth outfielder and occasional starter, thanks to his incredible power. Given 585 at-bats over the past two years, Thames has done the kind of things you'd expect from a borderline guy, with a sub-.300 OBP and 167 strikeouts, but he's also mashed 43 home runs. There's value there when used in the right spot—which for Thames is against fast-ball-reliant lefties—as pure 80 power on the 20-80 scouting scale is hard to find and almost always worth making room for.

Clete Thomas — OF — Bats: L — Throws: R — Height: 5' 11" — Weight: 195 — Born: November 14, 1983 — Age: 25

YEAR	TEAM	LVL	AGE	PA	R	2B	3B	HR	RBI	BB	SO	SB	CS	EqBRR	AVG	OBP	SLG	EqAVG	EqOBP	EqSLG	EqA	VORP	WARP	DEFENSE			
2006	LAK	A+	22	595	67	30	5	6	40	56	127	34	13	2.7	.257	.333	.367	.208	.274	.312	.208	-37.8	-1.6	131-CF	2		
2007	ERI	AA	23	599	97	30	6	8	53	59	110	18	11	0.0	.280	.359	.405	.229	.298	.346	.226	-19.4	-0.3	122-CF	4	4-LF	-1
2008	TOL	AAA	24	333	44	18	2	9	45	37	88	29	11	-1.3	.247	.333	.416	.242	.326	.416	.259	4.0	-0.3	75-CF	-12		
2008	DET	MLB	24	133	7	9	1	1	9	14	26	2	0	-1.0	.284	.366	.405	.278	.366	.400	.274	4.9	0.3	16-LF	0	13-CF	-2
2009	DET	MLB	25	443	49	21	3	8	39	39	115	19	7	1.1	.220	.294	.349	.220	.296	.361	.235	-8.8	0.3	105-CF	-4		

Breakout: 28% Improve: 51% Collapse: 29% Attrition: 15%   Comparables: Randy Salava, Scott Lusader, Rod Myers, Mark Little

Thomas was one of the biggest surprises to be found on Opening Day's rosters, as he took advantage of Granderson's hand injury to earn a job with an excellent spring. He then extended the surprise by being a spark at the top of the lineup, more than holding his own before Granderson's return. Unfortunately, it was all downhill from there, as he struggled with an ankle sprain during the second half of the season and then popped his elbow in September. A Tommy John procedure will keep him out until May at the very least, with no guarantees of returning to the majors when he's ready to play.

Casper Wells — OF — Bats: R — Throws: R — Height: 6' 2" — Weight: 210 — Born: November 23, 1984 — Age: 24

YEAR	TEAM	LVL	AGE	PA	R	2B	3B	HR	RBI	BB	SO	SB	CS	EqBRR	AVG	OBP	SLG	EqAVG	EqOBP	EqSLG	EqA	VORP	WARP	DEFENSE			
2006	ONE	A-	21	119	19	8	0	1	14	9	27	1	1	0.6	.229	.305	.333	.164	.218	.227	.142	-27.3	-1.5	16-LF	4	10-RF	-2
2006	LAK	A+	21	41	4	1	0	1	4	4	9	1	0	0.1	.152	.300	.273	.143	.268	.257	.198	-3.6	-0.3				
2007	ONE	A-	22	288	46	18	11	9	47	18	64	8	7	-0.9	.265	.323	.523	.185	.222	.365	.196	-38.1	-3.0	31-RF	-3	28-LF	-1
2008	WMI	A	23	211	30	7	0	10	26	22	39	17	5	1.4	.240	.351	.447	.180	.264	.333	.211	-13.2	-1.2	46-RF	-3		
2008	ERI	AA	23	313	60	18	6	17	53	30	66	8	3	1.8	.289	.376	.589	.257	.337	.540	.289	20.4	1.6	57-CF	-6	18-RF	1
2009	DET	MLB	24	523	56	26	4	16	62	37	136	11	5	1.4	.222	.286	.397	.222	.287	.410	.242	8.5	0.5	123-RF	2		

Breakout: 47% Improve: 66% Collapse: 18% Attrition: 11%   Comparables: Craig Monroe, Ken Gerhart, Kirk Asche, Nic Crosta

The Tigers' system has a number of power prospects, and Wells might be the toolsiest, because beyond his 27 home runs, he also stole those 25 bases and used the best arm in the system to rack up 19 outfield assists. Nevertheless, there are some questions on a scouting level about his pure ability to hit, in part due to a loopy swing, but also because of a hack-first approach. There's significant potential here, but a lot of work to be done for him to deliver on it.

PITCHERS

Jeremy Bonderman — Bats: R — Throws: R — Height: 6' 2" — Weight: 220 — Born: October 28, 1982 — Age: 26

YEAR	TEAM	LVL	AGE	W	L	SV	G	GS	IP	H	BB	SO	HR	GB%	BABIP	STUFF	WHIP	ERA	DERA	EqH9	EqBB9	EqSO9	EqHR9	DEF	VORP	SN/WX
2006	DET	MLB	23	14	8	0	34	34	214	214	64	202	18	50.3%	.323	31	1.30	4.08	3.96	9.5	2.7	7.8	0.7	-7	40.8	5.27
2007	DET	MLB	24	11	9	0	28	28	174¹	193	48	145	23	49.6%	.323	9	1.38	5.01	4.41	10.1	2.3	6.6	1.2	-14	12.4	2.36
2008	DET	MLB	25	3	4	0	12	12	71¹	75	36	44	9	48.1%	.297	-4	1.56	4.29	4.46	9.2	4.2	4.8	1.1	-1	7.8	1.21
2009	DET	MLB	26	7	7	0	28	19	122¹	128	44	88	15	46.0%	.300	16	1.41	4.50	4.40	9.2	2.9	6.1	1.0	-1	13.4	2.23

Breakout: 33% Improve: 60% Collapse: 17% Attrition: 22%   Comparables: Storm Davis, Larry Christenson, Larry Dierker, Barry Latman

Bonderman never seemed right from day one in 2008. His stuff was down across the board, and his once-plus command had completely disappeared. He finally admitted to some shoulder discomfort, and a diagnosis found not structural damage, but rather thoracic outlet compression syndrome, which pinches the nerves and blood flow to his arm, causing clotting. It's a serious condition that required season-ending surgery, and while Bonderman is optimistic and plans on reporting to spring training early to start his throwing program, we don't have enough historical evidence to predict a career path in any particular direction.

Eddie Bonine

Bats: R   Throws: R   Height: 6' 5"   Weight: 220   Born: June 6, 1981   Age: 28

YEAR	TEAM	LVL	AGE	W	L	SV	G	GS	IP	H	BB	SO	HR	GB%	BABIP	STUFF	WHIP	ERA	DERA	EqH9	EqBB9	EqSO9	EqHR9	DEF	VORP	SN/WX
2006	LAK	A+	25	4	4	1	41	11	106	108	27	83	9	44.8%	.309	-49	1.27	3.99	8.16	12.9	3.4	3.6	1.8	2	-26.4	—
2007	ERI	AA	26	14	5	0	25	25	154²	159	24	73	13	54.0%	.284	-23	1.18	3.90	6.42	11.1	1.8	2.3	1.3	10	-13.0	—
2008	TOL	AAA	27	12	4	0	17	17	106¹	107	18	69	10	56.6%	.295	-12	1.18	4.15	6.66	9.5	1.8	3.6	1.2	9	-12.1	—
2008	DET	MLB	27	2	1	0	5	5	26²	36	5	9	3	49.5%	.344	-11	1.54	5.39	4.56	11.9	1.8	2.8	1.1	-4	-2.0	0.13
2009	DET	MLB	28	4	8	0	35	18	102²	149	31	40	19	48.0%	.340	-11	1.74	7.08	6.85	12.8	2.4	3.3	1.6	-1	-20.1	-1.21

Breakout: 8%   Improve: 33%   Collapse: 32%   Attrition: 21%   Comparables: *Mike Rowland, Scott Randall, Paul Hartzell, Bob Tewksbury*

Never really seen as much of a prospect, Bonine won his first eight starts at Triple-A Toledo and thus put himself first in line when the Tigers finally pulled the plug on Dontrelle Willis in June. He got five starts for the Tigers—two good and three bad—but he never got another shot after the last two. Bonine is a strike-thrower who can put his pitches wherever he wants them, but that's really not enough, as his upper-80s fastball features little movement and his slider is average at best. He'll stick around for a while as an up-and-down type.

Freddy Dolsi

Bats: R   Throws: R   Height: 6' 0"   Weight: 160   Born: January 9, 1983   Age: 26

YEAR	TEAM	LVL	AGE	W	L	SV	G	GS	IP	H	BB	SO	HR	GB%	BABIP	STUFF	WHIP	ERA	DERA	EqH9	EqBB9	EqSO9	EqHR9	DEF	VORP	SN/WX
2006	LAK	A+	23	4	4	1	30	0	42¹	47	17	29	5	51.0%	.311	-48	1.52	4.06	7.30	13.9	5.1	2.9	2.4	-3	-7.0	—
2007	LAK	A+	24	5	3	23	48	0	51²	52	17	44	3	52.5%	.331	-30	1.33	3.48	6.46	10.8	4.0	4.4	1.3	1	-4.5	—
2008	LAK	A+	25	0	1	5	9	0	7¹	7	3	11	1	44.4%	.353	-14	1.37	6.16	8.10	13.5	4.1	8.1	2.7	-1	-1.9	—
2008	ERI	AA	25	0	0	2	3	0	3	1	1	1	0	37.5%	.125	-21	0.67	0.00	3.38	3.4	3.4	3.4	0.0	1	0.7	—
2008	TOL	AAA	25	0	0	1	4	0	9	5	3	7	0	65.2%	.217	-3	0.89	1.00	3.24	5.4	3.2	4.3	0.0	1	2.2	—
2008	DET	MLB	25	1	5	2	42	0	47²	50	28	29	3	53.2%	.303	-10	1.64	3.96	4.56	9.1	4.8	4.8	0.6	4	9.8	0.62
2009	DET	MLB	26	2	2	1	27	1	33²	37	16	21	3	50.0%	.300	-0	1.54	4.53	4.47	9.6	3.8	5.3	0.8	-0	4.2	0.33

Breakout: 27%   Improve: 44%   Collapse: 36%   Attrition: 38%   Comparables: *Joe Hudson, Warren Hacker, Mike Neu, Clint Sodowsky*

Dolsi's name is just close enough to *dosai* to provoke a craving for Southern Indian lentil crepes, but the Tigers had other cravings when they rushed him up after a grand total of three games at Double-A to replace Denny Bautista; his first big-league pitch was crushed for a home run by Manny Ramirez. He was inconsistent but at times dazzling for Detroit before shoulder soreness shut him down. Dolsi has an outstanding arm, consistently getting into the mid-90s with his fastball, but he's still rough around the edges, especially in terms of his secondary stuff and command. He's not guaranteed a big-league role in 2009, but he's still seen as an important bullpen contributor at some point down the line.

Kyle Farnsworth

Bats: R   Throws: R   Height: 6' 4"   Weight: 235   Born: April 14, 1976   Age: 33

YEAR	TEAM	LVL	AGE	W	L	SV	G	GS	IP	H	BB	SO	HR	GB%	BABIP	STUFF	WHIP	ERA	DERA	EqH9	EqBB9	EqSO9	EqHR9	DEF	VORP	SN/WX
2006	NYA	MLB	30	3	6	6	72	0	66	62	28	75	8	37.3%	.314	10	1.36	4.36	4.61	8.5	3.7	9.0	0.9	0	10.9	2.03
2007	NYA	MLB	31	2	1	0	64	0	60	60	27	48	9	30.2%	.288	-14	1.45	4.80	5.22	8.8	3.7	6.1	1.3	1	5.4	1.15
2008	NYA	MLB	32	1	2	1	45	0	44¹	43	17	43	11	41.9%	.294	-7	1.35	3.66	3.40	8.7	3.2	8.1	2.3	-1	10.6	1.94
2008	DET	MLB	32	1	1	0	16	0	16	27	5	18	4	26.4%	.469	2	2.00	6.75	4.30	16.6	3.1	9.8	2.5	-5	-3.6	-1.08
2009	KCA	MLB	33	2	3	3	48	0	54²	54	23	50	8	37.0%	.300	12	1.41	4.35	4.15	8.7	3.4	7.8	1.2	-0	7.8	0.66

Breakout: 20%   Improve: 59%   Collapse: 14%   Attrition: 19%   Comparables: *Scott Sullivan, Scott Service, Tim Worrell, Mike Trombley*

Farnsworth was his usual self in 2008, showing theoretically dominant stuff (upper-90s heat and a nasty high-80s slider) while also continuing an impressive career-long knack for blowing up at the worst of times. His rate of homers allowed per nine innings (2.24) was the second-worst in baseball for any pitcher with over 40 innings pitched, bowing only to that of his new Royals teammate, Joel Peralta (2.56). Farnsworth came to the Tigers in the Ivan Rodriguez trade and was just plain awful while dealing with a balky back. His power arsenal will always attract suckers, the Royals becoming the latest to answer to that description by signing him to a two-year deal; with Farnsworth and Peralta in the same bullpen, it's going to be like the *1812 Overture* out there.

Alfredo Figaro

Bats: R   Throws: R   Height: 6' 0"   Weight: 173   Born: July 7, 1984   Age: 24

YEAR	TEAM	LVL	AGE	W	L	SV	G	GS	IP	H	BB	SO	HR	GB%	BABIP	STUFF	WHIP	ERA	DERA	EqH9	EqBB9	EqSO9	EqHR9	DEF	VORP	SN/WX
2006	TGR	Ind	21	3	1	1	14	4	38²	29	12	31	0	51.3%	.257	-9	1.07	0.71	3.98	11.1	4.8	3.1	0.6	0	5.7	—
2007	LAK	A+	22	0	2	0	5	4	22²	26	6	6	0	60.7%	.313	-31	1.41	4.76	7.71	11.1	3.4	0.4	0.4	-2	-4.9	—
2007	ONE	A-	22	4	2	0	11	11	53¹	56	16	40	1	61.2%	.329	-18	1.35	3.38	6.75	13.1	4.0	2.7	1.0	1	-6.0	—
2008	WMI	A	23	12	2	0	19	19	123	99	30	96	0	55.1%	.277	1	1.05	2.05	6.11	10.2	3.4	3.2	0.4	14	-6.2	—
2008	LAK	A+	23	0	5	0	6	5	29¹	37	12	23	2	40.2%	.372	-29	1.67	4.91	10.08	15.5	5.0	4.0	1.8	0	-12.4	—
2009	DET	MLB	24	4	8	0	28	17	101¹	139	48	43	14	50.0%	.340	-8	1.85	7.14	7.02	12.1	3.9	3.6	1.2	-1	-19.2	-1.34

Breakout: 1%   Improve: 30%   Collapse: 37%   Attrition: 11%   Comparables: Alan Johnson, Kip Gross, Leo Estrella, Mike Christ

On a numbers level, Figaro was as good as anyone else in the Midwest League last year, with a season that included a pair of complete-game three-hit shutouts, almost unheard-of in Low-A. This short, skinny Dominican with a lightning-fast arm throws a low-90s sinker as well as a promising curve and changeup. He ran out of gas after a promotion to the Florida State League, and he doesn't project as a big star, but the Tigers thought enough of him to put him on the 40-man roster to avoid losing him in the Rule 5 draft.

Casey Fossum

Bats: L   Throws: L   Height: 6' 1"   Weight: 160   Born: January 6, 1978   Age: 31

YEAR	TEAM	LVL	AGE	W	L	SV	G	GS	IP	H	BB	SO	HR	GB%	BABIP	STUFF	WHIP	ERA	DERA	EqH9	EqBB9	EqSO9	EqHR9	DEF	VORP	SN/WX
2007	TBA	MLB	29	5	8	0	40	10	76	109	27	53	15	44.2%	.370	-30	1.79	7.70	7.55	11.3	2.9	5.1	1.7	-5	-21.0	-1.64
2008	TOL	AAA	30	3	0	0	11	4	46	21	19	48	4	56.7%	.170	5	0.87	1.96	4.95	4.5	4.1	6.4	1.2	9	3.2	—
2008	DET	MLB	30	3	1	0	31	0	41¹	44	18	28	4	46.2%	.317	-10	1.50	5.67	4.81	9.8	3.7	5.5	0.9	-2	0.6	0.22
2009	DET	MLB	31	2	3	1	33	4	50¹	55	23	34	6	45.0%	.310	-1	1.54	5.22	5.13	9.7	3.7	5.6	1.0	-0	1.4	0.26

Breakout: 34%   Improve: 60%   Collapse: 23%   Attrition: 40%   Comparables: Johnny Schmitz, Tom Bolton, Bob Shirley, Curt Young

When he was an up-and-comer in the Boston system, Red Sox fans labeled him "f-awesome," but by 2008, he was more focused on saving his f-ing career. Signed by the Pirates in January, he didn't make it out of spring training with them, but the Tigers gave him a shot because they needed an extra arm in Toledo. He pitched extremely well at Triple-A and did just enough in the big leagues to earn another shot somewhere with somebody. He's as far from overpowering as one can get, but his mix of different breaking balls might be enough to consistently retire lefties.

Armando Galarraga

Bats: R   Throws: R   Height: 6' 4"   Weight: 180   Born: January 15, 1982   Age: 27

YEAR	TEAM	LVL	AGE	W	L	SV	G	GS	IP	H	BB	SO	HR	GB%	BABIP	STUFF	WHIP	ERA	DERA	EqH9	EqBB9	EqSO9	EqHR9	DEF	VORP	SN/WX
2006	FRI	AA	24	1	6	0	9	9	41	56	13	38	5	53.3%	.398	-18	1.68	5.49	6.75	14.9	3.4	5.3	1.7	-11	-4.8	—
2007	FRI	AA	25	9	6	0	23	22	127²	122	47	114	14	45.6%	.306	-22	1.32	4.02	6.57	11.2	4.0	5.3	1.7	11	-12.3	—
2007	OKL	AAA	25	2	2	0	4	4	24²	23	11	21	1	44.7%	.293	0	1.38	4.74	7.03	8.9	4.1	5.2	0.4	5	3.9	
2007	TEX	MLB	25	0	0	0	3	1	8²	8	7	6	2	40.7%	.250	-14	1.73	6.21	7.27	8.3	6.2	5.2	2.1	1	-0.3	-0.12
2008	TOL	AAA	26	2	0	0	2	2	12	7	1	11	1	50.0%	.194	12	0.67	2.25	6.00	5.2	0.8	5.2	0.8	4	-0.5	—
2008	DET	MLB	26	13	7	0	30	28	178²	152	61	126	28	44.7%	.239	-1	1.19	3.73	5.03	7.2	2.7	5.5	1.4	20	33.2	3.71
2009	DET	MLB	27	6	7	0	29	17	110¹	124	43	73	16	44.0%	.300	8	1.51	5.25	5.10	9.9	3.2	5.5	1.3	-1	3.6	1.05

Breakout: 5%   Improve: 29%   Collapse: 38%   Attrition: 24%   Comparables: Brandon Duckworth, Charles Hudson, James Baldwin, Jack Armstrong

Little—aw hell, let's face it, *nothing* was made of the deal that sent Galarraga to Detroit from Texas for an anonymous minor league outfielder—but then he shocked everyone by turning out to be the Tigers' most consistent starter. He lives off a 90-93 mph fastball and a nice, hard slider, but this is as good as he's going to get, if not his out-and-out peak. He's a highly inefficient pitcher who often reaches 100 pitches before he's done with six innings, so he's really no more than a fourth starter in the end. Even so, during last year's nightmare, he was like an angel of mercy descended from Heaven.

Freddy Garcia

Bats: R   Throws: R   Height: 6' 4"   Weight: 260   Born: June 10, 1975   Age: 34

YEAR	TEAM	LVL	AGE	W	L	SV	G	GS	IP	H	BB	SO	HR	GB%	BABIP	STUFF	WHIP	ERA	DERA	EqH9	EqBB9	EqSO9	EqHR9	DEF	VORP	SN/WX
2006	CHA	MLB	31	17	9	0	33	33	216¹	228	48	135	32	41.8%	.285	1	1.28	4.54	4.65	9.2	2.0	4.9	1.2	3	32.7	3.77
2007	PHI	MLB	32	1	5	0	11	11	58	74	19	50	12	38.9%	.363	4	1.60	5.90	4.68	11.1	2.5	7.3	1.7	-4	-0.4	0.54
2008	DET	MLB	33	1	1	0	3	3	15	11	6	12	3	42.9%	.205	4	1.13	4.20	6.14	6.1	3.1	6.1	1.8	2	1.9	0.32
2009	DET	MLB	34	5	5	1	24	11	82	88	23	57	11	41.0%	.300	9	1.36	4.62	4.48	9.5	2.3	5.8	1.2	-0	9.1	1.31

Breakout: 19%   Improve: 44%   Collapse: 35%   Attrition: 24%   Comparables: Stan Williams, Rick Helling, Ted Power, Turk Farrell

After he had shoulder surgery in 2007, plenty of teams expressed interest in Garcia as a cheap pickup for the rotation, but the auditions and workouts were continuously delayed. After being rumored to be going to half the teams in baseball, Garcia finally signed with the Tigers, rehabbed his way back into action, and made three decent starts for them, but left his final outing with stiffness in his repaired shoulder. He's pitching in Venezuela this winter and looking for another job this year. Hopefully, this time he'll be able to show up before August.

Gary Glover

Bats: R   Throws: R   Height: 6' 5"   Weight: 225   Born: December 3, 1976   Age: 32

YEAR	TEAM	LVL	AGE	W	L	SV	G	GS	IP	H	BB	SO	HR	GB%	BABIP	STUFF	WHIP	ERA	DERA	EqH9	EqBB9	EqSO9	EqHR9	DEF	VORP	SN/WX
2006	YOM	JP	29	5	7	0	20	18	96	125	23	63	13	—	.349	-27	1.54	4.97	7.06	13.1	2.9	4.4	1.6	0	-14.3	—
2007	TBA	MLB	30	6	5	2	67	0	77¹	87	27	51	12	39.6%	.314	-17	1.47	4.89	3.84	9.0	2.9	5.1	1.4	-10	7.4	0.66
2008	TBA	MLB	31	1	2	0	29	0	34	42	18	22	3	41.7%	.339	-13	1.76	5.82	3.82	12.0	4.4	5.2	0.8	-7	-0.6	0.53
2008	DET	MLB	31	1	1	0	18	0	20¹	22	4	15	4	37.9%	.290	-5	1.28	4.43	4.05	9.4	1.8	5.8	1.8	-1	2.3	-0.91
2009	DET	MLB	32	2	2	1	37	0	46	53	16	29	7	41.0%	.310	-3	1.50	5.12	4.95	10.2	2.9	5.3	1.3	-0	2.2	0.15

Breakout: 34%   Improve: 58%   Collapse: 20%   Attrition: 36%   Comparables: Tom Buskey, Jim Coates, Don Lee, Ken Burkhart

Glover is a bouncer—a big righty who throws hard enough to keep getting chances and who has pitched for six different teams in his eight years. As long as he keeps throwing 92-95 mph, he'll keep getting more chances to be that 11th guy in the bullpen.

Jon Kibler

Bats: L   Throws: L   Height: 6' 5"   Weight: 210   Born: August 10, 1986   Age: 22

YEAR	TEAM	LVL	AGE	W	L	SV	G	GS	IP	H	BB	SO	HR	GB%	BABIP	STUFF	WHIP	ERA	DERA	EqH9	EqBB9	EqSO9	EqHR9	DEF	VORP	SN/WX
2007	TGR	Rk	20	3	2	0	7	5	29²	26	6	23	0	46.6%	.306	2	1.08	2.42	6.12	12.2	3.6	2.5	0.7	0	-1.4	—
2007	ONE	A-	20	0	0	0	2	2	11¹	8	3	11	0	56.8%	.205	10	0.97	2.39	6.52	9.3	3.7	4.7	0.9	2	-1.0	—
2008	WMI	A	21	14	5	0	23	23	154¹	103	32	126	4	58.6%	.248	13	0.87	1.75	5.62	8.6	3.0	3.5	0.9	17	-0.3	—
2009	DET	MLB	22	5	8	0	19	19	99²	124	42	47	14	50.0%	.320	3	1.66	6.29	6.21	11.1	3.4	3.9	1.2	-1	-9.9	-0.26

Breakout: 3%   Improve: 15%   Collapse: 51%   Attrition: 9%   Comparables: Andy Pettitte, Billy Traber, Dave Pyc, Tim Dillard

Evaluating prospects is a two-part process. You have to see what they're doing, and then you have to find out how they are doing it. What Kibler did was utterly dominate, but how he did it shows that he's not a big-time talent. He's a tall left-hander who throws downhill and pounds the strike zone with an upper-80s fastball, a nice curve, and a deceptive change—all of which he'll throw at any point in the count. That combination can give inexperienced Low-A hitters fits, but against more advanced competition, scouts anticipate he'll be no more than a middle reliever down the road.

Chris Lambert

Bats: R   Throws: R   Height: 6' 1"   Weight: 205   Born: March 8, 1983   Age: 26

YEAR	TEAM	LVL	AGE	W	L	SV	G	GS	IP	H	BB	SO	HR	GB%	BABIP	STUFF	WHIP	ERA	DERA	EqH9	EqBB9	EqSO9	EqHR9	DEF	VORP	SN/WX
2006	SFD	AA	23	10	9	0	23	23	120²	126	63	113	20	44.1%	.314	-33	1.57	5.32	7.45	11.5	5.2	5.3	2.2	-8	-23.1	—
2007	SFD	AA	24	0	2	0	5	5	26¹	24	8	17	5	34.6%	.250	-27	1.22	3.42	7.23	10.3	3.4	3.4	2.7	6	-4.3	—
2007	MEM	AAA	24	1	4	0	28	4	57²	74	29	50	10	41.6%	.372	-31	1.79	7.49	7.62	12.6	4.8	5.6	2.0	-5	-12.2	—
2008	TOL	AAA	25	12	8	0	26	26	149¹	143	48	124	7	37.7%	.313	4	1.28	3.50	6.06	9.2	3.1	4.8	0.7	10	-7.4	—
2008	DET	MLB	25	1	2	0	8	3	20²	31	7	15	3	41.0%	.378	-9	1.84	5.65	4.64	12.7	2.5	5.5	1.3	-6	-4.5	-0.39
2009	DET	MLB	26	5	7	0	31	17	94²	113	40	61	16	40.0%	.310	2	1.61	5.94	5.72	10.5	3.5	5.4	1.5	-1	-4.0	0.15

Breakout: 42%   Improve: 72%   Collapse: 6%   Attrition: 19%   Comparables: Darrell Akerfelds, Matt Williams, Greg Gohr, Brian Barber

A failed first-round pick by the Cardinals, Lambert moved to Detroit at the end of the 2007 season and had the best year of his career at Triple-A last year, getting his first taste of the big leagues as he tried to cover for Nate Robertson's collapse. Lambert doesn't throw as hard as he once did, as his formerly 92-94 mph fastball now sits in the 88-91 mph range, but he throws far more strikes than he used to, and his secondary pitches, especially his curveball, are solid. He'll get an honest shot this spring at earning that extra arm role on the Tigers' staff, but that's probably his ceiling.

Aquilino Lopez

Bats: R **Throws: R** **Height: 6' 3"** **Weight: 185** **Born: April 21, 1975** **Age: 34**

YEAR	TEAM	LVL	AGE	W	L	SV	G	GS	IP	H	BB	SO	HR	GB%	BABIP	STUFF	WHIP	ERA	DERA	EqH9	EqBB9	EqSO9	EqHR9	DEF	VORP	SN/WX
2007	TOL	AAA	32	3	5	26	48	0	53^2	46	11	58	5	34.2%	.306	-6	1.06	2.35	5.36	9.5	2.1	6.8	1.4	5	1.3	—
2007	DET	MLB	32	0	0	1	10	0	17^1	18	6	7	2	47.5%	.281	-22	1.38	5.20	5.29	9.0	3.2	3.2	1.1	1	1.7	0.06
2008	TOL	AAA	33	0	0	0	3	2	11	5	0	14	1	33.3%	.174	11	0.45	2.45	5.06	4.2	0.8	7.6	0.8	2	0.6	—
2008	DET	MLB	33	4	1	0	48	0	78^2	86	22	61	9	30.1%	.321	1	1.37	3.55	3.26	9.3	2.2	6.0	1.0	-3	18.0	0.18
2009	DET	MLB	34	3	3	1	34	1	51^2	56	15	39	9	35.0%	.300	5	1.38	4.81	4.60	9.6	2.4	6.3	1.4	-0	4.5	0.41

Breakout: 22% Improve: 47% Collapse: 32% Attrition: 39% Comparables: Bob Patterson, Russ Springer, John Wasdin, Dennis Cook

Lopez only made the team out of spring training thanks to injuries afflicting Rodney and Zumaya, but he ended the year with the best ERA among Detroit relievers. The Tigers responded by nontendering him in December, making him a free agent. It's a defensible move—sure, Lopez has a big-league arm, but only a very generic one. A classic fastball/slider combination serves him well, although he tends to work high in the zone and lefties pound him. If he's a reliever on your staff, that's not a bad thing. If he's your best reliever, you're in trouble.

Zach Miner

Bats: R **Throws: R** **Height: 6' 3"** **Weight: 200** **Born: March 12, 1982** **Age: 27**

YEAR	TEAM	LVL	AGE	W	L	SV	G	GS	IP	H	BB	SO	HR	GB%	BABIP	STUFF	WHIP	ERA	DERA	EqH9	EqBB9	EqSO9	EqHR9	DEF	VORP	SN/WX
2006	TOL	AAA	24	6	0	0	9	9	51^2	43	21	40	2	57.9%	.287	1	1.25	2.81	5.20	9.6	4.6	5.0	0.8	2	2.0	—
2006	DET	MLB	24	7	6	0	27	16	93	100	32	59	11	49.2%	.305	-7	1.42	4.84	5.06	10.1	3.1	5.2	1.0	1	9.9	1.48
2007	TOL	AAA	25	1	4	0	11	8	51^2	43	22	33	4	55.1%	.257	-22	1.26	4.87	7.88	8.8	4.3	3.8	1.1	4	-12.2	—
2007	DET	MLB	25	3	4	0	34	1	53^2	56	22	34	3	58.5%	.315	-4	1.45	3.02	2.92	9.5	3.4	5.0	0.5	-4	14.1	0.31
2008	TOL	AAA	26	0	1	0	4	2	10^2	11	3	15	0	25.9%	.423	10	1.31	3.36	2.79	12.1	2.8	9.3	0.0	-2	3.0	—
2008	DET	MLB	26	8	5	0	45	13	118	118	46	62	10	47.1%	.286	-8	1.39	4.27	5.25	8.6	3.2	4.2	0.8	11	17.0	2.69
2009	DET	MLB	27	4	4	1	35	7	72^1	78	28	43	8	47.0%	.300	1	1.47	4.68	4.59	9.5	3.2	4.9	0.9	-0	7.1	0.87

Breakout: 18% Improve: 46% Collapse: 31% Attrition: 32% Comparables: John Butcher, John Stuper, Bob Sadowski, Randy O'Neal

In 2006, Miner was a mediocre starter. In 2007, he was a mediocre reliever. Last year, he was mediocre in both roles, so I guess we can say he's, what, ambidextrous? He's a classic tweener type, without the power to be overwhelming or the command to be a pure finesse type. Still, there are roughly 360 pitching jobs in the big leagues, and he's generally worthy of one of them.

Rick Porcello

Bats: R **Throws: R** **Height: 6' 5"** **Weight: 200** **Born: December 27, 1988** **Age: 20**

YEAR	TEAM	LVL	AGE	W	L	SV	G	GS	IP	H	BB	SO	HR	GB%	BABIP	STUFF	WHIP	ERA	DERA	EqH9	EqBB9	EqSO9	EqHR9	DEF	VORP	SN/WX
2008	LAK	A+	19	8	6	0	24	24	125	116	33	72	7	65.7%	.275	1	1.19	2.66	6.07	10.3	3.1	2.4	1.2	4	-6.0	—
2009	DET	MLB	20	4	8	0	20	20	103^2	136	45	35	14	55.0%	.320	-4	1.74	6.74	6.69	11.5	3.5	2.9	1.2	-1	-15.6	-0.88

Breakout: 6% Improve: 18% Collapse: 42% Attrition: 6% Comparables: Roy Halladay, Matt Drews, Jamie Arnold, Sean Burnett

Porcello was universally seen as one of the top pitching prospects in the game before he threw a pitch as a professional, and in his pro debut, he led the Florida State League in ERA as a teenager. Yet, for some reason, his season was categorized by some as a disappointment, mostly due to a low strikeout rate. However, the Tigers limited him by only allowing a small number of breaking balls per start and had him focus on his low-90s sinker rather than his monster four-seam fastball. Despite this deliberate pair of handicaps, we repeat: he still led the league in ERA.

Clay Rapada

Bats: R   Throws: L   Height: 6' 5"   Weight: 200   Born: March 9, 1981   Age: 28

YEAR	TEAM	LVL	AGE	W	L	SV	G	GS	IP	H	BB	SO	HR	GB%	BABIP	STUFF	WHIP	ERA	DERA	EqH9	EqBB9	EqSO9	EqHR9	DEF	VORP	SN/WX
2006	WTN	AA	25	3	2	21	33	0	43^1	30	10	45	1	66.1%	.264	6	0.93	0.84	2.88	7.7	2.4	6.0	0.4	2	12.3	—
2006	IOW	AAA	25	3	2	0	28	0	23^1	27	15	21	0	54.8%	.412	-1	1.82	3.12	2.53	12.2	6.3	5.9	0.4	-3	7.3	—
2007	IOW	AAA	26	7	2	17	55	0	55^1	55	25	50	4	50.0%	.345	-9	1.45	3.58	4.97	9.8	4.4	6.2	0.9	3	3.5	—
2008	TOL	AAA	27	0	1	2	28	0	35	32	14	45	2	45.1%	.357	7	1.31	2.31	2.73	9.8	4.1	7.9	0.8	-3	10.5	—
2008	DET	MLB	27	3	0	0	25	0	21^1	19	14	15	0	52.3%	.302	-1	1.55	4.23	4.35	8.3	5.7	5.7	0.0	-1	2.8	0.21
2009	DET	MLB	28	2	2	2	48	1	41	44	21	32	4	47.0%	.320		4	1.57	4.82	4.73	9.5	4.1	6.5	0.8	-0	2.9	0.28

Breakout: 8%   Improve: 31%   Collapse: 38%   Attrition: 35%   Comparables: Scott Ruskin, Mike Myers, Hank Aguirre, John Cummings

Acquired from the Cubs for Craig Monroe, Rapada has some LOOGY possibilities in his future. He's not quite a pure side-armer, but he does release his upper-80s cut fastball from a very low three-quarters delivery that makes him very tough on lefties. That's the sum of his skills, but just making the majors is a nice accomplishment for a guy who wasn't even drafted.

Nate Robertson

Bats: R   Throws: L   Height: 6' 2"   Weight: 225   Born: September 3, 1977   Age: 31

YEAR	TEAM	LVL	AGE	W	L	SV	G	GS	IP	H	BB	SO	HR	GB%	BABIP	STUFF	WHIP	ERA	DERA	EqH9	EqBB9	EqSO9	EqHR9	DEF	VORP	SN/WX
2006	DET	MLB	28	13	13	0	32	32	208^2	206	67	137	29	48.0%	.281	1	1.31	3.84	4.39	9.3	2.9	5.4	1.2	6	43.3	5.60
2007	DET	MLB	29	9	13	0	30	30	177^2	199	63	119	22	46.6%	.315	-1	1.47	4.76	4.53	10.1	3.0	5.3	1.1	-4	21.5	2.67
2008	DET	MLB	30	7	11	0	32	28	168^2	218	62	108	26	46.7%	.343	-12	1.66	6.35	4.98	11.5	3.1	5.1	1.4	-22	-13.6	0.27
2009	DET	MLB	31	7	8	0	33	20	130	146	44	79	17	46.0%	.300		6	1.46	4.93	4.81	10.0	2.8	5.1	1.2	-1	8.2	1.69

Breakout: 25%   Improve: 63%   Collapse: 20%   Attrition: 28%   Comparables: Brian Bohanon, Terry Mulholland, Mike Flanagan, Darren Oliver

There is simply nothing positive to say here. The league hit .315/.373/.518 against him, and he got worse as the season wore on, his second-half ERA checking in at 8.77. Nothing positive happened when he moved to the bullpen. Want more good news, Tigers fans? He's owed $17 million over the next two years.

Fernando Rodney

Bats: R   Throws: R   Height: 5' 11"   Weight: 220   Born: March 18, 1977   Age: 32

YEAR	TEAM	LVL	AGE	W	L	SV	G	GS	IP	H	BB	SO	HR	GB%	BABIP	STUFF	WHIP	ERA	DERA	EqH9	EqBB9	EqSO9	EqHR9	DEF	VORP	SN/WX
2006	DET	MLB	29	7	4	7	63	0	71^2	51	34	65	6	58.4%	.238	5	1.19	3.51	4.84	6.6	4.2	7.3	0.8	3	12.7	2.28
2007	DET	MLB	30	2	6	1	48	0	50^2	46	21	54	5	49.0%	.306	9	1.32	4.26	4.18	8.0	3.3	8.2	0.9	-3	7.1	0.34
2008	DET	MLB	31	0	6	13	38	0	40^1	34	30	49	3	43.4%	.310	18	1.59	4.91	4.79	7.4	5.9	9.4	0.7	1	4.1	-0.11
2009	DET	MLB	32	3	3	9	45	0	52	48	27	51	5	46.0%	.300		14	1.43	4.17	4.09	8.1	4.2	8.2	0.9	-0	7.7	0.81

Breakout: 34%   Improve: 59%   Collapse: 21%   Attrition: 21%   Comparables: Mike Williams, Hoyt Wilhelm, Jim Hughes, Marshall Bridges

With Todd Jones retired, Rodney is likely to begin the year as the closer, which means Tigers fans should stock up on Mylanta. Rodney certainly looks the part, with the long beard and the intimidating upper-90s heat, but his severe control problems have him constantly teetering on the edge of disaster—and frequently going over it.

Kenny Rogers

Bats: L   Throws: L   Height: 6' 1"   Weight: 190   Born: November 10, 1964   Age: 44

YEAR	TEAM	LVL	AGE	W	L	SV	G	GS	IP	H	BB	SO	HR	GB%	BABIP	STUFF	WHIP	ERA	DERA	EqH9	EqBB9	EqSO9	EqHR9	DEF	VORP	SN/WX
2006	DET	MLB	41	17	8	0	34	33	204	195	62	99	23	50.1%	.265	-3	1.26	3.84	5.01	8.9	2.8	4.0	1.0	18	41.5	5.21
2007	DET	MLB	42	3	4	0	11	11	63	65	25	36	8	50.2%	.282	-8	1.43	4.43	5.74	9.0	3.3	4.5	1.1	6	6.5	0.81
2008	DET	MLB	43	9	13	0	30	30	173^2	212	71	82	22	43.2%	.327	-14	1.63	5.70	5.38	10.8	3.4	3.8	1.2	-7	-4.2	0.53
2009	DET	MLB	44	6	8	0	22	22	123^1	150	54	67	18	44.0%	.310		0	1.65	5.71	5.54	10.8	3.6	4.5	1.3	-1	-2.2	0.68

Breakout: 4%   Improve: 47%   Collapse: 30%   Attrition: 39%   Comparables: Warren Spahn, Jamie Moyer, Charlie Hough, Phil Niekro

Now well into his 40s, Rogers has been unable to match Jamie Moyer's success as a left-hander who simply gets by on throwing strikes and changing speeds. He got hammered with alarming regularity last year and, as of press time, is still deciding if he wants to give it one more shot.

Bobby Seay

Bats: L   Throws: L   Height: 6' 2"   Weight: 235   Born: June 20, 1978   Age: 31

YEAR	TEAM	LVL	AGE	W	L	SV	G	GS	IP	H	BB	SO	HR	GB%	BABIP	STUFF	WHIP	ERA	DERA	EqH9	EqBB9	EqSO9	EqHR9	DEF	VORP	SN/WX
2006	TOL	AAA	28	1	2	0	24	1	24²	25	6	14	3	44.8%	.313	-40	1.28	4.83	9.14	11.6	2.9	3.3	2.1	3	-8.5	—
2006	DET	MLB	28	0	0	0	14	0	15¹	14	9	12	1	36.2%	.295	-8	1.50	6.47	7.80	8.4	5.4	6.6	0.6	2	-0.6	0.04
2007	DET	MLB	29	3	0	1	58	0	46¹	38	15	38	1	39.8%	.289	11	1.14	2.33	2.78	7.5	2.8	6.6	0.2	2	19.1	2.23
2008	DET	MLB	30	1	2	0	60	0	56¹	59	25	58	4	40.4%	.367	11	1.49	4.48	3.64	9.6	3.8	8.4	0.7	-4	8.4	1.11
2009	DET	MLB	31	3	2	3	55	0	52	52	20	46	5	41.0%	.300	12	1.37	3.94	3.84	8.8	3.1	7.4	0.9	-0	9.3	0.81

Breakout: 28%   Improve: 54%   Collapse: 22%   Attrition: 19%   Comparables: Paul Assenmacher, Randy Myers, Will Ohman, Fred Gladding

After looking as if he might have broken through in 2007, Seay regressed, although he did at least lead the team in appearances. (Somebody has to.) He has above-average velocity for a southpaw and two decent breaking balls, and his fly-ball tendencies work well in his home park. At the same time, he doesn't give you the platoon advantage one normally expects from a left-hander, and his control disappears at times. He's nothing special, but he's usable.

Zach Simons

Bats: L   Throws: R   Height: 6' 3"   Weight: 200   Born: May 23, 1985   Age: 24

YEAR	TEAM	LVL	AGE	W	L	SV	G	GS	IP	H	BB	SO	HR	GB%	BABIP	STUFF	WHIP	ERA	DERA	EqH9	EqBB9	EqSO9	EqHR9	DEF	VORP	SN/WX
2006	ASH	A	21	6	9	0	26	21	111¹	134	49	60	14	39.1%	.315	-83	1.65	6.32	11.52	14.6	5.8	1.3	3.0	-6	-64.3	—
2007	ASH	A	22	8	2	1	42	0	69²	69	31	62	6	40.4%	.321	-31	1.43	4.52	6.75	11.4	5.6	3.8	1.8	-2	-7.8	—
2008	MOD	A+	23	1	0	0	7	0	13¹	12	9	14	1	41.7%	.344	-4	1.58	2.71	6.17	10.8	8.5	5.4	1.5	1	-0.7	—
2008	LAK	A+	23	5	2	2	39	0	53¹	29	30	61	2	34.7%	.241	2	1.11	2.36	5.51	6.8	6.3	6.5	1.0	6	0.5	—
2009	DET	MLB	24	2	4	0	23	6	50	60	38	34	10	38.0%	.310	-8	1.94	7.21	6.88	10.6	6.1	5.8	1.7	-0	-9.2	-0.67

Breakout: 20%   Improve: 49%   Collapse: 20%   Attrition: 11%   Comparables: Elvys Quezada, Dave Shipanoff, Kevin Joseph, Julian Vasquez

A second-round pick by the Rockies in 2005, Simons had been taking longer than expected to develop when he was sent to Detroit for Jason Grilli. The change of scenery did wonders, as he dominated coming out of the Flying Tigers' bullpen, limiting Florida State League hitters. While neither his fastball nor his curve is an overwhelming pitch, both grade as plus. If he can repeat anything like this kind of success at Double-A, he could be in line for a look by the end of the year.

Justin Verlander

Bats: R   Throws: R   Height: 6' 5"   Weight: 200   Born: February 20, 1983   Age: 26

YEAR	TEAM	LVL	AGE	W	L	SV	G	GS	IP	H	BB	SO	HR	GB%	BABIP	STUFF	WHIP	ERA	DERA	EqH9	EqBB9	EqSO9	EqHR9	DEF	VORP	SN/WX
2006	DET	MLB	23	17	9	0	30	30	186	187	60	124	21	42.6%	.297	9	1.33	3.63	4.27	9.7	3.0	5.6	1.0	10	48.3	6.13
2007	DET	MLB	24	18	6	0	32	32	201⁷	181	67	183	20	42.7%	.281	21	1.23	3.66	4.04	8.0	2.8	7.0	0.9	6	47.7	5.46
2008	DET	MLB	25	11	17	0	33	33	201	195	87	163	18	41.1%	.301	14	1.40	4.84	5.12	8.5	3.5	6.4	0.8	2	12.3	2.90
2009	DET	MLB	26	12	9	0	30	30	186¹	185	67	147	22	41.0%	.290	25	1.35	4.31	4.19	8.7	2.9	6.6	1.0	-1	24.7	4.09

Breakout: 28%   Improve: 60%   Collapse: 11%   Attrition: 11%   Comparables: Mike Moore, Jack McDowell, Josh Beckett, Dustin Hermanson

One could write a full-length book trying to document all of the disappointments to be found in the Tigers' 2008 season, and if some masochistic fool does it, Verlander will be the recipient of an early and very long chapter. Seen by some as a potential Cy Young contender entering the year, Verlander got off to a horrible start, but seemed to be straightening things out before falling off again down the stretch. His fastball is among the best in the business, and his curve is as well—when measured purely on break—but his inability to control any of his secondary offerings often leaves him behind in the count and forced to throw the heater. Big-league hitters can hit 98 mph when they know it's coming, and until they're afraid of something else entering the strike zone, they'll continue to sit back and wait for Verlander to back himself into a corner.

Dontrelle Willis

Bats: L   Throws: L   Height: 6' 4"   Weight: 225   Born: January 12, 1982   Age: 27

YEAR	TEAM	LVL	AGE	W	L	SV	G	GS	IP	H	BB	SO	HR	GB%	BABIP	STUFF	WHIP	ERA	DERA	EqH9	EqBB9	EqSO9	EqHR9	DEF	VORP	SN/WX
2006	FLO	MLB	24	12	12	0	34	34	223¹	234	83	160	21	49.2%	.316	15	1.42	3.87	4.14	9.1	2.9	5.9	0.8	2	41.5	5.36
2007	FLO	MLB	25	10	15	0	35	35	205¹	241	87	146	29	49.1%	.329	3	1.60	5.17	4.89	9.0	3.2	5.8	1.1	-8	2.6	1.98
2008	DET	MLB	26	0	2	0	8	7	24	18	35	18	4	41.2%	.219	5	2.21	9.38	10.50	6.8	12.0	6.0	1.5	5	-9.2	-0.09
2008	TOL	AAA	26	3	1	0	6	6	28¹	34	14	20	2	51.1%	.348	-18	1.70	4.45	6.84	12.0	4.8	4.1	1.0	1	-3.6	—
2008	LAK	A+	26	0	3	0	6	5	28	30	11	18	2	46.7%	.318	-28	1.46	4.50	6.57	12.4	4.7	2.9	1.5	-2	-2.7	—
2009	DET	MLB	27	4	6	0	26	16	83¹	99	43	50	11	47.0%	.320	-1	1.71	5.83	5.68	10.6	4.2	5.0	1.2	-0	-3.5	0.22

Breakout: 17%   Improve: 35%   Collapse: 33%   Attrition: 27%   Comparables: Tim Rumer, Bill Pulsipher, Alex Graman, Ryan Karp

When the Tigers traded for Cabrera and Willis and signed the latter to a three-year extension worth $29 million, we're guessing they were expecting more than zero wins. Willis hyperextended his right knee in April, and his attempts to pitch around having a sore landing joint led to mechanical issues that then morphed into a full-blown case of Blass disease. The knee is finally healthy, and Willis is promising to show up this spring in the best shape of his life. We're rooting for him, because when he's on, he's awfully fun to watch.

Joel Zumaya

Bats: R   Throws: R   Height: 6' 3"   Weight: 210   Born: November 9, 1984   Age: 24

YEAR	TEAM	LVL	AGE	W	L	SV	G	GS	IP	H	BB	SO	HR	GB%	BABIP	STUFF	WHIP	ERA	DERA	EqH9	EqBB9	EqSO9	EqHR9	DEF	VORP	SN/WX
2006	DET	MLB	21	6	3	1	62	0	83¹	56	42	97	6	34.9%	.254	42	1.18	1.94	3.02	6.3	4.3	9.3	0.6	7	36.7	4.96
2007	DET	MLB	22	2	3	1	28	0	33²	23	17	27	3	37.1%	.217	6	1.19	4.27	5.77	5.8	4.2	6.0	0.8	6	6.7	0.89
2008	DET	MLB	23	0	2	1	21	0	23¹	24	22	22	3	40.0%	.318	10	1.97	3.48	4.24	9.3	7.7	7.3	1.2	-1	1.9	-0.52
2009	DET	MLB	24	2	2	2	32	0	38	34	24	37	4	41.0%	.280	13	1.51	4.29	4.17	7.8	5.2	8.1	1.0	-0	5.6	0.44

Breakout: 21%   Improve: 36%   Collapse: 33%   Attrition: 27%   Comparables: Johnny Ruffin, Brian Bruney, Stan Belinda, Pete Cimino

Zumaya made a surprisingly quick return from shoulder surgery, and while his velocity wasn't all the way back to previous levels, he still sat at 96-98 mph with the occasional triple-digit reading on the radar gun. Still, his control declined to a nearly unacceptable level, and his season ended in September, when doctors found a stress fracture in his shoulder. If healthy, he might get some save chances, but it's possible that the flame that burned so brightly in 2006 will never return to that kind of luminance again.

LINEOUTS

Hitters

PLAYER	TEAM	LVL	AGE	PA	R	2B	3B	HR	RBI	BB	SO	SB-CS	EqBRR	AVG/OBP/SLG	EqAVG/EqOBP/EqSLG	EqA	VORP	WARP
OF J. Frazier	ERI	AA	25	484	55	22	1	6	55	31	51	1-1	-2.7	.303/.350/.397	.230/.271/.313	.201	-27.9	-3.3
OF F. Guzman#	ERI	AA	27	142	27	2	6	2	19	16	14	15-5	1.1	.281/.362/.446	.190/.262/.317	.212	-9.3	-0.3
	TOL	AAA	27	441	74	16	9	3	41	35	42	56-6	8.7	.270/.329/.378	.236/.292/.346	.239	-14.3	-1.2
OF J. Justice*	LAK	A+	23	313	46	18	5	10	37	29	77	3-9	-2.4	.298/.364/.504	.232/.290/.401	.233	-4.6	-0.6
	ERI	AA	23	175	15	5	1	3	16	14	41	1-1	-2.3	.153/.224/.255	.138/.201/.258	.149	-22.4	-1.6
OF J. Laster	LAK	A+	23	531	68	22	4	24	64	40	200	11-10	-2.0	.204/.268/.416	.167/.219/.333	.186	-48.6	-3.3
OF T. Perez*	TOL	AAA	33	488	56	30	2	13	63	48	43	19-6	-4.0	.302/.374/.473	.257/.327/.421	.260	8.4	0.0
INF W. Rhymes*	ERI	AA	25	576	76	21	7	3	60	44	66	17-6	-0.7	.306/.362/.391	.231/.281/.303	.209	-31.8	-1.5
	TOL	AAA	25	27	5	0	1	0	2	2	4	0-0	0.1	.320/.370/.400	.280/.333/.360	.244	0.1	0.0
2B S. Sizemore	LAK	A+	23	234	32	11	1	4	20	24	44	14-3	-1.6	.286/.365/.409	.224/.291/.338	.227	-9.3	0.5
SS D. Worth	ERI	AA	22	336	44	18	3	5	33	32	59	8-0	1.4	.254/.331/.386	.220/.291/.350	.230	-11.5	-0.7

Jeff Frazier, an older player with a lot of tools, finally started hitting at Double-A, but nevertheless lost his power stroke. ⊘ Bouncing from organization to organization, **Freddy Guzman** still possesses game-changing speed, covers whole hectares of ground in center, and is a fantastic basestealer with a career 84 percent success rate. If he could draw walks or hit for power, he'd be dangerous, but you can say that about a lot of guys. ⊘ A 31st-round draft-and-follow from 2003, **Justin Justice** has had to repeat every level exactly once; after showing platoon pop in High-A (.507 SLG vs. RHPs), he'll probably follow that pattern after a terrible Double-A debut. ⊘ **Jeramy Laster** has tremendous raw power, but 23-year-olds who strike out 200 times in the Florida State League rarely have much of a future. ⊘ That **Timo Perez** never showed up in the big leagues represents shrewd decision making. Had the Tigers been competitive, Perez, with the skills to be a solid bench outfielder, would have been on the roster. Out of it, the Tigers looked at youngsters like Joyce, and that allowed them to acquire Edwin Jackson. That's making the best out of a bad situation, and not enough teams do it. ⊘ Infielder **William Rhymes** can play three positions, makes contact, runs well, and could be a utility player down the road—but don't call him Buster. ⊘ An offense-oriented second baseman, **Scott Sizemore** lost half his season to a broken wrist and will have to make up for lost time—especially in the field—to have a shot. ⊘ If shortstop **Danny Worth** can figure out anything offensively, he'll reach the big leagues, because defensively, he's as good as anyone else in the system.

Pitchers

PLAYER	TEAM	LVL	AGE	W	L	SV	IP	H	BB	SO	HR	GB%	BABIP	STUFF	WHIP	ERA	DERA	EqH9	EqBB9	EqSO9	EqHR9	DEF	VORP
Y. Bazardo	TOL	AAA	23	4	13	0	130	177	44	75	19	52.9%	.371	-44	1.70	6.72	7.62	14.0	3.5	3.3	2.1	-16	-26.3
	DET	MLB	23	0	0	0	3	7	5	3	0	33.3%	.636	3	4.00	24.00	13.50	23.6	16.9	10.1	0.0	-3	-5.8
F. Cruceta	TOL	AAA	26	2	3	3	42²	39	24	61	0	48.5%	.402	22	1.48	4.22	3.69	10.4	5.8	9.2	0.2	-9	8.3
	DET	MLB	26	0	3	0	11²	13	10	11	2	51.4%	.355	-1	1.97	5.38	7.15	10.3	7.1	7.9	1.6	2	-0.4
S. Drucker	ERI	AA	26	0	0	0	12	11	6	7	0	55.3%	.289	-19	1.42	3.75	3.97	9.5	4.8	4.0	0.0	-1	2.0
G. Moscoso	LAK	A+	24	2	3	1	52	36	13	72	4	35.6%	.296	3	0.94	2.42	5.17	9.0	3.1	7.9	1.7	3	2.2
	ERI	AA	24	3	1	0	34²	24	8	50	4	27.3%	.278	31	0.92	3.11	4.09	7.6	2.2	9.5	1.4	-3	5.5
M. Robles*	WMI	A	19	5	3	0	91¹	54	54	79	2	34.0%	.235	18	1.18	2.66	6.34	8.1	7.7	3.9	0.8	11	-6.3
J. Tata	LAK	A+	26	1	3	0	27	28	26	20	5	41.2%	.311	-47	2.00	9.67	16.04	13.3	11.0	3.5	3.9	1	-26.7
V. Vasquez	TOL	AAA	26	12	12	0	159	179	37	115	27	39.8%	.310	-35	1.36	4.81	6.47	11.0	2.4	4.2	2.3	-3	-14.7
R. Weinhardt	LAK	A+	22	3	1	4	35¹	19	11	44	1	45.1%	.250	13	0.85	2.04	5.35	6.4	3.5	6.7	0.8	3	0.9

Though still relatively young and in possession of solid stuff, **Yorman Bazardo** had a miserable campaign at Triple-A. This year will be a make-or-break season for his prospect status. ⊘ The Indians, A's, Rangers, and Tigers have all seen **Francisco Cruceta** as a potentially dominating arm, and they've all been wrong. ⊘ Released by the A's after shoulder surgery, righty **Scott Drucker** headed for the indie leagues, where the Tigers found him; he showed good velocity out of the Double-A bullpen, so he's back in business. ⊘ Part of the package that netted Gerald Laird from the Rangers, reliever **Guillermo Moscoso** put up some eye-popping strikeout rates in the minors, but he's more deceptive than overpowering. ⊘ Smallish Venezuelan southpaw **Mauricio Robles** mixes in a nice curve to offset normal lefty velocity, but messy mechanics for the former outfielder contribute to command issues. ⊘ **Jordan Tata** had a lost season due to a fractured right hand, but he's nothing more than an extra arm in the first place. ⊘ As desperate as the Tigers were for help in their rotation, their never calling on **Virgil Vasquez** made it plain they had little interest in his modest command-oriented assortment; he was signed by Boston to a minor league deal. ⊘ **Robbie Weinhardt** was drafted in the 10th round last summer after showing improved velocity in his senior season for Oklahoma State and then used it to good effect in his debut.

MANAGER: JIM LEYLAND

YEAR	TEAM	W-L	Pythag +/−	Avg PC	100+ P	120+ P	QS	BQS	REL	REL w Zero R	IBB	Subs	PH	PH Avg	PH HR	SB2	CS2	SB3	CS3	SAC Att	SAC %	POS SAC	Squeeze	Swing	In Play
2006	DET	95-67	-2	94.0	68	2	83	9	390	238	35	51	81	.222	2	49	32	11	6	60	75.0%	44	2	151	116
2007	DET	88-74	-2	94.8	65	1	66	4	441	261	41	67	77	.246	2	86	25	16	4	42	73.8%	30	5	157	127
2008	DET	74-88	-4	94.9	68	2	63	13	440	237	63	66	66	.254	2	58	24	5	5	42	71.4%	27	0	148	122

No combination of tactics, lineups, or defensive alignments could have made the 2008 Tigers contenders, but Leyland wasn't satisfied until he had tried them all, just to be certain. Of course, he would have been roundly criticized had he watched the ship go down without pulling a few levers and twirling various dials, but Leyland's efforts, which have never strayed far outside the box, may have reached the point at which "trying" becomes "trying too hard." He attempted to cope with an ineffective pitching staff by walking anyone who looked dangerous with a bat in his hands (particularly Justin Morneau), dispensing a league-leading 63 IBB, but starters with shaky control and a

LOOGY who couldn't retire lefties was akin to pouring fuel on the fire. Leyland also deserves part of the blame for the evaluation failures that sent his first and third basemen ricocheting around the diamond. He attempted to stimulate the lineup by going through variants faster than Miguel Cabrera went through corn fritters, generating 110 unique permutations (the fourth-highest total in the American League) in an effort to recapture 2007's offensive mojo. Leyland's reputation for leadership remains intact, but if he made any contribution on the margins last season—precisely that to which most managers should aspire—it was probably a negative one.

Florida Marlins

In history's broad sweep, you can inevitably find a few whorls and eddies that seem like so many dead ends. The ephemeral and transient successes or failures can easily mislead us when it comes to larger, overarching considerations of what a team is doing badly or well. Given some of the ire being expressed this offseason over the Marlins and their thriftiness, it's important to identify whether this team is some sort of adaptive dead end or merely the latest iteration of Clark Griffith–style survivalism.

It's easy to get distracted when talking about the Marlins, because so many of the game's great themes, past and present, intersect in Miami. For example, the history of carpet-bagging owners coming in from out of town already has an honored spot in the game's history, while the shakedown of pliant municipalities to land publicly financed playpens has been one of the most spectacular near-universal achievements of the Selig Era. The Marlins are very much part of the program on both scores. Second, despite the accusation of cheapness that might attend this past offseason's latest round of arbitration avoidance, perhaps no team better represents the increasingly widely understood concept that when it comes to team construction, you pay premium talent top dollar while mercilessly exterminating the game's middle class. Finally, on the diamond, the team is equally representative of the trends that have captured imagination lately. While the Rays got all the attention for their rebuilt defense and attendant postseason breakthrough, the Fish also saw their defense do a radically better job in 2008, and the team made its own big move up in the standings. And while last year is seen as merely the start of something in St. Pete because of the

anticipated arrivals of a great deal of homegrown pitching, so too do the Marlins have outstanding young pitchers in the process of establishing themselves or moving on up. In short, if the Marlins have already been one of the game's most fascinating teams over the course of their brief existence because of rapidly generated titles punctuated by teardowns and cellar dwelling, it's an interesting franchise for other reasons as well and will continue to be interesting well into the future.

To answer the question of whether all of that fun and funky stuff actually translates into a worthwhile ballclub, let's tackle these themes as they affect the team's immediate future. We went into the team's ownership in some detail in this space last year—suffice it to say the Marlins' ownership is one of the less popular inventions of Bud Selig's team owners development program. But when ownership has turned over for more than half of the franchises in just the last 10 years and on 25 teams (counting expansion) in the last 20, lining up owners and ownership groups has been an important part of the industry's operations over the last two decades. The Lorians might not win any popularity contests, but who said owners were vying for popularity in the first place?

The developments on the ballpark side of things are a big part of Neil deMause's essay in the back of the book. However odious the final deal winds up being for a segment of the taxpaying public, the question for baseball is whether the new venue will alter the team's operating procedures and trajectory. Obviously, the new park can't hurt, and ideally, it will help them achieve better local revenues. Yet, the Fish need more than just a new venue. They also need the stability that the new stadium represents (perhaps symbolically

---

MARLINS PROSPECTUS

2008 record: 84-77; Third place in NL East

Pythagenport record: 81-80

Runs scored per game: 4.79 (5th in NL)

Runs allowed per game: 4.80 (11th in NL)

Team EqA: .265 (6th in NL)

2008 Batters Age: 28.3 (7th-youngest in NL)

2008 Pitchers Age: 26.6 (2nd-youngest in NL)

Ballpark: Dolphin Stadium; Slight pitcher's park; Park Factor of .981

2008: The Fish lose their two most recognizable players but gain 13 wins.

2009: The Marlins have found the youth that Ponce de León was looking for, but are they just spinning their wheels?

more than anything else). With construction only just beginning, the franchise should meanwhile focus on the product on the field. Delivering on this represents the Marlins' best promise that not only are they here to stay, but they're invested in the product as well.

In this already-hardened area of public antipathy and suspicion, last winter's run of arbitration-related deals and nontenders has elicited ire, because the team's actions on that front hardly seem designed to engender any trust. Instead, the moves seem a small-scale reenactment of the budget-slashing Huizenganation of 1998. A lot of the criticism is a response to the sheer scale of the problem, however; the Marlins had potentially as many as 15 arbitration cases to worry about, and rather than spend that much time arguing to panels about why most of their roster was worth only so much, they decided to divide that group into three piles: keepers, bargaining chips, and nontenders. It's easy to mistake gross scale for mere miserliness (Table 1).

Reflecting on how general manager Larry Beinfest handled this daunting slate of arbitration cases, it would be fair to say that the guys kept are generally the guys you'd want to keep, those who fall within the happy overlap of a Venn diagram as far as being relatively young, talented, and generally cheap compared with their value. Josh Johnson and Ricky Nolasco can be the front men in a very good rotation—you can't buy that kind of talent, even at the prices they'll reach through arbitration, and you almost never find stuff this good bobbing around on the waiver wire. Dan Uggla is oldish and a player you want to have control of for the tail end of his peak, after which you will just as certainly want to avoid making a big, multiyear commitment to him. As an outright purchase from the Reds in 2006 before he went through waivers, Cody Ross creates an already pretty tasty return on investment, and he's a younger and arguably better choice for your start-

ing left fielder than Josh Willingham, especially with Cameron Maybin on the way up and headed toward center field.

What about the cuts? Perhaps the drama of the late-November deadline for nontendering pressurized both actions and response, but in the broad view, the Marlins acted sensibly. Nelson and Treanor were both aging filler types, the sort you can find elsewhere, pay the minimum to, and get similar production. It's easy to get worked up over their acceptable performances and argue that it wouldn't necessarily have cost that much to retain them—the point is that they are quite fungible, they're not young, and why pay *anything* extra if you don't want to or have to?

The three trades might be seen as the most controversial element as well as the most obvious echo of 1998, but even here, the moves have a basic underlying logic. Dealing Kevin Gregg to the Cubs for Jose Ceda is a great move, adding a premium relief talent for somebody that general manager Beinfest scared up after the Angels wanted to get rid of him two years ago. Sure, Gregg has been useful, but with arms like Ceda or Matt Lindstrom or Ryan Tucker on hand, why pay an arbitration-set seven-figure salary for a useful utility pitcher who happened to be your closer only because somebody "must" close? Moving Mike Jacobs to the Royals for Leo Nuñez was a similarly frank recognition that Jacobs is basically filler-level talent at a premium position. If there's a dubious exchange in the pack, it's the deal with the Nationals, sending Willingham and Olsen to get Emilio Bonifacio and two prospects, but Olsen was more than a little lucky in 2008, and Willingham is already 30 and unlikely to get any better. As much as they were dumped, in light of what the organization has on hand, they were also replaceable.

Even with this bit of roster triage, there's no guarantee that the Marlins are necessarily done with their dealing.

Table 1. Flying Fish: The Arb-Eligibles

Kept in the Tank	Age	W/SX	Swapped	Age	W/SX	Non-Tender Fish	Age	W/SX
P R. Nolasco*	26	5.8	LF J. Willingham	30	4.0	C M. Treanor	33	0.2
2B D. Uggla	29	4.2	P S. Olsen	25	4.0	P J. Nelson	34	0.9
OF C. Ross	28	4.1	P K. Gregg	31	1.2			
3B J. Cantu	27	3.6	1B M. Jacobs	28	-0.8			
P J. Johnson	25	2.6						
RF J. Hermida	25	1.1						
UT A. Amezaga	31	1.0						
1/3 D. McPherson	28	0.3						
P L. Kensing	26	-0.7						

Age: Player age for the 2009 season.

W/SX: 2008 WARP for hitters, SN/WX for pitchers.

*Potential super-two arb-eligible.

They were shopping Jeremy Hermida and Jorge Cantu over the winter, but here again, that's because Florida should, considering that both aren't premium players or about to blossom into anything more than they are right now. Hermida's old-player skills as a hitter and probable upside have been the subject of much debate, but so far, the contras have to feel pretty good about their skepticism. Cantu was bobbing around on waivers for cause, given his fielding handicaps and his struggles to get on base; he's the sort of player who can prop up a team short of alternatives, but he's also the sort of regular you can't help but want to take a step up from.

While this all might seem a cavalier approach to asset management, where everyone and everything is for sale, the multitude of names in play doesn't obscure that the Marlins do have an actual, stable team core, and its name is Hanley Ramirez. While so much else was going well for the Fish during the 2008 season, perhaps the most important development for their future happened early on, when they came to terms with their star shortstop on a six-year, $70 million extension that will keep him in Miami through 2014, buying out not only his arbitration-eligible seasons but three more beyond. For all of the railing over the Marlins' retention of increasingly expensive mediocrities and how that's supposed to represent a commitment to something important (besides employing expensive mediocrities), Larry Beinfest did exactly what you're supposed to: not only did he discriminate among his middling talents, but he also paid top dollar for his top talent. We've been banging on this particular tocsin for more than a decade. Watching the Marlins do this in real-world operations in their pursuit of a policy of selective retention is just a matter of sound business practice.

Ramirez isn't simply a good player. His first three full years rank exceptionally well among the best from any young position players in the last 60 years of baseball history (Table 2). Keep in mind that WARP includes defense, and that's what *drops* HanRam to 13th in such excellent company. Among the shortstops, Ramirez's initial three-year mark in EqA is equal to Ripken's, better than Nomar's, and behind A-Rod. Is this somebody you spend to keep? Absolutely.

Change this sort of exercise to see where he ranks among all players (pitchers included) with the best three-year stretches without the player's being older than 24 in the third year—in other words, not necessarily these guy's first three seasons—and Ramirez's three-year run ranks 22nd overall over that same period (Table 3).

No doubt some of you have noticed the disappearances of Grich and Garciaparra from Table 3 after they

Table 2. Baseball's Best Three-Year Debuts, 1945–2008 (200 PAs minimum)

Player	Years	WARP	EqA
1. Cal Ripken Jr.	1982-84	31.8	.308
2. Bobby Grich	1972-74	31.6	.306
3. Johnny Bench	1968-70	27.9	.296
4. Dick Allen	1964-66	27.5	.339
5. Alex Rodriguez	1996-98	27.3	.311
6. Robin Ventura	1996-98	26.6	.311
7. Albert Pujols	2001-03	26.5	.339
8. Nomar Garciaparra	1997-99	25.6	.307
9. Grady Sizemore	2005-07	25.0	.299
10. Paul Molitor	1978-80	23.1	.289
11. Al Rosen	1950-52	23.0	.316
12. Tony Oliva	1964-66	22.9	.315
13. Hanley Ramirez	2006-08	22.8	.308

Table 3. The Genius of Youth: Best Three-Year Runs for Players Under 24, 1945–2008

Player	Years	WARP	EqA
1. Mickey Mantle	1954-56	32.7	.362
2. Cal Ripken Jr.	1982-84	31.8	.308
3. Eddie Mathews	1953-55	31.2	.349
4. Johnny Bench	1970-72	30.1	.308
5. Rickey Henderson	1980-82	29.0	.323
6t. Hank Aaron	1955-57	28.7	.331
6t. Albert Pujols	2002-04	28.7	.343
8. Dick Allen	1962-64	27.5	.339
9. Alex Rodriguez	1996-98	27.3	.311
10. Robin Ventura	1996-98	26.6	.311
11. Cesar Cedeño	1972-74	26.1	.324
12. George Brett	1975-77	25.6	.308
13. Willie Mays	1952-54	25.3	.341
14. Grady Sizemore	2005-07	25.0	.299
15. Frank Tanana	1975-77	24.0	—
16. Ned Garver	1948-50	23.9	.232
17. Roger Clemens	1985-87	23.8	—
18. Andruw Jones	1998-2000	23.6	.288
19t. Miguel Cabrera	2005-07	23.1	.325
19t. Ken Griffey Jr.	1991-93	23.1	.327
19t. Paul Molitor	1978-80	23.1	.289
22. Hanley Ramirez	2006-08	22.8	.308
23. Reggie Jackson	1968-70	22.4	.326
24. Bobby Grich	1971-73	22.3	.301
25. Jim Fregosi	1963-65	22.2	.298

showed up so prominently in Table 2; it just isn't easy to be this good this young. At any rate, the two tables reflect that Ramirez is a rare commodity, not simply because he's a shortstop, but also because he's an active ballplayer. The only active near contemporaries on this list are Pujols, Sizemore, and Cabrera—two first basemen and an older center fielder who doesn't hit as well as HanRam already has. Add in that his glove work improved last season, and it's not hard to see how he might not continue to rate with the Ripkens and the A-Rods of the world.

That defensive improvement is another echo of an industrywide trend that's in vogue, because while the Rays got all the media play for their massive upgrade on defense last year, the Marlins also made their own big improvement (Table 4). What's really interesting about the differences, however, is that where the Rays made several high-profile changes to their defensive alignment (even inspiring the odd MVP vote for Jason Bartlett), *the Marlins didn't*. Uggla and Ramirez were still their regulars in the middle infield, for example, and while both won't inspire paeans to slick work afield, they also were far better in 2008 than the year before. Although we take for granted that players have good and bad years at the plate or on the mound, we somehow seem less ready to work with the same assumption about a player's defense, which seems especially odd, given the team-level synergies intrinsic to the defensive arts.

Table 4. Making Leather Fashionable in the Gator State: Marlins and Rays Defensive Performance

Team	2007 DefEff	Rank	2007 PADE	Rank	2008 DefEff	Rank	2008 PADE	Rank
Rays	65.6%	30	-5.64	30	71.0%	1	1.26	3
Marlins	66.1%	29	-3.86	29	69.3%	13	0.96	4

The changes the Marlins did make were in center field—where Cody Ross absorbed a big chunk of utility-man Alfredo Amezaga's playing time—and third base, where Jorge Cantu stepped in to replace the departed Miguel Cabrera. In each instance, it wasn't a matter of bringing in great defenders as much as a case of replacing a pair who weren't assets with a more athletic and plausible pair at their respective positions. The Marlins' defense has the potential to get even better still if they really do move Ross to left while also shifting Uggla to

an infield corner to make room for the defensively gifted tandem of Cameron Maybin and Emilio Bonifacio. There's also a chance the team might just make do with Cantu and Dallas McPherson at the corners, and eventually Gaby Sanchez and Logan Morrison. Maybe the Marlins will leave their stars up the middle in place and use Bonifacio at third. All these things are being mooted, so we'll just have to see how it shakes out.

Lining up a quality defense could have the additional benefit of providing a soft landing for a young and improving pitching staff that won't simply be relying on Nolasco and Johnson from here on out. The Fish will also be counting on Anibal Sanchez to turn the corner in his comeback. A quality defense is going to make a big difference in whether Chris Volstad's second spin winds up as positive as his first or whether Adam Miller is finally going to live up to his initial billing. As is, this group of young starters won't have to go deep into games, not when Beinfest has been assiduously collecting a group of right-handed flamethrowers to comprise a no-stars bullpen with the talent to put a scare into people. The young pitching is the pride of the organization's player development program, but a combination of quality offense and an improving defense might give the club the platform to sustain what they've been building for a few years now.

Hope and faith is a theme we like to flog now and again. Part of that is a leftover brickbat, turning Bud Selig's words on him to highlight how many baseball teams did have hope that they might contend and who might engender faith that they'd put their best collective foot forward to get there if it wasn't within their immediate reach. While the Mets and Braves struggle to get their collective acts together, already choking on the Phillies' dust, the real fun begins now, because the Fish have put that best flipper forward. With the talent already on hand, they've got a reasonable hope of competing in their division and making a play at the wild card right now.

HITTERS

| Alfredo Amezaga | | | UT | | | | | | | Bats: S | | Throws: R | | Height: 5' 10" | | Weight: 180 | | Born: January 16, 1978 | | Age: 31 |

YEAR	TEAM	LVL	AGE	PA	R	2B	3B	HR	RBI	BB	SO	SB	CS	EqBRR	AVG	OBP	SLG	EqAVG	EqOBP	EqSLG	EqA	VORP	WARP	DEFENSE		
2006	FLO	MLB	28	378	43	9	3	3	19	33	46	20	12	0.7	.260	.332	.332	.264	.336	.335	.239	-0.4	-0.4	60-CF	-7	14-2B 1
2007	FLO	MLB	29	448	46	14	9	2	30	35	52	13	7	-1.3	.263	.324	.358	.270	.334	.375	.249	0.8	1.0	72-CF	4	14-SS -1
2008	FLO	MLB	30	337	41	13	5	3	32	19	47	8	2	1.1	.264	.312	.367	.268	.318	.380	.245	3.2	1.2	51-CF	4	14-SS 3
2009	FLO	MLB	31	262	30	9	3	2	19	19	33	7	3	1.1	.258	.315	.341	.261	.316	.355	.237	1.1	0.8	65-CF	3	

Breakout: 16% Improve: 39% Collapse: 35% Attrition: 28%   Comparables: John Moses, Quinton McCracken, Jose Macias, Dennis Hocking

Amezaga Anonymous warns you about a few symptoms of Amezaga addiction: it starts with enjoying something for its modest virtues, then deciding a little's not enough, and then getting hooked. Amezaga has played far too much center and gotten far too many at-bats for a nice little utility player. The Fish are slowly kicking the habit—giving Ross a shot last season cut into AA's playing time, and with Maybin on the horizon and Emilio Bonifacio potentially challenging him for a utility role, even his roster spot might get poured out. And if that doesn't work, there's always the Amezaga Patch, which has the dual benefit of curing the problem and keeping him safely tethered to the manager's arm.

Robert Andino   MI

Bats: R   Throws: R   Height: 6' 0"   Weight: 170   Born: April 25, 1984   Age: 25

YEAR	TEAM	LVL	AGE	PA	R	2B	3B	HR	RBI	BB	SO	SB	CS	EqBRR	AVG	OBP	SLG	EqAVG	EqOBP	EqSLG	EqA	VORP	WARP	DEFENSE		
2006	ABQ	AAA	22	549	70	18	6	8	46	33	100	13	11	-1.8	.255	.303	.363	.201	.248	.300	.190	-42.4	0.4	113-SS	20	4-2B	-1
2007	ABQ	AAA	23	644	85	25	13	13	50	40	129	21	13	0.0	.278	.322	.428	.211	.257	.334	.204	-39.2	-1.5	136-SS	-2		
2008	ABQ	AAA	24	204	28	14	3	6	26	18	31	9	5	-0.9	.287	.356	.497	.216	.284	.384	.232	-5.2	-0.2	42-SS	-4		
2008	FLO	MLB	24	68	7	2	0	2	9	4	23	0	0	1.5	.206	.254	.333	.206	.254	.333	.201	-2.6	0.0	10-2B	3		
2009	FLO	MLB	25	406	39	17	3	6	33	28	90	9	4	1.1	.224	.281	.336	.227	.282	.349	.219	-3.6	0.6	97-SS	4		

Breakout: 47%   Improve: 63%   Collapse: 21%   Attrition: 15%   Comparables: Danny Klassen, Johnnie LeMaster, Fran Mullins, John Kennedy

Andino has been projected to be an all-field, no-hit infielder for years now. While he posted a solid line in Triple-A this year, it was also his third year at the level. Now, with Bonifacio and Amezaga in the fold and Andino out of options, something's going to have to give, but faith in his fielding might make him a worthwhile pickup for teams that have been going shortstopless in public.

John Baker   C

Bats: L   Throws: R   Height: 6' 1"   Weight: 210   Born: January 20, 1981   Age: 28

YEAR	TEAM	LVL	AGE	PA	R	2B	3B	HR	RBI	BB	SO	SB	CS	EqBRR	AVG	OBP	SLG	EqAVG	EqOBP	EqSLG	EqA	VORP	WARP	DEFENSE
2006	SAC	AAA	25	340	49	19	1	4	38	40	77	6	0	4.6	.273	.361	.386	.237	.316	.343	.237	-6.9	-0.1	75-C	-7
2007	ABQ	AAA	26	303	35	15	0	8	41	28	58	2	0	0.0	.285	.360	.430	.208	.281	.325	.214	-15.6	-0.9	70-C	-5
2008	ABQ	AAA	27	221	35	14	1	6	31	24	34	1	2	0.9	.321	.398	.497	.217	.293	.343	.223	-7.9	0.1	48-C	1
2008	FLO	MLB	27	233	32	14	0	5	32	30	48	0	0	0.8	.299	.392	.447	.305	.397	.462	.301	17.5	1.6	56-C	-5
2009	FLO	MLB	28	276	31	14	1	5	27	28	65	2	1	-0.0	.248	.330	.377	.251	.331	.392	.251	6.9	1.3	68-C	-2

Breakout: 37%   Improve: 53%   Collapse: 29%   Attrition: 42%   Comparables: Sandy Martinez, Paul Bako, Dutch Dotterer, Ed Ott

You may remember him from *Moneyball*. Baker has seen his raw minor league numbers improve across three straight seasons, encouraging the Marlins to give him a chance when Matt Treanor went down. Baker's career had in part stalled thanks to his poor skills behind the plate, but he worked hard to improve during the season, even receiving assistance from the man he was replacing. Expecting Baker to continue to hit as well as he did for the Fish would be a bit much, but he's patient and his left-handedness gives him an advantage on most potential rivals. He'll get a shot at the starting job in 2009, though the Marlins have also shopped around for another backstop.

Jorge Cantu   3B

Bats: R   Throws: R   Height: 6' 3"   Weight: 200   Born: January 30, 1982   Age: 27

YEAR	TEAM	LVL	AGE	PA	R	2B	3B	HR	RBI	BB	SO	SB	CS	EqBRR	AVG	OBP	SLG	EqAVG	EqOBP	EqSLG	EqA	VORP	WARP	DEFENSE		
2006	TBA	MLB	24	448	40	18	2	14	62	26	91	1	1	-0.6	.249	.295	.404	.241	.292	.401	.239	2.6	-2.8	102-2B	-30		
2007	TBA	MLB	25	65	4	1	0	0	4	5	16	0	0	0.1	.207	.277	.224	.207	.277	.224	.178	-5.1	-0.5	6-1B	0		
2007	DUR	AAA	25	100	12	5	1	1	10	8	21	0	0	0.0	.242	.300	.352	.207	.260	.315	.199	-6.7	-0.5	8-1B	1		
2007	LOU	AAA	25	102	12	9	0	2	13	5	15	0	0	-1.0	.309	.363	.468	.274	.324	.453	.261	3.2	0.5	12-2B	3	10-1B	-1
2007	CIN	MLB	25	68	8	8	0	1	9	7	10	0	0	-1.1	.298	.382	.491	.281	.368	.456	.289	4.2	0.2	12-1B	-1		
2008	FLO	MLB	26	685	92	41	0	29	95	40	111	6	2	3.0	.277	.327	.481	.282	.331	.502	.280	30.5	3.6	120-3B	-3	32-1B	4
2009	FLO	MLB	27	583	67	33	2	20	79	41	104	4	2	-0.9	.269	.326	.454	.272	.327	.472	.269	20.5	2.3	137-3B	-2		

Breakout: 30%   Improve: 56%   Collapse: 14%   Attrition: 10%   Comparables: Joe Crede, Gary Gaetti, Mike Lowell, Tony Perez

The lack of a defensive home and inconsistent contact at the plate make Cantu's hold on any job precarious, but the Marlins reaped a big reward for giving him a shot at their opening at third, and though his fielding still isn't anything to get excited over, his bat returned for his best power output since 2005. Cantu isn't the most patient hitter, but as long as the ball leaves the park, he has value. The Marlins attempted to shop him this offseason, to no avail; now that Mike Jacobs has been sent packing, they're pondering switching him to first base.

Brett Carroll		OF										Bats: R		Throws: R		Height: 6' 0"		Weight: 190		Born: October 3, 1982		Age: 26	

YEAR	TEAM	LVL	AGE	PA	R	2B	3B	HR	RBI	BB	SO	SB	CS	EqBRR	AVG	OBP	SLG	EqAVG	EqOBP	EqSLG	EqA	VORP	WARP	DEFENSE			
2006	JUP	A+	23	244	31	12	1	8	30	18	48	9	3	0.1	.241	.324	.417	.201	.262	.353	.213	-13.5	-1.1	52-RF	-1		
2006	CAR	AA	23	280	29	15	3	9	30	18	62	4	1	-1.3	.231	.303	.422	.214	.276	.397	.231	-7.6	-1.2	46-CF	-7	27-RF	-1
2007	CAR	AA	24	117	9	13	0	3	12	12	20	0	2	0.0	.270	.359	.490	.231	.305	.423	.249	0.2	0.0	21-RF	0	8-CF	-1
2007	ABQ	AAA	24	346	60	21	6	19	70	18	69	0	4	0.0	.314	.361	.597	.243	.291	.480	.255	6.6	0.2	39-RF	0	34-CF	-3
2007	FLO	MLB	24	53	10	1	0	0	2	3	15	0	0	0.7	.184	.231	.204	.184	.231	.204	.134	-5.4	-0.7	9-CF	-1		
2008	ABQ	AAA	25	75	18	5	0	9	23	8	18	1	1	-0.0	.418	.480	.896	.324	.387	.676	.336	12.1	0.2	16-CF	-7		
2008	FLO	MLB	25	18	5	0	1	0	1	1	6	0	0	0.9	.059	.111	.176	.059	.111	.176	.000	-3.1	-0.3				
2009	FLO	MLB	26	353	31	16	1	11	41	24	103	2	1	0.1	.206	.268	.369	.208	.269	.384	.221	-9.6	-0.5	85-RF	0		

Breakout: 31%   Improve: 48%   Collapse: 34%   Attrition: 15%   Comparables: Jim Bennett, Andy Thompson, Randy Day, Keith Williams

Carroll is veering into fringy organizational guy territory; although he began the year on the big-league roster, a separated shoulder in May kept him out of the majors until September. He showed excellent power at Triple-A in 2007, but poor strike-zone recognition may forever keep him from wresting a job from the more established corner outfielders.

Chris Coghlan		2B										Bats: L		Throws: R		Height: 6' 1"		Weight: 190		Born: June 18, 1985		Age: 24	

YEAR	TEAM	LVL	AGE	PA	R	2B	3B	HR	RBI	BB	SO	SB	CS	EqBRR	AVG	OBP	SLG	EqAVG	EqOBP	EqSLG	EqA	VORP	WARP	DEFENSE			
2006	JAM	A-	21	111	14	5	1	0	12	13	9	5	2	-0.7	.298	.373	.372	.212	.279	.283	.202	-15.0	-1.7	19-3B	-6		
2007	GRB	A	22	360	60	26	4	10	64	47	43	19	4	0.0	.325	.419	.534	.228	.306	.369	.239	-6.6	-1.2	75-2B	-13		
2007	JUP	A+	22	148	17	5	3	2	18	15	19	5	1	2.1	.200	.277	.331	.180	.250	.301	.196	-12.5	-1.2	31-2B	-5		
2008	CAR	AA	23	565	83	32	5	7	74	67	65	34	10	2.2	.298	.396	.429	.250	.329	.371	.250	-0.9	1.0	114-2B	-2	9-3B	0
2009	FLO	MLB	24	602	73	34	4	8	49	55	100	20	7	2.0	.249	.323	.373	.253	.323	.388	.250	9.8	1.4	141-2B	-4		

Breakout: 42%   Improve: 72%   Collapse: 6%   Attrition: 4%   Comparables: Russ Adams, Steve Lyons, Andy Fox, Hiram Bocachica

A former first-rounder out of the University of Mississippi, Coghlan can work the count and knows what to do on base once he gets there. The knock against him is that none of his skills stand out and he doesn't have much projection left, but he has potential at second or as a frequently used utility infielder who can get on base.

Matt Dominguez		3B										Bats: R		Throws: R		Height: 6' 2"		Weight: 180		Born: August 28, 1989		Age: 19	

YEAR	TEAM	LVL	AGE	PA	R	2B	3B	HR	RBI	BB	SO	SB	CS	EqBRR	AVG	OBP	SLG	EqAVG	EqOBP	EqSLG	EqA	VORP	WARP	DEFENSE	
2007	MRL	Rk	17	22	0	0	0	0	2	1	2	0	0	-0.1	.100	.136	.100	.095	.130	.095	.000	-13.3	-0.7		
2007	JAM	A-	17	38	3	2	0	1	4	1	12	0	0	-0.1	.189	.211	.324	.162	.184	.270	.131	-10.2	-0.4	10-3B	1
2008	GRB	A	18	381	59	16	0	18	70	28	68	0	1	-2.7	.296	.354	.499	.231	.283	.399	.233	-7.2	-2.0	88-3B	-15
2009	FLO	MLB	19	572	46	26	1	14	54	43	127	0	1	-0.4	.221	.283	.352	.224	.284	.366	.222	-9.9	-0.6	134-3B	-4

Breakout: 47%   Improve: 64%   Collapse: 16%   Attrition: 3%   Comparables: Chris Marrero, Corey Smith, Brandon Wood, Darnell Coles

A first-round selection in 2007, last season Dominguez flexed some of the muscle that got him drafted twelfth overall, although he had to fend off mono early and elbow woes late. His instincts and a strong arm at the hot corner are already signs of a future Gold Glove candidate, but there is some concern that his bat is not on par with his glove—look no further than his road line of .246/.296/.392—but at least he crushed lefties, slugging .587. Given his age, he has plenty of time to sort his bat out.

Luis Gonzalez — LF

Bats: L   Throws: R   Height: 6' 2"   Weight: 210   Born: September 3, 1967   Age: 41

YEAR	TEAM	LVL	AGE	PA	R	2B	3B	HR	RBI	BB	SO	SB	CS	EqBRR	AVG	OBP	SLG	EqAVG	EqOBP	EqSLG	EqA	VORP	WARP	DEFENSE		
2006	ARI	MLB	38	668	93	52	2	15	73	69	58	0	1	2.1	.271	.352	.444	.259	.341	.421	.266	10.4	0.3	146-LF	-14	
2007	LAN	MLB	39	526	70	23	2	15	68	56	56	6	2	-0.5	.278	.359	.433	.278	.363	.443	.280	15.4	1.3	111-LF	-8	
2008	FLO	MLB	40	387	30	26	1	8	47	41	43	1	2	-3.7	.261	.336	.413	.268	.344	.431	.268	6.3	0.7	57-LF	1	17-RF -4
2009	FLO	MLB	41	314	36	16	1	6	36	35	37	3	1	-1.3	.262	.344	.391	.265	.345	.406	.263	4.8	0.3	76-LF	-6	

Breakout: 25%   Improve: 40%   Collapse: 43%   Attrition: 47%   Comparables: Enos Slaughter, Stan Musial, Carl Yastrzemski, Harold Baines

Gonzalez took a pay cut and signed for $2 million to play with the Fish in a backup role, but he ended up playing pretty often, thanks to Josh Willingham's spate of injuries. He did about as well as you can expect from a player who has been in decline for half of this century: he still drew walks, but he's a below-average stick in an outfield corner with declining defense. With the emergence of Ross and the arrival of Maybin, Gonzalez will be taking his mouthy (to the press, at least) veteran act elsewhere.

Brett Hayes — C

Bats: R   Throws: R   Height: 6' 1"   Weight: 200   Born: February 13, 1984   Age: 25

YEAR	TEAM	LVL	AGE	PA	R	2B	3B	HR	RBI	BB	SO	SB	CS	EqBRR	AVG	OBP	SLG	EqAVG	EqOBP	EqSLG	EqA	VORP	WARP	DEFENSE
2006	GRB	A	22	316	39	13	1	9	38	29	61	4	3	-1.8	.245	.321	.396	.169	.225	.272	.165	-35.2	-1.9	69-C 0
2007	JUP	A+	23	75	10	3	1	1	11	9	10	2	3	-0.7	.338	.413	.462	.284	.355	.403	.261	2.4	0.5	16-C 1
2007	CAR	AA	23	295	22	16	0	3	31	18	51	2	0	0.0	.234	.280	.326	.205	.244	.291	.182	-25.7	-2.7	71-C -14
2008	CAR	AA	24	194	19	8	0	6	18	10	43	1	4	-1.5	.232	.275	.376	.178	.211	.292	.160	-21.2	-1.6	47-C -3
2008	ABQ	AAA	24	126	21	3	1	5	17	4	23	1	1	0.3	.293	.331	.466	.220	.256	.364	.212	-5.7	-0.5	32-C -3
2009	FLO	MLB	25	313	21	12	1	5	27	18	79	2	1	-0.2	.195	.248	.297	.198	.249	.309	.187	-13.8	-0.3	76-C -2

Breakout: 37%   Improve: 51%   Collapse: 30%   Attrition: 23%   Comparables: Javi Herrera, Rick Guarno, Nick Trzesniak, Jason Hill

A heady receiver who gets high marks for his arm strength (he gunned down 33 percent of opposing thieves between Double-A and Triple-A), Hayes might end up getting a chance to stick as Baker's caddy if his fielding turns heads in camp. His hitting is what used to be politely referred to as "aggressive," so it won't be his bat that gets him up and keeps him up.

Wes Helms — 1B/3B

Bats: R   Throws: R   Height: 6' 4"   Weight: 220   Born: May 12, 1976   Age: 33

YEAR	TEAM	LVL	AGE	PA	R	2B	3B	HR	RBI	BB	SO	SB	CS	EqBRR	AVG	OBP	SLG	EqAVG	EqOBP	EqSLG	EqA	VORP	WARP	DEFENSE	
2006	FLO	MLB	30	278	30	19	5	10	47	21	55	0	4	-4.8	.329	.390	.575	.333	.391	.580	.316	26.2	2.0	49-1B -2	10-3B -2
2007	PHI	MLB	31	308	21	19	0	5	39	19	62	0	0	-0.6	.246	.297	.368	.243	.296	.361	.231	-4.8	-1.0	49-3B -4	11-1B 0
2008	FLO	MLB	32	278	28	11	0	5	31	17	65	0	0	0.3	.243	.299	.347	.248	.302	.360	.235	-5.1	-0.3	37-3B 2	24-1B -1
2009	FLO	MLB	33	186	19	10	1	4	22	15	37	0	0	-1.0	.264	.329	.408	.267	.330	.424	.259	5.1	0.4	47-3B -3	

Breakout: 23%   Improve: 50%   Collapse: 28%   Attrition: 39%   Comparables: Herb Perry, Walt Dropo, Tim Hulett, Mike Blowers

The last time Helms was a Marlin, he was a useful platoon piece that bashed left-handers to the tune of .301/.375/.506. That aptitude was nowhere to be found with the Phils in 2007, nor was it waiting to meet him when he bounced back to the Fish. Nevertheless, the Marlins re-signed Helms for two years and $1.9 million, something to remember next time they can't come up with a million bucks to keep an arb-eligible player around.

Jeremy Hermida — RF

Bats: L   Throws: R   Height: 6' 3"   Weight: 210   Born: January 30, 1984   Age: 25

YEAR	TEAM	LVL	AGE	PA	R	2B	3B	HR	RBI	BB	SO	SB	CS	EqBRR	AVG	OBP	SLG	EqAVG	EqOBP	EqSLG	EqA	VORP	WARP	DEFENSE	
2006	FLO	MLB	22	348	37	19	1	5	28	33	70	4	1	-0.6	.251	.332	.368	.250	.333	.373	.251	-0.2	-0.2	78-RF -5	6-CF 0
2007	FLO	MLB	23	484	54	32	1	18	63	47	105	3	4	-3.8	.296	.369	.501	.302	.377	.522	.299	24.9	3.8	111-RF 4	
2008	FLO	MLB	24	559	74	22	3	17	61	48	138	6	1	0.4	.249	.323	.406	.253	.327	.420	.260	3.3	1.1	123-RF 0	
2009	FLO	MLB	25	538	71	29	2	17	67	52	112	6	2	-0.5	.273	.350	.450	.276	.351	.468	.279	17.9	2.8	127-RF 3	

Breakout: 20%   Improve: 56%   Collapse: 12%   Attrition: 13%   Comparables: Ben Grieve, Mel Hall, Ed Kirkpatrick, Leron Lee

The oft-injured Hermida set a career high for plate appearances, but that was it for good news, as his power took a hit and he struck out more often while walking less. He displayed less patience with pitches outside the zone, but curiously also sat on more strikes than normal. The frequent comparisons to Ben Grieve are starting to look overstated, but only because at least Grieve was good in his early peak before fizzling, while Hermida has not even achieved "good" with any reliability. Appropriately concerned, the Marlins have shopped him around this offseason.

Mike Jacobs　　1B

Bats: L　Throws: R　Height: 6' 3"　Weight: 215　Born: October 30, 1980　Age: 28

YEAR	TEAM	LVL	AGE	PA	R	2B	3B	HR	RBI	BB	SO	SB	CS	EqBRR	AVG	OBP	SLG	EqAVG	EqOBP	EqSLG	EqA	VORP	WARP	DEFENSE	
2006	FLO	MLB	25	520	54	37	1	20	77	45	105	3	0	-0.6	.262	.325	.473	.263	.328	.480	.275	12.3	1.6	111-1B	0
2007	FLO	MLB	26	460	57	27	2	17	54	31	101	1	2	-1.8	.265	.317	.458	.269	.324	.472	.267	8.1	0.3	101-1B	-6
2008	FLO	MLB	27	519	67	27	2	32	93	36	119	1	0	-1.3	.247	.299	.514	.250	.302	.529	.275	17.1	-0.8	104-1B	-22
2009	KCA	MLB	28	469	53	26	1	19	72	37	93	2	1	-1.3	.258	.318	.459	.254	.316	.473	.268	6.1	0.2	111-1B	-9

Breakout: 23%　Improve: 44%　Collapse: 32%　Attrition: 16%　　　　Comparables: Tino Martinez, Greg Walker, Eddie Robinson, Gordy Coleman

Taking a look at Jacobs' numbers makes you wonder how he gets as much playing time as he does. His on-base rates have ranged from "good enough" to "abysmal," and his poor defense has not improved. Jacobs brings nothing to the table except for his power, and even that only shows up against right-handers (.266/.325/.504 from 2006 to 2008), though he has at least hit reasonably well on the road during the same stretch (.270/.335/.484). Since he was flipped to the Royals as arbitration boosted his paydays, you can expect more of the same. Jacobs is already in his peak years, and this is as good as he gets.

Cameron Maybin　　CF

Bats: R　Throws: R　Height: 6' 4"　Weight: 205　Born: April 4, 1987　Age: 22

YEAR	TEAM	LVL	AGE	PA	R	2B	3B	HR	RBI	BB	SO	SB	CS	EqBRR	AVG	OBP	SLG	EqAVG	EqOBP	EqSLG	EqA	VORP	WARP	DEFENSE	
2006	WMI	A	19	445	59	20	6	9	69	50	116	27	7	-0.2	.304	.387	.457	.230	.297	.368	.235	-10.4	1.3	87-CF	11
2007	LAK	A+	20	350	58	14	5	10	44	43	83	25	6	2.4	.304	.393	.486	.249	.330	.420	.264	6.3	-0.2	69-CF	-12
2007	ERI	AA	20	26	9	1	0	4	8	6	6	0	0	0.0	.400	.538	1.050	.333	.462	.810	.390	6.7	0.5	5-CF	0
2007	DET	MLB	20	53	8	3	0	1	2	3	21	5	0	1.0	.143	.208	.265	.143	.208	.265	.187	-3.9	-0.4	9-LF	0
2008	CAR	AA	21	459	73	15	8	13	49	60	124	21	7	3.5	.277	.375	.456	.236	.317	.392	.250	-1.2	1.5	101-CF	5
2008	FLO	MLB	21	36	9	2	0	2	3	8	4	0	2.1	.500	.543	.563	.500	.543	.562	.396	8.8	0.9	7-CF	2
2009	FLO	MLB	22	588	83	29	5	15	57	62	165	21	7	2.7	.265	.347	.429	.268	.348	.447	.275	23.5	4.5	138-CF	8

Breakout: 50%　Improve: 74%　Collapse: 3%　Attrition: 7%　　　　Comparables: Brad Komminsk, Kevin Dean, Dee Brown, Daryl Boston

The top prospect in the organization, Maybin looks at a ceiling that has been compared to that of a healthy Eric Davis, as he has the potential to be a 30-30 player. In the field, he has an above-average arm and uses his speed to cover a lot of ground in center. On the hitting side of things, Maybin has very strong, Davis-like wrists that give him great bat speed. There are roadblocks: He struck out more than a quarter of the time at Double-A this year, and he hit just .277 because of that, despite an above-average .375 BABIP. It's easy to envision a scenario where his batting average collapses because he can't stop whiffing, but should he learn to recognize the pitches that give him trouble, the result could be electrifying. He won't be a star in 2009, but few players have as much long-term potential.

Dallas McPherson　　3B/1B

Bats: L　Throws: R　Height: 6' 4"　Weight: 230　Born: July 23, 1980　Age: 28

YEAR	TEAM	LVL	AGE	PA	R	2B	3B	HR	RBI	BB	SO	SB	CS	EqBRR	AVG	OBP	SLG	EqAVG	EqOBP	EqSLG	EqA	VORP	WARP	DEFENSE			
2006	SLC	AAA	25	231	35	11	5	17	45	15	88	3	1	0.7	.250	.307	.596	.212	.263	.500	.252	1.3	-0.4	23-3B	-3	15-1B	-2
2006	ANA	MLB	25	121	16	4	0	7	13	6	40	1	0	0.6	.261	.298	.478	.254	.298	.465	.258	2.5	0.1	26-3B	-1		
2008	ABQ	AAA	27	530	94	22	3	42	98	76	168	14	6	1.5	.275	.379	.618	.197	.294	.433	.249	-3.6	0.3	103-3B	-3	13-1B	0
2008	FLO	MLB	27	15	3	2	0	0	0	4	5	0	0	-0.1	.182	.400	.364	.182	.400	.273	.264	0.4	0.0				
2009	FLO	MLB	28	448	51	21	2	20	57	48	160	9	4	-0.0	.207	.298	.422	.210	.298	.439	.250	2.3	1.0	106-3B	-2		

Breakout: 28%　Improve: 51%　Collapse: 20%　Attrition: 22%　　　　Comparables: John-Ford Griffin, Ozzie Canseco, Ryan Ludwick, Pat Dodson

The three words that come to mind when discussing McPherson are injuries, bombs, and strikeouts. Back surgery cost him all of 2007, but look on the bright side: he didn't strike out once the whole year. Given a chance by the Marlins, McPherson spent almost the whole season in Albuquerque making Three True Outcomes legends proud by delivering one of three (walks, homers, and punchouts) in almost 54 percent of his PAs and leading the minors in home runs. An August slump (.175/.245/.340) helped keep him down on the farm, but with Jacobs dealt and no clear choice at first or third, he might land a platoon role in camp, assuming his surgically repaired back holds up.

Jai Miller — OF

Bats: R Throws: R Height: 6' 4" Weight: 195 Born: January 17, 1985 Age: 24

YEAR	TEAM	LVL	AGE	PA	R	2B	3B	HR	RBI	BB	SO	SB	CS	EqBRR	AVG	OBP	SLG	EqAVG	EqOBP	EqSLG	EqA	VORP	WARP	DEFENSE			
2006	JUP	A+	21	401	40	16	2	0	24	45	115	24	10	-4.3	.209	.308	.267	.191	.273	.247	.189	-37.4	-2.8	100-CF	-5		
2007	CAR	AA	22	473	54	26	2	14	58	55	127	12	5	0.0	.261	.354	.438	.232	.310	.391	.246	-3.5	0.8	109-CF	5	4-LF	-3
2008	ABQ	AAA	23	498	67	22	5	19	56	52	133	20	6	1.4	.267	.349	.472	.205	.282	.361	.229	-18.3	-1.4	84-RF	-2	28-CF	-3
2009	FLO	MLB	24	486	53	24	3	11	48	47	150	13	5	0.6	.223	.304	.369	.225	.305	.384	.240	-3.9	0.8	115-RF	3		

Breakout: 39% Improve: 63% Collapse: 20% Attrition: 12%   Comparables: Scott Wade, Scott Lydy, Dominic Fucci, Brent Clevlen

Miller is a confusing prospect: he has six years of pro experience, but is still very raw and toolsy. He made progress at Double-A in 2007, bringing up his batting average and adding some power, but overall, it was just a baby step in the right direction, especially with that strikeout rate. He bumped his power up further in 2008 at Triple-A, but in center, his future is blocked by Maybin. With the frequency that players are jettisoned from the Fish, he may get a shot, but for now, he'll probably continue trying to tighten up his game in the minors.

Logan Morrison — 1B

Bats: L Throws: L Height: 6' 2" Weight: 215 Born: August 25, 1987 Age: 21

YEAR	TEAM	LVL	AGE	PA	R	2B	3B	HR	RBI	BB	SO	SB	CS	EqBRR	AVG	OBP	SLG	EqAVG	EqOBP	EqSLG	EqA	VORP	WARP	DEFENSE	
2006	MRL	Rk	18	99	10	4	0	1	7	10	12	1	0	-2.3	.270	.343	.348	.217	.273	.272	.187	-20.8	-1.6	19-1B	-2
2006	JAM	A-	18	88	6	3	0	1	11	11	17	0	0	-0.5	.203	.295	.284	.143	.227	.221	.147	-22.5	-1.6	20-1B	-1
2007	GRB	A	19	513	71	22	2	24	86	48	96	2	2	0.0	.267	.343	.483	.194	.255	.352	.208	-29.3	-5.0	111-1B	-18
2008	JUP	A+	20	555	71	38	1	13	74	57	80	9	3	-3.2	.332	.402	.494	.304	.364	.474	.287	39.0	1.6	118-1B	-9
2009	FLO	MLB	21	597	69	33	2	15	68	55	126	5	2	-1.3	.263	.333	.414	.266	.334	.431	.262	9.2	1.0	140-1B	-4

Breakout: 41% Improve: 67% Collapse: 10% Attrition: 7%   Comparables: Kent Hrbek, Greg Walker, Steve Cox, Justin Morneau

A 22nd-round pick in the 2005 draft, Morrison has been impressive the last two seasons. Thanks to his excellent plate coverage and textbook swing, the lefty was able to add power to his game in 2007 and drop his strikeouts considerably after a promotion to High-A in 2008. He's not going to be a power-hitting first baseman, instead profiling as a high AVG/OBP guy, but with his approach, he should succeed at the higher levels. He dominated the Arizona Fall League, hitting .404/.444/.667 in 99 at-bats, so if he adjusts to Double-A with little problem, the majors won't be too far out of reach for this polished hitter.

Mike Rabelo — C

Bats: S Throws: R Height: 6' 1" Weight: 200 Born: January 17, 1980 Age: 29

YEAR	TEAM	LVL	AGE	PA	R	2B	3B	HR	RBI	BB	SO	SB	CS	EqBRR	AVG	OBP	SLG	EqAVG	EqOBP	EqSLG	EqA	VORP	WARP	DEFENSE	
2006	ERI	AA	26	242	31	13	1	6	28	19	38	2	1	0.6	.277	.361	.432	.198	.264	.324	.203	-15.4	-0.2	54-C	2
2006	TOL	AAA	26	153	19	12	0	3	22	11	33	1	1	0.4	.270	.333	.423	.245	.301	.388	.239	-1.6	0.1	37-C	-3
2007	DET	MLB	27	185	14	10	2	1	18	6	41	0	0	-2.5	.256	.300	.357	.256	.296	.357	.229	-0.2	0.0	44-C	-1
2008	FLO	MLB	28	122	9	1	0	3	10	8	25	0	1	-2.7	.202	.256	.294	.202	.254	.294	.194	-6.0	-0.6	30-C	-2
2008	ABQ	AAA	28	30	2	1	0	1	2	1	8	0	0	0.1	.241	.267	.379	.172	.200	.310	.162	-3.2	-0.2	6-C	0
2009	FLO	MLB	29	154	13	7	1	3	15	10	37	0	0	-0.6	.229	.284	.354	.232	.285	.368	.223	0.2	0.4	40-C	-1

Breakout: 52% Improve: 61% Collapse: 28% Attrition: 45%   Comparables: Javier Valentin, Robert Machado, Mike Matheny, Russ Gibson

Rabelo has his uses, as he's solid behind the plate and capable of hitting well enough to back up at the position. However, the former Tiger could not put it together at the plate last year. Injuries (a left knee sprain before the season began and a sprained right wrist that ended his season in June) were at least partly to blame. With the release of Treanor, Rabelo is first in line to back up Baker.

Hanley Ramirez — SS

Bats: R Throws: R Height: 6' 3" Weight: 200 Born: December 23, 1983 Age: 25

YEAR	TEAM	LVL	AGE	PA	R	2B	3B	HR	RBI	BB	SO	SB	CS	EqBRR	AVG	OBP	SLG	EqAVG	EqOBP	EqSLG	EqA	VORP	WARP	DEFENSE	
2006	FLO	MLB	22	700	119	46	11	17	59	56	128	51	15	10.3	.292	.353	.480	.300	.361	.494	.291	54.9	5.8	150-SS	0
2007	FLO	MLB	23	706	125	48	6	29	81	52	95	51	14	2.3	.332	.386	.562	.343	.399	.594	.323	85.3	8.1	146-SS	-6
2008	FLO	MLB	24	693	125	34	4	33	67	92	122	35	12	3.0	.301	.400	.540	.312	.410	.574	.324	79.4	9.8	146-SS	12
2009	FLO	MLB	25	696	128	44	5	28	95	78	110	36	9	4.6	.318	.399	.548	.322	.400	.570	.324	86.2	8.7	162-SS	1

Breakout: 20% Improve: 71% Collapse: 3% Attrition: 0%   Comparables: Jim Fregosi, Alex Rodriguez, David Wright, Cesar Cedeño

Already one of the top offensive talents in the game, Ramirez improved the margins in order to raise his status further. His walk rate jumped significantly, though the hike in P/PA (3.6 to 4.1) also meant risking and receiving a few more strikeouts. His power was not affected with the change in approach, as he set a career high in homers while meaningfully increasing his HR/FB rate. Most important was the improvement in his defense: a butcher in the past, at the behest of infield coach Andy Fox, he worked on being aggressive and using his above-average arm to better effect. The lone negative was his oft-injured left shoulder, on which he had arthroscopic surgery after the season. As long as the defensive improvement is for real and the shoulder issues do not persist, you can safely shift his status from "great hitter" to "elite player."

John Raynor			**LF**							Bats: R		Throws: R		Height: 6' 2"		Weight: 185		Born: January 4, 1984				Age: 25				
YEAR	TEAM	LVL	AGE	PA	R	2B	3B	HR	RBI	BB	SO	SB	CS	EqBRR	AVG	OBP	SLG	EqAVG	EqOBP	EqSLG	EqA	VORP	WARP		DEFENSE	
2006	JAM	A-	22	223	36	8	4	4	21	17	51	21	2	3.6	.286	.356	.427	.192	.242	.303	.193	-37.3	-2.3		28-CF -2 15-RF -1	
2007	GRB	A	23	526	110	28	8	13	57	66	98	54	8	0.0	.333	.429	.519	.212	.290	.340	.226	-21.0	-1.9		106-LF -6	
2008	CAR	AA	24	534	104	29	6	13	51	62	122	48	11	6.1	.312	.402	.489	.245	.316	.392	.254	-0.7	0.1		89-LF -2 18-RF -3	
2009	FLO	MLB	25	541	62	29	5	11	47	47	160	21	8	2.9	.228	.302	.374	.231	.303	.390	.243	-6.7	0.9		127-LF 3	

Breakout: 36% Improve: 61% Collapse: 19% Attrition: 6%   Comparables: Richard Barnwell, Kevin Ward, Prentice Redman, Gary Redus

The MVP of the Sally League in 2007, this former ninth-round pick skipped High-A and went straight to Double-A without missing a beat: despite striking out a bit more, Raynor maintained his walk rate and held on to most of his power. Even with his patience, Raynor is sometimes overly aggressive early in the count, which is why he strikes out so often despite not being a power threat. His line-drive swing generates high batting averages, and that coupled with his ability to draw a walk is where his offensive value comes from. With Ross and Hermida already manning the corners, Raynor is bound for Triple-A, though a trade could open space for him.

Cody Ross			**CF**							Bats: R		Throws: L		Height: 5' 9"		Weight: 205		Born: December 23, 1980				Age: 28				
YEAR	TEAM	LVL	AGE	PA	R	2B	3B	HR	RBI	BB	SO	SB	CS	EqBRR	AVG	OBP	SLG	EqAVG	EqOBP	EqSLG	EqA	VORP	WARP		DEFENSE	
2006	LAN	MLB	25	14	4	1	1	2	9	0	2	1	0	0.2	.500	.500	1.143	.500	.500	.999	.474	5.9	0.5			
2006	LOU	AAA	25	64	11	1	0	3	6	13	12	0	2	0.0	.340	.484	.540	.294	.438	.490	.317	6.9	0.5		7-RF 0 4-LF -1	
2006	FLO	MLB	25	279	30	11	1	11	37	22	61	0	1	-0.7	.212	.284	.396	.216	.288	.408	.238	-5.6	-0.4		25-RF -3 23-LF 0	
2007	FLO	MLB	26	197	35	19	0	12	39	20	38	2	0	1.6	.335	.411	.653	.337	.416	.663	.348	28.0	2.6		27-CF -6 12-RF 1	
2008	FLO	MLB	27	506	59	29	5	22	73	33	116	6	1	-0.6	.260	.316	.488	.267	.323	.511	.280	22.5	4.1		97-CF 11 17-RF 3	
2009	FLO	MLB	28	404	55	24	2	18	61	36	88	6	2	-0.0	.272	.343	.497	.275	.344	.518	.288	24.1	3.1		96-CF -1	

Breakout: 17% Improve: 53% Collapse: 22% Attrition: 15%   Comparables: Shane Spencer, Benny Agbayani, Wes Chamberlain, Candy Maldonado

Until Ross joined the Marlins in 2006, he'd bounced all over the place without sticking. He got the Marlins' attention after his impressive (but short) 2007 campaign and eventually filled their gaping hole in center because nature abhors a vacuum. Though he was solid for most of 2008, it was his ridiculous May (14 hits, 10 of them homers) that guaranteed him job security, even though his walk rate plummeted and his whiffs rose. His bat should be good enough to play in a corner, meaning the Marlins have a younger, cheaper, and reasonably productive replacement for Willingham in Ross.

Gaby Sanchez			**1B**							Bats: R		Throws: R		Height: 6' 2"		Weight: 225		Born: September 2, 1983				Age: 25				
YEAR	TEAM	LVL	AGE	PA	R	2B	3B	HR	RBI	BB	SO	SB	CS	EqBRR	AVG	OBP	SLG	EqAVG	EqOBP	EqSLG	EqA	VORP	WARP		DEFENSE	
2006	GRB	A	22	237	43	12	0	14	40	39	20	6	2	-1.1	.317	.447	.603	.230	.329	.422	.261	3.3	-0.1		42-1B -5 8-C 0	
2006	JUP	A+	22	68	13	3	1	1	7	12	12	1	0	-0.2	.182	.324	.327	.158	.279	.316	.214	-4.7	-0.3		6-1B 0 5-3B 0	
2007	JUP	A+	23	547	89	40	3	9	70	64	74	6	6	3.2	.279	.369	.433	.234	.311	.374	.239	-7.3	-0.9		98-1B -1 7-3B 0	
2008	CAR	AA	24	557	70	42	1	17	92	69	70	17	8	-6.8	.314	.404	.513	.251	.323	.414	.256	6.7	1.6		66-1B 5 59-3B 1	
2009	FLO	MLB	25	543	62	29	2	13	59	56	103	7	3	-0.6	.244	.326	.394	.247	.327	.410	.255	4.8	1.4		128-1B 8	

Breakout: 35% Improve: 53% Collapse: 18% Attrition: 12%   Comparables: Garrett Atkins, Tom Evans, Jason Hart, Scott McClain

The shine came off the former fourth-round selection during his second full year in the minors, as he failed to hit for much power in High-A. Hitting is all Sanchez has going for him, however, so this was a problem for his prospect status. The Marlins promoted him to Double-A anyway, and it worked out to an extent: his power returned (but only against lefties, against whom he hit .374/.456/.680), and a permanent move to first base gave him a position where he could be a solid defender. Unless Cantu or Uggla shifts to first base, Sanchez will have a shot there in spring training; he will at least be useful as a lefty masher, which again makes one wonder why Helms was re-upped.

Kyle Skipworth   C   Bats: L   Throws: R   Height: 6' 3"   Weight: 195   Born: March 1, 1990   Age: 19

YEAR	TEAM	LVL	AGE	PA	R	2B	3B	HR	RBI	BB	SO	SB	CS	EqBRR	AVG	OBP	SLG	EqAVG	EqOBP	EqSLG	EqA	VORP	WARP	DEFENSE
2008	MRL	Rk	18	176	22	6	0	5	21	13	46	2	2	-0.7	.208	.263	.340	.164	.205	.261	.147	-60.4	-2.3	28-C 1
2009	FLO	MLB	19	479	31	20	2	6	35	28	146	3	3	0.5	.188	.239	.281	.191	.240	.292	.174	-27.2	-1.5	113-C -8

Breakout: 74% Improve: 81% Collapse: 9% Attrition: 7%   Comparables: Greg David, Rico Brogna, Tyler Houston, Mike Lieberthal

The Marlins' 2008 first-round pick was the top high-school catcher in the draft, but Skipworth struggled at the plate during his first taste of pro baseball. The Marlins were not deterred by his struggles; he's too young to worry about yet, especially with his plus-plus power potential and promising defense. It's tough to say just what kind of player he will be, but the potential to become an All-Star backstop is there.

Mike Stanton   OF   Bats: R   Throws: R   Height: 6' 5"   Weight: 205   Born: November 8, 1989   Age: 19

YEAR	TEAM	LVL	AGE	PA	R	2B	3B	HR	RBI	BB	SO	SB	CS	EqBRR	AVG	OBP	SLG	EqAVG	EqOBP	EqSLG	EqA	VORP	WARP	DEFENSE	
2007	MRL	Rk	17	28	6	2	0	0	1	1	6	0	0	0.2	.269	.321	.346	.222	.250	.259	.166	-6.7	-0.4	7-RF 0	
2007	JAM	A-	17	35	2	1	0	1	2	3	15	0	0	0.0	.067	.147	.200	.065	.118	.194	.000	-13.9	-1.1	9-RF -2	
2008	GRB	A	18	540	89	26	3	39	97	58	153	4	2	0.6	.293	.381	.611	.237	.316	.491	.270	18.7	1.5	63-RF -7	43-CF 2
2009	FLO	MLB	19	566	59	27	2	21	59	54	166	2	2	0.7	.220	.301	.405	.223	.302	.421	.244	-1.2	1.1	133-RF 2	

Breakout: 24% Improve: 47% Collapse: 25% Attrition: 3%   Comparables: Danny Tartabull, Manny Ramirez, Roberto Zambrano, Aramis Ramirez

Stanton was a second-round pick in 2007 who initially struggled to do anything with the bat after signing, but things came together for him in 2008. He started translating his tremendous power into game production, although there are some red flags: Stanton strikes out a ton, about a third of the time last year, and his improved walk rate was in part due to the league's respecting his status as a beast at the plate rather than an improved eye. Though a capable center fielder for now, his frame suggests he will fill out and have to move to right field permanently, but as long as he can cut down on the strikeouts and improve his strike-zone recognition, he'll have the bat to stick there.

Matt Treanor   C   Bats: R   Throws: R   Height: 6' 0"   Weight: 210   Born: March 3, 1976   Age: 33

YEAR	TEAM	LVL	AGE	PA	R	2B	3B	HR	RBI	BB	SO	SB	CS	EqBRR	AVG	OBP	SLG	EqAVG	EqOBP	EqSLG	EqA	VORP	WARP	DEFENSE
2006	FLO	MLB	30	185	12	6	1	2	14	19	34	0	1	-0.7	.229	.328	.318	.228	.326	.316	.232	-2.7	0.7	49-C 5
2007	FLO	MLB	31	198	16	7	1	4	19	19	29	0	0	-0.9	.269	.357	.392	.275	.362	.415	.273	7.2	0.5	50-C -6
2008	FLO	MLB	32	234	18	7	0	2	23	18	53	1	0	1.0	.238	.306	.301	.240	.310	.308	.224	-3.7	0.2	59-C 1
2009	DET	MLB	33	210	20	8	1	3	19	18	40	1	1	-0.6	.243	.317	.334	.243	.319	.345	.237	-0.2	0.7	53-C 0

Breakout: 19% Improve: 42% Collapse: 30% Attrition: 41%   Comparables: Steve Decker, Jerry McNertney, Andy Etchebarren, Al Evans

Yes, Treanor lost his job to a career minor leaguer after suffering a strained left hip in July, and yes, he was released by the Marlins to punt his arbitration eligibility and give Rabelo a shot as the backup. But things are not all bad, as the Tigers signed him to a one-year deal to back up Gerald Laird, and Treanor gets to go home to Misty May after work every day. Clearly, it's not all bad to be Mr. Treanor.

Dan Uggla   2B   Bats: R   Throws: R   Height: 5' 11"   Weight: 200   Born: March 11, 1980   Age: 29

YEAR	TEAM	LVL	AGE	PA	R	2B	3B	HR	RBI	BB	SO	SB	CS	EqBRR	AVG	OBP	SLG	EqAVG	EqOBP	EqSLG	EqA	VORP	WARP	DEFENSE
2006	FLO	MLB	26	683	105	26	7	27	90	48	123	6	6	1.1	.282	.339	.480	.287	.343	.489	.280	39.1	3.1	148-2B -9
2007	FLO	MLB	27	728	113	49	3	31	88	68	167	2	1	2.3	.245	.326	.479	.249	.332	.500	.280	26.4	1.0	155-2B -31
2008	FLO	MLB	28	619	97	37	1	32	92	77	171	5	5	1.1	.260	.360	.514	.268	.367	.538	.299	41.3	4.2	143-2B -8
2009	FLO	MLB	29	638	87	33	2	29	91	69	146	4	3	0.4	.262	.348	.485	.265	.349	.505	.286	38.2	3.3	149-2B -9

Breakout: 12% Improve: 43% Collapse: 19% Attrition: 9%   Comparables: Doug DeCinces, Tony Perez, Keith Ginter, Rico Petrocelli

Every year has been a surprise with Uggla: he exploded onto the scene after getting picked via the Rule 5 draft in

2006 and then followed that up by crossing the 30-homer mark in 2007. For 2008, the shock value was in his first-half line of .286/.374/.605, as it put him alongside Chase Utley as one of the position's premier sluggers. His second half did not go so well, with Uggla hitting just .225/.344/.398 from June 29 onward; if you listened to the man himself, a sprained ankle suffered the day before hampered his ability to hit the rest of the year. With a winter's rest, Uggla should be back to his old slugging self come Opening Day. Whether he remains at second for another year of poor fielding or moves to an infield corner is one of the Marlins' key decisions.

Josh Willingham — LF

Bats: R   Throws: R   Height: 6' 2"   Weight: 215   Born: February 17, 1979   Age: 30

YEAR	TEAM	LVL	AGE	PA	R	2B	3B	HR	RBI	BB	SO	SB	CS	EqBRR	AVG	OBP	SLG	EqAVG	EqOBP	EqSLG	EqA	VORP	WARP	DEFENSE	
2006	FLO	MLB	27	573	62	28	2	26	74	54	109	2	0	-5.8	.277	.356	.496	.281	.360	.509	.294	27.8	4.1	122-LF	5
2007	FLO	MLB	28	604	75	32	4	21	89	66	122	8	1	1.6	.265	.364	.463	.270	.371	.482	.293	24.2	1.9	132-LF	-16
2008	FLO	MLB	29	416	54	21	5	15	51	48	82	3	2	-2.1	.254	.364	.470	.262	.371	.493	.293	18.4	4.0	96-LF	13
2009	WAS	MLB	30	484	64	25	2	18	68	53	88	3	1	-1.1	.266	.358	.466	.269	.360	.487	.288	21.0	2.6	114-LF	-2

Breakout: 16%   Improve: 47%   Collapse: 20%   Attrition: 11%   Comparables: Bubba Trammell, Ryan Ludwick, Bill Renna, Leon Roberts

Willingham has never been a great bat, but he's a very good one that can take a walk, hit the occasional homer, and get in the way of a pitch. This knocked him out of the Marlins' price range this winter, and they sent their arbitration-eligible left fielder packing to the Nationals. At least the Nats know they are getting a good player, as Willingham has always been hampered by playing in Florida (.280/.373/.514 on the road, 2006-2008) and doesn't need a platoon mate. His lower back was a cause for concern, with Willingham missing most of May and June because of it, but there is no reason to believe that the injury is chronic.

PITCHERS

Burke Badenhop — Bats: R

Throws: R   Height: 6' 5"   Weight: 220   Born: February 8, 1983   Age: 26

YEAR	TEAM	LVL	AGE	W	L	SV	G	GS	IP	H	BB	SO	HR	GB%	BABIP	STUFF	WHIP	ERA	DERA	EqH9	EqBB9	EqSO9	EqHR9	DEF	VORP	SN/WX
2006	WMI	A	23	14	3	0	27	27	171	170	31	124	6	60.1%	.308	-25	1.18	2.84	5.91	13.9	3.1	2.8	1.4	-4	-4.9	—
2007	LAK	A+	24	10	6	0	23	23	135¹	130	34	78	5	58.4%	.287	-14	1.21	3.13	6.27	9.5	3.1	2.5	0.9	4	-9.5	—
2007	ERI	AA	24	2	0	0	3	3	18²	8	3	12	1	63.2%	.208	3	0.59	1.44	4.91	4.4	2.0	3.4	1.0	5	1.4	—
2008	FLO	MLB	25	2	3	0	13	8	47¹	55	21	35	7	55.3%	.324	-8	1.61	6.09	6.04	10.4	3.4	5.9	1.3	-1	-4.3	-0.30
2009	FLO	MLB	26	3	3	0	21	6	52	60	20	30	5	53.0%	.310	-3	1.53	5.20	5.69	10.5	3.0	4.2	0.9	0	0.2	0.25

Breakout: 16%   Improve: 44%   Collapse: 30%   Attrition: 45%   Comparables: Craig Anderson, Sergio Mitre, Jerry Janeski, Vince Colbert

An add-on from the Dontrelle Willis deal, Badenhop might be big, but he clocks in under 90 mph with his sinking fastball, and that's his most frequently used selection in a three-pitch arsenal (he also throws a change and a slider). His 2008 was forgettable, as he split time between the rotation and relief before going down for the rest of the season with right shoulder tendonitis in June. Never more than a middling prospect, Badenhop, even healthy, would have been in danger of being crowded out of the near-term picture by the homegrown talent.

Hector Correa

Bats: R   Throws: R   Height: 6' 3"   Weight: 165   Born: March 18, 1988   Age: 21

YEAR	TEAM	LVL	AGE	W	L	SV	G	GS	IP	H	BB	SO	HR	GB%	BABIP	STUFF	WHIP	ERA	DERA	EqH9	EqBB9	EqSO9	EqHR9	DEF	VORP	SN/WX
2006	MRL	Rk	18	1	2	0	10	5	41¹	38	15	38	1	48.7%	.316	5	1.29	1.75	6.27	14.2	5.7	3.8	1.6	0	-2.5	—
2007	GRB	A	19	1	5	0	8	8	31	55	16	20	7	39.3%	.436	-54	2.29	9.29	16.05	23.4	7.3	2.2	4.7	-4	-28.7	—
2007	JAM	A-	19	6	2	0	11	11	58²	61	13	83	5	43.4%	.384	18	1.26	3.22	4.53	14.9	3.3	6.9	2.7	-8	5.9	—
2008	GRB	A	20	0	1	0	4	4	10	15	1	9	1	32.4%	.389	3	1.60	6.30	8.68	16.4	1.9	3.9	1.9	-1	-3.2	—
2009	FLO	MLB	21	3	7	0	23	14	76¹	113	40	48	19	41.0%	.360	-10	2.01	8.43	8.80	13.5	4.1	4.6	2.2	0	-27.9	-2.14

Breakout: 30%   Improve: 69%   Collapse: 15%   Attrition: 18%   Comparables: Rick Siebert, Tim Scott, Leo Nuñez, Fernando Hernandez

After struggling in the Sally League in 2007, Correa was moved down to the New York–Penn League. There, the Puerto Rican import began to make adjustments to his raw secondary stuff and a developing fastball that's already capable of hitting the mid-90s. He was supposed to get his second chance at Low-A, but a tooth infection in April and a blister later on derailed his season. Given how much work his slider needs, that year of development will be missed, but he's still young enough to overcome that and get himself back on the Marlins' prospect radar, even if it's as a reliever.

Eulogio de la Cruz

Bats: R Throws: R Height: 5' 11" Weight: 175 Born: March 12, 1984 Age: 25

YEAR	TEAM	LVL	AGE	W	L	SV	G	GS	IP	H	BB	SO	HR	GB%	BABIP	STUFF	WHIP	ERA	DERA	EqH9	EqBB9	EqSO9	EqHR9	DEF	VORP	SN/WX
2006	ERI	AA	22	5	6	2	38	12	105¹	103	45	87	3	56.1%	.324	-4	1.41	3.43	6.17	10.5	4.8	4.2	0.7	5	-6.1	—
2007	ERI	AA	23	4	5	0	11	11	66	54	19	57	5	62.9%	.274	-2	1.11	3.41	6.18	9.5	3.2	5.1	1.2	5	-3.8	—
2007	TOL	AAA	23	3	0	0	22	1	38¹	41	18	25	0	44.3%	.336	-19	1.54	3.52	6.95	12.0	4.8	4.0	0.3	6	-5.1	—
2007	DET	MLB	23	0	0	0	6	0	6²	10	4	5	1	78.3%	.409	-20	2.10	6.72	6.00	15.0	6.0	6.0	1.5	-3	-3.6	0.00
2008	ABQ	AAA	24	13	8	0	25	25	147¹	139	60	118	13	60.3%	.301	-1	1.35	4.34	5.55	8.5	3.7	4.7	0.9	7	0.8	—
2008	FLO	MLB	24	0	0	0	6	1	9	15	11	4	2	47.4%	.382	-37	2.89	18.00	16.76	14.0	8.4	3.7	1.9	-3	-14.4	-0.20
2009	FLO	MLB	25	4	6	0	29	11	82²	91	41	57	8	54.0%	.310	0	1.60	5.56	6.10	10.0	3.9	5.0	0.9	0	-3.6	0.09

Breakout: 26% Improve: 63% Collapse: 14% Attrition: 21%   Comparables: Domingo Jean, Joaquin Andujar, Victor Cole, Hipolito Pichardo

De la Cruz's numbers trail behind his stuff, but that's because his high-velocity fastball runs flat, while his curve is often thrown out of the strike zone, which makes him less effective against more advanced hitters. Last year was no exception; he does not have the pitches to become an effective starter and will instead have to harness the ones he has in a relief role.

Kevin Gregg

Bats: R Throws: R Height: 6' 6" Weight: 240 Born: June 20, 1978 Age: 31

YEAR	TEAM	LVL	AGE	W	L	SV	G	GS	IP	H	BB	SO	HR	GB%	BABIP	STUFF	WHIP	ERA	DERA	EqH9	EqBB9	EqSO9	EqHR9	DEF	VORP	SN/WX
2006	LAA	MLB	28	3	4	0	32	3	78¹	88	21	71	10	35.4%	.335	6	1.39	4.14	4.09	10.3	2.3	7.4	1.1	-4	12.1	0.16
2007	FLO	MLB	29	0	5	32	74	0	84	63	40	87	7	29.7%	.264	19	1.23	3.54	3.32	5.7	3.6	8.4	0.6	0	20.3	3.49
2008	FLO	MLB	30	7	8	29	72	0	68²	51	37	58	3	46.7%	.253	8	1.28	3.41	4.11	6.6	4.0	6.6	0.4	3	12.8	1.24
2009	CHN	MLB	31	4	4	12	47	0	56²	52	25	52	6	40.0%	.290	7	1.36	4.06	4.26	8.0	3.5	7.0	1.0		110.3	1.10

Breakout: 12% Improve: 39% Collapse: 41% Attrition: 17%   Comparables: Ted Power, Mike James, Don Robinson, Matt Karchner

Gregg has his positives, starting with a low- to mid-90s fastball and supported by a slider and splitter, and he's also been relatively consistent, at least until a knee injury derailed his performance in the second half last year. Although his final WXRL total is mediocre, it crested at 2.54 through August 12 before the bum-kneed closer blew a trio of saves and saw his season derailed. Symptoms of his laboring through the year are also reflected in his walk and strikeout rates heading in the wrong direction. One area of improvement for Gregg was a better ground-ball rate, and if he keeps that and comes back healthy with the Cubs now that he's been dealt (for Jose Ceda), he might be an effective setup man for Carlos Marmol as well as veteran insurance for the youngster.

Mark Hendrickson

Bats: L Throws: L Height: 6' 9" Weight: 240 Born: June 23, 1974 Age: 35

YEAR	TEAM	LVL	AGE	W	L	SV	G	GS	IP	H	BB	SO	HR	GB%	BABIP	STUFF	WHIP	ERA	DERA	EqH9	EqBB9	EqSO9	EqHR9	DEF	VORP	SN/WX
2006	LAN	MLB	32	2	7	0	18	12	75	92	28	48	7	50.0%	.336	3	1.60	4.68	4.13	10.3	2.8	5.2	0.7	-7	4.8	0.49
2007	LAN	MLB	33	4	8	0	39	15	122²	142	29	92	15	48.0%	.335	5	1.39	5.21	4.85	9.6	1.8	6.2	1.0	-1	4.8	1.17
2008	FLO	MLB	34	7	8	0	36	19	133²	148	48	81	17	45.6%	.308	-9	1.47	5.45	5.55	9.8	2.8	4.8	1.1	0	-3.1	0.52
2009	BAL	MLB	35	3	5	1	29	8	68¹	80	23	39	9	45.0%	.310	-2	1.50	5.27	5.12	10.3	2.7	4.8	1.1	0	2.7	0.51

Breakout: 12% Improve: 36% Collapse: 32% Attrition: 38%   Comparables: Bill Krueger, Jason Johnson, Bob Walk, Ted Power

Though Hendrickson has never had the repertoire to be an effective starter, the towering southpaw has kept getting opportunities to start and keeps handing them back. Opponents hit just .240/.284/.347 in 2007-2008 when Hendrickson was in relief and .307/.360/.474 when he was the starter. As a lefty, he'll land with any team that wants to play along with the pretense that he can be an effective spot starter. This time, it was the Orioles, who signed him in late December.

Josh Johnson

Bats: L   Throws: R   Height: 6' 7"   Weight: 230   Born: January 31, 1984   Age: 25

YEAR	TEAM	LVL	AGE	W	L	SV	G	GS	IP	H	BB	SO	HR	GB%	BABIP	STUFF	WHIP	ERA	DERA	EqH9	EqBB9	EqSO9	EqHR9	DEF	VORP	SN/WX
2006	FLO	MLB	22	12	7	0	31	24	157	136	68	133	14	48.0%	.284	32	1.30	3.10	3.76	7.5	3.4	7.0	0.7	5	40.8	4.50
2007	FLO	MLB	23	0	3	0	4	4	15²	26	12	14	1	50.0%	.481	10	2.43	7.45	6.89	13.8	5.7	7.5	0.6	-4	-7.1	-0.20
2008	FLO	MLB	24	7	1	0	14	14	87¹	91	27	77	7	49.6%	.340	26	1.35	3.61	3.35	9.8	2.5	7.2	0.8	-3	19.1	2.60
2009	FLO	MLB	25	8	8	1	30	21	135	138	47	120	12	49.0%	.320	20	1.37	4.10	4.45	9.3	2.7	6.5	0.8	0	19.3	2.86

Breakout: 5%   Improve: 20%   Collapse: 44%   Attrition: 20%   Comparables: Jim Beattie, Carl Pavano, Jim Lonborg, Bob Anderson

Johnson missed over three months completing his recovery from the elbow surgery that cost him nearly all of 2007, but on his return, he showed flashes of his ace potential from 2006. His velocity was even up a few ticks from '06, and he had excellent command of all three of his pitches. The Marlins were understandably careful, allowing him to approach or surpass 110 pitches just three times, but even so, he managed to generate 11 quality starts through six innings in his 14 chances. We'll have to see if the big righty can handle a heavier workload; he ranked 25th in the majors in his rate of Lineup-Adjusted Support Neutral Value among all starters with 10 or more starts. Multiply that out to 30 starts or more, and that's a big boost on the Badenhops of the world.

Logan Kensing

Bats: R   Throws: R   Height: 6' 1"   Weight: 185   Born: July 3, 1982   Age: 26

YEAR	TEAM	LVL	AGE	W	L	SV	G	GS	IP	H	BB	SO	HR	GB%	BABIP	STUFF	WHIP	ERA	DERA	EqH9	EqBB9	EqSO9	EqHR9	DEF	VORP	SN/WX
2006	ABQ	AAA	23	1	1	2	13	0	18	11	5	18	2	60.5%	.220	3	0.89	3.00	5.40	5.9	2.7	6.5	1.6	4	0.4	—
2006	FLO	MLB	23	1	3	1	36	0	37²	30	19	45	6	30.9%	.282	14	1.30	4.54	5.02	6.9	4.1	9.8	1.2	3	5.8	-0.11
2007	FLO	MLB	24	3	0	0	9	0	13¹	11	7	13	0	32.4%	.306	14	1.35	1.35	1.98	6.6	4.0	7.9	0.0	1	6.7	0.60
2008	ABQ	AAA	25	1	0	3	13	0	12²	8	12	17	3	30.0%	.192	4	1.57	6.38	8.78	5.4	7.4	7.4	2.0	3	-4.7	—
2008	FLO	MLB	25	3	1	0	48	0	55¹	50	33	55	7	35.2%	.283	3	1.50	4.23	3.61	8.0	4.4	7.5	1.1	-3	8.3	-0.67
2009	FLO	MLB	26	2	2	2	43	0	48²	42	25	46	6	39.0%	.270	7	1.38	3.94	4.22	7.8	4.0	7.0	1.1	0	8.5	0.67

Breakout: 19%   Improve: 33%   Collapse: 41%   Attrition: 28%   Comparables: Jesus Colome, Travis Phelps, Charlie Hough, Bobby Castillo

Kensing did nice things with his low- to mid-90s fastball and slider during his brief stint with the Fish at the end of 2007, enough so that he was handed a job in the 2008 pen. Control issues saw him walk 5.7 per nine before earning a ticket back to Albuquerque, but he returned a month later with relatively better control, walking "just" 4.4 per nine while his strikeouts jumped to nearly 12 per, albeit in just 14 innings. If that is for real, Kensing might have a chance to be something more than a pitcher the Marlins have considered an extra reliever.

Matt Lindstrom

Bats: R   Throws: R   Height: 6' 4"   Weight: 210   Born: February 11, 1980   Age: 29

YEAR	TEAM	LVL	AGE	W	L	SV	G	GS	IP	H	BB	SO	HR	GB%	BABIP	STUFF	WHIP	ERA	DERA	EqH9	EqBB9	EqSO9	EqHR9	DEF	VORP	SN/WX
2006	SLU	A+	26	1	0	2	11	0	18²	14	7	16	2	68.6%	.250	-27	1.15	2.47	5.74	10.3	4.6	4.6	2.3	0	-0.2	—
2006	BIN	AA	26	2	4	11	35	0	40²	42	14	54	2	54.7%	.392	-6	1.39	3.81	5.60	13.8	4.1	7.9	1.0	-2	0.0	—
2007	FLO	MLB	27	3	4	0	71	0	67	66	21	62	2	48.0%	.333	24	1.31	3.09	2.63	7.8	2.4	7.6	0.3	-5	15.3	1.62
2008	FLO	MLB	28	3	3	5	66	0	57¹	57	26	43	1	48.6%	.335	6	1.45	3.14	3.11	9.3	3.6	6.2	0.2	-1	14.8	2.22
2009	FLO	MLB	29	2	2	3	41	0	44¹	46	18	38	4	49.0%	.320	6	1.44	4.08	4.44	9.4	3.2	6.3	0.7	0	5.9	0.55

Breakout: 10%   Improve: 28%   Collapse: 41%   Attrition: 33%   Comparables: Heathcliff Slocumb, Tim Crabtree, Warren Brusstar, Jay Ritchie

In the wake of the Gregg trade, Lindstrom's on the spot as the first in line to get a crack at closing in 2009. It's been a long road for him—in 2005, Lindstrom's arm suffered a stress fracture that messed with his release point and command of his pitches, but it looked as though he had overcome those issues by 2007. While the control issues have not resurfaced entirely, he posted an average walk rate this year, albeit next to a significantly lower strikeout rate.

Andrew Miller

| | | | | | | | | | | | | | | Bats: L | | Throws: L | | Height: 6' 6" | | Weight: 210 | | Born: May 21, 1985 | | Age: 24 |

YEAR	TEAM	LVL	AGE	W	L	SV	G	GS	IP	H	BB	SO	HR	GB%	BABIP	STUFF	WHIP	ERA	DERA	EqH9	EqBB9	EqSO9	EqHR9	DEF	VORP	SN/WX
2006	DET	MLB	21	0	1	0	8	0	10¹	8	10	6	0	69.7%	.242	0	1.74	6.12	7.84	7.0	8.7	4.4	0.0	0	-1.9	-0.04
2007	LAK	A+	22	1	4	0	7	7	41¹	43	15	28	1	65.2%	.313	-10	1.40	3.49	7.28	10.6	4.2	3.1	0.7	2	-7.1	—
2007	ERI	AA	22	2	0	0	4	4	30²	22	5	24	2	75.9%	.250	17	0.88	0.59	2.96	8.6	2.0	4.6	1.0	4	8.0	—
2007	DET	MLB	22	5	5	0	13	13	64	73	39	56	8	50.7%	.333	12	1.75	5.63	5.43	10.3	5.0	6.7	1.1	-3	0.1	0.78
2008	FLO	MLB	23	6	10	0	29	20	107¹	120	56	89	7	48.3%	.354	12	1.64	5.87	5.40	10.2	4.1	6.6	0.6	-10	-11.0	0.49
2009	FLO	MLB	24	6	7	1	35	17	109	106	48	99	9	51.0%	.310	15	1.41	4.20	4.59	8.9	3.4	6.6	0.7	0	13.5	2.07

Breakout: 47%   Improve: 68%   Collapse: 18%   Attrition: 21%   Comparables: Mark Mulder, Mike Pelfrey, Jon Garland, Mike Morgan

It's easy to get frustrated with Miller when you rate his lows against his highs, but try to remember that he's still just a kid learning on the job. He's trying to learn a third pitch to complement his fastball/slider combo, and there are going to be struggles as long as he's working on that. April was a terrible month, but in May and June, he shined, with 7.2 K/9, 3.6 BB/9, just 0.3 HR/9 and a 3.36 ERA over 61⅔ innings. Tendonitis in a knee interrupted this breakthrough, and Miller would subsequently appear in just nine more games as a reliever. With just two pitches at his disposal, he may be a better option from the pen in the short term, but he has too much potential as a starter for the Fish to give up on his rotation possibilities.

Justin Miller

| | | | | | | | | | | | | | | Bats: R | | Throws: R | | Height: 6' 2" | | Weight: 200 | | Born: August 27, 1977 | | Age: 31 |

YEAR	TEAM	LVL	AGE	W	L	SV	G	GS	IP	H	BB	SO	HR	GB%	BABIP	STUFF	WHIP	ERA	DERA	EqH9	EqBB9	EqSO9	EqHR9	DEF	VORP	SN/WX
2006	CHB	JP	28	0	1	0	12	0	11²	18	10	11	3	—	.385	-28	2.39	10.77	15.19	16.0	10.1	5.9	3.4	0	-11.4	—
2007	ABQ	AAA	29	0	0	6	11	0	12	9	4	20	0	50.0%	.346	12	1.08	1.50	1.54	8.5	3.1	10.8	0.0	-2	5.3	—
2007	FLO	MLB	29	5	0	0	62	0	61²	53	24	74	5	44.1%	.314	27	1.25	3.65	2.56	6.8	3.0	9.5	0.7	-8	12.9	1.18
2008	FLO	MLB	30	4	2	0	46	0	46²	46	20	43	4	31.6%	.321	4	1.41	4.24	4.76	9.1	3.4	7.5	0.8	0	3.1	0.27
2009	SFN	MLB	31	2	2	2	37	0	41¹	40	18	38	5	40.3%	.300	8	1.41	4.36	4.60	8.7	3.5	7.2	1.0	0	5.1	0.40

Breakout: 31%   Improve: 52%   Collapse: 30%   Attrition: 31%   Comparables: Doug Henry, Elmer Singleton, Wes Stock, Ricky Bottalico

After a dominant performance in situational relief in 2007, baseball's illustrated man kept the same approach he had in 2007, throwing sliders and fastballs. He didn't get nearly as many swings and misses in or out of the zone this time around, which cut into his strikeout rate, and elbow inflammation at midseason didn't help things, either. The Marlins designated him for assignment in August. He's signed a minor league deal with the Giants and rates as a potential steal, given the risk-versus-reward ratio.

Joe Nelson

| | | | | | | | | | | | | | | Bats: R | | Throws: R | | Height: 6' 1" | | Weight: 210 | | Born: October 25, 1974 | | Age: 34 |

YEAR	TEAM	LVL	AGE	W	L	SV	G	GS	IP	H	BB	SO	HR	GB%	BABIP	STUFF	WHIP	ERA	DERA	EqH9	EqBB9	EqSO9	EqHR9	DEF	VORP	SN/WX
2006	OMA	AAA	31	2	2	7	24	0	32	19	12	39	4	43.7%	.242	4	0.97	1.97	3.90	6.3	3.6	8.1	1.5	2	5.7	—
2006	KCA	MLB	31	1	1	9	43	0	44²	37	24	44	5	36.3%	.278	6	1.37	4.43	4.80	6.8	4.6	7.8	1.0	3	8.6	1.84
2008	ABQ	AAA	33	1	1	11	19	0	25²	17	6	36	1	41.8%	.296	24	0.89	2.10	3.33	6.7	2.2	9.2	0.4	3	6.1	—
2008	FLO	MLB	33	3	1	1	59	0	54	42	22	60	5	41.4%	.268	17	1.19	2.00	3.23	6.8	3.1	8.4	0.8	3	17.7	0.88
2009	TBA	MLB	34	3	2	3	46	0	47²	42	20	45	6	42.0%	.280	12	1.30	3.67	3.65	7.9	3.3	7.7	1.0	-0	9.4	0.86

Breakout: 13%   Improve: 25%   Collapse: 49%   Attrition: 14%   Comparables: Josias Manzanillo, Brendan Donnelly, Steve Reed, Jay Howell

After missing 2007 with a torn labrum and never rating as a great relief option in the past, Nelson managed to come back and punch out over three times as many hitters as he handed out unintentional walks to. He doesn't have great stuff, with a fastball that only occasionally clears 90, and he was hit-lucky on the statistical side of things—his BABIP is roughly 60 points too low, given his line-drive rate. Expect some ugly regression; the Marlins may well have, nontendering the journeyman this winter. He signed a one-year, $1.3 million contract with the Rays in December, and we'll see if maintaining his sunshine state of mind helps him maintain his luck on balls in play.

Ricky Nolasco

| | Bats: R | Throws: R | Height: 6' 2" | Weight: 220 | Born: December 13, 1982 | Age: 26 |

YEAR	TEAM	LVL	AGE	W	L	SV	G	GS	IP	H	BB	SO	HR	GB%	BABIP	STUFF	WHIP	ERA	DERA	EqH9	EqBB9	EqSO9	EqHR9	DEF	VORP	SN/WX
2006	FLO	MLB	23	11	11	0	35	22	140	157	41	99	20	41.0%	.319	3	1.41	4.82	4.56	9.6	2.3	5.8	1.2	-8	7.3	2.78
2007	FLO	MLB	24	1	2	0	5	4	21¹	26	9	11	3	39.7%	.343	-12	1.64	5.49	6.35	9.1	3.2	4.0	1.2	0	-2.5	0.04
2008	FLO	MLB	25	15	8	0	34	32	212¹	192	42	186	28	40.3%	.277	19	1.10	3.52	3.81	8.0	1.5	6.9	1.1	4	45.6	5.78
2009	FLO	MLB	26	11	9	0	27	27	176	178	41	146	21	42.0%	.300	23	1.24	3.93	4.22	9.2	1.8	6.1	1.1	0	28.7	4.38

Breakout: 19%   Improve: 43%   Collapse: 19%   Attrition: 15%   Comparables: Tom Poholsky, Eric Rasmussen, Reggie Cleveland, Scott Baker

It was difficult to pinpoint the primary source of Nolasco's pain in 2007—he was on the DL with elbow inflammation, and there was talk of bone spurs and shoulder issues as well—but it somehow healed itself without surgery before his AFL stint that winter. The positive steps taken there carried over to 2008, especially in the second half: from June 15 onward, Nolasco whiffed over a batter per inning while holding his walks to one per nine, a 140⅓ IP stretch of dominance that no pitcher in 2008 can claim. Given his rock-solid peripherals, Nolasco is primed to be a legitimate ace from here on out—with the obvious caveat of "if his elbow problems don't recur."

Scott Olsen

| | Bats: L | Throws: L | Height: 6' 5" | Weight: 215 | Born: January 12, 1984 | Age: 25 |

YEAR	TEAM	LVL	AGE	W	L	SV	G	GS	IP	H	BB	SO	HR	GB%	BABIP	STUFF	WHIP	ERA	DERA	EqH9	EqBB9	EqSO9	EqHR9	DEF	VORP	SN/WX
2006	FLO	MLB	22	12	10	0	31	31	180²	160	75	166	23	46.6%	.285	25	1.30	4.03	4.53	7.7	3.3	7.6	1.1	2	25.1	4.70
2007	FLO	MLB	23	10	15	0	33	33	176²	226	85	133	29	40.2%	.354	-2	1.76	5.81	5.67	10.0	3.6	6.2	1.3	-11	-20.8	-0.18
2008	FLO	MLB	24	8	11	0	33	33	201²	195	69	113	30	39.0%	.262	-6	1.31	4.19	5.10	8.5	2.6	4.5	1.3	12	20.7	4.04
2009	WAS	MLB	25	8	9	0	24	24	144²	150	49	93	19	42.0%	.290	13	1.37	4.42	4.79	9.4	2.7	5.0	1.2	0	14.8	2.67

Breakout: 18%   Improve: 44%   Collapse: 18%   Attrition: 16%   Comparables: Bill Travers, Randy Lerch, Joe Kennedy, Frank Viola

All season, analysts waited for the other shoe to drop on Olsen, but it never landed on its intended target. Somehow, despite losing even more strikeouts and three mph on his fastball, Olsen sliced a run and a half off his ERA. Yes, he also lopped over 1.5 UIBB/9 off his rates, but his homer rates were still bad, especially on the road, where opponents slugged .507. Olsen also had the benefit of great defensive support from an unreliable defensive unit; looking at his adjusted ERAs tells you how well he really pitched. That won't be the Marlins' problem in 2009, as he was sent to Washington in yet another arb-eligible salary dump; he's a classic example of the kind of starter Jim Bowden overrates and then is disappointed by.

Renyel Pinto

| | Bats: L | Throws: L | Height: 6' 4" | Weight: 215 | Born: July 8, 1982 | Age: 26 |

YEAR	TEAM	LVL	AGE	W	L	SV	G	GS	IP	H	BB	SO	HR	GB%	BABIP	STUFF	WHIP	ERA	DERA	EqH9	EqBB9	EqSO9	EqHR9	DEF	VORP	SN/WX
2006	ABQ	AAA	23	8	2	0	18	18	95¹	82	47	96	8	48.2%	.297	8	1.36	3.41	4.87	8.3	4.6	6.2	1.1	8	7.5	—
2006	FLO	MLB	23	0	0	1	27	0	29²	20	27	36	3	45.7%	.258	27	1.58	3.03	3.86	5.9	7.1	9.8	0.9	1	7.5	0.27
2007	FLO	MLB	24	2	4	1	57	0	58²	45	32	56	7	37.7%	.271	7	1.31	3.68	4.40	6.3	4.4	8.2	0.9	5	12.9	1.04
2008	FLO	MLB	25	2	5	0	67	0	64²	52	39	56	9	49.2%	.261	-5	1.41	4.45	4.98	7.2	4.6	6.8	1.2	4	7.3	1.72
2009	FLO	MLB	26	2	2	2	49	0	49	44	28	43	5	46.0%	.280	3	1.46	4.18	4.54	8.1	4.5	6.4	0.9	0	6.6	0.52

Breakout: 15%   Improve: 35%   Collapse: 45%   Attrition: 33%   Comparables: Drew Hall, Al Osuna, Jason Christiansen, Angel Miranda

Pinto is mostly a fastball/changeup guy with typical lefty velocity, but one who has trouble hitting his spots consistently. That's where the sky-high walk rates come from. Even though he's managed three straight seasons with a below-average BABIP, the walk rates cancel out the extra benefit. In a bullpen full of surprises and promising youngsters, Pinto is a placeholder.

Arthur Rhodes

| | Bats: L | Throws: L | Height: 6' 2" | Weight: 210 | Born: October 24, 1969 | Age: 39 |

YEAR	TEAM	LVL	AGE	W	L	SV	G	GS	IP	H	BB	SO	HR	GB%	BABIP	STUFF	WHIP	ERA	DERA	EqH9	EqBB9	EqSO9	EqHR9	DEF	VORP	SN/WX
2006	PHI	MLB	36	0	5	4	55	0	45²	47	29	48	2	39.1%	.346	15	1.66	5.32	4.02	8.8	4.8	8.4	0.4	-4	3.7	0.98
2008	SEA	MLB	38	2	1	1	36	0	22	17	13	26	0	32.1%	.347	20	1.36	2.86	4.29	7.3	5.1	9.9	0.0	3	5.9	1.17
2008	FLO	MLB	38	2	0	1	25	0	13¹	11	3	14	0	27.0%	.306	13	1.05	0.68	0.68	7.4	2.0	8.1	0.0	-1	7.4	1.03
2009	CIN	MLB	39	1	1	2	31	0	27²	26	14	29	3	38.0%	.310	12	1.45	4.20	4.18	8.4	4.0	8.1	0.8	-0	4.2	0.38

Breakout: 19%   Improve: 53%   Collapse: 23%   Attrition: 17%   Comparables: Mike Remlinger, Al Worthington, Jesse Orosco, John Franco

Following a disappointing 2006 campaign, Rhodes tore a ligament in his elbow and missed the entire 2007 season, but he returned to the Mariners in mid-April. Before and after being flipped to the Fish at the deadline (for Gaby Hernandez), he did the situational mastery thing that'll keep him in lettuce for years, holding lefties to .157/.253/.200 and allowing no home runs to batters of either persuasion, as he slips into the Fossas career path. The Reds signed him to a two-year deal, making them his sixth organization since 2004.

Anibal Sanchez

Bats: R   Throws: R   Height: 6' 0"   Weight: 180   Born: February 27, 1984   Age: 25

YEAR	TEAM	LVL	AGE	W	L	SV	G	GS	IP	H	BB	SO	HR	GB%	BABIP	STUFF	WHIP	ERA	DERA	EqH9	EqBB9	EqSO9	EqHR9	DEF	VORP	SN/WX
2006	CAR	AA	22	3	6	0	15	15	85	82	27	92	7	48.2%	.319	6	1.28	3.18	5.71	10.6	3.1	6.0	1.5	-4	-1.0	—
2006	FLO	MLB	22	10	3	0	18	17	114¹	90	46	72	9	43.5%	.243	26	1.19	2.83	3.71	6.6	3.2	5.2	0.6	9	36.6	4.78
2007	FLO	MLB	23	2	1	0	6	6	30	43	19	14	3	46.6%	.367	-6	2.07	4.80	2.87	11.2	4.9	3.7	0.9	-7	2.3	0.37
2008	FLO	MLB	24	2	5	0	10	10	51²	54	27	50	7	42.1%	.324	8	1.57	5.57	5.64	9.4	3.9	7.5	1.2	-1	-2.3	0.24
2009	CIN	MLB	39	1	1	2	31	0	27²	26	14	29	3	38.0%	.310	12	1.45	4.20	4.18	8.4	4.0	8.1	0.8	-0	4.2	0.38

Breakout: 19%   Improve: 53%   Collapse: 23%   Attrition: 17%   Comparables: Mike Remlinger, Al Worthington, Jesse Orosco, John Franco

Well-known as the kid who spun a no-hitter in 2006, Sanchez had a 2007 season that was a lost campaign, one in which he eventually went under the knife to repair his shoulder. Though 2008 was not a triumphant return the way fellow Fish Josh Johnson's was, there are positives: Sanchez's strikeout rate was higher than in '06, and at least his walk rate wasn't as ugly as it was in '07. He should do better over the course of a full season.

Brett Sinkbeil

Bats: R   Throws: R   Height: 6' 2"   Weight: 170   Born: December 26, 1984   Age: 24

YEAR	TEAM	LVL	AGE	W	L	SV	G	GS	IP	H	BB	SO	HR	GB%	BABIP	STUFF	WHIP	ERA	DERA	EqH9	EqBB9	EqSO9	EqHR9	DEF	VORP	SN/WX
2006	GRB	A	21	1	1	0	8	8	39¹	45	14	32	5	54.4%	.339	-31	1.51	5.06	8.72	16.0	5.3	3.4	3.4	0	-11.1	—
2006	JAM	A-	21	2	0	0	5	5	22²	14	8	22	1	52.8%	.260	-2	0.99	1.22	5.19	10.4	6.2	4.7	2.6	2	0.8	—
2007	JUP	A+	22	6	4	0	14	14	79	82	14	49	8	53.8%	.297	-30	1.22	3.42	8.04	11.6	2.4	2.9	2.3	4	-19.4	—
2008	CAR	AA	23	5	9	0	26	26	143¹	172	51	66	12	53.6%	.322	-36	1.56	5.02	7.27	13.0	3.6	2.1	1.5	6	-24.1	—
2009	FLO	MLB	24	4	8	0	19	19	94²	126	42	41	13	50.0%	.330	-6	1.78	6.58	7.09	12.1	3.5	3.2	1.3	0	-13.5	-0.74

Breakout: 9%   Improve: 42%   Collapse: 25%   Attrition: 17%   Comparables: Mark Petkovsek, Jon Perlman, Mike Christ, Jon Ratliff

A right-hander who relies on his low-90s sinker to induce grounders, Sinkbeil struggled during his first taste of Double-A; lefties were a particular problem, as they hit .329 and slugged .506. The good news for the oft-injured Sinkbeil is that he was mostly healthy for a change, with the exception of a blister that developed in August. To regain his prospect status, he needs to add something to stop lefties, because without it, he's just a groundballer with a nice move to first, a skill set that would limit him to the pen.

Taylor Tankersley

Bats: L   Throws: L   Height: 6' 1"   Weight: 220   Born: March 7, 1983   Age: 26

YEAR	TEAM	LVL	AGE	W	L	SV	G	GS	IP	H	BB	SO	HR	GB%	BABIP	STUFF	WHIP	ERA	DERA	EqH9	EqBB9	EqSO9	EqHR9	DEF	VORP	SN/WX
2006	CAR	AA	23	4	1	6	22	0	28²	11	14	40	0	49.1%	.229	20	0.89	0.96	3.62	4.6	4.6	7.9	0.3	4	6.0	—
2006	FLO	MLB	23	2	1	3	49	0	41	33	26	46	4	46.7%	.305	20	1.44	2.85	2.66	7.1	5.1	9.3	0.9	-2	13.1	2.05
2007	FLO	MLB	24	6	1	1	67	0	47¹	42	29	49	4	39.5%	.322	15	1.50	4.00	3.69	7.4	4.9	8.9	0.8	-1	8.6	1.35
2008	ABQ	AAA	25	2	1	0	29	0	31²	32	17	28	2	35.8%	.341	-9	1.55	1.70	3.52	9.4	5.0	5.3	0.6	4	7.1	—
2008	FLO	MLB	25	0	1	0	25	0	17²	22	8	13	6	29.0%	.291	-26	1.70	8.14	6.87	10.8	3.4	5.4	2.9	-2	-5.0	-0.35
2009	FLO	MLB	26	1	1	1	29	0	24¹	23	12	21	3	38.0%	.290	3	1.46	4.44	4.74	8.8	4.0	6.4	1.1	0	3.3	0.22

Breakout: 13%   Improve: 32%   Collapse: 51%   Attrition: 51%   Comparables: Mike Kekich, Dave LaRoche, Francisco Cordero, Bob Kipper

Tankersley's walk rates have always been problematic, but when he added mistakes up in the zone and a declining strikeout rate, you had a one-man big-inning generator. He spent much of the year in Triple-A working on his approach with his fastball/slider mix. That he's going to be 26 and still needs more time in the minors to work out the kinks doesn't bode well.

Ryan Tucker

| | | | | | | | Bats: R | | Throws: R | | Height: 6' 2" | | Weight: 190 | | Born: December 6, 1986 | | | Age: 22 |

YEAR	TEAM	LVL	AGE	W	L	SV	G	GS	IP	H	BB	SO	HR	GB%	BABIP	STUFF	WHIP	ERA	DERA	EqH9	EqBB9	EqSO9	EqHR9	DEF	VORP	SN/WX
2006	GRB	A	19	7	13	0	25	25	131¹	123	67	133	14	50.1%	.308	-38	1.45	5.01	9.27	13.0	6.8	4.4	2.8	-9	-45.1	—
2007	JUP	A+	20	5	8	0	24	24	138¹	142	46	104	6	48.4%	.319	19	1.36	3.71	6.21	11.3	4.1	3.6	1.1	-9	-8.5	—
2008	CAR	AA	21	5	3	0	25	12	91	64	37	74	2	46.6%	.247	22	1.11	1.58	4.30	7.3	3.8	4.4	0.5	16	12.7	—
2008	FLO	MLB	21	2	3	0	13	6	37	46	23	28	8	43.2%	.330	-4	1.86	8.27	7.30	11.2	4.9	6.1	1.9	-2	-11.0	-0.39
2009	FLO	MLB	22	6	9	0	41	22	131	141	68	97	17	44.0%	.310	4	1.58	5.37	5.77	9.7	4.0	5.4	1.1	0	-0.7	0.71

Breakout: 16%   Improve: 53%   Collapse: 15%   Attrition: 20%   Comparables: Kurt Ainsworth, Al Lachowicz, Jason Marquis, Chris Seelbach

Tucker's value was boosted by improved command in 2007, but his 2008 did not go nearly as well after he left the minors. The control problems resurfaced, and as he lacks a consistent second pitch—his changeup either is a plus or fails to do what it's meant to—continuing as a starter was a problem. If his changeup becomes a consistent offering, he's capable of starting, even more so if his slider stops being flat. Otherwise, he's on track to be a dominating, fireballing reliever—not a bad downside for the Marlins.

Rick Vanden Hurk

| | | | | | | | Bats: R | | Throws: R | | Height: 6' 5" | | Weight: 195 | | Born: May 22, 1985 | | | Age: 24 |

YEAR	TEAM	LVL	AGE	W	L	SV	G	GS	IP	H	BB	SO	HR	GB%	BABIP	STUFF	WHIP	ERA	DERA	EqH9	EqBB9	EqSO9	EqHR9	DEF	VORP	SN/WX
2006	MRL	Rk	21	0	0	0	5	5	15²	4	8	26	0	50.0%	.190	13	0.79	1.18	3.55	5.0	7.1	8.5	0.7	0	2.9	—
2006	JUP	A+	21	0	0	0	3	3	10¹	5	6	15	1	42.1%	.222	9	1.09	2.67	6.23	7.3	7.3	8.3	2.1	0	-0.6	—
2007	CAR	AA	22	2	2	0	9	9	53²	42	21	61	5	37.0%	.294	14	1.17	3.52	4.96	9.4	3.9	6.6	1.5	-1	3.5	—
2007	FLO	MLB	22	4	6	0	18	17	81²	94	48	82	15	31.3%	.354	9	1.74	6.83	5.64	9.3	4.6	8.2	1.5	-6	-10.5	0.17
2008	CAR	AA	23	3	3	0	10	10	55¹	49	19	55	8	40.6%	.291	-13	1.23	4.23	7.06	10.2	3.4	5.8	2.3	3	-8.3	—
2008	ABQ	AAA	23	2	1	0	4	4	17²	13	11	21	3	38.6%	.244	8	1.36	4.07	6.50	6.5	5.5	7.0	1.5	2	-1.8	—
2008	FLO	MLB	23	1	1	0	4	4	14	20	10	20	1	38.1%	.487	14	2.14	7.71	5.65	13.2	5.7	10.7	0.6	-2	-3.1	0.17
2009	FLO	MLB	24	5	6	1	32	12	91¹	93	47	85	14	40.0%	.300	9	1.53	5.30	5.63	9.2	4.1	6.9	1.3	0	0.9	0.55

Breakout: 29%   Improve: 58%   Collapse: 20%   Attrition: 20%   Comparables: Melido Perez, Fernando Cabrera, Duff Brumley, Sam Militello

The import from the Netherlands was not given much of a chance in the majors to prove he was better than his 2007 season. His admittedly raw approach consists mostly of throwing lots of low-90s fastballs and then occasionally mixing in something off-speed, but since his command is lacking, it doesn't really work. Things were fine at Double-A, but trips to both Triple-A and the majors saw more advanced hitters taking walks and waiting for mistakes. Given his later developmental curve, the Marlins could still have something here, but he's got to improve his command.

Chris Volstad

| | | | | | | | Bats: R | | Throws: R | | Height: 6' 7" | | Weight: 190 | | Born: September 23, 1986 | | | Age: 22 |

YEAR	TEAM	LVL	AGE	W	L	SV	G	GS	IP	H	BB	SO	HR	GB%	BABIP	STUFF	WHIP	ERA	DERA	EqH9	EqBB9	EqSO9	EqHR9	DEF	VORP	SN/WX
2006	GRB	A	19	11	8	0	26	26	152	161	36	99	12	61.4%	.314	-27	1.30	3.08	7.69	13.6	3.6	2.2	2.2	3	-29.9	—
2007	JUP	A+	20	8	9	0	21	20	126	152	37	93	8	56.8%	.345	5	1.50	4.50	7.65	13.3	3.7	3.5	1.5	-14	-26.3	—
2007	CAR	AA	20	4	2	0	7	7	42²	41	10	25	4	54.2%	.276	11	1.19	3.16	6.53	10.4	2.5	2.9	1.6	5	-4.1	—
2008	CAR	AA	21	4	4	0	15	15	91	86	30	56	0	59.9%	.301	17	1.27	3.36	5.78	9.9	3.2	3.2	0.3	9	-1.7	—
2008	FLO	MLB	21	6	4	0	15	14	84¹	76	36	52	3	55.8%	.279	37	1.33	2.88	3.71	7.9	3.3	4.9	0.3	5	23.4	3.21
2009	FLO	MLB	22	9	11	0	32	32	173¹	196	71	104	16	54.0%	.310	8	1.54	5.00	5.47	10.2	3.2	4.4	0.9	0	4.5	1.85

Breakout: 6%   Improve: 21%   Collapse: 39%   Attrition: 25%   Comparables: Jamey Wright, Brett Myers, Mike LaCoss, Jon Garland

Volstad is a finesse pitcher in a power pitcher's body: despite towering over opponents, he averages around 90 on his fastball, which he complements with a slow curve. As a result, he doesn't miss many bats, but this did not stop him from a successful debut—among all rotation men with 10 or more starts, he finished ninth in the majors in per-start rate of Support-Neutral Lineup-Adjusted Value. His success depends on his keeping his walks in check while inducing plenty of grounders, and although he did well on those fronts in his first go-round, he can't afford to see those slip.

Doug Waechter

| | | | | | | | | Bats: R | | Throws: R | | Height: 6' 4" | | Weight: 210 | | Born: January 28, 1981 | | | Age: 28 |

YEAR	TEAM	LVL	AGE	W	L	SV	G	GS	IP	H	BB	SO	HR	GB%	BABIP	STUFF	WHIP	ERA	DERA	EqH9	EqBB9	EqSO9	EqHR9	DEF	VORP	SN/WX
2006	DUR	AAA	25	1	12	0	17	15	79	129	24	45	7	41.5%	.407	-41	1.94	8.32	10.30	15.6	3.2	3.0	1.3	-16	-39.7	—
2007	VRO	A+	26	4	4	0	9	9	43²	53	5	34	6	47.1%	.356	-30	1.33	4.74	6.51	14.5	1.9	4.1	2.9	-2	-3.8	—
2007	HUD	A-	26	2	1	0	4	4	19	16	0	12	1	51.6%	.246	-15	0.84	1.42	3.63	10.4	1.0	2.1	1.6	-2	3.8	—
2008	FLO	MLB	27	4	2	0	48	0	63¹	63	21	46	7	34.0%	.287	-4	1.33	3.70	4.48	8.7	2.5	5.6	1.0	3	10.3	0.88
2009	KCA	MLB	28	1	2	1	27	0	35	42	11	19	5	40.0%	.310	-4	1.51	5.09	4.88	10.5	2.5	4.6	1.2	-0	2.5	0.14

Breakout: 34%   Improve: 60%   Collapse: 23%   Attrition: 45%   Comparables: Tom Buskey, Brian Stokes, Scott Winchester, Jon Adkins

The Marlins are not averse to turning starters into relievers, and Waechter was another of those experiments. He earned his check out of the pen, bumping up his strikeout rate by more than two per nine while maintaining the homer rate he established in 2006 with the Devil Rays. He benefited significantly from his defense, though, and his offerings—a low-90s heater and slider—are not the most impressive around. Most reliever performance is volatile, and Waechter's 2008 is a prime example of this. But that's now the Royals' problem, as they signed him to a one-year contract for 2009.

Sean West

| | | | | | | | | Bats: L | | Throws: L | | Height: 6' 8" | | Weight: 200 | | Born: June 15, 1986 | | | Age: 23 |

YEAR	TEAM	LVL	AGE	W	L	SV	G	GS	IP	H	BB	SO	HR	GB%	BABIP	STUFF	WHIP	ERA	DERA	EqH9	EqBB9	EqSO9	EqHR9	DEF	VORP	SN/WX
2006	GRB	A	20	8	5	0	21	21	120²	115	40	102	13	52.7%	.304	-27	1.29	3.74	7.18	13.2	4.8	3.5	2.9	0	-17.6	—
2008	JUP	A+	22	6	5	0	21	20	100²	79	60	92	3	51.1%	.296	6	1.38	2.41	5.65	10.2	6.9	4.9	0.9	3	-0.5	—
2009	FLO	MLB	23	4	7	0	17	17	85	96	67	72	10	49.0%	.330	6	1.90	6.24	6.72	10.2	6.1	6.2	1.0	0	-8.8	-0.31

Breakout: 4%   Improve: 17%   Collapse: 47%   Attrition: 13%   Comparables: Alan Newman, Brian Givens, Rich Scheid, Jeffrey Reece

West missed all of 2007 recovering from surgery on his labrum, but for the most part picked up where he left off in 2006. His velocity, which tops out in the mid-90s, was back by year's end, and his height helps to give his fastball some sinker-like qualities, but he needs a more consistent release point to cut down on the walks. His stuff was death on lefties, who managed all of 16 total bases off him in 105 at-bats. This year, he will get a shot at Double-A, where those extraneous free passes will break him if not taken care of.

LINEOUTS

Hitters

PLAYER	TEAM	LVL	AGE	PA	R	2B	3B	HR	RBI	BB	SO	SB-CS	EqBRR	AVG/OBP/SLG	EqAVG/EqOBP/EqSLG	EqA	VORP	WARP
1B T. Bozied	ABQ	AAA	28	484	86	28	3	26	80	50	76	7-2	1.6	.306/.382/.569	.204/.275/.384	.228	-15.7	-2.1
CF G. Burns*	JUP	A+	21	444	55	12	5	3	28	61	143	34-12	0.7	.244/.351/.326	.219/.311/.306	.227	-18.8	-1.1
OF S. Cousins*	JUP	A+	23	211	35	9	2	9	29	20	47	11-3	0.2	.304/.370/.513	.251/.308/.441	.257	3.3	0.1
	CAR	AA	23	103	15	7	1	1	9	10	28	4-1	-1.1	.264/.350/.396	.223/.291/.340	.222	-4.0	-0.5
OF I. Galloway	MRL	Rk	18	211	29	13	5	1	23	4	33	4-2	1.1	.286/.303/.417	.221/.233/.324	.186	-43.8	-3.2
OF J. Jones*	DET	MLB	33	90	10	2	1	1	5	8	18	0-1	-2.3	.165/.244/.253	.165/.253/.253	.177	-8.5	-1.2
	FLO	MLB	33	44	5	0	0	0	2	6	8	0-0	-0.2	.108/.227/.108	.081/.205/.081	.000	-5.8	-0.6
C P. Lo Duca	WAS	MLB	36	153	13	7	0	0	12	9	9	1-0	0.6	.230/.301/.281	.230/.301/.273	.206	-5.5	-0.9
	FLO	MLB	36	40	3	2	0	0	3	6	2	0-0	-1.2	.294/.400/.353	.294/.400/.353	.276	1.7	0.0

While you might expect there to be a Star Wars action figure named **Taggert Bozied**, there isn't, just a big minor league veteran, a professional hitter type who's already made the hyperspace jump to Oakland's farm system. ⊘ A young speed guy, **Greg Burns** is unlike most jackrabbits in that he doesn't get the ball in play all that often; whether that's equal parts Chuck Carr or General Wormwort is your call, but he'll need to make better contact to progress. ⊘ **Scott Cousins** could have been either a pitcher or an outfielder, and the Marlins decided to make him the latter. He was impressive in his stint in the Arizona Fall League (.297/.385/.624), but his work at Double-A reflects the need to refine his approach to be more than a fringe prospect. ⊘ Thanks to a poor senior season, **Ike Galloway** fell to the eighth round of this year's draft despite first-round tools. Though considered difficult to sign, he was nabbed by the Marlins; like most other youngsters, he will need to work on improving his strike zone recognition. ⊘ After coming over in a swap with the Cubs, **Jacque Jones** lost the Tigers' eye after a month, and it took the Marlins even less time than that to tire of him. ⊘ Even though he treats every at-bat as if he's double-parked, **Paul Lo Duca** had to deal with a couple of hand injuries, so it's no wonder he posted the lowest power numbers of his career. A healthy hand might mean a slightly more productive Lo Duca, but he's no better than a backup these days.

Pitchers

PLAYER	TEAM	LVL	AGE	W	L	SV	IP	H	BB	SO	HR	GB%	BABIP	STUFF	WHIP	ERA	DERA	EqH9	EqBB9	EqSO9	EqHR9	DEF	VORP
J. Delgado	CAR	AA	24	5	2	1	57¹	46	31	52	2	53.3%	.294	-9	1.34	3.46	6.19	9.1	5.2	5.3	0.7	4	-3.4
	ABQ	AAA	24	0	0	0	10²	17	4	6	2	58.5%	.385	-47	1.96	11.78	10.80	15.3	3.6	2.7	1.8	-1	-5.8
L. Gardner	FLO	MLB	33	0	0	0	6²	14	4	4	2	38.7%	.444	-37	2.70	10.75	6.43	18.0	3.9	5.1	2.6	-3	-3.9
C. Leroux	JUP	A+	24	6	7	1	74	60	26	78	6	45.1%	.295	-33	1.16	3.65	7.79	10.7	4.2	5.8	1.9	2	-15.7
C. Martinez	CAR	AA	26	2	2	3	38¹	38	16	33	5	41.2%	.324	-36	1.41	4.70	8.05	11.4	4.2	4.9	2.1	5	-9.4
	ABQ	AAA	26	2	2	0	14²	10	4	19	3	54.3%	.226	8	0.95	3.06	4.30	6.1	2.5	8.0	1.8	2	2.1
D. Trahern	ABQ	AAA	22	5	11	0	111	141	45	71	20	55.7%	.340	-25	1.68	6.16	6.56	11.4	3.8	3.6	1.8	-5	-11.4
T. Wood	JUP	A+	25	5	2	1	40	25	15	22	1	59.8%	.211	-29	1.00	1.80	5.94	7.2	4.2	2.5	0.7	7	-1.4
	CAR	AA	25	2	1	0	20¹	20	6	15	2	63.0%	.241	-30	1.28	5.76	9.31	10.7	2.8	3.7	1.4	4	-8.0

Part of the deal that put Hanley Ramirez in teal, **Jesus Delgado** is a live-armed Venezuelan who had to be converted to relief full-time, thanks to his limited off-speed selections, and his repeat of the Southern League was less than overpowering. ⊘ The live-armed **Harvey Garcia** didn't have much opportunity to show it in 2008, losing the year to a bum shoulder. ⊘ A 10-year minor league vet before finishing second in WXRL in the 2007 team's bullpen, **Lee Gardner** was knocked out for the season with shoulder surgery in mid-April. He already didn't have overpowering stuff. ⊘ Tall Canadian import **Chris Leroux** has been managed with great care, but basically has to rely on consistent low-90s heat to make up for a lack of consistent breaking stuff, and he struggles with left-handed hitters. ⊘ Tripped up by visa issues last spring after already missing most of 2007 because of elbow surgery, **Carlos Martinez** is nevertheless still hanging around on the 40-man after striking out enough people enough of the time in the minors. ⊘ The comeback of former Mets prospect **Henry Owens** from 2007 shoulder surgery will be delayed an extra 50 games after his suspension for performance-enhancing drug use. ⊘ Another bit received from the Tigers for Dontrelle Willis, **Dallas Trahern** was a radioactive isotope, getting lit up with an alarming regularity that might push the sinkerballer to the pen. ⊘ Although a bit old to be a prospect, **Tim Wood** pitched his way onto the 40-man by generating a ton of ground-ball outs and then shining in the Arizona Fall League.

MANAGER: FREDI GONZALEZ

YEAR	TEAM	W-L	Pythag +/−	Avg PC	100+ P	120+ P	QS	BQS	REL	REL w Zero R	IBB	Subs	PH	PH Avg	PH HR	SB2	CS2	SB3	CS3	SAC Att	SAC %	POS SAC	Squeeze	Swing	In Play
2007	FLO	71-91	0	91.0	50	3	48	11	560	375	60	54	284	.213	7	83	25	22	7	92	78.3%	24	4	135	90
2008	FLO	84-77	3	93.5	46	2	70	7	511	337	66	80	248	.211	7	69	25	7	2	80	61.3%	15	4	122	89

The *Sporting News* Manager of the Year, Gonzalez was at the helm of a team that outperformed its adjusted standings by three wins, though whether that was the result of his management skills is up for debate. He used some of his worst relievers (Taylor Tankersley, Logan Kensing) in situations they should never have approached, while some of the team's better relief options pitched in standard situations. He did, however, lead his relief prospects by the hand, giving them game scenarios with lesser importance to build their experience and confidence. Ditching Amezaga as the center fielder and giving someone with potential the job in Ross was an overdue move, as was giving Baker the keys to the catcher position once he came up and succeeded. Gonzalez rarely gave runners the green light, instead focusing on high-percentage basestealing with all his regulars (with the exception of Hanley Ramirez). He handled the rotation well, making adjustments when starters returned from injury and moving failed pitchers to the pen to get some use out of them (Hendrickson in particular). Gonzalez was also careful not to follow in the footsteps of the man he replaced two years ago, making sure not to abuse his young starters. Overall, he balanced the team's long-shot run at the division title with the organization's need to sort through its young talent, and considering where the Marlins finished, he did so admirably.

Houston Astros

It was a good year for Houston general manager Ed Wade. Not only did the Phillies, a team that he bossed from December 1997 through 2005, win the World Series with many players who had been acquired on Wade's watch (a fact acknowledged by the Phillies themselves during their celebrations), but the Astros, who were not a popular pick to contend, made a surprising run at the wild card. After a slow start, the Astros rose from well back of the pack at midseason to climb within two games of the leading Brewers. But in the wake of Hurricane Ike, the 'Stros were dealt Major League Baseball's decision to relocate two crucial home games with the Cubs to Milwaukee's Miller Park, practically home territory because of the proximity of Chicagoland.

The Astros lost both of the relocated games and, in the immediate aftermath of the hurricane, lost five straight contests by a combined score of 38-5. Though they recovered enough to win six of their final nine, it was too late—their momentum had been broken. Nonetheless, the season was viewed as a success, given that they had made the charge in the first place. Rising from the near dead, they enjoyed a 14-1 stretch from August 27 to September 11 (their last game pre-Ike), when their pitching staff (led by Roy Oswalt, who didn't allow a run in three consecutive starts) posted a 2.18 ERA in 136 innings. The offense helped out as well during this period, bashing 18 home runs. In the season that the perennial doormat Rays won a pennant, Wade couldn't rightly be called a miracle man, but plaudits for the team's 86-75 record were still sent his way. All things considered, it was widely felt that the Astros had done well for themselves. "I think it's been a successful year," manager Cecil Cooper told the *Hous-*

ton Chronicle after the team was eliminated. "What we wanted? No. I think any time you fall short of the post-season, you're disappointed. But all in all, I think a pretty successful year for us."

Cooper was wrong. If Wade took any bows, he was wrong. The Astros had not only fooled baseball, but also fooled themselves. That's because they fielded one of the worst 86-75 teams of all time. If you're reading this book, then chances are you already know that won-lost records in baseball are a reflection of runs scored and runs allowed. The more runs you score compared with those you allow, the more often you win. This is very basic stuff. Call it the Micawber Rule, after the character from Dickens' *David Copperfield*, who said, "Annual income twenty pounds, annual expenditure nineteen nineteen six, result happiness. Annual income twenty pounds, annual expenditure twenty pounds ought and six, result misery." In baseball, score three runs in a game and allow two, result happiness. Score three runs in a game and allow four, result misery.

Very often, a team's won-lost record will largely reflect this relationship. A team that scores a far larger number of runs than it allows will have a winning record, often a very good one. A team that scores far fewer runs than it allows will have a losing record. A team that breaks even will float somewhere in the vicinity of .500. Every season, however, a few teams seem to defy the Micawberishness of baseball. Rather than recognizing these teams for the fluke phenomena that they are, a person is tempted to look for some reason that they defy the basic laws of the game, for the quality that allows them to win while losing or lose while win-

---

ASTROS PROSPECTUS

2008 record: 86-75; Third place in NL Central

Pythagenport record: 77-84

Runs scored per game: 4.42 (11th in NL)

Runs allowed per game: 4.69 (8th in NL)

Team EqA: .257 (Tied for 10th in NL)

2008 Batters Age: 31.5 (Oldest in NL)

2008 Pitchers Age: 31.4 (Oldest in NL)

Ballpark: Minute Maid Park; Neutral park; Park Factor of .997

2008: Thirtysomething Miguel Tejada ages two years to avoid sitting at the kids' table during team meals, but the joke's on him—the Astros don't have kids.

2009: Undue praise is heaped on Ed Wade for the kamikaze run, as taking last year's W-L record at face value might prolong the inevitable rebuild.

ning. Frequently, the answer is some variation on "character" or, alternatively, the genius of someone connected with the team. The genius of the manager. The genius of the owner. The genius of Ed Wade.

Unfortunately, no reasons are the result of human agency. There is only random chance. No manager or general manager, no matter how intelligent, can defy physics. If you hurled any general manager off a bridge with great force, he would fly, but only for so long as it took gravity to get hold of him. Perhaps, on one throw out of a thousand, the genius would sail a few feet farther than he had the other 999 times. In 2008, the Astros scored 712 runs and allowed 743 runs, yet finished with a winning record. They were the equivalent of the falling genius, sailing just a few feet further into the void on the thousandth throw. Now it is gravity's turn.

On their merits, the Astros should have been a 76-86 club. When their hot streak began, they were 67-66, better than they deserved, but not so good that an objective observer would have mistaken them for achieving more than treading water. Over the next 15 games, they rampaged through the Reds, Cardinals, Cubs, Rockies, and Pirates. But for the sweep of the Cubs at Chicago, an achievement in the Cubs' strongest season in recent memory, they were not knocking off the 1927 Yankees. In the first game at Chicago, the Astros' starting lineup was Darin Erstad, Ty Wigginton, Miguel Tejada, Lance Berkman, Geoff Blum, Hunter Pence, Jose Castillo, and Brad Ausmus. The pitcher was Roy Oswalt, and he threw 8⅓ innings of shutout baseball. In the other two games, the lineup substituted Michael Bourn for Erstad, David Newhan for Castillo, and Humberto Quintero for Ausmus. In the series' second game, Brandon Backe got tagged early, but the Cubs didn't pitch well and the game went to extra innings. The Astros went ahead in the top of the 11th, when Blum hit a two-run go-ahead home run off Kerry Wood, after which closer Jose Valverde held the score. In the third game, late-July acquisition Randy Wolf pitched a shutout, striking out eight. Quintero gave the Astros all the offense they would need with an RBI ground single in the first, and later on, Wigginton hit a two-run shot for insurance.

These games simultaneously represent the high-water mark of the Astros' season and the reason their future is a moot point in spite of them. The lineups were laughable. Bourn and Castillo aren't good enough to be major league regulars and might not even be worthwhile reserves. Newhan and Quintero are what might charitably be called journeymen, Newhan not having topped a .300 on-base percentage since 2004 and Quintero's having batted .230/.271/.304 in 152 ma-

jor league games. Wigginton and Wolf aren't with the club anymore, the former having been nontendered and the latter having turned free agent. The quality that the Astros were putting on the field was so weak that the manager often considered Blum, a career utility infielder and .250/.310/.389 hitter, the team's best choice to bat fifth—both before *and* after Carlos Lee was lost to injury in early August.

Even the good stuff—or merely decent stuff—on the team is aging. The 2008 Astros were the oldest team in the National League. Lance Berkman, who tailed off badly in the second half, is 33, as is Kaz Matsui. Carlos Lee will reach the same birthday this June. Miguel Tejada is zooming through the years like H. G. Wells' time traveler shooting the Schrödinger wave, but as best we can tell, he will turn 35 in May. The club's off-season moves to date have consisted of bringing in even older men still. Mike Hampton, signed to bolster the rotation, is 36 and more fragile than a neurasthenic named Waterford Wedgwood von Dresden. Fellow winter import Aaron Boone, another 36-year-old reserve, just posted a .299 OBP for the Nationals. Imminent 33-year-old platoon outfielder Jason Michaels is coming off a .224/.292/.360 season split between the Indians and the Pirates.

As a result of the team's lack of motion in responding to what was realistically a losing season, it is difficult to tell what goal the team is moving toward. As the farm system is free of impact prospects and trending backward—with J. R. Towles' record-level hitlessness and Felipe Paulino's myriad health problems last year, the two players that both we and Baseball America identified as, respectively, the best hitter and pitcher in the system a year ago now see their futures in doubt. Help is not on the way.

Worse than Towles' and Paulino's failure to develop, no one else moved up to replace them. The currently anointed best prospect is another catcher, Jason Castro, who so far looks to have production that hews closer to the Astros' tradition of Brad Ausmus than that of Alan Ashby. (Joe Ferguson? Mitch Meluskey? Cliff Johnson? The Astros have heard that there are catchers who can play both sides of the game, but the club has almost never had one of its own.) The next-best prospect, Brian Bogusevic, is an outfielder recently converted from pitching and might not have the glove for center or the power for a corner. The Astros' third-best prospect, 2008 draftee Jordan Lyles, is just 55⅓ innings into his pro career. The paucity of talent on the farm is exacerbated by a longtime habit of giving up draft picks for free agents while also holding a hard line on bonuses. To date, Houston has still not given out a larger bonus than the $2.125 million handed to Chris Burke back in 2001; Castro, their top 2008 pick, signed for $2.07 million. The bonus policy resulted in outright disaster in 2007, when the club had forfeited its first- and second-round draft picks to free-agent compensation and then failed to come to terms with its third- and fourth-round picks.

We have now begun to probe into the weird operating methods of Astros owner Drayton McLane, a man at cross-purposes with himself. From time to time, McLane will rouse himself from his self-imposed austerity mode and allow his general manager to import an expensive veteran via trade or free agency. Most recently, Tejada was traded for last year; two years ago, the Astros signed Carlos Lee (to the largest contract in franchise history) and Woody Williams to big-money contracts; and the team traded for Aubrey Huff at mid-season in 2006. Back during their better days as a contender, the Astros spent to get Andy Pettitte and the un-retired Roger Clemens for 2004 and Jeff Kent for 2003. Additionally, McLane has authorized big contracts to keep Oswalt and Berkman in Houston.

It is impossible to say that the Astros have not been successful under McLane's ownership. Since he purchased the team in 1993, it has won four division titles, captured two wild-card entries into the playoffs, and, in 2005, the second of those wild-card teams reached the World Series. And yet, over the decade or so since the Astros won 102 games under Larry Dierker, the plan has frequently been compromised. Unsupported by the products of a robust player development system, the

veterans are reduced to mere tokens awash in a sea of submediocrity. Even the 2005 World Series team was something of a fluke, the best possible outcome for a team of its type. It was a subpar offensive collection powered into the playoffs by a congeries of strong pitching performances and then rising to the pinnacle through the magic of "the secret sauce"—strong starting pitching, a solid closer, and a tight defense. As Casey Stengel once said, "Sometimes it doesn't always work."

Similarly, recent seasons have been tossed away on pursuits that have little to do with winning. Consider Houston's allowing Craig Biggio to chase 3,000 hits when he was probably two seasons past what should have been a mandatory retirement. Or the unending embrace of Brad Ausmus. Then there's the recent indulgence of the general manager's fascination with Michael Bourn, a fetish that cost the team Brad Lidge—the reason that Phillies executives could afford to be so generous in the praise of Wade after the championship. Ed Wade had finally brought Philadelphia a title, but from the outside.

That's as close a brush to the World Series or any other postseason action as the Astros are likely to have soon. There is no Clemens to coax out of retirement, no stars in the system, and only Lidge's successor, Jose Valverde, to trade, though Wade's willful refusal to secure a real return for Lidge doesn't inspire much confidence in a big score when that deal inevitably goes down. Hurricane Ike was just the beginning. Après Wade, le deluge.

HITTERS

| Reggie Abercrombie | | | | OF | | | | | | | | Bats: R | | Throws: R | | Height: 6' 3" | | Weight: 220 | | Born: July 15, 1980 | | | Age: 28 |

YEAR	TEAM	LVL	AGE	PA	R	2B	3B	HR	RBI	BB	SO	SB	CS	EqBRR	AVG	OBP	SLG	EqAVG	EqOBP	EqSLG	EqA	VORP	WARP	DEFENSE			
2006	FLO	MLB	25	281	39	12	2	5	24	18	78	6	5	-2.1	.212	.271	.333	.214	.272	.346	.213	-10.7	-1.0	67-CF	-1		
2007	ABQ	AAA	26	379	71	23	9	17	55	11	95	41	6	0.0	.323	.361	.584	.237	.272	.439	.250	-2.7	-0.6	74-RF	-5	10-CF	-3
2007	FLO	MLB	26	80	16	3	0	2	5	2	22	7	1	2.3	.197	.238	.316	.197	.237	.316	.208	-3.2	0.4	14-CF	7		
2008	ROU	AAA	27	300	37	14	2	12	36	9	93	17	9	-2.8	.273	.297	.460	.227	.247	.368	.210	-15.3	-1.7	43-RF	2	24-LF	-3
2008	HOU	MLB	27	60	10	5	0	2	5	1	23	5	2	-1.0	.309	.339	.509	.327	.356	.564	.296	4.2	0.7	9-CF	3		
2009	HOU	MLB	28	370	38	19	3	10	37	15	118	18	6	1.0	.224	.263	.383	.227	.265	.393	.227	-8.9	-0.0	89-RF	2		

Breakout: 28% Improve: 45% Collapse: 31% Attrition: 26%   Comparables: Charlton Jimerson, Chris Jones, Jason Smith, Colin Porter

Pitchers love Reggie, as he treats the strike zone as though it were as wide as a church door and as deep as a well. That is more than enough to suck all the value out of his power and speed. It took a major injury (Carlos Lee's broken finger) to get him onto the roster as a fourth outfielder, and he beat up on some September call-up pitchers, but Houston was only impressed enough to keep him on a minor league contract and invitation to camp.

Brad Ausmus   C

Bats: R   Throws: R   Height: 5' 11"   Weight: 190   Born: April 14, 1969   Age: 40

YEAR	TEAM	LVL	AGE	PA	R	2B	3B	HR	RBI	BB	SO	SB	CS	EqBRR	AVG	OBP	SLG	EqAVG	EqOBP	EqSLG	EqA	VORP	WARP	DEFENSE	
2006	HOU	MLB	37	502	37	16	1	2	39	45	71	3	1	-1.1	.230	.308	.285	.229	.308	.281	.214	-18.2	0.4	125-C	5
2007	HOU	MLB	38	397	38	16	3	3	25	37	74	6	1	-0.5	.235	.318	.324	.235	.322	.332	.237	0.1	1.2	100-C	5
2008	HOU	MLB	39	250	15	8	0	3	24	25	41	0	2	-1.0	.218	.303	.296	.220	.308	.303	.217	-7.4	0.1	64-C	2
2009	HOU	MLB	40	196	18	9	1	3	18	20	32	1	1	-0.9	.238	.321	.340	.242	.323	.349	.235	1.9	0.8	50-C	-1

Breakout: 41% Improve: 59% Collapse: 24% Attrition: 47%   Comparables: Bob Boone, Tony Peña, Sandy Alomar, Benito Santiago

Ausmus's job last season was supposed to be tutoring Justin Towles on the fine art of catching. Mission accomplished—Towles hit just like Ausmus has for years, after which Ausmus was released. He's now looking for another team that values veteran mentorship. There's a word for "veteran mentorship"—it's *coach*, a guy you pay to sit in the dugout and be inspirational, not go out on the field and murder your offense.

Lance Berkman   1B

Bats: S   Throws: L   Height: 6' 1"   Weight: 220   Born: February 10, 1976   Age: 33

YEAR	TEAM	LVL	AGE	PA	R	2B	3B	HR	RBI	BB	SO	SB	CS	EqBRR	AVG	OBP	SLG	EqAVG	EqOBP	EqSLG	EqA	VORP	WARP	DEFENSE			
2006	HOU	MLB	30	646	95	29	0	45	136	98	106	3	2	-2.9	.315	.420	.621	.308	.416	.607	.336	68.7	7.2	102-1B	2	34-RF	-1
2007	HOU	MLB	31	668	95	24	2	34	102	94	125	7	3	-3.5	.278	.386	.510	.277	.391	.522	.308	44.8	4.3	118-1B	-3	25-RF	-2
2008	HOU	MLB	32	665	114	46	4	29	106	99	108	18	4	2.4	.312	.420	.567	.315	.423	.587	.336	72.5	9.4	148-1B	20		
2009	HOU	MLB	33	620	104	35	2	28	97	88	103	11	3	-1.5	.299	.402	.534	.303	.405	.549	.319	50.9	6.1	145-1B	6		

Breakout: 6% Improve: 38% Collapse: 16% Attrition: 6%   Comparables: Reggie Smith, Ken Singleton, Jeff Bagwell, Ryan Klesko

Berkman had a monster first half of the season (hitting .367/.451/.704 as of July 1) and seemed a shoo-in for the MVP award, but faded in the second half and collapsed in September. He did have a bout with pink-eye before slumping, and suffered a wrist injury a month later. This was the first year that he was exclusively a first baseman, and he excelled, although the +20 is probably excessively generous on the part of our system.

Geoff Blum   INF

Bats: S   Throws: R   Height: 6' 3"   Weight: 205   Born: April 26, 1973   Age: 36

YEAR	TEAM	LVL	AGE	PA	R	2B	3B	HR	RBI	BB	SO	SB	CS	EqBRR	AVG	OBP	SLG	EqAVG	EqOBP	EqSLG	EqA	VORP	WARP	DEFENSE			
2006	SDN	MLB	33	299	27	17	1	4	34	17	51	0	1	0.0	.254	.293	.366	.257	.299	.377	.235	-3.2	0.1	43-SS	0	22-3B	1
2007	SDN	MLB	34	370	34	21	1	5	33	32	52	0	0	1.1	.252	.319	.367	.258	.329	.380	.250	2.4	1.9	54-2B	9	10-SS	1
2008	HOU	MLB	35	356	36	14	1	14	53	21	54	1	2	-1.2	.240	.287	.418	.241	.287	.435	.245	-1.0	0.8	68-3B	7	5-2B	-1
2009	HOU	MLB	36	214	21	10	1	6	27	16	31	1	1	-0.6	.245	.305	.399	.249	.308	.410	.246	3.6	0.8	54-3B	3		

Breakout: 28% Improve: 45% Collapse: 26% Attrition: 47%   Comparables: Matt Williams, Bob Kennedy, Jim Morrison, Doug DeCinces

Blum's usefulness is in his flexibility; options-wise, you can't do better than a switch-hitter who can play anywhere on the field, though the "switch-hitter" part is purely nominal at this point, with Blum's ability to hit southpaws (.231/.296/.372 career) bordering on the mythical. After Lee's injury, the Astros employed Blum somewhat regularly at third while using Wigginton's flexibility to play left, which was strange but hardly crazy. This year, though, using Blum as the their third baseman now that Wigginton has been released—that's just plain nuts.

Brian Bogusevic   CF

Bats: L   Throws: L   Height: 6' 3"   Weight: 215   Born: February 18, 1984   Age: 25

YEAR	TEAM	LVL	AGE	PA	R	2B	3B	HR	RBI	BB	SO	SB	CS	EqBRR	AVG	OBP	SLG	EqAVG	EqOBP	EqSLG	EqA	VORP	WARP	DEFENSE			
2008	SLM	A+	24	28	4	2	0	1	6	4	1	1	0	0.4	.217	.357	.435	.167	.286	.417	.239	-0.6	-0.1	7-RF	-1		
2008	CCH	AA	24	145	21	10	2	3	20	16	24	8	1	0.8	.371	.447	.556	.287	.357	.465	.283	8.0	0.0	19-CF	-8	12-RF	-2
2009	HOU	MLB	25	429	53	24	4	9	43	37	94	10	4	0.8	.256	.324	.404	.260	.327	.415	.256	6.5	1.1	102-RF	1		

Breakout: 10% Improve: 33% Collapse: 45% Attrition: 10%   Comparables: Ty Gainey, Dave Clark, Val Majewski, Shane Mack

The Astros finally gave up on Bogusevic as a pitcher—he's got a translated line showing 17 starts and an 8.68 DERA at Corpus Christi—and moved him to the outfield. A two-way star in college, he picked up the offensive side as though he'd never put down the bat. He didn't show much power, though, and his speed was down from his college days; it's already marginal for a center fielder, and he may not have enough bat to merit everyday play at a corner spot. A strong showing in the Arizona Fall League should see him make Triple-A out of spring training, and from there it's just a short jump to the center fielder–less, Bourn-ful major league club.

Michael Bourn   CF

Bats: L   Throws: R   Height: 5' 11"   Weight: 180   Born: December 27, 1982   Age: 26

YEAR	TEAM	LVL	AGE	PA	R	2B	3B	HR	RBI	BB	SO	SB	CS	EqBRR	AVG	OBP	SLG	EqAVG	EqOBP	EqSLG	EqA	VORP	WARP	DEFENSE			
2006	REA	AA	23	361	62	5	6	4	26	36	67	30	4	7.1	.274	.350	.365	.243	.312	.326	.236	-10.6	0.4	78-CF	3		
2006	SWB	AAA	23	174	34	5	7	1	15	20	33	15	1	4.8	.283	.368	.428	.255	.339	.405	.270	3.1	1.6	27-CF	7	7-LF	0
2007	PHI	MLB	24	133	29	3	3	1	6	13	21	18	1	4.1	.277	.348	.378	.269	.346	.370	.277	6.4	0.8	24-LF	2	6-CF	1
2008	HOU	MLB	25	514	57	10	4	5	29	37	111	41	10	2.1	.229	.288	.300	.235	.294	.311	.227	-11.8	-0.9	114-CF	-3		
2009	*HOU*	*MLB*	*26*	*445*	*61*	*15*	*5*	*5*	*32*	*38*	*83*	*30*	*9*	*3.5*	*.258*	*.326*	*.361*	*.262*	*.329*	*.371*	*.253*	*5.4*	*2.1*	*105-CF*	*5*		

Breakout: 43%   Improve: 63%   Collapse: 14%   Attrition: 29%   Comparables: *Lance Johnson, Alex Sanchez, Al Pilarcik, Cory Sullivan*

Bourn should never, ever be allowed to face a left-handed pitcher, having now batted .182/.253/238 in 162 career plate appearances. Unfortunately, he doesn't swing with any authority against righties, either. Pitchers have learned that they can challenge him and get away with it. That puts the kibosh on trying to work out a walk, and so his speed doesn't get a chance to work. There's no way he should be a starting center fielder in the majors. Ed Wade got a lot of praise for the Astros' overachieving season, but without the manager's inexplicable desire to bring Bourn over from Philadelphia (for *Brad Lidge*) and play him every day, the Astros might have achieved even more without their GM's intervention.

Jason Castro   C

Bats: L   Throws: R   Height: 6' 3"   Weight: 210   Born: June 18, 1987   Age: 22

YEAR	TEAM	LVL	AGE	PA	R	2B	3B	HR	RBI	BB	SO	SB	CS	EqBRR	AVG	OBP	SLG	EqAVG	EqOBP	EqSLG	EqA	VORP	WARP	DEFENSE	
2008	TCV	A-	21	162	10	9	0	2	12	22	32	0	2	-1.2	.275	.383	.384	.193	.282	.297	.200	-19.8	-1.1	26-C	-2
2009	*HOU*	*MLB*	*22*	*530*	*40*	*25*	*2*	*10*	*52*	*48*	*140*	*3*	*2*	*-0.5*	*.210*	*.285*	*.334*	*.213*	*.288*	*.342*	*.216*	*-9.7*	*0.4*	*125-C*	*-10*

Breakout: 59%   Improve: 74%   Collapse: 15%   Attrition: 4%   Comparables: *Fredric Polka, Alan Zinter, Jeromy Burnitz, Shea Morenz*

Castro was the Astros' first-round pick last year (10th overall) and was the second catcher taken. Thrust into a rather arid farm system, he immediately became the club's top prospect. His outlook is good but not great: he should be a decent hitter, with good patience and gap power, and a bit of average as well. He's defensively solid and very baseball-smart. On the downside, he runs like a catcher, and none of his skills are so overwhelming that scouts say "star." He played much better in Hawaiian winter ball than he did at Tri-City, and he should make his full-season debut with High-A Lancaster, where he'll hit. But everyone does at Lancaster.

Koby Clemens   C

Bats: R   Throws: R   Height: 5' 11"   Weight: 193   Born: December 4, 1986   Age: 22

YEAR	TEAM	LVL	AGE	PA	R	2B	3B	HR	RBI	BB	SO	SB	CS	EqBRR	AVG	OBP	SLG	EqAVG	EqOBP	EqSLG	EqA	VORP	WARP	DEFENSE	
2006	LEX	A	19	352	40	19	1	5	39	32	67	2	1	-1.9	.229	.313	.346	.174	.234	.265	.169	-37.9	-4.6	81-3B	-16
2007	LEX	A	20	484	65	21	0	15	56	53	112	8	2	-4.1	.252	.344	.412	.200	.272	.318	.210	-28.7	-3.1	99-3B	-12
2008	SLM	A+	21	458	54	29	5	7	52	61	99	1	4	-0.8	.268	.369	.423	.244	.333	.399	.256	4.5	0.9	76-C	-6
2009	*HOU*	*MLB*	*22*	*546*	*57*	*31*	*2*	*15*	*60*	*56*	*134*	*3*	*2*	*-0.8*	*.235*	*.318*	*.401*	*.239*	*.321*	*.412*	*.253*	*9.0*	*1.5*	*128-C*	*-16*

Breakout: 56%   Improve: 82%   Collapse: 4%   Attrition: 7%   Comparables: *John Roskos, Randy Ready, Tom Redington, John Ackley*

To pull off a position switch, to catcher of all things, is difficult enough, but to do it while moving up a level and while your dad is in the headlines every day (in a bad way) is almost unimaginable. Clemens' arm was his best asset at third, and it plays well behind the plate. At the plate, when not behind it, he showed improved patience and moderate power; we do worry that the jump in batting average is an unsustainable, fluky spike. With the switch, he's solidly on a prospect's course—no nepotism required.

Collin DeLome　　　LF

| | | | | Bats: L | | Throws: R | | Height: 6' 2" | | Weight: 195 | | Born: December 18, 1985 | | | Age: 23 |

YEAR	TEAM	LVL	AGE	PA	R	2B	3B	HR	RBI	BB	SO	SB	CS	EqBRR	AVG	OBP	SLG	EqAVG	EqOBP	EqSLG	EqA	VORP	WARP	DEFENSE			
2007	TCV	A-	21	273	31	17	6	6	28	23	65	9	2	0.0	.300	.374	.494	.217	.270	.370	.221	-20.9	-2.4	33-CF	-4	11-LF	-5
2008	LEX	A	22	252	41	9	6	12	36	18	71	7	2	-0.6	.261	.329	.513	.211	.266	.409	.230	-7.2	-0.7	34-LF	-4	17-CF	1
2008	SLM	A+	22	267	40	14	3	10	35	17	57	7	2	2.8	.232	.305	.443	.213	.270	.414	.235	-6.0	-0.5	49-LF	-1		
2009	HOU	MLB	23	546	58	28	5	15	59	38	150	10	5	2.8	.227	.288	.395	.230	.290	.405	.237	-5.8	0.2	128-LF	0		

Breakout: 36%　Improve: 66%　Collapse: 13%　Attrition: 7%　　　Comparables: Brian Gordon, Jeff Key, Jeff Fiorentino, Ralph Bryant

DeLome, the Astros' fifth-round pick in 2007, was their highest pick who actually signed. They didn't have a number one or two, and both their number three and four guys rejected the strict slot money offered and went to college. DeLome is an athlete, not a ballplayer; he doesn't read the ball well, a failing that leads to strikeouts at the plate and bad routes in the field. But make a mistake, and he can crush it.

Darin Erstad　　　OF/1B

| | | | | Bats: L | | Throws: L | | Height: 6' 2" | | Weight: 220 | | Born: June 4, 1974 | | | Age: 35 |

YEAR	TEAM	LVL	AGE	PA	R	2B	3B	HR	RBI	BB	SO	SB	CS	EqBRR	AVG	OBP	SLG	EqAVG	EqOBP	EqSLG	EqA	VORP	WARP	DEFENSE			
2006	LAA	MLB	32	105	8	8	1	0	5	6	18	1	1	-0.1	.221	.279	.326	.211	.276	.305	.205	-3.6	-0.6	25-CF	-2		
2007	CHA	MLB	33	345	33	13	1	4	32	28	44	7	2	0.9	.248	.310	.335	.244	.310	.338	.232	-6.8	0.4	42-CF	6	20-1B	3
2008	HOU	MLB	34	342	49	16	0	4	31	14	68	2	3	1.2	.276	.309	.363	.280	.312	.376	.237	-2.6	0.7	34-CF	6	23-LF	3
2009	HOU	MLB	35	211	22	10	1	2	20	14	37	2	1	-0.1	.258	.312	.361	.262	.314	.371	.237	0.4	0.6	53-CF	1		

Breakout: 55%　Improve: 65%　Collapse: 19%　Attrition: 45%　　　Comparables: Gino Cimoli, Joe Orsulak, Hal Morris, Harry Walker

Healthy for the first time in three years, Erstad earned his way into playing time by virtue of defense, batting average, and a very weak starter ahead of him in Michael Bourn. His BABIP was the second-highest mark of his career—meaning that the average will come down—and his batting average is as empty as they come. Signed to an extension for 2009, he comes cheap, and, we might add, you get what you pay for.

J. R. House　　　1B/C

| | | | | Bats: R | | Throws: R | | Height: 5' 10" | | Weight: 210 | | Born: November 11, 1979 | | | Age: 29 |

YEAR	TEAM	LVL	AGE	PA	R	2B	3B	HR	RBI	BB	SO	SB	CS	EqBRR	AVG	OBP	SLG	EqAVG	EqOBP	EqSLG	EqA	VORP	WARP	DEFENSE			
2006	CCH	AA	26	423	58	23	2	10	69	32	44	2	2	-2.2	.325	.376	.475	.232	.274	.339	.213	-19.6	-2.4	65-C	-11	29-1B	-3
2006	ROU	AAA	26	128	25	15	0	5	36	9	15	0	0	-1.5	.412	.445	.675	.362	.395	.603	.331	18.6	0.9	24-1B	-4		
2007	NOR	AAA	27	471	52	32	2	11	66	43	59	1	5	-6.2	.298	.365	.463	.262	.322	.426	.256	8.7	0.5	50-C	-5	25-1B	-1
2007	BAL	MLB	27	41	5	2	0	3	3	1	11	0	0	-0.1	.211	.268	.500	.211	.268	.500	.253	0.6	-0.1	5-C	-1		
2008	ROU	AAA	28	513	63	25	0	18	60	53	52	1	2	-3.1	.306	.378	.480	.245	.308	.378	.239	-5.6	-0.6	70-1B	2	40-C	-6
2009	KCA	MLB	29	462	44	24	1	10	55	35	73	1	1	-1.7	.248	.308	.384	.245	.306	.397	.244	-2.1	0.7	109-1B	5		

Breakout: 28%　Improve: 53%　Collapse: 26%　Attrition: 16%　　　Comparables: Riccardo Ingram, Gary Bennett, J.T. Snow, Ron Johnson

The whole point of a good-hitting backup catcher is that he can be a good hitter, something that hasn't described House since, um, ever. Step back to 2001, and we thought his minor league numbers projected to his becoming a good hitter. But if you plot his Equivalent Averages out as is (not projected), they're always somewhere around .240. Some people just don't get better after age 20.

Chris Johnson　　　3B

| | | | | Bats: R | | Throws: R | | Height: 6' 3" | | Weight: 220 | | Born: October 1, 1984 | | | Age: 24 |

YEAR	TEAM	LVL	AGE	PA	R	2B	3B	HR	RBI	BB	SO	SB	CS	EqBRR	AVG	OBP	SLG	EqAVG	EqOBP	EqSLG	EqA	VORP	WARP	DEFENSE			
2006	TCV	A-	21	239	18	7	1	1	29	11	35	7	3	-0.4	.212	.251	.266	.150	.180	.198	.089	-74.1	-5.0	48-3B	-3		
2007	LEX	A	22	277	37	14	0	8	44	17	38	3	4	-1.5	.259	.304	.408	.188	.222	.291	.167	-27.7	-3.1	29-3B	-2	19-SS	-4
2007	SLM	A+	22	240	24	11	0	6	38	8	41	1	0	0.0	.263	.292	.393	.214	.233	.323	.188	-18.8	-2.2	53-3B	-6		
2008	CCH	AA	23	358	43	24	0	12	58	20	61	5	0	0.1	.324	.364	.506	.271	.307	.443	.257	6.9	0.0	82-3B	-8		
2008	ROU	AAA	23	107	10	2	1	1	9	5	25	0	0	-0.7	.218	.252	.287	.196	.224	.265	.158	-11.7	-1.2	26-3B	-2		
2009	HOU	MLB	24	488	35	21	1	9	47	24	115	2	1	-1.1	.215	.257	.326	.218	.259	.335	.199	-17.3	-1.7	115-3B	-2		

Breakout: 36%　Improve: 60%　Collapse: 28%　Attrition: 13%　　　Comparables: Tracy Woodson, Pedro Feliz, Don Sparks, Ryan Long

Johnson's 2008 at Double-A is one of the most out-of-context seasons in all of baseball. A BABIP 70 points above career high? All his offensive gain lies there, and it's an illusion, as quickly demonstrated by his stint in the Pacific

Coast League. He's a dead-red free swinger who'll chase a curve until it hits the backstop; the secret of success against him is simply don't give in.

Carlos Lee — LF

Bats: R Throws: R Height: 6' 2" Weight: 240 Born: June 20, 1976 Age: 33

YEAR	TEAM	LVL	AGE	PA	R	2B	3B	HR	RBI	BB	SO	SB	CS	EqBRR	AVG	OBP	SLG	EqAVG	EqOBP	EqSLG	EqA	VORP	WARP	DEFENSE
2006	MIL	MLB	30	435	60	18	0	28	81	38	39	12	2	-1.2	.286	.347	.549	.282	.346	.541	.298	26.6	0.2	95-LF -26
2006	TEX	MLB	30	260	42	19	1	9	35	20	26	7	0	-0.0	.322	.369	.525	.303	.358	.496	.295	20.4	0.1	48-LF -14
2007	HOU	MLB	31	697	93	43	1	32	119	53	63	10	5	-3.6	.303	.354	.528	.305	.358	.539	.298	45.6	5.1	152-LF 2
2008	HOU	MLB	32	481	61	27	0	28	100	37	49	4	1	-1.9	.314	.368	.569	.317	.371	.589	.316	44.1	2.5	103-LF -18
2009	HOU	MLB	33	572	81	32	1	25	91	49	60	8	2	-2.6	.296	.359	.508	.300	.362	.521	.297	34.2	2.9	134-LF -11

Breakout: 5% Improve: 36% Collapse: 21% Attrition: 6% Comparables: Juan Gonzalez, Kevin McReynolds, Albert Belle, Ted Kluszewski

Lee was leading the league in RBI when a Bronson Arroyo pitch hit squarely on the end of his bat, shattering the pinkie draped over it. The finger was broken in six places, requiring surgery, and Lee, who had never been on the DL in his career, missed the last seven weeks of the season. Like Manny Ramirez, "El Caballo" tempers his massive offensive production with poor defense, but at least without the drama of Carlos being Carlos.

Mark Loretta — INF

Bats: R Throws: R Height: 6' 0" Weight: 185 Born: August 14, 1971 Age: 37

YEAR	TEAM	LVL	AGE	PA	R	2B	3B	HR	RBI	BB	SO	SB	CS	EqBRR	AVG	OBP	SLG	EqAVG	EqOBP	EqSLG	EqA	VORP	WARP	DEFENSE
2006	BOS	MLB	34	703	75	33	0	5	59	49	63	4	1	-1.8	.285	.345	.361	.271	.337	.349	.246	13.2	1.0	132-2B 1 8-1B -1
2007	HOU	MLB	35	511	52	23	2	4	41	44	41	1	2	-4.8	.287	.352	.372	.290	.359	.381	.260	11.8	0.8	54-SS -5 22-2B -2
2008	HOU	MLB	36	297	27	15	0	4	38	29	30	0	0	-2.4	.280	.350	.383	.281	.350	.388	.264	7.3	0.5	42-2B -3 13-3B 0
2009	LAN	MLB	37	203	19	10	0	2	21	19	22	1	0	-1.0	.259	.331	.356	.264	.334	.373	.248	3.8	0.3	51-2B -3

Breakout: 14% Improve: 41% Collapse: 30% Attrition: 42% Comparables: Jeff Cirillo, Alan Trammell, Manny Trillo, Art Howe

Over the last four seasons, Loretta has been spectacularly consistent. Though the context changes the value of the numbers, in each season he's hit between .280 and .287, had an OBP of between .345 and .360, and slugged between .347 and .363. You might say that the guy is really in a rut, but that would imply highs and lows. Envisioned as the Astros' primary infield reserve, he wound up being limited to backing up Kaz Matsui's various injuries, as Cecil Cooper rode an idiosyncratic preference for Geoff Blum. A free agent, Loretta signed a one-year deal to work around the infield for the Dodgers. Watch out for the inevitable moment when Joe Torre decides he's a more reliable first baseman than James Loney.

Kazuo Matsui — 2B

Bats: S Throws: R Height: 5' 10" Weight: 185 Born: October 23, 1975 Age: 33

YEAR	TEAM	LVL	AGE	PA	R	2B	3B	HR	RBI	BB	SO	SB	CS	EqBRR	AVG	OBP	SLG	EqAVG	EqOBP	EqSLG	EqA	VORP	WARP	DEFENSE
2006	NYN	MLB	30	139	10	6	0	1	7	6	19	2	0	0.7	.200	.235	.269	.198	.234	.260	.166	-8.6	-0.9	31-2B 0
2006	CSP	AAA	30	129	26	4	0	3	16	9	20	3	1	0.9	.278	.328	.391	.203	.248	.305	.197	-9.6	-0.9	26-SS -4
2006	COL	MLB	30	126	22	6	3	2	19	10	27	8	1	1.1	.345	.392	.504	.327	.376	.469	.299	13.0	0.9	20-2B 0
2007	COL	MLB	31	453	84	24	6	4	37	34	69	32	4	6.7	.288	.342	.405	.277	.336	.399	.266	17.6	4.2	96-2B 21
2008	HOU	MLB	32	422	58	26	3	6	33	37	53	20	5	4.2	.293	.354	.427	.300	.360	.440	.281	21.4	1.3	91-2B -11
2009	HOU	MLB	33	480	63	24	4	6	41	40	66	18	5	2.5	.272	.336	.390	.276	.338	.400	.261	15.2	1.7	114-2B -2

Breakout: 17% Improve: 42% Collapse: 29% Attrition: 15% Comparables: Dave Collins, Tony Graffanino, Roberto Alomar, Rich Amaral

Matsui opened the season with one of the nastier-sounding injuries ever suffered by a baseball player. An anal fissure was followed up with a rather more prosaic list of back, groin, and hamstring ailments. This is a recurring problem; he hasn't had a 500-AB season since leaving Japan. He was reasonably effective in between all the injuries, dispelling our fears of Coors inflation, but "injury prone" and "reliant on speed" are an especially poor combination for the future.

David Newhan   UT

Bats: L   Throws: R   Height: 5' 10"   Weight: 185   Born: September 7, 1973   Age: 35

YEAR	TEAM	LVL	AGE	PA	R	2B	3B	HR	RBI	BB	SO	SB	CS	EqBRR	AVG	OBP	SLG	EqAVG	EqOBP	EqSLG	EqA	VORP	WARP	DEFENSE			
2006	BAL	MLB	32	143	14	4	0	4	18	7	22	4	2	-1.5	.252	.294	.374	.246	.294	.362	.231	-2.1	-0.9	18-CF	-5	14-LF	-2
2007	NWO	AAA	33	196	27	12	3	7	30	20	28	7	4	0.0	.347	.413	.572	.278	.342	.460	.273	8.6	0.6	28-2B	-5	7-LF	0
2007	NYN	MLB	33	83	9	1	1	1	6	8	19	2	0	1.3	.203	.289	.284	.203	.298	.284	.215	-2.9	0.0	8-LF	3		
2008	ROU	AAA	34	216	39	14	2	9	36	14	33	8	2	2.5	.308	.355	.535	.243	.284	.416	.241	-1.9	0.0	22-RF	-1	18-2B	1
2008	HOU	MLB	34	111	11	5	2	2	12	6	28	1	0	-2.1	.260	.297	.404	.260	.297	.404	.243	1.0	-0.6	20-2B	-5		
2009	HOU	MLB	35	248	28	13	2	6	28	16	52	5	2	0.3	.252	.304	.404	.256	.306	.415	.247	4.5	0.2	61-2B	-6		

Breakout: 25%   Improve: 47%   Collapse: 27%   Attrition: 43%   Comparables: Irv Noren, Curtis Pride, Gerald Williams, Chuck Hinton

Newhan was essentially the universal backup to the backup; when, say, Matsui was injured, Loretta would move from backup to starter and Newhan would move from Triple-A to the big-league bench. Offering versatility and little else, he was a poor fit for a team that already had multi-use players like Loretta, Blum, and Wigginton. A free agent, he'll try to find another team where the players have more solidly defined roles.

Jordan Parraz   OF

Bats: R   Throws: R   Height: 6' 3"   Weight: 220   Born: October 8, 1984   Age: 24

YEAR	TEAM	LVL	AGE	PA	R	2B	3B	HR	RBI	BB	SO	SB	CS	EqBRR	AVG	OBP	SLG	EqAVG	EqOBP	EqSLG	EqA	VORP	WARP	DEFENSE			
2006	TCV	A-	21	298	46	18	2	6	38	33	44	23	3	0.0	.336	.421	.494	.240	.306	.371	.242	-8.6	-0.1	67-RF	0		
2007	LEX	A	22	530	69	28	3	14	76	47	89	33	10	2.3	.281	.364	.446	.202	.265	.318	.206	-33.2	-4.0	108-RF	-10	11-CF	-4
2008	SLM	A+	23	504	82	31	3	6	42	64	79	21	10	-0.0	.289	.399	.419	.247	.339	.367	.252	0.8	0.2	68-RF	2	36-CF	-6
2009	HOU	MLB	24	559	67	30	3	11	54	50	123	14	5	0.1	.249	.323	.384	.252	.326	.394	.252	2.3	1.1	131-RF	0		

Breakout: 53%   Improve: 66%   Collapse: 19%   Attrition: 6%   Comparables: Chad Allen, Emil Brown, T.R. Lewis, Joel Wolfe

Parraz has been moved very slowly through the Houston system, and as a result, he's definitely old for his levels. His overarching skill is his arm, an absolute cannon, but the best use (pitching) is ruled out because he can't control it. That's pretty much the story for all his talents; he hasn't translated them into appropriate production. He's now the Royals' problem since getting traded to Kansas City for Tyler Lumsden.

Hunter Pence   RF

Bats: R   Throws: R   Height: 6' 4"   Weight: 210   Born: April 13, 1983   Age: 26

YEAR	TEAM	LVL	AGE	PA	R	2B	3B	HR	RBI	BB	SO	SB	CS	EqBRR	AVG	OBP	SLG	EqAVG	EqOBP	EqSLG	EqA	VORP	WARP	DEFENSE			
2006	CCH	AA	23	592	97	31	8	28	95	60	109	17	4	1.9	.283	.357	.533	.241	.306	.448	.259	8.4	0.7	105-RF	-5	20-CF	0
2007	ROU	AAA	24	106	17	11	1	3	21	10	15	2	0	0.0	.326	.387	.558	.292	.349	.510	.292	7.6	0.8	18-CF	-1	6-RF	1
2007	HOU	MLB	24	484	57	30	9	17	69	26	95	11	5	-0.1	.322	.360	.539	.328	.368	.559	.304	42.9	3.7	93-CF	-6	13-RF	2
2008	HOU	MLB	25	642	78	34	4	25	83	40	124	11	10	-0.8	.269	.318	.466	.274	.323	.488	.269	11.3	2.3	154-RF	2		
2009	HOU	MLB	26	603	86	35	3	24	86	48	114	12	4	0.9	.286	.346	.491	.290	.348	.504	.287	29.3	3.5	141-RF	0		

Breakout: 35%   Improve: 60%   Collapse: 11%   Attrition: 9%   Comparables: Derek Bell, Rondell White, Ollie Brown, Lee Walls

We've mentioned an unsustainable BABIP several times with the Astros, and Pence's 2007 and what followed in 2008 are a perfect cautionary example. Having seen the guy rocket fastballs all over the place in '07, pitchers threw him a lot more breaking pitches, and he spent the first half of the year chasing them before starting to hold back later in the year, culminating in a .302/.388/.581 September. He's a very good right fielder, with 16 assists in 2008, which helps balance out the offensive ups and downs.

Humberto Quintero   C

Bats: R   Throws: R   Height: 5' 9"   Weight: 215   Born: August 2, 1979   Age: 29

YEAR	TEAM	LVL	AGE	PA	R	2B	3B	HR	RBI	BB	SO	SB	CS	EqBRR	AVG	OBP	SLG	EqAVG	EqOBP	EqSLG	EqA	VORP	WARP	DEFENSE	
2006	ROU	AAA	26	322	39	21	2	4	37	19	48	4	0	0.5	.298	.352	.425	.255	.301	.379	.238	-3.8	1.4	78-C	5
2006	HOU	MLB	26	22	2	2	0	0	2	1	3	0	0	0.2	.333	.364	.429	.333	.364	.429	.275	1.1	0.3	6-C	2
2007	ROU	AAA	27	188	22	12	1	5	22	4	21	0	2	0.0	.333	.355	.497	.272	.296	.411	.240	0.3	1.3	45-C	7
2007	HOU	MLB	27	57	2	2	0	0	1	2	13	0	0	-1.4	.226	.281	.264	.226	.281	.264	.188	-2.2	-0.1	17-C	1
2008	ROU	AAA	28	124	13	2	2	3	18	5	15	0	2	-1.1	.237	.274	.364	.185	.218	.269	.151	-14.0	-0.7	30-C	1
2008	HOU	MLB	28	183	16	6	0	2	12	6	34	0	0	-0.0	.226	.270	.298	.229	.272	.306	.200	-7.0	0.3	51-C	6
2009	HOU	MLB	29	236	19	10	1	3	23	10	40	1	1	-0.8	.247	.288	.344	.251	.290	.353	.220	-1.1	1.0	59-C	3

Breakout: 42%   Improve: 59%   Collapse: 17%   Attrition: 38%   Comparables: Robert Machado, Russ Gibson, Ed Fitz Gerald, Jose Molina

Designated for assignment at spring's end, the perpetual Triple-A catcher-in-waiting seemed destined for another year in the minors, having been lapped by up-and-comer Towles. Then Towles flamed out rather spectacularly, and Quintero came along and did little better. Between the two, people see the 100-point gap in batting average and think Quintero was much better, but that advantage is mostly hollow. He did earn the manager's trust, though, and that bought him time.

Drew Sutton — 2B

Bats: S   Throws: R   Height: 6' 3"   Weight: 185   Born: June 30, 1983   Age: 26

YEAR	TEAM	LVL	AGE	PA	R	2B	3B	HR	RBI	BB	SO	SB	CS	EqBRR	AVG	OBP	SLG	EqAVG	EqOBP	EqSLG	EqA	VORP	WARP	DEFENSE			
2006	SLM	A+	23	551	65	27	2	15	48	69	84	20	15	-7.7	.263	.360	.430	.208	.283	.332	.217	-27.1	0.4	116-2B	8	5-SS	3
2007	CCH	AA	24	558	81	28	1	9	53	57	86	24	5	0.0	.269	.351	.388	.217	.287	.316	.219	-28.2	-2.3	89-3B	-7	26-2B	0
2008	CCH	AA	25	606	102	39	4	20	69	76	98	20	7	2.7	.317	.408	.523	.228	.307	.385	.242	-7.2	-1.1	94-2B	-10	15-3B	0
2009	HOU	MLB	26	549	55	28	2	10	51	51	124	10	4	0.3	.221	.298	.352	.224	.300	.361	.231	-2.8	0.0	129-2B	-8		

Breakout: 26% Improve: 51% Collapse: 14% Attrition: 10%   Comparables: Chris Clapinski, Freddy Sandoval, Brooks Conrad, Darrel Deak

Sutton gave a nice enough performance, but it came from a player way too old to still be at Double-A. Sutton is willing and able to play anywhere on the field, but his range and arm are both weak; for any lengthy usage, he's limited to second base. Houston's roster moves do seem to imply a competition between him and Chris Johnson for a major league spot; Sutton has a good chance of winning that.

Miguel Tejada — SS

Bats: R   Throws: R   Height: 5' 9"   Weight: 215   Born: May 25, 1974   Age: 35

YEAR	TEAM	LVL	AGE	PA	R	2B	3B	HR	RBI	BB	SO	SB	CS	EqBRR	AVG	OBP	SLG	EqAVG	EqOBP	EqSLG	EqA	VORP	WARP	DEFENSE	
2006	BAL	MLB	32	709	99	37	0	24	100	46	79	6	2	-0.3	.330	.379	.498	.318	.371	.486	.293	66.1	6.0	148-SS	2
2007	BAL	MLB	33	568	72	19	1	18	81	41	55	2	1	-0.5	.296	.357	.442	.287	.351	.444	.275	28.2	3.1	120-SS	-2
2008	HOU	MLB	34	666	92	38	3	13	66	24	72	7	7	-0.5	.283	.314	.415	.288	.319	.427	.253	19.4	2.4	153-SS	-1
2009	HOU	MLB	35	536	61	30	2	10	63	29	60	5	3	-1.2	.288	.331	.416	.292	.333	.427	.260	23.2	2.6	126-SS	1

Breakout: 5% Improve: 37% Collapse: 27% Attrition: 16%   Comparables: Alvin Dark, Dick Groat, Frank Malzone, Cal Ripken

The trade with the Orioles for Tejada came in for some criticism on its merits, but the information that came out afterward, with Tejada getting fingered in the Mitchell report and being revealed as two years older than previously reported, just made things worse. A year later, Tejada is continuing his decline, and there's nothing in the scouting reports to seize on and expect a reversal. With a year left on his contract, he'll be a very expensive option for 2009.

J. R. Towles — C

Bats: R   Throws: R   Height: 6' 2"   Weight: 195   Born: February 11, 1984   Age: 25

YEAR	TEAM	LVL	AGE	PA	R	2B	3B	HR	RBI	BB	SO	SB	CS	EqBRR	AVG	OBP	SLG	EqAVG	EqOBP	EqSLG	EqA	VORP	WARP	DEFENSE	
2006	LEX	A	22	321	39	19	2	12	55	21	46	13	5	-1.9	.317	.382	.525	.232	.276	.383	.228	-9.2	-0.1	58-C	-1
2007	SLM	A+	23	115	14	3	2	0	11	12	15	3	5	0.0	.200	.339	.278	.152	.243	.212	.156	-12.9	-0.9	26-C	-2
2007	CCH	AA	23	257	47	12	2	11	49	23	35	9	4	0.0	.324	.425	.551	.282	.361	.480	.286	15.7	1.5	46-C	-4
2007	ROU	AAA	23	50	5	0	0	0	2	4	7	2	4	0.0	.279	.354	.279	.250	.327	.250	.198	-2.3	-0.5	12-C	-3
2007	HOU	MLB	23	44	9	5	0	1	12	3	1	0	1	-0.2	.375	.432	.575	.375	.432	.550	.323	6.1	0.6	11-C	1
2008	ROU	AAA	24	192	28	8	2	7	28	13	31	4	3	-0.7	.304	.370	.500	.267	.326	.430	.258	4.2	0.8	45-C	-1
2008	HOU	MLB	24	171	10	5	0	4	16	16	40	0	0	-0.4	.137	.250	.253	.136	.253	.265	.183	-11.9	-0.7	46-C	0
2009	HOU	MLB	25	350	36	16	1	9	38	26	72	5	3	0.1	.231	.301	.383	.235	.303	.394	.240	3.8	1.6	84-C	-1

Breakout: 38% Improve: 50% Collapse: 21% Attrition: 19%   Comparables: Chris Stewart, Dave Sax, Tom Prince, Bill Bathe

Towles' failure at the major league level was historic: there hasn't been a player with more plate appearances and a lower BABIP (.157) since 1955. On the plus side, he did resume hitting when he went to the minors; on the minus, he stopped again as soon as he was brought back up. The Astros got caught up in his hot Texas League performance of 2007 and tried to jump him from the Sally League to the majors in only a year; give him some time.

Ty Wigginton — 3B

Bats: R Throws: R Height: 6' 0" Weight: 225 Born: October 11, 1977 Age: 31

YEAR	TEAM	LVL	AGE	PA	R	2B	3B	HR	RBI	BB	SO	SB	CS	EqBRR	AVG	OBP	SLG	EqAVG	EqOBP	EqSLG	EqA	VORP	WARP	DEFENSE			
2006	TBA	MLB	28	486	55	25	1	24	79	32	97	4	3	-2.9	.275	.330	.498	.268	.326	.490	.273	20.0	0.2	38-1B	-2	38-2B	-6
2007	TBA	MLB	29	417	47	21	0	16	49	28	73	1	4	-1.8	.275	.329	.458	.276	.331	.480	.271	11.6	-0.1	36-2B	-9	29-3B	-3
2007	HOU	MLB	29	187	24	12	0	6	18	13	40	2	0	0.6	.284	.342	.462	.286	.348	.476	.283	8.5	0.7	43-3B	-3		
2008	HOU	MLB	30	429	50	22	1	23	58	32	69	4	6	-2.8	.285	.350	.526	.294	.357	.551	.295	26.2	2.2	74-3B	-4	28-LF	-3
2009	HOU	MLB	31	459	56	25	1	19	69	36	83	4	3	-1.7	.272	.335	.477	.276	.337	.490	.277	21.0	1.6	109-3B	-8		

Breakout: 16% Improve: 43% Collapse: 30% Attrition: 14%   Comparables: Sean Berry, Richie Zisk, Tim Wallach, Bob Oliver

Wigginton had a fine year, punctuated by a remarkable August in which he hit more than half (12) of his season's home-run total. Houston cut him for purely financial reasons, unwilling to go to arbitration, but buyer beware— Wigginton was especially well suited to Minute Maid Park, with an OPS almost 400 points higher at home in 2008. His versatility, occasional power, and solid production against lefties (.288/.364/.514) make him a useful player to have around on a 400-at-bat basis for another few years.

PITCHERS

Alberto Arias

Bats: R Throws: R Height: 5' 11" Weight: 155 Born: October 14, 1983 Age: 25

YEAR	TEAM	LVL	AGE	W	L	SV	G	GS	IP	H	BB	SO	HR	GB%	BABIP	STUFF	WHIP	ERA	DERA	EqH9	EqBB9	EqSO9	EqHR9	DEF	VORP	SN/WX
2006	TUL	AA	22	8	6	0	49	9	111²	102	45	83	15	53.2%	.271	-34	1.32	4.37	6.95	10.4	4.1	4.1	1.8	9	-15.3	—
2007	CSP	AAA	23	2	2	0	10	3	26¹	32	8	15	1	57.3%	.365	-15	1.52	3.76	4.88	11.6	3.0	3.8	0.4	2	1.9	—
2008	CSP	AAA	24	3	4	0	30	0	45²	50	16	41	3	57.9%	.362	-8	1.44	4.73	5.02	10.7	3.3	5.7	0.8	0	2.8	—
2008	COL	MLB	24	0	0	0	12	0	13²	12	4	5	1	67.4%	.244	-13	1.17	2.63	2.63	7.2	2.0	2.6	0.7	1	4.7	-0.00
2008	ROU	AAA	24	1	0	1	8	3	23²	21	5	15	0	71.6%	.284	-2	1.10	1.52	2.82	8.9	2.0	3.6	0.4	2	6.9	—
2008	HOU	MLB	24	1	1	0	3	2	8	11	6	8	0	70.8%	.458	7	2.13	6.75	4.91	13.5	6.1	8.6	0.0	-1	-1.0	0.37
2009	HOU	MLB	25	3	3	1	43	4	55¹	62	26	37	6	56.0%	.320	-2	1.58	4.83	5.17	10.2	3.6	5.1	0.9	-0	2.9	0.41

Breakout: 2% Improve: 13% Collapse: 60% Attrition: 16%   Comparables: Julio DePaula, Julian Tavarez, Hipolito Pichardo, Jose Rodriguez

Arias was waived by Colorado in July to clear a spot on the 40-man roster and was subsequently claimed by Houston. It was a smart move for the Astros, given the thinness of their system, to acquire a serviceable player for no cost. Arias throws a pretty good sinker, but his struggles against lefties and low endurance tend to keep him in the pen.

Brandon Backe

Bats: R Throws: R Height: 6' 0" Weight: 195 Born: April 5, 1978 Age: 31

YEAR	TEAM	LVL	AGE	W	L	SV	G	GS	IP	H	BB	SO	HR	GB%	BABIP	STUFF	WHIP	ERA	DERA	EqH9	EqBB9	EqSO9	EqHR9	DEF	VORP	SN/WX
2006	HOU	MLB	28	3	2	0	8	8	43	43	18	19	4	38.3%	.275	-4	1.42	3.77	4.40	8.8	3.3	3.6	0.8	4	10.5	1.26
2007	HOU	MLB	29	3	1	0	5	5	28²	27	11	11	4	43.4%	.245	-6	1.33	3.76	4.03	7.8	3.1	3.4	1.2	1	5.7	0.77
2008	HOU	MLB	30	9	14	0	31	31	166²	202	77	127	36	39.2%	.328	-19	1.67	6.05	5.10	11.1	3.6	6.2	1.9	-12	-8.3	1.30
2009	HOU	MLB	31	3	5	0	22	9	63¹	70	28	46	10	40.0%	.300	1	1.55	5.45	5.68	10.0	3.5	5.6	1.4	-0	-0.3	0.31

Breakout: 11% Improve: 28% Collapse: 48% Attrition: 55%   Comparables: Jim Wilson, Johnny Beazley, Paul Wagner, Harry Byrd

Backe put together a tolerable two-thirds of a season in his comeback from Tommy John surgery, carrying a 4.73 ERA into August. Then, forearm problems precipitated a late-season collapse; he gave up 13 runs in his last three innings, and twice was left in to absorb 11 runs in a game. Because he is arbitration eligible, the Astros were on the verge of letting him go, but they are too thin in the rotation to do it.

Doug Brocail

Bats: L   Throws: R   Height: 6' 5"   Weight: 250   Born: May 16, 1967   Age: 42

YEAR	TEAM	LVL	AGE	W	L	SV	G	GS	IP	H	BB	SO	HR	GB%	BABIP	STUFF	WHIP	ERA	DERA	EqH9	EqBB9	EqSO9	EqHR9	DEF	VORP	SN/WX
2006	SDN	MLB	39	2	2	0	25	0	28¹	27	8	19	1	46.7%	.299	-2	1.24	4.77	5.14	9.0	2.2	5.5	0.3	1	2.6	0.35
2007	SDN	MLB	40	5	1	0	67	0	76²	66	24	43	8	44.0%	.243	-7	1.17	3.05	4.52	7.4	2.4	4.6	0.9	6	15.9	1.78
2008	HOU	MLB	41	7	5	2	72	0	68²	63	21	64	8	42.4%	.293	8	1.22	3.93	3.59	8.2	2.4	7.4	1.1	-1	13.1	1.65
2009	HOU	MLB	42	2	2	3	42	0	49	47	16	37	5	43.0%	.280	1	1.28	3.91	4.16	8.8	2.5	5.8	1.0	-0	7.9	0.68

Breakout: 7%   Improve: 43%   Collapse: 24%   Attrition: 19%   Comparables: Ron Reed, Roberto Hernandez, Mike Timlin, Don McMahon

The wily veteran surprised a lot of people, including us, by going from the best pitching environment in baseball to one of the worst and not missing a beat. He gave Houston a good setup option and was rewarded with another one-year contract. Twenty-two years and 14 major league seasons after being drafted by the Padres, Brocail is still looking to make his first postseason appearance.

Tim Byrdak

Bats: L   Throws: L   Height: 5' 11"   Weight: 195   Born: October 31, 1973   Age: 35

YEAR	TEAM	LVL	AGE	W	L	SV	G	GS	IP	H	BB	SO	HR	GB%	BABIP	STUFF	WHIP	ERA	DERA	EqH9	EqBB9	EqSO9	EqHR9	DEF	VORP	SN/WX
2006	BAL	MLB	32	1	0	0	16	0	7	14	8	2	2	53.1%	.429	-46	3.14	12.86	9.00	16.7	10.3	2.6	2.6	-2	-5.2	-0.06
2007	TOL	AAA	33	1	0	0	17	0	24¹	22	8	30	3	42.9%	.339	1	1.23	2.59	3.68	10.6	3.3	8.2	2.0	0	4.7	—
2007	DET	MLB	33	3	0	1	39	0	45	38	26	49	3	42.3%	.310	15	1.42	3.20	3.38	7.5	4.8	8.3	0.6	-5	7.3	0.83
2008	HOU	MLB	34	2	1	0	59	0	55¹	45	29	47	10	43.4%	.240	-11	1.34	3.91	4.39	7.2	4.1	6.7	1.6	4	10.8	1.14
2009	HOU	MLB	35	2	2	2	38	0	36²	35	18	35	4	44.0%	.300	6	1.44	4.43	4.67	8.7	3.8	7.2	1.1	-0	4.3	0.33

Breakout: 24%   Improve: 47%   Collapse: 40%   Attrition: 36%   Comparables: Pedro Borbon, Tom Martin, Mickey Harris, Lance Painter

Byrdak is ideally cast as a situational lefty, in the sense that he should never be allowed to face a righty, with an OPS difference of over 500 points last year. He was released by the Tigers after suffering through a terrible spring training, and Houston, which only had one lefty in its pen (rookie Wesley Wright), was happy to take the chance on him. At 35, the journeyman is pitching contract to contract, but then, aren't we all?

Jack Cassel

Bats: R   Throws: R   Height: 6' 2"   Weight: 215   Born: August 8, 1980   Age: 28

YEAR	TEAM	LVL	AGE	W	L	SV	G	GS	IP	H	BB	SO	HR	GB%	BABIP	STUFF	WHIP	ERA	DERA	EqH9	EqBB9	EqSO9	EqHR9	DEF	VORP	SN/WX
2006	MOB	AA	25	6	3	0	12	12	78	66	18	75	3	65.2%	.292	10	1.08	2.31	5.40	9.3	2.3	5.3	0.7	3	1.6	—
2007	POR	AAA	26	7	14	0	27	24	156²	203	42	117	13	58.1%	.369	-2	1.56	3.91	5.61	11.3	2.6	4.6	1.0	-8	-0.2	—
2007	SDN	MLB	26	1	1	0	6	4	22²	30	5	11	1	43.2%	.363	-2	1.54	3.96	3.80	12.2	1.7	4.2	0.4	-1	4.3	0.78
2008	ROU	AAA	27	9	5	0	19	17	107¹	113	30	72	10	56.4%	.311	-7	1.33	3.69	4.85	10.2	2.7	4.0	1.1	4	8.5	—
2008	HOU	MLB	27	1	1	0	9	3	30¹	38	8	14	5	45.9%	.320	-18	1.52	5.64	6.14	11.4	2.1	3.7	1.5	1	-1.5	-0.17
2009	HOU	MLB	28	6	8	1	42	18	121	141	40	70	14	52.0%	.310	1	1.50	4.97	5.29	10.6	2.6	4.4	1.0	-1	4.8	1.08

Breakout: 27%   Improve: 53%   Collapse: 20%   Attrition: 15%   Comparables: Dave Eiland, Rick Lysander, Lou Pote, A.J. Sager

Cast off by San Diego last December, Cassel is a fringe righty, liable to ride the Triple-A/major league border for the next several years. He's fairly conventional, with a fastball, a slider, and a palmy changeup, pitching to contact and taking his chances with the defense. His brother is Patriots quarterback Matt Cassel.

Shawn Chacon

Bats: R   Throws: R   Height: 6' 3"   Weight: 220   Born: December 23, 1977   Age: 31

YEAR	TEAM	LVL	AGE	W	L	SV	G	GS	IP	H	BB	SO	HR	GB%	BABIP	STUFF	WHIP	ERA	DERA	EqH9	EqBB9	EqSO9	EqHR9	DEF	VORP	SN/WX
2006	NYA	MLB	28	5	3	0	17	11	63	77	36	35	11	33.9%	.313	-22	1.79	7.00	6.64	10.7	4.9	4.2	1.4	-7	-12.5	-0.02
2006	PIT	MLB	28	2	3	0	9	9	46	47	27	27	12	36.2%	.261	-18	1.61	5.48	6.13	8.0	4.6	4.8	2.1	3	-1.3	0.62
2007	PIT	MLB	29	5	4	1	64	4	96	95	48	79	9	45.9%	.317	6	1.49	3.94	3.39	7.9	3.8	6.8	0.7	-2	20.4	2.15
2008	HOU	MLB	30	2	3	0	15	15	85²	88	41	53	16	38.7%	.280	-15	1.51	5.04	5.49	9.3	3.8	5.1	1.6	4	2.1	1.28
2009	HOU	MLB	31	3	4	0	22	7	56¹	60	27	41	10	41.0%	.290	-1	1.53	5.41	5.65	9.6	3.8	5.6	1.5	-0	-0.0	0.26

Breakout: 13%   Improve: 37%   Collapse: 49%   Attrition: 47%   Comparables: Steve McCatty, Dan Petry, Tom Griffin, Paul Wagner

In mid-June, upset about being removed from the rotation, Chacon refused to meet with general manager Ed Wade and manager Cecil Cooper in Cooper's office. That led to words between Chacon and Wade before Chacon grabbed

Wade by the neck and threw him to the ground; the other players had to pull him off. Despite the Astros' desperate need in the rotation and his solid work, he was released five days later. This wasn't his first disciplinary issue, and it's telling that nobody grabbed him.

Geoff Geary

													Bats: R		Throws: R		Height: 6' 0"		Weight: 180		Born: August 26, 1976			Age: 32

YEAR	TEAM	LVL	AGE	W	L	SV	G	GS	IP	H	BB	SO	HR	GB%	BABIP	STUFF	WHIP	ERA	DERA	EqH9	EqBB9	EqSO9	EqHR9	DEF	VORP	SN/WX
2006	PHI	MLB	29	7	1	1	81	0	91¹	103	20	60	6	51.5%	.331	9	1.35	2.96	2.68	9.6	1.7	5.5	0.5	-4	27.4	1.73
2007	PHI	MLB	30	3	2	0	57	0	67¹	72	25	38	8	52.7%	.308	-11	1.44	4.41	4.73	9.0	3.0	4.9	0.9	-4	0.1	0.74
2008	HOU	MLB	31	2	3	0	55	0	64	45	28	45	3	45.7%	.233	6	1.14	2.53	3.22	6.2	3.4	5.6	0.4	5	22.1	2.05
2009	HOU	MLB	32	2	2	2	45	0	53²	57	19	35	5	48.0%	.300	-2	1.41	4.19	4.47	9.6	2.8	5.0	0.9	-0	7.1	0.55

Breakout: 8%   Improve: 18%   Collapse: 53%   Attrition: 20%   Comparables: Tom Edens, Jack Aker, Ron Taylor, Clem Labine

Geary gave the best return of the players involved in the Lidge trade, holding down a middle relief role with quiet effectiveness all year. Geary isn't flashy, mixing up four pitches while pulling off the rare fly-ball-pitcher-who-keeps-it-in-the-park act. He suffered a couple of groin pulls during the year and had off-season surgery to repair hip and abdominal muscles. As generic righty middle relievers go, Geary is reliably nontoxic, about the most you can say for this normally volatile player subgroup.

Samuel Gervacio

													Bats: R		Throws: R		Height: 5' 11"		Weight: 160		Born: January 10, 1985			Age: 24

YEAR	TEAM	LVL	AGE	W	L	SV	G	GS	IP	H	BB	SO	HR	GB%	BABIP	STUFF	WHIP	ERA	DERA	EqH9	EqBB9	EqSO9	EqHR9	DEF	VORP	SN/WX
2006	LEX	A	21	7	5	10	47	0	83¹	58	28	89	8	39.3%	.249	-24	1.03	2.60	6.35	10.1	4.6	4.7	2.5	6	-6.0	—
2007	SLM	A+	22	1	3	18	39	0	55¹	42	15	80	1	47.7%	.328	17	1.03	2.44	3.93	9.8	3.4	7.9	0.7	-5	9.3	—
2007	CCH	AA	22	3	2	0	13	0	22²	15	11	24	1	38.9%	.275	9	1.15	1.98	5.85	7.7	5.4	6.8	0.9	4	-0.6	—
2008	CCH	AA	23	2	5	5	47	0	65¹	69	26	82	8	41.7%	.379	-11	1.45	4.13	5.46	11.8	4.2	7.6	1.8	-7	0.9	—
2008	ROU	AAA	23	1	0	0	3	0	8	6	3	14	0	37.5%	.400	7	1.13	2.25	2.45	9.8	3.7	11.0	0.0	-1	2.6	—
2009	HOU	MLB	24	3	4	1	25	6	57²	60	28	52	8	43.0%	.320	11	1.54	4.99	5.24	9.5	3.8	6.9	1.2	-0	2.8	0.47

Breakout: 22%   Improve: 47%   Collapse: 16%   Attrition: 8%   Comparables: Steven Quealey, Julio Machado, Kaz Tadano, Jimmy Serrano

Gervacio has a bizarre delivery that starts out more or less conventionally and then transmogrifies midstream into a side-armed release. He uses his fastball and slider very aggressively against righties, but as with most side-armers, left-handed hitters get a good look, unburdened by the sensation that the pitch starts out behind them. Whether he can limit the damage from lefties is one question for his future. Whether his elbow can stand the torque is another.

LaTroy Hawkins

													Bats: R		Throws: R		Height: 6' 5"		Weight: 215		Born: December 21, 1972			Age: 36

YEAR	TEAM	LVL	AGE	W	L	SV	G	GS	IP	H	BB	SO	HR	GB%	BABIP	STUFF	WHIP	ERA	DERA	EqH9	EqBB9	EqSO9	EqHR9	DEF	VORP	SN/WX
2006	BAL	MLB	33	3	2	0	60	0	60¹	73	15	27	4	46.6%	.325	-12	1.46	4.48	3.62	10.3	2.3	3.5	0.6	-4	11.1	1.81
2007	COL	MLB	34	2	5	0	62	0	55¹	52	16	29	6	62.8%	.269	-10	1.23	3.42	4.19	8.4	2.3	4.5	0.8	8	15.7	0.27
2008	NYA	MLB	35	1	1	0	33	0	41	42	17	23	3	48.9%	.307	-17	1.44	5.71	6.64	8.9	3.4	4.6	0.7	6	0.6	-0.46
2008	HOU	MLB	35	2	0	1	24	0	21	11	5	25	0	40.8%	.229	21	0.76	0.43	1.71	4.7	1.7	9.0	0.0	1	10.2	1.69
2009	HOU	MLB	36	3	3	3	49	0	57	56	19	40	6	49.0%	.280	0	1.30	3.80	4.06	8.9	2.6	5.3	0.9	-0	9.6	0.83

Breakout: 16%   Improve: 29%   Collapse: 40%   Attrition: 25%   Comparables: Mike Timlin, Dave Weathers, Tim Worrell, Dick Tidrow

In Yankee Stadium, Hawkins' platoon advantage (beats right, beaten by left) was compounded by a park that worked the same way, and he wound up getting killed by the southbats. In Houston, the park helped keep those left-handers in check, but he was used carefully by Cooper as the rare ROOGY. Add in differences in league quality, and the results seem obvious, if a tad extreme. He will return to Houston in 2009. Note the BABIP for last year's Astros segment and weep for what that portends for the future.

Brian Moehler

Bats: R   Throws: R   Height: 6' 3"   Weight: 235   Born: December 31, 1971   Age: 37

YEAR	TEAM	LVL	AGE	W	L	SV	G	GS	IP	H	BB	SO	HR	GB%	BABIP	STUFF	WHIP	ERA	DERA	EqH9	EqBB9	EqSO9	EqHR9	DEF	VORP	SN/WX
2006	FLO	MLB	34	7	11	0	29	21	122	164	38	58	19	46.8%	.340	-18	1.66	6.57	5.79	11.5	2.4	3.9	1.3	-9	-15.7	0.19
2007	HOU	MLB	35	1	4	1	42	0	59²	67	17	36	8	53.9%	.304	-9	1.41	4.07	4.05	9.4	2.2	5.1	1.0	1	10.0	-0.03
2008	HOU	MLB	36	11	8	0	31	26	150	166	36	82	20	45.1%	.296	-4	1.35	4.56	4.44	9.5	1.8	4.3	1.1	0	16.2	3.26
2009	HOU	MLB	37	3	5	0	25	9	68²	84	19	35	10	46.0%	.310	-6	1.50	5.34	5.62	11.1	2.2	3.9	1.3	-0	0.2	0.34

Breakout: 4%   Improve: 33%   Collapse: 55%   Attrition: 44%   Comparables: Cal McLish, Aaron Sele, Dick Donovan, Jim Lonborg

Moehler re-signed with Houston last January after finding no interest elsewhere. He started the season pitching long relief in meaningless situations, and not very well. Then, injuries forced him into the rotation, and for a good chunk of the year, he ranked as the Astros' top starter in ERA, relying on a sinker, a cutter, a slider, a changeup, and, above all, location, rarely breaking 90. He earned himself another year, with the Astros extending Scuffy's contract in August.

Fernando Nieve

Bats: R   Throws: R   Height: 6' 0"   Weight: 195   Born: July 15, 1982   Age: 26

YEAR	TEAM	LVL	AGE	W	L	SV	G	GS	IP	H	BB	SO	HR	GB%	BABIP	STUFF	WHIP	ERA	DERA	EqH9	EqBB9	EqSO9	EqHR9	DEF	VORP	SN/WX
2006	HOU	MLB	23	3	3	0	40	11	96¹	87	41	70	18	42.3%	.254	-10	1.33	4.21	4.86	7.9	3.4	6.0	1.5	10	18.7	1.81
2007	ROU	AAA	24	1	3	0	5	5	21²	30	15	13	1	30.3%	.397	-15	2.07	6.22	6.86	14.2	6.9	3.7	0.5	-4	-2.8	—
2008	ROU	AAA	25	2	5	6	36	7	72¹	87	27	63	13	39.8%	.341	-33	1.58	5.73	7.01	11.9	3.5	5.2	1.9	-1	-10.9	—
2008	HOU	MLB	25	0	1	0	11	0	10²	17	2	12	2	33.3%	.455	9	1.78	8.41	5.40	15.3	1.8	9.0	1.8	-3	-3.3	-0.33
2009	HOU	MLB	26	2	4	1	34	5	54¹	62	24	42	9	41.0%	.320	1	1.58	5.58	5.81	10.4	3.5	6.0	1.4	-0	-1.1	0.08

Breakout: 23%   Improve: 60%   Collapse: 17%   Attrition: 11%   Comparables: Manny Barrios, Luis Vizcaino, Santos Hernandez, Marino Salas

Nieve missed most of 2007 following Tommy John surgery and last year was diagnosed with a deviated septum that caused breathing problems. The Astros decided that this hard thrower with a fastball that reaches the mid-90s would follow his nose to the pen. Nieve struggled through most of the season, getting pummeled at Houston in a May call-up and in Round Rock (6.79 ERA in mid-July). Something changed about then; he started getting a lot more grounders, finished up at Triple-A with a 3.05 ERA over the last six weeks, and contributed a 4.70 to Houston in September. Left-handed hitters went 7-for-11 off him in the majors, too small a sample to be truly frightening, yet a decisive enough pounding to provoke worries that something in his approach to them is fatally faulty.

Bud Norris

Bats: R   Throws: R   Height: 6' 0"   Weight: 195   Born: March 2, 1985   Age: 24

YEAR	TEAM	LVL	AGE	W	L	SV	G	GS	IP	H	BB	SO	HR	GB%	BABIP	STUFF	WHIP	ERA	DERA	EqH9	EqBB9	EqSO9	EqHR9	DEF	VORP	SN/WX
2006	TCV	A-	21	2	0	2	15	3	38²	28	13	46	1	44.6%	.305	-6	1.07	3.77	9.46	11.7	5.6	5.3	1.7	0	-13.9	—
2007	LEX	A	22	2	8	0	22	22	96²	85	41	117	8	49.2%	.321	-15	1.30	4.75	8.36	11.7	5.5	5.9	1.8	-1	-25.8	—
2008	CCH	AA	23	3	8	0	19	19	80	89	31	84	8	50.0%	.370	-11	1.50	4.05	5.50	12.2	4.2	6.2	1.6	-6	0.8	—
2009	HOU	MLB	24	5	9	0	30	18	108	128	58	82	16	47.0%	.330	5	1.72	6.13	6.45	10.8	4.2	5.8	1.3	-1	-9.8	-0.27

Breakout: 25%   Improve: 62%   Collapse: 11%   Attrition: 17%   Comparables: Kip Yaughn, Steven Wolf, Wascar Serrano, Glen Cook

Norris's small size and the effort in his delivery suggest he won't hold up as starter, and as if to prove the point, he did go down with some elbow trouble last year. He was a reliever in the Arizona Fall League and excelled—his fastball, normally 92-95 mph, was hitting 97. While his curve is a plus pitch, his changeup is best left to theory. The Astros are strongly considering making that bullpen move a permanent one.

Roy Oswalt

Bats: R   Throws: R   Height: 6' 0"   Weight: 185   Born: August 29, 1977   Age: 31

YEAR	TEAM	LVL	AGE	W	L	SV	G	GS	IP	H	BB	SO	HR	GB%	BABIP	STUFF	WHIP	ERA	DERA	EqH9	EqBB9	EqSO9	EqHR9	DEF	VORP	SN/WX
2006	HOU	MLB	28	15	8	0	33	32	220²	220	38	166	18	50.4%	.310	28	1.17	2.98	3.03	9.1	1.4	6.4	0.7	3	71.9	7.47
2007	HOU	MLB	29	14	7	0	33	32	212	221	60	154	14	54.4%	.311	27	1.33	3.18	2.89	8.7	2.2	6.0	0.5	-6	59.0	6.70
2008	HOU	MLB	30	17	10	0	32	32	208²	199	47	165	23	51.6%	.293	18	1.18	3.54	4.06	8.5	1.7	6.3	1.0	9	43.3	5.73
2009	HOU	MLB	31	12	9	0	29	29	193	191	48	146	18	51.0%	.290	22	1.23	3.59	3.83	9.0	2.0	5.8	0.8	-1	36.7	5.53

Breakout: 6%   Improve: 31%   Collapse: 32%   Attrition: 11%   Comparables: Frank Lary, Doug Drabek, Steve Rogers, Andy Ashby

When Oswalt went on the disabled list in July with a herniated disk and a strained hip adductor, his ERA was an un-Oswaltian 4.56. After he came back, it was 2.24, including a 32-inning scoreless streak. Among his other qualities (95 mph fastball, a curve in the 70s, control), Oswalt has one of the fastest slide steps in baseball, with only two stolen-base attempts against him all season. He's had problems for several years with his hip/groin/lower back area; he's pitched through them before, and we shouldn't expect either trend to change in the near future.

Felipe Paulino

Bats: R　Throws: R　Height: 6' 2"　Weight: 180　Born: October 5, 1983　Age: 25

YEAR	TEAM	LVL	AGE	W	L	SV	G	GS	IP	H	BB	SO	HR	GB%	BABIP	STUFF	WHIP	ERA	DERA	EqH9	EqBB9	EqSO9	EqHR9	DEF	VORP	SN/WX
2006	SLM	A+	22	9	7	0	27	26	126	119	59	91	13	45.2%	.285	-46	1.41	4.36	7.90	12.2	5.4	3.5	2.4	2	-27.9	—
2007	CCH	AA	23	6	9	0	22	21	112	103	49	110	6	39.0%	.307	3	1.36	3.62	5.96	10.0	4.5	5.6	0.9	-2	-4.2	—
2007	HOU	MLB	23	2	1	0	5	3	19	22	7	11	5	49.3%	.283	-12	1.53	7.11	6.98	9.3	2.8	4.7	2.3	1	-2.4	0.27
2009	HOU	MLB	25	1	2	0	14	2	29	30	15	23	4	41.0%	.300	4	1.56	5.01	5.27	9.4	4.2	6.1	1.1	-0	1.6	0.19

Breakout: 49%　Improve: 63%　Collapse: 28%　Attrition: 50%　　　　Comparables: Jesus Colome, Don Cooper, Franklyn German, Calvin Maduro

Paulino faced four batters in 2008 and then became an episode of *House*, presenting with a pinched nerve, then elbow tightness, and then shoulder bursitis. He never pitched again. Before his arm trouble, his fastball could hit 100 mph, although it tended to come in flat and high (see his translated home-run rates for what happened next). After his arm trouble, well, who knows how hard he'll throw? He didn't pitch this winter, but the Astros believe he'll be fine for the spring.

Wandy Rodriguez

Bats: S　Throws: L　Height: 5' 11"　Weight: 160　Born: January 18, 1979　Age: 30

YEAR	TEAM	LVL	AGE	W	L	SV	G	GS	IP	H	BB	SO	HR	GB%	BABIP	STUFF	WHIP	ERA	DERA	EqH9	EqBB9	EqSO9	EqHR9	DEF	VORP	SN/WX
2006	ROU	AAA	27	2	2	0	5	5	26¹	32	13	13	2	43.6%	.333	-26	1.72	6.90	8.51	12.9	4.8	2.6	1.1	-1	-7.9	—
2006	HOU	MLB	27	9	10	0	30	24	135²	154	63	98	17	47.5%	.329	-1	1.60	5.64	5.09	10.4	3.7	6.0	1.0	-9	-5.0	0.88
2007	HOU	MLB	28	9	13	0	31	31	182²	179	62	158	22	43.6%	.299	19	1.32	4.58	4.23	8.2	2.6	7.2	1.0	-6	18.2	4.01
2008	HOU	MLB	29	9	7	0	25	25	137¹	136	44	131	14	41.3%	.316	23	1.31	3.54	3.95	8.9	2.4	7.6	0.9	-1	22.0	3.53
2009	HOU	MLB	30	7	8	1	30	19	123²	124	44	104	15	45.0%	.300	16	1.35	4.32	4.57	9.1	2.8	6.5	1.1	-1	14.8	2.35

Breakout: 24%　Improve: 51%　Collapse: 18%　Attrition: 23%　　　　Comparables: Denny Lemaster, Paul LaPalme, Billy O'Dell, Chris Hammond

Rodriguez continued to improve in everything but health, making two trips to the DL, one for a strained groin and one for an oblique, injuries that cost him about 10 starts. Wandy has a sneaky fastball; it's only about 90, but has late movement. He has an unusually small platoon split for a lefty, which last year was substantially backward; that probably has something to do with his by now well-known home/road splits, surprisingly better at home in front of the Crawford Boxes. He's not going to match Oswalt for innings, but is a very nice guy to have behind Oswalt in your rotation. The problem is that they need better than Moehler and Backe to round out the front four of a contender's rotation.

Chris Sampson

Bats: R　Throws: R　Height: 6' 1"　Weight: 190　Born: May 23, 1978　Age: 31

YEAR	TEAM	LVL	AGE	W	L	SV	G	GS	IP	H	BB	SO	HR	GB%	BABIP	STUFF	WHIP	ERA	DERA	EqH9	EqBB9	EqSO9	EqHR9	DEF	VORP	SN/WX
2006	ROU	AAA	28	12	3	4	27	18	125	110	14	68	12	59.9%	.249	-15	0.99	2.52	5.88	8.9	1.2	3.0	1.3	18	-3.8	—
2006	HOU	MLB	28	2	1	0	12	3	34	25	5	15	3	55.0%	.212	-4	0.88	2.12	5.35	6.4	1.1	3.7	0.8	11	12.8	1.36
2007	HOU	MLB	29	7	8	0	24	19	121²	138	30	51	20	48.2%	.294	-14	1.38	4.59	4.85	9.5	1.9	3.7	1.4	8	16.0	2.23
2008	HOU	MLB	30	6	4	0	54	11	117¹	118	23	61	8	57.4%	.293	3	1.20	4.22	3.87	9.0	1.5	4.3	0.6	-6	14.4	2.94
2009	HOU	MLB	31	4	4	1	37	7	74²	81	19	36	9	52.0%	.290	-5	1.34	4.29	4.58	9.9	2.0	3.7	1.1	-0	9.8	1.09

Breakout: 19%　Improve: 42%　Collapse: 37%　Attrition: 27%　　　　Comparables: Brian Lawrence, Jerry Staley, Mark Petkovsek, Scott Terry

Sampson won a spring training battle with Woody Williams for the fifth starter's job, forcing the latter into retirement, but however mighty that wee feat, Sampson soon found his Delilah. An ERA hovering around 6.00 at the end of May sheared him from the rotation. Bumped to the bullpen, Sampson was much better, as he has been in virtually all prior years—his career ERA as a starter is 4.63, but shrinks to 3.06 in 88⅓ career relief innings, the latter of which is notable for just one unintentional walk per nine innings. He tore an elbow tendon in September and may not recover from the surgery by Opening Day.

Polin Trinidad

									Bats: L		Throws: L		Height: 6' 2"		Weight: 170		Born: November 19, 1984		Age: 24	

YEAR	TEAM	LVL	AGE	W	L	SV	G	GS	IP	H	BB	SO	HR	GB%	BABIP	STUFF	WHIP	ERA	DERA	EqH9	EqBB9	EqSO9	EqHR9	DEF	VORP	SN/WX
2007	LEX	A	22	6	8	0	23	23	131¹	118	35	120	16	45.6%	.290	-37	1.17	4.18	7.34	11.4	3.7	4.1	2.5	8	-22.0	—
2007	SLM	A+	22	2	1	0	4	4	25²	23	3	23	4	39.3%	.250	-4	1.01	2.80	6.75	11.5	2.0	4.4	3.2	3	-2.9	—
2008	SLM	A+	23	4	2	0	10	10	62	46	11	34	2	46.7%	.229	2	0.92	2.32	4.22	7.4	2.0	2.7	0.6	4	9.2	—
2008	CCH	AA	23	6	5	0	18	18	107¹	109	21	75	13	40.5%	.294	-20	1.21	3.61	5.94	9.7	2.2	3.6	1.7	7	-3.9	—
2009	HOU	MLB	24	5	9	0	32	19	119¹	145	41	65	22	43.0%	.300	-1	1.55	5.96	6.21	11.0	2.7	4.2	1.7	-1	-7.1	0.03

Breakout: 6%   Improve: 23%   Collapse: 39%   Attrition: 21%   Comparables: Travis Blackley, Mike Farrell, Doug Simons, Pedro Martinez

Another prospect too old for his leagues, Trinidad is an extreme finesse pitcher who lives off his changeup. He also has a consistent history of reverse splits, doing a fair bit worse against left-handed hitters and allowing fewer hits than you'd expect. He'll float the occasional change for a home run. His future is likely to be in the bullpen, the Fiddler's Green of Left-Handed Persons.

Jose Valverde

									Bats: R		Throws: R		Height: 6' 4"		Weight: 255		Born: July 24, 1979		Age: 29	

YEAR	TEAM	LVL	AGE	W	L	SV	G	GS	IP	H	BB	SO	HR	GB%	BABIP	STUFF	WHIP	ERA	DERA	EqH9	EqBB9	EqSO9	EqHR9	DEF	VORP	SN/WX
2006	ARI	MLB	26	2	3	18	44	0	49¹	50	22	69	6	35.4%	.367	22	1.46	5.84	4.09	9.1	3.4	10.5	0.9	-6	2.0	0.87
2007	ARI	MLB	27	1	4	47	65	0	64¹	46	26	78	7	36.7%	.260	24	1.12	2.66	2.78	6.4	3.2	9.6	0.8	2	21.7	4.23
2008	HOU	MLB	28	6	3	44	74	0	72	62	23	83	10	39.5%	.284	15	1.18	3.38	3.19	7.6	2.5	8.8	1.2	-1	17.1	2.88
2009	HOU	MLB	29	3	5	25	51	0	57	49	22	62	6	40.0%	.290	19	1.25	3.56	3.75	7.8	3.1	8.3	1.0	-0	11.7	1.74

Breakout: 23%   Improve: 48%   Collapse: 33%   Attrition: 17%   Comparables: Todd Worrell, Lee Smith, Dick Radatz, Dan Wheeler

Valverde's year started poorly, with three blown saves in the first three weeks and an ERA over 12.00 as Cooper was figuring out Bullpen Usage 101. Concurrently, Valverde went to the videotape and made some mechanical adjustments. From July on, he was almost untouchable, with a stretch of 15 straight games with a save, helping him tie Billy Wagner for a team-record 44. A free agent after this season, he'll very likely be moved at the deadline should Houston's season start slowly.

Randy Wolf

									Bats: L		Throws: L		Height: 5' 10"		Weight: 200		Born: August 22, 1976		Age: 32	

YEAR	TEAM	LVL	AGE	W	L	SV	G	GS	IP	H	BB	SO	HR	GB%	BABIP	STUFF	WHIP	ERA	DERA	EqH9	EqBB9	EqSO9	EqHR9	DEF	VORP	SN/WX
2006	PHI	MLB	29	4	0	0	12	12	56²	63	33	44	13	39.0%	.305	-6	1.69	5.56	4.71	9.3	4.6	6.3	1.7	-3	0.9	0.97
2007	LAN	MLB	30	9	6	0	18	18	102²	110	39	94	10	42.9%	.334	24	1.45	4.73	3.94	9.0	2.9	7.5	0.8	-4	11.7	1.55
2008	SDN	MLB	31	6	10	0	21	21	119²	123	47	105	14	41.2%	.321	11	1.42	4.74	5.43	9.3	3.1	7.0	1.1	1	3.7	2.34
2008	HOU	MLB	31	6	2	0	12	12	70²	68	24	57	7	40.7%	.300	17	1.30	3.56	3.73	8.6	2.6	6.4	0.9	-1	13.9	1.97
2009	HOU	MLB	32	7	8	0	23	23	133	135	52	108	17	42.0%	.300	18	1.40	4.50	4.72	9.2	3.1	6.2	1.2	-1	14.1	2.46

Breakout: 12%   Improve: 56%   Collapse: 15%   Attrition: 13%   Comparables: Vida Blue, Ted Lilly, Gary Peters, Shane Rawley

On the face of it, the decision to get another Phillie whom Wade remembered fondly looked like a bad deal for the Astros, as they picked Wolf up at the trade deadline. But then they went 10-2 in his starts as they made their wild-card run. He made 30 starts for the first time in five years, which entitled him to be the bearer of the coveted "Temporarily Healthy Free Agent" card.

Wesley Wright

									Bats: R		Throws: L		Height: 5' 11"		Weight: 160		Born: January 28, 1985		Age: 24	

YEAR	TEAM	LVL	AGE	W	L	SV	G	GS	IP	H	BB	SO	HR	GB%	BABIP	STUFF	WHIP	ERA	DERA	EqH9	EqBB9	EqSO9	EqHR9	DEF	VORP	SN/WX
2006	VRO	A+	21	3	3	0	26	0	42	29	23	51	0	42.4%	.302	13	1.24	1.50	3.11	7.9	6.5	6.2	0.5	-4	10.4	—
2006	JAX	AA	21	1	1	1	15	0	21	14	11	28	2	42.9%	.273	11	1.19	4.71	6.52	8.8	5.1	7.9	1.9	-3	-2.0	—
2007	JAX	AA	22	6	2	2	30	1	61¹	45	31	68	4	47.8%	.275	2	1.24	2.50	4.60	8.0	4.8	6.0	1.1	3	6.5	—
2007	LVG	AAA	22	1	2	0	14	1	16²	28	18	18	4	41.1%	.511	-9	2.75	9.16	8.40	16.8	10.8	7.2	2.4	-7	-4.7	—
2008	HOU	MLB	23	4	3	1	71	0	55²	45	34	57	8	42.6%	.255	2	1.42	5.01	5.77	7.0	4.5	7.8	1.2	4	0.9	0.78
2009	HOU	MLB	24	2	2	1	30	2	35¹	32	19	32	4	43.0%	.280	8	1.44	4.21	4.46	8.2	4.2	7.0	1.0	-0	5.7	0.47

Breakout: 23%   Improve: 52%   Collapse: 31%   Attrition: 45%   Comparables: Tug McGraw, Dick LeMay, Jung Bong, Steve Blass

Wright is a Rule 5 pick from the Dodgers, who were afraid this would happen when they left him off their roster a year ago. As usual with Rule 5-ers, Wright was used carefully, only being allowed to go more than one inning eight times. He excelled as a lefty specialist, as expected; he also held right-handers to just a .220 batting average, but 14 of the 26 hits went for extra bases (.237 isso); he also walked righties twice as often. Now that he's survived the Prisoner of Rule 5 ordeal, he can get back to trying to conquer his control and figuring out what he wants to do with the rest of his life.

LINEOUTS

Hitters

PLAYER	TEAM	LVL	AGE	PA	R	2B	3B	HR	RBI	BB	SO	SB-CS	EqBRR	AVG/OBP/SLG	EqAVG/EqOBP/EqSLG	EqA	VORP	WARP
3B J. Castillo	SFN	MLB	27	420	42	28	4	6	35	25	71	2-2	-3.4	.244/.290/.381	.246/.295/.391	.234	-5.0	-0.6
	HOU	MLB	27	35	4	1	0	0	2	2	10	0-0	-0.3	.281/.314/.313	.281/.314/.312	.227	-0.7	0.3
1B P. Disher	TCV	A-	23	318	40	20	3	13	56	33	71	1-0	-1.6	.304/.381/.536	.188/.248/.338	.199	-41.2	-4.5
3B D. Flores	TCV	A-	21	236	34	17	0	11	37	12	35	5-0	1.6	.266/.319/.495	.192/.230/.375	.203	-28.1	-3.1
OF E. Iorg	CCH	AA	25	493	53	21	5	11	59	23	112	21-9	-3.5	.268/.308/.407	.194/.228/.310	.182	-43.0	-4.0
SS T. Manzella	CCH	AA	25	249	27	11	5	4	34	17	35	4-4	-3.4	.299/.346/.446	.217/.259/.335	.206	-14.2	-1.8
	ROU	AAA	25	247	19	15	1	0	15	17	39	0-4	-2.7	.219/.273/.294	.186/.233/.247	.148	-27.7	-1.2
SS E. Maysonet	ROU	AAA	26	466	59	24	1	6	34	44	70	4-3	1.7	.271/.343/.379	.225/.290/.314	.214	-22.2	-1.4
CF Y. Ramirez	ROU	AAA	23	457	50	23	3	12	52	11	65	19-9	-2.0	.231/.254/.382	.204/.224/.328	.191	-37.2	-1.0
UT M. Saccomanno	ROU	AAA	28	571	83	33	2	27	84	35	94	4-3	-1.5	.297/.339/.521	.231/.268/.399	.228	-15.1	-2.7
1B J. Van Ostrand	SLM	A+	23	406	41	28	1	7	64	30	45	1-3	-2.6	.292/.356/.433	.253/.304/.382	.238	-4.0	-2.0

You can find **Jose Castillo**'s picture in *Poor Richard's Almanac* immediately under the maxim "Necessity never made a good bargain" and just above the more obscure "There's not a lot of upside in snagging castoffs from the Pirates and Giants." The Nationals signed him to a minor league contract in December. ⊘ **Phil Disher**, a 15th-round pick in the 2008 draft, had as much power as any other Astros draftee—and almost no other baseball skill. ⊘ **David Flores** was a 2008 18th-round pick from Sacramento State; he's a glove-first defender who opened some scout's eyes with good performances against big competition. ⊘ Speedy center fielder **Josh Flores** missed the season after slipping on a curb and blowing out his knee last winter. His bat wasn't very good to begin with, and if his speed is at all compromised after the injury … but let us not think such thoughts; it's a bad time for anyone to be out of work. ⊘ **Eli Iorg** returned from the torn elbow ligament in 2007. If ever they developed a surgery for pitch recognition (Max Bishop surgery?), he'd be first in line. ⊘ **Thomas Manzella** fields like a shortstop, but hits like a pitcher. His glove is so good he still might make it to the big leagues on defense alone. ⊘ **Edwin Maysonet** is a minor league utility infielder; as a résumé item, that's right up there with "Atention to detale." ⊘ Although **Yordany Ramirez** is one of the top defensive center fielders in baseball, his bat will keep him in the minors. ⊘ An old corner hitter with some useful power, **Mark Saccomanno** could be a surprise contender for the third-base job this spring—not that he'd be very good at it. ⊘ **James Van Ostrand** was an old-for-his-leagues, slow Canadian Olympic player. On the bright side, he's the best badminton player in baseball.

Pitchers

PLAYER	TEAM	LVL	AGE	W	L	SV	IP	H	BB	SO	HR	GB%	BABIP	STUFF	WHIP	ERA	DERA	EqH9	EqBB9	EqSO9	EqHR9	DEF	VORP
D. Arguello*	SLM	A+	23	10	6	0	142	119	69	90	5	58.6%	.278	-5	1.32	3.30	5.54	9.2	5.0	3.4	0.7	8	0.9
D. Borkowski	ROU	AAA	31	2	2	2	402	40	7	26	3	48.1%	.301	-12	1.15	2.43	4.19	9.5	1.9	3.7	0.9	3	6.1
	HOU	MLB	31	0	2	0	36	54	14	24	9	42.6%	.369	-26	1.89	7.50	5.05	13.4	3.0	5.3	2.3	-8	-7.6
R. Hernandez	ROU	AAA	30	8	8	0	1242	120	43	95	18	39.9%	.286	-21	1.31	4.91	6.79	9.4	3.2	4.5	1.6	10	-15.8
	HOU	MLB	30	0	3	0	191	32	11	15	4	41.7%	.418	-5	2.22	8.39	5.21	15.2	4.3	6.2	1.9	-7	-6.9
J. Holloway*	TCV	A-	19	0	5	0	482	48	27	37	2	61.6%	.331	-15	1.54	4.07	8.93	12.7	7.4	2.5	1.6	0	-14.9
B. James	CCH	AA	24	6	6	0	93	107	35	45	9	57.2%	.323	-37	1.53	4.45	7.02	11.5	4.0	2.2	1.5	4	-13.4
J. Lyles	GRV	Rk	17	3	3	0	492	44	10	64	4	48.9%	.320	-7	1.09	3.98	8.52	12.3	3.7	4.6	2.3	0	-14.0
C. Paronto	ROU	AAA	32	0	2	3	522	61	14	57	2	57.0%	.391	9	1.42	3.07	2.19	12.0	2.6	6.9	0.5	-10	18.7
	HOU	MLB	32	0	1	0	101	11	2	4	2	45.7%	.281	-17	1.26	4.37	3.72	10.2	1.9	3.7	1.9	0	1.5
R. Seaton	GRV	Rk	18	0	0	0	4	8	2	4	1	41.2%	.438	-62	2.50	13.50	27.00	27.0	8.1	2.7	5.4	0	-7.8

A Nicaraguan player who first signed with the Astros as a 17-year-old in 2001, **Douglas Arguello** saw his career jumped forward with the development of a good sinker. He has big-league relief possibilities. ⊘ Though he struggled in his major league outings, **Dave Borkowski** pitched well enough in Triple-A to convince the Phillies to give him a shot this year. ⊘ And now, the end is near, and so **Runelvys Hernandez** faces the final curtain ... ⊘ **Jarred Holloway**, a 10th-round pick, is a big lefty with a good fastball and curve; he hasn't been able to control his pitches enough for success in college, let alone the pros. ⊘ **Brad James** enjoyed tremendous defensive support rising through the low minors, masking his inability to miss bats; they certainly didn't miss last year. ⊘ A first-round high school pitcher, **Jordan Lyles** is a classically tall, thin pitcher who can be projected to fill out and add oomph to his fastball. ⊘ A big guy who doesn't throw like one, **Chad Paronto** keeps riding the unlit nightmare highways that thread through the abandoned wastes that lie between the majors and Triple-A. ⊘ A third-round pick from the Houston area and the valedictorian of his high school, **Rod Seaton** is a projectable tall guy with a good fastball. He almost certainly would have headed to college had the team that drafted him not been the Astros.

MANAGER: CECIL COOPER

YEAR	TEAM	W-L	Pythag +/−	Avg PC	100+ P	120+ P	QS	BQS	REL	REL w Zero R	IBB	Subs	PH	PH Avg	PH HR	SB2	CS2	SB3	CS3	SAC Att	SAC %	POS SAC	Squeeze	Swing	In Play
2007	HOU	15-16	0	92.2	10	0	16	0	88	57	14	24	60	.265	0	11	5	2	1	16	81.2%	9	0	20	12
2008	HOU	86-75	9	90.0	45	1	67	7	488	325	53	69	252	.233	7	103	46	10	5	90	63.3%	32	2	125	92

Inflexible managing tends to elicit complaints about inflexible managers, but it often stems from suspect roster construction. It's easy for an outsider to insist that a manager "do something," but it's more difficult for the man in the dugout to determine whether a viable alternative exists in a club featuring few moving parts and even fewer worthy farmhands. In his first full year at the helm, Cooper found himself burdened with an aged, shallow roster, a meddlesome owner, and a GM who perpetrated his own managerial miscues. Despite occasionally strained media relations, Cooper's on-field performance was serviceable, if not inspiring. He featured the second-quickest hook among full-season NL managers, a strategy well suited to a team with the league's second-best WXRL and a comparatively weak starting staff. In general, Cooper erred on the side of inaction, but he did permit his runners to run—perhaps too often, as the 'Stros finished with one of the league's lowest stolen-base success rates. He also allowed his most prolific thief, Michael Bourn, to steal more at-bats in the leadoff slot than the outfielder merited. Cooper's off-season emphasis on pitching, to the exclusion of the team's even more problematic offense, betrays a weakness in evaluating needs, but the Astros pay him to reanimate the stiffs, not to disinter them.

Kansas City Royals

When Dayton Moore was hired as the Royals' general manager in the middle of the 2006 season, owner David Glass promised him complete autonomy and sufficient resources to execute the monumental task that lay ahead. Such talk, however, is as cheap as one of the budget warehouses that helped Glass earn a fortune. Judgment was rightfully reserved on Kansas City's supposed new leaf, as no Royals fan could put full faith and credit into the regime until seeing simultaneous proof of both divestiture and investment from above.

Nearly three years later, that proof has been obtained. Kansas City improved by six wins last year, the third straight season in which the club rose by at least six victories after crashing to the bottom with a third straight 100-loss campaign in 2005. But even more than on the field, the proof can be found on the bottom line, in the money that the Royals have become willing to spend.

The most visible sign of the paradigm shift on the plains is the team's expanded interest in free agents. It spent $55 million on Gil Meche before 2007 and $36 million on Jose Guillen before 2008, the largest contracts in each signing period handed out by any AL Central team. The financial commitment took a new direction this past offseason, as for the first time in recent memory, the Royals picked up the phone when teams called looking to dump salary, and aggressively moved to animate their moribund offense. While the two key trades made by Moore this winter are a mixed bag from a baseball standpoint, what cannot be questioned is the decision to pay the price for improvement (real or perceived) that each represented. In both deals, the Royals surrendered a reliever who is not yet arbitration-

eligible for a more expensive player—Mike Jacobs, whose gaudy homer total earned him a sizable chunk of change in arbitration, and Coco Crisp, who is guaranteed $5.75 million this season with an $8 million 2010 option. Those swaps were followed by Glass's announcement that payroll would increase by 20 percent in 2009 to a team-record $70 million, a hike made while most squads were tightening belts and selling parts to weather the recession.

While these transactions reveal a fresh financial outlook, a more important bellwether of change in Kansas City is the investment that, even should it prove sound, will not produce dividends for years. The only path to sustainable success for major league teams is opened on just two days a year in early June, and the Royals were presented with a critical opportunity to strike down that path last season, for they held three of the top 50 picks in the draft.

Kansas City started with a particularly bold stroke, using the third selection on Scott Boras client Eric Hosmer, the top high school hitter available, and then paying him $6 million to sign—$3 million above the MLB-recommended slot bonus. This was a far cry from two years earlier, when the team settled on Luke Hochevar with the first overall pick for $3.5 million. For the first time, the Royals then proceeded to spend big on securing premium talent in the later rounds. The best example of that new philosophy was the decision to snatch high school righty Tim Melville in the fourth; last year, the youngster was projected as a possibility for the Royals' *first* pick before slipping due to a subpar senior season and signability concern. Kansas City gave Melville $1.25 million to go pro, nearly $1 million above slot,

---

ROYALS PROSPECTUS

2008 record: 75-87; Fourth place in AL Central

Pythagenport record: 72-90

Runs scored per game: 4.27 (12th in AL)

Runs allowed per game: 4.86 (10th in AL)

Team EqA: .246 (13th in AL)

2007 Batters Age: 28.3 (6th-youngest in AL)

2007 Pitchers Age: 28.1 (5th-youngest in AL)

Ballpark: Kauffman Stadium; Slight hitter's park; Park Factor of 1.013

2008: Their record improves for the third straight season, but the underlying performance fails to go along for the ride.

2009: If the Royals don't develop and adhere to a coherent plan soon, even a federal bailout won't save DMGM.

adding another high-ceiling arm to a system now flush with an enviable collection of such commodities in the low minors.

All told, the Royals signed four players who were ranked among the top 50 amateur talents by Baseball Prospectus (no other team collected as many) and inked 32 of their selections for a total of $11.1 million, more bonus money than any team has ever distributed to its draft picks. Such expenditures alone do not guarantee a successful draft, but it does show that Moore is making good on his commitment to create a farm system that can produce the raw material needed for a perennial contender. Kansas City offered further validation of this promise in November by hiring Mike Arbuckle, the executive largely responsible for drafting the Phillies' championship core.

The results of the 2008 draft further emphasized that the Royals have entered a Brave new world—literally. It's no secret that Moore has targeted many of the players whom he helped draft and develop while with Atlanta (at the major league level, those include Tony Pena Jr., Brayan Pena, Kyle Davies, and Horacio Ramirez), and he carried along his former team's draft philosophy on his Midwestern migration. That philosophy favors high-ceiling players over those who are safer bets, which translates to a rule of *preps über alles*. Eight out of the first nine Royals picks last year came from high school, and six of the first seven the year before that. Compare this imbalance with the two Kansas City drafts before Moore took over: in 2006, 11 of the first 13 picks were from college, and the year before, 12 of the first 16. Players drafted out of high school are historically less likely to make the majors than collegians, so the last two Junes represent an extremely high-risk/high-reward proposition for the future of the franchise.

The money the Royals have spent on free agency, trades, the draft, and international talent (increasing a small footprint in Latin America) shows that Kansas City has emerged at long last from behind the great facade of competitive imbalance that for so long was used to hide the team's embarrassing effort and poor execution. What the Royals' late economic resurgence also reflects, in addition to the continual crumbling of the small-market lie, is the rising tide of cash that has lifted all major league boats. The recent economic downturn has stemmed that tide somewhat, but baseball is still flourishing as it never has in the past, with record revenues of $6.5 billion in 2008. For the Royals, this means record revenue sharing, and Glass has at last committed to consistently putting a healthy portion of his team's profit into the resuscitation of a franchise that has been continually in intensive care on his watch.

Could the spending help bring the Royals back to contention in the here and now, several years before their lower-level talent is ready to emerge? The weakened state of their AL Central peers has made that a legitimate question. Last season began with the division purportedly poised to serve as a battleground for two titans, but the swift overthrow of each has transformed the competitive landscape. Factor in reigning champ Chicago's decision to sell off veteran pieces and the Twins' perennially soft lineup, and as it stands now, no team in the Central has a clear path toward a 90-win season, meaning that anyone—yes, Virginia, even the Royals—has a chance to capture the flag.

While spending money is important, it is, of course, wise spending that brings division titles, especially in a division with no big-market giant. Heading into last offseason, the Royals had done a shrewd job of carefully apportioning funds for the pitching staff, which has improved drastically in the last two years: Kansas City's runs allowed dropped from 978 to 778 in 2007, then kept that weight off last year. The huge commitment to Gil Meche has proven to be an excellent investment, but the smaller sums used to completely transform the bullpen from a historic calamity into a core strength have stood out as Moore's strongest work. Kansas City relievers added exactly 10.4 wins above replacement level (WXRL) in each of the past two seasons. In the eight years before that, they topped out at 2.7 WXRL in 2001 and were a combined 4.2 wins *below* replacement level, thanks in large part to the worst single-season WXRL of all time, -7.7, in 1999. If Adjusted Runs Prevented is your favorite flavor, Royals' firemen combined for 72.3 from 2007 to '08, after racking up an absolutely stunning -263.5 from 1999 to '06.

Finding relief was therefore a daunting task, yet Moore did so with relative ease and at relatively low cost. After arriving in 2006, he took a stick of dynamite to what he'd inherited, dealing relievers Mike MacDougal, Ambiorix Burgos, Elmer Dessens, Andy Sisco, Jeremy Affeldt, and Denny Bautista to beef up the farm system (Daniel Cortes and Julio Pimentel), add a quality starter (Brian Bannister), and snag two first basemen (Ryan Shealy and Ross Gload). Among the departed, only Affeldt has pitched well. In 2007, Moore traded Octavio Dotel to the Braves for another starter, Kyle Davies, then picked up top prep lefty Mike Montgomery in the draft as compensation after the departure of one-year hire David Riske. The team's two best relievers last year, Joakim Soria and Ramon Ramirez, were acquired in the 2006 Rule 5 draft and a March 2008 trade for a player to be named later, respectively. Last May, Soria signed a three-year deal that includes club options stretching two years into free agency, a key first step toward locking up the club's young core talent, while Ramirez was flipped for Coco Crisp. Poised to step into Ramirez's cleats is Robinson Tejeda, who put up a 3.20 ERA with 41 Ks in 39⅓ innings after arriving off waivers from the Rangers in June.

This strong body of work led to optimism that Moore could efficiently replace the 120 innings of 2.78 ERA relief that were lost in the Jacobs and Crisp trades. Instead of going the low-cost route that had served the team so well, however, Kansas City elected to spend $9.25 million on a two-year deal for Kyle Farnsworth, a 32-year-old flamethrower coming off two subpar seasons. Coupled with the $1.8 million spent on ensuring the return of Horacio Ramirez, another scrap-heap relief find from last year, Farnsworth's signing essentially maxed out the team's payroll. Just several days after those two moves, the team announced that it did not have the funds to continue pursuing free-agent shortstop Rafael Furcal, a player who would have had an exponentially greater impact on Kansas City's fortunes than would Farnsworth and Ramirez.

While these signings did not help, what's seriously hamstringing Kansas City's novel financial flexibility is Jose Guillen's leaden albatross of a contract. That deal has turned out to be the most damaging of Moore's moves made in the name of building up a capable attack—moves that for the most part have failed to pan out. Beyond Guillen, there have also been the trades for Gload, Tony Pena Jr., and Joey Gathright, and then allowing them to eat up significant swaths of playing time. Not only has the offense failed to improve, but it has gotten worse: Kansas City's 4.3 runs per game in 2008 was its lowest average since 1992.

Lack of power is a huge part of that problem, as the team posted an eighth consecutive season without a 30-homer hitter (and fifth straight without a 25-homer man), a streak befitting the only major league team never to have a player hit 40 homers. But the even bigger issue is the squad's collective impatience. The Royals last season drew 392 walks, the lowest total in the majors. That averaged out to a free pass every 15.6 plate appearances, the fourth-worst total in AL history for the past 50 years, behind just the 2007 Mariners and the 2002 and 2005 Tigers. This problem has been endemic to the Royals throughout their history, as Kansas City has ranked no higher than 11th in the American League in OBP over the past five years and has not had a batter draw 90 or more walks in a season since Kevin Seitzer in 1989.

After the season, Moore spoke extensively about the importance of improving the team's OBP and backed up the talk by hiring Seitzer as the new hitting coach. However, that feel-good bubble was burst by the trade of Leo Nuñez for Jacobs, who drew 26 unintentional walks last year and put up a .299 OBP, the lowest for a regular first baseman in over a decade. First base has been an abyss for the Royals since Mike Sweeney's move to DH (see Table 1), so on paper, it looks as though Jacobs might solve two problems at once, giving Kansas City league-average production and the team's first 30-homer hitter since Jermaine Dye in 2000. Yet, the team had two cheaper options at the position in Ryan Shealy and Kila Ka'aihue, who, when accounting for defense—Jacobs is arguably the worst-fielding first baseman in the game—would together most likely produce at least as much value. If the club plays Jacobs every day, there is little hope for a significant rebound in the walks/OBP department, for Kansas City has already committed a large chunk of playing time to Miguel Olivo, perhaps the least patient hitter in the majors, and Jose Guillen, who drew the fewest passes of any qualifying outfielder last season.

Table 1. The First Shall Be Last: Royal Production at First Base, 2004–2008

Year	MLB 1B EqA	KC 1B EqA	KC 1B HRs	Regular(s)
2004	.279	.273	24	Ken Harvey, Mike Sweeney
2005	.282	.276	13	Matt Stairs, Mike Sweeney
2006	.281	.274	13	Doug Mientkiewicz, Ryan Shealy
2007	.279	.251	12	Ross Gload, Ryan Shealy
2008	.283	.257	14	Ross Gload

There's little help coming from the farm—other than Ka'aihue, the high minors have no impact bats—so the Royals will need to rely on the improvement of their current stock. Having Crisp in the everyday lineup will help on defense with some hope he'll improve on the Royals' collective .255 EqA from its center fielders in 2008. If Kansas City's offense is to improve to the point where the squad can challenge for the division crown, it will need twin phenoms Alex Gordon and Billy Butler to hit up to their billing.

If that happens, and the bullpen stays steady, and the young arms at the back of the rotation take a step forward … well, then Kansas City could end up hanging around long enough to strike, should no other team take charge in the Central. In all likelihood, however, KC's more patient fans will end up having to settle for having their cake slowly bake down on the farm, rather than eating it at Kauffman Stadium. For those who have already waited this long, another year spent looking ahead is only going to make the eventual reality, whenever it might come, taste that much sweeter.

HITTERS

Mike Aviles   SS

Bats: R   Throws: R   Height: 5' 9"   Weight: 205   Born: March 13, 1981   Age: 28

YEAR	TEAM	LVL	AGE	PA	R	2B	3B	HR	RBI	BB	SO	SB	CS	EqBRR	AVG	OBP	SLG	EqAVG	EqOBP	EqSLG	EqA	VORP	WARP	DEFENSE			
2006	OMA	AAA	25	502	52	21	3	8	47	28	48	14	5	1.9	.264	.307	.373	.228	.266	.331	.208	-27.7	-3.3	94-3B	-12	15-SS	-1
2007	OMA	AAA	26	581	78	27	6	17	77	30	59	5	5	-1.3	.296	.332	.463	.243	.279	.382	.227	-14.1	0.5	52-SS	2	47-3B	3
2008	OMA	AAA	27	227	42	21	6	10	42	11	23	3	0	-0.1	.336	.370	.631	.267	.298	.493	.267	7.7	2.5	32-2B	9	19-SS	2
2008	KCA	MLB	27	441	68	27	4	10	51	18	58	8	3	4.6	.325	.354	.480	.323	.354	.488	.285	35.2	4.8	84-SS	13	13-2B	1
2009	KCA	MLB	28	544	60	30	3	12	62	28	73	6	3	0.8	.268	.309	.409	.265	.307	.422	.251	10.8	2.3	128-SS	5		

Breakout: 19%   Improve: 48%   Collapse: 30%   Attrition: 16%   Comparables: Frank Malzone, Pat Meares, Ray Jablonski, Shea Hillenbrand

Behold, the mysterious power of age-27 seasons. Aviles entered 2008 with a line of .293/.334/.448 in over 2,300 minor league plate appearances; not even his mother would have predicted this sort of breakout. Happily, it spared the club from falling past the event horizon with Tony Pena at shortstop. Despite not being called up until late May, Aviles led Royals hitters in VORP and was nearly the best rookie bat in the league, finishing neck-and-neck with Evan Longoria in 67 fewer PAs. Although snubbed in the Rookie of the Year voting with a fourth-place finish, Aviles did at least get named KC's Player of the Year. Just as shocking as the offensive performance was how well Aviles played afield; not considered nimble enough to handle short every day at Omaha, he did fine in KC, showing strong instincts and good range to his right. It's doubtful whether Aviles can continue producing this well defensively or at the plate, but he'll give the Royals a significant bang for their pre-arb buck over the next two seasons.

John Buck   C

Bats: R   Throws: R   Height: 6' 3"   Weight: 220   Born: July 7, 1980   Age: 28

YEAR	TEAM	LVL	AGE	PA	R	2B	3B	HR	RBI	BB	SO	SB	CS	EqBRR	AVG	OBP	SLG	EqAVG	EqOBP	EqSLG	EqA	VORP	WARP	DEFENSE	
2006	KCA	MLB	25	409	37	21	1	11	50	26	84	0	2	-2.2	.245	.306	.396	.236	.300	.388	.237	-2.1	0.7	106-C	-1
2007	KCA	MLB	26	399	41	18	0	18	48	36	92	0	1	-0.1	.222	.308	.429	.214	.303	.431	.252	7.5	1.7	104-C	2
2008	KCA	MLB	27	418	48	23	1	9	48	38	96	0	3	-3.2	.224	.304	.365	.223	.306	.372	.236	-2.7	0.3	107-C	-5
2009	KCA	MLB	28	281	26	13	1	9	34	23	63	0	1	-1.2	.231	.303	.393	.229	.301	.405	.244	2.3	1.1	69-C	-1

Breakout: 25%   Improve: 47%   Collapse: 23%   Attrition: 39%   Comparables: Charles Johnson, Del Rice, Harry Chiti, John Orsino

While Aviles was showcasing what turning 27 can do for a career, Buck was emphatically reinforcing that not everyone gets that boost. Kansas City's former catcher of the future continued the free fall that began in June 2007, when the Royals eliminated Buck's high leg-kick trigger, even though he had 10 homers and an OPS near 1000 at the time. Since June 20, 2007, Buck has hit .210/.290/.339 in 637 PAs. Buck ceded the starting job to Olivo down the stretch and enters 2009 second on the depth chart. With his stagnation and no catching prospects in the minors, KC needs to find a long-term backstop.

Billy Butler   DH

Bats: R   Throws: R   Height: 6' 1"   Weight: 240   Born: April 18, 1986   Age: 23

YEAR	TEAM	LVL	AGE	PA	R	2B	3B	HR	RBI	BB	SO	SB	CS	EqBRR	AVG	OBP	SLG	EqAVG	EqOBP	EqSLG	EqA	VORP	WARP	DEFENSE			
2006	WIC	AA	20	535	82	33	1	15	96	41	67	1	0	-4.7	.331	.388	.499	.282	.330	.431	.263	15.0	0.4	95-RF	-2	20-LF	-6
2007	OMA	AAA	21	256	40	10	1	13	46	43	32	1	0	-3.8	.291	.412	.542	.256	.376	.478	.296	15.5	1.0	25-LF	-4	22-1B	-1
2007	KCA	MLB	21	360	38	23	2	8	52	27	55	0	0	-1.5	.292	.347	.447	.280	.341	.448	.271	11.0	0.4	9-1B	0	5-LF	-5
2008	OMA	AAA	22	115	18	6	1	5	13	14	7	0	0	0.0	.337	.417	.564	.291	.365	.476	.288	7.6	0.1	21-1B	-4		
2008	KCA	MLB	22	478	44	22	0	11	55	33	57	0	1	-0.5	.275	.324	.400	.272	.324	.413	.254	6.3	-0.3	29-1B	-4		
2009	KCA	MLB	23	506	60	28	1	15	70	42	65	0	1	-2.4	.291	.352	.457	.287	.349	.471	.282	19.3	1.8	119-DH			

Breakout: 39%   Improve: 70%   Collapse: 15%   Attrition: 11%   Comparables: Dave Winfield, Prince Fielder, Boog Powell, Joe Adcock

The numbers Butler served up in the first half left the Royals nonplussed, so the hefty hitting savant was dispatched to Omaha in late May with a 669 OPS, where he again proved his pedigree as the best pure hitter in the organization and then hit .305/.341/.476 for KC in the second half. The Royals continued to plug Butler in at first base on occasion, as they don't believe in having a player so young be a full-time DH, but his future will be *sans gants de cuir*. Butler should be the team's top hitter this year, but he does have things to work on, such as plate discipline and generating more lift from his swing. Jose Guillen's presence wore off on Butler last year: the DH saw the same amount of pitches per PA as the impatient outfielder (3.58) and grounded into the same number of double plays (23) in over 150 fewer plate appearances, the highest GIDP rate in the American League.

Alberto Callaspo   2B

Bats: S   Throws: R   Height: 5' 10"   Weight: 175   Born: April 19, 1983   Age: 26

YEAR	TEAM	LVL	AGE	PA	R	2B	3B	HR	RBI	BB	SO	SB	CS	EqBRR	AVG	OBP	SLG	EqAVG	EqOBP	EqSLG	EqA	VORP	WARP	DEFENSE			
2006	TUC	AAA	23	554	93	24	12	7	68	56	27	8	5	0.3	.337	.404	.478	.283	.347	.410	.264	15.2	3.7	68-2B	11	22-SS	-2
2006	ARI	MLB	23	47	2	1	1	0	6	4	6	0	1	-0.7	.238	.298	.310	.214	.277	.286	.194	-1.9	-0.3				
2007	TUC	AAA	24	261	48	15	2	5	30	28	17	1	2	-0.7	.341	.406	.491	.284	.352	.415	.269	8.5	0.9	33-SS	-1	17-2B	-2
2007	ARI	MLB	24	156	10	8	0	0	7	9	14	1	1	-0.1	.215	.265	.271	.215	.269	.264	.183	-10.7	-0.7	13-3B	1	8-SS	2
2008	KCA	MLB	25	234	21	8	3	0	16	19	14	2	1	-0.6	.305	.361	.371	.307	.365	.373	.263	7.7	0.7	41-2B	-4	9-SS	4
2009	KCA	MLB	26	350	39	15	2	3	30	29	28	3	1	0.6	.271	.334	.361	.267	.332	.372	.250	4.6	1.0	84-2B	0		

Breakout: 23%   Improve: 49%   Collapse: 26%   Attrition: 22%   Comparables: Luis Rodriguez, Omar Vizquel, Nelson Liriano, Walt Weiss

Callaspo was hitting .206 in 126 at-bats when he was picked up in late June on DUI charges, his second troubling incident in two years—he was arrested under suspicion of assaulting his wife in May 2007. After spending nearly two months on the DL with an "unspecified medical condition" following the DUI, Callaspo returned in late August in the wake of Grudzielanek's injury and became the team's starting second baseman, recording a .319/.371/.407 line in 125 PAs the rest of the way. He has the potential to be an above-average starter at the keystone should he stay off the blotter.

Shane Costa   OF

Bats: L   Throws: R   Height: 6' 0"   Weight: 190   Born: December 12, 1981   Age: 27

YEAR	TEAM	LVL	AGE	PA	R	2B	3B	HR	RBI	BB	SO	SB	CS	EqBRR	AVG	OBP	SLG	EqAVG	EqOBP	EqSLG	EqA	VORP	WARP	DEFENSE			
2006	OMA	AAA	24	224	35	12	4	10	29	13	25	4	0	0.3	.342	.398	.593	.309	.359	.544	.302	20.5	1.0	37-RF	-1	13-LF	-6
2006	KCA	MLB	24	252	23	20	1	3	23	6	29	2	0	0.4	.274	.304	.405	.266	.296	.392	.239	-0.4	0.4	35-RF	0	18-CF	2
2007	OMA	AAA	25	267	46	20	3	5	14	26	20	8	2	0.6	.326	.402	.502	.274	.348	.430	.272	9.2	0.8	37-RF	-2	7-LF	1
2007	KCA	MLB	25	109	13	6	1	0	12	5	23	0	1	-0.2	.223	.257	.301	.214	.248	.291	.179	-7.6	-0.5	11-LF	3	8-RF	0
2008	OMA	AAA	26	328	42	21	0	10	42	28	39	11	2	-0.5	.295	.354	.469	.242	.294	.372	.237	-6.8	-0.6	55-RF	-5	19-CF	1
2009	KCA	MLB	27	348	38	19	2	6	37	22	50	6	2	0.4	.263	.314	.392	.260	.312	.404	.250	-0.3	0.6	84-RF	0		

Breakout: 25%   Improve: 48%   Collapse: 31%   Attrition: 30%   Comparables: Bubba Crosby, Jacob Cruz, George Vukovich, Jay Payton

Kansas City should have cut costs in right field last season, but instead it decided to cut Costa and blow $36 million on Jose Guillen. Costa was shipped back to Omaha, where his numbers fell off before a wrist injury ended his season early. He's out of options, so if the Royals don't carry him, they stand a good chance of losing him on waivers. There's still some promise in Costa's bat, so bet on him making the squad as the Guillen implosion insurance policy.

David DeJesus   LF

Bats: L   Throws: L   Height: 6' 0"   Weight: 185   Born: December 20, 1979   Age: 29

YEAR	TEAM	LVL	AGE	PA	R	2B	3B	HR	RBI	BB	SO	SB	CS	EqBRR	AVG	OBP	SLG	EqAVG	EqOBP	EqSLG	EqA	VORP	WARP	DEFENSE			
2006	KCA	MLB	26	552	83	36	7	8	56	43	70	6	3	4.4	.295	.364	.446	.283	.356	.436	.275	21.4	4.5	62-LF	9	55-CF	10
2007	KCA	MLB	27	703	101	29	9	7	58	64	83	10	4	2.8	.260	.351	.372	.252	.345	.373	.256	11.4	3.5	152-CF	15		
2008	KCA	MLB	28	577	70	25	7	12	73	46	71	11	8	-1.5	.307	.366	.452	.307	.369	.466	.283	30.0	5.2	57-CF	3	54-LF	18
2009	KCA	MLB	29	557	71	27	5	8	53	43	72	8	4	1.7	.278	.343	.401	.275	.341	.414	.264	9.1	3.0	131-CF	5		

Breakout: 12%   Improve: 32%   Collapse: 29%   Attrition: 13%   Comparables: Del Unser, Dave May, Mark Kotsay, Steve Finley

We present to you the 2008 major league leader in Others Batted In Percentage. DeJesus topped all batting title qualifiers by cashing in 21.5 percent of the runners on base during his PAs. Unfortunately, he batted leadoff for most of the season, following out-factories like Pena, Gathright, and Buck at the bottom of the order, and therefore saw 80 fewer ducks on the pond than the average major league player with the same number of PAs. Such is the cruel irony that Royals fans have come to expect. DeJesus' average bounced back and he added some more power, producing his best campaign yet despite a renewal of being "day to day" with various nagging injuries. His undistinguished performance at center limits his value, but DeJesus did do outstanding work in left, where he will now be stationed full-time after the acquisition of Coco Crisp.

Joe Dickerson — RF

Bats: L   Throws: L   Height: 6' 1"   Weight: 190   Born: October 3, 1986   Age: 22

YEAR	TEAM	LVL	AGE	PA	R	2B	3B	HR	RBI	BB	SO	SB	CS	EqBRR	AVG	OBP	SLG	EqAVG	EqOBP	EqSLG	EqA	VORP	WARP	DEFENSE		
2006	IDA	Rk	19	272	36	14	3	7	38	19	34	9	8	-2.8	.281	.338	.450	.193	.231	.295	.178	-43.5	-4.2	60-CF	-11	
2007	BUR	A	20	466	50	23	2	3	43	38	76	26	13	1.5	.289	.354	.375	.230	.283	.304	.208	-27.2	-5.9	99-LF	-28	11-CF -6
2008	WIL	A+	21	353	39	10	10	5	45	31	48	24	14	-5.1	.297	.376	.442	.274	.339	.421	.262	9.9	1.1	79-RF	2	
2009	KCA	MLB	22	500	54	25	3	6	45	34	95	17	8	1.3	.248	.305	.361	.245	.303	.372	.238	-10.5	-0.5	118-RF	-5	

Breakout: 34%   Improve: 62%   Collapse: 16%   Attrition: 11%   Comparables: Jim Wawruck, Goefrey Tomlinson, Daniel Stryffeler, Jon Saffer

The Royals have a serious scarcity of offensive talent in the minors, which makes Dickerson one of the system's more promising bats. Considering that Wilmington is a pretty tough place to hit, his 2008 performance is more impressive than it seems. Dickerson has a great deal of speed, but without the ability to handle center, he currently projects as a fourth outfielder. He missed the last six weeks of the season with a broken finger, then hit just .269/.300/.433 in 110 Arizona Fall League PAs, so he has plenty to prove at Double-A.

Joey Gathright — CF

Bats: L   Throws: R   Height: 5' 10"   Weight: 170   Born: April 27, 1981   Age: 28

YEAR	TEAM	LVL	AGE	PA	R	2B	3B	HR	RBI	BB	SO	SB	CS	EqBRR	AVG	OBP	SLG	EqAVG	EqOBP	EqSLG	EqA	VORP	WARP	DEFENSE		
2006	TBA	MLB	25	182	25	6	0	0	13	20	30	12	3	2.4	.201	.305	.240	.191	.305	.224	.212	-7.9	-0.3	50-CF	1	
2006	KCA	MLB	25	263	34	6	3	1	28	22	45	10	6	-1.8	.262	.332	.328	.256	.332	.322	.237	-2.9	-0.2	66-CF	-2	
2007	OMA	AAA	26	277	44	10	4	0	25	43	24	25	8	0.5	.341	.457	.422	.275	.388	.341	.272	6.1	0.6	54-CF	-5	
2007	KCA	MLB	26	261	28	8	0	0	19	20	36	9	8	-1.0	.307	.371	.342	.308	.375	.339	.250	0.4	1.0	59-LF	7	6-CF 0
2008	KCA	MLB	27	315	41	3	1	0	22	20	40	21	4	2.8	.254	.311	.272	.255	.312	.273	.227	-6.0	-0.8	81-CF	-4	
2009	CHN	MLB	28	210	30	6	1	0	13	19	28	15	4	1.7	.264	.340	.309	.261	.337	.309	.242	0.8	0.6	53-CF	0	

Breakout: 34%   Improve: 53%   Collapse: 34%   Attrition: 44%   Comparables: David Hulse, Milt Thompson, Otis Nixon, Jason Tyner

Gathright picked up an extra-base hit once every 79 PAs during his time in the majors last year, the worst ratio in a season of at least 300 PAs since Rafael Belliard in 1988. Toss in his feeble work with Omaha, and a more punchless performance hasn't been seen since 1968. No one in the majors is faster, but that speed has not translated to good defense, making baserunning and the occasional bunt single his only tangible contributions. That's not a player worth the raise he would have seen in arbitration, and the Royals wisely nontendered him. Gathright was then picked up by the Cubs, who were worried they might not have enough outfielders to block Felix Pie.

Esteban German — UT

Bats: R   Throws: R   Height: 5' 9"   Weight: 195   Born: January 26, 1978   Age: 31

YEAR	TEAM	LVL	AGE	PA	R	2B	3B	HR	RBI	BB	SO	SB	CS	EqBRR	AVG	OBP	SLG	EqAVG	EqOBP	EqSLG	EqA	VORP	WARP	DEFENSE		
2006	KCA	MLB	28	331	44	18	5	3	34	40	49	7	3	-0.3	.326	.422	.459	.312	.415	.442	.300	25.3	1.2	21-3B	-5	19-2B -4
2007	KCA	MLB	29	405	49	15	6	4	37	43	60	11	7	-1.3	.264	.351	.376	.260	.351	.382	.258	4.7	-0.4	46-2B	-3	32-3B -5
2008	KCA	MLB	30	242	30	14	3	0	22	18	42	7	3	-0.1	.245	.303	.338	.247	.307	.344	.233	-4.4	-0.3	26-LF	0	24-2B 1
2009	KCA	MLB	31	217	26	9	2	1	18	20	34	5	2	0.6	.258	.330	.348	.255	.328	.359	.247	0.3	0.1	54-2B	-5	

Breakout: 7%   Improve: 33%   Collapse: 47%   Attrition: 29%   Comparables: Fred Marsh, Jamey Carroll, Junior Kennedy, Bubba Morton

German got off to a horrendous start, then failed again in his one shot at regular duty while playing second after Grudzielanek went down. As a utilityman who has played every position except right, catcher, and pitcher for KC, German has value, although he's below average with the glove at all of those spots, and last year, he brought a disturbing decomposition of his walk rate—from 2006 to 2008, it dropped from once every 8.3 plate appearances to once every 13.4, eroding his main contribution on offense. Nonetheless, if the Royals don't sign a second baseman, German will have a chance to unseat Callaspo for the job in the spring.

Johnny Giavotella — 2B

Bats: R   Throws: R   Height: 5' 8"   Weight: 185   Born: July 10, 1987   Age: 21

YEAR	TEAM	LVL	AGE	PA	R	2B	3B	HR	RBI	BB	SO	SB	CS	EqBRR	AVG	OBP	SLG	EqAVG	EqOBP	EqSLG	EqA	VORP	WARP	DEFENSE
2008	BUR	A	20	310	50	18	2	4	26	25	34	10	7	3.2	.299	.355	.421	.254	.303	.370	.233	-4.7	0.1	67-2B 0
2009	KCA	MLB	21	557	55	34	2	7	50	38	88	9	5	2.3	.248	.303	.364	.245	.301	.376	.237	-1.8	0.6	131-2B -1

Breakout: 29%   Improve: 65%   Collapse: 13%   Attrition: 5%   Comparables: Chuck Knoblauch, Brent Abernathy, Jason Hardtke, Jarrett Hoffpauir

Slowly but surely, the Royals are infusing offensive talent into the system. Giavotella signed quickly for around $800,000 five days after he was drafted in the second round (49th overall pick) last year, and he was therefore able to get in a solid chunk of time as Mike Moustakas's double-play partner. The diminutive second baseman handled the full-season league assignment with advanced bat control, which makes him the best middle-infield prospect in a system devoid of up-the-middle talent. Giavotella is an offensive-minded player, however. At this point, his glove needs more work than his bat.

Ross Gload   1B   Bats: L   Throws: L   Height: 6′ 1″   Weight: 190   Born: April 5, 1976   Age: 33

YEAR	TEAM	LVL	AGE	PA	R	2B	3B	HR	RBI	BB	SO	SB	CS	EqBRR	AVG	OBP	SLG	EqAVG	EqOBP	EqSLG	EqA	VORP	WARP	DEFENSE		
2006	CHA	MLB	30	167	22	8	2	3	18	6	15	6	0	-1.5	.327	.354	.462	.310	.341	.439	.275	8.5	0.1	28-1B -3	8-RF	-1
2007	KCA	MLB	31	346	37	22	3	7	51	16	39	2	2	-0.3	.288	.318	.441	.279	.312	.448	.259	5.4	-0.1	76-1B 0	6-LF	-4
2008	KCA	MLB	32	418	46	18	1	3	37	23	39	3	4	-2.2	.273	.317	.348	.274	.321	.354	.235	-7.2	-2.1	98-1B -10	7-LF	-2
2009	KCA	MLB	33	254	26	13	1	3	26	13	27	2	1	-0.5	.274	.314	.375	.270	.312	.386	.243	-2.3	-0.4	63-1B -2		

Breakout: 18%   Improve: 37%   Collapse: 36%   Attrition: 42%   Comparables: Larry Biittner, Scott Livingstone, Tim Thompson, Joe Orsulak

The Royals entered last season with Gload set to be their primary first baseman, and he was the worst regular at the position in baseball. But that statement doesn't do his year justice. How about this: the last time a first baseman had an OPS of 665 or below in 400 or more PAs was 1993 (Pittsburgh's immortal Kevin Young), and the last time a first baseman hit three or fewer homers in as many PAs was 1991—Todd Benzinger, coincidentally another Royal. Moore was so determined to not suffer a repeat episode that he overreacted by trading for Mike Jacobs. Gload is guaranteed $1.9 million in 2009, so he'll be *baa-ack* … but only as a pinch-hitter.

Alex Gordon   3B   Bats: L   Throws: R   Height: 6′ 1″   Weight: 220   Born: February 10, 1984   Age: 25

YEAR	TEAM	LVL	AGE	PA	R	2B	3B	HR	RBI	BB	SO	SB	CS	EqBRR	AVG	OBP	SLG	EqAVG	EqOBP	EqSLG	EqA	VORP	WARP	DEFENSE		
2006	WIC	AA	22	576	111	39	1	29	101	72	113	22	3	7.2	.325	.427	.588	.275	.361	.499	.293	38.2	5.0	119-3B 7		
2007	KCA	MLB	23	600	60	36	4	15	60	41	137	14	4	-1.0	.247	.314	.411	.240	.309	.415	.251	2.7	-0.2	128-3B -12	17-1B	2
2008	KCA	MLB	24	571	72	35	1	16	59	66	120	9	2	3.4	.260	.351	.432	.256	.351	.440	.276	20.3	2.1	132-3B -5		
2009	KCA	MLB	25	628	83	38	2	23	84	64	132	13	3	0.7	.258	.342	.457	.255	.340	.471	.280	20.2	3.1	147-3B -2		

Breakout: 25%   Improve: 62%   Collapse: 10%   Attrition: 8%   Comparables: Pat Burrell, Eric Chavez, Troy Glaus, Darrell Evans

George Brett's chosen heir has yet to claim the keys to Kansas City that were thought to be his birthright, with Gordon's having grown up a Royals fan and having starred at the University of Nebraska. Closer examination reveals that Gordon took a crucial step forward in year two, as his walk rate increased by 41 percent. He also closed the season well, putting up a 965 OPS in his last 32 games, which allays concern about the torn hip flexor that sent him to the DL in late August. On the other hand, Gordon's defense went in the opposite direction—his first-step quickness was not there—although the Royals still believe he can be a Gold Glove defender at the hot corner. Gordon needs to start translating his potential soon if any of the scenarios in which the Royals become surprise contenders in 2009 have legs.

Mark Grudzielanek   2B   Bats: R   Throws: R   Height: 6′ 1″   Weight: 200   Born: June 30, 1970   Age: 39

YEAR	TEAM	LVL	AGE	PA	R	2B	3B	HR	RBI	BB	SO	SB	CS	EqBRR	AVG	OBP	SLG	EqAVG	EqOBP	EqSLG	EqA	VORP	WARP	DEFENSE
2006	KCA	MLB	36	586	85	32	4	7	52	28	69	3	2	1.3	.297	.331	.409	.288	.326	.402	.253	16.2	2.3	126-2B 8
2007	KCA	MLB	37	486	70	32	3	6	51	23	60	1	2	1.5	.302	.346	.426	.296	.341	.430	.265	17.7	1.6	107-2B -2
2008	KCA	MLB	38	360	36	24	0	3	24	19	41	2	1	0.3	.299	.345	.399	.300	.346	.409	.264	11.6	1.6	80-2B 3
2009	KCA	MLB	39	259	26	14	1	3	26	14	34	1	1	-0.5	.277	.320	.373	.273	.318	.385	.246	3.7	0.4	64-2B -1

Breakout: 9%   Improve: 27%   Collapse: 42%   Attrition: 40%   Comparables: Jim Gantner, Randy Velarde, Dave Concepcion, Barry Larkin

Gload didn't settle for sabotaging first base; he also caused significant collateral damage to those in the vicinity as well: Grudz tore an ankle ligament in a collision with Gload on August 1, which ended his season and his career in KC. The 14-year veteran hit free agency coming off two league-average offensive seasons—his OPS+ was exactly 100 in both 2007 and 2008—which in addition to his solid defense certainly gives him value. The concern, of course, is his age and the ankle injury, both of which are notoriously difficult to overcome. Kansas City offered him arbitration, which Grudzielanek declined.

Jose Guillen — RF

Bats: R   Throws: R   Height: 6' 0"   Weight: 195   Born: May 17, 1976   Age: 33

YEAR	TEAM	LVL	AGE	PA	R	2B	3B	HR	RBI	BB	SO	SB	CS	EqBRR	AVG	OBP	SLG	EqAVG	EqOBP	EqSLG	EqA	VORP	WARP	DEFENSE	
2006	WAS	MLB	30	268	28	15	1	9	40	15	48	1	0	0.8	.216	.276	.398	.220	.276	.411	.238	-6.8	-0.1	61-RF	1
2007	SEA	MLB	31	658	84	28	2	23	99	41	118	5	1	-0.7	.290	.353	.460	.293	.356	.481	.286	26.6	3.6	144-RF	1
2008	KCA	MLB	32	633	66	42	1	20	97	23	106	2	1	-1.7	.264	.300	.438	.263	.300	.451	.254	6.5	0.9	60-RF	3 42-LF -1
2009	KCA	MLB	33	489	52	28	1	14	68	23	85	2	1	-1.2	.271	.313	.430	.268	.311	.444	.258	4.1	0.9	115-RF	-4

Breakout: 10%   Improve: 39%   Collapse: 33%   Attrition: 22%   Comparables: Rondell White, Jeffrey Leonard, Carl Furillo, Mickey Stanley

Well, *that* sure went well. Year one of Guillen's tenure was a doozy: he erupted in a profane tirade following the team's 10th straight loss in late May, had a verbal sparring match with pitching coach Bob McClure in early July, was forced later in the month to address an ESPN Deportes report that he wanted out of KC and was not speaking to his manager (Guillen denied it), blasted KC fans on multiple occasions, and then needed to be restrained from going into the stands to challenge a heckler in late August (those things aren't supposed to happen at home). All in all, just another typical season for everyone's favorite irascible outfielder. It was also typical at the plate—moderate power coupled with extremely poor plate discipline, in this case his worst walk rate since 1998. Guillen still managed to knock in almost 100 runs, taking a page out of the Joe Carter playbook. That superficial production didn't fool rival general managers, however, as Moore spent a good portion of the offseason futilely trying to undo his mistake. Between the two years and $24 million that remain on Guillen's contract, his poor reputation, and his deteriorating skills, who'd want him?

Eric Hosmer — 1B

Bats: L   Throws: L   Height: 6' 4"   Weight: 215   Born: October 24, 1989   Age: 19

YEAR	TEAM	LVL	AGE	PA	R	2B	3B	HR	RBI	BB	SO	SB	CS	EqBRR	AVG	OBP	SLG	EqAVG	EqOBP	EqSLG	EqA	VORP	WARP	DEFENSE
2008	IDA	Rk	18	15	2	2	0	0	2	3	2	0	0	-0.2	.364	.533	.545	.231	.333	.308	.232	-0.7	0.0	
2009	KCA	MLB	19	576	50	28	2	9	55	42	153	7	3	0.4	.222	.281	.335	.219	.279	.346	.218	-20.9	-1.2	135-DH

Breakout: 0%   Improve: 0%   Collapse: 0%   Attrition: 0%   Comparables: Joe Mauer, Adrian Gonzalez, Darryl Strawberry, Ben Grieve

The Royals took a prep infielder with their top selection in the draft for the second straight year, grabbing Hosmer, the best high school hitter in the country, with the third overall selection. He and agent Scott Boras agreed to a contract right before midnight on August 15 … *or was it right after?* The ridiculousness of the MLB-imposed signing deadline led to a pissing contest pitting Boras and the union against the Pirates and the commissioner's office over the contract of second overall pick Pedro Alvarez. To get his client more money, Boras declared that Alvarez's contract had been illegally submitted after the clock struck 12. That firestorm swept up Hosmer, as his contract was reported at the same time and he was thus pulled off the field until the grievance could be resolved—but only after already playing three games for the Chukars. All's well that ends with $6 million in the pockets of two young infielders. Some scouts grade Hosmer's power a perfect 80, and he's athletic enough to be above average on defense; while high school first basemen have historically been a bad bet in the draft, it looks like the Royals picked a winner.

Kila Ka'aihue — 1B

Bats: L   Throws: R   Height: 6' 3"   Weight: 233   Born: March 29, 1984   Age: 25

YEAR	TEAM	LVL	AGE	PA	R	2B	3B	HR	RBI	BB	SO	SB	CS	EqBRR	AVG	OBP	SLG	EqAVG	EqOBP	EqSLG	EqA	VORP	WARP	DEFENSE
2006	WIC	AA	22	395	40	15	0	6	45	49	73	0	1	-2.1	.199	.303	.300	.171	.258	.262	.186	-34.9	-3.8	87-1B -6
2007	WIL	A+	23	253	28	8	0	9	42	35	38	1	0	-2.1	.251	.360	.420	.191	.277	.309	.210	-15.8	-1.6	33-1B -2
2007	WIC	AA	23	288	37	13	0	12	40	41	40	0	0	-0.4	.246	.359	.447	.211	.310	.378	.241	-4.8	-0.3	35-1B 1
2008	NWA	AA	24	376	64	11	0	26	79	80	41	3	2	-0.9	.314	.463	.624	.248	.383	.492	.300	26.2	1.3	69-1B -10
2008	OMA	AAA	24	139	27	4	0	11	21	24	26	0	0	0.5	.316	.439	.640	.274	.388	.530	.309	12.8	1.1	25-1B 0
2008	KCA	MLB	24	24	4	0	0	1	1	3	2	0	0	-0.1	.286	.375	.429	.286	.375	.429	.281	1.1	0.1	
2009	KCA	MLB	25	531	56	22	1	15	60	65	101	1	1	-1.5	.225	.324	.375	.222	.322	.387	.250	-6.2	-0.0	125-1B -4

Breakout: 13%   Improve: 42%   Collapse: 34%   Attrition: 11%   Comparables: Sal Rende, Pat Dodson, Jeffrey Larish, Chris Carter

Before last season, Ka'aihue was just a second-tier power prospect with strong walk rates and a funky name. (The apostrophe represents the glottal stop of spoken language used in his native Hawaii.) He wasn't even on the 40-man roster; like Aviles, anybody could have snagged him in the 2007 Rule 5 draft. Then Ka'aihue went tribal on the Texas League and kept on hitting through Triple-A and up to "The Show." He finished second among all Double-A and Triple-A players in homers (37), first in OBP (.456), and second in slugging (.628), while leading the minors with 104 walks against just 67 strikeouts. While Ka'aihue should have gotten the chance to play in September, Hillman gave him only five starts, a poor reward for such a fine season. After the Jacobs trade, it appears that Ka'aihue will have to prove last year wasn't a fluke at Triple-A.

Mitch Maier CF

Bats: L   Throws: R   Height: 6' 2"   Weight: 210   Born: June 30, 1982   Age: 27

YEAR	TEAM	LVL	AGE	PA	R	2B	3B	HR	RBI	BB	SO	SB	CS	EqBRR	AVG	OBP	SLG	EqAVG	EqOBP	EqSLG	EqA	VORP	WARP	DEFENSE			
2006	WIC	AA	24	603	95	35	7	14	92	41	96	13	12	0.9	.306	.357	.473	.242	.286	.381	.230	-12.7	-1.7	114-CF	-10	20-RF	-1
2007	OMA	AAA	25	596	75	29	5	14	62	33	89	7	2	1.3	.279	.320	.428	.234	.274	.367	.223	-20.2	-1.0	82-CF	4	31-RF	-2
2008	OMA	AAA	26	383	57	24	1	9	41	29	42	12	3	-0.4	.316	.366	.470	.256	.302	.369	.238	-5.8	1.4	84-CF	10		
2008	KCA	MLB	26	97	9	1	1	0	9	2	18	0	2	-0.1	.286	.316	.319	.286	.316	.319	.217	-2.1	0.3	24-CF	5		
2009	KCA	MLB	27	379	36	20	2	7	39	23	69	5	2	0.4	.238	.287	.367	.235	.285	.379	.232	-5.5	0.7	91-CF	1		

Breakout: 31% Improve: 50% Collapse: 27% Attrition: 21%   Comparables: Midre Cummings, Bubba Crosby, Chris Singleton, Darrell Whitmore

After a decent performance for Omaha, Maier got off to a good start with Kansas City before August 20, when he was nailed in the face while trying to bunt a Zach Jackson fastball. The pitch broke three bones, but Maier was back on the field three and a half weeks later. The Royals left Maier off the 40-man in 2007, and he went unclaimed in the Rule 5 draft, but last year's modest breakout reserved him a spot.

Mike Moustakas SS

Bats: L   Throws: R   Height: 6' 0"   Weight: 195   Born: September 11, 1988   Age: 20

YEAR	TEAM	LVL	AGE	PA	R	2B	3B	HR	RBI	BB	SO	SB	CS	EqBRR	AVG	OBP	SLG	EqAVG	EqOBP	EqSLG	EqA	VORP	WARP	DEFENSE			
2007	IDA	Rk	18	47	6	4	1	0	10	4	8	0	0	-0.3	.293	.383	.439	.186	.255	.302	.191	-6.4	-0.3	7-SS	0		
2008	BUR	A	19	549	77	25	3	22	71	43	86	8	4	0.0	.272	.337	.468	.231	.285	.402	.235	-9.3	0.5	59-3B	8	56-SS	-6
2009	KCA	MLB	20	603	62	35	3	15	67	43	114	4	3	1.1	.239	.298	.397	.236	.297	.409	.243	1.1	1.0	141-3B	3		

Breakout: 49% Improve: 70% Collapse: 9% Attrition: 2%   Comparables: Ian Stewart, Darnell Coles, Adrian Gonzalez, Chris Lubanski

The second pick in the 2007 draft raised concern when he hit just .190 with a lone homer in 91 April plate appearances, but soon enough, Moustakas let the talent that had allowed him to set the California prep home-run record take over. In the second half, he raked at a .321/.392/.557 clip, smashing seven homers in August. While it may have been a coincidence, the torrid stretch roughly coincided with his switch from shortstop to third base in early June—Moustakas had to make the move at some point and seemed far more comfortable at his new position. PECOTA gave Moustakas a higher upside score than it did any other 2007 draftee, and there's plenty of reason to be excited for his future.

Miguel Olivo C

Bats: R   Throws: R   Height: 6' 0"   Weight: 220   Born: July 15, 1978   Age: 30

YEAR	TEAM	LVL	AGE	PA	R	2B	3B	HR	RBI	BB	SO	SB	CS	EqBRR	AVG	OBP	SLG	EqAVG	EqOBP	EqSLG	EqA	VORP	WARP	DEFENSE	
2006	FLO	MLB	27	452	52	22	3	16	58	9	103	2	3	-0.5	.263	.287	.440	.266	.289	.447	.247	5.8	1.9	111-C	5
2007	FLO	MLB	28	469	43	20	4	16	60	14	123	3	2	0.6	.237	.262	.405	.239	.267	.419	.230	-1.4	0.8	111-C	2
2008	KCA	MLB	29	317	29	22	0	12	41	7	82	7	0	-1.1	.255	.278	.444	.252	.277	.451	.249	7.2	1.8	55-C	9
2009	KCA	MLB	30	268	25	14	1	8	33	10	66	3	1	-0.5	.240	.273	.401	.237	.271	.414	.233	-0.8	1.0	66-C	-1

Breakout: 16% Improve: 41% Collapse: 32% Attrition: 32%   Comparables: Jeff Newman, Bill Schroeder, John Bateman, Jason LaRue

With apologies to Alec Baldwin, it takes brass balls to complain about playing time when your OBP is below .300, which is what Olivo did in the second half. To be fair, he *was* the best catcher on the team, outslugging Buck and gunning down 14 of 33 would-be thieves. Olivo became unhappy enough with Hillman's apportionment to publicly announce in late August that he was not going to exercise his $2.7 million option to return in 2009. The time-share behind the plate was evened out the rest of the way, and the Royals promised Olivo a starting job for 2009 after the season ended, convincing him to re-sign on a one-year deal with a mutual 2010 option. Giving Olivo most of the time at catcher isn't going to solve any of KC's problems: he had the lowest walk rate in the majors for those with more than 200 PAs, just ahead of teammate Tony Pena, and his .275 career OBP is the second-worst among active players with more than 2,000 PAs (Juan Castro wears the crown).

Tony Pena Jr. SS

Bats: R   Throws: R   Height: 6' 2"   Weight: 180   Born: March 23, 1981   Age: 28

YEAR	TEAM	LVL	AGE	PA	R	2B	3B	HR	RBI	BB	SO	SB	CS	EqBRR	AVG	OBP	SLG	EqAVG	EqOBP	EqSLG	EqA	VORP	WARP	DEFENSE	
2006	RIC	AAA	25	319	38	12	4	1	23	12	56	12	3	4.8	.282	.312	.359	.246	.273	.322	.210	-16.1	-1.1	81-SS	-7
2006	ATL	MLB	25	46	12	2	0	1	3	2	10	0	0	0.0	.227	.261	.341	.227	.261	.341	.204	-1.2	-0.4	9-SS	-2
2007	KCA	MLB	26	536	58	25	7	2	47	10	78	5	6	-3.0	.267	.284	.356	.265	.282	.361	.220	-7.9	1.5	144-SS	14
2008	KCA	MLB	27	235	22	4	1	1	14	6	49	3	1	-1.0	.169	.189	.209	.170	.193	.210	.113	-24.9	-2.9	66-SS	-5
2009	KCA	MLB	28	150	13	5	1	1	13	5	26	3	1	0.7	.234	.264	.307	.231	.262	.316	.200	-5.1	-0.3	39-SS	0

Breakout: 42% Improve: 58% Collapse: 32% Attrition: 54%   Comparables: John McDonald, Julio Gonzalez, Jackie Gutierrez, Craig Robinson

Those who regularly watched the Royals in 2008 saw one of the worst offensive performances of the past century. Pena's ineptitude was breathtaking—in a season of more than 200 PAs, no player since 1912 had produced a worse EqA. Pena couldn't even do the honorable thing and fall on his glove, as his normally outstanding defense went south as well. Perhaps the most mind-boggling aspect of Pena's tour de force, however, is that he drew two intentional walks. Thankfully, whichever divine force watches over the game made sure that appropriate punishment was meted out: against both the Blue Jays and Marlins, two runs came in to score immediately following the inexplicable act. Alas, Pena will be back, backing up Aviles at short.

Derrick Robinson CF

Bats: S   Throws: L   Height: 5' 11"   Weight: 170   Born: September 28, 1987   Age: 21

YEAR	TEAM	LVL	AGE	PA	R	2B	3B	HR	RBI	BB	SO	SB	CS	EqBRR	AVG	OBP	SLG	EqAVG	EqOBP	EqSLG	EqA	VORP	WARP	DEFENSE	
2006	ROY	Rk	18	208	25	6	3	1	24	24	55	20	14	-6.2	.233	.335	.318	.152	.210	.215	.133	-68.0	-5.2	46-CF	-9
2007	BUR	A	19	449	42	11	3	2	26	32	100	34	7	3.7	.243	.299	.300	.195	.240	.245	.171	-50.5	-6.0	101-CF	-24
2008	WIL	A+	20	556	69	22	8	0	34	51	97	62	17	-0.7	.245	.316	.322	.221	.283	.298	.216	-34.0	-1.8	114-CF	-4
2009	KCA	MLB	21	599	63	24	5	2	33	41	127	40	14	3.4	.227	.282	.300	.224	.280	.310	.216	-23.0	-0.7	140-CF	-3

Breakout: 71% Improve: 83% Collapse: 6% Attrition: 3%   Comparables: Will Taylor, Jerome Nelson, Milt Cuyler, Nathan Haynes

The Royals' farmhand among the position players, Robinson has the most impact potential other than Hosmer and Moustakas, although he's got miles to go. As a switch-hitter with blinding speed—he stole the third-most bases in the minors last year—and a true center fielder, he inspires visions of Willie Wilson, but at this point, he's far more athlete than baseball player. The Royals hope he plays his way to Double-A by season's end; to do so, Robinson will have to cut down on the strikeouts considerably.

Ryan Shealy 1B

Bats: R   Throws: R   Height: 6' 5"   Weight: 240   Born: August 29, 1979   Age: 29

YEAR	TEAM	LVL	AGE	PA	R	2B	3B	HR	RBI	BB	SO	SB	CS	EqBRR	AVG	OBP	SLG	EqAVG	EqOBP	EqSLG	EqA	VORP	WARP	DEFENSE	
2006	CSP	AAA	26	248	37	16	1	15	55	20	34	0	0	-1.5	.284	.351	.568	.221	.282	.460	.250	0.5	-0.4	44-1B	-3
2006	KCA	MLB	26	210	29	10	1	7	36	15	50	1	1	-1.3	.280	.338	.451	.271	.333	.438	.264	2.4	0.0	52-1B	-2
2007	OMA	AAA	27	139	14	7	0	7	24	15	28	0	0	-2.0	.262	.345	.492	.210	.288	.395	.236	-2.9	-0.6	16-1B	-3
2007	KCA	MLB	27	189	18	6	0	3	21	13	53	0	0	-2.8	.221	.286	.308	.215	.284	.308	.208	-9.7	-0.8	48-1B	1
2008	OMA	AAA	28	468	53	22	0	22	65	55	93	0	1	-2.9	.283	.376	.503	.213	.296	.378	.235	-10.6	-1.7	55-1B	-6
2008	KCA	MLB	28	79	12	1	0	7	20	5	19	0	0	-1.3	.301	.354	.603	.301	.354	.616	.313	7.5	0.5	19-1B	-1
2009	KCA	MLB	29	466	40	20	1	15	58	39	121	0	0	-2.8	.218	.291	.379	.215	.289	.391	.235	-10.8	-0.8	110-1B	-4

Breakout: 20% Improve: 41% Collapse: 34% Attrition: 20%   Comparables: Bucky Jacobsen, Jon Knott, Terry Lee, Brian Dorsett

Shealy served his time in the minors dutifully after getting banished in 2007 for the heinous crime of forcing Ross Gload into regular duty. Penance done, he was ready to hit when he finally got his next chance: Royals first basemen had combined for just seven homers when he arrived in September, but he doubled that total in short order. If left to his own devices, Shealy could likely provide league-average production for the next couple of seasons, but the presence of Mike Jacobs pushes him into a peripheral role, probably as the short side of a platoon.

Mark Teahen 4C

Bats: L   Throws: R   Height: 6' 3"   Weight: 210   Born: September 6, 1981   Age: 27

YEAR	TEAM	LVL	AGE	PA	R	2B	3B	HR	RBI	BB	SO	SB	CS	EqBRR	AVG	OBP	SLG	EqAVG	EqOBP	EqSLG	EqA	VORP	WARP	DEFENSE		
2006	OMA	AAA	24	98	14	8	4	2	14	19	12	0	0	0.9	.380	.500	.658	.333	.449	.580	.346	15.5	0.7	21-3B	-5	
2006	KCA	MLB	24	439	70	21	7	18	69	40	85	10	0	4.3	.290	.357	.517	.275	.350	.499	.291	26.2	1.0	105-3B	-17	
2007	KCA	MLB	25	608	78	31	8	7	60	55	127	13	5	3.2	.285	.353	.410	.275	.349	.410	.266	11.3	0.1	130-RF -12	6-1B	-2
2008	KCA	MLB	26	623	66	31	4	15	59	46	131	4	3	-1.8	.255	.313	.402	.253	.315	.413	.250	-1.0	0.3	85-RF -3	30-LF	7
2009	KCA	MLB	27	551	69	27	4	12	63	49	114	8	3	1.2	.265	.334	.412	.262	.332	.425	.263	4.1	1.0	129-RF	-4	

Breakout: 21%   Improve: 41%   Collapse: 23%   Attrition: 13%   Comparables: Todd Hollandsworth, Larry Bigbie, Mark Whiten, Harry Simpson

After 2006, it seemed that Teahen would be an important part of KC's future, but two years later, he's on the way out. Since Alex Gordon took his spot at third base in 2007, Teahen has roamed the edges of the diamond, shifting between all four corner positions, but the trades for Jacobs and Coco Crisp essentially eliminated his avenues to regular playing time. Given that Teahen's best season came while playing every day at the hot corner, some team desperate for help there could swing a deal to free him, and betting that a fresh start will help spark an age-27 rebound wouldn't be a bad risk.

PITCHERS

John Bale

Bats: L   Throws: L   Height: 6' 4"   Weight: 220   Born: May 22, 1974   Age: 35

YEAR	TEAM	LVL	AGE	W	L	SV	G	GS	IP	H	BB	SO	HR	GB%	BABIP	STUFF	WHIP	ERA	DERA	EqH9	EqBB9	EqSO9	EqHR9	DEF	VORP	SN/WX
2006	HRO	JP	32	1	2	6	30	5	43	45	11	46	5	—	.331	-2	1.30	2.93	4.02	10.9	3.1	7.4	1.3	0	7.1	—
2007	KCA	MLB	33	1	1	0	26	0	40	45	17	42	1	49.6%	.393	17	1.55	4.05	2.75	10.1	3.7	8.2	0.2	-4	8.9	-0.07
2008	KCA	MLB	34	0	3	0	13	3	26²	29	6	14	1	52.2%	.333	-4	1.31	4.38	3.51	9.8	1.8	4.2	0.4	-2	3.9	0.49
2009	KCA	MLB	35	2	3	1	28	4	45²	57	17	31	5	45.0%	.340	1	1.62	5.47	5.30	10.9	3.0	5.8	0.9	-0	0.4	0.18

Breakout: 12%   Improve: 32%   Collapse: 37%   Attrition: 41%   Comparables: Joe Grzenda, Jerry Don Gleaton, Buddy Groom, Joe Hatten

Bale won the fourth rotation spot in spring training, but came down with a dead arm after just three starts. Frustrated by the slow pace of his lifeless appendage's resuscitation, he decided to finish the job, breaking his pitching hand by punching a hotel door in early May. Shoulder trouble popped up again midsummer, but Bale managed to make it back to the Royals in September. He's a useful lefty piece to have as a swingman, so after nontendering him, the Royals re-signed him to a lesser deal.

Brian Bannister

Bats: R   Throws: R   Height: 6' 2"   Weight: 210   Born: February 28, 1981   Age: 28

YEAR	TEAM	LVL	AGE	W	L	SV	G	GS	IP	H	BB	SO	HR	GB%	BABIP	STUFF	WHIP	ERA	DERA	EqH9	EqBB9	EqSO9	EqHR9	DEF	VORP	SN/WX
2006	NOR	AAA	25	3	3	0	6	6	30²	34	5	24	4	41.4%	.319	-14	1.29	3.87	6.91	11.3	1.9	4.7	2.2	1	-4.2	—
2006	NYN	MLB	25	2	1	0	8	6	38	34	22	19	4	43.0%	.252	-5	1.47	4.26	4.15	7.8	4.4	3.9	0.9	1	6.7	1.01
2007	OMA	AAA	26	1	1	0	4	4	20²	16	4	14	4	54.8%	.211	-11	0.97	2.61	7.78	7.8	1.8	4.6	2.3	5	-4.8	—
2007	KCA	MLB	26	12	9	0	27	27	165	156	44	77	15	42.5%	.264	2	1.21	3.87	4.72	8.0	2.2	3.6	0.8	14	34.9	4.51
2008	KCA	MLB	27	9	16	0	32	32	182²	215	58	113	29	38.0%	.315	-12	1.49	5.76	6.20	10.4	2.6	4.9	1.4	5	-8.1	1.27
2009	KCA	MLB	28	6	9	0	23	23	129²	151	44	73	18	41.0%	.310	11	1.50	5.30	5.10	10.1	2.7	4.8	1.2	-0	4.2	1.44

Breakout: 7%   Improve: 45%   Collapse: 24%   Attrition: 25%   Comparables: Armando Reynoso, Art Ditmar, Josh Fogg, Jim Colborn

Voros McCracken had his revenge. After holding hitters to a .262 average on balls in play two years ago despite middling stuff, it was thought that Bannister's intelligence, pitching savvy, and fly-ball tendencies might allow him to defy the immutable balance between fielder and batted ball, but it was not to be. Bannister won his first three starts while allowing just 10 hits and three runs in 21 innings, increasing the perception that he had found a way to cheat the house. But the boom swung back hard: from that point forward, he was ripped for 11.4 H/9 and 6.90 RA, and his BABIP finished at .310. Having Crisp and DeJesus in the outfield on a regular basis should help him improve this year, but baseball's fundamental laws have proven that they aren't as willing to oblige.

Daniel Cortes

Bats: R Throws: R Height: 6' 5" Weight: 205 Born: March 4, 1987 Age: 22

YEAR	TEAM	LVL	AGE	W	L	SV	G	GS	IP	H	BB	SO	HR	GB%	BABIP	STUFF	WHIP	ERA	DERA	EqH9	EqBB9	EqSO9	EqHR9	DEF	VORP	SN/WX
2006	BUR	A	19	1	2	0	7	7	35	40	17	30	7	27.0%	.317	-35	1.63	6.69	13.98	17.8	7.3	3.5	6.0	1	-26.4	—
2006	KAN	A	19	3	9	0	20	19	107²	109	38	96	6	41.4%	.324	-2	1.37	4.03	8.87	12.4	4.7	3.5	1.6	-1	-34.6	—
2007	WIL	A+	20	8	8	0	24	24	123	102	45	120	7	39.4%	.293	8	1.20	3.07	6.35	11.4	4.6	5.2	1.4	4	-8.9	—
2008	NWA	AA	21	10	4	0	23	23	116²	103	55	109	13	37.5%	.290	1	1.35	3.78	6.49	10.0	5.0	5.5	1.7	15	-10.4	—
2009	KCA	MLB	22	5	11	0	24	24	125	147	79	90	20	38.0%	.320	10	1.81	6.52	6.21	10.2	5.0	6.1	1.4	-0	-11.8	-0.29

Breakout: 12% Improve: 48% Collapse: 22% Attrition: 13%   Comparables: Jason Schmidt, Scott Sobkowiak, Aaron Myette, Jason Bere

After Luke Hochevar graduated to the majors, Cortes became the Double-A club's top pitching prospect, and he had a season befitting that mantle (up until getting hammered in the Arizona Fall League). He's a fastball/curveball pitcher with a developing change and low- to mid-90s velocity. He works up in the zone and, as a consequence, has a pronounced fly-ball bias—last season, his G/F ratio was 0.76, up slightly from 0.71 in 2007. It's going to be tough for Cortes to keep his homer rate in check if that number stays in this range.

Kyle Davies

Bats: R Throws: R Height: 6' 2" Weight: 205 Born: September 9, 1983 Age: 25

YEAR	TEAM	LVL	AGE	W	L	SV	G	GS	IP	H	BB	SO	HR	GB%	BABIP	STUFF	WHIP	ERA	DERA	EqH9	EqBB9	EqSO9	EqHR9	DEF	VORP	SN/WX
2006	ATL	MLB	22	3	7	0	14	14	63¹	90	33	51	14	38.2%	.369	-2	1.94	8.39	6.82	12.1	4.0	6.4	1.7	-7	-18.4	-0.23
2007	ATL	MLB	23	4	8	0	17	17	86	92	44	59	12	42.6%	.300	-2	1.58	5.76	5.73	9.4	4.0	5.7	1.1	0	-5.5	0.88
2007	KCA	MLB	23	3	7	0	11	11	50	63	26	40	10	35.3%	.338	-11	1.78	6.66	6.62	10.9	4.3	6.1	1.8	-1	-7.3	-0.01
2008	OMA	AAA	24	6	2	0	11	11	57²	47	21	38	4	48.6%	.257	-5	1.18	2.03	4.97	8.1	3.5	4.0	0.8	6	3.8	—
2008	KCA	MLB	24	9	7	0	21	21	113	121	43	71	10	40.2%	.311	4	1.45	4.06	4.60	9.7	3.2	5.1	0.8	3	16.4	2.38
2009	KCA	MLB	25	5	8	0	28	17	102²	114	45	65	14	42.0%	.300	7	1.55	5.29	5.10	9.7	3.5	5.4	1.1	-0	3.3	1.00

Breakout: 23% Improve: 50% Collapse: 22% Attrition: 19%   Comparables: Mark Thompson, Stan Bahnsen, Steve Trachsel, Jim Hughes

Another one of the players whom Moore helped develop while with Atlanta, Davies finally showed batters some teeth after getting ripped apart in his first three major league seasons. The peripheral numbers were nothing to write home to John Schuerholz about, although Davies did manage to cut his homer rate down to a healthier level. Davies' performance was good enough to secure a rotation spot for 2009, but he will have to tune his command to repeat that ERA, for he threw a subpar 61 percent of his pitches for strikes last year.

Daniel Duffy

Bats: L Throws: L Height: 6' 2" Weight: 185 Born: December 21, 1988 Age: 20

YEAR	TEAM	LVL	AGE	W	L	SV	G	GS	IP	H	BB	SO	HR	GB%	BABIP	STUFF	WHIP	ERA	DERA	EqH9	EqBB9	EqSO9	EqHR9	DEF	VORP	SN/WX
2007	ROY	Rk	18	2	3	0	11	9	37¹	24	17	63	0	44.6%	.333	24	1.10	1.45	6.55	9.3	6.3	6.3	0.8	0	-3.5	—
2008	BUR	A	19	8	4	0	17	17	81²	56	25	102	4	37.1%	.283	24	0.99	2.20	5.60	9.0	4.1	6.0	1.4	2	0.0	—
2009	KCA	MLB	20	4	10	0	28	19	107²	135	65	78	21	37.0%	.330	5	1.85	7.16	6.79	10.9	4.8	6.1	1.7	-0	-18.1	-1.07

Breakout: 5% Improve: 20% Collapse: 48% Attrition: 8%   Comparables: Gio Gonzalez, Jake Stevens, Will Inman, Chuck Tiffany

The Royals might have found something when they selected this high school lefty in the third round two years ago. Duffy possesses a remarkably advanced feel for mixing pitches and setting batters up and was pretty much untouchable in his first full pro season, with Midwest League batters managing just a .193 average against his solid fastball, big-breaking slow curve, and well-controlled change. He's a bit like a left-handed version of Cortes, featuring a similar repertoire and batted-ball split (a 0.55 G/F ratio last year). Southpaws who can fan 11 batters per nine innings at any level are rare gems, and Duffy will get the chance to add more luster at High-A Wilmington.

Jimmy Gobble

Bats: L Throws: L Height: 6' 3" Weight: 200 Born: July 19, 1981 Age: 27

YEAR	TEAM	LVL	AGE	W	L	SV	G	GS	IP	H	BB	SO	HR	GB%	BABIP	STUFF	WHIP	ERA	DERA	EqH9	EqBB9	EqSO9	EqHR9	DEF	VORP	SN/WX
2006	KCA	MLB	24	4	6	2	60	6	84	95	29	80	12	39.6%	.339	0	1.48	5.14	4.63	9.7	3.0	7.5	1.2	-5	6.5	-0.36
2007	KCA	MLB	25	4	1	1	74	0	53²	56	23	50	6	36.1%	.342	2	1.47	3.02	2.61	9.6	3.7	7.5	1.0	-6	13.1	1.68
2008	KCA	MLB	26	0	2	1	39	0	31²	39	23	27	5	30.8%	.337	-13	1.96	8.80	6.61	10.7	5.8	6.6	1.4	-6	-10.6	-0.83
2009	KCA	MLB	27	2	2	2	43	0	42	43	21	37	5	37.0%	.310	10	1.50	4.71	4.51	8.9	3.9	7.5	1.1	-0	4.2	0.35

Breakout: 54% Improve: 75% Collapse: 12% Attrition: 35%   Comparables: Brad Havens, Bob Kipper, Dan Spillner, Bob Owchinko

After finally showing promise as a reliever in 2007, Gobble was gobbled up by hitters last year. His numbers look especially gruesome because of a historic 10-run top of the eighth against Detroit on July 21; no reliever in more than a half-century (at least) had ever before given up 10 runs while working an inning or less. Afterward, Gobble went on the DL with a bruised ego (and stiff back), but salvaged some pride by throwing seven scoreless September innings. Gobble is still an attractive option against lefties—he dropped his arm slot in 2007 and held his own kind to a 569 OPS in 69 PAs last year. Don't read on if you're faint of heart: righties hit .382/.517/.676 in 89 PAs. Consequently, he'll be the resident LOOGY this year.

Zack Greinke Bats: R Throws: R Height: 6' 2" Weight: 185 Born: October 21, 1983 Age: 25

YEAR	TEAM	LVL	AGE	W	L	SV	G	GS	IP	H	BB	SO	HR	GB%	BABIP	STUFF	WHIP	ERA	DERA	EqH9	EqBB9	EqSO9	EqHR9	DEF	VORP	SN/WX
2006	WIC	AA	22	8	3	0	18	17	105	96	27	94	12	44.0%	.297	-4	1.17	4.37	6.80	9.6	2.7	5.1	1.5	9	-13.2	—
2006	KCA	MLB	22	1	0	0	3	0	6¹	7	3	5	1	35.0%	.316	4	1.58	4.29	5.68	9.9	4.3	5.7	1.4	2	1.3	0.17
2007	KCA	MLB	23	7	7	1	52	14	122	122	36	106	12	32.6%	.321	13	1.30	3.69	3.37	9.0	2.5	7.0	0.9	-3	30.2	5.21
2008	KCA	MLB	24	13	10	0	32	32	202¹	202	56	183	21	43.3%	.312	22	1.28	3.47	3.52	8.9	2.3	7.2	0.9	-5	44.3	5.27
2009	KCA	MLB	25	12	10	0	30	30	192¹	191	57	164	22	41.0%	.300	31	1.29	3.96	3.81	8.7	2.4	7.2	1.0	-1	33.1	5.15

Breakout: 22% Improve: 51% Collapse: 16% Attrition: 13%   Comparables: Alex Fernandez, Joe Coleman, Kevin Appier, Denny McLain

It was worth the wait. After three trying seasons that featured adversity both on the mound and off it (in the form of social anxiety disorder and depression), Greinke fully seized his potential and delivered the season that people had been expecting since his scintillating 2004 debut. Few pitchers boast an arsenal that can approach the sophistication of Greinke's weaponry, as the young ace has tremendous control of a fastball, slider, curve, and change. The Royals' top priority should be getting Greinke inked to a long-term deal, but Greinke has already indicated that he's comfortable going year-to-year until free agency following the 2010 season.

Daniel Gutierrez Bats: R Throws: R Height: 6' 1" Weight: 180 Born: March 8, 1987 Age: 22

YEAR	TEAM	LVL	AGE	W	L	SV	G	GS	IP	H	BB	SO	HR	GB%	BABIP	STUFF	WHIP	ERA	DERA	EqH9	EqBB9	EqSO9	EqHR9	DEF	VORP	SN/WX
2006	IDA	Rk	19	0	4	0	14	9	49¹	74	21	36	6	56.5%	.415	-51	1.93	6.60	9.92	21.0	6.5	2.1	3.9	-15	-18.7	—
2007	BUR	A	20	1	2	0	7	7	31¹	32	12	27	2	40.0%	.326	-2	1.41	4.89	9.47	14.0	6.0	3.5	2.1	-1	-11.1	—
2008	BUR	A	21	4	4	0	19	18	90	83	25	104	7	53.4%	.329	0	1.20	2.70	5.63	12.4	4.0	5.6	2.0	-10	-0.3	—
2009	KCA	MLB	22	3	9	0	19	19	92¹	129	51	56	17	46.0%	.350	2	1.94	7.61	7.29	12.2	4.4	5.2	1.6	-0	-19.9	-1.43

Breakout: 27% Improve: 59% Collapse: 8% Attrition: 11%   Comparables: Greg Harris, Kevin Grater, Aaron Cames, Rob Henkel

Drafted in the 33rd round out of a California high school in 2005, Gutierrez emerged from obscurity last year. He made huge strides with his traditional three-pitch arsenal throughout the season and showcased outstanding command of both a mid-90s heater and a plus curve in the Midwest League playoffs, when he allowed just two runs in 12 innings with 17 strikeouts and just two walks in helping the Bees sweep to the championship. By the end of the year, the Royals felt he was by far the best pitcher they had at any minor league level.

Luke Hochevar Bats: R Throws: R Height: 6' 5" Weight: 205 Born: September 15, 1983 Age: 25

YEAR	TEAM	LVL	AGE	W	L	SV	G	GS	IP	H	BB	SO	HR	GB%	BABIP	STUFF	WHIP	ERA	DERA	EqH9	EqBB9	EqSO9	EqHR9	DEF	VORP	SN/WX
2006	BUR	A	22	0	1	0	4	4	15	8	2	16	2	39.5%	.167	-2	0.67	1.20	5.40	8.8	2.0	4.7	4.1	2	0.3	—
2007	WIC	AA	23	3	6	0	17	16	94	110	26	94	13	40.1%	.350	-18	1.45	4.69	6.90	12.6	3.1	5.8	2.0	-8	-12.6	—
2007	OMA	AAA	23	1	3	0	10	10	58	53	21	44	11	40.7%	.259	-15	1.28	5.12	6.42	9.4	3.5	4.9	2.1	4	-5.0	—
2007	KCA	MLB	23	0	1	0	4	1	12²	11	4	5	1	64.3%	.250	-5	1.18	2.13	1.42	7.1	2.8	2.8	0.7	-2	4.5	0.06
2008	OMA	AAA	24	1	1	0	3	3	17¹	11	6	12	2	70.6%	.191	-6	0.98	2.60	6.35	5.8	3.2	4.2	1.1	4	-1.4	—
2008	KCA	MLB	24	6	12	0	22	22	129	143	47	72	12	51.8%	.307	0	1.47	5.51	5.53	9.8	3.0	4.4	0.9	0	0.5	0.98
2009	KCA	MLB	25	6	8	0	28	19	117¹	131	43	70	14	48.0%	.300	9	1.48	4.95	4.82	9.7	2.9	5.1	1.0	-0	7.5	1.56

Breakout: 32% Improve: 61% Collapse: 22% Attrition: 29%   Comparables: Todd Stottlemyre, Steve Karsay, Gavin Floyd, Zach Miner

The first full major league season for the top pick in the 2006 draft was something of a dud. Still, it looked worse than it was: before suffering a season-ending rib-cage contusion in late August, Hochevar reduced his home-run rate. His overall numbers would have been better if not for poor timing—opponents hit .338 with runners in scoring position, as compared with .245 with nobody on. It wasn't a good enough performance to guarantee a 2009 rotation berth, as he'll have to battle Horacio Ramirez for the fifth spot.

Devon Lowery

Bats: L   Throws: R   Height: 6' 1"   Weight: 195   Born: March 24, 1983   Age: 26

YEAR	TEAM	LVL	AGE	W	L	SV	G	GS	IP	H	BB	SO	HR	GB%	BABIP	STUFF	WHIP	ERA	DERA	EqH9	EqBB9	EqSO9	EqHR9	DEF	VORP	SN/WX
2006	WIC	AA	23	5	1	4	24	0	33^1	29	19	31	5	40.7%	.260	-25	1.45	5.71	9.19	8.9	5.3	5.0	1.9	5	-12.9	—
2008	NWA	AA	25	1	0	2	9	0	13	8	5	17	0	29.0%	.258	9	1.00	0.69	2.84	6.4	3.6	7.8	0.0	1	3.9	—
2008	OMA	AAA	25	1	1	5	31	0	59^1	48	30	43	4	36.0%	.262	-11	1.32	2.12	4.31	8.0	4.6	4.3	0.8	6	8.1	—
2008	KCA	MLB	25	0	0	0	5	0	4^1	6	2	6	2	46.2%	.364	3	1.85	10.47	8.31	12.5	4.2	10.4	4.2	-1	-2.3	-0.01
2009	KCA	MLB	26	2	4	1	27	5	53	60	31	39	9	36.0%	.310	1	1.71	5.79	5.48	9.9	4.6	6.3	1.4	-0	-0.8	0.08

Breakout: 2%   Improve: 20%   Collapse: 53%   Attrition: 10%   Comparables: Jeff Bajenaru, Judd Songster, Jim Miller, Zach Schreiber

A consummate organizational soldier, Lowery finally broke from the ranks and charged up to Kansas City last year at the end of his eighth professional season. The Royals have shown a lot of faith in Lowery, protecting him on the 40-man roster through injury and mediocre results over the last several years, but his numbers don't inspire much confidence. With options remaining, Lowery is likely to be a regular on the shuttle between Omaha and KC.

Ron Mahay

Bats: L   Throws: L   Height: 6' 2"   Weight: 190   Born: June 28, 1971   Age: 38

YEAR	TEAM	LVL	AGE	W	L	SV	G	GS	IP	H	BB	SO	HR	GB%	BABIP	STUFF	WHIP	ERA	DERA	EqH9	EqBB9	EqSO9	EqHR9	DEF	VORP	SN/WX
2006	TEX	MLB	35	1	3	0	62	0	57	54	28	56	7	42.6%	.307	4	1.44	3.95	3.86	8.2	4.3	7.9	1.0	-3	9.1	0.20
2007	TEX	MLB	36	2	0	1	28	0	39	33	21	32	3	52.7%	.286	3	1.38	2.77	2.89	7.7	4.6	6.8	0.7	0	14.2	0.61
2007	ATL	MLB	36	1	0	0	30	0	28	19	16	23	1	47.4%	.243	6	1.25	2.25	4.18	6.1	4.5	6.8	0.3	6	10.2	0.46
2008	KCA	MLB	37	5	0	0	57	0	64^2	61	29	49	6	39.2%	.294	-5	1.39	3.48	4.24	8.3	3.7	6.1	0.8	4	14.5	3.58
2009	KCA	MLB	38	2	2	2	41	0	42^2	45	20	33	5	42.0%	.310	2	1.53	4.53	4.36	9.2	3.8	6.5	0.9	-0	5.4	0.41

Breakout: 11%   Improve: 21%   Collapse: 59%   Attrition: 28%   Comparables: Kent Mercker, Mike Myers, Mike Stanton, Ron Villone

Don't call me LOOGY: Mahay actually pitched better against righties (679 OPS in 168 PA) than against lefties (721 in 110) last year. Those numbers could be written off as a sample-size accident, but he also was more effective versus northpaws in 2005 and 2006. There was a great deal of demand for Mahay at the trade deadline, but the Royals decided to hang on for the back end of the two-year, $8 million deal the veteran signed before the season; however, if the Royals are out of contention at the deadline, he'll almost certainly be on the move.

Gil Meche

Bats: R   Throws: R   Height: 6' 3"   Weight: 220   Born: September 8, 1978   Age: 30

YEAR	TEAM	LVL	AGE	W	L	SV	G	GS	IP	H	BB	SO	HR	GB%	BABIP	STUFF	WHIP	ERA	DERA	EqH9	EqBB9	EqSO9	EqHR9	DEF	VORP	SN/WX
2006	SEA	MLB	27	11	8	0	32	32	186^2	183	84	156	24	45.1%	.298	7	1.43	4.48	4.56	8.8	4.0	6.8	1.1	-12	18.5	3.48
2007	KCA	MLB	28	9	13	0	34	34	216	218	62	156	22	47.6%	.301	12	1.30	3.67	3.85	8.8	2.4	5.7	0.9	0	47.4	5.19
2008	KCA	MLB	29	14	11	0	34	34	210^1	204	73	183	19	40.1%	.310	20	1.32	3.98	4.01	8.7	2.9	7.0	0.8	-1	30.9	4.61
2009	KCA	MLB	30	11	11	0	30	30	187^1	187	68	147	21	43.0%	.300	24	1.36	4.23	4.10	8.7	2.9	6.7	0.9	-1	27.4	4.38

Breakout: 13%   Improve: 55%   Collapse: 19%   Attrition: 11%   Comparables: Bob Rush, Mike Moore, Tim Belcher, Freddy Garcia

The Epic turned in another solid season, joining C. C. Sabathia, Bronson Arroyo, Ted Lilly, and Brandon Webb as the only other pitchers to make at least 34 starts in both 2007 and '08. This combination of durability and success places a feather in the cap of Moore, who was seemingly the only person in the universe who felt the injury-prone righty was worthy of a five-year, $55 million contract three offseasons ago. That deal now stands as a bargain. The Royals need to exploit Meche's transformation by putting together a contender soon, especially since a no-trade clause eliminates management's ability to cash in by selling high.

Tim Melville

								Bats:		Throws:		Height: 0' 0"		Weight:		Born:			Age: 19

YEAR	TEAM	LVL	AGE	W	L	SV	G	GS	IP	H	BB	SO	HR	GB%	BABIP	STUFF	WHIP	ERA	DERA	EqH9	EqBB9	EqSO9	EqHR9	DEF	VORP	SN/WX
2009	KCA	MLB	19	3	13	0	26	26	120	188	87	50	27	45.2%	.355	-15	2.29	9.53	9.09	13.6	5.8	3.5	1.9	0	-51.4	-4.50

Breakout: N/A   Improve: N/A   Collapse: N/A   Attrition: N/A   Comparables: Bob Keppel, Chris Tillman, Chaz Roe, Scott Garrelts

Melville was projected as a high first-round pick before his senior season, but then he struggled some and fell even further in the draft because of his expectation of getting paid as a top talent just the same. The Royals took him in the fourth round and gave him $1.25 million to sign, thus adding one of the top five prep pitching talents to their already formidable array of young arms. He'll start the year off in extended spring training, and he might get a chance to pitch in the Midwest League in his first pro season.

Michael Montgomery

								Bats: L		Throws: L		Height: 6' 5"		Weight: 180		Born: July 1, 1989			Age: 20

YEAR	TEAM	LVL	AGE	W	L	SV	G	GS	IP	H	BB	SO	HR	GB%	BABIP	STUFF	WHIP	ERA	DERA	EqH9	EqBB9	EqSO9	EqHR9	DEF	VORP	SN/WX
2008	ROY	Rk	19	2	1	0	12	9	42²	31	12	34	2	62.6%	.261	-14	1.01	1.69	5.14	9.8	4.6	2.3	2.8	0	1.8	—
2009	KCA	MLB	19	3	11	0	23	23	108	157	70	42	22	47.0%	.340	-12	2.10	8.57	8.24	12.7	5.2	3.3	1.7	-0	-35.4	-2.91

Breakout: 0%   Improve: 0%   Collapse: 0%   Attrition: 0%   Comparables: Ryan Feierabend, Ryan Morris, Scott Elbert, Nate Bland

The Royals have been searching for a solid reliever like Jeff Montgomery ever since the All-Star closer retired after the 1999 season. They might have found a good one in another Montgomery, young Michael, whom they snagged in the supplemental first round out of a California high school last year as compensation for losing free agent David Riske. (Thank you, Elias rankings!) The lanky southpaw pitches off his strong fastball and change and needs to find a new curveball grip after throwing a basic palm variety for years.

Leo Nuñez

								Bats: R		Throws: R		Height: 6' 1"		Weight: 165		Born: August 14, 1983			Age: 25

YEAR	TEAM	LVL	AGE	W	L	SV	G	GS	IP	H	BB	SO	HR	GB%	BABIP	STUFF	WHIP	ERA	DERA	EqH9	EqBB9	EqSO9	EqHR9	DEF	VORP	SN/WX
2006	WIC	AA	22	1	2	3	15	0	21²	18	12	22	3	47.4%	.278	-2	1.42	4.25	4.58	9.6	5.5	5.9	1.8	-2	2.2	—
2006	OMA	AAA	22	2	2	5	23	0	38²	37	13	33	5	35.7%	.299	-2	1.31	2.12	2.80	9.9	3.3	5.6	1.8	-2	11.0	—
2006	KCA	MLB	22	0	0	0	7	0	13¹	15	5	7	2	45.5%	.317	-7	1.50	4.74	4.26	9.9	3.6	4.3	1.4	0	2.2	0.05
2007	WIC	AA	23	1	0	0	6	5	20²	10	6	13	1	45.5%	.167	-6	0.77	0.87	4.19	4.7	3.3	3.3	0.9	5	3.0	—
2007	OMA	AAA	23	1	2	0	5	4	23	16	4	19	3	38.5%	.213	6	0.87	2.74	5.56	6.8	1.6	5.2	1.6	6	0.1	—
2007	KCA	MLB	23	2	4	0	13	6	43²	44	10	37	8	34.8%	.288	7	1.24	3.91	3.71	8.7	1.9	6.6	1.6	-1	8.6	0.85
2008	KCA	MLB	24	4	1	0	45	0	48¹	45	15	26	2	41.9%	.281	-3	1.24	2.98	2.79	8.0	2.6	4.3	0.4	-3	12.1	0.33
2009	FLO	MLB	25	2	2	2	38	0	44	40	15	35	4	42.0%	.280	6	1.25	3.64	3.94	8.3	2.6	5.8	0.9	0	9.5	0.72

Breakout: 19%   Improve: 30%   Collapse: 47%   Attrition: 27%   Comparables: Steve Kealey, Oscar Villarreal, Randy Moffitt, Steve Ontiveros

Nuñez had another solid season, sandwiched around a late-May lat strain that kept him out of action for two months. Seizing on the depth and strength of the bullpen, Moore sent Nuñez to the Marlins for first baseman Mike Jacobs in November. What's troubling is Nuñez's paucity of strikeouts; a fastball in the mid-90s along with a slider and change should lead to more whiffs than he generated last year. He is not a ground-ball pitcher, either, so he'll need to pump up those strikeouts in order to remain effective. Still, the Marlins did well in getting a cheap, young, hard-throwing set-up man who should be a significant part of their pen this year.

Joel Peralta

								Bats: R		Throws: R		Height: 5' 11"		Weight: 190		Born: March 23, 1976			Age: 33

YEAR	TEAM	LVL	AGE	W	L	SV	G	GS	IP	H	BB	SO	HR	GB%	BABIP	STUFF	WHIP	ERA	DERA	EqH9	EqBB9	EqSO9	EqHR9	DEF	VORP	SN/WX
2006	KCA	MLB	30	1	3	1	64	0	73²	74	17	57	10	32.0%	.299	-2	1.24	4.40	4.35	8.5	2.1	6.2	1.1	0	13.3	0.70
2007	KCA	MLB	31	1	3	1	62	0	87²	93	19	66	9	37.6%	.318	1	1.28	3.80	3.66	9.3	1.9	6.0	0.9	-1	20.1	0.81
2008	KCA	MLB	32	1	2	0	40	0	52²	56	14	38	15	37.1%	.272	-28	1.33	5.98	6.27	9.4	2.3	5.7	2.6	2	-2.8	-0.56
2009	KCA	MLB	33	2	2	2	41	0	49²	52	15	37	7	36.0%	.290	5	1.34	4.44	4.23	9.0	2.4	6.3	1.3	-0	6.4	0.54

Breakout: 28%   Improve: 47%   Collapse: 24%   Attrition: 34%   Comparables: Barry Manuel, Ted Wilks, Bob Wells, Jose Cabrera

Peralta was the one Royals reliever who was expected to be a major contributor but who did not perform well. The problem was home runs: like Nuñez, Peralta is far over on the fly-ball side of the divide, and last year, a few more left the park than usual. The stuff for the breaking-ball pitcher is still there, so expect a rebound this season.

Julio Pimentel

Bats: R   Throws: R   Height: 6' 1"   Weight: 190   Born: December 14, 1985   Age: 23

YEAR	TEAM	LVL	AGE	W	L	SV	G	GS	IP	H	BB	SO	HR	GB%	BABIP	STUFF	WHIP	ERA	DERA	EqH9	EqBB9	EqSO9	EqHR9	DEF	VORP	SN/WX
2006	VRO	A+	20	3	8	2	30	9	74¹	85	45	77	4	46.9%	.387	-6	1.75	5.71	8.45	13.3	7.3	5.1	1.4	-12	-20.6	—
2006	HDS	A+	20	2	1	2	12	0	22¹	21	10	26	3	47.7%	.323	9	1.40	3.26	4.43	10.6	5.3	5.8	2.2	0	2.6	—
2007	WIL	A+	21	12	4	0	27	22	152²	145	43	73	8	61.7%	.275	-22	1.23	2.65	5.90	12.1	3.7	1.7	1.4	5	-4.4	—
2008	NWA	AA	22	7	13	0	28	28	157¹	193	52	115	17	46.5%	.354	-23	1.56	5.38	7.23	13.6	3.7	4.0	1.7	-6	-25.5	—
2009	KCA	MLB	23	3	11	0	23	23	110	167	57	50	20	46.0%	.360	-5	2.03	7.91	7.55	13.2	4.1	3.9	1.6	-0	-26.9	-2.05

Breakout: 13%   Improve: 52%   Collapse: 21%   Attrition: 15%   Comparables: Les Straker, Ramon Bencomo, Cesar Mejia, Jose Ventura

Pimentel suffered a particularly hard shock when he moved from the pitcher-friendly Carolina League to the harsh, flat, forbidding landscapes of the Texas League. The hard sinker he'd bridled in 2007 spit the bit, for the new environment brought a drop in Pimentel's G/F ratio from 2.25 to 1.26, while his homer rate just about doubled. There was also some poor luck involved on balls in play. At least Pimentel's K/BB ratio improved, so a bounceback season should be in the offing.

Ramon Ramirez

Bats: R   Throws: R   Height: 5' 11"   Weight: 190   Born: August 31, 1981   Age: 27

YEAR	TEAM	LVL	AGE	W	L	SV	G	GS	IP	H	BB	SO	HR	GB%	BABIP	STUFF	WHIP	ERA	DERA	EqH9	EqBB9	EqSO9	EqHR9	DEF	VORP	SN/WX
2006	COL	MLB	24	4	3	0	61	0	67²	58	27	61	5	41.3%	.285	13	1.26	3.46	3.28	7.1	3.1	7.2	0.5	1	18.7	0.80
2007	CSP	AAA	25	4	0	0	25	0	27²	18	16	35	2	50.8%	.258	12	1.23	2.27	4.61	5.9	5.3	8.2	0.7	3	3.0	—
2007	COL	MLB	25	2	2	0	22	0	17¹	21	6	15	2	35.7%	.380	-3	1.56	8.32	6.35	11.1	2.6	7.4	1.1	-1	-4.2	-0.09
2008	KCA	MLB	26	3	2	1	71	0	71²	57	31	70	2	48.7%	.297	20	1.23	2.64	3.20	7.2	3.6	7.8	0.3	2	23.1	2.22
2009	BOS	MLB	27	3	2	3	52	0	57²	52	25	53	5	45.0%	.290	14	1.33	3.51	3.57	7.8	3.4	7.7	0.7	1	14.4	1.20

Breakout: 17%   Improve: 34%   Collapse: 31%   Attrition: 12%   Comparables: Eddie Watt, Curt Leskanic, Greg Harris, Jose Paniagua

As measured by Adjusted Runs Prevented, Ramirez was the team's most effective reliever last season; his 22.5 ARP was the sixth-best figure in the majors. A large part of that success was due to his extreme stinginess with the long ball—among pitchers with 70 or more innings, only Roy Corcoran and Jason Grilli had a lower rate of home runs allowed. Ramirez altered his pitch sequencing in 2008, throwing fewer fastballs and sliders and more changeups, a shift in philosophy that paid off. The solid season allowed Dayton Moore to take advantage of Boston's desperation to fulfill its Ramirez quota by trading Ramon for Coco Crisp, solving Kansas City's problem in center field.

Carlos Rosa

Bats: R   Throws: R   Height: 6' 1"   Weight: 185   Born: September 21, 1984   Age: 24

YEAR	TEAM	LVL	AGE	W	L	SV	G	GS	IP	H	BB	SO	HR	GB%	BABIP	STUFF	WHIP	ERA	DERA	EqH9	EqBB9	EqSO9	EqHR9	DEF	VORP	SN/WX
2006	BUR	A	21	8	6	0	24	24	138²	121	54	102	6	51.5%	.288	-24	1.27	2.54	6.55	12.3	5.8	2.8	1.7	0	-12.0	—
2007	WIL	A+	22	2	1	0	4	4	23	18	3	15	0	57.7%	.254	4	0.91	0.39	3.05	9.6	1.7	3.0	0.4	2	5.9	—
2007	WIC	AA	22	6	6	1	21	17	97	101	43	70	8	50.8%	.317	-17	1.48	4.36	6.85	11.0	4.7	4.0	1.3	7	-12.2	—
2008	NWA	AA	23	4	2	0	8	8	45	30	7	42	2	52.1%	.243	18	0.82	1.20	3.46	7.1	1.7	5.4	0.9	4	9.9	—
2008	OMA	AAA	23	4	3	0	11	11	50²	51	12	44	3	50.7%	.333	7	1.24	4.08	5.32	10.8	2.4	5.7	0.8	2	1.4	
2008	KCA	MLB	23	0	0	0	2	0	3¹	3	0	3	0	0.0%	.333	3	0.90	2.73	6.00	9.0	0.0	9.0	0.0	1	1.2	-0.28
2009	KCA	MLB	24	5	8	1	36	15	108¹	130	42	65	13	46.0%	.320	5	1.58	5.66	5.50	10.5	3.1	5.1	1.1	-0	-1.6	0.42

Breakout: 9%   Improve: 32%   Collapse: 36%   Attrition: 21%   Comparables: Tomo Ohka, Jae Kuk Ryu, Juan Dominguez, Vicente Padilla

One of the few prospects who found his way into the system from the Dominican before the Royals beefed up their presence there under Moore, Rosa had the best season of any KC pitcher in the high minors. The righty's fastball can get into the mid-90s and features natural sink, his slider gained consistency over the course of the season, and he possesses a decent change. With those kinds of tools and results that show he's figuring out how to pitch, Rosa is a dark-horse candidate to earn a few Rookie of the Year votes, provided he's healthy—a forearm strain ended his season a couple of weeks early, and it was rumored that the Marlins passed on him when discussing the Jacobs trade because of health concerns.

Joakim Soria

Bats: R   **Throws: R**   **Height: 6' 3"**   **Weight: 185**   **Born: May 18, 1984**   **Age: 25**

YEAR	TEAM	LVL	AGE	W	L	SV	G	GS	IP	H	BB	SO	HR	GB%	BABIP	STUFF	WHIP	ERA	DERA	EqH9	EqBB9	EqSO9	EqHR9	DEF	VORP	SN/WX
2006	MCD	MEX	22	0	0	15	39	0	37	37	11	30	2	49.2%	.325	2	1.30	3.89	5.15	8.8	3.2	5.9	1.0	1	1.8	—
2006	FTW	A	22	1	0	0	7	0	11¹	5	2	11	1	48.4%	.207	-9	0.63	2.43	7.20	6.3	2.7	4.5	2.7	2	-1.8	—
2007	KCA	MLB	23	2	3	17	62	0	69	46	19	75	3	41.1%	.256	31	0.94	2.48	3.25	5.7	2.3	8.4	0.4	6	26.4	4.80
2008	KCA	MLB	24	2	3	42	63	0	67¹	39	19	66	5	45.6%	.213	19	0.86	1.60	3.51	5.1	2.3	7.8	0.7	13	30.2	5.43
2009	KCA	MLB	25	4	5	32	54	0	60²	51	21	60	6	42.0%	.280	24	1.19	3.11	3.01	7.4	2.8	8.4	0.8	-0	18.2	2.68

Breakout: 5%   Improve: 23%   Collapse: 61%   Attrition: 16%   *Comparables: Huston Street, Gregg Olson, Ed Vande Berg, Scott Strickland*

Having a closer as ruthless as the Mexicutioner means you can afford to trade away two top setup men with little concern. Soria vaulted from dominant to sublime last season, giving up fewer hits per nine than any AL pitcher with at least 60 innings and posting the lowest WHIP in franchise history. His four-pitch arsenal includes a dizzying change of speeds: low-90s cutter, mid-80s change, upper-70s slider, and an unhittable 12-6 slow curve. Soria's varied repertoire and sheer domination have led to speculation that he might best be utilized as a starter, but for now, the Royals are keeping him in the pen. A good compromise would be to have him throw more innings—rolling out such a vicious late-game weapon for fewer than 70 frames a season represents a criminal underutilization, and Soria went more than an inning on just seven occasions last year after doing so 17 times in 2007. The Royals deserve better from Hillman this season.

Robinson Tejeda

Bats: R   **Throws: R**   **Height: 6' 3"**   **Weight: 230**   **Born: March 24, 1982**   **Age: 27**

YEAR	TEAM	LVL	AGE	W	L	SV	G	GS	IP	H	BB	SO	HR	GB%	BABIP	STUFF	WHIP	ERA	DERA	EqH9	EqBB9	EqSO9	EqHR9	DEF	VORP	SN/WX
2006	OKL	AAA	24	6	2	0	15	15	80	61	42	79	7	42.0%	.265	5	1.29	3.15	4.78	7.9	4.9	6.3	1.2	4	6.9	—
2006	TEX	MLB	24	5	5	0	14	14	73²	83	32	40	10	38.6%	.307	-9	1.56	4.27	4.46	9.5	3.8	4.3	1.1	-2	9.9	1.67
2007	OKL	AAA	25	1	3	0	5	4	18²	27	15	20	0	37.3%	.466	7	2.25	8.18	8.10	16.2	8.1	7.6	0.5	-3	-4.6	—
2007	TEX	MLB	25	5	9	0	19	19	95¹	110	60	69	17	36.1%	.317	-15	1.78	6.61	5.74	10.1	5.2	5.6	1.6	-13	-13.9	-0.33
2008	OKL	AAA	26	1	1	1	10	4	33	20	10	39	2	33.3%	.240	17	0.91	2.18	3.66	5.9	2.8	7.3	0.6	3	6.9	—
2008	TEX	MLB	26	0	0	0	4	0	6	5	5	4	1	25.0%	.222	-18	1.67	9.00	10.80	5.4	6.8	4.1	1.4	2	-2.1	-0.54
2008	KCA	MLB	26	2	2	0	25	1	39¹	22	19	41	3	33.3%	.209	12	1.04	3.21	5.03	4.8	3.9	8.2	0.7	6	8.4	0.88
2009	KCA	MLB	27	3	4	1	34	6	64²	61	34	55	8	38.0%	.290	10	1.46	4.72	4.55	8.2	4.1	7.2	1.0	-0	6.8	0.80

Breakout: 39%   Improve: 64%   Collapse: 20%   Attrition: 26%   *Comparables: Jim Britton, Joaquin Benoit, Rick Helling, Eric Plunk*

Fed up with a pitcher who seemed to be a Quad-A type after repeatedly failing in the majors, the Rangers designated Tejeda for assignment in June, despite his ability to blow people away with his mid-90s heat in the Pacific Coast League. That was a mistake. The Royals smartly snapped him up, and while Hillman used Tejeda almost exclusively when the Royals were behind—Kansas City was 4-21 in his appearances—this year, he should be elevated to a much more important role and a chance to join John Danks and Edinson Volquez as another pitcher the Rangers just plumb missed.

Kip Wells

Bats: R   **Throws: R**   **Height: 6' 3"**   **Weight: 205**   **Born: April 21, 1977**   **Age: 32**

YEAR	TEAM	LVL	AGE	W	L	SV	G	GS	IP	H	BB	SO	HR	GB%	BABIP	STUFF	WHIP	ERA	DERA	EqH9	EqBB9	EqSO9	EqHR9	DEF	VORP	SN/WX
2006	PIT	MLB	29	1	5	0	7	7	36¹	46	18	16	3	52.3%	.344	-10	1.76	6.69	5.30	10.6	4.0	3.8	0.8	-3	-3.1	0.14
2006	TEX	MLB	29	1	0	0	2	2	8	15	3	4	0	54.5%	.455	-7	2.25	6.75	0.00	16.4	3.5	3.5	0.0	-6	-0.6	0.15
2007	SLN	MLB	30	7	17	0	34	26	162²	186	78	122	19	49.5%	.329	3	1.62	5.70	5.14	9.9	3.7	6.2	1.0	-13	-10.8	0.74
2008	COL	MLB	31	1	2	0	15	2	27¹	29	19	22	3	58.3%	.333	-1	1.76	5.27	4.33	9.3	5.3	6.3	1.0	-3	-2.0	0.24
2008	KCA	MLB	31	0	1	0	10	0	10¹	10	11	9	1	48.3%	.321	5	2.03	8.74	7.45	9.3	9.3	7.4	0.9	0	-3.3	0.14
2009	KCA	MLB	32	2	5	0	25	7	60²	72	32	40	7	47.0%	.320	-1	1.71	6.04	5.90	10.4	4.2	5.5	1.0	-0	-4.2	-0.10

Breakout: 22%   Improve: 43%   Collapse: 34%   Attrition: 35%   *Comparables: Don Larsen, Jesse Jefferson, Jay Powell, Ed Whitson*

Heady with the theft of Ramon Ramirez from the Rockies in spring training, the Royals kept going back to the same well throughout the season, but to less effect. Wells became the fourth reliever to move from Colorado to KC in 2008 when he signed with the Royals in August after getting released by the Rockies. He made $3.1 million last year, but will be lucky to get a spring training invite in 2009, as he hasn't posted a WHIP below 1.5 in the majors since 2003.

Blake Wood

| | | | | | | | Bats: R | | Throws: R | | Height: 6' 4" | | Weight: 225 | | Born: August 8, 1985 | | | Age: 23 |

YEAR	TEAM	LVL	AGE	W	L	SV	G	GS	IP	H	BB	SO	HR	GB%	BABIP	STUFF	WHIP	ERA	DERA	EqH9	EqBB9	EqSO9	EqHR9	DEF	VORP	SN/WX
2006	IDA	Rk	20	3	1	0	12	12	52²	50	15	46	1	45.4%	.341	3	1.25	4.48	8.74	12.3	4.4	3.0	1.0	0	-15.8	—
2007	BUR	A	21	2	1	0	7	7	35²	32	14	26	3	38.5%	.276	-22	1.29	3.03	6.00	12.0	5.7	2.7	2.4	-1	-1.3	—
2008	WIL	A+	22	3	2	0	10	10	57¹	32	15	63	3	44.7%	.232	28	0.82	2.67	4.99	6.4	2.8	6.7	1.0	8	3.5	—
2008	NWA	AA	22	5	7	0	18	18	86²	96	32	76	7	48.8%	.357	-7	1.48	5.29	6.75	12.2	4.0	5.0	1.3	-5	-10.1	—
2009	KCA	MLB	23	4	8	0	18	18	93	111	45	62	12	44.0%	.320	12	1.67	6.00	5.80	10.4	3.9	5.6	1.1	-0	-4.6	0.24

Breakout: 25% Improve: 64% Collapse: 13% Attrition: 11%   Comparables: Robert Ellis, Jason Bell, Marc Barcelo, Matt Clement

Wood experienced the same rude hospitality from the Texas League that Pimentel did; also like Pimentel, he has terrific raw stuff, with a plus heater that reaches into the mid-90s. Finding a reliable third offering has been the problem: in 2007, he showcased a good power curveball yet was inconsistent with his changeup, while last year, his off-speed pitch came forward, but the breaker regressed. If Wood manages to saddle both at the same time, he could experience a breakout. If not, he might be bullpen-bound.

Yasuhiko Yabuta

| | | | | | | | Bats: R | | Throws: R | | Height: 6' 0" | | Weight: 190 | | Born: June 9, 1973 | | | Age: 36 |

YEAR	TEAM	LVL	AGE	W	L	SV	G	GS	IP	H	BB	SO	HR	GB%	BABIP	STUFF	WHIP	ERA	DERA	EqH9	EqBB9	EqSO9	EqHR9	DEF	VORP	SN/WX
2006	CHB	JP	33	4	2	1	47	0	55	43	26	48	3	—	.258	-6	1.25	2.62	4.85	7.8	5.4	5.7	0.9	0	4.3	—
2007	CHB	JP	34	4	6	4	58	0	62²	64	10	45	5	—	.292	-13	1.18	2.73	4.52	9.3	1.9	4.5	1.2	0	7.4	—
2008	OMA	AAA	35	4	3	3	20	0	40¹	46	16	33	3	47.3%	.352	-15	1.54	5.36	4.78	11.7	3.8	5.0	1.0	-5	3.4	—
2008	KCA	MLB	35	1	3	0	31	0	37²	41	17	25	6	50.0%	.297	-17	1.54	4.77	4.30	9.6	3.6	5.3	1.4	-2	3.2	-0.08
2009	KCA	MLB	36	1	2	1	32	0	35²	40	16	23	4	45.0%	.310	-3	1.56	4.97	4.83	9.7	3.6	5.6	0.9	-0	2.2	0.17

Breakout: 27% Improve: 37% Collapse: 39% Attrition: 37%   Comparables: Matt Herges, Jim Bruske, Giovanni Carrara, Joe Boever

The AL Central imported two-thirds of "YFK," the vaunted veteran relief trio from Bobby Valentine's Chiba Lotte Marines, but somewhere over the Pacific, the goods crossed the fine line from "well-aged" to "spoiled." Yabuta signed essentially the same two-year, $6 million contract as his Japanese teammate Masahide Kobayashi did with Cleveland, but had an even more forgettable American introduction, giving up 12 runs in 13 innings during April. Since he was designated for assignment in June, no one dared touch his contract, so Yabuta continued his tour of the Midwest in Omaha, where he did even worse. His track record in Japan didn't portend much better—his 50th-percentile PECOTA projection was very nearly a dead ringer for his actual line. The odds of his rebounding this year are poor.

LINEOUTS ━━━━━━━━━━━━━━━━

Hitters

PLAYER	TEAM	LVL	AGE	PA	R	2B	3B	HR	RBI	BB	SO	SB-CS	EqBRR	AVG/OBP/SLG	EqAVG/EqOBP/EqSLG	EqA	VORP	WARP
LF C. Lubanski*	OMA	AAA	23	438	51	20	8	15	54	38	130	5-1	-0.3	.242/.306/.448	.215/.273/.390	.229	-13.1	-0.8
OF P. Orlando	WNS	A+	22	489	73	15	12	9	42	22	97	28-9	3.5	.262/.308/.408	.228/.265/.367	.221	-20.8	-0.1
	WIL	A+	22	82	11	5	2	3	9	8	19	1-4	-1.3	.254/.325/.507	.233/.296/.438	.242	0.3	0.4
OF A. Ortiz*	BUR	A	21	446	50	10	7	3	33	15	68	29-15	-4.5	.308/.334/.386	.262/.285/.340	.217	-15.9	-1.5
	WIL	A+	21	118	10	5	2	0	12	9	11	5-5	-4.1	.311/.388/.398	.283/.345/.368	.249	1.4	-1.1
C B. Pena#	OMA	AAA	26	266	33	17	1	6	31	26	17	7-3	-3.9	.303/.376/.462	.246/.313/.375	.242	-2.4	-0.2
INF J. Smith*	OMA	AAA	30	459	52	20	7	20	62	23	128	3-1	0.5	.253/.289/.475	.195/.226/.355	.197	-32.3	-1.0
1B M. Stodolka*	OMA	AAA	26	259	32	12	0	5	21	27	42	0-1	0.4	.286/.366/.405	.232/.305/.326	.223	-8.8	-1.4
3B J. Taylor	BUR	A	20	533	79	17	4	17	58	81	97	40-14	0.8	.242/.372/.418	.206/.316/.356	.242	-11.7	-1.1

Chris Lubanski was taken fifth overall in 2003, but didn't hit well enough last year to shed his status as a prime example of the past regime's draft failures. ⌀ Acquired from the White Sox for Horacio Ramirez, **Paulo Orlando** is an excellent center fielder with plenty of speed. He fanned in 20 percent of his plate appearances last year and is vying to become the first player from Brazil to make the majors. ⌀ Another quick center fielder, **Adrian Ortiz** hasn't been able to manifest that skill on the bases so far, nor has he shown nearly enough patience, given his lack of pop. Ortiz will probably get to the majors, anyway, because of his wheels and defensive ability. ⌀ **Brayan Pena** became the latest addition to Moore's Atlanta-Midwest campus when the Royals claimed him off waivers; decent performance at Omaha was enough to earn a spot on the 40-man. He's out of options, so it's use him all season or (potentially) lose him. ⌀ Utilityman **Jason Smith** is on his sixth organization and heading for lucky number seven (the Astros) after getting nontendered. He's got pop, but also a .293 career minor league OBP. ⌀ **Mike Stodolka** is Rick Ankiel lite; the left-handed pitcher was taken with the fourth pick of the 2000 draft out of high school but switched to the outfield in 2006. He might yet turn out to be a decent bench bat, as he has shown great plate discipline since converting. ⌀ **Jason Taylor** was the 45th overall pick in 2006, and he came back after missing all of 2007 flashing an intriguing mix of power, patience, and speed, leading the Midwest League in walks and finishing fourth in steals. He's not going to stick at third (.904 fielding percentage), so his bat's his ticket.

Pitchers

PLAYER	TEAM	LVL	AGE	W	L	SV	IP	H	BB	SO	HR	GB%	BABIP	STUFF	WHIP	ERA	DERA	EqH9	EqBB9	EqSO9	EqHR9	DEF	VORP
J. Capellan	CSP	AAA	27	2	0	0	16	12	5	11	2	37.5%	.217	-7	1.06	3.94	6.75	6.2	2.8	3.9	1.1	5	-2.0
	OMA	AAA	27	2	1	0	37¹	35	14	20	3	33.3%	.281	-13	1.31	4.10	5.45	9.3	3.6	3.1	1.0	4	0.6
R. Colon	NWA	AA	28	2	0	1	17	18	4	8	1	43.3%	.298	-37	1.29	5.29	8.82	10.5	2.8	2.2	1.1	3	-5.8
	OMA	AAA	28	5	5	1	95	109	27	62	15	46.3%	.320	-30	1.43	4.64	6.06	11.7	2.8	3.9	1.7	6	-4.5
B. Duckworth	OMA	AAA	32	5	11	1	134²	132	49	103	23	52.7%	.280	-28	1.34	4.74	6.59	9.7	3.4	4.6	1.8	11	-14.1
	KCA	MLB	32	3	3	0	38	38	19	20	2	45.6%	.298	-3	1.50	4.50	4.91	9.1	4.2	4.2	0.5	1	4.5
J. Fulchino	OMA	AAA	28	3	4	5	61¹	71	27	53	2	46.6%	.367	-6	1.60	4.85	5.40	12.2	4.3	5.4	0.5	-5	1.3
	KCA	MLB	28	0	1	0	14	21	8	12	2	49.0%	.396	-16	2.07	9.00	6.28	13.2	4.4	6.3	1.3	-5	-5.7
B. Johnson	NWA	AA	23	10	9	0	143	168	38	86	20	48.5%	.321	-41	1.44	4.85	7.18	12.6	3.0	3.0	2.1	4	-22.9
T. Lumsden*	OMA	AAA	0	3	13	1	107¹	138	62	44	15	50.1%	.333	-47	1.86	7.21	8.97	13.0	5.4	2.1	1.5	5	-37.2
N. Musser*	OMA	AAA	27	3	5	6	56	47	37	64	9	36.0%	.271	-8	1.50	4.34	5.76	8.6	5.9	7.1	1.6	0	-1.0
C. Nicoll	WIL	A+	24	2	1	1	43¹	34	15	49	7	44.6%	.267	-17	1.13	2.91	4.15	9.5	3.7	6.9	2.8	0	6.3
	NWA	AA	24	4	1	3	43²	43	8	55	2	37.4%	.376	9	1.17	3.09	4.72	11.5	2.2	7.7	0.9	1	3.9
S. Runion	BUR	A	19	2	5	0	40²	54	9	11	7	51.9%	.320	-63	1.55	5.75	12.50	15.5	3.2	0.0	4.0	-3	-27.6

Leading off the parade of former Braves now toiling in the KC system is **Jose Capellan**, who was picked up from the Rockies in May. ⌀ Following him in line is **Roman Colon**, another former fledgling Bravo who failed to hatch and who has since bounced to the Tigers and Royals. ⌀ **Brandon Duckworth** delivered four quality starts in his seven turns in the Royals' rotation from late August through September. Kansas City signed him to a one-year deal following the season but wisely outrighted him to Omaha, eliminating the need to use a 40-man roster spot on their veteran rotation insurance. ⌀ The Royals tried **Jeff Fulchino** in relief after he had been used solely as a starter by Florida in seven years as a pro, but the new role didn't take; after a waiver claim, the Astros will try their luck with him next. ⌀ **Luke Hudson** underwent shoulder surgery in spring training and was expected back around a month later, but some continued soreness kept him out for the entire year. He refused an assignment to Triple-A after the season to become a free agent. ⌀ **Blake Johnson** came with Pimentel from the Dodgers in the deal for Elmer Dessens and, like his trade partner, hit a massive wall at Double-A. He has great command, but is just far too hittable to carve out a career at the upper levels. ⌀ **Tyler Lumsden** was swiftly removed from the 40-man roster after a second straight horrific season, but remarkably, the Royals found a taker for his services in Houston. ⌀ **Neal Musser** is a hard-throwing southpaw who could be in a big-league bullpen by now had he slightly better control, but it seems things are going in the wrong direction for Musser. He walked 10 in 10⅔ innings while pitching in the Dominican last winter. ⌀ **Christopher Nicoll** made the switch to relief full-time and struck out almost 10.8 per nine between the Carolina and Texas leagues, but as a fly-ball pitcher with a slight home-run problem, he will still have a tough time excelling in a major league bullpen. ⌀ The Royals' second-round pick in 2007, **Sam Runion** was held back in Rookie ball. Then, after eventually advancing to the Midwest League, he showed that he still has much to learn; he fanned just six percent of the hitters he faced, despite a good fastball.

MANAGER: TREY HILLMAN

YEAR	TEAM	W-L	Pythag +/−	Avg PC	100+ P	120+ P	QS	BQS	REL	REL w Zero R	IBB	Subs	PH	PH Avg	PH HR	SB2	CS2	SB3	CS3	SAC Att	SAC %	POS SAC	Squeeze	Swing	In Play
2008	KCA	75-87	4	98.2	73	2	76	3	438	277	15	52	71	.270	1	58	32	21	6	57	56.1%	28	0	122	97

In his first stateside season after coming back from Japan, Hillman displayed a pragmatism that KC's recent skippers have largely lacked. He was unafraid to utilize his second catcher as the DH to maximize a platoon advantage, plugging lefty-masher Miguel Olivo into that spot on 21 occasions, 15 of them against southpaws, and also pinch-hitting him six times. Most managers are loathe to use both catchers, fearing the unlikely embarrassment of being left without a backup should the starter get hurt. Less positive was Kansas City's work on the basepaths, as the Royals were successful on just 67.5 percent of their stolen-base attempts, the 26th-"best" ratio in baseball. Hillman showed an admirable aversion to the intentional walk, handing out just 15 all season, the third-lowest total in the last 50 years, although several of the free passes he did commission were head-scratchers. He established consistent usage roles for his top relievers and made the fourth-fewest pitching changes. Not having played in the majors sometimes makes earning the respect of major leaguers more difficult. The Royals lost 19 of their last 23 games in August, and it was thought that Hillman had lost the clubhouse, as manifested in the players' seeming apathy. The clubhouse tension was ascribed in large part to an alleged separate set of rules for the outspoken Jose Guillen, but Hillman stood up to Guillen in September, and the team went 18-8 in the final month. It's dangerous to ascribe too much to the manager, but that finish bodes well for the coming season.

Los Angeles Angels of Anaheim

The Angels don't get credit for whatever measure of unhappiness that attends rooting for them, not that they really should—after all, winning the World Series more recently than the Yankees, just six years ago, shouldn't be cause for despair. However, you can understand if there was some measure of anguish for Ana-heim-gelenos as a result of last season. Despite the early absence of staff ace John Lackey and an injury-wracked infield, for the first time in Halos history, the team won 100 games. Better still, with the team leading its division by almost a dozen games heading into the trade deadline at the end of July, general manager Tony Reagins refused to settle, instead gunning for everything by trading for Mark Teixeira to shore up a lineup in need of additional punch, reflecting a commendable determination not to make another blood-less exit from October baseball.

Unfortunately, all the Angels' efforts added up to "same result, different season," as they suffered their third League Division Series loss to the Red Sox in five years. It was an especially tight series, but a loss all the same. Moreover, as impressive as a 100-win season might be, the Angels were arguably the worst 100-win team of all time. That doesn't take 100 wins off the books, of course—*some* team from among all of them has to be the worst, after all. But the Angels' winding up a major-league-record 16 games better than their opponents-adjusted projected finish suggests that getting Teixeira might have represented more than just the cherry on top. His acquisition might have been a modest start to addressing a roster that simply still wasn't good enough to contend with the beasts from the AL East. Losing another season in the same fashion leaves

us with the question of whether the Angels' brand of baseball is no more a formula for postseason success than, say, Billy Beane's poopadoodle. Making good contact and running the bases effectively is all well and good, but is it really an operating philosophy, or is it instead a matter of fetishizing tactics in the absence of actual strategy?

While the Angels make a big deal out of baserunning and stretching opposing defenses, these aren't the Whiteyball Cardinals we're talking about—their results aren't really all that compelling. The Angels finished second in the American League and fifth in MLB in total steals and swiped them at a major league-average 73 percent clip. They rated fifth in their league and ninth in the majors in teamwide Equivalent Baserunning Runs (EqBRR), behind notionally "moneyball" teams like the A's and the Indians, no less. Nor is this a recent development—in 2007, the Go-Go Angels ranked just third in the American League and eighth in MLB in EqBRR. They're better than most, to be sure, but this isn't something significant that helps explain how they far surpassed their projected won-loss record, and it's not a tactical advantage of such heft that it leaves opponents in their dust. What's also important, for a team that supposedly places a premium on little-ball antics, the Angels do a great job of keeping notional speedsters like Erick Aybar nailed to the bases.

So where did they get those magic 16 wins that made the Halos not only history's weakest 100-win team, but also the going-away victors in a relatively pathetic division? Our starting point is right there—the AL West *was* a pathetic division, and the Angels got to tee off on it. Going 14-5 against the Mariners certainly wasn't an accident, and running off a 12-5 record against divisional

---

ANGELS PROSPECTUS

2008 record: 100-62; First place in AL West

Pythagenport record: 88-74

Runs scored per game: 4.72 (10th in AL)

Runs allowed per game: 4.32 (4th in AL)

Team EqA: .254 (10th in AL)

2008 Batters Age: 29.4 (7th-youngest in AL)

2008 Pitchers Age: 28.1 (6th-youngest in AL)

Ballpark: Angel Stadium; Slight hitter's park; Park Factor of 1.017

2008: Despite a teaspoon of Teixeira, another Angels season ends at the Fens.

2009: Don't let the hundred victories dazzle you: the Angels may be the team to beat, but they're far from immaculate.

foes in the final three weeks of the season helped pad things after the division's three dwarves had already packed it in. Equally predictably, the Angels were fortunate in one-run outcomes, going 31-21 in such contests. That represents almost a third of their schedule. Only four teams played in as many or more one-run games last season, and of those four, only one, the Giants, who matched the Halos by also going 31-21, enjoyed the Angels' good fortune: the Blue Jays (24-32), Twins (26-26), and Cardinals (24-28) were not so lucky. The Giants are ridiculously explicable: they preyed on an even more pathetic Padres squad by going an incredible 7-0 in one-run games en route to going 13-5 against their hapless divisional rivals.

Since the Angels weren't getting their big advantage from accumulating vast sums of tactical victories on the basepaths and weren't among the better offensive ballclubs in the league by any other standard and were also decidedly mediocre on defense (ranking 14th in the majors in both Defensive Efficiency and PADE), how *did* they do it? Perhaps we can chalk up one for the people who say pitching is 51 percent of the game or some other silly generalization, because it's there where the Angels start shining a wee bit better ... sort of.

Did the Angels have a great rotation? Again, not especially: the unit wasn't terribly impressive compared with those of other playoff teams, ranking ahead of only the White Sox in per-game rate for Support-Neutral Lineup-Adjust Value Above Replacement (SLNVA_R) among the eight that made it to October, although the White Sox led the majors with 101 quality starts plus blown quality starts. Table 1 shows the top 10 staffs of 2008 ranked by SNLVA_R, with LUCK being a measure of how many more wins the starters got than expected, on the basis of their support-neutral performance. The Angels were the "luckiest" rotation in 2008 and ranked an impressive 26th of the 1,348 team seasons from 1954 to the present. (For the curious, the 1982 Brewers were the luckiest-ever rotation, winding up 34.4 games better than they pitched.)

Table 1. MLB's Best Rotations of 2008

Rank	Team	QS+BQS	SNLVA_R	LUCK
1.	Blue Jays	96	.565	3.8
2.	Cubs	89	.562	12.0
3.	Dodgers	81	.554	-11.5
4.	Mets	92	.550	4.8
5.	Brewers	88	.549	0.1
6.	Red Sox	91	.547	13.3
7.	Rays	85	.545	7.4
8.	D'backs	98	.540	5.1
9.	Phillies	93	.536	5.8
10.	Angels	95	.535	25.9

The Angels' rotation did generate innings, delivering the second-highest total of any team's starters last season, with 1,012, finishing behind only the Blue Jays. Where the rotation's virtue of pitching deep into ballgames probably had an outsized synergistic effect was in the correspondingly lighter load carried by the unit that got the glory, at least for its closer: the bullpen.

While it would be easy to get frothy on the subject of how important Francisco "K-Rod" Rodriguez was to the team's success, it isn't quite that neatly a chicken-and-egg proposition. Because the Angels were a bad offensive ballclub hitched up to a rotation that was relatively solid and doing a good job of getting deep into low-scoring ballgames, it's no surprise that the Angels' pen wound up with the highest unit-wide leverage score in the major leagues. The pen was good but not exceptional when you view it through context-neutral standards: its Fair Runs Allowed (FRA) mark of 4.17 was a merely nice seventh in the majors, and the pen was seventh again in Adjusted Runs Prevented (ARP). However, because of the sheer volume of opportunities to pitch in tight ballgames (reflected in that MLB-leading leverage mark), the pen's execution in protecting those slender leads generated by the offense and rotation gets the pen up to fourth-best in WXRL, a mark that ranked behind the pennant-winning Phillies and Rays and the Mariano-enabled Yankees. And lest you missed it, this volume of opportunities also put Francisco Rodriguez in the record books at Bobby Thigpen's expense.

Now that K-Rod has left for the Mets, you might wonder if that's the end of this particular brand of magic. Coming to a sports page near you, you can expect to find a certain number of prepackaged stories about how an Angels team, suddenly struggling in the standings, misses that late-game mojo because the team somehow doesn't like the cut of free-agent import Brian Fuentes' jib. You can plan on wrapping tilapia with those stories—the problem isn't going to be Fuentes, any more than Scot Shields is going to fall into a funk because he's too busy keening for the man he used to set up so well. As the telling Diamondbacks drop-off from 2007 to 2008 illustrates, reliever performance in high-yield situations can fluctuate in terms of the impact on the outcomes. The best way to avoid that problem isn't to throw lots of money at relievers; it's to lower the impact of the vagaries of reliever performance one way or another, and there's no better way to do that than to build an offense that beats the opposition to bloody hell.

On the surface, this might seem a pretty simple order—the Angels' 2008 team EqA of .254 ranked 10th in the American League, so it would seem that upgrading the attack would be the obvious order of business. Consider the components of the team's offense (Table 2), and the range of prospective fixes gets narrowed down pretty fast. That's not to say this makes fixing things easy, however. Getting better production from their second and third basemen would be great, but is there really all that much that Reagins or Mike Scioscia can or should do, beyond hoping to get relatively healthy seasons from Howie Kendrick and Chone Figgins? Or Maicer Izturis? In any circumstance where any of these fragile fixes get refractured, that long-anticipated Brandon Wood breakout would obviously come in very handy.

Table 2. Angels 2008 Position Performance

Position	EqA	MLB Avg.
Catcher	.260	.253
First	.294	.284
Second	.251	.265
Third	.238	.270
Short	.245	.255
Left	.251	.275
Center	.272	.267
Right	.277	.279
DH	.265	.270

No, the real problem area, the action item that really needs addressing, is pretty straightforward: the Angels are yet again in danger of getting crummy production from the power positions, and not just from their left fielders and DHs, but now also from first base in the wake of Mark Teixeira's defection via free agency. While the club holds reasonable hope that Kendry Morales and a fully healthy Juan Rivera might make a difference at one or perhaps two of these slots, these represent fractional improvements over a broken-down Garret Anderson or free-agent boondoggle Gary Matthews Jr. Anticipating getting good work out of Morales and Rivera is like anticipating getting full seasons from Figgins and Kendrick—such fortunate developments would be nice enough, but still wouldn't come close to negating the damage done by losing a bat of Teixeira's caliber, especially in a lineup that is already hoping that Vladimir Guerrero and Torii Hunter will not lose too much too fast to Father Time as they head deeper into their 30s.

Losing Teixeira highlights another issue, one that goes back to the question of what the Angels actually do that's distinctive. For 2009, the once-touted farm system doesn't have the impact bat to replace Teixeira or a pitcher who will make all the difference in the rotation, meaning there isn't that much in the way of in-house reinforcements to secure the Angels' current roost atop the division. Since they failed to win the bidding on the one impact bat at a position where the team has a crying need, we're left asking whether the Angels are willing to settle for being the little engine that could but hasn't and doesn't, not on the bases, not in October, and not in their off-season shopping. The timing of opting out on Teixeira is especially unfortunate because it's long since time that the Angels accept their lot as a big-revenue franchise in a big market and start spending like it. While the disastrous decision to give Matthews $50 million suggests that the checkbook's been willing, they cannot let that expense price them out of pursuing difference-making bats like Teixeira's (or Manny Ramirez's).

The Angels may still have the talent to win the division for the time being, but by going cheap this past winter after their remarkable good fortune during the regular season, they stand a pretty good chance of being caught sooner rather than later and certainly rating no better than still-vincible foemen in the first round against better-balanced teams in the playoffs. If the standard in play is merely getting to the playoffs, it will represent a disappointing postscript to their best of intentions in bidding to win in 2008.

HITTERS

| Garret Anderson | | | | LF | | | | | | | | Bats: L | | Throws: L | | Height: 6' 3" | | Weight: 225 | | Born: June 30, 1972 | | Age: 37 |

YEAR	TEAM	LVL	AGE	PA	R	2B	3B	HR	RBI	BB	SO	SB	CS	EqBRR	AVG	OBP	SLG	EqAVG	EqOBP	EqSLG	EqA	VORP	WARP	DEFENSE
2006	LAA	MLB	34	588	63	28	2	17	85	38	95	1	0	-0.9	.280	.323	.433	.267	.316	.423	.256	9.5	2.7	91-LF 18
2007	LAA	MLB	35	450	67	31	1	16	80	27	54	1	0	0.7	.297	.336	.492	.287	.329	.489	.277	18.3	1.5	82-LF -3
2008	LAA	MLB	36	593	66	27	3	15	84	29	77	7	4	-4.4	.293	.325	.433	.288	.324	.441	.262	14.9	2.4	77-LF 12
2009	LAA	MLB	37	418	46	22	1	11	58	23	57	3	1	-1.4	.275	.316	.422	.274	.319	.440	.261	5.8	1.2	100-LF -2

Breakout: 18% Improve: 42% Collapse: 22% Attrition: 27%   Comparables: B.J. Surhoff, Dante Bichette, Dave Parker, Paul O'Neill

The Angels declined Anderson's $11 million option for 2009, potentially ending a 19-year stay in the organization, including 15 in the majors. He isn't worth $11 million, but as a platoon player, he still has the skills to hit somewhere in the .290-.300 range, with modest pop making up for few walks. The sum of his parts is something like an average player. His body is a little creaky at this point, and he's going to miss 15-20 games a year, but there are still far worse outfielders playing every day.

Erick Aybar   SS

Bats: S   Throws: R   Height: 5' 10"   Weight: 170   Born: January 14, 1984   Age: 25

YEAR	TEAM	LVL	AGE	PA	R	2B	3B	HR	RBI	BB	SO	SB	CS	EqBRR	AVG	OBP	SLG	EqAVG	EqOBP	EqSLG	EqA	VORP	WARP	DEFENSE			
2006	SLC	AAA	22	368	63	20	3	6	45	21	36	32	18	-1.5	.283	.327	.413	.230	.272	.344	.218	-16.3	-0.2	80-SS	-1		
2006	LAA	MLB	22	40	5	1	1	0	2	0	8	1	0	0.7	.250	.250	.325	.250	.250	.325	.199	-1.2	-0.5	9-SS	-3		
2007	LAA	MLB	23	211	18	5	1	1	19	10	32	4	4	-0.8	.237	.279	.289	.237	.282	.289	.199	-11.2	-0.6	36-2B	4	9-SS	-1
2008	LAA	MLB	24	375	53	18	5	3	39	14	45	7	2	3.6	.277	.314	.384	.278	.315	.394	.247	8.5	1.5	88-SS	4		
2009	LAA	MLB	25	390	43	16	3	3	33	20	48	12	5	2.4	.264	.306	.351	.262	.308	.366	.239	3.5	1.1	93-SS	4		

Breakout: 32%   Improve: 57%   Collapse: 22%   Attrition: 31%   Comparables: Sandy Alomar, Nelson Liriano, Neifi Perez, Jose Vizcaino

Aybar is a better player than he showed in 2008, but he was hampered by a dislocated pinky and later a hamstring strain, and with so many young middle infielders on the roster, he's going to have to hit more to keep his grip on an everyday job. In another organization, he'd have a better grip on a full-time gig; this, however, is not that organization. Aybar remains a good but impatient hitter with surprising pop for his size. On defense, he's as capable of provoking frustration, if not insanity, as any player in the biz, making a *SportsCenter*-worthy play one inning and booting a routine grounder the next.

Peter Bourjos   CF

Bats: R   Throws: R   Height: 6' 1"   Weight: 175   Born: March 31, 1987   Age: 22

YEAR	TEAM	LVL	AGE	PA	R	2B	3B	HR	RBI	BB	SO	SB	CS	EqBRR	AVG	OBP	SLG	EqAVG	EqOBP	EqSLG	EqA	VORP	WARP	DEFENSE	
2006	ORM	Rk	19	279	42	16	7	5	28	22	67	13	5	-0.2	.292	.354	.472	.206	.246	.321	.193	-36.2	-1.0	62-CF	5
2007	CDR	A	20	270	37	9	6	5	29	20	53	19	9	0.0	.274	.335	.426	.212	.262	.331	.211	-16.6	-0.3	61-CF	4
2008	RCU	A+	21	545	83	29	10	9	51	19	96	50	10	1.5	.295	.326	.444	.240	.268	.371	.225	-19.2	0.5	116-CF	9
2009	LAA	MLB	22	577	60	26	5	8	47	27	136	29	10	3.0	.239	.279	.349	.238	.281	.364	.230	-10.9	1.5	135-CF	9

Breakout: 48%   Improve: 69%   Collapse: 7%   Attrition: 9%   Comparables: Devon White, Ted Wilborn, Brian Hunter, Rusty Tillman

Normally, the image suggested by a player who is the son of a scout is that of a fundamentally sound grinder. In Bourjos's case, however, it's all about the tools: he's a plus-plus runner who covers a ton of ground in center and led the California League in stolen bases, but he'll swing at anything. A leadoff man's skill set without the walks makes him a fourth outfielder, but at 22, Bourjos has time to figure out which kind of player he can be.

Matt Brown   3B/1B

Bats: R   Throws: R   Height: 6' 0"   Weight: 200   Born: August 8, 1982   Age: 26

YEAR	TEAM	LVL	AGE	PA	R	2B	3B	HR	RBI	BB	SO	SB	CS	EqBRR	AVG	OBP	SLG	EqAVG	EqOBP	EqSLG	EqA	VORP	WARP	DEFENSE			
2006	ARK	AA	33	576	77	41	3	19	79	47	108	7	6	-0.9	.293	.362	.495	.167	.216	.275	.160	-65.6	-7.6	128-3B	-22		
2007	SLC	AAA	34	442	69	30	2	19	60	45	106	5	9	-5.0	.276	.358	.509	.195	.274	.371	.218	-17.5	-3.1	59-3B	-5	20-LF	-4
2008	SLC	AAA	35	437	75	33	4	21	67	32	80	4	2	-0.1	.320	.373	.580	.221	.268	.400	.227	-11.7	0.0	39-1B	5	33-3B	4
2008	LAA	MLB	35	20	0	1	0	0	3	1	10	0	0	-0.0	.053	.100	.105	.105	.150	.158	.000	-4.1	-0.5	5-3B	-2		
2009	LAA	MLB	36	239	19	13	1	5	29	15	63	2	1	-0.5	.209	.263	.351	.208	.265	.367	.217	-9.5	-0.6	59-3B	-3		

Breakout: 49%   Improve: 68%   Collapse: 29%   Attrition: 49%   Comparables: Jason Wood, Mike DiFelice, Ernie Young, Pedro Swann

Brown is your classic minor league performer. He's put up decent numbers at every level while playing every position but catcher and center field, but now that he's in his late 20s, he's limited to the two corner infield spots and he's been overmatched in a pair of very brief call-ups. He might get to make a few more cameos, but it's looking as if a spot on the 2008 Olympic squad is going to be his career highlight.

Hank Conger   C

Bats: S   Throws: R   Height: 6' 0"   Weight: 205   Born: January 29, 1988   Age: 21

YEAR	TEAM	LVL	AGE	PA	R	2B	3B	HR	RBI	BB	SO	SB	CS	EqBRR	AVG	OBP	SLG	EqAVG	EqOBP	EqSLG	EqA	VORP	WARP	DEFENSE	
2006	ANG	Rk	18	76	11	3	4	1	11	7	11	1	0	0.2	.319	.382	.522	.194	.237	.319	.180	-15.6	-1.2	8-C	-2
2007	CDR	A	19	320	33	20	0	11	48	21	48	9	4	0.0	.290	.336	.472	.229	.267	.370	.221	-13.1	-1.2	68-C	-10
2008	RCU	A+	20	318	47	20	2	13	75	14	55	2	1	-1.7	.303	.333	.517	.247	.277	.431	.240	-1.8	-0.7	9-C	-3
2009	LAA	MLB	21	536	51	30	1	15	67	29	111	3	2	-0.6	.245	.288	.401	.244	.290	.418	.243	-0.9	0.4	126-DH	

Breakout: 54%   Improve: 74%   Collapse: 11%   Attrition: 3%   Comparables: Neil Walker, Rafael Palmeiro, Brian McCann, Tim Thompson

Conger is at an extremely interesting place in his career. When he was drafted out of high school, everyone knew he could hit, but there were questions about his ability to stay behind the plate. Two and a half years later, we're in the same position. A laundry list of injuries has prevented him from playing the field of late, limiting him to just 10 games at catcher last year. At the same time, he keeps on hitting. If he can prove himself as a catcher, he could be a star. If not, he's just another bat.

Terry Evans   OF

Bats: R   Throws: R   Height: 6' 3"   Weight: 205   Born: January 19, 1982   Age: 27

YEAR	TEAM	LVL	AGE	PA	R	2B	3B	HR	RBI	BB	SO	SB	CS	EqBRR	AVG	OBP	SLG	EqAVG	EqOBP	EqSLG	EqA	VORP	WARP	DEFENSE			
2006	PMB	A+	24	263	43	10	1	15	45	20	50	21	1	3.5	.311	.373	.550	.237	.285	.429	.248	-1.3	0.2	41-RF	-1	18-CF	0
2006	SFD	AA	24	84	13	4	0	7	20	3	21	5	1	0.4	.307	.369	.640	.256	.306	.526	.277	3.9	0.3	21-RF	-1		
2006	ARK	AA	24	213	48	9	2	11	22	18	56	11	6	0.1	.309	.385	.553	.246	.308	.441	.254	2.9	-0.1	44-CF	-5		
2007	SLC	AAA	25	507	70	40	4	15	75	26	119	24	9	1.0	.316	.352	.512	.240	.278	.401	.234	-9.2	-0.9	59-RF	-1	46-CF	-3
2008	SLC	AAA	26	200	31	12	0	4	21	20	60	6	5	-0.2	.270	.345	.408	.213	.284	.315	.213	-10.0	-1.0	38-RF	-2		
2009	LAA	MLB	27	363	32	16	1	9	38	22	110	7	2	0.6	.207	.260	.341	.206	.262	.356	.215	-15.8	-0.8	87-RF	0		

Breakout: 13%   Improve: 30%   Collapse: 49%   Attrition: 21%   Comparables: Chris Jones, Scott Krause, Tim Unroe, Mark Brouhard

A late bloomer with power and speed whose 2006 bust-out elicited a lot of curiosity about what would come next, Evans has followed that up with an OK campaign in Utah and then an injury-filled 2008 season. With Garret Anderson's departure and questions in the corners for the Halos, he has a chance, but he's got to put himself back on the radar.

Chone Figgins   3B/UT

Bats: S   Throws: R   Height: 5' 8"   Weight: 180   Born: January 22, 1978   Age: 31

YEAR	TEAM	LVL	AGE	PA	R	2B	3B	HR	RBI	BB	SO	SB	CS	EqBRR	AVG	OBP	SLG	EqAVG	EqOBP	EqSLG	EqA	VORP	WARP	DEFENSE			
2006	LAA	MLB	28	683	93	23	8	9	62	65	100	52	16	9.6	.267	.336	.376	.258	.335	.370	.257	14.8	0.1	92-CF	-8	31-3B	-4
2007	LAA	MLB	29	503	81	24	6	3	58	51	81	41	12	7.6	.330	.393	.432	.326	.393	.435	.293	33.1	2.6	95-3B	-4	10-RF	-1
2008	LAA	MLB	30	520	72	14	1	1	22	62	80	34	13	7.7	.276	.367	.318	.276	.373	.318	.256	4.7	2.1	102-3B	9	7-2B	0
2009	LAA	MLB	31	484	68	18	4	4	35	49	74	29	9	3.8	.263	.340	.352	.262	.342	.368	.261	4.4	1.7	114-3B	2		

Breakout: 7%   Improve: 40%   Collapse: 26%   Attrition: 14%   Comparables: Don Buford, Dave Collins, Bip Roberts, Harold Reynolds

Figgins had a lot of value as a super-sub who could play anywhere on the field, draw same walks, run like the wind, and smack enough doubles and triples to get his slugging percentage up around .400. As an everyday third baseman who stopped hitting balls into the gaps, however, he's become something less than an asset. The Angels might try to fill their hole in left with Figgins, which really wouldn't be any better than playing him at the hot corner; they'd be best served by returning him to the superutility role.

Vladimir Guerrero   RF

Bats: R   Throws: R   Height: 6' 3"   Weight: 235   Born: February 9, 1976   Age: 33

YEAR	TEAM	LVL	AGE	PA	R	2B	3B	HR	RBI	BB	SO	SB	CS	EqBRR	AVG	OBP	SLG	EqAVG	EqOBP	EqSLG	EqA	VORP	WARP	DEFENSE	
2006	LAA	MLB	30	665	92	34	1	33	116	50	68	15	5	-0.6	.329	.382	.552	.313	.372	.534	.304	64.7	4.6	122-RF	-3
2007	LAA	MLB	31	660	89	45	1	27	125	71	62	2	3	-2.1	.324	.403	.547	.308	.392	.538	.311	56.7	5.7	105-RF	3
2008	LAA	MLB	32	600	85	31	3	27	91	51	77	5	3	-1.9	.303	.365	.521	.294	.360	.522	.295	40.5	2.8	94-RF	-8
2009	LAA	MLB	33	616	80	34	2	22	98	44	79	5	2	-2.3	.296	.351	.478	.295	.353	.499	.289	26.3	2.9	144-RF	-10

Breakout: 3%   Improve: 29%   Collapse: 26%   Attrition: 8%   Comparables: Dave Winfield, Jim Rice, George Scott, Joe Torre

Offensively, Guerrero arguably had his worst season since his rookie campaign in 1997, but he still ranked among the right-field leaders in VORP, EqA, and Equivalent Runs. Knee problems that had to be addressed with a minor surgery in the offseason have increasingly taken away what was once plus speed and made him a defensive liability despite his plus arm, but picking up his $15 million option for 2009 was really a no-brainer, and the Angels are hoping to work out a deal to keep him around even longer.

Torii Hunter — CF

Bats: R Throws: R Height: 6' 2" Weight: 225 Born: July 18, 1975 Age: 33

YEAR	TEAM	LVL	AGE	PA	R	2B	3B	HR	RBI	BB	SO	SB	CS	EqBRR	AVG	OBP	SLG	EqAVG	EqOBP	EqSLG	EqA	VORP	WARP	DEFENSE	
2006	MIN	MLB	30	611	86	21	2	31	98	45	108	12	6	0.7	.278	.336	.490	.269	.331	.485	.274	33.0	2.5	139-CF	-4
2007	MIN	MLB	31	650	94	45	1	28	107	40	101	18	9	-0.5	.287	.334	.505	.286	.335	.518	.283	40.3	3.3	148-CF	-5
2008	LAA	MLB	32	608	85	37	2	21	78	50	108	19	5	3.2	.278	.344	.466	.272	.342	.474	.279	32.0	2.1	133-CF	-10
2009	LAA	MLB	33	553	70	29	2	18	79	39	100	13	5	-0.2	.274	.330	.447	.273	.332	.466	.274	18.6	2.2	130-CF	-10

Breakout: 9%   Improve: 42%   Collapse: 25%   Attrition: 16%   Comparables: Dante Bichette, Dave Henderson, Brian Jordan, Rondell White

If you think that Torii Hunter wasn't worth $16 million last year, you're right, but don't say we didn't warn you, as PECOTA pegged both his on-base and slugging percentages within four points. We're not boasting; it wasn't a huge reach, but one right in line with Hunter's career rates. The Angels overpaid according to a career year, and they'll get to keep overpaying, as they're on the hook for a total of $36 million for Hunter's age-35 and age-36 seasons. We don't want to sound too negative here; Hunter is a good hitter and a wonderful defender and has clubhouse worth that we can't measure—but that doesn't excuse the Angels for signing a bad contract.

Maicer Izturis — INF

Bats: S Throws: R Height: 5' 8" Weight: 165 Born: September 12, 1980 Age: 28

YEAR	TEAM	LVL	AGE	PA	R	2B	3B	HR	RBI	BB	SO	SB	CS	EqBRR	AVG	OBP	SLG	EqAVG	EqOBP	EqSLG	EqA	VORP	WARP	DEFENSE			
2006	LAA	MLB	25	399	64	21	3	5	44	38	35	14	6	3.6	.293	.365	.412	.284	.363	.401	.269	14.3	1.1	79-3B	-2	6-SS	-1
2007	LAA	MLB	26	374	47	17	2	6	51	33	39	7	1	2.4	.289	.349	.405	.281	.346	.404	.267	10.4	0.8	51-3B	0	35-2B	-4
2008	LAA	MLB	27	321	44	14	2	3	37	26	27	11	2	3.4	.269	.329	.362	.267	.332	.368	.253	6.4	1.9	50-SS	7	21-2B	1
2009	LAA	MLB	28	416	54	20	2	5	37	37	43	11	3	2.3	.276	.342	.379	.274	.345	.395	.265	11.5	1.9	99-SS	-1		

Breakout: 24%   Improve: 51%   Collapse: 26%   Attrition: 19%   Comparables: Walt Weiss, Desi Relaford, Joey Cora, Don Buford

Izturis was the surprise winner of the shortstop derby in spring training, outplaying younger talents like Aybar and Wood, but it was all downhill from there, as he had back troubles early in the year, a strained hamstring in the middle, and surgery to repair a torn ligament in his thumb at the end of the season. His consequent lack of play time might have been for the best for the Angels (if not for Izturis), as he has fine skills for a utilityman but is stretched in an everyday role.

Howie Kendrick — 2B

Bats: R Throws: R Height: 5' 10" Weight: 200 Born: July 12, 1983 Age: 25

YEAR	TEAM	LVL	AGE	PA	R	2B	3B	HR	RBI	BB	SO	SB	CS	EqBRR	AVG	OBP	SLG	EqAVG	EqOBP	EqSLG	EqA	VORP	WARP	DEFENSE			
2006	SLC	AAA	22	312	57	25	6	13	62	12	48	11	3	0.5	.369	.408	.631	.303	.338	.537	.291	24.1	3.3	59-2B	5	7-3B	2
2006	LAA	MLB	22	283	25	21	1	4	30	9	44	6	0	0.4	.285	.314	.416	.274	.307	.410	.252	5.3	0.9	39-1B	-1	25-2B	7
2007	LAA	MLB	23	353	55	24	2	5	39	9	61	5	4	2.2	.322	.347	.450	.320	.344	.456	.270	15.8	1.5	85-2B	-1		
2008	LAA	MLB	24	361	43	26	2	3	37	12	58	11	4	2.7	.306	.333	.421	.303	.331	.426	.263	13.8	1.6	87-2B	2		
2009	LAA	MLB	25	427	49	22	2	7	46	15	67	11	4	1.3	.280	.312	.402	.279	.314	.420	.255	9.7	1.4	102-2B	0		

Breakout: 6%   Improve: 30%   Collapse: 38%   Attrition: 16%   Comparables: Mel Roach, Danny O'Connell, Jerry Adair, Yuniesky Betancourt

If Kendrick can stay healthy, he's going to win a batting title one of these days, but the problem is that more often than not, he's dealing with a hamstring injury. This is, unfortunately, the fate of many promising young second basemen; it's generally a difficult position at which to stay healthy, but even so, Kendrick's problems seem almost chronic. His bat speed and hand-eye coordination are so special, approaching Ichiro territory, that it would be a shame if we never found out what he could do with 650 plate appearances.

Jeff Mathis   C

Bats: R   Throws: R   Height: 6' 0"   Weight: 200   Born: March 31, 1983   Age: 26

YEAR	TEAM	LVL	AGE	PA	R	2B	3B	HR	RBI	BB	SO	SB	CS	EqBRR	AVG	OBP	SLG	EqAVG	EqOBP	EqSLG	EqA	VORP	WARP	DEFENSE	
2006	SLC	AAA	23	417	62	33	3	5	45	26	75	3	1	2.4	.289	.333	.430	.232	.273	.358	.219	-16.0	-0.1	83-C	0
2006	LAA	MLB	23	63	9	2	0	2	6	7	14	0	0	-0.1	.145	.238	.291	.130	.238	.278	.182	-4.6	-0.6	15-C	-3
2007	SLC	AAA	24	273	39	14	2	5	26	17	45	3	1	1.7	.244	.295	.376	.194	.245	.308	.191	-21.2	-0.4	58-C	4
2007	LAA	MLB	24	195	24	12	0	4	23	15	49	0	1	-1.0	.211	.276	.351	.206	.276	.359	.223	-4.7	0.1	53-C	0
2008	LAA	MLB	25	328	35	8	0	9	42	30	90	2	2	-2.1	.194	.275	.318	.189	.275	.317	.211	-12.0	0.3	89-C	5
2009	LAA	MLB	26	235	23	12	1	6	27	17	53	2	1	0.1	.227	.291	.381	.226	.293	.398	.240	1.5	1.2	59-C	1

Breakout: 50%   Improve: 62%   Collapse: 23%   Attrition: 42%   Comparables: A.J. Hinch, Mike Ryan, Steve Swisher, Mike Fitzgerald

Mathis began the year by sharing catching duties with Napoli, but the split shifted when Napoli hit and Mathis didn't, and when Napoli went down with shoulder issues, Mathis failed to take advantage of it. Once seen as one of the better catching prospects in the game, Mathis has now been given almost 600 PAs and his average is still below the Mendoza line. He's a good enough defender to hang around for the next decade as a backup, but that's well below where expectations were three years ago.

Gary Matthews Jr.   OF

Bats: S   Throws: R   Height: 6' 3"   Weight: 225   Born: August 25, 1974   Age: 34

YEAR	TEAM	LVL	AGE	PA	R	2B	3B	HR	RBI	BB	SO	SB	CS	EqBRR	AVG	OBP	SLG	EqAVG	EqOBP	EqSLG	EqA	VORP	WARP	DEFENSE			
2006	TEX	MLB	31	690	102	44	6	19	79	58	99	10	7	-1.0	.313	.371	.495	.296	.361	.478	.285	50.9	3.6	139-CF	-5		
2007	LAA	MLB	32	579	79	26	3	18	72	55	102	18	4	3.8	.252	.323	.419	.244	.320	.423	.260	12.0	1.6	129-CF	-1		
2008	LAA	MLB	33	477	53	19	3	8	46	45	95	8	3	-1.5	.242	.319	.357	.239	.319	.366	.243	-5.4	-0.7	38-RF	-3	35-LF	-3
2009	LAA	MLB	34	326	41	15	2	7	36	30	62	6	2	0.0	.265	.336	.395	.263	.339	.413	.265	5.6	1.0	79-CF	-5		

Breakout: 28%   Improve: 54%   Collapse: 26%   Attrition: 40%   Comparables: Gino Cimoli, Jerry Mumphrey, Stan Javier, Rico Carty

You know who one of the geniuses of the game is? Scott Leventhal. No, he's not some hotshot statistical analyst showing us the game in a new light—he's Gary Matthews' agent, and he got his client $50 million for a fluke year from a fourth outfielder. Even with left field open, the Angels are not talking about Matthews filling that hole, but they'll be weeping every month for the next three years when they sign that big check.

Kendry Morales   1B

Bats: S   Throws: R   Height: 6' 1"   Weight: 225   Born: June 20, 1983   Age: 26

YEAR	TEAM	LVL	AGE	PA	R	2B	3B	HR	RBI	BB	SO	SB	CS	EqBRR	AVG	OBP	SLG	EqAVG	EqOBP	EqSLG	EqA	VORP	WARP	DEFENSE			
2006	SLC	AAA	23	273	41	13	1	12	52	14	40	0	3	0.2	.320	.359	.520	.260	.294	.438	.246	2.3	-0.3	50-1B	-1		
2006	LAA	MLB	23	215	21	10	1	5	22	17	28	1	1	-2.1	.234	.293	.371	.226	.293	.359	.227	-7.2	-0.1	51-1B	5		
2007	SLC	AAA	24	275	42	20	1	5	37	15	30	0	2	-3.5	.341	.385	.486	.268	.313	.397	.243	1.0	-0.5	42-1B	-2		
2007	LAA	MLB	24	126	12	10	0	4	15	6	21	0	1	-2.7	.294	.333	.479	.286	.325	.471	.266	4.1	0.4	14-1B	1		
2008	SLC	AAA	25	340	46	19	0	15	64	19	43	1	3	-1.2	.341	.376	.543	.262	.297	.422	.245	1.3	0.0	60-1B	1	5-RF	1
2008	LAA	MLB	25	66	7	2	0	3	8	4	7	0	1	-1.2	.213	.273	.393	.213	.273	.393	.222	-2.4	-0.3	7-RF	-1	5-1B	0
2009	LAA	MLB	26	454	40	22	1	11	58	24	73	0	1	-1.9	.253	.295	.389	.252	.298	.406	.241	-5.8	-0.2	108-1B	0		

Breakout: 27%   Improve: 42%   Collapse: 28%   Attrition: 14%   Comparables: Kevin Grijak, Randall Simon, Carlos Rivera, Terry Tiffee

Morales hasn't lived up to expectations since the Angels signed him out of Cuba, but with Kotchman and Teixeira out of the way, he's finally going to get his chance. His minor league numbers have been consistently excellent, his brief big-league performances spotty. The Angels and scouts from outside the organization raved about his winter performance in the tough Dominican league, where Morales, in shape and focused, hit .404/.450/.778 in 26 games for the Gigantes. He could be a real sleeper in 2009.

Mike Napoli — C

Bats: R   Throws: R   Height: 6' 0"   Weight: 210   Born: October 31, 1981   Age: 27

YEAR	TEAM	LVL	AGE	PA	R	2B	3B	HR	RBI	BB	SO	SB	CS	EqBRR	AVG	OBP	SLG	EqAVG	EqOBP	EqSLG	EqA	VORP	WARP	DEFENSE			
2006	SLC	AAA	24	90	12	6	0	3	10	8	29	1	1	-0.5	.244	.344	.436	.213	.300	.375	.234	-1.9	0.2	17-C	1		
2006	LAA	MLB	24	325	47	13	0	16	42	51	90	2	3	-0.8	.228	.360	.455	.216	.358	.436	.273	13.2	2.1	80-C	2		
2007	LAA	MLB	25	263	40	11	1	10	34	33	63	5	2	1.9	.247	.351	.443	.239	.347	.440	.274	12.0	1.3	68-C	-3		
2008	LAA	MLB	26	274	39	9	1	20	49	35	70	7	3	-0.0	.273	.374	.586	.267	.371	.587	.312	28.6	2.3	70-C	-7		
2009	LAA	MLB	27	332	45	14	1	18	51	41	86	5	2	-0.1	.240	.344	.482	.239	.347	.503	.289	19.5	3.0	80-C	-2		

Breakout: 19% Improve: 48% Collapse: 28% Attrition: 19%   Comparables: Cliff Johnson, Dave Ross, Andre Thornton, Frank Fernandez

Even when Napoli hits in the .220s, he has value because of the home runs and walks, but when he hits .273, he's a legitimate offensive force. Last year's spike in batting average looks a bit fluky, as his BABIP took a huge jump, but he's still a fine, offense-oriented catcher with a ton of power. His poor defense requires a quality backup for those days when the 1985 Cardinals come to town, which is what Mathis provides. Combined, they're a cheap fix at a tough-to-fill position and should give the Angels years of worry-free catching enjoyment.

Robb Quinlan — 4C

Bats: R   Throws: R   Height: 6' 1"   Weight: 215   Born: March 17, 1977   Age: 32

YEAR	TEAM	LVL	AGE	PA	R	2B	3B	HR	RBI	BB	SO	SB	CS	EqBRR	AVG	OBP	SLG	EqAVG	EqOBP	EqSLG	EqA	VORP	WARP	DEFENSE			
2006	LAA	MLB	29	244	28	11	1	9	32	7	28	2	1	-0.1	.321	.344	.491	.312	.339	.491	.280	12.7	1.2	43-1B	1	15-3B	1
2007	LAA	MLB	30	194	21	9	0	3	21	14	27	3	2	-1.6	.247	.304	.348	.243	.304	.345	.227	-5.6	-0.8	26-1B	-2	9-LF	0
2008	LAA	MLB	31	181	15	1	2	1	11	14	28	4	2	-1.0	.262	.326	.311	.264	.331	.313	.232	-3.5	-0.5	29-3B	-5	13-1B	3
2009	LAA	MLB	32	172	17	6	1	3	17	11	26	2	1	-0.5	.253	.306	.349	.252	.309	.364	.237	-2.0	0.0	44-3B	-2		

Breakout: 23% Improve: 36% Collapse: 44% Attrition: 41%   Comparables: Art Schult, Lou Merloni, Hank Allen, John Wehner

Like a latter-day incarnation of Ron Jackson, Quinlan proved himself a useful commodity in the middle of the decade as a guy who could play both infield corners and bash lefties, but the offensive component of that equation has completely disappeared over the last two years. If first and third are your only positions and you're not hitting, you're going to have trouble sticking around. Appropriately, Quinlan will enter the spring with no guarantee of a job come April.

Juan Rivera — OF

Bats: R   Throws: R   Height: 6' 2"   Weight: 205   Born: July 3, 1978   Age: 30

YEAR	TEAM	LVL	AGE	PA	R	2B	3B	HR	RBI	BB	SO	SB	CS	EqBRR	AVG	OBP	SLG	EqAVG	EqOBP	EqSLG	EqA	VORP	WARP	DEFENSE			
2006	LAA	MLB	27	494	65	27	0	23	85	33	59	0	4	-1.4	.310	.362	.525	.301	.357	.517	.291	34.0	2.5	53-LF	0	27-RF	0
2007	LAA	MLB	28	44	3	1	0	2	8	1	4	0	0	0.1	.279	.295	.442	.279	.295	.442	.249	0.2	0.1	6-RF	1		
2008	LAA	MLB	29	280	31	13	0	12	45	16	33	1	1	-0.0	.246	.282	.438	.243	.282	.443	.248	-0.8	0.4	34-LF	4	13-RF	-1
2009	LAA	MLB	30	279	29	14	0	9	41	19	38	0	1	-0.6	.266	.318	.432	.265	.320	.451	.265	4.2	0.9	68-LF	-2		

Breakout: 35% Improve: 57% Collapse: 27% Attrition: 31%   Comparables: Mark Carreon, Wes Covington, Ellis Valentine, Keith Moreland

Rivera is a far better hitter than he showed in 2008 and is seen as such inside the industry. He was a hot commodity at the trade deadline and was on many teams' radars this winter as a cost-conscious free-agent alternative to many of the more expensive bats out there. Ultimately, the Angels gave him a three-year, $12.75 million deal with the promise that he'll get first crack at the everyday job in left field. A healthy Rivera—and "healthy" is the key caveat here, given Rivera's repeated problems on that score—should be up to the task with 20-25 home runs and solid on-base skills.

Sean Rodriguez — 2B

Bats: R   Throws: R   Height: 6' 1"   Weight: 198   Born: April 26, 1985   Age: 24

YEAR	TEAM	LVL	AGE	PA	R	2B	3B	HR	RBI	BB	SO	SB	CS	EqBRR	AVG	OBP	SLG	EqAVG	EqOBP	EqSLG	EqA	VORP	WARP	DEFENSE			
2006	RCU	A+	21	523	78	29	5	24	77	47	124	15	3	-0.5	.301	.377	.545	.238	.298	.428	.251	0.9	2.8	113-SS	7		
2006	ARK	AA	21	79	16	5	0	5	9	11	18	0	3	-2.7	.354	.462	.662	.294	.385	.574	.302	8.9	0.8	19-SS	0		
2007	ARK	AA	22	587	84	31	2	17	73	54	132	15	8	-2.8	.254	.345	.423	.217	.290	.363	.229	-18.5	1.4	125-SS	5	5-CF	2
2008	SLC	AAA	23	289	68	19	1	21	52	29	45	4	1	-1.4	.306	.397	.645	.244	.328	.508	.280	12.9	2.1	52-2B	6	8-SS	-4
2008	LAA	MLB	23	187	18	8	1	3	10	14	55	3	1	-0.7	.204	.276	.317	.205	.281	.331	.218	-7.1	-0.7	47-2B	-3		
2009	LAA	MLB	24	486	52	24	2	16	60	38	121	6	3	-0.1	.235	.304	.406	.234	.306	.423	.253	6.5	1.5	115-2B	-1		

Breakout: 26% Improve: 55% Collapse: 16% Attrition: 12%   Comparables: Scott Hairston, David Kelton, Ryan Raburn, Randy Asadoor

Rodriguez had a monster campaign at Triple-A last year, blasting 21 home runs in 66 games, but when he got his chance, thanks to Howie Kendrick's hamstring, he just didn't get the job done, paradoxically revealing the secret of his success: he was taking advantage of a great hitter's park in a great hitter's league at Salt Lake. Rodriguez has little shot at sticking in a utility job, as his range is stretched at shortstop and his arm is stretched at third. For now, he'll have to wait around for Kendrick to break again—which has been known to happen.

Freddy Sandoval   UT

Bats: S		Throws: R		Height: 6' 2"		Weight: 205		Born: August 16, 1982			Age: 26															

YEAR	TEAM	LVL	AGE	PA	R	2B	3B	HR	RBI	BB	SO	SB	CS	EqBRR	AVG	OBP	SLG	EqAVG	EqOBP	EqSLG	EqA	VORP	WARP	DEFENSE	
2006	RCU	A+	23	509	60	28	2	5	54	59	98	30	8	-1.2	.258	.343	.366	.183	.254	.265	.188	-45.9	-3.2	109-3B	-2
2007	ARK	AA	24	563	84	32	6	11	72	67	78	21	11	0.3	.305	.392	.468	.246	.322	.381	.248	-1.2	1.1	122-3B	3
2008	SLC	AAA	25	587	92	45	2	15	88	47	74	6	3	-1.4	.335	.389	.514	.256	.308	.393	.244	-1.6	0.0	76-3B 9 20-2B	-5
2009	LAA	MLB	26	525	50	27	2	7	52	40	98	7	3	-0.1	.235	.297	.348	.234	.299	.363	.234	-8.7	0.2	124-3B	-1

Breakout: 31%   Improve: 52%   Collapse: 26%   Attrition: 9%   Comparables: Jack Daugherty, Chris Saunders, Torey Lovullo, Royce Huffman

Sandoval has made slow and steady progress through the Angels' system, but the elevator stops here, as he has reached his ceiling. He's an adept hitter who should hit for a decent average, but his secondary skills are lacking for a corner infielder, he can't play short, and he's in a system that is loaded with players looking to fill the positions that he can play. He'll have more time to enjoy bopping at Salt Lake in 2009.

Mark Teixeira   1B

Bats: S		Throws: R		Height: 6' 3"		Weight: 220		Born: April 11, 1980			Age: 29													

YEAR	TEAM	LVL	AGE	PA	R	2B	3B	HR	RBI	BB	SO	SB	CS	EqBRR	AVG	OBP	SLG	EqAVG	EqOBP	EqSLG	EqA	VORP	WARP	DEFENSE
2006	TEX	MLB	26	727	99	45	1	33	110	89	128	2	0	-0.5	.282	.371	.514	.261	.362	.485	.290	38.3	4.4	158-1B 8
2007	TEX	MLB	27	335	48	24	1	13	49	45	66	0	0	0.9	.297	.397	.524	.282	.390	.514	.307	27.3	2.6	71-1B 2
2007	ATL	MLB	27	240	38	9	1	17	56	27	46	0	0	-0.8	.317	.404	.615	.319	.408	.628	.338	28.3	2.5	53-1B -1
2008	ATL	MLB	28	451	63	27	0	20	78	65	70	0	0	-1.0	.283	.390	.512	.287	.395	.534	.313	30.3	5.1	101-1B 14
2008	LAA	MLB	28	234	39	14	0	13	43	32	23	2	0	0.6	.358	.449	.632	.346	.442	.634	.355	34.9	3.6	49-1B 5
2009	NYA	MLB	29	647	93	33	1	28	100	83	106	2	0	-1.8	.281	.376	.495	.285	.383	.527	.308	36.2	5.1	151-1B 7

Breakout: 6%   Improve: 34%   Collapse: 15%   Attrition: 7%   Comparables: Eddie Murray, Bobby Bonilla, Boog Powell, Carlos Delgado

Right place, right time, right agent. After his trade to the Angels, Teixeira had 54 of the best games of his career, hit the free-agent market with Scott Boras on his side, and netted a huge eight-year deal from the Yankees. While eight years is a lot to give to anyone, Teixeira is a pretty safe bet; he stays healthy, and he's never had a bad season, never posting an OBP under .370 or slugging less than .514 since his rookie season. At the same time, he's never had that monster year, either. The Yankees are paying MVP money for a very good player, but he still needs to take a step forward to be the impact player you expect to be attached to $20 million a year.

Mark Trumbo   1B

Bats: R		Throws: R		Height: 6' 4"		Weight: 220		Born: January 16, 1986			Age: 23													

YEAR	TEAM	LVL	AGE	PA	R	2B	3B	HR	RBI	BB	SO	SB	CS	EqBRR	AVG	OBP	SLG	EqAVG	EqOBP	EqSLG	EqA	VORP	WARP	DEFENSE
2006	CDR	A	20	482	43	19	0	13	59	44	99	5	5	0.0	.220	.293	.355	.170	.228	.269	.167	-53.4	-5.6	110-1B -6
2007	CDR	A	21	516	57	27	2	14	76	34	98	10	8	0.0	.272	.326	.427	.207	.250	.327	.197	-37.6	-4.6	112-1B -9
2008	RCU	A+	22	438	70	28	2	26	68	26	67	7	3	0.7	.283	.329	.553	.231	.273	.447	.242	-2.3	-1.0	96-1B -4
2008	ARK	AA	22	134	13	7	1	6	25	7	29	1	2	-1.0	.276	.311	.496	.232	.263	.416	.231	-3.0	-0.4	28-1B 0
2009	LAA	MLB	23	582	49	29	1	16	72	35	137	4	2	-1.2	.227	.277	.376	.226	.279	.392	.231	-17.1	-1.3	136-1B -2

Breakout: 51%   Improve: 74%   Collapse: 11%   Attrition: 5%   Comparables: Tagg Bozied, Scott Thorman, Adam Hyzdu, Butch Garcia

Patience is a virtue (it also goes well with duck sauce). In 2004, the Angels gave Trumbo a record bonus for a 12th-round pick to steer him away from college. After two years of minimum production from a player who was limited to first base, many had already categorized Trumbo as a bust. Everything changed last year, as he got away from trying to hit everything out of the park, focusing on making natural contact and letting his strength work for him. The result was that he finished second in all the minors with 286 total bases, tearing through the Cal League and then doing well in his Double-A debut. Kendry Morales has the first-base job for now, but Trumbo is getting larger in his rearview mirror.

Reggie Willits   OF

Bats: S   Throws: R   Height: 5' 11"   Weight: 185   Born: May 30, 1981   Age: 28

YEAR	TEAM	LVL	AGE	PA	R	2B	3B	HR	RBI	BB	SO	SB	CS	EqBRR	AVG	OBP	SLG	EqAVG	EqOBP	EqSLG	EqA	VORP	WARP	DEFENSE			
2006	SLC	AAA	25	437	85	18	4	3	39	77	50	31	15	0.0	.327	.448	.426	.253	.372	.339	.260	4.3	3.1	75-CF	8	19-LF	7
2006	LAA	MLB	25	58	12	1	0	0	2	11	10	4	3	-0.0	.267	.411	.289	.250	.411	.273	.255	0.8	0.4	13-CF	3		
2007	LAA	MLB	26	518	74	20	1	0	34	69	83	27	8	-0.7	.293	.391	.344	.289	.393	.347	.274	11.8	3.5	58-LF	20	26-CF	-6
2008	SLC	AAA	27	43	7	2	1	0	4	5	6	1	1	0.1	.378	.452	.486	.263	.333	.368	.245	0.1	-0.1	4-RF	-1		
2008	LAA	MLB	27	136	21	4	0	0	7	21	26	2	1	1.5	.194	.321	.231	.187	.321	.224	.215	-7.5	-0.6	15-LF	0	10-RF	-1
2009	LAA	MLB	28	187	25	8	1	1	14	23	31	7	2	1.0	.256	.352	.347	.255	.354	.363	.264	1.9	1.0	48-LF	3		

Breakout: 27% Improve: 50% Collapse: 28% Attrition: 40%   Comparables: Jason McDonald, Gerald Young, Quinton McCracken, Jerry White

Willits was a revelation in 2007, filling in at all three outfielder positions while showing outstanding on-base skills, but 2008 was a disaster. Gallbladder surgery weakened him in spring training, and that set a theme of sorts, as his season was filled with injuries, including a pair of concussions and a torn-up hand from when he got spiked. That led to zero production, and as icing on the cake, he was cut from his Dominican winter league team when he started off 1-for-26. In 12 months, he's gone from a valuable player to one at a crossroads. It's a cruel game sometimes.

Bobby Wilson   C

Bats: R   Throws: R   Height: 6' 0"   Weight: 220   Born: April 8, 1983   Age: 26

YEAR	TEAM	LVL	AGE	PA	R	2B	3B	HR	RBI	BB	SO	SB	CS	EqBRR	AVG	OBP	SLG	EqAVG	EqOBP	EqSLG	EqA	VORP	WARP	DEFENSE			
2006	ARK	AA	23	418	45	26	0	9	53	33	47	1	6	-3.0	.286	.350	.428	.242	.297	.359	.227	-10.4	-0.1	80-C	-2		
2007	ARK	AA	24	204	24	9	0	6	27	22	26	5	3	-1.9	.271	.348	.420	.222	.289	.335	.220	-8.9	0.6	42-C	5	4-1B	0
2007	SLC	AAA	24	141	15	13	1	3	22	8	18	1	0	1.2	.295	.336	.477	.233	.277	.398	.232	-3.0	-0.7	36-C	-8		
2008	SLC	AAA	25	298	33	20	0	4	45	29	45	0	0	-2.8	.312	.386	.435	.241	.311	.335	.230	-7.4	0.8	57-C	6	9-1B	-1
2009	LAA	MLB	26	371	30	16	1	7	38	25	66	2	1	-1.2	.229	.285	.340	.228	.288	.355	.224	-5.6	0.9	89-C	0		

Breakout: 25% Improve: 42% Collapse: 35% Attrition: 20%   Comparables: Keith Osik, Jason Phillips, Chris Stewart, Tom Prince

A catcher with a solid offensive résumé, Wilson got a brief call-up in 2008, but he's in the wrong organization as a young catcher without obvious starting potential. It's not that he's bad; he's just merely average. He has some hitting skills, but not much power, and he's a good receiver with a decent arm, but there's no wow factor to his game. He's in danger of being an up-and-down Quad-A lifer.

Brandon Wood   3B

Bats: R   Throws: R   Height: 6' 3"   Weight: 185   Born: March 2, 1985   Age: 24

YEAR	TEAM	LVL	AGE	PA	R	2B	3B	HR	RBI	BB	SO	SB	CS	EqBRR	AVG	OBP	SLG	EqAVG	EqOBP	EqSLG	EqA	VORP	WARP	DEFENSE			
2006	ARK	AA	21	522	74	42	4	25	83	54	149	19	3	2.3	.276	.355	.552	.238	.305	.472	.266	11.6	1.6	115-SS	-12		
2007	SLC	AAA	22	488	73	27	1	23	77	45	120	10	1	3.7	.272	.338	.497	.220	.286	.410	.243	-7.2	-0.6	73-3B	-5	32-SS	-5
2007	LAA	MLB	22	33	2	1	0	1	3	0	12	0	0	0.0	.152	.152	.273	.152	.152	.273	.102	-4.1	-0.5	9-3B	-1		
2008	SLC	AAA	23	448	82	21	2	31	84	45	104	6	5	-0.8	.296	.375	.595	.234	.308	.458	.259	7.3	-1.5	88-SS	-31	13-3B	0
2008	LAA	MLB	23	157	12	4	0	5	13	4	43	4	0	1.0	.200	.224	.327	.200	.224	.340	.197	-7.8	-0.8	22-SS	-2	21-3B	1
2009	LAA	MLB	24	498	52	24	1	19	68	39	136	7	2	0.4	.227	.293	.417	.226	.295	.436	.252	6.0	0.5	118-SS	-13		

Breakout: 30% Improve: 58% Collapse: 17% Attrition: 14%   Comparables: John Russell, Gary Gaetti, Dean Palmer, Tim Pyznarski

Too many strikeouts at the upper levels have dimmed Wood's prospect star a bit, but he made some adjustments and hit .361/.448/.755 with 17 home runs in 147 at-bats at Salt Lake in the second half. This led to yet another call-up to the big leagues, and in his latest go-round, his bat finally showed some signs of life. Shortstops with this kind of power are hard to come by, and while the Angels still have no answer as to whether he's a shortstop or a third baseman, they're trying to figure out a way to get him into the lineup every day.

PITCHERS

Nick Adenhart

Bats: R   Throws: R   Height: 6' 3"   Weight: 185   Born: August 24, 1986   Age: 22

YEAR	TEAM	LVL	AGE	W	L	SV	G	GS	IP	H	BB	SO	HR	GB%	BABIP	STUFF	WHIP	ERA	DERA	EqH9	EqBB9	EqSO9	EqHR9	DEF	VORP	SN/WX
2006	CDR	A	19	10	2	0	16	16	106	84	26	99	2	52.5%	.283	30	1.04	1.95	5.75	10.3	3.7	4.0	0.9	2	-1.5	—
2006	RCU	A+	19	5	2	0	9	9	52	51	16	46	1	57.8%	.331	17	1.29	3.81	6.36	11.2	3.7	4.0	0.6	3	-3.9	—
2007	ARK	AA	20	10	8	0	26	26	153	158	65	116	7	51.8%	.332	17	1.46	3.65	6.09	11.9	4.6	4.3	0.9	5	-7.4	—
2008	SLC	AAA	21	9	13	0	26	26	145¹	173	75	110	15	46.4%	.357	6	1.71	5.76	5.99	12.0	4.9	4.6	1.1	-4	-5.8	—
2008	LAA	MLB	21	1	0	0	3	3	12	18	13	4	0	43.5%	.391	-10	2.58	9.00	7.36	14.7	9.8	2.5	0.0	-2	-4.1	-0.40
2009	LAA	MLB	22	6	11	0	34	23	135²	171	80	80	17	46.0%	.330	0	1.85	6.42	6.44	11.0	5.0	5.0	1.1	0	-16.3	-0.75

Breakout: 12%   Improve: 54%   Collapse: 12%   Attrition: 6%   Comparables: Joel Hanrahan, Chris Seelbach, Rob Woodward, David Cone

Adenhart lived up to expectations as one of the top pitching prospects in the game early on, putting up an 0.87 ERA in his first five Triple-A starts while limiting Pacific Coast League hitters to a .170 average. Then, called up for an emergency start in May against Oakland, Adenhart got ripped for five runs over two innings, and it was all downhill from there. He was sent down after three bad outings, and his ERA at Salt Lake was 7.08 the rest of the way. That's the kind of line that would point at something wrong healthwise, but that wasn't the case, as Adenhart's fastball stayed in the low 90s while touching 95, and both his curveball and his changeup maintained their signature bite. So what happened? Some think it's all between the ears, as Adenhart got hit hard, got scared, and started trying to get cute with his pitches instead of trusting his stuff, leading to hitters' counts and forced fastballs. That happens quite a bit with prospects, but rarely is the statistical drop so evident.

Jose Arredondo

Bats: R   Throws: R   Height: 6' 0"   Weight: 175   Born: March 30, 1984   Age: 25

YEAR	TEAM	LVL	AGE	W	L	SV	G	GS	IP	H	BB	SO	HR	GB%	BABIP	STUFF	WHIP	ERA	DERA	EqH9	EqBB9	EqSO9	EqHR9	DEF	VORP	SN/WX
2006	RCU	A+	22	5	6	0	15	15	90	62	35	115	4	39.4%	.299	20	1.08	2.30	4.76	8.7	4.7	6.8	1.0	4	7.4	—
2006	ARK	AA	22	2	3	0	11	11	60¹	80	22	48	8	45.9%	.367	-19	1.70	6.59	8.42	13.7	3.8	4.3	1.7	-3	-17.8	—
2007	RCU	A+	23	2	4	4	28	0	35	46	11	34	5	46.6%	.387	-40	1.63	6.43	8.62	15.5	3.7	4.6	2.3	-6	-10.5	—
2007	ARK	AA	23	0	1	10	23	0	25	16	12	28	2	40.3%	.246	-4	1.12	2.52	5.79	7.3	5.0	6.6	1.2	2	-0.5	—
2008	SLC	AAA	24	1	1	10	15	0	17	12	4	15	2	60.9%	.238	-3	0.94	2.12	3.31	6.6	2.2	5.5	1.1	2	4.1	—
2008	LAA	MLB	24	10	2	0	52	0	61	42	22	55	3	53.0%	.239	15	1.05	1.62	3.26	6.1	3.0	7.1	0.4	6	24.2	2.76
2009	LAA	MLB	25	3	3	3	50	1	60	57	25	51	5	47.0%	.290	13	1.35	3.88	3.94	8.3	3.4	7.1	0.8	0	11.5	0.97

Breakout: 26%   Improve: 50%   Collapse: 23%   Attrition: 21%   Comparables: Chuck Seelbach, Juan Rincon, Jorge Julio, Tom Walker

Arredondo began the year as a guy with a big fastball and little else, but then he proved that the pitch is more than good enough to get by on. He gave up a run in only eight of 52 appearances and picked up a fluky 10 wins that you just know won somebody their fantasy league. Not only does Arredondo's fastball sit in the 94-97 mph range, but it also features such excellent movement that at times he has control issues because of it. While the Angels have signed Brian Fuentes to close, if Arredondo can find a solid second offering, he might be ready to step in when Fuentes' two-year deal is done.

Chris Bootcheck

Bats: R   Throws: R   Height: 6' 5"   Weight: 200   Born: October 24, 1978   Age: 30

YEAR	TEAM	LVL	AGE	W	L	SV	G	GS	IP	H	BB	SO	HR	GB%	BABIP	STUFF	WHIP	ERA	DERA	EqH9	EqBB9	EqSO9	EqHR9	DEF	VORP	SN/WX
2006	SLC	AAA	27	4	3	1	40	5	65²	84	34	43	10	47.1%	.329	-43	1.81	6.76	8.31	12.9	5.0	3.9	1.9	0	-18.3	—
2006	LAA	MLB	27	0	1	0	7	0	10¹	16	9	7	3	36.8%	.382	-20	2.42	10.49	7.45	14.9	8.4	5.6	2.8	-3	-5.0	0.12
2007	LAA	MLB	28	3	3	0	51	0	77¹	81	24	56	7	44.7%	.318	-2	1.37	4.77	4.38	9.1	2.6	5.7	0.8	-4	8.9	0.50
2008	SLC	AAA	29	0	0	1	19	0	28¹	29	17	34	2	52.6%	.330	3	1.63	2.86	3.99	9.5	4.9	7.1	0.6	0	5.2	—
2008	LAA	MLB	29	0	1	0	10	0	16	30	12	14	2	39.1%	.452	-12	2.63	10.13	7.16	16.5	6.1	6.6	1.1	-5	-7.5	-0.50
2009	PIT	MLB	30	1	1	1	16	0	19	22	9	16	2	45.0%	.340	6	1.62	5.24	5.44	10.2	3.8	6.9	0.8	-0	0.3	0.01

Breakout: 37%   Improve: 58%   Collapse: 30%   Attrition: 57%   Comparables: Doug Linton, Charley Schanz, Alan Benes, Rodney Myers

Although he was a first-round pick eight years ago, the pro workload just never worked for Bootcheck, who failed to ever replicate the stuff from his college days at Auburn. In college, he showed a plus-plus fastball and good slider. As a pro, he merely had a good fastball and an average slider. Bootcheck made some progress with a move to the bullpen at Triple-A last year, so the Pirates are going to give him a shot at a relief role after signing him as a free agent.

Jason Bulger

| | | | | | | | | | | | | Bats: R | | Throws: R | | Height: 6′ 4″ | | Weight: 215 | | Born: December 6, 1978 | | Age: 30 |

YEAR	TEAM	LVL	AGE	W	L	SV	G	GS	IP	H	BB	SO	HR	GB%	BABIP	STUFF	WHIP	ERA	DERA	EqH9	EqBB9	EqSO9	EqHR9	DEF	VORP	SN/WX
2006	SLC	AAA	27	2	2	2	4	27	0	34¹	30	15	44	0	52.5%	.357	7	1.32	4.75	6.27	9.0	4.1	8.2	0.3	3	-2.5	—
2007	SLC	AAA	28	5	2	10	49	0	52²	51	24	81	4	51.2%	.392	21	1.42	3.76	3.51	9.5	4.2	10.3	0.9	-4	11.9	—
2007	LAA	MLB	28	0	0	0	6	0	6¹	5	3	8	0	57.1%	.357	6	1.26	2.86	1.59	7.9	4.8	11.1	0.0	0	2.3	-0.03
2008	SLC	AAA	29	4	0	16	37	0	43	25	22	75	0	57.1%	.347	37	1.09	0.63	0.92	7.6	4.8	11.0	0.2	0	20.4	—
2008	LAA	MLB	29	0	0	0	14	0	16	15	9	20	3	33.3%	.308	6	1.50	7.31	6.19	8.4	4.5	10.1	1.7	-1	-2.7	0.43
2009	LAA	MLB	30	2	3	3	50	1	48	46	29	55	4	46.0%	.330	20	1.55	4.58	4.62	8.3	5.0	9.7	0.8	0	4.4	0.43

Breakout: 10% Improve: 24% Collapse: 44% Attrition: 14%   Comparables: Mike Williams, Jim Gott, Derrick Turnbow, Jim Kern

Take Arredondo and subtract movement and command, and you've got Bulger. In the last three years at Triple-A, he's recorded 200 strikeouts in 129⅔ innings, thanks to easy mid-90s heat, but his marginal curveball and too many pitches out of the strike zone get him in constant trouble at the big-league level. His velocity is enough for him to last another five years as an up-and-down type, but it remains to be seen if he'll ever really stick.

Kelvim Escobar

| | | | | | | | | | | | | Bats: R | | Throws: R | | Height: 6′ 1″ | | Weight: 230 | | Born: April 11, 1976 | | Age: 33 |

YEAR	TEAM	LVL	AGE	W	L	SV	G	GS	IP	H	BB	SO	HR	GB%	BABIP	STUFF	WHIP	ERA	DERA	EqH9	EqBB9	EqSO9	EqHR9	DEF	VORP	SN/WX
2006	LAA	MLB	30	11	14	0	30	30	189¹	192	50	147	17	46.4%	.311	19	1.28	3.61	4.10	9.4	2.4	6.4	0.8	-5	35.0	4.83
2007	LAA	MLB	31	18	7	0	30	30	195²	182	66	160	11	44.4%	.304	27	1.27	3.40	3.33	8.1	2.9	6.5	0.5	-5	51.9	6.18
2009	LAA	MLB	33	5	4	0	19	12	75¹	78	25	57	8	43.0%	.300	14	1.36	4.26	4.28	9.1	2.7	6.4	1.0	0	11.5	1.50

Breakout: 12% Improve: 29% Collapse: 46% Attrition: 33%   Comparables: Tex Hughson, Mike Jackson, Burt Hooton, Bob Wickman

Escobar's 2008 season ended without ever getting started, as he bounced between rehabbing a bum shoulder and inactivity before finally going under the knife at the end of July. Best-case suggestions are that he might be back in action by May, but a return after the All-Star break seems more likely. Even if the Angels haven't found a fifth starter by then, the best spot for him at that point might be the bullpen, and with the Angels on the hook for this last year and $9.5 million, they should take whatever they can get.

Jon Garland

| | | | | | | | | | | | | Bats: R | | Throws: R | | Height: 6′ 6″ | | Weight: 215 | | Born: September 27, 1979 | | Age: 29 |

YEAR	TEAM	LVL	AGE	W	L	SV	G	GS	IP	H	BB	SO	HR	GB%	BABIP	STUFF	WHIP	ERA	DERA	EqH9	EqBB9	EqSO9	EqHR9	DEF	VORP	SN/WX
2006	CHA	MLB	26	18	7	0	33	32	211¹	247	41	112	26	43.5%	.315	1	1.36	4.51	4.12	10.5	1.8	4.3	1.1	-8	32.7	3.86
2007	CHA	MLB	27	10	13	0	32	32	208¹	219	57	98	19	41.4%	.288	-1	1.32	4.23	5.39	9.0	2.3	3.6	0.8	18	27.2	4.27
2008	LAA	MLB	28	14	8	0	32	32	196²	237	59	90	23	50.2%	.320	-9	1.51	4.90	5.22	10.8	2.5	3.7	1.1	3	11.6	1.93
2009	LAA	MLB	29	8	9	0	23	23	136²	163	39	67	16	47.0%	.310	8	1.48	4.89	4.92	10.4	2.4	4.1	1.0	0	8.1	1.86

Breakout: 7% Improve: 40% Collapse: 35% Attrition: 17%   Comparables: Jaime Navarro, Mike Witt, Jeff Weaver, Jack Fisher

As a pitcher who depends on location and changing speeds, Garland never inspired much confidence in the White Sox, even during his two 18-win seasons. They always thought he was just a few mistakes away from getting hammered, and those mistakes cropped up more than ever in 2008. Despite his 14-8 record, less than half his starts were quality, and he got worse as the season wore on. Still, he's made at least 32 starts in each of the last seven years, and that kind of durability alone should get him a nice deal with someone.

Kevin Jepsen

Bats: R Throws: R Height: 6' 3" Weight: 215 Born: July 26, 1984 Age: 24

YEAR	TEAM	LVL	AGE	W	L	SV	G	GS	IP	H	BB	SO	HR	GB%	BABIP	STUFF	WHIP	ERA	DERA	EqH9	EqBB9	EqSO9	EqHR9	DEF	VORP	SN/WX
2006	RCU	A+	21	4	4	16	47	0	50	51	34	46	2	50.3%	.348	-11	1.70	3.60	6.46	11.5	7.4	4.1	1.0	-1	-4.4	—
2007	RCU	A+	22	1	5	3	44	0	53²	61	38	50	2	52.8%	.376	-11	1.84	4.19	5.16	14.3	8.3	4.6	1.0	-7	2.2	—
2008	ARK	AA	23	2	1	11	25	0	31²	22	18	35	0	65.4%	.289	9	1.26	1.42	3.38	7.4	5.8	6.4	0.3	3	7.2	—
2008	SLC	AAA	23	1	3	2	15	0	23	17	12	21	3	62.5%	.259	-7	1.26	2.35	5.32	7.0	4.9	5.7	1.2	4	0.7	—
2008	LAA	MLB	23	0	1	0	9	0	8¹	8	4	7	0	44.0%	.320	-2	1.44	4.34	5.62	9.0	4.5	6.8	0.0	0	0.3	0.13
2009	LAA	MLB	24	2	3	1	27	3	48²	50	33	38	4	51.0%	.310	4	1.70	4.99	5.08	9.0	5.6	6.5	0.7	0	2.0	0.26

Breakout: 3% Improve: 18% Collapse: 65% Attrition: 14% Comparables: Craig Hansen, Gary Majewski, Jay Powell, Ron Willis

A second-round pick in 2002, Jepsen blew up his shoulder early in his career, and while it's been a long road back, he's starting to show the stuff that got him drafted so high in the first place. His 98 mph fastball got him a place on the Olympic team, but he still needs to throw more strikes to get a safe spot on the big-league roster.

John Lackey

Bats: R Throws: R Height: 6' 6" Weight: 235 Born: October 23, 1978 Age: 30

YEAR	TEAM	LVL	AGE	W	L	SV	G	GS	IP	H	BB	SO	HR	GB%	BABIP	STUFF	WHIP	ERA	DERA	EqH9	EqBB9	EqSO9	EqHR9	DEF	VORP	SN/WX
2006	LAA	MLB	27	13	11	0	33	33	217²	203	72	190	14	44.8%	.304	28	1.26	3.56	3.87	8.5	2.9	7.0	0.5	-3	48.6	5.46
2007	LAA	MLB	28	19	9	0	33	33	224	219	52	179	18	45.6%	.302	23	1.21	3.01	3.67	8.5	2.0	6.3	0.7	5	62.8	6.85
2008	LAA	MLB	29	12	5	0	24	24	163¹	161	40	130	26	45.5%	.292	4	1.23	3.75	4.46	9.0	2.1	6.5	1.5	11	35.3	4.54
2009	LAA	MLB	30	12	9	0	29	29	182²	185	53	139	20	45.0%	.300	23	1.31	3.92	3.94	8.9	2.4	6.4	0.9	0	30.9	4.68

Breakout: 2% Improve: 35% Collapse: 26% Attrition: 9% Comparables: Erik Hanson, Freddy Garcia, Frank Sullivan, Andy Benes

Lackey missed the first few weeks of the season with some arm soreness, but otherwise, he's been a workhorse who eats innings as an above-average starter. His stuff isn't awesome, but it's good, including a low-90s fastball and two solid breaking pitches. He doesn't have laserlike precision, but he does throw a preponderance of strikes. It's not his strengths, but rather his lack of weaknesses that make him so good, and the Angels smartly picked up his 2009 option while working behind the scenes to hammer out a long-term deal.

Shane Loux

Bats: R Throws: R Height: 6' 2" Weight: 235 Born: August 31, 1979 Age: 29

YEAR	TEAM	LVL	AGE	W	L	SV	G	GS	IP	H	BB	SO	HR	GB%	BABIP	STUFF	WHIP	ERA	DERA	EqH9	EqBB9	EqSO9	EqHR9	DEF	VORP	SN/WX
2006	OMA	AAA	26	2	5	2	31	0	54¹	74	15	23	2	60.5%	.355	-33	1.65	6.49	8.77	13.0	2.8	2.3	0.5	-3	-18.1	—
2008	SLC	AAA	28	12	6	0	22	22	138	154	40	77	14	51.6%	.309	-12	1.41	3.98	5.30	10.3	2.8	3.1	1.1	9	4.4	—
2008	LAA	MLB	28	0	0	0	7	0	16	16	2	4	1	60.3%	.268	-16	1.13	2.81	4.60	8.6	1.1	1.7	0.6	3	4.3	0.05
2009	LAA	MLB	29	4	6	0	29	12	91	118	31	36	11	50.0%	.320	-8	1.63	5.83	5.91	11.4	2.8	3.4	1.0	0	-5.1	-0.05

Breakout: 8% Improve: 23% Collapse: 42% Attrition: 27% Comparables: Mark Petkovsek, Lary Sorensen, Mark Johnson, Dave Eiland

Once a semihot prospect in the Tigers' system, Loux spent four years at Triple-A Toledo before becoming one of those guys who bounces from organization to organization because he's big, he throws strikes, and he can get ground-ball outs. That's really pretty much the sum of his skills: he has enough to pitch professionally, just not consistently at the highest level.

Dustin Moseley

Bats: R Throws: R Height: 6' 4" Weight: 215 Born: December 26, 1981 Age: 27

YEAR	TEAM	LVL	AGE	W	L	SV	G	GS	IP	H	BB	SO	HR	GB%	BABIP	STUFF	WHIP	ERA	DERA	EqH9	EqBB9	EqSO9	EqHR9	DEF	VORP	SN/WX
2006	SLC	AAA	24	13	8	0	26	26	149¹	164	51	114	18	52.9%	.317	-18	1.44	4.71	6.27	11.0	3.4	4.7	1.5	7	-10.4	—
2006	LAA	MLB	24	1	0	0	3	2	11	22	2	3	3	37.5%	.432	-38	2.18	9.00	6.30	19.8	1.8	1.8	2.7	-2	-3.6	-0.31
2007	LAA	MLB	25	4	3	0	46	8	92	97	27	50	7	48.8%	.307	-7	1.35	4.40	4.81	9.3	2.6	4.4	0.7	5	16.5	1.27
2008	SLC	AAA	26	7	10	0	20	20	116²	150	34	83	23	47.0%	.342	-34	1.58	6.94	7.47	12.5	2.9	4.3	2.0	2	-22.8	—
2008	LAA	MLB	26	2	4	0	12	10	50¹	70	20	37	6	48.9%	.381	-6	1.79	6.80	5.66	12.6	3.3	5.8	1.1	-4	-5.2	-0.40
2009	LAA	MLB	27	5	7	0	34	15	97¹	120	36	57	13	47.0%	.320	1	1.59	5.54	5.57	10.8	3.1	4.9	1.1	0	-1.9	0.35

Breakout: 40% Improve: 71% Collapse: 14% Attrition: 15% Comparables: Colby Lewis, Tony Brizzolara, Jon Ratliff, Jack Fisher

With the Angels' rotation banged up to begin the season, Moseley began the year as the team's fifth starter, but quickly pitched his way out of the job before hitting the DL with forearm soreness. Once he returned to action, he pitched no better. A highly regarded prospect when he was dealt to the Angels by the Reds for Ramon Ortiz, Mosely has a four-pitch mix centered on a cutter and a curve, but he doesn't have enough finesse to make it work at the big-league level. Last year was his big chance to establish himself, and he failed with sinking colors.

Darren O'Day

Bats: R   Throws: R   Height: 6' 4"   Weight: 220   Born: October 22, 1982   Age: 26

YEAR	TEAM	LVL	AGE	W	L	SV	G	GS	IP	H	BB	SO	HR	GB%	BABIP	STUFF	WHIP	ERA	DERA	EqH9	EqBB9	EqSO9	EqHR9	DEF	VORP	SN/WX
2006	ORM	Rk	23	0	1	7	14	0	14	11	5	15	1	41.0%	.270	-28	1.14	2.57	7.30	11.7	5.1	3.6	2.2	1	-2.3	—
2006	CDR	A	23	3	1	1	17	0	23	20	2	14	1	64.4%	.271	-33	0.96	2.74	6.64	10.6	1.8	2.2	1.3	2	-2.3	—
2007	RCU	A+	24	4	0	11	24	0	24	10	6	26	1	57.9%	.161	-2	0.67	0.75	3.09	4.6	2.7	5.0	0.8	2	6.5	—
2007	ARK	AA	24	3	4	10	29	0	29¹	27	14	22	3	56.8%	.293	-25	1.40	3.99	6.15	10.6	5.1	4.1	1.7	2	-1.6	—
2008	SLC	AAA	25	2	2	7	21	0	33	29	7	30	3	41.3%	.302	-4	1.09	3.27	5.28	8.8	2.1	5.9	0.9	5	1.1	—
2008	LAA	MLB	25	0	1	0	30	0	43¹	49	14	29	2	58.5%	.331	-1	1.45	4.57	3.74	10.0	2.7	5.2	0.4	-5	3.8	0.04
2009	NYN	MLB	26	2	2	2	42	0	47	47	15	33	4	52.0%	.300	4	1.33	3.77	4.23	9.1	2.6	5.4	0.7	0	8.7	0.66

Breakout: 27%   Improve: 59%   Collapse: 18%   Attrition: 20%   Comparables: Rich Loiselle, Jose Santiago, Dave Heaverlo, Matt Whiteside

Seen as little more than an organizational arm entering the year, O'Day was one of the more pleasant surprises during spring training, initially making the team and holding his own as an extra reliever. A sidearmer with the sinker/slider combination one normally expects from that type, O'Day had a slightly torn labrum at the end of the year, and when the Angels took him off the 40-man roster to protect others, the Mets called their bluff and snagged him in the Rule 5 draft. He'll compete for a similar spot in the Mets' pen and a chance to enjoy access to a far superior public transit system.

Darren Oliver

Bats: R   Throws: L   Height: 6' 2"   Weight: 200   Born: October 6, 1970   Age: 38

YEAR	TEAM	LVL	AGE	W	L	SV	G	GS	IP	H	BB	SO	HR	GB%	BABIP	STUFF	WHIP	ERA	DERA	EqH9	EqBB9	EqSO9	EqHR9	DEF	VORP	SN/WX
2006	NYN	MLB	35	4	1	0	45	0	81	70	21	60	13	49.8%	.248	-4	1.12	3.44	4.54	7.6	2.0	6.1	1.3	9	20.8	1.33
2007	LAA	MLB	36	3	1	0	61	0	64¹	58	23	51	5	48.0%	.283	1	1.26	3.78	4.41	7.6	2.9	6.1	0.7	1	12.2	1.21
2008	LAA	MLB	37	7	1	0	54	0	72	67	16	48	5	48.9%	.294	5	1.15	2.88	3.25	8.4	1.9	5.5	0.6	2	22.2	2.12
2009	LAA	MLB	38	3	2	2	46	0	53	56	16	34	6	46.0%	.290	-0	1.35	3.97	3.99	9.2	2.6	5.4	0.9	0	8.4	0.72

Breakout: 23%   Improve: 39%   Collapse: 42%   Attrition: 31%   Comparables: Buddy Groom, Al Brazle, Tom Burgmeier, Alan Embree

Oliver's big-league career is now at 15 years, and at this pace, he's got a good shot at getting to 20. He still has slightly above-average velocity for a lefty with good movement, as well as a tight slider that is a true weapon against left-handers. *Reliever* and *consistency* are two words that rarely go together, but Oliver has been pretty good for three years straight, and there's little reason to think it won't continue.

Francisco Rodriguez

Bats: R   Throws: R   Height: 6' 0"   Weight: 180   Born: January 7, 1982   Age: 27

YEAR	TEAM	LVL	AGE	W	L	SV	G	GS	IP	H	BB	SO	HR	GB%	BABIP	STUFF	WHIP	ERA	DERA	EqH9	EqBB9	EqSO9	EqHR9	DEF	VORP	SN/WX
2006	LAA	MLB	24	2	3	47	69	0	73	52	28	98	6	40.2%	.288	30	1.10	1.73	2.03	7.0	3.4	10.1	0.8	-1	33.6	7.29
2007	LAA	MLB	25	5	2	40	64	0	67¹	50	34	90	3	45.6%	.309	31	1.25	2.81	2.66	6.7	4.1	10.0	0.4	-2	23.1	4.24
2008	LAA	MLB	26	2	3	62	76	0	68¹	54	34	77	4	42.6%	.296	21	1.29	2.24	2.69	7.3	4.2	9.0	0.5	0	22.8	5.63
2009	NYN	MLB	27	5	5	45	56	0	61²	47	28	74	5	44.0%	.280	25	1.21	2.74	3.02	6.9	3.6	9.3	0.7	0	19.7	3.47

Breakout: 14%   Improve: 30%   Collapse: 43%   Attrition: 13%   Comparables: Dick Selma, Scott Williamson, Mark Littell, Rich Gossage

Rodriguez finished third in the American League Cy Young Award voting and sixth in the MVP race. The year before, he netted zero votes in either category. What a difference 62 saves makes, because let's be frank, he had much the same year. In 2008, Rodriguez faced a grand total of three more batters than he did the year before; he walked the same numbers of hitters, allowed four more hits, and struck out 13 fewer batters. In other words, he was a little bit *worse*, except for the saves. While the voters were fooled, the market was not, as the contract Rodriguez signed with the Mets falls in the reasonable range for a top-flight closer. Rodriguez's fastball was a bit off last year, but his changeup got much better to make up for it, and he should keep getting the job done.

Ervin Santana

Bats: R **Throws: R** **Height: 6' 2"** **Weight: 160** **Born: December 12, 1982** **Age: 26**

YEAR	TEAM	LVL	AGE	W	L	SV	G	GS	IP	H	BB	SO	HR	GB%	BABIP	STUFF	WHIP	ERA	DERA	EqH9	EqBB9	EqSO9	EqHR9	DEF	VORP	SN/WX
2006	LAA	MLB	23	16	8	0	33	33	204	181	70	141	21	38.6%	.272	12	1.23	4.28	4.84	8.1	3.1	5.6	0.9	6	31.5	4.11
2007	SLC	AAA	24	2	1	0	5	5	32¹	39	10	32	4	43.4%	.380	10	1.52	5.02	3.23	11.4	2.9	6.5	1.5	-7	8.1	—
2007	LAA	MLB	24	7	14	0	28	26	150	174	58	126	26	36.9%	.327	-7	1.55	5.76	5.44	10.1	3.2	6.6	1.6	-8	-1.9	1.46
2008	LAA	MLB	25	16	7	0	32	32	219	198	47	214	23	39.8%	.293	28	1.12	3.49	3.81	8.1	1.8	7.7	1.0	5	52.8	5.66
2009	LAA	MLB	26	13	9	0	30	30	198¹	193	56	173	23	40.0%	.300	30	1.26	3.88	3.88	8.5	2.4	7.3	1.0	0	33.5	5.20

Breakout: 31% Improve: 59% Collapse: 14% Attrition: 16% Comparables: Jake Peavy, Juan Marichal, Jack McDowell, Don Sutton

The Angels had been waiting for Santana to break out, but finally, as a 25-year-old, he was one of the top 10 starting pitchers in baseball. A closer look for the reasons behind the breakout provides some counterintuitive information. He didn't learn a new pitch; in fact, it was the opposite—Santana stopped throwing his curve and changeup, limiting his arsenal almost purely to his two plus offerings, a 94-98 mph fastball and a sharp slider with two-plane break. This less-is-more philosophy allowed him to throw more strikes, and the risk of giving hitters a far better shot at guessing what was coming was mitigated by the pure quality of what was coming out of his hand. This might be a model for some others to follow—worry more about quality of your arsenal rather than sheer quantity of offerings. Of course, as advice goes, it helps if you have stuff like Santana's to fall back on.

Joe Saunders

Bats: L **Throws: L** **Height: 6' 3"** **Weight: 210** **Born: June 16, 1981** **Age: 28**

YEAR	TEAM	LVL	AGE	W	L	SV	G	GS	IP	H	BB	SO	HR	GB%	BABIP	STUFF	WHIP	ERA	DERA	EqH9	EqBB9	EqSO9	EqHR9	DEF	VORP	SN/WX
2006	SLC	AAA	25	10	4	0	21	20	135²	117	38	97	12	53.2%	.269	-2	1.15	2.66	4.49	8.3	2.7	4.3	1.1	16	15.8	—
2006	LAA	MLB	25	7	3	0	13	13	70²	71	29	51	6	48.0%	.307	7	1.42	4.71	5.05	9.3	3.7	6.0	0.8	-1	5.6	2.16
2007	SLC	AAA	26	4	7	0	14	14	86¹	89	20	84	10	44.7%	.319	6	1.26	5.11	5.63	9.0	2.2	6.2	1.3	0	-0.3	—
2007	LAA	MLB	26	8	5	0	18	18	107¹	129	34	69	11	45.8%	.334	3	1.52	4.45	4.75	10.4	2.6	5.0	0.9	3	16.0	1.61
2008	LAA	MLB	27	17	7	0	31	31	198	187	53	103	21	47.7%	.269	2	1.21	3.41	4.14	8.5	2.3	4.2	1.0	10	46.6	5.38
2009	LAA	MLB	28	9	9	0	26	26	153¹	174	48	89	18	47.0%	.310	13	1.45	4.69	4.72	9.9	2.6	4.9	1.0	0	11.8	2.47

Breakout: 6% Improve: 33% Collapse: 25% Attrition: 15% Comparables: Paul Splittorff, John Halama, Kirk Rueter, Bud Black

Let's be frank: Saunders isn't this good. Seventeen wins, an All-Star Game appearance, and a top 10 ERA generally don't happen to you when you can't strike out even five batters per nine innings. Saunders is basically a left-handed version of Garland, mixing a deep arsenal of pitches and throwing strikes. Don't get us wrong—Saunders is awfully good at it, but he needs too much help to be able to put together these kinds of seasons consistently.

Scot Shields

Bats: R **Throws: R** **Height: 6' 1"** **Weight: 180** **Born: July 22, 1975** **Age: 33**

YEAR	TEAM	LVL	AGE	W	L	SV	G	GS	IP	H	BB	SO	HR	GB%	BABIP	STUFF	WHIP	ERA	DERA	EqH9	EqBB9	EqSO9	EqHR9	DEF	VORP	SN/WX
2006	LAA	MLB	30	7	7	2	74	0	87²	70	24	84	8	53.7%	.270	15	1.07	2.87	3.68	7.2	2.4	7.8	0.7	6	29.5	3.75
2007	LAA	MLB	31	4	5	2	71	0	77	62	33	77	7	46.6%	.278	8	1.23	3.86	5.00	7.1	3.6	8.0	0.8	7	15.6	2.60
2008	LAA	MLB	32	6	4	4	64	0	63¹	56	29	64	6	53.7%	.299	8	1.34	2.70	3.77	8.1	3.8	8.1	0.9	-1	11.9	3.21
2009	LAA	MLB	33	3	3	4	53	0	60¹	58	24	55	5	49.0%	.300	13	1.35	3.89	3.95	8.3	3.3	7.7	0.8	0	10.2	0.91

Breakout: 18% Improve: 38% Collapse: 35% Attrition: 13% Comparables: Hoyt Wilhelm, Mike Jackson, Jason Isringhausen, Dave Smith

It looked as if Shields was going to get a shot at picking up some saves with the departure of K-Rod, but the signing of Brian Fuentes means he'll return to the job he's had for most of the decade as one of the best and most consistent setup men in the game. He had some control problems in the second half last year, but they were attributable to a sore rib cage that altered his release point. Otherwise, Shields' plus fastball with sinking action and the slow, loopy curve that doubles as a change because of the velocity difference were as effective as ever.

Justin Speier

Bats: R   Throws: R   Height: 6' 4"   Weight: 205   Born: November 6, 1973   Age: 35

YEAR	TEAM	LVL	AGE	W	L	SV	G	GS	IP	H	BB	SO	HR	GB%	BABIP	STUFF	WHIP	ERA	DERA	EqH9	EqBB9	EqSO9	EqHR9	DEF	VORP	SN/WX
2006	TOR	MLB	32	2	0	0	58	0	51¹	47	21	55	5	31.7%	.300	14	1.32	3.16	2.63	8.2	3.5	8.6	0.9	-3	16.0	1.35
2007	LAA	MLB	33	2	3	0	51	0	50	36	12	47	6	38.5%	.240	9	0.96	2.88	3.96	6.1	2.0	7.4	1.1	5	16.4	1.94
2008	LAA	MLB	34	2	8	0	62	0	68	69	27	56	15	36.9%	.280	-20	1.41	5.03	4.93	8.8	3.1	6.4	1.9	-1	2.9	-0.32
2009	LAA	MLB	35	2	2	2	37	0	44²	45	16	35	7	36.0%	.290	4	1.37	4.39	4.34	8.9	3.0	6.6	1.3	0	5.6	0.45

Breakout: 18%   Improve: 40%   Collapse: 35%   Attrition: 27%   Comparables: Moe Drabowsky, Turk Farrell, Mike Trombley, Turk Wendell

Speier's deal with the devil must have reached its sunset clause in 2008. As a pitcher without overwhelming stuff, Speier's game is all about location. Last year, that location was consistently up in the zone, leading to that whopping total of 15 home runs in 68 innings, including 10 to left-handers in only 118 at-bats. The Angels voted no confidence by leaving Speier off their playoff roster, but they're still down for two more years of him at $10 million on their deal with him. They're hoping either he figures out what went wrong or that Beelzebub gives him an extension.

Rich Thompson

Bats: R   Throws: R   Height: 6' 1"   Weight: 180   Born: July 1, 1984   Age: 24

YEAR	TEAM	LVL	AGE	W	L	SV	G	GS	IP	H	BB	SO	HR	GB%	BABIP	STUFF	WHIP	ERA	DERA	EqH9	EqBB9	EqSO9	EqHR9	DEF	VORP	SN/WX
2006	ARK	AA	21	3	4	10	42	0	66	52	27	60	13	35.1%	.235	-16	1.20	5.18	8.29	8.0	4.0	5.1	2.6	11	-18.8	—
2007	ARK	AA	22	2	3	0	21	3	49¹	34	14	50	5	42.6%	.240	3	0.97	2.01	5.63	7.8	3.1	6.0	1.6	9	-0.2	—
2007	SLC	AAA	22	3	0	1	16	0	24²	17	6	32	2	44.1%	.278	25	0.93	2.19	3.65	6.2	2.2	8.4	0.7	3	5.4	—
2007	LAA	MLB	22	0	0	0	7	0	6²	10	3	9	4	30.0%	.375	6	1.95	10.75	9.95	14.2	4.3	11.4	5.7	0	-3.5	-0.00
2008	SLC	AAA	24	1	0	0	10	0	13¹	12	9	11	1	43.2%	.310	-10	1.58	4.06	3.46	8.3	6.2	4.8	0.7	-1	3.1	—
2008	LAA	MLB	24	0	0	0	2	0	2	4	2	1	0	66.7%	.444	-70	3.00	22.50	18.00	18.0	9.0	4.5	0.0	-1	-3.6	0.01
2009	LAA	MLB	24	2	4	1	46	4	53	63	28	36	9	43.0%	.320	-5	1.72	6.42	6.37	10.5	4.4	5.8	1.4	0	-6.4	-0.45

Breakout: 17%   Improve: 49%   Collapse: 19%   Attrition: 13%   Comparables: Gabriel Ozuna, Carlos Maldonado, Manny Barrios, Mike Perez

Thompson seemed to be on the precipice of a real job in the Angels' bullpen, even breaking camp with the big-league squad, but the bulk of his season was spent on the sidelines due to arm soreness. The affable Aussie (aren't they all?) has two plus offerings in his fastball and curve, but his age and two miserable showings in brief call-ups are working against him, making 2009 a pivotal season.

Jordan Walden

Bats: R   Throws: R   Height: 6' 5"   Weight: 220   Born: November 16, 1987   Age: 21

YEAR	TEAM	LVL	AGE	W	L	SV	G	GS	IP	H	BB	SO	HR	GB%	BABIP	STUFF	WHIP	ERA	DERA	EqH9	EqBB9	EqSO9	EqHR9	DEF	VORP	SN/WX
2007	ORM	Rk	19	1	1	0	15	15	64¹	49	17	63	3	56.6%	.271	12	1.03	3.08	6.91	9.6	4.2	3.7	1.4	0	-8.2	—
2008	CDR	A	20	4	6	0	18	18	107¹	80	32	91	3	64.0%	.263	27	1.04	2.18	5.80	9.3	4.0	3.6	0.9	10	-2.1	—
2008	RCU	A+	20	5	2	0	9	9	49	42	24	50	4	52.9%	.288	11	1.35	4.04	7.88	9.3	5.7	4.9	1.6	0	-11.6	—
2009	LAA	MLB	21	5	8	0	20	20	105¹	125	58	57	12	52.0%	.320	3	1.73	6.25	6.38	10.4	4.6	4.5	1.0	0	-11.5	-0.43

Breakout: 13%   Improve: 45%   Collapse: 19%   Attrition: 7%   Comparables: Ryan Kibler, T.J. Tucker, Nick Adenhart, Duane Ward

In the spring of 2006, Walden was the best high school prospect in the game, thanks to an upper-90s fastball, but his velocity disappeared during his senior year and he plummeted to the 12th round. The Angels followed him for a year at junior college, where he rebounded sufficiently to earn a $1 million bonus. With Adenhart's struggles, Walden has passed him as the top pitching prospect in the system, thanks to an outstanding fastball that is notable for both its plus velocity and its incredible sink. He's still rough around the edges in terms of secondary stuff and command, but all the ingredients are there for him to become a number two starter in a few years.

Jered Weaver

Bats: R   Throws: R   Height: 6' 7"   Weight: 205   Born: October 4, 1982   Age: 26

YEAR	TEAM	LVL	AGE	W	L	SV	G	GS	IP	H	BB	SO	HR	GB%	BABIP	STUFF	WHIP	ERA	DERA	EqH9	EqBB9	EqSO9	EqHR9	DEF	VORP	SN/WX
2006	SLC	AAA	23	6	1	0	12	11	77¹	63	10	93	7	32.7%	.318	31	0.95	2.10	3.15	8.6	1.4	8.1	1.1	4	19.4	—
2006	LAA	MLB	23	11	2	0	19	19	123	94	33	105	15	31.8%	.239	23	1.03	2.56	3.64	6.8	2.4	6.9	1.0	12	47.0	5.15
2007	LAA	MLB	24	13	7	0	28	28	161	178	45	115	17	37.7%	.319	9	1.39	3.91	3.75	9.4	2.3	5.5	1.0	-7	30.7	4.06
2008	LAA	MLB	25	11	10	0	30	30	176²	173	54	152	20	34.1%	.301	16	1.28	4.33	4.30	8.8	2.5	6.9	1.0	0	26.6	3.85
2009	LAA	MLB	26	11	9	0	28	28	172¹	177	51	136	22	37.0%	.300	24	1.32	4.25	4.23	9.0	2.5	6.6	1.1	0	23.0	3.81

Breakout: 8%   Improve: 43%   Collapse: 21%   Attrition: 11%   Comparables: Jack McDowell, Ben McDonald, Dustin Hermanson, Tommy Greene

The Angels have been waiting for Weaver's breakout for two years, and they're still waiting. One of the top pitchers in college baseball history and a former top prospect, Weaver wove a 2008 campaign filled with minor hiccups, including a sore shoulder, some gastrointestinal issues, and a bizarre late-season injury in which he ripped up his pitching hand when he snagged a staple while getting up from the dugout bench. Weaver never had ace-caliber stuff, but he has enough movement and command to be an above-average starter.

LINEOUTS

Hitters

PLAYER	TEAM	LVL	AGE	PA	R	2B	3B	HR	RBI	BB	SO	SB-CS	EqBRR	AVG/OBP/SLG	EqAVG/EqOBP/EqSLG	EqA	VORP	WARP
C R. Budde	SLC	AAA	28	186	16	8	2	2	23	10	47	3-0	0.5	.202/.258/.306	.136/.183/.205	.097	-28.5	-2.6
CF C. Fuller#	CDR	A	21	533	77	19	13	9	47	68	122	36-10	1.2	.260/.379/.425	.216/.314/.362	.242	-10.3	0.4
3B L. Jimenez	ORM	Rk	20	302	57	28	6	15	65	11	45	6-2	-0.0	.331/.361/.630	.216/.235/.381	.208	-28.4	-2.4
2B R. Mount*	RCU	A+	21	369	68	17	5	16	49	23	67	10-2	3.0	.290/.337/.512	.236/.280/.417	.239	-4.5	-1.9
OF C. Pettit	ARK	AA	23	251	27	12	2	6	26	16	39	5-2	-3.2	.248/.320/.401	.213/.269/.361	.218	-10.9	-1.5
SS P.J. Phillips	RCU	A+	21	521	68	22	11	8	55	24	125	35-9	3.0	.276/.313/.416	.226/.258/.348	.213	-27.3	-0.8
SS A. Romine#	CDR	A	22	543	79	21	4	2	34	55	76	62-18	0.3	.260/.347/.336	.200/.272/.262	.200	-45.0	-0.5
SS H. Statia#	ARK	AA	22	252	26	12	3	1	20	14	17	8-4	1.5	.242/.288/.336	.209/.249/.291	.190	-20.3	0.0

Ryan Budde has a career minor league OBP of .298 and spent the last five years at Triple-A for the Dodgers, Phillies, and Angels as that "just-in-case guy" because he can put on the mask and shin guards. ⊘ Speedster **Clay Fuller** made progress learning the left-handed half of switch-hitting and has the speed and OBP skills that might make a leadoff prospect of him. ⊘ **Luis Jimenez** is a bat-only prospect at the hot corner, but he has hit .322/.354/.583 in his first 133 pro games and the Angels are looking forward to seeing what he'll do in a full-season league as a 21-year-old. ⊘ Beset by injuries, **Ryan Mount** has taken four years to live up to some lofty expectations coming out of the draft; now he needs to prove that his 2008 showing was more than a Cal League mirage. ⊘ After hitting .327 in his full-season debut, **Chris Pettit** tanked at Double-A while coming back from a broken foot, but he recaptured a bit of his previous luster in the Arizona Fall League. ⊘ Brandon's younger brother, **P. J. Phillips** is plenty toolsy, but is still a long way from being a legit prospect. ⊘ **Andrew Romine** isn't much of a hitter, but there is hope that his speed, defense at short, and willingness to take a walk will be enough. ⊘ **Hainley Statia** has a big-league-ready glove at shortstop and a little-league-ready bat.

Pitchers

PLAYER	TEAM	LVL	AGE	W	L	SV	IP	H	BB	SO	HR	GB%	BABIP	STUFF	WHIP	ERA	DERA	EqH9	EqBB9	EqSO9	EqHR9	DEF	VORP
C. Alvarado	SLC	AAA	30	7	5	0	130²	123	64	131	14	35.3%	.303	1	1.43	4.27	4.90	9.1	4.4	6.1	1.1	0	9.9
M. Anton*	CDR	A	23	7	4	0	90	75	23	58	4	48.2%	.275	-20	1.09	2.40	5.26	10.3	3.5	2.4	1.3	5	3.0
	RCU	A+	23	6	5	0	81²	101	34	58	8	45.4%	.360	-34	1.65	5.51	7.64	14.0	5.3	3.3	1.9	-5	-16.0
T. Chatwood	ANG	Rk	18	1	2	0	38	25	36	48	1	58.5%	.304	-3	1.61	3.08	7.16	12.4	14.6	5.2	2.3	0	-4.8
R. Fish*	CDR	A	20	10	4	0	143	138	68	138	12	46.8%	.318	-22	1.44	4.85	8.68	13.0	6.3	4.3	2.1	-4	-41.9
N. Green	SLC	AAA	23	8	8	0	159	186	44	112	31	36.3%	.314	-25	1.45	5.32	5.80	10.9	2.6	4.1	1.9	-1	-3.4
R. Mosebach	ARK	AA	23	9	12	0	177¹	209	69	88	6	57.8%	.343	-17	1.57	4.62	7.47	12.2	4.2	2.4	0.7	4	-33.3
S. O'Sullivan	RCU	A+	20	16	8	0	158	167	50	111	8	50.6%	.315	11	1.37	4.73	7.44	10.8	3.8	3.0	1.0	-3	-30.2
A. Ortega	ARK	AA	22	9	7	0	135	124	49	83	11	46.7%	.277	-14	1.28	3.73	6.93	9.1	3.7	3.1	1.3	14	-18.8
	SLC	AAA	22	5	0	0	39¹	46	6	22	2	47.8%	.307	5	1.32	2.52	4.35	10.3	1.6	3.0	0.7	4	5.5
T. Reckling*	CDR	A	19	10	7	0	152¹	137	59	128	8	54.5%	.311	7	1.29	3.37	6.68	11.8	5.3	3.6	1.5	4	-15.5
R. Rodriguez	ARK	AA	23	2	4	11	53¹	46	11	48	3	60.4%	.282	-5	1.07	1.86	4.38	8.9	2.4	5.1	0.9	8	6.7
	SLC	AAA	23	2	0	0	14¹	20	6	8	2	62.7%	.383	-34	1.82	6.29	6.23	13.8	4.2	3.5	1.4	-2	-0.9
A. Serrano	SLC	AAA	27	2	0	0	18	26	5	12	7	35.9%	.333	-42	1.72	6.50	6.48	14.0	2.7	3.8	3.8	0	-1.6
M. Tobin	CDR	A	20	2	3	0	37¹	29	18	18	2	53.5%	.248	-16	1.26	3.14	7.11	9.7	6.3	1.4	1.4	6	-5.3

Minor league lifer **Carlos Alvarado** had a solid year at Triple-A, but that still wasn't enough to get him a big-league look. ⊘ After dominating at Low-A on location alone, **Michael Anton** found out that this wasn't enough to shine in the Cal League. ⊘ The Angels' top pick in the 2008 draft (second round), teenage righty **Tyler Chatwood** showed impressive velocity, a nice curve, and big-time control issues in his pro debut. ⊘ **Robert Fish** is a big-bodied lefty with good velocity and deceptive arm action; some in the organization see him as a major sleeper. ⊘ **Nick Green** has been durable, but as a finesse righty who survives on a plus change and otherwise decent stuff, he might find even a bid for the open fifth slot in the rotation beyond his reach. ⊘ The Phillies selected **Robert Mosebach** in the Rule 5 draft, but nobody is quite sure why. Maybe he does impressions or something. ⊘ **Sean O'Sullivan** is a finesse pitcher who struggled in the high-offense Cal League, but scouts still like him as a guy who can throw strikes and keep the ball in the park. ⊘ Venezuelan **Anthony Ortega** took a big step forward in 2008, but that only upgraded his outlook from organizational arm to potential middle reliever. ⊘ A seventh-round pick in 2007, **Trevor Reckling** looked to be worth much more than that during his pro debut, showcasing a curveball that some Midwest League scouts considered the best in the circuit. ⊘ Once upon a time, **Rafael Rodriguez** was a live-armed Dominican teen and recipient of the biggest bonus paid by the Angels to anyone from the island; more than seven years later, he's still throwing hard, and he pitched well enough to have finally been added to the 40-man. ⊘ On April 16, **Alex Serrano** pitched one scoreless inning against the Royals, in what might end up being the totality of his big-league career. Called up merely because he was the fresh arm at Triple-A, in the last two years at Salt Lake he's allowed twice as many hits (119) as strikeouts (58) in 87⅔ innings pitched. Still, it's probably one more inning than you or I will ever get, and his career ERA is lower than Bob Gibson's. ⊘ **Mason Tobin** entered the year as a potential breakout player, but that's still the case after he missed most of 2008 with shoulder issues.

MANAGER: MIKE SCIOSCIA

YEAR	TEAM	W-L	Pythag +/−	Avg PC	100+ P	120+ P	QS	BQS	REL	REL w Zero R	IBB	Subs	PH	PH Avg	PH HR	SB2	CS2	SB3	CS3	SAC Att	SAC %	POS SAC	Squeeze	Swing	In Play
2006	LAA	89-73	4	97.3	83	2	86	11	380	231	27	50	101	.171	4	123	45	23	6	42	73.8%	29	2	189	154
2007	LAA	94-68	4	97.4	85	0	85	2	396	245	22	31	101	.250	2	118	47	20	8	48	66.7%	31	3	170	142
2008	LAA	100-62	11	99.6	85	0	87	7	383	249	32	46	74	.182	0	109	38	19	8	46	69.6%	32	3	147	113

Whitey Herzog always said he'd like to show what he could do with a team of sluggers in a hitter's park, but the White Rat never did get the opportunity. Scioscia won't have to change organizations to find out for himself. As the Angels get older and slower and as replacements like Kendry Morales and Brandon Wood come aboard (or in Juan Rivera's case, come back), the skipper is being handed a different sort of ballclub than the much-discussed one focused on contact and speed. Scioscia isn't Chuck Tanner. Having already shown a steady hand with younger players, he'll adopt a willingness to create roles for youngsters on the margins, and he has avoided overmanagement of his bullpen. That's not to say he won't hit-and-run more than most, but he's not going to make people who can't run try to do so, and he's not likely to go bunt-happy. The interesting elective choices will be to see who he picks to fill Garland's slot in the rotation, who starts in the left side of the infield, and who winds up starting at first and left, but having signed a 10-year extension that gives him the sort of job security Herzog only dreamed of, Scioscia could pick wrong on all of them and still not have to worry about anything but his team.

Los Angeles Dodgers

There's never a dull moment for the Dodgers these days. Under general manager Ned Colletti, the club continues to exist in its bipolar state, having either fallen into some crisis or slump or else just emerged from one triumphantly—only to tumble into the next crisis. From an offseason that saw them axe manager Grady Little and flirt with trading blue-chip youngsters Matt Kemp and Clayton Kershaw to a first half filled with injuries, intrigue, and the team's usual streakiness, the 2008 Dodgers appeared headed for a sub-.500 finish in a mediocre division under new manager Joe Torre, a performance that may have threatened Colletti's job. Shockingly, the beleaguered GM pulled off a last-minute coup at the non-waiver trading deadline, acquiring Red Sox slugger Manny Ramirez in a three-team deal. Ramirez brought his dreadlocks, his star power, and no shortage of controversy to Los Angeles, but his big bat injected life into a moribund offense. The team rolled to its first division title since 2004 by winning 19 of the last 27 games and then swept the 97-win Cubs to capture the Dodgers' first postseason series since 1988.

On the surface, winning a division with an 84-78 team isn't a particularly impressive accomplishment, not for a team that PECOTA had forecast to win 87 games, the same total as that for the Diamondbacks and Braves—in other words, enough to contend for both the NL West flag and the wild card. Yet the Dodgers won in a year where they lost more dollars ($51.1 million) and a higher percentage of payroll (43.1 percent) to the disabled list than any other team did, a dubious honor owing to Colletti's tastes in free agents.

With the stupefying exception of Juan Pierre's five-

> ## DODGERS PROSPECTUS
>
> **2008 record:** 84-78; First place in NL West
>
> **Pythagenport record:** 87-75
>
> **Runs scored per game:** 4.32 (13th in NL)
>
> **Runs allowed per game:** 4.03 (1st in NL)
>
> **Team EqA:** .260 (8th in NL)
>
> **2008 Batters Age:** 27.2 (2nd-youngest in NL)
>
> **2008 Pitchers Age:** 29.8 (6th-oldest in NL)
>
> **Ballpark:** Dodger Stadium; Slight pitcher's park; Park Factor of .971
>
> **2008:** Manny arrives just in time to prevent Joe Torre's game of outfield roulette from ending in tragedy.
>
> **2009:** The home-grown core should keep improving if Ned doesn't deal it away. Oh, to be young and in the NL West!

year, $44 million deal, Colletti's best trait as GM is the modicum of restraint he's shown by going no longer than three years on any contract during his tenure. Even so, he has done a poor job of correctly valuing injury risk; his deals have been concentrated in fragile players. At one point or another, 10 of the 11 Dodgers making at least $2 million in 2008 saw time on the disabled list, the exception being the Paul DePodesta–signed Derek Lowe. In June, a perfect storm landed five of the team's six highest-paid players—Rafael Furcal, Nomar Garciaparra, Andruw Jones, Brad Penny, and Jason Schmidt, all Colletti signings—on the DL simultaneously.

Those five were all huge disappointments in 2008. Furcal got off to a torrid start in April, but missed over four months with a back injury that required surgery. Garciaparra served three separate stints on the DL for wrist, calf, and knee injuries, playing in just 55 games. Jones, coming off an injury-driven downer with Atlanta, arrived at camp at least 20 pounds overweight and hit an abysmal .158/.256/.249 while playing in just 75 games, thanks to knee problems. Penny tried to pitch through shoulder woes and put up a 6.27 ERA in 94⅔ innings. Schmidt didn't throw a single inning for the big club after undergoing two surgeries for a torn labrum in 2007; in December, the Dodgers exposed their idiocy by suing the insurance company on the grounds that *the rotator cuff injury that they knew about when signing Schmidt* was unrelated to the labrum woes, thus entitling them to recoup some of his salary. Anatomy is not Colletti's strongest subject.

Such injuries would have crippled most teams, but the Dodgers stayed afloat, thanks to an enviable nucleus of young, homegrown talent. Russell Martin, James Loney, and Matt Kemp may not have matched their promising 2007 performances, but all provided above-average production at their positions; all were under 25 years of age in 2008. Elsewhere in the lineup, Andre Ethier hit a searing .368/.448/.649 over the final two months, and Blake DeWitt began the year as the Opening Day third baseman and ended it filling in for the injured Jeff Kent at second. In the rotation, Chad Billingsley evolved into the frontline starter that talent observers had foreseen, while Clayton Kershaw emerged as the Dodgers' fourth-best starting pitcher. In the bullpen, Jonathan Broxton took over the closer duties when Takashi Saito went down at the All-Star break with a partially torn ulnar collateral ligament, and Cory Wade and Hong-Chih Kuo emerged as key setup men. Except for Ethier and Kuo, all were drafted by the Dodgers under the auspices of Logan White (currently the assistant GM for scouting), and all were 25 or under.

Fresh off the sting of having been lowballed out of his position as Yankee manager after 12 straight post-season appearances, Torre arrived to less-than-universal acclaim, given his strategic shortcomings and his predilection for veterans. Indeed, predecessor Grady Little had lost the clubhouse because of a generational split between the grizzled vets and the youngsters. And there was plenty of reason to fear the synergy between the new manager and Colletti, particularly in the wake of so many trial balloons being floated regarding potential trades of youngsters—trial balloons that apparently emanated from elsewhere in the front office, suggesting organizational disharmony.

Torre inherited two major question marks regarding his lineup: how to divide the outfield time between Kemp, Ethier, Pierre, and the newly arrived Jones (signed to a two-year, $36.2 million deal) and who would play third base. The new manager didn't acquit himself well in handling either problem, allowing injuries to dictate his choice for as long as possible.

Third base appeared to boil down to a decision between Garciaparra, who was coming off an uncharacteristically punchless season, and top prospect Andy LaRoche, who had failed to exert a hold on the job in 2007 because of a series of injuries. Instead, both players started the year on the DL, the former with a wrist fracture, the latter with a torn ligament in his thumb. Third option Tony Abreu, who'd missed most of 2007 with assorted lower abdominal ailments, also hit the DL with a groin strain. As a result, this war of attrition was initially won by DeWitt, a 2004 first-rounder who had split 2007 between High-A and Double-A, hitting a translated .248/.277/.400. After starting the year hot,

DeWitt predictably slipped as the league caught up to him. Amid that skid, LaRoche drew all of 12 starts spread out over a six-week span to reassert his claim, but hit just .203/.319/.322. Finally, Colletti traded two well-regarded prospects, pitcher Jon Meloan and catcher Carlos Santana, to Cleveland for Casey Blake, sending DeWitt back to Las Vegas and, at a rather steep price, providing Torre with exactly the kind of bland veteran-y goodness he understood. LaRoche and 2006 first-round pick Bryan Morris were subsequently sent to the Pirates in the three-team deal that netted them Ramirez, with Boston picking up the tab on the discontented slugger's contract.

This last points to another Colletti shortcoming: in all three summer deals (for Blake, Ramirez, and the Padres' Greg Maddux), he surrendered quality prospects left and right to avoid taking on additional payroll. The Dodgers, who opened with a $118.6 million payroll, have a much bigger dollar advantage over their division mates (who averaged $72 million in payroll) than they do a talent advantage, yet they risk stripping the next wave of talent from their system at the expense of a few million dollars.

As for the outfield, Torre shocked his longtime observers on Opening Day by breaking Pierre's streak of 443 consecutive games to start Ethier, Jones, and Kemp—at that junction the team's best offensive unit, at least on paper. Enamored of keeping his baserunners in motion, though, Torre soon began sneaking the weak-hitting Pierre back into the lineup at the expense of Kemp and Ethier. Through June, Pierre actually had more starts than any other outfielder (Table 1).

Table 1. Dodger Outfield Starts by Month

Month	Ethier	Kemp	Jones	Pierre	Ramirez
April	25	18	25	13	—
May	21	26	11	20	—
June	19	24	0	26	—
July	23	26	17	6	—
August	21	29	2	6	29
September	22	21	1	7	24

Injuries to Pierre and the cratering Jones alleviated the logjam somewhat, but not until a week after Ramirez's arrival did Torre find the courage to mothball the two expensive, unproductive free agents and move Kemp—who had been frozen out of center field in 2007—in between Ramirez and Ethier to create an outfield whose formidable offense compensated for its shaky defense. Indeed, the lineup, which hadn't seen a player hit more than 20 home runs in Dodger blue since 2005, had been wheezing prior to Ramirez's arrival, ranking in the NL's bottom quartile in scoring and homers. With Ramirez (and Blake and the full-time Kemp and Ethier), it was a different story (Table 2).

Table 2. Dodgers Performance Pre- and Post-Manny

Period	Games	RS	R/G	NL Rank	HR	NL Rank	AVG/ OBP/ SLG
Thru 7/31	108	450	4.17	13	74	15	.256/.321/.376
From 8/1	54	250	4.63	7	63	3	.281/.355/.443
Total	162	700	4.32	13	137	13	.264/.333/.399

At least Torre eventually stumbled on the right answer and, furthermore, let Manny be Manny as long as the team was rolling. Elsewhere, Torre went against his reputation by doing a laudable job of breaking in Kershaw and by relying on inexperienced relievers like Wade and Kuo, but he also made other mistakes. He wore Martin down to the nub and played Loney in all but one game despite a performance that cried out for a platoon partner. Giving up on shortstop Chin-Lung Hu when the slick-fielding 24-year-old prospect failed to hit in a brief trial, Torre unimaginatively wound up giving most of the playing time to Angel Berroa, the 2003 AL Rookie of the Year whose career had gone so downhill that he lost his job with the Royals to Tony Pena Jr. in 2007. Torre did show a spark of inspiration by turning back the clock to his days in the AL East and trying Garciaparra at shortstop, but that brief experiment ended with Nomar's recurring injuries.

The Dodgers entered the offseason with no fewer than 13 players, including Ramirez and three-quarters of their infield, filing for free agency. There was no shortage of posturing and hand-wringing regarding Ramirez, whom they initially offered a two-year, $45 million deal that elicited no response from the player or his agent. Word was, Ramirez and agent were seeking five years and more than $100 million. Complicating matters is what to do with Pierre and Jones beyond writing them off as sunk costs; bringing back even one

of them may mean a rerun of last year's overcrowded outfield.

The infield returned to its season-ending state, with Blake (three years plus option, $17.5 million) and Furcal (three years plus a vesting option, $30 million) both re-signing, the latter taking a 30 percent pay cut that at least acknowledges his risk. Those deals mean DeWitt will get first crack at retaining the second base job, with free-agent addition Mark Loretta (one year, $1.25 million) backing him up. Hu, Abreu, and prospect Ivan De Jesus Jr. appear to have been written out of the script except as fallback options, which is a bit disheartening.

As for the staff, the losses of Lowe, Penny, and late-season acquisition Greg Maddux (who retired) leave the Dodgers with a rotation of Billingsley, Kershaw, and Hiroki Kuroda, with rookie James McDonald and, less likely, Schmidt figuring in somewhere; the staff will need to add at least another innings eater. Meanwhile, Broxton remains the closer after the Dodgers non-tendered Saito, with whom they couldn't hammer out an incentive-based deal to account for his injury. With the departure of Joe Beimel, Kuo takes over as the top lefty specialist, with prospect Scott Elbert likely to join the bullpen as the second lefty.

Talent observers note that the team's vaunted player development system is starting to look thin, given the graduations and trades, but most teams would kill to get the types of contributions from the farm that the 2009 Dodgers expect, despite the obstacles in the infield. Indeed, most teams would kill to have the resources the Dodgers have, period—from the beautiful, renewed ballpark to the big-market revenue stream to the talent base largely under club control and thus suppressing the payroll for a few more years. With the economy taking a bite out of their competitors in Arizona and Colorado, the Dodgers retain a considerable advantage in the NL West, though all we really know is that they're a lock to lead the division in drama.

HITTERS

Tony Abreu **2B**   Bats: S   Throws: R   Height: 5' 11"   Weight: 200   Born: November 13, 1984   Age: 24

YEAR	TEAM	LVL	AGE	PA	R	2B	3B	HR	RBI	BB	SO	SB	CS	EqBRR	AVG	OBP	SLG	EqAVG	EqOBP	EqSLG	EqA	VORP	WARP	DEFENSE	
2006	JAX	AA	21	509	66	24	3	6	55	33	69	8	4	2.5	.287	.343	.392	.268	.316	.386	.246	0.5	2.0	110-2B	9
2007	LVG	AAA	22	253	48	22	5	2	18	14	34	5	0	0.6	.355	.399	.517	.275	.320	.415	.257	3.8	0.5	24-2B -5	17-SS 0
2007	LAN	MLB	22	178	19	14	1	2	17	7	21	0	0	0.3	.271	.309	.404	.271	.309	.422	.252	1.4	0.4	22-3B -3	13-2B 1
2009	LAN	MLB	24	374	40	20	2	5	38	24	56	4	1	0.8	.261	.314	.377	.266	.317	.395	.246	7.6	1.2	90-2B	2

Breakout: 16% Improve: 35% Collapse: 38% Attrition: 21%   Comparables: Yung-Chi Chen, Santiago Garcia, Carlos Guillen, Ray Olmedo

Abreu's 2007 was marred by Colletti's public skepticism regarding the abdominal and groin problems that curtailed his season; ultimately, Abreu underwent surgery for a sports hernia. As 2008 began, the Dodgers' rash of injuries at third base might have created an opening for Abreu, but his season ended early due to surgery for a torn hip labrum in late May. The Dodgers seem hopeful he can contribute in 2009; if healthy, he could find a role in their remade infield, but it remains to be seen how committed this regime is to him.

Pedro Baez — 3B

Bats: R Throws: R Height: 6' 2" Weight: 199 Born: March 11, 1988 Age: 21

YEAR	TEAM	LVL	AGE	PA	R	2B	3B	HR	RBI	BB	SO	SB	CS	EqBRR	AVG	OBP	SLG	EqAVG	EqOBP	EqSLG	EqA	VORP	WARP	DEFENSE	
2007	DGR	Rk	19	229	35	14	2	3	39	17	40	3	1	2.9	.274	.341	.408	.208	.252	.321	.200	-41.0	-3.3	53-3B	-9
2008	GRL	A	20	211	23	10	1	1	16	17	45	3	1	-0.4	.178	.244	.259	.153	.209	.226	.140	-29.6	-2.8	55-3B	-5
2008	OGD	Rk	20	268	37	20	1	12	50	18	69	2	2	-0.5	.267	.317	.502	.169	.205	.311	.167	-49.9	-3.2	58-3B	-1
2009	LAN	MLB	21	554	39	29	2	8	47	35	150	4	2	0.2	.199	.252	.307	.202	.254	.322	.195	-23.2	-1.7	130-3B	2

Breakout: 56% Improve: 69% Collapse: 17% Attrition: 14%   Comparables: Jose Bautista, Enrique Diaz, Carlos Villalobos, Jose Jimenez

This toolsy Dominican began the year at Great Lakes but was overmatched, lunging at pitches and giving away far too many at-bats. The Dodgers wisely extricated him, and he salvaged his season with a strong showing in Ogden. Baez has massive raw power and a fluid swing, but as his K/BB ratios suggest, his plate discipline needs major improvement. Defensively, he's got a great arm and good range, but his throwing can be erratic; he made 20 errors in 59 games at Ogden and fielded a Hobsonian .898. He'll start the year back at Great Lakes with hopes of reaching High-A by the end.

Josh Bell — 3B

Bats: S Throws: R Height: 6' 3" Weight: 205 Born: November 13, 1986 Age: 22

YEAR	TEAM	LVL	AGE	PA	R	2B	3B	HR	RBI	BB	SO	SB	CS	EqBRR	AVG	OBP	SLG	EqAVG	EqOBP	EqSLG	EqA	VORP	WARP	DEFENSE	
2006	OGD	Rk	19	276	45	17	3	12	53	23	72	4	0	2.6	.308	.367	.544	.203	.243	.356	.204	-30.7	-4.1	51-3B	-15
2007	GRL	A	20	438	65	21	3	15	62	39	109	5	1	0.0	.289	.354	.470	.224	.277	.366	.221	-16.4	-3.3	88-3B	-19
2007	SBR	A+	20	79	4	2	1	2	9	3	19	0	0	0.0	.173	.203	.307	.145	.165	.289	.127	-10.9	-2.2	17-3B	-12
2008	SBR	A+	21	220	34	12	2	6	21	31	56	4	2	-1.0	.273	.373	.455	.225	.318	.387	.249	-1.3	-0.4	32-3B	-5
2009	LAN	MLB	22	497	47	23	1	13	53	43	154	5	2	0.1	.220	.289	.364	.224	.292	.382	.230	-4.5	-1.1	117-3B	-16

Breakout: 35% Improve: 67% Collapse: 14% Attrition: 14%   Comparables: Shawn Bowman, Kevin Eberwein, Ryan Balfe, David Kelton

A 2005 fourth-round pick out of a Florida high school, Bell entered 2008 ranked sixth among Dodgers prospects, thanks to his plus-plus raw power from both sides of the plate. He arrived at camp 30 pounds lighter and, through the first two months, showed much-improved plate discipline and defense. After 35 errors and an .859 fielding percentage at Great Lakes in 2007, the result mainly of sloppy footwork, he made just five errors in 31 games. Alas, when the Dodgers discovered a cartilage abnormality near his kneecap, they shut him down for season-ending surgery. Expect him to be ready to go come springtime and to reach Double-A by the second half.

Angel Berroa — MI

Bats: R Throws: R Height: 6' 0" Weight: 195 Born: January 27, 1978 Age: 31

YEAR	TEAM	LVL	AGE	PA	R	2B	3B	HR	RBI	BB	SO	SB	CS	EqBRR	AVG	OBP	SLG	EqAVG	EqOBP	EqSLG	EqA	VORP	WARP	DEFENSE			
2006	KCA	MLB	28	503	45	18	1	9	54	14	88	3	1	-0.4	.234	.259	.333	.229	.256	.331	.203	-18.7	-2.1	127-SS	-11		
2007	OMA	AAA	29	352	47	17	0	8	40	25	44	2	2	-5.8	.300	.364	.433	.234	.295	.339	.223	-11.5	-0.2	67-SS	-2	7-2B	0
2008	OMA	AAA	30	201	34	13	0	10	27	8	25	4	2	-0.1	.291	.323	.519	.224	.249	.391	.217	-8.1	-0.4	34-SS	-4	16-2B	2
2008	LAN	MLB	30	256	26	13	1	1	16	20	41	0	0	0.5	.230	.304	.310	.232	.308	.311	.221	-2.3	-0.2	66-SS	0		
2009	LAN	MLB	31	191	16	8	1	3	19	10	32	1	1	-0.6	.240	.288	.343	.244	.291	.359	.223	1.8	0.1	49-SS	-1		

Breakout: 36% Improve: 50% Collapse: 34% Attrition: 46%   Comparables: Alvaro Espinoza, Hector Torres, Frank Duffy, Virgil Stallcup

When Furcal's injury and Hu's failure to hit pushed Colletti to look busy, he went dumpster-diving and snagged the 2003 AL Rookie of the Year from the Royals. Predictably, Joe Torre pounced on any aging alternative that freed him from pondering the matter, and Berroa held down the job for most of the final four months with all the panache of an "Occupied" sign on an airplane lavatory. That the Dodgers won a division title despite Berroa's drawing over 250 PAs rates among the year's bigger miracles.

Casey Blake — 3B

Bats: R   Throws: R   Height: 6' 2"   Weight: 210   Born: August 23, 1973   Age: 35

YEAR	TEAM	LVL	AGE	PA	R	2B	3B	HR	RBI	BB	SO	SB	CS	EqBRR	AVG	OBP	SLG	EqAVG	EqOBP	EqSLG	EqA	VORP	WARP	DEFENSE			
2006	CLE	MLB	32	456	63	20	1	19	68	45	93	6	0	-1.0	.282	.356	.479	.270	.352	.469	.284	21.8	1.6	93-RF	-4	7-1B	-2
2007	CLE	MLB	33	662	81	36	4	18	78	54	123	4	5	0.5	.270	.339	.437	.263	.336	.440	.265	11.8	1.6	134-3B	-3	6-RF	0
2008	CLE	MLB	34	368	46	24	0	11	58	33	68	2	0	-1.6	.289	.365	.465	.284	.362	.469	.287	20.1	1.7	72-3B	-3	18-1B	0
2008	LAN	MLB	34	233	25	12	1	10	23	16	52	1	0	0.2	.251	.313	.460	.251	.313	.469	.266	7.6	1.1	53-3B	3		
2009	LAN	MLB	35	444	50	24	1	14	62	37	88	3	1	-1.3	.261	.330	.435	.266	.333	.456	.267	14.8	1.5	105-3B	-5		

Breakout: 7%   Improve: 39%   Collapse: 28%   Attrition: 25%   Comparables: Doug DeCinces, Matt Williams, Brian Jordan, Jim Morrison

Whatever the virtues of Andy LaRoche, his uninspired performance and poorly timed injuries forced the Dodgers to scramble for third-base alternatives numerous times over the last two years. Casey Blake was acquired on July 26 to resolve that problem while providing Torre with a comforting if unspectacular blend of veteran herbs and spices (as well as enabling Colletti to trade LaRoche in the Manny deal). Nonetheless, the cost of acquiring Blake—catcher Carlos Santana and pitcher Jonathan Meloan, both solid prospects—was steep, and retaining Blake via a three-year, $17.5 million deal probably closes off DeWitt's future at his better defensive position. Nevertheless, Blake's ability to man any corner spot while providing 20-homers offers roster flexibility and increases the likelihood that some team will have interest in his services if the Dodgers need to punt.

Ivan De Jesus Jr. — MI

Bats: R   Throws: R   Height: 5' 11"   Weight: 182   Born: May 1, 1987   Age: 22

YEAR	TEAM	LVL	AGE	PA	R	2B	3B	HR	RBI	BB	SO	SB	CS	EqBRR	AVG	OBP	SLG	EqAVG	EqOBP	EqSLG	EqA	VORP	WARP	DEFENSE			
2006	CGA	A	19	563	65	17	2	1	44	63	85	16	5	-1.0	.277	.361	.327	.219	.284	.259	.196	-40.4	-5.6	114-SS	-33	7-2B	-2
2007	SBR	A+	20	502	69	22	3	4	52	57	64	11	6	0.0	.287	.371	.381	.239	.308	.311	.223	-18.3	-3.3	115-SS	-29		
2008	JAX	AA	21	560	91	21	2	7	58	76	81	16	2	3.4	.324	.419	.423	.286	.364	.383	.269	15.4	2.0	87-SS	-20	34-2B	12
2009	LAN	MLB	22	585	65	26	2	5	45	59	108	11	4	0.9	.259	.338	.346	.264	.341	.362	.251	13.3	0.7	137-SS	-12		

Breakout: 34%   Improve: 64%   Collapse: 15%   Attrition: 10%   Comparables: Wally Backman, Ricky Gutierrez, Brent Abernathy, Dave Hansen

De Jesus has an excellent chance to outdo his father, a glove-first shortstop who spent 15 years in the majors, and Junior's pedigree certainly factors into a basic baseball intelligence that raises every aspect of his game. For the second year in a row, his stock rose, and he earned the organization's Minor League Player of the Year honors for his season at Jacksonville. Though he doesn't project for much power, Ivan the Younger is a patient, contact-oriented hitter who works the count and sprays line drives to all fields. He's a strong defender as well, with steady hands, good range, and a solid arm; some feel that second base may be his ultimate destination even with Hu's fall from grace.

Blake DeWitt — 2B/3B

Bats: L   Throws: R   Height: 5' 11"   Weight: 175   Born: August 20, 1985   Age: 23

YEAR	TEAM	LVL	AGE	PA	R	2B	3B	HR	RBI	BB	SO	SB	CS	EqBRR	AVG	OBP	SLG	EqAVG	EqOBP	EqSLG	EqA	VORP	WARP	DEFENSE			
2006	VRO	A+	20	478	61	18	1	18	61	45	79	8	5	-5.1	.268	.339	.442	.221	.284	.377	.229	-14.6	-1.0	90-2B	-4	16-3B	-3
2006	JAX	AA	20	112	6	1	0	1	6	8	21	0	1	-0.3	.183	.241	.221	.171	.223	.210	.124	-14.9	-1.3	24-3B	0		
2007	SBR	A+	21	361	48	29	2	8	46	20	42	2	3	0.0	.298	.338	.466	.244	.275	.372	.220	-11.1	-0.6	79-3B	2		
2007	JAX	AA	21	187	20	13	1	6	20	7	26	0	1	-0.4	.281	.306	.466	.256	.278	.428	.237	-0.8	0.7	43-3B	6		
2008	LVG	AAA	22	124	16	4	2	4	18	10	14	1	0	-1.0	.306	.366	.486	.239	.298	.354	.234	-3.0	-0.1	20-2B	-2	5-3B	1
2008	LAN	MLB	22	421	45	13	2	9	52	45	68	3	0	1.9	.264	.344	.383	.264	.346	.390	.263	10.2	2.5	81-3B	13	22-2B	-2
2009	LAN	MLB	23	430	48	20	1	10	50	37	67	3	2	0.2	.264	.330	.401	.268	.333	.420	.258	12.1	2.1	102-3B	8		

Breakout: 50%   Improve: 75%   Collapse: 11%   Attrition: 26%   Comparables: Van Kelly, Dick McAuliffe, Rudy Meoli, Rance Mulliniks

A 2004 first-rounder, DeWitt had yet to impress in two Double-A stints, but a strong spring training and a rash of injuries helped make him the Dodgers' Opening Day third baseman. He hit .303/372/.465 through the first two months, but his performance cratered in June and July (.200/.263/.240), prompting the Dodgers to trade for Blake and farm DeWitt out. In Las Vegas, he resumed a none-too-successful 2006 attempt to convert to second base and wound up filling in for the injured Jeff Kent over the season's final six weeks and the postseason. He's a work in progress at second, but a plus at third base—his +11 via John Dewan's Plus/Minus system made him the only Dodger to crack a positional top 10—but it's not clear yet that his bat can carry a corner position or that it can overcome his deficiencies at the keystone. Furthermore, his high walk rate warrants skepticism, given pitchers' willingness to pitch around him at the bottom of the lineup (his line includes nine intentional walks) and his lack of plate discipline in the minors. Still, his was hardly a bad showing for a 22-year-old who didn't initially figure into the club's plans; he goes into 2009 as the starting second baseman after Blake's re-signing.

Andre Ethier   **OF**   Bats: L   Throws: L   Height: 6' 2"   Weight: 210   Born: April 10, 1982   Age: 27

YEAR	TEAM	LVL	AGE	PA	R	2B	3B	HR	RBI	BB	SO	SB	CS	EqBRR	AVG	OBP	SLG	EqAVG	EqOBP	EqSLG	EqA	VORP	WARP	DEFENSE			
2006	LAN	MLB	24	441	50	20	7	11	55	34	77	5	5	1.1	.308	.365	.477	.309	.365	.478	.286	17.9	1.4	99-LF	-8		
2007	LAN	MLB	25	505	50	32	2	13	64	46	68	0	4	-1.5	.284	.350	.452	.279	.349	.455	.275	13.3	2.7	87-RF	1	34-LF	6
2008	LAN	MLB	26	596	90	38	5	20	77	59	88	6	3	0.8	.305	.375	.510	.315	.385	.543	.310	43.2	4.8	99-RF	2	31-LF	-4
2009	LAN	MLB	27	608	85	34	3	17	81	63	88	6	3	0.4	.292	.368	.464	.297	.372	.486	.292	30.7	3.7	142-RF	-1		

Breakout: 12%   Improve: 45%   Collapse: 16%   Attrition: 3%   Comparables: Mel Hall, Norm Siebern, Lee Thomas, Johnny Grubb

Ethier got off to a hot start (.315/.400/.461 in April), but once he cooled down, he found himself as the odd man out in a crowded outfield. He brooded openly about playing time, something he's been prone to do throughout his Dodger tenure. Through the end of July, he hit just .274/.338/.442, but Torre's decision to play his best-hitting outfield in the wake of Manny Ramirez's acquisition provided Ethier with some job security. Ethier flourished, hitting a Manny-like .368/.448/.649 over the final two months, starting 33 of the team's final 36 games, and missing time only for the birth of his first child. In all, his performance nailed his 90th-percentile PECOTA projection, and while he's now squarely in his prime, he's going to have a tough time making an encore.

Rafael Furcal   **SS**   Bats: S   Throws: R   Height: 5' 9"   Weight: 195   Born: October 24, 1977   Age: 31

YEAR	TEAM	LVL	AGE	PA	R	2B	3B	HR	RBI	BB	SO	SB	CS	EqBRR	AVG	OBP	SLG	EqAVG	EqOBP	EqSLG	EqA	VORP	WARP	DEFENSE	
2006	LAN	MLB	28	736	113	32	9	15	63	73	98	37	13	-0.8	.300	.369	.445	.299	.371	.444	.283	45.1	4.7	153-SS	-5
2007	LAN	MLB	29	642	87	23	4	6	47	55	68	25	6	5.1	.270	.333	.355	.272	.339	.360	.252	11.1	3.1	135-SS	8
2008	LAN	MLB	30	164	34	12	2	5	16	20	17	8	3	2.6	.357	.439	.573	.371	.451	.608	.347	25.7	2.2	33-SS	-2
2009	LAN	MLB	31	469	68	21	2	7	46	47	53	17	4	1.9	.290	.363	.406	.295	.366	.425	.279	27.8	3.3	111-SS	2

Breakout: 8%   Improve: 36%   Collapse: 26%   Attrition: 3%   Comparables: Bip Roberts, Roberto Alomar, Tony Fernandez, Tom Herr

Furcal's torrid start fondly recalled his MVP-caliber 2006 second-half performance, but a strained sacroiliac joint sidelined him in early May. What was believed to be a minor injury ultimately resulted in a microdiscectomy on July 3, a surgery that's generally season ending. With the end of his contract on the horizon, Furcal rehabbed vigorously and beat long odds by returning to the lineup in the season's final week. He sparkled during the Division Series, reminding observers of how the Dodgers were simply a different team with him atop their lineup. Pursued heavily as a free agent, he re-signed with the Dodgers a day after appearing to have reached an agreement to return to Atlanta. It is a three-year, $30 million deal with a $12 million vesting option for the fourth year based on 600 PAs in year three. That's a pay cut from his old pact, and it's a relatively sensible deal, allowing the Dodgers to retain a player whose upside remains high.

Austin Gallagher   **3B**   Bats: L   Throws: R   Height: 6' 4"   Weight: 217   Born: November 16, 1988   Age: 20

YEAR	TEAM	LVL	AGE	PA	R	2B	3B	HR	RBI	BB	SO	SB	CS	EqBRR	AVG	OBP	SLG	EqAVG	EqOBP	EqSLG	EqA	VORP	WARP	DEFENSE			
2007	OGD	Rk	18	218	28	11	0	4	17	19	33	1	1	-1.8	.284	.346	.401	.187	.239	.256	.165	-41.9	-3.9	50-3B	-9		
2008	SBR	A+	19	344	36	33	1	5	55	29	73	1	4	-7.1	.293	.349	.456	.236	.291	.374	.229	-7.6	-1.7	55-3B	-8	20-1B	-2
2009	LAN	MLB	20	499	40	30	1	10	52	40	121	1	2	-2.0	.229	.292	.364	.233	.295	.381	.231	-5.2	-0.6	118-3B	-8		

Breakout: 64%   Improve: 82%   Collapse: 2%   Attrition: 3%   Comparables: Scott Cooper, Nick Castaneda, Steve Cox, Ronald Kelly

Gallagher is a behemoth with light-tower power that has yet to translate from batting practice to games. As befits a player from a cold-weather state (Pennsylvania) who played football as well as baseball in high school, his skills are raw, his strike zone judgment poor; before he was drafted in the third round in 2007, the scouting consensus was that he wasn't ready to face professional pitching. Despite those reservations, he made a strong showing for a teenager in High-A, manning the hot corner once Josh Bell went down. He's got a strong arm, but his defense is subpar, and his future probably lies at first base or an outfield corner.

Nomar Garciaparra　　　**INF**　　　Bats: R　　Throws: R　　Height: 6' 0"　　Weight: 190　　Born: July 23, 1973　　Age: 35

YEAR	TEAM	LVL	AGE	PA	R	2B	3B	HR	RBI	BB	SO	SB	CS	EqBRR	AVG	OBP	SLG	EqAVG	EqOBP	EqSLG	EqA	VORP	WARP	DEFENSE			
2006	LAN	MLB	32	523	82	31	2	20	93	42	30	3	0	-1.5	.303	.367	.505	.299	.363	.501	.294	26.3	3.0	114-1B	1		
2007	LAN	MLB	33	466	39	17	0	7	59	31	41	3	1	-1.4	.283	.328	.371	.282	.330	.375	.248	0.3	0.0	64-1B	-1	40-3B	0
2008	LAN	MLB	34	181	24	9	0	8	28	15	11	1	1	-0.8	.264	.326	.466	.272	.333	.481	.276	8.3	0.6	27-SS	1	8-3B	-3
2009	LAN	MLB	35	236	26	11	0	6	30	19	19	1	1	-0.7	.274	.335	.409	.279	.338	.428	.263	8.2	0.7	59-1B	2		

Breakout: 8%　　Improve: 38%　　Collapse: 36%　　Attrition: 36%　　　　Comparables: Bill Madlock, Rich Aurilia, Ray Boone, Pedro Guerrero

The second year of Garciaparra's two-year, $18.5 million deal went no better than the first. Given a shot at the team's third-base job in the spring, Garciaparra sustained a microfracture in his wrist, which sent him to the disabled list for the first of three stints, totaling 112 days. When he did play, he flashed the power that had deserted him in 2007, and he didn't embarrass himself in a return engagement at shortstop, though that inevitably ended with an injury. Garciaparra subsequently learned that he's got a congenital condition that manufactures excess scar tissue, which helps explain the frequency of his injuries. He may still have some use as a utilityman, but retirement looms as an option, a development that would quash his chance to round out a career that contained a peak superior to that of the average Hall of Fame shortstop.

Chin-Lung Hu　　　**SS**　　　Bats: R　　Throws: R　　Height: 5' 11"　　Weight: 190　　Born: February 2, 1984　　Age: 25

YEAR	TEAM	LVL	AGE	PA	R	2B	3B	HR	RBI	BB	SO	SB	CS	EqBRR	AVG	OBP	SLG	EqAVG	EqOBP	EqSLG	EqA	VORP	WARP	DEFENSE			
2006	JAX	AA	22	556	71	20	2	5	34	49	63	11	5	1.0	.254	.326	.334	.237	.300	.323	.221	-20.3	-1.3	119-SS	-11		
2007	JAX	AA	23	356	56	30	5	6	34	26	33	12	4	1.6	.329	.380	.508	.298	.341	.476	.278	20.1	2.1	77-SS	-4		
2007	LVG	AAA	23	200	33	10	1	8	28	6	18	3	4	-1.3	.318	.337	.505	.249	.270	.409	.228	-3.4	0.6	26-SS	3	17-2B	1
2007	LAN	MLB	23	31	5	0	1	2	5	0	8	0	0	1.0	.241	.241	.517	.233	.233	.500	.241	0.6	-0.4	8-SS	-4		
2008	LVG	AAA	24	168	21	5	3	1	15	7	19	2	0	-1.7	.295	.323	.385	.228	.255	.304	.196	-11.0	0.3	39-SS	6		
2008	LAN	MLB	24	129	16	2	2	0	9	11	23	2	0	2.2	.181	.252	.233	.171	.242	.222	.160	-7.6	-0.7	26-SS	2	12-2B	0
2009	LAN	MLB	25	422	43	19	2	4	36	27	58	5	2	1.3	.252	.304	.344	.257	.307	.360	.232	4.1	1.0	100-SS	3		

Breakout: 28%　Improve: 58%　Collapse: 25%　Attrition: 21%　　　　Comparables: Luis Sojo, William Bergolla, Mariano Duncan, Luis Rivas

An acrobatic defender whose hitting had progressed rapidly over the past year, Hu came into 2008 ranked as the Dodgers' third-best prospect. Injuries created a golden opportunity for him, first as a late-inning sub for Jeff Kent at second and then as the starting shortstop once Rafael Furcal went down. Given a month to make good in an unfairly short trial, he simply didn't hit; a recurrent problem with blurred vision in his right eye may have been a factor. In any event, he showed little evidence of 2007's developing gap power, and with Ivan De Jesus Jr.'s rapid progress, Hu's stock has taken such a hit that he may never again get a starting opportunity in LA.

Kenley Jansen　　　**C**　　　Bats: S　　Throws: R　　Height: 6' 2"　　Weight: 178　　Born: September 30, 1987　　Age: 21

YEAR	TEAM	LVL	AGE	PA	R	2B	3B	HR	RBI	BB	SO	SB	CS	EqBRR	AVG	OBP	SLG	EqAVG	EqOBP	EqSLG	EqA	VORP	WARP	DEFENSE	
2006	DGR	Rk	18	138	14	2	1	1	10	19	32	1	0	0.1	.248	.362	.308	.194	.275	.250	.183	-30.9	-0.6	33-C	1
2007	GRL	A	19	70	5	1	0	1	6	7	18	0	1	0.0	.102	.214	.169	.081	.169	.145	.000	-13.5	-1.1	19-C	-2
2007	OGD	Rk	19	215	26	5	1	2	22	28	50	0	0	-0.2	.240	.346	.311	.156	.242	.193	.142	-50.7	-3.0	39-C	-4
2008	GRL	A	20	277	31	15	0	9	27	23	72	3	0	0.9	.227	.298	.397	.198	.259	.344	.209	-16.9	-0.5	74-C	-2
2009	LAN	MLB	21	350	25	13	1	6	33	28	99	1	1	-0.1	.204	.273	.304	.207	.276	.319	.203	-9.7	0.5	84-C	2

Breakout: 70%　Improve: 81%　Collapse: 12%　Attrition: 19%　　　　Comparables: Jair Fernandez, Juan Apodaca, Jose Lobaton, Jose Monzon

The system was already thin at catcher before Carlos Santana was traded to Cleveland in the Blake deal, but with Lucas May's conversion going agonizingly slowly, the system's best hope as a backstop may be this hulking Curaçao native; like records of the rarely spotted giant squid, estimates of his size vary, running as high as 6-foot-5 and 245. Despite the unspectacular numbers, Jansen has tremendous raw power and a good throwing arm (catching 37 percent on attempted steals).

Andruw Jones   **CF**   Bats: R   Throws: R   Height: 6' 1"   Weight: 210   Born: April 23, 1977   Age: 32

YEAR	TEAM	LVL	AGE	PA	R	2B	3B	HR	RBI	BB	SO	SB	CS	EqBRR	AVG	OBP	SLG	EqAVG	EqOBP	EqSLG	EqA	VORP	WARP	DEFENSE	
2006	ATL	MLB	29	669	107	29	0	41	129	82	127	5	1	1.7	.262	.363	.531	.261	.363	.529	.300	50.9	7.2	148-CF	16
2007	ATL	MLB	30	659	83	27	2	26	94	70	138	5	2	-2.4	.222	.311	.413	.222	.314	.419	.255	7.2	1.1	150-CF	-5
2008	LAN	MLB	31	238	21	8	1	3	14	27	76	0	1	0.2	.158	.256	.249	.159	.261	.250	.178	-16.8	-2.4	56-CF	-8
2009	LAN	MLB	32	292	35	12	1	11	39	34	69	3	1	-0.6	.240	.333	.422	.244	.336	.442	.267	11.3	1.4	71-CF	-3

Breakout: 43% Improve: 63% Collapse: 20% Attrition: 32%   Comparables: Tom Brunansky, Jesse Barfield, Ellis Burks, Deron Johnson

Even amid a career-worst season in 2007, Jones retained some value, thanks to his defense and power and patience at the plate. Given that he'd played through a hyperextended elbow, his odds of rebounding appeared strong, and his two-year, $36.2 million Dodgers deal seemed a low-risk proposition. Alas, Jones arrived at Vero Beach tipping the scales at 240 pounds or so, started the regular season horribly, and missed six weeks after undergoing surgery to repair a torn meniscus in his right knee—from a hitting standpoint, the all-important back knee. Defying the odds, Jones' hitting declined on his return until continued knee soreness and a case of Mannymania sent him to the DL again in mid-August; he played just one more game. Nothing from his splits offers promise: he didn't hit against lefties, righties, at home, on the road, in a box, with a fox, in a house, or with a mouse. The Dodgers still owe Jones $22.1 million via his heavily back-loaded contract, and how they'll make him disappear remains as great a mystery as how a seemingly Cooperstown-bound 31-year-old center fielder could fall so far so fast.

Matt Kemp   **OF**   Bats: R   Throws: R   Height: 6' 2"   Weight: 230   Born: September 23, 1984   Age: 24

YEAR	TEAM	LVL	AGE	PA	R	2B	3B	HR	RBI	BB	SO	SB	CS	EqBRR	AVG	OBP	SLG	EqAVG	EqOBP	EqSLG	EqA	VORP	WARP	DEFENSE			
2006	JAX	AA	21	224	38	15	2	7	34	20	38	11	2	-1.3	.327	.402	.528	.310	.375	.537	.306	21.9	2.3	44-CF	2		
2006	LVG	AAA	21	202	37	14	6	3	36	17	26	14	3	1.1	.368	.428	.560	.297	.353	.476	.286	11.9	0.5	36-CF	-5	5-LF	-2
2006	LAN	MLB	21	166	30	7	1	7	23	9	53	6	0	2.0	.253	.289	.448	.248	.285	.438	.254	3.1	-1.2	20-CF	-9	8-RF	-1
2007	LVG	AAA	22	174	32	16	3	4	20	10	26	9	2	2.7	.329	.374	.540	.259	.305	.444	.258	2.6	0.5	18-RF	2	18-CF	-1
2007	LAN	MLB	22	311	47	12	5	10	42	16	66	10	5	-0.3	.342	.373	.521	.351	.383	.546	.306	22.9	2.5	69-RF	1		
2008	LAN	MLB	23	657	93	38	5	18	76	46	153	35	11	2.5	.290	.340	.459	.299	.349	.481	.282	35.6	3.3	92-CF	-4	54-RF	1
2009	LAN	MLB	24	574	85	34	3	19	76	45	114	26	9	2.3	.293	.352	.480	.298	.355	.503	.290	33.1	4.0	135-CF	-4		

Breakout: 31% Improve: 54% Collapse: 12% Attrition: 12%   Comparables: Hunter Pence, Rick Reichardt, Ellis Burks, Raul Mondesi

Kemp's first full season was uneven: while he continued to shred lefties (.369/.417/.571), his performance against righties tailed off dramatically, from .318/.340/.495 last year to .260/.309/.416. On the positive side, his unintentional walk rate improved (though it remains low), he flashed plenty of speed while improving his baserunning, and he handled center passably, enabling the Dodgers to play their best-hitting outfield on Manny Ramirez's arrival. The front office continually floats trial balloons about trading him, but without a massive return, such a move would be self-defeating. Kemp has the assets of a young Andre Dawson—a big power hitter's body, plus speed, and the ability to play center. He's still got tremendous upside.

Jeff Kent   **2B**   Bats: R   Throws: R   Height: 6' 2"   Weight: 210   Born: March 7, 1968   Age: 41

YEAR	TEAM	LVL	AGE	PA	R	2B	3B	HR	RBI	BB	SO	SB	CS	EqBRR	AVG	OBP	SLG	EqAVG	EqOBP	EqSLG	EqA	VORP	WARP	DEFENSE			
2006	LAN	MLB	38	473	61	27	3	14	68	55	69	1	2	-2.5	.292	.385	.477	.288	.381	.470	.293	31.7	2.5	99-2B	-6	5-1B	-1
2007	LAN	MLB	39	562	78	36	1	20	79	57	61	1	3	-1.3	.302	.375	.500	.303	.381	.513	.301	39.6	3.5	121-2B	-10		
2008	LAN	MLB	40	474	42	23	1	12	59	25	52	0	1	-1.7	.280	.327	.418	.284	.333	.430	.262	14.9	1.3	99-2B	-2		
2009	LAN	MLB	41	348	35	18	1	7	45	26	42	1	1	-1.9	.277	.332	.407	.281	.336	.426	.261	13.1	1.0	84-2B	-6		

Breakout: 6% Improve: 27% Collapse: 38% Attrition: 22%   Comparables: Gary Gaetti, Cal Ripken, Lou Piniella, Jeff Conine

Kent's least productive season since 1996 was marred by a torn medial meniscus in his knee that required surgery on September 2, costing him his starting spot in the playoffs despite a dogged rehab effort. He's pondered retirement this winter, and if we've seen the last of him for now, the all-time home-run leader among second basemen should have his day at Cooperstown eventually. Kent's prickly personality and businesslike approach often made him an easy target, but his humorlessness should never have been confused with a lack of passion for playing.

Andrew Lambo   **LF**   Bats: L   Throws: L   Height: 6' 3"   Weight: 190   Born: August 11, 1988   Age: 20

YEAR	TEAM	LVL	AGE	PA	R	2B	3B	HR	RBI	BB	SO	SB	CS	EqBRR	AVG	OBP	SLG	EqAVG	EqOBP	EqSLG	EqA	VORP	WARP	DEFENSE			
2007	DGR	Rk	18	218	38	15	1	5	32	29	34	1	2	-0.4	.343	.440	.519	.258	.327	.412	.256	8.3	0.3	35-RF	-1	13-1B	0
2008	GRL	A	19	518	58	33	2	15	79	41	110	5	2	-2.6	.288	.346	.462	.244	.295	.398	.239	-5.6	-2.7	99-LF	-21	5-1B	1
2008	JAX	AA	19	38	7	2	1	3	12	2	9	0	0	-0.2	.389	.421	.750	.324	.359	.703	.328	6.3	0.8	7-LF	3		
2009	LAN	MLB	20	600	58	33	2	16	69	48	152	3	2	-0.9	.242	.305	.399	.246	.308	.418	.246	-0.5	-0.2	140-LF	-11		

Breakout: 23%   Improve: 55%   Collapse: 18%   Attrition: 6%   Comparables: Mike Carp, Justin Morneau, Keith Hughes, Jason Kubel

Drafted in the fourth round in 2007 out of a Southern California high school, Lambo had the talent to go higher, save for a marijuana-related incident. As one of the youngest players in the minors' toughest offensive league, he stood out on a Great Lakes club that combined to bat just .241/.300/.354, then sparkled in a brief stint at Jacksonville. Though his lack of athleticism confines him to left field or first base, he has a plus arm and good hands and ranks as the system's best pure hitter. Note that in both years, he's shown a persistent reverse platoon split. He figures to return to Double-A to start 2009, perhaps playing under the name "Curly."

James Loney   **1B**   Bats: L   Throws: L   Height: 6' 3"   Weight: 220   Born: May 7, 1984   Age: 25

YEAR	TEAM	LVL	AGE	PA	R	2B	3B	HR	RBI	BB	SO	SB	CS	EqBRR	AVG	OBP	SLG	EqAVG	EqOBP	EqSLG	EqA	VORP	WARP	DEFENSE			
2006	LVG	AAA	22	406	64	33	2	8	67	32	34	9	5	2.0	.380	.426	.546	.307	.355	.458	.279	22.5	0.7	77-1B	-8	7-LF	1
2006	LAN	MLB	22	111	20	6	5	4	18	8	10	1	0	0.6	.284	.342	.559	.284	.342	.569	.299	6.2	0.8	25-1B	1		
2007	LVG	AAA	23	261	28	19	1	1	32	25	48	2	1	-2.4	.279	.345	.382	.217	.284	.302	.209	-14.2	-1.0	33-1B	2	22-RF	0
2007	LAN	MLB	23	375	41	18	4	15	67	28	48	0	1	-1.0	.331	.381	.538	.330	.384	.550	.311	30.1	2.5	87-1B	-3		
2008	LAN	MLB	24	651	66	35	6	13	90	45	85	7	4	-0.7	.289	.338	.434	.295	.344	.453	.274	20.9	0.5	153-1B	-12		
2009	LAN	MLB	25	595	74	34	3	15	78	49	76	6	3	-0.6	.286	.347	.445	.291	.350	.466	.277	21.0	1.9	139-1B	-2		

Breakout: 23%   Improve: 55%   Collapse: 17%   Attrition: 12%   Comparables: Chris Chambliss, Wally Joyner, Bruce Bochte, Jim Spencer

Despite leading the team in RBI, Loney's first full season in the majors was a significant letdown from his tantalizing showings in 2006 and 2007. His performance against lefties crashed through the floor, from .325/.381/.482 in 126 PAs in 2006-2007 to .249/.303/.361 in 189 PAs. He declined against righties as well, shedding 67 points of Isolated Power from 2007 to 2008. Fatigue may have been a factor; he hit .209/.229/.297 in September after starting all but six games prior to the final month. He's still young enough to rebound—25-year-olds with .303/.353/.480 performances in over 1,000 PAs don't grow on trees—but an occasional platoon partner wouldn't hurt.

Russell Martin   **C**   Bats: R   Throws: R   Height: 5' 10"   Weight: 210   Born: February 15, 1983   Age: 26

YEAR	TEAM	LVL	AGE	PA	R	2B	3B	HR	RBI	BB	SO	SB	CS	EqBRR	AVG	OBP	SLG	EqAVG	EqOBP	EqSLG	EqA	VORP	WARP	DEFENSE			
2006	LAN	MLB	23	468	65	26	4	10	65	45	57	10	5	0.2	.282	.355	.436	.278	.353	.430	.272	17.5	3.4	113-C	5		
2007	LAN	MLB	24	620	87	32	3	19	87	67	89	21	9	-1.6	.293	.374	.469	.299	.383	.489	.296	45.2	6.3	140-C	7		
2008	LAN	MLB	25	650	87	25	0	13	69	90	83	18	6	0.1	.280	.385	.396	.289	.394	.416	.288	37.5	5.4	139-C	3	8-3B	1
2009	LAN	MLB	26	579	86	29	2	12	64	69	75	14	6	0.3	.293	.382	.434	.298	.386	.454	.291	39.0	5.6	136-C	5		

Breakout: 25%   Improve: 56%   Collapse: 12%   Attrition: 10%   Comparables: Thurman Munson, Craig Biggio, Red Wilson, Smoky Burgess

In last year's book, we predicted Joe Torre would better manage Martin's workload to avoid late-season burnout as he had with Jorge Posada. Our bad. If anything, Torre exacerbated the problem by playing Martin at third base—his preconversion position—instead of resting him, sometimes shifting him back behind the plate late in games. Martin logged more innings than did any backstop other than Jason Kendall and slumped to a punchless .260/.371/.336 in the second half after a .294/.394/.436 first half. Furthermore, his caught stealing percentage slipped from 33 percent to 24 percent, and his brashness irritated the brass to the point that he became the subject of Hot Stove trade rumors. Martin is still an asset, but amid the bumper crop of good, young NL catchers—Brian McCann, Geovany Soto, and Chris Iannetta—future All-Star honors are not guaranteed.

Xavier Paul — OF

Bats: L   Throws: R   Height: 6' 0"   Weight: 200   Born: February 25, 1985   Age: 24

YEAR	TEAM	LVL	AGE	PA	R	2B	3B	HR	RBI	BB	SO	SB	CS	EqBRR	AVG	OBP	SLG	EqAVG	EqOBP	EqSLG	EqA	VORP	WARP	DEFENSE
2006	VRO	A+	21	520	62	23	3	13	49	38	114	22	15	0.0	.285	.343	.430	.233	.283	.368	.224	-16.7	-2.8	114-RF -12
2007	JAX	AA	22	482	64	21	2	11	50	48	112	17	9	-1.6	.291	.366	.429	.255	.319	.389	.247	0.5	-2.2	95-CF -24 5-RF 0
2008	LVG	AAA	23	506	82	28	5	9	68	43	96	17	7	-2.1	.316	.378	.463	.245	.305	.355	.236	-9.8	-3.2	104-CF -28
2009	LAN	MLB	24	498	55	24	2	10	51	41	115	13	5	1.0	.249	.314	.379	.253	.317	.397	.248	4.6	0.4	117-CF -12

Breakout: 41% Improve: 67% Collapse: 16% Attrition: 12%   Comparables: Mike Darr, Nic Jackson, Andre Ethier, Roy Johnson

Paul cut down his strikeouts and, like a silicone showgirl, put up superficially attractive numbers for Las Vegas. The 2003 fourth-rounder is a good athlete whose game doesn't have major strengths or glaring holes aside from problems hitting lefties. He makes solid contact with a line-drive swing, but has yet to translate that into real power, though for what it's worth, he showed more pop away from hitter-friendly Cashman Field (.306/.371/.472) than at home (.326/.385/.454). Paul's arm is considered the system's best, and he's got decent speed, but center is a stretch for him, and he'll have to be more productive to hold down a corner job on a first-division club. Right now, he looks like a Future Fourth Outfielder of America.

Jaime Pedroza — MI

Bats: S   Throws: R   Height: 5' 10"   Weight: 175   Born: September 12, 1986   Age: 22

YEAR	TEAM	LVL	AGE	PA	R	2B	3B	HR	RBI	BB	SO	SB	CS	EqBRR	AVG	OBP	SLG	EqAVG	EqOBP	EqSLG	EqA	VORP	WARP	DEFENSE
2007	OGD	Rk	20	239	33	18	1	8	40	14	44	4	4	-2.8	.360	.413	.569	.235	.274	.367	.222	-14.7	-2.1	49-SS -13
2008	SBR	A+	21	535	78	31	7	9	57	33	120	25	11	-2.7	.290	.342	.441	.237	.282	.371	.228	-14.5	-5.0	102-SS -39 23-2B -8
2009	LAN	MLB	22	568	54	32	3	11	57	35	146	13	7	1.3	.236	.288	.372	.240	.290	.390	.234	4.5	-1.1	133-SS -21

Breakout: 39% Improve: 61% Collapse: 18% Attrition: 9%   Comparables: Alfredo Diaz, Rich Casarotti, Chris Dean, Chad Curtis

Two years after the Dodgers tabbed Sergio Pedroza in the 2005 draft, they took his younger, less polished brother out of University of California–Riverside with a ninth-round pick. His 2008 season was a mixed bag; he hit for average and showed gap power and improved base-stealing ability, but his plate discipline was severely lacking. He won't make it as a shortstop, and his ability at second base has yet to wow anyone, which only makes an improvement in his approach at the plate even more of an imperative.

Juan Pierre — OF

Bats: L   Throws: L   Height: 5' 11"   Weight: 180   Born: August 14, 1977   Age: 31

YEAR	TEAM	LVL	AGE	PA	R	2B	3B	HR	RBI	BB	SO	SB	CS	EqBRR	AVG	OBP	SLG	EqAVG	EqOBP	EqSLG	EqA	VORP	WARP	DEFENSE
2006	CHN	MLB	28	750	87	32	13	3	40	32	38	58	20	4.0	.292	.330	.388	.288	.326	.386	.253	17.0	4.6	161-CF 26
2007	LAN	MLB	29	729	96	24	8	0	41	33	37	64	15	13.1	.293	.331	.353	.302	.341	.366	.257	15.3	1.5	158-CF -5
2008	LAN	MLB	30	406	44	10	2	1	28	22	24	40	12	2.1	.283	.327	.328	.294	.339	.342	.251	3.4	1.8	70-LF 12 13-CF 1
2009	LAN	MLB	31	443	62	15	3	0	30	24	25	39	10	3.2	.288	.330	.340	.293	.333	.356	.253	5.4	1.7	105-CF 2

Breakout: 17% Improve: 49% Collapse: 22% Attrition: 17%   Comparables: Lance Johnson, Luis Polonia, Ralph Garr, Tom Goodwin

Though Torre benched the $44 million man on Opening Day, Pierre found his way into the Dodgers' lineup all too often, thanks in part to Torre's traditionalist's perception of what makes a leadoff hitter. When he did play, Pierre was even less potent than usual, posting the lowest Isolated Power of any NL hitter with at least 400 PAs and again failing to get on base at a clip that maximized his primary asset, his speed. Acquiring Manny appropriately marginalized him; Pierre started just 20 times over the final three months, nine of them in the first two weeks after returning from an MCL strain. As much as Dodger fans and perhaps even Colletti wish he would go away, the three years and $28.5 million remaining on Juan-Be-Gone's contract will make that a dauntingly difficult task.

Manny Ramirez   LF   Bats: R   Throws: R   Height: 6' 0"   Weight: 200   Born: May 30, 1972   Age: 37

YEAR	TEAM	LVL	AGE	PA	R	2B	3B	HR	RBI	BB	SO	SB	CS	EqBRR	AVG	OBP	SLG	EqAVG	EqOBP	EqSLG	EqA	VORP	WARP	DEFENSE
2006	BOS	MLB	34	558	79	27	1	35	102	100	102	0	1	-2.6	.321	.439	.619	.290	.425	.571	.333	66.8	4.5	116-LF -14
2007	BOS	MLB	35	569	84	33	1	20	88	71	92	0	0	-2.0	.296	.388	.493	.275	.374	.475	.293	31.8	2.8	112-LF -5
2008	BOS	MLB	36	425	66	22	1	20	68	52	86	1	0	0.2	.299	.398	.529	.281	.387	.515	.306	34.3	3.2	60-LF 1
2008	LAN	MLB	36	229	36	14	0	17	53	35	38	2	0	0.0	.396	.489	.743	.398	.491	.763	.400	49.8	4.6	49-LF 2
2009	LAN	MLB	37	580	86	28	1	30	104	75	112	2	1	-2.7	.295	.391	.538	.300	.395	.564	.316	49.0	4.3	136-LF -13

Breakout: 9% Improve: 36% Collapse: 22% Attrition: 10%   Comparables: Frank Robinson, Gary Sheffield, Ellis Burks, Joe DiMaggio

A villain in Beantown, a hero in Tinseltown, Ramirez was the game's most controversial player in 2008. His efforts to get the Red Sox to exercise the first of his two $20 million options caused teammates, club officials, and some of the industry's most powerful writers to suggest that he faked injuries and ultimately quit on his team, as though he were some mutant cross between Derek Bell and the second coming of Hal Chase—never mind that he hit .347/.473/.587 in July as this drama unfolded. The Manny Show came to LA and provided a much-needed jolt to a flagging Dodger offense whose scoring rose from 4.17 runs per game to 4.63, helping them blow past the Diamondbacks to win the West. Facing pitchers who had more idea how to split the atom than to pitch to him, Ramirez used the whole field much more than in his Fenway days, doing absurd things like flirting with .400 and bashing towering opposite-field homers in Petco. Despite his production, the reports of his pretrade antics, Team Boras' aggressive negotiating stance, and the slow economy combined to suppress the market for his services. At this writing, he's still adrift, "Manny being Manny" costing him millions in lost contract offers.

Delwyn Young   OF   Bats: S   Throws: R   Height: 5' 10"   Weight: 210   Born: June 30, 1982   Age: 27

YEAR	TEAM	LVL	AGE	PA	R	2B	3B	HR	RBI	BB	SO	SB	CS	EqBRR	AVG	OBP	SLG	EqAVG	EqOBP	EqSLG	EqA	VORP	WARP	DEFENSE	
2006	LVG	AAA	24	583	76	42	1	18	98	42	104	3	4	-1.0	.273	.326	.457	.223	.274	.385	.226	-16.9	-2.3	89-RF -4	34-LF -4
2007	LVG	AAA	25	537	107	54	5	17	97	38	105	4	3	-0.5	.337	.384	.571	.257	.305	.451	.257	9.3	0.0	52-LF -6	51-RF -2
2007	LAN	MLB	25	36	4	1	1	2	3	2	5	1	0	0.3	.382	.417	.647	.382	.417	.647	.349	5.7	0.5	5-LF 0	
2008	LVG	AAA	26	56	14	5	1	3	10	7	8	0	0	0.4	.347	.429	.673	.260	.339	.480	.282	2.5	0.4	8-RF 1	
2008	LAN	MLB	26	143	10	9	0	1	7	14	34	0	0	-0.1	.246	.321	.341	.252	.326	.362	.243	-1.0	-0.5	10-LF -3	8-RF -1
2009	LAN	MLB	27	168	19	9	1	5	22	14	36	1	0	-0.1	.256	.320	.429	.260	.323	.449	.262	4.7	0.3	43-RF -2	

Breakout: 34% Improve: 57% Collapse: 27% Attrition: 36%   Comparables: Chris Magruder, Ryan Doumit, Joe Wallis, Bobby Clark

This former second baseman's migration across the defensive spectrum took so long that he's run out of options. With little shot at cracking the team's crowded outfield or passing through waivers, Young spent most of the year coming off the bench, where he fared better than Mark Sweeney in the pinch (.292/.393/.333 in 58 PA) and even worked as a bullpen catcher to keep himself busy. PECOTA sees him as useful enough to put up a handful of .330 OBP/.450 SLG or better seasons, which may not merit a starting job but could do wonders for some teams as a fourth outfielder/DH option. He'll need a trade to get that opportunity.

PITCHERS

James Adkins   Bats: L   Throws: L   Height: 6' 5"   Weight: 195   Born: November 26, 1985   Age: 23

YEAR	TEAM	LVL	AGE	W	L	SV	G	GS	IP	H	BB	SO	HR	GB%	BABIP	STUFF	WHIP	ERA	DERA	EqH9	EqBB9	EqSO9	EqHR9	DEF	VORP	SN/WX
2007	GRL	A	21	0	1	0	11	11	26	17	10	30	1	60.9%	.254	5	1.04	2.42	5.01	8.1	5.4	5.0	1.2	0	1.5	—
2008	SBR	A+	22	5	8	0	19	18	87²	106	38	75	6	51.9%	.360	-21	1.64	5.34	7.93	12.6	5.1	3.9	1.3	-15	-21.2	—
2008	JAX	AA	22	1	3	0	8	8	38	42	28	25	5	47.7%	.294	-24	1.84	4.74	7.54	11.7	6.6	3.2	2.2	-1	-8.0	—
2009	LAN	MLB	23	4	8	0	25	17	93²	114	57	60	13	47.0%	.330	-3	1.83	6.59	7.14	11.1	4.7	4.8	1.2	-0	-14.1	-0.90

Breakout: 41% Improve: 80% Collapse: 7% Attrition: 15%   Comparables: Chris Hancock, Kris Johnson, Sherman Corbett, Heath Murray

A polished southpaw out of the University of Tennessee who was chosen as a supplemental first-rounder in 2007, Adkins fared well in the Midwest League. His promotion to the Cal League didn't go so smoothly; Adkins was knocked around a bit, though he was a bit hit-unlucky. His fastball sits in the upper 80s, but features heavy sink and generates ground balls. Some consider his slider among the best in the system, but others say he lacks a true plus offering. He's a back-end starter unless he improves his secondary stuff.

Alberto Bastardo

Bats: L   Throws: L   Height: 6' 0"   Weight: 160   Born: April 6, 1984   Age: 25

YEAR	TEAM	LVL	AGE	W	L	SV	G	GS	IP	H	BB	SO	HR	GB%	BABIP	STUFF	WHIP	ERA	DERA	EqH9	EqBB9	EqSO9	EqHR9	DEF	VORP	SN/WX
2006	CGA	A	22	3	1	0	6	6	32	22	14	33	2	55.4%	.253	-3	1.13	1.41	4.40	8.5	5.7	4.4	1.9	-1	3.8	—
2006	VRO	A+	22	5	5	0	20	19	93	97	47	105	12	45.0%	.339	-30	1.55	4.55	7.20	12.1	5.9	5.5	2.6	-8	-15.1	—
2007	SBR	A+	23	6	5	0	16	13	69	73	25	73	8	40.8%	.350	-21	1.42	4.57	6.23	12.3	4.3	5.3	1.9	-7	-4.2	—
2008	SBR	A+	24	5	8	0	30	21	131²	152	51	109	9	46.3%	.345	-30	1.54	5.19	7.59	11.8	4.6	3.7	1.4	-18	-27.3	—
2009	LAN	MLB	25	3	6	0	25	13	78²	97	45	52	15	43.0%	.320	-5	1.80	6.67	7.10	11.2	4.4	5.0	1.7	-0	-12.6	-0.77

Breakout: 35%   Improve: 63%   Collapse: 17%   Attrition: 18%   Comparables: Victor Garcia, Edwin Hurtado, Yorkin Ferreras, Rafael Roque

A diminutive lefty who was signed out of Venezuela by the Orioles in 2002, Bastardo was plucked from them by the Dodgers in the Triple-A phase of the 2005 Rule 5 draft. With a combination of a low-90s fastball, an impressive slider, and a solid changeup, he whiffed more than one batter per inning at every stop until 2008, when his K rate fell off markedly on repeating at Inland Empire. He's shown a persistent reverse platoon split throughout his career—a shame, because growing up to be a situational lefty nicknamed "Albert the Bastard" is a fate worth aspiring to.

Joe Beimel

Bats: L   Throws: L   Height: 6' 3"   Weight: 215   Born: April 19, 1977   Age: 32

YEAR	TEAM	LVL	AGE	W	L	SV	G	GS	IP	H	BB	SO	HR	GB%	BABIP	STUFF	WHIP	ERA	DERA	EqH9	EqBB9	EqSO9	EqHR9	DEF	VORP	SN/WX
2006	LAN	MLB	29	2	1	2	62	0	70	70	21	30	7	58.2%	.274	-10	1.30	2.96	2.54	8.1	2.3	3.5	0.8	-4	20.8	2.45
2007	LAN	MLB	30	4	2	1	83	0	67¹	63	24	39	1	49.3%	.297	5	1.29	3.88	3.36	7.8	2.8	5.0	0.1	-2	13.8	2.23
2008	LAN	MLB	31	5	1	0	71	0	49	50	21	32	0	48.4%	.327	3	1.45	2.02	1.88	9.2	3.4	5.2	0.0	-2	19.6	1.32
2009	LAN	MLB	32	2	2	2	52	0	48	50	18	29	4	49.0%	.290	-5	1.42	4.09	4.48	9.5	3.0	4.6	0.8	-0	6.4	0.52

Breakout: 2%   Improve: 7%   Collapse: 79%   Attrition: 28%   Comparables: Steve Kline, Juan Agosto, Ray King, Mike Mohler

Don't be fooled by the low ERA; Beimel's 3.44 Fair Run Average was right in line with his 2006 and 2007 performances (3.39 and 3.33, respectively). He was less valuable than in years past, however, because where Grady Little used Beimel in multiple innings, Torre turned him into a traditional LOOGY while using Hong-Chih Kuo for longer stints. Just five of Beimel's appearances lasted more than one inning, while 30 of them were a third of an inning or less. Compare that with 2007, when he had 10 long appearances and 23 short ones, or 2006, with 18 long appearances and 11 short ones. Beimel showed a smaller platoon split than in years past; for his Dodger tenure, the numbers were .232/.274/.304 versus lefties, .280/.350/.397 versus righties. Kuo's emergence and Beimel's desire for a multiyear deal led to a parting of the ways.

Chad Billingsley

Bats: R   Throws: R   Height: 6' 1"   Weight: 245   Born: July 29, 1984   Age: 24

YEAR	TEAM	LVL	AGE	W	L	SV	G	GS	IP	H	BB	SO	HR	GB%	BABIP	STUFF	WHIP	ERA	DERA	EqH9	EqBB9	EqSO9	EqHR9	DEF	VORP	SN/WX
2006	LVG	AAA	21	6	3	0	13	13	70	57	32	78	7	47.8%	.289	22	1.27	3.99	5.45	8.0	4.3	7.0	1.2	7	1.1	—
2006	LAN	MLB	21	7	4	0	18	16	90	92	58	59	7	49.8%	.313	29	1.67	3.90	3.80	8.9	5.2	5.5	0.6	-2	16.9	2.66
2007	LAN	MLB	22	12	5	0	43	20	147	131	64	141	15	43.4%	.299	27	1.33	3.31	3.37	7.6	3.4	8.0	0.9	3	40.3	4.74
2008	LAN	MLB	23	16	10	0	35	32	200²	188	80	201	14	50.5%	.320	36	1.34	3.14	2.89	8.5	3.1	8.0	0.6	-11	50.6	6.16
2009	LAN	MLB	24	12	8	0	28	28	181²	165	73	175	16	47.0%	.300	30	1.31	3.55	3.86	8.2	3.1	7.3	0.8	-0	35.4	5.21

Breakout: 6%   Improve: 25%   Collapse: 44%   Attrition: 10%   Comparables: Kevin Gross, Aaron Sele, Jeremy Bonderman, Kevin Appier

Billingsley extended his 2007 performance level across an entire season in the rotation. Increasing reliance on the cut fastball that he learned in 2006 has led to greater pitch efficiency, more ground balls, and a lower home-run rate—the ninth-lowest in the league among ERA qualifiers last year. He became the first Dodgers pitcher to top 200 strikeouts since Chan Ho Park in 2001 and finished third in the league in strikeout rate, seventh in ERA, and 10th in SNLVAR. All in all, his progress makes for a textbook ideal of pitcher development. The only down note came during the League Championship Series, when Billingsley's emotions quickly got the better of him, leading to a pair of explosions and early exits. Billingsley sustained a spiral fracture of his fibula when he slipped on ice in mid-November, but should be healed in time for spring training.

Jonathan Broxton Bats: R   Throws: R   Height: 6' 4"   Weight: 290   Born: June 16, 1984   Age: 25

YEAR	TEAM	LVL	AGE	W	L	SV	G	GS	IP	H	BB	SO	HR	GB%	BABIP	STUFF	WHIP	ERA	DERA	EqH9	EqBB9	EqSO9	EqHR9	DEF	VORP	SN/WX
2006	LAN	MLB	22	4	1	3	68	0	76¹	61	33	97	7	41.3%	.303	36	1.23	2.60	2.35	7.0	3.4	9.9	0.7	-4	26.1	2.23
2007	LAN	MLB	23	4	4	2	83	0	82	69	25	99	6	48.3%	.312	32	1.15	2.85	3.21	7.4	2.4	9.6	0.6	2	23.4	2.82
2008	LAN	MLB	24	3	5	14	70	0	69	54	27	88	2	47.6%	.327	33	1.17	3.13	3.59	7.4	3.1	9.8	0.3	-1	13.9	1.83
2009	LAN	MLB	25	5	4	13	59	2	73	58	27	85	5	46.0%	.290	27	1.17	2.83	3.09	7.2	2.9	8.8	0.7	-0	22.6	2.30

Breakout: 21%   Improve: 51%   Collapse: 26%   Attrition: 7%   Comparables: Rich Gossage, Turk Farrell, Lee Smith, Ron Robinson

The future arrived more quickly than expected for the oversized closer of the future. After a slow start—a 4.94 ERA through May, perhaps linked to a strained lat—Broxton's performance improved markedly, and right after the All-Star break, he assumed the closer job after Saito broke down. His performance was uneven; he converted his first seven chances, was battered for two blown saves and two losses over his next eight appearances, and then saw little action as the Dodgers steamrolled their opposition down the stretch. The big boy experienced both the thrill of victory (closing out the Cubs) and the agony of defeat (Matt Stairs' pinch homer) in October. Given Saito's off-season departure, the closer's job is likely to be Broxton's going forward; with a fearsome fastball/slider combo, he's got the basic tools to succeed as long as he can put his last appearance behind him.

Jesus Castillo Bats: R   Throws: R   Height: 6' 1"   Weight: 190   Born: May 31, 1984   Age: 25

YEAR	TEAM	LVL	AGE	W	L	SV	G	GS	IP	H	BB	SO	HR	GB%	BABIP	STUFF	WHIP	ERA	DERA	EqH9	EqBB9	EqSO9	EqHR9	DEF	VORP	SN/WX
2006	OGD	Rk	22	2	5	0	14	14	72	65	25	55	3	49.3%	.292	-27	1.25	2.88	6.08	10.5	4.8	2.3	1.6	-3	-3.4	—
2007	SBR	A+	23	6	9	0	28	22	130	144	40	97	9	51.4%	.330	-26	1.42	4.78	7.42	11.4	3.6	3.1	1.3	-10	-24.5	—
2008	JAX	AA	24	7	4	0	23	23	114	123	33	76	7	48.8%	.325	-17	1.37	3.24	5.73	11.9	3.0	3.6	1.1	1	-1.5	—
2009	LAN	MLB	25	5	9	0	30	20	118²	151	51	66	18	47.0%	.330	-2	1.70	6.24	6.72	11.6	3.3	4.2	1.4	-0	-13.5	-0.59

Breakout: 6%   Improve: 33%   Collapse: 24%   Attrition: 15%   Comparables: Luis Mendoza, Jose Vargas, Ernie Carrasco, Mario Brito

A native of Nogales, Mexico, Castillo attended high school and junior college across the border in Arizona and was a 2003 draft-and-follow whose route thus far has included a summer in the Dominican league and a year lost to Tommy John surgery. Despite a dreadful second-half showing in 2007, he was promoted to Jacksonville last year and put together a pretty good season. Castillo's a sinker/slider control specialist who's got good command to both sides of the plate and velocity in the low 90s; he's not overwhelming, but he gets the job done. Triple-A will be the true test of his ground-balling ways; if he can keep the ball in the park, he stands a chance of seeing the big leagues by the end of the year.

Scott Elbert Bats: L   Throws: L   Height: 6' 2"   Weight: 190   Born: August 13, 1985   Age: 23

YEAR	TEAM	LVL	AGE	W	L	SV	G	GS	IP	H	BB	SO	HR	GB%	BABIP	STUFF	WHIP	ERA	DERA	EqH9	EqBB9	EqSO9	EqHR9	DEF	VORP	SN/WX
2006	VRO	A+	20	5	5	0	17	15	83¹	57	41	97	4	46.8%	.275	25	1.18	2.38	4.24	7.7	5.8	5.8	1.2	-4	11.5	—
2006	JAX	AA	20	6	4	0	11	11	62	40	44	76	11	32.9%	.254	9	1.35	3.63	6.79	9.1	7.1	7.3	3.2	7	-7.4	—
2008	JAX	AA	22	4	1	0	25	1	41¹	22	20	46	2	30.9%	.217	7	1.02	2.40	6.23	6.0	4.4	6.7	0.9	8	-2.7	—
2008	LAN	MLB	22	0	1	0	10	0	6	9	4	8	2	50.0%	.438	6	2.17	12.00	7.94	14.3	4.8	11.1	3.2	-2	-4.4	-0.18
2009	LAN	MLB	23	2	2	1	25	3	43¹	37	27	44	6	37.0%	.270	10	1.46	4.63	4.95	7.7	4.7	7.6	1.3	-0	3.8	0.40

Breakout: 32%   Improve: 58%   Collapse: 19%   Attrition: 18%   Comparables: Taylor Tankersley, Brandon Morrow, Kent Mercker, P.J. Bevis

Once regarded as just a notch below Kershaw in terms of stuff and projectability, this highly touted 2004 first-round pick lost most of 2007 to surgery to remove scar tissue from his labrum and didn't return to games until this past June. When he did, it was as a reliever, a role he took to quite well; he dominated hitters with a spiraling power curveball and an explosive low-90s fastball that can touch 95 with late life, and he showed better command than he did presurgery. Elbert figures to be the Dodger bullpen's second lefty behind Hong-Chih Kuo in 2009. The team hasn't ruled out a return to the rotation, where he profiled as a second or third starter before injury, but it wants to see him handle a more moderate workload first.

Steven Johnson

Bats: R | Throws: R | Height: 6' 1" | Weight: 185 | Born: August 31, 1987 | Age: 21

YEAR	TEAM	LVL	AGE	W	L	SV	G	GS	IP	H	BB	SO	HR	GB%	BABIP	STUFF	WHIP	ERA	DERA	EqH9	EqBB9	EqSO9	EqHR9	DEF	VORP	SN/WX
2006	OGD	Rk	18	5	5	0	14	14	78¹	79	25	86	4	40.3%	.364	-3	1.33	3.92	6.51	13.3	4.7	4.2	1.8	-8	-6.7	—
2007	GRL	A	19	3	6	0	18	16	81²	90	40	65	2	35.4%	.346	-5	1.59	4.85	8.96	12.9	6.9	2.8	1.0	-21	-26.2	—
2008	GRL	A	20	9	2	0	13	13	73	59	25	57	4	49.1%	.270	10	1.15	2.34	5.54	9.3	4.4	3.2	1.4	5	0.4	—
2008	SBR	A+	20	3	6	0	11	11	52	68	21	55	9	29.8%	.393	-13	1.71	7.10	10.68	15.7	5.2	5.6	3.2	-6	-25.2	—
2009	LAN	MLB	21	4	9	0	28	18	106	132	59	73	20	40.0%	.320	-0	1.80	6.83	7.24	11.3	4.3	5.2	1.7	-0	-17.0	-1.15

Breakout: 26% Improve: 62% Collapse: 12% Attrition: 10%   Comparables: Ken Cloude, Rafael Rodriguez, Leo Nuñez, Devon Lowery

The son of former major league pitcher Dave Johnson (1987-1993) was one of the top high school pitchers in Maryland state history when he was chosen as a 2005 13th-rounder. His progress up the ladder has been methodical, but even at Great Lakes, he was on the youngish side. He pitched reasonably well in the pitcher-friendly Midwest League, but struggled when promoted to the high-offense California League, as his lack of a plus pitch came back to bite him. He's got a deep arsenal, but he'll have to come up with an above-average offering to climb much higher.

Clayton Kershaw

Bats: L | Throws: L | Height: 6' 3" | Weight: 210 | Born: March 19, 1988 | Age: 21

YEAR	TEAM	LVL	AGE	W	L	SV	G	GS	IP	H	BB	SO	HR	GB%	BABIP	STUFF	WHIP	ERA	DERA	EqH9	EqBB9	EqSO9	EqHR9	DEF	VORP	SN/WX
2007	GRL	A	19	7	5	0	20	20	97¹	72	50	134	5	49.3%	.310	13	1.25	2.77	6.30	9.9	7.0	6.3	1.6	-7	-6.6	—
2007	JAX	AA	19	1	2	0	5	5	24²	17	17	29	4	41.0%	.236	22	1.38	3.64	6.94	7.7	6.6	6.6	2.7	1	-3.5	—
2008	JAX	AA	20	2	3	0	13	11	61¹	39	19	59	0	47.2%	.245	40	0.95	1.91	5.19	6.7	2.9	5.5	0.3	7	2.7	—
2008	LAN	MLB	20	5	5	0	22	21	107²	109	52	100	11	51.1%	.327	48	1.50	4.26	3.67	9.3	3.8	7.5	0.9	-5	16.5	2.95
2009	LAN	MLB	21	10	8	0	28	28	157	145	76	146	15	48.0%	.300	26	1.41	4.00	4.35	8.4	3.8	7.1	0.8	-0	23.9	3.61

Breakout: 23% Improve: 55% Collapse: 9% Attrition: 21%   Comparables: Dick Ellsworth, Milt Pappas, Mike McCormick, Mark Grant

Ranked fifth on our prospect list last year, Kershaw generated tremendous buzz from the outset of spring training; a YouTube clip of Vin Scully declaring his knee-buckling strike-three curveball "Public Enemy Number One" drew half a million visitors in just a few days. Kershaw debuted on May 25 and initially scuffled, putting up a 33/24 K/BB ratio in 38⅔ innings over eight starts before returning to Jacksonville in early July. Recalled three weeks later, he exhibited improved control—a 67/28 K/BB ratio in 69 innings—and his poise impressed observers as much as his stuff did. The Dodgers carefully monitored his workload all year, and if the final numbers didn't dazzle, they were great for a 20-year-old. There's no reason to get off this bandwagon; as the Dodgers have shown with Billingsley, they know how to handle a prized pitching prospect as well as any team.

Hong-Chih Kuo

Bats: L | Throws: L | Height: 6' 1" | Weight: 235 | Born: July 23, 1981 | Age: 27

YEAR	TEAM	LVL	AGE	W	L	SV	G	GS	IP	H	BB	SO	HR	GB%	BABIP	STUFF	WHIP	ERA	DERA	EqH9	EqBB9	EqSO9	EqHR9	DEF	VORP	SN/WX
2006	LVG	AAA	24	4	3	1	23	9	53¹	52	22	63	5	44.7%	.351	1	1.39	3.05	4.47	10.4	4.1	8.0	1.3	0	6.1	—
2006	LAN	MLB	24	1	5	0	28	5	59²	54	33	71	3	45.8%	.347	29	1.46	4.22	3.24	8.2	4.5	9.9	0.5	-5	9.8	1.03
2007	LVG	AAA	25	0	1	0	7	5	20	18	8	28	2	41.3%	.364	19	1.30	3.60	2.41	8.1	3.9	9.6	1.0	-3	6.6	—
2007	LAN	MLB	25	1	4	0	8	6	30¹	35	14	27	3	33.7%	.344	6	1.62	7.43	6.32	9.5	3.4	7.2	0.9	-2	-6.8	0.07
2008	LAN	MLB	26	5	3	1	42	3	80	60	21	96	4	47.1%	.289	37	1.01	2.14	2.34	6.7	2.0	9.1	0.4	0	29.2	3.14
2009	LAN	MLB	27	4	3	4	46	3	70²	62	27	74	6	45.0%	.300	19	1.27	3.43	3.72	8.0	3.0	7.9	0.8	-0	16.2	1.54

Breakout: 17% Improve: 40% Collapse: 37% Attrition: 9%   Comparables: Norm Charlton, Scott Stewart, Randy Myers, Mark Guthrie

Initially cast as a fifth starter/long man, Kuo pitched reasonably well, but his slow recovery times and history of elbow woes (four elbow surgeries, including two Tommy Johns) eventually pushed him into a more traditional bullpen role. There he finally delivered on the promise the Dodgers had long awaited, using his fastball/slider combo to hold hitters to a 447 OPS from the beginning of May to mid-August as he put up a 1.17 ERA and 62/9 K/BB ratio over 53⅔ innings pitched. A sore triceps limited him to just three September appearances and kept him off the Division Series roster, but he pitched well in the LCS. With Beimel's departure, he's now the bullpen's top lefty—if he can stay healthy. If Torre uses Beimel's absence as an excuse to cast Kuo in a LOOGY role, the manager will be forgoing some valuable innings.

Hiroki Kuroda

Bats: R **Throws: R** **Height: 6' 0"** **Weight: 189** **Born: February 10, 1975** **Age: 34**

YEAR	TEAM	LVL	AGE	W	L	SV	G	GS	IP	H	BB	SO	HR	GB%	BABIP	STUFF	WHIP	ERA	DERA	EqH9	EqBB9	EqSO9	EqHR9	DEF	VORP	SN/WX
2006	HRO	JP	31	13	6	1	26	25	189¹	169	21	144	12	—	.280	18	1.00	1.85	2.99	9.0	1.4	5.1	0.8	0	51.4	—
2007	HRO	JP	32	12	8	0	26	26	179²	176	42	123	20	—	.285	-5	1.21	3.56	4.66	9.8	2.5	4.5	1.2	0	17.5	—
2008	LAN	MLB	33	9	10	0	31	31	183¹	181	42	116	13	52.7%	.287	18	1.22	3.73	4.19	8.4	1.7	4.9	0.6	3	30.2	4.87
2009	LAN	MLB	34	8	7	0	22	22	132¹	141	33	80	14	49.0%	.290	12	1.31	4.16	4.54	9.7	1.9	4.6	1.0	-0	16.6	2.76

Breakout: 3% **Improve: 22%** **Collapse: 35%** **Attrition: 27%** **Comparables: Bob Friend, Ray Herbert, Andy Ashby, Cory Lidle**

Kuroda was just about everything the Dodgers could have wanted during his first stateside season. Occasionally he was unhittable, three times he took no-hitters into the fifth inning or later, and eight times he pitched at least six innings and gave up four hits or fewer. He ended the season ranked 22nd in the league in SNLVAR, and though he didn't strike out a ton of hitters, he got plenty of ground balls and ranked among the top 10 in K/UIBB ratio, fewest walks per nine, and fewest homers per nine. He closed the year on an 11-start roll in which he put up a 2.57 ERA. He may not be more than a third starter here, but if your number three is this good, you'll be a contender.

Derek Lowe

Bats: R **Throws: R** **Height: 6' 6"** **Weight: 230** **Born: June 1, 1973** **Age: 36**

YEAR	TEAM	LVL	AGE	W	L	SV	G	GS	IP	H	BB	SO	HR	GB%	BABIP	STUFF	WHIP	ERA	DERA	EqH9	EqBB9	EqSO9	EqHR9	DEF	VORP	SN/WX
2006	LAN	MLB	33	16	8	0	35	34	218	221	55	123	14	67.9%	.293	18	1.27	3.63	3.74	8.4	2.0	4.6	0.5	1	48.9	6.52
2007	LAN	MLB	34	12	14	0	33	32	199¹	194	59	147	20	66.3%	.292	18	1.27	3.88	4.11	8.2	2.3	6.2	0.8	0	30.0	4.58
2008	LAN	MLB	35	14	11	0	34	34	211	194	45	147	14	61.6%	.286	23	1.13	3.24	3.97	8.1	1.6	5.6	0.6	10	49.0	6.93
2009	ATL	MLB	36	11	8	0	27	27	175²	177	48	114	13	57.0%	.290	15	1.28	3.70	4.00	9.0	2.1	5.0	0.6	0	31.7	4.78

Breakout: 6% **Improve: 30%** **Collapse: 26%** **Attrition: 14%** **Comparables: Gaylord Perry, Andy Pettitte, Jerry Reuss, Larry Jackson**

Paul DePodesta's most enduring legacy as the Dodgers' GM may have been the four-year, $36 million deal to which he signed Lowe on the heels of the pitcher's ugly 5.42 ERA season in Boston. Lowe took to the easier league and ballpark like a duck to water, giving the Dodgers four very good campaigns notable for their consistency and his durability. Over that span, he ranked 11th in the majors in SNLVAR, 10th in innings, and 12th in ERA+. His final year was his best; he closed the season on a 10-start roll featuring a microscopic 1.27 ERA. The Dodgers would have paid handsomely to keep him around, but Lowe's preference was to return to the East Coast. Unsigned at press time, Lowe's new employer should be aware that he had a 3.47 RA at Dodger Stadium, but 4.89 on the road, and if they're wise, they already have a good inner defense with which to support this ground-ball artist.

Ethan Martin

Bats: R **Throws: R** **Height: 6' 2"** **Weight: 195** **Born: June 6, 1989** **Age: 20**

YEAR	TEAM	LVL	AGE	W	L	SV	G	GS	IP	H	BB	SO	HR	GB%	BABIP	STUFF	WHIP	ERA	DERA	EqH9	EqBB9	EqSO9	EqHR9	DEF	VORP	SN/WX
2009	LAN	MLB	20	4	11	0	24	24	121	163	79	66	25	46.1%	.331	-7	1.99	7.79	8.31	12.2	5.0	4.1	1.8	0	-33.2	-2.7

Breakout: N/A **Improve: N/A** **Collapse: N/A** **Attrition: N/A** **Comparables: Zach Miner, Scott Garrelts, Steve Maye, Steve Karsay**

For the fifth year in a row, the Dodgers tabbed a high school pitcher with their top pick, drafting Martin 15th overall. The Georgia native was a two-way talent who starred at third base—he was considered a potential first-rounder as a hitter—and pitched only as a closer until his junior year, when his upside on the mound could no longer be ignored. Considered one of the more athletic and projectable arms in the draft, he offers a mid-90s fastball with late sinking action and a sharp curve. His command is still a work in progress, due to his lack of experience. Martin didn't get a chance to make his pro debut, because he tore up a knee during fielding drills and needed season-ending surgery, but he was healthy enough to participate in the instructional league.

James McDonald

Bats: L   Throws: R   Height: 6' 5"   Weight: 195   Born: October 19, 1984   Age: 24

YEAR	TEAM	LVL	AGE	W	L	SV	G	GS	IP	H	BB	SO	HR	GB%	BABIP	STUFF	WHIP	ERA	DERA	EqH9	EqBB9	EqSO9	EqHR9	DEF	VORP	SN/WX
2006	CGA	A	21	5	10	0	30	22	142	119	65	146	15	46.3%	.290	-40	1.30	3.99	8.12	11.4	6.2	4.6	2.9	-4	-33.5	—
2007	SBR	A+	22	6	7	0	16	15	82	79	21	104	8	36.5%	.355	8	1.22	3.95	4.58	11.6	3.2	6.7	1.7	-10	8.2	—
2007	JAX	AA	22	7	2	0	10	10	52²	42	16	64	5	43.6%	.298	18	1.10	1.71	4.04	9.0	3.1	7.0	1.7	2	8.5	—
2008	JAX	AA	23	5	3	0	22	22	118²	98	46	113	12	35.8%	.281	-14	1.21	3.18	5.71	9.5	3.8	5.6	1.7	8	-1.3	—
2008	LVG	AAA	23	2	1	0	5	4	22¹	17	7	28	3	31.6%	.259	18	1.08	3.63	4.76	6.8	2.8	7.5	1.2	3	2.1	—
2008	LAN	MLB	23	0	0	0	4	0	6	5	1	2	0	19.0%	.250	-7	1.00	0.00	1.50	7.5	1.5	3.0	0.0	1	3.8	0.16
2009	LAN	MLB	24	6	8	1	36	16	114²	120	50	94	18	37.0%	.300	9	1.48	5.11	5.43	9.5	3.4	6.2	1.4	-0	3.2	0.96

Breakout: 14%   Improve: 34%   Collapse: 23%   Attrition: 16%   Comparables: Mark Kiefer, John Maine, Matt Kinney, Russ Springer

This slender 2002 draft-and-follow dabbled with a move to the outfield when he initially developed arm trouble, but since returning to pitching full-time in 2006, he's won the Dodgers' Minor League Pitcher of the Year award twice in a row. McDonald didn't dominate hitters to the same extent last year, but he was impressive in brief stints with Las Vegas and LA, including some long relief work in the NLCS. McDonald doesn't have a true out pitch, but he effectively mixes a fastball that ranges from 87 to 93 mph with great movement and command, a big-bending curveball, and a deceptive changeup with some sink. He'll be in the mix for a spot at the back of the rotation or in middle relief; hope he makes the team, because with his fly-ball rate, an extended stay in the PCL could get ugly.

Justin Orenduff

Bats: R   Throws: R   Height: 6' 2"   Weight: 205   Born: May 27, 1983   Age: 26

YEAR	TEAM	LVL	AGE	W	L	SV	G	GS	IP	H	BB	SO	HR	GB%	BABIP	STUFF	WHIP	ERA	DERA	EqH9	EqBB9	EqSO9	EqHR9	DEF	VORP	SN/WX
2006	JAX	AA	23	4	2	0	10	10	50	40	19	54	4	29.6%	.286	-3	1.18	3.42	6.85	10.0	3.9	6.3	1.6	2	-6.4	—
2007	JAX	AA	24	8	5	0	27	23	109	112	45	113	16	38.2%	.328	-40	1.44	4.21	5.49	11.7	4.1	5.8	2.4	-13	1.2	—
2008	LVG	AAA	25	3	7	1	31	21	110	142	66	95	25	37.3%	.356	-40	1.89	6.55	6.11	12.1	5.5	5.2	2.2	-10	-5.9	—
2009	LAN	MLB	26	3	6	0	25	11	74	89	41	58	16	38.0%	.320	-1	1.76	6.50	6.81	11.0	4.3	5.9	1.9	-0	-9.2	-0.51

Breakout: 17%   Improve: 50%   Collapse: 22%   Attrition: 22%   Comparables: Joel Hanrahan, Darrell Akerfelds, Rich Monteleone, Todd Worrell

Las Vegas is no place for an extreme fly-ball pitcher, so Orenduff's introduction to the rough justice of the PCL didn't go well at all. A 2004 supplemental first-rounder, Orenduff is a command/control guy with a low-90s fastball, a good slider, and a changeup that remains a work in progress. Unless he can miss more bats, his ceiling appears to be at the end of the rotation; a move to the bullpen may be in order, since his lack of stuff won't make getting over the Triple-A hump any easier.

Chan Ho Park

Bats: R   Throws: R   Height: 6' 2"   Weight: 210   Born: June 30, 1973   Age: 36

YEAR	TEAM	LVL	AGE	W	L	SV	G	GS	IP	H	BB	SO	HR	GB%	BABIP	STUFF	WHIP	ERA	DERA	EqH9	EqBB9	EqSO9	EqHR9	DEF	VORP	SN/WX
2006	SDN	MLB	33	7	7	0	24	21	136²	146	44	96	20	44.7%	.299	2	1.39	4.81	5.26	9.8	2.5	5.8	1.2	0	7.4	2.00
2007	ROU	AAA	34	2	10	0	15	15	84	100	24	70	18	47.7%	.323	-32	1.48	6.21	8.23	11.3	2.7	5.3	2.3	-3	-24.0	—
2007	NWO	AAA	34	4	4	0	9	9	51²	64	16	49	9	44.7%	.364	-9	1.55	5.57	6.13	13.0	3.3	6.5	2.1	-3	-2.8	—
2007	NYN	MLB	34	0	1	0	1	1	4	6	2	4	2	28.6%	.333	-18	2.00	15.75	13.50	13.5	4.5	9.0	4.5	-1	-4.7	-0.26
2008	LAN	MLB	35	4	4	2	54	5	95¹	97	36	79	12	52.6%	.307	-1	1.40	3.40	4.01	9.1	3.0	6.6	1.1	1	16.8	1.79
2009	PHI	MLB	36	3	3	2	36	3	60¹	64	21	45	8	46.2%	.300	2	1.40	4.47	4.66	9.5	2.7	5.7	1.2	0	6.8	0.70

Breakout: 30%   Improve: 56%   Collapse: 23%   Attrition: 39%   Comparables: Jim Clancy, Eddie Fisher, Stan Bahnsen, Todd Jones

Park turned in a reasonably effective season in a swing role, though he was knocked around for a 6.20 ERA over the final two months, when he was used more heavily. Overall, he finished second among the team's relievers in innings pitched, and in five starts, he put up a 2.16 ERA and 30/8 strikeout-to-walk ratio in 25 innings—all for a half million bucks after signing a minor league split deal. Seeking a rotation spot, he signed with the Phillies this winter; if he keeps the ball down, the next act of his career could be interesting. Note that his Dodgers career ERA is 3.77 in 275 games; in 103 games with three other teams, it's 5.63. His career ERA at Dodger Stadium is 2.96, and it's 5.16 everywhere else.

Brad Penny

| | | | Bats: R | | Throws: R | | Height: 6' 4" | | Weight: 260 | | Born: May 24, 1978 | | | Age: 31 |

YEAR	TEAM	LVL	AGE	W	L	SV	G	GS	IP	H	BB	SO	HR	GB%	BABIP	STUFF	WHIP	ERA	DERA	EqH9	EqBB9	EqSO9	EqHR9	DEF	VORP	SN/WX
2006	LAN	MLB	28	16	9	0	34	33	189	206	54	148	19	45.3%	.327	20	1.38	4.33	3.44	9.3	2.2	6.5	0.8	-14	32.5	4.50
2007	LAN	MLB	29	16	4	0	33	33	208	199	73	135	9	50.6%	.306	26	1.31	3.03	3.31	8.2	2.8	5.6	0.4	6	61.4	7.27
2008	LAN	MLB	30	6	9	0	19	17	94²	112	42	51	13	51.4%	.326	-15	1.63	6.27	5.90	10.5	3.5	4.4	1.3	-3	-9.3	0.48
2009	LAN	MLB	31	6	7	0	28	17	112²	120	42	80	12	48.0%	.310	8	1.44	4.47	4.85	9.7	2.9	5.3	1.0	-0	10.1	1.79

Breakout: 4%   Improve: 18%   Collapse: 54%   Attrition: 25%   Comparables: Doc Medich, Joey Hamilton, Jaret Wright, Sidney Ponson

Oh, the stupid things that come out of athletes' mouths. When sent to the DL for the third and final time in late September, Penny told reporters that the Dodgers' refusal to extend his contract in the spring prompted him to pitch while hurt, thus worsening his condition. Leaving aside the damage his wrong-headed machismo inflicted on his team's chances, we're left to believe Penny is unfamiliar with the customs of the free-agent market and hasn't followed the careers of A. J. Burnett and Carl Pavano, hurlers who've made a mint despite less-than-perfect attendance due to medical reasons. In any event, such acute observational skills made the Dodgers' decision to punt Penny's $9.25 million option a no-brainer; Boston followed up by spending $5 million to see a Penny and pick him up.

Scott Proctor

| | | | Bats: R | | Throws: R | | Height: 6' 1" | | Weight: 195 | | Born: January 2, 1977 | | | Age: 32 |

YEAR	TEAM	LVL	AGE	W	L	SV	G	GS	IP	H	BB	SO	HR	GB%	BABIP	STUFF	WHIP	ERA	DERA	EqH9	EqBB9	EqSO9	EqHR9	DEF	VORP	SN/WX
2006	NYA	MLB	29	6	4	1	83	0	102¹	89	33	89	12	34.8%	.273	5	1.19	3.52	3.46	7.8	2.8	6.9	1.0	-2	28.7	1.76
2007	NYA	MLB	30	2	5	0	52	0	54¹	53	29	37	8	26.7%	.280	-17	1.51	3.81	4.45	8.6	4.4	5.3	1.3	1	9.6	0.18
2007	LAN	MLB	30	3	0	0	31	0	32	25	15	27	4	37.0%	.247	1	1.25	3.38	4.13	6.3	3.6	6.9	1.1	2	7.0	0.73
2008	LAN	MLB	31	2	0	0	41	0	38²	41	24	46	7	38.6%	.327	0	1.68	6.05	5.98	9.1	4.4	8.9	1.5	-3	-6.1	-0.24
2009	FLO	MLB	32	2	2	2	43	0	50¹	48	23	45	7	37.3%	.286	4	1.40	4.28	4.56	8.6	3.6	6.6	1.2	0	6.3	0.50

Breakout: 27%   Improve: 52%   Collapse: 28%   Attrition: 29%   Comparables: Rich DeLucia, John Wyatt, Roy Lee Jackson, Kerry Ligtenberg

Torre had to lose one job and then move three thousand miles to take another, but he finally succeeded in pitching Proctor's arm off. After racking up more appearances than any other pitcher besides Jon Rauch in 2006–2007, Proctor got a lighter workload last year because he pitched poorly. Torched for 14 runs over an 11-game span in May and June, he was bound for Triple-A before disclosing that he'd been pitching through elbow soreness and thereby offering another data point as to how athletic machismo trumps common sense at the expense of winning. He underwent postseason surgery to repair a partially torn flexor tendon and remove a bone spur. Nontendered, his workhorse days have probably yielded to the avoid-the-glue-factory stage of life.

Takashi Saito

| | | | Bats: L | | Throws: R | | Height: 6' 2" | | Weight: 200 | | Born: February 14, 1970 | | | Age: 39 |

YEAR	TEAM	LVL	AGE	W	L	SV	G	GS	IP	H	BB	SO	HR	GB%	BABIP	STUFF	WHIP	ERA	DERA	EqH9	EqBB9	EqSO9	EqHR9	DEF	VORP	SN/WX
2006	LAN	MLB	36	6	2	24	72	0	78¹	48	23	107	3	36.8%	.280	41	0.91	2.07	2.21	5.7	2.3	10.0	0.3	0	33.5	5.43
2007	LAN	MLB	37	2	1	39	63	0	64¹	33	13	78	5	48.6%	.207	34	0.72	1.40	2.01	4.6	1.6	9.3	0.7	4	32.0	5.76
2008	LAN	MLB	38	4	4	18	45	0	47	40	16	60	1	45.4%	.336	34	1.19	2.49	2.12	7.9	2.7	9.8	0.2	-3	15.3	1.96
2009	BOS	MLB	39	3	3	14	40	0	46	37	15	48	3	42.0%	.281	21	1.14	2.93	2.99	7.0	2.7	8.7	0.6	1	14.2	1.80

Breakout: 0%   Improve: 3%   Collapse: 79%   Attrition: 18%   Comparables: Larry Andersen, Marv Grissom, Jesse Orosco, Tom Gordon

After leading the league in WXRL in 2007, age and mileage finally caught up to Saito last year. Slowed by a variety of lower-body ailments in spring training, he nonetheless pitched well in the first half. He then reported elbow tightness just before the All-Star break and soon underwent an experimental procedure in which team physician Neal ElAttrache attempted to repair his partially torn UCL by injecting platelet-rich plasma into the elbow. The jury is still out on the procedure's efficacy, but with the possibilities of Tommy John surgery and retirement looming, the Dodgers nontendered Saito when he wouldn't agree to an incentive-based deal. It will be a shame if he's done, because he's been downright dominant (1.95 ERA, 5.3 K/UIBB, and a .182/.246/.264 line by opposing hitters) during his short stateside stay.

Eric Stults

Bats: L   Throws: L   Height: 6' 0"   Weight: 215   Born: December 9, 1979   Age: 29

YEAR	TEAM	LVL	AGE	W	L	SV	G	GS	IP	H	BB	SO	HR	GB%	BABIP	STUFF	WHIP	ERA	DERA	EqH9	EqBB9	EqSO9	EqHR9	DEF	VORP	SN/WX
2006	LVG	AAA	26	10	11	0	26	26	153¹	153	68	128	10	47.9%	.331	1	1.44	4.23	5.60	9.9	4.3	5.2	0.9	3	0.0	—
2006	LAN	MLB	26	1	0	0	6	2	17²	17	7	5	4	42.6%	.236	-27	1.36	5.59	5.19	7.8	3.1	2.6	2.1	0	-0.2	0.25
2007	LVG	AAA	27	5	7	0	21	17	89¹	134	36	81	12	41.7%	.422	-17	1.90	7.56	5.82	13.4	3.8	5.8	1.5	-17	-2.1	—
2007	LAN	MLB	27	1	4	0	12	5	38²	50	17	30	5	43.5%	.363	0	1.73	5.81	4.19	11.2	3.5	6.5	1.2	-5	-0.8	0.48
2008	LVG	AAA	28	7	7	0	20	20	117²	118	35	102	14	43.3%	.305	-1	1.30	3.82	5.14	8.9	2.7	5.1	1.2	12	5.9	—
2008	LAN	MLB	28	2	3	0	7	7	38²	38	13	30	6	38.2%	.278	7	1.32	3.49	4.58	8.5	2.5	5.9	1.4	3	6.6	0.95
2009	LAN	MLB	29	6	7	1	45	15	108²	119	42	83	15	43.0%	.310	5	1.48	4.80	5.14	9.9	3.0	5.8	1.2	-0	6.5	1.15

Breakout: 14%   Improve: 41%   Collapse: 32%   Attrition: 16%   Comparables: Wayne Franklin, Kirt Ojala, Mickey Mahler, Gino Minutelli

Another fly-ball pitcher suffering the adverse atmosphere of Sin City, Stults has remained stuck in Vegas for the better part of the last four years, with results varying so widely that it's difficult to gauge his performance beyond pegging him as a Quadruple-A type. When injuries sidelined Kuroda and Penny in late June, Stults pitched as well as the Dodgers could have hoped, with three quality starts out of six, including a complete-game shutout of the White Sox. Caught in the numbers game, he didn't reappear in Dodger blue until after they'd clinched. With the departures of Penny, Lowe, and Maddux, he'll again be in the mix as a back-end rotation option.

Ramon Troncoso

Bats: R   Throws: R   Height: 6' 7"   Weight: 187   Born: February 16, 1983   Age: 26

YEAR	TEAM	LVL	AGE	W	L	SV	G	GS	IP	H	BB	SO	HR	GB%	BABIP	STUFF	WHIP	ERA	DERA	EqH9	EqBB9	EqSO9	EqHR9	DEF	VORP	SN/WX
2006	CGA	A	23	4	0	15	23	0	33	28	7	22	1	63.5%	.290	-33	1.06	2.45	7.07	10.3	3.2	2.6	1.0	4	-4.6	—
2006	VRO	A+	23	1	3	0	18	0	29²	43	14	31	1	54.1%	.457	-28	1.95	6.78	9.69	17.0	5.9	5.2	1.0	-7	-11.8	—
2007	SBR	A+	24	3	1	7	16	0	26	18	3	30	0	65.2%	.286	5	0.81	1.04	3.96	7.2	1.4	5.8	0.4	2	4.6	—
2007	JAX	AA	24	7	3	7	35	0	52	52	18	39	3	64.0%	.314	-23	1.35	3.12	5.48	10.6	3.4	4.0	1.1	4	0.6	—
2008	LVG	AAA	25	4	0	0	22	0	30²	43	16	18	1	61.6%	.385	-27	1.92	4.98	6.07	12.7	4.9	3.0	0.3	-3	-1.6	—
2008	LAN	MLB	25	1	1	0	32	0	38	37	12	38	2	61.7%	.357	15	1.29	4.26	4.42	9.1	2.5	8.1	0.5	0	4.8	-0.08
2009	LAN	MLB	26	2	2	1	35	1	39¹	42	17	29	3	56.0%	.320	3	1.51	4.30	4.77	9.8	3.4	5.6	0.6	-0	4.6	0.37

Breakout: 27%   Improve: 54%   Collapse: 19%   Attrition: 25%   Comparables: Jim Hannan, Aaron Small, Vince Colbert, Rick Bauer

Troncoso is a late-blooming Dominican with a low-90s fastball with heavy sink, plus secondary offerings that have improved as he has climbed the organizational ladder. He impressed the Dodgers' brass enough in spring training to break camp with the team, but was roughed up and sent down until late June, when he returned for good. He did a decent job in a low-leverage role, with plenty of ground balls and a strikeout rate that was off the charts relative to his track record. He did struggle with inherited runners (his Fair Run Average was 4.93), but if the K's are a true reflection of improved stuff, he's likely to work his way up the bullpen hierarchy.

Cory Wade

Bats: R   Throws: R   Height: 6' 2"   Weight: 180   Born: May 28, 1983   Age: 26

YEAR	TEAM	LVL	AGE	W	L	SV	G	GS	IP	H	BB	SO	HR	GB%	BABIP	STUFF	WHIP	ERA	DERA	EqH9	EqBB9	EqSO9	EqHR9	DEF	VORP	SN/WX
2006	CGA	A	23	6	5	2	23	14	94²	101	11	94	9	53.8%	.337	-44	1.19	4.97	8.67	13.7	2.2	4.1	2.5	-9	-28.3	—
2006	VRO	A+	23	2	4	0	7	7	39¹	52	13	32	9	40.0%	.350	-58	1.66	8.29	12.86	15.4	4.1	3.6	4.6	-5	-28.2	—
2007	SBR	A+	24	7	0	6	25	2	66	50	17	67	6	40.3%	.262	-15	1.02	2.45	4.96	8.0	3.1	5.0	1.5	6	4.4	—
2007	JAX	AA	24	0	1	0	14	0	33	22	11	33	2	41.3%	.233	-2	1.00	1.36	2.67	6.4	2.9	5.1	1.1	1	11.0	—
2008	JAX	AA	25	0	0	1	6	0	14²	14	1	13	3	50.0%	.282	-14	1.02	4.29	6.23	11.8	0.7	5.5	3.5	0	-0.9	—
2008	LAN	MLB	25	2	1	0	55	0	71¹	51	15	51	7	42.0%	.226	4	0.93	2.27	4.50	6.3	1.7	5.8	0.9	13	22.6	2.79
2009	LAN	MLB	26	2	2	2	39	0	47¹	45	14	35	6	43.0%	.280	5	1.24	3.92	4.25	8.7	2.2	5.6	1.1	-0	7.8	0.62

Breakout: 31%   Improve: 52%   Collapse: 20%   Attrition: 37%   Comparables: Steve Kealey, Jose Lima, Dick Marlowe, Bill Kunkel

The surprise of the Dodgers' bullpen last year was this 10th-round 2004 pick out of Kentucky Wesleyan who had plodded through the system until Inland Empire pitching coach Charlie Hough (the famous knuckleballer with less-famous perfect mechanics) helped him refine his curveball. Wade had less than 50 innings above A-ball under his belt when recalled in late April, but he became the rare rookie reliever to gain Torre's confidence. He's a command/control guy who navigates well with men on base; he led the league in double-play percentage despite being otherwise decidedly fly-ball-oriented and led the Dodgers in both relief innings and WRXL. His low BABIP suggests that regression is in order, but as a late bloomer, he may still have advances in store.

LINEOUTS

Hitters

PLAYER	TEAM	LVL	AGE	PA	R	2B	3B	HR	RBI	BB	SO	SB-CS	EqBRR	AVG/OBP/SLG	EqAVG/EqOBP/EqSLG	EqA	VORP	WARP
C D. Ardoin	LVG	AAA	33	114	14	6	0	4	16	8	24	0-0	1.8	.303/.369/.485	.204/.265/.330	.209	-4.7	0.0
	LAN	MLB	33	54	3	1	0	1	4	2	10	1-0	-0.6	.235/.278/.314	.235/.278/.314	.209	-1.1	-1.0
C A.J. Ellis	LVG	AAA	27	337	44	17	4	4	59	50	44	0-2	-4.9	.321/.436/.456	.228/.336/.326	.241	-5.6	1.4
OF J. Hoffmann	JAX	AA	23	544	64	20	3	10	71	54	73	28-9	1.2	.278/.350/.395	.245/.303/.353	.235	-12.4	-1.1
2B P. Mattingly	GRL	A	20	355	37	14	3	6	24	16	108	11-4	2.2	.224/.263/.337	.198/.229/.304	.179	-34.0	-4.1
C L. May	JAX	AA	23	441	54	27	1	13	54	32	112	6-1	1.7	.230/.294/.403	.208/.257/.361	.216	-21.9	-1.8
INF L. Maza	LVG	AAA	28	273	51	11	5	2	29	31	30	1-2	1.2	.378/.450/.492	.257/.327/.327	.235	-4.6	-0.6
	LAN	MLB	28	88	7	1	0	1	4	5	11	0-0	-0.4	.228/.282/.278	.237/.291/.287	.204	-3.2	-0.3
3B R. Mitchell	JAX	AA	23	542	65	22	4	16	75	42	95	8-4	-1.4	.264/.323/.425	.233/.280/.382	.229	-14.0	-2.3
UT P. Ozuna	CHA	MLB	33	69	5	3	0	0	6	2	3	0-2	-1.6	.281/.313/.328	.281/.313/.328	.217	-2.0	-0.2
	LAN	MLB	33	33	6	0	1	1	3	1	5	1-1	0.7	.219/.242/.375	.219/.242/.375	.206	-1.2	-0.3
OF J. Repko	LVG	AAA	27	535	89	26	7	12	50	50	108	20-6	3.8	.283/.373/.449	.200/.282/.321	.217	-26.1	-2.0
PH M. Sweeney*	LAN	MLB	38	108	2	3	0	0	5	15	28	0-0	-0.1	.130/.250/.163	.120/.241/.152	.125	-10.6	-1.2
OF S. Van Slyke	SBR	A+	21	192	29	9	2	5	26	11	35	7-4	-2.5	.261/.309/.420	.218/.260/.363	.212	-8.6	-1.2

Passing through seven organizations but playing in just 165 big-league games over 14 seasons, **Danny Ardoin** has created a solid consensus regarding his utility, or lack of same, although in about a season's worth of playing time, he's thrown out 37 percent of attempted basestealers. ⊘ At 28, **A. J. Ellis** is more suspect than prospect, but the defensively sound backstop (43 percent caught stealing) is on the 40-man roster, so the Dodgers may as well give him a shot at the backup job, particularly in light of his improved hitting. ⊘ Former hockey prospect **Jamie Hoffman** is toolsy and aggressive, but seems condemned to a future fourth outfielder's upside. ⊘ Things have yet to come together for Donnie Baseball's son **Preston Mattingly**, a 2006 supplemental first-round pick; he struggled both offensively and defensively while repeating at Great Lakes and now faces a steep climb to the big leagues. ⊘ **Lucas May**'s rocky conversion to catcher continues; he's down to one passed ball for every four games caught and up to 28 percent caught stealing, but a spiking strikeout rate and flagging power threaten to render him little more than a curiosity. ⊘ After languishing in the Twins' system for eight years, **Luis Maza**, by batting over .400 at Las Vegas, hit his way into an opportunity to claim the shortstop job once Furcal got hurt, but he soon hit his way out of it. ⊘ **Russell Mitchell** has some pop and made solid advances in his plate discipline at Jacksonville, but he's still short of good enough to hit at a premium position. ⊘ Speedy and capable of playing three infield positions as well as the outfield, **Pablo Ozuna** is indistinguishable from a whole army of utilitymen, most of whom don't cost $1 million a year. ⊘ A severe hamstring injury cost **Jason Repko** all of 2007 and downgraded his status from handy fifth outfielder— at least in this organization, with its excess of well-paid, unproductive outfielders. ⊘ Second on the all-time pinch-hit list, **Mark Sweeney** lacked no opportunities to add to his total, but he never came close to finding a groove. ⊘ **Scott Van Slyke**, son of Andy, was thought to be bound for Ole Miss when the Dodgers made him their 14th-round pick in 2005; progress has come slowly since, but some like his athleticism and the way his 6-foot-5 frame could fill out.

Pitchers

PLAYER	TEAM	LVL	AGE	W	L	SV	IP	H	BB	SO	HR	GB%	BABIP	STUFF	WHIP	ERA	DERA	EqH9	EqBB9	EqSO9	EqHR9	DEF	VORP
G. Aguasviva*	OGD	Rk	20	3	4	0	71¹	85	13	60	4	55.6%	.349	-12	1.37	2.90	8.50	12.6	3.2	2.1	1.5	0	-21.2
	GRL	A	20	1	2	0	19¹	34	6	20	1	48.6%	.478	-18	2.07	8.39	11.34	21.6	4.3	4.3	1.6	-8	-10.7
Y. Brazoban	JAX	AA	28	0	1	2	10²	7	2	13	1	63.0%	.231	6	0.84	2.52	3.48	7.0	1.7	7.0	1.7	0	2.4
	LVG	AAA	28	0	0	1	10	19	5	5	4	30.2%	.385	-57	2.40	10.80	7.20	16.2	4.5	2.7	3.6	-3	-1.8
V. Garate*	GRL	A	23	6	3	0	77²	61	28	103	4	47.0%	.322	2	1.15	1.85	4.03	10.5	4.8	6.6	1.5	-6	11.7
	SBR	A+	23	3	0	0	38¹	44	14	47	6	46.0%	.405	-11	1.51	4.70	5.61	13.9	4.5	6.7	2.9	-5	-0.0
J. Johnson	LVG	AAA	34	11	5	0	113	127	30	95	15	51.5%	.333	-5	1.39	3.82	4.46	10.0	2.5	4.9	1.3	0	14.1
	LAN	MLB	34	1	2	0	29¹	32	12	20	5	56.3%	.300	-13	1.50	5.22	5.28	9.6	3.1	5.6	1.6	-1	-0.5
B. Leach*	SBR	A+	25	0	1	3	13¹	11	4	13	0	52.9%	.333	-5	1.13	1.35	1.59	9.5	4.0	5.6	0.0	-1	5.0
	JAX	AA	25	2	2	12	59¹	44	34	49	2	49.4%	.273	-12	1.32	2.88	6.04	8.4	5.5	4.9	0.7	6	-2.6
J. Lindblom	GRL	A	21	0	0	0	29	14	4	33	2	52.2%	.179	19	0.62	1.86	5.20	5.5	2.0	5.2	1.6	4	1.2
T. Schlichting	JAX	AA	23	6	4	0	59²	58	18	49	4	45.9%	.318	-17	1.27	3.77	6.38	10.8	2.9	4.6	1.1	0	-4.8
J. Schmidt	SBR	A+	35	0	0	0	10¹	8	4	9	0	40.0%	.276	-19	1.17	3.50	6.10	7.0	4.4	3.5	0.0	-1	-0.6
	LVG	AAA	35	0	1	0	12¹	19	8	5	3	34.0%	.348	-46	2.20	7.32	8.76	13.1	5.8	1.5	2.2	-1	-4.3
J. Wall	SBR	A+	21	9	6	0	129	152	63	101	12	45.3%	.355	-28	1.67	6.28	8.01	12.9	6.0	3.6	1.8	-17	-30.7
M. Watt*	OGD	Rk	19	9	4	0	80²	91	21	79	7	52.5%	.360	-14	1.39	4.35	8.75	12.8	4.1	2.8	2.1	0	-25.2
C. Withrow	SBR	A+	19	0	0	0	4	2	6	1	0	54.5%	.200	-29	2.00	4.50	10.80	5.4	18.9	0.0	0.0	1	-1.9

Skinny Dominican lefty **Geison Aguasviva** put up a nice strikeout-to-walk ratio in his stateside debut, but he was old for his league and gave up more than his share of hits. ⊘ After Tommy John and labrum surgeries ruined his previous two years, **Yhency Brazoban** earned a brief return to LA, but pitched less than five innings after a bout of shoulder inflammation; the team's displeasure with his conditioning factored into a decision to nontender him. ⊘ Old for the Midwest League after knocking around the Astros' organization for three years, Venezuelan lefty **Victor Garate** was good enough as a strike-throwing control artist to be added to the 40-man. ⊘ After spending 2007 as a Seibu Lion, **Jason Johnson** returned stateside and bided his time in Las Vegas for half the season before joining the Dodgers as a long reliever/spot starter; if he didn't pitch all that well, at least he didn't pitch all that often. ⊘ A big lefty with better-than-average velocity for the type, **Brent Leach** has had to slowly work his way past a Tommy John surgery, a corrected problem with overly sweaty palms (no, really), and bad mechanics, but he's potentially a situational asset in the making. ⊘ Chosen in the second round of the 2008 draft, **Joshua Lindblom** was a closer at Purdue, but the Dodgers are trying him as a starter. He offers three solid pitches and dominated in his first taste of the pros. ⊘ **Travis Schlichting** washed out as a third-base prospect with the D-Rays, but he's taken up pitching with decent results and a power arm. ⊘ "Second surgery" isn't a phrase you want attached to your $47 million investment, but that's what **Jason Schmidt** underwent last September after a futile attempt to rehab from a 2007 labrum repair. Though his velocity had reached 92 mph before shutdown, scar tissue and arthritic changes in the acromioclavicular joint inhibited his delivery. The latest surgery was a last-resort modified arthroscopic Mumford procedure to try to salvage Schmidt's shoulder as much for throwing to his children as for throwing to Russell Martin. The Dodgers may wind up paying more than $1 million per big-league inning over the life of Schmidt's contract. ⊘ After a solid 2007 at Great Lakes, **Josh Wall** was knocked around in the California League. Scouts love his size (6'6") and his projection, but he has trouble keeping those long limbs in synch during his delivery. ⊘ Not the bassist of indie rock heroes the Minutemen, **Mike Watt** is a skinny southpaw with solid stuff and good command who was sent to San Diego as a PTBNL in the Maddux deal. ⊘ **Chris Withrow**, the Dodgers' top pick from the 2007 draft, had a hard-luck year, injuring his hand snorkeling and then being shut down due to elbow soreness after just four innings.

MANAGER: JOE TORRE

YEAR	TEAM	W-L	Pythag +/−	Avg PC	100+ P	120+ P	QS	BQS	REL	REL w Zero R	IBB	Subs	PH	PH Avg	PH HR	SB2	CS2	SB3	CS3	SAC Att	SAC %	POS SAC	Squeeze	Swing	In Play
2006	NYA	97-65	1	90.7	44	1	74	8	488	297	41	79	106	.231	0	121	30	18	4	50	68.0%	33	0	140	99
2007	NYA	94-68	-5	90.8	39	0	75	9	522	326	33	33	98	.221	1	113	35	10	5	52	78.8%	39	1	190	145
2008	LAN	84-78	-3	90.9	47	1	78	4	460	295	58	88	275	.233	2	102	40	24	2	85	75.3%	22	10	143	115

In his first year on the job, Joe Torre piloted the Dodgers to the NL West flag, the 13th straight postseason appearance for a Torre-led team. Returning to the National League, he was ever more Torre-esque, leading the majors in double switches and quick hooks and ranking second in stolen-base attempts and hit-and-runs. His low-key style provided an element of calm amid the Dodgers' daily soap opera. Derided for the team's lower-than-expected win total, he was handicapped by a roster that lost 1,377 days and an MLB-high 43 percent of its payroll to the DL while receiving subpar performances from expensive players not easily benched. He handled the bullpen well enough to finish third in the league in WXRL despite injuries and inexperience, and if he initially botched the logjams at third base and outfield, he also got his best team onto the field when it mattered most, contracts be damned. Years under George Steinbrenner have ingrained Torre's desire to look out for number one by making sure that he wins, even if that takes more flexibility than his critics give him credit for.

Milwaukee Brewers

Every Brewers fan knew the clip by heart. Big Pete Ladd delivers to Rod Carew, who smokes a one-hopper to Robin Yount, who throws over to Cecil Cooper, who clutches the ball in his glove and raises his outstretched arms as he heads toward the dog pile on the mound, where the Brewers celebrate their 1982 pennant. That final out stood as the pinnacle of the Brewers' success for over a quarter of a century, a moment to savor for a franchise that has enjoyed more bad times than good in 40 seasons of existence across two cities and two leagues. It defined not only the success of a pennant captured, but also the failure to top that with a world championship, and the epic, playoff-free drought that brought 25 seasons of frustration and occasional humiliation.

All of that changed on the final day of the 2008 season. The Brewers captured neither a pennant nor a division crown, but the pairing of their come-from-behind victory over the Cubs with a loss by the Mets earned them the NL wild-card berth and etched a fresh highlight reel into their fan base's collective unconscious. This one stars Ryan Braun's towering eighth-inning homer and C. C. Sabathia's bear hug of Jason Kendall upon inducing Derrek Lee to ground into a game-ending 4-6-3 double play. A new chapter has been written in Milwaukee baseball, and it's about damned time.

The Brewers' arrival in the playoffs continued a progression that began when they went 81-81 in 2005, their first year under new owner Mark Attanasio. After slipping to 75-87 the following year due to a slew of injuries, a rebound to 83-79 in 2007 gave them their first winning season since 1992. Despite missing the playoffs after a fast start, they had begun to emerge from

the shadow of the Selig Era. Now, with a wild card won while enjoying their first-ever attendance north of three million, they're squarely in a new light.

Not that the franchise has shed the Selig regime's stamp entirely, for the architects of the 2008 team predate Attanasio's arrival. General manager Doug Melvin, a late-2002 hire, and scouting director Jack Zduriencik, a late-1999 hire, have keyed the revival, with the latter responsible for drafting Corey Hart (2000, 11th round), J. J. Hardy (2001, second round), Prince Fielder (2002, first round), Rickie Weeks (2003, first round), Yovani Gallardo (2004, second round), and Ryan Braun (2005, first round)—major figures in the Brewers' renaissance thus far and key components of their future.

Zduriencik departed in October to take up the challenge of the Mariners' GM position, but not before watching another pick of his figure prominently in the Brewers' success, though he never took the field for them and is in fact no longer part of the organization. Matt LaPorta, the team's first-round pick from 2007, was the key asset in a four-for-one deal to acquire Sabathia from the Indians on July 7. LaPorta, a first baseman out of the University of Florida, had been considered an overdraft when chosen seventh, and an odd choice, given Fielder's presence at first base. In retrospect, it seems quite possible that Melvin and company realized they could grab a near-ready bat at a position (or three, if you include the outfield corners) that they had covered and parlay their surplus into just such a deal, on just such a near-term time horizon.

Sabathia's acquisition was necessary because the enviable surplus of starting pitching that the Brewers had begun the year with had already been thinned by major

---

BREWERS PROSPECTUS

2008 record: 90-72; Second place in NL Central

Pythagenport record: 87-75

Runs scored per game: 4.64 (7th in NL)

Runs allowed per game: 4.26 (4th in NL)

Team EqA: .262 (7th in NL)

2008 Batters Age: 29.0 (8th-oldest in NL)

2008 Pitchers Age: 29.8 (7th-oldest in NL)

Ballpark: Miller Park; Neutral park; Park Factor of .998

2008: Deadline deals end 26 years of wandering in the wilderness, as Dale Sveum plays Joshua to Ned Yost's Moses.

2009: Free agency foils an attempt at a repeat performance, but some of the 2034 playoff team's key contributors are already in diapers.

injuries to Chris Capuano (Tommy John surgery) and Yovani Gallardo (torn ACL). The Brewers had shaken off a 23-27 start to climb to 10 games over .500 and were in a virtual tie for the wild card when the deal went down. Melvin's message was clear: all in. The trade was a smash, as Sabathia went 9-0 with a 1.43 ERA in his first 11 starts while averaging eight innings per start and closed the season making his final three starts on three days' rest as the Brewers clawed for their lives. The big man posted the league's highest Support Neutral Winning Percentage (.724), finished with a 1.65 ERA, and received down-ballot support in both the MVP and Cy Young votes. Coupled with a big season from Ben Sheets, who threw more innings (198⅓) and posted his highest Support-Neutral Lineup-Adjusted Value Above Replacement (or SNLVAR) since 2004 before getting hurt in late September and being reduced to a forlorn cheerleader, the Brewers had one of the league's best one-two punches, and the rotation finished fourth in the league in SNLVAR.

Melvin had already done impressive work to position the team for success. The 2007 club's most glaring flaw was a defense that ranked 28th in the majors in Park Adjusted Defensive Efficiency (PADE), so over the winter, Melvin signed three-time Gold Glove center fielder Mike Cameron to a one-year, $7 million deal with an option, ending the unsuccessful experiment of playing Bill Hall in center. He moved Hall back into the infield at third base and shifted Braun away from a steady diet of "E-5" to left. Melvin also signed free-agent catcher Jason Kendall to replace Johnny Estrada, who had thrown out only 13 percent of intended basestealers while eliciting grumbles from the pitching staff over his game-calling. The Brewers vaulted to 10th in the majors in PADE—an improvement worth about five wins.

Melvin's smaller moves paid off as well. Outfielder Gabe Kapler was lured out of a managerial sabbatical in the Red Sox organization and was most productive during April in a platoon that covered for Cameron's 25-game suspension for testing positive for a banned stimulant. Russell Branyan arrived from Nashville in May to partner with Hall in a hot corner platoon and to provide some lefty sock, bopping 10 homers in his first 20 games as the Brewers climbed from three games under .500 to six games over. All told, however, the offense was middling, ranking seventh in the league with a .262 EqA and 4.63 runs per game. They had plenty of power (third in homers, fifth in slugging percentage), but finished just 10th in OBP. The root of the problem was a lineup that tilted even further to the right than Dick Cheney, with Fielder the only lefty-swinging regular. Lefty hitters drew a major-league-low 24.7 percent of

the Brewers' plate appearances. Not coincidentally, the team's showing against righty pitchers (.246/.317/.421) was the fourth-lowest in batting average and OBP, and the Brewers' 68-point deficit in OPS against righties relative to lefties was the third-largest platoon disadvantage in the majors.

The bullpen Melvin assembled was a mixed bag, too. After the departure of free-agent closer Francisco Cordero, Melvin signed closer Eric Gagné to a one-year, $10 million deal. The GM also signed David Riske to a three-year, $13 million deal to serve as a setup man, and traded little of consequence for the Pirates' Salomon Torres and the Mets' Guillermo Mota. Gagné blew a save on Opening Day, was asked to put his repaired elbow to the test with a heavy early workload, and blew four more before going on the disabled list in late May. Riske, whose contract included incentives in the event he wound up closing, was already on the DL at the time, so Torres wound up taking over closer duties. Despite a few high-profile blunders, Torres was serviceable; among the 22 pitchers who saved at least 20 games, he ranked 12th in WXRL with 2.9, and on the whole, the Brewers finished a none-too-shabby fourth in the league in that category.

Ironically, the mishandling of that bullpen was the proximal reason for manager Ned Yost's dismissal in mid-September, a nearly unprecedented move that came in the wake of Melvin's biggest blunder of the year (see the Brian Shouse comment, below). Yost's slavish devotion to Shouse for by-the-book matchups had been a defining trait of his tenure; thanks to that affinity, right-handers Gagné (who fared much better in a setup role), Riske, and Mota all averaged less than an inning per outing, and in too many games, the skipper often burned through his bullpen, leaving himself with only Shouse, who could be defeated by any right-handed bat.

Yost probably wasn't the right manager for the club at this stage of its development. He had shown patience in overseeing the development of the talented young nucleus during the lean years from 2003 to 2006, but his tactical abilities were already in question and his insistence on seeing Hardy and Weeks through extended slumps played a big part in the team's slow fade in 2007. The Brewers would have been better served changing managers at the end of the last season or, failing that, when they stumbled out of the gate in 2008. Waiting until mid-September to fire the manager while conceding that the move may not have been the right one, as Melvin did, flattered neither the GM nor the organization. Fortunately, Sveum was able to pilot the shell-shocked club to victory even as the ghost of Yost lingered.

After the season, Melvin bypassed making a commitment to Sveum to instead hire former A's manager Ken Macha to skipper the club in 2009. In Oakland, Macha chafed under Billy Beane's directions from the front office, and while Macha may have more latitude here to implement the occasional small-ball strategy (however ill fitting, given this roster), he's hardly the organization's biggest question mark. The departure of Zduriencik, who had the luxury of making seven picks among the first 100 of the 2008 draft, left West Coast cross-checker Bruce Seid to fill his oversized shoes. Seid's first major task will be to oversee a draft in which the Brewers have multiple high picks due to the free-agency departures of Sabathia, Sheets, and Shouse (two Type As and a Type B), though the Yankees' signing of Mark Teixeira bumped Milwaukee's compensation for losing Sabathia down to a second-round supplemental. Melvin's most daunting task, uncompleted at this writing, is to replace some 330 innings of ace-quality pitching. A healthy Gallardo may cover half of that, but among Jeff Suppan, Dave Bush, and Manny Parra, the Brewers have no aces up their sleeves—a shortfall that may doom their chances of contending.

Indeed, the real question is whether the Brewers' window of opportunity is already closing. Among the homegrown nucleus of their lineup—Fielder, Braun, Weeks, Hardy, and Hart—only Hardy had a clearly better season in 2008 than in 2007, an unsettling trend for a group of under-27 players (Table 1).

While the WARP totals are similar, much of that has to do with Braun's moving off third base and spending the full season in the majors. The four players besides Hardy all lost at least 23 points of EqA, and as a group, their EqA was 19 points lower while using up 320 more plate appearances—and 281 outs. This quintet can be expected to improve, given the players' position on the aging curve, but they're also getting more expensive. Braun is locked up through 2015 via a reasonable eight-year, $45 million deal, but the other four are all arbitra-tion-eligible at this writing. Their salaries could add up quickly for a cost-conscious small-market team.

While there are no impact bats at the immediate ready to join that fivesome, four players who spent much of 2008 at Double-A Huntsville—shortstop Alcides Escobar, third baseman Mat Gamel, catcher Angel Salome, and center fielder Lorenzo Cain—are roughly a year away. Escobar has Gold Glove potential in the field, but he's a bottom-of-the-lineup type who's got plus speed but little plate discipline. Some have suggested that the Brewers explore moving Hardy to third to accommodate Escobar, or else move Weeks to center field and either Hardy or Escobar to second, but after all of the shuffling of the last two years, the Brewers haven't seriously explored this. Gamel profiles as a worthy addition to the middle of the order, but he'll need to learn a new position, since his butchery at third base has drawn comparisons to Braun's notoriously poor play at the hot corner. Gamel represents a reprise of the LaPorta problem, since Braun and Fielder are blocking two of the three corner positions remaining; Hart would be wise to rebound if he wants to stay a Brewer. Salome is a fireplug who can hit but whose defense is below average. Both he and Cain might be ready to take over their positions from pending free agents Cameron and Kendall.

The Brewers are well fixed for position players, which means it all comes down to the pitching; 'twas ever thus. With no impact hurlers on the way, Melvin's job will be to scare up some quality innings, either on the free-agent market or in trade, which may mean breaking up that young nucleus. Parting with Fielder, a Scott Boras client whom the club has conspicuously not tied up in a long-term deal and with whom the team has already battled regarding prearbitration salaries, may be the best solution. One popular trade rumor had him going to the Giants for Matt Cain, and while that specific deal may not be viable, it could serve as a template. The Brewers have a lot going for them, but they'll need to rearm for further success.

Table 1. Strange Brew: The Cresting Wave of Milwaukee's Young Stars?

| Player | Age | 2008 | | | | | 2007 | | | | |
		PA	EqA	EqR	Defense	WARP	PA	EqA	EqR	Defense	WARP
Ryan Braun	24	663	.299	109	-6	4.1	492	.327	96	-36	1.8
Prince Fielder	24	694	.301	109	-11	3.1	681	.329	129	-11	5.6
J. J. Hardy	25	629	.284	89	20	6.8	638	.269	82	-5	2.9
Corey Hart	26	657	.266	85	2	2.0	566	.301	94	1	4.4
Rickie Weeks	25	560	.270	71	4	2.8	506	.293	74	-13	2.1
Total		3203	.285	463	9	18.8	2883	.304	475	-64	16.8

HITTERS

Russell Branyan   4C

Bats: L   Throws: R   Height: 6' 3"   Weight: 195   Born: December 19, 1975   Age: 33

YEAR	TEAM	LVL	AGE	PA	R	2B	3B	HR	RBI	BB	SO	SB	CS	EqBRR	AVG	OBP	SLG	EqAVG	EqOBP	EqSLG	EqA	VORP	WARP	DEFENSE			
2006	TBA	MLB	30	193	23	10	0	12	27	19	62	2	0	1.4	.201	.286	.473	.192	.286	.455	.254	0.0	0.1	41-RF	-1		
2006	SDN	MLB	30	89	14	1	0	6	9	15	27	0	0	-0.2	.292	.416	.556	.306	.433	.583	.340	7.9	0.8	20-3B	-3		
2007	SDN	MLB	31	146	16	5	1	7	19	21	48	1	0	-1.1	.197	.322	.426	.207	.336	.463	.275	2.1	0.5	17-3B	2	9-LF	-2
2007	SLN	MLB	31	39	4	0	0	1	2	7	15	0	0	-0.3	.188	.333	.281	.188	.333	.281	.228	-1.2	0.1	6-3B	2		
2008	NAS	AAA	32	179	24	15	0	12	36	25	49	4	1	0.5	.359	.453	.693	.297	.380	.551	.310	18.9	2.0	31-3B	3		
2008	MIL	MLB	32	152	24	8	0	12	20	19	42	1	0	0.9	.250	.342	.583	.250	.342	.598	.305	11.3	0.9	31-3B	-3		
2009	SEA	MLB	33	375	49	17	1	21	60	46	119	5	1	-0.5	.237	.335	.491	.240	.338	.519	.289	15.5	1.9	90-3B	-4		

Breakout: 18%   Improve: 48%   Collapse: 26%   Attrition: 26%   Comparables: Jim Spencer, Adrian Garrett, Charlie Keller, Wally Post

The nomadic Three True Outcomes hero passed through the hands of no fewer than four organizations between being released by the Brewers in early 2006 and returning from the wilderness in time to save their season. The Brew Crew was just 23-26 when Branyan arrived from Nashville to assume the long half of a third-base platoon with Bill Hall, and he opened up a can of Whoop-Ass on opposing pitchers, belting 10 homers over his first 20 games as the team went on a 16-7 tear. He cooled off markedly after that, and an oblique strain in mid-August effectively ended his season. In a smart low-cost move as the newly minted Mariners GM, Zduriencik made Branyan his first free-agent signing, paying him $1.4 million on a one-year deal and promising him a shot at Seattle's job at first base.

Ryan Braun   LF

Bats: R   Throws: R   Height: 6' 2"   Weight: 200   Born: November 17, 1983   Age: 25

YEAR	TEAM	LVL	AGE	PA	R	2B	3B	HR	RBI	BB	SO	SB	CS	EqBRR	AVG	OBP	SLG	EqAVG	EqOBP	EqSLG	EqA	VORP	WARP	DEFENSE	
2006	BRV	A+	22	260	34	12	2	7	37	23	54	14	4	0.1	.274	.346	.438	.236	.295	.382	.239	-5.0	-0.4	58-3B	-4
2006	HUN	AA	22	257	42	19	1	15	40	21	46	12	0	1.4	.303	.367	.589	.285	.340	.574	.303	24.0	1.0	57-3B	-11
2007	NAS	AAA	23	134	28	12	0	10	22	15	11	4	3	0.0	.342	.418	.701	.314	.388	.636	.324	19.4	1.3	29-3B	-2
2007	MIL	MLB	23	492	91	26	6	34	97	29	112	15	5	1.2	.324	.370	.634	.327	.374	.653	.326	58.5	1.8	106-3B	-36
2008	MIL	MLB	24	663	92	39	7	37	106	42	129	14	4	1.3	.285	.335	.553	.289	.339	.569	.298	45.0	4.1	146-LF	-6
2009	MIL	MLB	25	661	105	38	4	37	109	57	126	15	4	1.5	.296	.362	.560	.298	.360	.576	.307	51.4	5.4	154-LF	0

Breakout: 23%   Improve: 58%   Collapse: 12%   Attrition: 4%   Comparables: Ellis Valentine, Dusty Baker, Andre Dawson, Vernon Wells

Like Prince Fielder, the 2007 NL Rookie of the Year left himself a tough act to follow and put together a season that was productive if uneven. Braun ran hot and cold, with an OPS of 942 or above in three months and 784 or below in the other three months, with his September woes (.208/.304/.356) excused by lower-back problems that he played through after sitting just a week. He showed plenty of power, but his increased plate discipline was simply a by-product of the injury. His unintentional walk rate prior to getting hurt was 4.6 percent; afterward, it rose to 9.1 percent (he was at 5.7 percent as a rookie). The eight-year, $45 million deal he signed in May looks generous for a second-year player, but it's actually a steal: he'll make $6 million in 2012, which would have been his final year before free agency, and $20 million over the three years beyond that; he could easily be worth triple that money over the life of the deal, according to his Marginal Value Above Replacement Player (MORP).

Lorenzo Cain   CF

Bats: R   Throws: R   Height: 6' 2"   Weight: 185   Born: April 13, 1986   Age: 23

YEAR	TEAM	LVL	AGE	PA	R	2B	3B	HR	RBI	BB	SO	SB	CS	EqBRR	AVG	OBP	SLG	EqAVG	EqOBP	EqSLG	EqA	VORP	WARP	DEFENSE			
2006	WVA	A	20	603	91	36	4	6	60	58	104	34	11	2.5	.307	.384	.425	.232	.290	.325	.218	-26.4	-2.7	123-RF	-6	5-CF	-1
2007	BRV	A+	21	533	67	21	3	2	44	37	97	24	9	0.0	.276	.338	.344	.232	.285	.297	.207	-31.9	-2.5	84-RF	0	36-CF	-2
2008	BRV	A+	22	356	50	22	4	7	41	29	68	19	4	1.1	.287	.358	.448	.252	.309	.411	.252	1.4	0.5	64-RF	-2	13-CF	2
2008	HUN	AA	22	172	21	9	5	4	17	19	41	6	2	-0.8	.277	.363	.486	.234	.302	.422	.251	0.1	0.2	38-CF	-1		
2008	NAS	AAA	22	22	0	0	0	0	2	3	6	0	0	-0.0	.158	.273	.158	.150	.261	.150	.133	-3.0	-0.3				
2009	MIL	MLB	23	571	64	30	4	9	49	47	143	16	6	1.9	.241	.308	.367	.243	.307	.378	.239	-5.1	0.6	134-RF	2		

Breakout: 36%   Improve: 69%   Collapse: 16%   Attrition: 10%   Comparables: Kevin Romine, Reggie Hammonds, Don White, Kyle Washington

This toolsy 2005 draft-and-follow asserted himself as a legitimate prospect last year, showing enough improvement to rise from High-A to Triple-A. Cain is an excellent athlete whose top asset is his speed; he's got quick wrists and good bat speed, but his power is only starting to manifest itself. His big breakthrough was in learning to lay off of breaking balls out of the strike zone and waiting for pitches that he can drive. He still needs to refine his jumps and reads, but he's well positioned to become the homegrown successor to Cameron.

Mike Cameron   CF

Bats: R   Throws: R   Height: 6' 2"   Weight: 200   Born: January 8, 1973   Age: 36

YEAR	TEAM	LVL	AGE	PA	R	2B	3B	HR	RBI	BB	SO	SB	CS	EqBRR	AVG	OBP	SLG	EqAVG	EqOBP	EqSLG	EqA	VORP	WARP	DEFENSE	
2006	SDN	MLB	33	634	88	34	9	22	83	71	142	25	9	-0.1	.268	.355	.482	.282	.369	.509	.297	38.6	6.0	138-CF	10
2007	SDN	MLB	34	651	88	33	6	21	78	67	160	18	5	4.0	.242	.328	.431	.255	.344	.465	.277	22.8	2.7	146-CF	-6
2008	MIL	MLB	35	508	69	25	2	25	70	54	142	17	5	-0.8	.243	.331	.477	.248	.337	.499	.282	23.2	3.2	118-CF	2
2009	MIL	MLB	36	492	70	25	3	21	65	57	122	16	5	0.3	.254	.345	.472	.256	.343	.485	.281	23.4	3.1	116-CF	-2

Breakout: 10% Improve: 40% Collapse: 16% Attrition: 22%   Comparables: Ron Gant, Greg Vaughn, Reggie Sanders, Gil Hodges

Because center field was one of the weaker links in a porous defense in 2007, the Brewers signed Cameron to a one-year, $7 million deal, well aware that he would miss the first 25 games because of a suspension for testing positive for a banned stimulant. Though Cameron started slowly on returning, he had reeled off a fairly typical offensive season by the end. Cameron's low batting average and OBP are products of low contact rates; he more than compensates for his strikeout rates by rarely grounding into double plays (just four times last year) and a healthy blend of power and speed. As for his defense, he remains above average, with other metrics like Ultimate Zone Rating and Plus/Minus viewing him more charitably than our own. All in all, he remains a reasonable investment even at the $10 million price of his 2009 option, but teams should keep an eye on his production against right-handers.

Craig Counsell   INF

Bats: L   Throws: R   Height: 6' 0"   Weight: 175   Born: August 21, 1970   Age: 38

YEAR	TEAM	LVL	AGE	PA	R	2B	3B	HR	RBI	BB	SO	SB	CS	EqBRR	AVG	OBP	SLG	EqAVG	EqOBP	EqSLG	EqA	VORP	WARP	DEFENSE			
2006	ARI	MLB	35	415	56	14	4	4	30	31	47	15	8	-1.6	.255	.327	.347	.252	.324	.338	.235	-1.0	1.2	81-SS	7		
2007	MIL	MLB	36	334	31	12	2	3	24	41	47	4	2	-1.0	.220	.323	.309	.216	.326	.316	.234	-7.0	1.0	33-3B	3	22-2B	6
2008	MIL	MLB	37	302	31	14	1	1	14	46	42	3	1	0.9	.226	.355	.302	.226	.358	.302	.248	-0.6	1.1	30-3B	0	21-SS	5
2009	MIL	MLB	38	163	19	6	1	1	12	21	22	2	1	-0.2	.245	.349	.326	.247	.347	.336	.246	3.1	0.7	42-SS	0		

Breakout: 35% Improve: 56% Collapse: 29% Attrition: 54%   Comparables: Floyd Baker, Jeff Reboulet, Art Howe, Todd Zeile

For the second year in a row, Counsell found plenty of work at three infield positions, covering for Weeks and Hardy as they rested their ouchies, and—less ideally—assuming the right-handed half of the third-base platoon with Bill Hall once Branyan went down. Counsell has the batting stance of a stock boy desperately trying to dislodge a tin of beans from the uppermost shelf of the five-and-dime, but he can be a pest. His patience at the plate proved critical down the stretch for the Brewers; he drew 16 walks in 20 September games and wound up in the middle of some of the final week's crucial rallies. Not a bad utility infielder to have around, though he was a long way from justifying the two-year, $6 million deal that carried him through 2007-2008.

Callix Crabbe   2B/OF

Bats: S   Throws: R   Height: 5' 7"   Weight: 171   Born: February 14, 1983   Age: 26

YEAR	TEAM	LVL	AGE	PA	R	2B	3B	HR	RBI	BB	SO	SB	CS	EqBRR	AVG	OBP	SLG	EqAVG	EqOBP	EqSLG	EqA	VORP	WARP	DEFENSE			
2006	HUN	AA	23	571	59	18	2	5	46	71	62	32	13	-2.7	.267	.368	.345	.244	.333	.332	.244	-8.6	0.5	127-2B	-4		
2007	NAS	AAA	24	541	84	23	9	9	38	67	70	17	14	-3.7	.287	.377	.435	.256	.344	.391	.257	8.0	1.6	80-2B	-4	20-RF	2
2008	SDN	MLB	25	39	4	1	0	0	2	4	6	1	0	0.4	.176	.282	.206	.176	.282	.206	.183	-2.4	-0.3				
2008	NAS	AAA	25	254	32	9	3	1	18	40	41	9	5	-2.1	.270	.386	.358	.236	.341	.307	.242	-5.3	-0.8	32-2B	-2	14-LF	-4
2009	SEA	MLB	26	393	46	15	3	4	29	42	70	11	4	1.2	.239	.326	.335	.242	.330	.354	.248	-0.3	0.2	94-2B	-8		

Breakout: 23% Improve: 49% Collapse: 26% Attrition: 26%   Comparables: Luis Rodriguez, Jose Offerman, Jerry Browne, Luis Alicea

Everyone needs a Lilliputian switch-hitting utilityman from the Virgin Islands, or so the Padres thought when they netted Crabbe in the 2007 Rule 5 draft. Unlike most such picks, Crabbe made their Opening Day roster, but he found few opportunities before being returned to the Brewers six weeks into the season. Crabbe's 2007 breakout was illusory, founded on a bounty of triples that were the product of his speed, not newly developed power; when the triples dried up, his isolated power went into isolation. He's a fun little player whose destiny is to be organizational fodder.

Joe Dillon   UT   Bats: R   Throws: R   Height: 6' 2"   Weight: 215   Born: August 2, 1975   Age: 33

YEAR	TEAM	LVL	AGE	PA	R	2B	3B	HR	RBI	BB	SO	SB	CS	EqBRR	AVG	OBP	SLG	EqAVG	EqOBP	EqSLG	EqA	VORP	WARP	DEFENSE			
2006	YOM	JP	30	95	9	3	1	2	7	8	17	0	0	—	.195	.263	.322	.182	.242	.284	.171	-8.9	-0.9				
2007	NAS	AAA	31	378	69	28	2	20	73	50	34	6	1	1.7	.317	.405	.605	.254	.337	.477	.279	16.3	2.1	53-3B	9	17-LF	-6
2007	MIL	MLB	31	82	12	8	2	0	10	5	14	0	0	-0.1	.342	.390	.500	.342	.390	.500	.304	6.9	0.8	5-LF	2		
2008	NAS	AAA	32	206	35	8	1	5	23	29	30	1	2	-0.4	.263	.374	.409	.208	.304	.326	.225	-8.0	-0.4	35-3B	-2	7-2B	1
2008	MIL	MLB	32	90	13	3	0	1	6	13	21	1	0	0.2	.213	.337	.293	.213	.337	.293	.235	-1.4	0.1	5-2B	2		
2009	OAK	MLB	33	214	21	10	1	4	23	22	39	2	1	-0.1	.221	.306	.349	.226	.313	.372	.242	-1.8	0.6	54-3B	1		

Breakout: 22%   Improve: 35%   Collapse: 42%   Attrition: 49%   Comparables: Jim Dyck, Charlie Hayes, Dave Hollins, Razor Shines

The longtime minor league masher (.294/.379/.518 with 156 homers) couldn't come close to matching his sizzling late-2007 showing because he got so few opportunities early in the year. Instead of honing his swing at Nashville or picking up a start or two per week at a corner position to be named later, Dillon rusted on the bench, drawing just one start and 12 PAs in April, and only 80 PAs before being demoted in July. A 6-for-40 showing in the pinch didn't help his cause, either. Claimed by the A's after the Brewers DFA'd him, he won't be the next Jack Cust, but if anyone can take advantage of his abilities, the A's can.

Ray Durham   2B   Bats: S   Throws: R   Height: 5' 8"   Weight: 190   Born: November 30, 1971   Age: 37

YEAR	TEAM	LVL	AGE	PA	R	2B	3B	HR	RBI	BB	SO	SB	CS	EqBRR	AVG	OBP	SLG	EqAVG	EqOBP	EqSLG	EqA	VORP	WARP	DEFENSE	
2006	SFN	MLB	34	555	79	30	7	26	93	51	61	7	2	1.5	.293	.360	.538	.290	.359	.533	.298	47.7	4.5	129-2B	0
2007	SFN	MLB	35	528	56	21	2	11	71	53	75	10	2	-0.1	.218	.295	.343	.213	.295	.341	.230	-10.0	-0.9	115-2B	-6
2008	SFN	MLB	36	304	43	23	0	3	32	38	49	6	2	0.6	.293	.385	.414	.298	.391	.427	.289	15.9	0.4	60-2B	-13
2008	MIL	MLB	36	122	21	12	0	3	13	15	23	2	2	0.8	.280	.369	.477	.280	.369	.477	.283	7.1	0.6	23-2B	0
2009	MIL	MLB	37	316	43	19	1	6	32	38	49	6	2	0.0	.272	.360	.413	.273	.358	.425	.274	15.5	1.3	77-2B	-5

Breakout: 18%   Improve: 56%   Collapse: 19%   Attrition: 23%   Comparables: Jim Gilliam, Tim Raines, Phil Garner, Chris Speier

Durham's slow start made his poor 2007 look like the beginning of the end, but a sudden two-month surge (.311/.408/.439) piqued the Brewers' interest enough to trade two suspects (outfielder Darren Ford and pitcher Steve Hammond) to the Giants for him just after the All-Star break. With Weeks struggling against righties, Durham started 24 of the team's final 61 games. Despite the irregular schedule—or perhaps because of it—Durham continued to hit, with a slight return in the power department. Nonetheless, the shape of his last two seasons—not to mention his defensive shortcomings—suggests he's well into the decline phase of his career, and any new suitor expecting the 2006 model is likely to be disappointed.

Alcides Escobar   SS   Bats: R   Throws: R   Height: 6' 1"   Weight: 155   Born: December 16, 1986   Age: 22

YEAR	TEAM	LVL	AGE	PA	R	2B	3B	HR	RBI	BB	SO	SB	CS	EqBRR	AVG	OBP	SLG	EqAVG	EqOBP	EqSLG	EqA	VORP	WARP	DEFENSE	
2006	BRV	A+	19	386	47	9	1	2	33	19	56	28	8	5.0	.257	.296	.306	.221	.254	.268	.190	-36.2	-2.9	79-SS	-12
2007	BRV	A+	20	283	37	8	3	0	25	7	35	18	10	0.0	.325	.345	.377	.277	.295	.321	.217	-10.2	0.4	61-SS	4
2007	HUN	AA	20	245	27	5	4	1	28	11	36	4	3	-2.0	.283	.314	.354	.242	.269	.303	.198	-15.5	-0.6	59-SS	0
2008	HUN	AA	21	597	95	24	5	8	76	31	82	34	8	4.6	.328	.363	.434	.279	.307	.377	.243	-2.9	3.8	125-SS	18
2009	MIL	MLB	22	575	64	25	5	4	39	28	93	21	9	3.7	.264	.302	.351	.266	.300	.361	.231	4.4	2.0	135-SS	12

Breakout: 33%   Improve: 57%   Collapse: 13%   Attrition: 8%   Comparables: Joaquin Arias, Wilton Guerrero, William Bergolla, Erick Aybar

This nondrafted free agent from Venezuela already rates as the top defensive player in the Brewers' system and as one of the best in the minors, with great range and an excellent arm. His approach at the plate, on the other hand, draws mixed reviews. While he's got a quick bat, the ability to spray line drives from foul line to foul line, and plenty of speed, his approach is overly aggressive, with poor pitch recognition, and his power is minimal, leaving his offensive value tied up in whatever he delivers in terms of batting average. There's been talk that the Brewers could trade Hardy or Weeks to clear a spot for him, but it's only talk so far.

Prince Fielder 1B   Bats: L Throws: R Height: 6' 0" Weight: 260 Born: May 9, 1984 Age: 25

YEAR	TEAM	LVL	AGE	PA	R	2B	3B	HR	RBI	BB	SO	SB	CS	EqBRR	AVG	OBP	SLG	EqAVG	EqOBP	EqSLG	EqA	VORP	WARP	DEFENSE
2006	MIL	MLB	22	648	82	35	1	28	81	59	125	7	2	-2.0	.271	.347	.483	.268	.344	.477	.281	19.4	0.4	150-1B -19
2007	MIL	MLB	23	681	109	35	2	50	119	90	121	2	2	-3.0	.288	.395	.618	.283	.395	.620	.328	70.1	5.6	150-1B -11
2008	MIL	MLB	24	694	86	30	2	34	102	84	134	3	2	-7.1	.276	.372	.507	.275	.370	.517	.300	41.3	3.1	154-1B -11
2009	MIL	MLB	25	661	99	33	2	33	105	81	118	3	1	-3.6	.286	.380	.527	.288	.378	.542	.304	44.7	4.1	154-1B -6

Breakout: 17% Improve: 50% Collapse: 16% Attrition: 5%   Comparables: Boog Powell, Greg Luzinski, Jason Thompson, John Mayberry

Fielder had a hard time following up a season in which he became the youngest player ever to belt 50 homers in a season. Whether it was the controversy surrounding his self-imposed vegetarianism or his frustration over having his contract renewed at $670,000 instead of being offered a long-term deal akin to Braun's, he had his share of distractions early in the year and started slowly. Through April 22, he homered just once, and by Memorial Day, he was slugging a paltry .432. Like many a power hitter, his homers arrived in bunches, and he slugged above .550 in three of the final four months, including a season-high .600 in September with everything at stake. His performance fell off against lefties, from a respectable .261/.355/.479 in 2007 to .239/.313/.420 last year, a worrisome trend, and his defense is never a plus. He's still an asset, but it's no longer clear that the Brewers need to break the bank to secure him long-term.

Eric Fryer C   Bats: R Throws: R Height: 6' 2" Weight: 215 Born: August 26, 1985 Age: 23

YEAR	TEAM	LVL	AGE	PA	R	2B	3B	HR	RBI	BB	SO	SB	CS	EqBRR	AVG	OBP	SLG	EqAVG	EqOBP	EqSLG	EqA	VORP	WARP	DEFENSE	
2007	HEL	Rk	21	157	25	7	0	3	19	14	28	4	3	0.4	.209	.288	.324	.138	.197	.200	.111	-44.4	-3.2	30-C -6	
2008	WVA	A	22	437	76	26	5	10	63	43	74	15	3	1.8	.335	.407	.506	.251	.316	.392	.248	-0.1	-1.5	52-LF -11	38-C -8
2009	MIL	MLB	23	550	59	28	3	7	46	47	129	8	4	1.4	.238	.308	.352	.239	.306	.362	.232	-5.0	0.0	129-LF -2	

Breakout: 52% Improve: 72% Collapse: 14% Attrition: 6%   Comparables: Nevin Ashley, Benny Agbayani, Leverne Jackson, Jonathan Rivers

A 10th-round 2007 pick out of Ohio State, Fryer recovered from a poor debut to post a strong 2008 in the Sally League. With fellow receiver and 2007 pick Jonathan Lucroy joining him at West Virginia, Fryer adapted well to a shift to left field and then took over the bulk of the catching duties upon Lucroy's promotion. He's big and athletic, but his defense is suspect—he threw out just 19 percent of stolen-base attempts and made 12 errors in 39 games—and the Brewers' organization is getting a bit crowded behind the plate, but as long as Fryer continues to hit, he'll find a spot somewhere.

Mat Gamel 3B   Bats: L Throws: R Height: 6' 0" Weight: 205 Born: July 26, 1985 Age: 23

YEAR	TEAM	LVL	AGE	PA	R	2B	3B	HR	RBI	BB	SO	SB	CS	EqBRR	AVG	OBP	SLG	EqAVG	EqOBP	EqSLG	EqA	VORP	WARP	DEFENSE
2006	WVA	A	20	555	65	28	5	17	88	52	81	9	2	-3.0	.288	.359	.469	.219	.274	.354	.218	-24.4	-3.0	108-3B -13
2007	BRV	A+	21	534	78	37	8	9	60	58	98	14	7	0.0	.300	.378	.472	.256	.326	.417	.258	8.9	-1.4	112-3B -23
2008	HUN	AA	22	572	96	35	7	19	96	55	111	6	7	-0.7	.329	.395	.537	.273	.328	.461	.268	21.5	1.0	126-3B -11
2008	NAS	AAA	22	23	3	0	0	1	3	2	10	0	0	-0.0	.238	.304	.381	.238	.304	.381	.238	-0.3	-0.2	5-3B -2
2009	MIL	MLB	23	572	69	32	5	16	66	50	135	6	4	0.4	.258	.325	.431	.260	.323	.443	.259	15.0	1.3	134-3B -8

Breakout: 26% Improve: 59% Collapse: 16% Attrition: 7%   Comparables: Brandon Moss, Brendan Harris, Daryl Sconiers, Frank Catalanotto

A year after making 53 errors and fielding an impossibly low .826, Gamel improved his footwork under the watchful eye of Huntsville skipper and former Brewer infielder Don Money, cut his error total down to 30, and crossed the Hobson line, fielding .918. Nonetheless, the 2005 fourth-round pick still has no future at third base, though he continues to provide evidence that his bat will play anywhere. Gamel tore up the Southern League, finishing among the leaders in every major category and earning promotions to Nashville and Milwaukee despite a second-half slump caused by tendonitis in his right elbow. A move to an easier defensive position would seem to be in order, but with Braun, Hart, and Fielder blocking the obvious non-third corner destinations, the Brewers have their work cut out in trying to accommodate him.

Cole Gillespie   LF   Bats: R   Throws: R   Height: 6' 1"   Weight: 205   Born: June 20, 1984   Age: 25

YEAR	TEAM	LVL	AGE	PA	R	2B	3B	HR	RBI	BB	SO	SB	CS	EqBRR	AVG	OBP	SLG	EqAVG	EqOBP	EqSLG	EqA	VORP	WARP	DEFENSE			
2006	HEL	Rk	22	233	49	12	1	8	31	40	34	18	4	4.4	.344	.464	.548	.209	.289	.320	.218	-20.1	-1.6	27-LF	2	16-CF	-6
2007	BRV	A+	23	522	75	25	3	12	62	72	95	16	8	0.0	.267	.378	.420	.211	.308	.344	.232	-16.4	-1.5	122-LF	-6		
2008	HUN	AA	24	550	73	38	4	14	79	75	102	17	1	2.1	.281	.386	.472	.225	.308	.388	.246	-6.0	-2.1	98-LF	-18	30-RF	-2
2009	MIL	MLB	25	541	61	29	2	13	52	58	143	11	4	0.6	.229	.316	.380	.230	.315	.391	.247	-4.3	0.0	127-LF	-5		

Breakout: 42% Improve: 61% Collapse: 23% Attrition: 4%   Comparables: Chad Alexander, Scott Lydy, Mark Davidson, Gary Cooper

A Portland native who helped lead Oregon State to victory in the 2006 College World Series, Gillespie continued his steady rise through the system. After stumbling in early 2007 at Brevard County, Gillespie caught fire in the second half. He then carried that hot performance to Huntsville, where the only ding on his performance was a second-half power outage that saw his slugging percentage drop from .505 to .388. Gillespie is a polished professional hitter who works the count and draws plenty of walks, but his power is only moderate. Despite average speed and athleticism, he went 17-for-18 in steals last year and has stolen at an 80 percent clip as a pro. His lack of arm strength limits him to left, where Braun is already planted ahead of him, so his future may lie beyond Milwaukee.

Caleb Gindl   RF   Bats: L   Throws: L   Height: 5' 9"   Weight: 185   Born: August 31, 1988   Age: 20

YEAR	TEAM	LVL	AGE	PA	R	2B	3B	HR	RBI	BB	SO	SB	CS	EqBRR	AVG	OBP	SLG	EqAVG	EqOBP	EqSLG	EqA	VORP	WARP	DEFENSE			
2007	HEL	Rk	18	231	40	22	3	5	42	20	38	4	4	-2.0	.372	.420	.580	.249	.294	.380	.235	-7.1	-0.7	50-RF	-2		
2008	WVA	A	19	578	86	38	4	13	81	63	144	14	5	0.4	.307	.388	.474	.241	.316	.387	.246	-2.3	-0.2	116-RF	-4	17-CF	0
2009	MIL	MLB	20	615	68	38	5	12	55	59	167	9	5	1.3	.238	.314	.390	.239	.312	.402	.245	-3.6	1.2	144-RF	2		

Breakout: 32% Improve: 58% Collapse: 9% Attrition: 8%   Comparables: Rich Becker, John Csefalvay, Sil Campusano, Randy Washington

A fifth-round 2007 pick who drew draft consideration as a pitcher as well as a hitter despite his short stature, Gindl's an organizational favorite due to his strong work ethic, focus on fundamentals, and his ability to overcome a lack of vowels. He won the Pioneer League's batting title in his professional debut despite playing against much older competition, then made a successful jump to full-season ball, where he continued to demonstrate a mature approach at the plate and gap power. His strikeout rate is cause for some concern, and there's not much projection to him physically, but 20-year-olds with his advanced skills don't grow on trees.

Taylor Green   3B   Bats: L   Throws: R   Height: 5' 10"   Weight: 180   Born: November 2, 1986   Age: 22

YEAR	TEAM	LVL	AGE	PA	R	2B	3B	HR	RBI	BB	SO	SB	CS	EqBRR	AVG	OBP	SLG	EqAVG	EqOBP	EqSLG	EqA	VORP	WARP	DEFENSE	
2006	HEL	Rk	19	260	36	12	1	1	23	29	35	0	1	-3.1	.231	.328	.308	.165	.225	.224	.145	-57.1	-2.8	56-2B	2
2007	WVA	A	20	460	68	29	2	14	86	51	65	0	5	-4.2	.327	.406	.516	.252	.317	.392	.246	0.3	0.3	100-3B	-1
2008	BRV	A+	21	490	46	19	0	15	73	61	59	4	2	-2.6	.289	.382	.443	.260	.339	.415	.263	11.5	0.7	99-3B	-7
2009	MIL	MLB	22	553	58	27	2	11	55	55	99	2	2	-0.6	.250	.327	.382	.251	.325	.393	.248	6.3	1.0	130-3B	-2

Breakout: 33% Improve: 66% Collapse: 11% Attrition: 7%   Comparables: Rico Washington, Chris Alvarez, Walt McConnell, Travis Denker

This 2005 draft-and-follow won the organization's Minor League Player of the Year honors for a strong 2007 season in West Virginia, and while his raw numbers took a predictable hit in the Florida State League, the translations suggest that he continued to make progress. Green has very good plate discipline and contact skills, but he only projects to have average power. While he's not a butcher afield like Braun or Gamel at the hot corner, his range and arm strength at third base don't wow many observers, and if he has to move, the offensive bar will only be raised.

Tony Gwynn Jr.   CF

Bats: L   Throws: R   Height: 6' 0"   Weight: 190   Born: October 4, 1982   Age: 26

YEAR	TEAM	LVL	AGE	PA	R	2B	3B	HR	RBI	BB	SO	SB	CS	EqBRR	AVG	OBP	SLG	EqAVG	EqOBP	EqSLG	EqA	VORP	WARP	DEFENSE				
2006	NAS	AAA	23	494	73	21	5	4	42	42	84	30	11	3.1	.300	.360	.396	.268	.324	.358	.244	-2.8	2.8	91-CF	20	11-LF	-1
2006	MIL	MLB	23	80	5	2	1	0	4	2	15	3	1	-0.3	.260	.275	.312	.260	.275	.312	.210	-2.5	-0.4	15-CF	-1		
2007	NAS	AAA	24	138	19	3	3	0	13	9	14	4	3	-1.0	.286	.336	.357	.252	.299	.315	.216	-5.3	-0.8	27-CF	-4		
2007	MIL	MLB	24	135	13	3	2	0	10	12	24	8	1	1.2	.260	.326	.317	.254	.326	.311	.240	0.3	0.0	17-CF	1	7-RF	0
2008	NAS	AAA	25	412	47	9	3	2	26	29	54	20	6	-0.8	.275	.328	.331	.239	.288	.286	.208	-24.2	-0.8	83-CF	4	7-RF	0
2008	MIL	MLB	25	49	5	1	0	0	1	4	7	3	1	0.7	.190	.271	.214	.190	.271	.214	.194	-3.4	-0.1	5-CF	2		
2009	MIL	MLB	26	446	51	17	4	2	28	33	75	18	6	1.7	.249	.308	.329	.251	.306	.339	.230	-4.2	0.8	106-CF	3		

Breakout: 40%   Improve: 57%   Collapse: 25%   Attrition: 24%   Comparables: Jason Tyner, Jerry Owens, Tom Goodwin, Tyrell Godwin

Kid Gwynn was the team's Opening Day center fielder, thanks to Cameron's suspension, but after straining his hamstring during the season's first week, his fleeting opportunity in Milwaukee dissolved into another summer in Nashville. Given his lack of power and minimal patience, his combination of speed and defense is too slim to merit a starting role anywhere. He's fifth outfielder material, which at least means lots of late-inning work as a pinch-hitter (.273/.355/.345 career) or defensive replacement, but let's face it, if his name were Tony Jones, he'd hardly be worth a second look.

Bill Hall   3B

Bats: R   Throws: R   Height: 6' 0"   Weight: 210   Born: December 28, 1979   Age: 29

YEAR	TEAM	LVL	AGE	PA	R	2B	3B	HR	RBI	BB	SO	SB	CS	EqBRR	AVG	OBP	SLG	EqAVG	EqOBP	EqSLG	EqA	VORP	WARP	DEFENSE				
2006	MIL	MLB	26	608	101	39	4	35	85	63	162	8	9	-5.1	.270	.345	.553	.267	.346	.547	.290	43.7	5.2	124-SS	3	10-3B	0
2007	MIL	MLB	27	503	59	35	0	14	63	40	128	4	5	-2.4	.254	.315	.425	.256	.319	.436	.256	7.1	-0.4	115-CF	-15		
2008	MIL	MLB	28	448	50	22	1	15	55	37	124	5	6	-0.2	.225	.293	.396	.228	.297	.407	.239	-5.1	0.6	100-3B	6		
2009	MIL	MLB	29	468	60	24	2	19	62	47	117	7	4	-0.2	.253	.332	.459	.255	.330	.472	.271	18.3	2.3	111-3B	2		

Breakout: 28%   Improve: 63%   Collapse: 12%   Attrition: 14%   Comparables: Deron Johnson, Dean Palmer, Wally Post, Doug Rader

Hall hasn't come close to living up to the 2005 and 2006 performances that netted him a four-year, $24 million deal, though to be fair, being shifted around the diamond isn't helping. After his disappointing experiment in center field, the Brewers returned him to the infield at third base, where he provided a massive upgrade over Braun's butchery, but his bat was a major disappointment. An uncharacteristically abysmal .174/.242/.316 showing against righties played him into a platoon with first Branyan and then Counsell, and his opportunities diminished as the season went on. Some of his woes were attributable to a 45-point drop in BABIP despite an above-average line-drive rate, but he hasn't helped his cause by swinging at—and making contact with—a much higher percentage of balls outside the strike zone over the past two years. Still owed $15.7 million for the final two years of his deal, he's become a sizable problem instead of a handy solution.

J. J. Hardy   SS

Bats: R   Throws: R   Height: 6' 2"   Weight: 190   Born: August 19, 1982   Age: 26

YEAR	TEAM	LVL	AGE	PA	R	2B	3B	HR	RBI	BB	SO	SB	CS	EqBRR	AVG	OBP	SLG	EqAVG	EqOBP	EqSLG	EqA	VORP	WARP	DEFENSE	
2006	MIL	MLB	23	139	13	5	0	5	14	10	23	1	1	-1.4	.242	.295	.398	.242	.295	.391	.236	0.3	0.5	29-SS	3
2007	MIL	MLB	24	638	89	30	1	26	80	40	73	2	3	-1.1	.277	.323	.463	.277	.327	.474	.268	27.3	2.9	143-SS	-5
2008	MIL	MLB	25	629	78	31	4	24	74	52	98	2	1	-1.3	.283	.343	.478	.284	.345	.491	.283	40.4	6.8	141-SS	20
2009	MIL	MLB	26	621	78	32	2	21	79	50	89	2	2	-0.7	.284	.344	.459	.286	.342	.473	.275	36.3	4.6	145-SS	9

Breakout: 22%   Improve: 49%   Collapse: 18%   Attrition: 5%   Comparables: Davey Johnson, Bret Boone, Clete Boyer, Jay Bell

Good health becomes Hardy. For the second year in a row, he not only reached his 75th-percentile PECOTA projection as far as his rate stats were concerned, but also extended that performance across an extra 25 percent of playing time. He improved over 2007 in several areas, including his defense; beyond our own system's showing him love, he ranked second among shortstops via Ultimate Zone Rating (11.6) and third via Plus/Minus (+19). While his 26-point bump in BABIP may not be sustainable unless he increases his line-drive rate from a surprisingly low 15.5 percent, modest increases in walk rate and isolated power suggest he's recovering some of the development time lost to injury in his age-21 through age-23 seasons. On a team that saw Braun, Hart, and Fielder take steps backward last year, he's become a significant plus, and trading him simply to accommodate Alcides Escobar won't constitute a step in the right direction.

Corey Hart RF

Bats: R   Throws: R   Height: 6' 6"   Weight: 215   Born: March 24, 1982   Age: 27

YEAR	TEAM	LVL	AGE	PA	R	2B	3B	HR	RBI	BB	SO	SB	CS	EqBRR	AVG	OBP	SLG	EqAVG	EqOBP	EqSLG	EqA	VORP	WARP	DEFENSE			
2006	NAS	AAA	24	115	19	10	1	4	21	12	25	11	2	0.8	.320	.391	.560	.284	.353	.520	.297	8.4	0.8	17-LF	0	5-RF	0
2006	MIL	MLB	24	256	32	13	2	9	33	17	58	5	8	-3.1	.283	.328	.468	.284	.332	.479	.264	4.0	0.8	30-RF	-1	19-LF	3
2007	MIL	MLB	25	566	86	33	9	24	81	36	99	23	7	2.7	.295	.353	.539	.296	.355	.555	.300	40.2	4.4	97-RF	2	26-CF	-1
2008	MIL	MLB	26	657	76	45	6	20	91	27	109	23	7	3.7	.268	.300	.459	.271	.303	.474	.264	11.6	2.0	153-RF	2		
2009	MIL	MLB	27	612	89	38	4	23	85	42	103	23	8	1.9	.289	.343	.494	.291	.341	.509	.286	27.7	3.8	143-RF	3		

Breakout: 29%   Improve: 58%   Collapse: 8%   Attrition: 3%   Comparables: Joe Carter, Alexis Rios, Ollie Brown, Al Cowens

Hart went from being a key player in 2007 to a total mess in 2008; despite getting off to a solid start (.300/.348/.473 through May), he hit just .252/.275/.452 the rest of the way. His hacktastic approach at the plate caught up with him; he saw one of the heaviest diets of sliders of any player, and swung at far more pitches outside the zone than he had in the past. By September, he was a wreck, hitting just .173/.192/.245. He'll need to rebound to remain an asset as he becomes more expensive.

Hernan Iribarren 2B/OF

Bats: L   Throws: R   Height: 6' 1"   Weight: 180   Born: June 29, 1984   Age: 25

YEAR	TEAM	LVL	AGE	PA	R	2B	3B	HR	RBI	BB	SO	SB	CS	EqBRR	AVG	OBP	SLG	EqAVG	EqOBP	EqSLG	EqA	VORP	WARP	DEFENSE			
2006	BRV	A+	22	455	50	12	4	2	50	39	57	19	15	-3.5	.319	.376	.384	.273	.325	.334	.234	-6.8	-0.2	104-2B	-3		
2007	HUN	AA	23	542	72	23	12	4	53	44	109	18	16	-0.5	.307	.363	.430	.261	.312	.379	.239	-2.9	0.0	118-2B	-5		
2008	NAS	AAA	24	397	47	17	3	0	30	28	61	19	8	1.1	.277	.329	.341	.245	.292	.300	.212	-19.9	-1.0	53-LF	3	24-2B	0
2008	MIL	MLB	24	15	1	1	0	0	1	1	3	0	0	-0.0	.143	.200	.214	.143	.200	.214	.112	-1.6	-0.2				
2009	MIL	MLB	25	429	49	17	4	3	28	32	81	13	6	1.9	.253	.311	.341	.255	.309	.351	.232	-2.8	0.5	102-2B	-1		

Breakout: 32%   Improve: 57%   Collapse: 23%   Attrition: 13%   Comparables: Carlos Mendoza, Jose Herrera, Trent Oeltjen, Alexis Marte

After hitting a combined .323/.382/.436 during his first four minor league seasons, this Venezuelan speedster struggled on reaching Triple-A. While he's got quick wrists and excellent contact skills, his shortages of both power and plate discipline (and given his generally poor stolen-base percentages, may we also suggest a new term, poor speed discipline?) became glaringly apparent in the hitter-friendly Pacific Coast League. His offensive impact is almost entirely predicated on a high batting average. The combination of his defensive shortcomings and the Brewers' crowded middle infield led the Brewers to test him in the outfield, more as a warm-up for a utility role than as an eventual destination; he certainly can't hit well enough for an outfield corner. Since Escobar has the inside track on cracking the big club's middle infield, Iribarren will probably have to settle for honing his wares in Nashville again.

Gabe Kapler OF

Bats: R   Throws: R   Height: 6' 2"   Weight: 210   Born: July 31, 1975   Age: 33

YEAR	TEAM	LVL	AGE	PA	R	2B	3B	HR	RBI	BB	SO	SB	CS	EqBRR	AVG	OBP	SLG	EqAVG	EqOBP	EqSLG	EqA	VORP	WARP	DEFENSE			
2006	BOS	MLB	30	147	21	7	0	2	12	14	15	1	1	0.6	.254	.340	.354	.240	.333	.326	.236	-0.7	-0.5	20-RF	-2	11-CF	-4
2008	MIL	MLB	32	245	36	17	2	8	38	13	39	3	1	1.2	.301	.340	.498	.306	.344	.511	.287	14.8	1.5	28-CF	3	13-LF	0
2009	TBA	MLB	33	243	31	13	2	6	32	16	37	3	1	0.0	.282	.331	.442	.286	.335	.465	.274	9.2	1.3	60-CF	-2		

Breakout: 20%   Improve: 46%   Collapse: 28%   Attrition: 29%   Comparables: Gerald Williams, Brian Jordan, Roberto Kelly, Gary Ward

After spending 2007 managing Boston's Sally League affiliate in Greenville, America's favorite Jewish bodybuilding fourth outfielder came out of retirement to sign with the Brewers. Cameron's suspension and Kid Gwynn's injury opened up a larger share of the center field job in the first month, and Kapler responded by pounding four home runs before Tax Day. Though he cooled off, he remained an effective reserve, particularly useful against lefties (.354/.379/.622) and in the pinch (.323/.364/.548) as well as covering all three outfield slots. Assuming he heals properly from a lat he tore in September, he'll make a handy bench player somewhere.

Brendan Katin OF Bats: R Throws: R Height: 6' 1" Weight: 235 Born: January 28, 1983 Age: 26

YEAR	TEAM	LVL	AGE	PA	R	2B	3B	HR	RBI	BB	SO	SB	CS	EqBRR	AVG	OBP	SLG	EqAVG	EqOBP	EqSLG	EqA	VORP	WARP	DEFENSE			
2006	BRV	A+	23	496	64	34	3	13	75	34	112	4	6	-1.7	.289	.349	.464	.232	.278	.385	.227	-14.4	-2.3	88-RF	-9		
2006	HUN	AA	23	60	11	2	0	4	8	1	11	0	0	0.8	.224	.250	.466	.207	.233	.431	.220	-2.3	-0.9	10-LF	-6		
2007	HUN	AA	24	508	72	24	0	24	94	41	163	3	2	-1.0	.258	.329	.471	.224	.281	.407	.237	-9.3	-1.9	109-RF	-12		
2008	NAS	AAA	25	344	47	22	4	19	72	13	109	7	2	1.4	.271	.314	.542	.243	.279	.468	.252	3.0	-0.5	54-RF	-4	20-LF	-3
2009	MIL	MLB	26	390	38	19	1	14	49	23	129	5	2	-0.4	.221	.277	.399	.222	.275	.410	.232	-8.0	-0.5	93-RF	-4		

Breakout: 19% Improve: 41% Collapse: 36% Attrition: 18%   Comparables: Benny Colvard, Chris Hatcher, Terrel Hansen, Phil Hiatt

Three True Outcomes hitters have their uses, but Two True Outcomes hitters? Not so much. A former college teammate of Braun's, Katin has plenty of raw power, but as for the strike zone, he apparently saw it in a movie once and decided it wasn't for him. If he could learn to handle breaking balls, he might have a future; until then he's little more than a curio.

Jason Kendall C Bats: R Throws: R Height: 6' 0" Weight: 205 Born: June 26, 1974 Age: 35

YEAR	TEAM	LVL	AGE	PA	R	2B	3B	HR	RBI	BB	SO	SB	CS	EqBRR	AVG	OBP	SLG	EqAVG	EqOBP	EqSLG	EqA	VORP	WARP	DEFENSE	
2006	OAK	MLB	32	626	76	23	0	1	50	53	54	11	5	1.0	.295	.367	.342	.288	.365	.338	.256	14.8	3.0	140-C	4
2007	OAK	MLB	33	312	24	10	0	2	22	12	27	3	1	-0.7	.226	.261	.281	.226	.264	.281	.191	-12.4	-1.5	80-C	-7
2007	CHN	MLB	33	202	21	10	1	1	19	19	15	0	3	-0.4	.270	.362	.356	.263	.358	.349	.249	3.0	-0.2	48-C	-7
2008	MIL	MLB	34	587	46	30	2	2	49	50	45	8	3	0.5	.246	.327	.324	.247	.328	.332	.237	0.1	2.5	148-C	11
2009	MIL	MLB	35	309	31	14	1	2	24	25	29	3	2	-0.6	.251	.320	.323	.252	.318	.333	.229	0.8	1.2	75-C	1

Breakout: 18% Improve: 35% Collapse: 37% Attrition: 44%   Comparables: Brad Ausmus, Tony Peña, Joe Girardi, Mickey Owen

Even with a slight rebound at the plate, Kendall couldn't quite match predecessor Johnny Estrada's minimal contribution with the bat; he's got decent plate discipline and an admirable willingness to take one for the team, but you'll find more fearsome power threats in the Pony League. It was Kendall's stronger rebound behind the dish that turned his acquisition into an upgrade for the Brewers. Unlike Estrada, he elicited no public grousing from the pitching coach or staff, and he nailed a major-league-best 43 percent in 2008 after throwing out just 15 percent of stolen-base attempts in 2007. He was also durable, catching more innings than any backstop since Gary Carter in 1982, including the final 34 games of the season (which helps explain why he hit .202/.295/.298 in September). All that squatting vested his 2009 option at $4.6 million, a worthwhile short-term commitment, given that Angel Salome is on the way.

Mike Lamb 1B/3B Bats: L Throws: R Height: 6' 1" Weight: 190 Born: August 9, 1975 Age: 33

YEAR	TEAM	LVL	AGE	PA	R	2B	3B	HR	RBI	BB	SO	SB	CS	EqBRR	AVG	OBP	SLG	EqAVG	EqOBP	EqSLG	EqA	VORP	WARP	DEFENSE			
2006	HOU	MLB	30	421	70	22	3	12	45	35	55	2	4	-0.8	.307	.361	.475	.303	.359	.470	.281	16.1	2.2	56-1B	-1	28-3B	5
2007	HOU	MLB	31	353	45	14	2	11	40	36	45	0	0	1.9	.289	.366	.453	.288	.369	.460	.287	17.3	1.3	46-3B	-5	25-1B	1
2008	MIN	MLB	32	261	20	12	3	1	32	17	32	0	1	0.6	.233	.276	.322	.234	.280	.323	.214	-10.1	-0.9	51-3B	-2	6-1B	1
2008	MIL	MLB	32	11	2	0	0	0	0	0	1	0	0	-0.0	.273	.273	.273	.273	.273	.273	.180	-0.5	-0.1				
2009	MIL	MLB	33	209	24	10	1	4	23	19	26	1	1	0.0	.265	.333	.397	.266	.331	.408	.254	5.2	0.5	53-3B	-3		

Breakout: 22% Improve: 41% Collapse: 38% Attrition: 37%   Comparables: Joe Orsulak, Doug Mientkiewicz, Larry Biittner, Dane Iorg

After four serviceable years as a part-timer for the Astros, Lamb signed a modest two-year, $6.6 million deal to be the Twins' starting third baseman. Despite a bar set extremely low by Nick Punto's atrocious 2007 (.210/.291/.271), Lamb was an unmitigated disaster. He played his way out of the lineup by early June, then rode the pine for another 11 weeks before the notoriously pinchpenny Twins released him. There was no obvious cause for his offensive woes, but he had his share of bad luck; his 18 percent line-drive rate should have yielded a BABIP closer to .300 than .256, but that doesn't account for his loss of power. In any event, the Brewers picked him up too late for postseason eligibility, but they elected to retain him for 2009. He'll help out at both infield corners and provide a rare lefty bat off the bench, with the Twins on the hook for $2.6 million of his salary.

Brett Lawrie   C   Bats: R   Throws: R   Height: 5' 11"   Weight: 200   Born: January 18, 1990   Age: 19

YEAR	TEAM	LVL	AGE	PA	R	2B	3B	HR	RBI	BB	SO	SB	CS	EqBRR	AVG	OBP	SLG	EqAVG	EqOBP	EqSLG	EqA	VORP	WARP	DEFENSE
2009	MIL	MLB	19	490	33	20	2	6	39	30	137	5	2	0.6	.199	.252	.290	.201	.250	.299	.184	-22.3	-1.1	116-C -7

Breakout: N/A   Improve: N/A   Collapse: N/A   Attrition: N/A   Comparables: John Gibbons, Phil Clark, Mike Lieberthal, Derek Parks

Lawrie was a 16th-round pick in the 2008 draft—the highest spot ever for a Canadian position player. He's a natural hitter with excellent bat speed and plenty of power. Defensively, he's a project; he split time between third base and catcher as an amateur, and while he's got the build and the arm for the position, he'll need to improve his erratic throws and his game-calling. Learning the position will slow his timetable relative to his first-round peers, but with Angel Salome and Jonathan Lucroy ahead of him in the system, there's no rush.

Jonathan Lucroy   C   Bats: R   Throws: R   Height: 6' 0"   Weight: 185   Born: June 13, 1986   Age: 23

YEAR	TEAM	LVL	AGE	PA	R	2B	3B	HR	RBI	BB	SO	SB	CS	EqBRR	AVG	OBP	SLG	EqAVG	EqOBP	EqSLG	EqA	VORP	WARP	DEFENSE
2007	HEL	Rk	21	253	35	18	2	4	39	16	37	0	3	-4.8	.342	.383	.487	.221	.253	.312	.191	-33.0	-1.0	32-C 4
2008	WVA	A	22	274	45	16	1	10	33	30	39	8	1	2.9	.310	.391	.510	.236	.309	.402	.249	-0.8	1.1	47-C 3
2008	BRV	A+	22	272	31	12	1	10	44	28	45	1	2	-2.2	.292	.364	.479	.256	.317	.434	.258	5.0	1.6	48-C 4
2009	MIL	MLB	23	542	55	28	2	12	57	44	114	4	2	-0.4	.242	.307	.384	.243	.305	.395	.241	5.5	2.4	127-C -3

Breakout: 34%   Improve: 56%   Collapse: 14%   Attrition: 10%   Comparables: Brook Fordyce, Curtis Thigpen, Todd Zeile, Kiki Hernandez

Chosen in the third round in 2007 out of Louisiana-Lafayette, Lucroy was considered the second-best offensive catcher of the draft behind Matt Wieters. After a strong showing in the Pioneer League, he barely missed a beat as he zipped through the Sally League on the way to Brevard County, showing increased plate discipline as his power developed. Defense was what kept Lucroy from being a higher draft pick, and while his arm is considered only average, he threw out 45 percent of attempted basestealers. Along with Salome and Lawrie, he's helped the Brewers turn an organizational weakness into a strength, but he's behind both of them in the big picture.

Brad Nelson   4C   Bats: L   Throws: R   Height: 6' 2"   Weight: 220   Born: December 23, 1982   Age: 26

YEAR	TEAM	LVL	AGE	PA	R	2B	3B	HR	RBI	BB	SO	SB	CS	EqBRR	AVG	OBP	SLG	EqAVG	EqOBP	EqSLG	EqA	VORP	WARP	DEFENSE
2006	HUN	AA	23	332	47	14	1	6	39	63	62	6	3	-0.7	.264	.401	.392	.245	.367	.388	.272	8.2	0.8	65-1B -1
2006	NAS	AAA	23	152	22	10	0	3	17	18	36	4	3	-1.3	.215	.316	.362	.203	.289	.346	.226	-6.0	-0.6	34-1B -1
2007	NAS	AAA	24	445	54	23	1	20	65	31	98	9	6	0.1	.263	.317	.470	.234	.287	.420	.240	-3.5	-1.6	55-1B -5 19-RF -1
2008	NAS	AAA	25	553	78	36	1	18	78	73	77	13	8	-7.7	.286	.380	.480	.249	.334	.407	.259	8.1	-0.6	100-1B -9 7-3B -1
2009	MIL	MLB	26	496	59	24	2	14	55	55	106	10	4	-0.9	.240	.328	.399	.242	.326	.411	.255	2.0	0.3	117-1B -3

Breakout: 22%   Improve: 48%   Collapse: 21%   Attrition: 14%   Comparables: Ben Broussard, Paul Carey, Bob Hamelin, J.T. Snow

Once upon a time, before Prince Fielder was the overstuffed apple pie of the Brewers' eye, Nelson ranked as the team's top offensive prospect, but injuries stalled his progress and sapped his power. Though no longer a prospect, Nelson rekindled hopes of a big-league career in 2007, then built on that by restoring his plate discipline without surrendering any power, and wound up earning a September call-up. Blocked by Fielder, he has added the other corner positions to his repertoire to make himself a viable reserve; whether that happens in Milwaukee or elsewhere is the real question.

Angel Salome   C   Bats: R   Throws: R   Height: 5' 7"   Weight: 190   Born: June 8, 1986   Age: 23

YEAR	TEAM	LVL	AGE	PA	R	2B	3B	HR	RBI	BB	SO	SB	CS	EqBRR	AVG	OBP	SLG	EqAVG	EqOBP	EqSLG	EqA	VORP	WARP	DEFENSE
2006	WVA	A	20	467	63	31	2	10	85	39	63	7	3	-0.7	.292	.349	.447	.225	.270	.343	.214	-23.0	-1.0	76-C -3
2007	BRV	A+	21	276	33	20	0	6	53	12	32	1	0	0.0	.318	.341	.465	.280	.301	.425	.250	3.4	-0.8	38-C -12
2008	HUN	AA	22	411	67	30	2	13	83	33	57	3	2	-5.4	.360	.415	.559	.310	.354	.489	.288	28.8	2.1	76-C -10
2009	MIL	MLB	23	521	62	31	2	13	59	37	91	4	2	-0.5	.280	.333	.433	.282	.331	.446	.265	21.6	2.4	123-C -13

Breakout: 29%   Improve: 41%   Collapse: 15%   Attrition: 8%   Comparables: Brook Fordyce, Ivan Rodriguez, Adam Brown, Ron Jones

Salome began the year by serving the tail end of a 50-game suspension for a positive test for performance-enhancing drugs and ended it by confirming his spot among the game's top catching prospects. The squat fireplug—a

Bronx-raised Dominican drafted in the fourth round in 2005 and nicknamed "Pocket Pudge"—won the Southern League batting title while reassuring scouts that a catcher of his unique build could survive and thrive behind the plate. Defensively, Salome gets high marks for his mobility as well as his arm strength, but his footwork, blocking skills, and game-calling all need improvement. He'll start the year in Triple-A and may well get a chance to demonstrate whether he's ready to succeed Kendall as the starter.

Rickie Weeks 2B

Bats: R   Throws: R   Height: 6' 0"   Weight: 205   Born: September 13, 1982   Age: 26

YEAR	TEAM	LVL	AGE	PA	R	2B	3B	HR	RBI	BB	SO	SB	CS	EqBRR	AVG	OBP	SLG	EqAVG	EqOBP	EqSLG	EqA	VORP	WARP	DEFENSE	
2006	MIL	MLB	23	413	73	15	3	8	34	30	92	19	5	1.6	.279	.363	.404	.282	.362	.414	.276	17.9	1.7	90-2B	-4
2007	MIL	MLB	24	506	87	21	6	16	36	78	116	25	2	5.2	.235	.374	.433	.231	.375	.435	.291	26.6	2.1	110-2B	-13
2008	MIL	MLB	25	560	89	22	7	14	46	66	115	19	5	5.0	.234	.342	.398	.238	.345	.414	.268	13.8	2.8	118-2B	4
2009	MIL	MLB	26	594	94	28	5	17	59	72	121	20	6	3.0	.269	.373	.442	.271	.371	.455	.287	34.3	4.4	139-2B	3

Breakout: 30%   Improve: 66%   Collapse: 9%   Attrition: 5%   Comparables: Robby Thompson, Bump Wills, Joe Foy, Bobby Crosby

On the surface, 2008 appears to have been another disappointing season from Weeks as he dealt with injuries, but there is a messier reality. The knee sprain that sent him to the DL in June doesn't explain away his awful first-half showing (.217/.320/.367), and the thumb sprain that briefly sidelined him in mid-August didn't prevent a robust late-season performance (.253/.387/.471) over the season's final six weeks. The latter was actually abetted by mid-season acquisition Ray Durham, who started 12 of the team's final 22 games, all against righties. Weeks hit just .227/.319/.391 against righties last year, compared with .250/.391/.414 against lefties, a split that's persisted throughout his career and that crystallizes the true source of frustration with his development: he ought to be more than a lefty-masher at his age and with his gifts. There's a line of thinking that shifting him to center to make room for Escobar could aid his development while helping the team, but his keystone defense did improve last year, and the Brewers rose from 13th in the league to fourth in their percentage of double-play opportunities turned. Weeks is an enigma, but he retains enough value as it is to be a modest asset, and enough upside to be far more than that.

PITCHERS

Zach Braddock

Bats: L   Throws: L   Height: 6' 4"   Weight: 230   Born: August 23, 1987   Age: 21

YEAR	TEAM	LVL	AGE	W	L	SV	G	GS	IP	H	BB	SO	HR	GB%	BABIP	STUFF	WHIP	ERA	DERA	EqH9	EqBB9	EqSO9	EqHR9	DEF	VORP	SN/WX
2006	HEL	Rk	18	2	2	0	14	8	39¹	32	31	30	3	46.9%	.269	-31	1.61	5.52	12.09	11.8	10.4	2.2	2.5	4	-23.1	—
2007	WVA	A	19	3	1	0	10	9	47	28	15	68	1	44.4%	.276	42	0.91	1.15	3.67	8.2	4.1	7.3	0.6	6	8.9	—
2008	BRV	A+	20	4	7	0	21	11	65¹	55	42	80	7	34.9%	.308	0	1.49	5.51	9.78	10.9	7.1	6.8	2.3	2	-26.9	—
2009	MIL	MLB	21	3	6	0	24	12	71	80	60	67	13	41.0%	.330	2	1.96	7.19	7.49	10.2	6.2	7.2	1.6	1	-13.4	-0.92

Breakout: 24%   Improve: 64%   Collapse: 11%   Attrition: 13%   Comparables: Alexander Smit, Mike Megrew, Bill Cutshall, Terrell Wade

The grandson of "Cinderella Man" boxer Jim Braddock was dogged by arm troubles for the second year in a row, so he was kept on a short leash, pitching out of the bullpen in August after he returned from the DL. He had no problem missing bats in either role, but his walk rate was, shall we say, extreme. Braddock's fastball only sits in the low 90s, but his delivery is sneaky fast and his slider is sharp. Obviously, he'll need to improve his command as he jumps to Double-A, but the stuff is there.

David Bush

Bats: R   Throws: R   Height: 6' 2"   Weight: 210   Born: November 9, 1979   Age: 29

YEAR	TEAM	LVL	AGE	W	L	SV	G	GS	IP	H	BB	SO	HR	GB%	BABIP	STUFF	WHIP	ERA	DERA	EqH9	EqBB9	EqSO9	EqHR9	DEF	VORP	SN/WX
2006	MIL	MLB	26	12	11	0	34	32	210	201	38	166	26	48.7%	.289	19	1.14	4.41	4.66	8.2	1.4	6.5	1.0	9	30.6	3.99
2007	MIL	MLB	27	12	10	0	33	31	186¹	217	44	134	27	45.6%	.324	8	1.40	5.12	3.98	9.6	1.8	6.0	1.2	-16	12.4	2.66
2008	MIL	MLB	28	9	10	0	31	29	185	163	48	109	29	42.7%	.239	-2	1.14	4.18	4.69	7.9	2.0	4.7	1.4	9	25.8	3.79
2009	MIL	MLB	29	9	8	0	24	24	145	150	37	95	19	45.0%	.290	12	1.29	4.27	4.57	9.4	1.9	4.9	1.2	1	19.4	3.16

Breakout: 9%   Improve: 37%   Collapse: 29%   Attrition: 21%   Comparables: James Baldwin, Bobby Jones, Bill Wegman, Rick Langford

Bush's 2008 performance was really a tale of two seasons. Early mechanical struggles led to a brief exile to the bullpen and even a trip to Nashville; through May 22 he made just two quality starts out of eight (6.56 ERA, 4.6 K/9, 3.5 BB/9). Luckily, he turned things around, making 13 out of 21 quality starts with a 3.38 ERA, 5.5 K/9, and 2.0 BB/9. Don't take his tidy ERA as evidence that he's finally pitching up to characteristically strong peripherals; his already-problematic home-run rate soared, and his strikeout and walk numbers deteriorated. What changed was the defense behind him. Bush's BABIP dropped 85 points to an unsustainably low .238. He's a solid innings-eater, but when his luck evens out, next year's numbers might look more like 2007's than 2008's.

Chris Capuano

Bats: L   Throws: L   Height: 6′ 2″   Weight: 220   Born: August 19, 1978   Age: 30

YEAR	TEAM	LVL	AGE	W	L	SV	G	GS	IP	H	BB	SO	HR	GB%	BABIP	STUFF	WHIP	ERA	DERA	EqH9	EqBB9	EqSO9	EqHR9	DEF	VORP	SN/WX
2006	MIL	MLB	27	11	12	0	34	34	221¹	229	47	174	29	41.5%	.303	18	1.25	4.03	3.74	8.8	1.6	6.4	1.0	-5	40.6	4.79
2007	MIL	MLB	28	5	12	0	29	25	150	170	54	132	20	45.1%	.339	14	1.49	5.10	3.96	9.3	2.8	7.3	1.1	-17	5.7	2.01
2009	MIL	MLB	30	4	4	0	17	9	66¹	68	21	55	8	43.0%	.300	14	1.33	4.28	4.55	9.2	2.3	6.3	1.1	1	10.2	1.25

Breakout: 12%   Improve: 27%   Collapse: 47%   Attrition: 31%   Comparables: Joe Gibbon, Bob Kuzava, Don Mossi, Bill Henry

After Capuano closed 2007 on an extended bum note—a 6.08 ERA over his final 22 appearances, all Brewer losses—his luck didn't get much better in 2008. Soon after releasing Claudio Vargas, the Brewers discovered Capuano's torn ulnar collateral ligament. After two months of rehab, Capuano submitted to his second Tommy John surgery (his first was in 2002) and, barring complications, should be back with the Brewers midsummer. At anywhere near his 2005-2006 level, he'd be a boon to the rotation, but at his 2007 level, not so much. After the obligatory nontender in December, the Brewers re-signed him to a minor league deal.

Todd Coffey

Bats: R   Throws: R   Height: 6′ 5″   Weight: 255   Born: September 9, 1980   Age: 28

YEAR	TEAM	LVL	AGE	W	L	SV	G	GS	IP	H	BB	SO	HR	GB%	BABIP	STUFF	WHIP	ERA	DERA	EqH9	EqBB9	EqSO9	EqHR9	DEF	VORP	SN/WX
2006	CIN	MLB	25	6	7	8	81	0	78	85	26	60	7	51.8%	.321	6	1.42	3.46	2.77	9.3	2.7	6.3	0.7	-4	19.7	2.49
2007	LOU	AAA	26	2	0	1	19	0	27	17	5	25	0	56.3%	.254	7	0.81	1.33	3.81	6.2	1.7	5.5	0.3	5	5.2	—
2007	CIN	MLB	26	2	1	0	58	0	51	70	19	43	12	58.9%	.358	-12	1.75	5.82	3.81	11.2	2.8	6.9	1.9	-9	-2.0	-0.58
2008	CIN	MLB	27	0	0	0	17	0	19¹	25	6	8	4	56.9%	.318	-25	1.60	6.06	4.19	10.7	2.3	3.3	1.9	-2	-0.6	-0.01
2008	LOU	AAA	27	3	3	2	34	0	39¹	49	15	43	4	56.0%	.387	-15	1.63	4.35	5.35	13.1	3.9	6.6	1.5	-4	1.0	—
2008	MIL	MLB	27	1	0	0	9	0	7¹	6	2	7	0	65.0%	.316	7	1.09	0.00	0.00	7.7	2.6	7.7	0.0	-1	4.6	0.45
2009	MIL	MLB	28	2	2	1	38	0	39¹	42	16	30	4	54.0%	.320	3	1.48	4.21	4.55	9.7	3.0	5.9	0.9	0	5.1	0.45

Breakout: 16%   Improve: 44%   Collapse: 28%   Attrition: 35%   Comparables: Antonio Alfonseca, J.J. Putz, Adrian Devine, Esteban Yan

Free coffee can be a mixed blessing; you never know if it's the requisite octane level or how long it's been sitting on the burner. As for a free Coffey, the Brewers were in no position to complain when they claimed him on waivers from the Reds in early September. He'd emerged as a reliable reliever in 2006, but quickly returned to mediocrity, thanks to a Gap-induced gopher problem; nine of his 12 homers allowed in 2007 came at home, and continued problems with the long ball led the Reds to farm him out most of the summer. Milwaukee picked him up for the stretch run, despite his postseason ineligibility, and Coffey responded with a handful of spotless appearances. Freed from Cincy's bandbox and blessed with a legitimate defense behind him, he can be a useful part of the 2009 bullpen.

Mark DiFelice

Bats: R   Throws: R   Height: 6′ 2″   Weight: 190   Born: August 23, 1976   Age: 32

YEAR	TEAM	LVL	AGE	W	L	SV	G	GS	IP	H	BB	SO	HR	GB%	BABIP	STUFF	WHIP	ERA	DERA	EqH9	EqBB9	EqSO9	EqHR9	DEF	VORP	SN/WX
2007	HUN	AA	30	6	1	0	26	3	66²	50	6	60	3	44.3%	.264	4	0.84	1.62	3.79	8.3	1.2	5.0	0.9	8	12.4	—
2007	NAS	AAA	30	4	2	0	10	10	58	45	9	63	6	42.4%	.278	20	0.93	3.10	4.37	7.9	1.6	7.3	1.1	3	7.6	—
2008	NAS	AAA	31	5	1	0	13	12	64¹	50	8	65	5	38.1%	.271	17	0.90	3.22	4.35	7.7	1.3	6.2	0.9	1	8.6	—
2008	MIL	MLB	31	1	0	0	15	0	19	17	4	20	4	27.8%	.260	11	1.11	2.84	4.26	8.1	1.4	8.1	1.9	2	5.0	0.23
2009	MIL	MLB	32	5	5	2	41	9	92	90	20	75	14	38.0%	.280	9	1.19	3.99	4.21	8.8	1.6	6.2	1.3	1	17.0	1.92

Breakout: 10%   Improve: 29%   Collapse: 38%   Attrition: 30%   Comparables: Bret Saberhagen, Hideki Irabu, Scott Sanderson, Tom Sturdivant

A 15th-round pick by the Rockies back in 1998, DiFelice slogged through nine minor league seasons—including a 2005-2006 detour in the indie leagues—before joining the Brewers' chain. A cutter developed in the Atlantic League under the guidance of manager Sparky Lyle triggered eye-popping strikeout/walk ratios, and DiFelice's persever-ance was finally rewarded with a taste of "The Show." Though confined to low-leverage duty, he pitched well enough in two stints with the Brewers to merit a further look, particularly on a staff that spent $14 million on Gagné and Riske, whose injuries DiFelice helped cover for. He should be in the mix for a spot this spring.

Tim Dillard

Bats: S **Throws: R** **Height: 6' 4"** **Weight: 228** **Born: July 19, 1983** **Age: 25**

YEAR	TEAM	LVL	AGE	W	L	SV	G	GS	IP	H	BB	SO	HR	GB%	BABIP	STUFF	WHIP	ERA	DERA	EqH9	EqBB9	EqSO9	EqHR9	DEF	VORP	SN/WX
2006	HUN	AA	22	10	7	0	29	25	163²	167	36	108	10	54.9%	.301	-6	1.24	3.14	6.38	10.6	2.2	3.3	1.1	6	-13.6	—
2007	NAS	AAA	23	8	4	0	34	16	133	167	37	62	13	54.9%	.341	-25	1.53	4.74	5.62	12.9	2.9	2.8	1.2	0	-0.3	—
2008	NAS	AAA	24	6	1	2	37	0	63¹	57	28	55	5	57.5%	.299	-10	1.34	1.99	4.01	9.0	4.0	5.3	0.9	2	10.7	—
2008	MIL	MLB	24	0	0	0	13	0	14¹	17	6	5	2	44.4%	.294	-35	1.60	4.41	7.53	10.7	3.1	2.5	1.3	0	-2.8	0.28
2009	MIL	MLB	25	3	3	1	45	3	53¹	63	24	30	6	51.0%	.310	-9	1.62	5.34	5.74	10.7	3.3	4.2	1.1	1	0.3	0.13

Breakout: 17% Improve: 48% Collapse: 25% Attrition: 16%   Comparables: Lee Marshall, Rocky Childress, Steven Connelly, Greg Everson

A 2002 draft-and-follow—as a catcher—this son of former major league infielder Steve Dillard has seen his stock as a prospect fall in recent years. He's a sinkerballer who generates ground balls galore, but his mediocre secondary of-ferings made him all too hittable. A full-time shift to the bullpen helped him miss more bats, and like DiFelice, he wound up serving a couple of stints with the big club, first in May, when the injury bug bit, and again in September once rosters expanded. The Brewers could use a double-play specialist in their bullpen, but it remains to be seen whether Dillard has the stuff to succeed in that role.

Evan Frederickson

Bats: L **Throws: L** **Height: 6' 6"** **Weight: 240** **Born: September 23, 1986** **Age: 22**

YEAR	TEAM	LVL	AGE	W	L	SV	G	GS	IP	H	BB	SO	HR	GB%	BABIP	STUFF	WHIP	ERA	DERA	EqH9	EqBB9	EqSO9	EqHR9	DEF	VORP	SN/WX
2008	HEL	Rk	21	0	0	0	3	3	11²	13	5	16	1	71.0%	.429	-10	1.54	3.08	10.00	18.0	7.0	5.0	3.0	0	-4.4	—
2008	WVA	A	21	0	1	0	9	4	20¹	16	26	18	1	48.1%	.294	-7	2.07	6.21	12.94	10.7	17.4	3.9	1.1	1	-13.0	—
2009	MIL	MLB	22	3	9	0	31	19	98	128	102	60	17	48.0%	.340	-20	2.35	8.92	9.46	11.8	7.7	4.6	1.6	1	-35.5	-3.36

Breakout: 0% Improve: 0% Collapse: 0% Attrition: 0%   Comparables: Dennis Gray, Matt Young, Dave Kopf, Ryan Mills

A 2008 supplemental first-round pick out of the University of San Francisco, Frederickson is a big lefty who offers uncommon velocity for a southpaw—his fastball sits in the low 90s and touches 94-95 mph—as well as a good slider. Alas, his command is a bit lacking, and his low three-quarters delivery is a mess; he's experienced bouts of Blass-like wildness both in college and in the minors. He also threw 10 wild pitches in his Low-A stint, including five in his first outing and three in his third. As unsettling as all that was, at least he closed the year with four good relief appearances in five outings.

Eric Gagné

Bats: R **Throws: R** **Height: 6' 0"** **Weight: 240** **Born: January 7, 1976** **Age: 33**

YEAR	TEAM	LVL	AGE	W	L	SV	G	GS	IP	H	BB	SO	HR	GB%	BABIP	STUFF	WHIP	ERA	DERA	EqH9	EqBB9	EqSO9	EqHR9	DEF	VORP	SN/WX
2007	TEX	MLB	31	2	0	16	34	0	33¹	23	12	29	2	41.8%	.236	8	1.02	2.16	3.55	6.0	3.0	6.8	0.5	5	14.4	2.78
2007	BOS	MLB	31	2	2	0	20	0	18²	26	9	22	1	36.2%	.439	11	1.88	6.74	3.57	13.8	4.1	9.7	0.5	-5	-1.3	-1.40
2008	MIL	MLB	32	4	3	10	50	0	46¹	46	22	38	11	36.6%	.271	-20	1.47	5.44	5.76	9.1	3.8	6.6	2.0	3	1.1	0.19
2009	MIL	MLB	33	2	3	5	39	0	44¹	44	20	40	6	40.0%	.300	3	1.45	4.67	4.93	9.0	3.4	6.8	1.3	0	4.0	0.38

Breakout: 23% Improve: 50% Collapse: 27% Attrition: 34%   Comparables: Terry Mathews, Dan Miceli, Ricky Bottalico, Aurelio Lopez

Francisco Cordero's departure led the Brewers to venture into high-risk, high-reward territory by waving off Gagné's dismal Boston performance and signing him to a one-year, $10 million deal to close for them. The bad omens began on Opening Day, when Gagné blew a save, surrendering a three-run homer to Kosuke Fukudome. He blew four more saves before going on the DL in late May with a 6.98 ERA and rotator cuff tendonitis. When he returned six weeks later, it was in a setup role, and at the very least, the hemorrhaging stopped—Gagné put up a 4.33 ERA the rest of the way, with a 20/6 K/BB ratio. At this point, he's now had four seasons of shaky health; he may be worth an incentive-based gamble, but paying top dollar to entrust him with the closer's job is foolish.

Yovani Gallardo

Bats: R Throws: R Height: 6' 1" Weight: 210 Born: February 27, 1986 Age: 23

YEAR	TEAM	LVL	AGE	W	L	SV	G	GS	IP	H	BB	SO	HR	GB%	BABIP	STUFF	WHIP	ERA	DERA	EqH9	EqBB9	EqSO9	EqHR9	DEF	VORP	SN/WX
2006	BRV	A+	20	6	3	0	13	13	77^1	54	23	103	4	58.8%	.298	40	1.00	2.10	5.00	9.2	3.8	7.1	1.3	1	4.6	—
2006	HUN	AA	20	5	2	0	13	13	77	50	28	85	2	42.6%	.268	48	1.01	1.64	4.65	7.4	3.6	6.4	0.5	10	7.6	—
2007	NAS	AAA	21	8	3	0	13	13	77^2	53	28	110	4	44.0%	.295	57	1.04	2.90	3.98	7.4	3.4	9.5	0.6	3	13.4	—
2007	MIL	MLB	21	9	5	0	20	17	110^1	103	37	101	8	40.2%	.305	47	1.27	3.67	3.85	7.6	2.6	7.5	0.6	3	24.7	3.85
2008	NAS	AAA	22	0	1	0	3	3	15^2	20	5	18	2	35.6%	.419	14	1.59	5.16	5.27	14.5	3.3	7.9	1.3	-1	0.5	—
2008	MIL	MLB	22	0	0	0	4	4	24	22	8	20	3	38.6%	.302	23	1.25	1.88	1.99	8.7	2.8	7.1	1.2	0	10.4	1.21
2009	MIL	MLB	23	5	5	1	29	11	84	76	33	84	9	43.0%	.300	21	1.30	3.73	3.98	8.2	2.9	7.5	0.9	1	17.4	2.07

Breakout: 5% Improve: 25% Collapse: 50% Attrition: 25%   Comparables: Bob Welch, Danny Frisella, Bob Anderson, Dennis Martinez

Poised to build on his tantalizing 2007 debut and form a strong one-two punch atop the rotation with Ben Sheets, Gallardo tore up a knee shortly after pitchers and catchers reported, underwent arthroscopic surgery, and didn't make his first start until April 20. Less than two weeks later, he completely tore his right ACL via a collision with the Cubs' Reed Johnson in an apparently season-ending injury. Undeterred, Gallardo became the first player to return from such an injury in-season, a result owing at least as much to Milwaukee's crack medical squad and the state of the science as to his dogged rehab efforts; note that Milton Bradley's recovery from off-season ACL surgery was actually faster. With Sheets ailing, Gallardo made a four-inning start on September 25 and then two appearances in the Division Series. Though it was mostly a lost season, Gallardo remains more than capable of resuming his projected career path to the front end of a rotation.

Jeremy Jeffress

Bats: R Throws: R Height: 6' 0" Weight: 175 Born: September 21, 1987 Age: 21

YEAR	TEAM	LVL	AGE	W	L	SV	G	GS	IP	H	BB	SO	HR	GB%	BABIP	STUFF	WHIP	ERA	DERA	EqH9	EqBB9	EqSO9	EqHR9	DEF	VORP	SN/WX
2006	BRR	Rk	18	2	5	0	13	4	33	30	25	37	0	68.0%	.316	-14	1.67	6.00	13.21	11.5	8.9	3.2	0.9	0	-26.5	—
2007	WVA	A	19	9	5	0	18	18	86^1	62	44	95	8	45.2%	.263	-1	1.23	3.13	7.43	9.3	6.2	5.2	2.0	3	-15.5	—
2008	BRV	A+	20	4	6	0	15	14	79^1	65	41	102	5	53.9%	.333	27	1.34	4.09	7.27	10.6	6.0	7.4	1.6	1	-12.9	—
2008	HUN	AA	20	2	1	0	4	4	14^2	17	11	13	2	37.8%	.357	1	1.90	5.51	7.11	14.9	7.8	5.0	2.1	-1	-2.1	—
2009	MIL	MLB	21	5	9	0	21	21	112^2	116	79	107	14	48.0%	.320	16	1.73	5.86	6.24	9.3	5.2	7.2	1.1	1	-5.5	0.30

Breakout: 44% Improve: 72% Collapse: 4% Attrition: 15%   Comparables: Dody Rather, Clint Zavaras, Bill Mooneyham, Scott Scudder

The Brewers' top pitching prospect and their first-round pick from 2006, Jeffress began the year serving a six-week suspension for marijuana use. Upon returning, he stayed out of trouble—alleviating concerns about his makeup—and showed amazing raw stuff, blowing Florida State League hitters away with a fastball that touches triple digits and sits at 95-97 and a plus power curve. Jeffress's control and command still have a ways to go, but he's back on the right path and will return to Huntsville to continue his quest toward being a frontline big-league starter.

Seth McClung

Bats: R Throws: R Height: 6' 6" Weight: 260 Born: February 7, 1981 Age: 28

YEAR	TEAM	LVL	AGE	W	L	SV	G	GS	IP	H	BB	SO	HR	GB%	BABIP	STUFF	WHIP	ERA	DERA	EqH9	EqBB9	EqSO9	EqHR9	DEF	VORP	SN/WX
2006	DUR	AAA	25	1	0	5	14	0	16^1	16	2	26	1	35.0%	.385	16	1.12	2.24	3.45	10.9	1.7	10.3	1.1	-1	3.8	—
2007	DUR	AAA	26	1	5	5	40	0	58^2	38	43	68	3	50.4%	.259	9	1.38	1.99	4.58	7.4	7.0	7.4	0.8	6	6.2	—
2007	NAS	AAA	26	2	0	0	5	3	19	14	5	25	2	50.0%	.293	18	1.00	1.42	3.06	8.2	2.5	9.2	1.0	2	5.0	—
2007	MIL	MLB	26	0	1	0	14	0	12	11	5	11	0	55.9%	.333	7	1.33	3.75	5.40	7.7	3.1	7.7	0.0	-1	-1.1	0.00
2008	MIL	MLB	27	6	6	0	37	12	105^1	93	55	87	10	47.6%	.290	6	1.41	4.02	3.77	8.3	4.1	6.7	0.8	0	19.7	2.16
2009	MIL	MLB	28	4	4	1	31	7	66^2	64	35	58	7	45.0%	.300	7	1.48	4.51	4.84	8.7	3.9	6.6	0.9	1	7.7	0.91

Breakout: 20% Improve: 41% Collapse: 39% Attrition: 40%   Comparables: Steve Renko, Jeff Robinson, Jim Gott, Stan Williams

McClung didn't break out to the extent that the man he was traded for (Grant Balfour) did, but he turned into a pretty useful swingman for a guy who entered the year with a lifetime 6.15 ERA. As a reliever, McClung pitched mainly in low-leverage spots and lost causes; as a starter, he replaced Villanueva in late May and posted a respectable 4.24 ERA over an 11-start span, five of them quality starts. He returned to relief when Ned Yost scrapped a short-lived "rotation platoon" aimed at pitching Bush at home, and put up a 1.10 ERA in some meaningful September innings. McClung could crack the rotation or draw consideration for a late-inning relief role, though he'll have to overcome the departure of coach Mike Maddux, who helped iron out his mechanics and his ever-shaky control.

Guillermo Mota

| | | | | | | | | Bats: R | | Throws: R | | Height: 6' 6" | | Weight: 210 | | Born: July 25, 1973 | | | Age: 35 |

YEAR	TEAM	LVL	AGE	W	L	SV	G	GS	IP	H	BB	SO	HR	GB%	BABIP	STUFF	WHIP	ERA	DERA	EqH9	EqBB9	EqSO9	EqHR9	DEF	VORP	SN/WX
2006	CLE	MLB	32	1	3	0	34	0	37²	45	19	27	9	29.9%	.313	-24	1.70	6.21	6.21	10.0	4.3	5.7	1.9	-1	-1.6	-0.17
2006	NYN	MLB	32	3	0	0	18	0	18	10	5	19	2	47.7%	.190	18	0.83	1.00	2.00	5.0	2.0	8.5	1.0	2	10.0	0.82
2007	NYN	MLB	33	2	2	0	52	0	59¹	63	18	47	8	44.8%	.299	-3	1.37	5.77	5.49	9.2	2.4	6.5	1.0	0	-0.9	-0.41
2008	MIL	MLB	34	5	6	1	58	0	57	52	28	50	7	46.7%	.290	-3	1.40	4.11	4.69	8.6	3.9	7.1	1.1	3	7.8	0.43
2009	LAN	MLB	35	2	2	2	42	0	48²	49	21	38	6	43.0%	.290	-0	1.43	4.52	4.88	9.1	3.3	6.0	1.1	-0	3.8	0.34

Breakout: 20%   Improve: 39%   Collapse: 33%   Attrition: 32%   Comparables: Tanyon Sturtze, Stan Bahnsen, Roger Mason, Rick White

Acquired from the Mets for the similarly unpopular Johnny Estrada, Mota regained some of his former effectiveness, thanks to a mechanical tweak: bullpen coach Bill Castro noted he had resorted to hunching over during his delivery, causing his pitches to flatten out. The results of the correction were compelling, save for a five-week stretch prior to the All-Star break in which Mota resorted to his old habits and was bombed for an 11.81 ERA while allowing five homers in 10⅔ innings. Over the rest of the year, he put up a 2.43 ERA while allowing just two homers. Whether he can maintain consistency across a full season is anyone's guess, but as long as he has that mid-90s fastball, somebody will pay to find out.

Jake Odorizzi

| | | | | | | | | Bats: R | | Throws: R | | Height: 6' 2" | | Weight: 175 | | Born: March 27, 1990 | | | Age: 19 |

YEAR	TEAM	LVL	AGE	W	L	SV	G	GS	IP	H	BB	SO	HR	GB%	BABIP	STUFF	WHIP	ERA	DERA	EqH9	EqBB9	EqSO9	EqHR9	DEF	VORP	SN/WX
2008	BRR	Rk	18	1	2	0	11	4	20²	18	9	19	2	43.8%	.262	-28	1.30	3.48	8.00	13.0	6.5	2.5	5.0	0	-4.8	—
2009	MIL	MLB	19	3	11	0	23	23	103²	149	80	45	31	46.0%	.320	-23	2.21	9.19	9.46	13.0	5.7	3.3	2.7	1	-38.9	-3.51

Breakout: 0%   Improve: 0%   Collapse: 0%   Attrition: 0%   Comparables: Mike Henry, Jacob Brigham, Brian Edmondson, Wayne Dotson

A supplementary first-round 2008 pick out of an Illinois high school, Odorizzi is extremely athletic and projectable. His fastball sits in the low 90s while touching 94, but his secondary stuff remains a bit raw—not exactly a revelation among 18-year-old pitchers. He had a bit of trouble throwing strikes during his brief pro debut, but his command and control earned high marks prior to the draft. He'll start the year at Low-A Wisconsin.

Manny Parra

| | | | | | | | | Bats: L | | Throws: L | | Height: 6' 3" | | Weight: 200 | | Born: October 30, 1982 | | | Age: 26 |

YEAR	TEAM	LVL	AGE	W	L	SV	G	GS	IP	H	BB	SO	HR	GB%	BABIP	STUFF	WHIP	ERA	DERA	EqH9	EqBB9	EqSO9	EqHR9	DEF	VORP	SN/WX
2006	BRV	A+	23	1	3	0	15	14	54²	47	32	61	4	53.1%	.319	-11	1.46	2.99	7.85	11.1	7.1	5.7	1.7	0	-11.8	—
2006	HUN	AA	23	3	0	0	6	6	31²	26	8	29	0	54.0%	.370	12	1.09	2.88	4.45	9.5	2.5	5.4	0.3	-3	3.6	—
2007	HUN	AA	24	7	3	0	13	13	80²	70	26	81	2	48.7%	.315	13	1.19	2.68	4.82	9.8	3.3	5.5	0.5	4	6.5	—
2007	NAS	AAA	24	3	1	0	4	4	26	15	7	25	1	47.1%	.230	21	0.85	1.73	3.91	5.7	2.5	6.4	0.4	4	4.8	—
2007	MIL	MLB	24	0	1	0	9	2	26¹	25	12	26	1	36.8%	.338	19	1.41	3.76	3.67	7.7	3.3	8.0	0.3	-1	4.3	-0.10
2008	MIL	MLB	25	10	8	0	32	29	166	181	75	147	18	53.7%	.335	12	1.54	4.39	4.07	10.1	3.5	7.1	0.9	-10	14.3	2.98
2009	MIL	MLB	26	8	8	0	23	23	136¹	136	62	111	12	50.0%	.300	18	1.45	4.40	4.74	9.0	3.4	6.2	0.8	1	15.1	2.69

Breakout: 12%   Improve: 41%   Collapse: 22%   Attrition: 18%   Comparables: Joe Saunders, Matt Young, Darren Oliver, Zane Smith

Since lefties who throw in the low to mid-90s aren't exactly a dime a dozen, Parra was considered a promising prospect despite a history of shoulder woes. Making it through the season intact was a minor triumph, though the results weren't wholly positive: in-game stamina was an issue while averaging a staff-low 5.5 innings per start and yielding a .314/.373/.493 line to hitters after the third inning. He also ran out of gas down the stretch, putting up a 7.79 ERA in September. On the other hand, his strikeout rate was second only to Sabathia's among Brewer starters, and he was essentially a league-average pitcher despite a BABIP more than 30 points higher than the NL norm. His 32-inning increase from 2007 to 2008 puts him squarely in Verducci Effect territory, meaning that he may be in danger of underperforming again. But using him as a fifth starter, the Brewers could do far worse.

David Riske

Bats: R Throws: R Height: 6' 2" Weight: 180 Born: October 23, 1976 Age: 32

YEAR	TEAM	LVL	AGE	W	L	SV	G	GS	IP	H	BB	SO	HR	GB%	BABIP	STUFF	WHIP	ERA	DERA	EqH9	EqBB9	EqSO9	EqHR9	DEF	VORP	SN/WX
2006	BOS	MLB	29	0	1	0	8	0	9²	8	3	5	2	43.8%	.207	-15	1.14	3.71	5.40	6.3	2.7	3.6	1.8	2	2.6	-0.06
2006	CHA	MLB	29	1	1	0	33	0	34¹	32	14	23	4	36.7%	.272	-12	1.34	3.94	5.03	8.2	3.4	5.3	1.1	4	7.7	0.04
2007	KCA	MLB	30	1	4	4	65	0	69²	61	27	52	8	43.1%	.273	-4	1.26	2.45	3.03	7.6	3.3	5.9	1.1	4	27.8	1.10
2008	MIL	MLB	31	1	2	2	45	0	42¹	47	25	27	6	29.8%	.313	-19	1.70	5.32	5.88	10.2	4.6	5.2	1.3	4	1.5	0.55
2009	MIL	MLB	32	2	2	1	30	0	35²	37	18	26	5	40.0%	.290	-5	1.53	4.76	5.03	9.2	3.8	5.5	1.2	0	2.9	0.23

Breakout: 4% Improve: 19% Collapse: 62% Attrition: 37%   Comparables: Dyar Miller, Ricky Bottalico, Brian Boehringer, Felix Rodriguez

And the Milwaukee chapter's winner for groan-inducing pun of the year is the three-year, $13 million deal given to this reliever last winter: a Riske contract. Five straight seasons with ERAs under 4.00 made him seem like a fairly safe bet at the time, but Riske struggled with elbow woes, first serving a month-long DL stint due to a hyperextension and then being shut down in early September to remove a bone spur. The bum elbow compromised his command and velocity, so one shouldn't read too much into his declining peripherals beyond the fact that his numbers are generally all over the place, anyway. He should be ready to resume his role as an effective setup man.

C. C. Sabathia

Bats: L Throws: L Height: 6' 7" Weight: 290 Born: July 21, 1980 Age: 28

YEAR	TEAM	LVL	AGE	W	L	SV	G	GS	IP	H	BB	SO	HR	GB%	BABIP	STUFF	WHIP	ERA	DERA	EqH9	EqBB9	EqSO9	EqHR9	DEF	VORP	SN/WX
2006	CLE	MLB	25	12	11	0	28	28	192²	182	44	172	17	46.6%	.301	27	1.17	3.22	4.17	7.9	2.0	7.0	0.7	7	47.3	5.97
2007	CLE	MLB	26	19	7	0	34	34	241	238	37	209	20	47.6%	.316	29	1.14	3.21	3.19	8.9	1.3	7.0	0.8	-6	67.7	6.46
2008	CLE	MLB	27	6	8	0	18	18	122¹	117	34	123	13	46.4%	.317	26	1.23	3.83	3.84	8.6	2.3	8.1	1.0	0	25.5	3.07
2008	MIL	MLB	27	11	2	0	17	17	130²	106	25	128	6	52.6%	.291	45	1.00	1.65	2.74	7.6	1.5	7.9	0.4	8	51.9	5.61
2009	NYA	MLB	28	16	9	0	33	33	231	222	53	201	22	47.0%	.300	33	1.19	3.43	3.48	8.6	1.8	7.1	0.8	-2	48.0	7.02

Breakout: 8% Improve: 47% Collapse: 13% Attrition: 6%   Comparables: Don Drysdale, Steve Carlton, Roger Clemens, Frank Viola

After pitching deep into October the year before, the big man started slowly (13.50 ERA through four outings) and was traded to the Brewers as the Indians quickly faded. Like a cross between Hercules and Bob Gibson, Sabathia won his first nine NL decisions, cranking out a 1.43 ERA and eight innings per start, and then took his last three starts on three days' rest and tossed a complete game on the season's final day to clinch the wild card. His combined totals dominated the MLB leader board: first in starts, innings, complete games, and shutouts; second in strikeouts; fourth in ERA; fifh in K/9; and eighth in K/BB ratio. The Brewers made their best effort to retain him, but Sabathia couldn't resist the lure of big bucks in the big city: $161 million over seven years from the Yankees, with an opt-out after the first three. Critics may fear the way his unique physique could age, but Sabathia's athleticism and excellent conditioning habits count more than the prejudices about his bulk. Of more concern is how he'll hold up after logging 512⅔ innings (including playoffs) over the past two seasons.

R. J. Seidel

Bats: R Throws: R Height: 6' 5" Weight: 200 Born: September 3, 1987 Age: 21

YEAR	TEAM	LVL	AGE	W	L	SV	G	GS	IP	H	BB	SO	HR	GB%	BABIP	STUFF	WHIP	ERA	DERA	EqH9	EqBB9	EqSO9	EqHR9	DEF	VORP	SN/WX
2007	HEL	Rk	19	4	0	0	12	8	41	30	16	36	2	56.4%	.264	-1	1.12	3.07	7.71	9.5	5.9	3.1	1.5	0	-8.2	—
2008	WVA	A	20	9	5	0	26	25	121²	135	45	81	10	51.4%	.340	-22	1.48	4.51	7.94	13.7	5.1	2.6	1.9	-1	-27.1	—
2009	MIL	MLB	21	3	7	0	23	15	80	111	54	37	15	50.0%	.330	-17	2.05	7.96	8.38	12.5	5.0	3.5	1.7	1	-22.2	-1.78

Breakout: 15% Improve: 41% Collapse: 27% Attrition: 13%   Comparables: Brett Herbison, Michael Schlact, Carl Hanselman, Pedro Beato

Local ties and third-round money enabled the Brewers to convince this native of nearby LaCrosse—a 2006 draft-and-follow—to bypass a strong commitment to the University of Arkansas. Seidel is a sinkerballer who boasts a strong changeup and an advanced feel for pitching; as his big frame fills out, he's expected to add velocity. He struggled initially at West Virginia, with a 5.50 ERA before the break, but he missed more bats and got more help from his fielders to lower that to 3.68 after the break, allowing just two earned runs over his final five starts.

Ben Sheets

Bats: R Throws: R Height: 6' 1" Weight: 220 Born: July 18, 1978 Age: 30

YEAR	TEAM	LVL	AGE	W	L	SV	G	GS	IP	H	BB	SO	HR	GB%	BABIP	STUFF	WHIP	ERA	DERA	EqH9	EqBB9	EqSO9	EqHR9	DEF	VORP	SN/WX
2006	MIL	MLB	27	6	7	0	17	17	106	105	11	116	9	42.5%	.342	46	1.09	3.82	2.81	8.7	0.8	8.9	0.7	-10	23.8	3.18
2007	MIL	MLB	28	12	5	0	24	24	141¹	138	37	106	17	37.9%	.287	17	1.24	3.82	3.86	7.8	2.0	6.2	1.0	4	31.2	4.06
2008	MIL	MLB	29	13	9	0	31	31	198¹	181	47	158	17	42.9%	.285	25	1.15	3.09	3.20	8.3	1.8	6.4	0.7	-2	51.7	6.22
2009	MIL	MLB	30	11	8	0	27	27	173	168	44	134	21	43.0%	.280	19	1.22	3.77	4.03	8.8	1.9	5.9	1.1	2	32.2	4.81

Breakout: 0% Improve: 12% Collapse: 42% Attrition: 11% Comparables: Alex Fernandez, Jon Lieber, Ray Culp, Don Newcombe

In his walk year, Sheets made more starts and logged more innings than in any season since 2004. Furthermore, he lived up to his reputation as a frontline hurler, tossing a league-leading three shutouts and finishing in the NL top 10 in SNLVAR, ERA, walk rate, and strikeout-to-walk ratio. Unfortunately, he tore a flexor tendon in his elbow and was limited to just four innings after September 11, the time when the Brewers went into their tailspin. His timing was horrible, given his pending free agency; had he been hurt at the beginning of the year but healthy at the end, he might have snagged a Burnett-like deal. Instead, Christmas saw him unsigned and entertaining a fatal instinct flirtation with Texas, where pitchers go to die.

Brian Shouse

Bats: L Throws: L Height: 5' 11" Weight: 185 Born: September 26, 1968 Age: 40

YEAR	TEAM	LVL	AGE	W	L	SV	G	GS	IP	H	BB	SO	HR	GB%	BABIP	STUFF	WHIP	ERA	DERA	EqH9	EqBB9	EqSO9	EqHR9	DEF	VORP	SN/WX
2006	TEX	MLB	37	0	0	0	6	0	4¹	6	1	3	1	37.5%	.333	-12	1.62	4.19	4.15	12.5	2.1	6.2	2.1	0	1.0	-0.27
2006	MIL	MLB	37	1	3	2	59	0	34	34	17	20	3	53.2%	.292	-12	1.50	3.97	3.97	8.7	4.0	4.8	0.8	1	6.9	0.40
2007	MIL	MLB	38	1	1	1	73	0	47²	46	14	32	0	57.5%	.313	8	1.26	3.02	3.17	7.8	2.2	5.6	0.0	0	12.3	1.19
2008	MIL	MLB	39	5	1	2	69	0	51¹	46	14	33	5	63.0%	.265	-5	1.17	2.81	3.86	8.1	2.1	5.1	0.9	4	13.2	0.92
2009	MIL	MLB	40	1	1	1	30	0	27¹	30	10	17	3	54.0%	.310	-6	1.46	4.34	4.75	10.1	2.6	4.8	0.9	0	3.8	0.26

Breakout: 0% Improve: 8% Collapse: 72% Attrition: 52% Comparables: Mike Flanagan, Jeff Fassero, Gene Garber, Jerry Staley

One of the most cutting criticisms leveled at Ned Yost was for his slavish devotion to using this lefty specialist much too much, thereby cutting short his other relievers' appearances without significantly gaining the platoon advantage. Once again, Shouse wound up facing more righties (who touched him at a .301/.377/.452 clip) than lefties (.180/.196/.290), and once again, the Brewers wound up with a sub-.500 record in his appearances (34-35). Not surprisingly, Yost's overreliance on Shouse directly figured in his undoing: on September 14, in the third game of their four-game sweep at the hands of the Phillies, Yost had Shouse *intentionally walk* lefty Ryan Howard with a runner on second to face righty Pat Burrell and then left him in as Burrell singled and then Shane Victorino (batting righty, his stronger side) homered, turning a 3-3 tie into a 7-3 deficit. Yost was pink-slipped the next day. As for Shouse, he's a reasonably effective LOOGY who has carved a nice little niche for a guy who couldn't stick on a big-league roster until his age-34 season, but he's hardly sui generis.

Mitch Stetter

Bats: L Throws: L Height: 6' 4" Weight: 195 Born: January 16, 1981 Age: 280

YEAR	TEAM	LVL	AGE	W	L	SV	G	GS	IP	H	BB	SO	HR	GB%	BABIP	STUFF	WHIP	ERA	DERA	EqH9	EqBB9	EqSO9	EqHR9	DEF	VORP	SN/WX
2006	NAS	AAA	25	2	5	0	51	0	38	38	16	36	3	50.0%	.346	-16	1.42	4.50	5.80	10.9	4.0	6.1	1.0	0	-0.8	—
2007	NAS	AAA	26	1	0	1	24	0	14²	8	5	19	1	58.1%	.250	12	0.88	4.29	5.27	5.9	3.3	9.2	0.7	1	0.5	—
2007	MIL	MLB	26	1	0	0	6	0	5	2	2	4	0	41.7%	.182	5	0.80	3.60	5.40	3.6	3.6	7.2	0.0	1	1.3	0.08
2008	NAS	AAA	27	3	3	0	28	0	29	21	7	30	2	50.7%	.260	3	0.97	2.48	4.28	7.6	2.3	6.6	0.7	2	4.0	—
2008	MIL	MLB	27	3	1	0	30	0	25¹	14	19	31	2	42.1%	.231	22	1.30	3.20	3.28	5.5	5.8	9.9	0.7	0	7.0	0.65
2009	MIL	MLB	28	3	2	3	63	0	47²	42	25	48	4	44.0%	.290	11	1.38	3.86	4.15	7.9	3.8	7.6	0.8	0	8.8	0.77

Breakout: 21% Improve: 38% Collapse: 27% Attrition: 20% Comparables: Mike Mohler, Paul Assenmacher, Michael Wuertz, Paul Spoljaric

Beating the bushes as a lefty reliever is brief, glory-free work, but that has pretty much been Stetter's lot since the Brewers drafted him in the 16th round in 2003; coming into 2008, he'd totaled less than 300 minor league innings. After earning a September call-up in 2007, Stetter spent 2008 shuttling between Milwaukee and Nashville as the team's second lefty. Unlike Shouse, he held hitters on both sides of the plate in check, a minor trend that has persisted over the past two years. At the very least, he deserved better than pitching in so many lost causes; the Brewers were 10-20 in games in which he appeared. If Shouse moves on, Stetter may move up the pecking order, though he'll have to compete with R. J. Swindle.

Jeff Suppan

Bats: R   Throws: R   Height: 6' 2"   Weight: 220   Born: January 2, 1975   Age: 34

YEAR	TEAM	LVL	AGE	W	L	SV	G	GS	IP	H	BB	SO	HR	GB%	BABIP	STUFF	WHIP	ERA	DERA	EqH9	EqBB9	EqSO9	EqHR9	DEF	VORP	SN/WX
2006	SLN	MLB	31	12	7	0	32	32	190	207	69	104	21	47.5%	.299	2	1.45	4.12	4.65	9.6	2.8	4.5	0.9	6	26.1	4.30
2007	MIL	MLB	32	12	12	0	34	34	206²	243	68	114	18	47.8%	.329	10	1.50	4.62	4.21	9.6	2.5	4.6	0.7	-4	22.6	3.03
2008	MIL	MLB	33	10	10	0	31	31	177²	207	67	90	30	46.2%	.308	-19	1.54	4.96	5.62	10.8	3.0	4.2	1.5	8	3.1	2.58
2009	MIL	MLB	34	6	7	0	27	17	109²	125	38	61	14	46.0%	.300	-2	1.48	4.91	5.25	10.2	2.6	4.2	1.1	1	7.1	1.41

Breakout: 5%   Improve: 27%   Collapse: 41%   Attrition: 27%   Comparables: Walt Terrell, Aaron Sele, Pat Hentgen, Steve Trachsel

As the Brewers parted ways with Sabathia and Sheets, the $27 million still committed to Suppan through his 2011 buyout looked like an even worse investment than it did when the contract was inked. Suppan's low strikeout rate always portended the possibility of a performance like 2008's, but it was his sudden vulnerability to the long ball—posting his worst HR/9 since 2000—that did him in. His troubles worsened as the season went on and his velocity dropped. Through June, he'd put up a 4.05 ERA while allowing 0.9 homers and 5.1 strikeouts per nine; the rest of the way, his numbers deteriorated to a 5.98 ERA, 2.2 HR/9, and 3.9 K/9. Unless he can reverse those trends, this story won't end well.

Carlos Villanueva

Bats: R   Throws: R   Height: 6' 3"   Weight: 215   Born: November 28, 1983   Age: 25

YEAR	TEAM	LVL	AGE	W	L	SV	G	GS	IP	H	BB	SO	HR	GB%	BABIP	STUFF	WHIP	ERA	DERA	EqH9	EqBB9	EqSO9	EqHR9	DEF	VORP	SN/WX
2006	HUN	AA	22	4	5	0	11	10	62¹	60	14	59	6	48.6%	.303	-1	1.19	3.77	7.49	10.9	2.3	5.3	1.7	6	-12.1	—
2006	NAS	AAA	22	7	1	0	11	9	66²	42	26	61	6	41.4%	.210	15	1.03	2.72	5.17	6.9	3.7	5.9	1.1	11	3.0	—
2006	MIL	MLB	22	2	2	0	10	6	53²	43	11	39	8	44.7%	.230	23	1.01	3.69	4.00	6.7	1.7	5.8	1.2	4	14.0	1.40
2007	MIL	MLB	23	8	5	1	59	6	114¹	101	53	99	16	37.7%	.272	5	1.35	3.94	3.88	7.2	3.6	7.1	1.2	2	22.8	3.77
2008	MIL	MLB	24	4	7	1	47	9	108¹	112	30	93	18	48.8%	.303	-4	1.31	4.07	4.18	9.4	2.1	6.9	1.4	1	15.5	1.37
2009	MIL	MLB	25	5	5	2	41	7	85²	81	29	71	10	45.0%	.290	10	1.29	3.88	4.16	8.6	2.5	6.3	1.0	1	16.8	1.72

Breakout: 11%   Improve: 44%   Collapse: 25%   Attrition: 20%   Comparables: Esteban Yan, Rollie Fingers, Jeff Russell, Edgar Gonzalez

Villanueva split time between starting and relieving again, but this time around, his results were decidedly better as a reliever. He began the year in the rotation, but was rocked for a 6.43 ERA and 2.2 HR/9 through nine starts, four of them disasters and three quality starts. He found a groove upon moving into a middle relief role, often tossing multiple innings; his ERA dropped to 2.12 as his peripherals improved markedly: 0.9 HR/9 and a strikeout rate that rose from 5.6 as a starter to 9.4. The key was limiting hitters to one look at him. In their first PA, they hit .214/.276/.325, but thereafter, they seared him at a .369/.396/.681 clip. Not surprisingly, there's no talk about moving him back to the rotation.

LINEOUTS

Hitters

PLAYER	TEAM	LVL	AGE	PA	R	2B	3B	HR	RBI	BB	SO	SB-CS	EqBRR	AVG/OBP/SLG	EqAVG/EqOBP/EqSLG	EqA	VORP	WARP
SS B. Brewer	WVA	A	20	196	25	13	2	0	17	18	54	16-4	1.2	.213/.294/.310	.174/.246/.258	.180	-19.8	-1.2
•	BRV	A+	20	308	36	17	2	2	25	25	57	15-5	3.3	.251/.316/.349	.217/.272/.306	.208	-20.1	-1.1
CF C. Dykstra	HEL	Rk	19	166	24	9	0	5	17	21	30	4-4	-1.9	.271/.367/.438	.178/.247/.270	.171	-28.0	-2.2
1B C. Errecart	HUN	AA	23	411	57	22	1	15	46	33	109	1-2	-0.2	.247/.324/.439	.219/.278/.390	.230	-10.8	-2.8
OF L. Nix*	NAS	AAA	27	420	63	22	3	23	60	36	88	5-3	-1.4	.284/.348/.539	.227/.283/.426	.241	-3.9	-0.7
C L. Palmisano	BRV	A+	25	79	8	2	0	2	8	5	11	0-1	-1.9	.306/.367/.417	.230/.278/.324	.208	-4.2	-0.4
C M. Rivera	MIL	MLB	31	69	8	5	0	1	14	6	10	2-0	-0.1	.306/.377/.435	.306/.377/.419	.285	4.7	0.3
UT V. Rottino	NAS	AAA	28	477	59	30	3	7	55	31	72	9-4	-1.2	.260/.313/.392	.205/.250/.305	.194	-36.6	-3.1

The appropriately named **Brent Brewer** may have the highest ceiling of any player in the system, but he has yet to translate his outstanding athleticism and tools into the kind of on-field performance that suggests he can reach it. ⊘ Lenny's son **Cutter Dykstra** was the Brewers' second-round pick in the 2008 draft. He profiles as something of a right-handed version of the old man, a pesky hitter who works the count effectively, runs well, and plays with a max-effort style. ⊘ Prior to breaking a bone in his wrist in early July, **Chris Errecart** had restored some of the promise that led the Brewers to select him in the fifth round of the 2006 draft, hitting .291/.364/.519 for Huntsville. Alas, he returned too quickly and hit just .137/.224/.235 the rest of the way. ⊘ Bypassed during Cameron's suspension, **Laynce Nix** was consigned to Nashville for almost the entire season. There, he demonstrated his usual blend— some power, but only a dash of plate discipline, contact woes aplenty, and defense that may be slipping. ⊘ Once considered among the top catching prospects in the minors, **Lou Palmisano** had already seen his stock fall before he missed most of the season with a knee injury. The Orioles plucked him in the Rule Five draft and then traded him to the Astros, where he has at least a chance to figure into their wide-open catching situation. ⊘ **Mike Rivera** is the Maytag repairman of backup backstops, a lonely man because of starter Kendall's durability; Rivera is capable of a larger role, though he won't hit up to his 2008 level. ⊘ Racine's native son, utilityman **Vinny Rottino** has spent most of the last two years learning how to catch. The move hasn't done wonders for his hitting, but it may further his 25th-man aspirations.

Pitchers

PLAYER	TEAM	LVL	AGE	W	L	SV	IP	H	BB	SO	HR	GB%	BABIP	STUFF	WHIP	ERA	DERA	EqH9	EqBB9	EqSO9	EqHR9	DEF	VORP
O. Aguilar	BRV	A+	23	3	0	13	25²	13	10	25	0	42.6%	.220	-3	0.89	0.35	3.09	5.8	4.2	5.0	0.4	3	6.5
	HUN	AA	23	0	3	4	38	26	22	42	5	55.0%	.236	-15	1.26	3.08	7.30	8.0	5.1	6.3	1.9	-1	-7.0
B. Bramhall*	BRV	A+	22	5	4	1	111¹	91	32	106	5	45.0%	.289	-2	1.11	2.51	5.82	9.4	3.4	4.9	1.1	8	-2.5
C. Cody*	WVA	A	24	2	1	0	31	19	3	31	3	51.3%	.213	-1	0.71	1.74	5.08	7.6	1.6	4.4	1.9	4	1.6
	BRV	A+	24	4	5	0	83²	68	25	62	4	46.3%	.275	-12	1.11	1.83	5.45	9.1	3.6	3.6	1.2	16	1.3
L. Peña	NAS	AAA	25	2	3	15	49¹	54	47	49	4	49.0%	.365	-7	2.05	6.94	7.49	11.8	8.9	6.3	1.0	-4	-9.6
A. Periard	BRV	A+	21	9	6	0	112²	114	30	76	6	59.2%	.298	-5	1.28	3.51	6.45	10.9	3.1	3.0	1.2	-3	-9.9
	HUN	AA	21	2	4	0	38	42	16	20	3	48.1%	.317	-19	1.53	5.68	9.00	12.7	4.2	2.6	1.3	4	-12.8
C. Scarpetta	BRR	Rk	19	1	0	0	15²	8	8	27	0	56.0%	.320	12	1.02	0.57	2.25	9.8	8.2	7.5	0.8	0	4.5
	HEL	Rk	19	1	0	0	20²	18	8	31	2	52.2%	.372	7	1.26	3.48	7.88	14.6	6.2	6.2	2.8	0	-4.1
D. Turnbow	MIL	MLB	30	0	1	1	6¹	12	13	5	1	48.0%	.478	-12	3.95	15.71	12.79	18.5	15.6	5.7	1.4	-1	-6.9
	NAS	AAA	30	2	2	0	18	17	41	28	0	54.5%	.415	17	3.22	10.50	11.94	11.4	19.7	9.9	0.5	0	-12.2
N. Tyson	WVA	A	20	2	2	0	34	60	7	26	4	51.5%	.455	-23	1.97	8.74	9.32	22.8	3.2	3.2	2.6	-14	-11.6
	HEL	Rk	20	1	3	1	44	52	7	42	1	58.7%	.381	-1	1.34	3.48	7.12	15.5	3.2	2.9	1.0	0	-6.2

Omar Aguilar is a six-foot, 225-pound fireplug with mid-90s heat but violent mechanics, control problems, and secondary offerings that are a work in progress. ⊘ A 2007 18th-rounder out of Rice, **Bobby Bramhall** is an undersized lefty (5' 10", 170 lbs) with a high-80s fastball and a knee-buckling curve; after spending most of the year in the bullpen, he put up a 1.81 ERA and 40/5 K/BB ratio in 44⅔ innings as a starter late in the year. ⊘ A soft-tossing, undersized southpaw acquired from Detroit for Jose Capellan, **Chris Cody** puts up impressive numbers, but he's generally been old for his level. ⊘ **Luis Peña** can hit 99 on the gun, but an unsightly walk rate doomed his first taste of Triple-A; the Brewers like him as a bullpen arm, but he'll have to rediscover his control. ⊘ A groundballer whose fastball touches the mid-90s, **Alex Periard** was drafted as a 16-year-old out of Quebec and rewarded the Brewers' patience by reaching Double-A Huntsville at 21. ⊘ **Mark Rogers**, the Brewers' 2004 first-round pick, underwent surgery in June to remove scar tissue from his shoulder; he hasn't pitched in a game since mid-2006. The team nevertheless added him to the 40-man roster, so clearly they still think he has a future. ⊘ A torn finger tendon bumped **Cody Scarpetta** down to the 11th round in 2007; surgery cost him the season and additional bonus money while forcing the Brewers to protect him from the 2008 Rule 5 draft. His pro debut went well, as he missed plenty of bats with his low-90s fastball and power curve. ⊘ **Derrick Turnbow**'s fall from grace continued, as he pitched his way to the minors, still posted Dalkowskian strikeout and walk rates, and was finally discovered to have a slight tear in his rotator cuff, which he rehabbed without surgery. Signed by the Rangers on a minor league deal, they have to hope he doesn't do unto them what Gagné did unto Milwaukee. ⊘ A 2006 draft-and-follow who drew consideration as an outfielder as well, **Nick Tyson** is a pitch-to-contact type whose curve is considered the system's best—or it was, as he lost the feel for the pitch in Low-A before being demoted down to Helena.

MANAGER: NED YOST

YEAR	TEAM	W-L	Pythag +/-	Avg PC	100+ P	120+ P	QS	BQS	REL	REL w Zero R	IBB	Subs	PH	PH Avg	PH HR	SB2	CS2	SB3	CS3	SAC Att	SAC %	POS SAC	Squeeze	Swing	In Play
2006	MIL	75-87	5	94.6	67	3	77	13	427	257	34	20	235	.267	4	60	33	10	4	84	69.0%	20	1	134	96
2007	MIL	83-79	-1	94.1	56	3	75	12	492	305	37	50	253	.224	6	86	25	9	4	75	80.0%	22	1	125	100
2008	MIL	83-67	2	96.6	54	6	80	7	398	252	30	23	217	.208	7	85	27	20	7	68	67.6%	17	3	137	108

Yost went from potential Manager of the Year to former manager in the span of two weeks, a tumble that prevented him from entering October with many of the players whom he had first guided (to 68 wins) in 2003. One might presume such a dramatic reversal of fortune was precipitated by some fresh revelation of weakness, but the 3-11 start to September that sealed Yost's fate only intensified preexisting scrutiny of his tactical decisions. His periodic matchup miscues amounted to a relatively minor issue during seasons when no caliber of field generalship would have resulted in a playoff berth, but became an increasingly glaring fault as the marginal value of each Milwaukee win soared. Although Yost was better suited to a team in transition, Doug Melvin's postfiring endorsement of his former manager suggests that his historically late dismissal was less a commentary on his performance than an attempt to stave off a repeat of the 2007 collapse. Yost's in-house interim replacement, Dale Sveum, exuded calm and averted disaster in his 12-game stint, but Melvin chose to prioritize experience in his postseason search for a permanent successor, hiring former A's skipper Ken Macha, in whom Melvin had expressed interest prior to the 2003 season. Failures in clubhouse communication (some of them involving his once and future catcher, Jason Kendall) dogged Macha during his time in Oakland; Brewers fans will have to hope that his newfound autonomy doesn't prompt him to unleash a flurry of bunts signs restrained during four years under Billy Beane, on an unsuspecting National League.

Minnesota Twins

In 2007, the Twins finished 12th in the American League in runs scored, four games under .500, and 17 games out of first place in the AL Central. That winter, they lost their third-best hitter (who had been their most productive bat in '07) to free agency, and their fourth-best hitter lost much of the 2008 season to injury. Two high-profile attempts to trade pitching for hitting produced disappointing results, and the 2008 Twins wound up hitting fewer homers and stealing fewer bases (and at a lower success rate) than their punchless predecessors did. Yet, the 2008 Twins finished third in the American League in runs scored, sending 111 more men home than they had the year before, and got as far as a one-game playoff to determine the AL Central.

How did they do it? Luck would seem to have played a significant role. The Twins scored 829 runs in 2008, but their equivalent run total (derived from the component elements of run scoring such as hits, walks, steals, and outs) was just 764. That 65-run gap between the Twins' actual and equivalent runs totals was the largest in baseball; the only other team that came even close, the Red Sox, finished 55 runs *below* their equivalent run total. How does a team surpass its equivalent run total by so much? Whether you want to call it luck or timing, "it" was a key contributor, or, to use the baseball term for luck, "it" was clutch hitting. The Twins hit .279/.340/.408 as a team in 2008, but with men on base, they hit .298/.367/.443, and with runners in scoring position, they hit .305/.380/.446.

Clutch hitting is a touchy subject around these parts. It's not that we don't believe it exists—if a batter hits a two-run double to give his team a come-from-behind win in the ninth inning, that's obviously a clutch hit. It's

just that, on the basis of extensive research, we don't believe it's a repeatable skill. Hitting for power, drawing walks, stealing bases, playing good defense, even hitting for average (though to a lesser degree) are repeatable skills; a hitter's performance in any one of those areas is likely to be similar from one year to the next, and drastic changes in performance tend to either have ready explanations, such as injury or age, or represent a lasting change in his ability. The opposite holds for performance at the plate in what are generally described as clutch situations. Drastic diversions from a player's overall performance in such situations have historically proven to be unsustainable from year to year and are typically a statistical side effect of the small samples in which such clutch stats are compiled.

Take Twins Hall of Famer Kirby Puckett, for example. Puckett had a reputation for being good in the clutch, a reputation that held up under scrutiny in Nate Silver's study of clutch hitting in *Baseball Between the Numbers*. Over the course of his career, Puckett hit .322/.383/.496 in 2,146 plate appearances with runners in scoring position, compared with .318/.360/.477 overall. A year-by-year look at his performances with runners in scoring position, however, reveals the variability of clutch performance relative to that of overall performance. If one of the greatest hitters in Twins history couldn't sustain his clutch performance from year to year, there's very little chance that this deceptively mediocre Twins offense will be able to pull the same trick again in 2009. That means the Twins have some work to do where their attack is concerned. The good news is that while their offense was busy playing well over its head, the Twins' starting rotation was slowly but

---

TWINS PROSPECTUS

2008 record: 88-75; Second place in AL Central

Pythagenport record: 90-73

Runs scored per game: 5.09 (3rd in AL)

Runs allowed per game: 4.60 (8th in AL)

Team EqA: .264 (Tied for 4th in AL)

2008 Batters Age: 26.6 (Youngest in AL)

2008 Pitchers Age: 27.6 (3rd-youngest in AL)

Ballpark: Hubert H. Humphrey Metrodome; Pitcher's park; Park Factor of .961

2008: With Johan in Shea, the Twins finish one game away.

2009: Unless Bill Smith has discovered the secret to sustainable clutch hitting, things are going to get worse before they get better.

surely coalescing around a core of young, quality arms and is a unit likely to show significant improvement in 2009.

Trading Johan Santana to the Mets was largely a financial decision, but trading Matt Garza to the Rays in a package for Delmon Young and two other hitters was an example of the Twins' dealing from strength in an attempt to fix a weakness on the other side of the ball. In Francisco Liriano, Kevin Slowey, Scott Baker, Glen Perkins, and Nick Blackburn, the Twins have five starters between the ages of 24 (Slowey) and 27 (Baker), two of whom (Liriano and Perkins) are left-handed and all of whom pitched reasonably effectively in the major leagues in 2008. There's more where they came from: Anthony Swarzak (23) and lefty Brian Duensing (26) will start the year at triple-A; Jeff Manship (24), Tyler Robertson (21), and Alex Burnett (21) will line up behind them in Double-A; and David Bromberg (21) and Shooter Hunt (22) will begin 2009 in High-A Fort Myers. Altogether, that gives the Twins an even dozen starting pitchers under the age of 28, all with the potential to succeed in the major leagues and none more than two good years away from "The Show."

So, if the Twins have so much good young pitching, why did they need an unusually clutch offensive performance to lift them into contention in 2008? Because their current quintet of young arms needed most of the 2008 season to take shape—the Twins opened 2008 with a rotation that was headed by Livan Hernandez and that also relied on Boof Bonser. Liriano was attempting to jump right back in at the major league level after missing all of 2007 while recovering from Tommy John surgery. That didn't work out so well, as he made just three starts, giving up six runs in two-thirds of an inning in the last, before being demoted. The notional veteran duo did little better. Bonser was bad in 2007 and worse in 2008, lasting just 12 starts before being banished to long relief, sporting a 5.97 ERA. Hernandez made it all the way to the trading deadline before he and his 5.48 ERA were dumped on the Rockies.

Liriano had been replaced by Slowey the first time through the rotation and was replaced by him again when he was farmed out at the end of April. When Baker missed most of May due to a groin strain, he was replaced by Perkins; when Baker returned from the DL, he replaced Bonser. Finally, when Liriano eventually returned from an (overly) extended dominant stretch of Triple-A starts in August, he replaced Hernandez. From the beginning of the season through Bonser's last start on May 31, the Twins' rotation went 18-20 with a 4.58 ERA. From the trade of Hernandez through the end of the season, the Twins' rotation went 23-12 with a 3.87 ERA.

Absent Hernandez and Bonser (as a starter) and with a full season of Liriano, who went 6-1 with a 2.74 ERA after his return and was last seen dominating the Dominican winter league, the Twins stand to see a significant improvement in their run prevention in 2009 without having to make a single change to their pitching staff. That should have allowed second-year general manager Bill Smith to focus on shoring up the offense, which is due for a significant regression. Unfortunately, as we go to press, the only move he's made is to re-sign utility infielder Nick Punto with the intention of installing him at shortstop for another year. The decision is an exact repeat of the decision by Smith's predecessor Terry Ryan to re-sign Punto for two years after the 2006 season, only at twice the cost.

The organization has been down this road before, so if this seems familiar, there's a reason. The Twins had a sucking wound at third base in early 2006 in the form of reclamation project Tony Batista. Finally, in mid-June, they replaced Batista with Punto, who had been swinging a hot bat in a utility role. Punto hit .286/.340/.369 over the rest of the season while playing excellent defense, and the Twins surged up from fourth place to pass the Tigers and claim the division title. Thrilled that they had "solved" their third-base problems, the Twins signed Punto to a two-year deal and installed him at third base for 2007. Hitting .211/.312/.272 at the 2007 All-Star break, Punto gave the job back by the end of July. Last year, the Twins bounced between the slick-fielding but oft-injured and punchless Adam Everett and the stone-gloved, moderately productive Brendan Harris at shortstop before throwing up their hands and giving the job to Punto, who had been hitting .293/.347/.419 as a utilityman. Punto hit a mere .264/.336/.300 over the remainder of the season, but played his usual fine defense. Once again, the Twins have decided they've found the solution at a problem position, re-signing Punto, a .252/.319/.332 career hitter, in early December for $4 million a year after a brief glance at the pricier free-agent alternatives.

This is not progress. Punto should at least serve the purpose Everett was supposed to by replacing Jason Bartlett as the resident defensive wiz whose offense is an afterthought (if not outright offensive). If the Punto signing seemed like a wasted opportunity to upgrade the offense, it nevertheless reflects the Twins' consideration of the quality of the defense behind their young starters. We addressed this subject in detail in last year's annual, in our essay on the Tampa Bay Rays, who serve as a model for what the Twins are trying to do. Indeed, that model of young pitching and defense was key to both teams' desire to trade Delmon Young, then and now.

The primary return to the Twins in the deal that put Garza, Bartlett, and minor league reliever Eduardo Morlan with the Rays, Young was the top pick in the 2003 draft and was once considered the top prospect in all of baseball. When he finished as the runner-up in the 2007 AL Rookie of the Year voting, you might have thought he was headed in the right direction, but it was a fairly disappointing season in which he hit just .288/.316/.408. As a newly minted Twin, Young got off to a dreadful start in his sophomore season, hitting just .269/.320/.359 on the season on June 7. He rebounded from there, but not nearly enough. To make matters worse, Young was among the worst defensive left fielders in baseball last year, according to all the major defensive metrics, which express unanimity over Young's disastrously weak mitt and which don't quite convey the full extent of the poor judgment he exercises in choosing routes and diving after the uncatchable. In contrast, center fielder Carlos Gomez, the primary return for Santana, didn't hit much, either, but he did at least rank among the best defensive center fielders in baseball.

Young's miserable season presents the Twins with a problem in terms of which positions they might up-grade. With Gomez in place, the all-around excellence of Joe Mauer behind the plate, and Punto and second baseman Alexi Casilla representing a fine defensive double-play combo, they're set up the middle. Michael Cuddyer, one of the team's few reliably productive bats, will be returning from an injury-plagued year and seems likely to provide adequacy at the plate as well as strong play in right field. Justin Morneau is locked in at first base. The only slots where the Twins have an opportunity to upgrade their lineup *and* their defense are left field and third base. Denard Span's late-season emergence provided Minnesota with a better hitter and defender to replace Young in left—assuming Span's improvements stick. Setting aside the larger concern about lineup-wide regression in clutch situations, all the Twins need now, at least theoretically, is a third baseman who can provide strong play on both sides of the ball and to figure out what they're supposed to do with Young if he can't play ahead of Span.

It's possible that they could solve these problems with a move or two. The Twins are going to need to catch breaks with their younger cadre hitters recently arrived to reinforce Mauer and Morneau, specifically with the continuing development of Casilla, Gomez, Span, and perhaps even Young. If they do, they might have the right mix of pitching, defense, and just enough offense that they could find themselves right back in the thick of the race for the AL Central title.

HITTERS

| Brian Buscher | | | 3B | | | | | | | Bats: L | | Throws: R | | Height: 6' 0" | | Weight: 200 | | Born: April 18, 1981 | | | Age: 28 |

YEAR	TEAM	LVL	AGE	PA	R	2B	3B	HR	RBI	BB	SO	SB	CS	EqBRR	AVG	OBP	SLG	EqAVG	EqOBP	EqSLG	EqA	VORP	WARP	DEFENSE			
2006	NRW	AA	25	524	43	23	3	7	49	39	75	5	4	-2.8	.259	.321	.366	.221	.271	.312	.204	-32.6	-1.4	125-3B	6		
2007	NBR	AA	26	284	37	19	1	7	37	31	30	2	2	-3.8	.308	.391	.478	.222	.289	.358	.226	-9.5	-1.0	43-3B	-4		
2007	ROC	AAA	26	147	21	7	0	7	22	13	11	1	0	-0.7	.311	.374	.523	.269	.331	.463	.272	5.9	0.9	24-3B	3		
2007	MIN	MLB	26	94	8	1	0	2	10	10	16	1	0	-2.5	.244	.323	.329	.247	.333	.333	.244	-1.5	-0.5	23-3B	-5		
2008	ROC	AAA	27	214	27	12	0	8	30	20	21	1	2	-1.4	.319	.402	.514	.265	.344	.434	.267	6.8	1.4	36-3B	5	7-1B	1
2008	MIN	MLB	27	244	29	9	0	4	47	19	42	0	2	-0.3	.294	.340	.390	.300	.348	.410	.266	5.0	-0.2	58-3B	-9		
2009	MIN	MLB	28	330	31	16	1	8	40	26	54	1	1	-1.1	.250	.313	.388	.253	.317	.407	.252	3.4	0.7	80-3B	-1		

| Breakout: 34% Improve: 55% Collapse: 34% Attrition: 32% | Comparables: Bernie Allen, Dick Nen, Scott Cooper, Hal Rice |

After Mike Lamb pancaked as the Twins' starting third baseman, Buscher worked his way into a platoon role and got the bulk of the starts the rest of the way. His .205/.250/.205 line against southpaws in just 48 PAs didn't argue for expansion into a regular role (although he has hit lefties in the minors), and his .316/.362/.437 against righties seems like the gift of his .349 BABIP and a high line-drive rate, both of which might not last. In short, unless Buscher manifests some power to paper over those days in which the singles don't fall in, his career expectations are limited by when the Twins judge Luke Hughes or Danny Valencia ready for the majors.

Alexi Casilla 2B

Bats: S   Throws: R   Height: 5' 9"   Weight: 180   Born: July 20, 1984   Age: 24

YEAR	TEAM	LVL	AGE	PA	R	2B	3B	HR	RBI	BB	SO	SB	CS	EqBRR	AVG	OBP	SLG	EqAVG	EqOBP	EqSLG	EqA	VORP	WARP	DEFENSE		
2006	FTM	A+	21	359	56	12	6	0	33	30	36	31	6	8.5	.331	.390	.406	.285	.336	.367	.253	-2.7	0.3	43-2B -5	36-SS -2	
2006	NBR	AA	21	199	28	10	1	1	13	18	20	19	4	0.6	.294	.375	.382	.261	.330	.347	.249	-1.6	0.5	45-SS -2		
2007	ROC	AAA	22	365	53	13	1	3	20	34	50	24	12	-0.9	.269	.345	.344	.239	.312	.319	.228	-11.9	-2.1	41-SS -10	41-2B -9	
2007	MIN	MLB	22	204	15	5	1	0	9	9	29	11	1	1.5	.222	.256	.259	.223	.261	.261	.200	-10.7	-1.6	48-2B -8		
2008	ROC	AAA	23	121	11	3	0	0	2	18	18	4	3	-0.0	.219	.350	.250	.194	.322	.224	.209	-7.6	-1.1	20-SS -6	9-2B -2	
2008	MIN	MLB	23	437	58	15	0	7	50	31	45	7	2	0.4	.281	.333	.374	.287	.342	.392	.261	8.9	0.6	93-2B -8		
2009	MIN	MLB	24	466	53	18	3	3	36	36	62	15	5	2.1	.258	.319	.336	.260	.323	.352	.245	2.4	0.2	110-2B -8		

Breakout: 26%   Improve: 52%   Collapse: 20%   Attrition: 15%   Comparables: Maicer Izturis, Bernie Castro, Hanley Frias, Callix Crabbe

Sent out during spring training in favor of Brendan Harris, Casilla didn't hit at Triple-A, but was recalled on May 10 just the same when an injury crunch hit. Ron Gardenhire's dissatisfaction with Harris's defense eventually got Casilla a shot at the starting lineup, and when Casilla batted .340/.417/.520 over the balance of the month, the job was his. Batting .313/.351/.424 in late July, when he tore a tendon in his thumb, Casilla spent a month on the DL. Season-ending surgery had been an option, and given that Casilla hit .225/.302/.289 the rest of the way, it might have been the better choice. That's the benefit of hindsight, of course, and the longer Casilla stayed hurt, the longer Adam Everett persisted in the starting lineup, an argument for rolling the dice if ever there was one. It remains to be seen if Casilla can put together an entire season like the one he was having before he was injured.

Mike Cuddyer RF

Bats: R   Throws: R   Height: 6' 2"   Weight: 220   Born: March 27, 1979   Age: 30

YEAR	TEAM	LVL	AGE	PA	R	2B	3B	HR	RBI	BB	SO	SB	CS	EqBRR	AVG	OBP	SLG	EqAVG	EqOBP	EqSLG	EqA	VORP	WARP	DEFENSE		
2006	MIN	MLB	27	635	102	41	5	24	109	62	130	6	0	-1.3	.284	.362	.504	.272	.357	.493	.291	36.8	2.8	138-RF -8	6-1B 0	
2007	MIN	MLB	28	623	87	28	5	16	81	64	107	5	0	-0.6	.276	.356	.433	.274	.358	.445	.280	19.3	3.2	138-RF 3	4-1B 1	
2008	MIN	MLB	29	279	30	13	4	3	36	25	40	5	1	0.3	.249	.330	.369	.250	.333	.383	.254	-0.1	0.2	56-RF -1		
2009	MIN	MLB	30	412	52	22	3	11	52	39	79	5	2	-0.1	.261	.336	.423	.263	.341	.443	.272	7.3	1.4	98-RF -3		

Breakout: 15%   Improve: 42%   Collapse: 28%   Attrition: 20%   Comparables: Ellis Burks, Leon Roberts, Glenallen Hill, Jeffrey Hammonds

The M&M boys aside, most Twins are just good enough to play. They produce at a level designed to get the job done, no more, no less, like cogs in a bureaucratic machine staffed by the lowest bidders. At his best, Cuddyer can be, or at least has been, a little better than that, which is why having his year wiped away by multiple injuries was so disheartening—especially after the Twins took the rare step of committing to him financially. The only silver lining was that Cuddyer's absence resulted in the elevation of Denard Span. That leaves it to Cuddyer to heal up and justify the two years and 2011 team option remaining on his contract; over the last three seasons, the average right fielder has hit .277/.347/.452, rates Cuddyer has struggled to reach in most seasons.

Adam Everett SS

Bats: R   Throws: R   Height: 6' 0"   Weight: 170   Born: February 2, 1977   Age: 32

YEAR	TEAM	LVL	AGE	PA	R	2B	3B	HR	RBI	BB	SO	SB	CS	EqBRR	AVG	OBP	SLG	EqAVG	EqOBP	EqSLG	EqA	VORP	WARP	DEFENSE
2006	HOU	MLB	29	566	52	28	6	6	59	34	71	9	6	-0.9	.239	.290	.352	.237	.289	.351	.224	-9.6	4.2	142-SS 35
2007	HOU	MLB	30	236	18	11	1	2	15	14	31	4	2	-1.7	.232	.281	.318	.232	.284	.318	.210	-6.2	0.6	59-SS 8
2008	MIN	MLB	31	150	19	6	1	2	20	12	15	0	0	0.8	.213	.278	.323	.214	.285	.349	.229	-3.3	0.4	41-SS 3
2009	DET	MLB	32	172	15	7	1	2	15	10	22	1	1	0.3	.231	.281	.322	.231	.283	.332	.216	-2.8	0.5	44-SS 4

Breakout: 31%   Improve: 42%   Collapse: 41%   Attrition: 39%   Comparables: Larry Brown, Jose Pagan, Frank Duffy, Mike Mordecai

You know Everett's story: terrific glove, bat like the "before" picture in a Viagra ad. To that description we can now add "durability issues" after consecutive seasons with significant time on the DL, this time with a strained shoulder. The injury allowed Nick Punto to jump-start his Twins career, and the club was all set to release Everett when Casilla's own injury gave him a second life—for about two weeks, after which he served as a seldom-used defensive replacement. Everett's career rates now stand at .246/.298/.355, and he hasn't recorded an OBP above .300 since 2004. Over the offseason, Everett joined the defensively impoverished Tigers on a one-year, $1 million contract, where he will follow the examples set by former Tigers punchless shortstops like Ray Oyler and Eddie Brinkman.

Carlos Gomez   **CF**   Bats: R   Throws: R   Height: 6' 2"   Weight: 175   Born: December 4, 1985   Age: 23

YEAR	TEAM	LVL	AGE	PA	R	2B	3B	HR	RBI	BB	SO	SB	CS	EqBRR	AVG	OBP	SLG	EqAVG	EqOBP	EqSLG	EqA	VORP	WARP	DEFENSE			
2006	BIN	AA	20	486	53	24	8	7	48	27	97	41	9	0.8	.281	.350	.423	.252	.305	.394	.248	-2.3	1.3	115-CF	4		
2007	NWO	AAA	21	157	24	8	2	2	13	15	23	17	4	0.0	.286	.363	.414	.255	.331	.383	.258	0.8	0.6	35-CF	1		
2007	NYN	MLB	21	139	14	3	0	2	12	8	27	12	3	1.5	.232	.288	.304	.240	.300	.304	.230	-4.5	0.4	20-LF	6	15-RF	0
2008	MIN	MLB	22	614	79	24	7	7	59	25	142	33	11	2.2	.258	.296	.360	.267	.306	.380	.242	0.3	2.3	142-CF	16		
2009	MIN	MLB	23	463	58	21	5	8	45	24	96	29	10	3.5	.261	.310	.387	.264	.314	.406	.256	5.3	2.6	110-CF	8		

Breakout: 33%   Improve: 56%   Collapse: 19%   Attrition: 21%   Comparables: David Green, Mariano Duncan, Ruben Mateo, Lou Brock

The centerpiece of the Santana deal with the Mets, Gomez is the reason that Denard Span had to come up from the minors and mount an unlikely rescue of the Twins' offense. Until Span was locked into the leadoff spot in late July, Gomez had been its primary occupant, batting a self-neutering .246/.281/.345 in that capacity. Dropped to ninth in the order, he hit .286/.328/.400. Combine those latter rates with Gomez's speed and terrific defense, and you have a center fielder worth playing, though a central role in the offense may always be a reach unless the still-young Gomez can develop a hint of power and a modicum of selectivity—his 3.4 pitches seen per plate appearance ranked 62nd among 68 qualified AL hitters.

Brendan Harris   **INF**   Bats: R   Throws: R   Height: 6' 1"   Weight: 200   Born: August 26, 1980   Age: 28

YEAR	TEAM	LVL	AGE	PA	R	2B	3B	HR	RBI	BB	SO	SB	CS	EqBRR	AVG	OBP	SLG	EqAVG	EqOBP	EqSLG	EqA	VORP	WARP	DEFENSE			
2006	LOU	AAA	25	165	22	14	1	5	28	14	29	2	0	1.6	.324	.384	.534	.293	.352	.513	.292	12.4	0.9	20-3B	-2	9-2B	0
2006	NWO	AAA	25	257	37	14	0	5	32	26	56	3	2	1.4	.283	.379	.416	.252	.335	.372	.250	0.6	-0.3	34-3B	-4	14-SS	-2
2006	WAS	MLB	25	36	3	2	0	0	2	3	3	0	0	-0.1	.250	.333	.313	.250	.333	.312	.233	-0.2	-0.1				
2007	TBA	MLB	26	576	72	35	3	12	59	42	96	4	1	0.7	.286	.343	.434	.285	.345	.449	.273	25.2	1.0	85-SS	-15	46-2B	-5
2008	MIN	MLB	27	490	57	29	3	7	49	39	98	1	1	1.2	.265	.327	.394	.271	.336	.415	.262	10.7	0.2	52-SS	-5	36-2B	-6
2009	MIN	MLB	28	508	55	27	2	11	59	41	103	3	1	-0.2	.263	.328	.401	.265	.333	.420	.263	13.5	1.0	120-SS	-12		

Breakout: 19%   Improve: 40%   Collapse: 29%   Attrition: 19%   Comparables: Andre Rodgers, Tim Naehring, Hector Lopez, Hubie Brooks

Harris came over as an add-on to Delmon Young from the Rays in the borderline-disastrous preseason trade and presents a Derek Jeter problem in miniature. His bat plays well in the middle infield, but his glove does not. As such, the Twins quickly rethought the outcome of the spring competition between Harris and Casilla for the job at second, reducing the former to a utility role by mid-May. He acquitted himself ably, hopping on and off the Twins' merry-go-round at short and third while recovering from a slow start to bat .290/.356/.462 in 192 PAs from July through the end of the season. Unlike last year, Harris will probably begin this season on the bench, but given that the players in front of him are something less than Evers, Tinker, and Steinfeldt, he'll probably get his licks in ere long.

Luke Hughes   **3B**   Bats: R   Throws: R   Height: 6' 0"   Weight: 190   Born: August 2, 1984   Age: 24

YEAR	TEAM	LVL	AGE	PA	R	2B	3B	HR	RBI	BB	SO	SB	CS	EqBRR	AVG	OBP	SLG	EqAVG	EqOBP	EqSLG	EqA	VORP	WARP	DEFENSE			
2006	FTM	A+	21	368	31	15	0	4	37	23	72	6	2	-0.1	.231	.287	.312	.196	.243	.267	.175	-35.8	-2.0	81-3B	6	8-2B	-1
2007	NBR	AA	22	362	56	18	2	9	43	34	68	4	1	2.1	.283	.356	.438	.241	.304	.389	.242	-3.5	0.0	44-2B	6	19-LF	-8
2008	NBR	AA	23	319	53	15	3	15	40	28	70	4	1	1.5	.319	.385	.551	.298	.356	.536	.298	27.8	1.1	39-3B	-9	17-2B	-3
2008	ROC	AAA	23	117	17	7	1	3	21	7	30	2	0	1.1	.283	.325	.453	.262	.305	.430	.256	1.3	-0.2	26-3B	-4		
2009	MIN	MLB	24	483	50	24	2	13	59	33	121	4	2	0.9	.243	.301	.398	.245	.305	.417	.250	2.3	0.7	114-3B	-3		

Breakout: 16%   Improve: 38%   Collapse: 31%   Attrition: 13%   Comparables: Alfonso Soriano, Denny Gonzalez, Roberto Mejia, Jose Fernandez

For the first time since signing with the Twins as a nondrafted free agent in 2002, native Australian Hughes showed enough life with the bat to be interesting, but he was repeating Double-A, so it doesn't pay to get too excited. Given the organization's weak third-base options, if Hughes could play the position, he'd probably be on the verge of auditioning for the job, but 31 errors in 156 minor league games at the hot corner have probably put the kibosh on that. Hughes has put in extensive time at second and made cameos at first and all three outfield spots, so his path to the bigs is as a utilityman.

Jason Kubel   DH

Bats: L   Throws: R   Height: 6' 0"   Weight: 210   Born: May 25, 1982   Age: 27

YEAR	TEAM	LVL	AGE	PA	R	2B	3B	HR	RBI	BB	SO	SB	CS	EqBRR	AVG	OBP	SLG	EqAVG	EqOBP	EqSLG	EqA	VORP	WARP	DEFENSE
2006	ROC	AAA	24	134	18	7	2	4	22	12	23	2	0	-0.1	.283	.343	.475	.256	.313	.438	.260	2.3	0.0	22-RF -2
2006	MIN	MLB	24	235	23	8	0	8	26	12	45	2	0	-0.3	.241	.279	.386	.233	.275	.384	.228	-5.8	-0.6	23-LF 0 5-RF 0
2007	MIN	MLB	25	466	49	31	2	13	65	41	79	5	0	-3.4	.273	.335	.450	.269	.337	.464	.276	14.5	-0.2	79-LF -18
2008	MIN	MLB	26	517	74	22	5	20	78	47	91	0	1	-0.7	.272	.335	.471	.276	.342	.491	.282	21.3	2.0	27-RF 1 15-LF -3
2009	*MIN*	*MLB*	*27*	*494*	*58*	*25*	*3*	*15*	*69*	*42*	*88*	*4*	*1*	*-1.0*	*.265*	*.328*	*.438*	*.267*	*.333*	*.459*	*.273*	*11.4*	*1.2*	*117-DH*

Breakout: 19%   Improve: 46%   Collapse: 23%   Attrition: 10%   Comparables: Paul O'Neill, Eric Anthony, Harry Anderson, Dave Nilsson

Now years removed from being the exciting prospect who hit .323 and slugged over .500 in the minors prior to a career-altering knee injury, Kubel is firmly ensconced as a platoon DH who makes occasional appearances in the outfield corners. He boasts career rates of .275/.327/.464 against right-handers (and only .238/.324/.364 against left-handers), rates like those of an average DH over the last three seasons. As such, he is another Twin who is *comme ci, comme ça*, so-so. At different points in the last two years, Kubel has produced hot streaks that resemble his former prospect incarnation. Unless he can find that guy on a more regular basis—in his age-27 season, perhaps?—he's miscast as a run producer. The problem with reducing his role is that even the world's most overqualified fourth outfielder can play defense, and Kubel can't.

Matt Macri   INF

Bats: R   Throws: R   Height: 6' 2"   Weight: 200   Born: May 29, 1982   Age: 27

YEAR	TEAM	LVL	AGE	PA	R	2B	3B	HR	RBI	BB	SO	SB	CS	EqBRR	AVG	OBP	SLG	EqAVG	EqOBP	EqSLG	EqA	VORP	WARP	DEFENSE
2006	TUL	AA	24	326	35	12	2	8	35	22	66	2	4	-1.1	.233	.294	.372	.181	.232	.302	.181	-28.9	-3.5	77-2B -14
2007	TUL	AA	25	298	46	23	0	11	33	20	58	4	4	-0.9	.298	.349	.502	.224	.265	.381	.218	-11.3	-1.4	30-3B -3 20-2B 1
2007	ROC	AAA	25	50	5	1	0	3	6	3	13	0	0	0.2	.213	.260	.426	.191	.240	.404	.216	-2.5	-0.3	8-3B -1
2008	ROC	AAA	26	350	35	24	4	11	48	26	84	2	2	-1.1	.259	.323	.466	.224	.287	.413	.240	-4.3	1.4	33-SS 2 30-2B 6
2008	MIN	MLB	26	36	3	1	0	1	4	2	10	1	1	-0.1	.324	.361	.441	.324	.361	.441	.272	1.6	-0.3	7-3B -4
2009	*MIN*	*MLB*	*27*	*453*	*36*	*22*	*2*	*11*	*50*	*28*	*129*	*3*	*2*	*-0.2*	*.203*	*.259*	*.345*	*.205*	*.263*	*.362*	*.214*	*-12.8*	*-1.0*	*107-2B -7*

Breakout: 17%   Improve: 41%   Collapse: 37%   Attrition: 12%   Comparables: Mike Coolbaugh, Bob Brenly, Mike Gulan, Jeff Moronko

In 1928, the great John Ford directed *Mother Machree*, a film about a maternally inclined Irish immigrant forced to take work in a carnival, which really has nothing to do with Matt Macri, except that he hopes his blend of skills (capable glove, positional flexibility, and occasional power) will keep him in the majors long enough that he never has to work as a carny.

Joe Mauer   C

Bats: L   Throws: R   Height: 6' 5"   Weight: 215   Born: April 19, 1983   Age: 26

YEAR	TEAM	LVL	AGE	PA	R	2B	3B	HR	RBI	BB	SO	SB	CS	EqBRR	AVG	OBP	SLG	EqAVG	EqOBP	EqSLG	EqA	VORP	WARP	DEFENSE
2006	MIN	MLB	23	608	86	36	4	13	84	79	54	8	3	1.4	.347	.429	.507	.329	.421	.490	.316	67.4	7.1	119-C 6
2007	MIN	MLB	24	471	62	27	3	7	60	57	51	7	1	0.7	.293	.382	.426	.288	.382	.434	.288	31.1	4.3	88-C 8
2008	MIN	MLB	25	633	98	31	4	9	85	84	50	1	1	4.1	.328	.413	.451	.334	.423	.468	.314	57.1	7.1	134-C 5
2009	*MIN*	*MLB*	*26*	*612*	*88*	*32*	*4*	*10*	*68*	*70*	*59*	*6*	*2*	*0.2*	*.307*	*.388*	*.436*	*.309*	*.393*	*.457*	*.298*	*41.4*	*6.3*	*143-C 3*

Breakout: 8%   Improve: 35%   Collapse: 24%   Attrition: 6%   Comparables: Steve Kemp, Ken Oberkfell, Jason Kendall, Keith Hernandez

Last season, Mauer joined Hall of Famer Ernie Lombardi on the very short list of catchers to win two batting titles. In most regards, the year was a welcome return to form after the multiple injuries of 2007, although Mauer's power dropped again. In 2007, the outage was seen as a function of lack of leverage due to various leg problems, but at this stage, it seems more likely that unless Mauer radically alters a grounder-generating approach, he's never going to develop into a big-time home-run—or even doubles—producer. That's not a problem as long as he maintains his patience and doesn't have his footspeed completely eroded by catching. His defense speaks for itself, so he should have a long career as a backstop, even if his offense fades. Speaking of which, want to see something *really* scary? Through his just-completed age-25 season, Mauer has hit .317/.399/.457. Through *his* age-25 season, Jason Kendall batted .312/.399/.451. Just sayin'.

Justin Morneau   **1B**   Bats: L   Throws: R   Height: 6' 4"   Weight: 225   Born: May 15, 1981   Age: 28

YEAR	TEAM	LVL	AGE	PA	R	2B	3B	HR	RBI	BB	SO	SB	CS	EqBRR	AVG	OBP	SLG	EqAVG	EqOBP	EqSLG	EqA	VORP	WARP	DEFENSE	
2006	MIN	MLB	25	661	97	37	1	34	130	53	93	3	3	-1.5	.321	.375	.559	.308	.368	.547	.304	52.5	4.6	152-1B	1
2007	MIN	MLB	26	668	84	31	3	31	111	64	91	1	1	-2.9	.271	.343	.492	.266	.341	.501	.284	30.0	4.2	142-1B	12
2008	MIN	MLB	27	712	97	47	4	23	129	76	85	0	1	-2.5	.300	.374	.499	.303	.381	.523	.305	47.2	4.8	152-1B	-1
2009	MIN	MLB	28	655	84	36	2	24	101	64	91	1	1	-2.3	.281	.354	.475	.284	.359	.497	.291	26.4	3.3	153-1B	0

Breakout: 10%   Improve: 42%   Collapse: 24%   Attrition: 3%   Comparables: Kent Hrbek, Aubrey Huff, Wally Joyner, Dave Nilsson

As sure as night follows day, a player celebrated for his RBI total was also the man who led the majors in plate appearances with runners on base; Morneau had 400 such PAs, 25 more than runner-up David Wright. Morneau's season was unexceptional by the standards of first basemen; his RBI tally is the only way his work stood out. Consequently, we must conclude that the RBI stat was the major factor in his second-place finish in AL MVP voting. He did do a good job with men on, batting .330/.419/.574, though his percentage of baserunners driven in was just good, not great; Morneau's percentage of runners driven in was indistinguishable from, say, Nate McLouth's and fractionally inferior to that of Kevin Youkilis. Like crime, RBI are mostly a matter of opportunity, and focusing on them obscures other factors that might make a player less than MVP material—like, say, a first baseman who bats .320/.394/.532 through the end of July and who then goes into a long funk culminating in a .243/.298/.398 September, just as his club is losing a close pennant race.

Chris Parmelee   **1B/OF**   Bats: L   Throws: L   Height: 6' 1"   Weight: 200   Born: February 24, 1988   Age: 21

YEAR	TEAM	LVL	AGE	PA	R	2B	3B	HR	RBI	BB	SO	SB	CS	EqBRR	AVG	OBP	SLG	EqAVG	EqOBP	EqSLG	EqA	VORP	WARP	DEFENSE				
2006	TWI	Rk	18	179	29	7	4	8	32	23	47	3	3	-1.6	.279	.369	.532	.211	.279	.404	.235	-11.1	-1.4	30-RF	-4	10-1B	-1
2007	BLT	A	19	501	56	23	5	15	70	46	137	8	4	0.0	.239	.313	.414	.187	.248	.317	.193	-40.3	-4.4	103-RF	-9	4-LF	-2
2008	BLT	A	20	289	41	10	3	14	49	52	83	3	1	-0.3	.239	.385	.496	.207	.333	.414	.262	2.5	0.2	42-1B	-2	23-RF	-1
2009	MIN	MLB	21	505	48	24	3	16	57	55	155	3	2	-0.1	.208	.298	.383	.210	.303	.401	.246	-10.0	0.2	119-RF	-4		

Breakout: 49%   Improve: 66%   Collapse: 16%   Attrition: 5%   Comparables: Matt Winters, Manny Ramirez, Dave Kable, Jack Cust

Parmelee hit .239 in Beloit for the second consecutive season, but that's where the similarities in the seasons ended. The 2006 first-rounder's secondary skills kicked in with a vengeance, as he posted a decidedly un-Twinkie-like .146 Isolated Power and .257 Isolated Discipline before a broken wrist sent him home early. Still, his inability to make contact is a concern; even fellow Three True Outcomes (TTO) trooper Adam Dunn managed to surpass .300 in the Midwest League. Since his below-average speed is likely to keep him tethered to first base, his future in the organization will depend on an enlightened appraisal of his offensive talents, and his own capacity to put the ball in play.

Jason Pridie   **OF**   Bats: L   Throws: R   Height: 6' 1"   Weight: 190   Born: October 9, 1983   Age: 25

YEAR	TEAM	LVL	AGE	PA	R	2B	3B	HR	RBI	BB	SO	SB	CS	EqBRR	AVG	OBP	SLG	EqAVG	EqOBP	EqSLG	EqA	VORP	WARP	DEFENSE				
2006	MNT	AA	22	503	39	11	4	5	34	31	93	16	5	-0.9	.230	.281	.304	.210	.253	.287	.189	-42.5	-1.4	126-CF	10		
2007	MNT	AA	23	300	42	16	7	4	27	14	45	14	7	0.0	.290	.331	.441	.250	.286	.398	.234	-4.0	1.3	36-CF	0	27-LF	12
2007	DUR	AAA	23	274	47	16	4	10	39	22	47	12	3	0.0	.318	.375	.539	.282	.335	.500	.283	15.8	3.3	61-CF	13		
2008	ROC	AAA	24	603	84	21	16	13	61	30	152	25	9	5.5	.270	.305	.435	.249	.284	.417	.242	-4.3	2.3	105-CF	13	18-RF	1
2009	MIN	MLB	25	493	51	24	7	9	52	27	117	13	5	2.2	.243	.287	.387	.245	.291	.405	.242	-2.8	2.2	116-CF	11		

Breakout: 30%   Improve: 51%   Collapse: 18%   Attrition: 15%   Comparables: Brent Bowers, Mitch Maier, Pat Watkins, Kory DeHaan

A second-round pick of the Rays back in 2002, Pridie became part of the Twins' organization for the second time when he was included in the Delmon Young deal, a spin via the 2005 Rule 5 draft not having taken. As a prospect, Pridie has been up and down the charts faster than Rick Astley; he has great tools, but would he be able to overcome his poor strike-zone judgment and problems making contact? Until 2007, the answer appeared to be no. The test for 2008 was to see if his breakthrough of the previous season was for real. He failed. Pridie's speed and defensive abilities are such that he may yet have a career as a reserve, but anything more than that is doubtful, the high upside looking something like Corey Patterson 2.0.

Nick Punto | SS | Bats: S | Throws: R | Height: 5' 9" | Weight: 185 | Born: November 8, 1977 | Age: 31

YEAR	TEAM	LVL	AGE	PA	R	2B	3B	HR	RBI	BB	SO	SB	CS	EqBRR	AVG	OBP	SLG	EqAVG	EqOBP	EqSLG	EqA	VORP	WARP	DEFENSE				
2006	MIN	MLB	28	524	73	21	7	1	45	47	68	17	5	0.9	.290	.352	.373	.280	.349	.361	.259	9.3	1.5	86-3B	2	17-SS	2
2007	MIN	MLB	29	536	53	18	4	1	25	55	90	16	6	-0.6	.210	.291	.271	.209	.294	.273	.209	-26.3	-1.7	93-3B	5	24-SS	-3
2008	MIN	MLB	30	377	43	19	4	2	28	32	57	15	6	0.7	.284	.344	.382	.292	.355	.402	.266	13.4	2.8	59-SS	8	24-2B	1
2009	MIN	MLB	31	340	37	12	3	2	25	30	54	12	4	1.1	.241	.310	.318	.243	.315	.333	.236	-2.8	0.5	82-SS	-2		

Breakout: 17% Improve: 41% Collapse: 30% Attrition: 25%   Comparables: U.L. Washington, Dennis Hocking, Jose Uribe, Kazuo Matsui

Since becoming a Twins regular, Punto has had an every-other-year pattern of being mildly productive with the bat. In 2008, he rebounded from the worst offensive season of his career to have the best offensive season of his career. You don't need PECOTA to tell you what's likely to come next. Fortunately, Punto is a strong glove at second, short, and third in years both even and odd. Re-signed with the Twins for another two-year term (along with a 2011 club option), this time around he'll be cast as the starting shortstop, the position at which either flavor of his hitting is the least out of place.

Wilson Ramos | C | Bats: R | Throws: R | Height: 6' 0" | Weight: 178 | Born: August 10, 1987 | Age: 21

YEAR	TEAM	LVL	AGE	PA	R	2B	3B	HR	RBI	BB	SO	SB	CS	EqBRR	AVG	OBP	SLG	EqAVG	EqOBP	EqSLG	EqA	VORP	WARP	DEFENSE				
2006	TWI	Rk	18	172	18	12	1	3	26	12	14	4	2	0.3	.286	.339	.435	.225	.263	.363	.214	-20.2	-0.7	31-C	0	11-1B	-1
2007	BLT	A	19	316	40	17	1	8	42	19	61	1	1	0.0	.291	.345	.438	.221	.263	.344	.207	-17.4	0.2	50-C	8		
2008	FTM	A+	20	500	50	23	2	13	78	37	103	0	1	-5.0	.288	.346	.434	.251	.300	.394	.239	-4.0	1.0	74-C	4		
2009	MIN	MLB	21	493	37	25	1	10	56	30	123	0	0	-1.3	.233	.284	.360	.235	.288	.377	.230	-5.1	1.2	116-C	-4		

Breakout: 33% Improve: 45% Collapse: 27% Attrition: 11%   Comparables: Justin Huber, Francisco Cervelli, Jose Viera, Junior Ortiz

Ramos is a comer and would probably be even more of a hot prospect if he didn't have a Mauer-sized mountain of a roadblock in his way. As a hitter, he's developing power and holding his own as he moves up the ladder. As a catcher, he's already a great thrower, having gunned down 41 percent of attempted basestealers in 2007 and 43 percent in 2008. If he can improve his plate judgment, he'll be a star. If not, he's probably heading for a peak similar to that of fellow Venezuelan backstop Ramon Hernandez.

Mike Redmond | C | Bats: R | Throws: R | Height: 5' 11" | Weight: 200 | Born: May 5, 1971 | Age: 38

YEAR	TEAM	LVL	AGE	PA	R	2B	3B	HR	RBI	BB	SO	SB	CS	EqBRR	AVG	OBP	SLG	EqAVG	EqOBP	EqSLG	EqA	VORP	WARP	DEFENSE	
2006	MIN	MLB	35	191	20	13	0	0	23	4	19	0	0	-1.1	.339	.363	.411	.333	.358	.406	.268	9.5	1.5	43-C	4
2007	MIN	MLB	36	298	23	13	0	1	38	18	23	0	0	-2.6	.294	.346	.353	.295	.347	.354	.251	7.2	1.3	54-C	5
2008	MIN	MLB	37	137	14	6	0	0	12	5	11	0	0	-0.3	.287	.321	.333	.295	.328	.333	.235	0.9	0.0	28-C	-1
2009	MIN	MLB	38	166	11	7	0	1	16	8	15	0	0	-1.0	.252	.295	.310	.254	.299	.325	.218	-2.8	0.3	43-C	-2

Breakout: 11% Improve: 15% Collapse: 55% Attrition: 44%   Comparables: Joe Girardi, Don Slaught, Sandy Alomar, Bob Scheffing

Redmond, a career .292/.348/.365 hitter, is particularly solid against lefties, with career rates of .327/.382/.426. In a catching-scarce world in which the reserve backstop ranks are almost exclusively populated by catch-and-throw guys who check their bats at the door, Redmond's ability to chip in a few singles off the bench has disproportionate value. The Twins picked up his $950,000 option for 2009, and the only real worry is that at 38, he can't keep doing this forever.

Ben Revere | CF | Bats: L | Throws: R | Height: 5' 9" | Weight: 175 | Born: May 3, 1988 | Age: 21

YEAR	TEAM	LVL	AGE	PA	R	2B	3B	HR	RBI	BB	SO	SB	CS	EqBRR	AVG	OBP	SLG	EqAVG	EqOBP	EqSLG	EqA	VORP	WARP	DEFENSE			
2007	TWI	Rk	19	216	46	6	10	0	29	13	20	21	9	1.6	.325	.388	.461	.248	.284	.376	.229	-13.0	0.0	49-CF	1		
2008	BLT	A	20	374	51	17	10	1	43	27	31	44	13	1.8	.379	.433	.497	.311	.358	.415	.271	16.9	1.3	68-CF	-3	8-LF	0
2009	MIN	MLB	21	559	82	28	12	2	45	33	64	33	13	7.1	.297	.342	.410	.299	.347	.429	.273	19.5	3.8	131-CF	3		

Breakout: 51% Improve: 80% Collapse: 8% Attrition: 3%   Comparables: Johnny Damon, Trey Beamon, Len Dykstra, Mike White

Listen my children and you shall hear / Of the midnight ride of Ben Revere. And ride this Revere does, having stolen 65 bases in his first 133 pro games and legged out 20 triples. The downside is that "legging out" is not just a colorful turn of phrase—in 531 minor league at-bats, he has hit just 23 doubles and one home run, making Revere a one-base pony. Fortunately for him, when you lead the minors in batting average (as he did in 2008), win the Midwest League MVP award, and have the speed to play center, no one complains about that. He makes such good contact that he hasn't yet learned to let the bad pitches go by for walks, something the 2007 first-round pick will need to do to become a top-flight leadoff man.

Randy Ruiz DH Bats: R Throws: R Height: 6' 3" Weight: 235 Born: October 19, 1977 Age: 31

YEAR	TEAM	LVL	AGE	PA	R	2B	3B	HR	RBI	BB	SO	SB	CS	EqBRR	AVG	OBP	SLG	EqAVG	EqOBP	EqSLG	EqA	VORP	WARP	DEFENSE		
2006	TRN	AA	28	526	72	35	1	26	87	41	132	2	0	-2.1	.286	.361	.532	.186	.240	.329	.193	-39.0	-5.0	44-1B	-10		
2007	ALT	AA	29	185	20	9	1	7	30	18	32	0	1	-0.1	.290	.362	.488	.171	.227	.300	.176	-18.1	-1.9	15-1B	-2		
2007	REA	AA	29	89	16	10	0	3	12	6	21	1	0	-0.3	.378	.427	.610	.224	.258	.353	.207	-4.6	-0.2	13-LF	2		
2007	OTT	AAA	29	88	11	4	0	4	11	9	23	0	0	-0.1	.215	.295	.418	.188	.261	.375	.217	-4.2	-0.5	9-1B	1	5-LF	-2
2007	NRW	AA	29	165	25	6	3	8	27	11	40	0	0	0.0	.291	.352	.530	.192	.232	.321	.183	-14.2	-1.5	9-1B	-1		
2008	ROC	AAA	30	456	58	33	3	17	68	23	116	1	2	-3.9	.320	.366	.536	.260	.304	.449	.256	7.8	-0.7	40-1B	-8		
2008	MIN	MLB	30	68	13	2	0	1	7	6	21	0	0	1.0	.274	.338	.355	.274	.338	.355	.246	0.8	0.0				
2009	TOR	MLB	31	422	34	21	2	12	51	26	141	1	1	-1.3	.211	.267	.370	.212	.268	.379	.221	-13.4	-1.5	100-DH			

Breakout: 31% Improve: 48% Collapse: 30% Attrition: 26%   Comparables: John Lindsey, Luis Raven, Chris Truby, Brian Dorsett

Bronx native Randy Ruiz was born October 19, 1977, the day after Reggie Jackson hit three home runs to close out that season's World Series. Yes, it was a long time ago, but then Ruiz has been in baseball for a long time, joining the professional ranks when the Reds signed him as a nondrafted free agent in 1999. Despite career minor league rates of .302/.369/.524, it took him almost nine years to reach Triple-A. The reason is simple: if you want to make it to the majors as a clanky first baseman or DH, you'd better hit like Babe freakin' Ruth, and Ruiz falls well short of that standard, principally due to deficiencies in making contact and strike-zone judgment. After releasing Craig Monroe, the Twins gave Ruiz a shot at the right-handed half of the DH platoon. Ruiz was better than Monroe, but still less than might have been hoped. Cut loose after the season, Ruiz made his 10th change of organization, signing a minor league deal with the Blue Jays.

Denard Span OF Bats: L Throws: L Height: 6' 0" Weight: 195 Born: February 27, 1984 Age: 25

YEAR	TEAM	LVL	AGE	PA	R	2B	3B	HR	RBI	BB	SO	SB	CS	EqBRR	AVG	OBP	SLG	EqAVG	EqOBP	EqSLG	EqA	VORP	WARP	DEFENSE		
2006	NBR	AA	22	597	80	16	6	2	45	40	78	24	11	-0.4	.285	.340	.349	.251	.301	.311	.219	-24.0	-2.3	128-CF	-10		
2007	ROC	AAA	23	548	59	20	7	3	55	40	90	25	14	2.3	.267	.323	.355	.237	.290	.327	.218	-22.9	0.5	133-CF	13		
2008	ROC	AAA	24	184	32	11	1	3	14	26	36	15	8	-1.0	.340	.434	.481	.306	.404	.433	.290	13.0	1.4	32-CF	1	7-RF	0
2008	MIN	MLB	24	411	70	16	7	6	47	50	60	18	7	3.6	.294	.387	.432	.302	.398	.459	.295	21.2	2.6	77-RF	2	13-CF	-3
2009	MIN	MLB	25	439	57	18	4	4	39	37	75	16	6	2.6	.271	.337	.371	.273	.342	.389	.261	4.0	1.6	104-RF	5		

Breakout: 23% Improve: 48% Collapse: 25% Attrition: 28%   Comparables: Jerry Mumphrey, Mike Darr, Del Unser, Hosken Powell

A 2002 first-round pick, Span seemed like a bust until a promising second half at Rochester in 2007 and an eye-opening spring training. Called up in April after Cuddyer went down, he failed to impress, but back in Triple-A at the end of the month, he swung a mean bat both before and after a broken finger cost him almost a month of DL time. Finally back up on June 30, he took over in right field and, three weeks later, grabbed the leadoff spot, batting .297/.393/.449 the rest of the way. Can he do it again? Did he truly see plate judgment on the road to Damascus? Can the Twins find room for him, given that center field is blocked and Span lacks a corner man's power? Will he be able to sustain an unusually high (25.7 percent) line-drive rate and thereby keep his batting average up? Was it really all due to the LASIK surgery he had prior to the season? Stay tuned!

Matt Tolbert INF

Bats: S Throws: R Height: 6' 0" Weight: 180 Born: May 4, 1982 Age: 27

YEAR	TEAM	LVL	AGE	PA	R	2B	3B	HR	RBI	BB	SO	SB	CS	EqBRR	AVG	OBP	SLG	EqAVG	EqOBP	EqSLG	EqA	VORP	WARP	DEFENSE			
2006	FTM	A+	24	173	20	6	3	4	24	14	17	7	2	0.9	.303	.360	.458	.231	.277	.344	.220	-7.6	0.4	25-2B	3	8-CF	3
2006	NBR	AA	24	292	33	15	1	3	35	30	43	5	1	1.6	.258	.341	.363	.215	.287	.316	.217	-14.9	-1.1	26-2B	-6	25-3B	-1
2007	ROC	AAA	25	477	65	24	7	6	53	37	56	11	3	4.1	.293	.353	.427	.255	.311	.391	.247	-1.1	0.8	99-2B	-8	10-3B	5
2008	NBR	AA	26	57	6	3	0	0	6	1	6	3	3	-0.6	.250	.263	.304	.196	.211	.214	.135	-7.9	-0.3	9-SS	2		
2008	MIN	MLB	26	123	18	6	3	0	6	7	19	7	1	2.8	.283	.322	.389	.295	.339	.402	.269	4.1	0.0	10-3B	-1	10-SS	-1
2009	MIN	MLB	27	240	26	11	2	3	23	16	37	7	2	1.3	.250	.305	.358	.252	.309	.375	.244	1.6	0.6	60-2B	0		

Breakout: 35% Improve: 60% Collapse: 24% Attrition: 42%   Comparables: Matt Kata, U.L. Washington, Ted Kubiak, Jose Uribe

Tolbert has had an undistinguished minor league career since being drafted, showing minimal competence in most things aside from bunting. He made the club out of spring training, anyway, got the odd start early as the infield fell apart, and then tore ligaments in a thumb and vanished from mid-May until September. When he returned, he had a nice little 10-for-30 hot streak. The best endorsement one can give his season is that though not a speedster, he ran the bases well. Other than Gardenhire's liking the scrappy cut of his jib, there's little to recommend him over any other cadet utility infielder.

Steven Tolleson UT

Bats: R Throws: R Height: 5' 10" Weight: 180 Born: November 1, 1983 Age: 25

YEAR	TEAM	LVL	AGE	PA	R	2B	3B	HR	RBI	BB	SO	SB	CS	EqBRR	AVG	OBP	SLG	EqAVG	EqOBP	EqSLG	EqA	VORP	WARP	DEFENSE			
2006	BLT	A	22	204	23	8	2	2	16	27	34	7	9	-5.5	.287	.390	.392	.206	.289	.289	.205	-12.5	-1.4	17-3B	-3	16-2B	-1
2006	FTM	A+	22	186	23	8	1	4	23	22	24	3	1	-2.5	.268	.353	.408	.228	.306	.364	.239	-3.8	0.8	27-2B	7		
2007	FTM	A+	23	571	75	24	4	5	35	79	97	27	10	-1.5	.285	.388	.382	.223	.315	.313	.227	-21.1	-1.5	50-SS	-11	48-2B	1
2008	NBR	AA	24	397	54	28	1	9	50	44	74	12	6	-1.4	.300	.382	.466	.259	.332	.425	.263	8.8	1.5	33-2B	5	32-SS	-5
2009	MIN	MLB	25	466	44	22	2	7	43	42	113	9	4	0.0	.219	.294	.334	.221	.298	.350	.231	-6.5	-0.1	110-2B	-8		

Breakout: 12% Improve: 32% Collapse: 39% Attrition: 14%   Comparables: Doug Saunders, Billy White, Tim Barker, Mike Rouse

Tolleson did the best offensive work of his career at Double-A, but previous seasons may offer a better indication of his true talent level. Like his father (Wayne) before him, Steven has a future as a sometime middle infielder, though his contact skills should allow him to surpass his old man's meager efforts at the plate. He probably won't be his old man's equal as a basestealer, but he has sufficient speed to put in a center-field cameo without embarrassing himself, an important addition, given that utility infielders who can't play shortstop—and Tolleson really can't—don't get too many chances.

Danny Valencia 3B

Bats: R Throws: R Height: 6' 2" Weight: 200 Born: September 19, 1984 Age: 24

YEAR	TEAM	LVL	AGE	PA	R	2B	3B	HR	RBI	BB	SO	SB	CS	EqBRR	AVG	OBP	SLG	EqAVG	EqOBP	EqSLG	EqA	VORP	WARP	DEFENSE			
2006	ELZ	Rk	21	211	30	13	0	8	29	15	34	0	2	-3.2	.311	.365	.505	.206	.242	.317	.188	-33.0	-2.5	18-1B	-2	17-3B	0
2007	BLT	A	22	271	44	15	0	11	35	28	54	3	3	0.0	.302	.374	.500	.217	.278	.345	.217	-12.9	-0.8	46-3B	0		
2007	FTM	A+	22	250	28	8	2	6	31	16	48	1	0	0.4	.291	.332	.422	.245	.284	.361	.225	-7.8	-1.0	56-3B	-5		
2008	FTM	A+	23	251	35	19	3	5	44	27	43	2	2	-0.2	.336	.402	.518	.270	.331	.438	.264	7.8	0.7	52-3B	-1		
2008	NBR	AA	23	287	40	18	2	10	32	18	70	2	1	1.4	.289	.334	.485	.265	.307	.463	.260	7.6	1.6	56-3B	7		
2009	MIN	MLB	24	550	46	28	2	12	64	34	151	3	2	-0.3	.228	.279	.364	.230	.283	.381	.229	-10.1	-0.1	129-3B	-2		

Breakout: 16% Improve: 37% Collapse: 33% Attrition: 13%   Comparables: Jamie D'Antona, Adam Riggs, Brook Jacoby, Ken Shamburg

Since Gary Gaetti and his then-201 career home runs left town after the 1990 season, the Twins have seen a third baseman surpass the 15-homer mark just twice, Corey Koskie hitting 26 and 25 in 2001 and 2004, respectively. They haven't come close since, but that's not unexpected when you vent over 200 games on Nick Punto. Valencia has the power to end all that. What more he'll do is still open to question, as he's not selective, and although his work at third base is fundamentally sound, no one will ever mistake him for Brooks Robinson. He can also be a bit cranky and un-focused at times, which doesn't play well in the minors and doesn't work at all in the majors unless you're so good they can't get rid of you—and no one is saying Valencia rises to that level.

Delmon Young — LF

Bats: R Throws: R Height: 6' 3" Weight: 215 Born: September 14, 1985 Age: 23

YEAR	TEAM	LVL	AGE	PA	R	2B	3B	HR	RBI	BB	SO	SB	CS	EqBRR	AVG	OBP	SLG	EqAVG	EqOBP	EqSLG	EqA	VORP	WARP	DEFENSE		
2006	DUR	AAA	20	370	50	22	4	8	59	15	65	22	4	-0.9	.316	.341	.474	.280	.304	.446	.261	7.9	0.2	83-RF	-6	
2006	TBA	MLB	20	131	16	9	1	3	10	1	24	2	2	-1.5	.317	.336	.476	.317	.336	.476	.270	5.1	0.1	28-RF	-3	
2007	TBA	MLB	21	681	65	38	0	13	93	26	127	10	3	0.4	.288	.316	.408	.289	.318	.419	.255	5.9	0.6	129-RF	1	28-CF -6
2008	MIN	MLB	22	623	80	28	4	10	69	35	105	14	5	-1.9	.290	.336	.405	.297	.344	.426	.268	14.4	-0.5	148-LF	-21	
2009	MIN	MLB	23	577	70	31	3	12	68	30	99	16	5	0.2	.284	.325	.420	.286	.330	.440	.268	9.2	1.2	135-LF	-6	

Breakout: 27% Improve: 57% Collapse: 20% Attrition: 10%   Comparables: Jeff Francoeur, Shawn Green, Sean Burroughs, Darin Erstad

A year after Young was traded by the Rays due to mediocre production and an overweening sense of entitlement, rumors had him on the block again, especially after Gardenhire suggested that he ranked behind Cuddyer, Gomez, and Span on the outfield depth chart. Credit Gardy for seeing through a soft batting average, because Young might be the most useless .290 hitter in the game. Last year, the average left fielder batted .269/.344/.442; Young failed to break even while making a solid case for himself as the worst defensive outfielder in the majors. Having opened the season batting a homer-less .270/.321/.348 over his first 60 games, Young slugged his first homer on June 7, batting .304/.346/.443 over the remainder of the season. Still, he was as impatient as ever, drawing just 12 unintentional walks during that period, and a home run every 35 at-bats does not a power hitter make, so it's not clear that this was a turning point. Young is still young enough that he could start hitting and turn into anything from Jose Guillen to Dave Parker, but as of now, he's the farthest thing from a winning ballplayer.

PITCHERS

Scott Baker

Bats: R Throws: R Height: 6' 4" Weight: 210 Born: September 19, 1981 Age: 27

YEAR	TEAM	LVL	AGE	W	L	SV	G	GS	IP	H	BB	SO	HR	GB%	BABIP	STUFF	WHIP	ERA	DERA	EqH9	EqBB9	EqSO9	EqHR9	DEF	VORP	SN/WX
2006	ROC	AAA	24	5	4	0	12	12	84¹	77	25	68	4	42.4%	.303	3	1.21	2.68	4.73	10.0	3.2	4.8	0.8	7	7.5	—
2006	MIN	MLB	24	5	8	0	16	16	83¹	114	16	62	17	34.8%	.355	-7	1.56	6.37	4.88	11.8	1.7	5.9	1.7	-16	-7.2	0.17
2007	ROC	AAA	25	3	2	1	7	6	42²	34	4	41	3	48.3%	.779	14	0.89	3.16	5.72	8.7	1.1	6.2	1.1	6	-0.5	—
2007	MIN	MLB	25	9	9	0	24	23	143²	162	29	102	15	36.6%	.329	11	1.33	4.26	3.88	10.1	1.7	5.7	1.0	-7	25.0	3.22
2008	MIN	MLB	26	11	4	0	28	28	172¹	161	42	141	20	33.0%	.287	16	1.18	3.45	3.89	8.3	2.0	6.6	1.1	5	44.2	5.40
2009	MIN	MLB	27	9	8	0	25	25	153	164	39	113	20	38.0%	.300	21	1.33	4.28	4.31	9.5	2.1	6.0	1.1	0	19.1	3.27

Breakout: 17% Improve: 48% Collapse: 16% Attrition: 18%   Comparables: Kevin Millwood, Dustin Hermanson, Doc Medich, Jim McAndrew

The closest thing the Twins have to an ace in the post-Johan era, Baker ended the year with a flourish, delivering a 2.77 ERA in his final 10 starts. The only bump was a strained groin that cost him almost all of May. He boosted his strikeout rate in addition to delivering the solid control we've come to expect. Baker's predilection for allowing fly balls should be noted—he ranked seventh in the majors in lowest GB/FB ratio. Any change of environment, say, should Target Field prove to be windy fenceward when it opens in 2010, and Baker could look like a very different pitcher.

Nick Blackburn

Bats: R Throws: R Height: 6' 4" Weight: 230 Born: February 24, 1982 Age: 27

YEAR	TEAM	LVL	AGE	W	L	SV	G	GS	IP	H	BB	SO	HR	GB%	BABIP	STUFF	WHIP	ERA	DERA	EqH9	EqBB9	EqSO9	EqHR9	DEF	VORP	SN/WX
2006	NBR	AA	24	7	8	0	30	19	132¹	141	37	81	11	46.5%	.310	-35	1.35	4.43	7.18	11.6	3.3	2.8	1.5	1	-21.1	—
2007	NBR	AA	25	3	1	0	8	7	38	36	7	18	1	54.5%	.267	-16	1.13	3.08	7.34	8.8	1.9	2.1	0.5	3	-7.3	—
2007	ROC	AAA	25	7	3	0	17	17	110²	96	12	57	7	52.2%	.255	-4	0.98	2.11	5.16	8.9	1.2	2.8	0.9	18	5.1	—
2007	MIN	MLB	25	0	2	0	6	0	11²	19	2	8	2	38.6%	.405	-14	1.80	7.69	6.35	15.1	1.6	5.6	1.6	-3	-4.2	-0.55
2008	MIN	MLB	26	11	11	0	33	33	193¹	224	39	96	23	46.1%	.310	-3	1.36	4.05	4.56	10.2	1.7	3.9	1.1	-6	22.0	3.96
2009	MIN	MLB	27	6	8	0	29	17	113¹	140	30	53	15	46.0%	.310	0	1.50	5.22	5.32	11.0	2.1	3.8	1.1	0	1.5	0.87

Breakout: 8% Improve: 36% Collapse: 33% Attrition: 23%   Comparables: Mike Harkey, Billy Wynne, Mike Scott, Mark Clark

As Peggy Lee used to sing, "Is that all there is, is that all there is? If that's all there is, my friends, then let's keep dancing." Hyped pitching prospect Blackburn made it up and flashed excellent control, but he lacks a strikeout pitch and the league found him rather hittable. His ability to avoid ball four is nice, but unless he finds a way to induce more whiffs, he's going to be only as good or as bad as a light-footed defense makes him.

Boof Bonser

Bats: R　Throws: R　Height: 6' 4"　Weight: 260　Born: October 14, 1981　Age: 27

YEAR	TEAM	LVL	AGE	W	L	SV	G	GS	IP	H	BB	SO	HR	GB%	BABIP	STUFF	WHIP	ERA	DERA	EqH9	EqBB9	EqSO9	EqHR9	DEF	VORP	SN/WX
2006	ROC	AAA	24	6	4	0	14	14	86¹	68	35	83	4	38.3%	.272	7	1.20	2.82	5.58	8.7	4.2	5.9	0.8	9	0.2	—
2006	MIN	MLB	24	7	6	0	18	18	100¹	104	24	84	18	43.2%	.299	5	1.28	4.22	3.83	9.0	2.1	6.8	1.6	-6	17.4	2.35
2007	MIN	MLB	25	8	12	0	31	30	173	199	65	136	27	46.6%	.323	-5	1.53	5.10	4.79	10.3	3.2	6.2	1.5	-14	6.5	2.22
2008	MIN	MLB	26	3	7	0	47	12	118¹	139	36	97	16	42.0%	.328	-6	1.48	5.93	5.65	10.0	2.5	6.3	1.2	-13	-13.0	-0.32
2009	MIN	MLB	27	4	5	1	34	8	83²	88	27	64	10	43.0%	.300	10	1.38	4.58	4.67	9.3	2.7	6.2	1.0	0	8.2	1.04

Breakout: 46%　Improve: 75%　Collapse: 10%　Attrition: 25%　　Comparables: Ryan Rupe, Ron Robinson, Jim Nash, Jack Armstrong

Last year in this space, we pointed out that when right-handed hitters put the ball in play against Bonser in 2007, they hit only .231, whereas left-handers had a crazy-high .401 safety rate. The weirdness continued in 2008, with lefties hitting .374 on balls in play but righties batting only .287. The league-average figures were .297 for righty-on-righty action and .307 for lefty-on-righty. Roughly the same rates applied in 2007, so as Bob Dylan told Mister Jones, something is happening here. It seems that lefties see Bonser very well. Paradoxically, he strikes them out more often than he does right-handers, but when lefties make contact, they do so with vigor, batting .316/.375/.516. Righties have a harder time of it and are far less likely to hit the ball safely, or for extra bases when they do, or even to draw a walk. Now, we might have a chicken-and-egg problem, and the disparity is wholly the fault of the defense, but there's little evidence of that. The upshot is that the move to the pen was exactly the wrong way to handle Bonser, assuming the Twins should have kept using him at all. He pitched better as a starter, and the likely reason is that the killer lefties were washed out by the larger population of right-handed hitters. In a relief role, he was more vulnerable to concentrated doses of lefty lightning. There's never been a man more desperately in need of a cut fastball than Boof.

Craig Breslow

Bats: L　Throws: L　Height: 6' 0"　Weight: 185　Born: August 8, 1980　Age: 28

YEAR	TEAM	LVL	AGE	W	L	SV	G	GS	IP	H	BB	SO	HR	GB%	BABIP	STUFF	WHIP	ERA	DERA	EqH9	EqBB9	EqSO9	EqHR9	DEF	VORP	SN/WX
2006	PAW	AAA	25	7	1	7	39	0	67²	49	24	77	3	46.8%	.279	5	1.09	2.68	4.48	7.7	3.6	7.0	0.7	4	8.0	—
2006	BOS	MLB	25	0	2	0	13	0	12	12	6	12	0	36.1%	.353	6	1.50	3.75	3.65	8.0	4.4	8.0	0.0	0	3.3	-0.05
2007	PAW	AAA	26	2	3	1	49	1	68²	70	25	73	6	43.3%	.340	-13	1.38	4.06	5.71	11.0	3.6	6.5	1.3	-4	-0.8	—
2008	CLE	MLB	27	0	0	0	7	0	8¹	10	5	7	1	46.4%	.333	-6	1.80	3.25	2.08	10.4	5.2	6.2	1.0	-1	2.3	-0.03
2008	MIN	MLB	27	0	2	1	42	0	38²	24	14	32	0	43.7%	.238	12	0.98	1.63	3.35	5.5	3.1	6.7	0.0	4	15.6	0.86
2009	MIN	MLB	28	2	2	2	45	0	43¹	43	18	35	4	43.0%	.300	7	1.41	4.11	4.21	8.8	3.5	6.6	0.8	0	6.3	0.53

Breakout: 12%　Improve: 26%　Collapse: 42%　Attrition: 29%　　Comparables: Frank DiPino, Steve Mingori, Gary Lavelle, Mike Mohler

The Red Sox kept Breslow in the minors throughout 2007 and then waived him during spring training. Claimed by the Indians, he latched on as the last man in the pen, but LOOGYs are like placekickers in the NFL—miss a couple, and you're gone. In Breslow's case, he allowed a (nondecisive) homer to Jim Thome on May 21 and was almost immediately back on waivers. As the Twins bobbed their way next, Breslow did an excellent job for them, holding lefties to .183/.230/.232; Thome's was the only homer he allowed all season, and he tamed his walk rate. Now that Breslow has established himself, he'll probably appear in the next 12 editions of this book—which doesn't preclude a few more trips through waivers.

Jesse Crain

Bats: R　Throws: R　Height: 6' 1"　Weight: 205　Born: July 5, 1981　Age: 27

YEAR	TEAM	LVL	AGE	W	L	SV	G	GS	IP	H	BB	SO	HR	GB%	BABIP	STUFF	WHIP	ERA	DERA	EqH9	EqBB9	EqSO9	EqHR9	DEF	VORP	SN/WX
2006	MIN	MLB	24	4	5	1	68	0	76²	79	18	60	6	56.7%	.309	7	1.27	3.52	3.76	8.8	2.1	6.2	0.7	1	20.9	0.65
2007	MIN	MLB	25	1	2	0	18	0	16¹	19	4	10	4	48.2%	.294	-26	1.41	5.52	8.44	10.1	2.2	5.1	2.2	0	-5.3	-0.08
2008	MIN	MLB	26	5	4	0	66	0	62²	62	24	50	6	40.9%	.303	0	1.37	3.59	3.21	8.8	3.2	6.4	0.9	-7	10.5	0.08
2009	MIN	MLB	27	3	2	2	46	0	53	52	17	42	6	43.0%	.290	9	1.30	3.88	3.97	8.7	2.6	6.4	0.9	0	9.6	0.76

Breakout: 38%　Improve: 63%　Collapse: 20%　Attrition: 24%　　Comparables: Steve Foucault, Albie Lopez, Ron Taylor, Dave Smith

Given that Crain was coming back from surgery to repair both his labrum and his rotator cuff, it's hard to call his season anything but a success, especially since he got back in time to make the team out of spring training. Nevertheless, there were some concessions to the recovery, as the Twins were forced to carefully manage his workload, his usually excellent control had been dinged a bit, and his fly-ball rate was up. Still, by the end of the season, he was back in the setup role. We'll see if his second year back is even better.

Brian Duensing

Bats: L   Throws: L   Height: 5' 11"   Weight: 195   Born: February 22, 1983   Age: 26

YEAR	TEAM	LVL	AGE	W	L	SV	G	GS	IP	H	BB	SO	HR	GB%	BABIP	STUFF	WHIP	ERA	DERA	EqH9	EqBB9	EqSO9	EqHR9	DEF	VORP	SN/WX
2006	BLT	A	23	2	3	0	11	11	70	68	14	55	3	52.9%	.314	-21	1.17	2.96	5.72	12.5	3.2	2.9	1.5	-5	-0.8	—
2006	FTM	A+	23	2	5	0	7	7	40²	47	8	33	4	50.4%	.352	-26	1.37	4.25	8.21	15.1	2.9	4.0	2.4	-2	-9.9	—
2006	NBR	AA	23	1	2	0	10	9	49¹	51	18	30	6	57.4%	.304	-34	1.41	3.67	7.11	11.4	4.3	2.8	2.0	-3	-7.4	—
2007	NBR	AA	24	4	1	0	9	9	50²	47	7	38	2	43.8%	.288	1	1.07	2.66	6.06	9.2	1.7	4.0	0.7	8	-2.5	—
2007	ROC	AAA	24	11	5	0	19	19	116²	115	30	86	13	50.8%	.299	-20	1.24	3.24	6.60	10.8	2.7	4.5	1.7	15	-11.8	—
2008	ROC	AAA	25	5	11	0	25	24	138²	150	34	77	16	51.8%	.300	-27	1.33	4.28	7.33	10.6	2.5	3.0	1.5	21	-25.2	—
2009	MIN	MLB	26	5	9	0	32	17	110²	148	38	49	17	47.0%	.330	-7	1.68	6.22	6.29	11.8	2.8	3.6	1.4	0	-10.7	-0.43

Breakout: 10%   Improve: 41%   Collapse: 31%   Attrition: 18%   Comparables: Eddie Priest, Mark Thurmond, Blaise Ilsley, Clyde Wright

The Twins are like Chrysler in the K-car era, mass-producing a styleless but functional model that's just good enough to keep them in business—although the one thing Twins pitching prospects don't get is Ks. Duensing is another model off the assembly line, with standard-feature good control and let-'em-hit-it styling. He varies slightly from his fellow Twins pitchers in that he's not an extreme fly-ball pitcher, but his ceiling is still back-end starter or middle relief.

Eddie Guardado

Bats: R   Throws: L   Height: 6' 0"   Weight: 225   Born: October 2, 1970   Age: 38

YEAR	TEAM	LVL	AGE	W	L	SV	G	GS	IP	H	BB	SO	HR	GB%	BABIP	STUFF	WHIP	ERA	DERA	EqH9	EqBB9	EqSO9	EqHR9	DEF	VORP	SN/WX
2006	SEA	MLB	35	1	3	5	28	0	23	29	11	22	8	37.3%	.328	-15	1.74	5.48	3.91	11.0	4.3	7.4	2.7	-4	1.3	-1.16
2006	CIN	MLB	35	0	0	8	15	0	14	15	2	17	2	34.2%	.371	14	1.21	1.29	1.32	9.9	1.3	9.9	1.3	-2	4.5	0.54
2007	CIN	MLB	36	0	0	0	15	0	13²	16	4	8	2	22.4%	.304	-14	1.46	7.23	5.65	8.8	1.9	5.0	1.3	-1	-1.8	0.29
2008	TEX	MLB	37	3	3	4	55	0	49¹	38	17	28	3	28.9%	.246	-6	1.11	3.65	4.10	6.1	2.8	4.5	0.6	3	11.8	3.19
2008	MIN	MLB	37	1	1	0	9	0	7	12	2	5	1	23.1%	.440	-14	2.00	7.71	4.26	17.1	2.8	5.7	1.4	-3	-1.7	-0.20
2009	MIN	MLB	38	2	2	2	41	0	40¹	43	13	27	6	34.0%	.290	-4	1.38	4.49	4.51	9.4	2.7	5.4	1.2	0	4.1	0.37

Breakout: 14%   Improve: 30%   Collapse: 41%   Attrition: 39%   Comparables: Grant Jackson, Aurelio Lopez, Darold Knowles, Jeff Reardon

"Everyday Eddie" has fallen far enough from his former fame as a closer that last August, the Rangers traded him to the Twins for Mark Hamburger. Although Guardado did a fair job last year, picking up 25 holds, there's no reason to consider him a high-leverage reliever at this stage.

Deolis Guerra

Bats: R   Throws: R   Height: 6' 5"   Weight: 200   Born: April 17, 1989   Age: 20

YEAR	TEAM	LVL	AGE	W	L	SV	G	GS	IP	H	BB	SO	HR	GB%	BABIP	STUFF	WHIP	ERA	DERA	EqH9	EqBB9	EqSO9	EqHR9	DEF	VORP	SN/WX
2006	HAG	A	17	6	7	0	17	17	81	59	37	64	3	48.2%	.259	5	1.19	2.22	6.59	9.7	6.2	3.2	1.3	13	-7.5	—
2007	SLU	A+	18	2	6	0	21	20	89²	80	25	66	9	51.2%	.278	-2	1.17	4.01	7.52	10.1	3.4	3.7	2.1	8	-17.3	—
2008	FTM	A+	19	11	9	0	26	25	130	138	71	71	12	35.7%	.302	-31	1.61	5.47	9.03	12.2	6.1	2.2	2.1	-6	-44.5	—
2009	MIN	MLB	20	3	9	0	19	19	87²	125	61	41	22	38.0%	.330	-15	2.11	8.71	8.59	12.6	5.6	3.8	2.2	0	-30.7	-2.67

Breakout: 15%   Improve: 52%   Collapse: 10%   Attrition: 13%   Comparables: Jacobo Sequea, Robinson Tejeda, Jose Melendez, Greg Hansell

Part of the Santana payout from the Mets, Guerra is impossibly young and not getting any older, which is not to say that this is *The Curious Case of Benjamin Pitcher*, but rather that Guerra is not improving, but going backward. His fastball used to top out in the mid-90s, but he's lucky to reach 90 now. About the only aspect of his prospectdom that isn't in question: he's still quite tall.

Matt Guerrier

| | | | | Bats: R | | Throws: R | | Height: 6' 3" | | Weight: 195 | | Born: August 2, 1978 | | | Age: 30 | |

YEAR	TEAM	LVL	AGE	W	L	SV	G	GS	IP	H	BB	SO	HR	GB%	BABIP	STUFF	WHIP	ERA	DERA	EqH9	EqBB9	EqSO9	EqHR9	DEF	VORP	SN/WX
2006	MIN	MLB	27	1	0	1	39	1	69²	78	21	37	9	47.1%	.305	-15	1.42	3.36	3.93	9.7	2.6	4.2	1.0	1	18.1	0.79
2007	MIN	MLB	28	2	4	1	73	0	88	71	21	68	9	48.2%	.253	4	1.05	2.35	3.34	7.1	2.0	6.2	0.9	8	36.6	2.40
2008	MIN	MLB	29	6	9	1	76	0	76¹	84	37	59	12	47.2%	.308	-20	1.59	5.19	5.42	9.7	3.9	6.0	1.4	-2	1.0	0.76
2009	*MIN*	*MLB*	*30*	*3*	*3*	*2*	*48*	*0*	*57¹*	*61*	*21*	*42*	*7*	*45.0%*	*.300*	*3*	*1.43*	*4.42*	*4.51*	*9.4*	*3.1*	*6.0*	*1.0*	*0*	*6.2*	*0.50*

Breakout: 16%   Improve: 33%   Collapse: 42%   Attrition: 25%   Comparables: Dave Smith, Randy Moffitt, Dave Heaverlo, Dave Borkowski

It was no Guerrier and Ives print for Matt after three solid years in the Twins' pen. He was due for a comedown after a career-best 2007 fueled by an increased strikeout rate and favorable bounces on balls in play. Last year, he retained the former, but predictably lost the latter. Worse, Guerrier became vulnerable to the long ball down the stretch in 2007, and that carried over for a career-high home-run rate in '08. As in '07, Guerrier fell apart in the last two months, getting pounded for a 10.07 ERA in his final 25 appearances. His salary is now rising through his arbitration years, so the ever-frugal Twins will need to be sure that they're not sinking scarce resources into a failing arm.

Philip Humber

| | | | | Bats: R | | Throws: R | | Height: 6' 4" | | Weight: 225 | | Born: December 21, 1982 | | | Age: 26 | |

YEAR	TEAM	LVL	AGE	W	L	SV	G	GS	IP	H	BB	SO	HR	GB%	BABIP	STUFF	WHIP	ERA	DERA	EqH9	EqBB9	EqSO9	EqHR9	DEF	VORP	SN/WX
2006	SLU	A+	23	3	1	0	7	7	38¹	24	9	36	4	53.4%	.211	-9	0.87	2.36	5.40	8.2	3.1	4.6	2.1	2	0.8	—
2006	BIN	AA	23	2	2	0	6	6	34	25	10	36	4	41.9%	.239	-1	1.03	2.91	5.57	8.6	3.3	5.6	1.9	3	0.1	—
2007	NWO	AAA	24	11	9	0	25	25	139	129	44	120	21	42.0%	.278	-14	1.24	4.27	5.77	9.2	3.1	5.6	1.8	6	-2.5	—
2007	NYN	MLB	24	0	0	0	3	1	7	9	2	2	1	28.6%	.296	-29	1.57	7.71	7.36	11.0	2.5	2.5	1.2	0	-1.5	-0.17
2008	ROC	AAA	25	10	8	0	31	23	136¹	145	49	106	21	38.0%	.306	-36	1.42	4.56	6.43	11.0	3.6	4.6	2.0	7	-11.7	—
2008	MIN	MLB	25	0	0	0	5	0	11²	11	5	6	4	50.0%	.206	-29	1.37	4.62	7.94	8.7	4.0	4.0	3.2	4	1.4	0.05
2009	*MIN*	*MLB*	*26*	*5*	*7*	*1*	*38*	*13*	*96*	*111*	*39*	*61*	*16*	*40.0%*	*.300*	*-1*	*1.55*	*5.54*	*5.55*	*10.2*	*3.3*	*5.1*	*1.4*	*0*	*-1.4*	*0.36*

Breakout: 33%   Improve: 72%   Collapse: 13%   Attrition: 16%   Comparables: Mike Campbell, Greg Gohr, Darrell Akerfelds, Jeff Shaw

Getting this former first-rounder as part of the Santana ransom must have seemed like a good idea on paper, but Humber's curveball hadn't humped as much as it did before Tommy John surgery. Humber was hammered throughout the first half, but he righted himself in the second by going 6-1 with a 2.67 ERA in nine postbreak appearances. Most significantly, both his strikeout rate and his walk rate improved, jumping from 6.2 and 4.2, respectively, to 8.2 and 1.9. As with many pitchers who rely on a curve, Humber's homer rate is always going to be high, a reason why he's not meant for bullpen work, as he demonstrated in September. He's out of options, so if Humber's humper continues to hum, he could stick in the Hump Dome this year.

Francisco Liriano

| | | | | Bats: L | | Throws: L | | Height: 6' 2" | | Weight: 200 | | Born: October 26, 1983 | | | Age: 25 | |

YEAR	TEAM	LVL	AGE	W	L	SV	G	GS	IP	H	BB	SO	HR	GB%	BABIP	STUFF	WHIP	ERA	DERA	EqH9	EqBB9	EqSO9	EqHR9	DEF	VORP	SN/WX
2006	MIN	MLB	22	12	3	1	28	16	121	89	32	144	9	57.1%	.285	48	1.00	2.16	2.90	6.6	2.4	9.4	0.6	6	50.8	5.13
2008	ROC	AAA	24	10	2	0	19	19	118	102	31	113	8	42.9%	.294	9	1.13	3.28	5.32	8.9	2.7	5.8	0.9	14	3.5	—
2008	MIN	MLB	24	6	4	0	14	14	76	74	32	67	7	41.9%	.309	15	1.39	3.91	4.28	8.6	3.4	6.9	0.8	-5	7.9	1.38
2009	*MIN*	*MLB*	*25*	*9*	*8*	*1*	*35*	*24*	*145²*	*143*	*52*	*125*	*16*	*44.0%*	*.300*	*20*	*1.34*	*4.16*	*4.24*	*8.7*	*2.9*	*7.0*	*1.0*	*0*	*19.4*	*3.06*

Breakout: 7%   Improve: 34%   Collapse: 35%   Attrition: 9%   Comparables: Ken Holtzman, Chan Ho Park, Jim O'Toole, Steve Avery

Having missed 2007 recovering from Tommy John surgery, Liriano was understandably rusty initially, and the Twins farmed him out amid concerns about his location, the sharpness of his pitches, and—it was rumored—his running too much time off his arbitration clock. Recalled in mid-April, he was still obviously not ready, walking 13 in 10⅓ innings pitched. He was sent back down, and then began "The Wait," an excruciating drama during which Liriano pitched well in the minors while Livan Hernandez got sprayed with bullets like Edward G. Robinson at the end of *Little Caesar*. Liriano pitched well in June, pitched well in July, and sailed past the point where arbitration eligibility would be a problem for the penurious Twins. Meanwhile, Hernandez was allowing nearly seven runs per nine innings, a key handicap in a close race. Liriano finally returned on August 3; from then until the end of the season (when a bit of fatigue set in), the magic was back, the lefty making seven quality starts in 11 tries and striking out 60 against 19 walks in 65⅔ IP. It wasn't quite the old presurgical dominance, but it was good enough, and more efficient. Assuming his two fall shellings don't indicate a recurrence of anything medical, or the Twins don't get more bright ideas about how to keep him affordable, Liriano should be the staff ace in 2009.

Jose Mijares

Bats: L | Throws: L | Height: 6' 0" | Weight: 230 | Born: October 29, 1984 | Age: 24

YEAR	TEAM	LVL	AGE	W	L	SV	G	GS	IP	H	BB	SO	HR	GB%	BABIP	STUFF	WHIP	ERA	DERA	EqH9	EqBB9	EqSO9	EqHR9	DEF	VORP	SN/WX
2006	FTM	A+	21	3	5	0	27	5	63	52	27	77	10	42.6%	.301	-25	1.25	3.57	6.83	11.7	5.5	6.5	3.3	0	-7.4	—
2007	NBR	AA	22	5	3	9	46	0	61	40	48	75	7	47.3%	.243	3	1.44	3.54	4.85	7.1	7.4	7.0	1.7	-2	4.9	—
2008	FTM	A+	23	0	0	0	5	0	10¹	7	3	8	0	44.8%	.250	-15	0.97	2.62	5.59	7.4	3.7	3.7	0.0	1	0.0	—
2008	NBR	AA	23	1	1	2	11	0	15¹	16	7	17	2	28.9%	.326	0	1.50	2.94	3.52	10.0	4.1	7.0	1.8	0	3.5	—
2008	MIN	MLB	23	0	1	0	10	0	10¹	3	0	5	0	44.8%	.103	7	0.29	0.87	1.74	1.7	0.0	3.5	0.0	3	5.6	0.64
2009	MIN	MLB	24	2	3	1	32	3	52²	60	26	40	8	41.0%	.320	2	1.63	5.42	5.41	10.1	4.0	6.2	1.4	0	0.1	0.10

Breakout: 5% Improve: 22% Collapse: 45% Attrition: 14% Comparables: Pedro Viola, Josh Newman, Oneli Perez, Adam Butler

Fracturing one's pitching elbow in a car accident is rarely a good career move, but fortunately for Mijares, he came back from his January mishap in good form, rebounding to make the majors by September. Though he was a lefty, Gardenhire properly had him pitching whole innings, as he has the stuff to take on all comers. The only problem is that Mijares tends to put on weight; he doesn't throw meatballs, but he sure likes to eat them. He should take some of the setup innings this season, assuming he stays out of traffic, and White Castle.

Kevin Mulvey

Bats: R | Throws: R | Height: 6' 1" | Weight: 195 | Born: May 26, 1985 | Age: 24

YEAR	TEAM	LVL	AGE	W	L	SV	G	GS	IP	H	BB	SO	HR	GB%	BABIP	STUFF	WHIP	ERA	DERA	EqH9	EqBB9	EqSO9	EqHR9	DEF	VORP	SN/WX
2006	BIN	AA	21	0	1	0	3	3	13	10	5	10	1	61.1%	.257	7	1.15	1.38	3.97	9.5	4.8	4.0	1.6	-1	2.0	—
2007	BIN	AA	22	11	10	0	26	26	151²	145	43	110	4	55.7%	.305	11	1.24	3.32	6.18	9.2	3.0	3.8	0.6	6	-9.4	—
2008	ROC	AAA	23	7	9	0	27	27	148	152	48	121	16	40.6%	.312	-12	1.35	3.77	6.00	10.3	3.2	4.8	1.4	3	-6.3	—
2009	MIN	MLB	24	5	8	0	28	18	111	133	45	65	16	43.0%	.310	2	1.61	5.76	5.84	10.7	3.3	4.8	1.3	0	-5.3	0.20

Breakout: 12% Improve: 43% Collapse: 31% Attrition: 20% Comparables: Mark Thompson, Chad Durbin, Chad Ogea, Julio Valera

Yet another gift received for Santana, Mulvey was already the quintessential Twins pitcher, a guy with average stuff and above-average control who does just enough to get by. Last season largely brought more of the same, with the troubling development that his ground-ball rate plummeted, resulting in four times as many home runs allowed in about the same number of innings. This spring finds the generic Mulvey waiting for one of the generic pitchers in front of him to yield a spot somewhere on the staff, in the rotation or in middle relief.

Joe Nathan

Bats: R | Throws: R | Height: 6' 4" | Weight: 220 | Born: November 22, 1974 | Age: 34

YEAR	TEAM	LVL	AGE	W	L	SV	G	GS	IP	H	BB	SO	HR	GB%	BABIP	STUFF	WHIP	ERA	DERA	EqH9	EqBB9	EqSO9	EqHR9	DEF	VORP	SN/WX
2006	MIN	MLB	31	7	0	36	64	0	68¹	38	16	95	3	38.0%	.246	39	0.79	1.58	2.22	5.1	2.1	9.7	0.4	4	34.4	6.59
2007	MIN	MLB	32	4	2	37	68	0	71²	54	19	77	4	43.2%	.282	27	1.02	1.88	2.18	6.8	2.3	8.6	0.5	1	32.7	5.05
2008	MIN	MLB	33	1	2	39	68	0	67²	43	18	74	5	49.1%	.236	25	0.90	1.33	2.69	5.6	2.1	8.7	0.7	5	30.0	5.10
2009	MIN	MLB	34	5	4	31	55	0	61	48	19	64	5	44.0%	.270	22	1.08	2.54	2.61	7.0	2.5	8.5	0.8	0	21.0	3.14

Breakout: 8% Improve: 17% Collapse: 67% Attrition: 5% Comparables: Tom Henke, Mike Jackson, Lee Smith, Billy Wagner

We asked Minnesota housewife Betty Johnson to take this closer taste-test blindfolded. She slapped us and walked away, but you can still give it a try:

	G	W	L	SV	BS	IP	H	BB	SO	ERA	FRA	WXRL
Pitcher A	339	25	20	199	16	374	285	67	352	1.93	1.99	27.7
Pitcher B	342	20	10	199	20	350	229	98	429	1.83	1.85	28.8

Give up? "Pitcher A" is the leading brand, Mariano Rivera, while "Pitcher B" is Joe Nathan. One is going to the Hall of Fame. The other, unless he matches Rivera's unusual longevity, will go down as the best closer in Twins history and perhaps the second-best closer of the current epoch, and that's no small thing. If there was one blemish on Nathan's season, it was that abetted by some shaky defense, he packed his worst pitching of the season into a crucial three-week period between late August and mid-September, during which time he blew three of four saves.

Prior to the season, the Twins signed Nathan to a four-year extension with a club option for 2012, so he'll have plenty of chances to make up for it.

Glen Perkins

| | | | | Bats: L | | Throws: L | | Height: 5' 11" | | Weight: 200 | | Born: March 2, 1983 | | Age: 26 | |

YEAR	TEAM	LVL	AGE	W	L	SV	G	GS	IP	H	BB	SO	HR	GB%	BABIP	STUFF	WHIP	ERA	DERA	EqH9	EqBB9	EqSO9	EqHR9	DEF	VORP	SN/WX
2006	NBR	AA	23	4	11	0	23	23	117²	109	45	131	11	36.8%	.320	-13	1.31	3.92	6.52	10.9	4.3	6.2	1.6	-2	-10.9	—
2007	MIN	MLB	24	0	0	0	19	0	28²	23	12	20	2	40.7%	.273	-3	1.22	3.14	4.05	7.4	3.7	5.7	0.7	3	9.0	0.43
2008	ROC	AAA	25	2	1	0	7	6	33¹	28	19	27	2	36.3%	.265	-5	1.41	2.97	6.00	7.9	5.2	4.6	0.8	4	-1.5	—
2008	MIN	MLB	25	12	4	0	26	26	151	183	39	74	25	39.1%	.310	-17	1.47	4.41	4.88	10.5	2.1	3.9	1.6	-1	14.5	2.58
2009	MIN	MLB	26	4	6	0	28	14	89	103	34	49	14	41.0%	.300	-2	1.55	5.34	5.37	10.3	3.2	4.5	1.3	0	0.7	0.61

Breakout: 5%   Improve: 25%   Collapse: 47%   Attrition: 34%   Comparables: Allen Watson, Brian Anderson, Nino Espinosa, Neal Heaton

As Peggy Lee used to sing, "Is that all there …"—wait, we used that line for Blackburn, but it applies here as well. After an unimpressive camp, Perkins didn't come up until May, and, let's face it, with the exception of his low rate of walks per nine innings, he got his hat handed to him. Sure, in 21 starts through the end of August, he had an ERA of 3.96, but with few strikeouts and fly-ball-chuckin' ways, batters were hitting .287/.331/.454 against him, and his overall rate of homers per nine was the second-highest in the league for pitchers with 150 or more innings pitched. That he was completely lit up in September (7.45 ERA in five starts) was chalked up to fatigue, but more accurately could be ascribed to the results' finally catching up to his performance.

Dennys Reyes

| | | | | Bats: R | | Throws: L | | Height: 6' 3" | | Weight: 245 | | Born: April 19, 1977 | | Age: 32 | |

YEAR	TEAM	LVL	AGE	W	L	SV	G	GS	IP	H	BB	SO	HR	GB%	BABIP	STUFF	WHIP	ERA	DERA	EqH9	EqBB9	EqSO9	EqHR9	DEF	VORP	SN/WX
2006	ROC	AAA	29	1	0	0	4	3	18	11	3	13	0	61.2%	.234	5	0.78	0.50	4.41	6.6	2.2	4.4	0.0	6	2.2	—
2006	MIN	MLB	29	5	0	0	66	0	50²	35	15	49	3	72.3%	.254	21	0.99	0.89	1.66	6.1	2.8	8.0	0.6	0	26.4	2.20
2007	MIN	MLB	30	2	1	0	50	0	29¹	34	21	21	1	67.4%	.375	-3	1.88	3.99	2.86	10.8	6.0	5.7	0.3	-4	5.4	0.05
2008	MIN	MLB	31	3	0	0	75	0	46¹	40	15	39	4	59.1%	.283	6	1.19	2.33	2.62	7.9	2.8	6.9	0.8	0	17.4	0.57
2009	MIN	MLB	32	2	2	3	47	0	40	38	16	32	2	58.0%	.300	9	1.35	3.18	3.33	8.5	3.2	6.6	0.4	0	10.0	0.88

Breakout: 12%   Improve: 28%   Collapse: 50%   Attrition: 22%   Comparables: Terry Forster, Bob Wickman, Sparky Lyle, Mike Fetters

As we go to press, the rotund Reyes was out on the free-agent market looking for a team to hand him an equally rotund contract. That represents a big change of fortune from the previous fall, when elbow soreness had truncated his season and it was unclear if he would be pitching effectively or at all. Instead, he set a career high in appearances and had one of his best years as a situational specialist, holding southpaw swingers to .202/.250/.287. Most impressively, he walked just five of them in 101 PAs. Reyes hasn't always been this good or this durable, and a bit of knee soreness during the season hinted that his bulk may be a problem. Those caveats aside, he's a reasonably solid bet as lefty spot guys go.

Anthony Slama

| | | | | Bats: R | | Throws: R | | Height: 6' 3" | | Weight: 180 | | Born: January 6, 1984 | | Age: 25 | |

YEAR	TEAM	LVL	AGE	W	L	SV	G	GS	IP	H	BB	SO	HR	GB%	BABIP	STUFF	WHIP	ERA	DERA	EqH9	EqBB9	EqSO9	EqHR9	DEF	VORP	SN/WX
2007	BLT	A	23	1	1	10	21	0	24¹	15	9	39	0	52.4%	.295	5	0.99	1.48	4.71	9.4	5.1	7.7	0.4	3	2.1	—
2008	FTM	A+	24	4	1	25	51	0	71	43	24	110	0	47.7%	.322	23	0.94	1.01	2.95	8.2	3.9	9.0	0.4	-1	18.8	—
2009	MIN	MLB	25	3	3	2	29	4	58²	57	29	57	5	46.0%	.320	17	1.47	4.32	4.43	8.6	4.1	7.9	0.8	0	7.5	0.81

Breakout: 7%   Improve: 14%   Collapse: 69%   Attrition: 12%   Comparables: Geoff Combe, Connor Robertson, Mark Wohlers, David Riske

A fastball/slider guy who spent about 42 years in college and therefore has been quite old for his leagues, Slama throws a heavy fastball that is very hard to slam—in 102⅔ pro innings, he has yet to allow a home run. Sent to the Arizona Fall League, he struggled a bit with control, but otherwise did the things that had been successful for him, getting strikeouts and grounders. With success at Double-A, he's the kind of guy who could and should move up quickly—at 25, he's not someone you're waiting for to grow into a bigger pair of sneakers, but just someone to show you that his approach works at the higher levels.

Kevin Slowey

Bats: R		Throws: R		Height: 6' 3"		Weight: 195		Born: May 4, 1984		Age: 25												

YEAR	TEAM	LVL	AGE	W	L	SV	G	GS	IP	H	BB	SO	HR	GB%	BABIP	STUFF	WHIP	ERA	DERA	EqH9	EqBB9	EqSO9	EqHR9	DEF	VORP	SN/WX
2006	FTM	A+	22	4	2	0	14	14	89	52	9	99	2	42.5%	.230	31	0.69	1.01	3.55	7.1	1.5	5.5	0.6	0	19.1	—
2006	NBR	AA	22	4	3	0	9	9	59²	50	13	52	6	39.4%	.265	0	1.06	3.19	5.79	9.2	2.6	4.5	1.6	3	-1.2	—
2007	ROC	AAA	23	10	5	0	20	20	133²	110	18	107	4	43.3%	.277	22	0.96	1.88	4.06	8.6	1.5	4.8	0.5	14	21.6	—
2007	MIN	MLB	23	4	1	0	13	11	66²	82	11	47	16	30.1%	.297	-9	1.40	4.72	4.67	10.3	1.3	5.2	2.1	-4	5.2	1.08
2008	MIN	MLB	24	12	11	0	27	27	160¹	161	24	123	22	37.6%	.293	10	1.15	3.99	4.28	8.8	1.3	6.1	1.3	0	28.4	3.98
2009	MIN	MLB	25	10	8	0	26	26	159²	165	33	115	21	39.0%	.290	22	1.24	4.11	4.16	9.2	1.7	5.8	1.2	0	23.5	3.71

Breakout: 11% Improve: 41% Collapse: 22% Attrition: 10%   Comparables: Bob Sebra, Andy Sonnanstine, Scott Sanderson, Reggie Cleveland

Like Perkins, Slowey is a fly-ball pitcher with wonderful control—his 1.35 walks per nine innings was the lowest rate allowed by any MLB pitcher who threw over 80 innings. Unlike Perkins, he actually gets batters to swing and miss with some regularity; out of such differences are successful careers made. Slowed early by a strained biceps, Slowey pitched with solid efficiency (a 3.56 ERA in 24 starts) until September, when, as with many Twins pitchers, exhaustion seemed to set in. After lowering his troubling home-run rate in late 2007, Slowey continued to improve at keeping the ball in the park, but there are going to be days when the big blast bites him. Inventing some wrinkle to hold lefties at bay would help—they're slugging .506 against him in 431 career at-bats.

Anthony Swarzak

Bats: R		Throws: R		Height: 6' 3"		Weight: 195		Born: September 10, 1985		Age: 23												

YEAR	TEAM	LVL	AGE	W	L	SV	G	GS	IP	H	BB	SO	HR	GB%	BABIP	STUFF	WHIP	ERA	DERA	EqH9	EqBB9	EqSO9	EqHR9	DEF	VORP	SN/WX
2006	FTM	A+	20	11	7	0	27	27	145¹	131	60	131	8	40.2%	.300	4	1.32	3.29	5.68	11.4	5.2	4.4	1.4	-2	-1.1	—
2007	FTM	A+	21	0	0	0	3	3	15²	14	5	18	0	33.3%	.350	14	1.21	2.29	5.79	10.9	3.9	6.4	0.6	0	-0.3	—
2007	NBR	AA	21	5	4	0	15	14	86¹	78	23	76	6	34.0%	.299	22	1.17	3.23	4.29	9.7	2.9	5.1	1.1	-5	11.6	—
2008	NBR	AA	22	3	8	0	20	20	101²	126	37	76	12	35.3%	.350	-11	1.60	5.66	6.41	11.4	3.2	4.6	1.5	-7	-9.0	—
2008	ROC	AAA	22	5	0	0	7	7	45	41	14	26	4	44.5%	.266	-3	1.22	1.80	5.23	8.8	3.1	3.1	1.3	8	1.8	—
2009	MIN	MLB	23	5	8	0	20	20	104¹	125	43	62	17	37.0%	.310	6	1.61	5.91	5.92	10.7	3.4	4.8	1.5	0	-5.9	0.19

Breakout: 11% Improve: 42% Collapse: 18% Attrition: 10%   Comparables: Bobby Thigpen, Luis Andujar, Adam Peterson, Chad Ogea

Swarzak has apparently gotten past the drug use that earned him a 50-game suspension in 2007, but his effectiveness didn't come with him. Unlike most Twins pitching prospects, he actually has impressive stuff, but he's also a fly-ball pitcher short of a strikeout pitch. Right now, he has a fastball and a curve down pat, but might need a third pitch to make it as a starter in the bigs. His results at Triple-A were obviously greatly improved, but the low strikeout rate and still lower BABIP argue for some sample-size cynicism.

LINEOUTS

Hitters

PLAYER	TEAM	LVL	AGE	PA	R	2B	3B	HR	RBI	BB	SO	SB-CS	EqBRR	AVG/OBP/SLG	EqAVG/EqOBP/EqSLG	EqA	VORP	WARP
OF J. Benson	BLT	A	20	290	39	16	3	4	27	24	73	17-11	-3.5	.248/.326/.382	.206/.271/.328	.209	-16.7	-1.4
C D. Butera	NBR	AA	24	351	39	18	1	7	39	35	55	0-1	-4.6	.219/.308/.354	.190/.269/.323	.208	-21.3	-0.3
OF A. Hicks#	TWI	Rk	18	204	32	10	4	4	27	28	32	12-2	2.2	.318/.409/.491	.224/.296/.366	.232	-13.3	-0.7
1B G. Jones*	ROC	AAA	27	587	82	33	3	23	92	50	98	9-2	2.9	.279/.337/.484	.231/.290/.415	.244	-5.1	-0.8
OF A. Morales	ELZ	Rk	18	218	33	12	1	15	28	26	72	7-2	0.3	.301/.413/.623	.221/.303/.436	.253	1.6	0.1
C J. Morales#	ROC	AAA	25	208	18	8	1	4	15	8	28	0-1	-2.6	.315/.348/.426	.273/.304/.379	.234	-1.4	0.4
SS T. Plouffe	NBR	AA	22	249	32	17	3	3	21	16	43	4-2	-0.5	.269/.325/.410	.243/.293/.387	.234	-3.9	-1.0
	ROC	AAA	22	272	34	17	3	6	39	14	47	1-1	-0.1	.256/.292/.420	.234/.271/.397	.229	-6.6	0.8
3B D. Romero	BLT	A	21	162	21	8	1	3	18	7	38	1-2	0.1	.268/.309/.396	.217/.248/.342	.198	-10.3	-1.1
2B S. Singleton#	BLT	A	22	259	37	6	2	6	32	13	29	2-6	-1.1	.302/.348/.421	.236/.272/.343	.209	-11.9	-1.1
	FTM	A+	22	277	38	19	2	5	25	26	24	4-1	0.1	.295/.371/.452	.262/.326/.427	.260	5.9	1.3
OF R. Tosoni*	FTM	A+	21	170	27	7	3	1	19	21	30	3-5	-3.0	.300/.408/.414	.260/.349/.363	.253	1.4	-0.4
4C D. Winfree	NBR	AA	22	502	59	27	3	19	87	41	87	2-3	-2.4	.252/.319/.450	.233/.294/.431	.246	-0.1	-0.8

The Twins' second-round pick in 2006, **Joe Benson** is as toolsy as they come, but is still learning to apply those skills to baseball. Young and raw, he would still get the benefit of the doubt on athletic ability (for now), but the lower-back stress fracture that ended his season early could portend the erosion of the one thing he has going for him. ⊘ The Twins added **Drew Butera** to the 40-man this winter for his strong defense, but hitting .215/.302/.323 through 346 minor league games means he's a reach even by the low offensive standards of reserve catchers. ⊘ Center fielder, pitcher, deadly threat on the golf course—**Aaron Hicks** can do it all. The Twins made him their first-round pick in 2008; he comes with speed, power, and, most unusual for a player his age, patience. Time will tell us more, but right now, the package looks special. ⊘ **Garrett Jones**' 2008 resembled his 2007, minus the big-league call-up; consistency works for Albert Pujols, but not for 27-year-old Triple-A veterans. Jones signed a minor league deal with the Pirates, where he'll hope that a LaRoche quota violation forces them to open up a spot. ⊘ You don't often see massive power lines like that of **Angel Morales** in rookie ball. Clearly, he has the physical ability to hit the ball a long, long way, but he's going to have to cut his prodigious strikeout rate to keep producing at higher levels. ⊘ Puerto Rican backstop **Jose Morales** has struggled with repeatedly injuring his left ankle, but has inherited the roster spot that the Twins seem committed to devoting to aspiring third catchers. ⊘ More than ever, 2004 first-rounder **Trevor Plouffe** looks like a busted pick; he's begun shifting to utility work, but he may not have the bat for even that. Two years ago in these pages, we said that "Plouffe" is the sound a soufflé makes when it falls; it's not true, but it should be, because in this case, it's really appropriate. ⊘ **Deibinson Romero** is a toolsy prospect with the arm for third and a quick bat at the plate, but trouble staying healthy has hampered his development. ⊘ A car accident following the 2006 season initially sapped **Steve Singleton**'s power, but much of it returned last year. If he keeps hitting, he might have a future, but he'll have to show he can handle his former position of shortstop to make it as a utility infielder. ⊘ Before breaking his foot in May, **Rene Tosoni** showcased his on-base skills, but he'll have to develop more power to stick in an outfield corner. ⊘ First/third baseman **Dave Winfree** added the outfield to his repertoire, but his bat hasn't fully recovered from the jump to Double-A; he'll have to demonstrate that last year's improvement wasn't just a function of repeating the level.

Pitchers

PLAYER	TEAM	LVL	AGE	W	L	SV	IP	H	BB	SO	HR	GB%	BABIP	STUFF	WHIP	ERA	DERA	EqH9	EqBB9	EqSO9	EqHR9	DEF	VORP
D. Bromberg	BLT	A	20	9	10	0	150	149	54	177	10	47.1%	.364	4	1.35	4.44	7.12	13.3	4.9	5.7	1.8	-13	-21.6
R. Delaney	FTM	A+	23	1	2	13	31²	24	4	34	1	43.4%	.284	2	0.88	1.42	4.34	9.0	1.9	5.9	0.9	3	4.1
	NBR	AA	23	2	1	5	34¹	20	7	38	2	26.6%	.234	19	0.79	1.05	3.58	5.5	1.9	7.4	0.8	7	7.3
A. Gabino	NBR	AA	24	6	5	3	81¹	84	31	61	6	42.6%	.322	-13	1.41	3.10	4.19	9.7	3.4	4.8	1.0	4	12.1
S. Hunt	ELZ	Rk	21	0	0	0	19	4	6	34	0	71.4%	.148	18	0.53	0.47	3.50	3.0	4.5	6.5	0.5	0	4.2
	BLT	A	21	1	4	0	31¹	26	27	34	2	54.3%	.312	3	1.69	5.46	9.57	10.9	10.9	5.1	1.7	-1	-11.6
B. Korecky	ROC	AAA	28	6	5	26	74¹	66	22	71	3	53.7%	.309	0	1.18	2.91	4.69	9.0	2.9	5.7	0.6	6	7.2
	MIN	MLB	28	2	0	0	17²	19	8	6	2	51.7%	.293	-29	1.53	4.58	3.86	9.9	3.9	2.8	1.1	-1	2.3
J. Manship	FTM	A+	23	7	3	0	78²	68	20	63	0	55.8%	.294	6	1.12	2.86	6.03	9.8	3.0	4.0	0.4	1	-3.4
	NBR	AA	23	3	6	0	76²	90	24	62	8	53.4%	.345	-4	1.49	4.46	5.40	10.8	2.8	5.0	1.3	-7	1.7
M. McCardell	BLT	A	23	9	4	0	135¹	110	25	139	10	33.3%	.282	-15	1.00	2.86	5.34	9.9	2.6	4.5	1.8	-6	3.6
R. Mullins*	NBR	AA	24	9	9	0	148¹	169	59	99	18	46.8%	.321	-25	1.54	4.31	6.08	10.5	3.4	4.1	1.6	1	-7.7
P. Neshek	MIN	MLB	27	0	1	0	13¹	12	4	15	2	32.4%	.303	9	1.20	4.74	5.93	7.9	2.6	8.6	1.3	1	1.5
T. Robertson*	FTM	A+	20	5	3	0	82²	78	31	73	3	52.2%	.313	15	1.32	2.72	6.60	10.9	4.3	4.4	1.0	1	-8.3

Despite a ton of strikeouts in the Midwest League, **David Bromberg** isn't terrifically stuff-y and doesn't figure to be, despite his youth. He has the durability to start, but needs to develop more pitches to stay out of the pen. ⊘ Former NDFA **Rob Delaney** made the jump to Double-A with style; the only way to get a walk off him is to ask nicely and then make a sizable donation to his favorite charity. He should get a shot in the pen sometime this season. ⊘ However colorful his moniker, **Armando Gabino** is a generic righty middle reliever whose peripherals don't promise much beyond laboring in the back o' the bullpen. ⊘ After starring at Tulane, **Shooter Hunt** nevertheless saw control problems drop him down into the supplemental phase of the first round, where the Twins nabbed him last June. ⊘ **Bobby Korecky** has saved 131 minor league games, which is probably about 130 more than he'll save in the majors; workmanlike relief from the bottom of a bullpen is his ceiling. ⊘ **Jeff Manship** is another righty from Twins Central Casting, only this version's main pitch is a big curve. Depending on need, he could start or pitch middle relief, or the Manship could call him home. ⊘ On a team that births control pitchers as if they had Bob Tewksbury and Brad Radke mixing their DNA in the back room, **Michael McCardell** stands out as being sharper than most.

Somehow, the Twins didn't move him up to High-A last year, so he still has some time before the big Double-A test. ⊘ **Ryan Mullins** is much like every other pitcher described in this chapter, except his fastball and control are less impressive. Look for him as a fifth starter/long reliever when/if he arrives. ⊘ **Pat Neshek** underwent Tommy John surgery in mid-November 2008 and will probably miss the entire season. He's the owner of a .176/.229/.298 line against righties, and as the rare sidearmer who is not completely neutralized by lefties, he will be missed. ⊘ **Tyler Robertson**, a 2006 third-rounder, has just an OK fastball and poor mechanics, but his plus slider makes him very tough on lefties. He was shut down in July with tendonitis and hasn't pitched since, so his outlook for 2009 is cloudy.

MANAGER: RON GARDENHIRE

YEAR	TEAM	W-L	Pythag +/−	Avg PC	100+ P	120+ P	QS	BQS	REL	REL w Zero R	IBB	Subs	PH	PH Avg	PH HR	SB2	CS2	SB3	CS3	SAC Att	SAC %	POS SAC	Squeeze	Swing	In Play
2006	MIN	96-66	2	90.1	43	0	71	5	421	287	25	35	93	.143	2	88	36	13	6	59	52.5%	28	0	177	146
2007	MIN	79-83	-1	93.8	47	0	75	5	436	291	33	40	102	.250	1	94	29	18	1	55	61.8%	29	4	161	134
2008	MIN	88-75	-2	91.8	47	1	81	5	485	312	38	25	108	.247	3	86	37	16	5	85	61.2%	47	7	138	118

The Twins' unanticipated success in 2008 earned Ron Gardenhire his fourth runner-up finish in seven years of eligibility for the Manager of the Year Award, a sign of the esteem in which his work is held, even (or, perhaps, especially) outside Minnesota. The sentiment expressed by the Joe Posnanski–coined "Gardy Axiom," which suggests that the Twins' sustained competitiveness in spite of their perennially meager payroll can be attributed to a Gardy in the machine, offers one explanation for the manager's widespread support among the writers, as well as for the team's ability to surpass its combined Pythagorean record by 18 victories since Gardenhire took the reins. A closer examination, however, reveals some tactics that complicate this reputation for genius. Gardenhire's charges attempted 85 sacrifices in 2008, easily the most of any AL team, although one cannot entirely divorce his game-calling from a steady supply of worthy sacrificing lambs instead of lions in the lineup. In previous years, Gardenhire drew criticism for his reliance on experienced but mediocre bats, but he may have been simply going with the flow. This season, the Twins cut costs by more aggressively filling those vacancies with in-house alternatives. Regardless of whether he was responsible for the team's new, more efficient approach to roster construction, Gardenhire embraced the change, enhancing the team's performance in the short term without jeopardizing its future prospects.

New York Mets

The Mets' season ended with a ceremony, but its tenor was much more muted than what anyone involved had hoped for. All the team greats were on the field—Straw, the Kid, Keith, Tom Terrific, Piazza, even Doc, returning home for the first time in ages. They had come to celebrate the ballpark that had hosted so many of the amazing moments in franchise history, but the gathering felt more like a funeral. Shea should have seen one more October, yet all anyone could do now—the Mets past and present and the fans who stayed on in the drizzling rain—was pay final respects and lament the building's premature end.

Minutes earlier, the Mets had lost to the Marlins, 4-2, to miss the playoffs on the season's final day for the second straight year. Just as they had the previous season, the Mets played their final three games at home against the Marlins, attempting to salvage what had looked several weeks earlier like a sure ticket to postseason play. Just as they had the previous season, the Mets lost the first game, won the second behind an inspired pitching performance, and then dropped the season finale in dispiriting fashion. The "9" next to 3-1 MIL-CHC on the scoreboard turned to an "F" shortly before Ryan Church's drive died short of the warning track, officially administering another acute dose of agony.

That final out completed a repeat collapse and served as matching bookend to the other ugly ordeal endured by the Mets in 2008: Willie Randolph's firing. Randolph needed a strong start after the shock of suffering the second greatest swoon in baseball history in 2007, but instead, his team listed through the first three months. A five-game losing streak in early June dropped the team's record to 30-33, and by all accounts, Randolph

had become increasingly unable to communicate with his stars. Rather than fire the embattled skipper after that losing streak, the front office let the poison build, seemingly paralyzed, waiting while the Mets closed the homestand with three wins in five games, waiting while they flew cross country to Anaheim, and waiting while they won their next game against the Angels. Only then, in the dead of night, did there come the announcement that Randolph was being relieved, with a press release going out to the media just after 3 A.M. ET. The Randolph firing was embarrassingly unprofessional and reflected a division in the front office. Reports emerged that it was the team owners, the Wilpons, who wanted Randolph gone and who had consequently leaked information to the press to force general manager Omar Minaya's hand; other whispers surfaced about the role that Minaya's right-hand man, Tony Bernazard, played in the execution. Whatever the exact circumstances surrounding Randolph's dismissal, the Mets took a deserved beating, inside the game and out, for the poorly executed hatchet job.

Hatchets get buried by wins, however, and the Mets revived under interim manager Jerry Manuel, who was promoted from bench coach. From July 5 to September 10, New York went 40-19, moving from 5½ games behind Philadelphia to 3½ games ahead. With solid pitching fronted by Johan Santana and with the offensive core cranking out runs, it appeared that the Mets were headed toward a redemptive playoff berth. It was not to be.

Statistically, last year's collapse was not as bad as the 2007 meltdown, which rated as a 500-1 shot after New York's playoff odds peaked at 99.8 percent. The Mets

---

METS PROSPECTUS

2008 record: 89-73; Second place in NL East

Pythagenport record: 89-73

Runs scored per game: 4.93 (3rd in NL)

Runs allowed per game: 4.39 (5th in NL)

Team EqA: .272 (2nd in NL)

2008 Batters Age: 30.4 (2nd-oldest in NL)

2008 Pitchers Age: 29.1 (8th-youngest in NL)

Ballpark: Shea Stadium; Pitcher's park; Park Factor of .961

2008: A strong second half just sets up a second consecutive September meltdown.

2009: The extreme bullpen makeover provides sufficient surge protection to avert another disaster.

finished the 2008 season with a 7-10 record in their final 17 games, as opposed to 5-12 in 2007, and if not for the Brewers pulling out of their own tailspin to win six of their last seven, New York would have backed into winning the wild card. Last year's failure was still on the order of 12½ to 1 against, however, as the Mets reached their zenith on September 11 with a 92 percent shot. In many ways, however, the end to the 2008 season was even more damaging than the year before, because the later result was entirely predictable—perhaps even inevitable. The 2007 squad had fallen apart unexpectedly, heartbreakingly—these things sometimes happen. In contrast, the 2008 Mets were exploited. They had a fatal weakness, which eventually did them in. That weakness was the bullpen.

Placing the blame in any other bin would be an act of denial. True, the Mets scored just five runs in the final series against Florida, and several of the team's big guns failed to come up big in the last week (David Wright endured an especially vigorous backlash). Overall, though, they scored the second-most runs in the National League. And sure, the Mets dealt with a number of injuries, primarily to their corner outfielders, second baseman, and closer, a situation that later led team CEO Jeff Wilpon to claim that the squad had actually overachieved. But every team has injuries, and the Mets' core was, in fact, historically durable: New York became only the seventh team in baseball history (and the first since 1968) to have four players each appear in 159 or more games. Those four players were the team's offensive cornerstones—Wright, Jose Reyes, Carlos Beltran, and Carlos Delgado—and the Mets also got a career-high number of innings from their new franchise pitcher, Johan Santana.

No, the real problem was the bullpen. From that high-water mark on September 11 onward, Mets relievers were 2-5 with a 6.23 ERA and four blown saves, clocking in at two wins below replacement level as measured by WXRL. On the season, the Mets had the second-lowest WXRL in the National League, 4.93, and lost seven games in which they led at the start of the ninth inning, the most in baseball. Much of that was the fault of Billy Wagner, who blew five multirun save opportunities before going down for the year in early August. In contrast, the Phillies were, behind Brad Lidge, a perfect 79-0 when leading after eight.

Those numbers, however damning, only get the story started. The ineptitude of the Mets' bullpen last season was of a unique variety: after Wagner went down, New York had no one who could reliably pitch a full, clean inning of relief, because practically every one of their relievers was effective only as a specialist. Aaron

Heilman lost the feel for his changeup and, with it, the ability to retire lefties. Side-arming righty Joe Smith was also much worse against lefties. Lefty side-winder Pedro Feliciano, who in the past had held his own against righties, now was getting torched by them. Scott Schoeneweis was similarly helpless as anything other than a LOOGY. And while righties Duaner Sanchez and Luis Ayala did not show a dramatic split, they were hardly any more reliable for that fact.

Given those options, Manuel was forced to mix and match in the late innings, as the Mets' season descended to a lower rung of relief-pitching hell that previously had existed only in the far-flung reaches of Tony La Russa's subconscious. The Mets made 557 pitching changes, the third greatest total ever (also contributing to a mean game time of 3:05, the longest in the National League). New York's average relief outing lasted just 0.89 innings, the shortest in major league history. Five Mets firemen made 60 or more appearances while throwing fewer innings than games pitched; only the 1997 Giants had as many. (Speaking of creeping La Russanism: there have been 30 team seasons that had three or more pitchers fit this category, and 27 occurred from 2001 onward, with the other three in 1996-1997.) Furthermore, three Mets relievers threw at least 15 fewer innings than appearances. Only one other team can match that level of specialization: not surprisingly, La Russa's 2008 Cardinals.

Who deserves the blame for this disaster? The 2007 bullpen, which ranked 18th in WXRL, also faded at the most crucial point, going 2-6 with a 6.94 ERA and six blown saves in a brutal 15-game stretch starting September 11. That unit returned virtually intact for 2008; Minaya's major relief move was signing Matt Wise, who got hurt early on and was never a factor. It would be unfair to pillory the GM for Heilman's unexpected devolution, but the bullpen's failure nevertheless highlights the major issue with the Mets since Minaya has assumed control: broad strokes have been bold and usually brilliant (signing Beltran and Wagner, trading for Delgado and Santana), but the detail work of filling out the rest of the roster has too often been neglected. With a relief corps set to rely heavily on the 36-year-old Wagner, whose elbow had been hanging by a thread for years, and Duaner Sanchez, who missed all of '07 after separating his shoulder, Minaya should have added more depth in the offseason, when the pool of available relief talent is overflowing with quality options. Once the season starts, that pool dries up, as the Mets found the hard way. When the pen went to pieces, the trading deadline had already passed and it was all Minaya could do to dig up Luis Ayala and Al Reyes, neither of whom staunched the bleeding.

Last year's implosion served as the nadir of a particularly forgettable period of bullpen activity for Minaya. Since signing Pedro Feliciano and trading for Sanchez prior to the 2006 season, the Mets' bullpen moves had backfired: at the end of the '06 campaign, they dealt away both Heath Bell (to the Padres) and Matt Lindstrom (to the Marlins)—pitchers who will serve as the closers on their respective teams in 2009—and got no usable parts in return. Later that offseason, Minaya gave Guillermo Mota two years and $5 million after the pitcher tested positive for steroids, and Schoeneweis a three-year, $10.8 million deal, after the GM declined to bestow a similar pact on the more dependable Chad Bradford. In addition, he traded Brian Bannister for Ambiorix Burgos, who has, to say the least, failed to reach expectations.

The lack of depth exhibited in the bullpen's construction plagued the offensive roster, too. New York entered the season relying on injury-prone veterans in three spots—left and right field and second base—and had no strong options to back those players up. The Mets got lucky in the outfield with the remarkable reemergence of Fernando Tatis and the surprising contribution of Dan Murphy, but lacked similar fortune at second. The bench was a further weakness, as Mets pinch-hitters batted just .226, after hitting .228 in '07 and .187 in '06.

Besides the late-January trade for Santana (and scrounging up enough swag in a weak system to land the franchise arm was indeed a feat in itself), 2008 had not been a particularly good year for Minaya. Therefore, it was somewhat baffling why Wilpon handed his GM a contract extension for 2010-2012 less than a week after the season ended, before the smoke had even cleared from the team's second straight crash landing. That move proved again what the firing of Randolph had already made clear: the Wilpons are fully enamored of their GM, and this current Mets core will sink or swim with the Big O at the controls. While such a strong vote of confidence may not have been deserved at the time, Minaya swiftly went about justifying the ownership's faith. If last year the bullpen had been overlooked, Minaya now gave it his full attention.

While big moves don't normally equate with smart moves when it comes to the late innings (e.g., the Wagner deal), the Mets' brass was able to turn that unusual trick at the Winter Meetings. They identified Francisco Rodriguez and J. J. Putz as the top two late-inning options on the market and managed to snag both players through creative and savvy negotiation. After his record-setting 62-save campaign, K-Rod was purportedly looking for a five-year, $75 million deal, and it seemed the Mets would be desperate enough to approach that demand. But the combination of economic recession, uneasiness over Rodriguez's declining velocity and fastball usage, and general increase in prudence regarding big deals for relievers helped drive the price way down, leading to a much more reasonable three-year, $37 million pact (with a vesting fourth-year option). Then the Mets pried Putz away from the rebuilding Mariners, along with another usable bullpen arm in righty Sean Green, while simultaneously granting the disgruntled Heilman his wish for a change of role and scenery.

In Rodriguez and Putz, Minaya has added two power relievers capable of going full innings and retiring batters on both sides of the plate. If each stays healthy, the Mets will go from having practically no lead-protecting ability to possessing arguably the best back-end tandem in baseball, one that could effectively shorten the game to seven innings. Minaya did not stop there, continuing to reshape the pen by trading Schoeneweis to Arizona. Of the team's top six in relief innings from last season, only two, Feliciano and Sanchez, will return in 2009.

An added benefit of Minaya's major moves is that they have not cost the team its future. The two best minor leaguers lost in the Putz deal were well down on the organizational prospect list. Furthermore, while the Mets have forfeited a number of high draft picks to sign top free agents, those lost opportunities are not as costly for them, thanks to the team's cultivation of what has become the best Latin American pipeline in the game. The arrival of high-ceiling youngsters from the Dominican Republic and from Venezuela has allowed the Mets to focus on grabbing polished players in the draft: 44 of 52 New York draft picks last June were collegians, and the Mets signed 42 of their selections, tied with the Cardinals for the most of any team, to further bolster their improving talent stock.

The last two years have featured a disheartening waste of precious resources in Queens. New York's September struggles have squandered several fantastic seasons of peak production from the team's stars. While Wright and Reyes are just entering their primes, Beltran, Delgado, Santana, and Putz have a limited number of top-notch seasons left. The Mets will never have a better opportunity to win a World Series with their current core than they do now.

HITTERS

Moises Alou — LF
Bats: R Throws: R Height: 6' 3" Weight: 225 Born: July 3, 1966 Age: 42

YEAR	TEAM	LVL	AGE	PA	R	2B	3B	HR	RBI	BB	SO	SB	CS	EqBRR	AVG	OBP	SLG	EqAVG	EqOBP	EqSLG	EqA	VORP	WARP	DEFENSE			
2006	SFN	MLB	39	378	52	25	1	22	74	28	31	2	1	-0.9	.301	.352	.571	.299	.352	.564	.302	27.6	1.8	73-RF	-7	9-LF	-2
2007	NYN	MLB	40	360	51	19	1	13	49	27	30	3	0	0.4	.341	.392	.524	.347	.400	.543	.319	33.2	2.6	78-LF	-7		
2008	NYN	MLB	41	54	4	2	0	0	9	2	4	1	1	-0.1	.347	.389	.388	.367	.407	.408	.289	2.1	0.2	10-LF	-1		
2009	NYN	MLB	42	159	21	7	0	4	23	12	13	3	1	-0.7	.304	.360	.449	.309	.364	.471	.286	7.1	0.3	41-LF	-5		

Breakout: 19% Improve: 44% Collapse: 47% Attrition: 34%   Comparables: Andres Galarraga, Carlton Fisk, Enos Slaughter, Dave Winfield

The Mets knew that Alou would either be hurt or hitting; they just would have preferred a slightly better distribution of those outcomes. Hopes of coaxing another half-season from the veteran's bat were ended by a bodywide breakdown. A hernia and an ankle injury kept Alou out until May. He returned to the shelf with a calf strain, which he reaggravated in his first game back in June. Alou then tore a hamstring in his third minor league rehab start in July, ending his season and quite possibly his career. If 2008 was indeed the closing act, he heads to baseball's Elysian Fields as one of the greatest itinerant hitters of all time—only Al Simmons and Gary Sheffield have a higher career OPS than Alou's 885, among players employed by at least seven teams.

Marlon Anderson — UT
Bats: L Throws: R Height: 5' 11" Weight: 200 Born: January 6, 1974 Age: 35

YEAR	TEAM	LVL	AGE	PA	R	2B	3B	HR	RBI	BB	SO	SB	CS	EqBRR	AVG	OBP	SLG	EqAVG	EqOBP	EqSLG	EqA	VORP	WARP	DEFENSE			
2006	WAS	MLB	32	239	31	13	2	5	23	18	41	2	4	-0.4	.274	.331	.423	.282	.340	.444	.265	5.8	0.6	26-2B	0	8-RF	-1
2006	LAN	MLB	32	73	12	3	2	7	15	7	8	2	2	-0.0	.375	.431	.813	.375	.431	.812	.363	13.5	1.3	13-LF	1		
2007	LAN	MLB	33	29	3	0	0	0	2	3	5	1	0	-0.7	.231	.310	.231	.231	.310	.231	.206	-1.1	-0.1				
2007	NYN	MLB	33	77	14	7	0	3	25	5	12	3	1	-0.2	.319	.355	.551	.333	.368	.594	.310	7.0	0.7	7-LF	1		
2008	NYN	MLB	34	151	16	6	0	1	10	9	27	2	1	0.3	.210	.255	.275	.210	.255	.290	.191	-9.4	-0.1	18-LF	8		
2009	NYN	MLB	35	112	12	5	1	2	12	10	21	1	1	0.1	.240	.307	.361	.244	.310	.379	.240	-0.3	0.3	31-LF	2		

Breakout: 34% Improve: 50% Collapse: 26% Attrition: 54%   Comparables: Barney McCosky, Joe Orsulak, Mike Devereaux, Larry Biittner

The Minaya Mets have displayed a seeming inability to learn from past mistakes. After the 2005 season, they signed then 47-year-old Julio Franco to a two-year, $2.2 million contract to serve as pinch-hitter; Franco's performance dropped off in 2006 and bottomed out in '07, leading the Mets to cut him midseason and eat the remaining money. Two years later, when Marlon Anderson hit .319 in 69 at-bats after getting picked off the scrap heap midseason, Minaya gave the soon-to-be 34-year-old *the same contract*. Handing out multiyear deals to aging bench players is indefensible, and it wouldn't be surprising to see the Mets again swallowing cash this season to free up the roster spot wasted on their latest veteran pinch-hitter.

Carlos Beltran — CF
Bats: S Throws: R Height: 6' 1" Weight: 205 Born: April 24, 1977 Age: 32

YEAR	TEAM	LVL	AGE	PA	R	2B	3B	HR	RBI	BB	SO	SB	CS	EqBRR	AVG	OBP	SLG	EqAVG	EqOBP	EqSLG	EqA	VORP	WARP	DEFENSE	
2006	NYN	MLB	29	617	127	38	1	41	116	95	99	18	3	4.0	.275	.388	.594	.278	.394	.602	.327	69.4	8.5	132-CF	13
2007	NYN	MLB	30	636	93	33	3	33	112	69	111	23	2	4.7	.276	.353	.525	.280	.360	.547	.306	51.9	7.1	138-CF	13
2008	NYN	MLB	31	706	116	40	5	27	112	92	96	25	3	6.3	.284	.376	.500	.293	.385	.526	.311	57.3	9.2	156-CF	23
2009	NYN	MLB	32	652	106	36	3	27	96	84	96	18	4	1.9	.293	.385	.513	.298	.389	.538	.312	57.0	7.1	152-CF	5

Breakout: 13% Improve: 47% Collapse: 13% Attrition: 7%   Comparables: Andy Van Slyke, Larry Walker, Chipper Jones, Kirk Gibson

For a number of reasons—his huge contract, his poor first season, his quiet demeanor—Beltran has managed to be unappreciated while playing in America's largest city. He actively avoids New York's media glare while steadily producing at a Hall of Fame level. Last year was one of Beltran's best in the field, and by WARP, he was the best center fielder in baseball for the second time in the last three years (in 2007, he was only the best in the National League). He also did his best work in September, leading the club with a 1,086 OPS. The last two Mets collapses have squandered two sterling seasons from Beltran and prevented his return to the October stage on which he has performed so spectacularly. The good news is that his kind of dynamic power and speed combination promises to age well. By the time his seven-year, $117 million deal expires, it will be considered one of the best long-term commitments ever made.

Mike Carp   **1B**   Bats: L   Throws: R   Height: 6' 2"   Weight: 215   Born: June 30, 1986   Age: 23

YEAR	TEAM	LVL	AGE	PA	R	2B	3B	HR	RBI	BB	SO	SB	CS	EqBRR	AVG	OBP	SLG	EqAVG	EqOBP	EqSLG	EqA	VORP	WARP	DEFENSE			
2006	SLU	A+	20	573	69	27	1	17	88	51	107	2	1	-2.1	.287	.379	.450	.244	.316	.396	.248	-0.0	-0.8	134-1B	-5		
2007	BIN	AA	21	412	55	16	0	11	48	39	75	2	1	0.6	.251	.337	.387	.220	.292	.347	.224	-14.5	-1.7	95-1B	-2		
2008	BIN	AA	22	566	67	29	1	17	72	79	88	1	2	-4.9	.299	.403	.471	.275	.370	.451	.284	31.2	2.7	56-1B	0	49-LF	1
2009	SEA	MLB	23	571	59	26	1	16	67	58	115	1	1	-1.8	.247	.329	.395	.250	.333	.418	.262	1.2	1.2	134-1B	3		

Breakout: 22%   Improve: 50%   Collapse: 17%   Attrition: 7%   Comparables: Rusty Greer, Eddy Martinez-Esteve, Daryle Ward, Jon Tucker

Carp supplied the thunder to accompany April's showers, batting .356 with six homers in 101 at-bats to open his second season in Binghamton, and was thus one of the names mentioned as a potential replacement for Delgado during the latter's struggles. Those calls ceased as Carp floundered and Delgado flourished, but the youngster still ended up with a good season in a tough hitters' park after flopping in 2007. Shipped to Seattle as part of the Putz deal, Carp could be a passable option for the Mariners in time; he doesn't possess classic first-base power, so he'll need to continue to stay afloat against lefties (792 OPS last year).

Luis Castillo   **2B**   Bats: S   Throws: R   Height: 5' 11"   Weight: 190   Born: September 12, 1975   Age: 33

YEAR	TEAM	LVL	AGE	PA	R	2B	3B	HR	RBI	BB	SO	SB	CS	EqBRR	AVG	OBP	SLG	EqAVG	EqOBP	EqSLG	EqA	VORP	WARP	DEFENSE	
2006	MIN	MLB	30	652	84	22	6	3	49	56	58	25	11	-1.2	.296	.358	.370	.287	.355	.360	.256	21.5	1.0	140-2B	-8
2007	MIN	MLB	31	384	54	11	3	0	18	29	28	9	4	5.1	.304	.356	.352	.305	.361	.360	.258	9.5	0.5	82-2B	-6
2007	NYN	MLB	31	231	37	8	2	1	20	24	17	10	2	4.8	.296	.371	.372	.305	.383	.380	.277	9.8	0.4	48-2B	-7
2008	NYN	MLB	32	359	46	7	1	3	28	50	35	17	2	3.7	.245	.355	.305	.253	.363	.323	.261	4.1	-0.1	76-2B	-11
2009	NYN	MLB	33	421	55	11	2	0	26	44	39	16	4	1.5	.268	.347	.307	.272	.351	.322	.247	6.3	0.4	100-2B	-6

Breakout: 13%   Improve: 39%   Collapse: 27%   Attrition: 23%   Comparables: Mark McLemore, Tom Herr, Maury Wills, Tony Taylor

Well, at least he's not signed for the next three seasons at $18 million. Oh … oops. The decision to give Castillo a four-year deal after the 2007 season was met with stunned silence, and the first year of the ill-advised pact couldn't have gone much worse. In addition to the omnipresent issue of Castillo's balky knees, which required him to take frequent games off in the first several months, he suffered a hip flexor injury that wiped out nearly all of July and August. To make things more miserable, Castillo was reportedly also dealing with a painful divorce. He came back in late August and looked terrible, hitting .170 with a single extra-base hit in 65 PAs. That kind of power outage led Castillo to spend the season trying to snooker pitchers into giving him a free pass, resulting in the highest walk rate of his career. Minaya is attempting to short-sell his crippled stock, but the Mets will have to simply bite the bullet, play Castillo as often as his body allows, and hope their investment regains some value.

Ramon Castro   **C**   Bats: R   Throws: R   Height: 6' 3"   Weight: 255   Born: March 1, 1976   Age: 33

YEAR	TEAM	LVL	AGE	PA	R	2B	3B	HR	RBI	BB	SO	SB	CS	EqBRR	AVG	OBP	SLG	EqAVG	EqOBP	EqSLG	EqA	VORP	WARP	DEFENSE	
2006	NYN	MLB	30	144	13	7	0	4	12	15	40	0	0	-1.2	.238	.322	.389	.238	.326	.397	.254	1.2	0.9	34-C	3
2007	NYN	MLB	31	157	24	6	0	11	31	10	39	0	0	-3.2	.285	.331	.556	.294	.344	.580	.303	12.9	1.3	37-C	-2
2008	NYN	MLB	32	157	15	7	0	7	24	13	34	0	0	-0.9	.245	.312	.441	.252	.318	.455	.263	4.7	0.8	39-C	1
2009	NYN	MLB	33	218	26	10	0	9	31	20	47	0	0	-1.6	.260	.332	.462	.264	.335	.484	.275	12.9	1.7	55-C	-1

Breakout: 22%   Improve: 49%   Collapse: 30%   Attrition: 28%   Comparables: Gene Oliver, Mark Parent, Javy Lopez, Joe Oliver

There's no denying that Castro can hit, but every year, seemingly minor ailments shut him down for large stretches. He sat for the first 33 games of the year with a hamstring strain suffered in mid-March and then missed more time later in the year with a sprained ankle and strained quad. When he's healthy, he should be getting a majority of starts: the defensive drop from Brian Schneider to Castro is smaller than it is perceived to be and doesn't cancel out the significant offensive upgrade.

Endy Chavez — OF

Bats: L **Throws:** L **Height:** 6' 0" **Weight:** 165 **Born:** February 7, 1978 **Age:** 31

YEAR	TEAM	LVL	AGE	PA	R	2B	3B	HR	RBI	BB	SO	SB	CS	EqBRR	AVG	OBP	SLG	EqAVG	EqOBP	EqSLG	EqA	VORP	WARP	DEFENSE			
2006	NYN	MLB	28	390	48	22	5	4	42	24	44	12	3	0.0	.306	.348	.431	.308	.352	.440	.275	15.7	2.9	35-RF	4	29-CF	6
2007	NYN	MLB	29	165	20	7	2	1	17	9	16	5	2	1.6	.287	.325	.380	.296	.337	.388	.255	1.4	0.4	22-LF	-1	11-RF	1
2008	NYN	MLB	30	298	30	10	2	1	12	17	22	6	1	2.2	.267	.308	.330	.271	.314	.337	.235	-4.9	1.5	44-RF	7	22-LF	11
2009	SEA	MLB	31	239	27	9	2	1	19	14	22	5	2	1.0	.281	.324	.351	.285	.328	.371	.249	-0.8	0.8	59-RF	5		

Breakout: 23% Improve: 40% Collapse: 33% Attrition: 30% **Comparables:** *Jason Tyner, Jose Tartabull, Vic Davalillo, Manny Mota*

"The Catch" from Game Seven of the 2006 NLCS has forever endeared Chavez to Mets fans, and that play certainly wasn't a fluke: Chavez is among the best corner outfield defenders in baseball. But he hasn't carried over his career offensive production from '06, as his bat weakened considerably again last year. Chavez saw significant action in right when Church was out of commission, starting 40 games in June and July, but his tepid hitting earned him just 20 PAs (and zero starts) in the season's final month and a half. He's a decent fourth outfielder and will fill that role in Seattle after being moved in the Putz deal.

Ryan Church — RF

Bats: L **Throws:** L **Height:** 6' 1" **Weight:** 190 **Born:** October 14, 1978 **Age:** 30

YEAR	TEAM	LVL	AGE	PA	R	2B	3B	HR	RBI	BB	SO	SB	CS	EqBRR	AVG	OBP	SLG	EqAVG	EqOBP	EqSLG	EqA	VORP	WARP	DEFENSE			
2006	NWO	AAA	27	206	29	6	0	7	29	25	41	5	1	0.4	.246	.345	.400	.206	.291	.328	.223	-9.2	-0.2	27-CF	3	13-RF	-1
2006	WAS	MLB	27	230	22	17	1	10	35	26	60	6	1	0.4	.276	.366	.526	.284	.373	.543	.308	18.3	1.4	41-CF	-5	11-RF	0
2007	WAS	MLB	28	530	57	43	1	15	70	49	107	3	2	1.8	.272	.349	.464	.280	.358	.487	.287	23.7	4.4	81-LF	15	37-CF	-2
2008	NYN	MLB	29	359	54	14	1	12	49	33	83	2	3	0.8	.276	.346	.439	.285	.356	.464	.278	8.7	1.5	80-RF	0		
2009	NYN	MLB	30	317	37	15	1	10	40	32	72	3	1	-0.2	.254	.335	.421	.258	.338	.441	.267	8.8	1.2	77-RF	0		

Breakout: 13% Improve: 35% Collapse: 38% Attrition: 30% **Comparables:** *Bill Howerton, Jim King, Todd Hollandsworth, Joe Lefebvre*

Church was kneed in the helmet on May 20 while attempting to break up a double play and endured his second concussion of the season. Though initially listed as mild, it soon proved to be anything but and ended up destroying what had been shaping up as a career season. Church came back two days after being helped off the field, but was still dealing with the effects of postconcussive syndrome, which were exacerbated by chronic migraines. He went on and off the DL twice, with the second stint lasting nearly two months, and hit just .219/.305/.307 in 128 PAs after returning for the stretch drive. While serious concern for his health remains, especially in light of the increasing risk of recurrence associated with concussions, Church will begin 2009 as the starting right fielder.

Ike Davis — 1B

Bats: L **Throws:** L **Height:** 6' 5" **Weight:** 195 **Born:** March 22, 1987 **Age:** 22

YEAR	TEAM	LVL	AGE	PA	R	2B	3B	HR	RBI	BB	SO	SB	CS	EqBRR	AVG	OBP	SLG	EqAVG	EqOBP	EqSLG	EqA	VORP	WARP	DEFENSE	
2008	BRO	A-	21	239	17	15	0	0	17	23	43	0	0	-1.4	.256	.326	.326	.195	.251	.258	.172	-43.5	-3.5	55-1B	-3
2009	NYN	MLB	22	502	32	24	1	6	44	38	123	2	1	-0.7	.208	.270	.303	.211	.273	.317	.200	-25.9	-2.2	118-1B	2

Breakout: 64% Improve: 80% Collapse: 13% Attrition: 6% **Comparables:** *Chris Pritchett, Todd Sears, Shea Morenz, Mathew Kent*

Taken with the 18th pick of last June's draft as compensation for losing Tom Glavine, Ike is the son of former major league closer Ron Davis. Junior pitched, too, while at Arizona State, pumping heat in the mid-90s, but it was his bat that got him a $1.575 million signing bonus after producing 16 homers and a .742 slugging percentage for the Sun Devils last year. While college first basemen are generally the safest draft commodities, Davis struggled in his pro debut.

Carlos Delgado — 1B

Bats: L **Throws:** R **Height:** 6' 3" **Weight:** 240 **Born:** June 25, 1972 **Age:** 37

YEAR	TEAM	LVL	AGE	PA	R	2B	3B	HR	RBI	BB	SO	SB	CS	EqBRR	AVG	OBP	SLG	EqAVG	EqOBP	EqSLG	EqA	VORP	WARP	DEFENSE	
2006	NYN	MLB	34	618	89	30	2	38	114	74	120	0	0	0.4	.265	.361	.548	.266	.362	.556	.305	36.0	4.8	139-1B	4
2007	NYN	MLB	35	607	71	30	0	24	87	52	118	4	0	-7.5	.258	.333	.448	.261	.338	.463	.276	16.0	1.4	136-1B	-4
2008	NYN	MLB	36	686	96	32	1	38	115	72	124	1	1	-0.2	.271	.353	.518	.277	.358	.540	.299	38.2	4.6	152-1B	3
2009	NYN	MLB	37	583	77	27	1	26	96	59	103	2	1	-2.8	.277	.355	.486	.282	.358	.509	.289	27.6	2.8	137-1B	-1

Breakout: 11% Improve: 45% Collapse: 19% Attrition: 13% **Comparables:** *Fred McGriff, Andres Galarraga, Johnny Mize, Dave Parker*

After already slipping badly in 2007, Delgado was hitting .229/.306/.396 almost three months into the season. Throngs of Val Pascucci backers were set to march on Shea, but in the first game of a home-and-home double-header at Yankee Stadium on June 27, Delgado hit two homers and doubled while setting a club record with nine RBI. From that game onward, he put up a .308/.392/.626 line with 27 homers in 372 PAs, helping carry the Mets throughout the second half. The turnaround was attributed primarily to Delgado's going the other way with the high fastballs that pitchers had been tossing him. His unexpected surge made it an easy call for the Mets to pick up his $12 million 2009 option. He's 31 homers from 500, which, combined with the walk year, gives Delgado plenty of incentive.

Damion Easley — INF

Bats: R   Throws: R   Height: 5′ 11″   Weight: 195   Born: November 11, 1969   Age: 39

YEAR	TEAM	LVL	AGE	PA	R	2B	3B	HR	RBI	BB	SO	SB	CS	EqBRR	AVG	OBP	SLG	EqAVG	EqOBP	EqSLG	EqA	VORP	WARP	DEFENSE			
2006	ARI	MLB	36	220	24	6	1	9	28	21	30	1	1	-0.8	.233	.323	.418	.226	.317	.405	.251	2.1	-0.5	23-SS	-6	14-3B	0
2007	NYN	MLB	37	218	24	6	0	10	26	19	35	0	1	0.9	.280	.358	.466	.286	.364	.484	.288	11.1	1.7	37-2B	5	5-RF	-1
2008	NYN	MLB	38	347	33	10	2	6	44	19	38	0	0	1.5	.269	.322	.370	.278	.331	.389	.253	3.4	-0.4	60-2B	-9	5-SS	0
2009	NYN	MLB	39	192	20	8	1	4	22	14	26	0	1	-0.6	.266	.329	.392	.271	.332	.410	.256	6.4	0.4	49-2B	-3		

Breakout: 12%   Improve: 33%   Collapse: 39%   Attrition: 40%   Comparables: Dave Concepcion, Felipe Alou, Ken Griffey, Tony Taylor

One of the sad consequences of the Mets' two straight September collapses is that they denied Easley his first career playoff appearance. Easley is the active leader with an Ernie Banks Number of 1,706, the most career regular-season games played without experiencing the postseason. (Banks finished his career with 2,528.) Easley, pressed into semiregular service at second after Castillo went down, ended up with more PAs than he had seen since 2001, and he wilted under the heavier load. While Easley wants to continue his hunt for October, the Mets would like to have a backup infielder who is a better and more versatile defender and so have ended their association with one of the game's most well-respected players.

Nick Evans — OF/1B

Bats: R   Throws: R   Height: 6′ 2″   Weight: 180   Born: January 30, 1986   Age: 23

YEAR	TEAM	LVL	AGE	PA	R	2B	3B	HR	RBI	BB	SO	SB	CS	EqBRR	AVG	OBP	SLG	EqAVG	EqOBP	EqSLG	EqA	VORP	WARP	DEFENSE			
2006	HAG	A	20	565	55	33	3	15	67	45	99	2	0	-2.0	.254	.320	.419	.195	.244	.324	.193	-44.3	-4.0	127-1B	1		
2007	SLU	A+	21	440	65	25	1	15	54	53	64	3	0	0.1	.286	.374	.476	.240	.321	.412	.256	3.5	0.2	101-1B	-1		
2008	BIN	AA	22	326	52	18	7	14	53	26	64	2	1	-0.7	.311	.365	.561	.288	.337	.535	.290	24.7	0.8	52-1B	0	19-LF	-6
2008	NYN	MLB	22	119	18	10	0	2	9	7	24	0	0	-0.4	.257	.303	.404	.257	.303	.413	.248	0.3	-0.7	21-LF	-6		
2009	NYN	MLB	23	515	57	28	2	16	65	42	107	3	1	-0.1	.256	.319	.428	.260	.322	.449	.262	8.0	0.5	121-1B	-7		

Breakout: 34%   Improve: 56%   Collapse: 8%   Attrition: 6%   Comparables: Darren Reed, Steve Gibralter, Wes Bankston, Kevin Sliwinski

After excelling against Eastern League competition for the first two months, Evans made the leap to Queens to give the Mets some added outfield presence against lefties. In his debut, he rapped three doubles; Ben Grieve is the only other player to do so in the last 60 years. Evans did his job for the most part, strumming southpaws for an 894 OPS in 79 plate appearances. He collected just five hits in 40 PAs against righties; Evans will begin working on that latter issue at Triple-A to open the season.

Wilmer Flores — SS

Bats: R   Throws: R   Height: 6′ 3″   Weight: 175   Born: August 6, 1991   Age: 17

YEAR	TEAM	LVL	AGE	PA	R	2B	3B	HR	RBI	BB	SO	SB	CS	EqBRR	AVG	OBP	SLG	EqAVG	EqOBP	EqSLG	EqA	VORP	WARP	DEFENSE	
2008	KNG	Rk	16	265	36	12	4	8	41	12	28	2	1	0.1	.310	.352	.490	.214	.245	.345	.202	-34.5	-2.2	57-SS	-8
2008	BRO	A-	16	32	3	1	0	0	1	1	7	0	0	-0.1	.267	.290	.300	.226	.250	.258	.171	-5.5	-0.1	8-SS	1
2009	NYN	MLB	17	452	30	20	2	7	36	21	82	3	2	0.8	.206	.249	.308	.209	.251	.323	.192	-13.3	-1.0	107-SS	-2

Breakout: 34%   Improve: 46%   Collapse: 29%   Attrition: 10%   Comparables: Angel Villalona, Carlos Triunfel, Luis Gallardo, Felipe Gutierrez

If you believe the official listing, Flores was born on the same day that Tim Berners-Lee published the first papers on the World Wide Web. It's rare for a player to begin his pro career at 16, and in that small subset, the numbers put up by Flores have scarcely been seen before. He was signed out of Venezuela in late 2007 for $700,000, and given his big frame and tremendous offensive potential, Flores's top comp might just be another Venezuelan phenom, Miguel Cabrera, who also started his career at shortstop. Like Cabrera, Flores will grow out of the position, but the bat is good enough to play anywhere. Few 17-year-olds get the chance to play in a full-season league, let alone succeed in it, but Flores might be the prodigy who can do so.

Reese Havens · SS

Bats: L   Throws: R   Height: 6' 1"   Weight: 195   Born: October 20, 1986   Age: 22

YEAR	TEAM	LVL	AGE	PA	R	2B	3B	HR	RBI	BB	SO	SB	CS	EqBRR	AVG	OBP	SLG	EqAVG	EqOBP	EqSLG	EqA	VORP	WARP	DEFENSE
2008	BRO	A-	21	97	13	6	2	3	11	11	27	3	1	-0.1	.247	.340	.471	.205	.271	.386	.227	-6.4	-0.4	
2009	NYN	MLB	22	587	59	30	4	14	61	52	164	8	4	1.0	.218	.292	.370	.222	.295	.387	.235	-4.2	0.1	137-DH

Breakout: 42%   Improve: 60%   Collapse: 20%   Attrition: 4%   Comparables: Eric Valent, Ronnie Gideon, Geoff Jenkins, Louie Meadows

Havens was the only shortstop taken in last year's draft by the Mets, and while he played that position in college, the University of South Carolina product might shift to the keystone as soon as this season, given the intersection of the team's needs and his defensive abilities. Havens didn't produce much for the Gamecocks until last year, when he hit .359/.486/.645 and blasted 18 homers in 248 at-bats, rocketing his stock into the first round, where the Mets grabbed him with the 22nd pick. He doesn't have star-level potential, being more of a solid-across-the-board type, but he boosts a system sorely lacking in middle infielders.

Fernando Martinez · CF

Bats: L   Throws: R   Height: 6' 0"   Weight: 185   Born: October 10, 1988   Age: 20

YEAR	TEAM	LVL	AGE	PA	R	2B	3B	HR	RBI	BB	SO	SB	CS	EqBRR	AVG	OBP	SLG	EqAVG	EqOBP	EqSLG	EqA	VORP	WARP	DEFENSE	
2006	HAG	A	17	211	24	14	2	5	28	15	36	7	4	-3.9	.333	.389	.505	.253	.294	.389	.234	-2.7	0.1	43-CF	1
2006	SLU	A+	17	130	18	4	2	5	11	6	24	1	1	-0.4	.193	.254	.387	.164	.208	.344	.178	-12.3	-1.4	27-CF	-4
2007	BIN	AA	18	259	32	11	1	4	21	20	51	3	4	-2.8	.271	.336	.377	.229	.286	.329	.212	-11.6	-2.3	57-CF	-14
2008	BIN	AA	19	385	48	19	4	8	43	27	73	6	2	1.4	.287	.340	.432	.264	.312	.416	.252	3.8	0.5	82-CF	-3
2009	NYN	MLB	20	538	57	28	3	11	55	37	107	7	4	0.7	.253	.308	.388	.257	.310	.407	.245	6.1	0.8	126-CF	-9

Breakout: 46%   Improve: 67%   Collapse: 6%   Attrition: 10%   Comparables: Bobby Abreu, Ruben Mateo, Alex Fernandez, Carlos Gonzalez

Martinez elicits wildly divergent scouting reports, from potential MVP type to borderline starter. He improved only slightly in a repeat engagement with Double-A, but "showed flashes," to insert the requisite cliché. He also had a strong showing in winter ball. While Martinez boosted his power a tick, his walk rate remained stagnant, but equally troubling for the phenom's development have been persistent injury issues, as he has yet to play a full season, with a hamstring strain cropping up last year. Martinez will begin the season at Triple-A, patrolling center with the halo still above his head, and whatever questions persist about him, he's notably been on an extremely accelerated schedule, having just graduated out of teenagerdom. He should get a taste of the majors in September or perhaps sooner.

Daniel Murphy · LF

Bats: L   Throws: R   Height: 6' 1"   Weight: 210   Born: January 4, 1985   Age: 24

YEAR	TEAM	LVL	AGE	PA	R	2B	3B	HR	RBI	BB	SO	SB	CS	EqBRR	AVG	OBP	SLG	EqAVG	EqOBP	EqSLG	EqA	VORP	WARP	DEFENSE			
2006	KNG	Rk	21	37	2	0	0	2	7	4	1	0	0	-0.2	.273	.351	.455	.171	.216	.257	.148	-9.3	-0.6				
2006	BRO	A-	21	34	2	1	0	0	3	4	3	0	0	-0.1	.241	.324	.276	.200	.265	.200	.166	-7.2	-0.4				
2007	SLU	A+	22	559	68	34	3	11	78	42	61	6	3	-0.2	.285	.338	.430	.240	.288	.381	.233	-12.1	-0.2	131-3B	1		
2008	BIN	AA	23	407	56	26	1	13	67	39	46	14	5	-1.2	.308	.374	.496	.282	.342	.472	.279	20.6	2.4	60-3B	2	18-2B	2
2008	NYN	MLB	23	151	24	9	3	2	17	18	28	0	2	-0.4	.313	.397	.473	.321	.404	.504	.306	9.4	1.2	28-LF	1		
2009	NYN	MLB	24	548	62	28	3	12	62	46	76	9	4	-0.3	.263	.327	.405	.267	.330	.424	.259	11.5	1.8	129-3B	-3		

Breakout: 32%   Improve: 59%   Collapse: 11%   Attrition: 6%   Comparables: Frank Catalanotto, Brad Mills, Mike Lamb, Matt Stairs

Murphy was the third position player from the 2006 draft to make the majors, after Evan Longoria (third pick) and Manny Burriss (33rd), despite not being selected until the 13th round (394th overall). The Mets felt he was ready, because of an advanced plate approach; Murphy's pitch recognition skills ranked as tops in the system, and he demonstrated that ability in the majors: after getting called up on August 2, Murphy saw 4.25 pitches per plate appearance, a figure that would have ranked third in the National League over the full season. Finding a defensive position where he can stick has been a challenge. The Mets are hoping Murphy will improve to adequate in left field; they tried him at second in the Arizona Fall League, but that's just wishful thinking. As it stands now, he'll platoon with Fernando Tatis.

Angel Pagan — OF

Bats: S   Throws: R   Height: 6' 1"   Weight: 180   Born: July 2, 1981   Age: 27

YEAR	TEAM	LVL	AGE	PA	R	2B	3B	HR	RBI	BB	SO	SB	CS	EqBRR	AVG	OBP	SLG	EqAVG	EqOBP	EqSLG	EqA	VORP	WARP	DEFENSE			
2006	CHN	MLB	24	187	28	6	2	5	18	15	28	4	2	-0.3	.247	.306	.394	.241	.305	.382	.240	-2.9	0.1	24-LF	2	15-RF	0
2007	IOW	AAA	25	127	18	4	3	3	9	10	20	6	1	0.1	.250	.310	.414	.214	.270	.359	.222	-5.4	0.5	19-CF	4	6-LF	2
2007	CHN	MLB	25	161	21	10	2	4	21	10	32	4	1	-0.2	.264	.306	.439	.257	.304	.446	.259	3.0	0.4	26-CF	0	10-RF	1
2008	NYN	MLB	26	105	12	7	1	0	13	11	18	4	0	2.6	.275	.346	.374	.286	.356	.385	.273	2.6	0.2	19-LF	-1		
2009	NYN	MLB	27	188	23	9	1	3	19	16	31	7	2	1.1	.259	.321	.392	.263	.325	.411	.258	3.5	1.0	48-LF	3		

Breakout: 29%   Improve: 50%   Collapse: 26%   Attrition: 36%   Comparables: Scott Bullett, John Shelby, Mike Kingery, Stan Javier

Because of Alou's fragility, Pagan was the Mets' Opening Day starter in left field. On May 7, he injured his shoulder while falling into the stands to catch a fly at Chavez Ravine. The Mets initially asserted that he had only a bad bruise, but Pagan eventually revealed that his labrum was torn. He tried to come back in July without surgery, but a setback in Brooklyn forced him under the knife. Presumably healthy heading into camp, Pagan will battle with Jeremy Reed for the fifth outfielder's job.

Jose Reyes — SS

Bats: S   Throws: R   Height: 6' 1"   Weight: 200   Born: June 11, 1983   Age: 26

YEAR	TEAM	LVL	AGE	PA	R	2B	3B	HR	RBI	BB	SO	SB	CS	EqBRR	AVG	OBP	SLG	EqAVG	EqOBP	EqSLG	EqA	VORP	WARP	DEFENSE	
2006	NYN	MLB	23	703	122	30	17	19	81	53	81	64	17	4.8	.300	.354	.487	.305	.360	.495	.292	59.9	5.6	147-SS	-4
2007	NYN	MLB	24	765	119	36	12	12	57	77	78	78	21	9.9	.280	.354	.421	.292	.369	.447	.283	46.9	6.7	160-SS	8
2008	NYN	MLB	25	763	113	37	19	16	68	66	82	56	15	8.3	.297	.358	.475	.310	.370	.507	.297	62.6	5.8	157-SS	-11
2009	NYN	MLB	26	718	126	36	12	16	76	65	74	68	16	7.7	.309	.374	.478	.314	.378	.500	.304	68.4	7.2	162-SS	-1

Breakout: 40%   Improve: 71%   Collapse: 0%   Attrition: 3%   Comparables: Roberto Alomar, Jim Fregosi, Ryne Sandberg, Tony Fernandez

The Most Exciting Player in Baseball turned in a superlative season, becoming the eighth player in major league history to produce 50-plus steals and 70-plus extra-base hits in a year; Hanley Ramirez is the only other shortstop to do so. Reyes also led the National League in hits, posting the second 200-plus campaign in team history, and established new Mets career marks in both triples and steals. For the second straight year, he ranked second among major league shortstops in games played and, for the second straight year, had his worst offensive month in September. One of the priorities for the offseason was to find a backup capable of spelling "The Franchise" every now and again. Fresh legs in September might mean the difference in a playoff hunt for the Mets and an MVP award for Reyes.

Brian Schneider — C

Bats: L   Throws: R   Height: 6' 1"   Weight: 195   Born: November 26, 1976   Age: 32

YEAR	TEAM	LVL	AGE	PA	R	2B	3B	HR	RBI	BB	SO	SB	CS	EqBRR	AVG	OBP	SLG	EqAVG	EqOBP	EqSLG	EqA	VORP	WARP	DEFENSE	
2006	WAS	MLB	29	455	30	18	0	4	55	38	67	2	2	-2.6	.256	.320	.329	.254	.321	.322	.229	-5.1	0.8	112-C	3
2007	WAS	MLB	30	477	33	21	1	6	54	56	56	0	0	-1.9	.235	.326	.336	.236	.332	.340	.244	3.5	1.4	118-C	1
2008	NYN	MLB	31	384	30	10	0	9	38	42	53	0	0	-1.6	.257	.339	.367	.259	.343	.378	.256	7.8	2.3	98-C	7
2009	NYN	MLB	32	266	24	10	0	4	26	27	36	0	0	-1.4	.252	.330	.342	.256	.333	.358	.241	4.7	1.5	65-C	2

Breakout: 23%   Improve: 46%   Collapse: 30%   Attrition: 40%   Comparables: Ron Hassey, Brent Mayne, Johnny Oates, Jerry Grote

In his own understated way, Schneider was better than the Mets could have hoped for, improving at the plate from the previous two seasons and throwing out a third of attempted basestealers. Management was unmoved by his game calling, however, leading to efforts to bring in another backstop over the winter. The veteran catcher has a lot of limitations—for one, he can't make Mets fans forget about Lastings Milledge—but he's solid enough in a timeshare. New York shouldn't be too broken up about having him back in the final year of his four-year, $16 million deal, especially given the thin crop of alternatives available during the offseason.

Fernando Tatis — 4C

Bats: R   Throws: R   Height: 5' 10"   Weight: 175   Born: January 1, 1975   Age: 34

YEAR	TEAM	LVL	AGE	PA	R	2B	3B	HR	RBI	BB	SO	SB	CS	EqBRR	AVG	OBP	SLG	EqAVG	EqOBP	EqSLG	EqA	VORP	WARP	DEFENSE			
2006	OTT	AAA	31	368	44	15	2	7	37	36	56	8	2	1.3	.298	.372	.420	.241	.312	.355	.237	-6.9	-0.1	83-3B	0		
2006	BAL	MLB	31	64	7	6	1	2	8	6	17	0	0	-0.7	.250	.313	.500	.236	.312	.473	.269	1.7	0.1				
2007	NWO	AAA	32	572	90	31	5	21	67	62	103	8	6	0.0	.276	.359	.485	.219	.296	.382	.236	-11.3	-0.7	122-3B	-4		
2008	NWO	AAA	33	139	18	6	0	12	31	17	23	0	0	-0.4	.242	.345	.592	.194	.281	.444	.246	-1.4	0.6	26-3B	4		
2008	NYN	MLB	33	306	33	16	1	11	47	29	59	3	0	0.2	.297	.369	.484	.304	.378	.509	.302	18.4	2.0	32-RF	-3	31-LF	2
2009	NYN	MLB	34	220	25	10	1	6	27	22	47	2	1	-0.2	.245	.325	.402	.249	.328	.421	.259	4.6	0.7	55-3B	-1		

Breakout: 28%   Improve: 41%   Collapse: 37%   Attrition: 50%   Comparables: Don Zimmer, Billy Johnson, Robby Thompson, Wally Westlake

Forget Brad Lidge: Tatis was the real NL Comeback Player of the Year in 2008. Three years ago, after two full seasons away from the game, Tatis decided to return to raise money for the construction of a church in his Dominican hometown. By the time Tatis joined the Mets last year, the church had already been built, so he set about erecting something for himself: a new career. Tatis got back his late-1990s mojo, hitting for power against righties (.240 ISO) and OBP against lefties (.393), while also proving especially clutch, knocking in the game-winning or game-tying run(s) in the seventh inning or later five times. Tatis's season was ended early when he separated his shoulder diving for a ball on September 16, and the Mets missed him. He showed no lingering effects in the Dominican winter league and signed a one-year, $1.7 million contract to return.

David Wright — 3B

Bats: R   Throws: R   Height: 6' 0"   Weight: 215   Born: December 20, 1982   Age: 26

YEAR	TEAM	LVL	AGE	PA	R	2B	3B	HR	RBI	BB	SO	SB	CS	EqBRR	AVG	OBP	SLG	EqAVG	EqOBP	EqSLG	EqA	VORP	WARP	DEFENSE
2006	NYN	MLB	23	661	96	40	5	26	116	66	113	20	5	2.0	.311	.381	.531	.314	.385	.536	.311	55.3	5.0	152-3B -9
2007	NYN	MLB	24	711	113	42	1	30	107	94	115	34	5	2.7	.325	.416	.546	.334	.428	.576	.338	81.9	8.7	158-3B 0
2008	NYN	MLB	25	735	115	42	2	33	124	94	118	15	5	-3.1	.302	.390	.534	.315	.402	.568	.323	65.8	7.1	159-3B -6
2009	NYN	MLB	26	703	121	38	3	32	107	96	111	20	5	0.1	.302	.400	.538	.307	.404	.564	.324	72.3	7.6	162-3B -1

Breakout: 11%   Improve: 53%   Collapse: 16%   Attrition: 5%   Comparables: Ron Santo, Jim Ray Hart, Jeff Bagwell, Bobby Grich

Wright tied the franchise single-season record for RBI, matching Mike Piazza's total from 1999. He was excoriated by fans for failing to smash through that mark, however, because no one in the National League batted with more runners in scoring position (267 total), and the star third baseman hit .243/.328/.376 in those PAs. The criticism found focus in his ninth-inning at-bat on the final Wednesday of the season, when Wright came up with a runner on third and no outs in a 6-6 game and fanned feebly on several Bobby Howry pitches out of the strike zone. The Mets would fail to score and lost to Chicago in the 10th. Of course, blaming Wright for the team's failure is absurd, as is the suggestion that he needs to see a sports psychologist for his supposed clutch issue. Wright hit .340 in September and in 2007 put up a 976 OPS with runners in scoring position. He's the best player on the team, even if he doesn't deserve those Gold Gloves, and will continue to pump out superb seasons for years to come.

PITCHERS

Tony Armas

Bats: R   Throws: R   Height: 6' 3"   Weight: 225   Born: April 29, 1978   Age: 31

YEAR	TEAM	LVL	AGE	W	L	SV	G	GS	IP	H	BB	SO	HR	GB%	BABIP	STUFF	WHIP	ERA	DERA	EqH9	EqBB9	EqSO9	EqHR9	DEF	VORP	SN/WX
2006	WAS	MLB	28	9	12	0	30	30	154	167	64	97	19	41.0%	.307	-1	1.50	5.03	5.23	9.5	3.3	5.2	1.0	-1	5.3	2.84
2007	PIT	MLB	29	4	5	0	31	15	97	111	38	73	18	38.1%	.314	-12	1.54	6.03	5.63	8.9	3.0	6.1	1.5	-1	-4.7	0.42
2008	NWO	AAA	30	5	7	0	17	17	102²	85	20	88	9	46.0%	.273	9	1.02	2.54	4.53	8.8	2.0	5.5	1.0	11	11.3	—
2008	NYN	MLB	30	1	0	0	3	1	8¹	11	1	6	2	40.0%	.346	-6	1.44	7.59	6.48	11.9	1.1	5.4	2.2	-1	-1.8	0.01
2009	NYN	MLB	31	4	5	1	28	9	76¹	79	25	58	11	42.0%	.290	6	1.36	4.59	5.00	9.4	2.6	5.9	1.3	0	6.7	0.99

Breakout: 23%   Improve: 50%   Collapse: 31%   Attrition: 28%   Comparables: Moe Drabowsky, Victor Santos, Vicente Padilla, Jorge Sosa

Armas's career came full circle last year—by signing with the Mets, he became teammates with Pedro Martinez, for whom he was traded back in 1997. Armas had a better year than the future Hall of Famer, but his chance to help out down the stretch was ended when he became the third Mets player to suffer a hernia, missing the last two months. A free agent at press time, Armas proved that he's not yet washed up with his work in N'awlins, and he should get a shot with some team looking for rotational depth.

Luis Ayala

	Bats: R	Throws: R	Height: 6' 2"	Weight: 185	Born: January 12, 1978	Age: 31

YEAR	TEAM	LVL	AGE	W	L	SV	G	GS	IP	H	BB	SO	HR	GB%	BABIP	STUFF	WHIP	ERA	DERA	EqH9	EqBB9	EqSO9	EqHR9	DEF	VORP	SN/WX
2007	WAS	MLB	29	2	2	1	44	0	42¹	43	12	28	5	39.3%	.297	-5	1.30	3.19	4.01	8.9	2.1	5.5	1.1	4	11.2	0.73
2008	WAS	MLB	30	1	8	0	62	0	57²	63	22	36	6	47.2%	.311	-12	1.47	5.77	5.28	9.5	2.9	5.0	0.9	-3	-4.3	-1.26
2008	NYN	MLB	30	1	2	9	19	0	18	23	2	14	3	53.2%	.345	-3	1.39	5.50	5.00	11.5	1.0	6.0	1.5	-1	-1.0	-0.09
2009	NYN	MLB	31	2	2	3	39	0	44¹	47	14	29	5	46.0%	.300	-2	1.38	4.18	4.62	9.6	2.5	5.0	1.0	0	5.7	0.48

Breakout: 27% Improve: 44% Collapse: 36% Attrition: 41%   Comparables: Donn Pall, Doug Bird, Bill Long, Bill Fischer

Fed up with the repeated failures of their on-hand options in Wagner's absence, the Mets dealt Andy Hernandez for Ayala in mid-August out of sheer desperation. It just didn't work: Ayala proved adequate as the notional closer until mid-September, but then allowed eight runs in his last five innings, adding two crucial losses to his MLB-leading 10 relief defeats. The Mets understandably declined to offer him arbitration; relievers who strike out fewer than six per nine represent more risk than reward.

Pedro Feliciano

	Bats: L	Throws: L	Height: 5' 10"	Weight: 190	Born: August 25, 1976	Age: 32

YEAR	TEAM	LVL	AGE	W	L	SV	G	GS	IP	H	BB	SO	HR	GB%	BABIP	STUFF	WHIP	ERA	DERA	EqH9	EqBB9	EqSO9	EqHR9	DEF	VORP	SN/WX
2006	NYN	MLB	29	7	2	0	64	0	60¹	56	20	54	4	52.0%	.310	15	1.26	2.09	2.25	8.6	2.5	7.3	0.6	0	25.2	1.29
2007	NYN	MLB	30	2	2	2	78	0	64	47	31	61	3	57.9%	.257	16	1.22	3.09	3.70	6.4	3.7	7.8	0.4	2	15.3	2.03
2008	NYN	MLB	31	3	4	2	86	0	53¹	57	26	50	7	53.8%	.342	-1	1.56	4.05	3.33	10.2	3.9	7.7	1.2	-4	9.0	0.25
2009	NYN	MLB	32	3	2	3	53	0	47¹	45	21	40	4	51.0%	.300	6	1.38	3.63	4.04	8.6	3.4	6.5	0.7	0	9.0	0.79

Breakout: 10% Improve: 24% Collapse: 53% Attrition: 20%   Comparables: Jamie Easterly, Paul LaPalme, Tony Fossas, Paul Mirabella

Feliciano showed that he was not strictly a LOOGY in 2006 and 2007, but that ability completely vanished last year. While he remained solid against lefties (.210/.280/.295), right-handers hit .357/.453/.561. That huge split actually led to more frequent (if briefer) use, as Feliciano topped the majors in appearances; Manuel used Feliciano for less than three outs in his final 23 outings, the longest such streak in history. That resulted in the sixth-greatest-ever negative disparity between games and innings, behind seasons put up by notable LOOGIES Ray King, Mike Myers, and Jesse Orosco (and the less notable Sean Runyan).

Nelson Figueroa

	Bats: R	Throws: R	Height: 6' 1"	Weight: 180	Born: May 18, 1974	Age: 35

YEAR	TEAM	LVL	AGE	W	L	SV	G	GS	IP	H	BB	SO	HR	GB%	BABIP	STUFF	WHIP	ERA	DERA	EqH9	EqBB9	EqSO9	EqHR9	DEF	VORP	SN/WX
2006	NWO	AAA	32	3	5	0	16	11	76²	76	21	44	12	44.8%	.271	-33	1.27	4.37	6.90	10.0	2.7	3.3	2.0	7	-10.5	—
2007	CHH	MEX	33	8	6	0	19	19	153²	163	36	94	13	58.4%	.307	-16	1.29	3.86	6.03	9.8	2.8	4.1	1.4	7	-7.0	—
2008	NWO	AAA	34	4	7	0	20	16	113²	120	33	97	15	42.3%	.324	-12	1.35	4.43	5.74	11.2	2.8	5.4	1.5	-2	-1.6	—
2008	NYN	MLB	34	3	3	0	16	6	45¹	48	26	36	3	42.9%	.319	4	1.63	4.57	3.88	9.3	4.3	6.2	0.6	-6	2.1	-0.18
2009	NYN	MLB	35	4	5	1	33	10	71²	80	27	48	10	43.0%	.300	-3	1.48	5.10	5.54	10.1	2.9	5.2	1.2	0	1.8	0.47

Breakout: 14% Improve: 38% Collapse: 30% Attrition: 45%   Comparables: Doug Linton, Kevin Jarvis, Steve Parris, Frank Castillo

Figueroa made his first big-league appearance since 2004 when he was called up to replace the injured Pedro Martinez. Since Figueroa had spent 2005 rehabbing a torn rotator cuff, 2006 in Triple-A, and 2007 pitching in Mexico and Taiwan, his making it back to the bigs with his hometown team had to be satisfying. He opened with back-to-back quality starts, but faded immediately afterward, and the Mets outrighted him to Triple-A after the season.

Aaron Heilman Bats: R Throws: R Height: 6' 5" Weight: 225 Born: November 12, 1978 Age: 30

YEAR	TEAM	LVL	AGE	W	L	SV	G	GS	IP	H	BB	SO	HR	GB%	BABIP	STUFF	WHIP	ERA	DERA	EqH9	EqBB9	EqSO9	EqHR9	DEF	VORP	SN/WX
2006	NYN	MLB	27	4	5	0	74	0	87	73	28	73	5	47.6%	.286	16	1.16	3.62	3.80	7.7	2.5	7.0	0.4	2	20.6	3.28
2007	NYN	MLB	28	7	7	1	81	0	86	72	20	63	8	48.1%	.256	6	1.07	3.03	4.47	7.3	1.8	6.1	0.7	9	19.3	0.62
2008	NYN	MLB	29	3	8	3	78	0	76	75	46	80	10	43.9%	.323	0	1.59	5.21	5.59	9.0	4.5	8.1	1.2	1	-1.1	-0.35
2009	SEA	MLB	30	3	3	3	57	0	65	66	29	56	7	45.0%	.310	8	1.46	4.52	4.46	9.1	3.5	6.8	1.0	-1	6.4	0.52

Breakout: 29% Improve: 47% Collapse: 28% Attrition: 18%   Comparables: Lerrin LaGrow, Jay Witasick, Tyler Yates, Doug Brocail

Heilman always had a bumpy relationship with New York, and last year, he brought the storm that finally carried him out of the city. He completely lost command of his once-deadly changeup. Without it, he was unable to hold lefties at bay, and they thumped him for a .308/.425/.567 line with eight homers in 149 PAs. Heilman also displayed a knack for giving up huge long balls—nine of the 10 he allowed were hit with men on, the greatest number of multirun dingers ever surrendered by a reliever in club history. Heilman was long unhappy with relieving, and the team finally obliged him by sending him to Seattle as part of the package for Putz; with the Mariners, he'll get a chance to start.

Orlando Hernandez Bats: R Throws: R Height: 6' 2" Weight: 220 Born: October 11, 1965 Age: 43

YEAR	TEAM	LVL	AGE	W	L	SV	G	GS	IP	H	BB	SO	HR	GB%	BABIP	STUFF	WHIP	ERA	DERA	EqH9	EqBB9	EqSO9	EqHR9	DEF	VORP	SN/WX
2006	ARI	MLB	40	2	4	0	9	9	45²	52	20	52	8	32.8%	.373	21	1.58	6.11	3.89	10.4	3.5	9.6	1.4	-8	-0.4	0.71
2006	NYN	MLB	40	9	7	0	20	20	116²	103	41	112	14	36.8%	.287	23	1.23	4.09	4.17	8.0	2.8	7.9	1.0	-1	19.3	3.32
2007	NYN	MLB	41	9	5	0	27	24	147²	109	64	128	23	39.7%	.228	10	1.17	3.72	4.10	6.6	3.4	7.3	1.3	6	31.5	4.64
2009	NYN	MLB	43	3	3	0	15	8	55²	51	23	50	7	40.0%	.280	12	1.32	4.01	4.36	8.3	3.2	6.9	1.1	0	11.6	1.21

Breakout: 20% Improve: 47% Collapse: 25% Attrition: 56%   Comparables: Don McMahon, Jesse Orosco, Joe Niekro, Early Wynn

In spring training, *el Duque* revealed that he was still suffering from bunions; the painful deformity, caused by years of rising up on the ball of his right foot to execute that crazily high leg kick, had not been removed as originally reported. Instead, the surgery he had in the offseason was to fix a tendon strain in a toe. He attempted to alter his delivery to help take pressure off the toes, but the soreness lingered and he threw just 15⅔ innings of minor league rehab before aborting the comeback. Hernandez finally elected for bunion surgery in late August. His two-year, $12 million deal has expired, but the crafty old Cuban was spotted working out in Miami during the offseason.

Bradley Holt Bats: R Throws: R Height: 6' 4" Weight: 194 Born: October 13, 1986 Age: 22

YEAR	TEAM	LVL	AGE	W	L	SV	G	GS	IP	H	BB	SO	HR	GB%	BABIP	STUFF	WHIP	ERA	DERA	EqH9	EqBB9	EqSO9	EqHR9	DEF	VORP	SN/WX
2008	BRO	A-	21	5	3	0	14	14	72¹	43	33	96	3	45.6%	.263	13	1.05	1.87	5.52	9.0	6.0	5.8	1.5	7	0.6	—
2009	NYN	MLB	22	5	9	0	22	22	115¹	128	75	89	17	45.0%	.310	8	1.75	6.05	6.57	10.0	5.1	6.0	1.3	1	-10.0	-0.19

Breakout: 2% Improve: 8% Collapse: 68% Attrition: 19%   Comparables: John Ericks, Jay Witasick, Rich Lacko, Rick Huisman

Holt was perhaps the biggest late riser of the 2008 draft, as he suddenly started throwing mid-90s thunderbolts in his junior season at University of North Carolina–Wilmington. The Mets have a hankering for big college righties with top heaters (to wit: Mike Pelfrey), so they snatched up Holt with the 33rd overall pick. Holt's secondary pitches were initially considered suspect, but he made progress with his slider. In the pros, foes could only wait him out, because they couldn't hit him, as Holt led the circuit in both ERA and strikeouts. While his changeup needs a lot of work, Holt looks like a draft-day steal at this point.

Eddie Kunz Bats: R Throws: R Height: 6' 5" Weight: 250 Born: April 8, 1986 Age: 23

YEAR	TEAM	LVL	AGE	W	L	SV	G	GS	IP	H	BB	SO	HR	GB%	BABIP	STUFF	WHIP	ERA	DERA	EqH9	EqBB9	EqSO9	EqHR9	DEF	VORP	SN/WX
2007	BRO	A-	21	0	1	5	12	0	12	8	8	9	0	73.8%	.225	-24	1.33	6.75	10.97	8.4	7.6	2.5	0.8	0	-6.4	—
2008	BIN	AA	22	1	4	27	44	0	48¹	39	25	43	0	72.5%	.293	9	1.33	2.80	3.83	8.0	4.4	5.7	0.2	-2	9.2	—
2008	NWO	AAA	22	0	1	0	6	0	5²	9	2	4	1	54.5%	.381	-21	1.93	7.89	5.06	16.9	3.4	3.4	1.7	-3	0.3	—
2008	NYN	MLB	22	0	0	0	4	0	2²	5	1	1	1	81.8%	.444	-31	2.25	13.33	7.71	19.3	3.9	3.9	3.9	-1	-2.4	-0.14
2009	NYN	MLB	23	3	3	1	31	3	56	57	28	38	4	58.0%	.300	1	1.51	4.73	5.35	9.2	4.0	5.3	0.7	0	2.6	0.33

Breakout: 37% Improve: 61% Collapse: 13% Attrition: 10%   Comparables: Terry Adams, Barry Jones, Ed Farmer, Jim Hannan

When he was called up to the Mets in August, Kunz had yet to give up a home run in 60 innings of pro work, thanks to a hellacious low-90s sinker that produced a 3.6 G/F ratio in Double-A. Chase Headley broke that spell in Kunz's second game in the "The Show," welcoming Kunz with a deposit in Shea's bleachers. It seemed as though the brief big-league immersion shook Kunz up, for he ended his season by giving up a combined 33 hits, 22 runs, and four homers in 19⅔ innings between Triple-A and the Arizona Fall League. New York's 2007 first-rounder out of Oregon State, Kunz has the potential to be an excellent ground-ball reliever, but will need to work on his control at Triple-A.

John Maine

Bats: R   Throws: R   Height: 6' 4"   Weight: 200   Born: May 8, 1981   Age: 28

YEAR	TEAM	LVL	AGE	W	L	SV	G	GS	IP	H	BB	SO	HR	GB%	BABIP	STUFF	WHIP	ERA	DERA	EqH9	EqBB9	EqSO9	EqHR9	DEF	VORP	SN/WX
2006	NOR	AAA	25	3	5	0	10	10	56¹	55	20	48	2	52.3%	.317	0	1.34	3.53	6.17	9.5	3.7	5.0	0.7	1	-3.4	—
2006	NYN	MLB	25	6	5	0	16	15	90	69	33	71	15	40.9%	.225	6	1.13	3.60	4.75	6.9	2.9	6.6	1.3	9	19.1	2.35
2007	NYN	MLB	26	15	10	0	32	32	191	168	75	180	23	39.3%	.283	21	1.27	3.91	4.52	7.8	3.1	7.9	1.0	11	33.0	5.46
2008	NYN	MLB	27	10	8	0	25	25	140	122	67	122	16	42.2%	.276	11	1.35	4.18	4.89	7.8	3.6	6.8	1.0	7	18.3	3.00
2009	NYN	MLB	28	6	6	0	25	16	107	99	45	89	12	42.0%	.280	14	1.34	4.16	4.55	8.4	3.3	6.4	1.0	0	15.3	2.15

Breakout: 10%   Improve: 43%   Collapse: 33%   Attrition: 29%   *Comparables: Dick Woodson, Steve Bedrosian, Ernie Broglio, Steve Arlin*

For the second straight year, Maine wore down in-season. In 2007, it was a troublesome left hip, while 2008 produced a painful bone spur in his right shoulder. The injury affected Maine's control and durability, sent him on his first-ever DL trip at the end of July, and then sank his season completely three starts after his return. After having him pitch through pain during rehab with an eye toward helping out the bullpen down the stretch, the Mets activated him in the final week, but Manuel did not use him. Maine promptly underwent arthroscopic surgery to remove a lesion from the back of his shoulder socket after the season; the Mets badly need him to come back ready for a full season.

Pedro Martinez

Bats: R   Throws: R   Height: 5' 11"   Weight: 180   Born: October 25, 1971   Age: 37

YEAR	TEAM	LVL	AGE	W	L	SV	G	GS	IP	H	BB	SO	HR	GB%	BABIP	STUFF	WHIP	ERA	DERA	EqH9	EqBB9	EqSO9	EqHR9	DEF	VORP	SN/WX
2006	NYN	MLB	34	9	8	0	23	23	132²	108	39	137	19	37.1%	.266	23	1.11	4.48	5.20	7.4	2.3	8.4	1.1	9	15.3	3.10
2007	NYN	MLB	35	3	1	0	5	5	28	33	7	32	0	32.2%	.393	29	1.43	2.57	1.55	10.2	1.9	9.3	0.0	-6	7.1	1.01
2008	NYN	MLB	36	5	6	0	20	20	109	127	44	87	19	42.3%	.331	-6	1.57	5.61	5.27	10.6	3.1	6.4	1.5	-5	-2.2	0.98
2009	NYN	MLB	37	6	6	1	29	16	110	112	36	87	14	41.0%	.300	9	1.34	4.31	4.68	9.3	2.6	6.1	1.2	1	12.4	1.98

Breakout: 27%   Improve: 56%   Collapse: 25%   Attrition: 39%   *Comparables: Luis Tiant, Murry Dickson, Dave Stewart, Kevin Tapani*

Pedro is no stranger to injury, but he is a stranger to the numbers that appeared next to his name in 2008 box scores. Whether due to the hamstring that popped in his first start or simply the gradual erosion of greatness, the home-run issues of recent years got worse, and his famously precise control strayed. Velocity doesn't seem to be the problem—his fastball traveled at around the same speed that it did back in 2005—but something was certainly off, as Martinez posted his highest walk rate since he was a rookie. His four-year, $53 million contract has expired; during its duration, Martinez made 79 starts and pitched 486⅔ innings with a 3.88 ERA and a 464/137 K/BB. At the time, it was speculated that the Mets were paying Martinez for four years to get two good ones, but in the end, it was more like one. Chalk one up for the Red Sox.

Carlos Muniz

Bats: R   Throws: R   Height: 6' 1"   Weight: 180   Born: March 12, 1981   Age: 28

YEAR	TEAM	LVL	AGE	W	L	SV	G	GS	IP	H	BB	SO	HR	GB%	BABIP	STUFF	WHIP	ERA	DERA	EqH9	EqBB9	EqSO9	EqHR9	DEF	VORP	SN/WX
2006	SLU	A+	25	4	3	31	48	0	49¹	39	18	45	5	36.0%	.254	-39	1.16	3.12	7.05	10.1	4.4	4.2	2.2	4	-7.2	—
2007	BIN	AA	26	2	4	23	44	0	58²	43	17	62	2	34.4%	.266	2	1.02	2.45	4.32	7.1	2.9	5.9	0.6	0	8.3	—
2008	NWO	AAA	27	2	4	9	33	0	36²	30	14	31	5	33.3%	.258	-19	1.20	3.92	5.19	8.6	3.6	5.2	1.6	1	1.6	—
2008	NYN	MLB	27	1	1	0	18	0	23¹	24	7	16	4	26.7%	.286	-12	1.33	5.41	6.26	9.4	2.3	5.5	1.6	2	0.4	-0.08
2009	NYN	MLB	28	2	2	1	33	0	31²	31	12	22	4	34.0%	.270	-2	1.36	4.49	4.87	8.9	3.0	5.4	1.3	0	3.5	0.25

Breakout: 29%   Improve: 52%   Collapse: 29%   Attrition: 46%   *Comparables: Juan Acevedo, Darrel Akerfelds, Keith Creel, Floyd Chiffer*

Muniz is your garden-variety fastball/slider middle reliever. He came up and went down four times before rosters expanded in September and, with options remaining, is probably due for a similar fate in 2009. With the Mets' top affiliate having moved from New Orleans to Buffalo, at least Muniz's shuttling will involve less time aloft, but these days, we all know it's the time spent in the terminal that really kills you.

Jonathon Niese

| | | | | | | | | | Bats: L | | Throws: L | | Height: 6' 3" | | Weight: 190 | | Born: October 27, 1986 | | | Age: 22 |

YEAR	TEAM	LVL	AGE	W	L	SV	G	GS	IP	H	BB	SO	HR	GB%	BABIP	STUFF	WHIP	ERA	DERA	EqH9	EqBB9	EqSO9	EqHR9	DEF	VORP	SN/WX
2006	HAG	A	19	11	9	0	25	25	123	121	62	132	7	51.4%	.342	-13	1.49	3.95	7.88	14.2	6.9	4.9	1.8	-9	-25.8	—
2006	SLU	A+	19	0	2	0	2	2	10	8	5	10	0	50.0%	.296	6	1.30	4.50	11.17	9.3	5.6	4.7	0.0	0	-6.0	—
2007	SLU	A+	20	11	7	0	27	27	134¹	151	31	110	9	50.7%	.340	-3	1.36	4.29	7.32	12.9	3.0	4.2	1.5	-5	-22.8	—
2008	BIN	AA	21	6	7	0	22	22	124¹	118	44	112	5	53.4%	.323	30	1.30	3.04	4.15	9.8	3.2	6.0	0.6	-4	18.9	—
2008	NWO	AAA	21	5	1	0	7	7	39²	34	14	32	4	54.6%	.270	20	1.21	3.40	4.97	8.8	3.3	5.0	1.2	3	2.7	—
2008	NYN	MLB	21	1	1	0	3	3	14	20	8	11	2	50.0%	.383	11	2.00	7.07	5.14	12.9	4.5	6.4	1.3	-3	-2.4	0.12
2009	NYN	MLB	22	7	9	0	32	21	132	147	60	103	15	48.0%	.320	12	1.56	5.09	5.58	10.1	3.6	6.0	1.0	1	2.4	1.14

Breakout: 41% Improve: 83% Collapse: 6% Attrition: 14%   Comparables: Steve Searcy, Dave LaPoint, Andy Rincon, Dallas Braden

The strip-mining of the system to acquire Johan Santana left Niese as New York's top-rated young arm, and he did an excellent job carrying the organizational flag down on the depleted farm, rocketing through three levels and up to the majors. Niese was born on the same day that the Mets won Game Seven of the 1986 World Series, which suggests that the young southpaw is destined to help lead a renaissance. He has the ability to fulfill such expectations—a good low-90s moving fastball with sink, an excellent curve, and a solid change. While that stuff is not as dominant as that of his former high-school teammate, Chad Billingsley, it's good enough to help Niese become a third starter. He could win a rotation spot during the spring, but will most likely spend at least the first half fine-tuning in Buffalo.

Bobby Parnell

| | | | | | | | | | Bats: R | | Throws: R | | Height: 6' 3" | | Weight: 180 | | Born: September 8, 1984 | | | Age: 24 |

YEAR	TEAM	LVL	AGE	W	L	SV	G	GS	IP	H	BB	SO	HR	GB%	BABIP	STUFF	WHIP	ERA	DERA	EqH9	EqBB9	EqSO9	EqHR9	DEF	VORP	SN/WX
2006	HAG	A	21	5	10	0	18	18	93²	84	40	84	7	56.8%	.295	-27	1.33	4.06	8.89	12.4	5.8	3.8	2.2	2	-28.9	—
2007	SLU	A+	22	3	3	0	12	12	55¹	56	22	62	0	64.9%	.364	15	1.41	3.25	4.22	11.9	5.0	6.2	0.4	-1	7.5	—
2007	BIN	AA	22	5	5	0	17	17	88²	98	38	74	9	46.8%	.327	-15	1.53	4.77	6.94	11.2	4.4	4.6	1.6	-2	-12.6	—
2008	BIN	AA	23	10	6	0	24	24	127²	126	57	91	14	51.5%	.292	-17	1.43	4.30	6.02	10.0	3.9	4.5	1.5	9	-5.6	—
2008	NWO	AAA	23	2	2	0	5	4	20¹	25	9	23	0	46.8%	.410	6	1.67	6.65	5.68	13.7	4.3	7.1	0.5	-5	-0.2	—
2008	NYN	MLB	23	0	0	0	6	0	5	3	2	3	0	42.9%	.214	-13	1.00	5.40	7.71	5.8	3.9	5.8	0.0	1	0.1	0.02
2009	NYN	MLB	24	6	9	0	34	20	124¹	143	64	86	17	48.0%	.320	2	1.66	5.76	6.30	10.4	4.1	5.3	1.2	1	-7.3	0.03

Breakout: 12% Improve: 47% Collapse: 13% Attrition: 15%   Comparables: Scot Shields, Randy Bockus, Jack Nuismer, Reggie Patterson

The classic flame-throwing righty who lacks the third pitch needed to be a reliable starter, Parnell was converted to relief when he came up for a major league demitasse in mid-September. His fastball is a plus-plus offering that can reach into the high-90s in short bursts out of the pen and features late sink. Parnell backs that up with a good, hard slider, so he has the right combination to be a capable setup man. He has also shown the ability to retire left-handers—he actually held them to a lower OPS than he did righties, 732 to 760, at his three stops last year. If there are any spots left after *Omar's Extreme Makeover: Bullpen Edition,* Parnell will be first in line for one this spring.

Mike Pelfrey

| | | | | | | | | | Bats: R | | Throws: R | | Height: 6' 7" | | Weight: 215 | | Born: January 14, 1984 | | | Age: 25 |

YEAR	TEAM	LVL	AGE	W	L	SV	G	GS	IP	H	BB	SO	HR	GB%	BABIP	STUFF	WHIP	ERA	DERA	EqH9	EqBB9	EqSO9	EqHR9	DEF	VORP	SN/WX
2006	SLU	A+	22	2	1	0	4	4	22²	17	2	26	1	64.7%	.327	18	0.86	1.62	2.04	11.7	1.5	7.1	1.0	-3	7.0	—
2006	BIN	AA	22	4	2	0	12	12	66¹	60	26	77	2	49.7%	.347	20	1.30	2.72	4.53	11.5	4.7	6.7	0.6	-1	6.9	—
2006	NYN	MLB	22	2	1	0	4	4	21¹	25	12	13	1	49.3%	.353	6	1.73	5.49	5.75	11.1	4.4	5.3	0.4	0	0.0	0.15
2007	NWO	AAA	23	3	6	0	14	14	74	74	26	56	6	58.9%	.306	0	1.35	4.01	5.27	9.7	3.4	4.8	1.0	3	2.6	—
2007	NYN	MLB	23	3	8	0	15	13	72²	85	39	45	6	50.2%	.338	2	1.71	5.57	5.38	10.5	4.2	5.2	0.8	0	-0.5	0.30
2008	NYN	MLB	24	13	11	0	32	32	200²	209	64	110	12	50.9%	.310	14	1.36	3.72	3.73	9.6	2.5	4.5	0.5	-2	39.6	5.84
2009	NYN	MLB	25	10	9	0	27	27	163²	176	60	106	16	50.0%	.300	13	1.44	4.39	4.85	9.8	2.9	5.0	0.9	1	15.4	2.96

Breakout: 9% Improve: 29% Collapse: 38% Attrition: 14%   Comparables: Chris Carpenter, Ron Romanick, Jamey Wright, Brian Holman

Considered something of a bust heading into the season, Pelfrey bridled his powerful sinker and turned into the workhorse that the Mets envisioned when they took him ninth overall in the 2005 draft. After losing six straight starts from April 25 to May 26, Pelfrey had a 5.33 ERA and 4.2 BB/9, but then found the zone: his walk rate fell by two per nine and he posted a 3.20 ERA in 150 innings the rest of the way. Pelfrey relied more than ever on his hard sinker, earning the sixth-lowest home-run rate among qualified starters. The highlight of his year came in late August, when he saved the battered bullpen by throwing back-to-back complete-game victories, the first Mets pitcher to do so since Bret Saberhagen in 1995. Pelfrey's innings jumped by almost 50 last year, but his huge frame and sinkerball style suggest the ability to shake off any aftereffects. He'll have to, because suddenly he's being counted on as Santana's wingman.

Oliver Perez

Bats: L   Throws: L   Height: 6' 3"   Weight: 215   Born: August 15, 1981   Age: 27

YEAR	TEAM	LVL	AGE	W	L	SV	G	GS	IP	H	BB	SO	HR	GB%	BABIP	STUFF	WHIP	ERA	DERA	EqH9	EqBB9	EqSO9	EqHR9	DEF	VORP	SN/WX
2006	PIT	MLB	24	2	10	0	15	15	76	88	51	61	13	32.5%	.336	-3	1.83	6.63	6.75	9.4	5.1	6.4	1.3	-1	-13.1	0.20
2006	NYN	MLB	24	1	3	0	7	7	36²	41	17	41	7	30.8%	.358	16	1.58	6.38	5.35	10.7	3.8	9.4	1.5	-3	-2.0	0.42
2007	NYN	MLB	25	15	10	0	29	29	177	153	79	174	22	35.2%	.278	22	1.31	3.56	4.11	7.6	3.5	8.1	1.1	-3	23.8	3.99
2008	NYN	MLB	26	10	7	0	34	34	194	167	105	180	24	35.0%	.280	12	1.40	4.22	4.48	7.9	4.2	7.4	1.1	-2	21.5	4.42
2009	NYN	MLB	27	9	8	0	25	25	152¹	138	73	144	19	37.0%	.280	23	1.38	4.26	4.61	8.2	3.8	7.3	1.1	1	17.8	3.15

Breakout: 14%   Improve: 58%   Collapse: 18%   Attrition: 17%   Comparables: Tim Lollar, Barry Zito, Kevin Gross, Don Gullett

While he ended up with league-average numbers, the mercurial Perez took his own wild way getting there—he led the majors in walks and went as deep as seven innings in just seven starts. He also posted the lowest G/F ratio of any qualifying starter (0.67). Balls in the air are less likely to go for hits than grounders, so Perez has a greater ability to suppress BABIP than does the average pitcher, meaning his .276 mark from 2008 is not as flukish as might first be presumed. After taking over as pitching coach midseason, Dan Warthen had him pitch from the center of the rubber; from that point forward, Perez posted a 3.42 ERA and 2/1 K/BB in 110⅔ innings.

Duaner Sanchez

Bats: R   Throws: R   Height: 6' 2"   Weight: 210   Born: October 14, 1979   Age: 29

YEAR	TEAM	LVL	AGE	W	L	SV	G	GS	IP	H	BB	SO	HR	GB%	BABIP	STUFF	WHIP	ERA	DERA	EqH9	EqBB9	EqSO9	EqHR9	DEF	VORP	SN/WX
2006	NYN	MLB	26	5	1	0	48	0	55¹	43	24	44	3	54.1%	.274	10	1.21	2.60	2.50	7.2	3.5	6.7	0.5	-3	17.7	2.84
2008	NYN	MLB	28	5	1	0	66	0	58¹	54	23	44	6	44.6%	.271	-6	1.32	4.32	5.31	8.2	3.0	5.9	0.9	7	8.1	1.92
2009	NYN	MLB	29	2	2	1	39	0	43²	43	18	32	5	47.0%	.290	2	1.38	4.02	4.44	8.9	3.2	5.7	0.9	0	6.5	0.52

Breakout: 8%   Improve: 28%   Collapse: 40%   Attrition: 22%   Comparables: Matt Whiteside, Dave Smith, Barry Jones, John Frascatore

The separated shoulder that Sanchez suffered in a late-July 2006 taxicab accident led to two surgeries and cost him over a full season, but it also appears to have robbed him of some life on his fastball, and his slider has come down several pegs as well. He fought through the season and was still effective, at least for a Mets reliever, topping the bullpen in WXRL. The Mets believe his stuff will rebound this year and are counting on him to be the seventh-inning bridge to the Putz/K-Rod endgame.

Johan Santana

Bats: L   Throws: L   Height: 6' 0"   Weight: 210   Born: March 13, 1979   Age: 30

YEAR	TEAM	LVL	AGE	W	L	SV	G	GS	IP	H	BB	SO	HR	GB%	BABIP	STUFF	WHIP	ERA	DERA	EqH9	EqBB9	EqSO9	EqHR9	DEF	VORP	SN/WX
2006	MIN	MLB	27	19	6	0	34	34	233²	186	47	245	24	41.8%	.273	35	1.00	2.77	3.61	6.9	1.8	8.4	0.9	13	79.0	8.41
2007	MIN	MLB	28	15	13	0	33	33	219	183	52	235	33	39.5%	.275	21	1.07	3.33	4.01	7.5	2.0	8.5	1.4	8	57.1	6.41
2008	NYN	MLB	29	16	7	0	34	34	234¹	206	63	206	23	43.8%	.278	25	1.15	2.54	3.46	7.9	2.0	6.9	0.8	13	73.6	8.55
2009	NYN	MLB	30	15	8	0	31	31	216	189	58	200	23	43.0%	.280	28	1.14	3.14	3.44	7.9	2.1	7.1	1.0	1	52.1	7.35

Breakout: 5%   Improve: 46%   Collapse: 20%   Attrition: 12%   Comparables: Frank Viola, Mickey Lolich, Johnny Antonelli, Don Sutton

Many high-profile acquisitions wilt in New York, but Santana thrived in the Big Apple, leading the majors in ERA. Seven times, he left with the lead, only to have relievers give it back, which might have cost him the Cy Young Award. As usual, Santana got better as the season progressed, almost dragging the team into October by going 9-0 with a 2.09 ERA in his final 17 starts. The Mets were careful with Santana's workload throughout the first four months, but after several premature exits cost the team games against the Phillies, Manuel loosened the reins, allowing the ace to fire two complete-game shutouts. The result was a career high in innings pitched; that and the decline in his strikeout rate should be noted.

Scott Schoeneweis

Bats: L   Throws: L   Height: 6' 0"   Weight: 190   Born: October 2, 1973   Age: 35

YEAR	TEAM	LVL	AGE	W	L	SV	G	GS	IP	H	BB	SO	HR	GB%	BABIP	STUFF	WHIP	ERA	DERA	EqH9	EqBB9	EqSO9	EqHR9	DEF	VORP	SN/WX
2006	TOR	MLB	32	2	2	1	55	0	37¹	39	16	18	3	57.9%	.295	-24	1.47	6.51	6.06	9.6	3.8	4.0	0.8	0	-1.4	-0.01
2006	CIN	MLB	32	2	0	3	16	0	14¹	9	8	11	1	60.0%	.205	2	1.19	0.63	1.84	4.9	4.3	6.1	0.6	2	8.6	0.98
2007	NYN	MLB	33	0	2	2	70	0	59	62	28	41	8	53.4%	.300	-14	1.53	5.03	5.64	9.3	3.7	5.8	1.1	4	1.9	0.60
2008	NYN	MLB	34	2	6	1	73	0	56²	55	23	34	7	51.6%	.281	-14	1.38	3.33	4.23	8.8	3.3	4.9	1.1	4	12.1	0.02
2009	ARI	MLB	35	2	2	1	44	0	41	44	17	26	4	51.0%	.300	-6	1.49	4.64	4.73	9.4	3.3	5.0	0.9	0	4.6	0.39

Breakout: 18%   Improve: 33%   Collapse: 42%   Attrition: 35%   Comparables: Darold Knowles, Rheal Cormier, Frank DiPino, Steve Barber

On the season's final day, Marlins manager Fredi Gonzalez pinch-hit righty Wes Helms against Schoeneweis for lefty Mike Jacobs to open the eighth inning. Helms hit the ball over the left-field wall to put the Marlins up for good and kill the Mets' postseason hopes. That home run virtually assured that Schoeneweis would not be allowed to collect the final $3.6 million left on his contract in New York, as Minaya traded him to the D'backs for Connor Robertson in December. Hopefully, the Mets have learned that extreme specialists should never get three-year deals.

Joe Smith

Bats: R   Throws: R   Height: 6' 2"   Weight: 215   Born: March 22, 1984   Age: 25

YEAR	TEAM	LVL	AGE	W	L	SV	G	GS	IP	H	BB	SO	HR	GB%	BABIP	STUFF	WHIP	ERA	DERA	EqH9	EqBB9	EqSO9	EqHR9	DEF	VORP	SN/WX
2006	BRO	A-	22	0	1	9	17	0	20	10	3	28	0	60.5%	.233	9	0.65	0.45	4.42	7.4	2.5	5.9	0.5	1	2.4	—
2006	BIN	AA	22	0	2	0	10	0	12²	12	11	12	1	54.3%	.344	-5	1.89	5.90	8.44	12.7	10.1	5.1	1.7	1	-3.4	—
2007	NYN	MLB	23	3	2	0	54	0	44¹	48	21	45	3	62.9%	.354	15	1.56	3.45	2.84	9.9	3.7	8.5	0.6	-3	10.5	0.52
2008	NYN	MLB	24	6	3	0	82	0	63¹	51	31	52	4	64.3%	.267	2	1.29	3.55	4.69	7.2	3.7	6.5	0.6	5	11.3	1.74
2009	CLE	MLB	25	3	3	2	50	2	59	56	28	46	4	55.0%	.300	9	1.42	3.80	3.86	8.3	3.8	6.5	0.5	0	12.3	1.02

Breakout: 24%   Improve: 48%   Collapse: 24%   Attrition: 18%   Comparables: Pete Mikkelsen, Jim Hannan, Ricky Trlicek, Terry Adams

The side-winding Smith was the right-handed complement to Feliciano and Schoeneweis, holding righties to a .192/.286/.302 line (lefties put up a 903 OPS). Sensibly enough, Smith was managed carefully, facing righty batters much more frequently than southpaws (210 PAs to 61) while making the third-most appearances in the majors. He's an effective piece to have in the pen, especially at prearbitration prices, but there's reason to believe he could become more than a ROOGY: Smith's walk rate is what suffers against southpaws, as he's held them to a lone homer in 119 major league PAs. Any strides in that regard will be made in Cleveland, as Smith was shipped to the Tribe in the three-team, 12-player Putz bonanza.

Brian Stokes

Bats: R   Throws: R   Height: 6' 1"   Weight: 210   Born: September 7, 1979   Age: 29

YEAR	TEAM	LVL	AGE	W	L	SV	G	GS	IP	H	BB	SO	HR	GB%	BABIP	STUFF	WHIP	ERA	DERA	EqH9	EqBB9	EqSO9	EqHR9	DEF	VORP	SN/WX
2006	DUR	AAA	26	7	7	0	29	23	133	134	49	103	8	48.0%	.312	-12	1.38	4.13	7.11	9.8	3.8	4.5	1.0	6	-21.3	—
2007	TBA	MLB	27	2	7	0	59	0	62¹	90	25	35	11	49.8%	.366	-32	1.83	7.08	5.89	11.6	3.3	4.3	1.6	-7	-7.7	-1.28
2008	NWO	AAA	28	10	8	0	23	22	130²	124	48	97	7	44.4%	.300	0	1.32	4.41	6.51	9.7	3.5	4.4	0.7	6	-12.6	—
2008	NYN	MLB	28	1	0	1	24	1	33¹	35	8	26	5	41.3%	.319	-1	1.29	3.51	3.94	9.8	2.0	6.5	1.4	1	7.7	0.13
2009	NYN	MLB	29	3	4	1	39	6	65²	75	25	43	8	45.0%	.310	-3	1.52	5.09	5.57	10.3	3.0	5.1	1.1	0	1.2	0.28

Breakout: 8%   Improve: 40%   Collapse: 28%   Attrition: 18%   Comparables: Tim Redding, Shawn Holman, Reid Cornelius, Ron Mathis

Stokes was the chief offender in perhaps the worst bullpen of all time while pitching for Tampa Bay in 2007, so the Rays were no doubt happy to sell him to New York when Minaya came calling. It proved to be a decent pickup—the hard-throwing righty did a nice job after getting called up in August, allowing just nine runs in 27⅔ innings of relief to halve his ERA from the year before. Stokes throws in the mid-90s, but his heater runs straight and true to the target, allowing hitters to aim for the downs after triangulation. The high-paid, famous bullpen arms that were added over the offseason will likely consign him to Buffalo.

Claudio Vargas

Bats: R   Throws: R   Height: 6' 3"   Weight: 230   Born: June 19, 1978   Age: 31

YEAR	TEAM	LVL	AGE	W	L	SV	G	GS	IP	H	BB	SO	HR	GB%	BABIP	STUFF	WHIP	ERA	DERA	EqH9	EqBB9	EqSO9	EqHR9	DEF	VORP	SN/WX
2006	ARI	MLB	28	12	10	0	31	30	167²	185	52	123	27	41.5%	.300	5	1.41	4.83	4.15	9.0	2.3	5.8	1.2	-9	13.3	2.62
2007	MIL	MLB	29	11	6	1	29	23	134¹	153	54	107	23	36.2%	.319	-1	1.54	5.09	4.36	9.2	3.1	6.5	1.4	-7	7.9	1.53
2008	NWO	AAA	30	5	2	0	8	8	43¹	47	13	43	5	38.3%	.350	2	1.39	4.36	5.09	11.5	2.9	6.2	1.3	-4	2.3	—
2008	NYN	MLB	30	3	2	0	11	4	37	33	11	20	4	48.7%	.261	-6	1.19	4.62	5.30	8.1	2.3	4.5	1.0	2	3.3	0.78
2009	NYN	MLB	31	5	5	1	26	13	85¹	89	29	64	11	42.0%	.300	7	1.39	4.60	5.00	9.5	2.7	5.8	1.2	0	7.4	1.17

Breakout: 11%   Improve: 33%   Collapse: 42%   Attrition: 27%   Comparables: Kent Bottenfield, Mark Leiter, Don Lee, Jim Clancy

The Mets signed journeyman Vargas to a minor league deal in early April. He did his typical thing; after sopping up a few starts in late May until Pedro returned, Vargas then slid into the bullpen, but was designated for assignment after giving up four runs in a late-June outing. The Dodgers signed him to a one-year contract in December, and he'll compete for a utility pitcher's job.

Billy Wagner

Bats: L   Throws: L   Height: 5' 11"   Weight: 205   Born: July 25, 1971   Age: 37

YEAR	TEAM	LVL	AGE	W	L	SV	G	GS	IP	H	BB	SO	HR	GB%	BABIP	STUFF	WHIP	ERA	DERA	EqH9	EqBB9	EqSO9	EqHR9	DEF	VORP	SN/WX
2006	NYN	MLB	34	3	2	40	70	0	72¹	59	21	94	7	53.9%	.308	30	1.11	2.24	2.54	7.9	2.3	10.1	0.8	-1	25.9	5.96
2007	NYN	MLB	35	2	2	34	66	0	68¹	55	22	80	6	40.4%	.290	27	1.13	2.64	2.75	7.2	2.5	9.4	0.8	-1	22.1	3.69
2008	NYN	MLB	36	0	1	27	45	0	47	32	10	52	4	38.5%	.239	22	0.89	2.30	3.94	6.0	1.5	8.4	0.8	3	12.2	1.48
2009	NYN	MLB	37	4	4	25	49	0	49¹	43	16	50	4	43.0%	.290	16	1.20	3.02	3.33	8.0	2.5	7.8	0.8	0	13.5	1.96

Breakout: 15%   Improve: 33%   Collapse: 43%   Attrition: 19%   Comparables: Paul Assenmacher, Tug Mcgraw, Trevor Hoffman, Mike Remlinger

If Willie Randolph needed any help in his slow march to the guillotine, Wagner provided it. A week before the Mets messily dispensed with their embattled skipper, Wagner blew multirun leads in three consecutive outings, which resulted in two devastating losses. The blame for New York's second-half bullpen collapse cannot be placed entirely on Wagner's elbow injury, for despite gaudy overall statistics, he was not much better than his squad mates before going down on August 2, blowing seven save chances and giving up multiple runs seven times. Wagner has already said that he's played his last game for the Mets, even though he could conceivably make it back by late summer after undergoing September Tommy John surgery. The lefty's season proves once more that giving a long-term deal to a reliever is almost never a smart play, especially when that reliever is in his 30s, a lesson that the Mets will digest along with the $11.5 million that remains on Wagner's deal.

Matt Wise

Bats: R   Throws: R   Height: 6' 4"   Weight: 195   Born: November 18, 1975   Age: 33

YEAR	TEAM	LVL	AGE	W	L	SV	G	GS	IP	H	BB	SO	HR	GB%	BABIP	STUFF	WHIP	ERA	DERA	EqH9	EqBB9	EqSO9	EqHR9	DEF	VORP	SN/WX
2006	MIL	MLB	30	5	6	0	40	0	44¹	45	14	27	6	46.9%	.289	-11	1.33	3.86	5.11	8.8	2.5	5.1	1.0	4	5.8	0.77
2007	MIL	MLB	31	3	2	1	56	0	53²	61	17	43	5	36.6%	.337	6	1.45	4.19	2.96	9.2	2.5	6.6	0.8	-9	5.2	1.28
2008	NYN	MLB	32	0	1	0	8	0	7	10	3	6	2	48.0%	.348	-11	1.86	6.43	3.86	12.9	3.9	6.4	2.6	-2	-0.7	-0.26
2009	NYN	MLB	33	2	1	1	27	0	31²	33	11	24	3	42.0%	.300	2	1.38	4.26	4.67	9.5	2.6	5.8	1.0	0	3.8	0.30

Breakout: 10%   Improve: 27%   Collapse: 40%   Attrition: 33%   Comparables: Dyar Miller, Tom Buskey, Odell Jones, Ernie Johnson

"I've had three elbow surgeries, and this doesn't feel like anything," Wise said after getting shut down with right forearm stiffness in early April. Famous last words. He did make it back for six more outings, but then submerged again, this time with a weak right shoulder. That was the last anyone saw of him. Wise made $1.2 million last season, but his short-lived days of seven-figure salaries have passed. He'll probably have to settle for a minor league deal and a nonroster invite this year.

LINEOUTS

Hitters

PLAYER	TEAM	LVL	AGE	PA	R	2B	3B	HR	RBI	BB	SO	SB-CS	EqBRR	AVG/OBP/SLG	EqAVG/EqOBP/EqSLG	EqA	VORP	WARP
C R. Cancel	NWO	AAA	32	59	8	4	1	1	8	4	5	1-0	-0.6	.346/.397/.519	.278/.322/.463	.267	2.1	-0.1
	NYN	MLB	32	53	5	2	0	1	5	3	6	1-2	-0.1	.245/.288/.347	.265/.308/.367	.221	-1.3	-0.2
OF E. Carrera*	SLU	A+	21	494	61	11	12	7	29	46	86	28-9	1.0	.263/.344/.393	.223/.292/.354	.230	-17.1	-1.4
3B J. Marte	MTS	Rk	17	177	29	14	3	4	24	13	30	2-0	0.6	.325/.398/.532	.238/.284/.396	.235	-8.5	-1.8
OF T. Nixon*	TUC	AAA	34	222	39	15	0	10	31	40	25	1-0	-2.9	.309/.437/.558	.233/.350/.413	.268	4.7	-0.1
	NWO	AAA	34	49	9	1	0	4	13	8	9	1-0	0.2	.293/.408/.610	.233/.340/.465	.278	1.8	-0.2
	NYN	MLB	34	41	2	1	0	1	1	6	9	1-0	0.3	.171/.293/.286	.171/.293/.286	.215	-2.0	0.1
RF V. Pascucci	LEH	AAA	29	100	4	2	0	1	7	18	25	0-1	0.2	.232/.370/.293	.190/.320/.250	.208	-6.0	-0.7
	NWO	AAA	29	481	72	23	0	27	81	77	109	4-1	-3.9	.290/.410/.553	.233/.338/.432	.268	10.8	0.5
C F. Pena	SAV	A	18	426	34	22	3	6	41	25	95	0-0	-3.2	.264/.308/.380	.219/.260/.327	.200	-27.5	-2.3
2B A. Reyes#	NWO	AAA	25	353	41	11	1	0	22	31	47	13-6	-0.1	.283/.347/.325	.252/.309/.283	.216	-15.9	0.3
	NYN	MLB	25	121	13	0	0	1	3	4	20	2-0	1.2	.218/.259/.245	.223/.263/.250	.182	-6.9	-0.3
SS R. Tejada	SLU	A+	18	555	55	19	4	2	37	41	77	8-5	0.9	.229/.293/.296	.193/.246/.255	.172	-59.4	-3.9
C J. Thole*	SLU	A+	21	402	49	25	2	5	56	45	38	2-1	-3.2	.300/.382/.427	.258/.329/.381	.251	1.6	-0.3
2B G. Veloz#	SAV	A	20	501	68	25	5	6	52	32	93	28-12	0.3	.286/.339/.402	.239/.286/.347	.222	-18.6	-3.0
	SLU	A+	20	85	8	1	0	0	4	7	20	1-2	-0.2	.234/.298/.247	.192/.250/.205	.151	-10.8	-0.5

The primary New York comeback narrative was penned by Fernando Tatis, but **Robinson Cancel**'s encore also deserves recognition. He got a taste of the majors with Milwaukee in 1999, but hadn't made it back until the Mets called on him in June; strangely, New York kept him on the 40-man as the third catcher. ⊘ Part of the Putz package and now Mariners property, **Ezequiel Carrera** can fly in center and around the bases and has decent upside. ⊘ A Dominican third baseman named Marte, putting up big numbers as a teenager? Sounds familiar. The Mets hope **Jefry Marte** develops a little better than former phenom Andy has, but Jefry has true impact offensive potential, along with the athleticism and arm to stick at third. ⊘ So desperate were the Mets that they bought **Trot Nixon** from Arizona in mid-June to replace Church in right; he didn't hit (again), and got hurt (again), so at least he's consistent. The Brewers decided he was nevertheless worth a minor league deal this winter. ⊘ **Val Pascucci** has a career 928 OPS in 1,777 Triple-A at-bats and 174 career minor league home runs, yet he's gotten all of 74 major league PAs for his trouble. He played in Japan from 2005 to 2006, and that might be the only place where he's fully appreciated. ⊘ Another of the Mets' aggressive assignments to full-season action, **Francisco Pena** might have struggled behind the plate, but he didn't embarrass himself as an 18-year-old in the Sally League. ⊘ Some fuss was made about the solid job **Argenis Reyes** did, but his career-high minor league OPS is 700; the guy simply cannot hit. The Mets eventually recognized that they can find better backups, releasing him after the season. ⊘ On the strength of a fantastic 2007 debut in rookie ball, the Mets felt that Panamanian shortstop **Ruben Tejada** was ready for High-A, a tall task for an 18-year-old; he has an advanced offensive approach, but his lack of power and probable need for a shift off short seriously limit his upside. ⊘ In a perfect world, **Josh Thole** grows up to be the new Scott Bradley, a lefty-hitting backup backstop who gets on base a bit and makes contact. ⊘ With a big second half in the Sally League (861 OPS) and a big platoon split (775 OPS vs. right-handers, 662 vs. left-handers), **Greg Veloz** has enough promise beyond youth and tools to merit your notice.

Pitchers

PLAYER	TEAM	LVL	AGE	W	L	SV	IP	H	BB	SO	HR	GB%	BABIP	STUFF	WHIP	ERA	DERA	EqH9	EqBB9	EqSO9	EqHR9	DEF	VORP
M. Antonini*	SAV	A	22	4	4	0	73	63	16	61	2	49.5%	.284	0	1.08	2.71	5.54	10.1	3.0	3.5	0.8	-3	0.4
	SLU	A+	22	4	0	0	44	34	7	33	3	45.0%	.248	1	0.93	1.84	4.61	8.6	2.0	3.5	1.5	5	4.5
	BIN	AA	22	1	3	0	45²	43	16	32	10	34.7%	.250	-12	1.29	3.74	5.77	9.5	3.1	4.3	2.7	7	-0.8
D. Gee	SLU	A+	22	8	6	0	127¹	117	19	94	6	41.0%	.294	-1	1.07	3.25	5.85	10.4	2.0	3.6	1.1	4	-3.2
	BIN	AA	22	2	0	0	27	18	5	20	1	46.7%	.236	23	0.85	1.33	3.51	6.7	1.8	4.9	0.7	5	6.0
B. Knight	NWO	AAA	32	5	1	1	43¹	28	12	55	5	41.2%	.253	17	0.92	2.29	4.05	7.2	2.7	8.6	1.4	3	6.9
	NYN	MLB	32	1	0	0	12	14	7	10	0	52.6%	.378	0	1.75	5.25	5.40	10.8	4.6	6.9	0.0	0	0.5
J. Mejia	BRO	A-	18	3	2	0	56²	42	23	52	4	62.5%	.262	1	1.15	3.49	8.31	10.6	5.5	3.6	2.3	10	-14.4
S. Moviel	SAV	A	20	9	8	0	120	128	36	82	9	54.3%	.312	-16	1.37	4.43	8.61	12.7	4.1	2.6	1.7	-3	-35.7
D. Owen	SLU	A+	21	12	6	0	133²	135	33	116	12	47.6%	.323	-8	1.26	3.43	5.74	12.1	3.1	4.5	2.0	-1	-1.8
	BIN	AA	21	1	1	0	16¹	20	9	15	3	40.4%	.347	5	1.78	5.52	6.46	12.9	4.7	5.9	2.3	0	-1.5
A. Reyes	TBA	MLB	38	2	2	0	22²	21	10	19	2	34.8%	.306	-4	1.37	4.36	5.06	9.3	3.8	7.2	0.8	1	2.4
B. Rustich	SAV	A	23	3	4	0	49²	42	16	48	1	53.7%	.308	-16	1.17	3.62	7.74	10.9	4.4	4.4	0.6	1	-10.2

An 18th-rounder picked in 2007, **Michael Antonini** has already advanced through four levels of the Mets' system, but polished pitchers without great stuff often hit their ceiling there. ⊘ **Dillon Gee** doesn't have a great fastball and generates a lot of fly-ball outs, so no one is projecting stardom. Still, he clearly knows how to pitch, with just 1.4 BB/9 in more than 200 pro innings. ⊘ Since briefly showing up with the Yankees, **Brandon Knight** has pitched for the Fukuoka SoftBank Hawks, the Nippon Ham Fighters, Double-A Altoona, and the Somerset Patriots of the independent Atlantic League; on the verge of going into coaching, he was picked up by the Mets in May, and his perseverance not only led to his first major league victory but a bronze medal in Beijing. ⊘ Dominican righty **Jenrry Mejia** has the best pure arm in the system, with a fastball that regularly reaches the high 90s; he'll join Flores and Marte as part of the fearsome collection of talent at Low-A Savannah. ⊘ Towering righty **Scott Moviel** is vying to become the second 6' 11" player to pitch in the majors (Jon Rauch is the first). He's a project, but he improved throughout the season, posting a sub-3.00 ERA in 11 second-half starts. ⊘ **Dylan Owen** has pitched well in his first two years since getting drafted, but bears the stigma of being a short righty without great stuff, which means the trouble he ran into at Double-A will probably be endemic. ⊘ Less than a week after getting arrested in early April for a bar fight on his birthday, **Al Reyes** landed on the DL with a shoulder impingement, the first of two trips. The shoulder woes lowered his velocity several ticks, and the Rays DFA'd him in early August. The Mets kicked the tires but didn't use him, instead releasing him several weeks later. ⊘ **Brant Rustich** is a 6' 6", 230-pound righty who throws in the mid-90s with a strong slider. That sounds great, but he's managed fewer than 75 pro innings since getting drafted in the second round in 2007 and was shut down last August with a stress fracture in his pitching arm. ⊘ **Jason Vargas** missed all of last season with a hip injury, but came back to pitch in the Arizona Fall League, enough to earn him a ticket to Seattle as part of the Putz swap; he is likely to be tried as a reliever.

MANAGER: WILLIE RANDOLPH/JERRY MANUEL

YEAR	MGR	W-L	Pythag +/-	Avg PC	100+ P	120+ P	QS	BQS	REL	REL w Zero R	IBB	Subs	PH	PH Avg	PH HR	SB2	CS2	SB3	CS3	SAC Att	SAC %	POS SAC	Squeeze	Swing	In Play
2006	W.R.	97-65	5	96.0	79	1	78	4	473	330	39	32	246	.187	3	119	33	27	2	105	73.3%	38	1	127	101
2007	W.R.	88-74	1	99.0	83	4	84	0	499	319	40	36	264	.228	3	168	37	32	7	103	74.8%	32	2	145	114
2008	W.R.	34-35	-1	99.8	34	1	33	5	233	155	16	14	103	.200	2	55	15	12	2	48	75.0%	19	1	62	50
2008	J.M.	55-38	0	101.4	56	2	49	2	324	212	37	46	164	.245	2	54	16	16	3	64	57.8%	21	0	90	63

Willie Randolph endeavored to be a stolid, reassuring presence in the mold of Joe Torre, but Randolph's passivity had grown into a detriment. When Jerry Manuel signed a two-year deal with a club option shortly after the season's end, the new manager said (as reported in the *New York Times*), "You get so many statistical people together—they put so many stats on paper—and they say, 'Well, if you do this and you score this many runs, you do this that many times, you'll be in the playoffs.' That's not really how it works. And that's what we have to get away from." Manuel then went on to play the Eckstein card: "You don't see a lot of guys that have statistical numbers play well in these championship series. What you see is usually the little second baseman or somebody like that carries off the MVP trophy that nobody expected him to do. That's because he's comfortable in playing that form of baseball, so therefore when the stage comes, it's not a struggle for him." It would be foolish to blow these remarks out of proportion, but one has to be slightly wary of a philosophic shift toward smallball and the attempt to inculcate the offensive approach of "the little second baseman." Overreacting to the Mets' September struggles in the clutch or defining oneself as an activist anti-Randolph has the potential to do more harm than good. Fortunately, Manuel's comments often need to be taken with a grain of salt, like his statement in December that K-Rod and Putz would split closing duties 70/30.

New York Yankees

The Yankees' 13-year run of playoff appearances came to an end in 2008, and the way it happened accented just how remarkable that streak was. The Yankees didn't suffer a collapse; they just had one too many things go wrong while another team in the division had a similar amount of things go right, which, for the first time since 1993, left the Yankees on the outside looking in, come October.

The Yankees were almost able to make up their various in-season setbacks. When Chien-Ming Wang broke his foot running the bases in Houston in mid-June, Joba Chamberlain was just completing his transition to the rotation and more than compensated for the loss. As miserable as Robinson Cano's season was, his drop in production was more than compensated for by the upgrade that Jason Giambi provided over the assorted spare parts who manned first base for the team in 2007. Runs lost due to Hideki Matsui's nagging knee injury were recouped by the deadline addition of Xavier Nady and a nice rebound season from Johnny Damon. Derek Jeter's slight decline, compounded by his characteristic refusal to sit out a few games after being hit in the hand by a pitch in late May, was compensated for by another strong second half from Bobby Abreu. The runs lost to the expected regression from Alex Rodriguez coming off his 2007 MVP season were compensated for by the runs saved by a splendid season from the bullpen. Andy Pettitte's poor second half was compensated for by Mike Mussina's 20-win swan song. The team's lack of production in center field didn't actually differ significantly from its lack of production at the same position in 2007.

Had that been all that went wrong for the Yankees in 2008, they would have been able to repeat their 94-win

YANKEES PROSPECTUS

2008 record: 89-73; Third place in AL East

Pythagenport record: 87-75

Runs scored per game: 4.87 (7th in AL)

Runs allowed per game: 4.53 (7th in AL)

Team EqA: .262 (6th in AL)

2008 Batters Age: 32.0 (Oldest in AL)

2008 Pitchers Age: 31.0 (Oldest in AL)

Ballpark: Yankee Stadium; Slight hitter's park; Park Factor of 1.020

2008: Posada, the pitching, and a playoff streak go down with the stadium.

2009: Twenty feet's worth of premium free-agent starter only partly masks an aging lineup and a shoddy defense.

performance from 2007, which put them in a dead heat with the Red Sox for the wild card, but it wasn't. Unfortunately, not included in the above accounting is Jorge Posada's shoulder injury, which limited him to 28 starts behind the plate and ended his season just after the All-Star break. That left the team's catching duties in the hands of Jose Molina, whose −11.3 VORP (value over replacement player) was the sixth-worst in the American League, and whose −.317 MLVr (rate-based Marginal Lineup Value) was dead last in the majors among batters with 250 or more plate appearances in 2008. It wasn't Posada's injury that kept the Yankees out of the playoffs any more than it was any other single injury or disappointment, but rather the totality of injuries and disappointments that finally knocked the Yankees off their perch.

The misfortunes that befell the Yankees had every conceivable cause. Wang's was a freak injury. Rodriguez's regression had more to do with his otherworldly production in 2007 than any particular shortcoming in 2008; he still led the American League in VORP, despite falling 30.9 runs shy of his 2007 total, and in league EqA, he fell all the way down to second. Cano's and Melky Cabrera's struggles could be said to be of a piece, perhaps prolonged by new manager Joe Girardi and his coaching staff's tardy intervention with the two talented youngsters. Yet, despite the sheer variety of aforementioned miseries, the subtext to many of their problems was age. The roster didn't necessarily get old all at once. Chamberlain and a host of effective team-controlled relievers made significant positive contributions to the team, while Cano and Cabrera were unproductive, despite their youth. In the rotation, it was old horse Mussina who led the way while Wang, 28, got hurt; rookie starters Phil Hughes and Ian Kennedy opened the season in the rotation, but contributed just four quality starts all season because of injury and ineffectiveness. Nonetheless, the struggles of Posada, Jeter, Matsui, and Pettitte can all be attributed, at least in part, to age, as can the Yankees' decision after the season not to retain free agents Giambi and Abreu, despite the players' role as two of the team's most productive hitters in 2008.

For that last, general manager Brian Cashman deserves considerable credit, but not singularly. Hal Steinbrenner, the younger and more measured of George's two sons, officially succeeded his father as the team's general partner in late November, and his quieter brand of ownership (as compared with his more vociferous brother Hank) included empowering Cashman to do what was necessary this winter. This is critical, because Cashman has had to respond to Father Time's tax on aging talent. As we wrote in the Mets chapter in last year's annual:

> Older teams run an increased risk of injury or sudden erosion of skill, and that risk compounds with each additional elder added to the ranks. This is true if the players are coming off good or great seasons, if they are perennial All-Stars, or are just earning time toward their pension. Age doesn't care what a player did last year; past accomplishments are unable to slow the forward march of time that carries an athlete toward his competitive demise.

The team's response to its shortcomings in 2008 was surprisingly appropriate. Rather than fire the manager and the hitting coach, trade their disappointing prospects for "proven" veterans, and complement the latter by re-signing their few effective veteran free agents, the Yankees retained their coaches and youngsters, let their aging All Stars walk, and spent their money, and a few marginal trade chips, on making the team simultaneously better and younger.

That process actually began the previous winter, when the Yankees balked at a trade that would have sent some combination of Hughes, Cabrera, Kennedy, center-field prospect Austin Jackson, and/or a handful of lesser pitching prospects to the Twins for impending free-agent ace Johan Santana. With both Santana and that year's Cy Young Award winner C. C. Sabathia due to become free agents after the 2008 season, Cashman convinced the Steinbrenners to hold on to their prospects and gamble on trying to sign one of the two aces after the 2008 season.

To Cashman's credit, the strategy worked perfectly. While Santana went to the Mets in a preseason trade and signed the then-biggest pitching contract in major league history, Sabathia tested the market and landed in the Bronx via an even larger seven-year deal worth $161 million. In addition to keeping their prospects and landing perhaps the best pitcher in baseball, the Yankees got a pitcher a year younger than Santana and twelve years younger than Mussina, the man he's replacing.

Prior to signing Sabathia, Cashman also made a pair of trades that provided him with younger (though not necessarily young) short-term solutions for the impending departures of Abreu and Giambi. In both cases, he fleshed out the package he sent to his trade partner with second-tier pitching prospects who would have been exposed to the Rule 5 draft this past December, due to a lack of space on the Yankees' 40-man roster. In doing so, he properly turned an unfortunate side effect of the organization's glut of pitching prospects into a benefit.

That's not to say that both deals were clear winners. At the trading deadline, Cashman sent Jeff Karstens, Ross Ohlendorf, and Daniel McCutchen, along with 19-year-old outfield prospect Jose Tabata, to the Pirates for outfielder Xavier Nady and lefty reliever Damaso Marte. Cashman sold low on Tabata, a top hitting prospect who had suffered several hand injuries and was in the midst of a miserable Double-A debut compounded by a few behavioral problems, and bought high on Nady, a 29-year-old having a career year. The presence of Nady made the decision not to retain Abreu, who will be 35 this season and was absolutely atrocious in the field last year, easier to make.

In November, without the pressure of the pennant race driving up the price, Cashman sent middling pitching prospects Jeff Marquez and Jhonny Nuñez, along with square-peg utility infielder Wilson Betemit, to the White Sox for Kanekoa Texeira, a Hawaiian relief prospect considered superior to Nuñez and not yet Rule 5 eligible, and outfielder/first baseman Nick Swisher. This time, Cashman bought low on Swisher, who was coming off what was probably a fluky down year that had soured his relationship with ChiSox skipper Ozzie Guillen. Two years younger than Nady, Swisher is a superior player on both sides of the ball and provided Cashman with flexibility in his subsequent negotiations for a big bat to help ease the loss of Abreu and Giambi.

Naming Swisher the team's starting first baseman allowed Cashman to lie in the weeds while several teams played a very public tug-of-war over the top free-agent hitter on the market, first baseman Mark Teixeira. A young, Gold Glove–winning switch-hitter who does everything well except steal bases, Teixeira would have helped any team, but the Yankees were not only the oldest team in the majors in 2008, but also had the third-worst Defensive Efficiency in the American League, scored 179 fewer runs than in 2007 (dropping below 800 runs scored for the first time since 1995), and were intent on replacing their 37-year-old first baseman, Giambi. Two days before Christmas, Cashman pounced with an eight-year, $180 million contract. The signing allowed Swisher to move into a potential platoon with Nady in right field, a better solution to the loss of Abreu than playing Nady alone. What's more, despite the length of their contracts, Teixeira and Sabathia will, in the final year of their deals, still be younger than the men they're replacing, Jason Giambi and Mike Mussina, were in 2008. An additional five-year, $82.5 million contract for 32-year-old Blue Jays starter A. J. Burnett, inked in between the two larger deals, made less sense due to Burnett's history of injuries in non-walk years, questionable effectiveness, and age relative to the team's other new additions, though if Pettitte doesn't return, Burnett will make the team five years younger in his rotation spot.

Summed up, the Yankees committed $423.5 million to three players within the span of a couple of weeks in December, prompting cries of outrage about the rich getting richer. Such claims are not unfounded, as the Yankees will open 2009 in a new Yankee Stadium, a revenue-boosting gift from the city described by team chief operating officer Lonn Trost as "a five-star hotel [with] a ballfield in the middle of it." Designed for high-end luxury patrons, the new digs were financed in large part by public money and the exploitation of various revenue-sharing and tax loopholes, the latter of which are the subject of an ongoing congressional investigation. Still, with the eight-digit salaries of Giambi, Abreu, Mussina, Pettitte, and Carl Pavano coming off the books, the net result of the Yankees' December spending spree was a less-than-$4-million increase in the 2009 payroll prior to Nady's arbitration award (Table 1).

Though some have cited the Sabathia, Burnett, and Teixeira deals as evidence of the Yankees' abandoning their 2007 offseason commitment to youth, two of the three signings actually align with that commitment. After the coming season, the Yankees are expected to bid farewell to both Damon and Matsui, 35-year-old free-agents-to-be, replacing Damon with center-field prospect Austin Jackson, who will start 2009 in Triple-A. Though they were slow out of the blocks, the Yankees have finally built up a strong collection of catching prospects to replace Posada, starting with Francisco Cervelli and highlighted by 19-year-old Jesus Montero,

Table 1. More Bang for Their Buck: Yankee Payroll Change as of New Year's Day, 2009

Player	Age	2008 cost	2009 cost	Net
Credits				
Giambi	38	$21	$5**	$16
Abreu	35	$16	-	$16
Pettitte	37	$16	-	$16
Mussina	40	$11	-	$11
Pavano	33	$11	$1.95**	$9.05
I. Rodriguez	37	$4.3*	-	$4.3
Farnsworth	33	$3.7*	-	$3.7
Betemit	27	$1.165		$1.165
Total Credits				$77.215
Debits				
Teixeira	29	-	$25	-$25
Sabathia	28	-	$23	-$23
Burnett	32	-	$16.5	-$16.5
Swisher	28	-	$5.3	-$5.3
A. Rodriguez	33	$29	$33	-$4
Cano	26	$3	$6	-$3
Marte	34	$.667*	$3.75	-$3.083
Wang	29	$4	$5	-$1
Total Debits				-$80.883
Net Change				-$3.668

All amounts are in millions of dollars and include signing bonus payments; ages as of June 1, 2009; *estimated prorated portion of 2008 salary; **option buyout

who might not stick behind the dish, but is the organization's top hitting prospect.

Beyond that, the organization has a veritable conga line of pitching prospects, the front of which has started to emerge with Chamberlain, Hughes, and Kennedy. They could be followed by any of a group that includes Zach McAllister, George Kontos, Christian Garcia, Dellin Bentances, Andrew Brackman, Jeremy Bleich, Wilkin de la Rosa, and Jairo Heredia. Burnett's five-year deal, however, does make one wonder just how willing the Yankees are to endure the necessary growing pains of emerging starting pitching prospects after the struggles of Hughes and Kennedy. The same transformation began to take hold in the bullpen last year, the success of which was both the organization's and Joe Girardi's greatest accomplishment in 2008. Waiver claims, independent league finds, and minor league free agents such as Brian Bruney, Edwar Ramirez, Jose Veras, and Dan Giese, aided by cups of coffee from home-grown arms David Robertson and lefty Phil Coke, helped the Yankee bullpen finish third in the majors in WXRL last year. This largely minimum-wage relief corps should be supplemented this year by larger contributions from Robertson, Coke, Humberto Sanchez, and Jonathan Albaladejo, as well as the major league debuts of Mark Melancon and Steven Jackson, with only closer Mariano Rivera and re-signed lefty Damaso Marte earning more than six figures.

The Yankees are wealthier than ever, but they are also finally sweating the small stuff, be it the draft, the international amateur talent pool, the waiver wire, or even the independent leagues (which yielded Ramirez). Yet, even that deadly combination of wealth and wits doesn't guarantee them a return to the postseason in 2008, not in a division that also includes the ascendant Rays and the unshakable Red Sox, who may still be the better team. The organization is still thin on hitting prospects, increasing its reliance on the aging stars of the Joe Torre dynasty, and is still learning how or even if it's even willing to work its emergent young arms into the rotation. In addition, serious doubts have emerged about Girardi's militaristic approach to managing. The last of those problems is the only one that's easy to solve. Given the expectations created by the team's spending spree, anything less than a pennant is likely to result in such a solution. Of course, if one less thing goes wrong for the Yankees in 2009, a solution may not be necessary.

HITTERS

Bobby Abreu — RF

Bats: L　Throws: R　Height: 6' 0"　Weight: 210　Born: March 11, 1974　Age: 35

YEAR	TEAM	LVL	AGE	PA	R	2B	3B	HR	RBI	BB	SO	SB	CS	EqBRR	AVG	OBP	SLG	EqAVG	EqOBP	EqSLG	EqA	VORP	WARP	DEFENSE	
2006	PHI	MLB	32	438	61	25	2	8	65	91	86	20	4	3.9	.277	.427	.434	.265	.421	.417	.306	25.9	3.1	95-RF	-1
2006	NYA	MLB	32	248	37	16	0	7	42	33	52	10	2	1.6	.330	.419	.507	.316	.415	.485	.314	24.0	1.9	50-RF	-2
2007	NYA	MLB	33	699	123	40	5	16	101	84	115	25	8	0.1	.283	.369	.445	.273	.366	.447	.284	23.7	2.9	149-RF	-5
2008	NYA	MLB	34	684	100	39	4	20	100	73	109	22	11	-0.6	.296	.371	.471	.291	.373	.483	.289	32.6	4.1	147-RF	2
2009	NYA	MLB	35	574	87	29	4	13	66	67	99	19	7	0.7	.282	.368	.436	.287	.375	.464	.293	20.8	3.2	135-RF	-2

Breakout: 18%　Improve: 49%　Collapse: 24%　Attrition: 20%　　Comparables: Larry Walker, Enos Slaughter, Bernie Williams, Paul O'Neill

Our translations don't do justice to Abreu's peculiar brand of defense. He's like the star of a children's book: *The Outfielder Who Feared the Wall*. Abreu simply will not fade back on the ball, with the result that anything not hit directly at him or in front of him goes over his head. You know those long drives that seem like home runs, only to die on the warning track? Abreu watches them bounce. Ultimate Zone Rating, the Plus/Minus System, and the Probabilistic Model of Range all judge Abreu a major detriment. Abreu can still hit, though he has become less selective in recent years, with his 2008 walk rate being the lowest of his career. A team employing him as a DH should still get good value.

Wilson Betemit — INF

Bats: S　Throws: R　Height: 6' 3"　Weight: 230　Born: November 2, 1981　Age: 27

YEAR	TEAM	LVL	AGE	PA	R	2B	3B	HR	RBI	BB	SO	SB	CS	EqBRR	AVG	OBP	SLG	EqAVG	EqOBP	EqSLG	EqA	VORP	WARP	DEFENSE			
2006	ATL	MLB	24	219	30	16	0	9	29	19	57	2	1	-0.2	.281	.344	.497	.281	.347	.492	.283	12.8	0.6	23-3B	-1	10-SS	-3
2006	LAN	MLB	24	193	19	7	0	9	24	17	45	1	0	-1.9	.241	.306	.437	.237	.306	.422	.252	0.1	-0.5	44-3B	-7		
2007	LAN	MLB	25	192	22	8	0	10	26	32	49	0	0	-0.6	.231	.359	.474	.227	.365	.481	.291	7.5	0.3	39-3B	-7		
2007	NYA	MLB	25	92	11	4	0	4	24	6	33	0	0	0.2	.226	.278	.417	.214	.267	.429	.235	-1.3	0.0	8-1B	2	6-3B	0
2008	NYA	MLB	26	198	24	13	0	6	25	6	56	0	1	-1.7	.265	.289	.429	.259	.288	.434	.243	0.4	-0.6	23-1B	1	11-3B	-6
2009	CHA	MLB	27	199	23	10	0	8	28	17	53	0	0	-0.8	.253	.320	.451	.254	.321	.460	.267	6.2	0.5	50-3B	-4		

Breakout: 23%　Improve: 44%　Collapse: 32%　Attrition: 31%　　Comparables: Andy Tracy, Dallas McPherson, Wes Helms, Norm Zauchin

It was a disastrous season for Betemit. After he struck out seven times in his first 13 at-bats, it was revealed that he couldn't actually see the ball, because a case of pinkeye prevented him from wearing his contact lenses. A few days after returning from the DL, he strained a hamstring and disappeared again. Once he came back, Girardi kept trying to give him playing time, substituting him for A-Rod and Giambi, but Betemit consistently spit it back, striking out prodigiously and piling up errors at third. Traded to the White Sox for Swisher, he'll get a chance to win the third-base job. He has the pop for the position, but as a notional switch-hitter (.232/.276/.360 career vs. lefties) with a Swiss-cheese glove, he's only an asset if you're comparing him with Juan Uribe.

Melky Cabrera — CF

Bats: S Throws: L Height: 5' 11" Weight: 200 Born: August 11, 1984 Age: 24

YEAR	TEAM	LVL	AGE	PA	R	2B	3B	HR	RBI	BB	SO	SB	CS	EqBRR	AVG	OBP	SLG	EqAVG	EqOBP	EqSLG	EqA	VORP	WARP	DEFENSE			
2006	COH	AAA	21	135	19	6	2	4	24	10	9	3	1	-0.3	.385	.430	.566	.358	.404	.569	.323	18.9	1.3	27-CF	-2		
2006	NYA	MLB	21	525	75	26	2	7	50	56	60	12	5	2.3	.280	.360	.390	.268	.356	.375	.261	8.8	-0.9	112-LF	-17	8-RF	-1
2007	NYA	MLB	22	612	66	24	8	8	73	43	68	13	5	-0.1	.273	.327	.391	.267	.324	.394	.253	6.5	1.0	120-CF	4	16-LF	-6
2008	SWB	AAA	23	66	8	2	0	0	5	8	9	1	3	-2.9	.333	.409	.368	.316	.394	.351	.257	2.4	0.0	15-CF	-2		
2008	NYA	MLB	23	453	42	12	1	8	37	29	58	9	2	-1.0	.249	.301	.341	.245	.301	.342	.229	-5.7	1.4	109-CF	16		
2009	NYA	MLB	24	484	57	19	3	8	49	37	61	10	4	0.5	.267	.326	.376	.271	.332	.400	.258	6.5	1.8	114-CF	0		

Breakout: 30% Improve: 51% Collapse: 17% Attrition: 17% Comparables: Bernie Williams, George Wright, Hosken Powell, Rick Manning

A marginal player can fall hard and fast. After a .299/.370/.494, five-homer April suggested that Cabrera was the rare player who had developed new skills in the majors, he simply turned off, batting .226/.274/.293 over the next 90 games, at which point the Yankees finally, mercifully, sent him down. He was bad at home, bad away, bad against righties, and extra bad against lefties. Cabrera was more effective during a short stint at Scranton and in Dominican winter league action, and he remains a good defensive center fielder, but unless he can recapture the power he displayed in April or develop greater patience, he will need to contend for a batting title to avoid itinerant fifth outfielderdom—and there is no evidence that he can do these things.

Robinson Cano — 2B

Bats: L Throws: R Height: 6' 0" Weight: 205 Born: October 22, 1982 Age: 26

YEAR	TEAM	LVL	AGE	PA	R	2B	3B	HR	RBI	BB	SO	SB	CS	EqBRR	AVG	OBP	SLG	EqAVG	EqOBP	EqSLG	EqA	VORP	WARP	DEFENSE	
2006	NYA	MLB	23	508	62	41	1	15	78	18	54	5	2	-3.3	.342	.365	.525	.331	.357	.517	.294	50.4	5.5	113-2B	15
2007	NYA	MLB	24	669	93	41	7	19	97	39	85	4	5	-2.4	.306	.353	.488	.297	.347	.494	.281	36.4	6.5	157-2B	22
2008	NYA	MLB	25	634	70	35	3	14	72	26	65	2	4	-0.7	.271	.305	.410	.268	.303	.419	.246	6.2	2.2	155-2B	10
2009	NYA	MLB	26	594	66	33	3	12	72	29	70	3	2	-0.6	.284	.323	.419	.289	.328	.446	.265	20.7	3.3	139-2B	8

Breakout: 13% Improve: 43% Collapse: 22% Attrition: 7% Comparables: Tony Kubek, Carlos Baerga, Warren Cromartie, Al Oliver

A first-pitch swing at a ball out of the strike zone, popping it up to short left field, a disgusted shake of the head and dip of the shoulders, and a futile trot to first base; that was Cano's too-frequent contribution in 2008. He opened the season batting .151 in April, and "recovered" to bat .283/.311/.430 from then through late September. At that point, mechanical adjustments implemented by coach Kevin Long kicked in and Cano caught fire, batting .452 in a season-ending 11-game hitting streak. The Yankees believe that those changes will carry over, but if they don't, the Yankees will have to think about making a change, fast. When Cano isn't hitting for average, his on-field contribution is down to his glove, which is good but not in Mazeroski territory.

Francisco Cervelli — C

Bats: R Throws: R Height: 6' 1" Weight: 170 Born: March 6, 1986 Age: 23

YEAR	TEAM	LVL	AGE	PA	R	2B	3B	HR	RBI	BB	SO	SB	CS	EqBRR	AVG	OBP	SLG	EqAVG	EqOBP	EqSLG	EqA	VORP	WARP	DEFENSE	
2006	STA	A-	20	157	21	10	0	2	16	13	30	0	0	-0.6	.309	.397	.426	.243	.306	.354	.231	-6.2	-0.1	36-C	-2
2007	TAM	A+	21	348	34	24	2	2	32	36	59	4	3	0.0	.279	.387	.397	.232	.322	.338	.237	-7.0	1.3	88-C	4
2008	TRN	AA	22	88	8	5	0	0	8	11	14	0	0	-0.0	.315	.432	.384	.307	.409	.373	.285	4.5	1.0	16-C	3
2009	NYA	MLB	23	364	30	18	1	5	35	28	88	2	1	-0.7	.229	.302	.335	.233	.307	.356	.235	-2.5	1.3	87-C	-1

Breakout: 14% Improve: 27% Collapse: 47% Attrition: 14% Comparables: Omar Fuentes, Carlos Quintana, Jesus Flores, Chad McDonald

With Posada's injuries and Molina hitting as only he and your grandmother can, Cervelli might have gotten an early shot, but a fractured wrist suffered in a spring training collision kept him shelved for the bulk of the season. It is ironic that an accident that seemed inconsequential then—beyond the player's lost development time—could prove to have an outsized impact. Cervelli is a career .280/.381/.385 minor league hitter, with some walks, some doubles, a bunch of HPBs, and all of five home runs in 682 PAs. That suggests "future backup," but as Molina reflects, there are full-service backups, and then there are guys who are just jumped-up defensive substitutes.

Johnny Damon — LF

Bats: L   Throws: L   Height: 6' 2"   Weight: 205   Born: November 5, 1973   Age: 35

YEAR	TEAM	LVL	AGE	PA	R	2B	3B	HR	RBI	BB	SO	SB	CS	EqBRR	AVG	OBP	SLG	EqAVG	EqOBP	EqSLG	EqA	VORP	WARP	DEFENSE			
2006	NYA	MLB	32	671	115	35	5	24	80	67	85	25	10	5.1	.285	.359	.482	.273	.354	.472	.282	44.0	4.2	122-CF	4		
2007	NYA	MLB	33	605	93	27	2	12	63	66	79	27	3	7.5	.270	.351	.396	.261	.348	.395	.269	14.7	2.9	42-CF	5	30-LF	5
2008	NYA	MLB	34	623	95	27	5	17	71	64	82	29	8	1.9	.303	.375	.461	.298	.375	.470	.291	38.9	4.5	74-LF	7	32-CF	0
2009	NYA	MLB	35	549	80	26	4	12	62	55	77	22	6	1.8	.280	.354	.423	.285	.360	.450	.285	20.9	3.3	129-LF	1		

Breakout: 11%   Improve: 57%   Collapse: 14%   Attrition: 12%   Comparables: Kenny Lofton, Enos Slaughter, Mickey Vernon, Brady Anderson

Damon has been like his own action figure series in his three Yankee seasons. First there was "Oddly Slugging Damon," followed by "Injury-Action Slumping Damon," and finally "Classic Late-Career Peak Damon." Adjusted for context, Damon's 2008 ranked as the best offensive season of his career. Increasingly vulnerable to minor aches and pains (a bum shoulder produced his first career trip to the DL), Damon benefits from designated-hitting or the occasional day off, and if he misses the odd lefty pitcher, so much the better. He has retained his speed and could still play a decent center but for an arm that is to throwing what Jason Giambi is to interpretive dance. Damon has never been consistent, and it's not clear what this year's toy will be: "Old-Age Declining Damon," "Slowing Bat Work-the-Zone Damon," or even "Retro-Hirsute Caveman Stylin' Damon." He's in the last year of his contract, but lack of motivation has never been his problem.

Brett Gardner — CF

Bats: L   Throws: L   Height: 5' 10"   Weight: 180   Born: August 24, 1983   Age: 25

YEAR	TEAM	LVL	AGE	PA	R	2B	3B	HR	RBI	BB	SO	SB	CS	EqBRR	AVG	OBP	SLG	EqAVG	EqOBP	EqSLG	EqA	VORP	WARP	DEFENSE			
2006	TAM	A+	22	278	46	12	5	0	22	43	51	30	7	6.5	.323	.433	.418	.254	.354	.350	.258	1.3	-0.1	48-CF	-5	12-LF	-2
2006	TRN	AA	22	251	41	4	3	0	13	27	39	28	5	4.0	.272	.352	.318	.249	.320	.290	.236	-9.2	0.5	51-CF	4		
2007	TRN	AA	23	241	43	14	5	0	17	33	32	18	4	0.0	.300	.392	.419	.273	.354	.397	.270	6.2	0.8	50-CF	-2		
2007	SWB	AAA	23	207	37	4	3	1	9	21	43	21	3	4.7	.260	.343	.331	.239	.314	.310	.236	-7.0	1.0	42-CF	8		
2008	SWB	AAA	24	426	68	12	11	3	32	70	76	37	9	1.6	.296	.414	.422	.277	.396	.413	.290	22.2	3.5	72-CF	0	20-LF	5
2008	NYA	MLB	24	141	18	5	2	0	16	8	30	13	1	2.7	.228	.283	.299	.228	.288	.299	.232	-3.0	0.0	18-CF	2	16-LF	-1
2009	NYA	MLB	25	498	69	19	6	4	32	55	99	32	9	4.8	.253	.339	.351	.257	.345	.373	.265	4.8	2.4	118-CF	0		

Breakout: 18%   Improve: 46%   Collapse: 19%   Attrition: 13%   Comparables: Billy North, Kenny Lofton, Jason McDonald, Darrell Sherman

Gardner's first trial with the Yankees in late June was a bust, as the wannabe leadoff man batted just .153/.227/.169 in 17 games, though he did steal five bases in as many attempts. Recalled in mid-August, he was supposed to be given an extended trial in center, only to have Matsui's return push him to the bench within a few days; his next chance had to wait until he started 12 of the team's final 15 games. Gardner was far more successful in his second stint, batting .294/.333/.412 (73 PAs). Barring another acquisition, he'll have a chance to compete for the job in center this spring, but his chances of getting it and holding on to it depend on a high enough OBP to overcome his powerlessness; his baserunning and defense will speak for themselves.

Jason Giambi — 1B

Bats: L   Throws: R   Height: 6' 3"   Weight: 235   Born: January 8, 1971   Age: 38

YEAR	TEAM	LVL	AGE	PA	R	2B	3B	HR	RBI	BB	SO	SB	CS	EqBRR	AVG	OBP	SLG	EqAVG	EqOBP	EqSLG	EqA	VORP	WARP	DEFENSE	
2006	NYA	MLB	35	579	92	25	0	37	113	110	106	2	0	-6.1	.253	.413	.558	.233	.407	.527	.318	48.9	4.0	54-1B	-7
2007	NYA	MLB	36	303	31	8	0	14	39	40	66	1	0	-3.3	.236	.356	.433	.225	.352	.427	.273	5.8	1.0	14-1B	2
2008	NYA	MLB	37	565	68	19	1	32	96	76	111	2	1	-1.7	.247	.373	.502	.240	.371	.508	.299	29.8	2.7	101-1B	-6
2009	OAK	MLB	38	436	54	16	1	21	64	56	88	2	1	-2.7	.232	.346	.450	.238	.353	.480	.285	13.0	1.4	104-1B	-7

Breakout: 9%   Improve: 34%   Collapse: 35%   Attrition: 20%   Comparables: Darrell Evans, Willie Stargell, Willie McCovey, Ken Griffey

Giambi's season was a roller coaster that came to center on his upper lip. After beginning with what seemed like a .164/.315/.411 dare to get the Yankees to eat the last year of his contract, and having been failed by his usual slump-busting magic gold thong, he cultivated a mustache. With the caterpillar installed under his nose, Giambi busted out, hitting .310/.438/.613 with 12 homers in May and June. Mustache magic swept Yankee Stadium, but apparently it has a 60-day limit; Giambi cooled to .230/.349/.457 the rest of the way and the mustache went under the razor for dereliction of duty. A free agent after the Yankees bought out his $22 million option, his new/old employer the A's will get a DH whose walks and power make him productive in spite of his low batting average and who only needs occasional platooning. As for defense, Giambi enjoys putting on the glove and showed he could get through a season in the field without hurting himself, but you could kneecap a fire hydrant and it would still have more range.

Austin Jackson   CF   Bats: R   Throws: R   Height: 6' 1"   Weight: 185   Born: February 1, 1987   Age: 22

YEAR	TEAM	LVL	AGE	PA	R	2B	3B	HR	RBI	BB	SO	SB	CS	EqBRR	AVG	OBP	SLG	EqAVG	EqOBP	EqSLG	EqA	VORP	WARP	DEFENSE		
2006	CSC	A	19	611	90	24	5	4	47	61	151	37	12	4.6	.260	.340	.346	.203	.262	.271	.188	-51.5	-5.0	125-CF	-15	4-LF 0
2007	CSC	A	20	266	33	16	1	3	25	24	59	19	6	0.0	.260	.336	.374	.210	.268	.309	.205	-17.5	-1.4	56-CF	-4	
2007	TAM	A+	20	284	53	15	6	10	34	22	48	13	5	0.0	.345	.398	.566	.286	.335	.500	.280	17.3	2.1	63-CF	3	
2008	TRN	AA	21	584	75	33	5	9	69	56	113	19	6	-1.6	.285	.354	.419	.275	.338	.417	.264	15.2	1.1	111-CF	-8	
2009	NYA	MLB	22	595	68	32	4	11	60	48	138	17	6	2.0	.247	.311	.382	.252	.317	.407	.254	4.9	1.8	139-CF	-5	

Breakout: 37%   Improve: 62%   Collapse: 11%   Attrition: 8%   Comparables: Ellis Burks, Aaron Cunningham, Adam Jones, Paul Householder

Jackson's Double-A performance was a comedown from his 2007 High-A breakthrough, but was hurt by Trenton's Waterfront Park; he hit .311/.388/.496 on the road. He's still a work in progress, somewhat patient but not so much you'd be confident of his OBP in the majors. He hits for decent averages but is streaky and has some power but isn't a slugger. He has the speed to play center and run the bases, but isn't a prolific basestealer. With age, Jackson may slow enough that he'll be better suited for a corner, where his bat won't play nearly as well. In short, the Yankees may have a starting center fielder or a very solid fourth outfielder. Nevertheless, Jackson is also the only player in the system's upper levels close to being ready, and the two players in front of him are limited, so he'll get his chances.

Derek Jeter   SS   Bats: R   Throws: R   Height: 6' 3"   Weight: 195   Born: June 26, 1974   Age: 35

YEAR	TEAM	LVL	AGE	PA	R	2B	3B	HR	RBI	BB	SO	SB	CS	EqBRR	AVG	OBP	SLG	EqAVG	EqOBP	EqSLG	EqA	VORP	WARP	DEFENSE	
2006	NYA	MLB	32	715	118	39	3	14	97	69	102	34	5	1.2	.343	.417	.483	.329	.409	.470	.310	82.3	6.9	145-SS	-2
2007	NYA	MLB	33	714	102	39	4	12	73	56	100	15	8	2.2	.322	.388	.452	.316	.384	.457	.289	48.7	3.5	147-SS	-18
2008	NYA	MLB	34	668	88	25	3	11	69	52	85	11	5	1.0	.300	.363	.408	.298	.365	.413	.273	34.1	2.5	141-SS	-12
2009	NYA	MLB	35	599	78	25	3	6	56	49	84	13	4	0.2	.288	.353	.383	.293	.359	.408	.272	25.4	2.4	140-SS	-7

Breakout: 4%   Improve: 22%   Collapse: 36%   Attrition: 12%   Comparables: Dick Groat, Dave Concepcion, Julio Franco, Pete Rose

Slowed by age and nagging injuries, Jeter had his least productive offensive season in a decade. He was batting .306/.349/.419 on May 20 when he was hit on the hand by a Daniel Cabrera pitch; Jeter selfishly insisted on playing though it, and his production cratered, the Captain batting .203/.297/.278 over his next 20 games. He slowly recovered and finished strong, but by some accounts, he wasn't 100 percent until after the All-Star break. Regardless, Jeter's power never manifested, his .107 ISO being by far the lowest mark of his career, and his speed is ebbing. He's signed through 2010, a year short of when he'll be near the 3,000-hit mark; the Yankees will have a tough decision to make, because famous-player milestones sell tickets and merchandise, but as veterans of the Astros' *Biggioquest '07* can tell you, subjugating team goals to the greater glory of a fading star isn't conducive to winning. By 2010, Jeter's glove won't play in the infield and his bat won't play anywhere else. His 3,000th hit will have zero benefit to the winning effort.

Brandon Laird   1B   Bats: R   Throws: R   Height: 6' 1"   Weight: 215   Born: September 11, 1987   Age: 21

YEAR	TEAM	LVL	AGE	PA	R	2B	3B	HR	RBI	BB	SO	SB	CS	EqBRR	AVG	OBP	SLG	EqAVG	EqOBP	EqSLG	EqA	VORP	WARP	DEFENSE			
2007	YAN	Rk	19	178	27	14	1	8	29	6	26	0	0	0.7	.339	.367	.577	.244	.264	.424	.232	-7.1	-0.4	27-3B	3	12-1B	-3
2008	CSC	A	20	506	71	31	1	23	86	40	86	1	0	-2.5	.273	.334	.498	.235	.290	.425	.245	-2.1	-0.9	84-1B	-8	33-3B	2
2009	NYA	MLB	21	585	55	31	2	17	73	39	129	1	1	-1.0	.237	.291	.393	.241	.296	.418	.245	-6.0	0.3	137-1B	4		

Breakout: 37%   Improve: 57%   Collapse: 16%   Attrition: 4%   Comparables: Glenn Davis, Cecil Fielder, Aaron McNeal, Gabe Kapler

Laird led the Yankees' system in home runs; given that the total was 23, that fact is actually less exciting than it first appears. Originally a third baseman, the 2007 27th-rounder has the hands to play the hot corner, but not the athleticism. A grossly simplistic psychological reading would suggest he might know and worry about it: as a third baseman, he batted .171/.227/.287, but as a first baseman, he hit .310/.375/.579. That's a good sign for Laird, because though the Yankees are enamored of his personality, he's really going to have to slug.

Hideki Matsui   **DH**   Bats: L   Throws: R   Height: 6' 2"   Weight: 230   Born: June 12, 1974   Age: 35

YEAR	TEAM	LVL	AGE	PA	R	2B	3B	HR	RBI	BB	SO	SB	CS	EqBRR	AVG	OBP	SLG	EqAVG	EqOBP	EqSLG	EqA	VORP	WARP	DEFENSE	
2006	NYA	MLB	32	201	32	9	0	8	29	27	23	1	0	-0.4	.302	.393	.494	.282	.383	.476	.298	13.9	1.6	32-LF	3
2007	NYA	MLB	33	633	100	28	4	25	103	73	73	4	2	2.6	.285	.367	.488	.274	.362	.488	.290	28.2	2.8	109-LF	-7
2008	NYA	MLB	34	378	43	17	0	9	45	38	47	0	0	-0.5	.294	.370	.424	.287	.369	.427	.278	16.0	1.0	20-LF	-3
2009	NYA	MLB	35	403	49	18	1	10	52	42	55	1	1	-1.4	.275	.352	.417	.280	.358	.444	.279	12.3	1.4	96-DH	

Breakout: 13%   Improve: 40%   Collapse: 30%   Attrition: 23%   Comparables: Gates Brown, Paul O'Neill, Larry Walker, Harold Baines

Matsui was off to a great start, batting .337/.417/.495 through the end of May, when his knees started troubling him. His production fell off in June as he became too badly hobbled even to DH. After a month's rest, Matsui was offered season-ending surgery. Ever a gamer, Matsui rejected it and instead embarked on an intensive rehab program that succeeded in returning him to the lineup after nearly two months away. Unfortunately, he failed to realize that the truly dedicated professional knows when he will better serve his team by staying off the field; he batted just .209/.269/.326 in 24 games before being shut down for the inevitable surgery. Matsui is expected to be ready for spring training, but he will probably be restricted to DH in the last year of his contract, after which the Yankees should say good-bye, no matter how many caps "Godzilla" helps them sell in Tokyo.

Jose Molina   **C**   Bats: R   Throws: R   Height: 6' 2"   Weight: 245   Born: June 3, 1975   Age: 34

YEAR	TEAM	LVL	AGE	PA	R	2B	3B	HR	RBI	BB	SO	SB	CS	EqBRR	AVG	OBP	SLG	EqAVG	EqOBP	EqSLG	EqA	VORP	WARP	DEFENSE	
2006	LAA	MLB	31	245	18	17	0	4	22	9	49	1	0	-1.3	.240	.273	.369	.232	.269	.366	.222	-4.5	1.0	67-C	8
2007	LAA	MLB	32	131	9	8	0	0	10	3	30	2	1	-0.8	.224	.242	.288	.224	.242	.280	.178	-7.2	-0.4	37-C	1
2007	NYA	MLB	32	71	9	5	0	1	9	2	13	0	0	-1.2	.318	.333	.439	.303	.319	.409	.253	3.3	0.5	19-C	3
2008	NYA	MLB	33	297	32	17	0	3	18	12	52	0	0	0.1	.216	.263	.313	.216	.263	.317	.204	-11.4	0.7	83-C	11
2009	NYA	MLB	34	171	13	9	0	2	17	7	33	1	0	-0.9	.229	.271	.325	.233	.276	.345	.216	-3.5	0.6	44-C	2

Breakout: 40%   Improve: 61%   Collapse: 27%   Attrition: 51%   Comparables: Pat Borders, Mike DiFelice, Mike Matheny, Bill Haselman

Since 2001, 66 catchers, including Molina, have had a minimum of 750 PAs in the majors. Of those, exactly two—John Flaherty and Brandon Inge—have had lower OBPs than Molina's .275 (as a catcher only, Inge is lowest at .260). If OPS is your preferred stat, then just three backstops have been lower than Molina's 614. Compared to Molina, Henry Blanco is Mickey Cochrane. The wealthiest franchise in sports could have had anyone as their reserve catcher, but in December 2007, Cashman decided the Yankees would have Molina for two years. The GM then climbed Mount Sinai, shook his fist at the Almighty, and shouted, "I dare you to take Jorge Posada away from us, because we have JOSE MOLINA!" Thus goaded, the Almighty struck Posada with a bolt of lightning, and the Yankees hit the golf courses early. The moral of the story is that hubris sucks. P.S.: Molina threw out an excellent 44 percent of attempting basestealers, which is why he rates 0.7 of a win above replacement.

Jesus Montero   **C**   Bats: R   Throws: R   Height: 6' 4"   Weight: 225   Born: November 28, 1989   Age: 19

YEAR	TEAM	LVL	AGE	PA	R	2B	3B	HR	RBI	BB	SO	SB	CS	EqBRR	AVG	OBP	SLG	EqAVG	EqOBP	EqSLG	EqA	VORP	WARP	DEFENSE	
2007	YAN	Rk	17	123	13	6	0	3	19	12	18	0	0	-2.4	.280	.366	.421	.204	.260	.319	.197	-20.3	-1.6	21-C	-5
2008	CSC	A	18	569	86	34	1	17	87	37	83	2	1	-2.3	.326	.376	.491	.283	.327	.437	.261	17.2	1.6	70-C	-4
2009	NYA	MLB	19	622	57	30	2	13	66	38	113	2	2	-1.4	.252	.301	.381	.257	.307	.405	.245	3.3	1.6	145-C	-14

Breakout: 33%   Improve: 59%   Collapse: 17%   Attrition: 6%   Comparables: Ryan Klesko, Delmon Young, Richard Hidalgo, Chris Marrero

The anti-Molina, Montero is mediocre at throwing out runners (nailing but 26 of 105), but is a masher at the plate. This giant of a teenager may not forever be a backstop, but all credit to the Yankees for giving him every chance to show improvement before running him off the position. The good news is that if Montero does have to play first, his batting will carry the position.

Xavier Nady   OF

Bats: R   Throws: R   Height: 6' 2"   Weight: 210   Born: November 14, 1978   Age: 30

YEAR	TEAM	LVL	AGE	PA	R	2B	3B	HR	RBI	BB	SO	SB	CS	EqBRR	AVG	OBP	SLG	EqAVG	EqOBP	EqSLG	EqA	VORP	WARP	DEFENSE			
2006	NYN	MLB	27	292	37	15	1	14	40	19	51	2	1	-0.9	.264	.326	.487	.267	.329	.496	.277	9.9	1.1	69-RF	-1		
2006	PIT	MLB	27	220	20	13	0	3	23	11	34	1	2	0.2	.300	.352	.409	.299	.350	.412	.261	2.3	1.0	27-1B	6	26-RF	0
2007	PIT	MLB	28	470	55	23	1	20	72	23	101	3	1	0.8	.278	.330	.476	.283	.334	.492	.278	16.2	1.4	84-RF	-1	9-LF	-1
2008	PIT	MLB	29	360	50	26	1	13	57	25	55	1	0	-2.2	.330	.383	.535	.344	.396	.567	.322	31.6	3.4	80-RF	-1		
2008	NYA	MLB	29	247	26	11	0	12	40	14	48	1	1	0.4	.268	.320	.474	.263	.316	.482	.268	6.6	0.6	44-LF	0	6-RF	-1
2009	NYA	MLB	30	528	59	27	1	18	79	32	101	2	1	-1.5	.270	.323	.444	.274	.329	.472	.273	11.0	1.7	124-RF	-3		

Breakout: 5%   Improve: 31%   Collapse: 37%   Attrition: 12%   Comparables: Mike Marshall, Bill Robinson, Rondell White, Bob Oliver

Nady had the half-season of his life in Pittsburgh. Initially, it seemed as if the Yankees would get to enjoy their share of Nady's career year, as he hit .319/.385/.628 with eight home runs in his first 25 games in the Bronx, but he went ice-cold thereafter, his aggregate pinstriped production looking very much like typical Nady. At this writing, the X-Man looks like he'll share right field with Swisher, which would be for the best; Nady's combination of pop, impatience, and fielding in a corner make him a highly qualified bench player and an upgrade on a failing starter, but only that.

Jorge Posada   C

Bats: S   Throws: R   Height: 6' 2"   Weight: 205   Born: August 17, 1971   Age: 37

YEAR	TEAM	LVL	AGE	PA	R	2B	3B	HR	RBI	BB	SO	SB	CS	EqBRR	AVG	OBP	SLG	EqAVG	EqOBP	EqSLG	EqA	VORP	WARP	DEFENSE
2006	NYA	MLB	34	544	65	27	2	23	93	64	96	3	0	-5.6	.278	.375	.494	.264	.369	.475	.292	39.2	5.3	118-C	9
2007	NYA	MLB	35	589	91	42	1	20	90	74	98	2	0	-7.6	.338	.426	.543	.325	.419	.542	.326	69.6	6.5	124-C	-5
2008	NYA	MLB	36	195	18	13	1	3	22	24	38	0	0	-0.9	.268	.364	.411	.257	.362	.413	.273	7.3	0.2	26-C	-6
2009	NYA	MLB	37	257	28	13	1	7	33	28	50	1	0	-1.6	.249	.336	.406	.254	.342	.432	.269	9.3	1.5	63-C	-4

Breakout: 1%   Improve: 14%   Collapse: 55%   Attrition: 41%   Comparables: Alan Ashby, Ernie Whitt, Greg Myers, Mike Piazza

Take a glass still hot from its time in the dishwasher, fill it with ice water, and watch it shatter. The Yankees cracked under a similar strain in 2008, going from the heat of Posada's best season to the frigidity of Molina's replacement-level production. Posada's throwing shoulder troubled him from the outset, and though the Yankees tried to keep him in the lineup by giving him time at first and DH, they were eventually forced to bow to the inevitable. Posada couldn't throw and couldn't load his swing with any power, and he was miserable playing out of position. Surgery to repair labrum and capsule damage was performed in late July. Posada is expected to be ready for spring training, but what lingering effects the injury will have, now and in the three years remaining on his contract, are unknown. Posada will probably never get much respect from Hall of Fame voters, but those who failed to notice he was the Yankees' secret weapon all these years should heed what happened when this career .299 EqA hitter was removed from the lineup.

Alex Rodriguez   3B

Bats: R   Throws: R   Height: 6' 3"   Weight: 225   Born: July 27, 1975   Age: 33

YEAR	TEAM	LVL	AGE	PA	R	2B	3B	HR	RBI	BB	SO	SB	CS	EqBRR	AVG	OBP	SLG	EqAVG	EqOBP	EqSLG	EqA	VORP	WARP	DEFENSE
2006	NYA	MLB	30	674	113	26	1	35	121	90	139	15	4	-0.0	.290	.392	.523	.274	.386	.499	.303	53.3	4.8	145-3B	-4
2007	NYA	MLB	31	708	143	31	0	54	156	95	120	24	4	5.5	.314	.422	.645	.300	.414	.640	.342	91.5	10.3	149-3B	10
2008	NYA	MLB	32	594	104	33	0	35	103	65	117	18	3	3.0	.302	.392	.573	.294	.389	.576	.320	62.4	6.3	127-3B	2
2009	NYA	MLB	33	624	97	29	1	30	98	72	124	18	4	-0.2	.282	.373	.508	.287	.379	.541	.311	45.1	5.4	146-3B	-2

Breakout: 4%   Improve: 27%   Collapse: 27%   Attrition: 7%   Comparables: Sammy Sosa, Bobby Grich, Dave Winfield, Ken Caminiti

In 2007, A-Rod had one of the greatest seasons ever by a third baseman. Naturally, when his 2008 was merely average—by his own lofty standards—it seemed like a massive letdown. Add in his usual sub-Ruthian performance in the clutch, a rare visit to the DL due to a quad injury, and a very public divorce and apparent flirtation with Madonna, and it was another surreal year in which Rodriguez definitely wasn't appreciated and certainly wasn't loved (at least by fans—Madonna may be another matter). If there's any lesson to be drawn from Rodriguez's season, it's that even an inner-circle Hall of Famer can't carry a team and overcome three replacement-level players in the lineup.

Ivan Rodriguez   C   Bats: R   Throws: R   Height: 5' 9"   Weight: 195   Born: November 30, 1971   Age: 37

YEAR	TEAM	LVL	AGE	PA	R	2B	3B	HR	RBI	BB	SO	SB	CS	EqBRR	AVG	OBP	SLG	EqAVG	EqOBP	EqSLG	EqA	VORP	WARP	DEFENSE		
2006	DET	MLB	34	580	74	28	4	13	69	26	86	8	3	1.0	.300	.332	.437	.289	.323	.428	.259	21.4	3.3	118-C	9	6-1B -2
2007	DET	MLB	35	515	50	31	3	11	63	9	96	2	2	-2.2	.281	.294	.420	.275	.289	.428	.242	10.2	2.2	118-C	8	
2008	DET	MLB	36	328	33	16	3	5	32	19	52	6	1	-1.2	.295	.338	.417	.292	.338	.422	.266	13.6	2.1	79-C	3	
2008	NYA	MLB	36	101	11	4	0	2	3	4	15	4	0	1.3	.219	.257	.323	.208	.248	.333	.208	-2.6	-0.3	25-C	-1	
2009	NYA	MLB	37	289	29	13	1	4	31	14	50	5	1	-0.5	.263	.301	.364	.268	.306	.387	.242	3.1	1.3	70-C	-1	

Breakout: 12%   **Improve:** 38%   **Collapse:** 34%   **Attrition:** 37%   **Comparables:** Joe Girardi, Benito Santiago, Sherm Lollar, Elston Howard

Pudge hadn't posted an OPS+ over 100 since 2004, but the Yankees' catching situation in the absence of Posada was so wretched that they figured they could pick up the Cooperstown-bound Pudge from the Tigers and see if there was anything left in the tank. After all, the soft .295 he was hitting for Detroit meant he could at least be a boost on Molina, right? Wrong. Rodriguez's production was nigh-identical to Molina's, which argues either for immediate retirement or the possibility that bad hitting can be acquired via airborne transmission. Girardi didn't help matters with haphazardly handing out playing time, never starting Rodriguez more than two days in a row. Fortunately, the trade only cost the Yankees Kyle Farnsworth, relieverdom's top arsonist, and Rodriguez's contract would end with the season, so there was no lasting damage.

Austin Romine   C   Bats: R   Throws: R   Height: 6' 1"   Weight: 195   Born: November 22, 1988   Age: 20

YEAR	TEAM	LVL	AGE	PA	R	2B	3B	HR	RBI	BB	SO	SB	CS	EqBRR	AVG	OBP	SLG	EqAVG	EqOBP	EqSLG	EqA	VORP	WARP	DEFENSE
2008	CSC	A	19	436	66	24	1	10	49	25	56	3	0	-0.8	.300	.344	.437	.260	.300	.386	.237	-4.0	-0.6	51-C -6
2009	NYA	MLB	20	535	51	29	2	8	55	31	91	4	2	0.7	.248	.294	.365	.252	.299	.388	.238	-1.3	0.7	126-C -16

Breakout: 37%   **Improve:** 60%   **Collapse:** 17%   **Attrition:** 9%   **Comparables:** Dave Valle, Angel Salome, Bryan Anderson, Ricky Jordan

Montero's co-catcher at Charleston, 2007 second-rounder Romine has baseball bloodlines, with daddy Kevin a Red Sox outfielder and brother Andrew in the Angels' system. Unlike Montero, Romine has the physical tools to stay behind the plate, but he's no mere catch-and-throw type. Though slowed early by injury, he caught up to the league as the year went on, bashing eight of his 10 homers in the last two months. Catcher is the one nonpitching position at which the Yankees have depth in prospects, and part of the fun of the next few seasons will be seeing which of them gets to fill Posada's big cleats. Though still far away, Romine's combination of defensive tools and power gives him the inside track.

PITCHERS

Alfredo Aceves   Bats: R   Throws: R   Height: 5' 10"   Weight: 176   Born: December 8, 1982   Age: 26

YEAR	TEAM	LVL	AGE	W	L	SV	G	GS	IP	H	BB	SO	HR	GB%	BABIP	STUFF	WHIP	ERA	DERA	EqH9	EqBB9	EqSO9	EqHR9	DEF	VORP	SN/WX
2006	MTR	MEX	23	8	5	0	19	19	124¹	126	26	95	15	42.8%	.308	-17	1.22	4.50	7.35	10.9	2.6	6.0	2.0	10	-21.9	—
2007	MTR	MEX	24	11	5	0	18	18	106¹	96	33	70	6	54.8%	.280	-8	1.21	3.64	6.64	9.3	3.5	4.5	1.1	11	-11.4	—
2008	TAM	A+	25	4	1	0	8	8	47	32	8	37	1	46.6%	.235	1	0.85	2.11	6.65	6.9	2.0	3.8	0.6	8	-5.2	—
2008	TRN	AA	25	2	2	0	7	7	50	37	6	35	3	44.1%	.250	10	0.86	1.80	4.34	8.1	1.2	4.7	1.0	9	6.4	—
2008	SWB	AAA	25	2	3	0	10	8	43²	42	13	42	6	40.2%	.300	-9	1.26	4.12	5.44	10.5	3.0	5.9	1.7	0	0.7	—
2008	NYA	MLB	25	1	0	0	6	4	30	25	10	16	4	39.4%	.233	-3	1.17	2.40	4.30	7.1	2.8	4.3	1.2	6	11.4	.01
2009	NYA	MLB	26	6	7	0	34	18	106	119	36	65	15	42.0%	.300	5	1.45	5.03	5.05	10.0	2.7	5.0	1.3	-1	3.4	0.96

Breakout: 3%   **Improve:** 29%   **Collapse:** 35%   **Attrition:** 19%   **Comparables:** Manny Hernandez, Armando Reynoso, Felipe Lira, Wilton Chavez

The former Mexican Leaguer had a meteoric rise through the Yankees' organization last year, climbing four levels to reach "The Show" before September. Aceves doesn't throw hard, but he throws smart with a full assortment of pitches and had no trouble controlling lefties during his climb. In the majors, lefties did not hit Aceves often, but what they did hit they punished. Aceves' style was not meant for last year's defensively challenged Yankees, but this year's improved crew should support him better. He's in the mix for the fifth slot or Ramiro Mendoza's old utility role. Either way, kudos to Yankees scouts for the free-talent pickup.

Jonathan Albaladejo

Bats: R   Throws: R   Height: 6' 5"   Weight: 260   Born: October 30, 1982   Age: 26

YEAR	TEAM	LVL	AGE	W	L	SV	G	GS	IP	H	BB	SO	HR	GB%	BABIP	STUFF	WHIP	ERA	DERA	EqH9	EqBB9	EqSO9	EqHR9	DEF	VORP	SN/WX
2006	ALT	AA	23	1	2	1	18	1	36²	41	5	27	4	53.0%	.343	-24	1.27	3.98	5.46	14.1	2.0	4.0	2.0	-4	0.5	—
2007	HAR	AA	24	4	3	2	21	0	36²	30	15	35	3	54.8%	.278	-19	1.23	4.17	6.94	8.7	4.1	5.4	1.3	3	-5.2	—
2007	COH	AAA	24	3	0	0	15	0	24	14	7	21	2	57.8%	.194	-6	0.88	1.13	4.63	5.8	2.7	5.4	1.2	6	2.5	—
2007	WAS	MLB	24	1	1	0	14	0	14¹	7	2	12	1	61.1%	.176	14	0.63	1.89	3.21	4.5	1.3	7.1	0.6	2	6.3	0.40
2008	NYA	MLB	25	0	1	0	7	0	13²	15	6	13	1	43.6%	.378	9	1.54	3.94	2.84	10.7	3.6	7.8	0.7	-1	2.9	0.05
2009	NYA	MLB	26	3	3	1	33	3	51	55	20	37	6	47.0%	.310	5	1.47	4.58	4.63	9.7	3.1	5.9	1.1	-0	4.5	0.48

Breakout: 10% Improve: 37% Collapse: 43% Attrition: 36%   Comparables: Roman Colon, Dave Lemanczyk, Steve Crawford, Jose Capellan

Acquired from the Nationals for Tyler Clippard, Albaladejo was a successful dark-horse candidate for the pen, claiming the last spot in spring training. Twice optioned and twice recalled, in his third stint he made the painful discovery that it's difficult to throw your slider with a stress fracture in your pitching elbow, and he ended his year on the 60-day DL. He pitched as a closer in the Puerto Rican Winter League and will again compete for a spot this spring.

Dellin Betances

Bats: R   Throws: R   Height: 6' 7"   Weight: 185   Born: March 23, 1988   Age: 21

YEAR	TEAM	LVL	AGE	W	L	SV	G	GS	IP	H	BB	SO	HR	GB%	BABIP	STUFF	WHIP	ERA	DERA	EqH9	EqBB9	EqSO9	EqHR9	DEF	VORP	SN/WX
2006	YAN	Ind	18	0	1	0	7	7	23	14	7	27	1	38.0%	.271	11	0.91	1.17	4.26	10.4	4.7	5.2	2.4	0	2.8	—
2007	STA	A-	19	1	2	0	6	6	25	24	17	29	0	43.9%	.369	11	1.64	3.60	5.23	13.1	8.7	5.2	0.4	-5	0.9	—
2008	CSC	A	20	9	4	0	22	22	115¹	87	59	135	9	42.8%	.284	2	1.27	3.67	7.04	9.8	6.6	5.6	1.8	-5	-16.2	—
2009	NYA	MLB	21	4	8	0	19	19	90	105	73	72	15	41.0%	.320	6	1.97	7.17	7.18	10.4	6.5	6.6	1.5	-1	-18.3	-1.33

Breakout: 23% Improve: 56% Collapse: 15% Attrition: 9%   Comparables: Tyrone Hill, Eric Hurley, Boof Bonser, Floyd Youmans

Betances is a living monolith who throws in the 90s but is still trying to figure out his mechanics. He made significant strides toward that goal last season. He began the year by walking 40 and allowing eight homers in his first 55 IP. A quick demotion to the Gulf Coast League did wonders, and in the second half, his ground-ball rate doubled, he allowed but one home run in 60⅓ IP, and he walked 2.8 per nine. His strikeout rate led the Sally League. Should the new-look Betances hold on to his gains, he could shoot to the top of the Yankees' prospect heap.

Brian Bruney

Bats: R   Throws: R   Height: 6' 3"   Weight: 245   Born: February 17, 1982   Age: 27

YEAR	TEAM	LVL	AGE	W	L	SV	G	GS	IP	H	BB	SO	HR	GB%	BABIP	STUFF	WHIP	ERA	DERA	EqH9	EqBB9	EqSO9	EqHR9	DEF	VORP	SN/WX
2006	NYA	MLB	24	1	1	0	19	0	20²	14	15	25	1	34.7%	.271	20	1.40	0.87	0.90	6.3	6.3	9.9	0.4	-1	12.1	0.52
2007	NYA	MLB	25	3	2	0	58	0	50	44	37	39	5	33.6%	.285	-3	1.60	4.68	4.74	7.8	6.2	6.2	0.9	-1	6.7	-0.28
2008	NYA	MLB	26	3	0	1	32	1	34¹	18	16	33	2	43.7%	.193	11	0.99	1.84	3.60	4.1	3.6	7.5	0.5	6	15.1	.74
2009	NYA	MLB	27	2	2	1	36	1	44¹	41	27	39	5	41.0%	.290	7	1.54	4.47	4.50	8.3	5.0	7.3	1.0	-0	4.6	0.42

Breakout: 14% Improve: 36% Collapse: 51% Attrition: 25%   Comparables: Rich Garces, Jim Britton, Eric Plunk, Sammy Stewart

Sometimes, you do all the right things and the universe still bites you on the buttocks. Bruney came to camp determined to conquer his weight and his control problems, and he made major progress with both, but a Lisfranc fracture knocked him out late in April. Initially expected to miss the rest of the season, he battled back by early August and pitched well down the stretch, posting a 1.96 ERA in 23 innings and walking just 10, which for him is pinpoint control. He should be one of Rivera's primary setup men this season.

Joba Chamberlain

Bats: R   Throws: R   Height: 6' 2"   Weight: 230   Born: September 23, 1985   Age: 23

YEAR	TEAM	LVL	AGE	W	L	SV	G	GS	IP	H	BB	SO	HR	GB%	BABIP	STUFF	WHIP	ERA	DERA	EqH9	EqBB9	EqSO9	EqHR9	DEF	VORP	SN/WX
2007	TAM	A+	21	4	0	0	7	7	40	25	11	51	0	62.5%	.287	35	0.90	2.03	3.63	8.3	3.6	7.5	0.3	-1	7.6	—
2007	TRN	AA	21	4	2	0	8	7	40¹	32	15	66	4	54.2%	.364	35	1.17	3.35	3.60	11.3	4.1	10.8	1.8	-5	7.8	—
2007	NYA	MLB	21	2	0	1	19	0	24	12	6	34	1	38.0%	.229	24	0.71	0.38	2.25	4.9	2.2	9.8	0.4	4	14.1	1.83
2008	NYA	MLB	22	4	3	0	42	12	100¹	87	39	118	5	51.2%	.328	43	1.26	2.60	2.65	7.8	3.2	9.4	0.5	-2	32.9	.39
2009	NYA	MLB	23	9	6	2	37	17	124	107	47	133	8	48.0%	.300	34	1.24	3.09	3.15	7.7	3.1	8.8	0.6	-1	31.5	3.97

Breakout: 10%   Improve: 30%   Collapse: 35%   Attrition: 15%   Comparables: Roger Clemens, Aaron Sele, Don Newcombe, Bill Singer

Chamberlain was sent to the bullpen out of spring training with an amorphous promise that he would move into the rotation; the idea was to prevent injury by minimizing his workload. The highly anticipated move came on June 3, and Chamberlain pitched quite well as a starter, but he got hurt, anyway, missing most of August with rotator cuff tendonitis. There are many causes of pitcher injuries; some, though not all, can be mitigated, and until medical technology reaches a point when coaches can get live-action film from inside a pitcher's shoulder as he's working, it's very difficult to know which of the dozens of injury-causing variables is in play, or even if supposedly helpful things aren't actually harmful. Chamberlain was probably no safer in the pen than he was in the rotation, and his injury may have actually been caused by an awkward spill he took trying to get out of the way of a Pudge throw to second that came at him head-high earlier in the same inning that he was hurt. Nonetheless, upon his return, he was back among the relievers. The Yankees intend to restore him to the rotation this spring, but they have now set themselves up to be second-guessed anytime he has so much as a hangnail, as all manner of observers, qualified and un-, keep trying to assign blame.

Phil Coke

Bats: L   Throws: L   Height: 6' 1"   Weight: 210   Born: July 19, 1982   Age: 26

YEAR	TEAM	LVL	AGE	W	L	SV	G	GS	IP	H	BB	SO	HR	GB%	BABIP	STUFF	WHIP	ERA	DERA	EqH9	EqBB9	EqSO9	EqHR9	DEF	VORP	SN/WX
2006	CSC	A	23	0	1	1	5	2	17¹	10	4	19	0	67.5%	.250	4	0.82	0.53	1.84	8.6	3.7	4.9	0.6	0	6.1	—
2006	TAM	A+	23	5	7	0	22	18	110²	101	35	88	6	46.4%	.289	-23	1.23	3.59	6.99	10.6	3.9	3.5	1.2	2	-15.7	—
2007	TAM	A+	24	7	3	0	17	16	99	93	37	76	4	54.7%	.307	-12	1.31	3.09	5.38	11.5	4.7	4.0	1.1	3	2.1	—
2008	TRN	AA	25	9	4	0	23	20	118¹	105	39	115	7	50.2%	.308	13	1.22	2.51	3.88	9.9	3.1	6.6	0.9	0	20.8	—
2008	SWB	AAA	25	2	2	0	14	1	17¹	19	5	22	0	46.9%	.396	3	1.39	4.68	6.19	12.4	2.8	7.9	0.0	-1	-1.0	—
2008	NYA	MLB	25	1	0	0	12	0	14²	8	2	14	0	50.0%	.222	14	0.68	0.61	1.26	4.4	1.3	7.5	0.0	1	8.4	.79
2009	NYA	MLB	26	5	5	1	54	10	85²	96	35	62	10	47.0%	.320	5	1.52	4.99	5.07	10.0	3.3	5.9	1.0	-1	2.7	0.62

Breakout: 10%   Improve: 37%   Collapse: 33%   Attrition: 15%   Comparables: Dave LaPoint, Frank DiPino, Micah Bowie, Bobby Jones

Coke wasn't on anyone's prospect radar at the season's outset, but when he reached the majors in September, he proved to be the pause that refreshes. He'd failed to rise as high as Double-A until his sixth professional season, and nothing about him jumped out. But things began to click at Trenton and then downright gelled when he switched to the pen at Scranton. After narrowly avoiding losing him in the Nady trade, the Yankees called him up. Relying on his fastball/slider combo, he was unhittable in a way he probably never will be again, allowing just one run. With an eye toward a future relief role, he had a reverse split in Double-A and the majors, but for now Coke will compete for a starting spot in spring training. Should he fail at that, it's almost certain he'll be the pen's second lefty.

Dan Giese

Bats: R   Throws: R   Height: 6' 3"   Weight: 200   Born: May 19, 1977   Age: 32

YEAR	TEAM	LVL	AGE	W	L	SV	G	GS	IP	H	BB	SO	HR	GB%	BABIP	STUFF	WHIP	ERA	DERA	EqH9	EqBB9	EqSO9	EqHR9	DEF	VORP	SN/WX
2006	REA	AA	29	1	2	1	23	0	36	27	14	27	5	52.4%	.232	-35	1.14	2.50	6.25	9.4	4.5	4.0	2.3	6	-2.3	—
2006	SWB	AAA	29	2	2	0	25	0	35¹	46	4	33	3	40.2%	.394	-10	1.42	3.08	3.98	15.3	1.4	6.0	1.4	-8	5.7	—
2007	FRE	AAA	30	3	1	2	47	0	73¹	65	10	76	2	42.4%	.318	19	1.02	2.82	3.60	8.9	1.4	6.9	0.4	-1	15.6	—
2007	SFN	MLB	30	0	2	0	8	0	9¹	8	2	7	4	57.1%	.174	-8	1.07	4.84	5.79	6.8	1.9	6.8	3.9	1	1.0	-0.09
2008	SWB	AAA	31	4	2	0	13	10	59	43	14	51	2	49.1%	.255	9	0.97	1.98	5.04	7.8	2.4	5.2	0.5	10	3.4	—
2008	NYA	MLB	31	1	3	0	20	3	43¹	39	14	29	3	32.4%	.265	1	1.22	3.53	3.97	7.1	2.6	5.0	0.6	-2	6.2	.75
2009	NYA	MLB	32	4	5	1	34	9	73²	84	24	46	11	41.0%	.300	0	1.46	5.20	5.22	10.2	2.6	5.2	1.3	-1	1.0	0.38

Breakout: 4%   Improve: 12%   Collapse: 62%   Attrition: 33%   Comparables: Mark Leiter, Tim Worrell, Hal Brown, Chris Brock

Minor league vet Giese followed up his 2007 breakthrough to the bigs with solid swing work for the Yankees. The control artist occasionally lost his control, as in June 27's four-inning/four-walk start against the Mets, but otherwise did fine in trash-time relief appearances (Girardi generally called for him when trailing or way ahead) and emergency starts. The only note of caution for 2009 is that Giese was hammered in his final five appearances after a timeout for rotator cuff tendonitis.

Phil Hughes

| | | | | | | | Bats: R | | Throws: R | | Height: 6' 5" | | Weight: 220 | | Born: June 24, 1986 | | | Age: 23 |

YEAR	TEAM	LVL	AGE	W	L	SV	G	GS	IP	H	BB	SO	HR	GB%	BABIP	STUFF	WHIP	ERA	DERA	EqH9	EqBB9	EqSO9	EqHR9	DEF	VORP	SN/WX
2006	TAM	A+	20	2	3	0	5	5	30²	19	2	30	0	51.9%	.247	27	0.70	1.79	4.61	7.6	1.3	4.9	0.3	2	3.0	—
2006	TRN	AA	20	10	3	0	21	21	116¹	73	32	138	5	52.8%	.266	46	0.90	2.25	4.69	8.5	3.2	6.9	0.9	7	10.5	—
2007	SWB	AAA	21	4	1	0	5	5	28²	16	8	28	0	62.3%	.235	27	0.84	2.20	4.39	5.7	2.7	6.1	0.3	3	3.6	—
2007	NYA	MLB	21	5	3	0	13	13	72²	64	29	58	8	37.8%	.272	24	1.28	4.46	4.77	7.8	3.4	6.3	1.0	1	9.9	1.53
2008	SWB	AAA	22	1	0	0	6	6	29	34	9	31	2	42.0%	.364	11	1.48	5.90	7.24	12.8	3.3	6.6	1.0	0	-5.0	—
2008	NYA	MLB	22	0	4	0	8	8	34	43	15	23	3	35.6%	.360	4	1.71	6.62	6.35	10.9	3.7	5.3	0.8	-1	-3.6	.35
2009	NYA	MLB	23	5	5	0	26	14	84²	88	34	67	10	43.0%	.300	16	1.43	4.74	4.81	9.3	3.2	6.5	1.0		-1 5.4	1.03

| Breakout: 48% | Improve: 70% | Collapse: 13% | Attrition: 26% | Comparables: Pete Broberg, Roy Halladay, Joel Davis, Alan Wirth |

There was a lot of pressure on Hughes after the Yankees chose to retain him rather than package him in a deal for Johan Santana. He failed miserably, but the (sort-of) good news is that he was never healthy, having been pitching with a stress fracture in one of his ribs throughout the season. His rehab work was mixed, but his strikeout rate rebounded with the addition of a cut fastball to his repertoire. The rebound carried over to his brief return to the majors and in a very strong Arizona Fall League stint (38 strikeouts in 30 IP). After consecutive years with long DL stays, there's some concern that Hughes has trouble staying healthy, but he's still young enough and his arm is special enough that he deserves another trial or three before hope is allowed to yield to doubt.

Ian Kennedy

| | | | | | | | Bats: R | | Throws: R | | Height: 6' 0" | | Weight: 190 | | Born: December 19, 1984 | | | Age: 24 |

YEAR	TEAM	LVL	AGE	W	L	SV	G	GS	IP	H	BB	SO	HR	GB%	BABIP	STUFF	WHIP	ERA	DERA	EqH9	EqBB9	EqSO9	EqHR9	DEF	VORP	SN/WX
2007	TAM	A+	22	6	1	0	11	10	63	39	22	72	2	35.7%	.266	25	0.97	1.29	3.50	8.2	4.5	6.8	0.8	6	12.6	—
2007	TRN	AA	22	5	1	0	9	9	48²	27	17	57	2	41.8%	.234	24	0.90	2.59	5.11	7.0	3.7	7.4	0.8	6	2.4	—
2007	SWB	AAA	22	1	1	0	6	6	34²	25	11	34	2	43.8%	.267	23	1.04	2.07	4.50	7.6	3.1	6.2	0.8	5	3.9	—
2007	NYA	MLB	22	1	0	0	3	3	19	13	9	15	1	26.4%	.231	19	1.16	1.89	4.82	5.8	3.9	6.3	0.5	5	6.8	0.67
2008	SWB	AAA	23	5	3	0	13	12	69	52	17	72	4	41.7%	.282	18	1.00	2.35	4.36	8.0	2.5	6.3	0.8	7	9.1	—
2008	NYA	MLB	23	0	4	0	10	9	39²	50	26	27	5	42.9%	.346	-5	1.92	8.16	5.98	10.6	5.1	5.1	1.1	-9	-11.2	.47
2009	NYA	MLB	24	8	8	1	38	23	137¹	138	62	108	16	41.0%	.300	15	1.45	4.71	4.75	9.0	3.6	6.5	1.1	-1	9.5	1.82

| Breakout: 28% | Improve: 49% | Collapse: 25% | Attrition: 26% | Comparables: Shawn Hillegas, Pat Pacillo, Jaret Wright, Adam Eaton |

The award for most disappointing performance by a Yankee in 2008 has to go to Kennedy, a pitcher with average stuff but pinpoint control that disappeared in the majors and who seemed not to be too troubled by it. Kennedy's ability to locate had made him a 2006 first-rounder and a top prospect—his minor league ERA currently stands at 1.99 in 226⅓ IP. In the majors, he nibbled, got hammered, and alienated folks by saying things like, "I felt like I made some good pitches and competed, which is all that really matters. … What was it? A bunch of singles and three doubles, or so. I'm just not real upset about it." Girardi did little to hide his frustration with Kennedy throughout the season, which resulted in three demotions (one for an injured lat that the Yankees simply didn't bother to recall him from once his rehab concluded), the last of which came on August 10, two days after Kennedy made the comments above; he would not return, even when rosters expanded. He pitched well in the minors and in Puerto Rican action this winter, but Kennedy is going to have to fight numbers and organizational disenchantment to earn a spot.

George Kontos

Bats: R   Throws: R   Height: 6' 3"   Weight: 215   Born: June 12, 1985   Age: 24

YEAR	TEAM	LVL	AGE	W	L	SV	G	GS	IP	H	BB	SO	HR	GB%	BABIP	STUFF	WHIP	ERA	DERA	EqH9	EqBB9	EqSO9	EqHR9	DEF	VORP	SN/WX
2006	STA	A-	21	7	3	0	14	14	78¹	64	19	82	3	56.4%	.317	-10	1.06	2.65	6.93	12.7	4.4	4.5	2.3	-1	-9.4	—
2007	TAM	A+	22	4	6	0	19	17	94	95	30	101	15	44.4%	.321	-37	1.33	4.02	6.97	13.5	4.2	6.2	3.4	-3	-12.2	—
2008	TRN	AA	23	6	11	0	27	27	151²	134	57	152	14	40.1%	.300	5	1.26	3.68	5.17	9.9	3.4	6.8	1.3	-7	6.7	—
2009	NYA	MLB	24	5	7	0	25	17	97¹	115	47	73	18	40.0%	.320	8	1.66	6.20	6.16	10.6	3.9	6.1	1.6	-1	-9.5	-0.31

Breakout: 17%   Improve: 58%   Collapse: 13%   Attrition: 10%   Comparables: Duff Brumley, James McDonald, John DeSilva, Tommy Shimp

For the first time in his minor league career, Kontos impressed. He was initially reported to have been part of the Nady/Marte package, but the Yankees held on and got good results. This was the first time Kontos could say this without qualification, as his college career was unimpressive and his 2007 was interrupted by an arrest after he refused to leave a bar that had closed. His stuff isn't overpowering, and that in concert with a bias toward fly balls last season bodes ill. He'll move up to Triple-A, but with the Yankees rotation stocked, it's going to take excellent pitching and a clubhouse-wide case of stomach flu to get him into the picture.

Zach Kroenke

Bats: R   Throws: L   Height: 6' 3"   Weight: 210   Born: April 21, 1984   Age: 25

YEAR	TEAM	LVL	AGE	W	L	SV	G	GS	IP	H	BB	SO	HR	GB%	BABIP	STUFF	WHIP	ERA	DERA	EqH9	EqBB9	EqSO9	EqHR9	DEF	VORP	SN/WX
2006	CSC	A	22	8	6	0	25	20	113¹	124	41	86	9	52.2%	.326	-55	1.46	3.58	9.41	14.8	5.1	2.8	2.3	0	-40.5	—
2007	TAM	A+	23	2	2	0	29	0	43²	34	19	33	2	54.8%	.250	-23	1.21	2.27	5.83	8.6	5.0	3.5	1.1	3	-1.1	—
2007	TRN	AA	23	0	1	2	15	0	14¹	21	12	12	5	49.0%	.364	-42	2.31	9.44	10.03	19.3	9.3	5.4	6.2	-4	-5.8	—
2008	TRN	AA	24	6	0	1	37	0	43²	28	26	44	4	53.5%	.235	-3	1.24	3.09	4.46	7.0	5.1	6.6	1.3	1	5.4	—
2008	SWB	AAA	24	1	0	0	4	0	10	7	2	10	0	58.8%	.281	5	0.90	1.80	6.00	8.0	2.0	6.0	0.0	2	-0.4	—
2009	FLO	MLB	25	2	3	0	24	5	48²	56	30	38	7	48.0%	.330	-3	1.77	6.09	6.51	10.5	4.8	5.8	1.3	0	-4.5	-0.24

Breakout: 28%   Improve: 68%   Collapse: 12%   Attrition: 15%   Comparables: Mike Johnston, John Lepley, Todd Belitz, Jason Jimenez

If you say his name quickly, Kroenke can pass for a certain Royals ace, but he's actually a converted starter with a nasty slider who took a step toward curbing his control issues last season. More of those steps await him on the road to big-league LOOGYdom, but he'll have to take them fast if he hopes to stick with the Marlins, who selected him in the Rule 5 Draft. Kroenke actually had a reverse split last year, at Trenton and (to a lesser extent) at Scranton.

Damaso Marte

Bats: L   Throws: L   Height: 6' 2"   Weight: 210   Born: February 14, 1975   Age: 34

YEAR	TEAM	LVL	AGE	W	L	SV	G	GS	IP	H	BB	SO	HR	GB%	BABIP	STUFF	WHIP	ERA	DERA	EqH9	EqBB9	EqSO9	EqHR9	DEF	VORP	SN/WX
2006	PIT	MLB	31	1	7	0	75	0	58¹	51	31	63	5	40.1%	.326	14	1.41	3.70	3.97	7.3	4.1	8.7	0.6	-1	9.1	0.01
2007	PIT	MLB	32	2	0	0	65	0	45¹	32	18	51	2	43.2%	.280	27	1.10	2.38	2.38	5.8	3.2	9.1	0.4	-1	15.6	1.26
2008	PIT	MLB	33	4	0	5	47	0	46²	38	16	47	4	38.8%	.274	13	1.16	3.47	3.99	6.7	2.7	7.8	0.8	2	11.0	3.16
2008	NYA	MLB	33	1	3	0	25	0	18¹	14	10	24	1	24.4%	.302	17	1.31	5.41	4.34	6.8	4.3	10.1	0.5	-2	0.9	.49
2009	NYA	MLB	34	3	3	5	61	0	56¹	50	25	55	6	38.0%	.290	14	1.33	3.76	3.78	8.0	3.5	8.1	0.9	-0	10.3	0.95

Breakout: 26%   Improve: 48%   Collapse: 33%   Attrition: 10%   Comparables: Randy Myers, Dennis Cook, John Hiller, Mike Remlinger

The Yankees had coveted Marte for years—ironic, given that he was once their property but had been thrown away to get the immortal Enrique Wilson. The reality wasn't what the team had anticipated, but a good part of the blame goes to Girardi, who rode Marte through some long appearances; Marte was dealing with elbow soreness in short order. Marte remains a reliever who has held lefties to .200/.297/.287 over his career and can be trusted against righties as well. The Yankees declined his 2009 option, but quickly re-signed him to a three-year deal at a lower annual rate. Assuming his elbow worries are a thing of the past, he has shown the rare consistency that makes him one of the few relievers who makes a multiyear gamble worthwhile.

Mark Melancon

Bats: R   Throws: R   Height: 6' 1"   Weight: 175   Born: March 28, 1985   Age: 24

YEAR	TEAM	LVL	AGE	W	L	SV	G	GS	IP	H	BB	SO	HR	GB%	BABIP	STUFF	WHIP	ERA	DERA	EqH9	EqBB9	EqSO9	EqHR9	DEF	VORP	SN/WX
2008	TAM	A+	23	1	0	0	13	0	25¹	26	6	20	2	43.8%	.316	-23	1.26	2.85	5.79	11.2	2.7	3.9	1.5	2	-0.5	—
2008	TRN	AA	23	6	0	2	19	0	49²	32	12	47	3	64.1%	.232	10	0.89	1.81	4.37	7.0	2.3	6.3	1.0	5	6.5	—
2008	SWB	AAA	23	1	1	1	12	0	20	11	4	22	1	52.7%	.212	9	0.75	2.70	6.16	6.2	1.9	6.6	0.9	4	-1.2	—
2009	NYA	MLB	24	3	3	1	27	5	59¹	61	20	42	6	49.0%	.300	10	1.36	4.34	4.45	9.2	2.8	5.8	0.9	-1	6.9	0.77

Breakout: 23%   Improve: 50%   Collapse: 21%   Attrition: 10%   Comparables: Manny Corpas, Julian Tavarez, Arthur Martinez, Danny Graves

The Yankees have gone crazy trying to protect their young starters from overuse, but after missing 2007 recovering from Tommy John surgery, Melancon was allowed to throw 95 innings across three levels. Given that the inflection point for injury and/or regression for *healthy* relievers seems to be about 100 innings, this would seem to have been as imprudent a program as the team's handling of Joba Chamberlain was overcautious and ultimately irrelevant. In any case, Melancon did good work; he can still bust out a mid-90s fastball, and he has solid offspeed stuff. There's a long line of relievers ahead of him, but Melancon should leapfrog them no later than midyear.

Mike Mussina

Bats: L   Throws: R   Height: 6' 2"   Weight: 190   Born: December 8, 1968   Age: 40

YEAR	TEAM	LVL	AGE	W	L	SV	G	GS	IP	H	BB	SO	HR	GB%	BABIP	STUFF	WHIP	ERA	DERA	EqH9	EqBB9	EqSO9	EqHR9	DEF	VORP	SN/WX
2006	NYA	MLB	37	15	7	0	32	32	197¹	184	35	172	22	42.6%	.285	23	1.11	3.51	4.12	8.5	1.6	7.0	0.9	3	45.8	5.07
2007	NYA	MLB	38	11	10	0	28	27	152	188	35	91	14	43.5%	.348	4	1.47	5.15	4.26	11.3	2.0	4.8	0.9	-14	13.0	2.47
2008	NYA	MLB	39	20	9	0	34	34	200¹	214	31	150	17	49.7%	.327	21	1.22	3.37	3.86	9.4	1.3	6.1	0.8	3	45.1	.61
2009	NYA	MLB	40	12	8	0	28	28	181¹	189	39	122	17	47.0%	.300	20	1.25	3.67	3.72	9.3	1.7	5.5	0.8	-1	32.9	4.96

Breakout: 25%   Improve: 68%   Collapse: 6%   Attrition: 13%   Comparables: John Smoltz, Gaylord Perry, Dennis Martinez, Don Sutton

We rarely devote space to retired pitchers, but the circumstances of Moose's retirement were so unusual that we're holding on to the possibility that he might make a Clemens-like return (sans the congressional hearings). Having completed his long quest to win 20 games, Moose hung up his spurs, calculating that the quest for 300 wins would require another three seasons of high-level pitching, more of a commitment than he was willing to make. For years, sportswriters have made easy copy railing against the changes that big money has brought to the game, but one of the unremarked positives is that unlike the players of the past, Mussina has the freedom provided by his wealth to just go home, enjoy his family, and chase his bliss. That's something we should all empathize with.

Carl Pavano

Bats: R   Throws: R   Height: 6' 5"   Weight: 240   Born: January 8, 1976   Age: 33

YEAR	TEAM	LVL	AGE	W	L	SV	G	GS	IP	H	BB	SO	HR	GB%	BABIP	STUFF	WHIP	ERA	DERA	EqH9	EqBB9	EqSO9	EqHR9	DEF	VORP	SN/WX
2007	NYA	MLB	31	1	0	0	2	2	11¹	12	2	4	1	52.5%	.282	-5	1.24	4.78	4.09	9.0	1.6	2.5	0.8	-1	0.5	0.14
2008	NYA	MLB	32	4	2	0	7	7	34¹	41	10	15	5	42.4%	.316	-12	1.49	5.77	5.24	10.0	2.4	3.4	1.3	-2	-0.6	.25
2009	CLE	MLB	33	3	4	0	24	9	65¹	80	20	35	10	44.3%	.313	-4	1.53	5.60	5.50	10.8	2.4	4.4	1.3	0	-0.6	0.30

Breakout: 11%   Improve: 30%   Collapse: 54%   Attrition: 37%

Pavano made his last start of 2007 on April 9, and made his first start of 2008 on August 23. In between came Tommy John surgery and a rehab that seemed to stretch on endlessly, on account of the pitcher's ability to injure every part of his body, not to mention a reputation for malingering. Once "healthy," Pavano survived hittability despite complaints of a stiff hip. It's said the second year back from TJ surgery is the one to look forward to, but as Pavano has made just 26 appearances in the last three years, it's hard to know what he has left. The Indians, desperate for help at the back of their rotation, signed him to a one-year deal; they'd better have upgraded their whirlpool facilities since *Major League*.

Andy Pettitte

| | | | | | | | Bats: L | | Throws: L | | Height: 6' 5" | | Weight: 225 | | Born: June 15, 1972 | | | Age: 37 | |

YEAR	TEAM	LVL	AGE	W	L	SV	G	GS	IP	H	BB	SO	HR	GB%	BABIP	STUFF	WHIP	ERA	DERA	EqH9	EqBB9	EqSO9	EqHR9	DEF	VORP	SN/WX
2006	HOU	MLB	34	14	13	0	36	35	214¹	238	70	178	27	51.4%	.333	15	1.44	4.20	4.20	10.1	2.6	6.9	1.0	-3	29.6	4.06
2007	NYA	MLB	35	15	9	0	36	34	215¹	238	69	141	16	49.5%	.329	12	1.43	4.05	4.05	10.1	2.8	5.3	0.7	-5	39.0	5.30
2008	NYA	MLB	36	14	14	0	33	33	204	233	55	158	19	52.1%	.341	15	1.41	4.54	4.48	9.9	2.2	6.2	0.9	-5	20.5	.70
2009	NYA	MLB	37	10	9	0	27	27	168¹	187	53	119	17	49.0%	.320	19	1.42	4.41	4.48	9.9	2.5	5.8	0.9	-1	16.5	3.05

Breakout: 14% Improve: 43% Collapse: 22% Attrition: 20%   Comparables: Jerry Reuss, Frank Tanana, Jim Kaat, David Wells

Pettitte's season seemed to break down neatly into two halves, the first, in which he was generally effective, and the second, in which he was average at best. This is an incomplete reading; the Yankees' defenders were at their most butterfingered when he was on the mound. His strikeout rate was up for the season, and his overall line-drive rate didn't support the high BABIP he allowed. At the same time, Pettitte's rate for liners did rise to a dangerously high 26.3 percent in September (league average is roughly 19 percent). Pettitte blamed his weak second half on a lack of off-season conditioning, the result of his trying to keep a low profile after the release of the Mitchell Report. As we went to press, the Yankees were locked into a financial game of chicken with Pettitte, daring him to stay home or go to another team, even though his expressed desire was to return. The Yankees may not need him, but the market is undervaluing Pettitte's rebound chances if it limits his menu to the Bronx or nothing.

Sidney Ponson

| | | | | | | | Bats: R | | Throws: R | | Height: 6' 1" | | Weight: 260 | | Born: November 2, 1976 | | | Age: 32 | |

YEAR	TEAM	LVL	AGE	W	L	SV	G	GS	IP	H	BB	SO	HR	GB%	BABIP	STUFF	WHIP	ERA	DERA	EqH9	EqBB9	EqSO9	EqHR9	DEF	VORP	SN/WX
2006	SLN	MLB	29	4	4	0	14	13	68²	82	29	33	7	55.3%	.332	-6	1.62	5.24	4.04	11.3	3.5	4.2	0.8	-7	3.5	1.50
2006	NYA	MLB	29	0	1	0	5	3	16¹	26	7	15	3	45.8%	.411	-9	2.02	10.49	7.31	14.6	3.9	7.3	1.7	-7	-8.7	-0.49
2007	MIN	MLB	30	2	5	0	7	7	37²	54	17	23	7	53.6%	.359	-16	1.88	6.92	5.65	13.0	3.9	4.9	1.7	-7	-6.6	-0.20
2008	TEX	MLB	31	4	1	0	9	9	55²	71	16	25	3	56.0%	.335	1	1.56	3.88	4.89	10.3	2.4	3.5	0.5	-5	-0.2	0.19
2008	NYA	MLB	31	4	4	0	16	15	80	99	32	33	11	53.8%	.324	-21	1.64	5.85	5.88	10.7	3.3	3.2	1.3	2	-0.9	.93
2009	NYA	MLB	32	6	7	0	28	17	104²	129	40	48	12	50.0%	.320	-3	1.61	5.36	5.45	11.0	3.1	3.8	1.0	-1	-1.6	0.51

Breakout: 19% Improve: 49% Collapse: 24% Attrition: 29%   Comparables: Walt Terrell, Jaime Navarro, Joey Hamilton, Jeff Suppan

Sir Sidney had pitched superficially well for the Rangers when he was cut for being annoying in some unspecified way ("disrespectful," said Jon Daniels), putting up a 3.88 ERA despite miserable peripherals. His Yankees results were surprisingly equivocal, with Ponson making seven quality starts in 15 tries. Unfortunately, he also had six starts in which he failed to reach or survive the fifth inning. More than ever, Ponson is a ground-ball pitcher without the stuff to get more than a handful of strikeouts. With a pitcher like that, some days you get the bear, and some days the bear hits the ball in the general vicinity of Derek Jeter and it rolls into the outfield for a single. Then there's the third option—some days you piss off the bear by saying something out of line and he grants you your outright release.

Edwar Ramirez

| | | | | | | | Bats: R | | Throws: R | | Height: 6' 3" | | Weight: 155 | | Born: March 28, 1981 | | | Age: 28 | |

YEAR	TEAM	LVL	AGE	W	L	SV	G	GS	IP	H	BB	SO	HR	GB%	BABIP	STUFF	WHIP	ERA	DERA	EqH9	EqBB9	EqSO9	EqHR9	DEF	VORP	SN/WX
2006	TAM	A+	25	4	1	3	19	0	30¹	14	6	47	0	32.8%	.241	19	0.66	1.20	3.86	6.4	2.6	8.4	0.3	4	5.4	—
2007	TRN	AA	26	3	0	1	9	0	16²	6	8	33	1	56.0%	.208	16	0.84	0.54	1.69	5.6	4.5	10.7	1.1	1	7.0	—
2007	SWB	AAA	26	1	0	6	25	0	40	20	14	69	0	43.3%	.308	35	0.85	0.90	2.23	6.7	3.5	10.7	0.2	2	13.6	—
2007	NYA	MLB	26	1	1	1	21	0	21	24	14	31	6	36.4%	.383	12	1.86	8.14	6.10	10.9	5.7	11.3	2.6	-4	-4.8	-0.74
2008	SWB	AAA	27	1	0	0	8	0	9	2	1	13	0	50.0%	.125	9	0.33	0.00	3.12	3.1	1.0	8.3	0.0	3	2.4	—
2008	NYA	MLB	27	5	1	1	55	0	55¹	44	24	63	7	34.3%	.274	11	1.23	3.91	4.07	6.8	3.6	8.9	1.1	0	10.7	0.30
2009	NYA	MLB	28	3	2	4	54	0	58	49	25	62	6	39.0%	.280	21	1.28	3.51	3.53	7.5	3.5	8.7	0.9	-0	12.6	1.10

Breakout: 39% Improve: 69% Collapse: 12% Attrition: 19%   Comparables: David Riske, Dennis Higgins, Santiago Casilla, Frank Francisco

Changeup artist/stick figure Ramirez cemented his place in the majors with a generally solid campaign after coming up from Scranton at the end of April. However, his season breaks into two phases: the classic Blue period, comprising both his perfect minor league stint and his first 14⅔ IP in the bigs, during which he allowed not a single run; followed by the less-accessible Cubist period, which covered everything from there on—once the ice was broken, Ramirez pitched another 40⅔ IP and allowed 25 runs. Even within the later phase, he pitched 11 shutout innings in

July. The totality makes for one streaky pitcher; when he can locate the change, he's very hard to hit, and when he can't, he has little to fall back on and the home runs fly.

Mariano Rivera

														Bats: R		Throws: R		Height: 6' 2"		Weight: 185		Born: November 29, 1969		Age: 39

YEAR	TEAM	LVL	AGE	W	L	SV	G	GS	IP	H	BB	SO	HR	GB%	BABIP	STUFF	WHIP	ERA	DERA	EqH9	EqBB9	EqSO9	EqHR9	DEF	VORP	SN/WX
2006	NYA	MLB	36	5	5	34	63	0	75	61	11	55	3	57.7%	.269	18	0.96	1.80	1.99	7.5	1.4	6.0	0.4	0	35.1	5.35
2007	NYA	MLB	37	3	4	30	67	0	71¹	68	12	74	4	53.0%	.327	25	1.12	3.16	2.69	8.6	1.4	8.2	0.5	-3	22.9	3.71
2008	NYA	MLB	38	6	5	39	64	0	70²	41	6	77	4	54.6%	.220	34	0.67	1.40	2.14	4.8	0.8	8.3	0.5	5	34.3	.17
2009	NYA	MLB	39	5	4	36	58	0	65²	56	12	64	4	50.0%	.290	23	1.03	2.42	2.47	7.6	1.5	8.0	0.5	-0	22.8	3.59

Breakout: 7%   Improve: 30%   Collapse: 37%   Attrition: 14%   Comparables: Larry Andersen, Stu Miller, Hoyt Wilhelm, Marv Grissom

The closest thing baseball has to Fred Astaire, Rivera had an almost impeccable season, blowing just one save—trying to staunch a Twins rally enabled by Marte, he allowed a three-run homer to Delmon Young. More so than is his norm, Rivera had pinpoint control, walking just 0.76 batters per nine, the lowest walk rate in baseball in the 70-IP-and-up bracket. As has long been the case, Rivera's cutter allowed him to own left-handed hitters, limiting them to .147/.173/.194 rates. As measured by WARP, it was Rivera's best season; the more context-sensitive WXRL ranks it as only his fourth-best, but confirms that Rivera, not the record-setting K-Rod, was the most valuable closer in the American League. Rivera had minor shoulder surgery in October, so more than ever, our annual caveat applies: We don't know how many more years of this Rivera has in him, so enjoy it while you can still see him without having to schlep up to Cooperstown.

David Robertson

														Bats: R		Throws: R		Height: 5' 11"		Weight: 180		Born: April 9, 1985		Age: 24

YEAR	TEAM	LVL	AGE	W	L	SV	G	GS	IP	H	BB	SO	HR	GB%	BABIP	STUFF	WHIP	ERA	DERA	EqH9	EqBB9	EqSO9	EqHR9	DEF	VORP	SN/WX
2007	CSC	A	22	5	2	3	24	0	47	25	15	67	0	64.7%	.253	22	0.85	0.77	2.32	7.6	4.0	7.2	0.4	0	15.6	—
2007	TAM	A+	22	3	1	1	18	0	33¹	18	15	37	0	58.4%	.237	11	0.99	1.08	4.55	6.7	5.5	6.4	0.3	5	3.5	—
2008	TRN	AA	23	0	0	2	9	0	18²	8	6	26	0	54.3%	.235	17	0.75	0.96	2.12	5.3	3.2	9.5	0.0	1	6.6	—
2008	SWB	AAA	23	4	0	1	21	0	35	20	17	51	1	54.1%	.256	19	1.06	2.06	4.46	6.3	4.5	8.9	0.5	3	4.3	—
2008	NYA	MLB	23	4	0	0	25	0	30¹	29	15	36	3	41.3%	.351	14	1.45	5.35	5.16	8.8	4.2	9.7	0.9	0	1.6	.74
2009	NYA	MLB	24	4	3	3	49	3	62	52	32	68	4	48.0%	.300	24	1.34	3.62	3.73	7.5	4.1	9.0	0.6	-0	13.5	1.22

Breakout: 34%   Improve: 57%   Collapse: 17%   Attrition: 10%   Comparables: Byung-Hyun Kim, Ed Whitson, Mark Wohlers, Bruce Sutter

Robertson pitched his way from Double-A to the majors with some bodacious strikeout rates and followed up by allowing just two runs in his first 12⅓ big-league innings. Thereafter, previous problems with control reasserted themselves and thrashings ensued. Robertson's fastball/slider combo is tough to hit, but until such time as he achieves greater consistency, he's going to have a hard time escaping the low-leverage role in which Girardi utilized him.

Jose Veras

														Bats: R		Throws: R		Height: 6' 5"		Weight: 235		Born: October 20, 1980		Age: 28

YEAR	TEAM	LVL	AGE	W	L	SV	G	GS	IP	H	BB	SO	HR	GB%	BABIP	STUFF	WHIP	ERA	DERA	EqH9	EqBB9	EqSO9	EqHR9	DEF	VORP	SN/WX
2006	COH	AAA	25	5	3	21	50	0	59	49	19	68	3	46.5%	.311	2	1.15	2.44	4.26	8.4	3.3	6.9	0.8	2	8.5	—
2006	NYA	MLB	25	0	0	1	12	0	11	8	5	6	2	31.3%	.200	-23	1.18	4.09	6.30	7.2	4.5	4.5	1.8	3	2.5	0.21
2007	SWB	AAA	26	2	0	4	12	0	16	17	7	17	1	57.4%	.348	-8	1.50	4.50	4.20	11.4	4.2	6.6	1.2	-3	2.3	—
2007	NYA	MLB	26	0	0	2	9	0	9¹	6	7	7	0	40.7%	.222	-8	1.39	5.81	7.45	5.6	5.6	5.6	0.0	2	0.3	0.35
2008	NYA	MLB	27	5	3	0	60	0	57²	52	29	63	7	42.4%	.304	8	1.40	3.59	3.57	7.8	4.0	8.5	1.1	1	14.0	.93
2009	NYA	MLB	28	3	3	4	58	0	60	54	25	58	6	43.0%	.290	17	1.31	3.70	3.74	8.1	3.3	7.9	0.9	-0	11.6	0.98

Breakout: 26%   Improve: 40%   Collapse: 36%   Attrition: 16%   Comparables: Paul Shuey, Michael Wuertz, Jeff Nelson, Todd Worrell

Having spent most of 2007 on the DL after surgery to remove bone chips from his elbow, Veras began the season at Scranton, but was back up by May. As throughout his career, Veras fought his control, and his home-run rate was a bit high, though not Farnsworthian. Many of Veras's problems manifested in August and September, but no injury was reported. Assuming that this was no more than a blip on the radar, and further assuming no dramatic uptick in control, Veras would seem to have been placed in the role for which he is best suited, medium- to low-leverage relief work.

Chien-Ming Wang

													Bats: R		Throws: R		Height: 6' 3"		Weight: 225		Born: March 31, 1980		Age: 29

YEAR	TEAM	LVL	AGE	W	L	SV	G	GS	IP	H	BB	SO	HR	GB%	BABIP	STUFF	WHIP	ERA	DERA	EqH9	EqBB9	EqSO9	EqHR9	DEF	VORP	SN/WX
2006	NYA	MLB	26	19	6	1	34	33	218	233	52	76	12	63.8%	.293	3	1.31	3.63	4.62	9.9	2.2	2.8	0.5	18	55.7	5.75
2007	NYA	MLB	27	19	7	0	30	30	199¹	199	59	104	9	58.4%	.298	12	1.29	3.70	4.74	9.1	2.6	4.2	0.4	21	50.4	5.96
2008	NYA	MLB	28	8	2	0	15	15	95	90	35	54	4	55.0%	.284	13	1.32	4.07	5.04	8.0	3.0	4.5	0.4	11	17.7	.29
2009	NYA	MLB	29	8	7	0	30	19	126¹	141	42	67	10	56.0%	.310	7	1.45	4.39	4.53	10.0	2.7	4.4	0.7	-1	11.8	2.04

Breakout: 6%   Improve: 25%   Collapse: 43%   Attrition: 24%   Comparables: Dennis Lamp, Al Fitzmorris, Jake Westbrook, Mike Morgan

The best that can be said for Wang's injury-aborted season is that at least he didn't hurt his arm—halfway through a shutout of the Astros at Houston on June 15, Wang injured his foot running the bases. It was the dreaded "mid-foot sprain of the Lisfranc ligament and partial tear of the peroneal longus tendon of the right foot," and Wang spent the rest of the year getting around with various casts and crutches. Before the injury, his ground-ball rate was down a bit and his strikeouts and walks both up—pitching coach Dave Eiland had him going to his slider in strikeout situations instead of trying to induce grounders. The Yankees signed him to an arbitration-avoiding one-year contract, and he'll be back in the rotation, albeit now as an overqualified third or fourth starter.

LINEOUTS

Hitters

PLAYER	TEAM	LVL	AGE	PA	R	2B	3B	HR	RBI	BB	SO	SB-CS	EqBRR	AVG/OBP/SLG	EqAVG/EqOBP/EqSLG	EqA	VORP	WARP
OF J. Christian	SWB	AAA	28	297	48	17	1	6	45	20	34	22-4	4.4	.306/.357/.444	.254/.303/.382	.245	-2.9	0.3
	NYA	MLB	28	43	6	3	0	0	6	3	4	7-1	0.9	.250/.302/.325	.250/.302/.325	.248	0.4	-0.2
3B M. Cusick*	LEX	A	22	400	55	23	6	9	38	40	43	8-1	-0.9	.285/.356/.462	.225/.291/.372	.233	-10.8	-2.7
1B S. Duncan	SWB	AAA	28	252	38	14	0	12	44	41	55	6-1	-0.2	.239/.365/.483	.200/.319/.405	.256	-0.9	0.0
	NYA	MLB	28	65	7	3	0	1	6	7	13	0-0	0.0	.175/.262/.281	.175/.273/.281	.199	-4.7	-0.5
1B J. Miranda*	SWB	AAA	25	417	40	22	0	12	52	55	79	2-1	-1.7	.287/.384/.449	.265/.360/.429	.276	16.1	1.1
C C. Moeller	SWB	AAA	33	89	6	4	0	1	7	5	22	0-0	-0.4	.235/.270/.321	.195/.233/.268	.174	-8.7	-0.4
	NYA	MLB	33	103	13	6	0	1	9	7	18	0-0	-1.5	.231/.311/.330	.231/.311/.319	.226	-1.2	0.1
INF C. Ransom	SWB	AAA	32	481	69	24	3	22	71	50	115	9-5	2.2	.255/.338/.482	.214/.292/.412	.241	-5.8	1.6
	NYA	MLB	32	51	9	3	0	4	8	6	12	0-0	-0.1	.302/.400/.651	.302/.400/.628	.331	6.7	0.3
1B R. Sexson	SEA	MLB	33	292	27	8	0	11	30	37	76	1-0	-1.4	.218/.315/.381	.220/.322/.400	.254	-2.1	-1.1
	NYA	MLB	33	35	2	1	0	1	6	6	10	0-0	-0.0	.250/.371/.393	.250/.371/.393	.277	0.6	-0.2
3B B. Suttle#	CSC	A	22	428	63	23	7	11	44	45	93	2-1	-3.9	.271/.348/.456	.215/.285/.365	.225	-14.4	-0.2

Justin Christian's long journey from the independent Frontier League culminated in a call-up during an injury-inflicted roster crunch; nontendered in December, he's strictly reserve material. ⊘ The return for trading LaTroy Hawkins, **Matt Cusick** is a patient hitter with some power, but is limited by a lack of speed that makes his defense bad at any position, and that is a big part of why he wasn't drafted until 2007's 10th round. ⊘ Small-sample sensation **Shelley Duncan** was unable to hit in sporadic early playing time, got sent down, got hurt, got healthy, wasn't recalled, and was DFA'd in December. ⊘ Depending on your source, Cuban defector **Juan Miranda** is 26, 28, or 2,800 this year and has enough power that he might hold a job as a platoon DH, not that the modern, bullpen-heavy team has room for such a specialized creature. ⊘ **Chad Moeller** was signed to provide organizational depth; he could hardly have anticipated he'd spend a good part of the season in the majors while outhitting Jose Molina. ⊘ Minor league vet **Cody Ransom** has always had good power for a middle infielder; he'll compete for a bench spot with Angel Berroa, his polar opposite. ⊘ After earning his release from the Mariners, **Richie Sexson** signed with the Yankees, who were desperate for some pop against southpaws; six starts in less than a month was enough to convince them he wasn't going to give them what they needed. ⊘ **Brad Suttle**'s Sally League line wasn't that special, but hip and groin injuries hampered him, and a postseason MRI revealed that he had been playing with a torn labrum. If healthy, Suttle's contact skills, patient approach, and reliable glove could stand out.

Pitchers

PLAYER	TEAM	LVL	AGE	W	L	SV	IP	H	BB	SO	HR	GB%	BABIP	STUFF	WHIP	ERA	DERA	EqH9	EqBB9	EqSO9	EqHR9	DEF	VORP
C. Britton	SWB	AAA	25	3	1	0	27²	28	7	26	2	47.6%	.333	-5	1.26	2.27	2.84	11.0	2.5	5.7	1.1	-1	7.8
	NYA	MLB	25	0	0	0	23	28	11	12	4	26.8%	.312	-25	1.70	5.09	4.70	10.2	3.9	3.9	1.6	-1	1.8
A. Claggett	TRN	AA	23	4	2	9	58²	52	30	55	1	54.6%	.303	7	1.40	2.15	3.67	9.4	4.5	6.1	0.3	1	12.1
W. De La Rosa*	CSC	A	23	7	3	0	90¹	60	39	110	2	44.9%	.282	6	1.10	2.29	5.29	8.3	5.5	5.8	0.7	-2	2.8
	TAM	A+	23	2	1	0	16¹	12	5	15	0	55.6%	.267	5	1.04	1.10	3.52	7.6	3.5	4.7	0.6	-1	3.5
M. Dunn*	TAM	A+	23	4	7	1	124²	124	58	118	10	42.3%	.337	-28	1.46	4.55	7.75	11.7	5.4	5.0	1.8	-1	-26.3
C. Garcia	TAM	A+	22	4	2	0	49²	45	17	60	2	47.3%	.344	15	1.25	2.90	5.44	10.9	4.0	6.6	1.0	-1	0.8
E. Hacker	TAM	A+	25	2	2	0	53	38	9	31	1	56.8%	.242	-4	0.89	1.87	5.81	7.5	2.2	2.6	0.6	9	-1.1
	TRN	AA	25	7	4	0	91¹	83	28	84	3	49.0%	.313	16	1.22	2.76	5.29	10.2	2.9	6.3	0.5	10	2.9
A. Horne	TAM	A+	25	0	1	0	7	21	5	6	4	42.4%	.607	-97	3.71	23.14	27.00	48.2	11.6	5.8	15.4	-5	-11.2
	SWB	AAA	25	2	3	0	32	35	22	24	2	50.5%	.330	-16	1.78	5.63	8.60	11.6	6.5	4.2	0.9	0	-10.1
K. Igawa*	SWB	AAA	28	14	6	0	156¹	141	45	117	15	37.6%	.275	-11	1.19	3.45	5.73	9.6	3.0	4.4	1.3	14	-2.1
S. Jackson	TRN	AA	26	1	3	2	31¹	28	12	37	2	50.6%	.338	4	1.28	5.75	6.75	10.6	3.5	8.4	1.0	0	-3.6
	SWB	AAA	26	3	0	4	48¹	44	19	54	2	48.2%	.353	1	1.30	3.17	4.20	10.2	4.0	7.0	0.6	-1	7.0
J. Jones	TRN	AA	25	13	7	0	148²	146	49	91	11	47.2%	.284	-9	1.31	3.33	5.30	10.6	3.0	3.9	1.0	6	4.6
	SWB	AAA	25	0	1	0	11¹	6	1	11	0	41.4%	.207	11	0.62	2.39	4.91	5.7	0.8	5.7	0.0	2	0.8
J. Marquez	TRN	AA	23	1	1	0	15¹	12	7	12	0	53.8%	.304	7	1.24	2.94	3.21	9.0	3.9	5.1	0.0	-1	3.7
	SWB	AAA	23	6	7	0	80²	93	24	33	12	48.8%	.306	-39	1.45	4.68	7.21	12.2	3.1	2.1	2.1	1	-13.2
Z. McAllister	CSC	A	20	6	3	0	62¹	59	8	53	3	60.5%	.303	22	1.08	2.46	6.99	11.0	2.1	3.7	1.1	1	-8.8
	TAM	A+	20	8	6	1	88²	74	13	62	6	49.4%	.261	17	0.98	1.83	5.27	8.9	2.0	3.3	1.4	10	3.0
D. Rasner	NYA	MLB	27	5	10	0	113¹	135	39	67	14	42.9%	.319	-7	1.54	5.40	5.07	9.9	2.7	4.5	1.1	-6	-0.6
H. Sanchez	YAN	Rk	25	0	1	0	11²	9	4	15	0	50.0%	.321	-16	1.11	2.31	6.52	12.1	5.6	5.6	0.9	0	-1.0
P. Venditte	STA	A-	23	1	0	23	32²	13	10	42	2	41.6%	.171	-14	0.70	0.83	4.40	5.6	3.8	5.0	1.8	4	4.1
C. Wright*	TRN	AA	25	8	2	0	94¹	84	34	53	5	50.0%	.271	-6	1.25	2.96	5.81	9.5	3.3	3.5	0.8	14	-2.1
	SWB	AAA	25	2	1	0	37¹	27	9	19	1	53.7%	.234	-2	0.97	2.41	5.30	7.3	2.5	2.8	0.5	5	1.2

Midrotation stuff and nagging injuries made **Jeremy Bleich** a controversial 2008 supplemental pick, but he took his first step toward silencing critics by posting a sub-2.00 ERA in the Hawaiian Winter League. ⊘ The Yankees made **Andrew Brackman** their first-round pick in 2007, even though he was headed for Tommy John surgery and would miss 2008. He had poor control in college, something that carried over to his pro debut in the Hawaiian Winter League, where he walked 6.6 per nine. Brackman has tremendous height (6' 10"), a plus fastball, and a killer curve; to paraphrase Casey Stengel, Brackman has it in his body to be great, but whether or not he will be is anyone's guess. ⊘ For reasons that have never been made clear, the Yankees never gave **Chris Britton** much love, despite a fine rookie season in Baltimore and strong work at Scranton. Nontendered, he signed a minor league deal with the Padres. ⊘ The least-known part of the Gary Sheffield trade, **Anthony Claggett** polished his wares in High-A before returning to the pen at Trenton. Spotty control of his sinker got Claggett into jams, but inducing grounders at a 57 percent clip has a way of erasing mistakes. ⊘ Former outfielder **Wilkin de la Rosa** leveraged his powerful left arm into a pitching career, where a blazing fastball ensured success in his first full year on the mound; he'll have to refine his secondary offerings to avoid the bullpen at higher levels. ⊘ Formerly a college outfielder, **Mike Dunn** has a power fastball/slider assortment that needs some off-speed supplements if he's to improve on last year's beltings. ⊘ **Christian Garcia** returned from nearly two years in DL limbo (TJ and knee) with the curveball that has drawn favorable comparisons to those of Hughes and Betances; he could rise quickly if his fastball's velocity rebounds. ⊘ Before last season, 2002 draftee **Eric Hacker** had been equal parts injured and effective, losing time to elbow and shoulder surgeries. He made up for lost time in 2008, resurrecting a slow curve to pair with his lively fastball to earn a berth on the 40-man roster. ⊘ **Alan Horne**'s biceps and rotator cuff were only partially torn, but his season was irreparably damaged; suspect mechanics and persistent arm problems suggest it won't be his last season lost to injury, but it may have been his last as a starter. ⊘ **Kei Igawa** is a $20 million lemon whose fresh citrus smell the Yankees will enjoy through 2011, because there's no trade market for the import—even after the Yankees dropped him from the 40-man, no one put in a claim. ⊘ A move to the bullpen added velocity to **Steven Jackson**'s fastball, sink to his splitter, and control to his slider. According to StatCorner, Jackson led International League relievers in swinging strike-percentage, a sign that the sole remaining product of the second Randy Johnson trade may be ready to help. ⊘ Low strikeout totals and mediocre peripherals hamper **Jason Jones**'s ability to survive, but the Twins selected him in the Rule 5 draft hoping that a move to the bullpen would mask his shortcomings. ⊘ The White Sox got **Jeff Marquez** in the Swisher deal, but considering his abysmal peripherals not wholly ameliorated by his ground-ball rate or a shoulder injury that kept him out part of the year, it's hard to know what they saw in him. ⊘ A 2006 third-rounder, **Zach McAllister** hopes to ride good control and a low-90s fastball to the majors. ⊘ **Darrell Rasner**'s control act would have played in the National League or on a better defensive team, but he picked the Golden Eagles of the Japanese Pacific League. ⊘ Lumbering **Humberto Sanchez**, acquired in the Sheffield trade, arrived as a starter but has been remanded to the pen for fragility after Tommy John surgery; he was wild in Arizona Fall League action, so he'll need some work to inventory what's left. ⊘ Switch-pitcher **Pat Venditte** became an Internet sensation after he and Mets farmhand Ralph Henriquez reenacted Groucho's mirror routine from *Duck Soup*, prompting an in-season rule change. Novelty aside, Venditte throws a low-90s fastball and a plus slider. ⊘ **Chase Wright** got back on the horse after his famous four-homer Fenway debacle with a fine season split between Double- and Triple-A, but between shaky peripherals and bad memories, he didn't get recalled.

MANAGER: JOE GIRARDI

YEAR	TEAM	W-L	Pythag +/−	Avg PC	100+ P	120+ P	QS	BQS	REL	REL w Zero R	IBB	Subs	PH	PH Avg	PH HR	SB2	CS2	SB3	CS3	SAC Att	SAC %	POS SAC	Squeeze	Swing	In Play
2006	FLO	78-84	-2	94.9	74	3	86	9	436	270	58	96	247	.242	4	95	50	13	6	103	73.8%	42	4	145	104
2008	NYA	89-73	1	90.7	44	0	77	4	474	320	37	55	97	.256	4	107	36	11	3	39	79.5%	29	0	173	136

Girardi's inaugural season as Yankees manager can be summed up in one line: "Good at organizing a bullpen, bad at dealing with the press." Simply put, Girardi had problems with honesty, often refusing to admit that a player was injured, even when the general manager or the player himself was willing to confirm it. Clearly an intelligent student of baseball, Girardi often seemed to be bending under the pressure of his job, with the pointless falsehoods emanating from that insecurity. The nervousness was understandable—Girardi was about to go down in history as the man who landed the Yankees short of the playoffs for the first time since 1993, and he was following a tough act in Joe Torre. Yet, Torre's success was in large part due to his ability to defuse the tensions that surrounded the team, whereas Girardi seemed captured by them and even exacerbated them. This was a pity, because he has the makings of an excellent manager. Right off the bat, he did something Torre was unwilling or unable to do, turning to new or relatively unknown relievers. When several relievers among the team's Opening Day slate were ineffective or became injured, Girardi assembled an effective and almost entirely new pen outside of Mariano Rivera—who, coincidentally or not, had one of his best years for the new manager. Girardi was far less assertive with his lineup, letting Cano and Cabrera slump on endlessly, and playing Jose Molina even after the acquisition of Ivan Rodriguez. As an offensive manager, he clearly would like to have a faster team; he had the club stealing as often as the roster would allow, and he called for the hit-and-run more often than any other manager in the league.

Oakland Athletics

The A's went into the 2008 season with almost no expectation of sneaking up on anybody, let alone contending. General manager Billy Beane had already made a point of dispensing with many of the movable veteran components of the ballclub, dealing away Dan Haren (with Conor Robertson) for a package of prospects from Arizona, Nick Swisher for another gaggle of tyros from the White Sox, Mark Kotsay to the Braves for a pair of arms, and even shipping off Marco Scutaro to the Blue Jays for another pair. Netting 13 players—most of them quality prospects—for five with big-league experience was an aggressive bit of restocking for an organization whose self-help on the player development front had produced uneven results and served to pole-vault the club's farm system from one of the worst to one of the best. It might not have been the stuff that sells season tickets, but it was boldly done and was seen as necessary outside the organization as well as in.

Clearly, rebuilding was the standing order for the season to come; not even a modest little run at relevance in the season's opening months changed that. Although the A's managed to stay within four games of the Angels as the calendar flipped to July, there wasn't any real expectation that they'd keep pace. As the lineup struggled to plate runs all season, the rotation was the foundation of the team's modest success early on. This unit represented the team's transition from torn-down contender to retooled kiddie corps, a blend of veterans left over from the last A's division winner (Rich Harden, Joe Blanton, Chad Gaudin, and Justin Duchscherer) bolstered by a pair of pitchers brought over from Phoenix in the Haren trade (Dana Eveland and Greg

> ## ATHLETICS PROSPECTUS
>
> **2008 record:** 75-86; Third place, AL West
>
> **Pythagenport record:** 76-85
>
> **Runs scored per game:** 4.01 (14th in AL)
>
> **Runs allowed per game:** 4.33 (5th in AL)
>
> **Team EqA:** .244 (14th in AL)
>
> **2008 Batters Age:** 27.7 (3rd-youngest in AL)
>
> **2008 Pitchers Age:** 26.9 (Youngest in AL)
>
> **Ballpark:** McAfee Coliseum; Pitcher's park; Park Factor of .957
>
> **2008:** In a rebuilding year, Billy Beane's midseason machinations were the response to, not the cause of, the team's weaknesses.
>
> **2009:** After a fortifying winter Holliday, the team's first-half performance will determine whether it sets its sights on the Angels or on 2010.

Smith). Any bid to keep up appearances would depend on the rotation's performance, except that it was also the one resource likely to command additional depth in other teams' prospects. Even without getting into more fundamental concerns over whether the tragically fragile Harden would be able to last the year or if the merely workmanlike Blanton might not be good enough to keep his spot in the rotation, the commitment had been made to rebuild before the season, and the responsible choice was to stick with that plan.

There is a certain genius to being Orwellian as well as Orwell-like in the same instance. Orwell credited himself early on with "a power of facing unpleasant facts" and manifested this in his works, documenting in *Nineteen Eighty-Four* what we might glibly refer to as institutional spin-doctoring. Sure, it's just baseball, but for those ready to transform "Moneyball" into a slur (that's you, Mr. Morgan), they might credit the A's as baseball's answer to Oceania's dystopia, where objective truth and even ultimate success are warped by the need to service a purported ideology. In point of fact, the A's are an organization comfortable in the publicized awareness that, whatever the contingency generated by events, whatever unpleasant fact that Beane's crew is confronting within any particular season or with an eye toward the future, there is a plan, animated by reason, and guided by the fruits of research and careful consideration. An observer needn't be too much of a cynic to suggest that the A's fan base has been effectively indoctrinated to understand that, whatever the caprices of any one season, this guiding sense of mission is there. That's no small feat, whether we're talking Ingsoc or Moneyball. You don't need Minitrue-inspired confidence that the perpetual fight to build a better ballclub is the animating spirit of the Oakland A's, and that sacrifices, however terrible, invariably reflect that basic ambition.

As a result, there's no irony in suggesting that when the A's realized that they weren't really a contender after 2007, they sensibly began tearing down as soon as the opportunities to do so presented themselves. Tell A's fans that their ace might be dealt, and where the sports-radio scene and the local papers in most other markets might be awash with screams of outrage, in Northern California you get a measure of understanding and a concern for whether what came over in the deal serves the larger cause. Having managed expectations before the season and cautiously enjoyed the benefits of exceeding them, the A's are one of the very few organizations, perhaps the only organization, that can say that while transient overachievement was swell, it didn't really change matters any. When Team Beane communicates that there's a larger goal in play than finishing second in the AL West's short stack, it's accepted with a greater measure of faith than any other front office enjoys.

So it was no surprise that a week into July, Beane pulled off a trade with the Cubs that shipped Harden and Gaudin to Wrigley (aces as fragile as Harden perhaps need to be handcuffed to a spare, like the reproduction rules for royals). Subsequently, just after the All-Star break, Beane flipped Blanton to the Phillies. While the deals themselves weren't surprising, the return for these deals was surprising, especially from the Harden deal. As much as the A's might enjoy a deserved amount of confidence from their fans, the calculus of whether the team got value was complex and strained the comfortable faith the organization had cultivated.

Now, it's generally accepted that the A's aren't awash in cash and that they have to manage their talent and their money with the kind of care that most households can relate to. The problem is that dealing Harden (under contract for 2009) and Gaudin and Blanton (both arbitration-eligible but under team control through 2010) let the mask slip just that extra bit, leaving one to wonder if money wasn't just one of a number of considerations, but perhaps the main consideration. These weren't deals to dispatch veterans on the cusp of their free agency; this was five player-seasons of starting pitching beyond 2008 getting dealt. On the open market, five seasons' worth of that commodity, even involving pitchers as unpredictable as Harden or as merely workmanlike as Blanton and Gaudin, carries steep prices.

When you look at what the A's got from the Cubs, the concern is that instead of acquiring the talent they

needed, they acquired the talent they could settle for. It's unclear whether any of the four players brought over from the Cubs will ever contribute all that much or even outdo either of the top players coming from the Phillies in the Blanton trade. Eric Patterson's valuation swings wildly, depending on whether or not you consider him a second baseman; we've rated him among the best prospects at the position, but his defensive skills are in question, and if he can't play there, he becomes a low-powered left fielder who at best might flail a bit in center. Matt Murton is no better—slow left fielders with isolated power in the .150s had better get on base 40 percent of the time, and Murton doesn't. The prize from the swap, if anyone merits the term, was Sean Gallagher, but he's really like pitchers Greg Smith or Eveland—hurlers on the front edge of a wave of young pitchers rising up through the system, whose main virtue is that of being ready now.

To be fair, all of these hurlers have at one time or another been bandied about as onetime top prospects, and the shame of it is that the A's effectively reduced themselves to acting like a private equity firm, acquiring formerly buzz-worthy bits that might have value in some circles, and operating as a holding tank for prospects making their way from noted to middling to ex-prospects. That's all the balance of an active season plus three more starting pitcher-seasons gets you? Sounds like a pretty tough market—or a salary dump, and with Harden and Gaudin about to make $9 million in 2009 pitching for the Cubs, that may be the shoe that fits.

The question is whether the money saved was for savings' sake alone, or if there was some intent involved. As noted, the A's have a ton of young starting pitching on the way up, some of it homegrown and some of it brought in from various trades. Guys like Gallagher, Eveland, Gio Gonzalez, and Dallas Braden are only the first to arrive. But with a combination of homegrown talents like James Simmons and Trevor Cahill plus trade pickups like Brett Anderson and Josh Outman not far behind, the question isn't whether the A's have talent. It's how long they should stick with any one of them in the slots behind Duchscherer, should he or they struggle.

Similarly, the A's attention to detail has served them well in stocking the bullpen. Whether making something out of nothing in getting Brad Ziegler to change his arm slot, or getting useful types like Joey Devine, Andrew Brown, or Jerry Blevins in various deals, the A's seemed to put together a cadre of relievers out of nowhere at minimum expense. Ziegler and Devine set records for effectiveness in relatively modest amounts of playing time, headlining a unit that wound up fifth in the majors in WXRL and Fair Runs Allowed, and fourth in Adjusted Runs Prevented (ARP). Mix in Santiago Casilla's power potential in a high-leverage role among the adaptations and additions, and the A's have the makings of a no-stars relief cast that might do the job every bit as effectively as the more famous—and more expensive—assemblages. Even when or should some number of the initial crop falter, here again the organization has hard-throwing relief talent in spades, with kids like Andrew Carignan, Drew Bailey, or even Henry Rodriguez potentially capable of coming up fast if they overpower people with any consistency.

All of which leaves the question—if dealing Harden and Blanton and Gaudin was about money, and the A's are in pretty good shape with their pitching staff, where's the money supposed to go? The answer is, where it must, especially if you do want to sneak up on the league now instead of later: the offense. With a willingness to take on salary and trade depth from the bottom of their deck, the A's swapped nominal closer Huston Street, nominal rotation regular Greg Smith, and nominal outfield prospect Carlos Gonzalez to the Rockies to get Matt Holliday. There's plenty of potential for this deal to disappoint both parties. Holliday is leaving behind the easier league and one of the hittingest places in baseball to come to the tougher league and a tough park. For the Rockies, Street is a perfectly functional reliever pressed into the glory role early in his career, Smith is going to struggle putting as many people on base as he did last year while relying on a mediocre assortment of pitches, and CarGo cultism depends on a certitude that free passes are the devil's work. But Holliday is also not Emil Brown or Mike Sweeney, and while it's almost guaranteed that getting the Rockies' star is a one-year rental, adding a player due $13.5 million in 2009 suggests that the money saved is being spent with an eye to the present.

That wasn't the only move Beane and company made to fix the league's worst attack. In recognition of the crater at first base left by Daric Barton's disastrous rookie season, the A's spent $4 million to bring back their former MVP Award winner Jason Giambi, with a $6.5 million club option for 2010 for what would be the fragile slugger's age-39 season (with a $1.25 million buyout). The price was right—like past short-term commitments to Frank Thomas or John Jaha, there are risks involved, but Giambi retains enough upside to make them worthwhile. While Giambi and Jack Cust might seem to be mutually exclusive in any one team's lineup, Barton's spectacular failure and the question of how the A's outfield plays out creates overlapping op-

tions where either Giambi or Cust might play designated hitter, leaving the competition between Barton, the equally ill-starred Travis Buck, perhaps Patterson (the A's are short a leadoff hitter, after all), Murton, and Aaron Cunningham for a single lineup slot—if Barton wins, Giambi becomes the DH, and if any of the outfielders outplay Barton in camp, Cust will get the bulk of DH time.

The lineup is certainly not without its unresolved perils. The left side of the infield remains a toxic superfund site, with the A's effectively counting on Eric Chavez to be some significant fraction of his former self at third. An off-season pursuit of Raffy Furcal to address both the leadoff vacuum and Bobby Crosby's reliable absences from shortstop came to naught, leaving the question of whether settling for something in a short-term vein with Orlando Cabrera really helps the cause enough, or if trusting Crosby is worth one last roll of the dice. Similarly, center field is only notionally stocked for the time being, with a platoon of Ryan Sweeney and Rajai Davis (Ryjai Sweevis? Wasn't he in a Harry Potter book?) representing a surprising initial option instead of the 3 A.M. comfort call you might prefer it to be. In short, there's still plenty of danger that this might again be a lineup sorting through a couple of positions populated by "Staff" until the team gets a sense of where it is relative to the competition.

This last consideration is paramount, because the team is clearly taking last season's brief initial surprise flirtation with contention and the Angels' weakened Teixeira-less lot and extraordinary good luck last season as an indication that the AL West is there to be taken, even by a rebuilding team moderately stiffened with some veteran rentals. They're poised as ever in the realm of contingency, where players like Holliday or Duchscherer might be indispensable to a bid for contention or entirely available July headliners on the rumor circuit. It's a variable posture, of being ready to contend, sort of, in a weak division, and dependent on contingency. But is that any different from the A's past or future postures? As a franchise defined by its canny evaluations of value in the short, near, and long term, the A's aren't defined by Moneyball ideology, but are instead poised for whatever comes. As beaten to death as Moneyball has been, it is just a word with a life of its own, not an active faith beyond whatever its critics have imagined it to be.

On the more pragmatic level, it's perhaps best to keep in mind how Bruce Lee defined his own fluid form for victory, *Jeet Kun Do* (JKD): "Truth exists outside all molds; pattern and awareness is never exclusive … JKD is just a name used, a boat to get one across, and once across it is to be discarded and not to be carried on one's back" (Bruce Lee, *Artist of Life*, edited by John Little [Tuttle Publishing, 2001]). The A's will contend not because they adhere to some article of theory, but because they understand the need to do what it takes to get from an initial point to a better one. If there need be faith in any one thing, it's that, not Michael Lewis's best seller.

HITTERS

Jeffrey Baisley   3B

Bats: R   Throws: R   Height: 6' 3"   Weight: 210   Born: December 19, 1982   Age: 26

YEAR	TEAM	LVL	AGE	PA	R	2B	3B	HR	RBI	BB	SO	SB	CS	EqBRR	AVG	OBP	SLG	EqAVG	EqOBP	EqSLG	EqA	VORP	WARP	DEFENSE	
2006	KNC	A	23	545	86	35	1	22	110	62	86	6	1	1.0	.298	.382	.519	.198	.264	.342	.212	-30.5	-1.6	112-3B	2
2007	MID	AA	24	442	60	22	3	11	46	29	84	4	1	0.0	.257	.308	.408	.202	.244	.331	.197	-31.5	-4.1	96-3B	-16
2008	SAC	AAA	25	337	45	25	1	9	44	32	43	0	1	-1.2	.298	.374	.478	.262	.329	.413	.257	5.4	1.4	75-3B	5
2008	OAK	MLB	25	47	1	1	0	0	5	4	7	0	0	-0.0	.256	.319	.279	.256	.319	.279	.214	-1.5	-0.5	9-3B	-3
2009	OAK	MLB	26	467	35	22	1	9	47	32	106	2	1	-0.6	.205	.265	.327	.209	.270	.349	.214	-15.8	-1.1	110-3B	-4

Breakout: 26%   Improve: 43%   Collapse: 39%   Attrition: 11%   Comparables: Joe Dillon, Hunter Brown, Dave Doster, Marshall McDougall

Baisley is representative of what the A's used to do as far as player development—he's the classic polished college player who put up huge numbers in the Midwest League as a 23-year-old, but as he moved up the ladder, the power didn't come along for the ride. He has some solid on-base skills and still hits doubles, but in his brief major league debut, he was one of many to prove to the organization that he's not an everyday answer at third base. If Eric Chavez is hurt or hurting (again), a platoon with Jack Hannahan isn't out of the question, but with the platoon in center and multiple DH types hanging around, making space becomes a problem.

Wes Bankston   1B

Bats: R   Throws: R   Height: 6' 4"   Weight: 215   Born: November 23, 1983   Age: 25

YEAR	TEAM	LVL	AGE	PA	R	2B	3B	HR	RBI	BB	SO	SB	CS	EqBRR	AVG	OBP	SLG	EqAVG	EqOBP	EqSLG	EqA	VORP	WARP	DEFENSE			
2006	MNT	AA	22	183	20	7	1	4	19	12	37	4	1	-1.1	.263	.322	.389	.243	.291	.385	.235	-3.3	-1.4	29-3B	-11	4-1B	0
2006	DUR	AAA	22	207	22	13	0	5	29	10	40	0	1	-1.2	.297	.333	.441	.270	.308	.418	.247	2.1	-0.3	46-1B	-2		
2007	DUR	AAA	23	426	46	23	1	15	59	25	88	2	0	0.0	.238	.282	.418	.211	.251	.387	.219	-18.4	-1.8	77-1B	0		
2008	SAC	AAA	24	405	56	19	1	20	73	21	71	0	2	-3.1	.280	.328	.496	.251	.294	.430	.245	1.3	-0.4	54-1B	1	7-3B	-2
2008	OAK	MLB	24	63	4	3	0	1	4	2	15	0	0	-0.0	.203	.238	.305	.203	.238	.305	.185	-4.4	-0.5	12-1B	0		
2009	CIN	MLB	25	483	46	23	1	18	63	29	108	1	1	-1.2	.235	.287	.409	.234	.285	.410	.235	-4.4	-0.7	114-1B	-4		

Breakout: 28%   Improve: 50%   Collapse: 30%   Attrition: 15%   Comparables: Ryan Long, David Gibralter, Steve Dunn, Tommy Davis

Signed out of the Tampa system (where he'd stalled at the upper levels), Bankston was called up in an attempt to get some kind of run production out of the corners. But after a nice start, an 0-for-22 slump with 10 strikeouts got him sent back to Triple-A, and he wasn't heard from again. His up-and-down minor league career has shown some signs of life at times, but not enough for a player limited to first base. The A's had no more use for him, and the Reds signed him in the offseason.

Daric Barton   1B

Bats: L   Throws: R   Height: 6' 0"   Weight: 225   Born: August 16, 1985   Age: 23

YEAR	TEAM	LVL	AGE	PA	R	2B	3B	HR	RBI	BB	SO	SB	CS	EqBRR	AVG	OBP	SLG	EqAVG	EqOBP	EqSLG	EqA	VORP	WARP	DEFENSE			
2006	SAC	AAA	20	180	25	6	4	2	22	32	26	1	0	1.6	.259	.389	.395	.233	.356	.360	.258	1.0	0.4	36-1B	2		
2007	SAC	AAA	21	604	84	38	5	9	70	78	69	3	4	0.0	.293	.389	.438	.266	.359	.402	.267	16.2	1.6	111-1B	6	16-3B	-4
2007	OAK	MLB	21	84	16	9	0	4	8	10	11	1	0	0.4	.347	.429	.639	.347	.435	.653	.356	12.4	1.1	18-1B	0		
2008	OAK	MLB	22	523	59	17	5	9	47	65	99	2	1	1.6	.226	.327	.348	.226	.333	.360	.248	-7.9	-0.1	126-1B	1		
2009	OAK	MLB	23	467	56	22	3	11	52	55	75	3	2	0.1	.252	.344	.403	.257	.351	.429	.273	7.0	1.7	111-1B	3		

Breakout: 45%   Improve: 67%   Collapse: 17%   Attrition: 18%   Comparables: Keith Hernandez, Tookie Gilbert, Ken Oberkfell, Robin Ventura

Barton entered the year with high hopes, having posted a career batting line of .301/.414/.459 in the minors despite always being young for his levels. That and an impressive September 2007 showing had the A's confidently handing Barton the everyday first-base job, but then he got off to a bad start, suffered constant nagging injuries, and never found a groove. It's not that he was bad—he was downright awful. He ended the year on a high note, with four straight multihit games, and the A's are willing to give him a mulligan for the year and a second chance at the job—albeit with a much shorter leash.

Rob Bowen

| | | C | | | | | | | Bats: S | | Throws: R | | Height: 6' 3" | | Weight: 225 | | Born: February 24, 1981 | | Age: 28 |

YEAR	TEAM	LVL	AGE	PA	R	2B	3B	HR	RBI	BB	SO	SB	CS	EqBRR	AVG	OBP	SLG	EqAVG	EqOBP	EqSLG	EqA	VORP	WARP	DEFENSE	
2006	SDN	MLB	25	110	22	5	0	3	13	13	26	0	1	-0.7	.245	.339	.394	.255	.355	.426	.270	1.7	0.4	22-C	0
2007	SDN	MLB	26	98	12	8	0	2	11	13	28	1	2	-0.6	.268	.371	.439	.280	.388	.476	.287	5.1	0.5	23-C	-2
2007	CHN	MLB	26	36	3	1	0	0	2	4	13	0	0	0.2	.065	.167	.097	.065	.167	.097	.000	-5.7	-0.3	9-C	1
2007	OAK	MLB	26	54	6	1	0	2	5	10	20	0	0	0.2	.279	.415	.442	.279	.426	.442	.308	4.5	0.3	15-C	-2
2008	OAK	MLB	27	98	6	5	1	1	9	4	38	0	0	0.3	.176	.219	.286	.176	.219	.286	.167	-7.0	-0.7	25-C	-1
2009	OAK	MLB	28	153	15	7	1	4	16	15	48	1	1	0.0	.221	.305	.373	.226	.311	.397	.247	2.8	0.8	40-C	-2

Breakout: 57% Improve: 67% Collapse: 24% Attrition: 47%   Comparables: Tom Egan, Phil Roof, Dave Roberts, Tim Laudner

Bowen won the right to back up the young, durable Kurt Suzuki, who started 136 games last year. As a result, Bowen got little playing time and did little with it, but you can find plenty of regulars who do something like this in 100 at-bats or less. Bowen is better than this—switch-hitting backstops who draw the occasional walk, hit the occasional home run, and play solid defense have their uses. The A's recognized this and will bring him back in the same role for 2009.

Corey Brown

| | | OF | | | | | | | Bats: L | | Throws: L | | Height: 6' 2" | | Weight: 190 | | Born: November 26, 1985 | | Age: 23 |

YEAR	TEAM	LVL	AGE	PA	R	2B	3B	HR	RBI	BB	SO	SB	CS	EqBRR	AVG	OBP	SLG	EqAVG	EqOBP	EqSLG	EqA	VORP	WARP	DEFENSE			
2007	VAN	A-	21	256	31	18	4	11	48	37	77	5	3	-3.1	.268	.379	.545	.191	.266	.361	.216	-23.0	-2.5	36-CF	-6	17-RF	-4
2008	KNC	A	22	351	44	18	2	14	49	41	96	12	0	1.1	.270	.359	.483	.215	.292	.386	.239	-7.7	-0.8	72-CF	-8		
2008	STO	A+	22	214	34	9	0	16	34	17	72	4	1	0.8	.260	.322	.551	.216	.274	.442	.242	-2.1	-0.1	42-CF	-2		
2009	OAK	MLB	23	526	51	25	2	16	59	46	170	7	3	0.9	.213	.285	.378	.217	.291	.402	.240	-5.0	0.7	124-CF	-5		

Breakout: 45% Improve: 62% Collapse: 19% Attrition: 10%   Comparables: Eric Valent, Louie Meadows, Jason Cooper, Sergio Pedroza

A supplemental first-round pick in 2007, Brown is a bit of a strange bird. He's got plenty of tools, as evidenced by 30 home runs and 16 stolen bases in his full-season debut, and he plays a nice center while showcasing a solid arm. Then there are the strikeouts; 168 of them in 496 at-bats, 34 percent of his at-bats, 30 percent of his PAs—you get the point, a lot of strikeouts. Even still, it's quite common to see him shorten his swing with two strikes and use the opposite field. He's a difficult player to project because of the gap between what he is and what scouts see, but at the very least, there's something here to build on.

Emil Brown

| | | LF | | | | | | | Bats: R | | Throws: R | | Height: 6' 2" | | Weight: 210 | | Born: December 29, 1974 | | Age: 34 |

YEAR	TEAM	LVL	AGE	PA	R	2B	3B	HR	RBI	BB	SO	SB	CS	EqBRR	AVG	OBP	SLG	EqAVG	EqOBP	EqSLG	EqA	VORP	WARP	DEFENSE			
2006	KCA	MLB	31	601	77	41	2	15	81	59	95	6	3	0.3	.287	.358	.457	.274	.352	.443	.276	18.7	3.1	82-LF	-2	47-RF	9
2007	KCA	MLB	32	397	44	13	1	6	62	24	71	12	2	3.7	.257	.300	.347	.250	.297	.346	.232	-9.1	-0.7	68-LF	-1	17-RF	0
2008	OAK	MLB	33	438	48	14	2	13	59	27	65	4	2	-0.7	.244	.297	.386	.247	.301	.401	.243	-5.8	-0.2	49-RF	-2	46-LF	1
2009	OAK	MLB	34	270	28	11	1	6	32	20	46	4	1	-0.3	.247	.304	.378	.252	.310	.403	.250	-1.1	0.3	66-LF	-1		

Breakout: 23% Improve: 41% Collapse: 36% Attrition: 43%   Comparables: Gary Ward, Mike Devereaux, Brian Jordan, Gino Cimoli

The A's signed Brown to be a fourth outfielder and platoon partner against left-handers, but a combination of injuries and flameouts had him playing nearly every day between the two corners. He was stretched as a regular even in his prime (and we use that term loosely) during his Royals days, but declining skills in his early 30s have him barely worth a job anymore, let alone a regular spot. He's spending his offseason looking for work and will probably get no more than a nonroster invite.

Travis Buck OF

Bats: L   Throws: R   Height: 6' 2"   Weight: 225   Born: November 18, 1983   Age: 25

YEAR	TEAM	LVL	AGE	PA	R	2B	3B	HR	RBI	BB	SO	SB	CS	EqBRR	AVG	OBP	SLG	EqAVG	EqOBP	EqSLG	EqA	VORP	WARP	DEFENSE			
2006	STO	A+	22	145	24	17	3	3	26	14	18	2	1	1.2	.349	.400	.603	.277	.324	.500	.276	7.2	0.4	34-LF	-2		
2006	MID	AA	22	238	32	22	1	4	22	22	39	9	1	1.5	.302	.376	.472	.252	.315	.399	.251	0.5	3.2	50-LF	23		
2007	OAK	MLB	23	334	41	22	5	7	34	39	66	4	1	-0.1	.288	.377	.474	.290	.381	.495	.300	19.9	2.5	57-RF	1	14-LF	1
2008	SAC	AAA	24	197	28	8	2	2	17	25	34	4	1	2.1	.296	.396	.402	.266	.355	.364	.258	2.3	0.3	20-CF	-5	13-RF	0
2008	OAK	MLB	24	172	16	9	1	7	25	11	38	1	0	-1.7	.226	.291	.432	.232	.297	.452	.256	-0.7	0.7	32-RF	2	5-LF	2
2009	OAK	MLB	25	446	52	23	3	11	51	42	96	5	2	-0.1	.251	.328	.409	.257	.335	.435	.268	5.4	2.0	106-RF	5		

Breakout: 12%   Improve: 42%   Collapse: 29%   Attrition: 12%   Comparables: Bronson Sardinha, George Vukovich, Seth Smith, Ed Kirkpatrick

After an impressive rookie campaign, the wheels totally came off for Buck in 2008. He began the year in an 0-for-21 slump, hit the DL shortly thereafter due to shin splints, and never really got on track. Things got even worse after he suffered a concussion at Triple-A. Beyond the injuries, Buck did himself no favors by tinkering with his mechanics, which just led to further issues. The Holliday trade means that Buck is likely to be stuck in a reserve role this year, and he'll have to earn even that much.

Adrian Cardenas INF

Bats: L   Throws: R   Height: 6' 0"   Weight: 185   Born: October 10, 1987   Age: 21

YEAR	TEAM	LVL	AGE	PA	R	2B	3B	HR	RBI	BB	SO	SB	CS	EqBRR	AVG	OBP	SLG	EqAVG	EqOBP	EqSLG	EqA	VORP	WARP	DEFENSE	
2006	PHL	Rk	18	177	22	5	4	2	21	17	28	13	3	1.0	.318	.384	.442	.242	.294	.373	.233	-10.9	-0.9	41-SS	-7
2007	LWD	A	19	564	70	30	2	9	79	47	80	19	7	1.4	.295	.354	.417	.243	.291	.336	.223	-21.0	-2.3	123-2B	-14
2008	CLR	A+	20	293	44	11	6	4	23	28	42	16	0	3.2	.307	.371	.441	.270	.325	.408	.261	4.4	-0.2	64-2B	-11
2008	STO	A+	20	74	11	1	0	1	10	1	14	1	0	1.3	.278	.297	.333	.219	.240	.274	.173	-6.7	-1.2	12-2B	-6
2008	MID	AA	20	102	12	4	0	0	7	15	10	0	1	-1.8	.279	.392	.326	.236	.340	.270	.221	-3.5	-0.7	26-SS	-6
2009	OAK	MLB	21	577	59	26	4	8	48	43	106	13	5	1.9	.242	.300	.349	.247	.307	.372	.240	0.0	-0.2	135-2B	-12

Breakout: 36%   Improve: 68%   Collapse: 8%   Attrition: 4%   Comparables: Dave Hansen, Brent Abernathy, Jason Romano, Trey Beamon

Although Josh Outman was the player who reached the big leagues first, Cardenas was actually the key player in the Blanton deal. One of the best pure hitters in the minors, Cardenas has a textbook swing that has most scouts seeing him as a future .300 hitter in the big leagues with gap power, and the only question is where he'll end up defensively. He's playing shortstop for now, but most think he'll end up moving to the left or right, depending on how much power shows up. Either way, his bat should be enough for the position.

Christopher Carter 1B

Bats: R   Throws: R   Height: 6' 4"   Weight: 210   Born: December 18, 1986   Age: 22

YEAR	TEAM	LVL	AGE	PA	R	2B	3B	HR	RBI	BB	SO	SB	CS	EqBRR	AVG	OBP	SLG	EqAVG	EqOBP	EqSLG	EqA	VORP	WARP	DEFENSE			
2006	GRF	Rk	19	294	37	21	1	15	59	34	70	4	4	-3.1	.299	.398	.570	.211	.275	.389	.225	-16.3	-2.4	59-1B	-6		
2006	KAN	A	19	52	4	3	0	1	5	5	17	0	0	-0.8	.130	.231	.261	.104	.173	.208	.086	-9.4	-1.0	6-1B	-1		
2007	KAN	A	20	545	84	27	3	25	93	67	112	3	2	-0.7	.291	.383	.522	.222	.299	.392	.240	-8.1	-1.4	73-1B	-5		
2008	STO	A+	21	596	101	32	4	39	104	77	156	4	0	-4.3	.259	.361	.569	.212	.305	.454	.259	5.4	-1.4	38-3B	-14	38-1B	-5
2009	OAK	MLB	22	586	56	26	1	23	74	57	171	2	1	-0.9	.208	.290	.395	.213	.296	.421	.247	-6.7	-0.3	137-1B	-5		

Breakout: 29%   Improve: 54%   Collapse: 21%   Attrition: 9%   Comparables: Jonny Gomes, Kala Ka'aihue, Mike Bishop, Joe Citari

Carter had a busy offseason, moving from the White Sox to Arizona in the Carlos Quentin deal, and lasting a week or so there before moving on to Oakland as part of the Haren package. Oakland is glad he's with them after he led the minors in extra-base hits and total bases, despite hitting just .259—only 56 of his 131 hits were singles. He's an incredibly streaky hitter whose homers come in bunches, as do his strikeouts. The A's hope he can improve enough at third base to stay there, but most see him as a first baseman in the end, with some observers even throwing Ryan Howard comps out there.

Eric Chavez — 3B

Bats: L   Throws: R   Height: 6' 1"   Weight: 230   Born: December 7, 1977   Age: 31

YEAR	TEAM	LVL	AGE	PA	R	2B	3B	HR	RBI	BB	SO	SB	CS	EqBRR	AVG	OBP	SLG	EqAVG	EqOBP	EqSLG	EqA	VORP	WARP	DEFENSE	
2006	OAK	MLB	28	576	74	24	2	22	72	84	100	3	0	-3.2	.241	.351	.435	.228	.349	.418	.271	14.4	2.7	130-3B	4
2007	OAK	MLB	29	379	43	21	2	15	46	34	76	4	2	-2.6	.240	.306	.446	.239	.309	.457	.260	6.0	1.4	87-3B	3
2008	OAK	MLB	30	95	10	7	0	2	14	6	18	0	0	-0.1	.247	.295	.393	.247	.295	.416	.242	-0.5	0.0	15-3B	0
2009	OAK	MLB	31	331	36	15	1	11	43	35	70	2	0	-1.3	.238	.320	.408	.243	.326	.435	.263	6.5	1.3	80-3B	0

Breakout: 17%   Improve: 52%   Collapse: 28%   Attrition: 24%   Comparables: Leon Durham, Corey Koskie, Wayne Gross, Robin Ventura

Chavez didn't make his 2008 debut until the end of May while he recovered from back surgery, and he lasted a total of 23 games before his shredded shoulder went under the knife for major repair—the surgery was actually a "three-in-one" that attempted to fix a number of issues in the joint. He's expected to be done rehabbing by the time spring rolls around, and he's penciled in as the starting third baseman. The A's don't have many other worthwhile options, but Chavez is now five years removed from his classic seasons, and the chips are stacked against him.

Brooks Conrad — INF

Bats: S   Throws: R   Height: 5' 11"   Weight: 190   Born: January 16, 1980   Age: 29

YEAR	TEAM	LVL	AGE	PA	R	2B	3B	HR	RBI	BB	SO	SB	CS	EqBRR	AVG	OBP	SLG	EqAVG	EqOBP	EqSLG	EqA	VORP	WARP	DEFENSE			
2006	ROU	AAA	26	599	100	40	15	24	94	54	135	15	6	3.1	.267	.334	.534	.229	.290	.459	.254	4.4	2.6	97-2B	9	37-3B	-1
2007	ROU	AAA	27	605	85	36	3	22	70	63	144	12	3	0.0	.218	.305	.420	.177	.257	.337	.208	-39.2	-4.2	120-2B	-19	11-3B	-2
2008	SAC	AAA	28	517	86	29	5	28	91	46	127	4	1	1.4	.243	.313	.508	.191	.250	.387	.217	-23.7	-1.8	53-2B	-4	18-SS	-3
2008	OAK	MLB	28	19	0	1	0	0	2	0	9	0	0	-0.0	.158	.158	.211	.158	.158	.211	.000	-2.5	-0.3				
2009	ATL	MLB	29	474	45	24	3	15	53	42	136	6	3	1.0	.200	.274	.374	.200	.273	.385	.225	-7.1	-0.2	112-2B	-6		

Breakout: 32%   Improve: 62%   Collapse: 17%   Attrition: 16%   Comparables: Joe Dillon, Mike Coolbaugh, Chase Lambin, Dave Campbell

Despite hitting 69 home runs during his last three years at Triple-A for the Astros, Conrad got nary of whiff of the big leagues, being categorized as an undersized, light-on-tools hacker who plays four positions, but none of them well. He hit another 28 bombs last year to add to his Pacific Coast League star status in his first season with the A's organization and finally got the call for a couple weeks. He wound up showing that his reputation is there for a reason, and at 29, his window is closing. Hitting the road again, his next stop is Atlanta.

Bobby Crosby — SS

Bats: R   Throws: R   Height: 6' 3"   Weight: 215   Born: January 12, 1980   Age: 29

YEAR	TEAM	LVL	AGE	PA	R	2B	3B	HR	RBI	BB	SO	SB	CS	EqBRR	AVG	OBP	SLG	EqAVG	EqOBP	EqSLG	EqA	VORP	WARP	DEFENSE	
2006	OAK	MLB	26	398	42	12	0	9	40	36	76	8	1	0.8	.229	.298	.338	.220	.295	.327	.225	-3.3	0.1	92-SS	-1
2007	OAK	MLB	27	374	40	16	0	8	31	23	62	10	2	1.9	.226	.278	.341	.224	.280	.351	.223	-4.6	0.8	91-SS	6
2008	OAK	MLB	28	605	66	39	1	7	61	47	96	7	3	2.9	.237	.296	.349	.241	.302	.365	.234	-1.8	1.5	142-SS	5
2009	OAK	MLB	29	462	47	22	2	8	46	37	80	7	2	0.3	.240	.304	.356	.245	.310	.380	.243	4.6	1.1	109-SS	1

Breakout: 42%   Improve: 66%   Collapse: 21%   Attrition: 34%   Comparables: Scott Leius, Andre Rodgers, Frank Duffy, Mark Lewis

The A's finally got a healthy year out of Bobby Crosby in 2008, his first since his Rookie of the Year campaign in 2004. The problem was, his power completely disappeared. Even when he hit 22 home runs, he was overrated because of his lack of average and walks, but when he hits seven, he's downright valueless. Put it this way—if he'd hit that 40th double last year, he would have had the lowest slugging percentage of any player to hit 40, replacing Pete Rose's 1980 campaign for the honor. ("Hit King," indeed.) The A's tried to find a replacement this winter, even placing Crosby on outright waivers in December, but nobody bit and Rafael Furcal spurned them, leaving the A's to pay Crosby the $5.25 million due in the final year of his contract.

Aaron Cunningham — OF

Bats: R Throws: R Height: 5' 11" Weight: 195 Born: April 24, 1986 Age: 23

YEAR	TEAM	LVL	AGE	PA	R	2B	3B	HR	RBI	BB	SO	SB	CS	EqBRR	AVG	OBP	SLG	EqAVG	EqOBP	EqSLG	EqA	VORP	WARP	DEFENSE			
2006	KAN	A	20	402	58	26	3	11	41	34	72	19	10	2.9	.305	.386	.496	.235	.291	.384	.235	-7.9	-1.1	79-LF	-4	7-RF	-1
2007	WNS	A+	21	306	51	12	5	8	37	34	39	22	8	0.0	.294	.376	.476	.228	.296	.371	.238	-7.1	-2.0	36-RF	-6	26-LF	-9
2007	VIS	A+	21	135	25	11	2	3	20	5	23	5	3	-0.8	.358	.386	.553	.270	.295	.413	.240	0.2	0.0	16-CF	2	6-RF	1
2007	MOB	AA	21	132	25	8	3	5	20	12	27	1	3	-0.2	.288	.364	.534	.248	.311	.471	.257	3.7	-0.3	19-RF	0	9-CF	-5
2008	MID	AA	22	401	65	18	6	12	52	38	92	12	4	0.4	.317	.386	.507	.263	.324	.433	.262	8.4	0.7	59-CF	-11	22-LF	6
2008	SAC	AAA	22	89	21	5	0	5	14	11	16	3	1	0.1	.382	.461	.645	.346	.422	.590	.335	12.7	1.1	16-RF	0		
2008	OAK	MLB	22	87	7	7	1	1	14	6	24	2	0	-0.4	.250	.310	.400	.250	.310	.400	.250	0.5	0.2	17-LF	1		
2009	OAK	MLB	23	547	61	28	3	13	59	44	132	11	5	1.8	.247	.313	.399	.253	.320	.425	.259	2.7	1.3	128-LF	2		

Breakout: 28% Improve: 59% Collapse: 17% Attrition: 10% Comparables: Cody Ross, Paul Householder, Alonzo Powell, Randy Washington

Like Carter, Cunningham was originally drafted by the White Sox and came to Oakland through Arizona in the Haren deal. The quick changes of organizations mean he's played in seven minor league circuits in his short career, but he's hit in every one of them, producing a career minor league batting line of .311/.384/.496. In many ways, he's a righty version of a pre-2008 Travis Buck, where the batting average and on-base skills are there, but there are questions about his power ceiling as a corner outfielder. One of 12 players used in the outfield by the A's last year, the Holliday pick-up means he'll probably spend most of the year at Triple-A in preparation for a job in 2010.

Jack Cust — DH

Bats: L Throws: R Height: 6' 1" Weight: 230 Born: January 16, 1979 Age: 30

YEAR	TEAM	LVL	AGE	PA	R	2B	3B	HR	RBI	BB	SO	SB	CS	EqBRR	AVG	OBP	SLG	EqAVG	EqOBP	EqSLG	EqA	VORP	WARP	DEFENSE			
2006	POR	AAA	27	591	97	23	0	30	77	143	124	0	3	0.0	.293	.467	.549	.240	.402	.457	.300	36.4	1.8	117-LF	-20		
2007	POR	AAA	28	100	17	7	0	9	20	19	29	0	0	0.2	.300	.430	.725	.241	.366	.554	.305	8.0	0.8	14-LF	0		
2007	OAK	MLB	28	507	61	18	1	26	82	105	164	0	2	-3.8	.256	.408	.504	.254	.416	.522	.319	34.7	3.4	43-RF	-8	9-LF	-1
2008	OAK	MLB	29	598	77	19	0	33	77	111	197	0	0	1.5	.231	.375	.476	.234	.386	.497	.302	29.6	3.7	66-LF	-3	4-RF	0
2009	OAK	MLB	30	599	79	21	1	28	83	108	180	0	0	-2.3	.234	.375	.456	.240	.383	.485	.300	23.7	2.7	140-LF	-15		

Breakout: 12% Improve: 33% Collapse: 20% Attrition: 20% Comparables: Jim Thome, Jason Thompson, Ken Phelps, Erubiel Durazo

What's the difference between Cust and Adam Dunn at this point? Not really all that much—they're both horrible outfielders who don't hit for average, but both more than make up for it with home runs and tons of walks. Cust is almost comically bad defensively, and 2008 represented a small turn backward, so another step in that direction makes him a true liability. In any case, we're done betting against him and will simply book him for winding up with something like 30 home runs and 100 walks again.

Rajai Davis — CF

Bats: R Throws: R Height: 5' 11" Weight: 195 Born: October 19, 1980 Age: 28

YEAR	TEAM	LVL	AGE	PA	R	2B	3B	HR	RBI	BB	SO	SB	CS	EqBRR	AVG	OBP	SLG	EqAVG	EqOBP	EqSLG	EqA	VORP	WARP	DEFENSE			
2006	IND	AAA	25	417	53	17	1	2	21	27	59	45	13	6.9	.283	.335	.348	.250	.299	.312	.224	-17.1	-0.6	75-CF	3	17-LF	-3
2007	IND	AAA	26	239	31	12	4	4	30	21	25	27	9	-2.4	.318	.384	.469	.279	.340	.437	.271	8.4	0.8	26-LF	-4	26-CF	2
2007	PIT	MLB	26	57	6	2	1	0	2	7	3	5	2	-0.9	.271	.357	.354	.292	.386	.375	.273	1.5	0.1	9-CF	-1		
2007	SFN	MLB	26	162	26	9	1	1	7	14	25	17	4	3.5	.282	.363	.380	.289	.369	.387	.274	7.2	0.9	33-CF	2		
2008	SFN	MLB	27	19	2	0	0	0	0	1	6	4	0	0.6	.056	.105	.056	.056	.105	.056	.089	-2.7	-0.3				
2008	OAK	MLB	27	207	28	5	4	3	19	7	34	25	6	2.5	.260	.288	.372	.270	.301	.398	.253	2.5	0.3	52-CF	0		
2009	OAK	MLB	28	212	27	9	2	3	18	15	34	16	5	1.4	.254	.310	.359	.259	.316	.382	.252	1.6	0.7	53-CF	-1		

Breakout: 25% Improve: 47% Collapse: 31% Attrition: 33% Comparables: Jacob Brumfield, Jason Ellison, Gary Thurman, Jim Wohlford

Davis was released toward the end of April after getting off to a 1-for-18 start with the Giants, and the A's quickly snapped him up in their quest to find anyone who can play center field. Like Mayan agriculture, he's a hacker and burner whose impatient ways don't fit well with philosophies over what constitutes stable production, but he can go get it in the outfield, and his 25 stolen bases represented nearly 30 percent of the A's team total. He's got some use as an extra outfielder with wheels, and he'll probably retain that job this year, substituting for Sweeney in center.

Chris Denorfia   OF   Bats: R   Throws: R   Height: 6' 0"   Weight: 195   Born: July 15, 1980   Age: 28

YEAR	TEAM	LVL	AGE	PA	R	2B	3B	HR	RBI	BB	SO	SB	CS	EqBRR	AVG	OBP	SLG	EqAVG	EqOBP	EqSLG	EqA	VORP	WARP	DEFENSE			
2006	LOU	AAA	25	353	46	19	1	7	45	34	41	15	1	4.0	.349	.409	.484	.311	.371	.448	.289	22.4	1.2	59-CF	-7	12-RF	-1
2006	CIN	MLB	25	120	14	6	0	1	7	11	21	1	1	0.2	.283	.356	.368	.271	.350	.346	.248	0.8	0.6	13-RF	2	10-CF	3
2008	SAC	AAA	27	204	34	13	1	2	20	12	31	5	4	0.0	.302	.342	.413	.250	.286	.349	.219	-6.4	-1.9	37-CF	-13		
2008	OAK	MLB	27	71	10	3	0	1	9	6	16	2	0	-0.2	.290	.362	.387	.290	.362	.387	.271	2.8	0.0	8-LF	-3	8-CF	1
2009	OAK	MLB	28	320	33	14	1	4	29	23	62	6	2	0.4	.252	.308	.355	.257	.314	.378	.244	-0.9	0.0	77-CF	-8		

Breakout: 18%   Improve: 37%   Collapse: 44%   Attrition: 30%   Comparables: Jason Ellison, Marlon Byrd, Bruce Fields, Mike Brown

It's easy to forget Denorfia in the A's outfield shuffle, but he's still here, having spent 2008 proving he could still play after losing 2007 to the knee injury that made him available in the first place. His power potential was never all that great to start off with, so he's really only in the running for a reserve role, and if he can't play center reliably, even that's in doubt.

Sean Doolittle   1B   Bats: L   Throws: L   Height: 6' 3"   Weight: 190   Born: September 26, 1986   Age: 22

YEAR	TEAM	LVL	AGE	PA	R	2B	3B	HR	RBI	BB	SO	SB	CS	EqBRR	AVG	OBP	SLG	EqAVG	EqOBP	EqSLG	EqA	VORP	WARP	DEFENSE			
2007	VAN	A-	20	57	6	3	0	0	4	9	10	0	0	-0.5	.283	.421	.348	.216	.310	.255	.205	-6.2	-0.4	12-1B	0		
2007	KNC	A	20	222	23	10	0	4	29	24	40	1	0	0.0	.233	.320	.347	.175	.247	.265	.177	-22.0	-1.9	49-1B	1		
2008	STO	A+	21	384	64	25	3	18	61	46	99	7	3	-1.3	.305	.385	.560	.246	.323	.446	.264	8.6	0.0	64-1B	-6	7-LF	0
2008	MID	AA	21	219	25	15	0	4	30	17	54	1	1	-0.4	.254	.311	.388	.216	.265	.333	.206	-12.0	-1.1	40-1B	1	10-RF	0
2009	OAK	MLB	22	602	54	30	2	14	64	51	168	5	3	-0.3	.222	.290	.362	.227	.295	.386	.236	-14.9	-0.3	141-1B	5		

Breakout: 43%   Improve: 62%   Collapse: 15%   Attrition: 6%   Comparables: George Canale, Kevin Barker, Chris Weinke, A. J. Zapp

Doolittle entered the year as a Gold Glove–caliber first baseman with the ability to hit for average, but debatable power potential. He took steps toward answering that question by delivering 18 home runs in 86 Cal League games, then let the question crop up again with just four in 51 contests after a promotion to Double-A. He then answered it all over again with eight shots in 116 Arizona Fall League at-bats. What's real? Scouts aren't sure yet, and while his stock is up, nobody is throwing around a "strong buy" recommendation yet.

Mark Ellis   2B   Bats: R   Throws: R   Height: 5' 11"   Weight: 190   Born: June 6, 1977   Age: 32

YEAR	TEAM	LVL	AGE	PA	R	2B	3B	HR	RBI	BB	SO	SB	CS	EqBRR	AVG	OBP	SLG	EqAVG	EqOBP	EqSLG	EqA	VORP	WARP	DEFENSE	
2006	OAK	MLB	29	500	64	25	1	11	52	40	76	4	0	2.8	.249	.319	.385	.242	.317	.379	.248	8.4	1.6	119-2B	6
2007	OAK	MLB	30	642	84	33	3	19	76	44	94	9	4	-1.2	.276	.336	.441	.278	.340	.460	.273	26.2	6.6	148-2B	29
2008	OAK	MLB	31	507	55	20	3	12	41	53	65	14	2	1.1	.233	.321	.373	.237	.329	.396	.258	4.8	3.9	114-2B	20
2009	OAK	MLB	32	508	57	25	2	12	56	45	75	8	3	0.4	.248	.321	.394	.253	.328	.420	.262	12.6	3.0	120-2B	9

Breakout: 24%   Improve: 45%   Collapse: 25%   Attrition: 13%   Comparables: John Valentin, Phil Garner, Scott Brosius, Vance Law

While Ellis's batting averages have had a Saberhagen-like odd/even feel to them, his secondary skills remain consistently decent, with average power for the position and a solid share of free passes. Moreover, everything he does is made that much more valuable by absolutely flawless performance at second base. Dustin Pedroia won the Gold Glove there because of his offensive breakthrough, but Ellis is the best defensive second baseman in the game. Even after he struggled during the second half with shoulder problems, the A's brought him back for two more years at the same sort of money, figuring they can ride the ups and downs at the plate as long as they get the glove work.

Carlos Gonzalez CF Bats: L Throws: L Height: 6' 1" Weight: 200 Born: October 17, 1985 Age: 23

YEAR	TEAM	LVL	AGE	PA	R	2B	3B	HR	RBI	BB	SO	SB	CS	EqBRR	AVG	OBP	SLG	EqAVG	EqOBP	EqSLG	EqA	VORP	WARP	DEFENSE			
2006	LNC	A+	20	452	82	35	4	21	94	30	104	15	8	0.5	.300	.356	.563	.211	.255	.400	.225	-15.7	-1.6	95-RF	-4		
2006	TEN	AA	20	69	11	6	0	2	5	7	12	1	0	1.6	.213	.294	.410	.210	.279	.419	.241	-1.2	-0.4	15-RF	-3		
2007	MOB	AA	21	499	63	33	3	16	75	32	103	9	5	-0.9	.286	.330	.476	.247	.285	.423	.242	-2.5	-0.2	92-RF	-5	22-CF	3
2007	TUC	AAA	21	48	9	5	0	1	11	6	6	1	0	-1.4	.310	.396	.500	.262	.354	.429	.276	1.7	0.3	11-CF	1		
2008	SAC	AAA	22	189	23	9	1	4	28	16	35	1	1	-1.4	.283	.344	.416	.251	.307	.360	.232	-3.1	-0.6	31-CF	-4	11-RF	0
2008	OAK	MLB	22	316	31	22	1	4	26	13	81	4	1	1.3	.242	.273	.361	.243	.276	.369	.223	-6.6	-0.3	59-CF	3	18-RF	-1
2009	COL	MLB	23	487	58	31	2	14	62	32	107	6	3	0.5	.274	.323	.448	.257	.307	.424	.249	5.0	1.2	115-CF	-4		

Breakout: 44% Improve: 81% Collapse: 7% Attrition: 6%   Comparables: Pedro Valdes, Lloyd Moseby, Felix Jose, Alex Fernandez

Gonzalez's tools have always enamored scouts, but his effort has often left much to be desired. He got off to a decent enough start at Sacramento, which was enough for Oakland to give him a shot at the center-field job, which he really wasn't ready to handle at the plate. He's still young and immensely talented, but his problems are now Colorado's to handle, because after being the main cog in the Haren trade, he was a key factor in the deal that netted Matt Holliday for Oakland. For good as well as bad, this kind of talent's being on his third team in one calendar year does sort of tell you something about how much upside people anticipate for him.

Jack Hannahan 3B Bats: L Throws: R Height: 6' 2" Weight: 205 Born: March 4, 1980 Age: 29

YEAR	TEAM	LVL	AGE	PA	R	2B	3B	HR	RBI	BB	SO	SB	CS	EqBRR	AVG	OBP	SLG	EqAVG	EqOBP	EqSLG	EqA	VORP	WARP	DEFENSE			
2006	TOL	AAA	26	494	59	27	0	9	62	61	114	9	6	-5.0	.282	.379	.412	.248	.339	.378	.255	2.9	1.1	50-2B	2	40-3B	-3
2007	TOL	AAA	27	417	56	20	1	13	63	76	92	5	5	-2.1	.295	.422	.476	.251	.371	.428	.279	17.0	3.2	35-2B	4	20-3B	5
2007	OAK	MLB	27	169	16	12	0	3	24	21	39	1	0	-0.4	.278	.369	.424	.280	.375	.448	.288	7.4	0.5	41-3B	-5		
2008	OAK	MLB	28	501	48	27	0	9	47	55	131	2	0	-0.5	.218	.305	.342	.218	.311	.354	.238	-9.9	0.1	110-3B	2	9-1B	0
2009	OAK	MLB	29	318	32	14	1	9	36	38	83	3	1	-0.8	.224	.319	.375	.229	.325	.399	.255	2.7	1.0	77-3B	1		

Breakout: 21% Improve: 47% Collapse: 34% Attrition: 38%   Comparables: Jack Howell, Scott Cooper, Ed Bouchee, Jim Marshall

A career minor leaguer in the Tigers' system, Hannahan was acquired at the end of 2007 as an emergency pickup, and when you're a team with a multiyear commitment to Eric Chavez as the starter to observe, keeping someone around as an insurance policy is a necessity. Unfortunately, Hannahan was more like the agent who shows up at the scene of your car accident and promptly bashes out your headlights with a sledge hammer for getting him out of his cubicle. Nonetheless, the A's paid their premium to bring him back, 'cause when you've got Chavez, insurance isn't just a policy, but also maybe the law.

Matt Murton LF Bats: R Throws: R Height: 6' 1" Weight: 220 Born: October 3, 1981 Age: 27

YEAR	TEAM	LVL	AGE	PA	R	2B	3B	HR	RBI	BB	SO	SB	CS	EqBRR	AVG	OBP	SLG	EqAVG	EqOBP	EqSLG	EqA	VORP	WARP	DEFENSE			
2006	CHN	MLB	24	508	70	22	3	13	62	45	62	5	2	-0.5	.297	.365	.444	.289	.359	.434	.276	15.4	2.5	118-LF	5		
2007	IOW	AAA	25	172	30	16	1	6	27	18	18	1	0	0.5	.331	.407	.570	.281	.358	.497	.291	11.2	1.2	37-RF	1		
2007	CHN	MLB	25	261	35	13	0	8	22	26	39	1	0	-0.2	.281	.352	.438	.270	.349	.425	.269	6.9	1.0	32-RF	-4	21-LF	7
2008	IOW	AAA	26	225	26	11	1	1	15	29	20	4	2	-0.7	.298	.397	.382	.244	.330	.320	.234	-4.7	-1.2	47-LF	-8		
2008	CHN	MLB	26	42	2	2	0	0	6	1	5	0	0	-0.0	.250	.286	.300	.250	.286	.300	.202	-1.7	-0.2	7-LF	0		
2008	SAC	AAA	26	145	19	12	2	1	13	13	20	3	1	-0.5	.277	.345	.423	.233	.295	.353	.226	-4.1	-0.3	29-LF	0		
2008	OAK	MLB	26	31	1	1	0	0	2	1	7	0	0	-0.0	.100	.129	.133	.133	.161	.167	.000	-5.7	-0.1	7-LF	3		
2009	OAK	MLB	27	430	45	20	1	6	44	35	60	4	2	-0.7	.259	.323	.366	.265	.330	.390	.254	-1.3	0.7	102-LF	0		

Breakout: 23% Improve: 52% Collapse: 19% Attrition: 21%   Comparables: Terry Jorgensen, Pat Tabler, Lee Walls, Jacob Cruz

Murton is an ugly reminder for the Travis Buck fans of the world that there are lots of these guys around: "polished college hitter with a good swing who plays the game, blah blah blah." Then it turns out that defensively, they're limited to a corner and they don't have enough power for either position. Sure, sometimes you get some nice players, but more often than not, you get Matt Murton, who is now 27, fighting for a job, and about to tip into Triple-A journeyman status.

Eric Patterson — 2B/OF

Bats: L Throws: R Height: 5' 11" Weight: 170 Born: April 8, 1983 Age: 26

YEAR	TEAM	LVL	AGE	PA	R	2B	3B	HR	RBI	BB	SO	SB	CS	EqBRR	AVG	OBP	SLG	EqAVG	EqOBP	EqSLG	EqA	VORP	WARP	DEFENSE			
2006	WTN	AA	23	501	66	22	9	8	48	46	89	38	12	4.2	.263	.330	.408	.242	.301	.395	.247	-4.4	2.3	111-2B	11		
2006	IOW	AAA	23	76	14	1	1	2	12	6	9	8	0	3.0	.358	.395	.493	.324	.355	.456	.296	4.5	0.4	17-2B	-2		
2007	IOW	AAA	24	582	94	28	6	14	65	54	85	24	9	1.3	.297	.362	.455	.257	.321	.402	.253	4.2	0.8	79-2B	-9	23-CF	4
2008	IOW	AAA	25	220	33	16	3	6	28	12	45	11	0	2.6	.320	.358	.517	.267	.301	.427	.257	2.0	1.1	44-2B	4		
2008	CHN	MLB	25	44	5	1	0	1	7	5	12	2	1	0.6	.237	.318	.342	.237	.318	.342	.241	-0.8	-0.2	8-LF	-2		
2008	SAC	AAA	25	124	18	8	2	4	19	9	28	8	2	1.1	.330	.380	.550	.286	.333	.446	.272	4.2	0.2	22-2B	-3	4-CF	0
2008	OAK	MLB	25	104	11	3	0	0	8	12	24	8	0	1.5	.174	.269	.207	.165	.269	.198	.196	-6.0	-1.0	19-2B	-3	7-LF	-2
2009	OAK	MLB	26	472	56	23	4	10	45	38	99	18	5	3.0	.248	.311	.388	.254	.318	.414	.258	7.0	1.4	112-2B	-4		

Breakout: 31% Improve: 57% Collapse: 10% Attrition: 18%   Comparables: Scott Lusader, Jackie Brandt, Jake Wood, Tommy McCraw

Another part of the Harden trade whose acquisition just complicated things, Corey's younger brother lacks the athleticism of his older brother, but he's a better baseball player, one with gap power, plus speed, a proven track record at the upper levels of the minor leagues, and an idea of what he's doing at the plate. This Patterson's problem is defense, as he's sloppy at second base, and an attempted conversion to the outfield has been only a so-so proposition so far. His likely positions are now handled by a re-signed Ellis and a recently acquired Holliday, so it will be hard to find a role for him.

Cliff Pennington — INF

Bats: S Throws: R Height: 5' 11" Weight: 185 Born: June 15, 1984 Age: 25

YEAR	TEAM	LVL	AGE	PA	R	2B	3B	HR	RBI	BB	SO	SB	CS	EqBRR	AVG	OBP	SLG	EqAVG	EqOBP	EqSLG	EqA	VORP	WARP	DEFENSE			
2006	STO	A+	22	202	36	7	0	2	21	24	35	7	1	3.6	.203	.302	.277	.158	.238	.213	.154	-24.8	-2.3	43-SS	-8		
2007	STO	A+	23	333	50	17	3	6	36	43	54	9	2	-0.4	.255	.348	.399	.188	.266	.289	.198	-24.9	0.2	66-SS	8		
2007	MID	AA	23	314	41	13	2	2	21	38	35	8	2	0.0	.251	.343	.336	.216	.297	.295	.215	-16.9	-0.6	64-SS	-2	5-2B	-1
2008	MID	AA	24	244	42	7	2	0	18	39	36	20	1	-0.1	.260	.379	.314	.199	.305	.246	.214	-16.3	0.0	34-SS	7	17-2B	-4
2008	SAC	AAA	24	294	47	9	3	2	16	54	34	11	5	-3.0	.297	.426	.386	.266	.386	.344	.266	6.1	2.8	46-SS	11	15-2B	0
2008	OAK	MLB	24	117	14	5	0	0	9	13	18	4	1	0.9	.242	.339	.293	.245	.348	.296	.245	-0.6	-0.6	15-2B	-2	7-3B	-1
2009	OAK	MLB	25	524	53	21	3	4	35	58	96	12	5	1.3	.218	.307	.304	.223	.313	.323	.232	-6.2	0.9	123-SS	2		

Breakout: 38% Improve: 59% Collapse: 17% Attrition: 5%   Comparables: Trevor Crowe, Mike Watters, Ken Jackson, Adam Everett

A first-round pick in 2005, Pennington has had a slow rise through the system. Last year, he finally enjoyed an OBP-fueled breakout season at Triple-A, which earned him time in Oakland at the end of the year, when he filled in at all three non-first infield positions. Pennington has two big league-level skills: outstanding plate discipline and a very good arm. He's a bit stretched rangewise on the left side, but he holds his own there, and he has probably replaced Donnie Murphy as the primary infield reserve. With three injury-prone starters penciled in at second, short, and third, perhaps no utility infielder is guaranteed more playing time than Oakland's.

Gregorio Petit — SS

Bats: R Throws: R Height: 5' 10" Weight: 160 Born: December 10, 1984 Age: 24

YEAR	TEAM	LVL	AGE	PA	R	2B	3B	HR	RBI	BB	SO	SB	CS	EqBRR	AVG	OBP	SLG	EqAVG	EqOBP	EqSLG	EqA	VORP	WARP	DEFENSE			
2006	STO	A+	21	576	71	25	7	8	63	38	96	22	13	-3.0	.256	.310	.378	.200	.244	.301	.189	-45.8	-2.6	75-2B	4	61-SS	-6
2007	MID	AA	22	299	33	14	0	4	31	25	44	9	3	0.0	.306	.366	.403	.263	.316	.347	.235	-4.6	0.8	63-SS	2		
2007	SAC	AAA	22	260	20	12	0	2	28	16	48	1	2	0.0	.277	.327	.353	.256	.302	.324	.221	-7.8	0.4	57-SS	3	8-2B	1
2008	SAC	AAA	23	339	39	14	3	1	35	23	60	3	5	-3.0	.269	.322	.344	.242	.290	.306	.206	-15.6	0.0	68-SS	3	7-3B	0
2008	OAK	MLB	23	25	4	2	0	0	2	2	9	0	0	-0.1	.348	.400	.435	.348	.400	.435	.293	2.0	0.4	4-2B	2		
2009	OAK	MLB	24	399	30	16	2	4	32	23	85	5	2	0.1	.229	.276	.313	.234	.282	.334	.216	-7.2	0.3	95-SS	4		

Breakout: 32% Improve: 51% Collapse: 27% Attrition: 21%   Comparables: Luis Ordaz, Pedro Lopez, Fausto Cruz, Ray Olmedo

If Crosby continues to hit like a muscled-up Rey Ordonez, Petit might actually end up as the primary shortstop. The key here is defense, as Petit can really pick it, with the speed and instincts to reach plenty of balls, and the arm to take advantage of the other skills to good effect. He's no great shakes offensively, and his secondary skills are lacking. There will be worse shortstops out there with regular jobs in 2009, with Crosby perhaps among them.

Kurt Suzuki   C   Bats: R   Throws: R   Height: 6' 0"   Weight: 205   Born: October 4, 1983   Age: 25

YEAR	TEAM	LVL	AGE	PA	R	2B	3B	HR	RBI	BB	SO	SB	CS	EqBRR	AVG	OBP	SLG	EqAVG	EqOBP	EqSLG	EqA	VORP	WARP	DEFENSE
2006	MID	AA	22	444	64	26	1	7	55	58	50	5	3	-0.5	.285	.392	.415	.241	.333	.356	.245	-2.8	1.2	87-C -1
2007	SAC	AAA	23	240	32	9	0	3	27	21	41	0	0	0.0	.280	.351	.365	.257	.325	.336	.238	-3.5	0.6	43-C 2
2007	OAK	MLB	23	248	27	13	0	7	39	24	39	0	0	-0.8	.249	.327	.408	.250	.333	.420	.264	7.9	1.3	60-C 1
2008	OAK	MLB	24	588	54	25	1	7	42	44	69	2	3	-1.7	.279	.346	.370	.286	.355	.384	.260	14.9	3.2	136-C 5
2009	OAK	MLB	25	415	43	20	1	8	46	35	58	2	1	-0.9	.263	.335	.386	.269	.342	.412	.265	12.4	2.6	99-C 0

Breakout: 33%   Improve: 58%   Collapse: 17%   Attrition: 29%   Comparables: Cam Carreon, Jerry May, Jim Sundberg, Fred Kendall

There's something to be said for a Sundberg-style durable catcher who chips in on offense, and Suzuki is just that, as he played 141 games at the position last year. But at the same time, one does wonder at what cost. He was plainly out of gas in the second half, as the wear and tear of the season clearly took its toll down the stretch. While his defense is above-average across the board in terms of blocking pitches and controlling the running game, Oakland needs him to swing a fresh bat for a high average for him to have offensive value, as he's a bit of a hacker with a line-drive swing. As weird as this might sound, we're looking forward to seeing what he can do with *less* playing time.

Ryan Sweeney   OF   Bats: L   Throws: L   Height: 6' 4"   Weight: 215   Born: February 20, 1985   Age: 24

YEAR	TEAM	LVL	AGE	PA	R	2B	3B	HR	RBI	BB	SO	SB	CS	EqBRR	AVG	OBP	SLG	EqAVG	EqOBP	EqSLG	EqA	VORP	WARP	DEFENSE	
2006	CHR	AAA	21	492	64	25	3	13	70	35	73	7	7	-1.8	.296	.350	.452	.267	.320	.430	.255	10.0	0.6	57-CF -5	42-RF 1
2006	CHA	MLB	21	35	1	0	0	0	5	0	7	0	0	0.4	.229	.229	.229	.229	.229	.229	.130	-3.4	-0.4		
2007	CHR	AAA	22	450	50	17	2	10	47	48	71	8	5	-1.6	.270	.348	.398	.239	.314	.371	.240	-5.1	0.8	46-CF -1	34-RF 3
2007	CHA	MLB	22	49	5	3	0	1	5	4	5	0	1	0.3	.200	.265	.333	.200	.265	.333	.199	-3.2	-0.5	10-LF -2	
2008	OAK	MLB	23	433	53	18	2	5	45	38	67	9	1	2.7	.286	.350	.383	.291	.359	.393	.271	9.9	1.1	55-RF -3	41-CF -2
2009	OAK	MLB	24	454	53	21	2	9	49	40	73	7	3	0.2	.266	.333	.398	.272	.340	.424	.266	7.8	1.6	108-RF 2	

Breakout: 35%   Improve: 54%   Collapse: 18%   Attrition: 20%   Comparables: Bruce Bochte, Al Cowens, Norm Miller, Leon Durham

Sweeney just looks like he should be a star, and that is what has been so frustrating. He's tall, lean, strong, and athletic and has tools a-plenty, but the White Sox got understandably sick of waiting for his pretty swing to develop some power and included him in the package that got them Nick Swisher. Sweeney spent most of the year in the big leagues, and he did the same thing that he did in the past—hit for average, and little else. While he's still relatively young, it's time to give up on him as a future star. The A's believe in him enough that he is likely to begin the year as their starting center fielder (where his range is a bit short) and possible leadoff man (he's hardly a walk machine), but that's because you have to have one of each, and they don't have a lot of obvious alternatives.

Frank Thomas   DH   Bats: R   Throws: R   Height: 6' 5"   Weight: 275   Born: May 27, 1968   Age: 41

YEAR	TEAM	LVL	AGE	PA	R	2B	3B	HR	RBI	BB	SO	SB	CS	EqBRR	AVG	OBP	SLG	EqAVG	EqOBP	EqSLG	EqA	VORP	WARP	DEFENSE
2006	OAK	MLB	38	559	77	11	0	39	114	81	81	0	0	-3.4	.270	.381	.545	.259	.379	.535	.307	43.0	4.0	
2007	TOR	MLB	39	624	63	30	0	26	95	81	94	0	0	-4.3	.277	.377	.480	.268	.373	.482	.294	33.3	3.3	
2008	TOR	MLB	40	72	7	1	0	3	11	11	13	0	0	0.7	.167	.306	.333	.169	.319	.339	.237	-2.1	-0.1	
2008	OAK	MLB	40	217	20	6	1	5	19	28	44	0	0	-3.1	.263	.364	.387	.266	.373	.408	.277	6.1	0.7	
2009	OAK	MLB	41	326	29	11	0	10	40	41	62	1	0	-3.2	.225	.327	.373	.230	.334	.397	.259	1.5	0.1	79-DH

Breakout: 2%   Improve: 14%   Collapse: 48%   Attrition: 27%   Comparables: Andres Galarraga, Fred McGriff, Edgar Martinez, Darrell Evans

Watching Thomas last year provoked similar feelings to those of witnessing the final years of Steve Carlton, where all you could do was remember what once was one of the best players in the game. So let's forget about the drama surrounding Thomas's Toronto release or his second Oakland stint limited by bad wheels, and let's remember instead that for more than a few years, this guy was the most dangerous hitter in the game, a player everyone at the ballpark stood still to watch when he came to the plate. From 1991 to 1997, Thomas lead the American League in OPS four times, and in the other three years, he finished second twice and third once. In the shortened 1994 season, he reached base 252 times in 113 games while adding 73 extra-base hits. He was awesome, and we'll miss him.

Jemile Weeks   2B

Bats: S   Throws: R   Height: 5' 10"   Weight: 175   Born: January 26, 1987   Age: 22

YEAR	TEAM	LVL	AGE	PA	R	2B	3B	HR	RBI	BB	SO	SB	CS	EqBRR	AVG	OBP	SLG	EqAVG	EqOBP	EqSLG	EqA	VORP	WARP	DEFENSE
2008	KNC	A	21	90	11	3	1	1	8	13	12	6	2	0.5	.297	.422	.405	.247	.348	.351	.254	0.0	0.0	18-2B	-2
2009	OAK	MLB	22	604	61	26	4	6	44	54	123	15	6	1.8	.225	.299	.320	.231	.305	.340	.232	-7.0	0.3	141-2B	-2

Breakout: 6%   Improve: 19%   Collapse: 43%   Attrition: 1%   Comparables: Spike Owen, Joey Cora, Cliff Pennington, Chuck Knoblauch

The A's first-round pick last June, Weeks often gets compared with his brother Rickie, but strangely enough, only in terms of how different the two are. Rickie is thicker and stronger, while Jemile is lanky and much quicker. Like his brother, Jemile can be a bit sloppy at second base, but his athleticism gives him plenty of room for improvement, and he'll always have more range because of his speed. The one thing he does have like his brother is a good approach and tremendous bat speed, and some in the organization think he could move up quickly as a result.

PITCHERS

Brett Anderson

Bats: L   Throws: L   Height: 6' 4"   Weight: 215   Born: February 1, 1988   Age: 21

YEAR	TEAM	LVL	AGE	W	L	SV	G	GS	IP	H	BB	SO	HR	GB%	BABIP	STUFF	WHIP	ERA	DERA	EqH9	EqBB9	EqSO9	EqHR9	DEF	VORP	SN/WX
2007	SBN	A	19	8	4	0	14	14	81¹	76	10	85	3	60.7%	.335	16	1.06	2.21	5.12	12.2	2.3	4.5	1.3	-5	3.7	—
2007	VIS	A+	19	3	3	0	9	9	39	50	11	40	6	51.9%	.368	4	1.56	4.85	5.13	16.2	3.8	5.4	2.4	-7	1.7	—
2008	STO	A+	20	9	4	0	14	13	74	68	18	80	5	60.3%	.313	22	1.16	4.14	5.64	10.2	3.1	5.4	1.3	-3	-0.3	—
2008	MID	AA	20	2	1	0	6	6	31	27	9	38	3	55.8%	.324	28	1.16	2.61	5.14	10.0	3.2	7.7	1.6	3	1.4	—
2009	OAK	MLB	21	8	10	0	26	26	149²	167	56	103	17	51.0%	.310	19	1.49	5.08	5.27	10.1	3.0	5.7	1.0	-0	2.0	1.37

Breakout: 25%   Improve: 64%   Collapse: 11%   Attrition: 8%   Comparables: Charlie Kerfeld, Bill Pulsipher, Mark Gubicza, Kevin Morton

Carlos Gonzalez was the best prospect in the Haren deal when it was consummated, but it looks as if Anderson will turn out to be the best player brought to Oakland in the exchange. The son of a pitching coach, he was the most polished pitcher in the Arizona system as a teenager, but scouts were always turned off by his dumpy, unathletic frame. Last spring, he came to camp 25 to 30 pounds lighter and took another step forward because of it, with his low-90s fastball grading up because of its excellent movement and location. Unlike most pitchers his age, Anderson has advanced secondary offerings and an excellent feel for his craft. He's moving up rapidly, could be in Oakland by the end of the year, and has All-Star potential.

Jerry Blevins

Bats: L   Throws: L   Height: 6' 6"   Weight: 185   Born: September 6, 1983   Age: 25

YEAR	TEAM	LVL	AGE	W	L	SV	G	GS	IP	H	BB	SO	HR	GB%	BABIP	STUFF	WHIP	ERA	DERA	EqH9	EqBB9	EqSO9	EqHR9	DEF	VORP	SN/WX
2006	BOI	A-	22	1	2	0	16	0	22¹	27	8	19	3	53.2%	.333	-58	1.58	6.11	13.50	16.2	5.4	2.7	3.6	-5	-17.6	—
2006	DAY	A+	22	0	1	1	8	0	11²	18	4	9	0	47.6%	.450	-37	1.96	8.84	9.90	18.9	4.5	3.6	0.9	-4	-4.8	—
2006	WTN	AA	22	0	0	1	5	0	6¹	5	1	8	0	20.0%	.333	6	0.98	1.48	1.59	9.5	1.6	7.9	0.0	-1	2.5	—
2007	DAY	A+	23	1	0	6	15	0	23²	13	5	32	0	65.4%	.260	22	0.76	0.38	1.21	6.4	2.4	7.7	0.4	0	10.9	—
2007	TEN	AA	23	2	2	3	23	0	29¹	23	8	37	1	43.2%	.319	11	1.06	1.54	2.93	9.1	2.6	7.2	0.7	2	8.2	—
2007	MID	AA	23	1	3	1	17	0	21²	18	5	29	2	45.1%	.348	9	1.06	3.32	5.12	9.8	2.8	8.8	1.4	-2	1.0	—
2007	OAK	MLB	23	0	1	0	6	0	4²	8	2	3	1	10.0%	.368	-30	2.14	9.57	9.00	14.4	3.6	5.4	1.8	-2	-2.9	-0.22
2008	SAC	AAA	24	2	2	10	28	0	32¹	31	6	36	3	45.7%	.318	0	1.15	2.79	5.91	9.3	1.7	6.8	1.1	2	-1.1	—
2008	OAK	MLB	24	1	3	0	36	0	37²	32	13	35	2	42.9%	.294	11	1.19	3.10	3.72	8.2	3.0	7.7	0.5	1	9.9	0.89
2009	OAK	MLB	25	2	2	4	53	1	48¹	46	16	43	5	43.0%	.300	15	1.28	3.74	3.86	8.6	2.6	7.3	0.8	-0	9.8	0.84

Breakout: 46%   Improve: 78%   Collapse: 10%   Attrition: 22%   Comparables: Steve Wilson, Doug Bird, Mike Jeffcoat, Mike Stanton

Blevins was a breakout performer in 2007, and the Cubs figured they were selling high when they sent him to Oakland to acquire Jason Kendall for the stretch run. In the end, however, they gave up a nice bullpen arm. After he proved his massive step forward was for real at Triple-A, Blevins's combination of a 92-95 mph fastball and slow looping curve was more than enough for big-league success, as he fills the strike zone with both pitches. He's not a closer, but he's a quality seventh-inning type who should be a cheap, successful arm for Oakland well into the next decade.

Dallas Braden

| | | | | | | | | Bats: L | | Throws: L | | Height: 6' 1" | | Weight: 185 | | | Born: August 13, 1983 | | | Age: 25 | |

YEAR	TEAM	LVL	AGE	W	L	SV	G	GS	IP	H	BB	SO	HR	GB%	BABIP	STUFF	WHIP	ERA	DERA	EqH9	EqBB9	EqSO9	EqHR9	DEF	VORP	SN/WX
2006	ATH	Rk	22	2	0	0	6	6	21²	12	3	36	0	48.6%	.364	17	0.71	0.85	2.70	10.3	2.7	8.1	1.1	0	5.4	—
2006	STO	A+	22	2	0	0	3	3	13	12	5	17	3	27.3%	.300	-2	1.31	6.23	10.03	11.6	4.6	6.9	3.9	1	-5.8	—
2007	MID	AA	23	1	0	0	2	2	12	5	3	13	2	38.5%	.125	11	0.67	2.25	4.91	4.9	2.5	6.5	2.5	2	0.8	—
2007	SAC	AAA	23	2	3	0	11	11	64	51	18	74	4	44.0%	.292	28	1.08	2.95	4.19	7.9	2.7	7.7	0.7	2	9.8	—
2007	OAK	MLB	23	1	8	0	20	14	72¹	91	26	55	9	39.4%	.347	-4	1.62	6.72	6.12	11.2	3.0	5.9	1.1	-9	-12.3	0.14
2008	SAC	AAA	24	3	1	0	11	9	53¹	49	11	54	7	47.3%	.304	5	1.13	2.36	4.78	9.6	2.0	6.6	1.5	4	4.5	—
2008	OAK	MLB	24	5	4	0	19	10	71²	77	25	41	8	40.3%	.311	-7	1.42	4.14	3.80	10.4	3.1	4.9	1.1	-5	9.5	1.49
2009	OAK	MLB	25	5	6	1	33	14	93¹	99	31	65	11	42.0%	.300	10	1.39	4.54	4.64	9.6	2.6	5.8	1.1	-0	8.6	1.33

Breakout: 31% Improve: 51% Collapse: 21% Attrition: 24%   Comparables: Bob Ojeda, Dave Hamilton, Alex Kellner, Pete Filson

An obscure 24th-round pick in 2004, Braden had a minor league career ratio of more than 10 strikeouts per nine. This would make you think he's a power pitcher, but that's not the case; his big league rate of exactly six per nine is much more representative of his stuff. His fastball sits at a pedestrian 89-91 mph, but he's always doing something with it—he'll cut it in, sink it, add and subtract from it, and use it to try to set up his average slider and effective changeup. He'll never overpower people, but he's already exceeded all expectations. The A's are hoping he can fit into the back end of the rotation this year, with no need to believe that he'll ever be more than that.

Andrew Brown

| | | | | | | | | Bats: R | | Throws: R | | Height: 6' 6" | | Weight: 230 | | | Born: February 17, 1981 | | | Age: 28 | |

YEAR	TEAM	LVL	AGE	W	L	SV	G	GS	IP	H	BB	SO	HR	GB%	BABIP	STUFF	WHIP	ERA	DERA	EqH9	EqBB9	EqSO9	EqHR9	DEF	VORP	SN/WX
2006	BUF	AAA	25	5	4	5	39	0	62	52	36	53	5	46.4%	.276	-16	1.42	2.61	5.86	9.1	6.0	5.1	1.2	11	-1.7	—
2006	CLE	MLB	25	0	0	0	9	0	10	6	8	7	0	39.3%	.214	4	1.40	3.60	5.40	5.4	7.2	5.4	0.0	2	2.8	-0.17
2007	POR	AAA	26	2	3	0	32	0	35²	26	15	43	3	47.7%	.274	5	1.15	2.77	4.84	6.4	3.8	7.9	1.0	3	3.0	—
2007	OAK	MLB	26	3	3	0	33	0	41²	38	17	43	1	44.3%	.333	17	1.32	4.53	3.57	8.5	3.6	8.3	0.2	-4	6.3	-0.04
2008	OAK	MLB	27	1	0	0	31	0	35	23	21	28	3	37.1%	.217	1	1.26	3.09	4.15	6.0	4.9	6.2	0.8	3	9.0	0.19
2009	OAK	MLB	28	2	2	2	43	0	47¹	45	24	39	5	41.0%	.290	6	1.45	4.42	4.54	8.5	4.1	6.9	1.0	-0	4.7	0.38

Breakout: 13% Improve: 25% Collapse: 42% Attrition: 27%   Comparables: Jim Brosnan, Mike Adams, Marvin Freeman, Kevin Gregg

A big righty with a very live arm, Brown is already on his fifth organization in the last six years, having frustrated the previous four with his combination of plus-plus velocity, command problems, and some maturity issues. Limited last year due to an early-season appendectomy and some late-season shoulder problems, Brown still missed bats with his 92-96 mph fastball, although his walk rate remained a source of concern. Guys with his size and velocity get all sorts of chances, though; he will probably break camp as a middle man in the big-league pen.

Trevor Cahill

| | | | | | | | | Bats: R | | Throws: R | | Height: 6' 3" | | Weight: 195 | | | Born: March 1, 1988 | | | Age: 21 | |

YEAR	TEAM	LVL	AGE	W	L	SV	G	GS	IP	H	BB	SO	HR	GB%	BABIP	STUFF	WHIP	ERA	DERA	EqH9	EqBB9	EqSO9	EqHR9	DEF	VORP	SN/WX
2007	KNC	A	19	11	4	0	20	19	105¹	85	40	117	3	58.3%	.308	14	1.19	2.74	5.99	11.1	5.6	5.0	1.1	-1	-3.0	—
2008	STO	A+	20	5	4	0	14	13	87¹	52	31	103	3	64.4%	.254	42	0.95	2.78	4.95	6.8	4.3	6.2	0.8	5	5.8	—
2008	MID	AA	20	6	1	0	7	6	37	24	19	33	2	65.6%	.242	24	1.16	2.19	5.97	6.5	5.2	4.9	0.8	4	-1.4	—
2009	OAK	MLB	21	7	9	0	23	23	127²	122	76	94	9	54.0%	.290	18	1.54	4.75	5.01	8.6	4.7	6.1	0.6	-0	5.7	1.58

Breakout: 15% Improve: 46% Collapse: 20% Attrition: 9%   Comparables: Yovani Gallardo, Phil Hughes, Dennis Blair, Sean Gallagher

It's impossible to avoid comparisons between Cahill and Anderson. Both were second-round picks in 2006 out of high school, both are now in the A's system, and both pitched extremely well at High-A, Double-A, and for the U.S. Olympic team in China. On a stuff level, they're also similar. Although Cahill is right-handed, like Anderson he's not overpowering, but is hardly a soft-tosser, effectively mixing a low-90s sinker, outstanding curveball, and solid change, with good command and control of all three. If you saw one of the two pitchers, you saw the other last year, and one of the favorite debates among scouts this year was which one was better. The split of opinions was about 50/50, but agreement was universal that they both have star potential.

Santiago Casilla

							Bats: R		Throws: R		Height: 6' 0"		Weight: 200		Born: June 25, 1980			Age: 29	

YEAR	TEAM	LVL	AGE	W	L	SV	G	GS	IP	H	BB	SO	HR	GB%	BABIP	STUFF	WHIP	ERA	DERA	EqH9	EqBB9	EqSO9	EqHR9	DEF	VORP	SN/WX
2006	SAC	AAA	26	2	0	4	25	0	33¹	25	10	32	2	42.5%	.270	-3	1.06	3.26	5.18	7.1	2.7	5.7	0.8	3	1.5	—
2007	SAC	AAA	27	2	1	3	22	0	24	18	14	29	1	54.2%	.304	10	1.33	4.13	5.16	7.9	5.6	8.3	0.4	0	1.1	—
2007	OAK	MLB	27	3	1	2	46	0	50²	43	23	52	6	33.6%	.276	3	1.30	4.44	4.73	7.5	3.7	7.9	1.1	2	8.3	0.99
2008	OAK	MLB	28	2	1	2	51	0	50¹	60	20	43	5	44.8%	.359	0	1.59	3.94	2.76	11.2	3.3	6.8	0.9	-7	9.8	0.78
2009	OAK	MLB	29	3	3	4	51	0	57²	54	22	48	6	42.0%	.290	11	1.32	3.75	3.85	8.5	3.1	6.9	0.9	-0	10.7	0.91

Breakout: 30% Improve: 50% Collapse: 18% Attrition: 24%   Comparables: Jeff Brantley, Vicente Romo, John Wyatt, Marc Wilkins

When he was Jairo Garcia, he was one of the more exciting young relief prospects in the game, but becoming Santiago Casilla made him three years older, so he turned into a guy who's rawness was a matter of concern for a guy in his late 20s. His stuff is pure power, with a 96-98 mph fastball and an upper-80s slider, but the heater is straight, the slider flattens out, and he has trouble throwing strikes. It's big-league stuff, but it's not dependable enough for a late-innings role.

Joey Devine

							Bats: R		Throws: R		Height: 6' 1"		Weight: 225		Born: September 19, 1983			Age: 25	

YEAR	TEAM	LVL	AGE	W	L	SV	G	GS	IP	H	BB	SO	HR	GB%	BABIP	STUFF	WHIP	ERA	DERA	EqH9	EqBB9	EqSO9	EqHR9	DEF	VORP	SN/WX
2006	MYR	A+	22	1	3	0	13	2	18¹	13	11	28	1	30.8%	.343	11	1.33	5.97	8.82	9.9	6.6	8.8	1.1	-1	-5.8	—
2006	MIS	AA	22	2	0	0	6	0	11¹	2	4	20	1	30.8%	.100	10	0.54	0.81	3.60	2.7	3.6	9.9	1.8	2	2.2	—
2006	ATL	MLB	22	0	0	0	10	0	6¹	8	9	10	1	12.5%	.467	6	2.68	10.00	7.11	12.8	11.4	12.8	1.4	-1	-2.8	-0.35
2007	MIS	AA	23	2	4	16	33	0	35	26	13	51	1	50.7%	.352	15	1.11	2.06	3.45	9.2	3.7	8.9	0.6	-1	7.5	—
2007	RIC	AAA	23	3	0	4	17	0	22	15	6	27	1	51.9%	.333	16	0.95	1.64	2.49	7.1	2.5	7.5	0.8	-1	7.5	—
2007	ATL	MLB	23	1	0	0	10	0	8¹	7	8	7	0	58.3%	.318	8	1.80	1.08	1.08	7.6	7.6	7.6	0.0	0	4.4	0.26
2008	OAK	MLB	24	6	1	1	42	0	45²	23	15	49	0	38.7%	.221	29	0.83	0.59	2.86	4.9	2.9	8.8	0.0	6	22.1	2.25
2009	OAK	MLB	25	3	2	4	45	1	53¹	41	23	61	4	41.0%	.280	29	1.18	2.94	3.03	6.9	3.4	9.5	0.7	-0	16.7	1.43

Breakout: 26% Improve: 45% Collapse: 27% Attrition: 12%   Comparables: Danny Darwin, Gregg Olson, Steve Bedrosian, Mark Littell

Once the Braves' closer of the future, Devine never seemed truly recovered from Chris Burke's playoff home run off him a few years back. But it turned out that maybe a change of scenery was all he really needed. Utilizing a 93-96 mph fastball and wipeout slider, Devine regained his confidence with Oakland, as he didn't allow an earned run in his last 24 games of the season after missing a month with elbow soreness, limiting opposing batters to a ridiculous .097/.195/.097 line in the process. Ziegler got the saves at the end of 2008, but Devine will get them in 2009, as he profiles better for the role.

Justin Duchscherer

							Bats: R		Throws: R		Height: 6' 3"		Weight: 205		Born: November 19, 1977			Age: 31	

YEAR	TEAM	LVL	AGE	W	L	SV	G	GS	IP	H	BB	SO	HR	GB%	BABIP	STUFF	WHIP	ERA	DERA	EqH9	EqBB9	EqSO9	EqHR9	DEF	VORP	SN/WX
2006	OAK	MLB	28	2	1	9	53	0	55²	52	9	51	4	39.9%	.304	16	1.10	2.91	3.62	8.2	1.5	7.4	0.7	4	19.5	3.67
2007	OAK	MLB	29	3	3	0	17	0	16¹	18	8	13	3	51.9%	.313	-13	1.59	4.97	4.32	9.7	3.8	5.9	1.6	-2	1.8	0.03
2008	OAK	MLB	30	10	8	0	22	22	141²	107	34	95	11	43.0%	.238	18	1.00	2.54	4.26	7.0	2.0	5.4	0.7	18	45.7	5.47
2009	OAK	MLB	31	9	8	0	25	25	151	151	40	98	18	44.0%	.280	17	1.26	4.02	4.13	9.0	2.1	5.4	1.0	-0	21.5	3.48

Breakout: 1% Improve: 17% Collapse: 54% Attrition: 17%   Comparables: Sonny Siebert, Ken Johnson, Chris Bosio, Pat Dobson

Duchscherer carved himself a decent little career as a strike-throwing reliever, but nobody was expecting these kinds of results when he converted to starting, as he led the league in ERA for much of the year before missing the last six weeks of the season with a hip injury that ultimately required minor surgery. He's truly remarkable to watch, never touching even 90 mph with his fastball, but sinking and cutting it to all four corners of the zone and mixing in his curveball and slider more than half the time. A repeat performance is unlikely, but he does kick off 2009 as the only established pitcher in the Oakland rotation and is thus the de facto ace of the staff.

Alan Embree

Bats: L   Throws: L   Height: 6' 2"   Weight: 190   Born: January 23, 1970   Age: 39

YEAR	TEAM	LVL	AGE	W	L	SV	G	GS	IP	H	BB	SO	HR	GB%	BABIP	STUFF	WHIP	ERA	DERA	EqH9	EqBB9	EqSO9	EqHR9	DEF	VORP	SN/WX
2006	SDN	MLB	36	4	3	0	73	0	52^1	50	15	53	4	44.4%	.319	18	1.24	3.27	2.77	9.0	2.2	8.3	0.7	-5	13.3	1.40
2007	OAK	MLB	37	1	2	17	68	0	68	67	19	51	5	34.6%	.304	1	1.26	3.97	4.03	8.9	2.4	5.9	0.7	0	14.8	3.33
2008	OAK	MLB	38	2	5	0	70	0	61^2	59	30	57	8	45.1%	.304	-4	1.44	4.96	4.33	9.0	4.0	7.5	1.2	-7	2.8	0.26
2009	COL	MLB	39	2	2	2	46	0	44^2	50	18	37	6	42.0%	.320	2	1.52	5.19	4.88	9.3	3.2	6.7	1.1	0	4.3	0.35

Breakout: 16%   Improve: 40%   Collapse: 34%   Attrition: 33%   Comparables: Jeff Fassero, Dennis Cook, Mike Stanton, Buddy Groom

Embree is left-handed and still throws hard from a three-quarters delivery, so more often than not, he still gives lefties fits, although his command and the quality of his slider dipped a bit last year. He's good at what he's needed for, just not as good as he once was, so Oakland declined his $3 million option for 2009. The Rockies stepped in and signed him for only slightly less.

Dana Eveland

Bats: L   Throws: L   Height: 6' 1"   Weight: 240   Born: October 29, 1983   Age: 25

YEAR	TEAM	LVL	AGE	W	L	SV	G	GS	IP	H	BB	SO	HR	GB%	BABIP	STUFF	WHIP	ERA	DERA	EqH9	EqBB9	EqSO9	EqHR9	DEF	VORP	SN/WX
2006	NAS	AAA	22	6	5	0	20	19	105^2	71	41	110	4	55.1%	.275	32	1.06	2.74	4.62	7.4	3.7	6.7	0.5	4	10.8	—
2006	MIL	MLB	22	0	3	0	9	5	27^2	39	16	32	4	47.7%	.427	18	1.99	8.12	5.46	12.5	4.5	9.3	1.3	-5	-6.1	-0.97
2007	TUC	AAA	23	1	0	0	7	5	27^2	29	10	15	0	57.4%	.315	-6	1.41	1.95	3.29	8.9	3.3	3.3	0.3	1	7.0	—
2008	SAC	AAA	24	3	0	0	3	3	21	23	4	21	2	59.1%	.333	11	1.29	2.57	4.35	10.5	1.7	6.1	0.9	0	2.9	—
2008	OAK	MLB	24	9	9	0	29	29	168	172	77	118	10	49.1%	.316	13	1.48	4.34	4.53	9.8	3.9	5.8	0.6	1	24.6	3.93
2009	OAK	MLB	25	8	9	0	26	26	151	157	67	108	14	49.0%	.300	18	1.48	4.51	4.67	9.4	3.5	6.0	0.9	-0	12.4	2.49

Breakout: 16%   Improve: 50%   Collapse: 21%   Attrition: 13%   Comparables: Dave LaPoint, Bartolo Colon, Trevor Wilson, Wilson Alvarez

Almost a throw-in as part of the Haren deal, Eveland always showed plenty of potential on a pure stuff level, but he almost ate his way out of both the Milwaukee and Arizona organizations. Although he's still a big guy, he fit in much better with a team that knows it isn't selling jeans. He pitched like the steal of the century in the first half, putting up a 3.46 ERA in his first 19 starts, but the wheels fell off after the All-Star break, when he posted a six-plus ERA and took a brief trip back to the minors when the Red Sox hammered him for nine runs in two innings. His final line is actually representative of what should be expected of him. He's an average, usable starter, which is all that the A's are expecting from him at the back end of their rotation this year.

Keith Foulke

Bats: R   Throws: R   Height: 6' 0"   Weight: 210   Born: October 19, 1972   Age: 36

YEAR	TEAM	LVL	AGE	W	L	SV	G	GS	IP	H	BB	SO	HR	GB%	BABIP	STUFF	WHIP	ERA	DERA	EqH9	EqBB9	EqSO9	EqHR9	DEF	VORP	SN/WX
2006	BOS	MLB	33	3	1	0	44	0	49^2	52	7	36	9	24.4%	.293	-7	1.19	4.35	4.89	8.7	1.3	5.8	1.4	5	10.2	1.58
2008	OAK	MLB	35	0	3	1	31	0	31	28	13	23	7	33.3%	.244	-17	1.32	4.06	4.70	8.2	3.5	5.9	2.1	2	5.5	0.59
2009	OAK	MLB	36	1	1	1	24	0	30^1	31	9	22	5	36.0%	.290	2	1.34	4.36	4.38	9.4	2.4	6.1	1.4	-0	2.9	0.29

Breakout: 22%   Improve: 38%   Collapse: 43%   Attrition: 30%   Comparables: Josias Manzanillo, Steve Ridzik, Eddie Guardado, Floyd Bannister

After suffering through elbow issues in 2005 and 2006, Foulke retired, but he showed up in Arizona this spring looking for a job and throwing for whoever would look at him. The A's gave him a "no harm, no foul" deal, and he pitched fairly well when he wasn't dealing with calf, neck, or shoulder issues. His fastball is still in the mid-90s and his changeup is still a plus offering, so if he wants another chance in 2009, somebody's going to give him a look.

Sean Gallagher

| | | | | | | Bats: R | | Throws: R | | Height: 6' 2" | | Weight: 225 | | Born: December 30, 1985 | | Age: 23 | |

YEAR	TEAM	LVL	AGE	W	L	SV	G	GS	IP	H	BB	SO	HR	GB%	BABIP	STUFF	WHIP	ERA	DERA	EqH9	EqBB9	EqSO9	EqHR9	DEF	VORP	SN/WX
2006	DAY	A+	20	4	0	0	13	13	78¹	75	21	80	5	58.8%	.345	18	1.23	2.30	4.70	12.2	3.6	5.2	1.5	2	6.7	—
2006	WTN	AA	20	7	5	0	15	15	86²	74	55	91	4	51.5%	.326	30	1.50	2.71	4.58	10.3	6.5	6.2	0.9	0	8.7	—
2007	TEN	AA	21	7	2	0	11	11	61	54	24	54	3	48.6%	.291	18	1.28	3.39	5.08	10.0	3.8	4.8	0.8	2	3.3	—
2007	IOW	AAA	21	3	1	0	8	8	40²	33	13	37	1	45.5%	.308	29	1.13	2.65	4.23	7.5	3.1	6.1	0.5	4	5.8	—
2007	CHN	MLB	21	0	0	1	8	0	14²	19	12	5	3	41.1%	.308	-24	2.11	8.57	6.75	11.7	6.1	3.1	1.8	-2	-5.1	-0.17
2008	IOW	AAA	22	2	2	0	5	5	29	21	9	30	2	56.4%	.253	26	1.03	3.10	4.40	6.9	2.8	6.3	0.6	1	3.8	—
2008	CHN	MLB	22	3	4	0	12	10	58²	58	22	49	6	45.9%	.302	25	1.36	4.45	3.26	9.2	2.9	6.7	0.9	-7	6.7	1.03
2008	OAK	MLB	22	2	3	0	11	11	56²	60	36	54	7	27.6%	.329	14	1.69	5.87	6.04	9.8	5.2	7.5	1.1	-4	-6.7	0.31
2009	OAK	MLB	23	7	8	0	22	22	122	124	53	97	15	40.0%	.300	21	1.45	4.72	4.82	9.2	3.5	6.6	1.1	-0	7.8	1.78

Breakout: 36%   Improve: 63%   Collapse: 14%   Attrition: 24%   Comparables: Jeff Russell, Ryan Dempster, Jim Gott, Dave Borkowski

Another Cracker Jack prize from the Harden deal, the A's put Gallagher directly into Harden's rotation slot. While his numbers were unimpressive, he did impress at times, including seven two-hit innings in his Oakland debut and a late-season seven-inning, one-run showing against the Angels. A former 12th-round pick who found another four to six miles on his fastball since signing, Gallagher's heater now sits at 92-95, but his breaking balls have yet to come around, and when he misses, he misses up. Gallagher didn't turn 23 until the end of the year, and there's still growth potential in him, but the A's don't have enough ready arms for him to get some additional fine-tuning in the minors, so he'll get more of a trial by fire in the big leagues this year.

Gio Gonzalez

| | | | | | | Bats: R | | Throws: L | | Height: 5' 11" | | Weight: 185 | | Born: September 19, 1985 | | Age: 23 | |

YEAR	TEAM	LVL	AGE	W	L	SV	G	GS	IP	H	BB	SO	HR	GB%	BABIP	STUFF	WHIP	ERA	DERA	EqH9	EqBB9	EqSO9	EqHR9	DEF	VORP	SN/WX
2006	REA	AA	20	7	12	0	27	27	154	140	81	166	24	42.9%	.293	-12	1.44	4.68	7.58	11.5	5.9	5.9	2.6	1	-30.3	—
2007	BIR	AA	21	9	7	0	27	27	150	116	57	185	10	54.2%	.309	24	1.15	3.18	4.96	8.5	3.7	7.0	1.2	2	9.9	—
2008	SAC	AAA	22	8	7	0	23	22	123	106	61	128	12	42.0%	.298	13	1.36	4.24	5.65	8.8	4.6	6.6	1.1	0	-0.6	—
2008	OAK	MLB	22	1	4	0	10	7	34	32	25	34	9	43.6%	.258	-1	1.68	7.68	9.26	8.5	5.9	7.7	2.3	1	-12.7	-0.62
2009	OAK	MLB	23	6	10	0	40	22	128¹	129	71	103	18	42.0%	.290	10	1.56	5.37	5.50	9.1	4.4	6.7	1.3	-0	-1.8	0.62

Breakout: 51%   Improve: 75%   Collapse: 5%   Attrition: 20%   Comparables: Mike Kekich, Randy Wolf, Ray Sadecki, Frank Bertaina

A lefty with a monster curve and enough velocity to be really dangerous, Gonzalez came to Oakland in the Swisher deal, and while he limited Pacific Coast League hitters to a .233 average and struck out more than one batter per inning, his inconsistency was absolutely baffling. In late May, he struck out nine over six innings while allowing just one run; in his next start, he got hammered for 10 runs without getting out of the fourth. Five days later, he fired five shutout innings, but followed that by giving up seven runs and 10 hits over his next five frames. It was like that all year for him, because when he's throwing his low-90s fastball for strikes, he can dominate, and when he's not, it's a big ol' mess. The A's are hoping for more of the former as he enters the year with a clean shot at a rotation job.

Michel Inoa

| | | | | | | Bats: R | | Throws: R | | Height: 6' 7" | | Weight: 205 | | Born: September 24, 1991 | | Age: 17 | |

YEAR	TEAM	LVL	AGE	W	L	SV	G	GS	IP	H	BB	SO	HR	GB%	BABIP	STUFF	WHIP	ERA	DERA	EqH9	EqBB9	EqSO9	EqHR9	DEF	VORP	SN/WX
2009																										

Breakout: Improve: Collapse: Attrition: Comparables:

It's hard to get a PECOTA projection when you've yet to pitch a pro inning, and even more difficult when you've barely pitched a competitive inning at all. But Inoa is deserving of far more than just a comment at the tail end of the chapter. The talk of scouting circles all spring, the Dominican wunderkind signed for $4.25 million, more than doubling the previous high-water mark for a Latin American pitcher. Many who saw him called him the best 16-year-old arm they've ever seen; he already touches 94 mph, has a very good breaking ball, and with a long, loose six-foot-seven frame, his potential is almost immeasurable. Obviously he's very young, and countless things could go wrong between where Inoa is now and potential stardom, but his talent is borderline historic and deserves mention.

Vin Mazzaro

Bats: R Throws: R Height: 6' 2" Weight: 190 Born: September 27, 1986 Age: 22

YEAR	TEAM	LVL	AGE	W	L	SV	G	GS	IP	H	BB	SO	HR	GB%	BABIP	STUFF	WHIP	ERA	DERA	EqH9	EqBB9	EqSO9	EqHR9	DEF	VORP	SN/WX
2006	KNC	A	19	9	9	0	24	24	119²	146	42	81	7	57.1%	.363	-34	1.58	5.06	10.67	16.1	5.4	2.4	2.0	-3	-54.6	—
2007	STO	A+	20	9	12	0	28	28	153²	159	71	115	13	54.5%	.319	0	1.50	5.33	7.32	12.1	5.4	3.3	1.5	-7	-25.9	—
2008	MID	AA	21	12	3	0	22	22	137¹	115	36	104	3	53.9%	.283	29	1.10	1.90	4.90	8.1	2.8	4.1	0.5	16	10.1	—
2008	SAC	AAA	21	3	3	0	6	5	33²	49	9	27	3	46.2%	.389	12	1.72	6.14	6.82	14.8	2.6	4.8	1.1	-5	-4.3	—
2009	OAK	MLB	22	6	11	0	25	25	140¹	170	61	76	17	49.0%	.320	7	1.64	5.91	6.11	10.9	3.5	4.5	1.1	-0	-11.4	-0.15

Breakout: 5% Improve: 38% Collapse: 23% Attrition: 9% Comparables: Wally Whitehurst, Scott Chiamparino, Joe Johnson, Josh Hall

The A's always had faith in Mazzaro because of his one outstanding offering, and he finally began to put things together in 2008. He's a classic sinker/slider pitcher who can get both ground-ball outs and swings-and-misses from his two-seam dipper that touches 94, but he'll need to improve the rest of his arsenal to project as more than a third or fourth starter. There are a ton of young arms in the Oakland organization, so while Mazzaro led the Texas League in ERA last year, he still has work to do to distinguish himself from the pack.

Dan Meyer

Bats: R Throws: L Height: 6' 3" Weight: 210 Born: July 3, 1981 Age: 27

YEAR	TEAM	LVL	AGE	W	L	SV	G	GS	IP	H	BB	SO	HR	GB%	BABIP	STUFF	WHIP	ERA	DERA	EqH9	EqBB9	EqSO9	EqHR9	DEF	VORP	SN/WX
2006	SAC	AAA	24	3	3	0	10	10	49¹	63	20	29	10	36.7%	.332	-42	1.69	5.13	7.71	12.5	3.9	3.3	2.5	2	-10.9	—
2007	SAC	AAA	25	8	2	0	21	21	115¹	103	51	105	12	39.1%	.297	-1	1.34	3.28	4.46	9.2	4.3	6.1	1.3	3	13.6	—
2007	OAK	MLB	25	0	2	0	6	3	16¹	20	9	11	2	23.7%	.327	-22	1.78	8.83	8.47	10.6	4.2	4.8	1.1	-3	-8.6	-0.52
2008	SAC	AAA	26	10	5	0	22	20	122²	113	52	109	10	39.3%	.300	0	1.34	4.47	5.68	9.1	3.9	5.4	0.9	-1	-1.0	—
2008	OAK	MLB	26	0	4	0	11	4	27²	35	14	20	6	27.8%	.326	-24	1.77	7.47	7.48	11.7	4.2	5.5	2.0	-4	-10.5	-0.68
2009	FLO	MLB	27	4	6	1	36	13	88	91	42	71	12	38.8%	.300	3	1.51	5.22	5.57	9.4	3.8	5.9	1.2	0	1.4	0.60

Breakout: 44% Improve: 73% Collapse: 11% Attrition: 26% Comparables: John Cerutti, Jose Nuñez, Balor Moore, Pete Falcone

When the A's traded Tim Hudson to the Braves four years ago, Meyer was supposed to be the guy who was going to make it worth their while. He was a big-league ready, athletic, and highly projectable left-hander with excellent control of both a low-90s fastball and a solid slider. The second he got to Oakland, however, everything went backward, as his velocity dropped, his slider flattened, and he stopped throwing so many strikes. About once a month, he'd look like the Dan Meyer of old, but that wasn't nearly often enough. The A's just finally threw up their arms, took him off their 40-man roster, and let the Marlins pick him up, leaving the Hudson deal as one of the worst ever made by the Beane administration.

Josh Outman

Bats: L Throws: L Height: 6' 1" Weight: 180 Born: September 14, 1984 Age: 24

YEAR	TEAM	LVL	AGE	W	L	SV	G	GS	IP	H	BB	SO	HR	GB%	BABIP	STUFF	WHIP	ERA	DERA	EqH9	EqBB9	EqSO9	EqHR9	DEF	VORP	SN/WX
2006	LWD	A	21	14	6	0	27	27	155¹	119	75	161	5	47.4%	.288	2	1.25	2.96	7.41	11.3	6.5	4.6	1.2	7	-26.1	—
2007	CLR	A+	22	10	4	0	20	18	117¹	104	54	117	7	47.9%	.306	0	1.35	2.46	4.53	11.1	5.6	5.5	1.4	1	12.3	—
2007	RFA	AA	22	2	3	0	7	7	42	38	23	34	5	42.1%	.280	-5	1.45	4.50	6.34	10.3	5.6	4.7	1.9	-3	-3.1	—
2008	REA	AA	23	5	4	1	33	5	70¹	68	37	66	3	42.9%	.332	5	1.49	3.20	3.63	9.8	4.6	6.2	0.7	-3	14.7	—
2008	MID	AA	23	1	0	0	4	4	12²	13	3	5	1	63.0%	.273	-33	1.26	4.25	8.53	9.2	2.1	1.4	1.4	3	-4.1	—
2008	SAC	AAA	23	1	0	0	5	2	15¹	9	5	15	1	46.2%	.211	11	0.92	1.76	3.00	5.4	3.0	6.0	0.6	1	4.3	—
2008	OAK	MLB	23	1	2	0	6	4	25²	34	8	19	1	42.7%	.393	14	1.64	4.55	1.48	12.9	2.6	6.3	0.4	-10	2.3	0.53
2009	OAK	MLB	24	5	7	1	42	13	102²	117	57	70	15	43.0%	.310	1	1.69	5.59	5.68	10.3	4.4	5.7	1.3	-0	-3.5	0.12

Breakout: 10% Improve: 33% Collapse: 31% Attrition: 16% Comparables: Rick Krivda, Tom Fordham, Brad Woodall, Andy Pratt

We have to wonder how Outman's family life is. His father wrote a book on pitching mechanics, and as a youth, Josh followed his father's unique program, which employed no leg kick and an extreme back-to-forward rock. Once he got to college, coaches began to standardize his mechanics, and his pro stock took off. It's hard to find southpaws with mid-90s heat, but Outman has that and a sharp slider, to boot. His control is an issue, and while the A's made him a starter after acquiring him in the Blanton deal, most scouts see him as a late-inning two-pitch reliever in the end.

James Simmons

Bats: R   Throws: R   Height: 6' 3"   Weight: 205   Born: September 29, 1986   Age: 22

YEAR	TEAM	LVL	AGE	W	L	SV	G	GS	IP	H	BB	SO	HR	GB%	BABIP	STUFF	WHIP	ERA	DERA	EqH9	EqBB9	EqSO9	EqHR9	DEF	VORP	SN/WX
2007	MID	AA	20	0	0	0	13	2	29²	36	8	23	2	47.4%	.370	1	1.48	3.94	7.43	13.2	3.0	4.4	1.0	3	-5.4	—
2008	MID	AA	21	9	6	0	25	25	136	150	32	120	11	42.0%	.347	12	1.34	3.51	5.94	11.5	2.6	5.0	1.3	10	-4.7	—
2009	OAK	MLB	22	5	8	0	19	19	103	122	38	64	15	43.0%	.310	12	1.55	5.45	5.56	10.7	2.9	5.2	1.3	-0	-1.9	0.59

Breakout: 9%   Improve: 30%   Collapse: 29%   Attrition: 18%   Comparables: Al Lachowicz, John Wasdin, Josh Banks, Willie Fraser

When the A's drafted Simmons with their first-round pick in 2007, it was not for his upside; it was for his polish. Few scouts saw him as more than a fourth starter in the end, but at the same time, it was nearly impossible to see him not reaching that projection. In his full-season debut, he had little problem succeeding at Double-A, with his four average pitches playing up because of pinpoint command. Every team needs a dependable innings eater who keeps you in every game he starts, and Simmons is going to be one of those guys.

Greg Smith

Bats: L   Throws: L   Height: 6' 2"   Weight: 190   Born: December 22, 1983   Age: 25

YEAR	TEAM	LVL	AGE	W	L	SV	G	GS	IP	H	BB	SO	HR	GB%	BABIP	STUFF	WHIP	ERA	DERA	EqH9	EqBB9	EqSO9	EqHR9	DEF	VORP	SN/WX
2006	LNC	A+	22	9	0	0	13	13	88	57	31	71	3	54.5%	.239	8	1.00	1.64	3.84	6.0	4.0	3.6	0.8	7	16.0	—
2006	TEN	AA	22	5	4	0	11	11	60	65	23	38	4	35.2%	.326	-15	1.47	3.90	7.24	11.5	4.0	3.3	1.3	4	-10.0	—
2007	MOB	AA	23	5	3	0	12	12	69²	64	14	62	7	43.5%	.306	-6	1.12	3.36	6.25	10.1	2.1	5.0	1.7	7	-4.6	—
2007	TUC	AAA	23	4	2	0	10	10	52¹	61	18	34	4	40.7%	.339	-6	1.51	3.79	5.11	10.6	3.3	4.2	0.9	1	2.7	—
2008	OAK	MLB	24	7	16	0	32	32	190¹	169	87	111	21	36.0%	.263	-4	1.35	4.16	4.97	8.4	3.9	4.7	1.1	11	29.7	4.34
2009	COL	MLB	25	7	9	0	23	23	127¹	140	53	87	19	40.0%	.300	12	1.52	5.24	4.88	9.2	3.2	5.5	1.3	1	12.5	2.30

Breakout: 9%   Improve: 39%   Collapse: 34%   Attrition: 13%   Comparables: Ross Baumgarten, Alex Kellner, Angel Miranda, Jamie Moyer

Smith came over as an extra arm in the Haren deal, and it was a big surprise when he made the Opening Day rotation. Even more surprising, he held his own, at least on a runs-allowed level. The problem is that every other aspect of his game makes this look like a fluke, as his ratios are just not conducive to this kind of success. Last season was probably Smith's career year, and the trade to Colorado makes it even more unlikely that he'll top it.

Huston Street

Bats: R   Throws: R   Height: 6' 0"   Weight: 195   Born: August 2, 1983   Age: 25

YEAR	TEAM	LVL	AGE	W	L	SV	G	GS	IP	H	BB	SO	HR	GB%	BABIP	STUFF	WHIP	ERA	DERA	EqH9	EqBB9	EqSO9	EqHR9	DEF	VORP	SN/WX
2006	OAK	MLB	22	4	4	37	69	0	70²	64	13	67	4	39.4%	.303	26	1.09	3.31	3.41	7.8	1.6	7.4	0.5	-1	19.5	3.19
2007	OAK	MLB	23	5	2	16	48	0	50	35	12	63	5	43.5%	.259	26	0.94	2.88	3.38	6.4	2.0	9.2	0.9	-2	12.9	2.25
2008	OAK	MLB	24	7	5	18	63	0	70	58	27	69	6	37.9%	.292	11	1.21	3.73	4.01	7.9	3.2	8.0	0.8	2	15.2	1.94
2009	COL	MLB	25	3	3	10	45	0	52²	48	19	55	6	41.0%	.300	22	1.27	3.88	3.68	7.7	2.7	8.5	1.0	0	13.5	1.32

Breakout: 32%   Improve: 59%   Collapse: 26%   Attrition: 21%   Comparables: Cecilio Guante, Steve Foucault, Lindy McDaniel, Antonio Osuna

If you are compiling an all-time college baseball team, Street is unquestionably the closer, but he was miscast in the same role in the big leagues. Makeup and guile and good stuff are enough to get the job done where the bats go "ping," but if Street had never had a laundry list of legendary moments at the University of Texas and Team USA, he would never have been asked to save a game in the majors, because his is a setup man's skill set, and always has been. It's not that he isn't good; he's damn good. But as a closer, he's a bit short—as the Rockies will discover this year.

Brad Ziegler

Bats: R　Throws: R　Height: 6' 4"　Weight: 190　Born: October 10, 1979　Age: 29

YEAR	TEAM	LVL	AGE	W	L	SV	G	GS	IP	H	BB	SO	HR	GB%	BABIP	STUFF	WHIP	ERA	DERA	EqH9	EqBB9	EqSO9	EqHR9	DEF	VORP	SN/WX
2006	MID	AA	26	9	6	0	23	22	141²	151	37	88	17	45.9%	.307	-28	1.33	3.38	5.92	11.0	2.8	3.2	1.7	13	-4.6	—
2006	SAC	AAA	26	0	1	0	4	4	21¹	32	5	11	3	41.3%	.387	-29	1.75	5.97	8.38	14.9	2.3	2.8	1.9	-2	-6.0	—
2007	MID	AA	27	4	0	1	15	0	23²	19	4	18	0	62.5%	.275	-8	0.97	1.14	4.70	7.8	2.0	3.9	0.4	4	2.3	—
2007	SAC	AAA	27	8	3	1	35	0	54²	46	14	44	0	66.5%	.295	3	1.10	2.96	4.94	8.5	2.6	5.5	0.2	5	3.7	—
2008	SAC	AAA	28	2	0	8	19	0	24¹	15	4	20	0	68.7%	.227	6	0.78	0.37	2.28	5.7	1.5	4.9	0.4	2	8.7	—
2008	OAK	MLB	28	3	0	11	47	0	59²	47	22	30	2	65.3%	.269	-1	1.16	1.06	1.68	7.9	3.4	4.4	0.3	2	30.0	4.45
2009	OAK	MLB	29	2	2	5	42	0	45	48	16	25	4	53.0%	.300	-2	1.43	3.96	4.12	9.6	2.9	4.7	0.8	-0	6.6	0.62

Breakout: 10%　Improve: 23%　Collapse: 52%　Attrition: 26%　　Comparables: Jim Todd, Mike Fetters, Tim Crabtree, Warren Brusstar

Signed out of the independent leagues, Ziegler was an organizational arm who hit his spots and had a nice changeup, but everything changed when bullpen coach Ron Romanick, searching for the next Chad Bradford, thought Ziegler's mechanics were perfect for a conversion to side-arming. The rest is quite literally history after Ziegler began his career with 39 straight scoreless innings. While he occasionally mixes in a slider and changeup, 90 percent of his pitches are classic side-arm sinkers in the 84-88 mph range, leading to a ridiculous ground-ball ratio. His was one of the best stories of the season. He'll be setting up Joey Devine this year as part of the bullpen that nobody saw coming.

LINEOUTS

Hitters

PLAYER	TEAM	LVL	AGE	PA	R	2B	3B	HR	RBI	BB	SO	SB-CS	EqBRR	AVG/OBP/SLG	EqAVG/EqOBP/EqSLG	EqA	VORP	WARP
OF R. Dixon	ATH	Rk	17	201	32	3	10	8	42	18	68	5-2	-0.4	.263/.328/.525	.176/.219/.335	.184	-42.8	-2.7
C J. Donaldson	PEO	A	22	254	27	13	0	6	23	17	41	7-1	1.2	.217/.276/.349	.176/.224/.285	.170	-27.5	-1.5
	STO	A+	22	207	37	13	2	9	39	17	29	0-2	1.0	.330/.391/.564	.267/.324/.461	.264	6.9	1.1
INF J. Guzman	MID	AA	24	376	57	21	2	14	76	33	56	5-2	0.9	.364/.419/.560	.284/.335/.454	.270	15.0	0.0
	SAC	AAA	24	65	5	2	0	2	9	4	13	0-2	-1.5	.237/.281/.373	.217/.250/.350	.198	-3.5	-0.6
OF J. Herrera	MID	AA	23	281	44	13	2	9	36	22	71	8-4	-2.9	.267/.330/.439	.223/.279/.369	.223	-9.1	-0.8
INF D. Murphy	SAC	AAA	25	154	25	10	2	11	27	8	46	1-0	0.6	.270/.316/.603	.238/.281/.524	.264	4.4	1.3
	OAK	MLB	25	117	10	3	0	3	13	11	38	2-1	1.3	.184/.274/.301	.184/.780/.320	.215	-5.4	-0.2
C L. Powell#	SAC	AAA	26	367	42	11	0	15	53	63	85	0-1	-2.3	.230/.360/.417	.194/.308/.335	.231	-12.4	0.3
OF D. Putnam*	SAC	AAA	25	363	54	18	2	15	57	47	83	3-2	-0.1	.276/.384/.494	.241/.337/.421	.262	6.7	0.5
C A. Recker	MID	AA	24	482	57	29	4	11	64	43	140	1-2	-6.8	.274/.346/.437	.222/.283/.358	.222	-16.7	-0.4
OF R. Robnett*	MID	AA	24	104	13	6	0	1	8	17	24	1-0	-1.9	.259/.385/.365	.202/.314/.281	.222	-5.0	-0.4
	SAC	AAA	24	231	28	15	0	3	19	21	61	2-0	1.4	.236/.307/.351	.218/.281/.322	.212	-11.4	-1.4
OF M. Sulentic*	STO	A+	20	381	52	24	4	9	55	30	91	7-2	0.5	.309/.368/.481	.244/.298/.393	.238	-3.9	-0.8
DH M. Sweeney	OAK	MLB	34	136	13	8	0	2	12	7	6	0-0	-0.1	.286/.331/.397	.294/.343/.413	.264	2.6	0.3

Given $600,000 as a tenth-round pick last June, **Rashun Dixon** is already arguably the best athlete in the system, and A's officials were shocked at how un-raw his game was during his pro debut. ⊘ Also acquired in the Harden deal, catcher **Josh Donaldson** was suffering from lost-bat disease before the trade, but suddenly resembled an exciting offensive prospect again afterward. ⊘ **Jesus Guzman** is an offense-oriented second/third-base type who won the Texas League batting crown and had a huge winter in Venezuela, but the A's had no room to protect him; the Giants signed him in December. ⊘ Once a highly regarded five-tool stud, **Javier Herrera** has never gotten on track after missing the 2006 season due to Tommy John surgery, and his effort to do so has left much to be desired. ⊘ Passed up by younger, better players, utilityman **Donnie Murphy** hit his way back down to the minors and was signed by Baltimore over the winter. ⊘ **Landon Powell** combines impressive power and patience with a disturbing weight problem and two major knee surgeries in the past three years, endangering any faith in his ever panning out. ⊘ Dropped from the 40-man roster before the year, **Danny Putnam** is way down on the depth chart as an unathletic, undersized outfielder with modest on-base skills. ⊘ **Anthony Recker** hits well for a catcher, but not well enough for people to overlook his defense. ⊘ A former first-round pick, **Richie Robnett** has grown out of center field, but his power didn't come with him to Triple-A, and it was really his only plus tool. ⊘ A hit-only prospect who crashed and burned in 2007, **Matt Sulentic** got his blip back onto the prospect radar with a bounce-back season in the Cal League. ⊘ Veteran **Mike Sweeney** broke camp on the big-league roster as the designated clubhouse leader, but double knee surgery ended that, and perhaps his career.

Pitchers

PLAYER	TEAM	LVL	AGE	W	L	SV	IP	H	BB	SO	HR	GB%	BABIP	STUFF	WHIP	ERA	DERA	EqH9	EqBB9	EqSO9	EqHR9	DEF	VORP
A. Bailey	MID	AA	24	5	9	0	110¹	99	56	110	13	48.6%	.298	-27	1.41	4.32	7.31	9.3	5.1	5.6	1.7	6	-19.9
A. Carignan	MID	AA	21	3	3	24	52²	36	39	67	4	43.8%	.283	13	1.42	2.22	4.78	7.5	7.3	7.5	1.3	6	4.5
S. Demel	STO	A+	22	5	2	18	67	61	32	90	5	58.7%	.323	-2	1.39	3.36	4.73	10.2	5.4	6.7	1.4	-8	6.3
L. DiNardo*	SAC	AAA	28	6	5	0	71¹	107	16	49	7	56.8%	.403	-17	1.73	6.69	6.78	15.5	2.4	4.2	1.1	-11	-8.5
	OAK	MLB	28	1	2	0	23	31	13	12	3	55.2%	.337	-25	1.91	7.43	7.04	12.1	4.7	3.9	1.2	-2	-5.2
J. Gray	SAC	AAA	26	2	7	4	67²	86	23	50	9	48.3%	.353	-28	1.61	4.39	4.71	12.9	3.3	4.4	1.6	-4	6.2
	OAK	MLB	26	0	0	0	4²	8	1	4	1	27.8%	.412	-11	1.93	7.66	7.71	15.4	1.9	5.8	1.9	0	-1.1
C. Italiano	KNC	A	21	7	0	0	70	43	35	79	2	50.0%	.253	18	1.11	1.16	4.86	7.7	6.3	5.1	0.9	7	5.2
	STO	A+	21	1	4	0	30	44	26	33	7	42.2%	.394	-23	2.33	9.90	13.15	17.7	10.4	5.5	4.2	-5	-21.8
H. Rodriguez	STO	A+	21	2	3	2	75	57	40	104	5	50.9%	.315	13	1.29	3.96	5.54	9.5	6.3	7.6	1.4	-6	0.4
	MID	AA	21	2	7	0	41	51	44	43	1	56.7%	.400	4	2.32	7.46	9.08	13.4	10.8	6.0	0.5	-8	-14.6
T. Ross	KNC	A	21	0	1	0	19¹	16	5	16	1	66.7%	.268	-9	1.09	4.66	8.31	9.9	3.6	3.6	1.6	0	-5.2
K. Saarloos	SAC	AAA	29	9	4	0	140²	150	36	79	18	53.7%	.290	-20	1.32	4.22	6.10	10.1	2.5	3.1	1.4	8	-7.5
	OAK	MLB	29	1	0	0	26¹	37	4	12	2	54.9%	.357	-12	1.56	5.48	5.54	12.8	1.4	3.5	0.7	-1	-0.8
R. Webb	MID	AA	22	9	8	0	130	165	44	94	12	51.3%	.358	-21	1.61	5.19	7.97	12.8	3.6	3.8	1.4	1	-32.1

An older college product with a power arm, **Andrew Bailey** lacks control and secondary pitches. These limitations caught up with him starting at Double-A, but a move to the pen generated a 0.92 ERA in 39 IP. ⊘ A thickly built, short righty with mid-90s heat, **Andrew Carignan** combines setup man's stuff with massive control issues. ⊘ One of the stronger arms in the system, **Sam Demel** gets it up to 97 and has a plus slider, but he's still a few refinements away from being guaranteed a big-league career. ⊘ Always a pure finesse pitcher, **Lenny DiNardo** couldn't survive a velocity drop down to the mid-80s, but the Royals are going to give him another chance this spring. ⊘ **Jeff Gray** pitches in the middle to upper 90s, but he's still a player stuck in Triple-A in his late 20s because the pitch is straight and is his only decent offering. ⊘ A first-round talent who finished the year with elbow issues, **Brett Hunter** was drafted by the A's in the seventh round; his $1.1 million salary was based on his past ability to touch 100 mph. ⊘ Once a highly regarded prospect, strong-armed but frequently injured **Craig Italiano** dominated at Low-A in his fourth pro season, but ran out of gas in the second half, leaving many to project him as a reliever at best. ⊘ Blessed with one of the best arms in the game, **Henry Rodriguez** constantly hits triple digits with his fastball, the problem being that he has utterly no clue where it is going. ⊘ A second-round pick last June, **Tyson Ross** is a big, projectable power pitcher who never lived up to expectations during his college career at Cal. ⊘ We're as surprised as you are that **Kirk Saarloos** has gotten 500 big-league innings. ⊘ Added to the 40-man roster in the offseason, **Ryan Webb** has been slow to develop, but the club feared it might lose him in the Rule 5 draft to a team that saw potential in a tall, lanky pitcher with a loose arm.

MANAGER: BOB GEREN

YEAR	TEAM	W-L	Pythag +/−	Avg PC	100+ P	120+ P	QS	BQS	REL	REL w Zero R	IBB	Subs	PH	PH Avg	PH HR	SB2	CS2	SB3	CS3	SAC Att	SAC %	POS SAC	Squeeze	Swing	In Play
2007	OAK	76-86	-3	95.8	69	2	80	6	445	276	60	33	64	.175	0	51	17	1	3	31	58.1%	16	1	134	86
2008	OAK	75-86	0	93.6	48	0	69	6	441	289	45	54	91	.203	2	84	19	2	2	55	54.5%	27	2	109	74

While it would be easy to characterize Geren as the willing dugout executor of his master's operating philosophy, it would also be unfair and simplistic—having a GM and skipper who are on the same page seems like sound organizational management. Like a lot of skippers confronted with an unproductive lineup, Geren responded by running a bit more, especially in his using Rajai Davis to pinch-run, but also bunting a little more often. Sometimes, this can lead to a self-defeating cycle of managing for one run and getting less, but it seems less likely that this will become a problem here. On defense, Geren was more aggressive in his use of the intentional walk than you would expect, given the generally solid effort from the pitching staff. But having Huston Street issue a half-dozen walks is as much an indication of a questionable closer as it is a matter of questionable tactics. Sensibly enough, Geren relied on defensive replacements to get Emil Brown or Jack Cust off the field. All in all, you can consider 2008 an exercise in giving Geren experience in getting tactical in a tighter-run environment than he should have to operate in going forward. While that might seem a small thing, A's fans still wondering why Jeremy Giambi didn't get pinch-run for back in the 2001 ALDS understand that this sort of ticky-tack stuff matters in certain situations.

Philadelphia Phillies

In his book *Blundering to Glory*, the historian Owen Connelly advances the argument that Napoleon was less a genius than a brilliant improviser, noting that the Emperor was "not a seer who could ... plan his campaign flawlessly. He won because he never stopped going after the enemy." It's an important distinction worth appreciating because of the implied genius of a different sort in Connelly's observation: a genius born not of brilliantly executed perfect plans carried off without a hitch against feeble foes— that was the Yankees in the '30s—but of adapting to the challenge of operating on a field against other smart people who have smart plans of their own, and beating them just the same.

That can mean having the flexibility to accept that your best-laid plans can fall flat, and is perhaps the big thing that separates the Pat Gillicks of the world from, say, Bill Bavasi. Or Bond villains. Now that the Phillies have won it all in a league where the Mets or Dodgers or Cubs were the more obvious favorites, it's worth reflecting on how much Gillick's Phillies "blundered" their way into their own glory, by exploiting more than a few improvisations of their own, while overcoming the failure of so many of their more superficially impressive designs.

First, there's the question of how well the team regrouped after its humiliatingly quick exit from the 2007 playoff picture. They didn't really make that many major moves. They elected to go from stocking third base with "staff," to signing somebody they could write into the lineup card in ink; unfortunately, that somebody was Pedro Feliz. They lost an outfielder (Aaron Rowand) to free agency, and replaced him with Geoff Jenkins— that also didn't really turn out well, as Jenkins would eventually lose his job. They lost a starting pitcher in

PHILLIES PROSPECTUS

2008 record: 92-70; First place in NL East

Pythagenport record: 93-69

Runs scored per game: 4.94 (2nd in NL)

Runs allowed per game: 4.22 (3rd in NL)

Team EqA: .267 (4th in NL)

2008 Batters Age: 30.3 (5th-oldest in NL)

2008 Pitchers Age: 30.9 (2nd-oldest in NL)

Ballpark: Citizens Bank Park; Neutral park; Park Factor of 1.007

2008: A potent offense and surprisingly effective bullpen culminate in the Phillies' first championship since 1980.

2009: These aren't the 2007 Cardinals, but baseball's next dynasty won't hail from Pennsylvania.

Kyle Lohse, but anticipated replacing him by moving Brett Myers into the rotation after trading for Brad Lidge. Lidge's success got the headlines, but Myers' flexibility was part of what the Phillies did well that winter—repurposing pieces already on hand. Similarly, losing Rowand from center field was entirely survivable on defense because Shane Victorino's glove was somewhat wasted on right field.

Net, they didn't really wind up being a better team; by their Pythagorean projections, they were an 88-win team in 2007—and an 87-win team in 2008, and an 85-win team in 2006. This might seem a bit strange, but consider the performance of the major units of the team (see Table 1).

What exactly happened? The bullpen's received the lion's share of the credit for its huge turnaround in the wake of Lidge's redemption, and that's not entirely unreasonable—last year's Phillies pen wasn't just the league's best, it was the best bullpen in Phillies history, surpassing the previous all-time franchise-high WXRL tallies of the 2004 team (that made Tim Worrell briefly famous) and the 1987 team (Steve Bedrosian's Cy Young season). This was also a unit-wide feat, as Lidge's heroics only put an exclamation point to the exceptional work done by set-up men J.C. Romero, Ryan Madson, and Chad Durbin (two retreads and a homegrown reliever—we'll get to prove-

Table 1. Catching Up: Unit Performance in the Gillick Era

| Year | Offense | Rotation | Bullpen | Defense |
	EqA (NL Rank)	SNLVA_R (NL Rank)	WXRL (NL Rank)	PADE (NL Rank)
2006	.268 (3)	.491 (14)	8.75 (6)	-0.61 (12)
2007	.276 (1)	.498 (12)	7.34 (12)	0.15 (8)
2008	.267 (4)	.536 (6)	15.24 (1)	0.58 (4)

Table 2. Mommy, Where Do Phillies Come From? Finding the Studs for the 2008 Squad

Drafted/ Developed	Year (Round)	Cost	Free Agents	Year	Cost		Other Means	Year	How?
Pat Burrell	1998 (1)	$8 million ('98–'02)	Adam Eaton	2007	$24.51 million ('07–'09)		Brad Lidge	2008	Trade + Subsequent Extension
Brett Myers	1999 (1)	$2.05 million	Geoff Jenkins	2008	$13/$19.25 million ('08–'09/'10 option)		Jamie Moyer	2006	Trade + Subsequent Extension
Cole Hamels	2002 (1)	$2.0 million	Flash Gordon	2006	$18 million ('06–'08)		Joe Blanton	2008	Trade
Chase Utley	2000 (1)	$1.78 million	Pedro Feliz	2008	$8.5/$13 million ('08–'09/'10 option)		Shane Victorino	2006	Rule 5
Jimmy Rollins	1996 (2)	$340,000	So Taguchi	2008	$1.05 million		J.C. Romero	2007	Waivers, MLB min. + Subsequent Extension
Ryan Howard	2001 (5)	$235,000	Chad Durbin	2008	$900,000		Scott Eyre	2008	Trade + Subsequent Extension
Kyle Kendrick	2003 (7)	$135,000	Jayson Werth	2006	$850,000		Eric Bruntlett	2008	Trade
Ryan Madson	1998 (9)	$325,000	Rudy Seanez	2008	$400,000+Incentives				
Carlos Ruiz	1998 (NDFA)	$8,000	Gregg Dobbs	2007	$385,000				
			Clay Condrey	2006	MLB minimum				
			Chris Coste	2005	Minor League FA				

nance in a moment). But just as remarkable was the turnaround of the rotation—boosted by Myers, and shored up in-season with Joe Blanton's brand of adequacy, but not really *that* different a unit. It was still essentially reliant on Cole Hamels and Jamie Moyer, and had the benefit of some addition by subtraction by getting over Adam Eaton. And keeping with a theme for the 2008 season, the Phillies got a lot better defensively, though given the crude tools we have at our disposal on that score, it would be hard to suggest that this was the product of any one player—perhaps Chase Utley—as much as it appears to have grown out of a much more stable alignment.

If there was a quick lesson to be taken from the Gillick-era Phillies story, it's what transpired in 2006, Gillick's first year on the job. That was the season in which the Phillies punted early, dumping Bobby Abreu on the Yankees at the July trading deadline, only to veer back into the race two weeks later wondering how they were going to score enough runs. Since the warm bodies added to the organization in the deal haven't amounted to much, or were ever likely to, at best, the Abreu deal gave Gillick subsequent financial flexibility, but as we'll see, that wasn't necessarily employed to best effect. It would be a bit wildly optimistic to suggest that, if only they hadn't dealt Abreu, they might have pulled their first come-from-behind post-season berth in 2006 to make their current streak three in a row.*

_____

* Even so, there it is, and given the Cardinals' title from that year, it seems pretty clear just getting to that party could have led to bigger things.

Having blown that opportunity, Gillick didn't despair—as an aging exec with a win-now core, he simply went back to work and tried new combinations of supporting talent.

The pen was last year's bit of lightning in a bottle, but given how many constants this ballclub has relied upon over the last three seasons, it's important to review how it was painstakingly assembled, and by who—in the Phillies' brand of blundering to glory, credit really fundamentally belongs to the organization, and more usually in spite of Gillick's masterstrokes, not because of them, especially when the relative expenditures for the different kinds of risks can be so disproportionate (see Table 2).

Strictly speaking, this isn't an apples-to-apples comparison—the drafted/developed players would draw subsequent salaries, after all, but those were essentially limited under the umbrella of team control of players before they're eligible for any flavor of free agency or arbitration-related raises. Other expenses related to player development aren't shown here either—the franchise-record signing bonus ($4.1 million) given to Gavin Floyd in 2001, for example. No, in short, what this table shows us is just what it took in terms of an initial investment to get the guys who comprised the championship team.

Of course, the true source of joy and the genuine fount of glory is the left-hand column, and there, the men to credit are Ed Wade and, perhaps more specifically, director of scouting Mike Arbuckle (subsequently the assistant GM of scouting and player development). While Burrell didn't come all that cheaply, keep in mind that he was the first overall pick in the draft in '98—that's always going to cost you, and you can't say that the investment didn't turn out a whole lot better than, say, Reggie Taylor. On the low end, even if you discount players like Ruiz or Kendrick as filler organizational types, they represent the benefits of running a farm system—do some homework at the lower end of the amateur scene as well as at the top, and a few extras are bound to fall into your lap. Again, you can credit good scouting for all of these goodies—the list of people picked before Myers in '99 (Eric Munson and Kyle Snyder, among others) or Utley in '00 (Luis Montanez and Joe Borchard, anyone?) reflects how much these weren't all automatic or obvious, as perhaps Burrell was. Similarly, the Phillies being more or less unafraid of paying out seven-figure bonuses in the draft for more than a decade dovetails pretty neatly with their gift for finding the people worth paying them to.

Returning to the table, it isn't hard to see the mistakes, because they're right there in the middle, practicing the fine art of trying not to be seen; depending on your tastes in fifth outfielders, you can draw the line of regret above or below Taguchi. It would be easy to say that the expense of making big plans goes with the territory, but take a good look at the big-name quartet of free-agent additions: Eaton was unpredictable before he got expensive, Jenkins was old and losing ground, Feliz has never been all that useful, and Gordon was old, expensive, *and* unpredictable. Yet those are the guys, as far as initial investments go, that cost more than anyone to put in Philadelphia. If big-ticket expenditures in the free-agent market are supposed to yield instant gratification, you can forgive Phillies fans for finding little joy here. All of these were Gillick's signings, and *all of Gillick's big-ticket signings turned out badly*. We'll return to this in a moment, when we move on to some thoughts on the future that lies beyond the afterglow.

Things get happier when we move down below the line of regret in that middle group, where you find guys that you can credit Gillick for, and also some that Phillies player development staffers deserve props for bringing in. Werth was somebody Gillick's Orioles drafted in the first round in '97, and Dobbs is somebody that Gillick's Mariners signed as an undrafted free agent in 2001—in both cases, the Phillies subsequently took modest, affordable risks (on Werth's health and Dobbs' positionlessness), and employed each to better effect than anyone had before. Coste, the now-famous former indie leaguer, had bounced from organization to organization, as most felt his receiving skills left something to be desired. Durbin has been a utility arm

for a few years now; the price was right, and the results far exceeded reasonable expectations; nothing wrong with getting lucky now and again. These were players that anybody could have had, and anybody could have scouted, and anyone could have taken a chance on.

Now, let's skip over to the right-hand column. Let's be ungenerous, and say that we dismiss the addition of Lidge as a bit of taking advantage of Gillick's predecessor to add a quality pitcher who needed a change of scenery for shiny bits of roster flotsam that Ed Wade couldn't help but want because he was familiar with them. Not especially fair to Gillick, but here again, his familiarity with Moyer had to have helped. At the very least, you can collectively credit the organization's scouting effort for identifying and acquiring Victorino and Romero for next to nothing by today's standards for player acquisition—who says the wire and the Rule 5 draft have nothing to offer?

What isn't here, however, is any value received for the decision to dump Bobby Abreu, not to mention the absent regret over dealing Floyd (and Gio Gonzalez) for Chief Garcia in 2007. Both high-profile moves did nothing to help the Phillies win, and in Abreu's case, you can't even really suggest that the money saved was subsequently spent well, not when it was going to people like Eaton or Jenkins. The trade Gillick made in his first month on the job in November 2005, putting Jim Thome on the White Sox to make room for Howard at first base, also netted the Phillies payroll space, Aaron Rowand, Gonzalez, and Daniel Haigwood—which boiled down to more money poorly spent, two years of Rowand, and two draft picks from the Giants when Rowand signed with them. If this track record sounds somewhat spotty, it should, because it was.

What lessons are there to be learned for why it was sunny in Philadelphia in 2008, then? As we noted at the start, we should not judge too harshly the fact that Gillick made so many mistakes, because big plans have a nasty habit of going to pieces in contact with the realities of day-to-day baseball. Deals and moves cannot be fairly evaluated in terms of subsequent events, they can really only be treated on the basis of the information available at the time they get made. Gillick never ceased to try, whether in shoring up the rotation or assembling a pen, and if he had the benefit of a core of talent that had already been put together by the time he'd arrived, he also had the good sense to leave it be. For as badly as his big moves flopped with rather alarming reliability, they arguably never compromised the team's fundamental virtues, and for as badly as those moves flopped, they were also not the only moves made—familiarity helped bring players like Werth and Dobbs and Moyer into the fold, and elective additions like Romero and Victorino turned out more than a little well. As much as the Phillies of the Gillick era stumbled from one colossal mistake to the next in their major moves via free agency or in trades, they still found ways to add talent to the core, and when they got Lidge at a discount, they ran with it.

Now Gillick is gone, to another retirement involving another stint in an advisory capacity. Also gone is Arbuckle, the upshot of the decision to name front-office rival/assistant GM Ruben Amaro Jr. as Gillick's replacement. While Arbuckle has earned considerable credit for his work on the player development program, Amaro's credited with working on the team's arbitration cases (an odious yet necessary task) and consulting on trades and major free-agent contract negotiations, which, given the spotty track record of the organization in recent seasons, hardly seems like good news going forward. There's also the uncomfortable similarity between Amaro as an industry legacy groomed for front-office work and the last Gillick departure, which was for Bill Bavasi in Seattle—an industry legacy groomed for front-office work. This may not seem entirely fair to Amaro, but his initial work in the offseason hasn't given much cause for confidence. Letting Pat Burrell slip away so that he could be replaced with an older, more expensive, left-handed DH in Raul Ibañez not only ex-

accrbates the team's lineup lean, but at $31.5 million over three years, Ibañez is almost as unmovable from a roster as he is in left field. Signing Chan Ho Park isn't a bad move in itself, but banking on him as a starter seems like the worst sort of febrile wishcasting, between his massive (and career-long) platoon issues and his equally massive (and career-long) problems pitching away from Dodger Stadium.

So, the thing is done and the flag's been won. Even after Burrell's defection, the Phillies still have most of their core talent in place. Amaro's probably gotten off on the wrong foot with a couple of expensive mistakes, but they're his mistakes to make. What's going to be instructive as far as the Phillies' immediate future isn't how badly they did this winter, it's seeing if Amaro responds with Bavasi-like surprise over the inconceivable failure of his master plan and folds up, or if he manages to adapt and work around it while leaning on the same talent that's kept the Phillies within grabbing distance of a pennant for years. The National League hasn't given birth to a powerhouse ballclub in this decade, but four different senior circuit teams have been able to win the World Series in the last eight years despite the AL's generally assumed superiority. After blundering their way to glory last season, no team should better understand the virtue of keeping your head on your shoulders, because taking a shot can and does lead to outsized rewards.

HITTERS

Dominic Brown			OF								Bats: L		Throws: L		Height: 6' 5"		Weight: 204		Born: September 3, 1987		Age: 21
YEAR	TEAM	LVL	AGE	PA	R	2B	3B	HR	RBI	BB	SO	SB	CS	EqBRR	AVG	OBP	SLG	EqAVG	EqOBP	EqSLG	EqA	VORP	WARP	DEFENSE
2006	PHL	Rk	18	131	13	3	0	1	7	12	30	13	3	0.3	.214	.292	.265	.164	.215	.205	.136	-55.5	-4.2	14-CF -3 12-RF -6
2007	WPT	A	19	317	43	11	5	3	32	27	49	14	7	-2.5	.295	.356	.400	.248	.297	.354	.226	-15.3	-2.3	43-RF -5 29-CF -5
2008	LWD	A	20	516	77	23	3	9	54	64	72	22	7	-0.7	.291	.382	.417	.251	.333	.367	.250	-0.4	-0.9	65-CF -4 47-RF -10
2009	PHI	MLB	21	585	72	29	2	10	53	55	108	14	6	0.9	.256	.329	.379	.256	.329	.384	.249	3.3	0.9	137-CF -11

Breakout: 48%   Improve: 77%   Collapse: 10%   Attrition: 6%   Comparables: Mike Darr, Trey Beamon, Carlos Quintana, Peter Bergeron

Dominic Brown is a very good prospect with a lot of tools and a lot of potential, but the Darryl Strawberry comps being thrown around are a bit ridiculous. Yes, Brown is left-handed, tall, long, and an intriguing power/speed combination (not to mention African-American), but when Strawberry was the same age as Brown, he was putting up a 1021 OPS in the Texas League with 34 home runs, 45 stolen bases, and 100 walks. Brown has nothing close to that kind of power, and comparing nearly anyone to Strawberry, who had one of the best packages of tools in the last forty years, is more than a bit hyperbolic. Good prospect to be sure, but let's not get carried away.

Eric Bruntlett   UT

Bats: R   Throws: R   Height: 6' 0"   Weight: 190   Born: March 29, 1978   Age: 31

YEAR	TEAM	LVL	AGE	PA	R	2B	3B	HR	RBI	BB	SO	SB	CS	EqBRR	AVG	OBP	SLG	EqAVG	EqOBP	EqSLG	EqA	VORP	WARP	DEFENSE			
2006	ROU	AAA	28	93	11	3	1	1	7	17	13	3	2	0.0	.219	.380	.329	.182	.315	.286	.223	-4.5	-0.5	13-LF	-4	5-SS	1
2006	HOU	MLB	28	136	11	8	0	0	10	13	21	3	1	-0.0	.277	.351	.345	.267	.346	.325	.246	1.9	-0.2	16-SS	0	5-2B	-2
2007	ROU	AAA	29	262	31	10	4	1	21	31	36	13	4	0.0	.278	.365	.370	.216	.299	.297	.217	-13.3	0.7	34-CF	5	12-SS	3
2007	HOU	MLB	29	165	16	5	0	0	14	20	27	6	3	-0.4	.246	.346	.283	.252	.358	.288	.238	-0.9	0.0	39-SS	0		
2008	PHI	MLB	30	238	37	9	1	2	15	21	35	9	2	3.1	.217	.297	.297	.216	.298	.296	.218	-5.5	-0.6	31-SS	3	15-3B	-3
2009	PHI	MLB	31	149	17	6	1	1	11	14	23	5	2	0.6	.241	.319	.324	.241	.319	.329	.231	0.5	0.3	39-SS	-1		

Breakout: 34% Improve: 53% Collapse: 36% Attrition: 40%   Comparables: Terry Harmon, Jim Finigan, Fred Stanley, Alex Grammas

Nominally a utilityman, Bruntlett actually served in defined roles over long stretches. He started 28 straight games at shortstop in April and May in the absence of Jimmy Rollins. He then didn't get a single start anywhere from May 9 through June 20, primarily playing in blowouts and as a pinch-runner for Geoff Jenkins and Pedro Feliz. Later in the summer, he started a lot at third base when Feliz was injured, then finally settled in as Pat Burrell's legs in the season's last six weeks and the playoffs. Bruntlett runs well, can hit lefties a little, and play anywhere without killing you. He'll keep a job until he loses one of those skills.

Pat Burrell   LF

Bats: R   Throws: R   Height: 6' 4"   Weight: 235   Born: October 10, 1976   Age: 32

YEAR	TEAM	LVL	AGE	PA	R	2B	3B	HR	RBI	BB	SO	SB	CS	EqBRR	AVG	OBP	SLG	EqAVG	EqOBP	EqSLG	EqA	VORP	WARP	DEFENSE
2006	PHI	MLB	29	567	80	24	1	29	95	98	131	0	0	-5.6	.258	.388	.502	.248	.384	.484	.299	28.0	2.3	109-LF -13
2007	PHI	MLB	30	598	77	26	0	30	97	114	120	0	0	-1.3	.256	.400	.502	.249	.400	.500	.310	35.8	1.6	114-LF -28
2008	PHI	MLB	31	645	74	33	3	33	86	102	136	0	0	-1.2	.250	.367	.507	.250	.369	.520	.300	34.8	3.6	134-LF -8
2009	TBA	MLB	32	588	77	25	2	26	81	96	125	1	0	-2.9	.236	.364	.454	.240	.369	.477	.293	18.4	2.1	138-LF -11

Breakout: 6%   Improve: 31% Collapse: 34% Attrition: 13%   Comparables: Tim Salmon, Dwight Evans, Greg Luzinski, Danny Tartabul

The good kind of consistent, Burrell puts up .300 EqAs by drawing walks and hitting for power, and he plays almost every day. With no defensive value or speed, however, any loss in bat speed, any dip in walk rate, any drop in power is going to knock him out of the league in a hurry. The Rays have signed him to a deal—two years, $16 million—that seems like a bargain for what Burrell provides, and plan to make him a full-time DH. The short-term commitment is the key; Burrell's 2009 should be fine, but he won't hit enough to carry the DH slot much beyond that.

Chris Coste   C

Bats: R   Throws: R   Height: 6' 1"   Weight: 215   Born: February 4, 1973   Age: 36

YEAR	TEAM	LVL	AGE	PA	R	2B	3B	HR	RBI	BB	SO	SB	CS	EqBRR	AVG	OBP	SLG	EqAVG	EqOBP	EqSLG	EqA	VORP	WARP	DEFENSE			
2006	SWB	AAA	33	161	12	8	0	2	14	9	28	1	1	0.4	.177	.236	.272	.141	.193	.221	.117	-24.2	-2.3	25-1B	-3	12-C	0
2006	PHI	MLB	33	213	25	14	0	7	32	10	31	0	0	-0.4	.328	.376	.505	.322	.369	.487	.292	16.8	1.0	49-C	-6		
2007	REA	AA	34	116	14	5	0	5	31	5	13	0	0	0.0	.287	.319	.472	.171	.191	.288	.145	-13.9	-1.1	19-C	0	6-1B	-1
2007	OTT	AAA	34	102	8	5	0	0	10	10	14	0	0	0.5	.233	.317	.289	.185	.265	.239	.170	-9.7	-0.8	16-1B	1	6-C	-1
2007	PHI	MLB	34	137	15	3	0	5	22	4	20	0	0	0.7	.279	.311	.419	.277	.309	.408	.246	3.9	0.1	27-C	-1		
2008	PHI	MLB	35	305	28	17	0	9	36	16	51	0	1	-2.8	.263	.325	.423	.265	.325	.429	.259	8.7	1.1	69-C	0		
2009	PHI	MLB	36	141	12	6	0	3	15	8	23	0	0	-0.7	.247	.297	.373	.247	.297	.378	.231	1.0	0.5	37-C	-1		

Breakout: 37% Improve: 59% Collapse: 23% Attrition: 57%   Comparables: Ray Murray, Tom Pagnozzi, Joe Oliver, Bill Haselman

Coste came as close as he ever has to a full-time job last season, starting 19 of 34 games in one stretch, and never being out of the starting lineup in more than consecutive games. Whether cause or coincidence, Coste's performance slipped badly with the additional run of playing time, going .232/.308/.304 capped by an 0-for-14 that made it easy for Manuel to give the job back to Ruiz (who batted .283/.387/.396 in that same stretch). Coste is a plus backup catcher who needs to play for a manager, like Manuel, who is not afraid to use his backup as a pinch-hitter, so he's in the right place at the right time.

Greg Dobbs   4C

Bats: L   Throws: R   Height: 6' 1"   Weight: 205   Born: July 2, 1978   Age: 30

YEAR	TEAM	LVL	AGE	PA	R	2B	3B	HR	RBI	BB	SO	SB	CS	EqBRR	AVG	OBP	SLG	EqAVG	EqOBP	EqSLG	EqA	VORP	WARP	DEFENSE			
2006	TAC	AAA	27	421	60	19	3	9	55	37	58	14	5	-0.4	.314	.375	.451	.264	.318	.383	.247	0.0	0.5	42-3B	1	30-1B	1
2006	SEA	MLB	27	28	4	3	1	0	3	0	4	0	1	-0.3	.370	.393	.556	.370	.393	.556	.303	2.9	0.2				
2007	PHI	MLB	28	358	45	20	4	10	55	29	67	3	0	1.1	.272	.330	.451	.267	.330	.450	.269	10.8	0.2	46-3B	-6	11-1B	1
2008	PHI	MLB	29	240	30	14	1	9	40	11	40	3	1	-3.2	.301	.333	.491	.301	.333	.500	.281	13.3	0.3	37-3B	-7		
2009	PHI	MLB	30	219	28	12	1	7	28	18	37	3	1	-0.2	.276	.337	.451	.277	.337	.458	.271	10.0	0.8	55-3B	-4		

Breakout: 27% Improve: 48% Collapse: 23% Attrition: 27%   Comparables: Jerry Lynch, Rich Reese, Mike Lamb, Wayne Krenchicki

Dobbs has a pretty limited skill set—hitting right-handed pitchers for some average and power, surviving at third base—but it fits well on this Phillies' roster, enabling them to balance a bottom of the lineup that would list badly to the right otherwise. If you think pinch-hitting is a skill distinct from hitting, Dobbs' .314/.360/.526 career line in that role is impressive as well. He could do this for a while.

Jason Donald   SS

Bats: R   Throws: R   Height: 6' 1"   Weight: 190   Born: September 4, 1984   Age: 24

YEAR	TEAM	LVL	AGE	PA	R	2B	3B	HR	RBI	BB	SO	SB	CS	EqBRR	AVG	OBP	SLG	EqAVG	EqOBP	EqSLG	EqA	VORP	WARP	DEFENSE	
2006	BAT	A-	21	243	33	14	2	1	24	23	42	12	1	2.3	.263	.347	.362	.193	.255	.278	.188	-43.0	-1.9	58-SS	-4
2007	LWD	A	22	238	41	9	3	4	30	29	39	2	5	0.4	.310	.409	.447	.239	.318	.340	.233	-5.0	0.6	52-SS	2
2007	CLR	A+	22	336	48	22	5	8	41	35	70	3	2	-1.6	.300	.386	.491	.246	.320	.429	.257	5.1	0.4	79-SS	-9
2008	REA	AA	23	414	57	19	4	14	54	47	86	11	2	1.1	.307	.391	.497	.280	.357	.473	.286	23.5	1.5	90-SS	-16
2009	PHI	MLB	24	506	59	26	2	12	53	47	124	9	3	0.8	.248	.325	.397	.248	.325	.403	.254	14.1	1.2	119-SS	-6

Breakout: 20% Improve: 44% Collapse: 34% Attrition: 20%   Comparables: Scott Romano, Jim Opie, Brian Giles, Erick Almonte

Don't be alarmed by the low total of 93 games played; Donald missed time during the summer while playing for Team USA, which won bronze at the Beijing Olympics. He was, and is, healthy. Donald has a balanced skill set but not the athleticism of an everyday shortstop, although you might say the same of Troy Tulowitzki. He would be passable, but not that valuable, as an everyday third baseman. With second base and shortstop well occupied in Philadelphia, Donald's future involves incessant trade rumors and a starting middle-infield job on a different MLB team in 2010.

Pedro Feliz   3B

Bats: R   Throws: R   Height: 6' 1"   Weight: 210   Born: April 27, 1975   Age: 34

YEAR	TEAM	LVL	AGE	PA	R	2B	3B	HR	RBI	BB	SO	SB	CS	EqBRR	AVG	OBP	SLG	EqAVG	EqOBP	EqSLG	EqA	VORP	WARP	DEFENSE	
2006	SFN	MLB	31	644	75	35	5	22	98	33	112	1	1	-1.0	.244	.281	.428	.241	.281	.422	.239	-8.3	2.1	155-3B	17
2007	SFN	MLB	32	590	61	28	2	20	72	29	70	2	2	-5.0	.253	.290	.418	.252	.292	.423	.242	-2.0	3.1	136-3B	25
2008	PHI	MLB	33	463	43	19	2	14	58	33	54	0	0	-0.8	.249	.302	.402	.249	.304	.414	.247	0.6	0.9	109-3B	5
2009	PHI	MLB	34	338	35	16	1	10	43	23	46	0	1	-1.4	.261	.312	.409	.261	.313	.415	.248	6.1	1.4	82-3B	5

Breakout: 34% Improve: 54% Collapse: 26% Attrition: 37%   Comparables: Herb Perry, Ray Knight, Keith Moreland, Vinny Castilla

The other kind of consistent, Feliz has actually cut his strikeouts and bumped up his walks over the last two seasons, changes that have had no effect at all on his productivity. His very good glove work at third base makes this level of offense acceptable, especially given the left-handedness of the Phillies' rotation. However, the entire package is marginal, meaning that Feliz could fall out of the league at any time.

Greg Golson   CF

Bats: R   Throws: R   Height: 6' 0"   Weight: 190   Born: September 17, 1985   Age: 23

YEAR	TEAM	LVL	AGE	PA	R	2B	3B	HR	RBI	BB	SO	SB	CS	EqBRR	AVG	OBP	SLG	EqAVG	EqOBP	EqSLG	EqA	VORP	WARP	DEFENSE	
2006	LWD	A	20	419	56	15	4	7	31	19	107	23	7	1.4	.220	.258	.333	.181	.210	.267	.158	-48.8	-4.9	92-CF	-11
2006	CLR	A+	20	174	31	11	2	6	17	11	53	7	3	0.8	.264	.324	.472	.227	.276	.411	.235	-3.2	-0.2	37-CF	-2
2007	CLR	A+	21	449	66	27	3	12	52	21	124	25	8	0.8	.285	.322	.450	.238	.271	.392	.229	-11.9	0.6	98-CF	7
2007	REA	AA	21	158	20	5	2	3	16	2	49	5	0	1.4	.242	.255	.359	.208	.222	.331	.188	-12.9	-0.8	34-CF	1
2008	REA	AA	22	470	64	18	4	13	60	34	130	23	5	4.2	.282	.333	.434	.260	.306	.420	.254	3.4	1.6	101-CF	3
2009	TEX	MLB	23	534	59	26	4	13	55	31	157	20	7	2.5	.241	.288	.389	.238	.287	.394	.239	-5.2	1.3	126-CF	2

Breakout: 41% Improve: 71% Collapse: 16% Attrition: 7%   Comparables: Shane Mack, Hiram Bocachica, Dante Powell, Ty Gainey

A strong start earned Golson some attention and a slot at the Futures Game. By the end of the season, though, he had regressed to being the same disappointment he's been for years, including that wretched K/BB ratio at Triple-A. In November, the Phillies swapped him to Texas for John Mayberry Jr.; Golson should have a future as a fifth out-fielder and pinch-runner—he's stolen 120 bases at a 78 percent clip in the minors—but that's about as good as it will get.

Brad Harman — MI

Bats: R   Throws: R   Height: 6' 1"   Weight: 175   Born: November 19, 1985   Age: 23

YEAR	TEAM	LVL	AGE	PA	R	2B	3B	HR	RBI	BB	SO	SB	CS	EqBRR	AVG	OBP	SLG	EqAVG	EqOBP	EqSLG	EqA	VORP	WARP	DEFENSE
2006	CLR	A+	20	482	59	19	1	2	25	48	102	6	2	1.0	.241	.322	.305	.198	.268	.255	.185	-41.9	-3.2	111-SS -11
2007	CLR	A+	21	499	63	26	5	13	62	40	105	1	1	-1.6	.281	.341	.449	.235	.289	.388	.234	-9.5	1.4	110-2B 5 11-SS 4
2008	REA	AA	22	494	49	16	1	17	56	43	138	3	1	-0.8	.210	.280	.366	.196	.260	.350	.212	-26.9	-0.9	75-2B -1 38-SS 1
2008	PHI	MLB	22	11	1	1	0	0	1	1	1	0	0	-0.1	.100	.182	.200	.100	.182	.200	.087	-1.4	-0.2	
2009	PHI	MLB	23	544	52	26	2	15	55	45	140	5	2	0.2	.223	.290	.371	.223	.290	.377	.230	-0.4	0.7	128-2B 3

Breakout: 51% Improve: 75% Collapse: 15% Attrition: 6%   Comparables: Juan Espinal, Mario Lisson, Erick Almonte, Lance Madsen

Harman is one of those on-again, off-again prospects who alternates good seasons with bad ones, but in 2008 he had the best and worst of both worlds. He hit a career high 17 home runs and got his first taste of the majors, but he also struggled to keep his average above the Mendoza line while striking out once every 3.2 at-bats. With his pop and ability to play any position in the infield he has some utility possibilities, but few think he'll ever hit enough to be more than that.

Anthony Hewitt — 3B

Bats: R   Throws: R   Height: 6' 1"   Weight: 195   Born: April 27, 1989   Age: 20

YEAR	TEAM	LVL	AGE	PA	R	2B	3B	HR	RBI	BB	SO	SB	CS	EqBRR	AVG	OBP	SLG	EqAVG	EqOBP	EqSLG	EqA	VORP	WARP	DEFENSE
2008	PHL	Rk	19	129	14	7	1	1	9	7	55	2	0	-0.8	.197	.256	.299	.131	.171	.221	.101	-52.3	-3.9	19-3B -6
2009	PHI	MLB	20	462	34	23	2	6	32	26	169	7	4	1.0	.186	.236	.293	.186	.236	.298	.177	-27.8	-2.5	109-3B -7

Breakout: 92% Improve: 93% Collapse: 6% Attrition: 10%   Comparables: Kim Batiste, David Christensen, John Gumpf, Kieron Pope

It's impossible to consider Hewitt, a tools project who was the Phillies' first-round pick last year, without consider-ing the player listed above. Golson, taken with the 21st pick in 2004, and has never converted his speed and strength on the baseball diamond. Hewitt may have been the best athlete in the '08 draft pool—80 power on the 20-80 scout-ing scale, with excellent speed and a terrific arm—but he's just an athlete right now, and his pro debut is an indica-tion of the distance between him and a career.

Ryan Howard — 1B

Bats: L   Throws: L   Height: 6' 4"   Weight: 255   Born: November 19, 1979   Age: 29

YEAR	TEAM	LVL	AGE	PA	R	2B	3B	HR	RBI	BB	SO	SB	CS	EqBRR	AVG	OBP	SLG	EqAVG	EqOBP	EqSLG	EqA	VORP	WARP	DEFENSE
2006	PHI	MLB	26	704	104	25	1	58	149	108	181	0	0	-3.1	.313	.425	.659	.298	.413	.626	.339	82.3	7.2	157-1B -6
2007	PHI	MLB	27	648	94	26	0	47	136	107	199	1	0	-5.0	.268	.392	.584	.254	.386	.566	.316	55.2	4.7	138-1B -6
2008	PHI	MLB	28	700	105	26	4	48	146	81	199	1	1	-3.6	.251	.339	.543	.248	.337	.548	.292	36.6	4.5	157-1B 7
2009	PHI	MLB	29	631	96	25	1	40	110	86	161	0	1	-3.1	.270	.374	.547	.271	.374	.555	.305	40.2	4.4	147-1B -1

Breakout: 19% Improve: 40% Collapse: 17% Attrition: 13%   Comparables: Mike Epstein, Cecil Fielder, David Ortiz, Jim Gentile

When does it become all right to point out that despite having three straight top-five MVP finishes, Howard has been sprinting *backwards* for two seasons? His .313 batting average in '06 was a mirage driven by one of the best performances on contact (.455 BA) in history. In '08, his walk rate dropped off considerably, leading to a .339 OBP that simply isn't good enough for a no-defense first baseman in a hitters' park. Last season is the floor for this type of player; either Howard regains some ability to make contact, some batting average, or some walks, or he's headed for oblivion, no matter how many RBI he collects. Note to NL managers: he's a .231/.314/.471 career hitter against lefties, and getting worse by the year.

Tadahito Iguchi — 2B

Bats: R   Throws: R   Height: 5' 10"   Weight: 200   Born: December 4, 1974   Age: 34

YEAR	TEAM	LVL	AGE	PA	R	2B	3B	HR	RBI	BB	SO	SB	CS	EqBRR	AVG	OBP	SLG	EqAVG	EqOBP	EqSLG	EqA	VORP	WARP	DEFENSE
2006	CHA	MLB	31	627	97	24	0	18	67	59	110	11	5	-2.7	.281	.352	.422	.264	.343	.406	.262	25.4	0.2	135-2B -19
2007	CHA	MLB	32	377	45	17	4	6	31	44	65	8	1	2.7	.251	.340	.382	.240	.337	.378	.258	5.5	0.0	88-2B -11
2007	PHI	MLB	32	156	22	10	0	3	12	13	23	6	1	0.2	.304	.361	.442	.304	.365	.442	.284	8.8	1.2	30-2B 3
2008	SDN	MLB	33	330	29	14	1	2	24	26	75	8	1	1.1	.231	.292	.304	.241	.303	.323	.227	-6.3	-0.6	74-2B -4
2009	PHI	MLB	34	250	30	11	1	4	23	24	49	6	2	0.0	.251	.326	.368	.252	.326	.373	.248	5.4	0.4	62-2B -3

Breakout: 21% Improve: 38% Collapse: 36% Attrition: 43%   Comparables: Bobby Avila, George Strickland, Wayne Terwilliger, Tony Graffanino

Iguchi was a critical member of the 2005 World Champion Chicago White Sox. His second ring, however … Iguchi was released by the Padres on September 1 and joined the Phillies four days later. He pinch-ran once and pinch-hit twice over three weeks as the Phillies locked up the NL East, then started on the last day of the season after the division was clinched. A separated shoulder suffered in June ruined his year, and with no interest in his services as of mid-January, he appears headed back to Japan.

Jason Jaramillo — C

Bats: S   Throws: R   Height: 6' 0"   Weight: 200   Born: October 9, 1982   Age: 26

YEAR	TEAM	LVL	AGE	PA	R	2B	3B	HR	RBI	BB	SO	SB	CS	EqBRR	AVG	OBP	SLG	EqAVG	EqOBP	EqSLG	EqA	VORP	WARP	DEFENSE
2006	REA	AA	23	364	35	25	1	6	39	32	55	0	1	-1.9	.248	.320	.388	.223	.286	.360	.225	-12.3	0.0	81-C -2
2007	OTT	AAA	24	496	52	13	4	6	56	50	79	0	1	-2.3	.271	.350	.361	.252	.324	.342	.237	-7.3	-0.2	108-C -10
2008	LEH	AAA	25	473	48	20	0	8	39	42	82	1	1	-2.0	.266	.340	.371	.245	.314	.344	.233	-9.7	0.7	113-C -1
2009	PIT	MLB	26	359	32	16	1	6	34	31	67	0	1	-1.2	.238	.310	.349	.237	.310	.361	.232	1.0	1.3	86-C 0

Breakout: 27% Improve: 46% Collapse: 30% Attrition: 25%   Comparables: Koyie Hill, Alan Ashby, Brian Johnson, A.J. Hinch

Jaramillo is a gap hitter with a decent approach and a good arm, but there's nothing about his game that stands out. He's been stuck at the upper levels of the system for the last three years, but with two outstanding young catchers coming up through the system he was stuck between the proverbial rock and a hard place. Fortunately for him, he was traded to the Pirates in the offseason for Ronny Paulino, where he'll compete for the job of backing up Ryan Doumit this spring.

Geoff Jenkins — RF

Bats: L   Throws: R   Height: 6' 1"   Weight: 210   Born: July 21, 1974   Age: 34

YEAR	TEAM	LVL	AGE	PA	R	2B	3B	HR	RBI	BB	SO	SB	CS	EqBRR	AVG	OBP	SLG	EqAVG	EqOBP	EqSLG	EqA	VORP	WARP	DEFENSE
2006	MIL	MLB	31	555	62	26	1	17	70	56	129	4	1	2.0	.271	.357	.434	.267	.354	.426	.273	14.1	1.7	125-RF -2
2007	MIL	MLB	32	464	45	24	2	21	64	32	116	2	2	-0.4	.255	.319	.471	.251	.317	.475	.266	9.6	2.2	109-LF 9
2008	PHI	MLB	33	322	27	16	0	9	29	24	68	1	1	-0.4	.246	.301	.392	.243	.298	.394	.241	-3.9	0.5	72-RF 6
2009	PHI	MLB	34	243	29	12	0	9	35	21	52	1	1	-0.7	.267	.335	.454	.267	.336	.460	.270	7.9	1.1	60-RF 1

Breakout: 36% Improve: 57% Collapse: 23% Attrition: 42%   Comparables: Walt Moryn, Henry Rodriguez, John Mabry, Ed Kranepool

Signing Jenkins was an attempt to add lefty balance to the lineup, and while Jenkins did still bat from the left side, his skills were gone, his performance slipping towards replacement level. Jayson Werth's emergence and adequacy against righties salvaged what could have been a disastrous situation. Jenkins started just five times between August 8 and the season's final day; the Phillies went 29-18 and averaged 5.2 runs per game, about eight percent better than they did outside of that stretch. Jenkins may be under contract for '09, but he figures to be kept away from repeating any of that kind of damage to his own team.

Lou Marson — C

Bats: R   Throws: R   Height: 6' 1"   Weight: 200   Born: June 26, 1986   Age: 23

YEAR	TEAM	LVL	AGE	PA	R	2B	3B	HR	RBI	BB	SO	SB	CS	EqBRR	AVG	OBP	SLG	EqAVG	EqOBP	EqSLG	EqA	VORP	WARP	DEFENSE
2006	LWD	A	20	410	44	16	5	4	39	49	82	4	0	-1.5	.243	.343	.351	.196	.270	.280	.193	-31.3	-0.9	100-C 1
2007	CLR	A+	21	457	68	24	1	7	63	52	80	3	1	-0.1	.288	.373	.407	.241	.318	.357	.240	-6.6	1.1	106-C -1
2008	REA	AA	22	395	55	18	0	5	46	68	70	3	3	1.4	.314	.433	.416	.286	.397	.392	.284	18.9	2.7	85-C -2
2009	PHI	MLB	23	505	59	23	1	9	46	58	105	4	2	-0.1	.258	.346	.377	.258	.347	.382	.257	13.3	3.0	119-C 0

Breakout: 29% Improve: 58% Collapse: 22% Attrition: 7%   Comparables: Russell Martin, Jesse Levis, Phil Lombardi, Tom Redington

Marson did even less than Iguchi did to get a ring—he played in the last game of the regular season—and he may have lost the most to the title. Carlos Ruiz was already a Manuel favorite, and now has the glow of being a catcher for a title team, which will make it that much easier to justify his playing time. Marson is an OBP guy without a ton of power and just middling defense, and will likely spend most of 2009 at Triple-A. He'll be an asset come 2010.

Jimmy Rollins — SS

Bats: S   Throws: R   Height: 5' 8"   Weight: 175   Born: November 27, 1978   Age: 30

YEAR	TEAM	LVL	AGE	PA	R	2B	3B	HR	RBI	BB	SO	SB	CS	EqBRR	AVG	OBP	SLG	EqAVG	EqOBP	EqSLG	EqA	VORP	WARP	DEFENSE
2006	PHI	MLB	27	758	127	45	9	25	83	57	80	36	4	7.5	.277	.334	.478	.271	.328	.466	.277	45.9	4.3	154-SS -7
2007	PHI	MLB	28	778	139	38	20	30	94	49	85	41	6	7.7	.296	.344	.531	.293	.344	.536	.296	68.0	8.0	160-SS 8
2008	PHI	MLB	29	625	76	38	9	11	59	58	55	47	3	9.1	.277	.349	.437	.277	.349	.446	.285	44.4	5.2	131-SS 4
2009	PHI	MLB	30	656	102	36	6	16	68	59	65	37	8	4.4	.293	.360	.458	.293	.360	.464	.288	44.5	5.2	153-SS 3

Breakout: 14%   Improve: 49%   Collapse: 12%   Attrition: 5%   Comparables: Ray Durham, Brian Roberts, Rafael Furcal, Chuck Knoblauch

The ankle injury put Rollins on the DL for the first time in his career (in April) hindered him so much that he set career highs in steals and stolen-base percentage. More importantly, he posted career bests in walks, K/BB, strikeout rate, and OBP. So while no one was touting Rollins for MVP, he was showing the kind of development as a player that makes you think he'll be productive for a long time to come.

Carlos Ruiz — C

Bats: R   Throws: R   Height: 5' 10"   Weight: 200   Born: January 22, 1979   Age: 30

YEAR	TEAM	LVL	AGE	PA	R	2B	3B	HR	RBI	BB	SO	SB	CS	EqBRR	AVG	OBP	SLG	EqAVG	EqOBP	EqSLG	EqA	VORP	WARP	DEFENSE
2006	SWB	AAA	27	423	56	25	0	16	69	42	56	4	3	0.7	.307	.389	.505	.264	.339	.448	.270	15.3	2.7	78-C 3
2006	PHI	MLB	27	78	5	1	1	3	10	5	8	0	0	-0.5	.261	.316	.435	.257	.312	.429	.256	1.5	0.2	19-C -1
2007	PHI	MLB	28	429	42	29	2	6	54	42	49	6	1	0.3	.259	.340	.396	.251	.336	.393	.259	13.9	2.4	101-C 5
2008	PHI	MLB	29	373	47	14	0	4	31	44	38	1	2	1.9	.219	.320	.300	.218	.321	.302	.224	-6.6	0.2	93-C 2
2009	PHI	MLB	30	285	29	12	1	4	27	27	36	1	1	-0.6	.250	.331	.357	.250	.331	.362	.242	4.4	1.5	70-C 1

Breakout: 25%   Improve: 43%   Collapse: 28%   Attrition: 38%   Comparables: Jerry Grote, Gary Bennett, Kirt Manwaring, Brad Ausmus

The Phillies' top seven batters allowed Manuel the luxury of playing Ruiz' limp bat for most of the season and every day in October. Despite a reputation as a strong defensive catcher, Ruiz doesn't throw well (nabbing just 23.6 percent on stolen-base attempts last year, and 26.9 percent career), and no amount of other defensive skills sell his bat. Even the walks aren't real; outside of the eighth slot in the lineup, Ruiz has 12 unintentional passes in 182 PA. Nevertheless, the title means he'll play, and play a lot, in '09.

Matt Stairs — DH

Bats: L   Throws: R   Height: 5' 9"   Weight: 215   Born: February 27, 1968   Age: 41

YEAR	TEAM	LVL	AGE	PA	R	2B	3B	HR	RBI	BB	SO	SB	CS	EqBRR	AVG	OBP	SLG	EqAVG	EqOBP	EqSLG	EqA	VORP	WARP	DEFENSE
2006	KCA	MLB	38	261	31	14	0	8	32	31	52	0	0	-0.2	.261	.352	.429	.247	.349	.408	.267	4.9	0.4	9-1B -1
2006	TEX	MLB	38	88	6	4	0	3	11	6	22	0	0	0.7	.210	.273	.370	.198	.270	.346	.212	-3.4	-0.4	
2006	DET	MLB	38	44	5	3	0	2	8	3	12	0	0	-0.4	.244	.295	.463	.220	.273	.415	.233	0.2	-0.1	
2007	TOR	MLB	39	405	58	28	1	21	64	44	66	2	1	-2.7	.289	.368	.549	.279	.365	.549	.303	30.9	2.3	37-1B -2 32-LF -4
2008	TOR	MLB	40	368	42	11	1	11	44	41	87	1	1	-1.3	.250	.342	.394	.245	.342	.396	.260	5.9	-0.5	7-LF -8 5-RF 0
2008	PHI	MLB	40	19	4	1	0	2	5	1	3	0	0	0.1	.294	.316	.706	.294	.316	.706	.319	2.2	0.2	
2009	PHI	MLB	41	291	35	13	1	10	40	30	63	1	1	-1.5	.262	.344	.437	.263	.345	.444	.269	8.4	0.6	71-DH

Breakout: 19%   Improve: 53%   Collapse: 30%   Attrition: 25%   Comparables: Brian Downing, Willie McCovey, Tony Perez, Jose Cruz

If you didn't like Matt Stairs hitting a three-run homer to just about put away a pennant and get himself to a World Series for the first time ever … I mean, you're either a Dodgers fan or you're reading the wrong book. That was a great moment for a player who has been an underrated contributor to good teams—and bad ones—for a decade. Look for him to fill Jenkins' role for the Phillies in '09, getting 40 starts against tough righties in Jayson Werth's stead. However, keep in mind that Stairs may be just about done—his K/BB ratio fell apart last year, masked by a career-high nine intentionals.

Michael Taylor — OF

Bats: R   Throws: R   Height: 6' 6"   Weight: 250   Born: December 19, 1985   Age: 23

YEAR	TEAM	LVL	AGE	PA	R	2B	3B	HR	RBI	BB	SO	SB	CS	EqBRR	AVG	OBP	SLG	EqAVG	EqOBP	EqSLG	EqA	VORP	WARP	DEFENSE		
2007	WPT	A-	21	261	30	14	0	6	33	23	53	8	2	1.5	.227	.300	.365	.182	.234	.289	.180	-47.1	-5.7	43-LF -18	10-RF	-1
2008	LWD	A	22	288	40	12	3	10	50	31	43	10	3	-3.0	.361	.441	.554	.292	.361	.459	.282	16.3	0.9	46-LF -3	10-RF	-1
2008	CLR	A+	22	266	36	27	1	9	38	19	46	5	6	-0.7	.329	.380	.560	.286	.330	.504	.276	16.0	0.6	39-LF -4	13-RF	-1
2009	*PHI*	*MLB*	*23*	*609*	*68*	*33*	*2*	*17*	*74*	*46*	*136*	*9*	*5*	*-0.9*	*.257*	*.317*	*.416*	*.257*	*.318*	*.422*	*.253*	*3.8*	*0.5*	*142-LF -9*		

Breakout: 32% Improve: 59% Collapse: 18% Attrition: 4%   Comparables: Michael Restovich, Tydus Meadows, Matt Holliday, Alejandro Freire

Taylor was one of the best high school players in the county during his youth in Florida, but his stock went down during each of his three years at Stanford as his performances disappointed. After drafting him, the Phillies got him away from "The Stanford Swing," which focuses on one-plane contact, and told Taylor to return to his natural style. As you can see, the results were stunning and immediate. Built like Dave Winfield (only bigger), Taylor's ceiling rivals that of any prospect in the system, the only issue being that those three lost years in Palo Alto left him a bit behind the curve.

Chase Utley — 2B

Bats: L   Throws: R   Height: 6' 1"   Weight: 185   Born: December 17, 1978   Age: 30

YEAR	TEAM	LVL	AGE	PA	R	2B	3B	HR	RBI	BB	SO	SB	CS	EqBRR	AVG	OBP	SLG	EqAVG	EqOBP	EqSLG	EqA	VORP	WARP	DEFENSE	
2006	PHI	MLB	27	739	131	40	4	32	102	63	132	15	4	6.1	.309	.379	.527	.302	.373	.517	.301	65.9	7.3	152-2B	10
2007	PHI	MLB	28	613	104	48	5	22	103	50	89	9	1	3.1	.332	.410	.566	.330	.409	.575	.330	70.5	8.8	130-2B	14
2008	PHI	MLB	29	707	113	41	4	33	104	64	104	14	2	1.2	.292	.380	.535	.292	.378	.550	.311	63.7	9.0	156-2B	19
2009	*PHI*	*MLB*	*30*	*651*	*103*	*38*	*3*	*28*	*95*	*65*	*98*	*10*	*3*	*1.7*	*.295*	*.377*	*.522*	*.296*	*.377*	*.530*	*.305*	*55.8*	*6.5*	*152-2B*	*6*

Breakout: 8% Improve: 41% Collapse: 20% Attrition: 5%   Comparables: Chris Sabo, Leon Wagner, Rafael Palmeiro, Ken Boyer

Utley has essentially become this generation's Bobby Grich, the player who's so good that it should be impossible to overlook him, the sort of player whose gifts in the field and basic baseball intelligence should matter to people like the MVP voters who are supposed to see beyond the impressive counting stats. But because he's merely quietly excellent on a team loaded with more overstated talents, like Grich, the risk is that people will forget how much he's the single most important position player in the organization. How critical a role he plays could be made plain by his variable timetable for coming back from hip surgery in November; if it's four months, he won't miss much of the regular season, but if it's six, it might almost be June before he's making his impact on the Phillies' fortunes.

Shane Victorino — CF

Bats: S   Throws: R   Height: 5' 9"   Weight: 180   Born: November 30, 1980   Age: 28

YEAR	TEAM	LVL	AGE	PA	R	2B	3B	HR	RBI	BB	SO	SB	CS	EqBRR	AVG	OBP	SLG	EqAVG	EqOBP	EqSLG	EqA	VORP	WARP	DEFENSE		
2006	PHI	MLB	25	462	70	19	8	6	46	24	54	4	3	1.0	.287	.346	.414	.285	.341	.413	.261	12.4	1.6	61-CF 4	17-RF	3
2007	PHI	MLB	26	510	78	23	3	12	46	37	62	37	4	3.5	.281	.347	.423	.280	.348	.431	.279	18.1	2.7	102-RF	5	
2008	PHI	MLB	27	627	102	30	8	14	58	45	69	36	11	7.4	.293	.352	.447	.297	.357	.465	.282	34.2	3.5	134-CF -2	5-RF	1
2009	*PHI*	*MLB*	*28*	*565*	*84*	*27*	*4*	*12*	*53*	*42*	*65*	*26*	*8*	*3.4*	*.291*	*.352*	*.430*	*.291*	*.352*	*.436*	*.276*	*23.1*	*3.2*	*132-CF -2*		

Breakout: 12% Improve: 49% Collapse: 21% Attrition: 8%   Comparables: Billy Hatcher, Dave Collins, Coco Crisp, Dan Gladden

While the team has its share of celebs, Victorino's the fun scrapper who has responded to every challenge, from taking up switch-hitting down on the farm at the outset of his career, to moving from a reserve role to regularity in right to a star turn in center. Timing can be everything—keep in mind that he just had his age-27 season and it showed, dial your expectations down a notch, and enjoy the fact that between his work ethic and a friendly park, he'll be a relatively productive regular for several seasons to come.

Jayson Werth — RF

Bats: R   Throws: R   Height: 6' 4"   Weight: 210   Born: May 20, 1979   Age: 30

YEAR	TEAM	LVL	AGE	PA	R	2B	3B	HR	RBI	BB	SO	SB	CS	EqBRR	AVG	OBP	SLG	EqAVG	EqOBP	EqSLG	EqA	VORP	WARP	DEFENSE		
2007	PHI	MLB	28	304	43	11	3	8	49	44	73	7	1	1.0	.298	.404	.459	.292	.406	.462	.305	18.7	2.3	50-RF 4	14-LF	-3
2008	PHI	MLB	29	482	73	16	3	24	67	57	119	20	1	5.2	.273	.363	.498	.273	.364	.508	.301	31.5	4.1	74-RF 4	26-CF	1
2009	*PHI*	*MLB*	*30*	*500*	*83*	*25*	*4*	*22*	*67*	*66*	*116*	*14*	*5*	*2.4*	*.283*	*.380*	*.511*	*.283*	*.381*	*.518*	*.305*	*32.7*	*4.0*	*118-RF 0*		

Breakout: 26% Improve: 53% Collapse: 13% Attrition: 9%   Comparables: Jason Bay, Bob Allison, Tim Salmon, Chuck Hinton

There had to be something sweet about Werth winning a ring with the Gillick-era Phillies after starting out his career as Gillick's first-round pick in '97. Back then Werth was a gigantic catcher whose size caused concern for his long-term health, but his struggles with keeping healthy stayed with him even after he moved out from behind the plate. While something had to be done about Jenkins' slack bat, Werth's not really an effective everyday player. He doesn't hit for much power against right-handers, so his is the Gary Roenicke suite of skills—plus defense, good speed, and a bat stained by repeated lefty killing. Add in his earned reputation for fragility, and it's just as well that he'll get spotted by Stairs and perhaps even Jenkins in '09.

PITCHERS

Joe Blanton

Bats: R   Throws: R   Height: 6' 3"   Weight: 250   Born: December 11, 1980   Age: 28

YEAR	TEAM	LVL	AGE	W	L	SV	G	GS	IP	H	BB	SO	HR	GB%	BABIP	STUFF	WHIP	ERA	DERA	EqH9	EqBB9	EqSO9	EqHR9	DEF	VORP	SN/WX
2006	OAK	MLB	25	16	12	0	32	31	194¹	241	58	107	17	44.5%	.341	5	1.54	4.82	4.06	11.0	2.7	4.4	0.8	-21	18.9	2.90
2007	OAK	MLB	26	14	10	0	34	34	230	240	40	140	16	48.6%	.304	14	1.22	3.95	4.52	9.4	1.5	4.8	0.7	8	45.6	5.81
2008	OAK	MLB	27	5	12	0	20	20	127	145	35	62	12	47.1%	.304	-1	1.42	4.96	4.78	10.4	2.3	3.9	0.9	-7	5.9	1.66
2008	PHI	MLB	27	4	0	0	13	13	70²	66	31	49	10	42.4%	.268	0	1.37	4.20	4.61	8.3	3.3	5.5	1.2	3	8.9	1.49
2009	PHI	MLB	28	10	9	0	27	27	169²	182	49	117	20	46.0%	.300	17	1.36	4.43	4.62	9.6	2.3	5.4	1.1	-0	18.5	3.38

Breakout: 16%   Improve: 58%   Collapse: 16%   Attrition: 16%   Comparables: Danny Cox, Bobby Jones, Jose Mesa, Dick Fowler

It wasn't cheap to get Blanton from the A's, but he'll be under team control through 2010, so he wasn't going to be just a stretch rental. His workhorse rep took as much of a pasting as he did in the AL last season, and producing four quality starts in his Phillies stint didn't get him much of his former luster back, but he served his real purpose in the postseason by giving the team a fourth starter who wasn't named Eaton or Kendrick or Despair, and rose to the occasion with quality starts in the LDS clincher and the Game Four win that broke the Rays' back in the Series, the latter the game in which he jacked his first pro homer off of Edwin Jackson. Manuel seems to have his measure in terms of skipping the rep and hooking Blanton early when he gets in trouble, which should make for a solid couple of seasons at the tail end of the rotation.

Andrew Carpenter

Bats: R   Throws: R   Height: 6' 3"   Weight: 230   Born: May 18, 1985   Age: 24

YEAR	TEAM	LVL	AGE	W	L	SV	G	GS	IP	H	BB	SO	HR	GB%	BABIP	STUFF	WHIP	ERA	DERA	EqH9	EqBB9	EqSO9	EqHR9	DEF	VORP	SN/WX
2007	CLR	A+	22	17	6	1	27	24	163	150	53	116	16	40.9%	.275	-31	1.25	3.20	6.19	11.0	4.0	3.5	2.1	9	-9.5	—
2008	CLR	A+	23	3	3	0	8	8	52¹	44	9	32	2	33.9%	.264	-7	1.01	2.93	5.66	8.6	2.2	2.7	0.9	4	-0.3	—
2008	REA	AA	23	6	8	0	16	16	93²	114	30	69	13	45.1%	.346	-20	1.54	5.67	6.50	12.2	2.9	4.7	1.8	-8	-8.9	—
2008	PHI	MLB	23	0	0	0	1	0	1	1	1	1	0	33.3%	.500	1	2.00	0.00	0.00	9.0	9.0	9.0	0.0	0	0.6	0.01
2009	PHI	MLB	24	7	10	0	36	22	141	172	53	85	28	40.0%	.310	1	1.60	6.08	6.20	10.9	3.0	4.7	1.7	-0	-7.6	0.10

Breakout: 8%   Improve: 43%   Collapse: 24%   Attrition: 13%   Comparables: Zack Segovia, Kent Bottenfield, Joe Slusarski, Brian Sackinsky

Carpenter has five pitches, but the problem is none of them are especially good. He's a command/control type with little margin for error, and that margin disappeared when he moved up to Double-A and got hit around for a .305 batting average. Once seen as a possible back-end rotation piece, he needs to figure out some kind of something—better control, different pitch sequences, a trick offering—to recover even that modest status in a pivotal year in his development.

Carlos Carrasco

Bats: R   **Throws:** R   **Height:** 6' 3"   **Weight:** 180   **Born:** March 21, 1987   **Age:** 22

YEAR	TEAM	LVL	AGE	W	L	SV	G	GS	IP	H	BB	SO	HR	GB%	BABIP	STUFF	WHIP	ERA	DERA	EqH9	EqBB9	EqSO9	EqHR9	DEF	VORP	SN/WX
2006	LWD	A	19	12	6	0	26	26	159¹	103	65	159	6	50.4%	.254	8	1.06	2.26	6.75	9.4	5.4	4.3	1.3	15	-17.5	—
2007	CLR	A+	20	6	2	0	12	12	69²	49	22	53	8	47.4%	.222	8	1.02	2.84	6.57	8.8	3.9	3.9	2.5	13	-6.6	—
2007	REA	AA	20	6	4	0	14	13	70¹	65	46	49	9	37.6%	.273	-1	1.58	4.86	8.03	10.4	6.5	3.7	2.1	7	-17.6	—
2008	REA	AA	21	7	7	0	20	19	114²	109	45	109	13	46.9%	.313	11	1.34	4.32	5.15	10.0	3.5	6.4	1.5	0	5.3	—
2008	LEH	AAA	21	2	2	0	6	6	36²	37	13	46	1	49.0%	.356	37	1.36	1.72	3.44	9.3	3.4	7.4	0.5	-5	8.8	—
2009	PHI	MLB	22	7	8	0	22	22	126	129	59	107	18	44.0%	.300	20	1.49	4.96	5.14	9.1	3.7	6.6	1.2	-0	7.2	1.77

Breakout: 12%   Improve: 42%   Collapse: 15%   Attrition: 21%   Comparables: Jose Lima, Amaury Telemaco, Luis Vasquez, Anibal Sanchez

The top prospect in the system entering the year, Carrasco didn't make any great leaps forward in 2008 as much as he simply held serve. He took some time to made adjustments to the more advanced hitters at the upper levels, but those adjustments were made and he was once again dominating at the end of the year with his above-average fastball and outstanding changeup. He profiles as a solid third starter in the big leagues, with the potential to be a bit more, and he could be a key addition to the defending champs by midseason.

Clay Condrey

Bats: R   **Throws:** R   **Height:** 6' 3"   **Weight:** 215   **Born:** November 19, 1975   **Age:** 33

YEAR	TEAM	LVL	AGE	W	L	SV	G	GS	IP	H	BB	SO	HR	GB%	BABIP	STUFF	WHIP	ERA	DERA	EqH9	EqBB9	EqSO9	EqHR9	DEF	VORP	SN/WX
2006	SWB	AAA	30	4	2	6	39	0	51¹	41	15	28	1	57.2%	.267	-16	1.10	1.94	4.11	9.2	3.3	3.1	0.4	4	7.6	—
2006	PHI	MLB	30	2	2	0	21	0	28²	35	9	16	3	48.5%	.352	-9	1.53	3.14	3.33	11.0	2.7	5.0	1.0	0	8.1	0.03
2007	OTT	AAA	31	1	0	1	10	0	22	19	5	10	0	51.5%	.288	-18	1.09	2.45	5.40	8.1	2.2	2.7	0.4	3	0.4	—
2007	PHI	MLB	31	5	0	2	39	0	50	61	16	27	4	47.8%	.331	-8	1.56	5.04	4.59	10.1	2.5	4.6	0.7	-1	2.7	1.61
2008	PHI	MLB	32	3	4	1	56	0	69	85	19	34	6	54.8%	.328	-9	1.51	3.26	2.79	11.0	2.1	4.0	0.8	-3	17.5	0.30
2009	PHI	MLB	33	2	2	1	36	0	44¹	54	14	23	5	50.0%	.320	-8	1.52	4.78	5.03	10.8	2.5	4.1	0.9	-0	3.0	0.24

Breakout: 8%   Improve: 17%   Collapse: 57%   Attrition: 34%   Comparables: Dale Mohorcic, Mike Barlow, George Zuverink, Fred Gladding

Even the '27 Yankees had guys who could have been anybody, but Condrey's virtues are straightforward enough: he's a sinkerballer in a park where fly balls become souvenirs with an unnerving regularity, so even in a low-leverage sponge role, he helped keep things from getting out of hand. It's handy to have someone like that, even if it represents the back lot of a properly stocked roster, but there's no guarantee that the ring on his finger keeps him more than a bad week away from waivers.

Kyle Drabek

Bats: R   **Throws:** R   **Height:** 6' 0"   **Weight:** 185   **Born:** December 8, 1987   **Age:** 21

YEAR	TEAM	LVL	AGE	W	L	SV	G	GS	IP	H	BB	SO	HR	GB%	BABIP	STUFF	WHIP	ERA	DERA	EqH9	EqBB9	EqSO9	EqHR9	DEF	VORP	SN/WX
2006	PHL	Ind	18	1	3	0	6	6	23¹	33	11	14	2	54.9%	.408	-55	1.90	7.79	17.67	19.6	7.4	1.5	3.9	0	-24.5	—
2007	LWD	A	19	5	1	0	11	10	54	50	23	46	9	55.8%	.266	-14	1.35	4.33	9.44	11.9	5.5	3.6	3.4	7	-20.4	—
2008	WPT	A-	20	1	2	0	4	4	20¹	11	6	10	1	55.7%	.172	-10	0.84	2.22	7.58	5.7	3.8	0.9	1.4	5	-4.2	—
2009	PHI	MLB	21	4	11	0	24	24	116²	153	74	44	25	50.0%	.310	-15	1.94	7.90	8.19	11.7	5.0	2.9	1.9	-0	-30.9	-2.44

Breakout: 2%   Improve: 17%   Collapse: 48%   Attrition: 13%   Comparables: Jeff Perry, Richard Rice, Rob Wishnevski, Randy O'Neal

The team's first-round pick in 2006, Drabek missed most of the year recovering from Tommy John surgery, but was impressive upon his return. The Phillies completely revamped his mechanics, and while they still need to be smoothed out a bit, his arm action is much cleaner, his command is better, and both improvements came with no reduction in stuff, as his velocity worked its way back to his pre-injury levels, and his curve remains outstanding. The Phillies hope that his fourth pro season will be his first fully healthy one, and think he's poised for a breakout.

Chad Durbin

Bats: S   Throws: R   Height: 6' 2"   Weight: 200   Born: December 3, 1977   Age: 31

YEAR	TEAM	LVL	AGE	W	L	SV	G	GS	IP	H	BB	SO	HR	GB%	BABIP	STUFF	WHIP	ERA	DERA	EqH9	EqBB9	EqSO9	EqHR9	DEF	VORP	SN/WX
2006	TOL	AAA	28	11	8	0	28	28	185	169	46	149	17	42.3%	.283	-12	1.16	3.11	5.79	10.2	2.7	4.9	1.5	9	-3.6	—
2006	DET	MLB	28	0	0	0	3	0	6	6	0	3	1	42.9%	.250	-4	1.00	1.50	3.00	9.0	0.0	4.5	1.5	1	3.1	0.05
2007	DET	MLB	29	8	7	1	36	19	127²	133	49	66	21	46.3%	.274	-25	1.43	4.72	5.34	9.3	3.2	4.0	1.5	8	14.8	2.28
2008	PHI	MLB	30	5	4	1	71	0	87²	81	35	63	5	47.7%	.303	7	1.32	2.87	3.11	8.6	3.2	5.9	0.5	-1	22.1	1.83
2009	PHI	MLB	31	3	3	1	37	1	52¹	55	21	36	7	44.0%	.300	-1	1.44	4.44	4.62	9.4	3.1	5.4	1.1	-0	6.3	0.56

Breakout: 21%   Improve: 36%   Collapse: 40%   Attrition: 35%   Comparables: Juan Acevedo, Dave Borkowski, Donne Wall, Mike DeJean

It would be easy to throw the term "utility pitcher" at Durbin, but clearly some people are more useful to some teams than others, and while they mooted the idea, they never did need to have Durbin start, and once he made himself indispensable in the pen, it was increasingly out of the question. The Phillies needed someone who could handle different-length outings, and in the course of delivering a career year, he also gave them 33 multi-inning appearances. Not a classic ground-ball guy by any stretch, you can credit him with good situational pitching by finishing third among NL relievers in his percentage of double plays induced in DP situations (behind the Dodgers' Cory Wade and the Snakes' Chad Qualls). Like expecting him to repeat last season's success, counting on that might be a bit much.

Adam Eaton

Bats: R   Throws: R   Height: 6' 2"   Weight: 200   Born: November 23, 1977   Age: 31

YEAR	TEAM	LVL	AGE	W	L	SV	G	GS	IP	H	BB	SO	HR	GB%	BABIP	STUFF	WHIP	ERA	DERA	EqH9	EqBB9	EqSO9	EqHR9	DEF	VORP	SN/WX
2006	TEX	MLB	28	7	4	0	13	13	65	78	24	43	11	37.7%	.324	-7	1.57	5.12	4.81	10.3	3.3	5.2	1.4	-1	6.2	0.76
2007	PHI	MLB	29	10	10	0	30	30	161²	192	71	97	30	40.5%	.318	-15	1.63	6.29	5.31	10.1	3.5	5.1	1.5	-8	-10.8	0.66
2008	REA	AA	30	0	3	0	5	5	26²	34	4	23	8	54.3%	.306	-19	1.42	7.08	7.33	12.3	1.3	5.3	3.7	-5	-5.2	—
2008	PHI	MLB	30	4	8	0	21	19	107	131	44	57	15	44.1%	.330	-14	1.64	5.80	5.28	11.3	3.3	4.4	1.2	-3	-3.1	0.59
2009	PHI	MLB	31	3	4	0	20	9	61²	71	24	40	10	43.0%	.310	-1	1.53	5.48	5.66	10.2	3.0	5.0	1.4	-0	0.2	0.35

Breakout: 16%   Improve: 49%   Collapse: 37%   Attrition: 38%   Comparables: James Baldwin, Josh Fogg, Rich Dotson, Dustin Hermanson

To call Eaton's deal an unmitigated disaster might be too kind; the Phillies were reportedly willing to eat $8 million of the $9 million owed him in '09, and finding no takers. If there's a silver lining, it's his contributing 10 quality starts in his 19, but the electric fastball of his Padres days seems to have disappeared like so much medical waste, and the concern that Eaton can get to overthinking becomes that much more problematic when he's got no go-to pitch. If he has a third act, you can bet that it will be someplace where the situation is suitably desperate.

Scott Eyre

Bats: L   Throws: L   Height: 6' 1"   Weight: 215   Born: May 30, 1972   Age: 37

YEAR	TEAM	LVL	AGE	W	L	SV	G	GS	IP	H	BB	SO	HR	GB%	BABIP	STUFF	WHIP	ERA	DERA	EqH9	EqBB9	EqSO9	EqHR9	DEF	VORP	SN/WX
2006	CHN	MLB	34	1	3	0	74	0	61¹	61	30	73	11	44.8%	.342	11	1.48	3.38	3.03	9.4	3.9	10.0	1.5	-1	16.6	1.20
2007	CHN	MLB	35	2	1	0	55	0	52¹	59	35	45	3	40.9%	.366	9	1.80	4.13	3.47	10.9	5.7	7.7	0.5	-2	8.8	-0.64
2008	CHN	MLB	36	2	0	0	19	0	11¹	15	4	14	1	29.4%	.452	11	1.68	7.17	4.91	13.1	2.5	9.8	0.8	-2	-1.9	0.52
2008	PHI	MLB	36	3	0	0	19	0	14¹	8	3	18	1	45.2%	.233	14	0.77	1.89	1.98	5.3	2.0	9.2	0.7	0	6.0	0.63
2009	PHI	MLB	37	2	1	2	33	0	31	33	14	30	4	43.0%	.320	8	1.50	4.34	4.48	9.4	3.6	7.5	1.1	-0	4.2	0.35

Breakout: 21%   Improve: 37%   Collapse: 40%   Attrition: 29%   Comparables: Mark Guthrie, Frank DiPino, Arthur Rhodes, Cal Eldred

Frustrated by what they were seeing from their alternatives, and aware of how much they were counting on Romero, Gillick moved to add a token veteran to stock second lefty role. Their Eyre elicited, the Phillies liked what they saw from him having Cubby groin woes behind him so much, they gave him a $2 million extension to keep him in their employ for '09.

Tom Gordon

Bats: R   Throws: R   Height: 5' 10"   Weight: 200   Born: November 18, 1967   Age: 41

YEAR	TEAM	LVL	AGE	W	L	SV	G	GS	IP	H	BB	SO	HR	GB%	BABIP	STUFF	WHIP	ERA	DERA	EqH9	EqBB9	EqSO9	EqHR9	DEF	VORP	SN/WX
2006	PHI	MLB	38	3	4	34	59	0	59¹	53	22	68	9	46.9%	.293	15	1.26	3.34	3.54	7.4	2.8	9.1	1.2	3	17.0	3.35
2007	PHI	MLB	39	3	2	6	44	0	40	40	13	32	7	49.6%	.292	-3	1.33	4.73	4.05	8.3	2.5	6.8	1.4	0	5.1	1.25
2008	PHI	MLB	40	5	4	2	34	0	29²	31	17	26	3	40.6%	.304	-4	1.62	5.15	3.73	8.9	4.0	6.6	0.9	-5	-0.3	0.93
2009	PHI	MLB	41	2	2	2	27	0	31²	31	14	26	4	44.0%	.290	0	1.42	4.33	4.53	8.7	3.5	6.3	1.0	-0	3.9	0.34

Breakout: 17%   Improve: 56%   Collapse: 21%   Attrition: 30%   Comparables: Virgil Trucks, Jeff Fassero, Bucky Walters, Roy Face

Initially lined up to be Lidge's primary set-up man, Gordon labored through elbow woes in the first half before finally being shelved before the All-Star break, and going under the knife in October, and getting bought out by the Phillies shortly thereafter. While you can feel some small twinge of pity for Gordon's missing out on the chance to pitch in the World Series for the first time, he's going to keep at it. He may have to go through the rigmarole of a public workout at some point in the late spring, a la Freddy Garcia. With the clock running on down on Flash's career, it's worth remembering what a thing of beauty it's been to watch him snap off curves for more than 20 years.

Cole Hamels

Bats: L   Throws: L   Height: 6' 3"   Weight: 190   Born: December 27, 1983   Age: 25

YEAR	TEAM	LVL	AGE	W	L	SV	G	GS	IP	H	BB	SO	HR	GB%	BABIP	STUFF	WHIP	ERA	DERA	EqH9	EqBB9	EqSO9	EqHR9	DEF	VORP	SN/WX
2006	PHI	MLB	22	9	8	0	23	23	132¹	117	48	145	19	41.7%	.298	35	1.25	4.08	3.94	7.4	2.8	8.8	1.1	0	22.7	3.42
2007	PHI	MLB	23	15	5	0	28	28	183¹	163	43	177	25	44.2%	.282	31	1.12	3.39	3.14	7.5	1.8	8.0	1.1	-2	48.3	5.18
2008	PHI	MLB	24	14	10	0	33	33	227¹	193	53	196	28	41.1%	.263	20	1.08	3.09	4.05	7.5	1.8	6.8	1.0	16	55.5	7.21
2009	PHI	MLB	25	13	8	0	29	29	193	180	49	171	25	41.0%	.280	29	1.19	3.65	3.78	8.3	2.0	6.9	1.1	-0	39.6	5.70

Breakout: 14%   Improve: 41%   Collapse: 22%   Attrition: 10%   Comparables: Frank Tanana, Kevin Appier, Jim Merritt, Greg Swindell

Post-season performance has a way of cementing a reputation, and after a year to stew over that six-baserunner second inning against the Rockies in the opening game of the 2007 NLDS that led to another chorus of complaints about kids these days, there was something redemptive to Hamels' running the table all October long. He's moving out of the injury nexus with his reputation for inconsistency in history's wastebasket, and despite concerns over his fragility, that career-altering injury hasn't pounced. He may be high-maintenance in the immediate future, but the potential that he's just getting started staking his own claim to be the latter-day Lefty is there for all to see.

J. A. Happ

Bats: L   Throws: L   Height: 6' 6"   Weight: 200   Born: October 19, 1982   Age: 26

YEAR	TEAM	LVL	AGE	W	L	SV	G	GS	IP	H	BB	SO	HR	GB%	BABIP	STUFF	WHIP	ERA	DERA	EqH9	EqBB9	EqSO9	EqHR9	DEF	VORP	SN/WX
2006	CLR	A+	23	3	7	0	13	13	80¹	63	19	77	9	47.5%	.255	-24	1.02	2.81	6.97	10.1	3.2	4.8	2.4	5	-10.8	—
2006	REA	AA	23	6	2	0	12	12	74¹	58	29	81	2	41.2%	.298	15	1.17	2.67	4.32	9.7	4.5	6.1	0.7	-5	9.5	—
2007	OTT	AAA	24	4	6	0	24	24	118¹	118	62	117	12	33.8%	.335	-15	1.52	5.02	7.90	10.2	5.2	6.2	1.6	6	-27.9	—
2008	LEH	AAA	25	8	7	0	24	23	135	116	48	151	14	43.8%	.308	1	1.21	3.60	5.15	8.4	3.5	6.8	1.4	4	6.4	—
2008	PHI	MLB	25	1	0	0	8	4	31²	28	14	26	3	35.7%	.275	7	1.33	3.69	4.68	7.7	3.3	6.3	0.8	5	7.1	1.11
2009	PHI	MLB	26	7	7	1	36	18	111	108	49	97	15	40.0%	.290	13	1.42	4.63	4.79	8.7	3.5	6.8	1.2	-0	11.2	1.77

Breakout: 34%   Improve: 68%   Collapse: 14%   Attrition: 17%   Comparables: Chris Capuano, Mickey Mahler, David West, Lou Brissie

Happ took another step forward in 2008 thanks to improved command and a much better slider. He remains a finesse pitcher, but that's easier to swallow when the pitcher in question is a tall left-hander with naturally deceptive arm action. He pitched fairly well as both a starter and reliever at the end of the year, but there's no room for him in the Philadelphia rotation, making his best bet the idea that he sticks as a long reliever.

Kyle Kendrick

| | | | | | | | | | | | | | | Bats: R | | Throws: R | | Height: 6′ 3″ | | Weight: 190 | | Born: August 26, 1984 | | | Age: 24 |

YEAR	TEAM	LVL	AGE	W	L	SV	G	GS	IP	H	BB	SO	HR	GB%	BABIP	STUFF	WHIP	ERA	DERA	EqH9	EqBB9	EqSO9	EqHR9	DEF	VORP	SN/WX
2006	LWD	A	21	3	2	0	7	7	46²	34	15	54	0	51.7%	.291	23	1.06	2.14	6.07	10.6	4.5	5.4	0.7	2	-2.1	—
2006	CLR	A+	21	9	7	0	21	20	130²	117	37	79	15	40.9%	.260	-39	1.18	3.53	7.48	11.1	3.7	2.5	2.4	12	-23.9	—
2007	REA	AA	22	4	7	0	12	12	81¹	82	18	50	3	51.7%	.307	3	1.23	3.21	4.94	11.0	2.5	3.3	0.7	-5	5.5	—
2007	PHI	MLB	22	10	4	0	20	20	121	129	25	49	16	47.4%	.285	4	1.27	3.87	4.21	9.1	1.7	3.6	1.1	8	26.7	3.17
2008	PHI	MLB	23	11	9	0	31	30	155²	194	57	68	23	46.1%	.312	-16	1.61	5.49	6.11	10.8	2.7	3.4	1.3	10	-4.1	2.17
2009	PHI	MLB	24	5	6	0	25	13	88¹	103	32	43	13	48.0%	.300	-2	1.53	5.22	5.44	10.4	2.8	3.8	1.3	-0	2.5	0.79

Breakout: 13% Improve: 38% Collapse: 38% Attrition: 40%   Comparables: Esteban Loaiza, Joe Niekro, Brian Meadows, Bryan Rekar

His heroics in '07 were nice, but while he got to hold onto his rotation slot while Eaton lost his after the Blanton deal, the Phillies eventually pulled Kendrick from the rotation with the pressure on in September, slotting in Happ against the Braves for his next two turns (and winning both). In the age-old debate of nature vs. nurture to help sort out what can be done with Kendrick, it isn't the park that's killing him; more fundamentally, no matter where he calls home, he's not hard-wired with anything that works against lefties, who have slugged .544 against him in his brief career. That's all left-handers, so not just the ones who can hit. Boxed out of the rotation by Happ and the addition of Chan Ho Park, Kendrick's in danger of becoming a situational righty or extra arm.

Brad Lidge

| | | | | | | | | | | | | | | Bats: R | | Throws: R | | Height: 6′ 5″ | | Weight: 210 | | Born: December 23, 1976 | | | Age: 32 |

YEAR	TEAM	LVL	AGE	W	L	SV	G	GS	IP	H	BB	SO	HR	GB%	BABIP	STUFF	WHIP	ERA	DERA	EqH9	EqBB9	EqSO9	EqHR9	DEF	VORP	SN/WX
2006	HOU	MLB	29	1	5	32	78	0	75	69	36	104	10	47.4%	.335	19	1.40	5.28	4.42	8.4	3.6	10.5	1.0	-6	3.3	0.78
2007	HOU	MLB	30	5	3	19	66	0	67	54	30	88	9	45.5%	.300	20	1.25	3.36	3.18	7.1	3.4	10.1	1.1	-3	14.7	2.16
2008	PHI	MLB	31	2	0	41	72	0	69¹	50	35	92	2	48.2%	.302	35	1.23	1.95	1.82	6.9	3.9	10.0	0.3	-3	26.5	7.61
2009	PHI	MLB	32	4	4	25	53	0	60	52	29	71	6	46.0%	.300	21	1.34	3.49	3.64	7.7	3.8	9.2	0.9	-0	13.5	1.93

Breakout: 23% Improve: 59% Collapse: 21% Attrition: 16%   Comparables: Eric Plunk, Jim Gott, Lee Smith, Joe Page

Can you really be Comeback Player of the Year for coming away from a team that didn't know what it was doing? To some extent, what went Lidge's way was that a surprising number of his fly balls didn't hit the seats, where normally, you might have expected it. Everything else was the same or slightly better, but he wasn't hit-lucky, he was homer-lucky, despite moving from one bandbox to another. Maybe that's all it takes, leaving the scene of the much-belabored Pujols poke, and maybe that's what sells (fewer and fewer) newspapers. Given that Lidge never became ineffective as much as he had to deal with a few especially spazzy superiors in Houston, it looks like the proverbial change of scenery doing a player good, and not so much a "comeback" as a successful escape. It was a very good year, good enough to rank 18th-best on the all-time WXRL list. It also ranked behind all three years of Eric Gagne's 2002-04 run, Keith Foulke's big 2000—and his own first season as the Astros' closer in 2004.

Ryan Madson

| | | | | | | | | | | | | | | Bats: L | | Throws: R | | Height: 6′ 6″ | | Weight: 200 | | Born: August 28, 1980 | | | Age: 28 |

YEAR	TEAM	LVL	AGE	W	L	SV	G	GS	IP	H	BB	SO	HR	GB%	BABIP	STUFF	WHIP	ERA	DERA	EqH9	EqBB9	EqSO9	EqHR9	DEF	VORP	SN/WX
2006	PHI	MLB	25	11	9	2	50	17	134¹	176	50	99	20	44.7%	.364	-6	1.68	5.70	4.37	11.2	3.0	6.0	1.1	-16	-1.3	1.27
2007	PHI	MLB	26	2	2	1	38	0	56	48	23	43	5	49.1%	.269	5	1.27	3.05	3.63	7.1	3.2	6.3	0.8	5	17.6	1.63
2008	PHI	MLB	27	4	2	1	76	0	82²	79	23	67	6	52.8%	.307	11	1.23	3.05	3.24	8.7	2.1	6.6	0.7	2	23.0	2.01
2009	PHI	MLB	28	4	3	3	51	2	67¹	68	23	53	7	48.0%	.300	8	1.34	3.82	4.01	9.0	2.6	6.1	0.9	-0	13.2	1.15

Breakout: 25% Improve: 49% Collapse: 27% Attrition: 17%   Comparables: LaTroy Hawkins, Travis Harper, Ken Forsch, Dick Tidrow

Madson made a nifty return from the '07 season spoiled slightly by his strained shoulder. In an interesting twist, he alternated with Romero in the set-up responsibilities—where Romero's role was defined by interesting collections of circumstances and his ability to work without rest days, Madson's role was to do the more classic, static work eighth-inning assignment, getting entire frames to himself from start to finish. With his shoulder back in working order and his last arbitration coming up, it'll be interesting to see if the Phillies make a multi-year commitment, or if his oft-stated desire to start will make this season his swan song with the club.

Jamie Moyer

Bats: L   Throws: L   Height: 6' 0"   Weight: 185   Born: November 18, 1962   Age: 46

YEAR	TEAM	LVL	AGE	W	L	SV	G	GS	IP	H	BB	SO	HR	GB%	BABIP	STUFF	WHIP	ERA	DERA	EqH9	EqBB9	EqSO9	EqHR9	DEF	VORP	SN/WX
2006	SEA	MLB	43	6	12	0	25	25	160	179	44	82	25	38.7%	.296	-11	1.39	4.39	4.90	9.9	2.5	4.1	1.4	1	20.8	2.67
2006	PHI	MLB	43	5	2	0	8	8	51¹	49	7	26	8	50.3%	.255	4	1.09	4.04	4.47	7.6	1.0	4.1	1.2	3	9.4	1.22
2007	PHI	MLB	44	14	12	0	33	33	199¹	222	66	133	30	41.6%	.311	1	1.44	5.01	4.97	9.4	2.6	5.6	1.2	6	12.7	3.23
2008	PHI	MLB	45	16	7	0	33	33	196¹	199	62	123	20	45.2%	.291	9	1.33	3.71	4.15	9.0	2.4	5.0	0.9	10	39.7	5.01
2009	PHI	MLB	46	5	6	0	17	17	95²	105	39	54	17	44.6%	.282	-1	1.50	5.14	5.28	9.7	3.2	4.4	1.6	0	5.4	1.20

Breakout: 0%   Improve: 22%   Collapse: 39%   Attrition: 41%   Comparables: Phil Niekro, Hoyt Wilhelm, Satchel Paige, Nolan Ryan

Who knew he still had this in him? You can't exactly call him a workhorse, but what do we call a guy who takes his turns, isn't crushed if you pull him early, and knows how to cruise to give you innings on those days when you need him to? With 246 career wins and with 53.9 career WARP, he's still a bit out of reach for talking about the Hall of Fame, behind guys like Chuck Finley, Dave Stieb, and Charlie Hough, and nowhere close to Tommy John, but he's also into the range where you could see the Veterans Committee someday taking a shine to him. That's if his career ended today, and he's under contract through 2010. If, in 2004 after a seven-win season, you were told he'd have 54 wins left in him, you'd be doubtful; two years from now and with this team's lineup to help him, he'll be pushing 270 and 50, the sorts of things a boomer-age electorate might start taking notice of.

Brett Myers

Bats: R   Throws: R   Height: 6' 4"   Weight: 220   Born: August 17, 1980   Age: 28

YEAR	TEAM	LVL	AGE	W	L	SV	G	GS	IP	H	BB	SO	HR	GB%	BABIP	STUFF	WHIP	ERA	DERA	EqH9	EqBB9	EqSO9	EqHR9	DEF	VORP	SN/WX
2006	PHI	MLB	25	12	7	0	31	31	198	194	63	189	29	47.1%	.307	21	1.30	3.91	3.55	8.3	2.5	7.8	1.1	-5	40.2	5.41
2007	PHI	MLB	26	5	7	21	51	3	68²	61	27	83	9	48.4%	.308	19	1.27	4.32	3.99	7.6	3.0	9.6	1.0	1	12.0	1.33
2008	LEH	AAA	27	1	1	0	2	2	12¹	12	4	12	0	50.0%	.343	7	1.30	3.66	6.00	9.0	3.0	6.0	0.0	1	-0.5	—
2008	PHI	MLB	27	10	13	0	30	30	190	197	65	163	29	48.2%	.307	8	1.38	4.55	4.32	9.4	2.6	6.9	1.3	-5	18.4	3.64
2009	PHI	MLB	28	12	8	0	28	28	179¹	173	55	158	21	46.0%	.300	26	1.27	3.87	4.03	8.6	2.4	6.8	1.0	-0	30.8	4.78

Breakout: 18%   Improve: 58%   Collapse: 9%   Attrition: 7%   Comparables: Pete Vuckovich, Freddy Garcia, Larry Dierker, Jack Morris

If you really want a comeback player, just from this ballclub alone you might nominate Myers's coming back to the rotation as the upshot of the off-season addition of Lidge. His year wasn't without it's own odd wrinkles—how many eventual World Series winners send their Opening Day starter to A-ball in-season because he needed to work on his craft and rediscover his fastball, as opposed to a rehab assignment of some sort? After he returned in late July he rattled off ten straight quality starts (one was blown). Then his fastball took another powder in his last two games, but with solid touch on his curve and splitter, he wasn't disarmed and managed to muscle through the postseason well enough (and having that three-hit, three-RBI game at the plate against the Dodgers). At this point, there's nothing resembling a career trajectory as much as sporadic bouts of brilliance coupled with bizarre struggles. Perhaps part of the problem with calling this a comeback is that it's hard to say how long he'll stay.

J. C. Romero

Bats: S   Throws: L   Height: 5' 11"   Weight: 205   Born: June 4, 1976   Age: 33

YEAR	TEAM	LVL	AGE	W	L	SV	G	GS	IP	H	BB	SO	HR	GB%	BABIP	STUFF	WHIP	ERA	DERA	EqH9	EqBB9	EqSO9	EqHR9	DEF	VORP	SN/WX
2006	LAA	MLB	30	1	2	0	65	0	48¹	57	28	31	3	57.8%	.344	-13	1.76	6.71	6.27	10.8	5.1	5.1	0.6	-5	-7.4	0.03
2007	BOS	MLB	31	1	0	1	23	0	20	24	15	11	2	55.9%	.338	-12	1.95	3.15	2.41	12.1	6.8	4.3	1.0	-2	6.5	0.59
2007	PHI	MLB	31	1	2	0	51	0	36¹	15	25	31	1	64.7%	.169	16	1.10	1.24	2.80	3.3	5.6	7.4	0.3	6	18.7	2.30
2008	PHI	MLB	32	4	4	1	81	0	59	41	38	52	5	62.5%	.238	7	1.34	2.75	3.36	6.3	4.9	7.0	0.8	5	19.0	2.25
2009	PHI	MLB	33	2	2	2	55	0	49	46	29	40	4	54.0%	.290	0	1.53	4.19	4.45	8.4	4.7	6.3	0.7	-0	6.4	0.56

Breakout: 7%   Improve: 16%   Collapse: 49%   Attrition: 29%   Comparables: Curt Leskanic, Ron Perranoski, Mike Williams, Darold Knowles

One of the best dumpster discoveries of the last couple of seasons, the rubber-armed lefty logged his second 81-game season of his career while riffing on his particular three true outcomes: walks, strikeouts, and grounders. With a lively sinker/slider mix, he's not exactly a situational lefty as much as he's situational—seeing lots of runners aboard situations—in his usage pattern and he's also left-handed, but he's not really a LOOGY. Manuel would use him to turn around switch-hitters, or, a first lefty batter gotten, leave him in to intentionally walk a dangerous right-hander and then tackle the next lefty. Because Romero's a ground-ball guy who freezes the running game, Manuel could afford to take certain risks instead of pedantically alternating lefties and righties. Although Romero's protesting his innocence, a 50-game suspension in the offseason for use of a banned stimulant will put a crimp in his availability early on.

Joe Savery

| | | | | | | | | | | | | | | Bats: L | | Throws: L | | Height: 6' 3" | | Weight: 215 | | Born: November 4, 1985 | | Age: 23 |

YEAR	TEAM	LVL	AGE	W	L	SV	G	GS	IP	H	BB	SO	HR	GB%	BABIP	STUFF	WHIP	ERA	DERA	EqH9	EqBB9	EqSO9	EqHR9	DEF	VORP	SN/WX
2007	WPT	A-	21	2	3	0	7	7	26¹	22	13	22	0	51.9%	.272	-6	1.33	2.74	4.38	9.9	5.8	2.9	0.4	-3	3.3	—
2008	CLR	A+	22	9	10	0	27	24	150¹	171	60	122	10	51.4%	.346	-24	1.54	4.13	7.70	13.0	4.7	4.1	1.6	-5	-31.1	—
2009	PHI	MLB	23	4	8	0	19	19	96²	124	54	61	15	49.0%	.330	2	1.84	6.67	6.94	11.4	4.4	4.9	1.3	-0	-12.8	-0.64

Breakout: 33%　Improve: 70%　Collapse: 6%　Attrition: 9%　　　　Comparables: Scott Christman, Terry Mulholland, Chris Hancock, Justin Jones

Savery had some shoulder issues during his final year at Rice, but he looked fully recovered last fall after the Phillies used their first-round pick on him. Unfortunately, that stuff didn't hold up over a full season, as he lost considerable velocity and sat in the upper 80s with his fastball. He's a former power lefty now pitching with finesse stuff, and if the out pitches don't return in the next two years, maybe they can try him out as a hitter—he had third- to fifth-round potential as a slugging first baseman.

Rudy Seanez

| | | | | | | | | | | | | | | Bats: R | | Throws: R | | Height: 6' 0" | | Weight: 225 | | Born: October 20, 1968 | | Age: 40 |

YEAR	TEAM	LVL	AGE	W	L	SV	G	GS	IP	H	BB	SO	HR	GB%	BABIP	STUFF	WHIP	ERA	DERA	EqH9	EqBB9	EqSO9	EqHR9	DEF	VORP	SN/WX
2006	BOS	MLB	37	2	1	0	41	0	46²	51	26	48	6	31.2%	.336	3	1.65	4.82	5.13	9.1	4.8	8.0	1.0	0	4.2	-1.14
2006	SDN	MLB	37	1	2	0	8	0	6¹	7	6	6	2	38.1%	.263	-9	2.05	5.71	7.71	9.0	6.4	6.4	2.6	1	0.1	-0.86
2007	LAN	MLB	38	6	3	1	73	0	76	78	27	73	10	39.1%	.324	9	1.38	3.79	3.20	8.8	2.7	8.1	1.1	-3	16.4	0.77
2008	PHI	MLB	39	5	4	0	42	0	43¹	38	25	30	2	48.9%	.283	-6	1.45	3.53	5.44	8.0	4.4	5.4	0.4	4	3.3	0.07
2009	PHI	MLB	40	2	2	1	29	0	34¹	36	17	29	5	42.0%	.310	-1	1.54	4.94	5.14	9.3	3.9	6.5	1.2	-0	2.1	0.15

Breakout: 13%　Improve: 35%　Collapse: 49%　Attrition: 32%　　　　Comparables: Al Worthington, Jose Mesa, Mike Remlinger, Virgil Trucks

The permanently fragile fireballer has struggled for years with the challenge of pitching on consecutive days, but Manuel had Traction Action make an unusually long Saturday afternoon appearance (for Seanez), eight batters and 2⅔ IP on July 12, after already throwing an inning the night before in an extra-inning tilt. Seanez wasn't the same pitcher after, putting 13 of the next 21 batters he faced on base, with eight of them scoring. He departed for his roost on the DL shortly thereafter, came back in late August, blew a game against the Mets (pitching without rest again), and never saw much more than garbage time from there. Guys with as many warning labels as a fragile situational ROOGY can be hard to work around, but don't be surprised when he shows up in somebody's camp this spring.

R. J. Swindle

| | | | | | | | | | | | | | | Bats: L | | Throws: L | | Height: 6' 3" | | Weight: 190 | | Born: July 7, 1983 | | Age: 25 |

YEAR	TEAM	LVL	AGE	W	L	SV	G	GS	IP	H	BB	SO	HR	GB%	BABIP	STUFF	WHIP	ERA	DERA	EqH9	EqBB9	EqSO9	EqHR9	DEF	VORP	SN/WX
2006	CSC	A	22	4	2	2	21	0	44	35	5	46	0	50.8%	.289	5	0.91	0.61	2.72	10.4	2.0	4.5	0.5	0	12.7	—
2007	LWD	A	23	2	1	10	20	0	29	16	5	37	0	48.4%	.276	9	0.72	0.93	3.12	7.6	2.4	6.2	0.3	2	7.2	—
2007	CLR	A+	23	0	1	3	12	0	15	15	3	20	3	22.5%	.324	-9	1.20	4.80	7.11	14.2	2.8	7.8	4.3	0	-2.1	—
2008	REA	AA	24	1	0	0	11	0	16²	8	1	16	0	50.0%	.200	16	0.54	0.54	3.24	4.3	0.5	5.9	0.0	4	4.4	—
2008	LEH	AAA	24	2	1	1	27	0	36¹	33	7	51	1	36.4%	.376	21	1.10	1.98	3.93	9.2	2.1	8.7	0.5	3	6.4	—
2008	PHI	MLB	24	0	0	0	3	0	4²	9	2	4	2	16.7%	.438	-21	2.36	7.66	6.23	18.7	4.2	8.3	4.2	-1	-1.0	-0.19
2009	MIL	MLB	25	3	3	2	27	4	51¹	50	16	48	6	40.0%	.300	16	1.27	3.69	3.94	8.7	2.3	7.1	1.0	0	11.3	1.12

Breakout: 14%　Improve: 32%　Collapse: 37%　Attrition: 14%　　　　Comparables: Mike Stanton, Cliff Bartosh, Jim Poole, Joe Sambito

Swindle had a nifty little season, striking out 39 of 79 left-handed hitters among his 67 Ks in 53 IP, not too shabby for a Canadian who was drafted and quickly cut by the Red Sox, later washed out of the Yankees system after an initial spin through the indie leagues (with the Schaumburg Flyers), and followed that up with another successful indie stint with Newark, which got him to his shot with the Phillies. Signed by the Brewers to a guaranteed deal after the season, Swindle's shot at a job won't go uncontested, but his getting even this far is already an impressive story.

LINEOUTS

Hitters

PLAYER	TEAM	LVL	AGE	PA	R	2B	3B	HR	RBI	BB	SO	SB-CS	EqBRR	AVG/OBP/SLG	EqAVG/EqOBP/EqSLG	EqA	VORP	WARP
CF Q. Berry*	CLR	A+	23	590	63	24	1	3	43	65	103	51-14	1.5	.272/.360/.341	.222/.295/.286	.216	-34.0	-4.1
INF M. Cervenak	LEH	AAA	31	482	64	30	2	10	66	13	64	5-4	0.8	.311/.336/.452	.259/.282/.391	.231	-7.8	-1.6
OF Z. Collier*	PHL	Rk	17	150	15	9	1	0	19	17	28	5-0	1.6	.271/.347/.357	.184/.245/.257	.177	-38.3	-2.3
C T. D'Arnaud	LWD	A	19	70	12	5	0	2	5	5	10	0-0	-1.8	.297/.357/.469	.262/.314/.415	.251	0.7	-0.4
	WPT	A-	19	197	21	13	1	4	25	18	29	1-2	-2.3	.309/.371/.463	.267/.315/.406	.249	3.1	0.2
C J. Naughton*	LWD	A	21	316	29	17	0	2	33	27	39	1-1	-1.1	.275/.336/.359	.238/.294/.305	.214	-14.7	0.3
OF C. Snelling*	LEH	AAA	26	120	14	1	0	1	8	19	23	1-0	-0.0	.229/.367/.271	.204/.333/.245	.224	-6.1	-0.2
LF S. Taguchi	PHI	MLB	38	103	18	5	1	0	9	8	14	3-0	0.8	.220/.283/.297	.215/.277/.290	.208	-3.8	-0.6
1B A. Tracy*	LEH	AAA	34	507	71	34	0	22	85	65	96	5-0	-3.0	.288/.382/.521	.244/.334/.451	.271	15.0	1.5
OF B. Watson*	LEH	AAA	26	559	78	21	2	6	40	26	53	11-9	0.8	.305/.341/.388	.267/.302/.347	.225	-12.1	-3.2

Quintin Berry is the fastest player in the system and a ball hawk in center, but he's without any semblance of power and doesn't have enough on-base skills to be a leadoff hitter. ⊘ When **Mike Cervenak** could play some second base, he had potential to stick as somebody's infield reserve with a bit of sock, but now that he's reduced to playing the corners, he may have to settle for last year's late-career latte. ⊘ Selected ten picks after Anthony Hewitt, **Zach Collier** has only slightly less tools but far more polish. ⊘ Some see catcher **Travis D'Arnaud** as the best catching prospect in the system due to his power and superior defense. ⊘ Australian catcher **Joel Naughton** arguably has the best catch-and-throw skills in the system, but there are long-term questions about his bat. ⊘ **Chris Snelling** has always been as fragile as Meissen porcelain, but apparently the only pattern he comes in anymore is "broken." ⊘ You might feel for **So Taguchi**—if your calling card is glovework, and you lose your job as a defensive replacement in left field to a converted shortstop, it's a sign. ⊘ We suspect that **Andy Tracy** hasn't been hanging around this long just to achieve the honor of being an inaugural IronPig, but he did deliver the team's first-ever run, RBI, and home run in his first at-bat. ⊘ As slappy as ever, **Brandon Watson** dares to reach for the grass just beyond the infield dirt once in a while, but he's slowing down on the bases and he's no longer really playable in center.

Pitchers

PLAYER	TEAM	LVL	AGE	W	L	SV	IP	H	BB	SO	HR	GB%	BABIP	STUFF	WHIP	ERA	DERA	EqH9	EqBB9	EqSO9	EqHR9	DEF	VORP
J. Bisenius	REA	AA	25	3	3	0	42	33	24	33	5	44.1%	.262	-19	1.36	3.43	5.72	8.0	5.0	5.3	1.6	6	-0.5
	LEH	AAA	25	0	2	0	21²	24	18	21	1	41.8%	.390	-6	1.94	7.05	8.44	10.1	7.6	5.5	0.8	-1	-6.7
C. Chapman	LWD	A	24	7	7	0	139	133	37	118	6	52.0%	.315	-19	1.22	2.98	5.97	11.9	3.7	3.7	1.1	-2	-5.0
M. Cisco	LWD	A	21	2	1	0	35	22	0	30	0	64.3%	.227	21	0.63	0.51	3.55	7.1	0.8	3.5	0.3	5	7.5
	WPT	A-	21	1	0	0	19¹	18	5	22	1	56.6%	.327	0	1.19	1.87	4.32	12.4	3.8	4.9	1.6	-1	2.4
S. Escalona*	LWD	A	23	5	1	2	44²	36	18	60	1	63.1%	.350	1	1.21	3.42	5.59	11.4	5.6	7.1	0.7	-2	0.0
	REA	AA	23	0	1	1	24¹	27	14	29	3	52.9%	.375	3	1.69	2.22	3.57	11.9	5.2	7.9	1.6	-3	5.1
J. Knapp	PHL	Rk	17	3	1	0	31	26	12	38	1	40.3%	.333	5	1.23	2.61	6.29	14.1	6.7	5.2	1.8	0	-1.9
D. Naylor	LWD	A	22	5	3	0	87¹	69	21	97	8	56.1%	.280	-7	1.03	2.99	5.59	10.2	3.4	5.2	2.0	-1	0.1
	CLR	A+	22	3	7	0	78	86	31	59	8	40.4%	.328	-31	1.50	4.85	7.77	12.5	4.6	3.6	2.2	-1	-17.0
J. Sampson	LWD	A	19	11	4	0	135	152	52	69	5	54.3%	.320	-14	1.51	4.33	7.54	12.9	5.1	1.5	1.1	-6	-25.7
L. Walrond*	LEH	AAA	31	5	8	0	111	106	42	105	4	51.7%	.336	12	1.33	3.32	4.91	8.9	3.7	5.6	0.5	1	8.1
	PHI	MLB	31	1	1	0	10¹	13	9	12	0	53.6%	.500	9	2.13	6.12	2.89	13.5	7.7	9.6	0.0	-3	-0.7

Joe Bisenius still has plus velocity and a hammer curve, but his command has gone backwards in each of the last two years. ⊘ **Chance Chapman** has a chance of getting there due to his outstanding slider, but a long college career meant he was already 24 in his full-season debut. ⊘ Small right-hander **Mike Cisco** has average velocity but supernatural command, as evidenced by his zero walks in 35 innings just weeks after signing. ⊘ Venezuelan lefty **Sergio Escalona** has an excellent slider and enough velocity to get to be somebody's LOOGY at the very least. ⊘ A second-round pick last June out of a New Jersey high school, **Jason Knapp** is a raw, big-bodied right-hander who can got his fastball up to 97 mph in his pro debut. ⊘ Few in the system took a bigger step forward than Australian righty **Drew Naylor** after he led the organization in strikeouts, the products of his solid velocity and an outstanding curveball. ⊘ While the numbers didn't impress, **Julian Sampson** opened some scouts' eyes with a projectable frame and an outstanding sinker. ⊘ Journeyman southpaw **Les Walrond** cranked out 11 quality starts in his 17 at Triple-A, and used that to cash in by signing in Japan after the season. ⊘ Although **Mike Zagurski** lost all of 2008 to recovery from Tommy John surgery, "Bronko" should be back in action by the summer to take his shot at a spare lefty role in the pen.

MANAGER: CHARLIE MANUEL

YEAR	TEAM	W-L	Pythag +/−	Avg PC	100+ P	120+ P	QS	BQS	REL	REL w Zero R	IBB	Subs	PH	PH Avg	PH HR	SB2	CS2	SB3	CS3	SAC Att	SAC %	POS SAC	Squeeze	Swing	In Play
2006	PHI	85-77	-1	93.0	56	2	68	7	500	323	62	77	296	.209	3	87	25	5	0	82	69.5%	28	0	105	69
2007	PHI	89-73	1	92.8	55	1	72	8	498	310	62	121	262	.230	9	126	18	11	2	85	76.5%	26	1	146	113
2008	PHI	92-70	-2	96.0	62	3	86	7	468	319	64	98	281	.253	9	119	22	17	2	102	69.6%	25	1	131	99

Manuel may not be the classic, generalized ideal of a sabermetric manager, but if there's a good reason why not, we'd like to hear it. On offense, he runs with the people he should, avoids bunting with his position players over much, and pinch-hits aggressively with a bench full of players capable of delivering in different situations. On defense, he uses his bullpen creatively in a way that reflects an understanding of what his pitchers' specific skill sets are instead of following a more standard-issue platoon differential-driven playbook, he doesn't get overly cute with his rotation despite considerable in-season uncertainty. In short, he uses his entire roster, generally tries to sort out what people can do and sets them to it, and has gotten considerable good work out of other people's cast-offs. If that isn't sound management, what is? He will probably never win a Manager of the Year Award—setting aside any readiness for city slickers to get tripped up by the Appalachian accent, appreciation of his skill in game and roster management is probably best observed on the diamond, and not in the interview room.

Pittsburgh Pirates

It might be hard to remember, but the Pirates weren't always a laughingstock. They were the team of Wagner, Traynor, Waner, Kiner, Clemente, Stargell, and a skinny guy named Bonds. There has been plenty of proud history packed into the franchise's 122-year history. However, the chapter the Pirates are on the brink of writing in the coming season is not the type of history with which anyone wants to be associated. Another losing campaign would be the team's 17th consecutive season under .500; that would break the major league record of 16 set by the 1933–1948 Phillies. The losing streak started a year after former Pirate Sid Bream slid home with the winning run in the bottom of the ninth inning of Game Seven of the 1992 National League Championship Series, as the Braves completed a rally that was historic both in and of itself and in that it seemingly lowered a franchise into its grave. To put into perspective how long ago that was, Bream spent last season as the hitting coach for the Pirates' short-season A-ball club at State College after having been retired as a player for 13 years.

A cynic might say the Pirates' motto should be "Rebuilding Our Rebuilding Since 1993." The cynic would be right. But although the Pirates went 67-95 last season and lost one more game than they had in 2006—the final season guided by the bumbling triumvirate of Kevin McClatchy, Dave Littlefield, and Jim Tracy—there were finally some signs that the franchise might someday turn things around. The Nutting family, newspaper magnates from nearby Wheeling, had long been the money men behind the franchise, but they had entrusted the Pirates to McClatchy, the newspaper heir from Sacramento who put together the group that bought the team from a public/private consortium on the first day of spring training in 1996. McClatchy was able to get beautiful PNC Park built, but also made a number of dubious operational decisions, such as staying with general manager Cam Bonifay too long, then hiring Littlefield, and then giving Littlefield six years to do even more damage to the franchise with a series of bad trades, dubious free-agent signings, and awful drafts.

Understandably exhausted with failure, the Nuttings forced change. McClatchy was ousted, and Bob Nutting was installed as club president. He cleaned house, hiring Frank Coonelly, formerly Major League Baseball's chief labor lawyer and potential heir to Bud Selig, as president. Neal Huntington was brought in as GM from the Indians organization, a successful operation in a similar market. John Russell, a quiet, firm minor league manager from the Phillies' system, was hired to replace Tracy, who had been much more talk than action in his two seasons with the Pirates.

Running with much the same talent in 2008 as they'd fielded the year before, the Pirates were actually a respectable (for them) 50-57 through the end of July. Realizing, however, that building a team that could compete in the long haul was more important than attaining transient respectability and maybe even a winning record with a strong finishing kick, Huntington shopped his wares, dealing two-thirds of his starting outfield, sending Jason Bay to the Red Sox and Xavier Nady to the Yankees. While some felt he should have torn up the team as soon as he took over, Huntington shopped with more care, fully conscious of the need to restock an entire organization and not simply dumping salary for its own sake. Every little bit of talent had the

---

PIRATES PROSPECTUS

2008 record: 67-95; Sixth place in NL Central

Pythagenport record: 67-95

Runs scored per game: 4.54 (9th in NL)

Runs allowed per game: 5.47 (16th in NL)

Team EqA: .257 (Tied for 10th in NL)

2008 Batters Age: 29.0 (7th-oldest in NL)

2008 Pitchers Age: 26.9 (3rd-youngest in NL)

Ballpark: PNC Park; Pitcher's park; Park Factor of .965

2008: There appears to be a firm hand at the tiller, but abysmal pitching and defense leave the ship in dry dock.

2009: The foundations of the next successful Pirates team might be buried in here somewhere, but won't be unearthed for another few years.

potential to help, because the system had been left bare by the previous administration's ineptitude.

In return for Bay and Nady, Huntington acquired eight young players of varying potential and progress on the developmental path. Outfielder Jose Tabata, who had fallen out of favor in the Yankees' farm system despite reaching Double-A at the tender age of 19, was the centerpiece in the four-player package that arrived from New York. He was bundled with three-fifths of the Yankees' rotation at their Triple-A affiliate, Jeff Karstens, Ross Ohlendorf, and Daniel McCutchen. In the three-way Bay trade that included the Red Sox's sending Manny Ramirez to the Dodgers, the Pirates got third baseman Andy LaRoche and A-ball right-hander Bryan Morris from Los Angeles, and reliever Craig Hansen and outfielder Brandon Moss from Boston. Five of the eight immediately got a chance to contribute to the big-league team, but none who spent time with the Pirates after the trades played particularly well. In the lineup, Moss had a .247 EqA in 177 plate appearances, while LaRoche posted an anorexic .152 mark in 183 trips to the plate. On the mound, Karstens ran off 15 scoreless innings in his first two starts before the league caught up to him, while Ohlendorf and Hansen both took their lumps from the get-go.

Despite these initial disappointments, the Pirates believe that all five can be key contributors in 2009 and beyond. The biggest payoff, however, should come from Tabata and Morris, who join the homegrown center-field prospect Andrew McCutchen to give the system its best talents in an organization otherwise hampered by a dearth of quality prospects. McCutchen will challenge for a job in spring training, Tabata won't be too far behind (as he's expected to be in Triple-A), while Morris will open the year in the High-A Carolina League.

While the trades get headlines, the Pirates are really making the biggest strides in the first-year player draft and the signing of amateur free agents. This comes after years of making signability the primary consideration in determining their draft selections and subsequently taking an understandable beating from the media and fans for what came of that. The old regime saved the worst for last, passing on Georgia Tech's Matt Wieters with the fourth overall selection, instead picking Clemson left-hander Daniel Moskos. An elite prospect, Wieters will be the Orioles' starting catcher this year; Moskos, meanwhile, struggled with High-A competition.

In a refreshing reversal, the new leadership went for high-ceiling talent in the 2008 draft, spending over $10 million on signing its selections. Vanderbilt third baseman Pedro Alvarez, considered the top player in the draft, was taken with the second overall pick, and eventually signed to a four-year, $6.34 million big-league contract after predictably contentious negotiations with agent Scott Boras. Beyond Alvarez, the Pirates also signed a number of high school players for bonuses far above the selected slot price set by Major League Baseball (a system, ironically enough, devised and administered by Coonelly). Among those draftees were outfielders Robbie Grossman (sixth round) and Wesley Freeman (16th round), shortstop Jarek Cunningham (18th round), and right-hander Quinton Miller (20th round).

The Pirates also began building a new training academy in the Dominican Republic for an estimated cost of $5 million; the facility will be a huge improvement over what they currently have in that island nation. They also showed a willingness to spend in Latin America, where the Pirates were once pioneers, by signing a number of prospects, including Jonathan Barrios, a highly touted 16-year-old shortstop from Colombia. The Pirates also showed a willingness to be creative in pursuing foreign talent more obscure. They signed a pair of pitchers, left-hander Rinku Singh and right-hander Dinesh Kumar Patel, from India after the men appeared on a reality television show in their homeland called *Million Dollar Arm*. They also signed a South African, shortstop Mpho Ngoepe, after scouting him at Major League Baseball's training academy in Italy.

With the exception of Alvarez, none of these players brought into the organization will make an impact at the major league level for years. The Pirates will hope for improvement in 2009 from basically the same roster that finished last season by going 17-37 in the final two months after the trades of Bay and Nady. That doesn't mean that they're settling, however. Veteran pitching coach Joe Kerrigan has been brought in to try to fix a pitching staff that saw Paul Maholm be the only Pirates starter among the top 55 in the National League in SNLVAR. Manager John Russell says Maholm is the only starter assured of a spot in the rotation when spring training begins, as Tom Gorzelanny (0.8) and Ian Snell (1.5) were huge disappointments, contributing a combined 2.3 SNLVAR after delivering 10.4 in 2007. The Pirates did have some talent in the pen at least, with three relievers among the top 21 in the National League in WXRL last season, though left-hander Damaso Marte was packaged with Nady in the trade with the Yankees. Lefty John Grabow was fifth at 3.31, but will probably be traded at some point in the season as well, as he's eligible for free agency after the season. Closer Matt Capps's 2.04 WXRL was good for 21st, despite his missing nearly two months with a sore shoulder. For spring training,

Kerrigan plans to hold a daily drill in which pitchers will throw batting practice dummies standing in each side of the batter's box. Kerrigan's point is the Pirates need to pitch inside more after averaging a National League-worst 3.9 unintentional walks per nine last season.

The lineup struggled mightily after the trades of Bay and Nady, averaging 3.7 runs a game in the final third of the season after scoring 4.9 a game in the first 108 games. Center fielder Nate McLouth and catcher Ryan Doumit both had solid seasons after beating out Nyjer Morgan and Ronny Paulino, respectively, for starting jobs in spring training, and the Pirates now feel that McLouth and Doumit are both building blocks they can rely on into the near future. In contrast, Littlefield and Tracy felt that neither McLouth nor Doumit could handle a regular job in the major leagues.

Unfortunately, the bright spots are few and far between beyond McLouth and Doumit. First baseman Adam LaRoche was the only other regular to have an above-average season, although yet again, he punted the first two months of the season, hitting a .210/.288/.348 line through June 6 and then hitting .316/.381/.613 over the final 78 games. The Pirates will also hope for better production from their middle-infield combination of second baseman Freddy Sanchez and shortstop

Jack Wilson, although it's a matter of seeing them off fondly; both will probably be elsewhere in 2010, as they should become free agents after this season.

Although the Pirates' top three prospects entering the 2008 season all played at Triple-A, none clearly showed they are ready. McCutchen hit only one home run in his last 49 games after connecting eight times in his first 86. First baseman/outfielder Steven Pearce slipped mightily after what seemed like a breakout in 2007, while third baseman and 2004 first-round pick Neil Walker struggled to get on base at a clip that might demonstrate he'll inspire more than organizational regret in the future.

As a result, while there may be help coming down the road and the revamp of the player-development program proceeds apace, there is little help on the immediate horizon. Thus, it is hard to imagine the Pirates' not meeting their date with infamy and a record-setting 17th consecutive losing season sometime in the latter stages of this season. It's a pity that the new regime is going to have to live down this ignominious achievement, but the good ship *Pirate* wasn't merely taking on water; she had long since slipped from sight. Bringing back a once-proud franchise will take time, and not nearly as long as the time spent on sinking her.

HITTERS

Pedro Alvarez   3B

Bats: L   Throws: R   Height: 6' 3"   Weight: 235   Born: February 6, 1987   Age: 22

YEAR	TEAM	LVL	AGE	PA	R	2B	3B	HR	RBI	BB	SO	SB	CS	EqBRR	AVG	OBP	SLG	EqAVG	EqOBP	EqSLG	EqA	VORP	WARP	DEFENSE
2009	PIT	MLB	21	531	51	29	3	10	58	40	127	8	3	0.3	.238	.299	.375	.237	.299	.388	.237	-1.3	0.4	125-3B -2

Breakout: N/A   Improve: N/A   Collapse: N/A   Attrition: N/A   Comparables: Bob Horner, Ryan Zimmerman, Rick Nelson, Moises Alou

For once the Pirates did *not* take the cheap way out in the first-year player draft, selecting the best player available with the second overall pick in last June's draft. Alvarez's left-handed power stroke will play well at PNC Park, probably as soon as 2010; indeed, if he (or agent Scott Boras) hadn't dragged out negotiations last summer, Alvarez could have been the Opening Day third baseman this year. He may eventually move off the hot corner; he's fundamentally solid but not outstanding, and his size might hinder him. Regardless, he will provide star power to a franchise that desperately needs some.

Brian Bixler   SS

Bats: R   Throws: R   Height: 6' 1"   Weight: 195   Born: October 22, 1982   Age: 26

YEAR	TEAM	LVL	AGE	PA	R	2B	3B	HR	RBI	BB	SO	SB	CS	EqBRR	AVG	OBP	SLG	EqAVG	EqOBP	EqSLG	EqA	VORP	WARP	DEFENSE	
2006	LYN	A+	23	317	46	16	2	5	33	35	58	18	7	1.6	.303	.402	.434	.232	.306	.352	.231	-7.7	0.9	71-SS 4	
2006	ALT	AA	23	253	36	13	1	3	19	16	57	6	2	2.2	.301	.363	.407	.259	.310	.362	.238	-3.4	0.1	56-SS -3	
2007	IND	AAA	24	556	77	23	10	5	51	54	131	28	4	6.8	.274	.368	.396	.254	.339	.387	.260	5.7	0.9	111-SS -16	15-2B 2
2008	IND	AAA	25	364	44	8	5	7	36	27	107	23	7	-0.6	.280	.346	.402	.270	.331	.393	.256	4.2	2.6	73-SS 10	10-2B -1
2008	PIT	MLB	25	120	16	2	1	0	2	6	36	1	0	0.6	.157	.229	.194	.156	.227	.193	.132	-10.1	-0.7	31-SS 3	
2009	PIT	MLB	26	429	51	18	3	7	34	34	110	15	5	2.2	.246	.315	.362	.245	.315	.374	.243	6.5	1.4	102-SS 2	

Breakout: 30%   Improve: 60%   Collapse: 19%   Attrition: 17%   Comparables: Kiko Garcia, Bill Almon, Andy Sheets, Royce Clayton

Bixler has been a prospect of at least some note since being the Pirates' second-round pick in 2004, but he was terribly exposed in his first taste of the major leagues, overpowered at the plate by good fastballs and continually chasing sliders in the dirt. As a result, he struck out far too much for a player who relies on speed and has minimal power. Bixler did play good defense after a shaky start, but the trouble at the plate suggests his future lies not among the starting shortstops, but with the middle infield reserves.

Jason Delaney — 1B

Bats: R   Throws: R   Height: 6' 3"   Weight: 215   Born: November 9, 1982   Age: 26

YEAR	TEAM	LVL	AGE	PA	R	2B	3B	HR	RBI	BB	SO	SB	CS	EqBRR	AVG	OBP	SLG	EqAVG	EqOBP	EqSLG	EqA	VORP	WARP	DEFENSE			
2006	HIC	A	23	518	64	27	3	9	75	56	79	5	5	-6.1	.300	.379	.432	.203	.262	.294	.191	-40.1	-7.8	116-LF	-39		
2007	LYN	A+	24	296	39	16	3	9	44	38	52	2	1	-2.6	.340	.432	.536	.234	.307	.377	.239	-4.2	-1.2	45-1B	-5	19-LF	-2
2007	ALT	AA	24	262	25	10	0	7	35	38	52	0	0	-2.3	.265	.370	.404	.213	.305	.330	.226	-9.8	-1.2	29-1B	-8	21-LF	4
2008	ALT	AA	25	444	42	21	3	7	43	68	77	7	2	-1.4	.292	.403	.422	.237	.338	.355	.250	-2.3	-0.4	109-1B	-3		
2008	IND	AAA	25	119	18	6	1	0	8	17	25	0	1	-0.4	.255	.364	.337	.232	.339	.313	.238	-2.4	0.2	28-1B	3		
2009	PIT	MLB	26	503	44	23	2	7	43	51	121	3	2	-1.6	.218	.302	.325	.217	.301	.336	.224	-15.7	-1.3	119-1B	-2		

Breakout: 16%   Improve: 37%   Collapse: 36%   Attrition: 15%   Comparables: Eric Battersby, Vasili Spanos, Shawn Fagan, Mel Wearing

Delaney hits more like someone who plays an up-the-middle position than a first baseman or a left fielder, which is why his chances of ever getting anything more than a cup of coffee in the major leagues are slim. Seven home runs between Double-A and Triple-A won't get it done in a corner, and it was entirely unsurprising when he went unclaimed in the Rule 5 draft after being left off the 40-man roster.

Robinzon Diaz — C

Bats: R   Throws: R   Height: 5' 11"   Weight: 210   Born: September 19, 1983   Age: 25

YEAR	TEAM	LVL	AGE	PA	R	2B	3B	HR	RBI	BB	SO	SB	CS	EqBRR	AVG	OBP	SLG	EqAVG	EqOBP	EqSLG	EqA	VORP	WARP	DEFENSE			
2006	DUN	A+	22	447	59	21	1	3	44	20	37	8	1	-2.7	.306	.341	.383	.252	.283	.322	.211	-20.4	-1.1	88-C	-3	9-3B	-2
2007	NHP	AA	23	319	33	17	1	3	30	11	16	5	0	0.0	.316	.344	.409	.272	.296	.357	.229	-6.3	-0.6	49-C	-5	8-3B	-1
2007	SYR	AAA	23	69	4	3	0	1	10	1	6	0	0	0.1	.338	.358	.431	.303	.324	.379	.244	0.6	0.2	16-C	0		
2008	SYR	AAA	24	141	7	7	1	1	13	5	10	0	1	-0.5	.244	.266	.336	.220	.243	.311	.189	-10.6	-0.2	21-C	4		
2008	IND	AAA	24	14	0	0	1	0	3	0	0	1	2	-0.0	.357	.357	.500	.429	.429	.571	.282	2.6	0.1				
2009	PIT	MLB	25	348	27	14	1	3	31	13	34	2	1	-0.8	.246	.277	.320	.245	.276	.331	.205	-7.7	0.2	84-C	-3		

Breakout: 22%   Improve: 37%   Collapse: 42%   Attrition: 13%   Comparables: Einar Diaz, Humberto Quintero, Alex Delgado, Wil Nieves

The Pirates acquired Diaz from the Blue Jays in an August trade for third baseman Jose Bautista; he had been considered a decent prospect in a weak farm system. Diaz then spent September with the Pirates, but started only one game because of a hamstring injury. With a contact-oriented line-drive stroke and the requisite catch-and-throw skills, he projects as a decent backup catcher in the major leagues, but he'll have to compete with Jason Jaramillo, who was acquired from Philadelphia during the Winter Meetings.

Ryan Doumit — C

Bats: S   Throws: R   Height: 6' 1"   Weight: 220   Born: April 3, 1981   Age: 28

YEAR	TEAM	LVL	AGE	PA	R	2B	3B	HR	RBI	BB	SO	SB	CS	EqBRR	AVG	OBP	SLG	EqAVG	EqOBP	EqSLG	EqA	VORP	WARP	DEFENSE			
2006	PIT	MLB	25	178	15	9	0	6	17	15	42	0	0	-0.5	.208	.322	.389	.212	.320	.397	.252	-2.5	0.1	23-1B	0	10-C	0
2007	PIT	MLB	26	279	33	19	2	9	32	22	59	1	2	-1.2	.274	.341	.472	.279	.345	.498	.280	11.7	1.1	35-RF	1	25-C	-4
2008	PIT	MLB	27	465	71	34	0	15	69	23	55	2	2	0.2	.318	.357	.501	.330	.368	.530	.300	38.4	3.2	101-C	-10		
2009	PIT	MLB	28	426	53	26	1	13	56	32	67	3	2	-0.8	.281	.344	.453	.280	.344	.469	.275	21.4	2.4	101-C	-8		

Breakout: 11%   Improve: 31%   Collapse: 37%   Attrition: 17%   Comparables: Jason Varitek, Rich Gedman, Eddie Taubensee, Mike Macfarlane

Sometimes, finding a different way to skin a cat leaves you with something beyond an unhappy cat. Rather than settle for Paulino's incumbency, the new regime took Doumit seriously as a catcher after he'd wasted three years shuttling between that position, first, and right. Maybe it was Huntington's Cleveland experience—where the faith in Victor Martinez's virtues as an offense-first catcher has worked out more often than not—but Doumit responded with a fine season, hitting the most home runs by a Pirates catcher since Mark Parent also had 15 in 1995. He'll never be a great defender, but he worked his way up to adequate, giving the Pirates a source of strength at a tough position to find hitting talent. The Pirates further demonstrated their commitment to Doumit in December by signing him to a three-year contract with a single option for a two-year extension.

Shelby Ford   2B

Bats: S   Throws: R   Height: 6' 3"   Weight: 190   Born: December 15, 1984   Age: 24

YEAR	TEAM	LVL	AGE	PA	R	2B	3B	HR	RBI	BB	SO	SB	CS	EqBRR	AVG	OBP	SLG	EqAVG	EqOBP	EqSLG	EqA	VORP	WARP	DEFENSE
2006	HIC	A	21	249	43	16	3	6	27	14	51	4	3	-2.3	.265	.329	.444	.206	.247	.348	.202	-15.4	-0.4	54-2B	4
2007	LYN	A+	22	413	64	26	7	5	55	34	68	14	0	5.2	.281	.360	.433	.220	.279	.347	.223	-17.9	-0.9	88-2B	-4
2008	ALT	AA	23	349	43	23	10	4	32	20	49	19	5	2.0	.285	.338	.458	.263	.311	.440	.259	6.6	0.5	71-2B	-6
2009	PIT	MLB	24	485	56	31	5	8	46	29	93	16	6	2.1	.252	.305	.401	.251	.305	.414	.249	8.6	1.1	115-2B	-4

Breakout: 34% Improve: 67% Collapse: 14% Attrition: 16%   Comparables: Terry Shumpert, Keith Miller, Ben Francisco, Bob Grandas

Ford is unusually tall for a second baseman, but he's nevertheless one of the better prospects in a weak system—he's a dangerous hitter when healthy, hitting for gap power and chipping in with a few stolen bases. Ford will start this season at Triple-A, but he's in line to succeed Freddy Sanchez in 2010 if he can avoid the injury bug, as he missed time with back and hip problems the last two seasons. That's sort of the question, though; big men at the keystone make big targets, and while Ford has good range, he can be a bit clunky around the bag on the deuce.

Adam LaRoche   1B

Bats: L   Throws: L   Height: 6' 3"   Weight: 185   Born: November 6, 1979   Age: 29

YEAR	TEAM	LVL	AGE	PA	R	2B	3B	HR	RBI	BB	SO	SB	CS	EqBRR	AVG	OBP	SLG	EqAVG	EqOBP	EqSLG	EqA	VORP	WARP	DEFENSE
2006	ATL	MLB	26	557	89	38	1	32	90	55	128	0	2	-0.4	.285	.354	.561	.284	.355	.561	.302	34.7	4.2	130-1B	5
2007	PIT	MLB	27	632	71	42	0	21	88	62	131	1	1	-1.7	.272	.345	.458	.274	.351	.470	.280	21.7	3.2	146-1B	8
2008	PIT	MLB	28	554	66	32	3	25	85	54	122	1	1	-3.0	.270	.341	.500	.280	.350	.531	.294	27.0	2.7	126-1B	-3
2009	PIT	MLB	29	551	71	30	2	24	82	61	112	1	1	-1.2	.270	.353	.487	.269	.353	.504	.287	24.3	2.7	129-1B	0

Breakout: 13% Improve: 34% Collapse: 22% Attrition: 10%   Comparables: Jason Giambi, Johnny Briggs, Leon Durham, Paul Sorrento

Perhaps LaRoche should take a vacation at the start of every season and report to work right after the All-Star break, because it seems that he throws the first three months away every season. On his career, he has hit .253/.324/.447 in the first half over five years—or badly enough to lose his job perhaps anywhere but Pittsburgh—and .297/.360/.548 afterward, well enough to be a solid All-Star. Pile it all together in one lump, and you've got an immensely frustrating player who's pretty good in the aggregate, but keeps leaving you asking what would happen if he showed up earlier in the year.

Andy LaRoche   3B

Bats: R   Throws: R   Height: 6' 1"   Weight: 215   Born: September 13, 1983   Age: 25

YEAR	TEAM	LVL	AGE	PA	R	2B	3B	HR	RBI	BB	SO	SB	CS	EqBRR	AVG	OBP	SLG	EqAVG	EqOBP	EqSLG	EqA	VORP	WARP	DEFENSE	
2006	JAX	AA	22	277	42	13	0	9	46	41	32	6	3	-0.9	.309	.419	.483	.297	.394	.492	.304	23.8	3.3	60-3B	8	
2006	LVG	AAA	22	230	35	14	1	10	35	25	32	3	2	-2.8	.322	.400	.550	.263	.336	.463	.271	8.8	1.7	52-3B	6	
2007	LVG	AAA	23	311	55	18	1	18	48	39	42	2	2	0.8	.309	.399	.589	.249	.340	.483	.278	13.4	2.1	64-3B	6	6-LF	-2
2007	LAN	MLB	23	115	16	5	0	1	10	20	24	2	1	0.7	.226	.365	.312	.217	.365	.293	.247	-1.2	0.1	27-3B	0	
2008	LVG	AAA	24	166	35	3	0	5	28	37	14	2	1	1.6	.293	.452	.439	.227	.383	.336	.271	1.7	0.5	25-3B	0	7-2B	-1
2008	LAN	MLB	24	69	6	1	0	2	6	10	7	0	0	-0.3	.203	.319	.322	.203	.319	.322	.231	-1.3	-0.1	12-3B	0	
2008	PIT	MLB	24	183	11	4	0	3	12	14	30	2	0	1.0	.152	.227	.232	.152	.225	.242	.160	-16.2	-1.7	44-3B	-2	
2009	PIT	MLB	25	330	43	15	1	8	37	38	45	4	2	-0.2	.267	.359	.413	.266	.358	.427	.274	13.6	1.9	80-3B	1	

Breakout: 46% Improve: 68% Collapse: 11% Attrition: 28%   Comparables: Craig Worthington, Phil Gagliano, Dave Anderson, Kevin Youkilis

LaRoche may well have been a highly regarded prospect in the Dodgers' system, but he bombed with the Pirates, showing no plate discipline or power, no virtue in the field, no … anything, except giving them a murder of LaRoches. The Pirates had LaRoche the Younger visit hitting coach Don Long in Seattle over the winter in an effort to rebuild his swing and confidence. Despite his crash and burn, he's expected to climb back out of the crater and win the starting job at third, but he's going to have to show improvement in spring training, and the signing of Ramon Vazquez clouds the picture, pending Huntington's dealing one of the middle infielders.

Steven Lerud   C   Bats: L   Throws: R   Height: 6' 1"   Weight: 210   Born: October 13, 1984   Age: 24

YEAR	TEAM	LVL	AGE	PA	R	2B	3B	HR	RBI	BB	SO	SB	CS	EqBRR	AVG	OBP	SLG	EqAVG	EqOBP	EqSLG	EqA	VORP	WARP	DEFENSE
2006	HIC	A	21	446	45	28	0	12	57	40	146	4	3	-5.7	.239	.330	.402	.189	.251	.311	.191	-34.6	-2.7	92-C -9
2007	LYN	A+	22	328	27	17	1	4	31	31	63	3	2	-5.0	.202	.299	.310	.157	.228	.250	.157	-39.3	-2.6	80-C -5
2008	LYN	A+	23	273	36	14	0	8	40	26	65	1	1	-0.4	.256	.344	.419	.215	.287	.360	.227	-9.4	-0.1	56-C -2
2008	ALT	AA	23	163	17	7	0	4	18	14	42	1	0	-0.2	.233	.302	.363	.223	.288	.358	.227	-5.6	0.2	41-C 1
2009	PIT	MLB	24	428	35	20	1	9	41	35	122	2	1	-1.6	.213	.283	.336	.212	.283	.348	.216	-7.1	0.8	102-C 0

Breakout: 45%   Improve: 68%   Collapse: 13%   Attrition: 6%   Comparables: Eric Helfand, Jimmy Kremers, Paul Bako, John Baker

Lerud broke Matt Williams' Nevada high-school home-run record, but he struggled as a pro with injuries (and his confidence) until last season's big step forward. While he doesn't figure into the big-league picture and it's hard to project him as an eventual regular, he was added to the 40-man roster because there were clubs more than ready to take him in the Rule 5 draft. It's understandably hard to write off a left-handed hitting catcher who offers some pop and good defensive skills, and it's not as if the Pirates are awash in talent.

Andrew McCutchen   CF   Bats: R   Throws: R   Height: 5' 11"   Weight: 170   Born: October 10, 1986   Age: 22

YEAR	TEAM	LVL	AGE	PA	R	2B	3B	HR	RBI	BB	SO	SB	CS	EqBRR	AVG	OBP	SLG	EqAVG	EqOBP	EqSLG	EqA	VORP	WARP	DEFENSE
2006	HIC	A	19	503	77	20	4	14	62	42	91	22	7	1.4	.291	.356	.446	.224	.272	.350	.216	-23.1	-2.9	113-CF -15
2006	ALT	AA	19	87	12	4	0	3	12	8	20	1	1	-0.2	.308	.379	.474	.266	.333	.418	.258	2.0	-0.4	10-CF -3 8-LF -2
2007	ALT	AA	20	498	70	20	3	10	48	44	83	17	1	3.6	.258	.327	.383	.224	.284	.338	.223	-21.8	-0.1	116-CF 5
2007	IND	AAA	20	72	7	4	0	1	5	4	11	4	3	1.0	.313	.347	.418	.284	.319	.373	.243	0.1	0.3	15-CF 2
2008	IND	AAA	21	590	75	26	3	9	50	68	87	34	19	-5.1	.283	.372	.398	.266	.353	.386	.259	11.7	1.3	117-CF 0 7-LF -4
2009	PIT	MLB	22	577	74	30	2	10	52	54	97	20	9	2.2	.264	.336	.391	.263	.336	.404	.259	12.5	2.4	135-CF -1

Breakout: 42%   Improve: 67%   Collapse: 6%   Attrition: 9%   Comparables: Craig Landis, Scott Fletcher, Dave Martinez, Shannon Stewart

With outstanding speed, the potential to hit for average and some power, and Gold Glove–type range in center field, McCutchen has the gifts to become a bona fide exciting ballplayer, something the Pirates have had few of during their long stretch of futility. He had a decent season at Indianapolis, but last year's power outage, the product of intentionally cutting down on his swing last year, is a minor source of concern for scouts who used to project him to be a top-flight power/speed threat. The Pirates want him to initially return to Triple-A and dominate at that level before making him their starter, shifting Nate McLouth—Gold Glove or no—to a corner.

Nate McLouth   CF   Bats: L   Throws: R   Height: 5' 11"   Weight: 185   Born: October 28, 1981   Age: 27

YEAR	TEAM	LVL	AGE	PA	R	2B	3B	HR	RBI	BB	SO	SB	CS	EqBRR	AVG	OBP	SLG	EqAVG	EqOBP	EqSLG	EqA	VORP	WARP	DEFENSE
2006	PIT	MLB	24	297	50	16	2	7	16	18	59	10	1	4.2	.233	.293	.385	.235	.294	.393	.243	-1.3	0.1	39-CF 2 19-RF -1
2007	PIT	MLB	25	382	62	21	3	13	38	39	77	22	1	3.8	.258	.351	.459	.261	.357	.474	.293	23.2	1.8	55-CF -2 12-LF -1
2008	PIT	MLB	26	685	113	46	4	26	94	65	93	23	3	7.2	.276	.356	.497	.288	.366	.530	.303	50.9	5.4	145-CF -4
2009	PIT	MLB	27	612	93	38	4	21	78	62	93	20	5	3.4	.285	.365	.492	.283	.364	.509	.296	40.6	4.6	143-CF -5

Breakout: 24%   Improve: 52%   Collapse: 14%   Attrition: 8%   Comparables: Curtis Granderson, Bobby Higginson, Willie Kirkland, Andy Van Slyke

You wonder what the former Pirates regime thought during last year's All-Star Game when McLouth, who they felt was a bench player, made a game-saving play by throwing Dioner Navarro out at home in the 11th inning. McLouth beat out Nyjer Morgan for the starting center fielder's job with a fine spring training and never relinquished his grip on it, showing off the power, speed, and hustle that consistently impressed observers on his way up. His Gold Glove aside, McLouth is better suited to a corner spot and will move once McCutchen arrives.

Jason Michaels   OF

Bats: R   Throws: R   Height: 6' 0"   Weight: 205   Born: May 4, 1976   Age: 33

YEAR	TEAM	LVL	AGE	PA	R	2B	3B	HR	RBI	BB	SO	SB	CS	EqBRR	AVG	OBP	SLG	EqAVG	EqOBP	EqSLG	EqA	VORP	WARP	DEFENSE			
2006	CLE	MLB	30	548	77	32	1	9	55	43	101	9	5	1.9	.267	.326	.391	.259	.324	.380	.248	-2.5	1.3	115-LF	9		
2007	CLE	MLB	31	295	43	11	1	7	39	20	50	3	4	-0.8	.270	.324	.397	.267	.324	.402	.249	-2.2	0.8	55-LF	5	13-RF	1
2008	CLE	MLB	32	67	3	4	0	0	9	4	13	1	1	0.3	.207	.258	.276	.207	.258	.276	.197	-4.9	-0.4	11-LF	0	5-RF	0
2008	PIT	MLB	32	254	25	9	1	8	44	23	52	1	0	-0.1	.228	.300	.382	.237	.311	.404	.249	-2.4	0.4	28-RF	2	14-LF	-2
2009	HOU	MLB	33	189	22	9	1	5	22	16	36	2	1	-0.1	.253	.322	.411	.256	.324	.422	.257	2.9	0.6	48-LF	0		

Breakout: 36%   Improve: 61%   Collapse: 19%   Attrition: 45%   Comparables: Jeffrey Hammonds, Mike McCormick, Mark Smith, Emil Brown

Michaels washed out with the Indians last May and was promptly dumped on the Pirates. He started off decently, with a three-hit game in his first start and providing some late-game heroics, but he faded badly. Now far past the days when he could dream of being an everyday player, Michaels has a spot in Houston with his former Phillies because of his reputation as a lefty-masher—he's hit .286/.368/.433 against them for his career, but managed only .187/.267/.242 in 101 PAs last season.

Doug Mientkiewicz   4C

Bats: L   Throws: R   Height: 6' 2"   Weight: 205   Born: June 19, 1974   Age: 35

YEAR	TEAM	LVL	AGE	PA	R	2B	3B	HR	RBI	BB	SO	SB	CS	EqBRR	AVG	OBP	SLG	EqAVG	EqOBP	EqSLG	EqA	VORP	WARP	DEFENSE			
2006	KCA	MLB	32	360	37	24	2	4	43	35	50	3	0	-0.9	.283	.359	.411	.270	.352	.395	.267	5.1	0.9	82-1B	2		
2007	NYA	MLB	33	192	26	12	0	5	24	16	23	0	0	-0.2	.277	.349	.440	.267	.344	.442	.272	4.9	0.5	51-1B	0		
2008	PIT	MLB	34	334	37	19	2	2	30	44	28	0	0	-2.2	.277	.374	.379	.285	.382	.401	.281	9.2	1.2	32-1B	2	27-3B	-3
2009	PIT	MLB	35	199	26	12	1	3	23	24	21	1	0	-0.7	.287	.377	.423	.286	.376	.438	.284	9.3	1.1	50-1B	2		

Breakout: 35%   Improve: 59%   Collapse: 22%   Attrition: 39%   Comparables: Dave Bergman, Terry Puhl, Bruce Bochte, Bill Spiers

Mientkiewicz reinvented himself as a utility player last year, chipping in a bit at third base and the outfield corners. It can be a career-saving adaptation, at least in terms of getting him a few extra years of service time. He never had the power you want from a starter at a corner, but he can still pick it at first, work counts, and put the bat on the ball as a pinch-hitter. Add in utility ability, and he has his uses.

Nyjer Morgan   OF

Bats: L   Throws: L   Height: 6' 0"   Weight: 170   Born: July 2, 1980   Age: 28

YEAR	TEAM	LVL	AGE	PA	R	2B	3B	HR	RBI	BB	SO	SB	CS	EqBRR	AVG	OBP	SLG	EqAVG	EqOBP	EqSLG	EqA	VORP	WARP	DEFENSE			
2006	LYN	A+	25	274	43	7	3	0	22	20	40	38	11	3.4	.303	.390	.360	.202	.258	.242	.183	-25.3	-1.7	58-CF	0		
2006	ALT	AA	25	244	39	6	5	1	10	15	28	21	11	-0.5	.306	.359	.393	.243	.287	.319	.215	-11.1	0.2	37-LF	6	15-CF	2
2007	IND	AAA	26	184	30	4	2	0	10	15	28	26	7	3.7	.305	.374	.354	.263	.324	.317	.240	-4.1	0.2	32-CF	-1	9-LF	2
2007	PIT	MLB	26	118	15	3	4	1	7	9	19	7	3	-1.1	.299	.359	.430	.308	.373	.439	.276	6.3	1.7	25-CF	10		
2008	IND	AAA	27	352	54	13	4	1	33	18	47	44	8	4.0	.298	.349	.373	.251	.298	.321	.231	-12.9	-1.0	60-LF	0	16-CF	-4
2008	PIT	MLB	27	175	26	13	0	0	7	10	32	9	5	0.8	.294	.345	.375	.312	.362	.419	.268	3.3	1.4	19-LF	3	11-CF	4
2009	PIT	MLB	28	425	50	17	4	2	27	25	73	26	9	3.3	.248	.300	.327	.247	.300	.338	.229	-8.7	0.7	101-LF	8		

Breakout: 24%   Improve: 45%   Collapse: 29%   Attrition: 25%   Comparables: Bill Bruton, Eric Bullock, Marshall Edwards, Jeff Stone

Morgan is a late bloomer, having played junior hockey in Western Canada for four years, but he seems to have cemented a job on the Pirates' roster after having strong finishes in the big leagues in each of the last two seasons. He's the prototypical outfield reserve type, a speedy guy who can handle center, but who doesn't provide much pop or patience. To his credit, he is beginning to understand his limitations.

Brandon Moss   OF

Bats: L   Throws: R   Height: 6' 0"   Weight: 205   Born: September 16, 1983   Age: 25

YEAR	TEAM	LVL	AGE	PA	R	2B	3B	HR	RBI	BB	SO	SB	CS	EqBRR	AVG	OBP	SLG	EqAVG	EqOBP	EqSLG	EqA	VORP	WARP	DEFENSE		
2006	PME	AA	22	573	76	36	3	12	83	56	108	8	5	-2.0	.285	.357	.439	.251	.318	.397	.249	1.7	-0.1	128-RF	-4	
2007	PAW	AAA	23	559	66	41	2	16	78	61	148	3	5	-1.5	.282	.363	.471	.255	.331	.441	.263	15.1	1.0	99-RF	-3	12-CF -3
2007	BOS	MLB	23	29	6	2	1	0	1	4	6	0	0	0.4	.280	.379	.440	.240	.345	.400	.262	1.0	0.3	6-LF	2	
2008	PAW	AAA	24	182	29	8	4	8	30	16	47	2	0	-0.5	.282	.346	.528	.262	.328	.506	.281	9.2	0.8	36-1B	0	4-RF 0
2008	BOS	MLB	24	86	7	5	1	2	11	6	25	1	1	-0.4	.295	.337	.462	.282	.326	.449	.265	2.4	0.7	10-RF	1	9-LF 3
2008	PIT	MLB	24	177	12	10	2	6	23	15	45	0	1	-2.3	.222	.288	.424	.229	.294	.452	.253	-1.6	-1.0	24-LF	-10	17-RF -1
2009	*PIT*	*MLB*	*25*	*340*	*43*	*20*	*2*	*12*	*45*	*33*	*80*	*3*	*1*	*-0.3*	*.261*	*.338*	*.458*	*.260*	*.337*	*.474*	*.275*	*10.9*	*1.3*	*82-RF*	*-3*	

Breakout: 38%   Improve: 62%   Collapse: 24%   Attrition: 34%   Comparables: Curtis Granderson, Willie Kirkland, Graig Nettles, Jason Kubel

The Red Sox apparently didn't want to give Moss up in the Bay deal, but eventually accommodated themselves to his loss. In the end, Moss is really where he should be—as a corner outfielder with modest power, he wasn't really more than insurance for Boston, but he can work out more than reasonably well as a second-division team's starter in one corner or the other. He'll battle for a regular job this spring, a fight he should win.

Jim Negrych   3B

Bats: L   Throws: R   Height: 5' 10"   Weight: 180   Born: March 2, 1985   Age: 24

YEAR	TEAM	LVL	AGE	PA	R	2B	3B	HR	RBI	BB	SO	SB	CS	EqBRR	AVG	OBP	SLG	EqAVG	EqOBP	EqSLG	EqA	VORP	WARP	DEFENSE		
2006	WPT	A-	21	166	12	7	2	2	17	13	19	1	1	-0.7	.267	.327	.384	.211	.259	.303	.197	-23.0	-2.3	32-2B	-8	
2007	HIC	A	22	376	57	14	4	2	48	27	48	4	1	4.3	.282	.340	.365	.205	.251	.274	.178	-33.8	-3.2	81-2B	-8	
2008	LYN	A+	23	451	77	36	1	5	62	55	55	7	6	-1.3	.370	.448	.508	.305	.376	.431	.282	26.5	1.8	74-3B	-4	17-2B -2
2008	ALT	AA	23	102	10	5	0	0	10	11	14	5	1	0.7	.310	.394	.368	.281	.360	.337	.257	0.8	0.1	19-3B	-1	
2009	*PIT*	*MLB*	*24*	*586*	*65*	*33*	*3*	*6*	*52*	*50*	*93*	*7*	*3*	*1.3*	*.267*	*.333*	*.375*	*.266*	*.332*	*.388*	*.251*	*9.8*	*1.2*	*137-3B*	*-3*	

Breakout: 30%   Improve: 64%   Collapse: 15%   Attrition: 5%   Comparables: Bobby Morris, Dominic Rich, Chip Hale, Mike Rouse

Negrych is a one-tool player, but that tool, pure hitting ability, is rarer than you might think. He won the Carolina League batting title at Lynchburg and kept hitting after a late-season promotion to Double-A. The problem is finding Negrych a position, as he hasn't played well at second or third base. He will, however, keep getting chances because of his pesky, grinder's batsmanship, spraying line drives in all directions, a talent that made him the first baseball All-American in the history of the University of Pittsburgh.

Ron Paulino   C

Bats: R   Throws: R   Height: 6' 2"   Weight: 245   Born: April 21, 1981   Age: 28

YEAR	TEAM	LVL	AGE	PA	R	2B	3B	HR	RBI	BB	SO	SB	CS	EqBRR	AVG	OBP	SLG	EqAVG	EqOBP	EqSLG	EqA	VORP	WARP	DEFENSE
2006	PIT	MLB	25	481	37	19	0	6	55	34	79	0	0	-2.3	.310	.360	.394	.306	.358	.385	.263	15.9	2.3	119-C 0
2007	PIT	MLB	26	494	56	25	0	11	55	33	79	2	2	-1.0	.263	.314	.389	.266	.320	.407	.250	9.6	1.5	122-C -2
2008	IND	AAA	27	126	16	13	1	4	18	13	31	0	2	-1.0	.306	.373	.550	.268	.333	.500	.279	6.8	1.0	23-C 1
2008	PIT	MLB	27	130	8	5	0	2	18	11	24	0	0	0.0	.212	.277	.305	.212	.277	.322	.210	-3.9	-0.3	29-C -1
2009	*PHI*	*MLB*	*28*	*280*	*26*	*14*	*1*	*7*	*31*	*22*	*55*	*1*	*0*	*-1.5*	*.244*	*.306*	*.380*	*.244*	*.307*	*.386*	*.238*	*3.6*	*1.2*	*69-C -1*

Breakout: 29%   Improve: 41%   Collapse: 32%   Attrition: 37%   Comparables: Keith McDonald, Ramon Hernandez, Barbaro Canizares, Humberto Quintero

No Pirates player was hurt more by the franchise's regime change than Paulino, as he first lost his starting job to Doumit at the end of spring training, then moped and got out of shape, and then had even the dignity of being a big leaguer stripped from him with a demotion to Indy. Even upon his recall with roster expansion in September, Paulino started just one game. Clearly, a fresh start was called for, and he'll get it after being traded to the Phillies.

Steven Pearce — RF/1B

Bats: R Throws: R Height: 5' 11" Weight: 200 Born: April 13, 1983 Age: 26

YEAR	TEAM	LVL	AGE	PA	R	2B	3B	HR	RBI	BB	SO	SB	CS	EqBRR	AVG	OBP	SLG	EqAVG	EqOBP	EqSLG	EqA	VORP	WARP	DEFENSE			
2006	HIC	A	23	179	35	13	1	12	38	15	32	1	3	2.7	.288	.363	.606	.190	.240	.387	.207	-9.8	-1.2	39-1B	-1		
2006	LYN	A+	23	377	48	27	1	14	60	34	65	7	5	-2.0	.265	.348	.482	.203	.263	.369	.217	-17.5	-2.3	86-1B	-5		
2007	LYN	A+	24	85	19	4	1	11	24	8	13	2	0	1.0	.347	.412	.867	.244	.294	.615	.292	6.5	0.5	18-1B	0		
2007	ALT	AA	24	335	57	27	2	14	72	33	45	7	2	0.3	.334	.400	.586	.278	.334	.498	.282	18.9	1.7	78-1B	2		
2007	IND	AAA	24	131	18	9	1	6	17	6	12	5	0	2.0	.320	.366	.557	.301	.344	.561	.301	12.1	1.6	20-1B	4	9-RF	1
2007	PIT	MLB	24	73	13	5	1	0	6	5	12	2	1	0.5	.294	.342	.397	.294	.342	.397	.254	1.3	0.2	15-RF	1		
2008	IND	AAA	25	433	47	26	1	12	60	32	75	10	4	-1.0	.251	.312	.417	.233	.292	.402	.240	-5.3	-1.5	66-RF	-10	27-1B	0
2008	PIT	MLB	25	119	6	7	0	4	15	5	22	2	0	0.2	.248	.294	.422	.257	.303	.440	.258	0.6	-0.3	25-RF	-4		
2009	PIT	MLB	26	482	52	26	2	15	60	34	97	6	3	0.2	.246	.304	.412	.245	.304	.426	.250	-0.5	0.2	114-RF	-5		

Breakout: 20% Improve: 48% Collapse: 27% Attrition: 14%   Comparables: Craig Monroe, Jeff Baker, Mark Quinn, Marty Cordova

No doubt about it, Pearce was a massive disappointment last season. Making matters worse was his status as the Pirates' Minor League Player of the Year in 2007, when he'd begun the year at Lynchburg and finished it slugging his way all the way up to the major leagues. He had a good spring in 2008, but struggled in Triple-A after that good camp led nowhere but Indy. He experienced a curious power outage when called up, going 78 PAs before touching off a home run. But he did hit four of them in September, so while he'll be coming into his age-27 season without having really established himself, he'll get a shot at a starting corner outfield spot.

Jamie Romak — OF

Bats: R Throws: R Height: 6' 2" Weight: 220 Born: September 30, 1985 Age: 23

YEAR	TEAM	LVL	AGE	PA	R	2B	3B	HR	RBI	BB	SO	SB	CS	EqBRR	AVG	OBP	SLG	EqAVG	EqOBP	EqSLG	EqA	VORP	WARP	DEFENSE			
2006	ROM	A	20	420	55	26	2	16	68	59	102	3	1	0.2	.247	.369	.471	.200	.290	.359	.228	-15.2	-1.1	94-RF	-2		
2007	HIC	A	21	84	16	4	0	5	15	9	24	0	2	-0.4	.275	.393	.551	.230	.310	.432	.251	0.6	-0.3	17-RF	-3		
2007	LYN	A+	21	355	49	21	1	15	45	55	90	2	2	-1.3	.252	.380	.483	.203	.304	.384	.239	-6.8	-2.1	55-LF	-12	18-RF	-4
2008	LYN	A+	22	331	58	25	0	18	57	32	95	0	1	-2.8	.279	.360	.552	.259	.326	.512	.280	17.8	1.2	44-RF	-2	7-1B	-1
2008	ALT	AA	22	138	15	6	0	7	23	17	32	0	0	0.5	.208	.312	.433	.197	.290	.402	.238	-2.9	-0.2	33-1B	0		
2009	PIT	MLB	23	532	58	27	1	21	69	54	147	0	1	-1.3	.238	.321	.433	.237	.320	.448	.261	5.8	0.8	125-RF	-11		

Breakout: 31% Improve: 65% Collapse: 13% Attrition: 9%   Comparables: Kala Ka'aihue, Cesar Nicolas, Paul Russo, Dave Staton

Romak was surprisingly left off the 40-man roster by the Pirates after hitting a combined 25 home runs, but he went unclaimed in the Rule 5 draft. Like many Canadian amateurs, his skills are a little raw, but he has the power and plate discipline to make for a True Three Outcomes hitter. Romak began playing first base after being promoted to Altoona late last season; although he has a strong arm, he may be better suited to first because of his limited range.

Freddy Sanchez — 2B

Bats: R Throws: R Height: 5' 10" Weight: 185 Born: December 21, 1977 Age: 31

YEAR	TEAM	LVL	AGE	PA	R	2B	3B	HR	RBI	BB	SO	SB	CS	EqBRR	AVG	OBP	SLG	EqAVG	EqOBP	EqSLG	EqA	VORP	WARP	DEFENSE			
2006	PIT	MLB	28	632	85	53	2	6	85	31	52	3	2	1.6	.344	.378	.473	.343	.376	.468	.292	42.4	4.9	92-3B	15	27-SS	-5
2007	PIT	MLB	29	653	77	42	4	11	81	32	76	0	1	-2.7	.304	.343	.442	.308	.347	.454	.276	29.5	1.1	142-2B	-21		
2008	PIT	MLB	30	608	75	26	2	9	52	21	63	0	1	0.6	.271	.298	.371	.278	.306	.387	.241	1.1	-0.2	126-2B	-7		
2009	PIT	MLB	31	528	56	30	1	7	55	26	54	2	1	-0.4	.286	.324	.399	.285	.324	.412	.253	15.3	1.0	124-2B	-7		

Breakout: 9% Improve: 23% Collapse: 32% Attrition: 22%   Comparables: Joe Randa, Billy Moran, Frank Malzone, Mark Grudzielanek

Sanchez's fall has been steep since winning the NL batting title in 2006; to put up that final 2008 line, he needed a big second half, hitting .346/.378/.483 after the All-Star break just to get into mediocrity's general vicinity. In his defense, he did have shoulder surgery late in the 2007 season, but it's clear that his days as a regular are nearing their end. He can become a free agent after this season unless he gets 635 PAs to trigger a 2010 option, something the Pirates will probably try to prevent from happening.

Jose Tabata   OF

Bats: R   Throws: R   Height: 5' 11"   Weight: 160   Born: August 12, 1988   Age: 20

YEAR	TEAM	LVL	AGE	PA	R	2B	3B	HR	RBI	BB	SO	SB	CS	EqBRR	AVG	OBP	SLG	EqAVG	EqOBP	EqSLG	EqA	VORP	WARP	DEFENSE	
2006	CSC	A	17	363	50	22	1	5	51	30	66	15	5	-0.4	.298	.377	.420	.236	.291	.340	.222	-13.1	-1.4	68-RF	-3
2007	TAM	A+	18	456	56	16	2	5	54	33	70	15	7	0.0	.307	.371	.392	.252	.308	.329	.225	-13.1	-1.6	85-RF	-4
2008	TRN	AA	19	332	40	9	0	3	36	26	49	10	2	2.1	.248	.320	.310	.244	.307	.311	.227	-12.2	-1.0	67-RF	-2
2008	ALT	AA	19	97	16	6	2	3	13	8	18	8	0	2.4	.348	.402	.562	.322	.371	.567	.319	11.6	0.9	22-CF	-2
2009	PIT	MLB	20	557	64	25	2	6	46	39	84	18	6	1.9	.263	.321	.360	.262	.321	.372	.245	-2.4	0.5	131-RF	1

Breakout: 35%   Improve: 63%   Collapse: 10%   Attrition: 8%   Comparables: Raul Gonzalez, Roberto Zambrano, Ricky Otero, Francisco Melendez

The Yankees soured on Tabata last season when, frustrated by a slow start after clashing with coaches, he simply left Trenton in the middle of a game in May. That sort of Operation Shutdown capped questions about his effort at the plate and in the field. He played well after getting traded, and the basic skills—athleticism, great plate coverage, and quick wrists—are all still there. The Pirates feel he can achieve the superstar potential originally forecast for him, especially in light of his youth. If there's a danger, it's that he can play center in a pinch but he should wind up in a corner, and while he'll develop power, it might not play in left or right. He may end up being an underpowered corner outfielder with some pop, a good average, and enough walks. He has a high enough ceiling that it's possible, but lose any part of that proposition, and he'll come up short.

Neil Walker   3B

Bats: S   Throws: R   Height: 6' 3"   Weight: 210   Born: September 10, 1985   Age: 23

YEAR	TEAM	LVL	AGE	PA	R	2B	3B	HR	RBI	BB	SO	SB	CS	EqBRR	AVG	OBP	SLG	EqAVG	EqOBP	EqSLG	EqA	VORP	WARP	DEFENSE	
2006	LYN	A+	20	294	32	22	1	3	35	19	41	3	5	-2.4	.284	.345	.409	.234	.277	.343	.212	-12.8	-0.8	53-C	-3
2007	ALT	AA	21	490	77	30	3	13	66	53	73	9	4	1.7	.288	.362	.462	.250	.317	.411	.253	3.7	0.0	113-3B	-8
2007	IND	AAA	21	69	7	3	0	0	0	2	13	1	1	-0.8	.203	.261	.250	.185	.232	.231	.148	-7.9	-1.1	17-3B	-4
2008	IND	AAA	22	550	69	25	7	16	80	29	102	10	6	-1.3	.242	.280	.414	.230	.267	.402	.230	-14.1	0.0	124-3B	5
2009	PIT	MLB	23	554	62	32	3	14	64	39	100	8	5	0.5	.256	.312	.415	.255	.311	.429	.253	9.1	1.6	130-3B	1

Breakout: 62%   Improve: 81%   Collapse: 4%   Attrition: 4%   Comparables: Dmitri Young, Craig Worthington, Thomas Howard, Steve Hosey

Walker was named Indianapolis's MVP last season for the season listed above. Could there be a stronger indictment of the talent in the upper level of the Pirates' farm system? While Walker has made big strides defensively since being moved to third from catcher two years ago and has the strong arm and soft hands to make for a quality defender, his pitch-recognition issues haven't gotten better over time, and he has yet to have a truly good season at the plate. There comes a time where a prospect has to be more than athletic and needs to convert tools into skills; for Walker, that time is now.

Jack Wilson   SS

Bats: R   Throws: R   Height: 6' 0"   Weight: 195   Born: December 29, 1977   Age: 31

YEAR	TEAM	LVL	AGE	PA	R	2B	3B	HR	RBI	BB	SO	SB	CS	EqBRR	AVG	OBP	SLG	EqAVG	EqOBP	EqSLG	EqA	VORP	WARP	DEFENSE	
2006	PIT	MLB	28	594	70	27	1	8	35	33	65	4	3	-1.2	.273	.316	.370	.273	.317	.368	.240	3.9	1.6	127-SS	4
2007	PIT	MLB	29	535	67	29	2	12	56	38	46	2	5	0.5	.296	.350	.440	.299	.355	.454	.275	26.6	2.8	128-SS	-4
2008	PIT	MLB	30	330	24	18	1	1	22	13	27	2	2	-1.3	.272	.312	.348	.282	.321	.360	.237	2.7	1.8	78-SS	11
2009	PIT	MLB	31	387	39	19	1	4	37	22	37	3	2	-0.3	.272	.319	.367	.271	.318	.380	.242	8.6	1.3	93-SS	3

Breakout: 12%   Improve: 31%   Collapse: 33%   Attrition: 25%   Comparables: Rafael Ramirez, Deivi Cruz, Jerry Adair, Chris Gomez

Wilson is a likable guy and fan favorite in Pittsburgh, which makes it easier to forget that he's not among the top tier of big-league shortstops … or the second. While he's still good afield, he has lost all of what little power he had, was never one to take a walk, and has become injury-prone as he moves into his 30s. Eligible for free agency at the end of the season, surely his last with the Pirates, he will have to start adapting to life as a backup in anybody else's uniform in 2010. He'd have been gone already if not for the three-year, $20 million extension Littlefield gave him before the 2006 season.

PITCHERS

Jimmy Barthmaier

Bats: R   Throws: R   Height: 6' 5"   Weight: 220   Born: January 6, 1984   Age: 25

YEAR	TEAM	LVL	AGE	W	L	SV	G	GS	IP	H	BB	SO	HR	GB%	BABIP	STUFF	WHIP	ERA	DERA	EqH9	EqBB9	EqSO9	EqHR9	DEF	VORP	SN/WX
2006	SLM	A+	22	11	8	0	27	27	146¹	137	67	134	6	52.7%	.326	-4	1.40	3.63	6.40	12.4	5.5	5.0	1.2	-2	-11.0	—
2007	CCH	AA	23	2	9	0	24	16	90	116	44	73	11	51.8%	.365	-35	1.78	6.20	8.89	14.1	5.1	4.4	1.8	-8	-30.3	—
2008	ALT	AA	24	2	4	0	10	10	46¹	42	21	40	3	52.9%	.295	-4	1.36	4.86	6.25	9.1	4.0	5.4	0.8	1	-3.2	—
2008	IND	AAA	24	3	1	0	16	16	79	69	27	71	5	51.8%	.295	1	1.22	3.53	5.57	9.1	3.4	5.4	0.8	5	0.2	—
2008	PIT	MLB	24	0	2	0	3	3	10¹	16	8	6	3	41.0%	.371	-28	2.32	10.49	9.58	13.1	6.1	4.4	2.6	-1	-6.2	-0.25
2009	PIT	MLB	25	4	7	0	30	13	90¹	108	44	67	10	48.0%	.340	7	1.68	5.95	6.21	10.6	3.9	5.9	1.0	-1	-6.5	-0.15

Breakout: 64%   Improve: 85%   Collapse: 5%   Attrition: 23%   Comparables: Mike Fetters, Scott Roberts, Sean Douglass, Erik Schullstrom

Claimed off the waiver wire from the Astros, Barthmaier had a solid season in the Pirates' system last year, struggling only in his first taste of the major leagues (in part because of a bad case of nerves). A big guy who throws fairly hard, he has an out pitch that is actually an outstanding curve that he tightened up last season. Adding a serviceable changeup is the only thing keeping Barthmaier from being a serviceable big-league starter.

Denny Bautista

Bats: R   Throws: R   Height: 6' 5"   Weight: 190   Born: August 23, 1980   Age: 28

YEAR	TEAM	LVL	AGE	W	L	SV	G	GS	IP	H	BB	SO	HR	GB%	BABIP	STUFF	WHIP	ERA	DERA	EqH9	EqBB9	EqSO9	EqHR9	DEF	VORP	SN/WX
2006	OMA	AAA	25	2	5	0	10	10	44²	52	32	28	3	60.0%	.350	-16	1.90	7.33	8.77	12.1	7.0	3.8	0.9	-1	-14.1	—
2006	KCA	MLB	25	0	2	0	8	7	35	38	17	22	5	50.8%	.300	-10	1.57	5.66	5.86	8.9	4.1	4.8	1.3	1	-0.2	0.27
2006	CSP	AAA	25	1	4	0	6	6	36²	46	16	35	2	57.4%	.396	2	1.71	4.48	5.24	12.6	4.2	6.0	0.8	-5	1.4	—
2007	CSP	AAA	26	3	2	0	51	0	64²	54	31	63	1	52.8%	.306	7	1.31	2.92	4.16	7.6	4.5	6.3	0.3	7	10.0	—
2008	DET	MLB	27	0	1	0	16	0	19	15	14	10	1	35.1%	.259	-8	1.53	3.32	3.00	7.0	6.5	4.5	0.5	0	5.3	0.16
2008	PIT	MLB	27	4	3	0	35	0	41¹	46	28	34	5	39.7%	.350	-5	1.79	6.10	5.18	9.9	5.4	6.8	1.1	-3	-2.3	-0.39
2009	PIT	MLB	28	1	2	1	28	0	34¹	34	19	29	3	42.0%	.300	7	1.52	4.60	4.76	8.8	4.3	6.9	0.8	-1	3.6	0.23

Breakout: 34%   Improve: 55%   Collapse: 30%   Attrition: 46%   Comparables: Toby Borland, Todd Wellemeyer, Rodney Myers, Franklyn German

Bautista has a long, loose frame and a great arm that routinely delivers 95 mph fastballs, which might give you the impression he's a superstar waiting to happen. However, five teams have already taken a look—and a pass—in five seasons for two fundamental reasons. The first is that he can't throw strikes; the other is that he can't get anybody out. He was nontendered and then re-signed to a minor league deal, and if there's a safe bet in these times, it's that people will keep trying to harness his ability and will subsequently avail others of that same opportunity.

T. J. Beam

Bats: R   Throws: R   Height: 6' 7"   Weight: 215   Born: August 28, 1980   Age: 28

YEAR	TEAM	LVL	AGE	W	L	SV	G	GS	IP	H	BB	SO	HR	GB%	BABIP	STUFF	WHIP	ERA	DERA	EqH9	EqBB9	EqSO9	EqHR9	DEF	VORP	SN/WX
2006	TRN	AA	25	4	0	3	18	0	42²	26	12	34	1	36.6%	.231	-9	0.90	0.85	4.62	8.0	3.4	4.4	0.5	9	4.0	—
2006	COH	AAA	25	2	0	1	19	0	31²	16	13	37	1	50.0%	.221	9	0.93	1.73	2.97	5.0	4.2	7.1	0.6	1	8.9	—
2006	NYA	MLB	25	2	0	0	20	0	18	26	6	12	5	27.7%	.350	-24	1.78	8.50	6.23	13.5	3.1	5.2	2.6	-4	-4.8	-0.70
2007	SWB	AAA	26	4	3	3	29	0	47²	51	10	45	6	48.7%	.340	-17	1.28	3.58	5.48	11.4	2.2	5.9	1.8	2	0.6	—
2008	IND	AAA	27	2	1	5	30	0	43²	36	14	41	2	40.5%	.286	-3	1.14	3.09	4.07	8.4	3.2	5.6	0.6	0	7.1	—
2008	PIT	MLB	27	2	2	1	32	0	45²	43	20	24	6	37.3%	.262	-15	1.38	4.14	3.64	7.5	3.3	4.0	1.1	-2	7.3	0.17
2009	PIT	MLB	28	1	2	2	32	0	33²	35	13	24	4	39.0%	.290	2	1.42	4.48	4.58	9.2	3.1	5.7	1.1	-1	3.9	0.29

Breakout: 17%   Improve: 40%   Collapse: 36%   Attrition: 45%   Comparables: Mark Acre, Guillermo Mota, Mark Hutton, Adam Bernero

After getting hammered during his first taste of the majors with the Yankees, Beam washed up in PNC Park and pitched effectively at times. His sin has always been a fastball that has less movement than a spavined zebra. He really is just a 12th man on a pitching staff in an era where dialing past 11 might seem excessive.

Sean Burnett

Bats: L   Throws: L   Height: 6' 1"   Weight: 195   Born: September 17, 1982   Age: 26

YEAR	TEAM	LVL	AGE	W	L	SV	G	GS	IP	H	BB	SO	HR	GB%	BABIP	STUFF	WHIP	ERA	DERA	EqH9	EqBB9	EqSO9	EqHR9	DEF	VORP	SN/WX
2006	IND	AAA	23	8	11	0	25	24	120	136	46	46	13	46.5%	.301	-51	1.52	5.18	8.53	12.3	4.2	1.8	1.7	10	-35.7	—
2007	IND	AAA	24	4	5	0	15	15	70¹	83	39	31	4	48.2%	.336	-25	1.74	4.48	6.99	11.9	5.6	2.2	1.0	2	-9.9	—
2008	PIT	MLB	25	1	1	0	58	0	56²	57	34	42	7	50.8%	.311	-9	1.61	4.76	4.47	8.5	4.6	5.9	1.1	-2	4.0	0.78
2009	PIT	MLB	26	1	1	1	23	1	25¹	27	14	19	3	46.0%	.310	0	1.58	4.93	5.10	9.4	4.2	5.9	0.9	-0	1.8	0.12

Breakout: 28% Improve: 46% Collapse: 41% Attrition: 50%   Comparables: Wade Blasingame, Trever Miller, Jake Woods, Dan Serafini

Burnett spent four years rehabilitating from Tommy John and shoulder surgeries before finally getting another crack at the major leagues. Though he was once a promising prospect as a starting pitcher, his arm can no longer withstand the rigors of 100-pitch outings. Reinvented as a reliever, however, he still has just enough stuff to succeed, especially with last year's huge LOOGY-worth platoon split (limiting lefties to 514 OPS).

Matt Capps

Bats: R   Throws: R   Height: 6' 2"   Weight: 245   Born: September 3, 1983   Age: 25

YEAR	TEAM	LVL	AGE	W	L	SV	G	GS	IP	H	BB	SO	HR	GB%	BABIP	STUFF	WHIP	ERA	DERA	EqH9	EqBB9	EqSO9	EqHR9	DEF	VORP	SN/WX
2006	PIT	MLB	22	9	1	1	85	0	80²	81	12	56	12	43.4%	.292	7	1.15	3.79	4.32	8.1	1.1	5.6	1.2	5	17.0	0.68
2007	PIT	MLB	23	4	7	18	76	0	79	64	16	64	5	34.1%	.266	21	1.01	2.28	3.00	6.2	1.6	6.7	0.6	6	29.4	4.20
2008	PIT	MLB	24	2	3	21	49	0	53²	47	5	39	5	32.9%	.268	6	0.97	3.02	4.14	7.0	0.7	5.6	0.8	4	13.3	2.04
2009	PIT	MLB	25	3	4	16	50	0	57	54	12	45	6	39.0%	.280	14	1.16	3.44	3.53	8.4	1.7	6.3	1.0	-1	14.6	1.55

Breakout: 15% Improve: 29% Collapse: 43% Attrition: 19%   Comparables: Ron Davis, Steve Foucault, Ron Robinson, Rusty Meacham

The most questionable move John Russell made during his first season skippering the Bucs was using Capps for three innings of a tie game against the Cubs in late May. Already ridden hard by Jim Tracy in his first two seasons, he struggled afterward, allowing four of his five homers in June and eight of his 17 runs before a sore shoulder sent him to the DL for two months beginning in early July. The big man has the stuff to be a premier closer, except for the gnawing sense that his arm could fall off at any time.

Jesse Chavez

Bats: R   Throws: R   Height: 6' 2"   Weight: 175   Born: August 21, 1983   Age: 25

YEAR	TEAM	LVL	AGE	W	L	SV	G	GS	IP	H	BB	SO	HR	GB%	BABIP	STUFF	WHIP	ERA	DERA	EqH9	EqBB9	EqSO9	EqHR9	DEF	VORP	SN/WX
2006	FRI	AA	22	2	5	4	38	0	59¹	54	28	70	5	45.5%	.338	0	1.39	4.42	7.04	10.0	4.7	7.0	1.3	4	-8.8	—
2006	IND	AAA	22	2	1	0	12	0	17²	18	9	15	0	41.5%	.353	-5	1.57	4.19	6.32	11.5	5.7	5.2	0.6	0	-1.3	—
2007	IND	AAA	23	3	3	2	46	1	80¹	94	17	65	4	39.1%	.353	-9	1.38	3.92	6.25	11.7	2.2	4.8	0.8	1	-5.5	—
2008	IND	AAA	24	2	6	14	51	0	68²	58	22	70	8	43.2%	.278	-17	1.16	3.80	6.06	9.0	3.2	6.2	1.5	8	-3.3	—
2008	PIT	MLB	24	0	1	0	15	0	15	20	9	16	2	46.9%	.419	-2	1.93	6.60	5.17	10.9	4.6	8.0	1.1	-2	-1.8	-0.55
2009	PIT	MLB	25	2	3	2	48	3	52²	61	22	42	7	43.0%	.330	6	1.58	5.19	5.33	10.3	3.3	6.3	1.1	-1	1.3	0.20

Breakout: 35% Improve: 59% Collapse: 12% Attrition: 18%   Comparables: Jeff Gray, Steve Foster, Keith Troutman, Jeff Barkley

Chavez, a slender, late-round draft pick by the Rangers, was shipped to the Pirates in that rather forgettable trading deadline deal for Kip Wells in 2006. He's interesting nonetheless, because he throws very hard and has a decent slider, your classic reliever's assortment and the difference between his being just another arm and his status as a fringe prospect.

Zach Duke

Bats: L   Throws: L   Height: 6' 2"   Weight: 220   Born: April 19, 1983   Age: 26

YEAR	TEAM	LVL	AGE	W	L	SV	G	GS	IP	H	BB	SO	HR	GB%	BABIP	STUFF	WHIP	ERA	DERA	EqH9	EqBB9	EqSO9	EqHR9	DEF	VORP	SN/WX
2006	PIT	MLB	23	10	15	0	34	34	215¹	255	68	117	17	54.4%	.336	13	1.50	4.47	3.81	9.8	2.5	4.5	0.6	-14	27.6	3.72
2007	PIT	MLB	24	3	8	0	20	19	107¹	161	25	41	14	52.5%	.374	-11	1.73	5.54	4.31	12.5	1.9	3.4	1.1	-15	-4.2	0.67
2008	PIT	MLB	25	5	14	0	31	31	185	230	47	87	19	50.4%	.324	1	1.50	4.82	4.71	9.9	1.9	3.6	0.8	-11	5.3	2.41
2009	PIT	MLB	26	8	10	0	25	25	147²	178	41	74	16	49.0%	.320	13	1.48	4.83	5.00	10.7	2.2	4.0	1.0	-2	8.5	2.08

Breakout: 14% Improve: 47% Collapse: 29% Attrition: 20%   Comparables: Carlos Silva, Lary Sorensen, Neal Heaton, Fritz Peterson

Duke is running out of reasons as to why he has not repeated the success of his rookie season in 2005: He did not get along with pitching coach Jim Colborn in 2006, and he had arm problems in 2007, but last year, he just got hammered and there wasn't much to say or do other than strap on a helmet and take cover. Duke is going to have to start fooling some people some of the time in some of his starts lest he risk being remembered as a one-year wonder. Although he might plead for a bit of better defensive support, keep in mind that when a guy gets hit this hard this regularly for this many years, it's not all on the guys standing behind him.

Phil Dumatrait

Bats: R | Throws: L | Height: 6' 2" | Weight: 200 | Born: July 12, 1981 | Age: 27

YEAR	TEAM	LVL	AGE	W	L	SV	G	GS	IP	H	BB	SO	HR	GB%	BABIP	STUFF	WHIP	ERA	DERA	EqH9	EqBB9	EqSO9	EqHR9	DEF	VORP	SN/WX
2006	CHT	AA	24	3	4	0	10	10	49²	39	22	45	4	43.5%	.269	-11	1.24	3.66	6.07	8.8	4.3	5.1	1.4	-1	-2.4	—
2006	LOU	AAA	24	5	7	0	16	15	87²	104	36	58	10	48.8%	.338	-33	1.61	4.75	6.81	12.8	4.4	3.9	1.8	-1	-10.7	—
2007	LOU	AAA	25	10	6	0	22	22	125	114	49	76	10	44.0%	.269	-18	1.30	3.53	6.51	9.0	3.8	3.4	1.2	15	-12.2	—
2007	CIN	MLB	25	0	4	0	6	6	18	39	12	9	6	37.8%	.458	-44	2.83	15.00	11.09	17.8	4.8	4.3	2.4	-5	-17.9	-0.59
2008	PIT	MLB	26	3	4	0	21	11	78²	82	42	52	7	44.0%	.307	-3	1.58	5.26	5.47	8.7	4.1	5.2	0.8	1	1.5	0.55
2009	PIT	MLB	27	1	2	0	16	3	35	41	17	23	5	43.0%	.320	-2	1.66	5.85	6.05	10.5	3.9	5.3	1.2	-1	-2.6	-0.08

Breakout: 32%   Improve: 47%   Collapse: 34%   Attrition: 61%   Comparables: Paul Mirabella, Don Collins, Chris Welsh, Don Hood

The Pirates grabbed Dumatrait off waivers from the Reds after the 2007 season, and he wound up making the club in spring training as a reliever, moving into the rotation in May. There, he had moments when he looked like he might carve out some kind of career. However, three quality starts in 11 does not a fifth starter make, and after hurting his shoulder in July, he had surgery in September, which will make for a late start to his 2009 campaign.

Tom Gorzelanny

Bats: L | Throws: L | Height: 6' 2" | Weight: 220 | Born: July 12, 1982 | Age: 26

YEAR	TEAM	LVL	AGE	W	L	SV	G	GS	IP	H	BB	SO	HR	GB%	BABIP	STUFF	WHIP	ERA	DERA	EqH9	EqBB9	EqSO9	EqHR9	DEF	VORP	SN/WX
2006	IND	AAA	23	6	5	0	16	16	99	67	27	94	4	48.2%	.254	17	0.95	2.36	5.44	7.9	3.0	6.1	0.7	16	1.6	—
2006	PIT	MLB	23	2	5	0	11	11	61²	50	31	40	3	51.6%	.264	16	1.31	3.79	3.92	6.2	3.8	5.0	0.4	1	11.9	1.76
2007	PIT	MLB	24	14	10	0	32	32	201²	214	68	135	18	43.5%	.311	17	1.40	3.88	3.51	8.4	2.6	5.6	0.7	-4	41.5	5.13
2008	IND	AAA	25	3	1	0	7	7	35	28	4	33	1	46.4%	.281	16	0.91	2.06	4.36	8.5	1.4	5.7	0.5	2	4.5	—
2008	PIT	MLB	25	6	9	0	21	21	105¹	120	70	67	20	41.8%	.310	-20	1.80	6.66	5.79	9.5	5.1	5.0	1.6	-8	-13.2	0.78
2009	PIT	MLB	26	4	6	0	25	15	88²	95	43	63	10	42.0%	.300	9	1.54	4.92	5.06	9.5	3.8	5.7	1.0	-1	5.3	1.08

Breakout: 14%   Improve: 36%   Collapse: 34%   Attrition: 32%   Comparables: Mike Kekich, Frank Baumann, Jorge De La Rosa, Allen Watson

Gorzelanny looked like an emerging ace in 2007, but was worked too hard down the stretch to little point, came to spring training out of shape, and reportedly hurt his elbow at that point (if not earlier). Banished to the minor leagues after getting lit up in Milwaukee on the Fourth of July, he finally admitted at the end of the season that his elbow hurt more than he'd let on, as if the demonic ERA and the performance hadn't already clued everyone in. He pondered getting surgery on the aching middle finger of his pitching hand in the offseason, but avoided it, and should show up to camp with plenty to prove.

John Grabow

Bats: L | Throws: L | Height: 6' 2" | Weight: 205 | Born: November 4, 1978 | Age: 30

YEAR	TEAM	LVL	AGE	W	L	SV	G	GS	IP	H	BB	SO	HR	GB%	BABIP	STUFF	WHIP	ERA	DERA	EqH9	EqBB9	EqSO9	EqHR9	DEF	VORP	SN/WX
2006	PIT	MLB	27	4	2	0	72	0	69²	68	30	66	7	52.5%	.323	10	1.41	4.13	3.18	8.0	3.3	7.6	0.8	-6	12.7	1.25
2007	PIT	MLB	28	3	2	1	63	0	51²	56	19	42	6	52.4%	.325	0	1.45	4.53	4.39	8.6	2.7	6.6	1.0	0	6.5	0.79
2008	PIT	MLB	29	6	3	4	74	0	76	60	37	62	9	42.8%	.245	-2	1.28	2.84	3.56	6.3	3.6	6.2	1.0	5	22.3	3.31
2009	PIT	MLB	30	2	3	4	57	0	55²	56	26	46	5	44.0%	.300	7	1.46	4.22	4.35	8.8	3.7	6.7	0.9	-1	7.4	0.65

Breakout: 8%   Improve: 29%   Collapse: 48%   Attrition: 17%   Comparables: Dave Hamilton, Will Ohman, Mike Mohler, Paul Lindblad

Here's your surprise stat from the 2008 season: Grabow finished fifth in the National League in WXRL. While the Pirates have had constant roster turnover during the past five seasons, Grabow has weathered all the storms and quietly gone about his work as a situational specialist. While he may be anonymous outside Pittsburgh, he is the type of durable lefty reliever who could command a lot of money as a free agent after this season, making him a leading candidate for ex-Piracy.

Craig Hansen

Bats: R   Throws: R   Height: 6' 5"   Weight: 185   Born: November 15, 1983   Age: 25

YEAR	TEAM	LVL	AGE	W	L	SV	G	GS	IP	H	BB	SO	HR	GB%	BABIP	STUFF	WHIP	ERA	DERA	EqH9	EqBB9	EqSO9	EqHR9	DEF	VORP	SN/WX
2006	PME	AA	22	1	0	0	5	0	11	4	4	12	0	53.8%	.154	11	0.73	0.82	2.45	4.1	4.1	5.7	0.0	1	3.9	—
2006	PAW	AAA	22	1	2	0	14	4	36²	31	19	26	0	52.3%	.298	-2	1.38	2.73	5.73	9.0	5.5	4.4	0.3	3	-0.5	—
2006	BOS	MLB	22	2	2	0	38	0	38	46	15	30	5	46.5%	.353	0	1.61	6.63	6.57	10.1	3.3	6.1	1.2	-2	-5.8	-0.67
2007	PAW	AAA	23	3	1	3	40	0	51¹	58	32	48	2	65.9%	.348	-7	1.75	3.86	6.02	11.7	5.8	5.5	0.7	-2	-2.3	—
2008	PAW	AAA	24	1	0	0	11	0	16²	6	5	17	0	57.5%	.154	5	0.66	1.62	4.86	3.8	2.7	5.9	0.0	4	1.4	—
2008	BOS	MLB	24	1	3	2	32	0	30²	29	23	25	2	54.6%	.287	-2	1.70	5.57	4.83	8.2	6.0	6.3	0.6	-5	-2.8	0.15
2008	PIT	MLB	24	1	4	1	16	0	15²	11	20	7	1	58.0%	.213	-12	1.98	7.45	8.64	5.4	9.2	3.2	0.5	2	-4.2	-0.79
2009	*PIT*	*MLB*	*25*	*1*	*2*	*1*	*23*	*1*	*31*	*30*	*19*	*24*	*2*	*50.0%*	*.290*	*3*	*1.54*	*4.81*	*5.10*	*8.5*	*4.7*	*6.1*	*0.6*	*-0*	*2.2*	*0.18*

Breakout: 48%   Improve: 70%   Collapse: 20%   Attrition: 42%   Comparables: Rickey Clark, Terry Mulholland, Jerry Stephenson, Ron Willis

Any scout can watch Hansen throw three pitches and tell you he has a great arm, which is why he was once a first-round pick by the Red Sox. But Hansen has never been able to harness his pitches or his emotions and is thus still something of a project four years after starring at St. John's. He will get plenty of chances because of that arm, but he risks being eternally destined to be one more game away from his former promise every time he takes the mound.

Jeff Karstens

Bats: R   Throws: R   Height: 6' 3"   Weight: 185   Born: September 24, 1982   Age: 26

YEAR	TEAM	LVL	AGE	W	L	SV	G	GS	IP	H	BB	SO	HR	GB%	BABIP	STUFF	WHIP	ERA	DERA	EqH9	EqBB9	EqSO9	EqHR9	DEF	VORP	SN/WX
2006	TRN	AA	23	6	0	0	11	11	74²	54	14	67	4	46.9%	.248	7	0.92	2.30	4.28	9.0	2.2	4.7	1.0	1	10.2	—
2006	COH	AAA	23	5	5	0	14	14	73²	80	30	48	9	35.6%	.303	-31	1.50	4.30	8.01	10.7	4.3	3.6	1.9	7	-18.7	—
2006	NYA	MLB	23	2	1	0	8	6	42²	40	10	16	6	33.1%	.238	-10	1.17	3.79	5.65	8.2	2.1	2.9	1.3	7	8.8	0.86
2007	SWB	AAA	24	3	0	0	6	5	31	25	9	27	2	39.4%	.248	3	1.10	1.74	4.91	8.3	2.8	5.2	0.9	7	2.2	—
2007	NYA	MLB	24	1	4	0	7	3	14²	27	9	5	4	31.8%	.390	-49	2.45	11.02	9.60	15.6	4.8	2.4	2.4	-5	-10.8	-0.67
2008	SWB	AAA	25	6	4	0	12	12	68²	66	15	55	8	40.9%	.297	-9	1.18	3.80	5.57	10.4	2.3	4.9	1.6	3	0.2	—
2008	PIT	MLB	25	2	6	0	9	9	51¹	56	13	23	7	45.7%	.287	-5	1.34	4.04	4.44	8.7	1.9	3.4	1.2	-5	0.4	0.91
2009	*PIT*	*MLB*	*26*	*4*	*8*	*0*	*32*	*16*	*101²*	*123*	*32*	*61*	*15*	*41.0%*	*.320*	*4*	*1.53*	*5.71*	*5.88*	*10.8*	*2.5*	*4.8*	*1.3*	*-2*	*-3.6*	*0.22*

Breakout: 11%   Improve: 35%   Collapse: 30%   Attrition: 33%   Comparables: Donne Wall, Andrew Good, Tom Harrison, Shane Bowers

Karstens came to the Pirates from the Yankees in the Nady deal and shocked everyone by carrying a perfect game into the eighth inning against the Snakes after shutting out the Cubs over six innings in his Bucs debut. He never came close to pitching that well again, which was less surprising—his stuff is pretty ordinary, but he does know how to pitch. His best-case projection is that he winds up being a reliable fourth starter, but even that involves a good amount of wishful thinking. The most notable aspect to date of his brief Pirates tenure was the mellowing of his normally high fly-ball rate. Should that revert, it will be one more strike against him.

Paul Maholm

Bats: L   Throws: L   Height: 6' 2"   Weight: 230   Born: June 25, 1982   Age: 27

YEAR	TEAM	LVL	AGE	W	L	SV	G	GS	IP	H	BB	SO	HR	GB%	BABIP	STUFF	WHIP	ERA	DERA	EqH9	EqBB9	EqSO9	EqHR9	DEF	VORP	SN/WX
2006	PIT	MLB	24	8	10	0	30	30	176	202	81	117	19	55.2%	.334	6	1.61	4.76	4.40	9.6	3.7	5.5	0.9	-3	19.9	3.02
2007	PIT	MLB	25	10	15	0	29	29	177²	204	49	105	22	54.9%	.323	4	1.42	5.01	5.10	9.2	2.1	5.0	1.0	1	6.2	2.21
2008	PIT	MLB	26	9	9	0	31	31	206¹	201	63	139	21	55.3%	.298	12	1.28	3.71	4.31	8.2	2.4	5.4	0.9	10	40.8	5.29
2009	*PIT*	*MLB*	*27*	*10*	*11*	*0*	*28*	*28*	*177²*	*192*	*58*	*119*	*17*	*51.0%*	*.310*	*20*	*1.41*	*4.36*	*4.55*	*9.6*	*2.6*	*5.4*	*0.9*	*-3*	*18.7*	*3.46*

Breakout: 6%   Improve: 34%   Collapse: 21%   Attrition: 9%   Comparables: Bill Lee, Dave LaPoint, Scott Karl, Jim Abbott

Maholm was the only one of the team's touted stable of young starters to take a step forward last season, which is a reflection of how disappointing that particular bit of packaging was, sort of like actually getting a box of magazine sea monkeys and finding out it's not that happy family of finny anthropomorphic friends. He's not overpowering and lacks a dominant out pitch, but he's intelligent and knows how to work hitters, managing to deliver 20 quality starts through six innings in his 31. Maholm would make a solid fourth starter in a good team's rotation, but he'll almost certainly draw the assignment to be the Pirates' starter on Opening Day, which kind of explains why the Buccos are working on a 17th straight losing season.

Dan McCutchen

| | Bats: R | Throws: R | Height: 6' 2" | Weight: 195 | Born: September 26, 1982 | Age: 26 |

YEAR	TEAM	LVL	AGE	W	L	SV	G	GS	IP	H	BB	SO	HR	GB%	BABIP	STUFF	WHIP	ERA	DERA	EqH9	EqBB9	EqSO9	EqHR9	DEF	VORP	SN/WX
2006	CSC	A	23	1	0	1	7	0	21¹	13	5	18	2	43.4%	.220	-20	0.85	2.13	4.24	9.5	3.7	3.7	2.6	0	2.6	—
2007	TAM	A+	24	11	2	0	17	16	101	86	21	67	7	45.8%	.272	-22	1.06	2.50	5.32	10.5	2.8	3.4	1.6	10	2.7	—
2007	TRN	AA	24	3	2	0	7	7	41	30	12	36	2	40.8%	.268	3	1.02	2.41	5.06	8.7	3.1	5.3	1.0	6	2.2	—
2008	TRN	AA	25	4	3	0	9	9	53	43	18	52	4	45.8%	.279	12	1.15	2.55	3.86	9.2	3.1	6.6	1.1	2	9.5	—
2008	IND	AAA	25	3	3	0	8	8	48	49	7	41	12	37.8%	.274	-24	1.17	4.69	7.05	10.9	1.6	5.2	3.2	5	-7.2	—
2008	SWB	AAA	25	4	6	0	11	11	70¹	73	11	58	10	36.7%	.304	-12	1.19	3.58	6.02	11.3	1.7	5.0	2.0	6	-3.0	—
2009	PIT	MLB	26	5	9	0	29	18	113²	137	34	76	19	41.0%	.320	9	1.50	5.59	5.70	10.7	2.4	5.3	1.5	-2	-1.6	0.57

Breakout: 6%   Improve: 26%   Collapse: 40%   Attrition: 17%   Comparables: Brandon Knight, Brian Tollberg, Terry Gilmore, Nelson Figueroa

Of the three Scranton starters acquired from the Yankees as part of the package for Xavier Nady, McCutchen might be the one with the most upside. While Ohlendorf gets more touts, McCutchen throws hard and has a good competitive streak, although he tends to work a little more up in the zone than might make for a rotation regular. He'll get a shot to win a starting job in spring training, but some think that his velocity in the pen might make him a better option there.

Evan Meek

| | Bats: R | Throws: R | Height: 6' 1" | Weight: 190 | Born: May 12, 1983 | Age: 26 |

YEAR	TEAM	LVL	AGE	W	L	SV	G	GS	IP	H	BB	SO	HR	GB%	BABIP	STUFF	WHIP	ERA	DERA	EqH9	EqBB9	EqSO9	EqHR9	DEF	VORP	SN/WX
2006	LEL	A+	23	6	6	0	26	25	119	136	62	113	5	58.7%	.370	-11	1.66	4.99	6.73	13.6	6.1	4.5	1.0	-20	-13.1	—
2007	MNT	AA	24	2	1	1	44	0	67	74	34	69	2	54.2%	.392	-8	1.61	4.30	5.86	13.4	5.2	6.0	0.6	-3	-1.7	—
2008	ALT	AA	25	1	1	2	9	0	16	14	3	17	0	59.1%	.333	14	1.06	2.81	2.93	8.8	1.8	7.0	0.0	-1	4.5	—
2008	IND	AAA	25	0	0	2	23	0	41¹	30	14	34	2	60.5%	.239	-8	1.07	2.40	4.50	7.2	3.4	4.7	0.7	5	4.9	—
2008	PIT	MLB	25	0	1	0	9	0	13	11	12	7	3	56.1%	.222	-19	1.77	6.92	7.43	6.8	6.8	4.1	2.0	1	-3.1	-0.36
2009	PIT	MLB	26	2	3	1	42	3	49¹	60	27	36	5	53.0%	.340	-0	1.76	5.63	5.90	10.8	4.4	5.8	0.8	-1	-2.0	-0.09

Breakout: 29%   Improve: 64%   Collapse: 14%   Attrition: 15%   Comparables: Beau Kemp, Steve Schmoll, Jordan De Jong, Gary Ross

A Rule 5 pick from the Rays, Meek has inconsistent but occasionally outstanding velocity and equally inconsistent control. This inconsistency prevented him from sticking, but a deal was worked out with Tampa Bay where Meek could remain a Pirate, and he shined in the minors. Meek was subsequently so impressive in winter ball in Venezuela that it sparked talk he might make a good closer, and if he can consistently deliver mid-90s heat, it's not hard to understand why.

Bryan Morris

| | Bats: L | Throws: R | Height: 6' 3" | Weight: 200 | Born: March 28, 1987 | Age: 22 |

YEAR	TEAM	LVL	AGE	W	L	SV	G	GS	IP	H	BB	SO	HR	GB%	BABIP	STUFF	WHIP	ERA	DERA	EqH9	EqBB9	EqSO9	EqHR9	DEF	VORP	SN/WX
2006	OGD	Rk	19	4	5	0	14	14	59	64	40	79	3	50.9%	.386	-10	1.76	5.19	10.52	14.2	8.6	5.3	1.8	-6	-28.0	—
2008	GRL	A	21	2	4	0	17	17	81²	74	31	72	5	57.4%	.309	-11	1.29	3.19	6.78	10.8	5.0	3.8	1.6	1	-9.4	—
2008	HIC	A	21	0	2	0	3	3	14¹	17	12	11	2	49.0%	.326	-18	2.03	5.03	8.53	14.2	10.7	2.8	2.8	0	-4.1	—
2009	PIT	MLB	22	3	9	0	18	18	89²	119	60	51	14	50.0%	.340	-1	1.99	7.31	7.59	11.7	5.3	4.6	1.3	-2	-19.8	-1.39

Breakout: 15%   Improve: 38%   Collapse: 28%   Attrition: 11%   Comparables: Aaron Sele, Cliff Brantley, Johnny Ard, Jeff Marquez

A 2006 first-rounder for the Dodgers, Morris successfully bounced back from Tommy John surgery last season, doing so well that he was packaged to the Pirates in the deal that put Jason Bay in Boston and Manny in LA. Although Morris dealt with the typical postsurgery command issues, his reliable low-90s heat and plus curve make for the start of a top hurler's arsenal, with the question being whether his changeup develops to the point that he sticks as a starter, or if he winds up becoming a quality late-game reliever.

Ross Ohlendorf

Bats: R Throws: R Height: 6' 4" Weight: 235 Born: August 8, 1982 Age: 26

YEAR	TEAM	LVL	AGE	W	L	SV	G	GS	IP	H	BB	SO	HR	GB%	BABIP	STUFF	WHIP	ERA	DERA	EqH9	EqBB9	EqSO9	EqHR9	DEF	VORP	SN/WX
2006	TEN	AA	23	10	8	0	27	27	177²	180	29	125	13	48.7%	.317	-10	1.18	3.30	5.93	11.0	1.9	3.9	1.4	15	-5.8	—
2007	SWB	AAA	24	3	3	0	21	9	66¹	86	24	48	7	47.2%	.369	-31	1.66	5.02	6.86	13.7	3.7	4.3	1.6	0	-8.4	—
2007	NYA	MLB	24	0	0	0	6	0	6¹	5	2	9	1	53.3%	.286	6	1.11	2.86	4.26	7.1	2.8	9.9	1.4	1	2.3	0.13
2008	SWB	AAA	25	1	1	0	5	5	22¹	28	5	25	0	56.5%	.412	12	1.48	4.04	4.35	13.9	2.2	7.0	0.4	-3	2.9	—
2008	NYA	MLB	25	1	1	0	25	0	40	50	19	36	7	48.1%	.347	-11	1.73	6.53	5.58	10.7	3.8	6.9	1.6	-4	-5.0	-0.63
2008	IND	AAA	25	4	3	0	7	7	46²	46	8	40	7	41.7%	.302	-4	1.16	3.47	4.64	10.8	1.9	5.3	2.1	1	4.6	—
2008	PIT	MLB	25	0	3	0	5	5	22²	36	12	13	3	39.8%	.398	-17	2.12	6.34	5.87	13.3	3.9	4.7	1.2	-2	-4.1	-0.24
2009	PIT	MLB	26	3	5	1	30	7	67¹	78	23	50	8	46.0%	.320	9	1.49	5.00	5.18	10.3	2.7	5.9	1.0	-1	3.0	0.50

Breakout: 28% Improve: 59% Collapse: 17% Attrition: 39% Comparables: Russ Kemmerer, Adam Bernero, Roman Colon, Chad Durbin

Acquired from the Yankees in the Nady trade, Ohlendorf was a big disappointment in his September cup of coffee, failing to throw strikes with any consistency while tending to run out of gas early. The Pirates attributed the fatigue to his transition back to starting after bouncing back and forth between roles the last two years. While he has the type of power arm and sinking fastball action you'd hope might eventually front a rotation, he needs to develop durability and consistency to avoid falling back into a nice career as a classic sinker/slider power reliever.

Romulo Sanchez

Bats: R Throws: R Height: 6' 6" Weight: 208 Born: April 28, 1984 Age: 25

YEAR	TEAM	LVL	AGE	W	L	SV	G	GS	IP	H	BB	SO	HR	GB%	BABIP	STUFF	WHIP	ERA	DERA	EqH9	EqBB9	EqSO9	EqHR9	DEF	VORP	SN/WX
2006	HIC	A	22	0	3	4	21	3	40	51	18	28	4	54.5%	.343	-57	1.73	7.20	11.86	16.1	5.8	2.0	2.5	-8	-24.8	—
2007	ALT	AA	23	6	3	1	40	0	57²	43	17	52	8	49.4%	.232	-24	1.04	2.81	6.34	8.1	3.1	5.0	2.1	7	-4.5	—
2007	PIT	MLB	23	1	0	0	16	0	18	16	8	11	2	50.9%	.280	-8	1.33	5.00	5.29	7.4	3.7	5.3	1.1	2	1.6	-0.01
2008	IND	AAA	24	5	1	4	33	0	54²	50	19	32	5	42.8%	.273	-31	1.26	3.46	7.11	9.4	3.6	3.4	1.2	8	-8.5	—
2008	PIT	MLB	24	0	0	1	10	0	13¹	14	6	3	0	42.6%	.311	-27	1.50	4.06	4.26	9.2	3.6	2.1	0.0	0	2.3	0.11
2009	PIT	MLB	25	2	3	1	42	3	49²	61	23	25	7	44.0%	.310	-11	1.69	5.85	6.01	10.9	3.7	4.0	1.3	-1	-2.8	-0.15

Breakout: 14% Improve: 39% Collapse: 38% Attrition: 15% Comparables: Jose Garcia, Elio Serrano, Jeff McCurry, Hector Ramirez

Discarded by the Dodgers after one season in the Venezuelan summer league, Sanchez has spent parts of the past two seasons in the Pirates' bullpen. He's very large and throws hard, but until he learns to throw strikes with something other than the fastball, he will remain more intriguing than productive. Perhaps a cloaking device would help?

Ian Snell

Bats: R Throws: R Height: 5' 11" Weight: 190 Born: October 30, 1981 Age: 27

YEAR	TEAM	LVL	AGE	W	L	SV	G	GS	IP	H	BB	SO	HR	GB%	BABIP	STUFF	WHIP	ERA	DERA	EqH9	EqBB9	EqSO9	EqHR9	DEF	VORP	SN/WX
2006	PIT	MLB	24	14	11	0	32	32	186	198	74	169	29	44.4%	.327	11	1.46	4.74	4.44	8.7	3.1	7.4	1.2	-2	20.7	3.41
2007	PIT	MLB	25	9	12	0	32	32	208	209	68	177	22	46.5%	.315	23	1.33	3.76	3.53	8.1	2.5	7.1	0.9	-5	41.3	5.33
2008	PIT	MLB	26	7	12	0	31	31	164¹	201	89	135	18	39.9%	.360	5	1.76	5.42	5.15	10.4	4.1	6.5	0.9	-10	-3.9	1.53
2009	PIT	MLB	27	7	9	0	23	23	131²	139	58	108	15	43.0%	.310	22	1.50	4.83	4.98	9.4	3.5	6.5	1.0	-2	8.5	1.92

Breakout: 10% Improve: 37% Collapse: 29% Attrition: 21% Comparables: Diego Segui, Steve Mura, Eric Show, Bill Stoneman

Snell signed a three-year contract in the latter stages of spring training last year with the Pirates, made his first Opening Day start, and then promptly went off the rails from this seeming road to acedom. He was bothered by a sore elbow at times and did pitch better late in the season, but until he learns to pitch inside, his 95 mph heater and sharp slider won't be as effective as they should be.

Jeff Sues

Bats: R Throws: R Height: 6' 4" Weight: 228 Born: June 8, 1983 Age: 26

YEAR	TEAM	LVL	AGE	W	L	SV	G	GS	IP	H	BB	SO	HR	GB%	BABIP	STUFF	WHIP	ERA	DERA	EqH9	EqBB9	EqSO9	EqHR9	DEF	VORP	SN/WX
2007	HIC	A	24	3	2	0	8	8	31¹	37	19	26	9	31.0%	.308	-59	1.79	7.19	11.08	15.6	8.0	3.5	5.9	-1	-15.8	—
2008	LYN	A+	25	1	1	2	13	0	21¹	11	6	17	3	42.9%	.154	-20	0.80	2.11	6.20	5.3	2.7	4.4	2.2	6	-1.4	—
2008	ALT	AA	25	3	1	1	24	0	43	35	20	55	3	36.7%	.314	7	1.28	3.77	5.57	8.6	4.1	8.4	0.9	4	0.1	—
2009	PIT	MLB	26	2	4	1	28	4	56¹	57	27	48	9	39.0%	.300	8	1.51	5.08	5.18	9.1	3.9	6.9	1.4	-1	2.4	0.36

Breakout: 36% Improve: 69% Collapse: 8% Attrition: 16% Comparables: Jim Mann, Bob Ayrault, Aaron Rakers, Chris Demaria

Sues' pro debut was delayed for two years after he was drafted in the fifth round in 2005 because of shoulder surgery. But he turned himself into a prospect last season, when he was moved into the bullpen, routinely hitting 96 mph with his fastball and being named the organization's Minor League Pitcher of the Year. Sues is not a kid, and the Pirates will probably fast-track him to the major leagues by some point this season to get a closer look.

Ronald Uviedo

Bats: R   Throws: R   Height: 6' 2"   Weight: 150   Born: October 7, 1986   Age: 22

YEAR	TEAM	LVL	AGE	W	L	SV	G	GS	IP	H	BB	SO	HR	GB%	BABIP	STUFF	WHIP	ERA	DERA	EqH9	EqBB9	EqSO9	EqHR9	DEF	VORP	SN/WX
2007	SCO	A-	20	2	0	0	12	21	0	20²	16	3	26	4	39.2%	.273	3	0.92	3.91	5.94	13.0	2.7	6.5	5.9	-2	-0.6	—
2007	LYN	A+	20	0	0	0	4	0	11	9	3	7	2	38.2%	.226	-2	1.09	4.09	7.20	9.9	3.6	2.7	3.6	0	-1.8	—
2008	HIC	A	21	3	1	5	33	0	71²	70	15	76	8	36.4%	.313	-14	1.19	3.01	6.02	12.0	2.9	4.9	2.4	-1	-3.0	—
2008	LYN	A+	21	0	0	0	7	0	16	5	5	12	1	48.8%	.100	9	0.63	2.25	5.06	2.8	2.8	3.9	1.1	3	1.0	—
2009	PIT	MLB	22	2	4	1	27	6	59	71	25	40	11	41.0%	.310	2	1.62	5.91	6.00	10.7	3.3	5.4	1.6	-1	-3.2	-0.09

Breakout: 19%   Improve: 43%   Collapse: 26%   Attrition: 6%   Comparables: Sam Gervacio, Alessandro Maestri, German Marte, Luis Encarnacion

The Pirates haven't brought many Latin players to the major leagues in recent years, but have done a good job of picking up discards from other organizations and turning them into prospects. Uviedo was released by the Mariners in 2006 after three years in the Venezuelan summer league, but with a fastball that touches 95 mph, he's shown enough as a reliever with the Bucs during two seasons in the United States that they put him on the 40-man roster last fall.

Tyler Yates

Bats: R   Throws: R   Height: 6' 4"   Weight: 240   Born: August 7, 1977   Age: 31

YEAR	TEAM	LVL	AGE	W	L	SV	G	GS	IP	H	BB	SO	HR	GB%	BABIP	STUFF	WHIP	ERA	DERA	EqH9	EqBB9	EqSO9	EqHR9	DEF	VORP	SN/WX
2006	ATL	MLB	28	2	5	1	56	0	50	42	31	46	6	42.1%	.273	5	1.46	3.96	4.50	7.2	4.9	7.6	0.9	4	10.3	-0.67
2007	ATL	MLB	29	2	3	2	75	0	66	64	31	69	6	47.1%	.322	12	1.44	5.18	4.57	8.6	3.6	8.6	0.8	-6	-1.4	1.14
2008	PIT	MLB	30	6	3	1	72	0	73¹	72	41	63	6	50.0%	.308	1	1.54	4.67	4.52	8.1	4.2	6.5	0.7	-1	6.3	1.01
2009	PIT	MLB	31	2	3	3	49	0	56	55	27	47	5	46.0%	.300	7	1.46	4.27	4.46	8.7	3.8	6.6	0.8	-1	6.7	0.55

Breakout: 39%   Improve: 59%   Collapse: 23%   Attrition: 24%   Comparables: Matt Karchner, Don McMahon, George Frazier, Lerrin LaGrow

Rarely do the Braves give up on pitchers without a reason, and that was the case again last spring, when they traded Yates to the Pirates in spring training because he was out of options and wasn't going to make their club. The hard thrower pitched well early on, but his lack of command eventually caught up to him, as he worked his way down from a setup role to more of a middle-relief job by season's end.

LINEOUTS

Hitters

PLAYER	TEAM	LVL	AGE	PA	R	2B	3B	HR	RBI	BB	SO	SB-CS	EqBRR	AVG/OBP/SLG	EqAVG/EqOBP/EqSLG	EqA	VORP	WARP
OF A. Boeve	IND	AAA	28	294	37	16	3	12	46	24	89	13-4	-2.0	.251/.316/.471	.221/.281/.412	.240	-4.9	-1.6
C R. Chavez	IND	AAA	35	91	9	5	1	3	13	4	11	0-0	0.5	.306/.352/.494	.256/.297/.442	.250	1.0	0.9
	PIT	MLB	35	122	12	4	0	1	10	4	14	0-0	0.0	.259/.287/.319	.259/.287/.310	.208	-1.8	0.1
SS L. Cruz	ALT	AA	24	406	41	24	1	6	46	19	34	3-3	-1.4	.264/.303/.381	.232/.266/.347	.211	-19.7	2.4
	IND	AAA	24	127	19	10	0	3	15	3	14	2-4	-1.5	.325/.347/.483	.306/.328/.463	.258	5.9	0.2
	PIT	MLB	24	74	6	3	0	0	3	3	2	1-1	-0.7	.224/.278/.269	.235/.288/.279	.199	-2.9	0.0
INF J. Cunningham	PIR	Rk	18	174	20	11	1	5	22	14	26	2-1	-1.9	.318/.385/.507	.226/.274/.352	.220	-18.5	-0.5
SS C. D'Arnaud	SCO	A-	21	183	26	10	5	1	21	11	30	14-2	1.1	.286/.333/.423	.209/.246/.326	.200	-24.4	-2.6
SS B. Friday	LYN	A+	22	391	59	20	4	2	29	34	56	16-11	-3.3	.287/.365/.387	.251/.318/.345	.235	-6.7	2.5
INF C. Gomez	PIT	MLB	37	200	26	8	0	1	20	13	30	0-0	-0.6	.273/.322/.333	.279/.327/.344	.239	0.1	-0.9
CF R. Grossman#	PIR	Rk	18	21	3	1	0	0	1	4	7	1-0	-0.4	.188/.381/.250	.111/.238/.222	.129	-6.7	-0.5
3B M. Hague	HIC	A	22	242	25	14	0	6	29	20	28	1-0	0.9	.321/.384/.470	.249/.305/.371	.237	-3.5	-1.5
OF J. Keel	LYN	A+	23	496	76	24	2	20	81	65	89	16-5	-0.3	.237/.358/.451	.199/.301/.389	.243	-9.4	-4.8
INF L. Rivas	PIT	MLB	28	223	25	6	2	3	20	13	27	3-2	0.5	.218/.267/.311	.222/.270/.329	.207	-7.6	-1.3

Adam Boeve, a tools guy with power and speed, has never been able to translate them into production, which leaves him trapped in Triple-A. ⊘ **Raul Chavez** spent most of last season as the Pirates' backup catcher; the nicest thing you can say is that he's a decent defender, and pitchers like throwing to him. ⊘ **Luis Cruz** made it to the majors last September in his ninth pro season; he won't hit enough to be a regular, but is good enough defensively that he could carve out a career as a bench player. ⊘ **Jarek Cunningham** fell to the 18th round of last year's draft after suffering a knee injury during his senior season of high school, but drew high marks from scouts in the Gulf Coast League. ⊘ The brother of Phillies catching prospect Travis and the Pirates' fourth-round draft pick last year, **Chase D'Arnaud** was one of the few bright spots on a horrendous State College team that went 18-56. ⊘ Because of ankle and back problems, **Brian Friday** has yet to get his professional career on track since being the Pirates' third-round draft pick in 2007, but he has Eckstein-like batting skills with excellent glove work at short, making him the best internal candidate to be Jack Wilson's eventual replacement. ⊘ **Chris Gomez**'s offensive contributions have been whittled down to a few singles, and he no longer has the range to play shortstop except in emergencies. Having completed his stint in Pittsburgh on the elder statesman's tour, he's returning to Baltimore for more second-division fun. ⊘ **Robbie Grossman** was considered a potential second-round draft pick last season, but slipped to the sixth because of his commitment to the University of Texas. In a promising development, however, the Pirates lured the toolsy center-field prospect with an above-slot $1 million bonus. ⊘ The Pirates jumped ninth-round pick **Matt Hague** to full-season Low-A after just seven games at the short-season level; many scouts see him as an outfielder rather than a third baseman. ⊘ **Jared Keel** isn't considered a hot prospect, but he's bopped a bit since being drafted in the 31st round in 2006, while putting plans on becoming a game warden on hold. ⊘ **Luis Rivas** made the Pirates as a utility infielder to get his first full season in the major leagues since 2004, and he hit just well enough to earn himself another three years back in the bushes.

Pitchers

PLAYER	TEAM	LVL	AGE	W	L	SV	IP	H	BB	SO	HR	GB%	BABIP	STUFF	WHIP	ERA	DERA	EqH9	EqBB9	EqSO9	EqHR9	DEF	VORP
D. Davidson*	ALT	AA	24	4	2	0	64²	58	36	51	3	55.3%	.306	-7	1.45	3.34	4.95	9.4	4.9	5.2	0.8	3	4.3
J. Davis	IND	AAA	28	6	9	0	116¹	113	47	68	4	54.9%	.302	-7	1.38	4.41	7.00	9.9	4.1	3.3	0.6	12	-16.8
	PIT	MLB	28	2	4	0	34	38	17	13	2	54.5%	.321	-20	1.62	5.29	5.88	9.4	3.7	3.2	0.5	-1	-2.7
C. Hamman*	ALT	AA	28	5	6	0	70²	69	19	44	7	48.0%	.291	-15	1.24	3.18	5.35	10.0	2.5	4.0	1.4	6	1.8
	IND	AAA	28	4	3	0	62²	75	24	34	4	51.8%	.336	-21	1.58	5.02	6.41	12.1	3.8	2.9	0.9	-1	-5.3
Y. Herrera	ALT	AA	27	6	9	0	114¹	114	36	69	9	50.5%	.297	-10	1.31	3.46	4.95	9.8	2.8	3.7	1.1	3	7.9
	PIT	MLB	27	1	1	0	18¹	35	12	10	1	49.4%	.479	-17	2.56	9.84	5.79	15.9	4.8	4.3	0.5	-7	-8.6
B. Lincoln	HIC	A	23	5	5	0	62	72	6	46	8	51.9%	.327	-37	1.26	4.65	8.12	14.1	1.8	3.0	2.7	3	-15.2
	LYN	A+	23	1	5	0	41²	42	11	29	5	51.5%	.289	-16	1.27	4.75	5.49	10.3	2.7	3.7	1.8	-4	0.5
D. Moskos*	LYN	A+	22	7	7	0	110¹	124	43	78	8	56.0%	.331	-21	1.51	5.96	7.66	11.5	3.9	3.7	1.2	-6	-23.6
F. Osoria	PIT	MLB	26	4	3	0	60²	87	12	31	10	51.1%	.353	-21	1.63	6.08	4.75	12.0	1.5	4.0	1.5	-9	-5.5
M. Robles	HIC	A	24	1	1	6	27	23	1	19	2	51.2%	.263	-22	0.89	2.00	4.32	9.7	1.1	2.9	1.4	1	3.6
	LYN	A+	24	1	1	6	21¹	31	3	8	3	51.7%	.341	-46	1.60	3.80	6.86	13.7	1.7	1.3	2.1	-2	-2.9
	ALT	AA	24	1	1	0	18²	28	5	10	2	40.5%	.394	-31	1.76	6.26	5.89	14.2	2.5	2.9	1.5	-6	-0.6
J. Shortslef*	ALT	AA	26	5	2	3	62¹	59	25	51	3	52.6%	.306	-6	1.35	3.47	4.83	9.5	3.5	5.3	0.8	0	5.1
T. Taubenheim	IND	AAA	25	4	9	0	98	102	39	66	12	48.1%	.309	-32	1.44	5.60	7.92	10.8	4.0	3.8	1.7	4	-23.7
	PIT	MLB	25	0	0	0	6	7	3	4	0	15.0%	.368	6	1.67	3.00	3.00	10.5	4.5	6.0	0.0	0	1.7
J. Van Benschoten	IND	AAA	28	7	4	0	80¹	70	32	62	3	50.4%	.299	-6	1.27	3.92	6.26	9.2	4.0	4.7	0.6	10	-5.4
	PIT	MLB	28	1	3	0	22¹	37	20	21	7	43.2%	.411	-18	2.55	10.49	9.39	14.1	6.7	7.0	2.7	-4	-14.4
T. Watson*	LYN	A+	23	8	12	0	151²	149	36	104	16	33.3%	.292	-22	1.22	3.56	5.37	10.1	2.5	3.7	1.7	3	3.6

Armed with maximum redundancy and little else, **David Davidson** might only be notable for Dave Littlefield's getting fired the morning after Davidson got bombed in his 2007 debut. ⊘ **Jason Davis** has a good arm, but has never quite figured out how to use it, landing in Pittsburgh after failing to make the Rangers' suspect staff; released at the end of the season, he began looking at opportunities in Japan. ⊘ **Corey Hamman** is a journeyman who could wind up spending a little time in the major leagues if he catches a break. ⊘ The Pirates dropped **Yoslan Herrera** from the 40-man last season, less than two years after giving him a three-year, $1.92 million contract after his defection from Cuba. There's a good chance he will never see the major leagues again. ⊘ **Brad Lincoln** had an uninspiring 2008 after sitting out a year recovering from Tommy John surgery, but the bright spot for the Pirates' 2006 first-rounder is that he stayed healthy all season. ⊘ **Daniel Moskos** will be infamous in the organization for being picked directly ahead of Matt Wieters in 2007, but that might be better than being remembered for how he's pitched since. ⃠ **Franquelis Osoria** has a good sinker but no other pitch, but that's enough for him to get enough ground-ball outs to keep teams interested. ⃠ A Mets castoff, **Moises Robles** took off last season when he was moved to the pen. ⃠ **Josh Shortslef** is a big guy who throws soft and has spent enough time at Altoona that he could get elected as a Blair County commissioner. ⃠ **Ty Taubenheim** resurfaced in the major leagues last June to pitch one good game against the Rays before suffering a season-ending elbow injury. ⃠ The Pirates' first-round draft pick as a pitcher in 2001 after being college baseball's leading home-run hitter at Kent State, **John Van Benschoten** takes his 9.20 career ERA (MLB's highest ever by a pitcher with at least 90 career innings) to the White Sox. ⃠ **Tony Watson** is a gutsy soft tosser with a good idea of how to pitch, but weak stuff means that he'll need to prove himself over and over before getting a shot.

MANAGER: JOHN RUSSELL

YEAR	TEAM	W-L	Pythag +/−	Avg PC	100+ P	120+ P	QS	BQS	REL	REL w Zero R	IBB	Subs	PH	PH Avg	PH HR	SB2	CS2	SB3	CS3	SAC Att	SAC %	POS SAC	Squeeze	Swing	In Play
2008	PIT	67-95	1	92.5	57	1	59	6	497	307	31	21	289	.224	3	52	18	5	1	104	63.5%	36	1	92	72

Russell took over as a rookie skipper after a successful career managing in the minors, charged with changing the culture of a franchise that hasn't had a winning season since 1992. Russell did accomplish that much, as a team that quit on Jim Tracy the previous season played and worked harder and handled itself in a more professional manner. However, a lack of talent, especially after Bay and Nady were taken out of the heart of the order in late July, eventually caught up with the Pirates. While the quiet Russell made an impression in the clubhouse with his no-nonsense approach, he showed few real tendencies as far as running a game other than to protect his pitchers with low pitch counts—with the notable exception of allowing closer Matt Capps to pitch three innings in an extra-inning game in May. The Pirates hardly ran at all, but that was primarily because they had little speed; Russell made few substitutions, but didn't really have good reserves. There's really no way to judge Russell substantively until the Pirates build up their talent base; in the meantime, it's telling that Coonelly and Huntington stood firmly behind him, despite the 95-loss debut.

St. Louis Cardinals

The Cardinals have been run with an admirable stability. They'd had the same leadership on the field and in upper management from 1996, the first season under new owner Bill DeWitt Jr. and new manager Tony La Russa, through 2007, when general manager Walt Jocketty was fired after 13 seasons and replaced with assistant John Mozeliak. Only the Braves can boast that same level of stability over the past decade-plus. Not coincidentally, the Braves and Cardinals also rank first and second in wins in the National League during that span, with St. Louis averaging nearly 88 a season. DeWitt, La Russa, and Jocketty helped build the Cardinals into a franchise valued at $484 million last year by *Forbes* magazine, the eighth-highest total among major league clubs, a ranking that belies St. Louis's notional "small-market" status.

That difference between purported market size and economic performance is the product of the Cardinals' performance at the gate. While practically every team in every sport assures its backers that they're number one, Cardinals fans have legitimate claim to that title. The city of St. Louis has only 350,000 residents, and the metropolitan area contains 2.8 million people, a population base that ranks 22nd of the 30 baseball markets. A 2007 Baseball Prospectus study placed the team's "attendance sphere" at a little over three million, 24th largest in the majors. Yet the Cards punch above this weight class: Last year, 3.4 million paid to enter new Busch Stadium, the fourth straight season in which St. Louis was in MLB's top four in attendance. During La Russa's tenure, the Cardinals have ranked fourth or higher in NL attendance every season but one (2004, when they were sixth). This didn't begin with La Russa

or DeWitt; without exception, the Cardinals have finished in the top half of the National League since 1981.

Considering that attendance often lags behind on-field results, the team's consistent strong showing is related to the absence of any prolonged fallow periods. The Cardinals' only recent back-to-back losing seasons came in 1994-1995, a stretch complicated by the '94 strike and mitigated by the changes in ownership and management. The last time before '94-95 that they had consecutive losing seasons was 1958–1959. In short, Cardinals fans have never experienced the long losing stretches that sap support for the hometown nine. "Wait 'til next year" has almost always been informed by a reasonable expectation the team would return to contention.

In his first year as GM, however, Mozeliak faced the threat of that dangerous hangover effect. The Cardinals appeared to be caught in a downdraft: Stuck with a pair of injured aces as well as an aging, unproductive offense, they had been outscored by over 100 runs in 2007. The long run of relevance was apparently over. Ushering in a full-scale rebuilding effort would have led to a second straight losing campaign and the promise of continued growing pains, putting the Cardinals in uncharted territory regarding their famously faithful fan base. Yet spending aggressively in the effort to recreate their 2006 success was not an option, because the Cards were looking at a record payroll of over $100 million in 2008, due in large part to the $17.5 million owed to Chris Carpenter and Mark Mulder. St. Louis has been anything but cheap under DeWitt—from 2000 to 2008, its average payroll was $84 million, ranking no lower than 13th overall in any season—but even the golden goose of the Gateway City has its limits, as that permanent sea of red in the stands is, by ownership's lights, not enough to bankroll a vault into the highest spending tier.

So Mozeliak was stuck in the middle, tasked with building up a farm system that had gone partially to seed during the continual quest for red Octobers, while simultaneously working around the big contracts to invigorate a sagging major league roster. He embraced that position, hedging through the offseason without committing fully to youth or rearmament. Veteran pieces from the 2006 team were excised: David Eckstein was allowed to walk, Jim Edmonds was sent to San Diego, and Scott Rolen was exported to Toronto for Troy Glaus. In spring training, the club wavered over whether to promote its best youngster, Colby Rasmus, to replace Edmonds in center, eventually sending him down for more seasoning.

It didn't seem that those moves, coupled with the addition of mediocrities Joel Pineiro and Kyle Lohse to complete an unimpressive rotation, would do enough to prevent the Cardinals from continuing their downward flight. But true to historical form, they rebounded. Opening with an 18-11 month of April, the Cards stayed even with the Cubs into late May and tied for the NL wild-card lead at the trading deadline before falling back in the last two months.

A big part of the rebound was fueled by an improvement from 11th in the National League in runs two years ago to fourth, thanks partly to the new direction charted by Mozeliak. Rick Ankiel continued his triumphal transformation from failed pitching phenom to formidable masher, Glaus put up strong production at third, Ryan Ludwick exploded when bestowed with regular at-bats, and Albert Pujols won his second MVP Award. The rest of the squad didn't do much—no other player hit more than eight homers—but it didn't need to, as the fearsome foursome combined for 126, resulting in a circuit-leading EqA.

Just as critical to the Cardinals' unexpectedly strong season was their unexpectedly strong starting pitching. The rotation snipped over 100 runs allowed from its 2007 tally, as its total RA/9 dropped from 5.6 to 4.5. The credit for that belongs to La Russa and faithful pitching coach Dave Duncan, who have been together since 1983. Duncan is renowned for his ability to tease life from fading careers, and last season represented perhaps his best work, as he helped turn an unimposing crew into the 11th-best starting unit in the majors, with a .533 rate of SNLVA (after ranking 26th at .486 in '07), and that despite getting almost nothing from the rehabbing trio of Carpenter, Mulder, and Matt Clement.

The most remarkable aspect of that success is that four of last year's starters were converted from relief within the last two seasons. Braden Looper made 572 appearances out of the pen before St. Louis switched his role two seasons ago, Todd Wellemeyer was a fringe middle man who had already washed out of three organizations when the Cards stuck him into their rotation at the end of '07, Adam Wainwright was the team's best reliever in 2006 before moving back into a starting slot, and Pineiro had been banished to the bullpen for almost a year when St. Louis acquired him in late '07. Rounding out the rotation was Lohse, a free agent who'd found no market for his services before the season, but who posted a sub-4.00 ERA after signing late.

Moving from the bullpen to the rotation generally isn't reliably successful; not many relievers have the broad arsenal or stamina to combat hitters a second and third time through the order. But having already turned the trick in '07 with his move to the rotation, Looper actually increased his innings from 175 to 199 after never having thrown more than 86 from the pen, while Wellemeyer shook off some shoulder fatigue to throw 191⅔ innings one season after tossing just 80. Both pitchers also performed better in the second half en route to career years.

The Duncan/La Russa handling of the staff wasn't without a few wrinkles. Anthony Reyes chafed under the tutelage of his Cardinals coaches; Reyes views himself as a high-fastball power pitcher, while Duncan wanted him to be more of a two-seam groundballer. That prompted Mozeliak to deal Reyes last July for practically nothing. In addition, the magic that improved St. Louis's rotation did not reach the bullpen. Two years ago, the team's best unit was its relief corps. A repeat performance in 2008 would have resulted in a playoff berth, but the pen devolved, ranking 21st in the majors with 5.5 WXRL. The Cards struggled in the latter frames all season, blowing 31 saves, tied with Seattle for tops in the majors and losing 14 games in which they led at the start of the eighth inning, the most in baseball.

While St. Louis could use another bullpen arm, the late innings should not be its major concern. The team made noise about the need to add a closer in the offseason, with La Russa even advancing the possibility of using Carpenter in the ninth inning, but the Cardinals can cease their ninth-inning agita by simply turning to Chris Perez and Jason Motte, who could become the hardest-throwing relief tandem in baseball, and giving La Russa a power element that his recent bullpens have largely lacked.

One of the team's more pressing needs was addressed quietly and efficiently by the off-season trade of relief prospect Mark Worrell and a player to be named later to San Diego for shortstop Khalil Greene, who is entering his walk year. Playing in Petco Park has long depressed Greene's numbers, but his career road line of .270/.318/.484 suggests what he should do for St. Louis. That would represent a massive offensive upgrade; last year, St. Louis shortstops, led by Cesar Izturis, hit one home run and slugged .316.

Despite last season's results, the rotation could also use similar upgrading. Nearly every full-time starter in 2008 outperformed his PECOTA projection by a significant margin, with Wellemeyer making a particularly strong regression candidate. The Cards are currently penciling Carpenter into a rotation spot, unless they decide to convert him to closer. He has thrown 21⅓ innings over the past two seasons after Tommy John surgery, is coming off a second elbow operation this off-season, and is still dealing with a nerve issue in his shoulder, so it is uncertain whether he can pitch a full season, let alone return to his former level. The Cardinals also have little starting depth in the minors, and their best youngster, Jaime Garcia, is out for the year after Tommy John surgery, adding another to the gaggle of Cards pitchers who have experienced arm problems lately.

Barring a repeat miracle from Duncan, the Cardinals are thus still somewhere in the middle of the NL pack. They appear to be a piece or two away from becoming a serious contender, but they were reluctant to chase big game in the offseason despite the fact that their 2009 payroll, with Mulder and Jason Isringhausen off the books, currently projects to be at least $15 million less than last season's. Larger economic considerations might have been a factor; it's impossible to anticipate how much MLB attendance will be affected, but St. Louis, with its historically reliable base of support, should be able to weather the economic downturn better than most.

Perhaps Mozeliak is biding his time like last year, when he snagged Lohse on a one-year deal in mid-March. Or perhaps he plans to channel the skill of his predecessor, who was arguably best at adding talent for the championship drive with deadline deals; Mozeliak decided against doing so last season. Should he opt to sound the bugle in 2009, the Cardinals can deal from strength and depth in the outfield, particularly if and when Rasmus forces his way up from the minors and Chris Duncan returns from herniated disk surgery. Mozeliak also has a top-notch trade chit in young catcher Bryan Anderson, made expendable by the presence of Yadier Molina.

Whatever the plan of action, the St. Louis front office has an obligation not only to its loyal fan base, but also to its best player. Pujols is at his peak, which the Cards had better not waste, especially considering that his damaged right elbow still could blow at any point. If there were ever an instrument capable of busting recessions—and two straight years without a playoff berth certainly qualifies for a marquee franchise—it is the bat belonging to a player who might end up as the best right-handed hitter of all time. That bat pounded the Cards into the playoffs and to a title in '06, and there will be plenty of people at the park to see if it will do so again.

HITTERS

Bryan Anderson			C								Bats: L		Throws: R		Height: 6' 1"		Weight: 200		Born: December 16, 1986			Age: 22
YEAR	TEAM	LVL	AGE	PA	R	2B	3B	HR	RBI	BB	SO	SB	CS	EqBRR	AVG	OBP	SLG	EqAVG	EqOBP	EqSLG	EqA	VORP WARP	DEFENSE
2006	QUD	A	19	431	50	29	3	3	51	42	66	2	6	-3.8	.302	.377	.417	.239	.298	.340	.223	-14.0 -1.2	89-C -10
2007	SFD	AA	20	431	51	15	1	6	53	32	77	0	1	0.0	.298	.350	.388	.250	.295	.328	.219	-16.0 -1.0	99-C -9
2008	SFD	AA	21	86	12	5	0	2	14	4	12	0	0	-0.3	.388	.412	.525	.309	.329	.432	.263	3.0 0.8	16-C 3
2008	MEM	AAA	21	275	27	13	2	2	27	32	46	2	0	-4.3	.281	.367	.379	.249	.327	.336	.240	-4.2 0.6	66-C 0
2009	SLN	MLB	22	456	45	22	2	7	44	39	89	3	2	-1.0	.253	.319	.368	.256	.321	.387	.246	8.5 2.2	108-C 1

Breakout: 38% Improve: 66% Collapse: 17% Attrition: 16%   Comparables: Scott Hatteberg, Francisco Melendez, Doug McConathy, Andy Dziadkowiec

Mr. Anderson might not be The One, but he's arguably the best catching prospect in the league. The Cards are set behind the dish, however, so they might be open to dealing him for the right offer. Anderson had walked once in every 12 PAs on his career before arriving in Memphis, but he bumped that to once in 9.5 there. While knocked for his defense, Anderson increased his caught-stealing percentage from 27 in 2007 to 38 last year and has the potential to be adequate defensively. The last remaining question is whether the power will start to come.

Rick Ankiel CF

Bats: L   Throws: L   Height: 6' 1"   Weight: 210   Born: July 19, 1979   Age: 29

YEAR	TEAM	LVL	AGE	PA	R	2B	3B	HR	RBI	BB	SO	SB	CS	EqBRR	AVG	OBP	SLG	EqAVG	EqOBP	EqSLG	EqA	VORP	WARP	DEFENSE			
2007	MEM	AAA	27	423	62	15	3	32	89	25	90	4	3	0.0	.267	.314	.568	.218	.262	.457	.241	-4.0	-0.3	86-CF	-4	10-RF	-1
2007	SLN	MLB	27	190	31	8	1	11	39	13	41	1	0	0.3	.285	.328	.535	.292	.339	.556	.297	11.7	0.7	22-RF	-4	16-CF	-2
2008	SLN	MLB	28	463	65	21	2	25	71	42	100	2	1	-0.7	.264	.337	.506	.269	.343	.529	.291	25.4	2.4	85-CF	-2	15-LF	-4
2009	SLN	MLB	29	476	60	21	2	24	78	41	104	2	1	-0.3	.258	.327	.488	.261	.329	.513	.279	23.2	2.2	112-CF	-10		

Breakout: 18%   Improve: 53%   Collapse: 17%   Attrition: 15%   Comparables: Henry Rodriguez, Dan Pasqua, Franklin Stubbs, Geoff Jenkins

Forget those "comparables" names above: Perhaps Ankiel's top comparable from a historical perspective is Lefty O'Doul, who washed out as a pitcher by age 26 in 1923, returned five years later as an outfielder, and went on to hit .349 over seven seasons. Ankiel's numbers last year would have been even better had he not strained an abdominal muscle on July 26, after which he hit just .169 in 77 PAs before getting shut down in early September. His power is prodigious, and Ankiel also increased his unintentional walk rate by nearly 60 percent from 2007, a rise that could continue, given that his batting eye is probably still evolving. Thanks to Ankiel's formative years as a pitcher, he is now in his last season of arbitration eligibility, which is why the Cardinals were open to trading him over the winter. The front office couldn't find value, so he'll be back in center field for at least one more season.

Brian Barton OF

Bats: R   Throws: R   Height: 6' 3"   Weight: 187   Born: April 25, 1982   Age: 27

YEAR	TEAM	LVL	AGE	PA	R	2B	3B	HR	RBI	BB	SO	SB	CS	EqBRR	AVG	OBP	SLG	EqAVG	EqOBP	EqSLG	EqA	VORP	WARP	DEFENSE			
2006	KIN	A+	24	359	56	16	3	13	57	39	83	26	3	3.4	.308	.410	.515	.226	.300	.384	.243	-5.5	-0.5	24-CF	0	21-RF	-2
2006	AKR	AA	24	171	32	5	0	6	26	13	26	15	5	-1.5	.351	.415	.503	.297	.351	.439	.275	7.7	0.4	23-CF	-5	8-RF	-1
2007	AKR	AA	25	461	56	18	2	9	59	41	99	20	9	-4.1	.314	.416	.440	.237	.317	.344	.236	-9.0	-0.6	72-RF	0	14-CF	-2
2007	BUF	AAA	25	96	9	3	0	1	7	7	18	1	1	0.2	.264	.333	.333	.227	.284	.284	.198	-6.0	-0.3	22-CF	1		
2008	MEM	AAA	26	86	12	2	2	3	11	9	23	1	4	-0.8	.260	.349	.466	.213	.299	.347	.223	-2.7	-0.2	11-RF	0	6-CF	0
2008	SLN	MLB	26	179	23	9	2	2	13	19	39	3	1	-0.1	.268	.354	.392	.279	.367	.422	.278	3.9	0.5	23-LF	-1	5-RF	0
2009	SLN	MLB	27	162	20	7	1	4	18	15	39	4	2	0.1	.249	.327	.392	.251	.329	.412	.258	3.8	0.5	42-LF	0		

Breakout: 32%   Improve: 45%   Collapse: 40%   Attrition: 44%   Comparables: Dave Edwards, Adam Piatt, Luis Terrero, Chad Allen

Snagged from Cleveland in the 2007 Rule 5 draft, Barton proved to be an inspired pick, serving as La Russa's top pinch-hitter. He could continue to succeed in that role and be one of the better fourth outfielders in the business, as he plays plus defense in both corners and can hold the fort in center. La Russa used him primarily against lefties, but Barton's OPS was exactly 745 against both righties and southpaws last year, echoing his nearly even minor league splits.

Chris Duncan LF/1B

Bats: L   Throws: R   Height: 6' 5"   Weight: 230   Born: May 5, 1981   Age: 28

YEAR	TEAM	LVL	AGE	PA	R	2B	3B	HR	RBI	BB	SO	SB	CS	EqBRR	AVG	OBP	SLG	EqAVG	EqOBP	EqSLG	EqA	VORP	WARP	DEFENSE			
2006	MEM	AAA	25	206	23	11	0	7	31	25	53	1	2	-1.2	.271	.359	.448	.245	.325	.402	.251	1.5	-1.1	27-RF	-3	14-LF	-8
2006	SLN	MLB	25	314	60	11	3	22	43	30	69	0	0	1.3	.293	.363	.589	.294	.366	.591	.313	24.7	2.4	37-LF	-3	16-RF	1
2007	SLN	MLB	26	432	51	20	0	21	70	55	123	2	1	3.3	.259	.354	.480	.261	.361	.500	.290	18.8	-0.3	84-LF	-25		
2008	SLN	MLB	27	257	26	8	0	6	27	34	52	2	1	-1.6	.248	.346	.365	.253	.354	.376	.261	1.1	1.1	36-LF	2	16-1B	4
2009	SLN	MLB	28	314	41	13	1	14	46	39	73	2	1	-0.6	.260	.354	.463	.262	.356	.487	.286	13.2	1.4	76-LF	-4		

Breakout: 33%   Improve: 65%   Collapse: 14%   Attrition: 25%   Comparables: Dick Wakefield, Erubiel Durazo, Ryan Klesko, Gabe Gross

Duncan ended the 2007 season on the disabled list after surgery to repair a sports hernia, foreshadowing what came last year. Back and neck pain during spring training grew severe enough to leave his left arm and hand numb. Eventually, Duncan was diagnosed with a herniated cervical disk in his neck, a potentially career-threatening injury—Larry Walker hung up his spikes partly because of a related problem. Duncan had surgery in early August to replace the disk with a steel prosthetic, a relatively new procedure that avoids the limited range of motion that results from fusing the disks. The surgery went well, and Duncan was cleared to begin rehab over the winter. He should be ready to compete for the left-field job in camp.

David Freese   3B

Bats: R   Throws: R   Height: 6' 2"   Weight: 217   Born: April 28, 1983   Age: 26

YEAR	TEAM	LVL	AGE	PA	R	2B	3B	HR	RBI	BB	SO	SB	CS	EqBRR	AVG	OBP	SLG	EqAVG	EqOBP	EqSLG	EqA	VORP	WARP	DEFENSE	
2006	FTW	A	23	230	27	13	3	8	44	21	44	1	1	-0.3	.299	.374	.510	.207	.264	.362	.215	-10.9	-1.6	53-3B	-8
2006	EUG	A-	23	71	19	8	0	5	26	7	12	0	0	0.4	.379	.465	.776	.234	.296	.469	.255	1.8	0.0	8-3B	-1
2007	LEL	A+	24	592	104	31	6	17	96	69	99	6	1	0.0	.302	.400	.489	.211	.287	.333	.218	-25.2	-1.9	125-3B	-4
2008	MEM	AAA	25	510	83	29	3	26	91	39	111	5	2	-0.2	.306	.361	.550	.259	.308	.454	.259	10.7	1.3	113-3B	0
2009	SLN	MLB	26	505	51	24	2	13	58	39	131	4	2	-0.1	.235	.300	.382	.238	.302	.401	.241	1.2	0.6	119-3B	-1

Breakout: 29%   Improve: 50%   Collapse: 19%   Attrition: 14%   Comparables: Rob Sasser, Andy Phillips, Jose Fernandez, Chris Nyman

The Cards acquired Freese for franchise legend Jim Edmonds before last season. One might think being traded straight up for a potential Hall of Famer when you've yet to play above A-ball would put a lot of pressure on the kid, but Freese wasn't bothered at all, even after the Cardinals put him on a night train to Memphis that blew right past Double-A Springfield. You'd like to see a little more selectivity, but the real question is whether he can stay at third. The Cardinals think so, and he'll be back in Triple-A, insuring against a Glaus injury.

Troy Glaus   3B

Bats: R   Throws: R   Height: 6' 5"   Weight: 240   Born: August 3, 1976   Age: 32

YEAR	TEAM	LVL	AGE	PA	R	2B	3B	HR	RBI	BB	SO	SB	CS	EqBRR	AVG	OBP	SLG	EqAVG	EqOBP	EqSLG	EqA	VORP	WARP	DEFENSE			
2006	TOR	MLB	29	634	105	27	0	38	104	86	134	3	2	0.1	.252	.355	.513	.235	.349	.490	.284	29.8	3.5	133-3B	-1	6-SS	1
2007	TOR	MLB	30	456	60	19	1	20	62	61	102	0	1	-4.2	.262	.366	.473	.254	.364	.471	.287	21.6	2.5	104-3B	-1		
2008	SLN	MLB	31	637	69	33	1	27	99	87	104	0	1	-1.7	.270	.372	.483	.277	.379	.507	.301	36.2	4.9	139-3B	1		
2009	SLN	MLB	32	549	70	24	1	22	81	77	100	1	1	-3.0	.257	.366	.459	.259	.368	.482	.289	29.7	3.4	129-3B	-2		

Breakout: 12%   Improve: 43%   Collapse: 28%   Attrition: 12%   Comparables: Tim Salmon, Frank Thomas, Richie Sexson, Jose Canseco

Mozeliak's first challenging trade as general manager was a winner; the Cards and Jays swapped third basemen in January, and Glaus stayed healthy and produced a fine season, while Scott Rolen did neither. Glaus teamed with Ankiel, Ludwick, and Pujols to provide the pillars of the Cards' offense; each of those four players hit at least 25 homers, one of only two foursomes in the majors to do so last year (Florida had the other). He is in the $11.25 million player-option year of his contract and thus has extra incentive to turn in a repeat performance.

Jarrett Hoffpauir   2B

Bats: R   Throws: R   Height: 5' 9"   Weight: 165   Born: June 18, 1983   Age: 26

YEAR	TEAM	LVL	AGE	PA	R	2B	3B	HR	RBI	BB	SO	SB	CS	EqBRR	AVG	OBP	SLG	EqAVG	EqOBP	EqSLG	EqA	VORP	WARP	DEFENSE			
2006	SFD	AA	23	460	55	20	1	7	46	54	41	8	6	-1.4	.249	.345	.359	.214	.295	.313	.217	-22.0	-1.3	117-2B	-5		
2007	SFD	AA	24	236	23	16	0	7	33	26	18	3	1	0.0	.345	.420	.527	.286	.352	.433	.272	10.0	0.8	54-2B	-3		
2007	MEM	AAA	24	225	27	10	0	4	24	29	21	2	3	0.0	.300	.394	.416	.273	.363	.381	.262	5.4	0.5	40-2B	-3	6-3B	1
2008	MEM	AAA	25	475	48	31	1	4	45	49	45	2	4	-1.9	.273	.352	.383	.238	.308	.328	.226	-14.1	-2.2	100-2B	-15		
2009	SLN	MLB	26	472	42	22	1	6	43	44	57	2	2	-0.7	.240	.317	.341	.243	.319	.358	.237	2.3	0.3	112-2B	-5		

Breakout: 25%   Improve: 46%   Collapse: 26%   Attrition: 17%   Comparables: Joe Lis, Keith Luuloa, Jason Williams, Jason Hardtke

Hoffpauir is a small second baseman with outstanding bat control—he has walked more than he's struck out at every level. While he might provide an adequate facsimile of Adam Kennedy's offensive production this season, he needs to improve his glove work to be considered a defensive asset. Hoffpauir is likely to spend the year at Triple-A, but a solid season should put him in line to compete for the job in 2010.

Cesar Izturis   SS

Bats: S   Throws: R   Height: 5' 9"   Weight: 190   Born: February 10, 1980   Age: 29

YEAR	TEAM	LVL	AGE	PA	R	2B	3B	HR	RBI	BB	SO	SB	CS	EqBRR	AVG	OBP	SLG	EqAVG	EqOBP	EqSLG	EqA	VORP	WARP	DEFENSE			
2006	LAN	MLB	26	129	10	7	1	1	12	7	6	1	3	-0.9	.252	.302	.353	.252	.302	.353	.221	-4.7	0.2	28-3B	4		
2006	CHN	MLB	26	79	4	2	0	0	6	5	8	0	1	-0.2	.233	.282	.260	.233	.282	.260	.183	-4.7	-0.6	18-SS	-3		
2007	CHN	MLB	27	207	15	11	0	0	13	16	3	0	1.8	.246	.298	.304	.241	.296	.288	.210	-4.3	-0.5	51-SS	-1			
2007	PIT	MLB	27	130	16	3	2	0	8	6	3	0	3	-1.2	.276	.310	.333	.276	.315	.333	.220	-2.3	-0.4	23-SS	-2	6-3B	0
2008	SLN	MLB	28	454	50	10	3	1	24	29	26	24	6	-1.9	.263	.319	.309	.272	.329	.320	.240	2.6	1.6	112-SS	8		
2009	BAL	MLB	29	396	42	13	2	0	28	26	26	12	5	0.1	.259	.312	.310	.257	.313	.314	.226	-3.0	0.4	94-SS	1		

Breakout: 23%   Improve: 52%   Collapse: 30%   Attrition: 22%   Comparables: Cristian Guzman, Walt Weiss, Larry Milbourne, Aaron Miles

Izturis is an outstanding defender, but the Cardinals wanted more offense out of his position, pulling off their deal for Khalil Greene in early December; by that point, Izturis was in negotiations for a two-year, $5 million deal to be the Orioles' starting shortstop. Greene should be able to roughly approximate Izturis's defense while slugging close to 200 points higher, whereas Izturis has moved to one of the very few teams for which he will actually represent an offensive upgrade, as the multitude of O's shortstops combined for a 535 OPS last year.

Jon Jay — CF

Bats: L   Throws: L   Height: 6' 0"   Weight: 200   Born: March 15, 1985   Age: 24

YEAR	TEAM	LVL	AGE	PA	R	2B	3B	HR	RBI	BB	SO	SB	CS	EqBRR	AVG	OBP	SLG	EqAVG	EqOBP	EqSLG	EqA	VORP	WARP	DEFENSE			
2006	QUD	A	21	268	42	13	3	3	45	28	27	9	4	-0.2	.342	.416	.462	.276	.336	.387	.254	3.6	-0.1	49-LF	-3	7-CF	-1
2007	PMB	A+	22	134	19	8	0	2	10	5	25	5	2	0.0	.286	.321	.397	.250	.276	.359	.222	-4.7	-0.6	8-LF	-1		
2007	SFD	AA	22	117	17	4	2	2	11	11	19	4	1	0.0	.235	.333	.373	.198	.274	.330	.214	-6.6	-0.3	21-LF	1		
2008	SFD	AA	23	427	57	17	3	11	47	39	46	10	7	-0.7	.306	.379	.457	.250	.312	.378	.240	-3.2	1.0	91-CF	6		
2008	MEM	AAA	23	64	8	4	1	1	10	6	10	0	1	-0.0	.345	.406	.500	.305	.359	.441	.271	3.3	0.9	15-CF	5		
2009	SLN	MLB	24	542	64	27	4	9	54	41	83	10	5	1.6	.267	.327	.391	.270	.329	.411	.256	11.2	2.7	127-CF	5		

Breakout: 46% Improve: 72% Collapse: 9% Attrition: 8%   Comparables: Jim Wawruck, Billy Bean, Rob Richie, Trey Beamon

A second-rounder out of Miami in 2006, "Chief Justice" Jay took flight at Springfield and then had a fantastic debut in the Pacific Coast League. He has a classic left-handed stroke that sends balls rocketing into the gaps, and he has the speed and instincts to effectively patrol those gaps on defense. Jay is currently behind Rasmus in the line for work in center, but will slide back over from a corner to man that position for Memphis if the latter makes the big club.

Daryl Jones — OF

Bats: L   Throws: L   Height: 5' 11"   Weight: 180   Born: June 25, 1987   Age: 22

YEAR	TEAM	LVL	AGE	PA	R	2B	3B	HR	RBI	BB	SO	SB	CS	EqBRR	AVG	OBP	SLG	EqAVG	EqOBP	EqSLG	EqA	VORP	WARP	DEFENSE			
2006	QUD	A	19	92	15	5	1	1	7	6	23	2	2	0.1	.235	.308	.358	.188	.239	.306	.188	-7.7	-0.8	8-RF	-1		
2006	JCY	Rk	19	79	15	3	1	3	13	8	8	3	0	3.6	.265	.367	.471	.192	.253	.342	.202	-10.2	-0.9	10-CF	-2		
2007	QUD	A	20	481	71	15	3	4	31	41	94	22	12	0.0	.217	.304	.296	.170	.235	.232	.159	-56.7	-6.6	58-RF	-6	33-LF	-6
2008	PMB	A+	21	352	43	11	7	7	35	33	67	18	5	-0.7	.326	.406	.476	.278	.345	.432	.270	13.0	0.9	70-LF	0	13-CF	-3
2008	SFD	AA	21	151	19	6	1	6	14	22	30	6	1	1.0	.290	.409	.500	.233	.340	.403	.262	1.9	1.1	30-LF	6		
2009	SLN	MLB	22	560	64	25	4	9	50	49	126	18	7	2.9	.243	.316	.364	.245	.318	.382	.245	-3.9	1.1	131-LF	4		

Breakout: 52% Improve: 76% Collapse: 6% Attrition: 6%   Comparables: Jimmy White, Charles McGehee, Ryan Langerhans, Ray Lankford

There might not be a minor leaguer who took a bigger step forward last year. Jones was a great football player in high school, and his focus on pigskin meant he had less baseball experience than is typical for an upper-round draft pick. As a result, he needed more at-bats than the typical youngster needed to grow comfortable facing pro pitching. Now that's he's settled in, watch out. Right now, he projects as a corner outfielder in "The Show," and Cardinals fans can start dreaming of a home-grown tandem of Rasmus and Jones—a pair that could rival the Ray Lankford/Bernard Gilkey combo of the early 1990s.

Adam Kennedy — 2B

Bats: L   Throws: R   Height: 6' 1"   Weight: 195   Born: January 10, 1976   Age: 33

YEAR	TEAM	LVL	AGE	PA	R	2B	3B	HR	RBI	BB	SO	SB	CS	EqBRR	AVG	OBP	SLG	EqAVG	EqOBP	EqSLG	EqA	VORP	WARP	DEFENSE			
2006	LAA	MLB	30	503	50	26	6	4	55	39	72	16	10	-2.9	.273	.334	.384	.263	.330	.373	.247	11.4	2.1	127-2B	11		
2007	SLN	MLB	31	306	27	9	1	3	18	22	33	6	2	-1.5	.219	.282	.290	.216	.284	.295	.207	-12.4	-0.9	71-2B	0		
2008	SLN	MLB	32	365	42	17	4	2	36	21	43	7	1	3.2	.280	.321	.372	.284	.323	.385	.252	4.9	1.4	71-2B	7	6-RF	0
2009	SLN	MLB	33	234	26	10	2	2	22	16	28	6	2	0.3	.265	.320	.359	.267	.322	.378	.244	4.6	0.7	58-2B	0		

Breakout: 30% Improve: 55% Collapse: 22% Attrition: 37%   Comparables: Rob Wilfong, Denny Doyle, Jim Gantner, Glenn Beckert

Kennedy saw his bat revive a bit last year after losing its pulse in 2007, and he played outstanding defense; with Kennedy at second, Izturis at short, and Glaus and Pujols at the corners, the Cards might have had the best infield defense in the majors. The Cards' rotation is made up of fly-ball pitchers, however, which lessens Kennedy's value, but it wouldn't be the worst thing to keep him around as the starter in the last year of his $10 million, three-year pact. The Cards shopped him after the season, but they're likely to go into camp with Kennedy set to see the majority of starts after St. Louis parted ways with Aaron Miles.

Pete Kozma　　SS

Bats: R　Throws: R　Height: 6' 0"　Weight: 170　Born: April 11, 1988　Age: 21

YEAR	TEAM	LVL	AGE	PA	R	2B	3B	HR	RBI	BB	SO	SB	CS	EqBRR	AVG	OBP	SLG	EqAVG	EqOBP	EqSLG	EqA	VORP	WARP	DEFENSE	
2007	JCY	Rk	19	120	16	8	0	2	9	12	21	3	2	-1.4	.264	.350	.396	.188	.248	.286	.181	-22.1	-1.1	27-SS	-2
2008	QUD	A	20	434	58	20	4	5	40	45	69	12	5	-2.1	.284	.363	.398	.240	.307	.348	.232	-11.1	0.6	90-SS	1
2008	PMB	A+	20	94	4	4	0	0	10	10	27	0	1	-0.5	.130	.231	.182	.125	.215	.162	.131	-14.8	-1.3	21-SS	-4
2009	SLN	MLB	21	606	59	33	3	7	49	52	127	8	6	1.0	.231	.301	.342	.233	.303	.360	.231	0.9	1.1	142-SS	3

Breakout: 86%　Improve: 95%　Collapse: 2%　Attrition: 1%　　　Comparables: Trevor Plouffe, Jeff Blauser, Darnell Coles, David Corman

The 18th overall selection in the 2007 draft, Kozma recovered from a rough debut season to post solid numbers in the offense-suppressing Midwest League. He does just about everything well, but is not spectacular in any one facet, projecting to hit around 10 homers with a decent average and play solid defense as a major leaguer. He'll repeat at Palm Beach after a poor showing late last season.

Jason LaRue　　C

Bats: R　Throws: R　Height: 5' 11"　Weight: 205　Born: March 19, 1974　Age: 35

YEAR	TEAM	LVL	AGE	PA	R	2B	3B	HR	RBI	BB	SO	SB	CS	EqBRR	AVG	OBP	SLG	EqAVG	EqOBP	EqSLG	EqA	VORP	WARP	DEFENSE
2006	CIN	MLB	32	230	22	5	0	8	21	27	51	1	0	-1.0	.194	.317	.346	.181	.306	.326	.229	-4.7	0.7	57-C 5
2007	KCA	MLB	33	195	14	9	0	4	13	17	66	1	0	-0.4	.148	.240	.272	.143	.236	.274	.180	-13.2	-0.4	54-C 4
2008	SLN	MLB	34	189	17	8	1	4	21	15	20	0	0	0.4	.213	.296	.348	.218	.299	.370	.236	-2.1	0.4	46-C 2
2009	SLN	MLB	35	148	12	6	0	3	16	12	27	0	0	-0.5	.216	.293	.335	.217	.295	.352	.224	-0.3	0.6	39-C 1

Breakout: 43%　Improve: 58%　Collapse: 33%　Attrition: 54%　　　Comparables: Sal Butera, Joe Oliver, Danny Sheaffer, Larry Cox

LaRue bounced back from posting one of the worst batting averages in history to be merely miserable. He's a solid catch-and-throw guy, having nailed 36 percent of potential basestealers in the past three seasons, but perhaps his greatest contribution last year was conjuring up former Cardinals legend Al Hrabosky, the Mad Hungarian, by cultivating baseball's best Fu Manchu. That outstanding nod to history was almost worth the $950,000, one-year deal St. Louis gave him to return as Molina's backup.

Felipe Lopez　　2B

Bats: S　Throws: R　Height: 6' 1"　Weight: 185　Born: May 12, 1980　Age: 29

YEAR	TEAM	LVL	AGE	PA	R	2B	3B	HR	RBI	BB	SO	SB	CS	EqBRR	AVG	OBP	SLG	EqAVG	EqOBP	EqSLG	EqA	VORP	WARP	DEFENSE			
2006	CIN	MLB	26	394	55	14	1	9	30	47	66	23	6	1.2	.268	.355	.394	.260	.352	.380	.265	14.0	1.5	82-SS	-4		
2006	WAS	MLB	26	320	43	13	2	2	22	34	60	21	6	2.5	.281	.362	.365	.289	.372	.372	.271	12.7	0.6	68-SS	-11		
2007	WAS	MLB	27	671	70	25	6	9	50	53	109	24	9	-3.0	.245	.308	.352	.254	.319	.370	.244	1.7	0.8	104-SS	-5	42-2B	-1
2008	WAS	MLB	28	363	34	20	0	2	25	32	54	4	5	-4.8	.234	.305	.314	.237	.309	.323	.221	-10.0	-0.8	70-2B	-2	6-SS	0
2008	SLN	MLB	28	169	30	8	2	4	21	11	28	4	3	-0.8	.385	.426	.538	.397	.438	.571	.333	20.3	1.4	18-2B	1	10-3B	0
2009	ARI	MLB	29	538	75	26	4	9	50	54	82	17	6	0.8	.282	.357	.407	.275	.349	.398	.264	18.5	2.0	126-2B	-3		

Breakout: 37%　Improve: 63%　Collapse: 15%　Attrition: 8%　　　Comparables: Orlando Hudson, Tom Herr, Jose Vizcaino, Len Randle

Lopez hit just .250/.320/.344 in 1,354 plate appearances with the Nats after getting traded from Cincinnati in 2006, and he performed so poorly in the first half last year that GM Jim Bowden couldn't get anything for him at the trade deadline. So the Nationals released him and proceeded to watch, slack-jawed, as Lopez, on their dime, put up the best average in the National League from the time he signed with St. Louis on August 6 until the season's end (minimum 110 PAs). That toasty tear got him a one-year, $3.5 million deal to be Arizona's starting second baseman. Lopez made a wise career move, as the Snakebox is a tonic for sagging hitters' bats.

Ryan Ludwick　　RF

Bats: R　Throws: L　Height: 6' 3"　Weight: 220　Born: July 13, 1978　Age: 30

YEAR	TEAM	LVL	AGE	PA	R	2B	3B	HR	RBI	BB	SO	SB	CS	EqBRR	AVG	OBP	SLG	EqAVG	EqOBP	EqSLG	EqA	VORP	WARP	DEFENSE			
2006	TOL	AAA	27	571	81	34	2	28	80	48	167	2	6	-3.9	.266	.342	.506	.234	.302	.453	.254	6.9	0.3	92-RF	-2	18-LF	-1
2007	MEM	AAA	28	121	27	8	0	8	36	10	20	1	1	0.0	.340	.380	.642	.278	.322	.528	.283	7.3	0.8	21-LF	1		
2007	SLN	MLB	28	339	42	22	0	14	52	26	72	4	4	-3.0	.267	.339	.479	.274	.347	.502	.280	12.2	1.2	37-LF	0	29-RF	-2
2008	SLN	MLB	29	617	104	40	3	37	113	62	146	4	4	2.4	.299	.375	.591	.309	.383	.624	.324	54.8	6.5	107-RF	3	19-LF	-3
2009	SLN	MLB	30	527	70	27	2	26	86	52	124	3	2	-0.8	.264	.344	.500	.266	.346	.526	.289	26.1	3.1	124-RF	-3		

Breakout: 11%　Improve: 38%　Collapse: 31%　Attrition: 10%　　　Comparables: Gus Zernial, Dave Henderson, Al Ferrara, Jim Lemon

Ludwick's 2008 campaign is pretty far up the list of the best offensive seasons all-time for players who rode the bench on Opening Day. La Russa platooned him for the first month of the season, which was frustrating, given that the big slugger has consistently hit righties better throughout his career (and last year, as Ludwick had a 985 OPS vs. right-handed pitchers and 929 vs. lefties). Soon enough, Ludwick smashed his way out of part-time duty, and he continued to hit well throughout the season. He's a poor bet to have a sustained peak, given his late start, but in the short term, he should crank out a couple more 30-homer campaigns.

Joe Mather — OF
Bats: R Throws: R Height: 6' 5" Weight: 210 Born: July 23, 1982 Age: 26

YEAR	TEAM	LVL	AGE	PA	R	2B	3B	HR	RBI	BB	SO	SB	CS	EqBRR	AVG	OBP	SLG	EqAVG	EqOBP	EqSLG	EqA	VORP	WARP	DEFENSE			
2006	PMB	A+	23	494	64	33	1	16	74	36	91	9	0	2.5	.269	.332	.456	.219	.270	.379	.225	-18.1	-3.4	86-RF	-9	29-LF	-9
2007	SFD	AA	24	272	48	17	0	18	46	29	32	4	0	0.0	.303	.387	.607	.248	.320	.483	.273	9.9	0.7	39-1B	-3	24-RF	1
2007	MEM	AAA	24	288	32	10	1	13	31	23	51	6	0	0.0	.241	.329	.443	.218	.300	.401	.246	-3.2	0.3	63-RF	2		
2008	MEM	AAA	25	254	45	14	2	17	41	32	36	7	2	0.9	.303	.411	.630	.261	.358	.528	.296	17.8	1.6	49-RF	-3	5-CF	1
2008	SLN	MLB	25	147	20	7	0	8	18	12	32	1	0	-0.5	.241	.306	.474	.241	.306	.489	.268	3.5	0.6	14-LF	1	8-CF	-1
2009	SLN	MLB	26	423	51	21	1	15	57	36	84	6	2	-0.1	.248	.323	.433	.250	.325	.456	.266	8.6	1.5	101-RF	0		

Breakout: 27% Improve: 52% Collapse: 25% Attrition: 17%   Comparables: Ozzie Timmons, Scott Hairston, Ryan Ludwick, Sam Bowens

With a Jay, a McClellan, a Franklin, and more, the Cards lead the majors in potential U.S. History 101 name-tagging. "Increase" Mather looks a little like Ludwick, a hulking, slugging corner outfielder blooming relatively late in his career. It took Mather a long time to get going; it was not until his seventh pro season that he advanced above A-ball. He has come on quickly at the upper levels and did a fine job filling in for the Cards before going down in early September with a broken wrist. The organization's tremendous outfield depth is also Mather's curse; like Ludwick, he might need to wait before his playing time increases.

Aaron Miles — 2B
Bats: S Throws: R Height: 5' 8" Weight: 185 Born: December 15, 1976 Age: 32

YEAR	TEAM	LVL	AGE	PA	R	2B	3B	HR	RBI	BB	SO	SB	CS	EqBRR	AVG	OBP	SLG	EqAVG	EqOBP	EqSLG	EqA	VORP	WARP	DEFENSE			
2006	SLN	MLB	29	471	48	20	5	2	30	38	42	2	1	0.4	.263	.324	.347	.258	.323	.338	.236	1.3	-0.2	73-2B	-4	33-SS	1
2007	SLN	MLB	30	449	55	16	1	2	32	25	40	2	1	3.0	.290	.328	.348	.295	.336	.360	.246	4.2	-0.6	67-2B	-3	34-SS	-9
2008	SLN	MLB	31	408	49	15	2	4	31	23	37	3	3	0.3	.317	.355	.398	.325	.365	.415	.270	15.8	2.0	56-2B	3	19-SS	1
2009	CHN	MLB	32	266	27	10	1	1	21	17	25	2	1	0.1	.279	.327	.339	.276	.324	.339	.232	2.2	0.2	65-2B	-1		

Breakout: 6% Improve: 18% Collapse: 56% Attrition: 33%   Comparables: Larry Milbourne, Rey Sanchez, Jose Vizcaino, Denny Doyle

Miles had a career season, hitting almost identically well from both sides of the plate, with a .317 BA/752 OPS against right-handers and .315/755 against lefties. The Cardinals nevertheless decided to nontender him rather than risk paying a significantly larger sum than last year's $1.6 million in arbitration. That decision turned out well for Miles, who received a two-year, $4.9 million deal from the Cubs; he's likely to occupy the short side of a second-base platoon with Mike Fontenot.

Yadier Molina — C
Bats: R Throws: R Height: 5' 11" Weight: 220 Born: July 13, 1982 Age: 26

YEAR	TEAM	LVL	AGE	PA	R	2B	3B	HR	RBI	BB	SO	SB	CS	EqBRR	AVG	OBP	SLG	EqAVG	EqOBP	EqSLG	EqA	VORP	WARP	DEFENSE	
2006	SLN	MLB	23	461	29	26	0	6	49	26	41	1	2	-4.0	.216	.274	.321	.216	.274	.325	.207	-19.8	1.1	117-C	14
2007	SLN	MLB	24	396	30	15	0	6	40	34	43	1	1	-2.4	.275	.340	.368	.276	.344	.369	.253	10.6	3.1	97-C	15
2008	SLN	MLB	25	485	37	18	0	7	56	32	29	0	2	-5.0	.304	.349	.392	.309	.353	.401	.264	17.6	3.3	112-C	8
2009	SLN	MLB	26	348	30	16	0	5	40	26	31	0	1	-2.3	.273	.332	.375	.276	.334	.394	.251	10.4	2.3	84-C	4

Breakout: 31% Improve: 45% Collapse: 28% Attrition: 31%   Comparables: Bengie Molina, Ramon Hernandez, Joe Azcue, Michael Barrett

Molina didn't play as well defensively as in previous years, but finally got the Gold Glove that should have been his three seasons prior. Although his caught-stealing percentage dropped to 35 from 2007's awesome 54, Molina's formidable cannon served as a major deterrent to the running game: opponents attempted a steal fewer than once every 19 innings, the lowest rate among qualified catchers. Molina also continued to make strides in his offensive game, posting the lowest strikeout rate of any big-league backstop. That came after the Cards made the prudent investment of bestowing the youngest member of the Fraternal Order of Catching Molinas with a four-year, $15.5 million deal before the season that bought out his arbitration seasons and first year of free agency (with an option for the second).

Albert Pujols				1B							Bats: R		Throws: R		Height: 6' 3"		Weight: 230		Born: January 16, 1980		Age: 29

YEAR	TEAM	LVL	AGE	PA	R	2B	3B	HR	RBI	BB	SO	SB	CS	EqBRR	AVG	OBP	SLG	EqAVG	EqOBP	EqSLG	EqA	VORP	WARP	DEFENSE
2006	SLN	MLB	26	634	119	33	1	49	137	92	50	7	2	3.2	.331	.431	.671	.327	.431	.662	.352	85.1	9.7	140-1B 14
2007	SLN	MLB	27	679	99	38	1	32	103	99	58	2	6	-1.3	.327	.429	.568	.331	.436	.585	.336	74.9	9.5	150-1B 20
2008	SLN	MLB	28	641	100	44	0	37	116	104	54	7	3	-0.2	.357	.462	.653	.363	.468	.678	.371	98.7	11.3	135-1B 15
2009	SLN	MLB	29	663	126	40	1	35	124	101	57	7	2	-2.2	.339	.443	.609	.342	.445	.640	.352	87.8	9.7	155-1B 10

Breakout: 9%   Improve: 41%   Collapse: 6%   Attrition: 3%   Comparables: Frank Thomas, Jeff Bagwell, Boog Powell, Mike Piazza

It was perhaps Pujols' finest season. He set career highs in OBP and OPS and was over two wins above replacement more valuable than any other position player, despite a June stint on the DL with a calf injury. The two-time MVP is simply the best player in baseball and the finest first-base defender in the game. The tear in the ulnar collateral ligament of Pujols' right elbow, first sustained while playing the outfield in 2003, grew severe enough during the season to necessitate serious discussion of a Tommy John procedure at year's end. Pujols instead opted for an ulnar nerve transposition, typically a surgery performed on pitchers (Chris Carpenter had it done last winter as well) and not one that will keep Pujols from being ready for spring training. The need for an elbow reconstruction is potentially still present, but the troublesome joint has not kept Pujols from producing some of the best numbers in baseball history to this point.

Colby Rasmus				CF							Bats: L		Throws: L		Height: 6' 2"		Weight: 195		Born: August 11, 1986		Age: 22

YEAR	TEAM	LVL	AGE	PA	R	2B	3B	HR	RBI	BB	SO	SB	CS	EqBRR	AVG	OBP	SLG	EqAVG	EqOBP	EqSLG	EqA	VORP	WARP	DEFENSE
2006	QUD	A	19	341	49	22	3	11	50	29	55	17	5	0.4	.310	.373	.512	.246	.296	.419	.245	-0.4	-0.4	73-CF -7
2006	PMB	A+	19	225	22	4	5	5	35	27	35	11	3	-0.6	.254	.351	.404	.221	.305	.362	.236	-5.4	-0.1	51-CF -1
2007	SFD	AA	20	556	93	37	3	29	72	70	108	18	3	0.0	.275	.381	.551	.234	.324	.465	.270	15.8	1.9	120-CF -6
2008	MEM	AAA	21	387	56	15	0	11	36	49	72	15	3	2.9	.251	.346	.396	.221	.308	.342	.236	-10.8	0.3	83-CF 2
2009	SLN	MLB	22	534	67	26	2	16	63	55	108	18	5	1.0	.247	.328	.414	.249	.330	.435	.266	15.8	2.9	126-CF 2

Breakout: 40%   Improve: 66%   Collapse: 8%   Attrition: 5%   Comparables: Ed Kirkpatrick, Al Chambers, Chris Lubanski, David Justice

Rasmus was BP's number three prospect in the National League last season and was a candidate to break camp as St. Louis's starting center fielder. He had a strong spring, but the team opted for him to get some time in Triple-A, anyway. Memphis gave Rasmus the blues, however, as he was hitting under .200 toward the end of May. At that point, he heated up, hitting .331/.428/.514 in 173 PAs before a sprained knee set him down for a month. Rasmus came back at the end of the minor league season, but the Cardinals did not promote him during roster expansion, with La Russa saying, "he hasn't earned it." Rasmus then declined to play in winter ball. The knee should be sound, but Rasmus has a great deal to prove beyond his health this season; there's a chance he could make the club out of camp, but he will most likely need to hit his way up from Memphis. Note the baleful presence of Al Chambers among his comps; the first overall pick in 1979, Chambers is one of the most notorious prospect busts of the draft era.

Shane Robinson				OF							Bats: R		Throws: R		Height: 5' 9"		Weight: 160		Born: October 30, 1984		Age: 24

YEAR	TEAM	LVL	AGE	PA	R	2B	3B	HR	RBI	BB	SO	SB	CS	EqBRR	AVG	OBP	SLG	EqAVG	EqOBP	EqSLG	EqA	VORP	WARP	DEFENSE	
2006	QUD	A	21	281	41	9	2	0	21	20	20	13	3	2.4	.282	.346	.333	.230	.278	.272	.196	-19.9	-0.3	51-CF 9	8-LF -1
2007	PMB	A+	22	190	22	6	1	3	13	16	16	14	4	0.0	.253	.321	.355	.224	.283	.324	.221	-9.3	-0.5	38-CF -1	
2008	SFD	AA	23	271	46	17	3	4	32	17	34	13	5	2.8	.352	.396	.496	.288	.327	.416	.258	6.0	1.8	46-LF 7	7-RF 2
2008	MEM	AAA	23	151	10	4	1	1	10	5	24	2	3	-1.3	.220	.248	.284	.196	.220	.259	.152	-16.2	-0.7	30-CF 5	6-LF 1
2009	SLN	MLB	24	491	47	23	3	4	40	28	73	11	6	1.9	.242	.290	.331	.244	.292	.348	.223	-10.9	0.9	116-CF 7	

Breakout: 43%   Improve: 64%   Collapse: 12%   Attrition: 8%   Comparables: Dax Jones, Winston Ficklin, Robbie Katzaroff, Dana Williams

The Cardinals credit Robinson's breakthrough last year to a better understanding of what kind of offensive player he needs to be. The diminutive outfielder had a swing more befitting a slugger than a leadoff man, but adapting to his skills produced excellent results. Robinson's walk rate actually declined, however, and there's no way he can survive at the top of the order while drawing a free pass once every four games or so. It's hard to view his Double-A performance as fundamental improvement until he proves otherwise.

Brendan Ryan   INF

Bats: R   Throws: R   Height: 6' 2"   Weight: 195   Born: March 26, 1982   Age: 27

YEAR	TEAM	LVL	AGE	PA	R	2B	3B	HR	RBI	BB	SO	SB	CS	EqBRR	AVG	OBP	SLG	EqAVG	EqOBP	EqSLG	EqA	VORP	WARP	DEFENSE				
2006	SFD	AA	24	47	6	1	0	0	3	3	6	1	1	0.1	.302	.348	.326	.250	.283	.273	.194	-3.1	-0.2	10-SS	-1			
2006	MEM	AAA	24	27	4	0	0	1	6	1	3	1	0	0.7	.154	.185	.269	.154	.185	.269	.153	-3.6	0.0	6-SS	2			
2007	MEM	AAA	25	353	55	9	5	1	15	25	39	17	6	0.0	.272	.328	.341	.236	.290	.298	.212	-18.5	-0.4	76-SS	0			
2007	SLN	MLB	25	199	30	9	0	4	12	15	19	7	0	2.3	.289	.347	.406	.294	.355	.411	.275	8.9	1.8	19-SS	4	17-3B	3	
2008	MEM	AAA	26	88	13	5	0	3	10	4	17	1	0	-0.4	.238	.279	.413	.207	.241	.354	.207	-5.2	-0.5	6-2B	-2	5-RF	0	
2008	SLN	MLB	26	218	30	9	0	0	10	16	31	7	2	2.0	.244	.307	.289	.247	.310	.288	.218	-3.7	-0.5	28-SS	2	17-2B	-3	
2009	SLN	MLB	27	201	23	8	1	2	18	13	30	5	2	1.0	.256	.313	.347	.258	.315	.365	.239	3.5	0.6	51-SS	0			

Breakout: 55%   Improve: 66%   Collapse: 28%   Attrition: 40%   Comparables: Jerry Dybzinski, Kent Anderson, Terry Harmon, Lee Lacy

Entering last season, Ryan was thought to possess the potential to one day be an everyday middle infielder, but his 2008 campaign betrayed him as strictly utilityman material. He has little to no power, just a modest ability to slap some singles and provide speed off the bench. Ryan's real virtue is that he can play all over the diamond, including shortstop, and that'll keep him employed.

Skip Schumaker   OF

Bats: L   Throws: R   Height: 5' 10"   Weight: 195   Born: February 3, 1980   Age: 29

YEAR	TEAM	LVL	AGE	PA	R	2B	3B	HR	RBI	BB	SO	SB	CS	EqBRR	AVG	OBP	SLG	EqAVG	EqOBP	EqSLG	EqA	VORP	WARP	DEFENSE				
2006	MEM	AAA	26	403	47	13	3	3	27	23	48	11	4	1.2	.306	.348	.382	.264	.302	.333	.226	-11.0	-1.4	89-CF	-8			
2006	SLN	MLB	26	60	3	1	0	1	2	5	6	2	1	-0.5	.185	.254	.259	.185	.254	.259	.182	-5.0	-0.8	7-LF	-3			
2007	MEM	AAA	27	264	34	16	0	7	31	27	37	2	3	0.0	.306	.382	.466	.253	.326	.384	.247	0.6	-1.1	46-CF	-12	7-LF	-1	
2007	SLN	MLB	27	188	19	12	2	2	19	8	20	1	1	-1.8	.333	.358	.458	.339	.367	.480	.287	10.7	0.6	14-LF	-2	13-RF	-2	
2008	SLN	MLB	28	594	87	22	5	8	46	47	60	8	2	1.1	.302	.359	.406	.309	.367	.423	.276	21.7	1.9	62-CF	-7	38-LF	1	
2009	SLN	MLB	29	477	56	20	2	6	48	36	57	6	3	-0.2	.287	.343	.384	.289	.345	.404	.261	10.6	0.8	113-CF	-12			

Breakout: 16%   Improve: 46%   Collapse: 21%   Attrition: 31%   Comparables: Chris Gwynn, George Vukovich, Russ Snyder, Dave May

A La Russa blue-collar special, Schumaker won a platoon share of right field in spring training. He ultimately played nearly every day while moving among the three outfield slots, taking over for Duncan in left and then for Ankiel in center and exceeding his 75th-percentile PECOTA projection along the way. That breakout still represents below-average hitting for a corner, but Schumaker is a terrific defender in either left or right, if overmatched in center. That makes him a tweener, and he's a far better fourth outfielder than a starter. Batting lefty makes him incompatible for platooning with either Duncan or Ankiel, but their injury histories and his favorable standing with La Russa should get Schumaker plenty of playing time in '09.

Nick Stavinoha   OF

Bats: R   Throws: R   Height: 6' 2"   Weight: 225   Born: May 3, 1982   Age: 27

YEAR	TEAM	LVL	AGE	PA	R	2B	3B	HR	RBI	BB	SO	SB	CS	EqBRR	AVG	OBP	SLG	EqAVG	EqOBP	EqSLG	EqA	VORP	WARP	DEFENSE				
2006	SFD	AA	24	453	55	26	3	12	73	28	81	2	1	0.5	.297	.340	.460	.235	.272	.367	.220	-16.5	-3.1	84-RF	-8	13-LF	-6	
2007	MEM	AAA	25	539	50	17	0	13	49	31	81	7	1	0.0	.261	.309	.373	.228	.271	.327	.208	-28.5	-4.4	73-LF	-15	50-RF	-3	
2008	MEM	AAA	26	453	67	23	3	16	74	20	50	2	1	0.4	.337	.366	.518	.281	.308	.427	.252	7.1	-0.4	55-RF	-4	41-LF	-3	
2008	SLN	MLB	26	61	4	1	0	0	4	2	11	0	0	0.4	.193	.217	.211	.175	.200	.193	.106	-6.3	-0.9	6-LF	-1			
2009	SLN	MLB	27	461	40	20	1	9	52	26	82	2	1	-0.9	.238	.284	.358	.241	.286	.376	.226	-10.1	-1.2	109-RF	-8			

Breakout: 32%   Improve: 52%   Collapse: 26%   Attrition: 18%   Comparables: Jorge Toca, David Gibralter, Robb Quinlan, Bill Ortega

Stavinoha busted out at Triple-A, but in this crowded outfield, he's little more than an extra body. He has walked fewer than once every 17 PAs in his pro career, and his burly frame limits him to the corners, so it's not as if he's got a big upside as an everyday player. There won't be room for him on the Opening Day roster, but Stavinoha will probably shuttle back and forth from Triple-A once injuries strike.

Brett Wallace — 3B

Bats: L   Throws: R   Height: 6' 1"   Weight: 245   Born: August 26, 1986   Age: 22

YEAR	TEAM	LVL	AGE	PA	R	2B	3B	HR	RBI	BB	SO	SB	CS	EqBRR	AVG	OBP	SLG	EqAVG	EqOBP	EqSLG	EqA	VORP	WARP	DEFENSE	
2008	QUD	A	21	177	28	8	1	5	25	17	32	0	0	-1.9	.327	.418	.490	.277	.350	.434	.271	7.3	0.0	37-3B	-6
2008	SFD	AA	21	57	13	5	0	3	11	2	7	0	0	-1.0	.367	.456	.653	.308	.368	.558	.307	5.3	0.2	11-3B	-3
2009	SLN	MLB	22	553	66	29	3	15	67	45	113	4	2	-1.2	.267	.333	.426	.269	.335	.448	.267	18.2	2.0	130-3B	-5

Breakout: 16%   Improve: 39%   Collapse: 27%   Attrition: 6%   Comparables: Mo Vaughn, Sean Casey, Ryan McGuire, Travis Buck

Wallace won two Pac-10 Triple Crowns while at Arizona State and put up a 1,279 OPS for the Devils last season, but concern about the slugger's lumpy build and subpar athleticism kept him out of the draft's top tier. The Cardinals struck with the 13th pick, and Wallace rewarded them with what was unquestionably the most impressive pro debut of any 2008 draftee. He hit so well in the Midwest League that St. Louis jumped him past High-A up to the Texas League, where Wallace raked at an even more furious pace. His minimal range and questionable arm will most likely consign him to first base in the future, so he would be a better fit on a non-Pujols team, but he's hit so well that the Cardinals are content to let him slug first and ask defensive questions later, retaining him at the more difficult position until a move is truly necessary.

PITCHERS

Mitchell Boggs

Bats: R   Throws: R   Height: 6' 3"   Weight: 195   Born: February 15, 1984   Age: 25

YEAR	TEAM	LVL	AGE	W	L	SV	G	GS	IP	H	BB	SO	HR	GB%	BABIP	STUFF	WHIP	ERA	DERA	EqH9	EqBB9	EqSO9	EqHR9	DEF	VORP	SN/WX
2006	PMB	A+	22	10	6	0	27	27	145¹	153	51	126	7	45.1%	.338	-15	1.41	3.41	7.13	12.5	4.4	4.1	1.3	0	-21.9	—
2007	SFD	AA	23	11	7	0	26	26	152²	167	62	117	15	51.7%	.321	-23	1.50	3.84	7.70	11.7	4.2	4.2	1.5	13	-33.3	—
2008	MEM	AAA	24	9	3	0	21	21	125¹	107	46	81	11	50.1%	.264	-8	1.22	3.45	5.74	8.3	3.5	3.8	1.0	17	-1.8	—
2008	SLN	MLB	24	3	2	0	8	6	34	42	22	13	5	53.1%	.308	-23	1.88	7.41	7.08	10.7	5.0	3.1	1.3	-1	-7.5	0.04
2009	SLN	MLB	25	7	11	0	37	27	141	166	70	80	18	49.0%	.310	-1	1.67	5.87	6.33	10.6	4.0	4.5	1.1	-1	-10.8	-0.11

Breakout: 15%   Improve: 47%   Collapse: 15%   Attrition: 13%   Comparables: Scott Brow, Walt Terrell, William Brennan, Carlos Chantres

Boggs was called up in early June and thrust into the rotation after Wainwright's injury. He managed to survive until running into the Mets, who sent him back to Memphis for good with a 17-run barrage spread between two July starts. A fastball/curveball pitcher, Boggs doesn't have the stuff or command to maintain a spot in the rotation and will thus be shuttling back and forth between Triple-A and the majors again, as injuries necessitate.

Chris Carpenter

Bats: R   Throws: R   Height: 6' 6"   Weight: 230   Born: April 27, 1975   Age: 34

YEAR	TEAM	LVL	AGE	W	L	SV	G	GS	IP	H	BB	SO	HR	GB%	BABIP	STUFF	WHIP	ERA	DERA	EqH9	EqBB9	EqSO9	EqHR9	DEF	VORP	SN/WX
2006	SLN	MLB	31	15	8	0	32	32	221²	194	43	184	21	55.2%	.278	28	1.07	3.09	3.92	7.8	1.5	6.8	0.8	19	67.0	7.25
2007	SLN	MLB	32	0	1	0	1	1	6	9	1	3	0	66.7%	.391	4	1.67	7.50	4.26	12.8	1.4	4.3	0.0	-2	-1.2	-0.09
2008	SLN	MLB	33	0	1	0	4	3	15¹	16	4	7	0	55.8%	.327	-1	1.30	1.76	3.07	9.2	1.8	3.7	0.0	0	4.8	0.76
2009	SLN	MLB	34	6	5	0	22	14	92²	95	24	66	8	52.0%	.300	14	1.28	3.93	4.28	9.2	2.1	5.7	0.8	-0	14.2	2.05

Breakout: 4%   Improve: 23%   Collapse: 51%   Attrition: 29%   Comparables: Rick Reuschel, Bob Rush, Jon Lieber, Ken Forsch

Carpenter made his first rehab start on July 20, almost exactly a year after undergoing Tommy John surgery, but that didn't mark an end to his injury troubles, as he left his third start for the Cardinals with what was later diagnosed as a shoulder strain. He returned in early September to make a lone relief appearance, but had extreme difficulty recovering from that outing and was shut down a couple of weeks later with "nerve irritation" in the shoulder. Carpenter had ulnar nerve transposition surgery in November—that's on his elbow, not the shoulder; they're hoping that the damaged shoulder nerve will improve through rest and rehab. Carpenter was scheduled to begin a throwing program in January, but his days as a top gun might well be over. He's going to be paid like an ace over the next three seasons, regardless, with St. Louis on the hook for $44.5 million.

Randy Flores

				Bats: L			Throws: L		Height: 6' 0"		Weight: 190		Born: July 31, 1975			Age: 33	

YEAR	TEAM	LVL	AGE	W	L	SV	G	GS	IP	H	BB	SO	HR	GB%	BABIP	STUFF	WHIP	ERA	DERA	EqH9	EqBB9	EqSO9	EqHR9	DEF	VORP	SN/WX
2006	SLN	MLB	30	1	1	0	65	0	41²	49	22	40	5	41.4%	.355	-2	1.70	5.61	4.68	10.4	4.0	7.7	0.9	-5	-1.3	1.06
2007	SLN	MLB	31	3	0	1	70	0	55	71	15	47	2	44.7%	.383	14	1.56	4.25	3.04	11.0	2.1	7.0	0.3	-10	4.5	-0.46
2008	SLN	MLB	32	1	0	1	43	0	25²	34	20	17	2	50.5%	.360	-11	2.10	5.25	4.10	11.6	5.8	5.1	0.7	-4	-0.1	-0.58
2009	SLN	MLB	33	1	1	1	32	0	28¹	31	13	22	3	46.0%	.320	1	1.54	4.88	5.29	9.9	3.6	6.2	0.8	-0	1.1	0.08

Breakout: 19% Improve: 45% Collapse: 37% Attrition: 41%   Comparables: Rodney Myers, Buddy Groom, Ray King, Juan Agosto

The Cardinals gave Flores a two-year, $1.8 million contract to buy out two years of arbitration despite an ugly 2006 season. Pandering to La Russa's tactical proclivities with this particular situational lefty looked bad at the time, but at least the Cardinals could point to Flores's success as a LOOGY for justification—over the previous three years, he had held his own kind to a .222/.297/.341 line in 209 PAs. But from 2007 to 2008, he turned into a LNOGY, as lefties hit .322/.394/.473 against him in 170 PAs. Last year was particularly miserable; he pitched through arm soreness before undergoing shoulder surgery after his MRI showed a cyst and a fraying labrum. Deciding enough was enough, the Cardinals nontendered him in December.

Ryan Franklin

				Bats: R			Throws: R		Height: 6' 3"		Weight: 190		Born: March 5, 1973			Age: 36	

YEAR	TEAM	LVL	AGE	W	L	SV	G	GS	IP	H	BB	SO	HR	GB%	BABIP	STUFF	WHIP	ERA	DERA	EqH9	EqBB9	EqSO9	EqHR9	DEF	VORP	SN/WX
2006	PHI	MLB	33	1	5	0	46	0	53	59	17	25	10	48.1%	.278	-23	1.43	4.58	4.86	9.1	2.5	3.9	1.5	4	7.8	0.09
2006	CIN	MLB	33	5	2	0	20	0	24¹	27	17	18	3	48.7%	.343	-4	1.81	4.81	3.86	10.0	5.8	6.2	1.2	-2	1.5	-0.41
2007	SLN	MLB	34	4	4	1	69	0	80	70	11	44	8	49.4%	.251	0	1.01	3.04	3.84	7.5	1.0	4.6	0.8	8	23.9	3.05
2008	SLN	MLB	35	6	6	17	74	0	78²	86	30	51	10	44.3%	.306	-12	1.47	3.55	3.69	9.7	2.9	5.2	1.2	-1	15.0	3.20
2009	SLN	MLB	36	3	3	6	47	0	56²	61	19	34	6	45.0%	.300	-5	1.42	4.23	4.53	9.7	2.8	4.7	1.0	-0	6.7	0.65

Breakout: 13% Improve: 24% Collapse: 50% Attrition: 35%   Comparables: Rick White, Giovanni Carrara, Ron Kline, Brian Moehler

Franklin washed up on the shores of the Mississippi two years ago, having failed as both a starter and a reliever and carrying the black mark of a steroids suspension. An unexpected fit of control in 2007 revived his career, and he stayed on a roll until taking over as interim closer when Isringhausen got hurt last May. Franklin converted his first seven opportunities, but lost the job after allowing several big home runs. La Russa didn't really trust hard-throwing youngster Chris Perez, however, so he went back to Franklin in September. The veteran will again provide La Russa with a security blanket should the kids again not pass muster.

Jason Isringhausen

				Bats: R			Throws: R		Height: 6' 3"		Weight: 230		Born: September 7, 1972			Age: 36	

YEAR	TEAM	LVL	AGE	W	L	SV	G	GS	IP	H	BB	SO	HR	GB%	BABIP	STUFF	WHIP	ERA	DERA	EqH9	EqBB9	EqSO9	EqHR9	DEF	VORP	SN/WX
2006	SLN	MLB	33	4	8	33	59	0	58¹	47	38	52	10	44.5%	.247	-2	1.46	3.55	4.63	7.1	5.1	7.3	1.4	7	13.9	1.03
2007	SLN	MLB	34	4	0	32	63	0	65¹	42	28	54	4	46.4%	.215	11	1.07	2.48	4.03	5.4	3.2	6.7	0.5	9	21.4	4.24
2008	SLN	MLB	35	1	5	12	42	0	42²	48	22	36	5	52.6%	.328	-7	1.64	5.69	4.81	10.0	4.0	6.7	1.0	-4	-1.5	-2.32
2009	SLN	MLB	36	2	3	6	38	0	45	43	23	35	5	47.0%	.290	-0	1.46	4.31	4.64	8.6	4.1	6.2	1.0	-0	4.8	0.49

Breakout: 14% Improve: 34% Collapse: 43% Attrition: 27%   Comparables: Don McMahon, Mike Fetters, Dave Veres, Dave Weathers

Izzy pitched six straight scoreless frames to open the year, but then blew five of his next 11 save chances, picking up four losses in less than 10 innings. After a brief break from the closer role, he returned to give up four runs while recording only one out in his next chance. He then picked a fight with the clubhouse TV, lost, and went on the DL. Returning in June, he took back the closer role in August and then almost immediately lost it again with another spectacular combustion. Shortly thereafter, he was diagnosed with a partially torn tendon, undergoing surgery in mid-September. Now a free agent and seven saves shy of 300, Isringhausen should be healthy enough to show up at the start of spring training and probably won't break down until he actually pitches.

Kelvin Jimenez

Bats: R   Throws: R   Height: 6' 2"   Weight: 195   Born: October 27, 1980   Age: 28

YEAR	TEAM	LVL	AGE	W	L	SV	G	GS	IP	H	BB	SO	HR	GB%	BABIP	STUFF	WHIP	ERA	DERA	EqH9	EqBB9	EqSO9	EqHR9	DEF	VORP	SN/WX
2006	OKL	AAA	25	4	2	1	26	0	38²	40	24	40	4	45.2%	.333	-8	1.68	5.18	5.59	10.7	5.8	6.6	1.5	-2	0.0	—
2007	MEM	AAA	26	2	3	1	30	0	39²	46	11	34	2	66.4%	.358	-2	1.44	2.72	2.35	11.0	2.6	5.6	0.7	-8	13.8	—
2007	SLN	MLB	26	3	0	0	34	0	42	56	17	24	2	45.1%	.362	-11	1.74	7.50	6.00	11.6	3.2	4.9	0.4	-4	-9.1	0.30
2008	MEM	AAA	27	1	6	12	46	0	52¹	55	12	28	3	60.5%	.311	-19	1.28	2.93	4.86	9.9	2.2	3.1	0.7	2	4.1	—
2008	SLN	MLB	27	0	0	0	15	0	24	28	15	11	5	48.3%	.288	-29	1.79	5.63	5.55	10.0	4.8	3.7	1.8	0	-0.2	0.37
2009	CHA	MLB	28	2	3	1	47	3	55	68	25	28	8	50.0%	.320	-10	1.70	5.68	5.39	11.0	3.6	4.2	1.2	-1	-0.7	0.01

Breakout: 23%   Improve: 54%   Collapse: 17%   Attrition: 16%   Comparables: Edward Valdez, Miguel Saladin, Hector Ramirez, Roger Smithberg

Jimenez throws hard, but hasn't been able to translate that velocity into enough whiffs and consequently looks like a career mop-up man. In attempting to remove him from the big-league roster during the offseason, the Cardinals lost him to the claim-happy Blue Jays, who also tried to sneak him through waivers and saw him snatched by the White Sox. With another year of options left, Jimenez will probably spend the season bouncing between Charlotte and the South Side.

Josh Kinney

Bats: R   Throws: R   Height: 6' 1"   Weight: 215   Born: March 31, 1979   Age: 30

YEAR	TEAM	LVL	AGE	W	L	SV	G	GS	IP	H	BB	SO	HR	GB%	BABIP	STUFF	WHIP	ERA	DERA	EqH9	EqBB9	EqSO9	EqHR9	DEF	VORP	SN/WX
2006	MEM	AAA	27	2	2	3	51	0	71¹	46	29	76	2	58.1%	.263	10	1.05	1.52	3.59	6.7	3.9	6.8	0.4	6	15.1	—
2006	SLN	MLB	27	0	0	0	21	0	25	17	8	22	3	57.4%	.215	8	1.00	3.24	4.32	6.1	2.5	7.2	1.1	3	7.7	0.61
2008	SLN	MLB	29	0	0	0	7	0	7	3	1	8	0	75.0%	.188	7	0.57	0.00	1.29	3.9	1.3	9.0	0.0	0	4.4	0.13
2009	SLN	MLB	30	3	2	3	44	2	51¹	45	18	48	4	54.0%	.290	16	1.23	3.19	3.49	7.9	2.9	7.4	0.6	-0	13.3	1.24

Breakout: 7%   Improve: 17%   Collapse: 53%   Attrition: 12%   Comparables: Todd Frohwirth, Mike MacDougal, Lou Pote, Jim Mecir

Kinney was one of the unlikely heroes of the 2006 postseason, pitching 6⅓ scoreless innings after debuting that July. He underwent Tommy John surgery the following spring and took longer than most pitchers take to return from the procedure, suffering several setbacks during the 2008 season. Kinney finally made it back last September, 18 months after his surgery, and looked sharp in limited action. He should land a spot in the 2009 bullpen.

Kyle Lohse

Bats: R   Throws: R   Height: 6' 2"   Weight: 210   Born: October 4, 1978   Age: 30

YEAR	TEAM	LVL	AGE	W	L	SV	G	GS	IP	H	BB	SO	HR	GB%	BABIP	STUFF	WHIP	ERA	DERA	EqH9	EqBB9	EqSO9	EqHR9	DEF	VORP	SN/WX
2006	MIN	MLB	27	2	5	0	22	8	63²	80	25	46	8	39.0%	.350	-10	1.65	7.06	6.43	11.0	3.4	5.7	1.0	-3	-6.9	-0.43
2006	CIN	MLB	27	3	5	0	12	11	63	70	19	51	7	49.3%	.341	16	1.41	4.57	3.88	9.5	2.4	6.6	0.9	-1	9.3	1.40
2007	CIN	MLB	28	6	12	0	21	21	131²	143	33	80	16	37.3%	.307	9	1.34	4.58	4.33	8.7	1.9	5.1	0.9	-2	11.6	2.15
2007	PHI	MLB	28	3	0	0	13	11	61	64	24	42	6	42.9%	.315	7	1.44	4.72	4.60	8.9	3.1	5.8	0.7	2	6.8	1.42
2008	SLN	MLB	29	15	6	0	33	33	200	211	49	119	18	47.8%	.302	10	1.30	3.78	4.43	9.3	1.9	4.8	0.8	12	38.4	5.41
2009	SLN	MLB	30	10	9	0	26	26	161²	173	47	105	18	46.0%	.300	16	1.36	4.30	4.62	9.6	2.4	5.1	1.0	-1	17.5	3.17

Breakout: 16%   Improve: 42%   Collapse: 22%   Attrition: 16%   Comparables: Jaime Navarro, Jeff Suppan, Pat Hentgen, Steve Trachsel

What a difference a defense makes. Prone to the gopher ball, Lohse could attribute his smooth adjustment to the spacious confines of New Busch and the Cardinals' infield leather more to style than substance—he was generally the same old Lohse, albeit with a slightly better ground-ball rate. After turning down a multiyear deal with the Phillies and then being forced to settle for a below-market contract late in the offseason—Scott Boras doesn't win *all* his battles—Lohse was rewarded for his career season with a four-year, $41 million extension last September. (OK, maybe Boras does.) Lohse won't be worth the money or years on the deal, but he will continue to provide serviceable fourth-starter numbers.

Braden Looper

| | | Bats: R | Throws: R | Height: 6' 3" | Weight: 235 | Born: October 28, 1974 | Age: 34 |

YEAR	TEAM	LVL	AGE	W	L	SV	G	GS	IP	H	BB	SO	HR	GB%	BABIP	STUFF	WHIP	ERA	DERA	EqH9	EqBB9	EqSO9	EqHR9	DEF	VORP	SN/WX
2006	SLN	MLB	31	9	3	0	69	0	73¹	76	20	41	3	52.2%	.317	2	1.31	3.56	3.52	9.3	2.1	4.6	0.4	0	18.9	1.62
2007	SLN	MLB	32	12	12	0	31	30	175	183	51	87	22	44.4%	.281	-3	1.34	4.94	5.40	8.9	2.3	4.2	1.0	13	13.6	3.79
2008	SLN	MLB	33	12	14	0	33	33	199	216	45	108	25	49.3%	.298	1	1.31	4.16	4.70	9.6	1.8	4.4	1.1	6	24.6	4.21
2009	SLN	MLB	34	7	8	0	31	19	125²	141	34	70	14	47.0%	.300	4	1.39	4.62	4.98	10.1	2.2	4.4	1.0	-1	9.2	1.79

Breakout: 7%   Improve: 29%   Collapse: 36%   Attrition: 28%   Comparables: Mark Gubicza, Ken Forsch, Jim Lonborg, Bob Walk

In his second season as a starter, Looper completed his surprising transformation into a league-average innings muncher and, better still, further cut down his walk rate. Looper again substantially increased his reliance on his splitter, which is the major change in pitch selection that has accompanied his conversion to rotation work. As he headed into free agency, the Cardinals didn't offer Looper arbitration, a risk-averse but increasingly common maneuver. Having proven he can turn the trick, he'll no doubt be rounding out somebody's rotation.

Kyle McClellan

| | | Bats: R | Throws: R | Height: 6' 4" | Weight: 205 | Born: June 12, 1984 | Age: 25 |

YEAR	TEAM	LVL	AGE	W	L	SV	G	GS	IP	H	BB	SO	HR	GB%	BABIP	STUFF	WHIP	ERA	DERA	EqH9	EqBB9	EqSO9	EqHR9	DEF	VORP	SN/WX
2007	PMB	A+	23	4	1	0	16	1	29	22	4	24	0	54.9%	.272	-2	0.90	1.24	3.42	8.9	2.1	4.4	0.3	3	6.4	—
2007	SFD	AA	23	2	0	0	24	0	30²	24	6	30	2	55.7%	.266	-2	0.98	2.35	5.14	8.7	2.2	5.8	1.0	4	1.4	—
2008	SLN	MLB	24	2	7	1	68	0	75²	79	26	59	7	50.0%	.316	1	1.39	4.04	4.34	9.4	2.7	6.3	0.8	1	10.1	1.24
2009	SLN	MLB	25	4	3	3	48	2	65	62	21	50	5	49.0%	.290	10	1.27	3.54	3.83	8.5	2.6	6.1	0.8	-0	14.7	1.23

Breakout: 29%   Improve: 59%   Collapse: 26%   Attrition: 29%   Comparables: Jeremy Accardo, Ron Davis, Peter Munro, Brad Clontz

McClellan is a big right-hander with an even bigger arsenal: fastball, slider, cutter, curveball, and change. He quickly earned La Russa's trust, serving as the eighth-inning setup man for various closers for much of the final three months; his 30 holds tied him for the NL lead with Carlos Marmol. McClellan will probably return as a key setup man in 2009 and perhaps even earn some save chances if Chris Perez finds his way into the doghouse. He'll be a valuable piece while earning near the league minimum during the next two seasons.

Clayton Mortensen

| | | Bats: R | Throws: R | Height: 6' 4" | Weight: 180 | Born: April 10, 1985 | Age: 24 |

YEAR	TEAM	LVL	AGE	W	L	SV	G	GS	IP	H	BB	SO	HR	GB%	BABIP	STUFF	WHIP	ERA	DERA	EqH9	EqBB9	EqSO9	EqHR9	DEF	VORP	SN/WX
2007	QUD	A	22	0	2	0	10	10	40¹	44	8	45	2	62.6%	.372	-10	1.29	3.13	6.34	16.0	3.6	5.2	1.7	-3	-2.7	—
2007	BAT	A-	22	1	1	0	6	4	20¹	13	11	23	0	74.5%	.283	9	1.18	1.77	3.57	8.2	6.6	5.1	0.5	0	4.0	—
2008	SFD	AA	23	3	4	0	11	11	59²	59	22	48	6	61.2%	.301	-15	1.36	4.22	6.55	10.8	3.9	4.4	1.5	3	-5.8	—
2008	MEM	AAA	23	5	6	0	15	14	80	87	42	57	12	48.8%	.311	-22	1.61	5.51	7.56	10.8	4.9	4.2	1.7	8	-16.3	—
2009	SLN	MLB	24	5	7	0	18	18	97²	113	48	62	10	53.0%	.320	9	1.64	5.51	5.98	10.3	3.9	5.0	0.9	-1	-3.3	0.39

Breakout: 21%   Improve: 59%   Collapse: 15%   Attrition: 15%   Comparables: Marty Clary, Josh Rupe, Mitch Talbot, Andy Rincon

Mortensen was drafted as a college senior out of Gonzaga two years ago and was moved up a bit aggressively last season, skipping over High-A to open the season at Springfield. He was then promoted again, despite mediocre results. His sinker was perhaps the best in the system coming into the year, but it failed to do much sinking in Triple-A; he will repeat the level in 2009, but will be one of the first pitchers called on as need arises.

Jason Motte

| | | Bats: R | Throws: R | Height: 6' 0" | Weight: 200 | Born: June 22, 1982 | Age: 27 |

YEAR	TEAM	LVL	AGE	W	L	SV	G	GS	IP	H	BB	SO	HR	GB%	BABIP	STUFF	WHIP	ERA	DERA	EqH9	EqBB9	EqSO9	EqHR9	DEF	VORP	SN/WX
2006	QUD	A	24	1	1	0	8	0	12¹	16	3	13	1	45.5%	.372	-46	1.57	5.21	10.97	17.7	4.2	4.2	2.5	0	-6.4	—
2006	SCO	A-	24	1	2	8	21	0	26	30	4	25	1	43.5%	.358	-42	1.31	3.12	7.66	15.7	3.2	3.6	2.0	-3	-5.1	—
2007	PMB	A+	25	1	0	3	9	0	10	7	1	6	0	63.6%	.219	-18	0.80	0.90	4.35	7.0	1.7	2.6	0.0	1	1.4	—
2007	SFD	AA	25	3	3	8	44	0	49	36	22	63	3	39.5%	.325	7	1.18	2.20	3.50	9.1	4.7	8.2	1.0	0	10.2	—
2008	MEM	AAA	26	4	3	9	63	0	66²	64	26	110	6	35.9%	.400	20	1.35	3.24	3.03	11.0	3.8	10.7	1.0	-7	17.8	—
2008	SLN	MLB	26	0	0	1	12	0	11	5	3	16	0	47.6%	.250	11	0.73	0.82	1.69	5.1	2.5	10.1	0.0	0	4.9	0.61
2009	SLN	MLB	27	3	3	2	32	3	55	54	24	61	6	41.0%	.320	22	1.41	4.04	4.30	8.8	3.5	8.7	0.9	-0	8.5	0.84

Breakout: 35%   Improve: 61%   Collapse: 12%   Attrition: 14%   Comparables: Curt Kaufman, Kerry Ligtenberg, Doug Piatt, Pat Neshek

Motte entered the professional ranks as a catcher out of little Iona College in 2003, but, after hitting .188 in his first three seasons, decided that it might be worth switching to the other side of the battery. This wasn't a bad idea, considering he throws harder than most everybody else on the planet. Last year, Motte exploded for 14.8 strikeouts per nine, and his overall numbers would have been even more impressive if not for that grossly inflated BABIP. Motte's luck on balls in play started changing when he was called up in September, as he knocked the timber out of big-league hitters' hands with a fastball that sits in the 96-98 range and a vicious high-80s slider. Motte locked down the eighth inning in each of his final three appearances, which could be a preview of what's in store for him in 2009. At the very least, he should make the club in the spring, but he has a chance to steal away the closer role.

Mark Mulder

Bats: L   Throws: L   Height: 6' 6"   Weight: 215   Born: August 5, 1977   Age: 31

YEAR	TEAM	LVL	AGE	W	L	SV	G	GS	IP	H	BB	SO	HR	GB%	BABIP	STUFF	WHIP	ERA	DERA	EqH9	EqBB9	EqSO9	EqHR9	DEF	VORP	SN/WX
2006	SLN	MLB	28	6	7	0	17	17	93¹	124	35	50	19	56.8%	.339	-23	1.70	7.14	6.60	11.9	3.0	4.5	1.7	-2	-15.6	0.18
2007	SLN	MLB	29	0	3	0	3	3	11	22	7	3	4	35.4%	.419	-45	2.64	12.27	9.58	18.3	5.2	2.6	3.5	-5	-9.8	-0.61
2008	SFD	AA	30	3	0	0	3	3	16	14	7	9	1	53.1%	.271	-15	1.31	2.25	5.79	9.6	4.5	3.2	1.3	4	-0.3	—
2008	MEM	AAA	30	0	3	0	3	3	13¹	28	5	8	3	45.0%	.472	-51	2.48	13.53	15.63	20.6	3.6	2.8	2.1	-4	-14.2	—
2008	SLN	MLB	30	0	0	0	3	1	1²	4	2	2	0	28.6%	.667	-19	3.60	10.59	5.40	21.6	10.8	10.8	0.0	-1	-1.0	-0.25
2009	SLN	MLB	31	2	4	0	15	8	47²	58	20	25	7	49.0%	.310	-6	1.62	5.86	6.32	10.9	3.3	4.2	1.2	-0	-4.2	-0.07

Breakout: 46% Improve: 69% Collapse: 19% Attrition: 49%   Comparables: Steve Hargan, Don Johnson, John Farrell, Joe Magrane

Still far from sound after two shoulder surgeries cost him most of 2006 and '07, Mulder found his rehab shut down on several occasions, as he could not even get his arm fully into position. No doctor could figure out the exact problem, so Mulder took several cortisone shots and changed his arm angle to throw from a lower slot. Despite his being shellacked in his previous outing, the Cards called him up in late June, used him twice in relief, and then gave him a start a week later, which he left after just 16 pitches with a strained shoulder. In those three outings, Mulder threw 21 strikes and 22 balls and induced exactly one swinging strike. Dr. James Andrews told Mulder that only rest could fix the problem, so he sat for the remainder of the year. After off-season workouts, Mulder felt that he had gotten his arm angle almost all the way back up, but at press time, no team had made an offer to him. Between Mulder and Carpenter, the Cardinals got a grand total of 34 innings of 6.62 ERA ball from 2007 to '08, while paying their twin aces a combined $32 million.

Chris Perez

Bats: R   Throws: R   Height: 6' 4"   Weight: 225   Born: July 1, 1985   Age: 24

YEAR	TEAM	LVL	AGE	W	L	SV	G	GS	IP	H	BB	SO	HR	GB%	BABIP	STUFF	WHIP	ERA	DERA	EqH9	EqBB9	EqSO9	EqHR9	DEF	VORP	SN/WX
2006	QUD	A	20	2	0	12	25	0	29	20	19	32	0	53.4%	.296	0	1.34	1.86	6.29	10.0	8.9	5.2	0.7	1	-1.9	—
2007	SFD	AA	21	2	0	27	39	0	40²	17	28	62	3	29.7%	.200	26	1.11	2.43	5.12	5.1	6.8	9.3	1.2	6	2.1	—
2007	MEM	AAA	21	0	1	8	15	0	14	6	13	15	2	58.6%	.160	11	1.36	4.50	6.39	4.3	9.2	7.8	1.4	2	-1.1	—
2008	MEM	AAA	23	1	1	11	26	0	25¹	18	12	38	3	50.0%	.300	22	1.19	3.20	3.75	7.9	4.5	9.8	1.1	0	4.9	—
2008	SLN	MLB	23	3	3	7	41	0	41²	34	22	42	5	39.3%	.282	14	1.34	3.45	3.27	7.4	4.1	8.1	1.1	-3	8.0	0.47
2009	SLN	MLB	23	2	2	5	39	0	40	31	23	42	4	41.0%	.270	17	1.35	3.63	3.88	6.9	4.7	8.4	0.8	-0	8.0	0.75

Breakout: 19% Improve: 43% Collapse: 40% Attrition: 38%   Comparables: Armando Benitez, Jim Donohue, Esteban Yan, Mike Jackson

A supplemental-round pick in 2006, the 22-year-old Perez has seen a short pro career characterized by simultaneous wildness and dominance. He features one of the game's hardest fastballs and a plus-plus slider with devastating bite, drawing comparisons to the Dr. Jekyll versions of Kyle Farnsworth or Craig Hansen. Perez came up in May after overmatching the Pacific Coast League and, after a brief trip back to the bush, returned as the club's closer in August. He pitched well for the most part, although a couple of blown September chances caused La Russa to return to the devilringhausen he knew. The Cards made a show of looking for an established veteran to close this winter, but the team would be better served by giving its youngsters the responsibility: Between Perez and Motte, they have a pair of fireballing, high-upside hurlers well suited to the job.

Joel Pineiro

Bats: R Throws: R Height: 6' 1" Weight: 200 Born: September 25, 1978 Age: 30

YEAR	TEAM	LVL	AGE	W	L	SV	G	GS	IP	H	BB	SO	HR	GB%	BABIP	STUFF	WHIP	ERA	DERA	EqH9	EqBB9	EqSO9	EqHR9	DEF	VORP	SN/WX
2006	SEA	MLB	27	8	13	1	40	25	165²	209	64	87	23	48.3%	.331	-21	1.65	6.35	6.75	11.4	3.5	4.2	1.2	2	-14.2	0.65
2007	BOS	MLB	28	1	1	0	31	0	34	41	14	20	3	54.9%	.325	-16	1.62	5.03	4.24	11.1	3.4	4.5	0.8	-2	3.2	-0.38
2007	SLN	MLB	28	6	4	0	11	11	63²	69	12	40	11	47.8%	.296	4	1.27	3.96	3.94	9.6	1.5	5.5	1.5	1	12.4	1.70
2008	SLN	MLB	29	7	7	1	26	25	148²	180	35	81	22	49.1%	.319	-8	1.45	5.14	5.40	10.7	1.8	4.4	1.3	3	4.7	1.62
2009	SLN	MLB	30	6	7	1	30	16	111¹	127	33	65	14	48.0%	.310	4	1.44	4.72	5.07	10.3	2.4	4.6	1.1	-1	7.3	1.40

Breakout: 23% Improve: 58% Collapse: 22% Attrition: 27%   Comparables: Jack Fisher, Jim Colborn, Brett Tomko, Early Wynn

The Cardinals seem to be enamored with the two-year, $13 million contract, as one offseason after handing one to Mulder, they endowed Pineiro with the same investment. Pineiro came down with a DL-worthy case of shoulder stiffness in spring training and subsequently missed time with a groin strain, but when he did take the mound, he reverted to his old Seattle form and was the one rotation member who was below average. This earned him a brief trip to the bullpen in late August, but he returned to allow 19 runs in his final four starts. Pineiro is fifth-starter material, but St. Louis mistakenly valued him more highly than that after a decent run to end '07.

Russ Springer

Bats: R Throws: R Height: 6' 4" Weight: 225 Born: November 7, 1968 Age: 40

YEAR	TEAM	LVL	AGE	W	L	SV	G	GS	IP	H	BB	SO	HR	GB%	BABIP	STUFF	WHIP	ERA	DERA	EqH9	EqBB9	EqSO9	EqHR9	DEF	VORP	SN/WX
2006	HOU	MLB	37	1	1	0	72	0	59²	46	16	46	10	28.7%	.222	-3	1.04	3.47	4.10	6.8	2.1	6.4	1.4	6	16.9	0.57
2007	SLN	MLB	38	8	1	0	76	0	66	41	19	66	3	32.0%	.242	28	0.91	2.18	2.85	5.3	2.2	8.3	0.4	3	24.9	2.17
2008	SLN	MLB	39	2	1	0	70	0	50¹	39	18	45	4	33.1%	.259	10	1.13	2.33	2.68	6.8	2.7	7.0	0.7	1	17.5	1.16
2009	SLN	MLB	40	2	2	2	43	0	46	40	16	40	6	34.0%	.270	7	1.22	3.63	3.85	7.9	2.8	6.9	1.1	-0	9.5	0.79

Breakout: 4% Improve: 16% Collapse: 62% Attrition: 19%   Comparables: Don McMahon, Trevor Hoffman, Al Worthington, Jesse Orosco

This June, Springer will celebrate the 20th anniversary of signing his first pro contract. A thorough journeyman for most of that time, he has been a surprisingly effective reliever in the last two seasons, albeit in extremely low-leverage situations—roughly two-thirds of his appearances came when the Cards were either trailing or ahead by four or more runs. Still, Duncan can count another unlikely thirtysomething hurler redeemed. Not wanting to give a 40-year-old trash-timer a mandatory raise, the Cardinals didn't offer Springer arbitration. It was, perhaps incidentally, a generous gesture, as Springer was a Type-A free agent, and the required forfeiture of draft picks would have been an impediment to his getting an offer. Nonetheless, the old man remains on the market as we go to press.

Brad Thompson

Bats: R Throws: R Height: 6' 1" Weight: 190 Born: January 31, 1982 Age: 27

YEAR	TEAM	LVL	AGE	W	L	SV	G	GS	IP	H	BB	SO	HR	GB%	BABIP	STUFF	WHIP	ERA	DERA	EqH9	EqBB9	EqSO9	EqHR9	DEF	VORP	SN/WX
2006	MEM	AAA	24	2	0	0	14	5	42¹	36	6	33	3	60.8%	.282	-2	1.00	2.14	4.95	8.6	1.6	4.9	0.9	6	2.9	—
2006	SLN	MLB	24	1	2	0	43	1	56²	58	20	32	4	56.9%	.298	-4	1.38	3.33	3.56	9.2	2.7	4.7	0.6	1	14.8	0.68
2007	SLN	MLB	25	8	6	0	44	17	129¹	157	40	53	23	50.8%	.301	-26	1.52	4.73	4.77	10.5	2.5	3.6	1.5	-1	8.3	2.25
2008	SLN	MLB	26	6	3	0	26	6	64²	72	19	32	5	52.3%	.321	-7	1.41	5.15	4.82	10.2	2.3	4.1	0.7	-2	2.4	0.64
2009	SLN	MLB	27	3	3	1	27	5	56	63	18	30	6	51.0%	.300	-2	1.43	4.51	4.88	10.0	2.5	4.2	0.9	-0	5.0	0.61

Breakout: 16% Improve: 40% Collapse: 38% Attrition: 37%   Comparables: Tom Murphy, Al Fitzmorris, Jimmy Jones, Mike Wood

Thompson is a serviceable long man, although now that he's arb-eligible, that marginal value has dwindled. He's too homer-prone and hittable to pitch high-leverage innings, and he's a weak option to do more than spot work as a starter. Every team needs a guy who can soak up peripheral frames, and Thompson capably plays that role, but so could many other pitchers.

Jess Todd

Bats: R   **Throws:** R   **Height:** 5' 11"   **Weight:** 210   **Born:** April 20, 1986   **Age:** 23

YEAR	TEAM	LVL	AGE	W	L	SV	G	GS	IP	H	BB	SO	HR	GB%	BABIP	STUFF	WHIP	ERA	DERA	EqH9	EqBB9	EqSO9	EqHR9	DEF	VORP	SN/WX
2007	BAT	A-	21	4	1	0	16	7	58¹	48	14	69	2	55.5%	.319	14	1.06	2.78	5.68	10.7	3.4	5.5	1.2	-2	-0.5	—
2008	PMB	A+	22	3	0	1	7	4	27¹	18	7	35	0	52.3%	.286	25	0.92	1.65	2.49	8.2	2.8	7.1	0.4	-4	8.7	—
2008	SFD	AA	22	4	5	0	17	16	103	79	24	81	12	52.8%	.246	-6	1.00	2.97	5.59	8.6	2.6	4.5	1.7	13	0.1	—
2008	MEM	AAA	22	1	1	0	4	4	22²	19	11	20	4	45.3%	.259	5	1.32	3.96	5.82	8.3	4.6	5.4	1.7	3	-0.5	—
2009	SLN	MLB	23	5	6	0	24	16	99	105	39	69	13	48.0%	.300	10	1.45	4.98	5.38	9.5	3.1	5.5	1.1	-0	2.9	0.97

Breakout: 7%   **Improve:** 35%   **Collapse:** 28%   **Attrition:** 14%   **Comparables:** Marc Barcelo, Jason Bell, Ricky Nolasco, Justin Duchscherer

Todd possesses two strong pitches, a cut fastball and sharp slider, which each feature a good amount of movement (perhaps contributing to his 14 hit batsmen last season). That makes him especially nasty against right-handers, whom he held to a 600 OPS in 387 PAs last year, and a 481 OPS the previous season. Like many aspiring starters, he lacks a quality third offering, currently throwing the beta version of a changeup. The progress he makes with the off-speed pitch will determine his fate; even without it, he has enough stuff to be a solid reliever in the majors.

Ron Villone

Bats: L   **Throws:** L   **Height:** 6' 3"   **Weight:** 245   **Born:** January 16, 1970   **Age:** 39

YEAR	TEAM	LVL	AGE	W	L	SV	G	GS	IP	H	BB	SO	HR	GB%	BABIP	STUFF	WHIP	ERA	DERA	EqH9	EqBB9	EqSO9	EqHR9	DEF	VORP	SN/WX
2006	NYA	MLB	36	3	3	0	70	0	80¹	75	51	72	9	34.0%	.301	1	1.57	5.16	5.35	8.5	5.6	7.2	0.9	0	5.6	0.74
2007	SWB	AAA	37	0	1	1	17	0	23²	21	10	27	0	48.4%	.350	6	1.31	1.90	2.42	9.3	4.0	7.3	0.4	-2	7.9	—
2007	NYA	MLB	37	0	0	0	37	0	42¹	36	18	25	5	36.9%	.250	-18	1.28	4.26	5.98	7.7	3.8	4.6	1.1	8	8.5	0.18
2008	SLN	MLB	38	1	2	1	74	0	50	45	37	50	4	40.7%	.313	10	1.64	4.68	4.68	8.3	5.8	7.9	0.7	0	4.1	0.84
2009	SLN	MLB	39	1	2	1	32	0	30¹	30	19	26	3	41.0%	.300	-2	1.61	5.19	5.62	8.8	5.1	6.8	0.9	-0	0.1	-0.01

Breakout: 12%   **Improve:** 42%   **Collapse:** 33%   **Attrition:** 43%   **Comparables:** Jeff Nelson, Mike Fetters, Jim Bibby, Roberto Hernandez

Poor performance combined with a cameo appearance in the Mitchell Report (at least he was apparently smart enough to pay for his human growth hormone in cash) prevented Villone from securing a big-league deal in free agency last year. The Cardinals wanted to add a third lefty, so Villone eventually signed a minor league pact with them. He retired lefties well enough, holding them to a .176/.311/.318 line in 108 PAs. The veteran southpaw is on his last legs, although it's probable that some team will give him another shot; in the meantime, the Cards have changed over to Trever Miller, Charlie Manning, and Royce Ring to fill the LOOGY role.

Adam Wainwright

Bats: R   **Throws:** R   **Height:** 6' 7"   **Weight:** 230   **Born:** August 30, 1981   **Age:** 27

YEAR	TEAM	LVL	AGE	W	L	SV	G	GS	IP	H	BB	SO	HR	GB%	BABIP	STUFF	WHIP	ERA	DERA	EqH9	EqBB9	EqSO9	EqHR9	DEF	VORP	SN/WX
2006	SLN	MLB	24	2	1	3	61	0	75	64	22	72	6	49.8%	.290	19	1.15	3.12	3.03	7.7	2.3	7.9	0.6	1	24.1	2.78
2007	SLN	MLB	25	14	12	0	32	32	202	212	70	136	13	49.6%	.311	22	1.40	3.70	3.32	9.0	2.7	5.6	0.5	-12	38.4	5.84
2008	SLN	MLB	26	11	3	0	20	20	132	122	34	91	12	46.6%	.279	17	1.18	3.20	3.83	8.1	2.0	5.5	0.8	6	32.4	4.04
2009	SLN	MLB	27	8	7	1	33	20	132²	136	42	97	13	47.0%	.300	15	1.34	4.01	4.32	9.2	2.6	5.8	0.8	-1	18.6	2.86

Breakout: 2%   **Improve:** 15%   **Collapse:** 46%   **Attrition:** 27%   **Comparables:** Frank Sullivan, Ron Reed, Aaron Harang, Erik Hanson

What makes the Cardinals' overachievement last year even more improbable is that they managed to win 86 games despite getting only 20 starts from their best pitcher. Wainwright started out strong after signing a four-year, $15 million deal that includes options for his first two years of free agency, but then he missed two and a half months with a ruptured ligament in his right middle finger. The curveballer pitched well on returning, but supported by that .279 BABIP, last year's results might be the upper limit of Wainwright's range, as it's hard to do much better while fanning six men per nine.

Todd Wellemeyer

Bats: R   Throws: R   Height: 6' 3"   Weight: 225   Born: August 30, 1978   Age: 30

YEAR	TEAM	LVL	AGE	W	L	SV	G	GS	IP	H	BB	SO	HR	GB%	BABIP	STUFF	WHIP	ERA	DERA	EqH9	EqBB9	EqSO9	EqHR9	DEF	VORP	SN/WX
2006	FLO	MLB	27	0	2	0	18	0	21¹	20	13	17	1	44.6%	.317	1	1.55	5.49	4.57	7.9	4.6	6.2	0.4	-1	1.0	-0.40
2006	KCA	MLB	27	1	2	1	28	0	57	48	37	37	5	52.3%	.265	-2	1.49	3.63	4.04	7.1	5.7	5.2	0.8	2	14.0	0.49
2007	KCA	MLB	28	0	1	0	12	0	15²	25	11	9	4	41.3%	.362	-38	2.30	10.32	8.82	13.2	5.5	4.4	2.2	-2	-8.3	-0.23
2007	SLN	MLB	28	3	2	0	20	11	63²	52	29	51	7	42.2%	.259	7	1.27	3.11	4.08	7.0	3.5	6.8	0.8	0	10.3	1.50
2008	SLN	MLB	29	13	9	0	32	32	191²	178	62	134	25	40.2%	.270	6	1.25	3.71	4.41	8.1	2.5	5.5	1.1	11	36.3	5.12
2009	SLN	MLB	30	8	8	0	33	21	141¹	141	53	103	17	43.0%	.290	12	1.38	4.37	4.68	9.0	3.1	5.8	1.0	-1	15.0	2.48

Breakout: 8%   Improve: 28%   Collapse: 28%   Attrition: 18%   *Comparables: Cal Eldred, Mike Scott, Earl Wilson, Tim Wakefield*

Among the niftiest tricks of Duncan's lengthy coaching career (he's the longest-tenured pitching coach in MLB history) is the transfiguration of Todd Wellemeyer. Before arriving in St. Louis, Wellemeyer was a fringe reliever with a career 5.65 ERA and 1.68 WHIP in 178⅓ big-league innings. The chance that Wellemeyer would thrive as a starter might have seemed small on that basis, but Duncan recognized Wellemeyer's excellent fastball and nasty slider. Since becoming a Cardinal, Wellemeyer boasts a 3.56 ERA and 1.26 WHIP in 255⅓ IP, almost all of them in the rotation. He even fought through some midseason shoulder soreness to put up a 3.01 ERA over his final 13 starts. Even an extreme fly-ball pitcher like Wellemeyer cannot sustain a .270 BABIP, however, so expect regression in 2009.

Mark Worrell

Bats: R   Throws: R   Height: 6' 1"   Weight: 190   Born: March 8, 1983   Age: 26

YEAR	TEAM	LVL	AGE	W	L	SV	G	GS	IP	H	BB	SO	HR	GB%	BABIP	STUFF	WHIP	ERA	DERA	EqH9	EqBB9	EqSO9	EqHR9	DEF	VORP	SN/WX
2006	SFD	AA	23	3	7	27	57	0	61²	52	20	75	10	48.4%	.290	-16	1.18	4.56	6.21	9.5	3.3	7.3	2.2	-1	-3.9	—
2007	MEM	AAA	24	3	2	4	50	0	67	58	25	66	6	42.9%	.299	-3	1.24	3.09	4.09	8.0	3.4	6.3	1.1	1	11.1	—
2008	MEM	AAA	25	3	3	5	53	0	58²	45	31	80	2	35.0%	.326	19	1.29	2.15	3.56	8.2	4.9	8.9	0.5	-2	12.6	—
2008	SLN	MLB	25	0	1	0	4	0	5²	8	4	4	1	36.8%	.412	-6	2.12	7.89	6.75	13.5	5.1	6.8	1.7	-1	-1.4	0.04
2009	SDN	MLB	26	2	3	1	28	3	50²	47	25	50	6	40.0%	.300	13	1.43	4.19	4.76	8.7	3.9	7.4	1.0	-0	5.2	0.56

Breakout: 28%   Improve: 50%   Collapse: 26%   Attrition: 17%   *Comparables: Chad Orvella, Doug Piatt, Curt Kaufman, Dewey Robinson*

Worrell is not related to Tim and Todd Worrell, the brothers who combined for over 300 major league saves, but has the chance to make a similar name for himself. A side-arming righty, his career numbers include fewer than seven hits per nine and over 10.6 K/9, which led the Padres to covet him in the deal for Khalil Greene. Despite his delivery, there is evidence that Worrell could prove effective against all comers, as he held lefties to just two extra-base hits in 89 PAs last season. Worrell also generates a lot of fly balls, meaning that he should be an excellent fit for his new home, Petco Park.

LINEOUTS

Hitters

PLAYER	TEAM	LVL	AGE	PA	R	2B	3B	HR	RBI	BB	SO	SB-CS	EqBRR	AVG/OBP/SLG	EqAVG/EqOBP/EqSLG	EqA	VORP	WARP
INF B. Barden	MEM	AAA	27	456	60	21	4	9	35	38	72	3-3	-0.3	.285/.349/.421	.229/.285/.337	.217	-18.5	-1.5
1B A. Craig	SFD	AA	23	568	84	30	0	22	85	48	87	2-1	2.1	.304/.373/.494	.249/.310/.415	.249	2.9	0.7
SS T. Greene	SFD	AA	24	408	62	15	4	16	41	22	99	14-6	2.4	.259/.307/.449	.198/.239/.352	.202	-26.2	-2.9
	MEM	AAA	24	128	17	7	0	0	7	11	35	6-0	2.4	.234/.325/.297	.211/.291/.263	.207	-8.3	-0.1
LF C. Haerther*	SFD	AA	24	79	12	5	0	1	5	12	10	0-1	-0.8	.297/.423/.422	.224/.333/.328	.235	-1.5	0.4
	MEM	AAA	24	295	26	17	0	3	26	23	56	2-3	-2.5	.250/.311/.347	.224/.279/.305	.202	-16.7	-1.9
MI J. Martinez	SFD	AA	22	530	50	20	1	8	67	20	44	1-4	-2.4	.253/.292/.348	.208/.240/.295	.181	-43.3	-3.5
OF S. Peterson*	BAT	A-	20	275	35	20	2	1	39	39	65	3-2	-1.0	.291/.400/.409	.220/.312/.320	.228	-18.1	-1.5
1B J. Phelps	MEM	AAA	30	528	90	31	2	31	97	56	109	2-2	1.9	.291/.373/.568	.224/.296/.428	.247	-1.2	0.4
	SLN	MLB	30	36	4	1	0	0	1	2	11	0-0	0.1	.265/.306/.294	.265/.306/.294	.210	-1.1	-0.2
OF M. Shorey*	SFD	AA	23	432	49	28	2	11	66	29	110	1-0	-1.2	.304/.353/.472	.249/.294/.401	.241	-3.5	-1.3
SS N. Vasquez	JCY	Rk	19	246	42	16	1	4	25	29	52	8-2	-1.9	.317/.416/.462	.219/.296/.329	.223	-19.9	-0.3
UT R. Washington*	SLN	MLB	30	22	2	2	0	0	3	3	6	0-0	-0.0	.158/.273/.263	.158/.273/.263	.190	-1.3	-0.1
	MEM	AAA	30	314	54	15	0	13	40	52	49	0-2	0.4	.254/.392/.468	.197/.317/.348	.238	-7.6	-0.9

Brian Barden played shortstop in Memphis last year, but he's not slick enough to do the same in the majors, which is why he hasn't caught on as a utility infielder. ⌀ **Allen Craig** can hit, but has been clambering down the defensive spectrum ever since entering University of California–Berkeley as a wide-eyed freshman shortstop. ⌀ **Tyler Greene** put up almost the same OBP and SLG at Double-A last year that he did in 2007, and the 2005 first-rounder isn't even the best bit of Greene-ry at short after the acquisition of Khalil. ⌀ **Cody Haerther**'s problems are legion: He can really only play left, the Cards are stacked there, and he doesn't have nearly enough dynamite to blow through the logjam; he could turn into a decent pinch-hitter and reserve. ⌀ Entering the season as a decent middle-infield prospect, **Jose Martinez** saw his bat wilt with a prolonged exposure to the Texas League and lost his hold on playing short. ⌀ **Shane Peterson** was drafted in the second round last year out of Long Beach State, and the former Dirtbags star impressed with his advanced plate approach while playing all three outfield spots and first base. ⌀ Former hitting prodigy **Josh Phelps** found his first foray into the Pacific Coast League enjoyable, but didn't hit much in a late-season call-up. He signed a minor league deal with the Giants in the offseason. ⌀ Chunky platoon outfielder **Mark Shorey** won't catch many breaks in this organization, but slugging .498 against righties in Double-A might make for a reserve role somewhere someday. ⌀ Taken in the third round last year, **Nico Vasquez** had a strong debut in the Appy League. If he's a true shortstop, he could move up quickly, and if not, he can sing lead at the next Velvet Underground reunion. ⌀ Even if it didn't last, in a feel-good surprise **Rico Washington** made the Cardinals out of spring training, the culmination of 11 full seasons in the minors.

Pitchers

PLAYER	TEAM	LVL	AGE	W	L	SV	IP	H	BB	SO	HR	GB%	BABIP	STUFF	WHIP	ERA	DERA	EqH9	EqBB9	EqSO9	EqHR9	DEF	VORP
N. Additon*	QUD	A	20	9	5	1	119	92	35	108	12	32.0%	.259	-8	1.07	2.50	6.81	9.6	3.9	3.9	2.4	14	-14.2
	PMB	A+	20	2	0	0	18	11	5	13	1	41.7%	.243	17	0.89	0.50	3.12	6.7	3.1	3.1	1.0	1	4.8
R. Castillo	QUD	A	18	8	4	0	79	64	20	69	11	38.2%	.262	-8	1.06	2.62	6.31	10.9	3.6	3.9	3.4	6	-5.3
	PMB	A+	18	1	0	0	16	12	8	19	0	40.5%	.343	13	1.25	1.13	3.38	10.1	6.1	6.8	0.7	0	3.3
M. Clement	SFD	AA	33	1	0	0	10	12	3	5	1	56.8%	.306	-29	1.50	5.40	9.31	12.1	2.8	1.9	1.9	-1	-4.0
	MEM	AAA	33	1	0	0	16²	17	13	10	5	41.8%	.245	-34	1.80	7.01	9.37	9.4	6.6	3.3	2.8	1	-6.8
R. Flores*	MEM	AAA	28	7	4	4	63¹	71	33	58	6	33.0%	.351	-15	1.64	4.27	5.22	11.2	4.8	5.5	1.0	1	2.5
J. Garcia*	SFD	AA	21	3	2	0	35	26	16	41	0	62.8%	.306	31	1.20	2.06	4.50	8.7	4.8	7.0	0.3	3	3.9
	MEM	AAA	21	4	4	0	71	74	26	59	6	56.5%	.325	19	1.41	4.44	5.82	10.2	3.4	5.0	0.9	-1	-1.7
	SLN	MLB	21	1	1	0	16	14	8	8	4	61.5%	.208	-6	1.38	5.63	7.88	7.3	3.9	3.9	2.2	5	-0.1
B. Hawksworth	MEM	AAA	25	5	7	0	88²	111	38	83	12	48.9%	.372	-18	1.68	6.09	7.13	12.7	4.1	5.8	1.5	-11	-14.2
T. Herron	PMB	A+	21	2	2	1	56²	49	11	43	5	47.9%	.273	-4	1.06	2.70	6.26	10.5	2.5	3.8	2.0	7	-3.7
	SFD	AA	21	5	5	0	81¹	101	29	59	9	43.8%	.348	-10	1.60	5.20	7.21	13.8	3.9	3.9	1.7	2	-13.2
A. Ottavino	SFD	AA	22	3	7	0	115¹	133	52	96	16	46.5%	.339	-30	1.60	5.23	6.73	12.8	4.8	4.6	2.0	-8	-13.3
M. Parisi	MEM	AAA	25	8	2	0	84	80	33	58	7	52.5%	.290	-7	1.35	3.86	4.99	9.3	3.7	4.1	0.9	2	5.4
	SLN	MLB	25	0	4	0	23	37	15	13	2	43.0%	.402	-24	2.26	8.22	6.75	13.5	4.9	4.5	0.8	-6	-9.3
L. Perdomo	KIN	A+	24	3	1	18	39	19	17	43	0	49.5%	.218	5	0.92	0.92	3.35	5.0	4.3	6.2	0.2	4	9.4
	AKR	AA	24	2	0	1	15¹	12	7	17	1	38.5%	.297	1	1.24	3.53	5.02	8.2	3.8	7.5	0.6	2	0.9
	SFD	AA	24	2	2	1	18	18	6	22	2	45.1%	.327	-12	1.33	4.50	7.27	10.9	3.6	6.7	1.6	0	-3.2
F. Salas	SFD	AA	23	7	3	25	74	65	16	100	12	41.0%	.323	-9	1.09	3.65	4.81	10.6	2.5	8.4	2.4	-1	5.9
P. Walters	SFD	AA	23	1	2	0	36	35	8	34	5	47.6%	.300	-1	1.19	3.25	5.73	10.9	2.5	5.5	1.9	1	-0.5
	MEM	AAA	23	9	4	0	122	123	62	122	17	46.8%	.327	-7	1.52	4.87	5.97	10.2	4.7	6.2	1.6	-1	-4.8

Taken in the 47th round of the 2006 draft as a draft-and-follow pick, **Nicholas Addition** throws a fastball that barely rises above the mid-80s, but he has excellent command of his alternate offerings, especially a nasty changeup. ⌀ A short right-hander with an excellent curve, **Richard Castillo** made the huge jump from the Venezuelan summer league to High- and then Low-A and was very impressive at both stops, especially given he was one of the youngest players in full-season ball. ⌀ The Cardinals guaranteed **Matt Clement** $1.5 million after he missed all of 2007 after shoulder surgery, but Clement didn't begin a minor league rehab assignment until June and was released two months later. In their desperation, the Blue Jays have offered him another comeback shot. ⌀ Although they reunited **Ron Flores** with his older brother Randy, the Cardinals didn't have much other cause to employ him. ⌀ **Jaime Garcia** advanced from the 22nd round of the 2005 draft to become the team's best pitching prospect, but he failed to bypass the injury nexus unscathed—late-season elbow trouble led to Tommy John surgery. He was in line to compete for a rotation spot this season, but the sinkerballer will spend all of it rehabbing. ⌀ In the last two seasons, **Blake Hawksworth** has gotten repeatedly torched at Triple-A, but the Cards remain hopeful and are still carrying him on the 40-man. ⊘ Skinny **Tyler Herron** has average stuff but fantastic control; he bookended his season with strong work at Palm Beach in April and August, but in between had difficulty adjusting to Double-A. ⊘ The team's best left-handed reliever, **Tyler Johnson** had a strained rotator cuff that necessitated season-ending arthroscopic surgery in mid-May; he was nontendered in December. ⊘ Arguably the organization's best starting pitcher prospect entering the season, **Adam Ottavino** failed to keep the line moving at Springfield. He's a big righty (6' 5", 215) with one of the best heaters in the system, but he needs work on his slider and changeup. ⊘ Adding to the lengthening list of bum-winged Cardinals, **Mike Parisi** was diagnosed with a partial tear of his UCL in early August and underwent Tommy John surgery at the end of the season; he'll miss all of 2009. ⊘ Fringe righty reliever **Luis Perdomo** was the return from the Indians when the Cards sold low on Anthony Reyes; the Cards didn't think highly enough of Perdomo to protect him from the Rule 5 draft, where San Francisco snagged him. ⊘ Signed out of the Mexican League, righty **Fernando Salas** served notice in his second stateside season by fanning over 12 per nine with a greater than 6/1 K/BB as Springfield's closer, but he needs to work on cutting down the homers. ⊘ **P. J. Walters** had walked just two per nine in 217⅔ pro IP at the time he was called up to Triple-A, but saw his rate double with the Redbirds; while he did maintain his strikeout rate, he doesn't crack 90.

MANAGER: TONY LA RUSSA

YEAR	TEAM	W-L	Pythag +/−	Avg PC	100+ P	120+ P	QS	BQS	REL	REL w Zero R	IBB	Subs	PH	PH Avg	PH HR	SB2	CS2	SB3	CS3	SAC Att	SAC %	POS SAC	Squeeze	Swing	In Play
2006	SLN	83-78	1	92.7	55	2	74	5	468	294	35	69	271	.235	7	53	26	6	5	93	76.3%	32	4	135	110
2007	SLN	78-84	8	89.7	44	2	68	4	515	339	25	56	315	.296	5	50	26	6	3	93	73.1%	31	1	140	121
2008	SLN	86-76	-1	92.9	52	1	76	11	506	318	21	78	273	.239	6	63	27	9	3	109	65.1%	33	1	150	120

La Russa's 13th year with the Cards was one to take pride in, as he guided a projected second-division team into wild-card contention. The active leader in managerial victories, he needs to average 75.5 wins over the next four seasons to tie John McGraw for second on the all-time wins list (and first among all non–team owner/managers). The tendencies for which La Russa has earned fame (and infamy) were on exaggerated display last season. As is his wont, he used several relievers as extreme specialists, notably Villone, Flores, and Springer, giving the '08 Cardinals as carefully managed a tactical trio as only the '08 Mets have ever managed. Never one for the intentional walk, La Russa ordered the lowest total in the National League from the last nine seasons and the lowest total in franchise history in the 53 years for which records are available. La Russa batted the pitcher eighth in every intraleague game, ostensibly to get more runners on base for Pujols; nine-hole hitters put up an OBP around 70 points higher than the pitchers did, but it's hard to say exactly how much the gambit benefited the offense. La Russa called for the hit-and-run frequently, but the Cardinals did not execute well on the basepaths: Their -10.2 EqBRR ranked 22nd in baseball, and they were toward the bottom in both steal attempts (105, 23rd) and success rate (70, 21st).

San Diego Padres

As bad as the Padres' 2008 season was, the offseason that followed was worse, but in a way, it's in keeping with the franchise's history. Since their birth in the 1969 expansion, the Padres have had more than their share of odd ownership situations. To be sure, they have been treated far more gently by the fates than has their sister expansion franchise, the Montreal Expos/ Washington Nationals, but the latter's story is one of geographic and economic difficulties. In contrast, the Padres have all too often been kneecapped from above by the suits in the owner's suite.

Initial club owner C. Arnholdt Smith was undercapitalized, ran up a huge tax bill, entrusted the direction of the club to a series of Bavasis, and ultimately had to sell out to a Washington DC-based ownership group that intended to move the club to the capital city. That deal slowly fell apart, giving way to maneuverings that ended only when McDonald's magnate Ray Kroc stepped in and bought the club as a "hobby." Kroc was an upgrade over Smith, but was an autocrat who was used to being the command-and-control dictator of his company. The ups and downs of ballplayer performance was not something he really understood, and during an Opening Day drubbing in 1974 he famously grabbed the public address announcer's mic and said, "Ladies and gentlemen, I suffer with you . . . I've never seen such stupid ballplaying in my life." Kroc died in January, 1984, having left the club in much better shape than he found it (despite his eccentricities), and on the verge of fielding its first pennant winner. Ownership passed to his widow, Joan Kroc. Under Mrs. Kroc, the front office devolved into internecine squabbling, unable to agree on personnel decisions or cope with the drug scandals then rocking baseball. With the club spinning its wheels, Mrs. Kroc nearly sold out to Mariners owner George Argyros, a certain disaster that was narrowly avoided. Instead, the club was ultimately purchased by a group headed by TV producer Tom Werner, whose lasting monument in San Diego is the infamous 1993 fire sale in which Fred McGriff, Garry Sheffield, and others were dealt off to cut payroll.

The Werner group bailed out after 1994, selling to software entrepreneur John Moores, the author of their present difficulties. Moores' ownership has by any reasonable measure been the most successful in the history of the club. In his 14 years in control, the club has reached the postseason four times and reached the World Series once. The club also acquired a much-needed new stadium, Petco Park, breaking ground in 2000 and taking residence in 2004. That year, a franchise once thought permanently handicapped due to its being geographically trapped between Los Angeles to the north, Mexico to the south, a desert to the east, and an ocean to the west, drew three million fans for the first time.

The Padres' house was in order, but Moores' wasn't. In February, 2008, Moores' wife Rebecca filed for divorce. Normally, such an off-field development would not be the province of this book, but California is a community property state, and Mr. and Mrs. Moores' assets must be divided. The Padres are one of those assets. Certainly there is no good time for divorce, but the Padres found the improvement of the ballclub held hostage to the disillusion of the marriage. Since there is no good way to divide a ballclub down the middle, it was eventually decided that the club would have to be

---

PADRES PROSPECTUS

2008 record: 63-99; Fifth place in NL West

Pythagenport record: 67-95

Runs scored per game: 3.93 (16th in NL)

Runs allowed per game: 4.71 (9th in NL)

Team EqA: .257 (Tied for 10th in NL)

2008 Batters Age: 27.6 (4th-youngest in NL)

2008 Pitchers Age: 30.4 (3rd-oldest in NL)

Ballpark: Petco Park; Extreme pitcher's park; Park Factor of .903

2008: Petco makes the offense look worse and the pitching look better, but no ballpark yet devised would make either suitable for polite conversation.

2009: With an ace on the block and an owner in divorce court, even a weak division offers this squad no paths to glory.

---

sold. And at that point, for all intents and purposes, any possibility of the Padres becoming a competitive entity in 2009 ceased to be.

It was on this sort of consideration that the Padres frittered away the majority of the winter. Though the club's day-to-day leadership of CEO Sandy Alderson and GM Kevin Towers remained in place as Moores largely became an absentee owner, needed expenditures to upgrade or even maintain the club could not be made. In fact, the Padres were in cost-cutting mode despite a 2008 payroll of approximately $73.7 million, high by the franchise's historic standards but ranked only 11th in the National League and 19th in baseball. Khalil Greene, the 2002 first-round draft pick who once looked like he might be the best two-way shortstop in the history of a club that had failed to get the best out of Ozzie Smith or Garry Templeton, was dealt to the Padres for reliever Mark Worrell and a player to be named—which is to say, very little—in what was admittedly a salary dump. "In all candor," club executive vice president Paul DePodesta wrote on his blog, "part of this deal is the trade of Khalil's contract which was due to pay him $6.5 million in 2009. There are times when we have to make tough choices, and unfortunately finances do play a role." A widely publicized breakup between the club and all-time saves leader Trevor Hoffman, who had been with the club since 1993, was also attributed to the team's uncertain financial position. In both cases, the team parted with players whose sentimental value was perhaps greater than his actual value, Hoffman's powers having declined with age, and Greene having failed to top his rookie year in four years of trying. The moves nonetheless underscored the club's winter freeze-up. The only financially assertive move the club made at this time was to pick up outfielder Brian Giles' $9 million club option; given that Giles would have been due a $3 million buyout had the club declined, the actual cost of the decision, $6 million, was hardly a lavish investment.

Instead, the early part of the winter was dominated by the club's efforts to rid itself of Jake Peavy, the team's ace pitcher and, not coincidentally, its most expensive player. In December, 2007, Peavy had signed a three-year, $52 million deal extending his contract, which already covered 2008 and an $8 million club option for 2009, into 2012 or 2013, depending on whether a club option for the latter season was picked up. Flash forward less than a year, and a club that had been committed to having Peavy in Petco through at least his 32nd birthday was making every effort to unload him. Clearly something had changed, but the shift hadn't been engendered by the sore elbow that shelved the stopper for a month from mid-May to mid-June. Despite seemingly endless discussions with the Cubs and Braves and a quest for a dragnet search for a third trading partner to enable the deal, at this writing Peavy remains a Pad person.

Whatever the take from a Peavy trade might have been, the club desperately needs the influx of prospects and prodigies that such a deal might have provided. The Padres' downsizing would have been vastly aided by a productive farm system, but drafting and development has been problematic in recent years. Peavy was a find in the 15th round of the 1999 draft, and Chase Headley, a second-rounder in 2005, may yet establish himself as a quality left fielder or third baseman. Those two players aside, the bulk of the talent on the club—including Adrian Gonzalez, Kevin Kouzmanoff, Brian Giles, Heath Bell, and Chris Young—were acquired via astute trading by Towers.

Unfortunately, the drafts overseen by Towers and scouting director Chief Gayton (with the Padres since 2001) have been less successful. Towers has been GM since late 1995, so the first draft overseen by him came in 1996. During that time, the Padres have experienced some famous first-round busts, like 1998's ninth overall pick, Sean Burroughs, and 2004's first overall pick, Matt Bush—an occasion when Moores, trying to have it both ways, refused to pay the bonuses that attend such early selections in the draft. But other than Peavy, Headley, and perhaps Greene, the Padres have achieved little of note. A look through the draft rolls reveals 2000 second-rounder Xavier Nady, 2001 13th-round pick Jason Bartlett (traded as a minor leaguer to the Twins for outfielder Brian Buchanan in a move that Towers would probably like to have back), and a great many in-and-out players whose baseball cards will be considered four-for-a-dollar "commons" 150 years from now. It is an appallingly poor record. The team has also neglected to take part in the Latin gold rush, failing to mint even one everyday player from the Dominican Republic or Venezuela in franchise history. Recently, the team has reversed course, building a new complex in the Dominican in 2008, and went all in during the summer signing period, handing out seven-figure deals to three players, the most notable of which was a $2 million bonus to righty Adys Portillo, as well as Dominican outfielder Luis Domoromo ($1.25 million) and Venezuelan shortstop Alvaro Aristy ($1 million). However, these investments are still some time from paying off, if they ever do.

The combination cash freeze and barren farm leaves the club in the position of watching what was a 98 OPS+ offense stagnate—at best. Whereas last season catchers Josh Bard and Michael Barrett were never going to be confused with Yogi Berra and Johnny Bench, given health they had the potential to generate average to above-average offense at their position; not so with Nick Hundley. Opening Day second baseman Tadahito Iguchi isn't an impact player, but after a lost year at Triple-A, Matt Antonelli may not be a player at all. While Khalil Greene hadn't made any progress in years, Luis Rodriguez has no progress to make, being stretched as a utility infielder, let alone as a full-time shortstop. The outfielders remain of 2008 remain, but of the four only Headley has the possibility of real growth, while Brian Giles is in what will inevitably be his last year in a Padres uniform, and the productivity of the center field platoon may be a burn-after-seeing happenstance.

The bullpen is similarly stuck in a state of arrested development, with set-up man Heath Bell now promoted to closer. He should be able to perform decently in the role, but that leaves the remaining staff one pitcher thinner. As for the rotation, a version with Peavy present is obviously better than the alternative, but with or without him, the team will be counting on a recovery from Chris Young and untried hurlers such as Wade LeBlanc and Josh Banks to round out the rotation. If all goes well, the staff could hold its own, but as with the offense any bumps, injuries, or unexpected shortfall could provide the seeds of a freefall, even in so weak a division as the NL West.

In early January, a potential white knight emerged in the person of Diamondbacks CEO Jeff Moorad. The former player agent resigned his position with the Snakes, saying that he had reached an agreement in principle to purchase the Padres from Moores. However, although the deal seems to be moving forward on an expedited basis, the deal is not expected to be finalized until March. That means the club remains in stasis. "John and Becky [Moores] remain the primary owners of the Padres. I have no influence at all, nor will I have any influence on any of their personnel decisions," Moorad said when the deal was announced. Given that the season will be near to starting at the point that Moorad is picking out his wingback chair model—and that's if the deal goes through—it seems extraordinarily unlikely that the club will shake off its lethargy I time to retool for the coming season.

But even should Moorad take control of the club, a more intriguing question is this: even if 2009 is a loss, what of 2010? The farm system is hopeless and the free-agent class that follows this season is expected to be extremely thin, so even if Moorad deigns to up the budget, there will be few freely available players on whom to spend the dollars. Should Moorad retain the incumbent as his GM, Towers has made some excellent trades in his time, but he can't make enough good ones to overcome that kind of a handicap—can he?

HITTERS

Matt Antonelli — 2B
Bats: R   Throws: R   Height: 6' 0"   Weight: 203   Born: April 8, 1985   Age: 24

YEAR	TEAM	LVL	AGE	PA	R	2B	3B	HR	RBI	BB	SO	SB	CS	EqBRR	AVG	OBP	SLG	EqAVG	EqOBP	EqSLG	EqA	VORP	WARP	DEFENSE	
2006	EUG	A-	21	245	38	12	1	0	22	46	31	9	1	-0.4	.286	.426	.360	.209	.320	.262	.219	-22.6	-2.1	43-3B	-8
2007	LEL	A+	22	406	89	14	4	14	54	53	58	18	6	0.0	.314	.409	.499	.252	.333	.391	.254	3.3	-1.4	75-2B	-22
2007	SAN	AA	22	223	34	11	1	7	24	30	36	10	3	-2.0	.294	.395	.476	.269	.357	.440	.279	9.6	0.3	48-2B	-9
2008	POR	AAA	23	540	62	19	4	7	39	76	86	6	4	-0.8	.215	.335	.322	.190	.298	.281	.210	-31.0	-3.6	122-2B	-20
2008	SDN	MLB	23	65	6	2	0	1	3	5	11	0	0	0.8	.193	.292	.281	.193	.292	.281	.204	-2.4	-0.4	15-2B	-2
2009	SDN	MLB	24	536	58	23	2	9	45	63	107	8	3	0.3	.224	.321	.341	.234	.331	.372	.249	6.8	0.2	126-2B	-13

Breakout: 49%   Improve: 77%   Collapse: 8%   Attrition: 6%   Comparables: Adam Everett, Dan Cholowsky, Tim Hulett, Hiram Bocachica

After scoring 123 runs in 131 games across two levels, and also collecting 21 homers and 28 steals, Antonelli looked like one of the brightest prospects in the system coming into the year. Then he stumbled out of the gate at Triple-A after tinkering with his swing, and his game completely collapsed. The downward spiral was even worse than it appears; the horrible numbers in that slash line were only achieved with a surge in the final month. The tools are still there, but 2008 delayed his arrival for at least a year. The Padres are hoping he figures things out, because their alternatives at the keystone are few.

Josh Bard

C   Bats: S   Throws: R   Height: 6' 3"   Weight: 210   Born: March 30, 1978   Age: 31

YEAR	TEAM	LVL	AGE	PA	R	2B	3B	HR	RBI	BB	SO	SB	CS	EqBRR	AVG	OBP	SLG	EqAVG	EqOBP	EqSLG	EqA	VORP	WARP	DEFENSE	
2006	BOS	MLB	28	21	2	1	0	0	0	3	3	0	0	-0.2	.278	.381	.333	.222	.333	.278	.224	0.4	-0.3	6-C	-3
2006	SDN	MLB	28	263	28	19	0	9	40	27	39	1	0	-0.5	.338	.406	.537	.351	.420	.554	.329	29.1	3.3	55-C	2
2007	SDN	MLB	29	443	42	27	2	5	51	50	58	0	1	-4.2	.285	.364	.404	.295	.378	.422	.281	24.4	2.0	102-C	-8
2008	SDN	MLB	30	198	11	9	0	1	16	18	25	0	0	-0.3	.202	.279	.270	.202	.279	.275	.195	-7.5	-1.2	46-C	-6
2009	BOS	MLB	31	245	25	15	0	3	26	23	33	0	0	-1.2	.265	.336	.384	.257	.331	.387	.253	4.7	1.0	61-C	-3

Breakout: 17%   Improve: 34%   Collapse: 37%   Attrition: 26%   Comparables: Chad Kreuter, Jason Varitek, Alan Ashby, Brent Mayne

Bard's offensive explosion in '06 seems now more than ever like one of those flukes that takes hold of a part-time catcher now and then, though only cold-hearted Petco Park prevented him from putting together a similar encore in 2007, when he hit .330/.386/.456 on the road. Last year, though, it wasn't the park, it was *everything;* Bard suffered multiple injuries and never did get his bat on track, and since he's not very good controlling the running game, not much of value remained to him. The Padres waived him good-bye in October, and the Red Sox, who had dealt away a solid reliever in Cla Meredith just to be rid of Bard in the bundle two years ago, signed him to a one-year, non-guaranteed contract in January—his role to be determined pending the team's acquisition of a more qualified starter.

Michael Barrett

C   Bats: R   Throws: R   Height: 6' 3"   Weight: 210   Born: October 22, 1976   Age: 32

YEAR	TEAM	LVL	AGE	PA	R	2B	3B	HR	RBI	BB	SO	SB	CS	EqBRR	AVG	OBP	SLG	EqAVG	EqOBP	EqSLG	EqA	VORP	WARP	DEFENSE	
2006	CHN	MLB	29	418	54	25	3	16	53	33	41	0	1	-3.0	.307	.368	.517	.299	.362	.507	.293	30.5	2.0	96-C	-14
2007	CHN	MLB	30	231	23	9	0	9	29	17	36	2	2	-2.1	.256	.307	.427	.248	.303	.419	.246	4.8	0.4	53-C	-3
2007	SDN	MLB	30	136	6	8	0	0	12	2	21	0	0	-1.9	.226	.235	.286	.218	.228	.271	.159	-6.7	-1.1	32-C	-2
2008	SDN	MLB	31	107	9	3	0	2	9	9	16	0	0	0.5	.202	.274	.298	.202	.274	.298	.205	-3.2	-0.8	28-C	-6
2009	TOR	MLB	32	204	19	9	0	5	24	15	30	0	0	-1.0	.251	.312	.383	.253	.313	.392	.246	3.0	0.6	51-C	-4

Breakout: 30%   Improve: 58%   Collapse: 26%   Attrition: 37%   Comparables: Ray Fosse, Jim Essian, Joe Oliver, Scott Servais

Between a strained elbow early on and a fractured face and broken nose suffered when he was struck by his own foul ball in July, Barrett's season was a total loss. The Padres didn't exactly get what they expected when they traded for him; a concussion dropped him in August 2007, so in a season and a half all they got was 74 games and a .216/.252/.291 line. Despite three solid offensive years with the Cubs from 2004 to 2006 and his relative youth, it's not clear he has anything left. Like Bard, he's not much for throwing out baserunners, and Barrett is further handicapped by never having been named Mr. Personality, so if he hopes to play his bat will need to come alive. The Blue Jays signed him to a minor league contract, and if he can't cadge playing time from Rod Barajas, he may as well hang 'em up.

Kyle Blanks

1B   Bats: R   Throws: R   Height: 6' 6"   Weight: 281   Born: September 11, 1986   Age: 22

YEAR	TEAM	LVL	AGE	PA	R	2B	3B	HR	RBI	BB	SO	SB	CS	EqBRR	AVG	OBP	SLG	EqAVG	EqOBP	EqSLG	EqA	VORP	WARP	DEFENSE	
2006	FTW	A	19	359	41	20	0	10	52	36	79	2	0	-0.1	.292	.382	.455	.232	.301	.365	.234	-7.7	-1.9	51-1B	-9
2007	LEL	A+	20	531	94	31	4	24	100	44	98	11	2	0.0	.301	.380	.540	.241	.303	.425	.250	1.9	-0.4	59-1B	-3
2008	SAN	AA	21	565	75	23	5	20	107	51	90	5	4	-1.0	.325	.404	.514	.287	.352	.469	.280	30.0	2.5	123-1B	3
2009	SDN	MLB	22	613	71	28	2	19	76	54	132	5	3	-1.9	.259	.332	.424	.271	.341	.463	.273	17.2	2.4	143-1B	3

Breakout: 41%   Improve: 61%   Collapse: 13%   Attrition: 7%   Comparables: Cecil Fielder, Calvin Pickering, Joel Guzman, Daryle Ward

It's difficult for scouts to get past Fortress Blanks and his nearly 300 pounds; he is almost too big for his own good. However, he's also surprisingly nimble for his size, a good fielder, and he has hit everywhere he's ever played. Finishing in the Texas League's top five in each of the triple-slash categories, Blanks is more than just a one-dimensional slugger, but everything he does is overshadowed by that body, and despite the track record, he still doesn't have many believers.

Jody Gerut — CF

Bats: L Throws: L Height: 6' 0" Weight: 220 Born: September 18, 1977 Age: 31

YEAR	TEAM	LVL	AGE	PA	R	2B	3B	HR	RBI	BB	SO	SB	CS	EqBRR	AVG	OBP	SLG	EqAVG	EqOBP	EqSLG	EqA	VORP	WARP	DEFENSE	
2008	POR	AAA	30	123	22	9	2	5	18	13	11	4	1	1.3	.308	.382	.570	.245	.309	.445	.261	1.8	0.3	20-RF	0
2008	SDN	MLB	30	356	46	15	4	14	43	28	52	6	4	-1.6	.296	.351	.494	.320	.375	.546	.303	24.9	3.9	67-CF 9 7-RF	0
2009	SDN	MLB	31	455	68	27	4	15	63	40	63	8	5	0.3	.302	.365	.500	.315	.375	.545	.304	39.4	4.6	108-CF	2

Breakout: 25% Improve: 62% Collapse: 11% Attrition: 12%   Comparables: Irv Noren, Leon Wagner, Brian Jordan, Raul Ibañez

Gerut had quite the comeback season, and even though he'd been missing for two full years after knee surgery, he still put up overall rates that were the best of his career. He was helped some by Scott Hairston, who was used to protect him from those pesky left-handers, against whom Gerut has a lifetime line of .218/.299/.345. He was forced to abort his season after August 27 due to a strained finger ligament, so his fragility remains an issue. Still, he played a solid center field, and his production versus righties was not far off that of his pre-injury days, so if the Padres keep him in the platoon role he should continue to reward them.

Brian Giles — RF

Bats: L Throws: L Height: 5' 10" Weight: 205 Born: January 20, 1971 Age: 38

YEAR	TEAM	LVL	AGE	PA	R	2B	3B	HR	RBI	BB	SO	SB	CS	EqBRR	AVG	OBP	SLG	EqAVG	EqOBP	EqSLG	EqA	VORP	WARP	DEFENSE	
2006	SDN	MLB	35	717	87	37	1	14	83	104	60	9	4	-0.8	.263	.374	.397	.271	.384	.411	.282	16.6	3.3	155-RF	0
2007	SDN	MLB	36	552	72	27	2	13	51	64	61	4	6	1.1	.271	.361	.416	.286	.377	.449	.282	13.2	1.3	117-RF	-11
2008	SDN	MLB	37	653	81	40	4	12	63	87	52	2	2	0.8	.306	.398	.456	.332	.421	.503	.318	41.7	6.3	140-RF	5
2009	SDN	MLB	38	475	62	26	1	9	51	62	44	2	2	-1.3	.280	.376	.415	.292	.387	.452	.290	22.5	2.5	112-RF	-5

Breakout: 11% Improve: 31% Collapse: 29% Attrition: 25%   Comparables: Gene Woodling, Enos Slaughter, Mark Grace, Dixie Walker

Though the Padres picked up his $9 million option for 2009, Giles is in the last stages of a career in which he's shown himself to be a hitter superior to all but a very few in the history of the game—his carer OPS of 915 ranks 55th all-time. Last year represented a return to form after a couple of years that seemed to indicate a permanent state of decline. Given his age and contract status, personal distractions, likely regression, shrinking range afield, as well as the Pads' disarray, the team would be wise to get Giles fitted for a DH suit as soon as a suitable trading partner reveals itself—if he'll let them. He utilized his limited no-trade clause to block a trade to Boston last August.

Adrian Gonzalez — 1B

Bats: L Throws: L Height: 6' 2" Weight: 220 Born: May 8, 1982 Age: 27

YEAR	TEAM	LVL	AGE	PA	R	2B	3B	HR	RBI	BB	SO	SB	CS	EqBRR	AVG	OBP	SLG	EqAVG	EqOBP	EqSLG	EqA	VORP	WARP	DEFENSE	
2006	SDN	MLB	24	631	83	38	1	24	82	52	113	0	1	-3.9	.304	.362	.500	.313	.371	.518	.300	31.8	4.5	148-1B	5
2007	SDN	MLB	25	720	101	46	3	30	100	65	140	0	0	0.3	.282	.347	.502	.294	.363	.534	.300	41.3	4.6	161-1B	1
2008	SDN	MLB	26	700	103	32	1	36	119	74	142	0	0	-3.2	.279	.361	.510	.298	.378	.554	.311	45.8	5.2	157-1B	-1
2009	SDN	MLB	27	649	83	33	1	27	99	68	123	1	1	-2.4	.277	.356	.480	.289	.366	.524	.295	38.9	4.3	151-1B	2

Breakout: 6% Improve: 39% Collapse: 27% Attrition: 2%   Comparables: Willie Aikens, Mo Vaughn, Kent Hrbek, Justin Morneau

Amidst the wreckage that was the Padres' attack, Adrian Gonzalez stood like the Colossus of 10th Avenue. The opposition noticed, as he received 18 intentional walks, which was about as wide a berth as pitchers gave any NL hitter not named Pujols, who had 34; only Carlos Delgado and Prince Fielder, each with 19, had more than Gonzalez. In a typical Bud Black batting order, Gonazlez was followed by either Kouzmanoff or Headley, giving managers a strong case for bypassing the team's only full-service slugger. Gonzalez is at his peak now, and though he was an All-Star and first-time Gold Glove winner in 2008, the totality of his game is something short of unequivocal stardom. Lefties can shut him down (he hit .213/.287/.387 against them last year, albeit with 12 home runs), he's only moderately patient, and despite the fielding award he's not quite Keith Hernandez. He's the kind of player that could be mistaken for an MVP candidate in a big RBI year, but he's really in the next tier down. Signed for a total of $7.75 million this year and next, with a club option for $5.5 million in 2011, the one thing that *is* unequivocal is that he's a bargain.

Edgar Gonzalez   2B

Bats: R   Throws: R   Height: 6' 0"   Weight: 180   Born: June 14, 1978   Age: 31

YEAR	TEAM	LVL	AGE	PA	R	2B	3B	HR	RBI	BB	SO	SB	CS	EqBRR	AVG	OBP	SLG	EqAVG	EqOBP	EqSLG	EqA	VORP	WARP	DEFENSE		
2006	JUP	A+	28	83	10	8	0	2	10	6	18	1	3	-0.7	.293	.341	.480	.179	.217	.282	.163	-9.6	-0.9	17-2B	-2	
2006	CAR	AA	28	240	19	10	3	6	25	24	37	9	6	-3.9	.295	.371	.457	.186	.246	.295	.186	-21.4	-3.4	28-2B -15	14-SS	-1
2006	ABQ	AAA	28	170	29	10	1	5	36	20	32	1	1	0.9	.392	.473	.580	.270	.353	.426	.272	5.8	-0.8	35-2B	-14	
2007	MEM	AAA	29	519	64	34	3	8	53	50	69	15	4	0.0	.308	.377	.447	.245	.308	.360	.237	-9.1	-2.5	89-2B -21	21-3B	-2
2008	POR	AAA	30	97	10	1	0	4	12	12	12	0	4	-1.4	.293	.392	.451	.235	.320	.353	.229	-1.4	-0.2	8-RF 0	5-3B	0
2008	SDN	MLB	30	353	38	15	0	7	33	25	76	1	3	-2.9	.274	.329	.385	.289	.345	.412	.260	6.4	0.9	62-2B	1	
2009	SDN	MLB	31	189	18	8	1	3	18	16	40	1	1	-0.3	.240	.307	.357	.250	.316	.390	.243	4.5	0.0	48-2B	-4	

Breakout: 33%   Improve: 49%   Collapse: 32%   Attrition: 53%   Comparables: Chris Woodward, Randy Velarde, Wayne Terwilliger, Mark DeRosa

A 30th-round pick by the Rays in 2000, it took Gonzalez until he was a month shy of 30 years old to make it to the majors. In that time he's been Rule 5'd twice and released twice, moving through six organizations before finally finding one desperate enough to call him up. It just so happens that Edgar is Adrian's older brother, but Gonzalez's call-up wasn't solely the product of nepotism, as he had always swung a decent bat in the minors, but didn't quite have the bat for third or the glove for second. He filled in reasonably well enough for Tadahito Iguchi, though his bat cooled throughout the second half as he began to play sporadically around the field. Given his age, this probably represents the extent of his powers.

Khalil Greene   SS

Bats: R   Throws: R   Height: 5' 11"   Weight: 195   Born: October 21, 1979   Age: 29

YEAR	TEAM	LVL	AGE	PA	R	2B	3B	HR	RBI	BB	SO	SB	CS	EqBRR	AVG	OBP	SLG	EqAVG	EqOBP	EqSLG	EqA	VORP	WARP	DEFENSE	
2006	SDN	MLB	26	460	56	26	2	15	55	39	87	5	1	-0.0	.245	.320	.427	.255	.328	.449	.267	13.6	2.7	111-SS	3
2007	SDN	MLB	27	659	89	44	3	27	97	32	128	4	0	1.3	.254	.291	.468	.264	.302	.501	.270	25.4	3.9	153-SS	-1
2008	SDN	MLB	28	423	30	15	2	10	35	22	100	5	1	-1.4	.213	.260	.339	.219	.265	.358	.219	-7.1	-1.4	104-SS	-13
2009	SLN	MLB	29	517	58	27	2	18	69	38	100	5	2	-0.2	.253	.313	.434	.256	.315	.457	.262	20.6	1.8	122-SS	-6

Breakout: 32%   Improve: 65%   Collapse: 12%   Attrition: 9%   Comparables: Tony Batista, Alex Gonzalez, Dean Palmer, Gene Freese

The Pat Listach of his generation, Greene began retreating from the solid performance of his rookie year the very next season and hasn't stopped running since. Utterly defeated by Petco Park, he seems to have decided to try to overpower its distant fences with brute force. The result has been some decent home-run totals for a middle infielder, but too many strikeouts and a near-Dunstonian walk rate. That's when he's been healthy—durability is not one of his traits, and he exacerbated that last season by suffering a season-ending hand fracture in a brawl with an equipment chest. (He lost.) Greene was traded to St. Louis, where the park won't be anymore conducive to his lumberjack-it approach, but maybe the equipment chests are less combative.

Scott Hairston   OF

Bats: R   Throws: R   Height: 6' 0"   Weight: 200   Born: May 25, 1980   Age: 29

YEAR	TEAM	LVL	AGE	PA	R	2B	3B	HR	RBI	BB	SO	SB	CS	EqBRR	AVG	OBP	SLG	EqAVG	EqOBP	EqSLG	EqA	VORP	WARP	DEFENSE		
2006	TUC	AAA	26	440	83	22	1	26	81	52	78	3	0	0.7	.323	.407	.591	.259	.338	.485	.280	19.7	2.1	85-LF	0	
2007	ARI	MLB	27	199	21	13	1	3	16	19	37	2	0	-1.0	.222	.301	.358	.216	.299	.364	.235	-5.2	0.5	43-LF	7	
2007	SDN	MLB	27	95	16	5	1	8	20	7	18	0	0	-0.1	.287	.337	.644	.299	.347	.690	.325	9.6	0.7	20-LF	-3	
2008	SDN	MLB	28	362	42	18	3	17	31	28	84	3	1	-0.1	.248	.312	.479	.266	.330	.523	.284	14.5	3.0	42-CF 4	34-LF	6
2009	SDN	MLB	29	388	49	19	2	15	54	40	83	3	1	0.1	.254	.335	.455	.265	.344	.497	.282	18.5	2.6	93-LF	5	

Breakout: 18%   Improve: 49%   Collapse: 18%   Attrition: 18%   Comparables: Jeffrey Hammonds, Jason Lane, Wally Post, Greg Vaughn

Now several years removed from being a top prospect, Hairston has had two nigh-identical years in a row, although the underpinning changed—in 2007, he did all his damage against right-handed pitching and in the second half (really the last 26 games), whereas last year it was left-handers and the first half. Of course, his 2008 second half is missing a month because of the broken thumb suffered on August 27. Still, the overall consistency suggests that Hairston has finally identified the kind of player he's going to be, a solid defensive outfielder who has trouble getting on base but from time to time will sock the ball a long way. He and Gerut should have another year of productive platooning in them.

Chase Headley   LF/3B   Bats: S   Throws: R   Height: 6' 2"   Weight: 195   Born: May 9, 1984   Age: 25

YEAR	TEAM	LVL	AGE	PA	R	2B	3B	HR	RBI	BB	SO	SB	CS	EqBRR	AVG	OBP	SLG	EqAVG	EqOBP	EqSLG	EqA	VORP	WARP	DEFENSE	
2006	LEL	A+	22	571	79	33	0	12	73	74	96	4	5	-1.8	.291	.389	.434	.232	.312	.352	.234	-11.5	-1.9	124-3B -14	
2007	SAN	AA	23	522	82	38	5	20	78	74	114	1	0	-1.0	.330	.437	.580	.285	.377	.514	.302	44.3	3.6	118-3B -7	
2008	POR	AAA	24	295	49	24	1	13	40	31	65	0	0	-0.8	.305	.383	.556	.269	.339	.489	.279	14.7	0.5	56-LF -6	8-3B -2
2008	SDN	MLB	24	368	34	19	2	9	38	30	104	4	1	-0.5	.269	.337	.420	.288	.356	.458	.281	10.3	2.6	79-LF 7	6-3B 1
2009	SDN	MLB	25	491	60	25	2	16	61	52	116	4	2	-0.3	.258	.345	.436	.269	.354	.476	.282	19.7	2.5	116-LF 2	

Breakout: 21% Improve: 49% Collapse: 16% Attrition: 21%   Comparables: Carl Everett, Mike Young, Todd Benzinger, Mel Hall

San Diego's top prospect going into the season, Headley annihilated the ball in spring training but was optioned out anyway. A slow April delayed his return, but he soon caught fire. The Padres left him down as long as they could, giving the former third baseman time to adjust to outfield play, suppressing his service time, or both. When he finally did arrive in mid-June, Headley seemed lost. Selective in the minors, he went 88 PAs before drawing his first walk, but he did sock five homers. From then on, he was more representative of his apprenticeship, walking 30 times but hitting four times as many doubles as round-trippers. As much as the Padres need power, they need baserunners more, and it's the selective version of Headley that will help them spike their miserable team walk total of 2008.

Chad Huffman   OF   Bats: R   Throws: R   Height: 6' 1"   Weight: 217   Born: April 29, 1985   Age: 24

YEAR	TEAM	LVL	AGE	PA	R	2B	3B	HR	RBI	BB	SO	SB	CS	EqBRR	AVG	OBP	SLG	EqAVG	EqOBP	EqSLG	EqA	VORP	WARP	DEFENSE	
2006	EUG	A-	21	244	41	17	1	9	40	25	34	2	3	1.7	.343	.439	.576	.253	.322	.419	.258	5.5	-1.0	47-LF -10	
2007	LEL	A+	22	371	63	19	2	15	76	42	56	0	1	0.0	.307	.402	.522	.248	.323	.414	.255	3.9	0.6	82-LF 0	
2007	SAN	AA	22	197	28	4	1	7	28	22	44	0	0	0.4	.269	.362	.431	.249	.325	.405	.256	1.8	0.3	42-LF 0	
2008	SAN	AA	23	517	68	30	1	9	58	67	83	1	1	-3.0	.284	.383	.419	.248	.335	.373	.251	1.0	0.4	96-LF -3	6-RF 3
2009	SDN	MLB	24	550	62	27	2	14	60	55	118	3	2	-0.4	.251	.332	.400	.262	.341	.437	.268	11.2	1.8	129-LF -4	

Breakout: 37% Improve: 62% Collapse: 8% Attrition: 7%   Comparables: Carlos Quentin, Russ Morman, Glenn Braggs, Bronson Sardinha

Huffman hit 22 home runs in 2007, but experienced a power outage last year, which represents a huge problem for him, as his bat is the key to his future. Unathletic and limited to left field, Huffman is a polished hitter with a good approach who makes consistent hard contact, but if you want to be a corner outfielder in the big leagues, you have to be a power threat, not a doubles threat. This will be a make-or-break season for him.

Nick Hundley   C   Bats: R   Throws: R   Height: 6' 1"   Weight: 210   Born: September 8, 1983   Age: 25

YEAR	TEAM	LVL	AGE	PA	R	2B	3B	HR	RBI	BB	SO	SB	CS	EqBRR	AVG	OBP	SLG	EqAVG	EqOBP	EqSLG	EqA	VORP	WARP	DEFENSE
2006	FTW	A	22	248	29	19	0	8	44	25	45	1	1	-0.5	.274	.355	.474	.204	.269	.347	.215	-12.5	0.1	57-C 1
2006	LEL	A+	22	200	18	13	0	3	23	20	44	1	1	-0.8	.278	.357	.403	.220	.285	.330	.214	-8.8	-0.6	41-C -4
2007	SAN	AA	23	422	55	23	1	20	72	42	74	0	2	0.8	.247	.324	.475	.223	.290	.420	.242	-3.7	1.3	93-C 1
2008	POR	AAA	24	243	33	13	0	12	39	17	44	0	0	0.1	.232	.285	.451	.207	.255	.392	.220	-9.4	0.2	57-C 1
2008	SDN	MLB	24	216	21	7	1	5	24	11	52	0	0	0.4	.237	.278	.359	.249	.287	.386	.236	-1.4	0.5	54-C 1
2009	SDN	MLB	25	352	31	15	1	11	41	29	82	0	1	-0.5	.219	.287	.373	.229	.295	.407	.239	3.9	1.6	85-C 0

Breakout: 35% Improve: 59% Collapse: 19% Attrition: 23%   Comparables: Jeff Hearron, Giuseppe Chiaramonte, Joe Oliver, Chris Widger

Hundley looked like a solid catching prospect early in his career thanks to his power, his patience, and his solid defensive skills, but the questions about his ability to hit for average were being answered in an increasingly unsatisfactory manner as he made his weary way toward the upper levels, and his sisyphean struggles in the big leagues were, alas, predictable. His is a backup's skill set, but he's also very much all that the Padres have, so he'll likely be their starter in 2009.

Cedric Hunter — OF

Bats: L Throws: L Height: 6' 0" Weight: 185 Born: March 10, 1988 Age: 21

YEAR	TEAM	LVL	AGE	PA	R	2B	3B	HR	RBI	BB	SO	SB	CS	EqBRR	AVG	OBP	SLG	EqAVG	EqOBP	EqSLG	EqA	VORP	WARP	DEFENSE
2006	PDR	Rk	18	262	46	13	4	1	44	40	22	17	5	0.1	.371	.467	.484	.238	.302	.319	.223	-22.5	-1.7	23-CF -3
2007	FTW	A	19	549	53	20	2	7	58	47	78	8	9	-5.4	.282	.344	.373	.219	.271	.295	.196	-38.1	-2.8	108-CF -2
2008	LEL	A+	20	641	98	33	3	11	84	42	47	12	6	0.8	.318	.362	.442	.264	.305	.377	.238	-5.4	-0.3	125-CF -5
2009	SDN	MLB	21	620	59	30	2	8	53	44	79	7	4	0.7	.245	.300	.347	.255	.309	.379	.237	1.1	1.3	145-CF -1

Breakout: 49% Improve: 75% Collapse: 6% Attrition: 7% Comparables: Joe Orsulak, Dave Hansen, Will Smith, Don Mattingly

Hunter led the minor leagues with 186 hits last year, but there are grave doubts about his future that focus on his defense. Right now, he's a tick above average as a runner, capable as a center fielder. He's also only 21 years old, so if that body thickens up, or if he loses even half a step, he'll be sent to a corner where his value will plunge. Hunter is a slasher at the plate, whipping his bat through the zone and hitting nearly everything thrown at him, but the aggressiveness comes at the price of very few walks and only gap power. If he can't stay in center, he's a fourth outfielder.

Kevin Kouzmanoff — 3B

Bats: R Throws: R Height: 6' 1" Weight: 210 Born: July 25, 1981 Age: 27

YEAR	TEAM	LVL	AGE	PA	R	2B	3B	HR	RBI	BB	SO	SB	CS	EqBRR	AVG	OBP	SLG	EqAVG	EqOBP	EqSLG	EqA	VORP	WARP	DEFENSE	
2006	AKR	AA	24	276	46	19	1	15	55	23	34	2	3	-1.4	.389	.449	.660	.328	.380	.568	.313	32.5	3.4	54-3B 6	
2006	BUF	AAA	24	115	22	9	0	7	20	10	12	2	1	-0.2	.353	.409	.647	.330	.388	.621	.327	16.6	1.5	19-3B 1	6-1B 0
2006	CLE	MLB	24	61	4	2	0	3	11	5	12	0	0	-0.3	.214	.279	.411	.196	.274	.393	.228	-1.4	-0.2		
2007	SDN	MLB	25	534	57	30	2	18	74	32	94	1	0	-1.7	.275	.329	.457	.287	.341	.486	.281	20.8	2.7	125-3B 0	
2008	SDN	MLB	26	668	71	31	4	23	84	23	139	0	0	-0.3	.260	.299	.433	.274	.311	.465	.263	13.3	2.1	153-3B 0	
2009	SDN	MLB	27	639	76	34	2	24	92	43	117	2	1	-1.2	.275	.331	.465	.287	.341	.508	.282	36.0	3.8	149-3B -1	

Breakout: 24% Improve: 57% Collapse: 12% Attrition: 4% Comparables: Bob Oliver, Frank Thomas, Kelly Gruber, Tim Wallach

Until the very end of the season it was a solid year for Kouzmanoff. He's never going to be much in the on-base department due to his inability to believe himself when he whispers "take" as a pitch moves off the plate inside, but he has real power, and despite a defensive reputation that would seem to indicate he has hooves instead of hands, for the second year in a row he battled third base to a bloody draw. He slid off badly with the bat in September, and a couple of what proved to be minor injuries held him back; he should be good to go this spring. The park is never going to reward Kouzmanoff's approach, but he deserves to be counted among the team's limited assets.

Jose Lobaton — C

Bats: S Throws: R Height: 6' 0" Weight: 175 Born: October 21, 1984 Age: 24

YEAR	TEAM	LVL	AGE	PA	R	2B	3B	HR	RBI	BB	SO	SB	CS	EqBRR	AVG	OBP	SLG	EqAVG	EqOBP	EqSLG	EqA	VORP	WARP	DEFENSE
2006	FTW	A	21	77	15	3	1	1	11	12	12	0	0	-0.8	.279	.408	.410	.215	.316	.354	.236	-1.6	-0.2	19-C -3
2006	LEL	A+	21	145	12	7	0	4	15	20	42	0	2	-0.5	.213	.326	.369	.181	.271	.307	.202	-9.5	-1.3	33-C -8
2007	LEL	A+	22	357	50	15	3	10	47	41	79	0	0	0.0	.260	.346	.428	.208	.279	.341	.219	-15.8	-0.6	89-C -6
2008	SAN	AA	23	342	35	21	0	9	45	39	75	1	1	-3.4	.259	.338	.422	.228	.299	.364	.235	-8.0	0.8	80-C 2
2009	SDN	MLB	24	362	28	14	1	7	33	35	105	1	1	-0.6	.202	.281	.314	.211	.289	.343	.219	-5.0	0.8	87-C -1

Breakout: 24% Improve: 45% Collapse: 31% Attrition: 18% Comparables: Otto Gonzalez, Omar Fuentes, Vic Valencia, Al Pardo

While it doesn't exactly line up in our translation dictionary, we've been told that "Jose Lobaton" means the same thing as "Nick Hundley." They share the same profile—walks, a modicum of power, too many strikeouts to hit for average, and solid defense. Hundley has a few advantages, in that he's physically bigger and has a better health record; a variety of injuries have limited Lobaton to just 224 games over the last three years. Like Hundley, he's a backup, but he's unlikely to find the briefly cracked window of opportunity that Hundley did to prove the doubters wrong.

Drew Macias   OF   Bats: L   Throws: L   Height: 6' 3"   Weight: 175   Born: March 7, 1983   Age: 26

YEAR	TEAM	LVL	AGE	PA	R	2B	3B	HR	RBI	BB	SO	SB	CS	EqBRR	AVG	OBP	SLG	EqAVG	EqOBP	EqSLG	EqA	VORP	WARP	DEFENSE			
2006	MOB	AA	23	486	43	20	3	7	46	44	94	4	12	-4.0	.256	.334	.365	.235	.302	.355	.227	-12.3	-2.6	76-CF	-7	28-LF	-8
2007	SAN	AA	24	391	43	15	5	8	50	51	53	5	8	-3.6	.251	.355	.399	.216	.304	.341	.227	-12.7	-2.3	70-CF	-13	25-RF	-3
2007	POR	AAA	24	131	14	6	1	2	11	21	25	3	1	-1.5	.282	.397	.409	.252	.366	.369	.265	2.3	0.5	15-CF	3	11-RF	-2
2008	SAN	AA	25	603	92	27	4	11	66	83	81	18	6	0.8	.288	.393	.423	.224	.313	.334	.232	-16.6	-1.5	125-CF	-11		
2008	SDN	MLB	25	25	2	0	0	2	5	2	6	0	0	0.2	.200	.250	.500	.200	.250	.500	.257	0.3	0.0				
2009	SDN	MLB	26	524	49	22	2	7	43	52	110	8	4	0.4	.216	.298	.318	.225	.307	.347	.230	-7.6	-0.0	123-CF	-7		

Breakout: 30%   Improve: 49%   Collapse: 28%   Attrition: 9%   Comparables: Mike Hart, Terrmel Sledge, Terry Bradshaw, Rob Ducey

Credit Macias for disproving the skepticism inherent in being a 35th-round draft pick and making it to the majors, but even major league bench work may be a stretch due to his low batting averages. Macias's willingness to work a walk will be helpful, but when combined with averages that will need luck to overhaul .250 and no particular power potential, we're looking at fifth-outfielderhood as an aspiration.

Paul McAnulty   LF   Bats: L   Throws: R   Height: 5' 10"   Weight: 220   Born: February 24, 1981   Age: 28

YEAR	TEAM	LVL	AGE	PA	R	2B	3B	HR	RBI	BB	SO	SB	CS	EqBRR	AVG	OBP	SLG	EqAVG	EqOBP	EqSLG	EqA	VORP	WARP	DEFENSE			
2006	POR	AAA	25	552	76	34	5	19	79	62	79	1	2	0.0	.310	.388	.521	.273	.345	.471	.279	25.7	0.9	68-1B	-12	47-3B	-1
2007	POR	AAA	26	265	25	12	1	4	31	29	47	0	2	-4.3	.262	.347	.373	.219	.301	.321	.218	-10.4	-1.8	38-LF	-9	7-RF	1
2007	SDN	MLB	26	43	5	1	0	1	5	3	10	0	0	0.1	.200	.256	.300	.200	.256	.300	.189	-2.5	-0.3	4-RF	0		
2008	POR	AAA	27	225	34	14	1	13	50	35	38	0	0	-2.5	.343	.440	.646	.277	.369	.511	.300	16.1	1.4	48-LF	-2		
2008	SDN	MLB	27	164	9	7	1	3	13	26	41	0	0	1.4	.207	.341	.341	.215	.352	.370	.260	-0.4	0.5	30-LF	3	5-RF	-1
2009	BOS	MLB	28	404	47	26	2	13	53	44	83	1	1	-1.3	.251	.337	.441	.244	.331	.445	.269	3.9	1.1	96-LF	-3		

Breakout: 25%   Improve: 49%   Collapse: 20%   Attrition: 20%   Comparables: Phil Plantier, Randy Bass, Mike Maksudian, Tony Tarasco

McAnulty is a career .304/.395/.493 hitter in the minors who has made only brief and sporadic trips to the majors under difficult circumstances (the Padres always seem to have someone they like more). If he could just find enough playing time to get his wheels greased in the bigs, he could clearly provide the right team with 300 at-bats of good-ish platoon offense under the right circumstances. It's an uphill climb; he's limited to first base and the outfield corners defensively. He signed a minor league deal with the Red Sox over the winter, but their decision to re-sign Mark Kotsay probably eliminates any chance he had of breaking camp with the team.

Luis Rodriguez   INF   Bats: S   Throws: R   Height: 5' 9"   Weight: 190   Born: June 27, 1980   Age: 29

YEAR	TEAM	LVL	AGE	PA	R	2B	3B	HR	RBI	BB	SO	SB	CS	EqBRR	AVG	OBP	SLG	EqAVG	EqOBP	EqSLG	EqA	VORP	WARP	DEFENSE			
2006	MIN	MLB	26	132	11	4	0	2	6	14	16	0	0	0.5	.235	.315	.322	.219	.308	.298	.220	-3.1	-0.8	21-3B	1	8-2B	-5
2007	MIN	MLB	27	173	18	5	1	2	12	12	14	1	0	1.5	.219	.281	.303	.219	.285	.303	.211	-7.6	-0.5	26-3B	2	13-2B	-1
2008	POR	AAA	28	107	10	5	1	1	8	10	3	0	0	-1.2	.302	.368	.406	.245	.302	.337	.224	-3.0	0.1	25-SS	1		
2008	SDN	MLB	28	225	22	11	1	0	12	13	13	1	1	1.0	.287	.326	.351	.304	.339	.373	.253	4.9	-0.4	44-SS	-8	4-2B	-1
2009	SDN	MLB	29	223	20	8	1	1	18	18	19	1	1	-0.2	.255	.318	.325	.267	.327	.354	.239	4.0	0.1	56-SS	-4		

Breakout: 36%   Improve: 47%   Collapse: 29%   Attrition: 38%   Comparables: Marty Martinez, Brent Gates, Billy Moran, Walt Weiss

The Venezuelan took over shortstop for Khalil Greene when the latter was battered into submission by a hopped-up suitcase. Rodriguez isn't much of a shortstop, has all the home-run potential of Stephen Hawking, and is a "switch-hitter" who checks his bat against left-handed pitching. Unless the Padres have acquired another shortstop by the time you read this, Rodriguez will start. It's going to be a long year.

William Venable CF Bats: L Throws: L Height: 6' 2" Weight: 205 Born: October 29, 1982 Age: 26

YEAR	TEAM	LVL	AGE	PA	R	2B	3B	HR	RBI	BB	SO	SB	CS	EqBRR	AVG	OBP	SLG	EqAVG	EqOBP	EqSLG	EqA	VORP	WARP	DEFENSE
2006	FTW	A	23	541	86	34	5	11	91	55	81	18	5	3.2	.314	.389	.477	.217	.276	.334	.215	-26.9	-3.8	112-LF -15
2007	SAN	AA	24	572	66	19	3	8	68	38	84	21	2	1.5	.278	.337	.373	.238	.285	.323	.218	-26.2	-2.6	95-RF -3 18-CF -3
2008	POR	AAA	25	496	70	26	4	14	58	44	103	7	3	0.7	.292	.361	.464	.251	.313	.395	.246	-0.3	-0.9	98-CF -13
2008	SDN	MLB	25	124	16	4	2	2	10	13	21	1	1	0.0	.264	.339	.391	.282	.355	.436	.274	3.1	0.5	26-CF -1
2009	SDN	MLB	26	461	44	21	3	7	40	34	108	7	2	0.7	.226	.287	.340	.236	.295	.371	.230	-5.1	-0.3	109-CF -9

Breakout: 25% Improve: 46% Collapse: 27% Attrition: 16% Comparables: Jalal Leach, Ron Calloway, Pedro Swann, Kory DeHaan

The son of former big-leaguer Max, Will was better known for his basketball accomplishments as an amateur, where he was an all-Ivy League point guard at Princeton. He wasn't good enough for the NBA, but he was good enough for a shot in the minors, and it paid off for him when he reached the big leagues last year. He's a decent athlete with a nice feel for the game, but messing around on the boards kept him from playing a full season on the diamond until he was 23; for a player in his mid-20s, he could use some developing. There's a dusting of power, a smattering of speed, and the always-useful ability to play all three outfield positions, so he should find a spot on a bench somewhere, just like dad.

PITCHERS

Mike Adams Bats: R Throws: R Height: 6' 5" Weight: 190 Born: July 29, 1978 Age: 30

YEAR	TEAM	LVL	AGE	W	L	SV	G	GS	IP	H	BB	SO	HR	GB%	BABIP	STUFF	WHIP	ERA	DERA	EqH9	EqBB9	EqSO9	EqHR9	DEF	VORP	SN/WX
2006	NAS	AAA	27	1	1	2	15	0	16	17	8	18	2	48.9%	.349	-7	1.56	3.38	5.52	12.3	4.9	7.4	1.8	0	0.1	—
2006	NOR	AAA	27	0	0	0	13	0	14¹	13	7	12	0	42.9%	.317	-17	1.42	5.11	8.78	8.8	5.4	4.7	0.0	2	-4.7	—
2008	POR	AAA	29	3	1	0	12	0	14²	21	9	16	0	54.3%	.457	-7	2.04	5.51	4.85	15.9	6.2	6.9	0.0	-5	1.1	—
2008	SDN	MLB	29	2	3	0	54	0	65¹	49	19	74	7	44.6%	.273	21	1.04	2.48	3.20	6.8	2.2	9.0	1.0	4	22.2	1.88
2009	SDN	MLB	30	2	2	3	46	0	51	49	21	46	5	45.0%	.300	8	1.36	3.86	4.41	8.9	3.2	6.7	0.9	-0	7.1	0.59

Breakout: 17% Improve: 38% Collapse: 36% Attrition: 24% Comparables: Joe Beckwith, Doug Henry, Dave Baldwin, Ernie Johnson

Mike Adams had already been away from baseball for over a year thanks to surgery on his right knee, but he's already back in the same pickle jar, as shoulder surgery will keep him out until at least the All-Star break. There will be more reason to miss him this time; he finished second on the Padres in WXRL, striking out 10.2 per nine in the process, and he was particularly good against righties.

Cha Seung Baek Bats: R Throws: R Height: 6' 4" Weight: 220 Born: May 29, 1980 Age: 29

YEAR	TEAM	LVL	AGE	W	L	SV	G	GS	IP	H	BB	SO	HR	GB%	BABIP	STUFF	WHIP	ERA	DERA	EqH9	EqBB9	EqSO9	EqHR9	DEF	VORP	SN/WX
2006	TAC	AAA	26	12	4	0	24	24	147²	133	37	103	17	49.2%	.263	-13	1.15	3.00	5.07	8.9	2.4	4.2	1.5	8	8.3	—
2006	SEA	MLB	26	4	1	0	6	6	34¹	26	13	23	6	44.1%	.208	0	1.14	3.67	5.61	6.7	3.5	5.3	1.6	6	7.9	1.19
2007	TAC	AAA	27	1	1	0	6	6	31	33	10	18	1	40.6%	.314	-4	1.39	3.19	4.35	9.0	2.9	3.5	0.6	-1	4.3	—
2007	SEA	MLB	27	4	3	0	14	12	73¹	87	14	49	6	36.1%	.328	9	1.38	5.16	4.92	9.6	1.6	5.0	0.7	-5	3.5	0.89
2008	SEA	MLB	28	0	1	0	10	1	30	28	13	15	6	41.4%	.242	-23	1.37	5.40	5.76	7.9	3.6	3.9	1.8	1	1.0	0.19
2008	SDN	MLB	28	6	9	0	22	20	111	118	30	77	12	42.7%	.308	7	1.33	4.62	4.23	9.4	2.0	5.5	1.0	-9	6.9	2.58
2009	SDN	MLB	29	5	6	1	27	12	93²	98	28	63	11	43.0%	.290	6	1.34	4.39	5.00	9.7	2.4	5.1	1.1	-0	7.3	1.18

Breakout: 15% Improve: 51% Collapse: 22% Attrition: 33% Comparables: Roy Smith, Mike Scott, Jae Weong Seo, Shawn Boskie

Baek has four pitches that he throws consistently, though none are overpowering, a fact reflected in his strikeout rate. The Korean import wore out his welcome in Seattle and was dealt to the Padres in May, where he worked in the rotation and in relief. A fly-ball pitcher, Baek should have felt at home at pitcher-friendly Petco, but he was worse there (.298/.344/.449) than on the road (.239/.287/.410); given San Diego's above-average outfield crew, that seems more bad luck than trend. The Padres' front office seems to realize this, and Baek is one of the few pitchers penciled in for a rotation spot.

Josh Banks

Bats: R　Throws: R　Height: 6' 3"　Weight: 195　Born: July 18, 1982　Age: 26

YEAR	TEAM	LVL	AGE	W	L	SV	G	GS	IP	H	BB	SO	HR	GB%	BABIP	STUFF	WHIP	ERA	DERA	EqH9	EqBB9	EqSO9	EqHR9	DEF	VORP	SN/WX
2006	SYR	AAA	23	10	11	0	29	29	170¹	184	28	126	35	38.9%	.278	-48	1.25	5.19	8.10	11.0	1.9	4.2	2.9	10	-45.4	—
2007	SYR	AAA	24	12	10	0	27	27	169	192	24	101	22	46.8%	.307	-27	1.28	4.63	6.49	10.9	1.6	3.3	1.8	8	-16.0	—
2007	TOR	MLB	24	0	0	0	3	1	7¹	11	2	2	1	41.9%	.345	-30	1.77	7.40	4.91	13.5	2.5	2.5	1.2	-2	-1.0	-0.07
2008	SYR	AAA	25	0	2	0	3	3	16²	21	5	12	1	50.9%	.370	-11	1.56	7.01	7.31	11.8	2.8	3.9	0.6	-4	-3.0	—
2008	POR	AAA	25	1	1	0	9	4	30¹	39	8	22	3	42.5%	.356	-14	1.55	5.94	5.16	11.8	2.4	4.2	1.2	-6	1.5	—
2008	SDN	MLB	25	3	6	0	17	14	85¹	94	32	43	12	40.7%	.304	-13	1.48	4.75	5.27	9.8	2.9	4.1	1.3	2	6.0	1.36
2009	SDN	MLB	26	2	3	1	21	6	49¹	54	15	30	7	43.0%	.300	-0	1.40	4.74	5.40	10.3	2.3	4.6	1.3	-0	1.7	0.36

Breakout: 22%　Improve: 47%　Collapse: 22%　Attrition: 54%　　Comparables: Rod Nichols, Allen Ripley, Joe Slusarski, Brian Powell

Banks is an unusual pitcher. He seems overly attentive to his somewhat misnamed fastball even though he has a variety of other pitches, none of them very good. With his "heater" averaging around 87 mph, a cutter that doesn't cut enough to induce many ground balls, a poor strikeout-to-walk ratio, and far too many home runs allowed for a guy throwing half of his games in a park straight out of 1906, it's no surprise that his peripherals do not impress. San Diego was not fooled by his ERA, and has not guaranteed him a job for 2009.

Heath Bell

Bats: R　Throws: R　Height: 6' 3"　Weight: 225　Born: September 29, 1977　Age: 31

YEAR	TEAM	LVL	AGE	W	L	SV	G	GS	IP	H	BB	SO	HR	GB%	BABIP	STUFF	WHIP	ERA	DERA	EqH9	EqBB9	EqSO9	EqHR9	DEF	VORP	SN/WX
2006	NOR	AAA	28	3	3	12	30	0	35¹	27	8	56	1	54.5%	.356	28	1.00	1.28	2.43	8.6	2.4	10.0	0.5	-3	11.7	—
2006	NYN	MLB	28	0	0	0	22	0	37	51	11	35	6	53.3%	.398	2	1.68	5.11	4.89	13.1	2.6	8.2	1.3	-4	-0.6	0.30
2007	SDN	MLB	29	6	4	2	81	0	93²	60	30	102	3	60.5%	.259	37	0.96	2.02	3.04	5.9	2.6	9.1	0.3	9	39.4	5.69
2008	SDN	MLB	30	6	6	0	74	0	78	66	28	71	5	47.3%	.288	13	1.21	3.58	4.19	7.6	2.8	7.2	0.6	4	16.6	3.28
2009	SDN	MLB	31	3	3	4	54	0	61¹	56	22	56	4	50.0%	.300	12	1.27	3.24	3.75	8.5	2.8	6.9	0.7	-0	13.3	1.12

Breakout: 10%　Improve: 26%　Collapse: 46%　Attrition: 12%　　Comparables: Greg McMichael, Mike Timlin, Jay Howell, Fred Gladding

Bell came over from the Mets as a throw-in in a minor trade and ended up being a beast of a reliever for the Pads in 2007. The next year did not start the same way—Bell suffered from a dead arm that hindered his velocity and kept him from racking up strikeouts. Once he got those ticks back on his fastball, his strikeout rate rebounded, though he never regained his missing grounders. With Trevor Hoffman a casualty of age and marital strife, Bell was branded with the Scarlet C, which means the Padres' already lacking bullpen needs to find new help for the middle innings.

Matthew Buschmann

Bats: R　Throws: R　Height: 6' 3"　Weight: 209　Born: February 13, 1984　Age: 25

YEAR	TEAM	LVL	AGE	W	L	SV	G	GS	IP	H	BB	SO	HR	GB%	BABIP	STUFF	WHIP	ERA	DERA	EqH9	EqBB9	EqSO9	EqHR9	DEF	VORP	SN/WX
2006	LEL	A+	22	1	0	0	2	2	12¹	9	4	5	0	55.9%	.259	-21	1.07	3.72	7.71	6.9	3.9	0.8	0.8	2	-2.7	—
2006	EUG	A-	22	3	4	0	15	10	60¹	54	11	63	5	47.0%	.316	-25	1.08	3.14	7.92	13.3	3.2	4.5	2.7	2	-12.9	—
2007	LEL	A+	23	12	6	0	28	25	149¹	153	26	115	9	53.7%	.325	-10	1.20	2.89	4.88	11.1	2.3	3.5	1.1	-6	10.8	—
2008	SAN	AA	24	10	6	0	27	27	148	137	58	118	13	44.4%	.298	-19	1.32	2.98	5.83	10.0	4.2	4.5	1.4	7	-3.4	—
2009	SDN	MLB	25	5	9	0	29	18	114	132	51	72	15	46.0%	.310	1	1.60	5.49	6.25	10.7	3.5	4.7	1.2	-0	-7.3	0.00

Breakout: 5%　Improve: 27%　Collapse: 34%　Attrition: 16%　　Comparables: Matt Maysey, Jim Rasmussen, Rett Johnson, Paul Wagner

While Buschmann was among the Texas League leaders in ERA and strikeouts, scouts don't hold out much hope for him, and at times seem frankly baffled as to how he's found so much success with his average sinker/slider combination. It's certainly not his merely average command, but some aspect of a deceptive delivery that makes his release hand hard to pick up. Triple-A Portland is a tough place to pitch, and many think he'll meet his match there.

Cesar Carrillo

Bats: R　Throws: R　Height: 6' 3"　Weight: 175　Born: April 29, 1984　Age: 25

YEAR	TEAM	LVL	AGE	W	L	SV	G	GS	IP	H	BB	SO	HR	GB%	BABIP	STUFF	WHIP	ERA	DERA	EqH9	EqBB9	EqSO9	EqHR9	DEF	VORP	SN/WX
2006	MOB	AA	22	1	3	0	9	9	50²	45	15	43	5	57.8%	.286	-2	1.20	3.05	6.07	10.2	3.1	4.7	1.8	1	-2.4	—
2007	POR	AAA	23	0	2	0	5	5	15²	22	14	8	2	51.7%	.364	-22	2.29	8.60	9.00	12.6	8.4	3.0	1.2	-2	-5.7	—
2008	LEL	A+	24	3	5	0	15	14	57¹	69	33	32	6	54.1%	.328	-43	1.78	5.97	8.60	12.7	6.7	2.1	1.9	-6	-17.4	—
2009	SDN	MLB	25	2	6	0	23	11	69	88	51	32	11	48.0%	.320	-20	2.02	7.20	8.17	11.9	5.9	3.5	1.5	-0	-19.2	-1.51

Breakout: 17%　Improve: 53%　Collapse: 22%　Attrition: 28%　　Comparables: Troy McKay, Rod Boxberger, Nick Stocks, Ben Christensen

The club's first-round pick in 2005 and once the top prospect in the system, Carrillo is now the guy you point to every time someone tells you that Tommy John surgery isn't that big a deal any more. Once on the brink of the majors, Carrillo instead spent 2008 getting smacked around by California League hitters for a .301 batting average while walking more batters than he was able to strike out. If there's any silver lining here, it's that he was beginning to regain his low- to mid-90s velocity in the Arizona Fall League, but everything else is still a long way off.

Stevenson Garrison

Bats: S   Throws: L   Height: 6' 1"   Weight: 185   Born: September 12, 1986   Age: 22

YEAR	TEAM	LVL	AGE	W	L	SV	G	GS	IP	H	BB	SO	HR	GB%	BABIP	STUFF	WHIP	ERA	DERA	EqH9	EqBB9	EqSO9	EqHR9	DEF	VORP	SN/WX
2006	WVA	A	19	7	6	0	17	16	88	86	22	77	10	43.3%	.300	-17	1.23	3.48	7.22	13.1	3.7	3.6	3.0	2	-13.7	—
2007	BRV	A+	20	8	4	0	20	20	104²	105	28	74	6	47.1%	.296	7	1.27	3.44	7.54	11.6	3.4	3.4	1.3	-2	-20.8	—
2007	LEL	A+	20	2	3	0	7	7	42	32	6	28	2	44.6%	.270	21	0.90	2.79	4.57	7.2	1.7	2.6	0.9	-1	4.7	—
2008	SAN	AA	21	7	7	0	24	24	129²	123	37	108	13	43.5%	.295	2	1.23	3.82	6.88	9.9	3.0	4.6	1.6	13	-17.3	—
2009	SDN	MLB	22	7	10	0	25	25	142¹	159	55	92	21	44.0%	.300	11	1.50	5.21	5.90	10.4	3.0	4.9	1.3	-1	-3.7	0.73

Breakout: 19%   Improve: 55%   Collapse: 13%   Attrition: 10%   Comparables: Abe Alvarez, Jimmy Key, Andrew Lorraine, Darrell May

The Padres are loaded with finesse pitchers at the upper levels—good finesse pitchers mind you, but ones for whom it is difficult to project anything more than some back-end rotation possibilities. Garrison was probably the best of the group, with spotless command of a four-pitch mix. He threw a seven-inning no-hitter early in the 2008 season, but things began going slowly downhill from there, and he eventually required shoulder surgery. Garrison cannot afford to lose much more velocity, and we won't know if he did until some time around midseason.

Josh Geer

Bats: R   Throws: R   Height: 6' 3"   Weight: 190   Born: June 2, 1983   Age: 26

YEAR	TEAM	LVL	AGE	W	L	SV	G	GS	IP	H	BB	SO	HR	GB%	BABIP	STUFF	WHIP	ERA	DERA	EqH9	EqBB9	EqSO9	EqHR9	DEF	VORP	SN/WX
2006	FIW	A	23	6	2	0	12	11	72¹	72	13	46	3	51.9%	.307	-26	1.18	3.12	5.98	12.6	3.1	2.2	1.5	-5	-2.6	—
2006	LEL	A+	23	7	4	0	15	15	89²	116	16	56	7	50.4%	.354	-33	1.48	4.94	7.99	14.4	2.5	2.5	1.6	-5	-21.2	—
2007	SAN	AA	24	16	6	0	26	26	171¹	163	27	102	9	48.9%	.286	-6	1.11	3.20	5.79	10.3	1.9	3.1	0.9	8	-3.4	—
2008	POR	AAA	25	8	9	0	28	27	166²	187	45	107	22	43.7%	.313	-18	1.39	4.54	5.98	10.3	2.6	3.7	1.4	0	-6.8	—
2008	SDN	MLB	25	2	1	0	5	5	27	29	9	16	2	36.6%	.300	4	1.41	2.67	4.00	9.3	2.7	4.7	0.7	4	8.8	1.14
2009	SDN	MLB	26	6	9	0	36	23	127¹	150	40	71	16	45.0%	.310	1	1.49	5.10	5.81	11.0	2.5	4.2	1.2	-0	-2.0	0.63

Breakout: 9%   Improve: 42%   Collapse: 26%   Attrition: 15%   Comparables: Brian Powell, Scott Klingenbeck, Brian Meadows, Jeff Fischer

Geer got to the big leagues with the kind of stuff that leaves many players undrafted. His sinker parks in the mid- to upper 80s and his slider is fringy, but he does have a plus changeup and excellent command. Call it smarts or pitchability or confidence or whatever you like, but Geer has that little extra something that allows him to succeed at a limited level. He'll likely begin the year in the Padres rotation, and while there's no star here to wish upon, he just might stick around for a while.

Carlos Guevara

Bats: R   Throws: R   Height: 5' 11"   Weight: 190   Born: March 18, 1982   Age: 27

YEAR	TEAM	LVL	AGE	W	L	SV	G	GS	IP	H	BB	SO	HR	GB%	BABIP	STUFF	WHIP	ERA	DERA	EqH9	EqBB9	EqSO9	EqHR9	DEF	VORP	SN/WX
2006	CHT	AA	24	2	3	1	49	0	77²	74	27	89	6	47.5%	.335	-14	1.31	3.73	5.43	11.1	3.5	6.7	1.4	-3	1.3	—
2007	CHT	AA	25	1	2	16	51	0	62	51	23	87	4	41.4%	.348	7	1.19	2.32	2.68	9.6	3.6	8.2	1.1	-5	18.5	—
2008	POR	AAA	26	0	3	2	16	0	18	16	9	20	1	30.0%	.313	-8	1.39	6.50	6.50	8.5	4.5	6.5	0.5	-2	-1.8	—
2008	SDN	MLB	26	1	0	0	10	0	12¹	13	9	11	2	35.0%	.306	-7	1.78	5.85	6.23	9.0	5.5	6.9	1.4	-1	-1.7	-0.10
2009	SDN	MLB	27	2	2	2	29	1	32¹	30	16	32	4	39.0%	.290	10	1.40	4.06	4.61	8.5	3.9	7.4	1.0	-0	4.4	0.36

Breakout: 32%   Improve: 56%   Collapse: 30%   Attrition: 48%   Comparables: Floyd Chiffer, Tim Mauser, Dan Miceli, Bob Moorhead

While he's hardly the next Fernando Valenzuela, Guevara throws a screwball, and that's cool enough for us. A Rule 5 pick from the Reds last winter, the Padres were able to hide Guevara on the roster early in the season due to a groin strain, and they finally got permission from the Reds to keep him in exchange for "future considerations." Guevara's scroogie is actually a plus offering that makes hitters look silly, but it's also his only big-league caliber pitch, leaving him firmly in the one-trick Carlos category.

Justin Hampson

| | | | | Bats: L | | Throws: L | | Height: 6′ 1″ | | Weight: 200 | | Born: May 24, 1980 | | | Age: 29 |

YEAR	TEAM	LVL	AGE	W	L	SV	G	GS	IP	H	BB	SO	HR	GB%	BABIP	STUFF	WHIP	ERA	DERA	EqH9	EqBB9	EqSO9	EqHR9	DEF	VORP	SN/WX
2006	CSP	AAA	26	8	4	0	31	13	121¹	121	39	95	10	44.9%	.305	-8	1.32	3.34	5.28	9.3	3.1	4.7	1.0	8	4.1	—
2006	COL	MLB	26	1	0	0	5	1	12	19	5	9	3	31.1%	.381	-10	2.00	7.50	4.38	13.1	2.9	5.8	2.2	-3	-1.4	-0.22
2007	POR	AAA	27	1	1	0	10	0	12²	12	8	12	3	34.2%	.273	-15	1.57	3.54	5.54	8.3	5.5	5.5	2.8	1	0.1	—
2007	SDN	MLB	27	2	3	0	39	0	53¹	48	16	34	1	48.2%	.288	10	1.20	2.70	2.60	8.1	2.4	5.5	0.2	-2	17.2	0.84
2008	POR	AAA	28	1	2	0	10	0	10¹	11	3	16	1	37.0%	.385	10	1.36	3.50	4.35	10.5	2.6	9.6	0.9	-1	1.4	—
2008	SDN	MLB	28	2	1	0	35	0	30²	31	10	19	1	42.3%	.330	-1	1.34	2.93	2.48	9.3	2.5	5.3	0.3	-3	7.8	0.43
2009	SDN	MLB	29	2	2	2	40	0	36¹	35	13	27	3	43.0%	.290	2	1.32	3.63	4.15	9.0	2.9	5.6	0.9	-0	6.8	0.52

Breakout: 14%　Improve: 29%　Collapse: 42%　Attrition: 29%　　　Comparables: Paul Gibson, Al Aber, Mike Stanton, Ted Davidson

Hampson was a starter in the Rockies' organization who has pitched in relief since making it to the majors. He's an extreme fly-ball pitcher, a style that works well in the pitcher-friendly NL West. The Padres couldn't take advantage of his talents until June thanks to left-shoulder tendonitis; that's a shame, given he's a southpaw who can get right-handers out. With Adams now recovering from surgery and Bell the new closer, Hampson may see more work.

Dirk Hayhurst

| | | | | Bats: L | | Throws: R | | Height: 6′ 3″ | | Weight: 200 | | Born: March 24, 1981 | | | Age: 28 |

YEAR	TEAM	LVL	AGE	W	L	SV	G	GS	IP	H	BB	SO	HR	GB%	BABIP	STUFF	WHIP	ERA	DERA	EqH9	EqBB9	EqSO9	EqHR9	DEF	VORP	SN/WX
2006	LEL	A+	25	2	7	0	12	11	59¹	61	20	51	3	55.7%	.330	-20	1.37	3.96	7.00	11.7	4.0	3.8	1.2	-2	-8.4	—
2006	MOB	AA	25	3	5	0	12	10	52²	58	18	49	6	47.5%	.342	-24	1.46	4.83	7.28	13.0	3.6	5.4	2.1	-6	-8.8	—
2007	LEL	A+	26	0	1	0	13	0	20	23	6	16	0	60.9%	.359	-23	1.45	1.80	4.50	12.5	3.5	3.5	0.5	-5	2.2	—
2007	SAN	AA	26	4	1	2	32	1	59¹	54	9	55	6	49.2%	.282	-15	1.06	3.19	5.98	10.2	1.8	5.3	1.5	3	-2.4	—
2008	POR	AAA	27	2	3	2	46	2	84	84	28	98	7	40.2%	.352	5	1.33	3.75	3.90	9.9	3.1	7.4	1.0	-6	15.2	—
2008	SDN	MLB	27	0	2	0	10	3	16²	27	10	14	2	46.7%	.431	-12	2.22	9.70	7.31	15.2	5.1	6.8	1.1	-5	-8.1	-0.54
2009	TOR	MLB	28	3	4	1	26	5	55¹	67	24	44	9	44.0%	.330	3	1.64	5.50	5.51	10.7	3.5	6.3	1.4	1	0.7	0.25

Breakout: 32%　Improve: 68%　Collapse: 9%　Attrition: 15%　　　Comparables: Bret Prinz, Ken Crew, Aaron Looper, Brian Drahman

In his sixth minor league season, Hayhurst finally made it to The Show. He's a strike-thrower who mixes up four pitches to keep hitters guessing, and he receives high grades from coaches and teammates for his baseball intelligence and work ethic. Now entering the free-range portion of his career, he signed with Toronto in the offseason as a bullpen insurance policy.

Clayton Hensley

| | | | | Bats: R | | Throws: R | | Height: 5′ 11″ | | Weight: 190 | | Born: August 31, 1979 | | | Age: 29 |

YEAR	TEAM	LVL	AGE	W	L	SV	G	GS	IP	H	BB	SO	HR	GB%	BABIP	STUFF	WHIP	ERA	DERA	EqH9	EqBB9	EqSO9	EqHR9	DEF	VORP	SN/WX
2006	SDN	MLB	26	11	12	0	37	29	187	174	76	122	15	55.5%	.285	10	1.34	3.71	4.25	8.9	3.3	5.6	0.7	7	40.3	5.39
2007	POR	AAA	27	2	7	0	13	13	71	102	34	50	10	53.3%	.374	-26	1.92	6.72	7.23	12.7	4.4	4.3	1.6	-14	-12.6	—
2007	SDN	MLB	27	2	3	0	13	9	50	62	32	30	5	50.3%	.341	-8	1.88	6.84	6.02	11.1	5.1	5.1	0.9	-5	-8.5	-0.10
2008	POR	AAA	28	1	1	0	16	10	48	46	16	34	7	43.4%	.271	-21	1.29	3.94	6.17	8.9	3.1	4.0	1.5	6	-3.0	—
2008	SDN	MLB	28	1	2	0	32	1	39	36	25	26	2	51.6%	.296	-8	1.56	5.31	6.10	8.2	4.9	5.4	0.5	-1	-3.7	0.02
2009	HOU	MLB	29	4	6	1	34	10	81	90	38	54	9	49.1%	.308	-1	1.58	5.25	5.59	10.0	3.7	5.1	1.0	0	0.5	0.40

Breakout: 14%　Improve: 34%　Collapse: 36%　Attrition: 34%　　　Comparables: Doyle Lade, Rodney Myers, Ray Semproch, Kevin Blankenship

Though he was a promising tail-end starter a few years ago, Hensley's career has gone downhill over the past two seasons. The right-hander has been unable to find the plate pitching in the majors while failing to put up numbers worthy of notice at Portland, and a right shoulder strain before the year began didn't help his cause either. His fastball/slider combination helps him induce grounders and keep the ball in the park, though not nearly enough to counter all the free passes. He's no longer in the Padres' plans; he was non-tendered and signed a minor league deal with the Astros.

Trevor Hoffman

Bats: R   Throws: R   Height: 6' 0"   Weight: 215   Born: October 13, 1967   Age: 41

YEAR	TEAM	LVL	AGE	W	L	SV	G	GS	IP	H	BB	SO	HR	GB%	BABIP	STUFF	WHIP	ERA	DERA	EqH9	EqBB9	EqSO9	EqHR9	DEF	VORP	SN/WX
2006	SDN	MLB	38	0	2	46	65	0	63	48	13	50	6	33.2%	.236	9	0.97	2.14	3.61	7.1	1.6	6.5	0.7	8	25.6	6.05
2007	SDN	MLB	39	4	5	42	61	0	57^1	49	15	44	2	33.0%	.278	14	1.12	2.98	2.95	7.4	2.0	6.4	0.3	-3	15.3	2.88
2008	SDN	MLB	40	3	6	30	48	0	45^1	38	9	46	8	38.9%	.259	7	1.04	3.77	4.40	7.4	1.6	8.0	1.6	2	8.2	1.84
2009	MIL	MLB	41	3	3	19	38	0	43	40	10	36	5	38.0%	.280	6	1.16	3.41	3.65	8.3	1.8	6.3	1.1	0	9.8	1.50

Breakout: 7%   Improve: 35%   Collapse: 26%   Attrition: 24%   Comparables: Doug Jones, Dennis Eckersley, Ellis Kinder, Art Fowler

Hoffman followed his meltdown during the last two months of 2007 with his worst single-season ERA since 1995, but while he's clearly on the downside of his Hall of Fame career, he's far from done—in fact, the veteran closer recovered from a shaky April to record his best K/BB rates in years. In 2009, Hoffman will don a uniform other than that of the Padres for the first time since his brief turn as a Marlin in 1993, as the Brewers inked him to a one-year deal in an attempt to halt their closer carousel. Hoffman likely will fulfill that modest goal on reputation alone, but a BABIP correction is coming, and his fly-ball tendencies, which hampered him even in Petco, will hurt him even more in Miller Park, the site of one of the two blown saves which ended the Padres' playoff hopes in '07. Still, as long as Hoffman can maintain adequate separation between his fastball and changeup, and continue to limit the number of baserunners allowed through his own largesse, he'll succeed in reaching his stated goal of 600 saves.

Will Inman

Bats: R   Throws: R   Height: 6' 0"   Weight: 200   Born: February 6, 1987   Age: 22

YEAR	TEAM	LVL	AGE	W	L	SV	G	GS	IP	H	BB	SO	HR	GB%	BABIP	STUFF	WHIP	ERA	DERA	EqH9	EqBB9	EqSO9	EqHR9	DEF	VORP	SN/WX
2006	WVA	A	19	10	2	0	23	20	110	75	24	134	3	42.6%	.279	30	0.90	1.72	4.08	9.4	3.2	5.6	1.0	3	16.4	—
2007	BRV	A+	20	4	3	0	13	13	78^2	56	23	98	4	42.6%	.287	43	1.00	1.72	3.75	9.4	3.7	7.2	1.3	2	14.3	—
2007	HUN	AA	20	1	5	0	8	8	39^2	38	16	42	7	53.6%	.316	12	1.36	5.44	7.18	11.4	4.0	5.9	2.7	0	-6.4	—
2007	SAN	AA	20	3	3	0	7	7	41	33	19	40	6	26.1%	.267	20	1.27	4.17	5.84	9.5	4.9	5.8	2.2	-2	-1.0	—
2008	SAN	AA	21	9	8	0	28	28	135^1	119	71	140	10	36.6%	.304	4	1.40	3.53	6.98	9.5	5.3	5.9	1.2	9	-19.4	—
2009	SDN	MLB	22	6	9	0	23	23	129^1	126	76	115	17	40.0%	.300	17	1.56	5.17	5.85	9.1	4.6	6.7	1.2	-0	-2.6	0.74

Breakout: 12%   Improve: 46%   Collapse: 16%   Attrition: 14%   Comparables: Pat Hentgen, Paul Abbott, Lance McCullers, Paul Byrd

While Inman has a career minor league ERA of 2.82 and more than 10 strikeouts per nine innings, he's a deceptive pitcher, not an overpowering one. He's a little undersized, has a very good curveball with no more than average velocity, and command issues, but his unique motion allows all of his middling stuff to play up a bit. He could become a fifth starter if he can just learn to throw more strikes, but you've heard that about a hundred guys in this book already.

Wade LeBlanc

Bats: L   Throws: L   Height: 6' 3"   Weight: 202   Born: August 7, 1904   Age: 24

YEAR	TEAM	LVL	AGE	W	L	SV	G	GS	IP	H	BB	SO	HR	GB%	BADIP	STUFF	WHIP	ERA	DERA	EqH9	EqBB9	EqSO9	EqHR9	DEF	VORP	SN/WX
2006	FTW	A	21	4	1	0	7	7	32^1	31	10	27	1	46.8%	.303	-5	1.28	2.24	4.50	12.2	4.5	3.2	1.3	0	3.4	—
2006	EUG	A-	21	1	0	0	7	3	21^1	19	6	20	0	39.0%	.339	-9	1.18	4.27	9.35	12.5	4.7	4.2	0.5	2	-7.2	—
2007	LEL	A+	22	6	5	0	16	16	92	72	17	90	5	41.8%	.275	11	0.97	2.64	5.48	8.2	2.3	4.7	1.0	8	1.2	—
2007	SAN	AA	22	7	3	0	12	11	57^1	48	19	55	8	45.9%	.254	-5	1.17	3.46	6.79	9.9	2.7	5.7	2.1	9	-6.8	—
2008	POR	AAA	23	11	9	0	26	25	138^2	136	42	139	21	37.3%	.315	-6	1.28	5.32	6.58	9.5	2.8	6.2	1.6	2	-14.4	—
2008	SDN	MLB	23	1	3	0	5	4	21^1	29	15	14	7	44.0%	.328	-16	2.06	8.03	7.40	12.6	5.7	5.2	3.0	-2	-6.0	-0.11
2009	SDN	MLB	24	6	8	1	38	20	122^1	123	46	96	15	40.0%	.290	10	1.38	4.52	5.13	9.4	3.0	5.9	1.1	-0	7.3	1.47

Breakout: 54%   Improve: 83%   Collapse: 8%   Attrition: 22%   Comparables: Garrett Olson, Matthew Maloney, Frank Viola, Chris Haney

LeBlanc has one great pitch, and it's a doozy. His changeup is nearly perfect, thrown with the identical arm action of his fastball, but featuring a sizeable velocity difference and late drop. But will it be enough? His fastball's a high beeline of a pitch, always up and maxing out in the high 80s, his curveball doesn't really, and he needs to be more precise with those two pitches than he's currently able in order to set up the monster. Big-league hitters were not fooled the first time around, but he'll still get a shot at one of the last rotation slots this spring.

Cla Meredith

| | | | | | | | | | | | | | | | | | Bats: R | Throws: R | Height: 6' 0" | Weight: 180 | Born: June 4, 1983 | | Age: 26 |

YEAR	TEAM	LVL	AGE	W	L	SV	G	GS	IP	H	BB	SO	HR	GB%	BABIP	STUFF	WHIP	ERA	DERA	EqH9	EqBB9	EqSO9	EqHR9	DEF	VORP	SN/WX
2006	PAW	AAA	23	0	0	0	8	0	13	16	5	14	1	68.3%	.395	-9	1.62	5.54	5.84	13.1	4.4	6.6	1.5	-3	-0.3	—
2006	SDN	MLB	23	5	1	0	45	0	50²	30	6	37	3	70.0%	.199	17	0.71	1.07	3.28	5.7	0.9	6.2	0.5	11	27.8	3.70
2007	SDN	MLB	24	5	6	0	80	0	79²	94	17	59	6	72.2%	.348	8	1.39	3.50	3.36	10.7	1.7	6.4	0.7	-8	12.5	0.46
2008	SDN	MLB	25	0	3	0	73	0	70¹	79	24	49	6	69.4%	.336	-3	1.46	4.10	3.59	10.4	2.7	5.7	0.8	-7	8.7	0.04
2009	SDN	MLB	26	3	2	3	52	0	56²	55	18	38	3	62.0%	.300	4	1.29	3.18	3.76	9.1	2.5	5.0	0.4	-0	12.8	1.00

Breakout: 22% Improve: 33% Collapse: 33% Attrition: 19%   Comparables: Bill Castro, Hipolito Pichardo, Roger McDowell, Wayne Granger

Meredith's performance declined for the second consecutive year, though one can hardly take him to task for failing to duplicate the unsustainable BABIP and strand rate of his Ziegler-esque 2006. He remains a durable ground-ball artist, but has yet to address his vulnerability to lefties. As was the case in each of his previous two seasons, Meredith was plagued by an unusually high ratio of homers to fly balls, this despite the vast expanses of his home park. Normally we'd forecast a regression to the mean and a corresponding boost in performance, but since he's sustained the mark for over 200 innings in the Padres' pen, it's possible that Meredith's mean isn't quite the same as everyone else's. Of course, at least a few starters each season post comparable percentages in similar innings totals, and subsequently return to normal levels, so a correction may well be in the offing.

Scott Patterson

| | | | | | | | | | | | | | | | | | Bats: R | Throws: R | Height: 6' 7" | Weight: 227 | Born: June 20, 1979 | | Age: 30 |

YEAR	TEAM	LVL	AGE	W	L	SV	G	GS	IP	H	BB	SO	HR	GB%	BABIP	STUFF	WHIP	ERA	DERA	EqH9	EqBB9	EqSO9	EqHR9	DEF	VORP	SN/WX
2006	TRN	AA	27	0	1	1	26	0	38¹	26	8	44	6	31.7%	.221	-18	0.89	2.36	5.91	9.0	2.6	6.4	2.6	6	-1.2	—
2007	TRN	AA	28	4	2	2	43	3	74¹	45	15	91	1	33.0%	.257	23	0.81	1.09	2.84	7.2	2.2	7.5	0.4	2	21.4	—
2008	SWB	AAA	29	2	1	5	42	0	47¹	47	13	54	7	25.0%	.331	-13	1.27	3.81	5.36	11.3	2.9	7.2	2.1	0	1.2	—
2008	SDN	MLB	29	0	0	0	3	0	3¹	1	4	5	0	33.3%	.167	3	1.50	0.00	2.70	2.7	8.1	10.8	0.0	1	2.1	0.21
2009	SDN	MLB	30	2	3	1	25	3	49	47	19	47	7	34.0%	.290	11	1.34	4.09	4.57	8.9	3.1	7.1	1.3	-0	5.8	0.65

Breakout: 16% Improve: 43% Collapse: 38% Attrition: 21%   Comparables: Edwin Nuñez, Tom Niedenfuer, Cecilio Guante, Kevin Gregg

Signed out of the independent leagues, Patterson didn't make his organizational pro debut until he was 27, but he moved quickly through the Yankees' system before the Padres picked him up off of waivers when some difficult late-season 40-man decisions had to be made in the Bronx. He's a tall drink of water with a 90-94 mph fastball and a decent curve, but the lack of a horizontal element to his arsenal leaves him susceptible to left-handers. There's about 15 guys competing for a bullpen job with the Padres this spring, and what you can say about Patterson is that he's one of them.

Jake Peavy

| | | | | | | | | | | | | | | | | | Bats: R | Throws: R | Height: 6' 1" | Weight: 180 | Born: May 31, 1981 | | Age: 28 |

YEAR	TEAM	LVL	AGE	W	L	SV	G	GS	IP	H	BB	SO	HR	GB%	BABIP	STUFF	WHIP	ERA	DERA	EqH9	EqBB9	EqSO9	EqHR9	DEF	VORP	SN/WX
2006	SDN	MLB	25	11	14	0	32	32	202¹	187	62	215	23	39.8%	.307	31	1.23	4.09	3.64	8.8	2.5	8.9	1.0	-10	38.5	5.82
2007	SDN	MLB	26	19	6	0	34	34	223¹	169	68	240	13	45.4%	.279	47	1.06	2.54	2.96	6.8	2.4	9.0	0.5	3	76.0	9.13
2008	SDN	MLB	27	10	11	0	27	27	173²	146	59	166	17	43.2%	.284	26	1.18	2.85	3.60	7.7	2.6	7.7	0.9	8	50.6	6.25
2009	SDN	MLB	28	12	8	0	27	27	177	152	57	173	16	43.0%	.280	31	1.18	3.17	3.62	8.0	2.5	7.3	0.8	-1	39.8	5.55

Breakout: 7% Improve: 30% Collapse: 37% Attrition: 8%   Comparables: Don Sutton, Dave Stieb, Melido Perez, John Smoltz

Peavy's streak of three consecutive 200-inning seasons came to an end in 2008 after a sore elbow sidelined him for a month beginning in mid-May. His performance declined across the board after his Cy Young 2007, though all but seven other pitchers in the NL would have liked to experience the sort of decline which results in an eighth-place finish in SNLVAR. Even an improvement upon his previous season's statistics would have failed to result in additional hardware, however, since Peavy's offensive support evaporated last season, dooming him to a losing record. His teammates provided him with only 3.7 runs per start, nearly two runs fewer than they had a year earlier, and the sixth-lowest total among NL starters with a minimum of 100 IP. Whenever a few days elapsed between Yankees free-agent signings over the winter, Peavy trade rumors resurfaced, but as we go to press, he remains locked in the warm embrace of Petco Park.

Cesar Ramos

Bats: L **Throws:** L **Height:** 6' 2" **Weight:** 190 **Born:** June 22, 1984 **Age:** 25

YEAR	TEAM	LVL	AGE	W	L	SV	G	GS	IP	H	BB	SO	HR	GB%	BABIP	STUFF	WHIP	ERA	DERA	EqH9	EqBB9	EqSO9	EqHR9	DEF	VORP	SN/WX
2006	LEL	A+	22	7	8	0	26	24	141²	161	44	70	9	56.4%	.321	-32	1.45	3.70	6.19	12.6	3.8	1.7	1.4	-5	-8.2	—
2007	SAN	AA	23	13	9	0	27	27	163²	153	43	90	15	44.6%	.273	-24	1.20	3.41	6.84	10.4	3.0	2.8	1.5	18	-20.5	—
2008	POR	AAA	24	9	11	0	28	27	149²	183	57	105	17	45.8%	.349	-20	1.60	5.29	6.54	11.8	3.6	4.1	1.3	-15	-14.8	—
2009	SDN	MLB	25	5	8	0	20	20	109	130	46	67	15	45.0%	.320	6	1.61	5.54	6.28	11.1	3.3	4.6	1.3	-0	-7.4	0.08

Breakout: 21% **Improve:** 55% **Collapse:** 18% **Attrition:** 17% **Comparables:** Kevin Morton, Trever Miller, Bobby Sprowl, Larry Thomas

A supplemental first-round pick three years ago, Ramos has always earned praise for his aggressiveness and bulldog attitude, but he's a bit like the guy at the bar who gets some liquid courage and takes on the bouncer. Fearlessness is nice and all, but without much in the way of actual stuff, he's not exactly intimidating anyone. Average stuff and average command with equal a fifth starter at best, but last year's performance at Triple-A showed that he's not even there yet.

Chad Reineke

Bats: R **Throws:** R **Height:** 6' 6" **Weight:** 210 **Born:** April 9, 1982 **Age:** 27

YEAR	TEAM	LVL	AGE	W	L	SV	G	GS	IP	H	BB	SO	HR	GB%	BABIP	STUFF	WHIP	ERA	DERA	EqH9	EqBB9	EqSO9	EqHR9	DEF	VORP	SN/WX
2006	SLM	A+	24	6	5	0	17	17	99	82	29	87	5	52.9%	.275	-14	1.12	3.00	6.77	10.0	3.3	4.3	1.3	5	-11.9	—
2006	CCH	AA	24	1	3	0	15	4	44¹	33	26	45	3	45.6%	.264	-2	1.34	3.06	5.31	8.4	5.8	6.0	1.1	3	1.3	—
2007	ROU	AAA	25	5	5	0	32	16	100	99	52	95	7	38.2%	.332	-1	1.51	4.68	6.27	9.8	4.9	6.3	0.9	0	-7.0	—
2008	ROU	AAA	26	5	9	0	20	19	112¹	112	35	100	15	37.7%	.298	-8	1.31	4.41	5.37	9.7	2.9	5.4	1.4	-4	2.8	—
2008	POR	AAA	26	0	1	0	3	3	17¹	17	6	13	5	47.2%	.250	-17	1.33	4.16	6.61	9.4	3.3	4.4	2.8	3	-1.8	—
2008	SDN	MLB	26	2	1	0	4	3	18	14	12	13	1	31.5%	.260	3	1.44	5.00	5.50	7.0	5.0	5.5	0.5	0	1.0	0.37
2009	SDN	MLB	27	4	6	0	27	13	91	93	40	69	12	40.0%	.290	6	1.46	4.92	5.59	9.5	3.5	5.7	1.2	-0	0.8	0.60

Breakout: 25% **Improve:** 52% **Collapse:** 23% **Attrition:** 21% **Comparables:** Jason Johnson, Bob Long, Charlie Puleo, Gary Eave

The Padres got one of Houston's better pitching prospects at the deadline for Randy Wolf, but this is Houston we are talking about, so that's not saying much. A bit of a late bloomer (or slow developer for the less optimistic), Reineke is a big, burly righty with a solid fastball/slider combination but occasional control problems. Scouts like him better as a reliever, and that's where he was the best chance of pitching well in the big leagues this year. The Padres' needs might present them with a counter-argument.

Joe Thatcher

Bats: L **Throws:** L **Height:** 6' 2" **Weight:** 203 **Born:** April 10, 1981 **Age:** 28

YEAR	TEAM	LVL	AGE	W	L	SV	G	GS	IP	H	BB	SO	HR	GB%	BABIP	STUFF	WHIP	ERA	DERA	EqH9	EqBB9	EqSO9	EqHR9	DEF	VORP	SN/WX
2006	WVA	A	25	1	3	10	26	0	29	28	6	42	2	63.5%	.366	-17	1.17	2.48	6.12	14.4	3.2	6.8	1.8	-3	-1.4	—
2006	BRV	A+	25	3	1	2	16	0	30	12	9	32	1	60.6%	.162	-6	0.70	0.30	4.97	4.3	3.4	5.0	0.9	5	2.0	—
2007	HUN	AA	26	1	0	0	14	0	16¹	11	2	20	0	47.4%	.297	13	0.80	0.55	3.60	7.8	1.2	7.2	0.0	3	3.3	—
2007	NAS	AAA	26	2	1	1	24	0	21²	19	7	33	0	57.4%	.373	21	1.20	2.07	2.11	9.3	3.0	10.1	0.4	-2	8.3	—
2007	POR	AAA	26	1	0	0	8	0	8²	10	1	11	0	68.0%	.400	9	1.26	1.03	3.12	10.4	1.0	8.3	0.0	-2	2.4	—
2007	SDN	MLB	26	2	2	0	22	0	21	13	6	16	1	54.8%	.197	9	0.90	1.29	2.86	5.3	2.0	6.1	0.4	1	7.5	0.37
2008	POR	AAA	27	5	2	3	37	0	39	38	11	44	2	55.0%	.336	6	1.26	2.77	3.52	9.4	2.6	6.8	0.7	-5	8.9	—
2008	SDN	MLB	27	0	4	0	25	0	25²	42	13	17	4	44.9%	.427	-28	2.14	8.40	6.84	15.1	4.0	5.4	1.4	-5	-10.1	-0.99
2009	SDN	MLB	28	2	2	3	55	0	43	43	16	33	4	49.0%	.300	3	1.38	3.92	4.52	9.4	3.0	5.8	0.8	-0	5.4	0.47

Breakout: 35% **Improve:** 62% **Collapse:** 21% **Attrition:** 39% **Comparables:** Dave Tomlin, Justin Hampson, Mike Myers, Hank Aguirre

And independent league graduate and aspiring LOOGY, Thatcher looked like a steal when the Padres acquired him for a piece of Scott Linebrink in 2007, and pitched like one, too. Things went south for the southpaw last season, and while he wasn't really *eight-plus ERA* bad, he did lose his feel for the strike zone, rendering a stay in Triple-A inevitable. Thatcher straightened himself out in Portland, as minor league lefties stayed true to form by succumbing to his sweeping slider. It's only a matter of time—and probably very little of it—before their major league counterparts follow suit.

Chris Young

| | | | | | Bats: R | | Throws: R | | Height: 6' 10" | | Weight: 260 | | Born: May 25, 1979 | | Age: 30 |

YEAR	TEAM	LVL	AGE	W	L	SV	G	GS	IP	H	BB	SO	HR	GB%	BABIP	STUFF	WHIP	ERA	DERA	EqH9	EqBB9	EqSO9	EqHR9	DEF	VORP	SN/WX
2006	SDN	MLB	27	11	5	0	31	31	179¹	134	69	164	28	27.8%	.232	14	1.13	3.46	4.10	7.0	3.0	7.5	1.3	10	45.3	6.48
2007	SDN	MLB	28	9	8	0	30	30	173	118	72	167	10	30.3%	.246	36	1.10	3.12	3.84	6.1	3.3	8.0	0.5	7	44.9	5.98
2008	SDN	MLB	29	7	6	0	18	18	102¹	84	48	93	13	24.0%	.259	11	1.29	3.96	4.89	7.3	3.6	7.1	1.1	7	17.0	3.14
2009	SDN	MLB	30	6	7	1	27	17	111	97	47	100	14	33.0%	.270	16	1.30	3.93	4.42	8.1	3.4	6.8	1.1	-0	14.9	2.30

Breakout: 5%   Improve: 26%   Collapse: 41%   Attrition: 23%   Comparables: Ed Halicki, Steve Renko, Kerry Wood, Rick Sutcliffe

Albert Pujols has been punishing opposing pitchers for years, but the wounds he inflicts are generally of a statistical, and perhaps psychological, nature. His confrontation with Young last May 21, however, left the big righty in a heap on the mound, felled by a liner through the box. The impact dealt Young a broken nose, a deviated septum, and fractures of the skull and face, putting him out of commission for two months. When he did return, he manifested no lingering effects of his injuries, and actually pitched better than he had prior to the incident. He's still effective when available, but wouldn't be in a full season outside of Petco, as his fly-ball rates and dramatic home/road splits attest. What's most interesting about Young is that his towering height, delivery and environment appear to have made him the rare pitcher who can suppress BABIP; his .242 is the game's lowest over the last three seasons, below .260 in all three years whereas no other pitcher has done it twice. Filling Peavy's shoes as staff ace would be a stretch, but a return to his 2006-07 level is hardly out of the question.

LINEOUTS

Hitters

PLAYER	TEAM	LVL	AGE	PA	R	2B	3B	HR	RBI	BB	SO	SB-CS	EqBRR	AVG/OBP/SLG	EqAVG/EqOBP/EqSLG	EqA	VORP	WARP
OF C. Ambres	POR	AAA	28	476	82	27	7	22	77	56	89	8-3	1.9	.279/.368/.539	.216/.294/.407	.243	-5.8	-1.1
	SDN	MLB	28	48	3	1	0	0	0	7	15	1-0	0.4	.195/.313/.220	.195/.312/.220	.203	-2.2	-0.3
C M. Canham*	LEL	A+	23	488	65	28	5	8	81	66	73	13-1	1.6	.285/.382/.434	.219/.309/.340	.233	-13.5	-1.1
C L. Carlin#	POR	AAA	27	111	12	3	0	4	19	19	27	0-0	-0.5	.261/.396/.432	.217/.339/.337	.248	-1.5	0.1
	SDN	MLB	27	105	12	3	1	1	6	10	34	0-0	0.3	.149/.238/.234	.149/.238/.234	.156	-7.7	-0.7
OF J. Decker*	PDR	Rk	18	216	51	11	2	5	34	55	36	9-1	1.1	.352/.523/.541	.215/.346/.337	.248	-5.6	-0.8
OF L. Durango#	FTW	A	22	389	56	11	3	1	25	49	43	14-7	1.4	.305/.395/.365	.235/.313/.284	.217	-17.7	-2.3
	LEL	A+	22	87	20	4	1	0	10	13	7	1-1	-2.7	.431/.506/.514	.351/.425/.432	.304	7.5	-0.3
1B A. Dykstra*	LEL	A+	21	32	5	1	0	1	10	7	7	0-0	-0.1	.292/.469/.458	.240/.406/.400	.292	1.4	0.2
SS S. Kazmar	SAN	AA	23	433	53	21	3	3	39	38	66	7-4	-0.2	.264/.333/.359	.232/.291/.319	.216	-18.7	1.3
	SDN	MLB	23	46	2	1	0	0	2	5	14	0-0	0.3	.205/.289/.231	.205/.289/.231	.194	-2.2	-0.2
OF K. Kulbacki*	FTW	A	22	73	9	2	0	2	9	9	19	0-2	-1.2	.164/.260/.295	.127/.208/.190	.122	-10.8	-0.9
	LEL	A+	22	362	62	18	0	20	66	47	52	1-2	0.9	.332/.428/.589	.277/.365/.487	.290	22.2	1.8
C C. Morton	SAN	AA	26	177	18	8	0	3	18	11	55	1-0	0.3	.188/.243/.291	.137/.176/.202	.068	-28.9	-2.5
	POR	AAA	26	59	6	1	1	2	6	6	15	0-0	-1.4	.170/.254/.340	.148/.220/.315	.178	-5.6	-0.4
1B B. Myrow*	POR	AAA	31	417	60	23	1	12	59	81	72	0-1	0.4	.314/.451/.500	.244/.368/.381	.269	8.5	0.2
2B E. Sogard*	LEL	A+	22	622	97	42	3	10	87	79	62	16-7	2.0	.308/.394/.453	.254/.335/.381	.253	3.6	0.6

A first-round pick in the last century, **Chip Ambres** has a bit of pop but has never hit with enough consistency to convince that he could produce in The Show. ⊘ Catcher **Mitch Canham** has on-base skills and gap power, but his future relies on his ability to stay behind the plate, which is still anything but a sure thing. ⊘ **Luke Carlin** was called up in desperation when injuries decimated the Padres' catching corps. The above is a fair representation of his offensive potential. ⊘ One of the best high school hitters in the country last spring, **Jaff Decker** fell out of the first round because of his lack of athleticism, but won MVP honors in Arizona's complex league thanks in large part to that .523 OBP. ⊘ **Luis Durango** is a tiny water bug of an outfielder with speed, some decent on-base skills, and as much power as your great aunt Matilda. ⊘ A June 2008 first-round pick **Allan Dykstra** almost didn't sign because of a pre-existing hip condition, but he gives the system some much needed pop as a classic slugging first baseman. ⊘ **Sean Kazmar** profiles as a utility player at best, but the Khalil Greene trade might get him more at-bats than expected or preferred. ⊘ A name to remember (and one that is hard to forget), outfielder **Kellen Kulbacki** was the best hitter in the Cal League during the second half of the season, and while the bat is his only real tool, scouts think it's more than enough. ⊘ An absolutely massive catcher with an equally massive swing, catcher **Colt Morton** just doesn't make enough contact to be anything more than an insurance policy. ⊘ Minor league vet **Bryan Myrow** has shown some nice power and excellent selectivity in the minors, but not enough to get him work as a corner man. The Padres tried to leverage his skills in a pinch-hitting role, but three hits in 20 PA didn't get the job done. He'll go to camp with the White Sox. ⊘ One of those classic little college infielders without much in the way of tools, but tons in the way of effort and fundamentals, **Eric Sogard** can't play on the left side, so he'll have to keep hitting in order to reach the big leagues.

Pitchers

PLAYER	TEAM	LVL	AGE	W	L	SV	IP	H	BB	SO	HR	GB%	BABIP	STUFF	WHIP	ERA	DERA	EqH9	EqBB9	EqSO9	EqHR9	DEF	VORP
B. Corey	BOS	MLB	34	0	0	0	6	11	3	4	1	33.3%	.455	-32	2.33	10.50	7.94	17.5	4.8	4.8	1.6	-1	-3.3
	SDN	MLB	34	1	3	0	39	42	9	18	7	44.7%	.271	-26	1.31	6.23	6.58	9.1	1.8	3.6	1.6	1	-4.0
M. Ekstrom	SAN	AA	24	11	8	1	108	137	34	101	14	55.6%	.368	-41	1.58	4.58	7.04	13.8	3.4	5.2	2.0	-9	-16.0
	SDN	MLB	24	0	2	0	9²	14	7	6	2	47.1%	.375	-21	2.17	7.42	6.00	14.0	6.0	5.0	2.0	-1	-2.2
S. Estes*	POR	AAA	35	5	2	0	44²	45	10	29	3	58.9%	.298	0	1.23	3.62	4.57	9.1	2.1	3.7	0.8	-1	5.0
	SDN	MLB	35	2	3	0	43²	50	18	19	6	55.3%	.291	-16	1.56	4.74	5.89	9.7	3.0	3.5	1.2	2	1.0
E. Frieri	LEL	A+	22	8	6	0	123²	125	32	108	14	30.2%	.313	-30	1.27	4.00	5.85	11.2	3.3	4.2	2.1	-8	-3.1
	SAN	AA	22	1	0	0	11	7	2	10	3	34.5%	.160	9	0.82	4.09	8.10	7.2	1.8	5.4	3.6	2	-2.8
J. Germano	POR	AAA	25	2	9	0	98	119	25	67	12	51.0%	.336	-17	1.47	5.51	7.14	11.0	2.4	3.8	1.3	0	-16.6
	SDN	MLB	25	0	3	0	43²	54	13	17	8	49.7%	.303	-25	1.53	5.97	6.02	10.8	2.3	3.1	1.7	-2	-5.0
E. Gonzalez	POR	AAA	25	7	5	0	99¹	106	50	82	10	40.0%	.323	-16	1.57	4.44	5.47	10.0	4.5	4.8	1.1	-7	1.4
C. Haeger	CHR	AAA	24	10	13	0	178	167	77	117	13	39.6%	.287	-11	1.37	4.45	6.29	9.6	4.3	3.8	1.0	11	-12.8
M. Latos	PDR	Rk	20	1	0	0	14	12	2	23	0	65.5%	.414	11	1.00	3.21	6.55	14.7	3.3	7.4	0.8	0	-1.2
	EUG	A-	20	2	0	0	17¹	13	3	23	1	58.1%	.286	15	0.92	1.04	2.93	11.2	2.3	5.3	2.3	-1	4.5
	FTW	A	20	0	3	0	24²	24	8	23	3	51.4%	.300	8	1.30	3.28	6.95	11.9	4.5	4.1	2.9	-1	-3.3
J. Quezada	FTW	A	21	2	4	27	63²	42	19	79	1	46.8%	.268	18	0.96	2.12	5.95	7.8	3.8	5.6	0.6	7	-2.3

Former number one overall mistake **Matt Bush** missed all of 2008 recovering from Tommy John surgery, but the Padres had some hope for his conversion to the mound as he was touching the upper 90s before his elbow blew up. ⊘ One of an army of journeyman to march on San Diego, **Bryan Corey** was traded to the Padres by the Red Sox for a player to be named or cash considerations in May. Hopefully the Padres put that on their Visa so they got two percent cash back. ⊘ A bit of a system sleeper, righty **Michael Ekstrom** came alive with a move to the bullpen, where his sinker/slider combination worked much better in shorter stints. ⊘ **Shawn Estes**' battery died several years ago, and he's been coasting downhill ever since. After signing him as a free agent, the Dodgers will become the latest in a series of teams to pop his clutch and wait in vain for some sign of ignition. ⊘ Columbian righty **Ernesto Frieri** has a live arm and throws strikes, but his secondary stuff has lagged behind in his development, and most project him as a reliever. ⊘ **Justin Germano's** already-low strikeout rate collapsed in 2008, and right-handers teed off for a .330/.377/.528 line. This earned him an all-expenses paid trip to Japan, where he'll pitch for Fukoka. ⊘ Grabbed off of waivers from the Nats last February, **Enrique Gonzalez** was once a well-regarded prospect in the D'backs sytem but hasn't pitched well since Double-A in 2005. The Red Sox will try to sort him out in the minors. ⊘ **Charlie Haeger's** brief stint with the Padres got his name into this chapter, but accomplished little else. He continues to mark time until he's old enough to be a successful knuckleballer—age-wise, he's approaching his goal, but performance-wise, he's heading in the wrong direction. ⊘ While he missed a good chunk of 2008 with an oblique injury, right-hander **Matt Latos** has the highest ceiling of any pitcher in the system thanks to a perfect power pitcher's frame, mid-90s heat, and surprisingly good control. ⊘ Lanky righty **Jackson Quezada** was one of the best relievers in the Midwest League with a plus fastball/slider combination that was absolute murder on righties (.117/.199/.141). He's not overwhelming, but he has some middle relief possibilities.

MANAGER: BUD BLACK

YEAR	TEAM	W-L	Pythag +/−	Avg PC	100+ P	120+ P	QS	BQS	REL	REL w Zero R	IBB	Subs	PH	PH Avg	PH HR	SB2	CS2	SB3	CS3	SAC Att	SAC %	POS SAC	Squeeze	Swing	In Play
2007	SDN	89-74	-1	90.1	47	0	89	7	485	340	48	22	273	.187	3	50	16	5	7	88	72.7%	28	1	114	89
2008	SDN	63-99	-3	91.0	49	3	74	6	490	291	61	31	285	.198	3	34	17	2	0	83	71.1%	18	1	123	93

The list of ex-pitchers who have been highly successful as managers is largely limited to Tommy Lasorda, so Black already had history against him before he had even begun to cope with the Padres roster. A deluge of injuries didn't give him much of a chance, as the team's lack of depth gave him few options. On offense, his major accomplishment was constructing a center-field platoon of Gerut and Hairston that batted .304/.354/.547 after Jim Edmonds flunked out. The pitching staff ran through 32 arms, so that was more a case of day-to-day patching than an opportunity for a once well-regarded pitching coach to show his stuff. As a tactician, Black stays away from one-run strategies. Recognizing his team's lack of speed, Black didn't ask his club to run, despite which the team was better on the bases (10th in the majors in EqBRR) than many teams with faster legs. Black remains uninterested in one-run strategies and the rare times a position player sees a bunt sign, they probably look cross-eyed at the first base coach thinking someone made a mistake. Black has ability, but as he's going into the last year of his contract there have been the inevitable rumblings. If the Padres do him the favor of setting him free, a club with greater potential could do worse than giving Black a chance.

San Francisco Giants

The 2008 Giants can provide a number of lessons about team franchise management, but perhaps more than anything else, they provide us with a tale of the dangers as well as the hidden benefits of working with low expectations and then exceeding them. Like human beings, organizations don't self-evaluate perfectly well. Collective identity can mean bad things as well as good: a collective sense of responsibility, sure, and a collective sense of danger of course, but also a generalized sense of joy when things end up turning out a lot better than you expected. Instead of survivor's guilt, you wind up with a euphoric sense that you can do anything without hurting yourself—even playing people like Brian Bocock or Jose Castillo. Because if you did those sorts of things to yourself and you didn't finish in last place, how bad could it have been, right? And just imagine when you actually *try* to do better.

It's important to dial back to where the Giants were almost a year ago, before Tim Lincecum had a Cy Young Award in the trophy case, and when people were wondering if a young rotation might keep the club from 100 losses, or if the Giants would simply have to settle for being baseball's worst ballclub. Even with the decision to throw $60 million at Aaron Rowand, the club resembled little more than a holding tank for relatively unwanted veterans, an odd collection of dubious waiver-wire pickups to fill out the lineup, the always-sketchy products of the Giants' farm system, and that very nice pair of young hurlers that everyone admired.

Whether or not you want to characterize the Giants' possession of Matt Cain and Lincecum as a scenario involving a blind squirrel plus FedEx-delivered nuts in light of the modest talent on the rest of the roster is

more than a little fair—superficially, it seems hard to believe that picking Cain and Lincecum could be done by the same front office that signed Barry Zito to $126 million over seven seasons, or put together the Rowand/Winn/Roberts outfield for more than $9 million per player per player-season for 11 total seasons. But as we'll explain, even a team that does a remarkably bad job of picking free agents and setting prices for those free agents can still crank out some home-grown help, especially if they don't make the mistakes of the Astros or the Littlefield-era Pirates and sabotage themselves in the amateur draft.

Once camps opened, the Giants seemed well on their way to living down to expectations. Veteran shortstop Omar Vizquel was knocked out of action early with a bum knee, exposing the organization's galling shortage of remotely viable alternatives. Noah Lowry, the notional fourth horse in the rotation beyond Lincecum, Cain, and Zito, showed up with a bum arm that kept him out of action. The Giants presented a major league lineup featuring Bengie Molina batting cleanup, in no small part because they also had the aforementioned underpowered outfield of Rowand, Winn, and Roberts. Jose Castillo was patched in at third straight from the waiver wire. First base was a question mark. Ray Durham was collecting dust at second. Roberts banged up his knee a week into the season and disappeared for three months.

And as it turned out, predictions of 100 losses were overblown—in this small way, the Giants' season almost merits a passing grade. A big part of why was the convenience of the schedule—the Giants would get belted around by good teams, but then they'd catch the Padres (against whom they went 13-5, including an incredible

---

GIANTS PROSPECTUS

2008 record: 72-90; Fourth place in NL West

Pythagenport record: 68-94

Runs scored per game: 3.95 (15th in NL)

Runs allowed per game: 4.73 (10th in NL)

Team EqA: .247 (15th in NL)

2008 Batters Age: 30.3 (4th-oldest in NL)

2008 Pitchers Age: 27.2 (4th-youngest in NL)

Ballpark: AT&T Park; Neutral park; Park Factor of 1.002

2008: The clubhouse is quieter, but life without Barry meant the team's offensive innings were, too.

2009: Signing Edgar Renteria, 33, constitutes a youth movement for the offense, and Tim Lincecum and Matt Cain can't cover for the rest of the staff.

7-0 in one-run games) or the Nationals (sweeping all six games of the season series). Consider what that means—the team that tied for the 13th-best record in the league (with Atlanta) went 21-5 against the only two teams in the circuit with worse records. Against everyone else besides San Diego and Washington, the Giants were 51-85, a .375 winning percentage—that's a team that would have lost 100 games in a full season, exactly what was expected of them before the season.

The Giants weren't just lucky in getting to be the 16-year-old playing dodgeball against third-graders, however. They were also lucky in general, winding up tied with the Angels for the major league lead in one-run wins with 31 while losing 21. As noted, a big chunk of that came at the Padres' expense, but given that the Giants weren't a good team, this might seem a bit surprising. It gets even more surprising when you consider they had very few tactical options on offense. The Giants weren't just the team that finished last in home runs hit and the only team with fewer than 100 on the season (finishing with 94), they were the worst base-running team in total EqBRR, finishing 15th in the league in EqA and in unintentional walks drawn, and they were 14th in the NL in NetDP (measuring how many double plays they hit into in DP situations) and total baserunners caught stealing. In short, they didn't hit for power, didn't put people on base, and they were among the game's elite at wiping out the few baserunners they did have by hitting into twin killings or making gaffes on the bases—this last despite manager Bruce Bochy's enthusiastic embrace of the hit and run.

Taken as a group, the pitching staff supplied little basis for faith. Even with Lincecum's break-out campaign, the rotation finished ninth in the NL in its rate of Support-Neutral Lineup-Adjusted Value (SNLVA_R), and the bullpen finished last in WXRL, Fair Runs Allowed, Adjusted Runs Prevented—in short, it was a mediocre rotation backed by the league's worst bullpen. The defense was mediocre as measured by Defensive Efficiency or Park-Adjusted Defensive Efficiency, and yet the club still finished with the fourth-highest BABIP allowed in the National League. What the Giants' staff did do well was strike people out, trailing only the Cubs in the majors; practically speaking, the good news is that let them avoid the perils of trusting their defense over much.

So the Giants didn't really do any of the things you might expect a team with an insanely good record in one-run games: they didn't run well, didn't hit for power, and they didn't get great relief pitching. If you look at who started their one-run ballgames, you'll find the entirely unsurprising suggestion that Lincecum and Cain started 28 of them, going 16-12; the freak-show stat in this freak-show oddity was their going 6-1 in one-run decisions started by Jonathan Sanchez. Perhaps the best explanation can be found in the Giants' performance in the quality starts generated by their best three starters. They went 9-4 when Sanchez gave them a quality start, and while Cain got terrible run support on the season, the club did go 12-10 when he gave them a quality start; these are nice, but hardly the difference-makers. But when they got a quality start from Lincecum? They went 21-5. It wasn't quite Steve Carlton '72 territory, when Lefty famously won 27 games for a club that finished with 59 wins, but it might be about as close as we'll get for a while.

If there was an element of surprise in last year's Giants team, it was that a farm system that hasn't earned a ton of compliments of late actually cranked out some talent worth keeping an eye on, especially as the season progressed. Among the pitchers, Jonathan Sanchez did more than just replace the injured Noah Lowry, he handily surpassed him in terms of demonstrating the kind of effectiveness and upside that gives the Giants a third talented starter worth ranking directly behind Lincecum and Cain. Where the lineup started with a ghastly blend of overpriced adequacy and overripe waiver bait, Roberts' injury created the opportunity we thought Fred Lewis had long deserved, delivering a .281 EqA, speed, and good outfield defense. Young Pablo Sandoval might conjure memories of Bob Brenly's days of knocking around between the tools of ignorance and the infield corners, but whether or not he can play any of the three spots well, if he keeps raking, they'll find starts for him. We've been talking about Travis Ishikawa's ups and downs as a prospect for a half-dozen years now, but 2008 proved to be the year that he finally delivered on his power potential and broke through. Emmanuel Burriss, one of the club's top picks of 2006, showed leadoff skills from a middle infield slot TBNL. None of these guys are really blue-chip prospects, but when one of the most lightly regarded farm systems can crank out this many worthwhile supporting players, the organization deserves some measure of credit for doing something right, however belatedly in the cases of Lewis or Ishikawa.

The Giants responded to their large portion of good fortune aggressively. While it might not be a recognition of their relative weakness, they also aren't settling for what they had in house. General Manager Brian Sabean has spent the winter making a play for name free agents in a newly discovered yen for relevance. That's not as outlandish as it might seem at first blush—the NL West isn't especially strong, and clearly anybody in the senior circuit who can field 80-win talent in the first four months might be able to get a bit lucky to outstrip that pace, and then swing the right sort of deal at midseason to take their best shot at the wild-card slot or a division race that's short of a 90-win team. That's the nature of competitive balance in today's National League, and that can inspire ambition in just about every front office. (Outside of San Diego and the District of Columbia, of course.) And when you have gaping holes as large as the Giants had at short or the infield corners or in the bullpen, making substantive improvements isn't necessarily an exercise in adding premium ballplayers as much as finding people who can play.

While he lacked the freedom of action to play for really big stakes and make really big mistakes a la Zito or Rowand, Sabean did have the financial freedom of movement to add a gaggle of win-now free agents to short-term deals. While it didn't get the same sort of attention as Omar's Excellent Bullpen Bonanza, Sabean addressed the problem of a league-worst pen by quickly and quietly adding veterans Jeremy Affeldt and Bobby Howry, and he probably shouldn't stop there. To at least get blood flowing again at a position that had been a scar, he signed Edgar Renteria (no stranger to teams with delusions of grandeur) to a two-year, $18.5 million deal. While it's easy to laugh at the move because of Renteria's mediocre 2008 season with the Tigers, it's also important to note that even if he's merely adequate again, that's an enormous improvement, perhaps as many as three or four wins, over what they suffered through at short last season. They also brought in Randy Johnson on a one-year, $8 million deal (with as much as $5 million in various additional incentives). It seems clear that this won't simply mean that the Big Unit wins his 300th game in a Giants uni this summer, it means they're in it to win it. They may not exactly have all of the tools at their disposal—yet.

While the rotation was already anticipating getting Lowry back from his fall surgery to remove bone spurs, the decision to bring in the Big Unit means that Sabean decided to avoid betting too heavily on his recovery. Maybe this frees them to shop Sanchez, and maybe not; a lot will depend on what Lowry looks like in camp, but it isn't unreasonable for the Giants to wait for a quality offer, and failing that, push Lowry to the pen to start their best five until someone gets hurt. There was more than a little danger that the Giants might see themselves as sufficiently flush in starting pitching *before* the Johnson deal to be free to deal Sanchez for a temporary third-base fix, such as Jorge Cantu of the Marlins. Happily, that risk was avoided, at least initially, and while the Giants *do* still need help in the lineup, dealing a

power lefty for a bit of waiver bait isn't really optimal talent management.

That raises the question of whether or not Brian Sabean is really the GM who can turn things around. While the disappointments of the late Bonds period obscure the better days that came before, when Sabean had the best hitter in baseball history to build around, he initially did a good job of putting together a team worthy of him, assembling the team that won a title in his first season as GM in 1997. In that first year, Sabean effectively added half of his starting lineup—Jeff Kent, J. T. Snow, Jose Vizcaino, and Daryl Hamilton—for a single season's worth of Matt Williams and money. The problem from there wasn't that Sabean didn't have a creative streak when it came to making deals, it's that he had a tendency to load up on a few really big deals and then let it ride. You can say the same thing for the decision tree that put together the current low-powered outfield—spending money isn't the problem, but discrimination in picking who to spend big money on is, and doing something about it once the mistake has been made beyond displaying a stiff upper lip and living with them too often appears to be out of the question. When Jose Castillo failed to deliver as a starting third baseman, it was hardly Castillo's fault—he was just being the best Jose Castillo he can be. Instead, it had everything to do with the decision to put Castillo on the diamond in that role in the first place. If the GM can respond creatively and effectively to opportunities as they arise—and perhaps learn a thing or two about dipping into the free talent pool—he can make an outsized impact on a relatively talent-thin team. Sabean's track record on this score isn't especially good.

Because of their outsized achievements in one-run ballgames and winning at the expense of the league's even worse teams, it would be easy, not to mention sabermetrically orthodox, to write off the Giants as a club that should slip back below 70 wins. But by addressing some of their problems in the pen and the infield over the winter, and making space for younger talent to help patch some of the other gaps in the lineup and the pitching staff, it wouldn't be terribly surprising to see them ratchet their win tally up a few notches. A rotation with Lincecum, Cain, Randy Johnson, and Sanchez is awfully hard to write off, and if the club can add an impact bat at one of the infield corners, they might actually have enough stuff in the lineup to exploit their pitching assets. It won't be enough to contend with, but it also won't be a repeat of last year's scavenger-like survival via massacre of that handful of teams even weaker than they were.

HITTERS

Rich Aurilia — 1B/3B

Bats: R   Throws: R   Height: 6' 1"   Weight: 190   Born: September 2, 1971   Age: 37

YEAR	TEAM	LVL	AGE	PA	R	2B	3B	HR	RBI	BB	SO	SB	CS	EqBRR	AVG	OBP	SLG	EqAVG	EqOBP	EqSLG	EqA	VORP	WARP	DEFENSE				
2006	CIN	MLB	34	481	61	25	1	23	70	34	51	3	0	-0.1	.300	.349	.518	.292	.344	.506	.287	25.9	3.0	40-3B	-2	37-1B	0	
2007	SFN	MLB	35	358	40	19	2	5	33	22	45	0	0	0.4	.252	.304	.368	.250	.304	.372	.236	-4.4	0.0	41-1B	2	20-3B	0	
2008	SFN	MLB	36	440	33	21	1	10	52	30	56	1	1	-2.7	.283	.332	.413	.283	.334	.424	.262	8.5	1.3	54-1B	4	48-3B	0	
2009	SFN	MLB	37	241	24	13	1	5	30	18	31	1	1	-0.9	.268	.323	.400	.267	.322	.413	.252	3.4	0.6	60-1B	4			

Breakout: 13% Improve: 37% Collapse: 28% Attrition: 41%   Comparables: Lou Piniella, Vic Power, Sherm Lollar, Matt Williams

Aurilia's rebound from his miserable 2007 was largely the result of a correction in batting average and a few doubles that turned back into home runs. At 37, he's overextended as a regular, particularly at first base, but is no longer defensively viable elsewhere. The Giants nonetheless used him to spell Castillo at third while giving John Bowker most of the first-base starts against right-handers. Given that Bowker failed to out-hit Castillo, the arrangement was a net loss due to Aurilia's dismal defense. Aurilia can still do damage against lefty pitching (.321/.377/.526 last year), but unless your team has a lefty-hitting first-baseman or DH who needs a platoon partner, he doesn't have much remaining value.

Brian Bocock — SS

Bats: R   Throws: R   Height: 5' 11"   Weight: 185   Born: March 9, 1985   Age: 24

YEAR	TEAM	LVL	AGE	PA	R	2B	3B	HR	RBI	BB	SO	SB	CS	EqBRR	AVG	OBP	SLG	EqAVG	EqOBP	EqSLG	EqA	VORP	WARP	DEFENSE				
2006	SLO	A-	21	121	12	6	0	0	7	12	29	6	1	1.9	.223	.305	.282	.167	.229	.204	.151	-28.1	-0.7	17-2B	1	14-SS	3	
2007	AUG	A	22	178	24	9	1	1	20	16	19	26	8	2.4	.292	.354	.379	.223	.274	.295	.204	-11.8	0.7	39-SS	8			
2007	SJO	A+	22	398	42	19	3	4	37	35	105	15	10	0.0	.220	.293	.328	.196	.252	.283	.188	-32.8	-0.4	86-SS	8			
2008	SFN	MLB	23	93	4	1	0	0	2	12	29	4	2	-0.2	.143	.258	.156	.154	.275	.167	.168	-8.2	-0.8	26-SS	-3			
2008	FRE	AAA	23	141	14	3	0	0	3	14	39	7	3	0.6	.163	.254	.187	.143	.223	.167	.130	-20.4	-0.1	33-SS	9			
2009	SFN	MLB	24	351	27	13	1	3	23	28	97	16	7	0.6	.189	.259	.265	.189	.258	.274	.189	-15.4	-0.5	84-SS	4			

Breakout: 58% Improve: 72% Collapse: 19% Attrition: 14%   Comparables: Wayne Busby, Jason Knupfer, Mike Taylor, Jose Lobaton

It was evidence of how utterly unprepared the San Francisco Giants were for the 2008 baseball season that, when their 40-year-old shortstop was unable to answer the bell on Opening Day, their replacement was the slick-fielding Bocock, who hadn't even passed his brief High-A test the previous year. Not surprisingly, Bocock didn't hit, and it took the Giants three weeks to come up with another option for the position. Demoted only to Triple-A, Bocock was even worse there before his season was ended by a blood clot in his right middle finger.

John Bowker — OF

Bats: L   Throws: L   Height: 6' 2"   Weight: 190   Born: July 8, 1983   Age: 25

YEAR	TEAM	LVL	AGE	PA	R	2B	3B	HR	RBI	BB	SO	SB	CS	EqBRR	AVG	OBP	SLG	EqAVG	EqOBP	EqSLG	EqA	VORP	WARP	DEFENSE				
2006	SJO	A+	22	511	61	32	6	7	66	37	100	6	3	-1.1	.284	.337	.424	.236	.281	.354	.220	-18.1	-2.8	61-RF	-3	46-LF	-8	
2007	NRW	AA	23	587	79	35	6	22	90	41	103	3	7	-2.9	.307	.363	.523	.292	.338	.504	.282	38.2	2.0	85-RF	-4	23-CF	-1	
2008	FRE	AAA	24	102	13	3	1	2	9	7	23	2	0	1.0	.237	.304	.355	.202	.265	.319	.207	-6.3	-0.6	13-1B	-1	7-LF	0	
2008	SFN	MLB	24	350	31	14	3	10	43	19	74	1	1	-2.6	.255	.300	.408	.255	.300	.414	.245	-1.4	-0.6	62-1B	-3	10-RF	0	
2009	SFN	MLB	25	294	34	17	1	9	38	21	62	2	1	-0.3	.268	.326	.446	.268	.326	.460	.267	7.9	0.9	72-1B	1			

Breakout: 43% Improve: 58% Collapse: 24% Attrition: 37%   Comparables: Jerry Lynch, Cecil Cooper, Steve Whitaker, Lee Thomas

Bowker was called up in mid-April last year to make some starts in right field while Randy Winn replaced a banged-up Rowand in center. Bowker responded by cracking two home runs and driving in seven in his first two games. That prompted Bruce Bochy to make room for Bowker in the lineup as Aurilia's lefty foil at first base despite the fact that Bowker hadn't played the position since turning pro. From his first start at first base through an August demotion, Bowker hit .233/.285/.362. He was better as a September call-up, but has yet to prove the validity of his impressive Double-A debut in 2007. A lead-footed liability wherever he plays and a hacker at the plate, Bowker's major league career will hinge on his ability, or lack thereof, to turn his minor league doubles into major league homers.

Emmanuel Burriss　　MI

Bats: S　Throws: R　Height: 6' 0"　Weight: 170　Born: January 17, 1985　Age: 24

YEAR	TEAM	LVL	AGE	PA	R	2B	3B	HR	RBI	BB	SO	SB	CS	EqBRR	AVG	OBP	SLG	EqAVG	EqOBP	EqSLG	EqA	VORP	WARP	DEFENSE			
2006	SLO	A-	21	293	50	8	2	1	27	27	22	35	11	6.1	.307	.384	.366	.232	.287	.281	.207	-32.2	-0.9	59-SS	-1		
2007	AUG	A	22	405	64	14	4	0	38	28	49	51	15	3.8	.321	.374	.381	.241	.284	.286	.206	-24.4	-1.2	86-SS	-5		
2007	SJO	A+	22	160	23	2	0	0	8	12	20	17	3	0.0	.165	.237	.180	.146	.199	.153	.123	-25.9	-1.0	35-SS	4		
2008	FRE	AAA	23	64	6	1	1	0	6	2	6	2	2	-0.8	.258	.281	.306	.226	.250	.274	.170	-5.4	0.0	10-2B	2	4-SS	1
2008	SFN	MLB	23	274	37	6	1	1	18	23	24	13	5	2.9	.283	.357	.329	.289	.364	.335	.255	5.4	0.6	35-SS	-2	32-2B	1
2009	SFN	MLB	24	263	31	8	1	1	17	19	32	15	4	1.9	.252	.312	.304	.252	.311	.314	.229	-0.3	0.4	65-SS	1		

Breakout: 51%　Improve: 67%　Collapse: 17%　Attrition: 40%　　Comparables: Bip Roberts, Roger Metzger, Larry Milbourne, Billy Smith

By the end of April it seemed as if the Giants were filling out their roster by taking players in alphabetical order off of an organizational list. Bowker nearly skipped Triple-A to platoon with Aurilia at a position he'd never played in the minors, Bocock was their first attempt to stock short after Vizquel went down, and when Bocock didn't hit, they turned to Burriss, who flunked out of High-A in 2007 only to inexplicably start 2008 with Triple-A Fresno. The team's first compensation-round pick out of Kent State in 2006 acquitted himself surprisingly well. A speedy slap hitter with a decent plate approach and a good glove, Burriss will battle for the second-base job in spring training.

Travis Denker　　2B

Bats: R　Throws: R　Height: 5' 9"　Weight: 170　Born: August 5, 1985　Age: 23

YEAR	TEAM	LVL	AGE	PA	R	2B	3B	HR	RBI	BB	SO	SB	CS	EqBRR	AVG	OBP	SLG	EqAVG	EqOBP	EqSLG	EqA	VORP	WARP	DEFENSE			
2006	CGA	A	20	320	47	11	1	11	45	65	37	2	1	-2.3	.268	.420	.452	.216	.338	.362	.251	-1.9	-0.4	64-2B	-9		
2006	VRO	A+	20	220	24	6	0	5	25	24	36	0	2	1.3	.220	.309	.330	.179	.255	.281	.184	-20.4	-2.6	40-3B	-10	8-2B	0
2007	SBR	A+	21	461	65	27	3	10	57	48	65	8	2	0.0	.294	.369	.450	.242	.305	.367	.238	-7.8	-1.2	105-2B	-13		
2007	SJO	A+	21	32	7	3	0	1	9	7	2	1	0	0.0	.400	.531	.640	.385	.500	.577	.374	6.2	0.1	7-2B	-4		
2008	NRW	AA	22	91	4	4	1	0	6	14	25	1	1	-1.9	.184	.308	.263	.192	.304	.269	.211	-5.7	-0.6	21-2B	-3		
2008	FRE	AAA	22	253	42	20	0	7	30	31	46	2	0	0.3	.282	.373	.468	.244	.328	.391	.253	1.1	0.6	55-2B	0		
2008	SFN	MLB	22	42	6	4	1	1	3	5	10	0	0	-0.4	.243	.333	.486	.243	.333	.486	.277	1.8	0.3	8-2B	1		
2009	SDN	MLB	23	486	47	22	1	9	43	53	105	5	2	-0.0	.224	.313	.348	.234	.322	.380	.246	5.6	0.6	115-2B	-7		

Breakout: 30%　Improve: 56%　Collapse: 19%　Attrition: 7%　　Comparables: Pedro Castellano, Jesus Alfaro, Glenn Hubbard, Ralph Milliard

Claimed off waivers by the Padres in November, Denker was previously the player to be named later when the Giants sent Mark Sweeney to LA in late 2007. Denker rocketed from High-A to the big-league bench by late May of last year, then put together a solid showing at Triple-A after being demoted around the All-Star break. A short second baseman lacking in secondary skills, he does have a solid approach at the plate and doubles power. Given the quality of his competition, that might be enough to win him the Padres' second-base job this spring.

Kevin Frandsen　　2B

Bats: R　Throws: R　Height: 6' 0"　Weight: 180　Born: May 24, 1982　Age: 27

YEAR	TEAM	LVL	AGE	PA	R	2B	3B	HR	RBI	BB	SO	SB	CS	EqBRR	AVG	OBP	SLG	EqAVG	EqOBP	EqSLG	EqA	VORP	WARP	DEFENSE			
2006	FRE	AAA	24	328	46	25	3	3	30	12	30	7	4	-1.8	.304	.358	.440	.272	.315	.404	.249	2.5	-0.4	46-2B	-10	12-3B	-4
2006	SFN	MLB	24	102	12	4	0	2	7	3	14	0	1	-0.3	.215	.284	.323	.223	.284	.319	.207	-3.5	-0.3	19-2B	1		
2007	FRE	AAA	25	83	13	5	0	1	7	9	6	4	2	1.4	.403	.506	.522	.348	.451	.449	.315	8.1	1.1	10-2B	2	5-SS	0
2007	SFN	MLB	25	296	26	12	1	5	31	21	24	4	3	-1.1	.269	.331	.379	.269	.333	.386	.251	3.3	-0.4	38-2B	-5	15-SS	-2
2009	SFN	MLB	27	223	25	11	1	3	22	14	23	4	1	0.1	.273	.335	.379	.273	.334	.391	.254	6.7	0.7	56-2B	-2		

Breakout: 27%　Improve: 48%　Collapse: 26%　Attrition: 27%　　Comparables: Kevin Sefcik, Mark DeRosa, Steve Dillard, Joe Strain

Frandsen lost all but one at-bat of 2008 to a ruptured Achilles' tendon, but coming off a strong Arizona Fall League showing (.331/.392/.421) that mimicked his career minor league line (.327/.391/.458), he's the favorite to win the second-base job heading into spring training. It doesn't hurt that he's a local product with the kind of grinding, dirty-uniform approach that tends to win over fans and management equally. Unfortunately, while Frandsen makes a lot of contact, he'll be 27 in May, is an average fielder, is a poor basestealer, doesn't draw many walks, has middling power, and is likely to have trouble repeating his minor league averages in the majors or his AFL line in non-desert atmospheres.

Conor Gillaspie   3B

Bats: L   Throws: R   Height: 6' 1"   Weight: 195   Born: July 18, 1987   Age: 21

YEAR	TEAM	LVL	AGE	PA	R	2B	3B	HR	RBI	BB	SO	SB	CS	EqBRR	AVG	OBP	SLG	EqAVG	EqOBP	EqSLG	EqA	VORP	WARP	DEFENSE	
2008	GIA	Rk	20	25	2	3	0	0	7	3	1	0	1	0.4	.273	.360	.409	.174	.240	.261	.146	-6.4	-0.5		
2008	SLO	A-	20	80	4	4	0	0	8	9	13	2	0	0.3	.268	.350	.324	.187	.237	.227	.154	-17.2	-1.8	14-3B	-5
2009	SFN	MLB	21	550	38	28	2	5	45	40	126	7	3	0.5	.217	.278	.310	.217	.278	.320	.207	-18.4	-1.3	129-3B	-4

Breakout: 93%   Improve: 96%   Collapse: 4%   Attrition: 6%   Comparables: Mark Teahen, Chris Donnels, Sean Doolittle, Eric Sogard

A supplemental first-round pick out of Wichita State last June, Gillaspie is a polished college player without much upside. He's an ordinary defender with the ability to hit for average and get on base, but projects as more of a doubles hitter than any kind of home-run threat. The most notable thing about him is that he ended up as the first 2008 draftee to reach the big leagues when the Giants brought him up in a pinch-hitting role at the end of the season despite the fact that he was hardly dominating in the short-season leagues. Though that was more an oddity than anything else, he is a good candidate to advance quickly, but his legitimate arrival will produce a solid regular rather than the new face of the franchise.

Travis Ishikawa   1B

Bats: L   Throws: L   Height: 6' 3"   Weight: 225   Born: September 24, 1983   Age: 25

YEAR	TEAM	LVL	AGE	PA	R	2B	3B	HR	RBI	BB	SO	SB	CS	EqBRR	AVG	OBP	SLG	EqAVG	EqOBP	EqSLG	EqA	VORP	WARP	DEFENSE	
2006	NRW	AA	22	340	33	13	4	10	42	35	88	0	0	-1.2	.232	.316	.403	.227	.300	.388	.240	-5.2	-0.4	79-1B	1
2007	SJO	A+	23	222	35	15	1	13	34	19	78	0	0	0.0	.268	.342	.551	.210	.266	.415	.229	-5.6	-0.8	38-1B	-1
2007	NRW	AA	23	192	17	3	1	3	17	17	48	0	0	-0.5	.214	.292	.295	.205	.271	.284	.192	-14.7	-1.6	48-1B	-2
2008	NRW	AA	24	277	34	16	0	8	48	35	45	10	4	-3.6	.291	.382	.462	.279	.359	.450	.280	13.8	1.2	59-1B	1
2008	FRE	AAA	24	192	35	19	3	16	46	14	36	0	1	-0.4	.310	.370	.737	.264	.318	.603	.295	15.7	1.7	44-1B	4
2008	SFN	MLB	24	104	12	6	0	3	15	9	27	1	0	0.3	.274	.337	.432	.274	.337	.453	.272	2.7	0.6	24-1B	3
2009	SFN	MLB	25	551	62	31	2	18	72	51	138	6	3	-1.0	.246	.320	.428	.246	.320	.440	.260	5.0	1.4	129-1B	4

Breakout: 23%   Improve: 55%   Collapse: 18%   Attrition: 7%   Comparables: Garrett Jones, Mike Hocutt, Jim Adduci, Dan Johnson

Not long after the Giants nabbed the college-bound Ishikawa in the 2002 draft with a 21st-round pick and a big check, we said he "showed good plate discipline and developing power amidst the low batting averages." Five years later, not much had changed, and the power still hadn't developed save for a spike at High-A in 2005. Then last year, he finally hit in his third attempt at Double-A and unleashed a torrent of Triple-A homers, including seven in his first eight games in August, to earn a mid-August call-up. While the power went away upon his arrival in the majors, it could indicate that he's finally starting to harness his potential. Ishikawa is an excellent defensive first baseman who will work his share of walks. Given the Giants' lack of alternatives, he'll get a chance to build on his breakthrough season as the starter at first this year.

Fred Lewis   OF

Bats: L   Throws: R   Height: 6' 2"   Weight: 190   Born: December 9, 1980   Age: 28

YEAR	TEAM	LVL	AGE	PA	R	2B	3B	HR	RBI	BB	SO	SB	CS	EqBRR	AVG	OBP	SLG	EqAVG	EqOBP	EqSLG	EqA	VORP	WARP	DEFENSE			
2006	FRE	AAA	25	517	85	20	11	12	56	68	105	18	8	5.2	.276	.375	.453	.238	.329	.401	.257	3.7	-3.5	85-LF	-37	20-CF	-2
2007	FRE	AAA	26	191	31	8	6	8	32	19	36	9	1	2.4	.292	.366	.550	.237	.309	.445	.261	2.5	0.3	23-CF	-1	18-LF	-1
2007	SFN	MLB	26	180	34	6	2	3	19	19	32	5	1	0.4	.287	.374	.408	.287	.378	.427	.283	6.4	1.4	23-RF	0	13-LF	5
2008	SFN	MLB	27	521	81	25	11	9	40	51	124	21	7	4.9	.282	.351	.440	.287	.357	.458	.281	20.0	2.7	102-LF	8	8-CF	-5
2009	SFN	MLB	28	450	65	23	5	10	47	46	95	15	5	2.6	.277	.354	.436	.277	.354	.450	.278	15.1	2.3	107-LF	2		

Breakout: 27%   Improve: 53%   Collapse: 16%   Attrition: 23%   Comparables: Pat Kelly, Curtis Pride, Lee Maye, Larry Bigbie

An early April injury to Dave Roberts handed the athletic Lewis the bulk of the left-field job, and he seized his opportunity, hitting .363/.433/.588 through the end of the month. He cooled off after that, more closely approximating the line PECOTA had projected for him by hitting .269/.334/.418 over the remainder of the season. As evidenced by his double-digit triples and solid showing on the bases, his primary asset is his speed, so it will be interesting to see just how fast (or faster?) he'll be following September surgery to correct the painful bunion in his right foot that he'd lived with since childhood.

Scott McClain   3B/1B

Bats: R   Throws: R   Height: 6' 4"   Weight: 220   Born: May 19, 1972   Age: 37

YEAR	TEAM	LVL	AGE	PA	R	2B	3B	HR	RBI	BB	SO	SB	CS	EqBRR	AVG	OBP	SLG	EqAVG	EqOBP	EqSLG	EqA	VORP	WARP	DEFENSE			
2006	SAC	AAA	34	605	84	33	0	28	107	48	117	7	4	-1.1	.252	.313	.466	.204	.258	.378	.218	-25.9	-2.9	126-3B	-10	5-1B	-1
2007	FRE	AAA	35	533	69	24	0	31	100	59	98	1	2	-2.4	.267	.349	.517	.205	.282	.400	.234	-12.1	-2.2	93-1B	-5	14-3B	-4
2008	FRE	AAA	36	556	87	32	1	29	108	72	98	5	2	1.6	.300	.388	.553	.226	.306	.411	.248	-1.7	-0.7	63-3B	-6	52-1B	-2
2008	SFN	MLB	36	38	7	1	0	2	7	5	8	0	1	-0.7	.273	.368	.485	.273	.368	.485	.281	1.6	0.0	4-3B	-1		
2009	SFN	MLB	37	378	41	18	1	14	52	40	86	2	1	-1.1	.237	.318	.418	.236	.318	.431	.256	5.1	0.5	91-3B	-8		

Breakout: 43%   Improve: 74%   Collapse: 12%   Attrition: 39%   Comparables: Ernie Young, Matt Williams, Deron Johnson, Russ Morman

A late-round pick by the Baltimore Orioles way back in 1990, McClain reached Triple-A in mid-'95, just in time for the Orioles to start clearing third base for Cal Ripken. With the Mets in '97 he was stuck behind Edgardo Alfonzo's breakout season. With the Devil Rays in '98 and '99, it was Wade Boggs chasing 3,000 hits. After getting blocked by Jeff Cirillo in the Rockies' system in '00, McClain spent four years in Japan, hitting 39 homers for the Seibu Lions in 2001. Back in the States in '05, he landed behind Aramis Ramirez with the Cubs, then Eric Chavez in his last healthy season for the A's in 2006. By the time he finally arrived in the Giants' system in 2007, McClain was 35 and had just 24 major league games under his belt despite having hit a Crash Davis-like 251 home runs in nine and a half Triple-A seasons, and 357 between the minors and Japan. He finally got his first major league dinger as a September call-up last year at the age of 36. Brought back as a non-roster invitee, he finally has a fighting chance with a team lacking established starters in either infield corner. Better late than never, we suppose.

Bengie Molina   C

Bats: R   Throws: R   Height: 5' 11"   Weight: 225   Born: July 20, 1974   Age: 34

YEAR	TEAM	LVL	AGE	PA	R	2B	3B	HR	RBI	BB	SO	SB	CS	EqBRR	AVG	OBP	SLG	EqAVG	EqOBP	EqSLG	EqA	VORP	WARP	DEFENSE	
2006	TOR	MLB	31	458	44	20	1	19	57	19	47	1	1	-4.0	.284	.319	.467	.271	.309	.454	.259	15.7	1.2	96-C	-6
2007	SFN	MLB	32	517	38	19	1	19	81	15	53	0	0	-3.6	.276	.298	.433	.274	.298	.437	.249	15.0	2.3	123-C	5
2008	SFN	MLB	33	569	46	33	0	16	95	19	38	0	0	-7.0	.292	.322	.445	.294	.320	.455	.266	24.7	3.6	127-C	6
2009	SFN	MLB	34	389	35	21	0	10	53	16	35	0	1	-3.3	.276	.312	.416	.276	.312	.428	.251	12.5	2.4	93-C	1

Breakout: 12%   Improve: 37%   Collapse: 32%   Attrition: 23%   Comparables: Brian Harper, Darrin Fletcher, Bill Freehan, Jeff Conine

Bruce Bochy provided a case study on the importance of opportunity in hitting statistics by batting Bengie Molina in the cleanup spot last year. Molina had a fairly typical season by his own standards (from 2003 to 2007 he hit .282/.314/.440) but set career highs in RBI and double plays (23), both of which had more to do with having more runners on base ahead of him than with any change in Molina's game. Of course, those career highs were also the result of Molina's career highs in games and plate appearances, something of a red flag for a catcher who will turn 35 this July. Fortunately, Molina is in the last year of his contract, and Buster Posey should be ready to take over behind the plate in 2010.

Nick Noonan   2B

Bats: L   Throws: R   Height: 6' 0"   Weight: 180   Born: May 4, 1989   Age: 20

YEAR	TEAM	LVL	AGE	PA	R	2B	3B	HR	RBI	BB	SO	SB	CS	EqBRR	AVG	OBP	SLG	EqAVG	EqOBP	EqSLG	EqA	VORP	WARP	DEFENSE			
2007	GIA	Rk	18	224	33	11	4	3	40	12	20	18	3	1.6	.316	.357	.451	.224	.251	.322	.199	-35.9	-1.6	20-2B	-3	17-SS	2
2008	AUG	A	19	532	79	27	7	9	68	23	98	29	4	4.6	.279	.315	.415	.234	.266	.358	.218	-23.6	-2.1	116-2B	-11		
2009	SFN	MLB	20	616	64	38	5	9	55	31	114	18	7	2.8	.251	.292	.380	.251	.292	.392	.236	3.4	0.7	144-2B	-1		

Breakout: 68%   Improve: 86%   Collapse: 1%   Attrition: 6%   Comparables: Dave Hansen, Johnny Damon, Reid Brignac, Josh Barfield

Noonan could have used some college polish, but instead he took the Giants' supplemental-round money in 2007. As a result, he's a project, an unrefined athlete with great speed and gap power but poor instincts, a long, complicated swing, and poor pitch recognition. That would explain the spike in his strikeouts in his full-season debut last year.

Ivan Ochoa   MI

Bats: R   Throws: R   Height: 5' 9"   Weight: 160   Born: December 16, 1982   Age: 26

YEAR	TEAM	LVL	AGE	PA	R	2B	3B	HR	RBI	BB	SO	SB	CS	EqBRR	AVG	OBP	SLG	EqAVG	EqOBP	EqSLG	EqA	VORP	WARP	DEFENSE			
2006	AKR	AA	23	389	53	10	2	1	28	37	63	20	4	5.2	.251	.337	.301	.220	.294	.270	.210	-24.0	-0.7	103-SS	-2		
2006	BUF	AAA	23	47	4	2	1	0	2	4	5	4	0	0.5	.205	.326	.308	.175	.283	.275	.220	-3.2	0.1	11-SS	1		
2007	FRE	AAA	24	196	22	11	2	3	20	10	30	8	2	-1.5	.296	.337	.430	.260	.299	.387	.242	-1.7	1.1	43-SS	5		
2008	FRE	AAA	25	338	54	11	4	6	32	34	62	20	11	0.8	.318	.399	.445	.264	.336	.368	.250	1.2	0.5	48-SS	0	27-2B	-4
2008	SFN	MLB	25	134	7	8	0	0	3	4	28	0	1	-1.1	.200	.244	.267	.203	.246	.268	.173	-8.6	-0.5	27-SS	2	5-2B	1
2009	SFN	MLB	26	454	49	19	4	5	35	35	89	15	6	1.7	.240	.308	.342	.240	.308	.353	.234	1.4	1.0	108-SS	2		

Breakout: 39%   Improve: 65%   Collapse: 16%   Attrition: 17%   Comparables: Pedro Chavez, Edwin Rodriguez, Chico Fernandez, Ray Olmedo

Itty bitty Ivan Ochoa has enjoyed his time in the hitter-friendly PCL the last two years, hitting .310/.373/.439 for Fresno over that span, but in his major league debut he looked more like the all-glove, no-bat player who hit .242/.318/.296 over his first six minor league seasons. Ochoa has played just 36 games at a position other than shortstop in his professional career, all at second. Given Ochoa's utter lack of offense, a healthy Edgar Renteria should keep him out of the majors entirely.

Buster Posey   C

Bats: R   Throws: R   Height: 6' 2"   Weight: 195   Born: March 27, 1987   Age: 22

YEAR	TEAM	LVL	AGE	PA	R	2B	3B	HR	RBI	BB	SO	SB	CS	EqBRR	AVG	OBP	SLG	EqAVG	EqOBP	EqSLG	EqA	VORP	WARP	DEFENSE
2008	GIA	Rk	21	31	8	3	1	1	4	5	4	0	0	0.0	.385	.484	.692	.250	.323	.429	.258	1.3	0.0	4-C -1
2008	SLO	A-	21	14	2	2	0	0	2	3	0	0	0	-0.0	.273	.429	.455	.250	.357	.417	.251	0.8	0.0	
2009	SFN	MLB	22	561	55	30	3	12	60	46	132	7	3	0.7	.237	.304	.378	.237	.304	.390	.239	2.8	1.5	132-C -14

Breakout: NA   Improve: NA   Collapse: NA   Attrition: NA   Comparables: Randy Hunt, Eric Munson, Pat Burrell, Rick Nelson

The top player in college baseball last year, Posey hit .463/.566/.879 at Florida State, but some hefty bonus demands dropped him out of consideration for the top pick in the draft. While it wasn't surprising to see him fall a bit, it was a bit of a surprise to see the Giants take him with the fifth overall pick and give him a $6.2 million bonus. Posey is interesting in that it's hard to see superstar in his tool set, but it's also nearly impossible not to see him becoming an above-average catcher both offensively and defensively in short order. He should be an occasional All-Star rather than an occasional MVP candidate, which is just fine considering that the last Giants hitter other than Barry Bonds to make the All-Star team was Moises Alou in 2005.

Dave Roberts   LF

Bats: L   Throws: L   Height: 5' 10"   Weight: 180   Born: May 31, 1972   Age: 37

YEAR	TEAM	LVL	AGE	PA	R	2B	3B	HR	RBI	BB	SO	SB	CS	EqBRR	AVG	OBP	SLG	EqAVG	EqOBP	EqSLG	EqA	VORP	WARP	DEFENSE			
2006	SDN	MLB	34	566	80	18	13	2	44	51	61	49	6	5.6	.293	.360	.393	.305	.372	.415	.288	21.3	4.0	108-LF	5	11-CF	2
2007	SFN	MLB	35	442	61	17	9	2	23	42	66	31	5	7.4	.260	.331	.364	.261	.336	.372	.259	8.9	0.8	84-CF	-3	9-LF	0
2008	SFN	MLB	36	130	18	2	2	0	9	20	18	5	3	-2.4	.224	.341	.280	.224	.341	.280	.233	-3.6	-0.3	23-LF	-1		
2009	SFN	MLB	37	159	23	6	2	1	12	20	23	7	2	0.8	.269	.360	.363	.269	.360	.374	.266	3.4	0.8	41-LF	2		

Breakout: 24%   Improve: 54%   Collapse: 28%   Attrition: 42%   Comparables: Al Bumbry, Rick Miller, Rich Amaral, Lance Johnson

Roberts made just five starts last April before going under the knife for a degenerative condition known as "runners knee" that affects the cartilage on the back of the kneecap. When he returned, it was as a backup and pinch-hitter, but he notably made just one appearance as pinch-runner and went just 5-for-7 on the bases over his last 46 games. Roberts will be 37 at the end of May and will have consumed $13 million of the Giants payroll between last year and this one, not that the team was likely to do anything else constructive with that money.

Ryan Rohlinger 3B

Bats: R   Throws: R   Height: 6' 1"   Weight: 185   Born: October 7, 1983   Age: 25

YEAR	TEAM	LVL	AGE	PA	R	2B	3B	HR	RBI	BB	SO	SB	CS	EqBRR	AVG	OBP	SLG	EqAVG	EqOBP	EqSLG	EqA	VORP	WARP	DEFENSE	
2006	SLO	A-	22	273	34	13	1	3	28	27	27	0	2	-2.7	.252	.336	.355	.177	.239	.246	.164	-53.0	-0.9	61-3B	13
2007	AUG	A	23	586	86	31	3	18	78	62	83	3	3	0.0	.235	.332	.415	.162	.232	.276	.172	-60.8	-1.5	132-3B	24
2008	SJO	A+	24	322	45	16	0	7	46	34	50	5	1	1.5	.285	.368	.419	.220	.292	.314	.217	-15.1	-1.4	71-3B	-5
2008	NRW	AA	24	179	27	12	1	6	19	13	20	1	1	-1.0	.296	.358	.497	.284	.335	.500	.280	10.4	2.1	42-3B	9
2008	SFN	MLB	24	33	2	1	1	0	2	1	8	0	1	-0.8	.094	.121	.188	.125	.152	.219	.000	-6.0	-0.3	8-3B	2
2009	SFN	MLB	25	500	38	23	2	7	45	39	100	2	2	-0.1	.207	.275	.312	.207	.274	.321	.204	-18.4	0.2	118-3B	13

Breakout: 42%   Improve: 59%   Collapse: 23%   Attrition: 8%   Comparables: Adam Heether, Bo Robinson, Neil Sellers, Tony Woods

Yet another over-promoted infielder, Rohlinger didn't impress in the Sally League in 2007, and hit for less power in High-A in early 2008, but after 159 solid at-bats at Double-A, he was called up and installed at third, a solution that lasted all of six starts. An unspectacular player, Rohlinger profiles as something less than a major league starter, which given his almost complete lack of professional experience outside of third base means he may be something less than a major leaguer.

Aaron Rowand CF

Bats: R   Throws: R   Height: 6' 0"   Weight: 200   Born: August 29, 1977   Age: 31

YEAR	TEAM	LVL	AGE	PA	R	2B	3B	HR	RBI	BB	SO	SB	CS	EqBRR	AVG	OBP	SLG	EqAVG	EqOBP	EqSLG	EqA	VORP	WARP	DEFENSE	
2006	PHI	MLB	28	445	59	24	3	12	47	18	76	10	4	1.5	.262	.321	.425	.262	.315	.428	.256	9.3	0.5	101-CF	-6
2007	PHI	MLB	29	684	105	45	0	27	89	47	119	6	3	2.3	.309	.374	.515	.307	.372	.520	.299	53.5	4.3	153-CF	-10
2008	SFN	MLB	30	611	57	37	0	13	70	44	126	2	4	-2.7	.271	.339	.410	.274	.340	.422	.262	15.3	2.0	143-CF	0
2009	SFN	MLB	31	514	59	28	2	14	66	36	91	4	2	-0.8	.275	.336	.431	.275	.336	.444	.266	18.2	2.3	121-CF	-3

Breakout: 10%   Improve: 35%   Collapse: 29%   Attrition: 17%   Comparables: Rondell White, Cleon Jones, Mickey Stanley, Carl Furillo

PECOTA pegged Rowand for some serious regression in 2008, and he managed to fall short of even that. After banging himself up a bit in April with his aggressive play in center, he went on a tear, hitting .358/.435/.588 from April 19 to June 1, but hit just .235/.302/.338 over 398 plate appearances thereafter. The end result was a season that looked a lot like his 2005 and 2006 campaigns minus the stolen bases and plus a few extra intentional walks resulting from his being one of the few hitters in the Giants' batting order pitchers might recognize. To make matters worse, his defense isn't the asset it was made out to be. The Giants owe Rowand $48 million over the next four years, and he has a limited trade clause. If you don't think that contract could look much worse, just wait.

Pablo Sandoval 3B/C

Bats: S   Throws: R   Height: 5' 11"   Weight: 180   Born: August 11, 1986   Age: 22

YEAR	TEAM	LVL	AGE	PA	R	2B	3B	HR	RBI	BB	SO	SB	CS	EqBRR	AVG	OBP	SLG	EqAVG	EqOBP	EqSLG	EqA	VORP	WARP	DEFENSE			
2006	AUG	A	19	473	43	20	1	1	49	22	74	3	4	-0.3	.265	.309	.322	.211	.242	.260	.165	-47.5	-6.0	91-1B	-9	21-3B	-3
2007	SJO	A+	20	423	56	33	5	11	52	16	52	3	1	0.0	.287	.312	.476	.249	.269	.394	.226	-10.2	0.7	58-C	8	39-1B	0
2008	SJO	A+	21	301	61	25	2	12	59	23	39	2	1	-1.9	.359	.412	.597	.317	.364	.536	.300	28.8	3.1	49-C	2	10-1B	0
2008	NRW	AA	21	184	29	13	0	8	37	8	20	0	1	0.3	.337	.364	.549	.341	.364	.562	.305	21.6	2.2	30-C	2	7-1B	1
2008	SFN	MLB	21	154	24	10	1	3	24	4	14	0	0	0.0	.345	.357	.490	.347	.357	.514	.297	11.1	1.2	14-1B	0	10-3B	1
2009	SFN	MLB	22	565	64	38	3	15	74	30	82	3	2	0.4	.289	.329	.454	.289	.329	.468	.268	24.1	3.7	133-C	-5		

Breakout: 37%   Improve: 55%   Collapse: 16%   Attrition: 10%   Comparables: Arquimedez Pozo, Benito Santiago, Ruben Sierra, Leo Hernandez

Sandoval is a hitting machine. In fact, he's built like the WOPR mainframe computer from *WarGames*—calling him stocky would be charitable. His approach, however, is decidedly analog; the free-swinging Venezuelan never saw a pitch he didn't like or couldn't hit with authority. Sandoval crushed the California League repeating High-A to start the 2008 season, then did nearly as much damage at Double-A, prompting a mid-August call-up. Bouncing between catcher and the infield corners in the majors, he just kept on hitting before a strained quad limited his playing time in the season's final week. A true DH, he's a liability in the field regardless of position, but since the Giants have few other options, he'll be their starting third baseman this year for as long as Bruce Bochy can tolerate his fielding. Chances are he'll remain their number-three hitter longer than that.

Nate Schierholtz   RF

Bats: L   Throws: R   Height: 6' 2"   Weight: 215   Born: February 15, 1984   Age: 25

YEAR	TEAM	LVL	AGE	PA	R	2B	3B	HR	RBI	BB	SO	SB	CS	EqBRR	AVG	OBP	SLG	EqAVG	EqOBP	EqSLG	EqA	VORP	WARP	DEFENSE
2006	NRW	AA	22	510	55	25	7	14	54	27	81	8	3	0.4	.270	.325	.443	.262	.306	.437	.253	7.7	-0.8	112-RF -12
2007	FRE	AAA	23	439	67	31	7	16	68	17	58	10	4	1.3	.333	.365	.560	.292	.323	.500	.275	22.9	1.2	98-RF -6
2007	SFN	MLB	23	117	9	5	3	0	10	2	19	3	1	1.4	.304	.316	.402	.304	.316	.402	.252	1.0	0.0	26-RF -1
2008	FRE	AAA	24	377	62	22	10	18	73	21	51	9	3	1.6	.320	.363	.594	.274	.313	.497	.271	16.4	0.8	85-RF -5
2008	SFN	MLB	24	81	12	8	1	1	5	3	8	0	1	0.2	.320	.370	.493	.320	.370	.493	.289	4.6	0.7	18-RF 2
2009	SFN	MLB	25	488	63	31	4	15	65	27	75	8	3	1.2	.285	.331	.471	.285	.330	.486	.275	16.8	2.2	115-RF 0

Breakout: 29%   Improve: 62%   Collapse: 16%   Attrition: 16%   Comparables: Joe Pepitone, Steve Whitaker, Al Oliver, Terry Whitfield

To some extent, Schierholtz is the victim of Rowand's contract. Having been even more productive upon repeating Triple-A last year than he was in his successful age-23 debut at the level, Schierholtz was nonetheless stranded in Fresno until rosters expanded in September, and despite a solid showing in right field for the Giants that month, will remain on the bench to start 2009 despite the fact that either Randy Winn or Fred Lewis could play center were Rowand not clogging up the works. Schierholtz is not a future star, but he offers a nice arm for right field and is a minimum-wage player who is likely to be as productive as the rapidly-declining Rowand if given the chance.

Eugenio Velez   UT

Bats: S   Throws: R   Height: 6' 1"   Weight: 160   Born: May 16, 1982   Age: 27

YEAR	TEAM	LVL	AGE	PA	R	2B	3B	HR	RBI	BB	SO	SB	CS	EqBRR	AVG	OBP	SLG	EqAVG	EqOBP	EqSLG	EqA	VORP	WARP	DEFENSE	
2006	AUG	A	24	508	90	29	20	14	90	34	81	64	15	0.4	.315	.369	.557	.205	.241	.347	.205	-34.2	-2.9	64-2B -1	31-SS -9
2007	NRW	AA	25	411	55	17	9	1	25	26	66	49	17	0.1	.298	.344	.399	.247	.284	.335	.222	-17.0	-1.8	44-CF -2	29-2B -6
2008	FRE	AAA	26	188	25	11	4	5	15	17	32	13	9	-4.3	.310	.372	.509	.247	.303	.402	.240	-0.7	-1.0	24-LF -6	16-2B -3
2008	SFN	MLB	26	292	32	16	7	1	30	14	40	15	6	-1.6	.262	.299	.382	.265	.302	.389	.241	1.0	-1.1	51-2B -9	5-RF 0
2009	SFN	MLB	27	277	34	13	4	3	25	18	54	16	6	1.6	.259	.311	.380	.259	.311	.392	.247	4.1	0.3	68-2B -6	

Breakout: 45%   Improve: 74%   Collapse: 23%   Attrition: 42%   Comparables: U.L. Washington, Wilbur Howard, Juan Castillo, Al Weis

A speedy, slender, switch-hitting Dominican, Velez began 2008 in a second-base job-share with Ray Durham, but was demoted in late May after hitting just .207/.244/.322. He was recalled in early July and hit a hundred points better across the board, posting a .305/.341/.429 line the rest of the way and finishing the year as the Giants' everyday second baseman. The catch is that he's not much of a defender at the keystone. The Giants had him learn the outfield, discovering that he lacks the instincts for center as well. At best, Velez will compete with Frandsen and Burriss for the second-base job in camp, but seems better suited for a reserve role.

Angel Villalona   1B

Bats: R   Throws: R   Height: 6' 3"   Weight: 200   Born: August 13, 1990   Age: 18

YEAR	TEAM	LVL	AGE	PA	R	2B	3B	HR	RBI	BB	SO	SB	CS	EqBRR	AVG	OBP	SLG	EqAVG	EqOBP	EqSLG	EqA	VORP	WARP	DEFENSE
2007	GIA	Rk	16	224	40	12	3	5	37	15	42	1	1	1.4	.285	.344	.450	.190	.223	.308	.176	-49.2	-3.9	48-3B -7
2008	AUG	A	17	500	64	29	0	17	64	18	118	1	2	-2.9	.263	.312	.435	.226	.262	.378	.217	-19.7	-3.1	97-1B -7
2009	SFN	MLB	18	587	49	32	3	13	56	29	136	1	2	-0.5	.231	.275	.373	.231	.275	.384	.221	-14.5	-1.2	138-1B -1

Breakout: 66%   Improve: 83%   Collapse: 5%   Attrition: 0%   Comparables: Richard Hidalgo, Pedro Muñoz, Karim Garcia, Juan Gonzalez

Ignore Villalona's seemingly alarming 6.6 K/BB ratio from his full-season debut last year. What the Giants have here is a 17-year-old who hit his age in home runs in the Sally League when most his age would be high school juniors. His power grades out at an 80 on the 20-to-80 scouting scale, and he has plenty of time for his approach to mature. If there's any concern, it's that his already large frame was fleshed out by his introduction to American fast food last year. He'll move up to the High-A California League this year, where at least he can switch from McDonald's to In-N-Out Burger.

Omar Vizquel — SS

Bats: S | Throws: R | Height: 5' 9" | Weight: 175 | Born: April 24, 1967 | Age: 42

YEAR	TEAM	LVL	AGE	PA	R	2B	3B	HR	RBI	BB	SO	SB	CS	EqBRR	AVG	OBP	SLG	EqAVG	EqOBP	EqSLG	EqA	VORP	WARP	DEFENSE	
2006	SFN	MLB	39	659	88	22	10	4	58	56	51	24	7	-1.1	.295	.361	.389	.293	.359	.387	.267	27.8	3.4	145-SS	0
2007	SFN	MLB	40	575	54	18	3	4	51	44	48	14	6	0.9	.246	.305	.316	.246	.309	.322	.225	-8.4	4.2	136-SS	35
2008	SFN	MLB	41	300	24	10	1	0	23	24	29	5	4	-0.1	.222	.283	.267	.220	.283	.269	.197	-12.4	-0.6	74-SS	3
2009	SFN	MLB	42	124	11	4	0	0	10	10	11	3	1	-0.2	.227	.291	.284	.227	.290	.292	.204	-2.8	0.1	34-SS	1

Breakout: 18% Improve: 38% Collapse: 54% Attrition: 62%   Comparables: Dave Philley, Gary Gaetti, Steve Finley, Luke Appling

Dave Pinto's Probabilistic Model of Range listed Vizquel as the second-best defensive shortstop in baseball last year despite the fact that he was 41 and coming off of knee surgery that delayed the start of his season until May 10. Unfortunately, the days when Vizquel's bat was decent enough to be carried by his glove are over, as evidenced by the fact that the Giants were unable to find a taker for Vizquel at the deadline and, having failed to move him, benched him on August 1. A free agent, Vizquel may yet find a taker for 2009, but we're looking forward to the Hall of Fame debate that will arise once his retirement becomes official.

Randy Winn — RF

Bats: S | Throws: R | Height: 6' 2" | Weight: 195 | Born: June 9, 1974 | Age: 35

YEAR	TEAM	LVL	AGE	PA	R	2B	3B	HR	RBI	BB	SO	SB	CS	EqBRR	AVG	OBP	SLG	EqAVG	EqOBP	EqSLG	EqA	VORP	WARP	DEFENSE			
2006	SFN	MLB	32	635	82	34	5	11	56	48	63	10	8	-0.6	.262	.324	.396	.261	.324	.395	.249	0.6	0.2	74-RF	1	50-CF	-4
2007	SFN	MLB	33	653	73	42	1	14	65	44	85	15	3	0.6	.300	.353	.445	.301	.355	.456	.281	27.3	1.7	97-RF	-3	32-CF	-2
2008	SFN	MLB	34	667	84	38	2	10	64	59	88	25	2	5.9	.306	.363	.426	.309	.366	.436	.286	30.2	3.8	125-RF	3	12-LF	3
2009	SFN	MLB	35	508	70	29	3	8	52	43	64	14	4	0.4	.297	.359	.421	.297	.358	.434	.277	16.9	2.2	120-RF	-1		

Breakout: 18% Improve: 49% Collapse: 19% Attrition: 19%   Comparables: Jerry Mumphrey, Willie McGee, Stan Javier, Claudell Washington

Paying $8 million a year for a complementary player like Winn may make absolutely no sense for a team as far out of contention as the Giants, but at least he's doing his best to earn his keep, leading the team's hitters in VORP last year and finishing (a distant) second to Barry Bonds in 2007. Winn's defense in right got excellent marks last year, and his 25 steals in 27 attempts added considerably to his value. Entering the final year of his contract, Winn may actually find his way to a contender by the trading deadline, in which case he could become an important pennant-race patch or fourth outfielder. In the meantime, don't blame Winn for the fact that the Giants are one of the worst-run organizations in baseball.

PITCHERS

Tim Alderson

Bats: R | Throws: R | Height: 6' 6" | Weight: 217 | Born: November 3, 1988 | Age: 20

YEAR	TEAM	LVL	AGE	W	L	SV	G	GS	IP	H	BB	SO	HR	GB%	BABIP	STUFF	WHIP	ERA	DERA	EqH9	EqBB9	EqSO9	EqHR9	DEF	VORP	SN/WX
2008	SJO	A+	19	13	4	0	26	26	145^1	125	34	124	4	45.5%	.301	24	1.09	2.79	5.15	9.7	3.0	4.2	0.8	3	6.6	—
2009	SFN	MLB	20	4	8	0	18	18	95^2	112	38	61	12	44.0%	.320	11	1.56	5.77	6.12	10.4	3.2	5.0	1.1	-0	-4.3	0.28

Breakout: 5% Improve: 27% Collapse: 30% Attrition: 11%   Comparables: Adam Miller, Nick Adenhart, Shawn Hillegas, Don Schulze

The second of the Giants' three first-round picks in 2007, Alderson was excellent in his full-season debut at age 19 last year, though he doesn't project as more than a mid-rotation starter due to his approach. A finesse pitcher with only slightly better than average velocity, Alderson succeeds by pounding the strike zone, changing speeds, and hitting his spots. Still, he's remarkably good at it, particularly given his age and level, and could advance quickly, reaching the majors as soon as late 2010.

Madison Bumgarner

Bats: R | Throws: L | Height: 6' 4" | Weight: 215 | Born: August 1, 1989 | Age: 19

YEAR	TEAM	LVL	AGE	W	L	SV	G	GS	IP	H	BB	SO	HR	GB%	BABIP	STUFF	WHIP	ERA	DERA	EqH9	EqBB9	EqSO9	EqHR9	DEF	VORP	SN/WX
2008	AUG	A	18	15	3	0	24	24	141^2	111	21	164	3	43.4%	.303	42	0.93	1.46	4.01	10.4	2.3	5.7	0.7	8	21.8	—
2009	SFN	MLB	19	5	8	0	18	18	101^1	118	33	81	12	44.0%	.330	23	1.49	5.23	5.51	10.4	2.6	6.3	1.1	-0	2.0	1.00

Breakout: 0% Improve: 4% Collapse: 81% Attrition: 6%   Comparables: Steve Avery, Mark Grant, Phil Hughes, Rick Ankiel

Drafted ahead of Alderson with the tenth overall pick in 2007, Bumgarner made his pro-debut in the Sally League last year at age 18 and was even better than the year-older Alderson was a level above him. A tall lefty who throws with a low three-quarter delivery, Bumgarner showed up with a put-away curveball last year, which in combination with his mid-90s heat, solid changeup, and immaculate control made him downright dominant, as evidenced by his otherworldly 7.8 K/BB ratio. A potential ace, his promotions will be dictated by his performance, which means it's not unreasonable to expect him to join Alderson, Lincecum, and perhaps Jonathan Sanchez and Matt Cain in the major league rotation in 2011, giving the Giants two years to figure out how to assemble a major league offense.

Matt Cain

Bats: R   Throws: R   Height: 6' 3"   Weight: 235   Born: October 1, 1984   Age: 24

YEAR	TEAM	LVL	AGE	W	L	SV	G	GS	IP	H	BB	SO	HR	GB%	BABIP	STUFF	WHIP	ERA	DERA	EqH9	EqBB9	EqSO9	EqHR9	DEF	VORP	SN/WX
2006	SFN	MLB	21	13	12	0	32	31	190²	157	87	179	18	38.6%	.272	42	1.28	4.15	3.81	7.2	3.5	7.6	0.7	-4	34.6	4.70
2007	SFN	MLB	22	7	16	0	32	32	200	173	79	163	14	41.0%	.285	39	1.26	3.65	3.38	7.6	3.1	6.9	0.6	-1	47.2	6.46
2008	SFN	MLB	23	8	14	0	34	34	217²	206	91	186	19	34.6%	.304	24	1.36	3.76	3.61	8.3	3.2	6.8	0.7	-2	43.1	5.31
2009	SFN	MLB	24	11	11	0	30	30	190²	179	72	168	21	39.0%	.290	27	1.31	3.94	4.14	8.3	3.0	6.9	1.0	-0	30.5	4.87

Breakout: 8%   Improve: 28%   Collapse: 37%   Attrition: 11%   Comparables: Jim Palmer, Kevin Gross, Tony Cloninger, Gary Bell

Another former first-round pick out of high school, Cain was the unluckiest pitcher in baseball last year according to our Luck stat, which compares actual won-loss record to expected won-loss record. With average run support, Cain would have gone approximately 14-9. Instead, a mere 3.1 runs per game of support from his offense more than reversed that record. On the flip side, Cain was the tenth most fortunate pitcher in the majors when it came to having his bullpen strand his bequeathed runners, so his ERA was actually lower than it should have been. Still, it's to his credit that he pitched deep enough into most of his starts to keep the underside of the Giants' pen out of the game. Cain pitched a minimum of five full innings in 29 of his last 30 starts and pitched at least six full frames in 25 of those 30 starts. The dark side to that is that his workloads are slightly troubling for a pitcher who's just entering his age-24 season.

Kevin Correia

Bats: R   Throws: R   Height: 6' 3"   Weight: 205   Born: August 24, 1980   Age: 28

YEAR	TEAM	LVL	AGE	W	L	SV	G	GS	IP	H	BB	SO	HR	GB%	BABIP	STUFF	WHIP	ERA	DERA	EqH9	EqBB9	EqSO9	EqHR9	DEF	VORP	SN/WX
2006	SFN	MLB	25	2	0	0	48	0	69²	64	22	57	5	35.7%	.291	12	1.23	3.49	3.21	8.1	2.4	6.7	0.5	0	19.8	1.79
2007	SFN	MLB	26	4	7	0	59	8	101²	94	40	80	9	46.7%	.284	10	1.32	3.45	3.22	7.8	3.0	6.5	0.7	1	26.7	1.78
2008	SFN	MLB	27	3	8	0	25	19	110	141	47	66	15	39.7%	.337	-12	1.71	6.05	5.64	10.9	3.2	4.7	1.1	-5	-10.3	0.70
2009	SDN	MLB	28	4	5	1	31	9	77²	82	28	55	9	42.0%	.300	3	1.43	4.54	5.16	9.9	2.9	5.3	1.1	-0	4.5	0.76

Breakout: 5%   Improve: 18%   Collapse: 56%   Attrition: 38%   Comparables: Mike Scott, Joe Coleman, Phil Regan, Jay Tibbs

After a solid start to the season, Correia strained an intercostal muscle on his left side six pitches into his fifth start and missed a month and a half. When he returned, it took him nine tries to turn in a quality start, and he was ultimately pulled from the rotation in September having posted a 5.66 ERA with a 1.4 K/BB ratio in 14 starts since his return from the DL. Dropped from the 40-man after the season, he has caught on with his hometown Padres as a non-roster invitee and could benefit from the Padres' soft roster and big ballpark.

Jesse English

Bats: L   Throws: L   Height: 6' 2"   Weight: 215   Born: September 13, 1984   Age: 24

YEAR	TEAM	LVL	AGE	W	L	SV	G	GS	IP	H	BB	SO	HR	GB%	BABIP	STUFF	WHIP	ERA	DERA	EqH9	EqBB9	EqSO9	EqHR9	DEF	VORP	SN/WX
2006	SLO	A-	21	3	0	0	17	0	28²	21	18	40	6	33.3%	.283	-27	1.38	6.38	12.63	15.7	10.0	7.8	7.0	1	-16.2	—
2007	SLO	A-	22	5	0	0	10	0	26	14	5	46	0	42.2%	.311	22	0.73	0.69	1.25	10.0	2.9	7.9	0.8	-3	10.5	—
2007	SJO	A+	22	0	1	0	5	2	8¹	8	6	11	0	20.0%	.400	4	1.69	3.25	4.05	13.5	9.4	8.1	0.0	0	1.2	—
2008	SJO	A+	23	13	7	0	26	26	135¹	121	51	135	12	45.1%	.313	-22	1.27	3.19	5.99	10.8	4.8	5.2	1.8	-1	-5.1	—
2009	SFN	MLB	24	3	7	0	25	13	82¹	99	46	62	14	42.0%	.330	2	1.76	6.37	6.63	10.7	4.5	5.9	1.4	-0	-8.5	-0.36

Breakout: 17%   Improve: 44%   Collapse: 25%   Attrition: 14%   Comparables: Matt Beech, Dennis Cook, Ken Holubec, Lindsay Gulin

After having his progress slowed by problems of motivation and ulnar nerve surgery, the latter of which wiped out his 2005 season, English was converted back to starting at High-A last year and responded by nearly halving his walk rate while still striking out a man per inning. A lefty with an average fastball and a put-away changeup, he notably struck out nine men in a three-inning relief outing in 2007.

Geno Espineli

Bats: L   Throws: L   Height: 6' 4"   Weight: 195   Born: September 8, 1982   Age: 26

YEAR	TEAM	LVL	AGE	W	L	SV	G	GS	IP	H	BB	SO	HR	GB%	BABIP	STUFF	WHIP	ERA	DERA	EqH9	EqBB9	EqSO9	EqHR9	DEF	VORP	SN/WX
2006	NRW	AA	23	8	7	2	35	13	107	117	29	65	6	48.3%	.324	-29	1.36	4.12	6.84	12.0	3.1	2.9	1.1	-3	-13.4	—
2007	NRW	AA	24	8	10	0	29	24	141	142	37	105	8	50.9%	.315	-12	1.27	3.45	5.61	11.7	2.9	4.3	1.1	-6	-0.1	—
2008	FRE	AAA	25	1	1	1	38	0	61	56	11	48	2	52.9%	.303	1	1.10	2.66	4.12	8.7	1.8	4.7	0.5	2	9.7	—
2008	SFN	MLB	25	2	0	0	15	0	16	17	8	8	5	41.5%	.250	-35	1.56	5.06	7.04	9.4	4.1	4.1	2.9	3	-0.1	0.04
2009	SFN	MLB	26	2	3	1	49	3	48	57	19	29	6	48.0%	.320	-5	1.57	5.11	5.40	10.5	3.1	4.8	1.1	-0	1.6	0.22

Breakout: 17% Improve: 50% Collapse: 24% Attrition: 16%   Comparables: Alvin Morman, Cliff Young, Mark Malaska, Tom Thobe

Converted back to relief after a brief flirtation with starting, Espineli posted a 4.4 K/BB ratio in 38 games at Triple-A last year, but in 15 major league outings he walked as many as he struck out and was brutalized by right-handed batters (.333/.391/.667). The resulting image of a Quad-A reliever fits his marginal finesse repertoire. He was outrighted off the 40-man roster in October.

Brad Hennessey

Bats: R   Throws: R   Height: 6' 2"   Weight: 200   Born: February 7, 1980   Age: 29

YEAR	TEAM	LVL	AGE	W	L	SV	G	GS	IP	H	BB	SO	HR	GB%	BABIP	STUFF	WHIP	ERA	DERA	EqH9	EqBB9	EqSO9	EqHR9	DEF	VORP	SN/WX
2006	FRE	AAA	26	0	1	0	2	2	10	11	1	7	1	45.9%	.278	-13	1.20	2.70	9.82	9.0	0.8	3.3	0.8	1	-5.2	—
2006	SFN	MLB	26	5	6	1	34	12	99¹	92	42	42	12	44.7%	.256	-16	1.35	4.26	5.33	8.3	3.4	3.6	1.0	11	13.4	1.24
2007	SFN	MLB	27	4	5	19	69	0	68¹	66	23	40	7	47.1%	.281	-7	1.30	3.43	4.14	8.4	2.7	5.1	0.8	8	18.5	1.97
2008	FRE	AAA	28	7	10	0	21	21	132¹	157	37	69	22	41.1%	.316	-35	1.47	4.83	6.97	11.4	2.8	2.9	1.7	14	-18.9	—
2008	SFN	MLB	28	1	2	0	17	4	40¹	63	15	21	8	35.8%	.374	-26	1.93	7.82	5.09	13.3	2.9	4.2	1.8	-9	-9.3	-0.02
2009	BAL	MLB	29	3	5	0	33	10	73²	95	28	33	14	43.0%	.310	-12	1.66	6.19	5.90	11.2	3.1	3.8	1.6	0	-4.5	-0.11

Breakout: 17% Improve: 44% Collapse: 21% Attrition: 25%   Comparables: Don August, Brian Cooper, Matt Ginter, Jim Hunter

Eleven outings into his 2008 season, ex-desperation closer Hennessey had given up 38 hits in 16 relief innings and was sporting a 12.94 ERA, having allowed at least one run in all but two of those appearances. Returned to starting in Triple-A, he was subpar but no longer awful. Back in the majors in September, he turned in three quality starts in four tries, but was outrighted after the season and has since caught on as a non-roster invitee with the Orioles, who are sure to need a mid-season replacement in their rotation.

Alex Hinshaw

Bats: L   Throws: L   Height: 6' 4"   Weight: 190   Born: October 31, 1982   Age: 26

YEAR	TEAM	LVL	AGE	W	L	SV	G	GS	IP	H	BB	SO	HR	GB%	BABIP	STUFF	WHIP	ERA	DERA	EqH9	EqBB9	EqSO9	EqHR9	DEF	VORP	SN/WX
2006	SJO	A+	23	6	3	0	30	10	69	58	60	78	6	46.0%	.307	-17	1.71	4.30	9.19	10.8	9.5	5.5	1.9	-2	-24.6	—
2007	NRW	AA	24	3	1	0	17	5	41¹	22	19	50	2	45.7%	.222	5	0.99	1.96	5.35	6.5	4.7	7.2	0.9	4	1.1	—
2008	FRE	AAA	25	0	0	7	13	0	15²	5	4	21	0	43.3%	.167	15	0.57	0.57	1.76	2.9	2.3	8.2	0.0	2	6.5	—
2008	SFN	MLB	25	2	1	0	48	0	39²	31	29	47	5	27.0%	.292	15	1.51	3.40	3.35	6.9	5.6	9.1	1.1	-1	8.8	-0.31
2009	SFN	MLB	26	2	2	3	46	0	40²	34	26	43	5	37.0%	.280	12	1.46	4.02	4.22	7.4	5.2	8.4	1.0	-0	7.2	0.58

Breakout: 44% Improve: 59% Collapse: 23% Attrition: 28%   Comparables: Al Osuna, Mike Mohler, David Riske, Jack Meyer

Drafted out of San Diego State in the middle rounds of the 2005 draft, Hinshaw made his full-season debut in 2006 and walked people like he was going out of style, but adapted and got his walk and K-rates headed in the right direction both at Double-A in 2007 and Triple-A last year prior to his mid-May promotion, upon which he immediately became the team's top LOOGY. Though his walk rate crept back up in the majors, Hinshaw stranded 75 percent of his inherited runners and held lefties to a .205/.318/.274 line.

Tim Lincecum

					Bats: L		Throws: R		Height: 5' 11"		Weight: 170		Born: June 15, 1984			Age: 25	

YEAR	TEAM	LVL	AGE	W	L	SV	G	GS	IP	H	BB	SO	HR	GB%	BABIP	STUFF	WHIP	ERA	DERA	EqH9	EqBB9	EqSO9	EqHR9	DEF	VORP	SN/WX
2006	SJO	A+	22	2	0	0	6	6	27	13	12	48	3	50.0%	.246	25	0.93	2.00	3.24	6.8	5.0	9.4	2.2	-2	6.6	—
2007	FRE	AAA	23	4	0	0	5	5	31	12	11	46	0	53.6%	.218	29	0.74	0.29	2.15	4.3	3.4	9.5	0.3	4	11.2	—
2007	SFN	MLB	23	7	5	0	24	24	146¹	122	65	150	12	48.1%	.292	36	1.28	4.00	3.86	7.3	3.5	8.5	0.7	0	26.0	3.87
2008	SFN	MLB	24	18	5	0	34	33	227	182	84	265	11	44.7%	.312	49	1.17	2.62	2.70	7.2	2.9	9.3	0.4	-3	72.3	8.70
2009	SFN	MLB	25	13	9	0	30	30	206	169	77	220	16	45.0%	.290	37	1.19	3.25	3.47	7.3	3.0	8.4	0.7	-0	48.4	6.83

Breakout: 7%   Improve: 21%   Collapse: 42%   Attrition: 9%   Comparables: Johnny Antonelli, Jim Maloney, Andy Messersmith, Cliff Fannin

There was very little not to like about Lincecum's Cy Young season. His BABIP was an ordinary .310, yet he led the National League in fewest hits per nine innings, thanks in large part to his major league-leading strikeout rate. The worst stretch of his season lasted from mid-June into July and saw him post a 4.40 ERA and make just three quality starts in seven turns, but among those were dominant outings against the A's and Cubs. Thereafter, he turned in quality starts in ten of his last 13 games, going 7-2 with a 2.36 ERA. The only concern is his workload, as he surpassed his 2007 innings total (majors and minors combined) by 49⅔ innings (or 28 percent) and threw 120 or more pitches five times, including a four-start stretch as August turned into September in which he threw 132, 92, 127, and 138 pitches. He bounced back quickly from those high-stress outings, but how he bounces back from the accumulated strain of his breakout season will be more telling. If he survives 2009 intact, he may be unstoppable.

Noah Lowry

					Bats: R		Throws: L		Height: 6' 2"		Weight: 205		Born: October 10, 1980			Age: 28	

YEAR	TEAM	LVL	AGE	W	L	SV	G	GS	IP	H	BB	SO	HR	GB%	BABIP	STUFF	WHIP	ERA	DERA	EqH9	EqBB9	EqSO9	EqHR9	DEF	VORP	SN/WX
2006	SFN	MLB	25	7	10	0	27	27	159¹	166	56	84	21	38.3%	.288	-2	1.39	4.75	4.73	9.2	2.8	4.4	1.0	4	17.5	4.09
2007	SFN	MLB	26	14	8	0	26	26	156	155	87	87	12	47.6%	.295	8	1.55	3.92	4.36	8.7	4.4	4.8	0.6	7	26.1	3.63
2009	SFN	MLB	28	2	3	0	16	6	45	49	20	30	5	44.0%	.300	2	1.52	4.99	5.26	9.7	3.6	5.2	1.0	-0	2.7	0.45

Breakout: 11%   Improve: 20%   Collapse: 69%   Attrition: 54%   Comparables: Gerry Arrigo, Trevor Wilson, Monte Kennedy, Chris Nabholz

When Lowry had surgery to relieve exertional compartmental syndrome in his left forearm early last March, he was initially expected to return by the end of April. In mid-September, he was still trying to work his way back when it was discovered he needed another surgery to remove a bone spur from his left elbow. Though he's now expected to be ready for spring training, that promise should be taken with a large grain of salt. Whenever he does return, Lowry will have to fight his way back into the starting rotation now that Randy Johnson has taken his spot, as well as overcome that dangling plot thread from 2006-07, when his strikeout-walk ratio had reached an evil kind of equilibrium.

Joe Martinez

					Bats: L		Throws: R		Height: 6' 3"		Weight: 185		Born: February 26, 1983			Age: 26	

YEAR	TEAM	LVL	AGE	W	L	SV	G	GS	IP	H	BB	SO	HR	GB%	BABIP	STUFF	WHIP	ERA	DERA	EqH9	EqBB9	EqSO9	EqHR9	DEF	VORP	SN/WX
2006	AUG	A	23	15	5	0	27	27	167¹	156	26	135	9	58.5%	.296	-27	1.09	3.02	7.34	12.1	2.6	3.1	1.6	8	-28.2	—
2007	SJO	A+	24	10	10	0	28	28	162²	172	36	151	11	50.3%	.343	-15	1.28	4.26	6.40	12.9	2.9	4.6	1.3	-11	-12.6	—
2008	NRW	AA	25	10	10	0	27	27	148	131	37	112	6	58.3%	.286	10	1.14	2.49	5.31	8.8	2.2	4.8	0.6	10	4.6	—
2009	SFN	MLB	26	6	10	0	30	20	127	154	41	76	15	52.0%	.320	6	1.53	5.38	5.74	10.8	2.6	4.7	1.0	-0	-0.7	0.78

Breakout: 15%   Improve: 52%   Collapse: 10%   Attrition: 18%   Comparables: Bryn Smith, Dave McKae, Ben Hendrickson, Bob Bastian

The Boston College grad has methodically worked his way up the ladder since making his pro debut in the Sally League in 2005. Upon making the leap to Double-A last year, he saw his strikeout rate decline a bit, but otherwise had his best professional season. He's hell on right-handed batters and gets his share of ground balls, but as a 26-year-old sinker/slider guy who will be taking his first crack at Triple-A this year, he seems more like a future middle reliever than the sort of pitcher who will stick in a big-league rotation.

Osiris Matos

Bats: R   Throws: R   Height: 6' 1"   Weight: 180   Born: August 6, 1984   Age: 24

YEAR	TEAM	LVL	AGE	W	L	SV	G	GS	IP	H	BB	SO	HR	GB%	BABIP	STUFF	WHIP	ERA	DERA	EqH9	EqBB9	EqSO9	EqHR9	DEF	VORP	SN/WX
2006	AUG	A	21	7	3	13	44	0	61	42	12	81	3	40.0%	.277	4	0.89	1.77	4.70	9.7	3.0	6.4	1.5	3	5.4	—
2006	NRW	AA	21	0	0	2	6	0	9²	11	2	5	0	35.3%	.324	-22	1.41	3.91	8.00	12.0	2.0	2.0	0.0	2	-2.4	—
2007	AUG	A	22	0	0	4	7	0	9	1	1	9	0	31.6%	.053	9	0.22	0.00	3.12	1.0	2.1	4.2	0.0	4	2.4	—
2007	NRW	AA	22	5	0	4	35	0	56	50	21	43	3	38.7%	.288	-12	1.27	2.89	4.96	9.9	3.9	4.3	1.0	-1	3.7	—
2008	NRW	AA	23	0	0	8	27	0	36²	25	11	37	0	29.2%	.266	16	0.98	1.23	2.31	7.2	2.6	6.7	0.3	1	12.8	—
2008	FRE	AAA	23	1	0	1	5	0	9²	5	2	13	0	38.1%	.238	9	0.72	0.00	0.96	4.8	1.9	8.7	0.0	1	4.8	—
2008	SFN	MLB	23	1	2	0	20	0	20²	26	9	16	3	26.4%	.354	-9	1.69	4.78	5.48	10.5	3.4	5.9	1.3	-3	-4.1	-0.84
2009	SFN	MLB	24	2	3	2	48	2	52²	53	22	44	7	36.0%	.300	6	1.42	4.65	4.86	9.0	3.4	6.5	1.2	-0	5.2	0.49

Breakout: 11%   Improve: 35%   Collapse: 29%   Attrition: 13%   Comparables: Manny Sarmiento, Oneli Perez, Edwin Nuñez, Oscar Villarreal

Matos dominated in his repeat of Double-A last year, earning a call straight to the majors in early July. He can get his fastball up to 94 mph, but he lacks a solid secondary offering, and when his slider flattens out, as it often does, lefties feast. Matos also has a troubling fly-ball rate, and even though few of those fly balls turned into homers in the minors, that could change in a hurry in the major leagues. We're patiently waiting for the Giants to acquire Osiris's siblings, Horus and Anubis.

Pat Misch

Bats: R   Throws: L   Height: 6' 2"   Weight: 170   Born: August 18, 1981   Age: 27

YEAR	TEAM	LVL	AGE	W	L	SV	G	GS	IP	H	BB	SO	HR	GB%	BABIP	STUFF	WHIP	ERA	DERA	EqH9	EqBB9	EqSO9	EqHR9	DEF	VORP	SN/WX
2006	NRW	AA	24	5	4	0	18	17	103	95	24	79	7	48.5%	.294	-12	1.16	2.27	4.60	10.7	2.8	4.0	1.3	-2	10.2	—
2006	FRE	AAA	24	4	2	0	10	10	65²	74	11	57	7	44.0%	.327	3	1.30	4.00	3.94	11.4	1.8	5.4	1.5	-9	11.4	—
2007	FRE	AAA	25	2	5	1	34	3	66²	54	19	74	4	49.4%	.313	13	1.09	2.29	4.21	8.4	2.9	7.7	0.7	3	9.6	—
2007	SFN	MLB	25	0	4	0	18	4	40¹	47	12	26	3	44.9%	.338	1	1.46	4.24	3.86	10.2	2.3	5.4	0.7	-1	5.3	0.06
2008	FRE	AAA	26	6	5	0	20	13	87	101	27	56	15	47.5%	.319	-32	1.47	5.38	6.67	11.0	2.9	3.7	1.8	0	-10.0	—
2008	SFN	MLB	26	0	3	0	15	7	52¹	56	15	38	11	46.0%	.288	-11	1.36	5.68	6.20	8.9	2.2	5.5	1.7	4	-0.6	-0.27
2009	SFN	MLB	27	4	7	1	47	13	96²	115	31	60	13	46.0%	.320	-0	1.50	5.19	5.46	10.5	2.6	4.9	1.2	-0	2.3	0.71

Breakout: 17%   Improve: 38%   Collapse: 28%   Attrition: 32%   Comparables: Tom Urbani, Brad Woodall, Tom Bolton, Joe Kraemer

A career starter, Misch pitched well after being converted to relief in 2007, but after his first relief appearance of 2008 saw him pitch the equivalent of a quality start in relief of Barry Zito on April 27, Bochy stuck him back in the rotation as the replacement for the injured Correia. Misch responded with a 7.03 ERA in six May starts, all of them Giants losses. Thereafter he returned to relief and again pitched well in that role in both the majors and Triple-A. A finesse lefty who relies on a good changeup, Misch is more of a long man than a LOOGY, but he should continue to be valuable in that role now that the Giants have topped up their rotation.

Kelvin Pichardo

Bats: R   Throws: R   Height: 6' 0"   Weight: 160   Born: October 13, 1985   Age: 23

YEAR	TEAM	LVL	AGE	W	L	SV	G	GS	IP	H	BB	SO	HR	GB%	BABIP	STUFF	WHIP	ERA	DERA	EqH9	EqBB9	EqSO9	EqHR9	DEF	VORP	SN/WX
2006	AUG	A	20	2	4	0	12	5	36	31	17	35	1	46.6%	.286	10	1.33	3.25	6.34	11.0	6.1	3.9	1.1	-3	-2.7	—
2006	SLO	A-	20	2	0	1	6	0	15²	17	4	24	2	43.9%	.395	11	1.38	4.74	9.49	19.7	4.4	8.0	4.4	-2	-5.3	—
2007	SJO	A+	21	2	3	3	29	0	46²	37	17	71	2	40.2%	.361	20	1.16	3.08	5.53	10.2	4.3	8.1	0.9	-6	0.3	—
2007	NRW	AA	21	2	2	2	17	0	21	14	16	16	2	44.1%	.222	-10	1.43	3.86	7.45	7.9	7.4	4.2	1.9	3	-4.0	—
2008	NRW	AA	22	2	4	7	46	0	61²	49	33	62	4	38.5%	.276	8	1.33	2.48	3.30	8.2	4.5	6.4	0.9	-2	15.3	—
2009	SFN	MLB	23	2	3	1	22	5	49¹	52	28	40	6	40.0%	.310	6	1.61	5.29	5.56	9.3	4.5	6.5	1.1	-0	0.7	0.24

Breakout: 13%   Improve: 33%   Collapse: 36%   Attrition: 11%   Comparables: Sam Gervacio, Alfredo Gonzalez, Manny Barrios, Cesar Perez

Proof that the Low-A pitchers who get flipped in lesser deals don't always fade away, Pichardo is still climbing the Giants' ladder three years after he was acquired from the Phillies for the remains of Michael Tucker. Having made the leap to Double-A in mid-2007, Pichardo improved across the board upon his repeat of the level last year. The catch is that Pichardo's a small righty who throws 92 to 94 with a violent, maximum-effort delivery and complained of arm soreness last year, which suggests that his arm may give out before his stuff does.

Kevin Pucetas

Bats: R   Throws: R   Height: 6' 4"   Weight: 225   Born: November 27, 1984   Age: 24

YEAR	TEAM	LVL	AGE	W	L	SV	G	GS	IP	H	BB	SO	HR	GB%	BABIP	STUFF	WHIP	ERA	DERA	EqH9	EqBB9	EqSO9	EqHR9	DEF	VORP	SN/WX
2006	SLO	A-	21	7	1	0	15	15	70	57	19	60	2	51.2%	.283	-7	1.09	2.19	6.12	12.4	4.4	3.5	1.3	3	-3.3	—
2007	AUG	A	22	15	4	1	27	23	145¹	124	21	104	7	54.5%	.271	-10	1.00	1.86	5.01	10.6	2.2	2.9	1.2	8	8.5	—
2008	SJO	A+	23	10	2	0	24	24	125¹	115	27	102	6	51.4%	.300	-8	1.13	3.02	4.96	10.6	2.9	4.0	1.1	-5	7.9	—
2009	SFN	MLB	24	6	12	0	34	23	145¹	177	53	80	18	48.0%	.320	3	1.58	5.86	6.23	10.9	2.9	4.4	1.1	-0	-8.4	0.12

Breakout: 3%   Improve: 29%   Collapse: 28%   Attrition: 7%   Comparables: Matt Buschmann, Keith Brown, Travis Thompson, Tim Manwiller

A command/control righty out of South Carolina's tiny Limestone College, Pucetas has posted an outstanding 3.9 K/BB ratio in his three minor league seasons, but he has yet to pitch above High-A. As with all pitchers of his ilk, there are concerns that his ability to pound the strike zone won't be enough at the upper levels.

Sergio Romo

Bats: R   Throws: R   Height: 5' 11"   Weight: 185   Born: March 4, 1983   Age: 26

YEAR	TEAM	LVL	AGE	W	L	SV	G	GS	IP	H	BB	SO	HR	GB%	BABIP	STUFF	WHIP	ERA	DERA	EqH9	EqBB9	EqSO9	EqHR9	DEF	VORP	SN/WX
2006	AUG	A	23	10	2	4	31	10	103	78	19	95	9	36.4%	.255	-42	0.94	2.53	6.38	10.3	2.9	3.9	2.3	7	-7.8	—
2007	SJO	A+	24	6	2	9	41	0	66¹	35	15	106	4	34.8%	.264	15	0.75	1.36	3.30	7.2	2.8	8.9	1.2	3	15.3	—
2008	NRW	AA	25	1	3	11	24	0	27	22	7	30	1	30.4%	.323	5	1.07	4.00	6.84	9.0	2.5	7.6	0.7	1	-3.4	—
2008	SFN	MLB	25	3	1	0	29	0	34	16	8	33	3	32.6%	.163	16	0.71	2.12	4.58	3.8	1.8	7.4	0.8	5	8.2	1.94
2009	SFN	MLB	26	2	3	5	53	0	51²	44	15	49	6	36.0%	.270	16	1.14	3.65	3.86	7.6	2.3	7.5	1.0	-0	10.7	0.96

Breakout: 34%   Improve: 66%   Collapse: 16%   Attrition: 25%   Comparables: Trevor Hoffman, Keith Foulke, Jeff Reardon, John Wetteland

Romo is unique: a small righty with a funky, almost sidearm delivery, he's the rare reliever to feature a six-pitch arsenal (sinker, splitter, curve, slider, changeup, and a four-seam fastball that sits around 92 mph). None of those pitches are particularly impressive on their own, but the fact that the hitter never knows which one is coming, combined with Romo's great command and ability to hide the ball, makes him the rare finesse righty who is as good as his minor league numbers suggest and the rare low-angle righty who doesn't get hurt by lefties. After posting a 4.3 K/BB ratio as a Double-A closer last year, Romo came to the majors in late June and stranded 86 percent of his inherited runners over the season's final three months. The only man to score on his watch over his last 13 outings was an inherited runner who went home on a sac fly. He'll see late-inning work this year, whatever free agents Sabean brings in.

Billy Sadler

Bats: R   Throws: R   Height: 6' 0"   Weight: 200   Born: September 21, 1981   Age: 27

YEAR	TEAM	LVL	AGE	W	L	SV	G	GS	IP	H	BB	SO	HR	GB%	BABIP	STUFF	WHIP	ERA	DERA	EqH9	EqBB9	EqSO9	EqHR9	DEF	VORP	SN/WX
2006	NRW	AA	24	4	3	20	44	0	45¹	23	29	67	1	48.9%	.247	17	1.15	2.59	5.31	6.4	6.8	8.3	0.6	2	1.4	—
2006	FRE	AAA	24	2	0	1	7	0	10¹	5	2	12	1	43.5%	.182	9	0.69	1.78	4.15	5.2	2.1	8.3	1.0	2	1.4	—
2007	NRW	AA	25	0	0	1	9	0	12¹	3	6	18	1	55.0%	.118	11	0.73	0.73	3.97	3.2	4.8	8.7	1.6	2	2.0	—
2007	FRE	AAA	25	3	2	6	40	0	42¹	36	35	59	5	37.0%	.333	14	1.68	5.96	6.58	9.3	7.7	9.8	1.4	-3	-4.3	—
2008	FRE	AAA	26	1	0	1	22	0	33	19	21	41	0	57.3%	.257	18	1.21	1.09	3.13	6.0	5.7	8.0	0.3	2	8.7	—
2008	SFN	MLB	26	0	1	0	33	0	44¹	34	27	42	6	34.2%	.255	1	1.38	4.06	4.84	6.6	4.6	7.5	1.2	4	7.0	0.06
2009	SFN	MLB	27	2	2	2	37	0	39¹	35	23	39	4	42.0%	.290	11	1.46	4.08	4.29	8.0	4.7	7.8	0.9	-0	6.4	0.51

Breakout: 20%   Improve: 39%   Collapse: 38%   Attrition: 40%   Comparables: John Briscoe, Bob Gibson, Jeff Parrett, Dan Pfister

This Louisiana State product can get his fastball up to 95 mph when he isn't blowing people away with a vicious power curve. The problem is that he can't put the curve where he wants it, so batters spit on it and feast on his relatively straight heater. Still, he managed to dominate in Triple-A last year despite walking nearly six men per nine, and that earned him a pair of extended call-ups. The first, in May and June, didn't go particularly well, but the second, covering August and September, did. If he ever figures out how to get that curve over the plate, NL hitters are in trouble.

Jonathan Sanchez

Bats: L Throws: L Height: 6' 2" Weight: 165 Born: November 19, 1982 Age: 26

YEAR	TEAM	LVL	AGE	W	L	SV	G	GS	IP	H	BB	SO	HR	GB%	BABIP	STUFF	WHIP	ERA	DERA	EqH9	EqBB9	EqSO9	EqHR9	DEF	VORP	SN/WX
2006	NRW	AA	23	2	1	2	13	3	31²	14	9	46	0	49.2%	.250	24	0.74	1.15	3.77	6.0	3.1	8.5	0.3	0	5.8	—
2006	FRE	AAA	23	2	2	0	6	6	23¹	13	13	28	1	39.3%	.245	16	1.13	3.90	5.48	5.5	5.1	7.4	0.8	2	0.3	—
2006	SFN	MLB	23	3	1	0	27	4	40	39	23	33	2	36.0%	.306	7	1.55	4.95	4.17	8.6	4.4	6.6	0.4	-5	0.9	0.25
2007	FRE	AAA	24	0	0	0	6	3	20²	15	8	27	0	36.7%	.306	20	1.11	2.17	3.20	7.8	3.7	9.2	0.0	1	5.3	—
2007	SFN	MLB	24	1	5	0	33	4	52	57	28	62	8	43.4%	.374	14	1.63	5.88	4.06	10.1	4.2	10.1	1.2	-6	-0.3	0.31
2008	SFN	MLB	25	9	12	0	29	29	158	154	75	157	14	43.3%	.327	23	1.45	5.01	4.10	8.6	3.6	7.8	0.7	-12	10.9	2.95
2009	SFN	MLB	26	7	9	1	34	19	127²	120	56	122	12	43.0%	.300	21	1.37	4.25	4.50	8.4	3.5	7.5	0.9	-0	16.7	2.57

Breakout: 19% Improve: 41% Collapse: 25% Attrition: 21% Comparables: Erik Bedard, Pete Richert, Ken Kravec, Casey Fossum

After two years of jerking Sanchez between starting and relieving and the majors and the minors, the Giants finally just stuck him in the rotation and just let him pitch. Sanchez revealed himself to be a promising young lefty starter with a strong strikeout rate, though one prone to inconsistency and wildness. After blowing by his 2007 innings total (majors and minors combined) by 60 frames, Sanchez landed on the DL with a shoulder strain. He only missed the minimum, but when he hit the DL his ERA was 4.53, and in his five starts after returning it was 7.83. Altogether, Sanchez's innings more than doubled from 2007 to 2008 and surpassed his career high from three years prior by 32⅓. For a pitcher already struggling with control, that's worrisome.

Jack Taschner

Bats: L Throws: L Height: 6' 3" Weight: 210 Born: April 21, 1978 Age: 31

YEAR	TEAM	LVL	AGE	W	L	SV	G	GS	IP	H	BB	SO	HR	GB%	BABIP	STUFF	WHIP	ERA	DERA	EqH9	EqBB9	EqSO9	EqHR9	DEF	VORP	SN/WX
2006	FRE	AAA	28	6	7	14	45	0	49	49	17	68	5	41.6%	.389	6	1.35	3.67	4.57	11.1	3.4	9.3	1.4	-1	5.2	—
2006	SFN	MLB	28	0	1	0	24	0	19¹	31	7	15	4	28.6%	.380	-17	1.97	8.39	6.86	13.3	2.6	6.0	1.7	-6	-9.8	-0.19
2007	SFN	MLB	29	3	1	0	63	0	50	44	29	51	4	34.8%	.303	9	1.48	5.40	5.12	7.6	4.4	8.3	0.7	1	1.6	0.40
2008	SFN	MLB	30	3	2	0	67	0	48	57	24	39	5	41.4%	.344	-5	1.69	4.88	3.44	10.0	3.6	6.2	0.9	-7	3.1	-0.58
2009	SFN	MLB	31	2	2	2	45	0	41²	43	19	38	5	40.0%	.320	7	1.49	4.84	5.11	9.1	3.7	7.3	1.0	-0	2.5	0.21

Breakout: 32% Improve: 54% Collapse: 28% Attrition: 34% Comparables: Bob MacDonald, Fred Scherman, Yorkis Perez, Doug Henry

The arrival of Hinshaw made Taschner the second lefty in the Giants pen, but even that seemed too much for Taschner to do well at. From May 8 through the end of the season, nearly half of Taschner's inherited runners came around to score, he blew four saves in the first three weeks of August, and his second-half ERA swelled to 8.24 as opponents hit .380/.429/.598 against him. A high opponents' batting average on balls in play can be blamed for some of that, but not all. With the arrival of Jeremy Affeldt, Taschner may be out of a job.

Merkin Valdez

Bats: R Throws: R Height: 6' 3" Weight: 220 Born: November 10, 1981 Age: 27

YEAR	TEAM	LVL	AGE	W	L	SV	G	GS	IP	H	BB	SO	HR	GB%	BABIP	STUFF	WHIP	ERA	DERA	EqH9	EqBB9	EqSO9	EqHR9	DEF	VORP	SN/WX
2006	FRE	AAA	24	0	4	5	46	3	49	52	39	48	6	49.1%	.325	-19	1.86	5.88	8.03	10.2	6.9	5.7	1.5	-6	-13.3	—
2008	SFN	MLB	26	1	0	0	17	1	16	14	7	13	1	48.9%	.289	3	1.31	1.69	2.81	7.9	3.4	6.2	0.6	0	5.0	0.67
2009	SFN	MLB	27	2	2	1	30	2	41	41	19	33	4	47.0%	.300	5	1.45	4.29	4.57	8.9	3.7	6.3	0.9	-0	5.7	0.51

Breakout: 37% Improve: 57% Collapse: 25% Attrition: 35% Comparables: Brad Arnsberg, John Montague, Rodney Myers, Frank Reberger

Coming off a season lost to Tommy John surgery, Valdez made the Giants out of camp last spring and pitched well until pain in his pitching elbow pushed him to the DL in mid-May; he spent the rest of the season getting evaluated and rehabbing. When healthy, he can dominate with his high-90s heat, but entering his age-27 season, we're beginning to wonder if he'll ever be healthy again.

Tyler Walker

| | | | | | | | | | | | | Bats: R | | Throws: R | | Height: 6' 3" | | Weight: 275 | | Born: May 15, 1976 | | | Age: 33 |

YEAR	TEAM	LVL	AGE	W	L	SV	G	GS	IP	H	BB	SO	HR	GB%	BABIP	STUFF	WHIP	ERA	DERA	EqH9	EqBB9	EqSO9	EqHR9	DEF	VORP	SN/WX
2007	SJO	A+	31	0	0	0	3	10	0	10¹	9	2	15	0	41.7%	.409	9	1.07	1.75	2.00	12.0	3.0	8.0	0.0	-1	3.6	—
2007	FRE	AAA	31	1	2	7	20	0	23	25	10	23	5	43.7%	.308	-22	1.52	4.70	6.45	10.5	4.0	6.4	2.4	3	-2.1	—
2007	SFN	MLB	31	2	0	0	15	0	14¹	12	4	9	0	35.0%	.308	8	1.12	1.26	0.71	8.5	2.1	5.7	0.0	-1	7.4	0.91
2008	SFN	MLB	32	5	8	0	65	0	53¹	47	21	49	7	46.5%	.276	-1	1.28	4.56	5.50	7.5	3.0	7.2	1.2	5	4.6	1.06
2009	SFN	MLB	33	2	2	2	39	0	42¹	45	19	35	5	43.0%	.310	2	1.50	4.82	5.10	9.4	3.6	6.5	1.1	-0	2.6	0.21

Breakout: 6%　Improve: 28%　Collapse: 44%　Attrition: 28%　　Comparables: Matt Karchner, Terry Mathews, Tim Worrell, Jerry Spradlin

After working his way back from Tommy John surgery in 2007, Walker emerged as the Giants' primary set-up man in 2008 and pitched well save for a rocky May. Still, Sergio Romo began to intrude on his eighth-inning turf as the second half progressed, and the Giants opted to bring back Bobby Howry rather than re-sign Walker for 2009. Walker has since signed with the Mariners and will be in the mix for late-game innings once again.

Brian Wilson

| | | | | | | | | | | | | Bats: R | | Throws: R | | Height: 6' 1" | | Weight: 205 | | Born: March 16, 1982 | | | Age: 27 |

YEAR	TEAM	LVL	AGE	W	L	SV	G	GS	IP	H	BB	SO	HR	GB%	BABIP	STUFF	WHIP	ERA	DERA	EqH9	EqBB9	EqSO9	EqHR9	DEF	VORP	SN/WX
2006	FRE	AAA	24	1	3	7	24	0	28¹	20	14	30	2	48.1%	.253	0	1.21	2.88	4.10	7.5	4.8	6.8	1.0	1	4.4	—
2006	SFN	MLB	24	2	3	1	31	0	30	32	21	23	1	45.8%	.344	1	1.77	5.40	5.40	9.6	5.4	6.3	0.3	1	1.0	-0.08
2007	FRE	AAA	25	1	2	11	31	0	34¹	24	24	37	0	44.9%	.276	9	1.40	2.10	4.54	7.0	6.4	7.0	0.3	3	4.0	—
2007	SFN	MLB	25	1	2	6	24	0	23²	16	7	18	1	56.7%	.227	9	0.97	2.28	3.42	5.7	2.3	6.5	0.4	3	9.4	1.75
2008	SFN	MLB	26	3	2	41	63	0	62¹	62	28	67	7	51.7%	.340	10	1.44	4.62	3.92	8.9	3.5	8.6	1.0	-3	7.0	3.56
2009	SFN	MLB	27	3	5	25	53	0	57²	54	28	54	5	49.0%	.300	12	1.41	3.92	4.19	8.3	3.9	7.3	0.7	-0	9.6	1.35

Breakout: 10%　Improve: 34%　Collapse: 40%　Attrition: 19%　　Comparables: Paul Shuey, D.J. Carrasco, Jose Paniagua, Jack Baldschun

The Giants only won 72 games last year, but Wilson saved 41 of them. That's not all that unusual—he's just 17th on the list of percentage of team wins saved in a single season (Bryan Harvey's 45 saves for the 64-win expansion Marlins in 1993 tops the list)—but it's evidence that at least one San Francisco hurler actually benefited from his team's impotent offense. Wilson finished fourth in the NL in WXRL behind Brad Lidge, Carlos Marmol, and Brian Fuentes, and likely deserves an assist for Lincecum's Cy Young Award given the voters' focus on win totals and the fact that Wilson saved 12 of Lincecum's 18 wins. Wouldn't it be nice if he did it all again this year?

Keiichi Yabu

| | | | | | | | | | | | | Bats: R | | Throws: R | | Height: 6' 1" | | Weight: 200 | | Born: September 28, 1968 | | | Age: 40 |

YEAR	TEAM	LVL	AGE	W	L	SV	G	GS	IP	H	BB	SO	HR	GB%	BABIP	STUFF	WHIP	ERA	DERA	EqH9	EqBB9	EqSO9	EqHR9	DEF	VORP	SN/WX
2006	TIJ	MEX	37	0	0	5	11	0	12²	14	2	9	0	72.4%	.333	-8	1.31	2.95	5.73	11.5	2.5	5.7	0.0	1	-0.2	—
2008	SFN	MLB	39	3	6	0	60	0	68	63	32	48	3	47.7%	.288	2	1.40	3.57	4.43	8.0	3.5	5.5	0.4	3	9.7	0.28
2009	SFN	MLB	40	2	2	1	33	0	39¹	42	20	29	4	47.0%	.310	-4	1.57	4.94	5.30	9.6	4.0	5.8	0.8	-0	1.7	0.11

Breakout: 7%　Improve: 15%　Collapse: 65%　Attrition: 38%　　Comparables: Al Worthington, Jose Mesa, Virgil Trucks, Steve Reed

A veteran starter out of the Japanese leagues, Yabu came to America in 2005 to pitch in relief for the A's, but after a middling season in middle relief he failed to make the Rockies out of camp in 2006 and requested his release. He came to the Giants on a minor league deal with the Giants in late 2007, and then made the team out of camp last spring, only to get off to a rocky start complicated by a bizarre incident in which the elastic band he was using to stretch his arm came loose and scratched both of his eyes. After a brief demotion, he returned and pitched reasonably well in an early-inning set-up role despite middling peripherals. He'll return this year as a 40-year-old with just two major league seasons under his belt.

Barry Zito

							Bats: L		Throws: L		Height: 6' 4"		Weight: 210		Born: May 13, 1978			Age: 31

YEAR	TEAM	LVL	AGE	W	L	SV	G	GS	IP	H	BB	SO	HR	GB%	BABIP	STUFF	WHIP	ERA	DERA	EqH9	EqBB9	EqSO9	EqHR9	DEF	VORP	SN/WX
2006	OAK	MLB	28	16	10	0	34	34	221	211	99	151	27	40.0%	.287	3	1.40	3.83	3.94	8.5	4.0	5.6	1.1	-2	49.5	6.16
2007	SFN	MLB	29	11	13	0	34	33	196²	182	83	131	24	41.1%	.267	5	1.35	4.53	5.21	7.8	3.2	5.5	1.0	20	24.3	4.18
2008	SFN	MLB	30	10	17	0	32	32	180	186	102	120	16	37.8%	.307	5	1.60	5.15	5.26	8.8	4.3	5.2	0.7	-1	-1.0	2.03
2009	SFN	MLB	31	7	10	0	24	24	144¹	147	63	106	16	41.0%	.290	14	1.46	4.61	4.85	9.1	3.5	5.8	1.0	-0	12.7	2.51

Breakout: 12%   Improve: 37%   Collapse: 30%   Attrition: 20%   Comparables: Vinegar Bend Mizell, Doyle Alexander, Russ Ortiz, Darryl Kile

After declining in each of the previous three seasons, Zito's strikeout rate held steady last year, but he compensated for that by posting a career-high walk rate, which produced a miserable 1.2 K/BB and contributed to his career-high ERA and career-low innings total. Despite visions of a 2011 rotation of Lincecum, Cain, Sanchez, Bumgarner, and Alderson, the Giants still owe Zito $101.5 million on a contract that's guaranteed through 2013. They might want to start looking for a Mike Hampton-style trade (absorbing most of the expense) just to rid themselves of their mistake, though given how the Hampton trade worked out for the Braves, they're unlikely to find any takers. Now that Randy Johnson is on-board, Zito becomes the Giants' fifth starter and third-best lefty in the rotation. If you want to grasp at some very thin straws of hope, Zito did shave more than a run off of his ERA in the second half and pitched quite well in September.

LINEOUTS

Hitters

PLAYER	TEAM	LVL	AGE	PA	R	2B	3B	HR	RBI	BB	SO	SB-CS	EqBRR	AVG/OBP/SLG	EqAVG/EqOBP/EqSLG	EqA	VORP	WARP
C E. Alfonzo	NRW	AA	29	84	8	7	0	2	15	2	18	0-0	-1.6	.363/.393/.525	.247/.265/.370	.215	-3.0	-0.1
	FRE	AAA	29	125	17	10	1	5	24	7	30	1-0	-0.3	.310/.352/.543	.237/.278/.424	.240	-1.2	0.3
UT M. Downs	SJO	A+	24	489	74	30	1	17	75	34	57	24-13	-3.0	.304/.357/.494	.238/.284/.383	.230	-10.9	-1.0
	FRE	AAA	24	94	10	5	0	3	7	4	10	1-0	-0.1	.244/.298/.407	.218/.266/.356	.218	-4.1	-0.5
1B B. Harper*	FRE	AAA	26	370	48	32	0	20	59	13	57	0-1	-6.3	.315/.338/.577	.256/.278/.465	.248	3.7	-0.2
C S. Holm	FRE	AAA	28	79	7	4	0	0	11	10	12	0-0	-0.2	.273/.367/.333	.206/.291/.250	.200	-5.6	-0.2
	SFN	MLB	28	98	10	9	0	1	6	10	16	0-1	-0.4	.262/.357/.405	.262/.357/.429	.271	3.1	-0.1
UT B. Horwitz	FRE	AAA	25	302	40	11	1	7	29	31	42	1-1	1.2	.277/.353/.405	.230/.301/.341	.227	-9.2	-0.4
	SFN	MLB	25	42	5	0	0	2	4	5	10	0-0	0.1	.222/.310/.389	.222/.310/.389	.247	-0.3	0.6
C A. Witter*	NRW	AA	25	471	56	18	2	20	77	64	102	1-5	-4.8	.238/.345/.443	.209/.300/.391	.238	-8.1	-0.1

Previously suspended for a minor league substance violation in 2005, **Eliezer Alfonzo** served a 50-game suspension for testing positive for the steroid Stanozolol last year. Dropped from the Giants' 40-man roster after the season, he could land the Padres' backup catching job as a non-roster invitee this spring. ⊘ Utilityman **Matt Downs** has played everywhere but center field and catcher as a pro—he even worked as a relief pitcher at the University of Alabama—and offers power, speed, and a .310 lifetime average, though he's been old for his levels. ⊘ After seven years in the Mets' system, first baseman **Brett Harper** signed with the Giants and made a successful Triple-A debut at 26, continuing to display his excellent power and poor plate discipline. ⊘ Veteran minor league backup catcher **Steve Holm** put in for an apprenticeship en route to trying to get his union card in the International Brotherhood of Backup Catchers. ⊘ A marginal corner outfielder, **Brian Horwitz** could be useful as a bench bat, but failed to make an impression in his big-league debut during a brief mid-year call-up last year. ⊘ An undrafted graduate of East Carolina University, lefty-hitting catcher **Adam Witter** has shown some pop and a willingness to take a walk as a pro, but he's been consistently old for his level and has seen his batting average nosedive as he's advanced.

Pitchers

PLAYER	TEAM	LVL	AGE	W	L	SV	IP	H	BB	SO	HR	GB%	BABIP	STUFF	WHIP	ERA	DERA	EqH9	EqBB9	EqSO9	EqHR9	DEF	VORP
S. Barnes*	AUG	A	20	3	2	0	32²	15	7	41	0	39.4%	.198	31	0.67	1.38	5.58	5.9	2.9	5.9	0.3	8	0.1
V. Chulk	FRE	AAA	29	0	1	2	24²	25	13	21	3	37.8%	.324	-18	1.54	3.64	5.09	10.2	5.1	5.1	1.2	3	1.3
	SFN	MLB	29	0	3	0	31²	33	8	16	6	38.1%	.257	-18	1.29	4.83	4.86	8.4	1.9	3.8	1.6	1	2.0
J. Hedrick	NRW	AA	26	2	3	9	65²	41	21	74	4	29.8%	.239	12	0.94	1.37	3.13	6.5	2.8	7.5	0.9	4	17.4
W. Joaquin	AUG	A	21	1	2	2	52	49	20	49	1	49.0%	.324	-6	1.33	4.33	7.29	11.6	5.1	4.1	0.6	-7	-8.6
	SJO	A+	21	0	1	0	19¹	20	11	23	2	39.7%	.382	-4	1.61	4.66	7.88	13.5	7.3	6.8	2.2	-3	-4.1
M. Loree	SLO	A-	21	4	3	0	81	63	7	75	2	42.8%	.286	6	0.86	2.44	5.79	9.2	1.7	3.3	1.1	5	-1.5
D. Maday	AUG	A	22	9	4	0	104²	74	23	92	3	58.3%	.254	5	0.93	1.55	4.52	8.6	3.1	3.9	0.8	12	11.2
	SJO	A+	22	3	0	0	22	20	5	27	1	57.1%	.353	20	1.14	2.05	2.21	10.6	3.1	6.2	0.9	-5	7.6
	NRW	AA	22	1	1	0	18¹	31	8	11	2	40.0%	.426	-25	2.13	8.36	9.00	18.6	4.5	3.9	1.7	-3	-6.0
S. Palazzolo	NRW	AA	26	5	5	1	43	30	29	40	1	52.7%	.274	3	1.37	3.56	5.58	7.6	6.0	6.2	0.4	2	0.1
E. Quirarte	SLO	A-	21	3	3	14	29²	23	9	33	0	53.5%	.321	0	1.08	2.12	4.67	9.3	3.7	4.0	0.7	-2	2.8
B. Snyder*	SJO	A+	22	8	3	0	85²	79	18	73	2	47.6%	.308	13	1.13	2.00	3.40	10.4	2.8	4.2	0.7	-7	18.7
	NRW	AA	22	1	6	0	61²	77	23	44	9	38.4%	.345	-18	1.62	5.98	7.34	13.1	3.4	4.5	2.0	-3	-11.2
H. Sosa	SJO	A+	22	3	4	0	56¹	62	18	58	6	38.4%	.361	-12	1.42	4.32	6.00	13.9	4.3	5.4	2.2	-5	-2.1
C. Tanner*	SJO	A+	20	10	8	0	117	124	39	84	1	55.4%	.335	25	1.39	3.69	6.41	11.7	4.2	3.2	0.4	-11	-9.5
E. Threets*	FRE	AAA	26	4	5	0	66¹	53	36	46	5	57.5%	.247	-16	1.34	3.39	5.81	7.2	4.7	3.9	0.8	9	-1.6
	SFN	MLB	26	0	1	0	10	11	9	6	1	34.4%	.333	-3	2.00	3.60	2.79	10.2	7.4	4.7	0.9	-1	2.2

The Giants feel they got a steal in 2008 eighth-round pick **Scott Barnes**, a lefty out of St. John's who had no problems dominating in the full-season Sally League in his pro debut thanks to a three-pitch mix and an advanced feel for his craft. ⊘ A handful of rough relief outings last June got **Vinnie Chulk** dropped from the 40-man roster, and the fact that he slipped through waivers is an indication of his remaining value after his strikeout rate more than halved itself over the past four seasons. ⊘ A marginal fastball/slider reliever out of Northeastern University, **Justin Hedrick** has yet to reach Triple-A at age 26, though he did show progress repeating Double-A last year. ⊘ The Giants have been careful with **Waldis Joaquin** since Tommy John surgery wiped out his 2006 season, but he should ultimately settle in as a starter. He combines a mid-90s fastball with a plus slider, but needs a lot of work on his changeup and messy delivery. ⊘ Summit, New Jersey's **Mike Loree** has an insane 11.9 K/BB ratio as a pro, but he also has a fastball in the mid-80s. A Villanova grad pitching in the low minors, his stats will level out as he advances and those BP fastballs start getting turned around. ⊘ University of Arkansas product **Daryl Maday** (proposed nickname: "Make") pitched well in the Sally League last year, but struggled after a promotion to Double-A; he should ultimately settle in as a reliever. ⊘ Signed out of the independent leagues for the second time in the last three years, **Steve Palazzolo** gets a lot of velocity out of his 6-foot-10 frame, but he needs a lot of refinement. ⊘ A fifth-round pick last June, righty **Edwin Quirarte** is a strike-throwing college product without a ton of upside, but his sinker/slider combination could allow him to move quickly as a reliever. ⊘ The younger brother of former Indians prospect Brad, Ball State product **Ben Snyder** throws in the high 80s with a good change and slider, pounds the zone, and could be anything from a fifth starter to a LOOGY. ⊘ After a breakthrough year at High-A in 2007, **Henry Sosa** took a step backward last year, repeating the level with less success while fighting health and mechanical issues, though his mid-90s plus heat still intrigues. ⊘ Sinkerballing **Clayton Tanner** is one of the few high school pitchers in the Giants' system. Ironically, he offers the same low-ceiling finesse repertoire as his college-educated brethren but is more studious and obsessive in his preparation than his matriculated mates. ⊘ A lefty who can bring it in the upper 90s, **Erick Threets** sounds exciting until you discover he has no idea where his pitches are going.

MANAGER: BRUCE BOCHY

YEAR	TEAM	W-L	Pythag +/−	Avg PC	100+ P	120+ P	QS	BQS	REL	REL w Zero R	IBB	Subs	PH	PH Avg	PH HR	SB2	CS2	SB3	CS3	SAC Att	SAC %	POS SAC	Squeeze	Swing	In Play
2006	SDN	88-74	1	95.8	66	5	83	9	475	320	63	82	258	.260	8	111	26	12	4	79	74.7%	19	1	157	114
2007	SFN	71-91	-6	98.8	78	8	78	7	495	310	41	83	261	.268	5	106	29	13	2	94	71.3%	31	4	145	115
2008	SFN	72-90	5	99.9	91	8	80	9	478	287	59	60	273	.239	3	99	41	6	1	97	58.8%	26	3	161	133

Bruce Bochy couldn't have done anything to make the 2008 Giants something more than a last-place team, though it's troubling that he abused the only asset he had, his best young pitchers. Under Bochy, the Giants led the majors in pitching starts lasting 100, 110, and 120 or more pitches, and finished second only to the Mets in average pitches per start. Of the eight Giants starts that lasted more than 120 pitches, five of them were by Lincecum, and two of the other three were by Cain. If the Giants have any hope for the future, it's riding on those two arms, perhaps making those long outings about the worst thing Bochy could have done in 2008. The only other particularly notable thing about Bochy's management in 2008 was that his team ranked second to Lou Piniella's Cubs in swings with the runners in motion, our stat that approximates hit-and-run plays. The hit-and-run, while notionally effective at reducing double plays, also reduces batting average and slugging percentage by forcing the hitter to swing at a potentially bad pitch and try to avoid hitting it in the air. That makes it a play that reduces both risk and reward, not terribly unlike the sacrifice bunt, a strategy Bochy was far less inclined to employ. Such strategies make little sense for a high-scoring team loaded with power hitters like the Cubs, but aren't a bad way for a team with strong starting pitching that's far less likely to be rewarded by letting its hitters swing away to try to scratch out the extra run or two that could cash in a strong performance by one of those young starters. Intriguingly, the tactic worked well for the Cubs, but the Giants were one of the teams in baseball most likely to bounce into a twin-killing, suggesting that there's no avoiding the damage done by weak hitters.

Seattle Mariners

In baseball, as in urban nightlife, admittance to an exclusive club remains a cause for celebration. Despite the ravages of time and run scoring, groups beginning with the numbers "500," "300," and even "30/30" retain much of their cachet. The desire to classify "unique" talents according to their shared accomplishments extends even to the fabrication of ultraselective nonentities like the "20-20-20-20 Club," gerrymandered categories that hold little significance outside the minds of their creators. In light of the baseball community's fixation on largely arbitrary statistical designations, it should come as no surprise that the 2008 Mariners, finding themselves barred from the swankier establishments, founded their own: the 100-100 Club.

Also not surprisingly, the team's 2009 pocket schedule makes no mention of its status as a charter member. This lack of fanfare stems from the fact that membership in the 100-100 Club, like a subscription to Publishers Clearing House, rarely leads to a winning effort. Last season, the Mariners became the first team in baseball history to lose at least 100 games while spending a minimum of $100 million on player salaries. When the dust settled, the M's entered the history books with a 61-101 record and a $117.6 million payroll, a woeful return on investment. The team shelled out $7.3 million per marginal win, by far the highest total in the major leagues, where $2.4 million was the going rate. By way of comparison, the free-spending (and similarly playoff-missing) Yankees spent a mere $4.6 million per marginal win. For a team like the Mariners, which belatedly discovered that its assembled talent placed it near the bottom of the win curve—a state of affairs that de-

presses the value of each additional victory—this sort of profligacy constitutes especially glaring evidence of mismanagement.

The foundations for this disastrous campaign were laid during the Mariners' superficially successful 2007 season, when an 88-74 record ended a string of three consecutive sub-.500 finishes. The Mariners trailed the division-leading Angels by a single game as late as August 25 and maintained their precarious perch atop the wild-card standings four days later, convincing then general manager Bill Bavasi that his charges were poised to take the next step the following season. In reality, the Mariners weren't as good as their record indicated, outperforming their 79-83 Pythagorean mark by nine games.

The most momentous moves that Bavasi engineered over the 2007–2008 offseason, which were intended to put the finishing touches on a playoff contender, failed to pay dividends. Bavasi raised eyebrows across baseball by awarding middling free-agent right-hander Carlos Silva a four-year, $48 million contract and compounded that misguided decision by sending five players, including his top prospect, outfielder Adam Jones, to the Orioles for their talented but fragile lefty, Erik Bedard.

Silva arrived in Seattle with an "innings-eater" label in tow after averaging 193 frames per season during his four-year stint with the Twins. However, even this moderately valuable skill deserted him last season, as he logged just 153⅓ innings while being slowed by thigh, back, and elbow injuries. His new employers found that the innings he did consume did not agree with them, as

---

MARINERS PROSPECTUS

2008 record: 61-101; Fourth place in AL West

Pythagenport record: 67-95

Runs scored per game: 4.14 (13th in AL)

Runs allowed per game: 5.09 (11th in AL)

Team EqA: .250 (Tied for 12th in AL)

2008 Batters Age: 30.2 (7th-oldest in AL)

2008 Pitchers Age: 28.7 (5th-oldest in AL)

Ballpark: Safeco Field; Pitcher's park; Park Factor of .954

2008: Jim Riggleman thinks he's died and gone to the 1993 Padres, as the M's are hoisted by their own Bedard.

2009: Jack Z goes diving into the wreck looking for usable parts and finds only "a book of myths in which our names do not appear."

he finished with an awful .415 rate of Support-Neutral Lineup-Adjusted Value (or SNLVA_R, where .500 is average), the worst mark in the majors for anyone with 150 IP or more. Despite the size of his contract, Silva was never regarded as more than a complementary piece, however. Bedard was the guy ticketed for the vacancy at the top of the rotation. He, too, failed in convincing fashion, justifying every concern about his durability en route to making only 15 starts and accumulating a total of 81 IP. Bedard's lackluster spring training gave way to an absentee April, and shoulder problems felled him for good after July 4. He went under the knife in September after rest failed to fix what ailed him, and is now on track for a spring return.

On the other side of the ball, Bavasi wisely allowed the Royals to assume the burden of combustible outfielder Jose Guillen, but his replacement, free agent Brad Wilkerson, lasted just over a month in a Mariners uniform, posting a .243 EqA before being granted his release on May 7. Bavasi neglected to cut bait on some of the other sunk costs lining his roster, retaining the services of Richie Sexson, Jose Vidro, and Willie Bloomquist long enough for them to do considerable harm.

The failures of Bavasi's highest-profile acquisitions supplied the spark that ignited a tinder-filled roster. The Mariners floundered in all facets of the game, as their 4.1 runs scored per game, 5.0 runs allowed per game, and .682 defensive efficiency placed 26th, 24th, and 25th, respectively, in the major leagues. The team's comprehensive yet foreseeable collapse claimed its architect's job on June 16, when Bavasi was replaced with assistant GM Lee Pelekoudas, a veteran of almost 30 years with the Mariners' organization, on an interim basis. Pelekoudas fired manager John McLaren a few days later, replacing him with bench coach Jim Riggleman, again on an interim basis. These necessary changes produced few short-term improvements, as the damage had already been done, both on the field and during the previous offseason. By the time Bavasi and McLaren were removed, the team had fallen to 22 games below .500, and reports of indifferent players and a poisonous clubhouse atmosphere had begun to circulate.

Handcuffed by an indeterminate mandate from ownership, Pelekoudas did what he could to take out the trash. He released Sexson on July 10. Designated hitter Jose Vidro was put out of his misery on August 13, after his EqA had fallen to .220. Pelekoudas tried to apply his scalpel to other diseased portions of the roster, but his hand was stayed by team president Chuck Armstrong, who nixed trades that would have sent southpaw starter Jarrod Washburn to the Twins and left fielder Raul Ibañez to the Blue Jays. The departure of Washburn alone would have contributed $12.5 million to the team's rebuilding fund. Instead, barring a trade that does meet with Armstrong's approval, Washburn will spend the final year of his four-year, $37.5 million contract posting his usual unimpressive performance in Seattle. Though Ibañez's .296 EqA established him as the Mariners' most productive hitter in 2008, and he probably would have brought *something* in trade, he leaves under his own power, floating to Philadelphia as a free agent. The Mariners partly redeemed the situation by taking the increasingly rare step of offering Ibañez arbitration. The Phillies played ball, making the equally rare decision to sign him, despite the resultant forfeiture of draft picks, a rookie error by their new GM, Ruben Amaro, Jr.

Though Pelekoudas did little to betray their trust in his short time at the helm, Armstrong and CEO Howard Lincoln decided to make a complete break with the Bavasi era this offseason. After a lengthy search, the Mariners hired Jack Zduriencik to serve as their next GM. Zduriencik played an integral role in the Brewers' resurrection as the team's scouting director and has long been considered one of the top talent evaluators in the game, but his ascension to the top of the executive hierarchy had been hampered by his aversion to self-promotion. The well-regarded Pelekoudas remains with the team as an assistant GM.

In resolving his first order of business in picking a skipper, Zduriencik exhibited a rather unorthodox yet refreshing approach to managerial hiring. He interviewed seven candidates, none of whom had managed previously in the majors, and settled on a man after his own heart: Athletics bench coach Don Wakamatsu. Like Zduriencik, Wakamatsu not only defies attempts at proper spelling, but also has built a stellar reputation within the game, despite laboring in low-profile positions as a minor league manager and major league coach.

The addition of Zduriencik and Wakamatsu didn't represent the only change of gears, however. An unfamiliarity with contemporary performance analysis and sabermetrics was a charge that plagued the Bavasi regime. Though a product of the old school, Zduriencik moved quickly to allay any fears of deficiency in this respect, hiring Tony Blengino as his special assistant. A CPA in his prebaseball life, Blengino became the Brewers' assistant director of amateur scouting after he wrote a series of annual publications entitled *Future Stars*, statistics-friendly overviews of the top prospects in each organization, which appeared in the late 1990s and early 2000s. Blengino will head the team's newly created Department of Statistical Research, playing a vital role in player evaluation. The team has also secured the consulting services of noted sabermetrician Tom Tango, as well as those of former Baseball Prospectus contributor Mat Olkin, who has worked previously for the Mariners, but who can expect to find a more receptive audience in his new employers.

In an interview with BP's David Laurila, Blengino observed, "It was clear going in that [the previous regime] overrated their team from the last year," revealing a clear understanding of the predicament in which the current incarnation of the team finds itself. Frustrated Mariners fans may take solace in the knowledge that their unelected representatives are saying the right things and entertaining all approaches to successful team-building, but while the Mariners appear to have chosen the best available men for the job, transforming a last-place club into a pennant-winner does not necessarily follow from even an enlightened front-office reshuffling. Hiring executives from outside an organization is not unlike dipping into the free-agent market for established veterans, in that one pays for past performance in the hope that it continues. It remains to be seen whether Blengino's foresight will equal his hindsight in his new role, but the Mariners have done all they could off the field to improve their chances.

Zduriencik would like to continue Pelekoudas's efforts to offload bad contracts and has been promised ownership's cooperation in his attempts. Those who know Zduriencik say that they will be shocked if he doesn't eventually turn the Mariners into contenders with videogame giant Nintendo's resources at his disposal. One factor working in the Mariners' favor this season is that in a reversal of their 2008 plight, they are coming off a year in which they *under*achieved, finishing with a record six wins worse than their projected 67-95 Pythagorean mark. The most notable albatross contracts remaining on the books are those of Silva, who has $41 million coming to him over the next three seasons, and catcher Kenji Johjima, who signed a three-year, $24 million extension last April, which goes into effect this season.

Johjima's contract illustrates some of the pitfalls inherent in absentee ownership. Eighty-one-year-old former Nintendo president Hiroshi Yamauchi served as the team's principal owner from 1992 till 2004 and continues to exert a powerful sway over its operations, but has yet to witness his team's play in person. Multiple reports last year claimed that Yamauchi had forced Bavasi to sign Johjima to the aforementioned extension, despite criticism of his work as a receiver expressed by many of the Mariners' pitchers, particularly Bedard. In addition, the signing blocked a number of promising young catchers, including Jeff Clement, Rob Johnson, and Adam Moore, from the 40-man roster or the farm.

In addition to Silva, Johjima, and Washburn, third baseman Adrian Beltre ($12 million) and right-hander Miguel Batista ($9 million) represent extraneous expenditures that Zduriencik will almost certainly try to unload before the July 31 nonwaiver trading deadline. Bedard, who was eligible for arbitration at the end of last season and stands to test the free market at the conclusion of '09, may also find himself on the move if his surgically repaired shoulder proves sound.

And then, of course, there's Ichiro. While the star right fielder has managed at least 200 hits in each of his eight major league seasons, his teammates may not share the Seattle public's adoration for the Japanese import. The effects of clubhouse chemistry are often overblown and always unmeasurable, but Suzuki's production has never quite equaled his celebrity, as the scarcity of walks and home runs in his game ties most of his offensive value to his fluctuating batting average. Suzuki is in just the second year of a five-year, $90 million contract and, at age 35, constitutes a luxury item on a team in transition. However, Yamauchi's influence and Ichiro's marketability renders the possibility of a trade extremely unlikely.

Though the prospects for short-term success appear bleak, the Mariners aren't completely devoid of players with potential. Felix Hernandez possesses as much talent as does any starting pitcher in the game. He posted a .575 SNLVA_R last season and won't turn 23 until the first week of the season. Left-hander Ryan Rowland-Smith, 26, and right-hander Brandon Morrow, 24, both made seamless conversions from the bullpen to the starting rotation in the second half of last season. Morrow in particular has the stuff to fill the second slot behind Hernandez. Second baseman Jose Lopez is 25 and coming off a season in which he produced a much-improved defensive performance and a career-high .273 EqA.

Zduriencik also showed some creativity in his first trade, a three-team, 12-player extravaganza with the Mets and the Indians at the Winter Meetings in Las Vegas. From Seattle's perspective, the deal's key components were departing closer J. J. Putz, who was shipped to the Mets, incoming Mets right-hander Aaron Heilman, and outfielder Franklin Gutierrez, who migrated from the shores of Lake Erie to those of Puget Sound. The Mariners also netted a couple of usable spare parts for the big-league roster in left-hander Jason Vargas and outfielder Endy Chavez, along with three prospects who will fortify a farm system weakened by the Bedard trade.

Heilman needed a change of scenery, as he was unhappy working out of the bullpen with the Mets, and battled through knee problems while posting a -0.35 WXRL last season. The 26-year-old Gutierrez's EqA was a lackluster .247, but his tremendous range and defensive skills in center allow the team to put Suzuki in right for the foreseeable future. When the similarly slick-fielding Chavez mans left, the M's outfield trio will be one of the league's weakest offensive units but a true boon to the pitching staff in spacious Safeco Field.

Once the press conference announcing the complex trade had ended and most of those assembled had vacated the Bellagio press room, Zduriencik said with a smile, "That was a lot of fun, but there is still a lot of work to be done." For the first time in years, Mariners fans can contemplate the product of that labor with optimism.

HITTERS

Wladimir Balentien — RF

Bats: R   Throws: R   Height: 6' 2"   Weight: 190   Born: July 2, 1984   Age: 24

YEAR	TEAM	LVL	AGE	PA	R	2B	3B	HR	RBI	BB	SO	SB	CS	EqBRR	AVG	OBP	SLG	EqAVG	EqOBP	EqSLG	EqA	VORP	WARP	DEFENSE				
2006	SAN	AA	21	522	76	23	1	22	82	70	140	14	7	-0.7	.230	.337	.435	.210	.300	.386	.240	-9.9	0.5	94-RF	2	20-CF	3
2007	TAC	AAA	22	544	77	24	4	24	84	54	105	15	4	2.8	.291	.362	.509	.265	.333	.466	.274	20.4	1.6	106-RF	-6	5-LF	1
2008	TAC	AAA	23	275	49	20	0	18	55	32	49	3	4	-3.0	.266	.354	.584	.238	.316	.506	.272	10.3	1.3	24-LF	1	19-CF	-3
2008	SEA	MLB	23	260	23	13	0	7	24	16	79	0	1	-0.9	.202	.250	.342	.202	.254	.351	.205	-13.2	-1.4	33-RF	1	25-CF	-4
2009	SEA	MLB	24	477	48	22	1	15	58	41	125	5	2	-0.1	.226	.297	.392	.229	.300	.415	.247	-5.0	0.5	113-RF	-1		

Breakout: 19% Improve: 45% Collapse: 29% Attrition: 11%   Comparables: Justin Huber, Ozzie Timmons, Jose Malave, Richard Hidalgo

Pitchers exploited Balentien's lack of plate discipline in his first extended taste of the major leagues last season, continually enticing him to chase pitches out of the strike zone. A lack of patience has long been Balentien's bugaboo, but his Isolated Discipline recouped some of its 2007 losses in Tacoma last season, whereas his power reached heights unseen since his romp through the Arizona Fall League in 2003. Despite his struggles in the majors, he remains a safe long-term player. Balentien's struggles against righties in Seattle aren't reflective of his minor league splits, but, when coupled with his defensive inadequacies, make Endy Chavez the perfect caddy for the presumptive Opening Day left fielder.

Adrian Beltre — 3B

Bats: R   Throws: R   Height: 5' 11"   Weight: 220   Born: April 7, 1979   Age: 30

YEAR	TEAM	LVL	AGE	PA	R	2B	3B	HR	RBI	BB	SO	SB	CS	EqBRR	AVG	OBP	SLG	EqAVG	EqOBP	EqSLG	EqA	VORP	WARP	DEFENSE	
2006	SEA	MLB	27	681	88	39	4	25	89	47	118	11	5	-1.6	.268	.328	.465	.264	.328	.467	.270	20.6	5.1	152-3B	21
2007	SEA	MLB	28	639	87	41	2	26	99	38	104	14	2	-0.8	.276	.319	.482	.277	.323	.501	.278	27.1	2.9	145-3B	-3
2008	SEA	MLB	29	612	74	29	1	25	77	50	90	8	2	-2.3	.266	.327	.457	.271	.335	.479	.277	23.6	3.7	136-3B	7
2009	SEA	MLB	30	611	77	32	2	21	88	46	104	9	3	-0.8	.271	.330	.453	.274	.334	.479	.277	21.8	3.4	143-3B	4

Breakout: 15% Improve: 58% Collapse: 17% Attrition: 6%   Comparables: Travis Fryman, Gary Gaetti, Ken McMullen, Doug Rader

Beltre hasn't quite fulfilled the expectations placed on him when he debuted as a 19-year-old Dodger in 1998, but his brand of solidly above-average offense and superior defense has made him a valuable, if unspectacular, contributor for the Mariners. Beltre's recent performance level could be threatened by his surgery last September to remove bone spurs in his shoulder and replace a ligament in his thumb, though there's also a chance that he may again summon the magical powers that only come out his contract years. If he can stay healthy, Beltre will remain on track for membership in the Edgar Renteria/Johnny Damon Hall of Pretty Good Players, whose early career starts and consistent compiling may one day make voters for the real Hall of Fame distinctly uncomfortable.

Yuniesky Betancourt　SS

Bats: R　Throws: R　Height: 5' 10"　Weight: 190　Born: January 31, 1982　Age: 27

YEAR	TEAM	LVL	AGE	PA	R	2B	3B	HR	RBI	BB	SO	SB	CS	EqBRR	AVG	OBP	SLG	EqAVG	EqOBP	EqSLG	EqA	VORP	WARP	DEFENSE	
2006	SEA	MLB	24	584	68	28	6	8	47	17	54	11	8	0.5	.289	.310	.403	.288	.312	.406	.245	14.3	1.6	154-SS	-1
2007	SEA	MLB	25	559	72	38	2	9	67	15	48	5	4	0.7	.289	.308	.418	.292	.311	.436	.253	15.1	1.0	147-SS	-10
2008	SEA	MLB	26	590	66	36	3	7	51	17	42	4	4	-3.2	.279	.300	.392	.289	.310	.414	.248	11.9	0.3	150-SS	-14
2009	SEA	MLB	27	543	55	29	3	8	59	19	49	5	3	0.6	.272	.299	.388	.275	.302	.410	.245	9.8	1.2	128-SS	-2

Breakout: 18%　Improve: 35%　Collapse: 26%　Attrition: 12%　　Comparables: Rafael Ramirez, Deivi Cruz, Tommy Helms, Danny Thompson

After three seasons in the major leagues, Betancourt has established the type of player he's going to be: He'll swing at everything, hit most of what he swings at, draw a walk only when John Cleese sits behind the plate and says, "And now for something completely different," and hit enough doubles to keep pitchers honest. He can't hang his hat on his work in the field, either: the League of Extraordinary Defensive Metrics reveals him to be well below average at shortstop, despite all appearances to the contrary. To use one of the most abused phrases of the 2000s, Betancourt "is what he is," and what he is, is a marginal player.

Willie Bloomquist　UT

Bats: R　Throws: R　Height: 5' 11"　Weight: 195　Born: November 27, 1977　Age: 31

YEAR	TEAM	LVL	AGE	PA	R	2B	3B	HR	RBI	BB	SO	SB	CS	EqBRR	AVG	OBP	SLG	EqAVG	EqOBP	EqSLG	EqA	VORP	WARP	DEFENSE			
2006	SEA	MLB	28	283	36	6	2	1	15	24	40	16	3	2.0	.247	.320	.299	.241	.320	.293	.234	-2.1	0.5	36-CF	2	14-2B	0
2007	SEA	MLB	29	188	28	3	0	2	13	10	35	7	5	0.1	.277	.321	.329	.283	.330	.347	.236	-2.2	-1.1	16-2B	-5	15-3B	-1
2008	SEA	MLB	30	192	32	1	0	0	9	25	29	14	3	1.2	.279	.377	.285	.287	.391	.293	.265	4.2	0.4	18-CF	0	11-SS	0
2009	KCA	MLB	31	172	21	4	1	0	11	16	26	7	3	0.9	.251	.326	.299	.248	.324	.309	.234	-2.2	0.1	44-CF	-1		

Breakout: 15%　Improve: 34%　Collapse: 47%　Attrition: 38%　　Comparables: Lou Frazier, Brian Hunter, Terry Harmon, Mark Little

Bloomquist became a cult hero in Seattle on the strength of his history as a local boy who failed to make good, but succeeded in making the Mariners—for seven consecutive seasons. He showed more patience at the plate last season, but also experienced a truly historic power outage, as his lone extra-base hit placed him in a tie for the fourth-lowest isolated power mark among nonpitchers in history. In a pinch, Bloomquist can man any position that doesn't require a mask and a chest protector, but no matter where his managers choose to send him, he ain't nothing like the real thing. Credit the Mariners' new brass for realizing that and letting him walk to Kansas City.

Jamie Burke　C

Bats: R　Throws: R　Height: 6' 0"　Weight: 225　Born: September 24, 1971　Age: 37

YEAR	TEAM	LVL	AGE	PA	R	2B	3B	HR	RBI	BB	SO	SB	CS	EqBRR	AVG	OBP	SLG	EqAVG	EqOBP	EqSLG	EqA	VORP	WARP	DEFENSE			
2006	OKL	AAA	34	399	46	21	1	10	49	22	41	0	0	0.0	.278	.323	.422	.226	.264	.348	.210	-19.9	-1.8	53-C	-4	21-3B	-1
2007	SEA	MLB	35	129	19	8	0	1	12	7	17	0	1	-0.3	.301	.363	.398	.310	.371	.425	.275	6.1	0.3	36-C	-4		
2008	SEA	MLB	36	100	10	3	0	1	8	5	7	0	1	-0.6	.261	.303	.326	.272	.313	.337	.227	-1.4	0.1	28-C	1		
2009	SEA	MLB	37	179	14	6	0	2	17	9	20	0	1	-0.6	.241	.290	.313	.244	.293	.330	.217	-3.2	0.1	46-C	-3		

Breakout: 16%　Improve: 40%　Collapse: 40%　Attrition: 36%　　Comparables: Sandy Alomar, Joe Girardi, Clyde McCullough, Bob Scheffing

Here's a surprise: After 376 plate appearances, Burke remains a .301 career hitter in the major leagues. He has no power, but works the count and provides adequate defense. The Mariners nontendered him in December to avoid a potential salary arbitration hearing, but subsequently re-signed him to a minor league contract. He retains enough value to reprise his limited role and, as a result, won't finish his career above .300, a trade-off he's probably only too happy to make.

Miguel Cairo　INF

Bats: R　Throws: R　Height: 6' 1"　Weight: 210　Born: May 4, 1974　Age: 35

YEAR	TEAM	LVL	AGE	PA	R	2B	3B	HR	RBI	BB	SO	SB	CS	EqBRR	AVG	OBP	SLG	EqAVG	EqOBP	EqSLG	EqA	VORP	WARP	DEFENSE			
2006	NYA	MLB	32	244	28	12	3	0	30	13	31	13	1	0.9	.239	.280	.320	.227	.273	.305	.219	-4.1	0.4	36-2B	6	11-SS	2
2007	NYA	MLB	33	121	12	7	0	0	10	8	19	8	1	-0.3	.252	.308	.318	.243	.305	.299	.233	-1.9	-0.1	18-1B	-1	6-SS	2
2007	SLN	MLB	33	72	8	2	2	0	5	3	5	2	1	-0.2	.254	.296	.343	.269	.310	.358	.231	-1.3	-0.1	10-3B	0	5-2B	0
2008	SEA	MLB	34	250	34	14	2	0	23	18	32	5	2	-0.9	.249	.316	.330	.259	.325	.345	.240	-4.1	-0.7	45-1B	-6	13-3B	2
2009	SEA	MLB	35	116	13	5	1	1	9	8	17	3	1	0.2	.249	.311	.336	.252	.314	.356	.240	-1.6	0.1	32-1B	2		

Breakout: 33%　Improve: 46%　Collapse: 29%　Attrition: 55%　　Comparables: Darren Lewis, Gino Cimoli, Mike Devereaux, John Wathan

Cairo holds the bat with his hands far apart on the handle, but the Ty Cobb comparisons end there. Nevertheless, he's managed to carve out a 1,200-game career through a willingness to do whatever his managers ask of him, which can usually be described as "too much." Cairo manning first base regularly at his peak would have been a reach, but penciling him in at the game's premier offensive position 70 times in 2008 is nothing less than managerial self-flagellation. Even at the cold corner, Cairo was, at best, average on defense, casting doubt on his ability to maintain this charade for much longer.

Jeff Clement — C

Bats: L Throws: R Height: 6' 1" Weight: 210 Born: August 21, 1983 Age: 25

YEAR	TEAM	LVL	AGE	PA	R	2B	3B	HR	RBI	BB	SO	SB	CS	EqBRR	AVG	OBP	SLG	EqAVG	EqOBP	EqSLG	EqA	VORP	WARP	DEFENSE
2006	SAN	AA	22	70	7	6	1	2	10	7	8	0	0	-0.2	.288	.386	.525	.258	.338	.500	.280	3.7	0.4	12-C -1
2006	TAC	AAA	22	272	23	10	0	4	32	16	53	0	2	-3.0	.257	.321	.347	.240	.292	.328	.214	-10.4	-0.7	36-C -1
2007	TAC	AAA	23	530	76	35	3	20	80	61	88	0	0	1.2	.275	.370	.497	.249	.340	.449	.272	16.5	2.0	74-C -6
2008	TAC	AAA	24	211	40	17	0	14	43	35	30	0	0	-1.8	.335	.455	.676	.303	.412	.590	.331	26.9	2.3	29-C -3
2008	SEA	MLB	24	224	17	10	1	5	23	15	63	0	1	-1.1	.227	.295	.360	.232	.299	.379	.234	-2.3	-0.8	33-C -7
2009	SEA	MLB	25	426	50	22	1	16	58	42	91	0	0	-1.2	.258	.341	.449	.261	.344	.474	.280	17.8	2.5	101-C -12

Breakout: 29% Improve: 72% Collapse: 9% Attrition: 11%   Comparables: Ed Herrmann, Mo Vaughn, Charles Johnson, Jim Pagliaroni

Clement's 2008 was a tale of two seasons, with the "worst of times" coming at the highest level. He raked in Tacoma and did much of his damage against right-handers, alleviating fears that his previous offensive success had been a product of a southpaw feast unlikely to be repeated in "The Show." But his power and patience deserted him in major league competition, and the outgoing regime further jeopardized his future as an offensive difference-maker by relegating him to full-time DH duty. The new bosses appear more committed to the notion of Clement as a catcher, but a second knee surgery in three years performed last September suggests that Clement's body may soon leave them with little choice in the matter.

Greg Halman — OF

Bats: R Throws: R Height: 6' 4" Weight: 192 Born: August 26, 1987 Age: 21

YEAR	TEAM	LVL	AGE	PA	R	2B	3B	HR	RBI	BB	SO	SB	CS	EqBRR	AVG	OBP	SLG	EqAVG	EqOBP	EqSLG	EqA	VORP	WARP	DEFENSE	
2006	EVE	A-	18	123	19	6	4	5	15	3	32	10	4	-0.3	.259	.295	.509	.202	.221	.387	.203	-14.0	-0.9	25-CF -1	
2007	WIS	A	19	202	26	5	0	4	15	8	77	15	7	-0.4	.182	.234	.273	.151	.184	.229	.127	-31.7	-2.3	39-CF 1	9-RF -1
2007	EVE	A-	19	265	37	19	1	16	37	21	85	16	8	-4.3	.307	.371	.597	.225	.265	.414	.229	-11.6	-1.4	54-CF -7	
2008	HDS	A+	20	282	52	15	3	19	53	16	76	23	1	6.0	.268	.320	.572	.202	.249	.427	.237	-8.8	-0.7	54-CF -6	
2008	WTN	AA	20	256	43	14	2	10	30	16	66	8	6	-0.9	.277	.332	.481	.232	.273	.407	.230	-5.4	-1.5	57-CF -11	
2009	SEA	MLB	21	562	58	28	4	16	63	30	173	23	9	2.0	.225	.273	.387	.228	.275	.409	.236	-6.6	0.5	132-CF -4	

Breakout: 58% Improve: 75% Collapse: 13% Attrition: 5%   Comparables: Franklin Gutierrez, Wladimir Balentien, Braulio Castillo, Jose Gonzalez

Halman, a native Netherlander, was the MVP of his homeland's top league as a 17-year-old and appears to possess all the tools necessary to become a star. He held his own, despite two promotions last season, managing to reduce his lofty strikeout totals in the process. Halman must continue to work on pitch recognition, but his combination of power, speed, and defense could land him a regular gig in the majors as early as 2010, though he may ultimately profile as a right fielder.

Tug Hulett — MI

Bats: L Throws: R Height: 5' 10" Weight: 185 Born: February 28, 1983 Age: 26

YEAR	TEAM	LVL	AGE	PA	R	2B	3B	HR	RBI	BB	SO	SB	CS	EqBRR	AVG	OBP	SLG	EqAVG	EqOBP	EqSLG	EqA	VORP	WARP	DEFENSE	
2006	BAK	A+	23	361	46	19	7	2	37	61	61	15	5	-2.2	.291	.415	.426	.212	.316	.322	.233	-11.5	-0.6	32-3B 0	20-2B -5
2006	FRI	AA	23	223	36	8	4	0	15	31	36	9	2	0.2	.308	.405	.395	.260	.347	.328	.250	-1.4	0.3	47-2B -2	
2007	OKL	AAA	24	595	95	31	2	11	67	64	114	20	4	0.0	.275	.359	.406	.242	.324	.365	.247	-4.5	1.5	104-2B 3	18-SS -3
2008	TAC	AAA	25	400	71	22	5	14	47	49	73	10	5	-0.7	.298	.380	.518	.257	.332	.445	.268	11.0	1.5	43-SS -2	36-2B -2
2008	SEA	MLB	25	56	2	1	0	1	2	5	17	0	0	-1.5	.224	.309	.306	.224	.309	.306	.221	-1.3	-0.2		
2009	SEA	MLB	26	454	51	22	3	9	43	47	109	8	3	0.5	.231	.315	.367	.234	.318	.388	.250	3.3	1.0	108-2B -5	

Breakout: 22% Improve: 49% Collapse: 22% Attrition: 15%   Comparables: Kevin Melillo, Henri Stanley, Rob Ducey, Stuart Pederson

Hulett's Mariners debut was a triumph of guts and guile over natural ability, though his Pacific Coast League performance justified his call-up. The son of former utility infielder Tim Hulett, Tug has some pop from the left side, a rarity for an infielder, which makes him at least somewhat intriguing. His overall game is a little short for a big-league regular, however, and he'll most likely spend his career walking a fine line between major league role player and Triple-A regular.

Raul Ibañez — LF | Bats: L | Throws: R | Height: 6' 2" | Weight: 220 | Born: June 2, 1972 | Age: 37

YEAR	TEAM	LVL	AGE	PA	R	2B	3B	HR	RBI	BB	SO	SB	CS	EqBRR	AVG	OBP	SLG	EqAVG	EqOBP	EqSLG	EqA	VORP	WARP	DEFENSE
2006	SEA	MLB	34	699	103	33	5	33	123	65	115	2	4	-1.4	.289	.353	.516	.282	.353	.511	.289	38.6	3.6	156-LF -4
2007	SEA	MLB	35	636	80	35	5	21	105	53	97	0	0	-1.0	.291	.351	.480	.291	.354	.498	.289	29.9	1.1	126-LF -22
2008	SEA	MLB	36	707	85	43	3	23	110	64	110	2	4	-2.2	.293	.358	.479	.300	.368	.506	.293	38.5	3.9	151-LF -4
2009	PHI	MLB	37	577	77	33	2	22	88	53	89	2	2	-1.8	.289	.356	.485	.290	.356	.493	.285	26.1	2.2	135-LF -11

Breakout: 10% Improve: 39% Collapse: 25% Attrition: 15%   Comparables: Paul O'Neill, Ken Griffey, B. J. Surhoff, Fred McGriff

Ibañez defied Father Time again last season, posting a line almost identical to those of his previous two campaigns, along with slightly less horrendous defense than he provided in 2007, as his late-career peak rolls on. Despite being one of the oldest and least-talented of the various defensively challenged corner outfielders for sale to the highest bidder this offseason, Ibañez became the first to sign, fleeing Seattle's incipient rebuilding effort in favor of the greener pastures of the defending world champion. PECOTA foresees more of the same, as the move to the weaker league and the better hitter's park should offset any age-related slippage, but three-year contracts with 36-year-olds have a way of backfiring, even if the player in question has never been much better at the plate.

Kenji Johjima — C | Bats: R | Throws: R | Height: 6' 0" | Weight: 200 | Born: June 8, 1976 | Age: 33

YEAR	TEAM	LVL	AGE	PA	R	2B	3B	HR	RBI	BB	SO	SB	CS	EqBRR	AVG	OBP	SLG	EqAVG	EqOBP	EqSLG	EqA	VORP	WARP	DEFENSE
2006	SEA	MLB	30	542	61	25	1	18	76	20	46	3	1	-3.1	.291	.332	.451	.289	.332	.455	.269	24.6	3.3	131-C 1
2007	SEA	MLB	31	513	52	29	0	14	61	15	41	0	2	-4.1	.287	.322	.433	.288	.322	.451	.262	21.1	4.0	125-C 13
2008	SEA	MLB	32	409	29	19	0	7	39	19	33	2	0	-1.2	.227	.277	.332	.232	.282	.346	.219	-8.1	0.0	94-C 1
2009	SEA	MLB	33	290	25	13	0	5	34	13	29	1	1	-1.4	.254	.296	.359	.257	.299	.379	.234	1.2	1.1	71-C 0

Breakout: 10% Improve: 30% Collapse: 37% Attrition: 34%   Comparables: Danny Sheaffer, Sandy Alomar, Bengie Molina, Tony Peña

Johjima has never displayed anything close to the power he flashed for the Fukuoka Daiei Hawks while playing in a Mariners uniform, but he produced above-average offensive performances in each of his first two seasons in Seattle. The catcher's game headed south last season, as his offense ceased to resemble anything approaching an asset, his caught-stealing percentage declined, and his pitch-calling came under increased scrutiny. The Mariners are stuck with him through 2011; until then, he'll either be a welcome veteran presence in the event of a Clement malfunction or one of the league's best (and most expensive) backup catchers, though the M's probably could have filled the latter role from within at much less expense and without sacrificing much production.

Rob Johnson — C | Bats: R | Throws: R | Height: 6' 1" | Weight: 200 | Born: July 22, 1983 | Age: 25

YEAR	TEAM	LVL	AGE	PA	R	2B	3B	HR	RBI	BB	SO	SB	CS	EqBRR	AVG	OBP	SLG	EqAVG	EqOBP	EqSLG	EqA	VORP	WARP	DEFENSE	
2006	TAC	AAA	22	359	28	9	4	4	33	13	74	14	7	-0.1	.231	.261	.318	.214	.242	.293	.185	-29.8	-1.4	71-C 2	
2007	TAC	AAA	23	465	57	26	0	6	40	39	62	7	7	-0.6	.268	.331	.372	.246	.307	.343	.226	-11.0	-0.8	68-C -5	
2008	TAC	AAA	24	463	55	30	0	9	49	37	61	7	6	-2.5	.305	.363	.441	.276	.328	.392	.249	4.9	0.6	90-C -3	9-LF -4
2008	SEA	MLB	24	32	2	0	0	1	2	0	6	0	0	-0.0	.129	.129	.226	.129	.129	.226	.000	-4.4	-0.4	7-C 0	
2009	SEA	MLB	25	381	33	15	1	6	37	24	74	6	3	-0.1	.233	.284	.331	.236	.287	.350	.223	-6.2	0.4	91-C -6	

Breakout: 32% Improve: 47% Collapse: 28% Attrition: 25%   Comparables: Walt McKeel, Jim Gaudet, Ed Hearn, Bill Bathe

Johnson's third crack at the Pacific Coast League generated almost as much improvement as his second did, as his bat finally returned to its A-ball levels after the Mariners' curious decision to let him bypass the Southern League. His gap power and defensive prowess would make him a solid backup option now, but with Clement and Johjima ahead of him and Adam Moore hot on his trail, Johnson is at a career crossroad, asking the Lord above, "Have mercy, now trade poor Bob, if you please."

Bryan LaHair   1B

Bats: L   Throws: R   Height: 6' 5"   Weight: 215   Born: November 5, 1982   Age: 26

YEAR	TEAM	LVL	AGE	PA	R	2B	3B	HR	RBI	BB	SO	SB	CS	EqBRR	AVG	OBP	SLG	EqAVG	EqOBP	EqSLG	EqA	VORP	WARP	DEFENSE	
2006	SAN	AA	23	252	22	12	0	6	30	24	52	0	0	-2.9	.293	.371	.428	.259	.323	.382	.247	0.3	-0.5	57-1B	-3
2006	TAC	AAA	23	230	36	10	0	10	44	23	49	3	0	2.3	.327	.393	.525	.302	.365	.502	.296	17.9	1.6	52-1B	2
2007	TAC	AAA	24	606	79	46	2	12	81	49	126	0	1	-0.3	.275	.332	.431	.250	.305	.397	.243	-2.4	-1.0	132-1B	-3
2008	TAC	AAA	25	362	39	26	1	12	53	45	87	1	1	-1.4	.263	.356	.465	.226	.311	.387	.243	-3.3	-1.2	71-1B	-7
2008	SEA	MLB	25	150	15	4	0	3	10	13	40	0	1	-0.5	.250	.315	.346	.252	.322	.363	.239	-2.6	-0.7	31-1B	-4
2009	SEA	MLB	26	470	43	22	1	12	53	40	131	2	1	-0.9	.228	.297	.370	.231	.300	.391	.240	-8.6	-0.8	111-1B	-5

Breakout: 14% Improve: 39% Collapse: 38% Attrition: 17%   Comparables: Ray Brown, Kevin Burns, Todd Sears, Paul Carey

The Mariners put their LaHair up after releasing Richie Sexson last July, but the big lefty proved to be not only a few inches shorter than his predecessor, but also equally clueless at the plate. He's more of a gap hitter than an over-the-fence guy, which doesn't profile well for a limited defensive player at a power position. LaHair has never hit lefties, but he might have value as a part-timer. If everything goes his way, he'll be a poor man's Ben Broussard.

Jose Lopez   2B

Bats: R   Throws: R   Height: 6' 0"   Weight: 200   Born: November 24, 1983   Age: 25

YEAR	TEAM	LVL	AGE	PA	R	2B	3B	HR	RBI	BB	SO	SB	CS	EqBRR	AVG	OBP	SLG	EqAVG	EqOBP	EqSLG	EqA	VORP	WARP	DEFENSE			
2006	SEA	MLB	22	655	78	28	8	10	79	26	80	5	2	-1.7	.282	.319	.405	.280	.319	.407	.252	19.1	2.2	148-2B	5		
2007	SEA	MLB	23	561	58	17	2	11	62	20	64	2	3	-3.0	.252	.284	.355	.254	.287	.367	.225	-10.5	1.6	139-2B	18		
2008	SEA	MLB	24	687	80	41	1	17	89	27	67	6	3	-2.7	.297	.322	.443	.304	.330	.470	.272	28.0	6.9	139-2B	29	11-1B	3
2009	SEA	MLB	25	630	68	30	3	14	74	27	71	5	3	-0.3	.276	.312	.408	.280	.315	.431	.256	14.7	3.2	147-2B	11		

Breakout: 20% Improve: 44% Collapse: 22% Attrition: 10%   Comparables: Rennie Stennett, Rafael Ramirez, Bill Mazeroski, Jose Castillo

Lopez rebounded nicely from a disastrous '07 second half, setting career-high offensive totals across the board. His defensive work ranked somewhere near the middle of the pack, but the Mariners seem to view his long-term home as either first or third base, particularly if Adrian Beltre departs. Lopez has good power for a second baseman and the arm for third, but he'd be a lesser asset at another position. At the keystone, he's a fringe All-Star. At the hot corner, he's just a guy.

Mario Martinez   3B

Bats: R   Throws: R   Height: 6' 2"   Weight: 175   Born: November 13, 1989   Age: 19

YEAR	TEAM	LVL	AGE	PA	R	2B	3B	HR	RBI	BB	SO	SB	CS	EqBRR	AVG	OBP	SLG	EqAVG	EqOBP	EqSLG	EqA	VORP	WARP	DEFENSE			
2007	MRN	Rk	17	209	36	9	1	1	26	6	31	3	2	4.4	.281	.311	.352	.193	.208	.243	.136	-63.9	-4.3	28-SS	-4	15-3B	-2
2008	PUL	Rk	18	270	43	15	3	5	32	10	47	2	2	0.6	.319	.344	.462	.202	.225	.300	.176	-53.1	-3.3	61-3B	-3		
2009	SEA	MLB	19	491	31	23	2	4	34	18	120	3	3	0.9	.203	.235	.285	.205	.237	.302	.178	-30.1	-2.3	116-3B	2		

Breakout: 58% Improve: 71% Collapse: 21% Attrition: 6%   Comparables: Hector Gomez, Vilato Marrero, Luis Ordaz, Carlos Garcia

Martinez received a $600,000 bonus to sign out of Venezuela as a shortstop in 2006 and ranks as one of the Mariners' best long-term prospects. He's already outgrown his original position and held his own as an 18-year-old third baseman in the Appy League. The Mariners chose not to rush his development, allowing him time to adjust to his new spot in the infield. Raw and aggressive, Martinez has the time and ability to add power and patience and should get his first taste of a full-season league this year.

Adam Moore   C

Bats: R   Throws: R   Height: 6' 3"   Weight: 215   Born: May 8, 1984   Age: 25

YEAR	TEAM	LVL	AGE	PA	R	2B	3B	HR	RBI	BB	SO	SB	CS	EqBRR	AVG	OBP	SLG	EqAVG	EqOBP	EqSLG	EqA	VORP	WARP	DEFENSE			
2006	WIS	A	22	187	21	6	0	7	24	14	38	0	0	-1.8	.267	.342	.430	.202	.255	.329	.202	-12.5	-0.9	32-C	-3		
2006	EVE	A-	22	66	8	9	0	0	9	2	10	0	0	-1.0	.317	.348	.460	.203	.215	.312	.163	-11.7	-0.8	10-C	-1		
2007	HDS	A+	23	491	74	30	3	22	102	41	84	1	0	0.0	.307	.371	.543	.202	.257	.362	.214	-24.2	-1.6	98-C	-10	5-1B	0
2008	WTN	AA	24	490	60	34	2	14	71	40	77	0	1	-7.3	.319	.396	.506	.250	.309	.408	.247	1.1	0.6	105-C	-8		
2009	SEA	MLB	25	443	34	20	1	9	50	26	104	0	0	-1.8	.223	.278	.343	.226	.280	.363	.222	-7.6	0.5	105-C	-6		

Breakout: 20% Improve: 39% Collapse: 38% Attrition: 7%   Comparables: Pat Cline, Jim Campanis, Jake Fox, Brad Cresse

Moore is a prized rarity in baseball, now and forever: a slugging catching prospect. He duplicated his breakout '07 at a higher level last season and overhauled his defensive technique under the tutelage of roving catching instructor Roger Hansen, who gave him high marks. Moore's strong arm, game-calling, and work ethic should keep him behind the plate, although he's big for a catcher and has already survived one knee surgery. In a less catching-rich organization, he'd be a bigger name, but he deserves any hype he can get.

Mike Morse   UT   Bats: R   Throws: R   Height: 6' 4"   Weight: 225   Born: March 22, 1982   Age: 27

YEAR	TEAM	LVL	AGE	PA	R	2B	3B	HR	RBI	BB	SO	SB	CS	EqBRR	AVG	OBP	SLG	EqAVG	EqOBP	EqSLG	EqA	VORP	WARP	DEFENSE			
2006	TAC	AAA	24	228	23	15	1	5	34	14	46	0	1	-1.2	.248	.300	.403	.230	.276	.373	.225	-7.2	-0.8	15-3B	0	14-1B	-1
2006	SEA	MLB	24	48	5	5	0	0	11	3	7	1	0	0.1	.372	.396	.488	.372	.396	.465	.307	4.7	0.3	4-RF	0		
2007	TAC	AAA	25	324	48	26	0	6	39	26	47	5	3	-1.5	.309	.368	.460	.278	.333	.410	.258	6.5	0.6	52-3B	2	19-SS	-5
2009	SEA	MLB	27	253	20	11	1	4	26	16	57	2	1	-1.0	.225	.281	.333	.227	.284	.352	.222	-7.5	-0.4	62-3B	-3		

Breakout: 14% Improve: 33% Collapse: 48% Attrition: 35%   Comparables: Randy Johnson, Jim Wilson, Olmedo Saenz, Derek Wachter

Morse broke camp with the big club, but his season ended in mid-April, when he dislocated his nonthrowing shoulder while diving for a ball in left field and underwent surgery for a torn labrum. He should be healthy by the start of this season and could wind up filling the superutility role vacated by Willie Bloomquist, though like his predecessor, he's not much of an asset at any of the positions for which he owns a glove.

Jeremy Reed   OF   Bats: L   Throws: L   Height: 6' 0"   Weight: 200   Born: June 15, 1981   Age: 28

YEAR	TEAM	LVL	AGE	PA	R	2B	3B	HR	RBI	BB	SO	SB	CS	EqBRR	AVG	OBP	SLG	EqAVG	EqOBP	EqSLG	EqA	VORP	WARP	DEFENSE			
2006	SEA	MLB	25	229	27	6	5	6	17	11	31	2	3	0.6	.217	.260	.377	.213	.260	.374	.215	-6.4	-1.1	57-CF	-5		
2007	TAC	AAA	26	628	92	37	5	13	64	47	73	14	9	-3.3	.300	.354	.452	.257	.308	.393	.242	-1.6	-0.3	91-LF	-4	17-CF	3
2008	TAC	AAA	27	168	26	11	1	6	21	16	14	6	1	-2.0	.349	.413	.557	.288	.345	.464	.279	8.1	1.5	25-CF	6	6-RF	-1
2008	SEA	MLB	27	312	30	18	1	2	31	18	38	2	3	0.7	.269	.314	.360	.277	.324	.382	.245	-0.8	-0.3	51-CF	-4	11-RF	0
2009	NYN	MLB	28	237	29	13	2	4	26	17	32	4	2	0.4	.281	.333	.417	.286	.337	.437	.265	10.0	1.0	59-CF	-3		

Breakout: 43% Improve: 59% Collapse: 19% Attrition: 39%   Comparables: George Vukovich, Hosken Powell, Ted Uhlaender, Jim Holt

The offensive outburst in Tacoma with which Reed began last season summoned fond memories of his work in the White Sox system, but when given another extended trial in Seattle, he again failed to do anything at the plate. He retains his reputation as a plus gloveman in center, though when asked to comment, various defensive metrics emitted a collective yawn. After being sucked into the whirling vortex of the three-way, 12-player trade consummated at the Winter Meetings, he'll have a much-needed fresh start in New York this season, where he'll fill the outfielder-on-call role vacated by Endy Chavez. Reed should prove to be an asset as a part-time occupant of Citi Field's cavernous corners, with the potential to grab a bigger role if Safeco turns out to have been his offensive kryptonite.

Michael Saunders   OF   Bats: L   Throws: R   Height: 6' 4"   Weight: 205   Born: November 19, 1986   Age: 22

YEAR	TEAM	LVL	AGE	PA	R	2B	3B	HR	RBI	BB	SO	SB	CS	EqBRR	AVG	OBP	SLG	EqAVG	EqOBP	EqSLG	EqA	VORP	WARP	DEFENSE			
2006	WIS	A	19	416	48	10	8	4	39	48	103	22	7	1.4	.240	.329	.345	.193	.265	.284	.199	-33.9	-1.9	68-CF	0	23-RF	-2
2007	HDS	A+	20	507	91	25	4	14	77	60	116	27	10	0.0	.299	.392	.473	.209	.289	.332	.221	-21.6	-1.4	52-CF	2	33-RF	-2
2007	WTN	AA	20	60	8	1	2	1	7	7	20	2	1	0.0	.288	.373	.442	.259	.333	.426	.255	1.4	0.5	11-CF	3		
2008	WTN	AA	21	289	46	18	3	8	30	30	66	11	6	-2.8	.290	.375	.484	.239	.308	.413	.247	0.4	0.4	47-CF	0	5-RF	1
2008	TAC	AAA	21	105	12	4	1	3	16	9	30	1	2	-2.1	.242	.308	.400	.227	.286	.381	.226	-2.5	-0.1	15-CF	1	5-LF	0
2009	SEA	MLB	22	512	55	25	3	11	49	43	148	12	6	1.4	.232	.300	.369	.234	.303	.390	.242	-5.1	0.9	121-CF	-5		

Breakout: 48% Improve: 75% Collapse: 13% Attrition: 5%   Comparables: T. J. Staton, Rob Ducey, Ray McDavid, Jon Saffer

As a 19-year-old outfielder in the Midwest League in 2006, Saunders was an excellent hockey player, but the Canadian-born lefty has progressed quickly. A true five-tool talent, he needs to lay off breaking balls out of the zone to unlock his full potential. He's not a burner, but runs well enough to cover a fair amount of ground in center and could develop into a base-stealing threat as he refines his technique. Saunders underwent arthroscopic shoulder surgery late last season, but figures to make a run at earning a starting job left-field job in 2010, though his powerful arm makes him a better fit for right.

Ichiro Suzuki   RF   Bats: L   Throws: R   Height: 5' 9"   Weight: 170   Born: October 22, 1973   Age: 35

YEAR	TEAM	LVL	AGE	PA	R	2B	3B	HR	RBI	BB	SO	SB	CS	EqBRR	AVG	OBP	SLG	EqAVG	EqOBP	EqSLG	EqA	VORP	WARP	DEFENSE			
2006	SEA	MLB	32	752	110	20	9	9	49	49	71	45	2	7.4	.322	.370	.416	.315	.368	.412	.284	47.3	4.1	119-RF	-5	38-CF	7
2007	SEA	MLB	33	736	111	22	7	6	68	49	77	37	8	7.1	.351	.396	.431	.356	.403	.444	.299	61.7	4.9	151-CF	-6		
2008	SEA	MLB	34	749	103	20	7	6	42	51	65	43	4	12.7	.310	.361	.386	.319	.371	.404	.282	34.5	4.3	89-RF	-3	68-CF	7
2009	SEA	MLB	35	484	65	14	4	3	36	29	48	20	5	3.1	.292	.338	.359	.295	.341	.380	.259	6.3	1.6	114-CF	-3		

Breakout: 1%   Improve: 7%   Collapse: 54%   Attrition: 26%   Comparables: Lance Johnson, Matty Alou, Lou Brock, Al Bumbry

Suzuki had his worst season at the plate in 2008, though all that separated it from his successful 2007 was a 40-point drop in batting average. That decline stemmed from a BABIP that was below average by his standards, but it remains to be seen whether that was a one-year blip or an indication that Ichiro may have lost a step at age 34—a development that could augur his downfall, since a substantial portion of his hits never leave the infield. His work in the outfield also took a step back last season, supporting the deteriorating-wheels hypothesis, though he remains a plus defender. Suzuki reportedly took the Mariners' disastrous season hard, becoming less animated both on the field and in the clubhouse, but attributing his decline in performance to excessive team spirit (a quality his teammates have never accused him of possessing) when other factors can explain it is about as logical as believing that a player who only managed to top 20 homers twice in Japan could hit them at will in the majors, if only he could be bothered to.

Carlos Triunfel   SS   Bats: R   Throws: R   Height: 5' 11"   Weight: 175   Born: February 27, 1990   Age: 19

YEAR	TEAM	LVL	AGE	PA	R	2B	3B	HR	RBI	BB	SO	SB	CS	EqBRR	AVG	OBP	SLG	EqAVG	EqOBP	EqSLG	EqA	VORP	WARP	DEFENSE			
2007	WIS	A	17	164	18	8	2	0	14	5	23	4	8	0.0	.309	.342	.388	.239	.261	.297	.188	-11.7	-1.1	40-SS	-4		
2007	HDS	A+	17	225	32	10	2	0	22	12	31	3	4	0.0	.288	.333	.356	.198	.234	.241	.155	-24.2	-2.3	49-SS	-7		
2007	MRN	Rk	17	13	1	0	0	0	3	0	1	0	0	-0.1	.273	.231	.273	.250	.231	.250	.174	-2.9	-0.2				
2008	HDS	A+	18	479	75	20	4	8	49	30	52	30	9	1.7	.287	.336	.406	.207	.254	.309	.199	-34.8	-4.8	72-SS	-19	30-2B	-11
2009	SEA	MLB	19	583	52	25	3	4	43	31	83	16	8	2.3	.226	.270	.308	.228	.273	.326	.211	-15.7	-1.9	137-SS	-16		

Breakout: 69%   Improve: 78%   Collapse: 6%   Attrition: 4%   Comparables: Joaquin Arias, Junior Noboa, Luis Rivas, Jose Lopez

Triunfel spent last season in the California League, where he had finished his three-level 2007 odyssey. He was again the circuit's youngest player, but didn't look overmatched, a testament to his natural talent. The Mariners believed in Triunfel's power potential even after his homerless 2007, and he began to reward their faith by adding over 50 points to his isolated power in his second exposure to the level. His stocky build limits his range, and although the M's tried him at second base last season, his future may lie at third, where he could showcase his powerful arm. His immaturity may have played a role in a 10-day midseason suspension for undisclosed disciplinary reasons, but Triunfel will probably get a chance to add to his collection of leagues in which he's been the junior member in 2009.

Matt Tuiasosopo   3B   Bats: R   Throws: R   Height: 6' 2"   Weight: 210   Born: May 10, 1986   Age: 23

YEAR	TEAM	LVL	AGE	PA	R	2B	3B	HR	RBI	BB	SO	SB	CS	EqBRR	AVG	OBP	SLG	EqAVG	EqOBP	EqSLG	EqA	VORP	WARP	DEFENSE			
2006	SBR	A+	20	253	31	14	0	1	34	14	58	5	6	-1.2	.306	.359	.379	.238	.278	.297	.198	-14.6	-1.3	39-SS	-3	15-3B	-1
2006	SAN	AA	20	241	16	4	0	1	10	20	64	2	1	0.3	.185	.259	.218	.172	.233	.195	.133	-32.4	-3.4	56-3B	-7		
2007	WTN	AA	21	548	74	27	5	9	57	76	113	4	8	0.0	.260	.371	.404	.226	.322	.362	.244	-6.9	-0.2	127-3B	-5		
2008	TAC	AAA	22	500	87	32	2	13	73	47	104	4	0	0.7	.281	.364	.453	.251	.325	.397	.254	3.0	-1.5	105-3B	-22		
2008	SEA	MLB	22	47	1	2	1	0	2	2	16	0	0	-0.6	.159	.213	.250	.159	.213	.250	.143	-4.5	-0.3	12-3B	1		
2009	SEA	MLB	23	558	57	27	3	11	56	47	143	5	3	0.1	.237	.309	.366	.240	.312	.386	.245	-2.4	0.3	131-3B	-5		

Breakout: 45%   Improve: 66%   Collapse: 8%   Attrition: 4%   Comparables: Troy Tulowitzki, Phil Nevin, Ian Stewart, Benji Gil

Until 2007, Tuiasosopo's minor league performance had given him cause to regret his departure from the football track that carried his father and brother to the NFL, though the record $2.3 million signing bonus that the Mariners bestowed on him as a third-round pick in 2004 probably eased the sting of his on-field struggles. Something finally clicked, however, at Double-A in 2007, and the converted shortstop built on that progress in Tacoma last season. Although he looked lost at the plate in his first taste of the majors last September, Tuiasosopo's burgeoning power and smooth work at the hot corner will give the Mariners options in the event of Adrian Beltre's departure next winter.

Luis Valbuena — 2B

Bats: L   Throws: R   Height: 5' 10"   Weight: 160   Born: November 30, 1985   Age: 23

YEAR	TEAM	LVL	AGE	PA	R	2B	3B	HR	RBI	BB	SO	SB	CS	EqBRR	AVG	OBP	SLG	EqAVG	EqOBP	EqSLG	EqA	VORP	WARP	DEFENSE			
2006	WIS	A	20	373	45	16	6	3	38	44	44	21	7	-0.2	.286	.371	.400	.228	.298	.329	.224	-14.9	-0.9	80-2B	-4		
2006	SBR	A+	20	181	18	10	1	2	10	14	26	1	3	-1.2	.252	.315	.362	.202	.251	.304	.188	-13.6	-0.9	28-2B	1	10-SS	-1
2007	WTN	AA	21	505	55	23	3	11	44	48	83	10	6	0.0	.239	.311	.378	.206	.269	.333	.211	-28.0	-1.0	121-2B	1		
2008	WTN	AA	22	277	43	12	2	9	40	31	37	8	4	-3.2	.304	.381	.483	.257	.320	.414	.254	3.3	1.1	67-2B	2		
2008	TAC	AAA	22	246	41	9	0	2	20	28	32	10	4	-0.2	.302	.383	.373	.275	.350	.339	.249	0.5	1.0	58-2B	4		
2008	SEA	MLB	22	54	6	5	0	0	1	4	11	0	0	-0.1	.245	.315	.347	.245	.315	.347	.233	-0.2	-0.3	14-2B	-3		
2009	CLE	MLB	23	545	59	24	2	8	49	47	94	12	5	1.5	.248	.315	.354	.247	.314	.369	.242	0.9	1.4	128-2B	3		

Breakout: 35% Improve: 68% Collapse: 15% Attrition: 5%   Comparables: Danny Richar, Angel Gonzalez, Sandy Guerrero, Ramon Vazquez

Valbuena had his best professional season in 2008, and all it got him was a trip out of town, as he emerged from under the pile of bodies changing teams in December and discovered that he was an Indian. While still in the employ of the Mariners, he made regular contact, maintained his patient approach, and even exhibited decent power at Double-A, though most of his longest drives will settle into the gaps in the majors. Valbuena is rather short and stocky, and he'll have to watch his conditioning if he hopes to maintain his range as he ages. If he gives Indians fans a few Ronnie Belliard flashbacks over the next several years, he'll have done all that was expected of him.

Jose Vidro — DH

Bats: S   Throws: R   Height: 5' 11"   Weight: 195   Born: August 27, 1974   Age: 34

YEAR	TEAM	LVL	AGE	PA	R	2B	3B	HR	RBI	BB	SO	SB	CS	EqBRR	AVG	OBP	SLG	EqAVG	EqOBP	EqSLG	EqA	VORP	WARP	DEFENSE			
2006	WAS	MLB	31	511	52	26	1	7	47	41	48	1	0	-1.4	.289	.348	.395	.294	.354	.400	.266	17.0	1.1	102-2B	-7	6-1B	0
2007	SEA	MLB	32	625	78	26	0	6	59	63	57	0	0	-0.4	.314	.381	.394	.316	.387	.408	.284	23.0	2.4	8-1B	-1	6-2B	0
2008	SEA	MLB	33	330	28	11	0	7	45	18	36	2	1	-2.5	.234	.274	.338	.238	.280	.349	.219	-9.6	-1.3	6-1B	0		
2009	SEA	MLB	34	293	29	13	1	4	31	22	34	1	1	-0.9	.263	.320	.358	.266	.323	.378	.246	1.3	0.1	71-DH			

Breakout: 16% Improve: 37% Collapse: 42% Attrition: 42%   Comparables: Carlos Baerga, Eddie Waitkus, Jose Vizcaino, Tom Herr

Vidro's .314 batting average in 2007 kept up appearances, but other statistical and physical markers indicated that the end was near. He met his Waterloo last season, and while natural causes were the culprit, his demise was anything but dignified. Every time his name adorned one of John McLaren's lineup cards, an angel lost its wings, and the Mariners lost an opportunity to improve both their short-term and their long-term prospects. Mercifully, he was granted his sweet release in early August, almost certainly terminating his career. It's a shame that his premature collapse has overshadowed his valuable contributions during the first half of the decade, but he'll always be able to savor the honor of having been the last Montreal Expo to start an All-Star Game.

Mike Wilson — OF

Bats: S   Throws: R   Height: 6' 2"   Weight: 215   Born: June 29, 1983   Age: 26

YEAR	TEAM	LVL	AGE	PA	R	2B	3B	HR	RBI	BB	SO	SB	CS	EqBRR	AVG	OBP	SLG	EqAVG	EqOBP	EqSLG	EqA	VORP	WARP	DEFENSE			
2006	SBR	A+	23	226	38	15	3	9	38	22	59	4	6	-5.2	.315	.389	.555	.236	.295	.418	.242	-0.9	-0.4	44-RF	-3		
2006	SAN	AA	23	283	32	12	1	12	43	28	85	1	1	-2.9	.245	.336	.446	.223	.294	.402	.238	-3.8	-0.3	31-LF	-1	29-RF	0
2007	WTN	AA	24	235	30	7	2	10	28	17	89	3	0	0.0	.188	.272	.385	.167	.233	.330	.195	-18.9	-1.8	45-RF	-3		
2008	WTN	AA	25	485	76	26	2	27	84	62	117	9	0	1.9	.276	.388	.549	.207	.291	.412	.244	-7.0	-0.9	101-RF	-7		
2009	SEA	MLB	26	494	46	20	1	16	58	42	171	4	1	-0.7	.203	.278	.367	.205	.281	.388	.232	-15.9	-0.4	117-RF	-2		

Breakout: 27% Improve: 48% Collapse: 25% Attrition: 10%   Comparables: Jason Cooper, Kevin King, Dave Cochrane, Micah Franklin

Former Oklahoma linebacker recruit Mike Wilson has as much raw power as anyone else in the Mariners' organization, but hadn't fully harnessed it in competition until last season, when he launched 27 homers for the Double-A Diamond Jaxx. His patience and pitch recognition have improved over the years, but at age 25 and with little defensive value to augment his appeal, the reformed switch-hitter has seen his breakout performance come too late for him to fashion much of a career in the majors. He'd have to duplicate or improve on last year's performance in Tacoma this season to merit a sizable blip on the prospect radar.

PITCHERS

Phillippe Aumont

Bats: L   Throws: R   Height: 6' 7"   Weight: 220   Born: January 7, 1989   Age: 20

YEAR	TEAM	LVL	AGE	W	L	SV	G	GS	IP	H	BB	SO	HR	GB%	BABIP	STUFF	WHIP	ERA	DERA	EqH9	EqBB9	EqSO9	EqHR9	DEF	VORP	SN/WX
2008	WIS	A	19	4	4	2	15	8	55²	46	19	50	4	56.3%	.278	7	1.17	2.75	7.66	10.2	4.6	3.8	1.8	8	-11.3	—
2009	SEA	MLB	20	4	11	0	23	23	118¹	156	73	63	19	49.0%	.330	-1	1.93	7.45	7.38	11.7	4.9	4.2	1.4	-2	-27.1	-2.11

Breakout: 2%   Improve: 13%   Collapse: 36%   Attrition: 4%   Comparables: Matt Drews, Chris Carpenter, Jordan Walden, Jim Pittsley

Aumont's professional debut was put on hold for two months when he went down with a sore elbow, but the Mariners' 2007 first-round pick still managed to wow scouts and Midwest League batters with his fastball, which his 6-foot-7 frame can propel downward at speeds of up to 98 mph. Aumont needs seasoning, having had relatively little during his adolescence in Quebec. Nevertheless, he possesses the aptitude to reach the majors quickly, where he'll attempt to surpass the accomplishments of Jeff Francis and Adam Loewen, the only Canadians ever drafted higher.

Miguel Batista

Bats: R   Throws: R   Height: 6' 1"   Weight: 195   Born: February 19, 1971   Age: 38

YEAR	TEAM	LVL	AGE	W	L	SV	G	GS	IP	H	BB	SO	HR	GB%	BABIP	STUFF	WHIP	ERA	DERA	EqH9	EqBB9	EqSO9	EqHR9	DEF	VORP	SN/WX
2006	ARI	MLB	35	11	8	0	34	33	206¹	231	84	110	18	52.8%	.316	6	1.53	4.58	4.35	9.6	3.2	4.4	0.7	0	24.9	3.35
2007	SEA	MLB	36	16	11	0	33	32	193	209	85	133	18	45.3%	.315	6	1.52	4.29	4.14	9.0	3.6	5.3	0.9	-13	25.5	4.31
2008	SEA	MLB	37	4	14	1	44	20	115	135	79	73	19	46.5%	.318	-26	1.86	6.26	7.02	10.0	5.5	4.9	1.5	1	-16.7	-1.48
2009	SEA	MLB	38	4	6	1	31	10	76²	89	39	46	8	47.0%	.320	-5	1.66	5.36	5.31	10.4	4.0	4.7	1.0	-1	-0.2	0.36

Breakout: 13%   Improve: 37%   Collapse: 33%   Attrition: 30%   Comparables: Bob Buhl, Mark Langston, Sonny Siebert, Cal McLish

The pitcher/author/poet/musician may have developed as an artist last season, but he had a rough season on the mound, as a lack of command and a loss of velocity eventually cost him his rotation spot, returning him to a utility role he wasn't very useful in. A year ago in this space, we wrote that Batista's margin of error was "tiny," but now it's nonexistent. The Mariners plan to utilize the 38-year-old in short relief this season, hoping to salvage something worthwhile from their $9 million investment.

Erik Bedard

Bats: L   Throws: L   Height: 6' 1"   Weight: 195   Born: March 6, 1979   Age: 30

YEAR	TEAM	LVL	AGE	W	L	SV	G	GS	IP	H	BB	SO	HR	GB%	BABIP	STUFF	WHIP	ERA	DERA	EqH9	EqBB9	EqSO9	EqHR9	DEF	VORP	SN/WX
2006	BAL	MLB	27	15	11	0	33	33	196¹	196	69	171	16	49.9%	.314	23	1.35	3.76	4.22	8.5	3.1	6.9	0.7	3	41.0	5.46
2007	BAL	MLB	28	13	5	0	28	28	182	141	57	221	19	49.8%	.287	36	1.09	3.16	3.68	7.1	2.7	9.5	1.0	9	55.7	5.99
2008	SEA	MLB	29	6	4	0	15	15	81	70	37	72	9	39.6%	.275	12	1.32	3.67	4.44	7.4	3.7	7.0	1.0	1	13.2	2.32
2009	SEA	MLB	30	7	7	1	28	18	117	109	48	116	12	45.0%	.300	26	1.34	3.94	3.89	8.3	3.3	7.9	0.9	-1	19.9	2.77

Breakout: 11%   Improve: 41%   Collapse: 30%   Attrition: 23%   Comparables: Jack Harshman, Kelvim Escobar, Mark Langston, Andy McGaffigan

Bedard didn't pitch nearly often or effectively enough last season to justify the Mariners' decision to part with a substantial package of young talent in order to acquire him. He was plagued by a sore shoulder, which ended his season after an outing on July 4, and averaged just over five innings per start. When he was on the mound, Bedard was Seattle's second-best starter by a wide margin, but his peripherals paled in comparison with those of his 2007 campaign, when he recorded one of the best strikeout rates in AL history. His durability and willingness to pitch through minor pain and fatigue have been questioned throughout his career and drew added scrutiny after exploratory surgery on his shoulder last September revealed only minor structural damage.

Roy Corcoran

Bats: R **Throws: R** **Height: 5' 10"** **Weight: 170** **Born: May 11, 1980** **Age: 29**

YEAR	TEAM	LVL	AGE	W	L	SV	G	GS	IP	H	BB	SO	HR	GB%	BABIP	STUFF	WHIP	ERA	DERA	EqH9	EqBB9	EqSO9	EqHR9	DEF	VORP	SN/WX
2006	HAR	AA	26	0	2	16	21	0	26	12	10	40	1	54.2%	.239	13	0.85	0.35	4.18	6.1	4.2	9.1	0.8	2	3.7	—
2006	NWO	AAA	26	2	4	11	28	0	33²	24	25	37	0	66.7%	.293	10	1.48	2.44	4.09	7.4	6.5	6.8	0.3	1	5.5	—
2007	ABQ	AAA	27	4	4	15	53	0	61	63	33	52	1	61.4%	.344	-1	1.57	3.54	4.27	9.8	5.0	5.5	0.3	-1	8.7	—
2008	TAC	AAA	28	0	0	4	15	0	14¹	14	13	11	1	62.8%	.325	-12	1.89	5.03	5.40	9.4	8.1	4.7	0.7	-1	0.3	—
2008	SEA	MLB	28	6	2	3	50	0	72²	65	36	39	1	69.9%	.276	-1	1.39	3.22	3.65	7.3	4.0	4.1	0.1	-2	14.6	2.05
2009	SEA	MLB	29	2	2	2	41	0	48¹	53	25	31	3	58.0%	.320	-2	1.62	4.79	4.85	9.8	4.1	5.2	0.6	-1	2.5	0.18

Breakout: 17% Improve: 30% Collapse: 50% Attrition: 30%   Comparables: Gene Harris, John Riedling, Saul Rivera, Mike Koplove

Corcoran is the ultimate overachiever, a little guy who went undrafted after his career at Louisiana State and some-one who labored in a chemical plant until the Expos beckoned him to the exciting existence of a veteran minor leaguer. Ultimately, Corcoran broke through to the highest level, and thus far, he's continued to defy expectations by retaining his roster spot in spite of a 1.1 career strikeout-to-walk ratio. His astronomical ground-ball rates allow him to survive a certain amount of tightrope-walking, but his next 70 major league innings—assuming he has that many left in him—probably won't be so pretty.

R. A. Dickey

Bats: R **Throws: R** **Height: 6' 3"** **Weight: 220** **Born: October 29, 1974** **Age: 34**

YEAR	TEAM	LVL	AGE	W	L	SV	G	GS	IP	H	BB	SO	HR	GB%	BABIP	STUFF	WHIP	ERA	DERA	EqH9	EqBB9	EqSO9	EqHR9	DEF	VORP	SN/WX
2006	OKL	AAA	31	9	8	1	22	19	131²	134	46	61	17	46.2%	.283	-36	1.37	4.94	7.43	10.2	3.5	2.6	1.7	10	-24.9	—
2007	NAS	AAA	32	13	6	0	31	22	169¹	159	60	119	18	54.1%	.287	-13	1.29	3.72	5.90	9.7	3.5	4.6	1.3	17	-5.2	—
2008	TAC	AAA	33	2	5	0	7	7	49²	58	8	30	2	47.6%	.344	1	1.33	3.44	5.48	10.8	1.7	3.4	0.6	1	0.6	—
2008	SEA	MLB	33	5	8	0	32	14	112¹	124	51	58	15	47.3%	.299	-21	1.56	5.21	5.32	9.4	3.7	4.0	1.2	0	5.6	0.88
2009	MIN	MLB	34	4	5	0	30	9	76²	92	27	38	10	45.6%	.310	-8	1.56	5.44	5.53	10.7	2.9	4.0	1.2	0	-1.0	0.20

Breakout: 15% Improve: 44% Collapse: 26% Attrition: 38%   Comparables: Aaron Small, Roger Craig, Pete Walker, Kevin Jarvis

Dickey's knuckleball has yet to fool big-league hitters, as evidenced by the 5.82 ERA he's posted in 145⅓ innings since his conversion from a conventional pitching style prior to the 2005 season. The Triple-A results have improved steadily over the past four seasons, however, a trend that offers at least some hope that he can finally become a serv-iceable starter at the age of 34. In the unlikely event that he does, the Twins will reap the benefits, since they signed him as a free agent after the Mariners excised him from the 40-man roster at the end of last season.

Ryan Feierabend

Bats: L **Throws: L** **Height: 6' 3"** **Weight: 190** **Born: August 22, 1985** **Age: 23**

YEAR	TEAM	LVL	AGE	W	L	SV	G	GS	IP	H	BB	SO	HR	GB%	BABIP	STUFF	WHIP	ERA	DERA	EqH9	EqBB9	EqSO9	EqHR9	DEF	VORP	SN/WX
2006	SAN	AA	20	9	12	0	28	28	153	156	55	127	16	38.7%	.317	3	1.38	4.29	7.36	11.2	3.7	4.8	1.6	5	-27.2	—
2006	SEA	MLB	20	0	1	0	4	2	17	15	7	11	3	40.0%	.235	17	1.29	3.71	5.71	7.3	3.6	5.2	1.6	4	4.5	0.20
2007	TAC	AAA	21	6	4	0	19	19	108¹	131	33	70	9	39.2%	.349	12	1.51	3.99	4.96	11.0	3.0	4.0	1.0	-7	7.3	—
2007	SEA	MLB	21	1	6	0	13	9	49¹	73	23	27	10	37.4%	.371	-9	1.95	8.03	6.85	13.1	4.0	4.4	1.9	-6	-11.8	-0.25
2008	TAC	AAA	22	7	1	0	13	13	75	64	15	48	5	39.2%	.265	11	1.05	2.04	4.56	7.5	2.0	3.7	0.7	11	8.4	—
2008	SEA	MLB	22	1	4	0	8	8	39²	59	14	26	7	38.7%	.391	-2	1.84	7.71	6.21	13.6	3.1	5.5	1.7	-7	-9.2	-0.11
2009	SEA	MLB	23	6	11	0	36	25	136²	172	52	78	24	40.0%	.320	3	1.64	5.98	5.78	11.2	3.0	4.5	1.6	-2	-7.7	0.09

Breakout: 15% Improve: 45% Collapse: 26% Attrition: 17%   Comparables: Andrew Lorraine, Abe Alvarez, Chris Seddon, Wally Ritchie

Feierabend has always been considered a decent prospect, but those familiar only with his work in the majors have yet to see why, as he's struggled in all three of his trips to the big league jungle. His travails are understandable when one considers that he has been beaten up by the big kids at every stop along his route to the majors and won't turn 23 till the dog days of 2009. Feierabend's youth and inexperience have prevented him from posting eye-popping numbers at any level, but scouts agree that he'll be a successful starter in the majors, albeit one whose upside may be limited to the back end of the rotation. The southpaw throws a fastball that hovers around 90, an excellent changeup, a slider, and a curve, but without impressive velocity or a consistent third pitch, he needs to hit spots to be successful.

Sean Green Bats: R Throws: R Height: 6' 6" Weight: 230 Born: April 20, 1979 Age: 30

YEAR	TEAM	LVL	AGE	W	L	SV	G	GS	IP	H	BB	SO	HR	GB%	BABIP	STUFF	WHIP	ERA	DERA	EqH9	EqBB9	EqSO9	EqHR9	DEF	VORP	SN/WX
2006	TAC	AAA	27	4	1	5	15	0	24	18	11	12	0	63.6%	.243	-19	1.21	2.25	5.40	7.5	4.6	2.9	0.4	5	0.5	—
2006	SEA	MLB	27	0	0	0	24	0	32	34	13	15	2	59.6%	.305	-18	1.47	4.50	4.99	9.7	3.8	3.8	0.6	1	5.5	-0.04
2007	TAC	AAA	28	2	1	1	10	0	17²	13	8	10	0	74.1%	.250	-19	1.19	2.03	5.19	6.2	4.2	3.6	0.0	4	0.8	—
2007	SEA	MLB	28	5	2	0	64	0	68	77	34	53	2	63.1%	.369	5	1.63	3.84	3.41	10.0	4.2	6.3	0.3	-6	13.8	1.08
2008	SEA	MLB	29	4	5	1	72	0	79	80	36	62	3	63.9%	.320	5	1.47	4.67	4.98	8.4	3.7	6.0	0.3	-4	2.4	1.02
2009	NYN	MLB	30	3	3	2	53	0	61	60	27	46	3	58.0%	.300	3	1.43	3.75	4.25	9.0	3.5	5.8	0.5	0	10.6	0.83

Breakout: 22% Improve: 57% Collapse: 21% Attrition: 16% Comparables: Mike Fetters, Tim Crabtree, Jay Powell, Danny Kolb

Green is essentially a one-pitch pitcher, throwing sinker after sinker and hoping that batted balls don't find holes. As befits a pitcher who relies heavily on his defense, he experienced mixed results during the last three seasons with the Mariners. Green throws from a low arm slot, which leaves him with few effective weapons against lefties, who simply wait him out until they find themselves at first base. In need of bullpen help, the Mets acquired Green in a trade built around Putz, where Green will get a shot at riffing on the ROOGY stylings of the departed Joe Smith.

Felix Hernandez Bats: R Throws: R Height: 6' 3" Weight: 230 Born: April 8, 1986 Age: 23

YEAR	TEAM	LVL	AGE	W	L	SV	G	GS	IP	H	BB	SO	HR	GB%	BABIP	STUFF	WHIP	ERA	DERA	EqH9	EqBB9	EqSO9	EqHR9	DEF	VORP	SN/WX
2006	SEA	MLB	20	12	14	0	31	31	191	195	60	176	23	58.7%	.315	49	1.34	4.52	4.80	9.2	2.8	7.4	1.1	-3	22.5	3.76
2007	SEA	MLB	21	14	7	0	30	30	190¹	209	53	165	20	61.5%	.338	32	1.37	3.93	3.81	9.4	2.4	6.8	1.0	-8	37.0	4.32
2008	SEA	MLB	22	9	11	0	31	31	200²	198	80	175	17	52.2%	.319	32	1.39	3.45	3.81	8.7	3.3	7.0	0.8	-3	42.8	5.29
2009	SEA	MLB	23	12	10	0	30	30	192¹	190	67	170	16	51.0%	.310	33	1.34	3.81	3.78	8.8	2.7	7.0	0.7	-2	33.8	5.03

Breakout: 25% Improve: 45% Collapse: 18% Attrition: 6% Comparables: Dwight Gooden, Jeremy Bonderman, Carlos Zambrano, Joe Coleman

Hernandez has been pitching in the national spotlight for so long that it seems as if he's been around forever, but he's still younger than many pitchers who will be rookies this year. Last season, he added a willingness to pitch inside to his arsenal, which already included a high-90s fastball, a devastating slider, an above-average curveball, and an improving changeup. Although his ERA shrunk by a significant margin, Hernandez's peripherals essentially leveled off. His strikeout rate ticked upward slightly, and he allowed fewer homers, but he also induced fewer grounders, and his walk rate soared. Although any halt to a young player's forward progress represents a cause for concern, the damage was done in the second half, suggesting that the sprained ankle that sidelined the hurler in late June may have been the culprit. Hernandez will turn 23 during the season's first week and will use this temporary plateau as a base camp from which to ascend to even greater heights.

Gaby Hernandez Bats: R Throws: R Height: 6' 3" Weight: 215 Born: May 21, 1986 Age: 23

YEAR	TEAM	LVL	AGE	W	L	SV	G	GS	IP	H	BB	SO	HR	GB%	BABIP	STUFF	WHIP	ERA	DERA	EqH9	EqBB9	EqSO9	EqHR9	DEF	VORP	SN/WX
2006	JUP	A+	20	9	7	0	21	20	120	120	35	115	7	44.7%	.330	5	1.29	3.68	6.96	12.5	3.8	4.7	1.4	-8	-16.0	—
2007	CAR	AA	21	9	11	0	28	28	153²	144	56	113	14	39.5%	.282	-6	1.30	4.22	7.50	10.1	3.5	3.7	1.5	15	-30.9	—
2008	CAR	AA	22	3	0	0	4	4	23	21	4	17	3	40.5%	.261	-2	1.09	4.30	7.66	9.7	1.6	4.0	2.0	6	-5.1	—
2008	ABQ	AAA	22	2	8	0	13	13	64²	94	26	54	14	42.7%	.376	-18	1.85	7.23	7.41	13.0	3.6	4.8	2.0	-4	-12.9	—
2008	WTN	AA	22	1	1	0	6	6	32¹	38	15	23	3	49.5%	.343	-11	1.64	5.02	5.40	12.3	4.5	3.9	1.5	-5	0.7	—
2009	SEA	MLB	23	5	11	0	25	25	133¹	172	62	80	25	41.0%	.330	6	1.75	6.66	6.46	11.5	3.6	4.7	1.6	-2	-18.4	-0.89

Breakout: 26% Improve: 64% Collapse: 11% Attrition: 7% Comparables: Taylor Buchholz, Doug Waechter, Kent Bottenfield, Roy Smith

Ownership prevented interim GM Lee Pelekoudas from taking drastic measures to reshape the aging, underachieving roster of the club he inherited last season. One important move, however, was Pelekoudas's July acquisition of Hernandez from the Marlins for Arthur Rhodes. The durable curveballer morphed into a home-run dispenser in his first taste of Triple-A last summer, but at age 22, was still young for his league—an important point to consider when you are appraising the performance of that other Hernandez, who's already spent most of four seasons in Seattle's rotation, despite being Gaby's junior.

Cesar Jimenez

Bats: L   Throws: L   Height: 5' 11"   Weight: 180   Born: November 12, 1984   Age: 24

YEAR	TEAM	LVL	AGE	W	L	SV	G	GS	IP	H	BB	SO	HR	GB%	BABIP	STUFF	WHIP	ERA	DERA	EqH9	EqBB9	EqSO9	EqHR9	DEF	VORP	SN/WX
2006	SAN	AA	21	0	2	0	3	3	16²	10	5	10	0	69.6%	.217	9	0.93	2.78	6.60	6.6	3.0	3.6	0.0	4	-1.7	—
2006	TAC	AAA	21	5	10	3	24	19	107	107	55	66	8	50.5%	.307	-3	1.51	4.37	6.39	9.9	4.9	3.7	1.1	7	-8.8	—
2006	SEA	MLB	21	0	0	0	4	1	7¹	13	4	3	4	29.0%	.333	-33	2.32	14.79	13.50	16.0	4.9	3.7	4.9	-1	-7.4	-0.38
2007	TAC	AAA	22	2	1	2	16	0	25²	28	12	23	2	41.0%	.329	-3	1.56	3.50	5.47	9.2	4.1	5.5	1.0	-2	0.4	—
2008	TAC	AAA	23	1	3	3	29	0	38	37	8	47	3	45.4%	.324	11	1.18	3.55	4.66	8.8	1.9	7.4	0.9	-3	4.0	—
2008	SEA	MLB	23	0	2	0	31	2	34¹	32	13	26	2	39.6%	.313	4	1.31	3.41	3.58	8.3	3.3	6.3	0.6	0	8.6	-0.50
2009	SEA	MLB	24	3	3	3	58	3	58²	59	24	48	6	44.0%	.300	9	1.41	4.22	4.15	8.9	3.2	6.5	0.9	-1	8.3	0.83

Breakout: 37%   Improve: 68%   Collapse: 10%   Attrition: 16%   Comparables: Felix Heredia, Willie Hernandez, John Franco, Shane Rawley

Jimenez's stuff is a little short for the starting rotation, and he's shown a tendency to wear down after extended use, so the Mariners wisely shifted him to the bullpen on a permanent basis prior to the 2007 season. His average fastball and superb changeup gain effectiveness in short bursts, and he's exhibited improved control in the relief role. The lefty's changeup keeps right-handed hitters honest and gives him a future as something more than a specialist.

Stephen Kahn

Bats: L   Throws: R   Height: 6' 3"   Weight: 215   Born: December 14, 1983   Age: 25

YEAR	TEAM	LVL	AGE	W	L	SV	G	GS	IP	H	BB	SO	HR	GB%	BABIP	STUFF	WHIP	ERA	DERA	EqH9	EqBB9	EqSO9	EqHR9	DEF	VORP	SN/WX
2006	SBR	A+	22	2	0	8	20	0	27	16	15	35	1	41.3%	.250	8	1.15	2.00	4.97	7.1	6.0	6.4	0.7	4	1.8	—
2006	SAN	AA	22	1	3	0	31	0	39¹	50	31	33	3	46.8%	.385	-16	2.07	6.21	7.08	14.7	8.1	5.0	1.3	-8	-5.6	—
2009	SEA	MLB	25	1	2	0	14	4	33	38	20	24	4	44.0%	.320	0	1.75	5.80	5.71	10.2	4.9	5.7	1.1	-1	-2.4	-0.03

Breakout: 37%   Improve: 62%   Collapse: 26%   Attrition: 47%   Comparables: Dave Wehrmeister, Andy Larkin, Kurt Miller, Sean Douglass

The hard-throwing Kahn missed the last two seasons while recovering from reconstructive surgery on his left knee, but the Mariners still valued him highly enough to place him on the 40-man roster last November in order to avoid losing him in the Rule 5 draft. Kahn's fastball consistently sits in the mid-90s and occasionally touches 98, giving him the appearance of a future closer. He might be better off if he weren't so fixated on maintaining that appearance, as his fastball fetish causes him to neglect his mechanics and secondary offerings.

Mark Lowe

Bats: R   Throws: R   Height: 6' 3"   Weight: 190   Born: June 7, 1983   Age: 26

YEAR	TEAM	LVL	AGE	W	L	SV	G	GS	IP	H	BB	SO	HR	GB%	BABIP	STUFF	WHIP	ERA	DERA	EqH9	EqBB9	EqSO9	EqHR9	DEF	VORP	SN/WX
2006	SBR	A+	23	1	0	2	13	2	29¹	14	11	46	0	60.0%	.233	15	0.86	1.86	4.71	6.0	4.1	7.8	0.3	0	2.8	—
2006	SAN	AA	23	0	2	4	11	0	16	14	3	14	1	50.0%	.289	-6	1.06	2.25	4.91	9.2	1.8	4.9	1.2	2	1.1	—
2006	SEA	MLB	23	1	0	0	15	0	18²	12	9	20	1	47.7%	.262	18	1.13	1.93	3.06	6.1	4.6	9.2	0.5	2	8.6	1.61
2008	SEA	MLB	25	1	5	1	57	0	63²	78	34	55	6	44.3%	.364	-5	1.76	5.37	4.90	10.6	4.3	6.7	0.8	-9	-4.5	-1.64
2009	SEA	MLB	26	2	2	2	34	1	45²	47	22	40	5	44.0%	.310	10	1.50	4.65	4.58	9.2	3.7	6.9	1.0	-1	4.5	0.34

Breakout: 44%   Improve: 73%   Collapse: 8%   Attrition: 35%   Comparables: Vinnie Chulk, Elias Sosa, Pep Harris, Jose Paniagua

After trading Putz to the Mets and returning Brandon Morrow to his rightful place in the rotation, the Mariners find themselves in need of a closer. Lowe, who occupied the setup role at times last season, would be the logical choice, but for his propensity to allow walks and homers. His mid-90s fastball, biting slider, and lefty-killing changeup give him the necessary raw materials to be a dominant short reliever, but he needs to regain the feel for his pitches, which he possessed before undergoing two elbow surgeries in 2007. Perhaps another year removed from the knife will allow him to do so.

Randy Messenger

Bats: R **Throws: R** **Height: 6' 6"** **Weight: 240** **Born: August 13, 1981** **Age: 27**

YEAR	TEAM	LVL	AGE	W	L	SV	G	GS	IP	H	BB	SO	HR	GB%	BABIP	STUFF	WHIP	ERA	DERA	EqH9	EqBB9	EqSO9	EqHR9	DEF	VORP	SN/WX
2006	FLO	MLB	24	2	7	0	59	0	60¹	72	24	45	8	41.5%	.337	-9	1.59	5.67	4.82	10.1	3.1	6.0	1.0	-7	-2.6	-0.75
2007	FLO	MLB	25	1	1	0	23	0	23²	27	9	12	0	45.1%	.351	-3	1.52	2.66	0.76	9.1	3.0	4.2	0.0	-4	8.3	0.19
2007	SFN	MLB	25	1	3	1	37	0	40²	58	12	22	4	48.4%	.378	-10	1.72	5.09	2.90	12.5	2.2	4.7	0.9	-7	3.5	-0.87
2008	FRE	AAA	26	3	4	3	29	0	41	47	12	30	4	54.5%	.347	-19	1.44	4.83	5.02	11.5	2.9	4.5	1.2	-4	2.4	—
2008	TAC	AAA	26	6	0	1	12	0	22²	19	11	16	2	47.1%	.266	-14	1.32	2.38	4.50	7.4	4.5	4.1	0.8	2	2.7	—
2008	SEA	MLB	26	0	0	1	13	0	12²	16	5	7	1	27.3%	.349	-16	1.66	3.54	3.75	11.2	3.8	4.5	0.8	0	3.0	0.25
2009	SEA	MLB	27	2	3	1	48	1	55²	66	23	32	7	45.0%	.310	-5	1.59	5.22	5.13	10.6	3.2	4.6	1.1	-1	0.9	0.09

Breakout: 12% Improve: 39% Collapse: 30% Attrition: 12% Comparables: Mike Christopher, Aaron Small, Matt Karchner, Keith Brown

The Mariners signed Messenger after the Giants released him last July, and then Seattle stashed the hard-throwing reliever in Tacoma for six weeks before giving him a late-season look in the majors. Unfortunately, Messenger suffered from the same problem in Seattle that he exhibited with the Marlins, the Giants, and a host of their minor league affiliates: He couldn't consistently throw the ball across the plate. The Mariners need bullpen help, but Messenger won't fit that description unless he suddenly gains command of his pitches, an unlikely prospect at this stage of his career.

Brandon Morrow

Bats: R **Throws: R** **Height: 6' 3"** **Weight: 190** **Born: July 26, 1984** **Age: 24**

YEAR	TEAM	LVL	AGE	W	L	SV	G	GS	IP	H	BB	SO	HR	GB%	BABIP	STUFF	WHIP	ERA	DERA	EqH9	EqBB9	EqSO9	EqHR9	DEF	VORP	SN/WX
2006	MRN	Rk	21	0	2	0	7	4	13²	10	9	13	0	58.1%	.323	-5	1.44	2.73	5.59	12.1	10.2	3.7	0.9	0	0.0	—
2007	SEA	MLB	22	3	4	0	60	0	63¹	56	50	66	3	36.6%	.329	23	1.67	4.12	3.71	7.6	6.6	8.1	0.4	-3	12.8	2.34
2008	TAC	AAA	23	1	2	0	6	5	23¹	17	11	26	2	39.3%	.263	6	1.20	5.02	5.79	6.6	4.2	6.6	0.8	-1	-0.5	—
2008	SEA	MLB	23	3	4	10	45	5	64²	40	34	75	10	33.8%	.207	11	1.14	3.34	4.68	5.2	4.3	9.1	1.4	7	14.8	1.65
2009	SEA	MLB	24	4	5	5	41	7	72¹	63	40	77	8	38.0%	.290	19	1.43	4.28	4.19	7.8	4.4	8.4	1.0	-1	10.3	1.20

Breakout: 6% Improve: 13% Collapse: 69% Attrition: 28% Comparables: Matt Anderson, Steve Mura, Dave Morehead, Tracy Stallard

Morrow's return to the rotation was accompanied by much less fanfare than Joba Chamberlain's, in small part because it was accomplished behind the scenes. Last sighted throwing a single inning in relief on August 3, Morrow emerged from seclusion in his Pacific Coast League chrysalis to no-hit the Yankees for 7⅔ innings on September 6. His final four starts of the season included two clunkers, between which he allowed twice as many earned runs as he had all season out of the pen. Morrow spent most of the last two seasons utilizing only two pitches, and he'll need to refine his neglected changeup and improve his command to succeed as a starter. His developmental clock was frozen for nearly two years, so some struggles are inevitable, but the result will be worth the belated growing pains.

Eric O'Flaherty

Bats: L **Throws: L** **Height: 6' 2"** **Weight: 195** **Born: February 5, 1985** **Age: 24**

YEAR	TEAM	LVL	AGE	W	L	SV	G	GS	IP	H	BB	SO	HR	GB%	BABIP	STUFF	WHIP	ERA	DERA	EqH9	EqBB9	EqSO9	EqHR9	DEF	VORP	SN/WX
2006	SBR	A+	21	0	1	1	16	0	28¹	31	6	33	1	60.5%	.417	9	1.32	3.52	3.09	15.0	3.1	6.6	1.2	-6	6.5	—
2006	SAN	AA	21	2	2	7	25	0	39	45	15	36	0	56.4%	.391	17	1.54	1.15	2.14	13.6	4.3	5.6	0.3	-6	13.0	—
2006	SEA	MLB	21	0	0	0	15	0	11	18	6	6	2	40.0%	.381	-11	2.18	4.09	4.76	14.3	4.8	4.0	1.6	-3	-1.7	-0.46
2007	SEA	MLB	22	7	1	0	56	0	52¹	45	20	36	1	46.3%	.280	11	1.24	4.47	4.96	7.0	3.1	5.3	0.2	3	8.5	0.56
2008	SEA	MLB	23	0	1	0	7	0	6²	16	4	4	2	50.0%	.483	-51	3.00	20.15	15.43	20.6	5.1	3.9	2.6	-4	-11.1	-0.69
2008	IAC	AAA	23	1	0	2	14	0	16¹	23	9	19	1	49.0%	.449	-1	1.96	4.97	5.28	14.7	5.3	7.6	0.6	-1	0.5	—
2009	ATL	MLB	24	2	3	1	51	2	49¹	59	21	35	5	49.0%	.330	-0	1.62	5.55	5.91	10.6	3.4	5.5	1.0	0	-1.3	-0.07

Breakout: 42% Improve: 74% Collapse: 9% Attrition: 20% Comparables: Bob Allen, Dave Von Ohlen, Greg Langbehn, Cliff Bartosh

With George Sherrill closing in Baltimore, O'Flaherty began last season as the Mariners' situational southpaw. His work against lefties in 2007 fully qualified him for the role, but he made it only to mid-April before ineffectiveness landed him in Tacoma. His performance there represented only a moderate improvement over his major league meltdown, and O'Flaherty's '08 came to an end after a back injury suffered in June. Despite his struggles, the Mariners' decision to expose the talented 23-year-old to waivers came as a surprise. The Braves promptly claimed him and plan to give him another shot at the role he failed to fulfill last year.

J. J. Putz

								Bats: R		Throws: R		Height: 6' 5"		Weight: 250		Born: February 22, 1977			Age: 32	

YEAR	TEAM	LVL	AGE	W	L	SV	G	GS	IP	H	BB	SO	HR	GB%	BABIP	STUFF	WHIP	ERA	DERA	EqH9	EqBB9	EqSO9	EqHR9	DEF	VORP	SN/WX
2006	SEA	MLB	29	4	1	36	72	0	78¹	59	13	104	4	52.2%	.311	39	0.92	2.30	2.38	7.4	1.5	10.0	0.5	-1	32.7	5.60
2007	SEA	MLB	30	6	1	40	68	0	71²	37	13	82	6	44.2%	.201	26	0.70	1.38	3.55	4.3	1.5	8.6	0.8	15	36.6	7.40
2008	SEA	MLB	31	6	5	15	47	0	46¹	46	28	56	4	40.0%	.350	17	1.60	3.89	3.33	9.0	4.9	9.6	0.8	-3	9.1	-0.53
2009	NYN	MLB	32	4	3	15	48	0	55²	45	20	61	4	45.0%	.280	21	1.16	2.63	2.89	7.3	2.8	8.4	0.7	0	18.2	2.12

Breakout: 17%   Improve: 41%   Collapse: 32%   Attrition: 6%   Comparables: Roberto Hernandez, Eric Plunk, B.J. Ryan, Robb Nen

Putz injured his elbow during his first outing last season and landed on the DL. Although he didn't require surgery, he struggled to regain his health for much of the season and didn't appear to be back at full strength until September. As happens to most victims of elbow woes, Putz's control deserted him, though he retained his strikeout stuff. Part of his decline was attributable to an overcorrection in BABIP, as the flukily low .201 mark he posted in '07 ballooned to .350 last season. After an off-season trade spelled the end of his stay in Seattle, Putz will try to get back on track setting up for Francisco Rodriguez in New York. If he's healthy, he may prove to be the best closer the Mets acquired this off-season.

Juan Ramirez

								Bats: R		Throws: R		Height: 6' 3"		Weight: 175		Born: August 16, 1988			Age: 20	

YEAR	TEAM	LVL	AGE	W	L	SV	G	GS	IP	H	BB	SO	HR	GB%	BABIP	STUFF	WHIP	ERA	DERA	EqH9	EqBB9	EqSO9	EqHR9	DEF	VORP	SN/WX
2007	EVE	A-	18	3	7	0	15	15	75¹	61	43	73	3	47.0%	.272	-5	1.38	4.30	9.48	10.5	7.0	3.0	1.4	-6	-29.4	—
2008	WIS	A	19	6	9	0	25	22	124	112	38	113	9	49.0%	.298	1	1.21	4.14	8.16	11.1	4.1	3.9	1.8	-1	-31.4	—
2009	SEA	MLB	20	3	10	0	29	19	106¹	147	61	56	22	44.0%	.330	-7	1.95	8.03	7.86	12.4	4.5	4.2	1.8	-2	-30.6	-2.58

Breakout: 31%   Improve: 62%   Collapse: 10%   Attrition: 16%   Comparables: Jose Guzman, Beltran Perez, Amaury Telemaco, Calvin Maduro

Nicaragua has not been a fertile breeding ground for baseball talent in recent years, but the Mariners may have found a gem when they signed Ramirez in 2005. Prior to this season, the lanky right-hander's appeal stemmed primarily from projection and not performance, but Ramirez's command made great strides in the Midwest League last season, clearing an important hurdle on his path to a front-of-the-rotation future. His fastball has been clocked at 97 mph, and he also flashes a nasty slider. Ramirez remains a long way from the majors, but worth keeping an eye on, as he could cover ground fast.

Ryan Rowland-Smith

								Bats: L		Throws: L		Height: 6' 3"		Weight: 240		Born: January 26, 1983			Age: 26	

YEAR	TEAM	LVL	AGE	W	L	SV	G	GS	IP	H	BB	SO	HR	GB%	BABIP	STUFF	WHIP	ERA	DERA	EqH9	EqBB9	EqSO9	EqHR9	DEF	VORP	SN/WX
2006	SAN	AA	23	1	3	4	23	1	41²	38	18	48	2	46.1%	.333	-2	1.36	2.84	5.45	10.0	4.3	6.8	0.9	0	0.7	—
2007	TAC	AAA	24	3	4	1	25	0	41²	35	22	50	2	38.9%	.320	11	1.37	3.67	4.61	7.7	4.8	7.9	0.7	-3	4.5	—
2007	SEA	MLB	24	1	0	0	26	0	38²	39	15	42	4	35.2%	.354	13	1.40	3.95	3.05	8.7	3.3	8.5	0.9	-6	6.4	0.18
2008	TAC	AAA	25	2	0	0	3	3	18²	12	7	12	1	38.2%	.212	-4	1.02	2.89	5.79	5.3	3.4	3.4	0.5	5	-0.4	—
2008	SEA	MLB	25	5	3	2	47	12	118¹	114	48	77	13	40.9%	.280	-8	1.37	3.42	4.58	8.2	3.3	5.1	1.0	9	25.7	2.34
2009	SEA	MLB	26	4	6	2	43	9	85	88	37	60	11	42.0%	.290	5	1.47	4.59	4.48	9.2	3.4	5.6	1.1	-1	8.7	1.13

Breakout: 13%   Improve: 36%   Collapse: 40%   Attrition: 28%   Comparables: Bob Ojeda, Chris Haney, Gustavo Chacin, Hank Aguirre

The Mariners brought Rowland-Smith out of the bullpen for a spot start on July 1, and he entered the rotation for good five weeks later, posting a 3.50 ERA in 72 innings in his new role. However, the Aussie didn't show the peripherals normally associated with a figure that low, and he benefited from a lot of defensive support and a nice strand rate. He'll begin the season in the rotation, but might be destined to spend his days as a staff tweener—possessing four pitches might make him look like a starter, but unless one of them becomes a truly plus offering, he simply won't be able to keep up appearances.

Carlos Silva

Bats: R Throws: R Height: 6' 4" Weight: 245 Born: April 23, 1979 Age: 30

YEAR	TEAM	LVL	AGE	W	L	SV	G	GS	IP	H	BB	SO	HR	GB%	BABIP	STUFF	WHIP	ERA	DERA	EqH9	EqBB9	EqSO9	EqHR9	DEF	VORP	SN/WX
2006	MIN	MLB	27	11	15	0	36	31	180¹	246	32	70	38	45.6%	.320	-31	1.54	5.94	6.38	11.6	1.5	3.0	1.7	1	-8.4	1.40
2007	MIN	MLB	28	13	14	0	33	33	202	229	36	89	20	48.3%	.304	-2	1.31	4.19	4.87	9.9	1.5	3.4	1.0	10	34.7	4.93
2008	SEA	MLB	29	4	15	0	28	28	153¹	213	32	69	20	45.2%	.348	-15	1.60	6.46	6.22	11.9	1.7	3.6	1.2	-9	-17.7	0.26
2009	SEA	MLB	30	5	8	0	25	16	101¹	128	25	48	15	46.0%	.320	2	1.51	5.45	5.36	11.3	1.9	3.7	1.3	-1	-1.1	0.58

Breakout: 25% Improve: 53% Collapse: 21% Attrition: 29%   Comparables: Jim Barr, Jack Fisher, Lary Sorensen, Ed Lynch

Silva did nothing to dispel the perception that former general manager Bill Bavasi overpaid for him on the free-agent market. At his best, Silva is a fourth or fifth starter who doesn't walk or strike out anyone and who lives by getting batters to hit the ball on the ground, or would if his ground-ball rate wasn't unexceptional. Bavasi is gone, but this gift will keep on taking from the Mariners through 2011, after which they can pay him another $2 million to buy him out of his 2012 option. A signing like this one had so little chance of succeeding that if the Mariners franchise were a brand-new car, Bavasi's signing of Silva was tantamount to the GM's taking that car up to top speed and driving it into a wall. The real question isn't why he did it, but which smart guy gave him the keys?

Justin Thomas

Bats: L Throws: L Height: 6' 3" Weight: 220 Born: January 18, 1984 Age: 25

YEAR	TEAM	LVL	AGE	W	L	SV	G	GS	IP	H	BB	SO	HR	GB%	BABIP	STUFF	WHIP	ERA	DERA	EqH9	EqBB9	EqSO9	EqHR9	DEF	VORP	SN/WX
2006	WIS	A	22	5	5	0	11	11	61¹	69	17	51	4	57.9%	.349	-29	1.41	3.09	7.35	14.2	4.3	3.2	2.2	-4	-10.2	—
2006	SBR	A+	22	9	4	0	17	17	105¹	108	45	111	10	50.0%	.345	-17	1.46	4.11	6.88	13.4	5.3	5.5	2.0	-3	-12.7	—
2007	WTN	AA	23	4	9	0	24	24	119¹	147	61	100	11	44.8%	.372	-27	1.74	5.51	8.03	13.1	4.9	4.4	1.5	1	-30.0	—
2008	WTN	AA	24	7	7	0	25	17	118²	116	56	106	11	52.0%	.314	-20	1.45	4.32	6.14	10.3	4.4	5.0	1.5	-3	-6.7	—
2008	TAC	AAA	24	2	1	1	7	1	17	15	9	21	2	31.7%	.333	9	1.41	3.71	4.11	9.4	5.3	8.2	1.2	-1	2.5	—
2008	SEA	MLB	24	0	1	0	8	0	4	9	2	2	0	22.2%	.529	-36	2.75	6.75	4.91	22.1	4.9	4.9	0.0	-1	-0.5	-0.38
2009	SEA	MLB	25	3	6	0	33	11	80¹	105	47	53	13	46.0%	.340	-3	1.88	6.66	6.51	11.6	4.6	5.3	1.4	-1	-11.3	-0.75

Breakout: 18% Improve: 53% Collapse: 18% Attrition: 21%   Comparables: Ed Vosberg, Joe Ciccarella, Derek Root, Alex Graman

Thomas began the transition from starter to reliever at Triple-A during the second half of last season, eventually getting his first big-league action. He's a sinker/slider pitcher, the type most often associated with successful careers in the bullpen. He would seemingly have a future as a lefty specialist, except for the fact that big-league lefties went 8-for-14 against him. Fortunately, that's a small-sample fluke; Thomas does have a track record of retiring southpaw swingers in the minors.

Marwin Vega

Bats: R Throws: R Height: 6' 0" Weight: 175 Born: October 27, 1986 Age: 22

YEAR	TEAM	LVL	AGE	W	L	SV	G	GS	IP	H	BB	SO	HR	GB%	BABIP	STUFF	WHIP	ERA	DERA	EqH9	EqBB9	EqSO9	EqHR9	DEF	VORP	SN/WX
2006	WIS	A	19	5	10	0	20	20	97	111	37	71	4	52.9%	.343	-19	1.53	5.38	11.30	13.7	5.3	2.4	1.5	-8	-54.5	—
2007	HDS	A+	20	5	10	0	24	24	128²	149	43	82	14	54.2%	.332	-12	1.49	4.90	7.35	12.1	3.9	2.6	1.7	-2	-22.6	—
2008	WTN	AA	21	3	3	2	46	1	68²	67	44	50	3	50.5%	.324	-9	1.62	4.72	6.75	9.9	5.8	3.9	0.8	0	-8.3	—
2009	SEA	MLB	22	2	4	0	24	6	53	70	36	28	8	49.0%	.340	-12	2.01	7.27	7.19	11.9	5.4	4.2	1.3	-1	-12.0	-0.93

Breakout: 14% Improve: 42% Collapse: 29% Attrition: 19%   Comparables: Maximo Del Rosario, Aguedo Vasquez, Blas Cedeño, Julio DePaula

Vega was a surprise addition to the Mariners' 40-man roster last November, as he's not generally considered a prospect in many circles. He's a smallish reliever who throws a fastball in the low-90s, a slurvy breaking ball, and a tantalizingly slow changeup, but he has problems throwing strikes. Trivia: Vega could become the second Colombian to pitch in the major leagues, joining Emiliano Fruto. You knew that, right?

Jarrod Washburn

Bats: L   Throws: L   Height: 6' 1"   Weight: 190   Born: August 13, 1974   Age: 34

YEAR	TEAM	LVL	AGE	W	L	SV	G	GS	IP	H	BB	SO	HR	GB%	BABIP	STUFF	WHIP	ERA	DERA	EqH9	EqBB9	EqSO9	EqHR9	DEF	VORP	SN/WX
2006	SEA	MLB	31	8	14	0	31	31	187	198	55	103	25	40.8%	.284	-4	1.35	4.67	5.01	9.2	2.6	4.3	1.2	0	21.3	3.10
2007	SEA	MLB	32	10	15	0	32	32	193²	201	67	114	23	38.6%	.291	-2	1.38	4.32	5.15	8.5	2.9	4.5	1.1	8	25.2	3.37
2008	SEA	MLB	33	5	14	1	28	26	153²	174	50	87	19	37.9%	.309	-6	1.46	4.68	5.11	9.6	2.6	4.4	1.2	-1	10.3	2.50
2009	SEA	MLB	34	5	7	1	27	16	104	117	35	60	15	41.0%	.300	3	1.45	4.89	4.77	10.0	2.6	4.6	1.2	-1	6.7	1.32

Breakout: 15%   Improve: 44%   Collapse: 21%   Attrition: 34%   Comparables: Bud Black, Gary Peters, Ken Heintzelman, Rudy May

Washburn was a great story in 2002 when he won 18 games and helped the Angels win their only World Series title. He did so by using his fastball almost exclusively, baffling hitters by consistently changing speeds. Alas, major league starters cannot live by one pitch alone, and Washburn has been league-average at best since then. He has a $10.35 million salary this season in the final year of a four-year, $37.5 million contract, and it's safe to predict he will never make that kind of money again. In New York, Washburn-to-the-Yankees is a perennially popular rumor, but it's hard to know what the Yankees might see in him other than his career 2.56 ERA against them, his best versus any team against whom he's made 10 or more starts. Oh well; it worked for A. J. Burnett …

Jared Wells

Bats: R   Throws: R   Height: 6' 4"   Weight: 200   Born: October 31, 1981   Age: 27

YEAR	TEAM	LVL	AGE	W	L	SV	G	GS	IP	H	BB	SO	HR	GB%	BABIP	STUFF	WHIP	ERA	DERA	EqH9	EqBB9	EqSO9	EqHR9	DEF	VORP	SN/WX
2006	MOB	AA	24	4	3	0	12	12	61	53	27	49	4	48.1%	.283	-9	1.31	2.66	3.81	9.5	4.3	4.3	1.3	-3	11.3	—
2007	POR	AAA	25	3	7	9	47	10	92²	107	48	87	9	41.4%	.366	-12	1.67	5.24	5.28	10.2	4.7	5.9	1.1	-11	3.3	—
2008	POR	AAA	26	1	1	9	19	0	20	19	12	14	1	37.5%	.300	-24	1.55	5.85	6.86	8.7	5.5	4.1	0.5	0	-2.8	—
2008	SDN	MLB	26	0	0	0	2	0	3	4	1	2	0	36.4%	.400	-13	1.67	6.00	6.00	12.0	3.0	6.0	0.0	0	-0.3	-0.21
2008	TAC	AAA	26	0	4	11	33	0	40²	44	23	42	6	38.7%	.349	-17	1.65	6.41	7.91	10.7	5.1	6.5	1.6	1	-9.9	—
2008	SEA	MLB	26	0	0	0	6	0	5¹	7	6	3	2	42.9%	.278	-42	2.44	10.19	12.00	10.5	7.5	4.5	3.0	1	-2.7	-0.33
2009	SEA	MLB	27	2	4	1	45	4	50²	59	33	37	8	42.0%	.320	-6	1.81	6.30	6.17	10.3	5.2	5.8	1.3	-1	-5.6	-0.41

Breakout: 25%   Improve: 61%   Collapse: 18%   Attrition: 19%   Comparables: John Kiely, Joe Borowski, Doug Henry, Bobby Rodgers

The Mariners acquired the onetime promising prospect from the Padres last June in a swap for Cha Seung Baek. Although Wells served as the closer in Triple-A, he was disappointing both there and during a brief big-league stint in September. His fastball has a tendency to sail out of the strike zone, and Wells has never been able to correct the problem. Until he does, he will be perpetually stuck in the minors.

Jacoke Woods

Bats: L   Throws: L   Height: 6' 1"   Weight: 190   Born: September 3, 1981   Age: 27

YEAR	TEAM	LVL	AGE	W	L	SV	G	GS	IP	H	BB	SO	HR	GB%	BABIP	STUFF	WHIP	ERA	DERA	EqH9	EqBB9	EqSO9	EqHR9	DEF	VORP	SN/WX
2006	SEA	MLB	24	7	4	1	37	8	105	115	53	66	12	43.2%	.307	-9	1.60	4.20	4.28	9.7	4.5	5.0	1.0	-2	19.1	1.59
2007	TAC	AAA	25	5	7	1	25	18	114²	151	42	79	17	43.5%	.364	-34	1.68	6.90	7.55	12.4	3.6	4.4	1.8	-6	-23.2	—
2007	SEA	MLB	25	0	0	0	4	0	10²	9	7	4	1	35.1%	.222	-23	1.59	5.89	8.74	6.4	4.8	2.4	0.8	3	-1.0	0.03
2008	TAC	AAA	26	6	1	1	32	2	64	64	27	54	7	42.7%	.313	-17	1.42	4.08	5.22	9.5	4.0	5.2	1.2	3	2.5	—
2008	SEA	MLB	26	0	0	0	15	0	19	22	11	9	5	27.3%	.279	-32	1.74	6.16	5.89	10.3	4.9	3.9	2.5	-1	-1.0	-0.10
2009	SEA	MLB	27	2	3	1	34	4	52	59	26	35	7	41.0%	.310	-2	1.63	5.32	5.18	10.1	3.9	5.4	1.2	-1	0.6	0.17

Breakout: 29%   Improve: 56%   Collapse: 19%   Attrition: 15%   Comparables: Stan Clarke, Matt Perisho, Wally Ritchie, Neal Musser

Inconsistency has dogged Woods throughout his career. He has thrived at times as a long reliever, as his fastball, curveball, and changeup can flash as plus pitches. He does, however, go through spells during which he has trouble commanding all his offerings and either walks the park or becomes very hittable. He hasn't gotten major-league hitters with any regularity since 2006, which is why the Mariners dropped him from the 40-man roster last November.

LINEOUTS

Hitters

PLAYER	TEAM	LVL	AGE	PA	R	2B	3B	HR	RBI	BB	SO	SB-CS	EqBRR	AVG/OBP/SLG	EqAVG/EqOBP/EqSLG	EqA	VORP	WARP
DH V. Diaz	ROU	AAA	26	84	4	2	0	1	7	12	19	2-1	-0.1	.296/.398/.366	.247/.337/.301	.232	-2.0	-0.3
	TAC	AAA	26	473	65	38	0	24	100	49	149	7-2	0.6	.280/.362/.546	.245/.316/.465	.265	11.9	0.5
OF S. Garrett#	WTN	AA	29	97	16	8	2	1	14	7	21	1-0	1.3	.276/.333/.448	.165/.198/.275	.151	-12.1	-1.5
	TAC	AAA	29	418	50	24	1	10	62	26	75	5-4	0.0	.304/.349/.448	.239/.278/.350	.216	-15.6	-2.6
LF C. Jimerson	TAC	AAA	28	219	23	8	1	11	31	3	80	14-7	-1.0	.233/.250/.438	.189/.199/.344	.183	-19.0	-0.9
SS O. Navarro	TAC	AAA	23	395	47	21	1	1	31	31	71	2-3	0.2	.261/.326/.333	.231/.289/.295	.202	-20.8	-1.3
OF D. Raben*	EVE	A-	20	112	24	11	0	5	14	19	24	1-1	-2.5	.275/.411/.560	.210/.301/.400	.242	-2.7	-0.4
OF P. Redman	WTN	AA	28	165	24	8	0	6	25	24	23	2-3	0.8	.259/.377/.452	.143/.226/.238	.154	-20.5	-2.4
	TAC	AAA	28	365	73	22	2	19	51	37	45	7-6	-2.9	.310/.388/.571	.243/.312/.435	.254	4.3	-0.1
1B C. Wilson	TAC	AAA	31	207	30	11	0	12	40	23	51	0-0	-1.2	.287/.396/.557	.232/.327/.425	.261	2.7	0.1
	IND	AAA	31	251	27	6	0	10	27	21	60	3-2	-1.8	.230/.327/.396	.193/.277/.336	.214	-12.7	-1.6

Once a second base prospect, **Victor Diaz** is now a chunky minor league DH and a testament to the perils of bad conditioning. He's always been a good hitter, and after leading the Dominican winter league in homers, he will receive another shot somewhere. ⊘ **Shawn Garrett** has played for nine organizations during his 11 seasons in the minors, but hasn't yet lucked into so much as a shot glass of instant coffee, despite an occasionally capable bat. ⊘ Released by the Mariners, **Charlton Jimerson** failed to catch on elsewhere. The self-made product of a drug-tainted, single-parent household defeated far longer odds to reach Triple-A, but overcoming the poor plate judgment that resulted in Rolando Roomes' being his top PECOTA comp may be beyond even Jimerson's powers of determination. ⊘ **Oswaldo Navarro** reached the majors at age 21, a privilege normally reserved for real prospects. How he got confused with one of those is anyone's guess. ⊘ **Ronald Prettyman** is a third baseman without pop; he struggled in the Southern League at age 26. His baseball career may be nearing the end of its road, so making fun of his name would just be piling on. ⊘ The Mariners first signed **Dennis Raben** as a pitcher out of high school, but lost him to the University of Miami. Round two went to Seattle, however, as the second-rounder became the Mariners' highest draft pick to sign last season. The big lefty showed plenty of power in his Northwest League debut. ⊘ **Prentice Redman** played in 15 games for the Mets at the end of the 2003 season, which may turn out to be the extent of his big-league career. He raked in Tacoma last season, but might want to consider seeking instruction in another trade. ⊘ **Craig Wilson**'s bat awakened from its slumber when he arrived in Tacoma midway through last season, once more emitting a siren song audible only to general managers in search of a right-handed, defensively challenged first-base platoon partner to call their own.

Pitchers

PLAYER	TEAM	LVL	AGE	W	L	SV	IP	H	BB	SO	HR	GB%	BABIP	STUFF	WHIP	ERA	DERA	EqH9	EqBB9	EqSO9	EqHR9	DEF	VORP
T. Chick	WTN	AA	24	4	5	0	96²	92	44	80	7	39.7%	.314	-21	1.41	4.28	7.10	10.0	4.3	4.6	1.2	4	-15.0
	TAC	AAA	24	3	0	0	33	22	14	29	3	31.8%	.232	7	1.09	1.91	3.38	5.9	3.9	5.3	1.1	3	7.9
R. Dorman	WTN	AA	29	7	2	0	89¹	69	29	79	5	42.2%	.263	2	1.10	2.62	5.59	7.8	3.1	5.0	0.9	14	0.1
	TAC	AAA	29	2	4	0	37²	43	9	31	5	44.0%	.317	-11	1.38	4.77	5.73	10.3	2.2	4.8	1.4	-3	-0.5
L. Muñoz	ALT	AA	26	1	4	0	30²	41	16	14	4	49.1%	.359	-39	1.86	7.33	8.78	14.0	4.9	2.9	2.0	2	-9.8
	IND	AAA	26	3	3	0	69¹	78	26	42	13	32.5%	.295	-43	1.50	5.45	7.23	11.5	3.7	3.3	2.5	3	-12.0
	WTN	AA	26	1	2	0	29¹	38	15	22	2	48.7%	.374	-22	1.81	5.84	6.59	13.5	4.9	4.0	1.3	-4	-3.0
M. Piñeda	WIS	A	19	8	6	0	138¹	109	35	128	7	48.6%	.276	21	1.04	1.95	5.18	9.5	3.5	4.1	1.3	8	5.8
S. White	TAC	AAA	27	6	11	0	125	176	43	52	12	49.6%	.360	-28	1.75	5.47	6.77	13.2	3.3	2.2	1.1	-5	-15.2
J. Woerman	WTN	AA	25	1	3	0	29	27	12	20	0	47.7%	.286	-11	1.34	4.34	8.58	9.2	3.8	3.5	0.3	4	-9.4
	TAC	AAA	25	2	8	0	88	107	69	54	11	44.3%	.340	-27	2.00	7.47	9.04	11.5	7.1	3.4	1.4	-3	-32.0

Travis Chick once drew comparisons to Curt Schilling, but he'll be pitching for his fifth organization in 2009, after signing with the Dodgers as a free agent. Of course, Curt didn't really put it together till his age-25 season, so maybe this is Chick's year. ⊘ **Rich Dorman** has struggled at the Triple-A level in each of the past four seasons, which seems like a pretty strong indication that he's a Double-A pitcher. ⊘ **Luis Muñoz** made it to the majors with Pittsburgh last season, despite his ineffectiveness at Double-A, but didn't get into a game. Claimed off waivers, Muñoz bombed in the Mariners' organization and was dropped from the 40-man roster. A move to the bullpen couldn't hurt. ⊘ Dominican find **Michael Piñeda** was named the Mariners' minor league pitcher of the year after he employed a low-90s fastball, plus slider, and change to dominate the Midwest League. He worked out of the pen on occasion to limit his workload and capped off his season with a 14-strikeout one-hitter. ⊘ **Sean White**, a local kid from Mercer Island, has been plagued by injuries since he joined the Mariners as a Rule 5 pick in 2007. His groundball rate has fallen well off its peak, and as a result, White himself has fallen off the 40-man roster. ⊘ **Joe Woerman** bombed at Triple-A in his sixth professional season, solidifying his status as a fringe rotation prospect. He looked like something more than that as a reliever in 2006, so it may be that only delusions of grandeur are barring him from some form of success at the upper levels.

MANAGER: JOHN MCLAREN, JIM RIGGLEMAN

YEAR	MGR	W-L	Pythag +/−	Avg PC	100+ P	120+ P	QS	BQS	REL	REL w Zero R	IBB	Subs	PH	PH Avg	PH HR	SB2	CS2	SB3	CS3	SAC Att	SAC %	POS SAC	Squeeze	Swing	In Play
2007	J.M.	43-41	4	96.5	43	3	36	7	247	141	19	30	53	.260	2	35	12	5	3	20	80.0%	16	1	88	70
2008	J.M.	25-47	-2	95.6	36	0	31	7	197	114	12	10	31	.250	0	38	10	13	3	18	83.3%	15	1	68	57
2008	J.R.	36-54	-3	93.0	39	0	37	1	272	158	25	37	75	.235	0	32	15	6	2	37	56.8%	19	1	84	75

McLaren seemed to regard his team's failures as a personal affront, responding with puzzlement, anger, and many a closed-door meeting. After he lost his job on June 19, he regaled reporters with tales about the divisions between his former charges. Perhaps whatever issues had surfaced were truly insoluble products of excessive losing and the personalities involved, but McLaren demonstrated no more aptitude at addressing them than your typical replacement manager. Happily, the club had bench coach Jim Riggleman, an already-tested former skipper, on hand. Upon his ascension, Riggleman further tarnished McLaren's legacy by suggesting that his former boss had been seeing things, but the Riggs regime experienced its own share of relationship issues, perhaps the result of his heavy-handed approach to player relations. The team improved slightly under his guidance, and he took a more active in-game role, but he moved rather slowly—or not at all—to correct some of McLaren's more glaring mistakes. Vidro kept playing at DH for six interminable weeks on his watch, and Miguel Cairo kept getting starts at first base to the bitter end. Of course, Riggleman's ties to the old regime probably precluded him from retaining his post under any circumstances. **Don Wakamatsu**'s hiring to take up the reins was the product of an extended off-season managerial manhunt by new GM Jack Zduriencik, and the new skipper can lay claim to having worked for every team in the AL West in the 21st century, most notably as a bench coach in Texas and Oakland. As befits the hand-picked hire of the new GM, Wakamatsu is fully committed to implementing Zduriencik's long-term goals. As a former catcher, he plans to devote special attention to restoring Kenji Johjima's luster and could prove adept at evaluating and resolving the Mariners' glut of viable options at that position. If he can avoid the clubhouse turmoil and roster mismanagement overseen by his predecessors, his presence alone will impart some momentum to the fledgling rebuilding effort.

Tampa Bay Rays

The exorcism worked. After a decade in which they had won ballgames at a .399 clip, failed to top 70 wins in a single season, and escaped the AL East cellar just once, the Devil Rays announced in November 2007 that they were changing their identity by shortening their name to the Rays. While the 10,000-gallon "touch tank" of cartilaginous fish remained behind Tropicana Field's right-center field fence, majority owner Stuart Sternberg was clear about the luminous connotations of his team's new moniker, declaring the recast team "a beacon that radiates throughout Tampa Bay and across the entire state of Florida."

As hokey as that may have sounded at the time, the Rays *were* radiant in 2008, dazzling and shocking much of the baseball world by winning 97 games despite just a $44 million payroll. They captured the AL East flag, winning the game's premium division, and in the process ended the Yankees' 13-year streak of making the postseason. Furthermore, they bounced the White Sox from the Division Series and won the AL pennant by outlasting the defending World Champion Red Sox in a thrilling seven-game Championship Series before falling to the Phillies in a frigid World Series that was much closer than the 4-1 tally suggests. All told, their 31-win year-to-year increase tied for the fifth-largest turnaround since 1900, and the triumphs that followed made them the first team to improve by 30 games *and* win a post-season series. The run emphatically declared that the sour memories and humiliation of the Vince Naimoli/Chuck LaMar era were a thing of the past; the Devil got the hell out of Tampa Bay as though Charlie Daniels had kicked his ass.

This remarkable turnaround did not happen by accident, of course. Despite losing 197 games in his first two seasons on the job, Camus-quoting philosopher/manager Joe Maddon had already remade the clubhouse culture while demonstrating an aptitude for progressive thought from the dugout. General manager Andrew Friedman had already pulled off astute trades for players like Dioner Navarro, Edwin Jackson, J.P. Howell, and Grant Balfour, all of whom came into their own in 2008. He also picked up Carlos Peña, who bopped 46 home runs in 2007, straight off of the free-talent scrapheap.

More importantly, outstanding scouting, drafting, and player development laid the initial groundwork for the Rays' reinvention, giving credence to LaMar's much-ridiculed declaration at the outset of 2005, his final season as GM: "The only thing that keeps this organization from being recognized as one of the finest in baseball is wins and losses at the major league level.[9] While the Devil Rays' ineptitude at the major league level provided them with high draft picks year after year, such an opportunity hardly guaranteed automatic success in the draft, as the fate of the Pirates should remind. Upper-level LaMar-era picks Carl Crawford (second round, 1999) and B. J. Upton (first round, 2002) were key contributors to the team's 2008 success, as were lower-round picks James Shields (16th round, 2000) and Andy Sonnanstine (13th round, 2004). Meanwhile, Friedman used the first overall pick of the 2003 draft, Delmon Young, as the primary outbound player in the most important trade in franchise history. The deal of Young, Brendan Harris, and Jason Pridie for Matt Garza, Jason Bartlett, and Eduardo

---

RAYS PROSPECTUS

2008 record: 97-65; First place in AL East

Pythagenport record: 92-70

Runs scored per game: 4.78 (9th in AL)

Runs allowed per game: 4.14 (2nd in AL)

Team EqA: .265 (3rd in AL)

2008 Batters Age: 27.5 (2nd-youngest in AL)

2008 Pitchers Age: 26.9 (2nd-youngest in AL)

Ballpark: Tropicana Field; Slight pitcher's park; Park Factor of .973

2008: Perennial losers go from worst to first, but get caught in the rain just short of a Disney ending.

2009: "Rayhawks" were just the beginning. Despite their limited means, the Rays are in a position to be good for as long as they once were bad.

Morlan not only symbolized the franchise's evolution from a random assemblage of young talent with a few valuable assets to a functional team, it also provided the linchpin for one of the two historic turnarounds that the Rays pulled off in 2008.

Garza, the biggest name of the three ex-Twins, slotted nicely into the rotation (more on that momentarily), but it was shortstop Bartlett who anchored the most drastic defensive turnaround in more than a half-century. The 2007 Rays had set a record for modern-day futility with a .656 Defensive Efficiency, the lowest rate of converting batted balls into outs since at least 1954, the dawn of the Retrosheet era. With Bartlett effectively replacing Harris and Josh Wilson, the 2008 Rays led the major leagues with a .710 Defensive Efficiency, a 54-point year-to-year jump that outdistanced the rest of the historical field by six points (see Table 1).

Table 1: Defensive Turnarounds

Year	Team	DefEff	Prev	Diff
2008	Rays	.710	.656	.054
1980	Athletics	.728	.680	.048
1991	Braves	.714	.679	.035
1988	Brewers	.716	.683	.033
1971	Giants	.721	.689	.032
1978	White Sox	.714	.682	.032
2008	Marlins	.693	.661	.031
1955	Cubs	.735	.705	.030
1997	Tigers	.700	.671	.029
2001	Mariners	.727	.699	.028
1988	Reds	.726	.698	.028

This turnaround wasn't exactly unforeseen; in fact, the assumption of just such an about-face—well any expectation of simple regression to the mean—was the basis for an audacious 88-win PECOTA projection (later revised to 90) that put Baseball Prospectus on the spot; even last year's annual had hedged by admitting that the league and division made 2008 contention far-fetched for the Rays. "However, the .500 mark is a very achievable near-term goal..."

Bartlett's improvement over Harris and Wilson represented the Rays' largest swing in Fielding Runs Above Average (our new version, based on play-by-play) at any position, though other moves helped as well. The arrival of 2006 first-round pick Evan Longoria pushed incumbent Akinori Iwamura to second base, stopping the hemorrhaging at the keystone, while Upton's shift from second to center field (a transition begun in June 2007) began to pay off. In all, the defense improved at every position except pitcher, with six of the positions showing at least 10-run gains (see Table 2).

Table 2. Stopping the Bleeding

Pos	2008	2007	Diff	Principals (2007 to 2008)
P	-13	-9	-4	—
C	9	-7	+16	Navarro (-5 to +16)
1B	9	-7	+16	Peña (-5 to +5)
2B	-12	-27	+15	Motley Crew (-24 among the top four) to Iwamura (-12)
3B	9	2	+7	Iwamura (+6) to Longoria (+3)
SS	5	-33	+38	Harris (-15) to Bartlett (+10)
LF	17	-18	+35	Crawford (-8 to +14)
CF	7	-10	+17	Upton (+2 to +6)
RF	6	-3	+9	Young (+1) to Gross (+3)
Net	+37	-112	+149	

The upgraded defense as well as the addition of Garza combined to improve the starting rotation dramatically, as the BABIPs of every starter except Shields dropped precipitously, turning Sonnanstine and Edwin Jackson from punching bags to viable innings eaters (see Table 3).

Table 3: Rotation Situation

Pitcher	2007				2008				Improvement	
	GS	BABIP	ERA	SNLVAR	GS	BABIP	ERA	SNLVAR	BABIP	ERA
Shields	31	.284	3.85	5.8	33	.290	3.56	5.4	+.006	-0.29
Kazmir	34	.337	3.48	5.5	27	.267	3.49	4.8	-.070	+0.01
Jackson	31	.345	5.77	1.5	31	.303	4.37	4.2	-.042	-1.40
Sonnanstine	22	.328	5.85	1.3	32	.304	4.38	3.0	-.024	-1.47
Others	44	.356	7.33	-0.3	9	.284	4.82	0.5		
Garza	—	—	—	—	30	.271	3.70	4.9	-.082*	-3.40*
Total	162	.331	5.20	13.6	162	.289	3.95	22.9	-.042	-1.25

*2007 others, as compared to 2008 others plus Garza.

Garza's massive advantage over the 2007 rotation's dreck (Jason Hammel, J. P. Howell, Casey Fossum, and Jae Seo) bore additional fruit by not only subtracting these Fifth Horsemen of the Apocalypse, but via the moves of Hammel and especially Howell to the bullpen, the site of the team's second historic turnaround. The 2007 relief corps had finished in a virtual tie for the worst unit since 1954, as judged on the basis of their 6.80 Fair Run Average—their runs allowed per nine innings after adjusting for their performance in handling inherited runners. Roughly speaking, that's three runs allowed for every four innings, a long night of watching a bullpen fritter away a shaky starter's five-inning effort. All told, the 2007 relievers totaled -1.8 WXRL.

The 2008 unit trimmed their Fair Run Average to 4.17 while vaulting to a major league-best 15.4 WXRL; the 17.2-win turnaround ranked as the largest year-to-year bullpen upgrade in history. Howell led the way, with 4.7 WXRL (fifth in the AL) while putting up a 2.78 FRA.

Journeyman Grant Balfour, acquired from Milwaukee at the 2007 deadline for perennially disappointing Seth McClung, finished with 3.5 WXRL (10th in the AL), and a major league-low 0.96 FRA. Both pitchers struck out more than a hitter per inning, providing Maddon with dominant swing-and-miss set-up men from either side of the plate, and both proved adept at working multiple innings. Another 2007 deadline acquisition, Dan Wheeler, did good work as a set-up man but stumbled a bit while filling in at closer for Troy Percival, finishing with 2.3 WXRL (19th in the AL) and a 2.94 FRA. Chad Bradford added his worm-killing submarine style to the bunch with a 2.65 FRA upon being acquired during the post-deadline waiver period. Percival, who came out of retirement in mid-2007 and signed a two-year deal last winter, did excellent work through the season's first two months (2.95 ERA, 6.7 baserunners per nine) before hamstring, knee, and back problems sidelined him three times, diminished his effectiveness, and kept him off of the post-season roster. His absence offered a blockbuster opportunity for Maddon to demonstrate the fluidity of the team's late-game bullpen situation (mantra: get hitters out when called upon) while auditioning the game's top pitching prospect, David Price, in a few high-leverage situations.

At the outset of the year, Nate Silver noted that the 2007 club had five players with legitimate arguments for All-Star honors (Crawford, Upton, Peña, Kazmir, and Shields), but also 28 players who produced negative VORPs, collectively costing the Rays 157.9 runs below replacement level. With so much dead weight shed by the upgrades to the pitching and defense, the offense didn't require nearly as much work. In fact, their 2008 performance was within 0.05 runs per game and one point of EqA. Despite the team's success, the offense labored under a popular misconception that they were not a good-hitting team, thanks to a raw scoring level (4.8 R/G) which ranked just ninth in the AL, and a batting average that was second to last. Lost behind those numbers was the fact that they were fourth in on-base percentage, eighth in slugging percentage, and first in stolen bases. Also lost was that Tropicana Field ranked as the league's fourth-toughest park for hitters, behind Seattle, Oakland, and Minnesota's venues, depressing scoring by about three percent. The Rays' .265 EqA actually ranked third in the league behind only Texas and Boston, just a point below their 2007 mark.

Which isn't to say the offense was the same unit as the year before. Longoria hit .272/.343/.531 with 27 homers despite spending the first two weeks of the season in the minors and missing five weeks with a broken wrist; he was the unanimous selection for AL Rookie of the Year. Upton, despite dealing with a power-sapping shoulder injury that dropped his seasonal home-run total from 24 to nine, hit .273/.383/.401 and stole 44 bases; his seven post-season home runs allayed any concerns about the effects of the shoulder on his future. Despite dipping to 31 homers, Peña still led the team with a .306 EqA on the strength of a .247/.377/.494 performance. Navarro rebounded from a dreadful .227/.286/.356 showing in 2007 with a .295/.349/.407 line. Free agents Eric Hinske (20 homers, .281 EqA) and Cliff Floyd (11 homers, .286 EqA) both thrived in part-time roles, as did holdover Ben Zobrist (12 homers, .294 EqA) and winter trade acquisition Willy Aybar (10 homers, .262 EqA), who came back from a year missed due to personal problems; he filled in admirably for Longoria. Among the regulars, only Crawford disappointed, hitting .273/.319/.400 and missing seven weeks due to a hamstring strain.

The most exciting thing about the 2008 Rays is that they're just getting started. Longoria, Upton, Navarro, Crawford, the entire rotation (with Price replacing Jackson), and Howell are 27 years old or younger, as is Matt Joyce, the new right fielder acquired for Jackson. With their first pennant under their belts, the players are strapping in for the long haul as well. Longoria signed a six-year, $17.5 million deal with $30 million worth of club options for 2014-2016. Shields signed a four-year, $11.25 million deal with $28 million worth of club options for 2012-2014. Kazmir signed a three-year, $28.5 million extension which runs through 2011 and includes a club option. Peña is signed through 2010. Upton, Garza, and Sonnanstine have yet to reach arbitration eligibility, and Navarro's just getting there. This nucleus will stick around for awhile, allowing the club to control costs while pressuring the Yankees and Red Sox to keep pace via much more expensive free-agent signings. If the big-league talent isn't enough, the team can boast five players on our Top 100 Prospects list, starting with Price (#2), and including 2008 overall first pick Tim Beckham (#15), 2004 picks Wade Davis (#29) and Reid Brignac (#62), and 2006 pick Desmond Jennings (#40). Davis may find his way into the big club's bullpen at some point during the season, if not the rotation, as could Jeff Niemann, a power arm who ranked 25th on our 2007 list.

Furthermore, Friedman hasn't abdicated smart decision-making in the free-agent market. Not only did the Rays fill their right-field vacancy with Joyce, an excellent defender who hit .252/.339/.492 as a rookie last year, they also waited out the glut of outfield/DH types and snagged a deeply discounted Pat Burrell for two years and $16 million. They spent $1 million to sign fourth outfielder Gabe Kapler, who hit .301/.340/.498 for the Brewers last year, and $1.3 million to sign reliever Joe Nelson, a 33-year-old survivor of three labrum surgeries who put up a 2.00 ERA in a career-high 54 innings for the Marlins last year, striking out more than a hitter per frame. Burrell and Kapler are both righties, thus addressing the team's most glaring weakness: they went just 25-24 (.510) in games started against southpaws, compared to 72-41 (.637) against righties. Their .246/.330/.396 against lefties ranked 12th in the league in OPS and no better than 11th in any of the triple-slash categories.

All told, the 2008 Rays may have been the game's best story, better even than that of the World Champion Phillies. The work of Sternberg, team president Matthew Silverman, Friedman, and Maddon cast the Rays as one of the game's best-run teams, a braintrust that has drawn up a blueprint for attainable success while the rest of the baseball world viewed them as laughingstocks. Given the baggage attached to *Moneyball* and Oakland's more recent struggles, it is perhaps dangerous to invoke the Billy Beane-run A's of the early millennium, but the Rays appear to be the game's new textbook example of how to turn the fortunes of an organization around via smart, cutting-edge management. We can hardly wait to read the next chapter.

HITTERS

Willy Aybar — INF

Bats: S   Throws: R   Height: 5' 11"   Weight: 200   Born: March 9, 1983   Age: 26

YEAR	TEAM	LVL	AGE	PA	R	2B	3B	HR	RBI	BB	SO	SB	CS	EqBRR	AVG	OBP	SLG	EqAVG	EqOBP	EqSLG	EqA	VORP	WARP	DEFENSE	
2006	ATL	MLB	23	127	17	6	0	1	8	10	19	0	2	-2.7	.313	.373	.391	.313	.373	.374	.260	2.4	0.1	27-3B	-2
2006	LVG	AAA	23	222	30	12	1	10	41	22	24	1	3	-2.6	.315	.383	.538	.255	.323	.450	.262	5.6	1.0	25-3B 2	20-2B 0
2006	LAN	MLB	23	151	15	12	0	3	22	18	17	1	0	-1.1	.250	.356	.414	.248	.353	.411	.269	3.3	0.4	24-3B -3	11-2B 2
2008	TBA	MLB	25	362	33	17	2	10	33	32	44	2	2	-5.5	.253	.327	.410	.255	.331	.429	.260	5.3	1.7	40-3B 6	17-1B 2
2009	TBA	MLB	26	421	47	22	1	10	49	40	57	2	2	-1.2	.260	.335	.409	.264	.340	.430	.267	9.4	1.7	100-3B 0	

Breakout: 31%   Improve: 58%   Collapse: 21%   Attrition: 25%   Comparables: Luis Rodriguez, Scott Spiezio, Jose Vidro, Jeff Cirillo

Little was made of the deal that netted Aybar from the Braves for a pair of minor leaguers, but he turned out to be a key acquisition. Obviously, he's not a franchise cornerstone, and his is just a bench-level bat, but one of the most underrated properties in the game is the guy who can fill in at multiple positions when someone needs a rest without turning that lineup slot into a black hole. He'll have the same job next year, often against tough left-handers, filling in at any infield position without costing the team much in production.

Rocco Baldelli — OF

Bats: R   Throws: R   Height: 6' 4"   Weight: 200   Born: September 25, 1981   Age: 27

YEAR	TEAM	LVL	AGE	PA	R	2B	3B	HR	RBI	BB	SO	SB	CS	EqBRR	AVG	OBP	SLG	EqAVG	EqOBP	EqSLG	EqA	VORP	WARP	DEFENSE
2006	TBA	MLB	24	387	59	24	6	16	57	14	70	10	1	1.9	.302	.339	.533	.295	.332	.529	.289	32.6	3.1	86-CF 4
2007	TBA	MLB	25	150	16	6	0	5	12	9	35	4	1	0.8	.204	.268	.358	.204	.273	.365	.225	-4.5	-0.5	18-CF -2
2008	TBA	MLB	26	90	12	5	0	4	13	7	25	0	0	-1.0	.263	.344	.475	.262	.352	.500	.287	3.9	0.4	
2009	BOS	MLB	27	262	32	15	1	8	35	17	61	4	1	0.4	.263	.320	.443	.255	.315	.447	.262	5.6	0.9	65-DH

Breakout: 35%   Improve: 52%   Collapse: 25%   Attrition: 26%   Comparables: Leon Roberts, Sam Bowens, Glenallen Hill, Ivan Murrell

Once an up-and-coming superstar, Baldelli's career was derailed by injuries and an eventual diagnosis of a mitochondrial disorder that causes what is called "exercise intolerance," during which any physical exertion causes pain and/or extreme fatigue. That left Baldelli as a rarely used extra player in 2008, but doctors feel they've made some progress during the offseason, believing he can play more in 2009 with a different medical regimen. It was enough to convince the Red Sox to give him a shot at a bench outfield job, where he'll return to his hometown team (he's from Rhode Island) as a feel-good story to root for.

Jason Bartlett — SS

Bats: R   Throws: R   Height: 6' 0"   Weight: 185   Born: October 30, 1979   Age: 29

YEAR	TEAM	LVL	AGE	PA	R	2B	3B	HR	RBI	BB	SO	SB	CS	EqBRR	AVG	OBP	SLG	EqAVG	EqOBP	EqSLG	EqA	VORP	WARP	DEFENSE	
2006	ROC	AAA	26	250	42	23	3	1	20	10	28	6	3	-0.4	.306	.336	.443	.257	.284	.388	.232	-4.2	1.3	57-SS	8
2006	MIN	MLB	26	372	44	18	2	2	32	22	46	10	5	0.6	.306	.364	.390	.298	.358	.383	.264	16.3	4.6	99-SS	24
2007	MIN	MLB	27	570	75	20	7	5	43	50	73	23	3	6.3	.265	.339	.361	.264	.340	.366	.257	15.3	4.7	135-SS	21
2008	TBA	MLB	28	494	48	25	3	1	37	22	69	20	6	0.7	.286	.329	.361	.294	.337	.373	.254	13.6	3.0	122-SS	10
2009	TBA	MLB	29	480	54	21	3	4	35	29	65	16	5	1.7	.257	.310	.345	.261	.314	.363	.243	4.6	1.9	113-SS	9

Breakout: 6%   Improve: 29%   Collapse: 40%   Attrition: 23%   Comparables: Carlos Garcia, Alex Grammas, Eddie Kasko, Melvin Mora

We're not sure how it started, but certain segments of the media began pointing at Bartlett as the most valuable player on the team and the key reason for its turnaround. Maybe it was his modest level of experience, or that he was the one who played the biggest role on a much-improved defense (we can give him that), or perhaps he's just one of those grinders whose effort is visible. In reality, he's no more than a .280 hitter who doesn't walk, has no power, and is lucky he can handle a glove. They used to make fun of Royce Clayton for that combination of skills, and now they get in line to kiss the shoes of Bartlett? Explain that to us.

Tim Beckham — SS

Bats: R   Throws: R   Height: 6' 0"   Weight: 188   Born: January 27, 1990   Age: 19

YEAR	TEAM	LVL	AGE	PA	R	2B	3B	HR	RBI	BB	SO	SB	CS	EqBRR	AVG	OBP	SLG	EqAVG	EqOBP	EqSLG	EqA	VORP	WARP	DEFENSE	
2008	PRI	Rk	18	197	30	12	0	2	14	13	43	5	1	-0.3	.243	.297	.345	.170	.215	.242	.151	-54.7	-2.7	36-SS	-2
2009	TBA	MLB	19	546	44	23	3	5	37	32	147	11	5	1.7	.201	.252	.286	.204	.256	.300	.192	-24.0	-1.4	128-SS	-7

Breakout: 84%   Improve: 90%   Collapse: 7%   Attrition: 4%   Comparables: Mark Lewis, Jeff Blauser, Eddie Williams, Chris Nelson

There was no obvious slam-dunk first overall pick in the 2008 draft, and the Rays finally settled on Beckham and his tools as the best package available. An ultra-athletic shortstop with power, speed, and good instincts, he struggled during his pro debut, but scouts still brought up the Barry Larkin comparisons. His full-season debut with Low-A Bowling Green in the South Atlantic League will be one to watch if you're not distracted by Bowling Green of Ohio being in the South Atlantic League.

Reid Brignac — SS

Bats: L   Throws: R   Height: 6' 3"   Weight: 180   Born: January 16, 1986   Age: 23

YEAR	TEAM	LVL	AGE	PA	R	2B	3B	HR	RBI	BB	SO	SB	CS	EqBRR	AVG	OBP	SLG	EqAVG	EqOBP	EqSLG	EqA	VORP	WARP	DEFENSE		
2006	VIS	A+	20	455	82	26	3	21	83	35	82	12	6	0.7	.326	.382	.557	.246	.294	.429	.246	0.8	2.0	97-SS	5	
2006	MNT	AA	20	121	18	6	2	3	16	7	31	3	0	-0.7	.300	.355	.473	.277	.322	.473	.273	5.0	0.5	28-SS	-3	
2007	MNT	AA	21	596	91	30	5	17	81	55	94	15	5	0.0	.260	.328	.433	.226	.284	.382	.234	-14.9	1.2	126-SS	2	
2008	DUR	AAA	22	386	43	26	2	9	43	25	93	5	2	0.4	.250	.299	.412	.223	.270	.384	.226	-12.3	1.3	89-SS	9	4-2B 0
2008	TBA	MLB	22	11	1	0	0	0	0	1	5	0	0	0.0	.000	.091	.000	.000	.091	.000	.000	-2.4	-0.2			
2009	TBA	MLB	23	460	46	24	2	11	49	33	101	7	3	1.0	.233	.290	.385	.236	.294	.405	.242	3.4	1.5	109-SS	4	

Breakout: 38%   Improve: 57%   Collapse: 19%   Attrition: 10%   Comparables: Scott Cooper, Tony Manahan, Terry Shumpert, Myron White

Brignac was the California League MVP in 2006 because of his bat, but there were questions about his ability to stay at shortstop. Two years later, his bat has cooled off dramatically, but scouts now rave about his defense; his instincts and quickness give him plus range to both sides, and his arm is outstanding. He's also had above-average power for the position, but not enough hitting or on-base skills for that power to be of value. Because of the pretty wide back and forth, Brignac represents a pretty strange prospect at this point, and he'll have to do something astonishing for the Rays to push Barlett aside.

Carl Crawford — LF

Bats: L   Throws: L   Height: 6' 2"   Weight: 215   Born: August 5, 1981   Age: 27

YEAR	TEAM	LVL	AGE	PA	R	2B	3B	HR	RBI	BB	SO	SB	CS	EqBRR	AVG	OBP	SLG	EqAVG	EqOBP	EqSLG	EqA	VORP	WARP	DEFENSE	
2006	TBA	MLB	24	652	89	20	16	18	77	37	85	58	9	6.7	.305	.348	.482	.297	.345	.478	.287	40.5	4.2	144-LF	4
2007	TBA	MLB	25	624	93	37	9	11	80	32	112	50	10	6.7	.315	.355	.466	.317	.358	.484	.291	38.5	2.9	134-LF	-8
2008	TBA	MLB	26	480	69	12	10	8	57	30	60	25	7	4.2	.273	.319	.400	.277	.325	.417	.261	7.9	2.6	102-LF	14
2009	TBA	MLB	27	569	76	22	9	10	54	35	82	30	6	4.0	.276	.322	.409	.280	.327	.430	.268	6.6	2.2	133-LF	3

Breakout: 11%   Improve: 27%   Collapse: 28%   Attrition: 5%   Comparables: Deion Sanders, Darin Erstad, Terry Puhl, Johnny Damon

Formerly one of the most consistent performers in the game, Crawford's sudden downturn was one of the few low points in the Rays' season. He was suspended for his part in a fight with the Red Sox, suffered a hamstring strain, and had surgery to repair a tendon in his hand. Observers have been expecting a breakout performance from Crawford for years, but they may have to accept the fact that it may never come. Crawford is good, not great, and he needs to hit .300 to make up for his hacking style and average power. He can beat you in a number of ways, but it can cost a lot of outs to reap the benefits, an equation that the Rays might not always want to afford in the years to come.

Cliff Floyd   **DH**   Bats: L   Throws: R   Height: 6' 4"   Weight: 230   Born: December 5, 1972   Age: 36

YEAR	TEAM	LVL	AGE	PA	R	2B	3B	HR	RBI	BB	SO	SB	CS	EqBRR	AVG	OBP	SLG	EqAVG	EqOBP	EqSLG	EqA	VORP	WARP	DEFENSE	
2006	NYN	MLB	33	376	45	19	1	11	44	29	58	6	0	0.9	.244	.324	.407	.246	.323	.411	.259	1.7	0.7	85-LF	0
2007	CHN	MLB	34	322	40	10	1	9	45	35	47	0	0	-2.1	.284	.373	.422	.271	.364	.418	.274	9.2	1.3	46-RF	2 15-LF 0
2008	TBA	MLB	35	284	32	13	0	11	39	28	58	1	0	-1.3	.268	.349	.455	.269	.352	.465	.283	13.0	1.1		
2009	TBA	MLB	36	267	33	12	1	8	34	26	49	2	1	-1.2	.264	.341	.420	.268	.346	.442	.274	8.0	1.1	66-DH	

Breakout: 21%   Improve: 46%   Collapse: 32%   Attrition: 38%   Comparables: Harold Baines, Mike Easler, Chris Chambliss, Tino Martinez

Floyd was signed both as a designated hitter who would give the Rays a threat against righties, but also to be a solid veteran citizen in a pretty young clubhousr. As happens every year, he was moderately productive when he wasn't broken. He tore a labrum in his shoulder at the end of the season, threatening to hang them up if he needed another surgery. He's made nothing official yet, and he does have a bit of Eric Davis in him; a glance at his career line leaves one wondering what might have been had he not run into such a big hive full of injury bugs.

Jonny Gomes   **DH**   Bats: R   Throws: R   Height: 6' 1"   Weight: 225   Born: November 22, 1980   Age: 28

YEAR	TEAM	LVL	AGE	PA	R	2B	3B	HR	RBI	BB	SO	SB	CS	EqBRR	AVG	OBP	SLG	EqAVG	EqOBP	EqSLG	EqA	VORP	WARP	DEFENSE	
2006	TBA	MLB	25	461	53	21	1	20	59	61	116	1	5	-4.3	.216	.325	.431	.208	.326	.426	.258	-0.8	0.4	7-RF	0
2007	TBA	MLB	26	394	48	20	2	17	49	35	126	12	4	1.1	.244	.322	.460	.245	.325	.481	.274	7.8	0.2	29-RF	-2 21-LF -8
2008	DUR	AAA	27	123	19	11	0	2	14	12	32	0	1	-0.3	.252	.341	.411	.211	.293	.367	.228	-3.4	-0.2	12-LF	1
2008	TBA	MLB	27	177	23	5	1	8	21	15	46	8	1	0.5	.182	.282	.383	.182	.282	.396	.244	-2.2	0.0	14-RF	1 4-LF 0
2009	TBA	MLB	28	174	21	8	1	7	22	18	49	6	1	-0.2	.217	.309	.419	.220	.313	.441	.264	1.5	0.3	45-DH	

Breakout: 27%   Improve: 56%   Collapse: 25%   Attrition: 37%   Comparables: Kevin Maas, Marcus Thames, Bob Robertson, Bob Hamelin

He destroyed lefties early in his career, but never got the hang of hitting right-handers, and for the most part he's been a strange combination of a strikeout-prone slugger with a touch of speed and poor defensive skills who gets more at-bats than he deserves. Last year he finally stopped hitting everyone, being reduced to an occasional source of power off the bench forced to bounce up and down from the minors when there was simply no room for him on the roster. Non-tendered following the season, he'll get a shot from someone hoping he can muster some platoon value.

Gabe Gross   **OF**   Bats: L   Throws: R   Height: 6' 3"   Weight: 210   Born: October 21, 1979   Age: 29

YEAR	TEAM	LVL	AGE	PA	R	2B	3B	HR	RBI	BB	SO	SB	CS	EqBRR	AVG	OBP	SLG	EqAVG	EqOBP	EqSLG	EqA	VORP	WARP	DEFENSE	
2006	MIL	MLB	26	252	42	15	0	9	38	36	60	1	0	2.4	.274	.382	.476	.269	.382	.466	.295	15.5	1.5	29-CF	-2 14-LF 2
2007	NAS	AAA	27	90	13	3	2	4	10	14	14	2	0	0.0	.355	.456	.605	.295	.389	.513	.308	8.4	0.9	9-RF	1 6-LF 1
2007	MIL	MLB	27	210	28	12	2	7	24	25	37	3	1	1.6	.235	.329	.437	.231	.332	.445	.266	3.2	1.0	32-RF	5
2008	MIL	MLB	28	54	6	3	0	0	2	10	7	2	0	1.0	.209	.352	.279	.209	.352	.279	.250	-0.2	0.2	11-CF	1
2008	TBA	MLB	28	345	40	13	3	13	38	40	75	2	2	-1.0	.242	.333	.434	.243	.341	.453	.271	4.6	1.4	85-RF	3
2009	TBA	MLB	29	335	45	15	2	12	43	41	69	3	1	0.3	.256	.351	.448	.260	.356	.471	.285	10.7	1.8	81-RF	1

Breakout: 28%   Improve: 56%   Collapse: 19%   Attrition: 21%   Comparables: Len Gabrielson, John Vander Wal, Luke Scott, Mark Johnson

Last year, with Gomes struggling and Rocco Baldelli unavailable, the Rays acquired Gross from the crowded outfield situation in Milwaukee. As a corner guy who only hits righties (and those just adequately), he was basically the same kind of commodity as Eric Hinske, swapping defense for power and leaving you wondering what you really got in the exchange. Gross was never really equipped to be an everyday player, and he'll be a fourth outfielder this year, which is as it should be.

Eric Hinske   4C   Bats: L   Throws: R   Height: 6' 2"   Weight: 235   Born: August 5, 1977   Age: 31

YEAR	TEAM	LVL	AGE	PA	R	2B	3B	HR	RBI	BB	SO	SB	CS	EqBRR	AVG	OBP	SLG	EqAVG	EqOBP	EqSLG	EqA	VORP	WARP	DEFENSE		
2006	TOR	MLB	28	224	35	9	2	12	29	27	49	1	1	-1.2	.264	.353	.513	.246	.344	.492	.281	10.6	1.3	24-RF	2	7-3B 1
2006	BOS	MLB	28	88	8	8	0	1	5	8	30	1	1	1.3	.288	.352	.425	.278	.352	.392	.260	1.8	0.1	10-1B	-1	7-RF 1
2007	BOS	MLB	29	218	25	12	3	6	21	28	54	3	0	-0.1	.204	.317	.398	.189	.311	.389	.248	-2.4	0.5	31-1B	0	11-LF 5
2008	TBA	MLB	30	432	59	21	1	20	60	47	88	10	3	0.6	.247	.333	.465	.249	.340	.481	.279	14.1	1.8	38-RF	0	30-LF -1
2009	TBA	MLB	31	297	37	14	1	11	40	32	70	7	2	-0.5	.245	.332	.435	.249	.336	.458	.275	6.7	1.1	72-RF	-2	

Breakout: 21%   Improve: 49%   Collapse: 24%   Attrition: 30%   Comparables: Leon Durham, Dan Pasqua, Franklin Stubbs, Daryl Boston

With Hinske and Gross both impersonating the same guy—though with more athleticism from Gross and more power from Hinske—Maddon rode the hot hand and initially chose Gross for his playoff roster before deigning to bring Hinske aboard for the World Series as a replacement for Floyd. Hinske's 2008 season was perceived as a comeback campaign, with his good fortune to be playing for a winner garnering a bit more attention than it really merited. In the broad strokes, his season was just more of the same that we've seen from him since his distant and promising rookie season, and perhaps understandably that's why he roams the winter roads looking for work as we go to press.

Akinori Iwamura   2B   Bats: L   Throws: R   Height: 5' 9"   Weight: 175   Born: February 9, 1979   Age: 30

YEAR	TEAM	LVL	AGE	PA	R	2B	3B	HR	RBI	BB	SO	SB	CS	EqBRR	AVG	OBP	SLG	EqAVG	EqOBP	EqSLG	EqA	VORP	WARP	DEFENSE	
2006	YKL	JP	27	621	84	27	2	32	77	70	128	8	1	—	.311	.389	.544	.275	.351	.437	.273	24.3	1.8		
2007	TBA	MLB	28	559	82	21	10	7	34	58	114	12	8	1.5	.285	.359	.411	.287	.365	.426	.274	15.0	3.1	118-3B	6
2008	TBA	MLB	29	707	91	30	9	6	48	70	131	8	6	-1.3	.274	.349	.380	.278	.357	.393	.263	16.8	1.3	149-2B	-12
2009	TBA	MLB	30	598	73	26	5	9	51	59	114	8	4	1.4	.259	.336	.381	.263	.340	.400	.261	12.1	1.6	140-2B	-6

Breakout: 9%   Improve: 27%   Collapse: 33%   Attrition: 18%   Comparables: Mickey Morandini, Johnny Pesky, Todd Walker, Snuffy Stirnweiss

In 2007, Iwamura was a third baseman who hit like a second baseman. Noticing the resemblance, the Rays adroitly fixed that case of cognitive dissonance by moving him to second base. A fantastic defender, he had no problem transitioning to the middle of the infield, and he was the same hitter as last year, though slightly miscast as a leadoff man. With neither power nor speed and only a decent walk rate, Iwamura fits better toward the bottom of a lineup, but when things aren't badly broken, you don't really need to fix them.

John Jaso   C   Bats: L   Throws: R   Height: 6' 2"   Weight: 205   Born: September 19, 1983   Age: 25

YEAR	TEAM	LVL	AGE	PA	R	2B	3B	HR	RBI	BB	SO	SB	CS	EqBRR	AVG	OBP	SLG	EqAVG	EqOBP	EqSLG	EqA	VORP	WARP	DEFENSE	
2006	VIS	A+	22	406	58	22	0	10	55	31	48	1	2	-1.5	.309	.362	.451	.239	.283	.356	.222	-13.0	-1.6	21-C	-4
2007	MNT	AA	23	450	62	24	2	12	71	59	49	2	2	0.0	.316	.408	.484	.275	.356	.438	.276	18.9	2.6	68-C	0
2008	MNT	AA	24	356	51	13	2	7	43	62	33	1	0	-1.9	.271	.408	.405	.219	.329	.334	.241	-7.2	-0.7	69-C	-12
2008	DUR	AAA	24	118	14	7	0	5	24	10	14	1	1	-0.3	.278	.339	.481	.241	.305	.426	.249	0.6	0.0	25-C	-3
2008	TBA	MLB	24	10	2	0	0	0	0	0	2	0	0	-0.0	.200	.200	.200	.200	.200	.200	.079	-1.1	-0.1		
2009	TBA	MLB	25	466	46	20	1	9	48	45	70	2	1	-0.7	.234	.311	.353	.237	.315	.371	.242	-0.2	0.8	110-C	-13

Breakout: 20%   Improve: 42%   Collapse: 32%   Attrition: 16%   Comparables: Andy Abad, Mark Sweeney, Rusty Greer, Jamie Dismuke

One of the better offensive catching prospects around, Jaso is a solid hitter with a very patient approach and average power. The trouble is, he's not a very good catcher, especially when it comes to deterring the running game; he threw out only 25 percent of opposing basestealers last year, and that was with everyone and their mothers running on him. If you're not willing to start him and just live with that, he has little value as a backup, where glove over bat is the general philosophy. It's hard to see him finding any traction in Tampa; he's five months *older* than Dioner Navarro, but he could be a decent trade chip.

Dan Johnson — 1B

Bats: L Throws: R Height: 6' 2" Weight: 225 Born: August 10, 1979 Age: 29

YEAR	TEAM	LVL	AGE	PA	R	2B	3B	HR	RBI	BB	SO	SB	CS	EqBRR	AVG	OBP	SLG	EqAVG	EqOBP	EqSLG	EqA	VORP	WARP	DEFENSE	
2006	SAC	AAA	26	209	34	13	1	7	44	32	27	0	1	-1.4	.314	.426	.523	.277	.378	.475	.293	13.5	1.4	38-1B	2
2006	OAK	MLB	26	331	30	13	1	9	37	40	45	0	0	-1.4	.234	.323	.381	.223	.323	.369	.247	-4.7	0.3	80-1B	4
2007	OAK	MLB	27	495	53	20	1	18	62	72	77	0	0	-0.3	.236	.349	.418	.233	.354	.432	.275	10.0	1.0	96-1B	-4
2008	DUR	AAA	28	486	85	23	0	25	83	84	75	0	1	-1.2	.307	.424	.556	.243	.360	.449	.282	19.9	2.3	26-1B 2 10-3B	1
2008	TBA	MLB	28	28	3	0	0	2	4	3	7	0	0	-0.0	.200	.286	.440	.200	.286	.440	.246	-0.3	0.1	5-1B	1
2009	*TBA*	*MLB*	*29*	*476*	*54*	*20*	*1*	*14*	*58*	*62*	*86*	*0*	*0*	*-1.6*	*.241*	*.343*	*.403*	*.246*	*.350*	*.429*	*.273*	*7.3*	*1.4*	*113-1B*	*-2*

Breakout: 13% Improve: 43% Collapse: 24% Attrition: 16%   *Comparables: Mark Johnson, Paul O'Neill, Dave Hollins, Mark Leonard*

The A's were overflowing with power-hitting first base/DH types, so the Rays were able to pick Johnson up off of waivers to fill an organizational hole at Triple-A. He was Durham's player of the year, but the Rays had no use for his skill set until late-season roster expansion. Then, on September 9, in his first big-league at-bat with his new team, he took Jonathan Papelbon deep to help pull a win from the jaws of defeat in the ninth inning of a game that was the biggest win in franchise history at the time. It was one of those, "We'll always have Paris" moments; Johnson decided to go for the payday, signing a seven-figure deal to play in Japan this year.

Evan Longoria — 3B

Bats: R Throws: R Height: 6' 2" Weight: 180 Born: October 7, 1985 Age: 23

YEAR	TEAM	LVL	AGE	PA	R	2B	3B	HR	RBI	BB	SO	SB	CS	EqBRR	AVG	OBP	SLG	EqAVG	EqOBP	EqSLG	EqA	VORP	WARP	DEFENSE	
2006	VIS	A+	20	128	22	8	0	8	28	13	19	1	1	-0.5	.327	.402	.618	.252	.312	.487	.267	4.1	0.5	22-3B	0
2006	HUD	A-	20	39	5	1	1	4	11	5	5	1	0	-0.1	.424	.487	.879	.353	.410	.735	.360	15.8	0.7	6-3B	-1
2006	MNT	AA	20	109	14	5	0	6	19	1	20	2	1	0.1	.267	.266	.486	.248	.248	.457	.236	-1.1	0.5	25-3B	4
2007	MNT	AA	21	447	78	21	0	21	76	51	81	4	0	0.0	.307	.403	.528	.269	.350	.472	.282	22.3	2.7	96-3B	1
2007	DUR	AAA	21	128	19	8	0	5	19	22	29	0	0	0.0	.269	.398	.490	.236	.364	.443	.280	5.1	0.5	27-3B	-1
2008	TBA	MLB	22	508	67	31	2	27	85	46	122	7	0	0.4	.272	.343	.531	.274	.347	.553	.300	35.7	4.3	116-3B	3
2009	*TBA*	*MLB*	*23*	*604*	*80*	*31*	*2*	*27*	*88*	*58*	*133*	*7*	*2*	*0.5*	*.266*	*.342*	*.482*	*.270*	*.346*	*.507*	*.289*	*28.4*	*4.2*	*141-3B*	*4*

Breakout: 20% Improve: 59% Collapse: 14% Attrition: 8%   *Comparables: Ron Hansen, Eric Chavez, Jeff Burroughs, Ryan Zimmerman*

The Rays briefly kept Longoria down on the farm to start the season in order to manage his service time, but once he was up, he was as good as everyone thought he would be, hitting for average and power with hints of definite MVP possibilities down the road. The big surprise was his defense. He had received merely average reviews during his brief minor league career, but he was suddenly very good at the hot corner, making the highlight reels with his glove as often as with the bat. He's the total package, and the Rays wisely bought out his free-agent years, ensuring that he'll be with Tampa Bay through 2016.

Dioner Navarro — C

Bats: S Throws: R Height: 5' 9" Weight: 205 Born: February 9, 1984 Age: 25

YEAR	TEAM	LVL	AGE	PA	R	2B	3B	HR	RBI	BB	SO	SB	CS	EqBRR	AVG	OBP	SLG	EqAVG	EqOBP	EqSLG	EqA	VORP	WARP	DEFENSE	
2006	LAN	MLB	22	86	5	2	0	2	8	11	18	1	0	0.1	.280	.372	.387	.267	.360	.373	.264	2.8	-0.1	22-C	-5
2006	TBA	MLB	22	216	23	7	0	4	20	20	33	1	1	-1.3	.244	.316	.342	.236	.316	.340	.233	-2.7	0.5	53-C	1
2007	TBA	MLB	23	434	46	19	2	9	44	33	67	3	1	-0.3	.227	.286	.356	.225	.288	.368	.231	-3.8	0.0	108-C	-5
2008	TBA	MLB	24	470	43	27	0	7	54	34	49	0	4	-8.0	.295	.349	.407	.299	.355	.421	.267	18.4	4.3	112-C	16
2009	*TBA*	*MLB*	*25*	*381*	*38*	*18*	*1*	*7*	*43*	*32*	*52*	*2*	*1*	*-1.5*	*.259*	*.326*	*.382*	*.263*	*.330*	*.402*	*.256*	*8.4*	*2.4*	*91-C*	*3*

Breakout: 25% Improve: 53% Collapse: 18% Attrition: 26%   *Comparables: Buck Rodgers, Ramon Hernandez, Raul Casanova, Ellie Rodriguez*

Once seen as one of the better catching prospects in the game, Navarro had been written off after not getting it done for three years and moving to his third organization. With little to lose, the Rays gave him yet another opportunity, and he finally began to live up to expectations. It seems like he's been around forever, but he's only 25 years old. He has a great contact rate, but he also has a longer track record of struggles than of success. His defensive skills will give him value no matter what direction his bat takes this year.

Carlos Peña   1B

Bats: L   Throws: L   Height: 6' 2"   Weight: 215   Born: May 17, 1978   Age: 31

YEAR	TEAM	LVL	AGE	PA	R	2B	3B	HR	RBI	BB	SO	SB	CS	EqBRR	AVG	OBP	SLG	EqAVG	EqOBP	EqSLG	EqA	VORP	WARP	DEFENSE
2006	COH	AAA	28	462	65	17	0	19	66	63	89	4	0	-1.3	.260	.370	.454	.215	.316	.384	.250	-4.5	-1.4	86-1B -11
2006	PAW	AAA	28	44	7	3	0	4	8	5	5	0	0	0.1	.459	.523	.865	.368	.444	.737	.374	9.5	0.8	9-1B 0
2006	BOS	MLB	28	37	3	2	0	1	3	4	10	0	0	-0.6	.273	.351	.424	.242	.324	.394	.250	0.6	-0.1	9-1B -1
2007	TBA	MLB	29	612	99	29	1	46	121	103	142	1	0	-0.9	.282	.411	.627	.278	.414	.643	.342	68.6	6.6	138-1B -5
2008	TBA	MLB	30	607	76	24	2	31	102	96	166	1	1	-5.4	.247	.377	.494	.247	.383	.515	.305	33.0	4.7	130-1B 5
2009	TBA	MLB	31	600	80	24	1	30	91	89	158	1	0	-2.1	.239	.359	.476	.243	.363	.500	.294	20.3	2.9	140-1B -1

Breakout: 4%   Improve: 25%   Collapse: 36%   Attrition: 19%   Comparables: Jim Thome, Jim Gentile, Carlos Delgado, Mike Epstein

We had already witnessed endless years of Peña hitting right around .250 before his career year in '07, so it should not be a shock that he went back to doing what he'd been doing and regressed to the mean in 2008. Still, plus-plus power and 100 walks per year more than make up for that sort of batting-average issue, and Peña puts a cherry on top by adding outstanding defense to the equation. While many saw it as a down season, $18.25 million for two more years of this is more than a sound investment.

Fernando Perez   CF

Bats: S   Throws: R   Height: 6' 1"   Weight: 195   Born: April 23, 1983   Age: 26

YEAR	TEAM	LVL	AGE	PA	R	2B	3B	HR	RBI	BB	SO	SB	CS	EqBRR	AVG	OBP	SLG	EqAVG	EqOBP	EqSLG	EqA	VORP	WARP	DEFENSE
2006	VIS	A+	23	641	123	19	9	4	56	78	134	33	16	-4.4	.307	.398	.397	.215	.291	.283	.207	-37.1	-3.1	129-CF -9
2007	MNT	AA	24	476	84	24	10	8	33	76	104	32	18	0.0	.308	.423	.481	.246	.346	.394	.260	7.1	2.2	99-CF 5
2008	DUR	AAA	25	579	86	17	11	5	36	58	156	43	12	5.5	.288	.361	.393	.248	.321	.349	.243	-8.2	0.0	108-CF -2 11-RF 0
2008	TBA	MLB	25	72	18	2	0	3	8	8	16	5	0	1.3	.250	.348	.433	.250	.357	.433	.288	3.7	1.3	12-CF 8
2009	TBA	MLB	26	500	59	19	6	6	35	48	138	19	7	2.9	.233	.310	.342	.237	.314	.359	.242	-5.7	1.4	118-CF 2

Breakout: 27%   Improve: 50%   Collapse: 21%   Attrition: 9%   Comparables: Gary Pettis, Wayne Lydon, Chris Latham, Andres Torres

Perez is so cool. Even if this whole baseball thing doesn't work out for him, he'll be just fine—he spent three years at Columbia University studying creative writing, and when one scout was asked about his ultimate upside, his response was "President of the United States." He's pretty good at this silly game too, with speed, on-base skills, and the ability to play all three outfield positions. When either newly acquired Matt Joyce or Gabe Gross wins the right-field job this spring, the Rays will need a platoon partner against left-handers, and Perez will be the perfect fit. In a different organization, he'd get the chance to start in center.

Shawn Riggans   C

Bats: R   Throws: R   Height: 6' 2"   Weight: 210   Born: July 25, 1980   Age: 28

YEAR	TEAM	LVL	AGE	PA	R	2B	3B	HR	RBI	BB	SO	SB	CS	EqBRR	AVG	OBP	SLG	EqAVG	EqOBP	EqSLG	EqA	VORP	WARP	DEFENSE
2006	DUR	AAA	25	453	43	26	2	11	54	27	88	2	2	-1.0	.293	.341	.444	.252	.297	.404	.240	-2.3	0.1	85-C -6
2006	TBA	MLB	25	33	3	1	0	0	1	4	7	0	0	-0.5	.172	.273	.207	.138	.242	.172	.131	-2.8	0.0	7-C 2
2007	DUR	AAA	26	133	10	9	1	4	16	4	30	0	3	0.0	.281	.333	.471	.234	.278	.411	.231	-2.0	0.3	30-C 1
2008	TBA	MLB	27	152	21	7	0	6	24	12	30	0	0	1.1	.222	.287	.407	.224	.293	.418	.246	1.0	-0.3	38-C -7
2009	TBA	MLB	28	246	21	11	1	7	29	16	55	0	0	-0.6	.226	.282	.370	.229	.286	.389	.232	-1.0	0.4	61-C -5

Breakout: 37%   Improve: 56%   Collapse: 24%   Attrition: 42%   Comparables: Pete Daley, Brian Johnson, Bob Melvin, Jerry Moses

A total of 25 people tried to steal a base against Riggans in 2008, and he threw out exactly one of them (Joe Inglett, for you trivia buffs). That's not really what one looks for in a backup catcher, but Riggans does provide a little bit of pop on offense. He missed out on the postseason after his knee swelled up due to an infection, and the Rays re-signed his October replacement, Michael Hernandez, in the off-season to compete for the backup job in 2009. It's going to come down to personal preference for Maddon as to whether he wants runs or run prevention from the role.

Justin Ruggiano — OF

Bats: R   Throws: R   Height: 6' 2"   Weight: 205   Born: April 12, 1982   Age: 27

YEAR	TEAM	LVL	AGE	PA	R	2B	3B	HR	RBI	BB	SO	SB	CS	EqBRR	AVG	OBP	SLG	EqAVG	EqOBP	EqSLG	EqA	VORP	WARP	DEFENSE			
2006	JAX	AA	24	346	51	18	3	9	45	46	74	10	5	-1.3	.260	.367	.435	.233	.324	.399	.255	1.1	-0.4	64-RF	-8	6-LF	0
2006	MNT	AA	24	130	25	14	3	4	27	19	29	4	4	-1.3	.333	.442	.630	.286	.380	.589	.311	15.4	0.8	27-RF	-3		
2007	DUR	AAA	25	546	78	29	2	20	73	53	151	26	11	0.0	.309	.386	.502	.273	.345	.461	.276	24.7	2.7	74-RF	-1	40-LF	4
2008	DUR	AAA	26	289	49	18	3	11	51	22	77	20	3	1.1	.315	.374	.537	.269	.329	.473	.277	11.5	2.4	38-RF	3	16-LF	3
2008	TBA	MLB	26	81	9	4	0	2	7	4	27	2	0	0.9	.197	.247	.329	.197	.247	.355	.211	-4.0	0.1	10-RF	0	10-LF	4
2009	TBA	MLB	27	396	47	20	3	12	45	34	115	10	4	0.8	.240	.312	.413	.243	.315	.434	.260	0.7	1.4	95-RF	4		

Breakout: 12%   Improve: 37%   Collapse: 34%   Attrition: 19%   Comparables: Glenallen Hill, Alonzo Powell, Brent Cookson, Prentice Redman

Ruggiano was acquired from the Dodgers in 2006 as an extra body to even up the deal that also brought them Dioner Navarro. He's a tad old for a prospect, but he's also proven over the past three years that he can hit minor league pitching, though he failed to establish himself in an extended big-league look at the end of the season. He's an excellent athlete, with solid tools across the board, but scouts see him as a bad-ball hitter who didn't get enough of them in the majors while also swinging too often at pitches he shouldn't have. He's stuck behind a full depth chart 's worth of outfielders in Tampa, but the good news is that they have excellent barbecue up in Durham.

B.J. Upton — CF

Bats: R   Throws: R   Height: 6' 3"   Weight: 185   Born: August 21, 1984   Age: 24

YEAR	TEAM	LVL	AGE	PA	R	2B	3B	HR	RBI	BB	SO	SB	CS	EqBRR	AVG	OBP	SLG	EqAVG	EqOBP	EqSLG	EqA	VORP	WARP	DEFENSE			
2006	DUR	AAA	21	470	72	18	4	8	41	65	89	46	17	1.0	.269	.374	.394	.239	.343	.363	.256	0.4	-0.3	84-SS	-17	18-3B	-1
2006	TBA	MLB	21	189	20	5	0	1	10	13	40	11	3	0.7	.246	.302	.291	.241	.302	.282	.218	-7.8	-1.3	46-3B	-8		
2007	TBA	MLB	22	548	86	25	1	24	82	65	154	22	8	4.3	.300	.386	.508	.299	.389	.527	.307	47.4	4.6	75-CF	2	47-2B	-5
2008	TBA	MLB	23	640	85	37	2	9	67	97	134	44	16	3.3	.273	.383	.401	.280	.396	.423	.289	33.2	4.9	139-CF	6		
2009	TBA	MLB	24	558	90	27	3	14	58	73	124	40	12	2.7	.267	.367	.424	.271	.371	.446	.291	26.6	4.2	131-CF	-1		

Breakout: 21%   Improve: 56%   Collapse: 9%   Attrition: 8%   Comparables: Steve Kemp, J.D. Drew, Shannon Stewart, Rickie Weeks

Upton's remarkable post-season performance on the national stage nearly erased what had been a troubling and disappointing regular season. After slugging 24 home runs in '07, he hit only nine in '08; write part of that off to the torn labrum he played through, though that logic fades after the late-season power display. Of greater concern for his future going forward were the repeated mental lapses, the jogging on ground balls, and the occasional lack of effort. The regular season is a grind, but these things happen in 10-1 blowouts, not in key games for a team making a historic pennant run. With his shoulder now surgically repaired, he can be as good as he wants to be. There's no effort number to plug into PECOTA—even if he dogs it, he'll be good, but if he learned anything in October, he'll be great.

Ben Zobrist — UT

Bats: S   Throws: R   Height: 6' 3"   Weight: 200   Born: May 26, 1981   Age: 28

YEAR	TEAM	LVL	AGE	PA	R	2B	3B	HR	RBI	BB	SO	SB	CS	EqBRR	AVG	OBP	SLG	EqAVG	EqOBP	EqSLG	EqA	VORP	WARP	DEFENSE			
2006	CCH	AA	25	381	57	25	6	3	30	55	46	9	5	-3.2	.327	.434	.473	.247	.336	.355	.246	-1.7	-0.2	79-SS	-11		
2006	DUR	AAA	25	82	12	3	1	0	6	10	9	4	1	-1.0	.304	.400	.377	.254	.354	.324	.251	-0.4	0.4	18-SS	1		
2006	TBA	MLB	25	198	10	6	2	2	18	10	26	2	3	-0.9	.224	.260	.311	.220	.260	.308	.195	-9.8	0.2	50-SS	6		
2007	DUR	AAA	26	276	42	14	2	7	22	43	38	8	3	0.0	.279	.403	.455	.231	.347	.389	.263	3.0	1.3	52-SS	0		
2007	TBA	MLB	26	105	8	2	0	1	9	3	21	2	0	0.6	.155	.184	.206	.155	.184	.206	.123	-11.5	-1.7	26-SS	-7		
2008	TBA	MLB	27	227	32	10	2	12	30	25	37	3	0	0.8	.253	.339	.505	.254	.346	.533	.295	14.6	1.0	33-SS	-6	9-LF	-1
2009	TBA	MLB	28	267	32	12	1	6	27	28	46	4	1	0.2	.245	.328	.381	.248	.332	.401	.260	6.1	0.7	66-SS	-5		

Breakout: 36%   Improve: 54%   Collapse: 26%   Attrition: 33%   Comparables: Bob Meacham, Pumpsie Green, Bobby Crosby, Morgan Ensberg

Zobrist's miserable 2007 was the reason the Rays acquired Jason Barlett in the first place, but after returning from a nasty thumb injury early in the year, Zobrist refashioned himself as a future super-sub able to play six positions. He was pressing and swinging at everything in '07, but returned to his patient ways in 2008, drawing walks and waiting for pitches to drive. Expecting him to deliver a home run every 16.5 at-bats again is a bit of a pipe dream, but he's one of the more valuable reserve players around, one who can give a team reason *not* to panic if a starter is forced to the disabled list.

PITCHERS

Grant Balfour

Bats: R   Throws: R   Height: 6' 2"   Weight: 190   Born: December 30, 1977   Age: 31

YEAR	TEAM	LVL	AGE	W	L	SV	G	GS	IP	H	BB	SO	HR	GB%	BABIP	STUFF	WHIP	ERA	DERA	EqH9	EqBB9	EqSO9	EqHR9	DEF	VORP	SN/WX
2007	HUN	AA	29	0	0	2	8	0	11¹	8	4	21	0	50.0%	.381	11	1.06	2.39	3.38	9.3	3.4	10.1	0.0	0	2.6	—
2007	NAS	AAA	29	1	1	5	24	0	32	17	11	47	2	39.7%	.254	23	0.88	1.69	3.30	6.0	3.3	9.6	0.9	4	7.7	—
2007	TBA	MLB	29	1	0	0	22	0	22	26	16	27	1	46.7%	.455	21	1.91	6.14	3.38	10.5	6.3	9.7	0.4	-6	-0.3	-0.33
2008	DUR	AAA	30	1	0	8	15	0	23²	5	10	39	1	43.2%	.114	23	0.63	0.38	1.57	2.3	3.9	9.4	0.4	1	10.3	—
2008	TBA	MLB	30	6	2	4	51	0	58¹	28	24	82	3	29.7%	.225	32	0.89	1.54	2.70	5.2	3.5	10.0	0.5	6	27.2	3.48
2009	TBA	MLB	31	4	3	7	58	0	59¹	45	29	75	5	36.0%	.290	29	1.26	3.36	3.34	6.8	3.9	10.4	0.8	-0	14.4	1.37

Breakout: 27%   Improve: 49%   Collapse: 20%   Attrition: 12%   Comparables: Joe Nathan, Brendan Donnelly, Chad Fox, Francisco Cordero

It's easy to forget that Balfour could have been had by anyone. When Scott Dohmann beat him out for the final bullpen job last spring, the Rays passed Balfour through waivers to get him to Triple-A. He limited International League batters to just five hits in 23⅔ innings before his return, and then became a key part of the Rays much-improved relief corps the rest of the way as a dominating set-up man. He wears his heart on his sleeve; his yelling and screaming and fist-pumping are cause for friction when he's not your teammate, but that 94-98 mph fastball is lights-out and takes care of business.

Chad Bradford

Bats: R   Throws: R   Height: 6' 5"   Weight: 205   Born: September 14, 1974   Age: 34

YEAR	TEAM	LVL	AGE	W	L	SV	G	GS	IP	H	BB	SO	HR	GB%	BABIP	STUFF	WHIP	ERA	DERA	EqH9	EqBB9	EqSO9	EqHR9	DEF	VORP	SN/WX
2006	NYN	MLB	31	4	2	2	70	0	62	59	13	45	1	65.5%	.312	14	1.16	2.90	3.26	8.8	1.6	6.1	0.1	1	19.1	1.83
2007	BAL	MLB	32	4	7	2	78	0	64²	77	16	29	1	63.9%	.328	-3	1.44	3.34	3.03	10.1	2.1	3.4	0.1	-5	15.4	0.84
2008	BAL	MLB	33	3	3	0	47	0	40¹	41	7	13	2	70.5%	.295	-16	1.19	2.46	4.03	9.2	1.4	2.6	0.5	1	9.1	0.80
2008	TBA	MLB	33	1	0	0	21	0	19	18	8	4	1	61.8%	.266	-29	1.37	1.42	3.44	8.8	3.4	1.5	0.5	3	9.1	0.72
2009	TBA	MLB	34	2	2	1	35	0	38²	45	11	16	2	60.0%	.310	-8	1.44	4.18	4.32	10.4	2.2	3.4	0.5	-0	4.7	0.37

Breakout: 8%   Improve: 25%   Collapse: 57%   Attrition: 31%   Comparables: Dennis Lamp, Dale Murray, Dan Quisenberry, Clay Carroll

One might think that Bradford would be worth more than the ol' player to be named later, but that's all he cost Tampa for the stretch run. Sure, being a sidearmer isn't the sexiest thing in the world, but when it comes to getting right-handers out and keeping the ball on the ground, Bradford fills the role nicely, thank you. He hasn't had a bad year since settling into a full-time job earlier in the decade, and for the last three, he's been pretty damned good. The Rays will be happy to pay him the $3.5 million he's due in the last year of his contract.

Wade Davis

Bats: R   Throws: R   Height: 6' 5"   Weight: 220   Born: September 7, 1985   Age: 23

YEAR	TEAM	LVL	AGE	W	L	SV	G	GS	IP	H	BB	SO	HR	GB%	BABIP	STUFF	WHIP	ERA	DERA	EqH9	EqBB9	EqSO9	EqHR9	DEF	VORP	SN/WX
2006	SWM	A	20	7	12	0	27	27	146²	124	64	165	5	50.1%	.330	9	1.29	3.02	6.28	12.2	6.4	5.4	1.4	-9	-9.0	—
2007	VRO	A+	21	3	0	0	13	13	78¹	54	21	88	5	50.0%	.268	20	0.96	1.84	3.93	8.0	3.3	6.2	1.4	2	13.2	—
2007	MNT	AA	21	7	3	0	14	14	80	74	30	81	3	49.0%	.350	30	1.30	3.15	5.18	10.7	3.8	5.7	0.7	-3	3.4	—
2008	MNT	AA	22	9	6	0	19	19	107²	104	42	81	7	46.4%	.312	-3	1.36	3.84	5.47	10.8	3.9	4.3	1.2	1	1.4	—
2008	DUR	AAA	22	4	2	0	9	9	53	39	24	55	5	47.5%	.278	18	1.19	2.72	3.22	7.5	4.5	6.3	1.3	-1	13.3	—
2009	TBA	MLB	23	7	9	0	24	24	132	151	69	88	18	45.0%	.310	11	1.66	5.71	5.68	10.2	4.1	5.5	1.2	-1	-4.9	0.51

Breakout: 5%   Improve: 28%   Collapse: 37%   Attrition: 11%   Comparables: Rob Woodward, Robert Ellis, Shawn Chacon, Jason Bell

Davis has everything that scouts look for in a power-pitching prospect: an ideal frame, mid-90s heat, and a hard, heavy curveball. Those attributes alone are more than enough to pass the Triple-A test, and though his control and his changeup are just average, he's very close to a finished product. In a system without David Price, Davis would be a prize nearly guaranteed a rotation spot in the coming season, but in this crowded young rotation, he might, like Price, have to begin his career in the bullpen.

Scott Dohmann

Bats: R **Throws:** R **Height:** 6' 1" **Weight:** 200 **Born:** February 13, 1978 **Age:** 31

YEAR	TEAM	LVL	AGE	W	L	SV	G	GS	IP	H	BB	SO	HR	GB%	BABIP	STUFF	WHIP	ERA	DERA	EqH9	EqBB9	EqSO9	EqHR9	DEF	VORP	SN/WX
2006	CSP	AAA	28	0	0	1	10	0	10	6	1	12	2	38.5%	.167	4	0.70	2.70	5.91	5.1	0.8	6.8	1.7	3	-0.4	—
2006	COL	MLB	28	1	1	1	27	0	24²	26	15	22	4	36.5%	.324	-2	1.66	6.19	4.32	9.0	4.7	7.2	1.1	-3	-0.9	0.18
2006	KCA	MLB	28	1	3	0	21	0	23²	33	18	22	5	49.3%	.412	-3	2.15	7.97	6.14	13.1	7.0	7.8	2.0	-3	-4.6	-0.87
2007	DUR	AAA	29	4	1	5	37	0	48²	37	13	48	2	46.9%	.282	3	1.03	2.03	3.86	8.5	2.8	6.3	0.6	4	8.6	—
2007	TBA	MLB	29	3	0	0	31	0	32²	29	18	26	3	41.3%	.310	-3	1.44	3.30	4.02	7.5	4.9	6.3	0.9	1	8.8	1.15
2008	DUR	AAA	30	0	2	20	33	0	41²	35	12	49	2	37.8%	.321	6	1.13	3.45	4.58	8.7	3.0	7.3	0.7	2	4.5	—
2008	TBA	MLB	30	2	0	0	12	0	14²	18	7	12	2	57.4%	.364	-11	1.70	6.12	5.27	12.5	4.0	6.6	1.3	-1	-0.6	0.21
2009	TBA	MLB	31	2	2	2	39	0	38¹	39	18	32	4	43.0%	.300	6	1.48	4.50	4.48	9.2	3.6	6.8	0.9	-0	4.0	0.34

Breakout: 31% Improve: 61% Collapse: 27% Attrition: 20% Comparables: Don McMahon, Dave Borkowski, Vicente Romo, Curt Leskanic

Dohmann began the year in the big leagues while Balfour was in Triple-A, but the Rays reversed those assignments in early May and Dohmann ended up buried at Durham despite pitching well. With a 92-94 mph fastball that can touch 96 and a decent slider, he's got big-league stuff, but he also has a tendency to flatten his pitches when he overthrows. Instead of toiling away in the minors again, he signed a $650,000 deal to pitch one year with the Hiroshima Carp.

Matt Garza

Bats: R **Throws:** R **Height:** 6' 4" **Weight:** 185 **Born:** November 11, 1983 **Age:** 25

YEAR	TEAM	LVL	AGE	W	L	SV	G	GS	IP	H	BB	SO	HR	GB%	BABIP	STUFF	WHIP	ERA	DERA	EqH9	EqBB9	EqSO9	EqHR9	DEF	VORP	SN/WX
2006	FTM	A+	22	5	1	0	8	8	44	27	11	53	3	46.8%	.231	15	0.86	1.43	4.29	7.5	3.0	5.8	1.5	-1	6.1	—
2006	NBR	AA	22	6	2	0	10	10	57	40	14	68	2	39.9%	.271	27	0.95	2.53	5.33	7.8	2.8	6.5	0.7	1	1.6	—
2006	ROC	AAA	22	3	1	0	5	5	34	20	7	33	1	51.8%	.235	30	0.79	1.85	4.70	6.8	2.3	6.2	0.6	6	3.1	—
2006	MIN	MLB	22	3	6	0	10	9	50	62	23	38	6	37.4%	.346	10	1.70	5.76	5.22	10.8	4.0	5.9	1.1	-3	0.7	0.70
2007	ROC	AAA	23	4	6	0	16	16	92	93	31	95	5	42.6%	.341	12	1.35	3.62	5.32	11.1	3.3	6.5	0.8	-1	2.7	—
2007	MIN	MLB	23	5	7	0	16	15	83	96	32	67	8	47.7%	.351	14	1.54	3.69	3.15	10.6	3.3	6.5	0.9	-14	11.2	1.97
2008	TBA	MLB	24	11	9	0	30	30	184²	170	59	128	19	42.8%	.276	8	1.24	3.70	4.53	8.8	2.7	5.6	1.0	8	35.2	4.94
2009	TBA	MLB	25	9	8	0	25	25	151¹	157	54	111	18	43.0%	.300	21	1.39	4.46	4.45	9.3	2.8	6.0	1.0	-1	16.0	2.86

Breakout: 22% Improve: 52% Collapse: 21% Attrition: 13% Comparables: Matt Keough, Brian Holman, Jay Tibbs, Ron Kline

While Delmon Young and Garza were two of the top prospects in the game in 2007, both had failed to live up to expectations, and the Rays and Twins engineered a fascinating challenge trade that involved exchanging. So far, the Rays have certainly had the best of it, as Garza made slow yet steady improvements throughout the year, becoming their most feared starting pitcher in the postseason. He remains highly inconsistent, going six-plus innings while allowing one or zero runs in 11 of his starts, and also being hit for five or more runs six times, but his youth and a proven ability to dominate are enough to warrant the optimism. As with so many Rays, this is only the beginning.

Jason Hammel

Bats: R **Throws:** R **Height:** 6' 6" **Weight:** 220 **Born:** September 2, 1982 **Age:** 26

YEAR	TEAM	LVL	AGE	W	L	SV	G	GS	IP	H	BB	SO	HR	GB%	BABIP	STUFF	WHIP	ERA	DERA	EqH9	EqBB9	EqSO9	EqHR9	DEF	VORP	SN/WX
2006	DUR	AAA	23	5	9	0	24	24	127¹	133	36	117	11	47.8%	.335	-6	1.33	4.25	6.45	10.6	3.1	5.6	1.4	-3	-11.3	—
2006	TBA	MLB	23	0	6	0	9	9	44	61	21	32	7	42.9%	.375	-6	1.86	7.77	5.86	11.9	4.2	5.9	1.3	-8	-8.2	-0.25
2007	DUR	AAA	24	4	5	0	13	13	76¹	61	28	75	3	50.7%	.283	13	1.17	3.42	5.05	8.8	3.7	6.2	0.6	5	4.4	—
2007	TBA	MLB	24	3	5	0	24	14	85	100	40	64	12	41.4%	.333	-11	1.64	6.14	5.27	9.5	3.9	5.8	1.3	-7	-1.4	0.88
2008	TBA	MLB	25	4	4	2	40	5	78¹	83	35	44	11	47.2%	.288	-25	1.51	4.60	5.71	10.2	3.8	4.5	1.3	4	4.8	1.04
2009	TBA	MLB	26	3	3	1	33	4	59²	63	25	40	7	45.0%	.300	3	1.48	4.78	4.79	9.5	3.3	5.5	1.1	-0	4.0	0.48

Breakout: 36% Improve: 62% Collapse: 14% Attrition: 39% Comparables: Joe Kerrigan, Dustin Nippert, Rick Bauer, Dan Wright

Hammel is a talented young pitcher, but he's not talented enough to crack *this* rotation. He's put up consistently good numbers in the minors, thanks primarily to a fastball that is notable for both its sink and velocity, but his command and secondary offerings are merely average. In another organization he'd have a better chance as a back-of-the-rotation starter, but in Tampa Bay, he's stuck in a long-relief role.

Jeremy Hellickson

Bats: R   **Throws:** R   **Height:** 6' 1"   **Weight:** 185   **Born:** April 8, 1987   **Age:** 22

YEAR	TEAM	LVL	AGE	W	L	SV	G	GS	IP	H	BB	SO	HR	GB%	BABIP	STUFF	WHIP	ERA	DERA	EqH9	EqBB9	EqSO9	EqHR9	DEF	VORP	SN/WX
2006	HUD	A-	19	4	3	0	15	14	77	55	16	96	3	55.8%	.280	7	0.92	2.45	6.65	10.9	3.7	5.4	2.0	2	-7.7	—
2007	CGA	A	20	13	3	0	21	21	111¹	87	34	106	7	45.1%	.264	4	1.09	2.67	5.81	10.5	4.1	4.4	1.5	8	-2.2	—
2008	VRO	A+	21	7	1	0	14	14	76²	64	5	83	7	46.3%	.291	12	0.90	1.99	3.74	11.0	1.2	6.0	2.0	0	13.9	—
2008	MNT	AA	21	4	4	0	13	13	75¹	84	15	79	15	42.5%	.356	-10	1.31	3.94	5.62	13.9	2.2	6.8	3.4	0	-0.1	—
2009	TBA	MLB	22	7	8	0	23	23	131	152	39	89	21	43.0%	.310	18	1.46	5.25	5.18	10.4	2.4	5.6	1.4	-1	2.7	1.31

Breakout: 8%   **Improve:** 38%   **Collapse:** 19%   **Attrition:** 13%   **Comparables:** Luis Vasquez, Frank Castillo, Melido Perez, Andy Rincon

Hellickson has exemplary command of very good stuff, including a 91-94 mph fastball, a strong curveball, and a deceptive change, but he can be accused of throwing too many strikes. Just 20 walks in 152 innings is nice and all, but at some point you have to throw a chase pitch. Unless you're a pitching scientist a la Greg Maddux, hitters are going to hit you when they know that whatever you throw will be in the zone. It's hard to force a guy to throw fewer strikes—it goes against everything a pitcher is usually told—but it will be the key between Hellickson ending up in the back of someone's rotation or as just an unsolvable riddle.

James Houser Jr.

Bats: L   **Throws:** L   **Height:** 6' 4"   **Weight:** 185   **Born:** December 15, 1984   **Age:** 24

YEAR	TEAM	LVL	AGE	W	L	SV	G	GS	IP	H	BB	SO	HR	GB%	BABIP	STUFF	WHIP	ERA	DERA	EqH9	EqBB9	EqSO9	EqHR9	DEF	VORP	SN/WX
2006	VIS	A+	21	12	4	0	28	27	151	140	46	137	20	38.5%	.291	-23	1.23	4.41	7.03	11.1	3.8	4.3	2.5	3	-21.3	—
2007	MNT	AA	22	5	4	0	20	20	103²	88	39	90	10	39.1%	.276	-10	1.22	3.65	6.29	9.5	3.7	4.6	1.6	4	-7.5	—
2008	MNT	AA	23	3	3	0	20	20	94¹	69	40	76	9	42.9%	.238	-17	1.16	2.86	6.15	7.9	3.9	4.4	1.5	13	-5.5	—
2009	TBA	MLB	24	5	7	0	28	16	100	115	49	62	17	40.0%	.300	1	1.63	6.09	6.00	10.3	3.8	5.1	1.5	-1	-7.8	-0.11

Breakout: 7%   **Improve:** 34%   **Collapse:** 25%   **Attrition:** 18%   **Comparables:** Dan Meyer, J.A. Happ, Rob Henkel, Casey Whitten

It seems a bit odd to be calling a second-round pick a sleeper, but that's what Houser has become. He's had a few delays in his development over the past two years, including a controversial 50-game suspension last year for performance-enhancing drugs (based on a prescription he was taking), and minor knee surgery this year. He was having the best season of his career at Double-A in 2008, limiting Southern League hitters to a .205 batting average thanks to an average fastball and an outstanding curve. He's another Ray with solid fourth- or fifth-starter potential elsewhere, but in this system all he has are bullpen possibilities.

J. P. Howell

Bats: L   **Throws:** L   **Height:** 6' 0"   **Weight:** 180   **Born:** April 25, 1983   **Age:** 26

YEAR	TEAM	LVL	AGE	W	L	SV	G	GS	IP	H	BB	SO	HR	GB%	BABIP	STUFF	WHIP	ERA	DERA	EqH9	EqBB9	EqSO9	EqHR9	DEF	VORP	SN/WX
2006	OMA	AAA	23	3	2	0	8	8	36²	39	14	33	3	61.1%	.360	0	1.46	4.72	4.59	11.1	3.8	5.9	1.1	-4	3.7	—
2006	DUR	AAA	23	5	3	0	10	10	55¹	53	15	49	2	49.4%	.333	10	1.23	2.61	4.68	10.1	3.1	5.6	0.7	4	5.1	—
2006	TBA	MLB	23	1	3	0	8	8	42¹	52	14	33	4	46.7%	.366	11	1.56	5.11	5.09	10.8	3.1	6.4	0.9	-1	3.5	0.92
2007	DUR	AAA	24	7	8	0	21	21	128	110	34	145	16	56.8%	.301	-5	1.13	3.38	6.22	9.9	2.7	7.3	1.8	9	-8.2	—
2007	TBA	MLB	24	1	6	0	10	10	51	69	21	49	8	46.2%	.381	1	1.76	7.59	7.13	10.7	3.2	7.1	1.4	-4	-10.9	0.00
2008	TBA	MLB	25	6	1	3	64	0	89¹	62	39	92	6	54.7%	.252	18	1.13	2.22	3.77	6.7	3.6	8.2	0.6	7	27.8	4.72
2009	TBA	MLB	26	4	3	3	50	2	66¹	61	28	61	6	50.0%	.290	16	1.33	3.92	3.98	8.2	3.3	7.6	0.8	-0	11.4	1.07

Breakout: 39%   **Improve:** 63%   **Collapse:** 16%   **Attrition:** 22%   **Comparables:** Sparky Lyle, Tug McGraw, Jesse Orosco, Darold Knowles

There's more than smoke and mirrors going on here; Howell struck out more than a batter per inning despite rarely touching 90 mph with his sinking fastball. A failed starter, he had seemed for years to be better suited to a relief role. He's one of those players who wants the ball with the game on the line, and who thrives on pressure situations in a way that allows his stuff to play up. His fantastic slider and the solid changeup learned during his rotation days makes him equally dangerous against righties and lefties, and he should be a valuable set-up man for years to come.

Edwin Jackson

Bats: R   Throws: R   Height: 6' 3"   Weight: 210   Born: September 9, 1983   Age: 25

YEAR	TEAM	LVL	AGE	W	L	SV	G	GS	IP	H	BB	SO	HR	GB%	BABIP	STUFF	WHIP	ERA	DERA	EqH9	EqBB9	EqSO9	EqHR9	DEF	VORP	SN/WX
2006	DUR	AAA	22	3	7	5	22	13	73¹	84	35	66	7	47.6%	.352	-15	1.63	5.54	8.31	11.6	4.9	5.3	1.4	-4	-20.9	—
2006	TBA	MLB	22	0	0	0	23	1	36¹	42	25	27	2	52.1%	.348	4	1.84	5.45	5.40	9.6	5.9	5.9	0.5	-5	-2.5	-0.59
2007	TBA	MLB	23	5	15	0	32	31	161	195	88	128	19	46.0%	.349	1	1.76	5.76	5.84	9.5	4.4	6.0	1.1	-8	-8.5	1.43
2008	TBA	MLB	24	14	11	0	32	31	183¹	199	77	108	23	39.5%	.306	-8	1.51	4.42	4.40	10.8	3.7	4.9	1.3	-2	26.7	3.99
2009	DET	MLB	25	7	9	0	33	22	138¹	156	62	89	19	43.0%	.310	8	1.57	5.28	5.12	9.9	3.7	5.4	1.2	-1	3.7	1.33

Breakout: 14%   Improve: 44%   Collapse: 25%   Attrition: 16%   Comparables: Livan Hernandez, Steve Trachsel, Mac Suzuki, Stan Bahnsen

As a player entering his seventh season in the big leagues, it's easy to forget that Jackson is only 25 years old. He has frustrated the Dodgers and Rays for years; everyone expects that a monster athlete with a 93-97 mph fastball and plus slider should be way better than this, but he struggles with his changeup, his command, and his confidence. When he's on, he looks like an All-Star, and the Rays took a bit of a risk by dealing from a position of strength and sending him to the Tigers for Matt Joyce. He has a lot of breakout potential, but then again, we've been saying that for years.

Scott Kazmir

Bats: L   Throws: L   Height: 6' 0"   Weight: 190   Born: January 24, 1984   Age: 25

YEAR	TEAM	LVL	AGE	W	L	SV	G	GS	IP	H	BB	SO	HR	GB%	BABIP	STUFF	WHIP	ERA	DERA	EqH9	EqBB9	EqSO9	EqHR9	DEF	VORP	SN/WX
2006	TBA	MLB	22	10	8	0	24	24	144²	132	52	163	15	42.7%	.314	42	1.27	3.23	2.92	7.7	3.1	9.0	0.9	-11	38.6	4.81
2007	TBA	MLB	23	13	9	0	34	34	206²	196	89	239	18	43.8%	.339	36	1.38	3.48	3.00	7.8	3.6	9.0	0.8	-22	46.7	5.45
2008	TBA	MLB	24	12	8	0	27	27	152¹	123	70	166	23	31.2%	.271	14	1.27	3.49	4.14	8.0	3.8	8.8	1.4	7	36.8	4.84
2009	TBA	MLB	25	11	8	0	27	27	166	147	67	164	20	39.0%	.280	34	1.29	3.90	3.87	7.9	3.2	8.2	1.1	-1	28.6	4.31

Breakout: 10%   Improve: 34%   Collapse: 31%   Attrition: 10%   Comparables: Juan Pizarro, Johan Santana, Don Gullett, Frank Tanana

On the one hand, Kazmir is a great pitcher. On the other, in many ways he's becoming a right-handed version of Rich Harden—he's an ace as far as his numbers go, but he doesn't do many of the other things one expects from an ace. He regularly misses time here and there (in 2008 it was an early-season elbow strain), he's so inefficient that he often hits 100 pitches before he's made it to the fifth inning, and he can become a scheduled strain on the bullpen. Don't get us wrong, he's great, and clearly worth the nearly $40 million he'll receive over the next four years, but he's far from deserving of the "ace" designation.

Jacob McGee

Bats: L   Throws: L   Height: 6' 3"   Weight: 190   Born: August 6, 1986   Age: 22

YEAR	TEAM	LVL	AGE	W	L	SV	G	GS	IP	H	BB	SO	HR	GB%	BABIP	STUFF	WHIP	ERA	DERA	EqH9	EqBB9	EqSO9	EqHR9	DEF	VORP	SN/WX
2006	SWM	A	19	7	9	0	26	26	134	103	65	171	7	44.9%	.311	5	1.25	2.96	6.37	11.2	6.9	6.2	1.9	-4	-9.6	—
2007	VRO	A+	20	5	4	0	21	21	116²	86	39	145	8	43.1%	.289	31	1.07	2.93	5.43	8.7	4.1	7.0	1.4	3	2.0	—
2007	MNT	AA	20	3	2	0	5	5	23¹	19	13	30	2	42.5%	.333	21	1.37	4.25	6.53	10.5	5.7	7.8	1.3	2	-2.1	—
2008	MNT	AA	21	6	4	0	15	15	77²	65	37	65	6	43.9%	.278	7	1.31	3.94	6.91	9.2	4.5	4.8	1.3	9	-10.4	—
2009	TBA	MLB	22	6	10	0	34	23	134	155	87	94	22	42.0%	.310	4	1.80	6.42	6.34	10.3	5.1	5.8	1.4	-1	-14.9	-0.65

Breakout: 3%   Improve: 28%   Collapse: 33%   Attrition: 20%   Comparables: Cedrick Bowers, Rob Mallicoat, Daniel Haigwood, Erik Bedard

Of the myriad high-ceiling arms in the Rays system, McGee is the rarest of prospects. It's not that hard to find a guy who can touch 98 mph, but to find one who is left-handed? *That* is special. In 2008 though, he suddenly didn't look so special; the fastball lost a few ticks as the season wore down, his command disappeared, and the results were fairly predictable—a popped elbow and Tommy John surgery that will cost him most of 2009. The effort in his delivery and his inconsistent secondary offerings had many projecting him as a power reliever in the end, and this outcome may have sealed the deal.

Trever Miller

							Bats: R		Throws: L		Height: 6' 3"		Weight: 200		Born: May 29, 1973			Age: 36					

YEAR	TEAM	LVL	AGE	W	L	SV	G	GS	IP	H	BB	SO	HR	GB%	BABIP	STUFF	WHIP	ERA	DERA	EqH9	EqBB9	EqSO9	EqHR9	DEF	VORP	SN/WX
2006	HOU	MLB	33	2	3	1	70	0	50²	42	13	56	7	34.3%	.282	18	1.09	3.02	3.40	7.5	2.0	9.1	1.1	4	16.9	1.63
2007	HOU	MLB	34	0	0	1	76	0	46¹	45	23	46	6	37.7%	.302	4	1.47	4.86	4.28	8.0	3.7	8.0	1.1	-2	4.2	0.36
2008	TBA	MLB	35	2	0	2	68	0	43¹	39	20	44	2	31.9%	.322	9	1.36	4.16	5.01	9.1	3.9	8.3	0.4	3	6.5	1.35
2009	SLN	MLB	36	2	2	4	49	0	42²	38	18	42	4	39.0%	.290	12	1.30	3.71	3.97	8.0	3.3	7.7	0.9	-0	7.8	0.72

Breakout: 29% Improve: 49% Collapse: 27% Attrition: 21%   Comparables: Dennis Cook, Ron Mahay, Arthur Rhodes, Mark Guthrie

Sometimes it's hard to figure out just what makes a LOOGY. Just as Walter Sobchak can get you a toe by three o'-clock, we can find you a lefty with an upper-80s sinker and a decent slider. Maybe it's a release-point thing, maybe it's a movement thing, and maybe it just doesn't matter. Miller gets left-handers out, and if that's all you expect from him, you won't be disappointed. The Rays declined his $2 million dollar option for '09, but the Cardinals were more than happy to pay the same price for his services.

Jeff Niemann

							Bats: R		Throws: R		Height: 6' 9"		Weight: 280		Born: February 28, 1983			Age: 26					

YEAR	TEAM	LVL	AGE	W	L	SV	G	GS	IP	H	BB	SO	HR	GB%	BABIP	STUFF	WHIP	ERA	DERA	EqH9	EqBB9	EqSO9	EqHR9	DEF	VORP	SN/WX
2006	MNT	AA	23	5	5	0	14	14	77²	56	29	84	6	45.7%	.255	2	1.10	2.68	5.30	9.0	3.8	6.3	1.4	8	2.4	—
2007	DUR	AAA	24	12	6	0	25	25	131	144	46	123	13	42.9%	.341	-14	1.45	3.98	6.07	12.4	3.6	5.9	1.5	3	-6.3	—
2008	DUR	AAA	25	9	5	0	24	24	133	101	50	128	15	48.0%	.246	-8	1.14	3.59	6.12	7.5	3.7	5.7	1.4	19	-7.4	—
2008	TBA	MLB	25	2	2	0	5	2	16	18	8	14	3	47.2%	.313	-5	1.63	5.06	5.51	10.5	3.9	6.6	1.7	-3	-1.8	0.04
2009	TBA	MLB	26	7	8	1	37	18	127²	131	56	97	16	43.0%	.300	12	1.46	4.81	4.79	9.2	3.4	6.2	1.1	-1	8.4	1.60

Breakout: 43% Improve: 72% Collapse: 15% Attrition: 7%   Comparables: Chris Carpenter, Roger Salkeld, Craig McMurtry, Tommy Greene

While at Rice, Niemann was one of the best pitchers in college baseball history. An extreme workload there took it's toll, and while he's a very good prospect, he's not the pitcher the Rays thought they were getting when they made him the fourth overall pick in 2004. Built much like a right-handed CC Sabathia, Niemann has a 90-93 mph fastball (that used to sit in the mid-90s), a solid breaking ball, and decent control for such a gigantic pitcher. Still, as a merely good prospect who's big-league ready, he's lost in this system. He might have value as a bullpen guy, but he might have even more value on the open market; he'd be the top pitching prospect in plenty of weaker systems.

Troy Percival

							Bats: R		Throws: R		Height: 6' 3"		Weight: 240		Born: August 9, 1969			Age: 39					

YEAR	TEAM	LVL	AGE	W	L	SV	G	GS	IP	H	BB	SO	HR	GB%	BABIP	STUFF	WHIP	ERA	DERA	EqH9	EqBB9	EqSO9	EqHR9	DEF	VORP	SN/WX
2007	SLN	MLB	37	3	0	0	34	1	40	24	10	36	3	33.7%	.208	20	0.85	1.80	2.27	5.2	2.0	7.5	0.7	2	18.1	1.28
2008	TBA	MLB	38	2	1	28	50	0	45²	29	27	38	9	23.4%	.172	-14	1.23	4.53	6.07	5.9	4.7	6.5	1.8	5	2.7	1.65
2009	TBA	MLB	39	2	3	9	31	0	35¹	31	18	30	6	30.0%	.250	1	1.38	4.71	4.62	7.9	4.0	7.0	1.4	-0	3.2	0.36

Breakout: 9% Improve: 33% Collapse: 38% Attrition: 27%   Comparables: Don McMahon, Russ Springer, Diego Segui, Mike Remlinger

There's a theory out there that anyone can close, as long as they have the stuff and the numbers to back it up; it's just a matter of opportunity. For a team that receives plenty of praise for its new-school mode of thinking, the Rays went conservative with the save-garnering position, opting for the veteran who's been there before. There are pitchers in the bullpen with better stuff and better ratios, but Pervical's performance in the closer role was one of the key reasons that the Rays became the baseball story of 2008. Injuries kept him out of the postseason, and his availability for 2009 is in question after back surgery during the offseason, but in 2008, the Rays made some key decisions based on old-school mentality that worked out pretty well.

David Price

Bats: L   Throws: L   Height: 6' 6"   Weight: 225   Born: August 26, 1985   Age: 23

YEAR	TEAM	LVL	AGE	W	L	SV	G	GS	IP	H	BB	SO	HR	GB%	BABIP	STUFF	WHIP	ERA	DERA	EqH9	EqBB9	EqSO9	EqHR9	DEF	VORP	SN/WX
2008	VRO	A+	22	4	0	0	6	6	34²	28	7	37	0	50.0%	.311	24	1.01	1.82	4.20	10.5	2.7	6.0	0.3	4	4.7	—
2008	MNT	AA	22	7	0	0	9	9	57	42	16	55	7	57.7%	.246	8	1.02	1.89	4.67	8.5	2.8	5.7	1.9	10	5.4	—
2008	DUR	AAA	22	1	1	0	4	4	18	22	9	17	0	54.2%	.378	5	1.72	4.50	4.96	13.2	5.0	6.1	0.0	-2	1.2	—
2008	TBA	MLB	22	0	0	0	5	1	14	9	4	12	1	52.5%	.211	14	0.93	1.93	3.14	5.7	2.5	6.3	0.6	0	5.1	0.24
2009	TBA	MLB	23	6	6	1	28	15	102¹	106	37	78	10	50.0%	.310	18	1.39	4.20	4.23	9.2	2.8	6.3	0.8	-0	13.0	2.03

Breakout: 1%   Improve: 6%   Collapse: 77%   Attrition: 15%   Comparables: Mike Pelfrey, Paul Wilson, Justin Verlander, Mark Mulder

Everyone in the scouting community knew that he was the next best thing, and in October, Price proved it to the world. At this point, some feel that the Rays are in a bit of a Joba-style quandary with Price; he could easily be among the most dominant relievers in the game, but his long-term value clearly lies in his being a starter. If you want to nitpick a bit, the changeup is inconsistent, and as everyone saw, he can lose his command when he's jacked up and overthrowing, but everything else that you witnessed in October was real. Price is the best pitching prospect in the game, and he should be a perennial Cy Young candidate.

Juan Salas

Bats: R   Throws: R   Height: 6' 2"   Weight: 230   Born: November 7, 1978   Age: 30

YEAR	TEAM	LVL	AGE	W	L	SV	G	GS	IP	H	BB	SO	HR	GB%	BABIP	STUFF	WHIP	ERA	DERA	EqH9	EqBB9	EqSO9	EqHR9	DEF	VORP	SN/WX
2006	MNT	AA	27	3	0	14	23	0	34¹	13	14	52	0	56.1%	.197	21	0.79	0.00	3.24	4.9	3.8	8.6	0.3	4	8.7	—
2006	DUR	AAA	27	1	1	3	27	0	28²	15	11	33	3	44.1%	.185	-4	0.92	1.60	4.82	5.1	3.9	7.1	1.6	7	2.4	—
2006	TBA	MLB	27	0	0	0	8	0	10	13	3	8	1	43.2%	.343	-1	1.60	5.40	2.45	9.8	2.5	5.7	0.8	-4	-0.2	0.07
2007	TBA	MLB	28	1	1	0	34	0	36¹	36	17	26	7	31.7%	.259	-16	1.49	3.72	4.38	7.2	3.7	5.1	1.6	-1	5.1	0.03
2008	DUR	AAA	29	4	5	1	28	0	44²	32	11	53	2	42.2%	.288	12	0.96	2.62	3.89	7.6	2.6	7.3	0.6	3	7.9	—
2008	TBA	MLB	29	0	0	0	5	0	6¹	5	4	8	0	20.0%	.333	6	1.42	7.14	7.50	9.0	6.0	10.5	0.0	0	-1.1	0.03
2009	TBA	MLB	30	3	3	1	42	3	51²	50	23	43	7	39.0%	.290	6	1.41	4.54	4.49	8.7	3.4	6.8	1.2	-0	5.3	0.57

Breakout: 16%   Improve: 38%   Collapse: 36%   Attrition: 20%   Comparables: Joe Black, Jim Brosnan, Rich Monteleone, Mel Queen

Salas had spent portions of the last three seasons in the big leagues, but he was in Durham for most of 2008. A converted infielder, he has a lightning arm that delivers his mid-90s cutter with ease; lamentably, it's his only real pitch. He dares to mix in a slider on occasion, but it's a flat and sloppy thing, and if you're being pressed into surviving on cutters alone, they had better be in Mariano Rivera territory. The cutter that Salas has is good, but it's not *that* good, and that is why he's just an extra arm.

James Shields

Bats: R   Throws: R   Height: 6' 4"   Weight: 215   Born: December 20, 1981   Age: 27

YEAR	TEAM	LVL	AGE	W	L	SV	G	GS	IP	H	BB	SO	HR	GB%	BABIP	STUFF	WHIP	ERA	DERA	EqH9	EqBB9	EqSO9	EqHR9	DEF	VORP	SN/WX
2006	DUR	AAA	24	3	2	0	10	10	61¹	60	6	64	3	53.3%	.352	20	1.08	2.65	4.69	10.3	1.3	6.8	0.8	-1	5.6	—
2006	TBA	MLB	24	6	8	0	21	21	124²	141	38	104	18	43.8%	.334	8	1.44	4.84	4.56	9.7	2.7	6.7	1.3	-4	14.6	2.20
2007	TBA	MLB	25	12	8	0	31	31	215	202	36	184	28	45.3%	.287	17	1.11	3.85	3.99	7.2	1.4	6.5	1.2	-2	45.2	5.73
2008	TBA	MLB	26	14	8	0	33	33	215	208	40	160	24	47.4%	.290	14	1.15	3.56	3.64	9.5	1.6	6.1	1.1	-8	43.3	5.36
2009	TBA	MLB	27	12	8	0	28	28	183¹	186	43	135	21	45.0%	.290	25	1.25	3.92	3.92	9.1	1.9	6.1	1.0	-1	29.6	4.64

Breakout: 23%   Improve: 56%   Collapse: 11%   Attrition: 14%   Comparables: Danny Haren, Curt Schilling, David Bush, Chris Bosio

Few pitchers can produce the kind of numbers that Shields has by pitching his way. He throws his fastball less than 40 percent of the time, using it as more of a trick pitch to throw hitters off when they're looking for his changeup or slider. The scouting term for this is "pitching backwards," and even those that can do it well are generally relegated to back-of-the-rotation status. Shields is different than most backwards pitchers, however; he actually has good velocity, his command is impeccable, and his changeup really is that good. He makes it look easy, and he should be an above-average starter for quite some time.

Andrew Sonnanstine

Bats: L **Throws: R** **Height: 6' 3"** **Weight: 185** **Born: March 18, 1983** **Age: 26**

YEAR	TEAM	LVL	AGE	W	L	SV	G	GS	IP	H	BB	SO	HR	GB%	BABIP	STUFF	WHIP	ERA	DERA	EqH9	EqBB9	EqSO9	EqHR9	DEF	VORP	SN/WX
2006	MNT	AA	23	15	8	0	28	28	185¹	151	34	153	15	45.0%	.276	-8	1.00	2.67	5.70	9.9	2.0	4.7	1.5	20	-1.8	—
2007	DUR	AAA	24	6	4	0	11	11	71	60	13	66	8	47.8%	.275	0	1.03	2.66	5.45	9.4	1.9	5.9	1.6	10	1.1	—
2007	TBA	MLB	24	6	10	0	22	22	130²	151	26	97	18	39.9%	.333	4	1.35	5.85	5.23	9.2	1.7	5.7	1.3	-9	0.1	1.20
2008	TBA	MLB	25	13	9	0	32	32	193¹	212	37	124	21	43.3%	.309	7	1.29	4.38	4.22	10.5	1.6	5.2	1.0	-13	18.3	2.98
2009	TBA	MLB	26	10	9	0	26	26	161²	180	38	102	22	43.0%	.300	18	1.34	4.58	4.55	9.9	1.8	5.2	1.2	-1	14.8	2.84

Breakout: 38% Improve: 60% Collapse: 17% Attrition: 15%   *Comparables: Doug Drabek, Jose Lima, Ray Burris, Dick Drago*

He's a modern-day Bob Tewksbury! He mixes up four pitches, changes speeds, adds sink or cut when he can, and absolutely pounds the strike zone with all of them. The basic theory here is to trust your defense, understand that you are going to get hit, never give out a freebie, and keep your team in the game for six or seven innings. What makes Sonnanstine special is his understanding of the role. There's not a pitcher in the big leagues who wasn't utterly overwhelming as an amateur, and to not only adjust to being something far less than that, but to downright embrace it and find success in it ... that requires a very unique and underrated mind-set.

Mitch Talbot

Bats: R **Throws: R** **Height: 6' 2"** **Weight: 200** **Born: October 17, 1983** **Age: 25**

YEAR	TEAM	LVL	AGE	W	L	SV	G	GS	IP	H	BB	SO	HR	GB%	BABIP	STUFF	WHIP	ERA	DERA	EqH9	EqBB9	EqSO9	EqHR9	DEF	VORP	SN/WX
2006	CCH	AA	22	6	4	1	18	17	90	94	29	96	4	52.5%	.360	17	1.37	3.40	6.01	11.8	3.4	6.3	0.8	-4	-3.7	—
2006	MNT	AA	22	4	3	0	10	10	66	51	18	59	2	51.8%	.277	19	1.05	1.91	4.18	9.1	2.8	5.1	0.6	4	9.5	—
2007	DUR	AAA	23	13	9	0	29	29	161	169	59	124	13	56.0%	.333	-11	1.42	4.53	6.13	11.8	3.8	4.8	1.2	0	-8.6	—
2008	DUR	AAA	24	13	9	0	28	28	161	165	35	141	9	54.6%	.332	9	1.24	3.86	5.20	10.2	2.2	5.1	0.8	1	6.8	—
2008	TBA	MLB	24	0	0	0	3	1	9²	16	11	5	3	37.8%	.382	-24	2.79	11.13	9.35	17.7	10.4	4.2	3.1	-2	-5.7	-0.29
2009	TBA	MLB	25	6	7	0	35	16	114	131	44	75	13	50.0%	.320	8	1.53	5.11	5.14	10.3	3.1	5.4	1.0	-1	2.9	0.93

Breakout: 17% Improve: 43% Collapse: 29% Attrition: 14%   *Comparables: Jimmy Jones, Shane Reynolds, Chris Holt, Wally Whitehurst*

In 161 Triple-A innings last year, Talbot walked 35. Then, during a late-season call-up to The Show, he walked 11 in 9⅔. That, our friends, is called nerves. We're sounding like a broken record here, but it's hard to stand out as a young pitcher in this system, and the recoil from Talbot's first shot sent him back to the end of the line. He is, believe it or not, a strike-thrower with an average fastball, a decent slider, and a sweet changeup, but he's just in the wrong organization. When it comes to young pitchers in Tampa Bay, average, decent, and nice gets you thrown overboard.

Dan Wheeler

Bats: R **Throws: R** **Height: 6' 3"** **Weight: 220** **Born: December 10, 1977** **Age: 31**

YEAR	TEAM	LVL	AGE	W	L	SV	G	GS	IP	H	BB	SO	HR	GB%	BABIP	STUFF	WHIP	ERA	DERA	EqH9	EqBB9	EqSO9	EqHR9	DEF	VORP	SN/WX
2006	HOU	MLB	28	3	5	9	75	0	71¹	58	24	68	5	30.3%	.279	19	1.15	2.52	2.89	7.3	2.6	7.8	0.5	2	25.8	3.82
2007	HOU	MLB	29	1	4	11	45	0	49²	46	13	56	8	37.3%	.306	16	1.19	5.07	4.38	8.0	2.0	9.5	1.3	-1	4.6	1.10
2007	TBA	MLB	29	0	5	0	25	0	25	28	10	26	3	40.5%	.347	-1	1.52	5.76	6.67	8.3	3.0	7.3	1.0	-1	-3.3	0.18
2008	TBA	MLB	30	5	6	13	70	0	66¹	44	22	53	10	28.6%	.192	-8	0.99	3.12	5.05	6.3	2.7	6.3	1.4	12	17.2	2.29
2009	TBA	MLB	31	3	3	7	49	0	55¹	51	18	47	8	37.0%	.270	10	1.24	3.96	3.93	8.2	2.5	7.0	1.2	-0	9.3	0.91

Breakout: 22% Improve: 45% Collapse: 35% Attrition: 15%   *Comparables: Steve Bedrosian, Jeff Reardon, Justin Speier, John Johnstone*

Wheeler made a nice recovery from a tough 2007 campaign that was his only bad year in the last five. He lives off of his 88-92 mph cut fastball; if you're right-handed he mixes in a slider, for left-handers it's a changeup. If he has one weakness, it's location, and when he misses, he misses up, and the balls fly out of the yard. He's with Tampa Bay for the next two years with a club option for a third; consistently good relievers can be worth their weight in gold.

LINEOUTS

Hitters

PLAYER	TEAM	LVL	AGE	PA	R	2B	3B	HR	RBI	BB	SO	SB-CS	EqBRR	AVG/OBP/SLG	EqAVG/EqOBP/EqSLG	EqA	VORP	WARP
SS A. Cannizaro	BUF	AAA	29	91	15	4	0	3	14	7	7	0-0	-0.8	.321/.374/.476	.259/.308/.400	.244	0.0	-0.1
	DUR	AAA	29	198	16	8	0	1	14	17	18	1-0	-0.4	.240/.311/.304	.189/.256/.251	.182	-17.9	-2.3
1B J. Guzman	DUR	AAA	23	464	52	23	0	20	72	19	103	1-2	-7.3	.248/.276/.438	.222/.252/.407	.223	-15.1	-2.0
RF N. Haynes*	DUR	AAA	28	297	28	8	2	2	24	11	59	13-3	1.1	.253/.287/.318	.192/.224/.256	.165	-32.0	-2.9
	TBA	MLB	28	47	3	0	0	0	3	3	12	4-1	0.6	.227/.277/.227	.227/.277/.227	.195	-2.9	-0.2
C M. Hernandez	IND	AAA	29	271	29	14	2	3	17	17	35	0-2	-1.5	.266/.317/.373	.220/.267/.315	.198	-16.9	-1.5
C J. Jefferies*	HUD	A-	20	264	32	16	3	2	41	21	22	1-1	-1.7	.315/.379/.433	.265/.314/.376	.239	-2.2	-0.6
OF D. Jennings	VRO	A+	21	102	17	5	1	2	6	14	16	5-2	1.1	.259/.360/.412	.216/.307/.364	.242	-2.4	1.0
SS E. Johnson#	DUR	AAA	24	427	49	26	5	9	50	33	104	15-3	2.6	.261/.322/.424	.231/.291/.390	.237	-7.5	-0.3
3B C. Nowak	MNT	AA	25	535	80	35	4	15	77	55	78	6-5	-1.3	.295/.381/.486	.217/.284/.364	.226	-17.7	-1.8
	DUR	AAA	25	61	7	2	0	0	4	7	12	0-1	-0.7	.315/.393/.352	.259/.344/.296	.227	-1.2	-0.3
1B C. Richard*	DUR	AAA	34	539	82	32	4	26	88	55	127	5-0	0.5	.293/.375/.546	.231/.310/.443	.259	6.2	0.1

Andy Cannizaro is a 30-year-old organizational player who's served in four different organizations over the last two years; his ability to play anywhere on the infield will keep him employed. ⊘ Once the recipient of the biggest bonus in Dominican history, **Joel Guzman** grew his way out of shortstop and is now a sluggish, one-dimensional corner infielder whose approach at the plate is to swing at everything. ⊘ An undersized burner, outfielder **Nathan Haynes** is no more than a minor league insurance policy. ⊘ The ultimate minor league catcher, **Michel Hernandez** has toiled with six different organizations in the past six years; last season he saw his first big-league action in five years, and at least found some form of stability when the Rays re-signed him. ⊘ A third-round pick out of UC Davis, catcher **Jacob Jefferies** is an athletic defender with a good approach, outstanding contact skills, and questionable power. ⊘ While 2008 became a lost season due to his shoulder and back issues, outfielder **Desmond Jennings** remains one of the toolsiest players in the system, and the healthy version received raves from scouts in the Arizona Fall League. ⊘ Speedster **Elliot Johnson** bounced back a bit in his second Triple-A season, but not enough to bounce back onto the radar in an organization this deep. ⊘ **Chris Nowak** is a massive third baseman who has put up consistent numbers in the minors, but scouts would be higher on him if he wasn't 26 and barely out of Double-A. ⊘ Former Oriole **Chris Richard** has been reduced to Triple-A performer at this point in his career, but he's hoping that a 921 OPS at Durham will get him another chance.

Pitchers

PLAYER	TEAM	LVL	AGE	W	L	SV	IP	H	BB	SO	HR	GB%	BABIP	STUFF	WHIP	ERA	DERA	EqH9	EqBB9	EqSO9	EqHR9	DEF	VORP
N. Barnese	HUD	A-	19	5	3	0	66	52	24	84	1	53.1%	.319	23	1.15	2.45	6.94	10.0	4.8	5.2	0.8	2	-8.7
K. Birkins*	DUR	AAA	27	2	3	0	40²	57	28	29	4	56.8%	.381	-30	2.09	7.52	8.31	13.8	6.7	3.9	1.4	-1	-11.7
	TBA	MLB	27	0	0	0	10	5	5	7	0	56.0%	.208	2	1.00	0.90	2.00	5.0	5.0	6.0	0.0	1	5.4
A. Cobb	CGA	A	20	9	7	0	139²	113	35	97	16	58.7%	.248	-22	1.06	3.29	7.46	10.4	3.6	2.8	2.5	15	-24.9
J. Cummings	DUR	AAA	31	8	3	1	87²	76	23	77	10	44.6%	.286	-5	1.13	2.87	4.61	8.6	2.6	5.1	1.4	5	9.2
M. Moore*	PRI	Rk	19	2	2	0	54¹	30	19	77	0	63.6%	.254	21	0.90	1.66	6.98	7.7	5.5	5.0	0.7	0	-7.5
E. Morlan	MNT	AA	22	4	2	1	47	44	15	45	5	31.2%	.295	-8	1.26	3.64	5.64	10.1	3.0	5.4	1.6	2	-0.2
H. Rollins	VRO	A+	23	5	11	0	136¹	118	27	115	15	47.3%	.266	-32	1.06	3.30	6.68	10.8	2.5	4.3	2.3	9	-14.7
	MNT	AA	23	1	1	0	25	22	6	23	2	41.2%	.308	6	1.12	2.88	5.32	10.2	2.5	5.7	1.2	3	0.7
J. Ryu	DUR	AAA	25	1	2	0	24²	26	9	19	1	58.2%	.342	-6	1.42	4.37	5.32	10.3	3.4	4.6	0.8	0	0.7
D. Thayer	DUR	AAA	27	3	1	9	68¹	73	24	76	2	44.8%	.354	5	1.42	2.77	3.84	10.8	3.4	6.7	0.4	-2	12.8

A third-round pick in 2007, righty **Nick Barnese** has two plus pitches, a low-90s fastball and a plus curve, and the Rays think he has breakout potential in his full-season debut? ⊘ Left-hander **Kirt Birkins** got in some early-season innings as an extra lefty, but he's looking for work after Triple-A hitters smacked him around for a .331 opponent's average. ⊘ Undersized righty **Alex Cobb** has one of the better curveballs in the system, and just enough velocity to be seen as a real prospect and not just a trick pitcher. ⊘ After ten seasons in the minors without a single call-up, right-hander **Jeremy Cummings** considered retirement after pitching for the US Olympic team before re-upping with the Rays. ⊘ Entering the 2008 over-slot sweepstakes, the Rays gave $1.5 million to second-round pick **Kyle Lobstein**, who was seen by some as the top lefty high-schooler before a disappointing spring. ⊘ **Matt Moore** is a lightly regarded eighth-round pick out of a New Mexico high school, a beefy left-hander who opened eyes in 2008 by flashing 95 mph heat and a massive curveball; in a system that hardly needs one, he's a sleeper. ⊘ Seen as a top relief prospect when acquired in the Delmon Young deal, righty **Eduardo Morlan** lost some heat on his fastball and was left off of the 40-man roster, leading to Milwaukee's taking him in the Rule 5 draft. ⊘ Like many finesse pitchers, **Heath Rollins** took a small step backwards as he moved up a level—but he can't afford many more. ⊘ **Jae-Kuk Ryu** won't especially be missed, but he will miss most of 2009 after elbow surgery. ⊘ With a pro-career ERA of 2.34, right-hander **Dale Thayer** and his slider are going to get a look at some point, but scouts think his lack of velocity in a set-up pitch will hold him back in the big leagues.

MANAGER: JOE MADDON

YEAR	TEAM	W-L	Pythag +/–	Avg PC	100+ P	120+ P	QS	BQS	REL	REL w Zero R	IBB	Subs	PH	PH Avg	PH HR	SB2	CS2	SB3	CS3	SAC Att	SAC %	POS SAC	Squeeze	Swing	In Play
2006	TBA	61-101	-3	93.0	49	1	62	5	444	228	39	68	80	.225	1	109	45	24	7	64	54.7%	32	4	153	112
2007	TBA	66-96	0	97.1	80	0	69	12	483	258	31	16	80	.159	1	114	43	16	4	48	70.8%	33	4	129	92
2008	TBA	97-65	5	96.0	71	0	77	4	448	289	29	50	131	.186	3	113	38	28	10	41	56.1%	20	1	135	94

When Joe Maddon came to camp spouting his "9=8" slogan, it seemed like another version of Pancho Villa's supposed last words: "Don't let it end like this. Tell them I said something." After all, Maddon was entering his third year at the helm, and though the team's indisputable failures in the first two seasons were clearly more the fault of a neglected roster than anything he had done or failed to do, even as pragmatic a front office as that of the Rays might prefer to make a change after yet another flop season. The slogan meant that nine committed players could win one of eight playoff spots, and captured some of the "impossible dream" spirit of the effort of winning the team's first pennant; perhaps its true measure of success is that it grabbed the imagination of a group of players who had every right to be skeptical. However, it also shortchanged Maddon's own contribution, which was to guide the club to a 180-degree reversal in two key categories, WXRL and defensive efficiency. The Rays went worst-to-first in both categories from 2007 to 2008. Maddon the tactician was not always the equal of Maddon the motivator; handicapped by many injuries, he tried his best to patch by creating platoons at designated hitter and right field, but production at both positions was weak, and the usage required him to pinch-hit more often than any manager in the AL, although, try as he might, he could not find a successful pinch-hitter. The Rays were also a poor baserunning club (23rd in the majors in EQBRR) despite leading the league in steals with an acceptable success rate. Finally, his failure to use his lefty relievers in spot matchups opened him to criticism during the playoffs. However, Maddon did show imagination in embracing Ben Zobrist's unexpected power surge and in turning to the inexperienced David Price in key playoff situations in the absence of an experienced closer, reflecting an adaptability which suits a ballclub in transition on so many fronts at once.

Texas Rangers

When Justinian I ascended the throne of what we now call the Byzantine Empire in 527 AD, he didn't much care for the state of affairs he'd inherited. Rather than accept a world in which the heartland of the old Roman Empire had been overrun by barbarians for more than a century, he decided to ask for the impossible: he wanted it all back, to dial the clock back to the good old days. He snapped up a couple of effective leaders—the famed Belisarius, and the underrated Narses—to make it so, decided to hang the expense, and damned if they didn't do it, getting back all of Italy's boot and North Africa and almost making the Mediterranean a Roman lake all over again.

Now, history's always going to provide us with plenty of lessons about impossible challenges and the people foolish enough to take them up. They even turn the trick now and again, sometimes briefly, and sometimes with more lasting effect. And to their credit, the Rangers have decided enough's enough. The last year they had a rotation that ranked in the top half of the league in Support-Neutral metrics was in 1996, when they were fourth in the AL in the rate of Support-Neutral Lineup-Adjusted Value (or SNLVA Rate, or SNLVA_R). Since then, they've had the worst or next-worst rotation in the circuit in seven of the last ten years. The "exceptions" were in 2004-06, when the Rangers finished with the twelfth-best rotation in the league for three years in a row. Surely you remember those summers, Rangers fans—they were the salad days, when you just couldn't wait to go see Chan Ho Park give you five innings without doing too much harm.

As horrendous as the track record has been, it hasn't been because successive general managers haven't

tried to fix the problem. From among the high-profile moves of the last decade or so, they've signed Kenny Rogers, Mark Clark, Ismael Valdez, Jason Jennings, and John Thomson to seven-figure annual salaries, and traded for Aaron Sele, John Burkett, and Esteban Loaiza to do likewise. More steeply still, they've handed out contracts with average annual values of $10 million or more to Park and Kevin Millwood and Vicente Padilla. In short, it isn't like they haven't thrown money at the problem and called it management. Among the 20 best seasons for Rangers starting pitchers in franchise history, you'll find two from the last ten years, and just one delivered from among the big-ticket pickups: Rogers' 2002 campaign, when he went 13-8 with a 3.84 ERA, and the immortal Ryan Drese's 14-win season in '04. Both pitchers generated 5.4 SNLVAR in these solid yet subhistoric seasons. The best recent work's been done by Millwood and Padilla in 2006; they just barely get into the top 50, and you have to move down to the 105th rung to find the next starter season on the list from the last three years: Brandon McCarthy's 2007 introduction to pitching in Texas.

So, a massive amount of money has been paid out while bringing back so little return—that's the cost of doing business, right? If you're going to throw money at name pitchers, you take risks, and pitching's the most unstable commodity in the industry. Think again on what this means: not only have the Rangers' free-agent signings been bad news, mentioning McCarthy affords us the opportunity to note that their trades haven't turned out so well either. Trading for McCarthy is recent and galling in part because one of the men traded for him, power lefty John Danks, has already done more for the White Sox in one season than anyone really expects

---

RANGERS PROSPECTUS

2008 record: 79-83; Second place in AL West

Pythagenport record: 75-87

Runs scored per game: 5.57 (1st in AL)

Runs allowed per game: 6.04 (14th in AL)

Team EqA: .278 (1st in AL)

2008 Batters Age: 28.1 (5th-youngest in AL)

2008 Pitchers Age: 28.6 (6th-oldest in AL)

Ballpark: Rangers Ballpark in Arlington; Slight hitter's park; Park Factor of 1.018

2008: The Rangers discover that allowing 967 runs takes much of the fun out of scoring 901 runs.

2009: The cavalry's on its way, but continued run prevention problems head them off at the pass.

from McCarthy at any point in his career. Before giving current general manager Jon Daniels a mulligan for this move, you might have to ask yourself if he wouldn't rather apply it to the decision to trade away Armando Galarraga to the Tigers before camps opened last spring, to make space for Jennings on the 40-man roster. Here again, think on what this adds up to: not only have the Rangers' acquisitions via free agency and trades not delivered on the investments the organization has made on them, neither has a single product of the franchise's farm system done anything to pick up the slack in the last decade. That's not for lack of talent they've developed. Danks and Edinson Volquez (dealt to get Josh Hamilton, which is defensible enough) enjoyed fine years in other people's uniforms last season, seasons that would have ranked among the ten best in Rangers franchise history. And they're only just getting started, so at least somebody's done some good scouting in the organization.

So the Rangers have said enough, and it isn't a season too soon. The 2008 season had been barely dead a week when club president Nolan Ryan, famed almost as much for his almost-religious devotion to conditioning during his career as he was for his feats on the field, announced his decision to take personal responsibility for Rangers pitching at every level of the organization. As part of Ryan's new "get tough" mandate, he's stressing that pitchers need to build up arm strength, that pitchers won't be coddled, that risks will be taken, and innings will get pitched. It's the sort of tough talk that goes over well as a sound bite. The team followed up with a ten-day conditioning mini-camp in November that was attended by a number of the younger pitchers (and was apparently universally skipped by the veterans). We'll see what it adds up to; Ryan isn't wrong to want to see a more fit set of moundsmen, and the offseason chatter came after the club had already made a point of ratcheting up minor league workloads and getting more aggressive with in-season promotions. And in point of fact, when your pitching does as badly as the Rangers' has for as long as it has, it's time for public statements as well as comparatively quiet action.

The timing also seems convenient, in that while Ryan's talking tough, Daniels' player development program has been assiduously assembling pitching talent through the draft, signing overseas amateurs, and adding lesser-known live arms at the back end of the deals that have drawn so much fire down on Daniels. While fans will lock in on whether or not Matt Harrison makes the Teixeira trade of '07 look good or not, the real key to the deal is more likely to be Neftali Soto, as the trade blossoms into the gift that keeps on giving. While

Thomas Diamond tries to live down being the busted third of the once-famed "DVD" trio and the only one still in the house, the more noteworthy development is how he's about to be outstripped by arms like those of Feliz, Michael Main, Derek Holland, Tommy Hunter, and more besides. This is not to make excuses for dealing away Danks or Volquez, but to some extent Daniels' decision-making has been built on the bet that this player development program was going to bear fruit.

As part of the desire to make changes, they had indulged themselves in some in-season scapegoating by canning pitching coach Mark Connor, who was a holdover from the franchise's Showalter period, and bullpen coach Dom Chiti, part of former team president John Hart's clique. To find their new pitching coach, they looked forward to the offseason and finding the best possible candidate to participate in Ryan's new initiative. While they interviewed formerly well-regarded pitching gurus Rick Peterson (a colleague of Washington's from their days in Oakland, and an outspoken theorist when he was in vogue) and Dave Wallace, in the end they hired Mike Maddux away from the Brewers. Already familiar to Ryan from when Greg's older brother got his first break in coaching with a Ryan-owned farm team in 2000, Maddux arrives with an excellent reputation from his days in Milwaukee. Helping to identify who to round out the rotation with beyond Millwood and Padilla will be the noisy, obvious project, but it's notable that Maddux comes to town with more than a few relievers refurbished to utility to his credit.

That latter gift's going to matter more than a little for a Rangers team that did a horrifically bad job of managing the hand-offs of ballgames from its starters to its relievers. The term we like to use is "transition innings," those frames where a manager sends his starter out there, has cause to reconsider it, and has to go to the pen before the inning's done. If you remember that sport they play in suburban mallparks near you called hockey, you might compare this to a well-executed line change, or defending against a power play. However you wish to frame it conceptually, it's another something involving pitching that the Rangers do really badly. Last year, they were the worst team in the AL (see Table 1).

To some extent, this reflects a few different things at once—in managerial tendencies, we can see that the Orioles' Dave Trembley loved to grab a hook in the middle of an inning more than anybody, doing so 105 times, although with his rotation, you couldn't blame him. Similarly, Bob Melvin in Arizona was the most likely skipper in the game to hand his pen clean innings after letting his starters finish their own frames. Trembley and the Tigers' Jim Leyland saw these situations

Table 1. 2008 Transition Inning Performance, Starters and Relievers Combined

AL					NL				
Team	IP	R	RA/9	Leads Lost	Team	IP	R	RA/9	Leads Lost
Rays	65	75	10.4	1	Astros	64	95	13.4	3
Blue Jays	60	100	7	15.0	Cubs	55	82	13.4	7
Angels	65	117	16.2	8	Giants	64	109	15.3	6
Red Sox	56	105	3	16.9	Dodgers	60	104	15.6	3
White Sox	77	147	6	17.2	Marlins	54	96	16.0	5
Athletics	67	128	2	17.2	Braves	55	98	16.0	4
Royals	58	113	17.5	0	Mets	62	111	16.1	7
Indians	61	124	18.3	8	Cardinals	55	101	16.5	3
Tigers	87	184	19.0	12	Brewers	55	106	17.4	5
Orioles	104.1	234	20.2	10	Phillies	66	130	17.7	8
Yankees	65	148	20.5	4	Reds	59	121	18.5	4
Mariners	74	169	20.6	7	Pirates	61	126	18.6	3
Twins	62	146	21.2	5	Snakes	45	94	18.8	4
Rangers	66	156	21.3	5	Padres	52	109	18.9	6
					Nationals	58	125	19.4	9
					Rockies	68	165	21.8	9

blow up in their faces more than for anyone else; in contrast, the Royals' Trey Hillman didn't lose a single lead in these situations, and the pennant-winning Rays and Joe Maddon blew it just once. But to bring this back to the Rangers, this was the sort of thing where an already-poor rotation had to deal with the additional pain of seeing these situations go from bad to worse. While some of that's a matter of personnel—the "who" that gets pitched in these situations—some it is also on Washington for his in-inning management of his pen. The Rangers didn't do a good job of staunching the bleeding, and as we already know, this was working with the rotation equivalent of a hemophiliac. Since the Rangers haven't aggressively made over their pen this winter, improvement in this quarter is going to have to involve Washington and Maddux improving the unit's performance in these situations. That can be through a combination of hooking starters at the end of their frames (like Melvin) or finding ways to avoid blowing leads (like Hillman or Maddon or Geren).

The lineup will also require some sorting out, of course, especially in the wake of Milton Bradley's defection as a free agent. While Marlon Byrd, Nelson Cruz, and David Murphy might make for a nice rotation in the corners on either side of Josh Hamilton, it's also not exactly overpowering. Deciding that both Hank Blalock and Chris Davis shouldn't play third any more has a reasonable amount of sense to it—Davis was the team's first baseman of the future, and Blalock's body might not be up to the challenge. Unfortunately, by leaving third wide-open, Daniels created controversy by hauling shortstop Michael Young in to tell him that he'd be at the hot corner, apparently in anticipation of bringing up Elvis Andrus at short. While the Gold Glove Award isn't really a proof of defensive greatness, Young had just won it as a shortstop, and that's the sort of dignity that makes this more a matter of managing a perhaps understandably proud person and making a sales pitch. Young has understandably bridled and demanded a trade, which seems unlikely; barring the Rangers eating some large chunk of $16 million annual salary through 2013. Daniels has made the suggestion that Young's situation is like Cal Ripken's, but it's important to remember that was as much about Davey Johnson sending a message about who ran the team in 1996 as any other consideration, and was certainly not really all that much about how important it was to take Manny Alexander's future seriously. The point made, O's GM Pat Gillick picked up Mike Bordick in the offseason, and Ripken went to third. By picking this particular fight for prospect Andrus' benefit, the scenario only gets worse if Andrus struggles.

In the end, bringing change is as much about managing people and expectations as it is crafting overarching plans or issuing new edicts to reshape the order of things. The emperor Justinian may have demanded a return to the old days, and he may have seen it achieved in his lifetime. It also began to go to pieces as quickly as it was put together, because the Byzantines lacked the organizational strength—economic as well as in terms of manpower and talent—to make their efforts stick. What needs doing in Texas adds up to more than a few well-growled sentiments from one of the game's most readily identified greats, and they know it and have said as much; it will rely on much more than carefully executed planning, it will also require the sensible management of the assets the team has on hand. The Rangers are already working towards the day when they won't be a laughingstock, and with the rest of the division in various states of disrepair, it isn't implausible to suggest that they'll be confronted with the additional challenge of transitioning young pitching talent while climbing back into a title chase.

HITTERS

Elvis Andrus SS

Bats: R   Throws: R   Height: 6' 0"   Weight: 185   Born: August 26, 1988   Age: 20

YEAR	TEAM	LVL	AGE	PA	R	2B	3B	HR	RBI	BB	SO	SB	CS	EqBRR	AVG	OBP	SLG	EqAVG	EqOBP	EqSLG	EqA	VORP	WARP	DEFENSE	
2006	ROM	A	17	478	67	25	4	3	50	36	91	23	15	-0.4	.265	.324	.362	.209	.254	.292	.186	-39.3	-4.6	104-SS	-23
2007	MYR	A+	18	440	59	20	3	3	37	44	88	25	7	1.8	.244	.330	.335	.195	.260	.272	.190	-38.3	-1.7	98-SS	-2
2007	BAK	A+	18	123	19	2	0	2	12	10	19	15	8	-2.1	.300	.369	.373	.239	.295	.301	.215	-5.9	0.4	28-SS	4
2008	FRI	AA	19	535	82	19	2	4	65	38	91	54	16	6.5	.295	.350	.367	.247	.295	.316	.224	-21.8	1.1	108-SS	8
2009	TEX	MLB	20	586	66	25	4	4	42	38	119	33	12	2.9	.247	.299	.332	.243	.298	.336	.230	-5.5	0.7	137-SS	0

Breakout: 64%   Improve: 79%   Collapse: 5%   Attrition: 3.0%   Comparables: Luis Rivas, Edgar Renteria, Denny Gonzalez, Omar Infante

Andrus gets bandied around as one of the top shortstop prospects in the game, and it's easy to see why—he's loaded with defensive tools, runs extremely well, and he hit nearly .300 as a teenager at Double-A. That's a lot to be excited about, but it also ignores some massive holes in his game, including very little in the way of power and walks, and a consistently high error total due to sloppy play. He's got all the skills to be an everyday shortstop, but more the type that hits at the bottom of the order, as opposed to a future stud.

Joaquin Arias 2B

Bats: R   Throws: R   Height: 6' 1"   Weight: 165   Born: September 21, 1984   Age: 24

YEAR	TEAM	LVL	AGE	PA	R	2B	3B	HR	RBI	BB	SO	SB	CS	EqBRR	AVG	OBP	SLG	EqAVG	EqOBP	EqSLG	EqA	VORP	WARP	DEFENSE			
2006	OKL	AAA	21	525	56	14	10	4	49	19	64	26	10	-1.6	.268	.296	.361	.243	.269	.335	.213	-25.7	-1.2	122-SS	-7		
2008	OKL	AAA	23	460	59	15	9	7	49	19	53	23	5	0.8	.296	.329	.421	.256	.284	.362	.229	-12.2	-0.7	44-SS	-3	40-2B	-2
2008	TEX	MLB	23	120	15	7	3	0	9	7	12	4	1	0.1	.291	.345	.409	.291	.350	.409	.268	4.2	-0.3	25-2B	-7		
2009	TEX	MLB	24	498	56	21	6	6	43	21	67	19	6	2.2	.259	.293	.371	.255	.291	.376	.236	-0.8	0.1	117-2B	-6		

Breakout: 36%   Improve: 59%   Collapse: 16%   Attrition: 12%   Comparables: Alberto Gonzalez, William Bergolla, Miguel Cairo, Manny Alexander

Arias came back from a 2007 season lost to shoulder surgery to deliver much as he had before as a hitter—not walking much, pelting enough singles with a line-drive stroke, and trying to stretch defenses with a bit of basepaths derring-do. The problem is that the shoulder injury might effectively be the difference between a future as a second-division starter and that of a utilityman; he can no longer gun grounders from the hole with the same strength, and his bat won't carry him as a regular anywhere but short.

Hank Blalock DH

Bats: L   Throws: R   Height: 6' 1"   Weight: 200   Born: November 21, 1980   Age: 28

YEAR	TEAM	LVL	AGE	PA	R	2B	3B	HR	RBI	BB	SO	SB	CS	EqBRR	AVG	OBP	SLG	EqAVG	EqOBP	EqSLG	EqA	VORP	WARP	DEFENSE			
2006	TEX	MLB	25	646	76	26	3	16	89	51	98	1	0	-1.5	.266	.325	.401	.251	.317	.382	.245	0.7	-0.2	120-3B	-5		
2007	TEX	MLB	26	232	32	16	3	10	33	21	38	4	1	1.7	.293	.358	.543	.285	.353	.556	.301	17.7	1.6	38-3B	-1		
2008	FRI	AA	27	23	5	3	0	0	4	4	5	1	0	-0.1	.421	.522	.579	.250	.348	.350	.250	0.0	0.0	5-1B	0		
2008	TEX	MLB	27	281	37	19	1	12	38	19	40	1	0	-3.7	.287	.338	.508	.284	.338	.518	.287	14.0	1.6	33-1B	3	30-3B	-2
2009	TEX	MLB	28	431	51	22	2	15	60	35	71	2	1	-0.8	.265	.327	.442	.261	.326	.447	.266	8.0	1.2	103-3B	-5		

Breakout: 7%   Improve: 31%   Collapse: 35%   Attrition: 12%   Comparables: Chad Tracy, Roy Howell, Ed Kranepool, Jim Spencer

The saga of Blalock's peregrinations—from one infield corner to the other to DH, or from the DL and back again—on some level recall the equally unfortunate story of Larry Parrish, the star third baseman from the '80s who didn't really turn out quite as well as hoped. While there's some small hope that surgery on his shoulder might keep him in play for either corner, the Rangers expect he'll DH for them in the last year of his five-year deal. If they get 400 PA from him, they'll count themselves fortunate, but as PECOTA suggests, there's a reasonable chance that he outperforms that baseline projection.

Brandon Boggs   OF   Bats: S   Throws: R   Height: 6' 0"   Weight: 190   Born: January 9, 1983   Age: 26

YEAR	TEAM	LVL	AGE	PA	R	2B	3B	HR	RBI	BB	SO	SB	CS	EqBRR	AVG	OBP	SLG	EqAVG	EqOBP	EqSLG	EqA	VORP	WARP	DEFENSE			
2006	BAK	A+	23	327	48	20	4	8	37	40	63	13	4	-0.6	.261	.352	.444	.186	.260	.315	.203	-22.7	-3.1	64-CF	-16	10-LF	0
2007	BAK	A+	24	108	17	9	1	4	17	14	28	5	1	-0.1	.250	.361	.500	.186	.269	.371	.222	-4.8	-0.9	17-LF	-2	5-CF	-3
2007	FRI	AA	24	429	69	21	4	19	55	70	103	10	4	2.5	.266	.385	.508	.215	.321	.406	.255	0.3	0.7	93-CF	-1	6-LF	-2
2008	OKL	AAA	25	76	12	4	3	0	6	7	20	1	1	-0.0	.309	.368	.456	.261	.316	.377	.242	-0.3	0.1	13-LF	1	4-CF	0
2008	TEX	MLB	25	334	30	17	4	8	41	44	93	3	2	-1.4	.226	.333	.399	.225	.339	.418	.264	0.7	0.1	65-LF	-6		
2009	TEX	MLB	26	299	35	16	3	9	35	30	79	4	2	0.5	.234	.315	.419	.231	.313	.424	.256	0.6	0.6	73-LF	-1		

Breakout: 38%   Improve: 58%   Collapse: 23%   Attrition: 39%   Comparables: Duane Walker, Jose Cruz, John Lowenstein, Ruben Rivera

While more was expected as far as Boggs' upside when he was picked in the fourth round of the '04 draft as a toolsy prospect out of Georgia Tech, he's in danger of being an organizational soldier stretched to fulfill a utility outfielder role. Although a switch-hitter, his pop is really all from the right-hand side, and he can be overpowered by high-velocity offerings. He's stretched in center, leaving you with an outfield reserve who only sticks if he strikes his skipper's fancy.

Milton Bradley   RF   Bats: S   Throws: R   Height: 6' 0"   Weight: 225   Born: April 15, 1978   Age: 31

YEAR	TEAM	LVL	AGE	PA	R	2B	3B	HR	RBI	BB	SO	SB	CS	EqBRR	AVG	OBP	SLG	EqAVG	EqOBP	EqSLG	EqA	VORP	WARP	DEFENSE	
2006	OAK	MLB	28	405	53	14	2	14	52	51	65	10	2	0.8	.276	.370	.447	.265	.369	.435	.283	19.0	2.3	90-RF	3
2007	OAK	MLB	29	75	6	4	0	2	7	8	14	2	1	-1.2	.292	.373	.446	.292	.382	.477	.296	4.5	0.4	14-CF	-1
2007	SDN	MLB	29	169	31	5	1	11	30	23	27	3	1	-1.2	.313	.414	.590	.336	.441	.657	.353	20.1	2.1	36-LF	-2
2008	TEX	MLB	30	509	78	32	1	22	77	80	112	5	3	-1.8	.321	.436	.563	.315	.436	.571	.337	56.2	5.7	18-RF	2
2009	CHN	MLB	31	504	84	27	1	22	78	74	109	8	3	-1.4	.294	.402	.525	.291	.398	.524	.311	37.9	3.9	119-DH	

Breakout: 9%   Improve: 29%   Collapse: 36%   Attrition: 11%   Comparables: Ken Singleton, Bob Nieman, Travis Hafner, Erubiel Durazo

Signing Bradley to an incentive-laden one-year deal gave the Rangers exactly the sort of season we've always expected he had in him, although exploiting a hitter-friendly ballpark to slug .679 at home (against .462 everywhere else) boosted him from a good season to down-ballot MVP consideration. It also propelled him to a three-year, $30 million deal with the Cubs that is every bit the risk that it sounds like, while potentially giving them a game-breaking bat from the left side who should help resolve their lineup's heavy tilt to the right. It isn't that Bradley won't play a good right field—he's athletic, not crippled up—it's that he'll probably hurt himself doing it. Let's just say this now—it's a very good thing indeed that he's not playing for the Lou Piniella of 20 years ago. The mercurial Bradley needs a softer touch, and the combination of a mellower Lou, several established stars in the clubhouse, and an adoring fan base should give Bradley the cushion he needs to operate at his best.

Marlon Byrd   OF   Bats: R   Throws: R   Height: 6' 0"   Weight: 235   Born: August 30, 1977   Age: 31

YEAR	TEAM	LVL	AGE	PA	R	2B	3B	HR	RBI	BB	SO	SB	CS	EqBRR	AVG	OBP	SLG	EqAVG	EqOBP	EqSLG	EqA	VORP	WARP	DEFENSE			
2006	NWO	AAA	28	179	20	9	0	7	29	16	31	3	1	-1.9	.271	.363	.465	.219	.292	.369	.231	-4.7	-0.4	17-CF	1	14-RF	-2
2006	WAS	MLB	28	228	28	8	1	5	18	22	47	3	3	0.9	.223	.317	.350	.232	.325	.359	.241	-3.2	-0.7	45-CF	-7	9-RF	0
2007	OKL	AAA	29	195	29	15	2	6	32	13	30	3	2	0.0	.358	.415	.568	.279	.333	.458	.268	7.4	1.1	17-RF	1	12-LF	5
2007	TEX	MLB	29	454	60	17	8	10	70	29	88	5	3	2.9	.307	.355	.459	.300	.350	.465	.279	22.9	2.3	56-CF	-4	35-RF	-1
2008	TEX	MLB	30	462	70	28	4	10	53	46	62	7	2	-0.3	.298	.380	.462	.297	.383	.474	.295	25.7	3.0	49-CF	-1	31-RF	2
2009	TEX	MLB	31	411	53	20	3	10	48	32	73	6	3	-0.2	.271	.335	.426	.267	.333	.431	.266	7.3	1.5	98-CF	-4		

Breakout: 11%   Improve: 31%   Collapse: 34%   Attrition: 24%   Comparables: Shane Spencer, Derek Bell, Mike McCormick, Jason Michaels

Having resurrected his career with the Rangers so effectively, it seems harsh to start talking about him already heading toward his down slope, but he's not young, center isn't really a position he should play every day, and the speed from his days as a prospect has withered with age. He's an extremely useful fourth outfielder worth rotating in with some regularity to get a dose of OBP, and makes for a nice fall-back option on a team counting on Hamilton and Blalock.

Frank Catalanotto — DH

Bats: L Throws: R Height: 6' 0" Weight: 195 Born: April 27, 1974 Age: 35

YEAR	TEAM	LVL	AGE	PA	R	2B	3B	HR	RBI	BB	SO	SB	CS	EqBRR	AVG	OBP	SLG	EqAVG	EqOBP	EqSLG	EqA	VORP	WARP	DEFENSE			
2006	TOR	MLB	32	499	56	36	2	7	56	52	37	1	3	-2.8	.300	.376	.439	.284	.369	.425	.277	17.8	1.5	86-LF	-3		
2007	TEX	MLB	33	377	52	20	4	11	44	28	37	2	1	-0.4	.260	.337	.444	.254	.332	.453	.268	8.5	0.8	55-LF	-3	11-1B	1
2008	TEX	MLB	34	278	28	23	1	2	21	20	29	1	1	0.7	.274	.342	.399	.275	.345	.413	.264	3.6	-0.4	25-1B	-2	19-LF	-6
2009	TEX	MLB	35	181	22	10	1	3	22	15	22	1	0	-0.4	.280	.349	.412	.276	.347	.416	.268	3.5	0.3	46-LF	-4		

Breakout: 20% Improve: 46% Collapse: 26% Attrition: 49% Comparables: Russ Snyder, Larry Biittner, Johnny Grubb, Dale Mitchell

Credit Cat for being one of the very few offense-oriented second-base prospects who wasn't derailed by concerns over his glove work at the keystone. Instead, he hit well enough to employ in the corners in his peak seasons, and that got him into real money as a fill-in starter at first, left, or DH for the Jays and Rangers. He's long since declined to "professional hitter" batsmanship, but it isn't his fault the Rangers will be paying him $6 million ($2 million to buy out his 2010 option). A career .289 pinch-hitter, it might be nice to see him show up on a NL contender down the stretch for a taste of October.

Nelson Cruz — RF

Bats: R Throws: R Height: 6' 3" Weight: 225 Born: July 1, 1980 Age: 28

YEAR	TEAM	LVL	AGE	PA	R	2B	3B	HR	RBI	BB	SO	SB	CS	EqBRR	AVG	OBP	SLG	EqAVG	EqOBP	EqSLG	EqA	VORP	WARP	DEFENSE			
2006	NAS	AAA	25	423	68	22	1	20	73	42	100	17	6	2.4	.302	.378	.528	.267	.336	.479	.277	19.4	2.5	86-RF	4	8-CF	1
2006	TEX	MLB	25	138	15	3	0	6	22	7	32	1	0	-0.2	.223	.261	.385	.209	.254	.364	.213	-5.0	-0.6	35-RF	-1		
2007	OKL	AAA	26	187	32	9	1	15	45	21	34	1	2	0.0	.352	.428	.698	.297	.372	.594	.313	20.8	2.1	44-RF	3		
2007	TEX	MLB	26	332	35	15	2	9	34	21	87	2	4	-0.9	.235	.287	.384	.232	.287	.399	.231	-10.0	-0.4	69-RF	2	13-LF	-1
2008	OKL	AAA	28	448	93	18	3	37	99	56	87	24	8	0.8	.342	.429	.695	.268	.348	.532	.292	31.4	2.6	95-RF	-3		
2008	TEX	MLB	28	133	19	9	1	7	26	17	28	3	1	-0.1	.330	.421	.609	.325	.421	.623	.340	15.2	1.7	31-RF	1		
2009	TEX	MLB	28	534	73	26	2	25	83	51	135	14	6	0.1	.260	.335	.484	.256	.333	.490	.280	12.0	2.5	125-RF	0		

Breakout: 18% Improve: 48% Collapse: 22% Attrition: 13% Comparables: Ivan Calderon, Carlos Lee, Sammy Sosa, Richard Hidalgo

Cruz's up-and-down career hit one of its upswings, as he re-stated his case for a lineup spot after being taken off of the 40-man roster at the end of camp. Eventually, the Rangers saw the error of their ways and brought him back in August, well after he'd belabored the point. Don't get worked up about that comp to Sosa—it's a comparison to the Sammy Sosa before his big '98 and the attendant spike in walks in his age-29 season. That was a good ballplayer, a guy you could count on for 30-40 homers, a little bit more than you'll get from Cruz, but he's been given Ron Washington's endorsement as the cleanup hitter of the present.

Chris Davis — 1B

Bats: L Throws: R Height: 6' 3" Weight: 210 Born: March 17, 1986 Age: 23

YEAR	TEAM	LVL	AGE	PA	R	2B	3B	HR	RBI	BB	SO	SB	CS	EqBRR	AVG	OBP	SLG	EqAVG	EqOBP	EqSLG	EqA	VORP	WARP	DEFENSE			
2006	SPO	A-	20	280	38	18	1	15	42	23	65	2	3	-2.2	.277	.343	.534	.210	.260	.405	.225	-16.9	-2.7	33-LF	-5	29-1B	-5
2007	BAK	A+	21	418	69	28	3	24	93	22	123	3	3	-1.6	.298	.340	.573	.238	.270	.446	.241	-2.2	-1.6	90-3B	-15		
2007	FRI	AA	21	124	21	7	0	12	25	13	27	0	0	-1.2	.294	.371	.688	.250	.320	.562	.289	8.5	0.8	29-3B	-1		
2008	FRI	AA	22	202	43	14	0	13	42	13	44	5	1	1.9	.333	.376	.618	.280	.320	.524	.281	12.1	0.4	42-1B	-4		
2008	OKL	AAA	22	127	25	7	1	10	31	13	29	2	0	1.0	.333	.402	.685	.283	.346	.566	.303	10.9	0.7	28-1B	-2		
2008	TEX	MLB	22	317	51	23	2	17	55	20	88	1	2	0.3	.285	.331	.549	.282	.331	.568	.291	17.4	0.4	45-1B	-3	31-3B	-11
2009	TEX	MLB	23	574	70	31	2	29	93	39	156	4	2	-0.0	.259	.312	.490	.255	.311	.496	.272	12.0	1.4	135-1B	-1		

Breakout: 27% Improve: 55% Collapse: 18% Attrition: 11% Comparables: Kelvin Moore, Mike Laga, Ryan Klesko, Steve DeAngelis

Davis's game-breaking power didn't merely pound pitching, it beat back all comers in an accelerated climb through the upper levels of the system to claim whatever big-league corner Blalock wasn't in by late June. Mike Laga? Ouch, but I guess it beats a comparison to Dave Hostetler; use Klesko as your guide, and enjoy the bopping to come. Something of a piece of furniture at third despite a strong arm, the Rangers are moving him across the diamond to stay.

German Duran 2B/3B

Bats: R **Throws: R** **Height: 5' 10"** **Weight: 185** **Born: August 3, 1984** **Age: 24**

YEAR	TEAM	LVL	AGE	PA	R	2B	3B	HR	RBI	BB	SO	SB	CS	EqBRR	AVG	OBP	SLG	EqAVG	EqOBP	EqSLG	EqA	VORP	WARP	DEFENSE			
2006	BAK	A+	21	503	81	31	2	13	72	35	89	15	9	-8.0	.284	.331	.446	.222	.261	.350	.213	-24.9	-2.4	49-SS	-12	44-2B	0
2007	FRI	AA	22	529	81	32	5	22	84	34	77	11	2	-1.4	.300	.352	.525	.259	.304	.457	.259	11.1	2.3	124-2B	3		
2008	OKL	AAA	23	86	12	3	2	1	6	7	12	0	1	-0.3	.260	.318	.390	.231	.282	.359	.220	-2.8	-0.1	14-2B	1		
2008	TEX	MLB	23	158	22	6	1	3	16	7	32	1	1	0.4	.231	.275	.350	.231	.279	.371	.226	-4.9	-1.0	25-3B	-2	11-2B	-4
2009	TEX	MLB	24	319	37	18	2	9	38	20	61	4	2	0.1	.264	.314	.432	.260	.313	.437	.260	7.3	1.1	77-2B	-2		

Breakout: 49% **Improve: 66%** **Collapse: 12%** **Attrition: 25%** **Comparables: Bill Hall, Tony Batista, Frank Bolling, Scott Hairston**

Not to be mistaken for Deutschland's greatest cover band of New Wave's greatest band, Duran was sucked into the infield mess created by various injuries to the famous people. Gifted with a quick bat that can get a bit pull-happy and working with an aggressive approach, he's a hacker with line-drive power. He might end up getting another opportunity after heading to winter ball to hone his hot-corner glove work; he has the arm for it, if not the other gifts you'd like, but given they were grooming him for a utility role, it's his best shot.

Josh Hamilton CF

Bats: L **Throws: L** **Height: 6' 4"** **Weight: 235** **Born: May 21, 1981** **Age: 28**

YEAR	TEAM	LVL	AGE	PA	R	2B	3B	HR	RBI	BB	SO	SB	CS	EqBRR	AVG	OBP	SLG	EqAVG	EqOBP	EqSLG	EqA	VORP	WARP	DEFENSE			
2006	HUD	A-	25	55	7	3	1	0	5	5	11	0	1	0.3	.260	.327	.360	.154	.200	.192	.091	-17.0	-1.3	5-RF	-1		
2007	LOU	AAA	26	45	9	1	0	4	8	5	9	3	0	0.6	.350	.422	.675	.317	.378	.610	.331	5.9	0.6	7-CF	0		
2007	CIN	MLB	26	337	52	17	2	19	47	33	65	3	3	-0.9	.292	.368	.554	.284	.363	.551	.299	27.0	3.2	62-CF	5	9-RF	1
2008	TEX	MLB	27	704	98	35	5	32	130	64	126	9	1	1.7	.304	.371	.530	.300	.370	.540	.306	55.9	4.8	103-CF	-4	33-RF	-6
2009	TEX	MLB	28	642	91	33	3	25	94	57	125	8	3	0.7	.284	.351	.483	.280	.350	.488	.286	27.6	3.6	150-CF	-10		

Breakout: 5% **Improve: 34%** **Collapse: 22%** **Attrition: 7%** **Comparables: Walt Bond, Paul O'Neill, Matt Holliday, Harry Anderson**

While it's a bit much to call Hamilton's story heroic—the man did make his own problems—he seems to have them beaten to everyone's satisfaction, plating an excellent 20.7 percent of all baserunners on base when he batted, second only to David DeJesus among everyday players in the majors. That and his staying healthy were the achievements worth remarking upon; his counting stats added up as a result, and he had the benefit of a friendly park. The interesting in-season tweak was his spiking walk rate in the second half, almost one every 10 PA, fueled by seven intentionals as the league decided they'd seen just about enough of his dropping the boom on them. While he's not a strong center fielder, they really don't have an in-house alternative unless Pedro Borbon or Greg Golson comes along fast. Is there any player we know less about as far as what to expect from here? Probably not, and more power to him.

Ian Kinsler 2B

Bats: R **Throws: R** **Height: 6' 0"** **Weight: 200** **Born: June 22, 1982** **Age: 27**

YEAR	TEAM	LVL	AGE	PA	R	2B	3B	HR	RBI	BB	SO	SB	CS	EqBRR	AVG	OBP	SLG	EqAVG	EqOBP	EqSLG	EqA	VORP	WARP	DEFENSE	
2006	TEX	MLB	24	474	65	27	1	14	55	40	64	11	4	0.6	.286	.347	.454	.270	.338	.434	.269	24.8	2.2	117-2B	0
2007	TEX	MLB	25	566	96	22	2	20	61	62	83	23	2	6.2	.263	.355	.441	.254	.351	.446	.281	29.7	3.8	129-2B	3
2008	TEX	MLB	26	583	102	41	4	18	71	45	67	26	2	9.2	.319	.375	.517	.317	.376	.534	.310	53.7	4.6	120-2B	-10
2009	TEX	MLB	27	654	97	36	4	21	85	61	91	23	6	2.5	.284	.355	.472	.280	.353	.478	.289	34.9	4.4	152-2B	-1

Breakout: 14% **Improve: 39%** **Collapse: 20%** **Attrition: 5%** **Comparables: Dan Uggla, Toby Harrah, Willie Jones, Chris Sabo**

Where the Astros have famous second basemen like Bill Doran or Craig Biggio, the Rangers have never really had somebody like that—until now. The all-time franchise leader in games played at the keystone is Bump Wills with 697, a tally Kinsler should top sometime in 2011, assuming he stays healthy—which does seem to be the rub. Kinsler's lost a month or more to an injury in each of his first three seasons, and while none of them (broken thumb, stress fracture, and hernia repair) are career-altering, they do reflect that second is one of the most physically demanding positions on the diamond, perhaps matched only by catcher. The huge drop in his defensive performance might have been injury-related, but Kinsler also got considerable extra attention from Washington, the former infield coach, and there seems to have been an adjustment period involved. If he does keep struggling, however, an eventual move to third might not be the worst idea, especially now that Blalock and Davis have both slipped down the defensive spectrum and opened up the position for the long term.

Gerald Laird   C   Bats: R   Throws: R   Height: 6' 1"   Weight: 225   Born: November 13, 1979   Age: 29

YEAR	TEAM	LVL	AGE	PA	R	2B	3B	HR	RBI	BB	SO	SB	CS	EqBRR	AVG	OBP	SLG	EqAVG	EqOBP	EqSLG	EqA	VORP	WARP	DEFENSE	
2006	TEX	MLB	26	260	46	20	1	7	22	12	54	3	1	0.0	.296	.332	.473	.281	.320	.463	.267	12.6	2.1	66-C	6
2007	TEX	MLB	27	448	48	18	3	9	47	30	103	6	2	2.1	.224	.278	.349	.220	.278	.358	.223	-6.3	1.4	112-C	10
2008	TEX	MLB	28	381	54	24	0	6	41	23	63	2	4	1.2	.276	.329	.398	.280	.334	.420	.257	7.1	1.5	85-C	-1
2009	DET	MLB	29	327	35	16	1	8	37	21	61	4	2	0.2	.252	.304	.397	.252	.306	.410	.249	4.2	1.8	79-C	2

Breakout: 38%   Improve: 59%   Collapse: 20%   Attrition: 30%   Comparables: Phil Roof, Bob Boone, Rod Barajas, Matt Batts

The solid catch-and-throw young veteran placeholder in a system suddenly swarming with backstop promise, Laird shouldn't be confused with someone with hidden upside potential—he would be much better off in a job-share that hides him against the tougher right-handers. Unfortunately, the danger is that he's going to be treated as a regular by the Tigers, who dealt a pair of arms to find a patch to placate their angry Inge.

John Mayberry Jr.   OF   Bats: R   Throws: R   Height: 6' 6"   Weight: 230   Born: December 21, 1983   Age: 25

YEAR	TEAM	LVL	AGE	PA	R	2B	3B	HR	RBI	BB	SO	SB	CS	EqBRR	AVG	OBP	SLG	EqAVG	EqOBP	EqSLG	EqA	VORP	WARP	DEFENSE			
2006	CLN	A	22	533	77	26	4	21	77	59	117	9	3	-0.6	.268	.358	.479	.198	.268	.347	.215	-28.5	-2.5	90-RF	-12	25-LF	7
2007	BAK	A+	23	277	47	15	1	16	45	28	64	9	1	2.3	.230	.314	.496	.166	.232	.352	.199	-20.6	-1.9	58-RF	-3		
2007	FRI	AA	23	271	35	10	0	14	38	20	62	7	1	2.8	.241	.307	.453	.208	.263	.380	.223	-11.3	-1.2	68-RF	-4		
2008	FRI	AA	24	90	16	8	0	4	13	4	21	4	1	-0.2	.268	.322	.512	.226	.267	.429	.237	-1.4	-0.2	19-RF	-1		
2009	PHI	MLB	25	520	52	25	2	17	63	36	133	7	2	-0.6	.225	.485	.395	.225	.285	.401	.235	-9.1	0.4	122-LF	4		

Breakout: 41%   Improve: 66%   Collapse: 17%   Attrition: 12%   Comparables: Chad Mottola, Pete Tucci, Troy Afenir, Bob Zupcic

Twice a first-round pick (he didn't sign with the Mariners coming out of high school), Mayberry's skill set really hasn't advanced much since his Stanford days. Power at the plate and a big arm are his only tools, but he doesn't do enough other things to make up for it. He's absolute murder on lefties, batting .351 against them last year with nine home runs in 114 at-bats, but that's also probably his ultimate ceiling as a platoon partner at first base or either outfield corner. The Rangers traded him to the Phillies for Greg Golson, another player with tools and not a ton of skill.

Travis Metcalf   3B   Bats: R   Throws: R   Height: 6' 3"   Weight: 215   Born: August 17, 1982   Age: 26

YEAR	TEAM	LVL	AGE	PA	R	2B	3B	HR	RBI	BB	SO	SB	CS	EqBRR	AVG	OBP	SLG	EqAVG	EqOBP	EqSLG	EqA	VORP	WARP	DEFENSE	
2006	FRI	AA	23	477	51	16	2	8	37	45	112	9	7	-1.7	.221	.298	.325	.186	.251	.276	.183	-43.0	-4.3	116-3B	-11
2007	FRI	AA	24	226	38	18	0	7	34	21	44	2	1	1.0	.280	.345	.475	.229	.286	.385	.234	-5.3	-0.5	54-3B	-3
2007	OKL	AAA	24	70	2	3	0	0	6	7	17	0	0	0.0	.148	.232	.197	.129	.214	.161	.111	-10.6	-0.2	18-3B	5
2007	TEX	MLB	24	181	25	12	1	5	21	13	41	0	1	-0.0	.255	.307	.435	.250	.307	.444	.255	1.6	0.1	49-3B	-2
2008	OKL	AAA	25	288	36	14	1	5	37	18	59	0	1	-0.7	.253	.300	.370	.212	.253	.309	.192	-20.1	-2.0	71-3B	-4
2008	TEX	MLB	25	61	11	2	0	6	14	3	12	0	0	-0.4	.232	.279	.589	.232	.279	.589	.279	2.6	0.0	15-3B	-3
2009	TEX	MLB	26	444	34	20	2	9	45	30	121	3	1	-0.4	.199	.257	.324	.196	.256	.328	.201	-20.6	-1.7	105-3B	-5

Breakout: 36%   Improve: 49%   Collapse: 36%   Attrition: 11%   Comparables: Hunter Brown, Ron Coomer, Bob Brenly, Tim Olson

Having failed to build on his Cal League breakout in 2005, the Rangers might like to supersize their Unhappy Mc-Suspect Meal, but Metcalf doesn't seem like a good bet to comply. He has the arm that might make you squint and see a starting third baseman, but the Swiss are calling to ask for their holes back, because they'd be better found in cheese than a big-league swing. Hence the off-season suggestion that Young move to third, because Metcalf's just not going to turn into a worthwhile regular.

David Murphy   RF

Bats: L   Throws: L   Height: 6' 4"   Weight: 215   Born: October 18, 1981   Age: 27

YEAR	TEAM	LVL	AGE	PA	R	2B	3B	HR	RBI	BB	SO	SB	CS	EqBRR	AVG	OBP	SLG	EqAVG	EqOBP	EqSLG	EqA	VORP	WARP	DEFENSE				
2006	PME	AA	24	184	22	17	1	3	25	11	29	4	2	-0.2	.273	.315	.436	.224	.261	.379	.217	-7.5	0.0	41-CF	3			
2006	PAW	AAA	24	366	45	23	5	8	44	45	53	3	3	-0.7	.267	.355	.447	.241	.328	.416	.258	4.8	-0.1	61-CF	-8	15-RF	3	
2006	BOS	MLB	24	26	4	1	0	1	2	4	4	0	0	-0.0	.227	.346	.409	.227	.346	.409	.265	0.5	0.2	4-CF	1			
2007	PAW	AAA	25	444	50	20	5	9	47	41	68	8	1	-0.8	.280	.347	.423	.240	.304	.381	.240	-5.7	0.8	51-CF	-3	32-LF	10	
2007	TEX	MLB	25	110	16	12	1	2	14	7	19	0	0	0.2	.340	.382	.534	.330	.373	.553	.308	10.3	0.8	11-LF	-1	9-RF	0	
2008	TEX	MLB	26	454	64	28	3	15	74	31	70	7	2	1.2	.275	.321	.465	.274	.323	.482	.273	12.2	1.6	46-RF	3	46-LF	-2	
2009	TEX	MLB	27	428	52	23	3	12	54	33	76	6	2	0.1	.260	.320	.421	.256	.318	.426	.258	2.7	1.2	102-LF	1			

Breakout: 26%   Improve: 44%   Collapse: 31%   Attrition: 25%   Comparables: Paul O'Neill, George Altman, Ben Broussard, Jim Northrup

Part of the package received for flipping Eric Gagné to the Red Sox for the '07 stretch run, Murphy was enjoying a nice little bust-out season before a knee cost him the last third of the campaign. As a corner outfielder with platoon virtues but shy of massive power, he has his uses as someone to mix and match with Byrd and Cruz, but setting expectations higher than that would be a mistake—he's as good as he's going to get right now.

Max Ramirez   C

Bats: R   Throws: R   Height: 5' 11"   Weight: 170   Born: October 11, 1984   Age: 24

YEAR	TEAM	LVL	AGE	PA	R	2B	3B	HR	RBI	BB	SO	SB	CS	EqBRR	AVG	OBP	SLG	EqAVG	EqOBP	EqSLG	EqA	VORP	WARP	DEFENSE				
2006	ROM	A	21	326	50	17	0	9	37	54	72	2	0	-0.5	.285	.408	.449	.223	.319	.346	.238	-7.1	-0.6	36-C	-6			
2006	LKC	A	21	161	19	6	1	4	26	30	27	0	0	-0.9	.307	.435	.465	.235	.335	.353	.249	-1.3	-0.1	17-C	-3			
2007	KIN	A+	22	342	46	20	0	12	62	53	63	1	0	-2.9	.303	.418	.505	.245	.338	.398	.261	4.1	1.1	65-C	-4			
2007	BAK	A+	22	138	16	10	0	4	20	21	39	1	0	-1.5	.307	.420	.500	.250	.345	.408	.264	2.8	0.5	24-C	-1			
2008	FRI	AA	23	289	49	16	2	17	50	37	56	2	2	-2.5	.354	.450	.646	.298	.383	.567	.313	31.4	2.2	42-C	-9	8-1B	1	
2008	OKL	AAA	23	41	5	1	0	2	6	3	13	0	0	-0.3	.243	.293	.432	.237	.286	.421	.244	-0.3	0.0	7-C	-1			
2008	TEX	MLB	23	55	8	1	0	2	9	6	15	0	0	-0.3	.217	.345	.370	.217	.345	.370	.256	0.4	0.0	9-C	-1			
2009	TEX	MLB	24	461	51	20	2	15	55	50	128	2	1	-0.8	.236	.325	.406	.233	.324	.411	.257	5.6	1.7	109-C	-12			

Breakout: 8%   Improve: 24%   Collapse: 40%   Attrition: 10%   Comparables: Justin Huber, Mario Valdez, Erik Pappas, Leo Gomez

Max Ramirez can rake. Nobody doubts it, and he has a career batting line of .312/.413/.515 to make his case. He has big league-quality plate discipline, above-average bat speed, and plus power, but the questions remain as to what exactly to do with him. Defense has been his Achilles' heel throughout his career; he's something less than nimble behind the plate and opposing teams run on him with ease. That's always portended a future at first base or DH, positions where the offensive expectations suddenly increase at an almost alarming rate. We're not betting against him, but the odds become steep once he ditches shinguards.

Jarrod Saltalamacchia   C

Bats: S   Throws: R   Height: 6' 4"   Weight: 195   Born: May 2, 1985   Age: 24

YEAR	TEAM	LVL	AGE	PA	R	2B	3B	HR	RBI	BB	SO	SB	CS	EqBRR	AVG	OBP	SLG	EqAVG	EqOBP	EqSLG	EqA	VORP	WARP	DEFENSE				
2006	MIS	AA	21	377	30	18	1	9	39	55	71	0	1	-2.2	.230	.353	.380	.220	.326	.382	.250	-1.8	1.4	80-C	1			
2007	MIS	AA	22	94	18	7	0	6	13	13	17	2	0	0.0	.309	.404	.617	.277	.362	.554	.304	8.7	0.9	20-C	-1			
2007	ATL	MLB	22	153	11	6	0	4	12	10	28	0	0	-1.4	.284	.333	.411	.286	.340	.421	.264	4.8	0.2	21-C	-1	12-1B	-2	
2007	TEX	MLB	22	176	28	7	1	7	21	9	47	0	0	1.0	.251	.290	.431	.247	.290	.440	.246	1.8	-0.3	23-1B	-1	21-C	-4	
2008	OKL	AAA	23	64	10	3	1	2	13	7	15	0	0	-0.2	.291	.391	.491	.250	.344	.446	.272	2.1	0.4	15-C	0			
2008	TEX	MLB	23	230	27	13	0	3	26	31	74	0	2	-1.7	.253	.352	.364	.250	.357	.372	.258	3.2	0.2	52-C	-6			
2009	TEX	MLB	24	331	38	17	1	12	45	34	82	1	1	-0.7	.250	.333	.438	.246	.331	.443	.267	9.9	1.8	80-C	-5			

Breakout: 32%   Improve: 54%   Collapse: 17%   Attrition: 30%   Comparables: Jim Pagliaroni, Derrek Lee, Earl Battey, Ken Henderson

Salty might not have blossomed like the fully-finished prospect you might wish he was, but he's still relatively young, he's been bounced around more than a bit, and his 2008 was marred by injuries almost all the way along (a bruised hand early, a groin, a broken bone in a foot, and finally a disabling elbow problem). With Laird dealt, he heads into 2009 with a clean shot at the catching job. Given his significantly better performance against right-handers, you can probably expect a platoon or job-share with Teagarden, turning last year's revolving door into a more stable source of strength.

Chris Shelton — 1B

Bats: R   Throws: R   Height: 6' 0"   Weight: 215   Born: June 26, 1980   Age: 29

YEAR	TEAM	LVL	AGE	PA	R	2B	3B	HR	RBI	BB	SO	SB	CS	EqBRR	AVG	OBP	SLG	EqAVG	EqOBP	EqSLG	EqA	VORP	WARP	DEFENSE	
2006	DET	MLB	26	412	50	16	4	16	47	34	107	1	2	-1.4	.273	.340	.466	.262	.335	.451	.267	9.2	1.6	102-1B	7
2006	TOL	AAA	26	129	20	6	2	3	14	18	37	1	0	-0.4	.266	.372	.440	.243	.346	.414	.269	2.8	0.1	24-1B	-2
2007	TOL	AAA	27	594	75	31	1	14	65	83	141	4	2	-1.1	.269	.381	.420	.234	.335	.375	.252	0.1	-1.2	128-1B	-11
2008	OKL	AAA	28	291	38	22	2	11	51	31	54	0	0	-0.5	.340	.409	.570	.255	.318	.426	.257	4.1	-0.4	49-1B	-5
2008	TEX	MLB	28	117	14	5	0	2	11	17	33	1	0	0.3	.216	.333	.330	.208	.333	.344	.247	-2.0	0.0	28-1B	1
2009	SEA	MLB	29	373	34	17	1	10	40	38	111	2	1	-1.0	.211	.296	.361	.214	.299	.381	.238	-9.3	-0.3	89-1B	1

Breakout: 9%   Improve: 19%   Collapse: 43%   Attrition: 27%   Comparables: Reggie Whittemore, Trey McCoy, Russ McGinnis, Andy Phillips

Dial back to before Davis was up, and remember that the Rangers walked into camp with no set first baseman; in the meantime, they decided to let Jason Botts try fielding (he shouldn't), see if Ben Broussard had something left (he didn't), and find out if the player who had a 10-homer April back in 2006 might get that mojo going again with a change of scenery (he couldn't). Their curiosity satisfied and with Davis now set in stone at first, the can's been kicked to the Mariners, who will see if Shelton might earn a shot to platoon with Russell Branyan or Bryan LaHair.

Justin Smoak — 1B

Bats: S   Throws: L   Height: 6' 3"   Weight: 200   Born: December 5, 1986   Age: 22

YEAR	TEAM	LVL	AGE	PA	R	2B	3B	HR	RBI	BB	SO	SB	CS	EqBRR	AVG	OBP	SLG	EqAVG	EqOBP	EqSLG	EqA	VORP	WARP	DEFENSE	
2008	CLN	A	21	62	9	3	0	3	6	5	10	0	0	-1.0	.304	.355	.518	.263	.306	.456	.260	1.4	0.2	10-1B	1
2009	TEX	MLB	22	558	53	28	3	16	68	43	139	5	2	-0.2	.240	.304	.403	.236	.302	.408	.247	-7.2	0.5	131-1B	1

Breakout: N/A   Improve: N/A   Collapse: N/A   Attrition: N/A   Comparables: Michael Aubrey, Ryan Braun, Will Clark, Eric Munson

The 2008 draft was a strange one, certainly. Differences of opinion on talent as well as signing-bonus concerns meant that somebody who didn't deserve to was going to drop, and the Rangers could hardly contain their glee when Smoak fell to them with the 11th overall pick. While he's slow and limited to first base—which he plays well—some saw Smoak as the best pure hitter in the draft, with a picture-perfect swing, outstanding plate discipline, and big-time power to all fields. Think Justin Morneau with the ability to switch-hit—he could be that scary.

Taylor Teagarden — C

Bats: R   Throws: R   Height: 6' 1"   Weight: 200   Born: December 21, 1983   Age: 25

YEAR	TEAM	LVL	AGE	PA	R	2B	3B	HR	RBI	BB	SO	SB	CS	EqBRR	AVG	OBP	SLG	EqAVG	EqOBP	EqSLG	EqA	VORP	WARP	DEFENSE	
2006	RNG	Rk	22	29	4	0	0	0	1	9	7	1	0	-0.2	.050	.345	.050	.042	.207	.042	.000	-15.3	-0.7		
2007	BAK	A+	23	364	75	25	0	20	67	65	89	2	1	-1.4	.315	.448	.606	.235	.346	.439	.271	10.6	1.5	29-C	0
2007	FRI	AA	23	115	19	3	0	7	16	10	39	0	0	0.6	.294	.357	.529	.260	.313	.452	.262	2.7	0.0	14-C	-3
2008	FRI	AA	24	68	6	2	0	2	6	8	23	1	0	0.3	.169	.279	.305	.148	.246	.279	.186	-6.5	-0.2	10-C	1
2008	OKL	AAA	24	218	26	5	3	7	16	28	59	0	1	-1.9	.225	.332	.396	.199	.298	.340	.224	-8.1	0.3	55 C	1
2008	TEX	MLB	24	53	10	5	0	6	17	5	19	0	0	0.5	.319	.396	.809	.319	.396	.851	.371	9.9	0.9	11-C	-1
2009	TEX	MLB	25	354	37	14	1	12	41	39	121	1	1	-0.3	.212	.307	.389	.209	.305	.394	.244	-0.2	1.2	85-C	-4

Breakout: 30%   Improve: 49%   Collapse: 38%   Attrition: 32%   Comparables: Dave F. Schmidt, Kelly Shoppach, Ozzie Virgil, George Bjorkman

One of the best defensive catchers in the minors, Teagarden calls a game like a veteran, is agile behind the plate, and absolutely shuts down the running game. He's nothing close to a .319 hitter, though, although he more than makes up for it with plenty of walks and power. If you want to get really dreamy and optimistic, think Mickey Tettleton with Gold Glove–level skills, and you get the picture. Whether he or Saltalamacchia is the long-term answer for the Rangers is still the subject of debate, but better to have two good options when there are plenty of organizations with none.

Ramon Vazquez   **MI**   Bats: L   Throws: R   Height: 5' 11"   Weight: 170   Born: August 21, 1976   Age: 32

YEAR	TEAM	LVL	AGE	PA	R	2B	3B	HR	RBI	BB	SO	SB	CS	EqBRR	AVG	OBP	SLG	EqAVG	EqOBP	EqSLG	EqA	VORP	WARP	DEFENSE			
2006	BUF	AAA	29	123	19	2	1	2	11	22	27	2	1	0.0	.242	.377	.343	.186	.317	.284	.222	-6.1	-0.1	14-SS	-3	10-2B	3
2006	CLE	MLB	29	77	11	2	0	1	8	6	18	0	0	1.4	.209	.267	.284	.197	.267	.273	.197	-4.6	-0.8	11-3B	-1	5-SS	-4
2007	OKL	AAA	30	161	27	10	2	2	13	24	27	3	1	0.0	.258	.375	.409	.199	.306	.324	.229	-6.1	0.1	21-SS	2	13-2B	-2
2007	TEX	MLB	30	345	42	13	3	8	28	29	72	1	0	0.1	.230	.300	.373	.225	.300	.376	.239	-4.1	-0.5	61-3B	-2	13-SS	4
2008	TEX	MLB	31	347	44	18	3	6	40	38	66	0	1	-1.4	.290	.365	.430	.286	.368	.434	.280	14.1	1.1	60-3B	-7	16-SS	-1
2009	*PIT*	*MLB*	*32*	*240*	*29*	*12*	*1*	*5*	*23*	*26*	*49*	*1*	*1*	*0.3*	*.257*	*.342*	*.395*	*.256*	*.341*	*.409*	*.260*	*8.5*	*0.9*	*60-3B*	*0*		

Breakout: 25% Improve: 48% Collapse: 27% Attrition: 45%   *Comparables: Grady Hatton, Fred Hatfield, Ernest Riles, Floyd Baker*

So, you're wondering what a MI is, and that's short for middle infielder; call a guy a MINF and infielders or moms might take offense. It might seem strange that Vazquez elected to go to Pittsburgh as a free agent, but after getting punted before by other teams, a guaranteed $4 million probably trumped sorting out who else has to move and who plays where. It's a sensible choice for both player and team: he's not really a regular or a third baseman, and he's never again going to hit .300 or slug .500 and get people all worked up the way he did for a couple of months with the Rangers.

Mike Young   **SS**   Bats: R   Throws: R   Height: 6' 1"   Weight: 200   Born: October 19, 1976   Age: 32

YEAR	TEAM	LVL	AGE	PA	R	2B	3B	HR	RBI	BB	SO	SB	CS	EqBRR	AVG	OBP	SLG	EqAVG	EqOBP	EqSLG	EqA	VORP	WARP	DEFENSE	
2006	TEX	MLB	29	748	93	52	3	14	103	48	96	7	3	-0.5	.314	.356	.459	.299	.346	.442	.272	46.9	5.2	154-SS	8
2007	TEX	MLB	30	692	80	37	1	9	94	47	107	13	3	-0.2	.315	.366	.418	.308	.361	.419	.274	40.7	3.7	146-SS	-3
2008	TEX	MLB	31	708	102	36	2	12	82	55	109	10	0	3.9	.284	.339	.402	.284	.343	.412	.267	27.1	5.8	145-SS	20
2009	*TEX*	*MLB*	*32*	*539*	*64*	*27*	*2*	*8*	*55*	*40*	*84*	*7*	*2*	*-0.3*	*.279*	*.334*	*.393*	*.274*	*.332*	*.398*	*.257*	*15.0*	*2.6*	*127-SS*	*5*

Breakout: 9% Improve: 33% Collapse: 42% Attrition: 16%   *Comparables: Dave Concepcion, Dick Groat, Jeff Cirillo, Mark Grudzielanek*

You can relate to Young's frustration with the team's request that he agree to a move to third to make room for Andrus at short—he's worked hard to be a good middle infielder, and he's already had to agree to move off of second for Alfonso Soriano's brand of butchery around the bag. With his bat already come down from his days as a perpetual XBH machine now that he's out of his peak years, he isn't really an asset anywhere but up the middle.

PITCHERS

Joaquin Benoit   Bats: R   Throws: R   Height: 6' 3"   Weight: 220   Born: July 26, 1977   Age: 31

YEAR	TEAM	LVL	AGE	W	L	SV	G	GS	IP	H	BB	SO	HR	GB%	BABIP	STUFF	WHIP	ERA	DERA	EqH9	EqBB9	EqSO9	EqHR9	DEF	VORP	SN/WX
2006	TEX	MLB	28	1	1	0	56	0	79²	68	38	85	5	38.5%	.296	16	1.33	4.86	4.89	7.2	4.1	8.3	0.6	-2	5.8	0.20
2007	TEX	MLB	29	7	4	6	70	0	82	68	28	87	6	38.6%	.297	19	1.17	2.85	3.78	7.3	2.9	8.3	0.7	7	27.0	3.54
2008	TEX	MLB	30	3	2	1	44	0	45	40	35	43	6	28.0%	.276	2	1.67	5.00	5.21	7.1	6.2	7.3	1.2	-1	1.0	-0.29
2009	*TEX*	*MLB*	*31*	*2*	*2*	*2*	*42*	*0*	*50*	*48*	*25*	*49*	*6*	*37.0%*	*.300*	*13*	*1.45*	*4.40*	*4.08*	*8.3*	*4.1*	*8.0*	*1.1*	*-0*	*7.7*	*0.62*

Breakout: 33% Improve: 65% Collapse: 16% Attrition: 14%   *Comparables: Kyle Farnsworth, Charlie Hough, Russ Springer, Armando Benitez*

After giving the team two quality seasons in a set-up role, the Rangers had to suffer through a return to Benoit-related frustrations. Shoulder woes sapped the life on his fastball as well as discouraging him from using his slider as often, and that left him under-equipped. While the Rangers expect that his rehabbing the bum wing will bring him to camp in full operating order, believe it when you see it.

Thomas Diamond

| | | | | | | | | | | | | | | | Bats: R | Throws: R | Height: 6' 3" | Weight: 245 | Born: April 6, 1983 | Age: 26 |

YEAR	TEAM	LVL	AGE	W	L	SV	G	GS	IP	H	BB	SO	HR	GB%	BABIP	STUFF	WHIP	ERA	DERA	EqH9	EqBB9	EqSO9	EqHR9	DEF	VORP	SN/WX
2006	FRI	AA	23	12	5	0	27	27	129	104	78	145	14	39.8%	.285	-4	1.41	4.26	6.94	8.7	5.9	6.6	1.6	14	-18.0	—
2008	FRI	AA	25	3	3	0	12	11	53²	54	37	47	3	36.6%	.336	-10	1.69	6.20	9.12	11.1	7.1	4.9	0.9	1	-19.3	—
2009	TEX	MLB	26	3	6	0	22	13	71²	87	61	56	13	39.0%	.330	-3	2.05	7.78	7.25	10.5	6.9	6.5	1.5	-1	-15.0	-1.18

Breakout: 16% Improve: 45% Collapse: 37% Attrition: 26%   Comparables: Donnie Bridges, John Burke, Calvin Jones, Colin McLaughlin

Once the top pitching prospect in the system, Diamond has been passed up by younger and better players while also falling behind due to Tommy John surgery. In his return last summer, he got his low to mid-90s velocity back quickly, but like many in their first year after the procedure, his control went south. His lack of a solid breaking ball had many seeing him as a reliever down the road before the operation, and the time for that decision might come soon.

Scott Feldman

| | | | | | | | | | | | | | | | Bats: L | Throws: R | Height: 6' 5" | Weight: 210 | Born: February 7, 1983 | Age: 26 |

YEAR	TEAM	LVL	AGE	W	L	SV	G	GS	IP	H	BB	SO	HR	GB%	BABIP	STUFF	WHIP	ERA	DERA	EqH9	EqBB9	EqSO9	EqHR9	DEF	VORP	SN/WX
2006	OKL	AAA	23	2	2	4	23	0	27	20	9	24	2	51.2%	.250	-8	1.07	2.00	6.23	7.3	3.1	5.5	1.0	6	-1.8	—
2006	TEX	MLB	23	0	2	0	36	0	41¹	42	10	30	4	60.3%	.306	1	1.26	3.92	4.65	8.6	2.2	5.8	0.9	3	9.5	-0.03
2007	OKL	AAA	24	1	1	2	21	0	30	28	12	24	1	51.6%	.303	-14	1.33	4.50	6.83	9.0	3.7	5.0	0.3	2	-4.0	—
2007	TEX	MLB	24	1	2	0	29	0	39	44	32	19	3	58.0%	.308	-16	1.95	5.77	5.49	9.6	6.6	3.7	0.7	-1	0.2	-0.44
2008	FRI	AA	25	2	0	0	2	2	12²	11	2	4	0	64.4%	.250	-13	1.02	4.25	5.68	7.8	1.4	0.7	0.0	0	-0.1	—
2008	TEX	MLB	25	6	8	0	28	25	151¹	161	56	74	22	45.0%	.290	-16	1.43	5.29	6.07	8.9	3.1	3.9	1.3	3	-4.4	1.16
2009	TEX	MLB	26	5	7	0	33	14	98¹	117	38	51	14	46.0%	.310	-2	1.58	5.55	5.22	10.3	3.2	4.2	1.2	-1	1.2	0.66

Breakout: 15% Improve: 47% Collapse: 26% Attrition: 31%   Comparables: Jim Perry, Gary Glover, Brian Moehler, Steve Comer

The decision to move a guy like Feldman, one who throws from a pretty low arm angle, might seem strange; left-handed batters generally get the jump on those kinds of pitchers. But considering the Rangers' desperation and Feldman's broad (if unexceptional) assortment and sturdy frame, they gave it a shot and got adequacy for their trouble. They monitored his workload very carefully, and got 13 quality starts in 28. This does not mean he has a great future ahead of him as a rotation regular, but he's now a handy utility pitcher on a staff that always seems to need something.

Neftali Feliz

| | | | | | | | | | | | | | | | Bats: R | Throws: R | Height: 6' 3" | Weight: 180 | Born: May 2, 1988 | Age: 21 |

YEAR	TEAM	LVL	AGE	W	L	SV	G	GS	IP	H	BB	SO	HR	GB%	BABIP	STUFF	WHIP	ERA	DERA	EqH9	EqBB9	EqSO9	EqHR9	DEF	VORP	SN/WX
2006	BRA	Rk	18	0	2	2	11	5	29¹	20	14	42	0	51.9%	.346	20	1.17	4.02	8.22	11.7	7.4	7.0	0.8	0	-6.7	—
2007	DNV	Rk	19	2	0	0	8	7	27¹	18	12	28	0	50.7%	.273	8	1.10	1.98	6.23	10.0	7.1	3.7	0.8	0	-1.5	—
2007	SPO	A-	19	0	2	0	8	1	15	13	12	27	2	48.4%	.393	10	1.67	3.60	5.40	16.2	10.8	8.5	3.9	-3	0.3	—
2008	CLN	A	20	6	3	0	17	17	82	55	28	106	2	52.7%	.299	35	1.01	2.52	5.53	9.5	4.6	6.6	0.8	4	0.5	—
2008	FRI	AA	20	4	3	0	10	10	45¹	34	23	47	1	40.7%	.306	34	1.26	2.98	5.36	8.7	5.4	6.2	0.4	3	1.1	—
2009	TEX	MLB	21	4	7	0	24	16	88²	106	61	77	13	45.0%	.340	11	1.87	6.47	6.05	10.3	5.6	7.1	1.2	-1	-7.3	-0.16

Breakout: 5% Improve: 25% Collapse: 42% Attrition: 10%   Comparables: Hector Fajardo, Luis Andujar, Homer Bailey, Rich Harden

Prior to the 2007 season, we ranked Feliz as the third-best prospect in the Braves system, and people scoffed. Last year we had Feliz atop a talented Rangers system, and the laughter continued. And then, golly, this year everybody has him at the top of their lists. Go figure. Despite the high expectations, Feliz' full-season debut actually exceeded them, as he made the two-level jump to Double-A without missing a beat. The upper-90s fastball was always there, but Feliz made tremendous progress on his power breaking ball and suddenly big league–quality changeup in 2008, now looking like a complete pitcher with true ace potential. He's moving very quickly, and should be in line for a September call-up at the very least. Who knows, you may even have heard it here first.

Frank Francisco

| | | | | | | | | Bats: R | | Throws: R | | Height: 6' 2" | | Weight: 235 | | Born: September 11, 1979 | | | Age: 29 | |

YEAR	TEAM	LVL	AGE	W	L	SV	G	GS	IP	H	BB	SO	HR	GB%	BABIP	STUFF	WHIP	ERA	DERA	EqH9	EqBB9	EqSO9	EqHR9	DEF	VORP	SN/WX
2006	TEX	MLB	26	0	1	0	8	0	7¹	8	2	6	2	50.0%	.273	-3	1.36	4.93	3.52	8.2	2.3	5.9	2.3	-1	1.0	0.00
2007	TEX	MLB	27	1	1	0	59	0	59¹	57	38	49	3	38.5%	.320	3	1.60	4.55	4.45	8.6	5.4	6.4	0.5	-3	6.9	1.58
2008	TEX	MLB	28	3	5	5	58	0	63¹	47	26	83	7	33.5%	.276	20	1.15	3.13	3.60	6.2	3.3	9.6	1.0	2	16.7	2.15
2009	TEX	MLB	29	3	3	6	54	0	59²	52	26	66	7	38.0%	.290	22	1.30	3.84	3.58	7.6	3.6	9.0	1.0	-0	11.9	1.15

Breakout: 27% Improve: 55% Collapse: 26% Attrition: 12%   Comparables: Joaquin Benoit, Rich Garces, Trevor Hoffman, Kyle Farnsworth

Francisco's career seems to have suffered through so many interruptions it's as if he comes equipped with his own pop-up window; he had to open the year with the indignity of a return to Triple-A, but finished it back in the bigs and closing effectively. He has the power assortment to do perfectly well in the role, heat that's reliably mid-90s and power breakers that get lefties fishing. Now that he has enough time between his elbow's Tommy John and the present, he should be set to star in whatever high-leverage role they use him in, and he's still three years removed from free agency.

Kason Gabbard

| | | | | | | | | Bats: L | | Throws: L | | Height: 6' 3" | | Weight: 205 | | Born: April 8, 1982 | | | Age: 27 | |

YEAR	TEAM	LVL	AGE	W	L	SV	G	GS	IP	H	BB	SO	HR	GB%	BABIP	STUFF	WHIP	ERA	DERA	EqH9	EqBB9	EqSO9	EqHR9	DEF	VORP	SN/WX
2006	PME	AA	24	9	2	0	13	13	73¹	51	25	68	4	61.8%	.242	-2	1.04	2.59	5.45	8.2	3.9	4.9	1.1	4	1.1	—
2006	PAW	AAA	24	1	7	0	9	8	51¹	51	26	48	8	64.4%	.321	-18	1.51	5.28	7.66	11.5	5.6	6.0	2.4	2	-10.2	—
2006	BOS	MLB	24	1	3	0	7	4	25²	24	16	15	0	61.3%	.304	2	1.56	3.50	3.70	8.1	5.5	4.8	0.0	0	6.3	0.89
2007	PAW	AAA	25	7	2	0	14	14	75	66	25	64	10	61.1%	.271	-16	1.21	3.24	5.37	9.3	3.3	5.2	1.9	7	1.8	—
2007	TEX	MLB	25	2	1	0	8	8	40¹	40	23	26	5	56.7%	.292	-4	1.56	5.58	5.77	9.0	4.8	5.1	1.2	2	1.9	0.43
2007	BOS	MLB	25	4	0	0	7	7	41	28	18	29	3	53.5%	.225	8	1.12	3.73	5.82	6.8	4.0	5.8	0.7	9	10.8	1.12
2008	TEX	MLB	26	2	3	0	12	12	56	64	39	33	5	64.2%	.326	-3	1.84	4.82	5.14	9.5	5.6	4.7	0.8	-3	0.3	0.71
2009	TEX	MLB	27	5	6	0	27	16	94¹	107	46	59	10	54.0%	.320	4	1.63	5.33	5.10	9.8	4.0	5.1	0.9	-1	2.7	0.86

Breakout: 16% Improve: 38% Collapse: 34% Attrition: 30%   Comparables: Frank Baumann, Matt Young, Jim Shellenback, Bryan Clark

Gabbard spent a good chunk of the season sheathed by surgery to remove a bone spur from his pitching elbow. You can hope that this means he'll be healthy and recover a modicum of his control and make a solid bid for a spot in the rotation, but he wasn't able to participate in the initial round of the much-discussed "Nolan-style" winter workouts. If he's sound, he'll be in the running for one of the three open rotation slots in camp, but he'll have to be effective to stay ahead of the pack of youngsters nearing readiness.

Matt Harrison

| | | | | | | | | Bats: L | | Throws: L | | Height: 6' 5" | | Weight: 205 | | Born: August 16, 1985 | | | Age: 23 | |

YEAR	TEAM	LVL	AGE	W	L	SV	G	GS	IP	H	BB	SO	HR	GB%	BABIP	STUFF	WHIP	ERA	DERA	EqH9	EqBB9	EqSO9	EqHR9	DEF	VORP	SN/WX
2006	MYR	A+	20	8	4	0	13	13	81	77	16	60	6	50.2%	.297	13	1.15	3.11	5.83	11.5	2.5	3.7	1.8	2	-1.8	—
2006	MIS	AA	20	3	4	0	13	12	77	83	17	54	6	43.8%	.314	17	1.30	3.62	6.29	11.3	2.2	3.6	1.5	1	-5.6	—
2007	MIS	AA	21	5	7	0	20	20	116²	118	34	78	6	49.5%	.309	8	1.30	3.39	5.48	10.4	3.0	3.4	0.9	1	1.4	—
2008	FRI	AA	22	3	2	0	9	9	46	49	14	35	3	47.0%	.311	-4	1.37	3.33	5.98	10.9	3.3	3.9	1.0	-1	-1.8	—
2008	OKL	AAA	22	3	1	0	6	6	38	40	14	20	3	54.4%	.311	-4	1.42	3.55	3.86	10.3	3.6	3.1	1.0	-1	6.8	—
2008	TEX	MLB	22	9	3	0	15	15	83²	100	31	42	12	40.4%	.315	-6	1.57	5.48	5.92	9.9	3.0	3.9	1.3	1	-2.7	0.21
2009	TEX	MLB	23	7	12	0	42	27	153	201	60	78	26	44.0%	.320	-0	1.70	6.31	5.86	11.3	3.2	4.2	1.5	-1	-9.2	0.05

Breakout: 12% Improve: 42% Collapse: 23% Attrition: 19%   Comparables: Trevor Miller, Andrew Lorraine, Bobby Livingston, Billy Traber

Yet another player from the bounty received from Atlanta in the 2007 Teixeira deal, Harrison reached the big leagues as part of an impressive return from his injury-plagued '07 season, but like many young pitchers, he took some lumps once there. He's not a future All-Star, but he's a big-bodied lefty with average velocity, a plus slider, and a fearless mound presence. Despite the ugly total numbers, he had some moments of greatness, including eight scoreless innings against the Rays in August, and a five-hit shutout of the A's in September. He begins 2009 in the middle of the Rangers' rotation, and he should perform well in that role for years to come.

Derek Holland

| | | | | | | | | | | | | | | | | Bats: S | | Throws: L | | Height: 6' 2" | | Weight: 185 | | Born: October 9, 1986 | | Age: 22 |

YEAR	TEAM	LVL	AGE	W	L	SV	G	GS	IP	H	BB	SO	HR	GB%	BABIP	STUFF	WHIP	ERA	DERA	EqH9	EqBB9	EqSO9	EqHR9	DEF	VORP	SN/WX
2007	SPO	A-	20	4	5	0	16	14	67	57	21	83	7	41.4%	.303	-15	1.16	3.22	6.95	12.9	4.4	4.7	3.0	-4	-8.6	—
2008	CLN	A	21	7	0	0	17	17	93²	77	29	91	2	51.6%	.306	16	1.13	2.40	5.24	10.6	4.2	4.5	0.8	0	3.2	—
2008	BAK	A+	21	3	1	0	5	5	31	20	5	37	1	42.3%	.271	28	0.81	3.19	5.86	7.8	2.3	6.5	0.7	2	-0.8	—
2008	FRI	AA	21	3	0	0	4	4	26	14	6	29	0	50.0%	.211	24	0.77	0.69	4.94	6.1	2.7	6.8	0.4	7	1.7	—
2009	TEX	MLB	23	7	12	0	42	27	153	201	60	78	26	44.0%	.320	-0	1.70	6.31	5.86	11.3	3.2	4.2	1.5	-1	-9.2	0.05

Breakout: 12% Improve: 42% Collapse: 23% Attrition: 19%   Comparables: Trever Miller, Andrew Lorraine, Bobby Livingston, Billy Traber

Even the Rangers don't have a good explanation for what happened to Derek Holland last year, and frankly, they don't care, they're just enjoying it. One of the last of the draft-and-follows, Holland had signed with an average fastball, but he kicked off the year at Low-A Clinton touching 95 on the speed gun, and by the end of the season, it was there consistently while reaching as high as 99 mph, and he fills the strike zone with it. It's an absolute monster of a pitch, and he'll be a future stud if he can figure out a more breaking ball than his current slurvy offering. That will be his primary focus in 2009, and will determine his future as either a power starter or power reliever, but he'll be awfully valuable either way.

Tommy Hunter

| | | | | | | | | | | | | | | | | Bats: R | | Throws: R | | Height: 6' 3" | | Weight: 255 | | Born: July 3, 1986 | | Age: 22 |

YEAR	TEAM	LVL	AGE	W	L	SV	G	GS	IP	H	BB	SO	HR	GB%	BABIP	STUFF	WHIP	ERA	DERA	EqH9	EqBB9	EqSO9	EqHR9	DEF	VORP	SN/WX
2007	SPO	A-	20	2	3	1	10	0	17²	15	1	13	0	49.1%	.273	-8	0.90	2.54	7.31	10.1	1.7	2.2	0.6	2	-3.0	—
2008	BAK	A+	21	5	4	0	9	9	58¹	63	8	50	6	50.3%	.335	4	1.22	3.55	5.33	12.2	2.1	4.1	1.9	-2	1.6	—
2008	FRI	AA	21	4	2	0	8	8	52¹	52	17	28	5	46.5%	.290	-10	1.32	3.79	7.09	10.7	3.6	2.7	1.5	7	-7.8	—
2008	OKL	AAA	21	4	2	0	8	8	53	55	9	28	6	51.4%	.290	5	1.21	2.89	4.70	9.4	1.7	3.0	1.2	6	5.2	—
2008	TEX	MLB	21	0	2	0	3	3	11	23	3	9	4	32.7%	.422	0	2.36	16.36	14.59	16.1	2.2	5.8	2.9	-3	-12.4	-0.66
2009	TEX	MLB	22	5	9	0	27	19	112²	149	35	56	20	45.0%	.320	2	1.64	6.63	6.21	11.5	2.6	4.1	1.5	-1	-11.2	-0.42

Breakout: 20% Improve: 68% Collapse: 11% Attrition: 6%   Comparables: Brian Meadows, Mitchell Johnson, Garrett Mock, Joe Oliver

In his first full season, Hunter opened the year with an aggressive assignment to High-A, but he moved up on a nearly bi-monthly basis, and even saw a trio of big-league starts. He got hammered in the majors, but that doesn't lessen the accomplishment. While he's built more like a defensive lineman than a baseball player, he's hardly overpowering, relying on a low-90s sinker to either get ground balls or put him ahead in the count to set up one of his two breaking balls as a chase pitch. He projects as a durable back-end starter in the end, but he's got studs like Feliz and Holland already ahead of him, and a bounty of talented young arms coming up from behind.

Eric Hurley

| | | | | | | | | | | | | | | | | Bats: R | | Throws: R | | Height: 6' 4" | | Weight: 195 | | Born: September 17, 1985 | | Age: 23 |

YEAR	TEAM	LVL	AGE	W	L	SV	G	GS	IP	H	BB	SO	HR	GB%	BABIP	STUFF	WHIP	ERA	DERA	EqH9	EqBB9	EqSO9	EqHR9	DEF	VORP	SN/WX
2006	BAK	A+	20	5	6	0	18	18	100²	92	32	106	12	41.5%	.308	-3	1.24	4.13	6.56	10.0	3.8	5.0	2.2	-11	-10.0	—
2006	FRI	AA	20	3	1	0	6	6	37²	21	11	31	4	44.2%	.189	26	0.86	1.94	4.67	5.7	3.1	4.7	1.6	6	3.6	—
2007	FRI	AA	21	7	2	0	15	14	88²	71	27	76	13	38.2%	.247	0	1.10	3.25	6.81	9.1	3.3	5.0	2.1	11	-10.8	—
2007	OKL	AAA	21	4	7	0	13	13	73¹	65	28	59	13	35.9%	.255	6	1.27	4.91	6.69	8.6	3.5	5.2	1.9	4	-8.6	—
2008	OKL	AAA	22	2	5	0	13	13	74²	86	29	72	15	40.8%	.330	-7	1.54	5.30	7.16	11.4	3.6	5.9	2.1	2	-12.4	—
2008	TEX	MLB	22	1	2	0	5	5	24²	26	9	13	5	22.6%	.266	-3	1.42	5.47	5.84	8.8	2.9	4.0	1.8	1	1.0	0.26
2009	TEX	MLB	23	7	10	0	39	26	139¹	163	61	91	27	37.0%	.300	5	1.60	6.09	5.62	10.1	3.6	5.4	1.6	-1	-4.7	0.43

Breakout: 26% Improve: 57% Collapse: 19% Attrition: 19%   Comparables: Steve Dunning, Scott Scudder, Aaron Myette, Rick Rhoden

Once one of the top pitchers in the system, Hurley almost seems to be frozen in time, having made little progress in the past two years. His fastball hasn't lost its plus velocity or movement, but it also hasn't gotten any better. His slider remains good, but it's hardly a wipeout offering, and his changeup is still inconsistent. That's good enough to pitch reasonably well in the minors, but the leap forward to succeed in the big leagues hasn't occurred, and he's on the verge of being lost in the shuffle.

Jason Jennings

													Bats: L		Throws: R		Height: 6' 2"		Weight: 235		Born: July 17, 1978			Age: 30

YEAR	TEAM	LVL	AGE	W	L	SV	G	GS	IP	H	BB	SO	HR	GB%	BABIP	STUFF	WHIP	ERA	DERA	EqH9	EqBB9	EqSO9	EqHR9	DEF	VORP	SN/WX
2006	COL	MLB	27	9	13	0	32	32	212	206	85	142	17	45.4%	.295	17	1.37	3.78	3.53	8.2	3.2	5.5	0.6	4	50.3	5.59
2007	HOU	MLB	28	2	9	0	19	18	99	119	34	71	19	38.5%	.327	-9	1.55	6.45	5.72	10.0	2.6	5.9	1.6	-2	-8.4	0.74
2008	TEX	MLB	29	0	5	0	6	6	27¹	35	18	12	8	45.2%	.287	-33	1.94	8.57	9.10	10.0	5.0	3.1	2.5	2	-9.0	-0.61
2009	TEX	MLB	30	4	5	0	22	11	74	88	31	45	11	42.0%	.310	1	1.59	5.68	5.31	10.3	3.4	5.0	1.3	-1	0.2	0.46

Breakout: 12%   Improve: 33%   Collapse: 42%   Attrition: 33%   Comparables: Joey Hamilton, Ralph Branca, Moe Drabowsky, Jaret Wright

Jennings has now broken down in consecutive seasons with the same injury to the same flexor tendon—apparently the joint now comes in a nice tearaway version, like a high school football jersey. You might figure that Jennings is about as popular as Santa Anna after burning both Texas ballclubs in consecutive seasons, but there's talk that he'll be back in a Rangers uni as a non-roster invitee, because it couldn't tear a third time, could it? Can the next one involve some sort of solution with velcro?

Wes Littleton

													Bats: R		Throws: R		Height: 6' 2"		Weight: 210		Born: September 2, 1982			Age: 26

YEAR	TEAM	LVL	AGE	W	L	SV	G	GS	IP	H	BB	SO	HR	GB%	BABIP	STUFF	WHIP	ERA	DERA	EqH9	EqBB9	EqSO9	EqHR9	DEF	VORP	SN/WX
2006	FRI	AA	23	3	0	3	17	0	27²	13	7	25	1	64.3%	.174	4	0.74	0.66	3.29	4.3	2.6	4.9	0.7	5	7.0	—
2006	OKL	AAA	23	4	1	2	13	0	16	14	5	15	3	65.2%	.262	-7	1.19	2.25	3.52	8.8	2.9	5.9	2.3	1	3.5	—
2006	TEX	MLB	23	2	1	1	33	0	36¹	23	13	17	2	70.8%	.204	-8	0.99	1.74	3.67	5.2	3.4	3.9	0.5	7	17.8	1.61
2007	OKL	AAA	24	0	1	2	23	0	32¹	31	8	21	5	59.4%	.277	-27	1.21	5.02	7.20	9.6	2.4	4.2	1.8	4	-5.3	—
2007	TEX	MLB	24	3	2	2	35	0	48	48	16	24	6	56.2%	.275	-19	1.33	4.31	4.94	8.6	2.9	3.8	1.1	4	9.1	0.38
2008	OKL	AAA	25	7	1	6	44	0	58¹	55	25	58	3	54.9%	.322	-3	1.37	4.01	4.53	9.4	4.0	6.1	0.6	-2	6.6	—
2008	TEX	MLB	25	0	0	0	12	0	18	18	8	14	1	54.5%	.321	-4	1.44	6.00	5.60	8.7	3.6	6.1	0.5	0	-0.3	0.19
2009	BOS	MLB	26	3	2	2	58	0	54¹	55	24	37	4	53.0%	.300	1	1.44	4.27	4.37	8.7	3.5	5.8	0.7	1	8.4	0.68

Breakout: 21%   Improve: 49%   Collapse: 22%   Attrition: 16%   Comparables: Barry Jones, Fred Breining, Jesse Crain, Jack Aker

A side-armer who predictably generates the ground-ball outs you expect from the type, the athletic Littleton has never really had the stuff to fool enough right-handers to make it as a ROOGY, but he's also not had to deal with the kind of combustibility against lefties most of his ilk generally risk. Sold off to the Red Sox to make space on the 40-man, if Littleton sticks as an extra arm in the Beantown bullpen and does well, you can add his name to the list of arms rustled up by other teams, and undiscovered by the Rangers' APB to find some or any kind of pitching.

Warner Madrigal

													Bats: R		Throws: R		Height: 6' 0"		Weight: 200		Born: March 21, 1984			Age: 25

YEAR	TEAM	LVL	AGE	W	L	SV	G	GS	IP	H	BB	SO	HR	GB%	BABIP	STUFF	WHIP	ERA	DERA	EqH9	EqBB9	EqSO9	EqHR9	DEF	VORP	SN/WX
2006	ANG	Rk	22	2	1	5	12	0	12²	11	3	13	0	63.6%	.355	-26	1.15	3.69	7.20	13.5	4.5	3.6	0.9	0	-1.8	—
2007	CDR	A	23	5	4	20	54	0	61	44	23	75	3	56.1%	.293	-16	1.10	2.07	4.99	10.0	5.5	5.7	1.5	-2	3.5	—
2008	FRI	AA	24	1	0	10	14	0	15²	11	8	18	1	39.5%	.278	-1	1.21	1.72	4.40	8.2	5.0	6.9	1.3	1	1.9	—
2008	OKL	AAA	24	0	0	4	17	0	20¹	20	8	25	2	43.1%	.333	1	1.38	3.99	3.98	9.7	3.5	7.5	0.9	-2	3.7	—
2008	TEX	MLB	24	0	2	1	31	1	36	36	14	22	4	33.9%	.288	-14	1.39	4.75	4.95	8.2	3.2	4.7	1.0	-2	1.3	-0.76
2009	TEX	MLB	25	2	2	2	44	0	43¹	44	19	36	6	40.0%	.300	8	1.46	4.86	4.56	8.8	3.6	6.8	1.1	-0	4.4	0.32

Breakout: 35%   Improve: 50%   Collapse: 31%   Attrition: 37%   Comparables: Gene Pentz, Matt Ginter, Mac Suzuki, Dave Giusti

If you like your Madrigals classic instead of Rush'd, you should love Warner. The converted outfielder has the relief arsenal that sings like it's coming straight from the sheet music, with mid-90s heat alternating with solid sliders that wreak Trecento-style raucous havoc on the strike zone. The Rangers nabbed him as a minor league free agent before the season; he's not the mechanical mess that many conversion projects can be, which contributed to his quick rise through the system. He wasn't quite ready for a set-up role in "The Show," though the Rangers gave him the opportunity in the last month; the slider's still something of a work in progress. Still, he was a nice pickup, and will have a chance to stick.

Brandon McCarthy

Bats: R   Throws: R   Height: 6' 7"   Weight: 200   Born: July 7, 1983   Age: 25

YEAR	TEAM	LVL	AGE	W	L	SV	G	GS	IP	H	BB	SO	HR	GB%	BABIP	STUFF	WHIP	ERA	DERA	EqH9	EqBB9	EqSO9	EqHR9	DEF	VORP	SN/WX
2006	CHA	MLB	22	4	7	0	53	2	84²	77	33	69	17	39.3%	.260	-2	1.30	4.68	4.68	8.1	3.5	6.6	1.6	2	14.3	1.05
2007	TEX	MLB	23	5	10	0	23	22	101²	111	48	59	9	37.8%	.307	-2	1.56	4.87	4.32	9.4	3.9	4.4	0.8	-10	6.3	1.88
2008	OKL	AAA	24	1	1	0	5	5	26²	21	8	23	2	51.9%	.257	5	1.09	3.37	4.78	7.2	2.7	5.1	0.7	2	2.4	—
2008	TEX	MLB	24	1	1	0	5	5	22	20	8	10	3	27.0%	.246	-12	1.27	4.09	5.64	7.3	2.8	3.6	1.2	3	3.4	0.74
2009	TEX	MLB	25	3	4	1	32	8	68¹	73	27	45	10	39.0%	.290	3	1.46	5.09	4.75	9.3	3.3	5.4	1.2	-1	5.1	0.70

Breakout: 17%   Improve: 43%   Collapse: 34%   Attrition: 29%   Comparables: Arnie Portocarrero, Gary Glover, Bill Gogolewski, Phil Regan

While acquiring McCarthy doesn't represent Jon Daniels' original sin (or his last) where picking pitchers is concerned, the former White Sox prospect risks becoming a symbol for it. The problem is that McCarthy's the wrong kind of pitcher in the wrong kind of ballpark, and in an organization that *needs* him to be something, because they invested a lot—John Danks in particular—on the guess that he would be. In the end, McCarthy might just be a nice fourth or fifth starter with a low-powered assortment, and somebody who could pan out pitching someplace where the fences are a bit more remote (say, two counties over). After a season essentially lost to elbow woes, he'll get first crack at that fourth or fifth slot, but it's up to him to hold onto it.

Luis Mendoza

Bats: L   Throws: R   Height: 6' 3"   Weight: 180   Born: October 31, 1983   Age: 25

YEAR	TEAM	LVL	AGE	W	L	SV	G	GS	IP	H	BB	SO	HR	GB%	BABIP	STUFF	WHIP	ERA	DERA	EqH9	EqBB9	EqSO9	EqHR9	DEF	VORP	SN/WX
2006	WIL	A+	22	5	4	0	13	13	63¹	67	14	46	4	55.1%	.317	-14	1.28	3.14	5.24	12.5	2.9	3.5	1.6	-5	2.3	—
2006	PME	AA	22	1	5	0	9	9	48¹	73	14	29	4	56.1%	.401	-27	1.81	6.36	7.02	18.4	3.7	2.9	1.5	-11	-6.5	—
2006	FRI	AA	22	2	4	0	7	7	38¹	55	11	21	2	46.9%	.373	-22	1.73	7.80	10.06	14.0	2.9	2.5	0.7	0	-18.2	—
2007	FRI	AA	23	15	4	0	26	25	148²	145	48	93	11	46.7%	.289	-18	1.30	3.93	6.90	10.6	3.5	3.3	1.2	8	-19.8	—
2007	TEX	MLB	23	1	0	0	6	3	16	13	4	7	1	54.9%	.250	-5	1.06	2.25	4.02	6.9	2.3	3.4	0.6	3	6.7	0.57
2008	OKL	AAA	24	2	3	0	8	8	35	43	8	19	1	57.1%	.341	-10	1.46	5.14	4.81	11.5	2.1	2.9	0.5	-4	3.0	—
2008	TEX	MLB	24	3	8	1	25	11	63¹	97	25	35	7	48.2%	.373	-23	1.93	8.67	8.45	12.3	3.1	4.1	1.0	-12	-31.6	-2.03
2009	TEX	MLB	25	3	4	1	23	7	54¹	66	20	28	7	49.0%	.320	-2	1.57	5.50	5.22	10.5	3.0	4.3	1.0	-1	0.7	0.30

Breakout: 49%   Improve: 68%   Collapse: 13%   Attrition: 44%   Comparables: Bob Miller, Julio Santana, Luis Andujar, Andy Replogle

In their neediness, the Rangers had to turn to this Mexican sinkerballer no matter how unready he proved to be. The sinker didn't sink enough, and his secondary stuff lacked the movement and deception for him to do much more than hope he kept getting people to guess wrong; when so much is going amiss, it's hard to keep in mind what the guy does well, because you're seeing him working from the stretch non-stop. Once Mendoza improves his off-speed stuff, his low-90s heavy fastball is going to be able to deliver happy results. In the meantime, he really needs to be in Triple-A.

Kevin Millwood

Bats: R   Throws: R   Height: 6' 4"   Weight: 230   Born: December 24, 1974   Age: 34

YEAR	TEAM	LVL	AGE	W	L	SV	G	GS	IP	H	BB	SO	HR	GB%	BABIP	STUFF	WHIP	ERA	DERA	EqH9	EqBB9	EqSO9	EqHR9	DEF	VORP	SN/WX
2006	TEX	MLB	31	16	12	0	34	34	215	228	53	157	23	46.0%	.311	13	1.31	4.52	4.65	9.0	2.2	5.8	0.9	3	32.6	4.17
2007	TEX	MLB	32	10	14	0	31	31	172²	213	67	123	19	47.8%	.343	1	1.62	5.16	4.79	10.9	3.3	5.6	1.0	-12	4.4	1.51
2008	TEX	MLB	33	9	10	0	29	29	168²	220	49	125	18	42.0%	.359	8	1.59	5.07	4.59	10.8	2.3	5.7	0.9	-14	5.7	1.46
2009	TEX	MLB	34	8	9	0	24	24	141¹	166	45	98	19	45.0%	.320	16	1.49	5.09	4.78	10.2	2.6	5.7	1.1	-1	8.8	2.05

Breakout: 19%   Improve: 52%   Collapse: 19%   Attrition: 22%   Comparables: Mike Torrez, John Burkett, Jim Perry, Rick Rhoden

Millwood's somewhat under the gun to get his $12 million salary for 2010 guaranteed; if he fails to deliver 180 IP in '09, the team can void his deal. But for all of the constancy with which his name crops up in injury-related chatter, he has managed 60 starts the past two years, and with some moderate amount of adequate defensive support and better in-game management—he would have had 14 quality starts instead of 11 if Washington had a quicker hook—the results would look a lot better than they have. That's not to say they'd add up to the $24 million the Rangers paid over that time, but it wouldn't fit so easily within the litany of mound-y woe.

Dustin Nippert

Bats: R   Throws: R   Height: 6' 8"   Weight: 225   Born: May 6, 1981   Age: 28

YEAR	TEAM	LVL	AGE	W	L	SV	G	GS	IP	H	BB	SO	HR	GB%	BABIP	STUFF	WHIP	ERA	DERA	EqH9	EqBB9	EqSO9	EqHR9	DEF	VORP	SN/WX
2006	TUC	AAA	25	13	8	0	25	24	140	161	52	130	11	47.2%	.355	-2	1.52	4.89	5.88	11.7	3.6	5.9	1.0	-5	-4.1	—
2007	TUC	AAA	26	0	3	0	10	8	36	23	23	46	3	40.5%	.274	21	1.28	4.75	5.88	6.1	6.1	8.8	1.1	3	-1.0	—
2007	ARI	MLB	26	1	1	0	36	0	45^1	48	16	38	5	39.4%	.314	1	1.41	5.56	5.56	9.1	2.8	6.9	0.8	3	0.3	0.66
2008	OKL	AAA	27	6	2	0	12	10	63^1	65	16	43	8	43.6%	.302	-11	1.28	3.98	5.46	10.0	2.4	4.1	1.4	5	0.9	—
2008	TEX	MLB	27	3	5	0	20	6	71^2	92	37	55	10	37.9%	.350	-11	1.80	6.40	5.40	10.6	4.0	5.9	1.2	-7	-5.3	0.05
2009	TEX	MLB	28	4	5	1	29	8	76^2	87	32	53	10	43.0%	.310	5	1.54	5.21	4.87	9.8	3.4	5.7	1.1	-1	4.5	0.66

Breakout: 37%   Improve: 63%   Collapse: 24%   Attrition: 40%   Comparables: Jason Johnson, Rich Gale, Lerrin LaGrow, Jay Witasick

Snagged from the Snakes at the end of spring training, Nippert had an initial opportunity to stick in the pen but punted, spent two months starting for Oklahoma, came back to cool his jets for a six-week stint doing long relief after other people's disasterpieces, and then got a six-start audition for the rotation. It's a reflection of the local state of affairs that he managed one quality start in his six, and the Rangers thought that showed promise. Even so, there's enough upside here to keep him in mind for the rotation picture—low-90s heat and a plus curve capture the imagination very easily, and if you wrap it up in a Nippert-sized package, people stay interested.

Vicente Padilla

Bats: R   Throws: R   Height: 6' 2"   Weight: 220   Born: September 27, 1977   Age: 31

YEAR	TEAM	LVL	AGE	W	L	SV	G	GS	IP	H	BB	SO	HR	GB%	BABIP	STUFF	WHIP	ERA	DERA	EqH9	EqBB9	EqSO9	EqHR9	DEF	VORP	SN/WX
2006	TEX	MLB	28	15	10	0	33	33	200	206	70	156	21	45.2%	.310	14	1.38	4.50	4.48	8.8	3.1	6.2	0.9	-2	28.8	4.26
2007	TEX	MLB	29	6	10	0	23	23	120^1	146	50	71	16	47.0%	.323	-13	1.63	5.76	6.09	10.6	3.5	4.6	1.2	-2	-7.1	0.55
2008	TEX	MLB	30	14	8	0	29	29	171	185	65	127	26	42.7%	.306	-1	1.46	4.74	4.78	9.0	3.1	5.8	1.4	-5	10.3	1.72
2009	TEX	MLB	31	8	9	0	25	25	147^1	165	56	101	19	45.0%	.310	15	1.50	5.04	4.74	9.7	3.1	5.6	1.1	-1	9.6	2.21

Breakout: 24%   Improve: 68%   Collapse: 14%   Attrition: 22%   Comparables: Bobby Witt, Jim Clancy, Doyle Alexander, Mike Moore

Again, while it's easy to bash Padilla for his performance, he did pitch through pain in the second half; 16 starts into his season, he had a 3.74 ERA and had delivered quality starts in half of them. He provided just three more in his last 13, but with the benefit of better support than Millwood, he wound up with a superficially better-looking season in fantasy categories. If this was supposed to be an "up" year in his up/down pattern in recent years, the down's going to be pretty fugly this year, and you can pretty much write off the chances the Rangers will pick up their option on him for 2010.

Josh Rupe

Bats: R   Throws: R   Height: 6' 2"   Weight: 210   Born: August 18, 1982   Age: 26

YEAR	TEAM	LVL	AGE	W	L	SV	G	GS	IP	H	BB	SO	HR	GB%	BABIP	STUFF	WHIP	ERA	DERA	EqH9	EqBB9	EqSO9	EqHR9	DEF	VORP	SN/WX
2006	FRI	AA	23	0	0	0	6	0	6	7	4	3	2	60.9%	.250	-42	1.83	10.50	11.37	9.9	5.7	1.4	4.3	-1	-4.0	—
2006	OKL	AAA	23	1	1	2	12	0	13	13	6	4	0	67.3%	.309	-34	1.46	3.46	4.50	9.8	4.5	1.5	0.0	-1	1.5	—
2006	TEX	MLB	23	0	1	0	16	0	29	33	9	14	2	67.6%	.313	-8	1.45	3.10	2.83	9.7	2.8	3.8	0.6	-2	8.8	-0.15
2007	OKL	AAA	24	2	2	0	7	7	37	39	14	20	4	46.3%	.302	-20	1.43	4.62	6.95	10.7	3.7	3.5	1.3	5	-5.1	—
2008	TEX	MLB	25	3	1	0	46	0	89^1	93	46	53	8	48.8%	.320	-11	1.56	5.14	5.06	9.1	4.4	4.9	0.8	0	5.8	0.94
2009	TEX	MLB	26	3	3	1	33	2	54^2	60	25	33	6	49.0%	.300	-0	1.54	4.73	4.48	9.5	3.7	5.0	0.9	-0	5.9	0.48

Breakout: 20%   Improve: 38%   Collapse: 38%   Attrition: 40%   Comparables: Barry Jones, Gary Majewski, Jim Hannan, Vince Colbert

Alice Longworth used to say that if you can't say something nice about somebody, you needed to sit down next to her, but did she mean she wanted to hear about Josh Rupe? He spent the full season in the pen and generated the second-lowest Leverage score in the majors of any relief-only pitcher with 50 or more IP, ranking behind only the Royals' Joel Peralta. What does that make in today's era of over-managed pens? Mop-up Apprentice, first class? He must not have liked it very much, because his other major feat was tying for second on the team in hit batsmen with 10. He didn't have an exploitable split. He's still on the 40-man. No, there's no explanation.

C. J. Wilson

| | | | | | | | Bats: L | | Throws: L | | Height: 6' 1" | | Weight: 215 | | Born: November 18, 1980 | | Age: 28 |

YEAR	TEAM	LVL	AGE	W	L	SV	G	GS	IP	H	BB	SO	HR	GB%	BABIP	STUFF	WHIP	ERA	DERA	EqH9	EqBB9	EqSO9	EqHR9	DEF	VORP	SN/WX
2006	OKL	AAA	25	1	0	2	9	0	11	10	5	17	0	61.5%	.385	10	1.36	2.45	2.61	10.5	4.4	10.5	0.0	-1	3.4	—
2006	TEX	MLB	25	2	4	1	44	0	44¹	39	18	43	7	52.8%	.274	2	1.29	4.06	4.06	7.5	3.5	7.7	1.2	-2	7.4	0.31
2007	TEX	MLB	26	2	1	12	66	0	68¹	50	33	63	4	49.2%	.266	9	1.21	3.03	4.43	6.4	4.0	7.3	0.5	9	20.8	2.34
2008	TEX	MLB	27	2	2	24	50	0	46¹	49	27	41	8	47.9%	.306	-11	1.64	6.03	5.89	8.7	4.6	6.8	1.5	-3	-5.1	1.29
2009	TEX	MLB	28	3	3	14	50	0	49¹	49	24	42	5	47.0%	.300	9	1.47	4.38	4.15	8.5	4.0	7.0	0.8	-0	7.3	0.81

Breakout: 26% Improve: 63% Collapse: 15% Attrition: 18%   Comparables: Neal Cotts, Ray King, Paul Assenmacher, Mike Mohler

Pitching with "closer du jour" indecision dictating who might get saves any given night, Wilson gave it a good go, pitching through a bum elbow that required surgery to remove bone spurs in August; physical problems had already become apparent in March. There's no campaign medal for "Rangers Futilitarian Expedition 2008," so he has to settle for a scar, some saves, and a shot at a share of the role or setting up Francisco.

Jamey Wright

| | | | | | | | Bats: R | | Throws: R | | Height: 6' 5" | | Weight: 205 | | Born: December 24, 1974 | | Age: 34 |

YEAR	TEAM	LVL	AGE	W	L	SV	G	GS	IP	H	BB	SO	HR	GB%	BABIP	STUFF	WHIP	ERA	DERA	EqH9	EqBB9	EqSO9	EqHR9	DEF	VORP	SN/WX
2006	SFN	MLB	31	6	10	0	34	21	156	167	64	79	16	58.9%	.303	-5	1.48	5.19	5.42	9.9	3.4	4.3	0.8	8	9.7	1.71
2007	TEX	MLB	32	4	5	0	20	9	77	72	41	39	6	55.3%	.283	-7	1.47	3.62	4.54	8.5	4.7	4.0	0.7	5	16.8	1.72
2008	TEX	MLB	33	8	7	0	75	0	84¹	93	35	60	5	63.4%	.333	-1	1.52	5.12	5.21	9.1	3.4	5.5	0.5	-5	-2.6	0.11
2009	TEX	MLB	34	3	3	1	44	2	64¹	74	28	41	6	54.0%	.320	-2	1.57	5.01	4.80	9.9	3.6	5.2	0.8	-1	4.0	0.39

Breakout: 22% Improve: 42% Collapse: 29% Attrition: 24%   Comparables: Mike LaCoss, Dennis Lamp, Dave Weathers, Julian Tavarez

There isn't much glory associated with a classic middle-relief role, but it's the sort of thing we see less of in today's overbred bullpens. When you've got a rotation as up in the air as the Rangers' was, it makes sense to have a guy around who can squeegee the resulting mess into history's gutters, and Wright delivered on exactly that level, vulturing or soaking lots of decisions, and "blowing" a half-dozen saves, only one representing a true ninth-inning opportunity. Did we mention the relative absence of glory involved with the job? He's a free agent as we go to press, but he'll clearly do what he's asked to for a paycheck.

LINEOUTS

Hitters

PLAYER	TEAM	LVL	AGE	PA	R	2B	3B	HR	RBI	BB	SO	SB-CS	EqBRR	AVG/OBP/SLG	EqAVG/EqOBP/EqSLG	EqA	VORP	WARP
OF E. Beltre*	CLN	A	18	598	87	26	9	8	47	15	105	31-11	1.3	.283/.308/.403	.233/.253/.348	.207	-32.6	-2.3
CF J. Borbon*	BAK	A+	22	314	47	20	0	2	36	15	30	36-7	3.3	.306/.346/.395	.250/.284/.324	.222	-13.3	-0.7
	FRI	AA	22	280	40	12	2	5	22	14	32	17-11	-2.0	.337/.380/.459	.287/.322/.402	.248	3.9	1.6
OF B. Harrison	FRI	AA	26	392	66	23	0	17	66	42	99	18-2	1.6	.300/.385/.518	.214/.281/.366	.228	-13.7	-1.5
	OKL	AAA	26	98	6	3	1	1	7	10	28	0-0	-1.8	.221/.306/.314	.193/.265/.284	.193	-7.3	-0.7
SS M. Lemon*	BAK	A+	20	517	80	30	4	8	47	46	69	12-8	-6.1	.295/.374/.434	.237/.307/.362	.234	-9.3	-0.1
OF S. Murphy*	FRI	AA	24	557	84	35	9	20	87	36	125	15-3	0.0	.262/.311/.484	.208/.250/.396	.222	-22.8	-2.1
INF R. Roberts	OKL	AAA	27	529	71	28	8	10	66	67	78	15-3	1.4	.300/.388/.464	.236/.316/.367	.244	-6.4	-1.2
2B J. Vallejo	BAK	A+	21	344	48	14	2	9	50	26	46	27-3	-2.8	.287/.349/.432	.231/.288/.364	.232	-9.8	-1.0
	FRI	AA	21	283	34	15	2	2	31	15	45	15-1	2.4	.297/.341/.394	.250/.288/.341	.227	-9.7	0.3

Engel Beltre has the best package of tools of any hitter in the system while also possessing the highest ceiling, but it's not going to mean much if he doesn't improve his plate discipline. ⊘ Kind of the Elvis Andrus version of a center-field prospect, **Julio Borbon** has speed, defense, and the ability to hit for average, but he doesn't walk enough to be a leadoff man, and his power is limited. ⊘ A four-year college player who's subsequently too old to be considered a true prospect, **Ben Harrison** might have enough power and hitting skills to nevertheless make it as a bench outfielder. ⊘ The son of Chet, **Marcus Lemon** doesn't have enough of a bat to be an everyday player, but his defensive skills and baseball intelligence should help him land a utility role. ⊘ A good athlete with power and some speed, **Steven Murphy** doesn't have enough bat to be anything but a shuttle-worthy reserve. ⊘ After years spent in the Jays' system not having enough glove for second or enough bat for third, **Ryan Roberts** came back to his native Texas and delivered more of the same. ⊘ **Jose Vallejo** is among the fastest players in the system, but the jury is still out on whether he'll hit enough to play every day, as his lack of arm strength limits his utility possibilities.

Pitchers

PLAYER	TEAM	LVL	AGE	W	L	SV	IP	H	BB	SO	HR	GB%	BABIP	STUFF	WHIP	ERA	DERA	EqH9	EqBB9	EqSO9	EqHR9	DEF	VORP
J. Bannister	BAK	A+	24	4	6	2	63	63	29	51	5	55.7%	.319	-25	1.46	4.29	5.98	11.3	5.7	3.9	1.6	-6	-2.4
	FRI	AA	24	1	0	1	25²	26	22	15	1	54.2%	.309	-20	1.87	4.55	7.15	11.5	9.1	2.8	0.8	1	-3.9
B. Beavan	CLN	A	19	10	6	0	121²	105	20	73	12	48.8%	.256	-25	1.03	2.37	6.41	10.7	2.5	2.2	2.4	10	-9.6
J. Diaz	NWO	AAA	28	1	5	0	39	31	33	36	8	37.7%	.230	-18	1.64	6.69	9.23	7.8	7.2	5.3	2.1	3	-15.7
	FRI	AA	28	1	0	4	13²	10	11	13	1	45.7%	.265	-6	1.53	3.94	7.50	8.2	8.2	6.0	1.5	3	-2.5
	OKL	AAA	28	1	1	2	18	15	14	16	2	35.1%	.294	-13	1.61	5.50	8.31	8.3	6.7	5.2	1.0	3	-5.2
K. Fukumori	OKL	AAA	31	1	6	2	64	79	18	40	7	43.9%	.332	-28	1.52	5.48	6.46	11.7	2.6	3.5	1.2	0	-5.9
	TEX	MLB	31	0	0	0	4	11	4	1	2	42.9%	.474	-70	3.75	20.25	15.75	24.8	9.0	2.2	4.5	-2	-6.3
B. Gordon	FRI	AA	29	2	0	3	22	9	4	18	0	50.9%	.161	1	0.59	0.00	3.32	3.7	2.1	4.6	0.4	5	5.5
	OKL	AAA	29	4	5	0	71	85	15	51	14	43.0%	.326	-29	1.41	4.56	6.38	11.8	2.2	4.3	2.0	2	-5.7
	TEX	MLB	29	0	0	0	4	4	0	1	0	20.0%	.267	-18	1.00	2.25	4.50	6.8	0.0	2.2	0.0	1	1.6
K. Loe	OKL	AAA	26	3	5	1	58	70	20	31	7	56.3%	.321	-34	1.55	5.59	7.28	11.5	3.2	2.9	1.3	2	-10.4
	TEX	MLB	26	1	0	0	30²	36	8	20	3	51.9%	.324	-4	1.43	3.22	4.31	9.5	2.0	4.9	0.9	-3	1.7
M. Main	CLN	A	19	2	2	0	45¹	38	13	50	4	32.8%	.301	10	1.13	2.58	5.17	11.7	4.0	5.4	2.1	-2	1.8
D. Mathis	OKL	AAA	25	5	1	0	53²	51	14	36	7	55.6%	.278	-12	1.21	3.35	6.23	8.8	2.4	3.8	1.4	5	-3.6
	TEX	MLB	25	2	1	0	22¹	37	14	9	3	42.7%	.400	-28	2.28	6.86	6.65	14.5	5.4	3.3	1.2	-2	-5.6
M. Perez*	SPO	A-	17	1	2	0	61²	66	28	53	3	51.0%	.345	-18	1.52	3.65	8.53	16.2	5.9	2.8	2.0	-1	-16.5
O. Poveda	BAK	A+	20	4	4	0	90²	82	40	97	10	46.0%	.309	3	1.35	4.47	6.44	10.7	5.3	5.6	2.0	-11	-7.6
E. Ramirez	OKL	AAA	25	10	7	0	160	193	33	85	24	44.1%	.316	-26	1.41	4.50	6.49	11.2	2.0	2.9	1.6	5	-15.4
B. White*	OKL	AAA	29	4	1	6	53¹	45	30	62	4	45.7%	.323	1	1.41	3.55	5.51	8.7	5.2	7.3	0.9	5	0.5

After showing some promise early in his career, **John Bannister** lost the ability to throw strikes in 2008 and doesn't have enough stuff to make up for it, but the Rangers put him on their 40-man as part of the great Rule 5 scare of '08. ⊘ A first-round pick in '07, **Blake Beavan** doesn't throw as hard as he did in high school, but his immaculate control and heavy sink still allowed him to put up some impressive numbers. ⊘ Short and squat and built like a cube, **Jose Diaz** lights up radar guns, has no idea where anything's going, and lacks a second pitch. ⊘ After losing all of 2008 recuperating from a Tommy John surgery, **Willie Eyre** will be coming to camp hoping to reclaim his utility pitcher spot; although he got hammered in the AFL, he did strike out 33 in 26⅓ IP. ⊘ When people talk about exciting imports from Japan, they're probably not referring to **Kazuo Fukumori**, a sore-armed veteran signed to a two-year, $3 million deal before last season; his performance was more scaly than sushi-grade. ⊘ It's awesome that **Brian Gordon** finally got to the big leagues in his 12th pro season, but don't expect too much more from here. ⊘ In the legion of non-descript swingmen who've swung through the Rangers' roster, you can delete **Kameron Loe**—he was the tallish one, no the other tallish one—as he's been sold off to Fukuoka in the Japanese leagues. ⊘ While limited by a number of non-arm injuries in 2008, **Michael Main** is ultra-athletic, ultra-projectable, and already has plus stuff, making him a fantastic bet for a minor league breakout. ⊘ Seen as more of an organizational arm in the past, **Doug Mathis** could work his way into the big-league bullpen thanks to his ground ball-generating sinker. ⊘ One of many talented teenage Latin American arms in the system, **Martin Perez** has excellent mechanics, and his fastball and curve already rate as plus. ⊘ It's easy to forget about a guy like **Omar Poveda** in a system with this much pitching, but he still projects as an eventual fourth starter thanks to a good fastball and even better changeup. ⊘ **Elizardo Ramirez** has plus-plus control of minus-minus stuff, and no, that does not make him average. ⊘ **Bill White** is your classic Quad-A lefty with aggressiveness and guile, but not a whole lot of stuff.

MANAGER: RON WASHINGTON

YEAR	TEAM	W-L	Pythag +/−	Avg PC	100+ P	120+ P	QS	BQS	REL	REL w Zero R	IBB	Subs	PH	PH Avg	PH HR	SB2	CS2	SB3	CS3	SAC Att	SAC %	POS SAC	Squeeze	Swing	In Play
2007	TEX	75-87	-3	89.8	43	0	48	5	467	290	38	64	89	.215	4	76	23	12	2	82	69.5%	54	1	121	101
2008	TEX	79-83	4	91.3	54	1	52	11	457	261	44	38	117	.250	0	71	23	10	2	62	59.7%	33	0	132	93

"Wash" came into his second season of skippering already under a bit of a cloud of doubt, but it wasn't like Earl Weaver was going to win with this lot. You can find plenty of nits to pick in terms of in-game tactics, whether in the management of a bad bullpen, or trying to extend starters in their better outings, only to wind up with a generous blown quality start tally. Pen management wasn't a strength, but what did he have to work with? He probably deserves some credit for how he handled a club that brought in famous former problem children Josh Hamilton and Milton Bradley; nothing bad happened, and nobody's head exploded, after all. The shakeup of the coaching staff during and after the season involved unloading a lot of overlapping legacies and other people's hires. The new coaches reflect that Washington's not getting total authority over his own staff, which is neither a good thing or bad, but it does reflect that he's not solely responsible for how things are getting done. If and when he's scapegoated if and when the Rangers manage to disappoint people again, keep that in mind.

Toronto Blue Jays

In a long stretch of tough times to be a Blue Jays fan, 2008 was perhaps one of the toughest single seasons. In each of the first 11 years after the 1994 players' strike, the Jays finished behind both the Yankees and the Red Sox in the AL East. In all but one year from 1998 to 2005, they finished third in the division. In 2006, the Blue Jays finally broke the New York–Boston hegemony by sneaking past the Red Sox into second place. Perhaps the spell had broken. Perhaps the Blue Jays mattered in their own division.

Then the Jays fell right back to third in 2007, but they had (and made) excuses. High-priced closer B. J. Ryan recorded just three saves before having to undergo Tommy John surgery. All-Star center fielder Vernon Wells played with a torn labrum in his left shoulder and had his worst season. First baseman Lyle Overbay had his hand broken by a pitch on June 4 and hit just .225/.299/.321 after returning from a month on the disabled list. Slugging third baseman Troy Glaus was hampered by leg and foot injuries all year. Outfielder Reed Johnson landed on the disabled list in mid-April with a back injury that required surgery, and he hit just .232/.302/.307 after returning, while outfield prospect Adam Lind struggled in Johnson's stead.

Despite all of that, one very significant positive for the 2007 Blue Jays gave them hope for 2008. While the offense and bullpen were struggling to recover from their litany of injuries, an impressive young rotation was coalescing behind veteran ace Roy Halladay. When the Jays slipped past Boston in 2006, their rotation was bifurcated into a top three of Halladay, lefty Ted Lilly, and the oft-injured A. J. Burnett (who had just joined the team as a big-money free agent) and a bottom half of assorted ineffective starters who filled in the remaining two spots and the time Burnett lost to injury. Having feuded with manager John Gibbons late that season, Lilly left for a big free-agent payday with the Cubs that December, leaving the Jays with Halladay, the fragile Burnett, and thoughts of disabling the Rogers Centre's retractable roof and praying for rain.

The Blue Jays' Opening Day rotation in 2007 was Halladay, Burnett, 2005 one-year-wonder Gustavo Chacin, journeyman Tomo Ohka, and marginal strike-thrower Josh Towers. In May, Chacin, Ohka, and Towers were replaced by home-grown arms Dustin McGowan, Shaun Marcum (both in their age-25 seasons), and Jesse Litsch, who was then 22. All three of the kids pitched well, and as a result of their emergence, the Blue Jays' rotation jumped from 18th in the majors in SNLVAR in 2006 to second in baseball and tops in the American League in SNLVAR in 2007.

With Ryan due to return, Wells' shoulder surgically repaired, Overbay having had the winter to heal, Glaus replaced by Scott Rolen in an off-season deal, and Alex Rios appearing ready to make "the leap" heading into his age-27 season, the Blue Jays had high hopes heading into 2008, since their team was finally something more than a hasty assemblage of veteran parts. With a young five-man rotation that ranked among the major league's best and the taste of their second-place finish in 2006 still fresh in their mouths, the Jays hoped they could ride their young pitchers, their restored closer, and an anticipated offensive rebound into the hunt for the AL wild card and perhaps their first playoff appearance since 1993.

As it turned out, the Jays nearly did catch the Yankees

BLUE JAYS PROSPECTUS

2008 record: 86-76; Fourth place in AL East

Pythagenport record: 92-70

Runs scored per game: 4.41 (11th in AL)

Runs allowed per game: 3.79 (1st in AL)

Team EqA: .253 (11th in AL)

2008 Batters Age: 31.5 (2nd-oldest in AL)

2008 Pitchers Age: 28.9 (3rd-oldest in AL)

Ballpark: Rogers Centre; Neutral park; Park Factor of .991

2008: All pitching and no hitting make the Jays the hard-luck fourth-place finishers in baseball's best division.

2009: It'll take more than serendipity and Travis Snider to offset the pitching staff's problems. Fourth place is their story, and they're sticking to it.

in 2008, but that had less to do with the Blue Jays' surge than with the down-year experienced by their rivals. Both clubs actually slipped a rung in the division, passed by the Rays' long-term building project (you can't rebuild if you've never been on top, after all). The harsh realization was that 2006 was a false promise—it wasn't that the Jays were an up-and-coming team that year, but that the Red Sox were experiencing something of a lull while retooling between championships. Just like the Red Sox, who headed into 2007 by adding Daisuke Matsuzaka, J. D. Drew, Dustin Pedroia, and Hideki Okajima, the Yankees have since made significant upgrades to both their pitching staff and their lineup, changes that should put significant distance between them and the Blue Jays in 2009.

To make matters worse, the Blue Jays' outlook heading into 2009 would have been bleaker than it was a year ago, even without the Yankees' improvements or the Rays' arrival to truly upset the division's balance of power. It wasn't just a disappointing year for the Jays; it was a disastrous one. Not only did Wells suffer through another injury-marred season, but Rolen proved even more fragile than Glaus, Lind failed to realize his potential yet again, second baseman Aaron Hill lost half the season to postconcussion syndrome, and Jeremy Accardo, who had closed in 2007, switched places with Ryan by spending most of the season on the DL with a forearm strain. Worst of all, injuries decimated the Blue Jays' young rotation. Marcum hit the DL in late June with elbow pain, was awful after returning, and eventually underwent Tommy John surgery in September, thereby wiping out his 2009 season as well. McGowan hit the DL in late July, had season-ending labrum surgery, and will also start 2009 on the DL. Neither Marcum nor McGowan will have pitched a full season in the major leagues by the time they reach the 2010 season, which just happens to be the last year of Roy Halladay's contract.

Adding insult to injury, Burnett finally stayed healthy in 2008, just in time to opt out of his contract and sign a massive five-year deal with the Yankees. Suddenly, that young rotation around which the Jays had hoped to build is no more. As a result, the Blue Jays' projected Opening Day rotation for 2009 is now Halladay, Litsch (the team's fifth starter a year ago), and then probably big home-grown lefty David Purcey. Then they'll throw in more roof shenanigans. In anticipation of a fully functioning roof, they've been aggressive making waiver claims this winter, hoping to somehow fill out their staff with other people's leavings, a measure of the desperation forced on them by so many unproductive drafts and player-development mistakes.

Compounding those losses, general manager J. P. Ricciardi had made no significant upgrades to the team or the rotation over the winter. Then again, Ricciardi might be forgiven for his lack of reinvestment in the team he's haphazardly assembled over the past seven seasons. Prior to 2008, Ricciardi's existential crisis was that the club was at best an 87-win team trapped in a division with a pair of reliable 95-win teams in New York and Boston. This meant that even on the odd occasion when one of those teams had an off year—as Boston did in 2006 and the Yankees did last year—the Jays could still hope for no better than a second-place finish. Even if they did manage to finish in second, with nearly a quarter of their schedule coming against those two behemoths, the Jays stood little chance of winning enough games to make a run at the wild card. Now that another team in the division leapfrogged the Jays and their two reliable rivals to win the division and the AL pennant, the Jays now find themselves pondering their lot as a fourth-place team, because the Rays are unlikely to return to the depths of the division anytime soon.

The Rays achieved what the Jays had hoped to do, building around a good young rotation and a strong defense. A Jays' infield of Scott Rolen, John McDonald, Aaron Hill, and Lyle Overbay would have been outstanding defensively and a key component of a winning strategy behind the heavily ground-ball-oriented rotation with which they opened the 2008 season. That broad-brush characterization of the infield overlooks a few fundamentals. McDonald can't hit and never has, and he had lost the full-time job before he ever had it, once Ricciardi signed David Eckstein, a vastly inferior defender. Rolen can't stay healthy, and both Hill and Overbay have suffered season-ruining injuries in the last two years. The Jays will run three of the four back out there this year, with Marco Scutaro assuming the shortstop job, but they no longer have the young pitchers to support. Given Rolen's injury history, Overbay's lack of power, Scutaro's tepid production, and the big question mark hanging over Hill's ability to return to form, the Jays are giving up far too much on offense for an advantage that has lost its relevance to the construction of the team.

That absence of a hitting attack (the Jays were 11th in the American League in both EqA and runs per game in 2008) is exacerbated by the absence of a premiere slugger in his prime or a blue-chip prospect about to come into his own. Ricciardi deliberately chose to make Rios and Wells the centerpieces of his offense, but both have been merely very good in their best seasons instead of great, and Wells, coming off two injury-plagued seasons, just turned 30. The two most exciting hitters in the Jays' system are outfielder Travis Snider, who made his big-league debut at the age of 20 last year and is expected to mature into a star slugger, and last year's top pick in the draft, David Cooper, who could join Snider as a power-hitting upgrade on Overbay after the latter's contract expires in 2010. Both Snider and Cooper are legitimate prospects, but both are hulking corner men on a team short of any true star players up the middle. As we remarked in the last edition, Jays drafting has been very spotty during the Ricciardi era, and though they have developed some decent complementary players, there has been precious little for a ballclub that increasingly needs a lot more than that. Given that the Jays are not effective players on the free-agent market, the lack of home-grown stars puts them in an impossible position vis-à-vis the rest of the division.

The final blow in the Blue Jays' miserable 2008 came on December 2, when team owner Ted Rogers died of congestive heart failure at the age of 75. It was Rogers who had spearheaded his company's purchase of the team in 2000 and who approved the team's $26 million payroll increase in 2006 and 114 percent increase in payroll from 2005 to 2008. In last year's annual, we argued that the Blue Jays needed a change in leadership in the front office after six (now seven) years of mediocrity and lack of direction under Ricciardi. But now they lack the leadership in the owners' office to enact that change in a timely manner, leaving the team twisting in the wind to play out the string with an assemblage that's already proven to be short of contention.

Other than the Blue Jays themselves and their fans, no one expected them to contend in 2008, but at least at that point, they had hope. They had a good, young rotation around which to build and an owner willing to increase payroll to attempt to compete with his team's division rivals. Just twelve months later, both are gone, and the Blue Jays are little more than a fourth-place nothing with no hope on the horizon. It was a very bad year to be a Blue Jays fan, but this year could be even worse.

HITTERS

J. P. Arencibia   C   Bats: R   Throws: R   Height: 6' 1"   Weight: 210   Born: January 5, 1986   Age: 23

YEAR	TEAM	LVL	AGE	PA	R	2B	3B	HR	RBI	BB	SO	SB	CS	EqBRR	AVG	OBP	SLG	EqAVG	EqOBP	EqSLG	EqA	VORP	WARP	DEFENSE
2007	AUB	A-	21	249	31	17	1	3	25	14	56	0	0	-0.4	.254	.309	.377	.195	.232	.301	.178	-41.4	-2.2	54-C -4
2008	DUN	A+	22	262	38	22	0	13	62	11	46	0	0	0.9	.315	.344	.560	.271	.297	.498	.265	9.8	1.5	54-C 0
2008	NHP	AA	22	275	32	14	0	14	43	7	55	0	0	-0.6	.282	.302	.496	.262	.280	.471	.252	4.1	0.9	49-C 0
2009	TOR	MLB	23	555	51	32	2	18	75	25	137	1	1	-0.7	.246	.284	.420	.247	.285	.430	.243	3.6	2.1	130-C -4

Breakout: 40%   Improve: 63%   Collapse: 13%   Attrition: 5%   Comparables: Mike Fitzgerald, Greg Park, Joe Oliver, Glenn Wilson

The Jay's anointed catcher of the future, University of Tennessee product Jonathan Paul Arencibia was Toronto's first compensation-round pick in 2007 and lit up the Florida State League in the first half of 2008. He continued to hit for power after a midseason promotion to Double-A, but his poor plate discipline is an emerging concern. Still, few organizations can boast a 22-year-old catcher who slugged just shy of .500 at Double-A in his first full professional season. Arencibia's throwing could use work, but he held his own with a 25 percent caught-stealing mark. With little in his way, Arencibia could be the Jays' Opening Day catcher in 2010.

Rod Barajas   C   Bats: R   Throws: R   Height: 6' 2"   Weight: 230   Born: September 5, 1975   Age: 33

YEAR	TEAM	LVL	AGE	PA	R	2B	3B	HR	RBI	BB	SO	SB	CS	EqBRR	AVG	OBP	SLG	EqAVG	EqOBP	EqSLG	EqA	VORP	WARP	DEFENSE
2006	TEX	MLB	30	371	49	20	0	11	41	17	51	0	0	-0.5	.256	.298	.410	.246	.292	.401	.238	0.9	1.0	93-C 1
2007	PHI	MLB	31	146	16	8	0	4	10	21	24	0	1	-0.5	.230	.352	.393	.223	.352	.397	.262	3.6	0.9	34-C 3
2008	TOR	MLB	32	377	44	23	0	11	49	17	61	0	0	-4.9	.249	.294	.410	.249	.294	.421	.245	4.6	2.0	88-C 9
2009	TOR	MLB	33	243	23	13	0	6	30	17	42	1	0	-1.4	.241	.303	.392	.243	.304	.402	.245	2.8	1.3	60-C 1

Breakout: 24%   Improve: 44%   Collapse: 30%   Attrition: 35%   Comparables: Joe Oliver, Mike Macfarlane, Jeff Newman, Gus Triandos

When Gregg Zaun hit the DL in late May of last year, Barajas staked a claim on the starting job behind the plate, hitting .298/.375/.526 during Zaun's DL stay to keep the job on Zaun's return and then hit .227/.260/.366 as Gaston's preferred starting catcher until a hamstring tear ended his season two weeks early. Barajas threw out 34 percent of attempting basestealers on the season, but the extra outs he recorded with his arm were outnumbered by the extra outs he made with his bat. That the Jays picked up his $2.5 million option for 2009 and have slotted him as their starter is a sign of how little catching talent is available and how lost the Jays have become. Arencibia can't get to the majors fast enough.

Jose Bautista — UT

Bats: R Throws: R Height: 6' 0" Weight: 195 Born: October 19, 1980 Age: 28

YEAR	TEAM	LVL	AGE	PA	R	2B	3B	HR	RBI	BB	SO	SB	CS	EqBRR	AVG	OBP	SLG	EqAVG	EqOBP	EqSLG	EqA	VORP	WARP	DEFENSE			
2006	IND	AAA	25	119	12	9	0	2	9	14	19	2	1	-1.2	.277	.370	.426	.255	.339	.412	.263	2.4	0.1	23-3B	1	4-CF	-3
2006	PIT	MLB	25	469	58	20	3	16	51	46	110	2	4	-2.6	.235	.335	.420	.236	.333	.425	.260	3.9	-1.3	47-CF	-15	30-3B	-7
2007	PIT	MLB	26	614	75	36	2	15	63	68	101	6	3	-2.9	.254	.339	.414	.257	.347	.429	.270	10.9	1.8	119-3B	-3	15-RF	-1
2008	PIT	MLB	27	363	38	15	0	12	44	38	77	1	1	-4.2	.242	.325	.404	.251	.333	.429	.264	4.8	0.8	81-3B	-2		
2008	TOR	MLB	27	61	7	2	0	3	10	2	14	0	0	-0.1	.214	.237	.411	.214	.237	.411	.221	-1.8	0.0	5-3B	2		
2009	TOR	MLB	28	393	43	19	1	12	50	40	86	3	1	-1.0	.244	.326	.415	.245	.328	.425	.263	5.7	1.1	94-3B	-3		

Breakout: 21% Improve: 43% Collapse: 26% Attrition: 25%   Comparables: Steve Buechele, Leo Gomez, Keith Ginter, Fernando Tatis

Overextended as the Pirates' everyday third baseman the last three years, Bautista began to fulfill his utilityman potential after coming to the Jays in a late August swap, getting multiple starts at first, second, and third over the season's final weeks. Bautista can't hit for average and strikes out too much, but given his ability to play everywhere but shortstop and catcher, his walks and modest power make him a handy bench player.

Scott Campbell — 2B

Bats: R Throws: R Height: 5' 11" Weight: 190 Born: September 25, 1984 Age: 24

YEAR	TEAM	LVL	AGE	PA	R	2B	3B	HR	RBI	BB	SO	SB	CS	EqBRR	AVG	OBP	SLG	EqAVG	EqOBP	EqSLG	EqA	VORP	WARP	DEFENSE			
2006	AUB	A-	21	293	39	14	0	0	18	33	31	2	10	-2.6	.292	.397	.350	.225	.303	.275	.207	-30.4	0.2	59-2B	9	6-3B	-1
2007	LNS	A	22	468	68	17	4	7	43	68	56	4	5	-2.8	.279	.390	.397	.202	.293	.295	.210	-26.6	-2.7	102-2B	-13		
2008	NHP	AA	23	487	70	21	2	9	46	66	63	2	6	-4.3	.302	.398	.427	.273	.363	.407	.269	16.7	1.5	105-2B	-6		
2009	TOR	MLB	24	508	50	24	2	7	46	50	92	3	2	-0.1	.239	.318	.346	.240	.319	.355	.239	-1.0	0.8	120-2B	1		

Breakout: 30% Improve: 55% Collapse: 21% Attrition: 8%   Comparables: Armando Moreno, Marco Scutaro, Carlos Villalobos, Jesus Alfaro

New Zealand native Campbell is on a quest to become the first Kiwi to reach the major leagues. That he has walked 17 more times than he has struck out across his first three pro seasons bodes well for his chances. Campbell has modest power at best, but he hits for solid averages, rarely strikes out, and consistently gets on base at a .390 clip or better. He was working on diversifying his defensive portfolio in the Arizona Fall League in anticipation of being blocked by Aaron Hill and chased up the chain by Brad Emaus, but if Hill's comeback doesn't go as planned, Campbell will be ready to make history. Too bad it didn't happen in time for his baseball card to make its way into Murray's office in the second season of *Flight of the Conchords*.

David Cooper — 1B

Bats: L Throws: L Height: 6' 0" Weight: 175 Born: February 12, 1987 Age: 22

YEAR	TEAM	LVL	AGE	PA	R	2B	3B	HR	RBI	BB	SO	SB	CS	EqBRR	AVG	OBP	SLG	EqAVG	EqOBP	EqSLG	EqA	VORP	WARP	DEFENSE	
2008	AUB	A-	21	95	10	10	1	2	21	10	16	0	1	-1.9	.341	.411	.553	.261	.316	.443	.258	4.0	0.3	17-1B	1
2008	LNS	A	21	106	15	10	0	2	17	10	14	0	0	-0.8	.354	.415	.521	.296	.349	.449	.274	5.4	0.3	21-1B	0
2008	DUN	A+	21	102	10	9	0	1	13	10	16	0	0	-1.0	.304	.373	.435	.266	.324	.404	.252	1.2	-0.2	21-1B	-2
2009	TOR	MLB	22	540	53	35	3	12	62	42	117	3	1	-0.2	.253	.315	.407	.254	.317	.417	.254	-1.4	0.5	127-1B	-1

Breakout: 21% Improve: 40% Collapse: 27% Attrition: 7%   Comparables: Michael Aubrey, Ryan McGuire, Wally Joyner, Joe DeSa

David Cooper can hit. After a monster year at Berkeley, he was the Blue Jays' first-round pick in June and mashed everywhere the Jays put him. Although he managed just five home runs, he has plenty of power, and many of his doubles will turn into long balls as he adjusts to wood bats. That's important, because hitting is his only virtue—at best, he'll be an acceptable first baseman in the field. He could also afford to stand in a bit better against lefties, or he risks acquiring a platoon label very early on.

Brad Emaus 2B

Bats: R   Throws: R   Height: 6' 0"   Weight: 190   Born: March 28, 1986   Age: 23

YEAR	TEAM	LVL	AGE	PA	R	2B	3B	HR	RBI	BB	SO	SB	CS	EqBRR	AVG	OBP	SLG	EqAVG	EqOBP	EqSLG	EqA	VORP	WARP	DEFENSE			
2007	AUB	A-	21	152	21	6	0	2	14	12	26	2	0	-0.4	.228	.298	.316	.170	.224	.234	.151	-34.6	-1.9	26-3B	1		
2008	DUN	A+	22	543	87	34	3	12	71	60	56	12	4	1.5	.302	.380	.463	.260	.328	.414	.259	9.0	0.1	97-2B	-16	13-3B	2
2009	TOR	MLB	23	599	64	34	4	10	59	48	100	7	4	1.6	.244	.307	.378	.245	.309	.387	.244	1.4	0.8	140-2B	-5		

Breakout: 33%   Improve: 68%   Collapse: 17%   Attrition: 3%   Comparables: Tony Graffanino, Ian Kinsler, Danny Garcia, Rich Aurilia

Tulane product "Might" Emaus shifted back to second base from the hot corner for his first full-length professional season and made like Campbell in terms of his suite of offensive skills, only with significantly more power. Emaus has a quick, short stroke that makes his power come easily and naturally; in Hawaiian Winter Baseball, he hit .333 and drew 17 walks against just seven strikeouts. Another advantage he has over Campbell is that he's a solid defender at the keystone and could well be Toronto's next second baseman, although much depends on Hill's health, since the big-league starter is under contract through at least 2011.

Aaron Hill 2B

Bats: R   Throws: R   Height: 5' 11"   Weight: 195   Born: March 21, 1982   Age: 27

YEAR	TEAM	LVL	AGE	PA	R	2B	3B	HR	RBI	BB	SO	SB	CS	EqBRR	AVG	OBP	SLG	EqAVG	EqOBP	EqSLG	EqA	VORP	WARP	DEFENSE			
2006	TOR	MLB	24	606	70	28	3	6	50	42	66	5	2	1.2	.291	.349	.386	.278	.341	.370	.252	19.1	2.5	103-2B	12	49-SS	-5
2007	TOR	MLB	25	657	87	47	2	17	78	41	102	4	3	-0.3	.291	.333	.459	.284	.330	.463	.269	28.7	5.1	158-2B	18		
2008	TOR	MLB	26	229	19	14	0	2	20	16	31	4	2	1.9	.263	.324	.361	.265	.329	.373	.247	1.4	-1.1	54-2B	-14		
2009	TOR	MLB	27	457	47	23	2	8	50	32	65	5	2	0.0	.260	.317	.385	.261	.318	.394	.250	6.3	1.2	108-2B	1		

Breakout: 11%   Improve: 33%   Collapse: 33%   Attrition: 15%   Comparables: Mark Lewis, Pat Kelly, Ron Hunt, Tim Cullen

Last year was a complete wash for Hill. He followed three hot weeks with five bad ones, then suffered a season-ending concussion in a collision with Eckstein on May 29. Finally over his postconcussion symptoms, Hill should be back at the keystone for his age-27 season, but there's no telling where he'll pick up, now that he's a year removed from his 2007 power surge. Sometimes a lost season can completely derail a player's progress, particularly when that player was a late-bloomer to begin with.

Joe Inglett UT

Bats: L   Throws: R   Height: 5' 10"   Weight: 180   Born: June 29, 1978   Age: 31

YEAR	TEAM	LVL	AGE	PA	R	2B	3B	HR	RBI	BB	SO	SB	CS	EqBRR	AVG	OBP	SLG	EqAVG	EqOBP	EqSLG	EqA	VORP	WARP	DEFENSE			
2006	AKR	AA	28	77	20	9	0	3	9	11	4	7	3	-0.5	.516	.587	.797	.338	.408	.500	.305	8.2	0.9	16-SS	1		
2006	BUF	AAA	28	181	21	7	2	1	13	13	24	3	2	1.0	.299	.358	.389	.235	.290	.315	.216	-8.1	-0.8	15-2B	-1	12-SS	-3
2006	CLE	MLB	28	222	26	8	3	2	21	14	39	5	1	1.1	.284	.332	.383	.276	.329	.377	.252	5.6	0.2	47-2B	-3	5-LF	1
2007	BUF	AAA	29	455	45	15	9	4	57	40	62	7	12	-4.4	.253	.327	.367	.198	.266	.299	.197	-31.5	-1.8	56-2B	-1	25-LF	4
2008	SYR	AAA	30	62	12	2	2	1	6	7	7	1	2	-0.3	.407	.484	.574	.327	.403	.491	.295	6.2	0.1	9-2B	-3		
2008	TOR	MLB	30	385	45	15	7	3	39	28	43	9	2	2.5	.297	.355	.407	.298	.359	.418	.273	15.5	2.4	61-2B	4	10-RF	0
2009	TOR	MLB	31	286	32	12	3	3	24	22	43	4	3	1.1	.257	.318	.365	.258	.320	.373	.245	1.4	0.7	70-2B	0		

Breakout: 20%   Improve: 41%   Collapse: 31%   Attrition: 35%   Comparables: Herb Plews, Denny Doyle, Alex Cora, Marlon Anderson

In lefty-hitting Inglett and righty-hitting Bautista, the Blue Jays have a matched set of utilitymen. They're not a bad pair: Bautista has hit .256/.354/.461 against lefties in his career, and Inglett has swatted .300/.352/.414 against righties, and between the two of them, they can cover every position but catcher. The problem is that the Jays aren't using the flexibility these two offer to stay above replacement level, but maintaining nonhitters at short and third while pushing infield bats to the outfield, a recipe for failure.

Justin Jackson SS

Bats: R   Throws: R   Height: 6' 2"   Weight: 175   Born: December 11, 1988   Age: 20

YEAR	TEAM	LVL	AGE	PA	R	2B	3B	HR	RBI	BB	SO	SB	CS	EqBRR	AVG	OBP	SLG	EqAVG	EqOBP	EqSLG	EqA	VORP	WARP	DEFENSE	
2007	BLJ	Rk	18	188	20	1	1	2	13	20	44	7	4	0.4	.187	.274	.241	.139	.199	.191	.106	-70.7	-3.8	35-SS	-4
2008	LNS	A	19	528	74	26	6	7	47	62	154	17	8	-2.4	.238	.340	.368	.203	.289	.320	.216	-26.8	-1.6	119-SS	-12
2009	TOR	MLB	20	570	52	30	5	8	42	49	175	9	5	1.1	.210	.282	.334	.211	.284	.341	.220	-10.4	0.4	134-SS	4

Breakout: 71%   Improve: 87%   Collapse: 4%   Attrition: 3%   Comparables: Sean Rodriguez, Brent Brewer, Ken Jackson, Jason Woolf

One of three Toronto picks from the first compensation round in 2007, Jackson is a raw, toolsy shortstop who has yet to translate his natural ability into production at the plate. Though he runs well, he doesn't steal efficiently, and though he's adept at drawing walks, he too often will work his way into a bad count and strike out. Still, he is developing his doubles power, is a smooth, rangy defender, just turned 20 in December, and has a clear path to the majors.

Brian Jeroloman — C

Bats: L   Throws: R   Height: 6' 0"   Weight: 195   Born: May 10, 1985   Age: 24

YEAR	TEAM	LVL	AGE	PA	R	2B	3B	HR	RBI	BB	SO	SB	CS	EqBRR	AVG	OBP	SLG	EqAVG	EqOBP	EqSLG	EqA	VORP	WARP	DEFENSE	
2006	AUB	A-	21	169	27	10	1	0	21	26	38	0	0	0.1	.241	.363	.326	.176	.274	.250	.183	-29.2	-0.9	32-C	1
2007	DUN	A+	22	382	32	14	0	3	39	85	57	0	0	-2.9	.259	.421	.338	.215	.368	.291	.251	-5.7	0.3	92-C	-9
2008	NHP	AA	23	285	30	15	0	6	31	47	47	0	0	0.1	.270	.396	.416	.253	.369	.399	.275	8.3	1.3	64-C	-5
2008	SYR	AAA	23	88	5	2	0	0	5	11	17	0	0	0.1	.200	.302	.227	.184	.287	.211	.179	-8.2	-0.2	22-C	1
2009	TOR	MLB	24	416	37	17	1	6	36	53	94	1	0	-0.9	.213	.317	.321	.214	.318	.328	.234	-4.6	1.0	99-C	-4

Breakout: 21% Improve: 41% Collapse: 30% Attrition: 16%   Comparables: Bob Henley, Mark Johnson, Bo Dodson, Todd Betts

If Arencibia is the Jays' catcher of the future, this sixth-round pick out of the University of Florida in 2006 has his own destiny as his future backup. He's a strong defensive catcher with good receiving skills, footwork, and a quick release. Like many of the organization's other marginal prospects, Jeroloman has little power but a tremendous plate approach. The Mark Johnson comp fits neatly with what you might expect from him and should make him a useful enough caddy for Arencibia.

Adam Lind — LF

Bats: L   Throws: L   Height: 6' 2"   Weight: 195   Born: July 17, 1983   Age: 25

YEAR	TEAM	LVL	AGE	PA	R	2B	3B	HR	RBI	BB	SO	SB	CS	EqBRR	AVG	OBP	SLG	EqAVG	EqOBP	EqSLG	EqA	VORP	WARP	DEFENSE	
2006	NHP	AA	22	378	43	24	0	19	71	25	87	2	1	-5.1	.310	.357	.543	.270	.312	.486	.268	15.2	0.2	78-LF	-9
2006	SYR	AAA	22	137	20	7	0	5	18	23	18	1	0	0.9	.394	.496	.596	.355	.456	.573	.349	21.5	1.5	33-LF	-3
2006	TOR	MLB	22	65	8	8	0	2	8	5	12	0	0	-1.0	.367	.415	.600	.350	.409	.600	.333	8.6	0.7		
2007	SYR	AAA	23	190	20	8	2	6	28	14	42	0	0	-0.8	.299	.353	.471	.267	.319	.455	.264	5.5	-0.4	38-LF	-8
2007	TOR	MLB	23	311	34	14	0	11	46	16	65	1	2	0.4	.238	.278	.400	.232	.275	.401	.229	-7.3	-0.8	73-LF	-2
2008	SYR	AAA	24	213	24	17	2	6	50	19	36	1	1	-0.6	.328	.394	.534	.300	.366	.516	.297	17.9	1.1	37-LF	-3
2008	TOR	MLB	24	349	48	16	4	9	40	16	59	2	0	3.7	.282	.316	.439	.280	.316	.452	.263	8.1	0.2	66-LF	-5
2009	TOR	MLB	25	406	48	22	2	14	56	28	82	3	1	-0.1	.272	.326	.458	.273	.327	.469	.272	9.9	1.2	97-LF	-5

Breakout: 22% Improve: 50% Collapse: 28% Attrition: 25%   Comparables: Lee Thomas, Jim King, Leron Lee, Terry Whitfield

Ticketed for stardom after his brief, blazing introductions to Triple-A and the majors in his age-22 season, Lind failed to seize his opportunity in 2007, but didn't miss when the chance came again last year. Installed in left in late June, Lind hit .355/.377/.626 through the end of July to secure the job, but then cooled off over the final two months of the season. Beyond somewhat limited power potential (his ISOs aren't solid for a corner), Lind's plate approach in the bigs seems to be an issue; his K/UIBB was 2.1 at Triple-A last year and is a similar 2.2 over his minor league career, but in the majors, his career rate swells to 4.0, and during his poor August and September last year, it was up to an even six strikeouts for every unintentional walk.

John McDonald — SS

Bats: R   Throws: R   Height: 5' 11"   Weight: 185   Born: September 24, 1974   Age: 34

YEAR	TEAM	LVL	AGE	PA	R	2B	3B	HR	RBI	BB	SO	SB	CS	EqBRR	AVG	OBP	SLG	EqAVG	EqOBP	EqSLG	EqA	VORP	WARP	DEFENSE			
2006	TOR	MLB	31	286	35	7	3	3	23	16	41	7	2	1.3	.223	.271	.308	.213	.268	.295	.202	-10.2	-0.4	75-SS	1	5-2B	2
2007	TOR	MLB	32	353	32	20	2	1	31	11	48	7	2	0.5	.251	.279	.333	.248	.278	.333	.216	-7.1	1.2	89-SS	11	10-3B	4
2008	TOR	MLB	33	207	21	8	0	1	18	10	25	3	1	-0.8	.210	.255	.269	.211	.260	.276	.193	-10.6	-0.9	54-SS	-1		
2009	TOR	MLB	34	150	13	6	1	1	12	9	20	2	1	0.2	.223	.277	.301	.224	.278	.308	.209	-3.7	-0.0	39-SS	0		

Breakout: 41% Improve: 51% Collapse: 36% Attrition: 48%   Comparables: Bob Lillis, Luis Sojo, Chicken Stanley, Damaso Garcia

What happens when a player who has managed a ten-year major league career solely on the strength of his superb defense starts to slip in the field? Do teams notice, or does he get by for another five seasons on reputation alone? Most major fielding metrics (our own, Ultimate Zone Rating, Plus/Minus, and Dave Pinto's Probabilistic Model of Range) rated McDonald's 2008 defense as average to poor. It could have been a fluke—what, you think fielding doesn't vary just as hitting and pitching do?—or it could have been the beginning of his decline as a leather man. If the latter, all that's left is a career .236/.276/.310 hitter making $1.9 million in 2009.

Lyle Overbay — 1B

Bats: L   Throws: L   Height: 6' 2"   Weight: 235   Born: January 28, 1977   Age: 32

YEAR	TEAM	LVL	AGE	PA	R	2B	3B	HR	RBI	BB	SO	SB	CS	EqBRR	AVG	OBP	SLG	EqAVG	EqOBP	EqSLG	EqA	VORP	WARP	DEFENSE	
2006	TOR	MLB	29	640	82	46	1	22	92	55	96	5	3	-3.7	.312	.372	.508	.295	.363	.490	.289	36.9	3.9	140-1B	8
2007	TOR	MLB	30	476	49	30	2	10	44	47	78	2	0	-0.8	.240	.315	.391	.232	.313	.393	.247	-2.6	0.6	109-1B	7
2008	TOR	MLB	31	627	74	32	2	15	69	74	116	1	2	-1.5	.270	.358	.419	.267	.361	.429	.275	16.0	3.7	152-1B	17
2009	TOR	MLB	32	430	46	22	1	10	51	43	80	2	1	-1.9	.255	.332	.396	.257	.333	.405	.259	0.5	1.0	102-1B	4

Breakout: 6%   Improve: 26%   Collapse: 38%   Attrition: 28%   Comparables: Greg Brock, Dick Sisler, Gordy Coleman, Hal Morris

Overbay is in some ways the stereotypical Blue Jay. He's an adequate hitter and a fine fielder, but he's not productive enough to give his team an advantage at his position, he's not getting any younger, and he's signed for two more years at $7 million annually. Healthy again after a season ruined by a broken hand, Overbay failed to recover all of his 2006 production and doesn't seem likely to ever get it back. Overbay has always been an underpowered first baseman, and now there are signs that his defense is slipping as he advances into his 30s, which leaves you with … well, what exactly?

Alexis Rios — RF

Bats: R   Throws: R   Height: 6' 5"   Weight: 195   Born: February 18, 1981   Age: 28

YEAR	TEAM	LVL	AGE	PA	R	2B	3B	HR	RBI	BB	SO	SB	CS	EqBRR	AVG	OBP	SLG	EqAVG	EqOBP	EqSLG	EqA	VORP	WARP	DEFENSE			
2006	TOR	MLB	25	498	68	33	6	17	82	35	89	15	6	-0.5	.302	.349	.516	.289	.341	.503	.285	29.5	2.5	108-RF	-1		
2007	TOR	MLB	26	711	114	43	7	24	85	55	103	17	4	2.0	.297	.354	.498	.289	.350	.500	.289	40.9	4.5	140-RF	3	18-CF	0
2008	TOR	MLB	27	686	91	47	8	15	79	44	112	32	8	1.6	.291	.337	.461	.291	.340	.478	.280	31.5	2.9	92-RF	3	59-CF	-8
2009	TOR	MLB	28	643	87	37	7	19	83	49	111	21	7	2.0	.275	.332	.459	.276	.334	.470	.278	17.0	3.2	150-RF	3		

Breakout: 8%   Improve: 37%   Collapse: 19%   Attrition: 4%   Comparables: Garry Maddox, Roberto Kelly, Al Cowens, Dan Ford

After his breakouts in the previous two years, the Blue Jays had high hopes for Rios as he headed into his age-27 season. PECOTA knew better, calling for a .280/.339/.468 line. What it didn't see coming was Rios's nearly doubling his stolen-base tally while maintaining a fine 80 percent success rate. Rios's steals were split fairly evenly between his two managers, so the difference was in performance and not simply tactics. Still, his speed didn't help him avoid grounding into a career-high 20 double plays. That's a clue to what happened to Rios's production; after increasing his fly-ball rate over each of his last three seasons, he regressed in 2008, putting a higher percentage of his balls in play on the ground than in either of his two "breakout" seasons. As with Overbay, Rios is a complementary player miscast as a star.

Scott Rolen — 3B

Bats: R   Throws: R   Height: 6' 4"   Weight: 240   Born: April 4, 1975   Age: 34

YEAR	TEAM	LVL	AGE	PA	R	2B	3B	HR	RBI	BB	SO	SB	CS	EqBRR	AVG	OBP	SLG	EqAVG	EqOBP	EqSLG	EqA	VORP	WARP	DEFENSE	
2006	SLN	MLB	31	594	94	48	1	22	95	56	69	7	4	0.6	.296	.369	.518	.296	.369	.517	.298	36.5	5.5	137-3B	9
2007	SLN	MLB	32	441	55	24	2	8	58	37	56	5	3	1.6	.265	.331	.398	.269	.336	.415	.261	5.4	3.1	106-3B	17
2008	TOR	MLB	33	467	58	30	3	11	50	46	71	5	0	-0.9	.262	.349	.431	.259	.349	.438	.276	17.0	3.8	113-3B	15
2009	TOR	MLB	34	470	56	26	2	12	59	43	71	5	2	-1.0	.260	.335	.420	.261	.336	.430	.268	10.0	2.4	111-3B	7

Breakout: 6%   Improve: 27%   Collapse: 28%   Attrition: 16%   Comparables: Mike Lowell, Cal Ripken, Matt Williams, Kevin McReynolds

The Blue Jays got the notionally more talented and certainly the more famous player when they swapped third basemen with the Cardinals last January, but they also got the more fragile player. While Troy Glaus hit .270/ .372/.483 in 151 games for St. Louis, Rolen was doing his usual dance with the DL. A broken finger in spring training started him out on the shelf. He hit a meager .252/.349/.401 before going back on the DL in August with soreness in the same left shoulder that he'd had operated on three times in the previous three years. Having retooled his swing to accommodate the shoulder by dropping his hands, Rolen was able to hit .298/.350/.532 after returning at the end of the month, but he's averaged just 123 games a year since having the labrum in that shoulder repaired in 2005, he's had one good year in his last four, and he'll be 34 in April.

Marco Scutaro   SS   Bats: R   Throws: R   Height: 5' 10"   Weight: 185   Born: October 30, 1975   Age: 33

YEAR	TEAM	LVL	AGE	PA	R	2B	3B	HR	RBI	BB	SO	SB	CS	EqBRR	AVG	OBP	SLG	EqAVG	EqOBP	EqSLG	EqA	VORP	WARP	DEFENSE			
2006	OAK	MLB	30	423	52	21	6	5	41	50	66	5	1	1.0	.266	.350	.397	.256	.348	.386	.263	15.9	0.8	64-SS	-11	34-2B	3
2007	OAK	MLB	31	379	49	13	0	7	41	35	40	2	1	0.3	.260	.332	.361	.262	.337	.369	.251	3.6	1.0	39-SS	0	33-3B	-2
2008	TOR	MLB	32	592	76	23	1	7	60	57	65	7	2	-0.2	.267	.341	.356	.267	.345	.363	.255	9.2	4.9	53-SS	14	40-2B	3
2009	TOR	MLB	33	427	48	19	3	5	38	41	55	5	2	0.0	.255	.331	.358	.256	.332	.366	.250	4.1	1.6	101-SS	2		

Breakout: 18%   Improve: 38%   Collapse: 30%   Attrition: 24%   Comparables: Tadahito Iguchi, Jamey Carroll, Danny Murtaugh, Bobby Avila

Scutaro passed through three organizations before getting his first real shot in the majors at the age of 28, but he has made a nice little career for himself since. A splendid fielder, he has enough patience at the plate to make himself an acceptable middle-infield option despite a lack of power. Last year, he set career highs in games and PAs while bouncing between filling in for Rolen at third, platooning with Inglett at second, and ultimately taking over the bulk of the shortstop duties. As we go to press, he's penciled in as the starter at that last position. The Jays could do worse.

Travis Snider   LF   Bats: L   Throws: L   Height: 5' 11"   Weight: 245   Born: February 2, 1988   Age: 21

YEAR	TEAM	LVL	AGE	PA	R	2B	3B	HR	RBI	BB	SO	SB	CS	EqBRR	AVG	OBP	SLG	EqAVG	EqOBP	EqSLG	EqA	VORP	WARP	DEFENSE			
2006	PUL	Rk	18	226	36	12	1	11	41	30	47	6	3	0.1	.325	.412	.567	.214	.278	.369	.225	-16.3	-1.0	43-RF	-1		
2007	LNS	A	19	517	72	35	7	16	93	49	129	3	10	-1.7	.313	.377	.525	.229	.284	.393	.232	-10.7	-2.5	108-RF	-14		
2008	DUN	A+	20	66	15	5	0	4	7	5	22	1	0	-0.0	.279	.333	.557	.242	.288	.484	.260	1.3	0.1				
2008	NHP	AA	20	423	65	21	0	17	67	52	116	1	1	1.2	.262	.357	.461	.249	.335	.450	.270	13.0	1.8	37-RF	0	21-LF	4
2008	SYR	AAA	20	70	9	5	0	2	17	4	16	1	0	-0.1	.344	.386	.516	.328	.371	.531	.306	7.0	0.7	13-LF	1		
2008	TOR	MLB	20	80	9	6	0	2	13	5	23	0	0	0.4	.301	.338	.466	.301	.338	.493	.283	3.3	-0.1	11-LF	-3	7-RF	-1
2009	TOR	MLB	21	632	75	35	3	23	81	60	168	4	3	-0.2	.252	.326	.446	.253	.328	.456	.269	8.7	1.6	148-RF	-9		

Breakout: 36%   Improve: 69%   Collapse: 1%   Attrition: 3%   Comparables: Jay Bruce, Prince Fielder, Al Chambers, Sam Horn

The Jays' top prospect, Snider was the 14th overall pick in the 2006 draft, tore up the Midwest League in his age-19 season in 2007, and then picked up speed to race through three levels and register a solid major league debut last year. He'll open 2009 as Toronto's left fielder, a job he's likely to hold for a long time. He should turn in a solid rookie season combining a decent average, 20-plus homers, and more than his share of walks, and he should improve from there as he advances into his 20s.

Curtis Thigpen   C/1B   Bats: R   Throws: R   Height: 5' 11"   Weight: 190   Born: April 19, 1983   Age: 26

YEAR	TEAM	LVL	AGE	PA	R	2B	3B	HR	RBI	BB	SO	SB	CS	EqBRR	AVG	OBP	SLG	EqAVG	EqOBP	EqSLG	EqA	VORP	WARP	DEFENSE			
2006	NHP	AA	23	373	49	25	5	5	36	52	61	5	1	-1.8	.259	.370	.421	.233	.332	.387	.255	1.1	0.8	73-C	-6		
2006	SYR	AAA	23	56	3	3	0	1	9	2	9	0	1	-0.4	.264	.304	.377	.226	.268	.340	.196	-2.8	-0.5	14-C	-3		
2007	SYR	AAA	24	202	20	10	0	3	20	17	23	1	0	-0.4	.285	.348	.391	.258	.317	.357	.241	-2.3	-0.8	39-C	-10		
2007	TOR	MLB	24	110	13	5	0	0	11	8	17	2	0	0.8	.238	.294	.287	.228	.291	.277	.206	-3.5	-0.1	14-C	3	11-1B	0
2008	SYR	AAA	25	395	28	23	0	3	41	21	58	2	1	-0.8	.222	.267	.310	.200	.242	.288	.182	-34.6	-3.3	57-C	-6	31-1B	-4
2008	TOR	MLB	25	21	2	0	0	1	1	1	8	0	0	0.6	.176	.263	.353	.176	.263	.353	.221	-0.6	0.0	6-C	0		
2009	TOR	MLB	26	352	27	15	1	5	34	26	67	2	1	-0.4	.211	.274	.317	.212	.276	.324	.211	-12.3	-0.3	85-C	-7		

Breakout: 29%   Improve: 44%   Collapse: 39%   Attrition: 21%   Comparables: Mike Durant, Scooter Tucker, Lou Palmisano, Brian Johnson

With Arencibia and Jeroloman on the way, the Jays are making a desultory attempt at making Thigpen into a utility player who can catch. Over the past two seasons, he's seen time at second, third, and right field in Triple-A, though the only positions he's played more than four times are catcher and first. Of course, position flexibility won't matter much if he posts a sub-600 OPS at Syracuse again this year.

Vernon Wells — CF

Bats: R Throws: R Height: 6' 1" Weight: 225 Born: December 8, 1978 Age: 30

YEAR	TEAM	LVL	AGE	PA	R	2B	3B	HR	RBI	BB	SO	SB	CS	EqBRR	AVG	OBP	SLG	EqAVG	EqOBP	EqSLG	EqA	VORP	WARP	DEFENSE
2006	TOR	MLB	27	677	91	40	5	32	106	54	90	17	4	0.2	.303	.357	.542	.287	.349	.526	.294	59.5	7.1	146-CF 18
2007	TOR	MLB	28	642	85	36	4	16	80	49	89	10	4	1.3	.245	.304	.402	.239	.302	.408	.246	4.4	2.0	143-CF 10
2008	TOR	MLB	29	466	63	22	1	20	78	29	46	4	2	-1.1	.300	.343	.496	.296	.343	.506	.286	30.2	2.0	100-CF -8
2009	TOR	MLB	30	525	63	27	2	16	71	38	72	6	2	-0.4	.267	.323	.435	.269	.324	.445	.266	13.4	2.5	124-CF 0

Breakout: 7% Improve: 32% Collapse: 30% Attrition: 9% Comparables: Torii Hunter, Carlos Lee, Aaron Rowand, Derek Bell

Wells had the torn labrum that limited his 2007 performance repaired at the end of that season, but his opportunities to test out his repaired shoulder early last year were limited by two more injuries: a fractured wrist suffered in early May and a strained hamstring that put him back on the shelf barely a month after he had returned from the wrist injury. When Wells returned to action again on August 10, his season averages stood at .287/.329/.449 and he had hit just nine home runs, but he finally got going, hitting .318/.365/.566 with 11 homers in his final 44 games. He won't match those rates in 2009, but there's reason to be slightly more optimistic than PECOTA suggests if he can stay healthy.

Brad Wilkerson — OF

Bats: L Throws: L Height: 6' 0" Weight: 205 Born: June 1, 1977 Age: 32

YEAR	TEAM	LVL	AGE	PA	R	2B	3B	HR	RBI	BB	SO	SB	CS	EqBRR	AVG	OBP	SLG	EqAVG	EqOBP	EqSLG	EqA	VORP	WARP	DEFENSE
2006	TEX	MLB	29	365	56	15	2	15	44	37	116	3	2	1.1	.222	.306	.422	.208	.300	.404	.244	-5.0	-1.4	75-LF -12
2007	TEX	MLB	30	389	54	17	1	20	62	43	107	4	1	-0.4	.234	.319	.467	.227	.319	.472	.269	7.3	1.6	52-1B 2 31-LF 1
2008	SEA	MLB	31	68	1	4	0	0	5	10	15	1	2	-1.4	.232	.348	.304	.236	.364	.309	.238	-2.2	-0.2	17-RF -1
2008	TOR	MLB	31	241	20	8	2	4	23	25	53	2	3	-0.9	.216	.297	.332	.214	.301	.340	.226	-9.7	-0.9	38-RF 0 16-LF -3
2009	TOR	MLB	32	189	22	8	1	6	23	21	52	2	1	-0.2	.234	.320	.410	.235	.322	.420	.258	0.8	0.3	48-RF -2

Breakout: 39% Improve: 55% Collapse: 26% Attrition: 50% Comparables: David Dellucci, Roger Repoz, Mike Jorgensen, Larry Stahl

After being released by the Mariners, Wilkerson returned to Canada to platoon in right with Kevin Mench while Rios was covering for the injured Vernon Wells in center, but the Last Expo hit just .216/.297/.347 against righties as a Jay. It seems that despite his season-ending surgery in 2006, Wilkerson has never fully recovered from the problems with his right shoulder that began back in 2005. Last year, he compounded that preexisting condition by injuring his left shoulder on a dive in the outfield, and he later landed on the DL with a bad back. It's sad to say, but there's not much left here.

Gregg Zaun — C

Bats: S Throws: R Height: 5' 10" Weight: 190 Born: April 14, 1971 Age: 38

YEAR	TEAM	LVL	AGE	PA	R	2B	3B	HR	RBI	BB	SO	SB	CS	EqBRR	AVG	OBP	SLG	EqAVG	EqOBP	EqSLG	EqA	VORP	WARP	DEFENSE
2006	TOR	MLB	35	339	39	19	0	12	40	41	42	0	2	-1.8	.272	.363	.462	.254	.356	.436	.275	15.5	1.6	61-C -1
2007	TOR	MLB	36	391	43	24	1	10	52	51	55	0	0	-2.1	.242	.341	.411	.232	.338	.409	.264	13.2	1.2	94-C -6
2008	TOR	MLB	37	288	29	12	0	6	30	38	38	2	1	-0.4	.237	.340	.359	.235	.344	.366	.254	4.1	1.0	69-C 0
2009	TOR	MLB	38	176	16	8	0	3	19	20	29	1	0	-0.7	.222	.312	.343	.224	.314	.352	.237	-0.3	0.5	45-C -2

Breakout: 11% Improve: 32% Collapse: 42% Attrition: 57% Comparables: Rick Dempsey, Chad Kreuter, Alan Ashby, Tim McCarver

Elbow inflammation in May followed by a DL stint and a strong June performance from Barajas robbed Zaun of his starting job behind the plate last year. He made just 34 starts after returning on June 15 and hit the market as a catcher heading into his age-38 season after his batting average and isolated power had decreased in each of the last two seasons. If nothing else, his plate discipline remains excellent, and he performed adequately against opposing baserunners last year (26 percent caught stealing), but while he remains a practical backup, he's no longer practically perfect.

PITCHERS

Jeremy Accardo

Bats: R   Throws: R   Height: 6' 2"   Weight: 190   Born: December 18, 1981   Age: 27

YEAR	TEAM	LVL	AGE	W	L	SV	G	GS	IP	H	BB	SO	HR	GB%	BABIP	STUFF	WHIP	ERA	DERA	EqH9	EqBB9	EqSO9	EqHR9	DEF	VORP	SN/WX
2006	SFN	MLB	24	1	3	3	38	0	40^1	38	11	40	2	43.2%	.321	16	1.21	4.91	5.09	8.4	2.2	8.0	0.4	2	3.8	0.54
2006	TOR	MLB	24	1	1	0	27	0	28^2	38	9	14	5	44.2%	.337	-29	1.64	5.96	6.33	12.3	3.0	4.0	1.7	2	0.5	-0.90
2007	TOR	MLB	25	4	4	30	64	0	67^1	51	24	57	4	49.0%	.251	8	1.11	2.14	4.23	7.2	3.0	6.7	0.5	12	26.0	3.21
2008	TOR	MLB	26	0	3	4	16	0	12^1	15	4	5	1	45.7%	.318	-25	1.54	6.59	5.25	11.2	3.0	3.0	0.8	-2	-2.1	-0.38
2009	TOR	MLB	27	2	2	4	37	0	40^2	40	14	28	5	47.0%	.280	1	1.31	3.82	3.97	8.7	2.7	5.4	1.0	1	8.3	0.73

Breakout: 29%   Improve: 57%   Collapse: 25%   Attrition: 28%   Comparables: Randy Moffitt, Chuck Crim, Max Leon, Randy St. Claire

After returning the closer's job to B. J. Ryan, Accardo was supposed to become his primary setup man, but a forearm strain disabled him in mid-May and wound up essentially ending his season. Accardo never had surgery, and despite aborted rehab attempts in July and August, the injury supposedly healed completely with rest. Still, the proof is in the pitching. A year removed from his season as Toronto's closer, Accardo is unlikely to slot back in quite as high on the bullpen's depth chart.

A. J. Burnett

Bats: R   Throws: R   Height: 6' 4"   Weight: 230   Born: January 3, 1977   Age: 32

YEAR	TEAM	LVL	AGE	W	L	SV	G	GS	IP	H	BB	SO	HR	GB%	BABIP	STUFF	WHIP	ERA	DERA	EqH9	EqBB9	EqSO9	EqHR9	DEF	VORP	SN/WX
2006	TOR	MLB	29	10	8	0	21	21	135^2	138	39	118	14	52.9%	.317	21	1.30	3.98	3.76	9.4	2.6	7.1	0.9	-7	25.1	3.14
2007	TOR	MLB	30	10	8	0	25	25	165^2	131	66	176	23	55.8%	.262	17	1.19	3.75	4.64	7.7	3.4	8.6	1.3	13	36.6	4.18
2008	TOR	MLB	31	18	10	0	35	34	221^1	211	86	231	19	49.7%	.321	29	1.34	4.07	3.77	9.1	3.2	8.4	0.8	-14	34.1	4.82
2009	NYA	MLB	32	13	9	0	30	30	197	187	73	178	19	48.0%	.300	29	1.32	3.82	3.88	8.5	3.0	7.4	0.8	-1	31.4	5.03

Breakout: 33%   Improve: 69%   Collapse: 8%   Attrition: 12%   Comparables: Jack Morris, Mike Scott, Roger Clemens, Joe Dobson

That the only three 200-inning seasons of Burnett's career have been followed by either free agency or Tommy John surgery would seem to be a bad omen for the Yankees after giving him a five-year, $82.5 million contract. The Yankees were wowed by Burnett's dominating them in five starts last year (3-1, 1.64 ERA, 43 K, 6 BB, 38⅓ IP), but if you take those starts away, his 2008 ERA swells to a decidedly unimpressive 4.57, his WHIP gets up to 1.43, and his K/BB ratio shrinks to 2.4. Indeed, Burnett was sporting a 4.67 ERA on August 12 before making a strong contract push in his last eight starts, three of which came against the Yankees. He still has the high-90s fastball, the low-90s sinker, and the nasty knuckle curve, but despite press-conference claims that he learned a lot from Roy Halladay about how to use his stuff and keep his arm healthy, he has yet to prove it in a nonwalk year.

Shawn Camp

Bats: R   Throws: R   Height: 6' 1"   Weight: 200   Born: November 18, 1975   Age: 33

YEAR	TEAM	LVL	AGE	W	L	SV	G	GS	IP	H	BB	SO	HR	GB%	BABIP	STUFF	WHIP	ERA	DERA	EqH9	EqBB9	EqSO9	EqHR9	DEF	VORP	SN/WX
2007	DUR	AAA	31	0	1	4	12	0	15^1	13	2	16	0	58.5%	.327	13	0.98	1.18	1.29	9.6	1.3	7.1	0.0	-1	6.7	—
2007	TBA	MLB	31	0	3	0	50	0	40	63	18	36	7	57.4%	.438	-15	2.03	7.20	5.18	13.3	3.8	7.0	1.6	-9	-6.4	-0.83
2008	SYR	AAA	32	1	0	4	7	0	10	4	0	13	0	52.6%	.211	9	0.40	0.00	1.00	4.0	0.0	8.0	0.0	0	4.6	—
2008	TOR	MLB	32	3	1	0	40	0	39^1	40	11	31	2	55.7%	.319	5	1.30	4.12	3.58	9.8	2.4	6.5	0.5	-2	7.1	0.31
2009	TOR	MLB	33	2	2	2	35	0	38^2	40	12	32	3	53.0%	.310	5	1.33	3.73	4.16	9.3	2.4	6.1	0.7	1	7.7	0.64

Breakout: 43%   Improve: 70%   Collapse: 19%   Attrition: 24%   Comparables: Bob Locker, Larry Andersen, Matt Herges, Darren Holmes

Throw out one bad outing in which Camp allowed five runs in the 13th inning against the Rays (his former team), four coming on a Dioner Navarro grand slam, and Camp's 2008 ERA drops all the way to 3.05. That's bullpen life for you—discrete events can wreck an otherwise decent season. Overall, it was the journeyman's best year, as he also improved his K/BB ratio and posted a career-best WHIP. Not bad for a nonroster invitee, but the Jays should expect him to regress in 2009.

Jesse Carlson

Bats: L Throws: L Height: 6' 1" Weight: 160 Born: December 31, 1980 Age: 28

YEAR	TEAM	LVL	AGE	W	L	SV	G	GS	IP	H	BB	SO	HR	GB%	BABIP	STUFF	WHIP	ERA	DERA	EqH9	EqBB9	EqSO9	EqHR9	DEF	VORP	SN/WX
2006	FRI	AA	25	6	5	3	43	0	58²	65	18	45	7	47.7%	.314	-35	1.43	4.64	7.89	10.9	3.2	3.9	1.6	2	-14.5	—
2006	OKL	AAA	25	0	0	0	10	0	11	6	4	5	0	39.4%	.194	-20	0.91	0.00	3.38	5.1	3.4	2.5	0.0	3	2.6	—
2007	NHP	AA	26	8	2	6	58	0	70¹	77	18	81	4	38.6%	.388	-5	1.35	4.86	5.62	11.5	2.7	6.9	1.0	-6	-0.1	—
2008	TOR	MLB	27	7	2	2	69	0	60	41	21	55	6	35.4%	.236	9	1.03	2.25	3.28	6.6	3.0	7.5	0.9	5	22.3	2.26
2009	TOR	MLB	28	2	2	3	43	0	40	38	14	35	5	40.0%	.290	7	1.30	3.71	4.03	8.5	2.8	6.6	1.0	1	8.2	0.74

Breakout: 23% Improve: 36% Collapse: 34% Attrition: 41%   Comparables: Billy Brewer, Aaron Fultz, Lance Painter, Bob Mcclure

Carlson finally made it to "The Show" in his seventh professional season and with his fourth organization (not counting his previous stint in the Jays' system in 2005). He didn't just make it, either—he had an excellent rookie season as the second lefty in the Jays' pen, stranding 82 percent of his inherited runners (the fifth-best mark in the American League) and finishing third on the Jays in WXRL behind Downs and Ryan. The trio helped make the Toronto pen one of the 10 best in the majors in 2008. While it's great when a bunch of your marginal relief arms come through with strong seasons, it's a bad sign for the following year, because they're likely to regress.

Fabio Castro

Bats: L Throws: L Height: 5' 7" Weight: 185 Born: January 20, 1985 Age: 24

YEAR	TEAM	LVL	AGE	W	L	SV	G	GS	IP	H	BB	SO	HR	GB%	BABIP	STUFF	WHIP	ERA	DERA	EqH9	EqBB9	EqSO9	EqHR9	DEF	VORP	SN/WX
2006	FRI	AA	21	0	1	0	5	4	13²	14	8	10	1	45.5%	.302	-9	1.67	2.05	6.92	10.4	5.5	4.2	1.4	1	-1.9	—
2006	TEX	MLB	21	0	0	0	4	0	8¹	6	7	5	0	48.0%	.240	-1	1.56	4.34	7.56	6.5	7.6	4.3	0.0	2	0.8	0.02
2006	PHI	MLB	21	0	1	1	16	0	23¹	12	6	13	1	40.3%	.177	19	0.77	1.55	3.80	3.8	1.9	4.6	0.4	6	11.7	-0.59
2007	REA	AA	22	2	0	1	11	0	16²	12	6	24	0	39.5%	.316	15	1.08	2.69	4.11	8.8	3.5	8.8	0.6	0	2.5	—
2007	OTT	AAA	22	5	5	1	21	7	58¹	53	33	47	7	36.4%	.289	-16	1.48	4.01	7.35	8.6	5.3	4.6	1.8	5	-10.9	—
2007	PHI	MLB	22	0	0	0	10	1	12	9	13	14	2	41.4%	.259	12	1.83	6.00	6.75	6.8	8.2	9.8	1.5	2	-0.0	0.10
2008	REA	AA	23	8	2	0	27	16	110¹	109	46	95	14	39.9%	.302	-15	1.41	4.41	4.85	9.9	3.7	5.5	1.6	-4	8.8	—
2008	LEH	AAA	23	0	2	0	3	2	10	14	6	10	1	44.1%	.419	-10	2.00	8.10	8.10	12.6	5.4	5.4	0.9	-3	-2.8	—
2009	TOR	MLB	24	4	5	0	26	12	76¹	79	38	60	12	40.0%	.290	2	1.53	5.24	5.57	9.4	3.9	5.9	1.4	2	2.9	0.74

Breakout: 14% Improve: 39% Collapse: 30% Attrition: 15%   Comparables: Arnie Muñoz, Horacio Estrada, Rigo Beltran, Glen Perkins

The player to be named later received for Matt Stairs, this little Latin lefty arrived too late to pitch for the Jays at any level. Prior to that, the Phillies were attempting to convert him to starting, an experiment the Jays continued to let run in the Dominican winter league, but he had little success in the role at either location. It's just as well; as a hard thrower who dominates lefties, Castro is best suited for relief work. Unfortunately for him, the Jays are already up to their maple leaves in lefties, particularly in the bullpen.

Brett Cecil

Bats: R Throws: L Height: 6' 3" Weight: 220 Born: July 2, 1986 Age: 22

YEAR	TEAM	LVL	AGE	W	L	SV	G	GS	IP	H	BB	SO	HR	GB%	BABIP	STUFF	WHIP	ERA	DERA	EqH9	EqBB9	EqSO9	EqHR9	DEF	VORP	SN/WX
2007	AUB	A-	20	1	0	0	14	13	49²	36	11	56	1	60.9%	.268	21	0.95	1.27	4.20	9.2	3.0	5.0	0.8	3	7.0	—
2008	DUN	A+	21	0	0	0	4	4	10¹	6	2	11	1	72.0%	.208	9	0.78	1.75	5.79	6.8	2.9	5.8	1.9	3	-0.2	—
2008	NHP	AA	21	6	2	0	18	18	77²	66	23	87	4	59.8%	.310	37	1.15	2.55	3.49	7.7	2.6	7.1	0.7	2	18.1	—
2008	SYR	AAA	21	2	3	0	6	6	30²	28	16	31	1	68.2%	.314	16	1.43	4.10	6.00	8.7	4.8	6.0	0.6	1	-1.3	—
2009	TOR	MLB	22	8	5	0	20	20	118¹	103	44	109	8	57.0%	.290	26	1.24	3.54	3.97	7.8	2.9	6.8	0.6	2	23.8	3.51

Breakout: 9% Improve: 39% Collapse: 24% Attrition: 16%   Comparables: Tommy John, Mark Gubicza, Steve Barber, Dean Chance

The Jays nabbed Cecil out of the University of Maryland with a supplemental-round pick in 2007, and he's beginning to look like the organization's rare steal. A big lefty with low-90s velocity, a plus slider, and a decent changeup, Cecil excelled in Double-A for most of his first full pro season. His results after a late-season promotion to Triple-A were mixed, but he allowed just four runs in his last 19⅓ innings (over three starts), and he's young. He projects as a mid-rotation horse and could be in the Jays' rotation in relatively short order, and certainly by 2010.

Scott Downs

| | | | | | | | Bats: L | | Throws: L | | Height: 6' 2" | | Weight: 190 | | Born: March 17, 1976 | | | Age: 33 |

YEAR	TEAM	LVL	AGE	W	L	SV	G	GS	IP	H	BB	SO	HR	GB%	BABIP	STUFF	WHIP	ERA	DERA	EqH9	EqBB9	EqSO9	EqHR9	DEF	VORP	SN/WX
2006	TOR	MLB	30	6	2	1	59	5	77	73	30	61	9	56.4%	.287	-3	1.34	4.09	4.34	8.7	3.5	6.5	1.0	1	14.6	0.82
2007	TOR	MLB	31	4	2	1	81	0	58	47	24	57	3	61.1%	.291	14	1.22	2.17	3.07	7.9	3.6	7.9	0.5	5	23.8	2.29
2008	TOR	MLB	32	0	3	5	66	0	70²	54	27	57	3	67.8%	.263	12	1.15	1.78	2.48	7.2	3.1	6.5	0.4	3	30.2	3.77
2009	TOR	MLB	33	4	3	6	61	0	60	54	23	50	4	57.0%	.290	5	1.28	3.05	3.44	8.0	3.0	6.2	0.6	1	16.2	1.51

Breakout: 8% Improve: 24% Collapse: 51% Attrition: 12%   Comparables: Joey Eischen, Hal Woodeshick, Sparky Lyle, Mike Maddux

Sometimes, moving a pitcher into the bullpen can breathe life into his career. Downs was a 29-year-old starter with a 5.41 career ERA when he threw his first pitch for the Blue Jays four years ago. Though he was uninspiring that first year, the Jays thought they saw the makings of a good relief pitcher. The next season, Downs posted a 2.77 ERA in 54 relief appearances (against a 9.39 ERA in five starts). Made the team's primary LOOGY in 2007, Downs appeared in 81 games, held lefties to a .209/.294/.255 line, and pitched almost as well against righties. Last year, he moved to a more conventional setup role after Jeremy Accardo's injury and finished 10th in the majors in WXRL while posting a 1.78 ERA—not a bad second act for a guy who was once the "Who?" the Expos received when they finally traded Rondell White.

Jason Frasor

| | | | | | | | Bats: R | | Throws: R | | Height: 5' 10" | | Weight: 170 | | Born: August 9, 1977 | | | Age: 31 |

YEAR	TEAM	LVL	AGE	W	L	SV	G	GS	IP	H	BB	SO	HR	GB%	BABIP	STUFF	WHIP	ERA	DERA	EqH9	EqBB9	EqSO9	EqHR9	DEF	VORP	SN/WX
2006	SYR	AAA	28	3	1	1	18	0	20²	21	13	33	1	60.9%	.444	18	1.68	4.01	4.08	12.7	7.1	11.2	1.0	-4	3.0	—
2006	TOR	MLB	28	3	2	0	51	0	50	47	17	51	8	43.4%	.291	4	1.28	4.32	4.32	8.5	2.9	8.1	1.3	1	10.2	0.70
2007	TOR	MLB	29	1	5	3	51	0	57	47	23	59	3	47.5%	.289	14	1.23	4.58	4.45	7.8	3.3	8.1	0.5	0	8.9	0.68
2008	TOR	MLB	30	1	2	0	49	0	47¹	36	32	42	4	39.1%	.252	3	1.44	4.19	5.36	7.1	5.6	7.1	0.8	6	7.3	-0.20
2009	TOR	MLB	31	2	2	2	39	0	45	41	22	43	5	45.0%	.290	6	1.41	4.15	4.51	8.3	3.9	7.0	1.0	1	7.0	0.57

Breakout: 15% Improve: 45% Collapse: 34% Attrition: 22%   Comparables: Doug Bair, Curt Leskanic, Diego Segui, Don Elston

Now entering his sixth season as a middling reliever, Frasor managed to improve his performance with runners in scoring position last year, but it didn't have much effect on his overall performance, which was plagued by a spike in his walk rate, particularly against lefties. He's been trending toward becoming a full-on ROOGY over the last two years; his split in 2008 was striking, as righties hit .174/.276/.303 against him, but lefties hit .266/.420/.422 with nearly as many walks as hits.

Roy Halladay

| | | | | | | | Bats: R | | Throws: R | | Height: 6' 6" | | Weight: 225 | | Born: May 14, 1977 | | | Age: 32 |

YEAR	TEAM	LVL	AGE	W	L	SV	G	GS	IP	H	BB	SO	HR	GB%	BABIP	STUFF	WHIP	ERA	DERA	EqH9	EqBB9	EqSO9	EqHR9	DEF	VORP	SN/WX
2006	TOR	MLB	29	16	5	0	32	32	220	208	34	132	19	58.9%	.279	15	1.10	3.19	4.29	8.6	1.4	4.9	0.8	23	67.6	6.50
2007	TOR	MLB	30	16	7	0	31	31	225¹	232	48	139	15	54.8%	.304	14	1.24	3.72	4.33	10.0	1.9	5.0	0.7	9	49.9	6.65
2008	TOR	MLB	31	20	11	0	34	33	246	220	39	206	18	54.0%	.287	29	1.05	2.78	3.62	8.4	1.4	6.8	0.7	9	70.6	7.87
2009	TOR	MLB	32	14	8	0	29	29	196¹	188	44	159	17	54.0%	.290	18	1.18	3.31	3.68	8.6	1.7	6.0	0.8	4	45.2	6.46

Breakout: 15% Improve: 41% Collapse: 26% Attrition: 18%   Comparables: Chris Carpenter, Kevin Brown, Gaylord Perry, Rick Reuschel

It's a testament to how good Doc is when he's on his game that, in a season in which he completed an AL-leading nine games, the only two starts in which he surpassed 120 pitches were two of his worst. Halladay pitched six or more innings in all but one of his 33 starts in 2008, and lasted five full in the exception. He finished April with four consecutive complete games, three of which he *lost* as the Jays were outscored by a combined 10-4, and he finished the season by going the distance against the Yankees for his 20th win, completing the game with just 96 pitches. Overall, his season was a near-match of his 2003, which earned him the AL Cy Young, and if not for Cliff Lee's big season, he would have won the award again. He's a horse, a stud, and a bargain at $30 million over the next two seasons.

Casey Janssen

Bats: R   Throws: R   Height: 6' 4"   Weight: 205   Born: September 17, 1981   Age: 27

YEAR	TEAM	LVL	AGE	W	L	SV	G	GS	IP	H	BB	SO	HR	GB%	BABIP	STUFF	WHIP	ERA	DERA	EqH9	EqBB9	EqSO9	EqHR9	DEF	VORP	SN/WX
2006	SYR	AAA	24	1	5	0	9	9	42¹	47	8	32	3	55.9%	.336	-10	1.31	4.92	7.15	11.5	2.1	4.6	1.2	3	-6.7	—
2006	TOR	MLB	24	6	10	0	19	17	94	103	21	44	12	54.0%	.285	-8	1.32	5.07	5.40	9.6	1.9	3.7	1.1	1	5.8	1.25
2007	TOR	MLB	25	2	3	6	70	0	72²	67	20	39	4	48.9%	.276	-4	1.20	2.35	3.50	8.8	2.3	4.3	0.5	6	26.6	2.68
2009	TOR	MLB	27	4	3	1	28	7	62¹	64	18	39	7	51.0%	.290	0	1.30	3.87	4.28	9.2	2.2	4.6	1.0	1	11.2	1.35

Breakout: 16%   Improve: 47%   Collapse: 25%   Attrition: 27%   Comparables: Curt Barclay, Ben Flowers, Charlie Williams, Adrian Devine

One of the team's primary setup men in 2007, Janssen underwent surgery to repair a torn labrum in his pitching shoulder last March and missed the entire season. Labrum surgery isn't the death knell that it once was for a pitcher's career, so expect Janssen to be in the mix again this year, possibly even as a starter. As long as the drop returns to Janssen's low-90s sinker, he should pick up somewhere close to where he left off.

Brandon League

Bats: R   Throws: R   Height: 6' 3"   Weight: 190   Born: March 16, 1983   Age: 26

YEAR	TEAM	LVL	AGE	W	L	SV	G	GS	IP	H	BB	SO	HR	GB%	BABIP	STUFF	WHIP	ERA	DERA	EqH9	EqBB9	EqSO9	EqHR9	DEF	VORP	SN/WX
2006	SYR	AAA	23	3	2	8	31	1	54²	57	15	43	0	78.4%	.343	-2	1.33	2.16	4.38	11.1	3.1	4.9	0.2	0	6.7	—
2006	TOR	MLB	23	1	2	1	33	0	42²	34	9	29	3	76.5%	.244	5	1.01	2.53	4.19	6.9	1.9	5.2	0.6	3	12.0	0.55
2007	SYR	AAA	24	0	0	0	11	0	12	12	6	10	0	64.9%	.343	-20	1.50	3.00	7.71	10.0	4.6	4.6	0.0	0	-2.7	—
2007	TOR	MLB	24	0	0	0	14	0	11²	19	7	7	1	59.1%	.429	-18	2.23	6.15	3.38	16.9	5.1	5.1	0.8	-3	-0.2	-0.19
2008	SYR	AAA	25	2	3	2	20	0	34¹	36	10	32	2	69.4%	.327	-9	1.34	3.94	5.77	9.7	2.9	5.2	0.8	0	-0.6	—
2008	TOR	MLB	25	1	2	1	31	0	33	28	15	23	2	69.0%	.268	-3	1.30	2.18	3.09	8.2	3.9	5.6	0.6	2	12.1	0.62
2009	TOR	MLB	26	3	2	2	43	1	48²	47	20	33	3	63.0%	.290	1	1.36	3.45	3.92	8.6	3.1	5.1	0.5	1	11.9	1.00

Breakout: 22%   Improve: 47%   Collapse: 24%   Attrition: 19%   Comparables: Frank Linzy, Jim Acker, Steve Olin, Roger McDowell

When League is healthy, his upper-90s fastball is nearly unhittable. After spending most of the first half of last year pitching himself back into shape at Syracuse while he recovered from his 2007 injuries, League was called up at the end of June and posted a 1.78 ERA in 29 appearances over the remainder of the season, holding opposing hitters to a .230/.304/.319 line. It was almost an exact replay of League's 2006 season, which saw him arrive at the beginning of July and hold the opposition to a .214/.269/.283 line the rest of the way.

Jesse Litsch

Bats: R   Throws: R   Height: 6' 1"   Weight: 195   Born: March 9, 1985   Age: 24

YEAR	TEAM	LVL	AGE	W	L	SV	G	GS	IP	H	BB	SO	HR	GB%	BABIP	STUFF	WHIP	ERA	DERA	EqH9	EqBB9	EqSO9	EqHR9	DEF	VORP	SN/WX
2006	DUN	A+	21	6	6	0	16	15	89¹	94	8	81	5	58.6%	.333	12	1.14	3.54	4.80	12.0	1.6	4.4	1.3	-12	7.2	—
2006	NHP	AA	21	3	4	0	12	12	69¹	85	13	54	6	53.3%	.367	-2	1.42	5.08	7.61	14.3	2.4	4.2	1.6	-5	-13.5	—
2007	NHP	AA	22	7	2	0	10	10	61¹	51	14	46	5	55.9%	.253	4	1.06	2.35	5.07	7.8	2.4	3.9	1.2	2	3.6	—
2007	TOR	MLB	22	7	9	0	20	20	111	116	36	50	14	49.9%	.279	-4	1.37	3.81	4.71	9.9	2.8	3.5	1.2	4	18.1	2.92
2008	TOR	MLB	23	13	9	0	29	28	176	178	39	99	20	49.1%	.280	5	1.23	3.58	4.52	9.4	1.8	4.5	1.1	9	34.3	4.71
2009	TOR	MLB	24	9	8	0	24	24	143²	150	41	93	16	50.0%	.290	11	1.33	4.21	4.62	9.4	2.2	4.8	1.0	3	19.6	3.23

Breakout: 13%   Improve: 52%   Collapse: 22%   Attrition: 25%   Comparables: Paul Thormodsgard, Lary Sorensen, Dave Rozema, Kyle Kendrick

As a sophomore last year, Litsch improved his strikeout rate, cut his walk rate, and maintained the low BABIP from his rookie season. A .280 BABIP isn't extremely low, so it's possible that Litsch might actually be doing something that allows him to stay below the curve. Either way, his peripheral improvements suggest that whatever correction might come, it won't be as severe as we'd initially anticipated. Litsch finished his 2008 season by posting a 1.92 ERA over his last nine starts, a stretch that saw him pitch four games against playoff teams and shut out the Twins. He only just turned 24 and has just four pro seasons under his belt, so it could be that he's just getting better.

Shaun Marcum

Bats: R   Throws: R   Height: 6' 0"   Weight: 185   Born: December 14, 1981   Age: 27

YEAR	TEAM	LVL	AGE	W	L	SV	G	GS	IP	H	BB	SO	HR	GB%	BABIP	STUFF	WHIP	ERA	DERA	EqH9	EqBB9	EqSO9	EqHR9	DEF	VORP	SN/WX
2006	SYR	AAA	24	4	0	0	18	5	52¹	48	9	60	6	49.6%	.316	0	1.09	3.45	4.66	10.1	2.0	7.3	1.7	-1	5.0	—
2006	TOR	MLB	24	3	4	0	21	14	78¹	87	38	65	14	36.8%	.313	-7	1.60	5.06	4.21	10.1	4.3	6.7	1.5	-5	9.2	1.77
2007	TOR	MLB	25	12	6	1	38	25	159	149	49	122	27	42.4%	.271	-9	1.25	4.13	4.61	9.0	2.7	6.2	1.7	8	30.5	4.29
2008	TOR	MLB	26	9	7	0	25	25	151¹	126	50	123	21	43.1%	.248	9	1.16	3.39	4.08	7.7	2.7	6.4	1.3	8	37.9	4.57
2009	TOR	MLB	27	9	7	0	23	23	140²	132	47	124	18	43.0%	.280	19	1.27	3.94	4.25	8.4	2.6	6.5	1.2	3	24.2	3.72

Breakout: 11%   Improve: 41%   Collapse: 26%   Attrition: 22%   Comparables: Rodrigo Lopez, Brandon Duckworth, Tom Sturdivant, Adam Eaton

Marcum was sporting a 2.65 ERA, a 1.00 WHIP, and a 3.2 K/BB when he hit the DL in late June with discomfort in his elbow. A visit to Dr. James Andrews confirmed strained ligaments, but Andrews didn't think it was a major concern. After some rest and rehabilitation, Marcum returned to the rotation in late July, but over his next 10 starts, he posted a 4.78 ERA, a 1.46 WHIP, and a 1.6 K/BB. Shut down in mid-September, he went under Andrews' knife for Tommy John surgery and will miss all of 2009—the projection is just what might have been.

Dustin McGowan

Bats: R   Throws: R   Height: 6' 3"   Weight: 220   Born: March 24, 1982   Age: 27

YEAR	TEAM	LVL	AGE	W	L	SV	G	GS	IP	H	BB	SO	HR	GB%	BABIP	STUFF	WHIP	ERA	DERA	EqH9	EqBB9	EqSO9	EqHR9	DEF	VORP	SN/WX
2006	SYR	AAA	24	4	5	1	23	13	84	77	39	86	7	55.2%	.303	-8	1.38	4.39	5.96	9.6	4.7	6.2	1.2	-4	-3.2	—
2006	TOR	MLB	24	1	2	0	16	3	27¹	35	25	22	2	43.6%	.363	-2	2.20	7.25	7.24	11.5	7.9	6.3	0.7	-3	-8.5	-0.13
2007	SYR	AAA	25	0	2	0	5	5	22	16	9	29	0	53.8%	.333	21	1.14	1.64	3.48	7.8	3.9	8.3	0.4	0	4.9	—
2007	TOR	MLB	25	12	10	0	27	27	169²	146	61	144	14	53.8%	.276	19	1.22	4.08	4.52	8.2	3.0	6.8	0.8	7	33.3	4.26
2008	TOR	MLB	26	6	7	0	19	19	111¹	115	38	85	9	43.1%	.324	15	1.37	4.37	4.67	10.0	2.9	6.3	0.8	-1	11.6	1.92
2009	TOR	MLB	27	8	7	0	30	19	125¹	122	50	109	13	47.0%	.300	13	1.37	4.34	4.73	8.8	3.1	6.4	0.9	3	15.5	2.49

Breakout: 18%   Improve: 54%   Collapse: 16%   Attrition: 24%   Comparables: Tommy Boggs, Jim Gott, Kirk McCaskill, Paul Wagner

Just before Marcum returned from the DL in late July of last year, McGowan went on it. Surgery performed at the end of that month repaired a frayed labrum in McGowan's pitching shoulder, but did not repair a slight tear in his rotator cuff, damage that surgeon Dr. Timothy Kremchek deemed normal wear and tear. The surgery ended McGowan's season, but unlike Marcum, he should return to the Jays' rotation at some point during 2009, most likely in late May or June.

Brad Mills

Bats: L   Throws: L   Height: 6' 0"   Weight: 185   Born: March 5, 1985   Age: 24

YEAR	TEAM	LVL	AGE	W	L	SV	G	GS	IP	H	BB	SO	HR	GB%	BABIP	STUFF	WHIP	ERA	DERA	EqH9	EqBB9	EqSO9	EqHR9	DEF	VORP	SN/WX
2007	AUB	A-	22	2	0	0	6	2	18	9	6	21	0	52.4%	.214	5	0.83	2.00	4.76	5.8	3.7	4.8	0.5	2	1.6	—
2008	LNS	A	23	6	3	0	15	15	81¹	71	28	92	3	53.2%	.324	-2	1.22	2.55	5.07	11.2	4.7	5.3	1.1	-6	4.2	—
2008	DUN	A+	23	4	0	0	6	6	33¹	25	12	35	2	38.1%	.290	1	1.11	1.35	4.80	9.0	4.2	5.7	1.5	2	2.7	—
2008	NHP	AA	23	3	2	0	6	6	32²	24	12	32	2	32.6%	.265	16	1.10	1.10	4.50	6.5	3.1	6.2	0.8	3	3.9	—
2009	TOR	MLB	24	5	6	0	22	14	87	89	45	71	12	44.0%	.300	6	1.53	5.22	5.61	9.2	4.0	6.0	1.2	2	2.9	0.87

Breakout: 5%   Improve: 30%   Collapse: 41%   Attrition: 8%   Comparables: Jeff Musselman, Blaise Ilsley, Steve George, Scott Downs

A slim lefty starter taken out of the University of Arizona in the 22nd round of the 2007 draft following his senior year, Mills moved quickly in his first full season last year, excelling in the Midwest League and then making six strong starts in both High-A and Double-A. Since turning pro, he's gone 15-5 with a 1.96 ERA and struck out 180 in 165⅓ innings with just seven home runs allowed. He won't keep that up at the upper levels, but he has a decent assortment of pitches and a good approach and projects as a solid back-end starter; with the Jays' vacuum in the rotation, he could be rushed.

John Parrish

Bats: L   Throws: L   Height: 5' 11"   Weight: 210   Born: November 26, 1977   Age: 31

YEAR	TEAM	LVL	AGE	W	L	SV	G	GS	IP	H	BB	SO	HR	GB%	BABIP	STUFF	WHIP	ERA	DERA	EqH9	EqBB9	EqSO9	EqHR9	DEF	VORP	SN/WX
2007	BAL	MLB	29	2	2	0	45	0	41²	41	33	36	2	50.0%	.312	5	1.78	5.40	4.68	8.5	6.4	6.6	0.4	-3	1.9	-0.68
2007	SEA	MLB	29	0	0	0	8	0	10¹	22	4	5	0	69.6%	.489	-22	2.52	6.99	1.80	18.9	3.6	3.6	0.0	-6	-1.2	-0.12
2008	SYR	AAA	30	10	1	0	17	13	91	80	39	100	5	53.0%	.318	11	1.31	2.97	5.36	8.7	4.1	6.6	0.7	3	2.3	—
2008	TOR	MLB	30	1	1	0	13	6	42¹	47	15	21	5	38.5%	.307	-15	1.46	4.04	4.81	10.8	3.2	4.1	1.1	4	8.2	1.02
2009	TOR	MLB	31	3	3	1	43	4	60¹	62	29	46	6	48.0%	.300	-3	1.50	4.66	5.07	9.2	3.7	5.6	0.9	1	5.9	0.64

Breakout: 20%   Improve: 53%   Collapse: 28%   Attrition: 30%   Comparables: Paul LaPalme, Jim Davis, Scott Schoeneweis, Terry Burrows

The hard-throwing former Oriole arrived in Toronto at the end of June to provide some help as a swing man. As always, he was better in relief, in this case much better, posting a 1.46 ERA out of the pen compared with 5.10 in his six starts, though his peripherals were a mess in both roles. You can blame small samples, but we'll blame the fact that John Parrish just isn't that good. Special bonus fact: Lefties hit .305/.364/.525 against him last year, so however hard he's throwing, they're rocketing them right back out of the box.

David Purcey

Bats: L   Throws: L   Height: 6' 5"   Weight: 235   Born: April 22, 1982   Age: 27

YEAR	TEAM	LVL	AGE	W	L	SV	G	GS	IP	H	BB	SO	HR	GB%	BABIP	STUFF	WHIP	ERA	DERA	EqH9	EqBB9	EqSO9	EqHR9	DEF	VORP	SN/WX
2006	NHP	AA	24	4	5	0	16	16	88	101	44	81	9	43.1%	.351	-26	1.65	5.63	8.13	13.2	5.5	4.7	1.8	-6	-22.4	—
2006	SYR	AAA	24	2	7	0	12	12	51²	49	38	45	7	51.6%	.290	-19	1.70	5.45	9.80	10.0	7.4	5.2	2.0	2	-22.7	—
2007	NHP	AA	25	3	5	0	11	11	62	67	16	55	4	43.5%	.344	-6	1.34	5.37	7.29	11.0	2.8	5.0	1.1	-3	-10.9	—
2008	SYR	AAA	26	8	6	0	19	19	117	97	34	121	8	45.4%	.299	14	1.12	2.69	4.24	8.2	2.9	6.3	0.9	3	16.7	—
2008	TOR	MLB	26	3	6	0	12	12	65	67	29	58	9	32.8%	.315	5	1.48	5.54	5.12	9.8	3.7	7.2	1.3	-3	1.0	0.94
2009	TOR	MLB	27	7	7	1	32	19	115	112	51	102	15	41.0%	.300	9	1.42	4.65	5.01	8.7	3.4	6.6	1.1	2	11.0	1.88

Breakout: 33%   Improve: 63%   Collapse: 13%   Attrition: 24%   Comparables: Bruce Hurst, Mark Redman, Barry Zito, Jack Armstrong

The Jays' first-round pick out of the University of Oklahoma back in 2004, Purcey is a big, solidly built lefty who can throw in the mid-90s. He cracked the big leagues last year after finally getting his walks under control, first at Double-A in 2007 and again at Syracuse last year to prove he could keep it up. The latter stint represents Purcey's best showing as a pro. After an ugly spot-start debut, Purcey's results in his later 10-start stint were mixed, but he delivered 2.8 BB/9 while striking out 8.6, peripherals that suggest he was pitching better than his 3-5 record and 4.84 ERA would indicate. Given the injuries to Marcum and McGowan, he'll enter spring training with a rotation spot sewn up.

Robert Ray

Bats: R   Throws: R   Height: 6' 5"   Weight: 185   Born: January 21, 1984   Age: 25

YEAR	TEAM	LVL	AGE	W	L	SV	G	GS	IP	H	BB	SO	HR	GB%	BABIP	STUFF	WHIP	ERA	DERA	EqH9	EqBB9	EqSO9	EqHR9	DEF	VORP	SN/WX
2006	DUN	A+	22	2	4	0	14	9	48	59	13	37	2	43.1%	.370	-22	1.50	5.06	8.37	14.0	3.6	3.3	1.0	-6	-13.2	—
2007	DUN	A+	23	3	3	1	18	15	66²	83	24	57	3	50.7%	.376	-21	1.60	4.86	6.63	14.7	4.5	4.5	1.1	-8	-6.7	—
2008	DUN	A+	24	5	3	0	13	13	70²	71	18	60	6	48.6%	.310	-26	1.26	4.20	7.77	11.6	3.1	4.2	1.8	3	-15.4	—
2008	NHP	AA	24	8	6	0	16	16	96¹	108	27	72	6	48.3%	.334	6	1.40	3.18	4.37	10.0	2.5	4.7	0.9	-3	12.9	—
2009	TOR	MLB	25	5	7	0	23	16	95²	117	37	62	13	49.0%	.330	0	1.61	5.83	6.27	11.0	3.0	4.8	1.3	2	-3.6	0.28

Breakout: 10%   Improve: 54%   Collapse: 16%   Attrition: 14%   Comparables: Kevin Kloek, Garr Finnvold, Bryn Smith, Clay Christiansen

A storky righty drafted in the seventh round of the 2005 draft out of Texas A&M, Ray made a strong Double-A debut at New Hampshire in a half-season. He's taken his time because of injuries and comes at hitters with consistent low-90s heat, a good breaking pitch, and good command. But put it together, and it profiles more as a middle reliever or fifth starter type. With Ray added to the 40-man, who knows what a good camp might mean?

Scott Richmond

| | | | | | | | | Bats: R | | Throws: R | | Height: 6' 5" | | Weight: 225 | | Born: August 30, 1979 | | | Age: 29 | |

YEAR	TEAM	LVL	AGE	W	L	SV	G	GS	IP	H	BB	SO	HR	GB%	BABIP	STUFF	WHIP	ERA	DERA	EqH9	EqBB9	EqSO9	EqHR9	DEF	VORP	SN/WX
2008	NHP	AA	28	5	8	0	16	16	89²	89	30	84	14	42.9%	.292	-16	1.33	4.92	6.40	8.9	2.8	5.8	1.9	2	-8.0	—
2008	SYR	AAA	28	1	3	0	8	8	48	44	13	40	6	44.1%	.284	-3	1.19	3.56	4.50	8.8	2.7	4.9	1.6	-1	5.6	—
2008	TOR	MLB	28	1	3	0	5	5	27	32	2	20	2	37.1%	.349	20	1.26	4.00	2.45	11.2	0.7	6.0	0.7	-5	5.4	0.64
2009	TOR	MLB	29	6	6	0	27	18	99¹	103	32	76	15	42.0%	.290	5	1.35	4.63	4.96	9.3	2.5	5.6	1.4	2	10.1	1.69

Breakout: 27% Improve: 68% Collapse: 8% Attrition: 15%   Comparables: Jason Johnson, Garrett Stephenson, Claudio Vargas, Matt Kinney

Richmond's journey to the majors is far more interesting than his pitching. Born in Vancouver, a citizen of New Zealand via his father, and a graduate of Oklahoma State, the finesse righty was undrafted out of college and spent three years playing for Edmonton in the independent Northern League before being signed by the Jays. Richmond pitched poorly for Canada in the inaugural World Baseball Classic, but helped his homeland earn a spot in the 2008 Beijing Olympics; ironically, he got called up to the majors just in time to miss the actual Olympic tournament. His first four major league starts were nearly identical (five-odd innings, three runs), and the fifth was a rain-shortened six-inning shutout of the Orioles. In the majors and at Syracuse, he had pretty dramatic platoon splits, struggling to get lefties and shutting down righties; they're small samples, but something to keep an eye on.

Davis Romero

| | | | | | | | | Bats: L | | Throws: L | | Height: 5' 10" | | Weight: 170 | | Born: March 30, 1983 | | | Age: 26 | |

YEAR	TEAM	LVL	AGE	W	L	SV	G	GS	IP	H	BB	SO	HR	GB%	BABIP	STUFF	WHIP	ERA	DERA	EqH9	EqBB9	EqSO9	EqHR9	DEF	VORP	SN/WX
2006	NHP	AA	23	6	5	0	12	12	73¹	57	19	70	3	54.2%	.277	8	1.04	2.95	5.19	8.6	2.9	5.1	0.8	0	3.1	—
2006	SYR	AAA	23	4	4	1	18	3	44²	46	7	36	3	62.2%	.319	-8	1.20	3.87	6.49	10.3	1.9	4.6	1.0	-1	-4.3	—
2006	TOR	MLB	23	1	0	0	7	0	16¹	19	6	10	1	57.4%	.340	-2	1.53	3.87	2.35	11.2	3.5	5.3	0.6	-2	4.1	0.10
2008	SYR	AAA	25	5	9	0	25	23	106²	107	29	88	10	45.4%	.314	-11	1.27	3.71	5.68	9.7	2.8	4.9	1.2	10	-0.9	—
2009	TOR	MLB	26	5	5	1	29	12	81¹	83	27	59	10	47.0%	.290	5	1.35	4.31	4.71	9.2	2.6	5.4	1.0	2	10.8	1.58

Breakout: 20% Improve: 48% Collapse: 29% Attrition: 30%   Comparables: Israel Sanchez, Horacio Estrada, Byung-Hyun Kim, Gustavo Chacin

Davis Romero pitched pretty well for Syracuse, considering that he missed all of 2007 after labrum surgery; a 2.7 K/BB ratio isn't earth-shattering, but for a 25-year-old coming off surgery at Triple-A, it could have been a lot worse. Still, his ultimate destination would seem to be the bullpen. What is it with the Jays and this thing they seem to have for little lefties? Beyond Davis Romero, Fabio Castro is listed at 5 foot 7, and 2007 undrafted free agent Tim Collins is generously listed at 5 foot 7 as well.

Ricky Romero

| | | | | | | | | Bats: R | | Throws: L | | Height: 6' 1" | | Weight: 200 | | Born: November 6, 1984 | | | Age: 24 | |

YEAR	TEAM	LVL	AGE	W	L	SV	G	GS	IP	H	BB	SO	HR	GB%	BABIP	STUFF	WHIP	FRA	DERA	EqH9	EqBB9	EqSO9	EqHR9	DEF	VORP	SN/WX
2006	DUN	A+	21	2	1	0	10	10	58	48	14	61	5	41.8%	.291	14	1.07	2.48	5.30	9.7	3.1	5.1	1.9	5	1.8	—
2006	NHP	AA	21	2	7	0	12	12	67	65	26	41	7	47.7%	.282	-20	1.36	5.10	9.73	10.5	4.4	2.8	1.7	9	-28.5	—
2007	NHP	AA	22	3	6	0	18	18	88¹	98	51	80	9	45.6%	.340	-11	1.69	4.89	6.64	11.4	5.8	5.1	1.6	-8	-9.6	—
2008	NHP	AA	23	5	5	0	21	21	121²	139	55	78	9	52.6%	.337	-10	1.59	4.95	6.42	10.4	3.9	3.9	1.0	7	-10.6	—
2008	SYR	AAA	23	3	3	0	7	7	42²	42	20	38	3	57.3%	.328	5	1.45	3.37	4.08	9.8	4.8	5.4	0.9	-1	6.7	—
2009	TOR	MLB	24	5	7	0	19	19	98	117	50	58	14	50.0%	.320	1	1.70	5.86	5.96	10.6	4.0	4.7	1.2	2	-3.7	0.36

Breakout: 13% Improve: 35% Collapse: 24% Attrition: 14%   Comparables: Mike Mason, Sean Henn, Joe Saunders, Kevin Brown

Famously drafted ahead of Troy Tulowitzki in 2005, Cal State–Fullerton product Ricky Romero did at least finally make his Triple-A debut in 2008 and pitched reasonably well, which was a neat trick, considering he spent most of the year in Double-A pitching poorly. Romero throws in the low 90s with a good curve and change and gets a ton of ground-ball outs, which makes you think he really should do better, but he continues to struggle with both command and control, as evidenced by his walk rates.

B. J. Ryan

| | | | | | | | | | | | | | | | | | | | | | | | | | | | Bats: L | Throws: L | Height: 6′ 6″ | Weight: 260 | Born: December 28, 1975 | Age: 33 |

YEAR	TEAM	LVL	AGE	W	L	SV	G	GS	IP	H	BB	SO	HR	GB%	BABIP	STUFF	WHIP	ERA	DERA	EqH9	EqBB9	EqSO9	EqHR9	DEF	VORP	SN/WX
2006	TOR	MLB	30	2	2	38	65	0	72¹	42	20	86	3	39.0%	.245	34	0.86	1.37	2.60	5.6	2.5	9.3	0.4	8	37.3	6.06
2007	TOR	MLB	31	0	2	3	5	0	4¹	7	4	3	1	33.3%	.353	-28	2.54	12.56	11.57	13.5	7.7	5.8	1.9	-1	-4.2	-1.32
2008	TOR	MLB	32	2	4	32	60	0	58	46	28	58	4	40.3%	.278	11	1.28	2.95	3.45	7.5	3.9	8.0	0.6	1	16.1	3.16
2009	TOR	MLB	33	3	3	19	50	0	49¹	42	22	49	5	42.0%	.280	10	1.29	3.51	3.83	7.7	3.4	7.4	0.9	1	11.4	1.48

Breakout: 8%   Improve: 29%   Collapse: 45%   Attrition: 10%   Comparables: Doug Brocail, Roberto Hernandez, Norm Charlton, Eric Plunk

Though he missed the first couple weeks in April, Ryan returned from a year lost to Tommy John surgery much the same pitcher he was before the operation. His strikeouts were down only very slightly, and his walk rate up, but he was 32-for-36 in save opportunities and in the top 25 in the majors in WXRL. Having now had the surgery we all saw coming, he'd almost be worth his $10 million annual salary over the next two years, if the team had hope of contending.

Brian Tallet

| | | | | | | | | | | | | | | | | | | | | | | | | | | | Bats: L | Throws: L | Height: 6′ 7″ | Weight: 220 | Born: September 21, 1977 | Age: 31 |

YEAR	TEAM	LVL	AGE	W	L	SV	G	GS	IP	H	BB	SO	HR	GB%	BABIP	STUFF	WHIP	ERA	DERA	EqH9	EqBB9	EqSO9	EqHR9	DEF	VORP	SN/WX
2006	SYR	AAA	28	1	2	3	20	0	25	32	10	21	4	44.6%	.368	-34	1.68	5.76	6.75	13.9	4.4	5.2	2.4	-3	-2.9	—
2006	TOR	MLB	28	3	0	0	44	1	54¹	45	31	37	5	41.1%	.272	-3	1.40	3.81	4.26	7.8	5.3	5.7	0.9	2	13.1	1.46
2007	TOR	MLB	29	2	4	0	48	0	62¹	49	28	54	1	41.9%	.277	13	1.24	3.47	3.94	7.4	3.8	6.9	0.1	2	15.6	-0.08
2008	TOR	MLB	30	1	2	0	51	0	56¹	52	22	47	4	42.9%	.294	5	1.31	2.88	3.09	8.6	3.3	6.7	0.7	0	17.0	0.24
2009	TOR	MLB	31	3	2	2	49	0	50	46	21	44	5	44.0%	.290	5	1.33	3.78	4.14	8.3	3.2	6.6	0.9	1	10.2	0.83

Breakout: 20%   Improve: 41%   Collapse: 35%   Attrition: 22%   Comparables: Matt Thornton, Dan Plesac, Steve Hamilton, Doug Brocail

Another former Cleveland lefty, Tallet seems to have found his place in Toronto's pen. In each of his three years with the Jays, his walk rate and ERA have decreased and his K/BB ratio has increased. The changes are small, but they're good trends to have. Tallet doesn't have a significant split and is a converted starter, so he's best used as an old-fashioned multi-inning middle reliever, and given the holes in the Jays' rotation in 2009, this might make for a lot of work.

Brian Wolfe

| | | | | | | | | | | | | | | | | | | | | | | | | | | | Bats: R | Throws: R | Height: 6′ 3″ | Weight: 220 | Born: January 29, 1980 | Age: 29 |

YEAR	TEAM	LVL	AGE	W	L	SV	G	GS	IP	H	BB	SO	HR	GB%	BABIP	STUFF	WHIP	ERA	DERA	EqH9	EqBB9	EqSO9	EqHR9	DEF	VORP	SN/WX
2006	DUN	A+	26	1	4	0	5	5	24²	33	3	17	3	56.8%	.357	-35	1.49	5.95	9.00	15.1	2.0	2.9	2.5	-5	-8.3	—
2006	NHP	AA	26	1	3	0	24	2	42	54	15	34	5	44.6%	.350	-42	1.64	5.79	7.71	13.8	3.9	3.9	2.0	-7	-9.3	—
2007	SYR	AAA	27	2	0	0	17	0	26	18	6	23	1	46.5%	.243	1	0.92	1.04	3.24	6.5	2.2	5.4	0.7	3	6.6	—
2007	TOR	MLB	27	3	1	0	38	0	45¹	36	9	22	5	56.0%	.231	-12	0.99	2.98	4.22	7.6	1.7	4.0	1.1	4	13.3	0.40
2008	SYR	AAA	28	2	3	1	17	6	36²	39	10	29	2	58.3%	.336	-11	1.34	3.43	4.93	10.1	2.9	4.7	0.8	-1	2.6	—
2008	TOR	MLB	28	0	2	0	20	0	22	18	6	14	2	51.5%	.262	-3	1.09	2.45	3.05	7.8	2.2	5.2	0.9	1	8.0	-0.13
2009	TOR	MLB	29	3	3	1	34	3	50	51	16	35	6	51.0%	.290	-0	1.35	4.13	4.54	9.2	2.5	5.2	1.0	1	8.5	0.83

Breakout: 25%   Improve: 53%   Collapse: 28%   Attrition: 39%   Comparables: Kris Wilson, Mike Maddux, Cisco Carlos, Jay Aldrich

Wolfe pitched well in three stints in the Jays' bullpen last year. The catch is that he also "boasts" a career rate of 4.8 K/9 in the majors. To survive that, he induces grounders and doesn't walk many. While his minor league K/9 marks have been up over seven in the past two seasons, you can see what they translate into—straddling his big-league clip. He also has a consistently extreme platoon split, so he might be best deployed as a ROOGY in double-play situations. Then again, if that's your only claim on a roster spot, you're probably not going to last long.

LINEOUTS

Hitters

PLAYER	TEAM	LVL	AGE	PA	R	2B	3B	HR	RBI	BB	SO	SB-CS	EqBRR	AVG/OBP/SLG	EqAVG/EqOBP/EqSLG	EqA	VORP	WARP
UT R. Adams*	SYR	AAA	27	493	63	19	2	15	63	54	91	11-2	0.4	.259/.341/.417	.214/.295/.354	.231	-16.0	-0.7
3B K. Ahrens#	LNS	A	19	514	54	25	5	5	42	45	135	5-1	-1.9	.259/.329/.367	.213/.273/.309	.203	-32.3	-2.5
OF B. Coats*	SYR	AAA	26	493	67	23	5	7	44	36	89	14-7	-0.8	.286/.342/.407	.244/.299/.364	.232	-10.5	-0.4
C J. Collins	AUB	A-	22	164	20	13	3	3	21	7	17	0-1	-5.1	.326/.415/.525	.237/.291/.401	.236	-3.6	0.7
1B B. Dopirak	DUN	A+	24	463	77	25	2	27	88	47	100	0-0	-3.8	.308/.382/.577	.232/.294/.437	.249	0.9	-1.9
	NHP	AA	24	91	5	6	0	2	13	2	10	1-1	-0.8	.287/.297/.425	.253/.264/.402	.227	-2.0	-0.4
3B A. Hatch*	DUN	A+	24	201	25	12	1	7	27	28	39	2-4	-2.9	.329/.438/.539	.239/.332/.409	.256	2.4	-0.3
	NHP	AA	24	278	25	12	0	6	28	18	41	0-1	0.1	.235/.289/.353	.205/.252/.317	.194	-19.6	-4.0
INF K. Melillo*	SAC	AAA	26	169	21	4	2	5	17	21	32	1-0	-1.2	.260/.355/.418	.220/.306/.353	.234	-4.2	-1.1
	SYR	AAA	26	254	21	16	2	9	36	26	58	2-1	-3.4	.257/.332/.465	.219/.295/.408	.242	-2.9	-1.2
OF K. Mench	OKL	AAA	30	122	18	7	2	3	18	11	11	0-0	0.8	.282/.344/.464	.214/.270/.339	.212	-6.1	-0.5
	SYR	AAA	30	77	7	5	0	1	12	3	14	0-0	-0.4	.284/.312/.392	.230/.260/.324	.197	-4.7	-0.6
	TOR	MLB	30	131	18	11	1	0	10	14	18	2-0	1.5	.243/.321/.357	.237/.321/.360	.247	-0.8	-0.3
1B K. Phillips*	NHP	AA	24	301	33	16	0	8	34	27	41	0-2	-2.3	.306/.370/.455	.267/.326/.418	.255	5.5	-0.1
LF S. Stewart	TOR	MLB	34	200	14	4	2	1	14	22	18	3-1	-0.8	.240/.325/.303	.236/.328/.299	.232	-4.7	-0.3
2B J. Tolisano#	LNS	A	19	496	64	20	8	6	47	56	110	5-2	0.3	.229/.315/.354	.187/.264/.296	.197	-38.1	-3.8

Russ Adams was the Jays' first-round pick in 2002, was their starting shortstop in '05, lost the job in '06, lost his roster spot in '07, yet remains on the team's 40-man. ⌀ The 16th overall pick in the 2007 amateur draft, high school shortstop **Kevin Ahrens** has shifted to third, but has yet to begin to hit and is beginning to look as if he was significantly overdrafted. ⌀ Playing for his third organization in two years, **Buck Coats** spent 2008 playing center for Syracuse while roughly matching career rates that haven't earned him more than a cursory look; he's on the 40-man, for now. ⌀ While the system seems set for catching, Canadian **Joel Collins** nabbed 40 percent of attempted thieves and should make his full-season debut in '09. ⌀ Dunedin High hero **Brian Dopirak** was released by the Cubs last year after he failed to establish himself above A-ball; signed by the Jays, the local kid thrived in front of his home crowd, but foundered again in Double-A. ⌀ Like Dopirak, **Anthony Hatch** dominated in Florida in a repeat engagement as an old man on the circuit and then didn't hit a lick in his first crack at Double-A. ⌀ Only the latest A's player to bounce north of the border, **Kevin Melillo** was purchased from Oakland in June as infield insurance, but didn't get the call. ⌀ **Kevin Mench** had the audacity to complain about being platooned in Milwaukee; he didn't know how good he had it. The desperate Jays rescued him from Triple-A, but he didn't produce; he's moved on to the Hanshin Tigers in Japan. ⌀ A catcher moved to first, **Kyle Phillips** was in his third organization last year when he finally started to produce at Double-A at age 24, albeit in limited duty. ⌀ After a weak comeback with the A's in 2007, **Shannon Stewart** returned to the Jays as their starting left fielder, but nearly hit his way off the roster before a mid-June ankle sprain did the work for him. Released in August, he found no takers. ⌀ The Jays' second-round pick in 2007, **John Tolisano** struggled in his first full professional season last year and was probably overdrafted as well.

Pitchers

PLAYER	TEAM	LVL	AGE	W	L	SV	IP	H	BB	SO	HR	GB%	BABIP	STUFF	WHIP	ERA	DERA	EqH9	EqBB9	EqSO9	EqHR9	DEF	VORP
C. Beck	SBN	A	23	2	0	0	17²	13	3	19	0	43.1%	.255	-7	0.90	2.03	6.23	8.8	2.1	4.7	0.5	1	-1.2
	VIS	A+	23	6	5	1	95	86	25	89	8	42.9%	.297	-19	1.17	3.98	5.90	9.9	3.3	4.7	1.6	2	-2.9
T. Collins*	LNS	A	18	4	2	14	68¹	36	32	98	3	52.6%	.250	27	1.00	1.58	4.12	7.5	6.1	7.3	1.2	5	9.7
J. De Jong	SYR	AAA	29	6	2	5	71¹	70	37	71	8	48.8%	.328	-17	1.50	4.04	5.54	10.0	5.1	6.1	1.5	2	0.4
B. Murphy*	SYR	AAA	27	8	10	2	142	155	84	152	14	53.4%	.364	-4	1.68	5.32	5.74	11.3	5.9	6.6	1.4	-15	-2.0
L. Perez*	LNS	A	23	5	12	0	137¹	136	51	137	4	61.3%	.358	-10	1.36	3.61	6.81	12.7	5.0	4.5	1.0	-7	-15.8
K. Rodriguez	DUN	A+	23	8	8	0	111²	105	24	104	14	41.2%	.286	-15	1.15	3.14	6.97	10.9	2.6	4.7	2.5	4	-15.7
	NHP	AA	23	1	3	0	22¹	34	22	10	2	38.2%	.372	-24	2.51	11.30	13.30	12.9	7.8	2.3	1.2	0	-19.7
M. Rzepczynski*	LNS	A	22	7	6	0	121	100	42	124	2	68.8%	.316	10	1.17	2.83	4.62	10.6	4.7	4.8	0.7	-8	11.2
R. Santos*	AKR	AA	25	2	1	2	52¹	43	13	45	5	50.0%	.277	-7	1.07	3.79	4.86	8.3	2.3	5.6	1.3	2	4.1
	BUF	AAA	25	2	2	0	25	42	9	24	3	53.3%	.464	-23	2.04	7.20	5.01	17.4	3.5	5.8	1.5	-10	1.5
N. Starner*	LNS	A	24	1	4	0	43	37	8	45	1	46.1%	.321	2	1.05	1.67	4.10	10.8	2.9	4.8	0.7	-1	6.2
	DUN	A+	24	4	0	0	59¹	51	15	55	0	50.6%	.321	-1	1.11	1.82	3.50	9.7	3.0	4.8	0.3	-1	12.6

The return for Eckstein, big Texan **Chad Beck** started out primarily relieving, but was moved into the rotation last year. He posted a 4.46 ERA starting with an excellent 3.8 K/BB and a solid 1.17 WHIP. ⊘ Signed as an undrafted 17-year-old in 2007, **Tim Collins** is another tiny lefty (5' 7", 155) who utilizes a potent cocktail of pinpoint control, low-90s heat, a put-away curve, and two ounces of dry gin mixed with lemon juice and soda and served over ice. ⊘ Organizational soldier **Jordan De Jong** has been in-system since 2002 and has ROOGY potential as a bullpen bulldog despite a modest assortment. ⊘ After going 5-10 with a 5.73 ERA starting for Syracuse, hard-throwing journeyman lefty **Bill Murphy** was moved to the pen and became unhittable while striking out 19 in 13⅔ innings. ⊘ Lefty **Luis Perez** spins a nice sinker and had a strong full-season debut starting for Lansing last year, but he did it at the relatively advanced age of 23. ⊘ Cuban defector **Kenny Rodriguez** turned out to be 31 months older than initially reported, but his promising combination of a fastball that sits 89-93, a curve, and a change might be enough to get him on to people's radars (besides the Coast Guard's). ⊘ **Marc Rzepczynski** (pronounced rez-PIN-ski) is a lefty starter with a bowling-ball sinker, a good curve, and a decent change that also sinks, making it nearly impossible for hitters to get the ball in the air off him. ⊘ Claimed off waivers from the Indians, LOOGY wannabe **Reid Santos** was more heavily battered at his Triple-A debut than the fried cod special at Coronary O'Lardy's, and without the soothing benefit of tartar sauce. ⊘ Another undrafted lefty, **Nate Starner** was signed out of college and has since struck out 286 men in 269⅔ innings as a pro while bouncing between starting and relieving.

MANAGER: JOHN GIBBONS/CITO GASTON

YEAR	MGR	W-L	Pythag +/–	Avg PC	100+ P	120+ P	QS	BQS	REL	REL w Zero R	IBB	Subs	PH	PH Avg	PH HR	SB2	CS2	SB3	CS3	SAC Att	SAC %	POS SAC	Squeeze	Swing	In Play
2006	J.G.	87-75	0	90.2	54	2	63	9	480	282	56	59	112	.240	2	53	26	12	7	25	64.0%	16	3	164	140
2007	J.G.	83-79	-4	96.7	70	9	80	11	420	266	34	54	138	.226	4	47	16	9	6	43	76.7%	33	4	124	98
2008	J.G.	35-39	-3	98.7	39	1	38	6	205	145	26	25	53	.340	2	38	19	7	3	24	83.3%	18	0	70	59
2008	C.G.	51-37	-4	99.9	47	3	47	4	215	153	16	34	36	.333	0	26	4	7	0	44	63.6%	27	0	61	46

Having first joined the team as Bobby Cox's hitting coach in 1982, Gaston has been a member of the Blue Jays' organization for 25 of their 32 seasons. In his first stint as Toronto's manager, he led the team to four first-place finishes in his first five seasons, including the franchise's two championships, but those four years were followed by four years of mediocrity, leading to his firing in 1997. After two more seasons as hitting coach in 2000 and 2001, Gaston became a special assistant to president and CEO Paul Godfrey. Then, on June 20 of last year, he returned to the field as manager after a decade-long absence. Gaston made several immediate changes. He benched David Eckstein to get superior interior defense from Marco Scutaro and John McDonald, and got outfield prospect Adam Lind back up and installed him in left field in place of the washed-up veteran trio of Shannon Stewart, Kevin Mench, and Brad Wilkerson. He dropped the ailing Scott Rolen lower in the order and, soon after, moved replacement second baseman Joe Inglett into the leadoff spot. All but the last were worthwhile improvements. Under Gaston, the Jays went from Gibbons' 35-39 (.473) to a sparkling 51-37 (.580) run, despite injuries to Dustin McGowan, Shaun Marcum, and Vernon Wells, a turnaround that earned Gaston a two-year extension at the end of the season. Gaston 1.0 was noted for his aversion to young players and tactical reticence. The Jays' franchise is greatly changed from those days, so it will be fascinating to see if Gaston has acquired the flexibility to adapt to his new circumstances.

Washington Nationals

As a franchise, the Nationals have endured trying times over the past decade. Yet through thin and thinner—the purchase of the Expos by Jeffrey Loria in late 1999, their threatened contraction in late 2001, their unseemly relocation from Montreal to Washington in 2005, their half-decade as wards of the 29 other teams, the spotty track record of general manager Jim Bowden—the on-field product had always retained a modicum of dignity, a ball-club of modest means soldiering on gamely amid the chaos. Despite playing in outmoded facilities before just a smattering of fans and generating little revenue, never in that difficult stretch did the team lose 100 games or finish with the worst record in baseball. Never, at least, until 2008.

The Nationals hit rock bottom last year, losing 102 games, more than any team had since 2005, and more than any Expos/Nationals team had since 1976. This was no fluke; they finished with the majors' worst run differential, a 184-run deficit that rivaled only that 1976 club and their 1969 expansion forebears for futility. Injuries were a primary factor in the team's slide from the garden-variety 73-win mediocrity of 2007 to last year's debacle, for they exposed just how thin their minor league system is at its upper levels, the result of those years of neglect at the hands of their competitors. The team finished third in percentage of payroll lost to days on the disabled list (36.1 percent), seventh in salary lost and eighth in days lost. Injuries wracked the rotation, the bullpen and the offense, exposing some of Bowden's worst ideas, neutralizing some of his best ones, and initiating some bizarre decisions along the way.

As if that weren't bad enough, the team reached its nadir while inaugurating brand-new Nationals Park, a

---

NATIONALS PROSPECTUS

2008 record: 59-102; Fifth place in NL East

Pythagenport record: 62-99

Runs scored per game: 3.98 (14th in NL)

Runs allowed per game: 5.18 (15th in NL)

Team EqA: .244 (16th in NL)

2008 Batters Age: 28.0 (6th-youngest in NL)

2008 Pitchers Age: 27.6 (5th-youngest in NL)

Ballpark: Nationals Park; Hitter's park; Park Factor of 1.030

2008: The Nats put up their Dukes, but election year brings change for the worse.

2009: Opening Day inaugurates more baseball as usual in Washington.

$693 million boondoggle with a sordid history all its own. Ryan Zimmerman christened the ballpark with a walk-off homer on Opening Day, but the park's second game—admittedly, played eight nights later due to some scheduling quirks—drew fewer patrons (20,487) than any other modern park had in its second game, and the overall attendance of 2,320,400 was the lowest for any new ballpark in the post-Camden Yards era. Of course, it didn't help that the Nationals' record was the worst of the new-stadium bunch, even worse than the 1998 Devil Rays—they were that bad.

As a team, the Nationals allowed 5.1 runs per game, second-to-last in the NL. The rotation was third-to-last in SNLVAR, though the triumvirate of John Lannan, Tim Redding and a back-from-the-dead Odalis Perez were solid enough to combine for a 4.40 ERA and all crack the top 50 of the individual SNLVAR rankings; Lannan was 23rd. The remainder of the starters were rocked for a 5.80 ERA, with the trio of Shawn Hill, Matt Chico and Jason Bergmann, who had combined for 397⅔ innings of 4.27 ERA ball in 2007, managing just 230 innings of 5.60 ERA ball due to assorted injuries, and compiling a grisly 3-22 won-loss record. Tendinitis and a torn labrum limited Chad Cordero to just 4⅓ innings and prevented him from seeing a single save opportunity, while the bullpen finished second-to-last in the league in WXRL. On a positive note, once Bowden traded Cordero substitute Jon Rauch, Joel Hanrahan stepped in and did a more than serviceable job, striking out better than a batter per inning on the year, another dumpster-diving success for the GM.

The offense was 14th in the NL in scoring, eking out just 3.98 runs per game, and ranking last in the league in slugging (.373) and last in the majors in Equivalent Average (.244). Pick a position and you could find a problem. At catcher, 23-year-old Jesus Flores rightly got the nod over veterans Paul Lo Duca and Johnny Estrada, but he hit just .256/.296/.402, for a .243 EQA. At first base, Nick Johnson's return to activity after losing all of 2007 to a broken leg was curtailed by a torn tendon sheath in his wrist that limited him to just 38 games. Multiple injuries and complications from diabetes held Dmitri Young to just 50 games. Five-foot-eight Ronnie Belliard saw significant time at first, but it was Aaron Boone who wound up seeing the most time there. In all, Nationals first basemen hit .269/.360/.402. Belliard's services were in such demand at first and at third—where Zimmerman missed two months due to a torn labrum—that Felipe Lopez was allowed to fester at second base, hitting just .234/.305/.314 before being released on July 31. The entire outfield hit just .243/.330/.376, producing the second-lowest OPS of any team, and the Nats got just a .221/.303/.328 performance from their left fielders, mainly Wee Willie Harris and Wily Mo Peña. It's not as if this was a good-field, no-hit unit either; the Nats were 11th in the league in Defensive Efficiency (.689) and 14th in Park-Adjusted Defensive Efficiency.

To Bowden's credit, the outfield at least reflected an ambitious attempt to upgrade the ballclub. In the space of a single week of the 2007-08 offseason, the GM traded for two high-upside youngsters who had worn out their welcomes with their respective teams in Lastings Milledge and Elijah Dukes. The former commanded a more substantial package in Ryan Church and Brian Schneider, which is to say a tweener lacking the muscle for a corner position or the range to be an asset in center field, and a light-hitting but defensively sound catcher. Milledge's overall numbers weren't outstanding; he only hit to his 25th-percentile PECOTA projection and his defense was 11 runs below average, but the 23-year-old did hit .299/.355/.448 in the second half after losing a month to a groin pull. Dukes, acquired for 2006 fourth-rounder Glenn Gibson, benefited from the change of scenery and became the team's most potent bat, hitting .264/.386/.478. He stayed out of trouble, but he couldn't stay off the DL, making three separate trips and undergoing arthroscopic knee surgery in July. The overall first-year returns may not have been overwhelming, but both players are capable of joining Zimmerman as cornerstones of the rebuilding effort.

The infield was the other side of the coin as far as ambition, and coin is what it cost a team of such limited resources. Young's good work in covering for Johnson's absence in 2007 certainly merited a spot on our

Free Talent All-Star team, but the two-year, $10 million extension he received nonetheless seemed like a bad idea at the time given his age, condition and career pattern. Now, of course, it looks even worse given his time on the shelf. The $4.9 million spent on Lopez coming off a .245/.308/.352 campaign didn't exactly scream good sense given his spotty track record. Cristian Guzman gave the team great value (6.3 WARP) in the final year of his four-year, $16.8 million deal, but that only began to make up for the 2.1 WARP he produced in the deal's first three years, and doubling down via a two-year, $16 million extension for his age-31 and -32 seasons appears to have been a page torn from The Big Book of Bad Ideas. At least it can be said that the team more than got more than its money's worth from Belliard in the first year of his two-year, $3.5 million deal, though asking him to play first was a stretch, both literally and figuratively.

One of Bowden's more puzzling moves concerned the bullpen. On July 22, he traded Rauch, the towering (literally) mainstay of the bullpen who had already filled in ably for Cordero as closer, to the Diamondbacks for Emilio Bonifacio, a 23-year-old slap-hitting Triple-A second baseman who stands a very good chance of turning 33 in the year 2018. The move prefigured Bowden's futile attempt to obtain anything of value for Lopez and his subsequent release—which accompanied those of the similarly valueless Lo Duca and Estrada—but it did grant the Nats an even less imposing presence at the keystone while costing the team its most durable reliever. Soon Bowden would begin cornering the market on futility infielders, acquiring Alberto "Attorney General" Gonzalez from the Yankees and Anderson Hernandez from the Mets. One could almost picture the infomercial: Bowden in his trademark leather pants, promising buyers that he had a light-hitting second baseman or a shortstop to fit any budget.

The irony is that Bowden was able to flip Bonifacio in a rather impressive deal in early November, before the Hot Stove market had fully fired up. Taking advantage of the Marlins' need to clear out some of their arbitration-eligible players so as to continue crushing the souls of their few fans, the Fish parted with left fielder Josh Willingham and starter Scott Olsen for Bonifacio, second baseman Jake Smolinski (the Nats' second-round pick in 2007), and righty P.J. Dean (their seventh-rounder that same season). Willingham missed two months with a back injury, but even his .254/.364/.470 performance would have been an improvement. Whether he plays left field or first base, he should provide some of the muscle the lineup has been missing, though the team will have to figure out what to do with the contracts of other players (Johnson, Young, and Austin Kearns, who hit .217/.311/.316 while playing through injuries and who is still owed $14 million through 2010). Olsen will replace the departed Tim Redding; not that long ago, he was a promising power lefty who could miss bats, but he's lost some velocity, and his strikeout rate has fallen considerably. Also joining the rotation is Daniel Cabrera, who was non-tendered by the Orioles after years of frustrating performances; perhaps a change of scenery and a move from a hitter-friendly park in a grueling division to a pitcher-friendly one in the easier league can help unlock some of his potential. And perhaps a talking giraffe will sing the National Anthem on Opening Day—a GM can dream, can't he?

Another puzzling move was the club's failure to sign first-round draft pick Aaron Crow of Missouri, considered by some to be the top college right-hander in the draft. At last report, just $700,000 separated the two sides before they failed to reach an agreement by the August 15 deadline. Crow signed with the independent league Fort Worth Cats, and the Nats spent an extra million on 15th round pick J. P. Ramirez, an outfielder who slipped in the draft due to a commitment to Tulane. In all, while the team will get a supplemental pick after the ninth selection of the 2009 draft to replace the non-signing of Crow, not getting him was a major setback for a system that still needs rebuilding after years of MLB (dis)ownership. Furthermore, owning the first pick of the 2009 draft means picking San Diego State right-hander Steven Strasburg, dealing with Scott Boras, and wrapping up two high-dollar negotiations on a deadline after proving a lack of ability to get one deal done. Elsewhere, while the last two drafts have improved the system somewhat thanks to the team's willingness to go above slot, it's still a subpar system that saw three of its top five prospects—first baseman Chris Marrero, pitcher Josh Smoker, and outfielder Justin Maxwell—lose half their seasons to injury.

Aside from pitchers like Colin Balester and Garrett Mock possibly getting over the hump, the system won't be of much help for the 2009 Nats, and it remains to be seen what else they do to improve their lineup beyond praying for rain. Their interest in Mark Teixeira, who hails from nearby Maryland, demonstrated a willingness to spend money, but the team has little chance of wooing big-name free agents no matter how big a bankroll they flash given the decrepitude of the current squad. Furthermore, such a willingness means they run the risk of falling into the Oriole trap of signing mediocre stopgap free agents just because they're available. Come to think of it, Bowden's already done a good bit of that. What might have been interesting (and as we go to press it could still happen) would be if the team had taken advantage of the slow winter market and landed either Adam Dunn, who was drafted by the Reds during Bowden's tenure there, or Manny Ramirez, whose desires for a deal of longer than three years and higher than $20 million have yet to be sated. Neither would single-handedly turn the team into a contender, but either would improve the team's chances of escaping the NL East basement by the end of the decade—which at this point may be a necessity to win back disinterested DC fans.

Ultimately, the problem for the Nationals is that Bowden's core competency seems to be dumpster diving, and dumpster diving rarely leads to nutritious habits. Bowden has done an admirable job of finding free talent, but he's then spent bigger dollars to reward that talent just as it starts to regress. Not so free, not so talented. Free talent is great for filling out the margins of a team, and on a budget it's great to stumble across the odd Dmitri Young when the situation merits it. But the Nats have real work to do in building for the future, and if the cost of a Willie Harris or Ronnie Belliard winds up standing in the way of a signed first-round pick, they'll make little progress towards their goal.

HITTERS

Ron Belliard INF Bats: R Throws: R Height: 5' 8" Weight: 195 Born: April 7, 1975 Age: 34

YEAR	TEAM	LVL	AGE	PA	R	2B	3B	HR	RBI	BB	SO	SB	CS	EqBRR	AVG	OBP	SLG	EqAVG	EqOBP	EqSLG	EqA	VORP	WARP	DEFENSE		
2006	CLE	MLB	31	379	43	21	0	8	44	21	45	2	0	0.8	.291	.337	.420	.282	.332	.411	.259	15.3	1.1	87-2B	-1	
2006	SLN	MLB	31	211	20	9	1	5	23	15	36	0	3	-1.7	.237	.295	.371	.237	.299	.366	.226	-3.2	-0.5	50-2B	-3	
2007	WAS	MLB	32	557	57	35	1	11	58	34	72	3	0	0.9	.290	.332	.427	.297	.342	.442	.272	22.1	1.6	113-2B	-7	5-1B 0
2008	WAS	MLB	33	337	37	22	0	11	46	37	58	3	2	0.0	.287	.372	.473	.287	.374	.490	.292	19.1	1.6	26-2B	-6	24-3B -1
2009	WAS	MLB	34	343	38	18	1	8	41	30	53	2	1	-0.7	.267	.337	.410	.270	.339	.428	.264	12.6	1.0	83-2B	-6	

Breakout: 18% Improve: 46% Collapse: 30% Attrition: 30%   Comparables: Vern Stephens, Bill Madlock, Billy Johnson, Charlie Hayes

Even though Belliard had more innings at second base, he actually played in more games at both first and third. That's a harbinger for the future, as his declining range renders him increasingly unfit for the middle infield. His offense is just solid enough to make that a credible play in a reserve capacity, but not so much that you'd ever want to make him a corner starter.

Roger Bernadina   CF   Bats: L   Throws: L   Height: 6' 0"   Weight: 175   Born: June 12, 1984   Age: 25

YEAR	TEAM	LVL	AGE	PA	R	2B	3B	HR	RBI	BB	SO	SB	CS	EqBRR	AVG	OBP	SLG	EqAVG	EqOBP	EqSLG	EqA	VORP	WARP	DEFENSE		
2006	POT	A+	22	504	60	19	3	6	42	56	98	28	11	-3.0	.270	.355	.369	.222	.289	.311	.215	-25.9	-2.6	106-CF	-12	6-LF 1
2007	HAR	AA	23	415	58	15	2	6	36	38	80	40	13	0.3	.270	.340	.369	.227	.288	.322	.222	-19.6	-2.0	84-CF	-12	7-RF 1
2007	COH	AAA	23	53	6	3	0	0	1	9	11	0	1	-0.6	.167	.327	.238	.163	.308	.233	.197	-3.9	-0.5	12-CF	-2	
2008	HAR	AA	24	303	47	11	7	5	38	31	64	26	9	3.7	.323	.398	.474	.276	.346	.426	.270	10.2	0.7	56-CF	-6	7-RF 1
2008	COH	AAA	24	215	33	13	3	4	16	16	37	15	2	-0.4	.351	.404	.513	.325	.379	.490	.299	18.4	0.7	45-CF	-10	
2008	WAS	MLB	24	86	10	1	1	0	2	9	21	4	3	-0.0	.211	.294	.250	.224	.306	.263	.205	-5.2	0.0	12-CF	0	6-LF 3
2009	WAS	MLB	25	507	64	21	5	6	38	44	113	32	11	2.6	.254	.324	.361	.258	.326	.377	.252	5.5	1.4	119-CF	-5	

Breakout: 27% Improve: 51% Collapse: 18% Attrition: 12%   Comparables: Alexis Gomez, Dion James, Dwight Smith, Jason Conti

Bernadina logged a .335 batting average between Harrisburg and Columbus, displaying a never-before-seen ability to spray singles and doubles all around the park—and BABIPs some 75 points above his previous career highs. After being called up when Milledge went onto the DL, his numbers plunged right back toward his career norms. He has pretty good speed, but unfortunately it does not carry over into particularly good defense. You can consider him damned and doomed to the dreaded fate of any tweener, struggling to find work, but always getting short gigs.

Emilio Bonifacio   2B   Bats: S   Throws: R   Height: 5' 11"   Weight: 180   Born: April 23, 1985   Age: 24

YEAR	TEAM	LVL	AGE	PA	R	2B	3B	HR	RBI	BB	SO	SB	CS	EqBRR	AVG	OBP	SLG	EqAVG	EqOBP	EqSLG	EqA	VORP	WARP	DEFENSE		
2006	LNC	A+	21	608	117	35	7	7	50	44	104	61	14	4.4	.321	.375	.449	.219	.266	.320	.212	-35.1	-1.4	127-2B	0	
2007	MOB	AA	22	596	84	21	5	2	40	38	105	41	13	6.2	.285	.333	.352	.242	.283	.305	.211	-32.7	-1.5	75-2B	3	55-SS -7
2007	ARI	MLB	22	27	2	1	0	0	2	4	3	0	1	0.1	.217	.333	.261	.217	.333	.261	.207	-1.5	-0.2	5-2B	-1	
2008	TUC	AAA	23	402	49	18	5	1	29	27	64	17	8	-2.3	.302	.348	.387	.249	.293	.322	.219	-15.3	0.3	70-2B	5	10-LF 3
2008	ARI	MLB	23	12	3	1	0	0	2	0	5	1	0	0.4	.167	.167	.250	.167	.167	.250	.151	-1.2	-0.1			
2008	COH	AAA	23	36	9	2	0	0	3	4	4	4	2	-0.2	.452	.500	.516	.419	.472	.484	.327	5.6	0.2	8-2B	-2	
2008	WAS	MLB	23	174	26	5	5	0	12	14	41	6	4	1.0	.248	.305	.344	.250	.305	.353	.231	-2.9	-0.5	37-2B	-4	
2009	FLO	MLB	24	533	61	23	6	3	33	37	104	21	8	3.1	.250	.304	.341	.253	.305	.355	.234	0.6	0.7	125-2B	0	

Breakout: 49% Improve: 74% Collapse: 12% Attrition: 11%   Comparables: Anderson Hernandez, Alfredo Amezaga, Eider Torres, Hanley Frias

Bonifacio was acquired from Arizona straight up for Jon Rauch, and subsequently dealt to the Marlins in the Willingham trade. Why would they have wanted to pursue him in the first place is a good question; yes, having him around gave them an excuse to let Felipe Lopez walk, but that's an improvement in the clubhouse, not on the field. We'll give Bonafacio points for speed, and for being a better defender than the Nationals' alternatives, but in the end he's nothing more than the real-world picture of a replacement-level second baseman. While there's been some talk of making him a utilityman in Miami, the Marlins may use him to push Dan Uggla towards third base or as an outright replacement should they trade the slugger; even considering Uggla's shaky defense, it will be a big step down.

Aaron Boone   1B/3B   Bats: R   Throws: R   Height: 6' 2"   Weight: 200   Born: March 9, 1973   Age: 36

YEAR	TEAM	LVL	AGE	PA	R	2B	3B	HR	RBI	BB	SO	SB	CS	EqBRR	AVG	OBP	SLG	EqAVG	EqOBP	EqSLG	EqA	VORP	WARP	DEFENSE		
2006	CLE	MLB	33	392	50	19	1	7	46	27	62	5	4	-1.8	.251	.314	.370	.244	.312	.366	.237	-6.3	-2.0	96-3B	-18	
2007	FLO	MLB	34	228	27	11	0	5	28	21	41	2	0	0.6	.286	.388	.423	.291	.392	.444	.297	9.9	0.9	44-1B	-2	8-3B -2
2008	WAS	MLB	35	255	23	13	1	6	28	18	52	0	1	-0.9	.241	.299	.384	.241	.299	.392	.238	-3.6	-0.9	38-1B	-2	13-3B -3
2009	HOU	MLB	36	153	16	7	0	4	18	12	29	1	0	-0.5	.252	.319	.406	.255	.321	.417	.253	2.7	-0.1	40-1B	-2	

Breakout: 18% Improve: 40% Collapse: 33% Attrition: 48%   Comparables: Gary Ward, Bob Kennedy, Eric Karros, Mickey Stanley

The Nationals were suckers last year for taking on Boone after he had played a shockingly decent half-season for the Fish in 2007, and they inexplicably doubled down on the bet by also picking up his brother Bret after a two-year retirement. Mercifully, Bret never made it out of Columbus; unfortunately, injuries gave Aaron plenty of playing time.

A big drop in his K/BB ratio said "retire already," but Ed Wade and the Astros replied, "not just yet," figuring they needed Boone to help provide the leadership and character they weren't already getting from Darin Erstad and Jason Michaels, as the Astros assemble a bench that might have had a hard time cutting it in the old Senior League.

Mike Burgess — RF

Bats: L Throws: L Height: 5' 11" Weight: 195 Born: October 20, 1988 Age: 20

YEAR	TEAM	LVL	AGE	PA	R	2B	3B	HR	RBI	BB	SO	SB	CS	EqBRR	AVG	OBP	SLG	EqAVG	EqOBP	EqSLG	EqA	VORP	WARP	DEFENSE	
2007	NAT	Rk	18	154	22	6	3	8	32	25	37	1	2	-1.7	.336	.442	.617	.228	.312	.426	.252	2.4	-0.7	33-RF	-5
2007	VER	A-	18	81	10	1	1	3	10	10	23	1	1	-0.5	.286	.383	.457	.233	.300	.397	.236	-1.6	-0.4	18-RF	-2
2008	HAG	A	19	460	60	26	4	18	60	46	136	5	1	-1.8	.249	.335	.469	.212	.285	.399	.236	-9.9	-0.8	109-RF	-3
2008	POT	A+	19	83	12	3	0	6	19	9	26	0	2	-2.0	.225	.325	.521	.219	.301	.493	.262	2.0	0.0	17-RF	-2
2009	WAS	MLB	20	603	63	31	3	19	69	56	175	3	3	-0.1	.229	.305	.407	.232	.308	.425	.248	-2.2	0.5	141-RF	-4

Breakout: 34% Improve: 59% Collapse: 13% Attrition: 6%   Comparables: Rich Becker, Eric Duncan, Randy Washington, Nick Weglarz

If we were to run a translation without any adjustments for difficulty, and only adjusted the stats for the offensive levels of the league, then Burgess would get credit for 32 home runs last year, one of only three 19-year-olds (joining the Braves' Cody Johnson and the Royals' Mike Moustakas) to reach 30. That's also not his only tool—he has a cannon for an arm, and led all professionals in 2008 with 26 assists from right field. A supplemental first-rounder from 2007, he does have his flaws—he's kind of slow, with poor range, and with too many strikeouts—and he probably won't be able to get much bigger without also becoming a lot slower.

Kory Casto — 4C

Bats: L Throws: R Height: 6' 1" Weight: 195 Born: December 8, 1981 Age: 27

YEAR	TEAM	LVL	AGE	PA	R	2B	3B	HR	RBI	BB	SO	SB	CS	EqBRR	AVG	OBP	SLG	EqAVG	EqOBP	EqSLG	EqA	VORP	WARP	DEFENSE			
2006	HAR	AA	24	590	84	24	6	20	80	81	104	6	5	2.7	.272	.379	.468	.225	.320	.393	.250	-1.6	1.0	89-3B	-11	47-LF	13
2007	COH	AAA	25	472	56	20	2	11	55	54	106	4	4	-2.9	.246	.334	.384	.218	.299	.356	.230	-13.6	-1.5	59-3B	-11	46-LF	4
2007	WAS	MLB	25	57	1	2	0	0	3	2	17	0	0	0.1	.130	.158	.167	.130	.158	.167	.000	-9.0	-1.4	10-LF	-5		
2008	COH	AAA	26	149	19	5	0	6	26	19	27	1	2	0.9	.308	.396	.485	.267	.356	.435	.271	6.1	0.8	29-RF	2		
2008	WAS	MLB	26	182	15	10	0	2	16	19	36	1	0	-0.2	.215	.297	.313	.215	.297	.313	.217	-6.8	-0.5	20-1B	-1	12-3B	2
2009	WAS	MLB	27	192	22	9	1	6	23	21	40	1	1	-0.1	.245	.332	.408	.248	.335	.427	.262	5.3	0.7	49-3B	-2		

Breakout: 55% Improve: 70% Collapse: 15% Attrition: 44%   Comparables: Duane Walker, Preston Ward, Mark Leonard, John Vander Wal

His major league window is closing. The Nats had a DL lengthier than many Russian novels, giving Casto ample opportunities to get back up and stick, but his inability to do anything with them left him behind the likes of Willie Harris, Ryan Langerhans, and Aaron Boone. He does offer a team versatility, which might make him attractive to someone looking to get a head start on the coming of 13-man pitching staffs, but don't expect to see him get more than the occasional splash of java above Triple-A now that his power's gone out of his stroke.

Leonard Davis — LF

Bats: L Throws: R Height: 5' 10" Weight: 195 Born: December 24, 1983 Age: 25

YEAR	TEAM	LVL	AGE	PA	R	2B	3B	HR	RBI	BB	SO	SB	CS	EqBRR	AVG	OBP	SLG	EqAVG	EqOBP	EqSLG	EqA	VORP	WARP	DEFENSE			
2006	SAV	A	22	322	32	12	4	8	38	21	87	4	5	-3.5	.225	.284	.377	.170	.212	.270	.155	-38.1	-4.3	67-3B	-11	9-2B	-1
2007	HAG	A	23	385	47	29	4	16	56	25	86	7	6	-4.8	.290	.344	.534	.197	.238	.350	.200	-26.7	-4.0	56-3B	-15	18-2B	-3
2007	POT	A+	23	87	8	4	0	4	10	1	22	0	2	-0.2	.262	.267	.452	.200	.207	.329	.174	-8.0	-1.2	20-3B	-4		
2008	POT	A+	24	247	47	14	2	14	37	23	47	7	5	-1.2	.332	.403	.608	.268	.331	.496	.275	12.8	0.5	53 3B	-6		
2008	HAR	AA	24	48	8	1	0	4	10	6	5	2	0	0.4	.488	.553	.805	.429	.489	.738	.395	13.0	1.0	8-3B	0		
2008	COH	AAA	24	190	21	13	3	7	29	5	48	1	1	0.3	.239	.266	.461	.227	.250	.453	.232	-2.9	-0.4	26-LF	0	10-2B	0
2009	WAS	MLB	25	520	46	26	3	13	59	30	143	6	4	-0.2	.225	.275	.372	.228	.277	.388	.224	-7.7	-0.9	123-3B	-8		

Breakout: 22% Improve: 43% Collapse: 30% Attrition: 8%   Comparables: John Rodriguez, Jason Perry, Ryan Radmanovich, Jim Bennett

The Nationals' Minor League Player of the Year, Davis leapt from relative obscurity after cutting his K/BB rate in half. It's still awful, a translated 106/29, and at first Triple-A pitchers carved him up nicely, but after that bruising start (.187/.218/.293, .151 EqA), he came back with a month of .276/.303/.581, .274 EqA—production not too dissimilar from his Potomac line—and followed that with a similar level of production in the Arizona Fall League. Where he'll play remains an open question.

Ian Desmond   SS

Bats: R   Throws: R   Height: 6' 2"   Weight: 185   Born: September 20, 1985   Age: 23

YEAR	TEAM	LVL	AGE	PA	R	2B	3B	HR	RBI	BB	SO	SB	CS	EqBRR	AVG	OBP	SLG	EqAVG	EqOBP	EqSLG	EqA	VORP	WARP	DEFENSE
2006	POT	A+	20	408	50	20	2	9	45	29	79	14	8	0.7	.244	.313	.384	.203	.253	.327	.199	-27.7	-4.8	89-SS -34
2006	HAR	AA	20	132	8	4	1	0	3	5	35	4	1	-0.2	.182	.214	.231	.161	.194	.210	.121	-19.7	-2.1	36-SS -8
2007	POT	A+	21	536	69	30	4	13	45	57	99	27	11	-7.1	.264	.357	.432	.212	.282	.345	.221	-22.9	-1.4	127-SS -13
2008	HAR	AA	22	364	42	14	0	12	44	31	78	12	8	-1.5	.251	.318	.406	.229	.292	.381	.233	-7.7	0.6	91-SS 0
2009	WAS	MLB	23	474	46	22	2	10	47	35	107	16	7	-0.1	.227	.290	.356	.230	.292	.372	.231	1.7	-0.0	112-SS -8

Breakout: 43%   Improve: 67%   Collapse: 14%   Attrition: 5%   Comparables: Fran Mullins, Mike Lansing, Danny Klassen, Chad Spann

Formerly a touted teen, Desmond is a well-regarded fielder (a regard not shared by his statistical record), but his bat has been a little slow to develop. It is improving, at a roughly league-normal pace, and someday it should peak around major league average for a shortstop. The key, though, will be teaching him some semblance of control regarding his strike-zone judgment.

Elijah Dukes   RF

Bats: R   Throws: R   Height: 6' 2"   Weight: 250   Born: June 26, 1984   Age: 25

YEAR	TEAM	LVL	AGE	PA	R	2B	3B	HR	RBI	BB	SO	SB	CS	EqBRR	AVG	OBP	SLG	EqAVG	EqOBP	EqSLG	EqA	VORP	WARP	DEFENSE		
2006	DUR	AAA	22	334	58	15	5	10	50	44	47	9	4	1.9	.293	.401	.488	.261	.365	.453	.282	16.7	0.5	39-LF -7	26-RF -1	
2007	TBA	MLB	23	220	27	3	2	10	21	33	44	2	4	-1.1	.190	.318	.391	.192	.327	.412	.251	-2.1	0.0	38-CF -3		
2008	COH	AAA	24	57	8	3	1	1	6	8	17	2	2	0.3	.234	.368	.404	.229	.351	.396	.255	0.9	-0.3	8-LF -3		
2008	WAS	MLB	24	334	48	16	2	13	44	50	79	13	4	0.0	.264	.386	.478	.265	.389	.498	.303	18.2	3.3	68-RF 6	7-LF 1	
2009	WAS	MLB	25	507	82	26	3	19	65	69	98	17	10	0.0	.278	.386	.486	.282	.390	.508	.302	30.8	4.0	120-RF 2		

Breakout: 53%   Improve: 81%   Collapse: 3%   Attrition: 13%   Comparables: Mike Epstein, Austin Kearns, Adam Dunn, Ron Swoboda

Between injuries and issues both on the field and off, Dukes hasn't played anything close to a full season since 2005. Tampa Bay gave up on him for his off-field problems, trading him to Washington for a pitcher who had an untranslated ERA of 7.27 in Low-A. Dukes behaved himself in DC—his biggest faux pas was a run-in with Manny Acta for over-celebrating a home run—but he was still only a half-time player due to multiple injuries. When he was available he was quite impressive, so expect the Nats to roll with the wrinkles and try keeping him in their starting lineup. Anyone else find it ironic that both Kearns and Dunn show up in his comparables?

Jesus Flores   C

Bats: R   Throws: R   Height: 6' 1"   Weight: 185   Born: October 26, 1984   Age: 24

YEAR	TEAM	LVL	AGE	PA	R	2B	3B	HR	RBI	BB	SO	SB	CS	EqBRR	AVG	OBP	SLG	EqAVG	EqOBP	EqSLG	EqA	VORP	WARP	DEFENSE
2006	SLU	A+	21	480	66	32	0	21	70	28	127	2	0	-1.2	.266	.335	.487	.233	.284	.433	.244	-2.2	1.9	102-C 5
2007	WAS	MLB	22	197	21	9	0	4	25	14	48	0	1	-0.4	.244	.310	.361	.250	.318	.367	.238	1.2	0.4	44-C 2
2008	COH	AAA	23	69	8	3	0	1	7	8	20	0	0	-0.5	.153	.275	.254	.150	.261	.233	.172	-7.1	-0.7	15-C -3
2008	WAS	MLB	23	324	23	18	1	8	59	15	78	0	1	-2.9	.256	.296	.402	.257	.296	.410	.243	2.8	0.1	76-C -6
2009	WAS	MLB	24	314	32	17	1	11	41	23	71	1	1	-0.8	.252	.316	.432	.255	.319	.451	.260	13.5	2.2	76-C 0

Breakout: 45%   Improve: 71%   Collapse: 14%   Attrition: 29%   Comparables: Dann Bilardello, Randy Hundley, Jeff Torborg, Dick Brown

The original plan in '08 called for Flores, who'd been more or less buried as a Rule 5 pick in 2007, to spend the year in Columbus making up for his lost season while Lo Duca and Estrada managed the major league staff. That duo proved to be both fragile and inept, and it quickly became obvious that Flores was indeed their best backstop, for now and into the future. He's a good catcher with power, and there's a decent chance he'll be an All-Star if he can just learn to lay off those sliders low and away.

Alberto Gonzalez — SS

Bats: R   Throws: R   Height: 5' 11"   Weight: 165   Born: April 18, 1983   Age: 26

YEAR	TEAM	LVL	AGE	PA	R	2B	3B	HR	RBI	BB	SO	SB	CS	EqBRR	AVG	OBP	SLG	EqAVG	EqOBP	EqSLG	EqA	VORP	WARP	DEFENSE			
2006	TEN	AA	23	494	67	20	3	6	50	37	42	5	1	2.5	.290	.356	.392	.259	.317	.371	.242	-3.1	3.2	121-SS	16		
2007	TRN	AA	24	125	18	10	1	0	16	10	14	1	1	0.0	.330	.385	.440	.283	.331	.372	.249	0.8	0.8	27-SS	3		
2007	SWB	AAA	24	426	44	21	10	1	35	24	49	11	5	1.6	.247	.300	.362	.225	.271	.343	.214	-19.6	-0.4	99-SS	0		
2007	NYA	MLB	24	15	3	0	0	0	1	1	1	0	1	-0.0	.071	.133	.071	.143	.200	.143	.000	-3.3	0.1	4-SS	3		
2008	SWB	AAA	25	213	23	8	0	4	23	16	30	4	2	1.1	.250	.313	.356	.230	.288	.335	.222	-8.3	-0.2	33-SS	0	8-2B	-1
2008	NYA	MLB	25	58	4	2	0	0	1	4	8	0	0	0.9	.173	.232	.212	.173	.232	.212	.146	-5.3	-0.6	7-SS	0	6-3B	-1
2008	WAS	MLB	25	54	9	6	0	1	9	4	6	0	1	-0.0	.347	.407	.531	.347	.407	.510	.306	5.5	0.2	10-SS	-2		
2009	WAS	MLB	26	393	39	19	2	5	35	26	49	5	2	1.2	.250	.307	.351	.254	.309	.367	.235	4.0	0.9	94-SS	1		

Breakout: 38% Improve: 62% Collapse: 15% Attrition: 22%   Comparables: Julio Gonzalez, Rey Sanchez, Pedro Chavez, Domingo Ramos

Picked up in an easily overlooked deadline deal with the Yankees in exchange for pitcher Jhonny Nuñez, Gonzalez is the shortstop version of Emilio Bonifacio, picked up a week earlier in another trade for a pitcher. He's a slick fielder with a bat as soft as his hands. Call him Guzman insurance, expect him to spend the next year in Syracuse, and get on with your life.

Cristian Guzman — SS

Bats: S   Throws: R   Height: 6' 0"   Weight: 195   Born: March 21, 1978   Age: 31

YEAR	TEAM	LVL	AGE	PA	R	2B	3B	HR	RBI	BB	SO	SB	CS	EqBRR	AVG	OBP	SLG	EqAVG	EqOBP	EqSLG	EqA	VORP	WARP	DEFENSE	
2007	WAS	MLB	29	192	31	6	6	2	14	15	21	2	0	3.0	.328	.380	.466	.335	.391	.491	.305	17.1	1.4	42-SS	-4
2008	WAS	MLB	30	612	77	35	5	9	55	23	57	6	5	-3.0	.316	.345	.440	.318	.347	.451	.272	34.1	3.1	132-SS	-4
2009	WAS	MLB	31	625	87	38	6	8	70	33	58	10	4	1.4	.323	.361	.455	.327	.364	.475	.286	49.1	4.6	146-SS	-1

Breakout: 19% Improve: 52% Collapse: 7% Attrition: 3%   Comparables: Red Schoendienst, Julio Franco, Michael Young, Mark Grudzielanek

Perhaps it's time to give Guzman his due. He did a lot last year to demonstrate that what he had accomplished in 2007 was not just some fluke event, but a real departure from the Guzman of yore. There are two things we know that are different about Guzman now and Guzman pre-2007. First, he had LASIK surgery following the 2005 season, so maybe he was actually half-blind while he was hitting .219. Second, he's adapted from being a turf-aided slap-and-run speedster to a solid line-drive hitter. There's a better chance that he remains this kind of batsman for the next two years of his extended contract than there is of his remaining an adequate shortstop—his footspeed is declining rapidly.

Willie Harris — OF

Bats: L   Throws: R   Height: 5' 9"   Weight: 170   Born: June 22, 1978   Age: 31

YEAR	TEAM	LVL	AGE	PA	R	2B	3B	HR	RBI	BB	SO	SB	CS	EqBRR	AVG	OBP	SLG	EqAVG	EqOBP	EqSLG	EqA	VORP	WARP	DEFENSE			
2006	PAW	AAA	28	253	32	6	1	8	17	29	56	11	3	2.8	.220	.319	.367	.175	.266	.300	.204	-18.3	-1.9	21-2B	-5	19-LF	-1
2006	BOS	MLB	28	52	17	2	0	0	1	4	11	6	3	0.9	.156	.250	.200	.156	.250	.200	.179	-5.0	-0.7	10-CF	-3		
2007	RIC	AAA	29	70	17	7	2	1	7	8	6	7	3	1.1	.362	.457	.603	.283	.371	.517	.297	5.6	0.6	7-3B	2	5-2B	-2
2007	ATL	MLB	29	391	56	20	8	2	32	40	71	17	11	0.3	.270	.349	.392	.281	.363	.415	.265	5.3	1.6	69-LF	5	12-CF	0
2008	WAS	MLB	30	424	58	14	4	13	43	50	66	13	3	0.4	.251	.344	.417	.251	.346	.431	.272	10.4	3.3	63-LF	15	15-CF	0
2009	WAS	MLB	31	347	45	15	3	8	34	38	63	11	5	1.6	.249	.338	.396	.252	.341	.414	.264	7.1	1.8	84-LF	7		

Breakout: 22% Improve: 53% Collapse: 22% Attrition: 35%   Comparables: Eddie Milner, Michael Tucker, Rob Mackowiak, Jim Delsing

Just one more home run, and Harris would have tied for the team lead. The 13 that he did hit were a shocking number for a player who came into the year with a single-season high of two and a career total of seven; toss in the fact that as late as mid-June he was hitting all of .146 with two whole homers and the shock increases exponentially. For a team with fewer injuries, Harris would have been sent down if he was lucky, released if not; for a team that was missing its top four outfielders, he was in the right place when he got insanely hot in July and August, and he earned a two-year contract to try and keep it up.

Anderson Hernandez — MI

Bats: S   Throws: R   Height: 5' 9"   Weight: 170   Born: October 30, 1982   Age: 26

YEAR	TEAM	LVL	AGE	PA	R	2B	3B	HR	RBI	BB	SO	SB	CS	EqBRR	AVG	OBP	SLG	EqAVG	EqOBP	EqSLG	EqA	VORP	WARP	DEFENSE		
2006	NOR	AAA	23	444	44	11	4	0	23	21	70	15	5	-3.8	.249	.285	.295	.239	.274	.294	.199	-29.1	-2.0	70-SS -10	30-2B	3
2006	NYN	MLB	23	67	4	1	1	1	3	1	12	0	0	0.3	.152	.164	.242	.152	.164	.242	.091	-7.5	-0.7	12-2B	1	
2007	NWO	AAA	24	597	84	28	5	5	42	31	82	16	9	0.0	.301	.339	.397	.272	.308	.360	.234	-7.3	-0.9	108-SS -16	19-2B	1
2008	NWO	AAA	25	523	57	21	7	5	36	38	95	11	8	0.4	.203	.262	.307	.177	.228	.261	.164	-57.7	-4.3	114-SS -10	6-2B	0
2008	WAS	MLB	25	91	11	4	0	0	17	10	8	0	0	0.5	.333	.407	.383	.333	.407	.383	.285	5.1	0.7	16-2B	2	
2009	WAS	MLB	26	469	41	19	3	3	34	29	89	10	6	1.5	.223	.273	.305	.226	.275	.318	.205	-10.1	-0.8	111-SS -2		

Breakout: 40% Improve: 56% Collapse: 27% Attrition: 16%   Comparables: Jose Uribe, Ramon Santiago, Wilson Delgado, Alfredo Amezaga

Compared to what had gone before, the way that Hernandez hit down the stretch for the Nationals—along with the talk that accompanied it in the offseason—was strangely reminiscent of what Luis Hernandez did for Baltimore at the end of 2007. He's flirted with the replacement level for his entire career now (which is better than Luis, who had never even been introduced), and opening the season with him at second amounts to treating an open wound with prayer instead of sutures.

Nick Johnson — 1B

Bats: L   Throws: L   Height: 6' 3"   Weight: 225   Born: September 19, 1978   Age: 30

YEAR	TEAM	LVL	AGE	PA	R	2B	3B	HR	RBI	BB	SO	SB	CS	EqBRR	AVG	OBP	SLG	EqAVG	EqOBP	EqSLG	EqA	VORP	WARP	DEFENSE	
2006	WAS	MLB	27	628	100	46	0	23	77	110	99	10	3	-1.4	.290	.428	.520	.297	.435	.531	.330	50.4	6.9	142-1B	8
2008	WAS	MLB	29	147	15	8	0	5	20	33	25	0	0	0.5	.220	.415	.431	.211	.412	.431	.302	6.3	0.8	34-1B	-1
2009	WAS	MLB	30	430	66	22	1	15	58	80	71	4	0	-1.0	.266	.410	.472	.270	.414	.493	.312	26.2	3.1	102-1B	1

Breakout: 6% Improve: 42% Collapse: 18% Attrition: 14%   Comparables: David Justice, Randy Milligan, Erubiel Durazo, Mike Hargrove

Like the crystal egg from *Risky Business*, the leg lamp from *A Christmas Story*, the tablets in *The Ten Commandments*, or wind in a Kevin Smith movie, Nick Johnson always gets broken. In May he suffered torn ligaments and tendons in his wrist, and, as has often been the case with him, a seemingly straightforward injury took longer than expected to heal. The original timetable said "out six weeks," but he ended up needing further surgery after the cast came off, and he missed the rest of the season. His usual eye and power were still there during the brief time that he was. It's appropriate that Johnson came up as a Yankee—he's the Ron Blomberg of the *goyim*.

Austin Kearns — RF

Bats: R   Throws: R   Height: 6' 4"   Weight: 225   Born: May 20, 1980   Age: 29

YEAR	TEAM	LVL	AGE	PA	R	2B	3B	HR	RBI	BB	SO	SB	CS	EqBRR	AVG	OBP	SLG	EqAVG	EqOBP	EqSLG	EqA	VORP	WARP	DEFENSE	
2006	CIN	MLB	26	368	53	21	1	16	50	35	85	7	1	-0.1	.274	.351	.492	.265	.345	.481	.283	14.9	2.5	84-RF	6
2006	WAS	MLB	26	261	33	12	1	8	36	41	50	2	3	-0.4	.250	.381	.429	.259	.391	.453	.291	7.6	1.4	55-RF	-1
2007	WAS	MLB	27	674	84	35	1	16	74	71	106	2	2	0.9	.266	.355	.411	.272	.364	.428	.276	14.4	4.1	154-RF	13
2008	WAS	MLB	28	357	40	10	0	7	32	35	63	2	2	0.8	.217	.311	.316	.217	.311	.326	.226	-13.9	-1.0	82-RF	-3
2009	WAS	MLB	29	405	50	19	1	11	49	46	69	4	2	-0.7	.264	.355	.417	.267	.358	.436	.275	11.6	1.9	97-RF	1

Breakout: 29% Improve: 64% Collapse: 12% Attrition: 21%   Comparables: Michael Cuddyer, Glenn Braggs, Dwight Evans, Ollie Brown

That a player will suffer pain and have impaired hitting ability due to bone chips in his elbow is perfectly understandable. What is worrisome for Kearns (for his career) and for the Nationals (for all the money that they owe him in 2009-10) is that the elbow was still painful and impaired following surgery to correct the problem, thus robbing his swing of its drive. That the Nationals made the trade for Willingham cannot be seen as a vote of confidence.

Chris Marrero — 1B

Bats: R   Throws: R   Height: 6' 3"   Weight: 210   Born: July 2, 1988   Age: 20

YEAR	TEAM	LVL	AGE	PA	R	2B	3B	HR	RBI	BB	SO	SB	CS	EqBRR	AVG	OBP	SLG	EqAVG	EqOBP	EqSLG	EqA	VORP	WARP	DEFENSE		
2006	NAT	Rk	17	91	10	9	0	0	16	8	19	0	0	1.5	.309	.374	.420	.214	.264	.298	.195	-16.8	-1.4	21-LF	-3	
2007	HAG	A	18	243	31	14	0	14	53	14	39	0	4	-0.1	.293	.337	.545	.224	.259	.412	.225	-6.9	-2.6	35-LF -16	10-RF	-1
2007	POT	A+	18	290	40	11	3	9	35	32	63	0	0	-4.0	.259	.338	.431	.212	.276	.356	.219	-12.5	-1.7	53-LF	-6	
2008	POT	A+	19	289	40	15	2	11	38	25	55	0	0	2.2	.250	.325	.453	.229	.293	.424	.245	-1.3	-0.5	68-1B	-2	
2009	WAS	MLB	20	524	51	28	1	16	64	42	109	0	1	-0.6	.244	.308	.410	.247	.311	.428	.250	1.2	-0.3	123-1B	-7	

Breakout: 56% Improve: 76% Collapse: 3% Attrition: 2%   Comparables: Marc Newfield, Manny Ramirez, Tim Thompson, Matt Winters

The Nationals' top pick in 2006, Marrero continues to absolutely pound the ball—while his power doesn't quite rate with Burgess, he's still among the top ten or so for his age. The bad news is that he's still searching for a position, and with the shift to first base last year he's gone about as far to the right side of the defensive spectrum as he can go. The other bad news is that his season was cut short by a broken leg, with ligament damage in the ankle. It's not as if he had any speed to begin with, so there are no long-term worries there.

Justin Maxwell   OF   Bats: R   Throws: R   Height: 6' 5"   Weight: 225   Born: November 6, 1983   Age: 25

YEAR	TEAM	LVL	AGE	PA	R	2B	3B	HR	RBI	BB	SO	SB	CS	EqBRR	AVG	OBP	SLG	EqAVG	EqOBP	EqSLG	EqA	VORP	WARP	DEFENSE			
2006	SAV	A	22	68	8	2	2	1	7	8	23	1	0	0.8	.172	.294	.328	.145	.232	.274	.170	-7.4	-0.6	9-CF	0		
2006	VER	A-	22	306	36	11	3	4	33	27	61	20	5	2.4	.269	.346	.376	.184	.242	.269	.177	-59.3	-3.5	50-CF	-7	21-LF	3
2007	HAG	A	23	244	51	12	2	14	40	26	57	14	3	2.9	.301	.389	.579	.208	.278	.380	.230	-8.2	-0.6	36-CF	-2	9-RF	-2
2007	POT	A+	23	260	35	13	0	13	43	24	65	21	5	1.1	.263	.338	.491	.206	.264	.366	.224	-11.9	-0.6	54-CF	-2		
2007	WAS	MLB	23	27	5	0	0	2	5	1	8	0	0	0.1	.269	.296	.500	.269	.296	.500	.264	1.2	0.3	5-CF	2		
2008	HAR	AA	24	180	35	6	3	7	28	31	28	13	4	0.1	.233	.367	.459	.199	.320	.397	.256	-1.1	0.1	15-LF	-4	12-RF	0
2009	WAS	MLB	25	422	43	18	2	11	43	38	118	14	5	0.8	.204	.282	.352	.207	.284	.368	.228	-9.1	0.1	100-CF	-5		

Breakout: 32%   Improve: 47%   Collapse: 25%   Attrition: 13%   Comparables: Dominic Fucci, Ozzie Canseco, Anthony Sanders, Troy Hughes

Maxwell's season ended in May when he broke his right wrist trying to make a diving catch. Injuries are nothing new for him; they shortened his college career (at Maryland), and dropped him back to the fourth round of the 2005 draft. While he still gets high marks for power, speed, and maturity (which he should, given his age), he did have strikeout problems, though he had shown some dramatic improvement there before getting hurt. The lost time and the Nats' crowded outfield make him an even deeper sleeper than he was, but he's still a good candidate to come out of nowhere.

Lastings Milledge   CF   Bats: R   Throws: R   Height: 6' 0"   Weight: 205   Born: April 5, 1985   Age: 24

YEAR	TEAM	LVL	AGE	PA	R	2B	3B	HR	RBI	BB	SO	SB	CS	EqBRR	AVG	OBP	SLG	EqAVG	EqOBP	EqSLG	EqA	VORP	WARP	DEFENSE			
2006	NOR	AAA	21	367	52	21	4	7	36	43	67	13	10	0.1	.277	.388	.440	.272	.373	.450	.282	20.6	2.1	54-CF	-3	21-LF	3
2006	NYN	MLB	21	185	14	7	2	4	22	12	39	1	2	-0.3	.241	.310	.380	.240	.308	.377	.237	-3.7	0.2	23-RF	2	21-LF	1
2007	NWO	AAA	22	43	9	1	0	1	5	2	12	5	0	0.0	.333	.372	.436	.325	.364	.425	.293	2.2	0.2	8-RF	-1		
2007	NYN	MLB	22	206	27	9	1	7	29	13	42	3	2	-1.3	.272	.341	.446	.283	.351	.473	.278	6.6	1.2	25-RF	1	13-CF	1
2008	WAS	MLB	23	587	65	24	2	14	61	38	96	24	9	-0.4	.268	.330	.402	.271	.332	.414	.261	13.3	1.2	133-CF	-6		
2009	WAS	MLB	24	521	73	27	3	14	61	42	87	21	7	0.8	.281	.352	.442	.285	.355	.461	.281	25.5	3.3	123-CF	-1		

Breakout: 42%   Improve: 68%   Collapse: 10%   Attrition: 12%   Comparables: Rondell White, Vernon Wells, Ellis Burks, Andre Dawson

Plus/minus, plus/minus, which will win? The pluses are the five-tool talent that made him the key acquisition for the Nationals last offseason, which we all got a glimpse of in the second half of 2008, and that he's just turned 24 this spring. The minuses are the lack of maturity that led the Mets to deem him expendable and that are souring the Nats on him already; the lack of growth in his stats from 2004 (when he had a .259 EqA at age 19) until now; the defensive problems in center that are pushing him steadily into a corner; and the first half of 2008, when he had just a .245 EqA. Color us skeptical.

Luke Montz   C   Bats: R   Throws: R   Height: 6' 2"   Weight: 205   Born: July 7, 1983   Age: 25

YEAR	TEAM	LVL	AGE	PA	R	2B	3B	HR	RBI	BB	SO	SB	CS	EqBRR	AVG	OBP	SLG	EqAVG	EqOBP	EqSLG	EqA	VORP	WARP	DEFENSE			
2006	POT	A+	22	519	59	27	3	16	76	51	91	3	3	-3.7	.229	.313	.410	.192	.256	.337	.206	-33.2	-2.8	83-1B	-2	27-C	0
2007	POT	A+	23	253	43	15	1	7	39	45	54	3	2	-0.1	.269	.406	.458	.205	.315	.353	.238	-6.0	0.1	43-C	-2	8-1B	0
2007	HAR	AA	23	158	22	5	1	5	19	8	50	0	0	-0.6	.233	.274	.384	.203	.241	.351	.200	-10.3	-1.0	38-C	-6		
2008	HAR	AA	24	254	30	14	0	14	53	31	46	0	1	-2.0	.282	.368	.536	.244	.323	.476	.269	8.7	1.4	48-C	0		
2008	COH	AAA	24	181	18	8	1	2	18	13	37	1	1	0.2	.256	.309	.351	.232	.287	.327	.213	-8.1	0.0	42-C	1		
2008	WAS	MLB	24	26	2	0	0	1	3	5	9	0	0	-0.1	.143	.308	.286	.143	.308	.286	.219	-0.9	0.0	6-C	0		
2009	WAS	MLB	25	433	38	20	1	11	46	42	105	2	1	-0.7	.210	.290	.354	.212	.292	.370	.228	-3.8	1.0	103-C	-4		

Breakout: 28%   Improve: 46%   Collapse: 21%   Attrition: 11%   Comparables: Lloyd McClendon, Ozzie Virgil, B.J. Waszgis, Grant Psomas

Thanks to Chase Utley, Montz parlayed an early-season power streak at Double-A into a September call-up—Utley's collision with Flores knocked the Nats' regular catcher out for the final month, and Montz was an available option. He wasn't considered a prospect before this year, and there was nothing in his performance after June 1 to alter that. Feel free to recognize what he did at Harrisburg, but don't let it color your expectations.

Wil Nieves   C   Bats: R   Throws: R   Height: 5' 11"   Weight: 190   Born: September 25, 1977   Age: 31

YEAR	TEAM	LVL	AGE	PA	R	2B	3B	HR	RBI	BB	SO	SB	CS	EqBRR	AVG	OBP	SLG	EqAVG	EqOBP	EqSLG	EqA	VORP	WARP	DEFENSE	
2006	COH	AAA	28	348	29	13	0	5	34	18	29	2	1	-0.1	.259	.298	.346	.218	.255	.294	.189	-26.4	-2.0	79-C	-7
2007	SWB	AAA	29	98	5	1	2	1	8	6	10	1	0	-0.4	.256	.306	.344	.209	.255	.297	.193	-7.4	-0.1	26-C	1
2007	NYA	MLB	29	66	6	4	0	0	8	2	9	0	0	-0.1	.164	.190	.230	.164	.190	.230	.127	-6.6	-0.9	19-C	-3
2008	COH	AAA	30	29	3	1	0	0	2	3	6	1	0	-1.6	.240	.321	.280	.192	.276	.231	.194	-2.6	0.0	8-C	1
2008	WAS	MLB	30	196	15	9	1	1	20	13	29	0	1	-0.6	.261	.309	.341	.264	.311	.343	.230	-1.3	0.0	51-C	-1
2009	WAS	MLB	31	153	11	5	0	1	12	9	22	1	0	-0.5	.228	.278	.287	.231	.281	.300	.200	-4.3	0.0	40-C	-1

Breakout: 40% Improve: 54% Collapse: 40% Attrition: 58%   Comparables: Jerry Zimmerman, Mickey Grasso, Gary Bennett, Mike Roarke

After three years as the Yankees' third-string catcher, Nieves came to DC figuring to drop another spot—the intention was for him to back-up Flores at Triple-A Columbus. The organization wound up half right; the disappearance of Lo Duca and Estrada made him the backup in DC instead. Spotted against lefties, he has a semi-credible bat, albeit one driven entirely by an empty batting average.

Derek Norris   C   Bats: R   Throws: R   Height: 6' 0"   Weight: 210   Born: February 14, 1989   Age: 20

YEAR	TEAM	LVL	AGE	PA	R	2B	3B	HR	RBI	BB	SO	SB	CS	EqBRR	AVG	OBP	SLG	EqAVG	EqOBP	EqSLG	EqA	VORP	WARP	DEFENSE	
2007	NAT	Rk	18	151	16	6	2	4	15	25	38	2	1	-2.3	.203	.344	.382	.144	.245	.273	.178	-38.0	-2.5	13-C	-4
2008	VER	A-	19	302	42	12	0	10	38	63	56	11	9	-2.7	.278	.444	.463	.217	.358	.357	.259	1.7	1.3	46-C	-1
2009	WAS	MLB	20	534	54	23	1	12	47	71	122	8	5	-0.1	.209	.320	.346	.211	.323	.362	.240	0.6	1.6	126-C	-12

Breakout: 29% Improve: 56% Collapse: 16% Attrition: 3%   Comparables: Mike Whitlock, J.D. Closser, Nick Weglarz, Brian Deak

Norris drew 63 bases on balls in the New York-Penn League last year; that's the highest total in the league since Kevin Youkilis had 70 in 2001. Compared to Youkilis then, Norris is two years younger, hits for more power, and plays catcher—all to the good—but he struck out twice as often. Let's call him a Mickey Tettleton-style hitter, but remember that this is still just short-season ball and a very young player we're talking about. He's only been playing catcher for a couple of years since converting from third base in his senior year of high school; he has the arm for the job, but he still needs to work at the other aspects of catching.

Wily Mo Peña   OF   Bats: R   Throws: R   Height: 6' 3"   Weight: 245   Born: January 23, 1982   Age: 27

YEAR	TEAM	LVL	AGE	PA	R	2B	3B	HR	RBI	BB	SO	SB	CS	EqBRR	AVG	OBP	SLG	EqAVG	EqOBP	EqSLG	EqA	VORP	WARP	DEFENSE				
2006	BOS	MLB	24	305	36	15	2	11	42	20	91	0	1	1.3	.300	.348	.487	.284	.338	.465	.274	14.6	2.0	32-RF	0	22-CF	3
2007	BOS	MLB	25	172	18	9	1	5	17	14	58	0	1	-1.1	.218	.291	.385	.206	.285	.387	.229	-5.0	-0.7	23-RF	1	10-LF	-2
2007	WAS	MLB	25	145	24	4	0	8	22	8	36	2	0	0.8	.293	.352	.504	.301	.359	.526	.298	9.1	0.8	31-LF	-2		
2008	WAS	MLB	26	206	10	6	0	2	10	10	48	0	1	-1.7	.205	.243	.267	.205	.243	.272	.169	-16.5	-1.4	46-LF	2		
2009	WAS	MLB	27	178	18	8	1	6	23	14	45	0	1	-0.7	.253	.317	.415	.257	.320	.434	.256	4.4	0.4	46-LF	-1		

Breakout: 44% Improve: 58% Collapse: 29% Attrition: 46%   Comparables: Charlie Spikes, Wes Helms, Bob Zupcic, Russ Morman

Peña was never really healthy in 2008. He tore an oblique muscle in the spring, and probably returned from it too quickly. In June and July he tried to play through what turned out to be a torn labrum and rotator cuff. Trying to analyze his 2008 performance for clues to his future through the haze of all that hurting is a particularly pointless brand of navel-gazing; since he's supposed to be healthy by spring, expect him to recover his brute-force power and be limited to no more than half-time play.

Dmitri Young — 1B

Bats: S Throws: R Height: 6' 2" Weight: 220 Born: October 11, 1973 Age: 35

YEAR	TEAM	LVL	AGE	PA	R	2B	3B	HR	RBI	BB	SO	SB	CS	EqBRR	AVG	OBP	SLG	EqAVG	EqOBP	EqSLG	EqA	VORP	WARP	DEFENSE	
2006	DET	MLB	32	184	19	4	1	7	23	11	39	1	1	-1.5	.250	.293	.407	.240	.288	.398	.235	-2.5	-0.4		
2007	WAS	MLB	33	508	57	38	1	13	74	44	74	0	0	-2.8	.320	.378	.491	.328	.390	.514	.307	37.2	3.0	99-1B	-5
2008	WAS	MLB	34	180	15	6	0	4	10	28	28	0	0	-0.9	.280	.394	.400	.275	.394	.403	.286	6.6	0.4	33-1B	-3
2009	WAS	MLB	35	278	31	13	1	6	34	32	44	0	0	-1.8	.276	.361	.408	.280	.364	.427	.274	9.1	0.6	68-1B	-4

Breakout: 13% Improve: 36% Collapse: 35% Attrition: 34%   Comparables: David Segui, Bruce Bochte, Jerry Mumphrey, Bob Watson

Diabetic issues which helped force him out of action in 2006 resurfaced and kept him out for most of the year. The statistical outlook for Young as an African-American with fairly severe diabetes in his mid-30s, is unpleasant to say the least. The elevated glucose levels that define the disease weaken the blood vessels progressively over time. The earlier the onset, the earlier those vessels are liable to fail, leading to all of the worst results associated with diabetes—we're not just talking about ending a career, but blindness, amputation, or death. He did recover enough to see action in some minor league games in August, and he remains under contract for '09.

Ryan Zimmerman — 3B

Bats: R Throws: R Height: 6' 2" Weight: 210 Born: September 28, 1984 Age: 24

YEAR	TEAM	LVL	AGE	PA	R	2B	3B	HR	RBI	BB	SO	SB	CS	EqBRR	AVG	OBP	SLG	EqAVG	EqOBP	EqSLG	EqA	VORP	WARP	DEFENSE	
2006	WAS	MLB	21	682	84	47	3	20	110	61	120	11	8	-1.3	.287	.351	.471	.294	.361	.484	.285	26.4	4.1	155-3B	1
2007	WAS	MLB	22	722	99	43	5	24	91	61	125	4	1	1.5	.266	.330	.458	.274	.341	.482	.279	25.8	5.0	160-3B	12
2008	WAS	MLB	23	466	51	24	1	14	51	31	71	1	1	-2.2	.283	.333	.442	.281	.332	.447	.268	14.0	1.3	102-3B	-3
2009	WAS	MLB	24	597	78	35	2	19	84	56	91	4	2	-0.5	.289	.358	.471	.293	.361	.493	.289	36.3	4.2	140-3B	2

Breakout: 39% Improve: 64% Collapse: 11% Attrition: 4%   Comparables: Ken McMullen, Eric Chavez, Bob Horner, Larry Parrish

Every Nationals player except Nick Johnson started the season ice-cold; through April, Johnson was the only Nat regular with an above-average EqA. Zimmerman's was among the frostiest, mired at .224. For the rest of the year he hit at essentially the same level that he'd established in 2006-07; the downturn looks more severe because he missed nearly two months with a shoulder injury from a headfirst slide (why? why? why?), and never had sufficient time to balance out the cold start. Another year without noticeable improvement makes it seem more likely that he'll be just a very good third baseman, and not a David Wright-level star.

PITCHERS

Adrian Alaniz

Bats: R Throws: R Height: 6' 2" Weight: 200 Born: March 12, 1984 Age: 25

YEAR	TEAM	LVL	AGE	W	L	SV	G	GS	IP	H	BB	SO	HR	GB%	BABIP	STUFF	WHIP	ERA	DERA	EqH9	EqBB9	EqSO9	EqHR9	DEF	VORP	SN/WX
2007	VER	A-	23	8	2	0	13	8	60¹	42	8	62	2	49.7%	.248	-4	0.83	2.39	5.95	8.7	1.9	4.3	1.1	7	-2.2	—
2008	POT	A+	24	9	0	0	12	12	65¹	50	25	56	2	47.5%	.273	3	1.15	2.62	4.50	8.4	3.9	4.9	0.6	-1	7.3	—
2008	HAR	AA	24	0	5	0	13	13	66¹	61	30	47	10	42.0%	.264	-24	1.37	3.94	6.08	9.0	4.0	4.5	2.0	6	-3.4	—
2009	WAS	MLB	25	5	8	0	24	16	100¹	108	44	67	14	44.0%	.300	5	1.51	5.38	5.85	9.7	3.5	5.3	1.2	0	-1.3	0.53

Breakout: 5% Improve: 20% Collapse: 35% Attrition: 18%   Comparables: Ed Myers, Brian Bannister, Eric Show, T.J. Mathews

Alaniz was an eighth-round pick in 2007, a polished college pitcher taken out of the University of Texas. He had dominated (17-2) younger competition in the New York–Penn and Carolina Leagues, but began to run into trouble in Double-A. He's a command/control guy, mixing four pitches, with a fastball that barely breaks 90. Young hitters don't have the strength yet to really punish his mistakes; that luxury will run out as he advances.

Collin Balester

Bats: R   Throws: R   Height: 6' 5"   Weight: 190   Born: June 6, 1986   Age: 23

YEAR	TEAM	LVL	AGE	W	L	SV	G	GS	IP	H	BB	SO	HR	GB%	BABIP	STUFF	WHIP	ERA	DERA	EqH9	EqBB9	EqSO9	EqHR9	DEF	VORP	SN/WX
2006	POT	A+	20	4	5	0	23	22	117²	126	53	87	12	43.9%	.325	-18	1.53	5.22	7.98	13.0	5.2	3.6	2.4	-8	-27.2	—
2006	HAR	AA	20	1	0	0	3	3	19²	15	6	10	0	45.8%	.273	15	1.09	1.88	4.08	8.2	3.6	2.5	0.5	1	3.0	—
2007	HAR	AA	21	2	7	0	17	17	98²	103	25	77	9	45.7%	.314	5	1.30	3.74	5.17	11.2	2.7	4.3	1.5	-4	4.4	—
2007	COH	AAA	21	2	3	0	10	10	51²	49	23	40	3	35.0%	.309	11	1.39	4.18	6.80	9.7	4.4	4.6	0.9	3	-6.5	—
2008	COH	AAA	22	9	3	0	15	15	78²	79	23	64	14	40.9%	.293	-16	1.30	4.00	6.45	10.1	2.9	4.9	2.3	10	-7.0	—
2008	WAS	MLB	22	3	7	0	15	15	80	92	28	50	12	40.9%	.311	5	1.50	5.51	4.72	10.0	2.7	4.9	1.2	-6	-1.4	0.35
2009	WAS	MLB	23	7	12	0	40	27	157	180	60	104	26	42.0%	.300	5	1.53	5.49	5.87	10.4	3.0	5.2	1.5	0	-2.5	0.79

Breakout: 4%   Improve: 35%   Collapse: 24%   Attrition: 15%   Comparables: Bill Wegman, Steve Woodard, Rich Bordi, Sean Douglass

Balester has been on top of the Nationals' prospect list in recent years, but that's mostly involved being the best of a then-poor system rather than being a great prospect. He's a *good* prospect, spending half his age-22 season getting on-the-job training in the majors. Tall and (to date) durable, Balester relies on a fastball/curve/changeup package. He's successful when he keeps them down; when they get left up in the zone, which happens entirely too often, they end up as souvenirs. Don't expect him to automatically have a rotation slot this spring.

Jason Bergmann

Bats: R   Throws: R   Height: 6' 4"   Weight: 205   Born: September 25, 1981   Age: 27

YEAR	TEAM	LVL	AGE	W	L	SV	G	GS	IP	H	BB	SO	HR	GB%	BABIP	STUFF	WHIP	ERA	DERA	EqH9	EqBB9	EqSO9	EqHR9	DEF	VORP	SN/WX
2006	NWO	AAA	24	8	2	4	26	4	60²	54	20	62	5	27.2%	.314	-2	1.23	3.29	4.37	9.7	3.2	6.8	1.1	1	7.6	—
2006	WAS	MLB	24	0	2	0	29	6	64²	81	27	54	12	33.3%	.356	-10	1.67	6.68	5.68	11.1	3.3	6.8	1.5	-6	-6.9	-0.22
2007	COH	AAA	25	2	1	0	5	5	24	20	6	22	0	33.3%	.313	14	1.08	1.50	2.86	9.0	2.5	5.7	0.4	1	6.7	—
2007	WAS	MLB	25	6	6	0	21	21	115¹	99	42	86	18	36.3%	.249	3	1.22	4.45	4.70	7.6	2.8	6.3	1.3	4	15.0	3.17
2008	COH	AAA	26	2	2	0	5	5	29	26	11	27	2	34.9%	.300	3	1.28	3.72	4.76	8.6	3.5	5.4	1.0	0	2.6	—
2008	WAS	MLB	26	2	11	0	30	22	139²	153	47	96	25	31.8%	.299	-11	1.43	5.09	5.32	9.3	2.5	5.3	1.5	-2	-3.7	1.88
2009	WAS	MLB	27	4	6	1	28	11	81¹	85	28	58	12	38.0%	.290	6	1.39	4.75	5.09	9.5	2.7	5.6	1.3	0	6.2	0.98

Breakout: 19%   Improve: 44%   Collapse: 29%   Attrition: 33%   Comparables: Claudio Vargas, Shawn Boskie, Phil Ortega, Craig Swan

Bergmann made the squad out of spring training, but after giving up 12 runs in his first two starts they handed him a quick ticket back to Ohio. He returned a month later after Chico came up lame, but was finally dropped from the rotation for good in September. Attrition was the only reason he stuck in the rotation even that long, and if you see him starting with any regularity in 2009, that will probably be the reason once again.

Matt Chico

Bats: L   Throws: L   Height: 6' 0"   Weight: 205   Born: June 10, 1983   Age: 26

YEAR	TEAM	LVL	AGE	W	L	SV	G	GS	IP	H	BB	SO	HR	GB%	BABIP	STUFF	WHIP	ERA	DERA	EqH9	EqBB9	EqSO9	EqHR9	DEF	VORP	SN/WX
2006	LNC	A+	23	3	4	0	10	10	50²	48	11	49	5	43.5%	.293	-11	1.18	3.76	5.58	9.0	2.5	4.1	1.6	-2	0.1	—
2006	TEN	AA	23	7	2	0	13	13	81¹	62	21	63	6	40.6%	.249	-5	1.02	2.22	5.42	7.9	2.6	4.2	1.3	14	1.5	—
2006	HAR	AA	23	2	0	0	4	4	22²	28	8	13	3	46.7%	.347	-24	1.62	3.24	2.89	14.9	4.3	2.9	2.4	-5	5.6	—
2007	WAS	MLB	24	7	9	0	31	31	167	183	74	94	26	34.5%	.295	-12	1.54	4.63	5.19	9.7	3.5	4.8	1.4	6	10.5	2.94
2008	WAS	MLB	25	0	6	0	11	8	48	63	17	31	10	40.6%	.344	-13	1.67	6.19	5.29	11.5	2.6	5.1	1.7	-2	-3.3	0.06
2009	WAS	MLB	26	2	3	0	19	5	46²	50	17	31	7	41.0%	.290	1	1.44	4.92	5.30	9.8	2.9	5.2	1.3	0	2.9	0.41

Breakout: 14%   Improve: 36%   Collapse: 44%   Attrition: 56%   Comparables: Bob Sykes, Steve Rosenberg, Mike Kekich, Dave Hamilton

Chico struggled throughout the spring, but still managed to break camp in the rotation as the other candidates (Patterson, Bergmann) fared even worse. He was trying to return to a pitching motion that he'd used in high school in an attempt to improve his control, stop throwing across his body, and protect his shoulder; he wound up blowing out his elbow, and won't be ready to play until sometime during the 2009 season.

Tyler Clippard

Bats: R   Throws: R   Height: 6' 4"   Weight: 170   Born: February 14, 1985   Age: 24

YEAR	TEAM	LVL	AGE	W	L	SV	G	GS	IP	H	BB	SO	HR	GB%	BABIP	STUFF	WHIP	ERA	DERA	EqH9	EqBB9	EqSO9	EqHR9	DEF	VORP	SN/WX
2006	TRN	AA	21	12	10	0	28	28	166	118	55	175	14	44.4%	.258	4	1.04	3.36	6.98	9.6	3.9	5.9	1.5	13	-22.5	—
2007	TRN	AA	22	2	1	0	6	6	26²	22	12	28	5	28.2%	.273	-4	1.27	5.39	8.37	10.6	4.9	6.5	3.0	0	-7.3	—
2007	SWB	AAA	22	4	4	0	14	14	69¹	82	35	55	7	34.8%	.354	-12	1.69	4.16	6.54	12.6	5.1	4.8	1.6	-3	-6.6	—
2007	NYA	MLB	22	3	1	0	6	6	27	29	17	18	6	39.3%	.277	-2	1.70	6.33	5.40	9.4	5.4	5.1	2.0	-2	-0.9	0.24
2008	COH	AAA	23	6	13	0	27	27	143	129	66	125	15	38.2%	.291	-11	1.36	4.66	6.70	8.9	4.5	5.2	1.4	8	-16.6	—
2008	WAS	MLB	23	1	1	0	2	2	10¹	12	7	8	2	18.2%	.323	10	1.84	4.37	2.70	10.8	5.4	6.3	1.8	-1	1.5	0.02
2009	WAS	MLB	24	4	7	0	26	13	88¹	92	47	66	14	39.0%	.290	4	1.57	5.35	5.72	9.5	4.2	5.8	1.4	0	-0.0	0.52

Breakout: 23%   Improve: 64%   Collapse: 10%   Attrition: 18%   Comparables: Jamie Brewington, Mark Kiefer, Pat Mahomes, Russ Springer

Clippard was a Yankee prospect—if you have to use a noun—landed in a trade last offseason for reliever Jonathan Albaladejo. He made a big splash back in 2005; in retrospect, that appears to have been the product of some great defense behind him and a great deal of projection based on his age, a projection that has not extended into the real world. As an extreme fly-ball pitcher, he's had to nibble more to fend off the home runs as he's moved up.

Jesus Colome

Bats: R   Throws: R   Height: 6' 2"   Weight: 200   Born: December 23, 1977   Age: 31

YEAR	TEAM	LVL	AGE	W	L	SV	G	GS	IP	H	BB	SO	HR	GB%	BABIP	STUFF	WHIP	ERA	DERA	EqH9	EqBB9	EqSO9	EqHR9	DEF	VORP	SN/WX
2006	COH	AAA	28	1	1	0	25	0	33	35	15	25	3	47.3%	.308	-28	1.52	3.82	6.40	10.0	4.5	4.2	1.4	0	-2.9	—
2007	WAS	MLB	29	5	1	1	61	0	66	64	27	43	6	37.7%	.291	-4	1.38	3.82	4.07	8.5	3.1	5.4	0.8	1	12.2	1.69
2008	WAS	MLB	30	2	2	0	61	0	71	61	39	55	6	35.5%	.276	-3	1.41	4.31	4.88	7.4	4.1	6.0	0.8	4	7.1	0.84
2009	WAS	MLB	31	2	2	1	38	0	45²	46	23	35	5	41.0%	.290	-1	1.49	4.70	5.11	9.1	3.9	5.9	1.0	0	3.2	0.22

Breakout: 15%   Improve: 36%   Collapse: 37%   Attrition: 36%   Comparables: Brian Williams, Les Lancaster, Mike DeJean, Turk Wendell

Colome is a little better than he first appears, as his ERA was inflated by two outings in which he yielded a full third of his runs total on the season. Even so, he worked himself into the doghouse early by arriving in camp late with visa problems, and then found that the new park was not nearly so forgiving to fly-ball pitchers as was RFK. The Nationals used him in the furthest back of the bullpen, typically to finish out lost causes; he was released after the season rather than deal with the bother of an arbitration case.

Chad Cordero

Bats: R   Throws: R   Height: 6' 0"   Weight: 195   Born: March 18, 1982   Age: 27

YEAR	TEAM	LVL	AGE	W	L	SV	G	GS	IP	H	BB	SO	HR	GB%	BABIP	STUFF	WHIP	ERA	DERA	EqH9	EqBB9	EqSO9	EqHR9	DEF	VORP	SN/WX
2006	WAS	MLB	24	7	4	29	68	0	73¹	59	22	69	13	38.5%	.240	3	1.10	3.19	3.54	6.7	2.2	7.4	1.4	3	21.4	3.89
2007	WAS	MLB	25	3	3	37	76	0	75	75	29	62	8	38.7%	.306	3	1.39	3.36	3.89	9.0	3.0	7.1	1.0	3	17.1	3.62
2008	WAS	MLB	26	0	0	0	6	0	4¹	6	3	5	0	42.9%	.429	4	2.08	2.09	0.00	12.5	6.2	8.3	0.0	-1	1.7	-0.01
2009	WAS	MLB	27	2	2	3	42	0	48²	44	18	42	6	41.0%	.280	10	1.28	3.59	3.89	8.3	3.0	6.8	1.0	0	10.2	0.83

Breakout: 11%   Improve: 28%   Collapse: 47%   Attrition: 19%   Comparables: Jorge Julio, Steve Foucault, Jim Ray, Eduardo Rodriguez

Like GM at $80, Enron at $90, or Krispy Kreme at $45, Cordero's 2007 was a missed opportunity to sell high. These days GM and KK are around $3 a share, Enron is worthless, and Cordero was released last fall for nothing in return. His downfall was shoulder tendonitis early in the year; he came back, tore a lat muscle, came back again, and finally tore his labrum. A classic cascade sequence, he might make it back by the 2009 All-Star break, but it won't be in DC.

Ross Detwiler

Bats: R   Throws: L   Height: 6' 5"   Weight: 185   Born: March 6, 1986   Age: 23

YEAR	TEAM	LVL	AGE	W	L	SV	G	GS	IP	H	BB	SO	HR	GB%	BABIP	STUFF	WHIP	ERA	DERA	EqH9	EqBB9	EqSO9	EqHR9	DEF	VORP	SN/WX
2007	NAT	Rk	21	0	0	0	4	4	12	11	3	15	1	46.9%	.323	2	1.17	2.25	4.35	13.1	4.4	5.2	2.6	0	1.4	—
2007	POT	A+	21	2	2	0	5	4	21¹	27	9	13	1	50.7%	.356	-20	1.69	4.23	6.16	14.7	5.2	2.4	1.4	-3	-1.2	—
2008	POT	A+	22	8	8	0	26	26	124	140	57	114	8	54.9%	.357	-4	1.59	4.86	5.54	12.8	4.7	5.3	1.2	-16	0.7	—
2009	WAS	MLB	23	4	8	0	18	18	94¹	110	51	71	11	50.0%	.330	11	1.71	5.69	6.20	10.6	4.3	5.8	1.0	0	-5.0	0.22

Breakout: 28%   Improve: 61%   Collapse: 17%   Attrition: 9%   Comparables: Jeff Granger, Jeff Francis, Kyle Peterson, Ben Van Ryn

Nationals fans got all excited when Detwiler was called up back in September of '07, just three months after being drafted in the first round, but it was just a contractually-guaranteed gimmick. Coaches worked on his mechanics, trying to get him to stop throwing across his body, and he had trouble adapting; coincidence or not, he did pitch better after July 1 (3.85 ERA) than he had before (5.85), but not so much better that anyone's going to start casting a bronze plaque for him. His best pitch is a sinking heater that generates plenty of ground-ball outs.

Marco Estrada

Bats: R   Throws: R   Height: 6' 0"   Weight: 180   Born: July 5, 1983   Age: 25

YEAR	TEAM	LVL	AGE	W	L	SV	G	GS	IP	H	BB	SO	HR	GB%	BABIP	STUFF	WHIP	ERA	DERA	EqH9	EqBB9	EqSO9	EqHR9	DEF	VORP	SN/WX
2006	SAV	A	22	1	4	0	8	8	37¹	44	14	29	6	42.9%	.342	-47	1.56	5.58	9.00	16.5	5.4	3.0	4.5	-4	-11.3	—
2007	HAG	A	23	1	5	0	8	8	36	39	17	35	4	46.4%	.347	-27	1.56	5.25	9.28	12.9	5.9	4.2	2.2	0	-13.1	—
2007	POT	A+	23	5	3	0	11	11	58¹	67	17	54	7	51.1%	.355	-31	1.44	4.94	6.57	14.6	3.8	4.9	2.7	-8	-5.3	—
2008	HAR	AA	24	6	3	0	13	13	74¹	62	32	67	5	49.8%	.277	8	1.27	2.66	3.73	8.1	3.7	5.7	0.9	-1	15.0	—
2008	COH	AAA	24	3	3	0	12	12	65¹	73	21	52	3	44.1%	.352	1	1.44	3.58	4.65	11.2	3.3	4.8	0.8	-1	6.3	—
2008	WAS	MLB	24	0	0	0	11	0	12²	17	5	10	4	47.8%	.310	-18	1.74	7.80	6.75	11.5	2.7	6.1	2.7	-3	-4.9	-0.27
2009	WAS	MLB	25	4	8	1	37	15	105¹	125	47	72	17	46.0%	.320	0	1.63	5.89	6.34	10.7	3.5	5.4	1.4	0	-7.2	-0.15

Breakout: 9%   Improve: 31%   Collapse: 25%   Attrition: 19%   *Comparables: Don Cooper, Jim Farrell, Paul Fletcher, Glen Cook*

The only glimmer of notoriety this sixth-round pick from 2005 had in the prior three years was a good showing in the 2006 Hawaiian Winter League. He finally got the hang of pitching down in the zone last year, and the result was a four-month romp through the minors that ended with a promotion to Washington in August. A career starter, he basically took over Luis Ayala's slot in the bullpen—and stepped into it seamlessly by starting to suffer from acute gopheritis.

Joel Hanrahan

Bats: R   Throws: R   Height: 6' 3"   Weight: 215   Born: October 6, 1981   Age: 27

YEAR	TEAM	LVL	AGE	W	L	SV	G	GS	IP	H	BB	SO	HR	GB%	BABIP	STUFF	WHIP	ERA	DERA	EqH9	EqBB9	EqSO9	EqHR9	DEF	VORP	SN/WX
2006	JAX	AA	24	7	2	0	12	12	66	49	38	67	4	46.7%	.288	4	1.32	2.59	4.61	10.0	6.0	6.2	1.3	3	6.2	—
2006	LVG	AAA	24	4	3	0	14	14	74¹	70	39	46	7	41.5%	.269	-19	1.47	4.49	7.94	8.4	4.8	3.4	1.1	15	-19.2	—
2007	COH	AAA	25	5	4	0	15	15	75¹	65	36	71	10	39.3%	.266	-18	1.34	3.71	6.72	9.1	4.6	5.6	1.9	8	-9.0	—
2007	WAS	MLB	25	5	3	0	12	11	51	59	38	43	9	34.9%	.325	0	1.90	6.00	5.57	10.3	5.7	7.0	1.6	-2	-2.5	0.73
2008	WAS	MLB	26	6	3	9	69	0	84¹	73	42	93	9	43.9%	.303	13	1.36	3.95	3.81	7.7	3.8	8.6	0.8	-1	13.4	0.82
2009	WAS	MLB	27	2	3	3	33	3	51¹	47	27	47	6	43.0%	.290	9	1.44	4.28	4.65	8.3	4.1	7.2	1.0	0	6.7	0.66

Breakout: 24%   Improve: 39%   Collapse: 41%   Attrition: 44%   *Comparables: Shawn Hillegas, Jeff Parrett, Jim Britton, Mike Corkins*

Hanrahan was easily the Nationals' most pleasant surprise of the season. We had by and large given up on him last year ("a junkballer, having lost the plus stuff he had years ago with the Dodgers to injuries"), but lo and behold, he found it again in the bullpen, showing up in camp with a 96 mph fastball and a hard-biting slider. He earned a spot on the team by compiling one of the most impressive lines of anyone last spring: 13 IP, 2 H, 2 BB, 15 K, no runs. When Rauch was traded, Hanrahan took over as closer the rest of the way and performed credibly; the job is now his to lose this year.

Shawn Hill

Bats: R   Throws: R   Height: 6' 2"   Weight: 180   Born: April 28, 1981   Age: 28

YEAR	TEAM	LVL	AGE	W	L	SV	G	GS	IP	H	BB	SO	HR	GB%	BABIP	STUFF	WHIP	ERA	DERA	EqH9	EqBB9	EqSO9	EqHR9	DEF	VORP	SN/WX
2006	HAR	AA	25	3	3	0	10	10	50	46	5	32	2	63.0%	.275	-5	1.02	2.70	5.10	9.4	1.3	3.0	0.8	-1	2.7	—
2006	WAS	MLB	25	1	3	0	6	6	36²	43	12	16	2	50.8%	.323	0	1.50	4.66	4.71	10.4	2.5	3.7	0.5	0	4.2	0.94
2007	WAS	MLB	26	4	5	0	16	16	97¹	86	25	65	9	55.9%	.264	17	1.14	3.42	4.48	7.8	2.1	5.7	0.7	8	20.6	3.21
2008	WAS	MLB	27	1	5	0	12	12	63¹	88	23	39	5	48.9%	.374	4	1.75	5.83	3.98	12.2	2.8	4.8	0.7	-14	-6.7	0.24
2009	WAS	MLB	28	4	5	0	21	11	73²	83	22	44	8	51.0%	.310	5	1.41	4.65	5.12	10.2	2.3	4.7	1.0	0	5.6	0.94

Breakout: 14%   Improve: 35%   Collapse: 38%   Attrition: 44%   *Comparables: Vern Ruhle, Ray Bare, Al Fitzmorris, Tom Murphy*

There is a fairy tale about a princess on a glass hill that no suitor could climb. "Glass Hill" is a perfectly apt description for Shawn, who hasn't managed to pitch 110 total innings in a season since 2003. His forearm, which had caused trouble in '07, continued to nag him last year, and ultimately required surgery to clear out bone spurs and calcium deposits. The good news is that the ligaments which had been transplanted from his 2006 surgery were fine; if this clears up his problems—and with his track record, try not to place any bets—look for a lot more ground balls in Washington's infield this year.

Michael Hinckley

Bats: R   Throws: L   Height: 6' 3"   Weight: 170   Born: October 5, 1982   Age: 26

YEAR	TEAM	LVL	AGE	W	L	SV	G	GS	IP	H	BB	SO	HR	GB%	BABIP	STUFF	WHIP	ERA	DERA	EqH9	EqBB9	EqSO9	EqHR9	DEF	VORP	SN/WX
2006	POT	A+	23	6	8	0	28	28	148	178	63	79	18	47.6%	.326	-70	1.63	5.53	9.48	14.2	4.9	2.1	2.7	-6	-56.0	—
2007	HAR	AA	24	9	10	0	25	23	117^1	145	59	70	15	45.7%	.332	-49	1.74	5.83	8.02	13.4	5.2	3.0	2.0	-4	-29.0	—
2008	HAR	AA	25	5	3	0	23	6	65	79	40	53	6	52.2%	.369	-15	1.83	5.12	5.64	12.5	5.5	5.3	1.3	-4	-0.3	—
2008	COH	AAA	25	0	2	1	20	1	25^2	27	15	20	0	59.5%	.351	-9	1.63	3.15	5.32	10.6	5.7	4.6	0.4	1	0.7	—
2008	WAS	MLB	25	0	0	0	14	0	13^2	8	3	9	0	47.2%	.222	7	0.80	0.00	2.84	5.7	2.1	5.7	0.0	3	7.6	1.04
2009	WAS	MLB	26	2	4	1	43	5	51^2	61	30	31	7	49.0%	.320	-11	1.76	5.71	6.18	10.7	4.6	4.7	1.1	0	-3.1	-0.09

Breakout: 31%   Improve: 62%   Collapse: 12%   Attrition: 16%   Comparables: Augie Ruiz, Jim Hamilton, Darren Burroughs, Ramiro Martinez

Go back four years, back to when it was still the Expos farm system, and Hinckley was their top prospect. Shoulder issues—but no obvious, season-ending injuries—took the bite off of his curveball, and more than a little off of his fastball, which in turn made his change less effective. That brings us to today, where a former stud is trying to salvage himself a bullpen role, but finding that a left-handed pitcher who can't get left-handed hitters out is not in very high demand.

John Lannan

Bats: L   Throws: L   Height: 6' 5"   Weight: 200   Born: September 27, 1984   Age: 24

YEAR	TEAM	LVL	AGE	W	L	SV	G	GS	IP	H	BB	SO	HR	GB%	BABIP	STUFF	WHIP	ERA	DERA	EqH9	EqBB9	EqSO9	EqHR9	DEF	VORP	SN/WX
2006	SAV	A	21	6	8	0	27	25	138^1	149	54	114	11	52.2%	.332	-40	1.47	4.76	8.70	13.4	5.3	3.2	2.2	-13	-41.3	—
2007	POT	A+	22	6	0	0	8	8	50^2	31	15	35	3	61.9%	.207	-7	0.91	2.13	5.76	6.9	3.6	3.2	1.4	7	-0.8	—
2007	HAR	AA	22	3	2	0	6	5	36	31	15	20	2	57.5%	.261	-9	1.28	3.25	5.45	9.0	4.4	2.7	1.1	3	0.6	—
2007	COH	AAA	22	3	1	0	7	6	38	30	12	19	1	47.5%	.240	-2	1.11	1.66	5.40	7.6	3.2	2.7	0.5	10	0.8	—
2007	WAS	MLB	22	2	2	0	6	6	34^2	36	17	10	3	52.4%	.277	-7	1.53	4.15	4.28	9.4	4.0	2.7	0.8	0	5.6	0.95
2008	WAS	MLB	23	9	15	0	31	31	182	172	72	117	23	55.9%	.275	5	1.34	3.91	4.70	8.2	3.0	5.1	1.0	14	27.2	4.82
2009	WAS	MLB	24	6	7	0	26	17	110^1	113	46	72	11	52.0%	.290	8	1.44	4.38	4.81	9.3	3.3	5.0	0.9	0	12.0	1.89

Breakout: 6%   Improve: 31%   Collapse: 36%   Attrition: 26%   Comparables: Sean Marshall, Scott Olsen, Horacio Ramirez, Jason Davis

Lannan built off of a shockingly swift 2007 ascent with a solid 2008 that was both better and worse than his record made it appear. He was the fifth-unluckiest pitcher in the majors last year, differencing his actual and expected won/loss record (12-9 would have been more like it), but he also benefited from a +14 defense, as Guzman gobbled up the steady stream of ground balls that Lannan induced heading towards short. He's the only pitcher from their '08 rotation who comes in as a sure thing for '09.

Charlie Manning

Bats: L   Throws: L   Height: 6' 2"   Weight: 180   Born: March 31, 1979   Age: 30

YEAR	TEAM	LVL	AGE	W	L	SV	G	GS	IP	H	BB	SO	HR	GB%	BABIP	STUFF	WHIP	ERA	DERA	EqH9	EqBB9	EqSO9	EqHR9	DEF	VORP	SN/WX
2006	TRN	AA	27	8	3	1	48	1	83^1	60	28	81	5	48.2%	.249	-18	1.06	2.71	6.51	9.1	3.8	5.2	1.2	11	-7.7	—
2007	TRN	AA	28	1	0	1	7	0	9^2	4	2	9	0	48.0%	.160	3	0.62	0.00	2.79	4.7	1.9	4.7	0.0	2	3.0	—
2007	SWB	AAA	28	3	2	2	34	1	51^1	41	24	59	2	51.0%	.291	-2	1.27	4.39	7.28	8.2	4.4	6.9	0.7	6	-9.5	—
2008	COH	AAA	29	0	0	6	19	0	27^2	20	13	34	1	50.0%	.306	7	1.19	1.95	4.85	7.6	4.5	7.6	0.7	4	2.2	—
2008	WAS	MLB	29	1	3	0	57	0	42	35	31	37	8	39.7%	.243	-8	1.57	5.14	5.48	7.2	5.5	6.8	1.7	3	1.7	0.26
2009	SLN	MLB	30	2	2	1	37	0	31^2	31	17	26	3	44.0%	.290	2	1.50	4.70	5.07	8.6	4.4	6.6	0.9	-0	2.4	0.16

Breakout: 19%   Improve: 34%   Collapse: 39%   Attrition: 38%   Comparables: Billy Brewer, Stephen Randolph, Bobby Jones, Yorkis Perez

Manning was the team's designated lefty-killer, rarely lasting for even one complete inning. He was functional but far from spectacular at stopping his main targets. When right-handers came up he managed to keep them from hitting well enough, but he walked 22 of the 100 righties he faced—the equivalent of 10 walks per nine innings. Removed from the 40-man roster last fall, he was claimed by the Cardinals, who fancy situational assets the way some people go nuts for stamps.

Shairon Martis

Bats: R **Throws: R** **Height: 6' 1"** **Weight: 175** **Born: March 30, 1987** **Age: 22**

YEAR	TEAM	LVL	AGE	W	L	SV	G	GS	IP	H	BB	SO	HR	GB%	BABIP	STUFF	WHIP	ERA	DERA	EqH9	EqBB9	EqSO9	EqHR9	DEF	VORP	SN/WX
2006	AUG	A	19	6	4	0	15	15	76¹	76	21	66	3	35.5%	.322	6	1.27	3.67	8.59	13.0	4.0	3.4	1.4	0	-21.9	—
2006	SAV	A	19	1	1	0	4	4	21²	23	4	14	2	33.8%	.323	-5	1.27	3.82	7.13	13.8	3.1	2.5	2.5	1	-3.0	—
2006	POT	A+	19	0	2	0	2	2	12²	9	3	7	0	36.1%	.250	11	0.98	2.95	7.36	8.2	3.3	2.5	0.8	1	-2.2	—
2007	POT	A+	20	14	8	0	27	26	151	150	52	108	9	35.8%	.304	2	1.34	4.23	7.88	11.3	4.2	3.2	1.5	-5	-34.5	—
2008	HAR	AA	21	4	4	0	14	14	74²	73	28	57	5	42.7%	.308	21	1.35	3.98	4.65	9.5	3.3	4.9	0.9	-2	7.6	—
2008	COH	AAA	21	1	2	0	7	7	41²	42	17	42	2	32.0%	.342	22	1.41	3.02	4.76	10.0	4.1	6.1	0.7	1	3.7	—
2008	WAS	MLB	21	1	3	0	5	4	20²	18	12	23	5	33.3%	.255	21	1.45	5.65	5.48	7.6	4.2	8.4	2.1	0	-0.8	0.19
2009	WAS	MLB	22	7	12	0	41	27	153¹	159	70	122	22	39.0%	.300	11	1.49	5.19	5.58	9.4	3.6	6.3	1.3	0	2.4	1.27

Breakout: 16% Improve: 46% Collapse: 18% Attrition: 18%   Comparables: Cecilio Guante, Ramon Garcia, Jose Roman, Ugueth Urbina

This Curacao native provided the top highlight of the original World Baseball Classic by throwing a no-hitter against Panama, and he will settle in as the Dutch ace once again this spring. A change in his delivery, designed to slow him down and get more leg into it, added 5 mph to his fastball and helped him approach a league-average strikeout rate for the first time. Martis is not afraid to challenge hitters, which can get him into trouble. He impressed Manny Acta during a September call-up; while he could use a little more time in Triple-A, he should be up to stay very soon.

Garrett Mock

Bats: R **Throws: R** **Height: 6' 4"** **Weight: 215** **Born: April 25, 1983** **Age: 26**

YEAR	TEAM	LVL	AGE	W	L	SV	G	GS	IP	H	BB	SO	HR	GB%	BABIP	STUFF	WHIP	ERA	DERA	EqH9	EqBB9	EqSO9	EqHR9	DEF	VORP	SN/WX
2006	TEN	AA	23	4	8	0	23	23	131¹	144	50	117	14	50.6%	.339	-26	1.48	4.94	6.53	12.0	3.9	4.9	1.9	-14	-12.5	—
2006	HAR	AA	23	0	4	0	4	4	16	29	5	9	2	42.6%	.422	-55	2.13	10.69	15.60	19.2	3.6	2.4	1.8	-3	-16.7	—
2007	HAR	AA	24	1	5	0	11	11	51¹	66	28	41	5	50.5%	.367	-24	1.83	5.79	7.97	13.4	5.3	4.2	1.4	-7	-13.1	—
2008	COH	AAA	25	6	3	0	19	17	104²	98	25	96	9	45.7%	.309	2	1.17	3.01	5.01	9.1	2.4	5.4	1.2	7	6.6	—
2008	WAS	MLB	25	1	3	0	26	3	41	37	23	46	4	46.4%	.314	15	1.46	4.17	3.51	8.1	4.4	8.8	0.9	-2	6.2	0.28
2009	WAS	MLB	26	4	6	1	39	12	89¹	96	37	69	12	47.0%	.310	5	1.49	5.05	5.48	9.8	3.3	6.1	1.2	0	2.4	0.65

Breakout: 23% Improve: 60% Collapse: 11% Attrition: 25%   Comparables: Garr Finnvold, Oscar Muñoz, Ryan Nye, Eric Ludwick

Mock was able to pitch healthy and pain-free for the first time in four years, as he finally recovered from a 2006 surgery on his plant knee. That in turn allowed him to finish his pitches, and not leave them sitting high up on a tee for the hitters. After proving himself in Columbus, he wound up riding quite the yo-yo in mid-summer, being called up and sent back down three different times before being called up for a fourth time, to stay, in August. He was beaten up in three starts (7.20 ERA), but thrived in relief (2.42)—expect him to stay in the pen.

Michael O'Connor

Bats: L **Throws: L** **Height: 6' 3"** **Weight: 170** **Born: August 17, 1980** **Age: 28**

YEAR	TEAM	LVL	AGE	W	L	SV	G	GS	IP	H	BB	SO	HR	GB%	BABIP	STUFF	WHIP	ERA	DERA	EqH9	EqBB9	EqSO9	EqHR9	DEF	VORP	SN/WX
2006	NWO	AAA	25	1	0	0	6	6	26¹	21	11	28	2	45.6%	.292	6	1.23	2.76	4.81	8.9	4.1	7.0	1.1	1	2.1	—
2006	WAS	MLB	25	3	8	0	21	20	105	96	44	59	15	39.2%	.254	-7	1.33	4.80	5.35	7.8	3.2	4.6	1.2	5	7.3	2.48
2007	HAR	AA	26	3	7	0	15	15	71¹	86	19	46	21	30.7%	.283	-79	1.47	7.07	9.67	13.0	2.8	3.4	4.3	0	-30.3	—
2008	COH	AAA	27	5	3	0	16	16	99²	83	17	70	10	45.5%	.255	-5	1.00	2.17	4.96	7.9	1.8	4.1	1.3	16	6.7	—
2008	WAS	MLB	27	1	1	0	5	1	9	11	11	4	3	42.4%	.296	-28	2.44	13.00	12.54	10.6	8.7	3.9	2.9	1	-7.0	-0.27
2009	WAS	MLB	28	3	6	0	25	11	77	87	30	45	13	43.0%	.290	-4	1.51	5.49	5.89	10.2	3.1	4.5	1.5	0	-1.6	0.30

Breakout: 19% Improve: 43% Collapse: 28% Attrition: 33%   Comparables: Dennis Cook, Pete Filson, Ron Mahay, Matt Grott

The soft-tossing lefty proved he had recovered from the elbow surgery he had in 2006, which he now admits he came back from too soon—you can see that from looking at those 2007 numbers easily enough. He was the beneficiary of some fine defense at Columbus, so his numbers aren't quite as good as they might appear. He did get called up for a few weeks around the first of May, but after several flagrant beatings he was quickly sent back down. He'll have a tough time landing anything more than a long-relief spot, and even that will be an accomplishment.

Odalis Perez

Bats: L   Throws: L   Height: 6' 0"   Weight: 225   Born: June 11, 1977   Age: 32

YEAR	TEAM	LVL	AGE	W	L	SV	G	GS	IP	H	BB	SO	HR	GB%	BABIP	STUFF	WHIP	ERA	DERA	EqH9	EqBB9	EqSO9	EqHR9	DEF	VORP	SN/WX
2006	KCA	MLB	29	2	4	0	12	12	67	80	18	48	9	42.9%	.332	4	1.46	5.64	5.14	9.7	2.2	5.5	1.1	-3	1.9	0.70
2006	LAN	MLB	29	4	4	0	20	8	59¹	89	13	33	9	50.2%	.372	-12	1.72	6.83	5.16	12.7	1.7	4.6	1.2	-11	-9.7	-0.53
2007	KCA	MLB	30	8	11	0	26	26	137¹	178	50	64	14	46.3%	.341	-10	1.66	5.57	5.04	11.3	3.1	3.6	0.9	-7	2.6	1.10
2008	WAS	MLB	31	7	12	0	30	30	159²	182	55	119	22	47.8%	.324	4	1.48	4.34	3.88	10.0	2.6	5.9	1.2	-10	15.3	3.16
2009	WAS	MLB	32	6	8	1	32	17	117	128	36	76	14	46.0%	.300	6	1.40	4.44	4.82	10.0	2.4	5.1	1.1	0	11.9	1.91

Breakout: 19%   Improve: 49%   Collapse: 24%   Attrition: 31%   Comparables: Bob Knepper, Darren Oliver, Terry Mulholland, Dave LaPoint

The Nats' surprising Opening Day starter—on national television no less, and deflowering a new stadium—turned in his best year since 2004, despite a mid-season bout with tendonitis. He can carve up lefties with a wicked curve, but the trick is how to get all those nasty righthanders out—and unfortunately they creamed him for .306/.367/.507 rates. Perez filed for free agency after the season, and, just like earlier last year, interest was spotty, with everyone waiting until the higher-level guys clear out. He's the major league version of the last guy picked for kickball.

Tim Redding

Bats: R   Throws: R   Height: 6' 0"   Weight: 195   Born: February 12, 1978   Age: 31

YEAR	TEAM	LVL	AGE	W	L	SV	G	GS	IP	H	BB	SO	HR	GB%	BABIP	STUFF	WHIP	ERA	DERA	EqH9	EqBB9	EqSO9	EqHR9	DEF	VORP	SN/WX
2006	CHR	AAA	28	12	10	0	29	28	187	168	56	148	21	46.4%	.272	-21	1.20	3.42	6.01	10.2	3.3	4.8	1.7	16	-7.8	—
2007	COH	AAA	29	9	5	0	17	16	89²	110	24	63	9	46.0%	.348	-25	1.49	5.32	7.64	13.2	2.9	4.2	1.5	1	-18.4	—
2007	WAS	MLB	29	3	6	0	15	15	84	84	38	47	10	41.9%	.285	-2	1.45	3.64	4.59	9.0	3.6	4.8	1.0	9	19.0	2.77
2008	WAS	MLB	30	10	11	0	33	33	182	195	65	120	27	40.7%	.299	-3	1.43	4.95	4.74	9.4	2.7	5.3	1.2	-3	7.3	3.24
2009	NYN	MLB	31	5	6	0	26	14	94¹	102	34	63	13	42.6%	.298	3	1.45	4.83	5.25	9.8	2.8	5.1	1.2	0	5.7	1.10

Breakout: 10%   Improve: 31%   Collapse: 38%   Attrition: 37%   Comparables: Jim Wilson, Josh Fogg, Jim Colborn, Ramon Ortiz

Redding resurrected his career in Washington—all hail pitching coach Randy St. Claire—with a popularity around DC that belies his performance. Maybe it's because any performance at all was so completely unexpected, or that he did lead the team in starts and wins, or that he represents an Average Pitcher so well (actually, he's about one tick below average, straight across the board). Whatever it was, the laid-back Nationals' fans weren't happy with the financial decision to non-tender Redding rather than let him go through arbitration. They'll still get to see plenty of him, as he joined the Mets on a one-year, $2.25 million contract and figures to take a spot at the rear end of their rotation.

Saul Rivera

Bats: S   Throws: R   Height: 5' 11"   Weight: 155   Born: December 7, 1977   Age: 31

YEAR	TEAM	LVL	AGE	W	L	SV	G	GS	IP	H	BB	SO	HR	GB%	BABIP	STUFF	WHIP	ERA	DERA	EqH9	EqBB9	EqSO9	EqHR9	DEF	VORP	SN/WX
2006	NWO	AAA	28	1	1	1	12	2	28²	25	12	25	1	58.3%	.300	-3	1.31	1.60	3.25	8.8	3.9	5.2	0.7	0	7.2	—
2006	WAS	MLB	28	3	0	1	54	0	60¹	59	33	41	4	47.0%	.288	-4	1.52	3.43	4.14	8.3	4.1	5.3	0.6	1	11.8	1.10
2007	WAS	MLB	29	4	6	3	85	0	93	88	42	64	1	52.8%	.311	15	1.40	3.68	3.07	8.6	3.7	5.9	0.1	-5	20.8	2.57
2008	WAS	MLB	30	5	6	0	76	0	84	90	35	65	3	55.8%	.339	10	1.49	3.96	3.55	9.5	3.2	6.1	0.3	-4	12.1	1.73
2009	WAS	MLB	31	3	3	2	55	0	64	65	29	45	4	52.0%	.300	0	1.47	4.09	4.53	9.2	3.6	5.5	0.6	0	8.3	0.67

Breakout: 10%   Improve: 23%   Collapse: 51%   Attrition: 26%   Comparables: Dick Hyde, Hal White, Geoff Geary, Frank Williams

Sa-ool is 'salright, a short, stocky guy who has been thriving in a mid-inning role. Last year we worried that his home/road split (2.27/5.16 ERA) spelled trouble with the impending move out of RFK; this year that split was even more extreme, at 1.93 versus 6.51. The teams that saw him the most—the Mets, the Marlins, and the Phillies—were also the ones who did the most damage against him.

Chris Schroder

Bats: R   Throws: R   Height: 6' 3"   Weight: 210   Born: August 20, 1978   Age: 30

YEAR	TEAM	LVL	AGE	W	L	SV	G	GS	IP	H	BB	SO	HR	GB%	BABIP	STUFF	WHIP	ERA	DERA	EqH9	EqBB9	EqSO9	EqHR9	DEF	VORP	SN/WX
2006	HAR	AA	27	2	0	1	9	0	14	18	6	13	2	42.6%	.356	-28	1.71	5.14	6.92	14.5	4.8	4.8	2.1	-2	-1.9	—
2006	NWO	AAA	27	2	1	1	28	0	47¹	25	16	60	2	44.3%	.227	18	0.87	1.53	3.09	5.4	3.1	7.9	0.6	2	13.0	—
2006	WAS	MLB	27	0	2	0	21	0	28¹	23	15	39	7	29.4%	.281	10	1.34	6.36	5.90	7.4	4.0	10.2	1.9	-1	-2.5	-0.38
2007	COH	AAA	28	2	2	1	26	0	33	23	18	45	0	40.3%	.333	20	1.24	1.64	3.30	8.4	5.4	9.0	0.3	0	7.7	—
2007	WAS	MLB	28	2	3	0	37	0	45¹	36	15	43	2	35.6%	.266	20	1.13	3.18	2.85	6.8	2.5	7.6	0.4	-4	10.1	0.52
2008	COH	AAA	29	5	4	8	43	0	45¹	48	20	55	3	50.4%	.378	-1	1.50	3.97	3.98	10.9	4.4	7.3	0.8	-5	7.7	—
2008	WAS	MLB	29	0	0	0	4	0	5	6	6	3	2	50.0%	.267	-22	2.40	5.40	3.38	10.1	8.4	5.1	3.4	-1	0.2	0.03
2009	OAK	MLB	30	2	3	2	39	2	45¹	43	23	43	5	41.0%	.300	9	1.44	4.44	4.84	8.7	3.9	7.4	1.0	-0	4.4	0.46

Breakout: 17%   Improve: 44%   Collapse: 29%   Attrition: 16%   Comparables: Scott Dohmann, Rick Croushore, Joe Boever, Tyler Yates

A sometimes minor league closer, when Schroder began the season he was almost untouchable, allowing just one run in his first nine appearances. That was enough to draw the Nationals' attention, but in three separate call-ups he only saw action in four games. Eventually, the Triple-A hitters started catching up to him, and then the Nats stopped calling. He signed with Oakland as a free agent in November, where he might stick as a token veteran of sorts.

Steven Shell

Bats: R   Throws: R   Height: 6' 5"   Weight: 210   Born: January 1, 1983   Age: 26

YEAR	TEAM	LVL	AGE	W	L	SV	G	GS	IP	H	BB	SO	HR	GB%	BABIP	STUFF	WHIP	ERA	DERA	EqH9	EqBB9	EqSO9	EqHR9	DEF	VORP	SN/WX
2006	ARK	AA	23	1	2	0	3	3	18	20	4	10	1	51.7%	.322	-12	1.33	4.00	6.61	11.6	2.8	2.8	1.1	-2	-1.8	—
2006	SLC	AAA	23	5	9	0	24	22	122²	156	32	82	16	38.7%	.349	-23	1.54	6.19	6.31	12.9	2.6	4.1	1.7	-12	-8.9	—
2007	ARK	AA	24	0	0	0	5	0	13¹	10	1	19	1	35.5%	.300	13	0.83	0.68	2.13	9.2	1.4	8.5	1.4	1	4.9	—
2007	SLC	AAA	24	7	3	0	31	7	70¹	83	19	52	15	37.7%	.329	-32	1.45	4.74	4.98	11.1	2.8	4.8	2.4	-4	4.5	—
2008	COH	AAA	25	3	2	1	22	4	58¹	49	14	54	5	40.1%	.288	-2	1.08	2.62	4.31	8.4	2.5	5.6	1.2	3	7.8	—
2008	WAS	MLB	25	2	2	2	39	0	50	34	20	41	5	38.2%	.225	6	1.08	2.16	3.28	6.0	3.1	6.6	0.9	5	17.6	0.81
2009	WAS	MLB	26	3	4	3	45	3	62	62	23	51	9	39.0%	.290	7	1.37	4.35	4.65	9.1	2.9	6.5	1.3	0	7.2	0.78

Breakout: 15%   Improve: 25%   Collapse: 41%   Attrition: 27%   Comparables: Kevin Correia, Erik Bennett, Jose Capellan, Jay Baller

Shell escaped from the Angels' system as a minor league free agent, signing on with the Nationals. The Angels had been experimenting with switching him to relief, albeit half-heartedly; the Nationals were more aggressive about it. He was sensational out of the pen at Columbus; the stats don't look as impressive as they should, thanks to the four starts he made (with a reasonable 4.09 ERA) dragging down the excellent 1.73 he sported in relief. Called up in late June, he helped to solidify the pen in the second half.

Colton Willems

Bats: R   Throws: R   Height: 6' 3"   Weight: 175   Born: July 30, 1988   Age: 20

YEAR	TEAM	LVL	AGE	W	L	SV	G	GS	IP	H	BB	SO	HR	GB%	BABIP	STUFF	WHIP	ERA	DERA	EqH9	EqBB9	EqSO9	EqHR9	DEF	VORP	SN/WX
2006	NAT	Rk	17	0	1	0	5	5	16¹	23	3	8	1	51.7%	.373	-40	1.61	3.35	8.53	19.9	3.6	0.7	2.8	0	-4.1	—
2007	VER	A-	18	3	2	0	12	12	58²	55	26	31	2	57.0%	.285	-17	1.38	1.84	7.01	11.6	5.6	1.4	1.2	4	-8.0	—
2008	HAG	A	19	5	9	0	20	20	109¹	103	31	60	7	54.9%	.283	-13	1.23	3.71	7.98	9.9	3.8	1.8	1.4	7	-26.5	—
2009	WAS	MLB	20	4	11	0	23	23	118²	151	60	41	17	52.0%	.310	-9	1.78	6.95	7.64	11.5	4.0	2.7	1.3	0	-23.5	-1.68

Breakout: 3%   Improve: 24%   Collapse: 27%   Attrition: 11%   Comparables: Eric Ireland, Blair Johnson, Todd Noel, Sean O'Sullivan

Willems was the Nationals' number one pick in 2006, and the 22nd pick overall. His strikeout numbers have been nearly non-existent for his entire career, something exceedingly strange for someone who was supposed to throw 93-96 mph. This year he didn't approach that velocity, complaining of a dead arm until he was finally shut down in August. Pitchers who take this trajectory tend to crash.

Jordan Zimmermann

Bats: R   Throws: R   Height: 6' 2"   Weight: 200   Born: May 23, 1986   Age: 23

YEAR	TEAM	LVL	AGE	W	L	SV	G	GS	IP	H	BB	SO	HR	GB%	BABIP	STUFF	WHIP	ERA	DERA	EqH9	EqBB9	EqSO9	EqHR9	DEF	VORP	SN/WX
2007	VER	A-	21	5	2	0	13	11	53	45	18	71	2	48.8%	.347	11	1.19	2.38	3.71	12.8	4.7	6.8	1.4	-2	9.2	—
2008	POT	A+	22	3	1	1	5	4	27¹	15	8	31	1	55.0%	.241	24	0.84	1.65	4.44	6.7	3.3	7.0	0.7	4	3.1	—
2008	HAR	AA	22	7	2	0	20	20	106²	89	39	103	9	47.3%	.284	18	1.20	3.21	4.34	8.3	3.3	6.4	1.2	2	14.2	—
2009	WAS	MLB	23	6	7	0	19	19	110²	108	47	96	12	46.3%	.298	23	1.40	4.39	4.78	8.8	3.4	6.8	1.0	0	10.8	2.1

Breakout: 3%   Improve: 17%   Collapse: 34%   Attrition: 17%   Comparables: Bobby Jones, Erik Hanson, Terry Taylor, John Maine

After his junior year (non-arm) injuries dropped his stock, Zimmerman (no relation to Ryan) turned into a second-round steal for the Nats. As a collegiate pitcher, the Nationals have promoted him aggressively, and he has responded. His best pitch is a riding fastball which reaches the mid-90s; his curve, slider, and change are all good, at least some of the time. He's a very good athlete, he fields well, and he hits well (he was a DH in college when not pitching). By the numbers, he was arguably the best pitcher in the organization last year, leaving the team with decisions to make about how to handle him this year. While you would expect him to start in Triple-A, a strong spring could force their hand.

LINEOUTS

Hitters

PLAYER	TEAM	LVL	AGE	PA	R	2B	3B	HR	RBI	BB	SO	SB-CS	EqBRR	AVG/OBP/SLG	EqAVG/EqOBP/EqSLG	EqA	VORP	WARP
RF E. Baez	POT	A+	22	290	46	22	0	12	52	30	53	6-2	1.6	.286/.366/.514	.264/.333/.483	.276	13.7	0.7
	HAR	AA	22	185	22	9	1	2	13	15	50	5-3	0.5	.246/.311/.347	.225/.284/.325	.213	-8.9	-1.1
CF M. Daniel*	HAR	AA	23	557	61	12	2	14	56	59	126	19-11	-0.5	.256/.342/.375	.235/.314/.358	.238	-9.5	-1.4
3B S. King	HAG	A	20	364	39	21	1	6	33	22	75	4-4	-1.8	.284/.336/.406	.226/.272/.334	.209	-18.7	-1.7
	POT	A+	20	75	4	2	1	0	7	5	11	1-1	0.4	.214/.267/.271	.197/.240/.254	.162	-8.1	-0.5
UT R. Langerhans*	COH	AAA	28	257	40	16	2	3	31	40	57	12-3	2.0	.310/.418/.446	.248/.354/.367	.261	2.5	0.4
	WAS	MLB	28	139	17	5	2	3	12	25	31	2-0	0.9	.234/.380/.396	.234/.384/.396	.282	3.6	0.1
LF M. Lowrance*	POT	A+	23	292	39	17	0	12	39	37	59	2-2	-3.5	.268/.373/.480	.233/.322/.415	.254	2.4	-0.9
	HAR	AA	23	178	27	13	0	8	24	20	40	1-0	-1.1	.286/.376/.526	.268/.348/.497	.287	10.6	-0.2
UT P. Orr*	COH	AAA	29	316	46	16	11	2	33	21	56	19-4	4.4	.275/.331/.430	.221/.275/.360	.226	-12.4	-0.3
	WAS	MLB	29	79	10	2	1	0	7	2	16	1-0	-0.4	.253/.282/.307	.250/.278/.303	.204	-2.3	-0.4
RF A. Seuss	HAG	A	23	307	43	23	0	10	49	13	49	0-2	-2.5	.304/.339/.490	.216/.245/.357	.202	-18.0	-2.5
	POT	A+	23	214	32	14	1	4	21	4	42	2-2	-2.2	.245/.282/.385	.211/.235/.338	.193	-15.2	-1.7
2B J. Smolinski	HAG	A	19	210	28	12	1	4	22	19	33	1-2	-3.6	.261/.338/.402	.212/.282/.339	.216	-9.6	-0.2
	VER	A-	19	109	17	8	1	0	9	9	17	4-0	1.3	.306/.370/.408	.228/.278/.327	.212	-10.1	-1.0
3B S. Souza	HAG	A	19	89	14	4	0	2	10	8	26	8-2	0.5	.266/.348/.392	.222/.292/.333	.223	-3.7	-1.7
	VER	A-	19	207	27	7	0	5	25	24	54	14-7	1.6	.189/.296/.314	.153/.235/.257	.175	-41.7	-2.1

Edgardo Bacz showed a glimmer of life in his third try at A-ball, but he promptly went code-red at Double-A. ⊘ **Mike Daniel** has a good combination of skills, but they all tend to run a little below those needed in the majors. ⊘ **Stephen King** made excellent progress on his strikeouts, but was terror-stricken by left-handed pitchers. ⊘ An exceptionally and perhaps overly patient hitter, **Ryan Langerhans** only made it out of Columbus once the outfield injuries in DC were at their worst. ⊘ **Marvin Lowrance** was literally twice as good a hitter when playing the field (.322/.419/.601, combined and untranslated) as when he DH'd (.161/.220/.246). ⊘ A veteran utility player, **Pete Orr** brings a good glove and speed, but he might as well be hitting with a stale french baguette. ⊘ **Aaron Seuss** in the field, there is plenty to doubt; has some pop in his bat, but is prone to strike out. ⊘ **Jake Smolinski** is a line-drive hitter, not blessed with speed and not likely to develop much power, who was traded to Florida in the Willingham deal. ⊘ **Steven Souza** has one of the larger disconnects between his stats and his scouting reports, with some high expectations for him to develop more power and cut down on his strikeouts.

Pitchers

PLAYER	TEAM	LVL	AGE	W	L	SV	IP	H	BB	SO	HR	GB%	BABIP	STUFF	WHIP	ERA	DERA	EqH9	EqBB9	EqSO9	EqHR9	DEF	VORP
L. Atilano	HAG	A	23	0	0	1	25²	29	7	13	1	43.5%	.308	-36	1.40	3.15	7.50	11.2	3.8	1.5	1.1	0	-5.1
	POT	A+	23	5	2	0	62	50	14	39	5	52.8%	.255	-16	1.03	2.32	5.82	8.9	2.4	3.6	1.5	10	-1.4
	HAR	AA	23	0	1	0	6	6	2	3	0	55.0%	.353	-13	1.33	1.50	3.18	9.5	3.2	3.2	0.0	-1	1.5
W. Atwood*	VER	A-	21	2	1	0	52¹	40	9	60	2	40.4%	.286	11	0.94	2.41	5.17	10.0	2.5	4.6	1.3	0	2.2
M. Beno	HAG	A	21	0	1	6	18²	17	13	21	1	50.0%	.314	0	1.60	3.37	6.88	10.6	8.5	4.8	1.1	0	-2.4
	POT	A+	21	0	1	7	30	16	51	33	3	45.3%	.191	0	2.23	7.50	11.97	6.1	15.3	5.8	1.5	4	-20.7
P. Dean	VER	A-	19	4	1	0	46	26	16	34	2	44.6%	.203	5	0.91	1.57	5.49	7.3	4.6	2.7	1.4	7	0.5
C. Kimball	HAG	A	22	6	8	0	128¹	103	83	122	5	42.1%	.299	-3	1.45	5.05	7.86	9.5	8.3	4.3	1.1	-1	-27.9
B. Sanches	COH	AAA	29	2	1	13	33²	24	9	45	2	28.2%	.293	12	0.98	2.40	4.22	7.6	2.8	8.4	0.8	4	4.9
	WAS	MLB	29	2	0	0	11	16	5	10	2	42.1%	.400	-11	1.91	7.36	6.55	13.1	3.3	7.4	1.6	-1	-3.0
L. Speigner	HAR	AA	27	1	0	0	14²	8	5	4	0	68.1%	.174	-21	0.88	0.61	2.45	4.3	3.1	1.2	0.0	2	5.1
	COH	AAA	27	3	0	0	44²	36	8	36	3	54.7%	.268	-5	0.98	2.21	4.25	7.7	1.9	4.9	0.9	4	6.3
	WAS	MLB	27	0	1	0	8	13	6	1	1	68.8%	.400	-41	2.38	11.25	6.14	16.0	6.1	1.2	1.2	-3	-4.8
C. Stammen	POT	A+	24	4	2	1	69¹	59	17	62	6	53.8%	.276	-7	1.10	2.21	4.20	9.4	2.7	5.2	1.5	0	10.0
	HAR	AA	24	3	1	0	38¹	22	11	31	1	56.9%	.216	16	0.86	1.64	4.10	5.3	2.4	5.1	0.5	7	6.2
	COH	AAA	24	1	4	0	43	62	16	35	3	49.7%	.431	-17	1.81	7.33	7.51	15.3	4.0	4.9	0.9	-6	-8.1
C. Van Allen*	POT	A+	23	3	0	0	27¹	18	7	19	1	60.5%	.221	3	0.92	0.66	3.71	6.4	2.7	3.7	0.7	2	5.6
	HAR	AA	23	3	3	0	47¹	64	11	36	4	37.3%	.373	-3	1.59	5.14	4.66	12.8	2.1	4.7	1.2	-9	4.8
	NAT	Rk	23	0	0	0	4	3	0	2	0	33.3%	.273	-22	0.75	0.00	5.40	8.1	2.7	0.0	0.0	0	0.1

Former Braves prospect **Luis Atilano** is still trying to recover from TJ surgery in 2006; the Nationals have him on a very short pitch-count leash. ⊘ A twelfth-round pick last year out of South Carolina, **William Atwood** is yet another older finesse pitcher dominating rookie professionals. ⊘ A 36th-round pick from Oklahoma State, **Martin Beno** throws 97 mph gas with the pinpoint precision of a cattle stampede. ⊘ **Philip Dean** is a young pitcher who's still growing and gaining velocity; he'll need it. ⊘ **Cole Kimball** is a big, strong-armed guy from a small New Jersey college, and wilder than a drunken, tasered Tasmanian devil with anger-management issues. ⊘ Triple-A closer **Brian Sanches** got his third shot at the majors, and the major league hitters were quite pleased. ⊘ **Levale Speigner** stayed in the minors most of the year after being in Rule 5 limbo in 2007; an excellent reliever while in the minors, he may have been speignt by the time he was called up in September. ⊘ **Craig Stammen** (in his own words) began to pitch this year instead of throw, and he felt that it improved all of his pitches; it worked until Triple-A. ⊘ **Cory Van Allen** added a slider to his fastball/changeup repertoire, replacing a very bad curveball from his past.

MANAGER: MANNY ACTA

YEAR	TEAM	W-L	Pythag +/-	Avg PC	100+ P	120+ P	QS	BQS	REL	REL w Zero R	IBB	Subs	PH	PH Avg	PH HR	SB2	CS2	SB3	CS3	SAC Att	SAC %	POS SAC	Squeeze	Swing	In Play
2007	WAS	73-89	4	88.2	28	0	59	6	587	372	43	102	291	.198	5	59	20	10	2	90	70.0%	26	0	121	92
2008	WAS	59-102	-2	92.9	53	0	64	6	517	314	44	55	288	.237	7	74	36	7	7	106	60.4%	22	1	97	73

Of Casey Stengel's early managing days with literally bankrupt Dodgers and Braves teams, one contemporary observer said, "He reminded me of a guy who has made up his mind to force a pair of deuces to beat four aces, and can't stop trying." Acta's two years in Nationals harness have been a bit like that: he's an active, thinking manager who tries his best to gain an advantage using his roster. For the second year in a row, he was the major league runner-up in pinch-hitter usage, and he ranked third in relievers used after ranking first in 2007 (though this last may reflect the problematic pitching staff as much as his own preference). However, as the quote above suggests, the most frantic manager can't get too far if he's making moves with weak parts—Stengel's deuces are Acta's Castos and Lo Ducas. The flip side of Acta's activism is that he knows when to stay out of the way, not investing in one-run strategies; he disdains the hit-and-run and rarely asks his non-pitchers to bunt. Asked in January by the *Washington Post* how he had spent his winter, one of his answers was reading. "Just getting smarter," Acta said. He's smart enough now to handle a proper roster should Jim Bowden ever get around to furnishing him with one. Unfortunately, at the end of last season, the Nationals canned all of Acta's coaches except for pitching coach Randy St. Claire. Among the new crew is three-time loser/likely interim manager-in-waiting Jim Riggleman. If the Nats continue to struggle, Acta could quickly be gone. It happened to Stengel too. He eventually got the team his talents deserved; perhaps one day Acta will as well.

Discovering America, South to North

David Laurila

The number of Latin American players in professional baseball has grown exponentially in recent years, with more and more natives of the Dominican Republic, Venezuela, and other Spanish-speaking countries dotting the rosters of both minor and major league teams. Inked to contracts as teenagers, these young athletes come to the United States with untapped raw talent and a passion for the game, but there is more to their stories than aspirations and green cards. Often overlooked are the obstacles they face: not only the challenges of pro ball, but also those of learning a new language while acclimating to what is by and large a completely new culture. For most of them, it is not an easy transition.

A Whole New Language

Language is typically the biggest hurdle, as the majority of Latin American players speak little or no English when they are first signed. For some, like 20-year-old Red Sox outfield prospect **Ronald Bermudez**, a native of Venezuela who just completed his first season in the United States after two years in the Dominican Summer League, learning a new language has been a challenge.

"Not being able to speak English has been very difficult," said Bermudez, who offered his perspective with the help of a translator. "Other than that, everything has been the same as in other leagues; it's just baseball. But the English part has been difficult. My teammates try to help me out a lot, and they treat me the same, but the language is hard."

Carlos Carrasco, a top pitching prospect from the Phillies' organization, made his professional debut in 2004 at the age of 17. Nearly five years later, the native of Venezuela is still working to perfect his communication skills in his second language.

"When I come here for first time, I need to learn my English, I need to speak English," explained Carrasco. "Nobody here speaks Spanish. Some guys would try to, and we had a lot of things here, different in this country, like food, and everything. We need to stay like … it's too hard here in the USA, but before it was harder. Now I'm speaking more English. I'm trying; I'm trying to learn more English."

For young players like Bermudez and Carrasco, having someone like **Devern Hansack** on the team can be invaluable. A native of Nicaragua, Hansack was less of a student than a helping hand to Latin American teammates when he first came to the United States.

"For me, [communicating] wasn't that hard, because where we live, we speak English Creole," explained Hansack, a pitcher who spent last season with Boston's triple-A affiliate. "It is a Creole language; it is not complete English, but I could understand whatever it was you wanted to tell me, so picking up English was never that hard for me. I had some Dominicans in the group of guys that I was staying with—there were seven of us in one house—as well as from Venezuela and Columbia. I was the only one that could dominate it, so I had to step up in a lot of ways, like where we had to take care of the apartment with cable and water, and that stuff. I had to step forward, because I was the only one who could."

Another player who has acted as a liaison is Rays first baseman **Carlos Pena**, who had a head start with his second language. Because his family moved to Massachusetts from the Dominican Republic when he was 14, Pena learned English before playing professional baseball. There was still a learning curve, but Pena attacked it head-on.

"I was eager to take on the challenge, and enrolled myself in all English classes straight from the get-go," said Pena. "That wasn't easy, but I think it accelerated my learning of the language. I had taken classes in the Dominican Republic, but it's never the same when you get to the country and actually have to speak it for survival. As you talk to people and interact with teachers and classmates, that's how you really learn how to speak English. So it was a pretty big challenge, and I wasn't afraid of it, and I took it on. I was speaking fluently pretty quickly."

For **David Ross**, an American-born catcher who has seen action with five big-league teams, most recently with the Red Sox, communicating with Latin American players is both essential and a two-way street.

"By the time they get over here, they've usually had some English training," said Ross, "at least enough to know the basics, especially with pitchers. But as a catcher, you also learn real fast how to speak a little bit of Spanish, and how to get your point across the way you want to. I feel that it's definitely an adjustment in their everyday life, but the baseball is maybe a little easier, because the game has evolved to where you know enough Spanish to get your point across. If not, there was always somebody there that I could turn to. There is usually another Latin guy on the team that does understand, and you can call him over and have him help. And now, with [Latin] coaches and other staff people, there's usually not too much of a language barrier. We also had a third baseman [Mike Lowell] who, if I really needed to get my point across, I'd call him over and tell him exactly what I was thinking, and he would relay it in Spanish. So if you do have a problem, there are ways around it."

An increasing number of bilingual coaches and managers are easing the burden for Latin players, especially at the lower levels of the minor leagues, where they are most needed. One such person is **Juan Bustabad**, a native Cuban who manages the Dodgers' low-A affiliate.

"There are a lot more Latin coaches now, and also what we call roving instructors that go around and see the teams," explained Bustabad. "It's kind of easier for the players, because there are more instructors now. They learn a lot, kind of like the baseball language. Most all organizations have English classes for them, and as they go through those classes, they get better with their English. That's the beginning for many of them, and it's up to every individual how they take it from there. Some take out their teammates and try to learn, and some buy a dictionary that has English and Spanish, and they learn more words that way. They also watch TV. And being with their teammates, they like to joke around and might say something wrong in English, and the guys will laugh. But that's how they learn."

Communication can also be a problem for coaches who speak little or no Spanish. **Jon Matlack**, Detroit's minor league pitching coordinator, is sometimes frustrated by his inability to get his points across clearly.

"One of the drawbacks for me as a teacher, because I have such limited Spanish, is being able to communicate with them," explained Matlack. "If I don't have somebody in the area who can communicate to them, to translate, and if they don't understand my English, we have to do it by hit and miss. I have to show them and hope that they understand what I'm trying to show them, so the ones that pick up English quicker tend to

---

MELVIN MORA
THIRD BASEMAN, ORIOLES

"The first time I came here to the United States, it was kind of hard. There were just a couple of people who spoke Spanish. It was hard because sometimes they'd tell you to do something, and you didn't know what they say. You had to go learn English so you could understand what people tell you. I couldn't speak English; I'd just say 'yes'—that's it. They can tell me, 'You ugly,' and I'd say 'yes.' When it's time to go to the restaurant, you don't know what to say. You just point with your finger, even if you don't like that kind of food—when you go to a Chili's, or a Bennigan's, or a Kentucky Fried Chicken—you just see the plate with three pieces of chicken and you point to it. Even if you don't like that, you get it, because you don't want to go to the menu to try to read anything.

"But it didn't take me too long, because I'm the kind of guy who is always looking to communicate with people. I was watching a lot of TV, and trying to talk to a lot of American people. They'd be laughing at me, but I just wanted to know how they pronounced that thing. So they'd teach me, and they'd correct me at the ballpark. I never went to school to learn that. I just talked to the people on the field, and they were pretty good with me."

---

acclimate faster. What I find is that they're very good at fooling you about what they know. What I try to do when I'm getting this teaching thing going and trying to communicate with the kids, is that whenever I do it with a translator, I have the question repeated back so that they can tell me what they just heard. And a lot of times, I get back something completely different, where they haven't understood. That's one way of figuring out if they got it or not. And not in every case, but many, many times, I've come across kids who will 'yes, yes' you and smile, but they don't have the foggiest idea what I've told them. That's very difficult for us as instructors and developmental people, because we're trying to get them down the road a little bit, and it's detrimental to their progress."

Dick Scott, Toronto's director of player development, understands the importance of communication as well as anyone. Like Matlack, he recognizes that players have to be able to respond to instruction to take their game to the highest level.

"I think the guys want to learn English, and we recommend that they learn English," explained Scott, "but it's not so much that we're making them learn another language, but the higher they get up in the game, they really need to know English to make adjustments at the higher levels. Their ability allows them to play in the Gulf Coast League and Midwest League and make their way, but they don't learn the game, and the nuances, really, until they start to learn the language. Any directive from the manager, or one of the coaches, or the front office, they need to know that."

Arnie Beyler, who manages Boston's double-A affiliate and previously worked in player development for the Yankees, echoes Scott.

"To me, personally, what you see over here is that the Latin guys who are successful in the big leagues are smart, and they speak the language," said Beyler. "I don't think there are many Latin guys over here who are impact big league guys who really don't speak English, so that [reporters] can converse with them. That's a big deal, and I think that transfers out to the baseball field, too. You can't be a guy who's not very smart and play baseball. You have to know where to go, and which bases to back up, and how to do things over here and communicate. As you go higher in the game, and the guys start to dwindle a little bit, guys start to get weeded out based on that stuff."

Law and Order and Dealing with Performance-Enhancing Drugs

Language isn't the only hurdle for Latin American players. There are also a myriad of cultural challenges. As Carlos Pena has put it, "When a kid comes directly from the Dominican Republic, he's starting from zero. It's a totally different world." The differences in everyday life are many, ranging from food to the legal system.

Melvin Mora experienced the new set of rules and regulations firsthand when he came to the United States in 1992.

"An important thing for me to learn about the US is that they have a lot of security here," said Mora. "People follow the rules. You see a red light, or a stop sign, you have to stop. You go to jail if you don't, or they take your driving license. In Venezuela, it's kind of like people driving crazy—they might speed [through] the light. So it's a big difference. In Venezuela, you need to live the way the city is, how the country is. You have to be one thing; then coming here, you have to learn how to do what the American people do. I still have my Latin thing inside, but I had to learn about how the American people act. If you go to somebody's house, you see the house and know how the people live in there, and you need to get used to how they live in there. It's not your house. We're coming into a different country and learning how they live."

"Law enforcement is a big issue," added **Ed Romero Jr.**, who runs the Red Sox' Latin American program. "We have presentations in spring training where we bring in law enforcement officials to talk to the guys. It's not like Scared Straight, but we do have someone come in to talk to the players and emphasize how laws in the United States are different from the laws in Latin America. That's usually a pretty interesting presentation."

Performance-enhancing drugs (PEDs) are an important part of the message, as the majority of players suspended for PED use in recent seasons have been Latin. Quite often, the players have been unaware that they were taking a banned substance.

"The disadvantage down there is that they don't have the regulation," explained Romero. "You can go to a store down there and get something that's not labeled, and in reality it's a performance-enhancing substance and the kids don't know it. A lot of times, the street agents are giving something to kids that the kids think are vitamins, and it turns out to be a steroid. It can be tough for a player down there, because a person of confidence is giving them something and telling them to take it, and it ends up biting them in the rear. That's something we're trying to educate our players on. In the offseason, we keep in contact with them, telling them to be careful what they take; we keep reminding them to take things that are approved, and to run them by

---

NEAL HUNTINGTON
GENERAL MANAGER, PIRATES

"Unfortunately, we just had two players suspended for use [in 2008], and that is going to allow us to be even more aggressive, because our message is obviously not getting across as strongly as we had hoped. It is very important to have them realize that things that are available to them, that have been acceptable in the past, now aren't acceptable. The risks that they run in taking any supplements—it's the same education process as here in the United States. There used to be, and I believe there may still be, supplements on the market that have steroid traces that may trigger a positive. We need to make sure that [the players are] provided with a list of supplements that are approved and risk free. And that takes time; it takes time to get that all down there. Some of the things that are available here, that have been tested, aren't available there, in the Dominican or in Venezuela. And there's the risk that any player takes by injecting, or by using any of those unapproved supplements—the risk that they take, and the downside of potentially having a positive test when they thought they were doing everything right."

our Latin American trainers before they ingest something. We want them to be as careful as possible, and the more we educate them, the more careful they'll be."

What Teams Are Doing to Help

To varying degrees, every big-league organization is working to help Latin American players make the transition to life in the United States. While a comprehensive rundown of each team's efforts is impractical in this article, representatives of half a dozen ballclubs weighed in on their respective efforts.

"We've got English classes everywhere," said Jon Matlack. "Every location that has Latin kids that haven't picked up enough English, we have classes available. At the lower levels, we make it mandatory that they go. We also have [a bilingual coach] who can help at almost every location, but it's still an ongoing problem that we're trying to get sorted out. But we do have bilingual guys at most of our locations."

Pete Rancont, who manages Houston's low-A short-season affiliate, says that the Astros are also working to have at least one multilingual coach at each level.

"We're pretty easygoing, and our organization puts a Spanish-speaking coach with each club," said Rancont. "Here [at Tri-City], Joel Chimelis is Puerto Rican and speaks fluent Spanish. Donny Alexander, our pitching coach, and I both have a working knowledge of Spanish, so we don't feel that there's any isolation at all. Periodically, we'll fly some of our staff down to the Dominican and Venezuela, to see how the kids live, and some of the challenges they face when they come to the United States."

Like many teams, the Twins are focusing not only on language, but also on cultural issues. Twins manager **Ron Gardenhire** explained it this way: "There's obviously the language barrier, and I think that a lot of the Latin players understand that it is very important for them to be able to speak the language over here so that they get along. I think that we do a great job now of setting up academies and scouting down there. And we're not just developing players; we're also developing their skills as far as being able to come into this country and survive, and live day to day. As an organization, we have classes; we have everything set up for them so that we can help these young players get along. And it's very important that the organization is doing that, because it's not easy coming over here and not understanding."

According to Dick Scott, the Blue Jays are likewise extending the scope of their classroom sessions beyond English lessons: "We have a cultural diversity program that is kind of a multipronged attack at these players. Besides teaching them English, we help with the adjustment with housing and as many things as we can. The Dominican Republic is like a Third World country, and it's difficult for these guys to come to a place that has everything they could ever hope for. But they don't speak the language, and they don't understand the currency, and they don't understand about getting a rental house or apartment, or any of that stuff. So we try to get them acclimated as quickly as possible, and it's a bit of a process."

The Red Sox have been among the most active and aggressive teams in Latin America, and according to Arnie Beyler, education is a big part of their effort: "The way things have evolved, we have [Latin education coordinator] Duncan Webb over here, and we have classes for the guys. We also have classes for our [American-born] guys to learn Spanish in spring training. The kids are required to go to school in spring training for three weeks; the young kids are required to go until they get to a certain level. And Duncan goes down and spends a lot of time with the kids in the academy; they have an English class down in the academy. I was down there last winter for three weeks, because I had to go. Even the other organizations are going to the colleges in Santo Domingo at night. Each of them goes for a couple of hours a night, two or three nights a week to English class, just to try to learn stuff: how to get along, how to eat, how to order food. They learn the cultural differences, like dealing with women over here, and how to treat people—things that we kind of take for granted."

The Red Sox go even further in their attempts to acculturate the players in their organization, sending some of their American-born prospects to the Dominican academy for two weeks each winter. One of the players who went this past year was **Peter Hissey**, an 18-year-old outfielder from West Chester, Pennsylvania, whom Boston selected in the fourth round of the 2008 draft.

"I had a great experience going to the Dominican," said Hissey. "The culture was a lot different and took some getting used to, but I got to see how a lot of my teammates live. Communicating with the other players was always interesting. They would ask us questions using some English words they knew, but mostly they used hand motions. The entire trip was fun, and it was definitely something that I would recommend the Red Sox keep doing."

The Pirates are likewise committed to not only increasing their presence in Latin America, but also easing the transition of players they sign from south of the border.

"As we move forward, it's a work in progress," said Pirates general manager **Neal Huntington**. "We're building our academy down there, and once we get our academy going with dorms and classrooms, we'll be able to be much more aggressive in terms of how we're preparing players, not only in coming to the United States, but to be successful. Right now, we spend a lot of time educating them about similar things we educate our American-based players about, whether it is nutrition or the risk of steroids, but specifically about America—we're trying to expose them to what they're going to experience over here. We're talking about the changes in lifestyle; we're talking about changes in food; we're talking about the changes in experiences; we're talking about the difficulty of not knowing the language. We're trying to educate them in Spanish first, so they can learn in their native language before we can really begin to attack it, teaching them English. Right now, Spanish is their primary language and English is the second language, which is an important part of our package. But it's also trying to educate them about what is going to be expected of them over here, and what is different from how they play in the Dominican Republic, and what might be expected of them as they come to the United States and the opportunities that are available to them, and the potential derailers that they're going to face as they come over here—just the differences in cultures and the differences in baseball. I think it is important that we do that."

ED ROMERO JR.
LATIN PROGRAM COORDINATOR, RED SOX

"[Red Sox assistant general manager] Ben Cherington came up with the idea for the program a couple of years ago. He was looking to kind of turn the tables a little bit by having some of our American players go down to our Dominican academy and get a firsthand view of how things operate down there, not only from a baseball point of view, but also from a life point of view. It helps to give them an idea of how these kids are growing up and where they're coming from. The first year, we started off with a few guys; we had three guys go down there. And it turned out to be a good experience. They saw some of the country and kind of wore the shoes of how the young Dominican players feel when they come here to the States not knowing the culture or the language. But when they get on the baseball field, everybody speaks the same language. So it was a very positive experience, and we continued it last year, when we sent a couple more guys, and we'll do the same this year with a handful of guys. It's turned out to be a benefit to both sides, because the Latin guys have American guys coming to their turf and seeing what it's like from their point of view. When [the American-born] guys get back to the States, they talk to their teammates about it, so it becomes a positive experience to those guys as well. They learn more about what the Dominican is like, both the good and the bad. They give their teammates a semblance of where the Latin guys are coming from."

Something Old and Something New
Stadium Update

Neil deMause

On Opening Day of the 1989 season, baseball stadiums could largely be divided into two roughly even categories: the classic ballparks of the pre-expansion age, and the multipurpose "concrete donuts" of the 1960s and 1970s. In the previous decade, only one new ballpark had opened, the unloved and unlovely Minneapolis Metrodome. And while the Toronto Blue Jays were set to debut their new SkyDome that summer (with a roof that—wonder of wonders—could open and close depending on the weather), and new parks were underway in Chicago and Baltimore, these were viewed more as novelties than as the harbingers of a sea change.

Ten years later, the landscape had begun to shift. Nine teams (including the expansion Devil Rays, Rockies, and Diamondbacks) now played in stadiums less than a decade old. With parks like Camden Yards and Jacobs Field—dubbed "retro" for daring to feature exposed brick and steel, though in both acreage and amenities, they were more like SkyDome than like Ebbets Field—selling out nightly, more and more teams were looking to keep up with the Jacobses with new playpens of their own, funded wherever possible by local taxpayers. In the previous year, the Padres had won a public referendum for $225 million in funding for a new home, and the Yankees and Mets had unveiled plans for new stadiums they hoped to open by 2003, while the Red Sox were developing blueprints for a double-decked facility across Yawkey Way, with only the Green Monster to remain standing of the old Fenway.

Today, while Fenway still stands, thanks to John Henry and his ballpark director Janet Marie Smith (not to mention the unsung heroes of Save Fenway Park!—the community group that first proposed everything from seats atop the Monster to renovated concessions concourses), the transformation of the places where big-league baseball is played is all but complete. The Yankees and Mets will open their new stadiums this year, bringing to twelve the number of parks opened during the aughties, more than in any decade save for the expansion-era 1960s. As a result, since 1989, the av-

erage age of ballparks has dropped from 33 to 21. The Metrodome, which was baseball's newest stadium when today's rookies were toddlers, is today the majors' seventh-oldest—and it's already scheduled to be supplanted by the new Target Field next April.

The Metrodome cost $68 million to build; in contrast, Target Field is budgeted at $522 million, which even accounting for inflation is a nearly 250 percent increase. Of the new Twins park's cost, $387 million will come from public coffers, and unlike the Metrodome, which ultimately repaid its public owners through rent and concessions fees, taxpayers will see little of the stadium's new revenues. It's a growing trend: Harvard researcher Judith Grant Long has found that these types of "hidden" lease costs have grown over the years, as team owners learn that these leases attract less attention from policy makers and taxpayers than do outright cash grants.

Now that the Twins will no longer have to suffer the indignity of playing in a ballpark older than Joe Mauer, the list of teams demanding new homes has dwindled, though not entirely disappeared: the Florida Marlins, Oakland A's, and Tampa Bay Rays spent 2008 at work on new stadium plans, with varied results.

The Marlins' ever-changing cast of owners has been yearning for a new home almost as long as the team has been in existence: right after becoming the most freshly minted expansion team to win a world championship in 1997, the Fish became the fastest team to hold a fire sale, amid claims by then-owner Wayne Huizenga that the team had lost $30 million in its championship season. (Economist Andy Zimbalist promptly dismantled Huizenga's claims in the *New York Times Magazine*, noting the owner had failed to count profits from stadium operations and the team's cable outlet, each entirely Huizenga-owned.) For the next ten years, through two ownership changes, Marlins management steadfastly stuck to its insistence that the team couldn't possibly pay more than $192 million toward a stadium with construction costs upward of $400 million; despite increasingly urgent annual threats by team president David

Samson, culminating in a 2006 tour of potential relocation sites such as Portland and San Antonio, nothing shook loose any additional public funds.

The logjam finally broke in December 2007, when the city of Miami and Dade County concocted a convoluted deal whereby taxpayers would put up $360 million toward a stadium that would now cost $515 million to be built on the site of the Orange Bowl. (The city was also to build a $94 million parking garage with public funds.) The gimmick here was to take money from the city's "community redevelopment agencies"—money that was intended for impoverished communities—and use it to pay off debt on the city's performing arts center; this would free up tourist taxes that were being used on the arts center to go instead toward a new stadium.

Despite one county commissioner's calling the scheme "hijacking Peter to pay Paul," the city and county commissions each approved the stadium plan on February 21, 2008. In the meantime, though, an unexpected roadblock had appeared in the form of former Philadelphia Eagles owner Norman Braman, who'd filed suit to challenge the project on a variety of grounds, including the point that the project would redirect public money (both from the redevelopment agencies and from a proposed renovation of the Orange Bowl, which was instead demolished to make way for the new ballpark) without a public vote. The legal battles took up most of the year, but by November 2008, Judge Jeri Beth Cohen had dismissed all of Braman's objections, ruling that "the law in Florida is clear that retaining a professional baseball team in Miami satisfies a paramount public purpose." This assumes that the Marlins were going to leave town without a new stadium, but presumably Judge Cohen figured that one of these years, Samson's repeated threats would come true.

The delay did force the team to push back its planned opening date of its new digs. The new, not-yet-corporate-monikered stadium is set to open in 2012, at which point, as per its deal with the city, the team will become known as the Miami Marlins. Adjust your hats accordingly.

As the Marlins' stadium plans have seemingly come to fruition, the A's plans have run into difficulties. Lew Wolff, the real estate developer who took control of the franchise in 2005, had announced plans in November 2006 for a stadium seating 30,000 or so in the suburb of Fremont, about 30 miles south of Oakland, down I-880. (It's also conveniently as close as you can get to San Jose without treading on the Giants' MLB-designated territorial rights.) More than two years later, though, there

had been very little activity beyond a handful of press conferences, plus some renderings of a tiny 30,000-plus-seat park surrounded by a "ballpark village" of condos and upscale shops.

Wolff's proposed site, a 143-acre parcel owned by Cisco Systems to the west of what passes for Fremont's downtown, came under fire immediately from locals for both environmental concerns (the site abuts a wetland wildlife refuge) and traffic worries. When it's recognized for anything at all, Fremont is probably best known as the southern terminus of one of the Bay Area's BART light-rail lines; unfortunately, the proposed stadium site is about five miles away from the nearest train station, and while a proposed extension would bring BART closer, fans would still be facing a two-mile gap between the train station and the stadium gates. That was especially bad news because the only highway access would be via I-880; one regular East Bay commuter, asked to describe it at rush hour, replied, "Eeeagh, parking lot!"

Because it's in a redevelopment area, the Cisco site would be eligible to use "tax increment financing" (TIF), a relatively recent innovation in which any new property tax revenue gets kicked back to pay for construction costs—and since the land is currently undeveloped, almost any property taxes would be new. TIF critics have noted that new residents require services like police, fire, schools, and roads, but with TIFs in place, they no longer generate new taxes to pay for these services. Since Wolff has yet to publicly disclose a financing plan, though, it's been impossible to say whether TIFs would be part of the mix.

In any case, the economic meltdown may have put an end to Wolff's original plan. It's hard to raise money for a housing development when credit is at a standstill and condos in California are going for pennies on the dollar. At last word, Wolff was reportedly in talks with the city of Fremont to consider an alternate site adjacent to the planned Warm Springs BART station scheduled to open in 2014; given that the condo proceeds were supposed to help fund stadium construction, though, and that the new site may not be eligible for TIF money, he'd probably be back to square one in terms of financing. In December, Bud Selig wrote to Wolff that he was free to consider "other communities" if Fremont fell through, but didn't specify whether this was opening the door to a San Jose incursion or merely reminding him that there are plenty of other fish in the East Bay.

The third contestant in the new-stadium sweepstakes is a late entrant. The Tampa Bay Rays, whose Tropicana Field home was only completed in 1990 (and renovated in 1998 for the arrival of the expansion Devil Rays), announced in late 2007 plans for a 35,000-seat park along the Tampa waterfront on the site of the Rays' spring training home, Al Lang Field. (Because there isn't quite room for a big-league stadium, part of the shoreline would have to be filled in.) A retractable fabric "shade" would serve in lieu of a roof, being raised and lowered by pulleys attached to a vertical mast.

Since the Rays still have 19 years to go on their Tropicana Field lease, team execs—now including Michael Kalt, who helped the Yankees devise their stadium deal—turned to another development rights swap for their financing plan. The team's owners would put up about a third of the $450 million price tag, with much of the rest of the cash coming from developing the site of Tropicana Field, which for tax reasons is owned by the county but leased back to the city. Other revenue sources could include county hotel taxes, state sales tax funds currently being used to pay down the Trop's construction debt, and future parking revenues; asked how this latter would work, team president Matt Silverman replied, "The short answer is we don't know."

By mid-June, a developer had been lined up to build a mixed-use development on the Tropicana site, though its offer was only $65 million, far short of what would be needed to pay for a new stadium. Later that month, the Rays abruptly pulled their plan, apparently because the timetable was too short and Florida's budget woes too great. At last word, the team had commissioned a coalition of local business and political leaders to investigate alternate sites and gear up for a vote in 2010, though the way things are going, that year's state budget doesn't look likely to be much more flush.

Last year's other stadium-related drama took place in New York, where the Mets and Yankees were looking forward to counting down the days until Opening Day for their new homes in 2009, while wringing a bit of extra cash from nostalgic fans eager to visit Shea and Yankee stadiums one last time in the process. In the Yanks' case, though, their planned victory lap in the House That Ruth Built was disrupted by growing public controversy over their new stadium's funding.

In March, the city's Parks Department announced that the cost of tearing down Yankee Stadium, building new public parks to replace those demolished to make way for the new stadium, and providing such infrastructure as new underpasses and relocated sewer lines—all of which is being covered by the city—had nearly doubled in the course of two years, from $135 million to $242 million. (The new public parks, originally promised to open in 2009, now won't be available until 2011, leading to local news stories of forlorn high-

schoolers left with nowhere to play football.) At the same time, Yanks chief operations officer Lonn Trost revealed that the $1 billion stadium itself would need an additional $300 million in upgrades for such items as the scoreboard and concession stands. Trost didn't specify where the money would come from.

In June, it was revealed where: the Yanks would be asking for more than $300 million in new tax-exempt bonds to cover the added costs. While the team would pay off the bonds, it would be saving more than $50 million by avoiding the private taxable bond market. (The subsidy would cost taxpayers, mostly through loss of federal tax revenue, about $75 million.) While using public bonds for a private project was supposed to have been made illegal in 1986—precisely because local governments were handing out tax-exempt bonds like candy and fobbing off the cost of local projects onto the feds—the Yanks (and Mets) had obtained a so-called private-letter ruling from the Internal Revenue Service signing off on the deal, under the convoluted reasoning that the team's private construction bond payments were actually public property taxes. (Don't ask. Really. If you must know, go to fieldofschemes.com and search on the keyword *PILOTs*.)

While the first round of tax-free bonds had attracted little notice (outside of the city's Independent Budget Office, which called it "a very, very aggressive interpretation of the IRS code"), this round awoke the interest of state assembly member Richard Brodsky, who promptly hauled the city's development chief before his committee for two hours of questioning. Ohio congressman Dennis Kucinich followed with hearings in October to investigate how it was that the Yankees had valued the land under the new stadium at $21 million in documents submitted to the state (which needed to be convinced that the new parkland was worth at least as much), yet at $175 million for the IRS (which needed to confirm that the land value was high enough for the team's construction payments to qualify as property taxes).

While the hearings generated more heat than light, the resulting controversy put some tarnish on the Yankees' upcoming stadium opening, especially after it was revealed in November that city officials had traded parking revenues for a free luxury box to be used by elected officials. Meanwhile, the Mets largely ducked the controversy, despite being the recipients of several hundred million dollars in tax-free bonds themselves; their moment in the tabloids came in November, when the near-collapse of Citigroup left them insisting that their $400 million deal to name their new park Citi Field was not in jeopardy. This development led two Staten

Island council members to suggest that, in the wake of the government's bailout of Citigroup, the Mets' home be redubbed "Taxpayer Field."

It's an epithet that could have been applied just as reasonably before the bailout. Including parking garages and replacement parkland, the Yanks' stadium will cost an unfathomable $1.9 billion, making it easily the most expensive stadium ever built. Of that, city, state, and federal taxpayers will combine to pay about $860 million, while the team, after sundry tax breaks, will be on the hook for about $650 million; the rest will be covered by MLB (through deductions on the Yanks' revenue-sharing payments) and a private garage developer. The Mets' Citi Field is cheap by comparison, but only by comparison. At $830 million, it will still be the second-priciest ballpark in US history, and public subsidies will pay for more than half of the total costs. And here's something to chew on: between revenue-sharing deductions and federal tax subsidies, more than $600 million will come from other cities' fans and taxpayers, meaning that fans of the New York teams' rivals will end up putting in about two-thirds as much money as the teams do themselves.

For their money, fans will get a pair of ballparks that are undeniably more modern than the ones they replace. The new Yankees stadium (it's officially just Yankee Stadium, but that still sounds confusing, if not blasphemous, to many ears) is being touted as "moving the ghosts across the street," in Derek Jeter's famous line, with the same field dimensions and the same frieze atop the upper deck as the pre-renovation original. Of course, the field dimensions now set in steel-reinforced concrete were only in place since 1988 (when George Steinbrenner moved the fences in to make it easier for Jack Clark to reach them); and the frieze will be made of Plexiglas, not copper or the post-1976 concrete. As for outside the lines, the old three-tier stacked grandstand has been replaced by a more gradually sloping four-tier model. While this will benefit the claustrophobic (in the back of the lower deck) and vertigo-plagued (in the upper), setting back the upper deck by about 30 feet will mean a more distant view for fans there, not to mention a likely reduction in the stadium's signature roar. It also will see a reduction in seating, from 57,545 to about 53,000 plus standing room. Although the team has

promised to hold the line on upper-deck and bleacher ticket prices for 2009, it seems likely they'll rise soon thereafter, as increased ticket scarcity takes hold.

Then there are the other gewgaws: a scoreboard the size of Kentucky, a Hard Rock Cafe, and a 100-foot shopping concourse that fans will pass through on the way to their seats. "We tried to reflect a five-star hotel and put a ballfield in the middle," said Trost approvingly last spring; less approvingly, in June the newspaper *amNewYork* included the new Yankees stadium as one of its top ten "ugly buildings NYC would be better without."

For the Mets, Citi Field, or whatever its eventual name, is a sharp break with the hokey utilitarianism that was Shea, with an angular layout similar to other recent models like Turner Field and Citizens Bank Park, and a clutch of concessions facilities operated by Manhattan restaurant celeb Danny Mayer and located behind the center-field scoreboard. The seat reduction, meanwhile, is even more pronounced than in the Bronx, dropping from 55,601 seats to 42,500; Mets blogs have already begun worrying about whether the team's role as the affordable alternative to the Yankees may be in jeopardy. One thing they shouldn't expect is for the smaller capacity to translate into better nosebleed seats. While Mets management has touted the architectural similarity to Ebbets Field, the Dodgers' Brooklyn home stood just 60 feet tall; Citi Field tops out at 116 feet.

With the Twins' new home opening in 2010 and the Marlins likely to follow in 2012, could baseball's stadium boom finally be winding to a close? Perhaps, though there are still some potential candidates to go to the back of the line after the A's and Rays. The Blue Jays have been unhappy with SkyDome ever since it stopped drawing 4 million fans a year (coincidentally, about the same time the Jays stopped winning pennants). After new Cubs owner Sam Zell made an abortive attempt to get the state to foot the bill for a renovation of Wrigley Field last winter, mutterings began again about a possible replacement for the Friendly Confines. Heck, by 2012, Camden Yards will be 20 years old, and it doesn't even have a Hard Rock Cafe. Surely somewhere, a stadium architect and a bond lawyer are salivating.

An Unfair and Uneven Look at MLB's Marketing

Gary Huckabay

No One Likes Kudzu

About seven years ago, I had a phone conversation with author and editor Gary Gillette. I don't remember the reason that instigated the call, but the conversation has embedded itself in my consciousness, and I end up revisiting it at least once a year. Gary and I spoke at length about the relative futures and place in the American zeitgeist of various sports and entertainment ventures. We were in agreement about the constant and increasing encroachment of threats like NASCAR, the NFL, and even college basketball, which were being abetted by different parts of the entertainment industry, and ended up with those products overlapping big chunks of baseball's calendar, effectively putting the national pastime in the shade for long stretches. For me, all of this was further verification of two of my favorite hypotheses—first, that Europeans are right about the collective American palate, and second, that the world will always be getting worse, and not just because of the inexplicable popularity of Creed.

A few years later, I was contacted over the course of two years by five different television networks to do some consulting. There were some differences between what they were looking for, but at the core what they all wanted was a method to perform some hardcore measurement of the effectiveness of their ad spend. (Which is a little bit like the Holy Grail of advertising.) The people I spoke with at each network had a similar story, one that pretty much everyone knows. You're probably aware that there are a few more entertainment options available to people today than there were during the times when there were "three network stations and maybe three major independents" in each metro TV marketplace. The networks and advertisers have been in a deepening state of apoplexy and terror over this development for years. And so they should be. The mother's milk of network television is money from advertising. Advertisers are losing the ability to bludgeon people with their message, and networks are horrified of losing the money from selling advertisers the shillelagh.

How severe is the issue of viewer flight from the networks? To put a simple number or two on it, consider the case of the World Series. Over the past 25 years, the ratings (Nielsen/VNU) for the World Series have declined from a 23.3 rating and a 41 share to 10.6 and 18. There has been variance, partially explained in a given year by the size of the media markets involved, but the trend is pretty clear. Is it a case of baseball alone suffering the loss? No, because during the same 1983–2007 timeframe, the NBA Finals went from 32 million viewers to 20 million, with some years of retrenchment in there, presumably due to the league's signature player during the late '80s and early '90s, Michael Jordan.

So how does this affect baseball, and specifically MLB? What is going on in the marketplace? What's changing, and what are the likely effects on MLB? What are MLB's responses? And, realistically and practically, are they good responses?

Accountability Corner

We at BP have not been kind when we've examined MLB's marketing practices. Sometimes, MLB has been an easy target, playing follower and sycophant to partnerships large and small with organizations and products like NASCAR and various breweries. When I agreed to write this piece for the book, my opinion of MLB's marketing efforts were pretty much firmly set. I had assimilated and nearly perfected all the bad habits that I've spent nearly twenty years keelhauling the mainstream baseball press for—letting opinions and inertia guide my view and my writing, and I had prejudged baseball's response to changing competitive, technological, and economic factors.

In large part, my prejudice was borne from my narrow angle view. My view of baseball has been remarkably static for the nearly 20 years I've been examining it. From the first time that Sherri Nichols convinced me that I knew far less about the game than I thought, I've been focused on continually re-examining my view of the game—and when I say 'the game,' I mean precisely that, and no more. My attention and my eyes have been captured in using on-field performance as the driver for everything, from calculating how much a potential free agent is worth on an incremental basis to optimizing ticket-pricing mixes. But from a marketing perspective it's the on-field contests that are really the foundation upon which all other aspects of the customer's "purchase" of the product are constructed. That purchase doesn't have to be limited to an exchange of money for the right to watch a game; it doesn't even have to be an exchange between fan and baseball at all. That's all changed, and primarily for the better.

Old-Time Gospel from a True Believer

So let's start from the beginning, and with basics. Marketing is strategy. It's not simply advertising, branding, and spin, it literally means *everything* to a business. Everything. You can be a perfect organization in every other aspect of your business, but it doesn't matter if you don't make products that people want to buy, or they don't know about them. Having the world's best controller means approximately zilch if you don't have money coming in the door and you can't compete in the marketplace. Marketing is the battleground of the marketplace, and it's where you have to address the mixture and control of your product portfolio, distribution channels, pricing, and communication and interaction with the public. Most companies don't have enough quantitative marketing people, so some of these functions get shifted to other areas, which causes all sorts of interesting effects, but that's another article.

Like every business, MLB has a number of challenges in the marketing world. The sports media and even MLB's partners have not done them a whole bunch of favors in that area. The public square has been filled with some rather interesting notions that have become boring just because they've been beaten to death. For example, "The game's too long." Really? That's actually a pretty interesting idea, because it runs contrary to the available evidence. Baseball's revenues have been up, way up, and more people are consuming more MLB-based entertainment than ever before, from bad television to fantasy games. It makes you wonder about the process that generates this complaint: things are going well by every reasonable metric, and therefore, that's a problem, and the best way to deal with it is by reducing the amount of the core product? Interesting.

Can You Keep Them on the Farm?

For most of my lifetime, network television advertising revenues have been the big cash cow that everyone wanted a piece of, and one that advertisers and net-

works have been scrambling to protect. (The protection attempt is futile, much like the attempt of the traditional record companies' fight to stanch the bleeding of their own business model, but that's another piece, probably one for my massive contractual backlog of columns for BP.com.) The reason for this was simple: for a long time, the networks had an effective monopoly on the ability to reach consumers with rich media, and advertisers found that spending money on that was, by and large, a really good investment.

That may seem obvious, and it is, but until you really consider all the downstream effects and start putting some numbers around it, it doesn't really hit you in the sternum like it should. Only 30 years ago, there were three television networks. They provided somewhere around four to six hours of programming each weeknight. There was the national news broadcast, three hours of primetime programming, and late-night programming, dominated by Johnny Carson and *The Tonight Show*, followed up by Tom Snyder's occasionally coherent, nicotine-packed interview after Johnny and Ed bid goodnight to the nation.

Sports coverage, particularly nationally, was limited to the weekends, with the notable exception of the alcohol-fueled reverie of *Monday Night Football*. Baseball coverage on a national level was largely limited to the postseason, except for Saturday's *Game of the Week* broadcast. Obviously, coverage of athletics themselves and the rapidly bloating sports punditry industry has blossomed tremendously since these times. The issue is the scale of that expansion.

So how big is that scale? Is it big enough to invoke the cliché about a large enough quantitative change being, in fact, a qualitative change? You be the judge. Here are some quick Google searches, with the result counts:

Search Text	Google Result Count
Football Video	39,200,000
Baseball Video	16,200,000
Basketball Video	113,000,000
NASCAR Video	1,300,000
NASCAR Crash Video	404,000
Golf Video	259,000,000
Bowling Video	749,000
Olympics Video	4,030,000
Diet Coke and Mentos Video	
Hockey Video	4,090,000
Baseball blog	7,860,000
Football blog	28,650,000
Basketball blog	5,730,000
NASCAR blog	1,290,000
That thar's a left turn, Clem!	2
Porn	215,000,000

This is overkill, but you get the idea—your home entertainment options are more diverse than ever before. Even so, relative to the change that's taken place in terms of options available to consumers, there's still an awful lot of advertising revenue residing in network television. Naturally, the networks would prefer to keep it that way. (That too, is another piece.)

By the time you read this, MLB will have rolled out the MLB Network, part of its strategy to maintain and expand its marketplace performance in the face of increasing competition, a wide variety of new threats, partner relationships that are increasingly complicated, and the development of interest in the ill-based opinions of hundreds of thousands of on-line denizens who consider their innermost thoughts both relevant and interesting.

Rear-View Mirror

When Baseball Prospectus was in its infancy, before any of the initial contributors were even on board, there were several guiding principles I was absolutely determined to follow. One of these, still near and dear to my heart, is to never sugarcoat or deify the past. MLB is blessed and cursed by its incredibly rich history. It's comfortable with sepia tones, cults of personality, and easy icons that paint a whole picture by their mere inclusion or reference. It makes marketing the game relatively automatic in the short term. Just like Budweiser and GM sell patriotism instead of genuine comparative quality, MLB sells continuity. Under a lot of circumstances, it's a good strategy—chubby, balding, aging white guys who drive SUVs and wear badly trimmed goatees like continuity. For MLB, those guys represent a large and profitable market segment.

But looking backward always carries a price, in any industry you can name. Look at every major industry in American history. Just pick one. Take a look at that industry's history, and you'll find a number of places where a successful or dominant participant gets completely blindsided and takes a huge hit. Sometimes, they respond successfully, and re-invent themselves rapidly and well enough so they don't end up stuck in corporate amber. The more likely outcome is a state of increased inertia and sclerosis, followed by an orgy of frantic flailing, and eventually, excessive effort invested in assigning blame and wringing hands over a cruel reversal of fortune. Fortunately for MLB and its fans, the mediocre executives populating certain industries in the US have steered into enterprises other than baseball. MLB's working hard to avoid creating too many Ford Contours.

The Expanding Sea

Ultimately, baseball is simply an entertainment product. So is a movie, or a play, or a TV show. Or a street performer, or a local museum. A cat mixing Mentos and Diet Coke on YouTube. Playing cards. There's a nearly infinite number of options available for the enjoyment of the world's consumers of entertainment. Baseball isn't alone is facing the challenge of the shifting expectations and demands of the world's populace, but some of its adaptations have been remarkable, in their scope and in their execution. Whether you want to enjoy this product from the stands or in-house, baseball's improved delivery systems are outstanding developments for the fan and industry alike.

Built and Bought to Last

No matter what you think about how they were funded, you have to love the move of completely re-building baseball's storied physical plant. Almost every MLB city sports a new ballpark and supporting infrastructure. The multi-purpose concentric circle has been mercifully laid to rest in most locales, replaced by a multi-zoned cathedral worthy of the game. Even when the architecture won't age well and is reminiscent of one of those overly puffy exurb malls, these are still damn nice places to see a game compared to the parks they displaced.

This is a great thing for ownership, particularly if the cost of the park was in part paid by the local citizenry. Let's face it, there's no substitute for having two or three million folks come to see a game and drop some chunk of an ATM visit while doing so. The upgrade of the ballparks that's taken place over the last couple of decades has meant a dramatic improvement in the fan experience, and opened up marketing opportunities for clubs that were previously out of reach. Marketing components, like Price and Product, work best when they're in alignment. It's hard to sell a Kia as a Bentley; similarly, it was hard to market a visit to Veterans' Stadium in Philadelphia as a destination spot for out-of-town tourists. But make the ballpark newer, cleaner, more comfortable, with more amenities, and it's now possible that someone from outside Philadelphia may want to come into town for a ballgame, or stay in extra day in town and work it in. Try doing that with Al Davis's monument to Soviet management practices in Oakland. Приверженность к совершенству!

AOL Time Warner Domino's UPS

Other organizations have tried, but MLB has actually

done it: baseball has successfully created and integrated a specialized, customer-facing media arm. In other parts of entertainment, there's always a friction, and usually a dynamic churn of acquisition and divestment that takes place between content providers (like TV networks), and content delivery systems (like the incarnation of evil and incompetence that is Comcast). MLB's entry is something the typical Baseball Prospectus reader is already aware of—it's called MLB Advanced Media, LP, or MLBAM.

MLBAM is responsible for, among other things, MLB.com and MiLB.com. MLBAM has a solid technical infrastructure that it leverages in partnerships and sales with other sports and entertainment entities. If you deal with MLB on the web, you're dealing with MLBAM, and you're probably fairly happy with the arrangement, even allowing for the cursing over the occasional regional blackout. MLB.com and MLBAM provide a fantastic platform for product expansion on several fronts. The video processing, bandwidth, and content management at MLB.com allow them a great deal of flexibility in terms of addressing future problems as they arise. That doesn't just happen—it takes a commitment of cash, time, and a vision of what's possible down the road. How many large organizations can execute well on something like that?

One big problem that baseball's had in recent years is the public perception that the time investment necessary to attend or view a game is simply too much for potential customers to make room for in their busy lives. MLB's responded with the concentrated game on MLB.tv—a largely complete game in just a fraction of the time it takes to take in a full nine innings in real time. The production and high quality of the concentrated games allows for a dramatic reduction in the time investment necessary to take in a game, without significant quality loss for a large segment of MLB's target audience. The ability to time-shift and make a superior product for some market segment is a significant achievement for the marketing folks at MLB. Execution hasn't been perfect, but it's been very good, it's likely to get better, it will generate some very nice revenue, and it's an option for a large number of people who are simply incapable, by geography or time commitments to attend or view their desired games. Is this revolutionary or massively innovative? Not at all. But it is a well-considered response to a significant challenge, and it's executed well, two things that aren't as easy as they sound.

MLBAM also provides a very nice platform to acquire attractive properties that would fit in well with MLB's strategy and product offerings. But where to find such properties?

Open Source

Everyone's a control freak, and MLB is no different. Through a number of technological and legal means, they've tried like crazy to maintain control over what their customers consume. They've failed, like most entities not named De Beers. The result is a huge base of "Open Source" MLB entertainment, ranging from talk radio programs all over the world, to millions of doggerel-laden internet sites, to millions of fans competing in fantasy leagues. MLB wields remarkably little power over this amorphous mass of fanboy-driven enterprise. But that's not necessarily a bad thing.

Blogs, radio shows, fantasy leagues, and a million e-mail lists associated with fantasy leagues generate an enormous amount of opinion about the game. Fans get invested above and beyond the once-dominant local team. Outside of a few suffering fans in Kansas City, how many people would care about Mark Teahen if they weren't in a fantasy league? These ventures are driven by the passion and ego of individual, emotionally invested fans, and the networks they drive increase the overall passion of the entire fan base—all without MLB having to do much at all.

Open source has provided MLB with an entirely new engine for generating fan interest, one they could not have developed on their own. Why couldn't they, you ask? There are two reasons. The first is that it would be unbelievably bloody expensive. Acquiring a customer, a viewer, or a reader is a very expensive enterprise. Keeping them happy isn't cheap, either. Constant communication is difficult to manage; you need to know the size, preferences, and access channels for your customer segments, and you never know any of that as well as you'd like. With open source, the customers can seek out anything they want in terms of your product, and, wonder of wonders, even generate products for you, all for free or damn close to it.

The second aspect is one of knowledge and market research. I've spent most of my life working with marketing, numbers, and media, and one thing I can say with absolute certainty is that the vast majority of market research is awful. Pathetic. A complete and utter waste of time, energy, and money. Market research practiced badly is responsible for an enormous number of crappy, failed products. The explosion of technology, changing expectations about what media consumption really is, and the continued excellence of the core product on the field has created a tremendous crucible of creativity for MLB. New products pop up all the time, and radio and TV talent comes out of nowhere, all reflecting new, fresh ideas about how to look at the game. If they're good, they catch on, become popular, and increase both fan satisfaction and engagement. If not, the idea withers and dies without any loss of prestige, credibility, or cash.

The result is to leave MLB in the position of IBM and Oracle when it comes to open source—let people spend the time and money to ideate, develop, and improve. Then, you can pick and choose what you want to assimilate, controlling the timeline, terms, and integration. In some ways, MLB is even better off than the software companies, because software developers have been able to learn about business and obtain capital, thereby becoming potential threats to IBM and Oracle. As it's pretty unlikely that your typical baseball fan is going to start a credibly competitive rival baseball league, the core product platform remains unthreatened.

Where We Are

Business is a contact sport, and there is no time off. If you have a customer that you value, there will always be competitors busting their butt to try to take that customer away from you. There are always new threats, coming from a number of different directions, and even success poses its own unique challenges. People within the organization get complacent, competitors try to poach your key people, and sympathy is in short supply. Ultimately, businesses are about the livelihoods of individuals and their families, which is why it's so cutthroat to compete for the public's dollars.

MLB has faced a variety of obstacles and environmental changes over the past two decades. They've stumbled on a number of occasions, sometimes on real issues, sometimes on media vacuum-created pseudocrises. Yes, other sports and entertainment ventures have received a pass where baseball, bearer of the "National Pastime" tiara, has been held to scrutiny that any objective observer could only judge as ridiculous. But overall, MLB has done well in its marketing. Other ventures and institutions have fallen by the wayside or lay dead and bleeding as a result of failing to conquer less demanding foes. It's not as if ABC, NBC, CBS, and Fox aren't constantly fighting the same market forces, channel conflicts and changing tastes. And MLB has yet to foist the equivalent of *A Shot at Love* on an unsuspecting public.

Phil Gramm's not my idea of a beacon of wisdom, but his statement that economically we're a nation of whiners was probably resonant in large part because of its truth, especially where sports is concerned. Fans and talk radio hosts have to talk about something, so we whine about ticket prices, commercial breaks, and everything in between. We also have the nasty and unbecoming habit of bestowing unearned virtue on the past in order to have an invincible strawman to take on the reality of today. MLB owners and executives make easy foils; it takes someone with the visage and speaking style of a Don Fehr to give them a shot at sympathy. But realistically, what would or could anyone have done differently? MLB's Advanced Media venture has been, by any metric, a very big success, and is a heck of a model for other businesses to copy, even considering all MLBAM's blemishes and imperfections.

Baseball's adoption and integration of technology has been highly uneven. I remember thinking nearly 15 years ago that future TV coverage would be amazing, with new camera angles, split screens of live action, and we'd be freed of the tyranny imposed on television coverage by antiquated traditions like camera placement. I dreamed of split screens showing defender and umpire movement, and the real-time race between sprinting outfielders and baserunners, along with cool polygon analysis of pitching motion and velocity changes. I'm still waiting for anything remotely resembling technological advancement on the coverage side. So far, I've learned only about DirecTV's wanting an extra few bucks for inclusion of high definition in the Extra Innings package. (I warned you about the whining.) There's still a very long road to walk to really take advantage of the technological tools available. I am afraid that the change of the channel mix for baseball will mean less attention to high-end features for television as other channels increase their relative importance.

At the End of the Day, What Has MLB Done?
Faced with channel partners on television facing the eventual prospect of dramatically reduced advertising revenue, and increasing channel conflict, they've vertically integrated with the introduction of the MLB Network. As of this writing, MLBN has not launched, but based on the experience of MLBAM, it's unlikely the venture will fail because of a lack of vision. There will be some different challenges at MLBN than at MLB.com, and the impact of what promises to be a very challenging economic environment remains to be seen, but long term it's better to bet on a network that you know won't spend 40 percent of its time in August covering NFL minicamps rather than baseball.

In more general terms, MLB's done a very admirable job of reducing their critical vulnerabilities to the whims of their partners. To make a comparison, de Gaulle pushed France's nuclear weapons program because he didn't believe that the United States would go nuclear and commit suicide to defend France's sovereignty. Similarly, the MLB braintrust doesn't believe for a second that ESPN will act in MLB's best interest in the case of conflict with the 2011 AquaPoker Open in Dubai. Betting on perfect or favorable overlap of interests is a bad move—ESPN, Fox, CBS, ABC, NBC, or any other network would gleefully kick Maya Angelou down a flight of stairs as long as they had enough cameras set up, and Ryan Seacrest around host the event.

As people moved to the web, so did MLB, with a large investment and a pretty clear idea of what they wanted to accomplish. They've been able to take their signature, the in-person baseball game, and make it available at a lower time and money cost, reaching new customers and existing customers with a product offering that both find appealing. MLBAM's impact is far greater than merely maintaining MLB.com, but also serves as the intelligence engine for MLB's presence, diversification, and product development efforts off the field. I mean, this is an organization that has its act together to an extent that competitors outsource their media production and management to it. Can you imagine a circumstance where Google is so impressed with Microsoft's hosting technology that it outsources its hosting to Redmond? It's nice to make money as a service provider for your competitor, and if it actually comes to pass, you're doing something very right.

At the ballpark, the game's as strong as ever. Attendance is fine, considering ticket prices, the players on the field are paid exceptionally well, enough so that baseball remains an attractive career option for the very best athletes. The fields on which the game is played have never been newer, greener, or packed with more opportunities for profit, both in terms of concessions and out-of-home advertising.

In the media, MLB has responded to challenges like Pete Rose and the steroid scandal as well as any could reasonably expect. The bloviating punditry will continue to bring steroids up from time to time, but by and large, the response of MLB and the MLBPA has been very good. Reasonable policies are in place, and there's little perception among the public or the customers that steroids will be a problem in say, 24 months. That whole issue was exacerbated by the relationships between MLB, Congress, and the media—the last place you want to be is caught between a unipolar high-profile issue, hypocritical righteous indignation in Congress, and a camera. (One wonders whether, in retrospect, there might have been other issues that were worth attention on Capitol Hill.)

One thing that MLB never gets credit for, at least around the BP offices, is that they've actually undertaken and executed a lot of changes without really losing their soul. It would have been very easy over the past 25 years to really mess the game up. The 1994 season was effectively lost for many, but the reaction of all parties was pretty reasonable. The game on the field is so indescribably perfect as to allow the papering over of many mistakes, and the powers that be haven't really messed with it. For all the noise about stuff like the DH, ticket pricing, player salaries, and everything else, there's still a heck of a lot of baseball, it's still a daily narrative and addiction, and you just can't say that about most entertainment ventures. Yes, NASCAR's grown faster, but consider where MLB and NASCAR were starting from. There have been plenty of opportunities for MLB to completely implode from a public appetite standpoint, and they could well have messed up the game on the field. They haven't. That's worth something. That's worth a lot, actually, if you ask, say, a Lehman Brothers alum.

The next five or 10 years are, unfortunately, going to be very interesting. My own forecast for the American economy is considerably less sanguine than most people I speak with, and I'm counting on my consistent and prodigious ability to make forecasting errors to deliver our economy to a period of secular, robust growth. But if things are bad, there's going to be disparate impacts on different teams, and things like planning and budgeting will be increasingly difficult for those most severely affected. Some of this past winter's free agents are already seeing significantly lower contract offers than they expected, particularly players in the middle of the market. We can only hope that our biggest economic concern three years from now will be a glimmer of jealousy over the huge amount of money that A-Rod's being paid to be an average first baseman. From a marketing perspective, MLB's actions to date are responsible for the league being in a pretty good position to prosper no matter what the economy as a whole does.

The Baseball Prospectus
Top 100 Prospects

Kevin Goldstein

This is my third Top 100 Prospects list for Baseball Prospectus, and looking back at the last two versions, it seems we've done pretty well by our readers. Last year this list told you that Geovany Soto would be one of the best catchers in the National League immediately, and that Neftali Feliz was posed for a huge breakout in his full season debut. Still, prospect-ranking is not an exact science: I also said that J.R. Towles would be a .280-.300 hitter, a prediction by which I was only off by about half. Ranking prospects combines a number of factors. The first is combination of what a player is doing (performance), combined with knowledge of how the player is doing it (scouting). You can't rank prospects accurately without talking to people in the game, as two players with equal stats at the same level, position and age can both have vastly different projections based on how evolved their tools and skills are, and how much growth remains. The other major factor is one that doesn't always resonate well with some of our core readers, and that's instinct born of experience. You need to be around this for awhile, to be the kind of person who spends their free time looking at 20-year-old stats from the Pioneer League, or what a team has done in the fifth-round for the last decade to generate an understanding of who is a prospect and who isn't. It's not necessarily something that is totally quantifiable as much as it is identifying patterns in the sand. Nobody will ever get it totally right; the goal is only to get better every year.

1. Matt Wieters, C, Orioles
How many catchers in modern baseball history have profiled to hit third in the lineup of a championship club? Wieters does just that, and he has switch-hitting skills and well above-average defense.

2. David Price, LHP, Rays
What you saw in October was no mirage, as Price has two plus-plus offering and the makeup to close games in October despite having just 14 innings of big league experience. He's a true ace who will ensure that the Rays are here to stay.

3. Madison Bumgarner, LHP, Giants
A tall, power left-hander with mid-90s heat, a plus breaking ball, and impeccable command, Bumgarner was the best pitcher in the minors last year, with a nearly 8-to-1 strikeout-to-walk ratio, and with scouting reports as impressive as the numbers.

4. Pedro Alvarez, 3B, Pirates
More noted for his draft shenanigans than for his play in 2008, make no mistake—Alvarez is a massive talent who could move quickly, and he gives Pittsburgh the true impact bat they've been so desperately pining for.

5. Travis Snider, OF, Blue Jays
After moving from High-A to the majors in 2008, Snider might already be the best hitter in the Jays' organization, majors included. Once he reduces his strikeouts, he's an MVP candidate.

6. Neftali Feliz, RHP, Rangers
One of the best power arms around, Feliz supplements a fastball that can touch triple digits with a much-improved slider and a changeup, leaving no more room for debate as to whether or not he'll be a starter in the end. He will, and an ace-level one at that.

7. Rick Porcello, RHP, Tigers
Don't worry about the low strikeout rate, and remember that the Tigers forced Porcello to learn how to pitch in 2008, limiting his pitch counts and the use of his breaking balls. Even with those limitations, he still led the High-A Florida State League in ERA as a teenager.

8. Colby Rasmus, OF, Cardinals
His poor first half of last year isn't overly concerning; all of the tools that will make him become the National League's version of Grady Sizemore are still in place.

9. Buster Posey, C, Giants

The best player in college baseball this spring, Posey projects as an athletic .300-hitting catcher with average power and outstanding defense.

10. Jason Heyward, OF, Braves

This first-round pick from 2007 is a big, toolsy outfielder who displayed a professional approach and a feel for hard contact in his full-season debut; and at 6-foot-4 and 220 pounds, you know the power is coming.

11. Cameron Maybin, OF, Marlins

Sure he strikes out a lot, but he's still among the most dynamic players in the minors, showcasing true 30-30 potential and outstanding ball-hawking skills. With all of that, we'll live with the whiffs.

12. Dexter Fowler, OF, Rockies

One of baseball's most outstanding athletes, in 2008, Fowler proved that he's more than just another player with a box of potential tools—he's an on-base machine with developing power and Gold Glove–level talent in center field.

13. Tommy Hanson, RHP, Braves

After putting together one of the best seasons in the minors, Hanson made a historic showing in the Arizona Fall League, striking out 49 in 28⅔ innings while allowing just 10 hits and looking like he's nearly big-league ready. He'll be a consistent All-Star performer.

14. Mike Stanton, OF, Marlins

Forget about his power "potential"— Stanton slugged 39 home runs in his full-season debut as an 18-year-old, and if he can curb that propensity for swings and misses, the sky is the limit.

15. Tim Beckham, SS, Rays

The number one overall pick in the 2008 draft grades as above-average in power, speed, and defensive skills, leading some to compare him to a young Barry Larkin.

16. Chris Tillman, RHP, Orioles

The big prize in the Eric Bedard deal, Tillman dominated at Double-A before seeing his 21st birthday. He's one of many young arms in the Baltimore system that might make the O's yet another playoff contender in the American League East.

17. Lars Anderson, 1B, Red Sox

As far as one-dimensional sluggers go, Anderson is as good as they get. He projects for big numbers in all three triple-slash categories, and should come lumbering into the middle of the Boston lineup by 2010.

18. Eric Hosmer, 1B, Royals

No player in the 2008 draft even came close to matching Hosmer's monstrous power outlook, which earned him a $6 million bonus. He's more than just a slugger though, as he has the bat speed and the hand-eye coordination to make consistent contact as well.

19. Brian Matusz, LHP, Orioles

While some scouts bemoan Matusz's lack of a knockout offering, his fastball, curve, and changeup are all above average, as is his command. He's going to move quickly, and he'll form the back end of a very strong one-two punch with Tillman in Baltimore.

20. Michel Inoa, RHP, Athletics

Yes, there are eight million things that can go wrong between now and Inoa's arrival in the big leagues, but scouts that saw him were nearly universal in categorizing his talent as historic.

21. Mike Moustakas, 3B, Royals

Moustakas's slow start was attributed to bad weather and his adjusting to the pro game, but he was the most dangerous power hitter in the Midwest League in the second half, with one of the quickest bats around.

22. Justin Smoak, 1B, Rangers

The Rangers remain baffled as to how Smoak dropped to them in the 2008 draft, but they're not complaining about getting a powerful, switch-hitting, first baseman who is also an outstanding defender. He could be batting third in Arlington by 2011.

23. Trevor Cahill, RHP, Athletics

With a plus fastball, a plus-plus curve, and an advanced approach to the game, Cahill is just one of many outstanding young arms in the A's system that could give the club a rotation to rival that of the Hudson-Mulder-Zito years earlier in the decade.

24. Brett Anderson, LHP, Athletics

If I could rank him 23-A, I would. Cahill has a little more oomph, but Anderson has a superior changeup and excellent command. Scouts are split down the middle as to which one is better, and I'm riding the fence.

25. Andrew McCutchen, OF, Pirates

This toolsy center fielder made great progress at Triple-A on his plate discipline, and now profiles as a true leadoff man, but a dramatic cut in his strikeouts had the side effect of dramatically cutting his power.

26. Matt Dominguez, 3B, Marlins

Seen as a bit of an overdraft with the 12th-overall pick last year, Dominguez's advanced hitting skills and exemplary defense had some scouts comparing him to a young Eric Chavez.

27. Jhoulys Chacin, RHP, Rockies

Chacin is a skinny Venezuelan who pounds the strike zone with a remarkably deep five-pitch arsenal, and while he's not overpowering, he can carve up the plate and hitters never know what's coming next.

28. Gordon Beckham, SS, White Sox

This University of Georgia product has mind-blowing power for a middle infielder and had no trouble putting up an 1119 OPS in the Arizona Fall League shortly after signing. Even if he's forced to slide over to second base, he'll still be a run-producer in the mold of Chase Utley.

29. Wade Davis, RHP, Rays

As if Tampa Bay doesn't have enough young pitching, Davis's combination of mid-90s heat and a devastating breaking ball would likely work in the big-league bullpen right now. He may have to go there until a rotation slot becomes available.

30. Matt LaPorta, 1B, Indians

The big prize in the CC Sabathia deal, LaPorta should replace Ryan Garko at first base by the end of 2009, providing a significant offensive upgrade with plenty of power and walks.

31. Michael Bowden, RHP, Red Sox

Scouts don't care about Bowden's funky mechanics anymore, as he combines plus stuff with plus command and should be first on the list for a call-up to Boston should the need arise.

32. Jarrod Parker, RHP, Diamondbacks

Parker's stuff wasn't quite as good as advertised, and as he hails from chilly Indiana, he's still raw as compared to those Texas and California kids who practice year 'round, but he showcased mid-90s heat and a plus slider in his pro debut. Few were willing to lower his projection, conceding only that his development might take him a little longer than expected.

33. Carlos Santana, C, Indians

Stolen from the Dodgers for Casey Blake at the trading deadline, Santana has middle-of-the-order potential with the bat. He would rank higher if he had better defensive skills.

34. Josh Vitters, 3B, Cubs

The top prospect in the Chicago system by a mile, Vitters' swing is among the prettiest in the minors, and he'll either compete for batting titles in the future or hit a paltry .300 with 20 to 25 home runs.

35. Yonder Alonso, 1B, Reds

An offensive machine at Miami, Alonso is a classic slugging first baseman with tons of power and a patient approach. The only question is, where does he fit in an organization that has Joey Votto?

36. Ben Revere, OF, Twins

A surprise first-round pick in 2007, Revere flirted with .400 during much of his full-season debut, and for a little guy with top-of-the-line speed, his swing also packs a surprising punch.

37. Brett Wallace, 3B, Cardinals

Dubbed "The Walrus" by scouts for his thick, beefy build, Wallace might not be the prettiest player in the world, but he's one of the best hitters, and he had no problem raking at Double-A in his pro debut.

38. Jesus Montero, C, Yankees

A catcher in name only, nobody really cares that Montero will eventually be moved to first base. Competing for a batting title in a full-season league and showcasing plus power while most American kids his age are still in high school denotes a special hitting ability.

39. Aaron Hicks, OF, Twins

While some teams actually preferred him as a pitcher in last year's draft, Hicks is a true five-tool outfielder who was still thought to be raw when he signed, but was surprisingly polished in his pro debut.

40. Derek Holland, LHP, Rangers

Out of nowhere, Holland gained around eight mph on his fastball in 2008, transforming himself from just a decent pitching prospect into one of the most powerful southpaws around. The development of his secondary pitches will determine his ultimate upside.

41. J.P. Arenciba, C, Blue Jays

Who cares if he never takes a walk? Arencibia is an athletic defender with the ability to hit 25 home runs per year, and even without the walks, that's an All-Star.

42. Greg Halman, OF, Mariners

The toolsy Dutch native exploded in 2008 by reaching Double-A and falling just one home run short of a 30-30 season, though his plate discipline is still a bit of a concern.

43. Carlos Carrasco, RHP, Phillies

Some see Carrasco as a right-handed version of Cole Hamels, but with a tick less velocity and a very good changeup that's not quite as ridiculous. Carrasco's not an ace, but he's all but guaranteed to be a mid-rotation starter.

44. Fernando Martinez, OF, Mets

Scouts remain mixed on Martinez; for each one who sees him as an impact player down the road, there's another who sees him as merely average. A full healthy season (which he's yet to have) would do a great deal to clarify things.

45. Wilin Rosario, C, Rockies

No player in the short-season leagues opened more eyes than Rosario, an athletic Dominican who showcased big-time power and a strong arm in the Pioneer League; the Rockies think he has superstar potential.

46. Austin Jackson, CF, Yankees

The Yankees' center fielder of the future should be ready by 2010, and while he lacks any one blow-you-away tool, nearly every aspect of his game is above average.

47. Angel Villalona, 1B, Giants

Villalona's numbers might not impress, but remember that if he spent the next three years in the Sally League, he'd still be younger than most college draftees in 2011. Those are damned good numbers for a 17-year-old, and his potential remains enormous.

48. Christopher Carter, 1B, Athletics

The minor league leader in total bases, Carter has more power than anyone in the system, and he could be knocking on the door for a job in the big leagues if he can repeat his huge performance at Double-A.

49. Desmond Jennings, OF, Rays

This 2007 breakout player's progress was curtailed by numerous injuries in 2008. His tools are still the best in the system, and he displays a potent power/speed combination and a keen eye at the plate.

50. Jordan Schafer, OF, Braves

A mysterious suspension for involvement with HGH led to a slow start at Double-A, but Schafer rebounded with strong second-half lines. He'll be competing for the big-league center field job as early as this spring.

51. Alcides Escobar, SS, Brewers

Arguably the best defensive shortstop in the minors, Escobar could force the Brewers to slide J.J. Hardy to a new position once he proves that he can provide the level of offensive value that he did at Double-A in 2008.

52. Jake Arrieta, RHP, Orioles

A power righty who mysteriously fell to the fifth round in the 2007 draft, Arrieta's low- to mid-90s sinker allowed him to dominate at High-A. He joins a number of other young Orioles to make up one of the most impressive sets of starting pitching prospects in the game.

53. Logan Morrison, 1B, Marlins

The Florida State League batting leader has scouts deep in debate over his power ceiling, but even if it's on the low end, he's still similar in talent to John Olerud. If the power progresses the way some think it can, look out.

54. Wilmer Flores, SS, Mets

An ability to torch professional pitching at the age of 16 and a thick build that will move him off of shortstop sooner than later had some throwing around Miguel Cabrera comps for this high-priced Venezuelan wunderkind.

55. Michael Taylor, OF, Phillies

After three disappointing years at Stanford, this massive right fielder finally rediscovered his high school swing and had one of the minor league's biggest breakout seasons, being compared by one scout to a right-handed Dave Parker.

56. Jordan Zimmerman, RHP, Nationals

The Former Division-III star took a bigger step forward than anyone in the Washington system last year, handling Double-A with aplomb and setting himself up for a big-league look in 2009.

57. Brett Lawrie, C, Brewers

One of the best hitting prospects to ever come out of Canada, nobody questions Lawrie's plus-plus power, and he could rocket skyward this year if his conversion to full-time catching meets with success.

58. Mat Gamel, 3B, Brewers

The best hitter in the minors during the first half stumbled and became one of the worst in the second half;

even more concerning was his significantly subpar defense at the hot corner.

59. Ethan Martin, RHP, Dodgers

This 2008 first-round pick is already a pitcher, not a thrower, with three plus offerings and a level of athleticism that affords an abundance of projection.

60. Tim Alderson, RHP, Giants

The tall right-hander had no trouble getting out High-A hitters as a teenager in his pro debut, and while he lacks upside because of his average stuff, his control is impeccable, so good that he could be a big-league starter by the time he's 21.

61. Phillippe Aumont, RHP, Mariners

Aumont is a massive French-Canadian who has one of the heaviest fastballs around, but he's still an unfinished product. He'll need to improve his efficiency and command, or some may start to wonder if he'd be better off as a closer.

62. Reid Brignac, SS, Rays

Despite Brignac's offensive struggles at the upper levels of the Rays' system, he made great strides with the glove and is now expected to develop into a plus defender. He'll hit 20-plus home runs, but because of his low batting average and impatience the power will come at the cost of a lot of outs.

63. Jordan Walden, RHP, Angels

He's a pure power pitcher with one of the best sinkers in prospectville, a bowling ball that sits in the mid-90s. He could become a star if the rest of his arsenal comes around.

64. James McDonald, RHP, Dodgers

While McDonald's secondary stuff is better than his merely average fastball, his ability to change speeds and paint the corners earned him a spot on the postseason roster, and it will likely earn him a permanent spot on the big-league staff.

65. Michael Burgess, OF, Nationals

From the same high school that produced Gary Sheffield, Burgess's incredible bat speed and plus-plus raw power out of a smallish package drew the occasional Sheffield comparison, though he lacks the six-time All-Star's patience, his contact skills, and, luckily for Burgess, his temper.

66. Michael Main, RHP, Rangers

While a cracked rib limited Main to just 13 starts in 2008, he stepped forward with an abundance of right-now stuff and as much promise and athleticism as any pitcher around, making him one of 2009's best breakout candidates.

67. Chris Perez, RHP, Cardinals

The Cardinals' closer of the future has a classic plus-fastball/plus-slider combination; he's only a modicum of improved control away from being elite.

68. Engel Beltre, OF, Rangers

With plus-plus speed, Beltre covers an enormous amount of acreage in center, and he's a deadly weapon on the basepaths. His arm is above average and he has excellent raw power. He more than held his own in the tough Midwest League as an 18-year-old. So why isn't he higher? Because he'll swing at *anything*.

69. Mat Latos, RHP, Padres

Like many high-ceiling young power pitchers, Latos has the requisite big frame and equally big fastball, but what separates him from the pack is advanced command for his age.

70. Scott Elbert, LHP, Dodgers

It wasn't surprising to see Elbert struggle with his control following shoulder surgery, but his curveball is so good that he had little trouble advancing from Double-A to the majors shortly after his return.

71. Nick Adenhart, RHP, Angels

Scouts are confused about Adenhart's difficulties at Triple-A last year; his stuff didn't regress at all, but his confidence seems to be shot. It's hard to imagine where things go from here.

72. Jeremy Jeffress, RHP, Brewers

One of the hardest throwers in the minors, he's capable of touching 100 mph consistently and making hitters look foolish with his curve, but Jeffress is still held back by his command and makeup issues. He always seems to be on the verge of a huge step forward.

73. Elvis Andrus, SS, Rangers

The Rangers are already talking about moving Michael Young over (or out) in order to accommodate Andrus, who offers far-superior defense and remarkable speed, though his bat will fit better at the bottom of the lineup.

74. Aaron Poreda, LHP, White Sox

Few lefthanders in the game can match Poreda's upper-90s heat, and while he made some progress with his off-speed offerings in 2008, many still see him as a power reliever down the road.

75. Michael Saunders, OF, Mariners

A big, ultra-athletic Canadian with very good power and speed, Saunders lacks true impact potential, but his plentiful tools and his skills across the board should deliver him to the big leagues as an everyday starter by 2010.

76. Jason Castro, C, Astros

An overdraft with the 10th overall pick last June, Castro nonetheless profiles as a fine everyday backstop with both offensive and defensive value.

77. Andrew Lambo, OF, Dodgers

The best pure hitter in the Dodgers system, Lambo's bat is his only plus tool, and he'll have to prove himself at the upper levels to convince scouts that he has the ability to put up the numbers associated with a big-league left fielder.

78. Gorkys Hernandez, OF, Braves

Limited by a hamstring injury in 2008, the prize of the Edgar Renteria trade has outstanding wheels and fantastic defensive skills, and he's added an improved approach at the plate. Power, or rather the lack thereof, is his only weakness.

79. Angel Salome, C, Brewers

While a catcher with a nearly 1000 OPS at Double-A would normally rank higher, scouts have trouble getting past Salome's cube-like frame. At five-foot-seven and 200 pounds, he's a tree stump hampered by subpar defense.

80. Freddie Freeman, 1B, Braves

A hulking slugger with the ability to hit for both average and power, there is some concern about Freeman's hacking style and big frame, but many think he's one of the minor league's most underrated bats.

81. Ross Detwiler, LHP, Nationals

One of the top pitchers in the 2007 draft, Detwiler struggled with his mechanics during his full-season debut, but he got back on track late in the year, rekindling his low- to mid-90s velocity to go along with an outstanding curveball.

82. Kyle Skipworth, C, Marlins

This offense-oriented receiver has the kind of raw power and athleticism (for a catcher) that is rarely found in a backstop, but there are questions about his ability to stay behind the plate.

83. Nick Weglarz, OF, Indians

Weglarz has the plate discipline of a veteran and the ability to hit the ball out of the park to all fields, but he's also continuing to grow; that makes some fear he'll end up as a base-clogging designated-hitter type.

84. Kellen Kulbacki, OF, Padres

After a slow start while trying to play through minor injuries, Kulbacki was among the best hitters in the minors during the second half, batting .370/.449/.680 after the All-Star break. The bat is the lone tool, but it's a very good one.

85. Jeff Samardzija, RHP, Cubs

A much-improved slider rocketed Samardzija to the big-league bullpen, but he's still bafflingly inconsistent. He doesn't miss as many bats as a pitcher with his kind of stuff should.

86. Todd Frazier, SS, Reds

The former Little League World Series hero continues to hit wherever he goes, but he's been moved around defensively so much that nobody knows where his future lies, other than "not at shortstop." Oddly, "Not at shortstop" also describes all of the guys the Reds play there in the majors.

87. Josh Reddick, OF, Red Sox

A sleeper no longer, Reddick has all of the tools, including above-average power and a cannon for an arm, but he's going to have to tone down his aggressive batting approach at the upper levels.

88. David Cooper, 1B, Blue Jays

An offensive machine at Cal, the 2008 first-round pick hit over .300 at three different levels post-signing, and while he hit just five home runs in his 273 at-bats, many of those 29 doubles will go streaking over the fence as he adjusts to wooden bats.

89. Daniel Schlereth, LHP, Diamondbacks

The son of a former NFL lineman, Schlereth brings a football mentality to the late innings, as well as an upper-90s fastball from the left side and a knee-buckling power curve.

90. Brett Cecil, LHP, Blue Jays

With an above-average fastball for a southpaw and the best slider in the organization, Brett Cecil reached Triple-A in his full-season debut, and he could be a middle-of-the-rotation factor by the end of the year.

91. Jose Tabata, OF, Pirates

After a miserable two-thirds of a season with the Yankees' Double-A affiliate, Tabata came to life after the Xavier Nady trade, finally showcasing the outstanding bat speed that had made him such a highly regarded prospect in the first place.

92. Kyle Drabek, RHP, Phillies

This former first-round pick made an impressive return from Tommy John surgery, and showed improved mechanics and command. He could rocket up this list with a healthy full season.

93. Adrian Cardenas, SS, Athletics

Cardenas was the best prospect acquired in the Joe Blanton deal, and though most believe that he will eventually have to move off of shortstop, they also believe he'll hit .300 in the majors.

94. Jefry Marte, 3B, Mets

Yet another talented Latin American teenager in the Mets system, Marte doesn't have Wilmer Flores' offensive potential, but he's no slouch there either; he finished among the Gulf Coast League leaders in batting average and slugging, despite the fact that he was 16 years old at the start of the season.

95. Ivan DeJesus Jr., SS, Dodgers

Ivan's kid led the Southern League with a .419 on-base percentage, but his struggles against left-handers and the fear that his range is a tad limited for the left side of the infield are significant concerns.

96. Drew Stubbs, OF, Reds

The best defensive center fielder in the minor leagues has shortened his swing to cut down on his strikeouts, but sacrificed some power to do so, leaving him as more of a potential 15-30 asteroid than a 30-30 star.

97. Daniel Bard, RHP, Red Sox

This former first-round pick made an inspiring recovery from a case of the yips in 2007, blowing away hitters with a fastball that can reach 100 mph—and he can now actually keep in the strike zone. If he can make progress with the slider, he has shutdown closer potential.

98. Brandon Erbe, RHP, Orioles

Despite some struggles with control and location in 2008, Erbe still struck out more than a batter per inning as a 20-year-old at High-A, though scouts are mixed as to whether he'll end up as a starter or reliever.

99. Brandon Allen, 1B, White Sox

Built like a linebacker (which he once was) and loaded with pop, Allen has the best power in the White Sox system, and he's surprisingly athletic for his size. That high strikeout rate is his only problem.

100. Adys Portillo, RHP, Padres

The best pitcher on the Latin American market last year not named Inoa, Portillo signed for a $2 million dollar bonus. He already touches 93 mph as a 16-year-old, and he has a frame built for pitching success.

Team Name Key and Park Factors

Clay Davenport

League, Level, and Affiliation as of 2008

Abbr.	Team	League	Level	Affiliation	2006	2007	2008	Abbr.	Team	League	Level	Affiliation	2006	2007	2008
ABE	Aberdeen	NYP	A-	Orioles	967	949	954	COH	Columbus (OH)	INT	AAA	Nationals	979	988	983
ABQ	Albuquerque	PCL	AAA	Marlins	1118	1123	1126	COL	Colorado	NL	MLB	Rockies	1076	1066	1063
AGU	Aguascaliente	MEX	Mexico	—	1067	1045	999	CSC	Charleston (SC)	SAL	A	Yankees	968	949	938
AKR	Akron	EAS	AA	Indians	1015	1008	1008	CSP	Colo. Springs	PCL	AAA	Rockies	1078	1088	1096
ALT	Altoona	EAS	AA	Pirates	1001	997	990	DAY	Daytona	FSL	A+	Cubs	1053	1060	1079
ARI	Arizona	NL	MLB	Diamondbacks	1050	1054	1060	DEL	Delmarva	SAL	A	Orioles	960	933	916
ARK	Arkansas	TXS	AA	Angels	1025	1004	977	DET	Detroit	AL	MLB	Tigers	998	1015	1029
ASH	Asheville	SAL	A	Rockies	1100	1089	1076	DNV	Danville	APL	Rookie	Braves	919	939	961
ATL	Atlanta	NL	MLB	Braves	986	981	982	DUN	Dunedin	FSL	A+	BlueJays	1036	1022	1018
AUB	Auburn	NYP	A-	BlueJays	992	987	999	DUR	Durham	INT	AAA	Rays	1039	1050	1055
AUG	Augusta	SAL	A	Giants	958	970	968	DYT	Dayton	MDW	A	Reds	1014	1006	1016
BAK	Bakersfield	CLF	A+	Rangers	967	983	985	ELZ	Elizabethton	APL	Rookie	Twins	977	987	997
BAL	Baltimore	AL	MLB	Orioles	1001	1012	1023	ERI	Erie	EAS	AA	Tigers	1033	1056	1076
BAT	Batavia	NYP	A-	Cardinals	996	1020	1024	EUG	Eugene	NWN	A-	Padres	1006	997	988
BIL	Billings	PIO	Rookie	Reds	977	973	965	EVE	Everett	NWN	A-	Mariners	1016	985	967
BIN	Binghamton	EAS	AA	Mets	1014	1010	1013	FKU	SoftBank	JPL	Japan	—	973	995	1008
BIR	Birmingham	SOU	AA	WhiteSox	955	948	932	FLO	Florida	NL	MLB	Marlins	964	978	981
BLT	Beloit	MDW	A	Twins	1014	1017	1024	FRD	Frederick	CRL	A+	Orioles	1031	1029	1042
BLU	Bluefield	APL	Rookie	Orioles	1009	995	985	FRE	Fresno	PCL	AAA	Giants	970	971	984
BNC	Burlington (NC)	APL	Rookie	Royals	974	970	963	FRI	Frisco	TXS	AA	Rangers	1003	997	981
BOI	Boise	NWN	A-	Cubs	1047	1053	1052	FTM	Ft Myers	FSL	A+	Twins	980	974	963
BOS	Boston	AL	MLB	RedSox	1032	1041	1049	FTW	Ft Wayne	MDW	A	Padres	982	1006	1026
BOW	Bowie	EAS	AA	Orioles	971	967	960	GRB	Greensboro	SAL	A	Marlins	1048	1062	1070
BRI	Bristol	APL	Rookie	WhiteSox	978	967	949	GRF	Great Falls	PIO	Rookie	WhiteSox	989	1003	1000
BRO	Brooklyn	NYP	A-	Mets	973	971	965	GRL	Great Lakes	MDW	A	Dodgers	—	974	969
BRV	Brevard County	FSL	A+	Brewers	971	966	972	GRN	Greenville	SAL	A	RedSox	1022	1024	1025
BUF	Buffalo	INT	AAA	Indians	1040	1040	1031	GRV	Greeneville	APL	Rookie	Astros	980	1013	1024
BUR	Burlington (IA)	MDW	A	Royals	942	953	970	HAG	Hagerstown	SAL	A	Nationals	992	1013	1031
CAR	Carolina	SOU	AA	Marlins	1014	1019	1021	HAR	Harrisburg	EAS	AA	Nationals	1023	1028	1023
CAS	Casper	PIO	Rookie	Rockies	1031	1037	1038	HDS	High Desert	CLF	A+	Mariners	1108	1105	1107
CCH	Corpus Christi	TXS	AA	Astros	983	998	1012	HEL	Helena	PIO	Rookie	Brewers	975	974	959
CDR	Cedar Rapids	MDW	A	Angels	1019	1013	1024	HIC	Hickory	SAL	A	Pirates	995	1008	1015
CGA	Columbus (GA)	SAL	A	Rays	974	967	962	HNS	Hanshin	JCL	Japan	—	963	943	928
CHA	Chicago W. Sox	AL	MLB	WhiteSox	1032	1034	1039	HOU	Houston	NL	MLB	Astros	995	992	997
CHB	Chiba Lotte	JPL	Japan	—	946	974	997	HRO	Hiroshima	JCL	Japan	—	1070	1058	1039
CHH	Chihuahua	MEX	Mexico	—	—	1044	1039	HUD	Hudson Valley	NYP	A-	Rays	954	954	940
CHN	Chicago Cubs	NL	MLB	Cubs	1037	1042	1042	HUN	Huntsville	SOU	AA	Brewers	1009	1000	989
CHR	Charlotte	INT	AAA	WhiteSox	1022	1033	1038	IDA	Idaho Falls	PIO	Rookie	Royals	1013	1006	1028
CHT	Chattanooga	SOU	AA	Reds	1021	1024	1009	IND	Indianapolis	INT	AAA	Pirates	981	972	964
CHU	Chunichi	JCL	Japan	—	948	965	978	IOW	Iowa	PCL	AAA	Cubs	979	982	966
CIN	Cincinnati	NL	MLB	Reds	1035	1040	1031	JAM	Jamestown	NYP	A-	Marlins	1093	1079	1054
CLE	Cleveland	AL	MLB	Indians	987	1006	1010	JAX	Jacksonville	SOU	AA	Dodgers	968	951	949
CLN	Clinton	MDW	A	Rangers	1011	1004	1006	JCY	Johnson City	APL	Rookie	Cardinals	989	974	975
CLR	Clearwater	FSL	A+	Phillies	1008	989	971	JUP	Jupiter	FSL	A+	Marlins	906	912	923
CMP	Campeche	MEX	Mexico	—	930	932	926	KAN	Kannapolis	SAL	A	WhiteSox	1010	1013	1018

613

Abbr.	Team	League	Level	Affiliation	2006	2007	2008	Abbr.	Team	League	Level	Affiliation	2006	2007	2008
KCA	Kansas City	AL	MLB	Royals	1014	1018	1013	PME	Portland (ME)	EAS	AA	RedSox	1016	1006	996
KIN	Kinston	CRL	A+	Indians	981	980	982	POR	Portland (OR)	PCL	AAA	Padres	960	950	938
KNC	Kane County	MDW	A	A's	1051	1041	1027	POT	Potomac	CRL	A+	Nationals	974	971	974
KNG	Kingsport	APL	Rookie	Mets	1042	1054	1052	PRI	Princeton	APL	Rookie	Rays	1037	1020	1009
LAA	LA Angels	AL	MLB	Angels	986	1005	1017	PUE	Puebla	MEX	Mexico	—	1053	1063	1079
LAK	Lakeland	FSL	A+	Tigers	1030	1029	1032	PUL	Pulaski	APL	Rookie	BlueJays	1075	—	1088
LAN	LA Dodgers	NL	MLB	Dodgers	990	988	971	PZA	Minatitlan	MEX	Mexico	—	905	1033	1032
LEH	Lehigh Valley	INT	AAA	Phillies	—	—	964	QUD	Quad Cities	MDW	A	Cardinals	985	978	969
LEL	Lake Elsinore	CLF	A+	Padres	967	959	956	RAK	Rakuten	JPL	Japan	—	1009	1001	996
LEX	Lexington	SAL	A	Astros	1011	1004	996	RCU	R. Cucamonga	CLF	A+	Angels	979	972	963
LKC	Lake County	SAL	A	Indians	1017	1007	998	REA	Reading	EAS	AA	Phillies	1007	1018	1029
LNC	Lancaster	CLF	A+	RedSox	1103	1109	1106	RIC	Richmond	INT	AAA	Braves	1007	1012	1025
LNS	Lansing	MDW	A	BlueJays	1002	1016	1017	ROC	Rochester	INT	AAA	Twins	1022	1022	1021
LOU	Louisville	INT	AAA	Reds	994	1006	1024	ROM	Rome	SAL	A	Braves	960	971	980
LOW	Lowell	NYP	A-	RedSox	987	995	1008	ROU	Round Rock	PCL	AAA	Astros	938	943	945
LVG	Las Vegas	PCL	AAA	Dodgers	1086	1087	1091	SAC	Sacramento	PCL	AAA	A's	931	919	923
LWD	Lakewood	SAL	A	Phillies	927	932	945	SAN	San Antonio	TXS	AA	Padres	925	925	934
LYN	Lynchburg	CRL	A+	Pirates	1007	1022	1029	SAR	Sarasota	FSL	A+	Reds	1016	1021	1016
MCD	Mexico City	MEX	Mexico	—	1092	1103	1119	SAV	Savannah	SAL	A	Mets	972	972	967
MCL	Monclova	MEX	Mexico	—	992	988	992	SBN	South Bend	MDW	A	Diamondbacks	992	1011	1019
MCT	Tigres	MEX	Mexico	—	1036	921	927	SBR	Inland Empire	CLF	A+	Dodgers	948	937	931
MEM	Memphis	PCL	AAA	Cardinals	934	938	945	SCO	State College	NYP	A-	Pirates	984	993	1009
MHV	Mahoning Val.	NYP	A-	Indians	1030	1040	1036	SDN	San Diego	NL	MLB	Padres	917	907	903
MID	Midland	TXS	AA	A's	1010	1012	1007	SEA	Seattle	AL	MLB	Mariners	953	957	954
MIL	Milwaukee	NL	MLB	Brewers	1004	1002	998	SEI	Seibu	JPL	Japan	—	1007	1018	1020
MIN	Minnesota	AL	MLB	Twins	982	968	961	SFD	Springfield	TXS	AA	Cardinals	992	1012	1037
MIS	Mississippi	SOU	AA	Braves	964	965	970	SFN	San Francisco	NL	MLB	Giants	1000	998	1002
MNT	Montgomery	SOU	AA	Rays	1003	1007	1020	SJO	San Jose	CLF	A+	Giants	879	873	874
MOB	Mobile	SOU	AA	Diamondbacks	1008	1009	1012	SLC	Salt Lake	PCL	AAA	Angels	1085	1081	1077
MOD	Modesto	CLF	A+	Rockies	966	954	956	SLM	Salem (VA)	CRL	A+	Astros	962	971	976
MSO	Missoula	PIO	Rookie	Diamondbacks	1008	1005	998	SLN	St Louis	NL	MLB	Cardinals	979	975	975
MTR	Monterrey	MEX	Mexico	—	957	944	952	SLO	Salem-Keizer	NWN	A-	Giants	1000	1021	1047
MYR	Myrtle Beach	CRL	A+	Braves	974	978	984	SLP	San Luis Potosi	MEX	Mexico	—	1039	—	—
NAS	Nashville	PCL	AAA	Brewers	957	945	936	SLT	Saltillo	MEX	Mexico	—	1041	1048	1067
NBR	New Britain	EAS	AA	Twins	1016	1018	1014	SLU	St Lucie	FSL	A+	Mets	1003	1011	1020
NHP	New Hampshire	EAS	AA	BlueJays	996	1009	1018	SPO	Spokane	NWN	A-	Rangers	1053	1039	1004
NIP	Nippon Ham	JPL	Japan	—	974	964	963	STA	Staten Island	NYP	A-	Yankees	899	918	937
NOR	Norfolk	INT	AAA	Orioles	913	923	943	STO	Stockton	CLF	A+	A's	967	976	983
NRW	Connecticut	EAS	AA	Giants	884	878	888	SWB	Scranton/W-B	INT	AAA	Yankees	987	978	966
NWA	NW Arkansas	TXS	AA	Royals	—	—	1018	SWM	SW Michigan	MDW	A	—	1027	—	—
NWO	New Orleans	PCL	AAA	Mets	928	929	907	SYR	Syracuse	INT	AAA	BlueJays	1039	1027	1012
NYA	NY Yankees	AL	MLB	Yankees	997	1013	1020	TAB	Tabasco	MEX	Mexico	—	878	897	912
NYN	NY Mets	NL	MLB	Mets	964	961	961	TAC	Tacoma	PCL	AAA	Mariners	921	923	934
OAK	Oakland	AL	MLB	A's	970	956	957	TAM	Tampa	FSL	A+	Yankees	997	1006	1003
OAX	Oaxaca	MEX	Mexico	—	1052	1077	1085	TBA	Tampa Bay	AL	MLB	Rays	985	979	973
OGD	Ogden	PIO	Rookie	Dodgers	1055	1046	1036	TCV	Tri-City Val.	NYP	A-	Astros	1061	1075	1084
OKL	Oklahoma	PCL	AAA	Rangers	947	956	968	TEN	Tennessee	SOU	AA	Cubs	1042	1057	1065
OMA	Omaha	PCL	AAA	Royals	972	982	985	TEX	Texas	AL	MLB	Rangers	1024	1013	1018
ONE	Oneonta	NYP	A-	Tigers	1055	1047	1041	TIJ	Tijuana	MEX	Mexico	—	990	975	972
ORM	Orem	PIO	Rookie	Angels	923	946	976	TOL	Toledo	INT	AAA	Tigers	939	939	934
ORX	Orix	JPL	Japan	—	982	975	968	TOR	Toronto	AL	MLB	BlueJays	1011	996	991
OTT	Ottawa	INT	AAA	—	997	968	—	TRI	Tri-City	NWN	A-	Rockies	931	958	985
PAW	Pawtucket	INT	AAA	RedSox	1026	1034	1034	TRN	Trenton	EAS	AA	Yankees	949	947	930
PEO	Peoria	MDW	A	Cubs	979	965	953	TUC	Tucson	PCL	AAA	Diamondbacks	1036	1023	1015
PHI	Philadelphia	NL	MLB	Phillies	1022	1016	1007	TUL	Tulsa	TXS	AA	Rockies	1010	1015	1016
PIT	Pittsburgh	NL	MLB	Pirates	992	981	965	VAN	Vancouver	NWN	A-	A's	949	961	968
PMB	Palm Beach	FSL	A+	Cardinals	949	953	950	VAQ	Vaqueros Laguna	MEX	Mexico	—	1042	1001	966

Abbr.	Team	League	Level	Affiliation	2006	2007	2008
VER	Vermont	NYP	A-	Nationals	1038	1048	1044
VIS	Visalia	CLF	A+	Diamondbacks	999	1009	1024
VRC	Veracruz	MEX	Mexico	—	890	879	874
VRO	Vero Beach	FSL	A+	Rays	1039	1043	1038
WAS	Washington	NL	MLB	Nationals	950	946	1030
WIC	Wichita	TXS	AA	—	1003	1020	—
WIL	Wilmington	CRL	A+	Royals	984	985	970
WIS	Wisconsin	MDW	A	Mariners	991	997	993
WMI	W Michigan	MDW	A	Tigers	981	978	961
WNS	Winston-Salem	CRL	A+	WhiteSox	1051	1049	1040
WPT	Williamsport	NYP	A-	Phillies	954	925	906
WTN	W Tennessee	SOU	AA	Mariners	1006	1014	1024
WVA	West Virginia	SAL	A	Brewers	1020	1023	1039
YAK	Yakima	NWN	A-	Diamondbacks	956	955	972
YKL	Yakult	JCL	Japan	—	1066	1071	1076
YKO	Yokohama	JCL	Japan	—	1065	1057	1047
YOM	Yomiuri	JCL	Japan	—	950	949	950
YUC	Yucatan	MEX	Mexico	—	881	881	880

The Times, They Are A-Changin'

Clay Davenport

BP is pleased to present a couple of exciting new changes to this year's book, one of which has been long anticipated, and another which has been a source of some conflict between me and the not just the rest of the sabermetric world, but also many of my colleagues here at BP. We'll get to that one second; let's start with the changes in this year's book to how we evaluate defense.

Defense

The biggest change is the new defensive ratings, which are now running from play-by-play (PBP) data. Were we slow to adopt? Yes, but there is at least some reasoning behind it. I have always had a very strong bias in favor of using the same technique throughout the book. This means that I am very reluctant to derive one set of numbers for the majors and another, differently run set for the minors, or one set for 2006 and a different set for 2008; when I assemble the data, everything should be consistent with itself. The only exception has been for leagues where the data is significantly harder to come by, principally Japan, but also the occasional stats from Cuba, Korea, independent, or winter leagues. It has taken us until now to be able to achieve that consistency of data for all of the major and minor leagues we present, for all of the years which we include.

To review, the defensive methods we used before relied on the season aggregate totals. We knew how many putouts and assists there were for each position, and we knew how many hits there were in total. What we didn't know was how many hits went zooming by each player; we had to infer that in various ways. Unfortunately for all of baseball, hits go unnoticed in the traditional fielding records—an oversight of Harry Cartwright and the early scorekeepers that bothers us to this day. It is the hits that go by, more than the errors committed, that separate the bad fielder from the good. When we have a good PBP record, we can correct that oversight, and assign responsibility for every hit to the appropriate fielder. There are some other advantages, as well—the ability to distinguish unassisted putouts is a huge deal for rating first basemen, and you can derive opportunities for double plays and outfield assists. Those are nice, but they're as trivial as a haircut on "The Biggest Loser." It's knowing where the hits go that make the effort worthwhile.

The trick, though, is to have a good PBP record. A dirty little secret of our industry is that even the PBP record is far from clean and complete, and as with the traditional stats it is on the hits that the lapses tend to take place. Partly that's because we cannot make the assumptions we do of other plays. When you see '63' in a scorebook, you don't need to see a 'g' to be pretty sure it was a ground ball (although it could have been a dropped line drive). Too often, singles are recorded as nothing more than 'S'. For the last four years, that hasn't been a problem; there were less than a dozen uncoded hits in all four years combined. But something like 20 percent of the hits in our PBP database for 2004 don't tell us anything about how the ball was hit, and another five percent don't tell us who fielded it. There are a few years in the 1980s where about 75 percent of the hits have no other information about them. I'm still working on a solution I can be comfortable with for handling those.

The best PBP systems rely on highly detailed batted-ball data—a direction for where the ball was hit, some indication of how hard, and the result of the play, with the field broken down into many, fairly small zones. That data is typically available only for the majors. To keep the majors and minors on an even setting, we're dealing with a reduced set of data. Our system, then, is based around the following pieces of information:

- who fielded the ball, which stands in for direction;
- the type of hit, ground, fly, line, or pop;
- whether the pitcher was left- or right-handed;
- whether the batter was left- or right=handed;
- whether or not it was a bunt;
- whether or not there were men on base;
- the result of the play, be it an out, single, double, error, and how far runners advanced.

This leaves us, unfortunately, with a still significant inference problem to handle. The old system needed to distribute all hits to all fielders. The new system reduces those inferences to a smaller number, but still has to make them, because most ground-ball hits end up getting fielded by an outfielder. A ground ball to the left side can belong to either the shortstop or third baseman; a ground ball to center belongs to the shortstop, second baseman, or pitcher; those to the right side belong to either the first or second baseman. Line-drive hits are similarly nebulous; we can't always tell from the PBP who really had the best play on a liner, so the responsibility gets somewhat smeared out over adjacent positions. We do have some cases in our database with more specific hit information—say, a coded location of "5L," which means the ball went between the third baseman and the line—and I have used it to limit that ball to the third baseman. Most of the time, we don't enjoy this kind of specificity. This will create paired errors—a shortstop ranked too low matched with a third baseman ranked too high, for instance—if our assumed distribution is too far removed from reality.

For each possible combination of the events listed above, we want to define the average totals for the league as a whole. Actually, for any given year, I've summed across level; the American and National Leagues are combined into one "league," as the IL and PCL are at AAA, and all the AA leagues, and so on; excuse me for continuing to use the easier "league" to describe that. Consider a right-handed hitter facing a right-handed pitcher, swinging away with no one on, who hits a ground ball to third. That produced an entry in a table that looks like this:

Outs	Singles	Doubles	Triples	Homers	Errors	Total
3539	621	224	5	0	200	4589

Once that table is built, we run through the play-by-play data once again to rate individuals, comparing the results of every play they were involved in to the average expected result:

- If he makes the play, which an average player does 3539/4589, or .771 times, he is credited with +.229 outs, -.135 singles, -.049 doubles, -.001 triples, and -.044 errors.
- Allow a single, and the numbers are -.771 out, +.865 single, -.049 doubles, .001 triple, -.044 error.
- Allow a double, -.771, -.135, +.951, -.001, -.044

And so on. Repeat this for every play, and keep track of the sums for every individual. At the end we use something akin to linear weights to convert those plus/minus values into runs above or below average, the number that is presented to you on the charts.

But Wait! What About Ballparks!

There can be very large park effects on fielding data, especially for outfielders. For instance, here are ratings, in runs, for all outfielders (both teams), in games played by Boston, broken down by Boston home and road games:

	Fenway Park			Other Stadiums			Difference (Fenway-Others)		
	Left	Center	Right	Left	Center	Right	Left	Center	Right
2005	-87	-78	-17	24	-16	4	-111	-62	-21
2006	-39	-31	-10	21	7	4	-60	-38	-14
2007	-41	-29	-14	-2	21	17	-39	-50	-31
2008	-48	-50	-23	16	21	19	-64	-71	-42
Average	-54	-47	-16	+15	+8	+11	-69	-55	-27

To be fair, Boston is the most extreme case, but this means that a full-time left fielder in Boston can be expected to score around a -35 (since the numbers here combine both teams, you need to use half) thanks to the influence of the park. Thankfully, for infielders, the effects are much reduced; the biggest adjustment an infielder was -4.6 (for Texas third basemen), which is probably not even a real signal, just noise in the data.

For the purposes of the book, the defensive park factors were taken as a simple average over the 2005–2008 period (unless the park changed, as in Washington), and scaled to 100 balls hit to each position. A full-time left fielder will be charged with somewhere around 500 balls, so Boston outfielders get a credit of roughly 7 runs per 100 balls hit—a pretty significant adjustment for Manny Ramirez in recent years. The rest of the Boston outfield is similarly harsh. Houston's center field tends to play hard, San Diego's tends to play easy.

The best thing about having the PBP defense, though, isn't necessarily that it makes for better defensive ratings. I think the flexibility you get, the kind of breakdowns you can extract from the data, is just as valuable. For example, Jeff Keppinger had a +1 rating in April and May, before going down with a broken kneecap. He came back a month later, and was a -14 the rest of the way. That's a neat thing to know.

The more detailed PBP data allows us to break down the fielding ratings for every pitcher to create a customized DERA, not one that relies on the team's total defensive rating. We do recognize that this is not a perfect solution. There are certainly sample size issues that make the team numbers more reliable than those for individual pitchers. There are some discrepancies that result from the rather nebulous distinctions between "ground ball," "fly ball," and "line drive." The borders are fuzzy, and a hard-enough hit ground ball is effectively a line drive, as far as reaction times for infielders are concerned. I would guess that the defensive ratings will read as extra bad for a pitcher who gives up a lot of hard-hit balls (i.e., Nate Robertson of the Tigers, who had a defense rating of -22), and good for a pitcher who induces softer contact (Armando Galarraga, same team, but +20). The best and worst pitchers in the majors last year were

Worst		Best	
Nate Robertson, Tigers	-22	Tim Wakefield, Red Sox	+24
Javier Vazquez, White Sox	-19	Armando Galarraga, Tigers	+20
Garret Olson, Orioles	-15	Justin Duchscherer, Athletics	+18
A.J. Burnett, Blue Jays	-14	Cole Hamels, Phillies	+16
Shawn Hill, Nationals	-14	Tim Hudson, Braves	+15
Kevin Millwood, Rangers	-14	Jeremy Guthrie, Orioles	+15
Boof Bonser, Twins	-13	Justin Masterson, Red Sox	+14
Andy Sonnanstine, Rays	-13	John Lannan, Nationals	+14
Brandon Backe, Astros	-12	Cory Wade, Dodgers	+13
Livan Hernandez, Twins	-12	Joakim Soria, Royals	+13

New WARP calculation

Also new this year is that for the first time we are using WARP in the DT cards. WARP stands for Wins Above Replacement Player, and is intended to combine the player's batting, pitching, and fielding skills into one number. This is something we've had on the website for years, but haven't brought into the book before. There is one, very large difference between what we've presented in the book this year (and, by the time you read this, on the website), and what we have seen on the web before.

For years, I have had a peculiarly idiosyncratic way of defining what I meant by "replacement player." The part that threw most people was my definition of replacement defense, which was modeled on the way we defined replacement offense: if replacement-level offense is a level of hitting so bad that it gets you thrown out of the league, then replacement defense should be the level of fielding that gets you bumped to an easier position. My "replacement player" was a lousy hitter, pitcher, and fielder.

The consensus definition of replacement player throughout most of the sabermetric community, however, defined a replacement-level hitter as being an average fielder for his position. This created a discrepancy for a full season player of about 20 runs between my definition and that of the rest of the world—the difference between an average fielder and the typical "worst in the league" fielder. I have been convinced, however, to give up my quixotic definition and join the mainstream.

It is not a particularly willing decision, but there were some results of doing it my way that did not pan out. For instance, the theory behind doing it my way suggested that replacement-level defense should have a wider spread around average at the high-skill positions (C, SS, CF) than around the low-skill positions (1B, LF, RF). It also projected that the difference should have gotten wider—much wider—as you go further back in time, when there were more balls in play. I was running some tests last summer, and realized that these weren't so. The results in time did get a little bit wider, but not nearly as much as I would have expected. The bigger problem, though, was that the typical worst fielder in the league, at any position, in any era, was always on the order of -20 runs. There was no difference between worst shortstops and worst first basemen, nor any difference between shortstops in the 1890s or 1990s. Something around -20 was always the level that managers recognized as too bad to tolerate anymore. And on such a cruel fact, my theory must be rejected.

Our new WARP calculations, then, will use the concept of an average fielder for the position. This means that the calculation needs to know what the "average" hitting level is for each position. This is something I've resisted doing before; the entire reason for coming up with the alternate theory was to avoid using "positional adjustments," a concept I personally despise. The value that comes from a fielding position should properly be defined by the fielding, not by how well the players who play there hit. We would expect that that relationship should be fairly close, and perhaps in a perfect world with perfect information and zero response times the difference in fielding values between positions would exactly equal the difference in batting values between positions. It is a fact that in 1954 and 1955, when Willie, Mickey, and the Duke were in their primes, that the average center fielder in major league baseball was a better hitter than either the average left or right fielder, but I do not believe that the defensive responsibilities of the center fielder had fallen below those of a corner outfielder. I liked that the old system could give a designated hitter a defensive value of zero, and not have to find a way to make that compatible with a first baseman somehow. The difference in hitting between DHs and everybody else is not enough to make up for their defensive absence. Because I do feel so strongly about that, I am not using a strict "average hitter" definition when setting the expected performance level for a position. I am still trying to calculate a total defensive responsibility for each position, based on how many balls are hit to the position and what those results are; this is used to nudge the strict position averages up or down.

And yet, that may prove to be another mistake. The best way to explain it is to provide an example. Consider Jose Reyes of the Mets. Our key facts for him are that he's a shortstop, had a defensive rating of -11 in 2008, hit for a .297 Equivalent Average (EqA), with 121 equivalent runs. He played in 159 games and was responsible for 499 outs.

For our first step, we calculate the average team runs. In our equivalent environment (we've already translated), an average team scores 4.5 runs a game; so Reyes' team should have $159 * 4.5 = 715.5$ runs.

An average shortstop is defined to have an EqA of .251. This will change over time, as the offensive and defensive responsibilities change, but in the current era we're using .251 for shortstops. Catchers use a .234; first, second, and third bases are .275, .255, and .261, respectively; the outfield is .267 for left field, .251 for center, and .267 for right. Pitchers are .125; designated hitters, .285.

Reyes' Batting Runs Above Average, BRAA, equals 5, times outs, times $(eqa^{2.5} - poseqa^{2.5})$. That's a straightforward application of the EqA/EqR conversion. That would be $5 * 499 * (.297^{2.5} - .251^{2.5})$ equals 41.2 runs better than an average shortstop.

Since the average team would score 715.5, a team that had Reyes instead of their average shortstop would score $715.5 + 41.2 = 756.7$ runs.

The same team would allow 715.5 runs, minus the -11 for Reyes, for 726.5. I know I should lose a decimal place for precision there; just stay with me, please.

A team that scores 756.7 runs and allows 726.5 runs will have a winning percentage of .5204, using $R^2/(R^2 + RA^2)$.

Now we need to know what the winning percentage would be for an average team that replaced their shortstop with a replacement shortstop, instead of Reyes. Since we are defining the replacement shortstop to be an average fielder, we know this team will allow an average number of runs, 715.5. We need to know how many runs they will score.

In the past, I've defined a replacement player's EqA as a ratio from the average EqA for the position. This does cause problems, particularly when you get into pitchers, where the average position EqA actually approaches zero. I defined an average EqA, for any position, as .260; I defined replacement EqA as .230. For a full-time player who makes 486 outs per season (162 games, times 27 outs per games, divided by 9 players),

the difference between a .260 EqA and a .230 EqA is 22.11 runs. Replacement-level hitting is thus defined as 22.11 runs below average per 486 outs.

By this definition, since we have 507 outs to replace, the replacement level team will score 715.5 runs, minus (22.11 times 499/486), which is 692.8. A team that scores 692.8 runs and allows 715.5 will have a win percentage of .4839.

It then follows that Reyes' Wins Above Replacement will be his win percentage, .5204, minus the replacement win percentage, .4839, times the 159 games in which he played. That total is 5.8.

The same process for pitchers is very nearly the same, using an average DERA of 4.50 and a replacement level DERA of 5.75. Sticking with Mets, Johan Santana had a 3.46 DERA in 234 translated innings over 34 games. He also picks up a +3 for his fielding, and he hit for an .047 EQA with 69 outs.

His average team scores $34 * 4.5 = 153$ runs. His hitting will cost them 1.7 runs scored ($5 * 69 * (.047^{2.5} - .125^{2.5}) = -1.7$), so that's 151.3.

Defensively, we start from 153. He's +3 on fielding, and that takes us down to 150. His Pitching Runs Above Average (PRAA) = $(4.5 - 3.46) * 234/9 = 27.0$. Subtract that from the average, and the Santana team allows 123 runs. His win percentage, based on 151.3 runs scored and 123.0 allowed, is .6021. If Santana were a relief pitcher, which he's not, we would multiply his PRAA by his Leverage, a measure of the game conditions in which he appeared. Without doing that, closers would be substantially underrated.

The comparison replacement team will score $153 - 22.11 * 69/486$, or 149.9 runs. They will be credited as a zero (0) fielder, so they remain at 153, but they allow 1.25 more runs per nine innings than average. Over 234 innings that will add up 32.5 runs, so they're going to allow 185.5 runs. The replacement win percentage is based on 149.9 scored and 185.5 allowed, for a .3950. Santana's WARP is $(.6021 - .3950) * 34$, or 7.0.

You'll notice that pitchers tend to have a much larger spread between their winning percentage and a replacement player's percentage, than you'll find for position players; however, since it is spread over fewer games, the results tend to come out roughly even.

With that, I hope you enjoy the new way of doing things.

Pecota Leaderboards

Compiled by Ben Lindbergh

HITTERS

Batting Average

RANK	NAME	TEAM	BA
1	Chipper Jones	ATL	.341
2	Albert Pujols	SLN	.339
3	Cristian Guzman	WAS	.323
4	Hanley Ramirez	FLO	.318
5	Matt Wieters	BAL	.311
6	Jose Reyes	NYN	.309
7	Joe Mauer	MIN	.307
8	Dustin Pedroia	BOS	.303
T9	David Wright	NYN	.302
T9	Jody Gerut	SDN	.302
T9	Garrett Atkins	COL	.302
T12	Lance Berkman	HOU	.299
T12	Brian McCann	ATL	.299
14	Randy Winn	SFN	.297
T15	Vladimir Guerrero	LAA	.296
T15	Carlos Lee	HOU	.296
T15	Miguel Cabrera	DET	.296
T15	Ryan Braun	MIL	.296
T19	Manny Ramirez	LAN	.295
T19	Chase Utley	PHI	.295
T19	Conor Jackson	ARI	.295

Home Runs

RANK	NAME	TEAM	HR
1	Ryan Howard	PHI	40
2	Ryan Braun	MIL	37
3	Adam Dunn	ARI	36
4	Albert Pujols	SLN	35
T5	Prince Fielder	MIL	33
T5	Alfonso Soriano	CHN	33
T7	Miguel Cabrera	DET	32
T7	David Wright	NYN	32
9	Matt Wieters	BAL	31
T10	Carlos Peña	TBA	30
T10	Grady Sizemore	CLE	30
T10	Manny Ramirez	LAN	30
T10	Alex Rodriguez	NYA	30
T14	Pat Burrell	PHI	29
T14	Dan Uggla	FLO	29
T14	Mark Reynolds	ARI	29
T14	Chris Davis	TEX	29
T18	Hanley Ramirez	FLO	28
T18	Jack Cust	OAK	28
T18	Jay Bruce	CIN	28
T18	Lance Berkman	HOU	28
T18	Mark Teixeira	NYA	28

Runs Batted In

RANK	NAME	TEAM	RBI
1	Albert Pujols	SLN	124
2	Miguel Cabrera	DET	111
3	Ryan Howard	PHI	110
4	Ryan Braun	MIL	109
5	David Wright	NYN	107
6	Prince Fielder	MIL	105
7	Manny Ramirez	LAN	104
8	Alfonso Soriano	CHN	103
9	Matt Wieters	BAL	102
T10	Justin Morneau	MIN	101
T10	Aramis Ramirez	CHN	101
12	Mark Teixeira	NYA	100
13	Adrian Gonzalez	SDN	99
T14	Grady Sizemore	CLE	98
T14	Alex Rodriguez	NYA	98
T14	Vladimir Guerrero	LAA	98
T14	Adam Dunn	ARI	98
18	Garrett Atkins	COL	97
19	Lance Berkman	HOU	97
T20	Carlos Delgado	NYN	96
T20	Jason Bay	BOS	96
T20	Carlos Beltran	NYN	96

Runs

RANK	NAME	TEAM	RUNS
1	Hanley Ramirez	FLO	128
T2	Jose Reyes	NYN	126
T2	Albert Pujols	SLN	126
4	David Wright	NYN	121
5	Grady Sizemore	CLE	110
6	Carlos Beltran	NYN	106
T7	Ryan Braun	MIL	105
T7	Matt Wieters	BAL	105
T9	Lance Berkman	HOU	104
T9	Chipper Jones	ATL	104
11	Chase Utley	PHI	103
12	Jimmy Rollins	PHI	102
13	Prince Fielder	MIL	99
T14	Alex Rodriguez	NYA	97

RANK	NAME	TEAM	
T14	Ian Kinsler	TEX	97
T14	Adam Dunn	ARI	97
T17	Nick Markakis	BAL	96
T17	Ryan Howard	PHI	96
19	Brian Roberts	BAL	95
T20	Miguel Cabrera	DET	94
T20	Rickie Weeks	MIL	94

Stolen Bases, Major Leaguers

RANK	NAME	TEAM	SB
1	Jose Reyes	NYN	68
2	Jacoby Ellsbury	BOS	42
3	B.J. Upton	TBA	40
T4	Juan Pierre	LAN	39
T4	Willy Taveras	CIN	39
6	Jimmy Rollins	PHI	37
7	Hanley Ramirez	FLO	36
8	Josh Anderson	ATL	33
9	Brett Gardner	NYA	32
10	Brian Roberts	BAL	31
T11	Michael Bourn	HOU	30
T11	Carl Crawford	TBA	30
T13	Chone Figgins	LAA	29
T13	Carlos Gomez	MIN	29
15	Grady Sizemore	CLE	27

Stolen Bases, Minor Leaguers

RANK	NAME	TEAM	SB
1	Eric Young Jr.	COL	42
2	Corey Wimberly	COL	41
3	Derrick Robinson	KCA	40
4	Ben Revere	MIN	33
5	Roger Bernadina	WAS	32
6	Freddy Guzman	DET	30
7	Peter Bourjos	LAA	29
T8	Andrew Romine	LAA	27
T8	Jason Taylor	KCA	27
T10	Quintin Berry	PHI	23
T10	Greg Halman	SEA	23
T10	Ezequiel Carrera	NYN	23

On-Base Percentage

RANK	NAME	TEAM	OBP
T1	Albert Pujols	SLN	.443
T1	Chipper Jones	ATL	.443
3	Nick Johnson	WAS	.410
4	Todd Helton	COL	.405
5	Lance Berkman	HOU	.402
6	David Wright	NYN	.400
7	Hanley Ramirez	FLO	.399
8	Adam Dunn	ARI	.396
9	Matt Wieters	BAL	.395
10	Chris Iannetta	COL	.392

Isolated Power

RANK	NAME	TEAM	ISOP
1	Adam Dunn	ARI	.279
2	Ryan Howard	PHI	.277
3	Albert Pujols	SLN	.271
4	Ryan Braun	MIL	.264
5	Alfonso Soriano	CHN	.256
6	Mark Reynolds	ARI	.246
T7	Pat Burrell	PHI	.243
T7	Manny Ramirez	LAN	.243
9	Prince Fielder	MIL	.241
10	Carlos Peña	TBA	.237

Equivalent Average

RANK	NAME	TEAM	EQA
1	Albert Pujols	SLN	.352
2	Chipper Jones	ATL	.342
T3	Hanley Ramirez	FLO	.324
T3	David Wright	NYN	.324
T5	Matt Wieters	BAL	.319
T5	Lance Berkman	HOU	.319
7	Manny Ramirez	LAN	.316
T8	Carlos Beltran	NYN	.312
T8	Nick Johnson	WAS	.312
10	Alex Rodriguez	NYA	.311

Wins Above Replacement Player, American League

RANK	NAME	TEAM	WARP
1	Matt Wieters	BAL	7.9
2	Grady Sizemore	CLE	7.0
3	Joe Mauer	MIN	6.3
4	Alex Rodriguez	NYA	5.4
5	Mark Teixeira	NYA	5.1
6	Dustin Pedroia	BOS	4.7
7	Miguel Cabrera	DET	4.6
T8	Ian Kinsler	TEX	4.3
T8	Matt Holliday	OAK	4.3
T8	Nick Markakis	BAL	4.3

Wins Above Replacement Player, National League

RANK	NAME	TEAM	WARP
1	Albert Pujols	SLN	9.7
2	Hanley Ramirez	FLO	8.7
3	David Wright	NYN	7.6
4	Jose Reyes	NYN	7.2
5	Carlos Beltran	NYN	7.1
6	Chase Utley	PHI	6.5
7	Chipper Jones	ATL	6.3
8	Lance Berkman	HOU	6.1
9	Brian McCann	ATL	5.9
10	Geovany Soto	CHN	5.8

Value Over Replacement Player, All Hitters

RANK	NAME	TEAM	VORP
1	Albert Pujols	SLN	87.8
2	Hanley Ramirez	FLO	86.2

3	David Wright	NYN	72.3
4	Jose Reyes	NYN	68.4
5	Chipper Jones	ATL	65.0
6	Matt Wieters	BAL	59.6
7	Carlos Beltran	NYN	57.0
8	Chase Utley	PHI	55.8
9	Ryan Braun	MIL	51.4
10	Lance Berkman	HOU	50.9

Value Over Replacement Player, Catcher

RANK	NAME	TEAM	VORP
1	Matt Wieters	BAL	59.6
2	Brian McCann	ATL	48.8
3	Geovany Soto	CHN	42.5
4	Joe Mauer	MIN	41.4
5	Russell Martin	LAN	39.0
6	Chris Iannetta	COL	26.7
7	Pablo Sandoval	SFN	24.1
8	Angel Salome	MIL	21.6
9	Ryan Doumit	PIT	21.4
10	Tyler Flowers	CHA	19.7

Value Over Replacement Player, First Base

RANK	NAME	TEAM	VORP
1	Albert Pujols	SLN	87.8
2	Lance Berkman	HOU	50.9
3	Prince Fielder	MIL	44.7
4	Miguel Cabrera	DET	43.0
5	Ryan Howard	PHI	40.2
6	Adrian Gonzalez	SDN	38.9
7	Mark Teixeira	NYA	36.2
8	Joey Votto	CIN	32.4
9	Carlos Delgado	NYN	27.6
10	Justin Morneau	MIN	26.4

Value Over Replacement Player, Second Base

RANK	NAME	TEAM	VORP
1	Chase Utley	PHI	55.8
2	Kelly Johnson	ATL	41.2
3	Dan Uggla	FLO	38.2
4	Ian Kinsler	TEX	43.9
5	Rickie Weeks	MIL	34.3
6	Dustin Pedroia	BOS	31.8
7	Brandon Phillips	CIN	29.0
8	Brian Roberts	BAL	27.3
9	Robinson Cano	NYA	20.7
10	Orlando Hudson	ARI	20.4

Value Over Replacement Player, Third Base

RANK	NAME	TEAM	VORP
1	David Wright	NYN	72.3
2	Chipper Jones	ATL	65.0
3	Alex Rodriguez	NYA	45.1
4	Aramis Ramirez	CHN	37.8
5	Ryan Zimmerman	WAS	36.3
6	Kevin Kouzmanoff	SDN	36.0

7	Edwin Encarnacion	CIN	34.4
8	Garrett Atkins	COL	30.3
9	Troy Glaus	SLN	29.7
10	Evan Longoria	TBA	28.4

Value Over Replacement Player, Shortstop

RANK	NAME	TEAM	VORP
1	Hanley Ramirez	FLO	86.2
2	Jose Reyes	NYN	68.4
3	Cristian Guzman	WAS	49.1
4	Jimmy Rollins	PHI	44.5
5	J.J. Hardy	MIL	36.3
6	Stephen Drew	ARI	29.6
7	Rafael Furcal	LAN	27.8
8	Derek Jeter	NYA	25.4
9	Yunel Escobar	ATL	23.5
10	Miguel Tejada	HOU	23.2

Value Over Replacement Player, Center Field

RANK	NAME	TEAM	VORP
1	Carlos Beltran	NYN	57.0
2	Grady Sizemore	CLE	42.5
3	Nate McLouth	PIT	40.6
4	Jody Gerut	SDN	39.3
5	Matt Kemp	LAN	33.1
6	Josh Hamilton	TEX	27.6
7	Curtis Granderson	DET	26.8
8	B.J. Upton	TBA	26.6
9	Lastings Milledge	WAS	25.5
10	Chris Young	ARI	24.5

Value Over Replacement Player, Left Field

RANK	NAME	TEAM	VORP
1	Ryan Braun	MIL	51.4
2	Manny Ramirez	LAN	49.0
T3	Matt Holliday	OAK	34.6
T3	Adam Dunn	ARI	34.6
5	Carlos Lee	HOU	34.2
6	Alfonso Soriano	CHN	31.1
7	Pat Burrell	PHI	30.4
8	Raul Ibañez	PHI	26.1
9	Jack Cust	OAK	23.7
10	Jason Bay	BOS	22.0

Value Over Replacement Player, Right Field

RANK	NAME	TEAM	VORP
1	Jayson Werth	PHI	32.7
2	Elijah Dukes	WAS	30.8
3	Andre Ethier	LAN	30.7
4	Jay Bruce	CIN	29.4
5	Hunter Pence	HOU	29.3
6	Corey Hart	MIL	27.7
7	Vladimir Guerrero	LAA	26.3
8	Ryan Ludwick	SLN	26.1
9	Nick Markakis	BAL	23.5
10	Brian Giles	SDN	22.5

Value Over Replacement Player, Designated Hitter

RANK	NAME	TEAM	VORP
1	David Ortiz	BOS	28.7
2	Milton Bradley	TEX	28.0
T3	Billy Butler	KCA	19.3
T3	Jim Thome	CHA	19.3
5	Aubrey Huff	BAL	17.3

Rookie VORP

RANK	NAME	TEAM	VORP
1	Matt Wieters	BAL	59.6
2	Cameron Maybin	FLO	23.5
3	Angel Salome	MIL	21.6
4	Tyler Flowers	CHA	19.7
5	Ben Revere	MIN	19.5
6	Brandon Hicks	ATL	18.8
7	Brett Wallace	SLN	18.1
8	Kyle Blanks	SDN	17.2
9	Colby Rasmus	SLN	15.8
10	Todd Frazier	CIN	15.4

PITCHERS

Wins

RANK	NAME	TEAM	W
1	CC Sabathia	NYA	16
2	Johan Santana	NYN	15
T3	Brandon Webb	ARI	14
T3	Dan Haren	ARI	14
T3	Roy Halladay	TOR	14
T6	Rich Harden	CHN	13
T6	Tim Lincecum	SFN	13
T6	Josh Beckett	BOS	13
T6	Javier Vazquez	ATL	13
T6	A.J. Burnett	NYA	13
T6	Cole Hamels	PHI	13
T6	Ervin Santana	LAA	13
T13	Roy Oswalt	HOU	12
T13	James Shields	TBA	12
T13	Chad Billingsley	LAN	12
T13	Felix Hernandez	SEA	12
T13	Cliff Lee	CLE	12
T13	Brett Myers	PHI	12
T13	Jake Peavy	SDN	12
T13	John Lackey	LAA	12
T13	Justin Verlander	DET	12
T13	Zack Greinke	KCA	12

Strikeouts

RANK	NAME	TEAM	SO
1	Rich Harden	CHN	235
2	Tim Lincecum	SFN	220
3	CC Sabathia	NYA	201
4	Johan Santana	NYN	200
5	Dan Haren	ARI	189
6	Javier Vazquez	ATL	188
7	A.J. Burnett	NYA	178
8	Chad Billingsley	LAN	175
T9	Ervin Santana	LAA	173
T9	Jake Peavy	SDN	173
11	Cole Hamels	PHI	171
12	Felix Hernandez	SEA	170
T13	Max Scherzer	ARI	168
T13	Matt Cain	SFN	168
T13	Brandon Webb	ARI	168
16	Josh Beckett	BOS	167
T17	Scott Kazmir	TBA	164
T17	Zack Greinke	KCA	164
19	Roy Halladay	TOR	159
20	Brett Myers	PHI	158

Earned Run Average (min. 125 IP)

RANK	NAME	TEAM	ERA
1	Rich Harden	CHN	3.04
2	Johan Santana	NYN	3.14
3	Jake Peavy	SDN	3.17
4	Tim Lincecum	SFN	3.25
5	Brandon Webb	ARI	3.29
6	Roy Halladay	TOR	3.31
7	CC Sabathia	NYA	3.43
8	Dan Haren	ARI	3.53
9	Chad Billingsley	LAN	3.55
10	Javier Vazquez	ATL	3.58
11	Roy Oswalt	HOU	3.59
12	Cole Hamels	PHI	3.65
13	Derek Lowe	ATL	3.70
14	Josh Beckett	BOS	3.72
15	Max Scherzer	ARI	3.77
16	Ben Sheets	MIL	3.77
17	Felix Hernandez	SEA	3.81
T18	A.J. Burnett	NYA	3.82
T18	Randy Johnson	SFN	3.82
20	Brett Myers	PHI	3.87

WHIP (min. 125 IP)

RANK	NAME	TEAM	WHIP
1	Rich Harden	CHN	1.12
2	Johan Santana	NYN	1.14
3	Dan Haren	ARI	1.16
T4	Jake Peavy	SDN	1.18
T4	Roy Halladay	TOR	1.18
T6	Cole Hamels	PHI	1.19
T6	CC Sabathia	NYA	1.19
T6	Tim Lincecum	SFN	1.19
T9	Javier Vazquez	ATL	1.21
T9	Josh Beckett	BOS	1.21
11	Ben Sheets	MIL	1.22
12	Roy Oswalt	HOU	1.23
T13	Brandon Webb	ARI	1.24
T13	Ricky Nolasco	FLO	1.24

T13	Kevin Slowey	MIN	1.24
16	James Shields	TBA	1.25
T17	Ervin Santana	LAA	1.26
T17	Justin Duchscherer	OAK	1.26
T19	Aaron Harang	CIN	1.27
T19	Brett Myers	PHI	1.27

Saves

RANK	NAME	TEAM	SV
1	Francisco Rodriguez	NYN	45
2	Mariano Rivera	NYA	36
3	Jonathan Papelbon	BOS	33
4	Joakim Soria	KCA	32
5	Joe Nathan	MIN	31
T6	Brian Wilson	SFN	25
T6	Brad Lidge	PHI	25
T6	Jose Valverde	HOU	25
9	Brian Fuentes	LAA	23
10	George Sherrill	BAL	21
T11	B.J. Ryan	TOR	19
T11	Kerry Wood	CLE	19
T11	Trevor Hoffman	MIL	19
14	Bobby Jenks	CHA	18
15	Francisco Cordero	CIN	17
16	Matt Capps	PIT	16
T17	Takashi Saito	LAN	15
T17	J.J. Putz	NYN	15
19	C.J. Wilson	TEX	14
20	Jonathan Broxton	LAN	13

Win Expectancy over Replacement, Lineup-adjusted (WXRL)

RANK	NAME	TEAM	WXRL
1	Mariano Rivera	NYA	3.59
2	Jonathan Papelbon	BOS	3.54
3	Francisco Rodriguez	NYN	3.47
4	Joe Nathan	MIN	3.14
5	Joakim Soria	KCA	2.68
6	Jonathan Broxton	LAN	2.30
7	J.J. Putz	NYN	2.12
8	Brad Lidge	PHI	1.93
9	Takashi Saito	LAN	1.81
10	Brian Fuentes	LAA	1.75

Equivalent Strikeouts per Nine IP (50 IP Min.)

RANK	NAME	TEAM	EQSO9
1	Grant Balfour	TBA	10.4
2	Rich Harden	CHN	9.8
3	Joey Devine	OAK	9.5
4	Juan Cruz	ARI	9.4
T5	Francisco Rodriguez	NYN	9.2
T5	Carlos Marmol	CHN	9.2
T5	Brad Lidge	PHI	9.2

T5	Jonathan Papelbon	BOS	9.2
T10	Frank Francisco	TEX	9.0
T10	Dave Robertson	NYA	9.0

Stuff Score

RANK	NAME	TEAM	STUFF
1	Rich Harden	CHN	41
2	Tim Lincecum	SFN	37
T3	Joba Chamberlain	NYA	34
T3	Scott Kazmir	TBA	34
T5	CC Sabathia	NYA	33
T5	Felix Hernandez	SEA	33
T7	Edinson Volquez	CIN	31
T7	Zack Greinke	KCA	31
T7	Jake Peavy	SDN	31
T10	Ervin Santana	LAA	30
T10	Chad Billingsley	LAN	30

Value Over Replacement Player (VORP)

RANK	NAME	TEAM	VORP
1	Brandon Webb	ARI	56.0
2	Johan Santana	NYN	52.1
3	Rich Harden	CHN	51.0
4	Dan Haren	ARI	49.4
5	Tim Lincecum	SFN	48.3
6	CC Sabathia	NYA	48.0
7	Roy Halladay	TOR	45.2
8	Javier Vazquez	ATL	40.9
9	Josh Beckett	BOS	40.1
10	Jake Peavy	SDN	39.8
11	Cole Hamels	PHI	39.6
12	Roy Oswalt	HOU	36.7
13	Chad Billingsley	LAN	35.4
14	Max Scherzer	ARI	33.9
15	Felix Hernandez	SEA	33.8
16	Ervin Santana	LAA	33.5
17	Zack Greinke	KCA	33.0
18	Ben Sheets	MIL	32.2
19	Derek Lowe	ATL	31.7
20	Joba Chamberlain	NYA	31.5

Rookie Pitchers, VORP

RANK	NAME	TEAM	VORP
1	Brett Cecil	TOR	23.8
2	Mark DiFelice	MIL	16.9
3	Michael Bowden	BOS	15.3
4	Scott Lewis	CLE	14.5
5	David Robertson	NYA	13.5
6	Josh Kinney	SLN	13.3
7	David Price	TBA	13.0
8	R.J. Swindle	MIL	11.3
9	J.A. Happ	PHI	11.2
10	David Huff	CLE	11.1

Contributors

William Burke is part of the technical staff responsible for maintenance and development for Baseball-Prospectus.com and the other Prospectus sites. This is his second year coordinating statistical content for the annual book. William lives in suburban Chicago with his wife Amanda, son Joey, dog Natty, and child to be named later (Spring 2009).

Clifford J. Corcoran is a freelance writer and editor. The co-author of Alex Belth's Bronx Banter blog for the SNY Network, he also writes for SportsIllustrated.com and has contributed to *Fantasy Baseball Index*, the Baseball Prospectus books *It Ain't Over 'Til It's Over* and *Mind Game*, and the 2006 edition of *Baseball Prospectus*. He was the publisher's editor for the 2007 and 2008 editions of the annual as well as the editor of Howard Bryant's *Juicing the Game* and Brad Snyder's *A Well-Paid Slave*, among others titles. His earlier baseball writing can be found online on Clifford's Big Red Blog. A former music critic and lead singer, he lives in northern New Jersey with his very pregnant wife and their menagerie.

Clay Davenport is a meteorologist for the National Oceanic and Atmospheric Administration (NOAA) for whom he develops products to track rainfall from satellites so as to get an earlier jump on flash-flood warnings. He is one of the founding five of Baseball Prospectus and lives in Maryland with his wife, Susan.

Neil deMause is co-author of the book *Field of Schemes: How the Great Stadium Swindle Turns Public Money into Private Profit* (revised and expanded edition, University of Nebraska Press, 2008), and runs the stadium news website fieldofschemes.com. When not covering stadium shenanigans for Baseball Prospectus, he is an op-ed columnist for Metro NY and a regular contributor to the *Village Voice* and CNNMoney.com. He lives in Brooklyn with his partner, Mindy, and their six-year-old son, Jordan, who is unswayed by statistics in his conviction that Jose Reyes hits the most home runs ever.

Steven Goldman is a contributing editor to Baseball Prospectus. In addition to writing the historical analysis column "You Could Look It Up" for BaseballProspec-

tus.com, he has edited the BP-authored books *Mind Game* and *It Ain't Over 'Til It's Over*, and contributed to *Baseball Between the Numbers*. Steven is also the author of the biography *Forging Genius: The Making of Casey Stengel*. He has contributed to the BP annual since 2005 and has been co-editor of the last four editions. He is the creator of the long-running "Pinstriped Bible" column for the YES Network and is a commentator on the Network's *Hot Stove* television program. He was a baseball columnist for the *New York Sun* from 2004 to 2008, and blogs about politics and history at www.wholesomereading.com. Steven lives in New Jersey with his wife Stefanie, daughter Sarah, and son Clemens.

Kevin Goldstein covers baseball below the majors for Baseball Prospectus and is one of the nation's leading analysts on scouting, player development, and the draft. He lives in DeKalb, Illinois, with his one true love, Margaret, who hates baseball, as well as her two children, Xander and Cameron, a white pit bull named Otto, and a pair of cats, Henry and Pickles. Outside of BP, he has also written for ESPN.com, SportsIllustrated.com, *Baseball America*, and various annual publications.

Gary Huckabay is a founder and former CEO of Baseball Prospectus. He currently works in quantitative and strategic marketing for a large financial services company, and consults for MLB clubs and agents. Gary also serves as a lecturer and speaker on sports management and quantitative marketing at several universities. He lives in Northern California with his wife Kathy and son Charlie.

Derek Jacques resides in New York City, where he works with his wife, Paula, running an editorial services firm, Kepos Media. Derek writes the "Prospectus Toolbox" column for BaseballProspectus.com. This is his third time contributing to the annual. He has also written about baseball for *Bombers Broadside* and the *Colorado Rockies Magazine*.

Jay Jaffe is the founder of the eight-year-old Futility Infielder website (www.futilityinfielder.com), one of the oldest baseball blogs. In addition to covering the annual Hall of Fame ballot for BP, he writes the weekly columns "Prospectus Hit List" and "Prospectus Hit and Run" during the season. In recent years he's contributed work to *It Ain't Over 'Til It's Over*, *Mind Game*, Will Carroll's *The Juice*, *Bombers Broadside* and *Fantasy Baseball Index*. A graduate of Brown University who works as a graphic designer in New York City, he's married to Andra, the most supportive gal in the world, and once came in third in the famous Milwaukee Brewers sausage race.

Christina Kahrl is one of the founding quintet of Baseball Prospectus, the Managing Editor of BaseballProspectus.com, and was recently accepted into the ranks of the Baseball Writers' Association of America. Beyond her regular writing on player transactions on the site, she's written about baseball and football for *Playboy* and Playboy.com, Salon.com, Slate.com, Sports Illustrated.com, ESPN.com, the *New York Sun*, *Pride*, and *The Blade*, and has contributed to *Mind Game*, *It Ain't Over 'Til It's Over*, and the *ESPN Pro Football Encyclopedia*. A graduate of the University of Chicago with a graduate degree in History from Loyola University, she's settled into Edward Gorey's childhood neighborhood on Chicago's North Side with her Malinois, Argentina, where they romp through parks and beaches and destroy sticks with an alarming regularity.

David Laurila grew up in Michigan's Upper Peninsula and now writes about baseball from his home in Cambridge, Massachusetts. He authors the weekly "Prospectus Q&A" column at BaseballProspectus.com and has been a contributor to Baseball America, *Red Sox Magazine*, the *Boston Globe*, and other publications. A member of the Society for American Baseball Research, he has contributed to multiple SABR publications and to the Maple Street Press's *Guide to New England Ballparks*. The revised paperback edition of his first book, *Interviews from Red Sox Nation*, was published in March 2008.

Ben Lindbergh is a senior Manhattanite-in-residence at Georgetown University, and an intern at Baseball Prospectus. This is his first year contributing to the annual. He's also worked for the Yankees, the Nationals, and the Elias Sports Bureau.

Marc Normandin writes the "Fantasy Beat" and "Player Profile" columns at BaseballProspectus.com, and is in his third year of contributing to both the website and the annual. He also occasionally contributes to SportsIllustrated.com, and reviews video games and covers industry news at BlastMagazine.com. He lives in Boston, where he roots for the Red Sox and the cross-country Padres.

Caleb Peiffer graduated in 2007 with a degree in History from Harvard, where he covered sports for the university's daily, *The Crimson*. A Mets fan from birth on Long Island, he's now mourning the passing of Shea Stadium, particularly the upper deck. This is his rookie book effort after writing the "Prospectus Preview" column on BaseballProspectus.com during 2008, and he would like to thank the BP founders for graciously granting him the chance to help write the fantastic annual he first started reading eight years ago.

John Perrotto has covered Major League Baseball and the Pittsburgh Pirates in particular for twenty years. He began writing for Baseball Prospectus in 2007. He graduated from Geneva College, birthplace of college basketball, and lives in Beaver Falls, Pennsylvania, with his wife Brenda.

Nate Silver is the creator of the PECOTA projection system. IN addition to his duties for BP, Nate has written for Sports Illustrated, ESPN.com, and Slate.com. You may also know him from his politics blog, 538.com, or from his regular appearances on MSNBC in particular, but all across the dial during election season. He lives in Chicago, and his hobbies include poker, politics, eating burritos, and still making fun of Rex Grossman.

Acknowledgments

We would be ingrates of the first order if we didn't thank Sydelle Kramer, our agent, as well Cherise Fisher, our editor and champion at Plume, as well as Jennifer Risser of Plume. Promoting the book as a source of tremendous joy for all of us on the team, but it is especially the case because we get to work with Mary Pomponio, who handles our publicity at Plume.

The technical difficulty of laying this book out in short order would be impossible if not for the expertise and boundless energy of Christine Marra. Wherever she wants the bodies buried, we'll do the digging, because this book wouldn't *be* without her labors.

Self-love is something that draws more than a bit of public condemnation, but within BP's team, it's important for some of us to credit the people we work with, because there's the difference between doing the job and going above and beyond the call. Everyone who works for BP owes William Burke a big debt of gratitude, with so many of us syaing "Thank god for Bil" that you may as well figure we've all said it. There's also a general appreciation for Chris Schofield and Dana Glei, and now Joe Hamrahi, the people responsible for bookkeeping and payroll. Rany Jazayerli is much-loved for enthusiasm, both from his days as a more active participant in BP, and now that he's a semi-retired BP alum of sorts. On the web operations side of things, Christina Kahrl and the rest of the team owe a big debt to Dave Pease, Jeff Pease, Rick Lopez, John Erhardt, Caleb Peiffer, and Joe Sheehan for their work in keeping the big stage populated with articles and features that keep people engaged and entertained following the baseball the world over. Gary Huckabay was especially like to thank Chase Gharrity for his assistance, and Caleb Peiffer would like to especially thank Jason Paré for his. Christina and Steven would both like to thank Chase Gharrity and Ben Lindbergh for being outstanding interns who helped a ton. Will Carroll and Christina Kahrl would like to thank John Perrotto for his unstinting efforts on behalf of Baseball Prospectus.

Beyond these acknowledgments, there are more people that we should thank than we can fit into this space, but we will try, understanding that invariably there are going to be a oversights: Roman Abramovich, Ryan Alexander, R.J. Anderson, David Appelman, Andrew Baharlias, Jim Baker, Kevin Baker, Allen Barra, Maggie Barrett, Mark Bazer, Doug Behlmer, Alex Belth, Peter Bendix, John Blake, Tyler Bleszinski, Jon Boswell, Maury Brown, Larry Burke, John Burnson, Chris Cameron, Kathy Canavan, Shawn Carter, James Click, Steve Cofield, Dave Cokin, John Coppolella, Tod Crabtree, Jessica Curtis, Dan Dakich, Jayanthi Daniel, Paul DePodesta, the dingo, Bobbie Dittmeier, John DiTullio, Bob Dutton, Alex Early, John Erhardt, Bryan Evans, Diane Firstman, Tom Fontaine, Sean Forman, David Forst, Geoff Foster, Dan Fox, Lee Froehlich, Jeff Gambino, Pam Ganley, Brad Golder, Stefanie, Sarah, and Clemens Goldman, Gary Gillette, Michael Grady, Jimmy "The Greek," Thomas Grischany and Louise Kern, Dan Hart, Chad Hastings, Brian Hogan, Alan and Alexandra Houghton, Josh Kalk, Stan Kasten, Ted Keith, Geoff Ketcham, Marty Kobernus, Mat Kovach, Bob Kravitz, Scan Lahman, Jon Lane, Katie Laurila, Keith Law, Matthew Leach, Tim Lemke, Jane Levy, Chris Liss, Jacob Luft, Tim Marchman, Chris May, Peter McQuaid, Matt Melzak, Vinny Micucci, John Mirabelli, Dr. Richard Mohring, Devin Moss, Mike Murphy and Mike Murphy and another Mike Murphy (really, not all the same one), Jamey Newberg, Dave O'Brien, Jason Paré, Rodrigo Pereira, Dayn Perry, Dean Peterson, Picard, J.J. Picollo, Greg Pictrykiewicz, Steve Pijanowski, Mike Plugh, Jim Pollard, Peter Quadrino, Phil Rogers, Jeff Sackman, Eric SanInocencio, Keith Scherer, Diane Schroer, Cory Schwartz, Dan Scotto, Eric Seidman, Stu Shea, Dave Sheinin, Mike Siano, Eric Simon, David W. Smith, Jeff Smith, Michael David Smith, Casey Stern, Nick Stone, Kevin Sullivan, Bruce Taylor, Karen Turley, Jennifer VandenAkker, Chris Vernon, Chris Villani, Darren Viola, John Vuch, Norm Wamer, Bill Wanless, Craig Way, Jon Weisman, Eddie White, Brad Wochomurka, Keith and Kathy Woolner, Chris Caron, E.J. Argenio, Tom Spota, Jeff Erickson, Jason Grey, Louie Belina, Brad Davies, Craig Roberts, Michael Mazvinsky, Craig Elsten, Nicole Smith (and Kelli Jo Claxton and the entire Media3 staff), Bernie Miklasz, Randy Karraker, Benjamin Boyd, Michael Epstein, Bernie Ritter, Geoff Herman, Jeff Wheatley, David Lloyd, Steve Bunin, Brian Kenny, Bram Weinstein, Max Kellerman, Louie Gold, John Abbamondi, Alan Schwarz, Peter Kreutzer, Andy Andres, Chris Stone, Ben Reiter, Joe Lemire, Melissa Segura, Bill Simmons, Brian Parker, Ned Rice, Chaim Bloom, Paige

Beaudoin, Brent Gambill, Chuck Wilson, Dave Cokin, Ben Baumer, Omar Minaya, Brian Cashman, Fred Claire, Billy Beane, Jon Daniels, Manny Acta, Robby Artz, Chris Villani, Chris Curtis, Ferdinando DiFino, Jed Latkin, Darren Viola, Robbin Dunn, Danny Vara, Dan Rosenheck, David Leonhardt, Ed Randall, Erik Heiss, Eric Neel, Eric Karabell, Mike Ferrin, Shaun Clancy, Geoff Silver, Steve Hirdt, Gabe Goodwin, Gordon Damer, Jonathan Zaslow, Rob Leibowitz, Todd Zola, Jeff Passan, Nick Piecoro, John Donovan, Jason Romano, Jared Bodden, Jayson Stark, Peter Gammons, Brett Kaplan, King Kaufman, Lance McAllister, Laurence Kretchmer, Jay Levy, Jon Sciambi, Len Kasper, Robin Lundberg, Eric Lynch, Matthew Leach, Mike Smith, Owen Murphy, Rob Neyer, Pete Abraham, Steve Moyer, Ron Shandler, Todd Zolecki, Will Leitch

Christina offers a dedication to Franklin, who was there in dark times. I will always miss you.

"If you love college hoops, *College Basketball Prospectus* will take your appreciation to another level. The casual fan will really enjoy it, and the basketball junkie won't be able to live without it." —Fran Fraschilla, ESPN

College Basketball Prospectus

2008-2009

THE ESSENTIAL GUIDE TO THE MEN'S COLLEGE BASKETBALL SEASON

Featuring Tempo-Free Stats on All 31 D-I Conferences

Blake Griffin
Staying on at
Oklahoma

Billy Gillispie
Getting defensive
at Kentucky

Tyler Hansbrough
Returns for
senior season

Ben Howland
Building the new
UCLA dynasty

Raymar Morgan
Now "The Man"
at Michigan
State

Frank Martin
Is there life
after Beasley?

Ken Pomeroy, John Gasaway, and the authors of *Basketball Prospectus*

www.basketballprospectus.com

Plume
A member of Penguin Group (USA) Inc.
www.penguin.com